WORLD AUTHORS
1985–1990

Biographical Reference Books from
The H. W. Wilson Company

Greek and Latin Authors 800 B.C.–A.D. 1000
European Authors 1000–1900
British Authors Before 1800
British Authors of the Nineteenth Century
American Authors 1600–1900
Twentieth Century Authors
Twentieth Century Authors: First Supplement
World Authors 1950–1970
World Authors 1970–1975
World Authors 1975–1980
World Authors 1980–1985
Spanish American Authors: The Twentieth Century

The Junior Book of Authors
More Junior Authors
Third Book of Junior Authors
Fourth book of Junior Authors and Illustrators
Fifth Book of Junior Authors and Illustrators
Sixth Book of Junior Authors and Illustrators

Great Composers: 1300–1900
Composers Since 1900
Composers Since 1900: First Supplement
Musicians Since 1900
American Songwriters

World Artists 1950–1980
World Artists 1980–1990

American Reformers
Facts About the Presidents
Facts About the British Prime Ministers

Nobel Prize Winners

World Film Directors: Volumes I, II

WORLD AUTHORS
1985–1990

―――――――――

A Volume in the Wilson Authors Series

―――――――――

Edited by
VINETA COLBY

 THE H. W. WILSON COMPANY
NEW YORK   DUBLIN
1995

Library of Congress Cataloging in Publication Data
Main entry under title:
World Authors, 1985–1990 / editor, Vineta Colby.
p.   cm.—(Wilson authors series)
Includes bibliographical references.
ISBN 0-8242-0875-7
1. Literature, Modern—20th century—Bio-bibliography.
2. Literature, Modern—20th century—History and criticism.
I. Colby, Vineta.   II. Series.
PN451.W673   1995
809'.04048—dc20   95-41656
                                                        CIP

Acknowledgments for the use of copyrighted material and credits for photographs appear at the end of the volume.

PRINTED IN THE UNITED STATES OF AMERICA

Contents

Authors Included

PREFACE

WORLD AUTHORS 1985–1990 is the thirteenth volume in the on-going Wilson Authors Series. It adds 345 names of writers who have published a reasonably substantial and, within their genres, significant amount of work during the five-year period under survey. We cannot pretend to be comprehensive in our coverage, but every effort has been made to represent the multiplicity and the diversity of interests—literary and cultural, ethnic and national, scholarly and popular—that characterized these last decades of the twentieth century. Over the years our coverage of non-English language authors has kept pace with the increasing availability of translations; we are pleased to be able to offer an even wider coverage of them in this volume than in its predecessors.

More than one hundred of the authors in *World Authors 1985–1990* generously responded to our invitation to write autobiographical sketches. Many others sent biographical and bibliographical material. We are grateful to them, as well as to the contributors, many of them specialists in their fields, who are listed on page viii. We also acknowledge, with warm thanks, the cooperation of the editorial and production staffs of the H. W. Wilson Company—Elisa Ferraro, Susan Pavliscak, Norris Smith, Sandra Watson, Veronica Williams—and most especially Selma Yampolsky, who shared a considerable portion of the editorial responsibilities in the later stages of the making of this volume.

V.C.
September 1995

Contributors

Roger Allen, University of Pennsylvania
Lee Ambrose
Joachim T. Baer, University of North Carolina
Enikö Molnár Basa
Howard Batchelor
Joanne Bentley
Marianne Birnbaum, University of California at Los Angeles
Panayiotis A. Bosnakis, Princeton University
Graham Bottrill
Rachel Feldhay Brenner, University of Wisconsin-Madison
Robert A. Colby, City University of New York (Emeritus)
Verena Andermatt Conley, Miami University, Ohio
Rebecca L. Copeland, Washington University
Claire Cuccio, Washington University
Julia Cuervo-Hewitt, Penn State University
Joanne Long Demaria
Suzanne Erena
Tamara Evans, City University of New York
Margarite Fernández Olmos, City University of New York
Anita Gandolfo, University of West Virginia
Van C. Gessel, Brigham Young University
Zvia Ginor, Jewish Theological Seminary
W. Glyn Jones, University of East Anglia, England
Val Gough, University of Liverpool, England
Roger Greenwald, Innis College, University of Toronto
Lyubomira Parpulova Gribble, Ohio State University
Guneli Gunn
Lyn Jacobs, The Flinders University of Australia
Kathleen E. Kier, City University of New York
Lawrence Klepp
Stephen W. Kohl, University of Oregon
Jiri Kudrnc, City University of New York
Naomi Lindstrom, University of Texas
Gaetana Marrone-Puglia, Princeton University
Melissa Mcdaniel

Vasa D. Mihailovich, University of North Carolina
Diane Moroff
Catharine Nepomnyaschy, Columbia University
Viacheslav Nepomnyaschy
Anthony O' Brien, City University of New York
Krystyna S. Olszer, City University of New York
Kathleen Parthé, University of Rochester
Igela Pehrson
Janet Pérez, Texas Tech University
Giovanni Pontiero
David H. Richter, City University of New York
Andrew Riconda
Thomas Rimer, University of Pittsburgh
Gillian Rudd, University of Liverpool
Zeva Schapiro
George C. Schoolfield, Yale University
Joan Schroeter
Martin Schwabacher
Eric Sellin, Tulane University
Martin Seymour-Smith
Adam J. Sorkin, Penn State University
Herlinde Spahr
Drew Stevenson, Brooklyn Public Library
Dorothy Swerdlove
Edwin W. Terry, City University of New York (Emeritus)
Jon M. Tomman, University of New Mexico
John Whittier Treat, University of Washington
Luis Fernando Valente, Brown University
Alan R. Velie, University of Oklahoma
Charles Wagner
John Wakeman
Rhian Wakeman
Eleanor Wedge
Veronica Williams
Michiko Wilson, University of Virginia
Selma Yampolsky
Richard Zenith
David M. Zesmer, Illinois Institute of Technology (Emeritus)
Zhu Hong, Boston University and Institute of Foreign Literature, Chinese Academy of Social Sciences, Beijing

WORLD AUTHORS
1985–1990

*ABISH, WALTER (December 24, 1931–   ), American (Austrian-born) novelist, short-story writer, and essayist, writes: "I was born in Vienna into an insular middle class family that like so many other assimilated Jewish families at the time considered itself foremost Austrian. I think I am not distorting my past if I contend that I did not choose to become a writer—it was a role that was thrust on me. Looking back at my youth, I can only conclude from the way my father, a perfumer, a successful business man, radiating confidence and an eternal optimism, and my mother, many years his junior, drawn to the arts, an omnivorous reader, and at heart an unrelenting critic, nurtured my disquietude and, without communicating their intention to each other or to me, seemed to have gone out of their way to ensure that I would become a writer. I can see myself at the age of six, an only child, overprotected, egotistical, rebellious, already the writer-to-be, keenly assessing and questioning the veracity of everything that was taking place around me.

"In late 1938 we left Austria, going first to Italy then to France, where my father had business connections. After a year in Nice, where I attended a French school, we left in 1940 to join my uncle Phoebus in Shanghai, China, on what may have been one of the last passenger ships to leave before the outbreak of the war. During our eight-year stay in Shanghai from 1940 to 1948 I moved from school to school, first attending an English school and then, after the Japanese occupation, several Jewish schools. At the time, it seemed to me that China was a vast, forsaken terrain which other world powers could occupy and pillage at will. Growing up in Shanghai, I became inured to the abject misery I witnessed. I now consider my years in China as the most critical learning years of my life.

"In December of 1948, shortly before the Communist takeover, my parents and I left for Israel. It was there, while serving in the Israeli army, under the heady influence of a Hemingway novel I was reading, I first decided to be-

WALTER ABISH

come a writer, even though, except for a high school short-story competition I had entered and won, I had nothing to show that would indicate the slightest promise. After two years in the army, I worked for the American Library and the American Embassy and, preparing myself for an architectural career, attended Technosart where in 1954 I earned a diploma. In 1955 I spent a year working for an architect, feeling decidedly torn between my stated intention to become an architect and my desire to write. By then I had discovered Proust. When I stayed in Paris in 1956 I was elated to learn that the lady who ran the hotel where I was staying was none other than Celeste Alberet, Proust's former housekeeper. If anything, I saw this as further proof, if proof were needed, that I was destined to become a writer. In part, as a result of two theater productions, the Berlin Ensemble's *Mutter Courage*, in Paris, and later that year a performance of *Waiting for Godot* in London I became interested in the theater. During a lengthy stay in London, influenced by T. S. Eliot, I completed a long verse play, 'He Came to Witness'.

"After my arrival in the United States in 1957 I spent six months in a sanatorium in Denver where I continued to write plays. In 1958, now living in Brooklyn Heights, I translated several plays from the German and assisted in an off-Broadway production. A year later, I went to work for a New York planning consultant as a designer. In 1960 I quit my job in order to write 'On the Subject of Jochtan,' an autobiographical novel. It wasn't until the late sixties, after reading Borges, that I became interested in writing short fictions. In 1970, *Duel Site*, a book of my poems, was published by Tibor de Nagy Editions, and my stories began to appear in literary magazines, such as *Tri-Quarterly*, *Paris Review*, *Extensions*, and *Fiction Magazine*. I became a frequent contributor to the *New Directions Anthology*, and with James Laughlin's encouragement wrote *Alphabetical Africa*, which appeared in 1974. It was followed by *Minds Meet* in 1975 and *In the Future Perfect*, another collection of short fictions, in 1977. My novel *How German Is It* received the 1981 PEN/Faulkner Award and has since been translated into ten languages.

"For ten years, beginning in 1978, I was associated with the Writing Department in the School of General Studies at Columbia University. In 1977 I was writer-in-residence at Wheaton College, and in the fall of that year, visiting Butler Professor of English at the University of Buffalo. In 1986 I taught at Yale and in 1987 at Brown University.

"In the eighties I published a number of experimental texts that appeared in 1990 under the title of *99: The New Meaning*. I also published several autobiographical essays, 'Family' and 'The Fall of Summer' in which I describe my return to Vienna in 1982. In 1987 I received an invitation from the Deutscher Akademischer Austauschdienst to spend six months in Berlin where I intended to complete my novel, *As If*. By now [1992], at least six lengthy excerpts of the novel have appeared in *Conjunction*, *Antaeus*, *Granta* magazine, and *Facing Texts*, an anthology published by Duke University. However, since my stay in Berlin in 1987 had the paradoxical effect of stifling my imagination, I began another novel, *Eclipse Fever*, which was published in 1993 by Knopf in the United States and by Faber in England. Among the fellowships I have received are an Ingram Merrill Foundation Fellowship, 1977; a Guggenheim Fellowship in 1981; and two N.E.A Fellowships in 1979 and 1985. In 1987 I spent six months in Berlin as a fellow of the Deutscher Akademischer Aus-tauschdienst. That same year I received a John D. & Catherine T. MacArthur Fellowship, which enabled me to stop teaching for five years and concentrate, to the exclusion of everything else, on my writing. In 1991 I was the recipient of the Award for the Merit Medal for the Novel by the American Academy & Institute of Arts & Letters. In 1992 I received a fellowship from the Lila Wallace-Reader's Digest Fund.

"At present [1992] I am completing a collection of short fiction, a collection of essays, and *"As If."* the sequel to *How German Is It.*"

Walter Abish has on some occasions inspired, and on others provoked, his critics into blasts of rhetoric. Harold Bloom described *Eclipse Fever* in the *Washington Post Book World* as "one of the handful of essential American works emanating from the decade preceding the end of the second millennium." Writing of *Alphabetical Africa* in the *New York Times Book Review*, Richard Howard responded to what he called "an infuriating book" with: "Ideas and actions here are not developed, they are distributed; feelings are not dramatized, they are reified; the text is a kind of breviary of compulsive (and masturbatory) gratification." Paul West, in a review of *How German Is It* in the *Washington Post Book World*, says, "Like snow this novel accumulates delicately, lulling the mind with an inaudible dream . . . the novel drifts and swells into becoming a metaphor for postwar Germany . . . ." Earlier on, surveying Abish's fiction up to 1981, Jerome Klinkowitz wrote, in the *Georgia Review*, that his method has been "to treat the materials of fiction as objects in themselves—not as familiar cues to the reader (which trigger conventional responses and so set formulaic narrative to action) but rather as semiotic integers within the syntax of human behavior."

If "semiotic integers" rather than words that carry conceptual meaning are Abish's tools, then the result should be a fiction totally dissociated from the social realism and moral relevance that readers expect in conventional narrative. Yet, as Klinkowitz goes on to argue, *How German Is It* "shows how Abish has been writing about the ultimate reality all along." Even his radically experimental short fiction and his patently abstract novel *Alphabetical Africa* cannot properly be described as absurdist or irrational. On the contrary, Malcolm Bradbury writes in his introduction to the English edition of *In the Future Perfect*, "his work has an exactness and a clarity which is not always what we have grown used to in the chance-oriented free-style experimentation that has become almost a convention over recent years." The reader, unengaged with character or theme, is nevertheless caught up in the pursuit of elusive narrative threads: what is happening now? what happened in the past? what will happen in the future? Keeping himself as a writer aloof from the moral implications of what is going on in his fiction, Abish appears nevertheless to be probing beneath the surface "signs" of language for clues to meaning. "Whatever its reticence and indirection," Robert Boyers wrote of *How German Is It* in the *Columbia History of the American Novel*, "the novel is a work of intensely focussed moral energy." Abish offers no interpretation, no overt commentary on the "new" Germany trying to obliterate its Nazi history, but instead utilizes "enigma and obliquity . . . as reflections on pressing questions with which the novel is obsessed, as readers must be."

Abish's books *Minds Meet* and *In the Future Perfect* are more precisely described as collections of short fictions than as books of short stories because they defy all expectations about plot and character that readers customarily bring to short stories. Some seem to be the result of what Richard Martin, in the *Journal of American Studies* in 1983, called the "dictates of chance-become-system," a free fall, somehow landing within a structure that the author has under firm control. The scene is usually familiar—a recognizable American or German town, a shopping mall, a chic Manhattan apartment, the landscape of Southern California—but the familiar, Martin points out, is "a referent for defining the unknown." Writers define with words, language. Paradoxically, as Abish writes in the short fiction "Access" (in *In the Future Perfect*): "I'm not really concerned with language. As a writer I'm principally concerned with meaning." Interviewed by Jerome Klinkowitz in *Fiction International* in the early 1970s, he said: "In my writing I try to strip language of its power to create verisimilitude that in turn shields the reader from the printed words on the page that are employed as markers. Writing as close as possible to a neutral content, everything, the terrain, the interiors, the furniture, the motions of the characters are aspects of a topography that defines the limits of the situation being explored."

Aptly classified by Jerry A. Varsava in *Post-War Literature in English* as a " 'comic' meta-novel," *Alphabetical Africa* is a wildly experimental work. Though a tour de force of apparent absurdist and black humor, the book has the sting of the reality of postcolonial Africa in the late 20th century. Abish's choice of that continent as the scene was initially whimsical, but he recognized the implicit challenges involved—the mystery and romance that Africa holds for Westerners, its "distorted, unreliable history of colonialism," its disputed boundaries and clashing cultures. "Clearly there's a parallel to be drawn between my struggle to depict and, as a white writer, come to terms with the mysterious world of Africa and the intrinsic challenges of the text," he told Larry McCaffery in an interview in *Alive and Writing*. He credits the existence of the book to James Laughlin, who published many of the best avant-garde writers at his New Directions press. Laughlin had admired Abish's short piece "Minds Meet" and invited him to contribute to a New Directions anthology. What Abish expected to be a short fiction insisted on growing into a novel. He sent the first half to Laughlin who agreed to publish the book "if the second part is as strong."

Alphabetical Africa consists of fifty-two short chapters, divided exactly at the middle: twenty-six chapters headed A to Z, twenty-six Z to A. The novel moves by expansion and contraction. In the first chapter all the words begin with A: "Africa again: Antelopes, alligators, ants and attractive Alva, are arousing all angular Africans, also arousing author's analytically aggressive anticipations, again and again. Anyhow author apprehends Alva anatomically, affirmatively and also accurately." In the second, initial Bs are added: "Africa as before: Bantu also admire beauty and abduct agreeable Alva, astonishing Alva, and by all accounts, always adapting and bending, beguiled by Bantu bedtime behavior, and by beautiful, bedazzling bedding, authentic batik." By the I chapter the author can reveal his method: "Bit by bit I have assembled Africa." He proceeds to the end of the alphabet: "Zambia helps fill our zoos, and our doubts, and our extra-wide screens as we sit back." With the next chapter, the alphabet now in reverse, he can write freely: "Zanzibar is clearly marked on the map. It is an unforgettable island with picturesque clusters of whitewashed houses surfacing here and there among the giant mangrove trees." Contraction then sets in until, back to A, the novel ends:" . . . another awakening another awesome age another axis another Alva another Alex another Allen another Alfred another Africa another alphabet."

There are some fragments of plot with Alex, Allen, and Alva apparently involved in a jewel robbery, traveling to as many African countries as the alphabet allows from Angola to Zambia and along the way encountering an African queen named Quat and an army of ants. John Updike, who offered his own offbeat vision of modern Africa in *The Coup*, writes of *Alphabetical Africa* in *Picked-Up Pieces*: "Though the tale is murky as well as absurd, one is tempted to concede that Mr. Abish has performed as well as anyone could, given such extravagant handicaps. 'A masterpiece of its kind' does not seem too strong an accolade for a book apt to be the only one of its kind." The uniqueness of this novel, Kenneth Baker writes in *New Directions in Prose and Poetry*, is that "it acknowledges its complete dependence on the structure of the English language . . . .*Alphabetical Africa* is locked into English. No translation of it will be possible unless there is a language that is alphabetically and semantically congruent with English."

In 1978 Abish published an essay, "The Shape of Absence," introducing an exhibition of photographs made by his wife Cecile, a sculptor and photographer. Mounted in a gallery in Dayton, Ohio, this "project work," titled *Firsthand*, consisted of photographs of a brick house first seen whole, then in segments photographed at different times and separate views. Its theme, he wrote, is "the idea of an elusive tangibility," rendering the house a sign or "signification" rather than a house. "Elusive tangibility" describes his fiction as fittingly as it describes her work.

The central character of *How German Is It*, Ulrich Hargenau, once involved with a terrorist group, has returned to Germany from France. Arriving now as almost a stranger in his native land, he visits his brother, a prominent architect, in a new town, Brumholdstein, named in honor of an internationally famous German philosopher Brumhold, who is unmistakably modeled on the German philosopher, Martin Heidegger, known to have been a Nazi sympathizer. The town has been built near the site of a former Nazi concentration camp, leveled in 1956, and all the cosmetic efforts to conceal its past are shattered when, as the result of a break in a sewer pipe, the central street of the city collapses to reveal that it had been built over a burial ground for victims of the Holocaust.

A multiplicity of characters and a network of complicated events lead to a powerful conclusion in which Ulrich discovers his identity and his own unconscious relationship to Germany's past. The unique feature of the novel is its teasing ambiguity, its "elusive tangibility." Abish's, or Ulrich's, Germany is "real" in the sense that every detail of life is familiar, even commonplace; this Germany might be the reader's own country, Brumholdstein, the reader's hometown. But because Abish as narrator remains so distant from his characters, so nonjudgmental, offering no explanations, no interpretation, the familiar becomes mysterious, ambiguous. Richard Martin wrote of the novel in the *Journal of American Studies* in 1983 : "The term 'defamiliarization' is central to Abish's fiction; almost everything he

has written to date is finally bound up with the attempt to define the familiar—the world as we think we recognize it—through the fictional process of removing the known to regions of apparent mystery in order to create unease, the creative unease of the reader, who thus commences a questioning of the familiar for himself." As Abish told McCaffery: "My interest in Germany is not to explain it, but to highlight the German 'signs' that elicit a set response—a German truth—which in my book is either subtly questioned or negated or defamiliarized."

In his quest for "defamiliarization," Abish made it a point not to visit Germany until several years after completing *How German Is It*. The same impulse for distancing himself from his subject led to his choice of Mexico as the scene for *Eclipse Fever*, his next novel. He rejected his first plan to set the novel in Italy because, as he told the *Washington Post Book World*, he knew that country too well. Instead he chose Mexico, a country he had never visited. Amazingly, he evokes the Mexican scene in vivid detail. His characters, Mexican and American alike, are drawn into a maze of ironically comic intrigue involving the theft of pre-Columbian art objects, plans to build an elevator in the Aztec Pyramid of the Sun and a retirement colony for Americans on the site, and a frustrated attempt to witness the eclipse of the title. A heady combination of mystery, farce, and complex human relationships, *Eclipse Fever* covers an enormous amount of territory literally and figuratively. *Eclipse Fever*, Harold Bloom wrote in the *Washington Post Book World*, "is a profound analysis both of the immemorial malaise of Mexican society and cultures and, by juxtaposition, our own." It is also, he wrote, "disturbing and wildly entertaining." In the *New York Review of Books*, Diane Johnson linked the novel to Abish's earlier writings, pointing out that in all of them a foreigner or outsider confronts an alien culture that is American-dominated. The fine line between history and fiction disappears: historical Mexico yielding to Spanish conquest, contemporary Mexico embracing the cultural domination of the United States. The result, however, is not programmatical and didactic but, Johnson writes, a novel "organized like a fugue, a simple but pregnant melody in whose variations lie the pleasure and interest of the work."

Abish has published a large body of essays and experimental fictions in journals in the United States and abroad. He has also published *99: The New Meaning*, a collection of fragments from a variety of authors arranged, he writes, "to probe certain familiar emotional configurations afresh and arrive at any emotional content that is not mine by design." William Doreski suggests, in the *Literary Review*, that however arbitrary the choice and arrangement of the passages may be, "the strategies of design, the empowerment of context over content, dominates the book." Although defying the conventions of narrative fiction, Abish's juxtaposition of the passages evokes emotional and intellectual responses from the reader. Doreski writes: "Other authors, from Joyce through Beckett to our time, have asked something of the sort, but Abish, with a panache already familiar to admirers of his earlier work (especially the brilliant *How German Is It*), pushes the boundaries of fiction still further, challenging settled notions of language and structure and redefining the generic possibilities of his art."

Walter and Cecile Abish live and work in a loft in Manhattan's East Village, the center of New York's art scene in the 1990s. Cecile Abish is a sculptor and photographer and their studio is decorated with her large works. Though not actually collaborators, they share an approach to each other's work: "We have an ongoing dialogue and provide a kind of measure for each other."

PRINCIPAL WORKS: *Poetry*—Duel Site, 1970. *Short fiction*—Minds Meet, 1975; In the Future Perfect, 1977; 99, The New Meaning, 1990. *Novels*—Alphabetical Africa, 1974; How German Is It, 1986: Eclipse Fever, 1993.

ABOUT: Contemporary Authors 101, 1981; Contemporary Literary Criticism 22, 1982; Elliott, E., Columbia History of the American Novel, 1991; Karl, F. R. American Fiction 1940-1980, 1983; Klinkowitz, J. The Self-Apparent Word, 1984; McCaffery, L. & S. Gregory, Alive and Writing: Interviews with American Authors, 1987; New Directions Anthology 39, 1979; Tucker, M., Literary Exile in the 20th Century, 1991; Updike, J. Picked-Up Pieces, 1979. *Periodicals*—American Book Review March-April 1981; Anteaus 52, 1984; Contemporary Literature Winter 1989; Critique Studies in Modern Fiction Spring 1985; Fiction International Spring 1987; Georgia Review Summer 1981; Granta Review Summer 1979; Hudson Review Summer 1981; Journal of American Studies 17, 1983; Literary Review Fall 1991; New Directions in Prose and Poetry Fall 1977; New York Review of Books September 23, 1993; New York Times Book Review December 29, 1974; June 27, 1993; Novel Fall 1990; Post-War Literature in English December 1989; Salmagundi Winter–Spring 1990; Semiotext(e) Spring 1982; Thought 62, 1987; Washington Post Book World November 9, 1980; May 9, 1993.

*ALESHKOVSKY, YUZ (pseudonym of IOSIF YEFIMOVICH) (September 21, 1929–), Russian satirical prose writer, was born (September 21, 1929), in Krasnoyarsk. His

YUZ ALESHKOVSKY

youthful years coinciding with World War II, he was unable to obtain a formal education and is self-educated. During the period from 1949 to 1950, he served in the Soviet Navy. In 1950 he was sentenced to a four-year term of imprisonment for stealing a military truck and spent the years from 1950 to 1953 in the Gulag. Upon being released, he worked in Moscow as a truck driver and at other menial jobs. He turned to writing children's literature around 1955. However, unofficially, he became extremely popular as an unpublished—and unpublishable during the period—protest song writer. In 1970 he wrote a short novella called *Nikolai Nikolaevich*, which circulated in samizdat (the unofficial underground press) and became quite popular. The novella's plot revolves around the notorious but true story of the banning of a whole branch of biological science (genetics) in the U.S.S.R. in the mid-1950s; the story is seen through the eyes of a young thief hired to work as a sperm donor by a genetics laboratory chief prior to the laboratory's demise. Aleshkovsky's uncompromising stance, the satirical whimsy of this and all his subsequent works, and his use of obscenities assured that none of his works could be published in the U.S.S.R. despite their superior literary merit.

In 1979 Aleshkovsky was allowed to emigrate. His next major work, a novel titled *Ruka* (*The Hand; or, The Confession of an Executioner*), published in 1981, is an excellent illustration of its thesis that Communism was "an embodiment of absolute satanism." The protagonist of *The Hand* becomes a member of the Cheka (predecessor of the KGB) in order to avenge the death of his parents, who were murdered by a team of Cheka thugs during the campaign to exterminate "as a class" the kulaks (relatively well-off peasants). However, in the process he becomes as bloodthirsty as the Chekists themselves, and when finally he hears his murdered parents' voices begging him to abandon his path of revenge, murder, and mayhem, it is too late because his soul has been poisoned beyond redemption. Yet another short novella by Aleshkovsky called *Maskirovka* (Camouflage, 1980), portrays Soviet reality as a colossal Potemkin village. The supposedly peaceful city of Staroporokhov, where the novella takes place, is built over a huge underground military plant where most of its inhabitants are employed. The American spy satellite that passes over the city at regular intervals cannot detect the lack of bread and sausage in the city, and the main task of the police is to clear away the drunks passed out in the streets before the satellite's overflight.

The plot of the novel *Kangaroo*, 1981, is a grotesquely picturesque account of an old thief's participation in a show trial of a case (concocted by the KGB) of the rape and murder of the only kangaroo in the Moscow zoo. Material proof is presented at the trial in the form of a feature film and after the certain and predetermined verdict is reached, the hero is placed in a concentration camp where "honest communists" continue to engage in party demagoguery and reenact the class struggle by fighting the prison rat population.

The short novella *Sinenkii skromnyi platochek* (Modest blue kerchief, 1982), is written in the form of a letter by a schizophrenic Soviet World War II veteran to none other than Leonid Ilyich Brezhnev himself. In this letter the crippled veteran tells Brezhnev the story of his sad life and how he ended up in a mental asylum, showing how representative life in the asylum is of the life outside its walls. Addressing Brezhnev, he writes: "You really must be mad, and according to the dissidents' estimates, if you were admitted to the nut house now in order to have your mental capabilities, life goals, cultural level, and moral standards examined, it would turn out that it is you who should be locked up here." The novel *Karusel* (Merry-Go-Round), which appeared in 1983, supports the notion that in view of anti-Semitism and nature of the Soviet system itself, the only viable option for a Jew living in the U.S.S.R. was to emigrate.

Kniga Poslednikh Slov. 35 Prestuplenii (Book of Last Words. 35 Crimes, 1984) is a collection of short stories all written in the same form—as the last speech of an accused person standing trial. Each story is preceded by a quotation from an actual Soviet textbook on criminology, giving a brief description of an actual criminal case. The novel *Smert v Moskve* (Death in Moscow, 1985) is a satirical account of the life and death of a high-echelon Soviet villain named Lev Mekhlis, used as an illustration of the dog-eat-dog-all-eaten-by-Stalin life on the Soviet political Olympus.

The story told in Aleshkovsky's next novella, *Bloshinoye Tango* (Flea's Tango, 1986) takes place during the "period of mature socialism" (the early Brezhnev years); it describes the transition to the radiant Communist future in a research institution actively engaged in breeding a new type of flea, code-named "Hope for a new Afghanistan X6-X7." Capable of harboring a new and quite deadly strain of bacterial warfare, the flea is vicious and highly elusive, and has increased biting power, extraordinarily high mobility, and is capable of withstanding extremely high heat. The flea is supposed to play the role of a pivotal device that will turn the tide of the war in Afghanistan waged by the Soviet army against the Afghan rebels.

The collection of two novellas published together under the title *Slomannaya Sobaka* (The Broken Dog, 1989) consists of "A Small Novella About a Certain Madman and a Broken Dog" and "Lenin's Death." Both novellas mock the geriatric Soviet leadership of the latter day for the quagmire into which they had sunk the system and their own lives as well.

With the advent of *perestroika* and the demise of the U.S.S.R., publication of Aleshkovsky's works became possible in Russia, even though, in the spirit of the new Russian capitalism, quite a few of these editions were pirated. However, some were legitimate (sanctioned by the author and issued by legitimate publishers). Among these were two new novels: *RuRu* (Russian Roulette), published in the cinematographers' journal *Iskusstvo Kino* in 1991, which describes the living conditions of the rank-and-file inhabitants of the late U.S.S.R. during the period of stagnation, and *Persten v Futlyare* (The Ring in the Case), published in 1992 in the literary journal *Zvezda*, which dwells on the theme of the complicity of a certain part of the intellectual Soviet "intelligentsia" in the order of things in the U.S.S.R. in its latter days, when that part of the elite literally sold out to the Communist satan, and of their need for repentance. In 1994 an album CD *Okurochek* (Cigarette Butt) of Aleshkovsky's songs, performed by the author, was produced in Russia by a new Russian record-producing company called Sintez-Records. Most of the songs were the same ones that had circulated among the populace of the former U.S.S.R. on clandestantly copied tapes several decades before.

Aleshkovsky resides in Cromwell, Connecticut, and in 1995 was working on a new novel.

PRINCIPAL WORKS IN ENGLISH TRANSLATION:(tr. P. Meyer) "From the Book of Final Statements," *in Partisan Review* 5, no. 2, 1984; (tr. T. Glenny) Kangaroo, 1986; (tr. S. Brownsberger) The Hand; or, The Confession of an Executioner (introd. J. Brodsky), 1990.

ABOUT: Brown E. J. Russian Literature Since the Revolution 1982; Kasack, W. Dictionary of Russian Literature Since 1917, 1988. *Periodicals*—Library Journal April 1, 1990; New Republic August 25, 1986; New York Times November 11, 1981; New York Times Book Review April 27, 1986; May 6, 1990; New Yorker April 28, 1986; Partisan Review 50, no.4, 1983; Review of Contemporary Fiction Fall 1990; Slavic and East European Journal 28, Winter 1984; Stanford Slavic Studies 1, 1987; Washington Post May 4, 1986; World Literature Today Summer 1990.

EDWAR AL-KHARRAT

AL-KHARRAT, EDWAR (March 16, 1926–), Egyptian fiction writer, critic, and translator, writes: "I was born in Alexandria. My parents came from Akhmim, Upper Egypt, and from Al-Tarrana, Beheira. Raised and educated in Alexandria, I took a degree in law at its university, in 1946. Worked in a variety of jobs: storehouse-assistant at the Royal Navy Victualling Department, Alexandria (1944–1946) and bank clerk at the national Bank of Egypt up to 1948. During the late forties I was active in the revolutionary movement in Alexandria, and was held under Farouk, in concentration camps in Abiqir and El Tor, for two years. Released in 1950, I worked as an insurance clerk with the National Insurance Co., Alexandria and then as press and public-relations officer with the Romanian Embassy in Cairo. Married in 1958, I live in Cairo and have two sons and four grandchildren. In 1959, I worked with the Afro-Asian Peoples' Solidarity Organization and the Afro-Asian Writers' Association, eventually becoming Assistant Secretary General of both organizations. In 1983, resigned my post to devote myself to writing.

"I think that there are indeed constant elements that form—if I may use the expression—my concerns which have never left me since I started writing, and have been my companions since the beginning of my 'consciousness' even though, naturally, they were in a primary and embryonic form. One of these concerns, that would instantly be apparent to any reader who is interested in investigating what I am trying to

do, is the issue of man's loneliness or estrangement; whether it is his estrangement from himself, his estrangement and loneliness in society and in the company of others, among his companions, peers, and kin; his loneliness even in the most intimate relationships he creates, relationships that are the most close and inmost to himself, that in which, supposedly, all walls of loneliness should collapse. Then there is a man's loneliness in this universe, in a world that is made out of mute rocks, not carved out for him nor made to respond to his desires, urges, or passions. This estrangement, this loneliness, this isolation is what creates the fact that man is an island unto himself—this is a constant concern of mine. At the same time, you find an irresistible desire and a burning urge towards communication; towards breaking down these walls; towards communion—even more, infusion— with himself, between man and woman, between himself and his companions, comrades and peers in society, and finally between man and the universe. I imagine that these two courses, or concerns, are part of the constant elements in my writings. There are also other constant themes that complement these two elements, which propose other issues, I believe, such as the relationship between the temporal, transient, fleeting moment and the eternal, durable, and everlasting; or between what we can call the 'relative' and the 'absolute'; or in short, what has come to be known as the intimate, significant, burning relationship between the 'human' and what can be named as the 'divine'.

"As to the role of the artist, I will not broach

it here, except in a very simplistic manner. I do not think that the artist should be a publicist of anything; at least for me, I do not want to propagate, nor present, nor even deal with a cause in this abstract, simplistic or cerebral form.

"To my mind, art has a comprehensive, epistemological value that partakes in the human experience in all its complexity. Especially in this era, an era of electronics and mechanisms, programming and standardization. I believe that the artist's role nearly approximates that of the old prophets of the past: a role that transcends the philosophical, social, and even the esthetic techniques, to what almost reaches an experience of communication, revelation, and an ardent intimate creation that has the ecstasy of prophesy and also its illumination, and also verges upon a quality of knowledge that transcends—and incorporates also—intellectual cognition. Hence comes its particular esthetics, with its renewable laws, each and every time (in spite of the obvious importance of intellectual cognition, in its own field, of course, and I would not attempt, in any way, to belittle that).

"I am an Arab, Egyptian, Copt; that is, Coptic first and an Egyptian, writing in Arabic, and the whole of Arab culture has become one of the components of both my individual and collective life. Being Copt, this delineation points to the problem, which is not only an intellectual problem. The core of the Egyptian orthodoxy specifically is the incarnation of the absolute in man. The absolute in man, and man is the absolute without division: not even for one moment or a blink of the eye; it is the communion of the human and the divine. This is the issue, even more, the creed of Egyptian orthodoxy, and the essence of being a Copt. I claim that this also is basically the essence of being Egyptian. This differs from other Christian doctrines.

"Is it possible to say that besides the influences, the effort to return to ancient roots: the roots of ancient Egyptian art, and ancient Arab art, there are also obvious Western influences? A writer may feel that he is impressed or influenced by certain writers but his actual writings negate these feelings. For example, amongst the writers who very deeply influenced me—and I am not alone in this, but along with the whole of my generation—are the grand Russian writers, especially Dostoevsky, and later on D. H. Lawrence, the English Romantic poets—Shelley, Keats, Byron and so on. I even assiduously embarked upon a personal and private translation into Arabic of Shelley and Keats, followed by Baudelaire, during my early youth. I imagined at one time that I was greatly influenced by them, but does this show in my work?

"Is there a more obvious influence by James Joyce, for example, or Proust? These I read at a relatively late stage, so that I did not feel the same tumultuous effect that Dostoevsky and Lawrence, and before that Shelley and Keats, exercised on me in my early youth. It is possible that the influence of Joyce and Proust that I was exposed to immediately after this, was subtler and deeper. When I read *Ulysses*—which was an incredible thing at the time—I did not feel that tumultuous effect, but I was moved more by his collection *Dubliners*, since I wrote short stories at the time. But I think that *Ulysses* had its invisible, residual influence of a profound depth and a recurrent nature and a long-term resonance that comes back later. It is almost not consciously realized, sedimenting in some vicinity, a little beneath consciousness, and much deeper than it seems. But reading, influences, and the assimilation of artistic works are all part of life's work that, or course, never ceases.

"If we move from this interaction—I do not want to call it influence—but the interaction with the readings of Western works, which exists either in the area of the consciousness or the vicinity beneath it, is there some kind of interaction with the Arabic readings? Deep and basic. The Arabic heritage, for me, is something alive, potent and very contemporary: both on the popular level, where I read and lived the tales of *A Thousand and One Nights* as a child, and which has almost not left me till now, and on the classical level from the *jāhiliya* to *al-Qādai* and *al-Fādil* and *Subh al-'Ashā* that I read in secondary school. And of course there is the Christian and Coptic literature whose effect is, up till now, deep-rooted and lacerating."

———

Widely traveled in Europe, Africa, Asia, and North and Latin America, Edwar Al-kharrat has worked throughout his career to bridge cultures. With his translations from French and German into Arabic he has introduced Egyptian readers to the Western literature, and with his original writings, which have been translated into English, French, German, Spanish, Russian, Greek, and Japanese, he has introduced readers worldwide to the mind of contemporary Egypt. Al-karrhat has participated in many international literary conferences. He has lectured on modern Egyptian intellectual life at Oxford and in London; in the United States in 1992 he lectured at Yale, Princeton, Columbia, and the University of Pennsylvania.

There is a certain irony in the fact that a writer who is also a successful translator of foreign literature into Arabic should be relatively so little known to the English-language readers. With the English translation of *City of Saffron* in 1989, however, he has emerged as an important figure in modern Arabic literature. Edward Said, writing in the *Independent* in 1990, cited him as one of several writers whose works "are an accurate index of how excitingly far Arabic literature has come." Doris Lessing, responding to the *Independent* 's poll of favorite books of 1990, named *City of Saffron* as a novel worthy of comparison with the Alexandria quartet of novels by Lawrence Durrell as a portrait of that city and its life in the 1930s and '40s, and with Proust's *Remembrance of Things Past* as an evocation of the memories of a sensitive boy just coming to maturity.

Al-kharrat swims against the currents of realism and naturalism flowing through the writings of his fellow Egyptian Naguib Mahfouz, the Nobel laureate. Al-kharrat cites the limitations of such fiction. "I think that what we have begun to do in Egypt," he told an interviewer for *Al-Ahram* in 1991, "is to experiment in transgressing the imaginary boundaries between genres—the short story, poetry, the novel." The real nature of experience, he argues, is intangibility; and the memory—by which human experience is preserved—tends to erase the gaps between the past and present. In his work Al-kharrat favors subjectivity, drawing upon symbolism, dream sequences, and nonlinear narrative. Roger Allen reports, in *The Arabic Novel: A Historical and Critical Introduction*, that in an address to a writers' conference in Fez, Morocco, in 1979, Al-kharrat said that he uses his writing "as a weapon to bring about change, change both in the self and in others . . . for something better, more beautiful perhaps . . . something soothing in the oppressive heat of violence and suffocation. . . . " The rebellion he speaks of is more aesthetic than political. For a time in the 1960s, he edited an avant-garde literary magazine, *Galiri 68*, and wrote literary criticism in support of iconoclastic, experimental writing. Such work has not always met with favor from the political establishment; as recently as 1992 one of his favorite novels was banned from circulation in Egypt.

Al-kharrat began writing short stories early but pressures to earn a living prevented him from publishing until 1955. His first collection, *Hītān àliyya* (High walls, 1959) includes twelve stories set in everyday modern Alexandria, and its beaches and surrounding countryside, but their mood is intensely poetic and introspective. His principal characters are sensitive, alienated, and living in self-imposed isolation. In one story, "By the Water's Edge," a schoolteacher lives alone in a noisy, crowded apartment building.

But he has no part in his neighbors' lives, occupying "a solitary room on the roof with silent walls that hemmed in his days and, staring down on his loneliness, marked out the emptiness which was his life." With no companion but an affectionate puppy, he finally attempts suicide but is foiled, even in the act, by a vision of his dead sister. An Egyptian reviewer, Yusuf al-Sharuni, quoted in *Modern Arabic Literatue*, observed of the book: "The most obvious feature is that the author views his characters from the inside rather than from the outside. The psychological makeup of these characters is locked up within the high walls that prevent them from interacting with other people."

Al-kharrat's second collection *Sa àt al-kibriya* (Moments of Pride, 1972), won a state prize for short stories. Reviewers remarked once again upon the existential character of his writing. Like Albert Camus, to whom he has frequently been compared, he focuses on the struggle between the individual sensibility and the society in which the character exists. "[H]e is a loud paean to individualism, wherever it occurs," Sabri Hafiz wrote in *Al-Adab* in 1969 (quoted in *Modern Arabic Literature*), "to isolationism, to the process of switching off all events and societal values." The stories in this collection are heavily descriptive, drawing upon natural imagery of sky and sea as a background against which his characters move in confusion, torn between illusion and reality. His prose is sensuous: "Pools of light from the street-lamps are stagnant, a haze of gnats floating on their surface, undulating soundlessly." The lonely male protagonist often confronts visions of women in erotic dreams; and women, in often interchangeable rolls of mother, sister, wife, and prostitute, are treated worshipfully as icons to be both feared and revered.

Al-kharrat's most celebrated novel is his first, *Ramah wal-tinnin* (Ramah and the dragon, 1979), a book he himself calls "untranslatable." Drawing upon poetry, legend, history, and philosophy, chapters are seemingly unrelated yet thematically interlocked. The episodic quality of the novel derives from its origin as a short story, "Mikhael and the Swan." In the account that Al-kharrat sent *World Authors* he says that even as he finished the story he recognized it was the first chapter of a novel, to be followed by other episodes formulated somewhat as the intricate scrolls and arabesques of Arabic ornamentation incorporate "the accumulative infinite layers within a boundless circle that does not have a beginning, middle, or end, where subdivisions . . . episodes evolve from one subdivision to the second, to the third, and so on infinitely." Ramah is a mysterious female figure whom the author describes as "the other." It is Mikhael's goal to know her, or to become known to her, raising the question of whether indeed it is possible to transcend the self. The dragon is equally hard to define—certainly a symbol of evil, Satan, oppression, unfulfilled or frustrated love. Al-kharrat further suggests that "the dragon is the absolute, the divine, the consummate divinity, the consummately satanic within man. In this sense evil is absolute, in as much as good is absolute, but they are both human and relative also, contingent and eternal." Far more accessible to Western readers, *Turabuha Za 'faran* (*City of Saffron*, 1986), is also unconventional in its narrative structure, shifting back and forth among the memories of an imaginative boy who, like Al-kharrat is a Coptic Christian growing up in Alexandria during the late 1930s and the years of World War II. The city was often subjected to Nazi bombing raids, but the boy is sheltered by a loving family. The juxtaposition of the violent outside world and the security of his family life is rendered dramatically. Filtered through the memories and imagination of the boy, Alexandria and its inhabitants assume a symbolic dimension. "Alexandria, O Alexandria! Hard pearl of life within its unprised shell, and more" the book begins; "My hymn to you is yet a mumbled thing—a murmur." He recalls the miller to whose mill his mother sends him on an errand:

> It was run by an old Sa' idi with broken teeth. He wore a turban on his old gray head—and a muffler round his neck in winter and summer. He doled out the flour and the bran for me with a big iron scoop, fetching both from a tall wooden chest with a sloping lid and putting them in two buff paper bags. I could feel their weight on my arms as I picked them up to carry them against my chest; and I used to feel a bit embarassed. . . .

He also recalls the wildly mixed boyhood reading that shaped his imagination: the Bible, adventure stories, Arabic translations of Daudet's *Sappho* and Zola's *Nana*, but mainly the *Thousand and One Nights*, from which he experienced a veritable revelation: "And for the first time the world became bright with the fire of knowledge and the flood gushed out; and I became a vessel afloat, borne on the floodtide; and there is no road through the roaring waves of these high seas, where I rise and fall to this day."

Although Al-kharrat insists that *City of Saffron* is not an autobiography but a work of the imagination ("More, perhaps, a 'becoming' than a 'life'; not *my* life"), Robert Irwin, reviewing the novel in the *Times Literary Supplement*, was confident that "Mikhael and Edwar speak with one voice. *City of Saffron* is a feverish yet finely written exploration of certain mysteries. Mikhael is obsessed with something he cannot

name, but which is surely sex, but his creator is primarily preoccupied with past time and its recovery through memory and literary creation." Michael Moorcock, in the *Daily Telegraph*, called it work of "magic realism" that brings Alexandria and the boy through whom we see it vividly to life. For Christopher Wordsworth in the *Guardian*, "*City of Saffron* is a kaleidoscope of memories, apparently haphazard but transmuted into art as the author ponders and assembles them."

In his later writings Al-kharrat has moved from the radically experimental and even surrealistic quality that dominated his work in the 1950s and '60s to a more objective (though still unconventional) and socially committed fiction and criticism. He told his *Al-Ahram* interviewer in 1991, that he sees a new and independent spirit emerging among younger writers: "I very much like to see what is being written, especially writing which is not accepted by the establishment and is not welcomed by the publishers. Whatever looks odd or unorthodox to them intrigues and excites me. Imperfections are there, but I don't really care—on the contrary, these perhaps add to the richness. . . . And discoveries are there to be made."

PRINCIPAL WORKS IN ENGLISH TRANSLATION: By the Water's Edge (tr. N. Faraq and J. Wahba) in Manzalaoui, M. (ed.) Arabic Short Stories, 1945–1965, 1968; Birds Footsteps in the Sand (tr. D. Johnson-Davies) in Johnson-Davies, D. (ed.) Arabic Short Stories, 1983; Open Wound (tr. S. Magar and E. Al-Kharrat) in Kassem, C. and M. Hashem (eds.) Flight of Fantasy: Arabic Short Stories, 1985; City of Saffron (tr. F. Liardet) 1989.

ABOUT: Allen, Roger The Arabic Novel: An Historical and Critical Introduction, 1982; Liardet, F. Introduction to City of Saffron, 1989. Allen, Roger (ed.) Modern Arabic Literature, 1987, Periodicals—Al-Ahram Weekly May 23, 1991; (London) Daily Telegraph November 4, 1989; Guardian September 1, 1989; Independent August 12, 1990; November 24, 1990; Times Literary Supplement September 15, 1989.

*ANAYA, RUDOLFO A(LFONSO) (October 30, 1937–), Mexican-American novelist, playwright, poet, and writer of short stories writes: "I was born in Pastura, a very small village on the eastern plains of New Mexico. My family moved to Santa Rosa on the Pecos River, where I spent my childhood. During the Second World War, Santa Rosa, on the busy Highway 66, was a thriving town—the social, cultural and political center for the ranches and small communities which surrounded the town. My parents were both born and raised in the village of

°ah NY ah

RUDOLFO ANAYA

Puerto de Luna, a largely Hispanic farming community, which was destined to be deserted after the war.

"Puerto de Luna and Pastura figure large in my first novel, *Bless Me, Ultima*. I grew up in a Catholic household speaking only Spanish. Our family was large; the extended family of aunts and uncles and friends was even larger. Our home was a center of activity, a place where the extended family came to visit, to pause for rest during a trip, to tell stories.

"I now know that I received my instinct for storytelling from those early years when I listened to the simple stories of the friends of the family. The war made a deep impression. The people I knew were poor, hard workers, mostly unschooled and at the mercy of change. Moving into the English-speaking world was a difficult transition for the old Nuevo Mexicanos from the villages; my parents never quite made the adjustment. That pragmatic challenge was left to my generation.

"The suffering of the people was evident in their lives and stories. I listened to people; I was enthralled by their stories. It was a wonderful thing to be in that milieu receiving the word of the folk.

"I loved school, even though for someone like me who had lived in a Spanish-speaking world, it was a difficult journey. I loved nature. The hills surrounding the town and the river valley were my home. In my first novel I tried to capture the influence of nature, the church, family, good and evil, the nature of God, dreams, childhood friends, and the stirring of sexuality. I tried to capture the old values and heritage of a village culture which was threatened with extinction. I still use much of that worldview of my indigenous ancestors in my work; in fact my work portrays a clash of world views—the Anglo-American, in which I live and work, and the traditional Nuevo Mexicano culture of the region.

"In 1952 my family moved to Albuquerque. We lived in the Barelas barrio. Learning life on the urban streets was exciting, and sometimes dangerous. Two years later, while swimming in an irrigation ditch in the valley, I seriously hurt my back. I was in a hospital for the summer, and out of that experience came my third novel, *Tortuga*.

"I stayed close to my family, finished high school, then got a B.A. at the University of New Mexico. I became a teacher. During my time at the university I started writing. By the time the Chicano Movement came around in the mid-sixties, I had completed the manuscript *Bless Me, Ultima*.

"In 1966 I married Patricia Lawless. We began to travel. We both wanted to see the world, and fortunately we have. From China to South America to Europe to Africa, we've touched base with other cultures, other ways of seeing. Sooner or later all that goes into the novels, the stories, the plays.

"I now teach at the University of New Mexico. I feel very fortunate to have stayed close to home. My spirit is imbued by the people and earth of New Mexico. The majority of my work deals with the themes life had dealt me. I'm interested in the people, the changes which motivate peoples' lives, the various cultures of the Southwest, the folktales and folk wisdom, and the mythology of the Americas. I have taught myself to look within; a writer is a philosopher of life.

"My new work has taken me into a quartet of novels based in the city of Albuquerque, where I live. The first two novels, *Albuquerque* and *Zia Summer*, are written. I'm at work on the third. I'm also writing short stories and plays, and again the themes deal with indigenous cultural elements and the process of returning them to the community by creating art from them. As much as I can, I lecture nationally and internationally.

"Writing helps shape my universe. One works from experience into vision, from the way things are into what they might be. At the core of all good stories is an exploration of our human condition."

In 1981, Alan Cheuse pointed out, in the *New York Times Book Review* the irony of the fact that while Chicanos are descendants of some of the earliest immigrants to the United States, their culture was virtually unknown outside the Southwest until the first stirrings of multiculturalism in the 1960s. Among Chicano writers today, Rudolfo Anaya is one of the best, not only for his fiction, which is strongly rooted in his Mexican heritage, but also for his essays, lectures, and articles on his region and his people. He recalled that when he began his career, he had no Chicano models whose writing he could draw on. He had to emerge from that vacuum of influence on his own, drawing only on his own imagination and heritage.

Bless Me, Ultima, Anaya's first novel, is based upon its author's childhood memories. Like Antonio, his protagonist, Anaya was born and spent his early years on the llanos, the windswept plains of eastern New Mexico. His father, Martin, was a vaquero, a hardworking ranch hand; his mother, born Rafaelita Mares, was a farmer's daughter. The family spoke only Spanish at home; the children did not learn English until they went to school. Also like Antonio, Anaya had two older brothers who left home to fight in World War II. From his early childhood he absorbed the legends of His Mexican and Indian heritage as well as the strict Catholic teachings of his mother, who wanted him to become a priest. He had a happy childhood, roaming freely in the rugged Southwest countryside, and he early developed a passion for this region that is reflected in his writing—a sense of an animated nature, mysterious, challenging and dangerous, beautiful but demanding. Anaya excelled in his school studies and learned English quickly. He also learned his first lessons in self-consciousness, becoming aware that as a Mexican-American he was somehow different from the Anglos in the school.

The Anaya family moved to the barrio in Albuquerque when Rudolfo was fifteen; there he learned a totally new way of life—how to survive the street life of a city. These experiences figured in his second novel, *Heart of Aztlán*. He survived a serious spinal injury in a swimming accident that left him immobilized for months—yet he made a full recovery and graduated from Albuquerque High School in 1956. Already fascinated by books—everything from Dante, Shakespeare, and Milton to Walt Whitman and the moderns—he began to write poetry, but it was some time before he found his direction as a writer. From 1956 to 1958 Anaya attended business school planning to become an accountant, but in spite of financial problems, he decided to enroll in the University of Mexico to study English and American literature. He received his B.A. in 1963, then supported his graduate studies by teaching in the Albuquerque public schools. In 1968 he received an M.A. in literature; in 1972 he took another M.A., this one in guidance and counseling, working meanwhile as director of the Counseling Center of the University of Albuquerque. During these years, Anaya worked on a novel that was to become *Bless Me, Ultima*. Publishers showed little interest in the manuscript, but in 1972 he learned of a competition sponsored by a new press, Quinto Sol Publications, for the best novel by a Chicano. He submitted his novel, which won the Premio Quinto Sol and was published by that press. At first it was appreciated only by the Chicano community, but its fame spread quickly. Over the years it was reprinted many times; by 1990 it had sold well over 200,000 copies and won a place on the reading lists of many high school and college literature courses.

"This is a remarkable book," Scott Wood wrote in *America*, " . . . for its communication of tender emotion and powerful spirituality without being mawkish or haughty, for its eloquent presentation of Chicano consciousness in all its intriguing complexity; finally, for being an American novel which accomplished a harmonious resolution, transcendent and hopeful." Most remarkable about *Bless Me, Ultima* is its juxtaposition of the folklore of Indian culture with the realistic portrait of a Chicano boy in the years during and just after World War II. Often described as a bildungsroman (though in fact it ends when its central charter is only ten years old), it filters the child's memories through the consciousness of a mature narrator. This is no idyllic pastoral romance. The child Antonio grows up in a world always threatened by violence, superstition, and poverty. He is sheltered, however, by a loving family and by an old woman, Ultima, who comes to live with them. She is a *curandera*, a healer, possessing shaman-like powers to combat evil. Her gentle but firm guidance awakens the boy's sensitivity to nature and to humankind alike. "I felt more attached to Ultima than to my own mother," he recalls. Ultima told me the stories and legends of my ancestors. From her I learned the glory and the tragedy of the history of my people, and I came to understand how that history stirred in my blood." With her death at the end of the novel, the child grieves but knows that he had the strength that will shape his future: "Around me the moonlight glittered on the pebbles of the *llano*, and in the night sky a million stars sparkled. Across the river I could see the twinkling lights of the town. In a week I would be returning to school, and as always I would be running up the goat path and cross the bridge to go to church. Some time in the future I would have to build my own dream out of those things that were so much a part of my childhood."

The publication of *Bless Me, Ultima* marked the appearance of new spirit in Chicano literature. "It stood in stark contrast to the shrill polemics that emerged from the political cauldron of the 1960s and attempted to pass for literature," Antonio Márquez wrote in *The Magic of Words*. Reviewers noted the painstaking craft of the novelist here, but what impressed them most was what Vernon E. Lattin described, in *American Literature*, as "a new romanticism, with a reverence for the land, a transcendent optimism, and a sense of mythic wholeness."

Reviewing the reissue of *Bless Me Ultima* in 1994, Ray Gonzalez commented in the *Nation* that the novel "set the stage for the unique Chicano genre of Catholic-pagan fiction. The now-familiar elements include a supernatural environment, a questioning of traditional Christian values and the presence of a strong mother figure to perplex and guide the young protagonist through his life." He added that with the wisdom of hindsight, "it is clear that Antonio's apprenticeship at the hands of Ultima is part of the natural evolution of Mexican-American culture. The boy's awareness of good and evil still reverberates in our hearts. . . . Anaya recognizes that the Latino world is fluid and mysterious and can only be re-created by playing with time and the unpredictable environment that surreal-religious forces create in the lives of all, the young and the elderly, the isolated and the social, the powerful and the weak."

William Clark in *Publishers Weekly* termed *Bless Me, Ultima* "the seminal Chicano coming-of-age novel." Its themes, Clark noted, "spirituality and healing; Chicano tradition and myth; the sacredness of the land; the role of shaman-like figures as mentors and guides; and the quest for personal, communal and cultural identity," remained Anaya's concerns throughout his career.

In his preoccupation with the roots of his culture and its mythopoeic symbols, Anaya had clearly absorbed Jung's theory of the "collective unconscious." As he told an interviewer in *New America* in 1979: "One way I have of looking at my own work . . . is through a sense that I have about primal images, primal imageries. A sense that I have about the archetypal, about what we once must have known collectively. What we all share is a kind of collective memory."

Anaya addressed the problems of Chicanos transplanted from the plains to the urban barrios in his second novel, *Heart of Aztlán*, but—in the judgement of most of his reviewers—with less success. Márquez found the novel "less polished, less accomplished," noting its "disjointed and amorphous style which contrasts with the meticulous, controlled and carefully executed prose of Anaya's other works." The center of this novel is again a young boy who witnesses the struggles of his family when they move from a small farm which can no longer support them to Albuquerque in the early 1950s. As in *Bless Me, Ultima*, a visionary character, a blind street musician this time, saves them from complete destruction and points the way to a better future.

Tortuga, Anaya's third novel was based on his experiences after he suffered a severe back injury in a diving accident when he was a teenager. The novel is set in a sanatorium for crippled young people located at the base of a mountain call Tortuga (Turtle). Its central character, a teenage boy who has been injured in an accident, is given the name Tortuga because he must wear a huge body cast that covers him like a turtle's shell. Here, reviewers agreed, Anaya successfully blended the mythic and realistic. The mountain become a symbol of the independence that the boy will finally achieve when, after much suffering, he is freed from his cast and is able to walk. Around him are characters who represent real suffering victims but are also archetypal figures. They are all, in turn, surrounded by elemental nature—the mountain, the sky, changing seasons, and water, which becomes a spiritual agent in the boy's cure. *Tortuga* won the Before Columbus American Book Award in 1979.

Anaya has continued to write fiction, including a novel about the legend of Quetzalcoatl, *Lord of the Dawn*, and several plays, one a dramatization of one of his short stories, *The Season of La Llorona*, produced in Albuquerque in 1979; he has also written a screenplay on bilingual education that was produced on television. He has collected folktales from the Southwest and is the editor of several anthologies of stories and essays about this region. His poem *The Adventures of Juan Chicaspatas* is about a mythic quest for an Aztec goddess. It incorporates Spanish and local Chicano slang, the language of the barrio, into the lofty diction of the epic—an incongruous but effective technique that reminds readers of the color and vitality of the community. A Chicano "homeboy," the speaker celebrates María Juana, "diosa de los locos."

In addition to traveling widely in the United States and Europe, Anaya spent a month in China in 1984 on a W. F. Kellogg Foundation fellowship. His journal of that trip, published as *A Chicano in China*, reflects his ongoing quest for a common mythology that unites people of different cultures. He writes: "I know now why I went to China. I went to make those connections to points of love which exist in my soul. I went to connect my dream to the people of China . . . to share my love with them and to take their love. As I was taught, I hope to teach others to see into the soul of things, to make that simple, human connection, which unites us all."

In *Alburquerque*, the first of a quartet of "seasonal" novels, Anaya introduces a real-estate development scheme to divert the Rio Grande and create a southwestern "Venice" that endangers the way of life of the Hispanic and Indian communities in the region and threatens their traditions. Antonya Nelson, reviewing the novel in the *New York Times Book Review*, deemed it "lacking in specificity" and overladen with characters and points of view. She concluded, however, that some of the magical scenes involving a coyote spirit and various *curanderas* "are wonderfully told and mesmerizing."

Sonny Baca, Anaya's first P.I., confronts a terrorist cult responsible for the murder of his cousin and first lover in *Zia Summer*. She has been found with a *zia* sun sign carved on her body. The *Publishers Weekly* reviewer commented that "Anaya blends elements of nuclear wast-management and ancient tradition with considerable credibility . . . but best here is Sonny's convincing attachment to the land and the traditions that have shaped him."

Since 1974 Anaya has been professor in the English department of the University of New Mexico, teaching literature and creative writing. He lectures and publishes frequently on multiculturalism and bilingual education, emphasizing the importance of an all-embracing humanistic philosophy. While he urges his fellow Chicanos to "learn what you really are," he does not reject Anglo-American culture. Rather, he seeks to incorporate it into a worldview in which all cultures are components.

In his interview with William Clark in *Publishers Weekly* he summed up his views: "What I've wanted to do is compose the Chicano worldview—the synthesis that shows our true *mestizo* identity—and clarify it for my community and for myself. Writing for me is a way of knowledge, and what I find illuminates my life." The role of the writer, he concludes, may be to be the spiritual guide that his characters find in his novels.

PRINCIPAL WORKS: *Novels*—Bless Me, Ultima, 1972; Heart of Aztlán, 1976; Tortuga, 1979; Lord of the Dawn, 1987; Desolina, 1991; Alburquerque, 1992; Zia Summer, 1995. *Short stories*—The Silence of the Llano, 1982. *As editor-translator*—Cuentos: Tales from the Hispanic Southwest, 1980; (with A. Márquez) Cuentos Chicanos: A Short Story Anthology, 1984; Voces: An Anthology of Nuevo Mexicano Writers, 1987; (with F. Lomeli) Atzlán: Essays on the Chicano Homeland, 1989; Tierra: Contemporary Short Fiction of New Mexico, 1989. *Poetry*—The Adventures of Juan Chicaspatas. *Journal*—A Chicano in China, 1986. *Nonfiction*—A Ceremony of Brotherhood, 1680–1980, 1981. *Juvenile*—(with E. Gonzáles) The Farolitos of Christmas, 1995.

ABOUT: Bruce-Novoa, J. Chicano Authors, 1980; Contemporary Authors Autobiography Series 4, 1986; Contemporary Authors New Revision Series 1, 1981; Contemporary Literary Criticism 23, 1983; Contemporary Novelists 4th ed., 1986; Dictionary of Literary Biography 82, 1989; Lattin, V. E. Contemporary Chicano Fiction, 1986; Meier, M. S. Mexican American Biographies, 1836–1987, 1988; Mogen, D. (ed.) The Frontier Experience and the American Dream, 1989; Vassallo, P. (ed.) The Magic of Words: Rudolfo Anaya and His Writings, 1982; Who's Who Among Hispanic American Writers, 1992. *Periodicals*—American January 27, 1973; American Literature January 1979; Genre Fall 1988; Melus Winter 1984; Nation July 18, 1994; New American Spring 1979; New York Times Book Review October 11, 1981; November 29, 1992; Ploughshares 4, 1978; Publishers Weekly October 12, 1990; April 10, 1995; June 5, 1995; South Dakota Review Winter 1988.

ANTHONY, PIERS (August 6, 1934–), American (British born) science-fiction novelist, writes: "I was born in Oxford, England, in Aw-Ghost 1934. My parents both graduated from the University at Oxford, but I was slow from the outset. I spent time with relatives and a nanny while my parents went to do relief work in Spain during the Spanish civil war of 1936–1939. They were helping to feed the children rendered hungry by the devastation of the war. When that ended, my sister and I joined them in Spain. I left my native country at the age of four—and never returned. The new government of General Franco in Spain, evidently error-prone and suspicious of foreigners doing good works, arrested my father in 1940. They refused to admit that they had done so, making him in effect a 'disappeared' person, but he was able to smuggle out a note. Then, rather than admit error, they let him out on condition that he leave the country. World War II was then in progress, so instead of returning to England, we went to my father's country. In this manner I came to America at age six, on what I believe was the last ship out. Though I was too young to understand what was going on, in time I learned, and I retain an abiding hostility to dictatorships.

"My parents' marriage grew strained and finally foundered. Suffering the consequences of

PIERS ANTHONY

separation from my first country and my second country, as well as the stress of a family going wrong, I showed an assortment of complications such as nervous tics of the head and hands, bed-wetting, and inability to learn. It required three years and five schools to get me through first grade. I later gained intellectual ground, but lost physical ground. When I entered my ninth school in ninth grade I was at the proper level but not the proper size, being the smallest person, male or female, in my class. However, boarding school, and later college, became a better home for me than what I had had, and I managed to grow almost another foot by the time I got my B.A. in Writing at Goddard College, Vermont, in 1956. This was just as well, because I married a tall girl I met in college; I had to grow, literally, to meet the challenge.

"I had the hodgepodge of employments typical of writers. Of about fifteen types of work I tried, ranging from aide at a mental hospital to technical writer at an electronics company, only one truly appealed: the least successful. But the dream remained. Finally in 1962 my wife agreed to go to work for a year, so that I could stay home and try to write fiction full-time. The agreement was that if I did not manage to sell anything, I would give up the dream and focus on supporting my family. As it happened, I sold two stories, earning $160. But such success seemed inadequate to earn a living. So I became an English teacher, didn't like that either, and in 1966 retired again to writing. This time I wrote novels instead of stories, and with them I was able to earn a living. As with the rest of my

life, progress was slow, but a decade later I got into light fantasy with the first of my ongoing Xanth series of novels, *A Spell for Chameleon,* and that proved to be the golden ring. My sales and income soared, and I became one of the most successful writers of the genre, with twenty *New York Times* paperback best-sellers in the space of a decade. This enabled us to send our two daughters to college, and drove the wolf quite far from our door. We now live on a tree farm, and would love to have a wolf by our door, but do have deer and other wildlife. I am an environmentalist. My autobiography to age fifty, *Bio of an Ogre,* is now in print; there may be a sequel in time.

"But a writer does not live by frivolous fantasy alone. Today I am turning back to serious writing with direct comment on sexual abuse in *Firefly,* and on history in novels like *Tatham Mound,* which relates to the fate of the American Indians, and *Volk,* which shows love and death in civil-war Spain and World War II Germany. So I close the circle, returning in my writing to the realm I left as a child. My literary personality is splitting, with the fantasy paying my way in Caesar's coin, and the historical research addressing the god of this agnostic. There has always been a serious side to my writing, even in my fantasy, and my readers respond to it. I answer a hundred to two hundred letters a month, so remain in close touch with them. They tell me that I have taught many to read, by showing them that reading could be fun, and that I have saved the lives of some, by addressing concerns such as suicide. So I date my letters with my fantasy months, such as 'AwGhost,' 'OctOgre,' and 'FeBlueberry,' but take my readers as seriously as I take my writing. In fact I am a workaholic, and I love my profession. I have, of course, an ongoing battle with critics, who see only the frivolous level; it is doubtful whether my work will ever in my lifetime receive critical applause, but I believe in its validity for the longer haul. So do my readers."

———

Anthony is confident that his populist approach is the surest method of communicating his vision to a broad audience. He is proud to call himself a commercial writer. His devotion to his readers, and theirs to him, is extraordinary, as evidenced by his voluminous correspondence. In "Think of the Reader," an essay which concludes his short story collection *Alien Plot,* Anthony writes, "But I maintain that the essence of literature lies in its assimilation by the ordinary folk, and that readability is the first, not the last criterion for its merit . . . . I am successful in part because I make connections with my readers that bypass the editors as well as the critics." The respect Anthony has for his readers stands in stark contrast to the disdain he exhibits towards critics. While critics have accused Anthony of a multitude of sins—from an overfondness for puerile puns to a general hokeyness—the author remains undeterred, and rarely misses an opportunity to fire back. "I do know my market, and it is not the critics," he observes elsewhere in "Think of the Reader."

Chthon, Anthony's first published novel, was well-received, if not widely reviewed. The novel's protagonist, Anton Five, struggles to escape from the subterranean garnet mines of a hellish planet where he is a prisoner. The name of the planet, Chthon, comes from the Greek word for the infernal regions. Anton's ascent from the underworld of Chthon recalls mythic and religious accounts of such journeys. In the course of his trek, Anton encounters sundry monsters (giant jellyfish) and preternatural forces (scorching gale-force winds). Eventually, he makes contact with the planet Chthon itself, which he discovers to be a sentient mineral entity. Some of Chthon's problems, he learns, result from environmental disasters that could have been prevented. This theme—the fragile and symbiotic relationship between man and his environment—recurs in almost all of Anthony's work. *Publishers Weekly* (1967) called *Chthon* "a busy and ingenious combination of the elements of myth, poetry, folk song, symbolism, suspense story—a bursting package, almost too much for one book, but literate, original and entertaining." *Chthon* was nominated for two major science fiction awards, the Hugo and the Nebula.

The environmental theme is also prominent in *Macroscope*. The macroscope enables human beings to witness the entire space-time continuum as a single phenomenon. It unveils not only the "macro-" aspects of the universe, but the "micro-" ones as well, and has the power to reveal the depths of the subconscious mind and its myriad desires. The macroscope exposes human beings to a terrifying, sometimes mind-destroying, realization—their relative insignificance in the vastness of the universe. By suggesting parallels between the insignificance of humans in the universe and the insignificance of individuals in mass society, Anthony draws attention to the need for a humane human ecology. In *Twentieth Century Science Fiction Writers*, Craig Wallace Barrow says of *Macroscope*, "Not only does the novel deal with environmentalism on earth and the effects of disastrous population growth, but it shows the necessity for a mental environmentalism in the group's interactions." Although *Macroscope* re-

ceived little critical attention at the time of its publication, it was nominated for a Hugo Award and is now widely considered to be one of Anthony's most important novels.

Anthony is best known for his many series of science fiction and fantasy novels. The ongoing Xanth fantasy series is set in the magical kingdom of Xanth, a peninsular realm with a pronounced geographical resemblance to Florida, Anthony's home state for many years. Xanth is replete with fanciful flora (cookie bushes and shoe trees) and other-worldly fauna (dragons, centaurs, nymphs, and ogres). The outside, nonmagical, world is referred to as Mundania, with which Xanthians have occasional contact.

In *A Spell for Chameleon*, the first novel in the series, a young mortal named Bink sets out to discover whether he has magical powers. His special power, he learns, is that he cannot be harmed by magic. In the second novel, *The Source of Magic*, Bink is sent by the King of Xanth to find the provenance of the kingdom's magical powers. A *Publishers Weekly* (1978) reviewer said of *The Source of Magic*, "The characters and the prose have a penchant for cuteness; this is the central problem of the book. Nevertheless, the novel is redeemed by its inventiveness and charm." *Library Journal* reviewer Rosemary Herbert found the novel "a delightful sequel to *A Spell for Chameleon*," but expressed some concern over Anthony's use of sexual stereo-types. "Although female characterization is almost offensively stereotyped (Bink's wife has two distinct personalities: 'beautiful-stupid' and 'smart-ugly'!), nimble action makes this book a charmer."

One salient aspect of Anthony's writing is the prevalence of puns. Not only are the texts awash in puns, but many of the titles in series, such as the Xanth novels, are themselves puns: *Centaur Aisle*, *Crewel Lye*, and *Isle of View*. The Xanth novels, best-sellers, especially but not exclusively among adolescents, demonstrate that Anthony has evidently found a large and appreciative audience for his brand of humor. Some reviewers of books for young people have seemed almost insulted by Anthony's popularity. Reviewing *Ogre, Ogre*, the fifth Xanth novel, in *Voice of Youth Advocates*, Peggy Murray commented, "Those looking for the beauty and subtlety of high fantasy will not find it here, but Piers Anthony's stories, full of sophomoric humor and bad puns, have tremendous appeal with YA fantasy readers." Reviewing the sixth Xanth novel, *Night Mare* in *Voice of Youth Advocates*, Christy Tyson wrote, "More discerning readers may find that the humor is becoming just a bit strained and the action just a bit contrived."

While the Xanth series is quintessential fantasy literature, other series, such as Cluster and Bio of a Space Tyrant, are pure science fiction. In the Adept series, Anthony weaves together elements of both science fiction and fantasy. He does so by shifting his protagonist, Stile, between alternate worlds, Proton and Phaze. The former is ruled by science and technology, the latter by magic alone. Of the third novel in the Adept series, *Best Sellers* reviewer Paul Granahan remarked, "*Juxtaposition*, a work which combines both science fiction and fantasy, provides ample opportunity for [Anthony] to demonstrate his skill in each field." Although he deemed *Juxtaposition* "a lot of fun," Granahan wished "Anthony, with his obvious talent, would attempt deeper endeavors."

Roland Green, reviewing *Alien Plot*, a book of short stories with a nonfiction piece, pointed out Anthony's preoccupation with pleasing his audience, "The article is a cogent, sharply worded essay on authors keeping in touch with their readers" as well as his differences with critics and "persistent self-justification." He concludes that Anthony is "right in saying that critics have gone on dismissing him too long and too loudly." As Anthony himself said in an afterword to *Killobyte*, "Each novel is an adventure in itself, for the author as well as the reader...."

Anthony, the son of Alfred Bennis and Norma (Sherlock) Jacob, married Carol Marble in 1956. They have two daughters and live in Florida.

PRINCIPAL WORKS: *Novels*—Chthon, 1967; (with R. E. Margroff) The Ring, 1968; Macroscope, 1969; (with R. E. Margroff) The E.S.P. Worm, 1970; Prostho Plus, 1971; (with R. Fuentes) Kiai!, 1974; (with R. Fuentes) Mistress of Death, 1974; (with R. Fuentes) Bamboo Bloodbath, 1974; Rings of Ice, 1974; Triple Detente, 1974; Phthor (sequel to Chthon) 1975; (with R. Fuentes) Ninja's Revenge, 1975; Steppe, 1976; (with R. Fuentes) Amazon Slaughter, 1976; (with R. Coulson) But What of Earth?, 1976; Hasan, 1977; (with F. T. Hall) Pretender, 1979; Mute, 1981; Ghost, 1986; Shade of the Tree, 1986; (with R. Margroff) Dragon's Gold, 1987; (with R. Margroff) Serpent's Silver, 1989; (with R. Kornwise) Through the Ice, 1989; Pornucopia, 1989; Total Recall, 1989; Firefly, 1990; Hard Sell, 1990; Balook, 1990; (with R. Fuentes) Dead Morn, 1990; (with R. Margroff) Chimera's Copper, 1990; (with R. Margroff) Orc's Opal, 1990; Mercycle, 1991; Tatham Mound, 1991; (with P. J. Farmer) Caterpillar's Question, 1992; (with R. Margroff) Mouvar's Magic, 1992; If I Pay Thee Not in Gold, 1993; Isle of Women, 1993; Killobyte, 1993; (with R. Margroff) Three Complete Novels: Dragon's Gold, Serpent's Silver, and Chimera's Copper, 1993; Harpy Thyme, 1994. *Series*—"Apprentice Adept"—Split Infinity, 1980; Blue Adept, 1981; Juxtaposition, 1982; Out of Phaze, 1987; Robot Adept, 1988; Unicorn Point, 1989; Phase Doubt, 1990; Double Exposure (contains first three novels) 1982. "Battle Circle"—Sos the Rope, 1968; Var the Stick, 1972; Neq the Sword, 1975; Battle Circle (contains entire series) 1978. "Bio of a Space Tyrant"—Refugee, 1983; Mercenary, 1984; Politician, 1985; Executive, 1985; Statesman, 1986. "Cluster"—Cluster, 1977 (in U.K. Vicinity Cluster, 1979); Chaining the Lady, 1978; Kirlian Quest, 1978; Thousandstar, 1980; Viscous Circle, 1982. "Incarnations of Immortality"—On a Pale Horse, 1983; Bearing an Hourglass, 1984; With a Tangled Skein, 1985; Wielding a Red Sword, 1987; Being a Green Mother, 1987; For Love of Evil, 1988; And Eternity, 1990. "Magic of Xanth"—A Spell for Chameleon, 1977; The Source of Magic, 1979; Castle Roogna, 1979; Centaur Aisle, 1981; The Magic of Xanth (contains first three novels) 1981; Ogre, Ogre, 1982; Night Mare, 1983; Dragon on a Pedestal, 1983; Crewel Lye: A Caustic Yarn, 1985; Golem in the Gears, 1986; Vale of the Vole, 1987; Heaven Cent, 1988; Man from Mundania, 1989; (with J. L. Nye) Visual Guide to Xanth, 1989; Isle of View, 1990; Question Quest, 1991; The Color of Her Panties, 1992; Demons Don't Dream, 1993; "Mode"—Virtual Mode, 1991; Fractal Mode, 1992; Chaos Mode, 1994. "Omnivore"—Omnivore, 1968; Orn, 1971; Ox, 1976. "Tarot"—God and Tarot, 1979; Vision of Tarot, 1980; Faith of Tarot, 1980; Tarot (contains all three novels) 1988; Killobyte, 1993. *Short Stories*—Anthology, 1985; (with B. Malzberg et. al.) Uncollected Stars, 1986; Alien Plot, 1992. *Juvenile*—Race Against Time, 1973. *Autobiography*—Bio of an Ogre, 1988. *Correspondence*—Letters to Jenny, 1993.

ABOUT: Collings, M. Piers Anthony, 1983; Contemporary Authors New Revision Series 28, 1990; Contemporary Literary Criticism 35, 1988; Dictionary of Literary Biography 8, 1981; Twentieth Century Science Fiction Writers 1981. *Periodicals*—Best Sellers July 1982; Fantasy Review March 1984; Library Journal February 15, 1979; New York Times Book Review April 20, 1986; Publishers Weekly June 5, 1967; December 11, 1978; Voice of Youth Advocates April 1983; June 1983.

*ANTUNES, ANTÓNIO LOBO (September 1, 1942–), Portuguese novelist, was born and raised in Lisbon, and as a young boy, spent summers in the rural province of Beira Alta. Following in the steps of his father, a well-known neurologist and a professor at the Lisbon School of Medicine, Antunes took a medical degree with a speciality in psychiatry, a profession he still practices on a part-time basis. From 1971 to 1973 he served as an army doctor in Angola, where the Portuguese spent almost fifteen years fighting a demoralizing and ultimately unpopular war—similar in many respects to the Vietnam War—in a doomed attempt to maintain control over the centuries-old colony. The colonial war and his job at a psychiatric hospital, coupled with childhood memories and his expe-

°ahn TOO ness

ANTÓNIO LOBO ANTUNES

riences in relationships (he has been twice married and twice divorced), have provided most of the author's fictional raw material, particularly in his earliest books.

Antunes the writer began in verse, having published a poem in a Lisbon newspaper at age fourteen, and he is an assiduous reader of poetry to this day. He switched to writing fiction when he was studying at the university, producing and destroying various novels until he finally published *Memória do Elefante* (Elephant memory, 1979) at thirty seven. This book's protagonist, like the author, is a psychiatrist who did a stint as a medic in the colonial wars. Almost exactly in the middle of the narrative we learn that "between the Angola he had lost and the Lisbon he had not regained the doctor felt like a two-time orphan, and this initial sense of displacement had gotten progressively more painful, because much had changed in his absence." this anxious feeling of in-betweenness, of not really belonging anywhere except perhaps in the secure world of a childhood that exists only in memory, constantly plagues the main characters of Antunes's fictional world.

His second published novel, *Os Cus de Judas* (1979, *South of Nowhere*), brought him international recognition, with editions in more than a dozen countries and languages. Artur Lundkvist, of the Swedish Academy, said of the book: "Every page is an inspired prose poem which surpasses all ordinary storytelling. It is rare that a work of prose should be so rich in associations in all directions, with literary and artistic connections that so astonishingly widen our con-

sciousness and give fresh outlooks at every turn. When now a new Portuguese author such as this suddenly appears, he surprises us by his unusual experiences, his extraordinarily distinctive talent, by his bold style and sophisticated expressionism, by the combination of merciless realism and ever playful imagination."

The story is a restless monologue told by a lonely Angolan war veteran to a lonely woman he meets in a bar, "like a hermit who meets another hermit during a plague of locusts." As they drink Scotch after Scotch he tells his forever silent listener of the horrors of his military service, but more disquieting than the war's outward violence is the intimate horror of its stupidity, of the fact that thousands die or are maimed or return home—like the narrator—with a broken spirit to a broken marriage and slim hopes for the future merely because of a government's desire to preserve national honor. But if the war seems senseless, so do many interpersonal relationships, and the narrator weaves into his tale the accounts of his frustrated loves. Even the camaraderie he established with his fellow soldiers ends, on their arrival at Lisbon's airport, with "a handshake, a slap on the shoulders, a feeble embrace," and they go their separate ways, each man lugging his own baggage, "to vanish into the whirlwind of the city." The narrator, who has spent time in a mental hospital since his release from the army, is like a soul fallen through the cracks, with nothing solid to hang on to that might give him real or imagined meaning. Indeed, what could be more meaningless than his encounter with the silent woman, whom he eventually takes to his apartment for a perfunctory one-night stand?

Antunes was the first Portuguese novelist to describe in forthright detail the colonial war experience, but his critical success had less to do with what he said than with how he said it. Antunes broke radically with the traditional molds of Portuguese fiction, and if something of Faulkner and Céline can be found in his layering of times and places (Faulkner) and in his inventive and highly colloquial use of language (Céline), he had brought other things to his writing: a unique narrative voice, which is perhaps inevitable in any great writer, but also a new, highly visual prose style. Considering that he is sometimes cited in reviews as a successor to the mature James Joyce, not exactly light reading, it is remarkable that Antunes's books sell thousands of copies in a tiny country with one of Europe's highest illiteracy rates. In fact the kinship between *Ulysses* and *South of Nowhere* or Antunes's subsequent novels does not go very far beyond the so-called stream-of-consciousness technique. Joyce employs a battery of erudite references and difficult word games which, in their full-blown mode as found in *Finnegans Wake*, are apt to discourage even the well-informed and persevering reader. Antunes's fiction is culturally "lowbrow," requiring that the reader merely be able to visualize and take delight in the extravagant metaphors, such as the Angolan war veteran's remark to the woman he has just taken to bed: "I will penetrate you like a humble, mangy dog trying to sleep on a doorstep, searching hopelessly for comfort on the hard wood of the steps." Later novels become increasingly complex in their narrative structure, but they remain accessible, never presupposing special knowledge on the part of the reader.

Antunes's third published novel, *Conhecimento do Inferno* Welcome to Hell, (1980), completes what is a frankly autobiographical trilogy, revisiting the battlefront in Angola but delving more particularly into the microworld of the psychiatric hospital where the author himself works.

Explicacão dos Pássaros (1981, *An Explanation of the Birds*) charts new terrain, both thematically and stylistically. The antihero, Rui S., a dumpy and less-than-brilliant history lecturer, chooses no to follow in the steps of his father, a wealthy industrialist. After being rejected by his first wife, a woman of his own social class, Rui seeks meaning and solace in leftist politics, and takes up with lower-class Marilia, described by the ex-wife as "one of those pitiful Communists who wear red ponchos and clacking clogs." Despite this liaison, the party faithful never accept incurably bourgeois Rui into their midst. Realizing that they have little in common, Rui decides to dump Marilia, but she beats him to the punch, crowning his despair with humiliation. *Explanation* is on one level an anatomy of Rui's suicide, but the larger object of dissection is Portuguese society. This operation is masterfully achieved through what the author himself terms his "polyphonic" technique, in which crisscrossing voices belonging to various characters in various time periods constitute the narrative web. First applied in *Conhecimento*, the technique is perfected here and has become a hallmark of virtually all Antunes's later novels. David Unger, in the *New York Times Book Review*, called the novel "a richly imaginative work. . . . the timeless story of a man whose life has come unraveled." He concluded, "And as the story rushes to a close, its central, final act achieves an equally timeless and haunting power."

Fado Alexandrino (1983, translated *Fado Alexandrino*) is the author's most capacious work, inviting comparison with Tolstoy or Gogol, two of the writers Antunes most admires.

Like *War and Peace* or *Dead Souls*, *Fado* attempts to depict a nation and an age—Portugal in the transition years of 1972 to 1982—and the book is soberly divided into three twelve-chapter sections titled "Before the Revolution," "During the Revolution," and "After the Revolution." But within the bounds of this formal structure, which evokes the wistful *fados* sung in strict alexandrines by blind women on Lisbon's streets, the narrative pitches torrentially from voice to voice. Occurring within a time frame of less than twenty-four hours, this is not a sprawling fresco in the manner of the 19th-century Russian classics but a kind of obsessive *Guernica* set on paper, a chaotic record of war's ravages. Four war veterans representing diverse social strata meet at a military reunion in Lisbon, where they recall their time spent together in combat and recount their separate life stories since returning from Africa ten years earlier. The 1974 Revolution of the Flowers (so called because the soldiers who staged it fired no shot but placed carnations in the barrels of their rifles) brought democracy to Portugal, but the emotionally maimed war veterans feel even more out of place in the new society than in the old. Ariel Dorfman commented in the *New York Times Book Review* on the technique "which juxtaposes Africa and Portugal, a rape and a funeral, yesterday and today and anticipations of a possible tomorrow." Although such juxtapositions can be confusing, according to Dorfman, "it is crucial to the author's intention of revealing the hidden, mingled layers of his nation's subconscious. . . . What is miraculous in this novel . . . is that its readers are not themselves devoured by this chaos."

Antunes won the prestigious Portuguese Writers' Association Grand Prize for Fiction with *Auto dos Danados* (1985, *Act of the Damned*), his most Faulknerian tale, about the final dissolution of a decadent aristocratic family in post revolutionary Portugal. The domineering patriarch is on his deathbed, and his mentally deficient progeny dumbly look on as their greedy in-laws scramble for an inheritance which turns out to be nothing but debts. The bankruptcy of the family reflects the economic and spiritual poverty of a country that languished for decades in "the perfectly white peace—shapeless and flat—of the Salazar dictatorship." The narrative point of view shifts from character to character, but the state of the family and of the society that engendered it is desperate from every perspective.

As Naus (1988, several chapters published in English as *The Return of the Caravels*) closes a cycle in which Portugal may be considered the overriding protagonist. The specific of this novel is the *retornados*, the Portuguese who returned to the motherland in droves when the African colonies gained their independence in the mid-1970s. In this prose sequel to Camões' *The Lusiads*, the 16th-century epic of Portuguese conquest, Vasco da Gama and the other heroes of old find themselves in the less than glorious light of the modern colonial empire's collapse. Or is it the post revolutionary *retornados* who find themselves in the "Lixbon" that was the capital of the 16th-century realm? As if to suggest that nothing much has changed in the 400 years, the caravels are surrounded by Iraqi oil boats, while slave markets flourished side by side with duty-free shops.

Antunes refers to his next three novels as the "Benfica cycle," Benfica being the suburban neighborhood of Lisbon where he grew up. The landscape and atmosphere of this cycle recall his first novel, but the center stage is now occupied by the *world* of the author's youth rather than by the author himself. In *Tratado das Paixões da Alma* (1990; first section published in English under the title *Treatise on the Passions of the Heart*, two childhood friends meet years later as involuntary adversaries in the Criminal Investigation Department—one of them an examining magistrate, the other a terrorist who is to be examined and judged. As the interrogation proceeds they share memories of when they smoked cigarettes in secret, spied on bathing women and watched storks fly across the sky, arguing so passionately over the details and the significance of their past that the clerk-typist complains she can "no longer tell who's questioning and who's answering, it's all topsy-turvy." This confusion of voices, present in varying degrees throughout most of the author's work, makes the characters equal in a certain way, reinforcing this fictional universe's deterministic—we might say behavioristic—vision: the characters are products of the story, trying in vain to assert their individual importance or else resigning themselves to life's small pleasures. *Treatise on the Passions of the Heart*, like the author's other works, celebrates passions of whatever stripe or color, and in their motley combinations, as they exist in the human heart.

A Ordem Natural das Coisas (The natural order of things, 1992), is the closest Antunes has come to writing a detective story. It is also a novel within a novel, invented by a dying woman who lives alone, filling the solitude of her waning existence with ghosts that she molds and manipulates, to stave off the thought of her approaching death. Antunes's tenth novel, *A Morte de Carlos Gardel* (The death of Carlos Gardel, 1994), is concerned with the ordinary dramas of middle-class suburbanites, and most especially of the flawed or failed loves occurring and recurring over the course of several generations. The author has pruned some of the adjectives and elaborate metaphors from his baroque style, while the novelistic structure has become more complex.

Some critics have complained that there is little goodheartedness and no salvation in Antunes's novels, his characters being motivated by greed and envy, their relationships marked more by hatred than love. Reviewing *An Explanation of the Birds* in the *Times Literary Supplement*, however, Will Eaves commented "For every sacrificial myth—or rite of blood—there is a gentle comedy of transformation"—an observation which could apply to all of Antunes's works. In contemporary novels we are not used to receiving what we experience in life: love and hate mixed together, and envy or self-interest tainting even our high-minded acts. If Antunes's works do not "elevate" us in the traditional sense, they perhaps help us to accept and appreciate the complexity and ambivalence of our natural sentiments.

In an interview published in April 1994, Antunes announced that he had reached a terminus and would strike out in a brand-new direction, both stylistically and thematically. Though he had not begun writing it, he believed that his next novel would have something to do with the "new religions."

PRINCIPAL WORKS IN ENGLISH TRANSLATION: (tr. E. Lowe) South of Nowhere, 1983; (tr. G. Rabassa) Fado Alexandrino, 1990; (parts, tr. G. Rabassa in periodicals) The Return of the Caravels, 1991; (tr. R. Zenith) An Explanation of the Birds, 1991; (tr. R. Zenith), Act of the Damned, 1993; (parts, tr. R. Zenith in a periodical) Treatise on the Passions of the Heart, 1994.

ABOUT: *Periodicals*—Choice February 1992; Guardian July 20, 1984; Harper's August 1983; Independent October 17, 1993; Literary Review (London) December 1983; New York Times Book Review July 24, 1983; July 29, 1990; August 18, 1991; Times Literary Supplement September 11, 1992; October 22, 1993.

APPLEMAN, PHILIP (DEAN) (February 8, 1926–), American poet, novelist, and essayist, writes: "A lot depends on when you were born, and where. Being born in 1926 meant that my active memory began in 1929, just in time for the stock market crash and the ensuing twelve harsh years of depression. And it meant that I was of military age in time for World War II. Growing up in the gloom of the depression and the Great War wouldn't be any reasonable person's first choice, but there were compensations. Families pinched and squeezed by hard times often developed a defensive toughness, but just

PHILIP APPLEMAN

as often demonstrated the compassion that comes from being all-in-the-same-boat. And the war, terrible as it was, had a positive, unifying effect on a country that had, in its long economic extremity, become a house divided.

"Childhood, as often as not, is a case of such mixed blessings. My family was, on the one hand, shabby-genteel, but on the other hand, upwardly aspiring: wonderful things were always, supposedly, just around the next corner. My father, an orphan who was brought up on a farm and afterward variously employed, eventually developed his own business, manufacturing and selling, single-handedly, a powerful insecticide called Banol; unfortunately, it never made him rich, as he perpetually hoped. My mother, long-suffering and cheerful throughout the depression, managed, in spite of all odds, to come up with nutritious meals and moral support—until, at age forty-five, she was stricken (and often bedridden) with rheumatoid arthritis, which tormented her for the rest of her life. Having lost an older brother and an infant brother in the 1930s, my three sisters, Barbara, Ann, and Sara, and I grew up in a sheltered and nurturing household, constantly encouraged to do well, and to do good.

"The public school in our little town of Kendallville, Indiana was staffed by underpaid and overworked teachers, many of them (like our exacting English teacher, Eva L. Robertson) single women who would, in those days, have been fired for the sin of getting married. Most of them devoted themselves to their students with an intensity that made the job seem not only worth-

while but also admirable—which may have been one reason I later opted for a teaching career myself. Those teachers taught us well, but the best thing I remember their teaching us was to 'do things right'—or anyway, as well as we could. I recalled some of that in my third novel, *Apes and Angels*, and in a number of poems.

"After graduating from high school in 1944, I went (as virtually all able-bodied young men did then) straight into the army, where, as an aviation cadet, I was slated for pilot training. But given the glut of pilots at that late stage of the war, I was put on 'temporary' assignment as a physical training instructor, a job I held until the war ended. Discharged in November, 1945, too late for the start of the college year, I decided to make up for a rather dull army career by doing a hitch in the Merchant Marine in 1946, an experience so rewarding (both from the travel itself and from having plenty of time for serious reading) that I went back to sea again in 1948-49. My first novel, *In the Twelfth Year of the War* (a love story set against an endless jungle war in the Caribbean), drew heavily on those experiences.

"All of the above shaped my life, but what really changed my life, for two reasons, was college. Northwestern University had, at the time, a specially intergrated curriculum leading to the B.A. degree. It demonstrated the complex interrelations of all of the 'fields' of knowledge in a way that was intellectually exciting, and that made me understand, for the first time, what 'education' really means.

"The other reason college changed my life was that it was at Northwestern that I met Marjorie Haberkorn, who has been my wife, friend, companion, and collaborator ever since. We met in that same B.A. program (in French class, actually), and we've been a mutual-help team ever since. She spent her junior year in Paris at the Sorbonne (while I was again in the Merchant Marine), and after we graduated, married, and spent a year at the University of Michigan, we returned to France, on a year's Fulbright scholarship to the University of Lyon. Then we came back to Northwestern, where she taught grade school and high school to support us while I finished a Ph.D. (1955), with a dissertation on 'Darwin and the Literary Critics.'

"My first academic appointment was at Indiana University, where I went through the ranks from Instructor in English to Distinguished Professor, and now Distinguished Professor Emeritus. At various times I taught at Columbia University and the State University of New York at Purchase, as well as lecturing and giving poetry readings at dozens of other campuses. Margie also taught at Indiana University, first as an Associate Instructor in French and English, while earning her master's, and later as a faculty member in the French department.

"While teaching at I.U., I cofounded (in 1957) and for eight years coedited the scholarly journal, *Victorian Studies*; coedited and contributed to the literary/historical book, *1859: Entering an Age of Crisis*, and wrote and lectured on Darwin. Always deeply involved in civil liberties issues, I cofounded the Bloomington Civil Liberties Union, served as faculty adviser to the Indiana University Civil Liberties Union, and had the privilege of marching in the first civil rights freedom march in Bloomington in 1960. I was also president of the I.U. chapter of the American Association of University Professors, and served on the national AAUP Committee on Students' Rights, and on the National Council of that organization. I also served on committees of the Indiana Council on the Arts and the National Endowment for the Humanities, including an NEH supervisory committee for a pioneering course in medical ethics at the Columbia University College of Physicians and Surgeons. I mention all this to indicate that it is not a coincidence that much of my own writing, both poetry and fiction, has had a strong social orientation.

"In 1960-61 and 1962-63, Margie and I had one of the most demanding and rewarding experiences of our lives, directing and teaching in the International School of America (which is still operating, now called the International Honors Program)—a serious, hardworking school that spends an academic year flying around the world and spending two to four weeks in various countries of Asia and Europe. Three professors (of humanities, social science, and art and archaeology) and twenty-five college students (who live with local families in each country) study the cultures of Japan, China, Thailand, India, Iran, Israel, Egypt, Turkey, Greece, Italy, Germany, Poland, Russia, France, and England. That was an exhilarating experience, from which I wrote a nonfiction book, *The Silent Explosion*, a study of the moral, political, and economic aspects of overpopulation.

"I had been writing poetry since I was eight years old, and publishing it in the little magazines since 1956, but it wasn't until 1967 that my first volume of lyrical verse, *Kites on a Windy Day*, came out in England. The following year, the Vanderbilt University Press published a bigger book of my poetry, called *Summer Love and Surf*. In those days, I was also trying my hand at playwriting, in collaboration with Margie, but eventually gave it up, whereupon Margie went on to write some wonderful plays which have been produced often in New York, Los Angeles,

and elsewhere in the United States and Canada, and as far away as Finland.

"After the mid-sixties, my books appeared with a certain regularity; in 1970, two of them: my first novel, *In the Twelfth Year of the War* (described above) and the Norton Critical Edition *Darwin*, a much-used college textbook which has gone through in its second edition and 33rd printing. In 1975 I brought out an abridged version of the *Origin of Species*. 1976 was another two-book year: the Norton Critical Edition of Malthus's *Essay on Population*, still widely used in American colleges, and my third volume of poetry, *Open Doorways*.

"In 1981 I published my second novel, *Shame the Devil*, a fanciful exploration of what might have transpired if the Vikings, in their sundry travels, had picked up the mysteries of Mithra and transported them into limestone caves of the American heartland. My fourth book of poetry, *Darwin's Ark*, brought together two of my most intense preoccupations, Darwin and poetry, and was a collaboration with the fine artist, my old friend Rudy Pozzatti, who illustrated it beautifully. In 1986, Rudy created a series of exquisite lithographs on Japanese mulberry paper, and eleven of my poems were hand-set to appear with them, in a gorgeous limited-edition boxed folio called *Darwin's Bestiary*.

"*Apes and Angels* came out in 1989, and in 1991 I published *Let There Be Light*, a rewriting of the key Bible stories, some comic, some dead-serious, in dramatic monologues and narrative poems, along with a number of lyrical poems which were inspired by the humanistic joy that Margie and I have been privileged to share.

"All of my writing—poetry, fiction, and non-fiction—is born of the interplay, development, and clashing of perception: a threshing-out of understandings (not necessarily 'ideas' as such) that causes a certain exciting vibration in my head. The difference between poetry and every-thing else I do is that it is more emotionally en-gaged than prose, and comes to me in language that thrills me more than prose. And if all of that emotion and magic also happen to be socially en-gaged, then so much the better; I published an essay in *Poets and Writers Magazine* proposing that poets permit themselves to be more open to such social/emotional experiences than our cur-rent aesthetic orthodoxy allows.

"At age sixty-six [1992] I am still writing, and am more ambitious to write than ever, as is Mar-gie, whose plays have continued to prosper in constant productions on both coasts. We remain in-house critics for each other's work, which is both pleasant and helpful. And the social compo-nent of my poetry and fiction is important to me, the more so as the often-ignored problems of overpopulation and militant religious fundamentalism continue to obstruct social improvement. There is much to be done. I hope to be around, and helping to do it, well beyond the year 2000."

Appleman's writing, prose as well as poetry, but especially the poems in *Darwin's Ark*, demonstrate that the talents of the creative writer can flourish compatibly with the work of the scientist. Appleman still owns a worn and much underlined copy of a one-volume Modern Library Giant edition of *The Origin of Species* and *The Descent of Man*, which accompanied him on his tour of duty with the Merchant Marine, opening new vistas for a young man who had grown up in a small Baptist-dominated Indiana town. Reading Darwin, he discovered "the relief of being finally released from a constrained allegiance to the incredible creative myths of genesis, the profound satisfaction in knowing that one is truly and altogether a part of nature."

In one of the poems in *Darwin's Ark*, "Nostalgie de la Boue," Appleman writes: "We go back a long time together, / Hoosiers and mud." In "Black-Footed Ferret Endangered" he acknowledges the cruelty of nature—and of human nature:

> The taste in our mouths
> is the feeding of tigers:
> we're killing off eagles, too,
> and whales.
> How it all began: the way
> our thumbs slowly came round
> to grab for the throat. . . .
>
> —and then
> the clever tools: the hand-ax,
> the motor, more dangerous
> than tigers. . . .

In the title poem Darwin dreams of the biblical Noah and his family contemplating the Lord's resolution to destroy the world in flood. "He's going to drown us all? Japheth whispers," and he protests to his father about "useless trouble, the waste, / the genocide!"

Appleman's target however, is not the inexorable forces of nature but human ignorance and superstition, and he writes more in wry humor than in anger. His version of the Ark story, Stephen Jay Gould commented in *Parnassus*, makes us laugh, "but as we read on we slowly realize that the poem is also a thoughtful disquisition on Darwinian themes and their social meaning: the celebration of diversity and the problem of evil."

Appleman's first novel, *In the Twelfth Year of the War*, is a contemporary variation on the classic theme of good versus evil, full of echoes of Melville's *Billy Budd*. Thomas Lask wrote in the *New York Times*, " . . . though he is always serious, he is never grim." Even in his broadly farcical novel *Shame the Devil*, in which a pair of con men seek an ancient Norse settlement in a sleepy Indiana town, Appleman casts a satirical eye on the mores of small-town Middle America. While some reviewers found the novel too heavy-handed to be successful as satire, Art Seidenbaur wrote in the *Los Angeles Times*, "The happy ending makes no more sense than the murky, mythic middle. But who cares? Appleman wants to amuse and drop morals without moralizing; he's smart enough to do it swiftly, knowing the way of satire soon wears thin."

In *Apes and Angels*, he returns to provincial Middle America, this time an Indiana town called Kenton, clearly modeled on the town in which he grew up. On the brink of World War II, idyllic-seeming Kenton is a microcosm of America. Appleman draws on his rich store of memories of a small town wrestling with demons of ignorance and prejudice. Anti-Semitism, isolationism, religious opposition to the teaching of Darwin in the local high school, gossip, and scandalmongering seethe under the placid surface of life. From the point of view of an adolescent boy awakening to sex and falling in love for the first time, however, life is full of hope.

His work on Darwin led him to the study of Malthus. Appleman's travels in the Third World gave him a graphic picture of the miseries of poverty wherever the birthrate is unchecked and inspired him to write the short but compelling *The Silent Explosion*, which a *New Yorker* reviewer characterized as "a lucid, moving, and convincing discussion of the dangers of a continuing unchecked expansion of the world's population," and Sir Julian Huxley, who wrote a foreword to the book, felt "reveals the moral nature of the population problem."

For all its apparent lightheartedness, Appleman's is a poetry of commitment. In "Controversy, Censorship and Poetry," an essay in *Poets and Writers Magazine*, he urges poets to take stands on great public issues, "not as relentless ideologues, but as thoughtful people of good will." While Appleman's early work concentrated largely on personal experience—love lyrics and impressionistic responses to nature and to travel—he was always awake to the social and political causes of poverty and misery which he saw both in the Far East and in the United States. In his collection *Summer Love and Surf* he writes of America in "Remembering the Great Depression":

We were together then, islanded in the snow,
the dark, the dreams, the permanence of things:
cupboards always bare, shops on Main Street
closed, children fading into men—
men at the front door, waiting to be paid,
men at the back door, wanting to be fed—
island-people, huddled in the warmth,
dependable, the steady warmth of failure.

The poems Appleman collected some years later in *Open Doorways* show a similar concern for what Stanley Plumly, in the *American Poetry Review*, called "the darkly bad news of the world." There is nostalgia for the rapidly vanishing past: "But we are moving out now, / scraping the world smooth where apples blossomed, / paving it over for cars" ("Memo to the 21st Century") and uneasiness at the prospect of a dehumanized high-tech future. Reviewers praised the poems in *Open Doorways* for their craft and conviction: "He cares about what is true and good, and beauty follows," William H. Green wrote in *Kentucky Poetry Review*. Jay Parini, however, in *Poetry*, found that the poems "skitter over the surface of experience, which lies beneath them like a cold pond. He never breaks the crust; the shock of reality is missing."

Darwin's Ark was praised for its illustrations as well as its contents. "This is a poetry of current consciousness: awareness and celebration of life's fragility in the nuclear age," B. Wallenstein wrote in *Choice*. Many of Appleman's poems are both funny and disturbing at the same time. His humor is bold, unashamedly iconoclastic, with sometimes chilling effects. Nowhere is its sting more apparent than *Let There Be Light*—poems that the dust jacket frankly describes as a "satirical and polemical assault on the Judeo-Christian tradition." The "light" to which his title applies is less the "light" proclaimed by the Creator in Genesis than it is the "reason" of the 18th-century Enlightenment: the absolute rationality of the humanist confronting what he regards as the myth of Creation. William H. Green observed in *Kentucky Poetry Review*: "Though the God of Genesis has slipped away, Appleman's universe remains infused with value and purpose, no less real or spiritual because God is the Unknown, rather than an inscriber of tablets." Appleman's quarrel with orthodox religion dates back to his early conclusion that all religions "logically nullify each other." He expresses alarm over the rise of "right-wing fundamentalism" in the United States. In the end, as a humanist, Appleman protests against this world, while loving it, as he proclaims in "Lighting Your Birthday Cake," a tribute to his wife:

. . . Now
I can't believe in a world without

your bonfire of outrage, small flame of anguish,
pink glow of happiness.
Remember how I need your warmth:
As you blow out these candles, make a wish
to keep the fires burning.

Appleman has received many awards, among them the Midland Poetry Award and the Christopher Morley Award of the Poetry Society of America.

PRINCIPAL WORKS: *Poetry*—Kites on a Windy Day, 1967; Summer Love and Surf, 1968; Open Doorways, 1976; Darwin's Ark, 1984; Darwin's Bestiary, 1986; Let There Be Light, 1991. *Novels*—In the Twelfth Year of the War, 1970; Shame the Devil, 1981; Apes and Angels, 1989. *Nonfiction*—The Silent Explosion, 1965. *As editor*—(with W. M. Madden and M. Wolf) 1859: Entering an Age of Crisis, 1959; Darwin: Norton Critical Edition, 1970; Darwin: The Origin of Species, 1975; Malthus: An Essay on the Principle of Population, 1976.

ABOUT: Contemporary Authors New Revision Series 6, 1982; Contemporary Literary Criticism 51, 1989; Who's Who in America 1991–1992. *Periodicals*—American Poetry Review July–August 1977; Choice March 1985; Humanist March–April 1985; Kentucky Poetry Review Spring 1989; Los Angeles Times April 22, 1981; New York Times November 30, 1970; July 7, 1991; New Yorker June 26, 1965; Parnassus: Poetry in Review 14, #1, 1989; Poetry August 1977; Poets and Writers Magazine September–October 1992.

ARCHER, JEFFREY (HOWARD) (LORD ARCHER) (April 15, 1940–), British novelist and politician, was born in Weston-super-Mare, Somerset, the son of William and Lola (Cook) Archer. His father had been a professional soldier, his mother a journalist. He won a scholarship to Wellington School, a public school. After leaving Wellington he taught physical education for one year at Dover College before attending a one year program at Brasenose College, Oxford, for a certificate in education. He distinguished himself as captain of the university track and field team, setting a record for the 100-yard sprint. During a two-year period after completing his studies, he did research in the department of education and also became an aggressive and apparently tireless fund-raiser for university-supported charities; for one OXFAM event he secured the attendance of both Prime Minister Harold Macmillan and the Beatles. He was given the sobriquet "Mr. Four-and-a-Half Percent," based on the commission he charged.

After Oxford Archer became a professional fund-raiser and public relations adviser, setting up his own company, Arrow Enterprises. The

JEFFREY ARCHER

company's consistent success brought him a personal fortune and the residences, cars, and other accouterments to match. He went into politics as a member of the Greater London Council for Havering (1966 –1970), and then was elected Conservative Member of Parliament for Louth, Lincolnshire, despite a dispute with the United Nations Association, an Arrow client, over his expense accounts that resulted in his suing the Association chairman for libel. The suit was not settled until 1973, but in 1969 Archer defeated the Labour candidate by a huge margin and looked upon himself and was looked upon as a rising star in Tory politics, who "didn't enter Parliament with the idea of spending thirty-five years on the back benches," as he put it.

Archer had invested heavily in a Canadian industrial cleaning company called Aquablast. When it collapsed in 1974 he lost everything. Three of the company's directors were jailed for fraud; Archer's previous association with them brought his judgment into question, and he did not seek reelection to Parliament in 1974. This debacle caused him to begin his writing career. Determined to pay back his substantial debts but lacking capital or much in the way of job prospects, Archer decided to write a book loosely based upon his own experiences. His novel *Not a Penny More Not a Penny Less* concerns four men—an Oxford don, a society doctor, a Bond Street art dealer, and an aristocrat—who, having been defrauded by a dishonest businessman, join in an intricate series of maneuvers to recoup their losses. Published in 1976, the hardback edition sold a meager 3,000 copies. When published

in paperback, however, the novel became an instant bestseller, surprising everyone, not least the author, who found himself $50,000 richer.

Archer's next book, *Shall We Tell the President?*, is set in the United States in the early 1980s (the future) and concerns a plot to assassinate President Edward M. Kennedy. The manuscript cost Viking $250,000 (as well as the goodwill of Jacqueline Kennedy Onassis, who resigned from her editorial job with the company in protest), and film and paperback rights brought Archer an additional $500,000, enough to pay off the last of his creditors. The book was thus a success for him, though it did not become a best-seller. Reviews ranged from the mildly favorable ("fast-moving and somewhat suspenseful") to the savage ("a sick idea . . . a silly, imperceptive book"). In later editions Archer changed the name of the imaginary president.

In 1979 Archer published *Kane and Abel*. A lengthy novel, it concerns the strangely interlocking destinies of two quite different men— one a wellborn Boston banker, the other a Polish immigrant and self-made millionaire—who become, and remain, implacable enemies. His most successful book financially, it was followed two years later by a best-selling sequel, *The Prodigal Daughter*, in which the immigrant's child becomes America's first woman president. Jeffrey Archer's name was now established, and from this time on his career as a successful popular writer, constructing sagas of the rich and powerful, showed no sign of faltering. His books make no claim to being great literature, but their dynamic narrative qualities make them effective "page turners."

A. J. Anderson, writing in *Library Journal*, said of Archer's first novel, "The book forces us to accept the most outrageous unlikelihoods of plot, but, by the same token, it doesn't put us under the slightest cerebral strain," while E. S. Turner wrote in the *Times Literary Supplement*: "We have Jeffrey Archer's ingenious plot, with its echoes of Edgar Wallace and vintage Sexton Blake . . . It is told with that name-dropping and logging of train times that is thought to lend authenticity . . . there are walk-on parts for people as diverse as Lord Lichfield, Linda Lovelace and Harold Macmillan. Yet sophisticated it is not . . . The pace is quick, but would have been quicker if the author had not lingered to tell us irrelevant facts about the staffing of the *Times*, the square footage of the American Embassy in London and so on."

Most critics have agreed that Archer's commercial success derives from his mastery of the formulas of the popular novel: themes of wealth and power, melodrama, and a detailed series of events that keeps the plot moving. There is little attempt to analyze the underlying significance of those events. The language is comparatively simple, without the clumsy syntax or purple passages characteristic of much popular fiction, and the plots rattle along at a fast pace; his books are readable and undemanding. They are set in a simplified world in which good triumphs and evil is punished; a world in which characters representative of unambiguous values interact in straightforward ways to suggest, but not investigate, larger verities.

Archer retains an abiding love for the theater and in 1988 bought a controlling interest in London's Playhouse Theatre for $1.6 million. His own plays, however, have met with a mixed response. *Beyond a Reasonable Doubt*, a courtroom drama, opened in 1987 and ran for two years in London's West End, but its 1989 follow-up *Exclusive*, a drama about the inner workings of a newspaper, was a failure.

Politics has also remained a central issue in Archer's life, and despite his resignation from the House of Commons in 1974, he retained a significant presence in the Conservative Party, describing his dedication to Margaret Thatcher as "total," but he is not without political ambition for himself as well. In 1985, in recognition of his devotion, Margaret Thatcher made him deputy chairman of the Conservative Party. An unpaid but publicly prominent job, it drew upon his skills as a fund-raiser and popular speaker. Just over a year after assuming office his political career was again threatened with scandal. A British Sunday newspaper, the *News of the World*, published an article connecting Archer with a London prostitute. Another newspaper, the *Daily Star*, implied that the connection was sexual. Archer admitted having spoken to the women over the phone and giving her $2,800 to leave the country. He also admitted to paying a large sum of money to a third party to prevent her stories from reaching the press. However, he staunchly denied any sexual liaison and sued both publications. Despite complete vindication by the court ruling and the award of substantial damages (all of it donated by Archer to charity), he resigned his deputy chairmanship and did not run in any more elections.

In recent years Archer has moved into the top bracket of best-selling authors. He sold the British publishing rights of *As The Crow Flies* to Hodder and Stoughton for only £1 (90 pence after deducting his agent's commission) in order to demand a much higher level of royalties on sales and to reap tax advantages. Similarly, he sold the television rights to *Not a Penny More, Not a Pen-*

ny Less for £1. The result was a four-hour miniseries watched by eleven million people that greatly increased sales of the book.

The ingredients in Archer's 1993 thriller *Honor Among Thieves*—espionage involving the CIA and a beautiful Mossad agent, a plot by Saddam Hussein of Iraq to discredit President Clinton of the United States by stealing the original Declaration of Independence and burning it publicly on the Fourth of July—are brewed into a best-selling potion. Archer caps the book by presenting—in antique italic script—the treasure of political values itself—the Declaration of Independence. The Declaration probably provides the most exciting reading: most reviewers termed Archer's prose pedestrian and John Skow of *Time* called it a "frequent-flyer spy story."

Archer works hard on his novels: he shuts himself away for about eight weeks to complete a first draft and sometimes produces as many as eleven drafts before he is satisfied with a manuscript. The entire process takes about two years. As Joseph Lelyveld suggests, Archer has become a living exemplar of the rewards enterprise can bring.

Jeffrey Archer is a Fellow of the Royal Society of the Arts and was president of Oxford University Athletics Club in 1965. He has been president of Somerset Amateur Athletics Association, and a member of Carlton Cricket Club and of the Marylebone Cricket Club. He has also been an executive of the British Theatre Museum. In 1992 he was made a life peer—Baron Archer of Weston-super-Mare—and is thus assured of a seat in the House of Lords. He married Mary Weedon, a chemist whom he met at university in 1966; they have two sons and live in Grantchester. Archer also has a working home in London.

PRINCIPAL WORKS: *Novels*—Not a Penny More, Not a Penny Less, 1975; Shall We Tell the President? 1977; Kane and Abel, 1979; The Prodigal Daughter, 1982; First Among Equals, 1984; A Matter of Honor, 1985; A Twist in the Tale, 1988; As the Crow Flies, 1991; Honor Among Thieves, 1993. *Short stories*—A Quiver Full of Arrows, 1980; *Plays*—Beyond A Reasonable Doubt, 1987; Exclusive, 1989. *Juvenile*—By Royal Appointment, 1980; Willy Visits the Square World, 1980; Willy and the Killer Kipper, 1981.

ABOUT: Contemporary Authors New Revision Series 22, 1988; Contemporary Literary Criticism 28, 1984; Crick, M. Jeffrey Archer: Stranger than Fiction, 1995; Current Biography Yearbook 1988; International Authors and Writers Who's Who 1990-91; International Who's Who 1992-93, 1992; Richardson, S. Simply Wonderful: The Art of Jeffrey Archer, 1991; Seagrave, K. Sex and Politicians, 1990. *Periodicals*—Detroit Free Press September 5, 1985; Kirkus Reviews January 15,

1980; Library Journal May 1, 1976; Listener September 13, 1979; New York Times August 30, 1984; November 10, 1984; October 10, 1985; June 28, 1990; New York Times Book Review October 23, 1977; May 4, 1980; July 6, 1980; July 11, 1982; June 9, 1991; August 19, 1993; New York Times Magazine November 25, 1990; Times (London) October 27, 1986; Time July 26, 1993: Times Literary Supplement September 10, 1976; October 28, 1977; November 21, 1980; December 5, 1986; June 28, 1991.

*ARENAS, REINALDO (July 16, 1943–December 7, 1990), Cuban novelist, short story writer, poet, and playwright, was born in Perronales, a rural village in the province of Oriente, Cuba, the son of poor peasants. Abandoned by his father at birth, he was raised first by his mother and later by equally betrayed aunts and his maternal grandparents. He started his formal education when he was ten years old at a country school where he had to go on horseback. Later, when in 1955 his family moved to the town of Hologuín, he was able to go to a secondary school. These were difficult years of loneliness, despair, and extreme poverty that Arenas recalls with bittersweet memories in most of his early writings. The shadow of a lost father, which haunted him all of his life, and the love-hate relationship he had with his mother and aunts conditioned his personal relationship's with men and women for the rest of his life. For Arenas, writing soon became a way to escape his immediate reality. In 1958, lured by the idea of adventure, he ran away from home to join Castro's revolutionary forces. After the triumph of the revolution, he received a scholarship to study agricultural business in Holguín and, in 1961, he went to Havana where he took courses at the university and worked at the Institute of Agrarian Reform.

In the early 1960s the socialist government strongly encouraged cultural activities, and Arenas, like many other young writers, saw an opportunity to explore his talents. He decided to enter a storytelling competition sponsored by the National Library for which he wrote "Los zapatos vacíos" "Empty shoes," the first of a collection of stories for children of which only five were ever published, stories about the loss of innocence, the discovery of illusion and fantasy, the cruelty of a world obsessed with materialism, frustration, and death. Members of the jury were impressed, and he was offered a job at the National Library where he came in contact with other writers, participated in literary circles, and had time to read and to write. It was then that he met the two writers who, according to Arenas, had the strongest influence on him, José Lezama

REINALDO ARENAS

Lima and Virgilio Piñera, both homosexuals like Arenas and both in disfavor with the revolutionary government. Arenas's first novel, *Celestino antes del alba* (1967), for which he received an honorable mention, was immediately translated into English and French. It was the only one of Arenas's works ever allowed to be published in Cuba. Some years later, in 1982, it was published as *Cantando en el pozo*; translated as *Singing from the Well*, in order to distinguish Arenas's approved edition from the many pirated copies published abroad without his consent. *Celestino antes del alba* is a semi-autobiographical novel about the dreams and fantasies of a child raised in the hostile and isolated conditions typical of the countryside of prerevolutionary Cuba. The child narrator creates in his world of imagination his other, Celestino, a pure and innocent cousin, misunderstood and rejected by the family for being different. Celestino is the child-poet who finds his freedom and detachment from the world through writing, and who, much like Arenas when he was a child, resisted authority by following his urge to write poems on the bark of trees. Out of ignorance, his grandfather, Arenas's earliest symbol of repression, would cut down every tree with marks of writing. Celestino is the poet who even at death cannot be destroyed by the brutal surroundings that suffocate every character in the novel; he is a different being whose deviancy is to be himself in the midst of a repressive order that does not condone difference.

From this novel, Arenas's work is characterized by an obsessive search for freedom of expression and a defense of the imaginary in a barbaric world in which the writer is marginalized. The same rebellious character dies in one novel to reappear again, more mature, in a different or similar situation, in another one of Arenas's works, which have often been described as one continuous story in several parts, where one circumstance, event, or experience is seen from several points of view. *Celestino antes del alba* is a vision of a cruel and repressive world through the eyes of the child narrator while, in the second novel of the series, *El palacio de las blanquísimas mofetas* (1980, *The Palace of the White Skunks*), the same world is presented from the point of view of the adolescent Fortunato whose double is now not the poet within but the feminine within, his aunt Adolfina. In the third novel, *Otra vez el mar* (1982, *Farewell to the Sea*), the reader enters the inner world of a young revolutionary soldier who feels attracted to men, a feeling he must conceal from the homophobic militarized society of the postrevolutionary years 1959–1969, when nationalism, loyalty to the state, aesthetics, and sexual preference were rigidly prescribed by the political authorities. In *Farewell to the Sea*, the main character, Hector, who has seemed to follow convention as a way of survival, finds himself living in the loneliness of an internal exile, in a world as repressive and cruel as Celestino's prerevolutionary countryside.

From 1967 to 1968, Arenas worked as editor in the Cuban Institute of the Book under the Ministry of Culture, and on the staff of the literary journal *La gaceta de Cuba*, where some of his short stories and essays were published. In 1969, his second novel, *El mundo alucinante. Novels de aventuras* (1969, *Hallucinations*, also translated as *The Ill-Fated Peregrinations of Fray Servando*), was smuggled out of the country by a friend and immediately published in Mexico. Although this novel, as well as his collection of short stories *Con los ojos cerrados* (With closed eyes, 1972), had received an honorable mention in a literary competition, the Cuban government prohibited any of Arenas's works from being published because he wrote openly about homosexuality. In Cuba, Arenas was virtually unpublished, while abroad he had international recognition as an important proponent of the new Latin American narrative. *El mundo alucinante* was immediately translated to several languages and in 1969 shared the Prix Medici award in Paris with Gabriel García Márquez's *One Hundred Years of Solitude* for the best foreign novel. *El mundo alucinante* is a treatment and rewriting of the autobiography of Fray Servando Teresa de Mier, a Mexican priest who in the 19th century struggled for the independence

of his country and lived a rebellious life of continuous persecutions, incarcerations, and miraculous escapes. This hallucinatory book of adventures, of multiple realities, of history and fiction is, in Arenas's words, "the story of Fray Servando Teresa de Mier Noriega—just as it was, just as it might have been, just as I wish it had been. Neither a historic nor a biographical novel . . . " Fray Servando is not only an alter ego of Arenas himself, but he also uncannily foreshadows Arenas's own future years of persecutions, incarcerations, and escapes.

In the late 1960s and early 1970s the Cuban government began an inquisitory campaign to cleanse the country of all "undesirable elements." Already under surveillance for having smuggled his manuscripts out of the country, Arenas was accused of being a "counterrevolutionary" and an "immoral"—a sexual "deviant." In 1973 he was arrested but managed to escape and remain a fugitive at large in Havana's Lenin Park, on the outskirts of the city, where he hid for four months until he was caught and taken to El Morro prison. There he was kept incommunicado and tortured until he finally pleaded guilty to the charges against him, whereupon he was sent to a rehabilitation camp. His experience in prison and labor camps are candidly described in his autobiography, *Before Night Falls*, which Alastair Reid called, in the *New York Review of Books*, "a map of the reality" from which Arenas's fiction was made. During the years of persecutions and incarcerations, and later, of anonymity while being paid not to write, Arenas's reputation grew abroad.

In 1973 he smuggled out of the country the second novel of his five-novel series (which he called a *Pentagonia*, an "agony in five parts"), *The Palace of the White Skunks*, published first in French in 1975, and also *El Central* (1981), a long poem he wrote in 1970 while laboring in Manuel Sanguily, a sugar cane plantation in the province of Pinar del Río. In this poem, which he later combined with another two long poems under the title of *Leprosorio* (Leprosarium, 1990), Arenas mirrors two moments in Cuban history as a continuous never ending form of colonialism: the enslavement of Indians and Africans by Spaniards, and the present conditions of Cuban workers under Castro's style of socialism. The poem, as translated by Anthony Kerrigan, begins: Slave-hands

have turned up the land
have sown this land
have pressed those shoots
have milked the juice
so that the illustrious foreigner
armored with the vocabulary and guidelines
of his time may drop into the deeps

of his coffee the delicious cube,
stir with a silver spoon,
and sip. . . .

If the early *Singing From the Well* was a
semi-autobiographical novel from the point of
view of a child, for whom the symbols of authority were (as they were for Arenas) his mother,
aunts, and a terrifying grandfather who was always persecuting him, *The Palace of the White
Skunks* continues the saga from the point of view
of an adolescent of the same family, now living
in the city. The novel begins and ends with Fortunato's death. Like Arenas, Fortunato also
leaves home to join the rebels but cannot be admitted by the revolutionary forces unless he has
a rifle. He tries to steal one, is arrested, tortured,
and executed by government soldiers who make
him believe that he has been freed but shoot him
in the back, until "the river of dreams which had
seemed infinite stops. The interpreting ceases,
the fabulous voyages end, the transfigurations
and the imaginings, the invented consolations
grow dim and fade away." To Arenas, the moments of memory, clarity, and hallucination before death are the writer's life and work.

The third novel of Arenas's pentagony,
Farewell to the Sea, is written from the point of
view of the adult, a man who also leaves home
to join the rebels, and now, part of the new system, meditates on the political and social conditions of postrevolutionary Cuba. Unlike
Fortunato, Hector, the main character—whose
name echoes that of the Trojan hero in the
Iliad—chooses self-annihilation rather than a
life of lies, treason, deceit, and betrayal.
Farewell to the Sea, Arenas's most complex and
lyrical novel, is divided into two parts, six days,
and six songs. The first part is a meditation in
prose narrated by Hector's wife, an imaginary
Helen of Troy, in a fictional timeless Cuban dimension; the second one presents, through poetry, Hector's point of view as he reflects on his
life, his terrors, and the sixty-day vacation he, his
wife, and their eight-month-old baby have spent
at the beach living next door to an older woman
and her adolescent son, who may be a spy and
who sexually seduces Hector. This novel is,
above all, a meditation on sexuality and politics,
and sexuality as politics, contrasting a corrupt
political order, in a lyrical meditation, with the
once idealized revolution. Hector has been
forced into internal exile by political and sexual
repression. He is also the poet betrayed and
abandoned to the only space left in which he can
be free, his imagination. At the end of the novel,
the reader finds out that there was always only
one character, Hector, driving back to Havana;
the other characters—wife, son, mother, homo-

sexual adolescent, soldier, traitor, spy, poet—are
projections of himself. The structure of the novel
suggests a dance between prose and poetry, between a woman and a man. Hector's ambiguous
sexuality contrasts with the double genre, poetry
/ prose (in Spanish género means both "genre"
and "gender") of the text, and the double voice,
feminine / masculine, in which the novel is narrated. Thus, the book itself becomes an act of defiance and resistance against conventional
literary canons, and against the concept of truth
as absolute and inflexible. It becomes a defense
of individualism. The first manuscript of this
novel was destroyed when Arenas left it with a
friend for safekeeping, and, later, a second version was confiscated by the government and
used against him. With a borrowed typewriter
Arenas rewrote the novel a third time, sent it out
of the island, and, once out of Cuba, finally published it. This was Arenas's favorite novel perhaps because, as Roberto Valero, a friend of
Arenas, has said, Arenas's ideal was the ocean,
"uncontrollable, eternal, beautiful, impossible to
put in chains. . . . "

After several futile efforts to escape, Arenas finally was able to leave Cuba in 1980, passing un-
detected by government authorities during the
Mariel boat lift. Once in the U.S., and the recipient of Cintas and Guggenheim awards, Arenas
dedicated all of his time to writing although it
meant living at times in poverty. He was guest
lecturer at several universities, founded the journal *Mariel*, and became an outspoken voice
against Castro's regime and the plight of the
writer under Cuba's socialist government. Most
of his political essays have been published in a
single volume, *Necesidad de libertad. Mariel:
testimonios de un intelectual disidente* (Need for
freedom. Mariel: Testimonies of an intellectual
dissident, 1986).

In 1980 Arenas published a novella written
ten years earlier, *Vieja Rosa* (*Old Rosa*), about an
old woman who after a lifetime of hard work becomes a victim of the social changes brought
about by the revolution. Rosa is a symbol of the
old order, a conservative and superstitious matriarch who, like most of Arenas's characters, is
alone, with no other escape than death, the ultimate act of freedom for Arenas. Rosa chooses to
burn her house and herself rather than to be
forced to give away what she had earned with
her hard labor. Her oldest son, who, like Hector,
also fought with the revolutionary forces and is
now part of the new system, makes her turn her
land over to one of the cooperatives created by
the new government. Her daughter, disregard-
ing her mother's feelings, marries a black man.
At the end of the novel, Rosa discovers her youngest and favorite son actively engaging in a ho-

mosexual relationship and tries to kill him. Arenas presents Rosa as a symbol of an old order destroyed by revolution, but he creates in her character a profoundly complex woman who is the victim of two worlds, the traditional one that robbed her of happiness and the new world, equally unjust. In *Old Rosa* Arenas again sets forth the theme that there is no one single reality, that there are always many realities, many points of view, and that the only reality possible is the one found in "the play of human contradictions and human complexities." "We are cruel and tender," Arenas said, "greedy and generous, impassioned and meditative, laconic and rowdy, terrible and sublime, like the ocean. . . . "

Old Rosa includes a second novella, *Arturo, la estrella más hermosa* (1984, *The Brightest Star*), written in 1971, about Rosa's son, Arturo, an inmate in one of the rehabilitation camps that the Cuban government created for homosexuals. Like Rosa, and Fortunato, Arturo is also dying at the beginning and at the end of the novella, having been shot, not by his mother, but by a camp guard while attempting to escape. As he lies dying, he recounts his strategies for survival at the camp, and meditates on the nature of power and the demise of the weak. Like Arenas's own experiences in jail, which he candidly describes in his autobiography, Arturo does not belong to the official world nor to the world of the homosexual inmates. What makes Arturo different and a dissident in every aspect of the word is that he is a writer, and, like Fortunato, and before him Celestino, he finds his salvation and his freedom in writing.

In 1987 Arenas published *La loma del ángel* (*Graveyard of the Angels*), a transgressive and irreverent parody of Cirilo Villaverde's antislavery novel *Cecilia Valdés o la loma del ángel* (1882). Arenas indicated in his introduction to the novel that, in literature, "rewriting is as old as literature itself," and that, as he later observed, "one always writes about the present even when one writes about the past." This novel is a satire against 19th century literary realism and the "Socialist Realism" of the Cuban "official philosophy" of the 1970s. It slyly refers to Arenas's first novel, which won the highest honorable mention in the National Cirilo Villaverde Literary Contest in 1965 although his work was never allowed to be published in Cuba.

Arenas was infected with AIDS in 1983, In 1987, when the disease took a turn for the worse, Arenas began a race against time to finish his work before his death. Like Hector in *Farewell to the Sea*, he chose self-destruction and committed suicide in New York City four months after finishing his autobiography *Before Night Falls*, a candid, harsh, and honest map of his life, and an important key to understanding his work. The title refers to the agonizing days he spent hiding in Lenin Park, when the only escape from reality was writing and reading Homer's *Iliad*, an activity that necessarily ended everyday at nightfall; it is also a reference to the imminent nightfall—his death.

During his last years, Arenas finished his last two novels, *El color del verano o nuevo jardín de las delicias* (The color of summer, 1991), an irreverent book of personal vengeance in which he experiments with elements of science fiction, and in which he follows the chronology of his own life in hallucinatory fragments of apocalyptic and eschatological prophecies about Cuba's future. Making fun of political and literary figures, Arenas places the time of the action, the end of the dictatorship of Fifo (Fidel Castro) brought about by a mob of young people, in the year 1999, mixing literary genres, prose, theater, and poetry. Arenas images forth the hidden themes, metaphors, and symbols of colonialism, dictatorships, and exile in the history of Cuba in this novel, which is closer to Artaud's theater of the absurd than any experimental novel ever written in Latin America.

Arenas completed and published another book of poems, *Voluntad de vivir manifestándose* (*The will to live openly*, 1989), a play, *Persecución* (1986), and the last novel of the pentagony, *El asalto* (1991, *The Assault*), a hallucinatory meditation on power and authority, symbolized by the omnipresent figure of the mother, a symbol of Freudian complexities for Arenas as it was in *Singing From the Well*, and in his often anthologized short story "El hijo y la madre" ("Son and Mother"). *The Assault* is an Oedipal story in which the symbol of repression represented earlier by the grandfather's phallic ax, is now replaced by the son's phallic pen, with which he destroys the demons that have haunted him through life. It is also a detective story about the end of a political system that, like Arenas's father, like Castro's Revolution, abandoned its children.

In his writing, Arenas demanded total freedom of expression as he demanded sexual freedom in his personal life. "To write," said Arenas in 1980, "or to create is an act of irreverence, as much ethically as stylistic. . . . " He explained his motivation in *Before the Night Falls*:

> Two attitudes, two personalities, always seem to be in conflict throughout our history: on the one hand, the incurable rebels, lovers of freedom and therefore of creativity and experimentation, and on the other, the power-hungry opportunists and demagogues. . . . These attitudes have recurred over time: General Tacón

against Heredia, Martínez Campos against José Martí, Fidel Castro against Lezama Lima and Virgilio Piñera; always the same rhetoric, the same speeches, always the drums of militarism stifling the rhythm of poetry and life.

For Arenas, writing and sexuality are always closely linked—honest, open, sadistic, humorously cruel, transgressive, and vengeful—in the more subtle but deeply disturbing eroticism of his earlier work, and yet of a peculiar innocence and candor, in his later work. Whether in a pre or a post revolutionary Cuba, or even in exile, Arenas's characters are always in search of the other, the real friend, the innocent purity of the child-poet Celestino, the perfect lover, the loving mother, the caring father, always knowing that these dreams of a place and a time forever lost can only happen in the imagination of the writer. This is the theme of *El portero* (1989, *The Doorman*), which Arenas wrote while living in virtual poverty on the sixth floor of a walkup on New York's West Side. Like Arenas, Juan, a doorman at an elegant building in Manhattan, is a poor Cuban exile who fled in the Mariel boat lift and who is frustrated and perplexed by the incongruities of a materialistic land of equality for all where some are more equal than others. The building's pets "enlist their . . . doorman in their quest for liberation," according to the *New York Times Book Review*. Mauree Picard Robins said, "not since *Animal Farm* has a group so fervently argued the issue of their freedom." While trying to make sense of the absurd, the optimistic doorman "tries to escort the building's wacky tenants through the door to true happiness" to salvation, and out of the mental prisons humans have created for themselves. Only the animals succeed in returning to their own and true nature.

In the U.S., Arenas felt that he had been treated like a pariah in intellectual and literary circles because of his fierce anti-Castro sentiments. He criticized the leftists who, in the comfort of their homes and universities, supported a political system under which they would not want to live. Arenas was obsessed with freedom, whether personal, political, or social; a freedom based on individuality, risks, and choices. His life, like his work, is a story of internal and external exiles, ambiguities, and multifaceted realities. His works are transgressive and disturbing, as well as lyrical and poetic.

Facing an imminent death, but with a sense of completion, and thinking that his desire to die on the beach like his character Hector, was not possible, Arenas chose to take his own life. He left a letter in which he asked his friends to scatter his ashes on a beach in the Caribbean as his last farewell to the sea.

PRINCIPAL WORKS IN ENGLISH TRANSLATION: *Novels*— (tr. G. Brotherston) Hallucinations, 1971; (also tr. as Ill-Fated Peregrinations of Fray Servando by A. Hurley, 1987); (tr. A. Hurley) Farewell to the Sea, 1986; (tr. A. J. MacAdam) Graveyard of the Angels, 1987; (tr. A. Hurley) Singing from the Well, 1987; (tr. A. T. Slater and A. Hurley) Old Rosa: A Novel in Two Stories, 1989; (tr. A. Hurley) The Palace of the White Skunks, 1990; (tr. D. M. Koch) The Doorman, 1991; (tr. A. Hurley) The Assault, 1994. *Poetry*— (tr. A. Kerrigan) El Central, A Cuban Sugar Mill, 1984. *Autobiography*— (tr. D. M. Koch) Before Night Falls, 1993.

ABOUT: Flores, A. Spanish-American Authors: The Twentieth Century, 1992; Latin American Literature and Arts 44, 1991; Solé, C. A. and M. I. Abreu (eds.) Latin-American Writers III, 1989. *Periodicals*—Encounter January 1982; Journal of Evolutionary Psychology March 1984; Latin American Literary Review Spring-Summer 1980; Michigan Quarterly Review Spring 1984; Modern Language Notes March 1988; New York Review of Books March 7, 1991; November 18, 1993; New York Times December 9, 1990; New York Times Book Review September 1, 1991; October 24, 1993; October 16, 1994.

*AYALA, FRANCISCO (DE PAULA Y GARCIA DUARTE) March 16, 1906–), Spanish essayist, novelist, short story writer, critic, and journalist, was born in Granada. The firstborn son of Francisco Ayala, a liberal professional, and Luz Garcia-Duarte, a voracious reader and accomplished amateur painter, Ayala was reared in an intellectual and cultured environment. His maternal grandfather, a physician, was rector of the University of Granada. Like most upper-middle-class Spanish children, Ayala attended a Catholic private school (an experience remembered with distaste); otherwise, he recalls his childhood as idyllic. Ayala wrote poetry at eight, nine, and ten years old, and began writing articles and fiction at sixteen. He also tried painting. In 1921, the family moved to Madrid, where Ayala completed his *bachillerato* (secondary studies), beginning university studies in 1923. He received a law degree at the University of Madrid in 1929, and won a scholarship for graduate study in political philosophy and sociology in Germany. In 1931, he married Etelvina Silva Vargas in Berlin, and in 1932 earned his doctorate in law from the University of Madrid, winning posts in public examinations to teach in the law school there and serve as counsel to the Cortes (Parliament).

Ayala became a critic for Ortega y Gasset's prestigious *Revista de Occidente* (1927–1930) after publishing his first novel, *Tragicomedia de un hombre sin espíritu* (Tragicomedy of a man without spirit, 1925) when only eighteen.

*eye AH lah, frahn THEES coh

Both Ayala's fiction and essays, which illuminate and complement each other, reflect the tutelage of Ortega y Gasset, the model for Ayala's generation. A radically different novel, *Historia de un amanecer* (Story of a dawn, 1926), followed. Ayala and his critics have downplayed these early efforts, yet *Tragicomedia*, is an original European modernist experiment, interwoven with allusions to Cervantes, Calderón, Galdós, and Unamuno, reflecting Ayala's wide reading. *Historia*, a diffuse, quasi-allegorical treatment of conflicting ideologies, examines individual rights versus collective interests, resolving the conflict of pacifism versus violence with the willing sacrifice of a hero-victim. Both novels introduce enduring concerns reiterated throughout Ayala's subsequent work. In *Tragicomedia* he exploits characteristic Cervantine motifs, while in *Historia*, the themes of heroism and betrayal, violence and oppression, power and conspiracy, demagoguery and victimization all anticipate later Ayala essays, novels and tales.

Ayala was an editor of *La Gaceta Literaria*, the country's leading exponent of vanguardist aesthetics, and both *El boxeador y un ángel* (The boxer and an angel, 1929) and *Cazador en el alba* (Hunter at dawn, 1930), collections of stories and novelettes, are experimental. In them Ayala subordinates content to form and narrative to experimental imagery. Futuristic humanization of the technological, along with paradoxical Cubist dehumanization of man, predominate. Cinematographic touches abound, Ayala early enunciated technical and aesthetic concerns with the movie medium with *Indagación del cinema* (Inquiry into the cinema, 1929). This interest resurfaced in *El cine: Arte y espectáculo* (Movies: Art and spectacles, 1966), and *El escritor y el cine* (The writer and the movies, 1975). In Ayala's works surrealistic free association and metamorphosis reflect the techniques possible in cinema. Irony, fantasy, scraps of epics and myths—the juxtaposition of disparate elements typical of vanguardist discourse—heighten the strangeness of already disconcerting texts. Exotic linguistic elements include foreign words; onomatopoeia; technical jargon; startling, unexpected imagery, and syntactic dislocation. Ayala borrows from earlier movements (symbolism, impressionism), draws upon Cervantes, contrasts the worlds of childhood and adulthood, re-creates newsreel effects, and juxtaposes dream, memory, delirium, and reality, anticipating the coming Holocaust which he foresaw intuitively, during his stay in Germany.

While teaching at the University of Madrid in the late 1930s, Ayala abandoned fiction to write legal, sociological, and philosophical treatises, first publishing an extended study of the constitution of the newly instituted Second Republic. The Spanish civil war erupted during his absence on a lecture tour in South America in 1937; he returned to Spain, subsequently becoming secretary of the Spanish republic's diplomatic legation in Prague. His father was executed by the Franco military command in the early months of the war; his brother Vicente was among numerous republican youths forcibly mobilized into Franco's army (which paradoxically may have saved his life). Ayala went into exile in Argentina from 1939–1950, Puerto Rico from 1950–1958, and the United States, living first in Chicago from 1958–1966 and then New York. He returned to Spain for his first visit in 1960, visiting Madrid annually thereafter, but returning to live only in the mid-1980s, after Spain's transition to democracy.

Ayala established himself in Argentina first as a translator, rendering into Spanish works from English, Portuguese, Italian, and German, and soon became known as a journalist, sociologist, and author of treatises on political science; he lectured briefly at an Argentine university, but declined to formalize the arrangement. He spent 1945 in Brazil, teaching sociology in a special school for public servants in Rio, then returned to Argentina where he was involved with novelist Eduardo Mallea in founding the intellectual review *Realidad*; he also contributed to *Sur*, Latin America's premier literary journal, but eventually left Argentina for Puerto Rico because of the "abject totalitarian demagoguery" of the Perón regime. At the University of Puerto Rico, he was editor of the university press and founded the prestigious review *La Torre*. He then moved to New York, motivated partly by his daughter's decision to study architecture at Columbia University. In the United States, he taught at Rutgers University, Bryn Mawr College, the University of Chicago, and New York University. While the majority of his work was academic, including numerous literary studies and linguistic treatises, Ayala continued to write political philosophy and resumed his diplomatic career, serving the United States as representative to UNESCO.

Although there was a fourteen-year hiatus between *Cazador en el alba* and Ayala's return to fiction, he wrote assiduously, including studies of the 17th century Spanish historian, political theorist, and satirist Saavedra Fajardo, *El pensamiento vivo de S.F.* (The living thought of S.F., 1941), and of Jovellanos, the 18th-century Spanish encyclopedist, statesman, judge, civil theorist, and progressive intellectual. *Jovellanos* (1945), portrays a man whose interest in the role of public entertainment coincided with Ayala's own. A theoretical formulation of his fascination with Cervantes appears in *La invención del "Quijote"* (The invention of Don Quixote, 1950). Ayala further probed political philosophy with *El problema del liberalismo* (The problem of liberalism, 1941), *Historia de la libertad* (History of Liberty, 1942), *Los políticos* (Politicians, 1944), and *Ensayo sobre la libertad* (Essay on liberty, 1945). His preoccupation with Spain, echoing the "Generation of 1898" to a degree unmatched in his own generation of 1927, reappears in *Razón del mundo: La preocupación de España* (Worldly reason: Preoccupation with Spain, 1944), and *Una doble experiencia política: España e Italia* (A Double Political Experience: Spain and Italy, 1944), analyzing the two countries' institutionalization of Fascism. Ayala's delving into Spain's politics produced four more treatises during the 1960s, 1970s, and 1980s. While still in Argentina, he published *Histrionismo y representación* (Histrionics and performance, 1944), and *Tratado de sociología* (Treatise on sociology, 1947), in three volumes.

Ayala's next work of fiction, *El hechizado* (The bewitched, 1944), portrayed Spain's unfortunate Charles II, the last Hapsburg monarch, who was physically and mentally degenerate. This microcephalic head of a gigantic empire with an enormous bureaucracy symbolized many defects that Ayala perceived in contemporary Spain. Rejecting the carefree, ludic spirit of his early works, Ayala entered a period of a commitment, drawing implicit parallels between seemingly trivial, unrelated events and the Spanish civil war and its aftermath. His deceptively straightforward and seemingly documentary stories and novels carry tremendous subversive charges in their oblique, ironic exposure of the rancor, resentment, jealousy, pettiness, and cowardice of Franco's Spain. *La cabeza del cordero* (1949, *The Lamb's Head*) and *Los usurpadores* (1949, *Usurpers*) probe Spain's underlying discord and power struggles. *La cabeza* is about the civil war, concentrating less upon military aspects than on the human shortcomings of civilians and military alike. "*El Tajo*" (The Tagus) offers a psychological portrait of a Falangist officer whose unnecessary killing of an unarmed enemy springs from cowardice and fear of lower-class "bullies" dating from his childhood, while "*El mensaje*" (The Message) centers on a small town's fascination with an undecipherable note. In it, Ayala explodes fanaticism and claims of unique revelation. With irony artfully disguised as aesthetic distance, Ayala avoids partisan statements—to no avail, as the collection was banned in Spain for nearly three decades.

The eight short stories of *Usurpers* "illustrate the author's belief that every exercise of power is by nature a usurpation," according to William Ferguson, writing in the *New York Times Book Review* in 1987. Sibling rivalry, betrayal, jealousy, greed, envy, fanaticism, egotism, motivate familiar figures from Spanish history. "*El inquisidor*" (The Inquisitor) portrays a fanatic Inquisitor as driven by his own secret heresies. *Usurpers* was subsequently incorporated with *El hechizado*, a highly praised collection much admired by other major writers, including Jorge Luis Borges. Critics have deemed these tales masterpieces, establishing Ayala as Spain's foremost exponent of short fiction.

Ayala exploits numerous Borgesian literary tricks, including apocryphal sources, nonexistent "real-life" characters, the Cervantine "found manuscript" and textual commentary (actually the narrative), and unreliable narrators, as well as literary borrowings, imitations, parodies, and adaptations. Prologues, usually by imaginary friends of the author, receive original treatment from Ayala. Multiple narrative perspectives—inspired by Ortega's philosophy of perspectivism—serve to highlight paradoxical and contradictory aspects of human behavior. Like Unamuno (a major influence) Ayala rejects genre, distinctions, terming all of his fiction novels, regardless of length.

Tyranny and revolution in an imaginary Central American dictatorship (which in the second part becomes extremist "popular democracy") figure in Ayala's best-known novels, *Muertes de perro* (1958, *Death as a Way of Life*) and its sequel, *El fondo del vaso* (The bottom of the glass, 1962). The novelist refused to identify historical models for either government, although his experience with Peronism is an obvious influence. His postwar works, according to Ayala, reflect his reaction to exile and efforts to explain his own situation in the world. Existential alienation and inauthenticity, preoccupation with the mass media, corruption in government, the power of the press run amok, and terrorism by juvenile gangs, inform masterful portraits of society in crisis. Essays from the same period show similar preoccupations, including *Derechos de la persona individual para una sociedad de masas* (Individual rights in mass society, 1953), *El escritor en la sociedad de masas* (The writer in mass society, 1956), *La crisis actual de la enseñanza* (The current educational crisis, 1958), and *Tecnología y libertad* (Technology and liberty, 1959). In both essays and fiction, Ayala pursues his obsessive concern with relationships between the existential Self and the Other. Humanity's fundamental duties, Ayala suggests repeatedly, are summarized in the adages "Know thyself" and "To thine own self be true."

Ayala's later fiction abounds in picaresque elements and irony. The viler aspects, of social relations—humiliation, ridicule, debasement—are depicted in *Historia de macacos* (Monkey story, 1955). In *El As de Bastos* (Ace of Clubs, 1963) the decadence of consumerism, and varied moral and physical outrages are treated. *De raptos, violaciones y otras inconveniencias* (Concerning kidnappings, rapes, and other inconveniences, 1966), *El jardín de las delicias* (Garden of delights, 1978), and *El jardín de las malicias* (Garden of malice, 1988) sometimes echo brief news articles, almost telegraphically. Gardens recall the loss of paradise. The hellish atmosphere of Hieronymus Bosch's paintings underscores humanity's bestial side. Some tales echo baroque mannerism or *desengaño* (disillusionment). Evaluating his own work (in *El tiempo y yo*), Ayala stresses his wish to avoid both the esoteric or hermetic and the excessively facile. He conjectures that many readers' difficulties with his works spring from pervasive ambiguity, as well as his complex and contradictory characters.

Ayala has published eighteen novels and collections of stories, plus some fifty books of essays, literary criticism, sociological theory, and memoirs.

Important collections in Spanish of Ayala's ideas, life, and poetics include *Confrontaciones* (Confrontations: An intellectual autobiography, 1972); *Conversaciones con Francisco Ayala* (Conversations with Francisco Ayala, 1982), and *Recuerdos y olvidos* (Memories and Forgettings, 1982) memoirs in two volumes offering reminiscences of literàti from both sides of the Atlantic. *Las plumas del fénix* (Feathers of the phoenix, 1989), a collection of Ayala's most significant literary criticism, and *El escritor en su siglo* (The writer in his century, 1990), a compilation of his writings on social and literary theory, are indispensable references.

Belatedly, following decades of hostility by the Franco regime, he began harvesting his country's literary honors during the dictatorship's twilight years: the National Critics' Prize (especially prestigious because it represented neither commercial nor political interests) was awarded in 1972, and in 1983, Ayala received the National Literature Prize, the same year he was elected to the Spanish Royal Academy. In 1988, he garnered the National Prize of Spanish Letters for overall literary achievement, and in 1991, the Miguel de Cervantes National Literary Prize, winning out over Nobel Prize laureates Camilo José Cela and Gabriel García Márquez, as well as Mario Vargas Llosa. The Cervantes Prize, Spain's highest literary award, recognized a body of work which has "conspicuously enriched the literary patrimony" of the Spanish-speaking world.

PRINCIPAL WORKS IN ENGLISH TRANSLATION: *Fiction*—Death as a Way of Life (tr. J. Maclean) 1956; The Lamb's Head (tr. C. C. Fitzgibbons) 1971; Usurpers (tr. C. Richmon) 1987.

ABOUT: Columbia Dictionary of Modern European Literature, 2nd ed., 1980; Costa, L. (ed.) German and International Perspectives on the Spanish Civil War, 1992; Encyclopedia of World Literature in the 20th Century, rev. ed., I, 1981; Irizarry, E. Francisco Ayala, 1977; Moeller, H. B. (ed.) Latin America and the Literature of Exile, 1983. *Periodicals*—Discurso Literaria Spring 1989; Hispania May 1987; Hispanic Journal Spring 1989; Letras Peninsulares Spring 1990; New York Times Book Review June 21, 1987; PMLA January 1969; Revista Canadiense de Estudios Hispanicos Autumn 1981; Winter 1990.

AZUELA, ARTURO (June 30, 1938–), Mexican novelist and essayist Arturo Azuela told Reinhard Teichmann, in *La onda en adelante,* "I was born in the Santa María de la Ribera neighborhood of Mexico City. I had a good family life although we had many differences (political and religious). The first 15 years of my life were spent in my grandfather's house. He was Mariano Azuela, the great novelist of the Mexican Revolution. I was born in that house on Alamo Street, now Mariano Azuela Street. Then we moved to another neighborhood where I lived for four or five years. My early life was very comfortable. I wanted to be a violinist, and studied music from the age of 9 to the age of 18. At heart, I am nothing more than a failed violinist . . . . Then came a series of vocational searches: not only music, but civil engineering, mathematics, the history of science, politics, journalism . . . . I was abroad for a long time: first in Paris in 1960, then at the University of Texas in Austin ,where I got my master's degree in mathematical sciences, from 1962 to 1964. "My entry into literature came from an unconscious process: I began to tell my family stories in Austin. I returned to Mexico after getting my M.S. degree and dedicated myself to scientific journalism. I learned to dialogue with the typewriter keys and began to tell my tales as well. They were transformed; they were enriched; and they made up the first part of *El tamaño del infierno.* Then a lot of other things, little by little, led me to literature, and at 36 I published my first novel. It changed my life; it caused me to fix definitively on one vocation. It has been one of my greatest satisfactions. It has been a great deal of work and a great deal of historical and linguistic challenge in many different ways."

Azuela told J.H. Castro about what went into *El tamaño del infierno:* "I worked on that book with determination and effort. I revised it after completing arduous research. I interviewed a number of people of different ages; I frequently visited Los Altos in Jalisco, a region in which the major characters developed. There I conversed with very old people, monks, spinsters, widows, priests, old patriarchs, and cultured people, who told me countless stories about their lives. . . . Little by little I gave up mathematics, journalism, and the history of science and in a few years saw myself firmly fixed in the territory of literature. In the past, when I had no inkling that I would turn myself into a writer, I was introverted and silent. After writing my first novel, I lost my timidity and decided to tell stories."

A teacher, as well as a writer, Azuela taught mathematics and the history of science at the Autonomous University of Mexico. He was deeply affected by the events of 1968, when student demonstrators and their supporters where fired upon in the Tlatelolco plaza by the Mexican police. Many were killed, and many organizers of the demonstrations were jailed. Their demands had been for a greater voice in government.

El tamaño del infierno won the Xavier Villaurrutia prize in 1974 and has been followed by *Un tal José Salome* in 1975 and *Manifestación de silencios* which won the National Prize for the Novel in 1978 and was translated into English by Elena Murray as *Shadows of Silence*. George R. McMurray said in *Spanish American Writing Since 1941* that *Shadows of Silence* was Azuela's most important work. It "portrays a close-knit circle of beleaguered intellectuals who gravitate toward the fringes of radical politics but, out of justifiable fear, remain for the most part in the 'shadows of silence.'" The group is focused on one José Augusto Banderas, who has managed to publish a politically inflammatory article or editorial—it is not clear which. José Augusto is wanted for murder. As the novel follows members of his group in their coming together to speculate on the case, it becomes clear that each of them is truly unable to act in any significant sense, and, indeed, that the murder is not the political conspiracy that the newspapers have made it out to be, but a crime of passion committed on impulse when José Augusto finds another man with his lover. When Gabriel, one of the members of his circle, encounters him after a long search, he realizes that neither José Augusto nor his friends can put together a coherent personality among them, much less a revolution:

I didn't ask him a single question, making him feel as if I still acknowledged his natural superiority. At times, I had the feeling that the whole thing was unreal; that Banderas was, in fact, nothing but the sum total of all our blunders, or perhaps, only the projection of either my own fantasies or of my deeply buried complexes. . . . As

I left behind José Augusto's lanky figure with his cigarette dangling from his lips, I realized that his intelligence was way beyond mine, that he had read my mind and that, in fact, I didn't have the slightest idea as to what he had really gone through. . . . In any case . . . some of us bore a marked resemblance to a few of his personalities, and although it may not have seemed important, José Augusto knew that a Lunatic or an Unmentionable had, at some time or another, either lived in us or would eventually grow within each one of us . . .

It is only in Gabriel's vainglorious imagination that these Lunatics and Unmentionables exist. The entire group, in fact, is cynically manipulated by the real politcal powers of the country, who find them no threat at all to the established order. Mexico continues its sprawling life unconcerned with these people who are impotent to change anything.

Azuela's next two novels were published in Spain. *La casa de las mil vírgenes* chronicles the rise, prosperity, and subsequent decadence of Santa María de Ribera, the neighborhood of Mexico City where Azuela was born and raised. *El don de la palabra*, published in 1984, takes for its subjects the life of Spanish exiles in Mexico and women's liberation. The latter theme is developed through the character of a Mexican actress, the daughter of Spanish Civil War refugees. The fates of the Spanish and Mexican nations interlock in the novel.

Azuela was to make clear his belief in the value of political leadership—as opposed to torpor—in *La mar de utopías*, a series of autobiographical travel essays published in 1991. Writing about Salvador Allende, his political idol, he says:

In many senses politics is a spider's web, complex, labyrinthine; and there are politicians, authentic men of action, who know very well the meaning of leadership; perhaps more than anyone, leaders become collectors of enemies, true navigators on the long roads of calumnies, intrigues and low quarrels. Now, from a deep perspective, time is the best scout. Often, to be great is to be misunderstood. But sooner or later comes vindication. The visionaries' turn will come.

Azuela has, indeed, made the fate of nations his lifelong concern. He says of his childhood in *La mar de utopías*:

From the earliest conversations that I can remember in my grandfather's library . . . America was present, our America, from the ancient murals of Bonampak to Ercilla's *La Araucana*, and the America of the Jesuit missions of the Peruvian highlands, to that of Sor Juana Inez de la Cruz's romances, sonnets, and sayings up until the political differences of the last century and to the assassinations of leaders or revolutionary activists, bringing us to the first part of the 20th century. Our America was also there in the strings and keys, in the souls of our musical instruments; but above all in the word—not only in the written word, but in the declamations and recitals—in the poetry of our classics and in the immortal phrases of

our national heroes, even those laden with vulgarity and
unintentional humor.

Azuela set forth the purpose of his travels over
Latin America as not being for "reminiscences,
for shadows of memory, but for power over the
past—to make it more mine, more present, more
future."

PRINCIPAL WORKS IN ENGLISH TRANSLATION (tr. E.C. Murray)
Shadows of Silence,1985.

ABOUT: Castro, J.A. "Mi primero libro: Cambio mi vida"
in Los Libros September 1991; Flores, A. Spanish
American Authors: The Twentieth Century, 1992; Mc-
Murray, G. Spanish American Writing Since 1941,
1987; Teichmann, R. De la onda en adelante, 1987

BERNARD BAILYN

BAILYN, BERNARD (September 10,
1922–   ), American historian, was born in Hartford, Connecticut, the son of Charles Manuel
and Esther (Schloss) Bailyn. After a brief interruption for army service in World War II, he received his B.A. from Williams College in 1945.
In 1953 Bailyn received his doctorate at Harvard
and became a permanent member of the Harvard faculty.

Bernard Bailyn's works of historiography
have been called literature by many critics for
their elegant power of expression. As a social historian, Bailyn is famous as a principal modern
theorist of the American Revolution. As a coun-
terweight to the ideas of Charles Beard and his
followers that social and economic forces made
violent revolution inevitable, Bailyn's theory
posits that the Revolution was not at all the inevitable product of materialist concerns or of class
struggle, but "the product of human decision
and of the impact of personalities and ideas upon
the events of the time," as he says in the Preface
to *Faces of Revolution: Personalities and
Themes in the Struggle for American
Independence*. Bailyn believes that American
revolutionaries were responding to fears that
"irresponsible and self-seeking adventurers—
what the 20th century would call political gangsters—had gained the power of the British
government" and would quickly turn their predatory attentions on the colonies. Bailyn says that
"the theme of a radical revolution followed by
a conservative counter-revolution, the suppression of earlier aspirations, and the establishment
of a permanent struggle between conservative
forces on the one hand and populist impulses on
the other" has a dubious validity. Instead, he
chooses to depict a population not split between
haves and have-nots but more united by common interests. To Bailyn, the Constitution made

necessary compromises between the past and the
emerging needs of the modern world: "The essential spirit of the eighteenth-century reform—
its idealism, its determination to protect the individual from the power of the state—lived on,
and lives on still."

As a graduate student, Bailyn was influenced
by such distinguished teachers as Oscar Handlin,
the social historian, Charles Taylor, the medi-
evalist, and the American historian Samuel Eliot
Morison, noted particularly for his narrative
skills. His exposure to these masters persuaded
him in his writings to blend narrative and analysis.

Before Bailyn began work on his master's degree, he had decided to concentrate in American
colonial history, which became the subject of his
first three books. Bailyn's first book, *The New
England Merchants in the Seventeenth Century*,
details the growth of the merchant class. Bailyn's
central thesis involves the tension between mer-
cantile interests and the Puritan church. The
Massachusetts theocracy could not prevail
against the commercial forces that brought
about social change. Bailyn was writing not so
much economic history as social history in describing the influence of commercial activity on
the structure and functioning of New England
society. The volume was well received, both for
its ideas and Bailyn's narrative skills.

Bailyn's next book, *Massachusetts Shipping,
1697–1714*, written in collaboration with his
wife, Lotte Lazarsfeld Bailyn, is a solid statistical
study. One of the first pieces of historiography
in which quantitative methods of research are

employed to tabulate and assemble data, the book also illuminates the functioning of the commercial infrastructure of colonial days.

His third book established Bailyn as an authority on the social history of early America. *Education in the Forming of American Society* is a response to the early 20th century historians of education who were concerned mainly with formal schooling and less with the educational function of other social institutions. Bailyn contends that education is "the entire process by which a culture transmits itself across the generations." He demonstrates that in the early colonial period the formal school was less important in the education of the young than the family, work apprenticeship, the church, and the community. As time went on, because of such factors as changes in family structure, the abundance of land, the shortage of labor, and the lack of available private wealth, the formal school assumed more importance in the educational process. Lawrence A. Cremin observed in *The Transformation of Early American History* that the book "will prove sufficiently provocative to set in motion the kind of informed historical scholarship that . . . has been all too rare in the field of American education."

The 1960s saw Bailyn's writing career moving to a new, "middle" phase that lasted fifteen years. In the same period, Bailyn was promoted to full professor, and in 1966 he became Winthrop Professor of History. From 1962 to 1970 he served as editor-in- chief of the John Harvard Library, a collection of editions of classic works by American authors. In 1967 he became founding coeditor of *Perspectives in American History*, an annual published by the Charles Warren Center for Studies in American History at Harvard. Bailyn proved to be a master teacher on both undergraduate and graduate levels. Above all, he sought to develop a keen critical sense in his students, by providing challenging reading assignments with no syllabus or bibliography. Instead, each assigned book provided a launching pad for discussion of an important historical topic.

In the early 1960s Bailyn's scholarly investigations were concentrated on the origins of the American Revolution. He had been invited to edit a large collection of Revolutionary pamphlets for the John Harvard Library. Narrowing the collection down to seventy-two titles that had special value, he selected fourteen of these that would serve as the first volume of a projected four-volume work. The pamphlets selected covered the pre-Revolutionary years of 1750 to 1765. Each pamphlet has an introductory note giving a brief biography of the author, the intent of the document, and its influence. Bailyn supplied a long introduction to the work.

This introduction, "The Transforming Radicalism of the American Revolution," reflects Bailyn's thinking about the origins of American radicalism. He finds these origins not in social discontent or economic distress but mainly in the views of the English Radical Whigs of the 17th century, who wished to preserve English freedoms from what they perceived to be a corrupt and authoritarian government. Bailyn discerned that the Revolutionary pamphleteers used such terms as "conspiracy," "corruption," and "slavery" not as rhetoric and propaganda to influence a passive populace, but literally to describe existing conditions. The pamphleteers were applying the ideas of the English Radical Whigs to the American situation of the mid-1700s.

Volume One of *Pamphlets of the American Revolution* was awarded the Faculty Prize of the Harvard University Press in 1965. Bailyn's best-known and most influential work, *The Ideological Origins of the American Revolution*, a revision and enlargement of the introduction to *Pamphlets*, appeared two years later.

Ideological Origins is divided into three parts. The first, an overview of colonial political thinking from 1680 to 1760, presents the views of the Radical Whigs and the conspiracy theory, which the colonists used to explain English rule. The second part, treats the period from 1760 to 1776, when Americans opposed the supremacy of the English Parliament, desiring shared power with Parliament. In part three the ideas that motivated the rebellious colonists are shown to apply to the problems they would face in the post-Revolutionary period, such as chattel slavery, church-state relations, and the need for balanced government.

A companion volume, *The Origins of American Politics*, appeared a year after *Ideological Origins*. This book examined the peculiar nature of colonial politics and government, especially the office of the royal governor. While the governors enjoyed considerable theoretical powers, these were limited in practice because the governors lacked the power of patronage that might ensure political stability. As a result, factionalism ran rampant in the mid-18th century and dissenting ideas spread, in particular Radical Whig ideology. *Ideological Origins* and *The Origins of American Politics* established Bailyn's professional reputation, and he became the leader of the ideological school of historians of the American Revolution. *Ideological Origins* won the Pulitzer and Bancroft prizes for 1968. Several scholars, however, faulted Bailyn for not recognizing the importance of material concerns in his ideological interpretation of the causes of the Revolution. Others, themselves devotees of ideological origins, criticized him for giving little or no credence to the political theories of John Locke. Still others, historians of the New Left, objected that he paid insufficient attention to the discontent of the common people.

In 1974 Bailyn published his only book-length biographical work, *The Ordeal of Thomas Hutchinson.* Hutchinson was the American-born royal governor of Massachusetts from 1771 to 1774. A man of wealth, with good family connections, Hutchinson is portrayed by n as a person of ability and integrity. Like the colonial radicals, Hutchinson feared the excesses of political power, but he sincerely believed that the best interests of the colonists lay in loyalty to the English Crown. Hutchinson's problem with the colonial radicals was that he never really understood their discontent. Ultimately, the violent expression of this discontent drove him to leave Massachusetts for England where he died in 1780, a resentful, homesick, embittered man.

Bailyn is very sympathetic toward Hutchinson. In fact, as one of his former students, Gordon S. Wood, wrote in *The Transformation of American History,* Bailyn defended Hutchinson, in spite of claims to be nonpartisan in the book's preface. He intended to clarify the views of the loyalists, which enable one "to see the revolutionary movement from the other side around and to grasp the wholeness of the struggle."

The Ordeal of Thomas Hutchinson received numerous accolades including, a National Book Award. However, it also provoked the adverse criticism of Bailyn's favoring Hutchinson and having Tory leanings. Others accused him of an elite bias in presenting the loyalist view through the person of a man of wealth and influence, thereby discounting the poorer loyalists. New Left historians, considering themselves champions of an oppressed proletariat, were especially critical of Bailyn's apparent predisposition toward Hutchinson. Finally, there were those who contended that in upholding Hutchinson's life and ideas, Bailyn was subtly attacking the antiauthoritarianism of the Harvard student protests of the late 1960s.

Bailyn's presidential address to the American Historical Association in 1981 (published in the *American Historical Review,* February 1982) contains much of his philosophy of history. He favors comprehensive history that synthesizes and subsumes narrow, specialized segments of the subject, especially a fusion of manifest and latent events, the organization of large-scale systems and spheres as cores and peripheries, and the description of psychological states and their relation to the external world. Events such as the American Revolution in his system are "manifest," or clearly revealed. The migrations and settlements of the pre-Revolutionary years eventuating in a repressive government policy are "latent." The best history, Bailyn suggests, conjoins the two types of events. He identifies large central political cores such as eighteenth-century Britain in relation to the many peripheral settlements that resulted from migrations from the mother country. These outlying areas looked to the heartland "from which standards and the sanctioned forms of organized life emanated." There is a common shaping element between parent country and colony. Bailyn's writings also link the inner world of the human mind to the course of external events, influencing other historians to probe the minds of movers and shakers.

Bailyn's writings have returned to the colonial period. His principal, most ambitious project has the umbrella title, "The Peopling of North America," and the theme of European emigration to British North America in the mid-18th century. In the introductory volume *Voyagers to the West,* Bailyn examines the reasons for the migrations, the work the migrants found to do in America, how communities were organized, how social patterns developed, and how differences arose among the communities. Bailyn lays forth his data in broad brush strokes, summarizing numerous studies of European migration, supplemented by his own research in such sources as a British emigration register that listed every person who was known to have left England for America between December 1773 and March 1776, newspaper accounts, town records, local histories, and genealogical data.

Voyagers won Bailyn a second Pulitzer Prize, the Saloutos Award of the Immigration History Society, the Triennial Prize of the Society of the Cincinnati, and the Distinguished Book Award of the Society of Colonial Wars. Critics have been lavish in their praise of the work, calling it a "tour de force," "magisterial," and "gargantuan" in scope, method and analysis.

With two volumes remaining of the Peopling series, Bailyn has also managed to produce one book a year on other subjects since 1990.

Bailyn was Trevelyan Lecturer at Cambridge University in 1971. He has been awarded honorary degrees by Yale University and Rutgers University, among many others, and is a member of the American Academy of Arts and Sciences and the Royal Historical Society, as well as of the American Antiquarian and Philosophical Societies.

In 1981 Bailyn was president of the American Historical Association, and in the same year he was appointed Adams University Professor of History at Harvard. In 1983 he became a director of the Charles Warren Center for Studies in American History, and in the 1986–1987 academic year was Pitt Professor of American History at Cambridge University.

Bailyn married Lotte Lazarsfeld, a professor of psychology at Massachusetts Institute of Technology, in 1952. He has two sons and lives in Belmont, Massachusetts.

PRINCIPAL WORKS: The New England Merchants in the Seventeenth Century, 1955; (with L. Bailyn) Massachusetts Shipping, 1697–1714:A Statistical Study, 1959; Education in the Forming of American Society: Needs and Opportunities for Study, 1960; The Ideological Origins of the American Revolution, 1968; The Ordeal of Thomas Hutchinson, 1974; Voyagers to the West: A Passage in the Peopling of America on the Eve of the Revolution, 1986; Faces of Revolution: Personalities and Themes in the Struggle for American Independence, 1990. As editor—The Apologia of Robert Keayne: The Self-Portrait of a Puritan Merchant, 1965; (with D. Fleming) The Intellectual Migration: Europe and America, 1930–1960, 1969; (with D. Fleming) Law in American History, 1972; (with J. Hench) The Press and the American Revolution, 1980; (with P. Morgan) Strangers within the Realm: Cultural Margins of the First British Empire, 1991; The Debate on the Constitution, 1992.

ABOUT: Blackwell Dictionary of Historians, 1988; Contemporary Authors New Revision Series 8, 1984; Dictionary of Literary Biography 17, 1983; Henretta, J. A., Kammen, M., Katz, S. N. (eds.) The Transformation of Early American History: Society, Authority, and Ideology, 1991; International Who's Who, 1992–93; Who's Who in America, 1992–1993. Periodicals—American Historical Review October 1955; Journal of American History March 1961; Journal of Economic History March 1956; New England Quarterly March 1956; New York Times Book Review September 9, 1990.

BANVILLE, JOHN (December 8, 1945–   ), Irish novelist, was born in Wexford, the son of Martin Banville and Doris (Doran) Banville. He was educated in Wexford at the Christian Brothers School and at St. Peter's College, a secondary school. After short stints with Aer Lingus and the British postal service, Banville settled into a job with a London publishing house, in his free time writing short stories that began to appear in the daily Irish Press and in literary journals. Toward the end of the 1960s he moved back to Ireland and became a night copy editor with the Irish Press, a job he held until 1983, when he quit and attempted to get along as a full-time writer. He

JOHN BANVILLE

returned in 1986 to newspaper work, this time to the Irish Times, on a four-day-week basis; as he told an interviewer, "It means I don't have to make a huge effort to sell books to publishers. . . . one is just buying freedom." In 1988 Banville became literary editor of the Irish Times. He married Janet Dunham in 1969. They live in Howth, outside of Dublin, and have two sons.

His first book, Long Lankin, was composed of nine interrelated short stories followed by a novella, "The Possessed," which gathered many of the characters together at a party; Banville now considers "The Possessed" an embarrassment and has refused to reprint it. The title refers to a grisly old ballad, in which Long Lankin kills a woman and child and drinks their blood, trying to cure himself of leprosy. Desperate remedies and the fragility of the human bond—all too easily disrupted by an intruder—are motifs in the nine stories. "All of the pieces have a moody, enigmatic quality," according to Current Biography. A writer called Ben White, who is in search of escape from a land of make-believe, is a recurring figure in the book. Calling the work "a ray of hope for the future of fiction," Stanley Reynolds of the New Statesman wrote: "The theme is ambitious and the form . . . is far from usual, but Mr. Banville is masterly enough to carry both off." He summarized Banville's "overarching classical theme," according to Current Biography: "The loss of love and happiness is the price of freedom."

The semirealistic Nightspawn continues the story of Ben White, now living alone on an Aegean island. Dense with literary allusions and echoes ranging from Dostoevski's *Notes from Underground* to Eliot's "The Wasteland," sprinkled with puns, riddles, and anagrams, the book was recognized as a tour de force. Termed "metafictional," *Nightspawn* presents the surreal adventures of Ben White during a military coup in the form of parodies of such literary genres as the thriller. Thomas Lask in the *New York Times*, called the opening "grand" but felt that the story "never makes up its mind what it is."; In the *Progressive*, however, Elsa Pendleton, though conceding that the story was "chaotic and ambiguous," concluded that "Banville . . . achieved the result he wanted—an extended metaphor of trouble and despair as experienced by a sensitive man confronting a malignant universe."

Birchwood, a historical novel set in the mid-19th century, takes the form of a first-person narrative by Gabriel Godkin (the name has obvious symbolic connotations) and concerns the fate of the eponymous Godkin family estate in rural Ireland. Gabriel grows up in this decaying house in the company of his drunken father, his half-mad mother, his Machiavellian aunt, and his ruthless grandmother. "This, you might think, is really too much," wrote J. A. Cuddon in *Books and Bookmen*, "but the characters are wholly convincing and fully dimensional as human beings." The *Times Literary Supplement*'s reviewer remarked that the novel was "a jump . . . on to a fashionable bandwagon," but admitted that it did "achieve some moments of real gruesomeness." And most reviewers agreed about the precision and elegance of Banville's writing.

Commencing his mature period, Banville sought inspiration in the lives of scientists whose strivings to impose system on chaos seemed to Banville "desperate remedies," to carry forward one of his themes, because they had to struggle not only intellectually but against the negative weight of social pressures. In *Doctor Copernicus*, Banville brings to light the atmosphere of Renaissance Europe to which the Polish astronomer contributed the revolutionary turmoil of heliocentrism. "Banville's Copernicus is detached, reclusive, skeptical, and in his agonizing attempt to reconcile the beauty of his vision of the universe with the horrors of daily life in the sixteenth century, achingly human," *Current Biography* said. The *Times Literary Supplement* chose a scientist, Stephen Clark, to review the novel. "Psychological speculation on the roots of science do not make a novel," he wrote. "The strength of Mr. Banville's work lies in his pictures of Koppernigk [Copernicus] and Rheticus [the narrator]. . . . *Doctor Copernicus* is good

enough as a historical primer; as a novel it is better than most." The reviewer for the *Economist* also noted that few historical novels "illuminate both the time that forms their subject matter and the time in which they are read," but that "*Doctor Copernicus* is among the best of them." Julian Barnes, however, objected in the *New Statesman* to the novel's inelegant prose and its "great hulking metaphors."

Kepler, the story of the man who developed and confirmed the laws of planetary motion, like *Doctor Copernicus*, "focuses on the visionary scientist's lonely struggle against the received notions of his time," according to *Current Biography*, and "contrasts the exhilaration of intellectual discovery with what Banville called 'the sordidness of real life.' "Kepler, despite his bad eyesight, his lack of money, and his shrewish wife, pursued with exemplary zeal a "rage for order" (a phrase from Wallace Stevens, one of Banville's favorite poets).

Russell McCormmach, in the *New York Times Book Review*, said that "despite its shortcomings, *Kepler* is an informed and lively account of an important time and personality by an author of seriousness and talent." He describes how the reader encounters Kepler "at the moment of his . . . meeting with the Danish astronomer Tycho Brahe. . . . We leave him during his last illness as we met him. . . ."The novel opens:

> Johannes Kepler, asleep in his ruff, has dreamed the solution to the cosmic mystery. He holds it cupped in his mind as in his hands he would a precious something of unearthly frailty and splendour. O do not wake!

At the end of the book, at the end of his life, Kepler is awakened from a dream revelation:

> What was it the Jew said? Everything is told us, but nothing explained. Yes. We must take it all on trust. That's the secret. How simple! He smiled. It was not a mere book that was thus thrown away, but the foundation of a life's work. It seemed not to matter.
> "Ah my friend, such dreams . . . "

Paul Taylor commented in the *TImes Literary Supplement*: "Not the least of the pleasures to be derived from *Kepler* is the way Banville's tactile, sensuous prose coils itself confidently around everything. . . . It is Banville's achievement to charge each of Kepler's discoveries with the sublimity and the poetry that they held for the astronomer himself."

The Newton Letter owes much to two classic novels: Ford Madox Ford's *The Good Soldier* with its unobtrusively cunning narration and Goethe's *Elective Affinities*. In his choice of the names of its characters, Edward, Mittler, Charlotte, and Ottilie, Banville makes his debt to the latter explicit. The narrator, a modern historian, has been trying to explain the origins of Newton's disillusionment with scientific absolutes. He becomes involved with a neighboring family, the Lawlesses, abandoning his work on Newton. He fails to notice the parallels between Newton's crisis and his own misconceptions about the Lawlesses. *The Newton Letter* is an epistolary novel, addressed to Clio, the muse of history. Martin Swales, in the *London Review of Books*, remarking on how the narrative reveals the narrator's "moral growth" through his increasing feeling for the ordinary and commonplace, called the book "compassionate and vibrantly intelligent"; but Alan Brownjohn, in the *Times Literary Supplement*, thought the "unobtrusive symbolism" was cast in "all-too-delicate prose."

By the time *Mefisto*, the story of Gabriel, a mathematical prodigy, and his Mepistophelian mentor Felix, who strews obstacles in his path and may be his dead twin brother, was written, Banville had largely purged his language of extraneous rhetoric. Barbara Hardy, in *Books and Bookmen*, praised the "dazzlingly individual new novel." Banville himself had described the book as being about "the Yeatsian man caught between [perfection of the] life and [of the] work." Gabriel, the protagonist of *Mefisto*, Hardy continues, "can't be so reduced." William Kelly, in the *Irish Literary Supplement*, calls this *Tristam Shandy*–like narration (which traces the history of Gabriel from his conception) a "writer's rather than a reader's book," but "for all this, *Mefisto* succeeds in hauling the reader through moral horrors that seem anything but fictional. . . . If a book, as Kafka put it, should serve as an ice axe for the frozen sea within us, then this one is hard enough for the job."

The Book of Evidence, the most immediately accessible of all Banville's novels, deals with Freddie Montgomery, who is a bad son, a bad husband, a thief, an extortionist, and a murderer. The book consists of his prison testimony, given with the cool detachment of psychopaths like Dostoevski's Raskolnikov or Camus's Stranger. His one redeeming virtue is that he refuses to practice any kind of self-deception. Patricia Craig, in the *Times Literary Supplement* concluded that "given the terrible theme, the poor, mute, unreclaimable victim, the shocking randomness of things, banefulness has to win out over the novel's more diverting potential." Erica Abeel in the *New York Times Book Review* declared *The Book of Evidence* "coughed up from hell. . . . dynamiting received ideas and basic assumptions at every turn. . . . Banville dismantles conventional thinking about . . . the notion of motives."

Echoing the relationship between Banville's first and second novels, *Ghosts* continues Montgomery's story. He is stranded by shipwreck on a Hebridean island along with a group of fellow passengers. The resident "magician" of this island is a latter day Prospero. In the course of the novel the murderer finds a form of redemption. Once again Banville has written a novel replete with what Eric Korn, in the *Times Literary Supplement*, called "the dense but burdensome texture of reference." Unlike his earlier novels, which for some readers, in Korn's phrase, merely "lower the drawbridge of illumination over the moat of ambiguity," in *Ghosts* "Banville's tremendous adroitness ensures that the scholarship is not oppressive; and the wit, originality and resourcefulness of the diction are a constant pleasure."

Banville has often and understandably been accused of overwriting and undue obscurity. But his critics have seemed at one in attributing these faults not to pretentiousness or a wish to play to the gallery, but to seriousness and sincerity. As Marc Robinson, reviewing *Ghosts*, commented in the *New Republic*, "Banville writes deeply brewed fiction. From the mere water of sensation and contemplation he makes something dark, strong, bracing, warm."

The concluding novel of Banville's trilogy, after *Ghosts*, *Athena*, Michael Gorra said in the *New York Times Book Review*, may give the impression of a still life. "[M]ood becomes all—a mood sustained by a prose of idiosyncratic and appalling charm." The protagonist has taken a new name and set himself up as an art expert, authenticating paintings stolen from the house where he began. "*Athena* is as grotesque as a portrait by Arcimboldo, in which flowers and fruit and even fish can become the features of a human face, and every bit as beautiful," Gorra concluded. The *Publishers Weekly* reviewer cited the novel's "evocative physical detail and provocative metaphysical musings," and the "dreamlike world of pervasive unease and a sense of loss fueled by the narrator's unspecified guilt (he may also be responsible for a series of gruesome murders)," but concluded that Banville never quite justifies "all this angst."

Banville's work has won him several important literary awards. Among these are the James Tait Black Memorial Prize for *Doctor Copernicus*, the *Guardian* Fiction Prize for *Kepler*, and both the Allied Irish Banks Prize (from the Irish Academy of Letters) and the American-Irish Foundation Literary Award for *Birchwood*. In 1989 he received the Guinness Peat Aviation Book Award for *THe Book of Evidence*, cited as "the best in contemporary Irish writing."

PRINCIPAL WORKS: *Novels*—Long Lankin, 1970; Nightspawn, 1971; Birchwood, 1973; Doctor Copernicus, 1976; Kepler, 1981; The Newton Letter, 1982; Mefisto, 1987; The Book of Evidence, 1989; Ghosts, 1993; Athena, 1995.

ABOUT: Contemporary Authors 128, 1990; Current Biography Yearbook 1992; Duytschaever, J. and Lernout, G. (eds.) History and Violence in Anglo-Irish Literature, 1988; Imhof, R. John Banville: A Critical Introduction, 1989. *Periodicals*—Books and Bookmen September 1973; September 1986; Canadian Journal of Irish Studies July 1988; Economist December 18, 1976; Irish Literary Supplement Spring 1987; Irish University Review Spring 1981; London Review of Books July 15, 1982; New Republic February 21, 1994; New Statesman January 30, 1970; November 26, 1976; New York Times May 9, 1995; New York Times Biographical Service May 21, 1990; New York Times Book Review May 29, 1983; April 21, 1985; May 17, 1990; May 21, 1995; Newsweek May 2, 1983; April 23, 1990; Paris Review Winter 1989; Progressive February 1972; Publishers Weekly April 3, 1995; Spectator February 27, 1971; Times Literary Supplement February 5, 1970; February 16, 1973; December 10, 1976; January 30, 1981; June 11, 1982; March 31, 1989; April 9, 1993.

CLIVE BARKER

BARKER, CLIVE (October 26, 1952–   ), British horror and fantasy writer, playwright and filmmaker, was born in Liverpool, the son of Len Barker, a personnel director, and Joan Barker, a school welfare officer. His father's Irish Protestantism and his mother's Italian Catholicism, he told the *Chicago Tribune*, "canceled each other out," and he "wasn't raised as anything." His parents had insisted that his studies be more practical than art—his true interest at the time—so he studied English and philosophy, earning a degree in the latter in 1974 at the University of Liverpool. Never really enthusiastic, however, about his schooling, he continued to follow his own interests, which led to playwriting, a favored pastime since age eleven. After college he moved to London and wrote a number of plays that were produced for what he has described as London's "really fringe, avant-garde" theater, including such titles as *Frankenstein in Love*, *The History of the Devil*, and a very popular *The Secret Life of Cartoons*. But it was one of the "new voices" of horror that he came to prominence in the early 1980s with his grisly short story volumes *The Books of Blood*. Ironically, he wrote the stories at night as a mere distraction from his daytime playwriting.

The Books of Blood (volumes 1–3) appeared in England in 1984. Barker's graphic depiction of the violence of the supernatural coupled with his witty self-confidence made for a unique combination. Many reviewers have noted from his earliest publications up until his most recent work that Barker's prose is almost unreadable for its lurid content, and yet so ably handled that it is impossible not to follow through to the end of a story, however repulsive. Many of the stories are wildly imaginative, while still remaining in touch with the time-honored themes and conventions of horror—loss of identity, loss of life, ghosts, monsters in the attic. In "In the Hills, the Cities" a homosexual couple sojourning in Yugoslavia encounter giants, denizens of two rival cities whose populace are bound together by ropes and harnessed in order to stage a traditional mock battle which ends with the death of over 38,000 people. A encounter on a New York subway with a mad slasher in "The Midnight Meat Train" leads to a meeting with Lovecraftian, godlike creatures at the end of the rail line, and the initiation of a new mad slasher, an accountant merely trying to get home after working a late shift. In "Rawhead Rex" an ancient predatory monster unleashed from its grave terrorizes the English countryside in search of its favorite food, small children—a standard, recognizable horror plot—but what gives the story its novelty is Barker's willingness to allow for the creature's emotions—fear, embarrassment, anger over imprisonment, disdain for religion—and the townspeople's inhumanity. (Barker told *New York* magazine that if he had to choose between the Christians and the lions, he'd pick the lions.)

Barker was in turn praised and reviled for his graphic, show-all style, but many reviewers could not fail to recognize the intensity of the work. In *Fantasy Review* of June 1985 a reviewer commented: "All this carnality and mayhem is lovingly described in Barker's vivid, sensory cinematic style. . . . [y]et *Books of Blood* cannot be dismissed as mere splatter fiction; the philosophical and thematic content of these visceral stories elevates them from this category."

The first three volumes of *The Books of Blood* made such an impact that Barker was commissioned to produce three more volumes, which appeared in 1985 (in the U.S. they were published under separate titles rather than as *Books of Blood* volumes: *The Inhuman Condition, In the Flesh,* and *The Life of Death*). These, too, met with similar critical and public reception, but some reviewers noted more craft than gore in the second batch. Still, Barker maintained his very idiosyncratic and disturbing style: hands, feeling maligned and unfairly treated, sever themselves from the rest of their bodies in an act of grisly, rebellious secession in "The Body Politic"; a old-fashioned hook-armed bogeyman named the Candyman, haunting (and murdering) in a Liverpool ghetto in "The Forbidden," is chanted into existence by a child; and, in "The Age of Desire," a test drug produces a murderous, psychotic need for sex and leads, literally, to a sexual encounter with the Grim Reaper as the ultimate experience. Kim Newman, wrote in the *New Statesman,* "Having burrowed his way into the genre with his first books, Barker is now eating at it, *transforming* it from within." The reviewer concluded that, allowing for a few missteps, the tales "either tread new ground or seed the old spores that germinate into mutant blossoms." Ken Tucker, in the *New York Times Book Review,* (1986) praised Barker because he "avoids the breathless tone that makes most modern horror tales seem foolish, instead setting scenes in a measured voice with meticulous details that accumulate to create an atmosphere of dread and foreboding." He added, "Try to imagine the *Texas Chainsaw Massacre* with a screenplay by V. S. Pritchett and you have some idea of Clive Barker at his most effective."

Fantasy Review in September 1985 called Barker's first novel, *The Damnation Game* "important" for its "helping to establish links between graphic horror and high quality literature." A Faustian tale, it starts in the wartorn Warsaw ghetto and concludes, bloodily, forty years later, as Joseph Whitehead, a reclusive billionaire industrialist, tries to save his soul and flesh from Mamoulian, an inhuman gamesman who thrives on the consuming of human souls. The novel received many excellent notices, but some critics had reservations. Laurence Coven, in *Book World,* remarked: "Time after time Barker makes us shudder in revulsion. In pure descriptive power there is no one writing

horror fiction now who can match him. And to his credit, he does not write in a social vacuum. His terrors arise, at least in part, from a profound sadness and misery he perceives in the human condition. . . . " but added, "[T]here are only so many unspeakable acts one can speak about. No matter how brilliant the language, many readers will eventually be numbed by Barker's excess. His overkill deprives us of a sense of anticipation, and without anticipation there is no suspense."

Barker himself rails against the less-is-more criticism that has greeted his work. In an interview in *Faces of Fear,* he commented, "Horror fiction without violence doesn't do a great deal for me. I think that death and wounding need to be in the air. You've got to get the reader on this ghost train ride, and there's got to be something vile at the end of it, or else why aren't you on a rollercoaster instead? And I like to be able to deliver the vileness."

Reviewers have also complained about Barker's graphic linking of sex and death, but the connection is not without significance in the decade when AIDS came into the forefront of the world's consciousness. Barker maintained in *Faces of Fear* that a symbiosis of the two, sex and death, is at the root of all horror: "The postorgasmic sense of loss, or indeed the sense of escape or expulsion, seems to tie up very strongly with the preoccupations of horror, which are, very often, about the transformation of the body, which are about getting close to death but maybe avoiding it, which are about being out of control of oneself and one's feeling."

"Sex is about a little madness—how often is horror about madness? Sex is about a little death—how often is horror about death? It's about the body—how often is horror about the body?"

Barker prefers to be thought of as an author at work within the broad field of imaginative fiction. *Weaveworld,* though containing many horrific moments, was his attempt to extend his reach and perhaps, to escape the horror labeling that has caused him to bristle in interviews. Barker's second novel is an epic about men and magicians battling over possession of a carpet, a carpet made up of a fantastical universe of people, places, beauty, and dark magic. *Weaveworld* is perhaps Barker's best received work to date, with laudatory reviews in Britain and America. The *Kirkus* reviewer commented that the novel "manages via its powerful and giddy torrent of invention to grasp the golden ring as the most ambitious and visionary horror novel of the decade." John Calvin Batchelor wrote in the *New York Times Book Review,*

(1987): "Clive Barker reveals his prodigious talent for erecting make-believe worlds in the midst of Thatcher's tumbledown kingdom of Windsorian privilege and secretly policed ghettos. Reaching into its degraded and strangely fertile streets, he creates a fantastic romance of magic and promise that is at once popular fiction and utopian conjuring."

In 1987 Barker decided to test his mettle in a new medium—films. Several disappointing films had been made from screenplays he had written; he wrote the original screenplay "Underworld" and adapted his short story "Rawhead Rex" for the film version of the same title, but felt in both cases hardly any of what he had put on the page made the transition to celluloid. Barker took creative control and cast himself in the role of director for the feature *Hellraiser* in 1987, based on his novella, "The Hellbound Heart." The film, which even the author conceded was somewhat crude and rudimentary, nevertheless went on to make millions, inspired three sequels (Barker had a hand in making all), and brought the "Pinhead" Cenobites—well-mannered denizens from an alternate universe who enjoy tearing apart human flesh—into minor cult film status. Barker also turned his novella *Cabal* into the film *Nightbreed* in 1990. It starred blood-and-guts director—and obvious kindred spirit—David Cronenberg as a murderous psychiatrist who meddles in the netherworld and whose dead patient becomes a sort of Moses to a carnival of monster protagonists living beneath cemetery ruins. Given Howard Mittelmark's comments on the book in the *New York Times Book Review*, it is easy to see why Barker chose to adapt this story: "Filled with one ghastly, baroque effect after another, it's dazzling, captivating stuff, but finally it's all special effects. This is horror more cinematic than literary. . . . "

The Great and Secret Show, Barker's next ambitious novel and the start of a proposed trilogy called The Art, is over 700 pages long, and, in what *Time* termed its "kitchen sink ethic," throws into the mix a psychotic, evil postal employee who via the U.S. mail discovers a secret society enmeshed in a world of magic and the supernatural; a once-revered scientist who develops a cosmic altering substance that transforms life itself; a nubile teenager impregnated by lake spirits; a comedian whose primal fears are metamorphosed into tangible warriors of destruction; and a lot of ambiguous mysticism perpetrated in jargon such as "Quiddity," "the Ephermis," the "Metacosm," and the "Iad Uroboros." The *Book World* reviewer thought it "pretentious beyond belief," "too long by half," and "just silly," and hoped Barker would "return to the gooey enthu-

siasm for straight pop horror that made him an '80s staple." Ken Tucker, however, in the *New York Times Book Review*, commented that it was an allusive, mythic, complex, and entertaining pastiche of Thomas Pynchon's *Gravity Rainbow* and J.R.R. Tolkien's *Lord of the Rings*. "From *The Great and Secret Show*," Tucker wrote, "it is clear that Mr. Barker's intention is to force the horror genre to encompass a kind of dread, an existential despair, that it hasn't noticeably evinced until now. This is a tall order, one that this novel, which is skillful and funny but ultimately overwrought, doesn't quite accomplish."

Clive Barker, who claims his work as an illustrator and painter has always aided and abetted his descriptive panache, has received two British Fantasy awards and the World Fantasy Award for best anthology for *The Books of Blood*. While continuing to adapt his early tales of terror for the screen he has also adamantly refused to be typecast as just a horror writer. His 1991–1992 offerings included *Imajica*, an 800-page science fiction novel exploring man's contact with God and Earth's exclusion from and subsequent readmission into the "5 Dominions," a spiritual grouping of celestial bodies, which echoes C. S. Lewis's *Perelandra* space trilogy, and *The Thief of Always* (illustrated by Barker), which its publisher called a "fable for children of all ages," and *Publishers Weekly* described as being similar in spirit to the tales of the Brothers Grimm.

PRINCIPAL WORKS: *Novels*—The Damnation Game, 1985; Weaveworld, 1987; The Great and Secret Show, 1989; Imajica, 1991. *Short fiction*—The Books of Blood, Vol. I, 1984; The Books of Blood, Vol. II, 1984; The Books of Blood, Vol. III, 1984; The Inhuman Condition: Tales of Terror, 1986 (in U.K.); In the Flesh: Tales of Terror, 1986 (in U.K.: The Books of Blood, Vol. V); The Life of Death, 1987 (in U.K.: The Books of Blood, Vol. VI); Cabal (contains title novella and four short stories) 1988; The Hellbound Heart (novella) 1988. *Juvenile*—The Thief of Always, 1992.

ABOUT: Contemporary Authors 129, 1990; Winter, D. E. Faces of Fear, 1985. *Periodicals*—American Film September 1987; Booklist September 1991; Book World June 28, 1987; Books and Bookmen July 1985; September 1987; Chicago Tribune September 15, 1987, May 23, 1993; Fantasy Review June 1985; September 1985; Film Comment January/February 1990; Journal of Popular Culture Winter 1993; Kirkus Review August 1, 1987; Library Journal January 1990; New Statesman July 18, 1986; New York May 26, 1986; New York Times September 20, 1987; New York Times Book Review September 21, 1986; February 15, 1987; June 21, 1987; February 11, 1990; Omni October 1986; Publishers Weekly July 4, 1986; March 19, 1990; Rolling Stone February 11, 1988; Time March 19,

1990; Times (London) October 17, 1986; Times Literary Supplement October 11, 1991; Studies in Weird Fiction Spring 1991; Washington Post September 30, 1987; September 11, 1992.

*BAUDRILLARD, JEAN (1929–   ), French theorist and social critic, was born in Reims to working class parents who had moved to the city from the country where their parents had been peasants. "I was the first member of the tribe, so to speak, to do some studying," Baudrillard told an interviewer. "I was not brought up in an intellectual milieu. . . . It was not a cultural environment, so I had compensated for this by working extremely hard at the Lycée." This was the prestigious Lycée Henri IV in Paris, from which he moved on to study sociology at the University of Paris. For several years he taught German in the secondary schools. By the early 1960s Baudrillard was publishing translations into French of German authors, notably Bertolt Brecht and Peter Weiss, and contributing reviews to Jean-Paul Sartre's journal *Le Temps moderne* of works by Italo Calvino, Jorge Luis Borges, Uwe Johnson, and J. G. Ballard among others. In 1966 Baudrillard took his university degree and began teaching sociology at one of the newly established branches of the University of Paris at Nanterre, a position he held until 1987.

Already an affirmed Marxist, Baudrillard found himself in the center of the radical student movement that reached its climax in the tumultuous events of May 1968 and threatened to overthrow the government of President Charles de Gaulle. Baudrillard supported the students, but his own revolutionary radicalism has never conformed to any specific political ideology. He read extensively in the French intellectual Left—Sartre, Lévi-Strauss, Barthes, and somewhat later Foucault and Derrida. His thinking on consumerism and the impact of the mass media was heavily influenced by the writings of Herbert Marcuse and Walter Benjamin. Having apparently absorbed all of the major developments in contemporary European thought from neo-Marxism and Freudianism to structuralism and semiotics, he perversely but not uncharacteristically rejected them because they were based on assumptions of logic and rationality. The postmodern Western world, dominated by the technology of film, television, and computer-generated virtual reality, is, in his view, not a society reasoning about reality but one based on images, signs, simulacra—"hyperreality." Logic and rational analysis have become obsolete and irrelevant.

JEAN BAUDRILLARD

Baudrillard's first books, *Le Système des objets* (The Systematization of Objects, 1968) and *La Société de consommation* (The consumer society, 1970), are neo-Marxist in ideology, positing a prepatterned or coded response to the immensity of consumer goods that makes them into necessities. In the affluent society of postwar Europe and America, he argues, a technological revolution has taken place. He writes in *La Société de consommation* : "We are surrounded today by the remarkable conspicuousness of consumption and affluence, established by multiplication of objects, services, and material goods, all of which constitute a sort of fundamental mutation in the ecology of the human spirit." Increasingly, consumers become merely passive functions of the products they consume. These products have meaning themselves only as signs or codes, rather than as real things fulfilling real needs. The capitalism of the new society is based not on needs but on symbols or signs, "social signifiers" that dictate consumerism: advertising logos that signal a product, the "name brand," the social status implied in ever increasing consumption. In *La Société de consommation* he says: "The social logic of consumption is not at all that of the individual appropriation of the use value of goods and services . . . It is a logic of the production and manipulation of social signifiers."

His argument in *Le Miroir de la production* (translated as *The Mirror of Production*) is summed up in the book's subtitle, *L'Illusion critique du matérialism historique*—the critical illusion of historical materialism. As Douglas

°boh dree YAR, zhahn

Kellner explains it in *Jean Baudrillard: From Marxism to Postmodernism and Beyond*: "In *Mirror*, Baudrillard argues that Marx's categories and theories are too conservative to be useful to revolutionary theory, because they are too deeply imbedded in political economy to be of use in constructing a new social order free from the imperatives of production and political economy." In Baudrillard's words: "The super-ideology of the sign and the general operationalization of the signifier—everywhere sanctioned today by the new master disciplines of structural linguistics, semiology, information theory and cybernetics—has replaced good old political economy as the theoretical basis of the system."

Having broken with Marxism in the early 1970s, Baudrillard turned to an analysis of language as sign. Historically, he notes in *The Mirror of Production*, words had referents. In the postmodern age, however, signs have a significance of their own with no specific referent. Commercials on television, for example, "signal" now as language once did. Signs are codes for social values: the "good life" in a brand of beer, affluence in a make of automobile, social success in a style of clothing. The media have not only become the message, as Marshall McLuhan had predicted in *The Gutenberg Galaxy* in 1962, but they have created a new reality, "hyperreality," in which we experience events by looking at images, a simulated reality, on a television screen or a computer terminal. An illustration is Baudrillard's essay "La Guerre du Golfe n'a pas eu lieu" (The Gulf War never happened), published in *Libération*, a French daily, in February and March 1991, which explains by its title that for television viewers who watched news reports of it, the war was unreal. In *L'Echange symbolique et la mort* (Symbolic exchange and death, 1976) Baudrillard proclaims in a wildly revolutionary and nihilistic thesis that we have entered "the era of simulation"—involving, he argues, "the end of labor. The end of production. The end of political economy. The end of the dialectic signifier/signified which permitted the accumulation of knowledge and meaning, the linear syntagm of cumulative discourse . . . The end of the classic era of the sign. The end of the era of production."

Even Baudrillard's most sympathetic readers, such as Mark Poster (who edited an edition of his selected writings), are dismayed by his "bleak fatalism," his conclusion that only death survives "the discontinuous indeterminism of the genetic code that governs life—the teleonomical principle." Poster also notes his increasing obscurity: "[H]is writing style is hyperbolic and declarative, often lacking sustained, systematic analysis when it is appropriate; he totalizes his

insights, refusing to qualify or delimit his claims." On the other hand, Jorge Arditi says in his review in *Contemporary Sociology* of Mike Gane's *Baudrillard; Critical and Fatal Theory*, that Gane argues that "it is a common misconception to see in Baudrillard's oeuvre a total affirmation of nihilism . . . .for Baudrillard the fundamental question is how to resist the complacency of postmodern nihilism . . . ." The answer is to develop a "fatal" strategy to resist being entrapped by the sign—seduction, the "mastery of the symbolic."

Baudrillard challenges the leading French theorists of the day, terming them essentially reactionary. Michel Foucault, for example, who used the science of linguistics in the study of profound changes in human sexuality and social science over the course of centuries, is Baudrillard's target in *Oublier Foucault* (*Forget Foucault*). Foucault responded to this title with the comment, "I would have more problems remembering . . . Baudrillard."

Baudrillard faults Foucault for assuming that the agents of power in society are its institutions. "The universal fascination with power in its exercise and its theory is so intense because it is fascination with a *dead* power characterized by a simultaneous 'resurrection effect' in an obscene and parodic mode, of all the power already seen—exactly like sex in pornography."

By the 1980s Baudrillard's reputation as a controversial social theorist had been established in France and was beginning to spread to Britain and the United States. He provoked lively favorable response in some intellectual and academic circles, who applaud his call to deconstruct all traditional notions about art and aesthetics. Others who have commented on his work dismiss him as one of "the gimmick-mongers of contemporary French thought" who has "disqualified himself from serious intellectual regard" (Richard Vine in *New Criterion*).

With the publication of *Amérique* (*America*), Mark Poster's edition of his *Selected Writings*, and Mike Gane's collections of his essays and reviews in 1991, Baudrillard has become an international personality. He has lectured at universities and art museums in the United States and Great Britain and has appeared from time to time on the popular French television program "Apostrophes." He has also managed to provoke feminists with his book *De la seduction* (*Seduction*) in which he analogizes the seductive powers of signs with sexual seduction, representing the feminine as merely "appearance" in contrast to "the profundity of the masculine" and recommending that women "would do well to let themselves be seduced by this truth, because here is the secret of their power which they are in the process of losing by setting up the profundity of the feminine against that of the masculine." Some of his critics also find him homophobic and xenophobic, but most consider him a cultural gadfly who provokes readers in order to stimulate their thinking and undermine received assumptions. Describing the Centre Pompidou in Paris, for example, which he calls "a brilliant monument of modernity," he deconstructs the very concept of mass culture that it is intended to celebrate: " . . . this carcass of signs and flux, of networks and circuits . . . A monument to mass simulation effects, the Centre functions like an incinerator, absorbing and devouring all cultural energy, rather like the black monolith of *2001*—a mad convection current for the materialization, absorption and destruction of all the contents within it."

Like many European intellectuals, Baudrillard is both repelled and fascinated by America, which he uses as a paradigm for the society of hyperreality. Based on several visits he made to the United States in the 1970s and '80s, his *America* not only hails the "visceral, unbounded vitality . . . a metabolic vitality, in sex and bodies, as well as in work and in buying and selling . . . the only remaining primitive society"; but also proclaims—in the kind of paradox Baudrillard relishes—the country's imminent demise: "Can Reagan be the symbol of present-day America society—a society that having once possessed the original features of power is now perhaps at its face-lift stage?" Baudrillard saw much of America largely by flying from city to city or in an automobile racing down the superhighways with the car stereo blasting (Stephen Helmling, in the *Kenyon Review*, called him "a highbrow Hunter Thompson"). "Aeronautic missionary of the silent majorities," he rhapsodizes, "I jump with cat-like tread from one airport to the other."

The loud chorus of critical disapproval that greeted *America* in the United States was inspired by the hyperreality of the book itself—a series of mercurial images (James Marcus described it in the *New York Times Book Review* as "a mixture . . . of crazy notions and dead-on insights"), abstractions, and generalizations. *America*, in the view of some critics, is interesting as a demonstration of Baudrillard's solipsism. "Making America over into his image," Richard Poirier wrote in the *London Review of Books*, Baudrillard sees the country "as space waiting to be filled with thinking of his own."

In *Cool Memories 1980–1985* and its sequel, *Cool Memories II*, journals that Baudrillard describes as "a subtle matrix of idleness," he jots down aphorisms, some witty, some merely perverse: "Democracy is the menopause of Western society, the Grand Climacteric of the body social. Fascism is its middle-aged lust"; "Like dreams, statistics are a form of wish-fulfillment"; "Death too becomes conspicuous by its absence." Summing up his achievement in a review of his *Selected Writings* in the *New Republic*, Arthur C. Danto writes: "A lot of Baudrillard's prose is a mudge of pseudo-science enhanced by blague. My sense is that Baudrillard is less a writer than a performer of some kind, a sporadically brilliant illusionist whose feats of analysis are capable of making salient features of social reality that might never come to consciousness without him." But he warns the reader against reading him too much or too deeply: "At this point you are taking Baudrillard too seriously."

PRINCIPAL WORKS IN ENGLISH TRANSLATION: The Mirror of Production (tr. M. Poster) 1975; For a Critique of the Political Economy of the Sign (tr. C. Levin) 1981; In the Shadow of the Silent Majorities, 1983; Simulations (tr. P. Foss et al) 1983; Cool Memories (tr. C. Turner) 1988; Selected Writings (ed. M. Poster; tr J. Mourrain) 1988; The Revenge of the Crystal: A Baudrillard Reader (ed. M. Carter) 1989; Seduction (tr. B. Singer) 1990; The Transparency of Evil: Essays on Extreme Phenomena (tr. S. Benedict), 1994.

ABOUT: Contemporary Literary Criticism 60, 1990; Current Biography Yearbook 1993; Gane, M. Baudrillard's Bestiary, 1991; Gane, M. Baudrillard: Critical and Fatal Theory, 1991; Gane, M. Baudrillard Live: Selected Interviews, 1993; Kellner, D. Jean Baudrillard: From Marxism to Postmodernism and Beyond, 1989; Poster, M. *Introduction to* Baudrillard: Selected Writings, 1988: Stearns, W. and W. Choloupka (eds.) Jean Baudrillard: The Disappearance of Art and Politics, 1992. *Periodicals*—Art in America June 1988; Artforum April 1984; Contemporary Sociology January 1993; Kenyon Review Winter 1990; London Review of Books February 16, 1989; New Criterion May 1989; New Republic September 10, 1990; New York Review of Books June 1, 1989; New York Times Book Review February 12, 1989; Times Literary Supplement December 16, 1988.

BAUMBACH, JONATHAN (July 5, 1933–), American novelist and short story-writer, writes: "I was born in New York City, the first son, the only son for twelve and a half years, of Harold and Ida [Zackheim] Baumbach. My father was/ is a painter, and I grew up in a home in which the making of art took priority over all other concerns. My mother taught grade school, as many artists' wives did in those days, making it possible for my father to paint full time. I don't remember exactly when it started, but I had a sense of myself as a writer—the nature of what

JONATHAN BAUMBACH

it meant undefined—from virtually as far back as I can remember. It was a way of following in my father's footsteps while scratching in the sand to make my own.

"As an undergraduate, I wrote mostly plays, had a play of mine performed at college, briefly thought myself a playwright. On graduation from Brooklyn College [1955], I entered the M. F.A. Program in Theater Arts at Columbia University with a major in playwriting. The play I wrote at Columbia for my thesis, *The One-Eyed Man is King*, was produced at the Theater East the following spring. Although it was gratifying to have my play performed, it was in other ways a disillusioning experience. The play in performance seemed at best a distant relation to the one I had written. It wasn't theater that interested me, I discovered, but the writing of the play, the writing itself.

"Shortly after *The One-Eyed Man* completed its limited run, I was drafted into the army, let myself be drafted rather than stay in school. While in the army, I wrote some short fiction and a few film reviews for the magazine *Film Culture*. Film had always interested me more than theater and has been a major influence on my fiction. I've been an active film critic in one venue or another since 1973.

"Married now and with a child to support, I got an early release from the army to go back to school. Three years later [1961] I had a doctorate in English and American literature from Stanford University with a dissertation on the contemporary American novel, subsequently published as *The Landscape of Nightmare*.

Though I wanted nothing more than to write fiction, I had circumstantially postponed doing what mattered most to me for five years.

"I spent my first year as an instructor at Ohio State University, writing a novel—the novel, it seemed, writing itself—working in my office in a fever of necessity every free moment I could get. My first novel, *A Man to Conjure With*, was published by Random House in 1965; a few months after New York University Press had bought out *The Landscape of Nightmare: Studies in the Contemporary American Novel.* Though stylistically my own, *A Man to Conjure With* showed the influence of the books I had been reading. It was relatively conventional in form, was distinguished perhaps by its dream passages. My self-defining concerns as a writer have moved so far away from *A Man to Conjure With*, which was also published in England and Italy, I can barely remember at this point the self that wrote it.

"In 1968, I published my second novel, *What Comes Next*, with Harper & Row. In part a response to the Vietnam war, *What Comes Next* is a novel about public and private violence and is my darkest, most pitiless book—the manifest demon of my psychotherapy.

"My third novel, *Reruns*, which was not published until 1974, seemed to me at its completion in 1971 a notable advance over anything I had done before. The novel, composed of thirty-three cinematic dreams, was held together by recurring configurations—the same things happening again and again in metaphoric disguise. No one seemed to know what to make of it. My agent, Candida Donadio, sent it out for almost three years, and it collected something like thirty-four rejections. It was ultimately published by the Fiction Collective, a writers' cooperative I helped to found. Seventeen years after its first printing, *Reruns* is still in print, still in certain bookstores, is taught occasionally in universities courses, is written about in articles on the contemporary American novel. It has sold more than twice the combined sales of my first two novels. A further irony: publishers who rejected it in the first place turned down recent books of mine for not being in the 'same classic mode' as *Reruns*. The lesson is perhaps also classic. The new, the unexpected, is always suspect, in a culture that depends on sales receipts for its validation.

"After *Reruns*, I published most of my books with the Fiction Collective (*Babble, Chez Charlotte and Emily, My Father More or Less, The Life and Times of Major Fiction, Separate Hours*), which let me pursue my eccentric concerns as a writer without the deforming censorship of commercial constraint. Recently, I've completed a new novel called 'Flickers,' which, though innovative, seems nevertheless greatly accessible. My method as always is intuitive and nonrational. I continue to do as a writer what it seems to me I've always done: I continue to imagine language on a blank page."

In 1964 Jonathan Baumbach wrote: "To live in this world in which madness daily passes for sanity is a kind of madness in itself. Yet where else can we go?" This is the opening of his preface to *The Landscape of Nightmare*, his critical study of the post-World War II American novel. The statement may be read more broadly as a rationale of Baumbach's own fiction, for the novels and short stories that he has written since then have in common the assumption that novelists "have tried to make sense—to make art—out of what it's like to live in this nightmare."

Baumbach is an experimental novelist and founder of the Fiction Collective. Like a number of other young novelists working in nontraditional forms, abandoning conventional realism and linear narrative structure in an effort to reach more deeply into the human psyche, Baumbach discovered that commercial trade publishers were reluctant to handle such work. His own first two novels, though published by prominent trade publishers, were not widely promoted or reviewed, in his opinion, nor were they kept in print. Accordingly, he joined with Peter Spielberg and other writers (among them Raymond Federman, Ronald Sukenik, Walter Abish, and Russell Banks) in forming Fiction Collective, a cooperative self-publishing venture.

As Baumbach wrote in "Seeing Myself in Movies," "External reality, let me confess, for all its dazzle, has never seemed as charged to me as the unseen world." His interest in the psychological, Jerome Klinkowitz explains in *The Life of Fiction*, "is more properly a concern with liberated workings of the imagination, not with clinical abnormality. He is not interested in a character's curious behavior, except for the way it reveals itself in language; and even then *the* way, *the* manner, *the* form, is the important thing." Both *A Man to Conjure With* and *What Comes Next* have the quality of collage, organizing themselves around the consciousness of men who are alienated from reality, perceiving their lives as nightmares where memory and imagination reshape and frequently contort experience to the point where they—and the reader—cannot distinguish between the madness of dreams and the madness of reality in the modern world.

The working title of *Reruns* was "Dreambook." Its final title signals the special fascination that film has for Baumbach. Along with many other members of his pretelevision generation, he came under the shaping influence of movies of the 1930s, 1940s, and 1950s. Not only did their leading characters assume mythic proportions (especially those in horror films like *Dracula*, *Frankenstein*, and *King Kong*), but their kaleidoscopic images, their montages and flashing episodes, created a new kind of communication. The transferring of these effects to the written word produced a narrator who is watching a movie, losing himself in a world of flickering images, illusory, yet to him terrifyingly real. For Baumbach, movies and dreams intersect with reality, sometimes substituting for it, sometimes merging with it. As he writes in "Seeing Myself in Movies": "I use the shadowy logic (really illogic) of movie plots to simulate dreams. That is, I want to create fiction that has the logic and mystery of a dream while not seeming necessarily dreamlike." Made up of thirty-three episodes or sections, *Rerun* is an autobiography of a character whose name changes disconcertingly and who is so driven by the madness and absurdity of modern life that he can only reinvent himself in a movie:

> Separated at the present time from my third wife, Molly, to whom I am not legally married, unable to get a divorce from my second wife to whom I am still on the books husband, the father of four children (perhaps five), the son of at least two parents, Jewish on my mother's side, Italian lapsed Catholic on my father's, American, student, sometime soldier, comedian, film maker, revenger, driven in conflicting directions by dream-haunted ambition, I am here without wife or woman (no pleasant place to be), your guide and reporter, a hostage to the habits of rerunning the dead past in the cause of waking from the dream.

The pace is breathless—"The news had traveled so fast it had gotten to me before I had come to it," the narrator says. The effects are simultaneously grim and absurdly comic. The demands on the reader are enormous, but several reviewers felt that the novel repaid the effort. Michael Mewshaw, for example, observes in the *New York Times Book Review* that after a while "the reader loses a bit of his ability to respond or, worse yet, begins to suspect that Baumbach is spinning his wheels, not pursuing deeper meaning. Still, it can be funny . . . Jonathan Baumbach is much too talented to ruin his book—his prose has energy and acuity and he clearly has the technical facility to write this sort of novel. . . . "

Babble even more daringly flouts the conventions of realistic fiction. Its principal narrator is a baby, who tells his stories to his writer-father in a neat reversal of bedtime story logic. The stories he tells are funny and imaginative ones, including a private-eye detective story with a tough-talking baby detective named Spy Everest and a war story with a baby soldier ("'If someone comes to the door wearing a helmet and has a medal pinned to his shirt,' the young hero notifies his parents in a special delivery letter, 'that will be me. Don't accept anyone else.'") Thalia Selz commented in *Fiction International*: "Many modern writers have rendered simulacra of our contradictory universe by means of dreams. But few can rival Baumbach in wit, invention, and breadth of understanding. *Babble* is never strained and almost never private or cute." Some reviewers such as Joseph Epstein in the *Hudson Review* disagreed, however, finding that the novel requires too much energy from the reader, but that when the jokes are perceived, they fall flat.

Chez Charlotte and Emily carries to the limit the qualities of film montage. (Baumbach calls it "my most cinematic novel.") Scenes are shot and reshot; characters are named for movie stars—Francis Sinatra, Judith Garland, Bobby Mitchum, Maury Chevalier. The book opens with an epigraph from the French film maker Jean-Luc Godard, "Everything remains to be done," reminding us, as Irving Malin points out in the *Hollins Critic*, that "reality, like film, is never complete or perfect—it is on the contrary, *continually tentative*." The speaker (he cannot properly be called a narrator in a non-narrative novel) is a novelist introducing a novelist, Joshua Quartz, and his wife Genevieve. They communicate only through a story that the speaker is writing: "Joshua and Genevieve Quartz who, each in private crisis, are unable to talk to the other except in displaced language. From time to time, I stop work and read a paragraph to her, eliciting not so much response to my prose as acknowledgement of my presence."

"Each chapter of the book," Peter Quartermain wrote in the *Chicago Review*, "tends to be a more or less self-contained fantasy sequence belonging to one character . . . we meet cliché character after cliché character from movies, novels, TV, pulp magazines, etc." Quartermain found the overall effect of the book "politely boring; we have here an unfelt world, bookish and clever . . . a disguised, semi-allegorical essay on metaphor and identity, love and marriage." Don Skiles, writing in the *American Book Review*, finds in *Chez Charlotte and Emily* "a rich, positive ambiguity, the weird, quirky sense of senselessness, the incessant hunt for meaning, for definition, for the action that will shape, define, or transform." He regards Baumbach as "a true heir of the French existential writers."

The novel *My Father More or Less* explores the relationship between an unhappy eighteen-year-old boy and his father, a novelist living in England and writing a screenplay about a detective involved in murky conspiracies. Once again film and reality converge; "I have this idea off and on that my life is made up of pieces of old movies," says the boy, bitter at his father's abandonment of his wife and family yet hungry for his attention and love. Jerome Klinkowitz finds that although this novel, like its predecessor, is an experiment in intertextuality, *My Father* reads as accessibly as the most realistic fiction, indicating that Baumbach has found a useful device for bringing narrative fiction back within the literary mainstream." Equally accessible are many of Baumbach's short stories, most of which appeared first in periodicals such as *Esquire*, *Kenyon Review*, and *Partisan Review*. One of his stories, "The Return of Service," was reprinted in *Best American Short Stories*, 1978; two others, "Passion?" and "The Life and Times of Major Fiction," appear in the *O. Henry Prize Stories* of 1979 and 1984 respectively. With his 1990 novel *Seperate Hours*, however, Baumbach reverted to the more elusive manner of *Reruns* and *Chez Charlotte and Emily*. The couple here, both therapists, are experiencing the painful dissolution of their marriage. Each has a different version of the marriage, offering what Irving Malin characterizes in the *Review of Contemporary Fiction* as "an interpretation of interpretation, a fiction of fictions." Once again Baumbach is stressing the breakdown in communication, the failure of language, the hopelessness of separating truth from fiction. Even the text of the novel breaks down, with one section printed in two columns one containing side-by-side accounts from husband and wife. Writing in the *New York Times Book Review*, Steven Kellman is reminded of the characters' inability to perceive truths in Ford Madox Ford's *The Good Soldier*. For Kellman, *Separate Hours* is "a curiously bracing novel of dissolution."

Baumbach has taught creative writing since 1966 at Brooklyn College of the City University of New York and in 1972 became full professor and director of the college's M.F.A. program. He has been visiting professor at Tufts (1970–1971), the University of Washington (1977–1978, 1983–1984) and Princeton University (1990). He has received fellowships from Yaddo (1963, 1964, 1965), the National Endowment for the Arts (1969), the Guggenheim Foundation (1978), and the Ingram Merrill Foundation (1983). He has written film criticism for the *Partisan Review* since 1973 and has been a member of the National Society of Film Critics since 1976; from 1982 to 1984 he was its chairman. From his first marriage, to Elinor Berkman in 1956, he has a son and a daughter. They were divorced in 1967. In 1969 he married Georgia Brown, by whom he has two sons.

PRINCIPAL WORKS: *Novels*—A Man to Conjure With, 1965; What Comes Next, 1968; Reruns, 1983; Babble, 1976; Chez Charlotte and Emily, 1979; My Father More or Less, 1982; Separate Hours, 1990. *Short stories*—The Return of Service, 1980; The Life and Times of Major Fiction, 1987. *Criticism*—The Landscape of Nightmare: Studies in the Contemporary American Novel, 1966. *As editor*—(with A. Edelstein) Moderns and Contemporaries, 1968; Writers as Teachers/Teachers as Writers, 1970; Statements: New Fiction from the Fiction Collective, 1975; (with P. Spielberg) Statements Two, 1978.

ABOUT: Baumbach, J. Seeing Myself in Movies *in* K. Cohen (ed.) Writing in a Film Age: Essays by Contemporary Novelists, 1991; Contemporary Authors Autobiography Series 5, 1987; Contemporary Authors New Revision Series 12, 1984; Contemporary Literary Criticism 6, 1976; 23, 1983; Contemporary Novelists, 4th ed., 1986; Dictionary of Literary Biography Yearbook 80, 1981; Graham, J. (ed.) The Writers Voice, 1973; Klinkowitz, J. The Life of Fiction, 1977. *Periodicals*—American Book Review March–April 1981; Chicago Review Autumn 1980; Fiction International 1976; Hollins Critic February 1980; Hudson Review Winter 1976–1977; New York Times Book Review October 13, 1974; July 15, 1990; Review of Contemporary Fiction Fall 1990.

*BEI DAO (pseudonym of Zhao Zhengkai) (August 2, 1949–), Chinese poet and fiction writer, was born in Beijing to a family originally from the south of China. His father was a professional administrator and his mother a doctor. He was born in the year of the Communists' triumph in China, became a Red Guard, and enthusiastically supported Mao's Great Cultural Revolution that broke out when he was sixteen. After the initial euphoria of participating in the upheaval, he realized that it would end only in new forms of tyranny. Bei Dao's formal education had been disrupted, and now he was forced to endure stints of "reeducation" in the country and then to become a worker in Beijing. By 1974 he had written the first draft of his novella *Waves* and begun a sequence of poems. Those poems were to become a guiding beacon for the young people of the first—April 5th—Democracy Movement in 1976, in which thousands peacefully demonstrated in Tiananmen Square in Beijing. The movement was an abortive one, but Bei Dao won instant recognition and faithful following for his poetry, especially

BEI DAO

among young readers.

> Once I goosestepped across the square
> my head shaved bare
> the better to seek the sun
> but in that season of madness
> seeing the cold-faced goats on the other side
> of the fence I changed direction.

Jonathan Spence, reviewing *Waves* and the poems collected in *The August Sleepwalker* in the *New York Times Book Review*, said, "Thus did Bei Dao . . . gaze with sudden awareness at his once venerated leaders. . . . " In turn Bei Dao's followers, the young workers and students of the April 5th movement, seized on his words as their anthem:

> Debasement is the password of the base,
> Nobility the epitaph of the noble.
> See how the gilded sky is covered
> With the drifting twisted shadows of the dead.

In 1978, Bei Dao and another young poet, Man Ke, cofounded *Jintian* (Today), the first unofficial literary magazine in mainland China since 1949. This journal became the center for dissident voices that not only targeted the abuses of the past, but challenged the reformist government that followed them. It also provided space for the new kind of poetry that Bei Dao and other young poets were writing. Dubbed a "poetry of shadows" or "the misty school of poetry" for its elusive imagery and linguistic ambiguity, the new poetry was a clear break from official rhetoric. A liberation of the creative imagination, "misty" poetry was also the voice of the spiritual exiles alienated from the establishment, even before many of them were literally forced into exile after June 1989. Bei Dao and the "misty school of poetry" were attacked in the official press, and in 1980, *Jintian* was banned. But it had started an irreversible new trend in Chinese writing.

Since the middle 1980s, during periods of political relaxation, Bei Dao has traveled abroad to Europe and the United States on reading tours and writing programs. His writing has been translated into more than twenty languages. In March 1989, Bei Dao drew up a petition, signed by thirty-three intellectuals and writers in Beijing, calling for the release of political prisoners. It drew the wrath of the authorities and was actually the precursor of the June 4th Democracy movement, though during the demonstration in Tiananmen Square, brutally suppressed by government tanks, Bei Dao was abroad. A permanent exile since 1989, Bei Dao has divided his time between Oslo and New York, writing and editing *Jintian*, which continues to be a platform of creative and critical exploration for Chinese writers abroad and a growing influence worldwide.

As the work of an alien and an exile, Bei Dao's poetry reflects a sense of rootlessness:

On the map that covers over death
the terminal point is a drop of blood
the conscious stones beneath my feet
are forgotten to me.

China is always on his mind, but in perspective. The present, he says, "is a short period in a 5,000-year history. But I don't see much change." His poem *Zuguo* (Motherland) has only two lines: "She was engraved on a bronze shield / which leaned against a partition in a museum." "I don't think much of Chinese civilization is left," he said in an interview in 1990. "There is the food, and there is a little of the language. I am helping to preserve both. I cook with language." "Cooking with language" could describe Bei Dao's search for a new poetics, drawing on Western influences and modernist Chinese poetry of the 1930s and 1940s. Writing in free verse, Bei Dao is best known for intensely compressed images. To him, "Freedom" is "torn scraps of paper/fluttering"; "Labor" is "hands, encircling the earth"; and "Life" is "the sun has risen, too." These examples from *Notes from the City of the Sun* are typical of Bei Dao's cryptic style, which leaves the reader to supply the nuances in the empty spaces between the lines.

Bei Dao has gradually moved from his early exuberance and youthful defiance to a deepening pessimism, stamping his landscape with images of barrenness and making his language increasingly cold and clinical:

poverty is a blank
freedom is a blank
in the sockets of a marble statue
victory is a blank.

Throughout his development over some two hundred poems, the central force shaping Bei Dao's poetry, according to his translator Bonnie S. McDougall, is "his complex reaction to the pressures of a brutalized, conformist and corrupt society." Bei Dao's art is a commitment to communication between people and the expression of the self, transcending its political implications for the Chinese reader and imaging forth the human condition.

Though mainly known for his poetry, Bei Dao is also a writer of prose fiction. The novella *Waves* and other short stories have made Bei Dao one of the pathfinders in Chinese modernist fiction. In a series of seemingly disjointed scenes, *Bodong*, (translated as *Waves*) reveals the distortion of human feelings and the breakdown of communication that define contemporary Chinese society. The young intellectuals, workers and drifters, are viewed by the author with a cold detachment which matches their own cynicism, predictably eliciting comparisons with Hemingway's "lost generation." "Undistorted by propaganda or self-righteousness," Bonnie S. McDougall wrote, "the stories [in *Waves*] offer an unusually honest depiction of contemporary Chinese society by a native-born writer, and at the same time represent some of the finest writing to come out of China since the '40s. . . . The existential anguish that marks his characters off from the orthodox ensures their loneliness but also their unique identities."

The discouraged writer in Bei Dao's "Moon on the Manuscript" reflects: "How long can this voice linger in the world? . . . I write something, it is printed in a book, but who dares guarantee that twenty or thirty years later people will still be reading it?" Then he recalls a student aspiring to be a writer who has come to him for advice: "She had hope." And, his block broken, he begins to write again. In "Waves," a young man from a high-ranking family who has spent several years being "reeducated" in the country returns to Beijing as a factory worker and has difficulty adjusting to his circumstances. He meets a young woman from a family of intellectuals who recites a poem by Lorca to him. Their ensuing dialogue embodies the tentative yearning, and also the disillusionment of young China:

> "It's a beautiful dream. What a pity it lasts only an instant before it dies." "On the contrary, our generation's dream is too painful and too long. You can never wake up and even if you do, you'll only find another nightmare waiting for you." "Why can't there be a happier ending?" "Oh, you, always forcing yourself to believe in something: your country, hope, these pretty lollipops always luring you on until you bump into a high wall . . . " "You certainly haven't seen the end either." "That's right. I'm waiting for the end. I must see it, whatever it is, that's the main reason I go on living."

PRINCIPAL WORKS IN ENGLISH TRANSLATION: *Poetry*—Notes from the City of the Sun (tr. B.S. McDougall) 1983; The August Sleepwalker (tr. B.S. McDougall) 1988; Old Snow (tr. B.S. McDougall) 1991. *Fiction*—Waves (tr. by B.S. McDougall and S. Ternant) 1985.

ABOUT: Contemporary Authors 139, 1993; McDougall, B. S. *Introductions to* Waves, 1985; The August Sleepwalker, 1988; Old Snow, 1991; Martin, H., (ed.) Contemporary Chinese Literature, 1986; Soong, S. C. and J. Minford, (eds.) Trees on the Mountain, 1984; Spence, J. The Gate of Heavenly Peace, 1981; Tucker, M. (ed.) Literary Exile in the 20th Century, 1991; Who's Who in the People's Republic of China, 2nd ed., 1987; Yeh, M. Modern Chinese Poetry, 1991. *Periodicals*—Boston Globe April 7, 1991; Modern Chinese Literature Spring 1985; Spring 1989; New Republic November 19, 1990; New York Times Book Review August 12, 1990; Times Literary Supplement March 17, 1989; July 9, 1993.

BELL, MADISON SMARTT (August 1, 1957–), American novelist and short-story writer, writes: "Several years before I was born in 1957, my parents decided to move out of Nashville, where they had for the most part grown up, and buy a farm in Williamson County. I don't know if they originally intended to become scratch farmers to the extent that they eventually did; somehow I doubt it. But they did, within five or ten years, switch over almost entirely to an agrarian way of living. My father left his Nashville law firm and started a practice in Franklin, then a truly rural county seat. My mother ran a riding school to pay for fencing and with the help of our one black tenant grew a garden and froze and canned all our vegetables from it. We kept a milk cow and killed hogs. About ninety percent of what we consumed we raised or grew.

"Now my parents didn't do what they did for any ideological purpose, I am convinced, to whatever degree they ended up acting out a large number of the ideas and principles suggested by the Agrarian movement that sprang

MADISON SMARTT BELL

up among Southern writers in the thirties. They did it because it suited them, which is also a Southern prerogative. As much by accident as design they gave me a childhood which was sufficiently atavistic that in some ways I entered the modern world as a stranger. And that, to shoplift a phrase from Frost, has made all the difference.

"The way I grew up was curiously double from the very beginning. I belonged to a pair of working farmers who were also accustomed to the rights and privileges of the best education available. This meant that I would get up in the morning, feed the horses or milk the cow, and then be driven ten or fifteen miles to a private school in Nashville. But for twelve years, unlike most of the children I knew from town, I lived in two worlds instead of one. And of course, since it was my normal state to commute between these two quite different real world situations, I didn't see anything strange about it.

"I shuttled back and forth between the town and the countryside, generally happier and more at ease with the latter. I grew accustomed to a kind of reflexive hostility toward the encroachment of the town on the countryside, as the movement of progress dispossessed the farmers and chewed up the land and spat out more and more tract housing and office parks. In high school I read Flannery O'Connor and Faulkner and Robert Penn Warren and Andrew Lytle and Allen Tate, especially Tate's essays, and I read *I'll Take My Stand* as well. All this reading tended to underwrite the beliefs I had grown up on more or less unconsciously. In college I turned this subject into my academic specialty.

"But when I got my degree from Princeton, I did not return to the farm, as reason might have dictated I should. Instead I went to New York City and settled in one of grimiest and nastiest industrial slums to be found on the Brooklyn waterfront, where I remained in great contentment for almost seven years. Like other paradoxes in my life this one seemed natural enough to me at the time. I did not think about it much. What I did notice, though, was that I felt infinitely more comfortable in the ghetto, where everything was falling apart, than I did in parts of Manhattan where the metropolis was up and running with a well-tuned hum. That caused me to put myself the question I had first heard from Walker Percy: 'Why do people often feel bad in good environments and good in bad environments?' [From "The Delta Factor," in *The Message In the Bottle* (Farrar, Straus and Giroux, 1977)]

"A great many of my own aberrations seemed to yield themselves willingly to Walker Percy's reasoning. In one way I had become like those characters in *Love in the Ruins* who have to scramble through the swamp among the alligators and water moccasins to restore their sense of vitality. In another, I might argue that among the urban ruins I could see the forces of nature at work, for decay is a natural process, and that it made sense for me to prefer that to the picture of the city running the way it's supposed to—perfectly denatured.

"Since my marriage to Elizabeth Spires in 1985, I've lived a different kind of life, in different places. But it seems to me that most of my work so far has come out the friction between the liking I have for two very different things: big cities in their most degenerate state, and wild places at their most undeveloped. I don't live in any such place now. Still, some such theory seems best to account for the cycle of my first eight books of fiction, which is now, in my judgement, complete.

"Walker Percy also wrote that a great deal of human restlessness comes from our legitimate intuition that indeed we are *not* at home. Some such sense of dislocation causes a great many people, if not all people, to turn their lives into quests for something or other. Most of my novels, the best I can understand them myself, are in one way or another about spiritual pilgrimages. The purpose and motive of such pilgrimages is to try to repair what almost everyone, at one time or another, senses to be a seriously damaged relationship between oneself and oneself, oneself and the rest of humanity, oneself and the world. Some such vexation, and the effort to relieve it, is found at the core of all the world's religions, including psychotherapy, which has now become our culture's closest approximation to commonly shared and practiced religion.

"My books are all about people who knowingly or unknowingly tend to follow some religious doctrine (Islam, Santeria, Satanism, several variations of Christian mysticism, Christian Existentialism, Existentialism straight up, and most recently in *Doctor Sleep*, Renaissance Hermeticism). These characters are all in search of some viable way of faith which will offer them a credible explanation of creation and their place in it. The search goes on for them and for me, and probably, I believe, for most of the rest of us."

———

The "curiously double" upbringing Madison Smartt Bell says he has in many ways shaped his work. The two worlds of his fiction are the raw, menacing urban slum and the still rugged wilderness of backwoods Tennessee, although his characters are never completely comfortable in either. The son of Henry Denmark and Allen Wigginton Bell, Bell moved from the rural South to the Northeast when he entered Princeton University. As an English major he pursued his early loyalty to Southern writers, receiving his B.A. *summa cum laude* in 1979 with an honors paper on the Agrarian School. He went to live in Brooklyn and delved into the seamy side of life in the drug-infested slums of New York's East Village and Lower East Side and of Hoboken and Newark across the river in New Jersey.

Bell had written fiction while still in high school. During his undergraduate years at Princeton he wrote a novel, never published. In 1980 he enrolled in the creative writing program at Hollins College in Virginia, where he studied with the Southern poet and novelist George Garrett and received an M.A. in 1981. He worked there on a story that, with Garrett's encouragement, he developed into his first published novel, *The Washington Square Ensemble*. Back in New York he got by without "conventional employment," as he told Donna Seaman in *Booklist*, earning a living from his writing and having "a lot of time to stand beside characters like those I've written about without actually being one."

The Washington Square Ensemble attracted unusual attention for a first book. Like many other novels of the period it depicted the violent and sordid drug scene of the 1970s, but it did so with greater urgency and authenticity than most. Calling *The Washington Square Ensemble* "a tough-edged, streetwise novel" in the *Los Angeles Times Book Review*, Thomas Ruffen added that "Bell has that rarest of literary gifts: the ability to make word into flesh, to delineate compelling, vivid characters who bring to life the stark, horrowing world of tenements, derelict bars, shadowy alleyways, and inner-city parks where deviant behavior is the norm. . . . " The "ensemble" is a group of five heroin users and dealers, each of whom describes his own personal hell in lyrical stream-of-consciousness narrative that echoes the effect of a musical ensemble. As the novel unfolds, Mary Furness wrote in the *Times Literary Supplement* ( ), "the ensemble, tough and inured to the seamiest side of life, reveal themselves to have higher feelings and loyalties that are manifested in quiet, almost unnoticeable actions. Moments of tension turn almost imperceptibly into cool and sustained triumphs, like one of the passages of jazz which the author describes so well."

The leader of the group, Johnny Dellacroce, maintains a kind of integrity, not in spite of, but because he observes certain limits in the dealing of "pharmaceuticals," as he refers to illegal drugs:

> My true christened name is Enrico Spaghetti, or something like that, but I am known to my colleagues and business acquaintances as Johnny B. Goode. Because I love black people and their music and money, and because I do be good. I carry no I.D., my pockets are perennially empty of pharmaceuticals or anything else that you might want to find, and I do not do business with my relatives. Absolutely no way, not for years. I buy my pharmaceuticals from the Latinos in Alphabet Town, and what do I care if the Gambino family brings it all in from Turkey? Nothing, that's what I care, I care so little that most of the time I don't even know it. And I can afford the markup, because here in Washington Square Park we cater to classy clientele.

An even more sinister group of doomed and alienated deviates peoples Bell's second novel, *Waiting for the End of the World*; they are plotting their own version of Armageddon by conspiring to explode a nuclear bomb in Times Square. For Guy Davenport writing in the *Sewanee Review*, the novel carries alienation to its existential limits: "To conceive of a more nightmarishly meaningless world than the sleazy New York of Madison Smartt Bell's *Waiting for the End of the World* is difficult, and yet that extraordinary novel makes it clear that art can still make something out of nothing."

Straight Cut and *The Year of Silence* followed in swift succession. *Straight Cut*, a fast-moving suspense thriller, broke the New York pattern. The central character, as always in Bell's fiction, is a loner. Here he has retreated from a broken marriage and New York to an isolated Tennessee sheep farm. Nevertheless, he is swept into a wild adventure when he takes a job as a film editor in Rome and finds himself involved in a drug-smuggling scheme.

The Year of Silence is a skillfully constructed study of a group of lonely New Yorkers brought together by the suicide by one of them. The central scene (literally in the middle of the book) is narrated from the point of view of the suicide herself; the peripheral chapters are concentric circles of narrative. As Bell described the novel In a *Publishers Weekly* interview: "All the chapters are pairs, the first has a specific relationship to the last . . . .One of the problems with this, of course, is that you can't make sense out of the design until you've read the whole novel."

With *Soldier's Joy* Bell returned to the rugged rural scene of his childhood. Set in Tennessee in the early 1970s, its germ was Bell's own disgust with local Ku Klux Klansmen. His central character, Laidlaw, is a Vietnam veteran, returned from the war to find his family farm neglected and abandoned. Nevertheless he lives there contentedly, spending most of his time playing the banjo and slowly restoring the land. His lonely but idyllic existence is shattered when a black veteran who served in the same unit returns. The ties of loyalty that unite the two men force Laidlaw to take a stand against the bigots in the community. *Soldier's Joy* is not a political novel about the rapidly changing new South but rather a study of moral choices. David Bradley observed in the *New York Times Book Review* that the novel is set "just far enough in the past to have an undertone of the historical. His sets are luxurious in detail, painted from a palette of fecund earth tones, and his soundtrack has the clear acoustic ring of traditional bluegrass. These are perfect choices, for his tale is no clear-cut confrontation of cop and criminal but a complex conflict with elements as old as humankind."

As if deliberately resisting regionalism, Bell set his next novel, *Doctor Sleep*, in contemporary London. The scene, however—a shabby part of Notting Hill—and the ominous atmosphere of violence and drug dealing and the near delirium of its central character who suffers from insomnia recall the haunted spirit of Bell's earlier books. The narrator, a former heroin addict, who ironically practices as a hypnotist curing others of insomnia (hence "Doctor" Sleep) reads abstruse works of mysticism and philosophy by Hermes Trismegistus and Giordano Bruno, but finds himself involved in some deadly activities before he finally achieves sleep himself. To Elizabeth Tallent, writing in the *New York Times Book Review*: "Madison Smartt Bell renders the marginal, the underground, the twisted or seedy with quirky attentiveness. His array of lost souls gets onto the page without the least pre-emptive hint or authorial sympathy, yet he catches the poignant in the freakish."

Several of Bell's short stories have been included in the *Best American Short Stories* anthologies (1984, 1987, 1989). His first collection, *Zero db*, includes "Triptych I," a reworking of his very first short story about hog-butchering on a Southern farm as seen through the eyes of a little girl. Others range in scene from Princeton to a Puerto Rican slum in Hoboken to the Little Big Horn in 1876 ("Today Is a Good Day to Die," in which a young army officer sent out to fight the Indians rebels against the horrors he must witness). For Dean Flower in the *Hudson Review* this first collection "reveals a young writer experimenting expressively with different styles and genres (the flat monologue, the dialect yarn, the collage and various settings) . . . Bell has a fine ear for common speech and keeps his own language spare . . . the prose is full of poetic subtlety and the attention to detail is sharp." *Barking Man and Other Stories*, his second collection, ranges even wider. The haunts of the drug addicts and the homeless in Times Square and Tompkins Square Park are still there, but Bell also writes about the alienated and lonely in truck-stop diners and shabby motels all over America.

His compassion extends beyond human beings to animals: an intelligent white mouse used in laboratory experiments ("Holding Together"), gorillas in a London zoo ("Barking Man"), Sooner, the dog, in *Save Me, Joe Louis*. In a review of *Barking Man, and Other Stories* in the *New York Times Book Review*, Rick DeMarinis characterizes the world created by Bell as "a shifty, dangerous place, requiring of its inhabitants small acts of daily heroism. That these heroic deeds sometimes resemble madness or criminal mischief does not compromise their necessity or moral authenticity."

In *Save Me, Joe Louis*, Lacy, a young women companion of his childhood, tells Macrae, who has just left a life of crime in New York to return to his boyhood home in Tennessee, "You could do something. Be somebody." He is somebody, Macrae declares: "I'm the fruit of my actions." His existential moral authenticity is demonstrated by a final act of violence that enables him and Lacy to look "as if they were seeing each other for the first time in their lives."

It is the clarity of the light that Bell casts on such characters, as well as the compassion he extends to them, that typifies his work. Not for him "a tendency to ignore or eliminate distinctions among the people it renders," that he finds in "minimalism," as he wrote in an essay in *Harper's*. "I'm much more interested in the accomodations one individual makes to another," he told Laurel Graeber in the *New York Times Book Review*.

Bell is married to the poet Elizabeth Spires, who teaches along with Bell at Goucher College in Maryland. Bell received a Guggenheim Fellowship in 1991.

PRINCIPAL WORKS: *Novels*—The Washington Square Ensemble, 1984; Waiting for the End of the World, 1985; Straight Cut, 1986; The Year of Silence, 1987; Soldier's Joy, 1989; Doctor Sleep, 1991; Save Me, Joe Louis, 1993; All Souls' Rising, 1995. *Short stories*–Zero db, 1987; Barking Man and Other Stories, 1990.

ABOUT: Birkerts, S. American Energies: Essays on Fiction, 1992; Contemporary Authors New Revision Series 28, 1990; Contemporary Literary Criticism 41, 1987. *Periodicals*—Booklist April 15, 1993; Georgia Review Winter 1987; Harper's August 1986; Hudson Review Summer 1987; Library Journal December 1987; Los Angeles Times Book Review February 27, 1983; New York Times Book Review February 20, 1983; November 15, 1987; July 2, 1989; April 8, 1990; January 6, 1991; Publishers Weekly December 11, 1987; Sewanee Review Spring 1984; Fall 1988; Times Literary Supplement August 26, 1983; January 24, 1992.

BELL, MARTIN (February 2, 1918–February 1978), English poet and translator of French poetry, was born in Southampton to parents he described as "lower middle class." He was educated at Taunton School, and at the then University College of Southampton (later the University of Southampton), where he read English. His tutor there was the scholar and translator of Rilke, J. B. Leishmann, who took an interest in him, and who subsequently exercised some considerable influence on his earliest poetry, which was cast mainly in the manner of W. H. Auden, a poet whom he continued to admire. From 1935 until 1939 Bell was a member of the Communist Party. According to Peter Porter, Bell's literary executor and editor of his posthumously published *Complete Poems*, he did not make a full break with the party, however, "until the full horror of Stalinism was revealed in the immediate postwar period."

Between 1939 and 1945 Bell served in the Royal Engineers, for much of the time as an acting sergeant in Italy. From 1945 until 1964 he was a teacher in various primary and secondary schools in the London area. In the 1960's he became friendly with Anthony Burgess, whom he succeeded as opera critic for *Queen* magazine in 1965. Porter writes that Bell was "an idiosyncratic critic of music and opera, but, in many respects, a sound and unsnobbish one." Sent to Edinburgh that year to review the opera offerings at the Festival, he met and fell in love with a young woman, Christine McCausland, to

MARTIN BELL

whom a number of his later poems were dedicated.

Towards the end of his London years Bell conceived the character of an old man, "Don Senilio." Though himself only in his mid-forties, he made Don Senilio his persona, and the poems he collected as "The Irregular Stanzas of Don Senilio" reveal what critics consider his chief strength—the ability to modulate conventional poetic themes into a sardonic, regretful, self-satirical vernacular:

"It seems to me now a long time since
I was excited about anything.
I fill my insides with old man's bitter
And feel sour besides. How frail I feel.
And if I stammer now it's not young heat
Baffled, but an inefficient cricket
That never learned the use of its thin limbs
To make proper sounds. Fric, fric, hélas, fric, fric."
Thus Don Senilio scribbled a climacteric.

Characteristically, Don Senilio finds solace in alcohol:

Here's absinthe. You'd best booze it too
(The world can't last for I'm too mad)
Illumination could flash blue
To show what hopes are never had
And I might say a thing or two
(Before world ends. But I'm too mad).

In 1964, through the efforts of such admirers as the poet Peter Redgrove, Bell received the first Arts Council Poetry Bursary. Thereafter he became Gregory Fellow at Leeds University (1967–1969) and a part-time lecturer at the Leeds College of Art. In 1968 he received an award from the Arts Council to travel to Cyprus, the result of which was the part prose, part verse "Letters from Cyprus." They form a miscellaneous group—some inspired by Cyprus but others simply on any subject he chose to write about: the Woman he loved ("Although she causes poems, / And will again"), cats, French poets, alcohol ("The subtlest flatterer of them all, / Pool of Narcissus"), and politics,—on which he was cynical and despairing.

In the late 1950s, Bell was one of the leading spirits in the formation of the Group. This was a now almost forgotten association of poets (including Philip Hobsbaum, Edward Lucie-Smith and Peter Redgrove) whose rather vague poetics (outlined, if hardly defined, in the introduction to *The Group Anthology*) most nearly reflected the conservative ideas of the American poet Yvor Winters. More of an association of friends who met weekly to discuss their work than a meeting of like minds with a common program, the Group believed to have been influential. Bell's sardonic tone; however, was admired, and his reputation has subsequently been preserved by Peter Porter and others associated with the Group. Romer, reviewing *Complete Poems* in the *Times Literary Supplement* in 1988, suggested that Porter's introduction was "as full of human warmth and interest as any writer could wish." Nevertheless, he cautioned: "To attempt a just assessment . . . one has to evade a dragon at the gate in the form of Peter Porter." Romer did think, however, that "the best of Bell's poems justify the high claims Porter makes." These "best" poems, he finds, were written before what Porter called Bell's "long personal decline" after he moved to Leeds in the mid-1960s. "It is no secret," Porter writes of Bell, "that his later years were blighted by addiction to alcohol, and complicated by depression, lack of recognition, shortage of money and touches of paranoia." Bell described his state of mind in the witty and candid "Ode to Psychoanalysis," in which he refered to his "abortive analysis" with "Doctor Quackenbush" whose Freudian jargon about castration and negative transference left him "in the middle of several paths":

. . . suffering Hell because I'm always overdrawn
At the bank whose manager hovers
Clacking revengeful shears.
Hey there! Nobodaddy!
That's my flaming sword. . . .

In the later poems, printed for the first time in *Complete Poems*, Romer finds "the decline graphically traced": "it is here that Bell's imaginative sources ran dry, and alcohol didn't help." Criticisms of Bell's poetry have concentrated upon his lapses of taste (a pointlessly ugly and feeble poem about women writers and menstruation) and his over reliance on his wide reading: "the literariness of the poet's poet," says Romer, becomes, in his final years, a "brittleness because it lacks any matter to fix upon."

Some of Bell's translations, or more accurately, since they are not literal, adaptations from the French poets, notably Rimbaud, Corbière, Laforgue, and surrealists such as Max Jacob, André Brenton, Robert Desnos, and Pierre Reverdy appeared in his *Complete Poems*, but the major part of these remain unpublished—"a result," Philip Hobsbaum wrote in his obituary in the London *Times*, "not of the caution of editors but his own critical fastidiousness." Romer quotes his transformation of Laforgue's "La phtisie pulmonaire attrisant le quartier/Et toute la misère des grandes centres" ("L'Hiver qui vient") into "It's TB in the garden suburb,/All the sheer misery of satellite towns" with approval; but his work in this genre was too sparse and occasional to have attracted wide attention.

Bell died in Leeds at the age of sixty. From his first marriage, which ended in 1967, he had two daughters. Hobsbaum suggested that two lines from Bell's own rendering of Laforgue's "L'Hiver qui vient" provided the most "appropriate epitaph":

O let me every year, every year, just at this time
Join in the chorus, sound the right sour note.

PRINCIPAL WORKS: *Poetry*—(with George Barker and Charles Causley) Penguin Modern Poets 3, 1962; Collected Poems 1937–1966, 1967; Complete Poems, 1988. *Prose and Poetry*—Letters from Cyprus, 1970.

ABOUT: Hobsbaum, P. and Lucie-Smith, E. eds. A Group Anthology, 1963; Contemporary Poets, 1970; Porter, P. In Introduction to Complete Poems, 1988. *Periodicals*—Times (London) February 10, 1978; Times Literary Supplement December 30, 1988.

BENCHLEY, PETER (May 8, 1940–), American novelist, travel writer, and journalist, was born in New York City to Nathaniel Goddard Benchley, the writer, and Marjorie Louise (Bradford) Benchley. Benchley is famous for his first novel, *Jaws*, which was on the *New York Times* best-seller list for over forty weeks and made Benchley "the most successful first novelist in literary history," according to the *New York Times Book Review*. The movie *Jaws* created what *Newsweek* in 1975 called "Jawsmania."

Benchley is the third in a line of literary Benchleys. His grandfather was the well-known humorist and *Life* and *New Yorker* drama editor Robert Benchley. His father Nathaniel was a

PETER BENCHLEY

versatile writer on whose novel *The Off-Islanders* the 1966 movie *The Russians Are Coming! The Russians Are Coming!* was based. Peter and his brother, Nathaniel Robert, grew up on Manhattan's Upper East side in a brownstone in which John Steinbeck also lived, and which was visited by many writers and artists. "I guess it was inevitable that I should end up a writer," Benchley told interviewer Roy Renquist.

Like his father and grandfather, Benchley attended the Phillips Exeter Academy and Harvard University. He majored in English, graduating from Harvard *cum laude* in 1961.

Benchley's first book, *Time and a Ticket*, is the chronicle of an around-the-world tour he embarked upon after college, traveling on a "Family Fellowship" supplied by his parents. What he had going for him, he said in the foreword, was "an untutored, and thus open, outlook on the world" and a set of introductions and mode of travel which allowed him to meet an assortment of people—Prime Minister Nehru, a young Indian Communist, Peace Corps workers, and hotel pimps. As Charles Poore observed in the *New York Times*, Benchley tells us that what we really want when we seek a tropical paradise "is a place that *is* spoiled. No Benchley has ever written a more devastating analysis of hapless man in the toils of getting what he thought he wanted and then being dismayed by it."

During 1963, Benchley worked as a reporter and obituary writer for the *Washington Post* and wrote a children's story, *Jonathan Visits the White House*, for which Lady Bird Johnson wrote a foreword. He also served with the U.S. Marine Corps Reserves. After leaving the *Post*, he became an associate editor at *Newsweek*, where, he told Stuart Wavell in the *Guardian*, he wrote "the stories about the kangaroo which jumped into the women's bath" and rewrote the magazine's excess material for syndication to local papers and TV stations. He left *Newsweek* in early 1967 to join the speechwriting staff of President Lyndon M. Johnson, a job that ended with the inauguration of Richard Nixon, January 20, 1969. He returned with his family to New York City and began his career as a free-lance writer, contributing articles to such newspapers and magazines as *National Geographic*, the *New York Times*, the *New Yorker*, *Life*, and *Holiday*. He also worked during this period as a free-lance television news correspondent. According to several articles published after the success of *Jaws*, he was down to his last six hundred dollars and about to ask *National Geographic* for a job when, at a business lunch with an editor, he outlined his idea for "a novel about a great white shark that appears off a Long Island resort and afflicts it."

Bantam purchased the paperback rights for $575,000. The selling of *Jaws* continued with the release of the movie in 1975. Stuart Wavell commented that "nothing short of an atomic bomb can slow the momentum of the *Jaws* sales machine."

The story of *Jaws* is simple: a great white shark kills a swimmer at the beginning of the summer season in a resort town. The town officials, fearing the loss of revenue a shark scare will cause, refuse to let the chief of police close the beaches, and after two more attacks, the hunt is on. Many of the reviews praised Benchley's capacity to create suspense in these scenes of shark attack. For Andrew C. J. Bergman, writing in the *New York Times Book Review*, the shark is so menacing and its imagined malignity so well depicted that, "even though its attacks are telegraphed, they fix one's attention."

"The shark . . . is done with exhilarating and alarming skill and every scene in which it appears is imagined at a special pitch of intensity," John Spurling wrote, in the *New Statesman*, though he found the characterizations "rudimentary" and "ready-made."

Corroborating Michael Rogers's remark in *Rolling Stone* that "the shark was easily my favorite character—and, one suspects, Benchley's also" was a comment made by Benchley about his fear that *Jaws* might inspire "would-be Hemingways" to kill sharks: "I'd like to see two or three of these people get eaten and maybe that would put a stop to it." Few reviewers found the human characters of much interest, and many complained about the novel's other weaknesses in plot and prose style; the reviews were sometimes as savage in tone as Benchley complained they were. Calling *Jaws* "stunningly bad . . . a fish-opera featuring cardboard people and an overblown shark," *Village Voice* reviewer Donald Newlove wrote: "I think what hurts most is the shark. It lacks sharkness, a marvelous, strange sharkness to imperil my dreams." Yet for many readers, this imperilment is exactly what Benchley succeeded in creating.

As Benchley continued to publish novels, the terms on which he succeeded became clearer. His second novel, *The Deep*, the story of tourists who discover the wreck of a ship carrying drugs while looking for sunken treasure, was frankly reviewed as "a neat adventure novel." In the *New York Times Book Review*, Gene Lyons, calling Benchley "a very competent writer of fictional entertainments," put it this way: "What one gets from Benchley, and this, I think, is the essence of his commercial genius, is *escape*.

His third novel, *The Island*, about modern-day Caribbean buccaneers, is written according to a formula "that nobody seems to do quite as well as Benchley," observed Joseph McLellan in the *Washington Post*. Both *The Deep* and *The Island* were best-sellers, though they did not achieve the fame of *Jaws*.

In *Beast*, a giant squid, driven to unusual hunger because the fish banks off Bermuda have been depleted, attacks boats to get at the people inside. Christopher Lehmann-Haupt explained in his *New York Times* review (1991) why he found *Beast* an "astonishingly" satisfying read: "Benchley has sharpened his writing considerably. His descriptions of complex action, machinery and marine life are as colorful and vivid as a tropical reef before pollution set in. His characters are just subtle enough to make it hard to predict whether they are going to survive or not".

Benchley has also written three novels that do not match this "devil-in-the-deep" formula. The *Girl of the Sea of Cortez* is another sea story, but the protagonist is a young girl. The villain is her brother, a fisherman looking for a new fishing ground, and the hero a giant manta ray the girl has befriended. One enduring Benchley theme, also developed in *Beast* is that man's depredations are unsettling the balance of nature.

With *Q Clearance*, Benchley makes a greater departure—into political comedy. Calling on his experiences in Lyndon Johnson's White House, Benchley makes his hero Burnham a speechwriter who receives a top-secret clearance with a promotion and must fight off the Soviets and the disapproval of his liberal family. *Rummies*, too, was praised for its wit. In her review of the book in the *New York Times Book Review*, Anne Tolstoi Wallach called Benchley "a terrific writer of stripped-down prose, a funny and literate man" who "brilliantly gets us inside [the] befogged head" of his protagonist Scott Preston, a patient in a substance abuse center. These novels, while they are adventure stories, have established Benchley as a writer of comedy as well as what Donald Morrison, in *Time*, dubbed "sea-horse operas."

Benchley returned to the "devil-in-the-deep" mode with *White Shark*, which was criticized by Christopher Lehmann-Haupt in the *New York Times* for its lack of narrative drive. The hero of *White Shark* is an oceanographer trying to save white sharks, an endangered species in 1996, when the story takes place. The villains are dead Nazis whose superweapon has been buried at sea and is now loose.

Several of Benchley's interviewers have commented on his naturalness and appealing disingenuousness. It may be that Benchley's commercial genius is connected to his good nature in giving readers what they want on a summer's day.

Peter Benchley married Winifred B. Wesson on September 19, 1964; they have three children, Tracy, Clayton, and Christopher, and live in Princeton, New Jersey.

PRINCIPAL WORKS: *Novels*—Jaws, 1974; The Deep, 1976; The Island, 1978; The Girl of the Sea of Cortez, 1982; Q Clearance, 1986; Rummies, 1989; Beast, 1991; White Shark, 1994. *Nonfiction*—Time and a Ticket, 1964.

ABOUT: Contemporary Authors New Revision Series 35, 1992; Contemporary Literary Criticism 8, 1978; Current Biography Yearbook 1976. *Periodicals*—Guardian November 29, 1975; Los Angeles Times Book Review August 22, 1982; New Statesman May 17, 1974; New York Times August 15, 1964; June 27, 1991; May 30, 1994; New York Times Book Review February 3, 1974; May 16, 1976; July 8, 1979; July 27, 1986; December 17, 1989; July 7, 1991; New York Times Magazine April 21, 1974; Newsweek July 28, 1975; People November 24, 1975; Publishers Weekly February 11, 1974; Rolling Stone April 11, 1974; Time June 23, 1975; June 23, 1986; Village Voice February 7, 1974; Washington Post March 2, 1974.

BENFORD, GREGORY (ALBERT) January 30, 1941–), American physicist and science fiction writer, was born in Mobile, Alabama, one of identical twins of James Alton Benford, a colonel in the United States Army, and Mary Eloise (Nelson) Benford, a teacher. An "army brat," he lived in Japan, Atlanta, Germany, and Texas, be-

GREGORY BENFORD

fore entering the University of Oklahoma at Norman as a physics major. After taking his B.S. in 1963, he was a Woodrow Wilson Fellow from 1963 to 1964. Benford continued his studies at the University of California, San Diego, earning his Ph.D. in theoretical physics in 1967. From 1964 to 1967 he was a research assistant at the University of California, followed by two years as a postdoctoral fellow at the Lawrence Radiation Laboratory in Livermore, California, where he later served as a research assistant from 1969 to 1971. In 1971 he became a professor of physics at the University of California, Irvine. He was a visiting fellow at Cambridge University in England in 1976 and 1979. His specialties are plasma physics and astrophysics; he has written research papers and published articles in such magazines as the *Smithsonian* and *Natural History*, He is a grantee of the Office of Naval Research and the National Science Foundation, among others.

"I am a resolutely amateur writer, preferring to follow my own interests rather than try to produce fiction for a living," Benford told an interviewer. "And anyway, I'm a scientist by first choice and shall remain so." Despite his self-proclaimed amateur standing, however, Benford is viewed by critics and fans alike as a major writer of science fiction. "Benford's achievements in physics perhaps overshadow his accomplishments as an author, although his careers complement each other," Mark J. Lidman writes in the *Dictionary of Literary Biography Yearbook*. "His novels are characterized by thoughtful composition and scientific expertise, and his work experience lends authenticity to his perspective on science."

Benford started out as an enthusiastic reader of science fiction. For several years he was an editor of *Void*, a science fiction magazine. Benford honed his writing skills on short stories. His first published story, "Stand-In", appeared in 1965 in *Magazine of Fantasy and Science Fiction* and won second prize in a contest sponsored by that publication.

Early in his writing career, Benford began his exploration of that most classic of science fiction themes: contact between alien and human being. It is a theme that he has continued to develop in both short stories and novels. "Recognizing the statistical probability that there are intelligent aliens, and the improbability that we and they have actually met, he is also aware of the irrelevance of statistics to the actuality of possible contact, past or future, and to the desire for contact in the human imagination," David N. Samuelson says of Benford in *Foundation: The Review of Science Fiction*. "He is also concerned with the theme of the alien for its artistic potential, not only for word-pictures, but also as an index to human sensibilities. According to Samuelson, "Benford generally takes great care with verisimilitude, especially including the scientific factors. But he finds representing the alien more than a trick, more than putting human beings into funny costumes. Confronting the alien is in large part his rationale for writing. . . . "

In an afterword to his short story "And the Sea Like Mirrors," published in Harlan Ellison's 1972 anthology *Again, Dangerous Visions*, Benford explains: "The alien doesn't have to be some extraterrestrial life form. Every person on this planet is undergoing a continuous encounter with the incredibly strange world our technology is creating for us just around the corner. It is alien. We have to come to terms with it. So we adjust, we change, we accept. And often we don't know what price we have had to pay." Benford's own early aliens, however, were closer to the traditional kind that have been frightening, and fascinating, science fiction fans since the inception of the genre. In "Battleground," published in the June 1971 issue of *If*, Benford's alien is a huge time-traveling, man-eating insect. Mark J. Lidman, however, offers the reminder that "even at this early point in his career, Benford was intrigued by the alienness of mankind . . . In his later novels the human hero is also an alien, an outcast from his own society. . . . Benford often draws parallels between human and extraterrestrial aliens."

The Stars in Shroud, a rewrite of Benford's first novel, is set hundreds of years in the future when Earth's far-flung interstellar empire is being threatened by the Quarn. These aliens are demoralizing the Regeln colony with a disease that causes mass psychosis. Pitted against the Quarn is Captain Ling of Earth, who catches the disease himself and becomes a plotter against the Empire before recovering his sanity. The *Publishers Weekly* reviewer called it a "fine and superbly written science fiction novel. . . . Benford's imaginary worlds and imaginary people are fascinating as they carry on their lives in a, to us, surrealistic universe where empires crash and marriages crumble and human life goes on in much altered ways."

Benford's second novel, *Jupiter Project*, which has been called a "prequel" to Robert Heinlein's *Farmer in the Sky*, was aimed at the juvenile/young adult market. In 1977 Benford published the two novels that drew the attention of the science fiction world in earnest: *If the Stars Are Gods*, a collaboration with Gordon Eklund, and *In the Ocean of Night*. The former, an expansion of the authors' Nebula Award-winning novella of the same title, tells the story of astronaut/astronomer Bradly Reynolds's encounter, with two giraffe-like aliens who have arrived in our solar system to worship our sun. Reynolds is not a social man, and as David N. Samuelson describes him, his "objectivity is in doubt because more and more he comes to identify with what he thinks is the alien viewpoint, which progressively alienates him further from his fellow humans. . . . By the end of the story, meaning transcends for him the material quests of ordinary human beings," and he ultimately achieves his own kind of immortality.

The publication of *In the Ocean of Night* firmly established Benford's reputation. Started earlier than *If the Stars Are Gods*, it was finished later. Writing in the *Magazine of Fantasy and Science Fiction*, Algis Budrys termed it "a major novel." The protagonist is the only British astronaut in the American space program, an outsider who casts a critical eye on NASA and the United States and further seals his alienation when he refuses to destroy an incoming comet, which he discovers contains an alien ship with mechanical intelligence inside. The last section of the novel concerns an alien craft found wrecked on the Moon and the eventual discovery of a link between it and the legendary Bigfoot of the Pacific Northwest. Among the subplots of this complex novel is an influential charismatic religious group called the New Sons of God, who want to suppress information "that might damage man's mythological self-portrait." Lester del Rey was critical of the novel in his *Analog Science Fiction/Science Fact* review, noting that much of it has previously been published as short fiction in magazines: "That probably explains some of the trouble with the novel, since tying such material, written over several years, into a coherent whole is difficult." `In the same periodical, Spider Robinson declared that "*all* the characterization is first-rate; the dialogue is excellent; the writing itself is economical, vivid and quite literate. But what I think I liked most was that *Ocean* is one of the most successful attempts to infuse a work of with genuine spirituality. . . . "

In 1980 Benford published three successful novels: *Find the Changeling,* with Gordon Eklund; *Shiva Descending,* with William Rotsler; and *Timescape,* considered one of his best. Benford commented, "*Timescape* is rather different; it reflects my using my own experiences as a scientist." The premise of the story is that by 1998 the world is an ecological disaster; British theoretical physicists are trying to communicate back in time to warn scientists in the early 1960s of the experiments that will ultimately destroy the oceans. The message gets through to the University of California, La Jolla, in 1962, but it is garbled and puzzling. With the fate of the earth hanging on the outcome, Gordon Bernstein, an assistant professor of physics tries to decipher the true meaning of the message. David N. Samuelson, in the *Science Fiction Review,* remarked on the story's personal elements: "All of this is treated with loving, sensuous detail, much of it taken from life. . . . Benford is familiar with both Cambridge, where he has taught and studied, and La Jolla, where he was a graduate student at the time of the novel. Numerous real-life scientists make cameo appearances, including Benford and his brother (under another name) and a headline-hunting send-up of Carl Sagan." Samuelson declared it a "thoroughly engrossing novel." *Timescape* won Benford his second Nebula Award, as well as a British Science Fiction Association award, a John W. Campbell Award from the World Science Fiction Convention, and an Australian Ditmar Award.

In *Great Sky River,* Benford brings the reader into a future when intelligent machines are dominant and human beings, losers of the war with the machines, have a status akin to hunted insects. John G. Cramer wrote in the *Los Angeles Times Book Review* that here Benford turns for inspiration to Homer "for a wealth of literary allusions and resonances. . . . this motif creates an atmosphere. . . . which is an eerie synthesis of the high-tech neuro-circuitry of cyberpunk mixed with the Hades scene from Book XI of the *Odyssey.*" Cramer praised the book as an "ambitious work that sets new standards for hard science fiction," and offered an assessment of Benford's place in the hierarchy of science fic-

tion writers: "Benford's previous contributions to the S-F field include the highly acclaimed *Timescape,* the innovative *Against Infinity,* the splendid, underappreciated *Across the Sea of Suns,* and a very successful collaboration . . . to produce *Heart of the Comet.* With the publication of *Great Sky River* this impressive body of work must place Benford firmly among the new generation of masters of the S-F genre."

Gregory Benford makes his home in Laguna Beach, California, with his wife and two children.

PRINCIPAL WORKS: *Novels*—Deeper Than the Darkness, 1970 (rev. ed. as The Stars in Shroud, 1978); (with G. Eklund) If the Stars Are Gods, 1977; In the Ocean of Night, 1977; (with G. Eklund) Find the Changeling, 1980; (with W. Rotsler) Shiva Descending, 1980; Timescape, 1980; Against Infinity, 1983; Across the Sea of Suns, 1984; Artifact, 1985; (with D. Brin) Heart of the Comet, 1986; Great Sky River, 1987; Tides of Light, 1989; (with A. C. Clarke) Beyond the Fall of Night, 1990. *Juvenile*—Jupiter Project, 1975. *Short stories and novellas*—(with C. D. Simak and N. Spinrad) Threads of Time: Three Original Novellas of Science Fiction, 1974; In Alien Flesh, 1986; (with J. M. Ford and N. Springer) Under the Wheel, 1987. *As editor*—(with M. H. Greenberg) Hitler Victorious: Eleven Stories of the German Victory in World War II, 1986; (with M. H. Greenberg) What Might Have Been, 1989–1992.

ABOUT: Contemporary Authors New Revision Series 24, 1988; Contemporary Literary Criticism 52, 1989; Dictionary of Literary Biography Yearbook: 1982, 1983; Twentieth-Century Science-Fiction Writers, 1986; Who's Who in America 1994, 1993. *Periodicals*—Analog Science Fiction/Science Fact January 1978; June 1978; Foundation: The Review of Science Fiction September 1978; Los Angeles Times Book Review December 27, 1987; Magazine of Fantasy and Science Fiction July 1978; Publishers Weekly June 26, 1978; Science Fiction Review May 1977; August 1980; Washington Post Book World February 26, 1984.

*BENÍTEZ-ROJO, ANTONIO (March 14, 1931–), Cuban novelist, critic, short story, and screen writer, was born in Havana but has lived in exile since 1980. His international reputation rose rapidly during the 1980s and early 1990s, with translations of his work into English and many European languages. the first seven years of his life were divided between Panama, where his father was a theater manager, and Havana, which he visited every summer with his mother. His imagination was shaped first by his father's career promoting movie theaters. In these the impressionable young boy absorbed blood-and-thunder adventure films like *The Crusaders,*

°bay NEE tays-ROW ho

ANTONIO BENÍTEZ-ROJO

The Adventures of Marco Polo, and *Captain Blood*. From his mother's large family, dominated by a patriarchal grandfather who had fought in earlier Cuban struggles for independence, he absorbed a heritage of colonial Spanish culture. Cuba became his permanent home when his mother and father separated. "A very competent and modern woman for her era," as Benítez-Rojo recalls her, his mother worked as a secretary in the Cuban Ministry of Labor while he attended a Jesuit school in Belén. This solid traditional education and voracious reading on his own—Verne, Hugo, Dumas, Dickens and later Hemingway, Faulkner, Scott Fitzgerald— attracted him to a literary career. But his literary ambitions were not realized for a number of years.

Having studied finance and accounting at the University of Havana and at the American University in Washington, D.C., Benítez-Rojo entered government service, rising to a chief administrative position in the Bureau of Economic Planning of the Ministry of Labor. It was only as the result of a back injury that kept him bed-ridden for three months that he began to write. He prepared himself systematically by reading books on literary technique and imitating such Latin American authors as Borges, Carpentier, Rulfo, and Cortázar. His early narratives were all short stories. "Soon, it writing became an obsession . . . By the end of the year I had finished a book of fantastic tales. I gave it the title *Tute de reyes* and sent it to the Casa de las Américas contest. When I sent the manuscript, I made the following promise to myself:

'If I am a finalist, I will change professions and continue writing; in the opposite case, I will forget literature and continue my work in numbers and statistics'." *Tute de reyes* (1966; title story translated into English as "The Winning Hand"), won the annual first prize in the short story category from Casa de las Américas, the Cuban national publishing house and center for cultural activities.

Tute was followed in 1969 by *El escudo de hojas secas* (the titular story, whose Spanish title refers to a spurious coat of arms, was translated into English as "The Magic Dog"). While still in manuscript, the book had won the 1968 Luis Felipe Rodriguez award from the Union of Writers and Artists of Cuba. His second set of short narratives greatly resembles *Tute* in theme and approach, and the two have been reprinted in a single volume, the 1978 *La tierra y el cielo*, the title taken from a story translated into English as "Heaven and Earth," which gained fame in Cuba after it was filmed. There followed a long hiatus during which Benítez-Rojo published no substantial new creative writing, but in 1976 he published a single story in a very small volume, *Los inquilinos* (The tenants), which shortly after was included in his third short story collection, *Heroica* (1976). These more realistic stories, have fewer of the capricious and light-hearted touches that distinguish the first two collections, although an element of myth and magic is always present in Benítez-Rojo's writing.

A collection of Benítez-Rojo's short fiction, as rendered into English by various translators, was compiled by Frank Janney, who published it through Ediciones del Norte as *The Magic Dog and Other Stories*. This volume is made up of stories from *Tute de reyes*, *El escudo de hojas secas*, and *Heroica*, with the addition of a much later story, "Gentleman's Agreement," that the author had written after becoming an exile. From their original appearance in Spanish, Benítez-Rojo's stories were recognized as outstanding in new Cuban writing. They particularly drew the attention of Mario Benedetti, the noted Uruguayan writer who often participated in Casa de las Américas's literary contests and refereeing of manuscripts; later Benítez-Rojo collaborated with Benedetti on several editorial projects.

Seymour Menton, in his *Prose Fiction of the Cuban Revolution*, observed that "the stories of *Tute de reyes* and *El escudo de hojas secas* are distinguished from those of Benítez's contemporaries by their complexity." Although his short fiction has a strong fantastic vein running through it, it also offers an unmistakable comment on social history. This combination of myth with realistic elements and a critical view of society has been described as magical realism, the tendency made famous by such writers as the Columbian Gabriel García Márquez. In some of the tales, the backdrop is Cuba before the 1959 revolution. These stories allude to the most terrible conditions of life in that period, although their social criticism never overwhelms the telling of the story. There are references to the great gap between the poor and the wealthy, the obsession with skin color as a determinant of person's status, the decadence of the Havana entertainment world, and the police repression of the regime that Fidel Castro overthrew. Other stories are set during the time when Cubans were adapting to the 1959 Revolution. In these narratives, Benítez-Rojo focuses on individuals and groups who have not been able to accommodate themselves to the transition. Some of these odd-man-out characters become withdrawn and embittered, self-defeatingly designing their lives so as to participate as little as possible in society. Others join anti-Castro counterrevolutionary groups, who in Benítez-Rojo's stories appear as collections of aggrieved, perennially disaffected people, poorly adjusted to life with their fellow creatures.

At the same time that Benítez-Rojo's stories criticize pre-revolutionary Cuban society and Cubans who disdain the 1959 Revolution, they entertain readers with highly imaginative narrative inventions. Benítez-Rojo at times draws on the resources of classical myth and the 19th-century fantastic story. He includes in his tales such figures as that staple of Poe tales, the victim who comes back to drive a murderer mad ("Evaristo," from *Tute de reyes*) and an encounter between an elderly man and his younger self ("Tute de reyes"). Benítez-Rojo at times works with a notion, common in myth, that a statue may come to life or a living person may be transformed into a statue. The concept of luck, a mythical and magical idea, is deeply rooted in some Benítez-Rojo's characters—gamblers or speculators courting fortune with superstitious rituals. "The Magic Dog" is centered on a couple's shameless pursuit of material good fortune; in a bitter twist, their run of luck turns out to be accursed. Benítez-Rojo often endows an animal with mysteriously symbolic qualities, such as the lucky dog in "The Magic Dog" or the golden butterfly in "Estatuas sepultadas" ("Buried Statues").

During the same period that he shifted interests from economics to literature, Benítez-Rojo had different government positions; his new series of jobs was concerned with arts and culture. From 1975 to 1980 he held the important post of director of the editorial department of the

Casa de las Américas. He also compiled anthologies of Panamanian, Spanish American, and world literature, coediting some of these with Mario Benedetti. He carried out a number of writing assignments of the most varied sort, including occasional pieces and screenwriting; his *Los sobrevivientes* (The survivors) won the 1979 national prize for screenwriting. Some of his assignments involved research into Caribbean history and culture, and his knowledgeable and imaginative group of the region made him an important figure in Caribbean studies. In 1979 he was named to head the Centro de Estudios del Caribe.

A new direction in Benítez-Rojo's literary production was signaled by the 1979 publication of his novel *El mar de las lentejas*. Translated into English and published by the University of Massachusetts Press as *Sea of Lentils*, the novel refers in its title to the Caribbean, whose early colonial exploitation it examines. Whereas Benítez-Rojo had earlier focused on the period immediately before and after the 1959 Revolution, he now examined the era of Spanish colonization: the Caribbean in its frontier days, teeming with the sociopaths, misfits, and displaced people whose characterization is one of Benítez-Rojo's specialties. The novel was scrupulously researched; in particular, Benítez-Rojo had been a close student of the "chronicles of the Indies," the logs, memoirs, and histories left by contemporary explorers and colonizers. At the same time he drew upon his extensive studies of the Caribbean, Benítez-Rojo gave free play to his imagination, and elements of fantasy are often present in these writings.

Sea of Lentils is composed of four narratives designed so that they never coalesce into the type of unified whole that one might expect. As Frederick Luciani noted in the *New York Times Book Review*: "Each plot advances sporadically, in its own geographical and chronological frame. The stories are not woven together; when a character from one turns up in another, there is no satisfying sense of recognition. The novel refuses to be integrative. No sustainable ideology gives the events meaning. Nothing unites the character except, perhaps, the common experience of delusion and loss." The protagonists range in social class from a rapacious peasant who has come to Santo Domingo with Columbus to Phillip II, who, despite ruling over Spain, is no less out of step with his world than the other characters. Although the gold-seeking peasant is the only fictional protagonist, Benítez-Rojo exercises considerable license in recreating figures drawn from history.

The structure of *Sea of Lentils* corresponds to

Benítez-Rojo's often-stated ideas about the Caribbean, which were later formulated in his essay "The Repeating Island." He views the Caribbean as the "empty center" around which the Spanish New World Developed in its fluidly meandering way. As Sidney Lea observes in his Introduction to the English translation: "everywhere in *Sea of Lentils*, one can almost feel along the senses the instantaneous pulverization of certainty . . . *Sea of Lentils* shows froth the 'marine' character that its author ascribes to archipelagic cultures, not only because so many of its actions take place on or near water but also because fixity and definition are so persistently dissolved, as a sandcastle by wave or tide."

In 1980, Benítez-Rojo seized the opportunity of a trip to a scholarly convention in Paris to defect. His departure was notable not only because of his stature as a writer and intellectual, but because he had not been perceived as a dissident intellectual, had assumed key positions, and had been traveling with an official Cuban delegation when he defected. At this time Benítez-Rojo began to hyphenate his name in probably because foreigners are often confused by the double surnames that are common in Spanish. In Spanish-language publications, the author's name still generally appears as Antonio Benítez Rojo.

As a writer in exile Benítez-Rojo has been more easily accessible to literary people who had been taking an interest in him: interviewers, critics, translators, and editors on the international scene. He has held lecturing posts in Spanish American literature at the University of Pittsburgh and at the University of California at Irvine before assuming a regular position at Amherst College. Benítez-Rojo's work has been brought to the English language reading public by editors, among them Frank Janney and Sidney Lea, critic Roberto González Echevarría, and translator James Maraniss. Although his education had not been in literary criticism, Benítez-Rojo has become a proficient interpreter of Spanish-American literature. Once outside Cuba and in the U.S. academic circuit, he has published his studies in professional journals of literary criticism in both Spanish and English. Among these is a special Caribbean issue of the *New England Review and Bread Loaf Quarterly* (1984). The journal's editor, Sidney Lea, had been greatly struck by Benítez-Rojo's writing and his evolving thought about the Caribbean, and the special issue showcased both the Cuban author's vision of his region and his skill as a writer of fiction. Benítez-Rojo wrote his story "Gentleman's Agreement" for his issue which also included "The Repeating Island," an essay in which Benítez-Rojo interprets the Caribbean using concepts drawn from deconstructionism

and chaos theory. "The Repeating Island" shows the Caribbean as an apparent manifestation of chaos, with its haphazard history and islands strung out irregularity over vast spaces of liquid. Yet chaotic structures are known to reveal upon examination significant symmetries. Benítez-Rojo found meaningful recurring patterns, a "figure in the carpet," in the seeming disorder of the Caribbean.

Benítez-Rojo's work has appeared in *The Best American Essays 1986* and has earned a Pushcart Prize.

Interest in Benítez-Rojo and his work owes much to the originality with which he has been developing his vision of the Caribbean, drawing on his reading in history, literature, economics, deconstruction, theoretical physics, and other subjects. Yet the distinctive properties of Benítez-Rojo's though should not obscure the fact that he attracts readers with his skills as a writer: his literary language, ability to present his ideas persuasively, innovative means of constructing a narrative or essay, and, in the case of his early short fiction, the magical and fantastic strain he often introduces. Despite his late start in both fields, Benítez-Rojo has established himself as a significant figure in both the rising field of Caribbean studies and in Spanish-American literature.

PRINCIPAL WORKS IN ENGLISH TRANSLATION: *Novels*—(tr. Maraniss, J.) Sea of Lentils, 1990. *Short stories*—(Comp. Janney, F.) The Magic Dog and Other Stories, 1990. *Essays*—The Repeating Island, 1992.

ABOUT: Flores, A. Spanish American Authors: The Twentieth Century, 1992; Janney, F. *Introduction to* The Magic Dog and Other Stories, 1990; Lea, S. *Introduction to* Sea of Lentils, 1990; Martinez, J.A. (ed.) Dictionary of Twentieth Century Cuban Literature, 1990; Menton, S. (ed.) Prose Fiction of the Cuban Revolution, 1975. *Periodicals*—New England Quaterly and Breadloaf Review 6, 1984; New York Times Book Review August 26, 1990; December 16, 1990; SECOLAS 20, 1989; South Eastern Latin Americanist: Bulletin of the South Eastern Council of Latin American Studies 20, 1989.

BEN JELLOUN, TAHAR (December 1, 1944–   ), Moroccan novelist, poet, and journalist, was catapulted to international celebrity in 1987 when his seventh novel, *La Nuit sacrée* (*The Sacred Night*), was awarded France's prestigious Prix Goncourt. Two cities play a particularly important role in Ben Jelloun's work: Fez, where he was born, and Tangier, to which he moved with his family when he was eighteen years old and where he attended the French lycée. In *La Soudure fraternelle* (*Fraternal bonding*, 1994), a series of autobiographical sketches about friends and acquaintances of importance to his life from the early days at Koranic school to the present, Ben Jelloun provides new material about his childhood, youth, and young adult years.

In March 1965 student uprisings in Rabat, Casablanca, and other Moroccan cities were harshly suppressed by the authorities. The following year Ben Jelloun and a friend, having previously organized a student union, found themselves along with the ninety-odd other members of the union drafted into the army—although according to Ben Jelloun such military service did not exist at the time—and spent eighteen months at the El Hajeb base where they were "treated as prisoners."

After military service, Ben Jelloun returned to Rabat, where he studied philosophy at the Université Mohammed V and associated with the group of writers and intellectuals around the influential journal *Souffles* (*Breaths*), founded in 1966 by the poet Abdellatif Laâbi. Encouraged and inspired by Laâbi and Abdelkebir Khatibi, author of *La Mémoire tatouée* (*The tattooed memory*, 1971), Ben Jelloun published his first poems in *Souffles* and a collection of poems *Hommes sous linceul de silence* (Men under a shroud of silence, 1971).

In 1971, Ben Jelloun moved to Paris, where he earned a doctorate in psychiatric social work, his dissertation being based on the case histories of immigrant workers from North Africa whom he had counseled. His first novel, *Harrouda* (1973), a tale of two cities in which a sexual ogress named Harrouda hovers menacingly over the narrative, appears to have been partially inspired by Khatibi's *La Mémoire tatouée*, and contains traces of violence and sexuality reminiscent of those of the shocking novel *La Répudiation* (1968) by Algerian writer Rachid Boudjedra.

The overarching drama of the cases Ben Jelloun dealt with as a counselor is the sexual impotence that the male immigrant worker often experiences after coming to France. This material has found its way into several of Ben Jelloun's published works, notably his second novel, *La Réclusion solitaire*, (1976 *Solitare*), a fictionalized amalgam of some of these case histories, as well as the thesis itself, published in 1977 as *La Plus Haute des solitudes* (The deepest solitude). Other novels present and analyze characters who suffer crises involving yet other dysfunctions, such as *Moha le fou, Moha le sage* (Moha the mad, Moha the sage, 1978), ravings of an alleged madman, and *L'Ecrivain public* (The public scribe, 1983), the haunting account of a physical and mental invalid who pursues a quest for redemption and self-valorization.

Ben Jelloun's work has continued to attract many readers and extensive critical attention in the popular press as well as in scholarly journals throughout the world. As a result of the growing interest in the literature of the ex-colonies of France, as well as due to application of contemporary critical theories promoting a new "postcolonial" discourse, or counter discourse, Tahar Ben Jelloun has been lionized by traditional and poststructuralist critics alike; for example, his work has been endorsed by many feminists for its sensitivity to the problems of women's identity in the Maghrebian world, notably *L'Enfant de sable* (1985, *The Sand Child*), and *Les Yeux baisses* (With lowered eyes, 1991).

Inspired perhaps in part by understandable envy, some Maghrebian critics claim that Ben Jelloun is primarily a journalist bent on producing facile material of particular appeal to a French audience. To be sure, Ben Jelloun has written articles for magazines and some of his novels and stories contain material that borders on reportage; for example, *L'Homme rompu* (The broken man, 1994), a novel about widespread corruption in the Moroccan civil service; and *L'Ange aveugle* (Blind angel, 1992), a collection of quasifictionalized essays on the Italian Mafia that Ben Jelloun, with the assistance of his friend and translator Egi Volterrani, had written for the Naples daily *Il Mattino*. Keeping these cavils regarding Ben Jelloun's writings in perspective, one must acknowledge that Ben Jelloun inevitably spins a fascinating narrative, often couched in a haunting, oneiric, poetic prose—when not actually presented as poetry, for he is also an excellent poet—and there is ample evidence that he speaks neither solely to a French audience, nor solely to a Maghrebian audience, but to both, addressing the reader in consummate French which nevertheless contains many examples of intentional "interference" or bilingual wordplay, as in the humorous onomastics of "L'Assise" in *The Sacred Night*. Ben Jelloun tells us that she is thus nicknamed because of her large posterior, but the literal translation of l'Assise (the seated woman) in Moroccan Arabic is *gellasa*, the title for the superintendent seated at the entry to the women's bath, which is the job l'Assise holds in the novel. In Ben Jelloun's works, we also encounter numerous Islamic allusions (for example, in *La Nuit sacrée*, the interior of the baths is described as so murky that "good eyesight could scarcely distinguish a white thread, from a black thread," the ability to make that distinction being the criterion for beginning the daily fast during the holy month of Ramadan), as well as allusions to Moroccan proverbs and folktales. Although any reader can appreciate on an immediate level Ben Jelloun's bold and swiftly paced narratives, in order to derive the richest possible reading of one of Ben Jelloun's texts, one should acquire some familiarity with Morroccan language and culture.

Ben Jelloun has become more and more self-conscious of his cross-cultural role and recent novels have placed great emphasis on bilingualism. For example, in *Les Yeux baissés*, the female protagonist from a remote rural area of Morocco takes an itinerary that leads her to the city and ultimately to France, where she falls in love with the French language and aspires to be a writer in the acquired language; and the narrator of *L'Homme rompu*, has borrowed from work an old typewriter which is rusted and useless but which, after his wife has used it and a Larousse dictionary to prop up a broken bed, becomes magical and spontaneously writes surrealistic images reminiscent of those produced by a technique practiced by André Breton and the surrealists: *le cadavre exquis* (the exquisite corpse), a well-known party game process in which one person writes the subject of a sentence on a strip of paper, folds the latter over to hide what he or she has written, and passes the paper along to another person who supplies an adjective, and so forth, until a collective sentence is randomly formed, free of logic. Indeed, Ben Jelloun makes numerous allusions to Breton and surrealism in his work, notably in *La Soudure fraternelle, L'Homme rompu*, and *State of Absence*, in the last instance alluding in ludic fashion to "le cadavre exquis" in a threat sent to a criminologist who examines the bodies of Mafia victims: "Even if they are exquisite, you should not look at them too closely. The corpses, that is!"

The surreal quality in his writing lies not so much in automatic or trance writing, but in the transcription or creation of dream sequences, which occur in almost all his works, and in the cultivation of a "rational de-reasoning of meaning," to paraphrase Rimbaud. In *L'Homme rompu*, the protagonist Mourad writes of the magical typewriter what amounts to a succinct Ben Jellounian ars poetica:

For the time being, I dream the world since I cannot transform it. To dream is to assemble incongruous things and beings, and from that point of departure, to weave a trite or extraordinary story. I am simply following Schopenhauer's idea that "life and dreams are pages in a single book; to read the pages in order is life; to read them out of order is to dream.

For a long time I tried to follow the order of things. Now, thanks to the Olivetti-Larousse story, I place greater trust in disorder and the dream.

—tr. Eric Sellin

Nowhere is this fictive Schopenhauerian "manual" in which the order of life and the disorder of the psyche are in symbiosis or conflict more in evidence than in Ben Jelloun's tour de force, the diptych of *The Sand Child* and *The Sacred Night*, in which the "true" chronology and the "true" events are repeatedly placed in question by various characters who would "write" their interpretations on the blank pages of a mystical manuscript.

Although some critics feel that Ben Jelloun's best novel is *La Prière de l'absent* (Prayer of the absent, 1981)—a picaresque account of a quest journey made by a bizarre foursome from Fez to the southern reaches of Morocco in search of an ineffable salvation—the peak of Ben Jelloun's career to date has been, no doubt, the publication and enthusiastic reception of *The Sand Child* and *The Sacred Night*, which describe a young girl's development from psychological repression by the super- ego of male dominated Moroccan society (the girl is raised as a boy by her father, who is ashamed to have already sired seven daughters) to reclamation of her sexual and personal identity in a sequel of psychical liberation entailing sexual posturing, violence, and murder.

Jour de silence à Tanger (1990, *Silent Day in Tangier*), is a slim but compelling account based on the last years of Ben Jelloun's father. It is an interior monologue in which the protagonist spends his hours reminiscing about the erotic experiences of his earlier years; *Silent Day in Tangier* won critical praise. Aamer Hussein in the *Times Literary Supplement* commented: "Ben Jelloun's main concern is the passing of time, the nature of memory, and their link with the redemptive imagination. . . . Ben Jelloun's genius lies in evoking through language the grammar of existence, and the possibility of transforming with words the grimness of life's narratives." The *Economist* 's commentator noted that "Jelloun combines the gifts of the traditional Arab storyteller—that ability to play fantastic variations upon the simplest of themes—with remarkable philosophical insight, often reminiscent of the monologues of Samuel Beckett." This critic found "the intense probing of an individual mind" to "encompass the whole world of human preoccupations."

There followed *Les Yeux baissés*, about the "education" of a rural Moroccan girl; *L'Homme rompu*, in which a scrupulously honest but financially strapped government functionary finally succumbs to the temptation of corruption; and *La Soudure fraternelle*, an unpretentious and somewhat ingenuous reflection on various types of friendship, which nevertheless provides interesting insights into Ben Jelloun's personal and literary friendships with various men and women, including an account of his esteem for and ultimate break with Khatibi.

The Moroccan poet, Mohammed Loakira, has observed that virtually all Moroccan novelists are primarily poets. Indeed, Ben Jelloun's poems, from the brief concise maxim to the dithyrambic prose poem—a good selection of his poetry is found in *Les Amandiers sont morts de leurs blessures, suivi de A l'insu du souvenir* (The almond trees have died of their wounds, followed by Beyond the ken of memory, 1983)— are but miniatures or "narratemes" of the fictional works; and in them we encounter many of the same poetic elements as in the novels, such as intertextual nods to other writers, like Borges, references to *The Thousand and One Nights* (the frame story is perhaps the most salient structural component of Ben Jelloun's technique), and even an occasional wink at Ben Jelloun's own works (e.g., an oblique reference to *La Prière de l'absent* in *Les Yeux baissés*); and the digressions and the letters and dreams interpolated in the novels can often be read as self-sufficient prose poems. Conversely, a prose poem like the representative "Les Filles de Tanger" ("The Girls of Tangier"), contains in embryonic form most of the elements elaborated in Ben Jelloun's various novels:

> The Girls of Tangier have a star on each breast. Accomplices of the night and the wind, they live in seashells on the shores of love. Neighbors of the sun, that blows morning to them like a teardrop in the mouth, they own a garden. A garden hidden in the dawn, somewhere in the Old City where storytellers build boats for the giant birds of legends. They have braided a golden thread in their wild hair. Beautiful as a flame rearing up in the wilderness, like desire that raises the eyelids of night, like a hand opening for an offering, fish and shellfish from the sea and the sand. They go through town spreading the light of day and giving things to drink to the men suspended from the clouds. But the city has two faces: one for loving, the other for betraying. Its body is a labyrinth traced by the gazelle that has stolen honey from the lips of a child. A purple or ink-colored scarf tied over its forehead to protect the night's writing on the virginal body. A nameless flower has grown between two stones. An odorless flower has lit a fire in the veil of the rumpled day. A gap in the lips through which music slips and that rouses mirrors to dance. The girls, having descended from a nearby ridge, and naked behind the veil of the sky, bite into ripe fruit. Shells rain down on the veil. The veil becomes a stream. The girls become sirens who make love to the stars. The girls of Tangier awoke this morning with sand between their breasts, seated on a bench in the public garden. Orphans.
>
> -tr. Eric Sellin

Tahar Ben Jelloun, manages to write in French without abandoning his Maghrebian culture that permeates his discourse. After he was awarded the Prix Goncourt, a journalist asked him about the relative importance of French or Arabic to his writing, to which Ben Jelloun replied: "Arabic is my wife and French is my mistress; and I have been unfaithful to both!"

PRINCIPAL WORKS IN ENGLISH TRANSLATION: (tr. A. Sheridan) The Sand Child, 1987; (tr. G. Stanton) Solitaire, 1988; (tr. A. Sheridan) The Sacred Night, 1989; (tr. D. Lobdell) Silent Day in Tangier, 1991; (tr. J. Kirkeep) State of Absence, 1994.

ABOUT: Contemporary Authors 135, 1992; Contemporary World Writers, 2nd ed., 1993; Encyclopedia of World Literature in the 20th Century 5, 1993. *Periodicals*: Callaloo Summer 1990; *Economist* July 13, 1991; French Review February 1991; Itinéraires et Contactes de Culture 14, 1991; Middle East Report March–April 1990; Research in African Literatures Winter 1990; Studies in Twentieth Century Literature Winter 1991; Times Literary Supplement June 21, 1991; December 16, 1994.

BENNETT, ALAN (May 9, 1934–   ), British playwright, writer for cinema and television, actor and former revue artist, was born in Leeds, Yorkshire, the son of Walter Bennett, a butcher, and the former Lilian Mary Peel. He was educated at the Leeds Modern School, upon leaving which he went straight into the army, doing his national service (1952–1954) in the Intelligence Corps. He then went to Exeter College, Oxford, where he read history, receiving his B.A. in 1957. From 1959 to 1960 he held a post as a junior lecturer in medieval history at Magdalen College, Oxford.

By the end of 1961 he had become a celebrity: with Peter Cook, Dudley Moore, and Jonathan Miller he cowrote and performed in, the moldbreaking revue *Beyond the Fringe*, a series of satirical sketches which opened in Edinburgh on August 25, 1960, and transferred to London the following May. Drawing on traditional revue and music hall techniques, as well as on such American comedians as Lenny Bruce and Mort Sahl, they added a new and more intellectual dimension to the revue form. With its irreverent attitude towards the decline of religion, the nuclear threat, and the cold war, *Beyond the Fringe* enjoyed great success in England—and then in the United States when it opened in New York in 1962. Robert Coleman, commented in the *New York Mirror* that the "quartet is the epitome of versatility. It spoofs Prime Minister Macmillan, the royal family, religion, pompous academicians." Robert Brustein, conceding that *Beyond the Fringe* lacked "a firm moral centre" and was "immoderate, irresponsible, and totally destructive," nevertheless insisted that it was "violently funny": "if the young seem nega-

ALAN BENNETT

tive . . . then this may be because their positive
and responsible elders have left them such a poisoned inheritance. It is a measure of health, not
sickness, that their inevitable anger and resentment can still be disciplined within a witty,
sharp, and purgative art." Thus Bennett and his
three colleagues broke new ground.

With his first play, *Forty Years On*, produced
in Manchester and London (with Sir John Giel-
gud) in 1968, Bennett established himself as a
playwright. The sharpness and wit of *Beyond
the Fringe* have seldom been absent from his
subsequent work, but to these have been added,
cautiously but increasingly, a more serious and
nonsatirical element: what amounts to a lament
for the decline of English culture in the 20th
century. Irving Wardle, writing in the *New York
Times*, called *Forty Years On* "a mock-heroic
pageant of modern British myth": the school in
which it is set, he explained, represents "an image of Britain at the crossroads." The incoming
liberal headmaster of a small public school sa-
lutes his conservative predecessor by getting the
pupils to present an end-of-term revue-
entertainment, a picture of the past seen through
the hindsight of today, which parodies such figures as Oscar Wilde and Virginia Woolf. This,
like its successor *Getting On* (1971), about a
member of the British House of Commons who
expresses his hatred of new developments, was
closer in form to revue than to drama. *Habeas
Corpus* (1973), is a bedroom farce in the tradition of Georges Feydeau.

Towards the end of the 1970s Bennett's work
became both deeper and nearer to the conventional drama form. Meanwhile most critics, with
only a few dissenters—such as Clive Barnes in
the *New York Times*, who found *Forty Years On*
"cheap and nasty," full of "pretentiousness and
ineptness," and who felt that the
"anti-homosexual gibes" seemed "mildly
inappropriate," noted both that this earlier work
was wildly funny and that Bennett was essentially a traditionalist. As Julius Novick remarked in
the *Nation*, "the nostalgia seems to be essentially
genuine." A few of Bennett's critics—Donald
Campbell in *British Book News* for one—have
felt, though, that television and film offer Bennett the most fruitful media for the expression
of his genius. He has adapted many of his television plays for the stage.

The Old Country, produced in 1977, although
full of comic dialogue, is an essentially more serious and conventionally structured play than its
predecessors, with more deeply realized characters. In it a traitorous English civil servant and
his wife lead a paradoxically very English-style
life—in Russia. *Choice* found that there was "a
rejoicing in language for its own sake, which is
something of a mixed blessing inasmuch as motivation and psychology are not given the prominence probably needed to give the play more
substance." But *Choice* also found this treatment
of a British civil servant in exile ("for homosexu-
ality-linked security violation") "engrossing."

Many critics felt that Bennett took his first really "serious turn" with his script for Stephen Frears's film *Prick Up Your Ears* (1986), based on
the life of Joe Orton, the outrageous playwright
who was murdered by his homosexual lover.
Others trace the emerging seriousness of his
work back to Bennett's dark comedy of 1980,
Enjoy. As Thomas E. Luddy wrote of that play
in *Library Journal*, the "comic development is
wonderfully funny and touching" in this depiction of an old couple's awaiting the destruction
of their house, the last in a district under demolition; but the "end of the play slides into expres-
sionistic revelations of the severity of the
theme."

Aside from the obvious influence of the music
halls of both Great Britain and America (in
which he is taken rather more seriously than in
his own country), Bennett owes most to two contemporaries: Harold Pinter and Joe Orton. Undoubtedly he tried, in *Prick Up Your Ears*, to
represent Orton's life as Orton himself might
have represented it. Sheila Benson, in the *Los
Angeles Times*, wrote that the film had the
"rhythm and even the insolence of an Orton
play." Certainly in this script there is far less
sheer verbal playfulness than anywhere else in
Bennett, and as certainly the facts of Orton's

tragic story tended to steer him away from the merely comic. As for the squalor and lovelessness, or otherwise, of Orton's life, Bennett, as Desson Howe remarked in the *Washington Post*, tries to show "the beauty in 'dirtiness.'"

Although it casts no light on its subject, *Kafka's Dick*, produced in London in 1986, is an ingenious tilt at biographers: "Most of the action," Jim Hiley wrote in the *Listener*, "occupies the grey drawing-room . . . of Sydney, a spare-time Kafka scholar who would 'rather read about writers then read what they wrote'; a whining Kafka himself—perhaps deliberately not at all like the much more psychologically robust man of fact—metamorphoses from Sydney's tortoise, and proceeds to encounter both Max Brod, who failed to obey Kafka's wish that his work be destroyed, and his brutal father, who threatens to reveal the (miniscule) size of his eponymous "dick" if he does not deny that the father is a tyrant. The consensus among critics was that Bennett spoiled the seriousness of his play with cheap comic writing at odds with its subject. Thus Victoria Radin, in the *New Statesman*, observed that Sydney's remark that in Britain "gossip is the acceptable face of the intellect" "goes down rather oddly in a play in which the author gives his audience points for every name he drops. . . . "

Critics were unanimous in their praise of *Talking Heads*, a series of three adaptations of monologues from six originally commissioned by the British Broadcasting Corporation in the early 1980s. This was produced at the Comedy Theatre in 1992, with Bennett performing one of the pieces himself. "Bennett's genius," wrote Hugo Williams in the *Times Literary Supplement* in 1992, is that "he can people the stage with as many characters as he likes or needs for his strangely interior dramas, make them perform for him (and us) then engineer their departure without the audience's having to make the slightest effort of the imagination." More than one critic traced the origins of these brilliant sketches to Bennett's own performance as an Anglican vicar in *Beyond the Fringe*: "Although his self-caricature must be only a fraction of the whole picture," Williams commented, "Bennett has stuck to it over the years, to the point where the work itself seems to be the product of the public persona and sometimes, as here, indistinguishable from it."

The question of Bennett's status as a playwright has puzzled critics. Jim Hiley in the *Listener* complained that "you'll seldom find him registered among the best British scribes" and asks, "What's his offence?" His answer is that Bennett "collides with the class systems of both theatre and nation. . . . is difficult to categorize. . . . prefers comic elegance to the more familiar . . . rough strokes. He knows all about the parish pump but refuses to be parochial." Richard Christiansen, in the *Chicago Tribune*, wrote that "Alan Bennett is not as celebrated or prolific a playwright as his contemporaries Tom Stoppard and Simon Grey, but he ranks right up there with them as a witty and humane observer of England and of mankind in general."

Bennett made a successful adaptation of Kenneth Grahame's *The Wind in the Willows* for the National Theatre in 1990. His first film script, for *A Private Function*, starring Michael Palin and Maggie Smith, was particularly well liked in America, where, as an interviewer, J. B. Miller, said in the *New York Times Magazine* in 1990, he "is again a voice" owing to the PBS broadcasts of *Talking Heads*. His play about George III, *The Madness of George III*, produced in 1991 at the Lyttleton Theatre in London, starring Nigel Hawthorne, greatly added to his reputation: David Nokes, writing in the *TImes Literary Supplement*, was by now insisting (controversially but credibly) that he was "probably our greatest living dramatist," and described the new play as "an animated Rowlandson cartoon"; "like most of Bennett's best work," he asserted, "it appealed "not to the ear but to the eye." Of the episode when the king reads the lines, "but I am bound upon a wheel of fire," from Shakespeare's *King Lear*, Nokes writes: "It is as if Bennett is reminding himself, and us, of his own talent for poignant and profound human drama when not playing the showman's part as a crowd-pleasing latter-day Sheridan." But, as J. B. Miller observed, "There are, in fact, two Bennetts: the celebrated . . . playwright . . . who writes about spies and government ministers, actors and authors, and the Yorkshire Bennett who . . . [chronicles] the lives of quiet desperation so common to working-class families." The play was filmed and released in 1994 under the title *The Madness of King George*.

Stephen Schiff said of Bennett in a *New Yorker* article, "Bennett's renowned aversion to parties and opening nights, his shrinking violet manners, and his circumspect suspicion of praise are cherished by the English people. He is , to his dismay, a kind of cuddlesome love object. . . . Bennett is the 'National Teddy Bear'" —this last perhaps because generations of English children have listened to his narrations of Winnie-the-Pooh and *Alice in Wonderland* on the BBC.

In an excerpt from his journals published in the *New Yorker*, Bennett describes a visit to the doctor about what he thought was a tumor, but which turned out to be only a thrombosed vein: "Reprieved I bike back home thinking of the people who are not reprieved and do not bike back home, resolving to do better, work harder, behave. But it's such a precarious business, life's peaceful landscape suddenly transformed, what look like green fields suddenly a swamp of anxiety." Bennett concludes: "The majority of people perform well in a crisis and when the spotlight is on them; it's on the Sunday afternoons of this life, when nobody is looking, that the spirit falters."

Bennett, who is unmarried, has lived since 1967 in a part of Camden Town which is, as Miller explains, a " chic area in North London popular with film people and writers," near the house of his friend and colleague Jonathan Miller. He has received almost a score of awards, including three *Evening Standard* Drama Awards, the Guild of Television Producers Award, and the Hawthornden prize for *Talking Heads.*

PRINCIPAL WORKS: *Revue*—(with P. Cook, D. Moore, and J. Miller) Beyond the Fringe, 1963. *Plays*—Forty Years On, 1969; Getting On, 1972; Habeas Corpus, 1973; The Old Country, 1978; Enjoy, 1980; Office Suite (*contains* Green Forms, A Visit From Miss Prothero) 1981; Kafka's Dick, 1986; Single Spies (*contains* A Question of Attribution, An Englishman Abroad) 1988. *Teleplays*—Objects of Affection and Other Plays (three plays), 1982; The Writer in Disguise (five plays), 1985; Talking Heads, 1988; Images of Cornwall, 1992. *Screenplays*—A Private Function, 1984; Prick Up Your Ears, 1988.

ABOUT: Brustein, R. Seasons of Discontent: Dramatic Opinions, 1959–1965, 1965; Ryan, B. Major 20th Century Writers, 1991; Thwaite, A. (ed.) Larkin at Sixty, 1982. *Periodicals*—British Book News June 1985; Chicago Tribune April 12, 1985; Choice July–August 1979; Encounter December 1989; Hudson Review Winter 1990; Library Journal March 15, 1981; Listener October 2, 1986; Los Angeles Times May 1, 1987; Nation September 7, 1970; New Republic February 17, 1992; New Statesman November 7, 1986; New York Mirror October 29, 1962; New York Times November 5, 1968; April 13, 1989; New York Times Magazine September 30, 1990; New Yorker September 6, 1993; May 22, 1995; Newsweek January 21, 1991;Plays and Players November 1986; Times Literary Supplement June 12, 1991; February 7, 1992; Washington Post May 15, 1987.

*BERBEROVA, NINA (NIKOLAEVNA) (August 8, 1901–September 26, 1993), Russian fiction writer, poet, novelist, memoirist, biographer, and critic, was born in St. Petersburg. Even before the Revolution, which was to condemn her family as members of the bourgeois classes, she lived in two or more different worlds. Her father's Armenian family had Russified its name from Berberian to Berberova, but still maintained ties to the Armenian language and culture. Her father was in government service, a state councillor, trained as a mathematician. Her mother came from an upper-class Russian family with estates in Lithuania, where Berberova spent summers as a girl.

Berberova's maternal grandfather was a reformer, a liberal. While he tended to disdain formal society, he would receive the *muzhiks*, (peasants), who came to him for advice and to beg favors. She divided them into two opposite types: "Some muzhiks were demure, well bred, important-looking, with greasy hair, fat paunches, and shiny faces. They were dressed in embroidered shirts and caftans of fine cloth . . . .They walked in the church with collection trays and placed candles before the Saint-Mary-Appease-My-Grief icon. . . . The other muzhiks . . . were undersized, and often lay in ditches near the state owned wineshop. Their children did not grow because they were underfed . . . .in their homes, which I also visited . . . there was a sour stench." Berberova's grandfather was "visibly tormented by all this," she writes in her autobiography *The Italics Are Mine*, but from such experiences, she herself developed an unsentimental perception that some people's lives are fated. She sees her own life as impelled both by conscious decisions and by implacable forces—biology and sociology, she calls them—but it is her conscious choices that give her "a sharp sense of the 'electric charge' which one can call bliss . . . ." She determines to live by self-knowledge and choice, actively, not passively.

Berberova says that she knew the Russia she lived in before the Bolshevik Revolution was finished, and that the world of the intelligentsia "would in one way or another be destroyed."

Carol Rumens, reviewing *The Italics Are Mine* in the *New Statesman & Society*, found Berberova apparently aware of her own survival skills in a world that was crumbling: "The sense of herself as an amphibious being, able to breathe in two worlds, south and north, old and new, occurs early, linked to the other main theme of her life, the quest for an inner wholeness . . . ."

One quest began for her at the age of ten, when—feeling an urgent inner pressure to choose a profession—she became a poet, delighted by her own decisiveness. "Verses gushed from me. I choked with them. I couldn't stop," she writes in *The Italics Are Mine.*

Nina Berberova was in her last year at a progressive school in St. Petersburg when the Rus-

°bair BAIR uh vuh, NEE nuh

sian Revolution thrust her and her family from comfort and ease into poverty and misery. Her family began to wander, spending some time in the south, in Rostov, where she attended Rostov University for a year, involving herself in the literary and artistic circles that flourished there. When they returned to St. Petersburg, she continued to practice her chosen profession of poet and became acquainted with such other poets as Anna Akhmatova and Osip Mandelstam.

When she was twenty, she became the lover of Vladislav Khodasevich, a poet, leaving Russia with him in 1922 to live in exile in Berlin. There they were part of Maxim Gorky's entourage, the Russian exile community, that numbered among its members Vladimir Nabokov and Aleksandr Blok. In 1925 Berberova and Khodasevich moved on to Paris where she wrote for the Russian language daily *Poslednye Novosti*, producing two stories a month, as well as criticism and reportage. The money she earned often had to support both herself and Khodasevich. She considered him the greater writer, but describes their relationship as a friendship between equals. During this period, she wrote four novels and several widely praised novellas (*povesti*) and short stories (*rasskaz*).

In 1932 she left Khodasevich. In 1935 she began an affair with Nikolai Makeyev, a journalist whom she married in 1937. They moved to the French countryside where they renovated an old house. Berberova continued to cherish Khodasevich's poetry above her own, and she visited him when he was dying in 1939. Although in her fiction love is often evanescent and unconsummated, in fact Khodasevich loved her until the end (although he remarried). Berberova mentions other loving couples whom she knew, but she herself preferred "solitude in an anthill" to "solitude in a nest," and freedom to excessive domesticity.

In 1937 her biography of Tchaikovsky revealed the then-shocking fact of his homosexuality. She remained Khodasevich's editor and literary executor and wrote about Blok, the poet, and Aleksandr Borodin, the composer, as well. She expresses extravagant admiration for Vladimir Nabokov, whom she had read in Berlin and got to know in Paris. For Berberova, Nabokov is the "phoenix . . . born from the fire and ashes of revolution and exile. Our existence from now on acquired a meaning." She saw in Nabokov the salvation of the Russian community in exile. He was to her not merely a Russian but a universal writer whose immortality would ensure that their generation would never be lost to history.

The shabby Paris of nightclubs with their aging cabaret singers; American, French, and English tourists imitating Dmitri Karamazov in getting drunk, shattering their glasses, singing along; the cheap vodka and fat herrings consumed held no particular romantic charm for Berberova. She saw the factories where high-ranking officers of the White Army toiled. She looked down on the theatricality of weddings, funerals, and holiday celebrations, hating the ceremonies "even more than I hated the Christmas tree of my childhood." It was only the dinners honoring poets, the readings and the literary salons, that delighted her. Nevertheless, she remained in France during World War II. She only decided to leave in 1950 for the United States when the Russian exile community had dwindled away.

From 1950, Berberova worked in America as a file clerk, a language instructor, and a radio announcer, until in 1958 she was taken on by the Slavic Department at Yale as a lecturer. In 1963 she became a professor of literature at Princeton, remaining there until her retirement in 1971. She married a musician, Jorge Kochevitsky—and divorced him. During these years she was a guest at Yaddo, the artists colony, and lectured at such institutions as Columbia University, Indiana University, and the University of Pennsylvania.

One of the pervasive motifs in Berberova's writing is duality, contrast. Everything has its polar opposite. War, cataclysm, murder are seen in the light of people's opposite reactions. She proclaims hatred for dualism as well, announcing "that I myself am a seam, that with this seam, while I am alive, something has united in me, something has been soldered, that I am one of many examples in nature of soldering, unification . . . an example of synthesis in a world of antitheses."

In her memoir *The Italics Are Mine* she emphasizes her joy in life, which means more to her than literature: " . . . at my birth I was given an electrical charge, a colossal charge of tremendous strength." In *The Tattered Cloak*, a collection of six *povesti*, the lives of the characters mimic the lives of the Russian exiles Berberova knew in Paris, but the characters tend to react in opposite ways to her own healthy determination to survive and to gain self-knowledge. In the title story, Sasha, the narrator, lives in a slum, takes care of her aging, crumbling father, and works as a presser in a commercial laundry. Her father calls her his Cordelia. Reviewing the book in the *New York Review* Gabriele Annan remarked, "Cordelias don't survive. She pities but doesn't exalt them." Annan characterizes the alienation these people experience as numbness. Reviewing the book in the *New York Times*,

Michiko Kakutani finds "emotional precision" in the way Berberova conjures up the emigré world. "Whether they are fading courtesans, dronelike clerks or mousy servants, the people in . . . Berberova's stories all divide their lives into an after and a before: their exile marks a watershed from which they measure their subsequent lives . . . .World War II . . . will undermine their few remaining shreds of security and leave them with an even greater sense of dislocation." Berberova's characters, numbed though they may be, experience, according to Kakutani, "melodramatic events: A self-absorbed cad carelessly seduces a vulnerable spinster, who proceeds to kill herself in shame; . . . another despairing woman tries to stage the murder of her lover . . . . Though operatic in intensity, these events . . . feel like the inevitable outcome of that horrible spiral of emotions that turns hope into disappointment, expectancy into loss."

For Berberova an immense gulf yawns between those who achieve self-realization and those who merely survive or are ground under by circumstance. She sees the same gulf between herself and the pathetic Russian exiles, even between herself and such icons as Simone de Beauvoir, who, in her eyes, was overwhelmed by aging and fear of death. She describes in *The Italics Are Mine* how on her first trip back to Europe in 1965 she enters a restaurant and sees Simone de Beauvoir finishing dinner, but still sitting with her companion, another aging woman after Berberova has left. She thinks of the home she has achieved in Princeton, her interesting life as a professor and writer, not caring about her own aging as long as her students remain forever young, which of course they do. "My life awaits me there, in the small university town," she writes, "a spasm of joy grasps my throat." She walks past the Luxembourg Gardens where once she had awaited a lover eagerly. "Now I was eagerly setting off for home. It's still the same eagerness . . . . It has not changed, not worn out. It has not wasted away. It is still whole, like myself."

Berberova received honorary degrees in 1980 from Glassboro Teachers College, in 1983 from Middlebury College, and in 1992 from Yale University. The publication in France in 1985 of her stories of Russian emigre life in Paris brought her international recognition. She returned to Russia in 1989, and the relaxation of Communist control made her visit a triumph. The French government named her a Chevalier of the Order of Arts and Letters in 1989. Her story "The Accompanist" was made into a film in 1993 by the French director Claude Miller. Berberova spent her last years in Philadelphia, independent and strong-willed into her nineties. Joan Juliet Buck, who visited her in 1991, wrote in the *New Yorker*: "At ninety, walking with a cane for a broken hip on the slow mend, she radiated an intensity and a controlling will that were both fiercely touching and draining; she had the titanic strength of a pure, pitiless survivor and a hunger to talk."

Penelope Lively, reviewing *The Tattered Cloak* in the *Times Literary Supplement*, called Berberova " . . . one of those strange and miraculous writers who are, in a sense, the creation of the events to which they bear witness. Her gift is to reflect circumstance." Berberova speaks in *The Italics Are Mine* of her conviction "that my century is the only suitable century for me. I know that many judge our time differently. I speak now, however, not about world stability (was there ever such a thing?) or about the joy of living in one's own country (Russians flee theirs a good deal), but of something else. As a woman and as a Russian, where—in what time—could I have been happier?"

PRINCIPAL WORKS IN ENGLISH TRANSLATION: *Fiction*— (tr. M. Schwartz) The Accompanist, 1988; (tr. M. Schwartz) The Revolt, 1989; (tr. M. Schwartz) Three Novels, 1990; (tr. M. Schwartz) The Second Volume, 1991; *Memoir*— (tr. P. Radley) The Italics Are Mine, 1969.

ABOUT: Berberova, N. The Italics Are Mine (tr. P. Radley) 1969; Contemporary Authors New Revision Series 14, 1985; Slonim, M. Modern Russian Literaure, 1953; Tucker M. (ed.) Literary Exiles in the 20th Century, 1991. *Periodicals*—New Republic June 17, 1991; New Statesman & Society August 3, 1990; August 2, 1991; New Yorker October 25, 1993; New York Review of Books September 26, 1991; New York Times November 13, 1988; June 21, 1991; New York Times Book Review June 23, 1991; May 17, 1992; Times Literary Supplement August 9, 1991.

BIDART, FRANK (1939–   ), American poet, was born in Bakersfield, California, and grew up in the western California town of Bishop. He was educated at Bakersfield High School and the University of California at Riverside. His early ambition, fed by a boyhood infatuation with the movies, was to be a film director, making serious films, "as ambitious and complex as the greatest works of art—as Milton, Eliot, Joyce," he told Mark Halliday in an interview for *Ploughshares* in 1983. At the University of California he planned to major in philosophy, but, inspired by one of his teachers, the critic Philip Wheelwright, he switched to English literature. He had begun writing poetry early, but apart from a vague desire to be an "artist," he did not find his vocation until graduate school—Harvard, which he entered in 1962. There he took courses desultorily and "was scared, miserable, hopeful," but was now committed to writing.

In 1966, having already written some of the poems that were to appear later in his first volume, *Golden State*, he met Robert Lowell, whose *Life Studies* had been a model for his own work. He audited Lowell's creative writing classes regularly and soon became his close personal friend, assisting the older poet in editing and revising his works. In later years he played a similar role in his friendship with Elizabeth Bishop, winning a tribute from still another poet, Seamus Heaney, in 1992, as "one of the great mentors, a practical critic dear to the hearts of Robert Lowell and Elizabeth Bishop . . . an inimitable teacher and listener, as well as a definitive voice for the times." Transplanted from California to the East ("And so I made myself an Easterner . . . ," he writes in "California Plush," "finding it, after all, more like me / than I had let myself hope"), he has lived and worked in or near Cambridge, Massachusetts, ever since. He is a member of the English Department at Wellesley College in Wellesley, Massachusetts, and also teaches at Brandeis University in Waltham, Massachusetts. In 1979 he had a Guggenheim Fellowship.

The bare facts of Bidart's biography are generously fleshed out in his poetry. Richard Howard remarked, in an introductory note to *Golden State*, on "his convulsive pursuit of a voice which will, accountably, speak in the first person singular." The perils of inferring autobiography from literature are ever present, and Bidart himself admits to occasional "invention": "Confessional," a poem about his relationship with his mother, "begins with an anecdote about a cat that *didn't* happen to me." In this instance, he told Mark Halliday, "I felt, for complicated and opaque reasons, that the story was right at the beginning—that I needed it. Everything else in the poem," he added, "had to be 'true.'" That compulsion to be "true" drives his poetry. Howard describes his early work as "a poetry in search of itself." He appears also to be a poet in search of himself—a not unusual poetic pursuit, from that of such romantic poets as Wordsworth, and such 20th-century "confessional" poets as Lowell and Adrienne Rich. Painfully honest and self-revealing, his work spares neither himself nor the reader. In "Golden State IX" Bidart announces:

> in the awareness, the
> history of our contradictions and violence,

> insofar as I am "moral" at all,
> is the beginning of my moral being.

From the poems we infer that Bidart was ambivalent in his feelings for both his parents. His father, a farmer as depicted in "California Plush," was a heavy drinker and a poor manager of money:

> I look at my father:
> as he drinks his way into garrulous, shaky
> defensiveness, the debris of the past
> is just debris—; whatever I reason, it is a
> desolation
> to watch . . .

His mother divorced him, remarried, and later suffered a mental breakdown. Though more deeply attached to her than to his father, Bidart is equally ambivalent towards her, as evidenced by these lines from "Confessional": "I *did* love her . . . Otherwise / would I feel so guilty?" ("Confessional"). Later, in another personal crisis, he had to come to terms with his homosexuality. In "The Book of the Body," he writes of his struggle: "the NO which is YES, the YES which is NO."

Bidart creates in two voices: one the direct first person; the other various dramatic personae. These include a necrophiliac child murderer ("Herbert White"), an anorexic women ("Ellen West"), the great dancer Nijinsky slipping into madness ("The War of Vaslav Nijinsky"), a man who suffers the amputation of an arm ("The Arc"). Striving for the effects of human speech, his irregular prosody in "The War of Vaslav Nijinsky" is addressed to the reader's ear and eye alike:

> I can understand the pleasure of WAR,

> In WAR—
> where *killing* is a virtue; *camouflage*
> a virtue; *revenge* a virtue;
> *pity* a weakness—
> the world rediscovers

> a *guiltless* PRE-HISTORY

> "civilization" condemns. . . .

Writing in *Shenandoah*, Alan Williamson called Bidart "a consumate craftsman": "His fluid and inventive visual form, with its shifting margins and stanza shapes, its odd and profuse punctuation, is at the service of an ear exquisitely attuned to the rushes and hesitations of speech, the subliminally characteristic rhythms.

Only the real masters of the conversational mode—Frost, Jarrell—give us more of the unforgettable immediacy of the speaking voice. But Bidart's poems, unlike theirs, must often carry on voice alone, and on the naked importance of what is said."

James Atlas, similarly, notes of *The Book of the Body* in the *Nation* : "The sprawl and apparent randomness of Bidart's prosody belie an exacting sense of composition that has nothing to do with 'free verse'; every word, line and stanza is justified by Bidart's will to reproduce the character of speech, its cadences and hesitations. . . . There are a few striking lines in Bidart's poetry. It owes its effect to the cumulative intensity of the story he relates. . . . "

Even to those critics who find Bidart's typographic arrangements distracting, the emotional intensity the poetry evokes is paramount. "In the supreme poems . . . Bidart's spiritual force makes me forget the look and yield to the authority of the voice," Denis Donoghue wrote in the *New Republic.*

Bidart's dramatic monologues have been described as "case studies in verse." The speakers, even when based on real-life people, are imaginatively conceived; they are characters, complete in their individual identities. But in their suffering, or their inflicting of suffering upon others, they share with the poet a quest for some moral meaning to impose upon the chaos of their lives. In her review in the *New Republic* of his collection *The Sacrifice*, Helen Vendler writes, "In the harrowing poems . . . it is difficult to distinguish the cries of the saint from the shrieks of the damned." His anorexic Ellen West, who will commit suicide (based on an actual case study), is torn between the physical and the spiritual—her body with its demands for food and sex, her spirit seeking "weightlessness." It begins: "I love sweets,—/ heaven / would be dying on a bed of vanilla ice cream." She is indifferent to her sympathetic husband ("But he is a fool, He married / meat, and thought it was a wife"), disgusted by sex, fearful of aging, fascinated by the example of Maria Callas, who starved herself to slimness at the sacrifice of her art. But the main source of her anguish is her desire to understand her condition:

without a body, who can
know himself at all?
    Only by
acting; choosing; rejecting; have I
made myself—
    discovered who and what *Ellen* can be . . .

All these speakers are obsessed with guilt and need to expiate their guilt in some act of violence done to themselves or to others. In his own voice Bidart wrestles with his ambivalence towards his mother: "TO SURVIVE I HAD TO KILL HER," he writes in "Confessional." Herbert White's guilt is more horrifying to the reader: "When I hit her on the head, it was good," he begins his monologue. In his crazed mind there is beauty in the decomposing corpse of the little girl he has murdered and raped: "sometimes it was *beautiful*—; I don't know how / to say it, but for a minute, *everything* was possible." He also knows guilt: "and I knew I couldn't have done that,— / somebody *else* had to have done that,—." Guilt pervades Nijinsky's disintegrating mind—over his affair with Diaghilev ("in my soul, / I did *not* love him") and his betrayal of his wife. His awareness of the threat of insanity and doubts about the existence of God are mingled with a cosmic guilt for World War I:

. . . I am now reading *Ecce Homo.* Nietzsche
is *angry* with me—;

he hates "the Crucified One."

But he did not live through War—;
when the whole world painted its face

with blood.

Someone must expiate the blood.

Some reviewers of *In the Western Night*, Bidart's collected poems 1965 to 1990, cited his "typographic conceits," his "maddeningly disembodied narratives," the disturbing nature of much of his subject matter ("not for the faint-hearted," one wrote), but, at the same time, serious respect has been accorded Bidart's "acute intelligence, moral force and devoted skill at language," as Harold Bloom characterized Bidart's strengths in a review of *The Book of the Body* in the *New Republic.* Sven Birkerts in the *The Electric Life* noted Bidart's power to assail complacency: " . . . Frank Bidart's sharp, unlyrical, excruciatingly forthright work (I almost hesitate to call it poetry) assays our defended places. And though I do not 'like' it, though it does not give me pleasure, I *am* discomforted, challenged, and moved by it. I respect it as I respect anything that can rouse the inner man from his sleep of habit."

PRINCIPAL WORKS: Golden State, 1973; The Book of the Body, 1977; The Sacrifice, 1983; In the Western Night: Collected Poems 1965–1990, 1990.

ABOUT: Birkerts, S. The Electric Life: Essays on Modern Poetry, 1989; Contemporary Literary Criticism 33, 1985; Contemporary Poets, 5th ed., 1991; Hamilton, I.

Robert Lowell, 1982; Howard, R. *in* Bidart's Golden State; Miller, B. C. Elizabeth Bishop: Life and the Memory of It, 1993; Vendler, H. Part of Nature, Part of Us, 1980. *Periodicals*—Agni Review 36, 1992; Chicago Review Winter 1983; Field: Contemporary Poetry and Poetics Spring 1984; Nation June 18, 1977; New England Review and Bread Loaf Quarterly Winter 1981; New Republic November 26, 1977; October 10, 1983; May 14, 1990; Ploughshares 9, 1983 (rptd. *in* Bidart's In the Western Night, 1990); Shenandoah Winter 1974.

BINCHY, MAEVE (May 28, 1940–   ), Irish journalist, novelist, and short story writer, was born in Dun Laoghaire, near Dublin. Her father, William Binchy, was a lawyer, and her mother, Maureen Blackmore Binchy, was a nurse. They were very happily married, and Maeve Binchy, with her brother and two sisters, spent an idyllic childhood in the harbor town of Dun Laoghaire, where she attended St. Anne's Nursery School. At the age of eight she began school at the Holy Child Convent in Killiney, an institution she remembers with easy affection. She was somewhat lazy, bad at games and at math, but she was naturally intelligent, and despite her dismay at being overweight, she was very popular.

Throughout her youth Binchy had two ambitions, to become a judge and to become a saint. She decided instead on a teaching career, and took her degree at University College, Dublin. Graduating in 1960, she taught history at Dublin girls' schools for eight years, traveling extensively during the long summer holidays. Her father was so impressed by one letter that she sent him from kibbutz in Israel in 1963 that he edited it and sent it to a local newspaper. It was published, and so Binchy's journalistic career began. She wrote several travel articles, and became a successful free-lance columnist. In 1968 she resigned from her teaching post to join the *Irish Times* as an editor. When Binchy was twenty-eight years old she became London correspondent for the *Irish Times*, but maintained a connection to Ireland by buying houses in both London and County Dublin. In January 1977 she married the English writer and broadcaster Gordon Thomas Snell.

Binchy's "Saturday Column" formed the basis of *My First Book*, which was published in 1976, and *Maeve's Diary*, which appeared three years later. Both were amusing, lighthearted portrayals of the Irish and the English, and they sold well. Also in 1976 she wrote a one-act play, *End of Term*, which was produced at the Abbey Theatre in Dublin. Another play, *The Half Promised Land*, was set in a kibbutz and drew on her experience in Israel. It was staged in Dublin in 1979

MAEVE BINCHY

and in a small theater in Philadelphia in 1980. Binchy had considerable success also with two television screenplays, *Deeply Regretted By* (1979), which won awards in Ireland and in Prague, and *Ireland of the Welcomes* (1980).

Binchy's career in journalism was good training for short story writing, and although her short story collections have not sold as well as her novels, they have won her many admirers. As John Kenny crane observed in the *New York Times Book Review* in 1991, her talent is not for strong plotting but for "well-drawn characters and their dynamic interaction with one another." It is the simple yet—for these characters—complex circumstances of their lives, the fundamental weakness and moral decencies of human beings, that appeal to Binchy's readers. Each of the stories in her first collection, *The Central Line: Stories of Big City Life*, takes its title from a London tube station. A variety of characters, mostly female, are shown in differing states of dissatisfaction with their lives, with unresolved romantic and marital problems. One protagonist is drawn into the corruption of London's streets; another is an Irishwoman visiting England for an abortion. *Victoria Line*, a similar collection, focuses on the marriages of women from every social background, and the tedium or despair that characterizes their existence. It was published with *The Central Line* as *London Transports* in 1983, and received an enthusiastic response. Despite the bleakness of Binchy's themes, reviewers praised her fluency, her lively, assured style. Writing for the *Times Literary Supplement*, Helen Harris noted that the author's portrayal of the "small skirmishes of day-to-day urban survival is enjoyable, her wry observation of the different layers of London life is uncomfortably acute."

On the basis of the success of her first two short story collections, Binchy's publishers commissioned a novel, giving her a year to complete what appeared as *Light a Penny Candle*, her first novel, became a best seller. The story of a twenty-year friendship between an Irish girl and her English contemporary, it begins when Elizabeth White, the only child of an unhappily married couple living in London, is sent to stay with the Irish O'Connor family for the duration of the Second World War. Elizabeth grows up with Aisling O'Connor in a small rural town, and their friendship endures even after Elizabeth returns to England and her indifferent parents. She has an affair with an old boyfriend of Aisling's and both women have disastrous marriages. Although some reviewers found *Light a Penny Candle* contrived, it was generally commended for its narrative color, artistry, and honesty. Priscilla Johnson, in *School Library Journal* described it as "beautifully written . . . this dynamic novel has everything: romance . . . humor, outstanding characterization, sparkling dialogue and suspense."

Light a Penny Candle was followed by two further short story collections, *Dublin 4* and *The Lilac Bus*, set in Binchy's native Dublin. Many of the stories explore infidelity and unmarried pregnancy. The stories in *Dublin 4* are longer and more complex than those in the earlier volumes. "Flat in Ringsend," in which a painfully self-conscious eighteen-year-old country girl tries to come to terms with her new city surroundings, was admired for its irony. Patricia Ross, in *Library Journal*, found the collection "absorbing, entertaining reading with characters to care about."

The Lilac Bus consists of eight interconnected stories, each a portrait of one of the Dublin workers who travel home to rural Rathdoon every weekend in Tom Fitzgerald's minibus. The characters give their names to the stories in which they appear, and the collection coalesces into a coherent whole that has a greater depth and scope than one finds in the individual stories. In "Nancy," for example, a character named Dee asks Nancy Morris apparently irrelevant questions about her boss Mr. Barry; in "Dee," it emerges that Dee is having an affair with Mr. Barry.

Binchy's concern in *The Lilac Bus* is to portray the plights of ordinary people living ordinary lives against the backdrop of contemporary Ireland—a land struggling with political, economic, and religious oppression. Recurring issues are alcoholism, homosexuality, infidelity, and abortion. Tom, the minibus driver, has a bulimic sister; Judy lost her family in the sixties because of her drug dealing; Kev is a security guard, involved with a gang stealing materials from the site he is employed to protect. The dynamism of the stories lies in the interaction between the commuters. As in *Dublin 4*, plot is minimal, but critics found a surer touch and a sounder approach in *The Lilac Bus*, which Ross called "a showcase for her marvelous story telling ability."

Binchy's second novel, *Echoes*, is set like the first in rural Ireland. Clare O'Brien lives in the coastal resort of Castlebay, modeled on several towns Binchy had visited as a child—"where attitudes could be cruel, and tolerance was low." Clare, daughter of a humble shopkeeper, longs to transcend her own social status and the pettiness of small town life. Supported by a sympathetic teacher, she is accepted by a Dublin university, where she meets and marries the son of a prosperous doctor, but her marriage fails and she returns, defeated, to life in Castlebay. The teacher, in contrast, saintly stayed in the town to care for her crippled mother, is rewarded when she falls in love with the local reformed alcoholic. The rural and the urban are again contrasted in this book, and in spite of the narrowness of provincial life, it proves better than the big city where one can "die of loneliness." Reviewers were impressed with Binchy's descriptive power, and her eye for local detail.

In *Firefly Summer*, a novel inspired by Binchy's work on tourism for the *Irish Times*, an energetic and ambitious Irish-American millionaire, Patrick O'Neill, descends on a sleepy Irish town with plans to turn an old country estate into a luxury hotel complex. A series of accidents, and the prejudice and conservatism of the town's inhabitants, prevent him from fulfilling his ambition, and individual progress is again frustrated. Binchy's ability to evoke the people, the atmosphere, and the environment she knows so well was much admired; in the opinion of Michele Slung, in the *New York Times Book Review*, *Firefly Summer* was "the best Binchy yet."

Silver Wedding is an examination of the interactions and personal problems of the members of a single family. Each chapter focuses on one individual. In the first, Anna Doyle resents her parents for the social ambition that forces them, and her, to live a lie. Subsequent chapters explore the memories and feelings of other family members, creating a comprehensive view. In the final chapter all of the characters come together to celebrate the twenty-fifth wedding anniversary of the parents.

Circle of Friends, a stronger book than its predecessors, is the story of three young girls growing up in small-town Ireland. Benny Hogan is the only child of very normal parents, well adjusted but terribly conscious, as Binchy herself was, of her weight. Her best friend in Knockglen is Eve Malone, a slight, unconventional, and illegitimate child who is brought up by devoted nuns in the local convent. At University College, Dublin, during the 1950s, they meet Nan Mahon, the cold, beautiful, and socially ambitious daughter of a poor family. Benny is eventually betrayed by the man she loves and by Nan, whose aspirations, like those of the central character in *Echoes*, come to nothing. Benny and Eve find contentment in their friendship and with the men who love them—"all the friends sitting in a circle, looking as if they were going to sing forever." "A terrific tale, told by a master storyteller," Susan Isaacs wrote in the *New York Times Book Review*, "a wonderfully absorbing story about people worth caring about."

The tree in the title *The Copper Beech*, which like *Silver Wedding* consists of several interwoven narratives, is a unifying symbol. Standing near the village school, it bears the names of generations of children and their sweethearts. Some of the individual stories deal with sordid issues: murder, alcoholism, infidelity, illegitimacy, and guilty secrets. In one, a young woman falls in love with a priest and encourages him to fulfill his ambition to become a missionary in South America, and to leave the priesthood. He follows her advice, and returns to thank her for the love he has known with a younger woman. Binchy was again praised for her accuracy in depicting the emotional and everyday lives of her protagonists, and for her shrewd social analysis. As Anne Tolstoi Wallach wrote in the *New York Times Book Review*, *The Copper Beech* "tells the sort of tale that's almost impossible to abandon."

Maeve Binchy continued to contribute to the *Irish Times* and divided her time between London and Dalkey, County Dublin.

PRINCIPAL WORKS: *Nonfiction*—My First Book, 1976; Maeve's Diary, 1979. *Short stories*—The Central Line: Stories of Big City Life, 1978; Victoria Line, 1980; Dublin 4, 1982; London Transports, 1983; The Lilac Bus, 1984. *Novels*—Light a Penny Candle, 1982; Echoes, 1985; Firefly Summer, 1987; Silver Wedding, 1988; Circle of Friends, 1990; The Copper Beech, 1992; The Glass Lake, 1994. *Plays*—End of Term, 1976; The Half Promised Land, 1979; Deeply Regretted By, 1979; Ireland of the Welcomes, 1980.

ABOUT: Blain, V. ed., The Feminist Companion to Literature in English, 1990; Brady, A. M. and Cleeve, B. eds. Biographical Dictionary of Irish Writers, 1985; Buck, C. (ed.) Bloomsbury Guide to women's Literature, 1992; Contemporary Authors 134, 1992; Quinn, J. (ed.) A Portrait of the Artist as a Young Girl, 1986; Who's Who 1994. *Periodicals*—British Book News May 1986; Harper's April 1983; Library Journal December 1990; October 15, 1991; New York Times Book Review January 12, 1986; September 18, 1988; September 10, 1989; December 30, 1990; December 8, 1991; December 20, 1992; People Weekly March 11, 1991; Publishers Weekly October 26, 1992; School Library Journal August 1983; Today Autumn 1992; Times Literary Supplement November 28, 1980; April 1, 1983; March 30, 1984; Village Voice May 17, 1983; Washington Post Book World May 11, 1983; January 17, 1986.

BISSOONDATH, NEIL (DEVINDRA) (April 19, 1955–), Canadian novelist and short story writer, was born in Sangre Grande, Trinidad, to Crisen, a businessman, and Sati (Naipaul) Bissoondath, descendants of East Indians who had emigrated to the West Indies as indentured laborers on the sugar plantations. His maternal uncles are distinguished writers—V. S. Naipaul and his younger brother Shiva Naipaul, who died in 1985—both of whom left the island early in life. After completing his secondary education at St. Mary's College, Neil Bissoondath went to Toronto in 1973 to attend York University. He was acting on the advice of his uncle V. S. Naipaul, who had told him that England offered no future, and that the United States "was simply too big . . . So he suggested Canada as a good compromise."

Bissoondath became a Canadian citizen and has lived there ever since. He received a B.A. from York University with a major in French, in 1977 and worked for the next eight years teaching French and English as a second language at the Inlingua School of Languages and at the Language Workshop in Toronto. Evenings and holidays he wrote short stories, some of which were published in Canadian journals. In 1983 editors at Macmillan of Canada were so impressed with a collection of his stories that they recommended him for a writing fellowship at the Banff School of Fine Arts. Now working full time as a writer, Bissoondath completed his first collection of short stories, *Digging Up the Mountains*, which was published to favorable reviews and was short-listed for the City of Toronto Book Award. With a grant from the Canada Council for $12,000 he was able to complete his first novel, published as *A Casual Brutality* in 1988. Another collection of short stories, *On the Eve of Uncertain Tomorrows*, was published in 1990.

Bissoondath is now securely established as one of the most promising of younger Canadian writers, although he writes as a "transplanted" voice for the displaced and the dispossessed. His work, however, transcends the questions of ethnicity and racism. Although his principal subjects are the twice transplanted East Indians who moved from Asia to the Caribbean and then to Europe or North America, his canvas is large enough to include the displaced of the entire world. "The whole world, everybody's a refugee," a character in one of his short stories, "Veins Visible," reflects; "everybody's running from one thing or another." A young Canadian backpacking in Europe reflects (in "Continental Drift") on the rootlessness of modern humanity:

> The Arabs in England, the Turks in Germany, the Gypsies in Spain, the swarming lost of the bars, backrooms, and alleys of Amsterdam . . . There flows from their eyes the melancholy fear of those adrift, travel imposed not by desire, but by habit and circumstance, in what I have come to think of not as wanderlust but as wanderlost.

Bissoondath's "wanderlost" characters include not only West Indians with forebears from India, but an Afro-Caribbean working as a dishwasher in a Toronto strip joint ("The Power of Reason"), a young Japanese woman trying to live independently in Canada ("The Cage"), a white Canadian woman teaching school on a Caribbean island and discovering that "she had lost her sense of the picturesque . . . she had learnt quickly that the picturesque existed not by itself but in a quiet self-delusion" ("An Arrangement of Shadows"), Vietnamese and South American refugees awaiting in limbo their immigration hearings in Canada ("On the Eve of Uncertain Tomorrows"), an elderly Jewish survivor of the Holocaust choosing suicide rather than life in a nursing home ("Goodnight, Mr. Slade"). Even a white Canadian in his native Canada can be a displaced person when, like the lonely salesman in "Smoke", he realizes how empty and banal his narrowly conventional life is.

Because alienation, a condition common to modern life, rather than racial or ethnic identity, is the dominating theme of Bissoondath's fiction, he has met with some of the same kind of criticism that has been directed against V. S. Naipaul. As Victor J. Ramraj observes in an essay in *Writers of the Indian Diaspora*: "It would appear that Bissoondath—flying in the teeth of the postcolonial and postmodern theorists who demand of postcolonial writers an emphasis on separate identities and difference—consciously constructs his fiction without specific details of nationality and ethnicity to underscore the consciousness and universality of the emotional spiritual description of migrants and refugees."

The realization in postcolonial societies that independence has not only failed to bring desired goals of democracy and economic prosperity, but in fact has often led to chaos and bloodshed, pervades Bissoondath's work. "A Lot of Ways to Die," a shopkeeper who has returned from Canada to his native Caribbean island to open a business realizes that his workers are shiftless, the new independent government corrupt, and business failure is imminent: "I had some kind of crazy idea about starting a business, creating jobs, helping my people." In his ruin we see the despair of a whole society. Ramraj notes that while Bissoondath's books have had generally favorable reviews, some reviewers have commented upon his apparent coldness and detachment: "Bissoondath's relationship with V. S. Naipaul inevitably raised . . . the question of the anxiety of influence. His pessimistic outlook, his sense of placelessness, and his diagrammatic tone were perceived as Naipaulesque."

In his novel *A Casual Brutality* there is undeniably an element of portentousness—what John Lanchester, in the *London Review of Books*, described as "world-weary sententiousness" and Hanif Kureishi, in the *New Statesman & Society*, as "stern and over-controlled." To some extent the tone of the novel is inevitable because the narrator, Raj Raursingh, a native of an imaginary but representative Caribbean island that has newly won its independence, has experienced a ghastly tragedy. His Canadian wife and his young son are murdered by the lawless forces who have taken over the island. As the novel opens, widowed and childless, he is about to return to Canada:

> There are times when the word *hope* is but a synonym for *illusion*; it is the most virile of perils. He who cannot discern the difference—he whose perception of reality has slipped from him, whose appreciation of honesty has withered within him—will face, at the end, a fine levied, with no appeal, with only regret coating the memory like ash.

In a series of flashbacks—many of them drawn from Bissoondath's own experience—Raj recalls his childhood, his devout Hindu grandparents, his decision to study in Canada where he takes a medical degree and makes a good life for himself. With the recently won independence of his native island—ironically "on the day that Marilyn Monroe died and Nelson Mandela was arrested"—he returns, believing that he can make a real contribution to this new democratic state. It soon becomes apparent, however, that the island is totally unprepared for self-government, its only model the corrupt and exploitive colonial power that has now abandoned it. But Bissoondath does not assign the blame lightly. As the narrator's uncle explains, the failure is that of their own intellectuals, who have been "so busy looking backwards, so busy shouting the simple politics of blame . . . that they forgot to help prepare us for our chance." Given their chance for freedom, the islanders

> "blew it . . . we gave it away in bribes, we squandered it on useless projects. . . . Our leaders taught us how to blame, but not how to help ourselves. They gave us the psychology of the victim. So that when the money came we practiced the politics of greed. We acted like those who had ruled us before. As they exploited us, so we exploited each other.

Although reviewers expressed some reservations about the book, *A Casual Brutality* was almost universally recognized as a remarkable first novel: "a work of a sure hand and a disciplined mind," Marc Côté wrote in the *Canadian Forum*, praising Bissoondath as "a rare author who is able to write unforgettably well about a political situation without the sacrifice of his art to his beliefs." Even those who complained of its colorless characterization and "lack of focus" admired his "wonderful sensibility for capturing the complexity and paradoxes of island life" (Thomas Keneally in the *New York Times Book Review*).

On the Eve of Uncertain Tomorrows, another short story collection, was equally well received. Firdus Kanga, in the *Times Literary Supplement*, concluded that "Neil Bissoondath has kept the amazing promise he made with [his] remarkable novel." In the *New York Times Book Review*, Jim Shepard noted that "the best stories . . . provide us with those moments— glimpses into the heartbreaking and resilient worlds of these exiles—that are generous enough, and tender enough, to form the heart of what we carry away from the collection."

Bissoondath lives in Canada with Anne Marcoux, a lawyer, to whom he dedicated *A Casual Brutality*.

PRINCIPAL WORKS: *Short stories*—Digging Up the Mountains, 1986; On the Eve of Uncertain Tomorrows, 1990. *Novels*—A Casual Brutality, 1988; The Innocence of Age, 1992.

ABOUT: Canadian Who's Who 1993; Contemporary Authors 136, 1992; Howells, C. A. and L. Hunter (eds.) Narrative Strategies in Canadian Literature, 1991; Nelson, E. (ed.) Writers of the Indian Diaspora, 1993; Tucker, M. (ed.) Literary Exile in the Twentieth Century, 1991; Who's Who in Canadian Literature 1992–1993. *Periodicals*—Canadian Forum February / March 1989; London Review of Books January 5, 1989; Macleans October 3, 1988; New Statesman and Society September 16, 1988; New York Times Book Review August 16, 1987; February 26, 1989; May 26, 1991; Publishers Weekly January 6, 1989; Times Literary Supplement November 23, 1990; World Literature Today Spring 1991.

BLACK, DAVID (MacLEOD) (November 8, 1941–), Scottish poet who also publishes under the name D. M. Black, writes: "I was born in South Africa. My parents had met in Malawi (then Nyasaland) in 1936: my father a research chemist for the British Colonial Service, my mother a nurse. In 1941 my father left to join the Army in Europe, my mother, with one child age twelve months and four months pregnant with me, decided it was unsafe to remain in Malawi and moved to South Africa, where she spent the war living in a succession of hotels.

"My father returned in 1945; we spent a year in Malawi, then moved to Tanzania (then Tanganyika) and lived for four years on a small scientific research station at Amani in the Usumbara Mountains. My first coherent memories date from this time and are above all of the forest and its wild life. Later I went upcountry to boarding school in Lushoto, and for the first time, age seven, had the exciting experience of mixing with other children.

"I think the origin of my impulse to write lies in this period in Tanzania, when I coped with a huge amount of solitude by telling myself long, saga-like stories. My father, being a natural scientist, introduced me to plants, birds, rocks, etc; my first ambition was to be a geologist.

"When I was eight we moved to Scotland (my father's country), and thereafter the family was geographically stable. I grew up thinking of myself as Scottish. But in retrospect I see the strongest roots of my personality in Tanzania, with a father whom I admired, and a way of life (however weird the British Empire seems now) which I understood and felt at home in.

"One brother, private all-male schools, boarding from age thirteen: my upbringing systematically excluded girls, and I arrived in adolescence shy, frustrated, and extremely confused. Confusion became depression, I left school a year early and spent four years (1959-1963) adrift: in France, Edinburgh, London. In these years I did an immense amount of reading, including such unfashionable people as Bergson, Buber, Jung: I probably owe my sanity to the sense of purpose that these writers conveyed, as I earned my living at an essentially purposeless sequence of jobs as teacher, salesman, bank-clerk, security guard, etc. Meanwhile I was publishing my first poems, and when I finally decided to go to Edinburgh University at age twenty-one I suddenly had access to my first individual 'voice'—a teller of

DAVID BLACK

rapid, sardonic, rather bizarre short narrative poems, full of puns and sexual imagery. George MacBeth, who produced poetry programmes for the BBC, liked my work and quite suddenly I had a lot of outlets. I edited a small magazine, met the leading Scottish poets (of whom one in particular, Robert Garioch, became for me a model of poet as *craftsman*), and was greatly influenced by many people. Ian Hamilton Finlay, then doing typographical poems, was the first person who spoke to me of the importance of 'form'; Rick Ulman, a young American painter of enormous vitality, encouraged me to believe that creativity was precious and exciting.

"I published my first book, *With Decorum*, in 1967, shared a Penguin anthology, *Penguin Modern Poets 11*, with Peter Redgrove and D. M. Thomas in 1968, published my second book, *The Educators*, in 1969. I completed a philosophy degree in 1966 and took a job lecturing at Chelsea art college, London. It was the exciting time of the late sixties: sexual freedom, which for me as for many meant considerable confusion, drugs, which never greatly interested me, and 'new' forms of spirituality, which interested me a great deal.

"The only sense I can make of the next move is that it represented my need, because of my early history, to establish contact with something distant from the Europe of my conscious life. I went, not to Africa, but to Japan, and spent six months teaching in that fascinating and deeply foreign culture. I was greatly impressed by Buddhism; my horizons opened beyond the world of European Modernism, existentialism, etc., and

also beyond the European philosophy of my first degree. I returned to Britain, did a degree in Eastern Religions at Lancaster University, then went to live in a spiritual community in the North of Scotland.

"My father died at this time (1971). I was twenty-nine. I had become estranged from him in my teens, and had never really redeemed that estrangement. I think his death triggered a recognition that I needed to find a career I could view as solid and feel respect for, and (to cut the story short) I returned to London, did a psychotherapy training and then a full (Freudian) psychoanalytic training. I published two more collections of poems, *The Happy Crow* and *Gravitations*, and *Collected Poems 1964-87*. The long narrative poems in the last two of these books represent my most significant poetic achievement.

"There is a move throughout my writing history towards more formality and balance. I have a very great admiration for such writers as W. H. Auden and Richard Wilbur, and have made some attempt to translate Goethe. Professional life now takes up almost all my time, but if there is more poetry to come, it will, I think, continue in that direction."

————

David Black has been hailed as one of the most independent and original of contemporary Scottish poets. His mastery of his chosen poetic form plus his subject matter—sometimes contemporary but more often mythic and folkloric—and his relish for the grotesque have won him an enthusiastic readership among those who recognize, as Robin Hamilton writes, that "beyond all the masks and devices, Black is busy with the more sustained task of constructing an attitude toward reality—it's stranger than you think—by disturbing and rearranging our preconceptions." Relative neglect was Black's fate in the late 1970s and 1980s. Edwin Morgan tried to account for this neglect in his 1991 *Times Literary Supplement* review of Black's *Collected Poems*, noting that he published no poetry during the 1980s, devoting himself instead to study and to his practice of psychotherapy. A suggestion that poems written primarily in long narrative verse with the rarely used, classically formal hendecasyllabic line separate him from the mainstream of modern poetry is perhaps apt.

In a candid prefatory note to his *Collected Poems*, Black admits that writing poetry is not the center of his life but rather "an attempt to understand some area of feeling which has arisen and will be resolved elsewhere." He appears

to be seeking—and poetry is only one medium
for his quest—what he has called the "web of
connectedness," a link between the conscious
mind and the unconscious. Writing in memory
of his father, Ian A. Black, he recalls a walk they
took in the botanical gardens at Kew:

> and you walk always beside me, you with your knowl-
> edge of   names
> and your clairvoyant gaze, in what for me is sheer
> panorama seeing the net or web of connectedness.
>
>   ("Kew Gardens")

Through dreams, myth, and the surrealistic
worlds of fairy tales and Grand Guignol, Black
explores the buried inner life. James Greene
writes in his preface to the *Collected Poems* that
Black's concern is with "wholeness," bringing together "the human wisdom that has become
fragmented and abstracted into psychology, religion, politics and philosophy." Lofty as all this
sounds, the poetry is surprisingly accessible and
often wryly funny. In one of his earliest poems,
"The Rocklestrakes" (originally published as a
pamphlet in 1960), Black creates a Lewis Car-
roll-like monster, a metaphor for human needs
sometimes lodged, unacknowledged, in the dark
strata of the mind:

> A rocklestrake is neighing
>   Beside the autumn pond;
> A rocklestrake is baying
>   Across the vast immonde;
> The rocklestrakes are everywhere,
>   Born of gulping thirst,
> And though you trample on despair
>   The fate can never be reversed,
> Because it is yourself who make
>   The laughing, screaming rocklestrake.

Black's metrical narrative verse places him in
an English tradition from the "Gawain" poet and
Chaucer through the poetry of William Morris,
Tennyson and Browning. Whether narrating an
ancient Sumerian legend ("Urru and Uppu"), a
medieval tale of love and enchantment
("Melusine"), a Grimm fairy tale ("The Hands of
Felicity"), or contemporary stories of adultery
and incest ("Anna's Affairs" and "Peter Macrae
Attempts the Active Life"), he favors the eleven-
syllable (hendecasyllabic) line that is
"uninhibitedly accentual." Its dynamic effect
sweeps the reader up into the story, moving it
along at a dizzying pace. The narrator of "The
Hands of Felicity" is under a compulsion, but
not a very serious one:

> When the narrative demon sits astride my
> cerebrum and compels with yells and jeers these a-
> ppetitive cattle along some grass-less track I

find no pleasure in feeling bit and spurs! . . .

It is in fact pleasure in his tale he seeks, both for
himself and for the reader:

> unless, out of the wreck of sweat and flowers, I
> glimpse that body, the intangible and lovely
> woman's body again for whom I wayfare.

In *Lines Review*, Anne Stevenson, terms the
narrator's tone "self-contradictory—mocking
but sincere, over-literary but sympathetic," leading to a "predictably paradoxical" end in which
the reader, facing the dilemma of whether suffering or virtue leads to happiness, is forced to
the conclusion that neither does. She notes that
"the apparently (but not really) arbitrary line divisions . . . often leave the raw edge of broken
words hanging over the abyss of the right hand
margin," which may give the reader pause, but
she concludes that Black's technique is successful
and "themes of doubt and perplexity are handled with marvellous skill."

The familiar grisly folklore tale in "The
Hands of Felicity"—bargains with the devil, sadistic mutilation (but later miraculous restoration), marriage to a king, an evil mother-in-law
(the archetypal stepmother)—slips casually into
the modern world of politics and high-tech warfare—and feminism. The king's wicked mother
urges him to war with warnings against Felicity's advice:

> It is not for a King to be denied his will and
> to be governed by feminine complexity.
> All the glory of Europe's history could
> faint and sink in a dreary sunset while these
> pallid large-bottomed politicians and their
> chattering women go on mouthing opinion. . . .

The long line can also produce stately and sonorous effects. In "Melusine," the young narrator begins a fantastic adventure as he rides into
the woods on a white pony that his father has just
given him:

> In the glades of the greenwood bright with dew we
> paced and ambled. The wood was foetal, dawn and
> spring and birdsong, and all contained within that
> gravid weather.

Even the contemporary scene has its share of
hermits and enchanted dwarfs in Black's poetry.
In "Anna's Affairs," the very mortal Anna and
her crude lover ("he prefers mass to quality") are
spied on in their lovemaking by the narrator, a
voyeuristic dwarf: "I am not D. H. Lawrence.
Let me not / weary the daylights out of you with

/ two further repetitions." Like other narrators in Black's poetry, he remains at a chilly distance from the reader, but he is unabashedly self-revealing.

In a shorter poem, "From the Privy Council," the speaker is the state executioner:

> Delicacy was never enormously
> My style. All my favourite girls
> Walked at five miles an hour or ate haggis,
> Or swam like punts.

The executioner is a "quiet, conforming" man who has accepted the job simply because it was offered, but he becomes an efficient bureaucrat: "I hectored my hatchetmen into a spruce turn-out, / Insisted on a keen edge to their axes." The speaker in the longer "Notes for Joachim" is even more candid. A monk sworn to celibacy, he pours out to his confessor Joachim his anguish, his inability to subdue his sexual appetites or to erase from his memory his past active sex life. "True lust can / be a sort of reverence," he tries to persuade himself. Recalling the stone-carved saints in French cathedrals—"Tall men, with beards, and eyes enlarged with weeping / no doubt for the sins of the world and other virtuous causes. . . . " he sees the hypocrisy underlying the saints' tears. Each stands on an emblematic stone carving of an animal, "his private monster":

> poor crouching deformed beast, understandably angry!
> for human love stands on a monstrous pedestal,
> and gushing love abroad, gives little love
> to the beast who supports it.

As most of his critics have pointed out, Black's training in Jungian psychology has given him a heightened sense of the dark inner life of the mind, but it has also moved him, as he has said, "more and more into engagement with the real world." His poetry has a dual character, divided between those inner and outer voices. It finds its essence in lines from his short poem "For and Against the Environment," in which he celebrates the "wonderful world" of his North London garden: "great and more fragile is man than ant or earth or anemone / and in or out of the glass-house of nature, let him above all not be seduced."

Black's long narrative poems, Edwin Morgan writes, are his "special contribution to verse," but, as Andrew Greig writes in *Akros*, "These are not gratuitous stories or consciously symbolic creations; they endure because we feel a 'rightness' in them, and that 'rightness' lies in a half-recognized correspondence with fundamental movements of the human psyche."

PRINCIPAL WORKS: Theory of Diet, 1966; With Decorum, 1967; Penguin Modern Poets 11, 1968; The Educators: Poems 1969; The Old Hag, 1972; The Happy Crow, 1974; Gravitations, 1979; Collected Poems 1964-87, 1991.

ABOUT: Contemporary Authors 25–28, 1977; Contemporary Poets, 5th ed., 1991; Dictionary of Literary Biography 40, 1985; Fulton, Contemporary Scottish Poetry: Individuals and Contexts, 1974; Greene, J. *Preface to* Black's Collected Poems, 1991; Hamilton, R. Science and Psychodrama: The Poetry of Edwin Morgan and David Black, 1982. *Periodicals*—Akros December 1974; December 1978; April 1981; Chapman 1975; Autumn 1979; Lines Review December 1974; June 1979; June 1991; Literary Review October 5, 1979; Scotsman May 25, 1991; Scottish Book Collector August 1991; Scottish International February 1971; Swansea Review Spring 1993; Times Literary Supplement May 24, 1991.

---

*BLANDIANA, ANA (OTILIA-VALERIA COMAN) (March 25, 1942–), Romanian poet and prose writer, is fundamentally a nonpolitical writer who has been thrust into public life. She played a prominent role before, during, and after the December 1989 revolution that overthrew the Ceauşescu dictatorship, under which her work had been banned a number of times. In January 1990 she was briefly a member of the council of the provisional National Salvation Front government, from which she resigned in protest after only three weeks. From 1991 to 1993 she served as president of the Civil Alliance, a coalition of nonpartisan opposition interests which she helped found in November 1990, and she became president of the Romanian PEN Center, which she was instrumental in organizing after the revolution. The author of seventeen books of poetry (including three volumes of selected verse and three for children), six books of essays, and three books of prose fiction as well as a collection of tales, Blandiana has won two Writers Union prizes, the Romanian Academy prize, a fellowship to the International Writing Program in Iowa, the Herder Prize in Austria, and a grant from the German Academy of the Arts in Berlin.

Ana Blandiana was born Otilia-Valeria Coman in Timissoara, the cosmopolitan Western Romanian city that was once part of the Austro-Hungarian Empire and where, as it happened, the December 1989 revolt against the Ceauşescu dictatorship began. Her grandparents were Transylvanian peasants. She was the first daughter of Otilia and Gheorghe Coman; her father worked as a high school teacher first in Timissoara and later farther north near the border with Hungry in the city of Oradea, where (after

°blahn dih AH nuh

ANA BLANDIANA

he was forced to quit teaching) he served as an orthodox priest until he was arrested in 1959 by the Communist government and condemned to five years of forced labor because of his profession; he died in prison five years later at age forty-nine. The poet attended schools in Oradea and, from 1963 to 1967, the University of Cluj-Napoca. She then moved to Bucharest, where she worked for the next decade as an editor of the literary magazines *Viatsa studentlească (Student life) and Amfiteatro* (Amphitheatre) and also as librarian in the Institute of Fine Arts. In 1960 she married the journalist Romulus Russan.

Blandiana began to publish poetry at the age of seventeen in 1959, the year he father was imprisoned. From the beginning her work was signed with her chosen pen name Ana Blandiana, but immediately her work was banned as the product of the daughter of an enemy of the people. Her initial volume, *Persoane intiia plura* (First person plural), did not come out until 1964, during a brief period of liberalization between the postwar Stalinism (and propagandistic proletarian realism) of the Soviet occupation years and the Ceauşescu government's steadily intensifying control of the next two decades. Other important poetry titles included *Atreia taină* (The third mystery, 1969), *Octombrie, Noiembrie, Decembrie* (October, November, December, 1972), *Somnul din somn* (The sleep within sleep, 1977), *Ochiul de greier* (The cricket's eye, 1981), *Ora de nisip* (The hour of sand, 1983—from which the title of her collection in English was borrowed), *Stea de pradă* (Star of prey, 1985), and *Arhitectura valurilor* (The ar-

chitecture of waves, 1990), a collection completed in 1987 but unpublished at the time.

Beginning in 1968 Blandiana wrote weekly for the cultural paper *Contemporanul* (The contemporary), and from 1974 to 1991 for another major periodical, *România literară* (Literary Romania), with a few gaps during times the Ceauşescu government forbade the publication of her work. By the late 1980s, she had to write two, three, four, or more columns a week for just one to pass the censors.

She was banned for three months in 1985. European protests ended her relatively interdiction quickly, probably because President Ceauşescu had great concern at that juncture for Romania's image abroad. She was banned because of four outspoken poems in *Amphitheatre* the journal she once worked for. They included overt dissident comments such as that in "I Believe," in which she spoke of Romanians as "compliant" and concluded, characteristically, in a pointed question,

I trust we are a vegetal people
Has anyone ever seen
A rebellious tree?

Her most notable period of interdiction lasted for over a year from August 1988 until the revolution, after which she wrote her column again for about a year, giving it up in early 1991. Her silencing was the result of a witty fable in her third book of children's poems, *Intîmplări de pe strada mea* (Events in my street, 1988). The poem, about a vainglorious tomcat named Arpagic (the name is mock-heroic and belittling; it means "scallion"), was to a Romanian reader an unmistakably sly humorous reference to President Ceauşescu, the center of the nation's cult of personality. It was pointedly included in the book, according to Blandiana, more for the parent reading the story aloud, who would relish the satire, than for the child who would understand the animal fable on a different level. The cat fable was not out of character for Blandiana, many of whose much-read columns contained the kind of indirect, hidden allusions to the conditions of life and the political situation that Romanians called "lizards." During this, her third episode of proscription, the poet found a car stationed in front of her house day and night, watching and listening electronically, to her every conversation; her mail and phone service were cut off, and she received a number of death threats. But on December 22, 1989, the day the Ceauşescus fled Bucharest, she had the satisfaction of hearing demonstrators chant, "The cat is dead!"

The poet Mircea Ivănescu, has described Blandiana as "a Romantic so wounded by what she senses as disintegration and impurity in her contact with the actual . . . that she chooses to live in her nostalgia for innocence, for memory, as the more authentic experience." Her poetry has given new life to what might otherwise have seemed derivative or obsolete traditions. The Romanian critic Alexandru Stefanescu has written that "the verse of Ana Blandiana . . . is *beautiful*—in the old, pre-Baudelairean sense of the word—with a daring that is astonishing." Blandiana's poetry is in the tradition of the visionary late 19th-century Romanian romantic Mihaip Eminescu and the great metaphysical and philosophical Transylvanian poet Lucian Blaga, as well as the important late modernist, Tudor Arghezi. With a tone that is dignified, personal, but never intimately confessional, her poems celebrate the imagination and conceive of a kind of inward salvation, employing vivid imagery, often drawn from the natural world but transformed into her own symbolic vocabulary, and a melodious and evocative language.

Her work has been described by her English translators Peter Jay and Ana Cristofovici as "a poetry of epiphanies" that are "intimations of deeper, more secret and subterranean" apprehension's of "the ritual cycles of life. . . . " Some of her major themes involve the confluence of death with life, the latter frequently evoked with sensual natural imagery, often with erotic overtones:

> White bodies of poplars coming out of the water
> With Sleepy, slender forms,
> Beautiful adolescents or maybe women,
> Sweet confusion, moist locks
> Not daring to hide desire. . . .

But natural life is just as often presented as over-ripe and corrupt, albeit alluring. In "Bitter Body," Blandiana likens the body to the machinery of death and warns against the "Scent of a body abandoned by its soul / Under the shameless sun. . . . " She continues with urgency, "Don't come near me, don't touch me, / My body is poisonous and bitter . . . ", and concludes:

> Flee, flee!   From the arms of the defiling
>   cross
>   On which, happy, it's myself I despise.
>   Don't breathe in the intoxicating smell,
> When the soul forsakes me as the sun is high
> So I may capture you, and you crucify.

Elsewhere she contrasts physical existence and morality, in metaphysical imagery, as in the early poem "Purity, I know," published in her second book:

> Blue butterflies grow caterpillars,

> The flowers grow into ripe fruit.
> Only snow is immaculate white,
> The warm earth is impure at the root.

In a late poem, "So Must I Wait," procreation seems less important than decomposition:

> Now illness is more mine
> Than I myself have ever been.
> Just as rottenness
> Is more the fruit's
> Than its own seed.

Crucial to Blandiana's perceived moral imperatives is "the struggle," as defined by Marguerite Dorian in *World Literature Today*, "to remain faithful to a certain set of values in all circumstances, the responsibility toward her gift." But in "Purity, I know," "the word stays happy," and is at one with generation, sentience, and warmth. Dissolution for Blandiana is a release into the world of sanctity, free from the fallen world and from human consciousness:

> In just a millennium, or two,
> the rock will become sand,
> The iron links fine powder,
> My bones calcium molecules
> Dissolved in water,
> Suffering nothing.

Many of Blandiana's poems are parables of a fall, or paradise in destruction. Themes of guilt and complicity are often articulated in moral fables left for the reader to interpret. One relatively explicit work, "Portrait," envisions the corruption of the world on a city street, at once both the ontological universe and her own country:

> A sun of rats
> In a firmament of asphalt,
> An Apollo of filth . . .
> A rodent deity
> Ravenous of its age
> And haloed
> By garbage . . .

Eugen Simion, in the preface to a collection of her poems (in Romanian) in 1989, suggests that Blandiana's form of knowledge is "an architecture of questions." To Marguerite Dorian, similarly, from Blandiana's mid-career on, "Poetry becomes . . . a grave self-interrogation, . . . a severe scrutiny of life." Certainly from the mid 1980s (the period of the atypical protest poems noted earlier), the writer's language becomes tougher, an element of irony enters, the images turn troubling, the tone harsher, though never strident. Traditional pastoral and romantic elements become themes of despair and fatalism, as Blandiana bear's witness to the dire conditions of material and spiritual life in a police state controlled scarcity. They criticize the grotesque antipastoralism and antitraditionalism that led to the destruction of the historical core of Bucharest and the bulldozing of villages as part of a plan of systematic, forced resettlement. These concerns come together in Blandiana's "Ballad." Here, in a work almost folkloric, Blandiana reanimates the ancient Romanian story of the Master Builder Manole. He endeavors to build a monastery, but it crumbles every night. He vows, after a dream, to wall up the first person to appear that morning. Alas, it's his beloved and beautiful wife Ana who arrives, but he willingly sacrifices her. In Blandiana's poem, the poet-builder has necessarily taken on the anguished burden of self-sacrifice: "I have no other Ana: / My self I build into the wall." In "Ballad" the poet's dream is a "haunted" one, and her resources are diminishing:

> Ana has no other Ana
> And less and less often
> Even her own self
> Has Ana.

Blandiana's confidence in her beliefs and in the spiritual and social roles of art, as well as the obligations of her own creative work, produce an unshakable serenity in her work. In an essay of the 1960s, "The Poet's Luck," she says: "The only definition of poetry that didn't hurt me . . . was Carl Sandburg's sentence: "Poetry is the diary of a sea animal that lives on land and would like to fly." I saw these words as an almost sedative statement of fatality, as an act of gratitude signed by the poet for his destiny. . . . Loving the world he lives in, he will never stop anticipating another one superior to it. . . . This is his drama and his law. This is his luck." This notion of the fated poet is central to her self-conception. In "How I Became a Poet," from her book of essays *Autoportet cu palimpsest* (Self-portrait with palimpsest, 1986), Blandiana explained how she never swerved from her desire to make what she most admired: "I have never believed that I could become anything other than a writer (I say writer and not poet because I have always considered the condition of being a writer a profession, . . . while that of a poet seems to me, rather, a state, a state of grace. . . . " The poet being "a sacred monster," she defied censorship "because it was infinitely harder not to." Paradoxically when in the early 1980s she made a personal decision to be outspoken, it gave her an "inner freedom." The poetical novel she was writing roughly from 1983 on, though she believed it would never be published, did much to sustain her during the dark period of the late 1980s. (*Sertarul cu aplauze* [The drawer with applause] was published almost a decade after she began it, in 1992.)

Blandiana's prose has recently been translated as much as her poetry, with short stories and her novel appearing in Dutch, French, German, and Hungarian editions in the 1990s. Her intense, fantastic tales, such as those in *Proiecte de trecut* (Projects for the past, 1982) stem partially from Romanian tradition. They also embody aspects of a literary movement in European literature, especially that of Eastern Europe, which as Marguerite Dorian hypothesized, perhaps articulates a response to the absurdity of regimented life, a quest for a higher, invisible reality beyond the cruel and the banal. They come from a need to spin fabulous yarns to maintain sanity, or alternatively, to provide needed escape. Blandiana's tales, with their touches of satire, create a magical and meaningful universe. In one story, a philosophy professor tries to overcome food shortages by raising poultry on her balcony, but hard-to-get black-market eggs hatch not into chickens but into angels. In another, the birds nesting in a church tower take off with the church, bells, and bell ringer, a sign in the sky over Blandiana's imagined world that is, as the poet makes explicit in one of her poems, a dream within a dream within a dream—an inward striving for the ideal of eternity.

PRINCIPAL WORKS IN ENGLISH TRANSLATION: (tr. S. Avadanei and D. Eulert) Six poems and "The Poet's Luck" (essay) *in* 46 Romanian Poets in English, 1973; (tr. D. Duteseu, pref. D. Micu) Poeme/Poems, 1982; (tr. A. Deletant and B. Walker) Twenty poems *in* An Anthology of Contemporary Romanian Poetry, 1984; (tr. M. Cornis-Pop and R. J. Ward) six poems *in* Micromegas, 1984; Don't Be Afraid of Me: Collected Poems, *c.* 1985; (tr, A. Deletant and B. Walker) Thirteen poems *in* silent Voices: An Anthology of Contemporary Romanian Women Poets, 1986; (tr. P. Jay and A. Cristofovici) The Hour of Sand: Selected Poems 1969–1989, 1990; (tr. A. J. Sorkin with I. Ieronim and M. A. Tupan) Fifteen poems *in* Romanian Civilization, spring 1993; (tr. A. J. Sorkin) Ten poems *in* An Anthology of Romanian Women Poets, 1994.

ABOUT: Contemporary World Writers, 2nd ed., 1993; Journal of the American Romanian Academy of Arts and Sciences, 1993; Concerning Poetry Fall 1984; Index on Censorship August 1989; January 1991 Poetry Review Summer 1990; Romanian Civilization Spring 1993; World Literature Today Autumn 1989; Winter 1991.

BLOOM, ALLAN DAVID (September 14, 1930–October 7, 1992), American social philosopher, was born in Indianapolis, Indiana, the son of Allan and Malvina (Glasner) Bloom. Both parents were social workers of Jewish immigrant background and were, according to their son, interested in "the new intellectual life that was coming to America." Later in his life, Bloom commented on the fact that this heritage, combined with the fact that he grew up as a Jew during the emergence of the Nazi party in Germany, taught him to confront "serious issues about the world" at an early age.

Perhaps the major formative influence on Allan Bloom's intellectual life was occasioned by his family's move to Chicago in 1946. The young man soon learned that Robert Maynard Hutchins, as president of the University of Chicago, planned to enroll gifted students in a four-year liberal arts program beginning at the usual junior year of high school. Bloom, who "hated high school," found that the Great Books curriculum, rooted in a belief that universal truth and values underlie all authentic knowledge, was ideal for him. Bloom received his undergraduate degree in liberal arts from the University of Chicago in 1949 at the age of nineteen and immediately entered its elite department known as the Committee on Social Thought, an interdisciplinary program for talented graduate students. There Bloom came under the tutelage of Leo Strauss, a political philosopher, and absorbed Strauss's belief in "transcultural truth," bound by neither time nor cultural context. Bloom received his Ph.D. in 1955 from the University of Chicago with a dissertation on the political philosophy of the Greek rhetorician Isocrates.

For the next thirty-two years, Allan Bloom followed an academic career, publishing scholarly books, chiefly translations of classic works, in political philosophy and higher education and earning a reputation as an excellent lecturer. After receiving his doctorate, he briefly joined the faculty of the College of the University of Chicago as a lecturer in liberal arts. During the 1957–1958 academic year, Bloom was also a Rockefeller Fellow in Legal and Political Philosophy. In 1960, he published his first book, a translation, with notes and an introduction, of Rousseau's *Politics and the Arts: Letter to M. D'Alembert on the Theatre.*

Bloom taught at Yale in 1962, then accepted a position as assistant professor in the Department of Government at Cornell University. Two years later, following the publication of *Shakespeare's Politics*, a collection of essays written with Harry V. Jaffa of DePaul University, Bloom was granted tenure and promoted.

Shakespeare's Politics encapsulates Bloom's views on higher education, lamenting the decline of the Great Books approach and viewing the decline as the cause of the major ills of higher education. In his introductory essay "Political Philosophy and Poetry," Bloom affirms the need for a canon of literature, explaining that the aim of *Shakespeare's Politics* is to make "Shakespeare again the theme of philosophic reflection and a recognized source for the serious study of moral and political problems." Writing in the *New York Times Book Review*, Bernard Grebanier praised the "laudable intentions" of the authors but argued that the book "blossoms with assertions . . . which cannot be acceded to."

In 1967 Bloom further developed his critique of higher education in his essay "The Crisis of Liberal Education," in which he argued that modern universities fail to give students the philosophical foundation necessary for addressing fundamental questions. He called for a return to curriculum grounded in the "Great Books," since those texts, he asserts, are a profound testimony to the human spirit and provide an invaluable intellectual and moral experience for readers.

Bloom's predilection for bold assertions can be seen in his 1968 translation of Plato's *Republic*, for which he wrote an interpretive essay. Bloom's interpretation roused the ire of the classical scholar Gilbert Ryle, who wrote that the essay "constantly slides, without signal, into speculative elucidations, into objections, and into expressions of Bloom's own sentiments."

From his published writings, it might be expected that Allan Bloom would be out of step with the current of student unrest that swept through colleges and universities throughout the United States in the late 1960s. In 1969 gun-flourishing students at Cornell occupied administrative offices and forced their academic demands on the faculty. Although appalled by both the belligerence of the students and the nature of their demands, Bloom was most angered by the university's administrators who, he believed, capitulated to student demands and failed to support the faculty against capricious charges and threats of violence. In a 1988 interview Bloom explained: "There had been a policy for a couple of years . . . in which the university had tried to change itself to accommodate radical positions which simply couldn't be accommodated by the university . . . And then, of course, there was some very cowardly behavior . . . throwing to the wolves professors who had opposed these kinds of policies."

As a result of this experience, Bloom, who had been a popular lecturer at Cornell and recipient of the university's Clark Distinguished Teaching Award in 1967, left both Cornell and the country after 1969. From 1969 to 1970, he was a visiting professor at the University of Tel Aviv and the University of Paris. In 1970, Bloom officially resigned from Cornell and accepted a position at the University of Toronto. He continued his analysis of higher education in a 1971 essay, "The Democratization of the University," in which he denounced "the triumph of a radical egalitarian view of democracy" for its refusal to make judgments about the relative worth of ideas and values, thereby signaling the demise of the liberal university.

During his recuperation from a 1972 heart attack, he worked at another Rousseau translation, aided by an award from the Guggenheim Foundation. Bloom's choice of subject for translation reflected his continued preoccupation with the problems of higher education. His translation of *Emile; or On Education* was published in 1979 and was well received. That same year, Bloom returned to the University of Chicago and the Committee on Social Thought after an absence of nineteen years, now as a full professor.

Prompted by colleagues at Chicago, most notably the novelist Saul Bellow, Bloom developed an essay he had written some years earlier for the *National Review* into a book that was published in 1987 as *The Closing of the American Mind: How Higher Education Has Failed Democracy and Impoverished the Souls of Today's Students.* In it Bloom identifies "cultural relativism" as the disease that plagues American higher education. Succumbing to pressures from student activists in the late 1960s, the universities abandoned a splendid isolation that had facilitated the disinterested exchange of ideas and entered the arena of popular culture, which now determined educational criteria.

Most significantly for Bloom, in the name of "relevance" higher education had abandoned the "Great Books" that had nurtured his own intellectual development. To Bloom, the power of reason to pursue the common good is paramount. Openness to experiences and arguments "used to be the virtue that permitted us to seek the good by using reason," but tolerance, the only respected moral virtue, had come to mean "accepting everything and denying reason's power." Bloom asserts that in providing studies programs for women, blacks, and gays and lesbians, universities lost the critical distance needed "to question conventional wisdom [and] challenge conventional perspectives," which are the proper concerns of higher education.

The Closing of the American Mind elicited strong opinions. Christopher Lehmann-Haupt in the *New York Times* declared that the book "hits with the approximate force and effort of . . . electric-shock-therapy. . . . By turns passionate and witty, sweetly reasoned and outraged, it commands one's attention and concentrates one's mind more effectively that any other book

I can think of in the past five years." Writing in the *New York Times Book Review*, Roger Kimball hailed *The Closing of the American Mind* as "that rarest of documents, a genuinely profound book, born of a long and patient meditation on questions that may be said to determine who we are, both as individuals and as a society." Fueled by reviews that either lauded or challenged Bloom's ideas, sales soared. By June, *The Closing of the American Mind* was listed as number one on the *New York Times'* nonfiction best-seller list. Louis Menand complained in the *New Republic* that Bloom "wants the academy to be an ivory tower." What Bloom castigates as "relativism" Menand views as respect for another's belief or culture. Undeterred by his critics, Bloom said in a 1988 *Time* interview: "If we are not understood as believing in everything equally, we are depicted as believing in only one thing absolutely. There is no longer room for the theoretical middle ground. . . . American intellectual life has given us an easy way to believe anything we want." The controversy in the press and in academia initiated by *The Closing of the American Mind* was caused, to some extent, by Bloom's excessively polemical presentation. Although he praised the book Lehmann-Haupt remarked that it "is probably vulnerable to charges of elitism, antiquarianism, exaggerated subjectivity and skewed generalization from the particular." Bloom, in spite of his claim that higher education had lost the capacity for disinterested dialogue, seemed himself incapable of inhabiting the "theoretical middle ground" that he had always viewed as the appropriate place for educated discourse.

In 1990, Allan Bloom published *Giants and Dwarfs*, a book of essays, only one of which postdated *The Closing of the American Mind.* No longer were reviewers so overwhelmed by provocative assertions that they were willing to forgive lapses in logic and consistency. In the *New York Times Book Review*, Wendy Steiner accused Bloom of "insulting the reader with illogic, contradiction and infuriating double binds." In the *Times Literary Supplement*, Peter Brooks faulted Bloom for believing "there is a conspiracy by social and political radicals to practice thought reform through the curriculum," terming Bloom's apocalyptic warnings "lurid."

Shortly before his death in Chicago at the age of sixty-two, Bloom completed *Love and Friendship*, a collection of essays on the writers he most valued as guides to life: Plato, Shakespeare, Montaigne, Rousseau, Jane Austen, Stendhal—and, with reservations, Flaubert and Tolstoy. It is a passionately argued attack on contemporary mores, especially among the young, and on the psychologists and sociologists who have demythicized Eros, reducing idealistic love to sexual activity. ("Animals have sex," according to Bloom, "and humans beings have eros and no accurate science is possible without making this distinction.") The book reaffirms his conviction that great literature—in contrast to "the impoverished ugliness of our popular arts"—has the power to ennoble and elevate the human spirit.

Bloom's wide reading and his insight into individual works of literature were generally appreciated. "Bloom's patient attention to the text results in some brilliant readings," Roger Kimball remarked in the *Times Literary Supplement.* Unlike the deconstructionists, Kimball added, "his game is not to expose or subdue the 'text' but to understand and enter into the world the writer presents." He argued, however, that "*Love and Friendship* provides an inventory of false doctors and imperfect remedies." Michiko Kakutani, in the *New York Times,* thought Bloom "niggling and downright obtuse" in his judgement of such writers as Flaubert and Tolstoy. On the other hand, Kakutani found Bloom's appreciations of writers he favors— Rousseau and Shakespeare—"erudite, and sympathetic. . . . He deftly conveys . . . Rousseau's legacy of Romanticism" and the impact of *Emile* on the 19th century novel's "focus on the privileged and unconditional experience of love." But to Katha Pollitt, writing in the *New York Times Book Review,* Bloom's "Olympian disgust with modern mores" was unconvincing. She objected in particular to Bloom's attack on what he calls "radical feminism" and claimed he stacks the deck with "snide references to talk shows and cocktail party chit-chat. It isn't fair to contrast Rousseau with a sex manual or unnamed—and, I suspect, imaginary, 'radical feminists'."

Reviewing a book on Robert Maynard Hutchins for the *Times Literary Supplement* Allan Bloom criticized the author for his failure to understand either the man or his administration. Bloom wrote: "Hutchins intrigues and irritates him, but he almost never stops to question his own assumptions." The same might be said for Allan Bloom. The polemical excesses of Bloom's writings may have kept him below the empyrean regions of educated discourse, but his accomplishment was to shine a spotlight on what he and many others believed to be serious problems in contemporary American culture.

PRINCIPAL WORKS: *As editor and translator*—Jean-Jacques Rousseau, Politics and the Arts: Letters to M. D'Alembert on the Theatre, 1960; The Republic of Plato, 1968; Jean-Jacques Rousseau, Emil; or, An Education, 1979. *Nonfiction*— The Closing of the American Mind: How Higher Education Has Failed Democracy and Impoverished the Souls of Today's Students, 1987; Giants and Dwarfs, 1990; Love and Friendship, 1993.

ABOUT: Contemporary Authors 125, 1989; 131, 1991; Current Biography Yearbook 1988; Palmer, M and Pangle, T.L. Political Philosophy and the Human Soul: Essays in Memory of Allan Bloom, 1995. *Periodicals*—Chicago Tribune May 1, 1987; Harper's January, 1988; Los Angeles Times June 10, 1987; July 31, 1987; Los Angeles Times Book Review May 17, 1987; August 30, 1987; Nation May 30, 1987; New Republic May 25, 1987; April 4, 1988; Newsweek April 20, 1987; October 17, 1988; New York Review of Books November 6, 1969; November 5, 1987; October 7, 1993; New York Times March 23, 1987; January 3, 1988; October 8, 1992; June 29, 1993; New York Times Book Review July 10, 1964; April 5, 1987; November 4, 1990; August 8, 1993; Time April 13, 1987; August 17, 1987; October 17, 1988; Times Literary Supplement July 24, 1987; September 4, 1987; January 25, 1991; February 7, 1992; September 3, 1993; Washington Post June 18, 1987; Washington Post Book World April 19, 1987.

BOLAND, EAVAN (AISLING) (September 24, 1944–), Irish poet, writes: "I was born in Dublin. It was a green and secluded city then. We lived an a leafy road, almost beside the canal which cuts through the city. The lock was a splintery wood and boys dived off it in summer. It was a quite place and suggested the start of something closer to a rural childhood than an urban adventure.

"It didn't happen. In 1950 my father was posted to London and some of the counterarguments of my childhood appeared for the first time. My father was a diplomat: a true member of what may have been the last generation of European diplomats. Even now I see them standing on railway platforms, discoursing and wagering in first class carriages, taking unreliable planes to theatres of sudden crisis. It was a fellowship of pessimism which dispensed with barriers and languages. They offered to chaos their skills of rhetoric and their unending gifts for finding the appropriate dress.

"My mother possessed two identities which challenged all this. She was a painter and an orphan. She had studied in Paris with the cubist artist Leo Survage and met my father there. Her own mother had died shortly after she was born, in one of the fever wards in Dublin, at the age of thirty-one.

"As I grew up, it was my mother's image—the eloquent silences of her painting and an unspecified background of loss—which held my imagination. They still remain influences. When I left

EAVAN BOLAND

"In *Outside History* the argument is in the title. Much of what seems to me most memorable in the past also seems most imperilled: the oral tradition, the precious and fragile cargo of storytelling and unwritten perception. This not only stands outside history, it redefines it. Objects and narratives. A black lace fan. A broken mug. And the central sequence which tries to state my relation to an overbearing concept of official memory, an Irish inheritance, and my sense of something it occludes. All this is in the book.

"None of the themes and images in my work are either / or. The concept of history, and my quarrel with it, can illuminate something as small as a bright-cut spoon. The day-to-day life I live, on a street, under the Dublin hills, restate for me the concept of an oral tradition and sense of place. My children, my husband, the objects and elements of a home, are vivid fractions of theatre in and out of the poem. And I have faith that the poem itself—although perceptions of it have faltered in our time—is not an insular unit of expression but can widen out into a powerful and inclusive statement of a lived life."

———

Eavan Boland's poetry is an expression of her identity as a female poet of the nation of Ireland. Sometimes conceived as a journey, like that of Ceres or Aeneas, into the dark underworld of the mythic past, more often expressed in bold images of everyday domestic life, all her poems have in common what Brendan Kennelly describes as "a sustained formal beauty, a psychological astuteness, [and] a tone of calm yet intense intelligence."

The youngest of five children of Frederick and Frances (Kelly) Boland, she had some of her early schooling in London where, from 1950 to 1956, her father was Irish ambassador to the Court of St. James. Sensitive even then to her Irish identity in a country where anti-Irish feelings ran high, she suffered, she recalls in "An Irish Childhood in England," the pain of exile—"some malaise / of love for what I'd never known I had":

college and married and went to live in a suburb south of Dublin I thought I could glimpse, out of the corner of my eye—this makes it rational and decisive, which it was not—one of the difficulties in poetry. It is hard, especially for a women poet, to have the courage of individual experience. To claim the lyric moment inheres in experiences which had hardly seen the inside of a poem till this century. The routine day. Lifting a child. The shape of a kitchen. The feel of a kettle.

"In my case there was a complicating factor. I was Irish. Behind the challenge to put my day-to-day life, without compromise or reduction, into a poem and afford it visionary status, if it deserved it, was the additional claim of a powerful history. In my generation women poets in Ireland have gone from being the objects of the Irish poem to being its authors. With all the changes and stresses this implies.

"The work I have done—especially the books *Night Feed* and *The Journey* and *Outside History*—all revisit these themes and concerns. My mother's expressive gift and her inexpressive past. The images of a national identity. The intense moments of small children and making a home with my husband. All these have not only found their way into poems of mine, they have also made me aware of the way in which the poetry written by women in our time is forcing the ecosystem of poetry to redefine itself. Language. Image. Structure and cadence. These are all being turned and reshaped by the energies of new perspectives and a radical reexamination of a poem's purpose.

> barely-gelled, a freckled six-year-old,
> overdressed and sick on the plane
> when all of England to an Irish child
> was nothing more than what you'd lost and how . . .

In New York, "a beautiful, bizarre city," her father represented Ireland at the United Nations from 1956 to 1964 and she attended the Convent of the Sacred Heart. She returned to Ireland in 1960 and completed her formal education at the Convent of the Holy Child in County Dublin

(1960–1962) and at Trinity College, Dublin, (1962–1966) with first class honors in literature. In 1962, Boland published at her own expense a pamphlet, *23 Poems*. By 1968, after a year as a lecturer at Trinity, she decided to devote herself to writing, although from time to time she has lectured at the School of Irish Studies in Dublin and taught workshops for women poets. She has also been a member of the International Writing Program at the University of Iowa.

In 1969, Eavan Boland married the novelist and playwright Kevin Casey. The marriage produced two daughters—Sarah Margaret, born in 1975, and Eavan Frances, born in 1978. Motherhood and life in the suburbs of Dublin have helped to define her poetry as feminist. She acknowledges the wrenching difficulties of being a women and bridging the gulf between writing poetry and being a poet. Her poetry is drawn intimately and intensely from her own experiences as a women and a mother, but she draws equally from her struggle to "re-possess" Irish poetry and its traditions, both as a modern person and as a woman, outside "the Irish nation as an existing construct in Irish poetry." She chose to think of her womanhood, intertwined with her poetry, as a force for enlightenment, rather than as a window into sexuality.

In Ireland, even in the late 20th century, few women have won recognition as poets. Boland, however, has been criticized for being "destructively feminist" by Anne Stevenson. Reviewing *In Her Own Image*, Stevenson found Boland too steeped in "hips and breasts/ and lips and heat/ and sweat and fat and greed." Stevenson wished Boland had presented "a broader, more generous view of a women's life than that which centers on a frenzied preoccupation with her body." Reviewing *Outside History* in the *New York Times Book Review*, William Logan called Boland "domestic but not domesticated" and a true Irish poet, "formed by a national culture . . . however riven and violently marked. . . . " *Outside History*, however, "slants against that culture in its devotion to women. . . . " Logan finds her anger "bloodless": "She is expert in the passionless household poem, its subject the incident reminiscent, its tone the retrospect melancholy, its diction the vernacular significant." In "Suburban Woman," she traces "the quiet barbarities of the suburbs," the oppressive monotony of domestic duties:

Morning: mistress of talcums, spun
and second cottons, run tights
she is, courtesan to the lethal
rapine of routine. The room invites.
She reaches to flouoresce the dawn.

The kitchen lights like a brothel.

In such poems as "Anorexia," "Menses," and "Mastectomy"—cited as examples of what the French feminist critic Hélène Cixous has called *écriture feminine*—she has confronted female victimization in a male-dominated society. In "Mastectomy" she writes of the surgeons:

I flatten
to their looting
to the sleight

of their plunder
I am brute site
Theirs is the true booty.

In developing as a poet, Boland has come to reject many of the formalities of male-dominated poetry for a "radicalism" that comes from what she calls "primitive truth." Her declared intention is to bring the "sophisticated apparatus of poetry nearer to the less easily articulated human experience." Amy Klauke in *Northwest Review* finds in *Night Feed* a woman's perspective, but one in which "a sense of confinement is replaced by an appreciation of motherhood and celebration of "the nurturing instinct, with images of flowers and children . . . ":

This is dawn
Believe me
This is your season, little daughter.
The moment daisies open,
The hour mercurial rainwater
Makes a mirror for sparrows,
It's time we drowned our sorrows.

In a 1987 essay "The Woman Poet in a National Tradition" in *Studies*, Boland traces the almost simultaneous emergence of her sense of womanhood and her sense of nationhood: "A woman poet is rarely regarded as an automatic part of a national poetic tradition . . . I felt it vital that women poets such as myself should establish a discourse with the idea of nation, should bring to it a sense of the emblematic relationship between the feminine experience and a national past." Boland's later poems reflect the struggle to establish that relationship. Lachlan Mackinnon, reviewing *The Journey and Other Poems* in the *Times Literary Supplement* in 1987, observed, "When she conceals her art, Eavan Boland can be memorable and unnervingly honed, but when she does not she is hardly an artist at all." Writing about the same collection in the *Northwest Review*, however, Amy Klauke concludes; "Eavan Boland continues to express public realities through her uniquely personal perspective. In a voice both tender and intelligent, she is successfully widening the arena of viable poetry in Ireland."

In *Outside History*, Boland appears to have found her true voice as witness to what she has called "the lived life," both in her private experience as a woman and in her more public heritage of Ireland and its mythic past. Elsewhere, in her essay "The Woman, The Place, The Poet" (published in the *Georgia Review* in 1990), she cited Anna Akhmatova and Adrienne Rich as women poets who are "key witnesses to the fact that myth is instructed by history." Significantly she chooses the mythic image of Ceres (in "The Making of an Irish Goddess"), the mother who descended into hell in search of her daughter. This hell is Ireland: "the failed harvests, / the fields rotting to the horizon"; but in the title poem "Outside History," she accepts and embraces her Irishness:

I have chosen

out of myth into history I move to be
part of that ordeal
whose darkness is

only now reaching me from these fields,
those rivers, those roads clotted as
firmaments with the dead.

Raising rather than resolving questions, Mark Wormald commented in the *Times Literary Supplement* in a review of her seventh collection, *In a Time of Violence*, on Boland's special gift: "...no one map, no obvious political, poetic or philosophical agenda, can wholly explain her poetry's significance." For Denis Donoghue, writing in the *New York Review of Books*, "This book has many of Boland's recurring themes: her sense of things diminished by the thought of them; unlived lives; terrains of suffering not indicated by maps . . . ." In the *Nation*, Jan Garden Castro noted the "delicacy with which Boland dismantles icons associated with Irish tradition and culture. Boland . . . permits the voices in the poem to debate among themselves, to encompass visual arts, history, philosophy and other disciplines and to navigate the Irish past and present without reducing or compromising truths she discovers."

Boland herself cited Plato's warning against the poet's "irrational nature which has no discernment of greater or less," and prefaced this volume: "These poems try to take the gap between rhetoric and reality and study the corruptions and grief which happen in that space. . . . The time of violence in the title happens in the present and in the past. It happens in the soul and the event. It is that demanding state of process where things are revealed about woman-

hood and identity which lead on to an investigation—in the title sequence—of the poignant and dangerous mischances between expression and experiences."

Boland attempts to explore those spaces between the reality of experience and poetic rhetoric in the opening poem ' That the Science of Cartography is Limited":

—and not simply by the fact that this shading of
forest cannot show the fragrance of balsam,
the gloom of cypresses,
is what I wish to prove.

Standing in the woods bordering Connacht and recalling the ravages of the Irish famine of 1847, she understands the limitations of science, which can chart the site but never encompass the meaning of that catastrophe.

The subjects of the poems in *In a Time of Violence* range widely from the sufferings of displaced people to her own experiences—the nearly fatal illness of one of her daughters ("But I was Ceres then, and I knew/ Winter was in store for every leaf"), her memories of her mother ("There are dying arts and/ one of them is/ the way my mother used to make up a parcel"), her long, happy marriage, and in "What Language Did" her own aging:

I stood there and felt the melancholy
of growing older in such a season,
when all I could be certain of was simply
in this time of fragrance and refrain,
whatever else might flower before the fruit,
and be renewed, I would not. Not again.

In *Object Lessons* Boland seeks the meaning of being a woman and a poet in the context of the Irish tendency to regard women as icons. Lucy McDiarmid commented in the *New York Times Book Review* that Boland has been "criticized for creating a new piety." If this is true, McDiarmid noted, nevertheless "the object of *Object Lessons* and of much of . . . Boland's recent poetry is to wrest from Irish men the power of representing women in the Irish poem. . . . All the Irish women who never found a place in that [male]tradition make up . . . Boland's 'silent constituency,' a population remembered, created and summoned to assert the woman poet's entitlement to the Irish poem and to fight for lyric turf."

PRINCIPAL WORKS: *Poetry*—New Territory, 1967; The War Horse, 1980; In Her Own Image, 1980; Introducing Eavan Boland, 1981; Night Feed, 1982; The Journey and Other Poems, 1983; Selected Poems, 1989; Outside History, 1990. *Prose*—(with M. MacLiammoir) W. B. Yeats and His World, 1970; Object Lessons: The Life of the Woman and the Poet in Our Time, 1995.

ABOUT: Contemporary Literary Criticism 40, 1986; 67, 1992; Dictionary of Literary Biography, 1985; Kennelly, B. *in* Hogan, R., (ed.) Dictionary of Irish Literature, 1979. *Periodicals*—American Poetry Review January 1985; Colby Library Quarterly 27, March 1991; Concerning Poetry 18, 1985; Contemporary Literature Winter 1989; Georgia Review 44, 1990; Hudson Review 35, 1982; London Review of Books September 28, 1989; Nation June 6, 1994; New York Review of Books May 26, 1994; New York Times Book Review May 22, 1987; April 21, 1991; May 7, 1995; Northwest Review 25, 1987; Studies 76, 1987; Times Literary Supplement August 5, 1994.

MALCOLM J. BOSSE

BOSSE, MALCOLM J(OSEPH) (May 6, 1926–), American novelist, writes: "Throughout my life I have maintained a romantic belief in the power of the imagination. Life traps many of us, but the imagination, as an instrument of change and escape, enables us to break out into the larger world of possibilities. I think this is especially true for the lonely and the disaffected who can find a way through art, literature, and music to make their lives defiantly better.

"An only child, I grew up in Moline, Illinois, where I played football, ran track, and was lucky enough to study Latin. Immediately after high school I joined the Merchant Marine and commenced a routine of action that has taken me through six years of military service, war, and worldwide travel, especially in Asia.

"My first novel was about the Vietnam War, based in part on my own experiences. Thereafter, I have alternated between writing books for adults and for young people. The subjects have ranged from China in the 1920s to prehistoric America, from fourteenth-century Europe to modern India.

"Which is harder to write, a book for adults or for young people? For me the only significant difference is that the books for adults tend to be longer. The vocabulary I use is essentially the same for both, the plots are similarly intricate, the characters equally complicated. I don't believe in concessions to young readers in matters of style and difficulty of content. Some of the books I most fondly remember reading as a kid were beyond me in some ways, but the stretch it took to understand them contributed to their impact and lasting impression.

"But I do believe that narratives for either adults or young people must hold the imagination or there's no sense in asking readers to go on with them. Consequently, many of the settings for my books are exotic, involve a lot of action, move rapidly, and speak bluntly of the world as it was and as it is. My last adult novel was about the underbelly of life in 18th-century England.

The young adult book that came out [in 1993] describes Borneo after the First World War and the next one [*The Examination*, 1994] is set in Ming China.

"Obviously, I like to get around both in real life and writing. Yet I also believe that a writer can stay home, never travel, never have many experiences, and still create a rich world of fiction. Just look at Jane Austen!

"It all comes back to this concept of the imagination. If I have learned one thing during years of writing, it is the need to go beyond the facts into the heart of an experience; to do so involves taking chances and making mistakes and trusting ultimately in intuition. It is this sense of discovery through the imagination that keeps a lot of writers writing. It certainly works that way with me."

———

Born in Detroit and educated at Yale (B.A.), the University of Michigan (M.A.), and New York University (Ph.D.), Malcolm J. Bosse is the son of Malcolm Clifford Bosse, a stockbroker, and Thelma (Malone) Bosse. After a job at *Barron's Financial Weekly* and nearly a decade as a free-lance writer, in 1969, the year he got his Ph.D., Bosse joined the English Department at City College of The City University of New York. He has traveled and lectured extensively throughout Asia—in India, Bangladesh, Burma, Thailand, Singapore, Taiwan, and China. A long-time devotee of Asian culture—his avocational interests include t'ai chi, Oriental mythology, Asian history, and Chinese cooking—Bosse has used Asian settings, both contemporary and historical, in many of his novels.

The Journey of Tao Kim Nam, his first novel, is set in Vietnam during the 1950s, after the defeat of French forces at the hands of the Viet Minh, but before American military involvement. Distraught by the ascendancy of the Communists, Tao Kim Nam, the son of a farmer, sets out from his native village on a perilous trek toward Saigon; once there, he is reduced to begging in the streets until he consents to enter a French refugee camp. Well received by critics, *The Journey of Tao Kim Nam* was selected as one of the best novels of 1960 by the *Saturday Review*, and portions of it were later anthologized in *Vietnam Voices*. A *Christian Century* reviewer commented: "Sensitively written, capturing the poignancy of inarticulate people suffering in war, this novel comes very close to being a minor classic."

Bosse's next two novels, *The Incident at Naha* and *The Man Who Loved Zoos*, are mysteries with contemporary American settings. Both were nominated for Edgar Allan Poe Awards, the latter novel serving as the basis for the French film *Agent Trouble*. The Vietnam veteran protagonist, happening upon a busload of corpses, victims of a germ-warfare experiment gone awry, plunders the bodies for their personal possessions, and thereby becomes the unwitting target of a manhunt. "Mr. Bosse has put together a very strong plot," the *New Yorker*'s reviewer wrote, "and his characterizations are too convincing to be discounted, and much too real to be easily forgotten."

Bosse made his first foray into juvenile fiction with the publication of *The 79 Squares*, the story of an undisciplined fourteen-year-old on probation for vandalizing his school who meets an eighty-two-year-old ex-convict. Together, the boy and the old man embark on an unusual project: the creation of a garden composed of seventy-nine squares, where the boy learns to appreciate the beauty of what grows in nature. *The 79 Squares* was widely praised by critics and won a number of prizes, including the Library of Congress Best Books Award for 1980. Another of Bosse's novels for young people, *Ganesh*, the story of a young American born and raised in India who must adapt to life in the American Midwest, was equally successful. Nominated for a Parents' Choice Award, it was widely translated and published in seven foreign editions.

Bosse is probably best known for his historical novel *The Warlord* set in prerevolutionary China. Mixing fictional characters with historical figures (including Chiang Kai-shek and Mao Tse-tung), *The Warlord* chronicles the lives of a collection of people caught up in the long and bloody Chinese civil war: a mild-mannered graduate of the Yale Divinity School en route to his first Chinese mission, a Russian Comintern agent, a German weapons salesman, a White Russian woman living in Shanghai, and Tang Shan-teh, the fictional warlord of the title. Replete with action, violence, and sex, the novel is also punctuated with long meditations on Chinese history, philosophy, and religion. Finding the book's opening passages particularly bloody, Christopher Lehmann-Haupt noted in the *New York Times* that "surprisingly . . . *The Warlord* . . . succeeds because the invented characters who play the major roles are neither too specific nor too representative . . . yet all of them are wonderfully alive and complicated." "Bosse's best characters are fictive," the *Time* reviewer found. "As richly textured as a tapestry, *The Warlord* captures both the essence of Asia and the sweeping panorama of a people trapped between the ancient grinding forces of hollow tradition and heartless change."

Widely translated and featured as a Book-of-the-Month Club Main Selection, *The Warlord* was on the *New York Times* Bestseller List for five weeks. *Fire in Heaven*, the sequel to *The Warlord* also featuring a number of characters from *The Warlord* and set in post–World War II Asia, was not as successful, either critically or commercially, as its predecessor.

While Asia continues to be central focus of his fiction—the novel *Stranger at the Gate* takes place in Indonesia during the abortive Communist coup of 1965—Bosse has not hesitated to tackle new subjects and different themes. In *Mister Touch*, Bosse creates a post-apocalypse America in which V70, a deadly virus passed through casual contact, has ravaged the human population. The novel opens in a nearly deserted New York City, where packs of wild dogs roam the streets, and cutthroat bands of human survivors battle for food and other necessities. Mister Touch, the eponymous blind hero, is the leader, or "prez," of one such bedraggled group, the Skulls. Assuming leadership of the Skulls after the death of IRT, who named the group from subway graffiti of the 1970s, Mister Touch hopes to prove himself a different sort of leader and, despite his blindness, to bring the Skulls to a more healthful and tranquil environment, the Arizona desert.

Michael Bishop described *Mister Touch* in the *New York Times Book Review* as "an ambitious and peculiarly upbeat disaster novel." Notwithstanding its many grim scenes, Bishop finds the novel "life-affirming." The worldwide AIDS epidemic is an obvious inspiration for the novel, which Bishop considers a worthy successor of such dystopian classics as Nevil Shute's *On the Beach* and Anthony Burgess's *A Clockwork Orange*. He also detects links between *Mister Touch* and such American novels of migration as Larry McMurtry's *Lonesome Dove*. Yet, Bishop notes, "It is very difficult to communicate the richness of . . . Bosse's novel either by trying to pick out the many wayward plot threads from which he fashions his supple narrative or by pointing to his literary forebears." Bosse, Bishop concludes, "is very much his own man."

Bosse returned to the historical novel with *The Vast Memory of Love*, his first work set in 18th-century England. Once again, he brings together historical figures—among them, John Montagu, the fourth Earl of Sandwich, and Henry Fielding, author and magistrate—and fictional characters, this time in London during the 1750s. In the *New York Times Book Review*, Florence King observed, "Malcolm Bosse . . . re-creates the London of George II so vividly that his tale of avenging shepherds and blackmailed peers seems more a time capsule than a book."

Bosse, who has taught 18th-century literature, explains that he wrote *The Vast Memory of Love* because he perceived many parallels between 18th-century England and our own society. "What I tried to do was bridge the gap between that century and ours," he says. "Human nature doesn't change. What makes people different is the way they dress and build things and the way they go to church, but what makes them similar is emotion: the love and hate and greed, the same worries and hopes."

Bosse married Marie-Claude Aullas in 1969. They have two sons and are now divorced.

PRINCIPAL WORKS: *Novels*—The Journey of Tao Kim Nam, 1959; The Incident at Naha, 1972; The Man Who Loved Zoos, 1974; The Warlord, 1983; Fire in Heaven, 1985; Stranger at the Gate, 1989; Mister Touch, 1991; The Vast Memory of Love, 1992. *Juvenile*—The 79 Squares, 1979; Cave Beyond Time, 1980; Ganesh, 1981; The Barracuda Gang, 1983; Captives of Time, 1987; Deep Dream of the Rain Forest, 1993; The Examination, 1994.

ABOUT: Contemporary Authors 106, 1982; Something About the Author 35, 1984; Who's Who in America 1990–1991. *Periodicals*—Christian Century April 8, 1959; New York Times May 13, 1983; New York Times Book Review December 9, 1979; August 9, 1981; February 9, 1986; May 19, 1991; September 6, 1992; New Yorker September 9, 1974; Time July 4, 1983.

BRADLEY, MARION ZIMMER (June 3, 1930–), American science fiction writer, sends the following to *World Authors*: "For all of us born in the thirties—which seems to have been a regular heyday of dysfunctional families, and kids ostracized by their peers, mostly because they read with ease and pleasure and thought of schoolteachers as friends instead of enemies—from Nathan Leopold on down, we were regarded as somehow isolated from that educational sacred cow, the peer group. And for many of us, the only peer group we had was science fiction fandom, and all too often, our only friends were other fans.

"It is any wonder that that last generation of kids, without even penicillin, many of us with undiagnosed rheumatic fever or ear infections—grew up misfits? Or that when we discovered science fiction—the only kind of reading that doesn't demand you turn off your brain—other fans became instant family—often a family we'd never had, and the only family we ever acknowledged.

"The one great gift my mother gave me was to teach me to read when I was four, drawing criticism from the schools who then discouraged parents from self-educating their kids—probably because it taught them to be inwardly critical of their teachers. That wouldn't have mattered to my mother; in a better society she'd have had a diploma in early childhood education. She was the best teacher I ever had; by the time I was seven I read at an adult level-and therefore schools could do nothing for me but criticize. Constant criticism does warp a girl child; and I was duly warped.

"And so I never found anything I preferred to reading and writing. I became a writer literally before I could hold a pencil; my mother to this day keeps poems I dictated to her before I held a pencil. I live in fear someone in search of an original thesis will persuade her to unearth them. They were terrible poems, imitative and jejune, but they marked my path in life. I wrote my first fiction at eleven or so, and began a novel before I was eleven, in imitation of (who else?) Sir Edward Bulwer-Lytton; or Walter Scott. Or perhaps Charlotte Brontë. All of whom I'd read—I had no patience with school readers.

"Perhaps the less said about that first novel the better. I called it 'Last of the Stuarts' and it was about—of course—Charles Edward, the Young Pretender. Later, when I knew more history, I abandoned the project because—in my first real disagreement with my mother—I came to think of Scotland's getting rid of the Stuarts as the best thing that ever happened to that country. My first "real" novel was what later became *The*

MARION ZIMMER BRADLEY

Sword of Aldones; it was my equivalent of the Brontës' Gondal stories. I called it 'The King and the Sword' and it was a pretty shameless imitation of the books by Frances Hodgson Burnett (*The Lost Prince*), Rider Haggard (*She*), and Sax Rohmer (*She Who Sleeps*)—and the Graustark books of George Barr McCutcheon—which I still love—all of them. Later, at eighteen, when I began to read pulp fiction I encountered the work of Henry Kuttner and C. L. Moore and became a pretty shameless plagiarist of the pulp fiction I loved. My parents deplored it. Nowadays high school kids read and even take courses in science fiction; in those days I was always being told not to 'waste my good mind on that stuff,' and teachers would take the magazines away and consign them to the school furnace. But I persisted reading them and writing them. To this day I've never found anything I like better.

It did—and does—horrible things to my social life too; and it kept me having even one happy marriage. I married—what else—another loner, and in the isolation of fifties Texas became a writer; learned about culture shock so completely that I'm still writing about it. I put myself through college writing cheap romances (not nearly as sick as today's best-sellers) which in the Bible College I attended would have gotten me thrown out of school for reading, let alone writing them.

"My first published short story was in one of those ephemeral pulps; I followed it with others and attended my first science fiction convention in Cleveland, 1957 (so long ago that the membership fee was two dollars). In 1966 I met—also through fandom—one Walter Breen, and married him. I've nothing to say, at least in public, against Brad (Robert A. Bradley); he was a strictly honorable man and a great improvement on my parents. At least he believed in working steadily, feeding, supporting, and not abusing his family, and fathered my son David. David was the best thing to come out of that marriage. By Walter I had two other children, Patrick, born 1964, and Moira, born 1966.

"For a time I wrote several books a year; my favorites were the Darkover books, which in a very real sense were all descended from *The Sword of Aldones*. The best of them is perhaps *The Heritage of Hastur* or maybe *Stormqueen*. There are twenty-one Darkover novels now—the first six for Ace, then the rest for DAW (for my substitute father, as he was to a whole generation of fans, editor Donald A. Wollheim, who bought my first paperback novels.) In between the Darkover books came books such as *The Brass Dragon* and *Hunters of the Red Moon* and *The Survivors*, with my youngest brother Paul Edwin Zimmer. In 1982, by a lucky fluke I wrote probably my best book, a *New York Times* best-seller, *The Mists of Avalon*.

"This book has brought me in a lot of money and directly led to the sale of my second big historical, *The Firebrand*, a sort of feminine-based version of the Trojan War, which did not sell as well as the editor hoped because he forgot that American kids, unlike English ones, are not brought up on the Trojans and Greeks. Still, it has a very respectable sale, more in Europe, I think, than here. Currently I'm working on another historical novel with my sister-in-law Diana Paxson, whose first story I published. Diana is the best known of the young writers I've discovered, except Mercedes (Misty) Lackey, who has collaborated with me on the most recent Darkover book, *Rediscovery*. Another is Elisabeth Waters, first winner of the Gryphon award, and my secretary and housemate for many years. I've discovered several dozen young writers with the anthologies I started doing in 1979, with the *Sword and Sorceress* anthologies I began editing in 1983, and even more with my magazine started in 1988, *Marion Zimmer Bradley's FANTASY Magazine*.

"I don't use science fiction in my magazine, only fantasy. Science fiction, I say, is about technostructures, fantasy about our dreams and emotions. "And I still haven't found anything I like better than reading and editing science fiction and fantasy. Soon I'll be officially a senior citizen; and if I had my way I'd still be very much of a fan."

The 1962 publication of the long novelette *The Planet Savers* and the novel *The Sword of Aldones* marks the beginning of Marion Zimmer Bradley's complex, extended Darkover saga, "one of the most fully realized of the worlds of science fiction," according to Lester del Rey of *Analog Science Fiction/Science Fact* in 1978.

Favorably compared to other classic science fiction series, such as Frank Herbert's Dune books, the Darkover series likewise has garnered its own cult following; in the opinion of Roland Green in *Booklist*, her series is "beyond question one of the most notable feats of storytelling in the history of sf."

The planet Darkover, settled some two thousand years ago by earth colonists who crashed there, is anything but a utopia. As Susan M. Shwartz points out in *The Feminine Eye: Science Fiction and the Women Who Write It*, it is a "stark worlds of inbred telepaths, forest fires, blizzards, and a precariously balanced ecostructure. . . . on Darkover any attempt at change or progress carries with it the need for pain-filled choice." Despite their common roots, two cultures have evolved: the communal Terrans, with their advanced technology, and the self-reliant Darkovers, who are opposed to technology. Within this intriguing world Bradley has ample room to weavenumerous plots, subplots, and characters. Part of the interest here is Bradley's ability not to take sides openly when dealing with the two cultures, but rather to explore their ages-old conflict in all its complexity.

Bradley's fascination with dual conflict has been apparent from the very inception of Darkover. The protagonist in *The Planet Savers* is Jason Allison, who is afflicted with a personality disorder. Jason's dominant self is introverted and cold; Jay, his subordinate side, is just the opposite. It is Jay who procures the serum for a fever that is threatening Darkover, and ultimately there is an integration of the dual personalities, as well as a romantic union between Allison and Free Amazon Kyla Rainéach. *The Sword of Aldones* offers readers the most alienated of all of Bradley's heroes. Not only is Lew Alton physically scarred, but his father was a Darkovan and his mother a Terran. Alton finally leaves Darkover, unable to deal with the planet's violence and the continuing inroads of Terran technology.

Although it was published in 1975, the events of *The Heritage of Hastur* antedate those of *The Sword of Aldones*. Here are the roots of Lew Alton's alienation and his eventual disfigurement. The story offers Alton a foil in the form of Regis Hastur, a prince and another alienated character. While alton's path leads to bitterness, Hastur

discovers his heretofore absent telepathic powers and decides to accept his leadership role on the Comyn Council, realizing that "he, who had once sworn to renounce the Comyn, now had reform it from inside out, single-handedly, before he could enjoy his own freedom."

Bradley considers *The Heritage of Hastur* and *Stormqueen* the best of the Darkover books. The latter is set on a pre-Terran Darkover, a world of autocracy and violence. "The prose is quite clear, crisp and powerful, and Bradley's arguments are logical and reasonable," David A. Truesdale observed in the *Science Fiction Review* "She deals with the contemporary issues of genetic engineering, abortion, men and women as sex objects, what understanding, compassion and a call to reason can accomplish—all against a backdrop of feudal intrigue and inheritance by a people who are struggling and groping to understand and control their powers of telepathy, telekinesis and other psi powers. . . . A . . . thoughtful and detailed wonderment."

Bradley also considers *The Forbidden Tower* one of her best Darkover books. Paul McGuire III, in *Science Fiction Review* called it the "most psychological and sexual novel of the series" and the "most confined of . . . Bradley's novels, the isolation ultimately is that of a person within himself, separate in mind and body from others."

Given Bradley's proclivities it is not surprising that feminist concerns are part of the Darkover saga. Essentially limited to producing heirs or joining a sisterhood, the painful choices inflicted on Darkovan women by the rigid patriarchal society are especially evident in *The Shattered Chain*. Here a tribe of women, the Free Amazons or the Order of Renunciates, become, Susan M. Shwartz writes, a "metaphor for female and human conditions on Darkover and elsewhere of being bound by old choices, refusing to remain so, and—through enduring the pain of choice—arriving at new solutions and restories integrity."

Bradley has also been active in the area of homosexual rights. She wrote about homosexuality in *The Heritage of Hastur*. She has said that *The Catch Trap*, the story of two circus aerialists, was written while she having a love affair with a women. Bradley describes it as "probably the first full-length nonscandalous gay novel, which I . . . held back because I DIDN'T want to sell it as a cheap sex novel."

With the publication of the best-selling *The Mists of Avalon* in 1983, Bradley moved into the mainstream and a wider readership. "I've never been able to explain exactly why *Mists* was such a hit," she told *Writer's Digest*, "except maybe people felt like they were getting a different perspective, and were on the inside of what really happened during Arthurian times." Bradley wanted to show the women as liberated, and she re-created the legend of King Arthur and the Round Table from the perspective of its main women characters: Viviane, Gwenhwyfar, Morgaine, and Igraine. "This, the untold Arthurian story, is no less tragic, but it has gained a mythic coherence; reading it is a deeply moving and at times uncanny experience," wrote Maureen Quilligan in the *New York Times Book Review*. Likewise *The Firebrand*, Bradley's "feminine-based version of the Trojan War," features Kassandra as the chief protagonist, as well as a portrayal of a warm, loving Helen, rather than the "wicked adulteress of legend."

In addition to anthologies, Marion Zimmer Bradley has contributed to such science fiction publications as the *Magazine of Fantasy and Science Fiction*, *Amazing Stories*, and *Venture*. She makes her home in Berkeley, California.

PRINCIPAL WORKS: *Novels*—The Door Through Space, 1961; (as Lee Chapman) I Am a Lesbian, 1962; The Planet Savers, 1962; Seven From the Stars, 1962; The Sword of Aldones, 1962; (as Miriam Gardner) The Strange Women, 1962; (as Miriam Gardner) My Sister, My Love, 1963; (as Morgan Ives) Spare Her Heaven, 1963 (abridged as Anything Goes, 1964); The Bloody Sun, 1964; Falcons of Narabedla, 1964; Twilight Lovers, 1964; Castle Terror, 1965; Star of Danger, 1965; (as Morgan Ives) Knives of Desire, 1966; (as John Dexter) No Adam for Eve, 1966; Souvenir of Monique, 1967; Bluebeard's Daughter, 1968; The Brass Dragon, 1969; The Winds of Darkover, 1970; The World Wreckers, 1971; Dark Satanic, 1972; Darkover Landfall, 1972; (as Valerie Graves) Witch Hill, 1972; Hunters of the Red Moon, 1973; In the Steps of the Master, 1973; The Spell Sword, 1974; Can Ellen Be Saved?, 1975; Endless Voyage, 1975 (revised and reissued as Endless Universe, 1979); The Heritage of Hastur, 1975; Drums of Darkness, 1976; The Shattered Chain, 1976; The Forbidden Tower, 1977; The Ruins of Isis, 1978; Stormqueen, 1978; The Catch Trap, 1979; (with P.E. Zimmer) The Survivors, 1979; The House Between the Worlds, 1980; Survey Ship, 1980; Two to Conquer, 1980; Sharra's Exile, 1981; Hawkmistress, 1982; Web of Light, 1982; The Mists of Avalon, 1983; Thendara House, 1983; City of Sorcery, 1984; The Inheritor, 1984; Web of Darkness, 1984; Night's Daughter, 1985; Warrior Woman, 1985; The Firebrand, 1987; The Heirs of Hammerfell, 1989; (with J. May and A. Norton) Black Trillium, 1990; Leroni of Darkover, 1991; (with M. Lackey) Rediscovery, 1993; Ghostlight, 1995. *Short stories*—The Dark Intruder and Other Stories, 1964; The Jewel of Arwen, 1974; The Parting of Arwen, 1974; Sword of Chaos, 1982; Lythande, 1986; The Best of Marion Zimmer Bradley, 1988 (reissued as Jamie and Other Stories: The Best of Marion Zimmer Bradley, 1991). *Nonfiction*—(with G. Damon) Checklist: A Complete, Cumulative Checklist of Lesbian, Variant, and Homosexual Fiction in English, 1960; Men, Halflings, and Hero Worship, 1973;

The Necessity for Beauty: Robert W. Chambers and the Romantic Tradition, 1974; (with N. Spinrad and A. Bester) Experiment Perilous: Three Essays on Science Fiction, 1976. *As editor*—The Keeper's Price and Other Stories, 1980; Greyhaven: An Anthology of Fantasy, 1983; Sword and Sorceress: An Anthology of Heroic Fantasy 1-10, 1984–1993; Free Amazons of Darkover, 1985; Other Side of the Mirror, 1987; Red Sun of Darkover, 1987; Four Moons of Darkover, 1988; Spells of Wonder, 1989; Domains of Darkover, 1990; Renunciates of Darkover, 1991. *Juvenile*—The Colors of Space, 1963.

ABOUT: Arbur, R. Leigh Brackett, Marion Zimmer Bradley, Anne McCaffrey: A Primary and Secondary Bibliography, 1982; Breen, Walter. The Darkover Concordance: A Reader's Guide, 1979; Breen, W. The Gemini Problem: A Study in Darkover, 1976; Contemporary Authors Autobiography Series 10, 1989; Contemporary Authors New Revision Series 7, 1982; Contemporary Literary Criticism 30, 1984; Dictionary of Literary Biography 8, 1981; Paxson, D. Costume and Clothing as a Cultural Index on Darkover, 1977, rev. ed. 1981; Staicar, T. (ed.) The Feminine Eye: Science Fiction and the Women Who Write It, 1982; Twentieth-Century Science-Fiction Writers, 1991; Who's Who in America 1974, 1973; Wise, S. The Darkover Dilemma: Problems of the Darkover Series, 1976. *Periodicals*—Analog Science Fiction/Science Fact March 1977; August 1978; Booklist October 15, 1982; Foundation January 1979; New York Times Book Review January 30, 1983; Rigel Science Fiction Winter 1982; Science Fiction Review February 1978; September 1978; Writer's Digest June 1988.

*BRANDYS, KAZIMIERZ** (October 27, 1916–), Polish novelist, essayist, and playwright, was born into a well-to-do and assimilated family of Polish-Jewish professionals in the city of Lodz, Poland, where he and his older brother Marian, also a writer, spent their childhoods and received their primary education. In the early 1930s, the family moved to Warsaw where Brandys completed his schooling and graduated in 1939 with a law degree from Warsaw University. As a student he was active in a progressive, antifascist movement and distinguished himself by publishing an open letter protesting racial discrimination at Polish universities. Hitler's blitzkrieg attack on Poland in September 1939 and its dramatic consequences shocked Brandys. Five years spent under German occupation in Warsaw put an indelible mark on him: his secure and comfortable life was gone, and as a Jew he was forced to part with his family, change his name, move frequently, and live in constant danger of being discovered and arrested. Unlike his father, who died in a Gestapo prison, Kazimierz Brandys survived, assisted by friends, among them, Maria Zenowicz, whom he married in 1944.

*BRAHN dis, KAHZ im yairzh

KAZIMIERZ BRANDYS

Brandys began to write during World War II. The moral aspects of human behavior and the unpredictable reversals in people's fortunes, have engaged Brandys from the beginning. No less involving for him was the question of form. His writing underwent significant transformation from the traditional realistic novel to a new, postmodernist form of mixed genres.

Brandys's 1946 literary debut, the novel *Miasto niepokonane* (The invincible city), is a reflection on his wartime experience and an homage to the heroic struggle and ultimate destruction of Warsaw. The novel was well received in Poland and was subsequently translated into several languages. The war, often as a pretext for deliberation on moral dilemmas, surfaces in Brandys's work repeatedly. At the end of the war the country was in ruins; humanity was bankrupt. The destruction of the old world, however, created a unique opportunity for moral purification by rejection of the past and renewal. Disillusioned and emotionally broken, Brandys, like so many other European intellectuals of his generation, chose to believe that a better future depended on the success of Communism. He joined the Communist Party in 1946. His alliance with the Communists meant the acceptance of the official ideology both in the subject and the form of his writing. Soon he affiliated himself with the influential cultural weekly *Kuźnica* (The Forge). In articles published there, and later in *Nowa Kultura* (New Culture), he attacked Poland's pre-World War II system of social injustice, the country's cultural backwardness, and the moral weaknesses of its

intelligentsia. The cycle of novels *Między wojnami: Samson; Antygona; Troja miasto otwarte; Człowiek nie umiera* (Between the wars: Samson; Antigone; Troy, The open city; Man does not die), written between 1948 and 1952, embodies these themes. Brandys's aim is to reveal the fragility of the bonds in a typical "bourgeois" family, its fragmentation and ultimate destruction, rather than sustaining values and strength. The young hero , sensitive and morally upright, totters on the thin line between the old and new worlds and eventually leaves the "departing class" to join "the camp of common people."

Brandys was acclaimed for both his command of the language and his style, and for representing the new literary trend of "settling accounts" with the past. During the most repressive years, 1948 to 1956, referred to as the years of "domestic disgrace," the demands of official ideology forced Brandys to pay a heavy artistic and moral price. As a leading author and an activist in the highly political writers' union, he was obliged to conform to socialist realism, to glorify life under Communism, and to portray proletarian heroes.

Brandys's novel, *Matka Królów* (The Mother of the Krols, 1957; translated as *Sons and Comrades*) is enlivened by historical and psychological verisimilitude. Brandys depicts the life of a poor Warsaw neighborhood in which trials of the working class emerge in the story of Łucja Król, who loses all four of her sons, committed Communists, at the hands of Nazis or the sons' Communist comrades. The novel was popular, but was condemned by official critics who saw it as a libel on the allegedly ideal life in Communist Poland.

Sons and Comrades marked a new stage in Brandys's writing. His ideological conformism gave way to concern for his characters' inability to evaluate the intentions and deeds of others, making them victims of history. A film based on the novel, directed by Janusz Zaorski during the pre-Solidarity era, was a critical and popular success. This was confirmed later by the selection of the movie for the New Directors, New Films Festival at the Museum of Modern Art in New York

Unlike his failed theatrical ventures with the plays *Sprawiedliwi ludzie* (Righteous people, 1953 and *Inkarno* 1962), Brandys's other narratives were successfully made into movies, usually with the author as scenarist. One of them, *Samson*, directed by Andrzej Wajda, employs biblical allegories to depict the story of Jakub Gold, a Jew in hiding, who joins the Polish underground fighters and dies, gun in hand, under the symbolic ruins of the temple. Another, based on the short story, "Jak być kochana" (How to be loved), directed by Wojciech Has, portrays an actress who, during the occupation, jeopardizes her career in order to save a lover, an anti-Nazi hero.

Brandys has traveled widely and spent long periods abroad. He has frequently represented Poland at international gatherings of artists and intellectuals and has taught at several universities. A companion of the West European existentialists, he participated in their discussions and, like many of them, fell under the spell of Claude Levi-Strauss's *Tristes Tropiques* and books by Jean-Paul Sartre, Albert Camus, and Mircea Eliade. His 1966 visit to the United States resulted in travel notes, which he included in the novel *Rynek* (The square, 1968). America of the early post-Kennedy years is reflected there as a "country with a sin." Indians, blacks and the Japanese of Hiroshima are its victims; the author notes with satisfaction that Poland couldn't be blamed for similar crimes. On his second trip Brandys found himself in America in very different circumstances: as a political exile stranded abroad when martial law was declared in Poland. He was writer-in-residence at Columbia University from 1982 to 1983, a position which provided him with many opportunities to observe American society. Brandys used this experience in *Paris, New York: 1982–1984*, published in 1988. "In this modern Babylon slowly consumed by all kinds of moral and physical cancers, you often encounter—more often in fact than any place else—evidence of consideration for the underprivileged. The United States is one of the few ventures in human history that has proven to be successful."

Listy do pani Z. (Letters to Mrs. Z) was published in three parts between 1957 and 1961. It chronicles Brandys's life in Poland and abroad. Mrs. Z. is Brandys's typical reader, to whom he relates the events of his days and his nightly dreams with comments, reflections, and doubts. *Letters* can be seen as an inventory of Polish consciousness, dealing with such problems as political corruption, intolerance, a national inferiority complex, the low self-esteem of the Polish intelligentsia, and guilt towards the Jews.

It would be difficult to point to the particular event or to the moment in time when Brandys became disillusioned with the Communist system, converted to political dissent, and became a severe critic of the Communist system. He left the party in the late sixties, consequently becoming one of the most rigorously censored writers in Poland. For years, he was published only by the underground and foreign presses. Eventually he became a cofounder and editor of the independent quarterly *Zapis* (Record), where many Polish dissident writers have published. Perhaps the change in Brandys's ideas first became apparent in the form of his novels. Reality, differently viewed, demanded a different style. Once liberated from the obligation of creating fiction, Brandys experimented with forms of antinovel. The reflective monologue became a substitute for epic narration. Old stylistic divisions became vague. His new creations often are collages of mixed forms and genres; an excerpt taken from a newspaper, a historical sketch, a childhood memory—all of these were now incorporated into narration. Letters became one of his favorite forms, permitting him to reach deeper into the tormented conscience of an individual. *Wariacje pocztowe* (Correspondence variations, 1972) is composed of letters written by the fathers and sons of a family between the years 1770 and 1970. The characters evaluate their lives, posing constant yet never fully answered questions about the motive for their behavior and the validity of their choices: Was I right or wrong? Can I be forgiven? Am I good or evil?

Similar questions echo in many of Brandys's novels, repeated by characters living at different times but still facing the same moral dilemmas. The questions are posed by the "statistical Pole" from *Sposób bycia* (The way to be, 1965), the unattractive office worker in *Rynek* (The square, 1968), the visiting professor, lecturing on Polish literature at American and French universities — in *Pomsł* (An idea, 1974), and a theater director answering a Harvard professor's inquiry in *Nierzeczywistość* (A question of reality, 1977).

The young hero of the novel *Rondo* (1982) invents an imaginary wartime underground organization to raise the spirits of an actress with whom he is in love when the Nazi occupation closes theaters. This fabrication, however, attracts many, making the organization into "a considerable political and military force," according to Arthur Waldhorn writing in *Library Journal.* Waldhorn acclaimed *Rondo*, as did other critics, for its "complex discussions with sharply etched characters—about theater, religion, politics, love: which "compels attention to the stresses of selfhood, especially during times of political catastrophe."

Brandys's fascination with the influence of accidental events on human life is presented in *Rondo* in an almost musical fashion, according to Stanislaw Baranczak writing in the *New Republic*: "The recurring thematic refrains and the narrative method of circling around key events . . . convey a[n] . . . impression of a determined world in which . . . fate cannot be averted. . . . Once unreality is created, nothing can undo its very real existence." Although Philip Lopate, writing in the *New York Times Book Review*, thought the major ideas and dichotomies in the novel created a "rather feverish" effect, when the narrator of the novel calls it "impossible" to "explain my epoch to someone who lives in a different time," Lopate concluded that Brandys, with his "lush, caloric Polish generosity" has indeed "done the impossible."

The "real existence" of unreality surfaces in volume 4 of his diary *Miesiące*, when Brandys discusses the Moscow trials. "What's most fascinating for me is the fact that reality is set in motion by fiction," he writes. "In both cases, the phenomenon of fiction being incorporated into reality is similar. The invented scenario begins to function, becomes a source of collective determination and directs history."

Between 1978 and 1987, living in Poland under martial law, and in New York, and in Paris as a political exile, Brandys worked on his four-volume diary *Miesiące* (The months; translated in two volumes as *Warsaw Diary: 1978–1981* and *Paris, New York: 1982–1988*), a most original "auto-novel," as this new genre has been labeled. Brandys chronicles his and his wife's life during the dramatic years of growing anti-Communist sentiment in Poland, followed by the triumph of "Solidarity" and its subsequent repression by General Jaruzelski's martial law, his life as a political exile in New York, and the new beginning in Paris, conveying "the ambiguities of the period with striking accuracy and insight," Jaroslaw Anders said in *Newsweek*. R. Z. Sheppard, in *Time*, called Brandys "a moral . . . witness. . . . His steady voice . . . belongs wholly to the community of exiles that has quickened the conscience and enriched the writing of the 20th century."

In Paris Brandys continued to write in a variety of forms. In *Sztuka konwersacji* (The art of conversation), former lovers meet in Paris, and in a skillful semitheatrical dialogue, reveal the secrets and tragedies of their separate lives, which reflect their times. The piece, like several other novels by Brandys, was adapted for the stage, with considerable success.

Brandys wrote in the last volume of *Miesiące*: "I wanted to break away from a patriotic duty to write *de publicis*, from the chronicle of national tragedy. I wanted to reprivatize myself. . . . I was tormented, I felt form imposing itself on me; some of my sentences sounded like a press communique. I was unable to omit anything which had happened in Poland."

In a 1991 volume of essays, *Charaktery i pisma* (Characters and writings) the author suc-

ceeds, however, in distancing himself from the pressure of politics. Unlike his diaries, *Charaktery i pisma* has nothing to do with Polish reality. The essays resulted from long walks through Paris streets and meditations on literary personalities who once lived in this city—Oscar Wilde, Paul Leautaud, and Andre Gide. Since 1989 Brandys has been working on diary-essays, titled *Zapamiętane* (Remembered). Composed of comments on his readings, conversations with friends, letters, travels and musings on contemporary events, these essays are being published periodically by the quarterly *Zeszyty Literackie* (*Cahiers Littéraires*).

Brandys's books continue to enjoy great popularity in Poland, where they appear in frequent new editions. They have been translated into many languages. His international success was additionally confirmed by the popularity of his public lectures at the Ecole des Hautes Etudes en Sciences Sociales in Paris, his series on Radio France Internationale, and the 1992 award of the French government's order "des Arts et des Letters."

Explaining why he writes, Brandys said in *Miesiące*: "When I tell stories, I create connections between myself and the world. It is a substitute for faith and action. . . . I tell stories because I do not feel God strongly enough, and at the same time I don't want to provoke Satan. If everything were well in the world, we wouldn't have to tell stories."

PRINCIPAL WORKS IN ENGLISH TRANSLATION: *Fiction*— (tr. D. J. Walsh) Sons and Comrades , 1961; (tr. from French I. Barzun) A Question of Reality , 1978; (tr. M. Edelson) Letters to Mrs. Z , 1986; (tr. J. Anders) Rondo , 1989. *Memoirs*— (tr. R. Lourie) Warsaw Diary: 1978–1981 , 1984; (tr. B. Krzywicki-Herburt) Paris, New York: 1982–1988 , 1988.

ABOUT: Brandys, K. Warsaw Diary: 1978–1981, 1984; Paris, New York: 1982–1988, 1988; Columbia Dictionary of Modern European Literature 2nd ed., 1980; Contemporary Literary Criticism 62, 1991; Encyclopedia of World Literature in the 20th Century, rev. ed., 1981; Milosz, C. History of Polish Literature, 1969; Tucker, M. (ed.) Literary Exile in the Twentieth Century, 1991. *Periodicals*—New Republic September 1989; Newsweek January 30, 1984; New York Review of Books April 26, 1984; New York Times Book Review November 19, 1989, Time January 9, 1984.

BRENTON, HOWARD (December 13, 1942–   ), British playwright, novelist, and poet, was born in Portsmouth, England, the son of Donald Henry and Rose Lillian (Lewis) Brenton. His father was a police officer who became a Methodist minister. He was educated at Chichester High School and St. Catherine's College, Cambridge, where he graduated with honors in English. His first play, *Ladders of Fools*, was produced at Cambridge University in 1965. Immediately after graduation he worked as a theater stage manager and occasional actor; he began to have plays produced by semiprofessional and fringe groups.

Brenton has maintained the conviction that all drama is political, both in form and content; he has dedicated his dramas to the cause of socialism, writing to confront the traditional values of capitalist Britain. To challenge those values, Brenton incorporates into his plays theatrical shocks, verbal and visual humor, overt sexuality, and language that goes from the elevated to the crude. A dominant theme in Brenton's work is the corruption of British society: the abuse that decaying capitalism heaps upon its citizens. His targets are the representatives of British society's most powerful groups—political leaders, the police, the upper classes.

Brenton himself has said of his work: "The theatre is a bourgeois institution: you have to live and work against that." That attitude militates against his being readily absorbed into mainstream theater or becoming popular with the middle-class audiences. He remains a polemicist on the margin of English theatrical life. He has been compared with such other political playwrights as David Hare, Trevor Griffiths, Howard Barker, and Stephen Poliakoff, and has been identified as an inheritor of theatrical ground gained by such playwrights as David Storey, Edward Bond, and Tom Stoppard.

Brenton frequently portrays England in the grip of a terminal cultural crisis. Order and anarchy, individual experience and social need, historical inheritance and utopian vision, capitalism and socialism—all are intermeshed. Brenton has achieved mastery in demonstrating both meaningless violence and social anger, but has a more limited capacity to resolve the abrupt and brutal relationships they bring into being.

The year 1969 was crucial in Brenton's career as a playwright. No fewer than six of his plays were staged in that year. While four were produced outside London, the two London productions received special notice. *Revenge*, a seriocomic two-act play, juxtaposes a professional criminal recently released from prison and the Scotland Yard Assistant Commissioner responsible for the criminal's imprisonment. Brenton's intention is to undermine assumptions concerning social rectitude and the legitimacy of legal institutions by making law-breaker and law-enforcer equally corrupt and violent. The play also contains elements that have become charac-

teristic of Brenton's later work. The characters speak in slang, frequently repeating obscenities; serious ideas are conveyed in a comic manner; violent theatricalism is rampant, as when at the end of the play the characters all bite on blood bags and die. The criminal and the assistant commissioner are played by the same actor to emphasize the degree to which both sides of the law are playing the same game.

A similar theme is enacted in *Christie in Love*, a one-act play based on the life of the murderer John Reginald Christie. Christie is interrogated and finally hanged, by an inspector and a constable who are clearly as unstable and violent as Christie himself. The police act in a stylized, stereotypical manner, one of them endlessly repeating obscene limericks, while Christie behaves naturalistically. The effect is to dislocate the audience's assumptions concerning the legitimacy of the social order. Christie's behavior is not condoned, but his perverse violence and sexual confusion regarding women is mirrored in exactly those people and institutions who condemn him. A dummy is used to represent all of the female victims, symbolizing both all men's attitude toward women and Brenton's own inability to create female characters, as he claimed, before he was married. The play is staged on a set composed of pieces of old newspaper.

Brenton continued his theatrical experiments with *Wesley*, a play about the founder of Methodism, first performed in a church. *Wesley* includes narration, choir singing, and pantomime. *Scott of the Antarctic: What God Didn't See*, another experimental drama, was first produced on an ice-rink in the city of Bradford. English imperialist attitudes are lampooned through surrealistically simulated cannibalism. *Lay-By*, a collaboration with six other playwrights including Howard Barker, David Hare, and Stephen Poliakoff, exemplifies Brenton's continued willingness to experiment. Its explicit sexual content was condemned by many critics as gratuitous.

During the period 1972–1973, while Brenton was resident playwright at the Royal Court Theatre in London, he began work on a series of full-length plays constructed in short scenes. The series includes *Magnificence*, *Brassneck*, *The Churchill Play*, *Weapons of Happiness*, and *Epsom Downs*. In *Magnificence*, the first Brenton play produced on an important London stage, a cynical and entrenched power structure is confronted by immature political radicalism—one of Brenton's typical themes. A young political group has failed in its attempt to establish an illegal squat; their leader, Jed, whose wife has a miscarriage after brutal mistreatment from a bailiff, demands revenge upon the political establishment and chooses as victim a conservative cabinet minister. The plan misfires and both he and the minister wind up dead. It has been argued that in this play Brenton fails to give a clear ideological account of Jed's actions: they seem motivated as much by personal reasons as political ones. Peter Ansorge, however, has praised the play for connecting personal anger and frustration and their political causes: "Brenton's ability to bring Jed's frustration into the context of an increased sense of militancy marks out *Magnificence* as a key work of the period."

The Churchill Play, first produced at the Nottingham Playhouse in 1974, was to gain Brenton special notice and make him the first writer to have a play (*Weapons of Happiness*) commissioned and staged by the National Theatre in London. *The Churchill Play* continues Brenton's investigation of the relationship between those directing the forces and institutions that control society and those who are subject to those forces. In this fuller play, however, Brenton does more than oppose a crudely corrupt power system with a naive, if zestful, anarchism. The play is set in an Orwellian England, a country of militarized government and concentration camps. It opens with a play within the play (at first unknown to the audience) in which a recently dead Winston Churchill, lying in state on a catafalque, suddenly comes to life. The historical period of World War II, the time of the play within the play, the main play's setting in the future, and its actuality in production intersect, overlap, and blend in order to provide a complex comment on the political realities at the time of the performance. The dominant image is decay: decay in Churchill's body through death, decay in his reputation through revelation of an alternative version of his time in office, and his fear of the decay of syphilis from which his father died horribly. All these are paralleled with the political decay in 1984, our present. The play within the play is performed by the prisoners of one of the camps as a cover for an abortive escape attempt. They embody one of Brenton's recurring messages: hope for the future lies with the obscure, the survivors, those who live biding their time in the the cracks of a disintegrating society.

In the early 1980s Brenton was notorious for his long play *The Romans in Britain*, which had its premiere at the National Theatre in 1981. It is controversial because the invasion of Britain by the Romans is equated with the British "occupation" of Northern Ireland. Male nudity, graphic homosexual rape, and repeated obscenity on the stage resulted in the director of the play, Michael Bogdanov, being charged under the Sexual Offences Act of 1956. The production was attacked and defended in Parliament and in the press, arousing a greater popular interest in theater than Britain had seen in many years.

In 1989, Brenton published his first novel. According to Linda Taylor, writing in the *Times Literary Supplement, Diving for Pearls* is set in a "contemporary system that only respects money and power" and peopled by "a recognizable underworld of lefties, homosexuals, criminals, prostitutes and pimps, as well as the more insidious underworld of old school ties, Intelligence and politicians." Frank, the criminal employed by the British Secret Service to infiltrate the IRA by robbing banks for them, represents one of those underworlds while Cecily, the upper-middle-class woman who loves Frank, represents the other. Taylor points out that "the parallelism between varieties of nastiness makes [Brenton's] point. . . ." In this novel, she maintains, Brenton "manages to bring off some of the affronts and dislocations of his drama. . . . Brenton's sheer energetic bravado is impressive, and we are forced to recognize what he is getting at."

It has been said critically of Brenton that he is a politically committed playwright who cannot envisage change for the better and that he is something of an anomaly for being so. This is to ignore his rejection of easy utopian visions and his real efforts, albeit often through oversimplification, to elucidate the structures of political relationships.

The polemical character of his writing has not prevented Brenton from gaining official approbation for his work. In 1970 he received the John Whiting Award, and in the following years was given a bursary from the Arts Council of Great Britain for *Christie in Love*. He won the *Evening Standard* award in 1976 for *Weapons of Happiness*, and in 1985, the *London Standard* award and *Plays and Players* award for best new play for *Pravda: A Fleet Street Comedy*, a satire on contemporary British journalism which he wrote in collaboration with David Hare.

Reviewing *Hot Irons*, Brenton's collection of essays and diaries, in the *Times Literary Supplement*, Anne Varty commented that in one of the diaries, Brenton refers to himself as "'the stranger,' marking the self-conscious alienation which typifies his writing at home and abroad." She remarks, however, on Brenton's strenuous efforts to assist Michael Bogdonov and to fight censorship in general: "Brenton emerges from these pages as a writer whose compassion for his countrymen is matched only by his contempt for their government."

Brenton married Jane Margaret Fry in 1970. They have one son.

PRINCIPAL WORKS: *Published plays*—Revenge, 1969; Christie in Love and Other Plays, 1970; (with Howard Barker, David Hare, Stephen Poliakoff, et al.) Lay-By, 1972; Plays for Public Places (includes the one-act plays Gum and Goo, Wesley, Scott of the Antarctic) 1972; Hitler Dances, 1972; Magnificence, 1973; (with David Hare) Brassneck, 1974; The Churchill Play, 1974; Weapons of Happiness, 1976; Epsom Downs, 1977; Sore Throats and Sonnets of Love and Oppositions, 1979; Plays for the Poor Theatre, 1980; The Romans in Britain, 1980; Thirteenth Night, 1981; The Genius, 1983; (with Tunde Ikoli) Sleeping Policeman, 1984; Bloody Poetry, 1985; (with David Hare) Pravda, 1985; Brenton Plays: One. 1987; (with Tariq Ali) Moscow Gold, 1990; Berlin Bertie, 1992. *Unpublished plays* (with date of first production)—Ladder of Fools, 1965; Winter, Daddykins, 1965; It's My Criminal, 1966; A Sky-Blue Life, 1966; Gargantua, 1969; Fruit, 1970; How Beautiful With Badges, 1972; Measure For Measure (adaptation from Shakespeare) 1972; (co-author) England's Ireland, 1972; (with David Edgar) A Fart For Europe, 1972; The Screens (adaptation from Genet) 1973; Greenland, 1988; Berlin Bertie, 1992. *Poetry*—Notes from a Psychotic Journal and Other Poems, 1969. *As translator*—Bertol Brecht's Life of Galileo, 1980. *Fiction*—Diving For Pearls, 1989. *Essays*—Hot Irons, 1995.

ABOUT: Ansorge, P. Disrupting the Spectacle: Five Years of Experimental and Fringe Theatre in Britain, 1975; Boon, R. Brenton the Playwright, 1991; Contemporary Authors New Revision Series 33, 19 ; Contemporary Literary Criticism 31, 1985; Dahl, M. K. Political Violence in Drama, 1987; Dictionary of Literary Biography 13, 1982; Hayman, R. British Theatre Since 1955, 1979; Kerensky, O. The New British Drama: Fourteen Playwrights Since Osborne and Pinter, 1977; Mitchell, T. File on Brenton, 1988; Taylor, J. R. The Second Wave: British Drama for the Seventies, 1971; Worthen, W. B. Political Theatre: Staging the Spectacle, 1992. *Periodicals*—Chicago Tribune January 15, 1989; Drama 1981, 1985, 1989; Encounter January 1975; Harper's November 1985; Los Angeles Times April 6, 1984; Modern Drama June 1989; March 1990; September 1990; Nation August 13, 1973; July 12, 1986; New Society November 4, 1976; New Statesman July 4, 1980; October 24, 1980; July 10, 1981; New Theatre Quarterly November 1988; New York January 19, 1987; New York Times June 20, 1985; May 29, 1986; January 7, 1987; November 3, 1987; Newsweek May 1, 1989; Plays and Players February 1972; June 1974; September 1976; October 1979; November 19, 1983; December 1984; June 1985; August 1985; December 1985; Saturday Review July/August 1983; Sunday Times (London) May 19, 1974; November 26, 1978; Theater Spring 1981; Theater Journal March 1986; December 1987; Theatre Quarterly Summer 1979; Time June 10, 1985; Times (London) September 30, 1970; July 10, 1976; September 14, 1983; November 7, 1984; May 4, 1985; April 27, 1988; June 3, 1988; Times Literary Supplement March 30, 1984; May 17, 1985; September 12, 1988; June 23, 1989; October 5, 1990; April 24, 1992; July 7, 1995; World Literature Today Autumn 1981; Winter 1984.

BRIN, DAVID (October 6, 1950–), American science fiction writer and astrophysicist, was born in Glendale, California, the son of Herbert Brin, an editor, and Selma Brin, a teacher. Like his collaborator Gregory Benford, Brin brings impressive scientific credentials to his fiction, although he views his place in the scientific community with a modest eye and regards himself as more of a writer than a scientist. "I really don't consider myself to be a first-rate scientist," he told an interviewer in 1988. "I putter around the edges of subjects trying to point out things that I think some people have missed."

In 1972 Brin got his B. S. degree at the California Institute of Technology. His Ph.D. in applied physics and space science with a dissertation on comets and asteroids was awarded by the University of California, San Diego, in 1981. He worked as an electrical engineer in semiconductor device development from 1973 to 1977 and then as managing editor of the *Journal of the Laboratory of Comparative Human Cognition* from 1979 to 1980. From 1982 to 1985, Brin taught physics and writing at San Diego State University and was a postdoctoral research fellow at the California Space Institute, La Jolla, where he was a consultant for the U.S. space program. Since 1980 he has been a book reviewer and science editor for the Heritage Press in Los Angeles.

Among the modern writers Brin admires are Thomas Pynchon, Frederik Pohl, and Melvin Konner. He cites Aldous Huxley, James Joyce, and particularly Mark Twain as influences. Brin's first novel *Sundiver* introduces the unfolding universe of the Progenitors with its Five Galaxies inhabited by various races. The dominant races, the Patrons, claim to have been "Uplifted" by the Progenitors, the law-givers and first sapient species, who mysteriously disappeared long ago. This universe is ruled by zealots who make perpetual war and form entangling alliances to maintain the balance of power. In the novel, selective breeding and genetic engineering are supposed to uplift other species to higher status. "It has already begun with domesticated animals, such as cattle," Brin explains. "I wanted to explore the ethical problems involved in changing more sophisticated creatures such as dolphins or apes, to give them the capabilities to become fellow-citizens in our culture. Do we have the right to meddle with species that have their own dignity? These are serious ethical questions about this whole matter of uplift, of being patrons of a client species."

With the publication of *Startide Rising*, his second Uplift novel, Brin was catapulted to science fiction stardom; not only did it become a 1983 best-seller, . . . it swept both the Hugo

DAVID BRIN

and Nebula Awards the following year. *Startide Rising* traces the mission of the starship Streaker, with its crew of sapient dolphins, who communicate in language resembling haiku. Frank Catalano, in *Amazing* praised Brin's handling of the cetacean world: "a well-constructed dolphin psychology, society, and even religion that had me *believing* that's really how dolphins are."

Convinced that the "Universe" approach to writing is sometimes overused, Brin left the Progenitors to explore the realm of anomaly or parallel worlds in his third novel, *The Practice Effect.* A physicist becomes the first human to enter a parallel world. On the other side he finds Tatir, a feudal world where physical laws are different. Here objects do not wear out, but are improved by repeated use; this is called "practicing." Through this "practice effect" rough cloth becomes silk, primitive huts are turned into skyscrapers, and merchant signs proudly proclaim "Nothing New! All Old and Used!" "The conclusion of *The Practice Effect* is full of revelations," Donald L. Lawler wrote, "not the least of which is that Tatir is not an alternate world after all but rather a remotely distant earth future." Brin himself described the novel as a "light adventure-fantasy and romance. . . . a strict formula piece that was completely self-indulgent."

Brin's fourth novel *The Postman* is about a wandering storyteller who has survived a nuclear holocaust. After bandits steal his survival gear, he dons the uniform of a dead mail carrier and finds that the uniform is, as Gregory Frost of the *Washington Post Book World* points out, a

"symbol of civilization." Deciding to play the part, he tells the villagers he is there to establish mail service. He even begins carrying their letters, and, as he journeys west and other join him, his fictional position as an authority figure becomes a reality. The American Library Association recognized *The Postman* as a Best Book for Young Adults.

With the 1987 publication of *The Uplift War*, Brin returned to the universe of the Progenitors. The fate of the entire Five Galaxies is in jeopardy when the planet Garth, inhabited by humans and uplifted chimpanzees, is invaded by the Gubru, an arrogant birdlike race. The colonists are aided in their fight by the Tymbrimi, a race of practical joke lovers. As Tom Easton points out in *Analog Science Fiction/Science Fact,* "humans and neochimps and Tymbrimi together defeat the Gubru and score massive points in the Uplift culture with the aid of one of the grandest jokes in galactic history."

Brin's next novel *Earth*, takes place in the year 2038 on an Earth devastated by ecological irresponsibility, a world in which endangered animals cling to life in genetic laboratories and the greenhouse effect has made sunglasses and skin creams a necessity. A microscopic black hole has dropped into the Earth's core and the planet could be destroyed within two years. While scientists desperately look for a solution, the ultimate question is raised: Is the salvation of the Earth dependent on the extinction of the human race?

Glory Season introduces a planet dominated by women, most of them clones of their mothers. Men are "practically another species," used for such tasks as labor and breeding. "A man writing about an avowedly feminist society, . . . Brin has worked out the details of Stratoin life with considerable ingenuity," the *New York Times Book Review* noted.

Brin has published articles and stories in scientific journals and popular science fiction magazines, as well as a novella titled *Dr. Pak's Pre-School.* In 1985 he won a Hugo Award for his short story "The Crystal Spheres," collected in *The River of Time*, and another Hugo in 1988 for the *Uplift War.* He makes his home in Los Angeles.

In a postscript to *Earthclan*, which brings both *Startide Rising* and *The Uplift War* under the same cover, Brin writes "Perhaps we *are* the first to talk and think and build and aspire, but we may not be the last. Others may follow us in this adventure. Someday we may be judged on just how well we served, when alone we were Earth's caretakers."

PRINCIPAL WORKS: *Novels*—Sundiver, 1980; Startide Rising, 1983; The Practice Effect, 1984; The Postman, 1985; (with Gregory Benford) Heart of the Comet, 1986; The Uplift War, 1987; Dr. Pak's Pre-School, 1988; Earth, 1990; Glory Season, 1993. *Short stories*—The River of Time, 1986.

ABOUT: Contemporary Authors New Revision Series 24, 1988; Contemporary Literary Criticism 34, 1985; Something About the Author 65, 1991; Twentieth-Century Science-Fiction Writers, 1986. *Periodicals*—Amazing January 1984; Analog Science Fiction/Science Fact November 1987; Minneapolis Tribune December 25, 1983; New York Times Book Review July 8, 1990; July 134, 1993; Publishers Weekly August 12, 1983; Washington Post Book World December 22, 1985.

RITA MAE BROWN

BROWN, RITA MAE (November 28, 1944–   ), American novelist, poet, essayist, and screenwriter, was born in Hanover, Pennsylvania, and is the adopted daughter of Ralph Brown, a butcher, and Julia (Buckingham) Brown, a bakery and mill worker. Although raised in a loving family, Brown had to face the taunts of other children. It is not surprising, as Carol M. Ward points out in her book *Rita Mae Brown*, that the "themes of adoption, of finding one's place in a community, of coming home are important components of Brown's fiction."

In 1955 the family moved from York, Pennsylvania to Fort Lauderdale, Florida, where Brown graduated from Fort Lauderdale High School. She entered the University of Florida, but her scholarship was revoked in 1964 due to her involvement in the civil rights movement and the accusation that she was a lesbian. She hitchhiked to New York City and for a time lived in an abandoned car with a gay African-American man and a cat named Baby Jesus. Brown worked as a waitress and won a scholarship to New York University. She studied English and the classics, taking her B.A. in 1968. She also studied film at the School of Visual Arts, earning a certificate in cinematography.

Brown's years in New York were years of continuing activism as a feminist lesbian. She helped form the Student Homophile League at N.Y.U. and Columbia University, as well as New York City's first women's center. She was co-founder of the Radicalesbians and a theater group called the Feminist Repertory and Experiment Ensemble or FREE. "Brown disliked the student anti-war protesters and the self-righteous whites in the civil rights movement," Ward wrote. "She preferred to work on the grass roots level for feminist causes—establishing day care centers, schools, health care, and other services for women in the community."

In 1969 Brown became a photography editor. Her growing involvement with "radical lesbian separatism," however, took her to Washington D.C. in 1971. There she was an organizing member of the Furies, a feminist separatist commune, whose various members would make a significant impact on the course of feminist thought. From 1971 to 1972 she lectured in sociology at Federal City College. She was also a research fellow at the Institute for Policy Studies, where she later earned her Ph.D. in political science. Already a provocative essayist, she published political, feminist, and personal pieces in such forums as *RAT*, the *Ladder*, *Quest: A Journal of Feminist Liberation* (of which she was a founding editor), and the *Furies*. Twenty of her essays were later collected under the title *A Plain Brown Rapper*. Martha Chew, in *Southern Quarterly*, wrote: "The essays are important, not just as history and personal biography, but as ideology." Chew pointed out that "many of the essays offer perceptive insights into class divisions and other artificial categories dividing human beings," and concluded that they "reveal the intellectual basis of Brown's concern with problems of class, race, and gender categories that her fiction explores in the lives of Southern women and in the context of the Southern environment in which Brown grew up." *A Plain Brown Rapper* also details the reasons Brown was expelled from the Furies in 1972.

Brown was still with the collective when she published her first collection of poetry, *The Hand That Cradles the Rock*. It is not surprising that the poems reflect her radical feminist positions, as Ward points out: "Instead of the traditional female role as mother, ruling the world through procreation, modern woman must gain political power through activism or even through violence, if necessary. She criticizes the patriarchal system of institutionalized sexism for its oppression of the human spirit. . . . women are identified with nature, while men are defined by images of death, decay, and destruction." In *The New Lost Feminist: The Right Panel* Brown writes: "How this beast follows us / His leprous shadow blending with our own / And we fall to fighting among ourselves / Clawing the silk cheeks of other women." The poem ends with a tome of sadness and urgency: "Women, womenlimping on the edges of the History of Man / Crippled for centuries and dragging the heavy emptiness / Past submission and sorrow to forgotten and unknown selves. / It's time to break and run." In *The Arrogance of Immortality*, however, there is a touching melancholy: "The difference between / My little cat / And I / Is / That I / Know / I am going to die."

Ward describes the next phase of Brown the poet: "After this diverse volume of political diatribe, feminist anger, and Latin satirical influence . . . Brown's second volume of poetry explores the dimensions of romantic love." The poems are now more intimate and personal, for as Ward points out they were "inspired by Brown's relationship with a specific woman, the actress Alexis Smith."

It was Smith who encouraged Brown to write fiction; ready for a change from the polemical "fog," Brown started the creative process that had been "gnawing at her insides trying to get out." In her book *Starting from Scratch: A Different Writers' Manual*, she states: "I wanted my novel to be so witty that even Republicans would be forced to enjoy it. I think my reach exceeded my grasp—it still does—but *Rubyfruit Jungle* was an energetic beginning."

Rubyfruit Jungle, a semi-autobiographical coming-of-age novel, was enormous critical and commercial success. Rejected by all the major New York hardcover publishers, it was published in 1973 by the small feminist Daughters Press. It gained a cult following and, 70,000 copies later, was bought by Bantam; it has since sold in the millions and has been translated into almost every major language. "Despite the novel's overtly gay and lesbian polemics," Ward writes, "mainstream success was made possible by the book's humor, its daring heroine, and its reliance on traditional popular culture narrative formulae." Michael Bronski, in *Gay & Lesbian Literature*, calls it a cross between *The Adventures of Huckleberry Finn* and a lesbian *Tropic*

of Cancer with Brown serving up "her pungent social critique with bawdy humor."

Rubyfruit Jungle recounts the experiences of Molly Bolt who, as described by Bertha Harris in the *Village Voice*, was "born female, gay, illegitimate, poor, unloved, and white trash—but with enough courage, humor, and grit to get her from nowhere . . . to everywhere." *New Boston Review* reviewer Shelly Temchin Henge wasn't surprised to find that Mark Twain is Brown's favorite author: "Imagine, if you will, Tom Sawyer, only smarter; Huckleberry Finn, only foul-mouthed, female, and lesbian, and you have an idea of Molly Bolt." Molly narrates the story of her childhood in Pennsylvania and her family's move to Fort Lauderdale, Florida, where she ignores the boundaries of racial segregation and is defiant of sexual stereotypes. She is expelled from the University of Florida for political activism and continues her sexual odyssey and search for identity in New York, where two of her romantic interests are a black woman and an older white woman. Molly's experiences in the world of publishing and film are recounted, as well as her reconciliation with her mother and her return to New York at the end.

Writing in the *International Journal of Women's Studies*, Leslie Fishbein described the novel as "fundamentally amoral without being self-reflective about the consequences of its amorality." Fishbein also expressed concern that Brown substituted one kind of stereotype for another, pointing out that here everyone in a heterosexual marriage is miserable, heterosexual intercourse is on the dull side, and "Motherhood is portrayed almost as if it were a disease." Brown's lesbians, when they are portrayed in groups, are "viewed as butches and femmes, as sexual predators as in the bar and party scenes." Ultimately Fishbein found *Rubyfruit Jungle* "completely narcissistic and selfish. . . . an utterly individualistic tale that has no social consciousness or sense of commitment to a lesbian community." Bertha Harris, however, called it an "American primitive, whose predecessors have dealt only with male heroes. Although Molly Bolt is not a real woman, she is at least the first real *image* of heroine in the noble savage, leatherstocking, true-blue bullfighting tradition in this country's literature."

In 1973 Brown became a visiting member of the faculty of Goddard College in Plainfield, Vermont. She also helped with the planning of Sagaris College, an independent feminist institution, serving on the board of directors. In 1976 she published her second novel *In Her Day*. In the *Village Voice* Terry Curtis Fox called it the "story of two generations of lesbian women—a middle-aged, semi-closeted, premovement art historian and a hyper-politicized waitress/activist—who meet . . . and try to reconcile their up-and-down lives." Fox felt that Brown seemed to have "lost her style along with her theme," and declared that "if *Rubyfruit Jungle* succeeds as an outsider's first novel, *In Her Day* fails as an insider's second." In *Ms.* magazine Joan Larkin wrote that she missed the "complexity, the risks, the irreducible paradoxes in our human experiences that must be part of the novelist's seeing us whole in our time and place."

Brown was aware that she stood in danger of being stereotyped a "lesbian author," and bristles at the thought. "Look, calling me a lesbian writer is like calling Baldwin a black writer," she told Patricia Holt of *Publishers Weekly*. "I say no; he is not: he is a great writer." She went on: "My whole message is that we're *not* different. Sure, there are some things different about being gay or poor, or black or old, but they're not so monumental as to be impediments to human communications. Next time anybody calls me a lesbian writer I'm going to knock their teeth in. I'm a writer and I'm a woman and I'm from the South and I'm alive, and that is that."

In 1978 Brown returned to the South, moving to Charlottesville, Virginia; that same year she published her third novel, *Six of One*. Moving backward and forward in time between 1909 and 1980, Brown's revisionist history focuses on the women of Runnymede, a small town which includes two sisters who have been feuding for seventy-one years. "Disenfranchised and powerless, women have always been on the fringes of male history, often indirectly the victims of male actions," Carol M. Ward explained. "Brown attempts to correct that imbalance by looking at how women's lives are affected by the history that men create and by giving voice to the unrecorded history that women themselves create in the course of their daily lives." Liz Mednick, of the *New York Arts Journal*, quickly tired of Brown's unrelenting witticism: "The wise-cracks are fast enough, but no sooner sent off than they stop, drop, fizzle and fade into the next spurious remark." Mednick also found the story rather biased: "Brown's goal it appears is to show how wise, witty, wonderful and cute women really are. . . . Brown makes her men as flat as the paper on which they're scrawled." However, John Fludas, writing in the *Saturday Review*, found *Six of One* a "bright and worthy successor" to *Rubyfruit Jungle*. "If at times the comedy veers toward slapstick," he wrote, "and if there are spots when the prose just grazes the beauty of the human movement . . . the novel loses none of its warmth." *Bingo*, a sequel to *Six of One*, was published in 1988.

In 1979 Brown began a long and ultimately stormy romantic relationship with tennis star Martina Navratilova. With the break-up of the relationship in 1981, Brown moved to Los Angeles and worked as a scriptwriter. *Southern Discomfort*, her first novel without a lesbian theme, was published in 1983. "With her humor and outrageousness in tact," Ward wrote, "Brown manages in this romp through Southern history at the turn of the century to maintain her assault on social hypocrisy and sexual restrictions without direct reference to her lesbian identity." Brown sets her story in Montgomery, Alabama, in 1918 and 1928; her protagonist is Hortensia Reedmuller Banastre, wife, mother of two sons, and bastion of white society, who has an affair and a child with a sixteen-year-old black man. A scandal is created, as well as a daughter who is caught between two worlds. There are also subplots and, according to the *American Book Review*'s Charlotte M. Meyer, the "now-familiar Rita Mae Brown twists . . . incest, transvestism, adultery, homosexuality, miscegeny, filicide, suicide, alcoholism et al." Nevertheless, Meyer found it a "funny, vigorous, irreverent novel, as the earlier ones," although she felt "it needed more careful craftsmanship."

The 1983 novel *Sudden Death* was another departure for Brown. It is dedicated to sportswriter Judy Cook Lacy who encourages her to write a novel about tennis; shortly before Lacy's death from cancer Brown promised to do so. The plot concerns lesbianism and women's professional tennis. Elisabeth Jakab, in the *New York Times Book Review*, did not feel Brown was at her best: "The world of tennis does not seem to be congenial terrain for her, and her usually natural and easy style seems cramped." In the *Village Voice* Amy Wilentz quipped that "reading the religio-soap operatic finale, one is tempted to conclude that Brown had just one too many Martinas."

In 1986 Brown made a strong comeback with her sweeping Civil War novel *High Hearts*, in which a young woman cuts her hair, puts on men's clothing, and goes into battle with her husband. In *Ms.* Diane Cole called it an "entertaining historical tale that presents the war between men and women as a subplot to the War Between the States," and "at its best . . . a kind of feminist *Gone With the Wind*."

Brown entered the mystery field with the publication of *Wish You Were Here*, *Rest in Pieces*, and *Murder at Monticello, or, Old Sins*; her cat Sneaky Pie Brown is listed as co-author. Brown's leading human character is Mary Minor "Harry" Haristeen, the youngest postmistress in Crozet, Virginia, history; however, it is the anthropomorphic animals, especially Harry's cat

Mrs. Murphy, who plays key roles in solving the crimes. "The animal characters, in fact, are as clearly drawn as those of their masters," Mark Gerson pointed out in his *Quill and Quire* review of *Wish You Were Here*. "It could be cloying, but it's not. . . . All in all it's funny, original, and clever."

In her preface to *Rita Mae Brown*, Carol M. Ward stated that "although her novels, essays, poetry, and screenplays are not necessarily the most polished in terms of their artistic style, her treatment of the themes of contemporary feminism, lesbianism, and Southern identity makes her an important and influential author of her times."

Rita Mae Brown makes her home in Charlottesville, Virginia.

PRINCIPAL WORKS: *Novels*—Rubyfruit Jungle, 1973; In Her Day, 1976; Six of One, 1978; Southern Discomfort, 1982; Sudden Death, 1983; High Hearts, 1986; Bingo, 1988; Wish You Were Here, 1990; Rest in Pieces, 1992; Venus Envy, 1993; Dolley, 1994; Murder at Monticello, or, Old Sins, 1994. *Poetry*—The Hand That Cradles the Rock, 1971; songs to a Handsome Women, 1973. *Nonfiction*—A Plain Brown Rapper, 1976; Starting From Scratch: A Different Kind of Writers' Manual, 1988. *As translator*—Hrotsvitha: Six Medieval Latin Plays, 1971.

ABOUT: Contemporary Authors 1994; Contemporary Literary Criticism 18, 1981; 43, 1987; 79, 1994; Contemporary Authors New Revision Series 11 (1984); Current Biography 1986, 1987; Daly, B.O. and Reddy, N.T. (eds.) Narrating Mothers: Theorizing Maternal Subjectivites, 1991; Dynes, W.R. and Donaldson, S. (eds.) Homosexual Themes in Literary Studies, 1992; Gay & Lesbian Literature, 1994; Prenshaw, P.W. (ed.) Women Writers of the Contemporary South, 1984; Suleiman, S.R. (ed.) The Female Body in Western Culture, 1986; Ward, Carol M. Rita Mae Brown, 1993. *Periodicals*—American Book Review January/ February 1983; International Journal of Women March/April 1984; Los Angeles Times Book Review November 27, 1988; Ms. April 10, 1977; June 12, 1986; New Boston Review April/May 1979; New York Arts Journal November/December 1978; New York Times Book Review June 19, 1983; Publishers Weekly October 2, 1978; Quill and Quire December 1990; Saturday Review September 30, 1978; Southern Quarterly Fall 1983; Village Voice April 4, 1974; September 12, 1977; July 19, 1983.

*BUFALINO, GESUALDO** (November 15, 1920–), Italian novelist, essayist, and poet, writes (in Italian) [1993]: "I was born in Comiso (Ragusa) [Sicily], in 1920 to Biagio Bufalino, a blacksmith, and Maria Elia, a housewife. I began my studies in Comiso and fell passionately in love with writing at a very early age. I secretly

°boo fah LEE noh

GESUALDO BUFALINO

began to compose verses when I was ten and I continued until and after the war.

"My tumultuous and omnivorous reading habits were matched by my relentless experience as a cinematic spectator; an experience which I considered vital to escape from the provincial Sicilian life, and which taught me about Europe and the world.

"My school accomplishments (particularly, a first prize in Latin prose for high school students bestowed upon me by the Institute of Roman Studies in 1939) encouraged me to attend the university, but I was drafted into the Italian Army in 1942 and had to interrupt my studies. As part of my baggage, I brought along a big notebook of verses, a translation of Baudelaire (from Italian into French—to roughly recapture the rhythm of the original text, which was impossible to find in Sicilian bookstores), Montale, and Dante.

"On September 8, 1943, I found myself in Sacile, as a newly appointed second lieutenant. Talen prisoner by the Germans, I managed to escape and hide at first with a family of peasants and later in Scandiano (Emilia), where I stayed until the winter of 1944, when I contracted tuberculosis and had to be admitted to the local hospital. After Liberation, I went to a sanatorium, "La Rocca," situated between Monreale and Palermo. There I remained until February 1947, when I was fully recovered. Returning to my family, I took up private tutoring and acted as a substitute teacher until I was appointed to a permanent position in 1951. I taught humanities in a high school for twenty-five years. I also continued to write and, with the encouragement of a friend, Angelo Romano, I worked for various newspapers. I soon withdrew, however, from all public engagements and publishing chances. During these years I translated Baudelaire (from French into Italian, this time!) and Toulet.

"At the beginning of the seventies, I completed a novel *Diceria dell'untore* [*The Plague-Sower*], a kind of a fable which recounts my stay at the sanatorium. In 1978, I discovered some old photographs from the 19th century in an attic. I decided to organize an exhibition and write the introduction to the catalogue. The publisher Sellerio put them together as a book, *Comiso ieri* [Comiso yesterday], which I prefaced. Invited to submit my manuscripts, I reluctantly sent *Diceria*, which was published in 1981 and received the Campiello Prize. That same year, I lost my father. In 1982 I met and befriended Leonardo Sciascia, and I got married [to Giovanna Leggio] in December. During the past decade, I have published many books, among them essays, poems, novels, etc. With *Le menzogne della notte* [*Lies of the Night*], translated into sixteen languages, I won the Strega Priza in 1988. I currently live in Comiso in voluntary isolation."

When Gesualdo Bufalino's most celebrated book, *The Plague-Sower*, was published in Italy in 1981, it became the major literary event of the year, winning the Campiello Prize. A high school teacher—until his retirement in 1976—who had lived secluded from the literary world, the author captivated the Palermo publisher Sellerio with a photography book on his hometown. Eventually, he agreed to surrender a manuscript he had begun to write in 1950, completed in 1971, and subjected to several revisions.

Feverish, vibrant, sensuous, baroque, steeped in an atmosphere of hyperbole and excess, intemperance and passion; a striking blend of irony and theatricality: these are some of the distinguishing features cited by the reviewers of *The Plague-Sower*. The eminent author and critic Pietro Citati writes about Bufalino: "For him, only *the book* exists . . . The book is the supreme object, which encloses actual life—that kid who is crossing the street, that cloud that is shining under the rays of the sun—and fantastic life, that which is imagined, unreal, impossible; and such a mixture fascinates him like the most inebriating drink. . . . To read is to renounce living."

Thus literature eludes empirical existence. The artist stages a kind of personal resistance to the raw materials of life and stresses the limits of purposive action. As Bufalino writes in an autobiographical portrait in the *Antologia del "Campiello" 1981*:

> My life is like many others, two or three serious diseases, two or three half friends, a melancholic disposition tempered with bursts of hilarity; a Christian faith, fickle and atheistic, unfit to understand whether the universe is salvation or metastasis, grace or damnation; a hatred for History: paved with ideological fossils, an inert series of errors; a transport for what lasts and endures—places, sound jargons, honest customs, firm handshakes—in my secluded region. In literature, a love for the untrue and music, provided they are rooted in the fantastic and geometric dimension of suffering and memory.

Bufalino's literary production is remarkable for his self-integrated conception of life, and also because of his subject matter, Sicily, is so richly evoked through sensory perceptions: light, sound, and odor. In his first novel, he offers a poetic tribute to the memories of Sicily, her people and her traditions. The Mediterranean island becomes a mythic place where stories are construed in the expressive power of the word, a carefully designed rhetoric. As Bufalino explains in his "Instructions for the Use" of *The Plague-Sower*: "I must confess that the first chapter I wrote (it is not the first in the definitive order, and there is no need to say which one it is) was born of a serious game, the challenge of finding plausible interconnections among fifty words chosen beforehand for their common tone, color, and evocative charge."

Bufalino's constant preoccupation is with writing, an art he has mastered after a long apprenticeship in the skills of reading—primarily the work of Baudelaire, Proust, Montale, and Dante. While it maintains a certain ironic distance, his style—sometimes described as baroque—is whimsical, transparent, objective, and yet utterly personal. The plot of *The Plague-Sower* is typical of Bufalino's economy of style and thematic materials. In 1946, in a sanatorium near Palermo, an estranged group of people find themselves bound together by disease and destiny. All survivors from the war, they are kept waiting in the antechamber of death. In this condition of oblivion, life pulsates with a monotonous, wearisome beat. As the narrator-protagonist recalls at the end of chapter 2, "Ah yes, those were unhappy days, the happiest of my life." Bufalino conjures up extraordinary characters: Il Gran Magro (Longbones), a doctor / director who orchestrates the spectacle of life and death; Father Vittorio, the military chaplain; Sebastiano, who throws himself down a spiral staircase; Angelo, for whom "death is a mere screen of smoke between the living and the others"; Marta, the mysterious ballerina whom the protagonist passionately loves.

At the end, we are told why the protagonist is the only survivor:

A naked life awaited me, a nothingness of predictable days, without a sparkle or voice. I had to come out from the eye of my selfhood in order to be one of the many men in the street who humanly administer the petty wisdom of their breath and years. Like a retired actor putting back into the closet the bloody vestments of King Richard or Caesar, I would lay aside my buskins, and the soliloquies of the hero that I had pretended to be, in a corner of my memory. Perhaps this was why I had been granted a pardon, why I alone, and no one else, had survived the massacre: to bear witness to, if not denounce, a rhetoric and pity.

The Plague-Sower was followed by a number of remarkable books: the autobiographical prose of *Museo d'ombre* (Museum of shadows, 1982), a fantastic-historical portrait of Comiso and its vanishing past, and *Argo il cieco* (1984, *Blind Argus*), a story about love and memory, an elegant diary of the painfulness of aging; the short stories of *L'uomo invaso e altre invenzioni* (The man possessed and other inventions, 1986); the verses of *L'amaro miele* (Bitter honey, 1982); a collection of aphorisms, *Il malpensante* (The evil-minded, 1987); and a theatrical piece *La panchina* (The bench, 1989). Bufalino's essays and journalistic articles are collected in two volumes, *Cere perse* (The lost wax, 1985) and *La luce e il lutto* (Light and mourning, 1988). Among his later major works are *Calende greche* (On the Greek Calends, 1990) and *Qui pro quo* (1991). Although Bufalino's work has been translated into several languages, the first English edition, *The Plague-Sower*, appeared only in 1988, with a preface by Leonardo Sciascia.

In 1988 Bufalino returned to fiction with the widely acclaimed *Le menzogne della notte* (*Lies of the Night*), awarded Italy's most prestigious literary prize, the Strega. The novel, rich with intellectual subtlety, is especially interesting for its remarkable use of wordplay. *Lies of the Night* is set in an inhospitable island-fortress where four political prisoners—a baron, a poet, a soldier, and a student—await death for plotting against the Bourbon monarchy. On the eve of their execution, the governor proposes a last-minute reprieve: if one of them reveals the identity of their leader, they can all go free. The prisoners sit through the night telling stories of love and war, loyalty and revenge. As they see the scaffold being set up, each searches into his past for a memory that will give meaning to the approaching death. Bufalino's storytelling is deeply rooted in such narratives as Boccaccio's *Decameron* and the tales of the *Arabian Nights*. "This is fabulist territory," wrote the London *Sunday Times*, "Alexandre Dumas retold by Italo Calvino . . . this is metafiction of the most

ancient and honorable brand." M. J. Fitzgerald, in the *New York Times Book Review*, also pointed out Bufalino's debt to *The Thousand and One Nights*, but remarked, "The novel . . . is also linked to modernist fiction that is concerned with our conception of time, with the nature of history and the individual's perception of events, with the relationship between autobiography and fiction." Fitzgerald felt that the essence of the stories has to do with the revelation of "one unequivocal truth." This truth, according to Fitzgerald, "whether they betray their leader or not will rescue each of these men." "[N]one of the stories is quite what it seems," Peter Hainsworth commented in the *Times Literary Supplement* in 1990. "But the mystery is as much the mystery of life itself. Bufalino creates a remarkable atmosphere of death, while simultaneously instilling a sense of corrupt vitality, which is heightened by the intelligence and baroque sophistication of his style. All this is characteristic of his work as a whole." He added that in "Patrick Creagh's translation . . . the novel retains the quality of a political and metaphysical whodunit, written by a doleful, humorous and exasperated man of letters, who . . . can, like his characters, see the last morning approaching."

Gesualdo Bufalino's work stems from tradition peculiar to Sicilian narrative from Pirandello to Lampedusa and Sciascia. The theater of the world is played on anguish. It is a game: the labyrinth and the chessboard. "One writes," he says in *Cere perse*, "to give life to the desert; not to be alone in the voluptuousness of being alone; to divert from the temptation of nothingness or at least to postpone it."

PRINCIPAL WORKS IN ENGLISH TRANSLATION: (tr. S. Sartarelli) The Plague-Sower, 1988; (tr. P. Creagh) Blind Argus, or The Fables of Memory, 1989; (tr. P. Creagh) Lies of the Night (in U.K.: Night's Lies), 1991.

ABOUT: Barberi Squarotti, G. (ed.) Gli eredi di Verga, 1984; Nigro, S. Contemporary World Writers, 2nd ed., 1993; Who's Who in Italy 1988. Scrivere la Sicilia: Vittirino e oltre, 1985; Zago, N. Gesualdo Bufalino: La figura e l'opera, 1987. Zappulla Muscara, S. (ed.) Narratori siciliani del secondo dopoguerra, 1990. *Periodicals*—Financial Times June 23, 1990; Independent June 30, 1989; June 9, 1990; Listener June 21, 1990; Literary Review July 1990; Los Angeles Times April 25, 1991; New York Winter 1991; New York Times April 17, 1991; New York Times Book Review October 30, 1988; May 19, 1991; Observer June 17, 1990; Sunday Times (London) July 1, 1990; Tablet September 8, 1990; Times (London) June 21, 1990; Times Literary Supplement October 9, 1981; October 7, 1988; October 12, 1990; World Literature Today Autumn 1982; Summer 1983.

BURUMA, IAN (December 28, 1951–), British journalist and novelist, was born in the Hague, Netherlands, the son of Sytze Leonard, an attorney, and Gwendolyn Margaret Schlesinger, an Englishwoman. He was educated at Leiden University, from which he received an M.A. in Chinese history and literature, and lived for many years in Japan, first as a student of Japanese cinema and then as an editor and writer for the *Far Eastern Economic Review*. He has also worked as the foreign editor of *The Spectator*. He married his Japanese wife, Sumie Tani, on April 31, 1981. He has been a prolific contributor of political and cultural commentary on Japan, Korea, Burma (Myanmar), the Philippines and other Asian countries to numerous Western publications, including the *Economist*, the *New York Times, New York Times Magazine, Harper's* magazine, and the *New York Review of Books*.

Fluent in Japanese and thoroughly conversant with Japan's social mores and popular culture, Buruma, became known as one of the leading Western commentators on that country with the publication of *Behind the Mask*. The subtitle of *Behind the Mask*, "On Sexual Demons, Sacred Mothers, Transvestites, Gangsters, Drifters and Other Japanese Cultural Heroes," elucidates its subject matter. Writing from extensive acquaintance with Japanese films, comics, popular fiction, pornography, and child-rearing, Buruma offers an insider's account: "This book is an attempt to draw a picture of the Japanese as they imagine themselves to be, and as they would like themselves to be." His analysis, which takes into account both the visions of individual artists and the pulp entertainment created for the masses, is undertaken in the conviction that all art reveals something of the culture that created it: "Few Americans are really like John Wayne," he observes, "but many would like to be, which is significant."

In *Behind the Mask*, therefore, Buruma traces the influence on Japanese culture of Japanese heroes, both the mythical, religious, and historical figures who first exemplified Japanese values and the popular heroes of contemporary society. He scrutinizes the cultural role of women as well, believing that the traditional and honored roles of the Japanese man have forced women into two postures that are both opposed and complementary: the mother and prostitute. Buruma examines a third traditional role in popular entertainment, falling between the male and female roles, the transvestite, the paradigm of feminine behavior in which "cultural sex roles are most clearly defined." Many popular theater figures are men who play women's roles. He judges Japanese society to be not only self-

IAN BURUMA

consciously modern—in many superficial respects a far more advanced society than some European nations that have retained unbroken links with their cultural traditions—but also strangely anachronistic, "in many ways closer to the European Middle Ages." The achievement of this book, to use Buruma's own metaphors, is that it looks behind the mask of Japan's Western image to discover a mirror of universal human behavior that is disturbing to the outsider, especially one who seeks the accepted idea of Japan as a highly ordered and civilized society. "It is," Edward Seidensticker wrote in the *New Republic*, "a lively book about what we may call the dirty side of Japan, more interesting to some of us than the pretty side that has been so much more widely publicized by the Japanese information services and by those of us who write about Japan."

Those reviewers who, like Buruma himself, were Westerners well-acquainted with Japanese life, praised *Behind the Mask* for its originality and truthfulness. Dorinne Kondo in the *New York Times Book Review* was the only reviewer to question the justice of Buruma's portrait: "instead of complex, sensitive analysis, we are left with exaggerated portrayals of the Japanese as alternately irrational and slavishly conforming, a group of human automatons who, beneath their programmed politeness, harbor proclivities for lurid sex and violence." James Kirkup's *Times Literary Supplement* review, on the other hand, praises Buruma for his "sharp, unsparing reflections on the underside of Japanese society," especially because these counter Lafcadio

Hearn's "dreamy aetheticism." Joan Mellen, who has written extensively on the Japanese, singled out Buruma's analysis of the male character for praise in her *Nation* review and found his book notable for its revelations about the importance of violent pornography in a society where aggressive impulses are rigorously suppressed in daily life. Writing in the *New Statesman,* Justin Wintle allowed for a trace of "scabrous journalism" in Buruma's writing that results in an analysis of "limited scope," but could think "of no other account that will tell the reader so much in so little space."

In *God's Dust,* a composite portrait of modern Southeast Asia, Buruma describes visits to Burma, Thailand, the Philippines, Malaysia, Singapore, Taiwan, South Korea, and Japan. As D. J. Enright pointed out in the *Times Literary Supplement,* a sense of vertigo is the inevitable result of covering so much territory so rapidly, and the reader is left with mere glimpses of disparate societies. These were gathered, however, with a view to exposing the effects of change in a variety of social and political circumstances that range from extremely authoritarian (Singapore and Burma) to relatively liberal (Malaysia and Thailand). As in his earlier book, Buruma is out to challenge cliché, especially the assumption that the "real" East is to be found in rural settings away from the Westernized cities. This misconception, Buruma argues in his preface, is actually based on two false premises: that only in the cities has Western influence been deeply felt and that the Eastern character is in some way more "spiritual" than the Western. His challenge to the accepted view is based on the discovery that materialism appeals to both city and country dwellers, and that Asian peoples in general welcome improvements in their standard of living no matter what their religious beliefs. Although his book is composed of brief episodes and reveals its origin as a collection of magazine feature articles, it has the unity imposed by a good travel writer who is guided by a single thematic interest: "What has the process of Westernization brought about in Southeast Asian societies?"

Buruma also begins in *God's Dust* to explore political questions that he takes up later in a European context when writing about the effects of the collapse of the Soviet empire. Material progress, he observes, brings about a "crisis of identity" that is particularly acute in many Asian countries that have undergone a much more rapid process of modernization that Europe's. The old social order has been challenged often with violent results, and many of the scenes Buruma describes are those of extreme cultural dislocation in which new influences are mixed with old

traditions. The necessity to experiment, to redefine themselves, to find meaning in a world of conflicting values has made the capitalist countries of Southeast and East Asia extraordinarily dynamic. They are alive in a way that old Europe, complacently bearing the burden of its long, miraculously continuous history, is not.

God's Dust examines numerous clashes—and collaborations—between Western material progress and Asian tradition; it raises but does not answer Buruma's question about what happens to ethnic identity when it encounters modern machines and ideas of social progress. The result is not inevitably a loss of the spiritual or cultural values on which a sense of ethnic identity was based. Even when there is a loss, Buruma believes that the process of interchange between East and West cannot be arrested and may turn out to have more good consequences than bad: "Sealing off a culture from the corrupting influences of the outside world has a somewhat similar effect to shutting young girls up in a segregated boarding school—they fall in love with the first bit of corruption that comes their way." This point helps to underscore Buruma's own cultural neutrality: "It is hard to say which is worse, the tackiness of Coca-Colonization or the peculiar flowers that grow in a culture artificially but imperfectly isolated from the modern world."

Buruma also finds a reason for his fascination with Asian countries in his personal history. Born Dutch, but writing in his mother's language, and spending a large part of his life in Asia, Buruma portrays himself as a person so thoroughly deracinated that he is indefatigably curious about "other people's loyalties": "I have always wanted to know what it feels like to be entirely and unselfconsciously at home in one country."

In *Playing the Game,* Buruma transfers his interests in cultural identity and the influence that nations can exert on each other to a first attempt at fiction. His setting is India, a country that he has visited as a journalist, and his protagonist is an English writer in pursuit of the biography of a great Indian cricketer, Ranjitsinhji, who became the star player of the English national team during the 1890s, then fought in the British Army during World War I, and, finally returned to his own country to assume his hereditary role as maharajah of a small princely state before India's independence. Buruma's theme, announced by his title with its echo of the jingoistic English public school tag "play up and play the game," is the question of ethnic versus national identity: can an Indian, even of princely rank become an Eglishman simply by mastering an English game? The answer that the writer discovers is as ambiguous as his subject: in encouraging their colonial subjects to "play the game," the English were offering an idealized version of themselves, even a parody of their own behavior, a fiction to which they and the Indian master cricketer subscribed.

As Michael Gorra observed in the *New York Times Book Review*, the novel "is a curious hybrid of genres"—half biography, and half travel book. The passages in which Buruma's hero searches out information about his subject employ the author's considerable skills in depicting unfamiliar places, whereas his efforts to conjure up an English milieu are, as all reviewers note, less successful. Gorra pins what he sees as the failings of the novel on the lack of self-perception of its cricketer hero: he "doesn't have much to say about the issues his very existence raises." Richard Davenport-Hines, in the *Times Literary Supplement* (1991), cited Buruma's inability "to make a virtue of the confusion between fact and fiction." John Banville, in the *New York Review of Books* (1991), found *Playing the Game* "one of those novels that flow through the mind cool and savorless as water yet leave behind a tenacious silt. The portrait of Ranji, with its melancholy and its sly suggestiveness, tells us more about imperialism than would a shelf full of political histories."

The same concern lies at the center of Buruma's journalism and his fiction—the observation of the complex influences that make up cultural and national identity. His 1994 book *The Wages of Guilt* examines the questions of guilt and responsibility for World War II in both Germany and Japan. "I had for many years wanted to write a book on how the Japanese saw their recent history," he told an interviewer for the *New York Times Book Review*. "Then I began to find out that . . . a lot of Japanese nationalism and militarism in postwar Japan had come from Germany." Serge Schmemann, in the *New York Times Book Review*, quotes from *The Wages of Guilt*: "There are no dangerous peoples; there are only dangerous situations, which are the result, not of laws of nature or history, or of national character, but of political arrangements." Schmemann adds, "there are bound to be those who disagree with . . . Buruma's identification of flawed 'political arrangements' as the prime culprit in the great atrocities of our century."

Michiko Kakutani commented in the *New York Times* that Buruma exaggerates Germany's guilt consciousness, while presenting Japan as the product of a "shame culture." She faulted him for equating the wartime behavior of Germany and Japan and considered that he diminishes "the magnitude and specificity of the

Holocaust by repeatedly comparing it . . . to atrocities committed by the Japanese . . . . " In the *New York Review of Books*, Gordon Craig remarked that the distinction between guilt and shame may have "limited usefulness explaining the difference between the two societies." Craig cited the emergence of neo-Nazism in Germany and the " sacralizing of Hiroshima" as evidence of the contradictions which may complicate concepts of national guilt and shame. Both Schmemann and Craig concluded that Buruma offers a reconciling view, in Schmemann's words, "not an absolution, but a faith that there is no fatally or permanently flawed nation."

PRINCIPAL WORKS: *Nonfiction*—(with D. Richie) The Japanese Tattoo, 1981; Behind the Mask: On Sexual Demons, Sacred Mothers, Transvestites, Gangsters, Drifters, and Other Japanese Cultural Heroes, 1984; Gods's Dust: A Modern Asian Journey, 1989; The Wages of Guilt: Memories of War in Germany and Japan, 1994. *Novels*—Playing the Game, 1991.

ABOUT: Contemporary Authors 128, 1989. *Periodicals*—American Spectator October 1989; Film Quarterly Fall 1985; London Review Books June 14, 1990; May 9, 1991; Nation November 10, 1984; New Republic August 13, 1984; New Statesman February 17, 1984; October 27, 1989; April 19, 1991; New York Review of Books September 28, 1989; November 21, 1991; July 14, 1994; New York Times July 1, 1994; New York Times Book Review September 16, 1984; July 9, 1989; August 4, 1991; June 26, 1994; Times Literary Supplement March 9, 1984; October 6, 1989; April 5, 1991; Washington Post Book World May 6, 1984; June 25, 1989.

BUSCH, FREDERICK (August 1, 1941–), American novelist, short-story writer, and essayist, writes: "I was born in Brooklyn, New York, the first of two children of immigrants' children. So I'm a real American, pulsing the blood of Russians and Austrians, the descendant of a carpenter and a baker—meant from before my birth, I guess, to labor at structure and design, to compose ingredients and then turn on the heat. I continue to think of writing as intensely effortful manual labor that my grandfathers would respect.

"My father, a decorated veteran of the Tenth Mountain Division, which saw bloody action in the Second World War, was a well-known international lawyer. My mother taught biology in high school in Brooklyn, then taught at the college level, and wrote childen's books aimed at education in ecology and outdoor lore, still her occupation. My brother Eric, born in 1946, is an artist and a lawyer. He and I recall our father's father, in his dying days, writing poem after

FREDERICK BUSCH

poem: we had, I think, little choice but to be artists.

"I always wrote. I always read passionately—by which I mean deeply: by which I mean with a headlong, careless giving of the self to language and story. I was one of those kids who fell into what he read, who read adult books when he was too young to understand them, and who read—who still reads—enough escapist stuff (*John Carter of Mars, Navy Diver*, latterly detective novels and thrillers) to project me so far from actuality that I return, sometimes, to plan a seminar lesson, or answer a letter, or feed the dogs, only by virtue of strong effort.

"I was eight or so, I think, and in my room—a child of the rising middle class, I had a serene and spacious room of my own into which I could shut myself with all the books I asked for: how privileged I still feel!—I was reading *Robinson Crusoe*. In some passage I have not, on rereadings, been able to recover, Crusoe puts down a crucial implement—a knife, I think. I asked my parents if they knew the moment in question. I walked to the public library and returned with three other editions of the novel. I was discovered kneeling on the floor of my room, all four volumes open to the critical passage. You see, I explained to my parents, it doesn't say he ever picks it up. He might need it later. That faith in texts, that belief in the entire world Defoe had made for Crusoe (and me), that lust to reside in his world, and the sense of the need to take care of the details: they were—they are—the writers' insignia. If one cannot believe in an actual implement, available from a fictive world, one isn't an imaginative writer.

"I wrote bad poetry from the time I could write. I wrote prose narratives at Muhlenberg, and they turned to stories when I was a graduate student (for a year) at Columbia, replacing the long—the endless—bad poems I inflicted on editors and on women I loved. While I was supposed to be in Lionel Trilling's classroom, I was in my dim apartment on 114th Street, imitating the fiction of Bernard Malamud and William Faulkner. I was going to school in Hemingway. I was committed not to English poetry of the seventeenth century but to prose fiction. After Judy and I were married, in 1963, I typed while she slept; it seemed appropriate, since she worked while I from time to time only sought jobs (that, once I did land them, I quit or was fired from). In our one-room flat in the courtyard off Morton Street in Greenwich Village, while Judy lay on the bed that took up a quarter of the apartment, I sat on the edge of the bathtub and worked on the typewriter I had set on the closed toilet. In that apartment, and then in others, I wrote the three novels—and the dozens of stories—that were not (and never will be) published. When we were in Hamilton, New York, where I had been engaged on a two-year contract to teach freshman English at Colgate, my novel, *Coldly the Hand*, was accepted for publication (thanks to the efforts of the British writer Robert Nye) by Calder and Boyars. It was 1971, and I was in the soup for real and for keeps.

"Our sons are Benjamin and Nicholas. They're big and wonderful and they're on their way up and out. Which leaves Judy and me and a couple of Labrador retrievers and some accursed cats. We live on a wild ridge about five miles from the nearest town. On our land, some 50 yards from our old farmhouse, is a barn in which, in a weatherproofed room, I write. I can call out, but incoming calls won't ring in. I try to make language here most mornings. I keep the insulated curtains drawn so that I see only the keyboard and the wall behind my desk. On hand, in a single frame, two photos—one of a handsome woman in her youthful middle age, and the other of a pretty Irish-American girl of six or so. Their smile is identical, a continuum, a stay against time. Time is the enemy against which I work, and the pictures are my charm. On the screen of the word processor I'm trying to use, in the upper left-hand corner, I am asked to type in the key that unlocks my computer's memory. Every day, before I work, I type in Judy."

———

Frederick Busch once gave this definition of the category "writer's writer," "a nasty bouquet we throw to writers whose works are structurally or stylistically different, whose reviewers equivocate, whose admirers are said to be only other writers." Busch wrote these lines in 1973 when he had himself published just two books of fiction, and to a degree they have reflected the circumstances of his own career. Admired by a host of distinguished writers—Reynolds Price, John Fowles, Anne Tyler, Cynthia Ozick, and Raymond Carver, to name just a few—he is the recipient of an impressive list of honors.

Busch deals with the joys, sorrows, and violence of modern life, both in its domestic aspects and in the larger world. He takes Hemingway for a model in that he believes that the writer "must cause the reader to share the unstated emotion," as he says in an article on Hemingway in the *New York Times Book Review*. It is the writer's duty to unfold a world, a universe, so that the reader will be forced to confront unbearable pain, but will, at the same time, have an escape from that pain in the writing. Busch's peers largely judge him successful, but his success in an artistic sense, has perhaps limited his popularity.

With the exception of his imaginative re-creation of the last years of Charles Dickens's life in *The Mutual Friend*, Frederick Busch's fiction is drawn from the realities and immediacies of daily life. He is so close to his characters that it seems he cannot part from them when a novel closes, and he often carries them over into another book. The fiercely independent college counselor Lizzie Bean moves from a relatively small world in *Rounds* to the center of *Sometimes I Live in the Country*; the Sorensons, grieving for the loss of a child by miscarriage in *Manual Labor*, test the strength of their marriage and their commitment to an adopted son in *Rounds*; the journalist Harry, who tries to win back a former lover, Catherine, in the short story "The News" (in *Too Late American Boyhood Blues*), pursues her again in *Harry and Catherine*, a novel deemed by Ron Carlson in the *New York Times Book Review* to be "about rich, deep intimacy, about the larger loves that people come to in maturity."

Many of Busch's books are dedicated to his wife (Judith Burroughs), who is also the model for many of his strong women characters. Some of his sensitive portraits of children and adolescents draw their characteristics from those of his sons. Busch has put himself, as well, into his hardworking, dedicated male characters, many of them gifted amateurs in home repair, carpentry, plumbing, and nature lore. In *Rounds*, Dr. Eli Silver's practice as a pediatrician is described in clinical detail; the lawyer-protagonist of *Closing Arguments* displays Busch's inside knowledge of legal practice as the son and brother of lawyers. Busch insists, however, that his characters do not "come from life." Rather they come from "the writer's interior world."

Reviewing *Breathing Troubles* in 1972 a *Times Literary Supplement* critic called Busch "a spikey and demanding talent . . . [with] a remarkable ability to catch, to transcribe, the American voice and the indeterminations and discontinuities of conversation." In *Manual Labor*, the narrative point of view shifts from the voice of a miscarried fetus to the voices of his unhappy parents. With his maturing talent, according to Donald Greiner, reviewing *Manual Labor* in the *New York Times*, "Busch shows his mastery of familial frustration, his control of the sacrifices, misunderstandings and love which make up the daily routine for most of us."

Busch's language is lyrical, metaphoric, full of rich imagery. In "From the New World" (in *Absent Friends*) a Hollywood writer long estranged from his family, returns east for his father's funeral. In the cold, bleak house he reviews the circumstances of his alienation: "There he was, then, finally, alone in his aloneness, sitting in the darkness of his family's house, hearing it breathe, hearing the sighs, the little moans of its tentative repose. It was haunting itself. It was also haunting him. And, in a way, wasn't he its ghost?"

In *Invisible Mending*, those words on an advertising sign over a tailor's shop on New York's Lower East Side are used by the novel's protagonist, Zimmer, as the metaphor "for what love can do when applied to the world's sorrows," according to Norma Rosen writing in the New York Times Book Review. Zimmer is a Sartrean "inauthentic" Jew who is forced by a lover to search for Nazis. Rosen describes the novel as a failure because "narrative technique [is] used to avoid coming to grips with the moral implications of the story." She maintains that Busch has created a "nursery fictional world shielded from the terrors of the real world," in which "there are real Nazis and real Nazi-hunters."

Busch's fascination with Charles Dickens began while he was leading a study tour in London. He read Edgar Johnson's biography of Dickens, visited the Dickens homes in London and Gadshill, and did research at the Victoria and Albert Museum. *The Mutual Friend* is an imaginative re-creation of the last years of Dickens's life, when he undertook his exhausting tours of England and America giving highly dramatic readings from his novels to huge audiences. Framed in the narrative of George Dolby, Dickens's manager and companion on these tours, it is also Dolby's story, as he lies dying in a charity hospital, as well as that of Dickens and of others whose lives had been touched by him—his housekeeper, his wife, his mistress Ellen Ternan and the man she later married. As Nicholas Delbanco remarked in the *New Republic*, "Dickens . . . has stamped himself indelibly on every page. . . . the pastiche accumulates, at last, into something reverential. . . . the book is about one writer's God. . . . "

Many of Busch's themes—the endurance of marriage, the relationship of pain and pleasure, the difficulties of parenthood, the omnipresence of violence, and the degradations of war—are present in *Closing Arguments*. Patrick McGrath, in the *New York Times Book Review*, called it "a tight, dense, dark complicated novel about child abuse, sexual violence, war and law." Several narratives form a palimpsest: the stories of Estella Pritchett, a young social worker accused of murdering her lover, and Mark, her lawyer, a married man struggling with his marriage and children—and with his memories of a dreadful childhood and war—who engages in a passionate affair with her. "Spliced into this story, and counterpointing it to explosive effect, is an account of Mark's capture, interrogation and torture by the Vietcong some 20 years earlier, during the war in Vietnam," McGrath explained. "A design begins to emerge from these interwoven narratives, a three-tiered pattern of pain . . . evoking associations with an extended experience of torture in war, itself evocative of terrible abuse in childhood. . . . " According to McGrath, Busch's "difficult, idiosyncratic moral vision," suggests the work of Conrad and Faulkner; nevertheless, in the end, Busch's novel is derivative of nobody else's. . . . *Closing Arguments* traffics with despair without somehow ever becoming truly hopeless." McGrath concluded that "the sheer pleasure it offers as well-wrought story is immense."

Son of Benjamin Busch and Phyllis (Schnel) Busch, Frederick Busch spent his boyhood in Brooklyn, New York. He attended Muhlenberg College in Allentown, Pennsylvania, where he received a B.A. in 1962 and later was awarded a Litt.D. He took an M.A. at Columbia in 1967. He met Judith Burroughs in college and they married in 1963. They live in upstate New York, where since 1967 he has taught English at Colgate University, becoming Edgar W. B. Fairchild Professor of Literature.

Busch has been the recipient of many fellowships and awards, including Woodrow Wilson and Guggenheim fellowships, the PEN/Malamud Award for Excellence in the Short Story and an Academy and Institute of Arts and Letters award for the body of his fiction.

Invisible Mending received the National Jewish Book Award for fiction.

PRINCIPAL WORKS: *Novels*—I Wanted a Year Without Fall, 1971; Manual Labor, 1974; Domestic Particulars, 1976; The Mutual Friend, 1978; Rounds, 1979; Take This Man, 1981; Invisible Mending, 1984; Sometimes I Live in the Country, 1986; War Babies, 1989; Harry and Catherine, 1990; Closing Arguments, 1991. *Short Stories*—Breathing Trouble, 1973;Hardwater Country, 1979; Too Late American Boyhood Blues, 1984; Absent Friends, 1989; Long Way from Home, 1993; The Children in the Woods, 1994. *Nonfiction*—Hawkes: A Guide to his Fictions, 1973; When People Publish, 1987.

ABOUT: Birkerts, S. American Energies: Essays on Fiction, 1992; Busch, F. When People Publish, 1987; Contemporary Authors 33-36 1978; Contemporary Authors Autobiography Series 1, 1984; Contemporary Literary Criticism 7, 1977; 10, 1979; 18, 1981; 47, 1988; Contemporary Novelists, 4th ed. 1986; Dictionary of Literary Biography 6, 1980; Greiner, D. J. Domestic Particulars: The Novels of Frederick Busch, 1988; Who's Who in America 1990–1991. *Periodicals*—George Review 38, 1984; Gettysburg Review Autumn 1990; Iowa Journal of Literary Studies 3, 1981; Iowa Review Summer 1988; Literature and Belief 7, 1987; New Republic March 25, 1978; New York Times Book Review November 3, 1974; August 18, 1991; Publishers Weekly March 30, 1984; Times Literary Supplement February 22, 1974.

BUTLER, HUBERT (1890–1990), Anglo-Irish essayist, was born into a well-to-do Protestant family whose roots reached back into Norman Ireland. In common with many other Anglo-Irishmen of his time, he was educated at an English public school, Charterhouse, and then at Oxford University. As a young man he traveled extensively in Europe, in particular in Russia and Yugoslavia, acquiring a profound understanding of both countries. In 1941 he inherited a minor country house, Maidenhall, at Bennettsbridge, near the town of Kilkenny in the province of that name, and went to live there for the rest of his life.

Butler published essays in Seán O'Faoláin's famous dissenting and liberal-minded journal *The Bell* (1940–1954), and elsewhere. These essays did not attract wide critical attention, and he made a reputation only as a learned occasional essayist and as a spokesman for the Protestant minority. Then, during the 1980s, when Butler was in his mid-90s, the Lilliput Press, founded by Anthony Farrell, published three volumes of his essays: *Escape from the Anthill, The Children of Drancy*, and *Grandmother and Wolfe Tone*. "Farrell's small Lilliput Press had netted a giant," asserted Edna Longley in the *Times*

Literary Supplement, "and set in motion a wider retrieval." Longley maintained that Butler's essays "put back into currency ideas whose time in Ireland was supposed to have gone." Many other Irish critics have resisted this new assessment by ignoring it as irrelevant; but there can be no doubt that the recent collections of these essays have directed attention to an outstanding and humane talent, to which Roy Foster pays tribute in his eloquent and useful introduction to *The Sub-Prefect Should Have Held His Tongue.*

Butler was inspired by the Irish Literary Revival (or Renaissance). But the figure he most admired ideologically was not Yeats but AE (George Russell), now a much less fashionable writer in Ireland than he once was (at the turn of the century he was held to be Yeats's equal as a poet). AE was a Utopian as well as a mystic, poet, dramatist, and supporter of the Free State. Longley quotes from a key passage in a Butler essay of 1954, "Divided Loyalists," in which he explains, with some self-critical irony, how he became a Utopian: "AE had believed that, as the cooperative movement developed in Ireland, a real village community would grow round every creamery and that the principal of sharing would extend into every branch of life, spiritual, economic, cultural . . . . AE saw the hedges planted with apple trees and gooseberry bushes . . . . and gymnasiums and libraries, picture galleries and village halls, to which each man or woman made his contribution according to his powers . . . . Sixty years ago, an ingenious young person could really believe this would happen."

This Utopia, although hedged with ironic sophistication rather than with gooseberry bushes (as Longley explains), remained Butler's emotional ideal—the heart of Anglo-Irish, if not of Irish, nationalism, the latter being too Catholic in its metaphysic for Butler ever to be able to accept. Butler, who became a nationalist quite early in his life, did make what Longley calls "an unusual decision," certainly not that of a true cynic, or even one devoted to irony: to live, he said, by an ethic of "neighbourliness and shared experiences and common devotion to the land in which you live." He succeeded in keeping to this decision, and by the end of his very long life was revered by a small but distinguished band of devotees. "When you left Maidenhall it was Ireland outside the gates that seemed a museum," Longley gratefully exclaims.

The Catholics with whom Butler allied himself were, therefore, always such radicals and liberals and scourges of their church as Sean O'Faolain, Ireland's great keeper (and raiser) of literary standards, and Peader O'Donnell, who

took over the editorship of the *The Bell* when O'Faolain gave it up in 1946. O'Donnell's goal, like the one Butler pursued in his less strident manner, was always to improve conditions for the Irish poor. A number of the essays—and perhaps the most important of them—contest the many attacks that have been made upon the Anglo-Irish element that has been singled out from the Literary Revival. One of the most notorious of these attacks was made by the poet and literary journalist Patrick Kavanagh in John Ryan's influential magazine *Envoy* : he spoke contemptuously of the "pygmy literature" inspired by the revival. Butler answered him in "Envoy, and Mr Kavanagh," shrewdly and teasingly pointing out that, far from being "pygmy," Anglo-Irish literature was the "chief focus of psychological disturbance." Butler's urbane tone, because of its extremely civilized veneer, has reminded more than a few readers of that of the English poet and essayist C. H. Sisson, although the latter is apparently far to the political right of him.

The essays have a wide range of subject matter. Butler was a convinced nationalist, but one who expressed his belief in "ultimate unity and reconciliation," and he was nothing if not cosmopolitan. In the 1950s Butler was, in Longley's words, "ostracized at home" by Catholic elements: he had drawn unwelcome attention to the Croatian fascists' wartime persecution of Serbian members of the Orthodox Church, an action which he claimed was fully supported by the Roman Catholic Church. For the whole of his life this humane essayist sought, in one of the most violent countries of the world, reconciliation by means of straightforward, but peaceful, argument.

PRINCIPAL WORKS: Escape from the Anthill, 1985; The Children of Drancy, 1988; Grandmother and Wolfe Tone, 1990; The Sub-Prefect Should Have Held His Tongue, 1990.

ABOUT: Foster, R. *in* The Sub-Prefect Should Have Held His Tongue, 1990; Longley, E. in Newey, V. and Thompson, A. (eds.) Literature and Nationalism, 1991. *Periodicals*—Times Literary Supplement June 16, 1991.

CANNADINE, DAVID N. (September 7, 1950–), British historian, received a B.A. and Ph.D. from Cambridge University, where he taught history as a Fellow of Christ's College. From 1973 to 1974 he studied at Princeton University as a Procter Fellow under the guidance of Lawrence Stone, a historian noted for his meticulous studies of British social history. In 1982 Cannadine married Linda Colley, a British-born

DAVID N. CANNADINE

historian then teaching at Yale University. Like her husband, Colley is interested both in British social history and in historiography. Cannadine has acknowledged the influence of his wife's 1989 study of Sir Lewis Namier on his own biographical work on G. M. Trevelyan. Canadine is the editor of the New Penguin History of Britain, to which Linda Colley is a contributor. In 1990 he was appointed to a chair in history at Columbia University and in 1993 he was named Moore Collegiate Professor of history there.

As a writer of narrative history in a long British tradition that descends from Edward Gibbon and Thomas Macaulay through G. M. Trevelyan and J. H. Plumb (his Cambridge tutor), Cannadine is conscious of the impermanence of historical interpretation; of the fact that historians tend to interpret historical events in the light of their own times.

Although Cannadine has acknowledged that the vast growth of historical scholarship since World War II has made it impossible to write the kind of confident and sweepingly general narratives that his predecessors created, he still aspires to mediate as an interpreter between his contemporaries and this national history. Cannadine always seems to have an eye to the present, which is more comprehensible and less fleeting when founded in the past.

His ability to draw connections between current and historical events is most strikingly displayed in his review essays, which have appeared in the Times Literary Supplement, New York Review of Books, and other periodicals, since 1980. Prefacing a collection of these

occasional pieces, The Pleasures of the Past, Cannadine reflects on the relation between historical scholarship and the reading public. "Some tight-lipped colleagues," he observes, "dismiss the concern to reach a broad, nonprofessional audience as little more than self-indulgent exhibitionism." Cannadine defends his inclination to write for a general, educated audience by proclaiming that history has relevance and can give pleasure, and that "the fact that history is difficult, demanding and important is no reason for making it dull, or for taking it (or its practitioners) too seriously." Cannadine's discussions of Queen Victoria, the history of British cities, royal weddings, and of more general subjects such as time, sex, money, and food, are all informed by an interest in what the past has to say about the present. In his journalism, all history converges on the present moment, and is used to illuminate our current conditions and concerns.

Cannadine's style of historical writing differs from that of the "annalist" school, which is concerned not as much with interpreting the past as in presenting it, often in exhaustive detail, with the aim of re-creating it whole. The historian is supposed to be invisible, offering no clue as to outcome or the relative importance of events. Cannadine, by contrast, selects detail in order to trace continuity, or elaborate on a theme. He summarizes his compelling interests in the preface to The Pleasures of the Past: " . . . a variety of themes stand out and recur: the cult of the national heritage and of the country house, the increasingly critical attitude of writers on the monarchy, the decay of Victorian cities and the problems of urban blight, the first serious studies of the post-war conservative governments, and the diversities and doubts which characterize the contemporary historical scene. And behind all this lies the . . . climate of opinion current in Thatcher's England and Reagan's America, which has deeply influenced both the type and content of British history. . . . "

Several of the essays in this book are devoted to the subject on which Cannadine has expanded most of his labors as a researcher—the British aristocracy and monarchy. Writing on the marriage of the Prince of Wales to Lady Diana Spencer, he draws on the work of other historians, and on his own knowledge of the Victorian era, to reflect on the part played by ceremonial occasions in the evolution of the British monarchy from an autocratic to a constitutional role. Likewise, the current enthusiasm for the country house as a facet of the "heritage industry" is seen as part of a long process during which the social role of the aristocracy has vanished while the part played by their houses, as shrines to a lost culture, has been enlarged.

Canadine's interest in the relations between upper and middle classes, a subject that lies at the very center of British national life, was first announced in 1980 in *Lords and Landlords*, which shows, in its patient attention to the details of real estate transactions, marriages, and bank statements, the influence of the Princeton historian Lawrence Stone, who is noted for his ability to construct social history from the minutiae of domestic life as displayed in records. This work received no attention from popular reviewers, and it is clearly written primarily for professional historians. As an essayist and editor, however, Cannadine saw his own research as part of broader historical concerns that he and several colleagues addressed in collections of essays. In *The First Modern Society*, he writes on Queen Victoria's Hanoverian character. Later, in *Rituals of Royalty*, he summarizes the doctrine of "the divine rights of kings," exploring the connection between "power and ceremonial." "Ritual," he observes, "is not the mask of force, but is itself a type of power."

Canadine's knack of bringing "brio to Clio," as Stefan Collini put it in the *Times Literary Supplement*, is enjoyed by many historians and readers of historical and literary journals. Cannadine's major work is *The Decline and Fall of the British Aristocracy*, whose ambitious scope is announced by the allusion to Edward Gibbon in the title. This immense study is prefigured by the modest opening of the preface to Canadine's first book, *Lords and Landlords*: "It is arguable that the most fundamental changes to have occurred in Britain during the last two centuries concern the decline of the hereditary, aristocratic, landed elite on the one hand, and the rise of a mass, industrialized, urban society on the other." The foundation for the argument is laid down in the later volume:

> As the last quarter of the nineteenth century opened, the traditional, titled, landowners were still the richest, the most powerful and the most well-born people in the country. Today, they retain but a fraction of their once unrivalled wealth, their once unchallenged power, and their once unassailable status. . . . It is a broad and arresting subject, at once moving and infuriating, poignant and comical. . . .

Between the writing of the earlier book, which describes the gradual approach of the bourgeois landowner to the condition, though not the rank, of the titled peer, and the later, which depicts the aristocracy en route to its present role as barely surviving anachronism, there was a change in Cannadine's own stance as a historian. Whereas in *Lords and Landlords* he is present only as the virtually anonymous, dispassionate collector of information, in the later book he makes a well-rounded appearance as a personality whose assessment of his subject is inevitably affected by is own social milieu. Quoting an axiom by the historian E. H. Carr that "you cannot understand works of history without first understanding the historian who writes them," he declares his belief "that some of the most attractive and abiding features of life in Britain today are the legacy of those who form the subject of this book—a view that some may find intrinsically distasteful and implausible, and that others may feel makes the general tone far too indulgent and uncritical."

Alan Ryan wrote of *The Decline and Fall of the British Aristocracy* in the *New Republic*: "Cannadine's main aim is to paint a historical panorama of a social, economic, political, and cultural change that he thinks it quite apt to describe as a revolution. He declares himself against . . . 'tunnel history,' the sort of specialized history that separates social history from economic history, the history of departments of state from the history of elections, and so minutely on. As he elegantly says of his own account, 'The perspective that it offers on the aristocracy is unapologetically that of the parachutist, not the truffle hunter.'"

Noel Annan, on the other hand, in the *New York Review of Books*, characterized Cannadine's stance as that of the tiger hunter: " . . . No praise can be too high for the skill with which he has stalked his quarry. . . . but why did Cannadine go on stalking his tiger when it lay stretched out dead before him? The British aristocracy as an important political order and force did not survive the First World War. The Parliament Act killed it, democratic government and modern commercial and industrial society buried it." He answers the rhetorical question by declaring Cannadine's story "engaging," pointing out that the British aristocracy died during World War I, only to be reborn in fragmented form in what A.J.P. Taylor has called "the establishment"—a loosely connected ruling class that forms a social and intellectual meritocracy heavily influenced by the crasser manifestations of money and social privilege.

A. N. Wilson, reviewing *G. M. Trevelyan: A Life in History* in the *New York Times Book Review*, said: "If anyone wants to know why Britain was once a great world power and a great cultural influence, and why it has lost that position, many of the answers are to be found in . . . this work . . . I finished Mr. Cannadine's book in tears." Wilson identifies with the beauty of "the houses, values and way of life of the enlightened aristocrats of late Victorian England," doubting whether "an American audience will understand it: the extent of what we English have lost, and the way in which this great historian's life forces home that loss upon the reader." For Cannadine, however, according to Stefan Collini in the *Times Literary Supplement*: "a distancing self-consciousness must supervene, and with it . . . a sense of contingency of so much that a well-connected Victorian gentleman took to be natural. In practice this inescapable reflexivity has contributed to the manifold merits of the book." In his biography of G. M. Trevelyan, Cannadine describes his subject in terms that may well characterize his own work: "Like most historians, Trevelyan's life and work cannot be properly understood without reference to the time in which he lived. But like very few historians, the time in which he lived cannot be properly understood without reference to Trevelyan's life and work."

PRINCIPAL WORKS: Lords and Landlords: The Aristocracy and the Towns, 1774–1967, 1980; The Pleasures of the Past, 1989; The Decline and Fall of the British Aristocracy, 1990; G. M. Trevelyan: A Life in History, 1992; Aspects of Aristocracy, 1994. *As editor*—(with D. A. Reeder) Exploring the Urban Past: Essays in Urban History by H. J. Dyos, 1982; Patricians, Power, and Politics in Nineteenth-Century Towns, 1982; (with S. R.F. Price) Rituals of Royalty: Power and Ceremonial in Traditional Societies, 1987; (with A.L. Beier and James M. Rosenheim) The First Modern Society: Essays in English History in Honour of Lawrence Stone, 1989; Blood, Toil, Tears, and Sweat: The Speeches of Winston Churchill, 1989.

ABOUT: *Periodicals*—American Historical Review February 1992; Annals of the American Academy of Political & Social Science March 1992; Atlantic February 1991; Church History June 1992; Comparative Studies in Society & History October 1992; Contemporary Sociology September 1988; English Historical Review April 1989; January 1992; Historical Journal March 1992; History February 1989; History Today December 1982; June 1990; November 1991; Journal of British Studies April 1989; October 1991; Journal of Modern History June 1992; Journal of Social History Spring 1993; London Review of Books May 18, 1989; New Leader January 28, 1991; New Republic December 10, 1990; New Statesman & Society March 23, 1989; New York Review of Books December 6, 1990; New York Times Book Review November 19, 1989; November 4, 1990; May 30, 1993; Social History May 1992; Times Literary Supplement April 21, 1989; October 19, 1990; October 16, 1992; Victorian Studies Winter 1984; Winter 1992.

CANTOR, JAY (1950–), American novelist, literary critic, and essayist, was born in Great Neck, Long Island, the son of Eleanor Weschler and Alfred Joseph Cantor. He attended Harvard

JAY CANTOR

University, from which he graduated in 1970, and went on to study at the University of California at Berkeley before joining the faculty of Tufts University, where he became director of the creative writing program in 1977. He is married to Melinda Grace Marble, a fellow teacher. Cantor received a MacArthur Foundation grant in 1989.

Cantor's first book, *The Space Between: Literature and Politics*, is an ambitious collection of literary essays that deals with the political issues and social turmoil of the late 1960s and early 1970s. In considering the connections that may be found between literature and politics, Cantor examines works by Yeats, Shakespeare (*Hamlet*) and Samuel Beckett in the light of the teachings of several prominent Harvard professors of his time, including Stanley Cavell, Herbert Marcuse, Norman O. Brown, and Gregory Bateson. He explains in his preface that as a young student troubled by political events in American society he "wanted a political literature, and wanted to read literature politically." The search to find or create such a dimension in literature, he discovered, is misguided, because it leads to reductive readings that diminish all texts to allegorical shells interpreted merely as part of the "superstructure" of society. He concurs with Marcuse's statement that "the basic structure and dynamic of society can never find sensuous aesthetic expression," and cites Marcuse's *Eros and Civilization* in support of his belief that art is autonomous and independent of political struggle. It may, by forming visions, portray postrevolutionary society, but it cannot play a part in changing events except by accepting a lesser role as propaganda.

Cantor's choice of subject for his first novel is a logical extension of his interest in the relationship between literature and politics. *The Death of Che Guevara*, which took twelve years to write, is about Guevara, whose portrait, bearded, disheveled, and intensely romantic, adorned the walls of numerous student lodgings during Cantor's student days. Guevara, who died at the hands of Bolivian government forces in 1967, already existed in many fictional, biographical, and historical forms by the time Cantor chose to write about him, but what distinguished his effort from earlier biographical writing is that Cantor does not write from the outside as an impartial observer but from within Guevara's personality, filling the gaps between his protagonist's journal and his actions with thoughts that he imagines Guevara might have entertained. The Guevara of Cantor's novel is neither a fictional figure based on fact, nor a factual creation embellished by speculation; he is, rather, a complex amalgam in which readers may be uncertain, at any given moment, whether they are reading Guevara's own journals and political tracts, the reminiscences of his friend and fellow revolutionary, Regis Debray, the comments of political associates on Guevara's motives, or Cantor's words. In addition, Cantor has created Walter Ponco, a fictional fellow soldier who takes on the task of writing down his memories of Che during the Bolivian campaign, and these memoirs are in turn layered with the thoughts of the army officers who hunt Guevara down and execute him. Although Cantor often assumes the authority to write words for Guevara and to imagine what he may have thought, the reader is always brought back to the realization that these passages are speculations based on Cantor's reconstruction of his hero's biography, fragments of historical fact, and the writings of others. As a consequence, the authority of the author is deliberately questioned, and the existence of the fictional Guevara is constantly being challenged by the actual person. According to Welch D. Everman, writing about Norman Mailer's *The Executioner's Song* and Cantor's novel as examples of the new form of "docufiction," this uncertainty exemplifies Michel Foucault's point that in a novel the first-person singular does not represent the writer but a "second self whose similarity to the author is never fixed." From this critical perspective, which seems appropriate to Cantor's self-conscious style, the narrator is neither Cantor nor Guevara, but the result of a complex relationship between the two. The novel represents, therefore, the writer's efforts to understand what it might have been

like to be Guevara, an educated and sensitive man who felt compelled to take a side in the dialectic of political change and become a guerrilla fighter.

Some reviewers of *The Death of Che Guevara* observed that Cantor's immense effort to bring a personality to life in the context of political history is ultimately too self-reflexive, and too conscious of itself as a text to assume the full-blooded life of a novel. By making it impossible to move with certainty from fact to fiction, Cantor is effectively deconstructing all texts in his writing, whether created by him or borrowed from others, so that ultimately his intention is to break down the distinction between history and fiction and convince the reader that truth is not available. The character of Guevara has the last word on this point:

> "I had written me, and if I'd lied, were my lies, as I'd hoped, like some psychoanalytic symptom, an indirect way back to what was central? Had I, as I thought I wished, betrayed myself? Or was it just another story, one of so many possible with me (whoever that was) excluded, outside, just another reader of an arbitrary epic?"

Contributing a short statement to a *New York Times Book Review* "Symposium" (May 13, 1984), Cantor ascribes his taste for mixed, fragmented forms of fiction to the discovery of *Moby Dick* at age sixteen: "it had poetry in it, essays on metaphysics, pieces of zoological knowledge, songs, how-to manuals and plays. I knew soon enough that I couldn't attain a placid, unbroken form; all my positions were divided against themselves . . . I hope my novel *The Death of Che Guevara* has something of that quality." Dean Flower, in the *Hudson Review*, also draws this analogy, and suggests that "much of Cantor's success comes from the fact that he knows his subject the way Melville knew cetology." Michael Wood, summarizing the intricacy of Cantor's narrative in the *New York Times Book Review*, described the novel as "a lucid, compassionate work" and "a remarkable feat of the imagination." He found fault only with Cantor's inability to create different voices for different characters. He also wrote that "the novel takes us into the landscape of Guevara's politics rather than into the depths of his personality." Novelist Guy Davenport's article in the *Sewanee Review* contradicted this estimate by calling attention to Cantor's Guevara as a person. What interested him is the fact that Guevara's death is made to seem the inevitable outcome of his effort to act on his own revolutionary beliefs. His revolutionary idealism, his conviction that society ought be changed, is wiped out by the refusal of the Bolivian peasantry to take up arms. Robert Towers's consideration of the novel in the *New York Review of Books* concluded with the judgment that Cantor, trying to make biographical and political sense out of a life that was already well-documented, is simply overwhelmed by his material. Cantor, according to him, does not succeed in making a consistent whole out of his occasionally brilliant parts: "If the *Death of Che Guevara* were as successful in its larger perspectives as it is in its embellished parts, Cantor would have written a truly formidable book. But the novel is burdened, I think, by such a multiplicity of events, with such a throng of briefly encountered names and faces, that little momentum (as opposed to impact) is achieved."

Cantor's second work of fiction, *Krazy Kat: A Novel in Five Panels*, also borrows, exploits, and transforms a body of existing material and creates a new work from the interplay between the reader's expectations and his inventions. Again he is recycling folk material: the departure point is a popular comic strip whose last number appeared long before Cantor's own birth. Krazy Kat, the creation of George Herriman, was a regular feature of the various Sunday newspapers of the Hearst publishing company between 1913 and the artist's death in 1944. As Cantor explains at length in an essay reviewing Art Spiegelman's comic strip *Maus* (*Yale Review*, Autumn 1987), cartoon art, and popular art in general, has held an appeal for American artists and writers since the 1920s, when numerous painter, writers, and musicians began to appropriate the energetic imagery and forms of Broadway, commercial art, and jazz. Cantor's essay both aligns his interest in popular art with a long tradition and describes his strategy as a "postmodern ideological maneuver." Cantor defends his appropriation of a comic strip as a strategy that pays homage to the vitality of popular art. He also exploits its throwaway humor in order to make a serious point: in a "postmodern" world, Cantor asserts in his review of Spiegelman, everything, even serious political and social debate, is entertainment. The artist is therefore justified in subverting comical and trivial forms for serious purposes. In the process of deconstructing Herriman's technique, however, he burdens the original work heavily with modern philosophical and critical terminology. Describing the recurrent central action of the comic strip, in which Krazy Kat is continually hit on the head by a brick thrown by Ignatz Mouse, the object of her unrequited love, Cantor translates the action thus: "Perhaps this gadget's central motor is Krazy's recurrent Dionysian gesture, her affirmation of the brick. What we do with the pain is, of course, one facet of what we do with death, that 'nihilating negativity'

that hollows out the world, Hegel says, and makes time."

Krazy Kat is much more humorous and lighthearted than Cantor's critical translations suggest. In the first panel chapter Krazy expresses her love for Robert Oppenheimer, whose A-bomb takes the place of the brick that Ignatz Mouse usually throws; in the second Ignatz persuades Krazy to undergo the entire range of modern psychotherapeutic techniques; in the third Krazy attempts to secure a part in a movie; in the fourth Krazy is kidnapped by a parodic version of the Symbionese Liberation Army, which captured Patti Hearst, daughter of Krazy's original publisher; and in the fifth Krazy and Ignatz are reborn as a popular singer-pianist cabaret act, achieving "their desire to escape from a comic-book life into the roundness" of human life, as David Lehman wrote in *Newsweek*. "We . . . watch as they enter history, acquire memory and stride toward death."

Krazy Kat was found "sprightly, delightful and insightful" by Thomas Disch in the *New York Times Book Review* 1988. Maureen Howard, in the *Nation*, wrote that it "twinkles" and is "simply delicious." The complexities of Cantor's technique and range of ironic allusion were explored in an essay by Miles Orvell in *American Literary History* in 1992. Orvell claims that Cantor and Spiegelman, working on opposing sides of the merger between comic strip and novel, have created "hybridized forms that have no real precedent: "they have projected the mentality of the cartoon world with the complexity of high art, aiming at a broader-based audience, a middle space between high and popular culture . . . .What makes these works significant is that both *Krazy Kat* and *Maus* embody a seriousness of purpose that goes against the essential lightness of the cartoon mode, for both are attempting a literature that bridges the political and personal and establishes an exemplary posture toward twentieth-century history." He points out that in both *The Death of Che Guevara* and *Krazy Kat* Cantor is continuing to explore the connection between art and politics that he first examined in *The Space Between. Krazy Kat*, Orvell notes, offers a means to bridge the gap between political and artistic expression by using the territory of a comic strip as a "self-contained aesthetic universe."

The eight essays in Cantor's *On Giving Birth to One's Own Mother* explore Marx, Nietzsche, and Freud, whose work Cantor also explicates in the courses he teaches at Tufts University. In the title essay, Cantor discusses the difficulty an artist has in finding guiding principles in the "ironic, postmodern ethos," which tends to undermine the implications of all philosophical positions by its tendency to regard all messages as entertainment: "I'm looking for a clue to my *fate*—not who my wife should be, but what my next story should be, so that its theme might be mine, *inevitably*, to write." In these essays, Cantor has achieved a direct and passionate tone of voice that convinces the reader of his deeply serious engagement with the questions of style and content that have occupied him as a novelist. He portrays in his own uncertainties the condition of contemporary culture. Of his fiction, he has written: "the story is known before the reader picks up the book . . . .So the issue is, how can you make those plots alive again, interesting again? . . . I prefer that the readers and I start as equals so that they know everything I know, so they will be free—as free as I am . . . .My way of making them new is by going deeper into the psychology of the characters."

PRINCIPAL WORKS: *Fiction*—The Death of Che Guevara, 1983; Krazy Kat: A Novel in Five Panels, 1988. *Essays*—The Space Between: Literature and Politics, 1981; On Giving Birth to One's Own Mother: Essays on Art and Society, 1991.

ABOUT: Collins, J., Appropriating Like Krazy *in* J. Naremore and P. Brantlinger (eds.), Modernity and Mass Culture, 1991; Everman, W. D., "The Novel as Document: The Docufiction of Norman Mailer, Jay Cantor, and Jack Kerouac" *in* Who Says This? The Authority of the Author, the Discourse, and the Reader, 1988. *Periodicals*—American Literary History Spring 1992; Hudson Review Summer 1984; Journal of Modern Literature Summer 1990; Los Angeles Times Book Review May 23, 1982; Nation May 14, 1988; New Republic December 12, 1983; Newsweek February 29, 1988; New York Review of Books December 8, 1983; New York Times Book Review November 27, 1983; January 24, 1988; March 31, 1991; Publishers Weekly January 8, 1988; Sewanee Review Spring 1985.

*CAN XUE (pseudonym of DENG XIAOHUA) (May 30, 1953–   ), Chinese novelist and short story writer, writes (in Chinese): "Born to a family of revolutionary cadres, I am now [1992] thirty-nine years old, and have spent all these thirty-nine years in Changsha Hunan province, China. My father used to be head of the editorial staff at the *Hunan Daily* in the fifties. In 1957, both my parents were labeled 'rightists,' an enemy category, and our family was plunged into the depths of misery.

"I graduated from primary school in 1966, and that was the last of my school days. At first I stayed at home. In 1970 I joined a little neighborhood factory and from then on worked at

CAN XUE

heavy manual labor for eight years. I was married in 1979. My husband was a carpenter, a rusticated youth who made his way back to the city, and we now have a son. When my son was two years old, I and my husband stated to teach ourselves sewing to supplement our income. We finally succeeded in setting ourselves up as self-employed tailors. Since 1987 I have concentrated on creative writing.

"I started to write in 1983, and began publishing in 1985. Up to the present, I have written and published nearly 800,000 words, mostly novels or short stories. Most of them have been translated and published abroad, in English, French, Italian, German, and Japanese.

"When my works first appeared, most people in literary circles were puzzled. Now my works have been recognized in other countries. But I still feel neither readers at home nor abroad really understand the deeper emotional levels of my writing. Of my later works, only a few close friends can understand and empathize. To most readers, even the more sophisticated ones, my descriptions seem superficial and meticulous to the point of being boring. I am often depressed by the reception of my works. Even when some of them have elicited a strong reaction, I wonder what is the point of it all.

"I never brood over how to write, or how long I am going to keep on writing. Writing has become for me the only way of life. I just go on writing, though I also try to keep in touch with readers' response.

"I find it increasingly hard to find refuge against the all-enveloping darkness through writing, though I still write for an hour or two every day.

"I now live up in a seventh-floor apartment. I often feel threatened and do not wish to go out, especially when the sun is out."—tr. Zhu Hong

---

Can Xue erupted on the Chinese literary scene with bizarre images and evocations of fear and loathing which reminds her readers of Kafka. The reading world was stunned, but her talent was unmistakable, and she soon won recognition—on the mainland, in Taiwan, and abroad.

Canglao di Fuyun (translated as *Old Floating Cloud*) contains two novellas, "Yellow Mud Street" and the title story. The story of two neighboring families, vaguely located in a Chinese small town, is told in "Yellow Mud Street." the characters are presented mostly in terms of literally described bodily functions: licking, chomping, gulping, spitting, hiccupping, etc. Highlighted in loathsome detail, these people are barely human. One childless woman pats her belly: "It's nothing but a sheet of skin, some dirty intestines, and some other damnable unknown parts." The environment these people live in is defined by dirt and disease and sadistic images—sparrows nailed through their eyes, for example—evoking in the reader a sense of horror and disgust.

The two neighboring families live in fear and suspicion and mutual loathing. One of the men, Kuang, exorcises "evil spirits" behind closed doors. At work, he tries to prevent people from hearing his heartbeat. The other man, Geng, puts up iron bars in his house against unknown terrors. His wife, Mu-lan, on the other hand, sets up mirrors—she even hangs them on trees—to spy on her neighbors. When Geng and the neighboring woman Ru-hua have an affair, it is presented as a dream: "During the night amid the remaining fragrance, Geng Shan-wu and the woman next door had the same dream. Both saw a turtle with bulging eyes crawl toward their house. The front yard had turned into a mud hole. The turtle crawled and crawled along the edge of the mud on its muddy feet but couldn't reach its destination. . . ." The turtle, the Chinese symbol for a cuckold, here evidently suggests unsatisfactory intercourse. In the course of the narration, the characters become increasingly paranoiac, their interactions increasingly hostile, until they collapse psychologically and physically.

At first glance, the fictional world of Can Xue has no recognizable relationship to reality. These vaguely defined characters seem to move about in a timeless nightmare with no identifiable plot, but the striking images and ever-shifting moods and bursts of irrational dialogue hold the reader under a spell. There have been speculation that the writer herself was writing under the seizure of a form of madness. But others have suggested that the pervasive images of subhuman conditions suggest a bleak life of economic deprivation and political repression.

At a psychological level, the unusual imaging of the central female protagonist, Ru-hua, seems to hint at a new female assertiveness, albeit in gross and sickly distortion. For instance, Ru-hua not only carries on extramarital affairs, but grows sharp teeth like a rat and bites her husband every night, drawing blood. There is also deadly hostility between Ru-hua and her mother, a sharp inversion of the conventional mother/daughter relationship in women's writing. Highly suggestive too are the two sets of mother/son and father/daughter relationships, which hint at dark impulses.

Other representative works of Can Xue include short stories, notably *Tiantang di Duihua* (*Dialogues in Paradise*). In her forward to this book, Can Xue describes her life as an ongoing struggle to survive. At thirty, she says, "*I am in charge of the household, the child's education and a bit of dress design. A comfortable family, not very well-off, but cozy and passable.*" These italicized autobiographical passages are placed into impressionistic reveries about the meaning of her life. She concludes with a passage that explains her writing:

> I would like to be able to say that my work shines with a brightness that penetrates every word in every line. I would like to reemphasize that it is the beautiful blazing sun in the south that has evoked my creation. Because of the brightness in my heart, darkness becomes real darkness; because of the existence of paradise, we can have the deeply ingrained experience of hell; because of universal love, human beings can detach and sublimate themselves in the realm of art. Only mediocre and superficial persons can neglect this.

Can Xue was a participant in the International Writers' Project at University of Iowa in 1992. She is now actively writing and publishing.

PRINCIPAL WORKS IN ENGLISH TRANSLATION: (tr. R. R. Janssen and Jian Ziang) Dialogues in Paradise, 1989; (tr. R. R. Janssen and Jian Ziang) Old Floating Cloud: Two Novellas, 1991.

ABOUT: Tonglin Lu (ed.) Gender and Sexuality in Twentieth-Century Chinese Literature and Society, 1993. *Periodicals*—London Review of Books February 22, 1990; Modern Chinese Literature 4, 1988; San Francisco Review of Books Fall 1989; World Literature Today Summer 1990.

CARPELAN, BO (October 25, 1926–),
Finnish poet, novelist, and dramatist, is a member of an old Swedish-speaking noble family
(and, indeed, has the right to be called "baron");
however, blue-bloodedness did not necessarily
mean affluence, and Carpelan's father was a
modestly situated bank officer. Finishing the
Swedish Normal Lyceum, the oldest of Helsinki's Swedish-language boys' schools, in 1944,
Carpelan made his lyric debut with *Som en dunkel wärme* (Like a dark warmth) in 1946. In the
same year, he began his long career at the Helsinki City Library, employment which led to his
appointment as head of the department of foreign literature in 1964; he retired from the post
in 1980 when an "artist's professorship," awarded by the Finnish government, gave him the leisure to devote himself completely to his creative
work. (Carpelan was an ideal librarian; while
still a boy, he had acquired an enormous reading
background, and, with his open and friendly
personality, was vitally interested in the public
he served.) Concurrently, he pursued studies at
the University of Helsinki, ending in 1960 with
a doctorate for a dissertation on the Finland-Swedish modernist poet Gunnar Björling (1887–
1960). It did not get the warmest of critical receptions; although Carpelan once upon a time
had been a member of the circle around
Björling, for decades a guru of Finland-Swedish
youths with literary aspirations, the old poet refused to aid the research of his former disciple,
and Carpelan himself, with characteristic modesty, later called his scholarly product, and its
abstractions, evidence of "how confusedly inspired he was by the New Criticism." As a professional reviewer in his own right, working
principally for the leading Finland-Swedish paper *Hufvudstadsbladet* from 1950 to 1964, Carpelan demonstrated great acuity and fairness; in
an essay on Carpelan's reviews, which have fortunately never appeared in collected form, still
another critic, Sven Willner, saw that Carpelan's
strength lay precisely in his "New Critical" approach, basing analyses and evaluations as closely as possible on the text at hand. But he was an
eclectic in the best sense, "using, when needed,
historical, psychological, metaphysical, and, indeed, even socio-critical points of view." Willner
placed him in a venerable and admirable Finland-Swedish critical tradition, "orientating and
guiding" his readership, indulging neither in
savage attacks nor unnecessary mystifications,
and never following a rigid methodology.

As a poet, Carpelan was seen early on as the
heir to another great (and almost overwhelming)
tradition. During the 1920s, there had occurred
the surprising explosion of Finland-Swedish
modernism, comparable in its importance to

BO CARPELAN

what "Prague German" literature achieved at
about the same time—a linguistic minority in an
eastern outpost gave new impulses to the mother-literature of the west. The changes wrought
by Finland's young Swedish-language poets—
the abandonment of regular meter and rhyme,
the invention of new and startling images—did
not go unnoticed in Sweden proper (or, eventually, in Denmark and Norway); and the modernists themselves—Björling, Edith Södergran
(1892–1923), Elmer Diktonius (1896–1961),
Rabbe Enckell (1903–1974), Henry Parland
(1908–1930), and their critical champion, Hagar
Olsson (1893–1978)—gave Swedish-speaking
Finland, for a while, a primacy in the Scandinavian literary world it had never enjoyed before.
By the 1940s, however, exhaustion had set in:
some of the modernists were dead, others past
their prime, and only Enckell continued to produce lyric collections of major importance. It
was a time of numbing anxiety: Finland underwent the trauma of two wars with the Soviet
Union (1939–1940 and 1941–1944) and a briefer
conflict with German forces in the far north
(1944–1945); then it lived through years of uncertainty about the intentions of its victorious giant neighbor (and of the neighbor's supporters
inside Finland's boundaries), an uncertainty especially keen among members of the country's
Swedish-speaking intelligentsia, some of whom,
in fact, migrated to Sweden.

For those concerned about the vitality of
Swedish-language literature and mindful of its
prominence in the recent past, young Carpelan's
debut, at twenty, as a poet of obvious accom-

plishment, was a sign of revival. But what attracted reviewers' favor in the early collections—the sure-footed first book was followed by *Du mörka överlevande* (You dark survivor, 1947; a title particularly apt for the spirit of the times), and *Variationer* (Variations, 1950) —was a distinct voice that held promise of shortly becoming completely Carpelan's own, even though the heritage from the original modernists was plain enough. His language had a polish and richness, exceptional in a beginner, revealed in a poem from the initial collection, here quoted in its entirety: "In the evening's wool / someone wanders past with a lantern— / Like a dark warmth / until the dawn / is the pendulum's secret anticipation." A fondness for ellipses, omitted punctuation, and ecstatic outcries were habits acquired from Björling, as in the poem "Morning": "Beach sky not a shadow moves / the hand's distance blossoms here / grass silverclear— / Oh quiet silence / All is near the dream"; but Carpelan avoided Björling's flights into dadaism and demonstrative non sequiturs. Rather, his chiseled lines and muted elegiac tone were reminiscent of Rabbe Enckell. Futher, as Carpelan had readily admitted, he had learned from Wallace Stevens (whose *Man with the Blue Guitar*, published in 1937, had now reached Finland), and from the "image-laden" verse of the leading Swedish poets of the 1940s, especially Erik Lindegren (1910–1968)—poets who themselves, at the outset of their careers, had been inspired by Finland's modernists. However, Carpelan never set out to rival Lindegren or his fellow Swedes Karl Vennberg and Harald Forss in difficulty or obscurity; "August" in *Du mörka överlevande* is immediately accessible ("Who weaves upon your darkening loom, oh August, / and with his hand moves the distaff between all shadows / which sink into one another to be erased"). Likewise, throughout *Variationer*, a single attitude is readily discernible—the poet's affection for a world of beauty particularly to be found in nature, yet an affection troubled by intimations of pain or loss. Commenting on a poem from the collection, beginning "Confused the switchman spreads / his slumber over an autumn snow," Carpelan wrote in a Swedish anthology, *Diktaren om dikten* (The poet on the poem): "The basic tone is darker than that of resignation." Carpelan has scored his early lyrics for being "weighed down with symbols"; all the same, he can present complex emotional states succinctly and simply, as in a four-line poem from *Variationer:* "What is shadow? What is your longing? / The silence's rain, the autumn's beauty, / silvergray mist over flaming trees, / no pursuit, no death." Carpelan's early lyrics capture a peculiar postwar sensibility, a combination of thankfulness and despair.

Flashes of humor and topsy-turvy fantasy appear in the prose-poems of *Minus sju* (Less seven, 1952)—for example, in "The Night at the Opera," worthy of (and suggested by?) the Marx Brothers' famous movie; dreams—burlesque, touching, portentous—play a large part of now, as later on, in Carpelan's work. *Objkt för ord* (Object for words, 1954) is filled with an effort to render what the poet beholds in precise words; like Rilke in his early Parisian years, Carpelan "learns to see," and, like Rilke, he practices on *objects d'art*, as in the suite, "Upon Contemplating Some Old Flemish Masters." "Our blood takes its course" as we perceive the paintings, "moves quite quietly, / fulfilling our outer seeing in an inner reality." One of the paintings is of a woman: "She is aware of the suffering she will meet, / in her white ruff, nonetheless, she keeps her calm demeanor. / Her childlike hands rest too, thus touching us / where we hide ourselves in details, reminding us / of our childhood, of the future, like the master himself, unknown." In *Landskapets förvandlingar* (The landscape's transformations, 1957), the poet— who previously had talked for the most part to himself—began to posit a community of experience between the poetic voice and another being; the title poem opens passionately: "The landscape's transformations, / the sea's sleep; drunken cries by the bed / where love has already wakened," and forms a contrast to the collection's many lyrics about isolation, e.g. "He wanders alone / by the sea's silence" and "He who has walked paths, alone, / heard, received those meeting him, / is alone, simply alone / if a voice, a hand like fire has not laid waste / the silent hours, a life's fortifications." In 1954, Carpelan married, and the couple's first child was born three years later; in 1959, Carpelan surprised his sophisticated public by writing *Anders pa ön* (Anders on the island), followed by *Anders i stan* (Anders in the city), books for children about a little boy's growing awareness of the island where he vacations with his parents, and the friendly city where he lives the rest of the year.

With *Den svala dagen* (The cool day, 1960), Carpelan fully achieved the concision and precision at which he had long aimed; he had learned the art of producing the unforgettable line—for example, "for you, the springtimes' murmur is already past"—that is characteristic of Finland's great poet of its Golden Age Johan Ludvig Runeberg (1804–1877). The collection contains one of the best-known of Carpelan's poems, "Evening Walk," which encapsulates a human fate in a few lines: "A man walks through the forest / one day with shifting lights, / meets few people, / stops, observes the autumn sky. / He means to go to the churchyard / and no one follows him." And in "Old Woman and Path," Carpelan postulates an unquestioning, nonanalytical acceptance of events: after the old woman disappears into the forest, " . . . we heard the reeds before the wind had reached us. / Finally we saw the shine from the sky, / divined the light that comes from out of the darkness / and, smiling, goes out." The gnomic quality of *Den svala dagen* was summed up in the instruction: "Do not seek in the mute grass, / seek the mute grass." But pregnant brevity could be carried too far, and—always his own sternest critic— Carpelan has called some of the tiny verses in *73 dikter* (73 poems, 1966) almost incomprehensible, even to their creator. Nevertheless the poem: "All were not cast into the chambers, / the children were small and were thrown away directly," poses no mystery, nor does: "People foregathered with people / they are many in burning cities, / they are rinsed with oil, / arise again / in someone's words, in fire." Carpelan was all too aware of the 20th century's past horrors and horrors to come.

As if in reaction against the occasional riddles of the seventy-three miniatures, Carpelan's *Garden* (1969, *The Courtyard*), an album of views of apartment life during the 1930s, became his most widely read lyric collection; the perspective is that of a grown man remembering the family world of his childhood ("Saturday was best, / father and mother as if they / had been children / and I hear their voices / like a hand on my forehead"). The cycle was Carpelan's response to a decade that, in Finland as elsewhere, demanded social awareness from literature, and the courtyard and cramped flats can have shabby or ugly corners. Yet, at the same time, in its singular devotion to the speaker's parents, *The Courtyard* implicitly contradicts a common demand of the time, for hatred against the parental generation. Another symptom of Carpelan's discreet brand of social and human concern was his pair of books for young people, *Bagen* (1968, *The Bow*) and *Paradiset* (The Paradise, 1973; translated as *Dolphins in the City*), about a mentally retarded boy. Further, he treated the problems of age in *En gammal mans dag* (An old man's day, 1966), the most haunting of his several plays for radio and television. None of his work in a dramatic genre has ever been printed.

In the 1970s, Carpelan's narrative urge, having rather tentatively appeared in *The Courtyard*, found full expression in the novel. *Rösterna i den sena timmen* (1971, *Voices at a Late Hour*) depicts an atomic disaster, again from the standpoint of single family. The book's atmosphere may suggest such films as Stanley

Kramer's *On the Beach* (1959), Peter Watkins's *The War Game* (1967), and Ingmar Bergman's *Shame* (1968); indeed, Carpelan employs a cinematographic technique, now rushing forward, now lingering, now indulging in the movies' favorite device, the flashback. What intensifies the horror of the story is its location in time and place; shortly before midsummer the members of the extended family flee to an island vacation home, not to enjoy themselves but to die. If the terrifying novel has a weakness, it lies in the occasionally blurred characterizations (frequently expressed through interior monologues); but suspense, and the hope that the victims will escape, are maintained until the end. Suspense and atmosphere, now a seedy, down-at-the heels quality, are likewise created in Carpelan's psychological thriller *Din gestalt bakom dörren* (Your figure behind the door, 1975).

Carpelan came even closer to the detective story in *Vandrande skugga* (Wandering shadow, 1977), about arson and murder in a sleepy Finnish coastal town around the turn of the century. Although Carpelan, as already noted, is scarcely a social polemicist, the novel may have some relationship to the attacks made during the 1960s and 1970s, in fiction and the lyric, on the alleged whited sepulcher of the conservative Finland-Swedish establishment. As in his verse, Carpelan skillfully juxtaposes the idyll's undeniable charm with a sense of rot or doom; the Finnish civil war of 1918, a sideshow of the Russian revolution, lies in the offing; Dr. von Adler, the town's mortally ill physician (surely a descendant of Ibsen's Dr. Rank), tells Frid, the simple honest, and lower-middle-class police chief: "It looks to me as though the whole thing is a colorful balloon, slowly pumped up to capacity with poison gas, that sooner or later will get too close to a flame."

The 1970s may seem to have been a decade of concentration on prose, culminating in the dream book, in which Carpelan brought his gift for evocation most directly to bear. But he also continued his lyric production. In *Källan* (The source, 1973), he looked once more to the sources of strength (familial love, erotic love, love of nature) for which he was thankful; with the poem "In the North" he praised the unique magic of Scandinavian nature: "What one does not see sharpens the eye and the feeling / and most rowanberries are both bitter and lovely." At the same time, though, echoing his novel about the world's end, he repeated his vision of final disaster: "The cities stand with open walls / . . . And the people, where are the people?" In a suite, "Time is short," the collection's title-word appears: "Farewell to the simple source, the murmur, / the dreaming voices. / They were, existed, ceased to love." Then, in 1976, he published *I de mörka rummen, i de ljusa* (In the dark rooms, in the light), for which he received the Nordic Council's literary prize in 1977. The Council's citation praised him for his "lucid and taut lyrics in which [he] was able to express the interplay between the outer and inner reality in an exchange between an awareness of death and the sense of life."

The publication of the retrospective *Dikter från trettio år* (Poems from thirty years, 1980) might well have been regarded as the summation of a distinguished lyric career; *Dagen vänder* (The day turns, 1983) was made up of new poems but had the air of an envoy. Notably, Carpelan paid tribute to his affinitive spirits: to the Runeberg of *Idyll och epigram* (Idylls and epigrams, 1830) in "Did not know which bird it was there / in the thickets, cool with evening," to the Finnish artist Hugo Simberg (1873–1917) in the poem "The wingshot angel," to the sculptor Alberto Giacometti, and to Friedrich Hölderlin. The East Prussian poet, Johannes Bobrowski (1917–1965), whose lyric aims much resemble Carpelan's, had received a eulogy from him in the collection of 1976. Carpelan's cultural gratitude was also apparent in *Marginalia till grekisk och romersk dirktning* (Marginalia to Greek and Roman poetry, 1984), glosses on the poets of classical antiquity, whose "clarity and balance, but also passion and bold concentration of images" he admired. Then, in *Ar som löv* (Years like leaves, 1989), he turned to Hölderlin again, to Karen Blixen (Isak Dinsesen) and the house at Rungsted where she spent her last decades, and—most importantly—to his own parents. In his recollection of a childhood excursion to Turku Castle (called up by an old photograph), the sun is suddenly hidden by clouds, and his father complains about the way his son slouches besides his mother as their picture is snapped: "I remember that we took a taxi into town. / Everything was so strange, as if I had taken departure, the first one, without obvious causes. Now / the day was open, others followed."

It was inevitable that Carpelan, always fascinated by music, would turn to a member of his family, his great-uncle, Axel Carpelan (1858–1919), who had played a significant role in the career of Sibelius. When the novel *Axel* appeared in 1986, Carpelan recalled that the eccentric music-lover had never been mentioned in his boyhood home; as an adolescent, he came across the name—the composer dedicated his Second Symphony to this great and good friend—in Karl Ekman's *Jean Sibelius and His Work* (1935). The novel, a feigned diary of the clumsy outsider and would-be musician, contains portraits both of the shy admirer and the often brutal composer; further, it is a kind of history, told by the penurious nobleman, of Finland itself, from the middle 19th century (the diary starts with the great famine of 1866–1867) to the civil war of 1918. Beyond all this, *Axel* reflects as well the devotion of its author to the musical art: some of the diary entries are, in fact, small musical essays. Published by Gallimard in French translation, *Axel* was a great critical success. In England, Tom Aitken, reviewing it in the *Times Literary Supplement*, termed *Axel* a "poet's novel" and noted the "sharply pictorial, but also dream-like quality." He concluded that "Axel, the ridiculous man' . . . provides the book's central fascination. . . . [T]his part-real, part-invented man holds our appalled, admiring attention." A stage version, in which Sibelius and his drinking habits loomed larger than in the intricate diaristic text, had long runs both in Finland and Sweden.

In December 1993, Carpelan was given the most prestigious of Finland's literary awards, the Finlandia Prize, for his novel *Urvind*, in which, again, the reader confronts a single voice—that of the secondhand bookdealer Daniel Urvind, who writes fifty-three quasi-letters to his wife; she is away in America, doing research at Harvard. These letters are seldom weekly reports; rather, they are dips into the world of memory, into the correspondent's past, from childhood on. Naturally enough, reviewers spotted resemblances to *The Courtyard* and *Jag minns att jag drömde*; but the cast that inhabits Urvind's apartment house is much larger than before, and the number of literary and artistic allusions much greater; the title and the protagonist's name suggest Rilke's poem in the *Neue Gedichte*, "Uraltes Wehen vom Meer" (Age-old Blowing from the Sea)—the ancient, primal wind that both comforts mankind and blows it away into nothingness. Doubtless, the book has elements of a self-portrait, as in the passage when Daniel glides into sleep on his grandmother's couch: "Was it now, when I tried to capture the silence in my memory, that I was seized for the first time by the thought of writing, forming, setting down, seeking proper words which at least could give fragments of the image of myself for which I looked."

Carpelan is an artist of paradox: solipsistic in his poetic imagination but never egotistical, almost serenely in love with life's phenomena but beset by premonitions of catastrophe and obliteration, a busy man of letters who has created a life's work of an unusual solidity—but a life's work somehow fragmentary when it is at its finest: tiny lyrics, prose poems, dreams, diary entries, feigned letters that are no letters at all. Still, the whole career has been supported by a single belief in poetry's function: "The poet follows his own line, seeks his own voice, and rejoices, the older he gets, that human beings and things exist; theories and ideologies change, but the questions of existence remain. The good poem is forever topical, by refusing to renounce its innermost vision. It stands against what is evil, and for what is good. It opens our sense and always stands in the center of events: in the human heart."

PRINCIPAL WORKS IN ENGLISH TRANSLATION: *Poetry*—(tr. S. Charters) The Courtyard, 1982; (tr. A. Born) Room Without Walls (selected from Carpelan's first ten books of poetry), 1987; (tr. D. McDuff) Homecoming (contains The Courtyard, The Cool Day, and Years Like Leaves), 1992. *Novels*—(tr. I. M. Martin) Voices at a Late Hour (intro. G. C. Schoolfield), 1988; (tr. D. McDuff) Axel, 1988. *Juvenile*—(tr. S. La Farge) Bow Island: The Story of a Summer That Was Different, 1971 (in U.K.: Wide Wings of Summer); (tr. S. La Farge) Dolphins in the City, 1976. *Opera*—The Singing Tree, 1992.

ABOUT Contemporary Authors New Revision Series 27, 1989; Schoolfield, George C. *introduction to* Voices at a Late Hour, 1988. *Periodicals*—Books Abroad, 1963; Books from Finland, 1977; 1993; Times Literary Supplement June 14, 1989; World Literature Today Winter 1984.

CASEY, JOHN (DUDLEY) (January 18, 1939–), American novelist and short-story writer, was born in Worcester, Massachusetts, the son of Joseph Edward Casey, a lawyer and four-term member of Congress from Massachusetts, and Constance (Dudley) Casey, a political activist. He grew up in considerable affluence and was educated at private schools: St. Albans in Washington D.C. and Le Rosey in Switzerland. Until his teenage years, Casey was short, ungainly, and overweight; a life long battle with stuttering intensified his feelings of alienation and eventually pushed him toward writing. As he told an interviewer from *People*, "I became a writer, in part because I always had to think up lots of words to replace the ones I couldn't say." A bright but unruly student, he was often in trouble with school authorities. He was expelled from Harvard College in his sophomore year for bringing a girl to his dorm room. After spending six months in the army, he returned to Harvard, graduated in 1962, and planning to follow in his father's footsteps—enrolled in the Harvard Law School. He graduated from law school in 1965 and passed the Washington D.C. bar exam the same year.

Casey briefly practiced law with his father, but at the urging of the writer Peter Taylor, who was teaching at Harvard, applied for a one year fellowship to the Iowa Writers Workshop. He went to Iowa despite his father's objections, and spent not one year there but three, earning an M.F.A. in 1968. During much of his time in Iowa, Casey lived in near poverty. He and his first wife, Jane Barnes, whom he married in 1967, lived off their meager graduate fellowships and often dined on squirrels, rabbits, and other wild game that Casey hunted. Discussing his decision to forsake a law career for writing, Casey told *Newsweek*: "One of the things you try to do as a lawyer is drain away all the emotional coloration in order to see a factual skeleton. But what really interested me was how on earth someone got into that mess in the first place."

Using proceeds from story sales to the *New Yorker* and *Sports Illustrated*, Casey and his wife bought a four-acre island off the coast of Rhode Island, in Narragansett Bay. There Casey wrote, fished, and farmed, spending four years barely making ends meet. In need of a steady income, he applied for teaching jobs. In 1972, he became professor of English and creative writing at the University of Virginia in Charlottesville.

Casey did not publish his first novel, *An American Romance*, until he was in his late thirties. The novel is the story of a couple who are, in most respects, antitheses of one another. Anya is critical, analytical, and hyperintellectual. Mac, is quintessentially down-to-earth, a man who prefers to devote himself to the practical arts—carpentry, hunting, and fishing. John Leonard, reviewing *An American Romance* in the *New York Times*, declared the novel attended by "ideas that fight like trout. If Anya is the skull, the disembodied intelligence on the kitchen table, Mac the plant at the window or the wind outside, nature boy as tree. The combination is musical." Anya tries to transform Mac, though the results are rarely those she anticipates. Later, she realizes what separates the two of them:

> The great difference between Mac and her, she decided, was that she regarded Cervantes, Fielding, Tolstoy, and Melville . . . in retrospect, as builders of steps that led up to her own view of the world from above. But Mac was more like someone *in* these books—Don Quixote, Tom Jones, Pierre, and Ishmael—as they *started out* on their adventures. Mac had an anxious, sentimental freshness that made it easy for her to imagine him wandering blindly into the contrivances of these novels and getting hit on the head with the difficulties the author had in hiding around the bend.

An American Romance garnered favorable notice and was a runner-up for the 1978 Ernest Hemingway Award. In the *New York Times Book Review*, Anatole Broyard noted: "It is a mutant romance, Mac and Anya's, not for faint hearts. In his first novel, John Casey has unabashedly tacked the question that has tripped up so many novelists: Can we know the total self? . . . His unwinking eye sees just about everything. He is equally good in describing the grandeur and the dandruff of the self." Bruce Allen observed in Sewanee Review: "Casey won't allow either character to look good at the psychological or moral expense of the other. And that is an indication of an honest writer."

More than a decade passed before the appearance of Casey's second novel. In the meantime, he published Testimony and Demeanor, a collection of three short stories and a novella. The protagonist (and narrator) of each of the stories is a privileged young man facing potential crisis. While the novella "Connaissance des Arts" and the short story "Testimony and Demeanor" were singled out for praise, the collection as a whole received mixed reviews. "Connaissance des Arts" focuses on how a young professor of drama and composition copes with a young student who has a crush on him. New York Times reviewer John Leonard wrote "Academic politics, the nature of friendship, social insecurity, adolescent sexuality, literary criticism and art itself are explored with a passionate sophistication. 'Connaissance des Arts' belongs on the same shelf with [Thomas Mann's] 'Tonio Kröger.'" Roger Sale, in the New York Times Book Review, agreed that "Connaissance des Arts" was the strongest piece in the collection, but noted "[B]ecause these stories are all told in the first person by the heroes, Mr. Casey has stuck us with their lack of feeling or perception."

Not until the late 1980s, was Casey's work once again in the critical spotlight. His 1988 short story "Avid," first published in the New Yorker, was selected for an O'Henry Award. "Avid" centers on the emotional disintegration of a young Rhode Island woman who tries to leave home but cannot. Casey worked steadily throughout the 1980s on a trilogy set in Rhode Island. When he submitted part of that work to a Virginia fiction contest, his entry won third place; the top two prizes were claimed by two of his own students.

Casey's second novel, Spartina, is the story of Dick Pierce, a Rhode Island fisherman struggling to achieve economic and personal independence in a modern world that has not been kind to him. His family had been Rhode Island landowners since colonial times, but Dick's bleak economic future was sealed by his own father; lacking insurance, the old man had insisted on paying his final gargantuan hospital bill in full. Dick's beloved Rhode Island coastline, meanwhile, has become a playground for wealthy amateur yachtsmen, inflaming his antagonism toward the leisure classes. Dick's dream is to complete the Spartina, a diesel-powered fishing boat. The vessel's name refers to the hardy local salt grass, which thrives despite the scarcity of nutrients. The turning point in the novel comes when Dick navigates Spartina through a ferocious hurricane; he survives the storm but is forced to confront his wife—and himself—concerning an affair.

Casey based Dick Pierce on a number of individuals—most of them fishermen—he had known in Rhode Island. "I was impressed by what a full life of the mind they have," Casey told People.

Most reviewers found Casey's portrait of Dick Pierce not only convincing but compelling. "There is something so obsessive yet deeply unaware, even resistant, about his main character's struggle to come to terms with himself, his life, his lovers, his place in time and in the universe, that it can only be expressed in symbolic, even mythic terms," Susan Kenney wrote in the New York Times Book Review. "[t]his fearless romantic insistence on lyric, even mythic symbolism, coupled with the relentless salt-smack clarity of realistic detail . . . makes Spartina just possibly the best American novel about going fishing since The Old Man and the Sea, maybe even Moby Dick." In Time, Paul Gray said of Spartina: "Remarkable characters meet and clash on fields of social class, money and sex. They do not make novels like this very much anymore; John Casey deserves gratitude for being stubborn and talented enough to do so and succeed."

Casey received the 1989 National Book Award for Spartina. He had already begun the concluding work on the Rhode Island Trilogy. In 1980 Casey was divorced from his first wife and in 1982 he married Rosamond Pinchot Pittman, an artist and calligrapher.

PRINCIPAL WORKS: Novels—An American Romance, 1977; Spartina, 1989. Short stories—Testimony and Demeanor, 1979.

ABOUT: Contemporary Authors 69-70; Contemporary Authors, New Revision Series 23, 1988; Contemporary Literary Criticism 59 (Yearbook 1989), 1990; Who's Who in America 1990-1991. Periodicals—Chicago Tribune Book World May 28, 1989; Chronicle of Higher Education January 31, 1990; Los Angeles Times Book Review July 23, 1989; New York Times April 25, 1977; June 15, 1979; November 30, 1989; New York Times Book Review April 24, 1977; June 24, 1979; June 25, 1989; New Yorker April 18, 1988; Newsweek December 25, 1989; People January 22, 1990; Sewanee Review Fall 1977; Time July 17, 1989; Washington Post Book World June 4, 1989.

CASSIAN, NINA (November 27, 1924–),
Romanian poet, translator, and writer of fiction
and children's books, was born Renée Annie in
Galati, a major commercial center on the Danube between Bucharest and the Black Sea. Her
father, Iosif Cassian-Mătasaru, the pen name he
adopted and which she eventually took was a
self-educated writer, and an unsuccessful salesman and accountant. For a time in the 1930s he
worked as clerk for a businessman who roughly
half a century later became his daughter's benefactor when she sought political asylum in the
United States—Hermann Mayer, to whom the
poet's 1990 book, *Life Sentence*, is dedicated. Iosif Cassian-Mătasaru is known for one of the best
versions of Edgar Allan Poe's "The Raven" in
Romanian, reprinted even recently, but he
translated mainly French and German literature, publishing some fifteen books. He was also
a pianist who composed songs and tangos and accompanied his wife, the poet's mother, who was
a singer.

At the age of five, Nina Cassian began to
create, at first music—a waltz after beginning
piano lessons—and, after learning to read, poetry. "I wrote my first poem, and continued since.
Writing then was a kind of behavior like playing
or laughing, like breathing. As I said, it came in
a natural way, it wasn't a choice (it became one
afterwards)." However, no one in her family's
pre-World War II world could have guessed
how through her choices and the eventualities of
history her career would turn into an odyssey
representing many of the main patterns of 20th-
century literary achievement in Eastern Europe:
from enthusiasm for European modernism and
a political idealism that led to ideologically committed artistic production to Communist Party
disapproval and persecution, and subsequently
to a reemergence of individualistic, self-
expressive aesthetic intentions, private disillusion and dissidence, and finally exile abroad.

Cassian's early upbringing gave her a cosmopolitan perspective. When she was two, her family moved to the ancient Transylvanian city of
Brasov, an Austro-Hungarian center of culture
with a mix of populations—Romanian, German,
Hungarian, Gypsy, and, her own background,
Jewish. Though her parents were not observant,
she went to the primary school associated with
the city's synagogue. Cassian remembers her
childhood there, with the summers on the Black
Sea coast in Constanta (the Tomi where Ovid
was exiled), as making her Romanian and
"rather international" in psychological makeup:
"I was never religious. . . . I need to have faith,
not a religion, and I attribute to that necessity to
have a faith my early devotion to Communism,
which was a kind of a 'mystical crisis,' fortunate-

NINA CASSIAN

ly overcome." Cassian has said the main reason
that at sixteen she joined the then illegal party
was its "beautiful vision."

The poet's family had moved to Bucharest,
Romania's capital, five years before her political
activism began, living in boarding houses while
she attended an elite high school, where she excelled in languages, music, and drawing (later
she would also illustrate some of her volumes
and children's works). After Romania embraced
Fascism in 1940–1941, she was forced to transfer
to a school for Jewish girls. Cassian attended the
University of Bucharest as well as the Conserva-
tory of Music, but she never earned her degree.
In 1943 she married Vladimir Colin, a poet; the
next year she herself began to publish poetry,
first under the name Maria Veniamin. Her marriage lasted five years until she fell in love with
and married Al.I.("Ali," short for Alexandru
Iancu) Stefănescu, ten years her senior, later a
novelist and critic as well as an important editor.
This second marriage, to a man the poet considered the great love of her life, lasted until he
died in 1984. Meanwhile, Cassian's first volume,
La Scara 1/1 (On a scale of one to one), had been
published in 1947. As a young writer she admired the continental and avant-garde, including Max Jacob, Guillaume Apollinaire, Christian
Morgenstern (she translated the *Gallows Songs* as
well as numerous French poets), and—among
Romanian writers—the proto-surrealist Urmuz
as well as three major influences, the late 19th-
century romantic Mihai Eminescu and two more
contemporary figures, the hermetic and difficult
poet Ion Barbu and the often controversial but

always dazzling Tudor Arghezi, according to her assessment "the greatest modern Romanian poet." these influences—plus the need of the Party, which had just banned Arghezi's work as "the poetry of putrefaction and the putrefaction of poetry," "to demonstrate," in Cassian's words, "its intransigence by punishing not only a well-known exponent of 'decadent art' but also one of its own . . . who had been contaminated by the same 'illness'"—led to harsh attacks on her in the official paper *Scînteia* (the Spark) for the sins of elitism and modernism.

For ten years, although she tried—as she has avowed—"in good faith . . . to limit my fantasy and restrain my literary initiative so as to please those Party representatives I considered competent and honest," Cassian was repeatedly condemned for her "bourgeois addictions." Her sensibility and inventiveness, which delighted in devising an imaginary language, Spargan, and, to prove its viability, composing works such as a sonnet and rondeau in it, clashed with the colorless and rigid style of party-approved writing. Yet Cassian dutifully published four other volumes—including a 1955 selected poems—during the highly restrictive decade which came to a close roughly in 1956–1957, after Stalin died. This followed a lengthy period of personal disillusion: "My beliefs received blow after blow. . . . the Party has interposed, as a dark force. . . . My frame of reference, my criteria, the ideals of my conscience fell ill with doubt, indignation, amazement, and fear." In the mid-1950s, she found she could no longer write—"my milk stopped running"—and for two years she turned to music. With the relaxation of state control, however, she "could afford a certain naturalness and freshness" previously impossible and books began to flow, especially in the last half of the 1960s during the brief liberalized period of the early Ceauşescu years. In a decade and a half she issued over twenty books—mostly poetry, but also fiction and writing for children—until her pace slowed down in the progressively restrictive 1970s.

In Cassian's prolific career she has produced more than fifty books, including more than twenty-five of poetry, among them *Cronofagie* (Time devouring, 1969—a title suggestive of her central theme of morality) and the long-pending retrospective volume, *Cearta cu haosul* (The argument with chaos, 1994), for which her husband Ali Stefănescu had prepared introductory material more than a decade before politics allowed the book to appear; three volumes of fiction; over a dozen children's books; and four puppet plays. Notable individual poetry titles are *An viu, nauă sute si saptesprezece* (Vital year: 1917, 1949), *Dialogul vîntului cu marea*

(The dialogue of the wind with the sea, 1957), *Spectacol în aer libera* (Show in the open air, 1961—a title the poet borrowed for a book of selected love poems in 1974), *Sîngele* (The blood, 1966), *Ambitus* (Ambit, 1969), *Loto-poeme* (Lottery poems, 1972), *De îndurare* (Of mercy, 1981), *Numărătoarea inversă* (Countdown, 1983). Cassian has also written literary and film criticism. Important writers she has translated include Paul Celan, Yannis Ritsos, Bertolt Brecht, Molière, Vladimir Mayakovsky, and Shakespeare (both *The Tempest* and *Hamlet* as well as, most recently, a version of *A Midsummer Night's Dream*). Her musical compositions range from chamber pieces such as *The Magic Clarinet* for clarinet and piano and *Vivarium* for five voices and five instruments to large-scale works such as the *Processional Symphony*.

In 1985, while a visiting professor at New York University, Cassian learned that a long-time friend, Gheorghe Ursu, had been arrested. As a result of a meticulous diary in which he had imprudently recorded, with attribution, her satirical political verses, he was questioned extensively about her and tortured, a month after which he died. She knew it was unsafe for her to return to Bucharest. Indeed, two years later, her house was confiscated and her possessions removed with all her manuscripts, letters, art work, musical compositions, and notebooks as well as her library; her creative achievement was written out of her country's literary history and her books (even the children's works) removed from library shelves. After the revolution of December 1989, this official ostracism ended. Although Cassian visited Bucharest many times she made New York her home.

During the last decade, Cassian's work has been broadly disseminated in the English-speaking world, where she has variously been compared to Anna Akhmatova by Jane Kenyon, to Marina Tsvetayeva by Carolyn Kizer (one of her many eminent translators), and to Joseph Brodsky and Czeslaw Milosz by Howard Moss, who declared her "one of the best poets alive." Stanley Kunitz praised Cassian as "a world-class poet . . . at the peak of her power." Five books have appeared in English since 1981, translated by a number of prominent poets. Cassian's major collection in English, *Life Sentence*, which gathers some previously printed versions as well as many new ones, includes translations by Richard Wilbur, Dana Gioia, Christopher Hewitt, Fleur Adcock, William Jay Smith, and Ruth Whitman, as well as Kizer and Kunitz. The volume won the British Poetry Book Society's Translation Award. Since the late 1980s, Cassian has had a guiding hand in much of the translation of her work, and was the primary translator of her volume

Cheerleader for a Funeral (1992), in which the three-line poem "Language," written directly in English, wryly notes her double life in two languages: "My tongue—forked like a snake's / but without deadly intentions: / just a bilingual hissing." Currently, in fact, she is working on a long poem in English, "Inferno Lost."

William J. Smith, the editor of *Life Sentence*, describes Nina Cassian's poetry in his introduction as a passionate exploration of eternal themes such as love, loss, mutability, and death, all fundamental aspects of the "tragic sentence" of life. Human experience is approached with "tremendous range and vitality." Many of the poems are in fixed forms with intricate and subtly achieved rhyme patterns, balancing her joy at the richness of language with the intrinsically bitter timbre of her philosophical view. Her mood is never self-pity nor confessional, but intense, with what Fleur Adcock termed in *Poetry Review* an "uncompromising nakedness" of feeling conjoined with a quality Daniel Weissbort called an "hallucinatory force." In a *World Literature Today* review of *Call Yourself Alive?* (with many of Cassian's love poems), Marguerite Dorian, one of Cassian's translators, wrote: "Her poetry takes shape at the intersection of lucidity . . . with the games of imagination, the enticing, wonderfully shocking metamorphoses and mutations of words and feelings, of people and objects. . . . Cassian's world appears in savage flux and reflux, inventing, dismantling, and reinventing itself with mischievous and sober variations. . . . " These ever-changing changes are, to the poet herself, protean facets of life at its most essential. "Poetry is not to transcend life," Cassian has said, "or to transform it, but it *is* life."

A number of poems develop images that resemble still-life paintings of physical objects or static portraits of living creatures—or abstractions that seem to materialize and multiply—but more often than not, these are metaphors of change. Typical is a description in "The Couple" of swans that come into focus and are suddenly transformed into "giraffes!" In "Postmeridian," waiting, an "intermediary time," makes walls "pneumatic," deforms and "expands" chairs, "flattens the telephone." In other poems' mutations, a "big-billed swan," perhaps as the poet's shadow double, turns into "half-woman," and a fallen angel is perceived as a stork; arms seem "decapitated eels," dry leaves, birds, and the speaker's body, a "statue of insects."

The poet herself retains a stable presence as the emotional center of her thematic universe, emblematic of the human process of unceasing metamorphosis—from loss to fulfillment, despair to ecstasy. The illusion of a firmly anchored creative persona is fruitful and generative of much of the tension and dynamism in her poetry. Cassian admits: "I am constantly challenging myself, and that puts me in motion. I hate to exploit my own ability so I change domains, I change attitudes, I change points of view, style—which is harder, . . . but at least something pushes me forward. If I don't rise, at least I move on the horizontal if not on the vertical." She acknowledges the role of the unconscious, writing at times "as if an alien power did it through me": "Of course I believe in control and the author's intervention in the material . . . sometimes there are spontaneous things going on and sometimes mysteriously you take them as they come, a combination of spontaneity and lucidity and control—the real joy comes from that; I cannot impose spontaneity. . . . Art has so much to do with playing, with games, but there's also knowledge and lucidity and responsibility."

"The miracle of love," her poetry's core concern, is to Cassian an emotional force that can appear with "a vengeful smile." Love's physical intensity overwhelms space—the lover's "eyes make the air pulse, / they electrify the house, / . . . rugs flood / down the stairs like a river." The speaker promises that love will make wondrous her lover's perception: "you'll feel your pores opening / like fish mouths, . . . hear / your blood surging, . . . " and "feel light gliding across the cornea. . . . " The poet is "greedy . . . hungry . . . thirsty"; she refuses "to remain indebted for a kiss" and she proudly wears "a decoration" on her lapel: "rapture, that golden rosette." But in despair, she sits with a cigarette to "choke / in an Isadora-scarf of smoke / because you don't love me." Her physical being is tortured: "They cut me in two, the river and the moon, / and from my mouth the night pours forth like blood." In longing and loneliness, world and psyche turn "void," "pointless," dead: "How real are you? / How real were you?"

A perhaps equally compelling motivation for Cassian's poetic persona is her attempt to savor, control, and live through language, purified and intensified by the poet's voice. In "The Fourth Monkey," she is "the Monkey Who is Sentenced to Write": "I test between my teeth a syllable of eternity. . . . " In "Poetry," the word is "an inhabited homestead," but in "The Troubled Bay," from *Life Sentence*, the poet warns that "solid ground" is likewise "unsafe," and language is the ocean in which the poet finds she must venture:

I knew, as I swam at length far out from shore,
thinking of poets and so much in their debt,

having absorbed a hundred poems or more,
I'd have to write, or drown in one, myself.

"Licentiousness," begins, "Letters fall from
my words / as teeth might fall from my mouth."
In an interview in New York in 1993, the poet
spoke of being "very befriended with
dying . . . very familiar with that feeling," and
explained, "It's also related to losing my beloved,
my lover, who happened to be my husband:
when he died, I died." In "Cheerleader for a
Funeral," the title poem of Cassian's 1992 volume, she accepts the process of aging defiantly,
and wholeheartedly. "Everything was amazement / in that wretched adolescence," the speaker begins, but, "though the girl is now a hag,"
and despite her observing the "trash" and
"confused hatred" of a decayed, winter world,
"the great festivities of multiple decrepitude,"
she is able to declare, "Never mind, let's do it all
again, / let's get amazed, let's celebrate. . . . "
Although other poems lament a falling away,
Cassian's attitude is ultimately triumphant:
"And if the flesh is disappointed," she says in
"Dedication," a late work, nonetheless "the spirit
stays." The poem concludes with a paradoxical
challenge: "Read my book and get dizzy / on the
fragrance of my flesh."

Critics have pointed out that images of exile,
pain, nightmare, and imprisonment abound in
Cassian's work, partially at least a result of her
own difficult life under Communism and later
her forced emigration. Tam Lin Neville notes,
in *Hungry Mind Review*, that *Life Sentence* exhibits a population of caged, flightless, and sin-
gle-winged creatures, as in "The Bear" (pacing
its barred rectangle with "A frenzy for four
sides"), "The Kiwi Bird" ("the one without
wings" and "very very dumb"), and "Fable" (a
bitter tale about a graceless angel with "its wings
cut off" that God forces "to fly anyhow" as an
experiment); additionally, a number of other
works embody moods of oppression and entrapment, for example, Daedalus's labyrinth in
"Agoraphobia" or the "dangerous intimate zone"
between open portals in "The Doors." Many of
these images occur in Cassian's poetic bestiary.
"Art is as alive as an animal," she has said.
"Poetry is in the species. It is necessary for the
species as breathing and feeding and clothing itself when it's cold. The individual can do without books, art, creativity, but the species
cannot." As Cassian's animated word-animals
signify, the ultimate transformation is that of the
poet into her own words, into that mystery
which incarnates a writer's freedom, "the
Poem's afterlife."

PRINCIPAL WORKS IN ENGLISH TRANSLATION: (tr. E. Feiler) Six
poems *in* Blue Apple, 1981; (tr. L. Schiff with V. Nemoianu and E. Greavu) Lady of Miracles, 1982; (A.
Deletant and B. Walker) Eleven poems *in* An Anthology of Contemporary Romanian Poetry, 1984; (tr. A.
Deletant and B. Walker) Fifteen poems *in* An Anthology of Contemporary Romanian Women Poets, 1986;
(tr. F. Adcock, N. Cassian, A. Deletant, and B. Walker)
Call Yourself Alive?: The Love Poems of Nina Cassian,
1988; (tr. W. J. Smith with D. N. Cassian, D. Gioia, C.
Hewitt, C. Kizer, S. Kunitz, R. Whitman, and R. Wilbur) Life Sentence: Selected Poems (intro. W. J.
Smith), 1990; (tr. N. Cassian and B. Walker) Cheerleader for a Funeral (with three poems written in English), 1992.

ABOUT: Contemporary World Writers, 2nd ed., 1993;
Weissbort, D. (ed.) The Poetry of Survival, 1993.
Periodicals—Hungry Mind Review May 1990; Parnas-
sus: Poetry in Review 1988; 1991; 1993; Poetry Review
Summer 1990; World Literature Today Winter 1990.

CAVELL, STANLEY (LOUIS) (September
1, 1926–), American philosopher and literary
and film critic, was born in Atlanta, Georgia, the
son of Irving H. and Fannie (Segal) Goldstein.
Cavell recalls in "The Thought of Music" (in
Themes Out of School): "I spent my undergraduate years torn between the wish to be a
writer and the fact of composing music for the
student theater." He traces his interest in music
and literature to his parents—his immigrant father ("he who was in love with the learning he
would never have") and his talented mother,
who "made a living playing the piano for silent
movies and for vaudeville." After taking an A.B.
in music at the University of California in Berkeley in 1947, Cavell went to New York to study
composition at the Juilliard School of Music. He
returned to California for graduate study at of
the University of California at Los Angeles, and
choosing philosophy as his major field, he moved
on to Harvard University where he took a Ph.D.
in 1961. Cavell taught at Berkeley from 1956 to
1962, and since 1963 he has been the Walter M.
Cabot professor of aesthetics at Harvard. In 1992
he was named a MacArthur Fellow. From his
first marriage, to Marcia Schmid, in 1955, he has
a daughter. They divorced in 1961, and in 1967
he married Cathleen Cohen, with whom he has
two sons.

In the 1950s Cavell studied at Oxford with J.
L. Austin, the leading exponent of what was
known as "ordinary-language philosophy," a
kind of common sense philosophy. Through the
subtle, precise, and often witty articulation of
the manifold meanings and implications of common usage, Austin and his colleagues tried to
demonstrate that most of the epistemological

and metaphysical puzzles and quandaries of traditional philosophy were conjured up out of jargon, which is really a distortion of what language is about, a misunderstanding of what language does and can do. Cavell has adopted this approach as a way of extricating philosophy from academic specialization and finding a home for it not only in the ordinary language of common speech, but in the extraordinary language of literature and film. His concern is to repudiate the lonely metaphysical quest of modern philosophy since Descartes—and its even lonelier disillusioned residue, extreme skepticism, or nihilism—and to affirm the richness, intricacy, and ragged messiness of the world as it emerges in common speech and literature. In this way, philosophy, like language and literature themselves, can be rooted in and reconciled with community, shared experience, the commonplace and everyday. Cavell thus renounces the austerities of both traditional systematic metaphysics and the analytical school, whose narrow concentration on logic and scientific language has dominated Anglo-American academic philosophy since World War II. His approach and tone have been quirky, playful, polymorphous, and personal.

Another important influence on Cavell has been the great philosopher Ludwig Wittgenstein, who, after a heroic attempt to define the logical essence and metaphysical limits of language, arrived at his own reconciliation with ordinary language as embedded in practice and cultural "forms of life." Cavell's most extended treatment of Wittgenstein's ideas, *The Claim of Reason: Wittgenstein, Skepticism, Morality, and Tragedy,* weaves his own themes into a discussion that takes in Austin, Wittgenstein's student Norman Malcolm, John Rawls's *A Theory of Justice,* and literary theory, as well as Wittgenstein. Critics found these themes compelling, but also found the book self-indulgent. In the *New York Times Book Review,* Jonathan Lear wrote: "'Skepticism and solutions to skepticism,' says Stanley Cavell, 'make their way in the world mostly as lessons in hypocrisy: providing solutions one does not believe to problems one has not felt.' . . . Cavell . . . would like to provide a solution we do believe to problems we have felt. Skepticism, he thinks, can help us clarify our perceptions of personal and moral experience, and enable us to form a more mature view of the world . . . The main problem with this book is one of style. . . . Cavell is deeply concerned with finding a philosophical voice. Unfortunately, this concern undermines him, for while much of the book is charming, there is much that is overwritten and self-conscious." A similar note was struck in the *Times Literary*

Supplement by Anthony Kenny, who wrote that the book "possesses the rare ability to present Wittgenstein's thought in a manner that is philosophically accurate while making an immediate imaginative impact . . . Despite Cavell's philosophical and literary gifts his book as it stands is a misshapen, undisciplined amalgam of ill-assorted parts . . . *The Claim of Reason* is a worthwhile book, but it could have been much better had it been pruned of dead wood and over-exuberant foliage."

The book that probably best sums up Cavell's philosophical and literary concerns, beginning with its title, is *In Quest of the Ordinary: Lines of Skepticism and Romanticism,* a collection of lectures that enrolls his favorite American writers, Emerson and Thoreau, as well as Shakespeare, Wordsworth, and Coleridge, into his project of capturing the philosophical resonance of ordinary language and life. His title is, he acknowledges, paradoxical, suggesting "the sense that the ordinary is subject at once to autopsy and to augury, facing at once its end and its anticipation. The everyday is ordinary because, after all, it is our habit; but since that very inhabitation is from time to time perceptible to us—we who have constructed it—as extraordinary, we conceive that some place elsewhere, or this place otherwise constructed, must be what is ordinary to us, must be what ordinary—of course including both E.T. and Nicholas Nickleby's alter ego Smike—call 'home.'"

The literary critic George Steiner, writing in the *New Yorker,* used *In Quest of the Ordinary* as an occasion for mapping the confluence of literature and philosophy in Cavell's thought: "Cavell's entire work has been an argument on and for the interactions of philosophic speculation and the mirrorings of man and consciousness as we experience them in Shakespeare or in such Romantic masters as Wordsworth and Coleridge. Over and over, in phrasings at once elusive and poignant, Cavell invokes 'the recovery of the world' which only certain modes of philosophic discourse (those embedded in ordinary language) and certain orders of poetry (Shakespeare's tragedies and late redemptive dramas, Wordsworth's odes) can hope to achieve." Steiner also stressed the democratic inspiration of Cavell's work, and the importance of Emerson and Thoreau in sustaining it: "It is to Cavell and Harold Bloom that we owe much of the current revaluation of the genius—of the centrality—of Emerson, and it is Cavell who has done most to recuperate 'Walden' for serious philosophic notice . . . It is the utter indivisibility within Emerson of the speculative thinker and the language-maker, as it is the fusion in Thoreau of audacious abstraction and a most scrupulous at-homeness in the natural order, that abolishes any categorical separation between thinker and imaginer. And here Emerson's and Thoreau's Americanism and concomitant espousal . . . of democracy become paramount."

Noting Cavell's opinion that "Emerson and Thoreau, whom he regards as the founders of American thinking, are 'philosophically repressed in the culture they founded,'" Steiner concluded by declaring that, whatever the sources of academic resistance to Cavell, for the ordinary reader the chief obstacle will be the unordinary language with which he conducts his quest for the ordinary. Steiner objected to Cavell's "numerous tricks of style, at once coy and ceremonious, elusive and brusquely rhetorical" and to his "incessant self-reference," which included "citing . . . his own previous writings, moods, indecisions, idiosyncratic turns in exactly the same tone of canonic observance that he uses in discussing Descartes or Kant." But Steiner thought these obstacles were well worth climbing over: "At its best, his play of thought, his 'wordings of the world,' have a music, a stroke of wonder rare in current philosophical argument. Here is a harvest truly of the American grain and prodigality."

Writing about the same book in the *New Republic*, the American neo-pragmatist philosopher Richard Rorty found Cavell's conspicuously personal tone mostly a virtue: "Cavell is among professors of philosophy . . . the least defended, the gutsiest, the most vulnerable. He sticks his neck out farther than any of the rest of us. Who touches this book touches a fleshly, ambitious, anxious, self-involved, self-doubting mortal. Even readers who eventually get annoyed with the book's quirkiness, its unashamedly personal tone, will have to concede its entire honesty and self-awareness. They will have to admit that when Cavell becomes querulous or fey, he knows quite well what is happening. When he is allusive, he alludes to what moves him, not to what he thinks will impress us."

Rorty thought that some of Cavell's philosophical conjunctions were forced, "but sometimes . . . Cavell puts isms and textbook philosophical problems to one side. . . . Then he lets the members of his circle talk to one another without trying to pin labels ('philosopher' or 'literary artist') on them, and without arranging conversational groupings ('the skeptics,' 'the romantics'). At these times he is much more persuasive. He ties himself and his prose up into fewer knots."

Rorty singled out for praise a chapter in the book called "Being Odd, Getting Even," in which Cavell works variations on a theme that has preoccupied both Harold Bloom and Rorty himself: the "Promethean need to enact one's own existence, to invent a self rather than to play out a role embedded in ordinary forms of life," which, Rorty added, "is what makes odd people stop speaking Ordinary." Philosophers, "oddballs" by virtue of their detachment from ordinary concerns, are tempted to "get even by making everybody else seem, at least for a moment, out of it." They invent themselves in the process of "inventing a new vocabulary of praise and blame, . . . assuming a new (preferably 'transcendental') standpoint." The chief achievement of Cavell, according to Rorty, is his exemplary awareness and articulation of the philosopher's dilemma; his need for philosophical self-enactment draws him away from ordinary life, and his need for human understanding drags him (and sometimes his philosophy) back to it: "The conflict that Cavell splendidly dramatizes at his best, and fuzzes up with isms at his worst, is between the fact that life is hardly worth living without oddity and egoism, yet also hardly worth living without love and communion . . . His prose and his career both live out the conflict of which he writes. In the course of that career he has developed an increasingly distinctive and powerful mode of self-enactment. Emerson would have found Cavell as convivial as he would have found Wittgenstein."

Cavell's writings on film are as much about philosophy as they are about film. They often offer odd but intriguing insights. He writes, for example, in "The Thought of Movies" (in *Themes Out of School*):

> I discuss the blanket in *It Happened One Night* in terms of the censoring of human knowledge and aspiration in the philosophy of Kant; and I see the speculation of Heidegger exemplified or explained in the countenance of Buster Keaton; and I find in *The Awful Truth* that when the camera moves away from an imminent embrace between Cary Grant and Irene Dunne to discover a pair of human figures marking the passage of time by skipping together into a clock that has the form of a house, that in that image something metaphysical is being said about what marriage is, that it is a new way of inhabiting time, and moreover that that is a way of summarizing the philosophy, among others, of Thoreau and of Nietzsche.

Reviewing *The World Viewed: Reflections on the Ontology of Film* for *Library Journal*, J. A. Avant wrote that the essays "are full of observations (some of which are penetrating), but the observations are so undigested that hardly any of the essays builds to a discernable point . . . The author obviously loves the movies, but he loves his own words and thought processes more; and his words don't always make his thought processes comprehensible."

In his review of Cavell's second book on film,

Pursuits of Happiness: The Hollywood Comedy of Remarriage, in the *New York Review of Books,* Michael Wood found the philosophical tangents not so much obscure as pretentious: "His solemnity about film will be an obstacle for many readers. I find I'm mainly puzzled by the contrast with the intimate, murmuring style he uses for philosophy . . . What are we to think of the touch of a writer who can describe a beaming Cary Grant as 'a hieratic image of the human, the human transfigured on film,' or who sees in movie stars versions of what Matthew Arnold thought of as a person's best self? Isn't this just the gush of a film fan piped through abstraction and high culture? . . . Cavell has a way of making announcements like 'It is a leading thought of mine' and 'I wish to teach us to say' . . . These failures of tact are so large as to make one wonder whether they can be failures only of tact."

But, Wood conceded, "Cavell has a promising answer to some of these charges: He is trying to be outrageous, he says; his tactlessness is a tactic. Philosophy, he argues, is an outrageous activity." And some of the "lofty things" that Cavell has to say about *The Awful Truth,* the movie that is at the center of his discussion, are, Wood concluded, not outrageous at all: "The comedy of remarriage, as Cavell sees it, depends on the threat and legitimacy of divorce . . . *Pursuits of Happiness* is a book for anyone who is interested in film, or marriage, or philosophy, or any combination of them." Similarly, Noel Carroll, reviewing the book in the *Journal of Aesthetics,* found that his reservations about it were overcome by its basic soundness: "Though one may balk at many of the details of Cavell's interpretations, the general outlines of his approaches to each of the films seem sensitive and compelling, and in several instances authoritative." In the *Times Literary Supplement,* S. S. Prawer was not put off by Cavell's tendency to compare Hollywood comedies of the thirties with literary classics (the book "shows very well how such films . . . approach the spirit of late Shakespearian romance") and concluded by saying, "No book about the art of Hollywood that I have ever read can make its readers stop and think more effectively than this one—even if their aesthetic and moral valuation of some of these works differs from that of its author." It has been, in fact, Cavell's ability to make his readers stop and think, if only to disagree, that has drawn the most consistent praise throughout his career.

PRINCIPAL WORKS: Must We Mean What We Say? A Book of Essays 1969; The World Viewed: Reflections on the Ontology of film, 1971; The Senses of Walden, 1972;

The Claim of Reason: Wittgenstein, Skepticism, Morality, and Tragedy, 1979; Pursuits of Happiness: The Hollywood Comedy of Remarriage, 1981; Themes Out of School: Effects and Causes, 1984; Disowning Knowledge: In Six Plays of Shakespeare, 1987; In Quest of the Ordinary: Lines of Skepticism and Romanticism, 1988; This New Yet Unapproachable America: Essays after Emerson, after Wittgenstein, 1989; Conditions Handsome and Unhandsome: The Constitution of Emersonian Perfectionism, 1990.

ABOUT: Contemporary Authors New Revision Series 11, 1984; Mulhall, S. Stanley Cavell: Philosophy's Recounting of the Ordinary, 1994; Who's Who in America 1994. *Periodicals*—Journal of Aesthetics Fall 1972; Fall 1982; Los Angeles Times Book Review March 9, 1980; New Republic June 19, 1989; New York Review of Books January 21, 1982; New York Times February 9, 1982; New York Times Book Review December 2, 1979; New Yorker June 19, 1989; Times Literary Supplement April 18, 1980; February 26, 1982; (Village) Voice Literary Supplement March 1982; Washington Post Book world July 19, 1981; Yale Review June 1972.

*CHABON, MICHAEL (1963–   ), American novelist and short-story writer, was born in Washington D.C., the son of a pediatrician and a lawyer. He grew up in Columbia, Maryland, and spent summers and holidays in Pittsburgh with his father. He attended the University of Pittsburgh, where he received a B.A. in 1985, and the University of California at Irvine, where he received a Master of Fine Arts degree. Chabon achieved literary prominence at the unusually early age of twenty-four, when the publishing house of William Morrow paid $155,000, a near-record sum, for rights to his first novel *The Mysteries of Pittsburgh,* which was Chabon's master's thesis at Irvine. Morrow's strenuous efforts to support its investment in publicity raised critical expectations that inevitably placed reviewers on the defensive. . . . "Chabon needs to spend more time on structure," wrote Jonathan Keates in the *Times Literary Supplement* 1988. "He is not yet the master his publisher wish us to suppose him, but if he can keep off the hemlock and nepenthe of premature celebrity he should do very well indeed."

Chabon's subsequent writing, mainly short stories most of which first appeared in *The New Yorker,* have been collected in *A Model World.* They have tended to confirm the sense among reviewers that he is one of the most promising writers of his generation. His work has been praised for its very assured sense of structure, especially in the handling of Chabon's principal subject, the development of social consciousness in his young male narrators, Art Bechstein in

°SHA bun

MICHAEL CHABON

The Mysteries of Pittsburgh, and Nathan Shapiro, the subject of a group of stories in *A Model World*. As both novelist and short-story writer, Chabon has shown evidence of his ability to evoke the embarrassments, uncertainties, and humor of social situations in which the narrator, always looking onto a scene of which he is not yet a part and does not fully understand, strives to put himself at ease by choosing a posture that more often than not turns out to be inappropriate. In "S Angel," the opening story of *A Model World*, for example, the narrator makes preparations that presage comic misunderstanding: "On the morning of his cousin's wedding Ira performed his toilet, as he always did, with patience, hope, and a ruthless punctilio. . . . Ira never went anywhere without expecting that when he arrived there he would meet the woman with whom he had been destined to fall in love."

In this case, the object of his attentions turns out to be obsessed with selling her house following her divorce, and this sad discovery provokes Ira's solemn-comical reflections on the disparity between his fantasies and the realities of adult life: "He is mortified by the quickness with which his love affair with the sad and beautiful woman of his dreams had been derailed, and all at at once—the tequila he had drunk had begun to betray him—he came face to face with the distinict possibility that not only would he never find the one he was meant to find, but that no one else ever did either."

Chabon's wry, ironic tone of self-scrutiny that tends to deflate pretension and hold his subjects

at arm's length marks him out from other much-publicized authors of first novels. Art Bechstein, the narrator of *The Mysteries of Pittsburgh*, allows us to live through his experiences but also makes us aware that he lived beyond them, that he thinks they were important and formative, but not to be taken entirely seriously. We are also conscious, as Roz Kaveney pointed out in her *New Statesman* review, that Chabon is making a careful and self-conscious decision about his first appearance as a writer. He is well aware of the pitfalls of the first novel, which can easily seem gawky or pretentious, but he decides, as Kaveney puts it, to be "shameless": "Michael Chabon has decided to be the golden boy, and pretty much gets away with it."

Ever articulate but never quite as sophisticated as he would like to sound, Art Bechstein tells his story briskly:

> The last term in my last year of college sputtered out in a week-long fusillade of examinations and sentimental alcoholic conferences with professors whom I knew I would not really miss, even as I shook their hands and bought them beers. There was, however, a last paper on Freud's letters to Wilhelm Fliess, for which I realized I would have to make one exasperating last visit to the library, the dead core of my education, the white, silent kernel of every empty Sunday I had spent trying to ravish the faint charms of the study of economics, my sad and cynical major.

During this visit he encounters Phlox and Arthur, the opposing forces in a summer-long sexual contest for Art's affections. The "mysteries" of Pittsburgh, an industrial city that serves as an ironic counterpoint to Art's advenures, are in fact the hero's confusions and self-questionings about his identity—not only his sexual identity, which remains unresolved, but also his relations with his father and his dead mother, whose memory perplexes his sense of his own past. The rival attractions of Phlox, who presents in her obvious prettiness and altogether normal claims a paradigm of heterosexual identity, and of the poised and witty Arthur, whose allusive, teasing cleverness is a constant temptation to Art's intelligence, are deftly introduced at the very beginning of the novel, and thereafter balanced against one another.

The coming-of-age novel is one of the most popular fictional forms, especially for first novels, but what is notable about Chabon's contribution to this crowded genre is the adroitness with which he dramatizes the speech, actions, and interior life of Arthur in such a way as to define homosexuality as a culture and style of behavior. It is Arthur, with his slightly unexpected dress, choice of words, and quizzical reactions to emotional stress, who embodies romantic and social appeal, rather than Phlox. Chabon portrays the hero's growing love for and dependence on Arthur with scrupulous fidelity to his character's feelings, so that the reader also comes to see this as an inevitable choice between the heterosexual beauty in a studio apartment, where Phlox cooks sustaining but overpowering meals, and the prospect of footloose adventure with Arthur, who seems to promise a wider world of unrealized possibility. This choice is foreshadowed at the end of the first chapter, where Chabon displays his talent for ironic, mock-solemn narration:

> He made me afraid of seeming clumsy or dull. It was not as though I had any firm or fearful objection to homosexuals; in certain books by gay writers I thought I had appreciated the weight and secret tremble of their thoughts; and I admired their fine clothes and shrill hard wit, their weapon. It was only that I felt keen to avoid, as they say, a misunderstanding. And yet just that morning . . . hadn't I for the fiftieth time berated myself for my failure to encounter, to risk, to land myself in novel and incomprehensible situations—to misunderstand, in fact? And so, with a fatalistic shrug, I went to drink one beer.

Reviewers generally agree that Chabon displays an extraordinary command of style, and, in Jonathan Keates's words "a wealthier, more varied talent than those of other writers such as Brett Easton Ellis and Jay McInerney. . . . His style has an enviable suppleness and fluency which offers the perfect vehicle for the moral feints and shifts of the cool crowd he portrays. Carolyn Banks noted in the *Washington Post Book World* that "*The Mysteries of Pittsburgh* is a sad book at heart."

Chabon's 1991 short-story collection, *A Model World*, conveys the sharpness but also the evanescence of adolescent grief, especially in those stories that describe the coming of age of Nathan Shapiro, grouped under the title "The Lost World." What Nathan loses in these stories, is the quality of excited innocence, and what he gains is the discovery that life is more complicated and painful than a young person can imagine. The understated sensitivity of Chabon's style allows ludicrous social and moral dilemmas to be worked at in elegantly rounded anecdotes. In the title story of this group, a friend of the narrator plagiarizes his thesis in climatology, but the theft brings not retribution but a tenured job at a prestigious university. In "Blumenthal on the Air," a carefree disc jockey marries a casual acquaintance so that she can remain in the United States, then falls hopelessly in love with her. David Montrose noted in the *Times Literary Supplement* that this collection "is narrower emotionally than *The Mysteries of Pittsburgh* and more restrained artistically"; and, as one would expect of short fiction, the stories "offer

a lot more atmosphere than plot." Michiko Kakutani, writing in the *New York Times* calls several of the stories "overworked," but she describes Chabon as "one of his generation's most eloquent new voices." Elizabeth Benedict, a novelist writing in the *New York Times Book Review*, found *A Model World* an advance over *Mysteries of Pittsburgh* and offered the prediction that Chabon will eventually enter the pantheon of writers of "the best literature about boys growing up."

Before the publication of *A Model World* Chabon had begun his second novel, a project that remained mired in its excessively complicated plot, which, Chabon told Lisa See in *Publishers Weekly*, involved "Paris and Florida, utopian dreamers and ecological activists, architecture and baseball, an Israeli spy and a man dying from AIDS, a love affair between a young American and a woman 10 years his senior." As his somewhat messy personal life began to improve, Chabon gave up that project, which he had come to see as an albatross around his neck. Instead he published *Wonder Boys*, another novel set in Pittsburgh during a long-weekend writing festival, in which the main character is a novelist bogged down in the writing of his second novel. Robert Ward in the *New York Times Book Review* called him "an appealing hero," attracting our sympathy as he "struggles with his behemoth of a novel, as he broods about love and literature." Ward remarked that he "is a mess as a man and an artist . . . very much a lovable mess . . . .He can't bear getting older, doesn't want to become an official adult and is trying to find some way to hang on to the sweet anarchy of youth." Ward termed Chabon "an intelligent lyrical writer" and pointed out that his romanticism is held in check by the comic nature of his writing, causing his work "to reflect a nature that is at once passionate and satirical. The result is a tone of graceful melancholy punctuated by a gentle and humane good humor."

Chabon's first wife was a poet and his second an attorney.

PRINCIPAL WORKS: The Mysteries of Pittsburgh, 1988; A Model World and Other Stories, 1991; Wonder Boys, 1995.

ABOUT: Contemporary Authors 139, 1993; Contemporary Literary Criticism 55. *Periodicals*—Georgia Review Summer 1992; Los Angeles Times Book Review April 17, 1988; New Statesman May 13, 1988; New York May 2, 1988; New York Times Book Review April 3, 1988; May 26, 1991; April 9, 1995; Publishers Weekly April 10, 1987; April 10, 1995; Time May 16, 1988; April 8, 1991; Times Literary Supplement June 17, 1988; April 26, 1991; Village Voice April 19, 1988; Washington Post Book World April 24, 1988.

CHERRYH, C. J. (pseudonym of Carolyn Janice Cherry) (September 1, 1942), American science fiction and fantasy writer, was born in St. Louis, Missouri, the daughter of Basil L. Cherry, a Social Security representative, and Lois Ruth (Van Deventer) Cherry. While living in Lawton, Oklahoma, she watched the Flash Gordon serials and read what little the public library owned in the way of science fiction. She earned her B.A. in Latin from the University of Oklahoma in 1964, and her M.A. in the classics at John Hopkins University. From 1965 to 1976 she taught Latin and ancient history in the Oklahoma City public school system. In 1976 she published her first novel and embarked on a fulltime writing career, a goal she had aimed for since her adolescence.

Cherryh's fiction is well-served by her background in anthropology and classics, and by her wide range of interests, including ancient life and its artifacts. Cherryh's passion for ancient history has led to an impressive record of travels. She has journeyed through Italy, Switzerland, France, and England, retracing the campaigns of Caesar; she has explored the ancient sites of Thebes, Mycenae, Pompeii, Troy, Ephesus, Cnossus, and Sparta; she climbed Mt. Dicte on Crete, Zeus's birthplace; and she traveled to Rome, Istanbul, Pergamum, Athens, and Delphi and sailed the Adriatic. She was also at the maiden launch of the *Columbia* space shuttle.

Cherryh is a painter, as well as a writer. Her paintings often lead to ideas for a story. Susan Wells points out in the *Dictionary of Literary Biography* that "one such painting, a shadowy figure standing by a castle door, was the seed of Cherryh's first published novel, *Gate of Ivrel*," the first in her Morgaine trilogy. Morgaine, a beautiful warrior from a technically advanced civilization, is on a mission to close each of the Gates of Power which are being used by the Ghal civilization for time and interstellar travel with which they wreak havoc on other worlds. Along the way Morgaine gains the services of Vanze, a young male who is in disgrace and who becomes bound to her. "Like sword-and-sorcery, the trilogy draws on medieval romance, particularly the Grail legend—but in an inverted way," Mary T. Brizzi writes in *The Feminine Eye*. "Morgaine and Vanze are knight and squire . . . Don Quixote and Sancho Panza, but the truth is that the knight or king figure is Morgaine, female." *Gate of Ivrel* proved very successful and earned Cherryh a John W. Campbell Award for Best New Writer in Science Fiction. She kept Morgaine and Vanze closing gates through two sequels: *Well of Shiuan* and *Fires of Azeroth*. In a review of the former, Algis Budrys in the *Washington Post* called Cherryh the

C. J. CHERRYH

"best writer of this sort of adventure since the earliest days of C. L. Moore and the prime of Leigh Brackett," and concluded that "any reader who is willing to become lost in an alternate reality will find much to enjoy."

From the beginning of her publishing career, as Mary T. Brizzi points out, "Vivid characterization, indeed the sheer variety and number of characters in each novel, are a keystone to Cherryh's success. And basic to this success is her unconventional treatment of male and female personality traits. Her epic heroines are unswerving, rational, godly, dominant; her helpful males are confused, faulted, submissive, and emotional, opposite to traditional roles. . . . Role-reversed pairs make a statement about the complimentary nature of 'feminine' and 'masculine' traits, suggesting that a whole personality must partake of both. . . . "

Susan Wells called Cherryh's next novel, *Hunter of Worlds*, a "linguistic tour de force: three separate languages appear in the text, each with a distinct grammar and a specific history . . . creations of the three alien races of the novel." Set on the starship *Ashanome*, the plot concerns the efforts of the predatory humanoid Iduve race to bring vengeance on Tejef, one of their own, who has "betrayed an ancient rule" and is hiding in a human world. Brizzi calls it a "densely written study of cultural values, linguistics, and biology. More than an exploration of the Whorf hypothesis that language and thought are interdependent, the novel examines the cultural impact of the ecological role a species may have had before it evolved to sentience."

In 1978 Cherryh published *The Faded Sun: Kesrith*, the first in her Faded Sun trilogy; *The Faded Sun: Shon'Jir* and *The Faded Sun: Kutath* followed. In a paper on Cherryh reprinted in *Mythlore*, Paul Nolan Hyde states that the "driving force of *The Faded Sun* derives primarily from the exploration of the relationships between three distinct races . . . each of which, for the most part, have no idea what the others are about. The narrative focuses on the . . . hostilities . . . caused by an almost total lack of understanding between the parties." Susan Wells also points out that the trilogy contains Cherryh's recurring themes of the "woman in power and the centrality of culture." The plots follow surviving members of the mri race as they attempt to escape from their human captors, and their efforts to find and establish themselves on Kutath, their home world of legend. They are helped in their struggles by a human soldier named Sten Duncan, who becomes one of them, and forms a bridge between the two disparate cultures. In his paper on the trilogy Hyde notes that "Cherryh has taken the time to make her characters mythological; at least in the sense that the story line spends as much time revealing *why* the various characters are the way they are, as it does revealing *what* they are. Mythology tends towards the personal and the intimate; Science Fiction tends towards the cosmic and the empirical. It may difficult to imagine intimacy with the cosmic, but I think C. J. Cherryh approaches it."

In *Extrapolation* in 1986, Lynn F. Williams called Cherryh's 1981 *Downbelow Station* "one of her best novels," as well as "one of the best examples of the way in which the female leader takes care of her own people." The story concerns the rebellion of the Unio, made up of new colonies in deep space, against the Earth Company, the old established order. One of the keys to the struggle is control of Pell, the last neutral space station, where the beautiful captain Signy Mallory has taken refuge along with thousands of others. Williams points out that the "way in which violence destroys the fabric of civilization" is one of the major themes here. "In Cherryh's politically conservative view," Williams writes, "aristocratic power is not in itself evil as long as it is used well, and preservation of the status quo is preferable to violent change." She also describes Cherryh's female characters as not being "male heroes in drag, but distinctly feminine leaders who believe that power and responsibility go together, and that reform rather than revolution is the best solution to political problems."

Downbelow Station earned Cherryh a Hugo Award in 1982, the same year she started a new series with *The Pride of Chanur*. In his *Analog Science Fiction-Science Fact* review of *Chanur's Legacy*, the fifth Chanur novel, Tom Easton describes the overall story line of the series: "A single forlorn human had fallen into the midst of a complex multispecies, interstellar civilization beset by interspecies rivalries, and Cherryh showed it all from the viewpoint of the catlike hani, represented by Pyanfar Chanur, captain of the *Pride* and her crew of interstellar traders." By the time the reader finishes book four, *Chanur's Homecoming*, Pyanfar is the "head of the whole shebang known as Compact Space, stepping aside to pull strings from offstage and maintaining the peace." *Chanur's Legacy* continues the story through the trader Hilfy Chanur, niece of Pyanfar, who is now head of the clan, as well as captain of the Legacy. "Cherryh's tale has a straightforward core made complex by tangled motivations, political uncertainties, varied alien psychologies, and intercultural misunderstandings," Easton writes. "The result feels frantic, confused, bewildering—much like real life—but it also feels remarkably convincing."

In 1988 Cherryh continued the story of the *Downbelow Station* universe in her massive novel *Cyteen*; it was also published as three separate titles: *Cyteen: The Betrayal*, *Cyteen: The Rebirth*, and *Cyteen: The Vindication*. The saga begins with the tyrant Ariane Emory, who heads the Expansionist Party of the Multiworld Union and dominates the Council of Nine; she is subsequently murdered. The Project is a plan to replicate a genetic double for Ariane; that double turns out to be young Ari Emory, who must stop a sociogenetic flaw, uncovered by the original Ariane, which will lead to the destruction of humanity. The *Library Journal* reviewer wrote: "Murder, politics, and genetic manipulation provide the framework for the latest Union-Alliance novel. . . . Cherryh's talent for intense, literate storytelling maintains interest throughout this long, complex novel." In 1989 *Cyteen* earned Cherryh another Hugo Award.

Although known primarily as a novelist, Cherryh has published collections of her short stories. Colin Greenland, of the *New Statesman*, had mixed feelings about one of them, *Visible Light*, finding some of the short pieces "dispensable," but declaring the longer stories "excellent." He also stated, "In prose which is substantial if not always shapely, they demonstrate her characteristic hard, clear moral imagination." Cherryh is also a contributor to anthologies and magazines. Her short story "Cassandra," in *Visible Light*, was a Hugo Award winner in 1979.

Cherryh has created other worlds in other series, such as the Sword of Knowledge and Merovingen Nights, working with other writers as collaborator and editor. "We like to go *outside* our homes to meet strangers; those we invite inside are fewer," she writes in *Inside Outer Space.* "One wonders how we, ourselves, will react if others want to travel inside that space we define as ours—be it world or territory—to come and go at will. Then we may find out what we really are."

PRINCIPAL WORKS: *Novels*—Brothers of Earth, 1976; Gate of Ivrel, 1976; Hunter of Worlds, 1976; The Faded Sun: Kesrith, 1978; Well of Shiuan, 1978; The Faded Sun: Shon'Jir, 1979; Fires of Azeroth, 1979; Hestia, 1979; The Faded Sun: Kutath, 1980; Serpent's Reach, 1980; Downbelow Station, 1981; Wave Without a Shore, 1981; Merchanter's Luck, 1982; The Dreamstone, 1983; Forty-thousand in Gehenna, 1983; The Tree of Swords and Jewels, 1983; Chanur's Venture, 1984; Voyager in Night, 1984; Angel with the Sword, 1985; Chanur's Homecoming, 1986; (with J. Morris) The Gates of Hell, 1986; (with J. Morris and L. Abbey) Soul of the City, 1986; Glass and Amber, 1987; (with J. Morris) Kings in Hell, 1987; Legions of Hell, 1987; Cyteen, 1988; Exile's Gate, 1988; The Paladin, 1988; Smuggler's Gold, 1988; (with L. Fish) A Dirge for Sabis, 1989; (with M. Lackey) Reap the Whirlwind, 1989; Rimrunners, 1989; Rusalka, 1989; (with N. Asire) Wizard Spawn, 1989; Chernevog, 1990; Heavy Time, 1991; Yvgenie, 1991; Chanur's Legacy, 1992; The Goblin Mirror, 1992; Hellburner, 1992; Foreigner: A Novel of First Contact, 1994; Tripoint, 1994. *Short stories*—Visible Light, 1986; Festival Moon, 1987; Troubled Waters, 1988; Fortress in the Eye of Time, 1995; Rider at the Gate, 1995. *Nonfiction*—The Sword of Knowledge, 1995. *As editor*—Sunfall, 1981; Fever Season, 1987; Merovingen Nights, 1987; Divine Right, 1989; Flood Tide, 1990; Endgame, 1991. *As translator*—Barbet, P. Star Crusade, 1980; Henneberg, C. and N. Henneberg, The Green Gods, 1980; Walther, D. The Book of Shai, 1984.

ABOUT: Contemporary Authors New Revision Series 10, 1983; dictionary of Literary Biography Yearbook 1980; Jarvis, S. (ed.) Inside Outer Space: Science Fiction Professionals Look at Their Craft, 1985; Slocum, S. (ed.) Popular Arthurian Traditions 1992; Staicar, T. (ed.) The Feminine Eye: Science Fiction and the Women Who Write It, 1982; Twentieth-Century Science-Fiction Writers, 1991; Who's Who of American Women 1993. *Periodicals*—Analog Science fiction-Science Fact Mid-December 1992; Extrapolation Summer 1986; Library Journal May 15, 1988; Mythlore Spring 1992; New Statesman March 11, 1988; Washington Post March 5, 1978.

*CHEUSE, ALAN (January 23, 1940–   ), American novelist and writer of short stories, writes: "I was born in Perth Amboy, New Jersey, and attended public schools in north Jersey. Af-

ALAN CHEUSE

ter completing my bachelor's degree at Rutgers University (where I had the good fortune to have studied literature with such marvelous teachers and critics as Paul Fussell, John O. McCormick, and the late Francis Fergusson and Mason Gross) I worked as a toll-taker on the New Jersey Turnpike and then traveled in Europe. Upon returning to America I worked at a succession of jobs that included caseworker for the New York City Department of Welfare, bookstore sales clerk, speechwriter for an urban planner, and managing editor for a socialist quarterly journal. I married for the first time and a week after my first child, a son, Joshua, was born, my family and I left for Mexico where I taught literature and history in a private bilingual high school in Guadalajara.

"By 1968 I had returned once again to the United States, and began a doctoral program in comparative literature at Rutgers, under the direction of my former undergraduate teachers Fergusson and McCormick (along with literary critic and Dostoyevski biographer Joseph Frank, and comparativists Clauco Cambon and Joseph Wilhelm). A position in the literature division at Bennington College opened up and at the urging of Francis Fergusson, who had founded the drama program there, I applied for the job and was hired, teaching there from 1970 to 1978 (alongside critics Barbara Hernstein Smith and Harold Kaplan, poets Stephen Sandy and Dennis Browne, and novelists Bernard Malamud, Nicholas Delbanco and John Gardner).

"In the seventies I began to review fiction regularly for the *Los Angeles Times,* the *New York*

Times, and the *Nation*, and other places. But it wasn't until the autumn of 1978 that I left Bennington in order to write full-time, returning for a number of summers to serve on the staff of the Summer Writing Workshops (founded by Delbanco and Gardner) from a new home—and a new marriage—in Knoxville, Tennessee. Both my daughters—Emma Cordelia and Sonya Ruth—were born near the end of this decade. My first story was published—in the *New Yorker*—in December 1979.

"*Candace & Other Stories*, my first book of fiction, appeared in 1980. The title story was inspired by an appendix to his novel *The Sound and the Fury* which William Faulkner had written for *The Portable William Faulkner* edited by Malcolm Cowley and published in 1946. "Candace" tells the life of Candace Compson after she leaves Mississippi for the larger worlds of Hollywood and Europe. The other stories in the collection grew out of my own travels in Mexico and elsewhere.

"When I had been a teenager, my Soviet-born father had given me a copy of *Ten Days that Shook the World*, John Reed's book of reportage on the Bolshevik Revolution, suggesting to me at the time that it might help me to understand something of his own early life. With the images of that book in mind, I began to do research for a novel based on Reed's life, and the life of his wife Louise Bryant. The book, called *The Bohemians*, appeared in 1982. Four years later, I published *The Grandmother's Club*, my second novel, the story of a New Jersey rabbi who suffers a midlife crisis, leaves his congregation for the corporate world, and destroys himself and his family in the process, all of this told in the voice of his mother. My next book-length work was a hybrid of sorts, a book called *Fall Out of Heaven* that is part memoir, part history, part travel narrative, in which I attempt to give an account of my father's life as a flier in the Soviet Air Force and my life with him, and the story of the journey taken by my son and me across Soviet Asia on the trail of my father's adventures as a young man. This appeared in 1987. More stories appeared under the title *The Tennessee Waltz and Other Stories* in 1990, by which time I was teaching again and living in Washington, where I also continued to work for National Public Radio as book commentator for the evening news magazine "All Things Considered" and began to serve as host and coproducer of a new Syndicated Fiction/NPR coproduction called 'The Sound of Writing,' a short story magazine for radio. In the autumn of 1990 my novel *The Light Possessed* was published, a work about an American painter whose life resembles that of Georgia O'Keeffe. I am [1992] working on a new

novel and now married to dancer and choreographer Kristin O'Shee.

"Narrative fiction is my main passion as a reader, as it probably is for any prose writer, but I do manage to find the time to read my favorite contemporary poets as well as fiction (among them Philip Levine, C. K. Williams, Edward Hirsch, Robert Pinsky, who happens to be my friend since college, Sharon Olds, and Dorianne Laux). But music, movies, dance, painting, and sports engage me as well. Reviewing and teaching help me to engage myself with new work and revisit the old. As we lurch toward the millennium, I hope to go on living, writing, and reading as much as I can."

Alan Cheuse is the son of Henrietta (Diamond) Cheuse and Philip Cheuse, who had been born Fishel Kaplan in Russia. His father defected from the Soviet air force in the mid-1930s and changed his name when he came to the United States to protect himself from Soviet agents. Cheuse recalls in *Fall Out of Heaven* that his father was a commercial pilot in New Jersey and later worked for General Motors as a troubleshooter on the assembly line. The father-son relationship was stormy, and it was not until after his father's death and his reading of the older man's manuscript about his "wild and adventurous youth" in the Soviet Union that Cheuse came to understand the roots of their conflict: "old father, new son, man of Old World ways, and a boy trying to make an American life." *Fall Out of Heaven* is an homage to his father's memory and a message to his own son Joshua that, as he writes, "we're traveling light but we're encumbered, like all wanderers, with the ineffable but ever-present baggage of everything that's come before." Joshua, who was his companion on the trip to Russia recounted in the book, is the son of Cheuse's first marriage, to Mary Agan, in 1954, which ended in divorce in 1974. He has two daughters from his second marriage to Marjorie Lee Pryse, which lasted from 1975 to 1984.

Cheuse concludes *Fall Out of Heaven* with a resolution "to work hard in the world and at the same time try never to miss another beat of the life within." His fiction reflects his pursuit of that goal, mingling a vivid sense of place with a sensitivity to the deeper and darker undercurrents of the human spirit. In the short story "Sources of Country Music" in *The Tennessee Waltz* a bride leaves her husband sleeping in their motel room while she tours Nashville. At the Country Music Museum she sees Thomas Hart Benton's painting *Sources of Country Music*: "It's the finest work of art Brenda's ever seen! The banjo picker on the side, the women with their unfurled skirts before them, the steamboat churning down the river, the railroad train racing on the shore, its dark smoke steaming behind it like a flag—and on the right-hand side the cowboy twanging his guitar, the fiddlers, more women dancing, clap your hands, stomp your feet, the land coming up in spring." In her delight and enthusiasm, she rushes back to her husband who reluctantly follows her to the museum and responds to the painting with no more than an indifferent "Uh-huh." The story ends at that point—as the young bride feels "a little chill around her heart part of the chest."

Cheuse's characters are so deeply absorbed in themselves and in the sheer business of living that they cannot connect with each other nor can they grasp the meaning of what is going on around them. Lovers, husbands and wives, parents and children, strangers thrown together by chance, they are all "characters progressing through critical, often life-changing experiences," Dorothy Golden wrote of *The Tennessee Waltz* in *Library Journal.*

The reviewer of *The Tennessee Waltz* in *Choice* categorized Cheuse as "a minimalist somewhat in the Raymond Carver tradition." Although his stories have little plot, little or no final resolution, and no authorial voice to direct the reader, they are enriched by the personalities of the characters who reveal themselves spontaneously and unselfconsciously. Cheuse's ear for natural speech is sharp; he catches the rhythm and the idiom of every speaker. *The Bohemians*, with its subtitle *John Reed and His Friends Who Shook the World*, is the imaginary journal of the American journalist who moved from a sheltered boyhood in the woods of Oregon to Harvard, then to Greenwich Village in the yeasty days of the early twentieth century, and finally to Russia in the throes of the Bolshevik revolution. Cheuse writes short entries in Reed's voice, recalling his idyllic boyhood, his education at Harvard where he met William James and had Walter Lippman as a fellow student, and the beginnings of his career as a journalist on the radical paper the *Masses* in New York. Cheuse did not have to invent colorful characters; they crowded into Reed's life. He interviewed Pancho Villa, Theodore Roosevelt, and Leon Trotsky, and counted among his friends Lincoln Steffens and Eugene O'Neill. His lovers were the wealthy Mabel Dodge and the radical feminist Louise Bryant whom he married. Cheuse's imaginative re-creation of these personalities is the major strength of *The Bohemians*. In the *New York Times Book Review* Peter Andrews cited "many weaknesses," including its disorganized, chaotic narrative and its "florid" style.

Nevertheless, he conceded, the book "lives. And because it is alive with characters who dreamed great dreams as intensely as they made spectacular fools of themselves, it is a novel that transforms most of its vices into virtues and makes its failing become part of its triumph."

Talk—spontaneous and virtually unending—is the essence of Cheuse's long novel *The Grandmother's Club*. In fact, *The Grandmother's Club* is told in one voice; the speaker is Mrs. Minnie Bloch, mother of a businessman-rabbi, pouring out her family's history over coffee and full meals to her sister grandmothers. Because Minnie has such a huge, sympathetic imagination she can speak for all the other characters in the book, which becomes a kind of epic of Jewish-American life. She is the confessional voice of her son, whose driving ambition ultimately destroys him; of her unhappy daughter-in-law, carrying memories of childhood incest; and of her spirited granddaughter, trying to cope with the pressures of contemporary life:

> But at night, at times almost like these, when I close my eyes to see and try to contemplate the many sad mysteries of Jersey and New York, the stories I need to tell you, the stories you didn't know you needed until you heard them, then I call on the powers of my eyes and fingers, the strength of my old memory and deep heart feelings, whatever I have, whatever I give, to show you in your eyes inside the way things moved in this world where I once lived.

Christopher Lehmann-Haupt, in the *New York Times*, observed that the grandmother's endless stream of narrative can be wearing and that her humor is sometimes strained, but he praised "its powerful incantatory effects." While acknowledging the extreme length and the occasional melodrama of the book, Jerome Charyn, in the *New York Times Book Review*, found it "a bitter, brilliant series of songs . . . with a magical displacement of time and a language that rattles us and reminds us how close art and chaos really are."

Ava Boldin, the central character of *The Light Possessed*, is an artist celebrated for her paintings of the landscape of the American Southwest. She is also the widow of an equally celebrated American photographer, Alfred Stigmar. The identities of Georgia O'Keeffe and Alfred Stieglitz are barely concealed in these characters. Kit Reeves observed, however, in the *New York Times Book Review*, that biographical truth is less important here than psychological truth. Cheuse invents Ava's story and the characters who surround her "to tell not so much what his subject did as what she was like." The story has multiple points of view—Ava herself, her devoted older brother, her husband who loves her though he is not faithful to her, the young couple who care for the aged and nearly blind Ava in her last years, her closest woman friend. But it is the artist Ava's voice that resonates most clearly as the old woman reflects on her work: " . . . and so here they are: the products of all those days from all these years between, these images of time concentrated, as we might say that trees are concentrated sunlight, and when we burn them, they give off the light of the sun that has been stored within them, however long." S. I. Bellman, in *Choice*, found *The Light Possessed* "a brilliant evocation of the tortured, occasionally ecstatic life of the higly gifted artist, seen against the background that brings out the artist's best."

PRINCIPAL WORKS: *Short stories*—Candace and Other Stories, 1980; The Tennessee Waltz and Other Stories, 1990. *Novels*—The Bohemians: John Reed and His Friends Who Shook the World, 1982; The Grandmother's Club, 1986; The Light Possessed, 1990. *Nonfiction*—Fall Out of Heaven: An Autobiographical Journey, 1987. *As editor*—The Sound of Writing, 1991; Listening to Ourselves, 1994.

ABOUT: Contemporary Authors New Revision Series 27, 1989; Cheuse, A. Fall Out of Heaven, 1987. Choice September 1990; Library Jounral March 15, 1990; New York Times November 20, 1986; New York Times Book Review March 28, 1982; October 26, 1986; May 20, 1990; October 7, 1990; Publishers' Weekly January 15, 1982; August 22, 1986; Small Press Summer 1991.

CISNEROS, SANDRA (1954–   ), American poet and fiction writer, was born in Chicago to a Mexican father and a Mexican-American mother. She attended Catholic schools in Chicago, was graduated from Loyola University of Chicago, and in the 1970s attended the Iowa Writers Workshop, earning a master's degree. With the support from the National Endowment of the Arts and working a variety of jobs, she published three books of poetry and *The House on Mango Street* between 1980 and 1987. In 1991 Random House published *Woman Hollering Creek and Other Stories* and republished earlier work, making Cisneros "one of only a handful of Latina writers to make it big on the American scene," according to the *New York Times*; her six-figure contract allowed her to buy a Victorian house in San Antonio, Texas, where she was living. She has described herself as "nobody's mother and nobody's wife."

In "Only Daughter," in *Glamour*, Cisneros recalled that she once wrote, "I am the only daughter in a family of six sons. *That* explains

SANDRA CISNEROS

everything." She was both "the only daughter and *only* a daughter," so in college she could study what she wanted: "my father believed daughters were meant for husbands" and "it didn't matter if I majored in something silly like English. After all, I'd find a nice professional eventually, right?" She told the *New York Times's* Mary B. W. Tabor that after graduate school her father wanted her "stop all the foolishness" and come back home. Instead she worked as a teacher and a college recruiter, writing at night. A quotation from a Mary Cassatt calendar, "I can live alone and I love to work," she said, "become a mantra to me. I was trying to live alone, like all of these women in the calendar, and I was trying to work. But it's hard if you are a Mexican woman and used to living with your family and not estranging them." Cisneros credits her mother with supporting her: she told *Booklist* interviewer Raúl Niño: "I'm the product of a fierce woman who was brave enough to raise her daughter in a nontraditional way, who fought for my right to be a person of letters. And she did that in a household where she could have certainly trained me to be a housewife, but, instead, she let me go and study during times when perhaps I should have been helping her out." But both her parents, she said, "loved us all fiercely and gave us a stable environment and had a great deal of faith in us." One of the pleasures she reports in "Only Daughter" is showing her father a story which had been translated into Spanish and published in Mexico. "Where can we get more copies of this for the relatives?" he asked.

Much of Cisneros's childhood was spent moving between Mexico City, where her paternal grandmother lived, and Chicago. Her father's "bouts of nostalgia," she wrote in "Only Daughter," would cause the family to "let go our flat, store the furniture with mother's relatives, load the station wagon with baggage and bologna sandwiches and head south. . . . We came back, of course," she continued, "to yet another Chicago flat, another Chicago neighborhood, another Catholic school." *Notable Hispanic American Women* quotes Cisneros saying that her basic education in these schools was "rather sappy": "If I had lived up to my teachers' expectations, I'd still be working in a factory." (The humiliation she felt is registered in *The House on Mango Street*; Esperanza is accosted by a nun outside her flat: "You live *there*? The way she said it made me feel like nothing.") Tabor reported in the *New York Times* that Cisneros showed her fifth-grade report card to an audience of children and adults at the Brownsville branch of the Brooklyn Public Library, saying "I have C's and D's in everything. . . . The only B I had was in conduct. But I don't remember being that stupid." Yet it was a high school teacher who encouraged her to begin writing, and a college teacher who helped her enroll in the Iowa writing program.

The House on Mango Street is made up of vignettes, almost prose poems, spoken by Esperanza Cordero, a child-woman through whom the reader sees the life of the Chicago barrios Cisneros grew up in and the girl's emerging understanding of its social and sexual texture. First published by Arte Publico, the book established Cisneros's reputation among scholars of Chicano literature. Ellen McCracken, in *Breaking Boundaries: Latina Writing and Critical Readings*, prophesied that it would be denied "the wide exposure that admission to the canon facilitates" because it is "four times marginalized by its ideology, its language, and its writer's ethnicity and gender." In fact, according to Jim Sagel of *Publishers Weekly*, the novel has been read by students "from junior high school through graduate school in subjects ranging from Chicano studies to psychology to culture, ideas and values at Stanford University, where it has been adopted as part of the 'new curriculum'." Cisneros told Sagel how the story came into being. Studying Gaston Bachelard's *The Poetics of Space* with her Iowa classmates, Cisneros "felt foreign and out of place":

Everyone seemed to have some communal knowledge which I did not have—and then I realized that the metaphor of *house* was totally wrong for me. Suddenly I was homeless. There were no attics and cellars and crannies. I had no such house in my memories. As a child I had

read of such things in books, and my family had promised such a house, but the best they could do was offer the miserable bungalow I was embarrassed with all my life. This caused me to question myself, to become defensive. What did I, Sandra Cisneros, know? What *could* I know? My classmates were from the best schools in the country. They had been bred as fine hothouse flowers. I was a yellow weed among the city's cracks. It was not until this moment when I separated myself, when I considered myself truly distinct, that my writing acquired a voice. I knew I was a Mexican woman, but I didn't think it had anything to do with why I felt so much imbalance in my life, whereas it had everything to do with it! My race, my gender, my class! That's when I decided I would write about something my classmates couldn't write about.

Cisneros used the idea of the house to connect living alone as a woman and creative work; as she writes in "A House of My Own," a chapter typical of the book's lyrical mode:

Not a flat. Not an apartment in back. Not a man's house. Not a daddy's. A house all my own. With my porch and my pillow, my pretty purple petunias. My books and my stories. My two shoes waiting beside the bed. Nobody to shake a stick at. Nobody's garbage to pick up after. Only a house quiet as snow, a space for myself to go, clean as paper before the poem.

Told by Raúl Niño in *Booklist* that her work "hasn't been overtly political," Cisneros objected. "I think *House on Mango Street* is a very political work; it's really a book about a woman in her twenties coming to her political consciousness as a feminist woman of color." We can see the young Esperanza come into such consciousness both as she describes her house and as she defines her vision of herself in chapters such as this one, called "Beautiful & Cruel":

I am an ugly daughter. I am the one nobody comes for. . . . My mother says when I get older my dusty hair will settle and my blouse will learn to stay clean, but I have decided to not to grow up tame like the others who lay their necks on the threshold waiting for the ball and chain. . . . I have begun my own quiet war. Simple. Sure. I am one who leaves the table like a man, without putting back the chair or picking up the plate.

The realities of gender relations against which this passage is written can be seen in Cisneros's poem from *My Wicked, Wicked Ways*, "I understand it as a kiss":

but not a kiss. This
gesture, this burning.
But from an origin
furthest from the heart.

I recognize this
is for me, and yet
I sense I make no
difference. I know

if we say love
we speak of many things.

You mean the Buenos Aires moon,
the blond streetlamps,
the dance you danced.

But I know it as the wrist,
a shoe, a bruise,
a bone, a stick.

Literary agent Susan Bergholz reported to
Jim Sagel that she was so moved by *The House
on Mango Street* that she set out to find the author. Cisneros in this period had moved to Texas,
on a Dobie-Paisano Fellowship, and then, in
1987, when the fellowship ran out and she could
not support herself in Texas, moved on to a guest
lectureship at California State University at Chi-
co. Cisneros told Sagel that 1987 was the worst
year of her life: "I thought I couldn't teach. I
found myself becoming suicidal. Richard Bray
had told me Susan was looking for me, but I was
drowning, beyond help. I had the number for
months, but I didn't call. It was frightening because it was such a calm depression."
"Revitalized," according to Sagel, by a National
Endowment grant, her second—and by becoming Roberta Halloway Writer-in-Residence at
the University of California, Berkeley—Cisneros
sent Bergholz thirty-nine pages of new work,
which Bergholz sold. *Woman Hollering Creek*
was published in 1991, and a revised *The House
on Mango Street* issued; *My Wicked, Wicked
Ways* was republished in 1992.

With the publication of these books, Cisneros
began to receive attention from the press. Phoebe-Lou Adams reviewed *The House on Mango
Street* for the *Atlantic,* writing, "Cisneros has
compressed great force into this small, brilliant
work." Ilan Stavans, in *Commonweal* found the
book "at times amateurish," but "a composite of
evocative snapshots that manages to passionately
recreate the milieu of the poor quarters of
Chicago." Jenny Uglow, in the *Times Literary
Supplement* in 1992, appreciated Cisneros's
voice: "The reality of Hispanic life . . . rarely
enters mainstream American writing. Cisneros
sets out to fill the blank page and let her people
speak. There's much sadness here, but, paradoxically, the naiveté of her narrator is a bar to sentiment; the sharp child's eye sees even a dying
aunt as a figure of fun, mystery or awe, no more.
And her prose, with its Spanish rhythms and
lush, tumbling imagery, stays artfully this side of
over-ripe."

Reviews of *Woman Hollering Creek* were
even more enthusiastic. "Cisneros breathes narrative life into her adroit, poetic descriptions,"
Patricia Hart wrote in the *Nation,* "making them
mature, fully formed works of fiction."
Newsweek praised the playfulness, vigor, and
originality of Cisneros's feminist, Mexican-
American voice: "Noisily, wittily, always com-
passionately, Cisneros surveys woman's condition—a condition that is both precisely Latina
and general to women everywhere. Her characters include preadolescent girls, disappointed
brides, religious women, consoling partners and
deeply cynical women who enjoy devouring
men. They are without exception strong girls,
strong women. The girls who tell their brief stories are so alert they seem almost to quiver; the
mature women, in their longer stories, relish the
control they have painfully acquired. One, who
paints portraits of her lovers, says she is "making
the world look at you from my eyes." And if
that's not power, what is?"

In "Woman Hollering Creek," Cleofilas, a
young Mexican bride brought up on romantic
telenovelas, brought to a "town of dust and
despair" by her wife-beating, unfaithful Texas
husband, thinking about returning home to her
father's house, muses about who the woman in
the creek is:

> The stream sometimes only a muddy puddle in the sum-
> mer, though now in the springtime, because of the rains,
> a good-size alive thing, a thing with a voice all its own,
> all day and all night calling in its high, silver voice. Is it
> La Llorona, the weeping woman? La Llorona, who
> drowned her own children. Perhaps La Llorona is the
> one they named the creek after, she thinks, remembering
> all the stories she learned as a child. La Llorona calling
> to her. She is sure of it.

"How she sorts out her life, and the nice play
with metaphors that this involves," Peter S. Prescott and Karen Springen wrote in *Newsweek,*
"results in what may be the most appealing of
feminist stories."

Cisneros's feminism is always tied to her life
as a Chicana, a Latina woman. As Bebe Moore
Campbell wrote in the *New York Times Book
Review,* "In a land where our views of Hispanic
people are often limited or distorted, Sandra Cisneros offers precious glimpses of the internal
workings of their lives. She is an educator, unerring and relentless; she is not only a gifted writer
but an absolutely essential one." Aamer Hussein,
in the *Times Literary Supplement* in 1993 called
her "a quintessentially American writer" whose
work "bridges the gap between Anglo and
Hispanic." Cisneros agreed; as she told Tabor in
the 1993 *New York Times* interview, "I'm a
translator. I'm an amphibian. I can travel in both
worlds. What I'm saying is very important for
the Latino community, but it is also important
for the white community to hear. What I'm saying in my writing is that we can be Latino and
still be American."

Cisneros has lived in San Antonio, Texas, since
1984.

PRINCIPAL WORKS: *Fiction*—The House on Mango Street, 1984, rev. ed. 1991; Woman Hollering Creek and Other Stories, 1991. *Poetry*—Bad Boys, 1980; The Rodrigo Poems, 1985; My Wicked, Wicked Ways, 1987, 1992.

ABOUT: Calderon, H. and Saldivar, J. D. (eds.) Criticism in the Borderlands: Studies in Chicano Literature, Culture, and Ideology, 1991; Contemporary Authors 131, 1991; Horno-Delgado, A. et al. (eds.) Breaking Boundaries: Latina Writing and Critical Readings, 1989; Neito, E. M. and Telgen, D. (eds.) Notable Hispanic American Women, 1993; Saldivar, R. Chicano Narrative: The Dialectics of Difference, 1990. *Periodicals*—Atlantic June 1991; Booklist September 1, 1993; Commonweal September 13, 1991; Glamour November 1990; Nation May 6, 1991; New York Times January 7, 1993; New York Times Book Review May 26, 1991; Newsweek June 3, 1991; Publishers Weekly March 29, 1991; Times Literary Supplement May 15, 1992; September 13, 1993.

*CIXOUS, HÉLÈNE (June 5, 1937–), French novelist, essayist, and translator, was born in the colonial environment of Oran, Algeria, to a father of French-colonial background and to a mother of Austro-German origin. Her father died when she was a child. Early on Cixous was influenced by the environment in which she grew up. German, rather than French, is Cixous's native tongue. Members of her family were Sephardic Jews, and she lived through the persecutions of World War II. Sensitive to the influence of power at every institutional level— familial, academic, political—Cixous's fiction reflects a diverse desire to go beyond the horrors of 20th-century Europe and the trappings of the world into which she was born.

Cixous began her career as an academic. In 1959, at the age of twenty-two, she passed the prestigious *agrégation* in English. She married and had two children, a daughter and a son, born in 1958 and 1961. In 1962 she began teaching at the University of Bordeaux. In 1965 she and her husband were divorced and Cixous moved to Paris. She taught at the Sorbonne from 1965 to 1967 and at the University of Nanterre in 1967. Also in 1967 she published her first collection of writing, *Le Prénom de Dieu* (God's First Name). In 1968 she became *docteur és lettres*. The same year, in the aftermath of the student riots of May 1968, she was put in charge of the committee to found the experimental University of Paris VIII at Vincennes, now at Saint-Denis. An alternative to the traditional and, in the view of many, repressive French academic environment, Paris VIII was to be a center of learning where time-honored power structures and hierarchies would be kept to a minimum. Since 1967 Cixous has been professor of English literature at Paris VIII.

In 1969 Cixous, having become very active on the intellectual scene, founded with Tzvetan Todorov and Gérard Genette the review *Poétique*. The review was to be a forum for new ways of reading literary texts, a departure from the still largely literary-historical approach of 19th-century positivism. As a university professor of English literature, Cixous continued her career with the publication of her thesis, *L'Exil de James Joyce ou l'art du remplacement* (1968, The Exile of James Joyce). Though Joyce influenced her work through his insistence on the necessity to create new languages, on musicalizing literature and joining body and spirit, Cixous criticized him for his creative paradox. For Joyce, one must lose in order to have. In other words, one must kill in order to live. The movement to life starts with a killing of the other, with death, and guilt, a concept that differs significantly from Cixous's affirmation that loss and death are inevitable and necessary to life. In the United States, Cixous was first known for her work on Joyce and as an editor of *Poétique*. Subsequently, she made a name for herself as a feminist writer of fiction and plays. Cixous's abundant production can be divided into several groups, each loosely gravitating around a center of interest, along a path marked by Cixous's continued endeavor to push death back from the horizon of life.

The first texts are animated by a desire for autoanalysis in the wake of Cixous's discovery of Freud and such modern avatars as Jacques Lacan. Drawing her own portrait analytically, she works through her family structures, her childhood in Algeria, the death of her father, the influence of her German mother and grandmother, and her relationship with her brother. These familial structures are best rendered in *Dedans* (1969, Inside), which earned her the Prix Médicis and confirmed her reputation in literary circles.

The trilogy *Le Troisième Corps, Les Commencements*, and *Neutre* (The Third Body, Beginnings, and Neuter), published from 1970 to 1972, marks a period of great hope. In the aftermath of 1968, everything seemed possible. Students and professors had joined workers in the streets. Transformations in linguistic and ideological structures seemed unquestionable. Cixous's experimental texts of those years were written at the boundary of new theories and fictional invention. She developed her own fictions influenced by Derrida's theory, which transforms oppositions into differences; by Lacan's pronouncements on lanaguage as a chain of signifiers, a combination of metaphors and metonymies; and by Gilles Deleuze's texts undermining the logic of meaning, which put

°seek OO, eh LEHN

writing on the side of appropriation and death. The trilogy, like all of Cixous's subsequent work, is marked by an effort to undo repression, question power structures, and free writing and the self. Written at a time when the euphoria of new discoveries outweighed theoretical divergences, these texts combine many incompatible theories. The freeing of the subject and the undoing of repression go along with a reevaluation of what has been repressed: body, woman, writing. Cixous works through Lacan's pronouncements about the insistence of the letter in the unconscious and Derrida's affirmation about origin as repetition.

In 1974 Cixous established the Centre de Recherches en Etudes Féminines (Center for Research in Feminine Studies). The following year she published "Le Rire de la Méduce," translated in 1976 in the review *Signs* by Keith and Paula Cohen as "The Laugh of the Medusa." Cixous focuses on a small but crucial text by Freud that deals with castration, a founding concept of phallic society. Man, horrified by woman's genitals, turns to stone. The turning into stone, a defensive measure, becomes simultaneous with erection, or man's entrance into a symbolic system which excludes woman. Laughter, however, explodes that symbolic meaning; it is decentered toward something more positive, toward joy and an affirmation of life.

Affirmation of life functions as the most important concern of *La Jeune Née* (1975, *The Newly Born Woman*), a book cowritten with Catherine Clément. The title, *La Jeune Née*, plays at the same time on *Là-je-nais*, "there I am being born," and *La Genet*, a female version of the author Jean Genet, whose poetic writings assert the general equality of all human beings. In *The Newly Born Woman*, Cixous underscores the necessity of displacing the desire for recognition, always based on sexual war, which ends, symbolically, with the succumbing of one of the partners. To this, she opposes a process by which, through a journeying toward the other, through identification without fusion, the self goes as far as possible toward the other, lets herself be altered by the other, yet does not become the other. This desire keeps the other alive. To bring about change, Cixous urges women to break their silence, to "write themselves." They must write their bodies, their desires which heretofore have ony been talked about by men. Freud's Dora, the great hysteric of one of his case studies, is a central concern in *The Newly Born Woman*. *Portrait du soleil* (Portrait of the Sun, 1974) is a poetic rewriting of Freud's case study. A play, *Portrait de Dora*, performed at the Théâtre d'Orsay in 1975, published in 1976, and translated in 1977 as *Portrait of Dora*, put Freud on stage to show the analyst's own projections in his treatment of Dora and his writings on her.

Cixous's personal difficulties contributed to the 1977 text *Angst*, which deals with the breakdown of a love reltionship. The pain and anguish are not expressed in existential, representational terms, but in a metaphoric exchange of letters. The text, as always one of transformation, led Cixous to another phase in her consideration of women's issues. For the next few years Cixous espoused the cause of women in a more militant language and her work appeared almost exclusively under the imprint of the publishing house Des Femmes, where Cixous enjoyed a close relationship with Antoinette Fouque, cofounder of the Mouvement de Libération des Femmes (Women's Liberation Movement). She explained this decision in an interview (published in Verena Andermatt Conley's *Hélène Cixous: Writing the Feminine*) as reflecting her having attained an intellectual limit which, she felt, had to be surpassed. Consequently, she developed a more marked interest in relationships among women, though men are never completely absent in her writing.

In the 1970s Cixous discovered the Brazilian author Clarice Lispector. Influenced to a degree by the French new novel, but with a strong voice of her own, Lispector meditated on writing and on the relationship between life and writing. Lispector, in her interest in quotidian objects and preoccupation with passion and the flowing quality of the word, had already put into practice what Cixous had been seeking. Cixous's article in *Poétique*, "L'Approche de Clarice Lispector," appeared in 1979, the same year as the bilingual text *Vivre l'orange / To Live the Orange*. These texts play on fruit, but very differently from the earlier *Portrait du soleil*. There Cixous had punned in her opening statement: "D'Oran-je" (from Oran I am), linking her native city Oran to the orange. She had insisted on the cut made in the orange, on the gap or wound, from which the text had been written. Now, sweet nourishing juices replace the wound. The emphasis is on the metaphor of the world as fruit, as products, as something nourishing that one keeps alive: to live, not to consume; to keep alive, not to kill.

A break with Antoinette Fouque in the early 1980s prompted Cixous to leave Des Femmes temporarily. Her relationship with the publishing house had been increasingly strained. Cixous claims that she resented the limits a certain militancy imposed on her freedom. Another text, *Le Livre de Promethea* (1983, *The Book of Promethea*), written after her encounter with Ariane Mnouchkine, the director of the experimental Théâtre du Soleil, marks a turn. The book is a celebration of their encounter and a feminine rewriting of the Promethean myth, which, along with the myths of Orpheus and Ulysses, has figured prominently in literature. *The Book of Promethea* marks the culmination of a search for a positive passion, for a positive love and a language that touches lightly, intermittently, without seizing, appropriating, but infusing with life. The Promethean myth, from its epic dimensions of freeing the world and mankind, is transposed to quotidian passion, to detail, to a market scene, to fruits and flowers.

Cixous's encounter with Ariane Mnouchkine proved decisive. Mnouchkine was known for her innovative productions of Shakespeare, linking the Elizabeth stage with Far Eastern techniques. Cixous had already herself produced *Portrait of Dora* and was preparing *La Prise de l'école de Madhubaï* (performed in 1984; translated as *The Conquest of the School of Madhubaï*). With Mnouchkine, Cixous traveled to Cambodia to study a group of people that had been possessed by their neighbors. Cixous's play *L'Histoire terrible mais inachevée de Norodom Sihanouk roi du Cambodge* (performed in 1984; translated in 1994 as *The Terrible But Unfinished Story of Norodom Sihanouk, King of Cambodia*) is the story of a people that had lived happily, amid dancing, singing, and harmony. Such an overtly political play is a continuation of Cixous's fight against all forms of bodily and spiritual repression. The play is infused with a contemporary reading of the concept of freedom which, for her, is linked to poetry and writing. *L'Indiade ou l'Inde de leurs rêves* (The Indiade or India of their dreams), a play produced in 1986, deals with the problems of colonialism, the liberation of India, and pacifism.

Cixous's break with Ariane Mnouchkine in 1992 has made her write for a variety of theaters. An adaptation of the *Nibelungen* was produced in 1994, followed by a production for the Théâtre du Soleil, *L'affaire des sangs contaminés* (The Case of the Contaminated Blood) about French people who were given transfusions with HIV-positive blood. Next to plays, she continues her abundant writing of fictional text. A recent "autobiography," *Photos de Racine* (1993), assesses her own life and career as a writer.

In addition to writing for the theater, Cixous has continued to publish fiction. She has also produced *Entre l'écriture* (Between Writing, or Enter Writing, 1986) a collection of new and previously published meditations on writing and painting. Cixous has begun to focus increasingly on the relationship between history and writing. *Manne* (1988, *Manna*) is a lyrical text about the irruption of history in the personal lives of poets. It is a tribute to Osip Mandelstam, a victim of the Stalin regime, and Nelson Mandela, the fighter

against apartheid in South Africa, and also to women poets, from the Russian Marina Tsvetaeva to the concentration-camp victim Etty Heilsum. Her involvement in theater marks a new departure in Cixous's work which is likely to continue for some time.

For Cixous, it is a question of finding a language adequate to life, often in its smallest forms, but also of epic proportions. Cixous's writing is marked with passion, energy, and force. From fictional texts to theater and "theory," Cixous is always challenging and provocative. Situated in the mainstream of contemporary French thought of the last decades, Cixous manages to have a distinctive, slightly archaic, highly lyrical voice that is noteworthy for never being militantly strident.

PRINCIPAL WORK IN ENGLISH TRANSLATION: (tr. S. A. J. Purcell) The Exile of James Joyce, 1992; (tr. A. Barros) Portrait of Dora *in* Benmussa Directs, 1979; (tr. A. Liddle and S. Cornell) Vivre l'orange / To Live the Orange, 1979; (tr. J. Levy) August 1985; (tr. B. Wing) The Newly Born Woman (with Catherine Clément) 1986; (tr. C. Barko) Inside, 1986; Writing Differences: Readings from the seminar of Hélène Cixous (ed. S. Sellers) 1988; The Body and the Text (ed. H. Wilcox) 1990; (tr. V. A. Conley) Reading with Clarice Lispector, 1990; Coming to Writing and Other Essays (ed. D. Jenson), 1991; (tr. V. A. Conley) Readings, 1991; (tr. B. Wing) The Book of Promethea, 1991; (tr. S. Cornell and S. Sellers) Three Steps on the Ladder of Writing, 1992; (tr. J. F. MacCannell, J. Pike, and L. Groth) The Terrible But Unfinish Story of Norodom Sihamouh, King of Cambodia, 1994; The Hélène Cixous Reader (ed. S. Sellers) 1994; (tr. C. A. F. MacGillivray) Manna, 1994. *Periodical publications*—"The Character of 'Character'" *in* New Literary History, 1974; "At Circe's, or The Self-Opener" *in* Boundary, 2, 1975; "The Laugh of the Medusa" *in* Signs: Journal of Women and Culture in Society, 1976; "Fiction and Its Phantoms: A Reading of Freud's 'Das Unheimliche' ('The Uncanny')" *in* New Literary History, 1976; "Introduction to Lewis Carroll's Through the Lookingglass and The Hunting of the Snark" *in* New Literary History, 1982; "12 About 1980" *in* Boundary 2, 1984; "Reaching the Point of Wheat, or a Portrait of the Artist as a Maturing Woman"" *in* New Literary History, 1987.

ABOUT: Cixous, H. Writing Differences: Readings from the Seminar of Hélène Cixous (ed. S. Sellers) 1988; Cixous, H. The Body and the Text (ed. H. Wilcox) 1990; Conley, V. A. Hélène Cixous: Writing the Feminine, 1984, 1992; Conley, V. A. Hélène Cixous: Poetry and Politics, 1992; Eisenstein, H. and A. Jardine (eds.) The Future of Difference, 1980; Greene, G. and C. Kahn (eds.) Making a Difference: Feminist Literary Criticism, 1985; Moi, T. Sexual/Textual Politics: Feminist Literary Theory, 1985; Shiach, M. Hélène Cixous: A Politics of Writing, 1991. *Periodicals*—Boundary 2, 12, Winter 1984; Contemporary Literature 24, Summer 1983; Esprit Créateur 25, Summer 1985; French

Studies 7, Summer 1981; Signs 7, Autumn 1981; Sub-Stance, 5, 6, 10, 11, 16, 1976–1987; Theater Journal 37, 1985; Yale French Studies 75, 1988.

CLANCY, THOMAS (TOM) L., JR.

(1947–), American novelist, was born in Baltimore, Maryland, the son of a mailcarrier and a department store credit employee. He received his primary and secondary education at Baltimore-area Catholic schools and displayed an early interest in science fiction and military history. "I never read kids' books," he told *New York Times Magazine* interviewer Patrick Anderson. " . . . I remember reading Jules Verne in the third grade. I started on Samuel Eliot Morison in the fourth or fifth grade—he started me on military history." At Loyola College, a Jesuit liberal arts institution in Baltimore, Clancy majored in English, receiving his B.A. in 1969. As an undergraduate, he submitted a short story to the science fiction magazine *Analog*, but the work was rejected. Clancy was a strong supporter of the war in Vietnam, and served briefly in the ROTC while at Loyola College, but had to drop out because of poor eyesight.

Shortly after graduating from college, Clancy married Wanda Thomas and went to work as an insurance salesman. By 1980 he was able to purchase an insurance dealership in rural Maryland owned by his wife's grandfather. At the age of thirty-five, Clancy was by his own account financially secure, even prosperous, though terribly bored. His thoughts soon turned to fulfilling a long-standing ambition: writing novels.

Clancy had been mulling over a writing project for years, his imagination sparked by a news story about the Soviet frigate *Storozhevoy*, whose political officer, along with other crew members, staged a mutiny and attempted to defect to Sweden. To prepare for the writing, Clancy immersed himself in such works as Norman Polmar's *Guide to the Soviet Navy* and the British periodical *Jane's Defence Weekly*, learning as much as he could about the capabilities of Soviet warships. He also tried to imagine conditions under which a high-ranking Soviet officer might choose to defect. Many of his agency's clients were military people stationed in Maryland, and from them Clancy was able to obtain useful information about both the technology of modern warships and the psychology of those who serve on them. In plotting the battle scenes for his book, he made use of a commercially available war game called "Harpoon."

When it was completed, he presented the manuscript of *The Hunt for Red October* to the U.S. Naval Academy's Naval Institute Press in

TOM CLANCY

Annapolis which had only recently decided to publish fiction with a naval theme. A veteran submariner assigned to vet Clancy's manuscript found it not only "replete with errors," according to a *Newsweek* story, but also a source of classified information about American naval technology. After Clancy corrected the book's errors and convinced the editor that all his sources were nonclassifed, the Naval Institute Press cleared the novel for publication. An elaborate cat-and-mouse thriller, *The Hunt for Red October* pits the American forces attempting to guide the defectors aboard the submarine to U.S. territorial waters against the increasingly desperate Soviet fleet. The novel garnered much of its early popularity through word-of-mouth, often in military circles, bolstered by a number of early favorable reviews. In his *Washington Post Book World* review, Reid Beddow wrote, "It may be the most satisfactory novel of a sea chase since C. S. Forester perfected the form." In the *Times Literary Supplement*, U.S. Secretary of Defense Caspar Weinberger marveled, "The technical detail is vast and accurate, remarkably so for an author who originally had no background or experience." Soon it became obvious that *The Hunt for Red October* was a public relations boon for the U.S. Navy. Faced with selling a new attack submarine to Congress, Secretary of the Navy John Lehman, a former Clancy critic, hailed the novel as "a great service." The book found its way into the hands of President Ronald Reagan, who deemed it "the perfect yarn." It was equally popular as a film, starring Sean Connery as the commander of the defecting soviet sub.

The Hunt for Red October was not, of course, without its detractors. In his review in *Life* magazine, Loudon Wainwright remarked, "But surely one of the book's biggest selling points has to be that it all comes out right in the end. . . . [I]t reaffirms the comfortable convictions we have about ourselves and our superiority over the usual villainous Russians. . . . "

In the wake of the unexpected runaway success of *The Hunt for Red October*, Clancy was suddenly a celebrity. He was invited to the White House for a private meeting with President Reagan and was feted by military enthusiasts around the country. Now he had the opportunity to gain firsthand experience with the military operations and hardware he had known only from books and technical manuals. Clancy observed and participated in training exercises and spent a week at sea on a missle-carrying frigate, and another on a submarine. (Despite the detailed descriptions of life aboard a submarine in *The Hunt for Red October*, Clancy had never set foot on one until after the novel was published.)

Clancy incorporated much of his newfound knowledge of military hardware into his second novel, *Red Storm Rising*, about a full-scale, but non-nuclear war in Europe, terrorists' destruction of Soviet oil refineries in Siberia, which in turn triggered a massive Soviet strike against NATO forces in Western Europe. Like *The Hunt for Red October*, *Red Storm Rising* owes much to the war game "Harpoon," and in his preface to the novel, Clancy credits the game's creator.

Red Storm Rising was an enormous popular success. In the *Washington Post Book World*, the military historian John Keegan noting that there is "a long tradition of military futurology in Western literature," compared the novel with such works as Jules Vern's *Twenty Thousand Leagues Under the Sea* and H.G. Wells's *The War of the Worlds*, and predicted that *Red Storm Rising* would "take its place with those two triumphs. . . . .It is a brilliant military fantasy—and far too close to reality for comfort." The Naval War College apparently concurred and put the novel on its required reading list. Scott Shuger, a former naval intelligence officer, however, was uneasy about Clancy's acceptance in military circles. His fiction "dangerously inflated expectations about what the military can accomplish," he noted in the *Washington Monthly*. Shuger claimed that "Clancy's fantasies . . . fulfill the leaders' need to believe that a[n] . . . operation will be carried out exactly as ordered. Because he encourages complacency, Clancy's message is a threat to national security."

The subject of *Patriot Games*, Clancy's third novel, is international terrorism. The perpetrators are members of the ultra-radical group, the fictional Ulster Liberation Army. The hero of the novel is Jack Ryan, who helped to save the day in *The Hunt for Red October*. Ryan is Clancy's personification of intelligence, decency, and patriotism. A former marine who made a fortune on Wall Street, he is a CIA operative whenever he is called upon.

Patriot Games was as popular with the reading public as the earlier novels and became a popular film with Harrison Ford replacing Alec Baldwin as the stalwart hero, Ryan. The critical reception of the book, however, was mixed and some reviewers agreed with David Lehman's view of the novel's cold-war Manichaeanism. "There's no room for nuance or doubt in this universe of moral absolutes," he wrote in *Newsweek*. "What Clancy has to offer—and it makes his books seem emblematic of the Reagan administration's self-image—is an old-fashioned sense of certitude, righteousness and derring-do."

Clancy's penchant for technology-driven plots reasserted itself in his fourth novel, *The Cardinal of the Kremlin*, an espionage thriller set against the backdrop of a major U.S.-Soviet arms control negotiation, with Jack Ryan, once again at work for the CIA, as its hero. Robert Lekachman, in the *New York Times Book Review*, thought the novel "by far the best of the Jack Ryan series." Although he found Clancy's prose "no better than workman-like," Lekachman called the novel's "unmasking" of the Soviet agent "as sophisticated an exercise in the craft of espionage as I have yet to encounter."

Patrick Anderson's *New York Times Magazine* profile of Clancy was entitled, "King of the Techno-thriller." "Literature means a hundred years after you're dead they make kids read you in high school," Clancy told Anderson. "I'm in the entertainment business. . . . " But Clancy's choice of genre—the techno-thriller—does not stem from cold, commercial calculation. The scenarios of his novels and his unapologetic boosterism for the military and its high-tech weaponry are heartfelt expressions of his core beliefs.

The popularity of Clancy's first four novels is obviously predicated on rivalry between the U.S. and the U.S.S.R. As Evan Thomas noted in *Newsweek* in 1989, "the end of the cold war could be bad news for the techno-thriller business." In *Clear and Present Danger*, published shortly before the Berlin Wall came down, Clancy presciently turned his attention to a non-Soviet menace—the drug lords of the

South American cocaine cartel. Then, in *The Sum of All Fears*, in the aftermath of the Gulf War, Clancy has Jack Ryan, now in the post of deputy director of the CIA, assigned to organize Middle East peace talks at the same time a group of terrorists discover an Israeli nuclear bomb buried in the Syrian desert. However, Clancy's 1993 novel *Without Remorse* reverts to the earlier 1970s and the ever-menacing KGB.

Among the fruits of literary success was the Republican party's effort in 1990 to recruit Clancy as a candidate for a Maryland House or Senate seat. While Clancy declined to run, he told *U.S. News & World Report*: If I ever do this, it will be because I think I have an obligation to pay my country back for the success I've enjoyed. I guess I don't have the right to complain about the people in government unless I'm willing to take the plunge."

PRINCIPAL WORKS: *Novels*—The Hunt for Red October, 1984; Red Storm Rising, 1986; Patriot Games, 1987; The Cardinal of the Kremlin, 1988; Clear and Present Danger, 1989; The Sum of All Fears, 1991; Without Remorse, 1993.

ABOUT: Contemporary Authors 125, 1989; 131, 1991; Contemporary Literary Criticism 45, 1987; Current Biography Yearbook, 1988; International Authors and Writers Who's Who. *Periodicals*—Life April 1985; Nation's Business December 1987; New York Times August 15, 1991; New York Times Book Review July 31, 1988; New York Times Magazine May 1, 1988; New Yorker September 16, 1991; Newsweek August 17, 1987; August 8, 1988; August 21, 1989; Publishers Weekly August 8, 1986; Time August 21, 1989; Times Literary Supplement October 18, 1985; U.S. News & World Report September 15, 1986; March 26, 1990; Virginia Quarterly Review Winter 1993; Wall Street Journal August 18, 1986; Washington Monthly November 1989; Washington Post Book World October 21, 1984; July 27, 1986.

CLARK, MARY HIGGINS (December 24, 1929–), American writer of suspense fiction, was born in New York City to Luke Joseph Higgins and Nora C. (Durkin) Higgins. She grew up in New York City, in the Bronx, where her father owned Higgins Bar and Grill, a "wonderful, elegant Irish bar," she told a *Publishers Weekly* interviewer in 1989, where he "worked twenty hours a day and died young, trying to save his business." She was ten years old when her father died. . . . Unable to find a job, her mother worked as a baby-sitter and took in boarders. Mary attended the Villa Maria Academy as a scholarship student and worked afternoons and weekends as a telephone operator in a Manhattan hotel. She went on to secretarial school and

MARY HIGGINS CLARK

after graduation took a job in advertising at Remington Rand, working Saturdays at Lord and Taylor, the department store. She said about her jobs, "there were no 'woulds' or 'shoulds' or 'coulds' or 'ought to' about extra jobs. I *had* to." She was a Pan American flight attendant for a year before her marriage to an airline executive. That job provided the idea for her first story, "Last Flight from Danubia." She married Warren F. Clark in 1949. He died in 1964, leaving her to raise their five children. To support her family, Clark wrote scripts for radio shows. She also wrote her first book *Aspire to the Heavens*, a novel about George Washington, published in 1969. Though it sold poorly, "it proved I could write a book," Clark told a *Redbook* interviewer. "So I thought, 'now I'll try one that sells.'" Before getting the children to school and herself to her job, she wrote her first suspense novel, *Where Are the Children?*, published in 1975. It was a best-seller, as were her next five novels. Her seventh, *While My Pretty One Sleeps*, was the first book of a five-book contract for which Simon and Schuster paid a record-breaking advance. In 1992, Clark signed a $35 million dollar contract for four novels, a memoir, and a collection of short stories. *I'll Be Seeing You*, her tenth suspense novel, was published in 1993. When she sold the paperback rights to *Where Are the Children?* for a substantial sum and was thereby freed from "scrimping to educate the children," she decided that she could go back to school; she attended Fordham University three nights a week and earned a B.A. in philosophy, graduating summa cum laude in 1979. She was awarded the French Grand Prix de Littérature Policiére in 1980, an honorary doctorate from Villanova University in 1983, and an honorary doctorate from Fordham in 1988.

"I believe in good guys and bad guys and I plot for an emotional ending," Clark said in an interview with *Publishers Weekly*. One of her frequent devices for raising tension in her stories is to put a child in danger. *Where are the Children?* was turned down by two publishers who felt that women readers would be uncomfortable with the theme of murdered children, but Clark thought otherwise. When Nancy Harmon's children are kidnapped, she becomes a suspect. Under sympathetic questioning by a psychiatrist, her repressed memories lead to the identification of the murderer-kidnapper— her abusive ex-husband, whose suicide had thrown suspicion on her. Only in the last pages of the story does she realize that he must have faked his death, and that it is he who is threatening her new children. The novel uses several elements that have become characteristic of Clark's fiction: a short time-frame, in this case a single day: a woman whose memory of a crime is repressed or distorted; and a pathological killer whose guilt is established from the start. What creates the tension for which Clark's novels are known is a narration that shifts nervously among the characters, who separately come to realize the importance of the part of the story they know.

Clark is noted for the pace of her novels. In *A Stranger is Watching*, while a time-bomb ticks in an underground room in Grand Central Station, an innocent man convicted of another's crime is about to be executed, and the hero must both save his child and girlfriend *and* convince the governor to stay the execution before the bomb goes off. By her third novel, *A Cradle Will Fall*, a *Newsweek* reviewer noted the "familiar materials" with which Clark builds her novels, but conceded that the "hammering and joining are expertly professional." Elisabeth Jakab wrote in the *New York Times Book Review* that the plot of Clark's *A Cry in the Night*, in which the heroine, a mother of two is taken by her mysterious second husband to his isolated house, "appears to have been put together out of generous borrowings from many familiar sources, *Psycho, Gaslight, Rebecca, Jane Eyre*, among others"; but "the story sweeps rapidly along, and in spite of my sense of *déjà vu*, I was kept guessing for far longer than I care to admit." The novels that followed *Stillwatch, Weep No More, My Lady*, and *While My Pretty One Sleeps*, have glamourous settings—respectively, the Washington political scene, a posh California health spa, and the New York fashion world—and, like their predecessors, the tension-setting elements that drew millions of readers.

In his 1991 *New York Times* review of *The Anastasia Syndrome*, Herbert Mitgang gave what may be a fair appraisal of all Clark's fiction: "Mary Higgins Clark knows how to pull out the stops on the fiction organ, producing all the popular tremulous effects. . . . clean cut romance without parental guidance needed, royal characters, mysterious coincidences, glamorous clothing, perfect hairdressers, recognizable places in New York and London, moments of menace. *The Anastasia Syndrome* . . . is a perfect example of escape literature: undemanding, unbelievable and entertaining."

Several of her novels have been made into motion pictures—*A Stranger Is Watching* in 1982, *A Cry in the Night* in 1985, and *Where Are the Children?* in 1986. Two others were filmed for television—*The Cradle Will Fall*, in 1984, and *Stillwatch* in 1987.

PRINCIPAL WORKS: *Novels*—Aspire to the Heavens, 1969; Where Are the Children?, 1975; A Stranger is Watching, 1978; The Cradle Will Fall, 1980; A Cry in the Night, 1982; Stillwatch, 1984; Weep No More, My Lady, 1987; While My Pretty One Sleeps, 1989; Loves Music, Loves to Dance, 1991; All Around the Town, 1992; I'll Be Seeing You, 1993; Remember Me, 1994; Let Me Call You Sweetheart, 1995. *Collected short fiction*—The Anastasia Syndrome, 1989; The Lottery Winner, 1994. *As editor*—Bad Behavior, 1995.

ABOUT: Contemporary Authors New Revision Series 36, 1992; Current Biography Yearbook 1994; Twentieth-Century Crime and Mystery Writers, 3rd ed., 1991. *Periodicals*—Armchair Detective Summer 1985; Modern Maturity August-September 1989; New York Times December 6, 1989; June 4, 1991; New York Times Book Review November 14, 1982; December 3, 1989; June 16, 1991; Newsweek June 30, 1980; People November 2, 1992; Publishers Weekly May 19, 1989; October 19, 1992; Redbook March 1991.

CLIFTON, LUCILLE (SAYLES) (June 27, 1936–), American poet and children's author, whose works illuminate the experience of urban blacks in America. Whether dealing with the issue of racism, self-discovery, womanhood, African heritage, or family, Clifton's underlying theme is that it is good to be black. With short, economical, but passion-filled phrases, she affirms and humanizes in everyday language a sector of the population that is often ignored, patronized, feared, or underrated—the inhabitants of the inner city. Clifton admits that her definition of poetry differs greatly from that of many of her peers. "It's as if poetry started in the academy," she argued in an interview with Naomi Theirs for *Belles Lettres*. "But poetry didn't start at a desk; it didn't start at a computer. The

LUCILLE CLIFTON

first poem came from somebody walking out of a cave or off a savannah and looking up and seeing the stars and saying Wow!" She also writes in *Black Women Writers (1950–1980)*, "I have never believed that for anything to be valid or true or intellectual or 'deep' it had to first be complex. I am not interested if anyone knows whether or not I am familiar with big words. I am interested in being understood not admired."

Clifton was born in a working-class community in Depew, New York, just outside Buffalo. Her father, Samuel Louis Sayles, worked in a steel mill, and her mother, Thelma Sayles, worked in a laundry. Although neither parent finished elementary school, both were avid readers who passed on their love of reading to their daughter. "I saw reading as a natural part of life and grew up loving books and words," she told Harriet Jackson Scarupa in *Ms.* magazine. "How I do love words!"

In addition to being an avid reader, Clifton's father was also a weaver of tales who would tirelessly repeat stories about his ancestors to anyone who would listen. "My father told those stories to me over and over," Clifton told Theirs. "That made them seem important. He told the stories to whoever was present, but I was the person who listened." One of her father's favorite tales was about Clifton's great-great grandmother, Caroline. Born free among the Dahomey people of West Africa, Caroline was captured and enslaved as a little girl and forced to walk from New Orleans to Virginia. A native of a tribe in which the women were warriors, Caroline survived the horrors of slavery, becoming the myth-

ical family matriarch and role model whose legacy to her children and succeeding generations was "Get what you want, you from Dahomey women."

Clifton's mother was not a Dahomey woman, but her legacy was her poetry. "From Mama I knew one could write as a way to express oneself," Clifton told Scarupa. "My mother was a rather sad person. She had epilepsy and died, too young, at forty-four. A lot of feelings went into her poetry."

Clifton began writing poetry at an early age, but "I never thought of having a career as a poet," she explained to Theirs. "I hadn't thought it possible. . . . The only poets I ever saw or heard of were the portraits that hung on the wall of my elementary school—old dead white men from New England with beards. Of course it didn't seem a possibility for me."

In 1953 Clifton won a full scholarship to Howard University. "When I went away to college, well, that was some time," she writes in *Generations: A Memoir.* "People couldn't get it straight that I was going to Howard not Harvard. Nobody in our family had graduated from high school at that time. . . . We didn't know a thing about going to college." Clifton had a difficult time adjusting to college life and felt out of place among the black upper crust. She lost her scholarship after two years. "I didn't study," she admits in *Generations.* "I didn't have to I thought. I didn't have to know about science and geography and things that I didn't want to know." When her family expressed their dismay at her failure at Howard, her response was, "I don't need that stuff. I'm going to write poems. I can do what I want to do. I'm from Dahomey women."

In 1955 Clifton attended Fredonia State Teachers College (now the State University of New York at Fredonia), where with a group of fellow writers, she began finding her own voice as a writer. It was also here that she met Fred Clifton, an education and political writer, whom she would marry in 1958. At this point, Clifton had still not thought seriously about getting her poems published. "I had been writing with major intent—not the intent of publishing, which is what it often is today," she told Theirs. "But just trying to serve the poem well, trying to do the best I could." Clifton's friends, however, encouraged her to send her poems to the poet Robert Hayden. He sent them to another poet, Carolyn Kizer, who sent them to the YW-YMHA Poetry Center in New York, which gave Clifton its prestigious Discovery Award in 1969. The collection was published under the title *Good Times*, and was cited by the *New York Times* as one of the ten best books of 1969.

"When my first book was published I was thirty-three years old and had six children under ten years old," Clifton recalled in *Black Women Writers.* "I was too busy to take it terribly seriously. I was happy and proud of course, but had plenty of other things to think about."

Good Times paints a stark portrait of life in the inner city, where youths have forgotten their heritage and women "got used to making it through murdered sons / and . . . grief kept on pushing." Yet the everyday adversities are what compel inner city residents to live, dream, and "hang on":

> in the inner city
> or like we call it
> home
> we think a lot about uptown
> and the silent nights
> and the houses straight as dead men
> and the pastel lights
> and we hang on to our no place
> happy to be alive
> and in the inner city
> or like we call it
> home

Clifton's second volume of poetry, *Good News About the Earth*, suggests redemption from urban oppression. As she writes in the poem "good friday," "i rise up above myself / like a fish flying / men will be gods / if they want it." Black redemption, however, comes primarily through knowledge of self and history:

> listen children
> keep this in the place
> you have for keeping
> always . . .
> we have been ashamed
> hopeless tired mad
> but always
> all ways
> we loved us . . .
> pass it on

Clifton also suggests that black salvation and self-discovery will be achieved only by rejecting the images and perceptions that are not true reflections of African Americans. In the poem "after Kent State," from *Good News About the Earth*, she deals harshly with a major source of black oppression—racism:

> only to keep
> his little fear
> he kills his cities
> and his trees
> even his children oh
> people
> white ways are
> the way of death
> come into the black
> and live

Some reviewers concluded from this poem that Clifton hates whites. She denies this. "What I'm talking about is a certain kind of white arrogance—and not all white people have it—that is not good," she told Scarupa. "I think airs of superiority are very dangerous. I believe in justice. I try not be about hatred." Clifton is not only critical of certain "white ways," she is also critical of those self-destructive "black ways" that have hindered African-American progress. A poem in her third volume of poetry, *An Ordinary Woman*, illustrates this point:

> come home from the movies
> black girls and boys
> the picture be over and the screen
> be cold as our neighborhood
> come home from the show
> don't be the show
> take off some flowers and plant them,
> pick us some papers and read them,
> stop making babies and raise them . . .
> show our fathers how to walk like men,
> they already know how to dance.

Ordinary Woman is also Clifton's self-exploration and examination of her roles as woman and poet. "The thirty-eighth year / of my life, / plain as bread / round as cake / an ordinary woman . . . / I had expected more than this / I had not expected to be / an ordinary woman." Clifton's often optimistic and humorous writing style, however, transforms the ordinary into the extraordinary. As she writes in "Homage to my Hips," from *Two-Headed Woman*, "these hips are big hips . . . / these hips are mighty hips / these hips are magic hips / I have known them / to put a spell on a man and / spin him like a top!"

Although the issue of womanhood recurs throughout Clifton's poetry, she shuns being labeled a womanist, a term defined by Alice Walker as encompassing a black feminism that involves the "survival affirmation and empowerment of all persons." As Clifton explained to Scarupa: "The Movement is helpful to some women. It's good for them to realize they can be something or do something and not have to follow some prescribed role." Clifton has argued that love between the sexes can do more to heal the problems between them than animosity. "When people love each other, they'll accept a lot of things they wouldn't otherwise," she told Scarupa. "They can deal with things they couldn't deal with otherwise. It has to do with the nature of love."

Clifton has sought to make her poetry tools of understanding not only between the sexes but of the self, history, family, and religion. In her poems she wrestles with these issues while maintaining a sense of optimism. She insists, however, in *Black Women Writers*, "I am . . . much less sunny than I am pictured." Clifton is clearly pessimistic about the problem of drug addiction in the inner city. "We have a generation enslaving itself to drugs," she writes in *Essence* magazine. "Young men and women doing to our race what slavery couldn't." As she writes in the poem "White Lady" (a street name for cocaine), from *Quilting*:

> you have chained our sons
> in the basement
> of the big house
> white lady
> you have walked our daughters
> out into the streets
> white lady
> what do we have to pay
> to repossess our children
> white lady
> what do we have to owe
> to own our own at last

Clifton, however, is compelled to believe in triumph in the "long run." She writes in *Black Women Writers*: "I try to transmit the possible joy in my work. This does not mean that there have been no dark days; it means that they have not mattered."

The first of Clifton's children's books, *Some of the Days of Everett Anderson*, was published in the same year as her first volume of poetry, 1969. The mother of six children, Clifton has said that writing books for children came easily for her and that her first took about half an hour to write. "I must have been waiting to do it for a long time, although I'd never expressed that desire," she told Theirs. "I wanted to write a book about a child living in the projects to show that being poor—not having things doesn't mean being poor in spirit."

Audrey McCluskey, reviewing Clifton's books for *Black Women Writers*, commented: "She does not patronize the children for whom she writes. She gives them credit for being intelligent human beings who do not deserve to be treated differently because of their age. . . . [H]er respect for children as people and her finely tuned instincts about what is important to them—their fears—their joys . . . makes her a successful writer of children's literature."

Clifton has received many honors and awards, including a nomination for the Pulitzer Prize for poetry for *Two-Headed Woman* and a second nomination for *Good Woman: Poems and a Memoir* and *Next* (published concurrently in 1987). In 1970 and 1972 she received National Endowment for the Arts awards, and in 1979 was named Maryland's Poet Laureate. She received the Juniper Prize for Poetry in 1980 for *Two-Headed Woman*. A Distinguished Professor of Humanities at St. Mary's College in Maryland, she has nevertheless found it difficult to gain acceptance by her peers in education. As she told Theirs: "Sometimes my feelings are hurt when I think what I do is underrated by some people, especially because people know I didn't graduate from a four-year college. But I get over it. . . . I am very grounded in my own self. One of the blessings of being born an African-American woman is that I learned a long time ago not to buy other people's definitions of who I am and what I'm supposed to be like."

PRINCIPAL WORKS: *Poetry*—Good Times: Poems, 1969; Good News About the Earth: New Poems, 1972; An Ordinary Woman, 1974; Two-Headed Woman, 1980; Good Woman: Poems and a Memoir 1969–1980, 1987; Next: New Poems, 1987; Quilting, 1991. *Memoir*—Generations: A Memoir, 1976. *Juvenile*—The Black BCs, 1970; Some of the Days of Everett Anderson, 1970; Everett Anderson's Christmas Coming, 1971; All Us Come Cross the Water, 1973; The Boy Who Didn't Believe in Spring, 1973; Don't You Remember?, 1973; Good, Says Jerome, 1973; Everett Anderson's Year, 1974; The Times They Used to Be, 1974; My Brother Fine with Me, 1975; Everett Anderson's Friend, 1976; Three Wishes, 1976; Everett Anderson's 1 2 3, 1977; Amifika, 1911; Everett Anderson's Nine Month Long, 1978; The Lucky Stone, 1979; My Friend Jacob, 1980; Sonora Beautiful, 1981; Everett Anderson's Goodbye, 1983.

ABOUT: American Poets Since World War II, 1980; Black Literature Criticism 1, 1992; Black Women Writers (1950–1980), 1984; Clifton, L. Generations: A Memoir, 1976; Coming to Light: American Women Poets in the Twentieth Century, 1985; Contemporary Authors New Revision Series 24, 1988; Contemporary Literary Criticism 19, 1981. *Periodicals*—Belles Lettres Summer 1994; Essence November 1989; Ms. October 1976; New York Times March 1, 1992; School Library Journal February 1994.

CLIVE, JOHN LEONARD (September 25, 1924–January 7, 1990), American historian and educator, was born in Germany, one of two sons of Bruno and Rose (Rosenfeld) Kleyff. (His birth name, which he retained until 1941, was Hans Leo Kleyff.) A few dramatic details about his boyhood come to light in "The Use of the Past," the introduction to *Not by Fact Alone*. Clive recalled, "I grew up in Berlin, the son of Middle-class German-Jewish parents who were so 'assimilated' that they couldn't believe that the Nazis would retain power for more than a few years or were really serious about their anti-Semitic slogans, until shop windows were smashed, synagogues burned, and lawyers, doctors and businessmen carted off by thousands to concentration camps during and after the 'Crystal Night' of November 1938." The account tersely concludes that his father turned out to be one of the lucky ones: "He was arrested, then released on the condition that he and my mother and brother get out of Germany at once, leaving all their money and possessions behind."

However Clive's parents already had some idea of what lay ahead, because in 1937 they sent him off to boarding school in England. Joined in England by his parents and brother, Clive remained at Buxton College in Derbyshire until 1940, when the family emigrated to the United States. From 1943 to 1946 Clive served in the United States Army, attaining a commission as second lieutenant in the Office of Strategic Services.

Although his subsequent academic career was a transatlantic one, Clive's university education was entirely American; he earned his B.A. at the University of North Carolina and his M.A. (1947) and Ph.D. (1952) in history at Harvard. From 1948 to 1960 he taught at Harvard, where following an interlude on the history faculty of the University of Chicago (1960–1965) he was named William R. Kenan, Jr. Professor of History and Literature in 1979. He also served as visiting fellow at All Souls College, Oxford and visiting professor of biography at Dartmouth.

Clive was a cultural historian, his scholarly publications bridging the social sciences and the humanities. He specialized in what he called "cliography" (named for Clio, the muse of history), writing about personal influences that conditioned historians. He was particularly drawn to historians who wrote with literary distinction, notably Thomas Babington Macaulay, but also Edward Gibbon and Thomas Carlyle, as well as the American Henry Adams, and such continental figures as Karl Marx, Jakob Burckhardt, Alexis de Tocqueville, and Jules Michelet. He gained wide acclaim for the elegance and urbanity of his own writing.

Clive wrote in the introduction to his first book, *Scotch Reviewers: The Edinburgh Review, 1802–1815,* "If the dictum 'there is nothing deader than dead politics' can be applied even more forcibly to dead periodical literature, then any revivalist attempts must seek to surround the dry bones with the flesh and blood of personal context and contemporary setting." Accordingly, Clive vividly reconstructs the late 18th-century cultural ambience of the "Athens of the North" in which The *Edinburgh Review,* the first great 19th-century journal of critical opinion, emerged and developed. Consequently, Clive's book, *Scotch Reviewers* provides, as the *Spectator* reviewer wrote, "a footnote to intellectual history, to political history, and to literary history."

Thomas Babington Macaulay, with whose name Clive is mainly associated, was one of the leading early contributors to the *Edinburgh Review.* In introducing *Selected Writings of Macaulay,* which he edited with Thomas Pinney, Clive acknowledged that while this once-popular historian could never regain the "unchallenged eminence" he had held during the Victorian Age, "the strong individuality, originality, and, not least, the amusing and readable qualities of his work, give it a continuing interest, certainly enough to justify a fresh look."

This "fresh look" was provided in *Macaulay: The Shaping of the Historian,* the first extensive biography since Trevelyan's in 1876. Clive announced in his introduction: "The subject of this book is not the Eminent Victorian, the Macaulay of the collected *Essays and Speeches, The Lays of Ancient Rome,* the *History of England*—works that made him a household word in the English-speaking world, and gained him his country's first 'literary' peerage. It is rather the outsider, the 'parvenu,' (as he once called himself)—awkward, ugly, impecunious—who, by sheer talent and energy, won the respect of the Whigs and a seat in the cabinet by the age of forty." Clive focuses on Macaulay's character and inner life. A leading theme of Clive's narrative is the wresting free of the youthful prodigy from dominance by his evangelical father, who had hoped to turn his son's "rather disorderly genius" to the moral regeneration of the world.

Some fellow scholars questioned the proportions of the biography (the last four chapters, for example, are given over to a detailed exposition of Macaulay's educational and legal reforms as a government official in India), but all commended its scholarship, writing and human drama. The treatment of young Macaulay's relations with his father and younger sisters, in the words of John Robson, reviewer for *Victorian Studies,* "should win, among other honors, the Queen's medal for non-sexploitation." The book won the National Book Award for history, and was also nominated in the biography category. A number of reviewers were puzzled by the ending of Clive's narrative which left its subject at the age of thirty-eight, returned from India financially secure, and his monumental *History of England* as yet just a few jottings in a notebook. Conjectures arose about a possible forthcoming sequel, but Clive asserted that he never intended to carry the record further, having achieved his aim "to trace some of the forces—familial, intellectual, political, and personal—which helped to shape the man and the historian." Clive emphasized the novelistic vividness of Macaulay's characterization, his wealth of literary analogy, and the concreteness of his imagery.

Clive was instrumental also in reviving interest in another of his favorite historians, Edward Gibbon. Through his initiative, an international conference was held in Rome in 1976 to commemorate the bicentennial of the publication of *The Decline and Fall of the Roman Empire*. Clive was co-editor of the volume that grew out of this symposium; his own contribution, "Gibbon's Humor," stresses Gibbon's "grave and temperate irony," his footnotes alone constituting "a veritable academy of raillery and humor." Particularly in dealing with sex and Christianity, Gibbon is shown as a subtle ironist, concealing behind "a mask of credulity and devotion" his scepticism at vows of chastity and received traditions of miracles.

In "Amusement and Instruction: Gibbon and Macaulay," a paper presented at a meeting of the Massachusetts Historical Society early in 1975, Clive points out that as much as these two historians had in common—both corpulent, both bachelors, both rebels against domineering fathers, both having served in Parliament—in essential ways they were far apart. Gibbon's playfulness, mischievousness, and Voltairian anti-clerical tone, for example, were "miles away from Macaulay's straitlaced approach." Moreover, while both sought to amuse as well as instruct, Gibbon wrote for an elite circle, Macaulay for a more heterogeneous public.

For the series Classics of European Historians, Clive edited several landmark works, notably Thomas Carlyle's *History of Frederick II of Prussia, Called Frederick the Great*. Abridging Carlyle's text to about one-seventh of its original length, he selected what he regarded as its more accessible and colorful episodes, such as young Friedrich's apprenticeship and clash with his father, his relations with Voltaire, and the battle scenes. As with Macaulay, Clive brought out the paternal religious influence on Carlyle's idea of history. Recalling also in the introduction the little known fact that this had been a favorite book of Hitler's, Clive savored the irony that Goebbels read to Hitler just before his suicide the episode of the "seemingly miraculous salvation" of Frederick, owing to the sudden death of his enemy the Czarina of Russia.

Throughout his career, Clive habitually spent Christmas holidays, summers, and sabbaticals in England, where he was in great demand as a lecturer. He founded with fellow expatriates a German Club, "an idiosyncratic lunching group," according to an English friend Roy Foster, which "gave great scope to Clive's genius as a raconteur and to his Byzantine interest in social politics." At his home base Clive organized with a colleague, the Harvard Victorians, a convivial interdisciplinary circle that met monthly throughout the 1970s. On both sides of the ocean he enjoyed regaling colleagues at parties and dinners with comic verse of his own composition. A devotee of music as well, he frequently attended summer festivals on the continent, and was himself a talented jazz pianist. He was a Fellow both of the Royal Historical Society and of the American Academy of Arts and Sciences.

Clive's last book, *Not By Fact Alone*, brings together previously published essays under such rubrics as "Why Read the Great Historians?," and "Amusement and Instruction." Emphasizing the fundamental importance of the "historical imagination," Clive warns students to be on the lookout for "distortion, fantasy, and misrepresentation" among historians, pointing out that there is no such thing as an unbiased account of the past. He is distrustful also of so-called historical laws that eliminate "the unique, the contingent, the unforeseen." The tour de force of this collection is the concluding essay, "The Great Historians in the Age of Cliometrics," in which Clive turns the quantifying "New History" on its head by writing a hypothetical demographic study of mid-19th century watchmakers in southeastern Ohio in the styles of Gibbon, Macaulay, and Carlyle.

Not By Fact Alone was chosen by the National Book Critics' Circle as one of five nominees for distinguished criticism on the day after Clive's sudden death from cardiac arrest. In an obituary in the *Independent* that revealed a dark side of his temperament—intermittent but severe bouts of depression which may have accounted for the long intervals between books and the scattered nature of his output—Roy Foster wrote that his friend "brought to his social life, to his anxious interest in other people, and to the best of his writing, the quality which he defined in Macaulay: 'propulsive imagination.'"

PRINCIPAL WORKS: *Nonfiction*—Scotch Reviewers: The Edinburgh Review, 1802–1815, 1957; Macaulay: The Shaping of the Historian, 1973; Not By Fact Alone: Essays on the Writing and Reading of History, 1989. *As editor*—Thomas Carlyle, History of Frederick II of Prussia, Called Frederick the Great, 1969 (with Geofrey Best) R. W. Church, Oxford Movement: Twelve Years, 1833–1845, 1970; Henry T. Buckle, On Scotland—the Scottish Intellect, 1970; (with Thomas Pinney) Thomas Babington Macaulay, Selected Writings, 1970; (with Isaac Kramnick) Lord Bolingbroke, Historical Writings, 1974; (with G. W. Bowersock and Stephen R. Graubard) Edward Gibbon and the Decline and Fall of the Roman Empire, 1977. *As editor and translator*—(with Oscar Handlin) Gottlieb Mittelberger, Journey to Pennsylvania, 1960.

ABOUT: Clive, J., "The Use of the Past," *in* Not By Fact Alone, 1989; Contemporary Authors 85–88, 1980;

Who's Who in America 1988–1989. *Periodicals*—Atlantic Monthly April 1973; History and Theory 13; Independent (London) January 13, 1990; New York Times Book Review April 1, 1973; March 11, 1990; Spectator May 31, 1957; Times Literary Supplement February 2, 1990; Victorian Studies 17; Virginia Quarterly Review Spring 1974.

*CODRESCU, ANDREI (December 20, 1946–), American (Romanian-born) poet, fiction writer, and journalist, writes "I was born Andrei Perlmutter in Sibiu, Transylvania, Romania in 1946, shortly after Soviet tanks brought us 'Communism'. My father disappeared when I was six months old. I think I remember the smell of his leather jacket but I may be mixing it up with later leather jackets. When I was five a man with a similar leather jacket and a pistol in a holster appeared briefly in our lives. From five to seven I lived with a retired policeman who smelled similarly. When I was fourteen my mother dated an Army colonel who wore an ankle-length leather coat but I'm sure he was not in a position to confuse me because, by then, I was older and it was the smell of his boots that dominated our cramped Soviet-style interior with the communal kitchen. One time, I was standing in line at the 'Peace Cinema' to see the Soviet epic *Ivan the Terrible* when a woman in front of me turned around and said: 'Your father was a dangerous man!' I didn't know what she was talking about. I still don't.

"I grew up tenuously instructed in the educational platitudes devised by Stalin's ideologues. This narcoleptic vacuum was eminently conducive to dreaming so I spent most of my childhood and adolescence wandering about my medieval burg drawing inspiration from the same phantoms that educated other locals such as the poet Lucian Blaga (whose complete poetry I translated: *At the Court of Yearning*, 1986) and the philosopher E. M. Cioran, whose tonic nihilism I share. My first poems were published in Romanian literary journals under the pseudonym Andrei Steiu. I loved my first poems and knew them by heart. I was not surprised when the Sibiu cultural commissar called me to the Party headquarters and questioned my motives for writing such lines as: 'Under the red railroad men without faces gamble with the bones of the future.' I explained that such things cannot be easily explicated. He branded me an arrogant 'petty-bourgeois cosmopolitan.' I was thrilled, I had became a baby dissident. I was sixteen.

"I had two girlfriends: Marinella, who deflowered me in a hayloft above the goatshed on the grounds of the Sibiu mental hospital, and Aurelia, who wrote stories and tried to keep our

ANDREI CODRESCU

amour lofty. I married Aurelia, unfortunately. In 1965, after I finished the Gh. Lazar Lyceum, I was in imminent danger of being drafted into the Romanian army. Happily, Israel was buying Romanian Jews for $10,000 a head from the newly installed Ceauşescu regime, and my mother and I were among the first to be purchased. Christopher Hitchens once told me 'You're the only person I know who was bought and sold." But while I had been bought, my child-bride Aurelia had not because she was not Jewish. Faced with choosing between freedom on the one hand and marriage and the Romanian army on the other, I chose rock 'n roll.

"My mother and I never got to Israel but then we had no intention whatsoever of going there. During our six-month intransit in Rome, Italy, we applied for visas to several countries. We were accepted by Canada, Australia, and the United States. On March 28, 1966 we landed in New York with a plane full of Yugoslavs who were singing 'America the Beautiful' after finishing off all the slivovitz and sausages they had brought from home.

"I spoke no English when I arrived in Detroit, but far from being a handicap this blessed ignorance allowed me to absorb the language osmotically with all the body gestures that make words real. I was nineteen years old and so was America at that time. Happy coincidence? My first published work in the U.S. was a review of an imaginary film for *The Fifth Estate*, an anarchist newspaper. It was signed 'Andrew Codrescu,' a name rich in self-destructive implications (*Codreanu* was the founder of Romanian Fascism, my country's premier anti-Semite). Not long after, I met Alice Henderson, my future wife, at the 'Lost and Found' counter at Wayne State University. In 1967 we moved together to New York's Lower East Side. I worked at the 8th Street Bookstore and Alice went to the New York Studio School across the street. We lived on Avenue C between 5th and 6th Streets on a one-bedroom place that cost $65 a month. I frequented the poetry workshops at St. Mark's Church where I met many of the poets who taught me American poetry: Ted Berrigan, Allen Ginsberg, Anne Waldman, Joel Oppenheimer, Michael Stephens, Weatherly, Sam Abrams. My first book, *License to Carry a Gun*, won the Big Table Younger Poets award for 1970. It appeared that year, with a preface by the series editor, Paul Carroll. The book consisted of the work of three different imaginary poets whose careers I had hoped to launch, a la Machado, separately, but the economics of book-publishing prevented this venture in schizo-activism. (I did, eventually, launch a number of poets, in Romanian and in English, whose work has to date never been traced to me). In 1970 we moved from New York to San Francisco, a mystical and sexy place (then) that inspired my next three books of poetry, *The History of the Growth of Heaven*, *A Serious Morning*, and *Secret Training*. In 1973 I was awarded an NEA Fellowship and with the money we bought a perilously leaning shack in Monte Rio, California, a redwood paradise inhabited by people whose telephones were listed under pseudonyms. Here I wrote my first autobiography, *The Life and Times of an Involuntary Genius*, and two novellas 'Monsieur Test in America' (*Paris Review*, 1976) and 'Felicity' (unpublished). I also composed a novel, 'Meat from the Gold Rush,' a book about history and cannibalism. I met some of my dearest friends in these woods. Among them was the poet Jeffrey Miller who died in a car accident in 1977; we published his posthumous collection, *The First One's Free*. In 1977, driven away by Jeffrey's death and the general tedium of paradise, we moved to Baltimore where I began my teaching career. I taught in the Writing Seminars at Johns Hopkins University, then at the University of Baltimore where I began publishing my bimonthly journal of books and ideas, *Exquisite Corpse*. Also in Baltimore I started writing editorial pieces for the *Baltimore Sun* and the *City Paper*. In 1983 I read one of these pieces over the air on National Public Radio's program 'All Things Considered.' My contributions to A.T.C. led to a weekly radio column. Several books were published during this time, including *Selected Poems: 1970–1980* and my second autobiography (I suddenly had more

life to write about), *In America's Shoes*. In 1984 I was offered a job in the English Department at Louisiana State University in Baton Rouge. I have been teaching there ever since. In 1989 I went back to Romania for the first time after twenty-five years to cover, for NPR and ABC News, the bloody coup that toppled the dictatorship of Nicolae Ceauşescu. I wrote *The Hole in the Flag*, a book about that event and about my return. In 1989 I wrote and starred in *Road Scholar*, a movie shown nationwide on PBS in 1993. My collection of poetry, *Belligerence* was published in 1991. I now [1993] live in New Orleans and do what I have always been doing only more of it. There is nothing like evading the Romanian draft."

————————

When Andrei Codrescu arrived in the United States, the 1960s counterculture was in full swing, and he learned American English not only from the poets he sought out and studied under, but from an array of hippies, runaways, and street people he met in Detroit and New York City. Although he has spent more than half of his life in the United States and became a naturalized American citizen, Codrescu still maintains a wry, often mordant, perspective on his adopted homeland. "America is an incredible place for a writer," he told *Publishers Weekly* "because it presents the spectacle of continuously de facto surrealist reality, where seemingly incongruous things can exist right next to each other without apparent connection." Sensing perhaps that his keen awareness of the peculiarities of American life is dependent on his remaining, to some extent, an outsider, Codrescu has been in no hurry to remake himself in the image of an American. "I try hard not to lose my accent," he told a *New York Times* interviewer in 1993. "I have an accent-maintenance contract with my mother."

Codrescu published his first collection of poetry—*License to Carry a Gun*—within four years of his arrival in the United States. Reviewing the volume in the *Village Voice*, M. G. Stephens commented: "Codrescu has a mastery of English that comes from using a language essentially foreign to his experience. The beauty of his work lies in his usage of American idioms in metaphors and similes with an outsider's ear tuned to natural speech rhythms and patterns. . . . " For example, in his short poem, "for sarah," Codrescu employs the American vernacular to achieve a startling, eerie effect: "I can't empty myself of you / goddamn beatnick / I don't think you ever got to / rome. / Someone raped you and carved / your fine bones / with fertility masks. / it's what i should have done." While acknowledging that "the book as a whole has faults," Stephens maintained, " . . . the raw potential of the poet attests to his poetic sensibility."

The Life and Times of an Involuntary Genius, the first of Codrescu's several memoirs, deals primarily with his youth in Romania. Codrescu declares himself to be a "revolutionary" who nonetheless believes in monarchy. Certain critics took umbrage at such assertions; a reviewer for *Choice* called the memoir "a pretentious and foolish affair that will do little to enhance his reputation," and in *Best Sellers* Thomas A. Wassmer said, "It may be the greatest tribute to Codrescu that his prose drives a reader to the magical language of his poetry."

Codrescu's second book of memoirs, *In America's Shoes*, focuses on his experiences in the United States, and includes irreverent portraits of such figures as Robert Bly, Kenneth Rexroth, and Bob Dylan.

"What do you do if you're a masochist but have been placed / in a position of power?" Codrescu asks in "Dear Masoch," one of the poems in his collection *Comrade Past & Mister Present*. In the *New York Times Book Review*, Bruce Shlain marveled at the poet's skillful use of a variety of voices and his wide-ranging social and philosophical concerns. "In . . . Codrescu's native Transylvania," Shlain noted, "poets are social spokesmen, and that perhaps explains his fearlessness of treading on the language of philosophy, religion, politics, science or popular culture."

Codrescu's 1989 visit to Romania resulted in *The Hole in the Flag*. Part travelogue, part reportage, and part memoir of an exile's return, the book is his investigation of the 1989 bloody coup that toppled Nicolae Ceauşescu. Like most other observers, Codrescu believed that the revolution had been a more or less spontaneous uprising against a universally despised dictator, but after interviewing scores of Romanians, his sense of certainty began to waiver. The National Salvation Front, which had taken over in the name of the people, had exercised total control over the country's sole television station, making sure that only its official version of the revolution was disseminated. Codrescu began to suspect the machinations of the Soviet KGB, although he was never able to prove this. "Much of the evidence the author marshals to support his thesis consists of deduction and speculation," Alex Kozinski noted in the *New York Times Book Review*. In *New York Review of Books*, Istvan Deak expressed similar skepticism: "Codrescu . . . believes he can detect the shadow of the Soviet KGB in the planning and execution of the Romanian revolution. . . . Possibly so, but there is no proof of this."

Codrescu's cross-country drive from New York City to San Francisco was the basis for his book *Road Scholar* and a PBS documentary of the same title. Before embarking, the lifelong pedestrian had to learn to drive and get a driver's license. Codrescu remarks, "Learning to drive, the essential American rite of passage, will prepare me for the ultimate American ritual, the cross-country road trip." In the *New York Times Book Review*, Francis X. Clines found "rarely a dull moment" in *Road Scholar*. "Mr. Codrescu is the sort of writer who feels obliged to satirize and interplay with reality and not just catalogue impressions . . . [He] is a reminder that locomotion is not the heart of the matter; a decent imagination is."

Codrescu moved the bounds of his imagination by publishing his first novel, *The Blood Countess*, in 1995. The eponymous countess is a 16th-century figure from history who bathes in the blood of virgins in order to maintain her own youth. Her story alternates with that of a fictional modern descendant, a journalist who returns to Hungary to assuage his guilt at being absent from his country's agony. The two stories merge at the end, in the words of the *Publishers Weekly* reviewer, "in a scene of feverish melodrama . . . resulting in a neo-gothic tale" in which "Europe's social, political, intellectual and religious histories are skillfully interwoven with the more slippery threads of magic and myth. . . ." Nina Auerbach, in the *New York Times Book Review* deemed this "parable of atavism and possession" "chilling," but found the countess "closer to pornographic Victorian biters . . . than . . . to the cold hate at the heart of . . . Codrescu's historical horror." Auerbach concluded that "Codrescu writes splendidly about women as remote agents of fear, but when he tries to depict them, campy posturing undermines political dread."

PRINCIPAL WORKS: *Poetry*—License to Carry a Gun, 1970; The History of the Growth of Heaven, 1971; the, here, what, where, 1972; Secret Training, 1973; A Serious Morning, 1973; Grammar and Money, 1973; A Mote Suite for Jan and Anselm, 1976; The Marriage of Insult & Injury, 1977; The Lady Painter, 1977; For the Love of a Coat, 1978; Necrocorrida, 1980; Diapers on the Snow, 1981; Selected Poems: 1970–1980, 1983; Comrade Past & Mister Present, 1987; Belligerence, 1991. *Novels and Novellas*—Why I Can't Talk on the Telephone, 1971; The Repentance of Lorraine, 1976; Monsieur Teste in America & Other Instances of Realism, 1987; The Blood Countess, 1995. *Autobiography/memoirs*—The Life and Times of an Involuntary Genius, 1975; In America's Shoes, 1983;

The Hole in the Flag: An Exile's Story of Return & Revolution, 1991. *Nonfiction*—A Craving for Swan, 1986; Raised by Puppets Only to Be Killed by Research, 1989; The Disappearance of the Outside, 1990, *As editor*—American Poetry Since 1970: Up Late, 1987; The Stiffest of the Corpse: An Exquisite Corpse Reader, 1988; *As translator*—For Max Jacob, 1974; At the Court of Yearning: The Poems of Lucian Blaga, 1989.

ABOUT: Contemporary Authors New Revision Series 13, 1984; Contemporary Literary Criticism 46, 1988. *Periodicals*—Best Sellers June 1975; Choice July/ August 1975; Nation September 10, 1990; New York Times July 11, 1993; New York Times Book Review January 25, 1987; June 30, 1991; May 9, 1993; July 30, 1995; New York Review of Books March 5, 1992; Publishers Weekly May 24, 1991; May 1, 1995; San Francisco Review of Books Winter 1983–1984; Village Voice December 31,, 1970; World Literature Today Winter 1988; Summer 1990.

CONROY, PAT (DONALD PATRICK) (October 26, 1945–), American novelist and nonfiction writer, was born in Atlanta, Georgia, the first of seven children of Donald Conroy, a Marine Corps pilot, and the former Frances Dorothy Peek. While he was growing up, his parents moved frequently; Conroy has said that he and his siblings attended eleven schools in twelve years, yet all were A students and star athletes. "You hide in achievement and humor," he told Molly O'Neill in the *New York Times* in 1991, speaking of his emotionally devastating childhood. "You project strength and you lie. You lie all the time." Projecting strength was something Conroy learned from his violent, frequently abusive father; the covering up, or lying, he learned from his mother, who often succeeded in keeping the neighbors from knowing the family's dark secrets by hammering a false version of their father's abuse into her children, he told O'Neill.

While still a student at The Citadel, a military college in Charleston, South Carolina, where he received a B.A. in English in 1967, Conroy wrote a story about his grandmother who was an alcoholic, "the first crack in the family code of silence," he told O'Neill. He followed this up in 1970 with *The Boo*, a factual account (which he paid to have printed) of a colonel at The Citadel. Meanwhile, to earn a living, he taught English in public high schools, but the work was unsatisfying; what Conroy felt he needed was a new challenge. He found it teaching disadvantaged black children on an island he calls Yamacraw off the South Carolina coast. Some unorthodox and dramatic teaching method was needed, he felt, for children who did not know the name of

their country or that the world was round but did expect their teacher to know how to set a trap and skin a muskrat. Conroy saw his new job as an opportunity to obliterate the stain of the racism of his past while improving the lives of his students. Unfortunately, his determination to prove to his students that learning could be fun cost him his job, but the book that came out of this experience in 1972, *The Water Is Wide*, was the first to bring him to the attention of a national audience. The book was a success and was later made into the 1974 film *Conrack*, directed by Martin Ritt and starring Jon Voight.

Anatole Broyard described Conroy in the *New York Times Book Review* as "a former redneck and self-proclaimed racist," who brought to his teaching job in South Carolina "the supererogatory fervor of the recently converted"—while Conroy proclaims in the book that he had gone to Yamacraw Island for a "fallacious reason": "I needed to be cleansed, born again, resurrected by good works and suffering, purified of the dark cankers that grew like toadstools in my past." Broyard judged the book a "hell of a good story," while also commenting that the author was "not much of a stylist." He liked the fact that Conroy refused to "make a villain out of the school superintendent who fired him. Unlike many liberal do-gooders, Mr. Conroy does not see all conservatives, racists, reactionaries or rednecks as one-dimensional monsters. In his eyes, they are as much victims of their history . . . as the black people whose problems they haven't even begun to understand."

In 1969 Conroy married Barbara Bolling and became a stepfather of two daughters; the couple had a daughter of their own before they divorced in 1977. During this period he wrote his first novel, *The Great Santini*, which was regarded by several critics as an autobiographical account of his adolescence. The story, about family life on a military base and an authoritarian father who is unable to understand anything beyond military discipline, pits the father against the son, whose ambivalent feelings conflict with his longing for independence. Conroy later told the *Chicago Tribune* that his father recognized himself in the book and was furious. "Then people started telling him he actually was lovable. Now, he signs Christmas cards 'The Great Santini,' and goes around talking about childrearing and how we need to have more discipline in the home—a sort of Nazi Dr. Spock." *The Great Santini* was made into a movie starring Robert Duvall in 1979.

James Hutchins wrote in *Best Sellers*: "*The Great Santini* is a fine, sensitive novel that deserves to be read by all servicemen with families." The reviewer for the *Virginia Quarterly Review* enjoyed the book's realism—its dialogue, anecdotes, and "pure Marine" family atmosphere—but concluded that while the novel was a good one, the descriptive writing was "somewhat juvenile." In the opinion of Robert Burkholder, writing for *Critique: Studies in Modern Fiction*, the book is "a curious blend of lurid reality and fantastic comedy."

Conroy's next novel, *The Lords of Discipline*, takes place in a southern military institution and centers on the issue of racism and on four senior cadets who have roomed together since their plebe year. One of the cadets, the narrator, Will, is recruited to look after the academy's first black cadet and in the course of doing so, discovers a secret order to preserve the school's "whiteness." Much of the material comes from the author's experience at The Citadel, which he had written about earlier in *The Boo*. But this time, according to Frank Rose, in the *Washington Post Book World*, the fictionalized portrait of the institution "combines some of the more quaint and murderous aspects of The Citadel, West Point, and Virginia Military Institute." In Rose's opinion Conroy achieved two things in his book: it is "a suspense-ridden duel between conflicting ideals of manhood and a paean to brother love that ends in betrayal and death. Out of the shards of broken friendship a blunted triumph emerges, and it is here, when the duel is won, that the reader finally comprehends the terrible price that any form of manhood can exact." While commenting that the novel "virtually quivers with excitement and conviction," Rose complained that there are times when the book "develops the unlikely thrill quotient of a Hardy Boys adventure" and sometimes "sounds less like a work of fiction than like an anguished cry from the heart." Harry Crews, reviewing the book for the *New York Times*, commented that "the story has more twists than a snake's back. There are reversals inside reversals. Mysteries sprout like mushrooms after a summer rain." After at first feeling that Conroy had found "a great subject" and had "produced a book so superior to his other efforts that it might have been written by a different person," he concluded that Conroy, in the second half of the book, had become "more interested in posing and solving clever puzzles than in developing the character of the human beings inside those puzzles." The book was adapted for film in 1983.

The Prince of Tides, which followed in 1986, and which Conroy has described as being "the closest he's come to the truth," tells the story of Tom Wingo, an unemployed high school Eng-

lish teacher and football coach, who travels from the south to New York City after learning that his twin sister Savannah, a well-known poet, has been hospitalized there for a psychotic breakdown and suicide attempt. In the process of trying to help his sister, he becomes romantically involved with Savannah's tough-minded but caring psychiatrist who meets with him regularly in an effort to understand the Wingo family's bizarre history. Conroy admitted to using autobiographical material in the book and told the *Toronto Globe and Mail* that his family's reaction of anger was not unexpected to one who drew on his own life for his material.

Richard Eder, in the *Los Angeles Times Book Review*, criticized Conroy's inflated style. In his opinion, "the characters do too much, feel too much, suffer too much, eat too much, signify too much, and above all, talk too much." In contrast Judy Bass, in *Chicago Tribune Books*, found *Prince of Tides* "a brilliant novel that ultimately affirms life, hope, and the belief that one's future need not be contaminated by a monstrous past." Such differences of opinion were widespread, some reviewers citing such things as the author's "turgid, high-flown rhetoric," others admiring his prose as "spectacular and lyrical." Conroy cowrote the screenplay for *The Prince of Tides* (1992), which Barbara Streisand directed and costarred in with Nick Nolte as Tom Wingo.

In an interview with Sam Staggs for *Publishers Weekly*, Conroy said he thought the reason his books made such entertaining movies was "because I'm incredibly shallow. I write a straight story line, and I guess that's what they need. The dialogue also seems to be serviceable in a Hollywood way. But most important, I do the thing that Southerners do naturally—I tell stories . . . . Critics call me a popular novelist, but writing popular novels isn't what urges me on. If I could write like Faulkner or Thomas Wolfe, I surely would. I would much rather write like them than like me. Each book has been more ambitious. I'm trying to be more courageous." What does urge Conroy on, according to his own admission, is the hope of healing the wounds of his childhood. He uses writing, as he told Molly O'Neill, "to tell the truth, to avoid the truth, to tame the truth," even though each project elicits a despair that he and his family have to learn to live with.

In *Beach Music* a man living in Rome and trying to get over his wife's suicide is forced to return to South Carolina to attend his mother's deathbed. Tom Shone in the *New York Times Book Review* remarked that the book belongs in "the old Conroy credo: the novel as therapy, populated with characters who don't so much excavate their tortured past as explore it, re-explore it, map it out and then distribute tourist brochures."

Conroy lives in San Francisco with his second wife, Lenore Gurewitz, their daughter, an older daughter, and two adopted daughters from his former marriage. All his novels and the films made from them have been popular successes. His awards and honors have included the Anisfield-Wolf Award (1972), a National Endowment for the Arts award for Achievement in Education (1974) for *The Water Is Wide*, and the Lillian Smith Award for *The Lords of Discipline*. The latter was a also nominated for the Robert Kennedy Book Award in 1981.

PRINCIPAL WORKS: *Novels*—The Great Santini, 1976; The Lords of Discipline, 1980; The Prince of Tides, 1986; Beach Music, 1995; *Nonfiction*—The Boo, 1970; The Water Is Wide, 1972.

ABOUT: Contemporary Authors New Revision Series 24, 1988; Contemporary Literary Criticism 30, 1984; Dictionary of Literary Biography 6, 1980. *Periodicals*—Best Sellers September 1976; Critique: Studies in Modern Fiction 1, 1979; New York Times December 7, 1980; December 22, 1991; New York Times Book Review September 24, 1972; July 2, 1995; Publishers Weekly September 5, 1986; Virginia Quarterly Review Autumn 1976; Washington Post Book World October 19, 1980.

CORN, ALFRED (DEWITT) (August 14, 1943–), American poet, writes: "I was born in Bainbridge, Georgia. My mother, Grace Lahey Corn, died on my second birthday while my father A. D. Corn, Jr., was still in the Philippines with the Army Corps of Engineers. When he returned, we were reunited in Valdosta, Georgia, where he had grown up and where we lived throughout my childhood. South Georgia is associated in my mind with summer, either blazingly bright days spent at nearby lakes, or long dusty twilights scented with honeysuckle and punctuated by the eerily human cry of the whippoorwill.

"When I was five, my father remarried, his wife Virginia Whittaker MacMillan, a young World War II widow, who bravely and cheerfully assumed the role of mother to us half-orphans. During those early years, which were far from poverty if I compared our living standard to that of the black people who worked for us, I had much more trouble with my father (who was strict and sometimes used a belt) than my stepmother. He wasn't altogether satisfied with a son who read constantly, at the expense of making

ALFRED CORN

friends or playing sports. But at least no one could complain of my grades at school. By age sixteen my touchstone authors were Shakespeare, Whitman, and Wallace Stevens. A senior English honors paper took up the topic, unprecedented at Valdosta High, of Joyce's use of the stream-of-consciousness technique. I was the nearsighted, slump-shouldered valedictorian of my graduating class and had won a National Merit Scholarship, which sponsored my undergraduate studies at Emory University in Atlanta. Among the professors there were T. J. Altizer, the humanist theologian, and Walter Straus, who taught comparative literature. I chose French as my major on the basis of a certain knack for languages and the hardy assumption English literature was available enough to be learned on my own. The summer after my junior year was spent participating in a French language program in Avignon and then traveling in Italy and Greece. One of my liveliest, most intelligent, and prettiest fellow students was Ann Jones, to whom I was later married. We kept in touch during my last year at Emory and her last two at Berkeley.

"I read poetry just for pleasure throughout high school and college, and made strenuously awkward efforts at writing it as well. College courses added Baudelaire and Dante to the pantheon, as well as Tolstoy and Henry James. Fiction meant just as much to me as poetry, so there was no question of not signing up for the only creative writing course offered at Emory, a short-story workshop taught by H. E. Francis. Patricia Wilcox, the wife of my philosophy teacher, introduced me to contemporary

American poetry, Roethke in particular. We read what we wrote to each other as part of a solemn effort to make literary aspirations enter the realm of plausibility. I was at least practical enough to recognize that anyone who wanted to write would have to earn a living some other way. My plan was to continue French studies in graduate school, teach, and write on the side. Only some of the difficulties involved were then apparent to me, nor did it strike me that lack of sponsorship and a leaning toward unconventionality were also going to be obstacles. My senior thesis was a comparative study of Sade and the Symbolist-Decadent novelist Huysmans, an academic topic, certainly, but unusual for the time and place.

"I entered the graduate program in French literature at Columbia in the fall of 1965, choosing Columbia over Yale and Harvard because of its location in New York, which was unrivaled then as a city of the arts. New York quickly had a new defender: none of the usual complaints against it carried any weight when placed beside opportunities to see theater, opera, ballet, and classic movie revivals. Merely residing there was an endorsement of artistic ambitions. To stroll through Greenwich Village in an altered state of consciousness on your way to hear a blues concert was to feel righteously bohemian and to sense that you were part of a new cultural wave about to crest.

"In January of 1966, Ann Jones came for a visit during term break, and we thought of ourselves afterwards as a temporarily separated couple. She enrolled at Columbia as a comparative literature student the following fall, sharing an apartment with me in the West '80s. After a brief separation in the spring of 1967, we were reunited and were married in July that year before going off to Paris, where I had a Fulbright Fellowship. These were the years of the Vietnam conflict, and we opposed the war as actively we espoused the left or radical political discourse of our generation. Antiwar activities continued even in Paris where I also did half-hearted research on my dissertation topic, a comparison of Melville and Camus. My happiest moments were spent exploring obscure corners of this old capital city, sacred to me as the site of so many pivotal moments in literary history. It was this year that I finally read all of Proust.

"After our return, I taught first- and second-year French at Columbia as I tried to finish the dissertation. In fact, I never did so, abandoning the degree in the spring of 1970, and setting up as a free-lance writer while I worked as office manager at *University Review*, a tabloid-format literary journal aimed at graduate and undergraduate students.

"Ann and I separated in the fall of 1971. I moved in with Walter Brown, an architect whom I had met the previous spring. We lived in a loft in what had begun to be called SoHo, an old industrial district south of Houston Street then being colonized by artists and art galleries. Several years of intermittent employment followed, along with progress in my writing. I began publishing poems in magazines and, in 1975, my first collection, *All Roads at Once*, was accepted by Viking Press. Writer friends I was close to in those years included Edmund White, David Kalstone, and Richard Howard. At that time I was particularly interested in the poetry of Hart Crane, Elizabeth Bishop, James Merrill, and John Ashbery; the last two I had met at parties given by friends in common.

"In 1976, shortly after my first book was published, Walter Brown and I stopped living together. Later in the year I moved to New Haven to live with J. D. McClatchy, who was then an assistant professor at Yale. I taught my first creative writing course there and then took a two-year appointment at Connecticut College, an hour's commute away in New London. It was at first intimidating to meet luminaries like Robert Penn Warren and Harold Bloom or to call on James Merrill in Stonington, Connecticut, but enough indulgence was extended to a novice's lack of experience to make this new social life on some level plausible, and my four years in New Haven have a retrospective aura of distinction that I value.

"I came back to New York in 1982, my home base ever since, except for the autumns of 1986 and 1987 spent in London on a Guggenheim Fellowship and several terms of teaching at the University of Cincinnati, UCLA and the Ohio State University. During the early 80s J. D. McClatchy and I spent our summers in Vermont, after having bought a bright red 18th-century farmhouse in the upper reaches of the Connecticut Valley, what's sometimes called the Northeast Kingdom. Then, in 1989, he and I agreed to separate and set up independently.

"I have taught part-time in the writing programs at Columbia and CUNY over the last decade, while publishing several books of poetry and one book of collected critical writings. I am at work on a novel and continue to publish poetry—also, critical pieces in journals such as the *New York Times Sunday Book Review*, *Poetry*, *Washington Post Book World*, and the *Nation*. A number of prizes have come to me for my writing, including an Ingram Merrill Fellowship, the NEA, an award in literature from the Academy and Institute of Arts and Letters, and a Fellowship from the Academy of American Poets, unfortunately without confirming in me any sense of incontestable merit. Few writers claim to possess an objective view of what they've done. But there's no doubt that as I was writing my poetry it was also writing me into my present identity-which makes regrets or second thoughts pointless if not impossible.

"I live in New York with Christopher Corwin, whom I met in Cincinnati during my teaching appointment there. A good bit of the poetry in my six books is autobiographical, and, to all interested parties, I recommend them as a supplement to this statement."

In a conversation with fellow poet J. D. McClatchy published in the journal *Shenandoah* in 1983, Alfred Corn acknowledged that his work has "a strong autobiographical emphasis" and that it represents his "immediate response to 'real life'." Since poetry, like the other arts, seeks to render permanent what he calls "fluctuant reality," the poet begins with his own experience and through language, especially through metaphor, transforms it into "something immobile and permanent." In "Getting Past the Past," from Corn's first collection *All Roads at Once*, he remembers his family's black cook making biscuits:

> What was the source of that oven warmth,
> The starch and softness when I buried my head
> In the small of her back, hands almost
> Clasping around her waist?

Growing up in the South, he experienced racism, the bitter "revelations of anger." He acknowledges his own powerlessness in this struggle as he addresses black workmen:

> . . . I'm invisible to you
> And you can't hear the lines of friendship
> For her—and in general for you—
> That begin to form as I come closer.

He believes, however, in the inevitability of change. "Your children / ride the curve of history and will / Arrive, whether humanism approves or not."

In "Chinese Porcelains at the Metropolitan" he bridges "the trenches of time":

> . . . You've met the past and it is
> Present. The struggle has not ended,
> Will not end. Meaning is only a moment
> Contained; but form is legion. The rainbow lists
> Go on as new invasions spin up from dream.
> Everything still remains to be done.

The metaphoric bridge and the literal bridge meet in his tribute to the poet Hart Crane, one of his major poetic influences, in "The Bridge, Palm Sunday, 1973" as with a friend he walks across the Brooklyn Bridge to Crane's house: "Would we be joined with him and the voyagers before him? / Would a new sentence be pronounced, a living connection / Between island and island, for a second, be made?"

All Roads at Once won Corn the admiration of many poets, among them James Merrill and John Ashbery. Harold Bloom, writing in the *New Republic*, found it worthy of comparison with the work of Hart Crane himself: "Yet the effect is one of loving struggle, of the highest agony of identity and opposition and not of mere imitation." Richard Howard wrote in *Poetry*, "Corn breathes a good deal about the bush, trusting it will burst into flame, and it does so often enough, though the touch is sometimes very feathery indeed. . . . " He judges Corn's poems "like no one else's in their zealous disposition to let the world speak through them, to praise being. . . . "

A Call in the Midst of the Crowd, Corn's second collection, pays homage to Walt Whitman in its title and includes several short meditative lyrics. The long four-part title poem, which mixes introspection with prose collages about New York City from writers like Poe, Whitman, Henry James, and Edith Wharton, had a mixed reception. Its center is a lonely young poet wandering about the city over the course of a year (the four parts are the seasons), grieving over a broken relationship:

> Biography repeats itself. Couples break
> Apart. This could be that same winter spent
> Just down the street, a short walk from the grave
> Of Peter Stuyvesant; our divorce pending,
> Cheerless tippling, useless midnight phone calls,
> The commonplaces of pain—which makes us
> Anybody.

The quoted prose passages form an ironic counterpoint to the poet's self-absorption and link him to the outside world. As George Kearns wrote in *Canto*: "The relations between prose and poetry, various and witty, now clear, now elusive, suggest a game whose only rule is the poet's implicit meditation that *somehow* these other New Yorks converge upon him."

An even more concentrated experiment in autobiography is *Notes from a Child of Paradise*, a long narrative poem that traces in detail not only the complex relationship between the poet and his former wife ("*the incautious, starbright novel of our life / As sharers in a love. . . .* "), but also the romantic and rebellious lives of the whole generation of the 1960s ("With the dawn of the Aquarian Age / Peacepipes, buckskin, beads, Apache headbands / War paint and communal lodging"). Corn writes of the couple's "voyages of discovery"—as students traveling in France and in the Pacific Northwest, struggling to complete their studies in New York, and finally establishing new relationships: "For a long time / Separate paths had summoned us; a quiet past-tenseness / Already suffusing our sense of what our couple was." He cites the literary inspirations for the long poem. *The Prelude, Childe Harold*, and *The Bridge*, and echoes in its title and its text Dante's *Divine Comedy*: "You, a partner no more Beatrice / Carved in wax than I'm a Tuscan exile / Who never touched his muse."

Notes led Sven Birkerts to call Corn one of "the prophets of narcissism" writing a poem of "self-celebration," presumptuous in its references to Dante. (*Parnassus*) Alan Williamson, writing in the *New Republic*, connected the title to the French film *Les Enfants du Paradis* in that the generation of the 1960s indeed regarded themselves as "children of Paradise," but also as observers from the distant upper reaches of a theater, the ironic meaning of "the paradise." "No writer before Corn has captured so perfectly the poignant comedy of that little world: those American kids, some brilliant, some not, all sophomoric and a little scared, managing and mismanaging their love affairs in a blinding radiance of mythic parallel."

In "At the Grave of Wallace Stevens" in *The Various Light*, Corn displays a firmly controlled and almost classic simplicity:

> A cedar and a budding willow cast
> Shadows on the grave
>   And grass, the last patches of fluent snow
> Withdrawing into mud and air; as if
> To say, Poverty, be changed to Poetry:
> Let the veil be torn away, the weather cleared
> For a green metathesis where lucid leaves
> Damask this new ground!

A similar fascination with "the poetry of earth" is manifested in the poems in *The West Door*, some of them set in Vermont. One is a narrative, "An Xmas Murder," a poem which instead of sentimentalizing rural life confronts the brutality and prejudice of isolated country people. The settings of the poems move from Vermont to Maine to China to Ireland to a church in New York's Spanish Harlem. Everywhere in these poems reviewers noted a "finished" quality, a "mastery of rhythm and sound." The initial impulse in these poems is not the poet's mood but what Wayne Kestenbaum describes in the *Village Voice* as "calls from without . . . promptings from nature, history and art. . . ."

Corn's 1992 collection *Autobiographies* made it clear that his self-exploration, his detailed recording of personal experiences, is an attempt to project, through a rendering of his own experience, the sense of contemporary American society itself. Amy Clampitt commented that "Corn sees the very fact of American mobility and diversity as an epic theme, and he brings to it a discerning eye and ear . . . an exhilarating range of sympathy." Fred Muratori, writing in *Library Journal* deemed *Autobiographies* a reinforcement of Corn's "reputation for elegant eloquence, exemplifying . . . high income bracket poetry," until the reader comes to "1992." In that poem, according to Muratori, Corn's "mannerisms fade," and the poem is "a . . . journey through the American mosaic in which Corn sets out the 'content of the world that is my case'" in a "series of finely drawn vignettes illuminating the lives of men and women from a spectrum of regions, races, and economic circumstances."

In "1992" Corn moves through the periods of his life, to 1992, detailing the personal and social landmarks of each period. "Even now I dread these unmasked statements," he says in the opening section, but he persists:

> Yet can't deny the will to
> set out in search of what it is that shaped
> one witness's imagining of time
> and make available
> the content of the world that is my case—
> composed in part by all those I have met,
> thinking through the story of who we are.

David Kirby, terming "1992" a "stunning" poem in the *New York Times Book Review*, noted that the last section has updates on the lives of each of the characters he has introduced, and "each update ends in mid-sentence: the poem is not really unfinished; the lives go on outside its boundaries."

Corn's published prose includes criticism and fiction, as well as translations from Corneille, Proust, Rilke, Montale, and Neruda. *The Metamorphoses of Metaphor* is a collection of his essays on poets and two novelists, Proust and Elizabeth Bowen. He has published two stories: "Country Hosts" (*Ontario Review*, Fall-Winter 1988), a first-person account by a bookish ten-year-old boy of an unhappy summer spent on a farm, and "Part of His Story" (*Kenyon Review*, Summer 1991), excerpts from a novel-in-progress, narrated by a middle-aged American playwright grieving over the death of a lover who has found temporary solace in an affair with a younger man. Corn has also edited *Incarnation*, a collection of essays on the New

Testament by contemporary writers. Corn contributed an essay on Paul's Second Epistle to the Corinthians, in which he recalls that throughout his childhood reading of the Bible "I became aware that there are several kinds of language and that unaccustomed ways of putting things are often the most memorable and powerful."

PRINCIPAL WORKS: *Poetry*—All Roads at Once, 1976; A Call in the Midst of the Crowd, 1978; The Various Light, 1980; Notes from a Child of Paradise, 1984; The West Door, 1988; Autobiographies, 1992. *Essays*—The Metamorphoses of Metaphor, 1987; *As editor*—Incarnation: Contemporary Writers on the New Testament, 1990.

ABOUT: Contemporary Authors 104, 1982; Contemporary Literary Criticism 33, 1985; Contemporary Poets, 5th ed., 1991; Dictionary of Literary Biography Yearbook 1980, 1981; 120, 1992; Who's Who in America, 1992. *Periodicals*—Booklist January 1, 1988; Boston Review July-August 1984; April 1988; Canto Fall 1978; Library Journal November 1, 1992; Nation August 5, 1978; New Leader November 3, 1980; New Republic November 20, 1976; June 11, 1984; New York Times Book Review April 9, 1993; Parnassus Spring-Summer 1983; Fall-Winter 1984; Poetry January 1977, November 1978,; Shenandoah 345, 1983; Village Voice February 9, 1988; Washington Post Book World August 5, 1984.

CRACE, JIM (March 1, 1946–   ), British novelist, writes: "I was born at Brocket Hall, Lemsford, Hertfordshire, England, in a first floor bedroom which—before his wartime internment—Lord Brocket had reserved for his regular houseguest, von Ribbentrop, the Ambassador of Nazi Germany. The hall had been requisitioned during the war as a maternity hospital for London mothers. This is the single point of anecdotal interest in a childhood which, otherwise, was happy, balanced, and unspectacular.

"We lived in a rented ground-floor apartment in the north London borough of Enfield. My father worked for the Co-op, first as a milkman and then as an insurance agent and we were not wealthy. It was a socialist, atheistic and warm-spirited household—despite, on my father's part, a personal puritanism which would not allow television, for example, or jeans, or tinned food, or chewing gum, or comic magazines, into the home. Books, music, the theatre, the countryside were revered though my parents had no artistic skills of their own. To describe the preoccupations of my father's life when I was a child—family, politics, books, gardening, tennis, the countryside—is to describe exactly my own interests now. Even his personal puritanism is reasserting itself in me.

"Before 1986 I worked as a free-lance journalist, mostly for the weekend supplements. I was not one of those who considered journalism a second-rate craft. Indeed I still consider it more important and influential than fiction, and I might never have made the transfer to fiction, were it not for my editor and friend, David Godwin, who—admiring one of the few short stories I had written by that time—persuaded me (with a contract) to write *Continent*. That book won three of Britain's most prestigious literary prizes within a fortnight. I was able to give up journalism there and then, and to luxuriate in the unhurried if isolated pleasures of producing a new work of fiction every two or three years.

"*Continent*—a cycle of thematically linked stories set in an invented seventh continent which served as an abstraction for the Third World—investigated the impact of modern technologies and 20th century sensibilities on the more traditional ways of humankind. *The Gift of Stones*, located at the end of the Stone Age, was a political fable 'written' in the oral tradition. It explored how a work-obsessed, flint-knapping community might regenerate itself once its industrial skills were made redundant by the coming of metals—a modern, recessionary theme despite its prehistoric setting. *Arcadia*—perhaps my most accessible, generous-spirited and blemished novel so far—was a hymn to the life and wizardry of cities and a celebration of the resilience of urban communities, their capacity to regenerate themselves despite the deprivations of the street. My fourth, uncompleted, and as yet (1992) untitled novel is set in the 1830s. It takes emigration and dislocation as its major themes, but is also a love story. There is a fifth novel in preparation: it is called 'Quarantine' and takes place during the forty days in which Christ was tempted in the wilderness.

"I don't have conventional literary skills or preoccupations. I am not interested in photographic realism which holds a mirror up to the world. I prefer the powers and ambiguities of invention. Nor am I keen on self-revelation or self-analysis in my books. I am more concerned with the fate of communities than with catharsis of individuals. For these reasons I count myself to be a traditional storyteller, rhythmic, manipulative and moralistic, rather than the un-English modernist described by some of my critics. Indeed many critics in Britain are baffled by my work, justly finding it schematic and overwrought, while reviewers elsewhere in the world have been generally more receptive to my playful, contrived, disengaged and ornamented narrative manner. The fact is, however, that I take pleasure in writing as I choose. I won't adapt my literary style to suit dissenters, anymore than I will change my politics.

"I am not a particularly 'driven' novelist. I do not miss the nine-till-five of writing, in those liberating months between books, and—even mid-novel—I do not wake up in the small hours of the night feverish with paragraphs. I write because I can and not because I must."

The son of Charles Sydney and Edith Grace (Holland) Crace, Crace married Pamela Ann Turton, a teacher, in 1975. They have two children. After completing his B.A. at the Birmingham College of Commerce in London in 1968, Jim Crace went to Khartoum as a volunteer producer and writer for Sudanese Educational Television. A year later he went to Botswana to teach English in a secondary school. When he returned to England in 1970 he became a free-lance writer of educational scripts for BBC radio and television.

Continent, Crace's first book, was highly praised by reviewers and won several literary honors—the Whitbread Award for a first novel, the David Higham Prize for Fiction, the *Guardian* Fiction Prize, and the Primo Antico Fattore. Crace describes *Continent* as a group of "thematically linked stories," not a gathering of individual stories. The seven short narratives share a setting that is distinctly Third World, but although he writes after the experience of several years in Africa, this is no real country or continent. Unifying the stories is the theme of the impact of modern-day Western culture, its efficiency, its high technology, and its materialism, upon so-called "undeveloped cultures."

Continent takes place in a world where, Crace has said, "the didactic purposes of the book could flourish undisturbed by the facts of life." In "Talking Skull," the young son of a prosperous landowner returns home on holiday from his university studies abroad. He has seen and enjoyed the latest advances in Western society and is troubled by the superstition of his own people whom his father exploits by selling them ersatz milk believed to have magical powers. "People like to be reassured," the young man explains to a European visitor. "They like to believe that the solutions to problems can be bought by the jar." Forced to choose between his family heritage and "science and modernity," he listens to the advice of an older Westernized businessman:

"Don't sniff at money . . . especially your own. Remain intimate with your wealth. You want to be a city boy with an office, a bank account, and a Peugeot. You admire scientific curiosity, business initiative, modern industriousness. But all our business fortunes are based as much as yours on superstition. What is superstition but misdirected reverence? Your clients overvalue bogus milk. Ours overvalue transistors, motor cars, fashionable clothes, travel. This is the key to business. Unearth what is overvalued, amass it, and sell it at inflated prices. Your forefathers were the first of the modern businessmen. They grasped this basic principle of trade."

In other stories in *Continent* an aged artist sees his work sold at wildly inflated prices to Western markets. Forced by his government to continue to produce, although he is too old and tired, he passes off as his own the work of a forger. He is resigned to the inevitable: "The quest for meaning and form belongs to an age long past. I often draw a forest of trees, almost bare and leafless, with the moon hovering on the horizon. Is it dawn or dusk? Soon we shall know" ("Sins and Virtues"). In "In Heat," one of the few stories in the volume told from the point of view of an outsider, the elderly unmarried daughter of a distinguished anthropologist contrasts the coldness of her parents' marriage and of her own life with the natural expression of sexuality in the tribe her father has studied.

Writing in the *Hudson Review*, George Kearns differentiated these stories from the work of Borges and Calvino. "Crace's stories are delicately inventive elegies for the local, the odd, the inefficient, the native, as they give way before the international junk and its economic and ideological bases." Crace has, however, acknowledged the influence of magical realism, the mixture of realism and fantasy that marks much contemporary fiction, especially in Latin America. But he also cites as inspiration Samuel Johnson's 18th-century philosophical novel *Rasselas*, in which an imaginary adventure teaches its hero a moral lesson in stoicism and endurance. As Robert Olen Butler observed of *Continent* in the *New York Times Book Review*: "The forests and the villages and the cities on this continent are skewed just enough in their flora, their mores, their business pursuits to make us see our own world more clearly . . . This brilliant, provocative and delightful book shows us why progress must prevail, but it also shows us the terrible price that must be paid."

Crace lives in Moseley, a suburb of Birmingham, an industrial city that in recent years has suffered economically from foreign competition. More even than the immediate problems of unemployment and poverty, he sees such cities confronting the problem of regenerating themselves in the face of loss of the occupation or craft that has long sustained them. On a museum visit, he was struck by the beauty of the Stone Age implements and of the even better-crafted bronze artifacts which superseded them. This was the germ of *The Gift of Stones*, a short novel written in straight-forward but powerfully evocative prose. Jane Smiley described it in the *New*

York Times Book Review as "a modern poem, inviting concentrated attention upon meanings, juxtapositions, relationships, language, images, those things constant in human nature." The novel is set in a primitive community whose members have developed remarkable skills in stone work: "My father's generation was practised in the sorting of the stone. Its colour did not count. It was from weight and form that the villagers could tell from half a glance the way the stone would split, which piece would hold firm for an axe-head, which would fracture into scrapers, which were the most suitable for slingshot, what to keep for best, what to jettison at once, where the sharpest blade was seated in the planes and fissures of the stone."

The "stoneys" are destined to be superseded by another people who have "the gift of bronze": "Who'd go for flint, when tools in flint would flake with too much use? Now flint was only good for walls and tombs. For implements and arms, the world demanded bronze." But the crafts of stone and bronze are not the center of this book. It is the imagination of the narrator's father, crippled in boyhood by the loss of an arm and surviving in his community by his gift—the art of storytelling": "When he spoke he shaped the truth, he trimmed, he stretched, he decorated. He was to truth what every stoney was to untouched flint, a fashioner, a god. . . . My father's talent for inflating and for telling lies was always there, from birth. But no one guessed its power—until, that is, my father transformed his defect into a craft."

Richard Deveson suggested in the *Times Literary Supplement* that the real subject of *The Gift of Stones* is narrative itself: "Crace's main concern in describing the transition from one world to another is with the role of art and the imagination . . . he suggests at the end of this unusual book that the artist may, nevertheless, be the true progressive, and that it is the imagination, rather than economics, that will teach a society how to regenerate itself." At the novel's melancholy closing the stoneys move on to an unknown future, led by the storyteller:

> The stories that he'd told were now our past. His new task was to invent a future for us all. He closed his eyes and what he saw was the shingled margin of the sea with horses wild and riderless close by. He tried to place a sail upon the sea, but could not. He tried to fill the air with human sounds. But all he saw were horses in the wind, the tide in loops upon the beach, the spray-wet rocks and stones reflecting all the changes in the sky, and no one there to notice or applaud.

In *Arcadia*, Jim Crace's third book, he introduces what appears to be a realistic theme and setting: a large urban center and characters who are recognizable contemporary English men and women. But, as in the two earlier books, Crace's realism is itself an illusion. The city is Western, the time the present, but the purpose is to enhance Crace's version of allegory: stories that create "abstractions of the real world . . . [rather than] mirror the real world," as Crace has said. In contrast to the melancholy storyteller of *The Gift of Stones*, the narrator here is a journalist, "the mordant, mocking diarist on the city's daily." He tells the story of the octogenarian Victor, a self-made tycoon who began his life in abysmal poverty with his widowed mother carrying him, an infant, from their rural home to the cold, unwelcoming metropolis. To survive, she sits in the city's bustling food market begging, with her baby nursing at her breast. The rural-urban contrasts are richly drawn, with no element of pathos or sentimentality: "What of the free food of the countryside?" the narrator asks cynically. "The mushrooms and the nuts? The stubble grain left over by the thresher and the harvesters? Life's not like that, except in children's books. The free food of the countryside is high and maggotty before it's ripe; or else it's faster than the human hand and can't be caught. What's free and good is taken by the bully dogs and birds. What's left is sustenance for flies and mice."

At eighty, Victor's dream is to replace the old fruit-and-vegetable center with steel and glass towers that will bring the produce of the country into the heart of the city: "Arcadia. But modernised. Climate-controlled. Efficient. Accessible. Contemporary. Defended." He realizes his dream only to see it destroyed in a literally blazing climax. But the narrator anticipates its regeneration in a lyrical conclusion: "I used to think that buildings were all that could endure in cities. But people, it would seem, endure as well. They hang on by their nails. They improvise. They kick. They leave a legacy which is not brick or stone."

Reviewing *Arcadia* in the *Times Literary Supplement*, Adam Mars-Jones was struck by its "intense dream of a city" rendered in a prose that is almost poetry: "Not since *Moby Dick* has blank verse thrummed so relentlessly beneath the surfaces of prose." While "dazzling" and "thrilling in short bursts," the overall effect for Mars-Jones was "in quantity maddening." He summed up *Arcadia* as "a novel that poses as a meditation on cities but is actually a perverse idiosyncratic reconstitution, in a prose supersaturated with metre, of the pastoral."

Signals of Distress is laid in an English fishing village in the 1830s. A well-meaning, but bumbling, stranger, Aymer, arrives there, and a ship founders, disgorging its captain and crew in the same area. Aymer frees a slave from the ship, but he must dismiss a group of workers from his family enterprise because the industrial revolution has made them redundant. Despite his good intentions, he wreaks a certain amount of havoc. The *Publishers Weekly* reviewer remarked that "the narrative offers a glimpse of the social fabric of the mid-19th century. . . . Filtered through character motivations that include farcical misunderstandings, poignant self-delusions, wily chicanery, false hopes and true love, this novel about people dislocated from their milieu fixes a mesmerizing grip on the reader's imagination." T.J. Binyon observed, in the *Times Literary Supplement* that like Crace's earlier novels, *Signals of Distress* takes place at a transitional moment in human society, but unlike its predecessors, "there is much . . . that is comic, even farcical" here. Binyon considered it "an intriguing work; more approachable, being less schematic, than Crace's three earlier books."

Crace has been active in regional arts groups, including the Midlands Arts Centre, the Birmingham Festival of Readers and Writers which he founded in 1983, and in the International PEN. He lists his religion as "Humanist/Agnostic" and his politics as "Libertarian Socialist."

PRINCIPAL WORKS: *Fiction*—Continent, 1987; The Gift of Stones, 1989; Arcadia, 1992; Signals of Distress, 1994.

ABOUT: Contemporary Authors 135, 1992. *Periodicals*—Hudson Review Autumn 1987; New York Times Book Review June 28, 1987; July 16, 1989; Publishers Weekly February 13, 1987; July 10, 1995; Time July 27, 1987; Times Literary Supplement October 3, 1986; September 2, 1988; March 13, 1992; September 2, 1994.

CRAIG, GORDON ALEXANDER (November 26, 1913–), American historian, was born in Glasgow, Scotland, the son of Frank Craig, a compositor, and Jane Bissell Craig. He came to the United States in 1925 and attended local schools in Jersey City. He graduated from Princeton University with a B.A. in 1936, an M.A. in 1939, and a Ph.D. in 1941. As a Rhodes Scholar, he earned a Bachelor of Letters from Balliol College, Oxford University, in 1938.

During World War II, Craig served as a Marine Corps officer and was stationed in the Pacific theater between 1944 and 1946. In later years he was a research associate in the Office of Strategic Services, a special assistant in the U.S. Department of State, and a consultant to the U.S. Arms Control and Disarmament Agency.

GORDON CRAIG

Craig's career as professor of history spanned forty years, first at Princeton and later at Stanford, from which he retired in 1979. He was also for a brief time visiting professor at Columbia University and since 1962 has served as professor of modern history at the Free University of Berlin.

In a long and productive career as a historian, Craig has written mainly on modern Germany, military history, and diplomacy. While an undergraduate Craig visited Germany seeking information for a senior thesis on the Weimar Republic. He was fascinated by German art and music. "These masterpieces of high German culture made a deep and lasting impression on me." But, he added, "no more so than the many examples that I encountered of abuse of culture and, indeed, of inhumanity and barbarism." He was referring here to the spreading Nazism and anti-Semitism and to frequent "depressing symbols of eager obedience to authority."

In his foreword to *War, Politics, and Diplomacy*, a collection of essays, Craig described his own development as a historian. His interest in military matters was aroused as a young graduate student by his reading of Hans Delbrück's *History of the Art of War*, which made him aware of the close relationship and interaction between a society's military and its political establishment, a theme that runs through his works on Germany. While he was absorbed in Delbrück, he came under the influence of Edward Mead Earle, professor at the Institute for Advanced Study at Princeton and an authority on military history. On the eve of World War II

Craig collaborated with Earle and his close colleague Felix Gilbert in the editing of *Makers of Modern Strategy: Military Thought from Machiavelli to Hitler*, published in 1941 and reprinted many times. It contains contributions from twenty historians, including Craig, who analyzed the classic works of strategy by such authorities as Frederick the Great, Napoleon, Henri de Jomini, Carl von Clausewitz, Delbrück, Lenin and Alfred Thayer Mahan. Required reading for many years at the military academies and in ROTC programs, it has been praised as the best book on the subject and a "pioneering classic in the field."

The first book Craig wrote was *The Politics of the Prussian Army, 1640–1645*, which won for its author the 1955 Herbert Baxter Adams prize of the American Historical Association for the best book on European history by an American. This book deals with the influence of the German officer corps on domestic and foreign policy, first in Prussia and, after 1871, in a unified Germany. Craig examines the role of the German General Staff, which in successive regimes of empire, republic, and Third Reich neutralized political liberalism, buttressed an authoritarian regime, preempted civilian control, succumbed to Hitlerism, and eventually was destroyed.

In March 1958 Craig delivered the Albert Shaw Lectures on Diplomatic History at Johns Hopkins University. In these lectures, published as *From Bismarck to Adenauer*, Craig examines the evolution of German foreign policy from Bismarck and his Wilhelmine successors, through the chancellors of the Weimar Republic and the Nazi era, to Adenauer and his postwar espousal of European integration.

Craig's *magnum opus* is *Germany 1866–1945*, which begins with Prussia's victory over Austria in 1866. German political and social liberalism in the mid-19th century was never strong, and Craig shows how Bismarck's authoritarianism put the stamp on the structure and functioning of the newly formed German empire. The second part of the book deals with the Weimar regime, which spawned National Socialism and the Hitler phenomenon. Throughout, the book emphasizes the crucial role of the army in forcing political change.

In the *New York Times Book Review*, Hugh Trevor-Roper called *Germany* "a work of great erudition, packed with detail, and of wide range." In the *New York Review of Books*, Felix Gilbert wrote that "Craig's book certainly stands out from most of the literature on modern Germany as the best-informed and most reliable guide through the labyrinth of recent German history."

In *The Germans*, published in 1982, Craig devotes chapters to religion, Germans and Jews, money, women, the army, and other aspects of Post-World War II German life. Referring to Craig's "passionate insightfulness," Amos Perlmutter in the *New Republic* called *The Germans* a myth-destroying book, adding that it demonstrates "that Hitler was in fact representative of German romanticism, nationalism, and intolerance."

In *The Diplomats, 1919–1939*, edited by Craig and Felix Gilbert, seventeen writers comment on diplomatic history during the interwar period. The book is less a history of diplomatic events than a study of how individual diplomats conducted foreign affairs. William L. Langer, writing in the *New York Times Book Review*, said of *The Diplomats*: "Though a collaborative work, it is remarkably even and well-integrated . . . the best-informed, most authoritative and most provocative treatment of diplomatic history presently available for the period."

With Professor Alexander George of Stanford, Craig collaborated in *Force and Statecraft: Diplomatic Problems of Our Time*, a history of diplomacy over the last three hundred years, with an examination of the tools of international statecraft, including negotiation, deterrence, crisis management, and detente. Writing in *Political Science Quarterly*, Walter LaFeber cited one of the book's themes: "the growing power of public opinion after 1914 and the problems this and . . . multiple interest groups pose to democratic statecraft." LaFeber calls the book "an instructive discussion of why the world faces the dangers of a more chaotic international system."

In *The Triumph of Liberalism: Zurich in the Golden Age, 1830–1869*, Craig spotlighted a historic moment in which liberal leaders "developed industry, commerce, education, political freedom, civic spirit, entrepreneurial energy, and public welfare . . . immeasurably enriching the material and mental well-being of the citizens," according to Lionel Gossman in the *New York Review of Books*. In the *New York Times Book Review*, Raymond Grew found that "Craig uses his mastery of the techniques of diplomatic and political history" to describe how a zenith of high culture became "the achievement of moderate liberalism."

The wide critical respect accorded all of Craig's books and their popularity among general readers enabled many of his works to remain in print through more than one edition, affording him the opportunity to update prefaces and afterwords with analyses of recent events, like the reunification of Germany, in which he saw the country's return to the principles of the Enlightenment and Western liberalism.

As a teacher, Craig was regarded by students at both Princeton and Stanford as one of the top lecturers of any department. Among his many honors are membership in Phi Beta Kappa; Guggenheim Fellowships in 1969–1970 and in 1982–1983; and honorary doctorates from Princeton University in 1970, the Free University of Berlin in 1983, and Ball State University in 1984. He holds the Commander's Cross of the Legion of Merit of the Federal Republic of Germany 1984 and a doctorate of Humane Letters from Wake Forest University 1988. He is an honorary fellow of Balliol College, Oxford University, 1989, an honorary member of the Berlin Historical Commission 1975 and a fellow of the Center for Advanced Study in the Behavioral Sciences.

Gordon Craig married Phyllis Halcomb on June 16, 1939. He has three daughters and a son and lives in Menlo Park, California.

PRINCIPAL WORKS: The Politics of the Prussian Army, 1640–1945, 1955; From Bismarck to Adenauer: Aspects of German Statecraft, 1958; Europe since 1815, 1961; The Battle of Koeniggraetz: Prussia's Victory over Austria, 1866, 1964; War, Politics and Diplomacy: Selected Essays, 1966; Germany, 1866–1945, 1978; The Germans, 1982, 1991; (with A. George) Force and Statecraft: Diplomatic Problems Of Our Times, 1983, 1990; The End of Prussia: The Corti Lectures, 1982, 1984; The Triumph of Liberalism: Zurich in the Golden Age, 1830–1869, 1988; "Zurich" in Geneva, Zurich, Basel: History, Culture, and National Identity, (with N. Bouvier and L. Gossman), 1994. As editor—(with E. Earle and F. Gilbert) Makers of Modern Strategy: Military Thought from Machiavelli to Hitler, 1943; (with F. Gilbert) The Diplomats, 1919–1939, 1953; H. Rosinski, The German Army, 1966; H. von Treitschke, History of Germany in the Nineteenth Century; Selections from the Translations of Eden and Cedar Paul, 1975; Economic Interest, Militarism and Foreign Policy; Essays on German History, by Eckart Kehr, 1977; (with P. Paret and F. Gilbert) Makers of Modern Strategy: From Machiavelli to the Nuclear Age, 1986; (with F. L. Loewenheim) The Diplomats, 1939–1979, 1994.

ABOUT: Blue Book: Leaders of the English-Speaking World, 1974; Contemporary Authors 17, 1986; Foreign Affairs 50-year Bibliography:1920–1970; Institute for Advanced Study, A Community of Scholars, Faculty and Members, 1930–1980; Jessup, J. E., Guide to the Study and Use of Military History, 1979. Periodicals—American Historical Journal of Modern History June 1960; Journal of Modern History June 1960; New York Review of Books January 25, 1979; New York Times Book Review May 24, 1953; Political Science Quarterly Fall 1983; Times Literary Supplement October 6, 1978.

*CRASNARU, DANIELA (April 14, 1950–), Romanian poet, short story writer, and editor, is a former member of the national Parliament chosen in the first free elections after the 1989 revolution which overthrew the Ceauşescu dictatorship.

She was born in Craiova, an ancient regional capital and, in modern times, a small industrial city on the Wallachian plain between the Carpathian mountains and the Danube, the region Romanians call Oltenia. Her schooling took place in that city, and then she attended Craiova University, from which she graduated in 1973 with a degree in philology, majoring in Romanian and English. The same year as her graduation also saw the publication of Crašnaru's first volume of poetry, Lumin˘cit umbră (Light as much as shadow), by one of Romania's most prominent publishing houses for which the poet went on to work as an editor until two years before the revolution. This debut volume had been completed and accepted in 1969, near the close of a brief period of liberalization and relative freedom of expression, but although scheduled for 1971 publication, it was delayed two years more when the poet refused to accede to a request that she add ten to fifteen patriotic poems, a refusal that, she admits, was neither a political statement nor a protest of the changing political atmosphere, but a reflection of a simple fact: she did not write and thus did not have such poems. Both this first volume and her next, Spaţiul de graţie (The realm of grace, 1976), have been described by Romanian critics as highly skillful, and sentimental, "feminine" lyricism; in the descriptive terms of a 1978 Romanian dictionary of young writers, the works are "delicate," "candied," "artifical," "fragile," "diaphanous," and "angel-like." Their skill is notable but, in retrospect, they do not show the power, the thematic ambitiousness, and the personal frankness that became defining qualities in her later work.

Creative in language from a very young age—at three and four years of age, before she could write, she used to dictate poetry to her mother—Crăsnaru, according to family lore, was perhaps destined for a career as a writer. Her given first name was Carmen, "song," though she has always used the middle name she publishes under. Though her first volume was completed while she was still in high school and published before she graduated from the university, she never expected to become a professional writer. She participated actively in sport, was a gymnastics champion on the national team in her early teens, and played handball competitively, but she had to give up sports because of a gymnastics accident when she was fourteen. Her parents, Petre and Victoria Crăsnaru, both

°crahs NAH roo, dan YEL uh

had university degrees in pharmacy, as did her paternal grandfather; their own pharmacy was lost in the nationalization of 1948, and her first six years were spent moving from village to village with her parents, who were officially suspect because of their background as shop owners. Her mother and father believed that due to their dossier their only child had to master everything, and they were especially gratified at their daughter's interest in science and her academic accomplishments in such subjects as mathematics and physics, in the latter of which she excelled. As a teenager, Crăsnaru intended to go on the university to study biophysics, a career choice her family favored. Then, however, she fell in love, and her plans changed radically. Impulsively, she married after high school (this first marriage lasted only six months), and because the university in Craiova where she lived did not have the curriculum for her to go on in science, she applied instead to study literature and linguistics.

Despite her early dream of becoming a scientist, Crăsnaru remembers literary creation as something she was always aware of as a gift: "Somehow I realized very early I could have an artistic career . . . writing or drama or something concerning words. . . . You do not decide to be something. You are or you aren't. . . . Only those who weren't born so must decide." The concept of the artist born rather than made is a powerful notion in Romanian culture, and the writer Crăsnaru sees as having most influenced her, is the modern poet Tudor Arghezi, whom she values as likewise a "born poet." In prose, Crăsnaru cites specific writers she found most important, particularly Hemingway, Dostoyevski, Thomas Mann, Nabokov, Bulgakov, Borges, and García Márquez, but in poetry she believes nobody's work guided her in a specific manner. Besides Romanian writers, she acknowledges French, Italian, and a number of English and American poets (she knows English, French, Italian, and German, the first three fluently), singling out among writers in English Poe, Eliot, Elizabeth Barrett Browning, and Sylvia Plath, whose works had an important and widespread influence among Romanian women poets who began their careers in the late 1960s and the 1970s.

Plath's confessional style could be similar to Crăsnaru's own, although Crăsnaru's work, while often confessional in strategy and unflinching in its evocation of psychic pain and disturbing images, is less directly personal. For Daniela Crăsnaru, writing is a process of intense involvement, almost the opposite of "emotion recollected in tranquility." She states: "Poetry, for me at least, is therapy. When I'm overcharged

with impression and feelings, it's the most natural way to recover my balance. . . . When the interior pressure is too high, when I can't stand it any more, I write. . . . I wrote many poems crying, sometimes even canceling with my own tears the words I'd just written, and I had to reconstruct them." She compares her creative process to the antiquated medical procedure of "letting blood," but despite the success of her work, she admits to a discrepancy between intention and depth of feeling on the one hand and what words can capture on the other: "There's a very big difference between what I have in mind and what I am able to put on paper. All my life I've tried to diminish the distance. Somewhere on the way between my mind—arm—hand—pencil, I'm losing energy, I lose something. It's a betrayal." Seldom does she know the end as she begins. Occasionally she has the sense "that someone is dictating to me and I just have to follow this dictation." Such poems turn out most "flowing," she admits. Then Crăsnaru revises, with an eye for rhythm, repetition, stress, and the pruning of useless adjectives or redundancies. Given her fundamental conception of the act of writing as therapeutic and its outcome the pale or secondary transcription of an inward ideal, it is not surprising that one of Crăsnaru's major themes is the complex situation of the permanent but ornamental and ineffectual character of the work of art in contrast to the living intensities of a world of life and mutability.

This theme is particularly apparent starting with Crăsnaru's poetry of the 1980s. With the third volume, her work underwent what Mircea Iorgulescu called "a surprising evolution . . . a lyrical radicalization." In part the poet intentionally fashioned an elaborate and polyphonic style, "crowding, filling the page with very strong expressions" so as to defeat the censors by confusing them, but in part, as the greater substance of her work reveals, the style developed in response to growing metaphysical complexity. Despite greater and greater restrictions in Romanian society throughout the 1980s, and steadily increasing pressure at work at the publishing house which led her to quit (in part due to illness brought on by stress), the 1980s were a highly productive decade for Crăsnaru, with five books of poetry and two of short fiction. Her poetry includes four major individual volumes, *Vinzătorul de indulgente* (The seller of indulgences, 1981), *Şaizeci şi nouă de poezii de dragoste* (Sixty-nine love poems, 1982), *Niagara de plumb* (Niagara of lead, 1984), and *Hemisferele de Magdeburg* (The Hemispheres of Magdeburg, 1987), as well as her selected poems of 1988, *Fereastra in zid* (The Window in the Wall) which received the Eminescu Prize for poetry. But substantial portions of her prior work, although already approved by the censors for book publication, were not passed for reprinting in this collection, in which new work was also not permitted. The 1987 Magdeburg book met with high praise as "a piece of choice among the poet's books," Nicolae Manolescu, one of Romania's preeminent critics (and a leader of the political opposition), terming hers "a powerful natural talent and a vivid, versatile, brilliant intelligence." George Szirtes commented in the *Times Literary Supplement* on *Letters From Darkness*, a collection of her poetry translated by Fleur Adcock, that in them an "enormous longing for freedom . . . bounds and dances flexing its delicate well-practiced muscles. . . ." He termed Adcock's translations "excellent and sure-footed."

Crăsnaru has also written verse for children and two collections of short stories. *Marile reemiu* (The Grand Prize) came out in 1983 and *Pluta răsturnată* (The Toppled Cork Tree) in 1990. The latter dates from 1987 but was not published until after the revolution when the manuscript was discovered in the drawer of a Vice Minister of Culture's desk, where it had been relegated by the authorities.

Since the revolution, Crăsnaru has gone back to editorial work, in the spring of 1990 becoming director of Romania's leading publisher of children's literature, Ion Creangă Publishing House, which she is in the process of privatizing. Also in the spring of 1990, along with other writers and intellectuals, she ran for Parliament in the new government, but after serving on Parliament's Cultural Commission, she chose not to run again in the elections in 1992. She remains active in national politics, however, on the Executive Committee of the opposition Liberal Party, which favors rapid privatization, decentralization, and restitution of private property. Free to travel after the revolution, she has attended poetry festivals and given readings throughout Europe and in the United States. In 1993 she participated in the International Writing Program at the University of Iowa. She is married to Constantin Dragomir, who since the revolution, has been editor-in-chief of *Curierul national* (The National Courier) and a member of Parliament; they have one daughter, Alexandra born in 1979.

Daniela Crăsnaru's themes and subjects place her in the forefront of a remarkable group of postwar Romanian women poets who, in particular during the two decades subsequent to the creative renaissance of the 1960s, wrote with a sense of moral engagement and responsibility that played an important role in keeping truth,

justice, and freedom alive in Romania during these decades of oppression. In Crăsnaru, this is often expressed in the lyrical persona's ambivalence about love (usually portrayed as love lost or denied, or as an anguished eroticism) or about the interaction and personal cost of inward resistance with the mood of existential frustration that seems at once a correlative of, and commentary on, the poet's dispiriting place and time. Crăsnaru's concerns inevitably came into conflict with the censors. For a period of about a year in the early 1980s, after an ironic and angry speech at the Writers' Union convention, she was completely unpublishable. While retaining aspects of the verbal refinement and sensuality of her early work, as Adam J. Sorkin has observed in the *A.R.A. Journal*, "the poems became more sarcastic, more skeptical in tone, more disillusioned, more socially referential in their signification" with a "thickness of texture." Her poems from the 1980s on remain concrete and imagistic but are also intensely ironic, powerful in feeling, and highly concentrated. The poet Nina Cassian defines her achievements as "lucid, poignant poems, full of polemical verve and obvious freedom of expression."

Central to Crăsnaru's poetry is a drama of vividly evoked dichotomies and polarities, what Adam Sorkin called "an extension of the poetic voice's ambivalence as doubleness redoubled" and another commentator tallied up as "confession . . . in which the deep identity . . . is in fact the unity of diversity, the tension of an interior battlefield." These paradoxes are basic to her writing, and the poet herself has remarked that her "starting point" is inevitably "a kind of inner duality" for which she suggested two pairs of phrases: "spirit and body" and "lucidity and sensuality." Such dualities can be perceived in her combining of wit and a spiritualized sense of the carnal that Fleur Adcock saw, in understatement no doubt, as issuing in an "undercurrent of despair." The poetic voice of Crăsnaru's poems is characteristically dramatized both as isolated, solipsistic, and resigned to the "neurotic cage" of physical actuality in "The Thirty Year Old Body" encasing "a small incandescent crystal" but also to incorporeal existence, "a word in the belly of another word." In "Breath," the poet's putting her "hand that writes" to "the paper's whiteness"-her whole arm into "its cold, neutral / flesh" is

A suicide-
elegant
just about letter perfect.

—tr. Adam J. Sorkin

Manolescu, taking an image from the poem

"Tattooing," aptly observed that for Crăsnaru, "Life (love, disenchantment, fear) is tattooed with words, and in turn the words (lines of verse, texts) seethe with life's own blood, suffer and die."

Paradoxically, however, these words, which are the progeny of the woman-poet-creator, can do nothing, can make nothing living. An untitled poem begins,

> Let me confess
> words' uselessness.
> Their powerlessness
> in face of the real.
>
> —tr. Adam J. Sorkin

The poem alludes to writing as a "tragic utopia" which incarnates only "illusion," "imagination," and "irreality." But in a further antithesis, the imagination is what gives human beings freedom. Imagination, if a "wild beast which swallows me / each and every time I show fear," as the poetic persona says at the end of "The Raft of the Medusa," is ultimately inaccessible yet revolutionary and necessary.

Fundamental to Crăsnaru's work is concern with the central late 20th-century dilemma of individuality and marginalization, of power and powerlessness. She cannot change the threatening social and political atmosphere, even if she desires and imagines otherwise. She says of the sketched window that is at once fiction and overwhelming reality, "I don't have the courage to break through," and in the womb-like "interior waters," "this interior cosmos permeated / by my own image," her most terrible lament is

> Ah, how I hate this place where I feel so good
> as I've never felt there beyond
> in the physical landscape
> as I've never felt by the side of my child
> nor in the arms of any man.
> Ah, how I hate this place where I feel so good.
>
> —tr. Adam J. Sorkin and Ioana Ieronim

"Austerloo," a poem commencing with her historical confusion of where Napoleon lost and where he won suggests the poet's continual and self-aware struggle with some of the universal themes of literature: what is real and what is illusion, the value of illusion, individual sufficiency, the spectrum of life's basic experiences and essential meanings or meaninglessness, evoking in its meditation key lines from an earlier work, "Indigo, Violet," in *Letters from Darkness* where the poet writes of

> the smell of death,
> as close to the smell of love
> as violet to indigo
> in the spectrum of light.
>
> —tr. Fleur Adcock

If she often speaks as one of the powerless and alienated, Daniela Crăsnaru ends by celebrating the triumphant creative spirit's power to bring to us images of possible life and (to cite the end of the otherwise more somber "Scripta") simply to "be / abcdefg."

PRINCIPAL WORKS IN ENGLISH TRANSLATION: (tr. L. Ursu) Seven Poems *in* 15 Young Romanian Poets, 1982; (tr. A. Deletant and B. Walker) Eleven Poems *in Silent Voices: An Anthology of Contemporary Romanian Women Poets* (intro. F. Adcock), 1986; (tr. F. Adcock) *Letters from Darkness*, 1991; (tr. A. J. Sorkin with S. Celac, I. Ieronim, M. Nazarie, and M.A. Tupan) Ten Poems *in* An Anthology of Romanian Women Poets, 1994.

ABOUT: Sorkins, A. *in* An Anthology of Romanian Women Poets, 1994. *Periodicals*—Journal of the American Romanian Academy of the Arts and Sciences, 1993; Parnassus: Poetry in Review 1993; Times Literary Supplement March 27, 1992; World Literature Today Winter 1993.

CURLEY, DANIEL (October 4, 1918– December 30, 1988), American short story writer, novelist, and educator, was born in East Bridgewater, Massachusetts, and educated at the University of Alabama, where he received an M.A. He began his academic career at Syracuse University and Plattsburgh State Teachers College (now the State University of New York at Plattsburgh). From 1955 until his death he was a professor of English at the University of Illinois at Urbana-Champaign. In 1968 and 1982 he was named an Associate of the University of Illinois Center for Advanced Study.

His first book, *That Marriage Bed of Procrustes*, is a collection of short stories that focuses on unhappy marriages and crumbling relationships. "The central characters in three of the dozen stories are among the most unhappy, most unpleasant characters of recent fiction," William Peden wrote in the *New York Times Book Review*, "This joyless quality permeates most of Mr. Curley's stories. Whatever the scene, his characters are for the most part self-centered prigs or tormented masochists." For all that, Peden noted Curley's "palpable assets—honesty, intelligence, sincerity and technical adroitness."

Curley's first novel, *How Many Angels?*, is a portrait of a young man bored with his job and frustrated by his meddlesome fiancée. Reviewing it in the *New York Herald Tribune Book Review*, Gene Baro commented that Curley "enlists a clear, vivid style that can be colloquial, humorous, satiric, lyrical."

The protagonist of *A Stone Man, Yes* is the

head of the English department at an undistinguished university, whose wife, an alcoholic and a religious fanatic, withholds sex from him. He, in turn, pursues other women. However, he ultimately discovers, that his wife has been conducting a torrid affair with an instructor at the school. Most reviewers emphasized the literary qualities of the novel. In the *National Review*, Jeffrey Hart wrote: "Daniel Curley is a superb prose stylist, inventive in his use of language and skillful in his narrative. . . . His literary seriousness is almost overwhelming." The *Virginia Quarterly Review* called Curley's protagonist "a priceless contribution to any gallery of henpecked husbands and cuckolds." Martin Levin, however, wrote, in the *New York Times Book Review*, "The sinister carousel that . . . Curley depicts has an initial fascination as it begins . . . its hectic spinning. Interest dims rather than grows with each succeeding go-round."

After the publication of *A Stone Man, Yes*, Curley devoted much of the next twenty years to writing short stories and reviews that appeared in periodicals—among them *Playboy*, the *Atlantic*, the *Hudson Review*, *Epoch*, *Prairie Schooner*, and *Modern Fiction Studies*. His collection *In the Hands of Our Enemies* won a National Council of the Arts Award in 1971. His short stories were included in *Best American Short Stories*, 1955 and 1964, and the 1965 *O. Henry Prize Short Stories*. From 1955 to 1960, Curley served on the editorial board of *Accent*, a literary magazine featuring short fiction. The magazine was renamed *Ascent*, and Curly became editor in 1975. He remained in that position until his death.

Curley was also the author of several children's books, which grew out of stories he told to his own daughters, although he did not write then down until much later. The best known of these books is *Hilarion*.

In his short story collection *Living with Snakes*, which won a Flannery O'Connor Award, Curley again concentrates on analyzing the many varieties of unhappy relationships. "Christians don't face lions in these stories, but husbands, former husbands, and lovers do face lots of other animals—often with religious overtones," Christopher Benfey wrote in the *New York Times Book Review*: "Curley's characters see their fates and desires embodied in caged or wild animals." In "Trinity", for instance, the divorced parents of a dead child are reunited and take up their old habit of spending Sundays at the zoo, "their careful substitute for Mass," where they liturgically recites the names of the various birds in Latin. In the *Hudson Review* (1986), George Kearns wrote: "Curley's

stories of mid-America, unpretentious, highly crafted, generally comic or bittersweet, and closely observed, are representative of the best short fiction. . . . "

Magic and dreams are dominant elements throughout Curley's later fiction. In *Mummy*, Curley's last novel, an American vows to bring his mother's body home to Illinois for a proper burial, after it has been placed on exhibit in the mummy museum in Guanajuato, Mexico. But, according to Robert Plunkett in the *New York Times Book Review*, "Strange things begin to happen, Marc encounters Indians with sinister intentions and witches with magic potions. We soon realize we are on another kind of journey. It is not north to the border but rather through 'the blank spaces on the map,' a sort of literary twilight zone strewn with symbols and images and conceits."

In the *Hudson Review*, Dean Flower commented: "Curley makes all this extravagant material work by means of an imperturbable narrative detachment, an echo perhaps of the stoical skepticism his hero adopts about his own fate. He knows when to be deadpan, when hyperbolic, when terse. . . . We can laugh uproariously at Curley's macabre story because . . . it demands that we pass through 'the blighted gates' of death. In this, as in the mummy theft, he owes a considerable debt to Flannery O'Connor's *Wise Book*. But the voice is entirely, delightfully his own."

In the title story from *The Curandero*, a posthumously published volume, an American, traveling alone in Mexico, is convinced that he is dying. In his wandering, he finds himself in the home of a "curandero," a medicine man, who concludes that the man's "soul is loose" and effects a hallucinatory, sometimes comical reattachment. Cary Kimble termed the book "at once satisfying and acutely sad" in the *New York Times Book Review*. "If there is an autobiographical story, it is probably 'The Quilt'. . . . Here, a writer who published a fair amount, to small acclaim, returns to his hometown. . . . 'Even as a child he had practiced nostalgia, looking forward to looking back. He would sit in the window seat of the old house and imagine himself returning.'"

Reviewing *The Curandero* in *Choice*, S. I. Bellman said the "mood of sadness and regret . . . is enlivened by an obscure whimsy that marked his earlier work . . . and that set him apart from . . . other . . . successful fiction writers." The characters are "pathetic solitaries in adversity—sometimes pushed almost beyond their endurance—yet Curley manages somehow to soften for the reader the pain of their existence. . . . "

Curley was struck by a car and killed while vacationing with his wife in Tallahassee in 1988. Many reviewers have found in his work a kind of morbidly comic vision of what Cary Kimble calls "a man alone with himself, for better or worse, fighting off indifference and his own moral and physical decay."

PRINCIPAL WORKS: *Short Stories*—That Marriage Bed of Procrustes, 1957; In the Hands of Our Enemies: Stories, 1970; Love in the Winter: Stories, 1976; Living with Snakes: Stories, 1985; The Curandero: Eight Stories, 1991. *Novels*—How Many Angels?, 1958; A Stone Man, Yes: A Novel, 1964; Mummy, 1987. *Juvenile*—Ann's Spring, 1977; Billy Beg and the Bull, 1978; Hilarion, 1979. *Nonfiction*—(with R. Ebert) The Perfect London Walk, 1986. *As editor*—(with G. Scouffas and C. Shattuck) Accent: An Anthology, 1940–60, 1973. *Drama*—Invincible, 1970.

ABOUT: Contemporary Authors, 127, 1989; Contemporary Authors New Revision Series, 3, 1981; 18, 1986; Something About the Author 23, 1981; 61, 1990; Writers Directory 1988–90, 1988. *Periodicals*—American Book Review December–January 1991–1992; Choice September 1991; Hudson Review Spring 1986; Summer 1987; National Review August 25, 1964; New York Kerald Tribune Book Review February 23, 1958; New York Times January 3, 1989; New York Times Book Review September 22, 1957; July 19, 1964; November 10, 1985; April 26, 1987; May 26, 1991. Prairie Schooner Summer 1989; Virginia Quarterly Review Autumn 1964; Washington Post January 4, 1989.

*DAGAN, AVIGDOR (VICTOR FISCHL) (June 30, 1912–   ), Czech novelist and poet now living in Israel, writes: "I was born two years before World War I in Hradec Králové (known also under the German name Koeniggraetz), a town in Bohemia which at the time of my birth was a part of Austria, since 1918 a part of Czechoslovakia, and is at present [1993] in the Czech Republic. I studied at the University of Prague and became Doctor of Law and Political Science in 1938. Active since my early days in the Zionist movement, I was already during my university studies editor of the official organ of the Zionist Organisation in Czechoslovakia, as well as parliamentary secretary of the Jewish Party, a minority party represented in the Prague Parliament.

"In March 1939, a fortnight after Hitler's occupation of Czechoslovakia, I escaped to London where, caught by the outbreak of World War II, I remained for the next eight years. I became friendly with Jan Masaryk who, in 1940, became foreign minister in the Czechoslovak government-in-exile headed by President Beneš and who offered me a job in his ministry. I stayed in

AVIGDOR DAGAN

London even after the war's end as first secretary of the Czechoslovak Embassy and was recalled in 1947 to the Ministry of Foreign Affairs in Prague to head a department charged with preparing the Czechoslovak case for the peace treaty negotiations with Germany. However, after the Communist putsch and the tragic death of Jan Masaryk, I left Prague again, this time for the goal of my dreams, Jerusalem.

"In Israel I began almost immediately working again in the Foreign Office. Between 1955 and 1977 I served as chargé d'affaires in Japan and Burma, minister in Yugoslavia, and ambassador in Poland, Norway, Ireland, and Austria. I was also a member of the Israel delegation to the United Nations General Assembly, besides several other diplomatic missions. Between posts abroad I several times filled the job of head of the East European department in the Foreign Ministry. In 1977 I retired and have since then been living in Jerusalem as a writer.

"Literature was my first love. I started as a Czech poet and before living Prague for the first time, I had published four books of poetry, one of which, "Hebrew Melodies," was awarded the coveted Melantrich Prize in 1936. Before leaving finally for Israel, I had published four more volumes of poetry. By that time I had also written my first novel, "The Song of Pity," which won the ELK (European Literary Club) Prize in January 1948. A month later the Communists came to power and vetoed the publication of the book. It appeared first in Hebrew in 1952, in Czech, only thirty years later in Canada, and forty years later in Czechoslovakia, once again free from a totalitarian regime.

°dah GAHN, ah VIG dor

"For the next quarter of a century, fully occupied by my diplomatic work, I was able to write only sporadically, and so my next novel, *The Wisdom of a Rooster,* was published only in 1975. The book appeared later also in Hebrew and German.

"Since my retirement in 1977 all my time has been devoted to literary work. The result so far: eight novels, four books of short stories, two more books of poetry, and three children's books. One of the novels, *The Watchmaker from Zodiac Street,* I wrote together with my brother Gabriel Dagan. Practically all my books appear in Czech—under my original name Viktor Fischl, under which I have been known to Czech readers even before World War II—and Hebrew, but five of my novels have been translated into German, and one, *Dvorní šašci* translated as (*The Court Jesters*), also into English, French, and Dutch.

"I am also the author of two political books, namely *Conversations with Jan Masaryk,* published in Czech—five editions, the last one in a quarter of a million copies—and German, and *Moscow and Jerusalem,* written in English. I edited a 600-page volume on *The Jews of Czechoslovakia,* published in English.

"In 1992, on the occasion of my eightieth birthday, I was awarded two more literary prizes, namely the Czech Literary Fund Prize and the Hostovsky Prize. President Havel decorated me with the Thomas Masaryk Order.

"I still do not know the answer to the question, whether I am a Czech writer living in Jerusalem, or an Israeli writer working in Czech. Yet whatever the answer, I trust that in my Czech as well as in my Jewish themes—for Prague and Jerusalem are my two main fountains—the human voice is audible most of all."

Dagan is a nostalgic writer with deep roots in a Czechoslovakia of small country villages and the urban intellectual center of Prague, where Czech, German, and Jewish cultures were closely interwoven. His childhood was the era of the famous *Prager Kreis,* the Prague Circle, of such distinguished writers as Franz Kafka, Max Brod, Franz Werfel, and Rainer Maria Rilke. Although he has lived in Israel since 1949, Dagan continues to write mainly in Czech.

His earliest works were lyrical poems marked by traditional and spiritual themes, although clearly in the modern idiom. The poetry of the Hebrew Bible, most notably the Psalms, was a distinct influence, as witness his prize-winning *Hebrejske melodie* (Hebrew melodies) of 1936 and *Evropske zalmy,* (European Psalms, 1941).

His interest in the rural and folkloric traditions of Czech culture, later developed also in his fiction, is reflected in *Mrtva ves* (1943, *The Dead Village*). His first novel, *Piseň o lítosti* (The song of pity), was written in 1947 but not published until 1951 traces the coming of age of the central character against the background of the Holocaust. The narration becomes a catharsis for him, healing the traumas of his tragic past by breaking the seal of silence and examining them openly.

Some of the motifs of this first novel are developed in *Kuropění* (The song of the rooster, 1975). Like many writers in Eastern Europe during the years of Communist repression, Dagan uses allegory and fantasy as a cover for a thoughtful and serious examination of contemporary existence. The central character in *Kuropění* is a doctor who, after the death of his wife in childbirth, dedicated himself to curing the illnesses (spiritual as much as physical) of people in his village—through which he wanders as a pilgrim, staff in hand, with his rooster Pedro on his arm. The bird is his alter ego, a hedonistic, life-affirming spirit, with who, he has lively debates. More serious are his debates with God, whom he challenges forthrightly, raising ethical questions. The book ends on a note of reconciliation with God, affirming faith and the harmony of an eternal universe. With its precise language, almost biblical simplicity, and visionary spirit, *Kuropění* conforms to the more conservative traditions of modern Czech literature. It inspired a response from an underground Czech writer, Jan Křesadlo—author of *Zámecký pan aneb Antikuro* (The lord of the manor, or the anti-song of a rooster)—in 1992, who reacted against the subtle irony of *Kuropění* with a more crude and outspoken attack on the political corruption of the Stalinist era.

Almost as widely known and appreciated as *Kuropění* is the novel *Dvorní šašci* (*The Court Jesters*). The real world, rather than an allegorical country village, is far more palpable in this story of four Jews who survive in a Nazi death camp because the sadistic commandant, "lord of life and death in that place," uses them as entertainers (hence court jesters) in parties he gives for his Nazi friends. The narrator, a former judge and a hunchback from an accident at the time of his birth, has the gift of foresight: "Soon I began to believe that in my hump I carried a secret key to open gates for me that are locked to others, so that I can see what is invisible to everybody else and can guess what they can't." He serves his sadistic master as a clown–fortune teller, along with a dwarf, a juggler, and a scholar-astrologer. Brutally humiliated, forced to entertain even while starving and constantly aware of the imminence of the gas chambers, the four are finally rescued when the camp is liberated by the Russians. The narrator's faith has up until this time remained unshaken ("God was mother's skirt, the place where you're safe, the tree you touch when you're playing tag so they can't catch you—like the altar in a sanctuary.") But in later years, settled in Jerusalem and reflecting on his mission to bear witness to the atrocities he has seen ("to fight the battle against oblivion"), he traces the bitter fates of the other "jesters" and raises the central question of religious faith: "Has it ever occurred to you that he keeps us just like Major Kohl [the Nazi officer], just to amuse Himself? Maybe we're nothing but his court jesters." He never finds a direct answer, but walking out to the walls of Jerusalem to watch a sunrise, he experiences an epiphany and understands: "So much unimaginable beauty couldn't have been created without a purpose, and those who were allowed to stand and wonder at all this beauty couldn't have been created only to amuse their Creator. They weren't meant to serve Him as court jesters. More than that I didn't know. But that at least I knew."

Molly Abramowitz, in *Library Journal*, commented, "Dagan is a superb storyteller, detailing revenge, chance and divine purpose as he weaves together the shattered past and present of this unusual group of court jesters." Avery Rome, in the *New York Times Book Review*, praised Dagan's "modern fairy tale," created "to explore some of the important philosophical questions arising from the Holocaust: Is there a God? If so, what is His purpose for man? And how could He have permitted the atrocities of the concentration camps?" Rome, however, found that "Dagan's characters are less flesh-and-blood people than vehicles to probe his larger themes. . . ."

Kuropění and *Dvorní šašci*, Dagan's masterpieces, contain important motifs that recur in his other books. *Jeruzalémské providky* (The Jerusalem stories, published in Hebrew 1983 and in Czech 1985) is a mosaic of sketches and stories, evoking Dagan's vision of Jerusalem as a spiritual concept and a state of mind, both majestic and natural. "Sometimes it seems to me that Jerusalem is not a city at all, but a trace of God's pace. The only trace, before and after which there was none," says one of the characters. "But there are many things at which you would be amazed anywhere else; in Jerusalem, however, they do not particularly surprise you. . . . Jerusalem is not a city like other cities and that's why people who live here are different." In Jerusalem, the spiritual people know more about one another than anywhere else and cling to one another in a spiritual union. The book also depicts the cruel

reality of the Israeli-Arab war of 1967. The novel *Hodinář z uličky zvěrokruhu* (The watchmaker from Zodiac Street, 1992) is also about the spell of an Israeli city and about the victory of human goodness. In Jaffa, "almost everything is possible," and Viktor Blum, the watchmaker, overcomes, almost miraculously, the wounds from a concentration camp, with his kind wife by his side. *Figarova zlatá svatba* (Figaro's golden wedding, 1987) is a collection of playful sketches, in which philosophical motifs are treated with humor and irony. *Pátá čvrt'* (The Fifth Quarter, 1991), can be viewed as a counterpart of *Jeruzalémské povídky*: The Fifth Quarter was a place "where nothing was impossible. . . . Everything one can imagine was here, and even much more." The Prague Jewish ghetto is represented as a small enclosed world, whose very existence is, however, absurd and, indeed, open to question. Although tiny, it mirrors the whole world, and the author's love of the quarter is his love of the world.

Velocipéd pana Kulhánka (Mr. Kulhánek's velocipede, 1992), was inspired by the author's birthplace and is a sentimental series of vignettes of charming, eccentric characters whom we get to know through the adventures of a pilgrim, the cyclist Mr. Kulhánek.

Another of his books, *Moscow and Jerusalem: Twenty Years of Relations between Israel and the Soviet Union* (1970), with an introduction by Abba Eban was written in English and has not been published in Czechoslovakia. Dagan, working in the archives of the Israeli Foreign Ministry, discovered previously unpublished documents. From these, he traces the shifting positions of the U.S.S.R. towards Israel, from its initial support of the establishment of the state in 1947 to the complete breaking of relations in 1953 and the Soviet support of the Arab cause. In a closing note, he expresses some hope, based on Eban's diplomatic negotiations with the U.S.S.R., that a reconciliation might occur in the future, but emphasizes that responsibility for the Middle East conflict lies with the Soviet Union.

Dagan married Stella Berger in 1938. They had two sons. He told interviewers that he would not write his memoirs because he was too busy writing a variety of other books. Up to the restoration of democratic rule in the Czech Republic in 1989, he was best known in his native land not as a poet or novelist but for a book that circulated in samizdat (underground) publication—*Hovory s Janem Masarykem* (Conversations with Jan Masaryk, 1952). Since 1989, however, he has received increasing recognition both as a representative of pre-World War II literary culture and as a vital spokesman for contemporary Czech culture at home and abroad.

PRINCIPAL WORKS IN ENGLISH TRANSLATION: The Dead Village (tr. L. Lee) 1943; The Court Jesters (tr. B. Harshaw) 1989.

ABOUT: Contemporary Authors New Revision Series 30, 1990; Encyclopedia Judaica 1972; Who's Who in World Jewry. *Periodicals*—Library Journal October 1, 1989; New Leader May 3, 1971; New York Times Book Review November 12, 1989; Publishers Weekly September 19, 1989; Saturday Review February 6, 1971.

ROBERT DAHL

DAHL, ROBERT A(LAN) (December 17, 1915–　), American political theorist, writes: "I grew up in two small towns, one in Iowa, the other in Alaska. Because I spent the most formative years of my boyhood in Alaska, it was my life there, particularly in the little town of Skagway, that exerted on me, I think, the more profound and lasting influence.

"My father, the son of Norwegian immigrant farmers in North Dakota, had rejected farming for medicine. At the time of my birth in 1915 he, my mother (a South Dakotan), and my older brother were living in the town of Inwood (pop. 700) in northwestern Iowa. Although my father's medical practice was large, often even exhausting, when hard times hit the farmers of that region in the early 1920s his cash income began to vanish. As best I can recall, we never actually went hungry; in fact, we probably ate quite well, because the farmers often paid their bills in food—a year's supply of eggs and milk, a side of beef, a freshly butchered hog. But our clothes did get a bit threadbare at times; and to economize, my parents had to move into a house that even by the standards of that time and place lacked some pretty basic amenities: notably, indoor plumbing and potable water. (As to the first, we had an outhouse, and as to the second, a daily task of my brother and me was to haul buckets of water from the well of a friendly neighbor.)

"So it isn't surprising that when my father learned in the fall of 1924 that the only doctor in Skagway, Alaska, was leaving, he applied for his place and the regular salary guaranteed by the railroad company running north from Skagway to Whitehorse, Yukon Territory. I was just past my tenth birthday when we made the journey, perhaps the most memorable of my life, and reached Skagway in late January of 1925.

"With five hundred people, Skagway was even smaller than the Iowa town we had left. As thousands of tourists know, the town is situated in a spectacularly beautiful setting at the end of the long stretch of fjords called the Inside Passage, nestled in a narrow valley that runs between mountains down to the sea. There I acquired a love of nature and the outdoors—mountains, the sea, forests, rivers, lakes, glaciers and all—that I have never lost. Living there influenced me in other lasting ways as well: I developed a profound and enduring respect for 'ordinary people,' who, when you get to know them, are almost never ordinary. My later focus on questions of democratic theory and practice was, I suppose, one consequence. Because every boy was expected to work during summers—I spent mine as a longshoreman and a section hand—I acquired an enduring interest in the conditions under which people work, particularly their lack of power over crucial decisions in the firms where they work. Some of my earliest and latest writings, including *A Preface to Economic Democracy*, could be read as an expression of that interest. Finally, I have ruminated endlessly over the extraordinary advantages and disadvantages, opportunities and limitations, provided by living in a small town. I suppose *Size and Democracy* (which I wrote with Edward R. Tufte) was something of a by-product.

"I went to the University of Washington because it was the closest, requiring in those days (1932–1936) a five-day journey by ship down the Inside Passage to Seattle in September and back home in June. From Washington I went on for graduate work in political science to Yale, which I chose only because it provided me with the most generous fellowship. During my years as an undergraduate and graduate student, however, I felt not the faintest desire for an academic career, believing that my ideal future lay with a less contemplative and more active life in public service. It took some time for me to understand how wrong I was. After several years in Washington, mainly in the burgeoning war agencies of World War II, I spent almost three years in the infantry. Washington and military service not only provided me with experiences and insights that deeply influenced my view of the world, but it was in Europe in 1944 to 1945 that I came to realize that no career could satisfy me more than a life of teaching, scholarship, and writing.

"Luckily, after I returned from Europe in late 1945 a one-term substitute position opened up at Yale, beginning in January 1946. As it turned out, that one-term appointment was extended; one might even say that it did not end until I retired from Yale forty years later. I have never regretted my change in career at the age of twenty-nine, nor ceased to wonder at the element of sheer luck that helped to make it possible.

"What I have written here of my earlier life helps me, as it may the readers of this sketch, to account at least in part for my recurrent concern for questions in the theory and practice of democracy. Certainly I never set out as a young scholar to mine the field of democratic theory. Indeed, when I started, 'democratic theory' was not even a 'field' of political science. Yet I found myself drawn repeatedly to challenges in that undefined (and unbounded) area. Often, a question I had left in an unsatisfactory state in one book would become the subject of a later work. Yet it was only on looking back years later that I could see that without specifically intending the result, almost all my contributions bore on the subject of democratic theory and practice.

"A final note: The audience for which this brief sketch is intended made it inappropriate for me, I felt, to write of my family. But my narrative would be even more lopsided than it unavoidably is if I failed to say how central the members of my family have been. Important as my teaching and writing have been to me, I think my family has been the true core of my life."

In the citation attached to the Woodrow Wilson Prize awarded by the American Political Science Association to Robert Dahl on August 30, 1990 (his second), for his book *Democracy and Its Critics*, he is singled out as "a cautious and critical yet nevertheless ardent celebrant of democracy's many forms." Alan Ryan, who reviewed *Democracy and its Critics* in *New Statesman & Society*, praised its author as "one

of the great communicators," who has successfully reached . . . of a large audience encompassing journalists, political activists, and the wider public.

With the intention of becoming a lawyer, Dahl concentrated on political science and economics at the University of Washington and participated in a discussion group in which he detected "certain left currents." Yale, where he did his graduate work, had an especially strong faculty in international relations. His doctoral dissertation, "Socialist Programs in Democratic Politics," was a source he drew on for his later books. "I laid out five or six criteria that a program would have to meet in order to satisfy the requirements of a democratic order," he told Nelson Polsby in an interview for the Political Science Oral History Project, "Then I tested each of these."

After he received his doctorate in government and international relations in the fall of 1940, Dahl spent the next two years in government service, first as a management analyst for the department of Agriculture and, subsequently, as an economist in the Office of Production Management, and on the War Production Board. He voluntarily relinquished the draft deferment his position allowed him and entered military service during World War II. He won the Bronze Star with oak cluster, fighting with the Sixth Army in Alsace, Germany, and Austria. For a brief period after the war ended, he served with a "de-Nazification" unit under the United States Control Council.

Discharged from the army late in 1945, Dahl returned to New Haven to investigate teaching prospects. A "temporary" opening in the government department at Yale set him on his career path. He moved rapidly up, eventually retiring in 1986 as Sterling Professor of Political Science. For a five-year period (1957–1962), he chaired the department.

Dahl's first major publication, *Politics, Economics, and Welfare*, written in collaboration with Charles Lindblom, a colleague from the economics department, grew out of a graduate seminar they jointly conducted in the emerging field of labor economics. This book introduced the concept of "polyarchy," which has been characterized by James S. Fishkin in the *Routledge Dictionary of Twentieth Century Political Thinkers* as "a process in which nonleaders exert a high degree of control over leaders." Dahl sees polyarchy as a concomitant of democracy in large-scale governments, where political power is not confined to elected officials. Polyarchy, however, is a slightly lower step on the evolutionary scale toward "procedural democracy," according to Dahl.

A Preface to Democratic Theory focuses on the clash between majority and minority interests in the state. Democracy in America, Dahl asserts, is a "hybrid" form, neither "Madisonian" (which inherently distrusts the many) nor "Populistic" (which distrusts the few), but, according to Fishkin, "a system in which intense minorities tend to get their way, and in which there are many impediments to majority rule." *Who Governs?: Democracy and Power in the American City* which won Dahl his first Woodrow Wilson Award (in 1961), attempts to refute the charge that this American "hybrid" form of government is undemocratic on a local level because it tends to be dominated by a "ruling elite." Utilizing New Haven, Connecticut, during a period of vigorous urban renewal under the administration of Mayor Richard Lee as a case history, Dahl concludes that owing to competing elites—economic, social, and political— of relatively equal influence, power was more widely distributed in this city than critics of American urban government contended. *Who Governs?* was praised by Heinz Eulau in the *American Political Science Review* as "a sophisticated and undogmatic treatise on the democratic process," but it did not go unchallenged. While its findings were supported by two adjunct studies, Nelson Polsby's *Community Power and Political Theory* (1963) and Raymond E. Wolfinger's *The Politics of Progress*, (1973), the psychologist G. William Domhoff in *Who Really Rules? New Haven and Community Power Reexamined* (1978) disputed Dahl's basic thesis and faulted the methodology of all three books.

In *Polyarchy: Participation and Opposition*, another of his key books, Dahl set forth conditions for the achievement of democracy. These include elected officials who control government policy, frequent elections without coercion, nearly universal suffrage, elective office open to all the electorate, the right of free expression, the right to seek out alternative sources of information, and the right to form relatively independent associations or organizations, among which are political parties and interest groups.

The role of these last is the subject of *Dilemmas of Pluralist Democracy: Autonomy Versus Control*. Here Dahl's central concern is how much autonomy should be given to organizations of special interests within a democracy because of their potential "either to reduce injustice or to perpetuate it—to reduce it by creating an appropriate climate for change that enhances the lives of the majority or to perpetuate it by imposing the will of a minority that does not reflect the goals of the body politic." Dahl specifies criteria for the "ideal democratic process":

equality in voting, effective participation, enlightened understanding, final control over the agenda, and inclusion to the extent that "the demos ought to include all adults subject to its laws, except transients." To date, Dahl points out, no professed democracy has fully measured up to this ideal model.

Dahl's broad-based knowledge of the theory and the practice of popular government is reflected in *Democracy and its Critics*. In it, he reviews the evolution of democracy from its beginnings in the "demos" of ancient Greece to the modern refinements of representative government and the idea of political equality in the nation-state. From this vantage point, Dahl looks to a possible "third transformation" of democracy following upon the earlier city-state and nation-state models: its extension to such agglomeration as labor unions and corporations within nations as well as to international governing bodies. He warns, however, that if we overestimate the limits of democracy, we may "fail to try" new experiments, but if we underestimate them, "we shall probably try— and fail." He suggests that the domination of society by interest groups with a narrow focus can be overcome by creating a more informed citizenry, better able to participate in decision making, and sets forth ways of educating the public.

Reviewing *Democracy and Its Critics*, Alan Ryan in *New-Statesman & Society* thought it admirably balanced in its "tempering of theoretical claims with empirical evidence of their practicality or lack of it." Robert Bellah, in the *New York Times Book Review*, called attention to its timeliness, its publication coinciding with the prominence on the front pages of transitional political developments in Moscow, Warsaw, and Beijing. Jack Liveley's praise, in the *Times Literary Supplement*, was qualified. While he considered Dahl's defense of polyarchy and pluralist democracy cogent, he felt that his projections for the improvement of the democratic process through advances in telecommunications technology were sketchy. The book has since received the Elaine and David Spitz Book Prize of the Conference for the Study of Political Thought as well as the Woodrow Wilson Award, and has taken its place as one of the classics in its field.

In the preface to the fourth edition (1984) of his widely used textbook *Modern Political Analysis*, Dahl noted significant changes in his area of study since the first edition: a revival of "normative political theory"; an acceleration of empirical investigation; and "the increasing universality of political science," which heretofore had been almost exclusively confined to the

United States. Dahl himself has played an instrumental part in these developments, having lectured widely abroad as well as in America; his writings have been translated into French, German, Norwegian, Italian, Spanish, Portuguese, and Japanese. Among his numerous honors he has received an honorary Doctor of Laws degree from the University of Alaska in Anchorage and is a Cavaliere of the Republic of Italy. The citation from the Woodrow Wilson Award for *Democracy and Its Critics* eulogizes him as "political scientist whose distinguished career has helped us to define, at its best, our profession."

Dahl has been married twice. With his first wife Mary Louise Bartlett, whom he married in 1940 he had four children. She died in 1970. In 1973 he married Ann Sale Barber. He lives in North Haven, Connecticut.

PRINCIPAL WORKS: Congress and Foreign Policy, 1950; (with C. E. Lindblom) Politics, Economics, and Welfare, 1953; A Preface to Democratic Theory, 1956; A Critique of the Ruling Model, 1958; Who Governs?: Democracy and Power in the American City, 1961; Modern Political Analysis, 1963 (5th ed., 1991); Pluralist Democracy in the United States, 1967 (revised and reissued as Democracy in the United States: Promise and Performance; 4th ed., 1981); After the Revolution?: Authority in a Good Society, 1970 (rev. ed., 1990); Polyarchy: Participation and Opposition, 1971; (with E. R. Tufte) Size and Democracy, 1973; Dilemmas of Populist Democracy: Autonomy Versus Controlling Nuclear Weapons: Democracy Versus Guardianship, 1987; Democracy, Liberty, and Equality, 1986); Democracy and Its Critics, 1989. *As Editor*—Political Oppositions in Western Democracies, 1966; Regimes and Oppositions, 1973.

ABOUT: Baer, M. A., M. E. Jewell, and L. Sigelman (eds.) Political Science in America, 1991; Contemporary Authors New Revision Series 30; 1990; Contemporary Issues Criticism, 1982; Domhoff, G. W., Who Really Rules? New Haven and Community Power Reexamined , 1978; Lukes, S. Power: A Radical View, 1974; Power, Inequality, and Democratic Politics: Essays in Honor of Robert A. Dahl, eds. I. Shapiro and G. Reher; Routledge Dictionary of Twentieth-Century Political Thinkers, 1992; Who's Who in America, 1991. *Periodicals*—American Political Science Review September 1977; Commonweal October 18, 1985; January 2, 1990; National Review March 5, 1990; New Republic April 2, 1984; New Statesman & Society December 1, 1989; New York Review of Books October 21, 1971; New York Times Book Review November 12, 1989; Times Literary Supplement January 5–11, 1990.

DANTO, ARTHUR C(OLEMAN) (January 1, 1924–   ), American philosopher and art critic, writes: "My first career was as an artist, a call-

ARTHUR C. DANTO

ing in which I achieved a certain success, particularly in connection with some large black-and white woodcut prints which I exhibited through the fifties. These were inspired by the German expressionist artists I got to know at the Detroit Institute of Arts, a great museum, which had a great influence on me in my early years. Theses prints turn up, even today, when collections are given to museums, or at auction, and from time to time I encounter people curious to know if I am the same person who did them.

"I had no intention of becoming a philosopher, but I had some years left on the GI Bill, and when I decided to move from Detroit to New York in 1948 to pursue my career as an artist, I decided on impulse to apply to Columbia University as a graduate student in philosophy, which I thought would be interesting, not especially demanding, and that it would leave me ample time to make art. For some years I pursued two careers, for I turned out to be good at philosophy, and soon found myself an assistant professor. But I knew I would one day want to make a choice, and I recall vividly one night in the early sixties working at a large print, the thought welling up in me that I would rather be writing philosophy. Such inner voices are to be trusted: I immediately dismantled my studio, and have not so much as doodled ever since. I threw myself into philosophy with the full energy now available to me, and I like to think that the spirit of art infused my writing, for I aspired to a concreteness not typical of philosophical prose, as well as a clarity and even an elegance of style. I thought even philosophical writing could be a pleasure to read.

"The philosophy that engaged me was called analytical philosophy, which is concerned with certain questions of logic and language, inasmuch as the prevailing belief was that philosophical problems sooner or later must yield to one or another kind of linguistic analysis. I was enough of an enthusiast to have published three books with the expression 'analytical philosophy' in their titles: *Analytical Philosophy of History* (1965); *Analytical Philosophy of Knowledge* (1968); and *Analytical Philosophy of Action* (1973). I intended there to be five volumes in all, for a system had begun to emerge almost from the beginning. When, however, I came to write the volume on art, I felt the title 'Analytical Philosophy of Art' would badly misrepresent my views. I found instead the title *The Transfiguration of the Commonplace* in one of Muriel Spark's novels and appropriated it. My philosophy of art evolved not out of reading philosophy, but from the powerful experience in the art galleries, most particularly in connection with Andy Warhol's Brillo Boxes, in 1964. In fact I wrote a philosophical essay about the meaning of these works for the *Journal of Philosophy* that year, for they raised vividly the question of why they were art—I had no doubt of that—while the Brillo Boxes in the supermarket, which resembled them as closely as may be required, were not. In fact, this question in the philosophy of art seemed to me so central to philosophy as a whole, all of whose problems have that form, that I wrote a systematic text, *Connections to the World*, showing how this was true. I published two studies of continental philosophers, not ordinarily thought of as especially analytical—*Nietzsche as Philosopher* and *Jean-Paul Sartre*—in order to demonstrate the structures common to analytical and to continental philosophy, and in *Mysticism and Morality* I endeavored to show some of the logical architecture of Oriental philosophies. But with the appearance of the *Transfiguration*, as I call it, my life underwent a change.

"The book was widely discussed and reviewed in the art world, for the issues it discussed were the defining issues of the visual arts at that moment. This led to my being invited to contribute to various symposia in venues far removed indeed from those of professional philosophy, to which until then I had uniquely contributed, and finally, in 1984, to the invitation to write art criticism for the *Nation*, whose regular art critic I have been ever since. I had no more intended to be an art critic than to be a philosopher, but sometimes the world understands what we are before we do. It proved to be a happy connection, for in the *Nation* I had an intelligent readership, concerned with cultural issues, but in no sense was it part of the professional art world. I was honored for the essays I published there with the George S. Polk prize for criticism, in 1985, and, in 1990, by the National Book Critics Circle prize for criticism. I have published a number of larger essays on artists—on Cindy Sherman, Saul Steinberg, Mark Tansey, and Robert Mapplethorpe, among others. The essays on Mapplethorpe won the International Center for Photography Infinity Prize for writing on photography in 1993. The recognition has been exceedingly gratifying, of course, but the main reward has come from the sense that I have been able, in a way unusual for philosophers, to participate in the life of my times.

"I have become so committed a writer, as it turned out, that I retired early from my position as Johnsonian Professor of Philosophy at Columbia, to devote myself to it entirely. The demands from the art world have been difficult to resist, but I have the final volume of my philosophical system to write—which is to be on mental representation. I was widowed in 1978, but married the artist Barbara Westman in 1980, and with whom I have an entirely fulfilling relationship. This is one of the rewards of no longer being an artist myself.

"Since this essay is on me as a writer, I think a word or two on how I see that may be in order. I never have the sense that there is a book, or even an article, 'in' me, which the act of writing brings out and makes real. In fact I almost never think of writing in an introspective way. What I find is that when I sit down to write, something invariably appears on the paper which I had never thought of until it did so. Thinking, in my case, takes place at the ends of my fingers, rather than in my head. I write in a regular way, never more than three hours a day, and I use a typewriter rather than a computer. Friends point out how easy the computer makes revision, but I retort that I never revise. I only rewrite. And a computer might, in making revision easy, rob me of the extreme pleasure of finding what invention has brought to light requires by way of prose to make it worth reading. Rewriting is among the things I like best in the world."

Arthur C. Danto was born in Ann Arbor, Michigan, to Samuel Budd (a dentist) and Sylvia (Gittleman) Danto. After military service from 1942 to 1945, he took his B.A. at Wayne State University in 1948 and his M.A. at Columbia University in 1949. He spent a year of graduate study at the University of Paris, then taught philosophy for a year at the University of Colorado in Boulder. In 1951 he became an instructor in philosophy at Columbia, where he completed his Ph.D. in 1952. Danto rose to the rank of professor in 1966 and Johnsonian Professor of Philosophy in 1975. He was chairman of the department from 1979 to 1987 and in 1978 also became co-director of the Center for the Study of Human Rights. He has been a visiting lecturer and professor at many universities, among them Princeton, the University of California at Santa Barbara and at San Diego, and has had Fulbright, Guggenheim, and American Council of Learned Societies Fellowships. In 1976 he was a Fulbright Distinguished Professor in Yugoslavia. Danto has two daughters from his marriage in 1946 to Shirley Rovetch, who died in 1978. He lives in New York City with his second wife, the artist Barbara Westman, whom he married in 1980.

It has been observed that Danto came to art criticism as an outsider. Though his "first career" was that of an artist, it served in only a limited way to prepare him for what was to be his major vocation. Approaching art now not as a practicing artist but as a philosopher, he has brought rigorous analytical skills to aesthetic philosophy—raising the questions of what is art? and why create? Danto has rejected a purely aesthetical criticism that concentrates on form and line as opposed to subject. He described his goal as an art critic in his preface to a collection of his reviews in *The State of the Art*: "I am . . . ambitious to have it said of me that I have brought philosophy out in order to bring itself out of the precious precincts of the connoisseur, the collector, the dealer and the rebarbative art writings that obscure the place and importance of art. . . . "

Danto takes a synthesizing approach to philosophy and a historicist approach to aesthetic criticism. In 1989 he published *Connection to the World: The Basic Concepts of Philosophy*, in which he examines "theories of understanding, the mind/body problem, the connections between language and the world, and the relationship of mathematics to reality," according to Raymond Frey, writing in *Library Journal*. *Connections* grew out of and replaced *What Philosophy Is*. Julia Annas in the *New York Times Book Review* called it "an elegant, unifying overview of philosophical thought," addressed to "those who in . . . Danto's metaphor wish to climb above the tangled growths of particular arguments and get a view of the wide horizons . . . both sophisticated and accessible."

Danto writes with equal comfort on the latest trends in the art galleries of New York's Soho and on the paintings of pre-Renaissance Italy. In a single season, 1984–1985, he published reviews in the *Nation* of the Whitney Museum's BLAM!-exhibit of developments from Abstract expressionism to pop art—exhibitions of Van Gogh, Caravaggio, Henri Rousseau, Robert Motherwell, and a loan show of drawings from the Albertina in Vienna. Where Danto departs most from contemporary orthodoxy is in his conviction that art involves "more than meets the eye." As he wrote in an essay on the painter Mark Tansey ("The Case of the Sacred Cows," *Columbia*, Spring 1993): "[T]he 'test' for whether we understand a painting has less to do with our spontaneous, so to speak, 'animal' responses, than with our ability to reconstruct the meaning of the painting, construed as a kind of visual text."

The near-epiphany that Danto claims to have experienced when he first saw Andy Warhol's *Brillo Box* was important because it revealed the distinction between a banal material object displayed on the shelves of a supermarket and the work of art that Warhol had made out of it. "To see an artwork without knowing it as an artwork," he writes in *The Transfiguration of the Commonplace*, "is comparable in a way to what one's experience of print is, before one learns to read; and to see it as an artwork then is like going from the realm of things to the realm of meaning." In Danto's view, Warhol was here making a gesture, "a philosophical act": *Brillo Box* "does what works of art have always done—externalizing a way of viewing the world, expressing the interior of a cultural period, offering itself as a mirror to catch the conscience of our kings."

With the emergence of modernism in the early 20th century, artists abandoned the conventions of representing perceived reality, stripping their work down to a bare minimalism or literalism. As Danto puts it in his *Philosophical Disenfranchisement of Art*: "Having reached this point where art can be anything at all, art has exhausted its conceptual mission." He illustrates with examples from the Dadaists and singles out Marcel Duchamp's *Fountain*, an inverted urinal that, by an act of wit and daring, the artist transformed from a mere material object into a work of art—a gesture that became a philosophical act. At this point, Danto writes, art history ends: "[I]t is far from plain that we can separate art from philosophy, in as much as the substance is in part constituted by what it is philosophically believed to be." He writes in *The Transfiguration of the Commonplace*: "It [art] has not *stopped* but ended, in the sense that it has passed over into a kind of consciousness of itself and became, again in a way, its own philosophy."

Danto has been criticized for applying principles that are inappropriate or irrelevant to art criticism. Steven Goldsmith, writing in the *Journal of Aesthetics and Art Criticism* in 1983, finds him too subjective and idealistic: "For Danto, objects became art to the degree that their physical nature dissolves into pure philosophical idea, and he falls prey to the Hegelian puritanism which insists that the body and all its contingencies must be transcended as art evolves into spirit." Others maintain that Danto does not take art seriously enough. In a profile of Danto in the *New York Times Magazine*, Elizabeth Frank confirms Danto's ludic sensibility: "While Danto claims that he has no nostalgia for the days when he painted and made woodcuts, the fun he says he seeks in writing about art seems more than coincidentally to resemble the kind of non-serious play he thinks art has become."

Danto told Frank, "The main reason people read me is that they do not know what they will encounter. I do not predict my response, and have no line to argue. I am looking to explain what I am talking about, and the explanations come from all over the place, as would be expected if art is as complex as it is supposed to be."

Danto communicates his enthusiasm and exhilaration as effectively as he does his distaste. He reviews a contemporary artist whose "paintings are so anxious to please that it is as though they are wagging their tails." He dismisses the 1985 Whitney Biennial with scorn: "There is, I think, scarcely a single work here the world is better off for having, scarcely a single one whose disappearance would not contribute to the goodness of the universe at large." He can epitomize an artist's genius in a single sentence, as he does with an exhibition of Toulouse-Lautrec's posters at the Museum of Modern Art: "One cannot enter the galleries that house the famous and familiar posters without feeling, almost as a physical presence, the dense effluvia of sensual pleasure they distill: champagne, absinthe and dubonnet, rice powder and patchouli, dancers in frilled drawers and black stockings executing the manic steps of the quadrille . . . a brothel world of infinite ecstatic promise." Caravaggio leads Danto to an examination of the "ecstasy" a masterpiece evokes: "The Caravaggian blackness is not a naturalistic representation of night or shadow, but works instead a metaphoric division between our space and the space in which the martyrdoms and ecstasies and the violent adoration of Baroque art take place . . . Caravaggio's are spaces of encapsulated dark. . . . the extraordinary effect of a performer spotlighted not against but inside a surrounding darkness. . . .

In 1993 *Danto and His Critics*, a selection of essays by and about Danto was published. Reviewing the collection, J. White remarked in *Choice*: "The importance of Danto's contributions to epistemology, action theory, philosophy of history, and especially aesthetics is well established, but until the publication of these essays they have been neither presented nor criticized as an integrated body of work." In another review of the volume in *Library Journal* Leslie Armour further summed up Danto as "a self-confessed Cartesian who still believes that 'objective truth' exists, that people are not machines, and that every human activity (even—perhaps especially—bad art) can provide us with insight."

PRINCIPAL WORKS: Analytical Philosophy of History, 1965; Nietzsche as Philosopher, 1965; Analytical Philosophy of Knowledge, 1968; What Philosophy Is, 1968; Mysticism and Morality, 1972, 1987; Analytical Philosophy of Action, 1973; Jean-Paul Sartre, 1975; The Transfiguration of the Commonplace, 1981; Narration and Knowledge, (includes text of Analytical Philosophy of History) 1985; Connections to the World: The Basic Concept of Philosophy, 1985; The Philosophical Disenfranchisement of art, 1986; The State of the Art, 1987; Encounters and Reflections: Art in the Historical Present, 1990; Beyond the Brillo Box: Art in the Post-Historical Present, 1992; Mark Tansey: Visions and Revisions, 1992; Robert Mapplethorpe, 1992; Embodied Meanings, 1994; Playing with the Edge, 1995.

ABOUT: Contemporary Authors 17–20, 1976; Rollins, M. (ed.) Danto and His Critics, 1993; Who's Who in America 1990–1991. *Periodicals*—British Journal of Aesthetics July 1990; Choice June 1994; History and Theory 29, 1990; Journal of Aesthetics and Art Criticism Winter 1981; Winter 1983; Winter 1984; Winter 1987; Summer 1988; Library journal March 15, 1989; October 15, 1993; New York Times Book Review May 14, 1989; August 5, 1990; September 6, 1992; New York Times Magazine November 19, 1989.

DAVIS, DAVID BRION (February 16, 1927–) American historian, writes: "I was born in Denver in 1927 and then moved with my parents to eight cities or towns, from coast to coast, living in some fifteen rented houses and apartments during the next sixteen years. My father, Clyde Brion Davis, was a journalist who succeeded in becoming an independent novelist and the author of twenty books, but he also found it necessary to work for a time writing screenplays in Hollywood and serving as a part-time editor in New York. While my father was extremely mobile, we were also closely unified and did many things together. I'm sure that I learned more from my parents, from my pater-

DAVID BRION DAVIS

nal grandmother who usually lived with us, and from the family library, than I learned from the numerous schools I attended. My mother [Martha Wirt Davis], in particular, encouraged my scientific interests, exemplified in an ever-expanding chemistry laboratory in the basement.

"The shock of adjusting to one school after another reached a critical state in my junior year of high school. As my grades plummeted, I came close to rebellion and to joining the U.S. Marines, who were then recapturing islands in the South Pacific. I could easily have become a high-school dropout if my parents had not transferred me, in desperation, to the private McBurney School in Manhattan, where as a senior I won the coveted gold medal for best overall achievement. Immediately after graduation, in early June 1945, I shifted gears to infantry basic training in Georgia, learning how to shoot flamethrowers, machine guns, and mortars. Our preparation for the invasion of Japan in the fall was cut short by the atomic bombs in August. Much to my delight, I soon found myself bound for Germany and for a year of occupation duty which, at that impressionable age, became one of the formative experiences of my life. Aside from the opportunities to serve as a security policeman and German interpreter, traveling throughout Western Europe, sampling opera, ballet, Shakespearean plays, the Nuremberg trials, and excursions to medieval cloisters, I had the opportunity to meditate. In Nice, on a 'rest and recuperation' leave, I concluded that I would like to be a historian. The army was extraordinarily good to me. Yet it also

brought me into close contact with combat veterans, fugitive SS officers, thousands of displaced persons, and the appalling rubble and destruction of mass bombing. The German occupation also introduced me to the poisonous violence of racism in a segregated American army.

"In 1947, after returning from Germany, I entered Dartmouth College and soon settled into a major in philosophy. Finding that most of the history courses were dull and superficial, I tried to seek out the most stimulating teachers, regardless of subject—courses on Dante, Aristotle, 'philosophy of the mind,' Hegel, political theory. After being elected to Phi Beta Kappa in my junior year, I graduated from Dartmouth *summa cum laude* in 1950, but with new uncertainties about my future career.

"After taking time off to work on the assembly line and then as a scheduler at the Cessna Aircraft plant in Wichita, Kansas, I finally decided to pursue an academic career and applied to the Harvard program in the history of American civilization. Attracted by the idea of synthesizing history, philosophy, and literature, I had no knowledge of the Harvard faculty and no idea of what awaited me. Though greatly stimulated by a few brilliant teachers like Perry Miller and Howard Mumford Jones, I felt fortunate to escape Harvard after two years of course work, being chosen to teach at Dartmouth as a Ford Foundation teaching intern, an innovative program that examined the essence of successful teaching. During a third and final year at Harvard I completed a draft of my doctoral dissertation, later published as *Homicide in American Fiction, 1790-1860: A Study in Social Values*. I was also fortunate in publishing a number of term papers as scholarly articles. This put me in a position to win an appointment in 1955 as an assistant professor at Cornell. I remained at Cornell until 1969, teaching American intellectual history in addition to a survey course in American history and seminars on various topics.

"My early studies of homicide, capital punishment, movements of 'countersubversion,' and antislavery were all related to my desire to identify certain central 'problems' that would allow me to integrate philosophic and theological arguments with concrete social conflicts and issues of public policy. I had learned much from the history of abstract ideas, such as primitivism, progress, and nature, but I sought to anchor that kind of intellectual history in specific historical situations, viewing 'culture' as an always changing and contested terrain. This orientation guided my approach to *The Problem of Slavery in Western Culture*, a project greatly aided and influenced by a Guggenheim Fellowship in 1958–

1959, which allowed me to carry out sustained research in England. Because Cornell had generously granted me tenure at an early age, I felt under no compulsion to rush toward the publication of a second book, and was therefore free to expand the scope of the volume, which was eventually published in 1966 and which won a Pulitzer Prize and two other national awards. Though immensely pleased by the reviews and general response to this book, I also saw the need, in writing the sequel, to show how a momentous transformation in moral perception—the widespread realization that chattel slavery was an indefensible evil—came to be translated into specific acts of public policy.

"When I embarked on my study of 'the problem of slavery,' I had no idea that it would become a lifetime mission. While I've taken time off to write on other subjects, I'm still at work on the first volume of 'The Problem of Slavery in the Age of Emancipation.' Since 1970 I've been teaching at Yale, where I'm a Sterling Professor. I live in Orange, Connecticut with my wife Toni [Hahn] and two children, Adam and Noah. In 1988 I became a convert to Judaism."

In 1986, reviewing *From Homicide to Slavery*, a collection of David Brion Davis's essays written over a period of almost thirty years, Louis Rubin wrote in the *New York Times Book Review* that Davis "has been something of an iconoclast throughout his career." All of his writings share a common goal: what Rubin described as a study of "the extent to which social, political, and economic issues are shaped by—and help to shape—religious and philosophical belief."

Human aggression was the theme of Davis's first book, *Homicide in American Fiction*. Here, drawing on such writers as Charles Brockden Brown, Cooper, Hawthorne, Melville, and William Gilmore Simms, he studied the fictional representation of homicide in America in terms of "moral alienation."

Davis observed in his preface to *From Homicide to Slavery* that "an interest in social reform. . . . led me gradually into the origins of antislavery. . . . " The link between homicide and slavery, he points out, is dehumanization: "The killer literally reduces a human being into a nonbeing, removed from the flow of time. The enslaver reduces a human being to a state of 'social death,' to use Orlando Patterson's phrase, in which the captive is defined as an object, a thing without history."

In *The Problem of Slavery in Western Culture* Davis traces the religious and philosophical ideologies that had supported slavery up through the eighteenth century and the changing moral perceptions that produced the antislavery and abolition movements in Britain and America raising the question: "Why was it that at a certain moment of history a small number of men not only saw the full horror of a social evil to which mankind had been blind for centuries, but felt impelled to attack it through personal testimony and cooperative action?" Davis attributes this radical change in consciousness to such influences as the philosophy of the Enlightenment, the egalitarian principles behind the French and American revolutions, and the emergence of movements like Quakerism and Evangelicalism. "I . . . believe that . . . all liberations are won at a cost; that all choice involves negation. . . . Whatever one believes about historical progress—or the lack of it—we are the beneficiaries of past struggles, of the new and often temporary sensitivities of a collective conscience. . . . "

Ira Berlin, reviewing *Slavery and Human Progress* in the *Nation*, says Davis gives great "clarity and power" to his explication of "the ideological threads—Enlightenment ideas, evangelical religion, revolutionary republicanism, Smithian economics—that connected abolition to the rise of the capitalist order." According to Berlin, Davis points out that "'the very idea of progress owes much to ancient bondspeople who made manumission or escape the universal symbols for deliverance, redemption, resurrection, and divine mission.' This reminder is no codicil. Progress—like the relationship of freedom and slavery—had very different meanings to the slaves and enslavers."

In *Revolution: Reflections on American Equality and Foreign Liberations*, termed a "nuanced" and "complicated" study by Gordon Wood in the *New York Review of Books*, Davis reflects "on the theme of equality and foreign revolution in American history, concentrating on the era of the founding fathers and their 'exuberance and disillusion over the French Revolution. . . . '" Avoiding the ideologies of both the right and left, Davis associates the American ideal of equality with contradictory responses to foreign revolutions, from "remarkable receptivity to the idea of revolution" to being "the world's leading adversary of popular revolutions." "By looking at the Americans' responses to revolution through the complicated prism of equality," Wood remarks, "Davis has . . . placed an undue emphasis on the Americans' ambiguity and scruples concerning revolutions. He tends . . . to miss the full significance of their messianic aspirations to spread their republican revolution everywhere." John Dunn, however, in the *Times Literary Supplement* calls Davis "America's most distinguished historian of the intellectual impact of slavery . . . " and states that the most original quality of *Revolution* is "the power with which it focuses and explains America's distinctive unease in the face of modern revolution."

In addition to the Pulitzer Prize, Davis received the Annisfield Wolf Award and the National Mass Media Award from the National Conference of Christians and Jews in 1967 for *The Problem of Slavery in Western Culture*. In 1975 the American Historical Association awarded him the Beveridge Prize; in 1976 *The Problem of Slavery in the Age of Revolution* won the Bancroft Prize and the National Book Award for history and biography. He has been awarded fellowships by the Guggenheim Foundation (1958–1959), the Center for Advanced Study in the Behavioral Sciences (1972–1973), and the Huntington Library (1976); and received research grants from the National Endowment for the Humanities in 1980 and 1981, and a Fulbright Traveling Fellowship (1980–1981). Davis has lectured at many universities in the United States and abroad.

In April 1994, during what the *New York Times* described as a "roiling debate over the state of black-Jewish relations," Davis agreed to postpone a lecture on the Haitian Revolution of 1791, the first successful slave rebellion in the New World. According to the *Times*, University officials feared that he "would be subjected to heckling and harassment because he is Jewish."

PRINCIPAL WORKS: Homicide in American Fiction, 1790–1860: A Study in Social Values, 1957; The Problem of Slavery in Western Culture, 1966; The Clave Power Conspiracy and the Paranoid Style, 1969; Was Thomas Fefferson an Authentic Enemy of Slavery?, 1970; The Progress, 1984; From Homicide to Slavery: Studies in American Culture, 1986; Revolution: Reflections on American Equality and Foreign Liberations, 1990.

ABOUT: Contemporary Authors New Revision Series 26, 1989; Who's Who in America 1990–1991. *Periodicals*—American Historical Review June 1985; Atlantic August 1966; Journal of American History June 1985; December 1987; September 1990; Journal of Southern History August 1985; Nation December 7, 1984; New York Review of Books September 27, 1990; New York Times April 16, 1994; New York Times Book Review October 5, 1986; Times Literary Supplement February 1, 1985; May 31, 1985. *As editor*—Ante-Bellum Reform, 1967; The Fear of Conspiracy: Images of Un-American Subversion from the Revolution to the Present, 1971; Antebellum American Culture: An Interpretive Anthology, 1979.

DEGLER, CARL N(EUMANN) (April 28, 1917–), American historian writes: "I was born in Orange, New Jersey, but actually grew up Newark, New Jersey, where my parents were born. Both of my parents were children of German immigrants, and like so many migrants to America, they sought to provide for their children that which they themselves had lacked. My father, who was a firefighter in the city of Newark, was determined that I would attend college, even though neither he nor I really knew what went on in a college. And true to his determination, I entered Upsala College in the neighboring city of East Orange, close enough for me to save money by living at home.

"Although as an adolescent I harbored several ideas about what I might be when I grew up, being a writer never crossed my mind. It was there that I became concerned about the social inequities in American society, particularly social discrimination against African-Americans. My time at college also determined that I would become a historian. For at Upsala I found a model in a young teacher with whom I studied American history. By the time I had finished college, I knew I wanted to be a college professor, but I still did not see much connection between that and writing for the general public.

"Before I could begin my graduate education, the attack on Pearl Harbor virtually catapulted me into the army. My participation in World War II helped me shape my outlook as both a historian and as a writer. It took me out of the narrow geographical confines of the East Coast and transported me, as a weather observer in the U.S. Army Air Force, to Africa, India, and Burma. That experience brought me into contact with people I had never seen, much less met, before—like Indians and Africans—and with social conditions I had only read about.

"As a result of those years, by the time I entered graduate school at Columbia University in 1946 to study for a Ph.D. degree in U.S. history, I was committed to the idea that history was a genuinely necessary, rather than simply an interesting, subject. To recognize the connection between the past and the present now seemed to me to be the real key to understanding the present and to insuring that the future would be better. This idea assumed tangible form in the course of my teaching at Vassar College, where I wrote my first book *Out of Our Past*. Unlike most books by a young history professor, mine was not a work based on archival research. Rather, it was a highly interpretive, even personal, work that sought to account historically for how present American society had come to be. It was, in short, a frank attempt to demonstrate to the general reader how useful and practical history

CARL N. DEGLER

could be. It assumed that a knowledge of the past would help in solving the problems of the present.

"Since then, I have become considerably less sure that history can solve modern problems, though I have never lost my belief that a knowledge of history can elucidate the nature of a problem in the present and that it should be written for the general, as well as the academic, reader. Virtually all of the books I have written since have been shaped by that early conviction. In doing so, I have clearly set myself apart from those historians who emphasize the value of the past for its own sake and without reference to the modern world. I do not deprecate or seek to push aside that role for history. On the contrary, it provides much of the humanistic value, much of the poetry, much of the evocative power that the past always holds for us. It just is not the kind of history that I write.

"In retrospect, I recognize that it was the success of *Out of Our Past*, both commercially and professionally, that moved me to become a writer as well as a historian. For I then began to write for magazines like the *New Republic*, the *New York Times Magazine*, and the *Yale Review*. In almost all of those pieces, I sought to show how history could throw light on the present, that the present was frequently a prisoner of the past. Like *Out of Our Past*, the books that follow it have been only partly works of original research, being intended not to open up aspects of the past as yet unexplored, but interpretive studies of problems or social developments that have contemporary significance for the general public as

well as for historians. Thus my second book, *Neither Black Nor White*, which appeared in 1971, after I had moved to Stanford University, was in direct response to the ongoing concern in the 1960s about the relation between the character of slavery and modern race relations in this country. By looking at comparable race relations in another country—Brazil—I sought to throw light on the nature of race relations in the United States. My book *The Other South; Southern Dissenters in the Nineteenth Century* was a response to the growing recognition during the 1960s and 1970s that the white South was not a monolith, that there were historical roots for the racial changes that the South was undergoing during the civil rights era.

"Given my long-term concern with civil rights for blacks in American society and my having taught for sixteen years at Vassar College (then a women's college), it can come as no surprise that I was also a feminist in outlook even before I published in 1980 *At Odds: Women and the Family from the Revolution to the Present*. (In 1966, I had become a founding member of N. O.W.) Less easy to fit into the pattern, perhaps, is the origin of my book *In Search of Human Nature: The Decline and Revival of Darwinism in American Social Thought*. Yet, it too grew out of my interest in contemporary questions of equality and how social scientists have looked at those issues over the last century. It also reflects my commitment to bringing history to the general reader, for the book tells the story of the return of biological ideas to the social sciences in the 1980s.

"I retired from Stanford University in 1990, have been married to the same woman since 1948, and have a daughter and a son, and two grandsons—so far."

———

"An important justification of history is that it attempts to give to those who are alive today a sense of what it felt like to live at another time," Carl Degler writes in the preface to his *At Odds: Women and the Family in America from the Revolution to the Present*, "when different values an personal goals had to wrestle with the same timeless and insistent aspects of human existence—sex, birth worth, and the relations between the sexes—that engage the attention and energies of people today." His books deal with such issues as the emergence of America as a world power, the growth of big business, racial prejudice, women's rights, and, latterly, the nature-nurture controversy.

Out Of Our Past: The Forces That Shaped Modern America is neither an "arraignment" of

American society nor a "panegyric," he states in the preface. "One can stress the positive achievements of America without descending into the swamp of sycophancy or the desert of chauvinism." The book begins with the establishment of the American colonies in the 17th century and ends (in its first edition) at the brink of World War II. Our concepts of representative government, democracy, and social equality reached their fullest development in the New World, according to Degler, owing to unique social conditions: the abundance of land (the emphasis of Frederick Jackson Turner's famous "frontier theory"; the lack of a feudal tradition and a hereditary aristocracy; and the sanction of economic enterprise by both the Puritans and the Quakers.

Richard Morris wrote, in the *New York Herald-Tribune Book Review*, that "in the main [Degler's] opinions are fresh, sensible, scholarly, and persuasively argued." Charles Albro Barker, while commending the tone, style, and research of *Out of Our Past* in the *American Historical Review*, pointed out that as "aggregative social history" it was inevitably selective, omitting, for example, the influence of the military establishment and the accomplishments of a number of influential individuals (e.g., W.E.B. Dubois and John Dewey). The book has proved Degler's most popular, going into a third edition in 1983. In the latest edition, Degler added a chapter on foreign policy and carried the account forward to the Carter administration with its emphasis on human rights.

In *Neither Black Nor White: Slavery and Race Relations in Brazil and the United States* Degler refuted the thesis advanced by Frank Tannenbaum, which attributed the relative integration of blacks in Latin America (in contrast to the situation in the United States) to a more humanitarian attitude on the part of the Catholic Church than that which prevailed among the Protestant churches to the north. Degler concentrated on Brazil as the only country in the New World that rivaled the United States in size as well as in the importance of slavery in its history. A visit to Rio de Janeiro in 1967 to study original documents, as well as literature on the subject by native writers, led Degler to conclude that, contrary to the judgment of Tannenbaum as well as the Brazilian historian Gilberto Freyre, slaves were treated every bit as cruelly in Brazil as they were in the United States, and that, moreover, the Catholic Church had exerted little or no mitigating influence. He found the explanation for the superior economic and social status enjoyed by free blacks (especially mulattoes) in Brazil in their ready assimilation into the skilled trades that were rejected by Portuguese settlers.

Neither Black Nor White—its title is a double entendre relating both to the mixture of races and the complexity of the truth about race relations—found wide recognition as a groundbreaking book. It was nominated for a National Book Award, received both the Bancroft Prize from Columbia University and the Beveridge Prize from the American Historical Association, and was awarded a Pulitzer Prize in 1972.

The "peculiar institution" of slavery, which had figured peripherally in *Out of Our Past*, becomes central in *The Other South: Southern Dissenters in the Nineteenth Century*, Degler's study of the conflicts that developed in society below the Mason-Dixon line as a result of slavery. This book, as Degler characterizes it, is "about losers"—white southerners who throughout the nineteenth century stood up against the prevailing views of their region, adopting antislavery positions at the beginning, becoming pro-Union before the Civil War, turning to Republicanism during Reconstruction and joining the populist cause in the 1890s. Affirming that "the South is not and never has been a monolith," Degler again takes issue with fellow historians. In contrast to Eugene Genovese's projection of a unified planter class preoccupied with self-protection, Degler shows that opposition to slavery did not follow neat class lines, being found among planters as well as among small farmers and merchants. He further demonstrates that pro- and anti-abolitionists alike were prompted by a variety of motives—political, economic, ethnic, and humanitarian. At the same time he disagrees with Howard Zinn, who contends in *The Southern Mystique* that the South was not a truly distinct culture but shared the same values as other Americans "in weaker degree." Degler concludes to the contrary that the absence of urbanization, industrialization, and immigration set the South apart from he rest of the country. C. Vann Woodward, reviewing *The Other South* for the *New York Times Book Review* in 1974, hailed Degler among scholars "who have in recent years enlivened and invigorated the study of Southern history," but regretted that he had not included dissenters who left the South, some of whom Woodward felt were more interesting than those who remained behind. *Place Over Time: The Continuity of Southern Distinctiveness*, published three years later, grew out of a series of lectures Degler delivered at Louisiana State University in 1976. The title is derived from what he describes in the preface as the strong feeling for "roots, place, family and tradition" that he sees persisting from antebellum times into the second half of the 20th century.

In *Out of the Past*, Degler emphasized the

greater respect and rights enjoyed by American women in comparison with English women owing to their smaller proportion of the population than in England. In *At Odds* he expands on this theory. He attempts to connect women's studies with the equally proliferating research into the history of the family. "This book might be called an exercise in foolhardiness," Degler wrote in his preface, and indeed a number of reviewers, while impressed with the writing, felt that its subject was an unwieldy one. Lawrence Stone, in the *New York Times Book Review*, considered it "easily the most perceptive, the most thoughtful, the most balanced, and the most readable book" on the evolution of the family, but pointed out that by adducing literary, rather than statistical, evidence, and confining his sample to the white middle class, Degler constricted his field of vision. Christopher Lasch, in the *New York Review of Books*, commented that Degler's stress on the active part taken by women in the transformation of American life is sound, but concluded that the book as a whole "bogs down in confusion and contradictions."

Shortly after the publications of *At Odds*, Degler received a fellowship at the Center for Advanced Study in the Behavioral Sciences at Stanford, where he had been teaching since 1968, which provided him with the opportunity "to learn to think about the relation between animal and human behavior." This research culminated ten years later in the publication of *In Search of Human Nature: The Decline and Revival of Darwinism in American Social Thought*. In this densely packed study Degler traces the conflicts that arose between hereditarians and environmentalists as the different theories explaining human behavior alternately gained and lost popularity in the 20th century and recounts the shifts in theories of behavior from the biological explanation of social differences posited by Herbert Spencer and the Social Darwinists to the cultural determinism of anthropologists led by Franz Boas and Alfred Kroeber. After World War II the pendulum swung back to biology as "an attempt to place human beings properly in the framework of organic evolution"—the Synthetic theory of evolution and ethology, as N. C. Gillespie characterized it in *Choice*. Gillespie summed up the thinking of most reviewers in remarking that "the ideological dimension has been familiar in analyses of the first period, but is less discussed or acknowledged for the second." Dorothy Ross, in *The American Historical Review*, noted what she termed Degler's "judgment that sociobiology is concerned . . . with what is universal rather than differential in human behavior and that sociobiologists are now fully cognizant of the role of culture." She point-

ed out that many of the mistakes of the old sociobiology reappear in the new.

Stephen Sanderson, however, in the *American Journal of Sociology*, called *In Search of Human Nature* "an excellent book" and said, "Its most important message is that social scientists' antagonism to considering the biological foundations of human behavior is rooted far more in ideology than in science."

Concurrently with his scholarly works, Degler has produced textbooks for college courses, including *The Age of Economic Revolution 1876–1900* and its sequel, *Affluence and Anxiety*. He has contributed essays to *Philosophy and History*, edited by Sidney Hook and *The Woman in America*, edited by Robert Jay Lifton and has edited a number of volumes, such as *The New Deal*, a collection of articles by contributors to the *New York Times Magazine*; he has also been an active reviewer of historical journals. Colgate, Columbia, and Oxford are among the universities where he has been a visiting professor.

While holding National Endowment for the Humanities Fellowship (1983–1984) he delivered the Samuel Paley Lectures at Hebrew University in Jerusalem. He retired in 1990 as Mararet Byrnes Professor of History at Stanford.

PRINCIPAL WORKS: Out of Our Past: The Forces That Shaped Modern America, 1959; rev. eds. 1970, 1983; (with others) The Democratic Experience, 1963; The Age of Economic Revolution, 1876–1900; rev. ed., 1977; Affluence and Anxiety, 1968; rev. ed., 1975; Neither Black Nor White: Slavery and Race Relations in Brazil and the United States, 1971; The Other South: Southern Dissenters in the Nineteenth-Century, 1974; Place Over Time: The Continuity of Southern Distinctiveness, 1977; At Odds: Women and the Family from the revolution to the Present, 1980; In search of Human Nature: the Decline and Revival of Darwinism in American Social Thought, 1991. As editor—Pivotal Interpretations in American History, 1966; Charlotte Perkins Gilman, Women and Economics, 1966; rev. ed., 1970; The New Deal, 1970.

ABOUT: Contemporary Authors New Revision Series 3, 1981; Who's Who in America 1990–1991; Periodicals—American Anthropologist August 1972; The American Historical Review October 1959; June 1978; April 1992; American Journal of Sociology January 1992; Commentary November 1980; Journal of Negro History January 1973; Journal of Southern History February 1978; Library Journal June 15, 1971; December 1, 1973; Nation June 6, 1959' National Review April 26, 1974; New Republic May 10, 1980; New York Review of Books October 17, 1974; New York Times Book Review March 10, 1974; Saturday Review February 7, 1959; Science August 1, 1980; Virginia Quarterly Review Spring 1974; Washington Post Book World June 29, 1980.

DELBANCO, NICHOLAS FRANKLIN

(August 27, 1942–   ), American (British-born) novelist, short story, and travel writer, writes: "I was born in London, England, in 1942. My parents were German Jews who fled, separately, to England; there they were married in 1938. Ten years thereafter we came to this country—the 'we' consisting of my parents, my elder brother, Thomas, and me, who received his first pair of long pants at the halfway point to the voyage out. We settled in Larchmont, New York—and there, too, my younger brother Andrew, the family's 'American afterthought,' was born. I was educated at the Fieldston School, then Harvard University, then Columbia University. My mother died in 1974; the rest of us are alive and, as I write this [1993], well.

"That family of which I serve as titular head commenced in 1970, when Elena Carter Greenhouse and I were married. We have two daughters, Francesca (born in 1974) and Andrea (1978). They are, daily and yearly, a gift. We have a vast black dog, Major Scobie, a sleek tortoiseshell cat, Midnight, and the usual assortment of lawn mowers, lunchboxes, cars. In the early years of our marriage, Elena and I settled with some regularity in Provence. This location gave rise to my most recent work of nonfiction, an extended reminiscence masquerading as a travel text, *Running in Place: Scenes from the South of France*. The 'interested reader,' as they say, is referred to that autobiography for further details.

"Now, however—and somewhat to my surprise—home would appear to be the American Midwest. These issues of rootedness and rootlessness, of a self-engendered tradition, continue to concern me and therefore to compel imagination; my characters tend to be wanderers who hunt a provisional home. Or, alternatively, as in the Sherbrooke trilogy, they find themselves defined by—hemmed in and circumscribed by—the ancestral place. My first novel, *The Martlet's Tale*, appeared when I was twenty-three years old and was treated with that generous attention accorded the young; as a result I found myself poised in the role of writer and encouraged to continue with the work of words. Like most habits, this one has proved harder to break than to make, and I have published fifteen books by now. I am no longer 'promising' nor as yet 'distinguished'; the problem is how to negotiate the forty years or so that cause the former label to be replaced by the latter.

"I write this tongue in check because the task of self-assessment is a daunting one. My books are as different, one from the other, as it lay within my competence to manage; a summarial statement in this brief compass must necessarily

NICHOLAS FRANKLIN DELBANCO

exclude more than it can contain. So I'd prefer to leave assessment where it properly belongs—in the hands of others. We think about our manuscripts obsessively, or so I think; we should write about them rarely and at no great length.

"For nearly twenty years I was a member of the Bennington College faculty, in Bennington, Vermont—where, with the late John Gardner, I cofounded the Bennington Writing Workshops. The career of an author seems more and more often to be attached to the academy, and mine is no exception; I have taught at Skidmore, Trinity, and Williams Colleges, at Columbia and Iowa Universities. In 1985 my family and I moved to Ann Arbor, where I became the director of the MFA Program in Writing and a professor of English at the University of Michigan. It's a life like many others in this particular business; I edit magazines and anthologies, judge contests, am proud of those students who increase and multiply, mourn the loss of colleagues, am shocked at the passage of time. Having written at some length about the writer's trade, I don't propose to repeat that here; someday perhaps—the common plaint and dream—I'll produce something splendid, and not another two inches of iridescent mediocrity for the shelf. It's the sort of disease that writers call health to think each word written is rotten, but the next paragraph will surely be superb. . . . "

Nicholas Delbanco began work on his first novel, *The Martlet's Tale*, while still an undergraduate. In the summer of 1962 he enrolled in a Harvard Summer School course in fiction writing taught by John Updike, in one of Updike's rare forays into university teaching. Having made up his mind to write a novel, Delbanco plotted his course of action carefully. He had noticed that virtually all first novels are "either the myth of Narcissus or the parable of the Prodigal Son," and decided that he would take on the latter theme. He then searched for a setting and a voice which would distinguish his work. Since he had traveled in Greece the summer before, he set his rendering of the prodigal son story among modern-day Greeks in Athens and on the island of Rhodes. *The Martlet's Tale* proved to be an auspicious literary debut; it was published to mostly favorable reviews in the same year Delbanco received his M.A. from Columbia University. He dedicated the novel to the singer and songwriter Carly Simon, who was his girlfriend in the early 1960s.

Delbanco's next two novels, *Grasse 3/23/66* and *Consider Sappho Burning*, are audaciously experimental, full of verbal pyrotechnics, and—while ostensibly concerned with intimate human relationships—emotionally distant. For *New York Times* reviewer John Leonard, Delbanco's first three novels "seemed to refer to a world consisting wholly of words; to seek in language itself the solution to moral problems conceived of as perceptual problems. . . ."

His fourth novel, *News*, deals with the distorted political idealism of four expensively educated, well-to-do white men. Noting the author's apparent change of tack, John Leonard wondered facetiously whether Delbanco had been "set upon by Bennington Maoists and forced to sign an oath of relevance." Leonard welcomed the change: "The news of *News* is that an excellent writer is among us . . . and if we neglect him . . . we shall have to apologize to posterity." One of the novel's four protagonists is obsessed with the story of Tunis Gulik Campbell, a black man who ruled a short-lived black separatist state on the Georgia coastal islands in the nineteenth century. He is determined to convert three old friends to the gospel of Campbell. Delbanco weaves a historical account of Campbell's exploits into the story of the four friends, each of whom is in some way trapped inside a deteriorating dream. The *New York Times Book Review* named the novel one of its Books of the Year in 1970.

Delbanco's best-known work is known as the Sherbrookes trilogy: *Possession*, *Sherbrookes*, and *Stillness*. Once prosperous and illustrious, the Sherbrookes are a Vermont family whose fortunes and numbers have declined over the years. They retain some wealth, but little else. The first volume, *Possession* focuses on the lives of three of them and covers the day when Maggie, an unfaithful wife returns to Vermont to be with Judah, her much older husband, who has told her that he is desperately ill as a ruse to get her back. The plot centers on Maggie's interest in the estate, but much of *Possession* is devoted to Judah's and Maggie's reminiscences about their marriage.

Possession "is the boldest and most fully realized book Mr. Delbanco has written thus far," proclaimed the *New Yorker*. John Gardner wrote in a review of his favorite books of the year in the *New Republic*: "Here for the first time the rhetoric is in beautiful control, Delbanco holds himself in for most of the action, paying close attention to how people really speak, how things really look and feel."

In *Sherbrookes*, the second volume of the trilogy, old Judah Sherbrooke actually does die. Some months after his death, his and Maggie's twenty-six-year-old son Ian returns, and Maggie finds herself pregnant at the age of fifty-two.

The trilogy's concluding volume, *Stillness*, finds a reconstituted version of the Sherbrooke family living in the Big House. Maggie is there with her lover, Andrew, who is revealed to be the father of her new baby daughter. Ian, too, has remained in the house, writing about his deceased father. Frederick Busch noted in the *New York Times Book Review* that "Delbanco's . . . chief concern is history and its claims on a wealthy eccentric family." The trilogy ends "with a virtual prayer for resolution and a sad peace for the young writer Ian. The prose . . . is offered with the precision of heavy precious coins being counted on the palm."

About My Table, Delbanco's first collection of short stories, appeared in 1983 after he had already published ten novels. All nine of the stories chronicle the vicissitudes of successful professional men in their thirties. Delbanco dedicated the collection to the memory of his friend John Gardner, the novelist, poet, and playwright. Delbanco subsequently edited *Stillness and Shadows*, which contains two of Gardner's previously unpublished novels.

In "Remembering John Gardner," an article he wrote for the *New York Times Book Review*, Delbanco summed up the negative side of a writer's life: "Fame brings a constant, admiring assault, a request from civil strangers to be brilliant or outrageous or at least informed. It . . . forces one to substitute a mask for a face—sooner or later they fuse. This is doubly a danger for the writer since privacy is the *sine qua non* of his work, and he has had no training in the actor's life."

In *The Writers' Trade*, Delbanco's second collection of short fiction, he strips the veil of privacy from his characters' lives and thoughts. They are all professional writers who, except for "youthful summer jobs delivering fish or renting bicycles," according to Nancy Mairs in the *New York Times Book Review*, "have supported themselves by writing and perhaps teaching in prestigious colleges. . . . There's no juice in these tradesmen, no joy," Mairs declares, "and yet they ring true, I recognize them . . . and I have admired their work when they did it well." She cites Delbanco's accuracy as to how she herself would judge his work by quoting from one of the stories in *The Writers' Trade*: "His skill was a surveyor's skill, his habit that of witness . . . his habit was control. Reviewers praised his tact, his chilly noticing eye. They did so, however, in terms as measured as his own."

In the Name of Mercy, deals with the questions raised by euthanasia and assisted suicide. A young physician who has helped his terminally ill wife to commit suicide goes to work in a hospice, where he is visited by a woman famed for writing about how she helped her husband to end his suffering. When the hospice patients start to die at an accelerated rate, the narrative takes on a note of dark intrigue, which the *Publishers Weekly* reviewer termed "as appropriately elliptical as the rest of this well-written, well- considered work."

PRINCIPAL WORKS: *Novels*—The Marlet's Tale, 1966; Grasse 3/23/66, 1968; Consider Sappho Burning, 1969; News, 1970; In the Middle Distance, 1971; Fathering, 1973; Small Rain, 1975; Possession, 1977; Sherbrookes, 1978; Stillness, 1980; In the Name of Mercy, 1995. *Short Stories*—About My Table, and Other Stories, 1983; The Writers' Trade, and Other Stories, 1990. *Nonfiction*—Group Portrait: Joseph Conrad, Stephen Crane, Ford Madox Ford, Henry James, and H. G. Wells—A Biographical Study of Writers in community, 1982; The Beaux Arts Trio: A Portrait, 1985. *As Editor*—J. Gardner Stillness and Shadows 1986; Speaking of Writing: Selected Hopwood Lectures, 1990; (with L. Goldstein) Writers and Their Craft, Short Stories and Essays on the Narrative, 1991. *Autobiography*—Running in Place: Scenes from the South of France, 1989.

ABOUT: Contemporary Authors Autobiography Series 2, 1985; Contemporary Authors New Revision Series 29, 1990; Contemporary Literary Criticism 6, 1976; 13, 1980; Delbanco, N. Running in Place, 1989; Dictionary of Literary Biography 6, 1980. *Periodicals*—Nation August 31, 1970; New Republic March 19, 1977; December 3, 1977; New York Times June 12, 1970; New York Times Book Review June 28, 1970; December 6, 1970; April 3, 1977; November 9, 1980; September 18, 1983; July 20, 1986; July 23, 1989; March 18, 1990; New Yorker April 18, 1977; Publishers Weekly July 3, 1995; Saturday Review February 3, 1979; Times Literary Supplement April 17, 1987.

DEXTER, PETE (1943–   ), American novelist and journalist, was born in Pontiac, Michigan. His father died when he was two years old, and he moved with his mother to South Dakota. When she remarried, they moved to Milledgeville, Georgia, where his stepfather taught at the Georgia Military College. Milledgeville was the home of Flannery O'Connor, and as a boy he visited her farm to see the peacocks that she kept. When he was nine the family moved again, to Forest Park, Illinois, where he attended high school. He graduated from the University of South Dakota in 1970, having attended intermittently for eight years. During that period and later he worked at a variety of jobs—truck driver, gas station attendant, construction laborer.

Dexter became a reporter on the *West Palm Beach Post* in Florida in 1971. After a year there he went to Philadelphia where, until 1984, he worked for the *Philadelphia Daily News*. Since 1985 he has been a columnist for the *Sacramento Bee* in California. He has also written the "Sports Scene" column for *Esquire* and contributed articles to *Sports Illustrated* and *Playboy*. All this experience has served him as preparation for his hard-hitting, tough-talking novels with their emphasis on brutality and violence. As Robert Stone wrote in the *New York Times Book Review* (1991) of Dexter's novel *Brotherly Love*: "[T]he world in which its characters make their lives is as brutal, atavistic and unforgiving as that of any Elizabethan or Jacobean revenger . . . Few writers are better at describing the ways in which bad men do evil things and forgive themselves, while good men do nothing and suffer agonies of remorse." Dexter himself has said, "Violence is a great shaping thing. It shapes what follows for everybody. Not just as a literary device, but in real life."

One of Dexter's most frequently repeated stories attributes his becoming a novelist to a fight in a Philadelphia bar in 1982—"the most celebrated bar fight in the history of South Philadelphia," as he described it in a *New York Times* interview in 1988. An amateur boxer, he and a friend, heavyweight boxer Randy Cobb, got into a fight over a column he had written in the *Daily News* about neighborhood drug dealers. His leg and back were broken and his head smashed, but he survived to draw on the experience in his first novel, *God's Pocket*, a book rich in local color, authentic-sounding dialogue, and tough, ironic humor. His wryly comic attitude toward violence can be seen in the first paragraph of the novel: "Leon Hubbard died ten minutes after lunch break on the first Monday in May, on the construction site of the new one-story trauma wing at Holy Redeemer Hospital in South Philadelphia. One way or the other, he was going to lose the job." Leon has been killed by one of his coworkers. The structure of the novel is picaresque: Leon's stepfather, Mickey Scarpato, short of the money he needs for the funeral, loses what's been collected in the local bar betting on the horses; Smilin' Jack, the mortician, dumps Leon's body in the alley; Mickey puts the body in his refrigerated truck with stolen meat he's been unable to sell; when the truck is in an accident, the body is taken a second time to the morgue. Along the way, thugs sent out to find out about Leon's death are beaten up by the construction site foreman, who jabs out one of their eyes while a bystander applauds. Two other thugs are shot by seventy-four-year-old Aunt Sophie, whose son Bird is Mickey's boss in stealing meat trucks; and a newspaper man is beaten to death, a scene based on Dexter's own experience. But the plot, as Bill Ott wrote in *Booklist*, "is really just an excuse to let the characters talk." Amy Pershing wrote in *The Nation*, "Dexter's ear for Philly speech in uncanny . . . Everyone from truck driver to newspaper publisher talks the same way. Nonetheless, *God's Pocket* is a tough, funny, articulate book about violent, sad, tragically inarticulate people."

Deadwood, Dexter's second novel, published in 1986, shows what Robert Stone identified in Dexter's work as "a romantic element that's distinctly American." Set in South Dakota in 1876 during the Gold Rush into the Black Hills, the novel centers on Wild Bill Hickok, now in pain and going blind from syphilis and soon to be assassinated "holding aces and eights." But, according to Dexter, what attracted him to the story was Hickok's friend Charley Utter and the town of Deadwood itself:

Not counting tents or the Chinese establishments, where Captain Jack said he would not set foot, there were sixteen barrooms in the badlands. Some of them had been thrown together in a day, and the ceilings would shift in a wind or a fight. Some of them, like the Gem and the Green Front, were built more slowly, with a stage and a bar and little rooms upstairs closed off the hallway by curtains, and a girl's name written in chalk above each one. The prettiest ones and the singers got rooms with doors.

"You take care of people," one character says to Charley late in the book, after Hickok has been killed. "It's not that," he answers, "Amigos take care of each other." Charley, according to Ron Hansen, in the *New York Time Book Review* (1986), "is the oddly complacent picaro in this comic novel, a perplexed, ironical, lackadaisical

type"; but overall, Hansen found *Deadwood* to be "unpredictable, hyperbolic and, page after page, uproarious, a joshing book written in high spirits and a raw appreciation of the past."

Paris Trout, Dexter's third novel, won both the National Book Award in 1988 and a nomination for the National Book Critics Circle Award. Set in the fictional town of Cotton Point, Georgia, during the 1950s, it was regarded by many reviewers as a powerful indictment of racism. Paris Trout, a shopkeeper who sells on credit to the black community, is thwarted when he tries to collect a payment from a young black man he has cheated. He shoots the man's mother and kills the fourteen-year-old girl who is living with her. While the white community reluctantly moves to prosecute him for the crime, his pathological lack of guilt is underscored by his sadistic torture of his wife and his deepening paranoia, which ends in a rampage of killing. Deborah Mason observed, in the *New York Times Book Review*, that Dexter used "Trout's outcroppings of brutality and growing arsenal of guns to titillate rather than to advance the plot. It's as if he has to sell us on Trout's total depravity: being a racist killer isn't enough." Mason admired, however, Dexter's "exquisite understanding of the finely meshed engines of greed and self-interest that drive a small town." In particular she noted Dexter's characterization of Harry Seagraves, the lawyer who represents Trout, whose "steely assessment of his own interests when he takes on the case makes his slow, agonizing waking to the horror of Trout's actions and his own complicity all the more affecting." In the *New York Review of Books*, Robert Towers praised Dexter's evocation of the atmosphere of a small southern town, but wrote that the author "never takes his material beyond what is journalistically plausible. His characters stay on the surface, lacking distinctive voices or personalities."

The roots of *Paris Trout* lie in Dexter's own years in the South. The plot is based on the murder of a lawyer in Milledgeville, Georgia, where he had lived as a child. Nevertheless Dexter denies any specific southern literary influences. Much as he admires Flannery O'Connor, another Milledgeville resident, Dexter modestly observes, "[W]ho can touch the words she was putting down on the page. She's so good it's stunning. I wish some of it would rub off on me, but I don't see it." He also rejects any characterization of himself as a "southern" writer, telling Glen Collins in a *New York Times* interview in 1988: "I'm not a southern writer, and I would never presume to speak to, or for, the South." In response to comparisons that have been made between his work and Faulkner's he says, "The time in college I was supposed to be reading

Faulkner, I got the *Cliff Notes* for Faulkner, and I could not even understand *them*."

In *Brotherly Love*, Dexter moves beyond the easy barroom camaraderie on which much of the humor in *God's Pocket* and *Deadwood* is based, Male relationships again form the core of the story, but in this novel the emphasis falls on betrayal. Eight-year-old Peter Flood, frozen in fear of his neighbor's dog, watches as his baby sister is hit by the neighbor's car; Peter's father, a union officer connected to the mob, kills the neighbor in revenge against the orders of the mob bosses, and is killed in turn, perhaps lured to his death by his own brother. Abandoned by his mother, Peter lives with his uncle and his sadistic cousin, an accomplice in their criminal work. His only friend, Nick DeMaggio, a father figure, runs a local boxing gym where, as Jim Bencivenga wrote in the *Christian Science Monitor*, "Punching fists and butting heads replace understanding and tenderness." Flood is a "pathological masochist," wrote John Sutherland in the s Literary Supplement. "It is through his affectless gaze that the twenty-five years of ensuing graft, homicide and his own eventual self-destruction are viewed." Unlike the previous novels which were "dense, busy and energetic efforts, shot through with broad comedy," Sutherland described *Brotherly Love* as "all gaps, silences and dull, unreflecting surfaces." Robert Stone, however, in the *New York Times Book Review*, called *Brotherly Love* "a first-rate novel and masterly evocation of that undercivilized and unfree America in which millions of Americans still grow up and from which they wring their bread."

Dexter presents himself as someone who knows the world of work and violence. In interviews he refers to the numerous jobs he had during the eight years he took to earn a degree from the University of South Dakota. He told an interviewer for *Sports Illustrated*: "I was the one who just wanted to raise hell and shoot out the windows." He added, "The writing impulse took over when I found out what it was like to work for a living. As much as you bitch about all this stuff, and as many problems and irritations as you can run into with the writing, I promise you it's nothing like as irritating as having a keg of beer drop on your foot or driving out in the middle of nowhere on a hot day and having the heating system go out on the truck." The "attitude that writers are a special class, that really alienates me." he told *Publishers Weekly*. "I've seen people that actually worked themselves to death, people my age who are all used up from manual labor. I've had some of those jobs—luckily I didn't keep them too long—but I know what they are, and writing is nothing like it."

In 1991 Dexter wrote the screenplay for a television movie of *Paris Trout*, in which Dennis Hopper played the title role. The book's success made it possible for him to give up most of his free-lance magazine work, but he continues to write a weekly column for the *Sacramento Bee*. He lives on Whidbey Island, Washington, with his second wife Dian and their daughter Casey. He told Glen Collins that he would liked to have named his daughter after Flannery O'Connor, whose courage he admires for writing "so well while she was dying and she knew it . . . But my wife bridled at the idea she'd go through life with a handle like that. So we named her after someone whose use of the language I admired—Casey Stengel."

PRINCIPAL WORKS: God's Pocket, 1984; Deadwood, 1986; Paris Trout, 1988; Brotherly Love, 1991.

ABOUT: Contemporary Authors 131, 1991; Contemporary Literary Criticism 34; Yearbook 1984; Yearbook 1988; *Periodicals*—Booklist February 15, 1984; Christian Science Monitor October 28, 1991; Nation, March 3, 1984; New York Review of Books, February 16, 1989; New York Times December 5, 1988; October 17, 1991; New York Times Book Review September 2, 1986; July 24, 1988; October 13,1991, Publishers Weekly, October 4, 1991; Sports Illustrated, February 23, 1987; Times Literary Supplement February 21, 1992; Washington Post Book World June 1, 1986.

DIB, MOHAMMED (July 21, 1920–   ), Algerian French-language novelist, poet, and short story writer, was born in Tlemcen in western Algeria. After employment in a variety of capacities—teacher, accountant, weaver, interpreter, and journalist—Dib became a full-time writer. In 1959 he moved to France, where he has lived since. Dib has remained one of the most consistently excellent and prolific Maghrebian writers, producing more than twenty novels, books of poetry, and collections of stories, as well as two children's books and a play.

Dib was a member of a cohort of Algerian writers who exploded onto the literary scene in the early 1950s that has been called the "generation of '52" (the year in which first novels by Dib and Mouloud Mammeri appeared), consisting of Mouloud Feraoun, Dib, Mammeri, and Kateb Yacine. They are sometimes dubbed the "generation of '54" due to the historic importance of that year when, on November 1, the Algerian war of independence broke out.

Dib's writing falls into two essentially distinct paths, one poetry and the other fiction. These paths converge here and there (for example, poems are incorporated as songs into some of the early novels and some of the later novel assume the oneiric style characteristic of most of the poems), but they have tended to evolve in different ways over the fifty-year period since Dib began publishing. The poetry, from the earliest texts published in the mid-1940s to the most recent collections, has remained consistently enigmatic, with sensuous, even erotic nuances, rich with such tropes as the oxymoron and anaphora, and very hermetic, as in "L'Ombrage de l'éclair" ("Shadow of lightning") in *Formulaires* (1970; selections translated in *Omneros*, 1978):

to sculpt between your belly
and your legs in the yellow dust

the amnesia of august
its thirsty stillness
its carnivorous whiteness
its delicate black anger
its brief moment of burning

—tr. Eric Sellin

Dib's collections, which warrant him recognition as a major modern poet, include—besides *Formulaires*—*Ombre gardienne* (1961; Guardian shadow), *Omneros* (1975; selections translated in *Omneros*, 1978), *Feu beau feu* (1979; Fire beautiful fire), and *Ô vive* (1987); *Ô vive* is an untranslatable title punning on "Oh/*eau* (water)" and "*vive* (a fish / lively)" and *eau vive* (fresh spring water), with an underlying suggestion of *eau de vie* (aqua vitae). In his poetry, Dib contrives his special music with telegraphic, elliptical syntax—omitting logical narrative gambits or incipits and many customary connectives and articles—and he shrouds his poems with enigma by leaving much of the poetry's imagery to resonate in the unspoken spaces between the lines and in the margins of the page as well as with many deliberate ambiguities or multiple readings of the sort found in the titles *Omneros* (combining suggestions of man [*homo-/homme*], omni, and Eros) and *Ô vive* (see above). Dib's poems themselves fall into two categories: sparsely worded poems of the sort quoted above—what he has called "*poem* poems"—and brief prose poems, the latter usually composed through a process approaching automatic, of trance, writing. "I try each time to translate a vision; and I try in the most precise manner to approach that vision by means of the most exact words, the most precise and the most realistic. You will not find in my poems a single abstract of philosophical word," he told an interviewer in *CELFAN Review*.

Dib's novels, on the other hand, have evolved since 1952 from a naturalist-realist style reminiscent of that of Emile Zola—each novel in his early trilogy (unofficially called L'Algérie),

composed of *La Grand Maison* (The big house, 1952), *L'Incendie* (The fire, 1954), and *Le Métier à tisser* (The Loom, 1957), addresses a social problem such as hunger among the poor or the plight of peasants and the proletariat—to more and more intellectually challenging texts in which the reader is, albeit charmed by their brilliance and poetic energy, sometimes bewildered by their kaleidoscopic fragmentation, minimalization of traditional narrative action, lack of linear chronology, extensive use of interior monologue and interwoven levels of consciousness, and an eerie, metallic otherworldliness bordering on science fiction. An example is Dib's masterpiece *Qui se souvient de la mer* (1962, *Who Remembers the Sea*), to which the author appends a note defending his novel against the charge that although it deals with such a stark and epic tragedy as the Algerian revolution (1954–1962), it is overly concerned with abstractions and superficial aesthetic glitter. Dib cites in his defense the example of Picasso's powerful painting *Guernica* and the oneiric virtues of science fiction, which Dib claims never to have read before writing this novel, which marks a major turning point in the development of his novelistic technique:

I understand then that evil is not to be surprised amidst its ordinary enterprises, but elsewhere, in its true lair: man—and in the dreams, the deliria, that he feels blindly and that I have tried to dress in a formal structure. One will grant that such a thing could hardly have been done by means of traditional forms of writing. Let us return to *Guernica* not a single realistic element in the whole painting—neither blood nor dead bodies—and yet there is nothing that expresses so strongly the horror. Picasso has but fixed and given order to nightmares on his canvas; surely that was not for him a simple method of composition like any other.

—tr. L. Tremaine

Dib insists on the persistent value of traditional narrative techniques, "which continue to be indispensable for giving us the epic of cruel and terrifying tragedy, firsthand reports, documents for history," but claims that he found it impossible to convey by traditional means the horror requiring the "marriage of heaven and hell" without recourse to "oneiric and apocalyptic visions." Other novels, including *Cours sur la rive sauvage* (Run on the wild shore, 1964) and *La Danse du roi* (The dance of the king, 1968), also make use of the hard-edged, fragmented modernity of style found in *Who Remembers the Sea*. Thereafter we find periodic reinventions or adjustments of style without Dib's ever completely returning to the realistic mode.

Many of Dib's novels present archetypal characters who represent contrasting forces in society, such as good and evil, and explore dream worlds or Jungian strata of the human psyche, such as androgyny, or portend events which were soon to reverberate throughout Algeria and the Arab world. Thus *Un Été africain* (An African summer, 1959), *Dieu en Barbarie* (God in Barbary, 1970), *Le Maitre de chasse* (The hunt master, 1973), and *Le Désert sans détour* (The undeviating desert, 1992), speak variously of a summer in the life of a young woman who finds herself caught between her modern yearnings and the conflicting worldview of her parents' generation; of the imminent rise of Islamic fundamentalism; and of the sense of hopelessness and impotence sweeping Algeria in the 1990s. *Habel* (1977), Dib's one novel set in France, explores the question of androgyny.

From 1985 to 1994 Dib's major novels constitute what we may label a loosely knit "Nordic tetralogy," reflecting an episode in the personal life of the author. The characters' names vary from work to work, but there is a sense of cohesion and chronological order to the events, similar to the relationship in the early L'Algérie trilogy and in the first two volumes (*Dieu en Barbarie* and *Le Maitre de chasse*) of a trilogy Dib has said he will never finish, but which in some ways seems to have found its closure in *Le Désert sans détour*. The action of the first novel in the Nordic sequence, *Les Terrasses d'Orsol* (The terraces of Orsol, 1985), takes place in a fictitious Arab country by the sea (Algeria?) but introduces extensive passages describing a snowy country far to the north. The two novels that followed, *Le Sommeil d'Ève* (The sleep of Eve, 1989) and *Neiges de Marbre* (Marble snow, 1990), are set in a Nordic country (Finland?) and recount the advent and development of a sometimes turbulent romance between a Nordic woman and Mediterranean man who have a child and eventually become estranged. In a kind of reversal of *Les terrasses d'Orsol*, in which Dib insinuates the Nordic element into an ostensibly North African story, most of the action of the fourth novel, *L'Infante maure* (The Moorish infanta, 1994), takes place in a Nordic country and is the interior monologue of the couple's child, who is at one point taken to her father's homeland where she is introduced to the Arab part of her heritage, closing, as it were, a geographical parenthesis opened in *Les Terrasses d'Orsol*.

The novels, especially the more recent ones, indulge in the same brilliant wordplay as is found in the poems, especially 1) in place-names *Les Terrasses d'Orsol* we have a town names Orsol (*or* /gold) and (*sol* / earth, sun) in a fictitious country bearing the name Jarbher that combines the Arabic words for neighbor (*jār*) and seas (*bihār*); 2) in proper names: Dib's name (*adīb*

means "author") is almost the same as the word in Arabic for "wolf" (*di'b*), and in one novel there is a character known as "le Loup" (wolf); in another, a character actually bears the name Wolf; the name of another character in *Le Désert sans détour*—Hagg-Bar-suggests a semioxymoronic glossing of *baḥr* (sea) and *barr* (land) as well as contextual and religious inferences in the punning on *ḥājj* (pilgrim) and/or various verbal forms of the root *ḥajja* (pertaining to debate), the overall name being vaguely suggestive of *akbar*, as in *Allah akbar*, and 3) in titles: *L'Infante maure*, with the play on words in infante/enfante (child) and *maure* (moor, moorish) / *mort* (death). Indeed, in one copy of *L'Infante maure*, Dib inscribed to a friend the words: "*Cette parole d'enfant / Qui nous infante, / Qui nous invente*" (These words of the child / which make us royal heirs the [verb "infanter" is a neologism] / Which invent us).

Dib demonstrates in his works complete mastery of all minute possibilities of the French language from the exploration of the geology of meaning beneath the words to the creation of stunning neologisms, but his syntactical iconoclasm; his warps in traditional time projection; and his frequent recourse to bicultural content, stylistic parody, cultural and linguistic codemixing, and ludic linguistic winks at his sometimes oblivious Europhone reader all contrive to allow us to qualify Dib's texts since the early 1960s—poetry and fiction alike—as examples of what some postmodern theorists have termed postcolonial counterdiscourse.

PRINCIPAL WORKS IN ENGLISH TRANSLATION: *Novel*—(tr. Louis Tremaine) Who Remembers the Sea, 1985. *Short Stories*—(tr. L. Ortzen) "The Provider of All Good Gifts," "The End," and "Naema—Whereabouts Unkown" (from Le Talisman) *in* Ortzen, L. (ed.) North African Writing, 1970. *Poetry*—(tr. E. Sellin) Poems *in* The Contemporary World Poets, 1978; (tr. C. Lettieri and P. Vangelisti) Omneros (a selection of poems from Formulaires and Omneros), 1978; (tr. E. Sellin) Poem *in* The Worlds of Muslim Imagination, 1986.

ABOUT: African Literatures in the 20th Century: Bonn, C. Lecture présente de Mohammed Dib; Déjeux, J. Mohammed Dib, 1987; Déjeux, J. Mohammed Dib, écrivain algérien, 1977; Encyclopedia of World Literature in the 20th Century, 2nd ed., 1981; Khadda, N. L'Oeuvre romanesque de Mohammed Dib; Ortzen, L. (ed.) North African Writing, 1970. *Periodicals*—Francofonia Autumn 1991; Journal of the New African Literature and the Arts 9–10, 1971; Kalim 6, 1985; L'Esprit Créateur Spring 1986; Lotus: Afro-Asian Writings 30, 1976; Présence Francophone 34, 1989; Research in African Literatures Fall 1988; Summer 1992; CELFAN Review, February 2 1983; Stanford French Review Spring 1982; World Literature Today Winter 1984.

DICKSTEIN MORRIS (February 23, 1940–), American literary and social critic writes: "No one ever grew up with the dream of becoming a literary critic. Certainly not a boy born, as I was to immigrant parents Abraham and Anne Reitman Dickstein on the Lower East Side of New York, who went on to twelve years of schooling at an Orthodox Jewish yeshiva. In retrospect, a Talmudical education might orient one to textual commentary, but literary exegesis wasn't really what I wanted to do. I merely enjoyed reading and writing, and had a knack for talking about books.

"Early on I had a simple ambition: to know everything. With undiscriminating appetite, I devoured whatever I could lay my hands on: history, biography, fiction. Week by week, I read through whole sections of the local public library starting with art and anthropology. I looked for titillating details: I can still recall Margaret Mead's accounts of puberty rites in Samoa and New Guinea.

"Always in a hurry, I plowed through Somerset Maugham's egregious abridgments of the world's top ten novels: *Wuthering Heights, Old Man Goriot*, etc.—the classics with all the fat removed. I also had two exacting high-school English teachers, careful speakers, close readers, unsparing critics of my own hapless prose and poetry. Still, when I went off to Columbia in 1957 I thought I would become a lawyer or journalist, since I was a facile writer and had a big mouth—I edited the school paper and loved the debating team.

"All this changed during my first two years in college, My religious friends gave way to tough-minded intellectuals from the Bronx High School of Science who had already taken college-level courses and had read even more than I did. My freshman English teacher, Jim Zito, who would later become a legend at Sarah Lawrence, had the most dazzling mind and acid style I ever encountered. Writing had always come easily to me but he made me work at it, boil it down to essentials, make every adjective, every metaphor count. At the same time the famous Humanities course exposed me to world literature from Homer to Dostoyevski with an exhilarating intensity.

"At the end of my sophomore year I read Lionel Trilling's *Liberal Imagination* and got a glimpse of what critical writing could really be. I was hooked. For the first time I thought of staying on in a university so I could keep reading, keep writing, keep talking about the books I desperately loved. Good teachers reinforced this passion: Andrew Chiappe on Shakespeare, Trilling on modernism, Steven Marcus on the Ro-

MORRIS DICKSTEIN

mantic poets. They talked less like professional critics than as strenuous citizens of a community of letters. They preferred personal or historical insight to technical analysis. They were as much intellectuals as scholars, and the air was filled with politics, culture, and big ideas, not the safe prospect of graduate school.

"When I arrived at Yale as a graduate student in 1961 something else was in the air: an established critical formalism, demanding a kind of close reading I had never seen outside Cleanth Brooks's *The Well Wrought Urn*. It was a conservative department, best known for its medievalists and eighteenth-century scholars. But there were also vague stirrings from a junior faculty stocked with oppressed young romanticists like Harold Bloom, Geoffrey Hartman, and E. D. Hirsch, none of whom taught graduate students. After two years I got a fellowship to Cambridge, where I worked informally with F. R. Leavis and Raymond Williams, then returned to Yale to tackle Keats under the newly tenured Bloom, just admitted grudgingly to graduate teaching.

"Seeing Keats as a tragic realist, a poet of self-making, I could not have been further from Bloom's view of the Romantics as a 'visionary company.' But I got a delicious pleasure out of our working friendship and his always provocative mind. My book *Keats and His Poetry* appeared in 1971, when I was back teaching at Columbia. But by then the big carnival of the 1960s, especially the antiwar movement, the counterculture, the student uprisings, and new writers like Pynchon and Heller, had already drawn me to contemporary issues.

"For years I had been reviewing recent books for *Partisan Review, Commentary,* and *The New Republic,* more the pattern of a New York intellectual than the academic critic. Finally, after an essay on Allen Ginsberg, I saw a way of synthesizing the serious culture of the sixties, bringing the work of novelists, poets, journalists, and rock singers together with my own personal and political experiences, including the 1968 student uprising at Columbia. While teaching at Queens College after 1971, I wrote a series of review-essays for the *New York Times Book Review* on contemporary writers like Barthelme, Mailer, Malamud, Roth, then published my book on the sixties, *Gates of Eden,* in 1977. It began with Ginsberg and concluded with a chapter of autobiography, very much in the spirit of personal witness I identified with the sixties.

"Much of my later work followed from this book. One turn took me towards film and popular culture, another passion of the sixties that had been a real blind spot for older intellectuals I admired. Another took me back towards the 1930s, yet another decade of social crisis, political tension, and cultural ferment. I was especially fascinated by the films of the thirties—gangster films, dance musicals, screwball comedies, protest movies, creature features—with their mixture of escapism and social consciousness.

"Finally, the work of my academic colleagues shifted towards theory and criticism. I found myself trying to articulate the tradition behind my own blend of critical journalism, literary commentary, personal writing, and cultural history. Essays on practical criticism and book reviewing, polemics against post-structuralist theory, and reassessments of critics like Arnold, Trilling, and Kazin eventually led me to *Double Agent: The Critic and Society.* The book emphasized the critic's need to balance art and social concern, personal response and public discourse, both neglected by theorists caught up in academic jargon and professionalism.

"My favorite writers were displaced preachers, moral ironists as different as Wordsworth and Kafka, Blake and Benjamin, Hawthorne and Malamud, Henry James and Joseph Heller. To a remarkable extent, my values could be traced to those I had formed when young: the moral and textual exigency of my Jewish education, the urban cacophony and ethnic buzz of growing up in New York, my undergraduate faith in criticism as a form of *writing,* a branch of the intellectual life. I saw criticism, finally, as a visceral response to art in its moral and social complexity, at once personal and public, deeply attuned to how the imagination reshapes our common experience."

———

In an essay in *Partisan Review* (1984–1985), Morris Dickstein acknowledged the shaping influence of his religious heritage on his later work: "My immersion in The Book became a passion for books. The stress on right conduct, which Matthew Arnold called the essence of Hebraism, was gradually directed into a new framework—secular, moral, and political rather than religious." By his own account, Dickstein was now becoming a "double agent," the critic who combines "a deep feeling for art with a powerful sense of its changing place in human society."

Gates of Eden, nominated for a National Book Critics Circle Award in 1977, is a cultural history of the 1960s, written from the eyewitness point of view of a young graduate student and then college teacher. Observing the campus in his double role, Dickstein shared both the idealism of a generation inspired by the civil rights and other liberating movements and the bitter disillusion over the war in Vietnam. For him, as for so many others, the sixties was a period when the "search for personal authenticity" became identified with the "quest of social justice." In the 1968 student uprising on the campus of Columbia University he served on a faculty committee attempting to conciliate and mediate—an experience that "finally showed me that I *was* a liberal rather than a radical." Overall, Dickstein judged the decade as having "a liberating effect on many of our lives." Rethinking the decade in an introduction he wrote to the paperback edition of *Gates of Eden* in 1989, Dickstein reiterated his judgment that the sensibility of the American people had been profoundly changed: "Many of the fundamental rights we now accord to women, gay people, and blacks belong to the legacy of the sixties."

During the 1970s and 1980s he pursued his studies in literary and popular culture, lecturing and writing on contemporary fiction, Romantic and contemporary poetry, film, and such controversial questions of contemporary education as multiculturalism and revision of the literary canon. The course that Dickstein defined for himself in *Gates of Eden,* that "criticism, which is often tempted to be hermetic, can tell us something of the real world," led to his survey of criticism *Double Agent.*

The critic to whom Dickstein gives closest attention in *Double Agent* is Matthew Arnold, a Victorian, whose goal, Dickstein writes, "was not to create a timeless canon, a perfect society, or an absolute set of values, but to find whatever was needful for a given age." To that end "Arnold emphasized the reflection that should precede action: he insisted on the many-sidedness of the traditional humanist ideal."

Twentieth-century critics who have worked in the Arnoldian tradition are double agents—both intellectuals and public critics, academics and journalists. Among those Dickstein especially admires in *The Double Agent* are Lionel Trilling, Alfred Kazin, Edmund Wilson, and George Orwell. "Dickstein has a knack for getting at the heart of a critic's sensibility, even if on occasion he seems fair-minded to a fault," Arthur Krystal wrote in the *Times Literary Supplement*. "All too polite," John Sutherland wrote in the *New York Times Book Review*. "Diatribe rather than dialogue seems to be called for, assault rather than genteel subversion." In the *New York Review of Books*, Denis Donoghue judged the book "a little dispirited . . . *Double Agent* has the features of an epitaph. Dickstein does will to inform students that criticism was once a public art, reaching beyond the academy. . . . But he doesn't explain what precisely has changed and why." Christopher Lehmann-Haupt concluded his review of *Double Agent* in the *New York Times* with "Amen" to Dickstein's appreciation of literary journalism. "[He] strives to be the exemplar of his ideal, the balanced observer who strides multiple worlds and can discriminate between writers, their works and the implications of their utterances."

Dickstein began his teaching career at Columbia University (1966 to 1971). Since 1976 he has been professor of English at Queens College of the City University of New York and at the City University Graduate Center. He lectured in France and in England in 1980–1981 as a Fulbright fellow and in 1980 was also visiting professor of English and American Studies at the University of Paris. He had a Guggenheim Fellowship in 1973–1974, a Rockefeller Humanities Fellowship in 1981–1982, a Mellon Research fellowship in 1989–1990, as well as grants and fellowships from the Danforth Foundation, the ACLS, and the NEH. Her married Lore Wilner, a writer, in 1965. They have two children and live on the Upper West Side in New York City.

PRINCIPAL WORKS: Keats and His Poetry: A Study in Development, 1971; Gates of Eden: American Culture in the Sixties, 1977; Double Agent: The Critic and Society, 1992. *As editor*—(with L. Braudy) Great Film Directors: A Critical Anthology, 1978.

ABOUT: Contemporary Authors 85–88, 1980; Dickstein, M. Gates of Eden. 1977. *Periodicals*—Chicago Tribune January 10, 1993; New York Review of Books August 4, 1977; March 25, 1993; New York Times March 9, 1977; October 15, 1992; New York Times Book Review March 13, 1977; February 7, 1993; Newsweek March 28, 1977; Partisan Review 4, 1984–1985; Times Literary Supplement February 26, 1993.

*DINESCU, MIRCEA (November 11, 1950–), Romanian poet, was born and brought up in a working-class family in Slobozia, a small, rural town in the rich farming and grazing lands halfway between Bucharest and the Black Sea. Dinescu never attended college. He issued his first book at twenty-one, *Invocatie nimănui* (Invocation to no one, 1971), which won a Writers Union prize. Works of poetry followed regularly (he published four each decade in the 1970s and 1980s), with other important titles including dispozitia dumneavoastră (At your disposal, 1979), *Teroarea bunului simt* (The terror of being respectable, 1980), *Democratia naturii* (The democracy of nature, 1981), and *Rimbaud negustorul* (Rimbaud the merchant, 1985). In 1989, under house arrest, he wrote an additional volume which he has chosen not to publish, as he turned his attention to journalism, like many Romanian poets and novelists after the revolution. He is literary director of a popular satirical weekly, *Catavencu Academia*, for which he writes barbed prose pieces. In 1990, Dinescu served as a member of the provisional Romanian parliament after the 1989 change of government. In 1993, he was recipient of a year-long grant from the German Academy of the Arts in Berlin. Volumes of his work have been published in France, Germany, Holland, Hungary, Switzerland, the U.S.S.R., and in England, where sixty-one poems were put into English by Andrea Deletant and Brenda Walker as *Exile on a Peppercorn* (1985).

Dinescu made himself the most prominent public symbol of intellectual resistance in the years just before the overthrow of Nicolae Ceauşescu's totalitarian state in 1989. Only a little over two decades before, in 1967, the young man from the provinces, with his precocious poetic talent, had made his first appearance in print in a national literary journal. Two months shy of his seventeenth birthday, he was even then an identifiable voice and a charismatic figure. He moved from witty and graceful formal verse that seemed an ironic revitalization of older lyrical traditions to bitterly sardonic parables that were at the same time concrete and startling in their imagery and polemical, but still deftly formal in technique. By the late 1980s he made risk-taking public statements of undisguised protest and outrage. Dinescu fashioned himself, into the self-styled enfant terrible and angry young man of Romanian writing. As poet Nina Cassian (who had to seek asylum outside of Romania in the mid-1980s because of her own views), said in *Parnassus*, as unembarrassed . . . outstanding example of his generation" Dinescu had always adopted a variety of "shocking, rebellious, and defiant" postures, both aesthetic and actual:

*dee NESS coo, MEER chuh

"After his debut, Mircea Dinescu was never anonymous. . . . Though called a punk, a clown, a hooligan (etc.), Dinescu was actually acting responsibly, defending righteous causes and attacking some of the surrounding absurdities. . . . "

This close relationship between literary persona and real personality makes it hard sometimes to distinguish Dinescu the poet who was lionized in the poem, including one to the lack of heat in Romania's apartments and offices.

In an other poem, "Hunger" becomes the desired object of prayer—"God give us our daily hunger"—and "Epistle on Putting Up with the Fact of Life . . . " excoriates "you feather-brained Docs of the Ostrich Academy / there's not enough sand for all the heads we can bury." the systematic repression is attacked in "Pest Control," in which the exterminator "with a deadly smelling canister on his back" is after people, particularly old people—the elderly were often forcibly resettled in the countryside, where scant resources led to starvation—and in "Guernica," where victims are forced to the Danube-Black Sea Canal: "to dig their own graves in the rain / so we can find an outlet to the sea. . . . " In Dinescu's dystopia, "death is a homeland."

In "Walls," a poem less about physical things like "concrete, glass, and steel girders" than about intangible barriers such as fear and mental constructions, the poet indicts himself for sustaining his own fantasies of emotional release or escape:

What a stupid illusion:
to wall yourself in
and suddenly to feel
so free.

Dinescu the international celebrity who, after the flight from Bucharest on December 22, 1989, of Ceauşescu and his wife, found himself playing a triumphant hero's part. Ushered from his home in Bucharest, where he had been under house arrest for most of the year, to the television station nearby, he was the chosen spokesman of liberty, the first nonofficial face to appear on the nation's screens and proclaim, "Brothers, we are free." The poet's bravado, his self-created voice, and his personal bravery, his bold challenges to the state, are almost inseparable. Both as civic-minded citizen and severely censored but justifiably proud writer he used many of the same weapons, particularly irony, including sarcasm and satire, but also parables, allegories, absurdity, suggestive and reductive surreal images, epigrams, and taunts. Dinescu has stated that "irony really is a weapon, as long as the official power

is solemn and has an allergy to irony." The role of the classical *eiron*, the aloof, caustic observer of satire, allowed him to channel his indignation: "Oh God how I was born / red with anger," the poem "Travelling Players" begins. In 1986, interviewed on the publication in England of a book of his poems, Dinescu reflected on anger as a motivating force that "creates literature" and on sarcasm as a strategy natural to him: "I do not chose it on purpose, it is simply my way of writing. But besides sarcasm I also have an elegiac nature; maybe the sarcasm is just a disguised form of elegy after all."

This displacement of sentiment into irony is perhaps another reflection of the dualities of Dinescu's nature, which the Bulgarian literary critic Ognyan Stamboliev in *Concerning Poetry* sees as both guileless and guarded: "his almost childish simplicity and vulnerability coupled with his almost snobbish intellectual stance."

In an interview in London, in 1986, however, very little appeared in Dinescu's work to make a reader think the poet retained faith in the "Sweet innocence / to believe that poetry can improve the world" ("Absurd Chess"). Indeed, during the 1980s when Dinescu was working on *Moartea citeste ziarul* (Death reads the newspaper), the volume of poems that he could not publish in Romanian until after the downfall of the Communist government, Dinescu said unequivocally, "Nowadays we need poetry more than ever; of course, literature will not be able to save the world, but it can curse it here and there."

Soon after this, however, he turned his energies to public statements of opposition. His activism intensified throughout 1988 and 1989, beginning most markedly with his speech, "Bread and Circus," at a September 1988 colloquium in West Berlin and with a declaration to Radio Moscow in favor of Gorbachev (*glasnost* and *perestroika* were opposed by the Romanian Communist Party), and then continuing with a corrosive, widely circulated letter in March 1989 to the president of the Romanian Writers Union. After that he found himself followed everywhere by security operatives and discovered an electronic eavesdropping device in his plate in the Writers Union restaurant. Dinescu was forthwith dismissed from the union and from all gainful employment. At the same time, Dinescu gave an informative, wide-ranging, accusatory interview about Ceauşescu's terrorism and conditions in Romania to the French newspaper *Libération*; immediately the poet was placed under house arrest, along with his family—his wife Maria (always called Masa) and their two young children. Their phone was cut off as well. Dinescu also lost the right to publish, although for a year or more he had largely been silenced in domestic publications. Protest followed from both a small dissident group of Romanian writers and from numerous Western European writers, and in April 1989, in a barbed political gesture, a volume of Dinescu's poems was published in the Soviet Republic of Bessarabia (now Moldova). In June the poet was awarded the International Prize for Poetry of Rotterdam, with the jury's declaration that "through Mircea Dinescu, we honor all the Romanian writers who, with their work, defend the free spirit of a subjugated nation." Dinescu was not permitted to travel abroad in order to receive the prize.

An essay of this period, smuggled out of Romania in defiance of his house arrest and round-the-clock surveillance, is "The Mammoth and Literature." With Juvenalian invective and an unmuzzled frankness, it attacks the passivity of Romanian intellectuals and likens Romania's Stalinist state to a mammoth recently found frozen in Siberia—in its gut not the chamomile flower of that prehistoric creature's diet, however, but corpses. Amid Romania's chronic shortages and more and more widespread rationing of basic goods, he arraigns the state by remarking that "terror has become the national product which is offered abundantly without ration card, on any street corner in Romania." Had the revolution not freed Dinescu, his actions and attacks would have escalated to the point where he could well have been executed. the poet's personal jeopardy only underscores the witty but blackly humorless metaphors he devised in the first stanza of "Dance":

On the street death reads the newspaper
spread over the dead beggar's face
in neighborhood bars death fills its glass
death's in the open, death's under wraps.

The poet's ninth volume it was finally published in Romania in 1990, by which time it had already been printed in five European countries. It was joined by a selected anthology of works from 1968 to 1985, which recycled the title of Dinescu's third book, *Proprietarul de poduri* (The owner of bridges, 1976). This phrase most immediately suggests the rebel-poet-bum who is proprietor of bridges by dint of sleeping beneath them, but it also evokes more symbolic bridges and crossings; in the brief afterword called "In Lieu of a Postface," Dinescu playfully confesses, "I used to be a capitalist in the days of Communism. I was the owner of bridges."

The poems Dinescu is best known for show the combined talents that critics have defined as those of "both the poet and the antipoet." His work bristles with associations, some wild, fantastic, surreal, with a gift for metaphor as mordant and incisive as it is surprising. He uses traditional rhymed stanzaic forms, as in the lyric, "Not Today" from the early 1980s:

Reeling midst the empty glasses
over wine that's never there
I carouse with death—and so time passes
on this day for fast and prayer.
Worms come crawling on the lamp
doornails sizzle, the table thrashes
I breathe the perfume of that vamp
stripped naked of her robe of ashes.

Not today, perhaps tomorrow
(the devil knows what hour's mine)
young by moments snatched from sorrow
old all too soon in time's design.

Most of his unrhymed poems are also social and political commentaries with more existential overtones, usually slangy, inevitably defiant. Throughout his career he has flaunted more and more blatant challenges to authority, foregoing the self-protective subterfuges of indirection and obliqueness. For instance, in the four-line work "So?!"—a contemporary prophetic taunt—Dinescu swaggers, "Let me have my own way with a small-town newspaper," a place to work, and the most paltry publicity, "just a stained sign-board," and after just the requisite three days of mystery, there would be revolutionary plenty and sweet liberty: "the cities will reek of vanilla / and free ports." In "Epistle on Putting Up with the Facts of Life, With a Somewhat Metaphysical Postscript," he reveals the nakedness of the emperor's terrorism: "How can one man's bad temper / despoil such vast acreage of farmland, / how can his puny chill spread like ivy over blast furnaces?" This question is hardly rhetorical in its pinpointing the cause of Romania's agricultural and industrial disasters. The work wryly ends with the laughable image of God's allowing "the Pope's hiccup / to rock the Vatican bells," sly reference to Ceauşescu's obsessive hatred of religion. Another poem, "Cats of the Vatican," employs the same metaphoric geography "where autos and angels / dare not turn into forbidden streets" and closes with an allusion to the tight restrictions on travel by referring to "the insufferable stench of passports." It is in retrospect remarkable that such poetry was published, but some think the censors wanted to buy off writers with token freedom of expression, allowing in the realm of poetry a somewhat privileged area of permissible criticism, if not quite dissidence. By the mid-1980s, however, as émigré poet Dorin Tudoran put it, Dinescu's poetry was "radicalized" sufficiently to transgress the bounds of the dictator's censors. A few lines from "A Doctor's Advice" are a reminder that

"Tragedies don't hold out too long against the heat," referring to the ate of the iceberg which sank the *Titanic* and then floated to tropical waters and to the "scorching sentences of history." the poem closes ostensibly with advice: "Go north, further north, all you dictators, / you'll pass your doctorate in cold with highest honors." The insult is clear but there are more telling, complex allusions.

In a 1991 interview, Dinescu more directly observed, "From a certain point in time the conviction that you could resist through culture turned into a noble form of cowardice." Dinescu's poetry, though it can be hermetic and obscure in some of its imagery and connections, is in one sense as public as his forbidden interviews and secretly smuggled essays became. In another sense its inner truths, like those of much modern poetry, are concealed and indirect as well, and his oeuvre suggests a broader more complex commentary on the human condition than mere protest. Dinescu has been termed "a moralist of the modern age." It is in this sense that the Romania of his poetry is what symbolically he imagines as "the space from which God has fled."

PRINCIPAL WORKS IN ENGLISH TRANSLATION: (tr. L. Ursu) Seven poems *in* 15 Young Romanian Poets, 1982; (tr. M. Cornis-Pop and R. J. Ward) Five poems *in* Micromegas, 1984; (tr. A. Deletant and B. Walker) Exile on a Peppercorn: The Poetry of Mircea Dinescu, 1985; (tr. S. Deligiorgis, A. J. Sorkin, and S. Celac) Cummins, W. (ed.) Four poems *in* Shifting Borders: East European Poetry of the Eighties, 1993.

ABOUT: Deletant, D. *introduction* to Dinescu, M. Exile on a Peppercorn: The Poetry of Mircea Dinescu (tr. A. Deletant and B. Walker) 1985. *Periodicals*—Concerning Poetry Fall 1984; Index on Censorship August 1989; Liber October 1989; Literary Review Fall 1991; Parnassus: Poetry in Review 1993; Romanian Horizon / Orizont românesc January–March 1987; Times Literary supplement May 24, 1991; World & I February 1990.

DI PRIMA, DIANE (August 6, 1934–   ), American poet, writes: "I was born in Brooklyn, New York. Both my parents [Francis and Emma Malozzi di Prima] were Italian/American, my mother's family having come from Formia, and my father's from Sicily. The first strong influence on my life was my maternal grandfather, Domenico Mallozi, who was a passionate and committed anarchist, and friend of Carlo Tresca, Emma Goldman, etc. Domenico wrote for Tresca's newspaper, *Il Martello*.

"I myself began writing at the age of seven,

DIANE DI PRIMA

as an attempt to hold back or remember some important moments in my young life. I began reading the philosophers at the age of eleven, and had discovered poetry (particularly the Romantics) by the time I was thirteen. About a year later, at the age of fourteen, I had an intense experience in which I committed myself to a life of poetry, and began writing every day.

"In 1951 I briefly attended Swarthmore College on scholarship, but left in 1953 to take an apartment on the Lower East Side where I could write full-time. At about that time I began to correspond with Ezra Pound and Kenneth Patchen. The next three of four years were a writing apprenticeship: I wrote daily, studied languages and literatures, and investigated the burgeoning art forms around me: especially jazz, abstract expressionism, modern dance, and experimental theater. In 1955 I visited Ezra Pound for two weeks at St. Elizabeth's Hospital, staying with his good friend, the painter Sheri Martinelli.

"In 1958 I published my first book of poetry, *This Kind of Bird Flies Backward*. It was self-published, though released under the imprint of Totem Press (Amiri Baraka's newly founded publishing house). At this point I began to publish a book a year—some of the next important ones were *Dinners and Nightmares* (Corinth Press) and *The New Handbook of Heaven* (Auerhahn Press)—and became known as an important writer of the emerging 'Beat' movement. During that time I cofounded the Poets Theatre (1961–1965), and founded the Poets Press (1963–1969), which published the work of many new writers of the period. I also edited the influential literary newsletter *The Floating Bear* (1961–1969), which was coedited for the first two years by Amiri Baraka.

"In 1962 I met Shunryu Suzuki Roshi in San Francisco, and began what has become a life-long study of Eastern religion, an interest which has been reflected in my poetry ever since. In 1965, I left New York City for upstate New York, where I became actively involved with meditation and closer to the world of nature. My poetry of that period (e.g., *Kerhonkson Journal*, Oyez Press) reflects these influences which remained with me thereafter. For six months in 1966–1967 I participated in Timothy Leary's psychedelic community at Millbrook, New York. This was an exceptional situation in which to learn and experience the roots of creativity. By 1968, I had moved to Northern California where I still live, leaving behind the more active and public part of my life as an artist: producing plays, working in films, editing, publishing, etc., for a more exploratory phase.

"For the past twenty-four years I have lived and worked in northern California, where I took part in political activities of the Diggers (1967–1969), lived at a commune, Black Bear Ranch (1969–1970), studied Zen and Tibetan Buddhism, Sanskrit and alchemy, and raised my five children. In 1971, I began work on my long poem *Loba*, 'The She-Wolf'. This work brings together female figures from the animal, human, and mythological worlds, and synthesizes my work in the esoteric traditions of my own European background with the experience of meditation and the landscapes of the American West. *Loba Parts 1–8* was published in 1978 by Wingbow Press in Berkeley; a new edition with over 100 pages of additional material is planned.

"In 1973 I moved to Marshall, California, a small town on the coast of Tomales Bay, where I continued my work on *Loba*, and did a great deal of visual art: collage, photography, and assemblage. While there I founded the Poets Institute in Point Reyes, which included community classes in typesetting and pasteup and a graphics office open to local artists. I also taught many classes in writing, literature, collage, visualization, and qabalah at the Point Reyes Dance Palace. In 1976–1977 I was active in the first California Arts Council, Arts-in-Social Institutions program, teaching writing at Napa State Hospital (a facility for the mentally ill).

"In 1978 I returned to San Francisco, where I taught community writing classes in the Western Addition for The Neighborhood Foundation, and worked as a psychic and a healer. From 1980 to 1986, I taught Hermetic and Esoteric traditions in poetry in a short-lived but signifi-

cant Masters-in-Poetics program at New College of California. This program was spearheaded by myself, together with the important San Francisco poets Robert Duncan and David Meltzer. In 1983, together with three colleagues, I founded the San Francisco Institute of Magical and Healing Arts (SIMHA) to teach Western magical traditions. SIMHA ran a full curriculum in astrology, qabalah, tarot, healing, and ritual, from 1983–1990.

"At present [1993] I am working as a writer and privately seeing a few students of poetry. I am the author of thirty-one published books of poetry and prose. Among the most recent are *Pieces of a Song* (City Lights) and *Seminary Poems* (Floating Island Press). *Zip Code*, my collected plays, will be published by Coffee House Press this year. My work has been translated into twelve languages, and set to music by many prominent American composers. I have read and spoken at hundreds of colleges and universities in the United States and abroad."

————

In *Memories of a Beatnik* Diane di Prima recalls that a college freshman once asked her: "What do you suppose happened to all those beatniks?" She replied: "Well, sweetie, some of us sold out and became hippies. And some of us managed to preserve our integrity by accepting government grants, or writing pornographic novels."

Uncompromising, di Prima has made no concessions to Establishment codes of behavior, living and writing on her own terms. "Poetry is not a place where you can bluff," she told Ann Waldron in 1978 (*The Beat Road*). "You speak directly to the hearts of people . . . And there's way too much speech of the brain . . . So whatever else we do, the first thing is we reactivate the feeling, we reactivate the possibility of living a life of emotion and of flesh, as well as the life of the brain."

Di Prima's poetry traces the trajectory of her life—and, in a sense, of the American counter-culture that evolved from the Beatniks to the hippies of the 1960s: experimenting with psychedelic drugs and sex, protesting the Vietnam War and environmental pollution, and studying and practicing Buddhism, Hinduism, and Zen. In *Memoirs of a Beatnik* she recalls her early years in Greenwich Village, sparing no details of her sexual activity, keeping herself by modeling (at one time for the artist Raphael Soyer) and working at odd jobs. In spite of the hardships and risks (she added a footnote in the 1988 edition of *Memoirs* cautioning her readers against the threat of AIDS), she survived and kept writing.

In 1956 she read the newly published *Howl*, by Allen Ginsberg. The experience was an epiphany for her and for her generation:

> We had come of age. I was frightened and a little sad. I already clung instinctively to the easy, unselfconscious Bohemianism we had maintained at the pad, our unspoken sense that we were alone in a strange world, a sense that kept us proud and bound to each other. But for the moment regret for what we might be losing was buried under a sweeping sense of exhilaration, of glee; someone was speaking for all of us, and the poem was good. I was high and delighted. I made my way back to the house and to supper, and we read *Howl* together, I read it aloud to everyone. A new era had begun.

This Kind of Bird Flies Backward, the title of di Prima's first collection, suggests the boldly unconventional poetry she was writing. In "Poetics," she announces her mission:

> I have deserted my past, I can't hold it
> rearguard / to preserve the language / lucidity:
> it turned over god knows enough carts in the city streets
> its barricades are my nightmares . . .
> • • • •
>
> The language shall be my element, I plunge in
> I suspect that I cannot drown
> like a fat brat catfish, smug
>   a hoodlum fish. . . .
> let the language fend for itself

By the late 1950s di Prima was in the center of the Beat movement in New York. She met Ginsberg, Peter Orlovsky, Gregory Corso, and Jack Kerouac, and was active in experimental theater, which brought her into contact with such prominent writers and artists of the movement as Frank O'Hara and Michael McClure. Among them was the poet and playwright LeRoi Jones (now Amiri Baraka), with whom she had a daughter in 1961. With Jones she published *Floating Bear*, a mimeographed monthly newsletter, the title of which she took from the boat that A. A. Milne's Winnie-the-Pooh made out of a honeypot—"Sometimes it's a boat, and sometimes it's more of an accident." *The Floating Bear*, distributed free to writers, published everything from Keats to Kerouac—Jones, di Prima, Ginsberg, O'Hara, Charles Olson, Robert Creeley, an excerpt from King James VI's "Rules on Scottish Poetry," and song lyrics by Ma Rainey. In 1961 di Prima and Jones were arrested by the FBI for sending alleged obscenity through the mails. The October 1961 issue, which had a scatological satire by William Burroughs on Franklin D. Roosevelt and other political figures, was specifically charged. A grand jury declined to indict them, however, and *The Bear* continued publication until 1969. The issues were collected in a volume in 1973.

Aided by grants from the National Endowment for the Arts in 1973 and 1979, di Prima founded several small presses where she published her own poetry and the works of others. She continued to experiment in free form, sometimes in prose, sometimes in plays, most often in poetry. *The Calculus of Variation* is a surrealistic prose novel with large sections of poetry, much of it the hallucinatory visions of a woman, who, like di Prima, moved from New York to the West, bore children, and survived the breaking up of a marriage: "Stripped of all things I love," she writes in one passage, "loving all things. The brick wall in the sunlight, the blue sky, the black smoke I move through these, as I'd move through a picture book."

Larry Smith, in a review of *Pieces of a Song* in *Small Press*, noted di Prima's "dark humor and existential sarcasm." In "The Party" she demands recognition:

> I NEED TO BE LOOKED AT
>   be seen
> & not twice a week
> I'm not a Brancusi bird
>   not self-sufficient

And in "Four Takes in a Pregnant Spring" she confesses wryly:

> Now it's 10:45 & i'm tired, but not sleepy
> so i curl up on the couch w/ my stomach
> & somebody's poems
> & wonder why i haven't got the grace & sophistication
> of john ashbery
> & do i take myself too seriously

Di Prima embraced feminism as a link to universal spirituality. Writing in 1991 of *Pieces of a Song* in *American Book Review*, Carl Solomon observed that early on in her career her "particular wave of protest had a yea-saying, life-sustaining quality . . . and she appeared as a mother-figure to the often underweaned people of hippiedom. She appears less like a guerrilla matriarch, now, and more like a female seer or wise woman." The mystical poems of her ongoing *Loba* series evoke folklore and mythology to unite female images of all cultures—Earth Mother, Lilith, Persephone, Eve—in a single image:

> you are the hills, the shape and color of mesa
> you are the tent, the lodge of skins, the hogan
> the buffalo robe, the quilt, the knitted afghan

David Baker writes of the *Loba* poems, in the *Kenyon Review*, "The she-wolf provides di Prima with a fierce, elemental hero: a rapidly moving perspective able to maneuver from ecology and politics to erotics and religion, a perspective alternatively predatory and nurturing."

Di Prima was married to Alan S. Marlowe, an actor and director, in 1962; they were divorced in 1969. She married Grant Fisher, a poet, in 1972; they were divorced in 1975. She has five children. Her fellow poet Robert Creeley wrote of her in the foreword to *Pieces of a Song*: "She is an adept and flexible provider of the real, which we eat daily or else we starve. She is kind but will not accept confusion. She is beautifully warm, but her nature balks at false responses. She is true. . . . god bless her toughness and the deep gentleness of her hand!"

PRINCIPAL WORKS: *Poetry*—This Kind of Bird Flies Backward, 1958; Dinners and Nightmares, 1961; The New Handbook of Heaven, 1962; Poets Vaudeville, 1964; Hotel Albert, 1968; Earthsongs: Poems 1957–1959, 1968; L.A. Odyssey, 1969; Revolutionary Letters, 1971; Kerhonkson Journal, 1971; Loba, Part 1, 1973; Freddie Poems, 1974; Selected Pomes 1956–1975, 1975 (enlarged ed. 1977); Loba Part 2, 1976;Loba, Part 1–8, 1978; Wyoming Series, 1988; The Mysteries of Vision, 1988; Pieces of a Song: Selected Poems, 1990; Seminary Poems, 1991. *Plays*—Zip Code: Collected Plays, 1993. *Novel*—The Calculus of Variation, 1972. *Autobiography*—Memoirs of a Beatnik, 1969 (rev. ed. 1988).

ABOUT: Contemporary Authors New Revision Series 13, 1984; Contemporary Poets, 5th ed., 1991; di Prima, D. Memoirs of a Beatnik, 1969, (rev. ed. 1988); Dictionary of Literary Biography 5, 1980; 16, 1983; Knight, A. and K. (eds.) The Beat Road: Unspeakable Visions of the Individual, 1984. *Periodicals*—American Book Review June–July 1991; Kenyon Review Winter 1992; MELUS Fall-Winter 1987; Mother Jones March–April 1992; Small Press February 1991.

DIXON, MELVIN (WINFRED) (May 29, 1950–October 26, 1992), American poet, novelist, translator, scholar, and educator, was born in Stamford, Connecticut, the son of Handy and Jessie Dixon. He earned a bachelor's degree from Wesleyan University, Middletown, Connecticut, in 1971, and a doctorate from Brown University in 1975. Dixon was assistant professor of English at Williams College, Williamstown, Massachusetts from 1976 to 1980. In that year he joined the faculty of Queens College, of the City University of New York, where he was appointed full professor in 1986. He was elected Poetry Fellow of the National Endowment for the Arts in 1984 and Artist Fellow in Fiction of the New York Arts Foundation in 1988.

As early as 1969, Dixon's life work was well under way. In an article in *Negro Digest* he characterized a new black aesthetic as a phenomenon demanding "an organic, self-creating unity of forms," with the writer discovering his

form in the process of creating it. In *Moorings & Metaphors*, Karla F. C. Holloway characterized Dixon's reading and writing perspectives as a "utopic vision characteristic of a folkloric perspective."

Dixon's poems have appeared in numerous anthologies and journals, among them the *Southern Review, Kenyon Review, American Poetry Review*, and *Callaloo*, where he was a contributing editor. His first book of poetry *Change of Territory* was published in 1983. Using language of exile and return in a search for love and selfhood, Dixon set his poems in locales ranging from the sharecropping American south to the Paris of Montmartre, and from Harlem to Africa and the Caribbean. He is the wanderer in quest of a home and an identity. In France he recalls other searchers—black Americans like Jean Toomer and Richard Wright whom he calls "Kin of Crossroads":

> In silence I wonder how many of us
> came running fugitive
> to drink this wine, seed this history
> (not of Napoleon, Versailles, or Orleans) . . .

In *Going to Africa* he expresses uncertainty about where he belongs:

> I am not afraid of searching.
> But will she welcome me? I've left
> English grammar, French phonetics, history,
> anthropology notes, the King James Version.
>
> And if not the color of her soil,
> if my dance is toe-pointed and straight,
> will she know me even as one lost son?
> "I am not the prodigal," I said more softly.

Dixon's *Ride Out the Wilderness* a book of criticism discusses African American writings from slave songs and narratives to works by Toomer, McKay, Wright, Ellison, Jones, Baraka, Hurston, Walker, Gayl Jones, Baldwin, and Morrison. He notes in his introduction that the book was focused on the "ways in which Afro-American writers, often considered homeless, alienated from mainstream culture, and segregated in negative environments, have used language to create alternative landscapes where black culture and identity can flourish apart from any marginal, prescribed place.'" In *American Literature*, Cheryl A. Wall called *Ride Out the Wilderness* "a well wrought work" and "a 'singing book' " in which "Dixon's lyrical prose honors the tradition he defines." T. O. Mason, writing in *Choice*, called it a "persuasive, impressive, and valuable study," notable for "breadth of coverage more than depth of treatment." Nevertheless, he added, "Dixon's skill as a reader and critic overcomes whatever drawbacks his approach may have."

Dixon's first novel *Trouble the Water* won the Charles H. and N. Mildred Nilon Excellence in Minority Fiction Award. It is the story of a young man whose demented mother seemingly reflects the whole fallen world; her rehabilitation leads to the psychological salvation of her son. Henry Louis Gates, writing in *American Book Review*, characterized *Trouble the Water* as "a poet's novel: which means it's propelled by the lyricism of its language, carefully crafted imagery, and a wealth of perceptual observation. . . . " He concluded, however, that Dixon might "be betrayed by the generosity of his vision."

Vanishing Rooms, Dixon's second novel, is a study of three people tragically affected by the death of a homosexual man in New York City. The *Publishers Weekly* reviewer wrote: "Utilizing three different voices in alternating chapters, Dixon creates convincing psychological characterizations" in a "provocative" novel with "strong emotional resonance." Debbie Tucker said in *Library Journal*, "Dixon's powerful tale is rich in psychological insight, with action that is at times vividly brutal."

Dixon led a peripatetic life and made friends throughout the world. In *From Harlem to Paris*, the French critic Michel Fabre discussed Dixon's first trip to Paris in 1971, after he had been awarded a French government grant and the André Istel Fellowship of the Alliance Française. Dixon "came to France in search of his cultural ancestry just as he went to Africa to find his ethnic roots." He had expected more just treatment of people of color than he found in the United States, but he was disappointed to discover an inherent racial caste system even in ultrademocratic Paris. Nevertheless, he ingratiated himself with the French and formed lasting social and professional associations, including those with Fabre and his wife Geneviève, whose *Drumbeats, Masks, and Metaphor* Dixon translated for publication in English.

In Senegal in 1974 he met Félix Morrisseau-Leroy and Jean Brièrre, who encouraged his interest in West Indian and African poetry, particularly that of Jacques Roumain, the associate of Langston Hughes. In 1983 he went to Dakar, the home of the poet Léopold Senghor. In 1991, he published his translation of Senghor's *Collected Poems*.

By the end of his life, Melvin Dixon had turned most of his attention to the literature of AIDS, from which he suffered. In the *New York Times* (June 5, 1992) Bernard Holland reviewed a production of the "Aids Quilt Songbook: 1992," which included a musical setting of some of Dixon's poems. Holland regretted that the musical

score did not well serve Dixon's "biting texts . . . laconic in their gallows humor,"which were the products of his "tight-lipped inventiveness."

Dixon delivered the keynote speech at the Outwrite Conference in 1992, only a few months before he died of AIDS at the age of forty-two. The first major assessment of his work occurred at a conference at the Graduate Center of the City University of New York on March 4, 1994. Among the last of his published poems (*Kenyon Review*, Spring 1991) is "And These Are Just a Few," a warm tribute to friends he has already lost to AIDS, and an expression of hope for the future:

> This poem is for the epidemic dead
>   and the living. Remember
>   them?
> Your neighbors, your siblings, your
>   daughters and your sons.
>
> This poem is for the epidemic
>   living and the dead.
> Remember them, remember me.

PRINCIPAL WORKS: *Poetry*—Change of Territory, 1983. *Novels*—Trouble the Water, 1989; Vanishing Rooms, 1991; *Criticism*—Ride Out the Wilderness, 1991; "Singing a Deep Song: Language as Evidence in the Novels of Gayl Jones," in Evans, M. (ed.) Black Women Writers, 1984; "Singing Swords: The Literary Legacy of Slavery," in Davis, C. T. and Gates, H. L. Jr. (eds.) The Slave's Narrative, 1985; "Toward a World Black Literature and Community," in Harper, M. S. and R. B. Stepto (eds.) Chant of Saints, 1977. *Translation*—Fabre, G. Drumbeats, Masks, and Metaphor: Contemporary Afro-American Theater, 1983; Senghor, L. S. The Collected Poems of Léopold Sédar Senghor, 1991.

ABOUT: Contemporary Authors 132, 1991; Fabre, M. From Harlem to Paris: Black American Writers in France, 1840–1980, 1991; Holloway, K. F. F. Moorings & Metaphors: Figures of Culture and Gender in Black Women's Literature, 1992; Nelson, E. S. Contemporary Gay American Novelists, 1993; The Writers Directory 1992–1994. *Periodicals*—American Book Review July/August 1990; American Literature December 1988; Choice May 1988; Essence, 1991; Negro Digest July 1969; New York Times June 5, 1992, October 29, 1992; Publishers Weekly January 18, 1991; (Village) Voice Literary Supplement May 1990.

DIXON STEPHEN (June 6, 1936–), American novelist and writer of short stories writes: "There isn't much I can say regarding what I do and how I do it. I write a first draft of a story, when I'm writing stories, and after I

STEPHEN DIXON

finish the first draft, which usually takes me an hour or two (I'm a fast typist and the creation of the story comes quickly, almost at the speed I'm typing it), I start on the final draft the next day. I start with the first page of the initial draft and I work on that first page till I feel it's perfect, not a word wrong, every sentence coordinated with the sentences around it, every paragraph, if there's more than one (and lately there hasn't been), coordinated with the paragraph preceding and following it. That first page may take me a day or two to finish. I might work on it forty times, fifty, before I'm finished it, but I also might work on it only about ten times, though that's rare. after I have a completed final draft of a second page—page 2—and repeat the whole process. A fifteen-page story could take me anywhere from 20 days to write to 30. But it all begins with the initial outburst on the first day.

"My novels are written somewhat like that. Most of my novels started off as stories and just grew. By the time they approached page 50, I knew the work was outpacing me, wanting to run away from me, and I drew it in and started it again as a novel. I work a few pages at a time, scene to scene, in a way similar to my short story writing. I write a first draft of the scene, and then rewrite it till it's a final draft. Two of my novels took me just a year to write, though I worked on them every day and all day: I wrote while I was working as a bartender and waiter at a restaurant in New York City. I wrote early in the morning, took what I wrote to work, worked on it between customers and during slow periods, and actually used much of what was said by others in the restaurants in my novel. I didn't know where the book was going but I didn't have to; the workplace provided all the material I needed, even the bomb scares, hold-ups, and especially the characters.

"I like to keep the spontaneity of the initial draft of a story and scene. That's difficult, because the impulse is to refine; my trick is to refine the disorderliness of my writing, to make it almost orderly disorderliness. That goes with the prose and the way my characters speak. I have sort of made a career in writing on inexpressibility, inelegance, misusage, inarticulateness, gracelessness and unintelligibility. I find this to be much more interesting and realistic than elegance and eloquence, or simply put, the ability to express yourself clearly.

"I don't know where my ideas come from, my stories, my novels. Only rarely do I know what I'm going to write about once I finish a work. Most times I just sit down at the typewriter with a line that's been floating around in my head and start with that; almost always that grows into a story. Things just take off. I think that's what I love most about writing: to find out what's there inside my head. I also love words and sentences and love to fiddle with them till they read well aloud. I've never had trouble starting a story and never in finishing one, at least not in more than twenty years. I don't write two things at once; I start a story, work on it till it's finished. Most stories I start I finish. At the end of year I'll throw all my unfinished stories away. If there's something I haven't said, it'll come in something I'll say.

"*Fall & Rise*, a novel of mine, was started with the idea of writing a novel. I wanted to show how two people meet and later come together at the end of the day. A simple idea and I did it in only 450 manuscript pages. *Frog*, my novel, started as a story but by the time I started writing the succeeding story, I knew I had a novel. But I wanted a novel composed of stories, novellas, novels, in addition to letters, notebooks, announcements, anything to do with writing, including poetry, essays, reviews. It took me nearly six years of writing and I worked on it almost every day.

"I am now plumbing into my subconscious more, allowing, almost, my subconscious to write the initial draft of a story and seeing what I can make of it. It hasn't been too successful, I'd say none of my work has been to successful, but I enjoy doing it—the current phase and writing in general—and it's also what I've come to do and so will have a hard time not doing it. It will probably all end with lots of flops, since I'll probably continue writing long after I should have stopped. As for what my work means, I leave that to people who read it and might write about it. My credo regarding writing is to do it, copy it, send it out and leave the rest to the rest."

Stephen Dixon was born and educated in New York City, receiving his B.A. from City College in 1958. Except for a year at Stanford on a Wallace Stegner Creative Writing Fellowship and periods as a newsman in Washington, D.C., and as a technical editor in California, most of his early working career was spent in New York City where he was a salesman, a waiter, a bartender and, for seven years, a junior high school teacher in the public schools, all the while writing short stories that he began to publish in a number of magazines including *Harper's*, the *Paris Review*, *Playboy*, the *Yale Review* and *Triquarterly*. In 1974 he won a National Endowment for the Arts grant for fiction. His first collection of short stories, *No Relief* was published in 1976 to favorable reviews, but it was not until he published his first novel *Work* a year later that Dixon gained any kind of critical recognition.

Jerome Klinkowitz finds the major theme of Dixon's work to be "the fragility of human relationships, compounded by the danger of reality running off into infinite digressions and qualifications as stability collapses." An example is a short story in *Time to Go*, "Encountering Revolution", that begins flatly: "Georgia and I are getting our son dressed to go to the dentist when the doorbell rings. Jimmy wants to wear shorts and Georgia's insisting he wear slacks and I'm saying as I go to the door that I don't care what he wears so long as she gets him out of here and I can continue practicing for my recital tonight." A neighbor tells them that civil war has broken out, and a nightmare of violence and destruction follows. With the illogic of a nightmare, the story takes shape—at once terrifying, pathetic, and absurd. The obvious comparison is Kafka, but there are no symbols, no allegorical implications in Dixon's stories. The scene is vividly realized—most often a chaotic, bizarre urban center like New York—and the central character is a readily recognized vulnerable and anxiety-prone man doing the best he can to survive with a measure of integrity and grace.

Work, a short novel, traces first the efforts of an unemployed young actor to find a job and then, with minute detail, the work he finds as a bartender, a subject on which Dixon could write from personal experience. Thomas Stumpf wrote, in the *South Carolina Review*: "There is

an attractive aimlessness about all this, and it reflects the sort of structure that we all experience from day to day: actions that are dropped or begin again at unlikely times, digressions that are never wholly irrelevant, disappear . . . All this could be made more intense, but the lack of intensity is part of Dixon's truth. Life is neither the grand opera nor the babbling idiot's tale. Its rhythms and the rhythms of art are at variance."

Howard Tetch, the center of Stephen Dixon's novel *Frog*, is a struggling writer whose style is "undecorated, conversational, unstylized, spoken, even reads at times like quote unquote bad writing." Few reviewers of Dixon's fiction have ever accused him of bad writing, but over the years a number of them have commented upon his "splatter-style," his "unstoppable prose," what he himself calls "orderly disorderliness." In spite of its apparent randomness, however, his work always coheres. According to Klinkowitz, "Dixon manages to take the most familiar and even overexploited conventions and reinvest them with a sense of novelty unknown within contemporary realism." Klinkowitz refers to the stream of imaginative inventiveness that emerges from his detailed and minute realism, the spinning out of a small incident into a series of seemingly wild yet always just possible ramifications.

In *Garbage*, Dixon again catches the rhythm of the working life of a barkeeper, this one much harassed by mobsters in the garbage collection racket: "I call the police and tell them I want a tap on my home and business phones. Next day I awake the same time I do every morning and get set for work. I'll be in at nine-thirty and open by ten and work to the end. I do that seven days a week. Been doing it for eighteen years straight, not one day off for vacation or being sick or even when I had a hundred and three fever." This feisty, tough-taking character, Fleet, survives a brutal beating, the burning of his apartment, and the destruction of his bar. Indeed, Dixon's characters are usually survivors—of broken love affairs, failed careers, street violence. But unlike the indomitable Fleet, most of them are torn by the anxieties and uncertainties of everyday life. Howard Tetch in *Frog* is harassed not by mobsters but by the pressure of his writing, his teaching job, his family obligations. His imagination explodes with visions of disaster:

> He takes off the typewriter cover, picks up the first draft of a manuscript, bounces it on the table til it's stacked and squared, puts it down, reads the title page—okay, nothing much, but he'll make it better, turn it into something—puts paper into the typewriter and sits backs and thinks. Why did I shake the baby like that yesterday? I could hurt its brain. Bleeding in the brain. Some kind of hematoma. Subdural. Read about it in the paper last week. Mother's lover did it to her four-month-old baby.

Of Dixon's other novels, *Too Late* and *Fall & Rise* are quest novels, both urban nightmares. In *Too Late* the hero's girlfriend disappears and he pursues a frustrating search on the telephone, among her friends, in a police station, meeting an assortment of weird and menacing characters who might well have stepped out of the reality of New York City. In *Fall & Rise* the hero, a mild-mannered translator of Japanese verse, sees a woman at a party, falls madly in love with her, and encounters a nightmare of obstacles in the streets of Manhattan before he ends up finally in her apartment.

By far the most ambitious and, in the judgment of reviewers, the best of Dixon's novels is *Frog*, which received a nomination for the National Book Award in 1991. *Frog* is a huge (769 pages) and sprawling celebration of the creative energy that fuels a writer's mind. Strictly speaking, it is a collection of short stories, but since its center is the birth, life, death, and rebirth of a single character, it becomes a novel. Alan H. Friedman explained in the *New York Times Book Review* that, like its title (the name of the family's pet turtle), *Frog* "is a narrative that leaps forward and lands sideways and flops over backward, croaking in dissonant pitches from chapter to chapter and contradicting itself whenever it pleases." For Friedman, Dixon never achieves the "wizardry" of Joyce's Leopold Bloom or the range of experience of Updike's Rabbit, but relies "on the crude honesty of tomtom prose in a freewheeling structure. . . ."

The *Publishers Weekly* reviewer deemed *Interstate* the equal of *Frog* in exploring the "seemingly irrational and meaningless contemporary American universe." Probing an episode of random violence on an interstate highway in which one of the two young daughters of a man driving an interstate is shot and killed in the back seat, Dixon tells the story from eight viewpoints in order to challenge the reader to "leap imaginatively into the experience." The reviewer remarked that reading "*Interstate* is like being a passenger in a car speeding along the highway of the mind, swerving in and out of what is real and imagined, on the edge of losing control yet not losing it, because the driver knows what he's doing." George Stade in the *New York Times Book Review* noted Dixon's depiction of "the potential for psychopathology hidden in normal parental love . . . and . . . the madness and violence of America, past and present." Stade termed the novel "cruelly audacious" and praised its final "muted beauty."

Although Dixon notes wryly that his writing has not been "too successful" and has referred to his "worstselling books," he has received a number of honors for his work. His short stories have been widely anthologized, including two appearances in the *O. Henry Prize Stories* (1977, 1982), and several of them have been published abroad. *Too Late* has been translated into German (1987) and is scheduled for publication in Poland. In 1983 he received a literature award from the American Academy and Institute of Arts and Letters; in 1984–1985 he had a Guggenheim Fellowship. The *Paris Review* awarded him the John Train Humor Prize in 1986. Dixon taught creative writing at New York University's School of Continuing Education in 1979 and since 1980 he has been on the faculty of Johns Hopkins University teaching in the writing seminars. He lives in Baltimore with his wife Ann Frydman, a translator and teacher of Russian literature, and their two daughters.

PRINCIPAL WORKS: *Novels*—Work, 1977, Too Late, 1978; Fall & Rise, 1985; Garbage, 1988; Frog, 1991; Interstate, 1995. *Short stories*—No Relief, 1976; Quite Contrary, 1979; 14 Stories, 1980; Movies, 1983; Time to Go, 1984; The Play, 1988; Friends, 1990; All Gone, 1990; Long Made Short, 1994; The Stories of Stephen Dixon, 1994.

ABOUT: Contemporary Authors New Revision Series 17, 1986; Contemporary Literary Criticism 52, 1991; Klinkowitz, J. The Self-Apparent Word: Fiction as Language, Language as Fiction, 1984; Stephens, M. The Dramaturgy of Style: Voice in Short Fiction, 1986. *Periodicals*—Boston Review November–December 1991; New York Times Book Review October 14, 1984; July 7, 1985; June 4, 1989; November 17, 1991; May 21, 1995; Publishers Weekly May 5, 1995; South Carolina Review November 1977; Fall 1981; Fall 1984; Fall 1986; Time August 13, 1984.

DOBYNS, STEPHEN (February 19, 1941–), American poet and novelist, was born in Orange, New Jersey, to Lester L. and Barbara (Johnston) Dobyns. His father was an Episcopal minister whose duties kept the family on the move, and Stephen grew up in New Jersey, Michigan, Virginia, and Pennsylvania. He attended high school in Detroit, spent a year (1959–1960) at Shimer College in Illinois, then enrolled at Wayne State University in Detroit where he received a B.A. in English in 1964. Directed early toward a career in writing, he took an M.F.A. at the University of Iowa in 1967. After a year of teaching English at the State University of New York in Brockport, he returned to Detroit in 1969 as a reporter on the Detroit News. "I learned a lot at the newspaper," he wrote in an afterword to his novel *The House on Alexandrine*. "It taught me how to write (or started me on that path), and it showed me aspects of the world that I would never have seen in any other way."

STEPHEN DOBYNS

By 1970 Dobyns had written two novels and was at work on two others—"four books that never got anywhere," he recalled. As early as 1969 he had planned to write a novel about Detroit and its impact on a young country boy who comes to the city for the first time. He began writing that novel in 1971, after a five-month trip to Europe, but abandoned it altogether in 1977 after several publishers rejected it. Meanwhile, however, Dobyns was publishing poetry and other novels. He went back to teaching English at the University of New Hampshire from 1973 to 1975, the University of Iowa from 1977 to 1978, Goddard College in Vermont from 1978 to 1980, and Warren Wilson College in North Carolina in 1981. Since 1987 he has taught at Syracuse University in New York. In addition to a number of awards for his poetry, Dobyns has had grants from the National Endowment for the Arts and the Guggenheim Foundation, and fellowships at the MacDowell Colony and Yaddo. In 1987 Wayne State University Press asked if he had an unpublished novel in hand. Dobyns spent the next two and a half months rewriting his early Detroit novel, and it was published as *The House on Alexandrine* in 1989.

Dobyns's vision is a dark one, but one relieved by flashes of humor and warmth. His fiction ranges from the surrealistic and macabre of *Cold Dog Soup* and *The Wrestler's Cruel Study* to the realism of his novels of crime and suspense. His poetry, even when written in the first person and chronicling intimate personal experience, is emotionally controlled, cool and detached, rather than confessional.

His first collection of poetry, *Concurring Beasts*, won the 1971 Lamont Prize conferred by the Academy of American Poets. His verse line is the sentence, a series of prose statements that arrange themselves into poetry. In "Passing the Word," he compares poetry to "a mannequin . . . wig torn off,/ arms and legs/ piled on the floor. . . . "He goes on to describe the frightening vision of "The poem at your front door at three in the morning." The poem is like a disassembled mannequin, which takes possession of the poet entering him and becoming his skeleton, "a jumble of arms and legs for you to assemble." But the poet, with a somewhat mocking ruefulness, says,

> You are unnecessarily afraid. There is no harm here.
> You can refuse to accept it and in the morning
> it will be gone and you will have forgotten it. . . .

For Dobyns there has been from the beginning no refusal to accept and to express his vision as a poet, as he said in "The Ways of Keys":

> . . . Let me
> be the door and the lock. Let me
> learn the ways of keys.

Robert D. Spector noted in the *Saturday Review* that Dobyns's best work "suffers from a lack of human warmth and feeling . . . Nevertheless, Dobyns' accomplishment is remarkable. In his first book he has consciously created a poetic world whose values and sounds are uniquely his."

With later volumes of poems Dobyns continued to display what Ralph J. Mills, in *Poetry*, calls "the wit, intelligence, and surrealist obliquity" that marked *Concurring Beasts*. *Griffon*, Donald D. George wrote in the *Hollins Critic*, "is a remarkably sophisticated second book, the imagery spare, the language pared." In his afterword to *Velocities*, Dobyns described *Griffon* as "a breaking away, a discovery of metaphor in Anglo-Saxon riddles, an attempt to find a new language and a new subject" after "the Vietnam War and the domestic craziness that accrued to it. . . . " There are many riddles in *Griffon*. In "The Giver of Gifts," "These wounds/ are the eyes by which you see me. / Is it the night you ask? . . . " In "Seeing Off a Friend," as a man is falling from the twentieth floor, his friend stops him at the tenth and asks "What have you learned in your travels?" He gives no reply, but his fall is not unwatched:

> Beneath us
> the crowd is clamoring for his arrival. . . .
> Their mouths are open like pits in the earth.
> All his answers cover their faces.

With *Heat Death*, Dobyns "shapes definitive moments or states of mind into parables," according to *The Virginia Quarterly Review*. Death is a concern, as are "dreams, loss, cruelty . . . 'the deserted beaches of the heart.'" Many of the poems deal with the difficulties of emerging as a mature poet. In "Song of the Wrong Response," Dobyns sees the poem as a mugger assaulting its reader, striking "once above the heart." "The poem / touched you above the heart and you fled." J. D. McClatchy in *Poetry* found some "fine examples of the theme-and-variations format that Dobyns is best at—the theme providing control, the variations offering surprise." He felt the book to be overwhelmed, however, by poems "about Writing The Poem."

The French painter Balthus's works inspired Dobyns's *Balthus Poems*. "I tried to turn each painting into a personal metaphor to create narrative poems seemingly free from the lyrical first person voice," he wrote in an introductory note to that collection. He begins each poem with a description of a painting but then enters into the action, which takes place "within the minds of the characters described, but more importantly still in the mind of the author," according to Peter Stitt, writing in *Poetry*. In "The Card Game" a young girl and her brother play cards, she cheating shamelessly. Dobyns has thoughts of vengeance flash through the boy's mind, but:

> . . . At last the boy reaches to
> accept the card, allows himself to be beaten as she
> already knows he will do. And what has she won?
> What will she take from this brother she loves?
> She will place his moon face in the sky to watch
> over her, keep his cat body nearby to protect her.

Stitt said of *The Balthus Poems* in *The Georgia Review* that the poems are "deeply concerned not with the meaning of the lives we lead but with the nature and possibilities of the process of art. Each poem illustrates the . . . power . . . of the unfettered imagination by telling the story that seems to be suggested by a given painting. . . . "

In *Black Dog, Red Dog*, dramatic episodes—a theft and murder, a death in a foreign country, a broken marriage—provide poetic metaphors. Andy Brumer, in the *New York Times Book Review*, called *Black Dog, Red Dog* "a collection of quasi-narrative poems," which "may produce a trancelike state of narrative expectancy . . . but what follows is often as surprising and improvisational as the most abstract, nonsequential lyric poem. . . . a harrowing book. . . . " In "Under the Green Ceiling," a man is a mere fragment of the universe:

> he's like the quivering rodent under its
> protection of leaves, terrified when the chance
> rock crashes through its green ceiling, victim
> of a world that is endlessly random and violent.

Commenting on Dobyns' sixth collection of poems, *Cemetery Nights*, David Guillory, in *Library Journal*, called him "a born fabulator, a spinner of macabre or sardonic tales." In this volume Dobyns has an especially grisly subject: "the dead decide to have a party. Helter-skelter / they hurry to the center of the graveyard, / clasp hands and attack the possibility of pleasure." *Cemetery Nights* was awarded the Melville Kane prize by the Poetry Society of America.

In Dobyns's fiction, the themes are much the same. Elements of fable balance precariously with the routines of everyday life. The scales dip heavily towards the fabulous in novels like *Cold Dog Soup* and *The Wrestler's Cruel Study* in which, Dobyns's humor is black, but in the opinion of most of his reviewers delightfully so. In *Cold Dog Soup* a dog suddenly dies and the mother of a young woman whose pet it is insists that a young man dispose of its body immediately. Carrying the corpse in a plastic trash bag, he begins an absurdly comic journey into a modern-day urban *Inferno*.

An even more fabulous but more genial novel, *The Wrestler's Cruel Study* is a send-up of the sport of wrestling told as a fairy tale, with a handsome and morally impeccable hero, Michael Marmaduke, who wrestles as "Marduk the Magnificent." Sven Birkerts, in the *New York Times Book Review* found the book a bridge between high and low culture, entertaining and significant at the same time: "The novel is utterly preposterous, and quite serious; it is a philosophical inquiry dolled up in costumes from B-movie lots. Indeed, such is Mr. Dobyns's cunning that right when we think his novel has slipped into terminal silliness, he pulls us upright with some arresting metaphysical insight."

Another of Dobyns's experiments in the near-metaphysical is *The Two Deaths of Señora Puccini*. Set in an unnamed South American city, it is a mystery unraveled in the course of a single evening in which a group of middle-aged men, friends since boyhood, meet for an elegant dinner, while outside a revolution rages. All of the characters are either the perpetrators or the victims of sexual obsession; some are both. Weaving back and forth between past and present, presenting scenes that may or may not have actually happened, Dobyns skirts the edges of magic realism. As Susannah Herbert observed in the *Times Literary Supplement*: "Stephen Dobyns pays affectionate tribute to the grand old men of Latin American letters, avoiding

both slavish imitation and cheap parody. . . .
As self-consciously clever as the writers—Borges,
García Márquez, Vargas Llosa—he acknowledges, Dobyns's language is double-edged. . . .
old cycles of appetitie and apology, desire and
delusion, recommence."

In *After Shocks / Near Escapes*, Dobyns depicts the massive earthquake that struck Chile in
1960, telling his story from the point of view of
a thirty-eight-year old Chilean woman who recalls her childhood memory of the experience.
"This book is about memory as much as about an
earthquake," Dobyns has said. The memory is
his Chilean wife's, though she was not actually
a firsthand witness. The novel also draws on the
memories of many eyewitnesses whom Dobyns
interviewed on a trip to Chile in 1988.

Dobyns has shown a similar concern for realistic detail in his crime novels, knowledgeable
about the day-to-day operations of the police not
only in the United States but also in London,
where his first novel in this genre, *A Man of Little Evils*, takes place. He also displays detailed
knowledge of the activities of firefighters pursuing an arsonist in Boston in *Dancer with One
Leg* and of drug dealers smuggling contraband
in Maine in *A Boat Off the Coast*. His most commercially successful production is his Saratoga
series, featuring Charlie Bradshaw who has a
formidable memory for Saratoga history and
classic crimes of the past. Bradshaw is a mild-
mannered, middle-aged man who has won the
affection of many readers with his downright
decency and humanity—"a kind, inquisitive
man who liked children," as Dobyns characterizes him in *Saratoga Longshot*. Over the years
since his first appearance in *Saratoga Longshot*
in 1976, Bradshaw has grown—older, heavier,
and, in a moral sense, more mature. Of Dobyns's
detective stories, "There is absolutely no flab,"
Newgate Callendar said in the *New York Times
Book Review* in 1985. "Dialogue flows naturally,
characterizations are entirely convincing, plots
are well worked out, stereotypes are avoided."

In *Velocities*, published in 1994, Dobyns collected poems from *Concurring Beasts, Griffon,
Heat Death, The Balthus Poems, Black Dog, Red
Dog, Cemetery Nights*, and *Body Traffic*, added
several new poems, one an antiwar poem dealing with the Persian Gulf war. A number of the
new poems are set in Santiago, Chile. In one,
"Santiago: In Praise of Community," he provides
a poet's coda by describing how six blind women
are able to make their way safely amid the traffic of a crowded street while laughing at a joke:

But now come the sirens. How unfair! Have those

simple sightless souls been struck after all?

No, no, it was just an old poet whacked by a truck,
blinded by the excitement of completing his ode.

Dobyns was married twice and had children
from both marriages. His second wife, Isabel
Bize, is a biologist. He began teaching at Syracuse University in New York in 1987. In 1995,
he was suspended from his teaching position after throwing a drink in a graduate student's face
at a party. He admitted that he had thrown the
drink, because, according to the *New York
Times*, she insulted his writing.

PRINCIPAL WORKS: *Poetry*—Concurring Beasts, 1972;
Griffon, 1976; Heat Death, 1980; The Balthus Poems,
1982; Black Dog, Red Dog, 1984; Cemetery Nights,
1987; Body Traffic, 1990; Velocities: New and Select-
ed Poems, 1966–1992, 1994. *Novels*—A Man of Little
Evils, 1973; Saratoga Longshot, 1976; Saratoga Swim-
mer, 1981; Dancer with One Leg, 1983; Cold Dog
Soup, 1985; Saratoga Headhunter, 1985; Saratoga
Snapper, 1986; A Boat off the Coast, 1987; The Two
Deaths of Señora Puccini, 1988; Saratoga Bestiary,
1989; The House on Alexandrine, 1989; After Shocks/
Near Escapes, 1991; Saratoga Haunting, 1993; The
Wrestler's Cruel Study, 1993; Saratoga Backtalk, 1994;
Saratoga Fleshpot, 1995; Saratoga Trifecta, 1995.

ABOUT: Contemporary Authors New Revision Series 18,
1986; Contemporary Literary Criticism 37, 1986; Contemporary Poets, 5th ed., 1991. *Periodicals*—Georgia
Review Winter 1984; Hollins Critic April 1977; Library Journal November 1, 1986; New York Times
Book Review July 21, 1991; August 15, 1993; Poetry
May 1973; October 1983; Publishers Weekly June 21,
1991; Saturday Review March 11, 1972; Times Literary Supplement September 30, 1988; May 1, 1992; The
Virginia Quarterly Review Autumn 1980.

DOERR, HARRIET (April 8, 1910–),
American novelist and short story writer, was
born in Pasadena, California. She attended
Smith College for one year, transferred to Stanford University in 1928, and left without taking
a degree; she married Albert E. Doerr on November 15, 1930. Many years later, after the
death of her husband, she returned to school,
taking creative writing courses at Scripps College and was awarded a B.A. degree by Stanford
University in 1977. She attended the Stanford
Graduate School in Creative Writing and began
writing short stories some of which were published in the *New Yorker* and the *Atlantic*. Her
first novel, *Stones for Ibarra*, was published in
1984; it won the American Book Award for first
fiction and many other awards. The novel had
its origins in Doerr's short stories later collected
in *Under an Aztec Sun* when a New York editor
suggested that she develop some of these into a
longer single narrative.

HARRIET DOERR

The title *Stones for Ibarra* refers to the Mexican custom of leaving small stones in remembrance at the place where an accident has occurred. Sara and Richard an American couple, have gone to the remote village of Ibarra to reopen a copper mine Richard's family had abandoned during the revolution of 1910; Richard will soon be diagnosed as having leukemia and given six years to live. Doerr describes Sara as a woman "who imagines neither his death nor her own, imminent or remote as they may be." Doerr shows imagination and will, fate and accident meeting in mortality. In Mexico, "they will see everywhere—a disregard for danger, a companionship with death. By the end of a year they will know it well: the antic bravado, the fatal games, the coffin shop beside the cantina, the sugar skulls on the frosted cake."

Stones for Ibarra was widely praised for the clarity of both its vision and its prose. In a *Hudson Review*, essay, Wendy Lesser explains why Doerr's "enormous authorial omniscience" does not "diminish the characters' reality": the novel "manages to combine both a firm sense of destiny and a humble respect for accident; in the gap between the two lies the freedom she gives her characters." The Mexican setting creates a world which Julie Salamon in the *Wall Street Journal* saw as "legendary, and mystical"; but, as Jonathan Yardley pointed out in the *Washington Post Book World*, Doerr "neither sentimentalizes nor romanticizes her Mexicans . . . but rather sees them simply as ordinary people who happen to inhabit a world that is not the same as ours."

In *Stones for Ibarra*, Doerr weaves her story around vignettes of the Mexican people—stories "half heard and half invented," about José Reyes, in jail for a revenge murder; about Basilio, who killed his brother; about Chuy, whose partners in a taxi-buying scheme die in a mine explosion. In revising the stories into the novel, Doerr said, "I realized how much death there was in it, violent deaths and murders and suicides."

Under an Aztec Sun continues the pattern of alternating between stories about Mexicans and stories about Americans in Mexico. The Mexican protagonists are varied: a young boy witnesses his father's seduction of his slightly older cousin; a woman tells of the miracle cure of her child born deaf and dumb after she witnessed a murder on a train. Doerr's American protagonists are usually women, middle-aged or older and widowed or divorced, coming to Mexico to learn to cope with loss.

In 1993 Harriet Doerr published her second novel, *Consider This, Señora*, which, reviewers agreed, richly fulfilled the promise of her first book. The primary emphasis shifts here from Mexicans to North Americans, but the scene remains Mexico, the village of Amapolas, where a small colony of Americans work out their individual destinies. As in *Stones for Ibarra* there is authenticity of both character and place; Mexico and Mexicans are lovingly but also realistically portrayed. Sandra Scofield, writing in the *New York Times Book Review*, noted the novel's "deeper purpose," expressed perhaps most memorably by the elderly widow Ursula Bowles, as she contemplates her death: "She could see now that an individual life is, in the end, nothing more than a stirring of air, a shifting of light. No one of us, finally, can be more than that. Even Einstein. Even Brahms."

Much was made of the fact that Doerr was seventy-three when her first book was published. Of her life as a "wife and mother, all the usual things," Doerr has reported that several people have asked, "Were you happy all those years?" "I couldn't believe the question," she said, "Nobody could possibly be happy for forty years. And if you were happy for forty years, how could you write a book?" Yet in her essay for *The Writer on Her Work*, "A Sleeve of Rain," Doerr remembers the houses she has lived in, in details that suggest much happiness. (The title refers to a Mexican idiom for rain showers which fall "on isolated patches of the landscape.") Of a California adobe house she lived in with her husband and small children for five years, built in 1816 as the gristmill for a mission, she wrote:

"How is it to come in from the street and step through

the gate in your wall?" people asked us.

And we said, "Magic."

> For it was all enchanted. The high beams tied with leather thongs, the windows set in walls four feet thick, the whitewashed interior, the border that took the place of baseboards, painted with vegetable colors in an Indian design. . . . No matter that my first typewriter occupied a table in a bedroom or that a model airplane hung from a sycamore tree. No difference the diapers drying in front of the living room fire or the tricycle in the patio.

She wrote, too, of her childhood home in California, of the sleeping porch she shared with two sisters, of their parties and poetry recitations, of their teacher "Miss Harriet Hannah Hutchins, who traveled ten miles each way on the streetcar to fill our minds with words and numbers and how to find Vesuvius on a map."

Doerr's work is built on the differences between two cultures which, she said, "charmed and startled me. I still operate on that marvelous relationship of surprise on both sides." Though her stories are often about loss, they are also about imagination—both the imagination she sees in the rituals and magic of her Mexican characters and the imagination through which her American characters compose new understandings. Numerous critics have said of Doerr's prose that it is spare, and careful. Yet her vision is not bleak. "A Sleeve of Rain" ends:

> From the desk where I write today, I face a window three-quarters full of sky. At my left hand is a chip of copper ore that shows azurite. For no other reasons than these, I see all at once that everything is possible. I have recovered my houses. Now I can bring back the rest, picnics and circuses, train rides and steamers, labels on trunks, and wreaths for the dead on front doors.
>
> I have everything I need. A square of sky, a piece of stone, a page, a pen, and memory raining down on me in sleeves.

"The room you're in, the tree outside the window, the weather. They all affect me. But what affects me most is how small we are in all the vastness," she told an interviewer in *Modern Maturity*.

PRINCIPAL WORKS: *Novels*—Stones for Ibarra, 1984; Consider this, Señora, 1993. *Short stories*—Under an Aztec Sun, 1990.

ABOUT: Contemporary Authors 122, 1988; Contemporary Literary Criticism 34, 1984; Pearlmann, M. and K. U. Henderson (eds.) Inter/view, 1990; Sternburg, J. ed.) The Writer on Her Work Vol.II, 1991. *Periodicals*—Hudson Review Autumn 1984; Modern Maturity July-August 1994; New Republic January 30, 1984; New York Times Book Review August 15, 1993; Wall Street Journal January 23, 1984; Washington Post Book World December 25, 1983.

DORFMAN, ARIEL (May 6, 1942–), Chilean novelist, poet, playwright, and critic, was born in Buenos Aires, Argentina, the son of Adolf Dorfman, economist and engineer, and Fanny (Zelicovich) Dorfman, a Spanish literature teacher. Dorfman's grand parents were Jews who came to South America around the turn of the century after fleeing pogroms in Russia and Romania. Persecuted by the Argentine government because of his leftist views, Adolfo Dorfman left for New York in 1944, where he was joined by his family the following year, to work as an economist for the United Nations. Young Ariel learned English, and displayed an early talent for painting and music; he began writing stories at the age of seven. In 1954, distressed by the political climate in the United States that was dominated by Senator Joseph McCarthy, the family moved again, this time to Chile.

Initially, Ariel Dorfman was unhappy with his family's continual displacement, and recalls, as he wrote in *Spanish American Authors*, having "spent a considerable part of my adolescence looking back with nostalgia at my life in New York." Eventually, however, he says he was "seduced" by Chile. He completed his education there, earning a degree with honors from the University of Chile, in Santiago in 1965. In 1966 he married Maria Angelica Malinarich, an English teacher and social worker with whom he has two sons. In 1967, already embarked on a promising career as a professor of Spanish literature at the University of Chile, he became a naturalized Chilean citizen. He spent the 1968–1969 academic year as a research scholar at the University of California in Berkeley, where he witnessed the student antiwar movement.

Always interested in the theater (he had written his dissertation on Shakespeare), Dorfman chose British playwright Harold Pinter's work as the subject for his first book, *El absurdo entre cuatro paredes* (The absurd between four walls). He followed this with *Imaginación y violencia en América* (Imagination and violence in America), a collection of essays. Dorfman became a full professor at the University of Chile in 1970, the same year in which Salvador Allende Gossens, the first freely elected Marxist leader in the Americas, assumed the presidency of Chile. *How to Read Donald Duck*, written in collaboration with Belgian sociologist Armand Mattelart, was Dorfman's first book to appear in English translation. It examines the use of Disney characters and other cartoon figures as tools of cultural imperialism and capitalist propaganda. A *Times Literary Supplement* reviewer of the book noted that the authors "are writing out of Allende's Chile, with more than adequate reason to be daunted by their enemies' enormity within

ARIEL DORFMAN

and without, and by their own political precariousness. Their instructions on how to read Donald Duck . . . have an earnest vivacity and a hint of apocalypse." Dorfman returned to a consideration of the politics of pop culture in a subsequent collection of essays, *The Empire's Old Clothes.*

Dorfman wrote his first novel, *Moros en la costa* during the final tumultuous months of Allende's government. Published in Argentina in the 1970s, the novel appeared in English translation as *Hard Rain* in 1990. Taking its title and epigraph from Bob Dylan's song "A Hard Rain's A-Gonna Fall," the translation is a pared down and reorganized version of the Spanish-language original. The early rumbling of the CIA-inspired coup that destroyed Allende were already being heard when the novel was written, and the book is suffused with a mixture of apocalyptic dread and resilient hopefulness. As Dorfman noted in his introduction, "I wrote this novel while, outside in the streets and among the people of Chile, a battle raged for power, a battle to determine not only who would prevail in the country but also who would get the chance to tell its story, to write its history." In the place of any sort of conventional narrative, the novel presents an array of newspaper articles, editorials, student essays, book reviews, encyclopedia entries, and prefaces to anthologies. While all this material is made up, some of it is attributed to real writers. According to Richard Burgin in the *New York Times Book Review* (1990), most of the book's various pieces "grapple directly with the political reality of Chile in the last months of Sal-

vador Allende's Socialist Government and, specifically, with the way writers reacted to the reforms that provoked a military coup." Burgin found the novel "intellectually fascinating," but lacking in "narrative tension and a fully satisfying shape. . . . Nonetheless, it is eloquent in dramatizing both the inability of art to capture reality and the unthinkableness of life without art."

The violent coup that toppled Allende and brought Pinochet to power placed Dorfman, a left-wing intellectual, in immediate jeopardy. In his introduction to *Hard Rain*, he wrote, "The liberation that the novel promised turned out quite differently, as the circumstances of its very publication show. The day it was sent to the printer in neighboring Argentina, instead of celebrating the occasion, its author, having seen his own books burned on television, was going into hiding." He took refuge in the Argentine embassy in Santiago, but the Chilean government would not grant him safe passage out of the country. Ironically, his novel came to the rescue. When it was awarded the Premio Ampliado, a major literary prize, Dorfman was allowed to leave the country. After a brief stay in Argentina, he settled in France, where he taught literature at the Sorbonne and devoted himself fulltime to the Chilean resistance movement. Obsessed with the tragedy that had befallen his country, he wrote almost nothing for two years. He broke his silence with the collection *Missing*, poems which explicitly address the horror of torture, disappearance, and murder in Chile after the coup. Many of the poems in *Missing* also appear in a subsequent collection, *Last Waltz in Santiago.*

In 1976 Dorfman took a position as chief research scholar at the University of Amsterdam, remaining there until 1980. He then accepted a Woodrow Wilson Fellowship in Washington, D.C., moved to the United States for the third time in his life, and resumed writing fiction. His odyssey of exile only reinforced his focus on the problems of Chile. He devised a painstakingly complex scheme to have his second novel, *Widows*, published in Chile. Set in a Greek village occupied by the Nazis during World War II, *Widows* is a story of peasant women who confront the military authorities, demanding to know the whereabouts of their abducted husbands, brothers, and sons. Dorfman hoped his novel could slip past Chilean censors if it had been published first in Europe in a language other than Spanish. Using a pseudonym, Eric Lohmann, he concocted an elaborate history for the book and wrote a foreword, allegedly by Lohmann's son, explaining that its author, a Danish resistance fighter, had been killed by the Nazis.

He further claimed that its Greek setting was meant to disguise its real setting—Denmark! Dorfman hoped that *Widows* could appear first in Danish, German, and French, and only later be "translated" into Spanish. When one of the book's publishers would not cooperate, his plan fell through. *Widows* was first published in Mexico and Dorfman's name appeared on the title page.

In the *New York Times Book Review*, Alan Cheuse wrote of *Widows*: "The plot resounds with the moral thunder of classic drama, specifically that of *Antigone* and *The Trojan Women*. . . . Despite the fact that . . . Dorfman has transported his novel from his native Chile to other places and times, it gains . . . emotional amplitude and political resonance precisely because of the sharply observed details of the bereaved, who suffer no less painfully from the abuses of mortal rulers than they would have from the cruelties of vengeful or indifferent gods." In the *Times Literary Supplement*, Nicholas Rankin observed, "By taking on this subject, Dorfman runs all the risks of the political novel: rhetoric, didacticism, rant. But the literary man has the edge on the political animal. *Widows* . . . achieves its best effects by distancing itself from the author's historical situation and by exercising a powerful restraint."

The Last Song of Manuel Sendero, in contrast, is a sprawling work of magical realism in which fetuses stage a revolt, refusing to be born unless adults end political and economic repression. "I can almost say that it was my intention since before I was born to write *The Last Song of Manuel Sendero*, because I felt it was in me as a primeval memory of the race," Dorfman told *Publishers Weekly* interviewer Sybil Steinberg. The story of the fetuses, who finally consent to be born, is interwoven with the tale of two Chilean exiles living in Paris. In the course of their long discussions about their country's politics, the two conceive a plan to write an anti-imperialist comic book in which their homeland becomes "Chilex."

In weaving together the two stories, that of the fetuses and that of the exiles, one utterly fantastic, the other more or less realistic, Dorfman confronted a challenge facing all serious novelists: how to best apprehend and recount a turbulent and intractable reality. "Absolute realism I think is a trap," he told *Publishers Weekly*. Discussing his novels with another interviewer in 1988, Dorfman said: "For one thing, when I write, I don't think that I am writing fantasy; I think that I'm writing reality. This is very typical of Latin Americans. The babies in *Manuel Sendero* are no less real to me than the exiles in *Manuel*

Sendero. . . . I don't think that what happens in myth is any less real than what is historically recognizable, than what you can touch and photograph."

After ten years in exile, Dorfman was permitted to return to Chile as a visitor in 1983. He remained an unrelenting critic of Pinochet, writing articles in the *Nation*, the *New York Times*, the *Los Angeles Times*, and other publication exposing and denouncing the regime's atrocities. His trips to Chile did not proceed smoothly. At one point, news of his death was announced; in 1987 he was detained at the Santiago airport and expelled from the country. After spending 1983 as a visiting professor at the University of Maryland, he moved in 1984 to Duke University, where he teaches one semester per year. When Pinochet lost a 1988 referendum on his leadership and had to leave office, Dorfman began exploring the possibility of returning to Chile permanently.

The protagonist of *Mascara*, Dorfman's next novel, is a Kafkaesque figure, a nameless man with an unrecognizable face who toils in obscurity in an out-of-the-way government agency—the Bureau of Traffic Accidents. A photographer by trade, the faceless man possesses one very remarkable talent: he can recall every face he sees. He falls in love with a women with no memory, and imagines the two of them joined in a perfect union: "I with no face and she with no past, the two mirrors reflecting nothing more than each the other and the other again." As Robert Atwan observed in the *New York Times Book Review*: "*Mascara* . . . can be read as an ominous fairy tale, a literary horror story, a post-modern version of Jekyll and Hyde. But the book is also a parable of human identity and paranoia engendered by authoritarian politics. . . . Ariel Dorfman has handled these themes directly in his other works. In *Mascara* he takes a more oblique approach to capture the true face of political power."

My House is on Fire is a collection of eleven of Dorfman's short stories, all of which are set in a repressive military regime. One of the stories, "Reader", concerns a censor who begins reading a novel in which he discovers himself to be the main character. Dorfman adapted the story for the stage, and the play had its premiere in Santiago in 1989. He has also adapted his novel *Widows* for the stage. It won the Kennedy Center/American Express New Plays Award in 1988.

Dorfman's best-known play, *Death and the Maiden*, opened in London in 1991. In 1992 it came to Broadway, where it was directed by Mike Nichols and starred Glenn Close, Gene

Hackman, and Richard Dreyfuss. The play's precise setting is not identified, but its resemblance to post-Pinochet Chile is unmistakable. Gerardo, a lawyer who has just been appointed to a presidential commission assigned to investigate human-rights abuses under the old regime, has a flat tire on the way to his villa and is assisted by a Dr. Miranda, who drives Gerardo home. When Gerardo returns with the man he considers a kindly stranger, his wife, horrified, insists that the doctor participated in her rape and torture fifteen years earlier when she was a political prisoner. The play's American production received mixed reviews. In the *Nation*, Thomas M. Disch called it "a thriller for those who don't like thrillers. People who do will be apt to find it tame, predictable and preachy." Frank Rich, in the *New York Times* found the play itself "tautly constructed as a mousetrap." He faulted Nichols's production, however, as a "tedious trivialization of Ariel Dorfman's work. . . . " A film version of *Death and the Maiden* by Roman Polanski was released in 1994.

Dorfman cites Kafka, Faulkner, and Günter Grass as among his favorite 20th-century authors. "But the fundamental literary influences in my life have been the Latin American writers," he told an interviewer: Pablo Neruda, Julio Cortázar, Gabriel García Márquez. Contemporary Latin American fiction is the subject of the critical essays in his collection *Some Write to the Future*.

Konfidenz, Dorfman's 1994 novel, unfolds almost entirely by means of telephone conversations. A woman has come to Paris because she believes her lover, in flight from a right-wing dictatorship, to be in danger. She is telephoned in her hotel room by a man who claims to be a political colleague and friend of the lover, and who seems to know all about the woman. It is not until later that the reader learns that the time is not now, but 1939. "Suddenly," Sven Birkerts wrote in the *New York Times Book Review*, "we are on a revolving wheel of lies and concealments, and verifiable truth is nowhere to be found." The caller piles deception on deception. One lie is erased by another. Birkerts commented that if the book is seen in the light of an "allegorical conceit" Dorfman's "execution is deft." According to Birkerts, "*Konfidenz* looks to be a parable about kinds of truth—those of circumstance versus those of the exigent heart."

Dorfman's literary enterprise is a manifold one. In addition to being a noted critic and scholar, he has established a solid reputation as a novelist, poet, and dramatist. While his work is rooted in the experiences of one country, his vision has a universal appeal. His books have been translated into more than thirty languages. As he told *Publishers Weekly*, "[O]ur literature comes from an old Spanish tradition, but it's also created by all these voices which come from real people and from popular culture. This is one of the central issues of my generation, and it ends up being a question of: What is reality? How can you narrate a reality which has so many different fragments?"

Dorfman, speaking in the voice of the narrator in *Konfidenz*, answered the question of *why* he must attempt to convey his reality: "It would be a crime to steal . . . that faith . . . that faith which keeps on shouting silently from inside . . . that the world does not have to be the way it is. . . . "

PRINCIPAL WORKS IN ENGLISH TRANSLATION: *Nonfiction*—(with A. Mattelart) (tr. D. Kunzle) How to Read Donald Duck: Imperialist Ideology in the Disney Comic, 1975, 2d. ed. 1984; (tr. C. Hansen) The Empire's Old Clothes: What the Lone Ranger, Babar, and Other Innocent Heroes Do to Our Minds, 1983; Violence and the Liberation of the American Reader, 1990; Missing Continents, 1990; (with M. de la Parra and P. Errazuriz) Chile from Within, 1973–1988 (ed. S. Meiselas) 1990; (tr. G. Shivers and A. Dorfman) Some Write to the Future: Essays on Contemporary Latin American Fiction, 1991. *Novels*— (tr. S. Kessler) Widows, 1983; (tr. G. Shivers and A. Dorfman) The Last Song of Manuel Sendero, 1987; Mascara, 1988; (tr. G. Shivers and A. Dorfman) Hard Rain, 1990; Konfidenz, 1994. *Short stories*—(tr. G. Shivers and A. Dorfman) My House Is on Fire, 1990. *Poetry*— (tr. E. Grossman) Missing, 1982; (tr. E. Grossman and A. Dorfman) Last Waltz in Santiago and Other Poems of Exile and Disappearance, 1988. *Drama*—Death and the Maiden, 1991.

ABOUT: Contemporary Authors 124, 1988; 130, 1990; Contemporary Literary Criticism 48, 1988; Flores, A. (ed.) Spanish American Authors: The Twentieth Century, 1992; Tucker, M. (ed.) Literary Exiles in the Twentieth Century, 1991. *Periodicals*—Boston Review April 1987; Chasqui: Revista de Literatura Latinamericana May 1991; Los Angeles Times Book Review June 12, 1983; Nation May 11, 1992; New York Times July 31, 1991; March 8, 1992; March 18, 1992; New York Times Book Review July 24, 1983; February 15, 1987; November 6, 1988; December 16, 1990; December 25, 1994; Publishers Weekly October 21, 1988; Salmagundi Spring/Summer 1989; Times Literary Supplement February 23, 1973; December 9, 1983; (Village) Voice Literary Supplement April 1987.

DORRIS, MICHAEL (January 30, 1945–), American novelist and anthropologist, was born in Dayton, Washington, the only child of Jim and Mary Besy (Burkhardt) Dorris. After his father, a member of the Modoc Indian tribe, was

MICHAEL DORRIS

killed in World War II, Dorris and his mother
moved to Louisville, Kentucky, where they lived
with his aunt and grandmother. His family was
not well off, but he went to Georgetown University on a scholarship, graduating *magna cum
laude* in 1967 with a degree in English. He went
on to Yale to study the history of theater. While
a graduate student, he began taking classes in
American Indian ethnology, then switched majors, receiving a master's degree in anthropology
in 1970.

Following short stints teaching at the University of the Redlands (1970–71) and Franconia
College (1971–72) he jointed the faculty of Dartmouth College, where he founded and served as
chairman of the Native American Studies department. During the 1970s, he wrote *A Sourcebook for Native American Studies* and *Native
Americans: 500 Years After* as well as academic
articles and chapters of textbooks such as
Pre-Contact North America.

His ambitions became more literary, however,
when in 1979 he became reacquainted with
Louise Erdrich, a young writer who had been a
student of his at Dartmouth in the early 1970s.
In New Zealand for a year to do research comparing Native American and Maori peoples, and
without the burden of teaching, Dorris found
the time and the desire to try his hand at writing
fiction again, something he had given up fifteen
years earlier. Erdrich and Dorris exchanged stories and poems, and upon his return to the United States, they began collaborating on fiction for
magazines such as *Redbook* under the pseudonym Milou North. They were married in 1981,

and began to work closely together. "The person
whose name is on the book is the one who's done
most of the primary writing," Dorris explained
in *Publishers Weekly*. "The other helps plan,
reads it as it goes along, suggests changes in direction, in character and then acts as editor."

Dorris's first novel, *A Yellow Raft in Blue
Water*, is a story narrated by three generations
of Native American women: a fifteen-year-old;
her mother, a dying alcoholic; and the family
matriarch. Austin MacCurtain, in the *Times Literary Supplement*, called the differing versions
of the experiences that connect the three women
"a Faulknerian device." This device, according
to MacCurtain, gives "density and richness of
texture to the story." allowing its themes to
"emerge from the tale itself, without any need
for an omniscient authorial voice." Anatole Broyard, in the *New York Times*, thought the story
cinematic in its receding and advancing "as each
character goes further into the past and deeper
into motives. . . . The film runs in reverse and
the dead come back to life, the child re-enters
the womb. . . . " MacCurtain had one reservation —that the literary quality of Dorris's writing "betrays to some degree the integrity of his
characters" who are "semi-literate, the confused,
the wilfully blind."

The same objection was applied by Polly Shul-
man in the (Village)*Voice Literary Supplement*
to *Morning Girl*, a children's story of a Taino sister and brother who meet Columbus. She called
the writing "self-consciously beautiful." Most reviewers, however, were charmed: "The imagery
washes across the pages like the tides and shapes
a place that is far away in time and distance,"
Julie Cummins wrote in *School Library Journal*.

With *The Broken Cord*, Dorris returned to
nonfiction. The book is a moving personal account of his struggle to raise a son he had adopted before his marriage and a shocking exposé of
the ravages of alcohol on Native Americans. His
Sioux child Adam, as he is called in the book, was
diagnosed with fetal alcohol syndrome after a
long struggle with learning and motor problems.
Dorris "traveled the country collecting the bleak
stories. . . . babies born reeking of cheap wine,
babies born with delirium tremens," Patricia
Guthrie said in the *New York Times Book
Review*. "The alarming statistics and consequences of fetal alcohol syndrome are skillfully
interwoven with the human story of one of its
victims" in prose that is "clear and affecting,"
she added.

In 1989 *The Broken Cord* won the National
Book Critics Circle Award for general nonfiction. The book chronicles Dorris's "hopes and denial, frustration, rage and helplessness." wrote

Dulcy Brainard in *Publishers Weekly*, as it "describes a father's gradual acceptance of the shape of his child's life, a future radically different from the one anticipated." The book prompted U.S. Senate action on the problem of fetal alcohol syndrome and, reached a wide audience when it adapted into a television movie in February 1992.

In 1991, Dorris and Erdrich published *The Crown of Columbus*, their first collaboration under both their names. The story is alternately narrated by two college professors: Vivian Twostar, Native American single mother, and Roger Williams, a poet from an upper-class New England background. Vivian is writing an article from the Native American perspective on the quincentenary of Columbus's arrival in the Americas, and Roger has long been at work on an epic poem about Columbus's life. When Vivian stumbles across pages from Columbus's lost diary in a library she, Roger, their newborn daughter, and Vivian's unruly teenage son, head off to the Bahamas in search of the rest of the diary.

While many reviewers found *The Crown of Columbus* entertaining, some felt that Dorris and Erdrich tried to do too much. Robert Houston wrote in the *New York Times Book Review* (1991) that "it's as if in hoping to disguise any didactic intent, it tries on too many costumes—domestic comedy, paperback thriller, novel of character, love story—and finally decides that, unable to make up its mind, it will simply be them all at once." While troubled by a few historical inaccuracies, Kirkpatrick Sale wrote in the *Nation* that he found "some near interspersings of debunking and demythifying along with some artful presentations of Indian-angled perceptions of the Columbus legacy. Columbus, insofar as he matters at all, is rightfully treated as a 'naive innocent' in a world he could never understand, even as he set about laying waste to it."

Dorris and Erdrich live in an 18th-century farmhouse in Cornish, New Hampshire, with five children: Jeffrey Sava and Madeline, whom Dorris adopted while still single, and three younger daughters, Persia, Pallas, and Aza. Their oldest son Abel, the subject of *The Broken Cord*, died in September 1991 at the age of 23 after being struck by a car. Because of the success of his books, Dorris has been able to devote almost all of his time to writing.

PRINCIPAL WORKS: *Nonfiction*—Native Americans: 500 Years After, 1975; Native Americans Today, 1975; Man in the Northeast, 1976; A Sourcebook for Native American Studies, 1977; A Guide to Research in Native American Studies, 1984; The Broken Cord, 1989; Rooms in the House of Stone, 1993; Paper Trail, 1994;

Essays, 1994. *Short stories*—Working Men, 1993. *Novels*—A Yellow Raft in Blue Water, 1987;(with Louise Erdrich), The Crown of Columbus 1991. *Children's books*—Morning Girl, 1992.

ABOUT: Chaukin, A. & N., eds. Conversations with Louise Erdrich and Michael Dorris, 1994; Contemporary Authors New Revision Series 19, 1987; Reference Encyclopedia of the American Indian, 1990. *Periodicals*—Nation October 21, 1991; New York Times May 9, 1987; New York Times Book Review June 7, 1987; April 28, 1991; New York Times Magazine April 21, 1991; Publishers Weekly August 4, 1989; School Library Journal October 1992; Time April 29, 1991; Times Literary Supplement March 11, 1988; August 24, 1990; July 19, 1991; December 2, 1994. (Village) Voice Literary Supplement September 9, 1986; Writer's Digest June 1991.

DRAPER, THEODORE (September 11, 1912–), American historian, was born in Brooklyn, New York, the son of Samuel and Annie Draper. In 1933 he received his bachelor's degree from Brooklyn College, where he identified with the political Left. In his freshman year he joined the National Student League (NSL), most of whose leaders were members of the Young Communist League. Draper, however, did not belong to the Young Communist League, nor did he join the Communist party. Rather he chose to be a so-called fellow traveler. His first editorial job was at the helm of the *Student Review*, the organ of the NSL.

After graduating from Brooklyn College, Draper entered the graduate school of Columbia University. Though he early aspired to an academic career, when an editor of the *Daily Worker*, the official Communist party organ, offered him the job of assistant foreign editor of the paper, Draper accepted. He remained there for two years and then did a two-year stint as foreign editor of *New Masses*, a weekly of the intellectual Left.

In 1939 Draper published a book on the causes of World War II. In the following year, when France fell to the Nazis, he described the French collapse as signifying "new problems and new conditions" in Europe. This view brought Draper into the Communist party line, which held the Nazi–Soviet nonaggression pact to be in full force. Draper wrote: "The real issue for me was whether to change my mind or at least stifle what I believed. If I gave way now, could I ever think of myself and still remain a Communist?" Draper's answer was no; however, he did not break with the movement immediately.

In 1943 Draper was inducted into the army and, in his words, was "saved from thinking any

THEODORE DRAPER

more about American Communism, at least for the next three years." While in the army he wrote his first two books: a military and political history of the fall of France and a history of the role of his army unit in defeating the Nazis. Both volumes were well received.

After World War II, the Fund for the Republic, established by the Ford Foundation, engaged Draper to produce an extensive study of American communism from its beginning to the end of World War II. Draper completed *The Roots of American Communism* in 1957; he ended it with the year 1923, far short of the projected terminal date. The book's thesis is that the character, not controlled from Moscow, but was a response to economic inequality and political turmoil. Its strength came from immigrant labor and from attempts to organize workers into unions. Draper then recounts how in time the inchoate American Communist party became appendage of Russian Bolshevism.

Draper's book was well received. Arthur Schlesinger, Jr. wrote in the *New York Times Book Review* (1957) that it "provides the indispensable foundations for any understanding of American Communism." George Kennan then the country's leading authority on the Soviet Union, observed that the book was "an outstanding contribution to knowledge and understanding of the Communist movement in this country."

The Fund for the Republic approved Draper's request to produce a second volume that would cover the remainder of the period through World War II. This second volume, however,

completed in 1960, brought the history on the year 1929, still far short of the goal. *American Communism and Soviet Russia* developed more fully the theme of the Soviet domination of American Communism. Michael Harrington, wrote in *Commonweal* "It will long be a definitive source volume and analysis of the Stalinization of American Communism."

The Draper volumes on American Communism have enjoyed wide influence. In 1979 Draper's research files for these studies, comprising thirty-six linear feet, were purchased by Emory University for its library.

Draper next turned his attention to Fidel Castro and the Cuban revolution. Because Fund for the Republic was unable to finance a third volume on American Communism, Draper took a job as associate editor of the *Reporter*. The *Reporter* wanted an authoritative article on Cuba, where Fidel Castro had recently won political power, and commissioned Draper to write it.

Over the next five years, Draper produced two volumes: *Castro's Revolution: Myths and Realities*, in 1962, and *Castroism: Theory and Practice*, in 1965. Draper's thesis in the first volume is that Castro subverted the so-called peasant revolution and converted Cuba into an oppressive Marxist-Leninist state. The book includes an exchange of correspondence between Draper and the pro-Castro *New York Times* correspondent Herbert L. Matthews. In the second volume, Draper examines the first five years of Castro's rule, providing the sociological and economic background to, as well as the history of, the Castro regime. Draper's volume on Cuba were translated and widely distributed in Latin America and are still recognized as important primary studies of the Cuban revolution.

Draper then produced four books on such disparate topics as the Vietnam War, the American invasion of the Dominican Republic, Israel and world politics, and black nationalism. All four were for the most part well received.

In *Abuse of Power*, Draper contends that "the Vietnam War is on the Cuban and Dominican crisis writ large." He identifies a pattern in the three interventions, an abuse of power whereby the United States, failing in diplomatic negotiations, resorted to military might to gain its objectives. This, he holds is counterproductive and results ultimately in human calamity. In *Israel and World Politics* and in *The Rediscovery of Black Nationalism*, Draper is again concerned with antecedents—in the case of the former volume the roots of the Arab–Israeli war of June 1967, and in the case of the latter the 18th-century origins of black identity and self-determination.

In *The Dominican Revolt* Draper revised and enlarged essay he had written in 1965–1966. Draper maintains that the threat of a Communist takeover in the Caribbean republic was neither substantial nor genuine, and the United States was failed in not supporting Dominican moderates. The critic Irving Howe called it "intellectual journalism at its best," and Senator Ernest Gruening of Alaska wished that "copies could be sent to every member of the Foreign Affairs Committee of the Senate."

After *Rediscovery*, Draper produced no new book for thirteen years, but his output of magazine articles continued unabated. In 1983, Draper published *Present History. A Present of Things Past*, followed seven years later. Both books contained essays originally published in such periodicals as *Commentary, Dissent, New Republic, Encounter*, and *New York Review of Books*.

Present History, in which the essay treat mainly international affairs, produced praise from reviewers, but contradictory reactions to Draper's strengths as a writer. Richard Margolis, in the *New York Times Book Review*, wrote that the book deals with urgent dilemmas, using the light of history to dispel current murk. Draper, however, "seems less interested in policy than in personality," according to Margolis. Conor Cruise O'Brien, writing in the *New York Review of Books*, termed Draper "not at his best in dealing with personalities" but "fascinating and instructive . . . in the discussion of concepts and especially in the illustration, analysis, and assessment of key terms in the vocabulary of international affairs." O'Brien deemed Draper's prose full of "lapidary aphorisms."

Paul Berman, in the *New York Times Book Review* reviewing *A Present of Things Past*, another collection of essays many of which are book reviews, described Draper as "an investigative book reviewer" who draws on "broader research than is provided by the book in question." Berman added that Draper is a writer of great "moral power" which he "deploys in polemical volleys." Despite what Berman terms Draper's "frisky, vehement style," he found the author to be "a man of steady political judgment."

In *A Very Thin Line*, Draper applied his moral intelligence to a historical analysis of the Iran-contra affairs—a scandal of the Reagan administration in which arms were sold to an inimical Iranian regime in returnfor a promise of the release of hostages the Iranians were holding. The profits from the arms sales were to be used to fund rebels against the government of Nicaragua—the "Contras"—in defiance of the wishes of Congress. Many reviewers termed Draper's

"the definitive account" of these events. Tom Wicker, in the *New York Times Book Review* said that Draper demonstrates that an Iranian "con man . . . convinced them Poindexter and North, American security advisors and therefore President Reagan that he and they were dealing with moderates in Iran, though there was no evidence that any such moderates existed." According to Wicker, "The Iran-contra affairs were not aberrations unique to the circumstances and persons involved. In . . . Draper's meticulous and disturbing account, they show instead where arbitrary power can lead us." Anthony King, writing in the *Economist*, believed Draper's lesson is that it is a good idea to think through risky projects, and have them carried out by a cadre of reliable and responsible civil servants who "would not be so stupid as to be so deceitful. . . ."

Theodore Draper has been a Senior Research Fellow at the Hoover Institution on War, Revolution, and Peace, Stanford University, 1963–1974; member, Institute for Advance Study, 1968–1973; Research Fellow, Russian Research Center, Harvard University; Senior Fellow, Research Institute on Communist Affairs, Columbia University; member, American Academy of Arts and Sciences; member, Council on Foreign Relations. He has received fellowship awards from the National Endowment for the Humanities, the Guggenheim Foundation, the Lehrman Institute, and the Ford Foundation. In 1992 Draper was awarded the honorary degree of doctor of letters by Emory University.

Draper resides in Princeton, New Jersey. He is divorced and has son, Roger, who is also a writer.

PRINCIPAL WORKS: Six Weeks' War, 1944; The 84th Infantry Division in the Battle of Germany, 1946; The Roots of American Communism, 1957; American Communism and Soviet Russia, 1960; Castro's Revolution: Myths and Realities, 1962; Castroism: Theory and Practice, 1965; Abuse of Power, 1967; Israel and World Politics, 1968; The Dominican Revolt: A Case Study in American Policy, 1968; The Rediscovery of Black Nationalism, 1970; Present History, 1983; A Present of Things Past, 1990; A Very Thin Line: The Iran-Contra Affairs, 1991.

ABOUT: American Men and Women of Science: Social and Behavioral Sciences, 1973; Contemporary Authors 13–16, 1975; Draper, T. American Communism and Soviet Russia, reprint, 1986; Draper, T. preface to Present History, 1983; Draper, T. introduction to A Present of Things Past, 1990; Institute for Advanced Study, Community of Scholars . . . Faculty and Members, 1930–1980; Who's Who in America, 1992–1993; Who's Who in the World, 1974–1975. *Periodicals*—Commentary May 1966; June 13, 1991; Commonweal June 10, 1960; Economist, June 22,

1991; New York Review of Books September 29, 1983; March 15, 1990; New York Times Book Review March 10, 1957; May 22, 1983; January 28, 1990; May 26, 1991.

DUBERMAN, MARTIN (BAUML) (August 6, 1930–), American historian and dramatist, was born in New York, the son of Joseph, a Ukrainian Jewish immigrant garment manufacturer, and Josephine (Bauml) Duberman. He was educated at Yale University, where he received his B.A. in history in 1952, and at Harvard, where he received an M.A. in 1957. He taught at Yale from 1957 until 2962, and at Princeton from 1962 until 1972, when he joined the faculty of Herbert H. Lehman College of the City University of New York as Distinguished Professor of History. He is the founder and director of the Center for Lesbian and Gay Studies at the City University Graduate Center, and a member of the board of directors of the New York Civil Liberties Union. Martin Duberman has received a special award from the National Academy of Arts and Letters for contributions to literature; the Bancroft Prize for his first book, a biography of Charles Francis Adams; and the Vernon Rice-Drama Desk Award for his play *In White America*. He was nominated for the National Book Award for his biography of James Russell Lowell.

In an interview in *Radical History Review*, Duberman stresses that the theater "has always been part of my temperament." Although he abandoned his early intention to be an actor, he has continued to write plays, and has characteristically used the theater as a medium for combining scholarship with public presentation, and for exploring black and gay issues that also concern him as a historian and biographer. He describes himself in the same interview as a "malcontent," who has always been dissatisfied with conventional modes of explaining and interpreting the past, and one who has rejected history "as a vehicle for either self-expression or social change." Duberman's investigations of the historical past, which have concentrated first on black history and later on gay and lesbian history, illustrate his skepticism about the historian's ability to interpret personal motivation.

Although he doubts the ability of history to illuminate the causes of events and the nature of personalities, Duberman, who describes himself as a "nominalist," believes "there is more chance of knowing something if we deal with single individuals" and has primarily been engaged with personal history rather than with accounts of entire periods. He admits that much of his

MARTIN DUBERMAN

work has been inspired by the political concerns of his own time, and by his personal progress to self-discovery as a homosexual. The primary usefulness of history, Duberman seems to say, is that by attempting to understand it we can discover something about ourselves. It was therefore appropriate at the height of the civil rights movement to compose the documentary play *In White America* and in the 1990s to seek out the private and hidden lives of homosexuals in order to understand the cultural pressures that contribute to the search in contemporary society for recognition of homosexuality as a separate existence.

Although Duberman's two earliest books, biographies of Charles Francis Adams and James Russell Lowell, were not notable for revisionist attitudes toward the history they related, his interest in reexamining the past is plainly evident in his well-known essay "The Abolitionists and Psychology," which appeared in 1962 and was reprinted in the collection *The Antislavery Vanguard* in 1965. The essay did much to redeem the nineteenth-century predecessors of the civil rights movement from the charge that they were motivated by a kind of collective neurosis. It was also written to explain and justify contemporary agitation. Duberman wrote, in the preface to *The Antislavery Vanguard*: "For while the past should never be distorted to meet present needs, the focus of historical investigation will always reflect those needs; that is, inquiry will be directed, consciously or otherwise, toward those areas of past experience which seem to have most pertinence for our own." To acknowledge that a historian's work may be motivated by the perception that the past has urgent relevance to the present "is not presumptive proof," Duberman argues, "that his historical interpretations will be distorted." In fact, such a point of view may reveal connections that had been unnoticed, such as that the abolitionists made arguments for the freedom of black people which could serve the cause equally well at the time Duberman was writing: "If we once understood . . . how much the debate on the 'Negro Question' has already been rehearsed, we might not endlessly restage it."

Duberman's documentary play *In White America*, produced Off-Broadway in 1963, dramatized the long-ignored claims of blacks for equality by presenting their experiences in their words. In this assemblage of documents, which the *New York Times* drama critic compared to "a living newspaper," actors read from eyewitness accounts of slavery and segregation, and also from the writings of white figures such as Thomas Jefferson and Woodrow Wilson. Much of Duberman's energy during the 1960s and early 1970s went into the writing of plays for the Off-Broadway stage. Two of these productions, the double bill *The Recorder* and *The Electric Map*, performed in 1970, and *Visions of Kerouac*, performed in 1976, attracted critical attention. Both *The Recorder* and *The Electric Map*, which were performed together as *The Memory Bank*, reflect directly on the role of the historian in a way that is satirical and undermines the pretense of objectivity. In *The Recorder*, a young, nervous historian interviews an "Authority" and records his answers into a tape recorder. The machine, like the entire process of turning the subjective memory into a historical narrative, is faulty, and garbles the responses. By the time the play is over neither the two characters nor the audience is certain what has been said and the truth is lost, as Walter Kerr pointed out in the *New York Times*, "between tendentious questioning and faulty remembering." *The Electric Map* also explores the fallibility of history by exploiting another mechanical symbol, an electronic tourist map of the Battle of Gettysburg. As the two actors, brothers who quarrel about their past, dispute the meaning of certain events in their childhood, a tape recording describes the battle in the clichéd terms of official historical rhetoric as a conflict between brothers. Finally, the map itself, an image of events, collapses. Kerr found this play too determined to strain after symbolic significance: "Mr. Duberman has not been wise enough to let small enough alone." In his introduction to the published version of the play Martin Gottfried agreed: "The analogy between the Civil War and the war between these brothers is coy, even more so when it is extended as it is, implicitly, to the war between individualists and conformists . . .   homosexuals   and heterosexuals."

These plays dramatize the discontent with historical study that Duberman makes explicit in his essay "On Becoming a Historian," which he included in *The Uncompleted Past*, a three-part collection of articles written during the previous decade. The volume addresses the historical profession in general, the historical background to the civil rights movement, and, in a final section, the need for educational reform. The social historian Eric Foner, reviewing the collection in the *New York Times Book Review*, found Duberman's attack on his own profession to be merely personal: "Duberman's denial of the relevance of history seems misconceived. Indeed his conception of historical relevance strikes me as exceedingly mechanical—he denies that history can be relevant because he feels it can never aid directly in the eradication of social ills. In this formula there is no room for the imaginative use of historical analogies."

His various discontents—with his profession, his uncertain social identity, and the American political climate—were carried forward into the writing of *Black Mountain: An Exploration in Community*, an effort to convey a sense of the past through the consciousness of the historian, who openly describes his own sentiments while recounting the history of a radical educational institution. Although several critics commended Duberman for the vitality of his descriptions of the personal relations that influenced avant-garde artistic experiment at Black Mountain, the general view of he book was that the author's experiment had failed. Herbert Leibowitz's *New York Times Book Review* assessment was representative: "including his 'feelings, fantasies, and needs,' however sincere, ends up much ado about very little: Duberman has knocked down a methodological straw man. Ironically, *Black Mountain* is most valuable as documentary history . . . The book is disappointing—and alarming—because Duberman turns his back on the historical imagination itself."

What Leibowitz and Eric Foner found lacking in Duberman's writing is an unwillingness to present historical events so that the past appears to be not only completed but also subject to analysis in terms that satisfy the wisdom of hindsight. This is, however, the very aspect of historical writing that Duberman has consistently rejected. We should not study history, he believes, if our own experience does not prompt us to see a relevance between past and present. Since Duberman is a radical, constantly involved in social reform, he examines the past in order to lay the foundation for his views about the present. Duberman's own radicalism does much to explain his uneasy with traditional historiography, his virtual dismissal of his own work on Adams and Lowell, and the success of the documentary play *In White America*, in which his gifts for research and selection are displayed while his own judgment remains implicit.

Duberman's search for a style and subject that would allow him to re-create the past honestly while revealing truths that have profound implications for present social policy and thought was rewarded in his work on Paul Robeson. Robeson, a brilliantly successful student and athlete and later the most prominent black actor and singer of his generation, seemed to his contemporaries to embody the hopes of those who wished to create an egalitarian society. By openly associating himself with Communist ideology, in which he saw promise of true equality, Robeson earned the contempt and enmity of critics on both sides of the political spectrum: from McCarthy sympathizers of the early days of the cold war, who regarded him as a traitor, to the agitators for civil rights on the left wing, who disregarded his views as old-fashioned and turned to younger leaders in the black community. For Eric Foner, writing in the *Voice Literary Supplement* this book is "essential reading for anyone who would understand the racial history of our century . . . Duberman tells the story of Robeson's career as well as it is ever likely to be told." Duberman identifies with Robeson as a outsider in society but at the same time rigorously excludes his own feelings from the narrative and allows the complex facts to speak for themselves. He denies any understanding of Robeson's motivations, and Robeson himself left no personal memoirs to confirm such speculation. On the other hand, Duberman's painstaking re-creation of events, which involved suing the FBI under the Freedom of Information Act to obtain documentation, presents the reader with the framework in which Robeson made his unhappy choices. Nathan Higgins wrote in the *Nation* that Duberman recaptures "the greatness of Paul Robeson and the ambiguity and treacherousness of his time while guarding his own critical sense, avoiding many partisan and ideological traps."

In his later work Duberman has not excluded his personal feelings as a homosexual from his work as a historian and dramatist. The interviewer in *The Recorder* is at times probing for homosexual elements in his subject's personality; the historian-protagonist in *Black Mountain* speaks of his sexual identity and sympathy with the part-homosexual culture of the college; and

in *Visions of Kerouac*, a biographical drama staged in 1976, Duberman advances the thesis that Kerouac's unhappiness can be attributed to his repressed homosexuality. Mel Gussow wrote in his *New York Times* review that this was "a shaky amalgam of fact and fiction." Erika Munk, in the *Village Voice*, was much harsher, accusing Duberman of reductive stereotyping, poor writing, and general misunderstanding of the Beat culture in which Kerouac lived. It does not seem unjust to assume that Duberman's growing interest in the role of the homosexual in society, thoroughly explored in his later work, found an inadequate vehicle in this play. There is no adequate basis, as Munk points out, for Duberman's simple contention that Kerouac was a homosexual, or that he would have proved a better writer had he acknowledged the fact. Duberman's dramatic theme might be associated with a strategy that he identifies in the *Radical History Review* interview as part of homosexual culture during that time, which was to find the homosexual in everyone. In the preface to *Male Armor*, a collection of plays written between 1968 and 1974, Duberman describes this preoccupation in more general terms and his abiding interest in the question "What does it mean to be a man?" Reading the psychoanalyst Wilhelm Reich's concept of "character armor"—"the devices we use (and which then use us) to protect ourselves from our own energy, and especially from our sexual energy." Although his characters were not written to illustrate Reich's views, "the Reichian concept fits them because they're semi-automatons, men acting out roles they never designed and hardly notice."

Duberman's efforts to redefine the nature of a separate homosexual culture is based on the conviction that gays are not a population within the mainstream of heterosexual life but a separate "people" in the same sense that African-American are a people. That has been concealed by oppression because the option of leading an exclusively homosexual life was not then available," and this fact "had given us a different historical experience." Because of this essential difference, Duberman feels, gay people should resist pressures to become "homogenized" with the rest of the population.

Duberman spent a great deal of time in the 1980s researching the history of homosexuality in American life, reading extensively in archives and manuscript collections. This resulted in two publications in the new field of gay and lesbian history, which he has been instrumental in creating. As he makes clear in his autobiography *Cures: A Gay Man's odyssey*, his work as a historian in the field is directly motivated by compassion for those who, like himself, were compelled either to hide their sexual orientation in order to prosper or to seek treatment designed to correct what the medical profession regarded as a personality disorder. Duberman attempts throughout the book to present his own experience an example of a more general social phenomenon. Adam Mars-Jones, in the *New York Times Book Review* questions whether Duberman's experience is really representative of the lives of homosexuals had society seen them in a different light. In addition to his personal memoir, however, Duberman has encouraged pioneering research in what he calls "biographical reclamation." Some of the results were collected in *Hidden from History: Reclaiming the Gay and Lesbian Past,* which discusses the problems associated with this new field of investigation in the title essay and makes an attempt to compare human behavior across cultures and periods. The book demonstrates, as a reviewer in the *Journal of American History* remarked, "that gay and lesbian history is today among the most dynamic fields of historical scholarship."

PRINCIPAL WORKS: Charles Francis Adams: 1807–1886, 1960; James Russell Lowell, 1966; The Uncompleted Past: Collected Essays, 1961–1969, 1969; Black Mountain: An Exploration in Community, 1972; About Time: Exploring the Gay Past, 1986 (rev. ed., 1991); Paul Robeson, 1989; Cures: A Gay Man's Odyssey, 1991. *Plays*—In White America: A Documentary Play, 1964; The Memory Bank, 1970; Male Armor: Selected Plays, 1968–1974, 1975; Visions of Kerouac, 1977; Mother Earth: An Epic Play on the Life of Emma Goldman, 1991; Stonewall, 1993. *As editor*—The Antislavery Vanguard: New Essays on the Abolitionists, 1965; Hidden from History: Reclaiming the Gay and Lesbian Past, 1989; Lives of Notable Gay Men and Lesbians (40 vols.), 1993.

ABOUT: Aufderheide, P. (ed.) Beyond PC: Towards a Politics of Understanding, 1992; Contemporary Authors New Revision Series 2, 1981; Contemporary Literary Criticism 8, 1978; Duberman, M. Cures: A Gay Man's Odyssey, 1991; Mass, L. (ed.) Dialogues of the Sexual Revolution, 1, 1990; Simon, J. Uneasy Stages: A Chronicle of the New York Theater, 1963–1973, 1975. *Periodicals*—American History Review October 1961; July 1967; American Scholar Winter 1991; Commentary May 1989; Dissent Fall 1989; Journal of American History December 1990; June 1991; Journal of Ethnic Studies Summer 1990; Nation June 3, 1961; April 3, 1967; March 20, 1989; June 10, 1991; New England Quarterly December 1961; June 1967; New Leader February 20, 1989; New Republic November 4, 1972; New York Review of Books November 16, 1972; April 27, 1989; New York Times November 1, 1963; January 12, 1970; January 25, 1970; December 6, 1976; New York Times Book Review March 26, 1961; December 25, 1966; January 4, 1970; October 29, 1972; February 22, 1987; February 12, 1989; April 21, 1991; Psychology Today August 1987; Publishers Weekly January 13,

1989; Quill & Quire April 1989; Radical History Review Fall 198; Reviews in American History September 1974; December 1988; Salmagundi Spring/Summer 1991; Saturday Review December 3, 1966; January 3, 1970; October 21, 1972; Sewanee Review Fall 1992; Times Literary Supplement may 12, 1989; Village Voice December 20, 1976; (Village) Voice Literary Supplement April 1989; June 1991; Virginia Quarterly Review Spring 1967; Yale Review June 1961.

DUBUS, ANDRE (JULES, JR.) (August 11, 1936–), American short story writer and novelist, was born in Lake Charles, Louisiana, son of Andre Jules and Katherine (Burke) Dubus. He was raised in Lafayette, Louisiana, where his father was the manager of a local power company. Dubus was educated at a Christian Brothers school and, in 1958, received his B.A. degree from McNeese State College. That same year, Dubus married his first wife, Patricia Lowe, with whom he had four children. That marriage ended in 1970.

Dubus, who began writing in 1954, entered the U.S. Marines after college because "a writer has to have a job," as he explained, especially an unpublished writer with a growing family. Commissioned a lieutenant in 1958, he left the service as a captain in 1964. Shortly after receiving his first acceptance from the *Sewanee Review,* Dubus left the service and enrolled in the University of Iowa Writers' Workshop. Although acceptance of his story has been mentioned as a precipitating factor in Dubus's decision to leave the service for Iowa, he maintained that the immediate cause of his decision to resign his commission was a difference of opinion with a commanding officer. Dubus has also identified another factor, the death of his father, to whom he no longer had to prove his own manhood.

In 1966 Dubus received his M.F.A. from the University of Iowa, and in 1967 his first novel, *The Lieutenant,* was published. Although Dubus regarded it as something of a stepchild, his growing reputation resulted in a reprinting of *The Lieutenant* in 1986 after it had gone out of print. Since *The Lieutenant,* Dubus has published only novellas and short stories because he believes his forte is the art of compression.

Dubus also discovered the landscape for his fiction after leaving Iowa. In 1966, he settled in Haverhill, Massachusetts, and began teaching modern literature and writing at Bradford College, where he spent eighteen years, teaching four courses a semester, until he resigned in 1984 suffering from exhaustion. In this Merrimack Valley area of Massachusetts, "stubbornly pretty but economically troubled," Dubus found the ambience that pervades most of his fiction. His principal characters are bartenders, salesgirls, waitresses, and laborers of all kinds, those who scratch out a marginal economic existence. Commended by critics for his finely crafted, realistic fiction, Dubus establishes his characters as ordinary human beings frustrated by the problems of everyday life, who drink, smoke, and fornicate too much in an attempt to deal with those frustrations.

As early as his first short story collection *Separate Flights*, published in 1975, Dubus's fiction has been characterized as "mostly about spent and misspent love," and he has been praised for his ability "to dramatize love's counterfeit emotions: loneliness, jealously, and pity." Reviewing *Separate Flights* in Ontario Review, Joyce Carol Oates praised Dubus's "attentiveness to his craft and his deep commitment to his characters." The title of Dubus's 1977 collection, *Adultery and Other Choices*, reflects another pervasive theme in his fiction—the lack of understanding and miscommunication in the male female relationships. The title story, the novella *Adultery*, is emblematic of Dubus's obsession with unstable relationships that result in infidelity which only serves to intensify the partners' dissatisfaction. Dubus has himself acknowledged the autobiographical influences in his fiction, and *Adultery and Other Choices* was published in the same year as the dissolution of his two-year marriage to his second wife, Tommie Gail Potter.

However personally cathartic his fiction, Dubus at his best manages to refine personal emotion into powerful prose. Reviewing *Adultery*, Jonathan Penner commented in the *Washington Post Book World*, "The power of the story depends, not on any clever innovations of plot, but on something finer: the author's ability to notice what the rest of us merely see, to show us what important truths we never knew that we knew— and never *could* have known that we knew if we hadn't read this. Of the relationships between men and women, men and men, women and women, here is a wealth of understanding."

Dubus's 1980 short story collection, *Finding a Girl in America* was, not coincidentally, published the year after his third marriage, to the writer Peggy Rambach. Dubus credited that relationship with the development of a more positive outlook in his fiction.

The protagonist, Hank Allison, of *Finding a Girl in America* appeared in earlier Dubus stories ("We Don't Live Here Anymore" in *Separate Flights* and "Adultery" in *Adultery and Other Choices*). Many reviewers commented that the controlled distance Dubus achieved in "Adultery," a story narrated by the wife, is notably absent in "Finding a Girl in America." Reviewing the collection for *The New Republic*, Dorothy Wickenden commented, "Despite the implicit affinity Dubus himself feels for Hank Allison, he fails to convince us that this self-indulgent bore really can feel much about anything except his writings and his sex life. . . . Dubus takes his characters as seriously as they take themselves and the cumulative effort of all this earnestness is oppressive."

"Delivering," the story that received the most positive critical notice in the collection, reflects Dubus's ability to achieve distance with characters whose crises are not too close to his own. The narrative concerns two brothers, fifteen and twelve, who go out together to deliver papers the day their mother had left their father and return to "pick up the pieces of their lives and their father's," according to Julian Moynahan. "Without omitting any scabrous details . . . 'Delivering' somehow delivers an endorsement of the American family, from the standpoint of the children's need for it to survive, that is touching and oddly optimistic."

That same ability to evoke sentiment without sentimentality characterizes the highly praised 1984 novella *Voices from the Moon*, another story of a young boy struggling with the dissolution of his family. According to Dubus, it was the similarity to "Delivering" that impelled him to develop other perspectives in *Voices from the Moon*, "I was just doing to do it as a short story from the boy's point of view, but I realized I had written a story very much like that called 'Delivering.' I thought, I can't have another story about a boy overhearing something bad and dealing with it. So I decided to do each point of view."

Dubus's collection *The Times Are Never So Bad* was published in 1983. In its fifty-six-page novella *The Pretty Girl*, a young woman named Polly drinks and smokes too much and—like most Dubus protagonists—lives an almost purposeless existence, casually drifting from home to marriage and back to single life. Her estranged husband also drinks excessively and lifts weights compulsively. He rapes Polly at knifepoint, and she eventually becomes his killer. Joyce Carol Oates, writing in the *New York Times Book Review*, admired the technique in this story as Dubus builds his portraits "in a slow, detailed, fastidious way," but she admitted that Dubus's fiction is "perhaps an acquired taste, for his characters are resolutely ungiving and uncharming." *The Times Are Never So Bad* also marked the emergence of a thematic emphasis on Catholicism that had been submerged as a general religious sensibility in Dubus's prior fiction. In "A Father's Story" in that collection, the narrator, Luke Ripley, the divorced owner of a stable, leads a simple life, attends Mass every day, and seems unfailingly honest. Yet he deliberately obscures the evidence of the hit-and-run fatality for which his twenty-year-old daughter is responsible. He wrestles with God, but at the end of the story, he announces the achievement of a greater satisfaction than he had known in his former placid existence:

> I do not feel the peace I once did, not with God, nor the earth, or anyone on it. I have begun to prefer this state, to remember with fondness the other one as a period of peace I neither earned nor deserved. Now in the mornings . . . I say to Him: I would do it again. For when she knocked on my door, then called me, she woke what had flowed dormant in my blood since her birth, so that what rose from the bed was not a stable owner or a Catholic or any other Luke Ripley I had lived with for a long time, but the father of a girl.

Brian Stonehill, reviewing *The Times Are Never So Bad*, in the *Los Angeles Book Review*, compared Dubus with Flannery O'Connor in the power of his writing, his ability to command the reader's attention. Stonehill added that Dubus "focuses on the place of faith and grace in a Catholic heart. He hunts for purity's place in all of this, and it too clever and clear-sighted to settle for an easy answer."

For Dubus, the purity represented by Catholicism belongs to the innocent world of the virginal, the untested, those who have yet to encounter life's challenges. Religion can provide a locus of meaning for personal spirituality, as it does for Luke Ripley at the beginning of "A Father's Story," but its highest form is when it is redefined by human love, as it is at the end of that story.

In the novella *Voices From The Moon*, twelve-year-old Ritchie Stowe attends Mass daily and wants to become a priest. He fears a loss of spiritual purity when he learns of his father's plans to marry his older brother's former wife. The boy believes that the entire family will be "living in sin." Ritchie seeks the guidance of the parish priest, who advises, DdThink of love. They are two people who love each other, and as painful as it is for others, and even if it is wrong, it's still love, and that is always near the grace of God." As in "The Pretty Girl," there is a suggestion that Catholicism belongs to a world of innocence apart from human experience. The narrative ends with Ritchie experiencing his first kiss, entering the world of experience that the rest of his family inhabits.

Voices From The Moon shares with "A Father's Story" the explicit belief in the redemptive power of human love, whether it be erotic love or the love between parents and children. A compilation of Dubus's previously published fiction, *Selected Stories*, begins with *Voices From The Moon* and ends with "A Father's Story," narratives that chart his ideal of spiritual development from the untested purity of Ritchie Stowe to the mature parental love of Luke Ripley. Reviewing *Selected Stories* in the *New York Times Book Review*, Eva Hoffman noted, "Now that one has an overview of two decades of his work, it is evident that love is at the center of Mr. Dubus's fictional morality, its presence the greatest virtue, its corruption the only sin."

Selected Stories not only provided an overview of Dubus's work, it also marked a hiatus in his production of fiction. In 1986, returning to Haverhill from Boston in the early hours of a summer day, Dubus spotted some trouble on the road and, stopping to assist two accident victims, was run down by another car. One of the accident victims died, and Dubus lost the use of his legs; his left leg was amputated below the knee and the muscles of his right leg were destroyed.

Ironically, his accident brought Dubus into the limelight more than his fiction ever had. While he was admired by other writers, he was relatively unknown at the time of his accident. In 1987 a diverse group of well-known contemporary writers—among them John Updike, Gail Godwin, Stephen King, and Kurt Vonnegut—held a series of readings in Cambridge, Massachusetts to help raise money for Dubus's medical bills. In early 1988, his publisher, David R. Godine, brought out the *Selected Stories*, and in November of that year Dubus was profiled in the *New York Times Magazine*. The author's financial situation was considerably improved with a 1988 fellowship from the MacArthur Foundation. The $310,000 stipend, to be spread over five years, provided a measure of financial security.

Dubus continued working at his craft, although writing was understandably difficult during his convalescence and adjustment to his disability—an adjustment that included coming to terms with the dissolution of his third marriage in 1987, when he and Peggy Rambach separated following the birth of their second daughter. Dubus has chronicled his recovery in *Broken Vessels*, a group of autobiographical essays that he describes as "about a spiritual passage." Comparing that collection to Dubus's fiction in the *New York Times Book Review*, Leonard Kriegel commented that "Dubus captures the contradictory demands of being an American man more fully than any other contemporary writer I can think of. In the autobiographical essays of *Broken Vessels*, he captures those same contradictions."

PRINCIPAL WORKS: *Novels*—The Lieutenant, 1967; Voices From the Moon (novella) 1984. *Short Stories*—Separate Flights, 1975; Adultery and Other Choices, 1977; Finding a Girl in America, 1980; The Times Are Never So Bad, 1983; The Last Worthless Evening, 1986; Selected Stories, 1988. *Essays*—Broken Vessels, 1991.

ABOUT: Contemporary Authors New Revision Series 17, 1986; Contemporary Literary Criticism 13, 1980; 36, 1986; A. Dubus, Broken Vessels, 1991; A. Gandolfo, Testing the Faith: The New Catholic Fiction in America, 1992; T. E. Kennedy, Andre Dubus: A Study of the Short Fiction, 1988; I. Shafer (ed.) The Incarnate Imagination, 1988. *Periodicals*—America November 15, 1986; Book World December 18, 1977; Commonweal December 2, 1988; Critique Fall 1986; Georgia Review 43, 1989; Horizon April 1985; Los Angeles Times Book Review August 14, 1983; New Republic August 23, 1980; New York Times Book Review June 22, 1980; June 26, 1983; November 6, 1988; September 16, 1990; August 11, 1991; New York Times Magazine November 20, 1988; Ontario Review Fall–Winter 1976; Washington Post Book World December 18, 1977.

*DURYCH, JAROSLAV: (February 2, 1886–April 7, 1962), Czech prose writer, poet, dramatist, essayist, and journalist, was born in Hradec Králové in eastern Bohemia, into a family with both literary and religious inclinations. Rejecting his family's wish that he should study theology , he graduated in medicine from the University of Prague. As an army doctor he took part in World War I and then served in this profession for the better part of his life in several places in Czechoslovakia. He lived in Prague from 1937 until his death.

From the beginning of his literary career Durych integrated his literary and his religious impulses. He was influenced by *fin de siècle* literature, as well as by the literature of mystics such as the Spanish baroque saints Theresa of Ávila and John of the Cross. From the 1920s to the 1940s he was also a controversial Catholic journalist.

Until the Communist takeover in 1948 Durych was one of Czechoslovakia's most prominent writers, receiving several awards. After 1948 he was allowed to republish only several of his earlier works; his new books were published posthumously at the time of the Prague Spring in 1968, some of them only abroad.

As a young writer Durych collaborated with the movement *"Katolická moderna"* (the Catholic moderna movement), the goal of which was to enhance Czech Catholic culture by linking it more closely with modern democratic trends. At that time Durych published his first books: the lyrical symbolic prose *Svatý Jiří* (Saint Goerge), written in 1908, and the translation Výkřiky svaté Terezie de Jesu (The cries of Saint Theresa of Jesus, 1909), which was probably the first manifestation of the interest in baroque culture initiated by Czech Roman Catholic scholars and writers in the first half of the 20th century.

Durych acquired a considerable reputation with his four-volume cycle *Jamark života* (The fair of life, 1916). The first two volumes are prose works inspired by the evocative historical prose of Flaubert and Villiers de L'Isle Adam; the third and fourth volumes are ballads in verse, originating in the poetry of Czech Romanticists and the poems of Edgar Allan Poe. The cycle's story is set in the distant past, in which Durych created a model of a world full of contradictions. A beautiful young duchess with twin sons, cherished and admired, brings romance, adventure, and misfortune to her lovers and then to her husband.

Up to the second half of the 20th century Durych's works were basically romantic and poetic. He also wrote several works of nonfiction— essays on life, religion, and art—and short stories and prose poems—the Baudelairean *Kouzelná lampa* (A magic lamp, 1926). A collection of his short stories was published in 1932 under the title *Ohně v Mlhách* (Fires in the lists). They are mainly philosophical, pseudohistorical parables, showing the influence of early 20th-century expressionism and neoclassicism, and reflecting Durych's distinctly personal vision of a world divided between loathsome physical reality and the transcendence of God.

During the 1920s Durych also published four plays, the best of them being *Svatý Vojtěch* (Saint Adalbert, 1921), a tragedy about the Czech saint, who ultimately triumphs through his contempt for secular power. The others are the biblical *Lotr na pravici* (The thief on the right, 1924); *Svatý Václav* (Saint Wenceslas, 1925), based on the life of the national saint; and *Štědrý večer* (Christmas Eve, 1926), a mystical play.

The novella *Sedmikráska* (Seven beauties, 1925; translated as *The Daisy*), became the most popular of Durych's books. It is, according to the author, "a celebration of youth, beauty, poverty and joy." Like many of his other writings, it is a parable: a story of a young man who becomes enchanted with seven girls, one at a time, only to find out that the seven incarnations were one and the same person. Durych's lofty conception

*DOO Yeekh, Yoo ruh sluhf

of women concerns virgins as carriers of a part of God's mystery. In this book Durych's tendency towards naiveté or primitivism, which he shared with the avant-garde, probably reached its height.

In the 1920s Durych also wrote much poetry. This work was preceded by a thorough study of verse, especially of the rhythm of Czech folk poetry and its Romanticist adaptors—K. J. Erben and F. L. Celakovský—and also again showed the influence of Poe. *Panenky* (Maidens, 1923) depicted the manifestation of the spirit of the Virgin Mary in poor girls in a style that recalls the naive love poetry of the Czech National Revival of the early 19th century. *Zebrácké písně* (Beggar's Songs, 1925) and *Beskydy* (The Beskydy Mountains, 1926), on the other hand, show the influence of Villon and Poe, and resemble the poetry of the French symbolists Paul Claudel and Paul Valéry.

Along with Vladisav Vančura (1891–1942), Durych is regarded as one of the reformers of Czech historical prose, freeing it from 19th-century ideological traditions. His most influential historical novel, compared by Thomas Mann to *War and Peace*, is *Bloudění* (Wandering, 1929; translated as *Descent of the Idol*, a novel of the baroque. The background to this ambitious work is the career of the Bohemian general Abrecht von Wallenstein (1583–1634), a convert to Roman Catholicism and the protagonist of Friedrich von Schiller's great dramatic trilogy *Wallenstein*. Durych identifies him with the baroque zeitgeist, a period of bitter religious strife, turbulence, and suffering. He treats his subject with extraordinary imaginative sympathy. His main characters are two lovers—the Czech Protestant Jiří and the Spanish Catholic Andela, who wander about a large part of the then-known world from European battlefields to precolonial America. For Czech and other European readers the book was less a historical chronicle than a highly expressive symbolic affirmation of the Catholic roots of the Czech ethos. Readers of the English translation were impressed with its massive detail (the novel runs to 670 pages). Alfred Kazin wrote, in the *New York Times Book Review*, that "it represents the historical novel in the grand style . . . where the details do not confuse us, they add up into a naturalistic whole."

The relations and life stories of the characters are similarly, even bizarrely, intertwined in the novel *Masopust* (Shrovetide, 1938). The slow exposition of its story takes up the greater part of the book, and the characters are rendered with Kafka-like effects of the grotesque and ironic. The complicated story begins in Prague in 1611

during the night of Shrovetide when soldiers of the German bishop of Passau invaded the city and executed a massacre, and ends nineteen years later with the meeting of three of the four protagonists, all of whose deeds were seen to have been motivated by amorous desire. The omniscient narrator of this story penetrates the subconscious of the characters, and they become expressions of the zeitgeist turned upside down: "Indeed, things, and people as well, have been reordered and changed."

Boži duha (God's rainbow; the manuscript finished in 1955 and the book published posthumously in Prague in 1969) is sometimes regarded as the best of Durych's work. The pseudo-autobiographical novella, set in the Sudetenland after the end of World War II and narrated in the first person, is about the love between a sixty year-old Czech and a young German woman, each of them seeking their "lost wisdom." The book was first published in a German translation by the philosopher Jan Patočka, who interpreted the work in the light of Czech-German relations as a book about guilt, punishment and, above all, repentance.

Duše a hvězda (The soul and the star; the manuscript was completed in the 1950s, and published posthumously in Prague in 1969) is an allegorical novel about symbiosis of the masculine and the feminine principles, the former having diabolic, the latter angelic attributes. The main character is a woman—a poor factory worker—who meets the embodiment of her love first in her employer's son, whom she marries, and then, after her husband's early death, in his cousin who is indistinguishable from him.

In *Sluzebníci neužiteční* Karel Spinola, the Prague-born son of an Italian father and a Czech mother, is the main character, although a "collective hero" is represented by a group of Jesuit missionaries. It is a story about sacrifice. The Jesuits traveled throughout the world, seeking martyrdom, which they found at the stake in Japan in 1622 after having successfully spread Christianity there. Like *Bloudění*, *Služebníci neužiteční*, reflects the baroque spirit, but, unlike *Bloudění*, it is not concerned with Czech national historical "catastrophes" or "victories," instead dealing with the baroque unity of life and dream: "Why should one dream? Isn't reality a dream, much better and more interesting?"

The second of Durych's hagiographic works, *Světlo ve tmách*, 1988 (Light in the darkness, published in Prague in 1991) is about a Czech noblewoman of the 13th century, Blessed Zdislava of Lemberk, was another response to what Durych perceived as the Czechs' retreat from Catholocism and their historic past. As a Catholic and—though he expressed strongly liberal views on social reform—a political conservative, Durych was out of favor during the long years of Communist domination of Czechoslovakia. From 1948 to 1956 his works were formally banned from publication. When he died in 1962, there was some revival of interest in him, but with the deepening of Communist repression after 1968, publication of his work stopped again, except abroad where his books appeared in many European languages, including French, German, Polish, Hungarian and Danish. Since the early 1990s, however, there has been a wider demand for his work in his native land. His first book to be published after the advent of democracy was the treatise *Rytmus české prózy* (The rhythm of Czech prose, 1992), based on the study of the Czech Romanticist K. J. Erben. *Zlatý kočár*, (A Golden Coach; manuscript completed in 1962) consisting of voluminous scenes from the history of Durych's family and ancestors, and *Papežové a císaři* (Popes and emperors), a fragment dealing with the relations between spiritual and secular power, are still unpublished.

Durych was one of the most influential writers in Czech literature between the wars. Oppressed as a Catholic writer under the Communist regime, only in the last decade of the century is his image as a modern, versatile Central European writer being established. He is seen as a spiritual and also sensual, expressive, mystical, and dogmatic writer, an ironist, as well as a revealer of the subconscious.

PRINCIPAL WORKS IN ENGLISH TRANSLATION: "Wallenstein's Tomb," in Slavonic Review 11, 1932–1933; Descent of the Idol (tr. L. A. Hudson) 1935.

ABOUT: Columbia Dictionary of Modern European Literature, 2nd ed., 1980; Encyclopedia of World Literature in the 20th Century, rev. ed., 1981; Reader's Encyclopedia of Eastern European Literature, 1993. *Periodicals*—Books, November 22, 1936; New Statesman and Nation, May 4, 1935; New York Times, October 18, 1936; Times Literary Supplement, May 9, 1935.

EHRENREICH, BARBARA (August 26, 1941–), American essayist and novelist, feminist social critic, and political activist, was born in Butte, Montana, the daughter of Ben Howes and Isabelle Oxley (Isely) Alexander. Both her parents and their families had worked in and around the Butte copper mines for several generations. "These were not people who could be accused of questionable politics or ethnicity," Ehrenreich wrote in the introduction to her book

BARBARA EHRENREICH

The Worst Years of Our Lives. "Nor were they members of the 'liberal elite' so hated by our current conservative elite. They were blue-eyed, Scotch-Irish Democrats. They were small farmers, railroad workers, miners, shopkeepers, and migrant farm workers. In short, they fit the stereotype of 'real' Americans; and their values, no matter how unpopular among today's opinion-shapers, are part of America's tradition too. To my mind, of course, the finest part." The "unpopular" values Ehrenreich alludes to are political dissent, questioning authority, and atheism, none of which she remembers as being unique to her own family.

Ehrenreich received a B.A. from Reed College in Portland, Oregon, in 1963, and a Ph.D. in biology from Rockefeller University in 1968. From 1969 to 1971 she was a staff member of the Health Policy Advisory Center in New York City. She was an assistant professor of health sciences at the State University of New York College at Old Westbury from 1971 to 1974. Of her short-lived scientific career, Ehrenreich has said, "Vietnam made other concerns more politically and socially relevant." Since the mid-1970s, she has devoted the bulk of her time to writing and political activism. She has been a fellow at the Institute for Policy Studies since 1982, and a cochairperson of the Democratic Socialists of America since 1983. She was awarded a Guggenheim Fellowship in 1987.

Her first two books were written in collaboration with her first husband John Ehrenreich, whom she married in 1966. *Long March, Short Spring*, written while they were still graduate students, examines the student uprisings in Europe and the United States in the 1960s. Their second book, *The American Health Empire*, is a scathing dissection of a health care system more devoted to perpetuating its own interests than to treating people's illnesses. According to the Ehrenreichs, the United States health care system is devoted to three main goals: "increasing institutional profits and individual salaries, feeding medical research that often has only a tenuous relationship to any real medical needs, and insuring its own perpetuation by controlling medical education." In a *New York Review of Books* article, Michael G. Michaelson called it "the most solid criticism of American health care now available."

During the 1970s, Barbara Ehrenreich collaborated with Deirdre English on *Witches, Midwives, and Nurses: A History of Women Healers*, *Complaints and Disorders: The Sexual Politics of Sickness*, and *For Her Own Good: One Hundred Fifty Years of the Experts' Advice to Women*. *For Her Own Good* considers how an emerging class of professionals—pediatricians, home economists, psychologists, and gynecologists—set themselves up as powerful authorities on women's well-being, while at the same time they usurped many of women's traditional roles as healers and caregivers. In a review of the book in the *Annals of the American Academy of Political and Social Science*, J. L. Nelson wrote: "This is an intriguing, information filled, compelling excursion, using techniques of revisionist history, radical sociology, and interpretive essay writing, into the relations between women and the experts who have risen over time to analyze them and prescribe remedies. . . . a fascinating mixture of scholarship, interpretation, and wit."

The Hearts of Men: American Dreams and the Flight from Commitment is perhaps Ehrenreich's most controversial work. "This book is about the ideology that shaped the breadwinner ethic and how that ideology collapsed, as a persuasive set of expectations, in just the last thirty years," Ehrenreich wrote in her introduction. She scrutinizes the social phenomena from 1950 to 1980 behind the American man's flight from his "gray flannel" role as breadwinner, householder, husband, and father. Ehrenreich contends that *Playboy* magazine was instrumental in removing the stigma attached to bachelorhood (once closely associated with homosexuality), and giving it instead an aura of liberation from marriage. *Playboy*, according to Ehrenreich, announced to its readers that the pursuit of their own pleasure was every bit as important as supporting a wife and family. In the artists and writers associated with the Beat movement, Ehrenreich sees another group of men (albeit very different from the "playboys") who were zealous in their rejection of marriage, home, and family. In the human potential movement that flourished during the 1970s, she finds a theoretical justification for men's rejection of family life. She finds similar justifications at work in the men's liberation movement and the obsession surrounding Type A behavior; in both cases men were urged to opt out of a breadwinner role that was either psychologically crippling or overly stressful.

Ehrenreich concludes that the "breadwinner ideology," which esteemed the stable, responsible, family man, was the glue holding the American family in place. The rise of social phenomena like *Playboy* and the human potential movement both reflected and prompted men's revolt against the breadwinner ideal. Reviewing *The Hearts of Men* in the *New York Times Book Review*, Carol Tavris lauded Ehrenreich's incisive critique of contemporary American culture, but added that Ehrenreich's "analysis falters in its confusion of causes and effects. She continually implies a sequence (first came concerted pressures upon men to conform, then male protest, then scientific legitimation of male protest) when her own evidence shows simultaneity." *Village Voice* reviewer Judith Levine concurred, saying, "The ideology supporting men's abdication of family commitment is not new. It has coexisted belligerently with the breadwinner ethic throughout American history."

Nation reviewer Todd Gitlin, however, found Ehrenreich's focus on the collapse of the breadwinner ideology persuasive and useful. "This elegantly simple idea enables Ehrenreich to grasp a remarkable amount of recent cultural history," he noted. Gitlin faulted the book in only one respect, and this he termed "a quibble." "Attention to the psychology of male dependency . . . would have actually strengthened Ehrenreich's formidable analysis of the way culture is arrayed against love."

Fear of Falling: The Inner Life of the Middle Class is an exploration of contemporary American notions about class. Taking issue with the standard American definition of "middle class," which usually encompasses everybody who isn't extremely rich or poor, Ehrenreich argues that the real middle class is, in fact, the "professional class." Middle class people are those whose careers and positions depend directly on education and professional credentials, distinguishing them from the skilled and semiskilled members of the working class, and from the upper class, whose positions depend on the ownership of property and capital.

According to Ehrenreich, this professional

class is characterized above all by anxiety (the "fear of falling," or losing economic and political status) and complacency (a tendency toward political reaction and a reluctance to acknowledge the legitimacy of any needs but their own). Since members of the professional class dominate the ranks of government policy-making institutions and the media, these institutions can no longer represent the interests of the working class. As a consequence, the concerns and perspectives of the professional class are often presented to the public as questions of general or national interest. "When we see a man in work clothes on the screen," Ehrenreich writes, "we anticipate some grievance or, at best, information of a highly local or anecdotal nature. On matters of general interest or national importance, waitresses, forklift operators, steamfitter—that is, most 'ordinary' Americans are not invited to opine."

In the *New York Review of Books*, James Fallow wrote that *Fear of Falling* "is insightful and sensitive. . . . [I]t establishes two central points about America's productive culture. One is that people are devoting more and more energy to defending what privileges they have and to protecting their status with the class system, instead of creating new opportunities or strengthening the U.S. economic system as a whole." The other fundamental point, Fallow notes, "is that as professional-class consciousness has risen, the sense of the public good has declined." In *Newsweek* Laura Shapiro noted, "Reading Barbara Ehrenreich is always salubrious: here are genuinely left-wing political convictions, unfashionable but unflinching, tempered only by good humor. . . . it would be hard to find a wittier, more insightful guide to the last three decades than Ehrenreich."

In her introduction to *The Worst Years of Our Lives: Irreverent Notes from a Decade of Greed*, a short essay entitled "Family Values," Ehrenreich traces her own family's history of dissent, writing, "For dissent is also a 'traditional value,' and in a republic founded by revolution, a more deeply native one than smug-faced conservatism ever can be." This volume is a collection of essays, many of which originally appeared in *Mother Jones, Ms.*, the New Republic, and the *New York Times.* Among Ehrenreich's themes are politics, culture, religion, feminism, the war on drugs, and such fads of the 1980s as "the couch potatoes." Reviewing the collection in the *New York Times Book Review*, H. Jack Geiger wrote, "She may have Tocqueville's eye for political culture, but she has a marxist ear (Groucho, I mean) for its many forms of expression." Calling Ehrenreich "an up-front socialist" and an "an old-fashioned moralist," Geiger says, "she almost never preaches. She is

merciless—and mercilessly funny—on the Great Cultural Evolution of the 80s. . . . "

In 1993 Barbara Ehrenreich published her first novel, *Kipper's Game*, described by one reviewer as "a dystopian fantasy." Set in a reasonably close future plagued by environmental problems and social decline, it is the story of a woman who is seeking clues to the disappearance of her computer-genius son. In the course of her search she encounters mysterious and sinister scientific research complexes, intrigues dating back to the Nazi era, computer-hacking conspiracies, and an evangelical religious sect. Intellectually stimulating as the book undoubtedly is, it was faulted both for its colorless characterization and its vague and overly ambitious social criticism. "Ms. Ehrenreich heaps more on her plate than it can comfortably hold," Michael Upchurch wrote in the *New York Times Book Review*, "and the strongest impression her book leaves is of an undisciplined mind in intriguing ferment."

PRINCIPAL WORKS: (with J. Ehrenreich) Long March, Short Spring: The Student Uprising at Home and Abroad, 1969; (with J. Ehrenreich) The American Health Empire: Power, Profits, and Politics, 1970; (with D. English) Witches, Midwives, and Nurses: A History of Women Healers, 1972; (with D. English) Complaints and Disorders: The Sexual Politics of Sickness, 1973; (with D. English) For Her Own Good: One Hundred Fifty Years of the Experts' Advice to Women, 1978; The Hearts of Men: American Dreams and the Flight from Commitment, 1983; (with E. Hess and G. Jacobs) Re-Making Love: The Feminization of Sex, 1986; (with F. Block et al) The Mean Season: The Attack on the Welfare State, 1987; Fear of Falling: The Inner Life of the Middle Class, 1989; The Worst Years of Our Lives: Irreverent Notes from a Decade of Greed, 1990. Novel—Kipper's Game, 1993.

ABOUT: Contemporary Authors New Revision Series 16, 1986; Who's Who in America 1994. *Periodicals*—Annals of the American Academy of Political and Social Science March 1979; Humanist January/February 1992; Nation May 28, 1983; New York Review of Books July 1, 1971; March 1, 1990; New York Times Book Review June 5, 1983; May 20, 1990; August 8, 1993; August 14, 1989; Publishers Weekly August 24, 1990; Village Voice August 23, 1983.

*EKSTRÖM, MARGARETA (April 23, 1930–   ), Swedish novelist, short story writer, and poet, was born in Stockholm and grew up as the only child in a middle class family. Her father worked in an insurance company, and her mother was a housewife. Margareta Ekström graduated in the Faculty of Arts at the University of Stockholm in 1956, having studied litera-

*EK stroem

MARGARETA EKSTRÖM

ture, religion, psychology, and sociology. As a teenager Ekström devoted herself to painting, but eventually she became more interested in writing. When she decided to make writing her profession, her parents gave her their full support. In politics, too, she was free to follow her own convictions. In an interview in the Swedish periodical *Arbetet* in 1993 she reflected: "A middle-class upbringing offers a paradox: the parents give their children the means to break out of the middle-class frame. I had seen so much of . . . locked positions and did not want to end up in that situation myself. I have always looked upon myself as an oppositional woman. Politically I am a leftist. Today I call myself an 'undenominational socialist.'"

Ekström worked as a journalist and a book and film reviewer, and she published some short stories in various newspapers and periodicals before her real literary debut in 1960, with the collection of short stories *Aftnar i St Petersburg* (Evenings in St. Petersburg). During the 1960s, 1970s, and 1980s a new book appeared almost every year; up through 1994 Margareta Ekström published twenty-seven books. She has also translated a number of books from English into Swedish, among them works by Virginia Woolf, Eva Figes, Wole Soyinka, and Okot p'Bitek.

Six years before her literary debut, Margareta Ekström had married the writer and critic Carl-Eric Nordberg. After their divorce she formed a new family with the writer Per Wästberg, with whom she had two children. This relationship broke up in the early 1980s, a traumatic experience that forms the background to the themes of

sadness and loneliness in Ekström's subsequent works.

Recognized as a distinguished writer of short stories, Ekström has also published novels, collections of poems, diary notations, and stories for children. Her novels are: *Pendeln* (The pendulum, 1962), *Flickorna* (The Girls, 1963), *När de red omkring* (When they were riding about, 1969), and *Kvinnan som reste med Montaigne* (The woman who traveled with Montaigne, 1981). Her poetry begins with *Beringön* (Bering Island, 1965). When her daughter was three years old, she published a collection of poems to the child, *Ord till Jojanna* (Words to Johanna 1973), followed by *Under bar himmel* (Under the open sky, 1984), and *Skärmar* (Screens, 1990). *Om naturen pa Stora Skuggan* (On the countryside at Stora Skuggan, 1979), is a diary following the seasonal cycle in the surroundings of Stora Skuggan (Great Shadow), the country house where the author then lived with her family. Another diary is *Ord i det fria* (Words in Freedom, 1982). *Mat för minnet* (Food for memory, 1993), is both a cookbook and a biography. For children she wrote *Sagor fran Sjötullen* (Fairy tales from Sjötullen, 1972), *Katterna i Öregrund* (The cats of Öregrund, 1976) and *Katten som försvann* (The cat that disappeared, 1984). Ekström's *Olga om Olga* (Olga on Olga, 1994), is also a book about a cat, but this time not specifically for children. The narrator is a cat that tells anecdotes about her human friend. Both have the same the name and can be seen as different aspects of the author herself.

Despite this considerable production in other genres, Margareta Ekström is best known for short stories. Her collections are: *Aftnar i S:T Petersburg* (Evening in St. Petersburg, 1960), *Frukostdags* (Time for breakfast, 1961), *Överfallet och andra gränsintermezzon* (The assault and other border incidents, 1963), *Husliga scener* (Domestic scenes, 1964), *Födelseboken* (The book of birth, 1967), the anthology *Inte än—men snart* (Not yet—but soon, 1969), *Förhallandet till främmande makter* (The relationship to foreign powers, 1972), *Människodjuren* (Human animals, 1974), *Dödens barnmorskor* (1976, *Death's Midwives*), *Kärlekens utlan* (Love's foreign countries, 1982), the anthology *Den femte arstiden* (The fifth season, 1983), and *Skilda öden* (Divorced destinies, 1986). In English translation two volumes of short stories have appeared: *Death's Midwives*, translated by Eva Claeson, with a preface by Nadine Gordimer, and *The Day I Began My Studies In Philosophy*, translated by Eva Claeson, both containing short stories from several of the original collections.

Margareta Ekström prefers the short story genre, as she says in the interview in *Arbetet*, because it gives her the freedom to follow sudden impulses and rapidly mold them into literary form. She compares the swiftness that is required in writing short story with the art of painting a watercolor: just a few strokes of the paintbrush with a hand that does not hesitate or tremble, and the painting is completed. In a short story the writer cannot say everything; and must leave openings in the text, for the reader's imagination to fill in. In 1983, when she received an award for her mastery in the short story, she mentioned some authors in this genre whom she admired: Solveig von Schoultz, Ivan Turgenev, Katherine Mansfield, Ingeborg Bachmann, and Heinrich Böll.

As a Swedish reviewer observed of *Dödens barnmorskor* in 1976, there is a connection between the characteristics of the short story genre and one of the major themes of Ekström's stories: "The art of the short story is the art of abridgment. Many short story writers tell an anecdote. Margareta Ekström reproduces an atmosphere and sums up a life in a couple of conversations. . . . The form is also part of the content. The abridgment gives a picture of the life of human beings as a short whistle in emptiness, a lust that blazes up and is soon extinguished. . . . The stories get their life from the author's power of insight and the exceptional precision of her language." The experience at the center of Ekström's work includes the knowledge that is perishable and that an abyss may open under one's feet anywhere, anytime. There is a possible link between this theme and the fact that the author was born with a heart ailment and lived with a failing heart until 1982, when she underwent a successful operation. In an interview in *Manadsjournalen* in 1983, she formulated her attitude toward her heart disease: "Call it grief rather than despair. Death can be a kind of passe-partout; the shadows make you see things more clearly than otherwise. And when you think about it, what would become of joy and anxiety and vitality, all these things that are the essence of life, if life went on for ever?"

In her review of *Death's Midwives* in *Scandinavian Studies* (1987), Rose-Marie G. Oster emphasizes the close connection between form and content, language and the major theme in Ekström's stories: "In almost all of Margareta Ekström's stories there exists a precarious balance between the secure realities of everyday life that she describes so vividly . . . and the mysterious forces that are unleashed when she suddenly shatters the protective shell of such comforting routines. For almost all of her protagonists at some time come close . . . to the realm "where the wild things are," . . . until some are sucked into the great darkness. . . . The author's language reflects the tension between the many worlds in which the characters move. . . . There are few writers in Sweden who demonstrate this . . . ability to caress language until it opens up to new and mysterious depths, but who can also strip away all frills from sentence until the words lie sharp as the surgeon's knife. . . . "

The author's dual experience of life and death is admirably represented in the title story, "Death's Midwives," in which a woman is dying of cancer at a hospital and at the same time remembering the last time she was there, twenty years earlier, giving birth to her child. there is a confusion in her mind between the present and the past. Then she had the feeling of moving in a tunnel with no return—on the border between life and death—and now she has the same experience. Then she was creating life; now, as she is dying, she believes that she is hearing her little boy's voice through an open window:

> It prattled and babbled, it expounded and explained. And he couldn't say "s". She made an effort to stretch her neck and look up. The sun shone in through the window. The chestnuts on the horizon bowed to an imperceptible breeze. Their scent did not reach her. The light hit the shiny intravenous bottle, which reflected blindly.

All she saw was the sunshine bouncing against the nursery window, and his voice babbled on, and when she made an effort to somehow see his face the sun struck her with its double-edged axe.

In our predicament as perishable beings, the most important thing is to be alive, aware of living. Many lead mechanical lives, "darting back and forth between the supermarket and the meeting of the housewives' association, between filling in as a substitute at the druggist's and the more and more frequent dull, dreary hours watching television." This kind of life that threatens Ella in "Left Alone" after her sister has died:

> Better be completely dead than like a wound-up machine, merely playing a human role and pretending a human smile, while already half-dead and more a thing than a human being. Those are the sort of people who can hurt you in a crowd: they don't push with their elbows, they jab like table corners and cut like knives.

As Josephine Humphreys pointed out in her review of *Death's Midwives* in the *New York Times Book Review*, mechanical living is a danger especially in a rich and civilized country. But even in . . . Sweden it is possible to find a bench with a view of the river and the birds and "for a short while feel like a free human being."

Humphreys observed: "That brief chance is what life in a 'civilized' country can offer, and it is no mean gift. Ironically, it comes, these stories say, when death or an awareness of death is close—in old age, illness, childbirth, craziness, loneliness, love, all the uncivilized zones of human experience. . . . Miss Ekström's stories . . . ask an important question: what are the just concerns of a people who no longer need to worry about matters of life and death? And her answer is—matters of life and death. In these beautifully told stories, which linger in the memory, she finds that our oldest needs are also our hope and our human bond."

Happiness must include the painful awareness of illness, loneliness, and death. One must have courage to endure affliction. This is perhaps the very essence of human life, Ekström said in an interview in *Svenska Dagbladet* in 1990, on the occasion of publishing her collection *Skärmar*, poems that express her grief after the divorce from Per Wästberg: "Of course, death and forlornness and betrayal are nothing new in the history of mankind. . . . We are put to the test— we know that. And perhaps we are constructed for such strains. Perhaps we ourselves do not always want to remain in life, but something in ourselves, something in what happens strives towards survival."

Margareta Ekström is outspoken in her protest against cruelty and injustice. She is a member of PEN and is deeply engaged in work for Amnesty International. She calls herself a "natural feminist," and many of her stories depict women's lives with a wry irony directed against patriarchal society. Her protest extends beyond feminism, however, to the whole power structure. In her essay "The Big Sleep," in *The Day I Began My Studies in Philosophy*, as Molly Giles pointed out in the *New York Times Book Review*, (1990): "Ekström warns of the danger of another world war, and urges us to look at the "strange sleepiness" that silences those who try to object. "The only thing that can save us," she writes, "is total awareness," and yet we continue to dream, denying that our lives are in danger." In "Left Alone," (in *Death's Midwives*) Ella finds that life has lost its meaning after her sister's death, and she remembers what the two of them used to do:

When they had thought about such things, Sister and she, they had lit a candle and taken out a bottle of bourgogne [burgundy]. They had made a fire in the fireplace, even in the middle of the summer, and then read Dostoevsky aloud to each other, and household chores had had to wait. They had tried to go into a room that was their special common home, as Sister had called it, where they could warm themselves, and where Goethe had walked and Kant pondered, where Dickens had told tales, and Nijinsky had leapt. The common home was the little

house human beings helped each other to create to protect themselves from the icy winds of the inexplicable and the black holes of meaninglessness. It's a good thing we have learned to read, they had said, and had gone to the library the next day to get a new load of learning.

In Margareta Ekström's fiction literature functions as a consolation and a shelter against the cruelties of life. But the act of writing, she makes clear, is not a way of withdrawing from the evil aspects of life; rather, it is a way of offering resistance to them. Writing provides the courage to live) an authentic human life: "We are all going to die, of course, even one who enjoys life as much as I do. Writing is the pole that helps me keep my balance above the abyss."

PRINCIPAL WORKS IN ENGLISH TRANSLATION: Death's Midwives (tr. Eva Claeson) 1985; The Day I Began My Studies in Philosophy, and Other Stories (tr. Eva Claeson) 1989.

ABOUT: *Periodicals*—New York Times Book Review February 16, 1986; March 4, 1990; Scandinavian Studies 59, 1987; 63, 1991; World Literature Today 56, 1982; 63, 1989.

ELLIOTT, JANICE (October 14, 1931–   ), British novelist and journalist, writes: "I have always tried to avoid writing in a way that might invite categorisation in either subject-matter or treatment. The result is a body of work ranging from the bizarre and darkly magical (*Dr. Gruber's Daughter, Magic, The Sadness of Witches*) to the social realism of the 'England Trilogy' and the poignancy of *Secret Places*—set in the wartime Midlands where I grew up. I make frequent use of myth, which fascinates me (most overtly in *The Singing Head*). So does modern history (*Angels Falling*, set in Britain from 1901 to 1968; *Life on the Nile*, Egypt today and in the 1920s). The domestic scene has interested me only when it is set in, and interacts with, the larger, outer world (e.g., the menace of the authoritarian state in *Necessary Rites*). A sense of place is vital to me, even when I have invented a country (*The Country of Her Dreams*).

"I have been consistent only in my aspiration, my attempt each time to try something that will set me a fresh challenge as a writer. I am consistent, too, in my conviction that style is not the icing on the cake but an organic and essential element in a good novel. If there is one recurring theme, it may be the fall from grace, the image that of exile from the Garden.

"In the last decade I have felt an urge to get out of England (mentally, imaginatively, and physically), and so made use of a number of for-

JANICE ELLIOTT

eign settings (*The Italian Lesson, Life on the Nile, City of Gates*). I have also been more drawn by humour, sometimes to the forefront, more often as a bright, sharp thread in the weave. I believe that, as a result, my novels may have become more accessible to a wider audience.

"Given my inclination to dash off in different directions, I have been lucky in my critical reception. Not that I could have done otherwise. I am an entirely intuitive writer, often astonished to find myself where I am and in what company (e.g., with Hitler in an attic in North Oxford: *Dr. Gruber's Daughter*).

"Of my recent novels, *Secret Places* was the most successful. Set in a girls' school in the war. Best-seller. Made into a prize-winning film. For this I received the Southern Arts Award for Literature. Have always been lucky in critical success but commercial success has greatly improved in the last few years.

"I do not have any particular inspirations in the literary sense. The range of my novels is too great for that—sometimes very serious sometimes entertaining (like *The Italian Lesson*). An early influence when young was E.M. Forster. Inspiration has come increasingly from foreign settings, especially from the Middle East where I travel frequently.

"I am a compulsive and prolific writer. Very influenced by the visual—for instance, the work of the French painter, Marcel Mouly. I discovered his work at a summer show in Pont-Aven and have now used paintings of his on three book jackets—one of them on *Necessary Rites* (in

which I dressed Moira in the red dress Mouly uses in his painting)."

———

Janice Elliott was born in a rural village in Derbyshire, the daughter of Douglas John Elliott, an advertising executive, and the former Dorothy Wilson. She grew up in Nottingham, attended Nottingham High School for Girls, and studied English at St. Anne's College, Oxford, graduating with honors in 1953. At St. Anne's she was actively involved in the dramatics society and wrote four verse plays. In April 1959 she married Robert Cooper, a public relations officer. The couple have one son, Alexander.

Elliott began her journalistic career in 1954, working in London on the editorial staff of *House and Garden* and *House Beautiful*, on the woman's page of the *Sunday Times*, and as beauty editor of *Harper's Bazaar*. In 1962, when her first novel was published, she moved with her husband to a sixteenth-century cottage in Sussex. She continued to write, did some radio and television broadcasting, and contributed articles and reviews to publications including the *Times*, the *Sunday Times*, and *New Statesman*. She contributed regularly to *Twentieth Century Magazine* until 1972, and to the *Sunday Telegraph* until 1986.

Elliott's first novel, *Cave With Echoes*, is the story of a young man's unsuccessful search for love and acceptance. Jonah, the protagonist, looks back on his life and the emotional pain he has suffered, first at the hands of his mother, then at school. A friendship formed at Oxford University leads to a meeting with Agnes, with whom, briefly, he finds happiness. Then she too rejects him, and Jonah is on the verge of suicide. The *Times Literary Supplement* thought Jonah "too fluid and passive a personality. . . . He remains a sensitive pad absorbing pain and suffering, and dangerous to touch. . . . " The reviewer considered Elliott's style in the first person narration too "balanced and coherent" to portray a mind in dissolution.

In *The Somnambulists*, siblings are driven to a somnambulistic relationship with the world by being orphaned. The brother and sister, according to Bridget Brophy, writing in the *Sunday Times* (London), "move 'like dancers beneath the sea'. . . . Elliott's fabric is sprigged with knots of condensed observation and shimmers with lyrical metaphors. . . . through the sheer, unforced *bizarrerie* of her vision, which has the utter, almost alarming truthfulness only pure imagination can achieve." Elizabeth Jennings, in the *Listener*, found the tale "bizarre," as well, and noted "faults in design and treatment," but said that Elliott can write . . . with skill and perspicacity."

Since the early sixties, Elliott has produced novels at the rate of roughly one a year. Resourceful and adaptable, she has created an impressive range of characters and situation's, *The Godmother*, centers on an old woman nearing death. She has played the roles of a comforter and a destroyer, a benign magician and a malignant witch, although never a wife or mother, according to Nora Sayre in the *Nation*. "Elliott's . . . concern is the passive and almost arbitrary interaction of people who are far from fond of one another. . . . None of them wants to be an engine of control; hence their irritable insistence on making 'the godmother' a mythic figure from whom miracles are expected." The characters in *The Godmother* "are muted, respectable people who long for violence. They want to shout at and strike one another," according to Sayre. "The novel gives meticulous testimony that almost everyone feels—or is—insane at certain moments," she added.

The Buttercup Chain, a story of two college girls on holiday in Greece, which was filmed in 1970, was less successful. The *Times Literary Supplement* found it "bland and meaningless as the posed landscape with figures." Reviewers responded ambiguously to the extensive—some said superficial—use of allusion and symbolism in *The Singing Head*, a modern retelling of the orphans story, and its successor, *Angels Falling*, is a semimythic story of the decline of a well-to-do English family, in which the scene shifts cleverly both in time and place—Bloomsbury, Battersea, boarding school on the Downs, Oxford, Rome, East Africa. . . . Much of the zooming and fading, with elegantly blurred descriptions of the Blitz, snow over Oxford at Christmas gaiety in the Home Guard canteen or literary interviews at the Television Centre, succeeds in creating an authentic period mood," the reviewer in the *Times Literary Supplement* said, although caviling at an overliberal "use of the symbol [for the family] of gilded angels—sought for, unappreciated, and ultimately destroyed."

The Kindling marked a departure for Elliott from the middle- and upper-class milieu. The novel is set in an industrial town in the Midlands during the 1950s. The central character, Jack, is a working-class poet, a factory hand who "fences with the idea of total freedom and irresponsibility, but is enmeshed," according to Mary Borg, writing in the *New Statesman*. "Jack ends up giving himself to compromise, returning to his wife, beginning to write again and perjuring himself. . . . Jack's growth is at once delicately and remotely recounted, but one is deeply impressed with the reverberations of the story."

"England Trilogy"—*A State of Peace, Private Life*, and *Heaven on Earth*—which followed, centers on Olive, a dissatisfied urban housewife, and follows her through the collapse of her marriage after the war, a disastrous affair, and her retreat, in maturity, to rural Sussex. With these novels, Elliott was securely established as, in the words of a reviewer in the *Times Literary Supplement*, "a novelist with notable talent for recreating times past."

A Loving Eye, set in a mining community, was termed by Valentine Cunningham in the *New Statesman* a "dustbin-lorry" of a novel about "growing up in the provincial proletariat." Although such novels can be "wonderfully receptive grab-alls," Cunningham commented that perhaps "memories of bread and scrape and pikelets, of chapel picnics and the scholarship exam" might be a bit too rich a diet, but "happily, dustbin-lorries don't suffer indigestion. . . . The strain of making all this telling vividness coherent does . . . begin to tell a bit towards the end. . . . But . . . Elliott manages her people, grotesques and all with delightful skill. . . . " The protagonist "muses to his journal, 'if writing things down doesn't make them seem true—even make them happen like magic. . . . ' Indeed it does," Cunningham concludes, "at least Janice Elliott's writing does."

Secret Places, which was characterized by Lindsay Duguid in the *Times Literary Supplement* (1981), as a "saga of treachery and blood. . . . a novel of women without men," takes place during World War II in a girl's school. As the war progresses, one of the girls is persecuted for being a Jew and a German, and another girl "learns about love," according to Duguid. "Much of the book is funny. . . . But we are never far from a substratum of violence. . . . There are many references to blood": suicide, menstruation, a girl impaling herself on a railing, as well as a mother who is a morphine addict and a mad German in an internment camp. "All these details are woven to form a seamless and convincing whole," Duguid concluded. The novel was filmed in 1984.

With *The Country of Her Dreams*, Elliott left what Miranda Seymour, writing in *Books and Bookmen*, deemed "pleasantly anodyne autobiographical novels set in the fifties" to depict a world "fringed by menace and the unknown," towards which she had been moving in *Secret Places*. *The Country of Her Dreams* is set "in a country that sounds like Jugoslavia," according to Penelope Lively, writing in *Encounter*, "which is in a state of internal unrest; there is rioting, suggestions of a military coup." A British couple are there attending a congress on the preservation of key artifacts of European culture in the event of a nuclear war. Great pressure is placed upon their marriage, and indeed upon their psychic wholeness, by an outbreak of terrorism, in which the husband is taken hostage. The wife, Mary, responds to her husband's peril by having an affair. "Excessive circumstances, it is suggested, can unleash 'the serpents in oneself,'" Lively says. Savkar Altinel commented in the *Times Literary Supplement*, "There is no shortage of novels about happy couples who break up as soon as they step outside the confines of domesticity, or intellectuals who find themselves unable to cope with 'real' life, or smug Northerners who come to grief in Mediterranean lands." Altinel found Elliott's allusions to other novelists a strength, however. "The knowledge of literature she both displays herself and demands from her readers is a part of her defence of culture. . . . She knows that, however artificial happiness, order and rationality may be, the alternative, which is chaos, is only painful and unproductive."

In *Dr. Gruber's Daughter* Elliott returns to postwar England, "a time of dottiness and confusion," as Betty Pesetsky remarked in the *New York Times Book Review*. The scene is an Oxford hostel populated by a virginal Oxford don; a countess who feeds the mysterious denizen of the attic, Dr. Gruber; a woman who has an imaginary friendship with the new Queen Elizabeth and experiences phantom pregnancies; and others whom Pesetsky refers to as "stock characters." "Economy and wit mark . . . Elliott's prose. The characters are largely drawn with precision, using the busyness of people to illuminate the wondrous. . . . And the secrets of Radpole Road are an embarrassment to history," Pesetsky adds. The embarrassment turns out to be the fact that the attic denizen is Adolf Hitler. "Those who take their knowledge seriously have to be punished, for seriousness is out of order in Coronation year. . . . " Anita Brookner commented in the *Spectator*. Brookner found Elliott's farcical treatment "very well done. . . . [T]he reader is at last allowed access to grown-up world which might have seemed to be in danger of . . . total eclipse. Whether the grown-up world is more palatable than the world of surreal university junketings is something [the] reader will have to decide." Brookner says she finished the book with considerable admiration for Elliott's insight, overcoming "earlier impatience with her levity."

One of Elliott's recurring symbols, according to Jane O'Grady, reviewing *Necessary Rites* in the *Times Literary Supplement*, is "the lighted room motif." In *Sadness of Witches*, Martha the witch feels "shut out of the warm rooms of life"

as if she were outside during a party, with the curtains drawn against her. In *Life on the Nile* a woman looks into a room in which her husband is surrounded by other women. "But Martha . . . gains access to human warmth" and *Life on the Nile* ends with the couple "standing together in a dark garden that is suddenly illuminated as the lights indoors go off." O'Grady found that in *Necessary Rites* Elliott again achieved "the tantalizing dovetail between literal and metaphorical, inner and outer . . . typical of [her] satisfying literary agility." This time, however, the lighted room is seen from the inside, where the protagonists try unsuccessfully to exclude the chaos outside, "but, instead of being wistful archetype, it is negative and sinister." Living in the 1990s, the Franklands take in a girl who has been driven mad by watching her brother murdered by the IRA, and they are literally and metaphorically invaded. "The Franklands' ordered privacy is precarious and unhealthy, like that of England itself, now in possession of secret gulags and lethal-weapons installations, and imposing martial law and capital punishment in Northern Ireland. . . . As usual . . . Elliott is excellent on the trawled detritus of old marriages and the sense of place. The hint of magic she always gives, whether explicitly, or as here, through fairy tale allusions and people's free association, imbues even a menacing futuristic world with beauty as well as danger," O'Grady concluded.

In *City of Gates* Elliott attempts to evoke Jerusalem and to provide her protagonist, the modern pilgrim Daisy, with Christian redemption, which she achieves through acceptance of an immanent God. Daisy stays in the guesthouse of a woman for whom "'all times are one' and, as with the work as a whole, she constantly juxtaposes biblical and contemporary history," Bryan Cheyette wrote in the *Times Literary Supplement* (1992). He considered Elliott's invention of a character who encompasses all evil "clearly a device which enables Elliott to avoid any meaningful evocation of the real conflict in the Middle East." Nevertheless, he considered *City of Gates* "an accomplished and ambitious work with an admirably succinct and fast-moving narrative pace."

Anne Barnard, reviewing *The Noise From the Zoo*, a story collection, sums up Elliott's career: "[B]oth the author and her posse of woman-writer heroines nose along the boundaries between the world they live in and the ones they create. . . . Elliott . . . layers her spare, almost gaunt stories so that rather than repeating, they wind through a murky world where one object at a time looms large and distended, while the rest fade just out of reach. . . . Offering rich details in place and leaving tantalizing gaps in others . . . Elliott's own writing aims from a different angle at the themes of control and creativity her characters explore."

In 1981 Elliott and her husband moved from Sussex to a Georgian house on the water, in the small town of Fowey in Cornwall. For six years she worked as a tutor to a creative writing workshop there, and has reviewed books for the *Independent*. Elliott is a Fellow of the Royal Society of Literature.

PRINCIPAL WORKS: *Novels*—Cave With Echoes, 1962; The Somnambulists, 1964; The Godmother, 1966; The Buttercup Chain, 1967; The Singing Head, 1968; Angels Falling, 1969; The Kindling, 1970; A State of Peace, 1971; Private Life, 1972; Heaven on Earth, 1975; A Loving Eye, 1977; The Honey Tree, 1978; Summer People, 1980; Secret Places, 1981; The Country of Her Dreams, 1982; Magic, 1983; The Italian Lesson, 1985; Dr. Gruber's Daughter, 1986; The Sadness of Witches, 1987; Life on the Nile, 1989; Necessary Rites, 1990; City of Gates, 1992. *Short Stories*—The Noise From the Zoo and Other Stories, 1991. *Juvenile*—The Birthday Unicorn, 1970; Alexander in the Land of Mog, 1973; The Incompetent Dragon, 1982; The King Awakes, 1987; The Empty Throne, 1988.

ABOUT: Blain, V. etal. (eds.), The Feminist Companion to Literature in English, 1990; Brophy, B. Don't Never Forget: Collected Views and Reviews, 1967; Contemporary Authors 13–16, 1966; Contemporary Literary Criticism 47, 1988; Dictionary of Literary Biography 14, 1983; Todd, J. (ed.) Britis Women Writers, 1989. *Periodicals*—Books and Bookmen September, 1971; Encounter June/July, 1986; Listener April 23, 1964; November 2, 1978; Nation September 11, 1967; New Statesman June 12, 1970; July 16, 1971; July 29, 1977; New York times Book Review January 17, 1988; Saturday Review April 8, 1967; Spectator March 15, 1975; March 28, 1981; September 17, 1983; September 6, 1986; Sunday Times April 1964; Time and Tide September 13–20, 1962; Times (London) April 3, 1980; March 18, 1982; Times Literary Supplement July 21, 1966; October 13, 1978; March 13, 1981; March 19, 1982; September 20, 1991; October 9, 1992.

*****ESTERHÁZY, PÉTER** (April 14, 1950–), Hungarian novelist and essayist, is arguably the most important representative of contemporary Hungarian prose, and was one of the first to revolutionize and westernize the literary scene in the 1970s. His most fundamental contribution to modern Hungarian letters is his idiosyncratic, subversive view of history. Esterházy reexamines the entire notion of history, as well as the process of history. His use of "Borrowed material" (unacknowledged texts from other authors), creates a multilayered palimpsest of existential experience and demonstrates that, in Esterházy's judgment, history, like fiction, is just a text, a narrative.

Esterházy was born in Budapest and spent his early years in a small Hungarian village where his family, members of Hungary's aristocracy, were banned during the Stalinist terror. As he wrote, tongue in cheek, his father was "a martyr of the labor movement." During the "soft dictatorship" of János Kádár, the Esterházy family was permitted to move to Római Fürdö, a small community in the vicinity of the capital; its description can be found in his *Hrabal könyve* (1990, *The Book of Hrabal*). Esterházy completed his high school studies in 1968. He received his bachelor's degree in mathematics from Eötuös Loránd University and published his first short pieces in 1974. Esterházy's first volumes, *Francsikó es Pinta* (Francsiko and Pinta) and *Pápai vizeken ne kalózkodj* (Do not practice piracy on papal waters) appeared in 1975 and 1977, respectively. But it was his *Termelési regeny* (Production novel, 1979), which took its author nearly seven years to complete, that brought him national recognition. It is a parody, both ominous and hilarious, of an oppressive and obsessive system, and the response of the artist who refuses to be trapped by it. The two-way split between grotesque public life and the equally travestied private idyll of the hero is reproduced in the split format in the novel. The reader is directed by arrows and other graphic signals to convergences between the two segments.

In Esterházy's postmodernist works the form often underscores and esthetically supports the narrative. A case in point is the black-framed pages of his *A szív segedigéi* (1985, *Helping Verbs of the Heart*) as well as numerous books in which different typographies are juxtaposed. Esterházy isolates and validates each of his sentences, making them his moralistic and artistic center. He is primarily concerned with the sentence, the unit to which he professes his ultimate loyalty. He writes:

As opposed to their usual relationship, sentence and reality play a reversed role in my work. I measure each of my sentences against reality. Therefore, I remain unconcerned with my sentence's capacity of describing reality; instead, I seek to verify that reality indeed contains such a segment, i.e. to prove that my sentence is real. Consequently, without a sentence, there is no reality, at least I do not know what to do with it; I cannot relate to it. I do not claim that in the beginning there was the word, or intelligence, o strength, or action; I merely state my inability to deal with it. Even if the claim that I am choosing literature instead of life is exaggerated (or because, *ars longa, vita brevis est*), it seems to be a valid contention that I am happiest in paper-nearness, which I, of course, would not chalk up as pure gain.

°es tur HAZ ee

Indeed for Esterházy, home equals literature; his true *patria* is made up of bookshelves surrounding him in his study.

His fiction written in the 1980s—*Függo* (Dependent, 1981), *Kiszavatol a lady biztonságádért* (Who will vouch for the safety of the lady?, 1982), *Fuharosok* (1983, *The Transporters*), *Kis Magyar pornográia* (Short Hungarian pornography, 1984), *A szív segédigéi* (1985, *Helping Verbs of the Heart*), and *A kitömött hattyú* (The stuffed swan, 1988), first appeared separately, and subsequently, according to Esterházy's original design, in a massive on-volume edition titled *Bevezetés a szpirodalomba* (Introduction to belles lettres) in 1986.

A principal literary device in Esterházy's work is "the ultimate polyphony." He introduces into his novels multiple narrative voices and hides and juxtaposes the authorial "I." One of Esterházy's linguistic tours de force is his *Tizenhét hattyúk* (Seventeen swans, 1987) an "autobiographical novel" with contemporary Hungary as its background. The work is written in the language of the 18th century, yet it features a young proletarian girl as its heroine. It was first published under the pseudonym Lili Csokonai. A minor literary scandal erupted when it turned out that the author was not a young woman, some literary mogul's protégée, but Esterházy. The critics who did not discover the identity of the author until Esterházy himself revealed the truth were embarrassed. But Esterházy is always deceptive, especially when he uses the confessional first person singular or his initials, E.P., for his hero's name. He frequently includes his family members among his transformed literary subjects; a recent work, a three-act absurd comedy, *Bucsuszinfonia; A gabonakereskedo* (Farewell symphony; The grain merchant), features his father and brothers as its imaginary heroes.

Esterházy is especially admired for his use of language. The inimitable rhythm of his sentences is based on a combination of archaisms, slang, party jargon, and sophisticated prose. This characteristic of his work provides a great challenge to his translators. He uses language and reality as a conspirator uses his tools: secretively and cunningly, sharing a knowing glance with the initiated reader. A telling example of this method is his exploitation of the date June 16. While it is Bloomsday, the date that James Joyce jotted under the last line of *Ulysses*, it is also the date of the secret execution of Imre Nagy, the leader of Hungary's failed 1956 revolution. Esterházy often plays with the date, using it frequently in make-believe diaries, and in each case he leaves it for the reader and/or for the censor to decipher. He also amuses his readers by replacing phrases eliminated by the censor (or by himself, pretending to be the censor), in his text with ellipses.

In Esterházy's work time is central. He views time, like space, as empty and filled, at the same instant. He sees man imprisoned by time and space, even within a utopian framework. *Függo* (Dependent) also deals with time and memory. Esterházy agrees with Borges in that "the infinite can only be viewed at the same time" (a notion expressed in Borge's "Alef", and in Esterházy's *Függö*, and *The Book of Hrabal*. He addresses the same issue in *Kis Magyar pornógráfia* (Short Hungarian pornography), an ironical depiction of the "permanent" Hungarian ethos against the backdrop of Communist slogans and "red-white-green" nationalistic folklore.

Esterházy uses the discourse of Sartre, Camus, Gombrowicz, Joyce, Musil, Spinoza, Wittgenstein, and others, rejecting quotation marks and freely mixing their works into his own text, thus integrating his prose with the best known representatives of European literary tradition. In addition to "borrowing" individual words or phrases, Esterházy also works on a larger scale. In *The Book of Hrabal*, the Czech author Bohumil Hrabal's biography and some of his fiction appear as part of the novel.

The Book of Hrabal, the story of a Hungarian writer and his family, is told in three chapters: The Chapter of Faithfulness, The Chapter of Unfaithfulness, and untitled concluding chapter, with God as its principal character. The marital triangle is underscored by the tripartite arrangement of the book. The writer is working on a book about Hrabal, while his wife, Anna, is at first jealous of Hrabal, but later falls in love with him. Hrabal, the Czech author, is the pseudo subject of the novel. Three additional characters, God and two guardian angels, complete the cast. The plots may also be reduced to three: the rebuilding of the writer's house and Anna's fourth pregnancy, treated as one plot; her falling in love with Hrabal; and the Lord's falling in love with Anna. The stories are told in first and third person narrative, dialogue, epistle, and religious meditation forms. False perception again plays a major role; although the husband is supposedly writing about Hrabal, Anna is actually the one doing the writing. Perhaps the writer is still struggling with his first sentence. Thus, Esterházy's irony subverts the "omniscient" author image of the traditional novel. Phrases and situations borrowed from the real Hrabal's work, and the description of Hrabal, based on actual photographs, are added to amuse the reader.

Such an insider's joke is repeated in *Bevezetés a szépirodalomba* (Introduction to Belles Lettres), where Esterházy appropriates an entire short story written by Danilo Kiš, reasoning that its hero's name, Esterházy, makes the story his own intellectual property.

Recycling is another frequent feature of Esterházy's prose. Segments of his fiction that have appeared earlier resurface in new context. As in Cervantes' *Don Quixote*, the archetype of the text quoting itself, each self-quotation in Esterházy's prose takes an esthetically and ideologically new position. Since Esterházy views his own oeuvre as a single effort, he believes that by its transformed status, each new text also affects the original one.

Helping Verbs of the Heart is Esterházy's first book-length work to appear in English translation. It is a difficult test, dealing with a difficult time in the author's life. As the story unfolds, the narrator, an eldest son, describes his mother's last days in the hospital, surrounded by her confused family and an unsympathetic medical staff. This would be a straightforward narrative, a simple tale, about the death of a parent, had the author not been Esterházy. *Helping Verbs* is fragmentary and complex; the complexity of thoughts and feelings are reflected in the multilayered narrative which, with parts framed in black, is developed on different parts of the page, as well as on several planes of consciousness. At one point the roles reverse; it is no longer the son watching his mother die, but the mother mourning the death of her son. Without pathos and sentimentality—and with the intergeneration into the text of work of other authors such as Borges and Peter Handke, Esterházy epitomizes indignity and defenselessness of "all flesh" in the face of death.

In *Fuharosok* (1983, *The Transporters*), Esterházy confronts the issue of rape: the rape of women, and the rape of the country by its occupiers. He asserts that there are no pure victims: everyone is responsible, those who commit the crimes and those who permit them to happen. He also puts equal blame on his fictional alter ego, the "knight," the eternal intellectual who frequently and willingly succumbs to brute force and, seduced by it, will serve any perpetrator.

Esterházy continually reminds us that everything in the world is a matter of perspective. *The Book of Hrabal* is, in fact, Anna's book; the entire second part is written from her point of view. The critical importance of perspective is demonstrated by the various voices (one of them being that of God). Similarly in *Daisy* (1984), a bold and boisterous drama in a sleazy nightclub

in Berlin, an androgynous transvestite pair (Daisy and Robi) represent both the outrageousness of a divided Germany and the inexplicable mysteries of all human experience. *Hahn-Hahn grófnö pillantasa-lefelé a Dunán* (1991, *The Glance of Countess Hahn-Hahn*), a satire about Central Europe, can be read as a travelogue (subverting itself at every step), or a spy story in which agents and double agents are swept along by the River Danube—and the plot. It is however, also a historical novel, a 20th-century version of Theodor Fontane's 19th century novel *Ellie Briest*, a restaurant guide, a book about chaos, and a satire on a book by Claudio Magris, *Danubio* (1986). In this sense it is really a Danube book.

Esterházy insists that the reader take nothing for granted—not even where a book should begin. *Biztos kaland* (Safe adventure, 1989), a small volume of text and photographs (the latter by Balázs Czeizel) about an unknown young woman's life, can, be read from both ends of the book and seems to explode in the reader's face in the middle. But, perhaps, that is where the reader should have started reading. Furthermore, the story could be considered as a continuation of *Tizenhét hattyúk* (Seventeen Swans) but that is not the writer's concern.

Esterházy often combines text and illustration. *A vajszinü árnyalat* (The off-white shade, with Andraás Szebeni, 1993), approaches Hungary's recent history with a blend of provocative photographs and captions. Of the same type are his *Egy nö* (A woman, with Ferenc Banga), and *Amit a nyakkendörol tudni kell* (Everything you ever wanted to know about neckties), which appeared in 1993. While the former is designed as a scroll in the author's handwriting, accompanied by Banga's drawings (with the addition of a trilingual printed version), the latter not only describes all the intricacies of tying bow ties, but at the end rewards the reader with a detachable silk bow tie.

On a more serious plane, in Esterházy's works history has no purpose or direction and is often visually represented in the text by one of the author's favorite symbols, a snake biting its own tail. However, Esterházy' is not just another voice of nineteenth-century disillusionment, updated. The major difference between Esterházy and his pessimistic compatriots is his detachment. He places himself above the petty and biased nationalistic interpretations of Hungary's history. His memory—and his family's past— span much of the history of Europe over several centuries. His broad vision of the world and his gentle irony distinguish him from his fellow Hungarians. He is busy probing "the sources of existential disorder," is examining a world "wracked with terror, mistrust and isolation," trying to identify and define the artist's role in that world.

In the early 1990s Esterházy published three volumes of cultural and political sketches on life in Hungary after Communism. *A halacska csodálatos élete* (The miraculous life of small fry, 1991) *Az elefantcsonttoronyból* (From the Ivory Tower, 1991), and *Egy kekharisnya feljegyzesei* (The memoirs of a blue stocking, 1994), have a broad range. The individual pieces were first published in several periodicals and newspapers, but the volumes have a unifying feature: Esterházy's deep concern for Hungary's ethical and moral self-image. He pleads for more introspection, and for more balanced judgments of the past. His humanity and engaging wit make these writings enjoyable and thought-provoking.

Esterházy is an engaged writer, committed to language, to which he believes a writer is solely responsible. Therefore, he places words and their meanings, sentences and their semantic power, at the top of his responsibilities. "We cannot find words," he asserts, repeatedly in his writings. A writer blissfully unaffected by literary theories Esterházy has only amused scorn for those who theorize about his writings. He is in a permanent and passionate feud with language, and quotes more than a thousand writers—poets as well as thinkers. Perhaps he does this to underscore his basic concern: "Can any word be real enough to give us reality?"

Esterházy's work has been translated into about two dozen European languages. He has received a number of prestigious Hungarian and foreign awards, among them the Müvészeti Alap prize (1980): the Mikes Kelemen prize (Amsterdam, 1980); the Füst Milan prize (1983); the Dery prize (1984); the József Attila prize (1986); the Vilenica prize (Yugoslavia, 1988); the Krudy prize (1990); the Evropski Fejeton prize (Brno, 1991); the Soros Életmü prize (1992); "Premio opera di poesia" prize (Rome, 1993). He is married to Gitta Reén; they have four children.

PRINCIPAL WORKS IN ENGLISH TRANSLATION: (tr. M. H. Hein) Helping Verbs of the Heart, 1990; (tr. J. Sollosy) The Book of Hrabal, 1994; "The Transporters" in the Hungarian P.E.N. 26 (1985); *in* Hungarian Quartet, 1992; *in* The Kiss, 1993; (tr. R. Aczel) The Glance of Countess Hahn-Hahn, 1994

ABOUT: Contemporary World Writers, 2nd ed., 1993. *Periodicals*—Cross Currents Vol. 71, 1992; New York Times June 7, 1994; San Francisco Chronicle April 14, 1991; Times Literary Supplement December 31, 1993; April 15, 1994.

ESTLEMAN, LOREN D. (September 25, 1952–), American writer of mystery and Western novels and short stories, was born in Ann Arbor, Michigan, the son of Leauvett Charles Estleman, a short- haul truck driver, and the former Louise Milankovich, a postal clerk. Estleman's childhood holds clues to his fascination with the seamy side of life. He grew up hearing his father's stories of his rough-and-tumble past and his mother's near marriage to a member of the infamous Detroit Purple Gang. He had an Austrian-born grandmother, whose passion for gambling took her from job to job as a cook all over the country. One of her gambling acquaintances, she liked to recollect, was Al Capone.

From his childhood Estleman's favorite authors have been Edgar Allan Poe, Jack London, and Raymond Chandler, all of whom he cites as major influences. Another youthful influence was the television series "The Untouchables."

Early in his career Estleman worked on a number of Michigan newspapers. While in high school, he was a political cartoonist for Ann Arbor's *Michigan Red*, an AFL-CIO publication for federal employees. Later he was a reporter for the *Ypsilanti Press*. In 1974 he took his B.A. from Eastern Michigan University, where he majored in English literature and minored in journalism. After graduation, he continued to work on newspapers until 1980, when he embarked on his dream, a full-time literary career.

Estleman's goal was always to be a book writer. During his senior year in college, he published a gangster novel titled *The Oklahoma Punk*. Though undistinguished, this first book gave the writer an opportunity to develop his own style. The 1978 publication of *The Hider*, his second book and first western, marks the beginning of his dual career as mystery and Western writer. Since then Estleman has alternated between the two genres.

Estleman's journalistic experiences proved invaluable as he turned to writing detective fiction. Not only had he listened to the cops and their stories, while covering crime beats, but he sometimes went with them on arrests. Some of the stories as well as police jargon, cadences, and philosophy have made their way into his books. The clarity of style, eye for detail, and respect for research, demanded of good journalism helped Estleman bring a convincing sense to his prolific output.

With the encouragement of a group of Ann Arbor Sherlockians, Estleman joined the ranks of authors who have "unearthed" lost accounts of the master sleuth written by his associate Dr. Watson. The result was his first formal mystery,

LOREN D. ESTLEMAN

Sherlock Holmes Versus Dracula, published in 1978. As the title proclaims, the novel pits the world's most famous detective against the world's most famous vampire, who has come to England in search of fresh victims. A *Booklist* review declared that Estleman had created a "decent evocation of the Conan Doyle style in this sprightly pastiche." R. F. Grady, in *Best Sellers*, agreed that the "imitation of Watson's late-Victorian prose is admirably done," but found the ending "predictable . . . and unsatisfying." A year later Estleman followed with *Dr. Jekyll and Mr. Holmes*, with much the same results.

Estleman left the Victorian world of Holmes and Watson to start his popular Amos Walker series. Published in 1980, *Motor City Blue*, set in present-day Detroit, introduces Walker, a thirty-two-year-old Vietnam veteran and private investigator with a B.A. in sociology. Cynical, jaundiced, principled, a wearily compassionate loner, Walker hates crooks, cops, and phonies and is clearly in the Philip Marlowe/Sam Spade/Mike Hammer hard-boiled gumshoe tradition.

Estleman presents Detroit as a predator-filled place which gives Walker ample opportunity to be tough. "It's the place where the American dream stalled and sat rusting in the rain," Estleman says about Detroit. In *The Midnight Man*, he writes, " Warehouses and tenements wallowed in the mulch of decades . . . Yellow mortar oozes out of brick walls covered with obscenities . . . heaps of stale laundry shaped vaguely like human beings snores in doorways . . . their open mouths scooping black, toothless holes out of their stubbed faces."

Equally colorful are the perceptions Estleman gives to Walker about his fellow characters: "They got the bodyguard from central casting . . . He had no neck or maybe he did have and someone had accidentally chopped of his head and pasted a brown, gray-streaked wig on the stump and penciled on features to make it do for a substitute. Certainly they could have been penciled on, flat and lifeless as they looked, with bladderlike scar tissue over the eyes and a crescent of dead white skin on each cheek," Walker says in *Motor City Blue*, in which he is hired by an aging mobster to find his ward, a girl who disappeared from a fashionable finishing school. Working with only one clue, a nude photograph of the girl, Walker visits brothels, porn shops, and various denizens of the underside. The *New York Times* named it in a list of notable books of 1980. Jean M. White predicted in the *Washington Post Book World* that "Walker and Detroit could turn a winning combination." She noted, however, "lapses of florid overwriting that border on parody of the hard boiled style." *Angel Eyes*, the second Walker mystery, finds the sleuth hired by a nightclub dancer to find her in case she disappears. Newgate Callendar, in the *New York Times Book Review*, balked at Estleman's style: "Here is a tough, street-wise cop talking to Walker: ' . . . and that suit you're wearing went out with poems that rhyme.' Nice. Cute. But would that figure of speech have come out of the mouth of such a character? . . . Tough is tough, but inanity is also inanity." Fans of Estleman might argue that for every line that can cause a groan, such as "the air was as bitter as a stiffed hooker," there are little gems, like "the boundaries of Detroit are as vague as the mayor's morals."

Estleman has said that he has many more ideas for his alter ego and new directions for the series to take. Jean M. White, reviewing *Angel Eyes* for the *Washington Post Book World*, summed up the reasons for Amos Walker's continuing popularity: "Estleman knows the seamy underworld of Detroit's mean streets. He has a nice touch for its characters and language. His knife-sharp prose matches the hurtling pace of the action."

In 1984 Estleman introduced another Detroit tough guy to the mystery world. Peter Macklin is a hit man who has severed his ties to the mob but continues to free-lance. "He had sunk garrottes into fat necks in moving cars and heard arteries popping like corn in an oven when he applied pressure," Estleman writes in *Kill Zone*, using a third-person narrative for Macklin, rather than Amos Walker's first person. In this first Macklin yarn, a Lake Erie excursion boat is seized by terrorists demanding the release of "political" prisoners. Macklin is pitted against villains even lower than himself. Although not all reviewers believe that Estleman succeeded, several were willing to accept Macklin as he is and settled back to enjoy the action and colorful characters. "The plot twists and turns are dazzling," *Publishers Weekly* declared. "Macklin may seem a bit remote and shadowy, but that's not inappropriate in this whiz-bang of a book." Estleman followed with more Macklin adventures: *Roses Are Dead* and *Any Man's Death.*

Estleman's fast-moving style works with equal effectiveness in his Westerns. *The Hider,* his first Western, a blend of action and nostalgia, tells the story of a boy and an old man on a last buffalo hunt. In *The High Rocks,* Estleman introduces Page Murdock, a United States marshal in Montana, who plays by his own rules and falls short of the heroic lawman image. In *Private Eyes* Robert A. Baker and Michael T. Nietzel describe Murdock as a "man who can be purposefully brutal. He will kill for the sake of expediency and have few regrets afterward." Despite his brutality, Murdock is basically amiable and likable. *The High Rocks,* which has him trying to stop a childhood friend named Bear Anderson from causing unrest among Flathead Indians, was a nominee for the American Book Award.

Estleman has also written a number of novels re-creating famous characters and events of the American West. *Aces and Eights,* an account of the killing of Wild Bill Hickok and the trial of his murderer, was awarded the Golden Spur Award by the Western Writers of America for best Western historical novel. It is the first of a planned trilogy; the second, *This Old Bill,* is a fable based on the life of Buffalo Bill Cody; it was nominated for a Pulitzer Prize in Letters. The third volume is to portray George Armstrong Custer. In 1988, Estleman published *Bloody Season,* a gripping re-creation of the gunfight at the O.K. Corral. David Dary wrote on the *Los Angeles Times Book Review* that the "author's search for objectivity and truth, combined with his skill as a fine writer, have created a new vision of what happened in Tombstone. . . . "

Estleman has received nominations for the Shamus Award by the Private Eye Writers of America and A Michigan Arts Foundation Award for Literature. A prolific short story writer, he has appeared in such publications as *Alfred Hitchcock's Mystery Magazine* and *Pulpsmith,* and has often been included in anthologies. Among his favorite contemporary authors are Stephan Greenleaf, Bill Pronzini, Joe Gores, Donald Hamilton, Elmore Leonard and Douglas C. Jones.

In 1987, Estleman married Carole Ann Ashley, a marketing and public relations specialist. They make their home in Whitmore Lake, Michigan.

PRINCIPAL WORKS: *Novels*—The Oklahoma Punk, 1976; reissued as Red Highway, 1987); The Hider, 1978; Sherlock Holmes Versus Dracula; or, The Adventure of the Sanguinary Count, 1978; Dr. Jekyll and Mr. Holmes, 1979; The High Rocks, 1979; Motor City Blue, 1980; Stamping Ground, 1980; Aces and Eights, 1981; Angel Eyes, 1981; The Wolfer, 1981; The Midnight Man, 1982; Murdock's Law, 1982; The Glass Highway, 1983; Mister St. John, 1983; Kill Zone, 1984; The Stranglers, 1984; Sugartown, 1984; This Old Bill, 1984; Gun Man, 1985; Roses Are Dead, 1985; Any Man's Death, 1986; Every Brilliant Eye, 1986; Lady Yesterday, 1987; Bloody Season, 1988; Downriver, 1988; Peeper, 1989; Silent Thunder, 1989; Western Story, 1989; Sweet Women Lie, 1990; Motown, 1991; Sudden Country, 1991; King of the Corner, 1992; City of Widows, 1994. *Short stories*—General Murders: Ten Amos Walker Mysteries, 1988. *Plays*—Dr. and Mrs. Watson at Home *in* Greenberg, M. H. and Rössel-Waugh, C. L. (eds.) The New Adventures of Sherlock Holmes, 1987. *Nonfiction*—The Wister Trace: Classic Novels of the American Frontier, 1987.

ABOUT: Baker, R. A. and Nietzel, M. T. Private Eyes: One Hundred and One Knights: A Survey of American Detective Fiction 1922–1984, 1985; Contemporary Authors New Revision Series 27, 1989; Contemporary Literary Criticism 48, 1988; Pronzini, B. and Muller, M. 1001 Midnights: The Aficionado's Guide to Mystery and Detective Fiction, 1986; Twentieth-Century Crime and Mystery Writers, 1991; Twentieth-Century Western Writers, 1982. *Periodicals*—Best Sellers December 1978; Booklist September 15, 1978; September 1, 1985; Detroit March 8, 1987; Detroit News May 18, 1979; August 21, 1983; Los Angeles Times Book Review January 24, 1988; Monthly Detroit December 1981; New York Times Book Review November 1, 1981; Publishers Weekly July 13, 1984; August 23, 1985; Washington Post Book World September 21, 1980; October 18, 1981; Wilson Library Bulletin March 1985.

EXLEY, FREDERICK (March 28, 1929–June 17, 1992), American novelist, was born in Watertown, New York, the son of Earl, a telephone lineman, and Charlotte (Merkley) Exley. He had an older brother, Bill, as well as a twin sister and a younger sister. Although he was an all-state high school basketball player, Exley was never able to equal the success of his father, who had been a local sports hero. Following high school, Exley enrolled in Hobart College in Geneva, New York, where, thinking it would please his parents, he took courses to prepare for dental school. He soon transferred to the University of Southern California, however, where he ma-

FREDERICK EXLEY

jored in English. After completing his B.A. in 1953, he then returned east and drifted through various frustrating jobs including public relations and teaching high school. Meanwhile, the rest of his life was also in turmoil as he experienced alcoholism, failed marriages, and three short stays in mental institutions where he was diagnosed as paranoid and schizophrenic. All the while, however, he was writing, and it was his own troubled life that he would use as the basis for his trilogy of novels.

The main character in *A Fan's Notes*, the first of these autobiographical novels, published in 1968, is named Frederick Exley, but the book is subtitled "A Fictional Memoir." Exley explained in a prefatory note that although the episodes were somewhat similar to "that long malaise, my life, many of the characters and happenings are creations solely of the imagination." In an interview with the *New York Post*, Exley acknowledged that a few people had refused to sign releases so that he "had to build a kind of disguise around them." Still, he claimed that most of the book was true.

Whether authentic or not, the stories told by the narrator are vivid and energetic, evincing intelligence, insight, and ribald humor in the midst of madness. As Exley encounters obstacles at every turn, he becomes increasingly disillusioned and must eventually admit that he will never achieve success. Full of alienation and self-hatred, he spirals downward, stumbling drunkenly through dull jobs and unfulfilling sexual encounters. He ends up at one point spending months holed up in his mother's house, lying on the couch eating Oreo cookies and watching soap operas. His life is centered on the Sunday afternoon ritual of watching Frank Gifford achieve fame and adulation playing football for the New York Giants. After Gifford sustains a potentially career-ending injury, Exley picks a meaningless fight because he realizes "it was my destiny—unlike that of my father, whose fate it was to hear the roar of the crowd—to sit in the stands with most men and acclaim others. It was my fate, my destiny, my end, to be a fan."

Exley the author stated that the book took its unique form because he knew readers would not be interested in the autobiography of "a totally unknown man, a drunk, a wastrel, a lunatic." He told the *Village Voice* that "I knew that to pull the book off I'd have to employ the novelist's techniques of narrative, structure and so forth." Then he had the idea of using Gifford, who also graduated from USC in 1953, as an alter ego against whom he could compare his unfortunate life. "He went on to legend as a Giant halfback, and I went on to the bughouse," he reflected; "why was this? . . . *discipline.*"

Critical response to *A Fan's Notes* was almost universally favorable with several reviewers comparing Exley's writing to that of F. Scott Fitzgerald. Rudolph Wurlitzer noted in the *New Republic* (1968) that "Exley's social perception is as acute as Fitzgerald's." According to Derek Mahon of the *Listener*, "Exley-the-narrator seeks love and fame; like Gatsby, he believes in the green light of American romanticism; and he finds ashes." It is "a work of depth and seriousness," he continued, "a moving, richly humorous record of humiliation and perseverance." According to the *Times Literary Supplement* (1970), *A Fan's Notes* succeed because of its perceptiveness and self-mocking quality: "The book is not a manic cry of anguish and self-pity; self-examination is what Exley is about." Stanley Reynolds commented in the *New Statesman* that "the effect is rather like getting button-holed by a drunk in a bar who grips you by both lapels, breathing whiskey and polysyllables into your face, and never uses two words where he can possibly find 10 that'll do."

Exley garnered many awards for *A Fan's Notes*, including the William Faulkner Foundation award for the best first novel, a nomination for the National Book Award, and the Richard and Hinda Rosenthal Foundation Award from the National Institute of Arts and Letters, which is given to works which achieve critical but not commercial success. Initially the book only sold 8000 copies, but is has since been reissued in many different paperback editions. In the next few years, while working on his second book, Exley also received a Rockefeller Foundation award and taught at the Iowa Writers' Workshop. Published in 1975, *Pages from a Cold Island* was billed as nonfiction. Exley continues to denigrate himself despite the acclaim he had recently received for *A Fan's Notes.* This time the narrator Frederick Exley finds himself lacking not in comparison to an athlete, but to the American writer and critic Edmund Wilson. Wilson spent the last years of his life in Talcottville, in the same part of upstate New York where Exley lived; the two shared an affection for and identification with that region. In the book Wilson's last days are chronicled, and Exley's conversations with Wilson's daughter and secretary are reported. Although the two never met, Wilson epitomized for Exley the disciplined, dignified, literary figure that Exley was not. Exley's depression and aimlessness are compounded by his inability to complete the book that he is writing, also called "Pages from a Cold Island." Like his first book, *Pages* is full of detailed descriptions of Exley's random sexual encounters and alcohol-induced escapades.

The critical response to *Pages from a Cold Island* was mixed. Douglas J. Maloney, writing in the *Literary Quarterly,* reported that not only does Exley "maintain an infectious Rabelaisian humor," but "his writing is so beautifully structured that its effect is almost hypnotic." In the *New York Review of Books* (1975), however, Roger Sale wrote that "Exley is very much in need of a subject that is not himself." Ronald De Feo concurred in the *National Review,* noting that "the troubled, defeated, comic narrator of the earlier book has grown coarse and loud." According to Thomas Edwards of the *New York Review of Books* (1989), *Pages* lacks direction and, at its best, simply rehashed points made in the first book. "It's a sad, baffled book," he commented, "hard not to take as evidence of a talent in dissolution from rather ordinary causes."

In *Last Notes from Home,* the final part of the trilogy, Exley flies to Hawaii to visit his brother Bill, a retired colonel, who is dying of cancer. On the way, he meets Robin Glenn, a gorgeous flight attendant, and Jimmy O'Twoomey, a wealthy, drunken, verbose Irishman. After Bill's death, O'Twoomey takes Exley captive in an attempt to make him marry Robin and finish his book because he wants to be a character in it. Meanwhile, Exley is mourning his older brother, whom he idolized, and coming to terms with his belief that Bill was directly involved in planning the My Lai massacre. Also intertwined are reminiscences of high school, family, and sex, as well as opinions on subjects ranging from James Joyce to the women's movement to the internment of Japanese-Americans during World War II. The narrative jumps forward and back from one subject to the other; the result is a "surrealistic odyssey," as Paul Gray of *Time* magazine put it, in which Exley "demonstrates his skill at hallucinatory free association."

Gray echoed the comments of other reviewers, however, when he noted that "the point of the exercise may be lost on those who expect stories to make sense." Other reviewers were similarly ambivalent. David Montrose wrote in the *Times Literary Supplement* (1990) that, although *Last Notes From Home* occasionally recaptures the "spark of *A Fan's Notes,*" it lacks the "turbulence and poignancy" of the first novel. In the *Village Voice* (1988), M. George Stevenson declared *Last Notes* to be the most complicated of Exley's books, and also the most untidy: "There are too many loose ends for it to be the grandly overarching work it is so desperate to be," he wrote. Furthermore, "its narrative logic is sometimes maddeningly elliptical; some promising and promised avenues are not investigated."

Frederick Exley died in 1992 in Alexandria Bay, New York, after two strokes. He had two daughters, one from each of his two marriages, which both ended in divorce. Although he lived most of his life in New York's rural Thousand Islands region, he maintained telephone friendships with many literary figures, including William Styron and William Gaddis. Besides talking, his primary pastime was reading. "I read everything, but *everything,*" he told the *Village Voice* in 1975, "and I don't think I've ever read a book in which I didn't find something to admire." After Exley's death, his friend Mary Cantwell wrote in the *New York Times Book Review* that Exley "believed in the redemptive power of literature. There was no higher calling." Knowing writers was important to him because "it made him a member of their church." Cantwell wasn't surprised by Exley's death since "he smoked too much, he drank too much, he ate too little." Yet while he was alive he had tremendous energy: "His mind raced as furiously as a hamster in a cage, and just as circularly. I doubt if there was a moment in his life when Fred was free of himself."

PRINCIPAL WORKS: A Fan's Notes, 1968; Pages from a Cold Island, 1975; Last Notes from Home, 1988.

ABOUT: Contemporary Authors 81–84, 1979; Contemporary Literary Criticism 6, 1976; 11, 1979; Current Biography Yearbook, 1989. *Periodicals*—Listener January 29, 1970; Literary Quarterly May 15, 1975; National Review September 12, 1975; New Republic November 2, 1968; May 31, 1975; New Statesman January 30, 1970; New York Post October 5, 1968; New

York Review of Books June 26, 1975; January 9, 1989; New York Times December 23, 1968; New York Times Book Review September 25, 1988; September 13, 1992; People November 14, 1988; Time October 14, 1988; Times Literary Supplement January 29, 1970; August 31, 1990; Village Voice June 2, 1975, October 4, 1988.

RUTH FAINLIGHT

FAINLIGHT, RUTH (May 2, 1931–), British poet, fiction writer, and translator, writes: "I was born in New York City. My mother [Fanny Nimhauser] had been brought to America as a child of about six from what was then part of the Austro-Hungarian Empire, and is currently the newly declared state of Moldova. I think she never recovered from the shock of that original transplantation. My father [Leslie Alexander Fainlight] arrived in the mid-1920s from London via Montevideo. In 1936 he decided to take us back to England. I wondered for years whether he had considered the possible dangers for a Jewish family returning to Europe at that time. My mother seemed no more at ease in England than anywhere else. I suspect that my own sense of being an outsider was absorbed from her.

"I cannot remember when I wrote my first poem. Soon after the start of the Second World War, my mother, younger brother, and I were in New York again, this time as 'British refugees,' even though we all travelled on her American passport. The magazine of the British War Relief Society (where she worked as a secretary) printed some of my early efforts. But I still vividly recall the excitement of composing a whole poem in my head for the first time.

"The next years were spent in Virginia with my mother's elder sister. Aunt Ann's bookcase was the first private library I ranged through. She was the one who taught me about art and artists, and introduced me to opera and the beauty of spoken language.

"1946 saw us back in England with our father demobilised from the Royal Air Force. It was almost six years since we had been together as a family. The headmistress and teachers of my new school seemed surprised that a product of the American educational system could equal their pupils. I should have liked to stay on and prepare for university entrance. My father was a thoughtful man, proud when his son won a scholarship to Cambridge. But I was a girl— which at the time, in our world, was a decisive limitation.

"Because (like many small girls) I had said I wanted to be a dress designer, my father decided that the fashion industry would be a good way for me to earn my living. I was l allowed to attend the local College of Arts and Crafts to gain the relevant skills. I transferred myself into the Fine Arts Department for as many classes as possible, and escaped to the Reference Library rather than go to the others. Chanting 'The Love Song of J. Alfred Prufrock' and 'Byzantium' while walking home from the bus stop, I became the epitome of everything implied by the term 'art student' to nervous parents. By the age of eighteen I was married to another one.

"For the next few years I pursued what was then called a Bohemian existence in France and Spain with the writer Alan Sillitoe, whom I later married [1959]. In Majorca we became friendly with Robert Graves. My nearest approach to the tutorial system of English university life was when he would show me his current poem, and explain what he was doing. Books borrowed from his library became another important factor in my education. Many of my early poems reveal, by subject matter at least, the influence of this period.

"The birth of my son in 1962 marked an increase in output and intensity of writing. But although a 'chapbook' had been published in 1958, it was not until the mid-60s that my first collection, *Cages*, was brought out by Macmillan. The earliest poem included was written when I was seventeen.

"After literature, it has been the visual arts to which I have responded most strongly. Several of my poems have been inspired by specific works of art, or by the 'oeuvre' of an artist. Two from my next collection are: 'Chardin's *Jar of Apricots*,' and 'Arshile Gorky's *Mother*.' A sequence of eleven poems, *Climates*, with wood-cuts by the eighteenth-century Japanese artist Ki Batei, was published as a small book in 1983. And twice I have worked with a living artist, the sculptor and printmaker Leonard Baskin. In the 'Sibyls' section of my collection *Sibyls and Others* and in *Sibyls*, the verbal and visual works are the two sides of a dialogue. At times an image was the direct source of a poem. In other cases, the collaboration was more oblique.

"I feel that I can understand how a painter or sculptor works and what they are trying to achieve in a way close to me with regard to music. I cannot play an instrument nor read a score—a lack I became acutely conscious of recently, when I wrote the libretto for a chamber opera, *The Dancer Hotoke*, with music by Erika Fox, performed in 1991 as part of the Royal Opera's *Garden Venture*. We were delighted when it was nominated for the 1991 Laurence Olivier Awards. I started work on a new libretto for the Garden Venture season of 1993.

"In 1969, Alan Sillitoe and I published a version of Lope de Vega's *Fuenteovejuna* which had been commissioned by the National Theatre. My selection and translation of poems by the Portuguese poet Sophia de Mello Breyner was published in 1987. At the moment, the French poet Jean Joubert and I are translating a selection of each other's work. I have also edited and written the introduction for a selection of poems by my brother, Harry Fainlight, who died in 1982.

"My *Selected Poems* was published in 1987, and *The Knot* in 1990. My next book of poems, *This Time of Year*, has come out. I have recently completed a second collection of short stories, *Dr. Clock's Last Case*. The first, *Daylife and Nightlife*, was published in 1971.

"Everything that happens to me, whatever I read or hear about, can become material for a poem. The more I learn, and the longer I live, the more apparent become the connections between individuals and their environment, the past and the present. But the medium of poetry is language: poems are made with words. Poetry is a relationship between the writer and language and finally, that relationship is what involves me most deeply."

The title (and title poem) of Ruth Fainlight's second collection, *To See the Matter Clearly*, provides an image—the telescope—for her poetic concerns and method: "Through reason's telescope the figures / Seem distinct and small." When the focusing lens shifts, the images are transformed to "Huge soft pitted faces mouthing

/ Pain, and clumsy yearning gestures." The poet-observer draws back:

> Shift glass again, turn down the sound
> Retreat to that high vantage point
> And leave them thrashing in the undergrowth
> That through the telescope
> Shines beautiful as jewels.

She has written poems that are reflections on masterpieces of painting—"Velasquez's *Christ in the House of Martha and Mary*," "Titian's *Venus and Adonis*," and poems that reshape ordinary images into subjects for painting. In "Meat," published in *Sibyls and Others*, "a proper Chelsea lady / of a certain age" examines the offerings in a butcher's shop:

> He holds a tray of goblets out for her
> inspection almost deferentially,
> as though the relics of a martyrdom,
> some tortured part—and she bends forward, solemn,
> thoughtful, curious.
>
> . . . She's pondering, her vacant
> eyes reflective as a sphere of gristle,
> intent upon deciding what to choose.
> And in that chrome and crimson antiseptic
> antechamber to the slaughterhouse, they
> seem the natural focus of the composition.

Barbara Hardy, writing in the *New European Review*, says Fainlight transforms this "ordinary world and its little adventures" into "potent presences and significance." Fascinated with myth and ritual, she invokes the sibylline images. Her sibyl-poet is the classical tradition of mystery and omniscience ("Great Mother of the Gods, goddess / of caverns and wild beasts . . ."), but she is also Cassandra, a woman possessed by a burden of prophecy in "Introspection of a Sibyl":

> If only I could be aware of what is happening
> in that void, that gap, that murky, fathomless cleft
> where space and time must exist
> between inspiration and the sound of my own voice:
> the truth I never once have heard
> a moment earlier than my listeners

This sibyl is a woman burdened by her own aging body and failing powers: "But I am no more conscious of the prophecies / than I can understand the language of the birds." "The Delphic Sibyl" also professes ordinariness: "I was a simple woman / obedient, eager to please, and honoured / by the role."

Elaine Feinstein, in the *Sunday Times*, describes Fainlight's concerns as growing "naturally from a painfully honest self-scrutiny. . . ." Discussing *Another Full Moon*, Feinstein adds: "she accepts with irony the limit to her stern and obstinate spirit imposed by definitions such as 'Jew, woman, poet'. These are definitions that mark her as an outsider. . . . " In "My Position in the History of the Twentieth Century," Fainlight demonstrates that ironic stance: "Strange, how I've never lacked a certain confidence,

Fainlight had early (*The Region's Violence*) staked out a defiantly feminist position. In "Lilith," Adam's first companion is banished for assuming her own equality. "God had created her / From the same earth as Adam. / She stood her ground, amazed / By the idea of differences."

Mark Jarman, reviewing a later collection, *Fifteen to Infinity*, in the *Hudson Review*, considers that Fainlight "engages herself on any number of levels, in any number of ways, from the aging of her own body, to her interest in the classical world, to her Jewish background. . . . She is especially moving in her role as a daughter and as a mother, and as a sister, the elegist of her departed brother."

As Barbara Hardy points out, the knot is "a key image" in Fainlight's poetry, "created by joining apparently casual observation and pondered symbol." In "The Knot" one is formed by the twisted reeds of a hammock. Once in the sheltering retreat of the hammock, away from the distractions of daily life, the poet can function:

> . . . And sometimes there in my hammock,
> words would come and cluster together like wasps
> between the poles and matting of the roof
> as black as rotting fruit or drying membrane,
> a blossom of words in a dusty ray of light.
> Words would form a knot and start a story.

Several of the short stories in *Daylife and Nightlife* ponder the conflicts women suffer between their desire for privacy in which to create or simply realize themselves and their need for a lover. In "The Retreat," a woman literally retreats to a monastic cell in Spain for a few days but then returns to her lover: "By absenting herself she had created a vacuum into which any manifestation of the outer world might have rushed, pulled in by the force of her withdrawing action. But she hoped their life would continue as before,that although the complications of daily living would dilute and confuse what she brought down from the mountain, she would not forget it." In "Daylife and Nightlife," a woman suffers the agonies of writer's block. Although she is comforted by a sympathetic lover, also a writer—"She only knew that she was unhappy, that he was the most important, the most inaccessible, and the most troubling element of her unhappiness, and yet he was not really connected with it at all." As Fainlight observes in "The

Poet," a poem in *The Knot*, creativity is an endless struggle: "The torment starts whose cure is nothing less / than pen and ink and paper— / and the entire universe."

Fainlight's poetry has appeared in the *Times Literary Supplement*, *Southwest Review*, the *Yale Review*, and the *Hudson Review*. Her translations of selected poems by the Portuguese poet Sophia de Mallo Breyner, *Marine Rose*, was widely praised. She worked closely with the poet, who, she says, writes about elements and angels, conveying what *Choice's* reviewer called "the spirit of the original Portuguese poetry."

Fainlight lives in London and travels extensively. She has lived in France, Spain, Morocco, and Israel. In 1985 and in 1990 she was poet-in-residence at Vanderbilt University in Nashville, Tennessee. In 1994 she received the Cholmondeley Award for Poetry from the Society of Authors.

PRINCIPAL WORKS: *Poetry*—Cages, 1966; To See the Matter Clearly, 1968; The Region's Violence, 1973; Another Full Moon, 1976; Sibyls and Others, 1980; Climates, 1983; Fifteen to Infinity, 1983; Selected Poems, 1988; The Knot, 1990; Sibyls, 1991; This Time of Year, 1993; Selected Poems, 1995. *Short stories*—Daylife and Nightlife, 1971; Dr. Clock's Last Case, 1994. *Translations*—(with A. Sillitoe) Lope de Vega, Fuenteovejuna, 1969; Breyner, S. de Mellow, Marine Rose, 1988. *Libretto*—(for Garden Venture) The European Story.

ABOUT: Contemporary Authors New Revision Series 26, 1989; Contemporary Poets, 5th ed., 1991; International Authors and Writers Who's Who 1991–1992; Schlueter, P. and J. (eds.) Encyclopedia of British Women Writers, 1988; Todd, J. (ed.) Dictionary of British Women Writers, 1989. *Periodicals*—Choice December 1988; Hudson Review Summer 1987; Listener February 25, 1988; August 9, 1990; London Review of Books February 2, 1984; Poetry Review Summer 1988; Sunday Times March 13, 1988; Times Literary Supplement May 3, 1980; April 13, 1984; June 24, 1988; July 27, 1990.

FALDBAKKEN, KNUT (August 31, 1941–), Norwegian novelist, playwright, editor, and literary critic, was born in the ancient city of Hamar, Norway, on the banks of Lake Mjøsa. In 1960 he entered the University of Oslo as a student of psychology, only to abandon the academy two years later for what would become a life of writing. A self-proclaimed vagabond, at least in the early years, he worked first as a roving journalist and then in 1965 set out for Paris, the writer's city, with the intention of becoming an author. He made his literary debut a year later with a short story, "Sommerfuglene" (The

Butterflies), published in the debut issue of *Vinduet* (The Window), which became one of Norway's premier literary journals. Faldbakken himself assumed its editorship in 1975, his determination to write fiction fully realized.

The intervening ten years, however, were marked by experimentation and travel, both literary and geographical. Like so many Norwegian writers before him, including the most famous on the world stage, Henrik Ibsen, Faldbakken found it easier to write abroad than to write at home, living for protracted periods of time in France, England, Spain, Austria, Yugoslavia, and Denmark. As if returning the favor for his early travels, his books have been translated in more foreign countries—seventeen to date—than those of any other contemporary Norwegian writer. Indeed, the restless life seemed to suit him. He published his first novel, *Den gra regnbuen* (The gray rainbow) in 1967, two years after he had struck out for Paris. It was neither a critical nor a popular success. But when his second novel appeared, both the critics and the public took notice.

Sin mors hus (His mother's house) was published in 1969. With it, Faldbakken hit his stride as a storyteller, though he later remarked that during the writing of this story, he had no idea where it was leading him. In the novel, a young student abandons his studies in law at the University of Oslo and returns to his childhood home and to his widowed mother. At first joyful over his newly found freedom from societal pressure to become "someone," he takes ever more ominous steps into an incestuous relationship with his mother, becoming her lover and once again her baby, infantilized and finally at peace.

Sin mors hus heralded the quintessential Faldbakken novel: dramatic, seductive, gripping, and provocative, probing the psychology of a middle-class man brought up to be a good boy and a good citizen, but in fact deeply corrupted and crippled by a societal / familial ethic of relentless denial of needs, feelings, and desires. Fathers are missing. Mothers are all-consuming. Emotional deprivation masquerades as bourgeois well-being. The novel stirred up a storm of controversy in Norway that has swirled around Faldbakken ever since, though the focus of the controversy has gradually shifted from questions about taboo topics to questions about aesthetic excellence. But in 1969, living abroad and publishing at home, Faldbakken witnessed his star rising on the literary horizon.

In 1971 he published *Maude danser* (The Sleeping Prince), the suspenseful, disturbing story of another crippled being. Faldbakken narrates through the female voice of the virginal

Maude. Forty-seven-years-old and living in a boardinghouse, she is driven by a single traumatic event from her childhood when she confused her missing father with a dead man lying in the family garden. She thought she saw a prince, and she longed to awaken him with a kiss. Four decades later, desperately longing for love, sex, and—most importantly and most profoundly—a father, she pursues two middle-aged "princes" with the rage of Jack the Ripper, "kissing" them with catastrophic results. After the book appeared in English in 1988, Doris Lessing, writing in the *Independent*, praised Faldbakken for his depiction of the "lunacy [flickering] behind prim facades . . . the author draws you into familiar scenes and themes . . . he shifts the perspective, makes a scene-change, and you are watching a very different trauma." As in *Sin mors hus*, but with an even more grotesque twist, Faldbakken tells a tale of the abnormal in terms of the normal. For at its core, *The Sleeping Prince* too is about the trauma of the violated good child.

A year later, Faldbakken addressed the period of adolescence directly in *Insektsommer* (1972, Insect Summer). A young boy's erotic awakening clashes with the hard realities of the adult world one lush Norwegian summer. Peter, staying in the country with his aunt and uncle, is lured into Oedipal battle, competing with the uncle for the favors of a young woman. The uncle wins the girl. The aunt commits suicide. Peter's part in the crimes of the summer remains ambiguous, both as to what he willed to come about and what he has suffered as a consequence. Lessing said she couldn't think of a better book about adolescence. "Few readers will not wince, remembering and recognizing: the trouble is that adolescents are still children and do not really believe they have power to affect events as adults do. In fact, they have: suddenly or slowly they may understand that what they are observing, often with horrified helplessness, is partly their fault." Peter has been a master manipulator, but the question remains: has he taken revenge for the deep wounds he suffered at the hands of the adults?

As a consequence of these early novels, Faldbakken was recognized as a psychological realist to be reckoned with. His eye for both the dynamics and the details of everyday life was keen, insightful, sometimes wicked. His understanding of the relationship between the normal and the abnormal was intelligent and provocative. His instinct for the language and form of storytelling was superb. Yet some of the critics remained skeptical. To their minds Faldbakken skated too close to the edge of the popular.

Following these first novels, in which his vision was intensely interior, Faldbakken turned outward to the global, futuristic world of *Uar* (Lean years), published in two parts: *Aftenlandet* (1974, *Twilight Country*) and *Sweetwater* (1976). The epic, chronicling the collapse of Western technological civilization, was hailed by some as one of the high points of Norwegian literature in the 1970s. Apocalyptic in its portrayal of a group of people trying to make a life for themselves on a huge landfill, the "Dump," *Uar* probes relentlessly the brutalization of human beings living without any semblance of an ethical code. When Jonathan Bean, an officer in the Peacekeeping force, goes to the Dump in search of his missing brother in *Sweetwater*, he is forced to remain with the primitive residents. Faldbakken describes them as having become one: "the people themselves, their animal way of life, in a strange way harmonizing with their environment of garbage, decay and wretchedness. At that moment this unity with the 'landscape' became a confirmation of the security Bean was feeling, now he had at last given up resisting the fact that he lived there and lived together with them all, had abandoned his plans to escape and all hope of being rescued, abandoned memories of a definite order of things, cause and effect, the overriding system of logic and principle he had always called justice. Now that it was enough to feel satisfied after eating nauseating, semi-raw dog-meat, weariness after the day's toil, and the liquor. . . . "

Faldbakken's small band of refugees regresses ominously, inevitably to ever more infantile—that is, primitive—psychological and social states. The scenes of regression are shocking. And more questions arose about Faldbakken's agenda. The survivors are the strong, instinct-driven, sexually aggressive male and female, the Adam and Eve of the future. But are they new or are they old parents? Do they shed layers of inhibitions and taboos, only to be transformed into the rawest gender stereotypes of contemporary culture, macho man and earth mother? Is Faldbakken a visionary or a reactionary? Is he writing to shock or to enlighten?

Faldbakken had returned to Norway in 1975. Since 1972 he had been a literary critic for *Dagbladet*, the more liberal of Oslo's two leading newspapers, participating in the literary discourse from abroad. In 1975 he became editor of *Vinduet*, for five years steering the debate from within the boundaries of his own country. In 1978, having lived "at home" for three years and considered one of the major, if controversial, literary voices of his generation, Faldbakken published what most critics judge to be his finest novel, *Adams dagbok* (*Adam's Diary*). If he pub-

lished no other, this novel alone would secure his reputation as a consummate psychologist of the male psyche at the end of the twentieth century. Divided into three parts, the novel portrays the three "faces" of modern Adam—the Thief, the Dog, and the Prisoner—each in love with the same woman, Bel Ami, each named for his primary attachment to her. The Thief, her most recent lover, steals what emotion he needs from her and then abandons her, fearing involvement like death. The Dog, her former lover, is the Thief's nightmare, a helpless victim of his obsession for her. The Prisoner, her former husband, emasculated by her maternal eros, is literally and figuratively in prison for railing against her. *Adams dagbok* is a brilliant study of male rage, debilitation, and neurosis in a society in which social roles are changing, in which women are perceived to be gaining power and men to be losing it. Faldbakken was praised by female and male readers alike for the surgical precision with which he dissected the ailing male ego.

Others, however, grew somewhat wary of Faldbakken's focus on victimized males and victimizing women. Norwegian critic Janneken Øverland, in her review of the novel, expressed the fear that Faldbakken risked "peddling the hate and the uncertainty about 'the new woman' that lies latent in so many men." Indeed, in this novel as in others, there is an underlying glee in the violent acts of revenge against women exacted by the deeply wounded male characters. Does Faldbakken share that glee or not? Subsequent novels have not resolved the controversy.

After *Adams dagbok* Faldbakken's popularity grew. At the same time, his tenuous truce with the Norwegian critical establishment ended. In retrospect one newspaper called it a "permanent divorce." Readers at home and abroad embraced him, but the critics in Norway, particularly those in academia, judged him to be a greater exhibitionist than literary psychologist / satirist. Faldbakken scoffed, convinced that their censure belied discomfort, his provocative vision striking too close to the heart of the Norwegian society in which they were blindly embedded.

And, indeed, his major novels of the 1980s are double-edged social satires, each one examining the ever more precarious role of the man in the context of (Norwegian) institutions, past and present, that prove to be insidiously corrupting, deadly to any healthy notion of self, and repressing genuine creativity, sexuality, and love. In 1982 Faldbakken published *Bryllupsreisen* (*The Honeymoon*), about the breakup of the model marriage of a middle-class Norwegian couple, educated, intelligent, and capable, grounded in the moral values of the 1960s, bound for the material values of the 1970s, convinced of their rightness in the world. But in reality the wife is restless, the husband complacent, and in her effort to arouse him from the rut into which they have fallen, she challenges him sexually, shocking his puritan sensibility, destroying the bourgeois foundations on which his masculine identity rests. His only recourse, it seems, is violence. The novel became one of Faldbakken's most controversial, for his portrayal of the wife bordered dangerously on misogyny; but more provocatively, as far as the reading public was concerned, his portrayal of the erotic bordered on the pornographic. *Bryllupsreisen* was Faldbakken's greatest commercial success.

Three years later, in 1985, Faldbakken published *Glahn*, a unique challenge to one of Norway's most formidable literary institutions, Knut Hamsun (1859–1952), with whom all subsequent writers of Norwegian fiction—at least male writers—have had to contend. Faldbakken rewrites Hamsun's *Pan* (1984), denuding the novel's hero, Lt. Glahn, of his romance and his masculine mystique, suggesting that behind the bravado of one of Norwegian literature's most infamous fin de siècle lovers was homosexual desire. The demystification of the gender ethos of late romanticism in Norway was a fascinating experiment. At the same time, reviewers with roots in gay and lesbian criticism were as suspicious of Faldbakken's depiction of homosexuality as feminist critics had become of his depiction of women.

In 1989, as if to spite these very critics, Faldbakken published *Bad Boy*, about a middle-aged man, bound all his life by the repressive rules of being a "good boy"—particularly vis-a-vis his mother, and subsequently his wife and girlfriends—who takes revenge in what might be called virtual-reality fantasies of homosexuality, transvestism and sadomasochism. Faldbakken's flirtation with pornography was in this novel undisguised and unabashed.

In the late 1980s, as Faldbakken's confrontation with the Norwegian critical establishment intensified, foreign presses were coveting his fiction in ever greater numbers. He became well known in the English-speaking world. Doris Lessing, reviewing the English translations of *The Sleeping Prince*, *Insect Summer*, and *Adam's Diary* for the *Independent* in 1991, paid glowing tribute: "Faldbakken is a first-rate writer."

Faldbakken lives with his family in the small township of Ridabu, outside the city of Hamar, where he was born and raised and where he carries on his writing, both literary and journalistic. In 1990 he published *Evig din* (Forever thine), a novel in the tradition of the social / psychologi-

cal genre that has become his hallmark, once again confronting hidebound notions about the relationships between men and women. A year later he launched his first historical novel, *Til verdens ende* (To the ends of the earth), chronicling Christopher Columbus's voyage from medieval Europe to the New World. The author of a number of successful plays, he turned more of his attention to the stage over the years.

In 1992 the Norwegian educator and journalist Steinar Bjørk Larsen published an article in *Vinduet* contradicting traditional "wisdom" by suggesting that Faldbakken should be read in a modernist context along with his more acclaimed contemporaries, such as Dag Solstad and Hans Jørgen Nielsen. He has been one of the most passionate chroniclers of psychological repression, particularly in middle-class men, in contemporary Western society. He is among the most widely translated Norwegian writers of all time. Several of his novels have been made into films. His voice remains one of the liveliest, most articulate, most wicked voices participating in the cultural discourse of Norway.

PRINCIPAL WORKS IN ENGLISH TRANSLATION: (tr. L. Myhre) The Honeymoon, 1987; (tr. J. Garton) The Sleeping Prince, 1988; (tr. S. Lyngstad) Adam's Diary, 1989; (tr. H. Sutcliff and T. Støverud) Insect Summer, 1991; (tr. J. Tate) Twilight Country, 1993; (tr. J. Tate) Sweetwater, 1994.

ABOUT: Contemporary World Writers, 2nd ed., 1993. *Periodicals*—Independent (London) May 11, 1991; Scandinavian Review Autumn 1985; Scandanavica November 1983.

FALLON, PADRAIC (January 3, 1905– October 9, 1974), Irish poet and dramatist, was born in Athenry, County Galway—"fifteen miles from Yeats's tower," observed Dillon Johnston, in reviewing the *Collected Poems* in the *Times Literary Supplement*, thus emphasizing Fallon's early indebtedness to Yeats and his later struggle to emancipate himself. Fallon was educated at Mount Joseph's College in Roscrea, County Tipperary. For forty years he was a customs official, mainly in Wexford. He retired to Kinsale, in County Cork, and from there to Cornwall. In 1930, he married the former Dorothea Maher, by whom he had six sons. He died in Kent, England.

In his lifetime Fallon published very few books: a short story collection, *Lighting-Up Time*, in 1948, and an edition of the poems of Emily Lawless, the eccentric Irish friend of William Ewart Gladstone, in 1965. Although a contributor of poems and stories to Irish periodicals and anthologies, he was best known for his radio plays, particularly for two modernizations of old Irish tales, *Diarmud and Grainne* (broadcast in 1950) and *The Vision of Mac Conglinne* (broadcast in 1953). He also wrote two plays for the stage, *The Seventh Step* (produced in 1954) and *Sweet Love Till Morn* (produced in 1971 at the Abbey Theatre in Dublin). The claim made by his producer, Micheal O'hAodha, that his radio plays are "the most successful modernizations of ancient Irish literature," is challenged by the *Macmillan Dictionary of Irish Literature* as "highly extravagant"—but his power as a radio dramatist is nonetheless acknowledged. However, Maurice Lindsay's claim, made in the 1975 edition of *Contemporary Poets*, that, after Yeats, Fallon was "the most continuously exciting poet to come out of Ireland," now begins to look less and less exaggerated or eccentric, as increasing critical attention is given to his poetic work. Yet as Lindsay wrote, Fallon was in 1975 "almost unknown outside Ireland and America." A much-delayed volume of his poems was on press at the time of his death and was published soon after, but it was not until 1990 that a more complete collection was published, the immediately posthumous one having been widely criticized for leaving out much of the best work.

Fallon has joined the august band of poets, that includes Austin Clarke and Patrick Kavanagh whose work is compared to Yeats's. Johnston, in his *Times Literary Supplement* review, described Fallon, as a "salvaged" poet. In his introduction to the *Collected Poems*, Seamus Heaney writes that Fallon felt compelled "to establish his own poetic and political freehold in a territory where Yeats is still demanding the ground rents."

Yeats is prevalent in the early poems in Fallon's *Collected Poems*; no fewer than eight of them evoke him by name or place-name. Nonetheless, while conceding that Yeats is the "shade" lying "across the Irish literary scene" and that Fallon "does go in for a bit of Yeatsing," Maurice Lindsay thinks that "these poems push their way beyond the circumference of the shadow, and, indeed, throw by contrast a new kind of colouring upon the nature and achievement of Yeats." He quotes from the poem "Yeats at Athenry Perhaps": "But I'd never heard of him, the famous poet,/Who lived as the crow flies fifteen miles away . . . /Maybe he passed me by/In a narrow gutted street, an aimless/Straying gentleman, and I/The jerseyed fellow driving out the cows."

Fallon is now most regarded for the poems in the final section ("'Late Poems' 1960–1975") of the *Collected Poems*. Here, according to Dillon

Johnston, Fallon "reversed himself," and, instead of trying to find the transcendental in the local as he had in his earlier poetry, "abandons transcendent claims for . . . local [Galway] residents and sites." Rejecting the modernists' tracing of "local symbols towards universal roots," Fallon returned to the roots themselves: "Far from rendering local women 'anonymous' and transcendent, he can now localize and humanize the figure of Christ's mother. . . . can write a Catholic poem which is more European than Irish." He thus reached, Maurice Lindsay wrote, "a sense of contact with what matters most," as in "Mater Dei":

> Milk ran wild
> Across the heavens.
> Imperiously He
> Sipped at the delicate beakers she proffered him.
> How was she to know
> How huge a body she was, how she corrected
> The very tilt of the earth on its new course?

Fallon developed a formidable much-praised technique of employing novel rhyme patterns and, in particular, half-rhymes and off-rhymes, which convey a word-perfect effect. This technical achievement is based on Fallon's skillful manipulation of those rich overtones in Irish speech resulting from Gaelic, in which literature he was learned. His subject matter ranged from the intimately reminiscent and self-mocking, often cast in deliberately rude colloquial language, to the broadly descriptive, quite as often cast in an unashamedly purple rhetoric. There are also a number of dialogues with the blind 19th-century Irish oral poet Anthony Raftery, who inspired some of Fallon's best lines.

The *Macmillan Dictionary of Irish Literature* said of Fallon's as yet unpublished theater pieces: "The wit, the gusto, and the riot of rhetorical exuberance seem rarely paralleled and hardly excelled in modern Irish dramatic writing. . . . If any modern Irish writer cries out for proper attention and evaluation, then it is certainly Patrick Fallon." In his review of the *Collected Poems*, Johnston complained that Fallon's important translations from the Gaelic require more careful dating: "We need more information, some record of publication and revision, so that we can further assess Fallon's place among those poets we will soon carry with us into the next century."

PRINCIPAL WORKS: Poetry—Poems, 1974; Collected Poems, 1990. Fiction—Lighting-Up Time, 1948. As editor—The Poems of Emily Lawless, 1965.

ABOUT: Contemporary Authors 103, 1982; Contemporary Poets, 2nd ed., 1975; Fallon, B. (afterword) in Fallon, P. Collected Poems, 1990; Heaney, S. (introduction) in Fallon, P. Collected Poems, 1990; Hogan, R. (ed.) Macmillan Dictionary of Irish Literature, 1980. *Periodicals*—Eire-Ireland: A Journal of Irish Studies Fall 1986; Irish University Review Spring 1982; Times Literary Supplement November 23, 1990.

FARMER, BEVERLEY (February 7, 1941–), Australian novelist and short story writer, was born in Melbourne, educated at MacRobertson Girls High School and Melbourne University (B.A. in French and English) and has worked in restaurants in Greece, England, Melbourne, and the bush. She met her Greek husband-to-be at a chalet on the snowfields of the Victorian Alps, taught herself Greek while teaching French and English in secondary schools, and married in 1965. Her first story, "Evening," was published in *Westerly* in 1968. In 1969 she left Australia to live with her husband's family, who ran a small tobacco, wheat, and barley farm north of Thessaloniki. There, she rewrote *Alone*, a book that she says "took ten years to be brave enough to write and a further ten years to publish."

In *Alone* (Farmer calls it a *récit*), a young girl's recollections reveal the trauma of a lost love which leads to her suicide in Carlton, a Melbourne suburb. An innovative exposé of lesbian love, the novel attracted notice for its fine prose. Its artistic design, a considered reply to T. S. Eliot's *The Wasteland*, was largely overlooked. Farmer's immature, Eliot-obsessed protagonist, Shirley, finds her fruitless search for nourishment and fulfillment defined in Eliot's vision of a spiritual desert. The text is seeded with images and events taken from Eliot. The girl's lover exclaims, "After the event he slunk off," and she laments, "I cry much of the day and go out in the evening." Farmer thus demonstrates the unhealthy hold Eliot has on the "consciousness" of this would-be poet/writer. Shirley weds herself to the "rapt sterility of art" and ignores the inherent dangers of literary emulation. Farmer's novel offers ironic and poignant insights into the development of the artist as a young woman, but also demonstrates a unique ability to reconsider poetry and convention in the light of contemporary female experience.

In 1972 Farmer returned to Australia with her husband and had a son. That same year they opened a restaurant in Lorne, a seaside resort in southwest Victoria. After six years, a separation, and the deaths of her father and mother, Farmer went back to teaching and hotel work in Melbourne. It was not until 1979 that she wrote another short story for publication. In 1980 *Alone*

BEVERLEY FARMER

was published and she began *Milk*, her first collection of short stories, with the assistance of a Literature Board Grant. This collection, published in 1983, drew on her experience of Greek village life and won the New South Wales premier's award for fiction.

Milk is a collection of short stories about nurturing and formative influences, In them, children, parents, and grandparents interact to reveal cross-cultural tensions and human frailty, but also a universal need for love and consolation. The stories are notable for their sensitively and sensuously rendered portraits of people (alone and in families, loving, hating, working, or waiting) and places. In Farmer's fiction, description conveys perceptual experience, sensation, reaction, and significance. Social interchanges, like mealtimes or family gatherings with their commonplace rituals of eating and preparing food, offer a balance between physical and emotional action. In this way Farmer directs attention to unspoken agendas which are often the focus of the texts.

The collection of short stories Home Time was published in 1985, after Farmer had spent a term as writer-in-residence at the University of Tasmania. This is a companion volume to *Milk*: adult revaluations of origins, places of birth, family relationships, youthful or previous experience, and the concept of home are the dominant themes. These stories comment on innocence by their distance from it, and Farmer has suggested that here she was "not writing about love but the absence of it." She has claimed that she wrote these stories "in the key of loss." Reviews of the collection focused on the rendering of Greek experience, as noted in Willbanks's interview with Farmer in *Speaking Volumes*; the skillful portrayal of domestic circumstance; and a bleak realism. In *Home Time*, Farmer's experiments with form reach a new sophistication; narrative structures become more complex, stories continue or encapsulate other, intertextual references serve as subtexts, and images, motifs, and themes resonate as they do in poetry.

For example, in the title story of *Home Time* a couple, far from home, leave their apartment to share a drink at a nearby tavern, where *Casablanca* is being screened, examining their relationship as they view the fictional screen lovers. Within this narrative frame the older woman tells her life story (two love stories) but her toast to the younger woman, "Here's looking at you kid," is ironically offset by the speed with which "time goes by." Later that evening, the younger woman's interest in recording this narrative is seen by her partner as "scavenging" and the couple's relationship deteriorates in the time it has taken to tell the story. "A Man in the Laundrette," in the same collection, confirms the diagnosis of their dying relationship.

In many of Farmer's stories, home is no guarantee of security. In "A Woman with Black Hair," a victim of rape is forced to speak a text supplied by her attacker; in "Marina," an estrangement from home results in the tragedy of a young woman's inability to maintain a family life without support; and in "Fire and Flood" the belief in safety in stability is undermined by two tragedies and the emotional blockage of a survivor who, in the aftermath, "has nothing to say to anyone there." "Caffe Veneto" and "Matrimonial Home" are about instability and infidelity, but the collection, despite its evocations of absence, speaks eloquently of the need for "honour, endurance and love."

A Body of Water was described as "a collage-like compilation of writer's notes, short stories, poetry and textual reference." It was short-listed for the National Book Council Nonfiction Banjo award and for the New South Wales Douglas Stewart prize for nonfiction. This highly controlled stream of consciousness narration illustrates the wellsprings of writing. Five short stories emerge from the flow of diary entries, authorial responses to a year's events, review of formative influences and past performance and diverse appreciations of other texts. In this journal the seascape at Queenscliff is the setting for an investigation of the eddies and backwaters of an emotional and imaginative journey—to a "land of snows" beyond familiar terrain or personal history.

The Seal Woman, a novel, illustrates global environmental interdependencies, implying a continuity of mythic resources. The distance between the motif of the single self of *Alone* and *The Seal Woman*'s schemes encompassing history and change, indicates the extent of the journey being undertaken by Farmer:

> We who live on the green rim can put what is out of sight out of mind only for so long. This is the two-hundredth year that the land is in white hands, and the desert is twice the size it was in 1788. The rivers and seas are a swill of the excrement and silt, farm and factory waste. Ancient rain forests are felled and left lifeless, and the rain fails. The silt that runs off the old forest floor chokes the fish and coral reefs to death. The land withers under its white burdens of wheat and sheep, rabbits, foxes, dogs and cats, donkey, camels, water buffalo. From horizon to horizon vast lands are already dry dust under a white shimmer like ice, the death mask of the salt. A waste land where the salt crystals grow and grow, in the shade of skeleton trees. In the myth of the waste land, says the speaker, a curse was laid on the land.

The novel is about a Danish widow's attempt to come to terms with loss. She seeks refuge in Swanhaven, a sleepy backwater in Australia, but the issues of global warming, ozone depletion, the effects of chlorofluorocarbons and dioxins and the beleaguered world of animals close to extinction because of the blood bath of whaling, seal-hunting, and drift net fishing, impinge on the single life. In the dedication to *The Seal Woman* Don Anderson claims that Farmer "shows how to look at the world with fresh eyes, and how things thus seen are refracted by the mind." In *The Seal Woman*, the protagonist finds that words strung together may be either links or webs that ensnare; clearing encroaching gossamer threads away from her house to admit more light, she finds "Gossamer, goose-summer, the threads which connect with the past." In this, Farmer draws on a legacy of culture embracing the legends of Norse and Inuit cultures, ghost stories, the Finnish *Kalevala*, the Selchie legends, aboriginal creation and conception myths, Andersen's fairytales, the images of Coleridge, Eliot, and Australian evocations of bunyips and bad banksia men. Aptly, a final song celebrates a seal/woman's reclaiming of her own identity.

In "Preoccupations" in *Australian Literary Studies*, Farmer declares:

> The writer is not, or not necessarily, just manipulating structures, patterns, sequences of events in time; these can embody psychic states, show them forth, and therefore free the writer of them. These structures, patterns and sequences are metaphors, diagrams, mandalas. Maps of the islands of self. . . .

Farmer celebrates technique, which

> entails the watermarking of your essential patterns of

perception, voice and thought into touch and texture of your lines; it is that whole creative effort of the mind's and the body's resources to bring meaning of experience within the jurisprudence of form. . . .

PRINCIPAL WORKS: *Novels*—Alone, 1980; The Seal Woman, 1992. *Short stories*—Milk, 1983; Home Time, 1985; Place of Birth, 1990. *Nonfiction*—A Body of Water, 1990.

ABOUT: Ellison, R. Rooms of Their Own, 1986; Oxford Companion to Australian Literature, 1985; Willbanks, R. Speaking Volumes, 1992. *Periodicals*—Australian Book Review 1990, 1992; Australian Literary Studies May 1990; Island Magazine 25, 26, 1986; Times Literary Supplement September 14, 1990.

*FERRÉ, ROSARIO (September 28, 1942–), Puerto Rican novelist, poet, essayist, and literary critic, was born in the city of Ponce, Puerto Rico. With her father a wealthy industrialist and public figure (Luis A. Ferré, governor of the island from 1968 to 1972), and her mother a member of a prominent landowning family, Ferré grew up in a privileged world of private schools, exclusive clubs, and extensive travel. Following the custom of her social class, she studied in the United States at Wellesley and Manhattanville colleges, majoring in American and English literature. Her earlier childhood experiences, however, played an essential role in her literary development. In an autobiographical piece in *Spanish American Authors: The Twentieth Century*, Ferré recalls her mother's morbid obsession with an uncle who had died in a tragic accident, and remembers fondly her black, teenaged nanny, Gilda, who entered her life when she was seven and influenced the future direction of her work:

> Thanks to her I discovered that in the terrible world of Bluebeard a man could kill seven women out of jealousy before being punished by the law; that the Little Mermaid could have the courage to leave the ocean in search of her lover, even though she felt her feet destroyed by thousands of knives which sprang miraculously from the earth; and above all, that in the world of the Snow Queen, which was and still is my favorite story, a beautiful woman, but as cold as ice, kidnapped a child she could never love. Those stories, in short, helped reconcile me with my own destiny; if the terrible situations they described could happen in the real world, their heroes escaping nevertheless unharmed, the fact that my mother lived yearning for her dead brother, and that I felt devoured by jealousy, was not, after all, that extraordinary, and I ought to forgive her and forgive myself as well for it. That is why, in spite of the fact that my mother and Gilda have been dead now for many years, and that they never knew that I write fiction, it is them that I address when I write, or, what is the same thing, when I begin to tell myself a story.

The world of folklore and fairy tales of her youth lives on in Ferré's imaginative fiction.

In the late 1960s and early 1970s, Ferré attended graduate school at the University of Puerto Rico to study Latin American literature. There she came into contact with noted Hispanic scholars and authors, including the Uruguayan critic Angel Rama and the Peruvian novelist Mario Vargas Llosa, gaining as a result a renewed literary perspective and a desire to experiment with language and form. In 1972, Ferré's growing sense of artistic and social commitment led her to unite with a diverse group of writers to cofound and direct the literary journal *Zona de carga y descarga* (Loading and unloading zone). During its three-year existence, *Zona's* uncompromising commitment to artistic and social renovation reflected the literary and political momentum of its era.

Important changes were also taking place in Ferré's personal life. Despite the fact that her father espoused the cause of Puerto Rican statehood, Ferré denounced her family's political position and embraced Puerto Rican independence, identifying herself with left-wing groups that were traditionally suspicious of members of her social class. She also abandoned the stifling security of the role of dutiful wife and mother of three, divorcing her first husband and attempting to discover herself as a woman and as a member of a society with segments that her previously sheltered life had ignored.

Ferré's first successful story, "La muñeca menor" ("The Youngest Doll"), was published in *Zona*, and later included in her first book, *Papeles de Pandora* (Pandora's Papers, 1976). In an essay describing her creative evolution, "The Writing Kitchen," Ferré relates the initial literary attempts that took place in this transitional period of her life and the events that led to the writing of her first story. From Simone de Beauvoir she learned to approach important "external" subjects such as the great social and historical themes rather than concentrating on an internal world of emotions and intuition; from Virginia Woolf she learned the necessity of maintaining objectivity and distance, avoiding ire and querulousness, freeing herself from outrage and indignation.

The result was "The Youngest Doll," based on a true incident. The unusual story of a distant cousin who was abused by her husband and forced to live with relatives sparked Ferré's creative curiosity. The woman made honey-filled dolls for the young girls of the household, and was shamelessly exploited by a young doctor with whom she had fallen in love. The young physician cheated her out of her remaining money by falsely treating a strange ailment in her leg. Ferré's poetic retelling of the family anecdote evolved into her short story with the addition of the female character's retaliation against her abuser, an episode which Ferré later felt went against the standards of her feminist mentors. She confesses in "The Writing Kitchen": "I had betrayed Simone, writing once again about the interior reality of women; and I had betrayed Virginia, letting myself get carried away by anger, by the fury the story produced in me . . . Today I know from experience that it is no use to write by setting out beforehand to construct exterior realities or to deal with universal and objective themes if one doesn't first create one's own interior reality. It is no use to try to write in a neutral, harmonious, distant way if one doesn't first have the courage to destroy one's own interior reality."

Ferré left Puerto Rico in the mid-1970s, after *Zona* ceased publication, for a temporary stay in Mexico, taking along her manuscripts of stories and poems. There she published the collection of fourteen stories and six poems included in *Papeles de Pandora* in 1976, as well as many of her later works.

Rosario Ferré's writing began to attract critical attention almost immediately after her first publications appeared. *Papeles de Pandora* demonstrates Ferré's mastery of language in the unusual images and the distinctive combination of irony, humor, satire, and mystery that characterize her work. The central theme of the collection is the oppressive nature of the historically assigned roles of women in patriarchal cultures, and women's rejection of such roles. Most of the protagonists are women of the upper middle classes trapped in confining marriages, often aware of their oppressive situations. For some, the only escape is a retreat into fantasy; others rebel against their "bride-doll" existence. Ferré's social criticism is juxtaposed with elements of the fantastic and the grotesque, creating a mysterious, dream-like atmosphere:

Years passed and the doctor became a millionaire. He had gathered in all the patients in town who didn't mind paying exorbitant fees in order to get a look at a legitimate member of the extinct sugar-cane aristocracy. The youngest girl continued to sit on the balcony, motionless in her muslin and lace, always with her eyelids lowered. . . .

One thing disturbed the doctor's contentment. He noticed that as he grew older the youngest girl still kept the same firm and porcelained skin that she had had when he would call on her at the big house in the cane fields. One night he decided to go into her room and observe her in her sleep. He noticed that her chest wasn't moving. He then placed his stethoscope over her heart and heard a distant swirl of water. At that moment the doll opened her eyelids and out of the empty sockets of her eyes he saw the furious antennae of the prawns begin to emerge. ("The Youngest Doll")

Ferré deals with the theme of race and class differences among women in the story "Cuando las mujeres quieren a los hombres" ("When Women Love Men"), in which a white, middle-class widow meets her late husband's black mistress. In contrast to traditional literary presentations, however, in Ferré's story the black mistress thrives economically, becoming a "self-made" woman as she perfects the art of sex with the young white men of the town, eventually gaining a certain respectability and power, and even supplanting her late lover's widow at charitable and social functions. The widow, on the other hand, withdraws into an enclosed world of resentment and pain in which she clings to a imagined superiority based on marital status, social-class origins, and color. Ferré presents these very different women as mirror images, meshing their two voices in an interior monologue that combines their flow of consciousness to demonstrate the commonality of their roles as women—both exploited by a man of wealth and power. Without dismissing the social and economic advantages of the white middle-class wife, Ferré shows the hidden affinities between women who share a common victimization. According to the author, "Women are often willing to look at the truth of history as if it were made up of thousands of threads, or an infinite number of fragments. I believe it is because of how society has forced women to live that we are more able, like Penelope, to synthesize identities and weave our diverse threads into a tapestry which could perhaps save the homeland—as well as each of our personal Ithacas, from eventual destruction."

In 1980, Ferré published *Sitio a Eros* (Eros besieged), a collection of thirteen biographical essays of significant women writers of the nineteenth and twentieth centuries. The essays complement her imaginative work and examine the consuming and often forbidden passion of female creativity in such authors as Mary Shelley, George Sand, Flora Tristan, Jean Rhys, Anaïs Nin, Tia Modotti, Aleksandra Kollontai, Sylvia Plath, Julia de Burgos, Lillian Hellman, and Virginia Woolf. In 1982, her poetic works were collected in *Fábulas de la garza desangrada* (Fables of the bleeding crane). According to the critic Ramón Luis Acevedo: "The passion and expressiveness of her style are intensified in her poems, which almost always have a narrative or dramatic base. Thus *Fábulas de la garza desangrada* joins poems, love letters, and essayistic prose to point up the tragic condition of feminine existence, which oscillates between submission and rebellion, love and loneliness, alienation and the search for authenticity. The elaboration of Western Feminine myths with their roots in Greek antiquity confers density and projection on these poetic texts." In a review of Ferré in the *Nation*, Patricia Hart considers her to be, along with Isabel Allende, Luisa Valenzuela, and Clarice Lispector, one of Latin America's "magic feminists. . . . Latin America's male magic realists have long juxtaposed the impossible with the quotidian, so what sets these women apart is their feminist view of what we can and should call real."

Ferré has written several collections of children's stories in which her critical social vision persists; at the same time, however, the stories maintain an imaginative and poetic simplicity. She has also cultivated literary and artistic criticism. Her master's thesis from the University of Puerto Rico, an analysis of the works of Uruguayan author of fantastic literature Felisberto Hernández, was later published in book form, as was her doctoral dissertation from the University of Maryland, a study of Julio Cortázar.

The novel *Maldito amor* traces some one hundred years of Puerto Rican history, from the time of the United States' invasion of the island in 1898 to an imaginary future in the 1990s in which the United States "threatens" to force the island into becoming independent. The novel examines the changing social and economic relationships that evolve within several generations of plantation oligarchy, the "sugar barons." who are displaced by large United States' corporations and eventually become dependent on North American economic interests.

Included in the volume *Sweet Diamond Dust* are a short novella and three additional narratives, all tied together by a common motif: the revision and appropriation of official history by the marginalized sectors of society—women, poor, and people of color. Rosario Ferré's first collection had portrayed women in unhappy relationships with men; that theme is also found in *Sweet Diamond Dust*: "love, complaint, and— oh! I had to admit it—even vengeance. The image of that woman, hovering for years on end at the edge of that cane field with her broken heart, had touched me deeply. It was she who had finally opened the window for me, the window that had been so heretically sealed, the window to my story."

After living in Mexico and Washington, D.C., for several years, Rosario Ferré returned to Puerto Rico with her third husband, the architect Augustín Costa. In 1995 she published her first novel in English, *The House on the Lagoon*, the story of a Puerto Rican businessman who is on the side of Puerto Rican statehood and his Vassar-educated wife, a Puerto Rican nationalist. She begins to write a novel involving the history of their two families, and the two quarrel about the interpretation of that history, which includes tales of suicide, madness, passion, and political murder and betrayal. *Publishers Weekly* deemed the novel "a compelling panorama of Puerto Rican experience . . . rich in history, drama and memorable characters." The reviewer remarked that Ferré's narrative strategy serves her well as "the conflict over the past bleeds into a crisis in the present," dramatizing the issue of "who gets to write history."

PRINCIPAL WORKS IN ENGLISH TRANSLATION: Sweet Diamond Dust (tr. R. Ferré) 1988; Papeles de pandora: The Youngest Doll (tr. G. Rabassa et al.) 1991.in english: The House on the Lagoon, 1995.

ABOUT: Flores, A. Spanish American Authors: The Twentieth Century, 1992; Kanellos, N. (ed.) Biographical Dictionary of Hispanic Literature in the U.S., 1989; Martinez, D. (ed.) Spanish American Women Writers, 1990; Meyer, D. and Fernandez Olmos, M. (eds.) Contemporary Women Authors of Latin America: Introductory Essays, 1983; Meyers, E. and Adamson, G. (eds.) Continental, Latin American and Francophone Women Writers, 1987; Paravisini-Gebert, L. and Torres-Seda, O. (eds.) Caribbean Women Novelists, 1993; Rodriguez de Laguna, A. (ed.) Images and Identities: The Puerto Rican in Two World Contexts, 1987. *Periodicals*—Hispania March 1987; Lion and the Unicorn 10, 1986; Minnesota Review 22, 1984; Nation May 6, 1991; Publishers Weekly July 3, 1995.

*FISCHEROVÁ, SYLVA (September 24, 1963–), Czech poet, was born in Prague. She studied at the grammar school in Olomouc, a small town in Moravia where her father, Josef Ludvik Fischer (1894–1973), a philosopher and sociologist, was president of Palack University. In 1991 she graduated from Charles University in Prague, where she studied philosophy, physics, and classics. Fischerová had made several short trips abroad, including a brief visit to the United States; she took part in the Child of Europe readings at the Royal Festival Hall in London in 1988, and since the democratic takeover of her country in 1989, she has participated in a number of literary meetings on contemporary Czech literature. She teaches, with the rank of assistant professor, at the Institute of Classical Studies at Charles University and specializes in classical Greek literature.

Fischerová began to publish toward the end of the period of Communist domination in Czechoslovakia; her poems first appeared in periodicals and then, as was customary at that time, in almanacs or anthologies: *Zvláštní znamení* (Special Sign, 1985) and *Klíčeni* (Germinating, 1985). Reviewers observed that of the poets represented in these volumes, Sylva Fischerová was the most promising.

In 1986 she published her first book of poetry, *Chvění závodních koní* (*The Tremor of Racehorses*), which won the Czechoslovak Literary Fund Prize. With this volume Fischerová was established as one of the leading women writers of Czechoslovakia who brought new life into the often hothouse atmosphere of the poetry of the 1970s and 1980s. Others were Markéta Procházková, who had published her first collection—poems written in her childhood—when she was sixteen; Zuzana Trojanová, a disciple of the "beat generation" whose first book was published a year after her accidental death; and Marcela Chmarová, who later ceased publishing. Inspired by foreign women poets like Marina Tsvetayeva, Anna Akhmatova, and Emily Dickinson, Czech women writers, as Fischerová told Jim Grove in an interview in *Prairie Schooner*, have found no obstacle to publishing: "There are maybe more women poets in Czechoslovakia than men."

The poems in *The Tremor of Racehorses* are daringly imaginative, full of wit, irony, and irreverent satire. Fischerova writes with the exuberance and upredictability of the influential French poet Guillaume Apollinaire. Although, as some of her reviewers noted, Fischerová's verse has echoes of surrealism, she rejects its morbidity and seems to prefer a more whimsical, dadaist spirit. She cautiously balances cruelty and tenderness; indeed, some have called this collection her own "Songs of Innocene" and "Songs of Experience." If there is any analogy to painting here, it is close to the childlike and dreamlike works of Henri Rousseau with their appealing but menacing tigers and leopards and the recurring image of waves of the sea. A characteristic poem is "Poslední milovníci jasných obrazu" ("The Last Lovers of Bright Pictures") with its image of a girl who "was born to tie scarfs to waves of the sea." Among poets this mixture of naiveté and surprise comes closest to the poems and songs of the French Jacques Prévert or the Yugoslavian Vasko Popa. But added to this in Fischerova's work is a strain of sensuality in the spirit of fin de siècle poets such as Arthur Rimbaud, whom she cites in some of her poems.

Essentially, however, Fischerová is a philosophical poet, influenced most notably by the German philosopher Arthur Schopenhauer, on whom her father had published a distinguished monograph in 1921, *Arthur Schopenhauer: Genese díla* (Arthur Schopenhauer: The Development of His Work). In her best poems she has a broad philosophical vision, showing the influence of both classical Greek and ancient Chinese. But she can never quite abandon her sense of humor and of irony. Fisherova's "Pulnočni piják čaje" (Midnight Tea Drinker), with the classic figure of an intellectual contemplating in the night, but wryly aware of a "silly puddle," and "golden pigs," is probably the best illustration of her philosophical but often irreverent poems.

Fischerová's reading tastes are eclectic. As she told Jim Grove, her enthusiasms range from *Gone With the Wind*, which she read when she was fourteen or fifteen (and to which she alludes in several poems in *The Tremor of Racehorses*, to "German expressionists, dada, old Chinese poetry, Sylvia Plath, but above all I like Hölderlin. And the only principle, I think, is to listen to the things, to yourself, and to be sincere." At nineteen she wrote a love poems, "Black Tiger," which, she says, is really about "giving yourself to life."

Sometimes
there's only a black tiger
and a river with floating ashtrays.

And then
you discard everything,
including yourself, with such rapture
and you become
a black tiger on floating ashtrays.

tr. James Naughton

The Tremor of Racehorses was well received. Jef Wallace, in *Poetry Wales*, was impressed by a poetry thesis as "constantly renewed in an invention of fresh images"; he described her style as "ironical Surrealism." Michael Parker, in the *Times Literary Supplement*, noted the resemblance of some of her images to those of Sylvia Plath. Ian Milner, in an introduction to the volume, noted especially her poems of social protest which, thanks to their allegorical manner escaped the attention of the censors during the Communist dictatorship: "They have a strength of dramatic impact and a structural logic that one mightn't expect from and author so attached in other poems to fantasy and myth." Milner cites as an example the closing lines of "Give Me Ashes, Earth and my Dead":

There's still time—to withdraw as far as possible into oneself,
and take the ashes, earth and one's dead
the houses balance
in a fearful equilibrium.

—trs. J. and I. Milner

Fischerová's second collection, *Velká zrcad* a (Large mirrors, 1990), was received by critics as a more philosophical work than her first book, offering a vision of the world in the manner of Schopenhauer, in which images and material objects coexist. The poems are more intellectual and abstract, striking some reviewers as remote and abstract. But overall her poetry is impressive, as Jim Grove writes, for "its spare lyricism, its trenchant and sophisticated social / political component and its variety of forms."

Fischerova's poetry has been translated into English, French, German, Swedish, Danish, Latvian, Italian and Dutch.

PRINCIPAL WORKS IN ENGLISH TRANSLATION: (tr. J. Milner and I. Milner) The Tremor of Racehorses, 1990; Selections in Spafford, A. (ed.) Interference: The Story of Czechoslovakia in the Words of Its Writers, 1990; Selections in March, M. (ed.) Child of Europe: A New Anthology of East European Poetry, 1990; (tr. S. Fischerová, S. Friebert, J. Naughton, and V. Orac) Thirteen poems in Prairie Schooner, Winter 1992.

ABOUT: Milner, I. introduction to The Tremor of Racehorses, 1990. Periodicals—Poetry Review Summer 1990; Poetry Wales February 28, 1991; Prairie Schooner Winter 1992; Times Literary Supplement August 27, 1990.

FISH, STANLEY EUGENE (April 19, 1938–), American literary theorist, was born in Providence, Rhode Island, the son of Max and Ida Dorothy Fish. He grew up in Philadelphia, and was educated at the University of Pennsylvania, where he received his bachelor's degree in 1959, then went on to study English literature at Yale, where he received his doctorate in 1962. His dissertation on the Tudor poet John Skelton was published as *John Skelton's Poetry* in 1965. Fish's first academic post was at the University of California at Berkeley, where he rose to the rank of professor by 1969. From 1974 to 1985 he was professor and chairman of the English department at Johns Hopkins University. Since 1985, Fish has been chairman of the English department and professor of law at Duke University. Fish's first marriage—to Adrienne Aaron, in 1959—ended in divorce in 1980; since 1982, he has been married to Jane Parry Tompkins, who is also a professor of English at Duke University.

While Stanley Fish is renowned as a scholar of 17th-century English literature, the author of works on the poets John Milton and George Herbert, his national reputation outside this speciality rests on his lucid championship of reader-response theory, his investigations into the role of the reader within literature. Fish's notion of the role of the reader within the literary experience has evolved since his first important treatise, *Surprised by Sin: The Reader in Paradise Lost.*

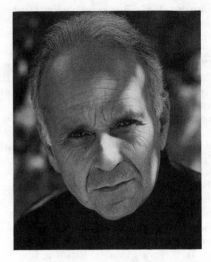

STANLEY EUGENE FISH

The topic of the reader in literature has a long history, going back to Book X of Plato's *Republic*, and rhetorical criticism flourished from Horace in the first century to Samuel Johnson in the eighteenth. The formalist New Criticism practiced in America after World War II, however, exalted the notion of the autonomous text, separated distinctly both from the authorial intention that had brought it into existence and from the reader's response to that text. Such essays as "The Affective Fallacy" (1947) by William K. Wimsatt and Monroe Beardsley argued against any attempt to define the text in terms of the emotions it aroused in the real audience.

The first major reaction to these strictures against the audience was in Wayne C. Booth's *The Rhetoric of Fiction*, which argued that all texts, even the most apparently objective, use a variety of rhetorical techniques to manipulate the audience, to make the reader more receptive to the values of the text, more (or less) sympathetic with its characters, more accepting of its worldview. Stanley Fish too argues that texts are designed to manipulate their readers. Where Booth portrays that manipulation as the friendliest of persuasions, Fish, characteristically sees the reader as the author's victim and the manipulative author as entangling readers within the contradictions of the text, splitting their sympathies, creating in readers a schizoid state for the sake of the author's didactic purposes. In *Surprised by Sin*, Fish argues that the center of reference in Milton's *Paradise Lost* "is its reader who is also its subject," that "Milton's purpose is to educate the reader to an awareness of his position and responsibilities as a fallen man, and to a sense of the distance which separates him from the innocence once his," and that "Milton's method is to re-create in the mind of the reader . . . the drama of the Fall, to make him fall again exactly as Adam did and with Adam's troubled clarity." When Adam chooses to disobey God in Book IX, for example, Milton forces the reader to experience two opposing impulses to do what Adam did and to reject it:

> . . . it would be a mistake to deny either of these impulses; they must be accepted and noted because the self must be accepted before it can be transformed. The value of the experience depends on the reader's willingness to participate in it fully while at the same time standing apart from it. . . . A description of the total response would be, Adam is wrong, no he's right, but, then, of course he is wrong, and so am I. The last is not so much a product of the scene itself as of the self-consciousness it encourages. . . . Moreover, the uneasiness [the reader] feels at his own reaction to the fact of sin is a sign that he is not yet lost . . . In the pattern I discern in the poem, the reader is continually surprised by sin and in shame, "sore displeased with himself," his heart "riseth against it."

The *Times Literary Supplement* review of *Surprised by Sin* called it an "extremely stimulating book," in that the epic "is in reality a vast trap repeatedly and expertly baited for the reader, who is necessarily of the devil's part," but observed that ultimately Fish fails to differentiate among the various voices of the poem, "and the reader flounders on."

For 1967, Fish had made a fairly radical argument in insisting that the meaning of *Paradise Lost* was not a single, complex but static meaning held in place by ironic balance of opposing forces (as the New Critics might have agreed), but a dynamic meaning that arises from the reader's being forced to see matters first one way, then another, then a third. But here this claim was being made only about a single poem, *Paradise Lost*. By 1970, in his article for "Literature in the Reader" for *New Literary History*, Fish was prepared to further generalize this method which he called "affective stylistics." While he admitted that there were comparatively straightforward texts that developed progressively, Fish suggested that some of the most interesting texts were "self-consuming artifacts" which apparently commit themselves to one conclusion, then reverse themselves. Fish gives the following sentence from Sir Thomas Browne as an example: "That Judas perished by hanging himself, there is no certainty in Scripture: though in one place it seems to affirm it, and by a doubtful word hath given occasion to translate it; yet in another place, in a more punctual description, it maketh it impossible and seems to overthrow it." Up to the first comma,

Fish claims, Browne seems to be claiming that it is a fact that Judas hanged himself; from then on, the author gradually and almost entirely takes it all back: "The prose is continually opening, but then closing, on the possibility of verification in one direction or another." Fish's method is to read the text slowly, word by word, alive at each instant to the shifts in apparent position and direction of the prose.

In *Self-Consuming Artifacts*, to which "Literature in the Reader" was published as an appendix, Fish appeals to the notion of the "informed reader," which he defines as a "hybrid" between the "ideal reader" of the New Criticism and "a real reader (me) who does everything within his power to make himself informed." Fish posits, in other words, that all competent readers have the experiences he discussed but that most of us are used to discounting our doubts and difficulties. He assumes, therefore, that literary texts have a single univocal meaning, an operational meaning within the reader, and that "each of us, if we are sufficiently responsible and self-conscious, can, in the course of employing the method, become the informed reader and therefore be a more reliable reporter of his experience." *Self-Consuming Artifacts* was nominated for a National Book award. The *Times Literary Supplement* called it "a book to set the mind racing, written for the most part in a splendidly plain style, and so enjoyable that its author might ask himself whether he has not signed against his own critical canon that a good book is one which leaves the reader feeling profoundly uncomfortable."

Fish discomfited the literary world in an article entitled "Interpreting the *Variorum*"—published in *Critical Inquiry* in 1975—which begins with a demonstration of "affective stylistics" and spells out some of the implications of locating the text within the reader. Fish examines three sonnets by Milton and discovers three difficult interpretive tangles that the combined wisdom of decades of Milton scholarship has been unable to untie. His conclusion is that the tangles are not merely an unavoidable part of the poems, but that the reader's vacillations between one possibility and the next, the experience of the undecidability of the meaning of the sonnets, in fact constitutes their meaning. But where Fish had earlier presumed that each poem defines an "informed reader" whose struggles to interpret the text constitute its poetic meaning, Fish here merely located meaning in the free actions of the reader. This effectively destabilizes the text, since any reader may perform slightly (or even grossly) different operations upon any given text.

In effect, Fish had recognized that the division between the "data" of the text and the "interpretation" that occurs within the reader was in danger of melting into the air. In the long run, Fish argued, there can be no hard "data" uncontaminated by a prior theory or interpretive practice. Features that we generally attribute to a text, like its genre, its individual metaphors and synecdoches, its rhyme and meter, even our recognition of individual words and letters within words, are not contained uncontroversially within the text but instead crucially depend on what the reader brings to the text. A formalist interpretive strategy views the poem in terms of its rhyme and meter, figures of speech, metaphor and irony; a psychoanalytic interpretive strategy sees the poem in terms of its core of fantasy and defense mechanisms. But the choice of interpretive strategy is entirely up to the reader, who is free to read any poem by any strategy: "If I read *Lycidas* and *The Waste Land* differently . . . it will not be because the formal structures of the two poems . . . call forth different interpretive strategies but because my predisposition to execute different interpretive strategies will produce different formal structures. That is, the two poems are different because I have decided they will be."

If the history of criticism contains countless contradictory opinions, it is not complete chaos either. Fish argues that the relative "stability of interpretation (at least among certain groups at certain times)" depends on the existence of what he calls *interpretive communities*: "Interpretive communities are made up of those who share interpretive strategies not for reading (in the conventional sense), but for writing texts, for constituting their properties and assigning their intentions." Those who share an interpretive strategy will need no theoretical explanation to be convinced of an interpretation; those who don't share one will not be convinced regardless of theory. And Fish therefore concludes that theory is unimportant: " . . . you will agree with me only if you already agree with me."

In the last four essays in *Is There a Text in This Class? The Authority of Interpretive Communities*, Fish describes how an interpretive community is formed, and how, once constituted, its members change their minds and the way they read (and thereby create) texts. He develops the idea that the interpretive communities existing at any given time constitute systems of beliefs. New communities develop owing to gaps between existing systems; the interpretive strategy of "affective stylistics," for example, filled a gap produced by the New Critics' rejection of the audience. New communities gain followers from preexisting communities by appealing to the deeper, more fundamental beliefs of interpreters; people change their interpretive communities as they discover conflicts between levels within their personal systems of belief. But is is not clear precisely what factors or beliefs contribute to allegiance to interpretive communities, and Denis Donoghue, reviewing the book for the *Times Literary Supplement*, jokingly suggested: "If you are, say, a man, a Catholic, a Sunday painter, a snooker-player, and a garage-mechanic, you have at least five communities, large or small, within which you interpret."

Is There a Text in This Class? is a collection of essays dating back to "Literature in the Reader," with prefaces in which Fish explains the transitions between his various theoretical positions. Denis Donoghue gently scoffed that "it is good to see that Fish has been arguing with himself and finding himself often unconvincing." In the *New Republic*, Gerald Graff, who was equally nonplussed at the idea of having to wade through Fish's discarded positions, traced Fish's later line of antifoundational argument "back to Kant," claiming that Fish's view of textual interpretation "has gained momentum in the last half-century, as many of the disciplines have reacted against the hubris of science's claim to discover a bedrock of hard fact on which knowledge is founded. There is no such bedrock, it is argued, since facts are already 'theory-laden.'" On the other hand, Alexander Gelley maintained in *Library Journal* that Fish does not "deal with an issue most pertinent to his position—the conflict of historical dimensions in any act of interpretation. . . . "

Since 1980, Fish has been extending his version of antifoundationalism—his notion that theory never constrains interpretation—from literature to law and other fields. In *Doing What Comes Naturally: Change, Rhetoric, and the Practice of Theory in Literary and Legal Studies*, he argues that our intellectual practices, including literary and legal interpretations, come not out of global theories but out of our personal systems of beliefs, that we are always free to interpret any text in accordance with those beliefs, and that therefore, "theory has no consequences." Fish concedes that there may be consequences to announcing that one has a theory: a circuit judge who claims to be a "strict constructionist" may attract a president's attention and wind up on the Supreme Court. Indeed, for Fish legal theories make sense precisely as announcements of political agendas or programs, rather than as effective methodologies; they are merely one more part of the rhetorical practice of law.

Fish's argument that we should just practice the art of interpretation, rather than wasting our time with theory, antagonizes some reviewers. John Ellis, in the *London Review of Books*, wrote: "To say that all one has to do is to ignore theory and do what comes naturally seems at the outset to be unable to deal with two most important facts of experience—that most of us find that reflecting on what we are doing is helpful, and that what comes naturally to many people can seem foolish or even horrendous to others. Can we really value reflection so little?" But Perry Meisel, in the *New York Times Book Review*, called *Doing What Comes Naturally* "a handy textbook for those who wish to catch up on the variety of questions to which literary criticism can usefully address itself today and to see a deconstructive method in action in various intellectual contexts, particularly in examining the similarities between questions of literature and law."

Stanley Fish might be described as the gadfly of contemporary literary theory. In an age that values consistency and coherence he has not only radically changed his literary theories many times but advertised his own disagreements with his earlier positions. In an era of theory, he has insisted that theory never constrains interpretive practice and has no important consequences. His influence is everywhere in that his skepticism has influenced the entire critical scene.

PRINCIPAL WORKS: John Skelton's Poetry, 1965; Surprised by Sin: The Reader in "Paradise Lost," 1967; Seventeenth-Century Prose: Modern Essays in Criticism, 1972; Self-Consuming Artifacts: The Experience of Seventeenth-Century Literature, 1972; The Living Temple: George Herbert and Catechizing, 1978; Is There a Text in This Class? The Authority of Interpretive Communities, 1980; Doing What Comes Naturally: Change, Rhetoric, and the Practice of Theory in Literary and Legal Studies, 1989; There's No Such Thing as Free Speech and It's a Good Thing Too, 1994.

ABOUT: Contemporary Authors 132, 1985; Dictionary of Literary Biography 67, 1988. *Periodicals*—Library Journal November 1, 1972; March 1, 1981; London Review of Books July 27, 1989; New Republic February 14, 1981; New York Times Book Review, May 21, 1989; New York Times Magazine May 3, 1992; Times Literary Supplement August 16, 1967; September 7, 1973; September 29, 1978; May 8, 1981; March 9, 1990; Virginia Quarterly Review Summer 1973.

FITZGERALD, PENELOPE (MARY) (December 17, 1916–), British novelist and biographer, writes: "Although I didn't start writing until quite late in life, I was born into a 'writing family,' in which everyone, including my brother and my cousins, worked hard for school and college scholarships. We received an old-fashioned (archaic might be a better word) classical education. My grandfather, who became a bishop of formidable learning, liked to remember that *his* whole education had cost his father one shilling (about twenty cents). This was the tip traditionally given by a new boy to the porter at St. Paul's School, then in the City of London.

"My father was editor of *Punch* from 1932 to 1945. His brother Dillwyn—my uncle Dilly—was a mathematical genius and expert decipherer of ancient Greek manuscripts. He was, perhaps, a little impatient with those whose minds worked differently from his own. To say you didn't understand mathematics seemed to him an absurd affectation, because it wasn't, after all, a question of understanding, but simply of seeing. He worked during the Second World War at the Department of Communications. There, by arriving at a method of solving Enigma, the German encipherment machine, he is said to have shortened the course of the war by about six months, with a corresponding saving of human lives. Two more uncles were priests, and to both of them writing came as naturally as breathing, though neither of them was very good with a typewriter. The youngest, Ronald Knox, believed that he had written so much that his bibliography had grown too complicated even for the Recording Angel. In the end, though, somebody, I'm glad to say, did undertake it.

"You can't escape your childhood, and I am grateful for mine, and particularly for the first few years, when my parents lived at Balcombe, in Sussex in the South of England. That was the time when I could run barefoot between the hen-coops, the raspberry canes, the white front gate, and the rose hedge. That was my kingdom, and it seemed quite large enough. Indoors I had another private territory under the dining-room table, since tables in those days were kept covered with substantial green cloths, which came down to the ground on every side.

"As to writing with the idea of publishing—I began as a biographer, with a life of the Victorian painter and designer Edward Burne-Jones. This was because one of my very earliest memories is being taken to Birmingham Cathedral and being held up to look at the West window, which was designed by Burne-Jones and installed in my grandfather's day. The subject is the Last Judgment, which I didn't take in, but the colours are a wonderful display of red, pink and rose, and it's the first time I remember seeing something which I recognised as a beauty, which of course when you're very young is the same thing as happiness. It was that memory that made up my mind to write about Burne-Jones.

"I have since done two other biographies, one of my family, and one of the poet Charlotte Mew. Certainly, she isn't widely known (my publisher referred to the book as 'Charlottee Who?') but she wrote at least three or four poems which I believe should truly be called great, and I wanted to get what was known about her sad life into print, before it all disappeared. All my other books have been novels. I began with a detective story, *The Golden Child*, about an exhibition of treasure in the British Museum. But the publisher warned me that it was necessary or at least advisable, to write at least another five stories with the same detective. I couldn't face this, so turned to straight novels, and—since I'd written about my family already—to my work situations. *The Bookshop* is about a bookshop in Southwold, on the east coast of England, where I had a job as a willing but not very efficient assistant. The shop is still there, in one of the oldest houses in the town, only a few yards from the sea. When I was there it was haunted by a noisy and unpleasant form of supernatural manifestation—a poltergeist. I heard it hammering and chuckling away almost as soon as I started work, and I thought at first it was the shoe-shop next door, not reflecting that shoe-repairers nowadays don't do any hammering, not even in While-You-Wait shops—perhaps least of all there. But the poltergeist represented for me a deep unease which I tried to get (although it's a comedy) into my novel, because Southwold at that time—I called it Hardborough—was a place of deep resentment and hostility to anything that was new. The struggle to keep the bookshop open, therefore, I hoped to make an image of much more important conflicts. At the same time it seems ironic—indeed, almost impossible—that such narrow-mindedness should go on in that boisterous fresh sea-wind, and under that shining sky. *Offshore*, which won the Booker Prize for fiction in 1979, was about life on an old wooden barge moored on the Thames at Chelsea Reach, not far above Westminster. We lived there because it was cheap, but not because it was safe, and in fact we went down twice, although Thames barges are constructed so that the deck always stays just above water. In *Human Voices* I recalled the peculiar, subterranean life at Broadcasting House, the headquarters of the BBC, during the bombing. *At Freddie's* is set in a theatrical school for stage children, where I used to teach, insofar as one could teach them anything. *The Beginning of Spring*, on the other hand, goes back in time beyond my own experience to a British household in Moscow before the First World War, at the end of winter, before the first ice breaks. For *The Gate of Angels* I stayed in the same period, about 1912, but moved to an imaginary college in Cambridge, very old, very small, very inward-looking. The debate in this novel is between those old friends and antagonists, soul and body, intuition and reason, although I think it doesn't work out quite as expected. I'm particularly fond of my protagonists in *The Gate of Angels*, Fred and Daisy. Fred is a research physicist of those early days; Daisy is a hospital nurse. As to what happens to them, I trust my readers, as indeed I've always trusted them, to finish the story for themselves in the only possible way.

"I try to work within closed areas, where moral and emotional problems will be intensified. I go back to times when prohibitions and social pressures were stronger so as to concentrate on difficulties which I profoundly believe have not gone away. I like to bring in children, because they introduce a different scale of judgement, probably based on the one we taught them but which we never intended to be taken literally. I feel drawn to people whom the twentieth century considers expendable, but who don't give up. As far as I'm concerned, they are not failures, for no one who shows courage can be considered a failure. I've heard my novels described as 'light,' but I mean them very seriously. If ever I see somebody reading one of my paperbacks on a bus or in the Underground I have to restrain myself from sitting down next to them and asking them whether they see the world as I do."

Penelope Knox took a degree in English literature at Somerville College, Oxford, in 1939 with first class honors. She went to work for the BBC as a program assistant after completing her education. In 1953 she married Desmond Fitzgerald, who died in 1976. They had one son and two daughters and she has eight grandchildren. Her writing career did not begin until the children were grown. In her novel *Human Voices* Fitzgerald recalled her experiences at the BBC during the grim years of World War II, somehow managing to find a matter-of-fact humor amid the tension and chaos: "When the Concert Hall was turned into a dormitory for both sexes, the whole building became a target for enemy bombers, and, in the BBC as elsewhere, some had to fail and some had to die." She later worked as a teacher in a theatrical school for children, drawing upon those experiences for *At Freddie's*, a novel about "the oddities and humanities of a stage school," as Penelope Lively termed it in *Encounter*. Freddie, the proprietress, one of nature's survivors, keeps both wrecks—herself and the school—afloat. Lively calls *At Freddie's* a "graceful and good-natured comedy. . . . particularly good on the wizened youth of theatrical children, corrupted by their trade. . . . " All of Fitzgerald's novels have a sharp but never corrosive note of satire and a striking evocation of scene. The chilly, damp provincial town of Hardborough in *The Bookshop*, where the heroine's determination to stock Nabokov's *Lolita* sets off a crisis, is caught in a few words: "survival was often considered all that could be asked in the cold and clear East Anglian air. Kill or care, the inhabitants thought—either a long old age or immediate consignment to the salty turn of the churchyard." In her first novel, *The Golden Child*, she captures the trendy 1970s with a casual reference to a restaurant near the British Museum that changes its name with every passing cultural season: "the Bloomsbury Group, Lytton Strachey Slept Here, the Cook Inn, Munchers, and Bistro Solzhenitzen now bore the name of The Crisis." In *The Beginning of Spring*, the story of a transplanted English family living in Russia in 1913, she re-creates a long forgotten past: "Up until a few years ago the first sound in the morning in Moscow had been the cows coming out of the side-streets, where they were kept in stalls and backyards, and making their own way among the horse-trams to their meeting point at the edge of the Khamovniki, where they were taken by the municipal cowman to their pasture, or, in winter, through the darkness to the suburban stores of hay. Since the tramlines were electrified the cows had disappeared." A Russian servant explains the fine distinctions of his religion to his English master: he is "Not an unbeliever, sir, a free-thinker. Perhaps you've never thought about the difference. As a free thinker I can believe what I like, when I like. I can commit you, in your sad situation, to the protection of God this evening, even though tomorrow I shan't believe he exists. As an unbeliever I should be obliged not to believe, and that's an unwarrantable restriction on my thought."

Penelope Lively observed that "the pleasures of Penelope Fitzgerald's novels are stylistic; there are few who can match her when it comes to the nailing of a character in a few words, the turn of phrase that brings a person or a place smoking off the page, the wry comment that sums up a situation." Unlike most satirists, Fitzgerald has a sympathetic imagination that enables her to get inside her characters, however distant they may be from her in time or personality.

John Ryle, in *New Statesman*, pointed up Fitzgerald's ability to limn the eccentric British: "Set in a houseboat community on Battersea

Reach in the 1960s, *Offshore* is full of richly eccentric characters who are terrifically English: a terrifically English estate agent trying to sell a leaking barge, a terrifically English layabout, a terrifically English male prostitute. . . . For them there is simply nothing like messing about in houseboats." In contrast her characters in *Innocence*, Italians living in contemporary Florence, are drawn with such fidelity to Italian mores, C. K. Stead writes in *London Review of Books*, "that when a young Englishwoman appears on the scene she really seems a foreigner and not as one might suspect, the focus of the novel's consciousness."

The Gate of Angels is "certainly about goodness," according to John Bayley, writing in the *New York Review of Books*. Laid in 1912 in "St. Angelicus College a small enclosed world embodying all the picturesque eccentricities . . . characteristic of academia. . . . this is far from being a campus novel. . . . " Bayley says. He attributes to Fitzgerald's "immense originality" the novel's lack of overt didacticism and avoidance of "any suggestion that she might have a feminist moral in mind, or a dig against science or a Christian apologetic." Fitzgerald's achievement, Bayley maintains, is in showing us "that the novel can still return . . . to its days of innocence, when it wished to show us what virtue was about. . . . "

PRINCIPAL WORKS: *Novels*—The Golden Child, 1977; The Bookshop, 1978; Offshore, 1979; Human Voices, 1980; At Freddie's, 1982; Innocence, 1986; The Beginning of Spring, 1989; The Gate of Angels, 1990. *Biographies*—Edward Burne-Jones, 1975; The Knox Brothers, 1977; Charlotte Mew and Her Friends, 1984. *As editor*—The Novel on Blue Paper: William Morris's Unfinished Novel, *in* Dickens Studies Annual 10, 1982.

ABOUT: Contemporary Authors 85-88, 1980; Contemporary Authors Autobiography Series 10, 1989; Contemporary Literary Criticism 19, 1981; 51, 1989; Contemporary Novelists, 4th ed., 1986; Dictionary of Literary Biography 14, 1983; Schlueter, P. and J. eds. Encyclopedia of British Women Writers, 1988; Todd, J., ed. Dictionary of British Women Writers, 1989. *Periodicals*—Encounter June–July 1982; London Review of Books October 9, 1986; New York Review of Books April 9, 1992; New York Times Book Review May 7, 1989; March 1, 1992; Times Literary Supplement November 17, 1978; September 26, 1980; April 2, 1982; Washington Post July 12, 1987.

FLEMING, BERRY (JILES) (March 19, 1899–September 15, 1989), American novelist, was born in Augusta Georgia, where his family, originally settlers in Virginia, had moved in 1790 as cotton traders. His parents, Porter and Daisy

BERRY FLEMING

(Berry) Fleming, were well-to-do, and they educated their son in private schools in the South (the Academy of Richmond County) and in New England (the Middlesex School in Concord, Massachusetts). Fleming entered Harvard University in 1918 and completed his bachelor of science degree there in 1922. While an undergraduate, he wrote for the *Harvard Lampoon* and began selling his light-humor pieces to the *New York Post*. Upon graduation he returned to his home town of Augusta to work as a reporter for the *Augusta Chronicle*.

Although there were periods of several years when Fleming lived in New York City and in Europe, he spent most of his life, and died in Augusta. His fiction often draws on Augusta, which he called "Fredericksville." Very different from the dark, guilt-haunted South of William Faulkner and other southern regionalists—it is more genial, more slyly humorous, though its portraits of provincial characters are realistic.

Journalism did not appeal to Fleming as a lifetime career, so in 1923, after a year of newspaper work, he moved to New York to study painting at the Art Students League. Although he showed distinct promise as a painter and in later years exhibited his paintings in Augusta, he found it easier to support himself by writing. He sold light verse and short essays to magazines, including the *New Yorker*, and—in England—*Punch*, and wrote his first novel, *The Conqueror's Stone*, a mystery-adventure yarn about piracy in the waters off the Carolinas in the late 18th century. Reviewers recognized humor and a promising talent in the book. Married

since 1925 to Shirley Molloy, Fleming felt encouraged enough by the sales of *The Conqueror's Stone*, to move with his wife to Europe where they lived for a year, mainly in France, while he divided his time between painting and writing.

Visa to France, his second novel, introduces a large international cast and weaves the characters together in a story involving some mystery and considerable humor. Once again reviewers responded favorably, finding the novel "engaging" if somewhat slight.

In 1931, Fleming and his wife returned to New York where he completed another novel, this one about a young bond salesman working in Wall Street—*The Square Root of Valentine*. By now Fleming had attracted notice as a writer of lightweight fiction, but with the coming of the economic depression of the early 1930s and his own maturity as a writer, he shifted his attention to more serious material. He returned to Augusta with his family (they had one daughter, Shirley), where he wrote a weekly column for the *Chronicle* and became increasingly interested in community affairs. In later years he administered a fund left by his father for civic and cultural activities in Augusta.

Siesta, published in the mid-1930s, reflects Fleming's more sober vision of a contemporary southern small town. More a series of sketches than a structured narrative, *Siesta* brings together the lives of the townspeople and a few outsiders from the North in a realistic portrait of a society struggling to define itself. Reviewers were struck by Fleming's fresh outlook on the South and by his dynamic narrative technique, which involved the use of local newspaper headlines, brief character profiles, and brisk dialogue. Howard Mumford Jones, in the *Saturday Review of Literature*, suggested that Fleming had proven himself "the most interesting southern novelist" of the time—this in 1935, when Erskine Caldwell was flourishing and William Faulkner had already published several of his major works.

Probably the most ambitious of Fleming's novels was *To the Marketplace*, published in 1938. His southern characters—bright, well-educated, and talented young people—are transplanted to the stimulating New York City of the 1930s. They make careers for themselves, fall in and out of love, fail, succeed, and some of them eventually return to their southern roots. Clifton Fadiman, in the *New Yorker*, pronounced Fleming "an honest writer . . . worth keeping an eye on."

Colonel Effingham's Raid, a gentle but ontarget satire on southern politics in

"Fredericksville," appeared when the country was engaged in World War II. This shrewdly observed picture of local petty corruption confronted by old-fashioned American idealism appealed to many readers. It was a Book-of-the-Month Club selection and in 1945 was released as a motion picture. Colonel Effingham is a retired U.S. Army officer who returns to his hometown and volunteers to write a column for the paper, ostensibly on the innocuous subject of military strategy. As the column rousingly retells the Civil War history of the town, the colonel awakens in the citizens a sense of pride in the local landmarks that greedy real estate developers and local politicians are planning to tear down. His story is narrated by his mousey young cousin, a reporter on the local newspaper, who gradually discovers his own independence and integrity in the older man's crusade to restore the town's pride in its past.

The critical and popular success of *Colonel Effingham's Raid* marked an ironic turning point in Fleming's career. Some of his best and most serious fiction was to follow. In 1944, his short story "Strike Up a Stirring Music," a sensitive account of a young army officer called up from the reserves for service in World War II, was included in both the *O. Henry Memorial Prize Stories* and the *Best American Short Stories* annuals. Three years later *The Lightwood Tree*, an ambitious history of a Georgia town related in episodic flashbacks to 1742, 1783, 1863, and World War II, was praised by Edward Weeks in the *Atlantic* as Fleming's "best novel and one of which Georgia should be proud." Both *The Fortune Tellers*, a mystery-suspense novel that confronts racial prejudice forthrightly but without sensationalism, and *Winter Rider*, the story of a middle-aged novelist who is stranded when his car breaks down in rural Georgia and finds new hope and inspiration for his work, had favorable reviews.

Although *The Fortune Tellers* was a Literary Guild selection, the sales of Fleming's novels dropped dramatically, and by the early 1970s he had trouble finding a publisher for his new work. Fleming stopped writing fiction altogether for almost twenty years and concentrated on painting and compiling local histories. He also ventured briefly into the theater with a dramatization of his 1953 novel *Carnival*, in which the central image, a carnival, is a metaphor for the human world and the central character is an "Everyman" who reminded some reviewers of a character in a morality play. Fleming turned *Carnival* into a two-act comedy called *The Acrobats*: It was given a colorful, imaginative production in 1961 by Lucille Lortel in which the audience was part of a carnival setting with sideshows and merry-go-round music.

In 1979 Fleming and a fellow Augustan, newspaper publisher Bill Harper, jointly founded Cotton Lane Press "to keep Berry Fleming before the reading public," as Fleming candidly admitted. Cotton Lane published several of his later novels and also a sixty-page paperback, *Notes for a Now-and-Then Painter*. These were not widely noticed, and Fleming's work might well have dwindled into total obscurity had it not been for a small publisher in Sag Harbor, Long Island, aptly named Second Chance Press. Fleming sent them a copy of his 1935 novel *Siesta*, which they liked well enough to reissue in 1987. "You know, I'm an old man," Fleming told his new publisher, "and if you publish one a year, I probably won't be around to see them." He lived, in fact, to see successful reprints of three more novels in 1988: *Colonel Effingham's Raid*; *Lucinderella*, a broadly comic novel about the return to the old homestead of an eccentric young woman who has become famous for revealing lurid family secrets in her novels; and the *The Make-Believers*. In 1989 Second Chance reissued *To the Marketplace* and *A Country Wedding*.

Fleming was eighty-nine years old when he completed the novel *Who Dwelt by a Churchyard*, a poignant memoir of an aged man, now widowed and alone, breaking up his home to move to smaller quarters and reviewing his life in the papers and photos he is forced to discard. In 1989, *Captain Bennett's Folly* was reissued. Described by Andy Solomon, in the *New York Times Book Review*, as "a zesty comic novel," it is the whimsical story of an old man outwitting his greedy relatives. "The plot's mystery," Solomon wrote, "lies in whether Captain Bennett's family will succeed. But the bigger mystery lies in how so entertaining a writer as Berry Fleming, now aged 90 and the author of 19 books, could have been publishing since 1927 without finding the wide and appreciative audience he deserves."

Fleming died in Augusta only a month after this review appeared.

PRINCIPAL WORKS: *Novels*—The Conqueror's Stone, 1927; Visa to France, 1930; The Square Root of Valentine, 1932; Siesta, 1935; To the Marketplace, 1938; Colonel Effingham's Raid, 1943; The Lightwood Tree, 1947; The Fortune Tellers, 1951; Carnival, 1953; The Winter Rider, 1960; Lucinderella, 1967; The Make-Believers, 1972; Two Tales for Autumn: Captain Bennett's Folly and The Inventory, 1979; The Affair at Honey Hill, 1981; A Country Wedding, 1983; Once There Was a Fisherman, 1984; The Bookman's Tale, 1986; Who Dwelt by a Churchyard, 1989. *Play*—The Acrobats, 1969. *Nonfiction*—(as compiler) One Hundred and Ninety-nine Years of Augusta's Library, 1949; Autobiography of a Colony, 1957; Autobiography of a City in Arms: Augusta, Georgia, 1861–1865.

ABOUT: Contemporary Authors New Revision Series 18, 1986; Current Biography 1953. *Periodicals*—New York Times September 16, 1989; New York Times Book Review August 6, 1989; New Yorker October 29, 1938; Publishers Weekly January 22, 1988; Saturday Review of Literature April 6, 1935.

*FONSECA, (JOSÉ) RUBEM, (May 11, 1925–   ), Brazilian novelist, short story writer, and scriptwriter, was born in Juiz de Fora, Brazil, the son of Portuguese immigrants. He came to Rio de Janeiro as a child and was educated there, securing a law degree from the Universidade Estadual do Rio de Janeiro (UERJ—State University of Rio de Janeiro). Married, he has three children and makes his home in Rio de Janeiro. He has published six novels and six collections of short stories that have put him at the forefront of contemporary Brazilian fiction. Although still little known in the United States, his novels and stories have been translated and published widely in Europe (France, Germany, Italy, and Spain—the latter in both Spanish and Catalan), and Latin America (Colombia, Argentina, and Mexico). One of his novels, *Augusto* (August) was made into a successful television miniseries in Brazil.

Fonseca is the best known of the generation of writers who came of age during the brutal dictatorship that ruled Brazil from 1964 to 1985, and his fiction if profoundly affected by the experience of censorship, ideological manipulation, torture, and arbitrary violence that characterized the period. The liberal economic policies of the regime created a short-lived boom that favored a small percentage of the population but impoverished millions. During the period, Brazil became one of the most unequal societies on the face of the earth, and the confident, expansive spirit of the 1950s that was expressed in vibrant poetry and fiction, exuberant painting, sculpture, and architecture, Bossa Nova, the creation of Brasília, and the belief that Brazil was destined for greatness gave way to a pervasive pessimism. In the "new democracy" that came to power in 1985, the country has struggled with the largest foreign debt in the developing world; incompetent, venal political leaders; galloping stagflation; and social malaise. In this climate it is hardly surprising that literary expression would favor irony, satire, and other genres of pessimism. Some critics have called this generation of writers "neo-naturalists" for their emphasis on man's inhumanity to man, and Fonseca's fictional world amply justifies such a description. The dramatic stage Fonseca has chosen for portraying such dynamics is Rio de Janeiro, former capital of the country and dysfunctional megalopolis of some 15 million citizens. Using experience he gained as a criminal attorney and former district attorney, Fonseca has concentrated his attention on the outer action of Rio's criminal element with the upper classes. His chosen narrators or protagonists are typically detectives or investigators who act as links between the rich and the poor. In a society as hierarchically stratified as Brazil's, these agents are uniquely situated to observe the real, as opposed to the idealized, rules of social interaction. One of his most successful creations, Mandrake, is not a detective, but a lawyer who is called upon in several narratives to get his rich clients out of scrapes with prostitutes, pimps, and other lowlifes. Other protagonists are police or amateur detectives who reflect middle-class values in their interactions with various denizens of the underworld. Often Fonseca's protagonists adopt a cynical or ironic pose as a way of distancing themselves from the crime and brutality they engage in or observe. In other cases, a detached third-person narrator relates urban social pathology in which the protagonists are unaware of the depravity of their actions. At other times, these actions are narrated in the first person, removing the possibility of any judgmental narrative voice.

The apparently nonjudgmental narrative stance adopted in stories like "Feliz Ano Novo" ("Happy New Year"), in which a gang of slum psychopaths invade an upper-class home during a New Year's Eve party and proceed to rape, pillage, and murder, coupled with Fonseca's use of street language, led to accusations that he was a pornographer. The collection *Feliz Ano Novo* (1975) was in fact censored by the regime and became a cause célèbre in the struggle for civil rights during the dictatorship. Fonseca's adoption of a popular narrative form, the detective story, and his objectified vision of urban pathology, have made him one of Brazil's most popular writers; ironically this popularity has been held against him by some critics, as if popularity and some serious intent were incompatible.

Fonseca's narrative incorporates urban slang and obscenity out of a concern with the contemporary debasement of language and with the way that euphemism disguises social exploitation. His anger at being labeled a pornographer led him to a spirited defense of so-called obscenities in the thinly disguised essay-story, "Intestino Grosso" ("Large Intestine"), in which an author defends himself against this accusation. This is the only source, beyond a close reading of his stories themselves, for any clue to the author's own moral vision. He resolutely refuses to grant interviews or to judge his own work or to engage in any way whatever with Brazilian literary society.

*fon SAY kah

What Fonseca creates in his short narratives is a complex tapestry or mural, or collective portrait, in which individual stories provide threads or elements of a larger picture—that of decadent urban society on the verge of breakdown. In fact, he has written several futuristic narratives in which this breakdown is expressed in horrifying terms. In "O Quarto Selo" (The fourth seal), for example, the protagonist is a government assassin, code-named "the exterminator," whose mission, the assassination of the head of the government is narrated dispassionately. In this story, Fonseca's concern with the misuse of language achieves full expression. The future depicted is one in which crime syndicates govern society and in which a vicious system of acronyms disguise brutality. Some of the acronyms, such as "BBBs," a term for pillaging gangs from the English "burn, baby, burn," express Fonseca's concern over the impact cultural imperialism has had on the Portuguese language. Debased Portuguese itself abounds. The word *love* (amor) is the most proscribed term in the CO (Code of Obscenities—pronounced *ku* in Portuguese, meaning *ass*) and God (*Deus*) is a governmental security agency. In "O Campeonato" (The championship) the narrator is an insect or an insectlike hominid historian or archaeologist who narrates a curious story mocking the culture of male sexual performance and the now familiar priapic saga of sports heroes.

Fonseca's concern with language has led him to create stories with surprise endings. Modern readers tend to be careless readers, and Fonseca has written many stories that require close attention or they make no sense. The hero of "O Gravador" (The recorder) is an alienated, sexually dysfunctional young man who records and replays obscene phone calls. When he goes too far and actually arranges a tryst with one of his telephone lovers, she comes to the assignation but doesn't see him: "I waited two hours, two hours by the clock, and George didn't show up. I checked out every inch of the square, expecting George to show up at any moment. . . . The rain wasn't enough to worry about. Well, there were a maid with two kids and a cripple in a wheelchair in the square . . . " What she does not know and what changes a banal story into a pathetic one is a seemingly innocent paragraph at the beginning of the story in which the reader learns that George, the recorder, is a cripple. In "A Matéria do Sonho" (The Stuff of a Dream) the levels of irony are dense with references to Shakespeare; in this case, however, the protagonist's lover, the stuff of *his* dreams, is a vinyl love doll whom he kills in a flight of passion by biting her on the ear! The problem is that the careless reader may miss crucial evidence of her true identity and be mystified at her demise.

Male sexual prowess or its lack is one of Fonseca's most important structuring elements. His narrators, like Vilela, the detective-protagonist narrator of his first novel, *O Caso Morel* (The Morel Case, 1973), and several short stories, and Mandrake, also the protagonist of several short stories and of his first novel translated into English, *A Grande Arte* (High Art, 1983), share the sexual frustrations and hangups of the men they investigate. For the men in his narratives, true intimacy is impossible, and mechanical, repetitive sexual athletics takes its place. Fonseca has portrayed a series of male characters, ranging from young to old, in various stages of alienation. Taken together, they offer the reader a portrait of social disintegration. The pivotal character in this series is Carlos, the protagonist-narrator of "O Relatório de Carlos" (Carlos's story), an authoritarian sexual athlete, affectless and manipulative in his social relationships, and incapable of dealing with women except as sex objects. His attitude barely conceals a profound misogyny:

> A man works like a dog, while his wife spends the day at the manicurist's, at the hairdresser's, at the pedicurist's, at the dress shop, at the doctor's, at a friend's house playing cards, at fashion shows, or just in bed sleeping like a retarded sloth. And when it comes time to separate, the idiot judge (like all judges) decides that half of everything that a man has earned belongs to that parasite.

It is hard for the reader to sympathize with Carlos when his "doll," his term for his latest conquest, betrays him with his best friend. It is also hard to determine whether he gets more pleasure from beating her or from sexual relations with her. His obsession with sex, his only real source of sensation, reveals itself to be as empty as everything else in his life: "Isn't sex the best thing there is? Pleasure in a world of palliatives? The only possible fruition reborn?" Given this belief, he cannot understand why, after fifteen days of uninterrupted copulation, he feels depressed. The source of his malaise, and that of other male characters in Fonseca's world, is his selfishness. He says, "I don't want to know anything about anybody's life, prostitute, housewife, president of the country, movie actor. Other people's lives aren't important to me. What is important to me is my own life. My own life."

Many of Fonseca's male characters, some in a pre-Carlos state miss the opportunity for real love in their anxiety and greed for power and sensation, others in a post-Carlos state of psychological depravity in which they murder, rape, and steal. There is a political dimension in some of these stories, as the sociopaths direct their violence against the upper classes. "O Cobrador"

("The Avenger"), for example, is the story of a sociopathic killer who is converted to an ideological cause and begins to kill for political reasons rather than mere hatred. It is stories like these that alarmed political authorities because the explicit language and violence in them were seen to be threatening the social order.

In his novels Fonseca explores these same themes and techniques in the greater depth that the novel format provides. In *O Caso Morel* (1973) (*High Art*) the protagonists are characters from short stories, Vilela and Mandrake. in *O Caso Morel*, a disillusioned Vilela has left the police force and become a private detective investigating the brutal sadomasochistic murder of a young socialite on a Rio beach. In *High Art*, Mandrake attempts to find out who is savagely murdering prostitutes, a quest which leads him to organized crime, a missing videotape, and his own attempted revenge on two thugs who beat him and sodomize his girlfriend. The high art of the title is the art of knife fighting, on which Mandrake propounds a great length. In *Bufo & Spallanzani* (1986), Fonseca builds a story around an arcane conundrum involving a sophisticated poisoning, and in *Vastas Emoções e Pensamentos Imperfeitos* (Vast emotions and imperfect thoughts, 1988) the story revolves around a missing movie script. *Vastas Emoções e Pensamentos Imperfeitos* ranges from Europe to Brazil, and gives Fonseca a much larger canvas on which to paint. In *Agosto* (August, 1990), Fonseca narrates the tortuous story of an honest, incompetent police investigator who gets involved in one of the defining moments of modern Brazilian history, the suicide of President Getúlio Vargas. August 1954 is as fraught with dreadful implications for Brazilians as November 1963, the date of John F. Kennedy's assassination, is for North Americans.

A defining characteristic of Fonseca's novels, as opposed to his short stories, is their erudition and intellectual challenge. With the exception of *O Caso Morel* and *Agosto*, they take readers into the realm of the arcane and are as concerned with mental puzzles and gymnastics as they are with the narrative line, although the story is never neglected. In his review of *High Art* in the *New York Times Book Review*, the Peruvian novelist Mario Vargas Llosa wrote: "In addition to being an amusing detective novel with all the devices typical of the genre and being accessible to all readers, it is elegant and subtle. Its microcosm of murderers, drug traffickers, prostitutes and ominous capitalists contains an ironic kaleidoscope of historical, literary and mythological allusions. These supplementary elements dignify the story and give it another esthetic dimension, which parodies the detective genre."

These two levels in the novel are not mutually exclusive. The perspicacious reader will quickly discover the system of allusions to which Vargas Llosa refers, but will not find the suspense of the main narrative diminished by it. The usual purpose of the novel—to tell exciting stories and narrate adventures—dovetails perfectly with the most demanding intellectual experimentation in Fonseca's work.

In *Romance Negro e Outras Histórias* (Novel noir and other stories, 1992), Fonseca returned to the short story format. One of these stories ("The Book of Panegyrics") continues the life of an earlier protagonist, the narrator of "The Stuff of a Dream." In "The Art of Walking in the Streets of Rio de Janeiro," Fonseca expresses his own frustrated love of this beautiful, ugly, mysterious, devastated city through the words of a narrator. "Novel Noir" is a tour de force in which the American protagonist, Peter Winner, best-selling crime novelist, engages his colleagues P. D. James, James Ellmore, Willy Voos, and Jean-Claude Billé, in a debate about the perfect crime during a "Festival International du Roman et du Film Noirs" in Grenoble, France. In a turn on the classic whodunit, Winner provides his interlocutors with three days to find out what crime has been committed by none other than Winner himself. Replete with erudition, outrageous puns, literary theory and philosophical speculation, the story is an excellent introduction to the mature Fonseca.

In 1994, Fonseca published his sixth novel, entitled *O Selvegan da Ópera* (The Savage of the Opera), which details with the life and times of opera composer Antonio Carlos Gomes (1836–1896). Gomes is thought of as Brazil's Puccini.

PRINCIPAL WORKS IN ENGLISH TRANSLATION: *Novels*—High Art (tr. E. Watson) 1986; Buto & Spallanzani (tr. C. E. Landers) 1990. *Short stories*—Stuff of a Dream (tr. E. Lowe) in Fiction, 1975; Large Intestine (tr. E. Lowe) in Review 76, 1976; Happy New Year (tr. P. J. Schoenbach) in Literary Review, 1984; The Avenger (tr. E. Lowe) in New World, 1986; Lonely Hearts (tr. C. E. Landers) in Colchie, T. (ed.) A Hammock Beneath the Mangoes, 1991; Mandrake (tr. A. Simpson) in Simpson, A. (ed.) New Tales of Mystery and Crime from Latin America, 1992.

ABOUT: Encyclopedia of World Biography 19, 1992. *Periodicals*—Comparative Literature Studies 28, 4, 1991; Latin American Literary Review July–December 1992; Luso-Brazilian Review Winter 1986; New World, 1986; New York Times Book Review September 7, 1986.

*FORNES, (MARIA) IRENE (May 14, 1930–), American playwright, director, and teacher, was born in Havana, Cuba, emigrated to the United States in 1945, and was naturalized in 1951. She began her career as a painter in Paris in the mid-1950s, and moved to New York City in 1957 where she worked as a textile designer for three years. She began writing plays in 1960, as a somewhat serendipitous result of an evening out with Susan Sontag, her friend and roommate at the time. Sontag was feeling frustrated and intimidated, anxious about being a writer. Fornes insisted they forego a party in the East Village and go home and write. Each woman unofficially began her career that evening.

A founding member and one-time president of New York Theatre Strategy, from 1973 to 1978, Fornes has always been very intimately involved with New York City's Off-Broadway theater. She has directed almost all of her own plays, as well as a few of some others, and has taught at the Theatre for the New City, at the Padua Hills Festival, and at INTAR (International Arts Relations), with which she has been associated since 1981. She is a member of the Dramatists Guild, ASCAP, the League of Professional Theatre Women, and the Society of Stage Directors and Choreographers. Her work has been honored by fellowships and grants, and by eight Obie Awards spanning two decades, including one for sustained achievement in the Off-Broadway theater.

Despite Fornes's commitment to the theater, and the many honors she has received, her career has not been without hurdles. While some critics have become champions of Fornes's cause, she has always found herself insufficiently funded and caught up in political battles. The politics of feminism have particularly had their impact on her career. When asked in 1985 by Scott Cummings for an interview in *Theater* whether there is a "tension between being feminine and being a feminist," Fornes explained that, to her, to be "a feminist I think means that you follow a political process that has a development and you are part of the development and you adhere to it. I am a feminist in that I am very concerned and I suffer when women are treated in as discriminatory manner and when I am treated in a discriminatory manner because I am a woman."

Fornes has avoided oversimplification of feminist issues, however. In her contribution to a special issue of the *Performing Arts Journal* (1983) consisting of statements by women playwrights, Fornes notes that most male spectators of her play *Fefu and Her Friends* responded with confusion because there is no male protagonist: "They cannot make heads or tails of it. The

only answer they have is that it is a feminist play. It could be that it is a feminist play but it could be that it is just a play. . . . The question of personal vision and imagery is for me more important than gender."

A year later in *Performing Arts Journal* Bonnie Marranca defended *Mud* as "imbued with a feminism of the most subtle order, feminism based on the ruling idea that a free woman is one who has autonomy of thought." This defense was in response to some critics who had condemned Fornes for allowing her female protagonist to be murdered at the play's end. To them this act perpetuated the status of Woman as Victim. Fornes herself denies that she has a specific agenda in mind. She told Ross Wetzsteon, in *New York* magazine: "I can't 'plant' things. . . . like a treasure hunt where you need a map. To me, a play is more like a path I just follow, never knowing where it's going to end up, letting the material guide me step by step." Even of a play as political as her *The Conduct of Life*, in which the wife of an army officer fears that her husband may be torturing prisoners and raping the servant girl, Fornes says: "I see political power in Latin America as orgiastic, sadistic, not from the head like the Nazis . . . But I don't believe that plays should analyze or make pronouncements; they should let you come close to the daily life of the characters, get to know them intimately—that way, the audience can decide for itself what it means." In that play rather than denouncing the officer who tortures political prisoners, Fornes simply lets his own words characterize him.

Politics have by no means been the only impediment to Fornes's success. Bonnie Marranca, who has been writing about Fornes for almost twenty years, noted in a recent essay in the *Performing Arts Journal* in 1992: "At her age, and with such a long record of distinguished achievement entirely within the medium of theatre, a fully elaborated directorial style, and a grand reputation as a teacher, Fornes should be given all that the American theatre has to offer in terms of resources. . . . Imagine what other artists might learn from Fornes." Her admirers agree that the problem lies in her audience's somewhat limited expectations. Fornes's reach is remarkably broad and her plays consistently diverse. It is difficult to characterize her work as a whole; among other plays, she has produced the Beckettian *Promenade* (1965); the quintessential romantic *Molly's Dream* (1968); the absurd *The Successful Life of 3* (1965), whose theme song demands, "Oh, let me be wrong, but also not know it"; the complex, gender-conscious *Fefu and Her Friends* (1978); the disturbing drama about Latin American political violence *The*

Conduct of Life (1985); and the metatheatrical *Mud* (1983). She writes both lyrical drama and political drama, making use of spectacle that resists immediate and easy comprehension. Plays like *Sarita* (1984) and *Tango Palace* (1963) combine very serious political concerns about society, poverty, and sexual relationships with playful song and dance. *Fefu and Her Friends* requires the audience to leave their seats and wander from room to room with the characters, as well as to untangle a moment of theatrical ambiguity at the play's end.

Fornes's plays are often termed realistic, though critics qualify the term: "hyper-realism," "surrealism," and "quotational realism"; all appear in Marranca's articles on her. Her own view, as she told Scott Cummings, is that "realism is just behavior. I like acting that is true, that I can see and believe something is happening to that character. You [the actor] have to be well grounded, grounded not with your intellect but with your humanity, your body, your carnality." Or as *Fefu*'s Emma describes the theater: "It's not acting. It's being. It's springing forth with the powers of the spirit. It's breathing." To those critics who find her work incoherent, Fornes would respond that she has not sought coherency; she has sought honesty, which can elude narrative coherency. In that vein, she defends the romantic lyricism for which she has been criticized. She asked Cummings: "Have you ever been with a person when just being with them makes you see everything in a different light? A glass of beer has an amber, a yellow that you've never seen before. . . . It *is* more beautiful. It isn't that you want it to be more beautiful."

While Fornes resists analyzing her own work, others have taken up her cause with fervor. W. B. Worthen, writing in *Feminine Forces*, considers Fornes's works as theater about theater, asserting that her plays, "precisely address the process of theater, how the authority of the word, the presence of the performer, and the complicity of the silent spectator articulate dramatic play." Toby Silverman Zinman, in an essay in *Around the Absurd*, totally rejects the idea that she is a realist and calls her an absurdist. Jill Dolan too denies that Fornes's plays are "realistic," insisting that she "implicate[s] the spectator[s] as witnesses to the unfolding narrative." Dolan, Deborah R. Geis, and Helene Keyssar have explored the feminist elements of Fornes's theater and find her work presents "a distinctly different way of thinking about both drama and its relation to gender," as Keyssar puts it.

In an article in the *Village Voice* in 1986, Ross Wetzsteon offered an overview of Fornes's achievement: "[The] very experiments in form and content that have made her career so compelling, the very changes in style that have kept her work so alive, are precisely the reasons she's received so little recognition. . . . Repetition would have made more comprehensible her discontinuities of language, character, space, and time, repeated exposure would have made accessible her matter-of-fact surrealism." But, he concludes, "There is . . . a Fornes signature after all—emotional complexity conveyed through ruthless simplicity, moral concern conveyed through a wholly dramatic imagination."

What Wetzsteon terms her "moral concern" situates Fornes in a spectrum of social dramas about the impact of society, culture, economics, and politics on women's lives, in the tradition of Rachel Crothers, Susan Glaspell, Lillian Hellman, right up to Caryl Churchill. Her "wholly dramatic imagination" has been realized in an intensely image-oriented element that unites her with such playwrights as Jean Cocteau and Samuel Beckett. She is also a social dramatist, sensitive to the power of social and political institutions. In all of Fornes's plays, the theater has its own foreboding and commanding life, and serves as a metaphor for the stages on which Fornes's spectators act out their own lives.

PRINCIPAL WORKS: Fefu and Her Friends *in* Performing Arts Journal, 1978; Drowning *in* Orchards, 1986; Maria Irene Fornes: Plays (*includes* Mud, The Danube, Sarita, *and* The Conduct of Life), 1986; Promenade and Other Plays (*contains* Tango Palace, Promenade, The Successful Life of 3, Molly's Dream, A Vietnamese Wedding, *and* Dr. Kheal), 1987; Abingden Square *in* Miles, J. ed. Womenswork: Five New Plays from the Women's Project, 1989; Springtime *in* Anteaus, 1991.

ABOUT: Austin, G. (ed.) Making a Spectacle: Feminist Essays on Contemporary Women's Theatre, 1989; Betsko, K. and R. Koenig (eds.) Interviews with Contemporary Women Playwrights, 1987; Brater. E. (ed.) Around the Absurd, 1990; Brater, E. (ed.) Feminine Focus, 1989; Contemporary Authors New Revision Series 28, 1990; Contemporary Literary Criticism Yearbook, 1985; Dictionary of Literary Biography 7, 1981; Dolan, J. The Feminist Spectator as Critic, 1988; Keyssar, H. Feminist Theatre, 1985; Krich Chinoy, H. and L. W. Jenkins (eds.) Women in American Theatre, 1964; Schlueter, J. (ed.) Modern American Drama: The Female Canon, 1990. *Periodicals*—Modern Drama 34, March 1991; New York Magazine March 18, 1985; New York Times January 14, 1978, January 22, 1978, March 13, 1984; Performing Arts Journal 2, 1978; 7, 1983; 8, 1984;14, 1992; Theater Winter 1985; Theatre Journal October 1990; Village Voice April 19, 1986.

*FUKS, LADISLAV (September 24, 1923–
August 19, 1994), Czech novelist and short story
writer, was born in Prague, the son of Vaclav
Fuks, a policeman, and Marie (Fryckova) Fuks.
He attended grammar school in Prague and during World War II was sent to work in Moravia.
After the war he studied at the arts faculty of
Charles University in Prague and graduated in
philosophy, psychology, and the history of art. In
1949, he earned a doctorate for a thesis on Bergson's concept of development. After that he
worked in a paper mill and then in the State Institution for the Maintenance of Historical
Buildings and Monuments, where he took special interest in Bohemian and Moravian castles
(in 1958 he published a monograph on one of
these, Kynžvart). He also worked in the Prague
National Gallery. From 1963 until his death in
1994 Fuks was a free-lance writer.

Fuks's first novel, *Pan Theodor Mundstock*
(1963, *Mr. Theodore Mundstock*), was published
at the beginning of the detente between Czechoslovakia and the U.S.S.R. An international conference on Franz Kafka in Liblice declared
Kafka's work acceptable for socialist society in
that same year, 1963. *Pan Theodor Mundstock*
takes place in Prague during World War II. It
is an absurdist parable about an older man, a
Jew, who tries to survive the Holocaust by decent individual behavior. Dismissed from his
longtime job as a clerk, Mr. Mundstock suffers
shock and a mental breakdown. Convinced of
his clairvoyance, he begins to assure his Jewish
friends of the early end of the war and then to
prepare himself for transport to a concentration
camp. He trains himself to live through the most
difficult circumstances, even the gas chamber or
the firing squad. After many of his friends commit suicide or are shipped to a concentration
camp, he finally gets a summons himself.
Trained and well prepared, accompanied by a
little boy admirer, he is approaching the meeting place when he is run over by a German truck
and killed.

Pan Theodor Mundstock is included in what
the Czech literary critics call the second wave of
prose dealing with World War II; the first wave
came immediately after the end of the war and
was marked by a relative perfunctoriness, largely as a result of Soviet pressure. The second wave
began at the time of the first political thaw in the
mid-1950s and was more varied from an ideological and literary point of view. The authors of
the second wave refrained from formal and impersonal treatment of history and returned to the
more probing psychological concerns of the
1930s and the 1940s. They also laid stress upon
feeling; although writing in a naturalistic style,
they rejected the stereotypes of socialist realism.

Pan Theodor Mundstock displays all of these literary traits. It has a bizarre and enclosed atmosphere, narrated from the point of view of a
madman whose madness dominates and absorbs
everything around him, producing what one,
Milan Suchomel, called "reality born of
illusions."

The novel has the quality of a stage play or a
film. The narration does not flow in a continuous
chronological stream, but follows a dramatic
curve. Pan Theodor fancies himself messianic
and harangues the living and the dead, as well
as his pigeon. Fuks devised a whole system of allusions, tags, and refrains, as well as using the
symbolism of numbers and colors. Fuks created
an atmosphere of uncertainty from the feeling
of nameless fear and its repression, an atmosphere fluctuation between terror and delusions
of a waxwork paradise.

Writing in the tradition of nineteenth-century
romantic and occult prose writers (from E.T.A.
Hoffman to Gustav Meyrink) and, of course,
Franz Kafka who exerted considerable influence
upon Czech literature in the 1960s, Fuks became
one of the foremost writers in contemporary
Czech literature, together with Milan Kundera,
Josef Skvorecký, Ivan Klíma, Ludvík Vaculík,
Arnošt Lustig, Vladimír Páral, Bohumil Hrabal,
and Jaroslav Putník. *Pan Theodor Mundstock*
was hailed as one of the major books of the "new
wave" and one of the best contemporary Czech
novels.

The collection of short stories *Mí černovlasí
bratři* (My black-haired brothers, 1962) though
published later, was written prior to *Pan Theodor Mundstock*, with which it has many features
in common. It consists of six short stories, narrated by a grammar school student (whose father,
like Fuks's father, is a police officer) and depicts
the tragic fates of the narrator's Jewish friends,
all between thirteen and sixteen years of age at
the time of the Nazi occupation of Czechoslovakia. Each short story contains a leitmotif:
"Sadness is yellow and six-pointed like the star
of David." The Jewish way of life and the authentic poetry of childhood and early adolescence are memorialized. As in *Pan Theodor
Mundstock*, Fuks's style is somewhat formal and
archaic, as a contrast to the usual language of
people the age of the narrator and his friends.
Evil is personified by an anti-Semitic Nazi professor of geography who is gradually driven to
insanity. The novel is permeated with melancholy, authentic sadness, in contrast to stories
about Jewish children written by other Czech
authors like Joseph Skvorecký and Arnošt Lustig
during the 1960s.

Fuks's second novel, *Variace pro temnou*

°FOOKS, LOO di sluf

strunu (Variations for a dark string, 1966), takes place largely in the same environment as these short stories and has the same narrator, the boy Michal. In the novel he is only eleven or twelve years old, which makes the atmosphere of the book all the more poignant. Like *Pan Theodor Mundstock*, this novel has a rambling structure, portraying the inner life of the narrator and introducing no outside ideological issues. Centered on Michal's mental life, the novel is filled with visions and grotesque experiences, which intersect with depictions of his relations with his environment and his policeman father, and with nostalgia for the past, the days of the old Austria-Hungary. The whole is pervaded by a strong odor of the grotesque and the phantasmagoric, like all of Fuks's works.

Fuks's novella *Spalocač mrtvol* (1967, *The Cremator*) is perhaps the most popular of his books, partly thanks to the film version made by Juraj Herz in 1969. This is a cautionary horror story of a maniacal employee of a crematorium in Prague whose messianic complex drives him mad. His madness is further fueled by Nazi ideology, with a strange overtone of Buddhist philosophy. He kills his Jewish wife and collaborates with the Nazis in their extermination activities.

The second of Fuks's collections of short stories *Smrt morčete* (The death of a guinea pig, 1969), written between 1953 and 1967, contains playful ironic stories full of grotesque absurdists and black humor, alternating between levity and a sense of ominousness. It also contains an Orwellian fable (written in 1953) about animals who destroy human order and tragically subservient people. Several tragicomic stories with Jewish characters are also included. The quiet face of the stories and their humor are deceptive as they gradually insinuate omens of evil and tragedy into the readers consciousness. The story, one of the author's best, is the mystical "Cesta do svaté země" (The Journey to the Holy Land) about Jews fleeing Austria after the Anschluss. *Smrt morčete* concludes the first period of Fuks's work, marked by an existential outlook and by the pathos of the world he depicts. With works like these Fuks established himself in Czechoslovakia—as well as abroad—as a writer of major importance.

The four books that followed are in much the same spirit as Fuks's ealier work, dealing sometimes whimsically, sometimes in deadly seriousness, with themes of fear, evil, justice, and injustice, but they are simpler in style and more direct. In *Myši Natálie Mooshabrové* (Natalia Mooshaber's mice, 1970), the dense atmosphere of fear and existential uncertainty typical of Fuks is replaced with a fantastic allegorical fairy tale with grotesque overtones about a deposed princess who lives in hiding incognito. *Pruíbeh kriminálnuího rady* (The story of a criminologist, 1971), is a psychological thriller about the criminal investigations of a police chief seeking to solve the murders of children; it also deals with this cold, efficient officer's relationship with his own son. *Oslovení z tmy* (Address from the darkness, 1972) is influenced by Fuks's study of Jewish mysticism. It conveys a fantastic vision of a boy confronting devilish temptation and the end of the world. *Nebožtíci na bále* (Dead men at the ball, 1972) is a macabre fable about two dead men unable to distinguish between life and death.

The three books Fuks published from 1974 to 1978 are characterized by the title of Josef Skvorecký's essay about the first of them: "A Kind Man at an Unkind Time." In *Návrat z žitného pole* (Return from the rye field, 1974) a student, under the influence of a visit to his native region, gives up his intention of emigrating. Czech official, as well as dissident, critics concurred that the book lacked conviction, but Skorecký pointed out that certain details of the text had oblique political meaning. *Pasček z doliny* (The shepherd boy from the valley, 1977) is an almost folkloric story about a little boy from eastern Slovakia that takes place immediately after the end of World War II. *Křišálový pantoflíček* (The crystal slipper, 1979) chronicles the childhood of Julius Fučuík, the hero of the Communist anti-Nazi resistance movement. Fuks quite deliberately abandoned the psychological experimentation of his earlier books to portray Fučuík.

The novella *Obraz Martina Blaskowitze* (The picture of Martin Blaskowitz, 1980), an intimate philosophical story of two men seeking but ultimately rejecting revenge for crimes committed during World War II, was critically well received.

Vévodkyně a kuchařka (The duchess and the cook, 1983) is a voluminous novel reflecting Fuks's nostalgia for the elegance and stylishness of the Austro-Hungarian monarchy, Vienna, and central European cosmopolitanism. A series of vignettes of the period before the end of the 19th and the beginning of the 20th centuries, it portrays society at a turning point when the constituents of the old and the new worlds coexisted temporarily, but were soon to come into tragic conflict. The two female characters of the title represent the extremes of the society: an Austrian duchess who founds a museum of the monarchy and writes a play about the end of the Roman empire at the opposite end of the social scale, and her cook. Through them Fuks represents both decadence and the beauty of a lost past. As a historical novel, it ranks with the fin de siècle of some of Austrian and German authors, such as Joseph Roth and Thomas Mann. Fuks's novel functions as a metaphor for the decadent society of the era.

Ladislav Fuks is one of the most admired of contemporary Czech writers, one who followed the traditions of central European culture—Czech, German, and Jewish—in Prague. Fuks was also one of the leading representatives of magical realism and postmodernism in Czech literature. Although his books were published in Czechoslovakia during the 1970s and the 1980s, some of his best works were not republished until after the democratic takeover in 1989. He completed his autobiography in 1994 shortly before his death in Prague at the age of seventy.

PRINCIPAL WORKS IN ENGLISH TRANSLATION: Mr Theodore Mundstock (tr. I. Urwin) 1968; The Cremator (tr. E. M. Kandler) 1984.

ABOUT: Contemporary Authors, 118, 1986; Birnbaum, H. and T. Eekman (eds.) Fiction and Drama in Eastern and Southeastern Europe: Evolution and Experiment in the Postwar Period; Proceedings of the 1978 UCLA Conference, 1980. Periodicals—Atlantic January 1968; Guardian Weekly February 6, 1969; Life January 26, 1968; New Statesman December 7, 1984; New York Times Book Review January 28, 1968; Times Literary Supplement January 23, 1969.

FULLER, CHARLES H., JR. (March 5, 1939–), American playwright, was born in Philadelphia to Charles Henry Fuller Sr. and Lillian (Anderson) Fuller. Fuller's father was a printer, one of the first black men to join the local printers' union. He started his own business, and moved his family from an apartment in a Philadelphia housing project to a home in an integrated community in North Philadelphia. Besides Charles Jr. and two younger sisters, the family included the elder Fuller's father and over the years about twenty foster children, two of whom were adopted into the family. Fuller remembers his parents as hardworking, unassuming people, supportive of their children's interests. Life at home was loving and "comfortable." Social problems were often discussed, and Fuller developed a concern about these issues, along with an interest in writing when he began to proofread galleys and set type for his father.

Fuller attended racially integrated Roman Catholic elementary and high schools. Tall, skinny, and unathletic, he played both flute and alto sax, and briefly considered becoming a musi-

cian. However, he was also an avid reader, and along with a classmate, Larry Neal (who also became a writer), he read everything he could find at school and in the public library. Fuller's introduction to live theater occurred in his early teens, when he saw a Yiddish comedy at the Walnut Street Theatre, which fascinated him, even though he could not understand a word of it.

After graduating from high school in 1956, Fuller attended Villanova University for two years, majoring in English. The difficulties of becoming an African American writer were brought home to him when a professor suggested that he give up his "foolish" literary ambitions, while his submissions to the student literary magazine were summarily rejected. He felt that he needed a break from schooling and enlisted in the U.S. Army in 1959, achieving very high scores on various tests. After six months of training in Virginia where, ironically, he went to school eight hours a day, six days a week, Fuller was sent to Japan and South Korea as a petroleum technician. He ran a laboratory that checked the quality of oil delivered to the army, a job that allowed him ample time to read and write. While he declines to talk about military life, some of his experiences, as well as his father's stories about the navy in World War II, have been incorporated into his plays.

Discharged from the army in 1962, Fuller returned to Philadelphia and married Miriam Nesbitt, a nurse and teacher whom he had met while at Villanova. He held a variety of jobs, including loan collector for a bank, minority student counselor at Temple University, and housing inspector in a very poor neighborhood, but continued writing whenever he could. He also began taking night courses at La Salle College in 1965, but stopped in 1967 without getting a degree.

During the 1960s, Fuller began to write skits about community problems, often involving the uneasy relationship between blacks and Puerto Ricans living in the same neighborhood. These playlets were performed under his direction by a local group that Fuller also helped to found, which became the Afro-American Arts Theatre of Philadelphia in 1967. In 1968, the troupe produced a set of six interconnected one-act plays by Fuller under the collective title of The Sunflowers, as well as a full-length drama called The Rise (or Brother Marcus), about black-rights advocate Marcus Garvey. Arthur Lithgow, director of the McCarter Theatre in Princeton, New Jersey, saw Fuller's work, and commissioned him to write a play for their 1968–1969 season. The Village: A Party concerns a superficially idealistic community of racially mixed couples which disintegrates into violence when its black leader, who has a white wife, is discovered to be in love with a black woman. Dan Sullivan, in the *New York Times*, praised the "intellectually provocative" concept and the sharply observed dialogue, but felt that the melodramatic ending was weak. He concluded that the drama's "originality and urgency are unquestionable and so is the talent of the playwright." The play opened under a new title, *The Perfect Party*, at an off-Broadway theater in New York in April 1969, where it received similarly mixed reviews. It closed after twenty-two performances. The McCarter experience had, nevertheless, proved to Fuller that he could be a writer, and it also provided him with valuable practical experience in play production.

In 1969, Fuller moved to New York City, where the New Federal Theatre presented his next professional production in 1972. *In My Many Names and Days* recounts the fifty-year history of a black family. This was followed by *The Candidate*, a play about a black, mayoral candidate, which the New Federal Theatre produced in 1974. That same year, Fuller began his long association with the Negro Ensemble Company, a group that he had encountered in 1968 at the McCarter Theatre. His first play to be produced under the NEC banner was *In the Deepest Part of Sleep*, a sequel to *In My Many Names and Days*. Set in Philadelphia in the mid-1950s, the drama unfolds through the eyes of an adolescent youth who watches the effects of his mother's mental illness on himself, his stepfather, and his mother's nurse. Once again, there were mixed reviews. The play was criticized for its overdrawn characters and predictable plot, a complaint that had also been made about *The Candidate*, but it was also noted that there were touching moments and some realistic scenes.

Fuller decided to reach beyond domestic drama for a historical subject. He dramatized an actual incident involving the dishonorable discharge of 167 black soldiers stationed in Brownsville, Texas, in 1906, based on a false charge that they had killed a man during a wild shooting spree. The hero of Brownsville Raid is Sergeant Mingo Saunders, a black career soldier, who is ordered by his white captain to find the culprit in his unit, and the strongest scenes take place in the army barracks as he tries to ferret out the truth. One of the soldiers is a ne'er-do-well whom the other men would be happy to sacrifice, but Mingo's belief in justice precludes furnishing a scapegoat to satisfy the white community's thirst for revenge. When no one confesses, Mingo and his men are discharged without a trial. (It was later proved that a white man did the shooting, and in 1972 the army ad-

mitted to a "gross miscarriage of justice" and cleared the men of all charges.)

The Brownsville Raid was Fuller's first major success. Reviews were generally favorable, with praise for the controlled way in which he handled his inflammatory subject, making the denouement even more poignant. The soldiers realistically submit to military segregation and unequal treatment, being proud of the army and their place in it. The white captain tries to protect his men from the racist forces confronting them until his own career is threatened. Flaws in the play were noted, however, by reviewers, including some extraneous romantic subplots, labored speeches, and underdeveloped subordinate characters. The play was produced off-Broadway by the NEC in December 1976 and ran for 112 performances.

In November 1978, Fuller ventured into the musical field when AMAS Repertory Theatre in New York mounted a showcase production of *Sparrow in Flight*, a musical biography of Ethel Waters written by Fuller with period songs arranged by Larry Garner. He returned to straight drama in 1980 with *Zooman and the Sign*, based on an actual incident that took place in Philadelphia. A young girl is killed by a stray bullet as she plays on her stoop. The white police officers seem indifferent to the family's pleas for justice, while the black community remains silent in order to avoid trouble. When the dead girl's father puts up a sign accusing his neighbors of protecting the gunman, they turn on him with threats of violence. Finally, the killer—a swaggering, homeless, possibly psychotic teenager named Zooman—is shot as he tries to tear down the sign, and violence has claimed another victim. Critical reaction was mixed. Some reviewers thought the play did not fully explore its promising theme, but others said that the play's shortcomings were outweighed by Fuller's effective use of understatement to depict the plight of deteriorating neighborhoods and disintegrating families. The play ran for only thirty-three performances after its opening in December 1980, but it was selected as one of the "Best Plays" of 1980–1981 for the Burns Mantle Theatre Yearbook series, and Fuller won both an Obie and an Audelco Award for playwrighting.

A Soldier's Play, Fuller's Pulitzer Prize-winning drama, was written in four months in 1981 as a tribute to his high school friend and fellow playwright Larry Neal, who had died earlier in the year. The play is set in an army camp in Louisiana during World War II. A black sergeant, Vernon Waters, has been murdered outside the camp confines, and suspicion falls on the local townspeople and the Ku Klux Klan. The army sends a black lawyer, Captain Richard Davenport, to investigate the death, over the objections of the unit's white commander, who is convinced that the white community will band together to frustrate Davenport's inquiries.

As Davenport delves into the case, a series of flashbacks reveals Waters to have been a tyrannical martinet, hated by all his men except the naive, easygoing C. J. Waters, burning with racial self-hatred, is determined to become as much like a white man as possible in order to get ahead in a white man's world, and C. J.'s stereotypical black behavior infuriates him. He goads C.J. into attacking him and then has the young man thrown into the brig, where C. J. hangs himself. Ironically, C. J.'s suicide triggers Waters's own disintegration, as he admits the futility of all his efforts to Pfc. Peterson one night in a drunken frenzy of rage and guilt: "You got to be like them! And I was! I was—but the rules are fixed . . . it doesn't make any difference. They still hate you." Peterson kills Waters, his violence motivated is at least in part by displaced rage at the army's segregation policy which will not allow black soldiers to fight alongside whites against the Germans or Japanese.

A Soldier's Play was produced by the Negro Ensemble Company at Theatre Four, where it opened on November 20, 1981, to almost uniformly favorable reviews. Frank Rich, in the *New York Times* spoke for the majority of critics when he termed it "in every way, a mature and accomplished work . . . [with a] remarkable breadth of social and historical vision." One of the few naysayers was Amiri Baraka, formerly LeRoi Jones, who conceded that the play was well-written but said that Fuller spoke for "the most backward sector of the black middle class." *A Soldier's Play* ran for 481 performances. Besides the Pulitzer Prize for drama, Fuller won the Audelco and Theatre Club awards for best play, the Outer Critics Circle Award for best off-Broadway play, and the New York Drama Critics Award for best American play. He adapted the script for a movie version called *A Soldier's Story*, directed by Norman Jewison and featuring many actors from the original cast. When the film was released in 1984, it was nominated for Academy Awards as Best Picture and Best Screenplay, and it also won the 1985 Edgar Allen Poe Mystery Award.

Fuller's next major project was a cycle of five plays, later expanded to six, under the collective title *We*, covering American history from the 1860s to 1900 from a black perspective. Starting in 1982, he read over a hundred books about the period, noting that the black experience was reported almost exclusively by white writers until

the late 1880s. *Sally*, the first play in the cycle, was written in 1986. It was followed by *Prince* in 1987 and *Jonquil* in 1988. *Sally* had its premiere at the National Black Arts Festival in Atlanta in July 1988 and opened in New York in November, where it was joined in repertory by *Prince* in December. The third and fourth plays in the cycle, *Jonquil* and *Burner's Frolic*, opened in 1990.

Sally takes place in South Carolina in 1862–1863, when the North is trying to aid displaced slaves whose plantations have been overrun by Union forces. The title character becomes involved with Prince Logan, an educated former slave who is now a sergeant in an all-black unit of the Union army. Prince's men strike for equal wages with the white soldiers, forcing him to identify the strike leaders or to face his own court-martial. Self-interest leads him to betray his men and to end the affair with Sally. *Prince* picks up the sergeant's life a year later, on a farm in Virginia where ex-slaves are still picking cotton. When they learn that they will not be paid for their work, one of the men protests and is thrown into jail.

Jonquil returns the action to South Carolina. It is 1866, the war is over, and the emancipated slaves are trying to become independent farmers and to exercise their political rights in the face of Southern white hostility and Northern indifference. After Sally is savagely beaten by members of the Ku Klux Klan, a blind and hardbitten ex-slave named Jonquil triggers a protest that ends in violence. *Burner's Frolic* is set in a small town in Virginia in 1876, when the former slaves have made some economic progress. Burner is a black businessman running for local office against a white opponent who is buying black votes, and the play concerns Burner's efforts to convince the people not to sell their votes or their hopes. The reception of all four plays was mixed, although *Prince* and *Jonquil* were deemed to have the strongest characters. Critics admired Fuller's awareness of personal motivations as well as the gulf between the promise of freedom and the political and economic realities, but they felt that the episodic style lacked dramatic intensity and failed to establish any cumulative impact.

Fuller has also written for television, starting with a series of twelve scripts for a weekly series called "Roots, Resistance and Renaissance" which was broadcast on WHYY in Philadelphia in 1967. Other scripts televised in Philadelphia include "Mitchell" (1968) and "Black America" (1970–1971). He adapted "The Sky Is Gray" by Ernest J. Gaines for "The American Short Stories Series" (PBS, 1980), and he adapted the Gaines novel *A Gathering of Old Men* into a television feature film for CBS (1987) which was selected for a special showing at the 1987 Cannes Film Festival. His short stories and articles have been published in various anthologies and periodicals. His honors include the Creative Artist Public Service Award in 1974; fellowships from the Rockefeller Foundation in 1975, the National Endowment for the Arts in 1976, and the Guggenheim Foundation, 1977–1978; the Hazelitt Award from the Pennsylvania State Council on the Arts in 1984; and a Monarch Award in 1985. Fuller has received honorary degrees from La Salle College (1982), Villanova University (1983), and Chestnut Hill College (1985). In addition to his writing, Fuller teaches African-American studies at Temple University. The Fullers have two sons.

PRINCIPAL WORKS: The Rise, *in* Bullins, E. ed. New Plays from the Black Theatre 1969; Zooman and the Sign, 1981; A Soldier's Play, 1982.

ABOUT: Black Playwrights, 1823–1977: An Annotated Bibliography of Plays, 1977; Contemporary Authors 112, 1985; Contemporary Literary Criticism 25, 1983; Contemporary Theater, Film and Television 7, 1989; Current Biography 1989; Demastes W. W., Beyond Naturalism: A New Realism in American Theatre, 1988; Dictionary of Literary Biography 38, 1985; Drama Criticism 1, 1991; Harriott, E., American Voices: Five Contemporary Playwrights *in* Essays and Interviews, 1988; Mapp E., Directory of Blacks in the Performing Arts, 2d ed., 1990; Peterson, B. L. Jr., Contemporary Black American Playwrights and Their Plays: A Biographical Director and Dramatic Index, 1988; Polak, M. L., The Writer as Celebrity: Intimate Interviews, 1986; Savran, D., In Their Own Words: Contemporary American Playwrights, 1988; Studies in American Drama, 1945–Present 2, 1987; Who's Who in America 1992–1993. *Periodicals*—New York Newsday December 12, 1988; New York Times November 13, 1968; January 11, 1982; December 18, 1988; Other Stages April 22, 1982; Seven Days January 18, 1989; Theater Week December 12, 1988.

*GALEANO, EDUARDO (September 3, 1940–), Uruguayan writer and caricaturist, writes (in Spanish): "Those who understand the ways of the heavens tell me that my tendency to get into trouble started with my first breath: on that morning at the end of the winter of 1940 the planets were in the house of Pisces. They also blame my sign, Virgo, for my mania for perfection, which obliges me to tear up a page for every one I keep. And they say my rising sign, Libra, is behind the hunger for beauty that has turned me into a glutton who devours people and words.

EDUARDO GALEANO

"I was born and grew up in Montevideo, on the coast between open fields and the sands of the beach. Now there are tall buildings here, and inside the buildings televisions, and around the buildings roaring automobiles. But this coast, where I walk every day in my comings and goings, is still the coast of my childhood.

"Back then I believed in God, and I wanted to be a saint. When I left my childhood behind, I lost God and my mystical fervor fell from heaven to earth. It's still here, searching for answers of flesh and bone.

"As a kid I also wanted to be a soccer player, even though everyone was convinced I wasn't even good enough to be the team's trainer. Neither a saint nor an athlete: I had no choice but to try my luck at other careers. In my early years I was a factory worker, a bill collector, a sign painter, a cartoonist, a messenger, a typist, and a bank teller. Such diverse activities only succeeded in proving my utter uselessness. But when I was barely out of childhood, I published by first articles: and from then on I've clung stubbornly to the hope that some day I'll learn to do it right.

"I've written several books, according to my private plan for vengeance. When I was a boy I swore I'd get back at the inedible alphabet soup I was forced to read. And back at the history courses that condemned me to remember dates and names my mind refused to store.

"That's why I'm always trying to undress the language, and why I work arduously to pull the clothes off rhetoric that muffles and conceals the naked word. I also try to bring together a past

°GAH lay ah noh

and present separated by an official history that reduces our collective memory to the feats of founding fathers in bronze who, galloping on marble stallions, poured immortal phrases of stone on the heads of the children of future generations. When I write I also try to marry the divorced, to put together pieces of myself: thinking and feeling, wakefulness and sleep, body and soul. I don't believe in the borders that separate literary genres, and I enjoy violating them. I also love to make fun of the customs officers who keep imagination and reality apart and raise a wall between literature called intimate and what they call socially concerned. The wars of the soul look too much like the wars of the street. I don't like it when they classify me or what I write. Borders enchain, labels lie.

"I'm a traveler. I walk freely on paths I recognize or invent. Walking on words, from book to book I go.

"A few months before the coup d'état in 1973, I was put in jail. I did not find the experience very enjoyable. When they let me out I went to Argentina. In Buenos Aires, I founded and edited a cultural magazine, *Crisis*, which lasted forty lovely months until a coup de'état swept Argentina too. My name turned up on the lists of those condemned by the death squads. I don't like being in jail; but I like being dead even less. I had no choice but to go to Spain, and there I lived in exile for eight years.

"Thanks to the Uruguayan and Argentinean generals, I found the time and perspective to write the trilogy "Memory of Fire." Under normal circumstances, that undertaking would have been impossible. I consulted over a thousand documentary sources and I wrote a thousand stories during thousands of hours of hard work and great pleasure. I hope readers find the books more pleasure than work.

"I returned to Montevideo at the beginning of 1985. Here I finished the final volume of "Memory" and I wrote *The Book of Embraces*, which combines words with pictures and is meant to be a feast for the eyes, not only a thing to read. Now [1992] I'm working on a new book, which for now is called 'Walking Words.' It's a book of stories, realities made delirious, delirium made real, to be published along with the engravings of a Brazilian artist, José Borges, who imagines with me."

—tr. Mark Fried

Eduardo Hughes Galeano was born in Montevideo, Uruguay, to Eduardo Hughes and Ester Galeano-Munoz. According to his rather Sartrean belief that identity is self-created, Galeano has himself published only a smattering of biographical facts. He has been married three times—in 1959 to Silvia Brando, in 1962 to Graciela Berro, and in 1976 to Helena Villagra—and has three children, but speaks only of his third wife, Helena, and of her lost child. Instead, he has given the world his impressions of it and of his place in it.

Starting his career as a political caricaturist, Galeano contributed cartoons to *El Sol*, the Socialist Party weekly. In his late teens he was already writing for and later became chief editor of *Marcha*, an influential weekly journal of opinion. Galeano sometimes used the pseudonym "Gius," a Hispanicized version of the name of his Welsh great-grandfather, but later dropped his paternal surname and used only his maternal surname. "Over the years, I have heard conflicting versions of this business about my chosen name," he said in *Libro de los abrazos* (1991, *The Book of Embraces*), calling the versions an offense to the intelligence: "the most screwed-up version makes me the red sheep of my family: it invents for me a hostile and oligarchic father instead of the actual father I have, a fabulous guy who always earned his living by his own work or good luck in the soccer pools."

Galeano's career in journalism also included a stint as editor of *Epoca*, a newspaper. His politics were always leftist and embraced a deep sympathy for and empathy with the dispossessed, the oppressed of the earth. As he said in *Nosotros decimos no* (1992, *We Say No*): "The true reality of the oppressor can only be seen from the point of view of the oppressed."

In "Are the Gods Crazy? Or Is It Me?" (published in the *Nation* August 31–September 7, 1992), Galeano describes his troubles understanding the United States. When he first applied for a visa twenty-five years previously, he regarded the question "Do you plan to assassinate the President of the United States?" as a joke. "I was so modest that I didn't even plan to assassinate the President of Uruguay, but I answered Yes." Galeano thought the question was "the brainchild of my teachers Ambrose Bierce and Mark Twain." The visa was refused. *La venas abiertas de la América Latina*, (*The Open Veins of Latin America*), was the first book by Galeano to be translated into English. It won a Casa de las Américas Prize in 1970 in Cuba. With it, Galeano embarked upon his lifelong attempt to arrive at a coherent interpretation of American reality. "I am not a historian. I am a writer obsessed with remembering, with remembering the past of America above all and above all that of Latin America, intimate land condemned to amnesia," he says in *We Say No*.

"I wanted to explore history in order to encourage people to make it, to help open up spaces of freedom in which the victims of the past can become protagonists of the present."

Driven to exile from Uruguay by the advent of a military dictatorship in 1973, Galeano settled in Buenos Aires, where he founded and edited *Crisis*, a journal of culture. Galeano told Sam Staggs in an interview in *Publishers Weekly* that *Crisis* was designed "to *show* popular culture alive and powerful, not merely to speak about it. . . . a stubborn act of faith in the creative and solitary work, the word that is not, nor tries to be neutral, the human voice that is not an echo or empty sound."

Argentina, however, was far from immune from the Latin American plague of military dictatorship. "The Argentine military whose atrocities would have given Hitler an inferiority complex," as Galeano says in *The Book of Embraces*, made it too dangerous for him to continue living there, and he had to depart for Spain in 1976. He spent the years from 1976 to 1984 (when he returned to Uruguay) living mainly on the Catalan coast. There, near Barcelona and the sea from which Galeano has said he cannot bear to be separated, he wrote his masterpiece, the trilogy "Memoria del fuego" ("Memory of Fire"): *Los nacimientos* (1985, *Genesis*); s caras y las máscaras (1987, *Faces and Masks*); and *El siglo del viento* (1988, *Century of the Wind*). He also found time during his exile in Spain to publish *Dias y nochas de amor y guerra* (1978, *Days and Nights of Love and War*). In that book, he told Staggs, he perfected the technique of what Gregory Rabassa termed "verbal collage": "I tried to create a structure from all the broken pieces of myself, like putting together a puzzle. *Days and Nights of Love and War* resulted from this open, free conversation with my own memory, as I tried to understand what had really happened and to guess who I really was."

In "Memory of Fire," Galeano narrates discontinuously the story of America (North and South) from the European conquest to 1984. The tables of contents listing the chapters in each of the three books are each about ten pages long and set in single-spaced, small type. Each small chapter is followed by a reference or two, and the reference lists take up about twenty pages in the back of each book. Characters—generals, peasants, workers, soldiers, revolutionaries, writers, artists, all real historic figures—appear and then reappear several chapters later, as though they were strands in an elaborate braid. The reader gets no sense of disjointedness, however, but rather the experience of a seamless whole.

"Memory of Fire," in small "takes" or chapters, most less than a page long, emblazons the history of the Americas on the memory of the reader. An extraordinary novel, or, rather, a new genre, it is made up only of fully documented history. The protagonists are the conquerors and the conquered and the plot is the wars, revolutions, uprisings, tortures, repressions, and political chicanery by which the conquerors have maintained their position throughout history. Galeano also tells stories of the creation of art, one means by which the oppressed hold at bay natural and unnatural death. Sor Juana Inez de la Cruz, Simon Bolívar, Walt Whitman, Alejo Carpentier, Juan Carlos Onetti, Julio Cortázar, Gabriel García Márquez—all are here, along with Alicia Moreau, encouraging the mothers of the Plaza de Mayo in Buenos Aires to demand word of their disappeared children. Alicia Moreau, nearly one hundred years old in 1977, is "as lively now as she was when the century began. . . ."

In a review entitled "Discovery is Theft" in the *Times Literary Supplement*, Ronald Wright said: "Great writers . . . dissolve old genres and found new ones. This trilogy by one of South America's most daring and accomplished authors is impossible to classify." Wright points out the poetic nature of Galeano's rescue "from the rubble of the big lies . . . battered bits of truth."

Galeano renders the real magical in "Memory of Fire." For the last volume, *Century of the Wind*, he uses the story of Miguel Marmol, the revolutionary and labor organizer born in El Salvador in 1905, as the "axis" of the book. He chronicles the successive "births" of Marmol, who survives first his illegitimate birth as an unwanted child, then starvation, then the destruction when he is thirteen of an army barracks in a massive earthquake, and then innumerable tortures and attempted executions at the hands of his political enemies. In *The Book of Embraces*, published after "Memory of Fire," and written in a somewhat similar if more personal style, Galeano describes celebrating with Marmol the fiftieth anniversary, when Marmol is eighty-two, of his escape from execution: " . . . Miguel is the truest metaphor for Latin America. Like him, it goes on being born. . . . I proposed that we jointly found Magical Marxism: one half reason, one half passion, and a third half mystery." Galeano thus slyly characterizes what he has already accomplished in "Memory of Fire."

The trilogy, completed in 1986, "captures the spirit that makes Latin American history and literature simultaneously disastrous and joyous, inhabited by tortured love songs and beheaded familiars," according to Thulani Davis in the

Village Voice Literary Supplement. Writing the book left Galeano, as he has said in *We Say No*, with a duodenal ulcer, and a herniated spinal disk that required surgery, but "happy as a dog with two tails."

"Memory of Fire" was followed by *We Say No*, a collection of pieces from Galeano's career in journalism. The essays date from 1963, and include Galeano's characterization of Jorge Luis Borges as "brilliant without a doubt." He says, however, that Borges regards life as a "labyrinth—the labyrinth of an endless library, which leads us nowhere. We are left with, at most, nostalgia: hope, never." Galeano's objective has been to share with everyone who will listen his own hopes for the world. In *The Book of Embraces*, he says, "The system feeds neither the body nor the heart: many are condemned to starve for lack of bread and many more for lack of embraces."

Galeano returned to Uruguay in 1984: "The Uruguayan generals were still in power, but on their way out. It was almost goodbye to the time of terror. I entered, crossing my fingers, and I was lucky," he said in *The Book of Embraces*. He suffered a heart attack, however, when he returned to Spain to settle his affairs. "Acute myocardial infarct, death clawing at the center of my chest. I spent two weeks in a hospital bed in Barcelona." During that period, he transferred the names from an old address book to a new one: "a prolonged mourning for the dead who had remained in the dead zone of my heart, and a long, much longer celebration of those still alive who fired my blood and swelled my surviving heart. And there was nothing bad and nothing odd about the fact that my heart had broken from so much use."

In 1984, Galeano's wife, Helena, had a miscarriage: "When Helena lost the child, the rosebush on the terrace shriveled up. The other flowers died one after another—all of them—though we watered them daily," he said in *The Book of Embraces*.

While still in exile, Galeano was contacted by Fico Vogelius, the publisher, who had been imprisoned and tortured "[f]or that crime, for the unforgivable crime of *Crisis*" by the Argentine military dictatorship. When the dictatorship came to an end, Vogelius decided to revive *Crisis*. Although Galeano says in *The Book of Embraces* that Vogelius was under sentence of death, this time from cancer, he lived until *Crisis* reappeared in April 1986. "The day following its rebirth, half a year beyond all prognostications, Fico allowed himself to die." Galeano is once again at the helm of *Crisis*.

In 1988, Galeano was awarded the José Car-

rasco prize, named for a journalist murdered in Santiago, Chile, by operatives of the dictatorial Pinochet regime. He became a kind of saint, according to Galeano in *The Book of Embraces*, for the poor people of the neighborhood where they dumped his body: " on the wall pitted by the shots, one can read thanks for favors received."

In Cedric Belfrage, the translator of "Memory of Fire" and *The Book of Embraces*, Galeano found his soulmate, his other self. "Each one of his translations increased our certitude of mutual identification. I would recognize myself in each of his translations and he would feel betrayed and annoyed whenever I didn't write something the way he would have," Galeano said in a dedication to *The Book of Embraces*, published after Belfrage's death.

In the *New York Times Book Review*, Jay Parini wrote that "*The Book of Embraces* moves beyond the stuffy confines of genre. . . . Of the almost 200 separate passages that make up this volume, a large number are accompanied by illustrative emblems. . . . Far from being merely decorative these images derive their power from specific contexts. . . . The author himself is one of the World's many 'flying creatures of beauty,' his typewriter a kind of flying machine." Parini terms the book "an argument for communal values, values like those practiced by some of the indigenous peoples of the New World before the conquistadors took over."

Las Palabras Andantes (1993, *Walking Words*) is "an anthology of stories about 'ghouls and fools,' derived from the urban and rural folklore of the Americas," according to John Leonard writing in the *Nation*. The stories are interspersed with "windows" for, as Leonard said, " the stray paradox and sneaky afflatus, and woodcut illustrations . . . by José Francisco Borges: a kind of commonplace book of mysterious transcendence." "Many of the tales have a populist cast as Galeano adopts the voice of shrewd peasant wit to take shots at a system that exploits the poor, "according to the *Publishers Weekly* reviewer, who found *Walking Words* laden with "intense lyricism, subversive humor and spellbinding storytelling," making for "lovely, resonant diversions." Louis de Bernières, in the *New York Times Book Review* remarked that Galeano's "dedicated and proselytizing readership" will be delighted with *Walking Words*, in which the themes "embrace the winning of love, double-edged miracles, poetic justice, portents and prodigies, metamorphoses, mystical occurrences and homespun theology."

According to Ronald Wright, "Galeano makes us appreciate the enormity of the task before modern Americans, whether North, Central, or South: the tasks of creating wholeness from the ruin of one world by another." It is by the embrace of contradiction, in a way, that Galeano sees salvation. He says in *The Book of Embraces*: "Turn loose the voices, undream the dreams. Through my writing, I try to express the magical reality, which I find at the core of the hideous reality of America . . . [W]e are the sum of our efforts to change who we are. Identity is no museum piece standing stock-still in a display case, but rather the endlessly astonishing synthesis of the contradictions of everyday life."

PRINCIPAL WORKS IN ENGLISH TRANSLATION: Guatemala, Occupied Country (tr. C. Belfrage) 1968; The Open Veins of Latin America (tr. C. Belfrage) 1973; Days and Nights of Love and War (tr. J. Brister, includes "In Defense of the Word" tr. B. S. Ortiz) 1983; Memory of Fire trilogy, I, Genesis (tr. C. Belfrage) 1985; II, Faces and Masks (tr. C. Belfrage) 1987; III, Century of the Wind (tr. C. Belfrage) 1988; An Uncertain Grace (with S. Salgado and F. Richin), 1990; The Book of Embraces (C. Belfrage with M. Schafer) 1991; We Say No (tr. M. Fried et al.) 1991; Walking Words, 1995.

ABOUT: Contemporary Authors New Revision Series 13, 1984; Flores, A. (ed.) Spanish American Authors: The Twentieth Century, 1991; Tucker, M. (ed.) Literary Exile in the Twentieth Century, 1991. *Periodicals*—Nation, August 31-September 9, 1992; New York Times Book Review October 27, 1985; March 1, 1989; April 21, 1991; New Yorker July 28, 1986; Publishers Weekly June 3, 1988; Times Literary Supplement October 20, 1989; (Village) Voice Literary Supplement May 1988.

GALVIN, BRENDAN (October 20, 1938–   ), American poet, writes: "I was born in Everett, Massachusetts, a suburb several miles north of Boston. There is little evidence of this in my poems, however, since I found Everett to be an extremely boring place and haven't set foot within the city limits in twenty-five years. I was more taken with the places out on the end of Cape Cod, where I spent childhood summers in an old house my family had purchased in the 1930s. Earlier in this century my grandfather had moved into that area, and now most of his grandchildren and great grandchildren live on the Cape too. So, as far as the psychic world of my poems is concerned, I grew up in South Wellfleet, and I now live in Truro, about eight miles away, when I am not teaching modern poetry and creative writing in the English Department of a state university in Connecticut.

"My poems are deeply involved in the sensory world of the outer Cape, and readers often note

BRENDAN GALVIN

the leap in subject matter between my second book and *Atlantic Flyway*, my third, in which the Massachusetts coast seems to have invaded my image bank to stay. My most recent book, *Saints in their Ox-Hide Boat*, is a poem spoken by my namesake St. Brendan, the sixth-century Irish monk and 'discoverer' of America. In part this is a rewriting of the eighth-century Latin *Voyage of Saint Brendan*, one of the most popular saints' tales of the Middle Ages and a late addition to the canon of Irish Immrama or magical voyage tales. This poem draws on the landscapes and seascapes I observed during several recent trips to Ireland. It allowed me to extend my narrative interests beyond anything I had done previously, and is full of riddles, prognostications based on the natural world, and an attempted recreation of what sixth-century Irishmen might have spoken like.

"I side with writers like William Faulkner and William Carlos Williams in their insistence that the universal in art derives from the local. Conversely, I hold no brief for most of the confessional, inner-life verse that's ubiquitous these days, feeling with La Fontaine via Marianne Moore that 'minds suffer disrepair / When every thought for years has been turned inward.'

"I suspect that as a biology major at Boston College I was building on an earlier interest in things that could be verified by the evidence of the five senses, but all those courses in the hard sciences made me a writer habituated to and attracted by accuracy of language. They also gave me a scientific vocabulary most poets don't have, as when I refer to a 'meniscus' of frost on a window pane.

"Beginning with *Atlantic Flyway* in 1980, I found I was increasingly writing poems about birds, and at that point I began to research and read up on what I write about. If possible, I want things in my poems to be scientifically correct, and I guess in this sense I'm an amateur naturalist, with an emphasis on the adjective. I've also found that reading around in a subject gives me information I can use in poems, and broadens my general knowledge as well. I think the poet should come away from the poem knowing things he didn't know when he began.

"It was in this way that my 1989 volume, *Wampanoag Traveler*, originated. I was reading a book on early American natural historians and their methods, adventures, beliefs, etc., when it occurred to me that I ought to write a book-length poem on one that I invented. Hence Loranzo Newcomb, the author of fourteen letters to members of the Royal Society in London, about life and times as a collector of flora and fauna in early eighteenth-century America. My undergraduate training as a biologist had come full circle in descriptions of alligators, hummingbirds and varieties of New World apples. I was also able to extend my knowledge of folklore in *Wampanoag Traveler*, since much of what passed for science in early America was in fact hearsay and supposition. *Saints in their Ox-Hide Boat* also trades in folklore, since sixth-century Irish monks seem to have been stuck part way between pagan and Christian sensibilities.

"Generally my poems are about an individual consciousness encountering something in the environment rather than, say, another person. In focusing outward, I seem to be able to touch the inner world without falling into the traps of victimhood and guilt-mongering I see all around contemporary poetry. I attain what feels like moments of revelation, though I wouldn't go as far as to say 'religious ecstasy,' as one commentator has. Certainly I'm out to surprise myself with what I see and say, and that may be the result of my childhood in Everett, that metropolis of boredom.

"One thing that perplexes me lately is that, although poets always claim to be the lightning rods of the race and so on, very few are writing about the natural world. I suppose this shouldn't be surprising, since most Americans live in cities anyway, but along with it comes the notion that the biosphere has been exhausted as a subject by earlier 'nature poets,' an idea that hardly holds water in the face of current ecological dangers. Contemporary poets, particularly the males, seem to have given up on the environment as a subject, even bought into the bourgeois notion that it isn't macho to write about it, or that it's a redundant exercise in nostalgia. So be it. I am happy to be one of George Oppen's 'legislators of the unacknowledged world,' and leave all navel-gazers to their own devices.

"In the meantime what continues to interest me in my own writing is the revelation to be found for both writer and reader in the unfolding on the page of a long sentence and the texture and flexibility of natural speech possible in the free-verse line. I am not interested in writing for any cause, including eco-politics, and intend for as long as I can to describe and celebrate the splendors of mere being, which I consider myself lucky to have participated in at all."

His work centers, Brendan Galvin has said, on the beaches, oceans and pine woods of the end of Cape Code. Peripheral to that enter, however, are worlds of the imagination large enough to span the North Atlantic to Ireland and stretch across history from the distant past to the present. Like other modern poets who express affinity with nature—Frost, (Roethke on whom Galvin wrote his doctoral dissertation), Elizabeth Bishop—Galvin writes with disarming simplicity about the most complex and mysterious of both natural and human phenomena. If he has given more attention in his poems to the natural world, it has not been at the price of humanity, for Galvin writes not only about people, real and imaginary, but he also, without being condescending or patronizing, humanizes nature.

"In the varied lives of birds, trees, raccoons, vegetables, oysters and scallops, Galvin finds metaphors for the human condition," Robert Gasper wrote in *Contemporary Poetry*. In *Atlantic Flyway*, his "Great Horned Owls" are models of domesticity; he sees them courting, mating, nesting:

In March
motherly, she'll ride
the jumble of sticks and pelts
she bumped a hawk for,
warming her egg
though she's sodden as a stump.

And their "Young Owls" are "trying deficient wings / and feet like goalies' mitts / at the nest's brink"

For Galvin the city is unnatural, and therefore antihuman, as he characterizes it in "Defending the Provinces" from *Atlantic Flyway*:

Sell the bridges for scrap
and let the rats clean up so in 200 years
guided tours can visit our national ruin
our own Macchu Picchu,
    and Americans, coming home
to their little towns, will tell how
last night on the highway, one star
over the bay seemed to move closer.

George Garrett, in *Three Rivers Poetry Journal*, describes Galvin's poetry as filled with "the sense of a truly imagined and awakened world . . . a sense of place (mostly Cape Cod) which rings true to memory even as it reinvents the turf and territory of it." Garrett notes that Galvin "trusts wholly the learned craft of poetry." He shuns academicism, mannerism, and obscurantism for an "anchor in reality." In "The Mumbling of Young Werther: Angst by Blueprint," an essay published in *Ploughshares* in 1978, Galvin broke ranks with many of his contemporaries, few of whom "write out of a sense of place . . . a concrete set of external circumstances which might tempt concentration on something other than their own cerebrations." He writes in "Proposals Made in the Name of Reason" in *No Time for Good Reasons*:

Let us no longer patronize the earth.
Uncapitalize all Nature;
not dreaming of abstract trees
but watching the blue smoulder
of certain pines.

Garrett also points out that Galvin often uses humor as bait "to lure the reader into a poem . . . then to shift to serious matters, leaving him wondering why he is laughing." In "Fear of Gray's Anatomy" in *The Minutes No One Owns*, Galvin writes:

The spinal cord is a zipper
& the lower digestive tract
has been squeezed from a tube like toothpaste.
All my life I had hoped someday to own
At least myself, only to find I am
Flood's ligaments, the areola of Mamma,
& the zonule of zinn.

The poem ends "I will ask my wife to knit a jacket for this book / & pretend it's a brick doorstop. / I will not open Gray's *Anatomy* again."

Galvin's most ambitious narrative poem is *Wampanoag Traveler: Being in Letters, the Life and Times of Loranzo Newcomb, American and Natural Historian*. Newcomb, Galvin's invention, travels through New England in the early 1700s. This is a world, Galvin writes, "in which science and superstition were interlocked and America beyond the Atlantic coast was truly a dark continent." Newcomb is a lonely man ("I do better / with vegetable kind than human / no easy admission. . . . ") who spares no effort to observe and record, even to the extent of taming a baby alligator and riding it "by throwing fishes before it" and letting himself be bitten by the rattlesnake he keeps in a rum keg.

Ben Howard, in *Poetry*, noted that the poem was stronger in its remarkable details than in any overall theme. Glyn Maxwell, in the *Times Lit-erary Supplement*, found it successful in "the intelligence and humanity Galvin breathes into this lonesome scientist . . . When so much contemporary poetry amounts to sinking a well just about anywhere and expecting a gush of universal significance, or not caring if nothing happens. Galvin triumphs the simplest way: creating and giving voice to a living character."

Inspired by reading the early medieval Latin *Voyage of Saint Brendan* and other accounts of bold monks who sailed off into unknown northern waters, Galvin wrote *Saints in Their Ox-Hide Boat*. Galvin re-creates their voyage in the words of St. Brendan himself. Like Loranzo Newcomb, his Brendan is an original—a brave, intelligent man driven by a passion to serve God in a remote spot where there will be no distractions to worship. The monks survive storms, bitter cold, and disease, and at the end, Brendan has a vision of God and the coming apocalypse, thus justifying his founding of St. Brendan's Isle as a sanctuary: "Call it the land beyond the wave. / You are the first I've led here, but others / will sail across centuries to it."

Galvin received a B.S. degree from Boston College in 1961, an M.A. from Northwestern University in 1964, and an M.F.A. 1967 and Ph.D. 1970 from the University of Massachusetts in Amherst. He was an instructor in English at Northeastern University in Boston from 1963 to 1965, an assistant professor at Slippery Rock University in Pennsylvania in 1968. Since 1968 he has been at Central Connecticut State University in New Britain where he has been professor of English since 1980. He married Ellen Baer in 1968; they have three children.

Among a number of other honors and awards, Galvin received a creative writing fellowship from the National Endowment for the Arts in 1974 and fellowships from the Connecticut Commission on the Arts in 1981 and 1984. In 1991, he received the first O.B. Hardison Jr. Poetry Prize from the Folger Shakespeare Library.

PRINCIPAL WORKS: No Time for Good Reasons, 1974; The Minutes No One Owns, 1977; Atlantic Flyway, 1980; Winter Oysters, 1983; Seals in the Inner Harbor, 1986; Wampanoag Traveler, 1989; Great Blue: New and Selected Poems, 1990; Saints in their Ox-Hide Boat, 1992.

ABOUT: Christina, M. Outer Life: The Poetry of Brendan Galvin, 1992; Contemporary Authors Autobiography Series 13, 1991; Contemporary Authors New Revision Series 24, 1988; Dictionary of Literary Biography 5, 1980; Holden, J. The Fate of American Poetry, 1992; Magill, F. N. ed. Critical Survey of Poetry, III, 1982. *Periodicals*—American Poetry Review January–February 1979; Boston College Magazine Winter 1988; Georgia Review Fall 1990; Hudson Review

Spring 1975; Magill's Literary Annual 1991; Midwest Quarterly 1976; New Review March 1992; Poetry September 1990; Shenandoah Winter 1991; Tar River Poetry Fall 1981; Fall 1987; Texas Review Fall–Winter 1987; Three Rivers Poetry Journal 19–20 1982; Times Literary Supplement May 31, 1991; Washington Times October 28, 1991.

GATES, HENRY LOUIS JR. (September 16, 1950–), American scholar and literary critic, was born in Piedmont, West Virginia, the son of Henry Louis and Pauline Augusta (Coleman) Gates. His father worked in the local paper mill during the day and moonlighted as a janitor for the telephone company. His mother, who worked as a housecleaner and a hairdresser, straightening the hair of her clients, was proud of her Coleman family heritage—"poor but talented and motivated," Gates called them in his memoir *Colored People*. Gates's family "carved out a dark- chocolate world, a world as nurturing as the loamy soil in Nemo's garden. . . . The tangle of family ties served as the netting that covered the garden's yield, setting it off from the chaos. . . . "

Young Gates entered the local Piedmont schools in 1955, just a few years after they had been racially integrated, and he grew up in an atmosphere where, in spite of still flagrant segregation in some areas, change was relatively painless. He and his family watched history as it emerged on their television screen: "the dawn of the Civil Rights era could be no more than a spectator sport in Piedmont. It was almost like a war being fought overseas." Years later, he writes, he realized " that for many of the colored people in Piedmont . . . integration was experienced as a loss. The warmth and nurturance of the womblike colored world was slowly and inevitably disappearing."

Gates attended nearby Potomac State College for one year to prepare for medical school. Here, however, under the influence of an English teacher, Duke Anthony Whitmore, he was inspired to study literature and encouraged to apply to Yale University. Although his good school grades alone might have won him admission, he strengthened his case when he wrote in the required personal statement:

My grandfather was colored, my father was Negro, and I am black. As always Whitey now sits in judgment of me, preparing to cast my fate. It is your decision either to let me blow with the wind as a non-entity or to encourage the development of self. Allow me to prove myself.

In 1970–1971 on a leave of absence from Yale, he worked as an anesthetist at a mission hospital in an Tanzanian village, and traveled extensive-

HENRY LOUIS GATES, JR.

ly in Africa before serving as director of student affairs in the West Virginia gubernatorial campaign of John D. Rockefeller, on which he wrote his undergraduate thesis. He graduated from Yale with a B.A. in history *summa cum laude* in 1973. He was enrolled between 1973 and 1979 at Clare College of Cambridge University in Great Britain, where he received his M.A. in 1974 and Ph.D. in 1979. He also served as a staff correspondent for *Time* magazine's London bureau from 1973 to 1975 and briefly as a public relations representative for the American Cyanamid Company in 1975.

Gates began his teaching career as an instructor at Yale in 1976, where he was promoted to assistant professor and director of the African American studies program in 1979 after he received his Ph.D. He has since held a succession of prestigious academic appointments as professor of English and director of African American studies at Cornell University from 1985 to 1988; as professor of literature at Cornell from 1988 to 1990; as professor of English at Duke University in 1990–1991. In 1991 he was appointed W.E.B. DuBois Professor of the Humanities and Chair of African Studies at Harvard University. The appearance of his seminal and influential book, *The Signifying Monkey*, which won an American Book Award in 1989, assured his scholarly reputation in the field of African American literature, while his copious popular writing, lecturing, and reviewing have made him a prominent commentator on contemporary black American culture and an advocate of a revised academic curriculum to include African-

American culture and tradition. His many fellowships, honorary degrees, and awards include the MacArthur Prize, in 1981. For identifying and decrying anti-Semitism among contemporary leaders of the black community in a *New York Times* Op-Ed piece in 1992, he received the Polk Award. Gates married Sharon Adams, a potter, in 1979. They have two daughters, to whom the preface of *Colored People* is addressed.

Gates is both a scholar, highly respected for his contributions to literary studies, and an activist in higher education, committed to reclaiming African-American literature and culture from its minority status within the academic curriculum. He has argued and campaigned for the establishment of African-American studies as a full-fledged discipline. Although Gates sees his academic policies as a tool for attracting more minority students to the universities, and believes that "decentering the humanities" can assist in "integrating the American mind," he claims that "blackness" is not innate to African-American culture. In all his critical writing he has explained the distinctive qualities of writing by black people as a response to the social and political conditions in which those writers lived. Since blacks have so long existed outside the mainstream of American culture, he argues, the study of their distinct modes of expression has as much right to an autonomous existence as the more traditional academic disciplines. Adam Begley's *New York Times Magazines* profile of Gates in 1990 quotes him as saying that African-American studies should not be "ghettoized," that the subject should be taught by both black and white professors and not treated from a "racialist" perspective. He wrote in *Time* magazine (September 23, 1991): "We do nothing to help our discipline by attempting to make of it a closed shop, where only blacks need apply. Nobody comes into the world as a 'black' person or a 'white' person: these identities are conferred on us by a complex history, by patterns of social acculturation that are both surprisingly labile and persistent."

The Signifying Monkey, which could be regarded as a treatise on how to read African-American literature, consists of two parts: a theoretical introduction to the context of African-American culture; and an examination of several works by African-American writers that shows how the complex web of influence that he has traced has shaped particular texts. The book, Gates explains in his introduction, "explores the relation of the black vernacular tradition to the African-American literary tradition," showing that African-American literature has "a two-toned heritage": "these texts speak in standard Romance or Germanic languages and literary structures, but almost always speak with a distinct and resonant accent, an accent that Signifies (upon) the various black vernacular literary traditions." The tradition is traced from the oral culture of slavery, which was rooted in the tribal cultures of West Africa, through the long process by which black society, deliberately deprived of literacy by its masters, first learned to speak, and then to write, in a dialect that it gradually appropriated from standard English and molded to its own purposes, which, as Gates demonstrates through quotations from slave narratives and early African-American texts, were defensive, subversive, and ironic. By reference to the culture of the slaves, Gates shows that West African culture was scattered in the brutal diaspora of American slavery, where it gradually evolved into "a truly Pan-African culture fashioned as a colorful weave of linguistic, institutional, metaphysical, and formal threads." Gates anchors his interpretations of both oral and literate African-American expression in observations of a crucial and constantly recurring trope, the Signifying Monkey. This figure is, on one side of the tradition, a descendant of the trickster figure of West African folktales, and on the other, a vehicle of mocking parody that he discovers in modern and contemporary black discourse, including popular music and street vernacular. "Signifyin[g]," a complex rhetorical strategy composed of irony and allusion, is, in Gates's account, both an element in black vernacular and a concept that can be used to read sophisticated literary texts such as Alice Walker's novel *The Color Purple*, a work that evokes the pioneering black writer Zora Neale Hurston, the epistolary novel in English, and the vernacular traditions of the Southern black family.

The act of signifyin[g], which Gates discovers everywhere in black expression, including jazz and demotic speech, supposes that black English is double-voiced. The audience hears the word as an embodiment of the original speaker's point of view and, simultaneously, as an expression of a second speaker's evaluation of that meaning from a different point of view. In simple instances of this technique (as exemplified by the black English use of the adjective "bad" to mean, approximately, "good") the word is seen to have mutable meanings of a variety that is determined by the verbal dexterity of the speaker. The recognition of this element of performance is essential to understanding black discourse, Gates claims. "Signifyin[g] is a principle of language use and is not in any way the exclusive province of black people, although blacks named the term and invented its rituals." By taking this position Gates can both demonstrate that there is an evolving tradition of black expression, a peculiarly black sense of a social and literary past, while at the same time recognizing that all words are common property, and that style can therefore be imitated.

Reviewing his first book, *Figures in Black*, and *The Signifying Monkey* in the *New Republic*, Andrew Delbanco praises the subtlety of Gates's reading of black texts, but questions the appropriateness of his methods. Delbanco points out that the special attributes of "signifying," when studied as purely literary qualities, are common to all literature, but his most serious reservation about Gates's argument is that, by applying insights derived from European criticism, he has undermined his own argument that black expression constitutes an independent tradition: "Gates tends to fall back into the portentous jargon of a literary criticism that is ill-suited to it. His analysis is murderously dissecting, a reductive translation of the living language of Ralph Ellison and Zora Neale Hurston into the taxonomies of Mikhail Bakhtin and Jacques Lacan."

Gates's meteoric rise to prominence began in 1982, the year after he received the MacArthur Foundation award, when he discovered *Our Nig*, a novel published in 1859 by Harriet E. Wilson, in a Manhattan bookstore. This forgotten work, which he was able to show was the first novel written by a black woman, was republished by Random House, and so lent support to his efforts to unearth and publicize the black literary tradition through two major scholarly enterprises: the Black Periodical Fiction Project, supported by grants from the Ford Foundation and the National Endowment for the Humanities; and the Schomburg Library of Nineteenth-Century Black Women's Writings, published by Oxford University Press. Gates's program for reassessing the place of African-American literature in the wider context of the national culture began to emerge in the 1987 volume *Figures in Black: Words, Signs, and the Racial Self*, which partly consists of essays published earlier in the 1980s, and was clearly announced in *The Signifying Monkey*, which appeared soon after. He sees these volumes as parts of a trilogy that will be completed by a projected third volume, "Black Letters and the Enlightenment."

The book *Loose Canons: Notes on the Culture Wars*, is a collection of essays in which Gates's "fault line," according to James Bloom, in the *New York Times Book Review*, "does not divide right and left or even Eurocentrists and their postcolonial antagonists so much as it separates 'vulgar cultural nationalists'(. . . Leonard Jeffries and Allan Bloom) from those for whom truly humane learning can't help but expand the constricted boundaries of human sympathy, of social tolerance." Gates reiterates his view that American culture should be regarded neither as a homogeneous monolith, nor as a host of competing fragments, but as a truly plural entity, "a conversation among different voices." He maintains the position that African-American culture has had a vital role in the shaping of American culture, being, according to Jack E. White in *Time*, "not a tangle of pathology." Rather, White said, Gates represents it as "the source of a strong and resiliant culture" that has enriched the world immeasurably.

PRINCIPAL WORKS: *Nonfiction*—Figures in Black: Words, Signs, and the Racial Self, 1987; The Signifying Monkey: Towards a Theory of Afro-American Literary Criticism, 1988; Loose Canons: Notes on the Culture Wars, 1992; The Amistad Chronology of African-American History, 1445-1990, 1993; Colored People: A Memoir, 1994; Speaking of Race, Speaking of Sex: Hate Speech, Civil Rights, and Civil Liberties, 11994. *As editor*—Black Is the Color of the Cosmos: Charles T. Davis's Essays on Black Literature and Culture, 1942–1981; Wilson, Harriet E. Our Nig; or Sketches from the Life of a Free Black, 1983; "Race," Writing, and Difference, 1983; (with Charles T. Davis) Black Literature and Literary Theory, 1984; The Slave's Narrative: Text and Contexts, 1985; (with J. Gibbs and K. Katrak) Wole Soyinks: A Bibliography, 1986; The Classic Slave Narratives, 1987; In the House of Osugbo: Critical Essays on Wole Soyinka, 1988; (as series editor) The Schomburg Library of Nineteenth-Century Black Women Writers (30 vols.), 1988; DuBois, W. E. B. The Souls of Black Folk, 1989; Johnson, James W. The Autobiography of an Ex-Coloured Man, 1989; Jonah's Gourd Vine, 1990; Mules and Men, 1990; Tell My Horse, 1990; Hurston, Zora N. Their Eyes Were Watching God, 1990; Voodoo Gods of Haiti, 1990; Reading Black, Reading Feminist, 1990; (with G. Bass) Mulebone: A Comedy of Negro Life, 1991; (as series editor) The Schomburg Library of Nineteenth-Century Black women Writers (10 vols.), 1991; (with K.A. Appiah) Critical Perspectives Past and Present (vols. on Zora Neale Hurston, Langston Hughes, Toni Morrison, Gloria Naylor, Alice Walker, and Richard Wright), 1993.

ABOUT: Contemporary Authors New Revision Series 25, 1989; Current Biography Yearbook 1992; Dictionary of Literary Biography 67, 1988; Who's Who in America, 1992–1993. *Periodicals*—American Literature October 1988; Black American Literature Forum Fall 1983; Spring/Summer 1986; Winter 1988; Chronicle of Higher Education July 15, 1992; Commonweal December 18, 1992; Contempoary Literature Spring 1986; Critical Inquiry Autumn 1985; English Language Notes December 1990; Modern Fiction Studies Spring 1988; Modern Philology November 1990; New England Quarterly December 1989; New Republic January 9, 1989; New York Times Book Review May 1, 1983; March 11, 1984; December 9, 1984; April 21,

1985; June 23, 1985; July 7, 1985; August 14, 1988; August 9, 1992; February 21, 1993; New York Times Magazine April 1, 1990; Sewanee Review Fall 1992; Southern Review July 1985; April 1986; Spring 1988; Time May 23, 1994; Times Literary Supplement May 17, 1985; December 29, 1989; World Literature Today Summer 1983; Fall 1983; Summer 1985; Yale Review Summer 1983. *Interviews with Henry Louis Gates*—Humanities Magazine July/August 1991; New Literary History Autumn 1991; Time April 22, 1991; US News & World Report March 16, 1992.

CARLO GÉBLER

GÉBLER, CARLO (ERNEST) (August 21, 1954–), Irish novelist and essayist, writes: "I was born in Dublin in the Republic of Ireland. My father Ernest Gébler was an already established author; a work called *The Plymouth Adventure* had enjoyed considerable success in the U.S. and been turned into a Hollywood film starring Spencer Tracy. My mother Edna O'Brien was an aspiring author, but had already published, I believe, before I was born, some stories in the *New Yorker* magazine. My parents' literary aspirations were antithetical; my mother favoured Chekhov and the communication of feeling, while my father preferred G. B. Shaw and literature with a didactic function. With differences like this, and my mother's success in the sixties, the marriage couldn't last. They separated in 1964, by which time the family were living in London. When I write I hope I sing in my own voice and not that of my parents, but they did teach me, my mother especially, something which has been invaluable to me as a writer; this was, if possible, never to work for anyone but only for yourself. My parents also revealed to me, at an incredibly early age, that it was possible to work an extraordinary miracle; you could write something, send it away, and someone would send you a cheque for it back in the post.

"I had a gloomy and miserable childhood. I went to a number of schools both state (i.e. public) and private, while my parents' marital relations were sorted out. Eventually, for which my brother and I gave our heartfelt thanks, custody was awarded to my mother. She sent me to a progressive boarding school called Bedales, where I felt isolated, and from where I went on to university, in the town of York in the north of England. I didn't like it; I am not a natural academic. But I graduated somehow, with a B.A. in English and Related Literature, and went on to what was then the National Film School (and is now the National Film and Television School) in Beaconsfield, outside London. This is where I feel I really got my education and it was here I began to write seriously, not just film scripts but also stories and plays.

"I also made two films—a documentary about a pilgrimage in the West of Ireland, *Croagh Patrick* and a fiction film based on a Chekhov story ('In the Ravine') relocated in the West of Ireland and called *The Beneficiary*. I graduated in 1979. I found myself somewhere to live in London and began to write full time. I was then lucky in that I was able to cut my teeth by publishing several short stories in a magazine called *The Literary Review*. In 1985 I published my first novel, *The Eleventh Summer*, a semi-autobiographical account of a young boy living with his grandparents on a farm in the west of Ireland. This has been followed by four further novels: *August in July*, *Work and Play*, *Malachy and His Family*, and *Life of a Drum*. I have also published two works of nonfiction, *Driving through Cuba*, a travel book about the country, and *The Glass Curtain*, an account of life and conflict in a contemporary Ulster rural community. In addition there are two published children's novels, and I have written and directed some films. I have now left London and returned to my island of origin; I do not, however, live in the Republic; I prefer to live in the north, and my home is in Co. Fermanagh. I am married and have three children."

———

Carlo Gébler's first novel, *The Eleventh Summer*, has a "melancholic sensibility," according to Richard Deveson, writing in the *New Statesman*. Anthony Daniels, in the *Spectator*, commented on the drabness and decay that Gébler observed in contemporary Cuba in

Driving through Cuba: "How to write about dreariness without being dreary? If Gébler does not manage it quite as well as Chekhov, he nevertheless maintains the reader's interest in the manifold varieties of awfulness that he encounters." Though *Driving through Cuba* is nonfiction, Daniels caught the essence of Gébler's quietly understated novels. His major characters, quite ordinary people, suffer sad but not tragic lives. Somewhat romantic, they live in a grubby, and frustrating, world. Their gray lives are, nevertheless, illuminated by a basic decency, a recurrent pattern in his fiction.

The Eleventh Summer is dedicated to Gébler's mother, Edna O'Brien, and draws on his memories of his Irish childhood. The novel is centered in the consciousness of a mature Paul Weismann, who is revisiting the Irish farm where he had spent a summer years earlier. This, however, is merely a frame for the point of view of the motherless young boy Paul who, within the span of a few months, confronts the mysteries of sex, the realities of old age and death, and the poignancy of separation from the one person who truly loves him, his feisty grandmother. He is a solitary, imaginative child, "father-to-the-man" Paul Weismann; the childhood that the adult recalls, however, is not a lyrical, Wordsworthian one. His mother's death was apparently a suicide. His father is cold and unloving yet insists on removing him from his grandmother's loving care. His grandfather is a violent drunkard who causes a fire that destroys the family's house. His surroundings are mean and sordid. It is little wonder that he will grow up emotionally alienated, having early on acquired the detachment that makes such life bearable:

As he stared across the fields towards the village perched on the hill, he recalled what had happened but without much emotion. He felt just commonly unhappy, rather than abjectly miserable. It was partly that his ability to forget and unknow was already beginning to operate and it was partly that he was no stranger to human ugliness and contrariness. He had already started the retreat from life back into himself, by which the passage to adulthood is achieved.

Reviewers in Great Britain and in the United States praised Gébler's sharpness of observation and his ability to evoke the child's world. Deveson wrote, in the *New Statesman*, "It is a remarkably good picture of the mind of a child, for whom, in his solitariness and vulnerability, one feels considerable compassion."

Gébler's more ambitiously conceived and structured second novel, *August in July*, is a first-person narrative by a man in late middle age, August Slemic, a Pole who had emigrated to England before World War II. He owns a successful real estate business; he has a wife he no longer loves and a grown son with whom he maintains a chilly, distant relationship. Slemic writes entries in a notebook covering the first part of 1981 until the wedding day of the Prince of Wales. Life has lost all flavor for Slemic: "All over London, all over England, all over the Western world, depression was descending like water spreading down a wall from a burst pipe." *August in July* probes Slemic's malaise, especially in a third-person narrative of his sheltered boyhood in Warsaw, during which his happiness shatters when he accidentally discovers his mother making love to his uncle. "Carlo Gébler's special subject, John Melmoth wrote in the *Times Literary Supplement*" "is proving to be the pain and unease that trickles into the space between the events of everyday life. He writes fetchingly about the unglamorous, the emotional underachievers. His prose is terse and functional."

Another study in alienation, this time of a young Irishman living in 1980s London, is *Work and Play*, which *Publishers Weekly* described as a "bleak but beautifully nuanced tale." The protagonist becomes involved with a group of heavy drinking, drug-using young people, but redeems himself when he comes to the aid of an Indian family victimized by racial prejudice. Although his act of heroism proves ineffectual, it leads to self-knowledge and the control he was seeking:

He had to take responsibility himself. Not only could he not let others shoulder his responsibility but, as he had been reminding himself, there was nothing other than his own self over which he had any influence."

In *Malachy and His Family*, Gébler returns to the diary or notebook form, in this case, a diary. Malachy, a young American who goes to England to meet his Irish father, his Hungarian wife, and their two children, records his impressions of a summer spent with his newly encountered family. Mark Wormold, in the *Times Literary Supplement* 1990, describes Malachy as, like Slemic in *August in July*, "a life split between countries and memories which he was trying to reconcile. . . . Malachy [is] also an exile from a past he can only partially untangle, and from feelings that an accidental birth and the accumulations of distance, psychological and geographical, have since imposed. . . . What emerges . . . from *Malachy and His Family* is a . . . sense that working through life's complications, on whatever scale, either by writing them or suffering them, can never mean working them out."

The central character in *Life of a Drum* is a

young woman whose jobs enable her to move from Iran to Lebanon to Cyprus. Forced back to England by conditions in those countries, she must make a new start. Marriage to a Polish immigrant to help him acquire citizenship results in their falling deeply in love. His sudden death devastates her, but she hangs on to life, takes a new lover, and recalls, more with resignation than with bitterness, her husband's observation: "What is born a drum is beaten till death." In this "short, deft novel," Lesley Chamberlain wrote in the *Times Literary Supplement*, "Gébler . . . makes his point by contradicting the social trend headlines. He reminds us that kindness could still be found in the yuppie years. . . . There is an unusual sweetness, not even bitter-sweet, about Gébler's writing. . . . " Chamberlain concludes that Gébler's heroine "remains   suspended   in . . .   angelic selflessness," and that in that almost timeless suspension, Gébler, he said, "has found the makings of a parable."

Driving through Cuba is an account of a trip Gébler made to Cuba in 1987 with his wife and young daughter, as a "tourist of the revolution." He went ill-equipped, in a rattling rented car, with little Spanish and no preparation for the bad roads, the crumbling towns, and the poorly equipped hotels. Nevertheless, he and his family emerged from their adventure with affection for the people and respect for their courage and good humor. Tad Szulc, a journalist with considerable expertise on Cuba, wrote in the *New York Times Book Review* that Gébler was "cavalier with basic events and dates in Cuban history," but, "has a good novelist's eye and ear, and his observations offer a painfully fair portrait of Cuba." Norman Lewis, another Cuba expert, said in the *Times Literary Supplement*, "Cuba offers a goldmine of potentially bizarre experiences for the . . . literary traveller. . . . The resulting   narrative   sparkles   with   fresh observations. . . . "

Also in 1987 Gébler visited Enniskillen in Northern Ireland, scene of a terrible bombing. Penetrating   what   is   called   "the   glass curtain"—the barrier "which you don't find out about until you walk into it and break your nose"—he talked to people, walked the streets, and gave his readers a good sense of the complexities of life in that troubled country. In the judgment of Tom Hadden in the *Times Literary Supplement*, the readers can get from *The Glass Curtain* "a far better understanding of the reality of life and death in Ulster . . . than from hours of portentous television pictures of murals and marches and murders."

PRINCIPAL WORKS: *Novels*—The Eleventh Summer, 1985;

August in July, 1986; Work and Play, 1988; Malachy and His Family, 1990; Life of a Drum, 1991; The Cure, 1994. *Nonfiction*—Driving through Cuba, 1988; The Glass Curtain, 1992; Murder of Bridget Cleary, 1994.

ABOUT: Contemporary Authors 133, 1991; Contemporary Literary Criticism 39, 1986; Gébler, C. Driving through Cuba, 1988. *Periodicals*—London Review of Books May 22, 1986; May 23, 1991; New Statesman February 1, 1985; New York Times Book Review March 11, 1990; March 18, 1990; Publishers Weekly August 9, 1985; March 4, 1988; January 5, 1990; Spectator August 13, 1988; October 26, 1991; Times Literary Supplement March 28, 1986; July 3, 1987; February 2, 1990; February 15, 1991; April 10, 1992.

GHOSH, AMITAV (1956–   ), Indian novelist, travel writer, and anthropologist, writes: "I was born in Calcutta. My family's origins lay in what is now Bangladesh, but my ancestors moved west, into India, in the nineteenth century. My father joined the army during the Second World War and saw action in North Africa and Italy. After the war he became a civil servant and was seconded to the Foreign Ministry. My childhood was thus spent outside India—for the most part, ironically enough, in the city that my family still called 'home,' Dhaka (which was then the capital of East Pakistan). My parents moved to Dhaka when I was about three and we lived there for six years. Dhaka was the setting for many of the most important formative experiences of my childhood: it was there for example, that I had my first experiences of religious and communitarian violence.

"My parents moved to Colombo in 1965 and three years later, to Teheran, but by this time I was away in boarding school in Dehra Dun, in North India. After school I went to Delhi University where I took an undergraduate degree in history. The end of my time in college coincided with Indira Gandhi's notorious State of Emergency, and immediately after graduating I joined the *Indian Express*, which was then the only newspaper that was outspokenly critical of her party and its leadership.

"Those were enormously exciting days at the *Indian Express*, with the police regularly raiding the newsroom and shutting down the presses, and they culminated eventually in Indira Gandhi's resounding defeat in the elections of 1977. However, it soon became clear to me that journalism of the kind I was practicing had no connection with the sort of writing I wanted to do and I spent my off-hours working towards a postgraduate degree in social anthropology and sociology. My efforts met with unexpected suc-

AMITAV GHOSH

cess, and in 1978, at the age of twenty-one, I won a scholarship to do a D.Phil. in social anthropology at Oxford.

"I was enrolled at Oxford for a period of three years and a few months, but much of that time was spent outside England. First I went to Tunisia to learn Arabic. After that I spent some time travelling slowly through Tunisia, Algeria, and Morocco: there are many echoes of that journey in my first novel *The Circle of Reason*. then, in 1980, I went to Egypt to begin my fieldwork, and moved into the village that I called 'Lataifa' in my third book, *In an Antique Land*. I went back to England in 1981 and the next year, after receiving my doctorate, I returned to India.

"My first job was a fellowship in Trivandrum, which is on the southernmost tip of the Malabar coast (India's western seaboard). The Malabar coast was a revelation: I discovered to my astonishment that the transcontinental, inter-cultural relationships of the old Indian Ocean trade are still a living part of everyday life there. It was there too that I began writing my first novel, *The Circle of Reason*.

"After a year I moved back to Delhi, and found a job as a 'research associate' in the university, a position that offered a monthly salary of six hundred rupees (about $20). Half that sum went on the rent of a tiny room (of a kind that is known as a 'servant's quarter'): a sun-baked enclosure on the roof which had just about enough room for a bed and a desk. It was only after my mother sold some jewellery and bought me a second-hand typewriter that I was able to begin typing up the final version of *The Circle of Reason*.

"In 1984, when I was about halfway through the book, Indira Gandhi was assassinated in Delhi. Thousands of Sikhs died in the riots that followed. Like many others in the university, I worked with groups that were attempting to provide relief to the victims. The experience was traumatic as well as revelatory and soon after finishing *The Circle of Reason*, the next year, I began work on another novel, *The Shadow Lines*, which deals in large part with the question of religious violence.

"*The Circle of Reason* was published in India and England in 1985, and in the U.S.A. in 1986. *The Shadow Lines* was published in India and England in 1988 and in the U.S.A. in 1989. They have both been translated into number of European languages. *The Circle of Reason* won the Prix Medicis Etranger in Paris in 1990, and *The Shadow Lines* has won the annual award of the Indian Literary Academy as well as the most important literary prize in Bengal.

"I taught in Delhi until the end of 1987. In 1988 I went to the University of Virginia for a year, to teach literature and anthropology. It was there that I began work on *In an Antique Land*, which was published in India and England in 1992 and in the U.S.A. in 1993.

"In February 1990 I was married, in Calcutta, to the American writer and biographer Deborah Baker. Our daughter, Lila, was born in 1991 and we now divide our time between Calcutta and Charlottesville, Virginia. My interests are cooking and sports, specifically squash, tennis, and badminton."

———

In cloth-weaving, the trade that brought East and West together over centuries, Amitav Ghosh found a metaphor for the fundamental unity of all things that pervades his first novel, *The Circle of Reason*, a rambling, whimsical fable of the adventures of Alu (which means "potato head"), an orphan boy adopted by a schoolteacher obsessed with the philosophy of rationalism and a passion for the scientific work of Louis Pasteur. A promising student, Alu suddenly decides to leave school at fifteen and become a weaver because, Ghosh writes: "Man at the loom is the finest example of Mechanical man; a creature who makes his own world as no other can, with his mind . . . [The machine] has created not separated worlds but one, for it has never permitted the division of the world . . . It has never permitted the division of reason." Although the loom has been superseded in the modern world by machines with destructive potential, Ghosh concludes that "Weaving is hope because it has no country, no continent. Weaving *is* Reason, which makes the world mad and makes it human."

The Circle of Reason is enormously ambitious, inspired, Ghosh has said, by his reading of *Moby Dick*. History and fantasy are generously mixed in the novel, creating a kind of magical realism. Alu is carried from India to Algeria and back at a dizzying pace. The bizarre characters include Alu's foster father Nury, an Indian egg salesman whose "trade was work of craftsmanship; a masterpiece in the art of staying alive. Nury's crossed eyes had the gift of looking not just ahead, but up and down, right into the heart of things" and an enormously fat madam who looks "as though her body had somehow outgrown her extremities." Living in what is in some ways a still ancient world, they are also entangled with modern technology and witness the chaos and warfare it brings in its wake. Though reason appears to fail every test, Alu survives with hope. "Hope is the beginning," the novel ends, on a note that Neville Shack described in the *Times Literary Supplement* as "poignant and thoughtful." Shack admired the novel but said, "This free-wheeling juggernaught of a story . . . inevitably generates more heat than light. A very lively style has it going in all directions, on escapades and wheezes, letting rip until some kind of rationale is added at the end to convey sobriety." In the *New York Times Book Review* Anthony Burgess found some faults, "divagations, episodic disquisitions . . . that hold up the narrative," but concluded, "[I]t is the intelligence manifested in the brilliant handling of language, that most impresses us. Many Western novels these days exhibit little more than the resources of a perverse sensorium. Here is a brain."

The promise displayed in *The Circle of Reason* was realized in *The Shadow Lines*, in which Ghosh moves from the timeless world of fantasy to the reality of modern post colonial India struggling to come to terms with independence. The novel deals with two cultures in portraying a solidly middle-class Indian family who have had a long and warm friendship with an English family. The story is a memory of a narrator haunted by the past—chiefly the history of his cousin, a brilliant young man whom he had idolized. He is also fascinated by an England he did not even know firsthand until he reached adulthood. Seen mainly through the eyes of the narrator as a child, the history of the two families, especially the child's own loving Indian one, is interwoven with the events of modern history—World War II, Indian independence, and, in the violent and tragic climax, the bloody warfare between Hindus and Pakistanis that Ghosh had witnessed himself as a child. In contrast to the grotesque characters of *The Circle of Reason*, the two cultures in *The Shadow Lines*, and the different age groups are portrayed with sympathy and understanding. When the narrator is taken as a child to visit some poorer relations, he is warned not to look out of the window at the spectacle of people scavenging for food: "I went willingly, I was already well schooled in looking away, the jungle-craft of gentility." In a household of people struggling to preserve their fragile class status, his mother reminds him that "the only weapon people like us had was our brains and if we didn't use them like claws to cling to what we'd got, that was where we'd end up, marooned in that landscape . . . the quicksand that seethed beneath the polished floor of our house, it was that sludge which gave our genteel decorum its fine edge of frenzy."

The Shadow Lines, Shakuntala Bharvani wrote (in the collection *Indian Women Novelists*) "transcends the narrow categorization of an Indian novel." Its scenes move back and forth from Calcutta and Dhaka to London; its characters are at home in both cultures. "It is clear," Bharvani writes, "that with Ghosh the Indian novel in English has surpassed the rigid barriers of time, place and action, thus making most earlier Indian fiction seem dated and simplistic." Nevertheless the barriers between cultures remain. They are the "shadow lines" of the title, drawn by people of goodwill who created the political borders between India and Pakistan "believing in that pattern, in the enchantment of lines, hoping perhaps that once they had etched their borders upon the map, the two bits of land would sail away from each other like the shifting tectonic plates of the prehistoric gondwanaland." But, Ghosh continues, there is irony in all this: "the simple fact that there had never been a moment in the 4,000-year-old history of this map when the places we know as Dhaka and Calcutta were more closely bound to each other than after they had drawn their lines . . . a moment when each city was the inverted image of the other, locked into an irreversible symmetry by the line that was to set us free—our looking-glass border."

Verlyn Klinkenborg, in the *New Republic*, called *The Shadow Lines* "a stunning novel, a rare work that balances formal ingenuity, heart and mind." Edward Howar, in the *New York Times Book Review*, termed the novel "amusing, sad, wise and truly international in scope . . . With this book Mr. Ghosh establishes himself as an accomplished artist, a master of style and insight."

In an Antique Land, the product of Ghosh's stays in Lataifa in 1980 and 1988, traces two stories interwoven, "the footsteps of Bomma, a 12th-century Indian slave, his Jewish master and their merchant friends . . . across . . . the Levant . . . [to] the western shores of India. . . . " Anton Shammas, in the *New York Times Book Review* said, "Ghosh also offers an enchanting, subtle glimpse into ordinary life in contemporary rural Egypt, in a manner that . . . rivals anything by the masters of social realism in modern Egyptian literature. . . . *In an Antique Land* uses conventional methods to blow away some historic, ethnographic and sociologic concepts." Shammas expresses admiration for Ghosh's "painstaking research and . . . astonishing attention paid to minute details," but adds, "the real achievement of . . . Ghosh's book is the way it deals with the poetics of current ethnography. Against the trend in which the ethnographer . . . is at the center of the writing . . . Ghosh . . . stays in the background . . . to create captivating vignettes of the Egyptian peasants among whom he lived."

In a Personal History piece in the *New Yorker*, "The Ghosts of Mrs. Gandhi," Ghosh describes how his marching against the violence that followed the assassination of Indira Gandhi influenced him as a writer. After the demonstrators faced down a crowd of "thugs," causing them to fade away, they formed an organization, the Citizens' Unity Front, to help those injured and dispossessed in the riots and to investigate the inciters. Ghosh did not participate in the investigation, deciding it "would be a waste of time because the politicians capable of inciting violence were unlikely to heed a tiny group of concerned citizens." The impact of the document the investigators produced forced Ghosh to declare "I was wrong." He then had to confront the problem of how to write about the events of 1984 without "re-creating them as a panorama of violence." He had a need to avoid "violence as an apocalyptic spectacle," as it has become in the modern world. Ghosh realized that he "had to resolve a dilemma, between being a writer and being a citizen." Ghosh was unable to resolve this dilemma satisfactorily until 1995 when he came to understand that a purpose of writing, like the purpose of demonstrating, could be "the affirmation of humanity." He concluded: "It is when we think of the world the aesthetic of indifference might bring into being that we recognize the urgency of remembering the stories we have not written."

PRINCIPAL WORKS: *Novels*—The Circle of Reason, 1985; The Shadow Lines, 1988. *Nonfiction*—In an Antique Land, 1992.

ABOUT: Contemporary Literary Criticism Yearbook

1986, 1987; Dhawan, R. K. ed. Indian Women Novelists I, 1991; Ghosh, A. In an Antique Land, 1992; Ghosh, A. "The Ghosts of Mrs. Gandhi" *in* New Yorker July 17, 1995; Kirpal, V. ed. The New Indian Novel in English, 1991; Nelson, E. ed. Writers of the Indian Diaspora, 1993. *Periodicals*—College Literature October 1992; Commonwealth Essays and Studies Autumn 1991; London Magazine March 1986; New Republic August 7, 1989; New York Times February 13, 1990; New York Times Book Review July 6, 1986; July 2, 1989; Times Literary Supplement April 11, 1986; May 3, 1991; January 15, 1993; Yale Review Spring 1990.

GIBSON, WILLIAM (FORD) (March 17, 1948–), was born in Conway, South Carolina, the son of William Ford, a contractor, and Otey (Williams) Gibson. He was raised in a small town in southwest Virginia, near the Appalachian Mountains. "A very backwater place, a detained backwater, by and large," he described Conway in *Interview* magazine. "There was no library, and science fiction books were the only source I had for subversive information. It was good escape, but I took some of it as a blueprint. It was as though I were hearing these lonely monsters from distance places."

Eventually Gibson turned from the more conventional science fiction writers to the darker visions of such iconoclasts as Philip K. Dick and J. G. Ballard. He also discovered William Burroughs and Thomas Pynchon. Burroughs in particular exerted a powerful influence on Gibson: it has been suggested that *Naked Lunch* be read before tackling Gibson's work. He stretches the fantasy of science fiction, as Burroughs stretched his drug-induced hallucinations to explore the depths of the human character.

Gibson attended a boarding school in Arizona. In 1967 he dropped out of high school and lived in Toronto, then the scene of an active counterculture. The Vietnam War and the draft in the United States kept him in Canada. There, in 1972, he married Deborah Thompson; the couple later settled in Vancouver. Gibson earned his B.A. in English at the University of British Columbia in 1977.

While at the university Gibson had taken a course in science fiction. In lieu of a term paper, he submitted a short story and launched his writing career. It was a precarious living at first, but one that enabled him to stay at home and care for his two young children while his wife worked as a language teacher.

By the early 1980s, his dark vision of the future, a world of high-tech villainy, was drawing attention with several short stories published in *Omni* magazine. Gibson, however, mistakenly believed his work was too disturbing to appeal

WILLIAM GIBSON

to a large audience. Both reviewers and audience proved him wrong. *Neuromancer* epitomizes a sub-genre of SF in which the interface of human and machine set amid the big-fish-eat-little-fish politics of corporation conglomerates threatens the very existence of the human spirit, but also provides humanity an escape from an overmechanized future." The novel also introduced the terms "cyberpunk" and "cyberspace" into the science fiction lexicon.

"Cyberpunk is science-fiction with an attitude," Gerald Jonas explains in the *New York Times Book Review;* "it imagines a future in which people use the latest technology to do nasty things to one another. Gibson's characters, who spend the better part of their lives literally plugged into supercomputers, experience electronic data-flow as sensory output; they live in a 'consensual hallucination' that Gibson has dubbed cyberspace." The antihero of *Neuromancer* is described as tomorrow's computer hacker, an interface or console cowboy, a data thief, and a cyberspace jockey. He is punished for his roguery with a nerve poison that prevents him from plugging into cyberspace. An enigmatic patron offers to help him to reenter cyberspace, in exchange for his services as an outlaw hacker and expert at invading electronic security systems. Accompanied by a biologically engineered female assassin, he ends up on a space station with two supercomputers. There he finds out that one computer, Wintermute, has hired him to help it dominate the other, Neuromancer. "The book's faults are glibness and a gimmicky use of farfetched gadgets," Charles

Platt wrote in the *Washington Post Book World.* "Gibson is no engineer, and doesn't even try to explain his pseudoscience. In visualizing the human impact of high technology, however, he is brilliantly perceptive. The resulting society is dehumanized and even repellent, but always derived from trends that are becoming apparent today."

Neuromancer garnered some of science fiction's most prestigious honors, including a Hugo Award, a Philip K. Dick Award, a Nebula Award, and a Ditmar Award from Australia. Gibson's antiestablishment jockeys continue to hack their way through computer space in the successful sequels *Count Zero* and *Mona Lisa Overdrive.*

In 1990 Gibson teamed with Bruce Sterling to publish *The Difference Engine.* The premise is that the inventor Charles Babbage built a steam-powered Analytical Engine in 1829, thereby starting the computer age a century early. Among the colorful characters are "neo-Luddite anarchist criminals," according to David Porush in *American Book Review.* Their program "almost succeeds in seizing London during an apocalyptic collapse of the local environment, a foul atmospheric inversion at the height of summer that is made lethal by technology Gibson and Sterling have unleashed." Porush calls the novel a "brilliant collaboration between . . . two luxurious and robust imaginations."

Gibson's fiction has attracted an enthusiastic, almost cultlike following. At a reading of his novel *Virtual Light* in 1993, the audience included computer hackers calling themselves Voxers, The *New Yorker* reported that one Voxer called Gibson the "Aesop of the computer age." Christopher Lehmann-Haupt, in the *New York Times,* called *Virtual Light* an absorbing thriller "driven by fascinating computer gimmicks. . . . a pair of glasses that enables the wearer to see the future cityscape of San Francisco as planned by a secret organization that is buying up real estate." Lehmann-Haupt faulted *Virtual Light,* however, for giving cyberspace short shrift: " . . . Instead of a vision of what lies beyond modernity . . . we end up with . . . a futuristic version of *It Happened One Night.*"

Gibson is also a screenwriter; his first film project was *Alien III.* In addition to his books, he contributes stories, articles and book reviews to such publications as *Omni, Rolling Stone,* and *Science Fiction Review.*

PRINCIPAL WORKS: *Novels*—Neuromancer, 1984; Count Zero, 1986; Mona Lisa Overdrive, 1988; (with B. Sterling) The Difference Engine, 1991; Virtual Light, 1993. *Short stories*—(with J. Shirley, B. Sterling and M. Swanwick) Burning Chrome, 1986.

ABOUT: Barron, N. ed. Anatomy of Wonder: A Critical Guide to Science Fiction, 1987; Contemporary Authors 133, 1991; Contemporary Literary Criticism 39, 1986; Gunn, J. ed. The New Encyclopedia of Science Fiction, 1988; Twentieth-Century Science-Fiction Writers, 1991. *Periodicals*—American Book Review December/January 1991-1992; Fantasy Review July 1984; Film Comment January/February 1990; Interview January 1989; New York Times August 29, 1993; New York Times Book Review August 29, 1993; New Yorker August 16, 1993; Washington Post Book World July 29, 1984.

GARY GILDNER

GILDNER, GARY (August 22, 1938–), American poet, novelist, and writer of short stories writes: "I was born in a small town in northern Michigan called West Branch. My father was born there too. His father, Edward, owned the lumberyard, where my parents and I lived for a while, in an apartment upstairs over the office, after we 'burned out,' as my mother put it. She says she wrapped me up in her muskrat coat and ran out through smoke and flame and continued on to Fred Dieboldt's garage two blocks away where my father was holding up the rear end of a Pontiac that had slipped off the jack so that the other mechanic who worked there could squeeze out from underneath. It may have been another make of car my father was holding up as he looked helplessly at my crying mother, but a Pontiac was what she seemed to remember him telling her. We couldn't confirm it because when she remembered this scene my father was dead. He'd been dead for several years, and she was reminiscing about West Branch, got around to the fire, how they lost everything, how she ran in the snow carrying me in the coat to find dad—all of which I'd heard before—and then suddenly here was this fresh, unlikely, *funny* detail. Forty years later. 'Oh you can laugh now,' she said, 'but that day you were bawling your head off. Your pants were full, which you hated, and you were hungry, mad too; I was holding you so tight—and I was bawling myself, yelling *Ted! Ted!* But he just stood there blue in the face, couldn't talk, couldn't move or that poor devil underneath would've got more than his ribs busted, and I didn't understand any of it.'

"That lumberyard—watching the men there make things, make them right, and hearing their talk—was a good classroom. As were the woods and lakes nearby. As was the farm twenty miles to the south of West Branch where my mother's parents lived, Steve and Nelly Szostak.

"My Polish grandfather was a great mystery to me: he didn't speak English; when he took his horses down to the creek for a drink he waded in with them and drank too, as they did; often he sat in his apple orchard—for hours, it seemed—gazing at the sky (what was he looking at?); at night after chores, after supper, he said his rosary kneeling beside the table, drank some whiskey, then read a book. No one I knew read as he did—and never books. He was buried on my eleventh birthday. Buried with the last book he was reading, the book he held when they found him. My grandmother slipped it in the coffin before Mr. Savage, the undertaker, closed the lid. She told me about this years later, but she couldn't tell me—didn't remember—the name of that book. Only that it was by this Korzeniowski. Korzeniowski (Joseph Conrad) was his favorite writer. I knew that. I also know that if I could choose one book for my grandfather to take into eternity—and I do choose—it would be *Heart of Darkness*.

"Just as World War II came to a close we left West Branch for Flint, where I attended Holy Redeemer Catholic School from the fourth grade to the twelfth. I was an alter boy, played baseball, basketball, and football. For several years—rich and confusing—we lived in a modest house on Buder Street, then my father built my mother her dream house in the country. I have written poems and stories about all of this: 'Wheat,' 'The Runner,' 'First Practice,' 'The House on Buder Street,' 'Nails,' 'They Have Turned the Church Where I Ate God,' 'Sleepy Time Gal.'

"In high school my ambition was to play professional baseball, but the curveball I learned how to throw too soon—and couldn't stop throwing—finally ruined my arm. Also, sliding into third base my senior year I broke my leg; a blessing, as things turned out, because slowed down by the cast I began to read, began paying a new kind of attention. In my memoir *The Warsaw Sparks*—which returns to baseball, Polish baseball, of all things—a homage to blessing continues.

"As a kind of postscript here, I went to the Carnegie Museum in Pittsburgh recently, to see an exhibit from Eastern Europe. Left on a bed in a small shack built from scraps of old lumber was a note: 'I need my memories. They are my documents.' I subscribe to that news."

Gary Gildner's first writings were short stories, and he did not begin writing poetry until he was in his late twenties. His early poems reflected his strengths as a writer of prose—a gift for narrative and characterization, an ear for natural idiomatic American speech, and a finely honed sense of place. In "First Practice" the poet recalls a boyhood memory of his athletic coach, one Clifford Hill "a man who believed dogs / ate dogs"), instructing the school team before a game. He lines up the boys to face each other; "across the way," he tells them,

> is the man you hate most
> in the world,
> and if we are to win
> that title I want to see how.
> But I don't want to see
> any marks when you're dressed,
> he said. He said, *Now.*

There is no moral or philosophical commentary in the poem. Yet, as James Coleman observed in *Centennial Review* in 1986:"Gildner's vision of the desert of American life and values places the battleground within our consciousness, where the banal and the vicious are the familiar, the easy to accept. Gildner's poetic world is then a world of values, received ones and truer ones."

Gildner's prose fiction examines our values just as candidly. Like his poetry, it records what simply meets the eye. A man who has drifted to Oregon to recover from a broken marriage reflects, in "A Million-Dollar Story" in *A Week in South Dakota*, "If you like rain and are inclined to put your feet up on a porch railing and look for meaning or at least interesting patterns in the way it falls and suddenly slants and bounces on things like tricycles left out and leaves and turned over flower pots, then Oregon may be the place for you." Many of Gildner's short stories are so short, sometimes only one page, and so compressed that they read like absurdist fiction. In longer stories Gildner offers a complex pic-

ture of modern marriage and a whole range of human experience. Reviewing his collection *The Crush* in the *Georgia Review*, Sterling Watson wrote, "This is a book of lovely, somber writing which remind us of Conrad's famous saying that the writer's job is 'to seize a passing phase of life from the remorseless rush of time.'" The protagonist of "Somewhere Geese Are Flying" is a middle-aged American alone in Paris, haunted by memories of his failed marriage. The scene shifts back and forth between the Left Bank, where he drifts around aimlessly, and his former home in the Middle West where, in spite of good intentions and genuine love, he cannot reestablish his once happy relationships with his wife and young daughter. He is the typical Gildner protagonist and, according to Watson, "a certain kind of modern man . . . a fellow who thinks too much too well, who is alternately feckless and endearing, a believer and a scoffer, a wit and a sentimentalist." He reappears in "The Burial," a story Gildner expanded into his novel *The Second Bridge*, where Bill Rau, a writer and college teacher, sees his happy marriage threatened and finds himself incapable of salvaging the values he cherishes. The novel is short but emotionally compelling, sketching first the rift in the Raus' marriage, then their reconciliation. Their renewed happiness is shattered by the death of their teenage daughter in a fire. Unable to confront his grief, Rau leaves his wife for several days and travels aimlessly about the country. When he returns he learns that she has disappeared. His search for her through the snow-covered wilderness of northern Michigan provides more than a mere suspenseful climax. Richard Goodman commented in the *New York Times Book Review* that Gildner "draws his characters distinctly. He knows what he wants to say well enough to say it simply. Ultimately this evocative novel offers many lessons about the fear and beauty of giving yourself over to another person."

Poetry and prose converge in *The Warsaw Sparks*, a record of a year that Gildner spent in Poland as a Fulbright lecturer and part-time coach of the Warsaw Sparks baseball team. His ethnic roots in Poland had figured from time to time in his poetry—notably in "Szostak," his tribute to his maternal grandfather, a Polish immigrant and farmer, who "died / at one A.M.—reading Conrad / in the can by kerosene." Thomas S. Gladsky points out in his study of ethnicity in American literature, *Princes, Peasants, and Other Polish Selves*, that one of Gildner's recurrent characters is a "deethnicized ethnic . . . disguised as the all-American boy." Gladsky believes that his time in Poland gave Gildner's writing a whole new dimension: "Gildner discovers a new American self and an old Polish one, transforms his American poetry into multicultural one, and bridges the chasm between the ethnic and nonethnic voice in his previous writing." A remark by a Polish student, "Primarily we miss ourselves as children," overheard by Gildner, gave him the necessary connection between his American past and his Polish present. A poem with that quoted remark in its title, makes the connection: "I am now in a house in Poland, I had / oatmeal for breakfast, I had oatmeal for breakfast / in America in 1942." Thus he returns to the past and his memory of his Polish grandfather:

> In the late sunlight I followed him down to the creek.
> In the late sunlight minnows skittered away.
> Like little brown clouds they all moved away.
> In the honeyed glow of a kerosene lamp on the table
> he opened his book and we all moved away.
> He lay his face on the water.
> In the last light he entered the water.

The Warsaw Sparks are literally the young Polish ballplayers but figuratively, as Albert E. Stone points out in his introduction to the book, they are "sparks of memory" for Gildner. His midwestern boyhood is illuminated by his experience in the Polish present. For him, as with many other American boys, baseball was a passion and it became so for these Polish youths. The prose text of the book, a lively account of his teaching, his personal life, and his coaching of the amateur but ardent Polish team, and the constant battle with government bureaucracy, is sprinkled with poems. One, "In a Warsaw Classroom Containing Chairs," suggests the challenge an American teacher faces with his students who search in the books they are reading with him for "the American character"—"its here and there or its wide / and lonely and rich and two-fisted / get up and go. . . ." Other poems depict the hardships of daily life in Poland and the indomitable spirit of the Polish people.

Although in both his prose and poetry Gildner has concentrated primarily on the present and on the past as it related to his own condition, he has written two narrative poems that evoke the historical past. One is "Johann Gaertner (1793–1887)" in *The Runner*, an account of the life of a man who at nineteen was a starving veteran of the Napoleonic wars and emigrated to America where he became a prosperous farmer in "Little Festine, Iowa"—

> where Anton Dvorak came to drink
> local Bohemian beer,
> and hear the Turkey River;
> and where rosy Johann Gaertner
> dug down deep in the rich black dirt
> to make his own hole

and one for his wife as well.

Another evocation of the distant past is a sequence of eighteen sonnets, *Letters from Vicksburg*, inspired by a collection of letters that John Blood, a young Union soldier from Iowa, wrote home to his wife in 1863. Gildner describes these poems as "translations, even though I did not use all of the original material and departed from it whenever it seemed necessary or fruitful." He did retain the semiliterate spelling of the originals, with the result that the soldier speaks directly in his own voice to the reader. He describes the hunger and exhaustion of the men as they near a plantation house and the reactions of the women living there:

> . . . when they
> saw us standing at the dore they jumped
> and screamed I told them they neat not be scart
> for we was only yankey soldiers only
> hungry and was never nowen to hert
> the ladies so we took posesion of
> the tabel ate a harty dinner then
> helpt ourselfs to other things we wanted

The soldier recounts the horrors of battle and of disease—" . . . my feet / steped over deat and wounted thick as sheep." The closing sonnet, written in correct and formal English, is from his commanding officer, informing his wife that he has died of typhoid fever:

> . . . I have sent
> his final statements and his military
> history on to Washington D.C. Truly
> I assure you, Madam, I was hurt,
> for John was hardy, in the best of health—
> but O alas! in life we are in death.

Gary Gildner is the son of Jean Szostak and Theodore Gildner. He received B.A. (1960) and M.A. (1961) degrees from Michigan State, the latter in comparative literature. He has been writer-in-residence at Reed College (1983–1985), Michigan State (1987), and Davidson College (1992); and Fulbright lecturer at the University of Warsaw (1987–1988). After a twenty-five-year association with Drake University, in 1991 he resigned his position to give more time to writing and to travel. He is married to Elizabeth Sloan, an artist. He has a daughter, Gretchen (Gildner) Demkiewicz, from an earlier marriage to Judith McKibben, and two grandchildren, Gabriel and Joanna. He has received the National Magazine Award for Fiction, a Pushcart Prize for Fiction, grants from the National Endowment for the Arts, the Robert Frost Fellowship from Breadloaf, the Helen Bullis and Theodore Roethke prizes from *Poetry Northwest*, and the William Carlos Williams

Prize from *New Letters.* He is a Yaddo and Mac-Dowell Colony Fellow. He has read his poems at the Library of Congress, the YM-YWHA in New York, the Academy of American Poets, and at more than two hundred colleges and schools in the U.S. and abroad.

PRINCIPAL WORKS: *Poetry*—First Practice, 1969; Digging for Indians, 1971; Nails, 1975; Letters from Vicksburg, 1976; The Runner, 1978; Jabon, 1981; Blue Like the Heavens: New and Selected Poems, 1984; Clackamas, 1991. *Novels*—The Second Bridge, 1987. *Short stories*—The Crush, 1983; A Week in South Dakota, 1987. *Memoir*—The Warsaw Sparks, 1990. *As editor*—(with J. Gildner) Out of This World: Poems from the Hawkeye State, 1975.

ABOUT: Contemporary Authors New Revision Series 12, 1984; Contemporary Poets, 5th ed., 1991; Gildner, G. The Warsaw Sparks, 1990; Gladsky, T. S. Princes, Peasants, and Other Polish Selves, 1992; Janeczko, P. B. Poetspeak, 1983. *Periodicals*—Centennial Review Spring 1986; Georgia Review Fall 1984; Hungry Mind Review May/June 1990; Library Journal March 15, 1975; New Letters Summer 1981; New York Times Book Review April 26, 1987.

FRANK GILROY

GILROY, FRANK D(ANIEL)

(October 13, 1925–), American playwright, screenwriter, and novelist, was born in New York City to Frank B. Gilroy and Bettina (Vasti) Gilroy. Gilroy's father was an Irish-American coffee broker, while his mother came from German and Italian stock. The family lived in the Bronx and young Gilroy was educated in the public school system, graduating from DeWitt Clinton High School, despite poor grades, in February 1943. He worked for a few months as a runner on Wall Street, before being drafted into the army in December 1943 and sent to Europe during World War II. He was able to use the G.I. Bill to get a college education, after his discharge in 1946, when Gilroy sent applications to forty colleges, assuring them that "I have the stuff to reach my goal." He was turned down by thirty-eight institutions, but was accepted by Dartmouth, where he majored in sociology and minored in psychology and English. Gilroy had been writing stories since the age of fourteen, but a playwriting course in his junior year convinced him that drama was his vocation. During his final two years at Dartmouth, he had several plays produced, and he won the Eleanor Frost Playwriting Award in both his junior and senior years. He also edited the college newspaper, *The Dartmouth*, and played jazz trumpet in a student band.

Gilroy graduated with a B.A. magna cum laude in 1950, and won a scholarship to the Yale School of Drama, but had to drop out after six months when he ran out of money. He then tried his hand at selling beach cabanas and working as a copy boy at the Young & Rubicam advertising agency in New York City. In 1952, Gilroy sold a ten-minute sketch to the Kate Smith television show. Realizing the medium's potential, he decided to concentrate on free-lance work for television until he had earned enough money to back to his real interest, playwriting. This was the start of the Golden Age of television, and Gilroy wrote scripts for all of the major shows that specialized in presenting drama. Critics praised *A Matter of Pride*, adapted in 1957 from John Landon's story "The Blue Serge Suit," and *Far Rockaway* in 1965. Reminiscing in 1986, Gilroy said, "I did about 40 [or] 50 of those shows . . . you could walk right into the office of *Studio One* and just give the script to them. . . . If you had any talent, you could show it. Today there's no place to show talent. If you do anything different, you'll never get it on the air."

Gilroy moved to California to write scripts for films and television programs, including Western series such as "The Rifleman" and "Have Gun, Will Travel." His 1954 teleplay *The Last Notch*, about a "high noon" gunfight, was made into a 1956 film, *The Fastest Gun Alive*, adapted by Gilroy and Russell Rouse, who also directed. It received respectable reviews. Gilroy's first major film success was *The Gallant Hours*, written in collaboration with Beirne Lay Jr. and released in 1960. The movie showed no actual battle scenes, but concentrated on the ordeal of command, as James Cagney in the role of Admiral William F. Halsey Jr. planned the strategy for the Battle of Guadalcanal in World War II. Both the star and the script were praised for restrained characterization and compelling depiction of events.

Thanks to the income from his various film and television projects, Gilroy felt able to devote some time to playwriting. He completed *Who'll Save the Plowboy?* in 1957, although it was not until January 1962 that the drama had an off-Broadway production at the Phoenix Theater in New York. The plot centers on the reunion of two veterans several years after Larry's dangerous battlefield rescue of Albert, nicknamed "the plowboy" because of his dream of owning a farm. Larry, who is dying from complications caused by the wound he suffered in the rescue, wants reassurance that his sacrifice was not wasted. He hopes to find Albert happily married and to meet the little boy who is his godson and namesake. Albert tries to hide the truth that he and Helen are embroiled in a bitter, loveless marriage and that, as Helen tells Larry privately, their child is severely retarded and has been institutionalized. Not knowing of this conversation, Albert introduces a neighborhood boy as young Larry, and the older Larry "saves" the plowboy once again by pretending to believe the lie.

In spite of his grim theme, Gilroy managed to inject a great deal of humor as well as rage into the lean dialogue of his Ibsenesque characters. The maturity of his writing and the psychological truths he revealed about his unhappy trio impressed virtually all the critics, who hailed the arrival of a new young playwright. *Who'll Save the Plowboy?* won the 1961–1962 Obie (off-Broadway) Award as the season's best American play. It was produced in London in 1963 and has had other foreign productions.

Gilroy came back to New York in 1961, and his second play, *The Subject Was Roses*, was completed in 1962. Although producers expressed interest, it took two years for a production to materialize. After several false starts, described in his book *About Those Roses, or How Not To Do a Play and Succeed*, Gilroy persuaded two friends, Edgar Lansbury and Ulu Grosbard, to serve respectively as producer/designer and director, and the drama opened on Broadway at the Royale Theater on May 25, 1964. The play is a family triangle involving Nettie and John and their 21 year-old son, Timmy, who has just been mustered out of the army following World War II. The setting is a middle-class Bronx home on the morning after a welcome-home party that turned into a father-and-son beer-drinking binge, which the mother blames

on her husband. John and Nettie rage at each other. Timmy is caught on this domestic battlefield, at first siding with his mother as he gently teases her into a better mood, but later becoming sympathetic to his father's point of view. Occasionally, John and Nettie try to reach out to one another, but the moment passes before they can express their feelings, giving way to misunderstanding and resentment. The play ends a few days later as Timmy is about to move out. He has finally been able to tell John that he loves him, and he has come to another realization which he admits to his mother: "When I left this house three years ago, I blamed *him* for everything that was wrong here. When I came home, I blamed *you*. Now I suspect that no one's to blame. Not even me."

Both of Gilroy's parents were dead by the time he wrote the play. When asked to comment on its autobiographical aspects, he said that while the physical details of time and place were similar: "The actual story as such did not take place. It has taken me twenty years to understand all it was based on. I was not as wise as a boy, twenty years ago, as the boy in the play—unfortunately. But it's the first attempt to deal directly with my own material, my own lifetime story." Reviewers were divided in their estimate of the play, with some calling it an impressive and honest naturalistic drama, while others considered it an unexciting play about three dull people. Nevertheless, although the play had opened with no advance sale, it ran for 832 performances and won the Pulitzer Prize, the New York Drama Critics Award, the Outer Critics Circle Award, and the Antoinette Perry (Tony) Award. Gilroy's film adaptation, using some of the original Broadway cast, was released in 1968. In 1988, Gilroy gave permission to the directors of the George Street Playhouse in New Brunswick, New Jersey, to adapt the play for a black cast. A revival, directed by Jack Hofsiss, had a limited run in 1991.

Gilroy's next play, *That Summer—That Fall*, was a modern version of the Phaedra legend, set in a rundown Manhattan neighborhood with an Italian-American family as the protagonists. It opened on Broadway in March 1967 to generally negative reviews, which criticized the dramatist for draining away the tragedy and force of the original in his moody adaptation. The play closed after twelve performances.

In a marked change of pace, Gilroy wrote a romantic comedy called *The Only Game in Town*, which had its Broadway premiere in May 1968. The setting is Las Vegas, where a compulsive gambler meets a third-rate dancer. She throws over her longtime lover, a wealthy businessman, for the gambler, but cannot throw off his gambling habit. After losing almost all his money, he makes one last lucky bet, and the curtain comes down on a happy ending as they decide to marry. While criticizing the hackneyed plot, most reviewers liked the repartee and one-liners sprinkled throughout the dialogue. The play ran for only sixteen performances on Broadway, but Twentieth-Century Fox had already agreed to buy Gilroy's film adaptation as a vehicle for Elizabeth Taylor and Frank Sinatra (replaced by Warren Beatty because of scheduling conflicts); the picture was filmed in France and Las Vegas, and released in 1970. Also in 1970, Gilroy published a war novel titled *Private.*

Desperate Characters, was a 1971 film written, produced and directed by Gilroy from the novel by Paula Fox. Taking its title from Thoreau's dictum, "The mass of men lead lives of quiet desperation," the movie starred Shirley MacLaine in a story of personal anxiety and despair amid the material luxuries of upper-middle-class life. While some reviewers called the film "stagey," the majority praised its realism and subtlety. The movie won the 1971 Berlin Film Festival Silver Bear Award for best screenplay and best picture.

Gilroy returned to the stage briefly in July 1972 with four short plays—*Come Next Tuesday, 'Twas Brillig, So Please Be Kind,* and *Present Tense*—dealing with a variety of family problems. The program was presented off-Broadway under the collective title *Present Tense.* Unlike his usual "flat-out realistic" style, Gilroy said, these plays were "grounded in reality, but . . . there's more going on than what's apparent." In 1973 he published a novel *From Noon Till Three,* which he later adapted and directed as a film, released in 1976. The comic plot, verging on farce, deals with a small-time bank robber's seduction of his prisoner, an attractive widow he is guarding while his gang pulls off a bank heist. The widow later writes an exaggerated and colorful account of their three-hour tryst, turning the seduction into a popular romantic legend. A few reviewers enjoyed the spoof, but others considered it an intriguing concept gone awry. Gilroy's next film, which he distributed in addition to producing, directing, and writing, was *Once in Paris,* based in part on his experiences while filming *The Only Game in Town.* Released in 1978, this romantic comedy involving a scriptwriter in Paris, his chauffeur, and a beautiful Englishwoman, was poorly received.

Television was still important in Gilroy's career. He wrote several episodes for *The Dick Powell Show,* including a script called "Who Killed Julie Greer?" in 1961. The hero was a millionaire private detective named Amos Burke, and the episode developed into the popular action-adventure series "Burke's Law." In 1975 he wrote and directed *The Turning Point of Jim Malloy,* based on John O'Hara's autobiographical short stories, which became the basis for the "Gibbsville" series. He was also involved in writing and directing for the "Nero Wolfe" series in 1979.

Gilroy returned to Broadway in November 1979 with *Last Licks.* In some ways it was a sequel to *The Subject Was Roses,* and the playwright acknowledged that *Last Licks,* another three-character play about family tensions, also contained a "kernel" of autobiography. The mother is dead and her widowed husband has become a recluse. The son hires a live-in housekeeper over his father's strenuous objections. She turns out to be the old man's former mistress, however, eager to resume their affair. The son, who had no suspicion of this relationship, confronts them in a fury. The father then sends his son away so that both men can live their own lives. Most reviewers thought the joke was thin to begin with, and that it definitely soured by the end of the evening. The play closed after a brief run, and a London production as *The Housekeeper* in 1982 received a similar negative critical reaction.

In 1985, Gilroy wrote and directed *The Gig,* a film which harked back to his college days as a jazz trumpeter. A group of middle-aged, middle-class men who have been playing together for years as an amateur combo are suddenly offered the opportunity of a two-week "gig" at a Catskill hotel. When one of their number has to drop out, they hire a professional black musician, and the movie concerns the interaction and understanding which gradually develops. Many critics considered *The Gig* a warm and humorous venture into wish fulfillment. In 1989, a film, *The Luckiest Man in the World,* again written and directed by Gilroy, opened to mixed reviews. In it, a man has who alienated all his friends and family misses connections for a plane that crashes on takeoff; as a result he resolves to change his life and treat people better. But he has a problem: nobody will believe him.

In 1987, Gilroy returned to the one-act play format, which some consider his forte. For Marathon '87, Ensemble Studio Theater's annual one-act play festival, he wrote *Real to Reel,* a comic sketch involving a female film critic and an actor. For Marathon '91, he presented *A Way with Words,* in which a man who is planning to remarry fears that his ex-wife will seek a recon-

307   GÖNCZ

ciliation. Frank Rich, reviewing a revival of *The Subject Was Roses*, which opened in 1991 in *The New York Times*, said of *Roses*: "people don't . . . write plays like this one anymore, in which a plain-spoken Mom, Dad and Son settle every score . . . in two acts that leave no psychological threads untied." He contrasted *A Way With Words*, calling it, "as wry and elliptical as this youthful hit [*Roses*] is prosaic." Marathon '92 featured *Give the Bishop My Faint Regards*, a comedy about the film industry, and Marathon '93 offered *Fore!*, another sketch of Hollywood life.

Gilroy returned to Broadway briefly in November 1993 with *Any Given Day*, a prequel to *The Subject Was Roses*, in which the three characters of the earlier play reappear. This family drama is set in a drab apartment in the Bronx with a "host of regretful characters," according to Ben Brautley in the *New York Times*, who described it as Gilroy's bid to write something like a Cheklovian tragicomedy of withering expectations.

Also in 1993 appeared *I Wake Up Screening! Everything You Need to Know About Making Independent Films, Including a Thousand Reasons Not To*, an account in diary form of his making of *Desperate Characters, Once in Paris, The Gig*, and *The Luckiest Man in the World*. Gilroy laconically recounts his difficulties with using Jack Lenoir, a nonactor with an ego problem, in *Paris* and recollects the musical highs of *Gig*. Gilroy felt himself inured to the difficulties of filmmaking, however, by his wartime experiences. He remembers recounting war stories to friends: "viewing Ohrdruf Nord, the first concentration camp overrun in April 1945: 3,200 matchstick corpses that made Patton puke, etc. . . . Their attention . . . drew me out so that I felt drained at the end." Although Gilroy was drained by his experiences in film, as well, he begins his brief epilogue to the book by saying, "I've made a solemn vow to my family that I will never again raise money for an independent film." He concludes, however, "I've written a new script. . . . Stay tuned."

Gilroy married Ruth Dorothy Gaydos in 1954; they have three sons. He is a member of the Writers Guild of America, the Dramatists Guild (which he served as President from 1969–1971), and the Directors Guild of America. In 1966, Dartmouth College awarded him an honorary Doctor of Letters degree.

PRINCIPAL WORKS: *Plays*—Who'll Save the Plowboy?, 1962; The Subject Was Roses, 1962; Far Rockaway, 1967; That Summer—That Fall, 1967; The Only Game in Town, 1968; Present Tense, 1973; The Next Contestant, 1979; Dreams of Glory, 1980.

Nonfiction—About Those Roses, or How Not To Do a Play and Succeed, and the text of The Subject Was Roses, 1965; I Wake Up Screening! Everything You Need to Know About Making Independent Films, Including a Thousand Reasons Not To, 1993. *Novels*—Private, 1970; (with Ruth Gilmore) Little Ego, 1970; From Noon till Three: The Possibly True and Certainly Tragic Story of an Outlaw and a Lady Whose Love Knew No Bounds, 1973.

ABOUT: Contemporary Authors 81–84, 1979; Contemporary Dramatists, 4th ed., 1988; Contemporary Literary Criticism 2, 1974; Current Biography 1965; Dictionary of Literary Biography 7, 1981; Notable Names in the American Theatre, 1976; Who's Who in America, 1992–1993. *Periodicals*—Action November–December 1971; Hartford Times April 22, 1966; Hollywood Drama-logue May 8–14, 1986; New York Herald Tribune March 21, 1965; New York Post June 9, 1964; New York Times November 18, 1979; November 17, 1993; Newark Evening News July 12, 1964; Newsday December 2, 1985.

*GÖNCZ, ARPÁD (February 10, 1922–), Hungarian playwright, fiction writer, and political leader, was born and educated in Budapest. Göncz completed secondary school in 1939 and enrolled in the faculty of law of the Pázmány (later Eötvös) University, receiving his law degree in 1944. His political activities were the focus of his early life, and he did not embark on a literary career until he was politically silenced by the Communist regime.

Göncz was a member of the liberal opposition as early as 1938 and later joined the resistance movement. Wounded in a skirmish with German soldiers in the last days of World War II, he joined the Independent Smallholders Party and served as private secretary to Béla Kovács, head of the party. He also edited the youth journal *Nemzedék*. Upon the arrest of Kovács by the Communists in 1947, Göncz withdrew from politics and became a laborer in the steel industry, and later, a skilled worker. Eventually he went to work for the Agricultural Ministry and enrolled in the Agricultural College of Gödöll''o. While he was there the revolution of 1956 broke out. His chief contribution in that period was enabling Imre Nagy's papers to be removed from Hungary and published in the West. In 1957, after a secret trial, he was sentenced to life imprisonment for his involvement in the events of 1956. Following the general amnesty in 1962, he was released.

In prison, Göncz learned English. Upon his release he was able to find employment as a translator, all other jobs being barred to him. After a brief stint as a technical translator, he turned to belles lettres, and, between 1965 and the elec-

°GAHNJ

tions of 1989 that made him president of Hungary, he worked as a free-lance translator and writer. His novel *Sarusok* appeared in 1974, and in 1975 he turned it into a drama, translated into English was *Men of God* in 1990. In 1983 he received the József Attila prize, in 1989 the Wheatland Prize, and in 1991 the Paul Harris and Albert Schweitzer prizes.

When the democratic opposition began to form in Hungary in the late 1970s, Göncz became involved as an editor of the Bibó memoirs. On May 1, 1988, he became a founding member of the Network of Free Initiatives and later joined the Alliance of Free Democrats. Concerned with historical accuracy, he was a founder of the Committee on Historical Revisionism, while in the wider sphere of human rights he helped establish the Hungarian branch of the League of Human Rights. The climax of political activity came on August 3, 1990, when he was elected to a five-year term as president by the Parliament. In literary circles he was recognized by being elected president of the Writers' Association in December 1989, and while he had to resign as active head upon his election to national office, he has remained honorary president since then.

Göncz first made his name as a translator. While still in prison he sent out a translation of Galsworthy as an anniversary present to his wife. He was later to translate such American writers as James Baldwin, Truman Capote, E. L. Doctorow, John Updike, William Styron, William Faulkner, Ernest Hemingway, Arthur Miller, Edgar Allan Poe, and Edith Wharton. His plays have been performed in Eastern and Central Europe and in Germany, but are not well known in the United States, although four have been published in translation. Sensitive to the problem of translation, Göncz seeks to "transplant experience" rather than merely reproduce the text. As his American translators Katharina and Christopher Wilson point out in *Plays and Other Writings*, he is aware of the translator's problems in rendering cockney or Westminster English, or in conveying, as he puts it, "Brautigan's English? Sailor's English? Sheepraiser's English? Coalminer's English?"

Favoring drama, short story, and essay, Göncz has written only one novel. His style emphasizes drama over narrative, and his short stories have a particularly dramatic flavor. "Homecoming" and "Encounter" are in the form of short dramatic scenes. "The Front" and "Old People" are essentially dramatic monologues rather than narratives. Spare dialogue and the power of what remains unsaid propel the dramatic situation. His effective psychological dramas are of-

ten enacted on an inner stage, whether formally plays, such as *Hungarian Medea*, or short stories. The extensive stage directions of his plays often establish the universality or timelessness of the drama, and he uses the choice of the chorus to frame the action. As E. L. Doctorow writes, "[Göncz] has found two different forms to carry the burden of his perceptions, the dramas and the story; the high tormented life of the mind exquisitely rendered in classical theatrical strategies and the low life of the body's ordinary suffering, rendered with brutal honesty, in the prose of the realist."

Hungarian Medea (1976) is a dramatic monologue which allows the viewer to follow the existential struggles and compromises of a young woman in the upside-down world of post–World War II Hungary. The accommodations of the 1950s, however, do not fit with the political and economic changes of the 1970s, so that Medea is left alone and betrayed. As the daughter of a military officer, she and her family had been deported to the countryside where their only means of survival lay in Medea's job of cleaning stables. In order to provide food for them, along with a measure of protection, and security, she befriended and eventually married an ambitious young peasant, Andrew Jason. While she tutored him and helped him get his university degree, she also moved into his world of the opportunistic technocrat, betraying her own middle class origins. She feels this betrayal most strongly when her husband divorces her to marry his boss's daughter. This background is, however, only a framework for the play. As Göncz notes in his introduction, "Everything—night and day, light and shadow, modern furniture and old, picture and reflection, the modern preface and the classic text, the past and the present, the good and the bad—all emphasize both the irreconcilability and inseparability of male and female."

The skillful combination of Hungarian East European realities with universal themes characterizes Göncz's work. As his translators Katharina and Christopher Wilson point out, *Hungarian Medea* is a "post–World War II and post-1956 transplantation of Euripides' play into Hungarian soil. As does Euripides' play, *Hungarian Medea* also explores the psychological struggle of a woman caught in the clash between two worlds: two social, historic, and cultural realities as well as the internal struggle of her soul between love and hate for her husband who deserted her." Göncz's 1988 essay "Medea változatok" (Medea variations) explains this conflict by seeking the origins of the Medea legend upon which Euripides based his play and which in turn was to inspire Göncz himself. In analyzing the classical model, he casts light on the motivation of his own heroine: the Greek Jason's sense of justice is flawless, he points out, because an oath made under duress is not binding. Medea, moreover, is a traitor *even if* her treason was for his sake. His new marriage is purely dynastic, for it is not Creon's daughter whom he loves but the position this marriage will secure for him. The tragedy lies in Jason's lack of moral fiber: he looks for excuses and fails to own up to his deeds. Similarly, Medea put her knowledge at the disposal of this adventurer and in doing so had renounced her family. Now she seeks revenge for the wrong inflicted on the daughter of Helios, as if the first betrayal had not been her own. Similarly, Mrs. Medea in Göncz's play had betrayed her family for the ambition of a young man. She symbolically "sacrifices" on the altar of her past, burning photographs of her parents and of her husband. Ironically, as she tells a friend over the phone, "I killed Andrew and my parents today . . . It's only my son whom I did not kill," her son is committing suicide because of her self-absorption, self-pity, and concern with the past have made her ignore him when he needed her most.

In recent writings, Göncz has made it clear that his plays always concern present-day problems. In the essay, "politika és irodalom" (Politics and literature, 1991) he states: "My first work, *Sarusok*, appeared—after a delay of five years—when I was fifty-two . . . This book is the history of a 15th-century Hungarian heretic's trial, but in reality it is not a historical novel, but the summary of my prison experiences. This was recognized at the time not only by my readers, but also by the 'literary office,' although no one wrote it down at the time." This pivotal essay is a statement of the author's experience of Central and Eastern European literature as the vehicle of self-expression when most other forms of self-expression were denied. In the Renaissance and baroque periods, poets were also soldiers defending the country against the Turks; thus, in their commitment to the national cause, the literary and the political became fused. In the 19th century it was again a poet, Sándor Pet´ofi (1823–1849) who best formulated the ideals of the revolution and who served again as inspiration in 1956. The tradition continued in the years of Communist rule when the poet's opinion was sought, while the politician was ignored.

Rácsok (1986, *Iron Bars*) depicts the poet's role. The author calls it "a black comedy," a drama of the absurd, limning the senselessness of the communist system. The characters are divided into "Those who have names," "Those who have faces," and "Those who have neither names nor faces; who only exist." The "hero" is a political prisoner, a minor poet, whose chief work, the national anthem, has been "appropriated" by a megalomaniac dictator. Because he refuses to give up his claim to the poem, he had been imprisoned for many years, but is now free. His old friend, the dictator, suddenly showers favors and presents on the poet's wife and son who had been ostracized all these years. All he has to do is accept the dictator as the author of the national anthem and he will be made poet laureate. He refuses, for as laureate he could write only what the dictator approved. Upon his refusal, the poet is taken to an insane asylum. Ironically, a tacit agreement with his physician seems to suggest that life can go on under such a dictatorship, provided everyone observes unwritten rules and remains under the dictator's (i.e. Communist Party's) control. These "rules" echo the Hungarian system of censorship—self-censorship by the author, the editor, the publisher, and all involved in literary production—rather than an official censorship. The informed reader cannot miss the negative reflections on the notorious system, which also categorized authors and works as "Supported," "Tolerated," and "Forbidden," guaranteeing respectively honors and an assured income, the occasional royalty to supplement another job, or the unwelcome attentions of the secret police.

In some short stories and in *Mérleg* (Balance, 1985), Göncz examines the trauma of the revolution of 1956 when families and lovers were separated. Reunions came about only in the 1970s, when those who had fled to the West returned for visits. The play is a dialogue between two former lovers. She had gone to the United States, married, and sought to forget her past, only to find that it cannot be shaken off so easily. He had stayed, married within the old circle, and made a reasonably successful career. Complicating their relationship is the memory of the gulf that existed between them because they had come from different social classes. Their failure to communicate in the past haunts their conversation. "Can you separate the two?" the man asks early in the conversation. "Separate them? The girl and history?" she answers. The exchange reveals much about Hungarian life in the mid-twentieth century.

In his Foreword to *Homecoming and Other Stories* Göncz makes a tally: "The man who has risked his skin once for democracy is likely to do so a second time. The revolution put an end to my studies. . . . Our experiment failed. It was at that point I served *my* six years, the years—which I believed—I owed the devil. . . . It was in prison that I learned the English language, and I still feel that for this, if nothing else, my confinement was worthwhile."

In *Persephone*, a light play, Göncz explores the dilemma of a new generation, which has to choose between a vital hedonism and a pessimistic authoritarianism. The protagonists: Deo, the goddess of light, and Hecate, the manipulator of the underworld, both different aspects of the same reality. The Hades here is the rather benevolent one of the later years of the Communist regime, yet it is clear that the risk associated with the sunshine of Deo is worth infinitely more than the "security" of Pluto's underworld.

In the essay "Politika és irodalom" Göncz sought to answer the question: "Are you a politician or a writer?" His simple answer is "politician *and* writer" because the two are inseparable in his person. He can thank the imprisonment that was a result of his political activities for having become a writer, and thus was known by a fairly large segment of the population. The writer, the observer and commentator on human behavior, stores experience, Göncz explains. In the final analysis, however, he refuses to choose between being a writer and a politician, and affirms merely that he seeks to lead his life as he had always, honestly and simply. In 1947 Göncz married Zsuzsanna Göntér, and had four children.

PRINCIPAL WORKS IN ENGLISH TRANSLATION: *Drama*—(tr. K. M. Wilson and C. C. Wilson) Voices of Dissent: Two Plays (includes Hungarian Medea and Iron Bars) 1989; (tr. K. M. Wilson and C. C. Wilson) Plays and Other Writings (includes the plays Men of God and Persephone and eight short stories) 1990. Short stories—(tr. K. M. Wilson and C. C. Wilson) Homecoming and Other Stories, 1991.

ABOUT: Doctorow, E. L. *postscript to* Göncz, A. Voices of Dissent, 1989; Göncz, A. *foreword to* Homecoming and Other Writings, 1991; Wilson, C. C. and Wilson, K. M. *Afterword to* Göncz, A. Plays and Other Writings, 1991. *Periodicals*—U.S. News and World Report October 28, 1991.

GOWING, LAWRENCE (BURNETT)

(April 21, 1918–February 5, 1991) British educator, art historian, and painter, who was knighted for his services to art in 1982, was born in Stamford (Lincolnshire, England), into a Norfolk farming family of no particular artistic sympathies. He was educated at Quaker schools, the Downs, and Leighton Park. At the Downs he was taught by Maurice Feild, who encouraged him to paint in oils and also to paint directly what he saw, and to whose influence and example he ever afterward paid tribute. Upon leaving school he wanted to become a filmmaker, and tried to enlist the aid of poet W. H. Auden, who was working for the GPO film unit. Auden discouraged him from taking this step, but did introduce him the the the painter William Coldstream, ten years his senior, who became his mentor, teacher, and lifelong friend—and who, like Feild, was always an advocate of the kind of monumental naturalism which insists above all upon the primacy of what is seen by the painter.

Gowing was only in his early twenties when he became a precocious member of Coldstream's so called "Euston Road" school, along with such painters as Victor Pasmore and Graham Bell. The style cultivated by this school, which sought to return to realism and to eschew both surrealism and abstraction, left its mark on his aesthetic, but was eventually modified by another influence, the most powerful in Gowing's career as a critic and teacher: that of the painter, sculptor, poet, and critic Adrian Stokes. Richard Wollheim, in his memoir of Gowing in the *Times Literary Supplement*, reported that the difference between the unrevised and the revised versions of Gowing's book *Vermeer* was that the text of the former had been "transposed into the key of Adrian Stokes" in order to reach its final form. Stokes, who as an art critic championed "carving" as opposed to "molding" values, also influenced Gowing in the way in which he developed his own personality. In such books as *Inside Out* (1947) Stokes powerfully advocated the building of the inner self through passionate study of the outside world: "the utmost drama of the soul as laid-out things," he wrote in an essay on Giorgione's *Tempestà*. Thus, in Wollheim's words, Gowing "revelled in controversy, in dissent, in outcry."

Gowing would have been happiest, his (London) *Times* obituarist thought, to have been remembered as a painter; but though his painting was respectfully received, right up to his last grand retrospective at the Serpentine Gallery, "his real talents lay more in art history and especially in conveying to others what he had discovered." In the 1940s he had been much in demand as a portraitist (Isaiah Berlin, Cecil Day-Lewis, and many others), and he later made a number of interesting and applauded experiments, the most famous of which was the series of figure-paintings in which, says Wollheim, "tied up naked in various postures," he either had paint "sprayed around his body on to a canvas behind or on to his body which was then rolled on the canvas." The astonishing results were shown at the Serpentine in 1982. But it was as an exhibition organizer and writer on painters that he became most celebrated and most valued. In particular, his descriptions of works by painters as varied as Vermeer, Turner, and Cézanne were found as useful by the viewer as they were brilliantly evocative. His television programs on Masaccio, Cézanne, Matisse, Goya, and others were widely watched, and were preferred by some to the more numerous and more widely ranging ones of Kenneth Clark—not a figure with whom he was in much sympathy.

During World War II, Gowing was a conscientious objector. In 1948, at the age of twenty-nine, he became Professor of Fine Arts at Durham University. His writings had become known earlier, when his *Notes of a Painter* appeared, over a number of years, in *Penguin New Writing*. In 1958 he went on to become principal of the King Edward VII School of Fine Art at Newcastle upon Tyne. Ten years later he became principal of the Chelsea Art School. From 1953 he was a trustee of the Tate Gallery, thus beginning an association which continued until his death, He was Professor of Fine Art at Leeds University from 1967 until 1975, when he became Slade Professor at University College, London. He retired ten years later, but remained active, both as Research Fellow at the Washington National Gallery and as a curator of the Phillips Collection in London—he commuted between these two jobs until doctors forbade him to fly lest it put too severe a strain upon his heart. In addition to all this, he served on and chaired many committees, such as the Arts Film, the Arts Council, and the Gulbenkian Painting.

Among Gowing's most outstanding achievements Wollheim mentions his "Thomas Jones lecture, many of the Vermeer descriptions, the Turner catalogue, the Chelsea syllabus, the body art, the Masaccio film (for BBC television, 1984), the early Cézanne exhibition [Edinburgh and the Tate Gallery, 1954]. . . . the great arabesques he wove round his stammer." The first Cézanne exhibition, to which Wollheim referred, was both a triumph for Gowing and an apt demonstration of his brilliant and correct intuitions. In it, he boldly challenged the accepted dates of several important and well-known works. This provoked a furor, until the world's leading Cézanne expert, John Rewald, confirmed Gowing's painter's judgment by producing documents supporting his position. "Few writers on painting," the *Times* obituarist declared, "have matched his expression, subtle in insight, precise in analysis, colourful in its rhetoric, unbounded in its generosity." And Wollheim commented in his memoir on how his "extraordinariness" could be studied in many ways, "but in none so clearly, so authoritatively, as in his preoccupation with creativity as he found it among the dead and the living, among his idols and his mentors, among his favourites and his friends."

Gowing was married three times and had three daughters.

PRINCIPAL WORKS: Renoir, 1947; Vermeer, 1952, rev. ed. 1961; Cézanne (catalogue) 1954; Constable, 1960; Goya, 1965; Turner: Imagination and Reality, 1966; Matisse: 64 Paintings (catalogue) 1966; Hogarth (catalogue) 1971; Watercolours by Cézanne (catalogue) 1973; Matisse, 1979; Lucian Freud, 1982; The Originality of Thomas Jones, 1986; Paintings in the Louvre, 1987; Paul Cézanne: The Basel Sketchbooks (catalogue) 1988; Cézanne: The Early Years (catalogue) 1988.

ABOUT: Contemporary Authors 11–12, 1965; Who's Who, 1990. *Periodicals*—Los Angeles Times February 7, 1991; New York Times February 7, 1991; Times (London) February 7, 1991; Times Literary Supplement April 5, 1991.

GRAFTON, SUE (April 24, 1940–), American crime novelist, writes: "I write about a hard-boiled private eye because those are the books I was raised on. Raymond Chandler, Dashiell Hammett, Ross Macdonald, Mickey Spillane, and Richard Prather. My father, C. W. Grafton, was a municipal bond attorney all his life, but he also wrote and published three mystery novels . . . *The Rat Began to Gnaw the Rope, The Rope Began To Hang the Butcher,* and *Beyond a Reasonable Doubt.* Because of him, I developed a real passion for the genre.

"When I started work on *'A' Is for Alibi,* I wasn't even sure what a private investigator did. In the process of writing that first book in the series, I began the long (and continuing) task of educating myself. I've studied police procedure, forensics, toxicology, books on burglary and theft, homicide, arson, anatomy, poisonous plants. I elected to write about a female protagonist because I'm female myself and I figured it was my one area of expertise.

"I made the decision to use 'Santa Teresa' instead of 'Santa Barbara' when I first wrote 'A' . . . more as a psychological device than anything else. I am, in essence, the Goddess of Santa Teresa. I control the weather. I can move real estate at will. I can change the coastline, if it suits my purpose. If I tell a story about police corruption in Santa Teresa, I don't have to worry about the local cops suddenly refusing to take my calls. Also, I fancy, it cuts down on lawsuits . . . I've had none to date. It feels freer to me and I'm less self-conscious in the writing. I really don't want to write about the town I live in. I want to write about one very similar, but where the homicide rate is much higher than it is here.

SUE GRAFTON

"The cases I write about are invented, though some of the side stories and the back stories I collect from the newspaper. I like looking at the dark side of human nature, trying to understand what makes people kill each other. In my soul, I'm a real law-and-order type and I don't want people to get away with murder. In a mystery novel there is justice and I like that a lot.

"Kinsey Millhone is my alter-ego . . . the person I might have been had I not married young and had children. I think of us as one soul in two bodies and she got the good one. The '68 VW she drove (until *'G' Is for Gumshoe*) was a car I owned some years ago. In *'H' Is for Homicide*, she acquires the 1974 VW that's sitting out behind my house. It's pale blue with only one minor ding in the left rear fender. (I don't mind her driving the car, but with her driving record, I refuse to put her on my insurance policy.) I own both handguns she talks about and, in fact, I learned to shoot so that I would know what it felt like. I own the all-purpose dress she refers to. I've also been married and divorced twice, though I'm now married to husband number three and intend to remain so for life.

"What's interesting about Kinsey's presence in my life is that since she can only know what I know, I have to do a great deal of research and this allows me, in essence, to lead two lives . . . hers and mine. Because of her, I've taken a women's self-defense class and a class in criminal law. I've also made the acquaintance of doctors, lawyers, P.I.s, cops, coroners, all manner of experts. I would be a lesser writer if it were not for the generosity of those I call on in the course of a book."

Sue Grafton's mystery writing may be inextricably linked to the alphabet, but her literary career did not start with the letter "A." In the late 1960s, she published two mainstream novels: *Keziah Dane* and *The Lolly-Madonna War*. During this period, she and a friend founded a women's consciousness-raising and counseling group called Homemakers Unlimited. Although the group disbanded, Grafton's own confidence was raised enough for her to break into screen and television writing. One of her projects was to coauthor the screenplay of her second novel. The story deals with a modern-day feud between backwoods families and was filmed by MGM as *Lolly Madonna XXX*.

For eight years Grafton worked under the constraints of writing "by committee." According to a profile in *Bestsellers*, "She had already decided to return to writing books when her second divorce provided her with a plot for her mystery. Engaged in a bitter custody battle, Grafton fantasized about poisoning her ex-husband." Grafton admits this is true, but tempers the story: "I am personally such a law-abiding bun that I knew I would never actually act it out. . . . So the next best thing was to put it in a book and get paid for it." From Grafton's divorce came a most profitable marriage to hard-boiled detective Kinsey Millhone.

In a scene from *'A' Is for Alibi*, Millhone is hiding in a trash dumpster while being stalked by a killer: "He lifted the lid. The beams from his headlights shone against his golden cheek. He glanced over at me. In his right hand was a butcher knife with a ten inch blade. I blew him away." Clearly the reader is not in the presence of Miss Marple; just as clear are Millhone's roots in the fictional world of macho private eyes who have names like Mike Hammer and describe the world in pithy, first-person prose. Ed Weiner, in the *New York Times Book Review*, states that Millhone's creator may be the best of a group of recent women writers who are placing "women operatives in the traditionally male-dominated genre of American private eye fiction." He goes on to note that "none of them . . . have gone so far as to redefine the genre. They play it fairly conservative and conventional. But in their work there is thankfully little of the macho posturing and luggish rogue beefcake found so often in the male versions, no Hemingwayesque mine-is-bigger-than-yours competitive literary swaggering."

Readers and critics alike find Kinsey Millhone's peppery personality extremely engaging and, even more than Grafton's skillful plotting, Millhone is the main drawing card of the series. *People* magazine described Millhone as "California casual—a 32 year old divorcee who lives in a one-room 'bachelorette' in Santa Teresa . . . drives a beat up old VW, eats olive-pimento cheese spread on whole wheat toast and cuts her own hair with nail-scissors. She's got a foul mouth and wry, descriptive eye." Grafton told Enid Nemy, interviewing her for the *New York Times*, "I work to keep her flawed and inconsistent." Nemy's comment: "[W]ho can resist a character who sometimes lies 'just to keep my skills up'?"

In *'A' Is for Alibi*, Millhone is hired to prove the innocence of a woman who has served eight years in prison for poisoning her husband. Grafton followed with *'B' Is for Burglar*, in which Millhone's efforts to find a missing woman of wealth lead to a complicated murder case. Weiner called it "one of the best written crime novels by anybody in recent memory, followed closely by *'D' Is for Deadbeat*." His opinion of *'F' Is for Fugitive*, in which Millhone investigates a seventeen-year-old murder, was less enthusiastic: "Atypically slow-paced, it uncertainly backs into its central story. . . . Even in a less than top-notch performance, Ms. Grafton's work surpasses most of what limps along as detective fiction these days."

Sue Grafton has won a number of awards for her teleplays and novels, including a Shamus Award from the Private Eye Writers of America for both *'B' Is for Burglar* and *'G' Is for Gumshoe*, and the Falcon Award from the Maltese Falcon Society of Japan for *'F' Is for Fugitive*. According to *Bestsellers*, she delivers another completed manuscript for another letter to her publisher every August 15th. Grafton figures she will be sixty-eight years old when *'Z' Is for Zero* is published, but Kinsey Millhone will only be forty.

PRINCIPAL WORKS: *Novels*—Keziah Dane, 1967; The Lolly-Madonna War, 1969; 'A' Is for Alibi, 1982; 'B' Is for Burglar, 1985; 'C' Is for Corpse, 1986; 'D' Is for Deadbeat, 1987; 'E' Is for Evidence, 1988; 'F' Is for Fugitive, 1989; 'G' Is for Gumshoe, 1990; 'H' Is for Homicide, 1991; 'I' Is for Innocent, 1992; 'J' Is for Judgment, 1993; 'K' Is for Killer, 1994; 'L' Is for Lawless, 1995. *As editor*—Writing Mysteries: A Handbook, 1992.

ABOUT: Blain, V., P. Clements, and I. Grundy. The Feminist Companion to Literature in English: Women Writers from the Middle Ages to the Present, 1990; Contemporary Authors New Revision Series 31, 1990; Twentieth-Century Crime and Mystery Writers, 1991. *Periodicals*—Bestsellers 3, 1990; New York Times August 4, 1994; New York Times Book Review May 21, 1989; People July 10, 1989.

GREENBLATT, STEPHEN (JAY) (November 7, 1943–   ), American historian and literary critic, writes: "I was born in Boston, Massachusetts. My parents were also both born in Boston, children of Jewish immigrants from Lithuania who came to America in the late nineteenth century. My maternal grandparents escaped from the Russian authorities by hiding in the bottom of a hay wagon; in this country they had a small hardware shop. My paternal grandfather was a ragpicker, complete with horse and wagon. My father chose not to take up the reins but went to law school instead.

"I grew up in the suburbs, in a town with a fine public school system. Many of the names and faces, small triumphs and grand adolescent heartaches from my school years have been swallowed up in the dark backward and abysm of time, but I remember being passionately involved in drama, and I vividly remember my senior-year English teacher, a man of wry intelligence and unusual intellectual integrity. The most exquisite expression of that integrity—or the one I recall best—came toward the end of the year during the last class he taught on *King Lear*. After explicating and excavating that great text more than I had ever imagined to be possible, after struggling to awaken in us what the philosopher Richard Rorty celebrates as 'the imaginative ability to see strange people as fellow sufferers,' our brilliant teacher humbly expressed defeat in the face of something that continued to elude him, something ineffable at the heart of Shakespeare's tragedy. I knew that this defeat, if it could be called that at all, was the triumph of literature. And I began to have an inkling of how I might want to spend my life.

"I was an undergraduate at Yale in the early sixties, the last years of a postwar American optimism soon to be crushed by the Vietnam War. These were also, as it turned out, the last years of the virtually uncontested authority of New Criticism, then at its height in the Yale English department. My undergraduate honors thesis, on Huxley, Waugh, and Orwell—published as *Three Modern Satirists*—reflected that authority. It also reflected my admiration for my thesis director, Alvin Kernan, whose lively prose style I shamelessly imitated.

"In two years as a Fulbright Scholar at Cambridge University, I learned to distance myself a bit from my models and my methods. I read widely and unsystematically, traveled, and wrote comedy sketches as a member of the cele-

STEPHEN GREENBLATT

brated Footlights. I returned to Yale for graduate school, determined to figure out a way to do
a different kind of criticism, one that would reflect my sense that art could not be separated
from the conflicts and impurities and mixed motives of life. If I thought of this project as a daring rebellion against my New Critical teachers,
the rebellion cannot have seemed all that threatening to them: Alvin Kernan agreed once again
to be my thesis director. I wrote on the functions
of art in the career of Sir Walter Ralegh; the thesis was published as *Sir Walter Ralegh: The Renaissance Man and His Roles*.

"In 1969, fresh from graduate school and just
married, I took a job at the University at Berkeley, then convulsed (like the rest of the country,
only more so) by an amazing succession of crises,
antiwar demonstrations, riots, teach-ins, sit-ins,
strikes, and protests. The first four or five years
at Berkeley were a remarkable period that has
set a permanent mark on my work. The intense
political and theoretical ferment of that time,
exhilarating and challenging and at times maddening,   helped   to   shape   *Renaissance
Self-Fashioning* and is reflected and refracted in
my   subsequent   books,   *Shakespearean
Negotiations, Learning to Curse*, and *Marvelous
Possessions*. These books have shared an obsession with the place history in cultural studies, an
engaged concern with colonialism and literature, and a deep longing for Shakespeare. I have
also tried to think of myself as a writer—
something curiously difficult sometimes for
English professors to do.

"For more than two decades I have lived in

Berkeley, where my wife and I have raised out
two sons. But I am by nature restless, have traveled widely, and currently divide my teaching
duties between Berkeley and Harvard."

Stephen Greenblatt has become identified in
academic circles with the movement known as
the New Historicism, a term he coined for an approach to literary interpretation. In his introduction to *The Power of Forms in the English
Renaissance*, a volume of essays he edited to
which scholars from universities in America and
abroad contributed, he distinguishes this method
from both traditional historical scholarship and
formalist criticism (or the New Criticism, as it is
known in America). Basically the New Historicism, as Greenblatt enunciates it, "challenges the
assumptions that guarantee a secure distinction
between 'literary foreground' and 'political
background,' or more generally between artistic
production   and   other   kinds   of   social
production."

Greenblatt was raised in Newton, Massachusetts, a suburb of Boston, in what he described
as a "passionately Jewish household." However,
he told Adam Begeley, who interviewed him for
the *New York Times Magazine*, that the Judaism
of his parents—Harry J. and Mollie (Brown)
Greenblatt—"wasn't authentic because it wasn't
theological." In the course of his academic career he has lectured in Israel, and in a personal
note in his book *Marvelous Possessions* he professes still to feel "in the midst of deep moral and
political reservations, a complex bond" towards
the strong Zionism imbued in him by his parents.

He spent two years at Pembroke College,
Cambridge on a Fulbright Scholarship. He
earned a second B.A. in 1966, then returned to
Yale, where he received a Ph.D. in English in
1969. His doctoral dissertation on Sir Walter Ralegh was awarded the John Addison Porter
Prize.

Greenblatt's first major book, *Sir Walter Ralegh: The Renaissance Man and His Roles*, an adaptation of his doctoral dissertation, anticipates
in its fusion of literature, history, and politics the
path he was to follow as a cultural critic. In Ralegh's career, according to Greenblatt, "the
boundaries between art and life completely
break down"; writing for this adventurer-
courtier-man of letters was a form of "surrogate
action," the role-playing central to his life
"ranging from a deliberate and prearranged performance to an all but unconscious fashioning of
the self."

This concept is expanded in *Renaissance Self-
Fashioning: From More To Shakespeare*, in

which Greenblatt contends that the sixteenth century was a period of "increased self-consciousness about the fashioning of human identity as a manipulable, artful process." He suggests that all six writers considered in this book—the poets Edmund Spenser and Sir Thomas Wyatt, the dramatists Christopher Marlowe and William Shakespeare, the theologian William Wyatt, and Sir Thomas More—felt the necessity to remake themselves, for they were all "displaced in significant ways from a stable, inherited social world." Greenblatt argues that role-playing and theatrical metaphor came naturally to Renaissance figures conditioned to institutions that partook of staged performance—the church with its rituals and ceremonies and the court with its pageants and processions. *Renaissance Self-Fashioning* received the British Council Prize in 1982 for the best book in British Studies by a North American Scholar.

At the University of California at Berkeley, where he arrived in 1969 to begin his teaching career, Greenblatt became the leader of a lively group of humanists who included the art historian Svetlana Alpers, the cultural historian Thomas Laquer, and the scholar of French literature Dennis Hollier. To provide a forum for the contextual scholarship promulgated by this circle he launched in 1983 the journal *Representations* (he had nicknamed his colleagues "The Reps"). The contents of *Representing the English Renaissance*, a collection of essays culled from the journal, and edited and introduced by Greenblatt, range through Elizabethan and Jacobean poetry, theater, art, religion, politics, and mapmaking. Greenblatt's own contribution, "Murdering Peasants: Status, Genre, and the Representation of Rebellion," examines the effect of "social constraints" on the various depictions of lower-class political protest in monuments by Dürer, Sidney's *Arcadia*, Spenser's *The Faerie Queene*, and Shakespeare's *Henry VI: Part II*. Basic to all these essays is the assumption that the "aesthetic realm" is not "autonomous," as Greenblatt puts it, but interconnected with the entire culture of which it is a part.

Accordingly, Greenblatt's two books that followed the inauguration of his journal develop its central thesis that during the Renaissance, literary and artistic representation appropriated and transformed the language, sign systems, and gestural vocabularies of the court, the church, and the marketplace. In *Shakespearean Negotiations: The Circulation of Social Energy in Renaissance England* (published as part of the University of California series The New Historicism: Studies in Cultural Poetics), Greenblatt sets out to examine "how collective belief's and

enterprises were shaped, moved from one medium to another, concentrated in manageable aesthetic form, offered for consumption." Shakespeare's history plays, for example, confirm Machiavelli's hypothesis that the success of a monarch lies in winning the concent of the governed to power that originated in force. In the recurrent disguise motifs of the comedies, Greenblatt detects the subliminal influence of popular treatises on transvestitism and hermaphrodites. *King Lear* (particularly Edgar's feigned madness) is related to *A Declaration of Popish Impostures*, a contemporaneous exposé of demonology and exorcism that Shakespeare is assumed to have read. The disguised duke in *Measure for Measure* "fuses the strategies of statecraft and religion," and can be taken at the same time as a surrogate for the playwright; *The Tempest* appropriates "the powerful social energy of princely paradoxes." *Shakespearean Negotiations* received the 1988 James Russell Lowell Prize awarded by the modern Language Association of America.

In 1988 Greenblatt delivered the Clarendon lectures at Oxford, followed by the Carpenter Lectures at the University of Chicago, which grew into *Marvelous Possessions: The Wonder of the New World*, his most ambitious book in scope, and his most widely read one. Published the year before the quincentenary of Columbus's first voyage, *Marvelous Possessions*, according to its introduction, is a probing of "the representational practices that the Europeans carried with them to America and deployed when they tried to describe to their fellow countrymen what they saw and did, "devices to which Greenblatt attaches the shorthand label "mimetic capital." The main figures he studies are the pilgrim-adventurer Mandeville, the seamen-explorers Columbus and Frobisher, and the conquistador Cortés. The language ("symbolic technology") of the various records left behind by these and other invaders of the New World all reflect for Greenblatt a conflict on the part of Europeans between erasing and preserving differences between themselves and the alien peoples they encountered—they saw them, that is, as both "others" and "brothers."

Simon praised *Marvelous Possessions* in the *New Republic*, (1992) as "by far the most intellectually gripping and penetrating discussion of the relationship between intruders and natives . . . Nothing else in the entire literature of the Columbus quincentennial approaches his vivid engagement with the crucial issues of cross-cultural perceptions." On the other hand, Roberto González Echevarria, (writing in the *New York Times Book Review*), thought that what begins as a systematic study of acculturation "eventually disintegrates into a scattershot commentary on the atrocities visited on the natives, and how these were rationalized." Anthony Pagden, in the *Times Literary Supplement* (1991), found the book "compelling" and "powerful," but pointed out Greenblatt's lack of strict attention to chronology, ethnocentrism (e.g., implying that Europeans alone were guilty of acquisitiveness), and occasional anachronism—reading Montaigne, for example, through twentieth-century rather than contemporaneous eyes.

Generally the response to Greenblatt's publications, and to the school of criticism associated with him, has been ambivalent. E. Pearlman, reviewing *Renaissance Self-Fashioning* in *Library Journal* (1988), for example, was impressed with its "high intelligence, considerable learning, and acute sensitivity," but concluded that "readers may occasionally find themselves less enlightened than dazzled by the author's ingenuity." Of *Shakespearean Negotiations*, Frank Kermode remarked in the *New Republic* (1988): "Despite the charm of the peripheral detail, I couldn't help feeling that there was a weakening of interest when the plays themselves were addressed. There is a great quantity of sexological or political sack, but only a pennyworth of interpretative bread." The claims of the New Historicism itself to originality have been contested. E. Pearlman has described their methodology as "an eclectic blend of annals, history, and anthropology." Their rhetorical approach to the study of literary texts has long been utilized by social scientists in content analysis propaganda, and their techniques of exegesis are standard procedures of classical and biblical scholars. Greenblatt has acknowledged such influences as the Renaissance historian Jakob Burkhardt on his idea of *self-fashioning*," of the French social theorist Michel Foucault on what he calls in *Shakespearean Negotiations* "the circulation of social energy," and of the linguistic theories of the Bulgarian semiotician Tzvetan Todorov's *The Conquest of America* on *Marvelous Possessions*.

During the 1980s, according to Adam Begely in his *New York Times Magazine* article ("The Tempest Around Stephen Greenblatt"), the New Historicism, once sparked, "spread like a California brush fire from Renaissance studies to American studies, from English departments to history departments, from art history to film studies." Its impact has been felt in the proliferation of programs at universities bearing the umbrella label of cultural studies—though the tern Greenblatt prefers for his approach is "cultural poetics," a borrowing from Todorov. However, it has not met with universal approval among

critics. Camille Paglia, the most extreme denigrator, has dismissed the New Historicism as a scholastic equivalent of junk bonds. More restrained skeptics have questioned the tendency to overpoliticize literature, reducing it to a verbal battleground of ideologies, to scant the original genius of the author, or to collapse qualitative distinctions between "high" and popular art. A fundamental concern has been raised by Frederick Crews, a colleague of Greenblatt's at Berkeley, and one of his staunchest admirers, who has pointed out, "To do it [the New Historicism] well, you have to be very good." Clearly, here is a field where little learning is a dangerous thing, a caution that has not deterred all-too-many neophytes from rushing in, reviewers have complained. As Edward Pechter, a Canadian professor of English, has summed up the situation: "Between Greenblatt bashing and Greenblatt cloning, we are dealing with a magnitude of critical power it would be hard to exaggerate."

The wide dissemination of the New Historicism undoubtedly owes much to Greenblatt's charisma as a teacher, to which many have attested. His fame has spread abroad through visiting professorships at Oxford, the University of Bologna, the University of Florence, the University of Trieste, and the Ecole des Hautes Etudes in Paris. In America he splits the academic year between the University of California at Berkeley, where he holds the Class of 1932 Chair, and Harvard, which long sought to lure him away full time. He is a Fellow of the American Academy of Arts and Sciences. The publishing firm of W. W. Norton has appointed him general editor of its Shakespeare series.

In *Learning to Curse*, a collection of essays on modern culture published between *Shakespearean Negotiations* and *Marvelous Possessions*, Greenblatt affirms that even if it means disturbing received opinion and knocking down the classics from their pedestals, "I am committed to the project of making strange what has become familiar."

PRINCIPAL WORKS: Three Modern Satirists: Waugh, Orwell, and Huxley, 1965; Sir Walter Ralegh: The Renaissance Man and His Roles, 1973; Renaissance Self-Fashioning: From More to Shakespeare, 1980; Shakespearean Negotiations: The Circulation of Social Energy in Renaissance England, 1988; Learning to Curse: Essays in Early Modern Culture, 1990; Marvelous Possessions: The Wonder of the New World, 1991. *As editor*—Allegory and Representation: Selected Papers from the English Institute, 1979–80, 1981; The Power of Forms in the English Renaissance, 1982; Representing the English Renaissance, 1988; (with G. Gunn) Redrawing the Boundaries: The Transformation of English and American Studies, 1992.

ABOUT: Contemporary Authors 49–52, 1975; Montrose, L. "New Historicism" in Redrawing the Boundaries, 1992; Who's Who in America, 1994. *Periodicals*—Choice May 1981; May 1988; History Today May 1992; Library Journal March 15, 1981; April 15, 1988; London Review of Books December 5, 1992; Nation October 19, 1992; New Republic February 29, 1988; January 6–13, 1992; New York Review if Books March 31, 1988; New York Times Book Review February 16, 1992; New York Times Magazine March 28, 1993; Times Literary Supplement September 4, 1981; December 13, 1991; (Village) Voice Literary Supplement December 1991.

GREER, GERMAINE (January 29, 1939–), Australian feminist writer, educator, art historian, and literary critic, was born into a conservative middle-class family that lived near Melbourne. Her father, Eric Reginald Greer, was away in the military for the first six years of her life. Her mother, Margaret May Mary (Lanfrancan) Greer claimed to have given birth to her on a cattle station during a bushfire. After her father's return from the service, a brother and a sister were born. Her father, the advertising manager of a newspaper, was still away from home much of the time, however. In *The Female Eunuch*, she referred to hers as an "unbroken home which ought to have been broken." In *Daddy, We Hardly Knew You*, written after her father's death, Greer attempted to make peace with the man, who, she had learned, suffered from anxiety neurosis incurred in the military. Greer told Andrea Chambers in an interview in *People*: "Our house had no books, no paintings, no culture." She attempted to run away at the age of seventeen and did so successfully the following year.

Greer began her education at Star of the Sea Convent, near Melbourne, and then won government scholarships to the University of Melbourne, where she received an honors B.A. in English and French literature in 1959. At Melbourne she was active in theater groups, wrote drama criticism, and served on the aboriginal scholarship committee. She earned a first class honors M.A. in 1961 at the University of Sydney, becoming a senior tutor. She did odd jobs and taught at a working-class girls' school until 1964, when she won a Commonwealth Scholarship to Newnham College, Cambridge. She received a Ph.D. degree in 1967.

In 1968 Greer married Paul de Feu, but they separated after a few weeks. They were divorced in 1973, and he later married Maya Angelou. Until 1973 Greer was a lecturer in Elizabethan and Jacobean drama at the University of Warwick in Coventry, ninety miles north

GERMAINE GREER

of London. During this time she became a self-confessed "groupie" of counterculture popular music, appeared in dramatic productions and television discussions, and wrote articles for the *Listener*, the *Spectator*, and underground journals. She also helped found a pornographic publication, *Suck*, with other Australians in England. She wrote a column for the *London Sunday Times* from 1971 to 1973 and has written gardening articles for *Private Eye* under the pseudonym "Rose Blight."

Greer became a widely recognized celebrity upon publication of *The Female Eunuch* in 1971, which Janet Todd called a "classic text of the later twentieth-century feminist movement" and an "outrageous and supremely readable critique of the role of women in western society." The carefully researched and documented book became a best-seller in Britain and the United States and was translated into many languages. In it, Greer presented housewives as passive creatures untouched by the women's movement and needing to slough off their "timidity, plumpness, languor, delicacy, and preciosity." They should learn that the word "feminine" need not mean "without libido." In *The Female Eunuch*, Greer argues that women are encouraged from childhood to stand for the "Eternal Feminine," which disgusts her:

I'm sick of pretending eternal youth. I'm sick of belying my own intelligence, my own will, my own sex. . . . I'm sick of pretending that some fatuous male's self-important pronouncements are the object of my undivided attention. . . . I refuse to be a female impersonator. I am a woman, not a castrate.

Greer also attacked the myth of machismo, which she believes turns men into competitive and aggressive opposites of "feminine" women, and thus creates a polarity that distorts our ideas about love, resulting in a mutual dependency and making marriage "a pernicious institution" wherein women fear abandonment and "bind their children to themselves by self-sacrifice intended to induce feelings of guilt." True love, Greer said, is only possible between true equals secure in their own self-love. Although she rejects the ideal of the nuclear family, preferring extended or communal groupings, she does not see a solution in the hatred of men expressed by some radical women's groups. *Newsweek* pronounced *The Female Eunuch* the "most realistic and least anti-male" manifesto of the women's movement. Greer has never concealed her preferences for male sex partners, and she places blame for inequities on women, on capitalism, and on history. The revolution she called for in *The Female Eunuch* was a radical change of spirit in women.

A coast-to-coast American promotion tour in the spring of 1971 resulted in magazine covers, television and radio appearances, and Town Hall debate against self-declared male chauvinist Norman Mailer. Greer shocked audiences at the National Press Club and elsewhere by charging pharmaceutical companies with selling deodorant products to women by persuading them that their body odors were naturally offensive.

Her second book, *The Obstacle Race*, asks why no women artists from the Middle Ages to the 19th century reached the stature of their male counterparts. Because Greer found that internal psychological factors and not social pressure explained the absence of great female artists, some critics charged that she was abandoning feminism. Janet Todd defended Greer, finding this accusation merely "an unfortunate symptom of the media-created 'decline of feminism' in the 1980's." It was a charge that was to stick in the United States, however, especially given her next outspoken book, *Sex and Destiny*, in which Greer argues that Western efforts to limit population in less developed countries are racist. Greer had by this time failed to bear a child of her own, and her argument proclaims the value of having children, as opposed to having sex. In the *Nation* Linda Gordon said that Greer's case was strong but "antifeminist and condescending toward people who aspire to greater wealth and more independence." Judith Levine, in the *Village Voice*, feared that Greer wished women once again to be "barefoot and pregnant." American feminists saw *Sex and Destiny* as a turnabout from *The Female Eunuch*, which had proclaimed their right to enjoy sexual activity without the obligation to have children. But feminists outside of the United States were more accepting of Greer's seemingly modified stand. Greer remarked to Gillian MacKay of *Maclean's*: "People are saying I am against sex. I am not."

The Madwoman's Underclothes, a collection of journalistic short pieces on such diverse topics as rock music, advertising, Norman Mailer, abortion, legalization of marijuana, and the problems of nations such as Ethiopia and Cuba, was bound to provoke reviewers who had originally referred to Greer with the meliorative term "saucy." In the *New Statesman* Sara Maitland referred to the collection as "libertarian individualism running amok and ending up . . . in a manic individualism which is frequently charming, occasionally brilliant and fundamentally arrogant and patronizing."

Daddy, We Hardly Knew You was the result of Greer's two-year search for her father's character and identity. Christine M. Hill praised it in the *London Reveiw of Books* as "a risky, flamboyant, long-sustained star performance, complete with pratfalls, and buffoonery, self-mockery and self-mockery and self-castigation."

The Change, a study of the menopause that downplayed the importance of sexual activity, was characterized by Rosemary Dinnage in the *Times Literary Supplement* as a "mix of argument, medical history, literary interpretation, information, anthropological pickings, and personal philosophy—never boring, invigoratingly wrong-headed." In the *New York Times Book Review*, Natalie Angier noted that the material was "haphazardly presented," but called *The Change* a "brilliant, gutsy, exhilarating, bruising, exasperating fury of a book, broadly researched, boundlessly insightful." Angier praised in particular the "glorious" final chapter, "Serenity and Power," in which Greer suggests that "only when a woman ceases the fretful struggle to *be* beautiful can she turn her gaze outward, find the beautiful and feed upon it."

Among Greer's critical studies, *Shakespeare* brought little acclaim because it was a mere introduction (in the Oxford Past Masters series). Her most praised academic work was a book she coedited: *Kissing the Rod*, an anthology of annotated poems and biographical material on fifty (mostly unknown) 17th-century women poets, derived from research in archival and manuscript sources. The *Times Literary Supplement* praised it for the "absence of the kind of ideological exaggerations that frequently mar the efforts of feminist campaigners in the field of literary history."

Greer traveled widely and did free-lance journalism in the early 1970s. She taught poetry from 1979 to 1982 at the University of Tulsa, where she founded and directed the Tulsa Oklahoma Center for the Study of Women's Literature. She has projected an edition of the works of the 17th-century playwright Aphra Behn. In 1994 she hosted a late- night talk show for the BBC.

Greer is an accomplished cook and gardener and has homes in England and in Tuscany, Italy. She has been criticized for her refusal to espouse current literary and feminist ideas, but she remains a self-avowed anarchist and atheist and an unorthodox independent thinker.

PRINCIPAL WORKS: The Female Eunuch, 1971; The Obstacle Race: The Fortunes of Women Painters and Their Work, 1979; Sex and Destiny: The Politics of Human Fertility, 1984; Shakespeare, 1986; The Madwoman's Underclothes: Essays and Occasional Writings, 1987; Daddy, We Hardly Knew You, 1989; The Change: Women, Ageing and the Menopause, 1991. As editor—(with J. Medoff, M. Sansome, and S. Hastings) Kissing the Rod: An Anthology of Seventeenth-Century Women's Verse, 1989.

ABOUT: Contemporary Authors New Revision Series 33, 1991; Current Biography Yearbook 1988; Ryan, B. (ed.) Major Twentieth-Century Writers, 1991; Todd, J. (ed.) British Women Writers: A Critical Reference Guide, 1989; Who's Who, 1988. Periodicals—London Review Books April 20, 1989; Maclean's April 15, 1984; Nation May 26, 1984; New Statesman November 21, 1986; New York Times Book Review October 11, 1992; Newsweek March 22, 1971; People December 17, 1979; Times Literary Supplement June 17, 1988, October 25, 1991; Village Voice, May 15, 1984.

GRIMES, MARTHA, American mystery writer, was born in Pittsburgh, Pennsylvania, the daughter of D. W. Grimes, a city solicitor, and June (Dunnington) Grimes, a hotel owner, and grew up in Garrett County, western Maryland. She took her B.A. and M.A. degrees at the University of Maryland and then taught English at the University of Iowa, Iowa City; Frostburg State College, Maryland; and Montgomery College, Takoma Park, Maryland.

In 1981, Grimes published her first mystery novel. "I was sitting in a Hot Shoppe in Bethesda, looking at a book about English pub names, and I came across 'The Man with a Load of Mischief,'" she said in the Washington Post. "Suddenly I knew that's what I wanted to do: write books set in English pubs . . . Now, unless I have the pub name first, I can't write the book." Grimes clearly understands the importance of the pub in the social fabric of rural life. "The English inn stands permanently at the con-

MARTHA GRIMES

fluence of the roads of history, memory and romance," she writes in her first novel.

Her traditional English setting in place, Grimes chose a classic English mystery protagonist to anchor her series: a Scotland Yard detective, Inspector Richard Jury. He is quiet, clever, and cultured. "I wanted him to be a man who really liked women—I mean, *liked them as people*," she told Susan Clark in the Armchair Detective in 1988. "He was to be the very opposite of a chauvinist." Jury is assisted in his cases by a colorful supporting cast. Immediately at hand is the nose-blowing, hypochondriacal Sergeant Wiggins—"likable enough, and efficient, but always on the verge of keeling over," she describes him in The Man with a Load of Mischief. Jury's unofficial assistant is the urbane, intelligent—he can master the Times crossword puzzle in fifteen minutes—Melrose Plant, who has renounced his title of earl, and who holds a university chair in French romantic poetry. If Jury bears a resemblance to P. D. James's Adam Dalgliesh and Ngaio Marsh's Roderick Alleyn, Plant is cousin to Dorothy Sayers' Lord Peter Wimsey and Margery Allingham's Albert Campion. "While the poetically romantic Jury is forever plucking burrlike women off his ankles," Marilyn Stasio wrote in the New York Times Book Review in 1991, "the dapper Mr. Plant, who seems to spring from more tensile literary stock . . . moves more comfortably among the idiosyncratic characters that are . . . Grimes's most beguiling contribution to the genre."

"Grimes's books are powerful comedies of non-manners, of the assumed gaps between the blue-blooded and the red-blooded people, and tell how both types flow through the same channels in rural England," Ray B. Browne wrote in the *Armchair Detective* in 1985. "Her people are delineated in Hogarthian outlines, vitalized by Dickensian gusto, but characterized by a detached humor and understanding that make them distinctly Grimesian." Despite her humorous bent, however, Grimes's children, as well as her animals, often fall victim to murder or psychological damage. Nevertheless, Grimes insists that they are portrayed as intelligent and resourceful characters—more so than many of her adults.

The Man with a Load of Mischief opened the Jury series in 1981. The setting is the village of Long Piddleton, where two separate murders have occurred at two pubs. One victim has been found with his head in a keg of ale and the other hanging on the signpost of the Jack and Hammer—unusual murders are another Grimes trademark. Since the killings took place during the Christmas revelries of Long Pidd's most prominent citizens, Jury and Plant have all the local gentry on the suspect list. It soon becomes apparent that the quiet village harbors many secrets. More murders follow before Jury finally confronts the murderer in a darkened church.

Carpenter described Grimes's novels as being "essentially contrapuntal. . . . The murders are grisly, bizarre, the investigation plodding with immumerable interviews and speculations, the comedy light and sparkling, or amusingly outrageous. She works these elements back and forth, gradually weaving them all together."

In *The Old Silent*, the reader knows something unusual is coming when Grimes acknowledges a host of musicians from Miles Davis to Jimi Hendrix, "and Melrose Plant *especially* wants to thank Lou Reed." While on a rest and recreation leave in West Yorkshire, Jury witnesses a woman kill her husband. After learning that the woman's son, a musical prodigy, was presumed dead after a kidnapping years before, Jury wonders if the two crimes are related. Carpenter points out that "throughout the story there are phrases from popular songs, and the movement of the novel resembles that of jazz, with shifts of perspective, more 'riffs.' The plot is as complex as ever, and the problem of identity crucial as it often is, but the music motif makes this novel unique among her works."

Comparisons between Grimes and the Christie/Sayers/Allingham tradition of mystery writing are inevitable. Despite her obvious affection for that Golden Age and her skill at evoking the proper English settings and characters, Grimes has created her own niche. Ray B. Browne describes her as a "writer who mixes her love for the tradition with a healthy touch of the 'mean street' philosophy of Raymond Chandler; she mixes her Agatha Christie with warm suds from the pubs."

An odd addition to the Grimes mystery canon is *Send Bygraves.* It is a story of murder, told in free verse.

After eleven Jury mysteries, Grimes set *The End of the Pier* in a small American town, where the Rainbow Cafe is the main hangout. The chief characters are Maud Chadwick, a moody and depressed waitress at the cafe, and Sheriff Sam DeGheyn, a married man who is attracted to her. Four local women have been murdered in three years and Sam believes the wrong man has been imprisoned, leaving the real killer at large. Michiko Kakutani, in the *New York Times*, praised Grimes's deft handling of the suspense part of the novel, but pointed out that it "aspires to be more than a simple murder mystery, and considerable energy is expended on delineating the characters' inner lives and psychological drives." For Kakutani, the author is overly obsessed with the relationships between parents and children. "In the end, Ms. Grimes's insistence on hammering home this theme pulls the novel down," she concludes.

The Horse You Came In On includes a newly unearthed Edgar Allan Poe story that may not be a fake; a triple murder; and an author, a friend of Melrose Plant's, who feels she is a victim of a plagiarist. The novel has been considered a thinly veiled attack on Elizabeth George, another American mystery writer whose stories have English settings. No serious charges of plagiarism have been raised, however, according to Sarah Lyall, in the *New York Times*.

Martha Grimes lives in Washington, D.C., and is the divorced mother of a son, Kent Van Holland, who works in publishing.

PRINCIPAL WORKS: *Novels*—The Man with a Load of Mischief, 1981; The Old Fox Deceiv's, 1982; The Anodyne Necklace, 1983; The Dirty Duck, 1984; Jerusalem Inn, 1984, The Deer Leap, 1985; Help the Poor Struggler, 1985; I Am the Only Running Footman, 1986; The Five Bells and Bladebone, 1987; The Old Silent, 1989; The Old Contemptibles, 1991; The End of the Pier, 1992; The Horse You Came in On, 1993; Rainbow's End, 1995. *Verse*—Send Bygraves, 1989.

ABOUT: Contemporary Authors 117, 1986; Pronzini, B. and Muller, M. 1001 Midnights: The Aficionado's Guide to Mystery and Detective Fiction, 1986; Twentieth-Century Crime and Mystery Writers, 1991. *Periodicals*—Armchair Detective Summer 1985; Spring 1988; Bestsellers 1, 1990; New York Times July 14, 1993; New York Times Book Review January 27, 1991; April 10, 1992; Publishers Weekly June 23, 1989; Washington Post October 3, 1983.

GROSSMAN, DAVID (1954–), Israeli novelist, journalist, and children's storywriter, was born in Jerusalem, to Yizchak Grossman, a native of Austria who taught David to love Yiddish literature, and his wife Michaela, a Jerusalemite. Thanks to his knowledge of Yiddish literature, Grossman became, at the age of nine, a youth reporter on the radio. After his military service, he continued his radio work in the news department and studied initially law and then philosophy at Hebrew University. In 1988, Grossman resigned his radio post to protest against censorship of Palestinian issues. "I refuse," wrote Grossman in his letter of resignation, "to collaborate in laundering the reality as it is imposed on me . . . this would be an act of irresponsibility toward the public that we are obligated to serve."

Grossman is well known for his liberal political views. He has always promoted the end of occupation of the territories conquered in the 1967 Six Day War and recognition of the Palestinian national entity. Three of Grossman's works deal directly with Israel's predicament as an occupying nation: the novel *Hiyukh Ha-Gedi* (1982, *The Smile of the Lamb*) and two nonfiction books, *Ha-Zeman Ha-Tzahov* (1986, *The Yellow Wind*) and *Nokhemim Nifkadim* (1992, *Sleeping on a Wire: Conversations With Palestinians in Israel*).

Smile of the Lamb is about a loss of innocence, the end of trust in invincible moral values. Uri, a young idealistic Israeli, lets himself be persuaded by Katzman, an army commander, to serve in the administration of the West Bank to help defend the rights of the Arabs. Katzman, a survivor of the Holocaust, does not believe in the value of justice, as demonstrated by his own violence toward the Arabs. A murderous conflict between Katzman and Khilmi, a half-mad old Arab whom Uri has befriended, and Uri's discovery that his wife is involved with Katzman, destroy his hope. Innocence withers in the face of brutality and deceit. *The Smile of the Lamb* was made into a film which received an award at the Berlin Film Festival in 1990.

The theme of the corrupting influence of occupation on both the occupier and the occupied reemerges in *The Yellow Wind*. Grossman describes his meetings with both Jews and Palestinians in the West Bank. He interviews refugees in camps, Israeli soldiers on the bridges, Palestinian students and nursery teachers, and Jewish settlers. He shows the powerlessness, destitution, and frustration of the Palestinians as well as the unfairness of the sentences meted out by the Israeli military court in the territories. Grossman argues passionately that occupation cannot be just or moral, that it causes ethical disintegration

DAVID GROSSMAN

and erosion of human rights on both sides. Grossman's warning against Israel's denial of the Palestinian problem presaged the intifada of the early 1990s. *The Yellow Wind* was adapted into a play and staged in Tzavta, the best-known experimental theater in Tel Aviv. The play was well attended and well received. Translated into Arabic, the book was enthusiastically received by the Israeli Arab community.

Grossman's heartfelt engagement with the Israeli-Arab issue resurfaces in *Sleeping on a Wire*. In the *New York Times Book Review* (1993) Robin Wright compared this book to John Howard Griffin's *Black Like Me*, the 1961 report of a white man who changed his color to experience personally the plight of the African-Americans. Grossman's book focuses on the Israeli Arab population. In a mode similar to that of *The Yellow Wind*, the author punctuates the transcripts of his interviews with his own commentaries on the plight of Israel's Arab citizens. As he sees it, this Arab community is doubly marginalized. These are second-rate citizens, deprived of many of the privileges enjoyed by their kin in the occupied territories, who see them as opportunists who have betrayed the Palestinian cause. "Who are they, really?" asks the author. "Arabs? Israeli Arabs? Palestinians? Torn between contradictory identities . . . they are trapped in an impossible situation." Writing in *Library Journal*, James Rhodes commented, "Grossman . . . shows how these people have learned the difficult tasks of not only walking the tightrope, but also of 'sleeping on the wire in midstep.'" Grossman sees his country endangering its own existence by "creating an enemy it will run against after its other enemies have made their peace with it."

Polemical writing represents only one aspect of Grossman's literary output. His career as a fiction writer began with short stories. One of his first stories, "Yani on the Mountain," was awarded the Neuman Prize in 1978, and in 1980 his story "Donkeys" was awarded the Harry Hirshon Prize by the Hebrew University. *Ratz* (The jogger), a collection of Grossman's short stories, was published in 1983. The book was critically appraised as coming from a promising voice in Israeli literature. According to Dov Vardi in *World Literature Today,* "The vitality of talent and the quality of [Grossman's] writing seems to equal and even surpass his predecessors'." Grossman's psychological insights, especially in the title story, demonstrate the author's understanding of the world of childhood, especially in the context of difficult intergenerational relationships.

Grossman continued to explore the complexities of parent-child relationships in *Ayien Erekh: Àhava'* 1986, *See Under: Love,* which was compared by Edmund White in the *New York Times Book Review* to "the small but awesome canon" of "a few nearly mythic books, such as Faulkner's *The Sound and the Fury,* Gunter Grass's *The Tin Drum,* Gabriel García Márquez's *One Hundred Years of Solitude* [in which] large visions of history get told in innovative ways." The novel was translated into English, German, Italian, French, Swedish, and Norwegian.

See Under: Love is an imaginatively represented story of a child of Holocaust survivors who tries to come to terms with the parental experience of the Holocaust. The various attempts to penetrate the unfathomable world of horror are represented in four sections. In the first, Momik—a nine-year-old boy growing up in Jerusalem—tries to devise ways to defeat the "Nazi Beast" that destroyed the lives of his strange parents and of his senile great-uncle, Wasserman, a famous writer of children's stories before the war. In the second section, Momik, now a married man and a father, goes to Warsaw in search of the Polish-Jewish writer Bruno Schulz, who was shot by the Nazis. Momik imagines that Shulz escaped the Nazis by jumping into the sea transforming himself into a salmon. The third section reconstructs Wasserman's life in a concentration camp. Though he wishes to die, Wasserman is coerced into telling stories to the concentration camp commander who, as a boy, used to admire Wasserman's writing. The fourth section is entitled "The Complete Encyclopedia of Kazik's Life." Kazik is the hero of one of Wasserman's stories. The encyclopedia is a glossary whose entries are intended to draw together all the previously told and the so far untold stories that pertain to the Holocaust.

In response to the camp commander's declaration "I like simple stories," Wasserman says, "There are no simple stories anymore." Denis Donoghue, in the *New York Review of Books,* commented: "One of the many remarkable features of the novel is Grossman's control of the multiplicity of styles and emotional tones his several stories require, from the demotic to the sublime. Some of the episodes . . . show a rich and uncruel comedy in an otherwise appalling dance of death. . . . On every questionable occasion his sense of the issue involved is exact; his moral taste seems impeccable." Madeline Marget, in her *Commonwealth* review, agreed that Grossman "is a difficult writer, and yet he does not spare us the weight of his oppressive subject . . . [yet] he transcends the horror of his story with the evidence of . . . human potential and its realization." In the *Times Literary Supplement,* however, S. S. Prawer criticized Grossman for the novel's final section: "A sequence in which a Jewish captive is depicted as soliciting ghastly tortures from an SS interrogator in order to find his own essential self will seem to man . . . not only psychologically unconvincing but also lacking in the taste and tact needed for so sensitive a subject."

Grossman himself is aware of the difficulty in treating the subject of the Holocaust. In a 1987 interview with *Ha-Aretz,* he admitted that only when the book was completed did he grasp his inadequacy to confront the issue and said that he hoped to return to the Holocaust theme. Meanwhile, Grossman published another novel, *Sefer Ha-Dikduk Ha-P'nimi* (1991, *The Book of Intimate Grammar*), in which he continued to explore the complexity of parent-child relationships in modern Israel. Aaron, the young, sensitive protagonist becomes the victim of the oppressive atmosphere of his home. Aaron's stunted growth is a symbolic response to the cruelty of the parental generation. The mediocrity of Israel's society in the 1950s and 1960s is represented by Aaron's materialistic, mundane parents—a domineering mother and a vulgar, brutish father. The novel, which ends on the eve of the Six Day War in 1967, culminates with Aaron's disappearance and possible suicide.

Alfred Kazin, reviewing the novel in the *New York Review of Books,* found the conclusion in which Aaron is about to enter an abandoned refrigerator an "extraordinary denouement, ambiguous and frightening. Will the boy deliberately or accidentally commit suicide?" Kazin found a difficulty in that "since everything is now imaginary"—the friends and family watching his Houdini escape—"shouldn't Aaron also want to revenge himself on them by killing himself—not altogether voluntarily—right in front of their eyes?" Kazin, however, took a laudatory tone toward all of Grossman's writings: "There is an obvious connection between the stark, dramatic reportorial style of *The Yellow Wind* and the virtuosity demonstrated in *The Book of Intimate Grammar*. . . . Grossman is as stimulating artistically as he is brave in reporting the true relations between the occupied and the occupiers, between the Jewish family and those, like Aaron Kleinfeld, who, against their will, fall out of it."

Grossman's pessimistic view of the process of maturation and socialization has not prevented him from becoming a successful writer for children. His first children's book, *Du-K'rav* (Duel, 1982), focuses on a friendship between a twelve-year-old boy and a young-in-spirit seventy-year-old man. It was praised in *Ha-Aretz* (1984) as "vibrant, suspenseful and full of good humour." The story was adapted into a play. *Gan Riki* (Riki's Kindergarten, 1988), is a play set in a nursery school. Despite its all-child cast, the play is actually an astute investigation (and indictment) of Israeli society. It was staged in the Habima, a major Israeli theater, in 1989.

Grossman is also the author of a series for children about the boy Itamar. A play based on the first story, "Itamar M'tayiel al Ha-Kirot" (Itimar Is Climbing the Wall) was staged in a children's theater.

In 1988, Grossman received the Har Zion Prize in recognition of his efforts to enhance understanding between Arabs and Jews and his contributions to peace. In 1991, he was awarded the prestigious Nelly Sachs Prize for his literary oeuvre. Grossman lives in Jerusalem with his wife and two children.

PRINCIPAL WORKS IN ENGLISH TRANSLATION: *Novels*—(tr. B. Rosenberg) See Under: Love, 1989; (tr. B. Rosenberg) The Smile of the Lamb, 1991; (tr. B. Rosenberg) The Book of Intimate Grammar, 1994. *Nonfiction*—(tr. H. Watzman) The Yellow Wind, 1988; (tr. H. Watzman) Sleeping on a Wire: Conversations with Palestinians in Israel, 1993.

ABOUT: Blackwell Companion to Jewish Culture, 1989; Ramras-Rauch, G. The Arab in Israeli Literature, 1989; Sokoloff, N. Imagining the Child in Modern Jewish Fiction. *Periodicals*—Commentary June 1988; July 1989; Commonwealth September 8, 1989; Ha-Aretz November 30, 1984; April 9, 1987; November 11, 1988; New York Review of Books December 22, 1994; New York Times Book Review April 16, 1989; September 28, 1989; March 7, 1993; Times Literary Supplement January 26, 1990; September 2, 1994; World Literature Today Summer 1984; Spring 1992.

GURGANUS, ALLAN (June 11, 1947–), American novelist and writer of short stories writes: "My work acknowledges the difficulty of the average day (there is no average day) of the typical human life (is yours typical?). My sense of humor and co-dependency on the lilt and sway and lavish compensations of language itself, these help get my characters through; these get me by, with glee. I don't think any writer with a single authorial third-person voice, detached and impartial as a weather satellite (and about that emotional) has much to tell me. Sometime just before the Holocaust, sometimes just prior to our perfecting of the Nuclear Bomb, the possibility of assuming God's eye-view of our struggle stopped being aesthetically enlivening or ethically possible. (Many of us believe that, at this time, or certainly by late November 1963, God took early retirement, to Boca Raton). What is left? Witnesses witnessing. Workers speaking toward truth out of the factuality of shoptalk. History's victims blowing the whistle on History. The world now: a choir of soloists.

"I have faith in people's ability to tell their own truth eloquently. Un-grammar is often no impediment to eloquence. It can become the very source of originality, perspective, purity, innocence. The operative verb in the title of my first novel remains 'Tell.' That is a direct order and our only hope. What scares me in the political cruelty of Bush-Reagan reality: how few people really feel free to say what they're thinking and, therefore, how few people now know what they think. Sexual candor has ceased, without quite being missed. Truth-telling is considered whining. By preventing TV cameras from showing soldiers' coffins returning from the ill-advised Persian Gulf War, our president intended to prevent people from believing in these deaths. What's scariest, he did just that.

"We have carved out our consciences and installed, in that sanctified hollow, media centers. Our gift for listening has been consumed by our need to consume. The survivors, the troublemakers, the cut ups, the bad kids, the outsiders, the secret sharers, the investigated, the unaffiliated—these are my people. These are the witnesses I listen to, and by seeming to speak for them, by speaking *as* them. Along with the demise of fresh water you can drink without filtering or boiling or dying quick, with the end of fresh air one can breathe without carcinogenic threat, along with the end of going out for a walk

ALLAN GURGANUS

at midnight without fear, we have lost our unalloyed, trusting capacity to listen. My writing describes, by inversion, a fascination with listening. It is the work of someone who can recount others' talk, not simply his own. There are only a few notable qualities that make me feel, on my best days, reasonably well-equipped to at least begin to undertake my apprenticeship as a storyteller. One is my memory which, while not photographic as to name and date, can replicate the shoe size, mole patterning, and vocal tones and motives of a cross-the-street neighbor who played catcher on the semi pro ballteam in Rocky Mount, North Carolina, in 1950 when I was three. His dog was named Ginger and he sold office equipment on the side. This is not inherently important unless it feeds an advancing invention. Autobiography ain't fiction; and a lot more people in this world can 'write up' what literally befell them than the handful of derangos who can make up the fated events with a force that outstrips and out-reals and outlasts anything that is merely and often dully Actual. The tilt toward the mythic, the tall tale that stands one head higher than anyone in the story actually could, the exaggeration that scares and delights us into true belief—these color-cakes in my Woolworth's watercolor kit fascinate me. I use them by the gross, scrubbing, repainting till I get the lewd and lurid tints just right. I write dozens of drafts of every page I release. Conrad told us that the meaning of a novel must exist in every granular particle of that work, every sentence. When I first read this, I thought, 'Man, you got to be joshing me.' But I eventually found that the guy was earnest, that his admonition was not only possible but essential if literature is the goal.

"My great god is Chekhov. Like me, his dad was a grocer who beat him a bit too often. Like me, he grew through cringing to the far side of that and went on on toward a certain simple bravery. This bravery involves a reticence regarding any orthodoxy. Though I am a white man, a favorite character I've created to date is Castaliz, a black slave in *Oldest Living*. Though my forebears were slave owners, I found it easier to identify with the slave. Though I am a gay male, I often write in the voices of heterosexual women and, for them, I feel an admiration and a delight and a sad identification. Though I've enjoyed a superb literary education, some of it institutional and much of it self-induced, I admire the intensities I find in the voices of those, like the heroine of my first novel, who stopped school at age fourteen. I tend to admire wisdom more than mere smartness.

"My history, my ancestry as a scion of nothing much but little farms and semi-prosperous stores—has given me a subject endlessly rich because endlessly ordinary. Writing about very rich people and very poor people is easier than chronicling the woes and hopes of middle-class ones. The middle class—so endangered and neutered so willingly under the Republican administrations—is the major consumer of Novels as a form, and that form's major subject.

"In the first volume of my Falls Trilogy, *Oldest Living Confederate Widow Tells All*, and in my book of stories and novellas, *White People*, I have told the stories of some ninety striving folks from a small town called Falls, North Carolina. Since the city limits sign I see in my head tells me there are twelve hundred souls in this Bird Sanctuary, I feel sure that I will be kept productive and off the streets for years to come; I'll do that by being productively on the streets of this town I keep imagining, lot by lot, garage by garage, soul by soul. It is adamantly not the town I grew up in. Then I would be merely a rememberer. What thrills me is finding the lives and lies and reasons of people who look and sound utterly unlike me. The farther I throw my voice, the richer the echo grows in its terrible nearness, its scary familiarity. I am working now on the second book of my trilogy, a novel, 'The Erotic History of a Southern Baptist Church.' The blinded son of the '*Oldest Confederate Widow*' and her oldest Confederate becomes the preacher of the country parish. I feel I am being given, one at a time, fragments of some parchment map that, once assembled, will be seen to form, not merely a little town in the middle of nowhere, but a forlorn a weedy kind of earthly paradise. I am happiest when there; I am happiest when then; I am happiest when, in offering myself up to the seeming arbitrariness of invention, I strike my own moral principles like artesian wells that bring to the surface of the Local buckets of waters too cold and pure and sweet to be merely Local.

"My fascination is with the worst one human can do to one other and to place that alongside the best that we can hope from one another. I want to write the funniest books possible about the worst things that can happen to people. I want to earn honest laughs even from death itself.

"In the terrible desert of American letters known as Minimalism, we were told that emotion is remote to modern life, that numbness is our lot. Hooey. Never have so many people felt so very many contradictory symphonic inflationary emotions in so short a span of office hours. The swings are Wagnerian and disruptive and yet richly deep and vivid. Our novels and stories should reflect, and brave, our age's emotional wallop. I want to make my readers' emotional equipment remember its being virtuosic and wise. I want tears the way a seducer insists, against better judgment. By guilelessly pushing and pulling at my readers' hearts and funny bones and ticklish armpits and especially at their vulnerable needy responsive genitals—(all is fair in the war of love which we call narrative)—I remind them of their own value as they're driven to pity and despise or desire someone I create from twenty-six possible squiggles on a white page made of refined wood pulp, a page bound in a pile of such pages by glue made from horse hooves and blackened by ink that is varnish, minerals, tar, ash. The first requirements of a writer: a sense of humor, a horny love of words for their own colors, shapes and gonging magic, plus the dead certainty that the writer himself/ herself is going to die. How to enjoy the hours prior to death, how to survive historical forces that are drumming us, enlisting us, marching us toward enemies we do not hate . . . how to love our lives and feel their force in the minutest particle of their temporal pounding toward an end?—these queries make reading and living so urgent, so joyful and important. Lucky is the person who finds him/herself in exactly the correct occupation.

"I talked long before learning to take that first step I so viciously disparaged, 'Why should I walk?' I hope I can write long after I lose the power to walk far. Writing novels offers a much better job than being a dancer, say, somebody whose working life is done-for at age thirty— five. Time makes fools of us all but meantime, it should make us philosophers too. Novelists avenge time by making novels of it. This is why novelists only just get started at age forty; just when lyric poets have shot their bolt. Time is fiction's subject; that is how we presume to endure, however temporarily, the temporality that's killing us; how does the meat come to love the meat grinder; how does a mortal soul see Time so clearly that his/her vision of Time outlives her/ his mere embarrassment of a single frail ended body. To justify itself, literature must be useful. That is what I hope for my own books. My great good luck is that I am a composer who deals in melody; I am a bitterly well-informed person, a news junkie, in fact, who loves and trusts stories to tell all, or as much of 'all' as I can perceive. Some writers suspect stories; they are snobbish about mere tales; they snub Story and make the reader beg for a moment's melody among the astringent scratchings and complaints. I think the old songs are best. Schubert is greater, finally, than Schoenberg. The Gershwins will outlast Roger Sessions, already have, and he's still technically alive; they're gone. Though Beckett is , doubtless, a great writer, Dickens will always have more readers because he is a bigger writer and a greater one; because his hope, earned hope, not assumed hope, is greater.

"Maybe I believe that daily gesture is inherently meaningful; maybe that allows me to try to make something, for myself and my reader out of such seemingly mundane chores as grocery shopping, getting the Buick a lube job, going on a bus tour, taking care of one's own children.

"For me, Vermeer remains one of the greatest painter-writer-artists our species has yet produced. He often shows us women alone at home in the mid-to-early afternoon. They sit facing windows; they are pouring milk, reading letters, or playing a keyboard instrument for themselves alone. Some are just sitting there in some specific thought, a thought so specific, so emblematic of the wise dailiness of human existence that we rush toward them, without knowing the thought's exact content but feeling utterly for this one thought's form, the pome-like, pear-like rounded pleasing weight of it in another human head. We cannot guess which gentleman she expects to see tonight, which grocery list item she now adds to the mental list, which upcoming walk across town she is imagining—no, but we rush toward what is rendered—the act of having to be only one person, in one place, at one chore, in one nation and century, on this single wintry afternoon. Getting to imagine our lives as they are and as we wished they were—and as we live our own lives falteringly, fierce, stuck somewhere in between.

"I live there. I write there. I will die there, busy. The subject is inexhaustible. I want, in a few created lives, to provide some few moments' justice in a world that's running out of it."

Allan Gurganus describes his writing as "the work of someone who can recount others' talk, not simply his own." Filtered through what he calls a "tilt to the mythic," his massive novel *Oldest Living Confederate Widow Tells All* and his shorter fiction collected in *White People* have established him as an important figure in contemporary American fiction. In awarding him the Sue Kaufman Prize for Best American First Fiction of 1989, the American Academy and Institute of Arts and Letters cited his "storytelling gift of astonishing scope and plenitude, and an equally astonishing vernacular agility. What might in less responsible hands have been merely a stunt . . . becomes a meditation on human cussedness and endurance that is at once comically alive, wrenching and profound."

Lucy Marsden, the ninety-nine-year-old widow—narrator of his 718-page novel shares with the Ancient Mariner the gift of holding the listener spellbound. Christopher Lehmann-Haupt, in the *New York Times* (1989), while confessing that Lucy's "tidal sense of narrative" left him somewhat hypnotized, "like her nursing-home companions going for their daily doses of soap opera," said "Of all the long (and possible overlong) novels I've read in the past few years, this long novel pays back most for the time and energy you give it."

Gurganus has said that Lucy, his "Southern Scheherazade," was inspired by his paternal grandmother, "who was crippled with arthritis and rarely spoke." To make up for her silence about what must have been her rich memories of the Reconstructionist South and the many Confederate veterans she must have remembered, Gurganus says he invented Lucy as "an attempt to tell myself what my grandmother might have told me." In fact, his own boyhood was not as far removed from the distant past as it might have been in any other part of the United States. Born in Rocky Mount, North Carolina, the son of M. F. and Ethel (Morris) Gurganus, he grew up in a small town where Civil War memories were kept alive by custom and tradition. Still it was a shock to him when he learned, years later, that his forebears had been slave owners.

Gurganus's first career interest was in art, and he studied painting at the Pennsylvania Academy of Fine Arts in 1966 and 1967. Threatened with the military draft during the Vietnam War and rejected for conscientious objector status, he enlisted in the U.S. Navy. He spent four years in the service, most of them as a message decoder on an aircraft carrier that fortunately had a large library. His reading was so thorough and extensive that upon his discharge from the navy in 1970 he received two years of liberal arts credit from Sarah Lawrence College, where he completed his B.A. in 1972. Encouraged by Grace Paley, who had been one of his writing teachers at Sarah Lawrence, and a Danforth fellowship, Gurganus went to the Writers Workshop at the University of Iowa to study for an M.F.A., which he received in 1974. A guest writer-in-residence there at that time was John Cheever, who took an immediate interest in his work. Without Gurganus's knowledge, Cheever sent one of his stories, "Minor Heroism," to the *New Yorker*, which promptly accepted it. This stunning first success—all the more remarkable became it was the first story with a homosexual subject that the *New Yorker* had published—launched his professional career.

In 1974, Gurganus went to Stanford University on a Wallace Stegner Fellowship and taught there for two years. In 1976 he received a grant from the National Endowment for the Arts. During those years he was publishing stories in anthologies and magazines, including the *Atlantic*, *Harper's*, and *Granta*. In 1981, while working on a novel at Yaddo, the writers' colony in Saratoga Springs, New York, he read a newspaper story about the surviving widows of Confederate veterans, women who had married men much older than they and who had therefore outlived them by many years. One phrase "stopped my breath: 'oldest living Confederate widow.' " He abandoned the novel he had been working on and devoted himself for the next seven years to the new book, living in a small apartment in New York City to give himself needed distance from the South. At that time he also taught writing courses at Sarah Lawrence. *Oldest Living Confederate Widow Tells All* was heralded by enormous publicity. A month before the official publication, articles on the author and his novel appeared in the *New York Times*, *New York* magazine, and *Publishers Weekly*. Gurganus and his publisher proudly described *Confederate Widow* as "maximalist": "I would be extremely happy if my book were seen as one of the nails in the coffin of minimalism," he told Sam Stagges in *Publishers Weekly*. "I think there is a great appetite, and a great need, for Stories with a capital S."

Story there is in good measure— Lucy's long life, the lives of her parents, friends, her nine children, neighbors, the residents in the state-run home for the aged where she now survives, and the near-mythic black woman Castalia who was her servant, her moral guide, and devoted friend. Lucy is also the medium for her husband's vivid memories of the Civil War, which he entered as a thirteen-year—old child and left, after Appomatox, as a soberly mature man of sixteen:

> My man's peacetime memory lost many a house key but it recollected the whereabouts of every roadhouse in either Carolina. A tale-telling vet could get free bourbon after dark. Captain Marsden's peacetime memory forgot to pay our grocery bills on time, but, child, his wartime one was a Dewey decimal system of musket balls. Every minute from '61 to '65 had schooled Cap in how to tell it true.

Most remarkable about Lucy—besides her longevity and her relentless memory—is her capacity for hope:

> The odd part stays: happiness. How stubborn it is, whatever bracket you land in. When I think over the list of my losses and time's take-backs, the household accidents, small everyday betrayals, the way your genius kids turn out to be just regular, if nice. Times, happiness surprises me. It keeps you as its hobby. Lord be praised. For some of us lucky ones, child, happiness stays our daily habit like any other. Happiness: that beautiful duty.

Some reviewers found the novel "trite and soggy and the voice of the narrator . . . irritatingly folksy," as Nick Hornby put it in the *Times Literary Supplement*. Peter Prescott, in *Newsweek*, found much of the book "sentimental stories [that] tend to resolve themselves around grotesque, or at least extravagant, characters." Although Jay Tolson, in the *New Republic*, admired Gurganus's writing, he judged the novel "troubling . . . because his view of war's causes draws so deeply on a resilient American myth—on the myth of the American Adam, a creature at once natural and fully realized, at peace with the world and with his neighbors."

A humane spirit informs the shorter fiction collected in *White People*. Contemporary in setting with the exception of "Reassurance," in which Walt Whitman appears as a nurse caring for a young Union soldier dying of his wounds, and a fantasy, "It Had Wings," about an angel who falls, quite naked, into the backyard of a lonely old lady, most of the stories take place in the same small North Carolina town where Lucy Marsden spent her life and are peopled with her neighbors. Included here is Gurganus's first published story, "Minor Heroism," subtitled "Something About My Father," a sensitive memoir told by a homosexual son, an artist and writer estranged since childhood from his father, a World War II hero, and by the father. The father says, confessing his inability to understand his son: "You might say Bryan and I have never really seen eye to eye. He had always had certain mannerisms and his talents are unlike my own."

Henry Louis Gates Jr. wrote of *White People* in the *Nation*, "Most of these stories are narrated by people who want some sort of forgiveness—it's what fuels their loquacity, speeds along their confessions." Part of their problem, Gates concluded, may lie in their being "white" people, emotionally repressed, unable to release or express their genuine selves. Gates concluded his review with praise for Gurganus's talent for making the reader "squirm with recognition" and for his courage in taking "no precautions . . . against pathos, bathos, authorial indignity. As a result, his best stories command a sort of sublimity of the mundane; they locate the dangerous glamour in ordinariness."

Gurganus divides his time between Chapel Hill, North Carolina, and an apartment in New York City. In addition to his ambitious writing schedule with plans for more novels, a collection of essays, and an autobiography, he devotes much time to raising money for AIDS research and to protesting governmental attempts to censor the arts. In 1994, *Oldest Living Confederate Widow* was adapted for a four-hour television miniseries. Gurganus did not do the adaptation, but he played a small role in it as a Confederate officer leading 150 men into battle.

PRINCIPAL WORKS: Oldest Living Confederate Widow Tells All, 1989; Blessed Assurance, 1990; White People, 1991.

ABOUT: Contemporary Authors 135, 1992. *Periodicals*—House and Garden May 1989; Lost Angeles Times January 18, 1991; Nation April 15, 1991; New Republic October 30, 1989; Newsweek September 25, 1989; New York August 21, 1989; New York Times August 14, 1989; May 1, 1994; New York Times Book Review August 13, 1989; February 3, 1991; (London) Observer November 5, 1989; People September 18, 1989; Publishers Weekly June 23, 1989; August 11, 1989; November 27, 1990; Times (London) November 8, 1989; Times Literary Supplement September 19, 1991; The Writer October 1991.

HADAS, RACHEL (November 8, 1948–   ), American poet, essayist, and translator, writes: "I was born in New York City and grew up on Riverside Drive in the apartment my parents had moved into the year before and which I emptied out only last summer (1992) after my mother's death. My father, Moses Hadas, taught classics at Columbia for many years; my mother, Elizabeth Chamberlayne Hadas, who had been Daddy's student before becoming his second wife, taught Latin at the Spence School in New York.

RACHEL HADAS

"It was a bookish family all right—my older sister Beth now heads the University of New Mexico Press, and I now teach English at the Newark campus of Rutgers. But our way (or ways) with words didn't necessarily add up to openness. 'None of us was afraid to put a name/ to anything, but neither did we lift/ our faces from the pages of our books,' I wrote in 'Learning to Talk.' Putting names to feelings, learning the truth through testing its sounds, has been a consistent effort of my work.

"Reeling off the facts of college—travel— marriage No.1—separation—graduate school— marriage No.2—motherhood—teaching is a routine task, one which others besides myself could perform. But to say how these things really felt, what they meant and how their meanings continue to develop—this is the task of my unabashedly personal poems and essays.

"It's possible to assign themes to my separate books: life in Greece to *Slow Transparency*, motherhood to *A Son from Sleep*, teaching to *Pass It On*. But the how is always as important as the what, and a lot of the same preoccupations continue to operate throughout my work via style rather than subject matter. I try to write as beautifully and precisely and truthfully as I can. Poetry is the place in life where I have courage to see and say painful things; it's also the best way I know of to catch happiness on the wing. Poetry and, in the last few years, essays and translations as well, are how I make sense of the world; these, and teaching, which I feel lucky to get paid for doing.

"I majored in classics at Radcliffe, lived in Greece, married Stavros Kondylis, lived on Samos, returned to the U.S., got an M.A. in poetry at Johns Hopkins and a Ph.D. in comparative literature at Princeton, married George Edwards, a composer who teaches at Columbia, teach English (despite my lack of any degree in it) at Rutgers, as I've said. George's and my son Jonathan was born in 1984. As in any life, the facts are bony and dry as a skeleton, only language and hindsight—adding up in my particular case to poetry—flesh out the scaffolding. I feel this with special acuteness now that what I have of both my parents, other than memories, is paper and ink. I've recently been going through some of the papers of my maternal grandfather, Lewis Parke Chamberlayne (1879–1917), a classicist, poet, and translator. I wouldn't be surprised if it's a common experience for poets to discover in middle age that they're not the self-created wonders they used to suppose, but that writing is in their blood."

Rachel Hadas's three themes—Greece, motherhood, teaching—represent stages but not unrelated subjects in her work. Greece is not only the country where she lived for five years and discovered her vocation for literature, but is part of the rich background of knowledge that was her heritage. Motherhood and teaching figures in her work not only as personal experiences but as metaphor's for continuity and growth in nature and in human life.

Her earliest published collection, *Starting from Troy*, dedicated to her father, is a tribute to him in both form—most of the poems are strictly metrical—and content, reshaping the ancient legend of Troy into an expression of grief at his death.

> What rests with us?
> How did he say goodbye? Did he say it?
> Or must we build what was by tearing down
> what is, beat down our celebrated towers
> to our own stature, shut our eyes, and sing?
>
> All fighters, fathers, all departed heroes,
> our house cries out for you.
> ("That Time, This Place")

Greece became reality for Rachel Hadas when in 1969 she traveled there on an Isobel M. Briggs fellowship. In Athens she met a number of poets, among them James Merrill, Chester Kallman, W. H. Auden, and Alan Ansen, whom she describes in an essay, "Mornings in Ormos," as "a portly polymath, expatriate American writer, and delightfully eccentric man." Living with Ansen at that time was a handsome young Greek, Stavros Kondylis, with whom she fell in love. They married in 1970 and went to live on the island of Samos. She learned to speak demotic Greek and for a while lived happily in the seaside village of Ormos. She describes the marriage, which ended after four years, candidly in "Mornings in Ormos": "Stavros was as confused as I was. The fact of our marrying one another testifies to the mutuality of our befuddlement." The young couple bought a disused olive press and went into business, arousing the hostility of their business-competitor neighbors. When the press was destroyed by fire of mysterious origin, they were accused of arson, brought to trial, and acquitted. Her trial for arson was a portent of her alienation: "Head hanging, I'm accused by those in power / of being who I am; of being here," she wrote in "Mornings in Ormos." "When I left the village, and soon after that the marriage, it was not like emerging from a cocoon; neither was it like leaving paradise behind. Both images have tempted me, and both are false. What's true is that adult life was beginning."

She returned to the United States to resume her life as a graduate student at Johns Hopkins, from which she received an M.A. in poetry in 1977, and at Princeton, where she took a Ph.D. in comparative literature in 1982. Her doctoral dissertation, *Form, Cycle, Infinity: Landscape Imagery in the Poetry of Robert Frost and George Seferis*, published in 1985, was a work of literary scholarship and criticism, as well as a personal expression. As she wrote in an introductory note, the study "is my attempt to eat my cake and have it too. The stuff of which it is made is not only the words of Frost and Seferis but also the accumulation of mornings and afternoons, seasons and weathers, that I lived through in Samos and Vermont." Sunbathing in Samos, she read Wordsworth's *The Prelude* (a work that she said in "The Dream Machine" influenced her own "growth of the poet's mind." Later, staying in Vermont, she remembered the Aegean Sea. The juxtaposition of the New Englander Frost and the Greek Seferis, contemporaries who "wrote in different languages and knew little or nothing of one another's work," proved illuminating. Her analysis of their love for specific qualities of place, such as walls, stones, sea, sun, and light, becomes a study of "the balance between inner and outer worlds in each poet's work."

The poems in *Slow Transparency*, Hadas's second collection, are the fruit of her years in Greece. They trace her growing ambivalence —her love for Greek culture and the beauty of the country clashing with her sense of estrangement as in "The Colors of the Place":

> Brave
> new world gone dry and flyblown in September
> that gleamed in June. . . .
> * * *
> Where is the olive green, unsullied island
> I had imagined, silver toes dipped in a sea
> of perfect crystal?

Reviewers found her work impressive for its technical mastery, but several noted formalism—what Jorie Graham described in the *New York Times Book Review* (1984) as "Hadas's unwillingness to let a poem fly." At times, Graham noted, "the poems freeze into . . . intellectualized posturing . . . But in those poems where thinking is not inflated to fit shapeliness . . . Hadas confronts the details of her life with some genuine power." Anne Stevenson said in the *Times Literary Supplement* "there is intelligence here, and imagination which augurs well for the future,"

In her later work, however, reviewers noted a greater spontaneity and accessibility. Robert B. Shaw wrote in *Poetry* that *Pass It On*, "without ceasing to be personal in theme and tone, gives voice to some of the deepest concerns of a generation." He observed that Hadas's "themes of family and cultural transmission come together deftly in poems which consider the role of language in life through observing a child learning to talk." Liz Rosenberg wrote of the same volume, in the *New York Times Book Review* that "there is no sentimental gloss" in her poems on motherhood and "very little superficial or facile in [her] thought." Though Rosenberg detected an occasional "intellectual archness" in Hadas's poems about teaching, she praised her "wry, unexpected humor" and her "brilliant gift for metaphor."

The poems in Hadas's 1992 collection, *Mirrors of Astonishment*, display a more mature voice. Middle-aged herself now, she had intimations of her won mortality. The grief of her mother's recent death and the memory of her father's death years earlier still haunt her. In *In the Middle*, she recalls her physical closeness to them as a child, sitting between the two of them, "sensing myself even then in a not so permanent / crack of creation. I would never stop / issuing from, but the place was mortal." She writes of family life, her parents, her sister, and her young son—all devotees of language: "None of us was afraid to put a name / to anything. . . . " and of her husband in "Love,"

> It took me years to learn to sleep with you—real sleep,
> not euphemism, sinking back on one another's silence.
> The centripetal centrifugal juggle of two matched affections.

Michael Klein, writing in *Kenyon Review*,

found "a rough music that drifts in and out . . . like an impatient breeze, lyrical and quick-minded," in *Mirrors of Astonishment.* He found that Hadas "shines when she lets things get strange. Her poems 'Visting the Gypsy' (which beautifully incorporates a seer's forecast into how the speaker sees herself) and 'Roadblock' both get tougher as they travel further into the heart of the unfamiliar."

Many of the qualities that distinguish Hadas's poetry are carried over into her informal essays collected in *Living in Time* (which also includes her long poem "The Dream Machine"). Some of these, such as "Mornings in Ormos," and memories of her childhood reading which she now shares with her own child, "The Cradle and the Bookcase," might serve as complements to her poetry.

Rachel Hadas has been a volunteer leader in poetry workshops conducted by the Gay Men's Health Crisis. "The whole thing was my idea," she wrote in "The Lights Must Never Go Out," an essay in *Living in Time*; "no one was making me do it; yet I couldn't help envisioning any poetry group with PWAS [Persons with Aids] as an uncomfortable alternation of compassion and stimulus—a use of poetry both to soothe and prod."

In *Unending Dialogue: Voices from an AIDS Poetry Workshop*, a collection of her students' verse along with a group of her own poems, the students' poems are starkly powerful. Her own poems are compassionate, eloquent, and restrained. In "Taking Sides" she contrasts life and death using the image of a quarrel between speech and silence, which is death:

Our task today: to write against the clock.
Hush. The makework pastime
darkens to divination as we sit.
Can you make out the mortal combat between twin wishes,
opposing poles of dumbness and of speech?

° ° °

Dumbness desires the paper to stay white.
Language longs for dumbness
to open his mouth for once . . .

Rachel Hadas has followed her father and maternal grandfather—of whom she wrote in the acknowledgments to *Other Worlds Than This* that he "convinced me from beyond the grave . . . that the love of translating must be an inherited trait"—as a translator. *Other Worlds Than This* includes translations from the French poets Charles Baudelaire, Arthur Rimbaud, and Paul Valéry, as well as from the classical Latin and the modern Greek. Translating, especially Baudelaire, required "monumental selflessness," as she remarks in the introduction

to the volume. "What I had been doing in working on Baudelaire was exchanging one kind of challenge, one kind of exploration, for another. The process wasn't always delicious. . . . I sometimes felt tucked too snugly into the bed of the poem." James Merrill praised the "ease and mastery of her renderings" as "breathtaking."

In 1976 Hadas was a fellow at the MacDowell Colony and a scholar at the Bread Loaf Writers Conference. She won a Guggenheim Fellowship in 1988 and in 1990 an award in literature from the American Academy and Institute of Arts and Letters.

PRINCIPAL WORKS: *Poetry*—Staring from Troy, 1975; Slow Transparency, 1983; A Son from Sleep, 1987; Pass It On, 1989(with others) Unending Dialogue: Voices from an AIDS Poetry Workshop, 1991; Mirrors of Astonishment, 1992. *Prose*—Form, Cycle, Infinity: Landscape Imagery in the Poetry of Robert Frost and George Seferis, 1985; Living in Time, 1990. *As translator*—Other Worlds Than This, 1994. *As editor*—(with others) Saturday's Children: Eileen W. Barnes Award Anthology, 1982.

ABOUT: Contemporary Authors New Revision series 29, 1990; Dictionary of Literary Biography 120, 1992; Hadas. R. Living in Time, 1990. *Periodicals*—Kenyon Review Winter 1993; New York Times January 4, 1992; New York Times Book Review March 4, 1984; May 6, 1990; Parnassus: Poetry in Review 16, 1991; Poetry June 1990; Times Literary Supplement July 20, 1984.

HAMILTON-PATERSON, JAMES (November 6, 1941–), British novelist, journalist, and poet was born in London, the son of John and Ursula (ImThurn) Hamilton-Paterson. Both of his parents were doctors. He was educated at Kings School, Canterbury, and at Oxford University where he took his M.A. and was awarded the Newdigate Prize for poetry in 1964. He taught in Tripoli, Libya, in the early 1960s. Later in that decade he became a free-lance journalist and worked in Vietnam. He wrote for the *Sunday Times* (London), for the *Times Literary Supplement* as science fiction editor, and for the *New Statesman*, from 1968 to 1974. For a time he was features editor at *Nova* magazine.

As a direct result of his experience in Vietnam, he published *A Very Personal War: The Story of Cornelius Hawkridge*, simultaneously a biography and an exposure of corrupt United States governmental practice in Southeast Asia. It combines investigative journalism, narrative drive, and a poetic sensibility—an eclecticism that has continued to characterize Hamilton-Paterson's work. It also reveals his love of exotic locations. A habitual traveler, Hamilton-Paterson incorpo-

JAMES HAMILTON-PATERSON

rates the results of his wanderings into novels and nonfiction investigations. He resides alternately in a small mountaintop house high in the Italian province of Tuscany and a bamboo hut on a small island in the Philippines, and spends most of his time alone, visiting family and friends in England only occasionally. He considers it vital to his writing to live abroad and see his own culture only from the outside, and finds a self-imposed solitary routine crucial to his productivity. In an interview in the *New York Times Book Review* in 1990, Hamilton-Paterson said he was joining an expedition out of Woods Hole, Massachusetts in search of "sunken things." "I'm interested in the search for a lost object . . . I think I've always wanted to become lost in some way."

Gerontius, Hamilton-Paterson's first novel, is the imaginative recreation of a voyage up the Amazon presumably but never actually made by the British composer Edward Elgar. The life of the river is backdrop to personal drama, as Elgar enters the poignant territory of his later years having outlived his friends, his wife, and his ability to compose. Elgar inhabits a psychological fantasy world, a maze of lost emotions, as old age attacks his aesthetic principles, as well as his body. *Gerontius* won the Whitbread Prize for first novel and was runner-up for the Book of the Year, 1989.

Reviewers have noted Hamilton-Paterson's skillful use of language alternatively to discover himself and escape from himself. Several, however, have pointed out the risks in such linguistic play. In *Playing With Water: Passion and Soli-*

tude on a Philippine Island, where he describes Philippine cultural and political life, David Chandler, in the *Times Literary Supplement*, finds a tentative quality: "Its form derives from its being pushed along by stretches of lyrical writing, rather than by thematic developments. These, in turn, are held in place by rumination, á la Thoreau, about large themes and about Hamilton-Paterson's early life."

That Time in Malomba (published in England as *The Bellboy*) is a satire, termed "delightful" by Michael Malone in the *New York Times Book Review*. It is the story of a young Englishwoman who goes to the Far East with her two children. She is looking for spiritual enlightenment in the "holy" city of Malomba, but finds fake mysticism and exploitation. "Hamilton-Paterson makes us feel the mysteriously powerful, ominous, somnambulent physicality of places like Malomba, with its sheen of brilliant colors, sounds and smells where the 'madonna with a faulty neon halo' winks," Malone wrote. He deemed "this resonant, beautifully nuanced novel" destined to become a classic.

The Great Deep: The Sea and Its Thresholds is a collection of linked essays reflecting on diverse aspects of the world's oceans—reefs, islands, charts, wrecks, fishing, pirates, and monsters. In the *New York Times Book Review*, Alexander Frater described a lone fisherman whose outrigger canoe vanishes. The "abandoned increasingly desperate figure" of the fisherman recurs at intervals in the book. "In the end the canoe reappears, the fisherman clambers aboard and returns . . . to the refuge of his island shack." Frater noted that by the end the reader realizes that the fisherman is Hamilton-Paterson himself, and Frater speculates on "whether he got the idea for his book during those lost, scary hours in the water." In any case, Hamilton-Paterson's personal "reflections on every conceivable aspect of the oceans serve to underpin this intricate and scholarly survey." Rosemary Dinnage, in the *Times Literary Supplement*, described the best effects of the book as "liberation into a magical element."

In the novel *Griefwork*, Leon, the central character, is curator of a palm greenhouse in a European city at the close of the Second World War. With single-mindedness and hard work Leon has preserved his crystal palace of glass, with all its exotic species intact, despite the destructive horrors of the war. As the novel opens, he struggles to keep his boilers fed in a fuel-starved Europe deep in winter. The Palm House is an anachronism, yet a defiant symbol of the natural and the elemental. All of the novel's action takes place within the Palm House, where

Leon also lives; it is for him, a refuge of beauty and order in an ugly and cynical world.

Hamilton-Paterson's handling of the narrative never allows the novel to become sentimental. Leon rejects the patronizing aesthetics of visitors; crucial to conception of his own efforts is his "grasping the idea of an unsubjective taxonomy." The plants speak their minds through Leon's fantasies, providing a critical commentary at the close of each chapter upon the human behavior they observe. The pressure of outside events, Leon's physical and mental decline, and a remarkable act of generosity ultimately result in the destruction of the Palm House, but it has served as a metaphor to illustrate the progress, or decline, in economics, ecology, and modern Western culture.

Equally ambitious as a commentary on contemporary life—here the Philippines under the corrupt and ruthless rule of the Marcoses—Hamilton-Paterson's *Ghosts of Manila* is a grisly novel of murder and mayhem. Described by Giles Foden in the *Times Literary Supplement* as "his plump story of ritual murder, shantytown life, archaeology, vampires, cannibalism and graft in the Philippines," it piles horrors on horrors. The central character, a British archeologist, writes his thesis on the Philippine concept of "amok" in the form of a novel within the novel. "What emerges is a gruesome portrait of contemporary Manila, filled with corruption, drugs, violence, murder, crooked land deals, vampirism and the generally bizarre. . . . This postmodernist sleight of hand is only partly successful," Stephen Dobyns observed in the *New York Times Book Review*, "since it hinders one's ability to see the characters as people. . . . Hamilton-Paterson's gifts seem more journalistic than novelistic." He gave Hamilton-Paterson credit, however, for the "many pleasures in the book, mostly connected to the strangeness of the author's depiction of Manila. . . . "

Hamilton-Paterson summed up his credo in an interview with the (London) *Sunday Times*: "The thing I feel now more than anything is an astonishing freedom and power. But I know what I'm doing and what I want to do. I can go anywhere. It's not the freedom that cash brings you, disproving the Thatcher creed, because I've never had a bean. It's extraordinary what you can do on nothing. You don't need all those things you're told you need."

James Hamilton-Paterson has also published volumes of poems, short stories, and books for children. In addition to the Whitbread Prize he won the Gold Medal at the International Radio Festival of New York in 1990, for a radio play adapted from *Gerontius* for the BBC in the same year. He is a member of the Royal Geographic Society and an accomplished pianist.

PRINCIPAL WORKS: *Novels*—Gerontius, 1989; That Time in Malomba, 1990 (in U.K.: The Bellboy); Griefwork, 1993; Ghosts of Manila, 1994. *Short stories*—The View from Mount Dog, 1986. *Nonfiction*—A very Personal War: The Story of Cornelius Hawkridge, 1971; (with Carol Andrews) Mummies: Death and Life in Ancient Egypt, 1978; Playing With Water: Passion and Solitude on a Philippine Island, 1987; The Great Deep: The Sea and its Thresholds (in U.K.: Seven Tenths) 1992. *Juvenile*—Flight Underground, 1969; Hostage!, 1978. *Poetry*—Option Three, 1974, Dutch Alps, 1984.

ABOUT: Contemporary Authors 137, 1992. *Periodicals*—New York Times Book Review October 5, 1980, April 29, 1990, October 14, 1990, August 9, 1992; November 27, 1994; Observer (London) January 21, 1990; Publishers Weekly July 6, 1990; September 21, 1990; Sunday Times (London) November 12, 1989, January 21, 1990; Times (London) January 25, 1990; Times Literary Supplement July 2, 1970, March 10, 1972, February 28, 1975, April 7, 1978, August 14, 1987, March 24, 1989, January 26, 1990, July 17, 1992; May 14, 1993; May 20, 1994; Washington Post October 26, 1990; Washington Post Book World May 5, 1991.

HANRAHAN, BARBARA (September 6, 1939–December 1991), Australian painter, print maker, and fiction writer. Her companion Jo Steele sent *World Authors* an extract from some notes found among her papers after her death in 1991: "I am not satisfied to be predictable, to write as thousands of others could. I must push into myself enough, dare to be original and individual enough to find my own viewpoint. As an artist I must believe in myself enough to be selfish. I must be selfish enough to push my writing into regions that are not neatly labelled. Doing this is not a comfortable business.

"Australia has shaped me. I am an Australian writer. The images of Australia that are mine—summer, Adelaide, the natural world—are part of my own private mythology. I carry them with me wherever physically I settle. They are with me in Australia, they are with me in London. Distanced physically from Australia I am able to see it more vividly. All the little hindrances and annoyances dissolve all that remain are the potent *big* things. This is why I feel it's of value to divide my life between England and Australia, which to me are summed up by London and Adelaide. Two places so different that one illuminates the other. London so large that I may lose myself, which means find myself because I can be anonymous. Adelaide—smaller, strange, the place where I began from, the place of childhood, of legend.

BARBARA HANRAHAN

"The foundations of all I write are buried deep in my childhood. Adelaide creeps through all my writing. I see the city with my own eyes. Then and Now fuse—the *real* city becomes a dream city. The people of my childhood are important, too. The big earthy grandmother, so strong, so basic, so soft; the stories of her past. Iris Pearl was the baker's daughter . . . Charles Ebenezer the dead grandfather, the policeman. My mother, butterfly—delicate, dabbing April Violets scent behind her ears . . . my father who read the newspaper at the dance, who won the scholarship to Christian Brothers College—who looked like Tyrone Power, who died. . . . All this is *my* Adelaide. Adelaide is a strange place. I want to write of it as the writers of the Deep South wrote of their America.

"I wrote *The Scent of Eucalyptus* out of an inner need. Adelaide and my past came tumbling down onto paper. I remembered. Writing in London while snow flew at the pane, I sweated in the heat wave.

"No creative artist realises a potential. Only the *little* people, the second-raters do that. The future is the present is the past. I am stocking up past for my future now. I will just write on, I will grow stronger, learn to channel my power, learn to recognize my own bad writing, my bad prints and outgrow them.

"When I am seventy I hope to be nicely wrinkled. There won't, however be much point to me living on to seventy if I am not still fresh and young and a child, still inside myself. Chronological age to me is unimportant. I think of all those bold girls I knew in the Primary School—

so bold and vivid at twelve, so fixed and dead at twenty. Society deadens us. The individual is not important to society. All the little quirks must be flattened out. So early we are neatly slotted into our official identities. Only a few escape. When I was twenty-one I was older than I am now. I was riddled with guilt. I worried because I did not fit into a tidily gift-wrapped world. I was always pretending. Yet I could never truly see myself as a wife, as someone's mother. I was always surprised at the daring of all these girls who, so young, tended a shell-stitch bundle, who were confident enough, perfect enough, to play mama to another human being. All this cosy materialism was always something repugnant. More than that, I have always felt that to marry, to have a child, would be for me a wicked thing. These things were never meant to happen to me—my part in life was meant to be different. For twelve years I have lived with the sculptor Jo Steele. Our life together is lived in perfect accord. We are both creative artists; we are both individuals, we respect each others' identities. He does not serve me; I do not serve him. We are a pair of people, we are ourselves. Because we trust each other we are free to reach back to the children we once were. I feel that to grow older, perfectly, is to grow closer to the child within us. Often the inner child is strangled out of existence by life. The wiser we become, the more childlike we are."

————

It was not Barbara Hanrahan's fate to become a "nicely wrinkled" seventy-year-old, but into her fifty-two years of life she crowded two successful careers—artist and writer—and fulfilled her ambition to be an original. Central to her work in printmaking and in fiction writing alike is a unique blend of fantasy and realism. "I'm not interested in going into a fantasy world that isn't linked strongly with an earthy material world," she told a radio interviewer in 1980. For that reason she preserved her child's vision, a worldview that is innocent but also knowing, simple but also complex. "A child looks at things clearly, directly. You get a strange straight-on view, so intense that it takes in all the little details to the side as well."

Her disarmingly honest and appealing first novel *The Scent of Eucalyptus* is an autobiographical memoir only thinly disguised as fiction. The only child of Maurice William and Ronda (Goodridge) Hanrahan, she was born in Adelaide. Her father, a factory worker, died when she was only three, and she grew up in a household of women: her pretty mother, who worked as a secretary and later as a commercial artist; her Aunt Reece who remained a child all her life; her strong-willed grandmother—all of whom are richly realized as characters in *The Scent of Eucalyptus*. Hanrahan herself was an imaginative child, living in a world that was sharply divided between illusion and reality:

> I was the one who wandered in the garden and talked with the flowers; I was the one who raced with the others across the asphalt and limped home with bloody knees.

> And as I grew older I became adept at leaping quicksilver from one of my selves to the other. And as I grew older the split grew deeper, yet I forgot that it was there.

The novel ends with her mother remarrying and the young narrator on the brink of her mature life. Her family, though all originals themselves, hoped for a sheltered bourgeois future for her—marriage, children, and domesticity—without realizing, she writes, that "they were different—that they had made me different by my upbringing in that house of the red verandah, where beauty lay all about: in Reece's ugly face, Tinker's [her blind and beloved cocker spaniel] milky gaze, my grandmother's wrinkles, the lilac shadows beneath my mother's eyes; where like, under its sham layer of studied conformity was strangely original, strangely unworldly."

Early discovering her artistic talent, Barbara Hanrahan attended the South Australian School of Art in Adelaide from 1957 to 1960. She then taught art for four years. In 1964, having already won recognition of her work in Australia, she went to London to continue her studies at the Central School of Art. Her early years there were the inspiration for two more deeply personal novels, *Sea Green* and *Kewpie Doll*. In the latter she describes her discovery of the joys of printmaking: "I had escaped to a world of my own. All the insect bite worries fell off me. Nothing counted but my hand with the crayon marking marks on the stone . . . The creamy limestone surface was so sensitive, it seemed a living thing. . . . [I]n the Printmaking Room I found a new world."

By the early 1970s Barbara Hanrahan was exhibiting her etchings, silk-screen prints, and woodcuts in all the major cities in Australia and in galleries in Italy and England. Her art, like her fiction, has the stamp of originality, evoking a sense of childlike innocence penetrating into a sinister and corrupt world. In an article in *Quadrant* Annette Stewart writes: "Nearly all of the prints appear to have been 'done by a child, if an incredibly sophisticated one . . . most of the figures are simplified, stiff, doll-like, as in children's drawings. This delicate 'simplicity' masks deeper meanings, but is important in itself, a child's way of looking at the world."

Barbara Hanrahan's fiction centers on women; men figure only peripherally. Although she had kept journals since childhood, she did not begin writing fiction until after her grandmother's death in 1968. Living in London at the time, she found herself increasingly absorbed with recreating her own past and her relationship to her grandmother.

Hanrahan sets most of her novels in the Victorian or Edwardian past, reflecting perhaps the influence of her grandmother, who had told her many stories of her own early life. In that past of a still-colonial Australia dominated by the strict conventions and social codes of Victorian England, she found a combination of innocence and repressed evil that fascinated her. *The Peach Groves* and *The Frangipani Gardens*, generally regarded as her two best novels, offer detailed picture of the clothes, furnishings, houses, and gardens of the lost past and center on children who innocently stumble upon scenes of sex and imminent violence. In *The Peach Groves*, an Adelaide mother takes her two young daughters to visit her brother and his wife in New Zealand. The comfortable and protected characters might be living in a Garden of Eden, but gradually they make a series of shocking discoveries—incest, pedophilia, violence, suicide: "All the old certitudes meant nothing. Under the layers of elegant clothes were bodies that lusted and cried in the night. An uncle could still be a man who was worthless . . . and not Mama, but a matron with a mouth that pouted to be kissed, not Auntie, but the little match girl, crying to come in from the cold."

The Frangipani Gardens introduces two pairs of young people, one already tainted with evil, the other innocent orphans living with an eccentric aunt who paints strange, visionary scenes that foretell the future. The struggle between good and evil takes on elements of fantasy here with spell casting, Tarot cards and fetish dolls. Nevertheless the novel remains based in the reality of early twentieth-century Adelaide, ending with an account of the visit of the Duke and Duchess of York to Adelaide in 1901. Though good and evil are primary forces in these novels, Hanrahan scrupulously avoids making moral judgments on her characters: "I'm interested in opposites, art and poetry come out of these inconsistencies. I like my angels weighed down in marble."

In her later novels Hanrahan turned from these semimystical themes to a more straightforward realism. These are shorter books, narrated by women who have quietly accepted the hard terms that life has imposed upon them. They are not represented as noble and heroic, but neither are they merely passive victims. *Flawless Jade* stands out from the others, all set in Australia or England, because its scene is modern China. Here Wing-Yee survives the hardships of the Sino-Japanese War and the Cultural Revolution only to suffer a more painful personal blow—the loss of a chance for a career in films because her old-fashioned mother opposes it.

Generally, Hanrahan remains close to home. Annie Magdalene, in the novel of that title, lives her uneventful life working in factories, caring for her parents, her neighbors, and the birds and insects in her garden. She grows old uncomplainingly, satisfied to live in memories and enjoy the natural rhythms of life like the bees who sit on her arms but never sting her: "They don't worry me at all, I think they love me; I just let them stay (if you brush them off they get cross), they're only sitting there to have a rest." Alexandra May (named for the Duchess of York because she was born on the day of the royal visit to Adelaide) chronicles her uneventful life in *Good Night, Mr. Moon*—a less than idyllic marriage, financial hardships, the birth of her children, the loneliness of her later years, and her difficulties in adjusting to the changing conditions of modern life. Interspersed with this running account are her addresses to the moon before she falls asleep at night and Hanrahan's small decorative engravings that mark divisions in the text. Like *The Scent of Eucalyptus*, these are memory novels recording the past as graphically and imperishably as the stone impressions of her prints.

At the time of her death Hanrahan was writing another autobiographical novel, *Michael and Me and the Sun*, which was published posthumously with sixteen prints she had made years before as an art student in London.

PRINCIPAL WORKS: *Novels*—The Scent of Eucalyptus, 1973; Sea Green, 1974; The Albatross Muff, 1977; Where Queens All Strayed, 1978; The Peach Groves, 1979; The Frangipani Gardens, 1980; Dove, 1982; Kewpie Doll, 1984; Annie Magdalene, 1985; A Chelsea Girl, 1988; Flawless Jade, 1989; Good Night, Mr. Moon, 1992; Michael and Me and the Sun, 1992. *Short stories*—Dream People, 1987; Iris in Her Garden, 1991.

ABOUT: Contemporary Authors 127, 1989; Contemporary Novelists, 4th ed., 1986; Oxford Companion to Australian Literary, 1985. *Periodicals*—Australian Literary Studies May 1983; May 1990; New York Times Book Review March 9, 1986; Publishers Weekly, December 20, 1985; Quadrant January–February 1988; Southerly December 1992; Times Literary Supplement May 20, 1977; May 30, 1980; January 20, 1984; October 18, 1985; September 14, 1990; Westerly September 1982.

HARDISON, O(SBORNE) B(ENNETT) JR. (October 28, 1928–August 5, 1990), American scholar, educator, library director, poet and essayist, was born in San Diego, California to Osborne Bennett Hardison,, who served as a naval commander in World War II, and Ruth (Morgan) Hardison. He entered the Massachusetts Institute of Technology with the intention of becoming a biophysicist, but switched his interest to literature. His university degrees were earned at the University of North Carolina (B.A., 1949; M.A. in English literature, 1950) and the University of Wisconsin (Ph.D., 1956). Prior to his appointment to the Folger Shakespeare Library in Washington, D.C., his main career position, he taught in the literature departments of the University of Tennessee, at Knoxville; Princeton; and, for the longest period (1957–1969), at the University of North Carolina at Chapel Hill, where he also served as co-chair of the Duke University-University of North Carolina Program in the Humanities. Essays by students in one of his seminars at North Carolina on contemporary criticism make up the contents of a collection that he edited under the title *The Quest for Imagination*.

Hardison may be characterized as a Renaissance man in a double sense. As a scholar he published original interpretations of the literature of the Renaissance. As a writer he bridged what C. P. Snow has dubbed "The Two Cultures"—art and science. "My method is simple," he wrote in the preface to his *Disappearing through the Skylight*. "I have tried to listen carefully to what people involved in creating and interpreting cultural change say about what they are doing. The testimony of artists has been as important in this respect as the testimony of scientists." As familiar with the world of quasars and black holes and the International Style of architecture as he was with Elizabethan prosody—and equally at home with modern film and medieval church drama—he reached out to a cultivated readership beyond the confines of academic specialism.

Hardison made his debut as a writer with a collection of poems, *Lyrics and Elegies*, part of the Poets of Today Series edited by John Hall Wheelock, who characterized Hardison as "a philosopher, indeed a metaphysician, by temperament." He termed Hardison's poetry "implicitly, and often explicitly . . . a criticism of contemporary life" in his introduction to the volume. "A certain austerity and coldness of tone sometimes mask . . . a great charge of feeling." Some of the poems, such as "Star Chamber" (on the trial and death of Sir Thomas More) utilize Renaissance subjects as ironical comment on shifting moral values. In others he emulates the witty juxtapositions of metaphysical poetry, as in "Leibniz to His Coy Mistress," which concludes:

O. B. HARDISON JR.

Therefore, my dear, do not resist
The fires that sear your troubled dust;
Of all the worlds that may exist
This is the only world that must.

The longer poem "Bernini's Colonnade" illustrates "the relativity of truth as we know it" through the image of the famous entrance to St. Peter's as viewed from various vantage points. It anticipates Hardison's later humanist/technophile essays. The enigmatic "Spieltrieb" looks forward to one of the focal concepts of *Disappearing through the Skylight*—the "playfulness" of modern literature, painting, and architecture.

During his years as a professor of literature, Hardison distinguished himself as an editor of critical texts (including a commentary on Aristotle's *Poetics* and anthologies of medieval and Renaissance rhetorical treatises) and particularly as an author of scholarly monographs. A year in Rome on a Fulbright Fellowship (1953–1954) produced *The Enduring Monument: A Study of the Idea of Praise in Renaissance Theory and Practice.* Relating Renaissance theories of poetry to rhetoric, Hardison analyzes and justifies the didactic emphasis traceable from Dante's *Canzonieri* to Donne's *Anniversaries* in reaction against the "aesthetic" bias of his predecessors (notably Joel Spingarn). A grant from the Guggenheim Memorial Foundation (1963–1964) gave him the leisure to complete *Christian Rite and Christian Drama in the Middle Ages,* in which he reconstructs "the shift from ritual to representational modes" that marks the transi-

tion from medieval to modern drama. In this landmark study Hardison takes issue with such earlier scholars as E. K. Chambers and Karl Young, who tended to separate literature from religion, by demonstrating that religious ritual *was* the drama of the early Middle Ages. With the decline of classical drama, the ceremony of the Mass in particular exemplified the principles of tragedy set forth in Aristotle's *Poetics.* This book was awarded the Haskins Medal of the Medieval Academy of America in 1967.

In 1969 Hardison was appointed director of the Folger Shakespeare Library, where he had previously been a Fellow. His term in this post, extending to 1983, saw a remarkable period of growth for this institution, which had been somewhat isolated. Hardison not only made the library a center of international scholarship with the establishment of the Folger Institute of Renaissance and Eighteenth-Century Studies, but he made it more accessible to the public through founding the Folger Theatre Group (now the Shakespeare Theatre), and initiating a program of literary readings and a series of concerts of medieval and Renaissance music by the group known as the Folger Consort. He also organized docent tours and helped to start the Folger's program for teaching Shakespeare in public schools in the Washington area. Another scholarly accomplishment was bringing the *Shakespeare Quarterly* to the Folger. From the material standpoint, he raised eight million dollars, making possible physical expansion and renovation, including the introduction of advanced temperature and humidity controls.

During his tenure at the Folger Library, Hardison embarked on explorations of contemporary culture in *Toward Freedom and Dignity: The Humanities and the Idea of Humanity,* a collection of lectures originally delivered at the annual Humanities Forum sponsored by Elon College in North Carolina. Drawing on both traditional and contemporary concepts of humanism, Hardison pleads for the recognition of the humanities as not merely luxuries, but "central to the preparation of human beings for the kind of society that is possible if we manage to avoid an Orwellian technocracy." These lectures were written in a despairing mood when he was beset by fear of imminent "atomic annihilation and population explosion", he told the *New York Times Book Review.* This disposition had obviously been dispelled by the time he undertook his later works of popularization, notable for their upbeat tone and exuberance, indicating that he had established a modus vivendi with the new technology. "I just got tired of being a pessimist," he confided in the same interview. "You can only live so long with the notion that humanity will destroy itself."

Entering the Maze: Identity and Change in Modern Culture had its inception in a series of lectures delivered at Clemson University in 1978, and was shaped during the course of a fellowship at the Aspen Institute in Colorado during the summer of 1979. The title, as indicated by the epigraphs, echoes both Milton's *Paradise Lost* ("And found no end, in wand'ring mazes lost") and Pope's *Essay on Man* ("A mighty maze! but not without a plan"). "The central concern of this book is the relation between contemporary culture and the mental ecology of those who, for better or for worse, inhabit that culture," Hardison explains in its preface. "In the metaphor of the title, contemporary culture is a maze, a tangle of paths that seem to lead everywhere and nowhere at the same time."

A linking theme for *Entering the Maze* arises from the odd juxtaposition of the statue of George Washington contemplating the swing of a Foucault pendulum in the Museum of American History, suggesting to the author in his essay "America as Europe" an "emblem of the contrast between the glories of the past and the realities of technological culture." "Taking Bearings," the first group of essays, illustrates the persistence of anachronistic art forms, particularly classical architecture, in American monuments. "In Mazes Lost" is a consideration of the disturbing influences of contemporary technology, such as the clash between medical progress and ethics and the effects of computer science on the classification of knowledge. "Mirrors on the Wall," concerned with media art created by technology, includes a pithy survey of Alfred Hitchcock's oeuvre ("the film artist as rhetorician") and a searching appraisal of Laurence Olivier's adaptation of *Henry V*—which Hardison had previously edited for a collection of published film scripts.

The last group, appropriately titled "The Thread of Ariadne," proposes ways out of the maze, including retention of a core curriculum in modified form in our schools. The concluding essay, rather misleadingly called "The Future of Poetry," finds the makings of a "Fourth World, Art-timeless and universal" in image-based media like photography, sound recordings, film, and television, rather than in poetry which, being dependent on language, had since the Romantic period to become nationalistic or ethnocentric.

"He must tell us more about his Fourth World," remarked Murat Williams in his review of *Entering the Maze* in the *Virginia Quarterly Review*. Hardison obliged with *Disappearing through the Skylight*, a collection of essays published the year before his death, bearing on its title page a quotation from Thomas Jefferson: "I

am captivated more by dreams of the future than by the history of the past." Accordingly, this second part of what was conceived as "a trilogy on identity in modern culture" really looks towards the twenty-first century. The title alludes to modern banks, "airy structures of steel and glass" whose tops seem to soar out of sight, by contrast with their symmetrical, low-lying neoclassic predecessors. This image is expanded in the essays that follow to describe changes that have taken place in our conceptions of nature and of human evolution, as well as in history, language, and art—all areas of knowledge which have burst out of their traditional boundaries and in effect, "disappeared" beyond our ready grasp.

Such phenomena as the double helix, the geodesic dome, cubistic art, concrete poetry, "chance music," cylindrical architecture, and computer-generated languages—all manifestations of Heisenberg's uncertainty principle—lead Hardison to compare the 20th century transformation of culture to the conversion from paganism to Christianity of the the third century. Converts then spoke in "figures and paradoxes", he points out, as do present-day artists and scientists. "At no other time in history have conditions been more exciting—or more filled with promise for beings on a small planet hurtling through the vast darkness of space toward an unknown and unimaginable future which they themselves are creating," he concludes in the prologue to the book. Essentially *Disappearing through the Skylight* registers and celebrates the end of the Renaissance and the advent of postmodernism.

The style of these essays dazzled most reviewers, and Hardison's elucidation of recondite discoveries in mathematics and physics made the book a bestseller. Malcolm Bradbury said ,in the *New York Times Book Review*, that "we require a vast and varied assessment of a long century of fundamental and irrevocable transformations. This by large, splendidly illustrated synthesis is . . . more than a start."

Hardison left the Folger Library in 1983 to have more time to write and "to be a bohemian, my secret proclivity," but soon thereafter he accepted an appointment to the English faculty of Georgetown University, where he taught for his remaining years. As a young professor at the University of North Carolina he had been featured in an article in *Time* magazine (and on its cover) titled "To Profess with a Passion," which profiled a group of outstanding American college teachers. At Georgetown he acquired a similar reputation; his courses on Milton, Shakespeare and the Renaissance lured numerous students away from their favorite television programs. True to the spirit of his favorite age, the Elizabethan, he was famous for his bawdy language, as well as for his eloquence. In the course of a busy professional life he was at various times president of the Renaissance Society of America, The Shakespeare Association of America, and the Washington English-Speaking Union. He was also active in the Quark Club, a group of scientists and humanists who met at the Smithsonian Institution to discuss cultural change. Among the scholastic honors, he received from more than twenty universities and societies were the Cavaliere Ufficiale from the Italian Government in 1974 and the Order of the British Empire in 1983. The largesse he enjoyed as the beneficiary of scholarly foundations is wryly alluded to in "Finis" the poem that concludes his volume *Pro Musica Antiqua:*

So rent me a house on Naples' bay
Where I can feel the tears of things
And think what song the siren sings
And how to make you, patron, pay.

Hardison died suddenly at the age of 61 of a blood clot caused by a cancer that had been diagnosed just a month before. Just a few hours before he died, he exchanged a ritual handshake with friends assembled at his bedside and cheered them all up with his witticisms. He was survived by his wife, the former Marifrances Fitzgibbon (whom he married in 1950), four daughters, and two sons. Left on his computer disks at his death was the text of a book in progress that he intended to be the final volume of his trilogy on cultural change. However, in the last year of his life he managed to bring out another scholarly monograph in his field of specialization, *Prosody and Purpose in the English Renaissance.* This book received laudatory posthumous reviews, notably in an homage issue of the *Sewanee Review,* which included a tribute by the poet Anthony Hecht, a colleague at Georgetown University, and a poem by George Garrett, another colleague and one-time collaborator. "O. B. Hardison lived in the past, the present, and in what is to come," concludes the anonymous obituary in the *Renaissance Quarterly.* "Perhaps it is that ability to achieve temporal concordance that makes him seem to be still with us." The Folger Library established an annual poetry award in his honor.

PRINCIPAL WORKS: *Poetry*—Lyrics and Elegies (*in* Poets of Today) 1958; Pro Musica Antiqua, 1977. *Scholarly monographs*—The Enduring Monument: A Study of the Idea of Praise in Renaissance Theory and Practice, 1962; Christian Rite and Christian Drama in the Middle Ages, 1965; Prosody and Purpose in the English Renaissance,1989. *Cultural criticism*—Toward Freedom and Dignity: The Humanities and the Idea of Humanity, 1971; Entering the Maze Identity and Change in Modern Culture, 1981; Disappearing through the Skylight, 1989. *As editor*—Modern Continental Literary Criticism, 1962; Renaissance Literary Criticism, 1963; (with A. Preminger and F. Warnke) The Princeton Encyclopedia of Poetry and Poetics, 1965, abr. ed.: The Princeton Handbook of Poetic Terms, 1986; (with L. Golden) Practical Rhetoric, 1966; Aristotle's Poetics (tr. L. Golden) 1968; (with George P. Garrett and J. R. Gelfman) Film Scripts One, 1971; The Quest for Imagination, 1971; (with others) Classical and Medieval Literary Criticism, 1974 abr. ed. 1985.

ABOUT: Who's Who in America, 1990–1991; Contemporary Authors New Revision Series 6, 1982; 132, 1991. *Periodicals*—AB Bookman's Weekly December 17, 1990; America January 16, 1982; March 3, 1990; Books Abroad Summer 1963; Critical Quarterly Spring 1965; English Language Notes March 1967; Library Journal October 15, 1989; New York Review of Books April 26, 1990; New York Times August 7, 1990; New York Times Book Review December 31, 1989; Renaissance Quarterly Spring 1991; Sewanee Review July 1978; Winter 1991; Shakespeare Quarterly Winter 1990; Smithsonian November 1990; Time May 26, 1966; Virginia Quarterly Review Summer 1982; Washington Post August 7, 1990.

HARRIS, MACDONALD (September 7, 1921–July 24, 1993), American novelist and short story writer, sent the following to *World Authors* in 1992:

"I was born in South Pasadena, California, a suburb of Los Angeles, in 1921. At that time Los Angeles was still a big village, and I lived an idyllic and uneventful childhood, marked by a good deal of inner storytelling and reverie-making about the world around me. As a child I was an insatiable reader, and there was hardly a time when I didn't write. In high school I published stories and sketches in the local newspaper. I broke off college to go to sea as a merchant marine cadet in 1942, and later became a naval officer; I served in the European Theater and in the South Pacific, and ended the war in Japan. All during these years I continued to read and to write, and several of my stories appeared in a magazine published by the U.S. Merchant Marine Academy.

"After the war I enrolled at the University of Redlands, a small college set in the orange groves in Southern California. There I met my future wife, took the one and only creative writing course of my life, and sold my first story to a national magazine; 'The Sad Lady' appeared in *Esquire* in 1947. I went on to graduate work at the University of Southern California, and continued to write stories. One of them, 'Second Cir-

MACDONALD HARRIS

cle,' originally published in *Atlantic Monthly*, was reprinted in *Prize Short Stories* (*The O. Henry Collection*), and another, 'Trepleff,' from *Harper's* (a chapter of the novel by the same title), was included in *The Best American Short Stories* in 1967.

"My first novel, *Private Demons*, was published by Houghton Mifflin in 1961. It was juvenile and rather light in tone, influenced by my years of writing magazine stories. *Mortal Leap*, in 1964, was better; it came out of my war experiences and was an adventure tale with metaphysical implications, an identity story. Both of these novels were tentative and preliminary. With *Trepleff*, published by Gollancz in London in 1968 and Holt, Rinehart & Winston in 1969, I expressed myself for the first time in an authentic voice that was to continue, with evolution and change, through the rest of my work. By this time I had a Ph.D. and I was teaching in the Writing Program at the University of California, Irvine, where I remained until 1991.

"My work came to the attention of serious critics in 1976, when *The Balloonist* was nominated for a National Book Award and widely reprinted and translated. By this time I had dropped the vein of autobiography I had experimented with briefly in *Mortal Leap* and, to a degree, in *Trepleff*; *The Balloonist*, based on the historical attempt of the Swedish Andrée Expedition to teach the North Pole in a free balloon, came frankly out of my reading and my interest in arctic exploration, although my naval training in navigation and my experience as an amateur sailor played a part. As everyone knows, there is

an autobiographical element in all fiction, however disguised, and on the other hand there is no 'true' or autobiographical account of a human life that is not fictional to some extent. This theoretical point has always fascinated me, and the fictive nature of consciousness and the relation between fact and artifact play a part in such 'metafictional' novels as *Screenplay*, *Glowstone*, and *Glad Rags*.

"I have always been interested in travel and especially in Europe. I know Italian and French well, Spanish less well, and German a little. Starting in the sixties, I have spent long periods in Europe with my family: two separate years in Italy, a year in Paris, and other shorter stays of several months. This encounter with Europe has played a large part in my fiction from *Trepleff* through *Glowstone*. More recently, with *Hemingway's Suitcase* and *Glad Rags*, I have sought consciously to express the American experience, and my own American experience, although there are still European elements in both these later novels. As an American writer I am a Jamesian rather than a follower in the steps of Mark Twain. My other literary affinities are, chiefly, Dickens, Proust, Virginia Woolf, Thomas Mann, Hemingway, and, especially Nabokov. I am impressed by Jung, although a little wary of Jungians, and an avid reader of biographies of writers, whether or not I like their writing.

"My legal name is Donald Heiney. The use of a fictional pseudonym, which I began with my earliest stories, has provided a convenient form of controlled schizophrenia which has enabled me to cling to an artistic temperament and a creative outlook even though I've lived most of my life in a banal bourgeois atmosphere. The problem for a writer in those circumstances, I think, is to resist the forces that attempt to make him normal and to remain a little crazy. In this, at least, I think I have succeeded. If I could characterize the development of my writing over the years, I would say that it has become odder and more idiosyncratic, and at the same time more accessible to larger numbers of readers. I find that a difficult achievement, and one that I am pleased with."

⸻

MacDonald Harris dates the emergence of his "authentic voice" as a novelist to *Trepleff* in 1968. In fact, he has many authentic voices. Irving Malin in *Review of Contemporary Fiction* suggested that Harris's "Polo's Trip" in *Cathay Stories* shows an obsession with Coleridge's "Kubla Khan." The central character, a wealthy young modern-day Venetian begins a quest that takes him totally out of measurable time and recognizable space. He ends up a prisoner on the borders of Cathay some time around 1380. The story is told in the form of a letter the young man addresses to "His Excellency, the Consul General of Venice, Xanadu, Celestial Kingdom of Cathay"—a plea for help that deconstructs itself even as he writes it: "For how can one hope to succeed in a petition when he does not know the name, the correct title, or the address of the person to whom he is writing, and cannot even be sure of his existence? Such metaphysical doubts, quite at odds with my normal rational personality, have begun to assail me lately. Perhaps I have imagined all this, I tell myself, or perhaps I am only a character in a work of fiction I am writing down on this rice-paper in order to while away the hours in this hopeless place." As Malin suggests, Harris appears to be writing fiction about fiction and "Kubla Khan" is an apposite allusion "because he recognizes that he is in a miracle world of 'rare device.'"

Literary references both direct and oblique abound in Harris's fiction. In *Trepleff*, his first novel to achieve wide critical attention, he set a pattern for his later work, although each subsequent book has its own distinctive stamp and has challenged the reader to explore a different area of human knowledge or experience:—science in *Glowstone*, aeronautics in *The Balloonist* and *Herma*, music in *Herma* and *Tenth*, history in *Pandora's Gallery* and *The Treasure of Sainte Foy*, mythology in *Bull Fire*, film in *Screenplay*, folklore and fantasy in *The Little People*, literary satire in *Hemingway's Suitcase*. *Trepleff* takes its title from the name of the young protagonist of Chekhov's *The Sea Gull*. Its 20th-century American hero-protagonist acts in that play in college and is haunted by the role thereafter. Although he in no way imitates Chekhov's character and indeed resists it by launching a promising career as a psychiatrist, he drifts into a series of irresponsible actions that perversely mirror those in the play and leave him in the end in an insane asylum. Like most of Harris's novels, *Trepleff* balances its potentially tragic subject with irony and wit. Robert Maurer in *Saturday Review* found this combination somewhat disconcerting: "[I]ts tone sways hither and yon from dead seriousness to slapstick comedy, from high lyricism down to existential coolness, with intermittent squiggles of mood as unexpected as they are indescribable. . . . " Still, he conceded, the book is full of energy and intelligence: "For such traits a reader should be willing to be a bit out of kelter, to live in a house of fiction where, as Trepleff puts it, the walls are not quite straight."

While Harris's use of the outright supernatural is infrequent ("the little people" in his novel of that title are fairy spirits of ancient Britain who communicate with an American scholar recuperating from a nervous breakdown; the contemporary hero of *Screenplay* follows a rabbity-looking old man right through the movie screen into the Hollywood of the silent film era), he stretches the imagination to its limits. He switches time, places, sexes, and introduces historical figures as characters: Caruso, Puccini, Marcel Proust in *Herma*, Monet at Giverny in *Glowstone* Henri Rousseau in *The Balloonist* Thomas Mann in *Tenth*. His male characters turn into women: one of the polar explorers in *The Balloonist* proves to be a glamorous adventuress with whom the central character has had a passionate love affair in Paris. Perhaps the most remarkable of these instances of androgyny is the heroine of *Herma*, a brilliant young American opera singer who survives the San Francisco earthquake and becomes the toast of belle époque Paris. Herma's alter ego is the young man who manages her career, Fred Hite—the name an obvious pun.

At the base of these novels is a recognizable reality, often portrayed in precise factual detail. Steven G. Kellman observed in *Western Humanities Review* that Harris may be subverting the pride we take in our technical mastery, noting "a playful skepticism about the contribution factual information makes to out ability to understand and govern ourselves." Harris acknowledged that his work was moving in the direction of "magical realism."

Elements of the fabulous mingle with the factual in *The Balloonist*. Set in 1897 as the memoir of a Major Gustavus Crispin, a Swede who actually perished in a balloon expedition to the North Pole, and told in the first person as an exciting adventure tale, it intersperses Crispin's memories of a passionately romantic love affair in belle époque Paris at the turn of the century with an account of harrowing polar experiences *The Balloonist*, nominated for a National Book Award in 1976, was widely praised for its elegant writing, as here, the narrator beings his ascent:

> I feel the gondola stir, lurch to one side and rise slowly. The white faces below are a clump of strange flowers, damply pale against the brown of the beach, following our motions as sunflowers follow the sun. Everything below us, the sheds of the camp, the white faces looking upward, dwindles and shrinks as if pulled to a center by invisible lines of force. I look over the side to be sure the guide ropes are trailing properly. They slither over the beach and enter the sea, where they follow behind us leaving three snaky furrows on the water.

P. L. Adams in the *Atlantic* called the novel "a bittersweet fantasy about man's struggle with his assorted enemies: machines, nature, women and his own intelligence . . . an ironic comedy which ultimately becomes truly moving."

Harris's last novel, *A Portrait of My Desire*, is the story of a wealthy widower who becomes involved with his sensualist housekeeper. He attempts to get hold of a painting, with which he is also besotted. Donna Seaman commented in *Booklist*, "Harris's send-up of epicurean insularity, lust-inspired foolishness, and ruthless pragmatism is stylishly wry." Rachel Billington spoke for other reviewers, however, when in the *New York Times Book Review* she found the novel labyrinthine and its characters not "weighty enough to bear their symbolic purposes." Nevertheless, Billington deemed it "gripping, clever and original . . . a convincing hybrid of novel and thriller. . . ."

Harris received the Award in Literature from the American Academy and Institute of Arts and Letters in 1982 and grants from the American Council of Learned Societies and the American Philosophical Society. In 1985 he received a special citation from PEN for his novel *Tenth*. He taught comparative literature and creative writing at the University of California, Los Angles (1949–1953), the University of Utah (1953–1965), and the University of California, Irvine (1965–1991). Harris married Ann Borgman in 1948. They had two sons to whom he dedicated one of his works of nonfiction, *They Sailed Alone: The Story of the Single Handers*, an account of voyagers who sailed the oceans alone in small boats. Harris died at his home in Newport Beach, California, of a heart attack.

PRINCIPAL WORKS: *Novels*—Private Demons, 1961; Mortal Leap, 1964; Trepleff, 1968; Bull Fire, 1973; The Balloonist, 1976; Yukiko, 1977; Pandora's Galley, 1979; The Treasure of Sainte Foy, 1980; Herma, 1981; Screenplay, 1983; Tenth, 1984; The Little People, 1986; Glowstone, 1987; Hemingway's Suitcase, 1990; Glad Rags, 1991; A Portrait of My Desire, 1993. *Short stories*—The Cathay Stories and Other Fictions, 1988. *Nonfiction*—(as Donald Heiney)—America in Modern Italian Literature, 1964; Three Italian Novelists, 1968. Juvenile—They Sailed Alone: The Story of the Single Handers, 1972.

ABOUT: Contemporary Authors New Revision Series 3, 1981; Contemporary Literary Criticism 9, 1979; White, J. Mythology in the Modern Novel, 1971. *Periodicals*—Atlantic October 1976; Booklist March 1, 1993; Hudson Review Winter 1992;; New York Times July 13, 1980; March 18, 1984; June 17, 1990; May 19, 1991; July 27, 1993; New York Times Book Review April 11, 1993; Newsweek October 25, 1982; Publishers Weekly September 18, 1981; Review of Contemporary Fiction Summer 1989; Saturday Review December 20, 1969; Times Literary Supplement November 28, 1968; August 22, 1980; April 22, 1983; Western Humanities Review Spring 1982.

HARRISON, BARBARA GRIZZUTI (September 14, 1934–   ), American journalist, essayist, novelist, and critic, was born in Brooklyn, New York, the daughter of Italian immigrants—Dominick Grizzuti, a printer, and Carmela (Di Nardo) Grizzuti. In 1944, a door-to-door proselytizer converted Carmela Grizzuti to the Jehovah's Witnesses. Nine-year-old Barbara joined also, and spent much of her youth and adolescence proselytizing for the apocalyptic sect. Harrison left the sect in 1955 and published a well-regarded memoir of her involvement with Jehovah's Witnesses, *Visions of Glory*, more than twenty years later.

Despite her youthful immersion in the world of the Witnesses (who eschew most civic and secular activities, and have an obligation to convert others), Harrison was an avid reader, excelled in school, and claims that she knew that she would eventually become a writer. She credits a high school English teacher with having changed her life. "He knew I was talented and encouraged me," Harrison told an interviewer in 1985.

She went to work immediately following high school. In 1960 she married W. Dale Harrison, an official with the world-relief agency CARE. Most of their eight-year marriage was spent overseas, primarily in Libya (where their son Joshua was born) and in Bombay, India (where their daughter Anna was born).

It was not until after her divorce in 1968 that Harrison made a serious attempt to become a professional writer. She wrote an article for the *New Republic* which chronicled a struggle to incorporate feminist demands into the curriculum of her daughter's school in Brooklyn. The owner of the *New Republic* and Liveright publishing company, Gilbert Harrison (no relation to her husband), urged her to expand the article into a book, even offering her an advance. Calculating her living expenses for the following six months, she asked for and received a $4,000 advance on what was to become her first book, *Unlearning the Lie: Sexism in School*. The book highlights the heated debates surrounding the creation of the sex-roles committee at the Woodward School, a progressive parent-teacher cooperative for kindergarten through the eighth grade. "One great virtue of Harrison's book is that it documents a process of changing an institution, however small," Florence Howe wrote in the *American Scholar*. "We have too few such histories, too few lessons from the efforts of feminists to achieve at least change, if not power."

Harrison's second book, *Visions of Glory: A History and a Memory of Jehovah's Witnesses*, is, as the title suggests, both a history of the religious sect and a personal account of her own

BARBARA GRIZZUTI HARRISON

eleven-year involvement with it. Reviewing it in the *Nation*, Lisa Gubernick noted that "the autobiographical fragments give the book balance and weight. Through them she can convey what this peculiar theology feels like." Although she deemed it "a very badly organized book," Vivian Gornick, in the *New York Times Book Review*, found much of value in *Visions of Glory*: "It is . . . quite well written, contains a mass of absorbing information, and the personality of its author is extremely appealing." Gornick did not find the autobiographical portions of the book convincing: "Yet, when I closed the book I found myself thinking: I still don't know what it's like inside the skin of a Jehovah's Witness. I still don't know what it is that pierces and holds those who are converted, what the quality of their passion is. I can't taste it or feel it."

Very near the end of *Visions of Glory*, Harrison makes a surprising revelation: she has returned to the Catholic church. "When I compare the Church with the Witnesses, I think: The Witnesses explained everything, and explained everything legalistically. The Church does not attempt to explain everything: triumphant, militant, glorious, it is humble enough to get on its august knees and say 'We do not know'. . . . The Church has room for everything, including, God knows, vulgarity. That is what I love about it—that it is catholic, universal."

Off Center is a collection of essays, reviews, and interviews that originally appeared in the *New Republic*, *Ms.*, *Ladies' Home Journal*, the *Village Voice*, and other publications. Harrison's topics and targets are diverse; she examines her own moral ambivalence toward abortion, race riots in her old high school, and popular cult movements such as "est" (a form of marathon group therapy) and the Moonies. In a section of the book entitled "Culture Heroes," she dissects Jane Fonda, Dick Cavett, and Joan Didion. Her skewering of the essayist and novelist Didion, which was first published in the *Nation*, is especially savage. She describes Didion as a "neurasthenic Cher," whose prose style is "perversely sentimental, dismissing the truth in order to achieve effect." According to Lore Dickstein in the *New York Times Book Review* (1980), "These essays exhibit Mrs. Harrison's ability to pass beyond the shibboleths of celebrity to the person behind the myth." Praising Harrison's integrity, Dickstein wrote: "Many writers of personal journalism use their work as occasions for self-promotion: The author becomes the subject of the piece. Barbara Grizzuti Harrison does not fall into this swamp of indulgence; her feminist politics and personal responses, always present in her writing, serve as backdrop for the more important matter—her subject. Her essays are sharp and well-written; she has a taste for the absurd, a distrust of idealism, and affection for people. Mrs. Harrison claims she loves her work; it shows."

Harrison's novel *Foreign Bodies* was markedly less successful than her other work. The novel's protagonist, a journalist in her thirties, falls madly and impossibly in love with a homosexual Pakistani painter. "Harrison's fine ear and sharp eye as a journalist-essayist are rarely evident in her novel," Clancy Sigal wrote in the *New York Times Book Review*. "It is pretentious, flagrantly overwritten and essentially humorless. What a wonderful comedy lurks behind the interminable dialogue and random peregrinations of the heroine!" Harrison acknowledged in a *Publishers Weekly* interview that "maybe half a dozen people in the whole country liked it," and that her editor urged her to "bury" the novel. Harrison has also written many (as yet uncollected) short stories.

She made an extensive and leisurely journey through Italy in the mid-1980s, beginning in the northern cities (Milan, Venice, and Florence), spending some time in Rome, and then venturing into the more remote, less often visited regions of Abruzzi and Calabria. *Italian Days*, her meditation on this journey through the homeland of her parents, won critical approval everywhere. Reviewing it in the *Atlantic*, Corby Kummer wrote, "*Italian Days* is a rich account of a long stay in Italy, visiting monuments, conducting brief and intensive friendships, eating, following the tracks of writers and historians, and everywhere looking for her place in the

Church in which she was baptized but which she left in childhood, returning only as an adult." In the *New York Times Book Review*, Eva Hoffman said, "The spirits of Montaigne, Goethe, Stendhal, Hawthorne and Henry James, among others, hover over her narrative, and Ms. Grizzuti Harrison generously interweaves the impressions of these illustrious fellow travelers into her own." Although she found some of the family anecdotes "repetitious," Hoffman was particularly impressed by Harrison's accounts of her meetings with long-lost relatives: "She is honest enough to convey the full ambivalence of these meetings, the mingling of great expectations, misunderstanding, some illumination, disappointment and finally reconciliation."

Harrison's *The Astonishing World* features interviews with Mario Cuomo and Gore Vidal. A resident of Manhattan since the success of *Italian Days*, she continues to be a regular contributor to such periodicals as *Mademoiselle*, the *New York Times Book Review*, and the *New York Times Magazine*. The subject matter of her journalistic writing is diverse and usually topical; in addition to book reviews and interviews with celebrities and writers, Harrison has written about phone sex, the men's movement, breast implants, and designer handguns for women. Although she had admitted to being "the least disciplined person I know," her journalistic output is prodigious. "I don't know how I learned to write, but it was terribly important to me," she told *Publishers Weekly*. "Language was both my way out of my difficult life, and my way in—to myself."

PRINCIPAL WORKS: *Nonfiction*—Unlearning the Lie: Sexism in School, 1973; Visions of Glory: A History and a Memory of Jehovah's witnesses, 1978; Off Center: Essays, 1980; Italian Days, 1989; (with S. Nardulli) The Islands of Italy: Sicily, Dardinia, and the Aeolian Isles, 1991; The Astonishing World: Essays, 1992. *Novel*—Foreign Bodies, 1984.

ABOUT: Contemporary Authors New Revisions Series 15, 1985. *Periodicals*—American Scholar Autumn 1973; Atlantic August 1989; Nation January 13, 1979; New York Times August 23, 1989; New York Times Book Review November 19, 1978; June 15, 1980; July 1, 1984; Publishers Weekly July 27, 1992.

HARWOOD, GWEN (GWENDOLINE NESSIE FOSTER) (June 8, 1920–), Australian poet, essayist, short story writer, and librettist, was born at Taringa in Brisbane to Joseph Richard and Agnes (Jaggard) Foster. She was educated at Michelton and Toowong State Schools and Brisbane Girls Grammar School and took a

degree in music performance in 1936. She has lived and worked in Hobart, Tasmania, since 1945.

Harwood developed an early passion for poetry and music (especially opera) and studied piano and composition with the Handel scholar Dr. Robert Dalley-Scarlett, with whom she taught, after attaining her music teacher's diploma in 1939. She became the organist at All Saints' Church in Brisbane after a seven-month novitiate in the Anglican Franciscan convent in Toowong (August 1941–January 1942). *Blessed City*, a collection of her letters to Thomas Riddell in 1943, is filled with wit, shrewd observation, and love of language. At the time she wrote those letters she was a somewhat rebellious public servant in the War Damage Commission in Brisbane. The letters show how her home life and interactions with other musicians, poets, artists and intellectuals of the day were formative.

She married a graduate of Melbourne University, Bill Harwood on September 4, 1945, and moved to Hobart, where Bill Harwood was appointed as lecturer in the department of English at the University of Tasmania. Harwood later observed, in an essay in the CRNLE Essays and Monographs Series that "in my husband's luggage lay the *Tractatus Logico-Philosphicus.*". She writes:

> In the *Tractatus*, Wittgenstein separates descriptive language, "reports about the world" in the scientific sense, from metaphor, fantasy, the sphere of what can only be shown in the way poetry shows us a sense life. . . . when Wittgenstein says "Ethics and aesthetics are one and the same" (*Tractatus* 6.421) he is surely referring to the power of poetry to infuse experience with value.

In his essay "Voices from the Mirror" (in Robert Sellick's *Gwen Harwood*) Vincent O'Sullivan cites Harwood's poem "Hesperian" as evidence of her debt to Wittgenstein: "'Essence is expressed by *grammar*'/ an aged philosopher sighed, 'My God!'" A line in another poem further demonstrates the diversity of Harwood's investigations of relationships between experience and speech: "since man's a language user / he must *say* things are, or cannot speak at all."

In *Boundary Conditions*, Jennifer Strauss says, "In art and life, Harwood seems to concede, language may be surpassed in some functions by music or painting." Her tribute to the pianist, Rex Hobcroft "Four Impromptus," while articulating Harwood's assertion of the comparatively "modest" potential of language, paradoxically demonstrates its power:

> But for this hour I offer you,
> whose warmth and words and skill renew
>
> the heart, a poem, though words can never

contain, as music does, the unsayable
grace that cannot be defined
yet leaps like light from mind to mind.

Gwen Harwood delights in and exploits the ambiguities of language. Her poetry shifts from the graceful or playful, to the wicked or intellectually serious, with often surprising deftness. The range within one poem can be complex, despite her disarming directness. For example, an observation about birdsong in "Blackbird" acknowledges the ambivalence of nature's gifts and simultaneously serves as a wry comment on the Christian faith:

In the morning my blackbird sings
   "Believe in the Trinity."
In the evening he seems to say
   "Abandon all property."
Song, faith and ethics from one beak—
   what a divinity!

Words and music are central preoccupations, but a feature of Harwood's poetry is the diversity of approaches to the subject. Jennifer Strauss writes:

The boundaries that are drawn sharply in one poem are in others stormed by intellect, dissolved by tenderness, laughed out of their power to harm. And all this is reflected in the technical management of line and stanza, where a new order grows out of the contest between the conservative impulse of formal structures of metre, rhyme and stanza length and the energising thrust or gentle flow of particular utterances which break the notional bounds of stanzas and other formal units of division.

A search for the harmony that music represents also provides a rationale for her poetry. In "They Trust Me with the Axe: the Poetry of Gwen Harwood" in Brooks and Walker's *Poetry and Gender*, Elizabeth Lawson cites Harwood's claim that "the nearest expressive correspondences to human experience are always found, not in language but in music;" in her "Postlude: Listening to Bach," music has the power to "bridge the cryptic spaces / between us and the peace—giving solution / to what our nature is, how the world's made." Harwood has consistently paid tribute to a range of composers and musicians and her songs and humorous "replays" of her own performances express her abiding interest in music as a source. "Beyond Metaphor," from *The Lion's Bride*, deals lightly with serious issues:

Only Mozart, perhaps, found the right tone
to make things bearable. Who was it said
at the end of *Tractatus*: What you can't say
you can't say, and you can't whistle it either.

In "Wittgenstein and Engelmann,": Harwood observes the dichotomy between language and reality, an unbridgeable gap, that nevertheless is bridged:

how propositions cannot state
   what they make manifest;
of the ethical and mystical
   that cannot be expressed;

how the world is on one side of us,
   and on the other hand
language, the mirror of the world;
   and God is, *how things stand.*

Harwood's belief in the "limitations of a scientific, logical positivist view of the world," according to Alison Hoddinot in *Gwen Harwood: The Real and The Imagined World* is shown in "Thought Is Surrounded by a Halo," which links language, word, and body in a manner reminiscent of the metaphysical poets:

Language is not a perfect game,
and if it were, how could we play?
The world's more than the sum of things
like moon, sky, centre, body, bed,
as all the singing masters know.

Picture two lovers side by side
who sleep and dream and wake to hold
the real and the imagined world
body by body, word by word
in the wild halo of their thought.

As a librettist of renown, Harwood has worked with prominent Australian composers: James Penberthy, Larry Sitsky, Ian Cugley, and Don Kay. She once wrote to Larry Sitsky claiming that "Usher" [Poe's "The Fall of the House of Usher,"] was "inoperable," and then proved herself wrong by writing the libretto for Sitsky's opera, produced in Hobart in 1965. In a radio interview after the publication of *Blessed City* she spoke of the complex relation between words and music, maintaining, "that text and music were integral but that the text should not be set free 'to go about alone in the world.'" This has been confirmed by her refusal to publish her libretti separately, and her claim that "the words are merely the concrete slab for the composer's glorious superstructure." Harwood's music master character, Professor Kröte (German for "toad"), a homesick exile—romantic—and drunken; The Kröte poems explore the pathos of the musician's thwarted potential as in "A Music Lesson":

Kröte's not well. His mood is bloody. A pupil he can
hardly stand attacks a transcendental study—Lord, send
me one real pianist. Soul of a horse! He slaps her hand
and breathes apologies to Liszt.

The poem ends: "If God exists / then music is his love for me."

Gwen Harwood published her first poem (as "Gwendoline Foster") in the journal *Meanjin* in 1944. With four children born between 1946 and 1952 to care for, she did not publish again until 1956; thereafter, under pseudonyms, her poems appeared mainly in *Meanjin* and *The Bulletin*. Her first collection, *Poems*, was published in 1963, and she then published steadily—poems, essays, book reviews, and opera libretti. By the early 1970's she was recognized as one of Australia's foremost poets. She has received numerous honors, including the *Meanjin* Poetry Prize (1959 and 1960), the Grace Leven Poetry Prize (1975), the Robert Frost Award of the Fellowship of Australian Writers (1977), the Patrick White Award (1978), and an honorary doctorate of letters from the University of Tasmania (1988). In 1988 she was writer-in-residence at Monash University, and in 1989 she was made an Officer of the Order of Australia. Her volume *Bone Scan* won the 1989 Victorian Premier's Prize for Poetry. At the Adelaide Festival of 1990 she received the J. J. Bray Award, and her *Blessed City: Letters to Thomas Riddell 1943* won the *Age* Book of the Year Award. The Australian Society of Arts and Letters awarded her its gold medal in 1992.

Harwood was treated for breast cancer in 1985, an experience she confronted in a number of her later poems, among them "Bone Scan":

In the twinkling of an eye,
in a moment, all is changed:
on a small radiant screen
(honeydew melon green)
are my scintillating bones.
Still in my flesh I see
the God who goes with me
glowing with radioactive
isotopes. This is what he
at last allows a mortal
eye to behold: the grand
supporting frame complete
(but for the wisdom teeth),
the friend who lives beneath
appearances, alive
with light. Each glittering bone
assures me: you are known.

Although her later years have been darkened by illness and the death of close friends, Harwood has retained her sense of the harmony of humanity and nature. Fleur Adcock observed, in a review of her *Collected Poems* in the *Times Literary Supplement*, that Harwood has many voices, many "poetic selves": "the philosopher, the ecstatic celebrant of life, love, nature and are . . . and (increasingly evident as the years go by) the elegist." One of her most moving elegies, "A Feline Requiem," is for her cat Tiglath-Pileser, "named for the grand Assyrian kings":

Death lays his icy hand
on kings of any kind.
Now yours is the first grave
in our arcadian grove.
It will be as beautiful
as old Anacreon's.

We outlive so many loves.
In shade a royal presence
watches the sunlit lawn
and the unsuspecting doves.

PRINCIPAL WORKS: *Poetry*—Poems, 1963; Poems / Volume Two, 1968; Selected Poems, 1975, rev. ed. 1985, 1990; The Lion's Bride, 1981; Bone Scan, 1988; Collected Poems, 1991. Nonfiction—Blessed City: The Letters of Gwen Harwood to Thomas Riddell January to September 1943, 1990.

ABOUT: Brooks, D. and B. Walker (eds.) Poetry and Gender, 1989; Buckley, V. Cutting Green Hay, 1983; Contemporary Authors 97–100, 1981; Contemporary Poets, 5th ed., 1991; Hoddinott, A. Gwen Harwood: The Real and the Imagined World, 1991; Lawson, E. The Poetry of Gwen Harwood, 1991; Oxford Companion to Australian Literature, 1985; Sellick, R. (ed.) Gwen Harwood (Centre for Research in New Literature in English Monograph Series), 1987; Strauss, J. Boundary Conditions: The Poetry of Gwen Harwood, 1992; Taylor, A. Reading Australian Poetry, 1987; Who's Who of Australian Writers 1991. *Periodicals*—Australian Literary Studies May 1976; Times Literary Supplement January 24, 1992.

HAWKING, STEPHEN W(ILLIAM) (January 8, 1942–), British theoretical physicist, was born in Oxford, England, the first of four children of Frank and Isobel Hawking. His father was a doctor who specialized in tropical diseases and spent many months each year doing research in Africa. In 1950 the family moved to St. Albans, a just north of London, where Hawking spent the rest of his childhood. He attended the St. Albans School, a private school affiliated with the local cathedral, where he quickly fell in with a group of bright boys. Always curious to find out how things work, he developed a passionate love for the sciences at an early age. Although his father wanted him to study medicine, Hawking was uninterested in biology, considering it too descriptive and concerned primarily with categorization. Instead, he was fascinated by mathematics and physics, which he though could lead to underlying truths about the universe.

Hawking attended Oxford University, where he quickly became known as a brilliant but lazy student. Because of his acute intuitive understanding of physics, he seldom had to do any work. His advisor at Oxford, Robert Berman, later recalled that "it was only necessary for him to know that something could be done, and he could do it without looking to see how other people did it." In 1962 he took a B.A. with high honors, later estimating that he had spent only one hour a day studying during his time at Oxford. He arrived at Cambridge University to begin doctoral studies in cosmology in the fall of the same year.

During Hawking's first few months at Cambridge, he noticed that he was having difficulties in movement. In January of 1963, his illness was diagnosed as amyotrophic lateral sclerosis (ALS), an incurable progressive disease that affects the nerve cells in the spinal cord and parts of the brain, causing loss of control of muscle movement. The body gradually becomes immobilized and death usually occurs when the respiratory muscles are affected and the patient contracts pneumonia and suffocates. ALS does not affect the mind, however, and the disease is painless. Given only two years to live, Hawking quickly slipped into a deep depression, unable to progress with his research. He eventually realized, however, that if he had only a short time to live, he must use the time constructively. A further incentive was that he had fallen in love with Jane Wilde, a young language student who, he said, gave him "the will to live." He returned to his research determined to work hard for the first time in his life. In his chosen field, the work could be done almost entirely mentally.

Hawking received his Ph.D. in 1965 with a thesis that established his scientific reputation. In his thesis, "Properties of the Expanding Universe," Hawking adapted intricate mathematical methods recently developed by his colleague Roger Penrose to Einstein's general theory of relativity, which explains the effect of gravity on large objects. By imagining the reverse of the process of matter falling into a black hole, he demonstrated that if one went backwards in time to the big bang, one must find a singularity, a point of infinite density and zero volume, that contained all of the matter in the universe. "There is a singularity in our past," he wrote in his thesis, which presented his first singularity theorem for the origin of the universe. Hawking spent the next few years collaborating with Penrose in the study of the properties of singularities and black holes.

Throughout his career, Hawking has produced a steady stream of articles for scientific journals. The most renowned of these is "Black Hole Explosions?" published in *Nature* in 1974, in which he explained a method by which black holes could emit radiation. Previously, it was thought that this was an impossibility, that nothing could escape from a black hole. To explain how black holes could emit energy, Hawking relied upon quantum mechanics, the field which describes the behavior of subatomic particles. Quantum theory posits the existence of virtual particles and antiparticles which are created in pairs and then immediately annihilate one another. Hawking determined that if one of these pairs materialized right on the boundary of a black hole, it was possible for one of the particles to fall into the black hole, allowing the other to escape in the form of radiation. By wedding general relativity and quantum mechanics in the discovery of what became known as Hawking radiation, Hawking took a first step toward the unification of these two great accomplishments of theoretical physics in the 20th century. This search for the grand unification theory, a law from which all other laws of physics could be derived, continues to obsess theoretical physicists.

Hawking's professional writing is known for its clarity and elegance. Dennis Sciama, Hawking's adviser at Cambridge, described Hawking's paper on black hole radiation as "one of the most beautiful in the history of physics." Because of Hawking's disability, he is unable to scribble down notes and equations as do most theoretical physicists. Instead, he relies more on visualizing four-dimensional geometry in his head. As a result, remarked Jeremy Bernstein in the *New Yorker*, his scientific papers "are full of ideas and relatively free of equations. They read more like prose than like mathematics."

In collaboration with George Ellis, Hawking published his first book, *The Large Scale Structure of Space Time*, in 1973. Aimed at professional physicists, it was a treatise on classical cosmology that contained none of Hawking's current research. Although it is now considered a classic in the field, it is incomprehensible even to many professionals. In 1981, *Superspace and Supergravity* was published, another highly technical monograph aimed at the professional physicist.

Hawking's deteriorating physical condition put an increasing financial burden on him. He had been in a wheelchair since 1970, and by the early 1980s he was capable of only slight movement. His speech had become so slurred that only a few close friends could understand him. In order to pay for the private nursing that he required, Hawking decided to write a book on cosmology intended for mass audiences. By 1985 Hawking had finished a draft of his book. That same year he contracted pneumonia, which necessitated a tracheostomy that completely removed his ability to utter any vocal sound. His wheelchair was then fitted with a computer, enabling Hawking to write or speak in an easily understandable computer-generated voice. The only voluntary muscle movement remaining for Hawking is the use of three of his fingers, which allows him to operate his wheelchair and to click on the words he chooses with his computer.

The publication of *A Brief History of Time: From the Big Bang to Black Holes* in 1988 made Hawking an international celebrity. In it, he gives background on classical cosmology, and also describes his own work on the nature of black holes, their relationship to the big bang, and the conditions necessary for both. He also discusses the most recent work being done in search of a grand unification theory. According to Hawking, finding such a theory would enable everyone to engage in a discussion of why the universe exists at all. "If we find the answer to that," he wrote, "it would be the ultimate triumph of human reason—for then we would know the mind of God."

Written in clear prose carefully intended to be understood by the layman, Hawking's book received mixed reviews but was immensely popular. Jeremy Bernstein, in the *New Yorker*, found it a "charming and lucid book" which has a "sunny brilliance." Bernstein also noted, "The most original parts of Hawking's book consist of the description of his own work. Since this has been of such great importance in modern cosmological theory, and since he describes it so lucidly, this gives the general reader an opportunity to learn some deep science directly from the source." The reviewer for the *Economist* complained, however, that Hawking did not provide "much sense of the process of physics," nor "an analysis of how different ages foster different ideas." "In the end," remarked David Blum in *New York*, Hawking "has written what amounts to a graduate-school textbook, albeit a breezy one."

Although some claim that few people who bought the book actually read it, *A Brief History of Time* has, nevertheless, sold over five million copies and has been translated into thirty languages. Biographers Michael White and John Gribbin observed in *Stephen Hawking: A Life in Science* that even though many of the books were barely opened, there are probably millions of people "who have learnt more about the Universe we all live in through reading his words. With this alone he has achieved astounding success by awakening a skeptical public . . . to the beauty of science." They concluded, "The popularization of science has seen a new renaissance, thanks in large measure to his efforts."

Hawking's personal story also intrigued the public. According to the reviewer in the *Economist*, "It is the contrast between the body trapped in a wheelchair, able to speak only through a computer system, and the mind that ranges the cosmos which has caught the public imagination: the king of infinite space, bounded in a nutshell." In 1992, this fascination with Hawking the man produced the uncommon occurrence of a commercial film being made from a science book. While the film version of *A Brief History of Time* provides an introduction to Hawking's work and the basic concepts of cosmology, it is more biographical than the book. Most of the film is composed of interviews with Hawking and his family, friends, and colleagues. Vincent Canby wrote in the *New York Times* that "they are variously serious, funny, brilliant, caustic and, from time to time, eccentric in a way that evokes memories of more than one novel about England's academe." According to Stanley Kauffman in the *New Republic*, being in the presence of such agile minds and Hawking's own towering intellect makes the film "viscerally and intellectually thrilling."

Coinciding with the release of the film was the publication of *Stephen Hawking's A Brief History of Time: A Reader's Companion*, edited by Hawking. It is a companion not to the book but to the film. As Hawking explained in the foreword, "this is The Book of The Film of The Book. I don't know if they are planning a film of The Book of The Film of The Book." The companion consists of all of the interviews in the film plus much that was edited out, as well as biographical sketches of the speakers.

Hawking has spent his entire professional career at Cambridge University, where he is currently the Lucasian Professor of Mathematics, a position once held by Isaac Newton. In 1965, Cambridge had awarded him a fellowship; in 1973, he was made a research assistant in the department of applied mathematics and theoretical physics. He was promoted to Reader in Gravitational Physics in 1975 and two years later he was offered a chair in gravitational physics, a position the university created specifically for him. He has won virtually every prize in physics, including the Albert Einstein Award, the Wolf Foundation Prize, the Hopkins Prize, the Maxwell Prize, and the Dannie Heinemann Prize. He also became a Fellow of the Royal Society in 1974, one of the youngest scientists ever to be so honored, and in 1988 he was made a Companion of Honour, one of Britain's top distinctions.

Hawking and Jane Wilde, who married in 1965, separated in 1990. They have three children: Robert, Lucy, and Timothy. Although Hawking spent a great deal of time travelling around the world giving lectures and attending symposia, his students regarded him as an excellent adviser, much more available to them than most professors. High-spirited, witty, yet intensely stubborn, Hawking had an extraordinarily powerful presence.

PRINCIPAL WORKS: (with George Ellis) The Larger Scale Structure of Space Time, 1973; A Brief History of Time: From the Big Bang to Black Holes, 1988; Black Holes and Baby Universes, and Other Essays, 1993. *As editor*—(with W. Israel) General Relativity: An Einstein Centenary Survey, 1979; Superspace and Supergravity, 1981; Stephen Hawking's A Brief History of Time: A Reader's Companion, 1992.

ABOUT: Contemporary Authors 129, 1990; Current Biography Yearbook, 1984; Overbye, D. Lonely Hearts of the Cosmos, 1991; White, M. and Gribbin, J. Stephen Hawking: A Life in Science, 1992. *Periodicals*—Economist June 25, 1988; New Republic September 28, 1992; New York October 24, 1988; New York Times August 21, 1992; New York Times Magazine January 23, 1983; New Yorker June 6, 1988; Newsweek June 13, 1988.

WILLIAM HEINESEN

*HEINESEN, WILLIAM (January 15, 1900– March 12, 1991), Faroese poet and novelist was born in Thorshavn, Faroe Island, the son of Zacharias Heinesen, a merchant and shipowner, and Caroline Jacobine Restorff. On his father's side he belonged to an ancient Faroese family and could count on the national freebooter hero Mogens Heinesen (1545–1589) among his forefathers, while his mother belonged to an immigrant family and spoke Danish in preference to Faroese. This mixed marriage, and more particularly the bilingual nature of his upbringing, had a fundamental significance for Heinesen, who, while being firmly Faroese in outlook, always wrote in Danish.

At his father's behest, Heinesen reluctantly left home for Copenhagen at the age of sixteen to study at the College of Commerce, but he lacked interest and turned to writing, first to journalism, then to "serious" writing. In 1919 he made contact with a group of Denmark's leading poets and authors, notably the left-wing Otto Gelsted and Hans Kirk, who were to have a lasting importance for him. Gelsted was for many years something of a mentor for him, while Kirk, the author of the novel Fiskerne (The fisherfolk, 1928), provided the model for Heinesen's own Noatun (1938, Niels Peter). Heinesen returned to Thorshavn and settled there in 1932, living partly by writing and partly by painting. (Although his international reputation derives from his writings, he is equally famous as an artist in his native Faroe Islands, and indeed he claimed that painting was for many years his main source of income). He was a serious contender for the Nobel Prize for literature, but he made it clear

that he would not accept such an honor, convinced that if the prize were to be awarded to a Faroese language. On his eightieth birthday in 1980 he was made a citizen of honor in his native Thorshavn.

Heinesen started his career as a writer of poetry, publishing in all seven volumes. His first, Arktiske elegier (1921, Arctic Elegies) is as elegiac as its title suggests, an offshoot of symbolism of the turn of the century. Ultimately, these poems, which echo the religious crisis Heinesen admitted to having in his childhood, reflect a young man's effort to come to terms with his own mortality, and the solution he reaches— almost certainly deriving from Camille Flammarion's La fin du monde—is the renewal of life by all chemical components of living organisms being reincorporated into new life forms:

See, I am life to all time,
a seed borne hither by the birds,
transformation that will never die,
I remember that I grew before.

The poetry from the end of the 1920s and beginning of the 1930s retains the elegiac tone, reinforced by renewed metaphysical speculation occasioned by the death in 1927 of the poet's brother, Heine. However, by the mid-1930s, Heinesen's poems show a growing left-wing political awareness partly resulting from the emergence of Nazism in Germany and partly from a sense of indignation at social ills. A tendency to experiment with poetic form and to leave behind the elegiac and symbolist nature of the early work appears. The experimental and satirical

°HY nuh sen

poetry emerges again in the sole volume of poems from the 1960s, *Hymne og harmsang* (Hymns and songs of indignation 1961), but it is largely dropped again in the final *Panorama med regnbue* (Panorama with rainbow) from 1972, with its cosmic vision, summing up the philosophy of a lifetime and coming to terms with the mortality Heinesen had faced already in the first volume.

His first published novel, *Blaesende gry* (Windswept Dawn 1934), partly echoed the religious preoccupations of the previous years, but it is also a portrait of Faroese society in transition from an essentially medieval pattern to the modern community of today. At the same time it contains a hint of the dichotomy between realism and fantasy which was to become a feature of Heinesen's prose, and even here, in the shape of the solicitor Morberg, the author shows his predilection for caricature. *Blaesende gry* is written in the style of the Danish "collective" novel, being without a principal character, but instead using a social group as its central feature. It also shows the first signs of Heinesen's creation of a cosmic myth with Simona, the wife of the shipowner and subsequently of sectarian Sylverius, portrayed as a symbol of woman raised above ordinary mortals. This tendency is continued in *Noatun*, despite this novel's being the closest approach to social realism in the entire corpus of Heinesen's work. A group of Poor Faroese settle in and out-of-the-way valley known as Dodmandsdal (Dead Man Valley) and the novel depicts their struggle to establish themselves. A girl by the name of Maria is persuaded to join Samson, and she gives birth to a child. The biblical names suggest the parallel with the Bible story, and this attempt to demythologize the biblical account and give it a new, humanist, significance is further developed in the rest of Heinesen's work. At the same time, *Noatun* marks the first stage in the creation of a myth based on the confrontation of life and death forces that was later to become the essential component in Heinesen's work. An outsider joins the group, but is arrested as a wanted criminal. He is carried out of the village and across the mountains tied to a stretcher. As the party walks close to the cliff edge, he manages to throw himself over, and a few days later the party that had been carrying him alive, carried his body to the grave. The novel contains other episodes with a similar implication.

The confrontation between life and death, or life-asserting and life-denying forces, has its fullest development in the novels *Den sorte gryde (1949, The Black Cauldron)* and *De fortable spillemaend* (1950, *The Lost Musicians*). The Faroese see them—like much else that Heinesen

wrote—as romans à clef, but this will scarcely concern the non-Faroese reader. Different as they are, these two central novels both reflect the conflict between forces representing life and death. The first is set during the British occupation of the Faorese during World War II. An offshoot of the collective novel again, it depicts a community on one of the Faroese islands, but many of the characters are caricatured to a greater or lesser extent, and the confrontation is reflected in the conflict between ordinary people who are being exploited and the exploiters themselves, now of whom, Opperman, is clearly identified with death. He finally succeeds in seducing the main female character, Liva ("life"), while his own wife lies dying in a nearby room. Liva suffers a breakdown and goes out of her mind; she is finally incarcerated in an asylum founded by Opperman in memory of his now-dead wife. The "ordinary" characters are also in conflict with the life-denying dominant sectarians. The sectarian leader, Simon the baker, rejects Liva, despite a clear erotic attraction between them, and is thus also partly responsible for her subsequent mental breakdown. Like many others of Heinesen's fanatical sectarians, he devoted himself to religion as recompense for profound family tragedy, in this case the death of his entire family.

The life/death confrontation continues in *De fortabta spillemaend*, now in the setting of the struggle for total prohibition, achieved in 1907. Again, the sectarians lead the antilife forces, this time under the tutelage of the bank director, Ankerson, while the representatives of life are poor members of society who seek solace in music. One by one, the musicians come to grief, the result partly of narrow-minded sectarianism, partly of scheming on the part of Ankersen's putative son, partly because the arrogant and snobbish police chief—an immigrant Dane—is intent on pinning a bank robbery on a "cap man," not a "hat man." The central feature of the novel is a rowdy Faroese wedding in which the two factions literally do battle in the streets on Thorshavn. Comedy and tragedy blend in this novel, which ends on a note of hope, as Orfeus, the boy prodigy, goes off to Copenhagen to further his career in music, the symbol of life.

With these two novels, Heinesen left the path of social realism and moved into magic realism. His next two novels suggest a further move into the realm of myth. This is particularly obvious in *Moder Syvstjerne* (1952, *The Kingdom of the Earth*), which is a sequel to *De fortabte spillemaend* in that the two books have characters in common, while the second refers back to the first. In mood, however, it is totally different, and the main character, Antonia, is a symbol of motherhood, portrayed on one occasion very much as the Virgin Mary in paintings of her as Queen of Heaven. Here, Heinesen advances his attempt to create a humanist myth with cosmic overtones to take the place of Christianity. Antonia, warmly lauded as the archetypal mother figure, gives birth to a child, but falls into the clutches of the narrowly religious Trine, who proceeds unintentionally to inflict suffering on both Antonia and her son, symbolically being the first person to separate mother and son when the child is to be baptized in a dark church, surrounded by symbols of death. It is an intricate and many-faceted novel in which the main tendencies of Heinesen's work become clear as never before.

Unique among Heinesen's works was his next, and longest, novel *Det gode hab* (1964, *The Good Hope*), a historical novel set in the 17th-century Faroes and written in a pseudo-17th-century Danish. In its account of the most oppressive period of Faroese history, it seems to be an allergy of a concentration camp. At the same time it also suggests a life-death confrontation, and contains a biting criticism of the representatives of the state church, an element that had already been apparent in earlier work. Caricature gives way here to the creation of characters who are larger than life.

In the 1960s Heinesen moved into the third phase of his prose work, in which social realism and magical realism were subsumed into the creation of myth. This stage is dominated by the short story form, which had already made its appearance in two volumes in the late 1950s and early 1960s. Indeed, it could even be argued that *Moder Syvstjerne* forms a transition to this phase with its slender action forming the frame for a large number of brief accounts. This, certainly, is the structure of the late novels arnet ved verdens ende (1976, *The Tower at the Edge of the World*) and, even more, *Laterna magica* (1985), this latter being only a series of short stories told by an aging narrator on his way to Grey Skull Wharf, where a ferryman awaits him. Even with a good deal of humor, there is a certain elegiac element to be felt again as the author looks back and reflects on the way in which his ideas and concepts have developed. Obsession and the incomprehensibility of human nature are themes taken up in these books, together with a portrayal of the way in which a child seeks to understand the world by creating a series of its own fantasies and myths. Incipient erotic urges in children are suggested, the children themselves being largely unaware of them. The introductory piece in *Her skal danses* (Here let us dance, 1980) actually shows the narrator discovering his own mother before he was born; time, we are

told in *Laterna magica*, is all in one pool—everything exists already. The influence of Chinese Taoist philosophy seems evident in these aspects oh Heinesen's work, and there are also references to Karma in *Blaesende gry* and *Den sorte gryde*, which reappear in the late work, where references to Fate abound. There is throughout a sense of Cosmos, a non-Christian transcendentalism, which accepts no tangible explanation to existence. Cosmos, the Universe, is a mystery that can be sensed but not explained. At the center of it, Life is the most important thing of all, and those who transgress it or reject it for religious intolerance are guilty of offending against it.

Virtually all Heinesen's work is set in the Faroes and clearly reflects Faroese culture. However, it has universal perspective and validity and is in no way inward-looking. Nor does it in any way presuppose familiarity with the Faroe Islands and their way of life. Nevertheless, *Her skal danses*, which many people (wrongly) thought was a farewell, contains the most moving and dignified homage to Faroese culture in the title story, which in a way typical of Heinesen, juxtaposes life and death with a Faroese wedding on an isolated island interrupted by a shipwreck and ensuing death. When the wedding guests nevertheless insist on continuing their traditional ring dancing, they are forbidden to do so by the representatives of the official church. They withdraw and continue their dance at the home of an aged couple who prepare a simple, almost medieval Faroese meal, and where the wife is graced with a pagan name. The ritual meal, the life/death confrontation, the dignity of the entire account, raise this story to a mystical level not seen anywhere else in Heinesen's work. It is a homage to Faroese culture, a homage to life, a homage to humanity, all in one, and in its way it sums up everything that Heinesen wrote.

PRINCIPAL WORKS IN ENGLISH TRANSLATION: *Novels*—(tr. J. Noble) Niels Peter, 1939; (tr. E. J. Friis) The Lost Musicians, 1971; (tr. H. Brnner) The Kingdom of Heaven, 1973; (tr. J. F. West) The Good Hope, 1981; (tr. M. Jackson) The Tower at the Edge of the World, 1981; (tr. T. Nunnally) Laterna Magica, 1987; (tr. W. G. Jones) The Black Cauldron, 1992. *Short Stories*—(tr. H. Brnner) The Winged Darkness, 1983. *Poetry*—(tr. A. Born) Arctics, 1980.

ABOUT: Brnner, H. Introduction to The Winged Darkness and Other Stories, 1983; Three Faroese Novelists, 1973; Columbia Dictionary of Modern European Literature, 2nd ed., 1980; Dansk Biografisk Leksicon, 1980; Jones, W. W. William Heinesen, 1974. *Periodicals*—American-Scandinavian Review June 1973; New York Times March 14, 1991; Scandinavian

Studies August 1969; Winter 1978; Scandinavica November 1970; Times Literary Supplement March 2, 1973; World Literature Today Winter 1988.

HEMPEL, AMY (December 14, 1951–), American short story writer, was born in Chicago, Illinois, the eldest of the three children of Gardiner and Gloria Hempel. When she was in third grade the family moved to Denver and later, when she was in high school, to San Francisco—both moves precipitated by her father, who was a successful businessman. What Hempel recalled about her childhood, in an interview with Michael Schumacher, was having had "a lot of fun . . . terrific brothers, a terrific father," but a rocky relationship with her mother, who was unable to communicate with her except through books. "How we communicated, when we did, was to talk about the books we read. I read as a way to talk to her." To try to keep up, she read above her level, consulting the dictionary whenever her mother used words she didn't understand. Hempel excelled in English at school and knew early that she wanted to become a writer, though she now regards her first writing efforts as "pathetic." Her experiences, she maintains, have made her into the writer she has become.

Some of those experiences were traumatic. When Hempel was eighteen, her mother committed suicide. Around the same time Hempel was involved in two serious accidents, one on a motorcycle, the other in a car. She was "in a pretty morbid state of mind for some time . . . afraid of dying and being injured." Wanting to get past those fears, she watched several autopsies and enrolled in an anatomy class where she dissected cadavers. "I thought I'd be better off if I could make myself view the whole thing from a scientific side . . . It absolutely worked."

For thirteen years, from 1969 to 1982, Hempel drifted from one place to another, doing odd jobs, attending several California colleges, studying journalism, and working briefly on two separate occasions for publishers in New York City. She attended for a time the Bread Loaf Writers Conference at Middlebury College in Vermont, where John Gardner and Stanley Elkin were teaching. She worked for a time in a counseling group for terminally ill people in Berkeley. But finally, after the wrenching experience of watching her best friend die of cancer, she "got serious": she moved to New York and began writing for a fiction workshop at Columbia University.

Hempel has since described her time in California as "lost years," although they supplied her with much of the material for the short stories she wrote for the workshop. Her instructor Gordon Lish liked the stories and arranged for them to be published in 1985. "All of the stories," Hempel has said, "are set out West, and come from missing the west coast, trying to find value in the time spent there."

The characters in Hempel's first collection, *Reasons to Live*—"composites" she calls them of people she knew in California—are often wounded or bereaved but always struggling to find resilience and wit in an alienating world. Though all are scarred by loss or overwhelmed by getting through their days, they keep searching for reasons to live—the presence of someone, some mindless activity, or a joke that will momentarily alleviate the pain. Describing her work in a *New York Times Book Review* interview, Hempel quoted the famous heart surgeon, Christian Barnard: "'Suffering isn't ennobling, recovery is.' If I have a motto for this particular bunch of stories, that's what it is."

In learning her craft, Hempel has said that she was influenced by "Mary Robison, Barry Hannah, Leonard Michaels, Raymond Carver—contemporary short story writers who 'reinvent' the language, who tell the truth in shocking ways." She views these writers as using "a kind of compression and distillation in their work that gets to the heart of things and gives the reader credit for being able to keep up without having everything explained."

It is "compression and distillation" rather than bare-boned minimalism that characterizes Hempel's fiction. Some of her stories cover no more than two pages, leading Sheila Ballantyne, in the *New York Times Book Review*, to complain that the pieces in *Reasons to Live* are "so truncated and incomplete [that] they are interesting only as snapshots." She concedes, however, that they are "tough-minded, original and fully felt." *Reasons to Live*, as its spare title suggests, examines the resilience of the human spirit in the face of loneliness, physical pain, bereavement, madness, and death. Michiko Kakutani wrote, in the *New York Times*, that Hempel's characters are often "too wise, too damaged or maybe just too skeptical to hold out for anything so luminous as hope or faith." Yet most of them respond to their unhappiness with defensive humor, sometimes self-mocking, sometimes plainly absurd. Other characters are numbed into sheer "disconnectedness." Whatever their pain, "they get by." Hers is "a gift for empathy," Kakutani wrote, observing: "Rather than trivializing their efforts to get by . . . Hempel writes of her characters with charity and understanding."

Many of Hempel's stories are set in the California of Joan Didion—a landscape of freeways, fast food restaurants, and "apartments done in fake Spanish colonial": bright sunshine, and the ever-present threat of natural disasters; populated by affectless characters drifting passively rather than directing their own lives. "What you forget living here, " the narrator of "Tonight Is a Favor to Holly" says, "is that just because you have stopped sinking doesn't mean you're not still under water." The voice that speaks lines like these is never tearful and self-pitying. To the contrary, she is wryly humorous. "Tonight Is a Favor to Holly" begins: "A blind date is coming to pick me up and unless my hair grows an inch by seven o'clock, I am not going to answer the door. The problem is the front. I cut the bangs myself, now I look like Mamie Eisenhower."

In a review of *Reasons to Live* in *Commonweal*, Dawn Ann Drzal recalled Freud's observation that the basic aim of psychoanalysis is "transforming hysterical misery into common unhappiness." This is a formulation, Drzal writes, that Hempel's characters "would be more than willing to settle for . . . " One of the most moving stories in *Reasons to Live*, "In the Cemetery Where Al Jolson Is Buried," is told by a woman watching a close friend dying of cancer. In a hospital room filled with state-of-the-art equipment that prolongs dying, she responds to her friend's request: "'Tell me things I won't mind forgetting . . . Make it useless stuff or skip it.'" What follows is a stream of trivia, absurdities, wisecracks: "She laughs and I cling to the sound the way someone dangling above a ravine holds fast to the thrown rope." The terrible responsibility of friendship at this moment of dying tests her courage. Her honesty prevails: "I see fear in her now and am not going to try to talk her out of it. She is right to be afraid." What redeems Hempel's stories from morbidity is her firm control, her assured technique, what Howard Nemerov described in a dust jacket endorsement of *Reasons to Live* as "the terse elegance of their composition and the elegiac sorrows of their substance."

At the Gates of the Animal Kingdom demonstrates the same skills. In these stories, Hempel displays a technique that Robert Towers, in the *New York Times Book Review*, called "miniaturist" rather than minimalist, implying a depth of observation that belies its small scale: "to call them sketches or fragments is to overlook the elegance and compactness of their style and the unsettling impact of the feelings conveyed." Readers who come to Hempel's work expecting a developed plot will be frustrated, Towers remarked, yet "what one cherishes in Amy Hempel are not her plots but her quirky sensibility and the beautifully honed verbal craft she brings

to bear on the situations and themes that have attracted her amused and rueful eye."

Hempel told Michael Schumacher that she has always been interested in people who have responded to stringent trials. "Extremity—that's what I respond to. I'm endlessly, endlessly interested in people who have *come through* something, and the more they have come through, the more interested I am in them and their stories." The trick in writing, she says, "is to find a tiny way into a huge subject. In my case, it's loss." She collects scraps of information and phrases and pieces them together as though working on a quilt. If she does it "right," the pieces accumulate and take on significance by the end of the story. "One of the good things about writing is that I'm different on the page than I am in person. One the page, I get to be precise, cool, tough—things that I'm really not. In life, I'm all over the place: I'm vague, not defined, and full of fear. But what people see is the end result, this precisely honed story. You get to be known that way and it's wonderful."

Hempel's stories have appeared in anthologies, including *Best American Short Stories, 1986* and the *Norton Anthology of Short Fiction*. She is a contributor to several periodicals, among them *Vanity Fair, Harper's, Mother Jones, Vogue*, and the *New York Times Magazine*. She was contributing editor of *Vanity Fair* from 1985 to 1986. She won the Pushcart Prize and the Silver Medal, Commonwealth Club of California in 1986 for *Reasons to Live*.

She lives in a New York City apartment where one of her chief enjoyments is caring for her two cats. "If I were not a writer," she told Schumacher, "I would be a veterinarian."

PRINCIPAL WORKS: Reasons to Live, 1985; At the Gates of the Animal Kingdom, 1990.

ABOUT: Contemporary Authors 137, 1992; Contemporary Literary Criticism 39, 1986; Contemporary Literary Criticism Yearbook 1985; 1986; Schumacher, Michael Reasons to Believes, 1988. Periodicals—Commonweal September 20, 1985; New York Times April 13, 1985; New York Times Book Review April 28, 1985; March 11, 1990.

*HIJUELOS, OSCAR (August 24, 1951–), American novelist, was born in New York City, the younger of two children of Pasqual Hijuelos, a cook and dishwasher, and Magdalena (Torrens) Hijuelos, a homemaker with a secret passion for writing poetry. His parents emigrated to New York from Oriente province in eastern Cuba in the 1940s. They settled on the West Side of Manhattan where Hijuelos grew up in a work-

*ee HWAY lowss

ing class neighborhood of mixed ethnicity. Because of Hijuelos's heritage, he is often categorized as a Cuban-American writer, but in April 1993, he told Esther B. Fein of the *New York Times* that he considers himself "a New York writer of Cuban parentage, with different influences. My background is an important element, the most important, but not the only one." Just as important as being Latino, Hijuelos argued in an interview with Marifeli Perez-Stable in *Culturefront: A Magazine of the Humanities*, are his working-class identity and his heterogeneous childhood. "My memories of childhood are mostly about what I experienced in the world outside of my house," he explained. "How would you describe a twelve-year-old kid who goes down to the Village to listen to jazz on a Sunday afternoon? Or who went to the Apollo theater in Harlem to watch James Brown or played softball in Harlem, alongside a Dutch-Italian friend? These experiences were not specifically Cuban, at all, but simply part of being raised in New York."

Hijuelos went to the City College of New York where he studied writing with Donald Barthelme, receiving a B.A. in 1975 and an M.A. in 1976. After graduation, he worked for several years researching advertising trends while writing on the side. One of his early stories, "Columbus Discovering America," was included in the *Best of the Pushcart Press* anthology for 1978. By the time Hijuelos began writing a novel, he had become interested in questions of identity, and his first novel, "Our House in the Last World," published in 1983, was about Cubans who emigrate to America. A careful mixture of realism and surrealism, the novel tells the story of Alejo and Mercedes Santinio, who arrive in New York in 1944. Although the Santinios are ambitious, they are never able to move beyond menial jobs and poverty. As Alejo's dreams continue to be frustrated, he descends into drunkenness and despair. Meanwhile, Hector, the sickly younger son of the family, is struggling to find his own identity while caught between his father's commitment to an ideal of virile masculinity and his mother's excessive attention and anxiety. The older son accepts his father's promiscuous, violent vision of manhood and escapes the pressures of the family by joining the air force. All the while, the Santinios remember Cuba as a lost paradise. Edith Milton wrote in the *New York Times Book Review* (1983) that because the word "last" in the title means "both final and previous, the novel's central tension is between the lost, misremembered Eden and the ultimate reality, first of contemporary life and in the end of death." Milton also noted that the strengths of this "novel of great warmth and

tenderness" lie in its touching evocation of character and in "the sheer energy of its narrative." She also credited Hijuelos with never losing "the syntax of magic, which transforms even the unspeakable into a sort of beauty."

In Hijuelos's younger years, he played in bands that performed popular and Latin music, and he incorporated his passion for music into his second novel, *The Mambo Kings Play Songs of Love.* Consciously trying to avoid a traditional narrative line, Hijuelos organized his novel like the music that provides its center. "The formal idea was sort of like having a record going round and round. You know how sometimes when you listen to music and the song cuts off and you're into another feeling? I wanted to move atmospherically. I saw the chapters as different songs," Hijuelos explained in *Publishers Weekly.* In the novel, this form is manifested by having Cesar Castillo holed up in a seedy motel, recollecting events in his life, and preparing to drink himself to death while listening to old records of the Mambo Kings, the band in which he and his brother played. Hijuelos explained that as Cesar puts on different records, "he has different thoughts, going forward, going back. It does drift around, I have to admit; the reader is not always aware of being with Cesar, but I wanted that improvisational feel in part of the book, like a horn line."

In the novel, Cesar and his brother Nestor arrive in America from Cuba in 1949. Throughout the next decade they work in low-paying, dreary jobs, but spend their evenings playing with the Mambo Kings, consumed by the flashy world of music and dance. Hijuelos crams the book with rich, lyrical detail about both the Latin music scene of the 1950s and the drudgery of the Castillos' daily lives. Cesar is a classic portrait of hypersexual machismo, while Nestor is more sensitive, pining for a lost love back in Cuba for whom he wrote twenty-two different versions of the band's only hit, "Beautiful Maria of My Soul." The culmination of the brothers' career occurs when Desi Arnaz invites them to appear on the "I Love Lucy" show, an event that is remembered and replayed throughout the novel. Nestor eventually dies an early death and Cesar lives out his life as a building superintendent, left with nothing but his memories.

Most critics applauded Hijuelos's depiction of the Castillos' exuberant yet melancholy world. Joseph Coates of the *Chicago Tribune* praised Hijuelos's use of the "I Love Lucy" show: "This apparently trivial 24 minutes of entertainment, reprised throughout the book, becomes the mythical hinge of a considerable epic. And it is Hijuelos's achievement to make clear both the silliness and seriousness of this consummately American apotheosis: the Guest Appearance on National TV." Coates also remarked, "The novel leaves one with the same chill, a sense of some voracity at the heart of the American dream that chews up talented people and spits out what's left, that magnifies personal faults, along with rewards, and turns them into self-destruction, into the litany of missed chances and bad choices that Cesar recites in his final agony." Margo Jefferson, in the *New York Times Book Review* (1989), noted that the novel's strength is "that it doesn't center on the Castillos' longing to cross over into the American dream; it leads us across into their dreams instead. . . . The novel alternates crisp narrative with opulent musing—the language of everyday and the language of longing. Some reviewers felt that Hijuelos's ironic attitude toward Cesar's machismo and sexual exploits did not come through clearly. Grace Edwards-Yearwood remarked in the *Los Angeles Times Book Review*, however, that "Hijuelos has painted an erotic and desolate landscape where people surge to life and diminish with terrifying exactitude."

The novel won the Pulitzer Prize for fiction in 1990, making Hijuelos the first Latino to be so honored. The book was also nominated for the National Book Award and the National Book Critics Circle Award. Hijuelos served as a consultant during the production of the motion picture version of *The Mambo Kings*, which was released in 1992. Although he had hoped that the film would break new ground for Latino moves, he was disappointed in the final product. In *Culturefront*, he described the film as "a very watered down version of the book," in which the characters lost their complexity and his subtle examination of the American dream became "a cliché."

In Hijuelos's third novel, *The Fourteen Sisters of Emilio Montez O'Brien*, he moved from a macho world to a predominantly feminine one. The novel tells the story of an Irish immigrant, Nelson O'Brien, who travels to Cuba during the Spanish-American War to take photographs. In Cuba he meets the beautiful young Mariela Montez, who returns with him to a small Pennsylvania town to live. They proceed to have fourteen daughters and then finally, miraculously, a son. Throughout the tangled, abundant narrative, Hijuelos describes all of the children, but concentrates primarily on the eldest, Margarita, and young Emilio. Margarita devotes her early life to caring for her sisters in their chaotic, loving household, but then enters an emotionally vacant marriage. At the age of ninety, she finally reclaims happiness when she remarries and rediscovers her sexuality and self. Emilio, mean-

while, escapes this feminine world by fighting in Italy during World War II and then becoming a small-time movie star in Hollywood.

Many reviewers compared Hijuelos's novel to those of Gabriel García Márquez. Michiko Kakutani wrote in the *New York Times* (1993) that the novel was "more redemptive" than *The Mambo Kings* and, like García Márquez's *Love in the Time of Cholera*, was primarily concerned "with the cyclical nature of time, and the enduring possibilities of love." Kakutani was particularly impressed by Hijuelos's ability, despite the multitude of character, "to implant a firm sense of each and every one of them in our imaginations." In the *New York Times Book Review* (1993), Thomas Mallon disagreed, claiming that the daughters are "inevitably reduced to overly vivid shorthand characterizations. [Hijuelos] usually relies on a single trait to keep each sister distinct." Mallon acknowledged, however, that once Hijuelos "has the whole operetta going, the effect seems marvelously complicated." He also marveled at Hijuelos's sensuous, exuberant prose. The novel "is overstuffed to the point of giddiness," he wrote. Through the use of "Rabelaisian catalogues" and period detail, "the overall effect is luscious and life-loving. There are moments when one has to laugh, appreciatively, at the book's sheer plenitude."

Oscar Hijuelos lives on the Upper West Side of Manhattan, only a few blocks from where he grew up. In 1985, he received fellowships from both the National Endowment for the Arts and the American Academy in Rome

PRINCIPAL WORKS: Our House in the Last World, 1983; The Mambo Kings Play Songs of Love, 1989; The Fourteen Sisters of Emilio Montez O'Brien, 1993.

ABOUT: Contemporary Authors 123, 1988; Contemporary Literary Criticism 65, 1991. *Periodicals*—Chicago Tribune August 13, 1989; Culturefront: A Magazine of the Humanties Winter 1993; Los Angeles Times Book Review September 3, 1989; New York Times March 2, 1993; April 1, 1993; New York Times Book Review May 15, 1983; August 27, 1989; March 7, 1993; Publishers Weekly July 21, 1989.

*HILDESHEIMER, WOLFGANG (December 12, 1916–August 20, 1991), German short story writer, playwright, novelist, biographer, essayist, critic, librettist, translator, and painter, was born in Hamburg. The son of a Jewish chemist, he attended German schools until 1933 when his family emigrated first to England and subsequently to Palestine. There he trained to become a carpenter while also taking drawing

°ilda SHY mer

lessons and studying interior design. He attended the central School of Arts and Crafts in London from 1937 to 1939, receiving instruction in graphic arts and stage design. Following his return to Palestine he taught English for the British Council in Tel Aviv from 1940 to 1942 and served the British government as information officer in Jerusalem from 1943 to 1946. From 1946 to 1949 he was an interpreter at the Nuremberg war crimes trials, and from 1948 on, the editor of all the trial proceedings. For the following eight years Hildesheimer lived in Amback (Bavaria). During this period he began to write and caught the attention of critics in 1952 with a collection of short stories. For nearly thirty years there followed a steady stream of publications in a variety of genres. In 1957 he moved to Poschiavo, a town in southeastern Switzerland. In the late 1960s and in the 1970s he also lived intermittently in Urbino (Marches, Italy). In 1983, Hildesheimer quit writing literature, having stated as early as 1976, in "The End of Fiction," that "the attempts of literature, including the littérature engagée, to master our situation by setting fictitious models, have failed, which does not necessarily mean that they will not figure in the history of literature. but they are a matter of the past. No form of novel will do to express our situation." In the last years he dedicated his time partly to writing speeches, essays and reviews—in response to specific commissions—and partly to his collages and other works of art, which were shown at various international exhibitions. Wolfgang Hildesheimer died of a heart attack at his home in Poschiavo.

Hildesheimer was a member of PEN of the Federal Republic of Germany, of the Academy of the Arts in Berlin, and corresponding member of the German Academy for Language and Literature in Darmstadt. He was awarded an honorary doctorate from the Unversity of Giessen in 1982 and received numerous prestigious prizes: the Blind Veterans' Prize for Radio Plays in 1954; the Prize for Literature from the Free City of Bremen (1966); the Georg Büchner Prize in 1966; and the Prize for Literature by the Bavarian Academy for the Arts (1982).

Hildesheimer arrived on the German literary scene with *Lieblose Legenden* (Loveless Legends, 1952; revised and expanded in 1962), a collection of satirical tales mostly about phony intellectuals and artists. Writing mock obituaries, inventing biographies of famous people who never existed, and concocting grotesquely pedantic lectures that ring all too true, Hildesheimer consistently undermines academic and journalistic lingo with deadpan humor. The lives he imagines for his wacky characters seem predictable at first, but slyly introduced non sequiturs and ruptures in logic that rendered them ultimately absurd. These "legends" are indeed "loveless" because they are not imbedded in some divine plan that promises salvation in the end; rather, they present lives disrupted by irrational events that never begin to make sense; everyday life is a sum of frustrations and absurdities echoing the predicament of so many characters in Kafka and anticipating Paul Auster's postmodern nightmares. Some of these stories have become textbook classics in intermediate German courses in the United States, and most of them are now available in English in *The Collected Stories of Wolfgang Hildesheimer*.

Whereas his 1953 novel, *Paradies der falschen Vögel* (Paradise of Fake Birds; rewritten as a radio play with the title *Begegnung im Balkanexpress*—Encounter on the Balkan Express) satirizes the "culture industry," subsequent plays and radio plays such as *An den Ufern der Plotiniza* (1956, On the Banks of Plotiniza), *Prinzessin Turandot* (1955), and *Opfer Helena* (1960, *The Sacrifice of Helen*) satirize political power. In *Paradies der falschen Vögel* the narrator's uncle, an art forger, invents the artist Ayaz Mazyrka (1579–1649), along with a collection of his paintings. The local art historian in the tiny kingdom of Procegovina, where the action takes place, then invents a four-volume biography of this created individual that is, the narrator says, a work of astonishing scientific fantasy. In *Opfer Helena*, Helen of Troy becomes a positive figure of indentification. Far from being an unscrupulous temptress, she is, as the German title suggests, the victim of men obsessed with power who, in order to start a war, abuse Helen and her ability to love. Although she sees through these typically "male" power games and is a morally superior human being, she herself remains powerless: thus the resigned conclusion of *Opfer Helena*.

By the late fifties, Hildesheimer abandoned his predominantly satirist mode and emerged as one of the best-known German proponents of the theater of the absurd. In his widely acclaimed Erlangen address, "Über das absurde Theater" (Concerning the Theater of the Absurd, 1960) Hildesheimer explained that "the absurd play confronts the spectator with the incomprehensibility of life . . . a spectator waiting for an interpretation waits in vain." In contradistinction to the theater of the absurd, not only Aristotelian but also epic theater always either provide or intimate answers, and adherence to catharsis signifies faith in the mission of the theater. According to Hildesheimer, however, "the Absurd Theater admits that theater does not have the power to purge people. Powerlessness, doubts, and the world turned alien are the crux of every absurd play, and thus it becomes a contribution to the clarification of man's predicament."

To Hildesheimer every absurd play is a parable. Sutart Parkes points out that this parabolic element is particularly clear in *Pastorale oder Die Zeit für Kakao* (Pastorale or Time for Cocoa, 1957) where a strange quartet of singers gathers in the open air and talks an outrageous mixture of business and artistic jargon. As summer turns to winter and two of them die, "the connection between bourgeois business and cultural life and death and decay is shown." Those who survive are as cadaverous as those who died. The message is stressed by the title Hildesheimer gave to the cycle of plays to which *Pastorale* belongs: *Spiele, in denen es dunkel wird* (Plays in which darkness falls), in which the stage lights gradually fade to emphasize the finite limits of human imagination.

As Martin Esslin explained, the thorough blending of comic and tragic elements is one of the most important characteristics of the absurd. In this sense, Hildesheimer's grotesque tragicomedy, *Die Verspätung* (1961, The Delay), one of his greatest stage successes, is indeed a fully absurdist work: The "hero" of the play is, on the surface, a silly professor and charlatan in search of a miraculous bird, the Guricht, from which the human species allegedly descends. The Guricht, as it turns out, does exist but altogether fails to correspond to the fantastic expectations of the professor, who does not survive this disillusionment. As ridiculous a figure as the professor may be, there is also a tragic side to his search: his absurd idée fixe is a parable of human hopes, dreams, and wishes transcending a reality that is both trite and alien.

With *Mary Stuart* (1970), a one-act, one-set play re-creating the last hour of Mary Queen of Scots, Hildesheimer, according to his "Anmerkungen zu einer historischen Szene" (Notes to a Historical Scene) wants to demonstrate that the reconstruction of inner motivations of persons involved in events of the distant past is an impossibility since history itself is absurd. Anticipating his Mozart biography, Hildesheimer suggests that "historical biography is a pastime . . . at best conjecture, at worst *kitsch.*" His play runs counter to Friedrich Schiller's canonized version of the same subject matter, *Maria Stuart* (1800), in which the heroine is imbued with Kantian Idealism; her motivations for her opposition to Queen Elizabeth I are made clear, and she achieves tragic dignity in the end. In contradistinction, Hildesheimer decenters and deconstructs Mary Stuart step by step. Since she never listens to what others tell

her, a meaningful dialogue cannot develop. The audience's attention is constantly diverted from Mary, focusing instead on the executioner's know-how and his macabre concerns, the doctor's and the apothecary's deliberations on how to drug her, and her servants's quarrels, and lewd actions on stage. Mary's beauty is fake; her composure is the result of heavy sedatives; she is robbed of her jewelry piece by piece; the seat of her throne is perforated so she can perform her bodily functions; over her bald head she wears a wig which, as the executioner fears, will probably fall off after decapitation—a serious flaw to *his* perfectionist performance. And what should the audience make of this? Hildesheimer's answer is simple: "Whoever leaves the theater with the question what was Mary really like, has at least grasped my intention in representing her."

Hildesheimer's vast, book-length monologue, *Tynset* (1965), elaborates on the monologic predicament of isolated and lonesome insomniacs he first explored in two plays, *Nachtstück* (1963, Night Piece) and *Monolog* (1964). In *Tynset*, the first-person narrative voice belongs to a sleepless, depressive man who remains nameless. He spends a nasty November night in the isolation of his house to protect him from the hostile world outside. The source of the narrator's anxiety is brought out more clearly than elsewhere in Hildesheimer's work: the narrator's father was killed by the Nazis. The murderers, however, got away and are lying in wait. The narrator is "afraid of the silence of the night in which those are at work who are not afraid." Tynset, a small Norwegian town whose name the narrator comes across while reading train schedules—his favorite nighttime reading—and the yearning fantasies attached to that name are to rescue him from his anxieties. Tynset suggests the possibility of an escape to the unknown. But as the night progresses, the narrator comes to the conclusion that the real Tynset would disappoint him; he abandons the idea of going there and remains in his bed. Tynset is to be the place of his unlimited imagination. In *Tynset*, with its skillfully interwoven complex themes and motifs, conventional narrative style and plot development have given way to a highly differentiated polyphonic architecture, which sets Hildesheimer's technique apart from the psychological naturalism of interior monologues.

Hildesheimer's monologic phase culminated in 1973 with another fictional work, *Masante*. The first-person narrator is at an inn in the desert outpost of Meona. Masante is the name of a house he left behind and to which he will never return. Here, the escape the narrator dreamed about in *Tynset* has taken place. As forlorn and rundown a place as Meona turns out to be, it offers everything to the imagination: "all wishes remain open here. . . . imagination rather than satisfaction rules here." The monologue, however, has a longer span than that in *Tynset*. It is, according to Peter Wapnewski, "a poetic encyclopedia," including a plethora of geographic, historical, and topical references. Unlike *Tynset*, the play with imagined episodes now points to depressing possibilities that lie well along the lines of what might happen in reality. At the close of *Masante*, the narrator is sent "into the desert," and the monologue "dissolves." Since the reader has been told that no one ever returns from the desert, it must be accepted that the monologist will die there. We witness, in other words, the demise of the fictive "I." The shift away from the singular focus on the isolated narrator to external reality signals the end of the monologic form, and it comes as no surprise that since *Masante*, the majority of Hildesheimer's work has been nonfictional.

Hildesheimer's skepticism about biographical "truth" affected not only his portrayal of historical figures such as Mary Queen of Scots but also that of exceptional artists. "Who was Mozart?" he asked in a lecture given in 1966, and in a 1971 speech on Albrecht Dürer, "Bleibt Dürer Dürer?" (Does Dürer Remain Dürer?) he maintained that we cannot know who Dürer really was. Hildesheimer's greatest commercial success, his biography of Mozart (1977) on which he worked for twenty years, is based on the same premise—namely, that genius is incomprehensible: "Because I cannot entireely imagine him, either, and if I have succeeded in imparting something of this unimaginability, of demonstrating that Mozart is not one of us, then my book has succeeded." Marion Faber, the translator of the English edition writes: "The book is a theoretical speculation on the nature of genius . . . Hildesheimer is writing a self-conscious biography, and in its self-conscious preoccupation it approaches meta-biography." At most Hildesheimer can offer "single aspects of a possible reality," while allowing for contradictions and openly admitting to speculation for what it is. In addition, Hildesheimer's *Mozart* differs from many previous biographies of the composer by acknowledging that while he was a musical genius, he had notable character flaws. His Mozart is not the domesticated hero previous generations have made him. According to Hildesheimer, Mozart revealed himself only in his music; but his music should not be taken as a key to the different stages of his life and to his experiences. Marion Faber praises Hildesheimer for avoiding "the trap of trying to explain or understand Mozart's music *through* the biographical context in which it was written. He does not look for causal connections between Mozart's emotional life and his compositions. . . . Furthermore, Hildesheimer's biography never loses sight of the fact that it is his *music*, not his life, that makes Mozart great."

In 1981—in the manner of Virginia Woolf's mock-biography *Orlando*—Hildesheimer published *Marbot*, a fictional biography about a young British aristocrat, Sir Andrew Marbot, living in the early 19th century. *Paradies der falschen Vögel* is an early precursor of the goal Hildesheimer wanted to realize with *Marbot*. Sir Andrew is portrayed as a genial dilettante, an art connoisseur and theoretician who, in his analyses of great works of art, anticipates the insights of psychoanalysis into aesthetics. Marbot owes his deeper understanding of the hidden sources of beauty to the central upheaval in his own life, his incestuous relationship with his mother, Lady Catherine. Following their inevitable separation, his desire to get to the heart of painting is a sublimation of his passion for his mother. When he realizes, once and for all, that he himself has been denied what he longs for and admires most—that is, creativity—he coolly opts for suicide.

Hildesheimer said in an interview that while working on his Mozart book, he discovered that biography can be written only about persons "who did not exist." Thus *Marbot* is the exact reversal, a kind of mirror-book, of *Mozart*. Whereas he destroyed the legend surrounding Mozart, the legend, in the case of Marbot, was firmly implanted in a sociohistorical setting: Hildesheimer makes him an acquantance of Goethe, Schopenhauer, Byron, Leopardi, and others. Destructive analysis in *Mozart* was followed by synthetic construction in *Marbot*. The result, according to Gert Schiff, is "a sustained illusion of authenticity." In 1986, as Patricia H. Stanley discovered, the fall catalog for Daedalus Books had to make the following apology in its listing of *Marbot*: "We are extemely embarrassed to admit that we have been selling this very interesting work of fiction as a historical biography. . . . We were flummoxed by that fact that Hildesheimer is the author of the well-known biography of Mozart. . . . "

Mitteilungen an Max über den Stand der Dinge and anderes (1983, "Missives to Max") developed out of a contribution Hildesheimer wrote for a festschrift on the occasion of Max Frisch's seventieth birthday in 1981. In these texts Hildesheimer seeks to reveal the missing substance not only of the rhetoric of high culture but also of proverbs, colloquialisms, and commercial and public labeling. Their images and metaphors are threadbare and have degenerated into stereotypical speech patterns. The same applies to all too frequently quoted lines from the Bible and from such canonized authors as Rilke, Hölderlein, Schiller, and Kant. Reminiscent of his practice in *Lieblose Legenden*, Hildesheimer submits these phrases and texts to grim and witty puns that help to dissolve intellectual pretensions into nothingness. He finds in contemporary speech piles of ready-mades that can be used at random and that do not connect with reality. Given this linguistic inventory and the author's disillusion with the language, the true "state of things" referred to in the original title cannot be grasped, as proven by the missives themselves, which do not attempt at any point to provide a concrete definition of the "state of things."

His farewell to literature in 1983 is just the final consequence of Hildesheimer's ever-growing doubts that literary form can capture the world—given its overwhelming complexities and the irreversible environmental catastrophes of our time. In an interview in 1984, Hildesheimer declared his belief that the end is here, that the artist has no posterity.

PRINCIPAL WORKS IN ENGLISH TRANSLATION: *Short Fiction*—(tr. P. H. Stanley) "I Find My Way" in Dimension 8, 1975; (tr. P. H. Stanley) "The Vacation" *in* Gargoyle 6, 1977; (tr. P. H. Stanley) "Why I Became a Nightingale" *in* Gargoyle 9, 1978; (tr. P. H. Stanley) "The Summer Bed Fugue" (*excerpt from* Tynset) *in* Literary Review 27, 1984; (tr. J. Newgroschel) The Collected Stories of Wofgang Hildesheimer (includes "Missives to Max"), 1987. *Novel*—(tr. P. Campton) Marbot, 1983. *Biography*—(tr. M. Faber) Mozart, 1982. *Drama*—(tr. J. L. Rose) The Sacrifice of Helen, 1968. *Essay*—(tr. P. H. Stanley) "The Absurd I" *in* Denver Quarterly 15, 1980.

ABOUT: Cambridge Guide to World Theater, 1988; Contemporary Authors 101, 1981; 1992; Contemporary Literary Criticism 49, 1988; Dictionary of Literary Biography 69, 1988; 124, 1991–1992; Encyclopedia of World Literature in the 20th Century, vol. II, 1981; Esslin, M. The Theater of the Absurd, 1961; Faulhaber, U. et al. (eds.) Exile and Enlightenment: Studies in German and Comparative Literature, 1987; Fehn, A. et al. (eds.) Neverending Stories, 1992; Hartigan, K. V. (ed.) From Pen to Performance: Drama as Conceived and Performed, 1983; Hayman, R. (ed.) The German Theater: A Symposium, 1975; Mc-Graw-Hill Encyclopedia of World Drama, vol. 2, 1984; The Oxford Companion to German Literature, 1986; Stanley, P. H. The Realm of Possibilities: Wolfgang Hildesheimer's Non-Traditional Non-Fictional Prose, 1988; Stanley, P. H. Wolfgang Hildesheimer and His Critics, 1993. *Periodicals*—Art in America February, 1984; Atlantic April 1983; October 1983; Biography Summer 1980; Booklist September 15, 1983; Choice April 1983; Comparative Literature Studies 23, 1986; Current Musicology 35, 1983; Denver Quarterly 15, 1980; Deutsche Vierteljahrsschrift für Literatur-

wissenschaft und Geistesgeschichte 64, 1990; Economist October 1983; Encounter June 1983; Forum for Modern Language Studies January 1983; High Fidelity 33, 1983; Kosmos March 1967; Library Journal October 1, 1983; May 15, 1987; Modern Language Studies 19, 1983; Monatshefte 71, 1979; Nation 27, 1982; New York Review of Books November 18, 1982; May 12, 1983; New York Times Book Review October 9, 1983; May 10, 1987; Opera Journal 16, 1983; Publishers Weekly July 30, 1982; August 5, 1983; April 24, 1987; Quill and Quire, September 1987; Seminar 5, 1969; Time October 4, 1982; Times (London) June 1, 1961; Times Literary Supplement May 18, 1973; May 26, 1978; October 7, 1983; World Literature Today Autumn 1982; Summer 1984; Summer 1985; Yale Review 73, 1983; Yearbook of Comparative and General Literature 32, 1983.

HILLERMAN, (ANTHONY GROVE) TONY (May 27, 1925–), American mystery novelist, journalist, and educator, was born in Sacred Heart, Oklahoma, the son of August Alfred and Lucy Mary (Grove) Hillerman. Sacred Heart was a dust-bowl town where August Hillerman ran a general store and worked a farm without a tractor. The house had no indoor plumbing or electricity, and the family struggled, as did their Seminole and Blackfeet neighbors. There was no library and movies were expensive, so Hillerman learned early in life the value of storytelling. He was sent to St. Mary's Academy, originally a boarding school for Potawatomi and Seminole girls. "The nuns forgave us for not being Potawatomies. . . . But they never forgave us for not being boys," Hillerman told Alex Ward in an interview in the *New York Times Magazine*. He began to attend Oklahoma State University in Stillwater after his father died in 1941, but he returned home to run the farm when his brother went to war. He too joined the army in 1943. After two years fighting in Europe he stepped on a concussion mine behind German lines, suffering burns, two broken legs, and partial blindness. He came home decorated with the Silver Star, the Bronze Star, and the Purple Heart.

In 1946 he was awarded a B.A. at Oklahoma University, where he met his wife, Marie Unzer. Hillerman's first job after college was writing three original Purina Pig Chow radio commercials each day. After a few weeks he left to work for the Borger, Texas, *News Herald*, covering crime stories in a town dominated by petroleum and rubber factories. He continued a career in journalism, becoming first a writer for, then editor of, and finally, executive editor of the Santa Fe *New Mexican* (1954–1962).

He resigned his position to study literature and creative writing at the University of New

TONY HILLERMAN

Mexico, where he earned an M.A. in 1966 while
serving as an assistant to the university's president. Hillerman steeped himself in Graham
Greene, Dashiell Hammett, Raymond Chandler,
and Ross MacDonald, but the mystery writer
with the greatest influence on him was Arthur
Upfield, an Australian, whose books Hillerman
had read in his youth; they are set in the outback
and feature a half-French, half-aboriginal policeman.

Hillerman's University of New Mexico master's thesis was "The Great Taos Bank Robbery,"
later the title essay of a successful nonfiction
book. He became a professor in the journalism
department there in 1965 and remained until
1987.

His affinity for Native American culture developed in 1945 when he witnessed a Navajo Enemy Way ceremony held to restore a solider
freshly returned from the war to harmony. As he
told Catherine Breslin of *Publishers Weekly* in
June 1988, he was fascinated by seeing "people
with a living culture still affecting how they
live." As a student of Navajo, Zuni, and Hopi culture, he reads anthropology texts and doctoral
dissertations and travels throughout the rugged
Southwest, stopping at trading posts and auc-
tions with Native Americans who are his frequently consulted "experts"—one a female
shaman. Ironically, however, when he sent the
manuscript of his first novel, *The Blessing Way*,
to a literary agent in 1970, he was advised to "get
rid of all that Indian stuff." He did not do so, and
achieved success with his novels precisely for
their *for* their "deep-rooted sense of place and

people." As Alex Ward observed in the *New
York Times Magazine*, Hillerman "may be the
only writer who has been compared to both Raymond Chandler and Carlos Castaneda,"

Hillerman's main character is Lieutenant Joe
Leaphorn, a Navajo tribal policeman: a mature,
sophisticated, somewhat poetical, but highly logical skeptic educated in anthropology and
caught between white, Native American, and
Mexican American cultures, and obstructed by
federal, state and local bureaucracies. In his fifth
novel, *People of Darkness*, Hillerman introduced a contrasting Navajo policeman: Sergeant
Jim Chee, younger, more intuitive and more
spiritual, but also well educated. Chee retains his
Navajo beliefs and is in training to be a shaman.
Although tempted to join the FBI, he does not
wish to leave the reservation. Both en are contemplative, introspective, and low-key, even
when under fire. An occasional glimpse into
their respective private lives rounds out the two
characters but never interferes with the plot.
The reader usually knows more than either of
the detectives, because they work separately and
have but a grudging alliance.

Hillerman's books have steadily gained in
popularity and positive critical attention. His
first novel, *The Blessing Way*, met with encouraging reviews, especially for the character of Joe
Leaphorn, but it contained more errors of fact
than his later mysteries would. He temporarily
abandoned the Navajo policeman for his second
novel, *The Fly on the Wall*, creating a political
reporter based in Albuquerque and involving
him in what the *New Yorker* called "a thriller
that is not merely thrilling . . . but also a provocative ethical conundrum." The big question
in a Hillerman novel is not really "Who done it?"
but *why*? Like the Navajo, he sees unhappiness,
chaos, and crime as the results of ruptured social
patterns and alienation of individuals.

Dance Hall of the Dead (which won the Mystery Writers of America's Edgar award for 1973)
depicts the disruption of harmony brought about
by alienated Native Americans, white drug culture denizens, and other social renegades. His
next novel, *Listening Woman*, focuses on broken
taboos. In solving the central crime Leaphorn
passes through his own mythological ordeal in
order to right the perverted worlds of both Indian and Anglo.

Reviewers called *People of Darkness* Hillerman's best work yet. It introduces Chee as the
seeker not only of the criminal but of what Robin Winks in the *New Republic* called "the human mystery . . . how do Anglo values differ
from Navajo values?"

The fact that in Hillerman's books there are

"worlds," rather than "a world," highlights another issue: racism, by which no Hillerman characters is untouched. Racism in these novels is a pervasive evil, ranging from the subtle to the malignant. As Jane S. Bakerman wrote in *Melus*, Hillerman "dramatizes the presence of racist behavior in our society by consistently showing its effects as they are linked to other traits of character and social behavior." Leaphorn and Chee, although pragmatic and imperfect, have a Navajo perspective that precludes taking of vengeance.

In *The Dark Wind*, Chee is guilty of the exploitation of another world: that of the Hopi. This novel, in Bakerman's view, raises "entertainment fiction to the level of valid social commentary without for a moment sacrificing either objective."

The great success of *Skinwalkers*, which won the Golden Spur Award of the Western Writers of America, enabled Hillerman to leave teaching to write full-time, and two years later *A Thief of Time* became his first best-seller. In the *New York Times Book Review* (1988), Michael Dorris said, "A sense of place and character often takes precedence over the story," which tells of "the search for a missing archaeologist. . . . [a] specialist in Anasazi pots . . . on the verge of . . . the identification of a specific artist, dead a thousand years," who "beneath a full desert moon" has vanished.

Talking God is set in Washington D.C.,where the Smithsonian Institution's collection of Indian skeletons was, in the 1980s, causing much displeasure among Native Americans. Hillerman's carefully researched fictional treatment resulted in the return of some of the bones to their rightful burial places.

Coyote Waits has one of Hillerman's crowded plots, involving the murder of a police officer and a history professor, as well as long-lost burial places and shamanistic lore. In the *New York Times*, Robert F. Gish pronounced Hillerman "one of the nation's most convincing and authentic interpreters of Navajo culture. . . . An extra payoff of *Coyote Waits* is an . . . utterly convincing advocacy of Native American culture and an enchanting depiction of the spirit of the Southwest."

Other reviewers find Hillerman excessively reverent toward the Navajos, however, and lacking in humor. In the *New York Times Book Review* Verlyn Klinkenborg called *Sacred Clowns* Hillerman's "most pallid" novel. "Hillerman does not allow himself satire or irreverence or even vulgarity," Klinkenborg maintained. "He has taken laughter—one of the Navajo's strongest traits—away from them"

Spiritual issues are central to Hillerman, a Roman Catholic, who especially admires Navajo antimaterialism, strong family ties, love of language, sense of humor, distaste for obscenity, and belief that evil exists.

In *Talking Mysteries* he says of his writing method: "I never being a chapter without a detailed and exact vision of the place it will happen, the nature of the actors in the scene, the mood of the protagonist, the temperature, direction of the breeze, the aromas it carries, time of day, the way the light falls, the cloud formations."

Hillerman and his wife live modestly in Albuquerque, but he travels frequently in his secondhand car all over New Mexico, Arizona, Utah, and Colorado, where he does his best research, in situ.

PRINCIPAL WORKS: *Novels*—The Blessing Way, 1970; The Fly on the Wall, 1971; Dance Hall of the Dead, 1973; Listening Woman, 1978; People of Darkness, 1978; The Dark Wind, 1981; The Ghostway, 1984; Skinwalkers 1986; Talking God, 1988; A Thief of Time, 1988; Coyote Waits, 1990; Sacred Clowns, 1993. *Nonfiction*—The Great Taos Bank Robbery, and Other Indian Country Affairs, 1973; (text) New Mexico, 1975; (text) Rio Grande, 1975; Indian Country: America's Sacred Land, 1987; Hillerman Country, A Journey Through the Southwest, 1991; (with E. Bulow) Talking Mysteries: A Conversation with Tony Hillerman, 1991; *As Editor*—The Spell of New Mexico, 1976. *Juvenile*—The Boy Who Made Dragonfly, 1972.

ABOUT: Balassi, W., J. F. Crawford, and A. O. Eysturoy (eds.) This is About Vision: Interviews with Southwestern Writers, 1990; Bargainnier, E. F. and G. N. Dove (eds.) Cops and Constables: American and British Fictional Policemen, 1986; Contemporary Authors New Revision Series 21, 1987; Contemporary Literary Criticism 62, 1991; Current Biography Yearbook 1992; Hillerman, T. "Making Mysteries with Navajo Materials," in P. A. Dennis and W. Aycock (eds.) Literature and Anthropology, 1989; Hillerman, T. and Bulow, E. Talking Mysteries: A Conversation with Tony Hillerman, 1991; Magill, F. (ed.) Critical Survey of Mystery and Detective Fiction, 1988; Something About the Author 6, 1974; Reilly, J. M. Twentieth Century Crime and Mystery Writers, 1980; Who's Who in America, 1994; Supplement 1991–92; Winks, R. W. (ed.) Colloquium on Crime: Eleven Renowned Mystery Writers Discuss Their Work, 1986. *Periodicals*—Library Journal February 1, 1970; Melus Fall 1984; New Republic December 13, 1980; New York Times August 16, 1988, June 24 1990; New York Times Book Review July 3, 1988, June 18, 1989, October 17, 1993; New York Times Magazine May 14, 1989; New Yorker September 25, 1971; Publishers Weekly June 10, 1988, October 24, 1988; Southwest Review Spring 1982.

HIRSCH, E(RIC) D(ONALD), JR. (March 22, 1928–   ), American critic and educator, was born in Memphis, Tennessee, to Eric Donald and Leah (Aschafenburg) Hirsch. He grew up in Marvell, Arkansas, where his father ran a general store, but the family moved back to Memphis where the elder Hirsch prospered in the cotton business. (*Cultural Literacy*, Hirsch's best-known book, is dedicated to his father, from whom he claims to have learned "the courage to follow ideas whither they lead.") He attributes his precocity to both "a traditional education and rebellion against Southern ethos." An influential book was Gunnar Myrdal's study of racism, *An American Dilemma*.

At Cornell University, his undergraduate institution, Hirsch had difficulty at first in finding his direction. After deciding that the family cotton business was not for him, and discovering that he was not cut out to be a chemist, he heard Vladimir Nabokov (then a professor at Cornell) lecture on Russian literature and became "hooked on English." He received his B.A. in 1950. Following a tour of duty in the United States Naval Reserve (1950–1952), during which he took postgraduate courses in Paris and Berlin, he entered Yale University, earning his M.A. in 1955 and his Ph.D. (on a Fulbright Fellowship) in 1957.

Hirsch began his teaching career at Yale as an instructor in English in 1956, rising to the rank of associate professor by 1964. In 1966 he was appointed to a professorship in English at the University of Virginia, Charlottesville, which remained his principal academic base. In 1973 he was named Kenan Professor of English, and in 1989 Linden Kent Professor.

Hirsch's work spans literary theory and educational practice. The books by which he established his reputation among academic colleagues are in hermeneutics, but as Brian G. Caraher observed in the *Dictionary of Literary Biography*, behind his diversity of interests lies "an unending concern for *types* and for the *typicality* of expressive and interpretive behavior." This preoccupation led him eventually from the study of the foundations of literature to the exploration of the bases of literacy."

Hirsch's purely literary interests were introduced in his first book, *Wordsworth and Schelling: A Typological Study of Romanticism*, revised from his doctoral dissertation. In this study Hirsch investigates the kinship between Wordworth's *Lyrical Ballads* and other early poems and Schelling's *Naturphilosophie*, based, he is quick to point out, not on direct influence but on a shared worldview (weltanschauung). In common with Schelling's idealism, Words-

E. D. HIRSCH, JR.

worth's "structure of experience" is informed by what Hirsch labels "enthusiasm" or "panvitalism," the assumption of a reciprocity between the mind and nature (subject and object in philosophical terms). For both the poet and the philosopher, "by striving to unite with things of the world, man is striving towards God.

During a year as a Morse Fellow at Yale, Hirsch conceived his second book, *Innocence and Experience: An Introduction to Blake*. Centered on another poet of the Romantic Age who found God manifest in nature, this study is connected with the Wordsworth book and is also typological in dealing with Blake as a prototype of the romantic. While the earlier book drew on the findings of previous Wordsworth scholars, in his second book Hirsch took issue with previous Blake scholars who had assumed a continuity between Blake's early and late writing. Instead, Hirsch contends that the Poems of Experience represent a complete alteration in spiritual outlook from the Poems of Innocence, signified by an "expanded perception of the actual world." In the *Times Literary Supplement*, a reviewer noted that "scholars cannot afford to ignore" Hirsch's "convincing" explication of the discrete periods of Blake's works. The poem-by-poem commentary that takes up the second half of *Innocence and Experience* was especially welcomed by teachers, and it received the Explicator Award for 1964.

With his next two books, *Validity in Interpretation* and *The Aims of Interpretation*, Hirsch attempts a theoretical groundwork for what he calls "authorial will" and "shared types." *Validity in Interpretation* was written in reaction against what Hirsch calls scholars of the "radical historical" persuasion—historical, legal, biblical—who deny the stability of meaning of a text as it passes from one generation to another, as well as critics and poets—notably T. S. Eliot and Ezra Pound—who would "banish the author" in favor of poetry that is "impersonal, objective, and autonomous." Even if an author comes over time to reevaluate the significance of work previously produced, Hirsch argues, its "original meaning" is not altered. Against those who maintain that an author's meaning is inaccessible, he poses a distinction between "the public facts of language and history," which are retrievable, and "a private world beyond the reach of written language." In *The Aims of Interpretation*, made up largely of articles that had appeared in learned journals, Hirsch develops his dichotomy of "meaning," derived from a careful reading of a text, and "significance," which relates meaning to various historical and topical contexts—the first the province of interpretation, the second the province of criticism.

"Mr. Hirsch has performed a monumental service . . . that of reinstating the credentials of objectivism and defining the limits of the aesthetics of truth," wrote the reviewer of *Validity in Interpretation* for the *Virginia Quarterly Review.* "This study is a necessary tool for anyone who wants to talk sense about literature." Some other reviewers of this book and its successor, *The Aims of Interpretation*, complained of Hirsch's repetitiousness and occasional contradictions, and readers untrained in philosophical discourse were warned that the going could be rough. Nevertheless, these two treatises established their author in the vanguard of literary theory.

Hirsch's subsequent remarkable descent from theoretical criticism to the elementary school classroom is anticipated in chapter 8 ("Some Aims of Criticism") of *The Aims of Interpretation.* Here he urges as a step towards a "multidisciplinary humanistic philosophy of literature" the cultivation of a plain style of prose, "the most important style in literature because it is so widespread and contains so much of the best that is said and thought in the world." Above all, Hirsch saw in plain style "the chief vehicle of mass literacy in modern cultural life." In *The Philosophy of Composition*, the book that followed *The Aims of Interpretation*, Hirsch follows up his concern for mass literacy with more emphasis on "relative readability," the effect of conventional style that fulfills the "patterns of expectation" that writers and their readers have in common. Hirsch had confronted student deficiency in writing and reading during a brief stint

as director of composition at the University of Virginia in the early 1970s. However, a turning point when "my life changed" (as he told Christopher Hitchens, who interviewed him for the *New York Times Magazine*) occurred in 1978 when he discovered that students at both the University of Virginia and at a nearby community college, while equally adept at "decoding" words, broke down in background comprehension at their respective levels, the university students unable to interpret a passage from Hegel, the community college students stumbling over name recognition of central figures connected with the Civil War. This experience led Hirsch to conclude that the fundamental problem of education in America lay in the lack not of basic literacy but of what he came to label "cultural literacy."

Hirsch's engagement with this problem culminated in *Cultural Literacy: What Every American Needs to Know*, the book that extended his reputation far beyond academic circles. "For reasons explained in this book, our children's lack of intergenerational information is a serious problem for the nation," he announces in the opening chapter. "The decline of literacy and the decline of shared knowledge are closely related."

Cultural Literacy was conceived when Hirsch came upon a finding by the National Assessment of Educational Progress (NAEP) that between 1970 and 1980 seventeen-year-olds declined in their ability to read written materials, and that the decline was especially striking in the top group—those supposedly able to read at the "advanced" level. The investigators were appalled to discover that these young people were ignorant of essential facts of geography and history (not only of the Civil War, but of the two World Wars), nor could they recognize references to literature, mythology, and the Bible formerly taken for granted as common knowledge. Conversation with the educator Mina Shaughnessy encouraged Hirsch to pursue the issue on his own, and his ideas were introduced at a conference held in her memory in 1980. His "seeds," as he refers to them, were further germinated at the Center for Advanced Study in the Behavioral Sciences at Stanford, where he was a fellow in 1980–1981.

In *Cultural Literacy*, Hirsch attributes the decline of literacy in America and the fragmentation of the school curriculum to the "ever growing   dominance   of   romantic formalism"—the stressing of reading skills over content—in educational programs. He traces this decline to the theories of John Dewey and ultimately back to Rousseau's *Emile*, with its idea of "natural development." Hirsch contends, that contemporary educators, in their continuing emphasis on words and sounds in the reading process, have ignored the latest research by cognitive psychologists into the function of schemata (categorization) in the retention of knowledge, as against memorization of words, which tend to be quickly forgotten. These schemata make possible the "shared knowledge" that Hirsch urges as a way out of our educational abyss, a pedagogical application of the "shared types," or universal mind-sets, central to his literary theory.

The coincidence of the recent publication of another educational polemic, Allan Bloom's *The Closing of the American Mind*, inevitably brought the two professors into juxtaposition in reviews, a coupling that made Hirsch uneasy. *Cultural Literacy* is far more temperate in tone and less dogmatic than Bloom's book. Moreover, as against Bloom's emphasis on select college students, Hirsch pointed out that he is antielitist in his attention to the ordinary student in the lower grades. Furthermore, unlike Bloom's concentration on the humanities, especially the classics, Hirsch's curriculum is broadened to take in the social sciences, biology, medicine, and the physical sciences, as well as the popular arts.

While Hirsch's program was applauded by a number of educational reformers, it met with some resistance from the field, notably from Herbert Kohl, author of *The Open Classroom*, which promotes the "progressive" system of teaching by demonstration and the acting out of situations. It was also opposed by representatives of the "cultural left" in educational circles who objected to the Western bias embedded in the list of names, words, and phrases ("What Literate Americans Know") that makes up the appendix to *Cultural Literacy*. Among literature professors, George Steiner, who reviewed the book in the *New Yorker* ("Little-Read Schoolhouse"), commended it as a "brief, crystal-clear and condignly urgent tract," if solemn and humorless. Though he questioned the originality of Hirsch's diagnosis of our educational malady, Steiner was impressed by the background of psychological and sociological research that he brought to its proposed cure.

The appendix to *Cultural Literacy* was expanded into a thick volume titled *The Dictionary of Cultural Literacy*, which provides a technical explanation for the 5,000 terms in the list. Compiled with the collaboration of two colleagues at the University of Virginia, the dictionary is divided into twenty-three sections—among them, "The Bible," "Mythology and Folklore," "Literature in English," "Fine Arts,"

"World Politics," "American Politics," "Earth Sciences," "Life Sciences," and "Technology." Altogether, this "collective memory," as Hirsch refers to it, "forms the basis for communication, and if it is shared by enough people, it is a distinguishing characteristic of a natural culture." (In *Cultural Literacy*, Hirsch pointed out that 80 percent of the items on his list have been a part of common culture for more than 100 years.)

Along with the considerable interest it stirred up in educational circles, this compendium has had its denigrators—notably Mortimer Adler, who dismissed it as an intellectual game of Trivial Pursuit. Others have noted arbitrariness of inclusion and omission (Dickens is in, but not Thackeray, even though *Vanity Fair* is among the titles "every American" should know; Matthew Arnold is invoked in Hirsch's *The Aims of Interpretation*, but the Arnold who makes the list is Benedict). Ironically, factual errors were detected by some discerning readers of the first edition, not all of them corrected in the revision. Daniel Seligman, in his "Keeping Up" column in *Fortune*, characterized the whole as "great fun to read and full of mistakes," in particular "truly terrible in business and economics."

Cultural Literacy and its offshoots made Hirsch a media celebrity. To his deeper satisfaction, his work has had a significant, if as yet slight, impact on teaching. A conference on the core curriculum conducted by Hirsch in Charlottesville attracted public school principals, as well as professors of education. A promotional tour for the first edition of the *Dictionary of Cultural Literacy* took him to the Miami Book Fair, where he addressed a group of school department heads. The outcome was the establishment of an experimental core curriculum in the first six grades of schools in Dade County. The first of these so-called core knowledge schools was visited by Jeff Litt, newly installed principal of a public elementary school in the South Bronx, who shortly thereafter introduced this curriculum. According to Hirsch's article "Teach Knowledge, Not Mental Skills," in the *New York Times* of September 4, 1993, the reading level of these students, mainly African-American and Hispanic, was raised by 12.5 percent. Over 100 schools throughout the U.S. have adopted this program.

These programs are monitored from the Core Knowledge foundation, established in 1986 by Hirsch. The Foundation disseminates information, conducts seminars and workshops on how to get "shared content" into the schools, and has produced several textbooks.

Hirsch married Mary Monteith Pope in 1958, and they had three children.

PRINCIPAL WORKS: Wordsworth and Schelling: A Typological Study of Romanticism, 1960; Innocence and Experience: An Introduction to Blake, 1964; Validity in Interpretation, 1967; The Aims of Interpretation, 1976; The Philosophy of Composition, 1977; Cultural Literacy: What Every American Needs to Know, 1987; (with J. Kett and J. Trefil) The Dictionary of Cultural Literacy: What Every American Needs to Know, 1988. As editor—A First Dictionary of Cultural Literacy: What Our Children Need to Know, 1989; What Your First Grader Needs to Know: Fundamentals of a Good First-Grade Education (The Core Knowledge Series) 1991; What Your Second Grader Needs to Know: Fundamentals of a Good Second-Grade Education (The Core Knowledge Series) 1991; What Your Third Grader Needs to Know: Fundamentals of a Good Third-Grade Education (The Core Knowledge Series) 1992; What Your Fourth Grader Needs to Know: Fundamentals of a Good Fourth-Grade Education (The Core Knowledge Series) 1992; What Your Fifth Grader Needs to Know: Fundamentals of a Good Fifth-Grade Education (The Core Knowledge Series) 1993; What Your Sixth Grader Needs to Know: Fundamentals of a Good Sixth-Grade Education (The Core Knowledge Series) 1993.

ABOUT: Contemporary Authors New Revision Series 27, 1989; Dictionary of Literary Biography 67, 1988; Lentricchia, F. After the New Criticism, 1980; Madison, G. The Hermeneutics of Postmodernity, 1988; Ray, W. Literary Meaning: From Phenomenology to Deconstruction, 1984; Who's Who in America 1994. Periodicals—Bulletin of the Center for Children's Books January 1992; British Journal of Aesthetics Summer 1981; Change August 1988; College English November 1977; Commentary July 1987; Commonweal September 25, 1987; Critical Inquiry December 1982; Education Digest October 1989; Fortune December 19, 1988; October 18, 1993; Journal of Aesthetics and Art Criticism Fall 1984; Nation May 30, 1987; New York Times Book Review April 26, 1987; New York Times Magazine May 13, 1990; New Yorker June 1, 1987; Newsweek November 14, 1988; November 2, 1992; Time August 17, 1987; Times Literary Supplement February 11, 1965; Virginia Quarterly Review Summer 1967.

HIRSCH, EDWARD (MARK) (January 20, 1950–), American poet, writes: "Poetry is so marginal in our country that almost all American poets have had to invent themselves from scratch. I am no different. We begin writing in secret out of emotional desperation, we recreate the idea of poetry for ourselves, we project a life, a community, and a culture that we aren't really sure exists. Books are our only beacons, our imaginative guides through the labyrinths of human experience.

"I was born in Chicago, Illinois, and grew up in a middle-class Jewish family. We are thoroughly American. It wasn't until I began writing

EDWARD HIRSCH

in high school that I remembered—it must have lodged in my unconscious—that my grandfather had also written poetry. I soon discovered that no one recalled whether he wrote in English, Hebrew, or Yiddish, but they did remember that he copied his poems into the backs of his books. After he died my grandmother, whom I adored, gave all his books away. The work was lost. It did not occur to me for another twenty years to try to imagine the actual character of those poems.

"All poetry is imaginative and emotional reclamation. I love the sheer intensity of the lyric, its ecstatic and outsize passion. I believe that 'only emotion endures,' as Ezra Pound said, and I take entirely seriously the idea that writing poetry is a means of soul-making. At the same time one does not forget that feeling in poetry can only be expressed through precise language. A poem is something made out of words, a formal event, a durable construction. It is stamped with the personality of its maker, and yet there is always something impersonal about it.

"I began writing earnestly in college and have never stopped. At first I apprenticed myself to the Metaphysical Poets because I admired the playful and crafty way they used the language of argumentation to articulate emotional concerns. I still like a poetry of conceits that brings together intellect and passion. Later, however, I fell in love with a more modern and romantic poetry that created a wilder logic, that invented its own forms, that treated poetry as a means of redemption.

"I think of my poems as 'memorandums of my affections'—to borrow John Clare's phrase. I write to recall the failed, the marginal, the forgotten, to explore and recover fluctuating states of mind and feeling. Much of my work seems to me about history and posterity, about what gets passed on and what gets lost over time. We Americans are great forgetters, but my poetry tries to remember intense instances of human suffering. And it memorializes the process and project of various artists and poets, visionary exemplars of the imagination, Virgilian guides. I see an ongoing argument throughout about the longing for transcendence and the need to live on earth as it is."

———

The lost poems of Edward Hirsch's grandfather have been a shaping influence on his poetry. "They are always before me," he wrote in "My Grandfather's Poems" (in *Conversant Essays*), "an unnamed presence, a spiritual ideal . . . by turns wry, tender, passionate, playful, modest, heartfelt; the voice of a quiet intellectual who understands that he lives inside history, who tries to speak with true feeling."

Living "inside history," Hirsch acknowledges the need for a "poetry more distanced from the self, where the self wasn't the only subject." Questioned by an interviewer in 1986 in *The Post-Confessionals* as to the distinction between his poetry and the "confessional" poetry of writers like Robert Lowell, John Berryman, and Sylvia Plath, whom he much admires, he replied: "I became uncomfortable with the fact that there weren't enough other people in that poetry, and there were ways in which poets were prizing their own experience over other people's experience . . . I dislike the activity of centering your own suffering above the suffering of all others."

Hirsch's first collection, *For the Sleepwalkers* drew some criticism for its own self-involvement. J.D. McClatchy remarked in *Poetry* that some of the poems were "vitiated by a coy or dizzying self-indulgence,"and Hugh Seidman in the *New York Times Book Review* found some of the poems marked by "narcissistic invention." In "Song Against Natural Selection," which opens the collection, wounds draw pity:

The weak survive!
A man with a damaged arm,
a house missing a single brick, one step
torn away from the other steps
the way I was once torn away
from you. . . .

But the poem affirms the first line: "The weak survive!" It closes with firm resolution and a sig-

nificant shift from the singular "I" to the universal "we":

. . . we survive
so that losing itself becomes a kind
of song, our song, our only witness
to the way we die, one day at a time;
a leg severed, a word buried; this
is how we recognize ourselves, and why.

In the same volume Hirsch appears in various personas of writers and artists: Rimbaud in a drugged and drunken nightmare; Isaac Babel witnessing a pogrom; Paul Klee creating art out of "Oblongs and squares patches of ground, / Constellations over mean houses, and an / Orange balloon on a courtesan's window"; Matisse, a color-intoxicated young boy watching his sister dressing for a country dance, "trying on her pink shoes / And red slip, and her red shoes and / Pink slip, and her orange dress"; García Lorca visiting New York, writing "the poetry / that matters, the loneliness of America."

Phoebe Pettingell, in the *New Leader*, praised Hirsch's first collection for his daring, "his willingness to face up to failure." The failures, she wrote, "suggest promise, and at his best he speaks with authority." Jay Parini, in the *New Republic*, noted "a slight, somewhat self-conscious formality, as if he wishes to hold his material in place by distancing himself from it," but admired his attention to technique and diction. Hirsch has said of his poetics: "I view free verse . . . as a continual struggle between freedom and control, a search for a new, articulate and governing shape in language, a passionate American syntax and speech," he wrote in an essay on William Carlos Williams in the *Ohio Review* in 1987.

Wild Gratitude, Hirsch's second collection, includes a number of poems about his boyhood in Chicago, such as "The Skokie Theatre," which describes how at twelve, sitting next to a girl and watching a movie he first becomes aware of his sexuality; the death of a close friend in "Omen"; and his insomnia in "The Night Parade: Homage to Charles Ives." In several poems Hirsch uses insomnia as a metaphor for a suffering that stretches from his own condition to one common to his readers. In "I Need Help," which he addresses to all the insomniacs of the world, he pleads for help "to fly out of myself":

Because I can't do it alone. It is
So dark out here that I'm staggering
Down the street like a drunk or a cripple;
I'm almost a hunchback from trying to hold up
The sky by myself. The clouds are enormous
And I need strength from the weight lifters.

The title poem of *Wild Gratitude* pays homage to the 18th-century British poet Christopher Smart, who suffered periods of madness. (Smart was the subject of an earlier poem in *For the Sleepwalkers*: "I am a wild ass galloping through the streets / Trailing the dog star, the mad gull.") In "Wild Gratitude," contemplating his own cat Zooey, Hirsch recalls Smart's "I Will Consider My Cat Jeoffrey," with its eloquent tribute to Jeoffrey, "servant of the Living God," even as Smart was himself:

Who wanted to kneel down and pray without ceasing
In every one of the splintered London streets,

And was locked away in the madhouse at St. Luke's
With his sad religious mania, and his wild gratitude. . . .

David Wojahn commented on Hirsch's deep feeling in *Wild Gratitude* as well as his "technical prowess." Where at times emotion veers dangerously toward sentimentality, he observed in the *New York Times Book Review*, "he can usually avoid bathos because of his prosodic skill and his gift for engaging metaphor." In the *Hudson Review*, Liam Rector noticed Hirsch's tendency in *Sleepwalkers* to use adjectives "as poetic buzz-words . . . a kind of predictable straining after affability," but wrote that in *Wild Gratitude*, Hirsch "has a coherent sense of restraint in its baroque effusiveness."

The poems in *The Night Parade* strike a balance between the personal and the universal. In *The Night Parade* a Murphy bed is a source of wonder. "It was like putting the night away / When we closed the wooden doors again / And her bed disappeared without a trace," and in "My Grandfather's Poems": "I remember that he wrote them backwards, / In Yiddish, in tiny, slanting, bird-like lines. . . . " In "Proustian" Hirsch celebrates childhood memories: "Sometimes it is enough just to remember / There was once a time before we knew about time / When the self and the world fit snugly together."

Other poems in *The Night Parade* treat more ambitious themes. "When Skyscrapers Were Invented in Chicago" recalls the devastating fire that destroyed the city but also created the need for a new city: "It couldn't have happened without a democratic vision / Of time, the present finally equal to the past." "And Who Will Look Upon Our Testimony" is a terrifying vision of the Black Plague leaving its heritage of suffering to the future: "Oh happy posterity / who will die in its own time / with its own wondering tales of woe."

Helen Vendler, in the *New York Review of Books*, said Hirsch "wants to be sad on behalf of the world," but that when he assumes a more emotionally restrained voice, "he is capable of quiet, believable poems." She admires especially "Infertility,"—also singled out for praise by Stephen Dobyns in the *New York Times Book Review*—a contemplative poem on the never-conceived whose souls drift through space:

We don't know how to name
    the long string of zeroes
Stretching across winter,
    the barren places,
The missing birthdates of the unborn.

The poem, Dobyns wrote, "combines what is best in . . . Hirsch's work: strong emotion and exactness of language. There is the sense that the poem forced itself into being, that silence was no longer possible, that the emotion derives from the deepest core of the human animal."

Margo Jefferson, reviewing *Earthly Measures* in the *New York Times*, said Hirsch "examines ecstasy and delight . . . through the medium of art and landscape: Dutch paintings, the poetry of Wallace Stevens, the anguished consolation of Simone Weil's philosophy. . . . *Earthly Measures* is a kind of fine-art exhibition, filled with the objects and subjects . . . Hirsch treasures most." He returns frequently to images of the city, as a metaphor for both the height of civilization and its dark underside, so that he can sing the city as "a net of stars / spreading out before us" in "Roman Fall," as "the long-awaited sublime" of Henry James's Rome in "The Italian Muse," but refer to his friend in "Apostrophe (In Memory of Donald Barthelme, 1931–1989)" as "collagist of that mysterious overcrowded muck / we called a city," like himself, and, perhaps, as in "Orpheus Ascending," like the universal poet:

Inconsolable Orpheus, who cannot decide
To sing, who never expected to find
A world above so much like the world below.

Edward Hirsch is the son of Kurt and Irma (Ginsburg) Hirsch. He has two sisters. He received his B.A. from Grinnell College (1972) and his Ph.D. from the University of Pennsylvania (1979). He also received an honorary degree form Grinnell College in 1989. Hirsch taught at Wayne State University from 1978 to 1985. Since then he has been teaching in the Creative Writing Program and the department of English at the University of Houston. He is married to a museum curator, Janet Landay; they have one child.

Hirsch has received an Amy Lowell Traveling Fellowship (1978), an Ingram Merrill Foundation Award (1978), a National Endowment for the Arts Creative Writing Fellowship (1982), the Lavan Younger Poets Award from the Academy of American Poets (1983), the Delmore Schwartz Memorial Award from New York University (1985), a Guggenheim Fellowship (1986), the National Book Critics Circle Award (1987), and the Rome Prize from the American Academy and Institute of Arts and Letters. His poems and reviews appear regularly in a wide variety of literary magazines and periodicals—among them, the *New Yorker*, the *Nation*, and the *New Republic*.

PRINCIPAL WORKS: For the Sleepwalkers, 1981; Wild Gratitude, 1986; The Night Parade, 1989; Earthly Measures, 1994.

ABOUT: Contemporary Authors New Revision Series 20, 1987; Contemporary Literary Criticism 31, 1985; 50, 1988; Dictionary of Literary Biography 120, 1992; Ingersoll, E. G. (ed.) The Post-Confessionals: Conversations with American Poets, 1989; McCorkle, J. (ed.) Conversant Essays: Contemporary Poets on Poetry, 1990; Who's Who in America 1990–1991. *Periodicals*—Georgia Review Summer 1982; Hudson Review Autumn 1986; New Leader March 8, 1982; New Republic April 14, 1982; New York Review of Books January 28, 1990; New York Times August 3, 1994; New York Times Book Review September 13, 1981; June 8, 1986; January 28, 1990; Poetry September 1982, May 1986; Virginia Quarterly Review Summer 1986.

HITCHENS, CHRISTOPHER (1949–   ),

British journalist and writer on political and literary affairs, was born in Portsmouth, England, where his father, a commander in the Royal Navy, was stationed following active service in World War II. Although his writing is almost invariably inspired by his personal reactions to public events, Hitchens has revealed few factual details of his biography. He attended a British private school before entering Balliol College, Oxford, where he joined the International Socialist party, and from which he graduated with a B.A. about 1970. He lives in Washington, D.C., with his wife and son. In essays and reviews he occasionally refers to his own views as "socialist" and "radical."

From the essay "On Not Knowing the Half of It, which appeared in *Grand Street* in 1988 and was reprinted in *Prepared for the Worst*, we learn that his father had a distinguished naval career, that Hitchens is the older of two sons, and that his family moved frequently during his early years on account of his father's naval service. But this essay, like much of Hitchens's writing, uses personal experiences as an occasion for meditation on larger issues. Hitchens's discov-

ery, shortly before his father's death, that his mother, who died in 1973, had concealed her Jewish identity, even from her husband, in order to become assimilated in English society, provokes a lengthy discourse on the situation of English Jews in the context of Western anti-Semitism. What distinguishes the Jews, Hitchens finds, and what makes him grimly pleased to be among their number, is the sense that "the worst can happen." It is as if he discovered a social and philosophical basis for his acerbic nonconformism that justifies and explains his predilection for irony and satire. Like the classical Roman satirist Juvenal, whom he frequently quotes approvingly, or his near-contemporary, the American journalist and novelist Tom Wolfe, whose novel *Bonfire of the Vanities* he has praised, Hitchens prides himself on his ability to puncture cant and pretension and debunk social eminence. He is at his entertaining best when complaining about the popularity of the British royal family, the intellectual failings of the American political right, or the sentimental, mock-patriotic postures of Oliver North and Ronald Reagan. His most characteristic writing, and his most significant achievement, is the weekly column "Minority Report," which has appeared in the *Nation* since 1983. His unswerving dissent and wide knowledge of contemporary politics and literature have made him a prominent reviewer of political books and a frequent guest on late-night talk shows, about which he has written disparagingly in the essay "Blabscam," which appeared in *Haprer's* magazine in March 1987. Inevitably, he has assumed a reputation as a scourge of American conservatism and the bete noir of those who write in two of its leading publications, *National Review* and *Commentary*. His arguments, however, invariably draw on an impressive array of knowledge and are replete with historical comparison and reference. As Tom Bethell observed in the *National Review* (April 7, 1989) "the Hitchens style is relentlessly argumentative and analytical, rarely expository."

Hitchens's earliest publication was an introduction and preface to an edition of Karl Marx's classic work *The Paris Commune*, but his first widely noticed book (written with Peter Kellner) was a straightforward, factual account of the career of then British prime minister James Callaghan. In *James Callaghan: The Road to Number Ten*, described in the London *Times* by Paul Johnson as an "excellent little book," Hitchens and his coauthor trace Callaghan's rise to the top of the British Labour party through the structure of the Trades Union Congress, which is the British equivalent of the AFL-CIO. Like it American counterpart, the TUC had often found itself in conflict with conservative political interests. The chief interest of Hitchens's study, therefore, was the question of whether Callaghan, a former union official, would be able to reconcile the concerns of national government with the priorities of organized labor, or whether, in bending too far towardhis former constituency, he would be rejected by the majority of voters. The book was prescient in predicting that Callaghan would not be able to master this conflict of allegiances, for his government was soon driven from power by the Conservative party under the leadership of Margaret Thatcher, who took a firmly anti-Union stand.

No trace appears in *Callaghan*, a factual, sober book, of the Hitchens who emerged in *Cyprus*, written, as Hitchens acknowledged in the preface to a 1989 reissue of the book, "in a fit of bad temper in order to commemorate the tenth anniversary of the 1974 invasion of Cyprus." His purpose there was, more accurately, to express his moral outrage at the injustice done to the island by a succession of non-Cypriot overloads, including the Turks and British, for whom it has been a pawn in political maneuvering that had little to do with the needs of the island's inhabitants. the book traces the history of Cypriot affairs back to the Roman Empire and earlier, but concentrates primarily on the events immediately preceding and following 1974, when the Turks occupied the island in order, ostensibly, to protect the Turkish minority from the Greek majority. This state of affairs exists in defiance of Hitchens's view, which is that "the island has been, since the Bronze Age, unmistakably Greek." While allowing that he writes with "intense emotion" that excuses his exaggeration oversimplification of some circumstances, P. J. Vatikiotis, in the *New Republic,* was critical of Hitchens's historical account and especially with this estimate of the potential for Greek/Turkish independent state on the island: "An independent Cyprus . . . was never really on." But he agreed that "its undoing was callous and disgraceful" and that it came about as a result of the foreign policy of Henry Kissinger, long a butt of Hitchens's ridicule and moral condemnation.

The idea of a book on the long-disputed case of the "the Elgin Marbles," sculptures removed from the Parthenon in Athens by Lord Elgin in 1800 during the Turkish occupation of Greece, grew from an essay by Hitchens published in the *Spectator* on January 1, 1983. *The Elgin Marbles: Should They Be Returned to Greece?* (1987, U.S. title *Imperial Spoils*), with essays by Robert Browning (on the Parthenon's influence on material and intellectual culture) and by Graham Binns (on the continuing efforts to conserve

and restore the Acropolis), appeared four years later, after the Greek government had submitted a formal request for the restitution of the sculptures from the British Museum to the Acropolis. Hitchens's essay, *The Elgin Marbles,*" deliberately and studiously avoids stridency, patiently laying out the cases for and against restitution in order to analyze both the logical and emotional bases for the Greeks' claim and the British government's refusal. The story, which begins with a detailed account of Elgin's actions based on his own words and those of his associates, concludes with a description of Melina Mercouri's efforts, as Greek minister of culture, to reclaim the works of art as part of the Greek national heritage. Because, Hitchens explains, the Elgin Marbles are the most celebrated and by far the most precious example of artifacts removed from their place of origin, they have become "a species of test case":

> If possession is nine points of the law, the how many is it, or should it be? Can we continue to justify an act—the amputation of sculpture from a temple—that would be execrated if committed today? And are there any standard, apart from national egoism or entrepreneurial reach, that should govern the apportionment of cultural property?

Hitchens rests his case for giving the marbles back to Greece on the grounds that their removal violated the integrity of a great work of art that must be seen entire and in its original context in order to be appreciated. The British Museum's proudest possession is therefore, in Hitchens's phrase, "a repressed and guilty secret."

James Gardner, in his review of the book in the *National Review* asserted that because Hitchens is a socialist he was, therefore, sympathetic to socialist Greece and opposed to right-wing Turkey, whose permission Elgin secured in 1800 to remove the sculptures; Gardner cast the suspicion thatHitchens succumbed to "the middlebrow temptation to see the whole issue as politics through other means." Gardner argued that since the modern Greeks are not direct descendants of the original creators of the works, they are not entitled to them.

Blaming the Victims, a collection of essays edited with Edward W. Said, the prominent literary critic and advocate of the Palestinian Arab cause, attempts to set the political cause of the Palestinian Arabs in a historical context. Hitchens's contribution to this volume is the essay "Broadcasts," which questions the frequently made assertion that in 1948 Arab forces fighting Israeli troops exhorted Palestinian Arabs to leave their homes. Hitchens's interest in and knowledge of Middle Eastern affairs is evident in *Prepared for the Worst,* a collection of short political and literary essays drawn from *Grand Street*, the *Nation*, the *London Review of Books*, and other periodicals. These pieces exhibit the full range of their author's sympathies and interests, which include the writers Thomas Paine, Evelyn Waugh, George Orwell, Paul Scott, and Tom Wolfe, but the book is dominated by a single political concern—American policy toward the Middle East and South and Central America during the Nixon and Reagan eras. Hitchens has nothing approving to say about American foreign policy, and he is especially angered by the support of Nixon and Reagan for totalitarian regimes in Chile, Guatemala, and El Salvador. Nor does he confine his animus to Republicans. He asserts, in a notably lively piece, "Kennedy Lies," that the face-off between Nikita Khrushchev and John F. Kennedy over the Cuban missiles was a dangerous instance of American saber rattling, and that respect for Kennedy has been kept alive by a cleverly constructed public relations campaign. Hitchens' writing on the Reagan era, the demise of which he predicted some years before it actually occurred, is even more plainspoken:

> Ronald Wilson Reagan is not (just) a hapless blooper merchant. He is a conscious, habitual liar. . . . How can you tell when he's lying and when he's just making it up? No easy answer here. A rule of thumb is when he's lying, his lips move.

Since *Prepared for the Worst* has no unity other than that imparted by its author's style and opinions, critical reactions, whether approving or hostile, focused on a few essays at the expense of the rest. Tom Bethell, in the *National Review*, accused Hitchens of being "fashionable whether he likes it or not," whereas Hanif Kureishi, in *New Statesman & Society* complimented Hitchens for his originality and independence from received opinion. the Irish diplomat and writer Conor Cruise O'Brien, who is treated roughly in one of Hitchens's essays, acknowledged in his *Times Literary Supplement* review that "when not carried away by various temptations, he is a good writer."

Monarchy: A National Fetish, is a scathing diatribe against the British habit of paying sentimental obeisance to its Royal Family. Hitchens dislikes inherited wealth and social position, but what distinguishes his brief book is his deflation of the arguments for preserving the monarchy. He cites two favorite points of promonarchists: that the stable tradition of the monarchy guarantees against the danger of the "imperial presidency" courted by the American style of republicanism; and that the office of a monarch with no formal power acts as a check on an elected Parliament. Hitchens response to the first by

citing the reigns of George III, George IV, and Edward VIII, all kings who, in his judgment, subverted principle and attempted to influence politics in evil ways. He addresses the second argument by pointing out that it was the Republican Cromwell, and not the monarchical state, who created the present system by executing King Charles II. Hitchens's argument against monarchy is summed up in the following passage:

> What is this? Why, when the subject of royalty of monarchy is mentioned, do the British bid adieu to every vestige of proportion, modesty, humour, and restraint? Why, in this dubious and sentimental cause, will they even abandon their claim to a stiff upper lip? We read with revulsion about those countries where the worship of mediocre individuals—the Ceauşescu dynasty in Romania comes to mind—has become even more of an offense than it has abore. We are supposed to know enough to recoil from sickly adulation, and from its counterpart, which is hypocrisy and envy. We learn from history the subtle and deadly damage that is done to morale by the alternation between sycophancy and resentment. Yet the unwholesome cult of the Windsors and the Waleses is beginning to turn morbid before our eyes.

"Is this an argument of abolition?" Hitchens concludes, "Of course it is." Jack Lively's response in the *Times Literary Supplement* objects that Hitchens blames the monarchy unfairly for much that he fins wrong with Britain, namely class distinction, snobbery, and the failure to address social issues. Lively points out that the monarchy is a convenient symbol of these things, but not their cause, and complains that Hitchens does not fully understand the political role of the monarchy.

Hitchens deployed his talent for satirical exposition at book length in *Blood, Class, and Nostalgia: Anglo-American Ironies*, much of which is devoted to the thesis "that the reverse and affection for things English has increased in direct proportion to the overshadowing and relegation of real British power." This is, as he admits, a shadowy and amorphous subject, since the very existence of the "special relationship" between Britain and the United States is acknowledged by those who have invoked it to be an elusive reality. Hitchens believes that it does in fact exist, and owes its solidity to a host of political, racial, and social factors that can be glimpsed in diplomacy, in advertising, and in the manners and behavior of the American ruling class, which is usually, as he points out, a white Anglo-Saxon Protestant class. Alan Brinkley wrote in the *New York Times Book Review* that "although Hitchens is himself a by-product of the 'special relationship . . . ' he is not at his best in this ambitious book. He falls back too often on extended analyses of obvious literary and political figures . . . without creating a coherent framework for his discussion. . . . Much of this book is a diffuse and shapeless as the complicated subject it addresses." Several reviewers who did not enjoy Hitchens's generally Anglophobic animus complained, like Alan Ryan in the *New Republic* of a lack of "theme," while others, such as Peter Brimelow in *National Review* (1990), seemed angered by the very suggestion that American behavior is influenced by the British at all. Brimelow observes in the course of his review that the book is a "buoy marking the submerged shoals of the left-wing psyche," more informed by social dislike than serious historical analysis. Hugh Brogan's assessment in *New Statesman & Society* (1990) is the most measured and accurate in pointing out the book is slapdash history but entertaining gossip—"both interesting and infuriating."

PRINCIPAL WORKS: (with P. Kellner) Callaghan: The Road to Number Ten, 1976; (with D. Stephen) Inequalities in Zimbabwe, 1979; Cyprus, 1984 (reissued as Hostage to History: Cyprus from the Ottomans to Kissinger, 1989); Imperial Spoils, the (in U.K.: The Elgin Marbles: Should They Be Returned to Greece?); Prepared for the Worst, 1988; Monarchy: A National Fetish, 1990; Blood, Class, and Nostalgia: Anglo-American Ironies, 1990; For the Sake of Argument, 1990; (with E. Kashi) When the Borders Bleed, 1994; International Territory, 1994. *As editor*—Karl Marx: the Paris Commune, 1971; (with E. Said) blaming the Victims: Spurious Scholarship and the Palestine Question, 1988.

ABOUT: American Spectator September 1990; Christian Science Monitor August 15, 1990; Christianity Today February 19, 1988; Commentary November 1990; Economist July 28, 1990; Encounter March 1990; London Review of Books June 1, 1989; August 16, 1990; Mother Jones May/June 1991; National Review April 7, 1989; October 27, 1989; August 6, 1990; New Republic July 9, 1990; New Leader August 6, 1990; New Republic October 8, 1984; July 9, 1990; New Statesman & Society April 21, 1989; July 20, 1990; New York Review of Books July 20, 1989; New York Times Book Review November 11, 1984; June 24, 1990; Raritan Summer 1990; (London) Times September 28, 1976; Times Literary Supplement August 14, 1987; April 14, 1987; April 28, 1989; March 16, 1990; August 10, 1990; (Village) Voice Literary Supplement May 1989.

HOGAN, DESMOND (December 10, 1950–), Irish Novelist and writer of short stories writes: "I'm a very solitary person. In my life, I have been involved with people emotionally and those emotional things have been destroyed in time. It has tended to make me philosophic and solitary. If you meet a few people who are nice, that's miraculous to me. I'm shrouded but I'm not suspicious. It's partly the nature of the times. You have to be wary of

DESMOND HOGAN

opening yourself too much. You find yourself being profoundly self-protective.

"I come from a hard Catholic background with quite a repressed adolescence. I suppose I'm always in flight, in terror from it. The worst of Ireland will never leave you alone. It always demands that you are part of some structure, a family or whatever. That I hate. That's my real contention. It always tries to implicate you in its darkness, not just Catholicism. It imposes hangups on you. The important thing is to grow, to be allowed to grow, independent of those structures.

"To make one's little impression, that's important. Also to recognise the brevity in life. Being true to something. To believe in the idea of purity which, I know, alot of people would ridicule. My work . . . it's neither smart nor fashionable. It attempts to be about the verities-love, life, sex.

"The works of mine which I stand over are *The Ikon Maker*, *A Curious Street*, *A New Shirt*, my two books of stories *The Mourning Thief* and *Lebanon Lodge*, collected in the United States as *A Link wit the River*, and my book of travel and documentary *The Edge of the City*.

"My fiction is an attempt to describe people without country, without family, who are themselves, who are travelers. It's appropriate that I should have, outside my fiction, a travel book.

"But generally you write things, you don't intellectualize about what you write. Always on my mind once, as I wrote, was the image of myself as I appeared on a black and white picture postcard, by chance, in 1959-a boy standing on a street in Ballinasloe, working out for myself a world apart.

We used to perform plays around that time. Dressing up as Our Lady of Fatima and Our Lady of Lourdes and Dracula, and have gangs coming in and breaking up our theatre. The performances were eventually banned by my mother, who thought that, after a certain age, I shouldn't be running around dressed as Our Lady of Fatima. I began writing short stories then and going to Dublin to see films.

"The mental hospital made a very big impression when I was growing up. all those people looking out at you from behind bars. There were also very romantic things about Ballinasloe, like the October Fair Week. That was a very powerful thing, the travelers coming and the Fair Green filled with caravans. On one hand there was the mental hospital, and on the other hand the tinkers. I grew up with a terrible fear of being put in the mental hospital, then the tinkers gave the idea of running away, of escaping.

"There is something about writing that is special. All those people who survived Stalinist Russia when books were destroyed, but they kept books in their heads. Learnt them off by heart and kept them, in that way, for thirty-five years. It seems to be what keeps the imagination and the soul alive—literature. There are triumphs of survival. Like Etty Hillesum being brought to Auschwitz who threw part of her diaries out the window. Her diaries were published in 1981. In one of the last entries in her diaries she says she's **really** glad someone like Rilke lived. The idea of him writing those beautiful poems enables her to go through the Holocaust.

'All that really matters is the inner light. This, and only this, is important,' Nadezhda Mandelstam wrote

That's what one aims for.
Nothing happens unless one is brave.

Desmond Hogan was born, the second of five sons, in Ballinasloe, County Galway. His father owned a drapery store. From the local Catholic secondary school he went to University College, Dublin, in 1969; after taking his B.A. he stayed on for a year for his M.A. (1973). At twenty he won the Hennessy Award for a short story, and, although for several years he devoted most of his time to travel in the United States, Egypt, and Greece and to work in street theaters in Dublin, he was primarily interested in writing fiction. His first novel, The Ikon Maker, as the Macmillan Dictionary of Irish Literature noted, like his early short stories and plays, sets forth the

main themes of his work: "the traumas of early adolescence and a somewhat ambiguous preoccupation with homosexuality."

The central character of The Ikon Maker is a widowed mother of a son, totally devoted and dedicated to him but unable to break down a wall of silence that exists between them. Living in a small town in the west of Ireland, clearly the Ballinasloe of Hogan's boyhood, she "watched him grow in a harsh environment of loss, of alcoholic fathers, of stone walls." From childhood, the boy's only interest is constructing figures, ikons, out of bits of cardboard, eggshells, fluff, anything which might give shape and form to life. Against the 1960s to 1970s of drugs and turmoil in northern Ireland, he grows up estranged from her and goes off to London. She struggles to understand and accept his disaffection and his homosexuality without ever achieving any real communion with him: "She'd given birth. She'd loved her son. He'd gone from her now, indeed far from the land, but always inside he'd wear the camouflage inside him, behind the barrier of social rejection, of casting off society, he'd wear a very private idea of love, an idea amounting to teddy bears when he was two and the grey ikons he created at seventeen."

While impressed with the sensitivity and grace of Hogan's writing (Victoria Glendinning found in his work "a lyricism that is beautifully controlled," reviewers had reservations about some stylistic self-indulgence—fragments of sentences, shifting points of view, careless use of language. His second novel, the more ambitiously conceived The Leaves on Grey, traces the lives of two upper middle class Irish boys through their university educations into maturity. Drawn closely from Hogan's experiences of growing up in modern Ireland—"maker of wounds, tormentor of youth, ultimately breaker of all that was sensitive and enriched by sun, rain, and wind"—it is a melancholy story concluding with a legend that seems to haunt Hogan's work. This is the tale of the "Children of Lir" who are transformed into swans. "And those swans will always represent to me the grief of Ireland, the human spirit freeing itself from human form, the pain of a nation distilling itself into tenderness."

Even more ambitious in its scope, a novel within a novel that moves from Belfast in the troubled 1970s to 17th-century Ireland under the occupation of Oliver Cromwell, A Curious Street established Hogan (in the words of a reviewer for the Observer) as "a striking figure in the exciting new wave of Irish fiction." The narrator, half-British, half-Irish, is a soldier in the British army discovering his own Irish roots. He becomes fascinated with the life and mysterious death of a homosexual who had once been loved by his mother and who had left behind him a manuscript of a historical novel. The subject of that novel—the inevitable frustration of romantic and political ideals both in Ireland's past and its present—is "the curious street" that is Ireland. "Hogan's major accomplishment," Paul Deane wrote in *Notes on Modern Irish Literature*, "lies in communicating the degree to which time and history circle about the present. . . . The effect is, on the one hand, that history in Ireland is alive and constantly duplicating itself in present events, and, on the other hand, that history, in doing so, stifles and holds back the present from any change or growth or improvement." Hogan's characteristiclly impressionistc and poetic style, with its lack of transitions and its abrupt shifts in time and scene, creates, in Dean's words, "a design from bits and pieces of Irish history, character and psychology." Theo L. D'haen, in *Anglo-Irish and Irish Literature*, found the novel a model of postmodernism: "It explodes the very myths, the received ideas, the popular and canonized 'truths' of Irish history it is appealing to."

It is for his short stories, however, rather than his novels that Hogan is primarily known. The several collections that have appeared in recent years continue to focus on the Irish, exiles even at home and certainly abroad. "His major theme," D. W. Madden wrote of *A Link with the River* in *Choice*, "is pain, usually emotional or psychological, sometimes reconciled, other time festering and ceaseless. He consistently depicts a world of unspoken, intuitive, intimacies as the characters struggle for dignity in their thwarted lives." The American novelist Louise Erdrich, in the preface to that volume, praised Hogan's "rich and fractured vision, the quiet troughs in a hopelessly frustrated history that led to explosions of madness, but also contain the impetus for change, which is what in the end makes . . . Hogan's work so valuable. In his hands, fiction becomes transformative."

As a writer preoccupied in his fiction with themes of displacement, it is appropriate that Desmond Hogan has chosen the anonymity of a great metropolitian city like London for his home. In a note to his collection of short nonfiction pieces *The Edge of the City*, he wrote that he settled there after traveling from Dublin to San Francisco in 1976: "I never really returned to Dublin from San Francisco. In a sense I wandered. From address to address to London. London is a city of cheap flights and when I had money I used it for that." His travels have taken him from Santa Cruz, New Orleans, and Memphis (for a visit to the Elvis Presley shrine at Graceland), to North Yemen, South Africa, Israel, and innumerable points between. He has visited the United States many times, and he lived for a year (1989) in Tuscaloosa as writer-in-residence at the University of Alabama. Several of his plays have had stage productions: the one-act *A Short Walk to the Sea* and *Sanctified Distance* at the Peacock Theatre in Dublin in 1975 and 1976. He has also dramatized some of his fiction: the short story "Jimmy" for BBC Radio 3 in 1978, another story, "The Mourning Thief," for BBC Television in 1984. His dramatization of *The Ikon Maker* was staged in London in 1981.

PRINCIPAL WORKS: *Novel*—The Ikon Maker, 1976; The Leaves on Grey, 1979; A Curious Street, 1984; A New Shirt, 1986: *Short stories*—The Diamonds at the Bottom of the Sea, 1979; Children of Lir, 1981; The Mourning Thief, 1987; Lebanon Lodge, 1988; A Link with the River, 1989. *Nonfiction*—The Edge of the City: A Scrapbook 1976–91, 1993.

ABOUT: Binding, T. J. (ed.) Firebird I: Writing Today, 1982; B. Bramsback Anglo-Irish and Irish Literature (ed.) 1988; Contemporary Authors 1994; Dictionary of Literary Biography 14, 1983; Macmillan Dictionary of Irish Literature, 1979. *Periodicals*—Choice November 1989; New York Times Book Review July 16, 1989; Notes on Modern Irish Literature 6, 1994.

HOLDEN, URSULA (August 8, 1921–   ), British novelist, writes: "I was born in Bridport, a seaside town in the south of England. I was one of a family of five and our upbringing was middle class with strong Victorian overtones. There was an emphasis on fearing and loving God, on stoicism and obedience. Family prayers took place each morning with the servants kneeling in their corner of the room. I rarely saw my father, who worked abroad in the Egyptian Civil Service, and my mother spent part of each year with him. She ruled the roost. I and my young brother were taught lessons by a governess who when our mother was away took over the household reins.

"From an early age I felt overshadowed by the rest of the family and I was known as 'the quiet Holden.' I acquired a low self-esteem early in life, never feeling able to compete with my elder sisters and my brother. Academically I failed to reach the high standards that they did. This may be the reason that—in my early fiction particularly—I was drawn towards inadequacy in various forms: underdogs, losers, the disadvantaged interest me more than the successful. I often think of C. G. Jung's advice to an artist: 'It is vital that your creative endeavour should appear to-

URSULA HOLDEN

tally beyond your capacity.' These words inspire me when I'm in a blue funk about my work.

"At eleven I went to a day school where I found it difficult to make friends after those secluded lessons with my governess. The friends I did make were not approved by my mother, whose values tended to be snobbish, in accordance with those times. Later, at my boarding school, and when both parents were in Egypt, the family home was closed. The servants and the governess were disbanded. We stayed with friends during the holidays, and for one fearful Christmas my brother and I went to a holiday home for children with parents abroad. I missed my mother dreadfully but we had been brought up never to complain.

"The war came and with it came more change. The old class system was rocked. Servants disappeared never to reappear as they were before. I joined the W.R.N.S. to work in a signals office alongside or under those who had once waited on me. My nervousness was a handicap but eventually I learned the importance of total accuracy; anything else was castigated. I also learned to mix, to sink myself into another's personna, to empathise. Being a good listener is vital if you want to write.

"After the war I lived in Dublin where I married, rather unhappily. It was not until 1962 and back in London with three children that I was seriously bitten by the writing bug. I joined a class where my jejune efforts received encouragement. I learned the necessity of daily application to both reading and writing and to reach beyond my seeming range. Also I was advised to

regard myself as a professional at once, although the world did not, and it was in fact eleven years before I became one. But I got an agent, John Johnson, earlier than that, who stuck with me and eventually placed my second novel, *Endless Race*, which in 1975 the *Times* hailed as a contribution to English writing. Such praise, coming so late, made me quite ill. Since then I have written twelve more novels on one of my five manual typewriters.

"Through my work I have been to the States, staying as a fellow at Millay, MacDowell and Yaddo artist centres. There is also the lovely Tyrone Guthrie in Ireland where I have stayed many times. Ireland plays a large part in my fiction.

"Some of my recent books have been translated into Dutch and one, *Penny Links*, went into Russian.

"I listen to a lot of music; the peace and order of Bach never fails. I practice yoga seriously and I'm a movie addict. I like reading about other writers. Recently I've been reading biographies on Nijinsky, the Russia dancer. I'm inspired by his dedication.

"I am often asked for advice from people wanting to write. I tell [them] never to miss a day's stint and, having received encouragement from an informed source, never to give up hope."

In 1976, having just launched her literary career, Ursula Holden wrote in an essay for *New Fiction* that her novels were "in part a compensation or justification for sorry relationships, for which I seem doomed." Victoria Glendinning, reviewing *The Cloud Catchers* and *Fallen Angels* in the *New York Times Book Review* in 1980, described Holden's characters as "emotional refugees" and commented: "All the novels have the black reek of cyclic deprivation and cyclic cruelty. Every character is a sad leech, looking for someone to belong to, while longing to shake off the unwanted ones who doggedly try to hang on." Most of the characters in her novels survive with the promise of a bearable if not necessarily happy future.

Reviewers have remarked on the black, more accurately gray, humor of her books. "Cheerfulness," Walter Clemons wrote of her work in *Newsweek*, "keeps breaking in—along with robust bawdiness, acid wit and sharp observation." Like Muriel Spark and Beryl Bainbridge, to both of whom she has often been compared, Holden is an ironist with a sense of illogicality of life and the absurdity of fate. ("If . . . Holden is like anyone, however, it is

Jean Rhys, " Glendinning declared, noting that Holden has said of Rhys, "I feel like her.") As Neil Hepburn wrote of Holden's *String Horses* in the *Listener*: "[T]errible things happen, but they are recounted with such bubblings of wit, such charming eccentricities of detail, such greedy fascination for bizzarreries that it is all very like good gossip. It is only when you finish her admirable novel that you become aware of how serious she really is, about dependence, of course, and about birth, and copulation, and death."

Parents are dead, absent, abusive, or, at their worst, indifferent in Holden's work. In a trio of novels—*Tin Toys*, *Unicorn Sisters*, and *A Bubble Garden*, three young sisters are adrift amidst the horrors of wartime England. Their father is dead. Their beautiful and selfish mother lavished presents on them but sends them away to school while she pursues her own career, singing to the troops and trying to get into the movies. The eldest daughter, Ula, the narrator of *Tin Toys*, is sent off for Christmas to Ireland with a servant on a home visit. There, in a squalid house with the servant's noisy and sloppy mother, Ula briefly enjoys the joy of at least belonging to a family. That happiness ends abruptly when an older son in the family abuses her and she runs away. By a quirk of fate she finds a place in another family, but not until she has accidentally killed their bullying daughter.

In *Unicorn Sisters* another sister, Bonnie, is the central consciousness. She struggles to hold her little family of siblings intact at the boarding school to which they have been sent. The staff has all but disappeared, and anarchy ensues when a group of London slum children join them as refugees from the blitz. The innocence of childhood is brutally dispelled as the children confront death, sexual intercourse, and the cruelty of other children. Holden writes about childhood with much sympathy but no sentimentality. As Ula observes in *Tin Toys*, "Being cruel gave you power." But it is Bonnie in *Unicorn Sister* who recognizes the terrible consequences of her mother's neglect:

> While I had been worrying about our future, Mamma had been spending foolishly. We still had nothing to wear. I wanted to hit her; as if my sisters weren't babyish enough . . . Was I the only one with sense? You couldn't control grownups, you could only get attention by being ill or unpleasant, they did as they wished in the end.

The third novel, *A Bubble Garden*, begins as the narrative of the third sister, Tor, but shifts, to the third person. The scene is County Armagh, Ireland, which figures often in Holden's work. The mother is now remarried to an alcoholic army officer. The family is trying to sur-

vive on a run-down farm, a hopeless task, until a young stranger appears and begins to rehabilitate the property. The prospect of a happier fate for the farm and the family is never realized, however. Once again an arbitrary stroke of fate, an accident, shatters their hopes. But as is often the case in Holden's fiction, the gloom is relieved by the author's control of her technique. Patricia Craig wrote in the *Times Literary Supplement*: "The frightful things that happen in Holden novels are recounted with boldness and exuberance, and with a feeling for the picturesque element in doom and disagreeableness. The author has a sharp eye for disquieting detail and an economic way with her plots."

Holden's adults fare no better than her children, whom they much resemble in their innocence and helplessness. *Turnstiles*, for example, suggests by its title the series of blows that assail its central character, an artist's model. Deserted by her husband and pregnant, she gets loving care from a homosexual brother-in-law, but he dies violently. Her child shows signs of autism, and her long-absent mother appears only to torment her further. Even admirers of Holden's novels considered the calamities of *Turnstiles* excessive, yet in almost every instance they found redeeming features in the novel. Neil Hepburn, in the *Listener*, compared it to the earlier *String Horses* in which two sisters share a loving relationship that survives the trials of their lives. In *Turnstiles*, he wrote: "The characters are too much larger than life to be lively, the symbolism of irreversible and progressive change and decay too heavily spread to convince—but not because Miss Holden cannot write well. The technique remains; but the fermenting misanthropy that was so creative in *String Horsees* has somehow soured."

Help Me Please was Holden's twelfth novel in fifteen years and brought her considerable attention. Somewhat longer and more ambitiously structured than her earlier books, *Help Me Please* has seven narrators—all of them centering on a single character, Hattie, a pretty sixteen-year-old. Among these are her adoptive parents, a drab, middle-aged pair whose marriage is empty and who cannot communicate their love to their adoptive daughter; the unmarried and sexually inhibited librarian for whom Hattie works; and the librarian's assistant, a middle-aged bachelor who falls passionately in love with her. The novel builds on a series of simple but richly observed details—lovers meeting in a fast food restaurant, the obsessive housecleaning of Hattie's mother; the clumsy but well-meaning efforts of her father to amuse and entertain her. With the exception of Hattie's school friend who comes from a happy-go-lucky and loving Irish

Catholic family, all the characters in the novel, Ann Duchêne noted in the *Times Literary Supplement,* "are suffering from some kind of emotional deprivation." Yet, as in the earlier novels, they learn to accept if not to triumph over their unhappy lot. Robert Sproat wrote in the *Literary Review* that apart from the bare account of Hattie's life and love affair, "very little actually happens other than people unwittingly revealing to us what their lives are like, what they themselves are like, which looks easy to write but in nothing of the kind. It is something Holden does as well as anyone currently writing."

PRINCIPAL WORKS: Endless Race, 1975; String Horses, 1976; Turnstiles, 1977; The Cloud Catchers, 1979; Penny Links, 1981; Sing About It, 1983; Wider Pools, 1984; Eric's Choice, 1986; Tin Toys, 1986; Unicorn Sisters, 1988; A Bubble Garden, 1989; Help Me Please, 1991. *Collection*—Fallen Angels (*includes* Endless Race, String Horses, *and* Turnstiles), 1981.

ABOUT: Contemporary Authors Autobiography Series 8, 1989; Contemporary Authors New Revision Series 22, 1988; Contemporary Literary Criticism 18, 1983. *Periodicals*—Independent January 27, 1981; Listener April 1, 1976; May 26, 1977; Literary Review January 1991; New Fiction July 1976; New York Times Book Review February 17, 1980; Newsweek January 21, 1980; Observer April 6, 1986; People January 1988; Spectator February 19, 1977; June 23, 1979; Times (London) January 16, 1991; Times Literary Supplement March 19, 1976; February 18, 1980; February 3, 1989; January 18, 1991.

HOLMES, RICHARD (GORDON HEATH)

(November 5, 1945–   ), English biographer, was born in London, the son of Dennis, a lawyer, and Pamela (Gordon) Holmes, a children's writer. He attended Downside, a Roman Catholic private school, and Churchill College, Cambridge University, where he received a B.A. in 1967. Holmes, one of the leading literary biographers of his time, is noted for his radical opinion that a just biographical account of a dead writer can only be the result of the biographer's "love" or "hero-worship" for his subject. Such a strong compulsion is an essential qualification, Holmes argues in his part-autobiographical work *Footsteps: Adventures of a Romantic Biographer,* for the task of reconstructing the connections between the circumstantial details of a writer's life and his creative work. In *Footsteps* he describes his search for biographical detail as a personal quest, but he also recognizes that the pursuer will never attain complete knowledge: "Somehow you had to produce the living effect, while remaining true to

RICHARD HOLMES

the dead fact . . . You would never catch them; no, you would never quite catch them. But maybe, if you were lucky, you might write about the pursuit of that fleeting figure in such a way as to bring it alive in the present." Like Boswell writing on Johnson, Holmes relies in part on his own exuberance and air of tireless curiosity to persuade his readers to share his interest. According to James Atlas, profiling Holmes in the *New Yorker* in 1994, his writing has a hypnotic quality: "The reader sinks into his narrative as if into a dream. The endless detail, instead of overwhelming us, has an almost incantatory effect. Characters who have been dead for hundreds of years rise before us like apparitions: Coleridge in Dorothy Wordsworth's garden at Dove Cottage, drinking tea in the moonlight; Shelley declaiming to his friend Hogg, 'without order, and with his natural vehemence and volubility.' Holmes's paragraphs teem with life, like a cell culture on a microscope slide." He begins his biography of Coleridge, for instance, by offering the reader what is almost a challenge to take up the pursuit with him: "If he does not leap out of these pages—brilliant, animated, endlessly provoking—and invade your imagination (as he has done mine), then I have failed to do him justice."

After graduation from university, Holmes immediately began to write reviews and historical feature articles for the *Times* of London, and imagined that he would become a poet writing about the experience of outdoor physical activity. His first publication was, in fact, a volume of poems, but already he had experienced an impulse that was to prove more permanent. While still a student he had walked through the Cévennes Mountains of France in an attempt to emulate the journey that Robert Louis Stevenson had made in 1878 and described in *Travels with a Donkey* (1879). This was a deliberate effort not only to recapture Stevenson's experience of scenery and rural life, but also to follow the writer's path in throwing off the constraints of a strict religious upbringing. Holmes, the skeptical Roman Catholic, admired Stevenson, the doubting Calvinist. Instead of writing poems as he intended he found himself composing "prose meditations" about his growing "friendship" with Stevenson. This feeling of identification with a figure in the literary past intensified when, in the late 1960s, Holmes experienced the turmoil of the student uprising in Paris and began to feel an affinity with William Wordsworth and Mary Wollstonecraft, who had been in Paris at the time of the French Revolution in the 1790s. When the student uprising and its ideals were put down by force, Holmes experienced a profound sense of disillusionment that he compared with Wordsworth's reaction to the events that betrayed the purpose of the French Revolution. This, in turn, led him to seek out the scenes of the lives of those who had, he felt, gone before him, and eventually to become curious about the poet Shelley.

Before beginning the long pursuit of Shelley that was to result in his much-praised biography of 1974, he had published biographical speculations on another poet, Thomas Chatterton, who had died a suicide in 1770 at the age of seventeen. Chatterton's early death, which came before he could realize his brilliant promise, had provided several writers of the Romantic movement with a powerful image of a young genius cut down by social circumstance. For Holmes, the meteoric career of Shelley, dead at twenty nine, exercised an even more powerful fascination, especially since Shelley's life, which continually brought ideals and principles into conflict with social convention, recalled the frustrations of his own generation. Holmes became obsessed with Shelley and, as he recalls in *Footsteps*, followed his hero's path around Italy before returning to England to write his biography. Holmes warns in the preface however, that the book is not "for Shelley lovers." Peter Conrad pointed out in his 1974 *Times Literary Supplement* review that Holmes "feels it his duty to be caustically, unsentimentally modern," and, instead of a Romantic hero presents "an existential hero," to make "Shelley acceptable to an anti-Romantic aesthetic of dry, tough, hard style." Despite his praise for Holmes's insights, Conrad felt that the biographer had overstated the case against Shelley's self-dramatizing tendencies in a way that

"tempts him to mistrust the poet's imagination and to punish its audacity." Conrad compares Holmes with Lytton Strachey, an earlier biographer celebrated for his reductive and debunking attitude to his subjects.

The recognition that a biographer must rely both on objective documentation and a sense of personal affinity caused Holmes to abandon a project on which he spent great effort in the mid-1970s. Returning to Paris after completing his pursuit of Shelley, he became fascinated with the poems of Gérard de Nerval(1808-1855), an insane writer who composed remarkable hallucinatory works. The difficulty of writing about such a subject, Holmes explains in *Footsteps*, is that lack of evidence outside the work itself can drive the biographer into a solipsistic identification with the subject: "Self-identification—the first crime in biography—had become my last and only resort." His work on Nerval, entitled "A Dream Biography," remains unpublished, but years of immersion in the French literature of that period did result in a translation of Théophile Gautier and an essay on Nerval published with a translation by Peter Jay in 1984.

Holmes's growing interest in another English Romantic poet, Samuel Taylor Coleridge, was announced by the publication of a short critical study in 1982, but he collected his thoughts on the craft of biography in *Footsteps* before embarking on the full-length biography of Coleridge. *Footsteps*, which is part autobiography, part travelogue, primarily consists of four essays: on Stevenson, Wordsworth and Mary Wollstonecraft, Nerval, and Shelley. Each essay traces Holmes's own search for the writer, conveying the excitements and frustrations of the quest. Holmes describes, for example, his momentary vision of the Shelleys' infant son in the garden of the house where Shelley had lived, and depicts, with self-mocking frankness, his fall through the skylight of a Paris building while trying, like Nerval, to meditate on the stars. Peter Quennell, who described this book in his *Times Literary Supplement* review (1985) as "a diverting blend of biography and autobiography," observed that Holmes's "romanticism colours not so much the subjects he pursues as the story of his own pursuit."

Coleridge: Early Visions, which was conceived as the first of two volumes on the poet's life, was praised as the first biography to present Coleridge's extraordinarily diverse intellectual life as a coherent whole. For John Bayley, writing in the *London Review of Books* (1989), the effort to understand Coleridge the person was an excellent strategy for assembling the often conflicting strands in the poet's complex intellectual life: "The life in Coleridge seems permanently, confusedly, perpetually present—and never more so than in this almost incredibly vivid biography. . . . [I]n this compelling narrative of those early years of the poet Holmes makes us seem actually to be living with him, sharing in the stream of his consciousness in a way that would be quite unthinkable with Wordsworth."

Although he finds Holmes sometimes "a shade too dispassionate," and prone to present insufficient evidence, Stephen Gill, reviewing the book in the *Times Literary Supplement* (1989), found Holmes successful in capturing Coleridge's many facets: "poet, theologian, philosopher, political commentator and activist, husband, father—which does one stress in shaping a narrative?. . . . Richard Holmes rightly and bravely asserts there can be only one answer. All must be stressed." Robert Bernard Martin in the *New York Review of Books* asked, —"How does one give shape to a cloud of smoke? Or how to put the pieces of Coleridge together to make it credible that his works proceeded from one man?"—and finds Holmes's approach appropriate.

Holmes won the Whitbread Book of the Year prize for *Coleridge: Early Visions* and was awarded the Order of the British Empire in 1992.

PRINCIPAL WORKS: *Biography*—Thomas Chatterton: The Case Reopened, 1670; Shelley: The Pursuit, 1974; Coleridge, 1982; Footsteps: Adventures of a Romantic Biographer, 1985; Coleridge: Early Visions, 1989; Dr. Johnson and Mr. Savage, 1994. *As editor*—Shelley on Love, 1980; Wollstonecraft, M. A Short Residence in Sweden, Norway, and Denmark, 1987. *Poetry*—One for Sorrow, Tow for Joy, 1970. *Drama*—Inside the Tower (BBC Radio 3) 1977.

ABOUT: Contemporary Authors 133, 1991; Holmer, R. Footsteps: Adventures of a Romantic Biographer 1985; Who's Who 1993. *Periodicals*—American Scholar Summer 1991; Atlantic June 1990; Hudson Review Spring 1991; London Review of Books October 21, 1982; December 7, 1989; New Republic June 25, 1990; New Statesman November 17, 1989; November 17, 1975; April 7, 1986; July 2, 1990; September 19, 1994; New York Review of Books June 12, 1975; April 10, 1986; December 6, 1990; New York Times July 2, 1975; May 24, 1990; New York Times Book Review June 22, 1975; October 20, 1985; June 17, 1990; New Yorker Nineteenth Century Literature December 1991; Time June 30, 1975; Times Literary Supplement August 9, 1974; July 19, 1985; November 3, 1989.

HONGO, GARRETT (KAORU) (May 30, 1951–   ), American poet, writes (in 1992): "I was born in the village of Volcano in Hawaii and

GARRETT HONGO

grew up on the North Shore of Oahu and in southern California. I attended Pomona College, graduating with honors, and spent a year touring Japan and writing poetry on a Thomas J. Watson Fellowship (1973–1974). I did graduate work in Japanese language and literature at the University of Michigan, and while there in 1975 I won first prize in poetry in the Hopwood Writing Contests. I held several academic fellowships at Michigan—a Horace H. Rackham School of Graduate Studies Award, the William T. Honnold Fellowship (for Pomona College alumni), and a grant from the School of Arts and Sciences.

I left Michigan and spent three years working in community and regional theater in Seattle, Washington, and served for a time as director of an inner city arts center. I was founding director of The Asian Exclusion Act, a theater group devoted to staging plays of interest to Asian Americans. 'Nisei Bar & Grill,' my full-length tragicomedy, premiered as a work-in-progress at the University of Washington's Ethnic Cultural Theater in 1976 and was restaged in San Francisco by the Asian American Theater Workshop in 1980. During this time, I was also Poet-in Residence at the Seattle Arts Commission and an instructor in Asian American Studies at the University of Washington.

I returned to graduate work in 1978, studying English and critical theory at the University of California, Irvine, until 1982. I received the M. F.A. in English in 1980.

In 1982, Wesleyan University Press published *Yellow Light*, my first book of poetry. Poems from that book had been appearing in the *New*

Yorker, the *Nation, Antaeus,* and *Harvard Magazine,* and have been frequently anthologized. Wesleyan first reprinted *Yellow Light* in 1984, and it has subsequently gone into four printings.

The River of Heaven, my second book of poems, was published by Alfred A. Knopf in 1988. Poems from it appeared extensively in magazines and have also been frequently anthologized. *The River of Heaven* was the Lamont Poetry Selection of the Academy of American Poets in 1987 and one of the three finalists for the Pulitzer Prize in Poetry last year.

I've taught poetry at the University of Southern California, The University of California, Irvine, the University of Houston, and the University of Missouri-Columbia, where I was poetry editor of *The Missouri Review* for four years. At Missouri, I was awarded three fellowships by the Research Council of the Graduate School for summer projects in 1985, 1986, and 1987 (essentially, work on *The River of Heaven*). I am now associate professor of English and director of creative writing at the University of Oregon.

I've received a Guggenheim Fellowship and two fellowships from the National Endowment for the Arts (1982 and 1988). My other awards include the Discovery/*The Nation* Award from the Poetry Center for the 92nd Street Y (1981), a MacDowell Colony Residency Fellowship (1986), a Pushcart Selection (1986), and the David Prescott Barrows Centennial Medal from Pomona College (1987).

I'm currently working on two prose books I hope to finish by the end of this year. One is an essay on the Japanese-American internment during World War II and the recent movement for redress. It's called 'Shining Wisdom of the Law' and is under consideration at Alfred A. Knopf. The other project is 'Volcano Journal,' a book of personal essays that combine family, geologic, and natural histories. Both of these works evolve out of long-standing interests.

"As a fourth-generation Japanese-American, I've looked upon the mass evacuation of Japanese from the West Coast as both a communal shame and a kind of folkloric legacy to be honored and disseminated. The experience and its remembrance has been crucial to my identity as a writer for a multitude of reasons. Historically, the 'Exclusion,' as many attorneys prefer to call it, functions as the most crucial event in the history of the Japanese in America after the immigration itself. Yet, it has remained a mystery in a multitude of ways—legally and morally, as an administration of injustice from our government; historically, as an event and chain of events unchronicled by historians; psychically, as a communal trauma suffered by a mass of people who have socially repressed its memory; and spiritually, as the experience of pain, loss, and tragedy among each of the excluded individuals and their descendants. In my book, I'm trying to write an extremely personal accounting for this social and political experience. I've interviewed survivors, legislators, attorneys, artists, historians and sociologists, government officials, and community activists, trying to glean from each of them their personal version of what the experience has meant. And, in writing their stories, I'm trying to write my own story too, situating myself and my writing within the history of the Japanese in America.

"'Volcano Journal,' is also a book of situating as well, but rather than approaching the historical and social, it is a book situating the geologic, geographic, and mythological dimensions of my life. I was born in the village of Volcano in Hawaii, at the summit of Kilauea and under the shadow of Mauna Loa, the two active volcanoes of the Hawaiian chain. I was born in a tropical rain forest above the lava fields, in the back room of the general store built by my grandfather to serve the community of Japanese-American truck farmers who worked the thin soil around the volcano. As soils go, it is geologically the newest piece of earth on our planet. I'm writing about the natural world of my birth and its mythological dimensions. I'm writing about finding the place of the self within the context of an immensely sublime landscape.

"For 1992–1993, I want to begin work on 'Gods of Luck,' my third book of poems, which will be narratives and lyrics concerning the new immigrants to America, many of them Asian— that is, the Southeast Asians and Chinese from Taiwan and Hong Kong—against the psychic and cultural backdrop of my own awareness of descent from the Japanese who immigrated to America over one hundred years ago. I'm thinking about travelling to some of these 'homelands' myself, perhaps making an excursion through Asia. But my main focus will be Asians in America, particularly in the cities. As with my second book, *The River of Heaven,* I'll be working with themes of dislocation and identity, exploring uprootedness within the underclass, trying to portray feelings of loss and separation from cultural memory. I want to think about the making of beauty in difficult circumstances, the impermanent founding of civilization in a work of art or in a moment of consciousness rescued from savagery. I want to render what I know about these various Asian and Asian-American histories into poetic language, into certain poetic structures I've been meaning to try but haven't.

Garrett Hongo grew up yearning for assimilation into American culture but discovered as he matured that he was denying a vital part of himself. In high school in California, he writes in "96 Tears" (in *The River of Heaven*), he attended advanced placement classes where "the idea of hierarchies, / 'rank' was finally made clear / to me," and he considered himself "pridefully among the sullen elite."

Phoebe Pettingell noted in her *New Leader* review of *The River of Heaven* that "Hongo's verses become an elaborate ritual of atonement for leaving behind his culturally ambiguous background." In his mature poetry, however, Hongo embraces that background. He is never estranged from his Asian roots, even as he sees them now firmly planted in America. "Roots," in his first volume, *Yellow Light*, expresses his ambivalence when he visited Japan, "the country my ancestors had called their own," and became aware of that other world which until then he had not perceived as his own:

> I learned there was a signature to all things
> the same as my own, and that my own sight
> sanctified streetlights and stalled cars
> the same as ceremonies in solitude.

He celebrated the beauty of this land in "To Matsuo Basho and Kawai Sora in Nirvana," a fantasy in which he imagines the two seventeenth-century Japanese poets in a Japanese landscape:

> Then, near moonrise,
> yawning and half-asleep,
> they walked through the rising smoke
> of leaves and pine cones,
> the watchfires of the village,
> and made the past their hermitage.

The poems in *Yellow Light* reflect the wide range of Hongo's feelings—from tenderness and nostalgia for an idealized Japan of the past to rage at the mistreatment of Asian Americans in the United States. "Stepchild" expresses his outrage at the Asian-American Exclusion Act of 1882, the Anti-Alien Law of 1913, the Exclusion Act of 1921, and the internment of Japanese Americans in World War II. "Our history is better," he reflects. In his later volume *The River of Heaven*, his anger is spent, and he writes in an almost elegiac mood. Most of the poems here are narratives spoken by Asian Americans who see themselves realistically as part of the cultural diversity that is America—Jews, Italians, African-Americans, Latinos.

Robert Schultz, writing about *The River of Heaven* in the *Hudson Review*, noted that in spite of a certain prosiness inevitable in narrative-monologues where the speakers do not always speak as poets, "Hongo's rich vocabulary and undulant syntax holds his stories of loss and remembrance in a secure, distinctive music." Schultz found some of the poems "Whitmanesque" in their long lines, their use of catalogues and parallelism:

> I want the cold stone in my hand to pound the earth,
> I want the splash of cool or steaming water to wash my feet,
> I want the dead beside me when I dance, to help me flesh the notes of my song, to tell me it's all right.
> —"*O-Bon*: Dance for the dead"

Among contemporary poets, Philip Levine—who writes of the poor and underprivileged himself—has most influenced him. Hongo dedicates "Choir" to Levine. It is a monologue spoken by an Asian American gas man reading the meter in an empty ghetto church. He recalls singing hymns in his childhood "with a black kid, a white one, and another Japanese": "We make up myths for what we don't know, / ways to excuse our own failure to turn from / ignorance and our own cruelty."

Garrett Hongo's father, Albert Kazuyoshi Hongo, an electrical technician, figures in many of his poems. He experienced loneliness and humiliation and found some release for his unhappiness in gambling: "For splendor, for his cheap fun . . . [he] would go to the track." In a statement sent to *World Authors* summing up his feelings about his own work, Hongo writes of his father: "He was a great example to me of a man who refused to hate, or, being different himself, to be afraid of difference, who accepted the friendship of all the strange and underprivileged ostracized by the rest of 'normal' society—Vietnamese, southern blacks, reservation Indians relocated to the city—and I want my poems to be equal to his heart."

In *Volcano* Hongo profiled his father—and his grandfather— in what David Galef in the *New York Times Book Review* termed "part naturalist's notebook, part family chronicle and part a record of soul-searching." Galef concluded that *Volcano* "sucessfully recaptures . . . 'a way to belong and a place to belong to.'"

PRINCIPAL WORKS: Yellow Light, 1982; The River of Heaven, 1988; Volcano, 1995. As editor—The Open Boat: Poems from Asian America, 1993.

ABOUT: Contemporary Authors 133, 1991; Contemporary Poets, 5th ed., 1991. Periodicals—Antioch Review Spring 1983; Hudson Review Spring 1989; New Leader June 13, 1988; New York Times Book Review July 16, 1995; Poets and Writers Magazine September–October 1992; Publishers Weekly February 12, 1988; Sewanee Review Spring 1983; Virginia Quarterly Review Winter 1983.

HORNE, ALISTAIR (ALLAN) (November 9, 1925–   ), English historian, journalist, and biographer, was born in London, the son of Sir James Allan and Auriel Camilla (Hay) Horne. He was sent to Ludgrove School when he was eight. He described it in his memoir *A Bundle from Britain* as "a Belsen of the spirit . . . a place of rampant unchecked bullying." He was relieved to be sent on to Le Rosey in Switzerland, but returned to the horrors of English public school life at Stowe. Oddly enough, the onset of World War II rescued him from his harsh life. He was sent to the United States as a "bundle from Britain" and spent the years from 1940 to 1943 as the guest of an upper-class American family who gave him the affection he had never received at home and sent him to the Millbrook School, a place he deemed paradise compared to the English schools he had attended. Patriotism, however, drove him to return to England when he was seventeen, instead of attending Harvard. He joined the Royal Air Force, but poor vision prevented him from becoming a pilot; he became instead an officer in the Coldstream Guards attached to M15 and served in Egypt. He received his M.A. from Jesus College, Cambridge in 1949.

Horne began his career as a journalist, writing for the *Cambridge Daily News*, in 1950. From 1952 to 1955 he was foreign correspondent in Germany for the *Daily Telegraph*. In 1955, Horne became a free-lance writer, a career he has maintained ever since.

In 1953 he married Renira Margaret Hawkins. They had three daughters. This marriage was dissolved in 1982. In 1987 he married the Honorable Mrs. Sheelin Eccles.

The bulk of Horne's work has been in military history and he has written on a wide variety of subjects ranging from the Napoleonic era, the Paris Commune, World War I and II, the Algerian War of 1954–1962, as well as biographies of generals and statesmen. Horne's first book to receive wide popularity was *The Price of Glory*, first published in 1962 and reissued with a new preface in 1993. *The Price of Glory* is an account of the World War I battle of Verdun, which, as Horne says, was "the longest battle of all time," lasting ten months, and Verdun became "the battlefield with the highest density of dead per square yard that has probably ever been known." In his 1993 preface, Horne describes the genesis of his book, dating to the period when, as a young correspondent in Germany in the 1950s, he saw the remnants of the "lethal course" of Franco-German relations over the past century:

[T]he sinister hills of Verdun engendered emotions that

were never quite to leave me alone—fascinated by the story and its profound historic consequences, admiring of the staggering courage of those, on both sides, who fought there, but appalled by the waste and sheer stupidity. . . . No other book I have ever written affected me quite so deeply; the tears came again and again. It was, unashamedly, an *anti-war* book.

With *The French Army and Politics, 1890–1970*, published in 1984, Horne completed a series of three books that included *The Fall of Paris, 1870–1871*, and *To Lose a Battle: France, 1940*, concerning the cultural and military relationship between France and Germany. His compendious approach combines social themes and historical facts to make a compelling story. Horne has described his inspiration for this trilogy as "Franco-German relations, the root of evil in the world I grew up in." He charted the nadir of Franco-German relations with the Nazi invasion of 1940. *To Lose a Battle* is essentially a military history, but Horne gives due regard to the vacuum left in French government after World War I, which, together with the mistakes of Versailles, led France into a hapless confrontation with a relentless and vengeful Hitler.

In this, as in most of his work, Horne incorporates a colorful narrative style with encyclopedic information emphasizing nationalism, myth, race, and tradition. Thomas Molnar, in the *National Review*, commented that Horne's method was to give his "watchful attention" to practically everything: "the ups and downs of soldiers' and officers' pay, the relationship of social class to officer recruitment, the pros and cons of a conscripted versus a professional army. . . . It is a very estimable achievement to untangle . . . the many threads that compose the agitated existence of the French army."

Horne believes that French military history is paramount because of French memories of defeat which have reverberated into modern times. As he said in the epilogue to *The Price of Glory*:

The years when Britain was bowing to the inevitable have seen successive weak French Governments goaded on by an army desperate for *la Gloire*—anxious to win a war, any war—to committing themselves irrevocably to military "solutions" in their overseas territories. There was first Syria and Madagascar, then Indo-China and Algeria. . . . Dien Bien Phu was chosen as a fortress where the resurrected French Army would stake its honour and fight, if necessary, to the last man. . . . Once again, as the Viet Minh swarmed over the hastily constructed bunkers, the cries of *'on les aura!'* and *'Ils ne passeront pas!'* were heard.

Horne was chosen as the official biographer of Harold Macmillan, prime minister of England from 1957 to 1963, and later Lord Stockton. The two-volume biography gained full cooperation from its subject (on the proviso that nothing would be published until after his death) which provided Horne with unique access to Macmillan's copious papers. Kenneth Minogue, reviewing the first volume for *Encounter*, concluded: "Alistair Horne's treatment of Macmillan is a brilliant account of a political education. It is, however, almost entirely blind to what might be called the Machiavellian dimension of his political skill. There is no sense of the mechanism of support on which the successes depended . . . What Horne has made clear, however, is the almost stoic virtue with which a long career of disappointments was turned to success." Peter Jenkins, in the *New York Times Book Review*, wrote: "His book is particularly good on the subtleties of Macmillan's introverted, fastidious and elusive character. . . . Horne, a military historian by trade, is more at home with the war years in the Mediterranean and with the Suez incident which forms the climax of the book, than with the radical Macmillan of the 1930s. . . . " Reviewers praised Volume II of *Macmillan* for the "aplomb" with which Horne used "Macmillan's own brilliant diaries and conversation" (the *Economist*) and for being "perceptive and exceptionally well informed" (Piers Brendon in the *New York Times Book Review*), although all noted Horne's extraordinary "affection for his hero," as Brendon terms it. Ben Pimlott wrote in the *New Statesman*: "Macmillan's departure as Prime Minister came at the right historic moment—marking the effective end of noblesse oblige in British politics. Horne's elegant volume captures the strangely distant feeling of that sunset age."

Horne chronicled his own early life in *A Bundle from Britain*, which Francine du Plessix Gray in the *New York Times Book Review* called "a poignant, deftly written memoir of his youth, focusing on the wartime years he spent in the United States." Gray noted the accuracy of his portrayal of the way émigrés saw the "differences between the American and the European character, contrasting the Old World's aloof, jaded mannerisms with Americans' forthrightness. . . . Anyone who felt the pulse of New York between 1940 and 1942 will be poignantly thrust back into the curious blend of Pollyanna jollity and growing doom that suffused those years. . . . Horne's youth was so marked by the events of World War II, and his political sense so precocious that *A Bundle from Britain* is inevitably shaped by his mini-history of the war."

Horne published *Monty: The Lonely Leader, 1944–1945*, written with David Montgomery, Field Marshal Montgomery's son, in 1994. The story of the famously arrogant European commander in the last year of World War II, *Monty* was reviewed in conjunction with a book about Eisenhower and Montgomery in the *Economist*. "Horne's judgments, naturally enough, are a mite more in favour of Montgomery's actions," the reviewer noted. "The Englishman, Mr. Horne, is the shrewder military commentator, though he may stray too far in emphasizing how close run a thing the battle of Normandy was."

Horne's wide-ranging interests have extended to North Africa about which he has produced *A Savage War of Peace: Algeria 1954–62*, and articles in the *New York Review of Books* and *Smithsonian*. In one article, he laments Churchill's destruction of the French fleet at Mers-el-Kebir in 1940 to prevent its falling into Hitler's hands. In another he describes modern Algeria (1985) as a relatively serene and stable nation after its decades of bloody war. His political sympathies, which tend toward the right, emerge in articles in the *National Review*, in one of which, "New Hope for Chile?" (1988) he supports Pinochet in Chile, believing the dictator unjustly maligned by leftists.

Alistair Horne was a director of the Ropley Trust Ltd. from 1948 to 1977 and a founder of the Alistair Horne Residential Fellowship in Modern History at St. Anthony's College, Oxford, in 1969. He became supernumerary fellow of St. Anthony's College in 1978. He was a Fellow of the Woodrow Wilson Center in Washington D.C. in 1980 and 1981.He presented the Lees Knowles Lectures at Cambridge University, England, in 1982 and the Goodman Lectures at the University of Western Ontario, Canada, in 1983.

Horne served as a member of the Management Committee of the Royal Literary Fund from 1969 to 1991 and became a member of the Franco-British Council in 1979. He was a member of the Committee of Management of the Society of Authors from 1979–1982 and a trustee of the Imperial War Museum from 1975 to 1982. He is a Fellow of the Royal Society of Literature.

In 1963, Horne won the Hawthorndon Prize for *The Price of Glory: Verdun 1916*. In 1978 he was awarded the Yorkshire Post Book of the Year Prize for *A Savage War of Peace: Algeria 1954–62*. For this work he also won the Wolfson Literary Award. In 1985 he was awarded the Enid Macleod Prize for *The French Army and Politics, 1870–1970*. In 1992 he was made a Commander of the British Empire, received a Litt. D. from Cambridge University, and was awarded the French Legion d'Honneur.

PRINCIPAL WORKS: Back Into Power, 1956; The Land is Bright, 1958; Canada and the Canadians, 1961; The Price of Glory: Verdun 1916, 1962; The Fall of Paris:

The Siege and the Commune 1870–1871, 1976; To Lose a Battle: France 1940, 1969; Death of a Generation, 1970; The Terrible Year, 1971; Small Earthquake in Chile, 1972; A Savage War of Peace: Algeria 1954–62, 1977; Napoleon, Master of Europe 1805–07, 1979; The French Army and Politics, 1870–1970, 1984; Macmillan, 2 vols., 1988–89; A Bundle from Brian, 1993; (with D. Montgomery) Monty: The Lonely Leader, 1944–1945, 1994.

ABOUT: Who's Who, 1993. Periodicals—Choice February 1985; Economist July 1, 1985; June 4, 1994; Encounter April 1989; History June 1985; National Review February 1985; New Leader February 5, 1990; New Statesman October 14, 1988; June 23, 1989; New York Times Book Review March 5, 1989; November 26, 1989; September 11, 1994; Times Literary Supplement October 14, 1988; June 23, 1989.

HOURANI, ALBERT (HABIB) (March 31, 1915–January 17, 1993), British historian, was born in Manchester, England, the son of a prosperous Christian Lebanese merchant. He was educated in London and later attended Magdalen College, Oxford, where in 1936 he took first-class honors for the B.A. degree. Upon completing his education at Oxford, Hourani taught for two years at the American University of Beirut, Lebanon; and with the outbreak of World War II in 1939 he joined the research department of the British Foreign Office. In the same year he became a member of the Royal Institute of International Affairs. The historian Arnold Toynbee was director of studies there, and Hourani acknowledged that Toynbee had a profound influence on him.

During the war Hourani went to Cairo, Egypt, where he worked in the office of the Minister of State. He traveled widely in the Arab world and made many acquaintances among younger Arab officials, teachers, and politicians. After the war he was sought out by British authorities for his counsel on Palestinian refugees.

Giving up what may have become a promising career in politics, Hourani accepted a teaching position at his alma mater, Magdalen College, in 1948. He lectured at Magdalen in modern Middle Eastern history and later at the newly founded St. Anthony's College until his retirement in 1980. At various times during this period he lectured at Harvard and at the University of Chicago. He also lectured at universities in Europe and in the Arab world. At St. Anthony's College Hourani was instrumental in establishing and developing a Middle East Center, and with the aid of fellow historian Elizabeth Monroe he built an important collection of papers on the modern Middle East.

Hourani's chief scholarly interests were the impact of Europe on the development of Arab thought and Arab nationalism and the perceptions of Western scholars and travelers on the Islamic world. He wrote widely on both subjects. Syria and Lebanon: A Political Essay, Hourani's first book, summarizes the history of the two countries and discusses the peace settlement of World War I, leading to an examination of the impact of Westernization and the concomitant growth of nationalism in the countries of the eastern Mediterranean. He then examines the French occupation and the early years of World War II, finally going on to take up the relations of France and Britain with Syria and Lebanon to the end of World War II. The book concludes with some prognostications for the region. Hourani discusses three choices facing the people of those two countries: rejecting the Western influence, accepting Western ideas selectively without altering the Arab culture, and reconstructing Arab society by accepting the best of Western culture.

Produced during World War II and concluding with the year 1945, the work has been characterized as a classic. Anticipating its importance, Kenneth Williams in the Spectator hailed it as an "admirable book, which should run to several revised editions"

Another influential book was Hourani's Arabic Thought in the Liberal Age, 1798–1939. In this work he considers the impact of Western liberal thought, mainly that of Britain and France, on a few principally Egyptian and Lebanese writers of the 19th and early 20th centuries. Hourani identifies certain changes in Arabic political and social thought as the result of the European ascendancy and the decline of Ottoman influence. Arabic thinkers wished to accept some Western ideas and tailor them to the needs of Arab society.

Hourani identifies two streams of Arabic thought on Western ideas. One is to restate Islamic precepts as they relate to Islamic society; the other seeks the separation of religion and politics and advocates a secular society. While the two seem to be in conflict, Hourani's book seeks to show that the two trends were actually confluent and spawned Arab nationalist feeling in the 20th century. Hourani traces the lines of thought in four generations of Arabic-speaking writers. In the first period, roughly from 1830 to 1870, the writers saw the West as a model to be followed without the risk of losing the Arab-Muslim identity. In the second generation, from 1870 to 1900, the Arab-Muslim identity was perceived as threatened. The West occupied certain Arab countries, and its political influence was growing in the declining Ottoman Empire. Arabs were forced to accept change, but they felt impelled to hold on to something of their past. The third period, roughly from 1900 to 1939, witnessed a separation of Islam from secular principles and the espousal of nationalism. In the epilogue of his work Hourani identifies a fourth phase characterized by a revival of Islam, social reform, and an expanded Arab nationalism.

The editors of *Foreign Affairs 50-Year Bibliography*, writing ten years after the book's appearance, called it a "product of mature reflection with breadth and balance of historical judgment. . . . " Edward Said called both *Arabic Thought in Liberal Age* and the earlier *Syria and Lebanon,* "classics", mined by both scholars and general readers for their scope and their fastidiously refined attention to the fabric of Arab life."

A History of the Arab Peoples covers Arab history, from the seventh century to the present. Part 1, spanning the seventh to the tenth centuries, details the birth and growth of Islam. Part 2—the 11th to the 15th centuries—describes the consolidation of Arabic societies, in which Islam and the Arabic language are unifying forces. Part 3, the Ottoman ascendancy, from the 16th to the 18th centuries, describes the Arab peoples under Turkish domination. Part 4, the history of the decline of the Ottoman Empire (1800–1939) depicts the age of European hegemony. In part 5, the period since 1939, the Arab nation-states assume center stage in a time of expanding nationalism.

Shaul Bakhash stated in the *New York Review of Books* that Hourani's interests are not mainly in political events, dynasties, rulers, or battles. His concern is the "style of politics in the Arab world and the manner in which power was won, held, and used"—the social and cultural history. The high Islamic culture, and the Arabic language as the means of transmitting this culture, is the dominant theme. The common culture defined and went beyond local politics and dynasties. Hourani returns again and again to the concept of the unity of the Arab world within the crucible of the common religion and language. While recognizing that there are local differences within Islam, he is primarily concerned with the commonalities.

Robert Irwin commented in the *Times Literary Supplement*: "Hourani has not written an event-based narrative. . . . The virtue of this . . . lies in the amount of space . . . made available for discussion of the broader themes of social and cultural history. . . . For Hourani poets have been the unacknowledged legislators of

the Arab world. . . . Again and again, our attention is drawn to the importance of poetry and prose . . . and . . . the history of the Arabs is shown to be unintelligible unless full weight is given to the role of the Arabic language in unifying the culture and in shaping the way a community thought about itself." L. Carl Brown, reviewing *A History of the Arab Peoples* in the *New York Times Book Review*, also found Hourani "strong on the evolution of political, theological and philosophical ideas in the Arab world from the seventh century to the present." Brown noted, however, that "he gives almost equal space to social and economic developments, especially to the texture of city life and urban ties to the countryside (strongly tilted in favor of the former) and to the evolving role of women throughout the centuries."

Islam in European Thought is a compilation of essays on European studies of Islam from the Middle Ages to modern times. The second part of the book deals with the 18th and 19th-century responses of Islam to Western influence. Robert Irwin in the *Times Literary Supplement* found the book "tantalising," noting Hourani's "almost mystical chains of initiation and transmission by which orientalists passed on their methodologies and skills from one generation to the next. . . . " Nisid Hajari in the *(Village) Voice Literary Supplement*, however, found Hourani to be "proposing an ideology of scholarship" wherein masters pass on to disciples "the 'right' methodologies, epistemologies, and values. . . . " Malise Ruthven, on the other hand, in the *New Statesman & Society*, found Hourani's a wise voice, "uncontaminated by religiosity or lust for power."

PRINCIPAL WORKS: Syria and Lebanon: A Political Essay, 1946; Minorities in the Arab World, 1947; A Vision of History: Near Eastern and Other Essays, 1961; Arabic Thought in the Liberal Age, 1798–1939, 1962; Europe and the Middle East, 1980; The Emergence of the Modern Middle East, 1981; A History of the Arab Peoples, 1991; Islam in Europe thought and Other Essays, 19991. As editor—St. Anthony's Papers 11: Middle Eastern Affairs 3, 1961; St. Anthony's Papers 16: Middle Eastern Affairs, 1963; St, Anthony's Papers 17: Middle Eastern Affairs 4, 1965; (with S. M. Stern) The Islamic City, A Colloquium, 1970; (with S. M. Stern and V. Brown) Islamic Philosophy and the Classical Tradition: Essays Presented by His Friends and Pupils to Richard Walzer on His Seventieth Birthday, 1972; (with T. Mostyn) Cambridge History of the Middle East and North Africa, 1988; (with N. Shehadi) The Lebanese in the World: A Century of Emigration, 1992; (with P. Khoury and M. Wilson) The Modern Middle East: A Reader, 1993.

ABOUT: Contemporary Authors 140, 1993; Foreign Affairs 50 Year Bibliography, 1972; Spangnolo J. (ed.)

Problems of the Modern Middle East in Historical Per-
spective: Essays in Honour of Albert Hourani, 1992.
Periodicals—International Journal of Middle East
Studies, November 1984; Journal of Politics February
1947; Los Angeles Times February 17, 1991; January
23, 1993; Middle East Journal January 1947; New
Statesman and Society April 26, 1991; New York Review of Books September 26, 1991; New York Times
Book Review March 31, 1991; Political Quarterly
April/June 1963; Spectator April 26, 1946; Times
(London) January 26, 1993; Times Literary Supplement February 22, July 5, 1991; Voice Literary Supplement June 1990; Washington Post January 22,
1993.

HOVE, CHENJERAI (February 9, 1956–   ),
Zimbabwean poet and novelist, was born at
Mazvihwa in Zimbabwe. He has been a teacher
of literature in rural high schools, a literary editor at Mambo Press (1981–1985) and Zimbabwe
Publishing House (1985–1987), chair of the Zimbabwe Writers' Union (1984–1989), and Writer-
in-Residence at the University of Zimbabwe in
Harare. Hove is married with five children. His
work is strongly marked by the African struggle
for liberation from the white settler regime of
Ian Smith's Rhodesian Front, which had declared its independence from Britain in 1965.
Gathering strength in the early 1970s, the guerrilla war, or "bush war," led by Robert Mugabe
and Joshua Nkomo, gradually wore down the
grim counterinsurgency tactics of the Smith regime, until Mugabe's wing of the Patriotic Front
won an absolute majority in the supervised election of 1980.

Hove's works in Shona and in English began
to appear shortly after an independent, majority-ruled Zimbabwe set out to construct a nation.
Flora Veit-Wild wrote in *Research in Africa
Literatures* that Hove "holds an important place
in Zimbabwe's post-Independence literary
scene. In the early 1980s he emerged as a major
poetic observer of the war of liberation." He belongs to the second generation of Zimbabwean
literature, a generation known among African
writers for their lyrical, hard-hitting, eloquent
fiction; his contemporaries include Charles
Mungoshi, Dambudzo Marechera, the feminist
Tsitsi Dangarembga, and Shimmer Chinodya.
Among them, Hove is distinguished by the beautiful Shona-inflected English of his prose style,
saturated in the proverbs, stories, oral history,
and spirituality of the country people. The language of his fiction recalls what earlier African
writers had done with English, notably the Nige-
rians Amos Tutuola and Chinua Achebe, whose
first novel *Things Fall Apart*, Hove has said, was
"like meeting my own face in the mirror for the

CHENJERAI HOVE

first time." Veit-Wild describes this style as "a
fairly literal translation of Shona sentence-
structure, proverbs, terminology, and imagery."
Hove, recalling what the Caribbean poet-critic
Kamau Brathwaite calls "nation language"—an
infusion of the energies of creole and indigenous
"suppressed languages" into postcolonial English—speaks of "cleansing the colonial languages . . . a task which we can only achieve
with the inspiration of the great masters of oral
narrative."

Much of Hove's poetry and fiction is a retrospective meditation on the experience of the
Zimbabwean people—particularly the rural
Shona people, peasant farmers, squatters, or laborers on large (often white-owned) commercial
farms—during the ten years of fierce fighting,
and the years of independence, which for Hove
are still haunted by memories of the bush war.
As the Zimbabwean novelist Charles Mungoshi
said in the introduction to Hove's first book of
poems, *Up in Arms*: "The voice is Zimbabwean . . . born out of Zimbabwe's short painful
history. . . . These poems ring with the self-
evident truth of one who had suffered and survived, one who has been there." The tone of this
poetry is lyrical, elegiac, close to the ground of
experience, somewhat disabused, and skeptical
about the outcome of the struggle. Hove might
well be called a nationalist writer in several
senses (Shona, Zimbabwean, Pan-Africanist), but
his spokesperson and representative of the new
nation is not the official but the poorest citizen,
the "povo" (from the Portuguese *viva o povo*,
meaning "long live the masses").

In an early poem, the speaker is a homesick farmer who identifies "Africa" with the countryside: "Don't close the window / . . . For Africa speaks outside: / The spatter of raindrops on the heart / Sings eternal songs: / Would my drummer were here" ("Exiled Farmer"). There is a war-weary, even antimilitarist ring in images such as "loaded guns wait like dormant snakes / at the but stop." It is a world "Where, to the hungry, / We donate guns!", where "Gunbills strange food bills" ("Uprising"). This last poem echoes the book's title to protest the way the past struggles the present: "Yes, I am up in arms, / with this wounded ghost

The typically acerbic, epigrammatic irony appears already in an earlier poem, "Dreams," which Hove contributed to *Samora! Tribute to a Revolutionary* (1980): "Arm the cripples / the battle starts." The imagistic spareness of Hove's early verse is well caught by Mungoshi's remark, made about poems like "War-Torn Wife," that he "uses silence to speak to him." Hove's later poem "Nursery Rhyme after a War" captures the mood of many in the region wrestling with what is lost and what is not yet gained by their sacrifices: "fig tree fig tree / where are the figs? / fig tree fig tree1 / where is my brother? / I will come at sunrise / to sing this song/for my brother / for my fig." His second volume of English verse, *Swimming in Floods of Tears*, is dedicated to "the people as they search for themselves / in the ceasefire of life." At this stage, and in his third book *Red Hills of Home*, Hove begins to address the problems of "development," and the social policies of austerity urged on developing countries by international aid sources. He writes in "Independence Song," from *Red Hills of Home*, that "Independence came, / but we still had the noose / around our neck, / . . . So we carry the noose / and beg to be dragged again / in the name of development." The quandary of economic dependency continuing after political independence, the povo's rage at neocolonialism, has never been more succinctly stated. The speaker in "A Letter from a Cane Cutter to a Tourist" enacts the object-like fate of cultures commodified for tourism, so often a priority for development strategists: "I stand dark as a shadow, bowed. / Black charcoal soot embalms me/ with my panga [machete] in my claw / . . . I am tourism / for your sole speculation / as my blood oozes / like some paint."

Hove's poetry is in revolt against this commodification; like the antinationalist foe of official Zimbabwe, Dambudzo Marechera, he is a writer who refuses. His elegy for Marechera celebrates the writer's autonomy and critical political thinking: "My friend this is for you who refused/You who refused all shackles/

Preferring to walk in the shadow of your own world/Calling the world your shadow." His later poem "To the Wielders of Flags," published in the 1988 BBC anthology *The Fate of Vultures: New Poetry of Africa*, echoes the title poem by the Nigerian Tanure Ojaide about the "vultures" and "flash millionaires" of neocolonial Africa whom, Ojaide promises, the poets of Africa will never praise. Hove's wielders of flags, the power brokers of Zimbabwe, are not quite written off; rather, the poem addresses them in the voice of one who watches the world closely, and sees primarily the urgency of good leadership. Those who are "leaning on the rock of the republic . . . leaning on the rock of state" are urged to "listen to deserted hearts/ . . . weary soles walking the bush path"; to "burn the flag of poverty on infants' faces/and tread the thorns of your people." The rhetoric invokes a rural world (in contrast to the city where new wealth is flaunted), and its image of leadership is the traditional authority of the chiefs, close to and open to the people, not the alienated modern State. Like so many African writers of his generation, Hove looks to writing itself as a form of power able to contest the power of the authorities. His mastery was acknowledged by special commendations from the judges of the Africa-wide Noma Award for both *Up in Arms* and *Red Hills of Home*.

After 1985 Hove turned mostly to fiction, with a novel in Shona and two in English. *Bones* won the Noma Award in 1989, marking Hove's first major publication, to enthusiastic reviews, outside Zimbabwe; it has been translated into seven languages. Jane Bryce in the *New African* review called it "a truly African novel," and Emmanuel Ngara named in a "milestone" in Zimbabwean literature. Dedicated to "those who gave their bones/to the making of a new conscience," *Bones* disseminates the image of its title through the whole narrative, with a backdrop of drought, massacre, death, and resurrection, which recalls the prophet Ezekiel as well as Shona proverbs and the rural landscape. Don Mattera, the South African poet, wrote in the *Weekly Mail* that Hove's "village is the world and its simple and unsophisticated peasants are actors who portray our roles under oppression today." Split in time between the days of the bush war and independence, and in place between farm and city, the story is told in retrospect by several characters, principally the two women whose relationship frames the novel. It is a notable example of woman-centered fiction by a male African writer. Kaizer Nyatsumba in the *Star* called it "a heart-rending account of woman's courage." In the novel, two women, workers on a settler's farm, connected by a young man, the son of one woman and the fiancé of the other. The young man has joined the guerrillas. After the war is over and he has not returned his mother leaves the farm to try to find him in the city. Both women suffer cruelly after this break. The city scenes portray a place of cold institutions and hostile men in uniform, where, again, the two women form a defensive alliance. The son/fiancé is left at the end facing the loss of both mother and lover, and musing like the speaker of Hove's poem "Nursery Rhyme after a War" on the fruits of the struggle: "'I went to fight with guns, but the fight which I have now is bigger than the fight of guns and aeroplanes,' he says, his eyes cutting through the sky like a knife cutting through things that are hard and soft at the same time."

The chapter entitled "The Spirits Speak" begins with a hallucinatory prophecy of skies crowded with vultures, the symbols of massacre:

> Arise my children. Do you not see the vultures flying over the corpses that are not yet? See the clouds which fake the flight of the vultures. Many clouds hiding many vultures with large beakes, all waiting for the many corpses that are not yet. Do you not see the corpses when there are vultures in the sky? Look at the sky and tell me if you see the sun? The large wings of the vultures are like shady clouds so that you cannot read the pattern of the sky. The sky, so old and with so many eyes that you do not see.

Shadows continues in the same idiom ("the novel of my idea of our collective memory"), but is a significant use of it for other purposes, examining new themes such as the history of ethnicity in the bicultural nation—what the Ndebele scholar Luke Mhlaba calls "the linguistic-cultural pluralism which forms the reality of present-day Zimbabwean societies"—and the cultural basis for development schemes like the resettlement of farmers in the purchase areas. The novel also explores religious practice in relation to politics and people's identification with the land. *Shadows* is still inscribed "for those killed in wars," but these are the "bigger fights" presaged at the end of *Bones*, the undeclared wars of development and social conflict.

Like *Bones*, *Shadows* has at its core a simple, tragic story. As Hove describes its genesis, it "was born many years ago when I saw two young people, lovers, opt for death instead of life." Johana's and Marko's double suicide—a shocking event in Shona culture—is recounted early in the novel, which then expands into a sustained meditation from multiple points of view on its meaning, and its consequences for those close to the pair, "as other events have forced it to be not only their story, but the story of others." In a prologue, Hove complicates the genre of the book by distinguishing it from "fiction . . . tall tales . . .

history . . . politics." In their place, his use of the word "tale" suggests that he has in mind the model of the oral storyteller: "This is their tale. One day they will read it, or hear rumors of it. They cannot read. They will never read. The world of written words is hidden away from them." The continued use of the interior monologue confirms this intention. Lamenting that written words are "hidden away" from his rural people, Hove has brought *their* hidden words into print. Linear narrative and chronology are abandoned in *Shadows* for the montage of different times, places, and points of view that, to a Western reader, has a cinematic quality, like a poetic documentary—the quality, in fact, of the new African cinema. Like that cinema in West Africa, Hove's storytelling has adapted the role of the oral storyteller to modern cultural forms, constituting himself as "the guardian of popular memory."

In *Shadows* the oral history of the precolonial past of southeastern Zimbabwe enters—the story of how the Ndebele under Mzilikazi moved into Shona areas and set up a powerful state, absorbing some Shona as a subject caste, from 1940 to 1980. This story is told from the Shona side as the history of "Gotami's lands." Johana's family and Marko have been resettled in the 1970s as smallholders in a modernizing agricultural development scheme. The new farmers come from different places and cultures and are thrown together as neighbors on land whose "laws" they do not know: the sacred sites, the rules for when not to work, the chief Gotami's *mhonodoro* spirit to be propitiated. The original inhabitants, Gotami's people, had been moved off the land by the British at the turn of the century, but their descendants return for religious observances, and are angry that the "strangers" from Shona and other ethnicities (Johana is infatuated with a boy who sings Ndebele herding songs) now occupy their land in ignorance of its laws. The ethnic interactions—the theme of displacement and alienation from religious ties to the land—become the background for the unlucky love of Johana and Marko, and for the coming of the guerrillas. In *Bones* the spirits of 1897 speak on the margins of the tale as a chorus; Veit-Wild, not sympathetic to this feature of *Bones*, calls it a "mythologization of national history" and a "mystification" of the war. In *Shadows*, with more specificity and perhaps less romanticism, Hove weaves the spirit of Gotami, and his resourceful leadership of the Shona in difficult times before the coming of Rhodes, into the tale of love, death, madness, war—and the words, songs, stories, and dances that allow his people to cope with them. This dimension of the novel follows Achebe's prescription for African writing to go back behind the colonial period to find out "where the rain began to beat us," and so guide the way forward again to cultural recovery.

PRINCIPAL WORKS: *Poetry*—Matende mashava, 1982; Up in Arms, 1982; Swimming in Floods of Tears, 1983; Red Hills of Home, 1985. *Novels*—Masimba avanhu, 1986; Bones, 1988; Shadows, 1991.

ABOUT: "Introduction" to *Up in Arms*, 1982. *Periodicals*—Weekly Mail (Harare) 1988; Guardian, (Lagos) August 15, 1988; New African, September 1990; Research in African Literatures, Fall 1993; Southern African Review of Books, February/May 1990; Star, (Johannesburg) February 7, 1989; Sunday Mail (Harare) 1991.

HOWARD, MICHAEL (ELIOT) (SIR MICHAEL HOWARD)

(November 29, 1922–   ), British historian, was born in London, England, the son of Geoffrey Eliot and Edith (Edinger) Howard. He attended Wellington College (1936–1940), and began his undergraduate studies at Christ Church, Oxford, before joining an elite British regiment, the Coldstream Guards, in 1942. He served with distinction in combat in Italy, was twice wounded, attained the rank of captain, and received the Military Cross in 1943. Returning to Oxford after the war, he graduated and joined the faculty of the University of London, where he lectured in history, and then in war studies, until 1980, becoming Chicele Professor of the History of War in 1977. In 1980 he was appointed to the prestigious position of Regius Professor of Modern History at Oxford University, which he occupied until 1989, when he accepted the position of Robert A. Lovett Professor of Military and Naval History at Yale University. He is also the president and co-founder of the International Institute for Strategic Studies in London, has received honorary doctorates from the Universities of Leeds and London, and is a fellow of All Souls College, Oxford. He became a Commander of the British Empire in 1977 and was knighted in 1986.

Michael Howard's contributions to the study of modern history have reached a wider audience since he has occupied prominent teaching positions at Oxford and Yale and published his general reflections on the relationship between military and civilian affairs in *The Lessons of History*. His earlier work and writing was virtually unknown outside the small circle of military historians. In a brief essay on his own profession that appeared in *History Today* in December 1984 he explains why military affairs have only recently been assimilated to the general study of social and political history. In an age of nuclear weapons that can be transported across great distances, war is no longer, for advanced societies, a remote event conducted by volunteer armies, but a phenomenon that must be studied in the context of international relations. In this respect, Howard believes, historians are "doing no more than returning to an older tradition": "There is no 'military history' as such of classical antiquity, or even of the Middle Ages. These were societies organized for war, constantly at war, and their structure and their activity cannot be dissociated." The view of military history as a very narrow subject concerned only with the study of armies and the movements in wartimes, he argues, "is a luxury which can be enjoyed only by atypically peaceful societies, and it is perhaps an indication of how peaceful our own society is today that military history in its narrowest operational sense should be enjoying so remarkable a boom."

Howard traced the origins of his strategic thinking back to Clausewitz and Jomini, the 19th-century writers who first studied war as an activity of advanced, industrialized societies. Clausewitz, he has written, is one of the very few "who have penetrated below the ephemeral phenomena of their own times and considered war, not just as a craft, but as a great socio-political activity, distinguished from all other activities by the reciprocal and legitimized use of purposeful violence to attain political objectives." Howard also admired the synthesizing idea that is original to Clausewitz, of war as a "remarkable trinity, in which the directing policy of the government, the professional qualities of the army, and the attitude of the population all played an equally significant part." Since Howard believed, as Clausewitz, that warfare is "an instrument of policy," he argues that it should be studied as a rational act, not as the failure of human values. As he has shown in his studies of European war, societies may be analyzed on Clausewitzian principles that reveal their predisposition to war. This quality, which Howard grimly terms "bellicity" to distinguish it from mere belligerence, he posits, existed in German society before World War II and rendered British efforts at appeasement futile.

Because of these scholarly views, Michael Howard's opinions and insights into contemporary international affairs guaranteed him a certain amount of odium in public, journalistic debate. He was an adviser to the British government during the 1960s and 1970s, when the Campaign for Nuclear Disarmament (or CND) was at its height, and was gradually drawn into a frequently abusive public argument that ranged those who advocated Britain's unilateral disarmament and defection from NATO against those who, like Howard himself, believed such a policy would be naive and disastrous. In 1981 he took the side of *realpolitik* in a debate at the Oxford Union in which his opponent was the even more celebrated E. P. Thompson, a leading figure in the CND. The result of this debate, according to the (London) *Times Higher Education Supplement*, was that the great majority of the audience, who came as vigorous advocates of disarmament, left questioning their views.

Though he profoundly disagrees with what he regards as the naive attitudes of liberals, believing that a stable, peaceful society must be able to defend itself against attack, Michael Howard is equally outspoken in his dissent from the diametrically opposed point of view, that Western nations must be committed to an arms race that will ensure superior destructive power. He therefore found himself attacked on both sides; by Thompson on the left, and by Colin Gray, the American director of National Security Studies at the Hudson Institute, on the right. His exchange of views with Gray appeared in the journal *International Security* between 1979 and 1981. Although much of this debate was conducted in the arcane terms of nuclear war planning, Howard's views on nuclear war centered once again on the Clausewitzian principle that wars are fought for social and political reasons with the consent of populations. He therefore found that planning for nuclear war ignored the question of what such a war would be about and had become a hermetic subject. His recommendation that Britain should preserve strong conventional forces while remaining within the American shield of nuclear deterrence seems to justify his insistence in *The Causes of War*, that planning for defense should take account of the roots of conflict in social inequalities. In writing about the history of Soviet expansion in scattered essays, he observed that there was no good reason for the Soviet Union to attack the West. He has also shown, throughout his writing, that war has always been caused, not by the clash of empires, but by the rivalries and hatreds of nation-states.

Writing in the (London) *Sunday Times* at the height of his involvement in the British controversy over national defense policy, Michael Howard took up the disagreement between "hawks" and "doves" to describe himself as an "owl":

> There remains no way to save the unspectacular program of what I would term the "owls": the patient negotiation of multilateral arms control, based on a sympathetic but reciprocal understanding of the adversary's own security problems combined with a prudent awareness that nu-

clear power, even if it is not used, is . . . a formidable weapon of intimidation in international politics.

In wars, Howard has written, "the element of force is controlled and channeled along certain conduits. However intense its degree of violence, that element is used instrumentally by legitimized authorities." This point of view is central to his conviction that war, at least in its postmedieval form, is not a condition opposed to civilized order. War is "a highly social activity" that "demands from the groups which engage in it a unique intensity of societal organization and control," he said in "Can War Be Controlled." He goes on to comment: "One still occasionally comes across the old-fashioned liberal stereotype of the soldier as a stupid and brutal *Untermensch* dedicated to random violence. Such characters can indeed be found in most armies, but equally most armies go to great lengths to discipline and if possible eliminate them." Howard's study of history, therefore, is informed by an interest in war as a deliberate social act, a strategic choice exercised by a society in pursuit of its interests, which have been implicitly endorsed by the majority of its members, who would not otherwise be willing to engage in violence.

An understanding of the causes of war is, for Michael Howard, an essential condition of negotiation for international peace because they are a part of what he terms the "historical process" of physical improvement and moral growth. This imperative, he said in his 1989 valedictory lecture as Regius Professor of Modern History at Oxford University, "provides indeed the real justification for the study of history as process." In that lecture he depicts armed struggle as a quest to redress grievances, not as a Machiavellian pursuit of power.

The ending of the cold war, accompanied by the emergence of intertribal strife and local conflicts between long-suppressed ethnic groups, has done much to vindicate Michael Howard's policy of patient and thorough analysis of historical process as a basis for strategic planning. The essay "Structure and Process in History" in *Lessons of History* places his work within the long tradition of European historiography as opposed to the newly prominent French structuralist school represented by Emmanuel Le Roy Ladurie, which dwells on the resemblances between human actions irrespective of time and place. For Howard, history is a succession of "freely willed human activities," not repetitive actions in which mankind is a passive victim. James Sheehan, in the *New York Times Book Review*, found *Lessons in History* a reminder that the world "is a perilous place, filled with

people who are prepared to gain their ends."
Sheehan regards Howard as delivering a warning that "peace and prosperity . . . may tempt
its beneficiaries to forget this unhappy fact and
cause them to lose the virtues and values necessary to defend themselves. . . . "

PRINCIPAL WORKS: (with J. Sparrow) The Coldstream
Guards: 1920–1946, 1951; Disengagement in Europe,
1958; The Franco-Prussian War: The German Invasion of France, 1870–1871, 1961; Lord Haldane and
the Territorial Army, 1967; (with R. Hunter) Israel
and the Arab World: The Crisis of 1967, 1967; Strategy
and Policy in Twentieth-Century Warfare, 1967; The
Mediterranean Strategy in the Second World War,
1968; Studies in War and Peace, 1970; Grand Strategy
(U.K. History of the Second World War, vol. 4), 1971;
War in European History, 1976; War and the Nation
State, 1978; War and the Liberal Conscience, 1978;
Clausewitz, 1983; The Causes of Wars, 1983; British
Intelligence in the Second World War (vol. 5), 1990;
The Lessons of History, 1991; The Continental Commitment, 1989; Strategic Deception in the Second
World War, 1992; The Mediterranean Strategy in the
Second World War, 1993. editor—Soldiers and Governments: Nine Studies in Civil-Military Relations,
1957; Wellingtonian Studies: Essays on the First Duke
of Wellington, 1959; The Theory and Practice of War,
1965; (with P. Paret) Clausewitz on War, 1977; Restraints on War, 1979.

ABOUT: Contemporary Authors New Revision Series 2,
1981; Who's Who, 1993. Periodicals—American Political Science Review September 1992; Annals of the
American Academy of Political and Social Science
July 1992; Armed Forces and Society Summer 1985;
Canadian Journal of History December 1991; Contemporary Review December 1990; English Historical Review January 1984; Historian Winter 1992;
International Affairs July 1991; New York Times April
3, 1991; New York Times Book Review March 24,
1991; Political Science Quarterly Summer 1984; Social
Science Quarterly June 1992; (London) Sunday Times
November 9, 1980; (London) Times Higher Education
Supplement February 20, 1981; Times Literary Supplement September 20, 1991.

SUSAN HOWATCH

HOWATCH, (STURT) SUSAN (July 14,
1940–   ), British novelist, writes: "I was born in
England in 1940 and took a degree in law at
London University. In 1964 I emigrated to
America where I met my husband [Joseph
Howatch]. My daughter was born in 1970, and
my husband and I separated in 1975 after eleven
years of marriage. During the 1960s I produced
six paperback originals, all mysteries, which
were later published in hardback. They were
The Dark Shore, The Waiting Sands, Call in the
Night, The Shrouded Walls, April's Grave, and
The Devil on Lammas Night.

"In 1971 the first of my long intergeneration-
al, multinarrator novels emerged and was an international success. The title was Penmarric.
This was followed by Cashelmara, The Rich Are
Different, Sins of the Fathers, and The Wheel of
Fortune. All five were based on true stories taken from history and updated to the 19th and/or
20th centuries. Penmarric, Cashelmara, and The
Wheel of Fortune mirrored the lives of the Plantagenet kings of England; The Rich Are
Different and Sins of the Fathers were based on
Roman history at the time of Julius Caesar and
the Emperor Augustus, with the United States
representing imperial Rome and England representing the Greek culture of Egypt in the first
century B.C.

"In 1975 I returned to Europe with my daughter and we lived for four years in the Republic
of Ireland before settling in England. It was
while living in Salisbury, by the cathedral, in the
early 1980s, that I conceived the idea for my
present series of six novels about the Church of
England in the 20th century. Each book is designed to stand independently of the others, but
the more the books are read, the wider becomes
the reader's perspective on the multidimensional
reality which is being presented as I explore
Christian themes and worldly conflicts. The novels are: Glittering Images, Glamorous Powers,
Ultimate Prizes, Scandalous Risks—which won
the Winfred Mary Stanford Memorial Prize—
and Mystical Paths. Absolute Truths is the final
novel in the series. I now live in London.

Although Susan Howatch refers to her first six books as mysteries, they also contain enough elements of Gothic romance to place them in that genre. In these early novels, as in her later ones, setting plays an important role, with Britain being a Howatch favorite for the proper mix of Gothic atmosphere and history. "The most important part of the story is to get the setting and background right," she told the Newark *Star-Ledger*. "Just being in the place, soaking up the setting helps." No less important are Howatch's characters, who find themselves in dire predicaments on seaside ancestral estates or remote farms in the Scottish highlands.

The Devil on Lammas Night, the last title from her mystery/Gothic phase, is the occult tale of a young woman who unwittingly falls under the spell of a handsome Satanist and a coven of witches. Ruggiero and Weston point out that "Howatch's skillful interweaving of realistic characters and complex situations makes a bizarre theme plausible and frightening."

Howatch's already successful literary career took on new proportions when she moved from Gothics to immense family sagas with the publication of *Penmarric* in 1971. In the *Writer*, (1977) she pointed out that both *Penmarric* and *Cashelmara*, her second saga, contain Gothic and historical elements, but differ from her earlier novels both in their length and their concentration on character development over a much longer period of time. "A span of thirty years enables you to follow characters if not from the cradle to the grave, at least from immaturity to maturity," Howatch explained. "With the challenge of charting their psychological development comes the challenge of knitting their lives into historical background to give the saga its 'epic' effect. Ideally the characters should be people of their times to the extent that the era is no mere backdrop but an unobtrusive additional character permeating every turn of the story." Spanning three generation's (1890–1945) and narrated by a succession of five characters, *Penmarric* centers on the large family estate in Cornwall, which gives the novel its title.

Cashelmara took Howatch two and a half years to research and write. This time six narrators (1859–1891) tell another complex story of an estate, this one in Ireland, with another collection of passionate characters, the wealthy de Salis family, who range from Ireland to England and America. Susan Cooper, in the *Christian Science Monitor*, called the novel an "unwieldy mammoth." For Cooper the different narratives create so many shifts in focus that all sense of unity is destroyed. But she acknowledged that "it's an achievement to envisage and accomplish any work of this size however flawed. The historical background is accurate and its small details effectively vivid."

Howatch completed her family saga phase with *The Rich Are Different, Sins of the Fathers,* and *The Wheel of Fortune*. These novels are all set in the 20th century.

By the early 1980s Howatch was undergoing a "constructive mid-life crisis" as she described it to Amanda Smith in *Publishers Weekly*. While some "people quit their jobs or do something quite different," Howatch continued to write, but moved into a new phase of her career: novels about the Church of England in the 20th century. Long attracted to Victorian literature and its "strong moral theme" that, Howatch recognized, "has now rather gone out of fashion," she was no longer writing specifically for the popular market but "for my own pleasure." In *Christianity Today*, Donald McCullough pointed out that Howatch has been called the 20th century's Anthony Trollope. "The Church of England—its liturgical and theological controversies and political skulduggery—provide the backdrop for these stories, and the cathedral in fictional Starbridge is the center around which they revolve." Among Howatch's main characters are men of God with human emotions and weaknesses. "I was so tired of seeing clergymen, priests, portrayed as caricatures," she told *Publishers Weekly*. And while she acknowledged that many would question how much interest can be generated in the Church of England, she explained that the "main issues are moral and spiritual, which, of course, are timeless."

Glittering Images, the first in the series, concerns a young, widowed minister named Charles Ashworth, who is sent by the Archbishop of Canterbury to discreetly observe a bishop who may be involved in a menage à trois. This potential clerical scandal proves of less significance in the novel than the exploration of the character of the young minister himself, tested against a background of the divisions within the Anglican church in the 1930s. Subsequent novels in this series became bestsellers, refuting the notion that there was no popular audience for such subjects. *Glamorous Powers*, set in the early 1940s, deals with spiritual healing. *Ultimate Prizes*, in the later 1940s, examines the spiritual, and sometimes material, ambitions of the clergy. With *Scandalous Risks* in 1990, Howatch brought her series to the year 1963. The story centers on the love and burgeoning sexual involvement of twenty-six-year-old Venetia Flaxton and the sixty-one-year-old Neville Aysgarth, who is the Dean of Starbridge Cathedral, her father's closest friend, and a married man. Joan Mooney, in the *New York Times Book Review*, said the book had potential as a story, "but it contains too many stock figures and obvious ironies." *Mystical Paths* is set in 1968; the next book in the series, *Absolute Truths*, was published in 1994.

Donald McCullough described Howatch's Church of England books as "ecclesiastical mysteries, with serviceable language that neither ascends the heights of great prose nor descends into the pits of poor usage. Occasionally her dialogue is strained, but for the most part, her characters are well-rounded, complex people."

"It's an author's primary duty to entertain," Howatch told *Publishers Weekly*. "Sling in all the philosophical terms, but keep the reader turning the page."

PRINCIPAL WORKS: The Dark Shore, 1965; The Waiting Sands, 1966; Call in the Night, 1967; The Shrouded Walls, 1968; April's Grave, 1969; The Devil on Lammas Night, 1970; Penmarric, 1971; Cashelmara, 1974; The Rich Are Different, 1977; Sins of the Fathers, 1980; The Wheel of Fortune, 1984; Glittering Images, 1987; Glamorous Powers, 1988; Ultimate Prizes, 1989; Scandalous Risks, 1990; Mystical Paths, 1993; Absolute Truths, 1994.

ABOUT: Contemporary Authors New Revision Series 24, 1988; Twentieth-Century Romance and Historical Writers, 1990. *Periodicals*—Christian Science Monitor July 3, 1974; Christianity Today October 28, 1991; Library Journal March 15, 1971; New York Times Book Review November 11, 1990; Publishers Weekly October 16, 1987; (Newark) Star-Ledger June 13, 1974; Writer June 1977; June 1980.

HOWE, TINA (November 21, 1937–), American playwright, was born in New York City to radio and television commentator Quincy Howe and his wife Mary (Post) Howe, an artist. Howe found her father gentle and shy but "I grew up in a household that was dominated by large, ferocious women," she said in a panel discussion in which four women playwrights were interviewed by Mervyn Rothstein in the *New York Times* in May 1989. In a family that included a Pulitzer Prize-winning biographer (her grandfather, Mark Anthony DeWolfe Howe), an uncle (also Mark Howe) who was dean of the Harvard Law School, and an aunt (Helen Howe) who was a professional monologist, Howe often felt inferior. She considered herself an outsider. Although the "bloodlines were perfect," as Howe told Ross Wetzsteon in *New York*, the Howes were not wealthy. Still, Tina was educated at private girls' schools in Manhattan, and she soon discovered that the liberal views she had absorbed from her father were not shared by the

TINA HOWE

other students. In desperation, she decided to become the class clown, although her antics were frowned upon by the school authorities.

In the early 1950s Quincy Howe moved the family to Urbana, Illinois, where he had been appointed professor of journalism at the University of Illinois. Both Tina and her brother were enrolled in the progressive University High School. She told Lou Ann Walker, in an interview in the *New York Times* in April 1989, that the school was filled with "'geniuses'. Everyone around me was shockingly verbal. . . . For me, it was . . . always being cowed and humiliated." She became interested in theater and music, however, and studied piano for several years. Howe attended Bucknell University in Lewisburg, Pennsylvania, for two years before transferring to Sarah Lawrence College in Bronxville, New York, where she graduated with a B.A. in 1959. For a short story course at Sarah Lawrence, she handed in a play called *Closing Time* instead of the regular assignment. Her friend and classmate Jane Alexander directed and starred in the play for a school production, which was a hit with the student audience. Howe later described the work as an "incredibly pretentious piece about the end of the world," but "something happened in that moment of acclaim" and she decided to become a playwright.

As a graduation gift, Howe's father gave her money for a year in Europe. She went to Paris with the thought of studying at the Sorbonne, an idea which she soon abandoned in favor of finishing a never-produced full-length play.

(Friends have said that this "closet play" is about her parents, with a great deal of implied violence.) While in Paris, she attended a performance of Eugéne Ionesco's *The Bald Soprano*, and this ignited her interest in absurdist theater.

When the year was up, Howe returned to New York where she met Norman Levy. They were married in 1961. While Levy studied for his Ph.D., Howe took a few graduate courses at Chicago Teachers College (1963–1964) and later at Columbia University. She also supported them both by working at various jobs, including department store sales clerk, newspaper reporter, editor at Scott, Foresman, and teacher. She taught high school English in Bath, Maine, and in Madison, Wisconsin, where she headed the drama department and directed student productions of her own plays. Howe has said that this period was the start of her practical training as a playwright, because she had to learn how to keep the attention of an audience of restless teenagers.

Howe's first professionally produced play was *The Nest*, a comedy about three young women living in a duplex apartment who entertain two men friends at a dinner party. The influence of Ionesco and Beckett can be seen in the jokes and sight gags, including a scene in which two of the women leap into a two-foot tall wedding cake and emerge covered with whipped cream. The play received scathing reviews and closed after one performance, but it was early evidence of Howe's extravagant imagination and her absurdist sense of humor.

Undeterred by the critical trouncing, she wrote *Birth and After Birth*, a savage satire that juxtaposes birth rituals in so-called "primitive" societies and child-parent relationships in an "enlightened" middle-class American family. When the play was completed in 1973, it fared worse than *The Nest*—producers were afraid to touch it, Howe's agent refused to represent her any longer.

Continuing her self-described "antic version" of women in modern society, Howe turned her attention to women as artists in *Museum*, which explores the interdependence of the artist, the actual work of art, and the reaction of the viewer as a consumer of art. The setting is an art gallery, and three large exhibits occupy the stage: a series of blank white canvases by a "reductionist" painter, which an ardent student tries to copy; a group of soft portrait sculptures hung on a clothesline, the clothespins for which are continually being pilfered by visitors; and several sculptures made of bird and animal bones of somewhat grisly origin. The fourth exhibit is the audience. *Museum* "gives us the pictures' point

of view," Richard Elder said in the *New York Times* in 1978. "It is the people who flash by and blur." The play's off-beat humor, with a sense of menace lurking just beneath the surface, had a mixed critical reception, ranging from enthusiastic to lukewarm.

The Art of Dining, presented in December 1979 by the New York Shakespeare Festival, explores art of a different sort and its literal consumption. The stage is divided into the kitchen and dining room areas of a restaurant just opened by a young couple. The wife is the chef, but her maitre d' husband keeps sampling her culinary efforts while an assortment of customers waits to be served. Similar to *Museum* in that it consists of a series of vignettes, some poignant and some savagely satirical, *The Art of Dining* also embodies Howe's confessed fascination with food and the ritual of eating. The play did not please the majority of New York critics, and it closed after six performances before moving to the John F. Kennedy Center for the Performing Arts in Washington, D.C., for a five-week run.

At this point, Howe felt she had to write more conventional plays. In 1982, her one-act play *Appearances*, about a lonely saleswoman and her customer, was performed at the Ensemble Studio Theatre's Marathon '82 festival. *Painting Churches*, which Howe had been working on since 1979, was her most successful play, in terms of critical response. The play was directed by Carole Rothman, coartistic director of Second Stage; the partnership proved so successful that Rothman directed Howe's next four plays.

Painting Churches is the most autobiographical of Howe's plays and was, she says, the most difficult to write, even though her parents had been dead since the mid-1970s. The plot concerns Mags Church, an artist who returns to her once-elegant Boston home to visit with and paint her elderly parents, Fanny and Gardner Church, as they are going into retirement. Gardner is a gentle, prize-winning poet who has become slightly senile, while Fanny is initially presented as an eccentric and selfish woman. In the second act, however, there are glimpses of the passionate marriage that the Churches once enjoyed, and Mags begins to understand the burdens that Fanny carries in coping with her husband's senility and her daughter's insecurities.

Howe won several awards: an Obie for distinguished playwriting (for a trio of plays—*Painting Churches*, *The Art of Dining*, and *Museum*); an Outer Critics Circle Award for outstanding off-Broadway play, as well as their John Gassner Award to a promising playwright; a Rosamund Gilder Award for creative achievement from the New Drama Forum; and a

Rockefeller grant to become playwright-in residence at Second Stage. *Painting Churches* was produced on public television's *American Playhouse* series in 1986, and in 1993 it was presented on cable television under the title *The Portrait*, with Gregory Peck and Lauren Bacall in the leading roles.

Coastal Disturbances, another Second Stage production directed by Carole Rothman, moved to Broadway for a run of 350 performances. Howe described this play as a love story and a valentine to her husband. She said: "I wanted to redress the way men are perceived onstage these days, . . . as being filled with self-hatred that spills out. . . . I think the play is . . . about falling in love from a woman's point of view, but what animates the story is my desire to put the tenderness of men onstage. . . . " The setting is a New England beach, and her artist protagonist is a young woman photographer who has a brief fling with a handsome lifeguard. Once again, Howe tells her story in a series of vignettes, as other characters appear on the beach and provide glimpses into their lives. The critical reception was mostly favorable, with praise for Howe's unsentimental humor and vivid imagination, coupled with her affection and sympathy, although some reviewers dismissed the plot as thin.

Approaching Zanzibar, Howe's third Second Stage production to be directed by Carole Rothman reunited Howe with her friend and Sarah Lawrence classmate, actress Jane Alexander, for their first professional collaboration. *Approaching Zanzibar* follows the Blossom family on an automobile trip across the United States, during which they play the game geography (which accounts for the play's title) as they combine a vacation with a visit to Mrs. Blossom's dying aunt, an eccentric artist. It is another examination of parent-child relationships and the efforts of different generations to come to terms with aging and death.

Howe was again praised for her humor, her sensitive characterization and her ear for dialogue. However, several critics also noted that despite the attractive writing and the serious theme, the play was lacking in drama. Both *Painting Churches* and *Approaching Zanzibar* were presented in England in 1991, where Howe was praised for her graceful writing and her wit, but criticized for her "obsessive domesticity and Pollyannaesque passion for uplift," a quality which the critic felt was characteristic of most modern American playwrights.

Howe's next play, *One Shoe Off*, her fourth collaboration with Carole Rothman and Second Stage, marked a return to the absurdist style of her early works. Two couples and a male friend are gathered for a dinner party in a decrepit farmhouse that is literally being invaded by nature—trees poke their leaves through floors and ceilings, and vegetables are sprouting in closets, under beds, behind the stairs, and in every available damp corner. In sharp contrast to the fecund plant world are the barren lives of the humans, who have as Frank Rich put it in the *New York Times*, "[s]terile marriages, bankrupt friendships, empty bank accounts, vanished children, grotesque highway accidents, kitchen fiascos," and other disasters. Rich found that *One Shoe Off* "never offers the terrifying glimpse into the abyss that its set and its 'Job'-like parade of catastrophes promise."

Howe lives with her husband, historian and novelist Norman Levy, and their two children in Manhattan. She holds adjunct professorships in dramatic writing in both New York University and Hunter College (City University of New York). In 1991, the Whitney Museum of American Art published an oversized album called *Swimming*, consisting of nine photographs by Tina Barney and a play Howe wrote to accompany them. She received a grant from the National Endowment of the Arts in 1984, and was awarded an honorary doctorate of letters from Bowdoin College in 1988.

Lou Ann Walker in the *New York Times* in 1989 described Howe's writing trademark as "the contrapuntal technique, characters speaking in parallel, nonintersecting lines, each lost in . . . reverie. As the dialogue crosscuts and overlaps the humor—or pathos—grows, until finally the missed connections are caught. . . . "

PRINCIPAL WORKS: Birth and After Birth, *in* Moore, H. (ed.) The New Women's Theater, 1977; Museum, 1979; The Art of Dining, 1980; Painting Churches, 1984; Three Plays)includes Museum, The Art of Dining, Painting Churches), 1984; Coastal Disturbances: Four Plays (*includes* Museum, The Art of Dining, Painting Churches, Coastal Disturbances), 1989; Swimming, 1991.

ABOUT: Betsko, K. and Koenig, R. Interviews with Contemporary Women Playwrights, 1987; Contemporary Authors 109, 1983; Contemporary Dramatists, 4th ed., 1988; Contemporary Literary Criticism 48, 1988; Contemporary Theatre, Film, and Television 7, 1989; Current Biography 1990; Feminine Focus: The New Women Playwrights, 1989; Notable Women in the American Theatre, 1989; Studies in American Drama 1945–Present 4, 1989. *Periodicals*—American Theatre September 1985; May–June 1993; Guardian March 28, 1991; New York Times November 28, 1983; New York Times November 16, 1986; April 30, 1989; May 7, 1989; April 14, 1993; Theater Week June 12, 1989.

HUMPHREYS, JOSEPHINE (February 2, 1945–   ), American novelist, writes: "I was born in Charleston, South Carolina. We lived in the old part of the city, and I grew up under its influence. My mother worked at the Charleston Museum, and my sisters and I often played in the museum's hidden back rooms among bottled reptiles, antique dolls, apothecary jars, and cast-off dioramas showing how Indians welcomed the first white Charleston settlers. The very miscellany of history struck me as fascinating and frightening. Sometimes my mother brought home stuffed specimens that moths had eaten into; we had a cockatoo, a turkey, a seal, a bear, and a twelve-foot-long alligator.

"We lived for a while with my grandmother in the big house that was her only souvenir of a bad marriage to a rich doctor. From my grandmother and my mother I gathered that women were meant to be 'proper' in public, but at home they could be smart, funny, a little bit wild, a little bit crazy. My father had no wild bone in his body. Having left Harvard Business School after one year, he worked most of his life for the Charleston Development Board, his mission to lure northern industry into the South. He loved the creeks and woods of the low country. He was an almost stern man, almost gruff—but his household of five women mellowed him. He was teased and tricked and argued into laughter. Jokes were very important in the family, and maybe too important. We tended not to discuss anything too intimate or serious.

"I think I saw my parents' jobs as opposites—one looking back and one looking forward—and so, early on. I was aware of the dichotomy of the South, its twin obsessions with the past and with the future.

"My parents had no money when they married. But they both worked hard, and they spent very little. We ate a lot of 'free food'—fish we caught, deer and ducks my father hunted, collards and tomatoes from the fields of friends. My mother never bought a new dress for herself until I was in high school, and my sisters and I often wore hand-me-downs from other families. My father saved every extra penny he had, and went into debt the first year of his marriage in order to invest in some land across the river. He feared another depression, I believe; he was also determined to send us all to college. In my parents' eyes, education was the single most important provision they could make for their daughters.

"I went to a variety of public and private schools—public until 1957 when I suppose I became part of the first 'white flight' into private schools, even before the public schools were integrated.

"From my earliest years I loved books, teachers, the classrooms, the pencils, paper, desks, tests, everything about school. Most of all I loved writing stories and poems and plays. After graduation from an all-girl, all-white high school, I went to Duke University (my father had sold his property to pay the tuition). My freshman class was the first integrated undergraduate class at Duke; there were three black women and maybe five black men in a class of seven hundred.

"It's hard to examine your own youth for formative influences; there are so many possibilities. Certainly the city itself, Charleston, had an effect on me, and so did my education-oriented family. I grew up shy, bookish, but secretly in love with just about everything: men, poetry, nature, stories—and secretly frightened of all the same things. I think my love, this passion for the real world, came from inside me, if one can be genetically programmed to become engaged with reality; I think my fear may have also been genetic, part of my nature, but was certainly nourished by the atmosphere of Charleston in the fifties and sixties, when there was a stultifying pressure on young people to choose the safe course, avoid risk, and stifle any kind of aberrant behavior or expression.

"My adult life has consisted of a campaign to eliminate the fear and follow the passion. And I believe it began that first year at Duke, when I enrolled in a writing class taught by Reynolds Price. I had always wanted to be a writer. But not until that class did I understand how powerful that desire really was. I also studied with the great writing teacher William Blackburn, who had been Price's teacher, as well as William Styron's and Anne Tyler's. The two teachers, Price and Blackburn, encouraged me to write; but what may have been more important was the fact that I lost my heart to them. I adored them. They were the first men I had ever met who themselves loved literature. My father did not love literature; he loved me. He thought fiction was useless, because you couldn't learn anything from it—how to plant a tree, for instance, or keep bees or make wine. He was a little worried about how I meant to earn a living.

"My years at Duke were also crucial to my understanding of race in the South. Until then, that understanding had been limited, as our segregated lives were limited. When I was little, I occasionally thought how strange segregation was, and (less occasionally) I thought how unfair it was. But at Duke I began to think of it as a perversion. And I began to look at southern history in a different light. I remember a moment of sudden illumination, too, when it occurred to me that the black presence—the African heritage as well as the living people—was what made the South the place I loved, and was in fact the South's most promising and interesting feature.

"I met my husband at Duke, also during that first year. He was from Illinois, he was a Catholic, and he played the guitar—three strikes against him by Charleston standards and probably why I fell for him. He also loved literature, and he was infinitely kind. After graduating, he went to law school in Texas; I finished my last year at Duke, and went to Yale graduate school. But New Haven turned out to be a nightmare for me, and my year there the loneliest and second-most-desperate year of my life. The next fall, it became unbearable. Martin Luther King was killed, and the whole world looked increasingly dismal. I knew I couldn't go back home; Charleston represented to me the kind of southern society I couldn't live in. And I couldn't live in the North. Snow fell and turned gray in piles along the streets, and I sank into one of my worst bouts of depression, unable to think my way out. Finally I made a long-distance call to Texas and proposed marriage; the proposal was accepted, and we were married two months later.

"Texas and marriage saved me. My husband and I spent two idyllic years living south of Austin on Onion Creek. Texas was the South, in a way, but it was raucous and courageous, and Austin had a healthy share of liberals, Jews, hippies, and musicians. We had lots of friends, mostly crazy law students. We had a cow and two geese and a Triumph motorcycle. I attended classes at the university, and began a dissertation on the works of William Cowper, unbalanced British poet of the pre-Romantic era (author of an epic poem about a sofa, as well as the hymn 'There Is a Fountain Filled With Blood'). We protested against the Vietnam war and against the removal of oak trees at the site of a new football stadium. From time to time friends were arrested for marijuana possession, and got off. We drove to Mexico with fifty dollars and spent a week in a hotel with parrots in the courtyard and Jesus on the wall, and came home with ten dollars left over. We studied, fished in Onion Creek, outfitted ourselves in Mexican or Neiman-Marcus clothes from the Austin Thrift Shop, and ate barbecue. I remember those Texas days as sunny and free, almost perfect.

"But not perfect, because I was not writing fiction. Even under the happiest of conditions, I've never been happy unless I'm writing. The best reality is not enough for me; I need it to be also reflected in story, my story, whatever I'm working on. Cowper's 'The Sofa' struck me more and more as unrelated to reality. But I wasn't ready to write fiction. We were faced with the problem of settling down somewhere after my husband finished law school.

"He wanted to move to Charleston. He loved the place. I tried to explain why I didn't want to move back; but he suggested we try it for a while. Maybe it had changed, or maybe I had changed enough to see it in a new way.

"So we tried it. And almost immediately I could tell that it would be all right. Charleston had indeed changed, with an extraordinary influx of newcomers, with integration, and increase in black political power, and a surprising economic boom due to new industry, the development my father had worked so long for. Everything I liked about Charleston was still there, and the things I didn't like seemed to be on the way out.

"I took a teaching job at the Baptist College, twenty miles outside the city. We had two children. Almost every day I vowed to begin writing fiction again, but those years passed so quickly that it was actually 1978 before I began, and it took another slide into depression to bring me to the first page of my first novel. I believe those slides have always resulted, finally, in major forward steps for me, as if the long, awful term of melancholy has its own secret purpose, and that is to force me forward into something bright and new. At any rate, after a particularly bad sink, one day I quit my job and sat down to write.

"I was thirty three years old.

"That first book, *Dreams of Sleep*, took five years to write, since I worked only when my children were in school. I think it's clear from the novel, especially the opening chapters, that I wasn't yet out from under the effects of the cloud. It's a rather depressing story. My second novel, *Rich in Love*, is a completely different world, a much rosier picture. I don't know yet what *The Fireman's Fair* is; it takes me several years to get a clear look at the published book, to separate it from the book I envisioned as I was writing.

"My children are grown now. My husband and I moved to Sullivan's Island last year, out of the city to a quieter existence. But paradoxically I haven't become more withdrawn from the world; I'm more connected to the place and the people than I've ever been before. It's an energizing, inspiring connection; it's what keeps me writing. Writing is for me a sort of translation, but all I can say in explanation is that it's just the translation of one mystery into another."

With its concern for deteriorating families, Josephine Humphreys's fiction has a disarmingly modest scope, yet her work is distinguished by its deft characterizations, unerring presentation of southern manners, sly humor, and carefully honed writing. In 1984 her first novel, *Dreams of Sleep*, created much excitement, winning the PEN/Hemingway prize for first work of fiction and being cited by some reviewers as one of the most accomplished first novels in years.

The novel revolves around the failing marriage of Alice and Will Reese, a couple in their mid-thirties living in Charleston, South Carolina. Will, a gynecologist, had grown distant from Alice and is having an affair with the receptionist in his office. Alice had become depressed, lethargic, and isolated at home. Into this world enveloped in sadness comes Iris Moon, an impoverished seventeen-year-old, who had already braved many difficulties in her short life. When Alice hires Iris as a baby-sitter, Iris brings a small spark of hope into the house, reminding the Reeses of the possibility of renewal.

Most reviewers agreed that Humphreys imbued a well-worn subject with new life. In the *Washington Post Book World*, Jonathan Yardley observed that Humphreys "writes about familiar and durable subjects, most particular among them the fragility of love and what she calls 'the loneliness of marriage,' but she approaches them with a refreshing desire to see them as if they were new." Reviewers also praised Humphreys's uncanny understanding of characters and their motivations. Yardley particularly noted the way Humphreys "writes about men, gets into their minds and hearts, with a knowledge that any man will recognize as acute." In the *New York Times Book Review*, Ellen Douglas commented on "Humphreys's sure grasp of human psychology. She works out for us a complicated story of shifting allegiances, of despair and hope, and she almost always makes us believe her characters had to act just as they do."

Douglas also noted that Humphreys "writes as if she has been meditating for years not only on the vagaries of human characters and destiny but on the uses of the English language." Indeed, it is her writing ability that most impresses reviewers. In the *Nation* Michael Malone observed that "In finding words, joining them into sentences, crafting sentences into paragraphs, she shows an often exquisite judgment, a tone of almost perfect pitch and rhythm, a feel for metaphor and image that is always sure and sometimes stunning." Humphreys herself agrees that her primary concern is the use of language. In an interview with *Publishers Weekly*, she said: "It was quite a shock to me when reviewers spoke of the novel's characters as though they were flesh and blood. I never—never!—looked at them that way. I was much more interested

in words. Storytelling is not my biggest talent, I'm afraid. It's necessary, of course, but I think of the story as a vehicle for words."

Because Iris was Humphreys's favorite character in *Dreams of Sleep*, in her next novel, *Rich in Love*, she created another seventeen-year-old girl, Lucille Odom, to function as the narrator. Humphreys said she wanted "to imagine a girl so connected to her place that it becomes more than a setting." Lucille is an insightful, irreverent girl who sees everything clearly, deeply. She observes the world carefully, overwhelmed as "beauty doubled and tripled around" her. At the beginning of the novel, Lucille's mother abruptly abandons the family, leaving Lucille's father reeling and depressed. Meanwhile, her beautiful older sister returns home, newly married and pregnant, wanting neither husband nor child. To her surprise, Lucille realizes she is falling in love with her brother-in-law. As the family seemingly disintegrates, Lucille finds herself quite naturally playing the role of caretaker, trying to hold everything together. As each of the characters exhibits some self-awareness, a minor though significant movement towards healing results.

Many reviewers admired the way Humphreys realistically yet humorously depicts an unsettled world, while retaining a glimmer of hope. In the *Times Literary Supplement*, Jenny Abbott wrote: "Humphreys dissects sultry Southern life acutely and comically, yet maintains a fundamental belief in renewal. Paying attention to her characters' emotional and geographical restlessness, she employs a downbeat and laconic tone which makes the depth and detail of the picture all the more surprising. . . . " In the *New Republic*, Dorothy Wickenden reiterated the importance of humor in what is essentially a coming-of-age novel, remarking that it "could easily have slipped into the trite and saccharine, but once again Humphreys reveals an extraordinary ability to explore inner lives with subtlety, originality, and deadpan humor. *Rich In Love* avoids banality by ironically exploiting the catalog of clichés about unhappy families." Wickenden was less impressed with Humphreys's resolution of her plot, saying: "She is more adept at conveying people in turmoil than she is at rendering their recovery. Her satiric vision gives way at the end to a mannered sentimentality and a tendency to succumb to pat psychology."

Humphreys's third novel, *The Fireman's Fair*, takes place in the aftermath of the hurricane that battered South Carolina in 1989. In an interview with the *Southern Review*, Humphreys explained that the hurricane hit just as she was finishing the novel, so "all of a sudden the settings that I was dependent on for the spirit of the book were not there. And I thought, well, that doesn't matter; that shouldn't affect the book. But it really did. Reality affects your whole vision of what you're working on." Rather than writing in the hurricane at the end, she rewrote the entire book so that the action occurred after the hurricane. "It didn't take much rewriting because the book was already filled with images of ruin and disaster—which my books are all full of. For the first time they had an excuse," Humphreys recalled.

On the morning after the storm, the novel's protagonist, Rob Wyatt, decides to quit his job as a lawyer to become a "free spirit," saying to himself: "Now was the time to do it. With the whole place thrown into confusion, one man's leap into a small personal chaos would be less noticeable." Rob is burdened by his unrequited love for Louise, the wife of his old boss. But now into his life comes nineteen-year-old Billie, a waiflike girl who needs his professional assistance. The two become entangled, and through Billie, Rob's life is revitalized and he realizes that being connected to someone is preferable to dropping out of the world.

Although she mentions the "folksy, story-telling tone," Abigail Levene wrote in the *Times Literary Supplement*: "The book casts a powerful spell. All is drawn tightly together by a fine use of metaphor, in particular the recurrent sea-related images which serve as a reminder that natural forces may strike whenever and however they please. Human behaviour is equally incomprehensible." This confusion and instability is the norm for Humphreys whose domain, observed Levene, "is a hazy grey area, where we must open our eyes and our minds in order to see clearly." According to Anthony Quinn of the *New Statesman*, Humphreys' "comic technique derives from a remarkable ear for inner outer speech: the language people use as they ponder what they are actually doing, contrasted with the language they use when talking to others about what they ought to be doing." In *Time*, John Skow observed that "her style is subdued and swiftly illuminating. She is also a witty observer of regional manners" and "a virtuoso of intimation. Her insights and ironies cause twinges rather than shocks of recognition." In the *New York Times Book Review*, however, Frank Conroy was more critical, finding the book "entertaining, nicely sprinkled with intelligent *aperçus*, warm and comfortable in its tone," yet " certainly not high art." Nevertheless, Conroy concedes, "it is good craft, and good craft has its pleasures."

Josephine Humphreys is one of the three daughters of William and Martha (Lynch) Humphreys. She earned an A.B. from Duke University in 1967 and an M.A. from Yale in 1968, was a Guggenheim Fellow in 1984, and received the Lyndhurst Foundation Prize in 1985. Humphreys married Thomas Hutcheson, a bond lawyer, in 1968. They have two sons, Allen and William.

PRINCIPAL WORKS: Dreams of Sleep, 1984; Rich in Love, 1987; The Fireman's Fair, 1991.

ABOUT: Bosworth, S. A World Unsuspected: Portraits of Southern Childhood, 1987; Contemporary Authors 121, 1987; Contemporary Literary Criticism 34, 1984; Pearlman, M. and Henderson, K. U. Inter/View: Talks with America's Writing Women, 1990. *Periodicals*—Nation October 10, 1987; New Republic October 19, 1987; New Statesman November 1, 1991; New York Times Book Review May 13, 1984; May 19, 1991; Publishers Weekly September 4, 1987; Southern Review Autumn 1991; Time May 27, 1991; Times Literary Supplement August 26, 1988; November 29, 1991; Washington Post Book World May 6, 1984.

HWANG, DAVID HENRY (August 11, 1957–), American playwright and opera librettist, writes: "My father arrived in the United States from Shanghai, my mother is an ethnic Chinese raised in the Philippines. I was born in 1957 in Los Angeles. My work to date has been shaped by the dilemma of living simultaneously inside and outside the culture of my homeland. That the reader, upon perusing the previous sentence, may ask, 'To which homeland does Mr. Hwang refer—China or the U.S.?' quite nicely sums up my problem. I consider myself undeniably American, yet the fact that my immigrant forbears came from Asia calls up a contradiction that those with ancestors from, say, Germany or England do not face.

"I am often asked, 'Do you consider yourself an Asian-American playwright or simply a playwright?' That strikes me as a bogus opposition, a fact evident if the subject of the question is changed: Is Tennessee Williams a southern White-American playwright or simply a playwright? In Williams's case, we do not perceive the two possibilities to be in contradiction. Therefore, I truthfully reply, 'I consider myself an Asian-American playwright *and* simply a playwright.' My way of seeing the world is undeniably influenced by my ethnic heritage. Like all humans, however, I have also been shaped by the other facts of my life: gender, class, education. Furthermore, the fact that race has influenced my worldview does not imply that I would always choose to write about Asian or Asian-American characters.

DAVID HENRY HWANG

"When I began playwriting, I *did* feel compelled to write about being Chinese-American. *FOB* was written to be staged in my dormitory, an Asian-American theme house at Stanford University. It was later produced by the late Joseph Papp at the New York Shakespeare Festival, where it won the 1981 Obie award for Best American Play. Mr. Papp was an important influence on my development, producing my first five plays between 1980 and 1983, while I was still in my mid-twenties.

"After writing what I now refer to as my Chinese-American trilogy (*FOB*, 1980; *The Dance and the Railroad*, 1981; *Family Devotions*, 1981), I wanted to address some themes not directly connected to issues of race. At the same time, however, I was wed to working primarily with Asian actors, since we have rarely been represented as more than caricatures, cruel or sweetly subservient, on America's screens and stages. My compromise was to write two tragic love stories set in Japan (*The House of Sleeping Beauties*, 1983; *The Sound of a Voice*, 1983). This was followed several years later by my first play having nothing to do with Asians (*Rich Relations*, 1986). That this last work was deemed a failure by critics did not prevent me from realizing that it was now possible, indeed imperative to my growth as an artist, that I address characters from the many different groups that make up America and, indeed, the world.

M. Butterfly (1988) was inspired by actual newspaper accounts of a French diplomat who carried on a twenty-year affair with a Chinese actress, whom he later discovered to be both a spy and, more significantly, a man in drag. Boursicot, the real-life Frenchman, tried to account for the fact that he'd never seen his Chinese sweetheart naked: "I thought she was very modest. I thought it was a Chinese custom." Reading this, I began to suspect that he had fallen in love not with an actual person, but with the West's fantasy stereotype of the submissive Oriental woman. Writing *M. Butterfly* gave me the opportunity to put some of my personal themes onto a wider international canvas. With the premiere in Vienna of *1000 Airplanes on the Roof* (1988), my collaboration with composer Philip Glass and designer Jerome Sirlin, I also explored cross-cultural misunderstandings on an extraterrestrial scale, through the story of a man who believes himself visited by beings from another planet.

"In more recent work, I continue to explore the fluidity of personal identity, particularly in the context of race. Where do racial mythologies come from? Why do we assume we can infer information about a person's interior self from their exterior features? In this shrinking world, is race still a useful construct, or is it simply a fantasy that we've agreed to invest with meaning? In *Bondage* (1992), a man and a woman, skins covered head to toe in black leather, fantasize about belonging to any number of races during a sadomasochistic bondage session. Similarly, in my play *Face Value* (1993), mistaken racial identity triggers the same comedy of misperceptions that gender confusion has wrought in past sex farces.

"Through writing, I play out on an external stage the conflicts and debates that rage within my own mind. Mystery and confusion seem to me an integral part of the human experience; I attempt as best as I can to confront them with both intellectual rigor and emotional compassion."

David Henry Hwang's experiences as the American-born and educated son of Chinese parents have enabled him to portray cultural clashes and expose racial stereotypes in over a dozen plays and film and television scripts, as well as in librettos for two science fiction operas. Whether exploring the effect of East-West confrontations or the impact of contact with extraterrestrial forces, Hwang uses the stage as a call for compassion and understanding of the "other."

His first play, *FOB*, was written for a student production during Hwang's senior year at Stanford University. It was accepted for a summer 1979 workshop presentation at the O'Neill Center in Waterford, Connecticut, and Joseph Papp offered it at the New York Shakespeare Festival's Public Theater the following year. The play takes place in a dingy Chinese restaurant outside Los Angeles, and deals with three characters who represent different stages of assimilation. Steve is a self-assured, fresh-off-the-boat ("FOB") immigrant from China, whose wealthy father has sent him to the United States for an education. Dale is an American-born Chinese ("ABC") who had embraced the American lifestyle of fast cars and rock music, and is embarrassed by the "yellow ghosts" who are his tradition-bound parents. Between them stands Dale's cousin Grace, a UCLA student whose family has lived in America for ten years. Although she understands Dale's point of view, she has not renounced her Chinese heritage, and she tries to act as a bridge between the two men. The play veers from a realistic situation in the first act to a Chinese dance-drama in the second, where Steve and Grace perform a stylized battle between a Chinese god and a woman warrior. When the action reverts to the original scene, Dale has become the "outsider."

Reviewers were in general agreement that the play was flawed, but that Hwang made effective use of both realism and fantasy to tell his story. John Simon ended his review in *New York* with the prescient comment, "We should be hearing more from Mr. Hwang. . . . " *FOB* won a 1980 Drama-League Award and an Obie (off-Broadway) Award as best new play of the 1980–1981 season, and it became the first part of what Hwang refers to as his Chinese-American trilogy.

His second play *The Dance and the Railroad* is set in 1867, when Chinese workers building the transcontinental railroad went on strike for higher pay and shorter hours. Lone is a former member of the Peking Opera who was sold into slavery by his parents. He has been working on the railroad for two years, using his off-hours for meditation and dance in order to feel some control over his life. Ma is a naive newcomer, having arrived a few weeks earlier with plans to get rich working on the "Golden Mountain" and return home a wealthy man. While waiting for the strike to be settled, Ma is intrigued by Lone's dancing, and the latter reluctantly agrees to teach him the art. As they perform exercises and scenes from the Peking Opera, their dialogue is often coarse and hilarious, with Ma unwilling to spend hours pretending to be a duck or a flea; but beneath the comedy is a profound sadness, as they recall their lives in China and the terrifying voyage to America. The play ends when the strike is settled, leaving the workers little better off than they were before. Each man realizes

that he will never return to China, neither wealthy (Ma) nor a star of the Peking Opera (Lone).

Reviewers found this play, consisting of five short scenes, a further refinement of Hwang's exceptional ability to fuse Western naturalism and Eastern ritual with beauty and simplicity. The *New Yorker's* Edith Oliver, who had been one of his mentors at the O'Neill Center, was particularly impressed by Hwang's vivid imagination and the hypnotic effect of the drama. *The Dance and the Railroad* earned a Drama Desk nomination and a CINE Golden Eagle Award. A television adaptation was broadcast in 1982.

In October 1981, while *The Dance and the Railroad* was still running there, *Family Devotions* opened in another section of the Public Theater. In this play, an affluent Chinese-American family living happily in the luxury of their Bel Air home are visited by an elderly uncle from China who forces them to reevaluate their lives. The title is a "triple entendre" which refers to the family's worship of material things, their fundamentalist Christian beliefs, and the traditional Chinese reverence for family. Hwang said that he had tried to write a Kaufman-and-Hart type of comedy, based loosely on his own family (who were affluent and practiced Christian fundamentalism), and the play careens between satire and farce before its startling ending wherein family skeletons are revealed. This time, reviewers thought that despite many funny bits, the comedy was thin and did not fulfill its promising intentions. However, the play did receive a Drama Desk nomination.

The collective title *Sound and Beauty* was given to a pair of one-act plays produced at the Public Theater in October 1983. *The House of Sleeping Beauties* was adapted from a novella by Nobel Prize-winner Yasunari Kawabata, who committed suicide in 1972. Hwange makes Kawabata a character in this play about elderly men who visit a mysterious brothel to sleep beside drugged, naked virgins in order to come to terms with death. Its companion piece, *The Sound of a Voice*, is based on a Japanese folktale of a samurai who sets out to gain glory by killing a reputed witch, but finds himself falling in love with her. Reviewers rated *The Sound of a Voice* the better play, but thought both plays weak. Frank Rich said in the *New York Times* that the plays seemed less mature than Hwang's earlier efforts.

In 1986, Hwang wrote his first play about an all Caucasian family, an absurdist comedy called *Rich Relations*, which had a brief run. A disillusioned son (instead of an elderly uncle) returns to his wealthy home with disruptive results, but reviewers considered it a rehash of *Family Devotions*, even to the sitcom dialogue of the first act and the mysticism of the second.

At this time, Hwang began to write for film and television. For film, he adapted *Seven Years in Tibet* by Heinrich Harrer and Dostoevski's *The Idiot*. He wrote an original screenplay for the film *Golden Gate*, released in early 1994, about a romance between and FBI agent and a young Chinese woman. Hwang's television scripts include *My American Son*, a piece about the Iran-Contra scandal. Meanwhile, his plays opened in London in 1987 with *The Dance and the Railroad* and *The House of Sleeping Beauties* produced as a double bill called *Broken Promises*. Reviews were mixed, but Paul Arnott, in the *Independent*, remarked on Hwang's facility with absurdist techniques, and said that although his characters and problems were Oriental, "his drama has a tragi-comic force akin to Edward Albee."

Hwang's first play to reach Broadway was *M. Butterfly*, based on a true incident involving a French diplomat's conviction for espionage, for passing information to his Chinese mistress. In reality the mistress is a male spy masquerading as an actress in the Peking Opera. In the diplomat's insistence that he did not realize the deception because he always respected his consort's modesty, Hwang saw parallels with the Puccini opera, *Madama Butterfly*. In *M.Butterfly*, however, according to Frank Rich in the *New York Times*, it is Hwang's premise that the "sexist and racist roles that burden Western men" are inherited from a "cultural icon like *Madama Butterfly*." Hwang overturns the stereotypes, and the diplomat eventually becomes the doomed butterfly, while the "actress" spy gloats triumphantly.

Clive Barnes, in the *New York Post*, and Edith Oliver, in the *New Yorker*, were both enthusiastic about the play, Barnes saying that "*M. Butterfly* sizzles with the immediacy of theater at its most challenging and entertaining," while Oliver applauded "the richness and resourcefulness of [Hwang's] plays and the steadiness of his complex plots." Other reviewers praised the imaginative concept of the play, but felt that it was not fully realized in the execution. Frank Rich called it "a sweeping, universal meditation on two of the most heated conflicts—men versus women, East versus West—of this or any other time," but he felt that Hwang indulges in "thesis mongering" when he posits macho posturing as a cause of imperialism. John Simon, in *New York*, thought that Hwang had settled for too many complications and superficialities, rather than exploring the deeper psychological impli-

cations of the relationship. Some reviewers also criticized the use of American slang by all the characters, regardless of their nationalities. However, Hwang explained to an interviewer for *Drama* that he likes to "take the crassest type of sitcom and butt it up against high culture like opera and find a relationship between the two. . . . [in order] to cut through . . . misconceptions . . . [about Asian character]. Asians can be just as crass as [other] people." *M. Butterfly* ran for 777 performances. It won the 1988 Tony Award for best play, as well as Drama Desk and Outer Critics Circle awards for outstanding play. Hwang also won the John Gassner playwriting award and a Pulitzer Prize nomination. Productions were mounted throughout the world, and Hwang adapted his play for a film version.

Also in 1988, Hwang worked with composer Philip Glass and designer Jerome Sirlin to produce a science fiction music-drama called *1000 Airplanes on the Roof*. Hwang's libretto is a ninety-minute monologue for a character called M who believes that he (or she) was kidnapped repeatedly by extraterrestrial beings, whose presence is announced by the roar of a thousand airplanes—a description of the sound of UFOs used by many who have claimed sightings. M is torn between the need to tell someone about his experiences at the risk of being judged insane, and his fear that silence and repression of the memories will almost certainly lead to real insanity. Sirlin's projected scenery made M appear to move easily in and out of buildings and to leap off a roof into the starry sky. The work had its premiere in a hangar at the Vienna International Airport during the 1988 Donau Summer Festival before beginning a tour of the United States and Canada, where the hypnotic effects of the repetitive music and the projected scenery were deemed impressive.

Hwang participated in the 1992 Humana Festival in Louisville, Kentucky, with the one-act play *Bondage*, which M.S. Mason in the *Christian Science Monitor*, called "a bizarre sexual metaphor for the complexity of race relations and the sad contemporary incapacity to love. . . . "

In 1992, Philip Glass invited Hwang to work with him again, this time an opera called *The Voyage*, commissioned by the Metropolitan Opera Company to commemorate the 500th anniversary of Columbus's discovery of America. Hwang's libretto depicts exploration in various eras and the newcomer's predicament in a strange land. In the opera's prologue, a crippled scientist contemplates the universe from his wheelchair, praising the courage of those who follow their vision into the unknown. Act I takes place toward the end of the Ice Age aboard a spaceship from another planet that is hurtling out of control toward Earth. Each crew member imagines what life will be like in this unknown place. Act II is set in 1492 aboard the *Santa Maria*, as Columbus contrasts the harsh realities of the voyage with Queen Isabella's lavish promises when he set sail. Act III takes place in the year 2092, when two crystals left by the Ice Age explorers are found; these pinpoint the planet where the original space voyage originated. The epilogue finds Columbus on his deathbed in 1506, disillusioned with Isabella and preparing for his greatest adventure as he is transported into the star-strewn night. The opera received mixed reviews, both for Glass's score and Hwang's libretto.

Hwang played an active role in the conflict over the selection of a British actor to play the Eurasian "Engineer" in a Broadway musical, *Miss Saigon*. He felt that the real problem lay in the perpetuation of racial and sexual stereotypes. He dealt with the subject in *Face Value*, a farce involving a white actor made up in yellowface to play the title role in a musical called "The Real Manchu." Asian actors plan to put on white makeup and disrupt the opening night as a protest against the casting. (The *"Manchu"* actors speak broken English with "Oriental" accents, while the Asians speak correctly.) Meanwhile, a white supremacist who is convinced that Asians are stealing jobs from whites, kidnaps the white actor in the belief that he is really Chinese. Numerous complications ensue, with people falling in and out of love because of mistakes based solely on race, but all ends happily with a series of interracial marriages. Unfortunately, the early reviews were uniformly negative, and when the play came to Broadway in April 1993, it was forced to close after a few previews.

David Henry Hwang is the son of Henry Yuan Hwang, a banker, and Dorothy (Huang) Hwang, a piano teacher. He married Ophelia Chong, an artist, in 1985. They were divorced a few years later. Besides the honors awarded to his individual plays, Hwang has received fellowships from the Guggenheim and Rockefeller foundations, the New York State Council on the Arts, and the National Endowment of the Arts.

PRINCIPAL WORKS: Broken Promises: Four Plays (*includes* FOB, The Dance and the Railroad, Family devotions, The House of Sleeping Beauties) 1983; The Sound of a Voice, 1984; M. Butterfly, 1989; 1000 Airplanes on the Roof, 1989; FOB and Other Plays (*includes* Rich Relations) 1990.

ABOUT: Contemporary Authors 132, 1991; Contempo-rary Dramatists, 4th ed., 1988; Contemporary Literary Criticism Yearbook 1988; 55, 1989; Current Biography 1989; International Authors and Writers Who's Who 1991–1992. *Periodicals*—American Theater April 1993; Christian Sciences Monitor April 2, 1992; Drama Review Fall 1989; Independent April 9, 1987; Modern Drama March 1990; New York June 23, 1980;April 11, 1988; January 11, 1993; New York Post March 21, 1988; New York Times November 7, 1983; March 21, 1988; New Yorker July 27, 1981; April 4, 1988; Stage-bill October 1992; Theater Spring 1989.

HYNES, SAMUEL (LYNN) (August 29, 1924–) American literary historian and educator, was born in Chicago, one of two sons of Samuel Lynn and Margaret (Turner) Hynes. The family moved to Minneapolis where he received his early schooling. In his memoir *Flights of Passage: Reflections of a World War II Aviator*, Hynes recollects as a boy watching biplanes landing and taking off at a naval reserve air station. "But for all the romance of the Navy field, I didn't want to be a pilot." he recalls. "I was not, even in imagination, a pilot, but I was a true believer in the religion of flight."

Reaching young manhood with America's entry into World War II Hynes, at the age of eighteen, interrupted his education at the University of Minnesota, where he had been in attendance for four months, to enter a civilian pilot training program at North Texas State Teachers' College in Denton. This was a first step towards the Navy flight training recorded in the early chapters of *Flights of Passage*. "We grew upon active duty," he writes of himself and fellow cadets. "The years that in peacetime we would have spent in college we spent instead first in learning to fly, and then to fight a flying war, and then in fighting it." From 1943 to 1946 Hynes served as a bomber pilot in the United States Marine Reserve Corps, participating in more than a hundred missions against the Japanese at Okinawa and Ulithi. He rose to the rank of major, and was decorated with both the Air Medal and the Distinguished Flying Cross.

After his discharge from military service, Hynes resumed his university education, receiving his B.A. from the University of Minnesota (1947) and his M.A. (1948) and Ph.D. (1956) in English literature from Columbia University. A teacher at Columbia he recalled with particular warmth was Lionel Trilling. In 1949 he was appointed to the English faculty at Swarthmore College. This post was followed by professorships at Northwestern University from 1968 to 1976 and Princeton. He retired from Princeton as Woodrow Wilson Professor of Literature in 1990.

"I do not believe that literary history can be

separated from social and political and economic history," he writes in the preface to *The Auden Generation*. He established his reputation with *The Edwardian Turn of Mind*, centered on "a brief stretch of history," as he notes in the preface, "but a troubled and dramatic one—like the English Channel, a narrow place made turbulent by the thrust and tumble of two opposing tides. "The decade when Edward VII reigned in England, as Hynes sees it, was poised uneasily between nostalgia for the Victorian age and anticipation of the modern age that was to supersede it. To the privileged and the affluent, this period must have seemed "like a long garden party on a golden afternoon," he observes in the opening chapter, but "a great deal that was important was going on outside the garden."

The main part of the book is a reconstruction of what was taking place "outside the garden" in politics ("The Decline of Fall of Tory England," "The Fabians"); science ("Science, Seers, and Sex"); the arts ("The Theatre and the Lord Chamberlain," "The Organization of Morality"); and relations between sexes ("The Trouble with Women"). Such colorful nonconformists as Beatrice Webb, H. G. Wells, George Bernard Shaw, Havelock Ellis, and Elizabeth Robins exemplify the "sense of the time as one of liberation from the Victorian past." By the concluding chapter ("The End of the Party"), the death of Edward VII has broken the last link with Victorianism, and the guns of August 1914 bring the book to a resounding close.

Among reviewers, Steven Marcus, in the *Atlantic*, considered *The Edwardian Turn of Mind* "a most impressive survey," which succeeds in "bringing coherent conceptual organization to a formidable mass of material that hitherto has been dealt with in separate and related categories." To the contrary, Gertrude Himmelfarb, in the *New Republic*, suggested that the book zig zagged too much in time to define what was unique to the decade it covers. Margharita Laski, in the *Saturday Review of Literature*, praised it as "a delightful book to read, often witty in its turn of phrase and often original in its own turn of mind," but thought it "idiosyncratic," and warned readers against taking the author's selective account of this era as the whole story.

A kind of addendum to *The Edwardian Turn of Mind*, centering more on the creative writers of the period, is *Edwardian Occasions*, a gathering of essays on such figures as Frank Harris, Ford Madox Ford, E. M. Forster, T. E. Hulme, Ezra Pound, Rupert Brooke, and Maurice Hewlett. In this collection, Hynes attempts to isolate the particular tone of Edwardian literature as "one of social awareness and anxious concern," in reaction against the ivory tower view from Bloomsbury in Virginia Woolf's famous essay "Mr. Bennett and Mrs. Brown."

For his next monographic study, *The Auden Generation*, Hynes turned to the 1930s, studying writers who were born in England between 1900 and World War I, came of age during the 1920s, and matured during the Depression. Their writing consequently was pervaded by the shadow of a war past, leaving a bitter feeling of "depletion, disillusionment, resentment against the 'Old Men' who had brought it about," and the specter of another war looming ahead which they felt powerless to prevent. With the prototype of T. S. Eliot's stark vision of modern society in *The Waste Land* before them, these Oxbridge-educated, socially conscious writers produced what Auden termed "parable-art" (as exemplified by his own *The Dance of Death*), replete with Marxian allegory and Freudian symbolism, aiming to make poetry "a mode of action." While the book takes its title from the greatest and most enduring poet of this decade, numerous surrounding figures, famous and obscure, proclaim poetry "an instrument of change." The entry of German armies into Poland, the occasion for Auden's poem "September 1, 1939," "marks the violent end of the decade and the climax towards which the book builds."

Stephen Spender, one of the survivors of "The Auden Generation" when the book was published in 1976, greeted the book , in the *New Statesman*, as "an extremely lucid, reasonable, and intelligent study" which "greatly enlarges the reader's view of the generation." To John Fuller, in the *Times Literary Supplement*, the book not only verified Auden's centrality in the poetry of the 1930s, but was valuable also for "its many corrective and judicious estimates of minor writers." The American reviews were more qualified. Ronald Berman, in *Commentary*, questioned Hynes's having confined himself to "a small and unrepresentative group of privileged people, bourgeois, literary, homosexual, radical." In the opinion of Diana Trilling, in the *New York Times Book Review*, Hynes displayed insufficient knowledge of the political background of the decade, and overemphasized the influence of T. S. Eliot and I. A. Richards. The English writer Christopher Sykes, in the *New Republic*, also suggested that Hynes exaggerated the prescience of these poets. Sykes contended that they were as much taken by surprise by the coming of World War II as were contemporary statesmen. However, reviewers were unanimous in praise of Hynes's critical acumen and his skillful marshaling of his complex material.

A *War Imagined: The First World War and English Culture* is the culmination of what Hynes conceived in retrospect as a trilogy tracing the cultural history of England from the death of Queen Victoria to the beginning of World War II. Because this last book is set chronologically between *The Edwardian Turn of Mind* and *The Auden Generation*, the three works are not "systematically continuous," as Hynes concedes, but "they share one conviction—that art and history are not to be separated, that art exists in time and is shaped by time." Drawing on a rich trove of sources—literary, documentary, graphic—*A War Imagined* vividly recapitulates shifting attitudes towards "the war to end wars," beginning with euphoria, dampened by disillusionment as eyewitness accounts from the battlefields came through (an exposure initiated by artists like William Orpen and C.R.W. Nevinson, rather than by writers), followed by the bitter postwar aftermath with England standing "shakily and gloomily on the rubble of the war's destruction." The ultimate effect of this conflagration was "a sense of radical discontinuity of present from past," what Hynes labels "The Myth of the War." The book generally won favorable response, notably from Noel Annan, in the *New York Review of Books*, who was impressed by its vitality and thoroughness of research.

War experienced directly, rather than vicariously, is the subject of Hynes's autobiographical *Flights of Passage*, published two years before his retirement, but marked, as reviewers observed, by the freshness of youth. Fusing his romantic awakening with his baptism by fire, *Flights of Passage* is an impressionistic coming-of-age memoir at once candid and sensitive. In one episode Hynes recalls meeting Elizabeth Igleheart, sister of a fellow cadet at whose wedding in Birmingham he acted as best man. They married when Hynes was nineteen, while he was awaiting orders to be sent overseas to the Pacific Theatre. They have two daughters, Miranda and Joanna, and *Edwardian Occasions* is dedicated to "Liz."

Apart from his own books, Hynes has been a prolific editor of Edwardian and contemporary authors who figure in the background of his historical studies. His three-volume edition of the complete poems of Thomas Hardy grew out of his first book *The Pattern of Hardy's Poetry*, for which he won the Explicator Award in 1962. In the course of his academic career he has been a Fulbright Fellow, and has received grants from the Guggenheim Foundation, Bollingen Foundation, American Council of Learned Societies, and National Endowment for the Humanities. In Noel Annan's judgment, he has established himself as "among the foremost critics of English culture in the first half of this century."

PRINCIPAL WORKS: The Pattern of Hardy's Poetry, 1961; William Golding, 1964; The Edwardian Turn of Mind, 1968; Edwardian Occasion: Essays on English Writing in the Early Twentieth Century, 1972; The Auden Generation: Literature and Politics in the 1930s, 1976; A War Imagined: The First World War and English Culture, 1991. *As editor*—Further Speculation by T. E. Hulme, 1955; English Literary Criticism: Restoration and Eighteenth Century, 1963; (with D. G. Hoffman) English Literary Criticism: Romantic and Victorian, 1963; Great Short Works of Thomas Hardy, 1967; Arnold Bennett, the Author's Craft and Other Critical Writings, 1968; Christopher Caudwell, Romance and Realism, 1970; Twentieth-Century Interpretations of *1984*: A Collection of Critical Essays, 1971; Graham Greene: A Collection of Critical Essays, 1973; The Complete Poetical Works of Thomas Hardy (Vol. 1, 1982; Vol. 2, 1984; Vol. 3, 1985); The Complete Short Fiction of Joseph Conrad (Vol. 1, 1991; Vol. 2, 1992). *Memoir*—Flights of Passage: Reflections of a World War II Aviator, 1988.

ABOUT: Contemporary Authors 105, 1982; Hynes, S. Flights of Passage, 1988; Who's Who in America, 1992–1993. *Periodicals*— Atlantic October 1968; Commentary September 1977; Encounter July 1976; National Review June 24, 1988; New Republic July 20, 1968; April 16, 1977; New Statesman July 1976; New York Review of Books June 9, 1977; March 26, 1992; New York Times Book Review May 22, 1977; April 24, 1988; June 2, 1991; Saturday Review of Literature July 6, 1968; Time March 7, 1988; Times Literary Supplement June 18, 1976; Virginia Quarterly Review Autumn 1968.

ISAACS, SUSAN (December 7, 1943–), American novelist and screenwriter, was born in Brooklyn, New York, to Helen and Morton Isaacs (an engineer.) After attending Queens College (City University of New York), she worked as an editorial assistant at *Seventeen* magazine where, among other tasks, she wrote advice to the lovelorn under the house name of Abigail Wood. In 1968 she married Elkan Abramowitz, a trial lawyer. She subsequently became a senior editor at *Seventeen* but left the magazine in 1970 when her son was born. During his infancy, and for a time while she was pregnant with her second child, she took a part-time job writing political speeches for several Brooklyn Democrats and also worked with the community boards on women's and cultural issues. Having sharpened her powers of observation while interacting with many kinds of people in her various jobs, she decided in 1975 to try her hand at novel writing, a decision that resulted in *Compromising Positions*, a whodunit about a

SUSAN ISAACS

bored housewife who escapes from her dull husband and daily routine by playing detective when her periodontist is found murdered in his office.

Compromising Positions, a main selection of the Book of the Month Club when it was published in 1978, received several favorable reviews for its fast action and wisecracking dialogue, but was criticized by others for its clumsily contrived plot. Jack Sullivan, in the *New York Times Book Review*, was charmed by Isaacs's initial "verbal dexterity and sheer cleverness," but was disappointed by her inability to sustain the "deliciously mean stuff" of her early chapters. In his view, Isaacs's heroine becomes "bogged down in an elaborate murder case that is as tedious as her laundry and her husband."

Katha Pollitt, who found Isaacs's first novel "a perfect read," was distressed by the author's viewpoint in her second one—*Close Relations*, a love story set against a background of New York Democratic politics. Reviewing the book for *New York* magazine, Pollitt commented that "in the world of *Close Relations*, only the very wealthy are reasonable and humane, able, say, to enjoy classical music—everyone else is an ethnic grotesque . . . A novel—even a fluent, frequently clever one like this—needs more to sustain it than the protagonist's realization that having lots of money is heaven on earth. . . . If I didn't remember that the heroine of *Compromising Positions* cast her lot with a lowly policeman, I'd suspect Isaacs of being a bit of a snob." Other less socially sensitive critics fond the book a delightful romp.

Class differences are indeed almost always central in Isaacs's novels. In her ambitious third novel, *Almost Paradise*, about a marriage between a Yankee WASP from a wealthy family and the insecure daughter of a vaudeville and burlesque performer, the author goes into great detail about the diverse family backgrounds and the elements that go into making the marriage both good and bad. The book "may aspire to being a consideration of the cords and discords of contemporary marriage," Jonathan Yardley commented in the *Washington Post Book World*, "but it's really just another good read." Crediting Isaacs with being a "perceptive observer of social customs," and for knowing "how to keep a story rolling along," he nevertheless found the main characters "improbable" and the novel "weighted down with the clichés of schlock fiction." Though his view was echoed by several others, *Almost Paradise* was an enormous popular success, reaching best-seller status even before its official publication date.

Shining Through also achieves its dramatic punches through a carefully observed focus on class difference. It is the story of an ordinary woman, a secretary, who begins by feeling dazzled by her wealthy but insensitive WASP boss, but comes to value herself as a World War II spy and discovers the she loves and is loved by a man who treats her as an equal. Isaacs contrast the moral characters of her two male protagonists, both of them wealthy, upper-class lawyers. The boss whom the narrator admires at the book's beginning turns out to be weak, fickle, and selfish; the man she ends up with is strong, determined, kind, and caring, proving Isaacs does not automatically assign perfection to upper-class characters.

Isaacs returned to the detective genre in *Magic Hour*. Her narrator this time, a Bridgehampton, Long Island, detective, sets out to solve the mystery of a murdered movie producer but along the way falls in love with his chief suspect, the victim's wife. Helen Dudar, in the *New York Times Book Review*, commented that "it takes a while for the story to develop the kind of narrative drive a light novel of this sort wants. After the first swift pages, the novel really clunks around the Hamptons for a while. Still, Ms. Isaacs is sos deft at creating a personalized imagery of Hollywoodized Hampton and at skewering tribal customs that you find yourself developing a fondness for the author even as you grumpily wonder when she will get on with it. What allows her to lead the reader on so happily is her wicked eye for small, telling detail."

After All These Years enters the world of a Queens housewife whose husband suddenly gets rich. After his announcement that he is leaving her for a younger woman, she trips on his murdered corpse and becomes the chief suspect. "Susan Isaacs doesn't romance her readers, she performs for them," Barbara Raskin commented in the *New York Times Book Review.* "For the most part her characters are fairly stock characters doing shtick," she said, but concluded, "Still you gotta laugh, and why not?" Amelia Weiss in *Time* pronounced Isaacs's heroines "never the usual trophy wives," but a "prize greater than rubies. . . . "[W]oe to the Richies, those slobs who can't appreciate them. . . . Because . . . Isaacs plays God, her vengeance is swift and funny, and her heroines live happily ever after."

All of Susan Isaacs's novels have been best-sellers, and two (*Compromising Positions* and *Shining Through*) have been made into movies. (In 1993 she was writing the screenplay for her novel *After All These Years.*) In addition to writing fiction and films, Isaacs also reviews books for the *New York Times*, the *Los Angeles Times*, the *Washington Post*, and *Newsday*. She is a member of the National Book Critics Circle, Poets and Writers, The Creative Coalition, PEN, Mystery Writers of America. She lives on Long Island with her husband.

PRINCIPAL WORKS: *Novels*—Compromising Positions, 1978; Close Relations, 1980; Almost Paradise, 1984; Shining Through, 1988; Magic Hour, 1990; After All These Years, 1993. *Screenplay*—Compromising Positions, 1985.

ABOUT: Contemporary Authors New Revision Series 20, 1989; Contemporary Literary Criticism 32, 1985; Current Biography Yearbook 1993. *Periodicals*—New York October 6, 1980; New York Times June 16, 1993; New York Times Book Review April 30, 1978; January 20, 1991; July 11, 1993; Time August 9, 1993; Washington Post Book World February 12, 1984.

*ISER, WOLFGANG (July 22, 1926–), German literary critic, was born in Marienberg, the son of Paul Iser, a businessman, and Else Steinbach Iser. He was educated at the University of Leipzig and the University of Tübingen, and received his Ph.D. from the University of Heidelberg in 1950, where he had studied with the philosopher Hans-Georg Gadamer and absorbed his phenomenological approach to hermeneutics, or textual interpretation. Iser specialized in English literature and in the early 1950s taught at Heidelberg and the University of Glasgow. He married Lore Reichart, a translator, in 1952. Iser rose through the academic ranks at the universities of Würzburg and Cologne, and in 1967 became professor of English literature at the University of Constance in Germany. Iser has

WOLFGANG ISER

also taught at American universities, including Wesleyan and Princeton. He has been permanent visiting professor of English at the University of California at Irvine, as well.

Wolfgang Iser began his career by publishing two scholarly books, his dissertation on the eighteenth-century English novelist Henry Fielding's worldview, and a study of the aesthetic theories of the Victorian critic Walter Pater. Along with his colleague at the University of Constance, Hans Robert Jauss, Iser became renowned as one of the principal practitioners of "reception theory," a mode of literary criticism that has been highly developed on the European continent and has some importance as a mode of literary theory in America and England. The difference between Iser and Jauss is primarily one of emphasis: Jauss's interest has been primarily the *history* of reading and the contribution that a theory of reception can make to the broader concerns of literary history. Iser's attention has been on the act of interpretation itself as it happens within the minds of each of us as we "perform" the text.

Iser understands the relationship of the author and reader as being like that of the composer and performer of a piece of music, in terms of the creative collaboration between the two. Although the composer is clearly the primary genius whose intentions must be respected, without the performer the composer's genius would remain forever mute. Furthermore, just as two virtuoso pianists will create quite varied interpretations of the same Beethoven sonata, so different readers will produce different interpretations of the same story by Hemingway or novel by Woolf.

Following the terminology of phenomenologist Roman Ingarden, Iser speaks of the text as being "concretized" by the reader: in the reading process, the abstract is made concrete, the vague is visualized, the spirit is made flesh. For Iser, the reader's interpretative activity is called into play by the gaps (*Löcher*) that every text contains. No text could possibly be completely explicit about every detail of the events of a narrative (Even Joyce's *Ulysses*, nearly a thousand pages about the experiences of three Dubliners on a single day, necessarily leaves out a great part of their experience.) Nor would complete explicitness be desirable: if a text could fill in every gap so as to leave nothing to the inference and imagination, it would be insufferably tedious to read. The reading process involves filling these gaps, and we do so, most of the time, without even being aware of the activity. In the process of reading, for example, we imagine what the hero and heroine look like, in ways consistent with the descriptions we are given in the text; nevertheless, no two readers' mental pictures of Robinson Crusoe or Elizabeth Bennett would be exactly alike. This, Iser says, is one reason why film adaptations are almost invariably disappointing to readers of novels: they have usually pictured things and people very differently. The other reason film adaptations are often disappointing is that films, in their visual explicitness, deprive the audience of much of its role as a "producer" of the text: a reader is required to imagine scenes that the text leaves out, dialogue the text leaves unspoken, and so on. Watching a film is a far more passive experience than reading a novel.

Another important issue for Iser is that in the course of the reading of a narrative, readers are not merely processing the words on the page. We read in the context of memory and in terms of the expectations and desires we have been led to form—both in the short and long terms—about what is going to happen. At each moment of the experience, the narrative has a past, present, and future that, like our sense of our own lives, changes as we move through it. Details that are brilliantly etched as they are read may become hazy in the memory later on, while an event that seemed unimportant when we read about it may suddenly loom with greater significance. And a text on second reading will certainly have a different shape than on first reading because, knowing what is ultimately going to happen, we are in less doubt about which lines of action are going to be significant.

In terms of the reader's freedom to "create"

the text, Iser's position is midway between that of Wayne C. Booth (who views the text as quite strictly molding the reader's response) and Stanley Fish (who asserts that the meaning of a text is completely indeterminate, since readers in fact create the texts they read). In a debate with Fish, Iser argued that the author's words were "given," that many interpretations were "determinate," and that the gaps between words and interpretations were "indeterminate." There might be many legitimate readings of a particular text, but there would also be "misreadings," performances of a text that violated either the author's words or interpretations the author could reasonably presume from a reading public familiar with the conventions of the time. (For Fish, by contrast, "misinterpretation" would be a contradiction in terms, since in his view readers create the text in the process of reading.)

What determines these interpretations, for Iser, is what he calls the "repertoire" of previous literary models and contemporary social and cultural norms. Experienced readers are familiar with the repertoire; students learn it in the course of interpreting texts in the classroom. The repertoire changes over time, and there are periods when the repertoire of norms is strongly determinative of interpretation, intermixed with other periods when the norms are weak and susceptible to a great deal of literary innovation and experimentation. And thus the reader's role too evolves over time. Iser is aware that much twentieth-century fiction—along with some experimental earlier works, like Sterne's *Tristram Shandy*—has chasms, as well as the usual gaps, abysses that defy the reader's ability to fill in, and that problematize the entire reading experience.

Much of this theory began to take shape in Iser's inaugural lecture to his professorship at the University of Constanz, "Die Appelstruktur der Texte," in 1970 (published in English as *Indeterminacy and the Reader's Response in Prose Fiction* in 1970). He developed and elaborated it in two books, *Der Implizite Leser* (1972, *The Implied Reader: Patterns of Communication in Prose Fiction from Bunyan to Beckett*) and *Der Akte des Lesens* (1976, *The Act of Reading: A Theory of Aesthetic Response*). The latter presents his theory of reader response in its deepest detail; the former uses the theory to interpret representative texts from three centuries of prose fiction, and to demonstrate how the role of the reader has shifted over that period.

Reviewing *The Implied Reader* for *Library Journal*, Bernard Zaidman said that Iser "succeeds in offering a basic framework for a rational theory of literary effects and responses based on the novel"; and Frank Kermode, in the *Times Literary Supplement*, while criticizing the "occasionally repetitive" structure of the book (which had been assembled from separate articles), viewed it as "a strong and important book." *The Act of Reading*, in which Iser becomes most technical and abstract, was less well received, partly because of his use of the unfamiliar terminology of German phenomenological studies, partly because of the translation from the German. William Bache, in *Modern Fiction Studies*, complained that "*The Act of Reading* is not so much an act as a chore . . . , a book that I didn't so much read as slog my way through." Walther Hahn, in *Comparative Literature*, who found *The Act of Reading* "challenging" and "amazing," was irritated by Iser's esoteric perspective: "the impression is created that the entire study is intended only for those 'in the know.'" Terence Hawkes, in the *Yale Review* stated that Iser is "at his best when he gives an account of [the] phenomenology of reading. . . . The operation of the 'wandering viewpoint,' the activity of *gestalt*-building by means of creative selectivity, and the use of memory as an 'ordering' filter—all encourage the reader finally to beget something that isn't objectively inherent in the linguistic signs that confront him." He complained that "Iser's jaw- (or *gestalt*-) breaking style could make a happy man very old."

For about fifteen years, Iser continued along this line of research, not only producing many articles and a book on Sterne's *Tristram Shandy* but stimulating a good deal of work by others along similar lines. Beginning around the mid-1980s, however, Iser began to shift the focus of his research from the structure of literature to its function, from the question of *how* we read literature to that of *why* we read it. Perhaps the key essay signaling this alteration in Iser's interests is his 1986 piece titled "Changing Functions of Literature," which is reprinted in his 1989 collection of essays, *Prospecting*. The essay is informed by Iser's sense that literature itself was in a state of crisis. Iser does not believe that literature itself was dead or dying, as so many avant-garde theorists have announced, but that the social *functions* of literature are no longer clear and for the moment it seems to have lost its role in contemporary culture.

Iser suggests that, beginning with Immanuel Kant, art was seen as providing a world of beautiful appearance outside of and opposed to the world of reality. In entering that world one transcends and is set free from the limitations of an ugly and contingent world. Culture (as Matthew Arnold believed) could be an antidote to social anarchy; art (as Walter Pater believed) could give us both ecstasy and immortality. All through Europe—and nowhere more so than in Germany—art was placed at the highest pinnacle of human achievement, and given a role in society to which, Iser feels, it could never measure up. "Autonomous art did not ennoble man, as is all too clear from the appalling slaughter that has taken place in this century," he writes in *Prospecting*. Disappointed with this failure to control anarchy and monstrosity, our culture has exiled literature to the fringes of culture. What is needed, Iser argues, is a different and more apt sense of what its function might be: "Two answers can be excluded: [literature] is neither an escape from reality nor a substitute for it. Instead it reacts to reality and in so doing interprets it. . . . Interpretation is a never-ending process of directing ourselves in the world, and literature provides an exemplary form of this process in that it is a reaction to the world accompanying its ever-changing situations."

Iser is not merely arguing that learning to read literature is a preparation for the interpreting, guessing, and gap-filling that we all have to do in real life—though this is indeed a part of its function. But Iser thinks that literature has a more crucial role because of the fact that our worldviews, the systems we create to edit reality and make us secure in it, are never complete and always leave aspects of experience that are "ungraspable." Literature "deals with the inescapable residue that escapes the mastery of the systems." And something always does get left out because of "the decentered position of man: he is, but does not have himself." Literature, Iser argues, continues the work that myth performs in less-developed cultures, giving us images and narratives that can express our self-understanding and thus bridge the otherwise uncloseable gap between life-as-process and life-as-meaning.

Iser thus believes that literature functions within developed societies as myth does in primitive ones, as a storehouse of hypotheses, of guesses, of alternative worlds of "as if" that humankind can try out in order to explain those aspects of life for which culture has no systematic answer. This leads Iser in the direction of what he calls a "literary anthropology." Anthropology itself in its current methods, Iser argues in *The Fictive and the Imaginary: Charting Literary Anthropology*, account for the need, in every society, to create a literature, "cannot explain why literature seems to be necessary as a continual patterning of human plasticity."

Iser begins his exploration by making a distinction between three categories: the "real," the "fictive," and the "imaginary." The "real" is not only the world of experience but the discourses and systems of thought (law, science, economics, and so on) by which a given society orders that world. The "imaginary" is the product of that human faculty behind desire, dream, and play, to which philosophers and psychologists have given words like "fantasy" or "imagination." For Iser the "fictive" is not identical with the imaginary but rather the product of an interplay between the imaginary and the real: "without the imaginary," fictionality remains empty, and without fictionality, the imaginary would remain diffuse. "Out of their interplay emerges the staging of what is unavailable to us," he writes in *Prospecting*. The fictive transgresses the current categories of thought and allows us to think of ourselves in new ways. The interplay also functions as games do: we play the text and the text, in turn, plays us. Iser identifies several different ways of playing that correspond to the uses of literature: as "the search for meaning as a game that ends when meaning has been found"; as a mode of "gaining experience" that requires us to "expose ourselves to the game," putting "out own norms and values. . . . at stake"; as a source of "pleasure" in "the activation of our faculties" by the "extraordinary demands" the game puts on us; and finally in the deconstructive "bliss" described by Roland Barthes, where the reader "plays" the text rather than the other way about.

In the *Times Literary Supplement*, Terry Eagleton praised the "concluding, richly suggestive chapters" of *Prospecting* for their "strikingly original meditations on the ontology of fiction. . . . Literature is a ritual of reconciliation, a form of therapeutic adaptation by which we 'overcome our own duality. . . . '" Eagleton, a Marxist critic, saw little social change resulting from these meditations: "Like hermeneutics in general, reception theory tells us less how to read than what happens anyway when we do so. As such, it runs the risk of leaving everything exactly as it was." Terence Cave, reviewing *The Fictive and the Imaginary* for the *Times Literary Supplement*, admired Iser's "complex, dense and often abstruse argument" but felt its Germanic difficulty was insufficiently controlled by the translators (David Henry Wilson and Iser himself), and concluded that, for those of us who are not professional phenomenologists, "the essays in part Three of *Prospecting* will continue to afford a more accessible view of [Iser's] latest moves in the game of reading."

Iser is concerned with the historical determinants of fiction making, with the question of how certain modes of fictional creativity (such as the Renaissance fixation on the pastoral) met social needs of the particular culture. These change, of course, throughout history, in tandem with the discursive systems in the realm of the "real," altering what each successive moment in the culture finds "ungraspable"—and thus what it needs fictions to help it grapple with. Iser's work develops his "literary anthropology" along these lines: toward a literary history that explains the modes of creativity in terms of such cultural fault lines.

PRINCIPAL WORKS IN ENGLISH TRANSLATION: (tr. W. Iser) Henry Fielding's World View, 1952; (tr. D. H. Wilson) Walter Pater: The Aesthetic Moment, 1988; (tr. W. Iser) The Affective Structure of the Text, 1970; (tr. W. Iser) Spenser's Arcadia: Fiction and History in the English Renaissance, 1970; (tr. W. Iser) The Implied Reader: Patterns of Communication in Prose Fiction from Bunyan to Beckett, 1974; (tr. W. Iser) The Act of Reading: A Theory of Aesthetic Response, 1978; (tr. W. Iser) Laurence Sterne: Tristram Shandy, 1988; (tr. W. Iser) Prospecting: From Reader Response to Literary Anthropology, 1989; (tr. W. Iser and D. H. Wilson) The Fictive and the Imaginary: Charting Literary Anthropology, 1993.

ABOUT: Contemporary Authors 57-60, 1976; Eagleton, T. Literary Theory: An Introduction, 1982; Holub, R. C. Reception Theory: A Critical Introduction, 1984; Jauss, H. R. Aesthetic Experience and Literary Hermeneutics, 1984; Makaryk, I. R. Encyclopedia of Contemporary Literary Theory, 1993; Richter, D. H. (ed.) The Critical Tradition, 1989; Turner, R. (ed.) Thinkers of the Twentieth Century, 1987; Wer Is Wer 1993–94. *Periodicals*—Criticism Summer 1979; Library Journal February 15, 1974; Modern Fiction Studies Summer 1980; Times Literary Supplement July 11, 1975; August 5, 1988; March 16, 1990; December 24, 1993; World Literature Today Spring 1990; Yale Review Summer 1975; Summer 1980.

ISHIGURO, KAZUO (November 8, 1954–), British (Japanese-born) novelist, was born in Nagasaki, one of three children of Shizuo, an oceanographer, and Shizuko (Michida) Ishiguro. "I still have a picture of myself at 10 months old, sitting in front of the family swords and banner," he told an interviewer for *Newsweek*, referring to his samurai ancestry. In 1960, at the age of five, he was brought by his parents to England, along with his two sisters, for what was expected to be a temporary assignment for his father in the exploration and development of the oil deposits in the North Sea. He intended to go back to Japan with his family when the job ended. "Japan was a place I was going to return to and live in, and it never happened,DD Ishiguro recalled. By 1970 his parents decided to settle permanently in England, Shizuo Ishiguro having found the new land more "liberating."

KAZUO ISHIGURO

Ishiguro accounts for the vividness and intimacy with which he later portrayed Japan, a country he knew only from fleeting childhood impressions, in his first two novels (*A Pale View of Hills* and *An Artist of the Floating World*) by his immersion in Japanese culture. Only Japanese was spoken at home even after the family resettled, and he has continued to speak to his parents only in their native language, though he admitted that "my Japanese isn't very good, like a five-year old's Japanese mixed with English vocabulary, and I use all the wrong forms." He was raised in the Japanese style, and while he was educated in English schools, his parents kept him regularly supplied with Japanese books imported from the mother country. Concurrently young Ishiguro grew up in the affluent London suburb of Guildford, in accordance with what he has characterized as "a very typical southern English upbringing." As the only Japanese student at the English school he attended, he was inevitably an object of attention, but, according to his testimony, he did not suffer from racial discrimination. As a schoolboy he was struck particularly by one difference in the two cultures: "I always used to think that my English friends' parents were terribly rude to them. Very rarely does a Japanese mother shout and yell and order around a child."

During his teens Ishiguro learned to play the piano and guitar, performed in London pubs, and aspired to be a rock star. He went so far as to audition for record companies, but received no encouragement. His life for the next few years was peripatetic. Following his secondary school graduation in 1973, he served for a brief period as a grousebeater for the Queen Mother at Balmoral Castle. He then hitchhiked around the United States and Canada. Back in Scotland in 1976, he was employed briefly as a social worker before deciding to take up study at the University of Kent.

After earning his B.A. with honors in philosophy and literature at the University of Kent in 1978, Ishiguro went back to social work in London, working among the homeless for an organization known as the Cyrenians. During this period, entertaining literary ambitions, he submitted a radio play he had composed to the creative writing program at the University of East Anglia, into which he was accepted. Unsure of his prospects as a writer at the time, fearful in fact of being "exposed as a fraud," he spent the summer before entering the program at a farmhouse in Cornwall preparing himself by writing four short stories. Contrary to his self-doubts, Ishiguro enjoyed immediate recognition. Three of his first stories were published by Faber & Faber in their anthology *Introduction 7: Stories by New Writers*. Prior to completing his M.A. at East Anglia in 1980 (among his teachers here were Malcolm Bradbury and Angela Carter), he had already signed a contract with Faber & Faber for a novel then in progress, *A Pale View of Hills*.

As Ishiguro sums up his literary preoccupation: "I am interested in England and Japan; in memory and self-deception; in people who believe thier lives a failure." Etsuko, the central character and narrator of *A Pale View of Hills*, is a former Japanese housewife who has emigrated from Nagasaki to England and is a survivor of the atomic bomb attack that ended World War II. She has had a tangled domestic life—divorced from her first Japanese husband, since remarried to an English journalist, but now living in isolation—circumstances that give her story its particular psychological tension, poignancy, and enigmatic mood. The sense of a woman torn between worlds is conveyed by the opening sentence, where we are told that the name of her younger daughter Niki "had some vague echo of the East about it," a compromise between the English father's wish for a Japanese name and her own preference for an English one. It is gradually revealed in the narrative that follows, weaving between past and present, that Etsuko's first marriage was an oppressive one, and that Keiko, her daughter from this marriage, has committed suicide. Furthermore, Etsuko's sorrows have been bound up with those of a war widow named Sachiko, a latter-day Madame Butterfly deserted by an American G.I., and burdened also by a disturbed daughter.

A *Pale View of Hills* is evocative but puzzling, and in the end unresolved. We never learn, for example, exactly why Keiko commits suicide, though it is implied that she could not adjust to life in a strange, new country. Etsuko's second husband is only referred to, and it is not clear whether she is presently widowed or divorced. Furthermore, it is matter for conjecture whether Sachiko's misfortunes actually happened or are projections of Etsuko's own. "It is possible that my memory of these events will have grown hazy with time." Esuko herself admits in an early chapter "that things did not happen in quite the way they come back to me today." The very title of the book is ambiguous—referring literally to Etsuko's distant surroundings, but implying dimness of perception. Ishiguro acknowledged (in an interview with Gregory Mason for *Contemporary Literature*) that he deliberately intended to "leave a big gap in the narrative." Because Etsuko is dealing with a painful period of her life, he continues, she "talks all around it . . . I was trying to explore . . . how people use the language of self-deception and self-protection." Basically, Ishiguro explains, Etsuko both nourishes guilt feelings and is trying to ease them.

Ishiguro told Mason that at this initial stage of his career he lacked the technical sophistication to bring off so convoluted a narrative. He felt in particular that he had not adequately prepared for the rather abrupt ending in which Etsuko is estranged from her younger daughter Niki. While noting structural faults, reviewers generally greeted *A Pale View of Hills* as an impressive first novel. Francis King, in the *Spectator*, described it as "a memorable and moving work, its elements of past and present, of Japan and England, held together by a shimmering, all but invisible, set of images linked to each other by filaments at once tenuous and immensely strong." To Edith Milton, writing in the *New York Review of Books*, in this "delicate, ironic, elliptical" novel, "Sachiko and Etsuko become minor figures in a greater pattern of betrayal, infanticide, and survival played out against a background of Nagasaki, itself the absolute emblem of our genius for destruction." *A Pale View of Hills* received the Winifred Holtby Award from the Royal Society of Literature in 1983. Although it was selected by the American Library Association as one of the "notable books of 1982" and was favorably received in the American literary press, it did not fare as well commercially in the United States as in Great Britain. It has since been translated into thirteen languages.

An unreliable narrator is also at the center of Ishiguro's next novel, *An Artist of the Floating World*, but this time one whom the reader can readily recognize. Unlike its predecessor, this novel takes place entirely in Japan, its title evoking at once a tradition of Japanese art depicting evanescent reality (*ukiyo-e*), and a nation in transition. The narrator, a retired artist named Masuji Ono, had indeed studied under a master, Seiji Moriyama, whose intention was to "modernize" the *ukiyo-e* artist Utamaro:

> Mori-san . . . had, for instance, long abandoned the use of the traditional dark outline to define his shapes, preferring instead the Western use of blocks of color, with light and shade to create a three-dimensional appearance, And no doubt, he had taken his cue from the Europeans in what was his most central concern: the use of subdued colours.

This synthesis of tcechniques aptly describes Ishiguro's aim as a novelist. The sharp, terse description of the roof of Ono's house looming up between two gingko trees with which the novel opens suggests placid old Japanese woodblock prints. However, Ono's subsequent reminisces, rendered as they are in "subdued colors" and tinged with "light and shade," reverberate with implication.

The occasion for Ono's dredging up of his past is the Japanese custom of *Miai*—the preengagement exchange between the families of his marriageable younger daughter and a prospective groom. His daughter has already lost out on one marriage opportunity, so Ono is especially concerned to put the best face on his history; nevertheless, his evasions and rationalizations expose compomising situations, such as his having turned his art to propaganda for the euphemistically titled Committee on Unpatriotic Activities during the late war, and even having betrayed one of his favorite students, turned dissident, to the authorities. The reader infers eventually from this memoir, spread out over a year and a half from the fall of 1948 to the summer of 1950, that Ono is out of tune with the new age, and that, while still respected, he has had his day. The novel ends on a note of resignation and reconciliation as Ono gazes wistfully at the pleasure district he had known as a youth, now converted to an industrial complex:

> I smiled to myself as I watched these young office workers from my bench. Of course, at times, when I remember those brightly-lit bars and all those people gathered beneath the lamps, laughing a little more boisterously perhaps than those young men yesterday, but with much the same good-heartedness, I feel a certain nostalgia for the past and the district as it used to be. But to see how our city has been rebuilt, how things have recovered so rapidly over these years, fill me with genuine gladness. Our nation, it seems, whatever mistakes it may have made in the past, has now another chance to make a better go of things. One can only wish these young people well.

An Artist of the Floating World received glowing reviews in both England and America. The author's erstwhile teacher Malcolm Bradbury in particular singled it out as "an extraordinary novel, never dramatic and never direct, played by the complex rules of deference and shame, nuance and indirection." It was shortlisted for the Booker Prize, won the Whitbread book of the Year Award for 1986, and has been translated into fourteen languages.

With his next novel, Ishiguro was determined, as he told his interviewer from *Newsweek*, "to try and do without the Japanese thing. It's incredible the way people reach for the same limited number of similes, about cherry blossoms and carp in still waters." *The Remains of the Day*, his best-known novel, is accordingly set entirely in England and stretches in its time span from 1923 until the mid 1950s.

Like its predecessors, *The Remains of the Day* is a first-person narrative alternating between past and present, in the form of a log of a country holiday kept by an aging butler once in the employ of Lord Darlington, "a great man close to the center of history." Remote as the locale and period are from the author's own experience, he found similarities between British and Japanese upper-class mores, such as polished manners coupled with moral obliquity, strict protocol, blind devotion to "superiors," and emotional reserve. Moreover, Stevens, the narrator of *The Remains of the Day*, like Masuji Ono, is a remnant from a vanished way of life. He too tries to justify reprehensible conduct, in this instance Lord Darlington's anti-Semitism and Nazi sympathies. Ultimately, Stevens inadvertently exposes his own obtuseness, having failed, for example, to recognize that Lord Darlington's capable housekeeper Miss Kenton loved him, thereby causing her to make an unhappy marriage, and leaving him with an emotionally bereft vicarious life. His account ends with his returning to a much depleted Darlington Hall, now owned by an American multimillionaire whom he hopes to serve as efficiently as he did its previous master.

The Remains of the Day was widely praised not only by reviewers but also by fellow writers like Salmon Rushdie, Maxine Hong Kingston, and Doris Lessing, as both a tour de force and a moving tragicomedy. As reported in the *Observer*, Ishiguro was especially gratified to receive three letters from a seventy-year old butler once in the employ of Lord Londonderry, who, like Lord Darlington, had entertained Hitler's ambassador Joachim von Ribbentrop. According to this butler, his master "who had always tried to do his best died a sadder and a wiser man."

Ishiguro was pleased to be told by his correspondent not simply that he "got the social details right," but that "the book's emotional content had touched a nerve." It achieved bestsellerdom and received the Booker Prize. A further reward was the opportunity to return for the first time to his native land in the fall of 1989, courtesy of the Japan Foundation.

The Remains of the Day has since reached even wider audiences as the first of Ishiguro's novels to be filmed. It was made by the producer Ismail Merchant, the director James Ivory, and the writer Ruth Prawer Jhabvala. In the two principal roles, Anthony Hopkins proved the perfect embodiment of Stevens, and Emma Thompson, though not the ideal physical type, brought the headstrong Miss Kenton vividly to life. The adaptation does not fully replicate the novel, but it does penetrate to Stevens's emotional core.

The Unconsoled can be called a dream, or, rather, nightmare, novel. A concert pianist arrives in a mysterious European city to give a concert and to rescue the city from its strangely terrible past. The pianist is oddly disoriented, and it becomes clear that he has been here before. The *Publishers Weekly* reviewer remarked that "almost every turn of the plot concerns a failure of communication and a stifling of emotional responses. Children are profoundly wounded by their self-absorbed and insensitive parents; lovers alienate each other across an emotional abyss." To the reviewer this nightmare atmosphere is a "journey through life: . . . its events capricious and inexplicable, its destination undoubtedly 'the vast, dark, empty space' of the soul's extinction." *Publishers Weekly* termed the novel "stunning."

Ishiguro attributes his success to such international writers as Rushdie, Kundera, and García Márquez having prepared the way. Malcolm Bradbury considers him one of several émigré writers to have rescued the British novel from its provinciality and sentimental "nostalgic mode." Ishiguro, however, thinks of himself as very much in the Western tradition of Dostoevski, Chekhov, and Dickens, though he also cites the influence of the Japanese novelists Tanizaki and Kawabata, as well as of the domestic films of Ozu and Naruse. Despite his success, he continues to live modestly in an ordinary semidetached house in the London suburb of Sydenham with his wife, the former Lorna Anne Macdougall, a social worker whom he met while engaged in community activity in London on behalf of the homeless. They have one daughter. He generally shuns participation in literary life. For recreation, he still plays the piano and guitar, though not for public performance. He prides himself on his leisurely pace of writing, claiming to have "anguished for weeks" over just one line of *The Remains of the Day*. In 1990 he was awarded an honorary D.Litt. by the University of Kent.

PRINCIPAL WORKS: *Novels*—A Pale View of Hills, 1982; An Artist of the Floating World, 1986; The Remains of the Day, 1989; The Unconsoled, 1995 *Short Stories*: Three stories *in* Introduction 7: Stories by New Writers, 1981. *Television scripts*: Profile of Arthur J. Mason, 1984; The Gourmet, 1986.

ABOUT: Bradbury, Malcolm No, Not Bloomsbury, 1987; Contemporary Authors 120, 1987; Contemporary Literary Criticism 27, 1984; 56, 1989; Current Biography September 1990; Rushdie, S. Imaginary Homelands, 1991; Who's Who, 1994. *Periodicals*—Atlantic November 1989; Contemporary Literature Fall 1989; East st Film Journal June 1989; Encounter June–July 1982; Harper's Bazaar February 1990; London Review of Books February 6, 1986; New Statesman April 4, 1986; New York Review of Books December 7, 1989; New York Times January 24, 1993; New York Times Book Review May 9, 1982; June 8, 1986; October 8, 1989; New York Times Magazine April 29, 1990; Newsweek October 30, 1989; Observer (London) May 14, 1989; October 29, 1989; Publishers Weekly July 3, 1995; Spectator February 27, 1982; Times Literary Supplement February 19, 1982; February 19, 1982; February 14, 1986; May 19–25, 1989.

*IVANESCU, MIRCEA (March 26, 1931–), Romanian poet and translator, was born in Bucharest. He attended schools there and went on to the city's university, earning a degree in French in 1954. He then proceeded to work in Bucharest for nearly two decades in a variety of editorial positions: on the board of the Romanian press agency Agerpress; as an editor of the foreign policy weekly *Lumea* (The World); as head of the department of literary criticism for Romania's main publishing house of foreign literature in translation, Universe; and as English-language editor of the monthly periodical, *Romanian Review*. He became an editor of the literary magazine *Transylvania*, published in the cultural center of Sibiu, where the poet has lived since the early 1970s. Ivănescu's awards include prizes both for poetry and for translation from the Romanian Academy, the Romanian Writers' Union, and the Writers' Association of Bucharest. As a poet, he has also composed works directly in English, enough to make up a small volume, and he has written verse in French as well.

Ivănescu's first book, *versuri* (lines), came out relatively late for the usual pattern of a poet's career, in 1968 when the poet was thirty-seven, but he has published books at a steady pace since then. The list of subsequent books of poetry, sixteen in total—all of his individual volumes follow the same quirky, all-lowercase, antimetaphoric style in their titles—includes the following: *poeme* (poems, 1970), *poesii* (lyrics, 1970), *alte versuri* (further lines, 1972), *alte poeme* (further poems, 1973), *amintiri* (memories, 1973; also contains poems by Leonid Dimov and graphics by Florin Pucă), *poesii nouă* (new lyrics, 1982), and *poeme vechi, nouă* (new old poems, 1989). In 1983, *other poems, other lines* was published by Eminescu Publishing House in Bucharest and became the first major representation of Ivănescu's poems in English. It was also his first selected volume, the poet having a hand in choosing the 120 works that Stefan Stoenescu translated, representing a limited portion of his output. In 1992, *would-be poems*, 45 works Ivănescu wrote in English, was published in Sibiu. The collection contains both fixed forms such as balladlike blues and sonnets (Stoenescu observes that Ivănescu more than any contemporary poet has naturalized this latter form in modern style in Romanian), and also looser free verse, sometimes epistolary, as well as occasional pieces and speculative ruminations. This diversity represents the poet's formal range in his native tongue as well, although none of the English-language poems is as ambitious nor as colloquial and sinuous in linguistic medium as Ivănescu's works in Romanian.

Ivănescu's translations into the Romanian language include some of the major American and British novelists and poets of this century, as well as books such as Franz Kafka's *Diaries* and *Letters to Milena*, Henri Perruchot's *Life of Gauguin*, Hannah Arendt's *The Origins of Totalitarianism*, and Leonard Bernstein's *Young People's Concerts*. He has translated five novels by William Faulkner, including *The Sound and the Fury, Absalom, Absalom!*, and *The Reivers*, and F. Scott Fitzgerald's *The Great Gatsby* and *Tender is the Night*. He has also translated James Joyce's *Ulysses* and a book-length volume of T. S. Eliot's poems as well as his *Murder in the Cathedral*, in addition to novels by Truman Capote and Peter Beagle. A 1980 volume of poetry by Frank O'Hara, of which he was one of two translators with Constantin Abăluță, became particularly influential among the younger, 1980s generation of self-consciously postmodern poets in Romania, as were as well Ivănescu's own long-lined, vernacular, intellectually playful, often ironic, and always self-consciously literary poetical texts. His important anthology *Poezie americană modernă si contemporană* (*Modern and Contemporary American Poetry*) published in 1986, offered Romanian readers generous

* eve ah NES koo, MEER cha

helpings of major American voices of the modernist period such as Robert Frost, William Carlos Williams, and Wallace Stevens (to whose intellectually challenging poems Ivănescu's are not unrelated), and two writers who, according to Ivănescu, influenced him as a poet despite his avoidance of imagism and its techniques, T.S. Eliot and Ezra Pound (the latter "when he's not being too erudite," Ivănescu stipulated in an interview in *Cross Currents*). The volume also included a variety of other figures, among them a fellow disdainer of capital letters, e.e. cummings, and a number of midcentury and confessional poets—Denise Levertov, Sylvia Plath, Robert Lowell, and John Berryman, whose *Dream Songs* especially influenced Ivănescu's work. Also of importance to Ivănescu was Rilke's rejection of formal rhyme for assonance, consonance, and internal echo, which "freed" him, he has said, "in the way I was writing, but more important, in the way I was thinking." Ivănescu published a volume of Rilke translations in 1993.

The linguistic fabric of a Mircea Ivănescu poem has often been described as prose-like. Indeed, his characteristic effect is a contemplative spontaneity that appears essayistic and discursive. His most successful artifice is perhaps his ability to conceal artifice. Writing in a deliberately parenthetical, digressive, syntactically complex style, he achieves a subdued, disguised lyricism. Ivănescu's pages are filled with parentheses and dashes, and seemingly casual asides to the reader: "perhaps it is," "as if," "if all of us were to go," "what if now there came," "suppose he's right," "now, let us leave fiction aside," "so, let us take a look," "that is, how can I really know," "what else could we add," " the beginning—if we believed that the beginning of an event / could ever be found," "a comma, here, between the subject of this / convoluted sentence." Many of Ivănescu's poems appear to be chance or meandering elaborations of a pensive and ironic speaker's suppositions and hypotheses—"the game in which i compose my feelings." His conversational style comes across as kind of learned, culturally allusive, and pleasurably intricately nuanced interior utterance (often seeming to intend, as one work begins, "to compound a state of mind"), and his expression retains a quaint and appealing privacy. Despite Ivănescu's bookishness, however—poem after poem betokens the eclectic postmodernist's purposeful intertextuality, an ever-present self-awareness of the literary and other artistic sources of his inspiration as in titles like "portrait of a lady," "joyce in trieste," "pseudo-gogh," and "winter light"—both his translator, Stoenescu, and the American scholar Virgil Nemoianu, find willful, auto-ironic defensiveness and secretiveness here. Nemoianu writes, "His poetry refuses the outside world so decisively that its very absence becomes meaningful." Stoenescu remarks likewise on Ivănescu's skeptical posture and concludes that the impression is not the poet's derivativeness but a sense that he knows, and everywhere communicates, "his belatedness, . . . his having been anticipated." Ivănescu's is thus an evanescent, melancholy, fallen world in which being "innocently original" is no longer possible, an inherently elegiac verbal universe in which "originality, therefore, is pure fiction." It has been suggested as well that the poet writes as if poetry itself is in dissolution, a condition which makes it no longer directly possible to create what most readers think of as poetry.

The novel, the modern age's quintessential medium of fictiveness, was an important formative influence on Ivănescu's poetic development, and as his copious translation indicates, he is widely familiar with the variety of Anglo-American and European stylistic experiments. An important prose writer for Ivănescu was Malcolm Lowry, particularly his *Under the Volcano*. Another was the Romanian novelist Camil Petrescu: "the man who influenced me most regarding style, and made me believe I could write poetry." In his interview with Thomas C. Carlson, in *Cross Currents*, the poet cites a Petrescu passage in which the narrator tells a woman character to write like she speaks, without literariness. Ivănescu adds, "Ever since, . . . I have tried to imitate the natural sound and cadence of my own voice." This seeming lack of sophistication, of "conventions or tricks," is a subterfuge, of course. Not surprisingly, for a writer who questions the very idea of originality, who began composing poetry at twenty-seven only after a dare from a woman friend at work to write some poems about her, he does not believe, or pretends not to believe, in the importance of inspiration. He admitted as a mature writer in 1983 that "much of my poetry even now is written on a bet." Many of his quotations and textual allusions proceed with what can only be intentional misprision and sometimes a partial counterfeiting. Text, like the world, is malleable to the mind that apprehends it and reshapes it. The Ivănescu poem progresses by fits and starts, with the flexible copositional method of the stream-of-consciousness novel (e.g., interruption, commentary, subjectivity, fantasy, self-reflection, flashback, montage, recursion) in continual process, both forwarding the poetic movement and foregrounding its limitations, what the poet termed "the imperfect medium of language."

An example of what Stoenescu defines as

Ivănescu's imperturbable solipsistic reflexivity" can be seen in one of his many works about language itself,"is poetry something different?" This apparent treatise about poetry and inwardness embodies Ivănescu's typically sharp, if spare, sensory detail in a situation in which nothing hapens and which refers, as is often the case, to an offhanded, offstage, prior drama. The poem begins:

> in poetry you shouldn't do any telling—i've read somewhere
> this piece of advice to a young poet—therefore let me not tell
> about the way she used to wake up so early in the morning, and sit up
> in her bed, waiting for her breathing to calm down, her face buried in
>   her hands—

It goes on, rephrasing the negation,"let me not confess the dread i was in, . . . " but then shifts the level of attention while maintaining the ostensible parallelism:

> . . . let me not
> hold poems in my hands, the way i walk with the mirror
> which reflects those mornings with their greyish light
> just before dawn. poetry should not be representation,
> a series of images—so it's written. . . .

The voice immediately continues in two modalities essential to the poet's discourse—defining and asking questions. Ivănescu writes:

> poetry
> should be an inner utterance. so should i again be
> speaking about her face choking, gasping
> for breath?

The poem, however, at once shifts so as to undercut the emotional content by treating it as a dilemma of aesthetics and a sign of the futility of seeking truth about reality: "that would only be my way of speaking / about her face," which the poet sees "through layers of turbid regrets, of thoughts which are mine only," and "about her image—it would only be a mask, only an image." He comes to a stop upon a biting question: "while she—her own true self, what about that?" The use of the closing interrogative, the unanswerable question or the feint into self-doubt, is frequent in Ivănescu's self-denying closures that are habitually evasive and resistant to finality while, paradoxically, communicating inward doubts, personal and philosophical apprehensions, and nostalgia for memories that are often moments of mystery, awe, and existential terror.

Ivănescu's predominant concern in his work has variously been seen as the tension between the ongoing flux of present time and the haunting fixedness of the past moment retrieved from (or reimagined as the content of) memory, or the irresolvable gap between the contemplating subject and the object of perception and thought. The Ivănescu poem is usually a structure of feelings in which the poetic voice, while not denying the realm of empirical reality though nonetheless suspicious of his medium, remembers an event or person (in both instances very frequently involving an unnamed, absent *she* or *her* in an experience psychologically shared by the poet in the second person, or the first person plural as *we*, with the *you*-reader). To Ivănescu, "the act of remembering is central to human understanding." But human memory with its present consciousness and the past partakes of the dialectivcal nature of his poetic "inner landscape." His poems have the tenuousness of processes rather than the solidity of products. He reminds the reader that the world we think we know is provisional, conditional, unreal. Ivănescu has stated that "the most a writer can hope for is to suggest . . . an alternative reality, an *imagined* reality." "But any book / is a lie," to use the words of one of his poems, and time (or reality-in-time—"the time right here") "eddies around you" and "glides in its passing / on one side, on the other." Some of his titles confirm the centrality of this dialectic within his work: "on the unreality of memory," "on the unreality of literature," "but there are also true memories," "in the corridor of time," "time must have a stop," "time has no stop."

These concerns have been elucidated by Romanian critics as a kind of inverted Proustianism, in which recovery of lost time brings not joy but a reiterated sense of the void. Implicit in this are fear in the poet's contemplation of the human condition defined by mutability and death (one poem speaks of "this dread, which i have felt in my bones, for such a long / time," another of time, like partings, as "estrangement"), a fundamental acceptance of the futility of communication (novels' and movies' untruth, fictive senses and hypothetical events, games and fakes are part of the poet's quiver), and an intrinsic solitude associated with images of winter and cold pale light seen from an enclosed room ("outside it was also winter then. rainy weather. / and her face, alien").

Antithetical to these moody expressions, however, are more optimistic or positive emotions like loyalty and love, which, as Stoenescu argues in his prefatory essay to *other voices, other lines*, the poet refuses to debunk, as similarly he refrains from either the straighforwardly pathetic, or the universally ironic with its corrosion of all value structures. Most of Ivănescu's books are dedicated simply to Stela, his wife of many years, and one teasing work, "a lie?"—though the poem opens, "how beautiful death is—isn't it?"—nonetheless closes in the elliptical three-word coda to the last line, "hell is the inability to love—to feel—and how beautiful—." Ivănescu's irony is gentle, muted, despite such imagery as the arbitrary hopelessness of "everything . . . like a game" in the somewhat sardonically entitled poem "jocularities." The games aren't unremittingly somber and for keeps. As in his 1970 book *poeme* (poems), his world can be droll and comically exotic. The volume contains the fantastic (and more than a bit campy) chronicle of the character Mopete, a kind of alter ego—in fact Muppet-like, an association his name elicits. Ivănescu's Mopete has a dog of air; he and his friends drink, philosophize, and go walking; there is a blond owl who evokes an aura of power; Mopete reads detective stories and writes poems; in one sequence, "Heraldic Animals," somewhat akin to Morgenstern, the reader can find a catdog, a frogpig of indolence, and a friend whose name translates as Mr. Benighted.

Typically, Ivănescu has described in *Cross Currents* another extended work, *poem* (1973), as

"nothing more than a detective novel in verse, complete with murders,
mystery, hidden bodies, and so forth. Yet some critics saw it as a
profound commentary on the nature of poetry itself, the ultimate
failure of communication, and so on. All this was very flattering,
but as far as I was concerned, untrue. . . . So what we are left with, it
seems to me, is the poem on the page. It must speak for itself."

But the poet cautions:

"this memory you can treasure as long as /
you yourself can manage to keep within the boundaries of time— . . .

But "time too, must have a stop"—and, in the poet's universe, that is what memories and works of art implicitly strive to overcome.

WORK IN ENGLISH: would-be poems, 1992.

PRINCIPAL WORKS IN ENGLISH TRANSLATION: (tr. S. Stoenescu) *other poems, other lines*, 1983; (tr. M. Cornis-Pop and R. J. Ward) Four poems *in* Micromegas, 1984; (tr. A. Sorkin and L. Ursu) Four works *in* Focuri pe apă: 7 Poeti din Sibiu / Fire on Water: 7 Poets from Sibiu, 1992.

ABOUT: Stoenescu, S. *Foreword to* Ivănescu, M. other

poems, other lines (tr. S. Stoenescu) 1983. *Periodicals*—Cross Currents 1985; Times Literary Supplement January 2, 1987.

JACOBSEN, ROLF (March 8, 1907–February 20, 1994), Norwegian poet, was born in Oslo (then called Kristiania), the son of Martin Julius Jacobsen, who completed both medical and dental school, and Marie (Nilsen) Jacobsen, a nurse. The couple had one other child, Rolf's younger brother, Anton Martin. Jacobsen described his parents' marriage as unhappy; his mother left his father in the late 1920s.

The publication in 1933 of Jacobsen's first book, *Jord og jern* (Earth and Iron), marked the debut—largely ignored at the time—of Norway's first fully-fledged modern poet. Fifty-two years later, his twelfth and final volume of poems, *Nattapent* (Night Watch), was a bestseller. In the course of his long career, Jacobsen received many honors, including membership in the Norwegian Academy of Language and Literature; the Doubloug Prize (1968) and the Grand Nordic Prize (1989) from the Swedish Academy; and a nomination for the Neustadt International Prize for Literature (1990). His work has been translated into over twenty languages. Writing in *Stand*, David McDuff called Jacobsen "one of the world's greatest twentieth-century poets, who may be ranked on a par with Auden, Eliot and Montale."

Jacobsen's work has been translated into over twenty languages. H. K. Sehmsdorf commented in *Choice* on the translation, *The Silence Afterwards*, "Poet Roger Greenwald . . . has succeeded in rendering Jacobsen's work in readable English that preserves a good deal of the tonality and texture of the originals. . . . Most of Greenwald's translations are not only accurate but good poems and a pleasure to read." In *Scandinavian Studies* Frankie Shackelford termed them "exceptionally accurate and uniquely inspired" and concluded they were "as close to the originals . . . as translations of poetry can possibly be."

Many motifs in Jacobsen's life and work appear during his formative years. He was to work mainly as a journalist and newspaper editor, and would become a poet whose distinctive perspective can be located in complex relations to both the rural/natural and the urban/technological. Nature made an early, strong impression on him when he was six and the family moved to Asnes, a community in Hedmark County where his father had obtained a post as a school dentist thanks to a socialist victory in local elections. Jacobsen spent seven years in the country; for five

ROLF JACOBSEN

of these he and his brother were educated by their mother, who had completed one year of teacher's training. When he was thirteen, Jacobsen was sent to Oslo to attend a private school. The uncle he stayed with was a railway engineer, head of the bridge division of the Norwegian State Railway, giving Jacobsen now a firsthand source of insight into new technologies.

Jacobsen attended the university in Oslo for about five years, but completed only the preparatory examination in philosophy. Politically he seemed comfortable on the left; he joined a socialist intellectual group, Clarté. In 1934, upon his return to Asnes to care for his father, he became a member of the Labor Party leadership for Hedmark County and took over the local office of a daily newspaper, the *Kongsvinger Arbeiderblad*, that was allied to Labor. But he was to be deeply disillusioned by a Labor government that failed to mobilize against an expected German invasion, which came on April 9, 1940.

On December 21, 1940, Jacobsen married Petra Tendø, who worked as a postal clerk and a seamstress. Despite years of hardship and trial during and after World War II, the couple enjoyed a long and harmonious marriage (Petra Jacobsen died in 1983). They had two sons. After the war, Jacobsen settled in Hamar, where he worked as a bookseller for ten years, then for another ten as a journalist and night editor at a daily newspaper, the *Hamar Stiftstidende*. Around 1950 he converted to Catholicism. The fine old wooden house where he lived, with its view of the railroad line and Lake Mjøsa, eventually became a well-known landmark, thanks to Jacobsen's memorable use of his surroundings in his poems.

Literary and other artistic influences on Jacobsen were diverse. Among his sources he named the poetic *Edda*, "everything that could be sung," Faroese dance rhythms, Karel Capek's play *R.U.R.*, and Carl Sandburg's poetry; and one can infer that his familiarity with painting and his feel for the concision of good journalism played a role as well. Yet none of these can account for the abiding freshness of his work. That freshness springs not from sources, but from a combination of gifts: a talent for memorable images and an ear that gives a large number of his poems a "rightness" as musical structures of feeling; insight into the relation of humans to nature and culture; a receptive attitude toward both phenomena and writing that is non-Romantic and marked by humility; and an irony that can be scathing but is often warm and humorous. Along with these gifts, Jacobsen's work also displays a continual awareness of the key role of language in consciousness.

In Norway, where modern trends arrived late, Jacobsen's first book attracted attention mainly for the free form of many of the poems and for the introduction of motifs from technology and from modern urban life. "Byens metafysikk" ("The Metaphysics of the City") begins:

Under the gutter gratings,
under the moldy stone cellars,
. . .
the telephone cables' nerve fibers.
The gas pipes' hollow veins.
Sewers.

After further elaboration, Jacobsen takes this poem to an unexpected conclusion. Returning to street level, he describes an active, but perhaps figuratively blind, "you" rushing around the city with "silk against your navel's / white eye and a new coat in the sunshine," and an observing "I":

And up in the light somewhere I, of course, stand and watch how
the cigarette's blue soul flutters like a chaste angel
through the chestnut leaves toward eternal life.

The placement of humans in a middle realm (here, as in Norse mythology, between an underworld and the heavens) is typical of Jacobsen, for whom "between" is a recurrent word in both spatial and temporal dimensions.

This poem shows a complete penetration of the natural by the man-made; yet, as Erling Aadland pointed out in his essay in *Rolf Jacobsen*, the metaphors work in both directions, technifying the natural even as they animate the technical. This mingling, which the book title *Jord og jern* suggests—since iron ore comes from the earth and iron returns to it as rust—runs throughout Jacobsen's work and gives the lie to oversimplified interpretations that make nature "good" and technology "bad." Per Thomas Andersen noted in his essay in *Frøkorn av ild* (Kernels of fire) that Jacobsen is fascinated by technology, but not euphoric over it. On the one hand, Jacobsen has written the best poems with a certain element of futurism that are to be found in Norwegian. On the other hand, Andersen says, "one need not for that reason see any ghosts of Marinetti." That judgment is borne out by a poem from *Vrimmel* (Swarm) (1935) called "Arv og miljø" ("Heredity and Environment"), in which an opening description of a childlike dancer leads to a parallel account of a different kind:

Now
with innocent pupils
and frightened eyebrows
the gas mask stares out over the world
with its snout a curious point
like a child.

Then we begin to dance
under cold spotlights, white spotlights.
Tango and
Cucaracha
to machine guns, like this:
Arms raised. Two steps to the side.
Awkward bend in the knees.

That the gas mask and the machine gun first came into use during World War I makes the "Now" at the turning point of this poem especially ominous.

We can see here the beginning of a historical awareness in the poems that was to become deeper as Jacobsen's work progressed. *Vrimmel* shows clearly Jacobsen's interest in the long temporal scale of history, the large spatial scale of astronomy, and scale in general. In "Gummi" ("Rubber"), Jacobsen moves from the large to the small—and the viewpoint of the small—in breathtaking fashion. Describing a main road "still gray and wet in [its] endless tunnels of forest," he follows the progress of an ant that wanders into the imprint of a car tire's brand name, carrying a pine needle. The poem concludes:

Pine needles are heavy.
Time after time it slid back down with its tottering load
and worked its way up again
and slipped back again.
Outward bound across the great, cloud-illumined Sahara.

The last word suggests that even when driving our powerful machines, we too are *between* something smaller and something larger.

His publisher launched Jacobson as Norway's first modernist; Jacobsen never accepted this label, associating it with a hermeticism that ran counter to his ambition of presenting accessible surfaces. Poul Borum pointed out in his foreword to *The Silence Afterwards* that Jacobsen shares certain features with objectivist poets like William Carlos Williams, and also displays a "cosmic sensuality" like D. H. Lawrence's and a calm irony reminiscent of Bertolt Brecht's. But if these traits qualify him as a member of the "realist" branch of modernism, with respect to the Symbolist mainstream, the poet was right. He shared few of its concerns and used few of its techniques. As to form, one might call Jacobsen a classical poet in modern dress. But in other ways—with respect to the issues that engaged him and the type of insight he brought to them—he was not a half-step behind, but a half-step ahead.

After a hiatus of sixteen years occasioned by World War II, the poet published his third book, *Fjerntog* (Express train) (1951), which can be seen as transitional. The interpenetration of the natural and the technical remains striking, as in the final stanza of "Koks" ("Coke"):

It was an Age of Steam. Under the white cherry blossoms
it sent toward the sky
and between the dark trunks of its columns of smoke, I
had my childhood. In their
    forests
I found the first cold flowers: Coke
in Theater Street.

Likewise, Jacobsen's use of animation continues to reflect a characteristic type of thought, as in the opening lines of "Cobalt": "Colors are words' little sisters. They can't become soldiers. / I've loved them secretly for a long time." These short sentences say something about ideologically driven speech, about the poet's relation to painting, and perhaps about a hesitant, adolescent desire.

Jacobsen also develops further in this book the notion of operations—usually coherent—that are at work beyond people's awareness. "Solsikke" ("Sunflower") reads:

What sower walked over the Earth,
which hands sowed
our hearts' kernels of fire?

Like rainbow bands they went out from his fists
to frozen soil, young loam, hot sand;
they will sleep there,
voracious, and drink our life
and blast it to pieces
for the sake of a sunflower you don't know about
or a thistle head or a chrysanthemum.

Come, young rain of tears,
come, gentle hands of sorrow.
It's not as terrible as you think.

The conclusion sounds a note of acceptance that is in accord with Jacobsen's receptive posture as a poet: he is one who observes, who listens (even to silence), who, as he said, uses his "antennas." Many of his poems remind us not merely of what we have failed to notice, but *that* we are failing to notice. Andersen, invoking Heidegger, says Jacobsen reminds us of "the forgetting of being." In "Dag og natt" ("Day and Night")—in which people are again "between"—neither day nor night ever ends; each "just goes off to another place / for a little while" and then returns, wondering if we'll be waking soon, or why we aren't yet asleep. The poem concludes:

There is no end to delight, none to pain,
none to death, none to life.
They just go off for a little while. . . .

There is no end to the stars and the wind.
There is only you yourself,
who aren't who you think you are.

The "forgetting of being" is here described in a direct relation between people and a natural order—just as it was described, in "Byens metafysikk" ("Metaphysics of the City"), in a relation between people and both natural and technical orders. But Jacobsen sometimes evokes this "forgetting of being" in a more pointed way, by having nonhuman elements, whether natural, mythical, or technological, "talk" to one another above people's heads (a variant, Andersen remarks, on the Jobean and Faustian theme of the divine wager). In *Vrimmel*, the poem "Odda" has columns of smoke from factories "greeting" the earth's best-known volcanoes. In *Hemmelig liv* (Secret Life) (1954)—a breakthrough for Jacobsen and undoubtedly one of his finest books—the poem "Den ensomme veranda" ("The Lonely Balcony") has the balcony ask the western wind to see if God might have a use for it; then the poet tells us that the balcony gets cut down by men putting up a neon sign for Scotch whiskey. Both forms of "reminder" appear throughout Jacobsen's work.

In the three books published from 1954 to 1960, Jacobsen carries out what Aadland calls his greatest task: "to interpret the realization of the earth under the imperatives of the heavens." These books, Aadland writes, "are among the richest, strangest and most thoughtful in Norwegian literature. Only on the surface are they simple and easily accessible poetry—and making them seem so is [a] feat."

Sometimes, in high spirits, Jacobsen suggests

that meaning makes itself apparent to whoever attends: in the title poem of *Brev til lyset* (Letter to the light) (1960), a tractor is a lumpy fist writing a letter "that anyone who wants to can read." But more often, the reading is problematical. In "Grønt lys" ("Green Light"), from *Sommeren i gresset* (Summer in the grass) (1956), in which the earth itself is "between" ("I felt it lie down heavily on its side in the evening like a buffalo, / in the darkness between the stars, where there is room"), Jacobsen's reminder suddenly sprouts a complex metatextual comment:

But why it has such great patience with us
deep down in its iron core, its huge magnesium heart, we
are far from
    understanding.

For we have forgotten this: that the Earth is a star of grass,
a seed-planet, swirling with spores as with clouds, from sea to sea,
a whirl of them. Seeds take hold under the cobblestones
and between the letters in my poem, here they are.

This offers a striking image of Jacobsen's receptive method: the seeds give the letters their meaning, and ultimately they have greater power, as in "Solsikke" ("Sunflower"). Only poetic language can approximate or remind us of the nonverbal meanings of seeds. As Aadland remarks, "words are not reality, but without reality, words are not worth anything. Jacobsen writes his way into this intellectual interstice: writing is a battle against the tyranny of reality on the one hand and irresponsible aestheticism on the other. Language . . . is neither reality nor aesthetics, but something in between. . . . "

In the title poem of *Stillheten efterpa (The Silence Afterwards)* (1965), the poet's exhortation to be done with the distractions of commerce yields an even clearer sense of the medial position of language, which occurs between two silences—those before and after our noise:

be done and come home
to the silence afterwards
that meets you like a warm spurt of blood against your forehead
and like thunder rolling
and like strokes of mighty bells
that set your eardrums quivering,
for words don't exist anymore,
there are no more words,
from now on everything will speak
with the voices of stone and tree.

Jacobsen insists that we need to listen to such silences, though we cannot easily interpret them, that an important meaning resides in places and at levels we customarily ignore. This theme is beautifully distilled in the poem "Blinde ord" in *Pusteøvelse* (Breathing exercise) (1975):

Blind Words

—are words that lovers say with their skin
inside night's space, where thoughts are without form.

—are words the dying person forms in his throat
and never gets said before the candles have burned
down.

—are words the fetus says when it dreams
about sounds it cannot hear and colors it doesn't know.

—are words the wind says to the tree and sorrows
say to our heart.

—words that were here before words were created,
words that the earth is made of
and that the stars exhale as light
in their timeless breathing.

Such poetry suggests not only humility, but patience. Like "the silence afterwards," Jacobsen "waits in the stairwell till everyone's left," in the hope that his subject will reveal itself. This poet who all his life maintained a lively interest in everything new nonetheless has a gaze that hangs back, as Asbjørn Aarnes wrote in his essay in *Frøkorn av ild*—a gaze that remains behind. As a result, Jacobsen sees things in a way that at first seems out of kilter to us. Only when we have allowed his quiet perceptions to sink in do we realize, says Aarnes, that it is we who are out of kilter:

Hundvako, Hangur and Skriulaupen.
Peculiar names we have in this country of ours,
as if hacked out of the mountains, just as they are,
or chipped out of old tree stumps.

But it seems like they no longer fit anything.
Perhaps they're avoiding us,
and we them. Our motels. Our gas stations,
and what we talk or think about.

Framrusthovdi, Uppnostindann', Tindulvstølane.
People must have lived here before
who were familiar with the place in a way we've lost,
and took the words right out of the rock face
and carved them for us like runes.
Will they last?

This poem, "Hundvako," from *Tenk pa noe annet* (Think About Something Else) (1979) ingeniously uses dialectal place names—and simply the emotional suggestiveness of certain sounds—to draw from readers a feeling that they barely knew they had. One does not need to take the reference to a better prior age literally to acknowledge the power of the statement; nor can one miss the relevance of the closing question to poetry itself. The poem places modern life between an almost timeless past and a vast, unknowable future. In other poems, Jacobsen uses specific historical references to create a similar scale, as in "—Mere fjell" ("—More mountains"):

Think of it:—That old round-top has stood as it stands
now
all the time since King Harald's day.
It stood here when they nailed a poor wretch to the cross.
As it stands now. As it stands now.
Wearing trickling streams and heather scrub and that
large
steep brow
without any thoughts in it. It stood here
through Belsen and Hiroshima. It stands here now
as a landmark for your death, your unease,
perhaps your hopes.
So you can go over there and hold onto something hard.
Some old something. Like the stars.
And cool your forehead on it,
and think your thoughts through.
And think for yourself.

Often, as here, Jacobsen likens both man-made and natural objects to humans, or has them feel, observe, speak or write; sometimes his images ascribe agency without ascribing human-like actions. Jacobsen's poems share this manner of expression with the work of two of his great Norwegian contemporaries, the poet Olav H. Hauge and the novelist and poet Tarjei Vesaas. No doubt it emerges from the intimate contact with nature that Norwegians—writers and readers alike—have had for centuries and still have now. It would be a mistake to regard such use of animation as literary naiveté on the one hand or as evidence of "animistic" belief on the other. Jacobsen grasps profoundly the degree to which our being in the world is an interaction with our environment, and how all meaning derives ultimately from that interaction. Ascribing an active role to elements of the environment is an effective way of conveying a certain form of knowledge—not mysticism. In "—Mere fjell" ("—More Mountains"), the word "brow" marks the qualities of our relationship to the unthinking that help us to think, marks the role the mountaintop has in a dynamic interaction.

The depth of Jacobsen's poetry, then, must be located not in the philosophical or psychological dimensions, but in what we must call the spiritual dimension, though it has little to do with religion. Such poetry challenges modern criticism insofar as our critical terms still reflect a conceptual framework developed in the 19th century: because God is dead, nature must be inanimate (without spirit). Jacobsen understood that nature is animate. In fact, it was because he looked hard at the universe as a living system that he was able to see our own creations play a role in shaping who we are, and was therefore able to make them vivid in poems long before they acquired the sorts of cultural accretion that (as Susanne Langer suggested in *Philosophy in a New Key*) they must have before they can be employed symbolically. Thus, we must think twice when Jacobsen's concern and compassion for human life move us to call him a humanist. For his view is in fact much broader than one that puts humans at its center and makes them the source of all values. He reminds us in "Hyss—" ("Hush—"), from *Headlines* (1969), that the waves breaking on the shore are telling us not to be so proud:

> . . . Hush
> they say to us—
> it's *our* world
> *our* eternity.

In his last three books, Jacobsen published poems in which he gradually came forward after a lifetime of personal reticence. Such poems are like summings-up, touching in their explicit acknowledgment of themes implicit in earlier work, such as his lifelong obsession with railroads and his fondness for clouds and gray weather. In "Til deg" ("To you"), from *Tenk pa noe annet*, he writes one of his few love poems, addressed to his wife in the knowledge that one of them must die first, before too many years have passed: "Surely this / is the only thing we've never / wanted to talk about."

Unexpectedly, it was Petra Jacobsen who died first. Jacobsen's suite of poems about their life together and her death closed his final book, *Nattapent* (Night Watch, 1985), and probably accounted for its great popular appeal. In spare, moving poems, Jacobsen mourns and remembers, questions and affirms. The last poem is "Ildfluene" ("The Fireflies"):

> It was the evening with fireflies
> while we were waiting for the bus to Velletri
> that we saw two old people kissing
> under the plane tree. it was then
> you said, half to the air
> half to me:
> Whoever loves for years
> hasn't lived in vain.
> And it was then I caught sight of the first
> fireflies in the darkness, sparkling
> with flashes of light around your head.
> It was then.

It must inevitably come as a shock to readers moved by Jacobsen's humane and humble poetry to learn that after World War II the poet was convicted of treason for having supported the Nazis and was sentenced to three-and-a-half years at hard labor (he spent over a year as a prisoner awaiting trial, then served the balance of the sentence, mainly cutting timber). There has been considerable debate in Norway about the fairness of the legal proceedings undertaken after the war. Moreover, Jacobsen's case is still controversial and requires further research. It raises two main questions: first, to what extent was Jacobsen guilty of betraying his country by lending support to the Quisling regime or the German occupiers; and second, did he in fact embrace Nazism?

The evidence on the first question is too complex to present here. It would seem that Jacobsen thought he could walk a fine line between the Nazis' requirements and his obligations to his conscience and his countrymen. In effect, Jacobsen tried to pursue an individual solution to a problem that called for an unambiguous choice of sides. He was convicted of having been a member of the Norwegian National Socialist party (Nasjonal Samling, hereafter NS) and with having carried out certain duties for it; and with having written editorials that supported some of the actions taken by the NS and the German occupiers (the extent to which he wrote these on his own initiative is difficult to establish). The trial did not reveal a complete picture of Jacobsen's motives; it did establish, however, that he never acted *qua* NS-supporter vis-a-vis his colleagues, that he turned a blind eye to their ignoring of directives from the NS, that he never informed on anyone, and that he engaged in no dealings with the NS that yielded personal financial gain. The court's sentence was widely regarded as unduly harsh.

The second question—whether Jacobsen in fact embraced Nazism—is undoubtedly the main issue for readers outside Norway, and is somewhat easier to answer than the first question. It is clear that Jacobsen never embraced any of what we now regard as the main elements of Nazism: the cult of the Führer, the mythology of racial "purity," and the extermination of Jews, gypsies, homosexuals, and others labeled "undesirable." He was never so much as accused by anyone of writing or uttering a single sentence in support of such doctrines.

(All translations of quoted material are by Roger Greenwald. Translations from *The Silence Afterwards: Selected Poems of Rolf Jacobsen* are used by permission of Princeton University Press. "The Fireflies" appeared in *WRIT* 18 and is used by permission of the translator.)

PRINCIPAL WORKS: (tr. R. Bly) *Twenty Poems*, 1977; (tr. R. Greenwald); *The Silence Afterwards: Selected Poems of Rolf Jacobsen, WRIT 18, 1987;* (tr. R. Hedin) *Night Music: Poems by Rolf Jacobsen*, 1994.

ABOUT: Bly, R. Introduction to *Twenty Poems*, 1977; Borum, P. Foreword, to *The Silence Afterwards*, 1985; Greenwald, R. Introduction, The Silence Afterwards, 1985; Naess, H. S., ed., A History of Norwegian Literature, 1993; Zuck, V., ed., Dictionary of Scandinavian Literature, 1990. *Periodicals*—Choice October 1986; Scandinavian Studies 74,3; Stand Magazine Autumn 1988, World Literature Today Autumn 1988; Winter 1990. *In Norwegian*—Frøkorn av ild: Om Rolf Jacobsens forfatterskap, ed. Karlsen, O.; Vesaas, O. Rolf Jacobsen—en stifinner; hverdagen, 1994.

JAMESON, FREDRIC R. (April 14, 1934–), American literary critic, was born in Cleveland, Ohio, raised in New Jersey, and educated at Haverford College (B.A., 1954) and Yale University, where he received his Ph.D. in 1960. He taught at Harvard University from 1959 to 1967, at the University of California at San Diego from 1967 to 1976, at Yale University from 1976 to 1983, and at the University of California at Santa Cruz from 1983 to 1985. In 1986 he became Lane Professor of Comparative Literature at Duke University.

Jameson's doctoral dissertation on Jean-Paul Sartre, the philosopher and, like himself, Marxist, became his first book, *Sartre: The Origins of a Style.* In a review, "On Aronson's Sartre," Jameson recounted something of his intellectual development: "I came to Marxism *through* Sartre and not against him; and not even through the later, Marx-oriented works such as the *Critique*, but very precisely through the 'classic' existential texts of the immediate post-war period. . . . [I was] a *Time-Life* reading student of the Eisenhower era . . . [who would] occasionally, unexpectedly, stumble across peculiar and alien references to taboo realities—sudden digressions about the 'proletariat,' . . . allusions to Marx (of whom we had been taught that his economics was completely disproven and out of date), to 'surplus value,' 'commodity reification,' etc. . . . Later on, these became mysteries to explore, as one begins to shed one's local Americanisms."

In his second book, *Marxism and Form: Twentieth-Century Dialectical Theories of Literature*, Jameson presented "a general introduction" to the sort of Marxism he considered most vital for the post–World War II, post-industrial West. He followed not the tendentious Stalinist tracts of the 1930s, what might be called Russian Marxism, but a Western, "relatively Hegelian kind of Marxism" using dialectical thought in an effort to show how complex social structures, which were glossed over by the mass media, relate to literary production. For Jameson the seminal texts of this movement are Georg Lukacs's *Theory of the Novel*, Walter Benjamin's *Origins of German Tragedy*, Theodore W. Adorno's *Philosophy of the New Music* and *Negative Dialectics*, and Jean-Paul Sartre's *Critique of Dialectical Reason*. Most of *Marxism and Form* is an exposition of these texts.

In his climactic fifth chapter, "Towards Dialectical Criticism," Jameson sets forth his own ideas of what a genuine dialectical-materialist criticism would be like. Most important is the notion of criticism as "metacommentary" that must always "include a commentary on its own intellectual instruments as part of its own work-ing structure." Jameson points out that for a formalist the concept of "point of view" is a neutral tool of analysis without historical content: after all, any narrative, whenever written, must be told from *some* point of view. For Jameson, on the other hand, the notion of "point of view" is not timeless at all; it reflects the specific historical situation of Henry James (who invented the term) and the "lived experience" of the middle class in the late 19th century: "seeing life from the relatively restricted vision of our own monad." A genuinely dialectical criticism, for Jameson, would be self-conscious about the terms and structures that it assumes, would attempt to understand these tools in their historical contexts.

The last part of the chapter presents a complex "allegorical" notion of literary interpretation in which form and content are seen as interchangeable. For Jameson, in addition to the usual "form" and "content" of any literary text, there is the "form of the content" and the "content of the form." Jameson claims that the "content" of a literary work "never really is initially formless . . . but is rather already meaningful from the outset, being . . . the very components of our concrete social life itself: words, thoughts, objects, desires, people, places, activities." It is the lived experience of the social world. On the other side "form" itself has its "content": styles and plots encode ideas about the material world. One obvious example would be the love sonnet of the Renaissance, whose importance underscores the dynastic or commercial character of the marital bond in that era. (In our own era, men and women who can marry for love as a matter of course do not need to create such formal objectifications of feeling.) Sometimes the "content of the form" operates in surprising ways. For example, Jameson views the surface violence and anxiety of science fiction movies of the 1950s not merely as a covert reference to the terror of nuclear annihilation during a period of escalation in the cold war, but as also encoding a collective wish-fulfillment fantasy on the part of postwar society, a utopian fantasy about genuinely gratifying work, personified in the ubiquitous scientist hero whose activity—empowering, untrammeled by routine, rewarded by deep self-satisfactions rather than by cash—suggests "a return to older modes of work organization, the more personal and psychologically satisfying world of the guilds." In *Marxism and Form* Jameson presents a new dialectical criticism to interpret literature in such a way as to penetrate to the repressed collective political desires of the society in which it is produced.

Many reviewers, including those not particularly sympathetic to Marxism, were deeply impressed by Jameson's achievement in *Marxism and Form*. Theodore Fielder, in *Library Journal*, called the book "not just a major contribution to the theory of literary criticism [but] an intellectual event of the first order." And René Wellek said that Jameson had "succeeded in . . . convincing us that Marxism is an omnipresent, living mode of thought in Western and Central Europe" and that his book was "a challenge also to the American intellectual to come to terms with Marxism." The reviewer for *Choice* argued, however, that by limiting his analysis to the Western, Hegelian type of Marxism, Jameson "conforms to the needs of monopoly capitalism and U.S. imperialism, making 'Marxism' a safe, respectable, nonrevolutionary hobby for unwitting professors."

In *The Prison-House of Language: A Critical Account of Structuralism and Russian Formalism*, Jameson attempts to come to terms, as a Marxist critic, with Russian formalism and its outgrowths, structuralist and poststructuralist literary theory, which had swept through France and, even as he was writing, was becoming a major influence on American academic thought. Like *Marxism and Form*, *The Prison-House of Language* is partly a summary of structuralism and poststructuralism, partly a critique. As one would expect from *Marxism and Form*, Jameson approaches formalism and structuralism from the standpoint of what it leaves out: history, and particularly social history, as a determinant of literary texts. Jameson objects to the structuralist tendency to present socially conditioned forces as a synchronic system (like the rules of a language at a given time) rather than as a narrative. He sees this as a way of evading history, but he is also aware that the structuralist rejection of narrative in favor of fragmented, rule-bound systems is appealing in the contemporary critical climate.

The Prison-House of Language was welcomed by critics for its elucidation of French structuralism and the tracing of its Russian roots, even as its Marxist biases were noted. The *Virginia Quarterly Review* called it "a brilliant and provocative book"; W. L. Ballard in *Library Journal* noted that Jameson's "grasp and presentation of fundamentals in his materials are awe-inspiring in their breadth and clarity" and said the book "should be read by everyone interested in modern thought." In *Yale Review*, however, Jonathan Culler—then engaged in his own book on structuralism—stated that Jameson's book recorded "his struggles toward a statement that has not yet taken shape, a pattern that will not form."

What would help to make the statement take shape, however, was the fact that Jameson's encounter with structuralism in *The Prison-House of Language* had introduced him to the so-called "structural Marxists," Louis Althusser and Pierre Macherey. In particular, Jameson had absorbed Althusser's sense of ideology. In traditional Marxist thought, ideology is the false consciousness that a society creates in order to hide from itself the unpalatable truth about real economic and political relationships. As such, ideology is expected to "wither away" after the proletarian revolution that leads to the worker's state, since it will be unnecessary in a completely just society. Althusser, on the other hand, views ideology as a "representational structure" that allows the individual to consider his or her own lived experience in relation to the social structure or to history. Ideology in this sense would always be necessary, no less after the revolution than before. Also in contrast to other Marxists, Althusser and Macherey do not present ideology as completely coherent, a seamless web. The contradictions between the way things work and what a given society says about the way things work create "gaps" and "fissures," but we are not necessarily aware of these gaps. In portraying lived experience, however, literature often brings these gaps to the foreground by its inner contradictions. Society represses its internal contradictions, but by carefully reading literary texts we are often able to witness the "return of the repressed," the surfacing of the fissures in the ideology of a society. Here we see the working of the "political unconscious."

Thus, in 1981, when Jameson finally presented his own dialectical theory of literature in his most celebrated and to date most important book, *The Political Unconscious: Narrative as a Socially Symbolic Act*, he was developing and working out motifs and lines of thought that had already appeared in his two previous works explicating Marxist and structuralist theory, and in his 1979 book *Fables of Aggression*, on the modernist Wyndham Lewis. The notion, originally in *Marxism and Form* and *The Prison-House of Language*, of literature as an "allegory" in which texts encode both the "false consciousness" of their age and its "utopian" dreams is here elaborated into a fourfold system of meanings which, as in medieval hermeneutics or in the scheme of Northrop Frye, holds literal, allegorical, moral, and anagogical levels of meaning. In addition, Jameson adds two other methodological figures of speech to assist in the analysis of texts. One is the "rectangle" of the structural linguist A. J. Greimas. The rectangle systematizes the narrative text the way an equation systematizes relationships between numbers. For example, in

Conrad's *Lord Jim* Jameson sees various characters and their actions embodying "value" and "activity" in all the possible combinations. Jim himself embodies both value and activity; the pilgrims to Mecca on the Patna represent value combined with nonactivity; the buccaneers (such as Jim's nemesis, Gentleman Brown) represent nonvalue combined with activity, and the lazy, exploitative "deck-chair sailors" who briefly appear combine nonvalue with nonactivity. The other new element in Jameson's repertory of critical techniques is what he calls the "molecular" and "molar" aspects of the allegorical representation of ideology in narrative. Generally, Marxist critics have dealt with the large-scale features of a text—plot and themes—to the exclusion of its fine structure. Jameson calls this the "molar" level ("molar" referring to the overall mass of a substance). Jameson believes, however, that the political thematics of narratives can also be found at the "molecular" level of the structure of individual sentences and demonstrates, in passages from Balzac's "La Vieille Fille" Dreiser's *Sister Carrie*, and Conrad's *Lord Jim* and *Nostromo*, that the political unconscious operates at the level of the style of individual sentences.

The reception of *The Political Unconscious* was very favorable: it quickly became the critical text most frequently cited in other criticism. The reviewer in *Choice* (1981) called the book "monumental": its "learning and range of reference are exceeded only by the imperial embrace of its complex argument." David Punter in *Criticism* judged it a "vital contribution to cultural study, packed with solid argument yet glittering with energy and urgency." Jonathan Arac, in *Modern Fiction Studies*, found Jameson's results going "decisively beyond" other commentators on Conrad and the other novelists he discusses. William E. Cain, in the *Sewanee Review*, while complaining of "dense and clotted prose" that "tests the reader's patience from beginning to end," called *The Political Unconscious* "a rich, provocative, and important study of several of the most pressing issues in contemporary criticism: the relation between theory and practice, the meaning and relevance of literary history, and the 'politics' of literature." A few post-Althusserian Marxists disagreed with the favorable assessment. For example, Terry Eagleton, in the *New Left Review*, suggested that Jameson's subtle analyses of the "utopian moment" in various nineteenth-century texts, while transcending the tendentious arguments of "vulgar Marxism," seemed to have also transcended its revolutionary spirit and its identification with the oppressed: "The question irresistibly raised for the Marxist reader of Jameson is simply this: how is a Marxist-Structuralist critique of a minor novel of Balzac to help shake the foundations of capitalism?"

After *The Political Unconscious*, Jameson, perhaps considering his mapping of the historical basis of literary narrative essentially complete, and perhaps feeling literature is no longer the chief mode of expression of culture, became more a cultural than a literary critic. The "texts" upon which he works are much more likely to be films or buildings than novels stories. *Signatures of the Visible* and *The Geo-Political Aesthetic: Cinema and Space in the World System*, collect Jameson's essays on film written between 1979 and 1992. Many of these essays attempt to demonstrate by using popular films some of the same insights he had presented in *The Political Unconscious*: that "all contemporary works of art . . . have as their underlying impulse—albeit in what is often distorted and repressed unconscious form—our deepest fantasies about the nature of social life, both as we live it now, and as we feel in our bones it ought rather to be lived," as he said in *Signatures*. Thus the Mafia family in Coppola's *Godfather* films is simultaneously an unconscious distortion, an allegory of modern life and a utopian fantasy. The study of film also allows Jameson to compare and contrast with Western cinema the films of Russia, China, and the Third World, and the differences in "cognitive mapping" in these cultures at disparate levels of development.

Jameson's film criticism received mixed reviews from the professionals. In *Film Quarterly* Richard Allen accused him of displaying "all the narcissistic scholarly and writerly failings of his . . . mentor in critical theory, Jean-Paul Sartre," but after attacking Jameson's manner, Allen praised his "sensitivity to both history and aesthetics," a combination "too rare in an era of increasing specialization." John Higgins applauded the "unusual vigour and agility of Jameson's readings" of Western, Soviet and Third World cinema, though in the long run he suggests that Jameson's "allegorical method constantly threatens repetition and reduction," so that it is the "instance of reading" rather than Jameson's "system" that inspires confidence in its value.

The most ambitious of Jameson's books after *The Political Unconscious* is clearly *Postmodernism; or, The Cultural Logic of Late Capitalism* (1991). Assembled from essays published since 1984, *Postmodernism* shows the contemporary world suffering from a crisis in which our cultural representations parody and subvert themselves. Painting seems to consist of random gestures, pillaging or burlesquing various moments of the artistic past, an artistic scene in which "there is no there there," no anchoring contemporary style. Architecture evokes the past in its details, but creates new forms of space that disorient and immobilize the individual trapped within them. The contemporary media present the various levels of the past simultaneously: children can watch cartoons from the 1940s and television situation comedies from the 1950s; rock stations play "golden oldies" from the 1960s and 1970s along with the music of today. The audience response to what Jameson calls the "spatialization" of culture is a "waning of affect." Modernist angst disappears with the disappearance of the monadic bourgeois "self," but so does all other intense emotion: cultural products are received instead with "free-floating and impersonal" feelings, a mild collective euphoria.

The ultimate cause of these cultural and psychological phenomena is what Jameson calls "late capitalism," its unfathomable bureaucratic web and the fragmented social system that it fosters. In many ways the individual today is even more alienated from any vision of supportive community and rewarding work than the wage slave of the Industrial Revolution. In the post-industrial West, factories have often been moved by multinational corporations to the Third World, where wages are low, leaving service industries and the large-scale corporate activities of finance and marketing. But at the same time in late capitalism the traditional Marxist distinction between economic base and cultural superstructure begins to dissolve, as the primary business of the First World becomes the creation of culture itself for everyone: designs for manufactured objects, architectural planning, media programming, information and information systems.

Postmodernism drew a mixed response from its reviewers, who were generally overawed by Jameson's "easy mastery of the vocabularies of so many expert cultures—architecture, philosophy, literary theory, political economy, film theory among them," as the reviewer for *Choice* (1991) put it. The book's being assembled from previously published articles gave some readers the sense of reading the same chapter over and over again. Stephen Howe, in *New Statesman & Society,* suggested that Jameson's is "at worst . . . a cheap magician's trick in which the dialectic becomes the fairy wand that transmutes all oppositions into some grand but misty totality." And Geoffrey Galt Harpham, writing in the *Times Literary Supplement,* felt that, after the "spectacular" opening chapter, the book became "sporadic, more personal, more loosely structured, less compelling," concluding as it

does with "a 110-page essay that one feels might have gone on for ever."

Jameson described *Postmodernism* as "the third and last section of the penultimate subdivision of a larger project entitled 'The Poetics of Social Forms.' " We can therefore expect further volumes from Jameson on the other two major style systems of recent times, realism and modernism—in addition to whatever Jameson will want to study in the other subdivisions. His cultural criticism, however, will probably continue to explore the political unconscious of artistic representations—the truth behind the false consciousness of ideology that is allegorically expressed in fictions, and its utopian fantasy rooted in eternal human desire.

PRINCIPAL WORKS: Sartre: The Origins of a Style, 1961, 2nd ed. 1984; Marxism and Form: Twentieth-Century Dialectical Theories of Literature, 1972; The Prison-House of Language: A Critical Account of Structuralism and Russian Formalism, 1972; Fables of Aggression: Wyndham Lewis, The Modernist as Fascist, 1979; The Political Unconscious: Narrative as a Socially Symbolic Act, 1981; The Ideologies of Theory: Essays 1971–1986 (Volume I: Situations of Theory; Volume II: The Syntax of History) 1988; Modernism and Imperialism, 1988; Late Marxism: Adorno in the Stream of Time, 1990; Signatures of the Visible, 1990; Postmodernism; or, The Cultural Logic of Late Capitalism, 1991; The Geo-Political Aesthetic: Cinema and Space in the World System, 1992.

ABOUT: Dictionary of Literary Biography 67, 1988; Dowling, W. C. Jameson, Althusser, Marx: An Introduction to "The Political Unconscious," 1984; Frow, J. Marxism and Literary History, 1986; MacCabe, C. preface to Geo-Political Aesthetic, 1992; White H. The Content of the Form, 1987. Periodicals—Choice June 198, April 1991, September 1991; College Literature Spring 1983; Contemporary Review June 1981; Criticism Fall 1981; Diacritics 12 1982; Film Quarterly Summer 1991, Summer 1993; Journal of American Culture Spring 1993; Library Journal May 15, 1972; October 15, 1972; Modern Fiction Studies Winter 1982; Modern Language Review June 1994; Nation October 15, 1990; New Left Review May–June 1981; New Republic February 19, 1990; New Statesman March 1980, New Statesman & Society March 15, 1991; Sewanee Review October 1981; Southern Humanities Review Summer 1993; Times Literary Supplement June 8, 1973; August 28, 1981; May 24, 1991; June 28, 1991; August 13, 1993; Virginia Quarterly Review Spring 1973; Yale Review October 1972, December 1972.

JANOWITZ, TAMA (April 12, 1957–), American novelist and short story writer, was born in San Francisco, California, to Julian Frederick Janowitz, a psychiatrist, and Phyllis (Winer) Janowitz, a poet. When Janowitz was

TAMA JANOWITZ

five her family moved to Amherst, Massachusetts, where her father had been appointed head of the mental health department at the University of Massachusetts. After her parents divorced, she and her young brother lived with their mother, who supported them with poetry grants before eventually becoming an assistant professor of English and poet-in-residence at Cornell University. With little money and no television, the family read voraciously, but talked little. Janowitz often accompanied her mother to poetry readings, and afterwards would criticize the other poets. "She was really very clever," her mother recalled in a 1986 *New York* interview. "What she was objecting to was anything phony, pretentious, you know, saying nothing and trying to make it sound like something very important." The family moved frequently, but eventually settled in Lexington, Massachusetts, where Janowitz graduated from high school in 1973, a year ahead of her class.

At Barnard College in New York City, Janowitz majored in creative writing and became a prolific short story writer. Her work won many awards, including a Bread Loaf Writer's Conference scholarship in 1975, the Elizabeth Janeway Fiction Prize in 1976, the Amy Loveman Prize for Poetry in 1977, and a guest editorship of *Mademoiselle* in 1977. After earning her B.A. in 1977, she worked for a short period as an assistant art director at an advertising agency, and then won a fellowship at Hollins College in Virginia, where she received an M.A. in 1979. While at Hollins, she wrote her first novel, *American Dad*, and sent out portions of it under

the name Tom A. Janowitz because she had gotten no response using the name Tama. The *Paris Review* accepted a section of the novel, and the entire work was published under Janowitz's real name in 1981.

With *American Dad*, Janowitz displayed an energetic flair for satire which would become her trademark. Modeled on her own family, the novel is narrated by Earl, the elder of two sons of Robert Abraham Przepasniak, a domineering, oversexed psychiatrist, and Mavis, a late-blooming, eccentric poet. During an argument long after their divorce, Robert accidentally kills Mavis when he breaks down the door she has barricaded herself behind, causing a postage meter to fall on her head. Robert is jailed on manslaughter charges, and Earl takes off on a coming-of-age journey through Europe. Reviewers universally praised the first half of the book which focuses on the parents, but found the second half, in the words of Garrett Epps of the *New Republic*, to be "thin gruel." Although Epp's praised Janowitz's "precious satirical eye" and "sensuous writing," he complained that "Earl's adventures are mostly filler, marring what is otherwise one of the most impressive first novels I've read in a long time." David Quammen wrote in the *New York Times Book Review* that "Janowitz has a fine comedic inventiveness, especially as applied in light dabs to character," but her "inventiveness is consistently undermined by the lack of grace—and even more so, precision—in her language."

Despite the generally positive reviews, *American Dad* sold fewer than a thousand copies. By 1984, Janowitz had written four more novels, but could get none of them published. Frustrated, she decided to focus on short stories. By this time, she was a habitué of the downtown Manhattan art scene, and she began taking notes at parties and art openings, recording conversational tidbits and odd details that illuminated the milieu. Incorporating these details imbued her new stories with vitality, and the *New Yorker* soon published *The Slaves of New York*, about Eleanor, a passive jewelry designer who lives with a volatile artist named Stash. More of Janowitz's stories appeared in the *New Yorker*, as well as in *Mississippi Review*, and *Harper's*.

A collection of these and other stories, *Slaves of New York*, was published in 1986. Eleanor and many other characters are made "slaves" by the cost of housing in New York, living with people they do not love simply because they cannot afford to live alone. Janowitz explained in an interview with the *Washington Post*: "When I say slaves of New York, I mean people come here as slaves to something. They're a slave to their sis-

ter's apartment. They're a slave to ambition—
they want a job in publishing at the best salary.
Or they don't fit in their hometown and they're
a slave to that. Everyone in this country who was
a misfit in their hometown comes to New York."
Like Eleanor and Stash, who reappear in many
of the stories, most of the characters are artists,
designers, models, or artdealers. With a satirical
eye and deadpan voice, Janowitz constructs vivid portraits of such odd characters as a Jewish
southern belle, who is making a living as a prostitute, and a pompous painter, Marley Mantello,
who plans to construct his own chapel next to the
Vatican. Despite their pretensions, the characters are often insecure or awkward, always feeling a bit outside of or behind the trendy world
they inhabit.

Because of Janowitz's sardonic style and evocation of the New York scene, many reviewers
compared her to Fran Lebowitz and Jay McInerney. R. Z. Sheppard of *Time* found Janowitz's
work less accomplished than Lebowitz's, saying
Lebowitz has "more and better one-liners,"
while Janowitz "piles on more bizarre details
with a heavy hand." Although "her stories can
have arresting beginnings," he continued, she
"has no follow-through. Part of the problem is a
lack of structure that presumably is meant to
mirror the shapelessness of her characters' lives.
Also her language is grating and imprecise." But
in the *New Statesman* (1987), Victoria Radin
wrote that "the book could easily serve as a document of the mores of the New York art scene in
the late Eighties." Radin complimented Janowitz's balance, observing that she "writes
about people who are not terribly nice with an
underlying hopefulness that they'll get nicer;
and she shows how little control they have over
themselves or their lives without pitying or inflating them." Alice H. G. Phillips concurred in
the *Times Literary Supplement* (1986), noting
that Janowitz "observes everything with a sharp
eye but with a New York bohemian's true affection for her world." Others, however, felt that
the distance with which Janowitz views her
characters makes the stories shallow. In the *New
York Times Book Review* (1986), Jay McInerney
remarked that the stories were "fun" because
they "reflect a downtown esthetic, a campy
postmodernism," but regretted that the characters never "experience catharsis or epiphany."
Similarly, Carol Anshaw observed in the *Village
Voice* that Janowitz "takes the comfy chair just
above the action and chooses as protagonists the
one-dimensional foible-filled sorts who used to
turn up as side characters. . . . While this
makes for breezy, amusing stories, it keeps her
from reaching in, pulling out the really interesting stuff—passion and fear and heartbreak."

Even before *Slaves of New York* was published, Janowitz had become a celebrity. Her
youth and style made her a member of the
"literary brat pack" that included McInerney,
Bret Easton Ellis, and other writers who actively
courted fame. Janowitz became a close friend of
Andy Warhol, who told her, "Don't pay attention to *what* they write about you. Just measure
it in inches." She became involved in the flamboyant promotion of *Slaves,* handing out excerpts on the streets and starring in the first
"literary video" on MTV, intended to sell the
book to young viewers. The advertising campaign was so successful that *Slaves* became the
first short story collection to reach the best-seller
list since 1959. It fared less well as a film, in
1989, for which Janowitz wrote the screenplay.
Produced by Merchant and Ivory, distinguished
for their screen adaptations of Henry James and
E. M. Forster, it was directed by James Ivory and
starred Bernadette Peters as Eleanor. Released
with a splashy advertising tie-in with Bloomingdale's fashion boutiques, it received unfavorable
reviews and did poorly at the box office.

A Cannibal in Manhattan, Janowitz's second
novel, was a revised version of one of her earlier,
unpublished novels. More farcical than her previous work, the novel is a picaresque tale of a
"noble savage" among the real savages of New
York. Mgungu Yabba Mgungu, the president of
a South Pacific island, is brought to New York
by Maria Fishburn, an heiress who saw his picture on the cover of *National Geographic* years
earlier and fell in love with him. The couple
marry, Maria is murdered, Mgungu unwittingly
eats her, and then traverses the various social
strata of New York. In the *TImes Literary
Supplement* (1988), Peter Reading called the
novel "amusing" and wrote that it "is at its best
when dealing with the seedy. The cartography
of garbage-and-stray-dog waste land is impeccable. Mgungu's sojourn with the winos is funny
compassionate and productive of a humane
Dickensian character-sketch." Most reviewers
were less generous. "Narrated by a cartoon, populated by cartoons, the book has no emotional
center, no depth, little engages or moves us,"
Francine Prose wrote in the *New York Times
Book Review* (1987). According to Victoria
Radin, in the *New Statesman* (1988), "Glib cynicism cancel out the jokes and there is simply too
much knowingness." Although Radin believed
that "the book is rescued by a high-spirited sympathy for its hero and the author's eye for sensuous detail: smells, colors, and tastes," she
dismissed the novel as "a private joke that should
have stayed in the closet." Even more critical
was Jonathan Yardley of the *Washington Post
Book World* who wrote that the novel "is utterly

devoid of originality, energy, thematic purpose, charm—you name it, *A Cannibal in Manhattan* hasn't got it."

Janowitz rebounded from this critical drubbing with her 1992 novel, *The Male Cross-Dresser Support Group*. Pamela Trowel, a single, jaded Manhattanite who sells advertising for *Hunter's World* magazine, is surrounded by lascivious men, shrewish women, and garbage. She befriends a young boy named Abdul and takes him in, making no attempt to find out where he came from. After getting fired and fearing that Abdul will be taken away from her, she hits the road "in the time-honoured, wide-horizoned, strike-out-for-the-gold tradition of disaffected America," wrote Giles Foden in the *Times Literary Supplement* (1992). Because she is wanted by the police, when Pamela returns to New York she disguises herself as a man to hunt for the disappeared Abdul, eventually becoming involved in the eponymous group. In the *New York Times Book Review* (1992), Robert Plunket called Janowitz's comic voice "one of the best in the business," noting that "it is instantly recognizable—precise, fearless, with the intuitive rhythm of someone who was born funny. Not a syllable is out of place. She goes off on tangents, to be sure, but with such authority that the reader follows her everywhere, fascinated." Foden agreed, praising the "many hilarious set-pieces which give the novel it anarchic feel." Recognizing he compassion, Foden also wrote, "Relentless in her satirical portrayal of the hunters in the 'hunter's world,' it is remarkable that, while going through so many fictional hoops, Tama Janowitz can still keep back some pity for the hunted. She shows that there can be deviancy without depravity and that America's most peculiar citizens may yet be its most precious cultural assets. Sceptics . . . will discover in this funny, disturbing anti-*Bildungsroman*, something more than literary junk food."

Tama Janowitz and her husband Tim Hunt, a curator for the Andy Warhol estate, live on the Upper West Side of Manhattan. In 1985, Janowitz earned an M.F.A. from Columbia University, and the following year she was a fellow at Princeton University. She has received two National Endowment for the Arts grants and was writer-in-residence at the Fine Arts Work Center in Provincetown, Massachusetts.

PRINCIPAL WORKS: American Dad, 1981; Slaves of New York, 1986; A Cannibal in Manhattan, 1987; The Males Cross-Dresser Support Group, 1992.

ABOUT: Contemporary Authors 106, 1982; Contemporary Literary Criticism, 43, 1987; Current Biography Yearbook 1989; Schumacher, M. Reasons to Believe:

New Voices in American Fiction, 1988. *Periodicals*—Esquire November 1988; New Republic June 6, 1981; New Statesman February 27, 1987; March 4, 1988; New York July 14, 1986; New York Times September 6, 1992; New York Times Book Review May 17, 1981; July 13, 1986; October 4, 1987; August 30, 1992; Time June 30, 1986; Times Literary Supplement December 12, 1986; March 4, 1988; October 30, 1992; Village Voice August 5, 1986; Washington Post August 30, 1986; Washington Post Book World September 25, 1987.

JOHNSON, CHARLES (RICHARD) (April 23, 1948–   ), American novelist and writer of short stories writes: "From the day in 1970 when I dedicated myself to writing fiction I had one intention only: the creation of a body of work that would develop the wing on American literature known as 'philosophical fiction.' As a lifelong student of philosophy, Eastern and Western, and as someone drawn to Buddhism since the late age of nineteen, this orientation was probably inevitable. In my late teens and early twenties I often relaxed from the study of philosophy by reading fiction—Sartre's novels and plays, the fiction of Camus, Santayana, Herman Hesse, Thomas Mann, Aldous Huxley, and Jack London were some of my youthful favorites because here the perennial questions of philosophy were dramatized. I was also drawn to the works of Richard Wright, Ralph Ellison, and Jean Toomer for the same reason, but beyond these three I saw nothing in African-American literature that approached what we might call the 'novel of ideas.'

"It's is worth pointing out, I suppose, that before making a commitment to this species of literature I was a professional cartoonist. In elementary school in Evanston, Illinois, where I was born in 1948, my art teachers had all praised my drawing ability. I must confess that from childhood forward art was a refuge for me, an experience so necessary—like breathing—that, at age ten or eleven, I'd spend my Sunday mornings sketching on the streets of downtown Evanston; I raided the public library for every book on painting I could find, and pored over every printed image that came my way.

"So by age fourteen I was determined to pursue a career as a commercial artist. After completing a course in cartooning taught by the prolific, New York-based writer/artist Lawrence Lariar, I began publishing both stories and drawings when I was seventeen. During the seven years I devoted to comic art I published over 1,000 drawings in a variety of publications, worked as an editorial cartoonist and journalist, sold one-page scripts to comic books, created and

CHARLES JOHNSON

hosted an early PBS series on how to draw, and published two collections of black political drawings. But by 1970 I began to feel I'd pretty much exhausted my expressive and exploratory capacities in this medium, and my interest shifted to the philosophical possibilities of the novel.

"I wrote six novels in two years, one every academic quarter I was in college from 1970 through 1972. I often refer to these a 'apprentice' (or learning) novels. The first was a precursor to *Oxherding Tale* and a story I wrote in the 1980s called "China," insofar as it concerned the progress of a black American martial artist through Eastern philosophy (I've been in the martial arts since I was nineteen and now codirect a Seattle school that teaches the Choy Li Fut system of grandmaster Doc-Fai Wong). The second was about the African slave trade, and it was in this 1971 manuscript that I began the research for *Middle Passage*.

"But, as I've said, none of these early novels— which were more or less influenced by some of my favorite writers at the time (John A. Williams, Baldwin, Wright)—achieved what I wanted; I had yet to find a satisfying way to interface philosophy and black fiction. Fortunately, as I was completing my last year in the master's program in philosophy at Southern Illinois University, novelist John Gardner was teaching his last year there in English. We met in his office and at his home to go over what became my seventh novel, *Faith and the Good Thing*. All in all, this became a very important friendship for me. Not only was I exposed to Gardner's highly original ideas about art as he

developed them (they appear later in such works as *The Art of Fiction* and *On Moral Fiction*), but through him I was exposed at an impressionable age to the highly disciplined habits of a *total* writer. He was one of two or three (if that many) American novelists who can be said to have had an aesthetic position; he was a fiction writer with whom I could discuss intellectual history from the pre-Socratics to R. G. Collingwood; a man who lived for literature as I had previously lived for drawing, and who left us before his death in 1982 one of the most diversified and complex bodies of work in American literature.

"Gardner was a guide and model then, but only up to a point. As I moved through the Ph.D. program in philosophy at SUNY-Stonybrook, where I concentrated on phenomenology and aesthetics, and completed everything except my dissertation (I wrote two drafts, and this later became the critical book *Being and Race*), I found that we differed in many ways in our interpretations of black life, black literature, the proper relationship between fiction and philosophy, and on the value of Eastern thought, which became increasingly important to me as a way of life after the publication of *Faith and the Good Thing*, the birth of my son Malik a year later, and when I accepted the responsibilities of a professor at the University the year after that. In other words, I needed in my late twenties a Way (or *do*, as the Japanese say) to bring every aspect of my life—art, fatherhood, profession—together in a spiritually satisfying manner, and it was in the tradition of Buddhism (one of the world's most demanding religions, intellectually and ethically) that I found the means to do this. To a certain extent, *Oxherding Tale*, which was composed between 1975 and 1980 (I threw out 2,400 pages to realize the 350 pages of the finished manuscript) was the novel where I took my first steps away from Gardner and developed the courage to write about what concerned me most: namely, questions of cultural identity.

"In that novel, in *Middle Passage*, and in the short stories I've published, the central question—the most driving concern—is the mystery of the self and personal identity. It's true that the novels and stories throw a wide net over many philosophical issues (the nature of art, of desire, scientific problems, ethical dilemmas, ontology, perception, our experience of wealth, the epistemology of film), but at the heart of all these fictional meditations the foundational question is, who am I? What is consciousness? What is the self? It is not a question for which I seek a final answer. In philosophy, especially phenomemnology, and in science, we can only achieve provisional answers; we can explore a theme or a problem through character and situations, come to a conclusion in a particular work, but in the *next* work we must resume the unearthing process again, going back to reexamine all our conclusions and premises.

"Thus, when I write I try in each work to appropriate a different literary form (or tradition), sometimes using the tale, sea story, slave narrative, parable, fable, or science fiction tradition. Formal variations, I've come to see, allow different avenues or approaches to age-old questions and force me to explore these problems in a different way with each new fictional project. This same interest in formal virtuosity has also led me to write in other genres—screenplays for television and motion pictures, criticism, essays, and a great deal of book reviewing—in order to discover to greater and greater degrees the possibilities of expression through the forms of language we inherit from so many cultures.

"Strange to say, though, I only reluctantly call myself a writer. As when I was in my teens, I simply say I'm an artist who sometimes will body forth what he has to disclose through drawing, sometimes through fiction, and most often—or so I hope as a lay Buddhist—through the smallest details of daily life."

Accepting the National Book Award in November 1990 for his novel *Middle Passage*, Charles Johnson paid tribute to Ralph Ellison, whose *Invisible Man*, he said, set a new path for black American fiction. For the decade of the 1990s Johnson envisioned "a fiction of increasing intellectual and artistic generosity, one that enables us as a people—as a culture—to move from narrow complaint to broad celebration."

As a student of philosophy as well as a writer Johnson has been concerned with examining basic assumptions about African American writing. In his critical study *Being and Race: Black Writing Since 1960* he rejected naturalistic fiction—"misery-filled protest stories about the sorry condition of being black in America"—because it constricts the imagination, perpetuating stereotypes and confining the writer to a "splintered perspective." Johnson pleads for "whole sight," which he defines as "both the promotion of a 'black' or 'female' perspective in fiction and a *broadening* of our expressions and vision of these perspectives. What is at stake is the fundamental question of how we see life in general and black life in particular." He told the *New York Times* in 1991 that he sees black writers of the future moving "from ideology in the narrowest political sense" to broad philosophical questions like "what it means to be a human being who is black."

Johnson's novels make no concession to easy popularity. They are unconventional in plot, combining graphic detail (his early career as a cartoonist has left its mark on his fiction) with wild flights of the imagination. He sprinkles his generally brisk, straight forward prose with startling diction: anachronisms (his early 19th-century characters often have distinctly 20th-century voices); archaisms; and mouth-filling, dictionary-daunting words—*ostrobogulous, pungled, mubblefuddled, refocillated.* He introduces magic into the grim realities of human suffering, mingled terror and tragedy with light-hearted, sometimes burlesque humor. Reviewing *The Sorcerer's Apprentice*, his collection of short stories, in the *New York Times* in 1986, Michiko Kakutani praised Johnson's "narrative finesse—his ability both to rework old legends and to create a glowing alloy of the colloquial and the mythic, the naturalistic and the surreal."

In *Faith and the Good Thing*, Johnson's first published novel, the technique shows less "finesse" than in his later fiction, but Johnson was clearly on the path. Faith Cross, his heroine, whom John Skow described in *Time* as "a rural Candide," pursues her quest for the "Good Thing" from the Georgia swampland where she grew up to the brothels of Chicago's ghetto where she meets her fiery death and an apotheosis, reincarnated in Georgia as the swamp witch who had initially sent her out on the quest, a conjure woman spouting philosophy, Skow observed, "as if she were Hegel." The "Good Thing," Faith eventually learns, is the discovery of oneself as a whole person. Part folktale and legend, drawing on both African tradition and European philosophy from Plato to Sartre, the novel had mixed reception from reviewers. For Pearl K. Bell in the *New Leader*, "[H]omiletics drown out the fictional vitality, and the result is less art than sermon." But Annie Gottlieb in the *New York Times Book Review* found it "a flawed yet still fabulous book, at its best as a many-splendored and ennobling weaving-together of thought, suffering, humor and magic." Like the protagonist of Ellison's *Invisible Man*, Elizabeth A. Schultz observed in the *College Language Association Journal* in 1978, Faith travels the path of the American black experience; but unlike him, "she envisions a way to reconcile the many with the one."

Johnson defies the conventions of storytelling even more boldly in *Oxherding Tale*. His primary medium is the slave trading narrative: a first-person account of a slave who, after many adventures both terrible and comic, achieves freedom in the antebellum South. Along the way the light-skinned young narrator, conceived in a drunken joke when the plantation master and his slave switched places in their wives' beds, has experiences that fall somewhere between those of Fielding's Tom Jones and those of the real Frederick Douglass. "When I look back on my life," he reflects, "it seems that I belonged by error or accident—call it what you will—to both house and field, but I was popular in neither, because the war between these two families focussed, as it were, on me, and I found myself caught from my fifth year forward in their crossfire." The young man is physically attractive, hardy, resourceful, fortified with a sense of humor and an extraordinary education, supplied by his tutor, a transplanted New Englander named Ezekiel Sykes, who teaches him Greek, Latin, mathematics, music, literature, and, above all, philosophy. Part of the young man's education comes from an imaginary visit to the plantation by Karl Marx, who scorns Ezekiel's philosophy and speaks with a comedian's German accent: "'You vant to say that the Transcendental Ego is empty—correct?—and exists only through vhat is conscious of, which means, as in Hegel, that alienation in the Other is necessary in every act of perception?'"

Oxherding Tale (its title alludes to a group of pictures by a twelfth-century Zen artist), though not widely reviewed, won critical approval as a successful blending of "allegorical satire" with "historical realistic fiction." Steven Weisenburger wrote in *Callaloo*: "The writing moves in a middle ground between the cultures of the East and West, between realism and parable . . . Johnson's real gifts are a sense of voice and a delight in skewing one's formal expectations." In the *Village Voice* Stanley Crouch concluded that "Charles Johnson has enriched contemporary American fiction as few young writers can, and it is difficult to imagine that such a talented artist will forever miss the big time that is equal to his gifts."

Johnson reached that "big time" in 1990 when his *Middle Passage* won the National Book Award for Fiction, the first time a black writer had been so honored since Ellison won the award in 1953 for *Invisible Man*. The selection of the book was not unanimous, however, and reflected some division among the award jurors, one of whom was quoted in the *New York Times* as saying that "ethnic concerns, ideology and moral self-righteousness" had compromised their considerations.

Middle Passage is a first-person narrative, in the form of the journal of Rutherford Calhoun, a freed slave, recording his adventures from June 14 to August 20, 1830, on a slave ship sailing the middle passage from New Orleans to the West Coast of Africa to pick up a cargo of slaves.

Young and extremely well educated, Calhoun seeks to escape gambling debts and a forced marriage by impulsively stowing away on the ironically named *Republic*. Not until the ship is well out of harbor does he discover that it is a slaver and a death ship: "a kind of fantastic Black Maria, a wooden sepulcher whose timber moaned with the memory of too many runs of black gold between the New World and the Old." The captain is a sadistic but intelligent and well-read dwarf on a mysterious quest for an African god, and most of the crew are drunk, diseased, and depraved:

> We were forty of a company. And we'd all blundered, failed at bourgeois life in one way or another—we were, to tell the truth, all refugees from responsibility and, like social misfits ever pushing westward to escape citified life, took to the seas as the last frontier that welcomed miscreants, dreamers and fools.

In the end, Calhoun returns to America—"this land of refugees and former indentured servants, religious heretics and half-breeds, whoresons and fugitives—this cauldron of mongrels to all points on the compass"—and calls it "home."

Clearly, the *Republic* is on an allegorical voyage, its reality as a slave ship layered with literary echoes. Johnson acknowledges in an introductory note "many sea stories and histories of ships from many cultures." Thomas Kenneally wrote in the *New York Times Book Review* that despite "a frequent straining for meaning, an unnecessary portentiousness . . . this is a fiction that holds the mind."

Middle Passage, like Johnson's earlier novels, troubled some reviewers with its unorthodox technique and frequently mannered language. As the story of a slave ship that spares no gruesome detail of the sufferings of its human cargo, its swings into swashbuckling adventure and almost slapstick comedy are at times disconcerting. John Haynes, in the *Times Literary Supplement*, remarked on the shifts of mood: "It would not be difficult to take a solemn view of Johnson's book on the grounds that slavery, like the Holocaust, is much too serious to be used as for the purposes of entertainment, that the novel is a deflection rather than a penetration of the past." But Johnson takes a broader perspective in this novel. The humor, he told a reporter for the *New York Times*, as well as the florid diction and the anachronisms were intended as an effort "to close the distance between the past and present . . . a kind of ironic winking at the reader."

In addition to the National Book Award, Johnson received a grant from the National Endowment of the Arts while he was working on *Oxherding Tale*; that novel won the Callaloo

Creative Writing Award in 1983. The same year he also received the Governor's Award for Literature from the State of Washington. His short story "China" won a citation from the Pushcart Press in 1984 and another story, "Exchange Value," appeared in the *Best American Short Stories of 1982.* His work for Public Television, which began with "Charlie's Pad," his how-to-draw show, includes the film *Charlie Smith and the Fritter Tree,* written in 1978 for the PBS Visions Series. This is the story of a 135-year-old former slave who had been brought to America from Liberia as a child and lived through the Civil War into the Civil Rights movement. In 1983 he collaborated with John Alman on the PBS program *Booker.* Johnson is the son of Benjamin Lee and Ruby Elizabeth (Jackson) Johnson. He married Joan New, a teacher, in 1970; they have a son, Malik, and a daughter, Elizabeth.

PRINCIPAL WORKS: *Novels*—Faith and the God Thing, 1974; Oxherding Tale, 1982; Middle Passage, 1990. *Short stories*—The Sorcerer's Apprentice, 1986. *Cartoons*—Black Humor, 1970; Half-Past Nation Time, 1972. *Nonfiction*—Being and Race, 1988. *Drama*— Olly Olly Oxen Free, 1988; All This and Moonlight, 1990.

ABOUT: Contemporary Authors 116, 1986; Contemporary Literary Criticism 7, 1977; 51, 1989; Dictionary of Literary Biography 33, 1984; LaBlanc, M. L. (ed.) Contemporary Black Biography 1, 1992. *Periodicals*—Callaloo October 1978; Fall 1984; Winter 1984; College Language Association Journal December 1978; September 1986; New Leader December 23, 1974; New York Review of Books January 17, 1991; New York Times February 5, 1986; November 28, 1990; January 2, 1991; New York Times Book Review January 12, 1975; March 30, 1986; July 1, 1990; Obsidian 1980; Studies in American Fiction Autumn 1991; Time January 6, 1975; Times Literary Supplement June 7, 1991; Triquarterly Fall 1991; Village Voice July 19, 1983.

JOHNSON, PAUL (BEDE) (November 2, 1928–), British historian and journalist, was born in Barton, England, to William Aloysius and Anne Johnson. His father (memorialized in the dedications of *A History of the Modern World* as "artist, educator, and enthusiast") was proprietor of a small art school. From him Johnson acquired a lifelong interest in painting, particularly landscapes, and he himself is an amateur watercolorist. He was brought up in what he describes as "a strictly Catholic household." According to his own testimony he planned to be a historian from his earliest years, but his mother hoped he would become a priest, and towards

that end his first education was conducted by Jesuits at Stonyhurst College in Lancashire. Subsequently he entered Magdalen College, Oxford, where he was awarded a B.A. with honors in history in 1950.

Johnson began his professional career as a journalist, first in Paris from 1952 to 1953 on the multilingual journal *Réalités,* and subsequently in London on the *New Statesman* when that paper was edited by Kingsley Martin. In his essay "The Art of Political Journalism," which introduces his collection of pieces from the *New Statesman* titled *Statesmen and Nations,* Johnson acknowledges in particular the influence of Aylmer Vallance, who taught him the art of writing effective editorials, stressing succinctness and specificity ("workable conclusions in persuasive language," in Johnson's words). From 1965 to 1970 he was the editor of the *New Statesman,* a period which saw its widest circulation and influence. He espoused socialism and mingled freely with Labor politicians. The pressures of the post led him to resign to devote himself to his own writing.

In 1957 Johnson married Marigold Hunt, a book reviewer and public affairs administrator. They raised their family (three sons and a daughter) in a rural 18th-century house in Buckinghamshire far from the "seedy materialism of London," as he told an interviewer. There he wrote most of the books for which he became famous, at the rate of one a year. Concurrently he maintained a flat in London to consult libraries and write his columns for the *Spectator* and other papers to which he continued to contribute after he left the *New Statesman.*

In the prologue to one of his first historical studies, *The Offshore Islanders,* in which he attempts to trace the origins of the English nation, Johnson denies any sharp distinction between the journalist and the historian. For him, both are equally involved with "the discovery and elucidation of truth," and with clarifying human events. "A good journalist casts anxious and inquiring glances over his shoulder," he writes, "and a good historian lifts his eye from the page to look at the world around him." His extensive output indeed displays remarkable versatility. Descriptions of great landmarks are presented in *A Place in History* (written as text to accompany a series of documentary films presented by Thames Television), *The National Trust Book of British Castles,* and *British Cathedrals* (some of which he sketched). His strong religious faith is conveyed in *Pope John XXIII* and *Pope John Paul II and the Catholic Restoration. Elizabeth, Ireland: Land of Troubles,* and *A History of the English People* are explorations of the British heritage begun with *The Offshore Islanders*. He even has one novel to his credit, *Left of Centre*. However, he established his reputation and reached his widest readership with a group of more historical works, cosmopolitan in scope: *Enemies of Society, A History of the Modern World from 1917 to the 1970s* (retitled *Modern Times* in America), *A History of Christianity*, and *A History of the Jews*.

Johnson's break with the *New Statesman* signaled a shift in his political position from socialism to conservatism, which became increasingly evident in his polemical writings. From the mid-seventies on (in the words of Robin Blackburn in "The End of the Tether," which appeared in the *New Statesman* after Johnson's departure), he "unloosed a series of extraordinary vicious attacks, first on the trade unions and the Labour Party, and then on an ever widening range of targets from ecology to modern art, from the philosophy of Herbert Marcuse, to the Notting Hill carnival."

These views are distilled in *Enemies of Society*, an inquiry into "the basic causes of the decline of civilizations." Here Johnson traces a succession of "take-offs and collapses" throughout history, from the Graeco-Roman period to the 1970s, when he detects "a new and sombre mood of introspection," indicative of a need to reexamine our values. The lifeblood of civilizations for Johnson springs out of "the spirit of economic and political liberalism, embodied in an urban middle class." Decline sets in when this healthy situation is tampered with in any way: monarchy and slavery destroyed ancient civilizations; in the Middle Ages, society regressed from urbanism to an agricultural economy; modern industrialism and capitalism have been threatened by collectivism and excessive government regulation. "The prose is lucid, the tone is forthright," wrote the playwright Tom Stoppard in the *Times Literary Supplement*, "which may be a polite way of saying there is something to infuriate almost everybody." Other reviewers were impressed by Johnson's grasp of social ills, but felt that his diagnosis of them was simplistic, and his cures were vague.

In 1980 and 1981, Johnson was a Resident Fellow and De Witt Wallace Visiting Professor of Communications at the American Enterprise Institute in Washington, D.C., a conservative think tank. The principal product was *A History of the Modern World from 1917 to the 1980s*, which focuses on the impact of what Johnson calls "statism." World War I, the event that sets off this study, is especially significant for Johnson because, unlike wars of the nineteenth century which restored the status quo, it marked the dis-

integration of the old order, substituting the "shibboleths" of nationalism and self-determination. Furthermore, the Treaty of Versailles, intended to secure world peace, sowed the seeds of World War II. Concurrently, in the realm of ideas, Johnson singles out as key modern figures Marx, Einstein, and Freud, who "combined to undermine, in their different ways, the highly developed sense of personal responsibility, and of duty towards a settled and objectively true moral code," that had been central to European civilization. The bulk of the book traces the consequences of bureaucratic bungling and moral confusion from the New Deal to "The Collectivist Seventies."

Some scholars found Johnson's perspective constricted and questioned his assumptions, but the book was widely praised in the popular press. The poet Stephen Spender, in his review in the *Atlantic*, hailed it as "a work of intellect and imagination"; to the sociologist Robert Nisbet it was "truly a distinguished work of history" (*New York Review of Books*. The American edition of *A History of the Modern World, Modern Times*, was named among the Best Books of 1983 by the *New York Times*. According to Melik Kaylan ("The Chutzpa of Paul Johnson," *Connoisseur*, February, 1989), its author became "the toast of Reagan's Washington." An especially ardent admirer of the American edition was Richard Nixon, on whom Johnson wrote a tribute in *Commentary* in October 1988.

Religion and politics are interwoven for Johnson as early as *The Offshore Islanders*, in which he traces the roots of the breaking off of what became the British nation from the Roman Empire to the Pelagian Heresy. This connection is intensified in *A History of Christianity* and *A History of the Jews*. In *A History of Christianity*, taking issue with those who regard the critical methods of historical research incompatible with religious faith, Johnson argues that Christianity, "by identifying truth with faith, must teach—and, properly does teach—that any interference with the truth is immoral." In its 2,000-year span, the book vividly recalls the various epochs of the Christian Church from its origins in "the Jesus sect" (considered its best part by some reviewers), to its dissemination by Paul, to its spread ("From Martyrs to Inquisition"; "Mitred Lords and Crowned Ikons") and splintering ("The Third Force"; "Faith, Reason, and Unreason"), carrying the record forward to the Second Vatican Council and its aftermath. Feeling that by the mid-1970s, when the book was published, the predominance of Christianity was on the wane as an influence on human destiny, Johnson was prompted to write the book, as he states in its preface, by the need for "a retrospect and balance sheet." Accordingly, accomplishments are weighed against failures. The religion inspired by Jesus "has not made man secure or happy or even dignified," Johnson concludes. "But it supplies a hope. It is a civilising agent. It helps to cage the beast. It offers glimpses of real freedom, intimations of a calm and reasonable existence."

Some reviewers of *A History of Christianity* felt that Johnson fell short of the highest scholarship. Philip Toynbee, writing in the *Critic*, thought it "a very able history of Christianity in relation to the political and intellectual history of Western Europe," but "the essence of true Christianity has simply been left out." The theologian Martin Marty observed in the *New York Times Book Review* that Johnson had read widely but not deeply in the sources, concluding that "newcomers may be stunned by the clusterings of proper names, far too many of them misspelled. . . . But it is hard to picture newcomers or professionals losing interest or failing to be informed along the way."

Shortly after *A History of the Jews* was published, Johnson confided to an interviewer that as a boy in Lancashire, red-haired, Catholic, and left-handed, he knew what it was to be a pariah, making him especially sympathetic to victims of anti-Semitism. Spread out over four millennia beginning with Abraham, and ending with "the role of secular Zionism today," the book thoroughly bears out its opening statement: "The Jews are the most tenacious people in history." Johnson finds the Jews remarkable because, having survived through three-quarters of the history of civilization, they "stand right at the centre of the perennial attempt to give human life the dignity of a purpose."

A History of the Jews was generally well received, though some historians spotted gaps or faults of emphasis. Melik Kaylan pointed out in *Connoisseur* that Johnson left out the atypical relations of the Jews with Islamic Spain and Ottoman Turkey. Arnaldo Momgliano in the *New York Review of Books* noted Johnson's failure to consider the mystical side of Judaism. Martin Gilbert (in *Commentary*), while welcoming Johnson's "powerful reminder of the Jewish achievement throughout the ages," thought that he made the Jews out to be too passive under the Nazi regime in Germany.

Intellectuals, Johnson's next book, is an examination of a group of "free spirits, adventurers of the mind," ranging from Rousseau to Noam Chomsky linked rather tenuously as geniuses who promoted "themselves as possessing the moral authority to transform society, a claim that Johnson disputes," according to T. L. Cooksey in *Library Journal.* Jaroslaw Anders, in the

Times Literary Supplement, noted that "Johnson believes that the seeds of intellectual error are to be found in defects of character. . . . He seems so eager to condemn his subjects . . . that he confuses his evidence and often succumbs to trivial sensationalism."

The Birth of the Modern: World Society 1815–1830, the longest of Johnson's synchronic histories, covers the shortest period of time, a decade and a half which he views as especially significant for having launched both England and America as world powers. Some scholars felt that Johnson did not really define "modernism," ad found *The Birth of the Modern* rambling.

"Writing is a matter not of inspiration, but of application," is Johnson's response to interviewers who have expressed wonder at his prodigious output, which he attributes to efficient work procedures acquired from journalism and preparing scripts (more than forty) for television documentaries. In particular he has found the television writer's technique of blocking out scenes on index cards useful in organizing his books. He claims that once he has done his requisite research and worked out his structure (the most important stage for him), the writing proceeds with relative ease: "By the end, it becomes a visual process which I often do on the floor."

Apart from labor unions and government interference, Johnson's favorite targets are tabloid journalists who go after scandal rather than news. (On one occasion he successfully sued *Private Eye* for libel.) In the interest of improving newspaper standards, he has served on the Royal Commission of the Press and remains a member of the national Union of Journalists. Among honors he has received are the Francis Boyer Award for Services to Public Policy (1979) and the King Award for Excellence in Literature (1980). Robin Blackburn sums up his politics as an evolution from "reactionary radical" to "radical reactionary." "A leftist turned rightist, a Catholic who is a fierce Zionist, a journalist who advocated censorship," in the word of Malik Kaylan, "Johnson is a controversial and contradictory figure."

PRINCIPAL WORKS: The Suez War, 1957; Journey into Chaos, 1960; Merrie England, 1964; Statesmen and Nations, 1971; The Offshore Islanders: England's People from the Roman Occupation to the Present, 1972 (in U.K.: From Roman Occupation to European Entry); (with G. Gale) The Highland Jaunt, 1973; The Life and Times of Edward III, 1973; Pope John XXIII, 1974; Elizabeth I: A Biography, 1974 (in U.K.: Elizabeth I: A Study in Power and Intellect); A Place in History, 1975; A History of Christianity, 1976; Enemies of Society, 1977; Britain's Own Road to Serfdom, 1978; The Civilization of Ancient Egypt, 1978; Civilizations of the Holy Land, 1979; A Tory Philosophy of Law,

1979; British Cathedrals, 1980; Ireland: Land of Troubles, 1980 (title varies in subsequent editions); (with I. Kristol and M. Novak) The Moral Basis of Democratic Capitalism, 1980; The Things That Are Not Caesar's, 1980; The Recovery of Freedom, 1981; Pope John Paul II and the Catholic Restoration, 1982; Modern Times: The World from the Twenties to the Eighties, 1983 (in U.K.: A History of the Modern World from the Twenties to the Eighties); The Aerofilms Book of London From the Air, 1984; A History of the English People, 1985: Saving and Spending: The Working-Class Economy in Britain, 1870–1939, 1985; A History of the Jews, 1987; Intellectuals, 1988; Castles of England, Scotland, and Wales, 1989; Cathedrals of England, Scotland and Wales, 1990; The Birth of the Modern: World Society 1815–1830, 1991; Wake Up Britain! A Latter-Day Pamphlet, 1994. *Novel*—Left of Centre, 1960. *As editor*—The Oxford Book of Political Anecdotes, 1986; (with others) Unsecular America, 1986; Stravinsky Retrospectives, 1988; Workers Versus Pensions; Intergenerational Justice in an Aging World, 1990; American Government: People, Institutions, and Policies, 2nd ed., 1990.

ABOUT: Contemporary Authors New Revision Series 34, 1991; Current Biography Yearbook, 1994; Johnson, P. *Introduction to* Statesmen and Nations, 1971; Who's Who 1991; *Periodicals*—Atlantic August 1983; Commentary June 1987; Connoisseur February 1989; Critic Winter 1976; Critical Quarterly Winter 1989; Economist October 8, 1988; October 7, 1989; Economist October 8, 1988; October 7, 1989; Harpers, September 1977; Library Journal march 1, 1989; Nation September 17, 1977; national Review June 24, 1983; April 21, 1989; New Statesman December 14, 1979; October 17, 1988; New York Review of Books August 5, 1976; October 27, 1983; October 8, 1987; July 20, 1989; New York Times April 14, 1988; New York Times Book Review January 28, 1973; October 20, 1974; July 16, 1976; June 26, 1983; March 26, 1987; March 12, 1989; June 23, 1991; New Yorker September 6, 1976; November 26, 1979; Newsweek August 22, 1983; Publishers Weekly May I, 1987; Times Literary Supplement may 28, 1971; September 15, 1972; May 11, 1973; July 12, 1974; June 3, 1977; April 21, 1978; July 8, 1983; May 30, 1986; October 17, 1986; April 22, 1988; January 26, 1990; February 23, 1990; September 6, 1991; U.S. News & World Report March 27, 1989.

JOSEPH, JENNY (May 7, 1932–), English poet, novelist, and children's writer, was born into a Jewish family in Birmingham, the second daughter of Louis and Florence Joseph. She was, she tells *World Authors*, originally named Jenny. She went up to St. Hilda's College, Oxford, in 1950, where she gained favorable notice from Dame Helen Gardner, the literary critic. She graduated from there with Honours in English in 1953. From 1953 until 1957 she worked in newspaper journalism. She lived in South Africa (1957–1959), working as a journalist (Drum Pub-

JENNY JOSEPH

lications) and teaching; this experience, in particular, the observation of apartheid, a system of rigid racial segregation and discrimination against the black majority, was intellectually formative. It caused her to develop the humane attitudes expressed in such poems as "Living Off Other People—Welfare," which has been printed separately in the United States. Asked to leave South Africa, she returned to Great Britain, married, and with her husband, Anthony Coles, operated a pub until 1972. Her husband, by whom she had three children, died in 1985. She taught languages from 1972 until 1974, and thereafter worked in adult education and extramural departments. Since the late 1980s she has lived in a small village near Gloucester.

Jenny Joseph began publishing her poems in periodicals while still a student. Her first collection, *The Unlooked-For Season*, was well-received, and won the Eric Gregory Award in 1961. But it was with *Rose in the Afternoon and Other Poems* that Joseph really made her mark, especially since this included the first printing of her best-known poem, "Warning," particularly admired in the United States, where it has been taken up by feminists and groups concerned with aging:

When I am an old woman I shall wear purple
With a red hat which doesn't go, and doesn't suit
me. . . .
shall sit down on the pavement when I'm tired
And gobble up samples in shops and press alarm
bells
And run my sticks along the public railings
And make up for the sobriety of my youth. . . .

This is an example of a thoroughly worthy "popular poem." Nevertheless, in its bitterly ironic last three lines it does begin to approach her best:

> But maybe I ought to practise a little now?
> So people who know me are not too shocked and surprised
> When suddenly I am old, and start to wear purple.

Such love-poems as "The Sun Has Burst the Sky", which begins

> The sun has burst the sky
> Because I love you
> And the river its banks.
>
> The sea laps the great rocks
> Because I love you
> And takes no heed of the moon dragging it away
> And saying coldly "Constancy is not for you."

were applauded for their directness of expression and lyric energy. As Joseph makes eminently clear in "The Life and Turgid Times of A. Citizen" and its subtitle "PROEM: *Against metaphor—but how then?*":

> I am not going to talk to you about islands
> Or about waving grasses.
> I am not going to mention the lakes that the moon fills
> (Although there was a moon this morning, a very fine one) . . .
>
> Oh no, if I want to say louse, pig or bastard
> That people are bullies and like to watch others fall
> On these broken pavements, and never lend a hand
> Except to keep themselves up, I should say their names.

Joseph's popular touch is clearly seen in her (only occasionally expressed) critical opinions. She admires such writers as the popular historical novelist Margaret Irwin and the even more popular science writer R. M. Dawkins. Yet along with this appreciative "ordinary-person" warmth towards the superficial or modish, goes a keen interest in such unfashionable but certainly not superficial thinkers as Hans Vaihinger, author of *The Philosophy of "As If"* (1916). It is in "as if" fiction that, as a prose writer, Joseph is most interested. Although her work it has become more colloquial over the years, Joseph has still to reconcile her feelings toward the currently "acclaimed" as opposed to the truly lasting. Of postwar English woman poets she is certainly one of the most widely read, and this depth and breadth of her reading shows, although quite unobtrusively, in her compassionate and subtle work, in particular in her poems. She is at her best in such powerful and deeply personal poems as "Lure," in which she perfectly achieves her own voice:

> Someone a long way off is using my blood.
> Maybe sip-sipping it when they lap the rain,
> Maybe not getting the extra nourishment,
> Maybe not tasting, in glasses they drink, the iron. . . .

Jenny Joseph has said that "the work of mine that comes nearest to writing what I wanted is *Persephone.*" The book alternates between verse accounts of the mythic story of the goddess Demeter, who must share her daughter for part of the year with Hades, the god of the Underworld, and prose pieces set in contemporary times. The main line of the narrative is carried by the verse: "Powerful, efficient, Demeter is wearied by / The help men need from her, her endless journeys / To barren pathetic farms to make things grow. . . . " Her search for her lost daughter is paralleled with vignettes of troubled mother-daughter relationships in the shifting values of modern society. The book has been praised for Joseph's ongoing concern for women. Beyond its feminist implications, however, it reconstructs a timeless ancient myth in a modern domestic setting. Joseph writes in a note appended to *Persephone*: "The suggestion is not only that every disaster has its counterpart in its due season but the more fatalistic one that without time in the Underworld, without surrender to the powers of darkness, without loss, there can be no birth or fruition: no winter—no summer."

Robert Nye praised *Persephone* in the London *Times* in 1986, but with some reservations. Calling it perhaps "a female counterblast to the works of D. M. Thomas" (widely regarded, whether fairly or unfairly, as a misogynistic writer), Nye felt that the prose parts of the work were "light." Other readers have felt that the verse is dilute by Joseph's own best standards, and that the prose, in its attempt to link the grandeur of myth with the "ordinary life," is a little sentimentalized and lacking in sharp descriptions of the vices that beset even the most "banal" of people—meanness and envy being two universal ones in particular that she seems not (in her work as yet) fully to acknowledge. This volume required special printing and presentation; this kind of production its British publishers, unfortunately, were unable to provide. But *Persephone* means much to her, and, in a projected work on lines at least roughly similar (certainly, as she has remarked, it will be "fiction"), provisionally entitled "Extended Similes," she will perhaps surprise her small but now growing audience of serious readers.

Reviewing *Selected Poems* in the *Times Literary Supplement*, George Szirtes remarked on the "crisp and crystalline" qualities of Joseph's best poems. "They discover a world living in the clutches of disappointment and mortality, but open to the possibility of intense delight in minute but dazzling particulars of nature and in rare acts of human kindness. . . . her nervous energy works on substantial experience with a vast appetite."

Joseph herself in "The Inland Sea," from *Beyond Descartes* has provided a kind of poetic raison d'etre. She speaks of a dream in which she is reassured by the fact that old sages "journey ever" to seek the inland sea. But she asks, "Why do I, a life time late, these years after / Talk of dreams, fabricating premises / . . . when the direct truth / And the direct lie are muddied by convenience / And compromised." Her answer:

The hidden, ancient, still-fructifying source
Silent shines in sunlight.
Can you see? Come a bit nearer then. Now.
Look: we have come to the inland sea.

PRINCIPAL WORKS: *Poetry*—The Unlooked-For Season, 1960; Rose in the Afternoon and Other Poems, 1974; The Thinking Heart, 1978; Beyond Descartes, 1983; The Inland Sea: A Selection from the Poetry of Jenny Joseph, 1989; Selected Poems, 1990; (with R. Mitchell) Beached Boats, 1991; Selected Poems, 1992; Ghosts and Other Company, 1995. *Juvenile*—Nursery Series: Boots, Wheels, Wind, Water, Tea, Sunday (6 vols.), 1966–1968. *Fiction*—Persephone, 1986.

ABOUT: Contemporary Poets, 5th ed., 1991; Dictionary of Literary Biography, 1985. *Periodicals*—Times (London) September 19, 1976; June 18, 1986; December 3, 1991; Times Literary Supplement May 28, 1993.

JUST, WARD (SWIFT) (September 5, 1935–), American novelist, short story writer, and journalist, was born to Franklin Ward and Elizabeth Swift Just in Michigan City, Indiana, and grew up in Waukegan and Lake Forest, Illinois, north of Chicago. He attended two private high schools: Lake Forest Academy in Illinois and the Cranbrook School in Michigan. At the former, he has recalled, a remedial English teacher wryly encouraged him to become a writer, despite his "dismal" grades. F. Scott Fitzgerald was the literary hero of his adolescence, as later he would lionize Ernest Hemingway, Henry James, and William Faulkner.

After attending Trinity College in Hartford, Connecticut, from 1953 to 1957, Just returned home to write for the *Waukegan News-Sun*, an influential conservative newspaper published by his father's family. To his family's consternation, he left in 1959 to become a reporter for *Newsweek* in Chicago and Washington. Covering the capital in the early days of the Kennedy administration deeply influenced Just's fiction writing. He remained in Washington from 1962

WARD JUST

to 1963 as a political correspondent for *Reporter* magazine, then joined the London Staff of *Newsweek*. During a six-month stay in Spain in 1964, Just made an unsuccessful attempt an fiction writing. This failure, confirmed by a caustic editor, convinced him that "I was not finished with journalism, nor journalism with me; that would take another five years, and Vietnam."

Just went to Vietnam in late 1965 as a newly hired *Washington Post* correspondent. His affecting stories about ordinary soldiers enhanced his reputation as a journalist and won him the Washington Newspaper Guild Award in 1966 and 1967 and the Overseas Press Club Award in 1967. Despite a serious grenade injury in June 1966, Just did not leave Vietnam permanently until the following May. Before returning to Washington, he took a leave of absence in Ireland and wrote *To What End: Report from Vietnam*. John Sack, also a Vietnam reporter, writing in the *Washington Post*, called the nonfiction work "a panorama of Vietnam's people, politics, and meaningless disasters in a picture built of the most delicate of pointillist dots." Like Sack, *Newsweek* and *New York Times* reviewers admired Just's journalistic style: unpolemical, reasoned, and cool, allowing the story to tell itself.

Just told a reporter for the *Times* that being a war correspondent was "as good as it was ever going to get for me. I could go out and cover other stories or political campaigns, but it was like running the same horse around the same track." He again attempted the leap from news to novel with *A Soldier of the Revolution*, about an

American who sides with his guerrilla captors during a Latin-American insurrection. Some critics praised the work's intelligence and evocation of bungled American intervention abroad. Others, however, thought the book self-conscious and lacking in artistic perception. After *Soldier*, Just reverted to nonfiction with *Military Men*, a study of the United States Army and the changes it underwent in the Vietnam era. The piece originally appeared as two long articles in the *Atlantic* and won the National Magazine Award for nonfiction in 1970. Richard R. Lingeman, in the *New York Times*, called the book a "sharp, discerning portrait" and a "fine, taut, involved job of reporting."

Despite the mixed reception of *A Soldier of the Revolution*, Just made a decision to forsake journalism for fiction writing. He resigned from the *Washington Post* in 1970 and made "a sort of living" by writing short stories. The *Atlantic* magazine, where he served as contributing editor from 1971 to 1984, published many of his early stories. In 1973, nine of them were collected in *The Congressman Who Loved Flaubert and Other Washington Stories*, which won the 1974 Washington political book award and extensive critical acclaim. *Los Angeles Times* reviewer Charles Solomon praised Just's "crisp, straightforward style" and the book's success in portraying American government better than "many civics texts." Other reviewers, noting Just's admiration of Ernest Hemingway, suggested that Just might follow Hemingway's path from journalism to short stories to novels.

Not surprisingly, Just did exactly that. Finding Washington inhospitable to fiction writing, he moved to rural Vermont. In his first post-Washington book, *Stringer*, Just revisited the Vietnam experience. The title character, an intelligence agent sent on a guerrilla mission, loses his sanity after being captured by the enemy. The *New Republic*'s reviewer praised the book for sorting out the "ironies growing out of the Vietnam imbroglio." Although many criticized the book's unanswered moral questions and frustratingly obscure surrealism, *Time* called Just "one of several promising American writers now creeping up on the big novel."

Just appears to have woven autobiographical threads into his next two novels, *Nicholson at Large* and *A Family Trust*. *Nicholson at Large* chronicles the personal and professional crisis of a Washington journalist who has become so consumed by previous relationships and events that he can't function in the present. Finally, he chooses to battle his past by writing about it, "cold in the knowledge that he could survive history." In the *New York Times Book Review*, Christopher Lydon termed the novel "puzzling and incomplete." Alan Cheuse, in *Nation* (1976), complimented Just's expression of "deep, credible feelings in a political novel" but regretted that Nicholson and the book remain "at large." In *Newsweek*, Arthur Cooper praised Just for his understatement and promoted him from a "promising" to a "heavyweight" novelist.

A Family Trust relates the demise of a family newspaper. Its three "heroes," according to Doris Grumbach in the *Saturday Review*, are "the newspaper itself; the town . . . fighting against the advances of progress and development; and the . . . family; held together for a while . . . until without the founder's unilateral vision, it finally disintigrates." Grumbach's comments conclude, "for towns like Demeut, the war against ugliness and bigness is over, but we can enjoy accounts of the battle in novels like Ward Just's." *A Family Trust* pleased most reviewers with its ambiguous storytelling. Some noted the novel's slow pace, but found Just's prose, like his characters, controlled and energetic. In *Newsweek*, James N. Baker praised especially the novel's "ironic and touching" resolution of the conflict between change and tradition.

Along with novels, Just continued to write short pieces, three of which merited inclusion in *Best American Short Stories* in 1972, 1973, and 1976. Later stories won a National Magazine award for fiction in 1980 and O. Henry awards in 1985 and 1986. Just collected six of his short works in *Honor, Power, Riches, Fame, and the Love of Women*. The main characters include war correspondents, a truce-negotiator, a CIA agent, and a congressman, all of whom "survive by mobilizing a pragmatic cynicism," according to D. Keith Mano in the *National Review*.

Just next published another Washington novel, *In the City of Fear*, set during a Georgetown dinner party in which the moral and political predicaments of several characters and of Washington itself in the Vietnam era are delineated in flashbacks. Arnold Klein, in the *Nation* (1982), called the flashbacks "tortuous" and the language "rambling [and] thinky," despite some shrewd aphorisms. Jonathan Yardley concluded in the *Washington Post Book World* that "Just is a writer of considerable sophistication, but in his earnest desire to teach the lesson of Vietnam—and the lesson that moral commitment must not be shied away from—he resorts to a clumsy apparatus."

Just perhaps sought a resolution to his own Vietnam conflict, as well as his main character's, in *American Blues*. An unnamed journalist writing a history of Vietnam cannot compose the final chapter until he returns to Saigon. There he realizes that he cannot simply summarize and give meaning to such an absurd, inextricable event, but can only attach importance to abstract ideas like honor and hope. Just's strengths of style and political and historical knowledge impressed reviewers, though they found his characters superficial and the ending inconclusive.

With *The American Ambassador*, Just stepped away from both war and Washington, but continued to sound the depths of senseless violence and the tension between public and private responsibility. Bill North, a patriotic American diplomat, finds his son has joined a German anti-American terrorist group. Reviewers declared the novel convincing in its complexity: a successful interweaving of political intrigue, emotional conflict, and psychological stress. Comparisons with Joseph Conrad stemmed from Just's ability to integrate politics and characterization and to keep the novel going at several levels; another literary comparison suggested by the book's title and its examination of American and European differences was to Henry James. In the *New York Times Book Review*, Robert Stone described *The American Ambassador* as Just's best work, "charged with authenticity. There is a wide variety of splendid portraits foreign and domestic; Mr. Just can create characters more effectively in a paragraph than some do in an entire volume."

Just wrote *the American Ambassador* while writer-in-residence at Phillips Andover Academy in Massachusetts from 1982 to 1984. Two years later, while reading in Paris, he wrote his most acclaimed Washington novel, *Jack Gance*. As he maneuvers Gance from his first job as a pollster in Chicago to a seat in the U.S. Senate, Just examines the conflicts between political ambition and personal ethics and loyalties. Tom Dowling of the *San Francisco Examiner* cited Just's functional but elegant portrayal of "real people driven by ordinary passions," In the *New York Times* Judith Martin crowned him the "Washington novelist's Washington novelist," a label that Just has rejected as limiting and incorrect. "They are novels that happen to take place in Washington, that often have political or journalistic context to them. They are not Washington novels any more than they are Chattanooga novels or Philadelphia novels," he told Elizabeth Mehren of the *Los Angeles Times* in 1983. "*Jack Gance* is at least as much a Chicago book as it is a Washington book." The *Chicago Tribune* agreed with this assessment and gave Just the 1989 Heartland Award for fiction, which recognizes outstanding writing about the midwest.

In 1990, after sifting through thirty-three pieces he had written over two decades, Just compiled *Twenty-one: Selected Stories*. Through a wide range of places, circumstances, and characters, Just explores the themes of public versus private life, ethical quandaries, and interpersonal relationships. The spectrum of his work led commentators to proclaim him stronger on the subjects of men, Saigon, and Washington than on women and Europe, but nonetheless a masterful storyteller. *New York Times* reviewer Herbert Mitgang noted that Just is the rare writer who successfully moves from reporting to fiction: his stories "go beyond colorful journalism; they have something vital to say about our striving, sometimes disappointing style of life."

In *The Translator*, Just portrays the thwarted lives of German translator Sydney van Damm and his American wife Angela. The novel is set primarily in Paris from 1989 to 1990, amid the turbulence of the Berlin Wall's collapse and German reunification. Angela wants to leave Paris to quell her own turmoil, as Sydney explains to his old friend Junko Poole:

> "We have a word for it in German, *Entzauberung*. Truly, German is the language of anxiety. It means disenchantment and melancholy, a profound sense of the falseness of things. It is the sense that life falls short."

When Junko offers lucrative pay for translating documents related to the illicit sale of Warsaw Pact weapons, Sydney ill-advisedly accepts. In the *Dallas Morning News*, Philip Selb applauded Just's "splendid ability to show how moments in the continuum of world history become interwoven with events in individuals' lives." Robert Towers, in the *New York Review of Books*, found the male characters uncompelling, on the other hand, and the prose often "too worldly, too allusive, too obviously rhetorical."

Best known for his Washington novels and stories, Just broaches compelling and often unsettling subjects. "The working life, the [Vietnam] war, political, love affairs, and marriage," he wrote in the preface to *Twenty-one*, "seem to be the waters on which my boats set sail, men and women glaring at their compasses and navigating home—or anyway a port of convenience, some consoling anchorage, someplace *else*."

Just has two daughters, Jennifer and Julia, by his first wife, Jean Ramsay, and a son, Ian, by his second wife, Anne Burling. With his third wife, Sarah Catchpole, he now divides his time between Paris and Martha's Vineyard, Massachusetts.

PRINCIPAL WORKS: *Novels*—A Soldier of the Revolution, 1970; Stringer, 1974; Nicholson at Large, 1975; A Family Trust, 1978; In the City of Fear, 1982; The American Blues, 1984; The American Ambassador, 1987; Jack Gance, 1989; The Translator, 1991; Ambition & Love, 1994. *Short stories*—The Congressman Who Loved Flaubert and Other Washington Stories, 1973; Honor, Power, Riches, Fame, and the Love of Women, 1979; Twenty-one: Selected Stories, 1990. *Nonfiction*—To What End: Report from Vietnam, 1968; Military Men, 1970.

ABOUT: Contemporary Authors New Revision Series 32, 1991; Current Biography Yearbook 1989; Who's Who in America 1992–1993. *Periodicals*—Atlanta Journal April 15, 1990; Common Cause Magazine, March/April 1989; Dallas Morning News October 27, 1991; Los Angeles Times, January 29, 1989; Los Angeles Times Book Review June 10, 1990; Nation February 7, 1976; October 30, 1982; National Review October 26, 1979; New Republic April 6, 1974; New York Review of Books January 16, 1992; New York Times January 1, 1971; May 9, 1990; New York Times Book Review December 20, 1970; October 26, 1975; September 9, 1979; March 15, 1987; Newsweek October 13, 1975; April 24, 1978; Publishers Weekly March 13, 1987; San Francisco Examiner January 3, 1989; Saturday Review April 15, 1978; Time July 8, 1974; Virginia Quarterly Review Summer 1971; Washington Post April 7, 1968; Washington Post Book World September 26, 1982; Washington Times September 24, 1991; October 14, 1991.

ISMAIL KADARE

*KADARE, ISMAIL (January 28, 1936–), Albanian novelist and poet, was born in Gjirokastër, in the south of Albania. His father worked in the civil service. The boy grew up during the turbulent years of World War II in a country occupied successfully by fascist Italy, Nazi Germany, and the U.S.S.R. His novel *Kronikë në qur* (1971, Chronicle in stone) is told from the point of view of a child who might well be Kadare himself remembering his early years—children playing games against a background of blackouts, searchlights, aerial bombardments, witnessing the arrests (and usually executions) of neighbors suspected of working with the resistance movement. During the German occupation he fled with his family to the mountains; they returned when the fighting ended to find their town ravaged. "It was not easy to be a child in that city," he writes. Eight at the time hostilities ended, he attended primary and secondary schools in Gjirokastër and went on to study languages and literature at the University of Tirana from which he received a teacher's diploma in 1956. He began publishing poems and journalism and attended the Gorki Institute in Moscow for advanced study in world literature. In 1961, after Stalin's death and the cooling of relations between Albania and the U.S.S.R., he returned to his homeland where he soon won recognition as a poet and novelist.

Kadare's most popular novel in Albania—and,

after its translation into French and English his best known novel abroad—was *Gjenerali i ushtrisë së vdekur* (*The General of the Dead Army*), published in 1963. Although endorsed by the rigidly Communist Albanian state, the novel is not polemical or propagandistic. Its success in Albania was the result of Kadare's portrait of the Albanian people. Their suffering and their endurance under foreign occupation are graphically presented. Robert Escarpit wrote in his preface to the American edition of book: "A country of feudalism and serfs, without roads or schools, forgotten on Europe's fringes, the Albania of yesterday had scarcely any literature at all; though she had always had, and still retains, a strong tradition of oral poetry. Now, on the twenty-fifth anniversary of his country's liberation, Ismail Kadare is presenting his readers not merely with a novel of world stature . . . but also . . . with a novel that is the voice of ancient Albania herself, speaking to today's world of her rebirth."

The general of the title is Italian (though his nationality is never stated) on a mission to Albania, years after the occupation and war, to repatriate the remains of his fellow soldiers. For him the country is especially bleak and sinister, but he is dedicated to his grisly duties, seeing himself "like a new Messiah, copiously provided with maps, with lists, with the infallible directions that would enable him to draw them up out of the mud and restore them to their families." Gradually, however, his disgust with his work overwhelms him. "I have a whole army of dead men under my command," he observes bitterly.

°keh DAH ray

"Only instead of uniforms the are all wearing nylon bags." He is also increasingly aware of the implacable resistance of the Albanian people. "Do you know what the Albanian people remind me of?" he asks the priest who accompanies him on the mission. "They remind me of the sort of wild beast that at the approach of any danger, before leaping or charging, freezes into immobility in a state of extreme tension, muscles coiled, every sense on the alert. This country, I feel, has been exposed to so many perils for so long that a state of extreme alert like that has become second nature to it." The general completes his work, but not before he has suffered an almost total nervous breakdown and moral collapse, and the novel ends with a sense of frustration and futility. The Communist authorities regarded *The General of the Dead Army* as a powerful nationalistic statement. But, as Janet Byron suggested in an article in *World Literature Today* in 1979, the novel invites other readings: "Kadare weakens the allure of this notion by showing that while vice is unevenly distributed, suffering is not. The wartime intruders and their descendants do not suffer any more on account of their corruption, nor do the Albanians suffer any less because of their virtue."

Kadare consistently approached Albania's national identity with a subtlety—some have called it an ambiguity—rare in Communist-approved literature. Though a committed Marxist he is no ideologue. He was in fact accused in 1982 by the president of the League of Albanian Writers and Artists of deliberately evading politics by cloaking much of his fiction in history and folklore, writing in a deliberately oblique style that some have described as Kafkaesque.

In the novel *Dasma* (1968, *The Wedding*), the heroine is rescued from a traditional arranged marriage in the backward north by government orders assigning her to factory work in the south. There she meets and marries a man she loves, defying her father and ancient tradition. This novel was received in Albania as a tribute to the "enlightened" dictatorship of Enver Hoxha, who came to power in 1944 and died in 1985. But the same decade Kadare was also publishing short stories of a more politically subversive character. A collection of these, *Qyteti i jugut* (The southern city, 1964) juxtaposed scenes of peasants blinded by superstition and tribal feuding with stories that depicted state officials as persecutors of even the mildest political dissenters. Fundamentally Kadare is concerned with the liberation of Albania from its backward past. He supported communism to the extent that it promoted such liberation. He served as a delegate to the People's Assembly in 1970 and—rare in Communist states—he was given freedom to travel and to publish abroad. He offended the authorities, however, in 1975 with a politically satirical poem and for the next three years was forbidden to publish.

With *Keshtjella* (1970, *The Castle*), a story of Albania's struggle against the Ottoman Turks in the 15th century, and *Ur me tri harge* (The three-arched bridge, 1978) Kadare returned to the politically safer historical mode. Both novels portray a feudal Albania threatened by a foreign conqueror. The narrator of the later novel is a priest who is represented sympathetically (significant because modern Albania is an atheist state), and the plot involves the ancient custom of immurement. It is framed as a mystery with the narrator gradually unravelling dark secrets of corruption not only in the ruling classes and the foreign invaders but rooted also in the ignorance and superstition of the Albanian people themselves. Nowhere in Kadare's fiction is the haunting presence of medieval legend more impressive than in *Invitation was Doruntine* (1986, *Doruntine*). This too is a mystery story with a medieval sleuth, not a clergyman here but the secular chief constable of his region.

> He [the officer] headed for the door of the house to go inside. 'The Vranaj are no more!' another voice said. He raised his head to see who had uttered these words, but his eyes, instead of seeking out someone in the small crowd, rose unconsciously to the eaves of the house, as though the voice had come from there. For some moments he did not have the strength to tear his eyes away. Blackened and twisted by storms, jutting out from the walls, the beams of the wide porches expressed better than anything else the dark fate of the line that had lived under that roof.

A widowed mother's six sons have died in war; her only daughter, Doruntine, is married to a foreigner who has taken her to a distant land. The novel begins with the simultaneous deaths of the mother and daughter, who has obviously fled her husband accompanied by a mysterious figure, reported to be her elder brother risen from the dead. The officer's unenviable task is to solve the mystery of Doruntine's return and identify her companion while steering clear of the divisions that existed within the Albanian church. Medieval Albania caught in a struggle between Byzantium Rome, East and West, resonated with political implication for Kadare's 20th century Albanian readers.

Even more pointed in its challenge to political orthodoxy was *Nëpunësi i pallatit të ëndrrave* (The employee of the palace of dreams, 1981; translated as *The Palace of Dreams*), a political allegory and Kadare's most daring novel. The central character is a young man, the descendant of a long line of distinguished civil servants, who goes to work in the Tabir Sarrail, "one of our great imperial state's most important institutions . . . the first in the history of the whole world to have institutionalized the interpretation of dreams. . . . " His job in this vast bureaucracy is to select, sort, and interpret the dreams of the populace for the purpose of capturing for the rulers the signal dream presaging their overthrow. For some unknown reason, while a purge of top officers takes place around him, he is singled out for promotion to chief of the whole operation. At the end the passive young man accepts his fate: he walks about the city, but it is beginning to pale for him. "A few years hence neither the wonders nor the horrors of this would have any effect on him; they were, after all, pale copies of the wonders and horrors *there*, in the Tabir. . . . "

This time there was no mistaking the anti-Establishment thrust of the novel. Almost immediately after its publication *The Palace of Dreams* was banned. Kadare told an interviewer for *Vanity Fair* in 1991 that he could not himself explain why he had been so oblivious to the government's reaction. "How had I done this? Because I was always buried in literature, and I did not imagine the danger." He continued to publish, however, returning once more to the historical mode with *Prilli i thyer* (1982, *Broken April*). This is a romantic story of the blood-vengeance feuds that were part of life in northern Albania well into the twentieth century. Set in the early 1900s, in pre-Communist days, the novel contrasts a rugged peasant fatally committed to a vow of vengeance and an over-refined man from the south who brings his wife to this savage backward country on their honeymoon. Savkar Altinel wrote of the book in the *Times Literary Supplement* in 1990: "Kadare has produced not just a sad and beautiful tale, but also a powerful allegory about pre-Communist Albania with its downtrodden masses, its ineffectual men of science in the service of feudal institutions, and its cloistered intelligentsia ignorant of social realities."

In the late 1980s, as former satellites of the U.S.S.R. moved toward independence, Kadare found himself drawn into a confrontation with the Albanian secret police. It was apparent to him that Hoxha's more moderate successor Ramiz Alia was not keeping pace with the liberating forces sweeping eastern Europe. In October 1990 Kadare defected and found political asylum in France. Although Albania rejected the Communist Party in an election a year later, Kadare remained in self-imposed exile in Paris with his wife, Elena, and their two daughters.

Although Kadare's literary reputation had been high in France since the early 1970s, he had enjoyed little recognition from the English-reading public until the late 1980s when translations of his work began to appear in numbers. Probably his most admired book in Great Britain and in the United States is his fictionalized memoir *Chronicle in Stone*, which won high praise from John Updike in the *New Yorker* in 1988. Most remarkable in this novel is the child's narration, "the voice of innocence," as Updike describes it, reporting the tragedy of his country. "Although on one level the boy misunderstands the events that shape his life," Leonie Caldecott wrote in the *New York Times Book Review*, "the very lack of adult prejudices guarantees a clear-sightedness that conveys the pain of his people more vividly than anything else could hope to do." In November 1990 Kadare's American publisher reported that *Chronicle in Stone* was being read in American college courses in Eastern European literature, and plans were under way to issue translations of many of his other works.

An additional novel by Kadare is *The Concert*. One of the notable perversities of the Albanian situation, according to Robert D. Kaplan in the *New York Times Book Review*, has been its successive breaking off of relations with its protectors. *The Concert* is laid against Albania's break with China. The characters, mainly Albanian, range from a family with a nurturing mother and a sane father to a writer resembling Kadare, to assorted spies, government officials, and even Mao and Lin Biao. Bill Marx, reviewing *The Concert* for the *Nation* found that Kadare's attempt "to celebrate the quiet heroism of Albanians who persevered under the hammer-blows of politics" led him to "a cheap sentimentality that his other novels, steeped in history and hallucination, handily escape." He, nevertheless, characterized Kadare's strengths as a writer in his ability to depict a scene where "acts of explanation, of detection, of *knowing*, are fruitless in a world where phantoms, in the guise of human beings, dispose of their victims in mysterious ways." According to Kaplan, on the other hand, "Kadare makes us understand the secret of how a totalitarian regime survives: terror breeds isolation, and that isolation denies the inhabitants a crucial perspective, without which it's hard for them to realize just how abnormal their society really is."

PRINCIPAL WORKS IN ENGLISH TRANSLATION: (tr. A. Cungo from J. Vrioni's French version) The Wedding, 1968; (tr. D. Coltman from J. Vrioni's French version) The General of the Dead Army, 1972; (tr. P. Qesku from J. Vrioni's French version) The Castle, 1980; Chronicle in Stone, 1987; Broken April, 1990; (tr. B. Bray from J. Vrioni's French version) The Palace of Dreams, 1993; (tr. B. Bray from J. Vrioni's French version) The Concert, 1994.

ABOUT: Contemporary Literary Criticism 52, 1989; Current Biography Yearbook 1992. *Periodicals*—Nation December 19, 1994; New York Times October 26, 1990; November 14, 1990; December 6, 1990; New York Times Book Review January 24, 1988; June 28, 1991; September 26, 1993; November 6, 1994; New Yorker March 14, 1988; Times Literary Supplement July 3, 19087; December 7, 1990; February 2, 193; Vanity Fair May 1991; (Village) Voice Literary Supplement February 1988; World Literature Today Autumn 1979; Winter 1981; Spring 1987; World Press Review July 1991.

JEROME KAGAN

KAGAN, JEROME (February 25, 1929–), American psychologist and educator, writes: "I grew up as the eldest of two sons in Rahway, New Jersey, a small, industrial town about twenty miles south of New York City. My parents owned a small business and I am a typical member of that generation whose childhood was made apprehensive by the decade of depression that ended with the onset of World War II.

"The subjective construction of my life rests on the assumption, hopefully valid, that four relatively independent classes of events had to be joined to understand why I have spent the last three decades as a professor of psychology at Harvard.

"The choices of an intellectual career required both early success in school, which was made easier by some verbal talent and the good fortune to be in a school system in which the majority of children came from working class homes that did not value academic achievement. The early praise by devoted teacher persuaded me that analysis and inference were domains of special competence. This conclusion was aided immeasurably by the fact that I did not perceive any other special talent. As a result, I entered college attracted to a life of ideas rather than business which I regarded as unsafe given my father's misfortune, or law which my adolescent prejudices regarded as cooked rather than raw.

"A third factor, somewhat harder to understand, was a curiosity about nature centered on the mystery of bodies and the variation in human moods and beliefs, rather than on stars, rocks, or the sea. I suspect the former concern has a partially sexual origin. The latter is partially derived from being a victim of prejudice and attempting to understand why people who seemed so same and civil in their everyday behavior could hold groundless, irrational hostility.

"Historical factors comprise the final influence. I took seriously a professor's comment in an undergraduate psychology course that I would make a good psychologist and applied for graduate work in psychology as well as biochem-

istry. In the spring of 1950, I received an invitation from Frank Beach, a comparative psychologist at Yale, to become his research assistant should I decide to matriculate in psychology at Yale. I had been reading Donald Hebb's book, *The Organization of Behavior*, and Hebb's high praise for Beach, wedded to the inherent attraction to human nature, pulled me to psychology rather than biochemistry.

"After receiving my Ph.D. in 1954, I taught briefly at Ohio State University. Although I was drafted into the Army in 1955, I spent most of the time as a member of a research project stationed at the U.S. Army Hospital in West Point as part of a team studying the reasons for the high rate of attrition among the cadets. The most important historical event was an invitation to join the staff at the Fels Research Institute in Yellow Springs, Ohio, after my discharge in January 1957. The director, Lester Sontag, gave me access to the files of over 150 individuals who had been studied intensively since their birth in 1929. In collaboration with Howard Moss we interviewed and assessed these subjects who were then in their third decade. The results of this investigation, published in 1962 in the book *Birth of Maturity*, had a profound influence on my subsequent scientific career for it reinforced the long-standing motivation to explain the development of a personality. The unexpected acclaim that followed publication of the work led to the award of the Hofheimer Prize of the American Psychiatric Association and an invitation to join the Harvard faculty. After prolonged vacillation because of the totally gratifying life in Yellow

Springs, I decided to come to Cambridge in 1964.

"I have worked on three major problems during my 28 years in Cambridge. The first project probed the bases for psychological variation for the first few years of life. The resulting monograph, *Change and Continuity in Infancy*, taught me that a major maturational change occurred during the last few months of the first year but, less happily, if there were preservation of traits from early infancy through childhood they were subtle and not easily discerned.

"The successful application of a Baconian strategy in this first project motivated a similar style of investigation of the next 12 months. The results of this effort, published in *The Second Year*, revealed the emergence of the first signs of a moral sense and of self-consciousness in the middle of the second year and provided a basis for a continuing interest in human morality. The chapter on moral development in *The Nature of the Child* remains a source of pride.

"In the mid-1970s, the potential influence of infant day/care was a national concern and in collaboration with Richard Kearsley and Philip Zelazo I studied the effect of day care on young infants in the first three years. The book that summarized this project, called *Infancy* and published in 1978, indicated that attending a well-staffed day-care center was not potentially harmful. The unexpected and more interesting result formed the basis for our current work on temperament. The Chinese infants attending our day-care center were, like those who were raised at home, more timid, restrained, and apprehensive than were the Caucasian children who were observed under the same conditions. This intriguing observation was the basis for our interest in temperament over the last 13 years. The study of children who are shy, timid, and restrained, on the one hand, or sociable, bold, and affective, on the other, has persuaded me to award more power to biology than I had during the first decade of my postdoctoral work.

"I often ask old friends I have not seen for a long time which of their old ideas have changed most since our last conversations. My answer to that question is that I now award considerably more power to biology and the historical moment in which a life is led and a little less to the patina of daily interactions that social scientists are so found of celebrating."

"I celebrate nature," Jerome Kagan told two interviewers from the *Journal of Counseling and Development* in 1990. "My joy comes from making discoveries about nature, not uncovering

beautiful objects in my mind. Therefore I've always been an empiricist, a Baconian who believed—this is a deep belief—that humans are so vulnerable to illusion and self-deception that trying to discover the basic categories in a new science by thought alone is not likely to be profitable." In the course of his career as a developmental psychologist, Kagan has always tried to follow the data, even when those data disrupt his hypotheses. For much of his career, he has been evaluating and reevaluating the relative importance of biological factors, on the one hand, and environmental factors, on the other.

From Birth to Maturity, written with Howard Moss, is the report of a long-term developmental study of eighty-nine people begun in 1929, when all of the subjects were infants. Although the group under observation was hardly a typical cross section of American society (almost all were white Protestants with above-average intelligence and highly educated parents), Guy E. Swanson, writing in the *American Sociological Review*, praised the book as "a report of exceptional interest to sociologists."

Change and Continuity in Infancy reports the results of Kagan's first large-scale project at Harvard, a longitudinal study in which he observed and assessed the development of 180 infants at four, eight, thirteen, and twenty-seven months of age. "In addition to presenting a variety of new findings," Walter Emmerich wrote in *Science* in 1971. "This work is s a bold and imaginative search for psychological structures which organize the infant's rapidly developing behavioral repertoire."

Kagan's studies of infants were beginning to suggest that genetic/biological factors (not environmental ones) predominate in the early stages of mental development. In order to further test this hypothesis, Kagan traveled to Guatemala to observe the child-rearing practices of the Mayan Indians there. He found that during the first two years of life, Mayan infants are routinely left alone in dark rooms for much of the day. Nonetheless, by the time these infants reach later childhood, they are as alert, intelligent, and psychologically well-developed as children from other cultures who spend their first two years in more "stimulating" pursuits.

Kagan and his colleagues Richard Kearsley and Philip Zelazo begin their book *Infancy: Its Place in Human Development* with a long discussion of a belief cherished by both popular wisdom and orthodox psychology: that the experiences of the first two years of life are so critical as to virtually determine long-term development; and that those first two years are best spent in the nurturing company of one's biological mother. Insisting that these beliefs are based on cultural values, not on empirical evidence, the authors proceed to disclose the results of their study of the effects of day care on a group of Chinese American and Caucasian American babies. They concluded that there are no perceptible developmental differences between infants in high-quality day care and those reared exclusively at home. "One innovative feature of this study was its simultaneous assessment of the contributions of social class and ethnicity to early patterns of development," Susan Goldberg wrote in a review of the book in *Science* in 1978.

Kagan continued to court controversy in *The Nature of the Child*, in which he wrote, "Every society needs some transcendental theme to which citizens can be loyal." For Kagan, that theme in secular America is that the bond between infant and mother is sacrosanct and irreplaceable. Moreover, the absence or weakening of this relationship is often seen as resulting in grave developmental problems, leading inexorably to permanent psychological impairment to the child. Kagan's research at Harvard and in Guatemala found little evidence to sustain such beliefs. Rather than uncovering a strong link between the various stages of childhood development, Kagan found the links between earlier and later stages of development to be weak. In short, he posits that early deprivation of maternal love does not lead inevitably or necessarily to a maladjusted child or a disturbed adult.

The Nature of the Child was the first of Kagan's books to receive widespread notice (most of it favorable) in general interest publications, even earning its author a profile in *Time*. With recognition and popularity, however, came the possibility that Kagan's theories would be oversimplified, misunderstood, or misapplied. "Parents who hope that a book with this title will provide a blueprint for child-rearing will be disappointed," British psychoanalyst Anthony Storr warned in the *New Republic*. "Kagan is neither a Spock nor a Freud. On the other hand, those who really want to know what modern research into infant and child development has to say will be amply rewarded. Kagan is a skeptical, conscientious scientist who is reluctant to go beyond the facts, and who constantly questions received opinion, with illuminating result."

In 1987, Kagan was the recipient of an Award for Distinguished Scientific Contributions from the American Psychological Association. In its citation, the association noted, "As much as any American, Jerome Kagan has led the great growth of developmental psychology in our time."

In *Unstable Ideas*, largely an epistemological treatise, Kagan attempts to establish a new conceptual framework through which the science of psychology might escape the imprecise models and vague terminology—that is, the unstable ideas—that have mired it in the past. For Kagan, always the empiricist, the progress of psychology has been hindered by a tendency on the part of researchers to reify human mental processes, a tendency characterized by the overuse of such "unstable" concepts as "consciousness" and "self." Although the term is ubiquitous in psychological literature, Kagan finds little evidence that "consciousness" (however defined) is a significant determinant of human behavior. Because it is vague to the point of ineffability (and thus useless for scientific inquiry), "self" is another "unstable" idea Kagan thinks psychologists should dispense with entirely. In place of such imprecise, metaphysical terms, Kagan proposes the master concept "temperament," which, he argues, can better link the research of psychologists (and other behavioral scientists) to the work of "hard" scientists, especially biologists and neurologists.

"The proposed change in emphasis is quite radical," Richard M. Restak wrote in the *New York Times Book Review*. "Psychology, in contrast to the 'hard' sciences and even psychiatry, has, on the whole, continued to speak of mental events as if they were things. Attempts are still being made to graft terms like 'instinct' or 'drive' onto new findings in the neurosciences. But, if we accept . . . Kagan's approach, psychologists may have to change direction in regard to subject matter, terminology and research methods to account for the more dynamic nature of internal processes."

Kagan's developmental studies now take careful account of both environmental and biological factors. He has recently been studying how the home environment can modify an infant's temperament in the first year of life. As always, nature is his obsession. "I . . . confess to a flaw that may be fatal to empirical scientists," he writes in *Unstable Ideas*. "I so revere nature that sometimes I suspect I do not want to understand her too completely. If I am too successful, she will lose all of her mystery. I poke and prod her but, with e. e. cummings, smile privately in celebration of her perennial answer—Spring."

The son of Joseph and Myrtle (Libermann) Kagan, Jerome Kagan did his undergraduate studies at Rutgers University, taking a B.S. degree in 1950. He married Cele Katzman in 1951. They have a daughter and live in Belmont, Massachusetts.

PRINCIPAL WORKS: *Psychology*—(with G. Lesser) Contemporary Issues in Thematic Apperceptive Methods,

1961; (with Howard Moss) Birth to Maturity: A Study in Psychological Development, 1962; (with P. Mussen and J. Conger) Child Development and Personality, 1963, 7th ed. 1991; (with E. Havemann) Psychology: An Introduction, 1968, 7th ed. 1991; (with R. McCall et al.) Change and Continuity in Infancy, 1971; Personality Development (ed. I. Janis) 1971; Understanding Children: Behavior, Motives, and Thought, 1971; (with Richard Kearsley and Philip Zelazo) The Effects of Infant Day Care on Psychological Development, 1976; (with A. Rossi and T. Hareven) The Family, 1978; The Growth of the Child: Reflections on Human Development, 1978; (with Richard Kearsley and Philip Zelanzo) Infancy: Its Place in Human Development, 1978; (with C. Lang) Psychology and Education: An Introduction, 1978; (with E. Lomax and B. Rosenkranz) Science and Patterns of Child Care, 1978; (with O. Brim) Constancy and Change in Human Development, 1980; (with P. Mussen and J. Conger) Essentials of Child Development and Personality, 1980; The Second Year: The Emergence of Self-Awareness, 1981; The Nature of the Child, 1984; (with A. Skolnick) The Psychology of Human Development, 1986; Unstable Ideas: Temperament, Cognition, and Self, 1989; (with M. Small) Cognitive Development, 1990. *As Editor*—(with J. Wright) Basic Cognitive Processes in Children: Report of the Second Conference Sponsored by the Committee on Intellective Processes Research of the Social Science Research Council, 1963; (with P. Mussen) Readings in Child Development and Personality, 1965, rev. ed. 1970 (reissued as Basic and Contemporary Issues in Developmental Psychology, 1975); Creativity and Learning, 1967; (with N. Talbot and L. Eisenberg) Behavioral Science in Pediatric Medicine, 1971; (with M. Haith and C. Caldwell) Psychology: Adapted Readings, 1971; (with R. Coles and J. Tanner) Twelve to Sixteen: Early Adolescence, 1972; (with P. Mussen and J. Conger) Readings in Child and Adolescent Psychology: Contemporary Perspectives, 1980; (with S. Lamb) The Emergence of Morality in Young Children, 1987; (with R. E. Izard and R. B. Zajonc) Emotions, Cognition, and Behavior, 1988; (with R. B. McCall) Fundamental statistics for Behavioral Sciences, 1990.

ABOUT: Contemporary Authors New Revision Series 24, 1988; Who's Who in America 1991–1992. *Periodicals*—American Psychologist April 1988; American Sociological Review October 1963; Journal of Counseling and Development July/August 1990; New Republic November 5, 1984; New York Times September 14, 1984; New York Times Book Review November 18, 1984; May 28, 1989; Science December 10, 1971; December 15, 1978; Time October 22, 1984.

---

*KANIUK, YORAM (1930–   ), Israeli novelist and journalist, was born in Tel Aviv to a Zionist family, but one intensely tied to the Jewish communities of Europe whence they had recently emigrated. Growing up in the free yet sheltered environment of the first Hebrew city, in a community that was becoming aware of the

looming shadow of Nazism, he served in the Haganah, the underground army of Jewish Palestine. He became an adult as what began as a struggle against British rule assumed the proportions of a war against seven Arab nations. His coming of age paralleled the emergence of Israel as a nation, and Kaniuk, like many other soldiers who had fought in the War of Independence began his search for personal autonomy. His own particular war trauma had occurred when he and his comrades ran out of ammunition on a hillside during the Battle for Jerusalem in the 1948 war. The Arab soldiers, thinking they were dead, casually drank coffee and practiced target shooting at the "corpses." "I was executed every two minutes," Kaniuk told Penny Kaganoff in an interview in *Publishers Weekly*.

He looked for an artistic voice that would reflect the absurdity and the cruelty of the new reality. A move away from socially relevant literature with an ideological agenda was almost inevitable. Like other young Israelis recovering from the physical and emotional trauma of war, he began to travel and explore foreign cultural horizons, his focus shifting to the individual and his private concerns. Early on it was Kaniuk's style that distinguished him from the other young writers of his generation and placed him in its avant-garde. Typically, Kaniuk writes with little concern for consistencies of time and place. Dislocated heroes are central to his narratives' with events unfolding around them as if to validate their identity rather than provide social context.

Kaniuk came to the United States via Europe in 1951. He was an accomplished painter when he arrived in New York, but in the ten years that followed he became more and more devoted to writing, producing a body of prose that continued to convey painterly sensibilities.

Kaniuk's work has been widely translated; his first novel, *The Acrophile*, was published in English in 1961, several years before it was published in its original Hebrew (*Hayored Le-Ma'Lah*, 1963), because Kaniuk commissioned his own translation and then sold the novel to an American publisher. Dan Miron observed of the English language version in *Haaretz*,: "The translation is no less revolutionary than the story itself . . . refined, transparent, unmannered."

In *The Acrophile* Dani, a lonely, comic, often pathetic hero, is haunted by an ironic turn of events during which he killed an arab boy as he struggled frantically to convince his fellow soldiers to spare the child. In the course of this often whimsical novel, Dani, who has come to New York from Israel to study ancient languages,

°kan YOOK, yuh RAHM

achieves academic success. He chooses, however, to abandon this career and sell ice cream instead, explaining his decision:

> "Professors, did you ever climb a mountain that had no peak, open a package and find in place of the anticipated gift a small box, within it another, and another, in the end—nothing? No, you wouldn't understand, because you are the salt of the earth. . . . "

Dani's intense but fleeting human connections are reflected in the final pages of *The Acrophile*: "I met myself at the halfway mark, between the clouds and the murky streets, alone, related to all things and remote.." He decides to become a guide in the Empire State Building—"atop the tallest monument, erected to itself by the tallest city"—a choice that leads to the novel's eloquent conclusion:

> This far we have soared—from here on, the winged world. This is man's realm—beyond it the realm of the fly. I can see the people, tiny, less than themselves, at the mercy of the traffic lights, and in the evening at seven, when the avenues are almost cleansed of people, I walk home. By the river I have my room, a few books, a small kitchen and cool, dreaming beauty under my window. I write sometimes and drink to myself, each day melting into another in dreary beautiful succession. I like it this way.

Kaniuk's work is laced with autobiographical material, recurring events and characters that make his eight novels and assorted short stories into a kind of saga. *Himmo Melekh Yerushalayim* (1966, *Himmo, King of Jerusalem*) is set in a convent converted into a hospital in besieged Jerusalem in 1948, where lies a young Israeli horribly wounded in the war for independence. Hamutal, a passionate nurse, obsessed with her love for Himmo, struggles to keep him alive and then, defiantly, helps him in his wish to die. The book is rich with the landscape of Jerusalem, evoking a timeless dimension that reflects and deepens the highly charged human drama.

In *Sussetz* (1973, *Rockinghorse*), Kaniuk leads his hero, Aminadav Sussetz, through a series of events and relationships that loosely parallel those of his own life, but transcending the restrictions of real time and space. The tale begins with a recapitulation of Aminadav's life in New York in the 1960s, ranging from Greenwich Village to Harlem, from the high culture of the art world to the free and easy jazz scene. Here the aspiring young painter embarks on his amorous and artistic adventures. He decides to abandon his wife and child and return to Israel where his quest for identity impels him to make a film about both his own birth and his father's death. This raw and rather literal reading of the Oedipal drama assumes more and more absurd di-

mensions as he begins to deconstruct and fantasize his parents' lives. Beginning with an epigraph from Jorge Luis Borges—"Life is but a guided dream," Kaniuk constructs a novel that, as George Klin wrote in *World Literature Today*, "reads like the notes of an endless nightmare." Klin commented, "If it were possible to sum up . . . Kaniuk's complex novel, teeming with ideas, moods and events, it would be in the narrator's bitter observation as he gazes upon the world: 'I'm not at home. I'm a long way from home.'"

Aminadav appears again in *Ha-sipur al doda Shlomtsion ha-gedola* (1975, *The Story of Aunt Shlomzion the Great*). In it, he re-creates the landscape of his childhood, focusing on a grand old lady who embodies the history of early Zionism and dominates the intricate and extended web of his family's life. Aminadav's ambivalence toward Shlomzion and the world she represents is relieved by an undercurrent of compelling nostalgia as he explores his fascination with this formidable woman:

> I wonder what motivates Aunt Shlomzion—Sound and fury, said Macbeth. I am sitting in the yard. The rains are over and gone. Pain appears in our land. The dog houses are gone, the little foxes are gone. The houses crumble in tired dignity, beggar-kings on new streets ruled by formica potentates. The elite of Tel Aviv lived here once. Spider webs and rust remain. . . .

Aunt Shlomzion's personality unfolds through a series of striking images, romantic, yet often bizarrely detailed with warmth and color that make the portrait alive, immediate, a source of sheer fun. "The character works," Alan Mintz wrote in the *New York Times Book Review* in 1979, "because she is an archetype: the Great Mother. . . . Like the land of Israel . . . though she requires continual sacrifice she is never appeased."

In *Adam Ben Kekev* (1969, *Adam Resurrected*) and *Haeyhudi Ha-Ahron* (1982, *The Last Jew*), Kaniuk's nonlinear prose meanders through vast expanses of history and geography, projecting ideas and emotions on to a dazzling array of character. The central figure in *Adam Resurrected* is Adam Stein, a clown and musician who survives a Nazi extermination camp through a humiliating relationship with the commandant. Choosing life, though this means descending to a subhuman level, he entertains fellow Jews—his own family included—on their way to the ovens. He is required to "play dog" to amuse his master, reverting to this role later in life, when he suffers a mental breakdown. After the war he builds a successful career as a clown and moves to Israel, where the madness of his earlier life overcomes him. He spends time in a hospital, forms a liaison with the head nurse, and, ultimately, regains his sanity. Adam is cured, resurrected, finds asylum—a metaphor that serves as a savage representation of the State of Israel. In Kaniuk's view, it must transcend its role as a haven for a physically and emotionally battered refugee population to move ahead.

The Last Jew, an elaborate phantasmagoria of events and personalities, spans several generations, ignoring the conventions of chronology and time. Here again a survivor, Ebenezer Shneurson, becomes a noted circus performer. The relationship between Shneurson and Sam Lipker, his adopted son who lives in New York and turns Shneurson's accounts of Jewish history into a play there before bringing it to Israel, recalls Aminadav in *Rockinghorse* and his bizarre autobiographical film. Henkin, a teacher along with the narrator, from whom Henkin hopes to learn details of his son's death in the recent war, engage in an elaborate attempt to process the past and relate it to the present. The common enterprise of this complex collage of characters is perpetuating the memory of the dead. A blurred image that seems charged with meaning, emerges though the elements of the image as well as its message are often elusive.

Kaniuk's later works move away from the wildly imaginative toward the more immediately relevant, with characters who have a more particular social and political identity than the archetypal figures that inhabit his earlier novels. This is not a surprising development for a writer who has been a popular journalist and political commentator.

Over the years Kaniuk has written for several Israeli newspapers and been a popular lecturer on the kibbutz circuit, questioning the moral implications of political decisions criticizing the basic fabric of Israeli society, becoming a "guru" of sorts for the younger generation. In "The Plastic Flower Children," which appeared in *Life* magazine's *Special Reports—The Spirit of Israel,* in 1973, Kaniuk said of Israel's cultural climate:

After the last war, Sabra left the game. He wandered off to care for himself and trusted the moves to his parents and grandparents . . . Around him he sees an active society . . . that demands justice everywhere in the world, but he doesn't rise up at the lack of it in his own home . . . On the razor edge of the Judean Hills . . . a remarkable culture could have arisen. . . . But we are creating today a culture of plastic flowers.

Aravi Tov (1984, *Confessions of a Good Arab*) and *Bito* (1987, *His Daughter*) pursue these issues in Kaniuk's characteristic fashion—employing the technique of magical realism but with a more coherent plot line than was offered

in his earlier works. *Confessions* is narrated by Yosef Sherara, the son of an Arab father who has been the object of Franz's emotional attachment. Franz marries a woman who looks like the young Arab and the young Arab, now a distinguished historian is fated to marry their daughter. The product of this union is the half-Jewish, half-Arab Yosef, who in Gabriele Annan's words "can't face 'the daily round of persecution and discrimination which an Arab in Israel is supposed not only to accept, but even to excuse.' So he decides to grow up a Jew with his grandfather rather than an Arab with his father." Annan characterized the novel in *The New York Review of Books* in 1988, as a "romantic tale of a love begotten by despair upon impossibility, and an elegy not only for the Middle East, but for the past in general. . . .

Yosef's father, an expert on the Arab-Jewish conflict, asserts " . . . that there is no hope at all, that the tragedy begins long before the historians can locate it. That everything seems to have been preordained. That the fanaticism was inevitable. That the country was foreign to both nations, which invented national movements which did not stem directly from their histories, but only from their sufferings." The narrator, Yosef, has a parallel view of his personal predicament;

I don't expect anything good to happen and I have no desire to know about bad things before they happen. I try to hold on to the image of Franz . . . Life seemed to him like an intricate and terrifying maze from which he had extricated himself only by the sacrifice of everything dear to him. . . . I had always understood his fear of me, he was afraid that my art would try to express what had happened to us and that would be a catastrophe.

In *His Daughter* we follow Joseph Krieger, a retired brigadier in the Israeli army, in a search for his missing daughter. A series of complex but misleading clues turns this novel into a detective story. The problematics of Krieger's life—his failed marriage, his inadequacy as a father, his emptiness as a person—are articulated with a vividness that provides the reader with the pleasure of recognition but falls short of providing real enlightenment. Krieger's brilliant military career has led to to neither wisdom nor satisfaction. He laments: "My whole life was one long gruelling preparation for an event which never happened. The wars that I had fought were just the minor fulfillment of a dream (something to be placed in parentheses); they were never the war I wanted." Denis Donoghue, reviewing *His Daughter* in the *New York Review of Books,* commented that Krieger may be "a representative figure, an extreme instance of the sabra and of the price a country pays for producing such men as Moshe Dayan or Ariel Sharon." Donoghue's conclusion, however, is that "Krieger never becomes what he is evidently intended to be, a character richer and more diverse than the mere sum of the attributes he is given."

Reviewers agree that Kaniuk's work is highly original, imbued with a macabre humor that lends charm, even magic to his often absurd and startling imagery. Thomas Edwards, in the *New York Review of Books* in 1978, called Kaniuk "essentially a comic writer, for all the grimness of his subjects." Edwards found Kaniuk's characters moving "from uneasy failure to uneasy success . . . from a sense that they have been betrayed by God, man and themselves, to a sense, which . . . lies at the center of serious comedy, that since betrayal is part of the continuing order of things, even it somehow sustains us. . . . Kaniuk's way of apprehending . . . them savingly asserts that intelligent, sensitive people can survive, if just barely, the guilt that life and history impose on them, that the duties of the imagination are longer than the duties of social and political identity."

Kaniuk's disquieting sense of reality has encouraged younger writers to explore new literary horizons, to replace ideas with ideals, to go beyond the prevailing limits of psychological and moral consciousness in order to engage in the quest for a single truth and a single unfragmented self.

PRINCIPAL WORKS IN ENGLISH TRANSLATION: *Novels*— (tr. Z. Shapiro) The Acrophile, 1961; (tr. Y. Shachter) Himmo, King of Jerusalem, 1969; (tr. R. Flantz) Rockinghorse, 1977; (tr. S. Simckes) Adam Resurrected, 1978; (tr. Z. Shapiro) The Story of Aunt Shlomzion the Great, 1979; The Last Jew, 1982; (tr. D. Bilu) Confessions of a Good Arab, 1988; (tr. S. Simckes) His Daughter, 1989.

ABOUT: Contemporary Authors 134, 1992; Contemporary Literary Criticism 19, 1981. *Periodicals*—Haaretz February 23, 1962; Modern Hebrew Literature Fall–Winter 1982–1983; Spring–Summer 1984; Spring 1989; New York Review of Books February 9, 1978; August 18, 1988; September 28, 1989; New York Times Book Review November 20, 1977; January 21, 1979; September 18, 1988; Publishers Weekly April 28, 1989; World Literature Today Autumn 1978; Spring 1980.

*KAPUŚCIŃSKI, RYSZARD (March 4, 1932–), Polish journalist, was born in Pinsk, a small impoverished town in eastern Poland. His parents, Jozef and Maria (Bobka) Kapuściński, were school teachers. During World War II the family moved to Warsaw and back to the countryside, trying desperately to escape the Nazi

*ka poosh CHEEN skee, REE shahrt

RYSZARD KAPUŚCIŃSKI

depredations. Young Kapuściński watched Jews being led to execution in the Warsaw Ghetto. He watched firing squads that operated in the countryside, at first by night, then all day. His early years were filled with the horrors of war—bombings, homelessness, poverty, and starvation. Early on, as he wrote in the essay "1945," published in the *New Republic* in 1986, he learned "that the world had suddenly become dangerous, foreign, and evil, that one must be on one's guard." His exposure to the brutality and suffering of those years was, ironically, prophetic of his chosen career in later life as a reporter on the wars that have ravaged Third World countries since the "peace" of 1945. "Because, in a certain but essential sense, the war did not end for me in 1945, or even soon thereafter. In many ways something of it endures even today, because for those who live through it, war never finally ends."

Living under Communist rule in postwar Poland, Kapuściński developed a pronounced distaste for a career in politics although he had been a member of the Communist Youth league. At the University of Warsaw, which he entered in 1950, he studied history, taking an M.A. in 1955. Academic life, however, did not appeal to him, and he refused an offer of a teaching post at the university to work as a reporter for a youth magazine, *Sztandar Miodych*. Here he did his first investigative journalism, writing a series of controversial articles about the exploitation of workers in a steel factory. The articles stirred up a scandal, but when an official investigation confirmed his allegations, Kapuściński was honored by the authorities with the Golden Cross of Merit. But chafing under the restrictions of the Communist government in Poland, he became a foreign correspondent for *Polityka*, a weekly which sent him to Africa. In 1962 he joined the Polish Press Agency and reported on Third World news in Asia, Africa, the Middle East, and Latin America. Kapuściński may truly claim that he witnessed "the birth of the Third World," having been present at more revolutions and civil and colonial wars than probably any other contemporary reporter.

Kapuściński cabled his reports back to Poland in short, objective news stories. Sensing somehow the inadequacy of such bare facts to communicate the history-making events he was covering, he began to rewrite and expand these reports, giving more color to his impressions. His first book, a best-seller, was a report on rural conditions in his homeland, *Busz po polsku* (The Polish Bush, 1962), but thereafter his books were drawn from his foreign experiences. The first of these to be translated into English in 1982 was *Cesarz The Emperor: Downfall of an Autocrat).* This was an account of the last years of Emperor Haile Selassie of Ethopia. Based on Kapuściński's interviews with those surrounding the old emperor, it reports with mordant humor and shrewd political insights the final decay of an autocracy. "This is not simply a history of the Ethiopian crown," Neil Ascherson wrote in *New York Review of Books.* "It is something much rarer in our time: the record of an imperial court, the dying years of the monarchy as they were seen by courtiers." Ascherson was not disturbed by the author's, impressionistic version of the facts. "In Kapuściński's rendering the fallen Emperor's men speak with the periods of Tacitus, the melancholy retrospection of Gibbon . . . If Kapuściński did some 'shaping' of their testimony, this does not invalidate this sensitive, powerful, and surprisingly merciful book."

Kapuściński's tendency to convert the hard facts of journalism into metaphor and allegory has been attributed by several of his reviewers to the pressures of the Communist party who scrutinized everything he wrote. For Polish readers, Haile Selassie was a mask, a symbol of the repressive and sterile Polish state under Communism. "In East Europe allegory is the name of the political correspondent's game," Xan Smiley observed of the book in the *New York Times Book Review* , while Peter S. Prescott suggested in *Newsweek* that the Emperor was "a stand-in for Stalin, Big Brother, the ruler who brings his country to a condition of nearly perfect stasis."

Kapuściński found another symbol of state au-

thoritarianism in Shah Mohammed Reza Pahlavi of Iran. In *Szachinszach* (1985, *Shah of Shahs*), his observations on the revolution that overthrew that ruler's tyranny only to replace it with the equally repressive religious dictatorship of the Ayatollah Khomeini, was read by his Polish audience as immediately relevant to their own condition. "People in Poland look for these extra meanings," Kapuściński told an interviewer for the *New York Times* in 1985. "I write about men who merely wear the costumes of the Shah of Shahs, the Lion of Judah, or, yes, Polish First Secretary Edward Gierek. Everything is a metaphor." Thin as the veil of allegory was, it allowed Kapuściński to remain on the best-seller lists in Poland.

In 1960 Kapuściński was one of the few European journalists covering the war for independence in the Congo. In 1964 he covered revolts in Zanzibar and Tanganyika, and in 1965 observed the overthrow of President Ben Bella in Algeria. He moved on to Latin America in 1970 to report on the war in El Salvador, and in 1975, he almost single-handedly reported the beginnings of the prolonged struggle in Angola. In between he was on the scene for the Arab-Israeli war in 1973.

Africa has been the principal scene of Kapuściński's reporting because it is a whole continent caught up in the anticolonial struggle and its aftermath. In the 1960s he wrote in *The Soccer War:*

A new Africa was being born, and this was not a figure of speech or a platitude from an editorial. The hour of its birth was sometimes dramatic and painful, sometimes enjoyable and jubilant; it was always different (from our point of view) from anything we had known, and it was precisely that difference that struck me as new, as the previously undescribed, as the exotic.

Kapuściński's personal and impressionistic prose captures the essence of the history-making events he covered. *Jeszcze dzien zycia* (1987, *Another Day of Life*) and *Wojna futbolowa* (1991, *The Soccer War*) won the admiration of such writers as Salman Rushdie and John Updike. Reviewers described his work as merging the terse realism of Ernest Hemingway with the imagination of Gabriel García Márquez. First, however, Kapuściński is a reporter with a passion, as he writes in *The Soccer War*, "to experience everything for myself." As a result, he has put his life routinely at risk, undergoing hair-raising and harrowing experiences. Redeeming his work from the merely sensational and self-serving (one minority view belongs to Ian Walker, who, in the *New Statesman* refers to Kapuściński's "temptation to portray himself as the Boy's Own hero risking his life to get the story . . . romantic self-mythologizing") is his sympathetic imagination, his ability to identify with the lives of the people he writes about. He plunges into the interior of Angola in the midst of the war "because, as I see it, it's wrong to write about people without living through at least a little of what they are living through," he writes in *Another Day of Life*. Yet he recognizes the ultimate futility of what he is doing:

> The world contemplates the great spectacle of combat and death, which is difficult for it to imagine in the end, because the image of war is not communicable—not by the pen, or the voice, or the camera. War is a reality only to those stuck in its bloody, dreadful, filthy insides. To others, it is pages in a book, pictures on a screen, nothing more.

The Soccer War takes its title from internecine struggle in the Third World—a conflict that began in the World Cup soccer competition between Honduras and El Salvador in Mexico in 1969. Out of a sporting event riots erupted and the game became politicized into a destructive war between the two countries. Suddenly the attention of the news media was concentrated in Latin America. "The only chance small countries from the Third World have of evoking a lively international interest is when they decide to shed blood," Kapuściński remarks bitterly. "This is the sad truth, but so it is." The same bitter irony echoes in *Another Day of Life*, his report on the confused and bloody warfare in Angola, newly liberated from Portugal but ravaged by civil war, a pawn in the Soviet-Cuban clash with South Africa.

Kapuściński enjoyed relative freedom as a reporter for the Polish Press Agency because the anticolonial struggles in the Third World were strongly supported by the U.S.S.R. But with the steadily growing power in Poland of the Solidarity party, which Kapuściński supported, he fell into disfavor and in 1981 his press credentials were revoked. By this time, however, translations of his books in Western Europe and the United States had won him an international reputation as a powerful spokesman in the cause of human freedom. Like Graham Greene and V. S. Naipaul, Peter S. Prescott wrote in a review of *The Soccer War* in *Newsweek*, "he makes literature out of journalism."

In 1994 Kapuściński published *Imperium*, a record of "his journalistic travels into Russia and its colonies from 1958 until the early 1900's," according to Bill Keller writing in the *New York Times Book Review*. Keller noted that *Imperium* contains "treasures": "His visit to Vorkuta, the arctic mining and gulag city is a triumphant combination of bleak history and black comedy. His account of feckless coal miners try-

ing to organize themselves, but failing because only the bosses know how to run meetings, is a wonderful miniature of Russia's pratfalls in the theater of new democracy." Keller found, however, that "because he believes Russia is inexorably mired in its history," Kapuściński concentrated on the past, and its terrors and "communed more with spirits of the dead than with the living."

Keller sums up Kapuściński's achievement by calling him "a kind of mosaicist, piecing together vignettes and encounters and trip notes and snippets of history until they add up to something rich. . . . Kapuściński is an enchanting guide, combining boundless stamina, felicitous, writing, childish curiosity and the literate authority of a true intellectual."

Adam Hochschild, in the *New York Review of Books*, saw *Imperium* as a work of "magic journalism." Hochschild singled out Kapuściński's "ability to capture the historically telling image," his "acute sense of what the former Soviet bloc and the Third World have in common," and his "unerring moral radar for detecting the abuses and delusions of every sort of autocracy and nationalism whether in Moscow, Yerevan, Teheran, Johannesburg." He concluded that "beneath the seductive dazzle of his prose, the questioning moral imagination of this truly original writer makes his work a whole."

Kapuściński lives in Warsaw. He married Alicja Mielczarek, a pediatrician, in 1952; they have one daughter.

PRINCIPAL WORKS IN ENGLISH TRANSLATION: (tr. W. Brand and K. Mroczhowsha-Brand) The Emperor: Downfall of an Autocrat, 1983; (tr. W. Brand and K. Mroczhowsha-Brand) Shah of Shahs, 1985; (tr. W. Brand and K. Mroczhowsha-Brand) Another Day of Life, 1987; (tr. W. Brand) The Soccer War, 1991; (tr. K. Glowzewsha)Imperium, 1994.

ABOUT: Contemporary Authors 114, 1985; Current Biography Yearbook 1992. *Periodicals*—New Republic January 27, 1986; New Statesman November 2, 1990; New York Review of Books August 18, 1983; August 15, 1991; November 3, 1994; New York Times April 12, 1985; New York Times Book Review May 29, 1983; February 2, 1987; April 14, 1991; Newsweek April 11, 1983; April 15, 1991; Vanity Fair March 1991.

KAUFFMAN, JANET (June 10, 1945–), American poet, novelist, and writer of short stories writes: "I was born in Lancaster, Pennsylvania, and grew up on a tobacco farm in a predominantly Mennonite community. I graduated from Juniata College, Huntingdon, Pennsylvania, in 1967, and from the University of

JANET KAUFFMAN

Chicago, with a Ph.D. in English, in 1972. But more than academic work, it was my early and continued involvement with farming, with the natural world, the social action and pacifism of the Mennonites, followed by the civil rights and women's movements, that affected my work and writing in crucial ways. I think of writing as action. Literally. Of language as physical, political, human action.

"After graduate school, I wrote poetry for ten years, before writing fiction, and in fact an emphasis on language, on spoken words, ordinary or extraordinary talk, is central to both my fiction and poetry. I like the blur of those categories, and often don't make a distinction in my mind between short story, or even novel, and poem. The short novels *Collaborators* and *The Body in Four Parts* have many short prose poem sections, and I'm interested in evolving, chance, organic structures that defy the linearity and conclusiveness of traditional narratives. A mix of things, and things mixed up, makes real sense to me.

"In many of my stories, the outside world enters or matches or overlaps the human world. It's important to me that nature not be a background for character development—not just scenery— but a complex part of human identity. I'm sure the handwork of some of the farming I've known—tobacco, hay—has something to do with my determination as a writer to attend to the physicalities of place, person, and language.

"I'm not a good storyteller; I have a terrible memory for plot. But the simple and complex physicality of language, of talk—air out of a human mouth—interests me tremendously. I can listen to anybody say anything.

"From 1986–1988 I taught at Jackson Community College in Jackson, Michigan, and since then have taught at Eastern Michigan University in Ypsilanti, Michigan."

Janet Kauffman's parents, Chester Kauffman and Thelma (Hershey) Kauffman, worked a tobacco farm near the southeastern Pennsylvania town of Landisville. After earning a Ph.D. from the University of Chicago (where she wrote a dissertation on the poetry of Theodore Roethke), Kauffman settled on a farm in southern Michigan. Because her poetry and fiction is usually set in rural Pennsylvania, Ohio, or Michigan, some critics have labeled her a regional writer. Whether or not Kauffman is a true regionalist, all of her writing is informed by a strong sense of place and by an abiding attachment to the rhythms of farm life and the natural world. While men are hardly absent from her world, most of her poems and stories center on the lives of women. In "Mennonite Farm Wife," a poem in her collection *The Weather Book*, Kauffman writes: "She hung her laundry in the morning / before light and often in winter / by sunrise the sheets were ice. / . . . I never doubted they thawed / perfectly dry, crisp / the corners like thorn."

When she turned to writing prose fiction, in the early 1980s, Kauffman had already been writing and publishing poetry for nearly a decade. Her first short story collection, *Places in the World a Woman Could Walk*, contains a dozen tales, most of them about, and narrated by, rural women. These women are apt to be put-upon, heartbroken, or poverty-stricken, but they are almost invariably resilient and resourceful, and many of them display a stoic sense of humor. The narrator of the story "Patriotic," for example, tries to manage her farm chores with the help of a fat neighbor lady and a teenage boy, while her husband works on a construction job. Although he found several pieces in the collection "too programmatic in their feminism," Robert Towers noted in *The New York Review of Books* that "Janet Kauffman achieves her effects with light, deft touches, and a minimum of explanation." The men in her fiction, he observed, "have mostly gone off to find paying jobs or have simply gone off, leaving the women to do the heavy as well as the light work on the home place." Nonetheless, he wrote, these women remain "extremely susceptible to men, no matter how unreliable (or indeed dangerous) they may be."

"Kauffman doesn't fool around," Bob Shacochis wrote in a highly enthusiastic *Saturday Review* notice of *Places in the World a Woman Could Walk*. "She dives for the mystery within each personality, the surprise that jolts every narrative track." Kauffman, he suggested, "is a regionalist only in the sense of setting, of stage . . . [She] is, to my taste, more delicious than the usual fare, cherries and figs and exotic soup to the biscuit and peas of other, less visionary, regional writers." In the *New York Times Book Review* (1984), Wendy Lesser commented: "The forceful women who occupy Janet Kauffman's short stories about rural and small-town America do not fit any of the stereotypes we have come to expect from much modern urban fiction. These women are strong without being self-sufficient, knowing yet not sophisticated, accustomed to long silences but delighted at the least chance for conversation."

Kauffman's first novel *Collaborators* grew out of her short story "My Mother Has Me Surrounded" in *Places in the World a Woman Could Walk*. In the short story, a Mennonite woman and her young daughter sunbathe and swim at a Delaware beach in August. Both the story and the novel are narrated by the daughter, whose chief concern is an account of her relationship with her mother, who emerges as a complex, enigmatic, and seemingly all-powerful figure. "I'm small enough to lie beside her and use her shade," the narrator recalls early in the story. "There, I am invisible; I am in hiding, in the only darkness she offers me." In the novel, the narrator's recollection of that one day at the beach becomes the foundation for a lyrical reminiscence about life on a Bucks County, Pennsylvania, tobacco farm. Although various characters—the father, a brother, a few farm helpers, and a friend of the mother—play some part in her tale, the narrator focuses throughout on her mother, the epicenter of her girlhood universe. The mother is at once a hardworking Mennonite farm wife and a feisty, irreverent freethinker. She shocks her daughter with stories about youthful sexual adventures and tells her "[o]n the sly . . . , and more than once, that the world had nothing to do with God." She has named her daughter not from the Bible, but after a sunken ship—the *Andrea Doria*. "She said she liked the sound of it, that's all. I tried to believe her," Andrea says.

But Andrea has come to an earthshaking realization, one that colors every aspect of her extended reminiscence: She cannot believe much of what her mother said. "My mother lied to me about everything," she notes dryly in the opening line of the novel's brief introductory chapter. About halfway through the novel, the mother

suffers a stroke; although she makes a partial recovery, the once indomitable woman is noticeably changed and diminished. Eventually, she dies of a second stroke, leaving the twelve-year-old Andrea stranded on the brink of maturity.

In the *New Republic* Anne Tyler wrote that Kauffman had taken one of the few "less than perfect" stories from *Places in the World a Woman Could Walk* and fashioned it into a novel of "compelling strength." Noting that the portrait of a single "complicated character" had been transformed into a novel about "the sinewy, tough, often bitter relationship between the mother and her daughter," Tyler concluded: "In *Collaborators*, the daughter has it in her to fill the mother's shoes someday. . . . That's what makes her story so important, so painful, and so deeply satisfying." In the *New York Times Book Review* (1986), Ursula Hegi hailed *Collaborators* as a "stunning novel." "[It] is a novel that needs to be read slowly, word by word, image by image, to allow Janet Kauffman's extraordinary gift for language and character development to unfold. She brings a poet's sensitivity to her prose. . . . " *New York Times* reviewer Michiko Kakutani agreed to some extent, calling *Collaborators* "essentially a long tone poem," and praising its "incantatory language." "Too often, however," Kakutani wrote, "the finery of . . . Kauffman's language simply results in wordy passages, freighted with ambiguity and a kind of portentous symbolism."

Obscene Gestures for Women, Kauffman's second collection of short fiction, had a mixed reception. "What strikes the reader of this slender book is the amazing generosity of the writer," Robert Kelly wrote in the *New York Times Book Review*. "In this second collection, Janet Kauffman . . . offers fifteen stories of spare elegance, revealing crannies full of unexpected details." Reacting, in the *Georgia Review*, to what he called "the bombastic hyperbole" of the book's dust-jacket blurbs, Greg Johnson observed: "Kauffman is a writer of modest but genuine talent who was probably embarrassed to find herself hurled toward 'the end of speech'. . . . these brief pieces show Kauffman as a wily experimenter in technique and form who nonetheless writes within a consistently narrow emotional range."

The Body in Four Parts, Kauffman's second novel, provides ample evidence of her experimental technique. Like her earlier work, it is built on the slimmest of plots—in this case, a drive through the Pennsylvania countryside in search of watercress. The narrator-protagonist is actually four people in one; each "part" is represented by one of the four fundamental elements:

earth, air, fire, and water. "Ms. Kauffman's pantheistic conceit is not quite as whimsical (or off-putting) as a description of it might suggest," Jonathan Baumbach wrote in the *New York Times Book Review*. According to Baumbach, *The Body in Four Parts* "is a book that adorns itself in words. Words make up its parts: words in virtuoso display come first and last. . . . Behind earth, air, fire, and water is a fifth element, the poet's language, the words that imagine into clarity the invisible world."

PRINCIPAL WORKS: *Poetry*—(with J. McGann) Writing Home, 1978; The Weather Book, 1981; Where the World Is, 1988. *Short stories*—Places in the World a Woman Could Walk, 1984; Obscene Gestures for Women, 1989. *Novels*—Collaborators, 1986; The Body in Four Parts, 1993.

ABOUT: Contemporary Authors New Revision Series 43, 1994; Contemporary Literary Criticism 42, 1987; Dictionary of Literary Biography Yearbook 1986. *Periodicals*—Georgia Review Spring–Summer, 1990; New Republic April 21, 1986; New York Review of Books May 31, 1984; New York Times February 19, 1986; New York Times Book Review January 8, 1984; April 20, 1986; September 24, 1989; August 29, 1993; Saturday Review January–February 1984.

KAYE, M. M. (MARY MARGARET) (August 21, 1908–), British author of mysteries, books for children and historical novels, was born in Simla, India, the second of the three children of Margaret Sarah Bryson, a missionary's daughter, and Cecil Kaye, a British officer in the Indian army. In her 1990 memoir, *The Sun in the Morning: My Early Years in India and England*, Kaye described her early childhood in Simla, the mountainous summer capital of the Indian government in the days of the Raj, as "enchanted." She adored her father, who spent hours reading to her and sharing with her his interest in history, languages, and wildlife. She was fond too of her Indian nurse, who told "enthralling tales about the doings of gods and heroes," unlike the British nannies who raised the children of richer British officials on such stories as *Peter Rabbit*. Their nurse, Kaye recalled, "would sing us to sleep with the age-old nursery songs of Hindustan, and let us run wild in a way that no British nanny would have permitted." Given an abundance of freedom, and frequently separated from her father whose work took him to Delhi during the winter months, she spent her time exploring the countryside and talking with the proprietors of the Indian-owned shops along Simla's Mall. From an early age she came to feel herself a part of India.

Somewhat later in her childhood, after her older brother had been sent to England to be educated, she and her sister spent winters with their parents in Delhi, where Kaye became fascinated by India's history, an interest that was to last all her life and to inspire many of her novels:

> The Delhi of my childhood, my Delhi, was not the great sprawling city so well known to hosts of tourists who call it New Delhi: for New Delhi had not been built then, and the site that it now occupies was a stony, treeless plain . . . My Delhi was the old walled city of the Moguls and the British-built Cantonment area that lay beyond it in the shadow of the Ridge—that long spine of rock which juts up from the surrounding plains like the back of a basking whale from a barely ruffled sea. The Ridge is steeped in history, and from its crest you could look down on Shah Jehan's walled city with its battered outer gateways, close-packed houses, bazaars, palaces and great Red Fort.

Her chief childhood memory of her Scottish mother was "of her rushing in to say good-night to us before going out to a party, looking perfectly beautiful in a shimmering ball-dress and smelling divinely of a special scent." Kaye resented her mother as a "nitwit," and modeled herself on her father, whose love for India and its people matched her own.

Kaye was sent "home to England" to be educated after World War I ended, when she was ten. Despite some lonely times in English boarding schools and an occasional fear that she might never see India or her parents again, her interest in her new surroundings and a discovery of the pleasure of reading poetry helped to assuage a seven-year separation from her parents.

In 1925, when she was seventeen and her father retired from service in India, the family returned to England, and Kaye began studying at an art studio in London. She had been praised for her art work and having won an award for it at boarding school, she thought of becoming an illustrator of children's books. But two years later, her father was asked to return to India to do government work and took his family with him. Kaye recalled that on hearing of their return to India, "it was like winning the Calcutta Sweep or being given the most marvellous present in the world. I remember wanting to cry and then wanting to run out onto the lawn and scream for joy . . . to stick flowers in my hair and dance bare-foot between the trees in the park."

Kaye remained in India until her father's death, and then with her mother went back to England where she set herself up in a studio to paint and illustrate childrens' books, eventually writing some of her own. In 1942, having returned again to India, she met and married Godfrey John Hamilton, a major general in the

British army. During the war years she did volunteer work while her husband often was away
in Burma. The couple left India in 1947 when
the country achieved independence; for many
years thereafter they and their two daughters
were constantly on the move. Kaye, who enjoyed
the opportunity to visit many countries, did not
begin publishing the novels for which she is best
known until she was forty-five. But since then
she has published prodigiously.

Her three mysteries written in the
fifties—*Death Walked in Kashmir, Death
Walked in Berlin* and *Death Walked in
Cypress*—were not much reviewed, but when
she published the first of her three historical novels *Shadow of the Moon*, in 1956 she began to
achieve popularity. The book takes place during
the time of the 1857 Indian Mutiny when the sepoys (native soldiers) of the Bengal army revolt-
ed against their British officers. Seen through the
eyes of an orphaned Anglo-Spanish girl who, like
Kaye, had been raised in India but educated in
England, it interweaves the story of her return
to India and eventual marriage with the story of
the mutiny, at the same time giving a vivid picture of life in that country in the nineteenth century. As David Tilden wrote in the *New York
Herald Tribune Book Review*, "Kaye pictures
[India's] welter of races, religions, ideals and su-
perstitions; its fragrances and stench, beauty and
horror. Nor does she shrink from showing the
short-comings of all but a few of its British
overlords." In the *Spectator*, John Bayley termed
the book "excellent because . . . Kaye has a real
historical conscience, a sense of impartiality and
a great many old mutiny records to draw upon."
His cavil was that Kaye "cannot refrain from exploiting the amorous and horrific side of the
business—dashing officers with moustaches, and
screaming ladies in crinolines having their heads
hacked off by sepoys." The *Times Literary
Supplement* reviewer argued that the author's
characters were "wooden and unconvincing,"
but gave her credit for an "unbiased picture of
India at the time of the Mutiny."

Kaye wrote three more mysteries, *Later Than
You Think; House of Shade*; and *Night on the
Island*, before publishing her second historical
novel, *Trade Wind*, in 1963. The first of these
mysteries, set in the Rift Valley fifty miles from
Nairobi just after the Mau-Mau uprising, was described as a "routine mystery-romance" by Anthony Boucher in the *New York Times*. The
second, which takes place in Zanzibar, was described by James Sandoe in the *New York Herald Tribune Book Review* as "a pleasant piece of
work, striving a little hard for its thrills but keeping one diverted well enough."

Trade Wind takes place in nineteenth-
century Zanzibar at a time when the island was
a center of the African slave trade. It combines
a history of the time with romantic clashes between two social outcasts—an orphaned aboli-
tionist from Massachusetts and a piratical slave
trader, who first meets the heroine when she is
washed overboard near Zanzibar. Walter Shapiro, in the *Washington Post Book World*, noted
that Kaye's "narrative indicts hypocrisy, intolerance and the inability of many westerners to appreciate or understand local customs. But she
carefully avoids blanket indictments or the shrill
rhetoric of anti-colonialism." While commenting that a few of her European characters "come
across as one-dimensional windup toys," he
found the book "carefully researched" with sufficient action "even for sensibilities jaded by
television."

When *The Far Pavilions*, Kaye's most popular
work of fiction, came out in 1978, Francis King,
writing in the *Spectator*, made clear the reason
for Kaye's popularity as a novelist: "[H]er book
is a triumph of narrative, perseverance and hard
work . . . The result could best be described as
an Indian *Gone with the Wind*." Kaye spent fifteen years writing *The Far Pavilions* while raising her two daughters, fighting a successful
battle against cancer, and maintaining a household for her family in such trouble spots as Ken-
ya, Northern Ireland, Germany, Egypt, and
India.

The protagonist of *The Far Pavilions* is a 19th-
century British boy, raised in India and England,
who finds himself torn between his two heritages
when he returns to India as a soldier. He becomes embroiled in various adventures while
wooing an Indian princess who must choose between her heritage and the man she loves. Brigit-
te Weeks, in the *Washington Post Book World*,
found that the novel's most impressive achievement was "its balanced insight into the contemporary confusion and ancient order of 19th-
century India. On one hand Kaye shows
tremendous affection, sensitivity and understanding of the Indian people, their culture, religion and traditions, as they attempt to live in an
imposed British environment with all its narrowness and blunderings. Yet at the same time she
gives full credit to those colonialists, both civilian
and military, who make the best of an unheroic
situation, whose sense of duty—however odd in
retrospect—is strong and whose courage is
unfailing," For Rahul Singh, in *Punch*: "[T]he
significance of [Kaye's novels about India] lies in
her attitude. . . . There is none of the romantic
sentimentality that saw India as a country of
snake charmers and bejewelled princes, with the
faithful Gunga Din thrown in. Nor the view of

it as one vast, multiplying, putrefying sewer for which there was no possible hope. Ms. Kaye sees India as many Indians do, and for this one must applaud her."

Kaye wrote in *The Sun in the Morning* that she was blessed with "two invaluable gifts—an excellent memory and what I can only describe as a personal video set," which imprinted scenes and settings so vividly in her mind that she was able to recall them years later when writing her novels. It had been her "great good fortune to see India when that once fabulously beautiful land was as lovely, and to a great extent as peaceful and unspoiled, as Eden before the Fall." Geoffrey Ward, in the *New York Times Book Review*, noted regretfully that the India Kaye describes in her memoir "does seem paradisiacal" and that her "found nostalgia for the Raj seems untroubled by a single second thought." He found particularly irritating Kaye's insistence that her parents were not racists, that they were devoted to their Indian servants, and that her best friends were Indians, even though she "does not trouble to include any of the servants' real names." Kaye did not fail to recognize, however, that some Britons in India regarded Indians as inferior, and she acknowledges their unfair bias in her novels.

Kaye's first two historical novels were reprinted and became best sellers after *The Far Pavilions* established her reputation as an accomplished novelist. *The Far Pavilions* was produced as a television mini series in 1984.

PRINCIPAL WORKS: *Historical Novels*— Shadow of the Moon, 1956, (rev. ed. 1979; Trade Wind, 1963, (rev. ed. 1981; The Far Pavilions, 1978. *Mysteries*—Death Walked in Kashmir, 1953; Death Walked in Berlin, 1955; Death Walked in Cypress, 1956; (reissued as Death in Cypress, 1984); (as Mollie Hamilton) Later Than You Think, 1958; House of Shade, 1959; Night on the Island, 1960. *Juveniles*—(as Mollie Kaye) Potter, Pinner Meadow, 1937; The Animals Vacation, 1964; Thistledon, 1982; The Ordinary Princess, 1984. *Memoir*—The Sun in the Morning: My Early Years in India and England, 1990. *As editor*—The Golden Calm: An English Lady's Life in Moghul Deli, 1980. *Other*—The Far Pavilions Picture Book, 1979.

ABOUT: Contemporary Authors New Revision Series 23, 1988; Contemporary Literary Criticism 28, 1984; Kaye, M. The Sun in the Morning. *Periodicals*—New York Herald Tribune Book Review September 1, 1957; September 20, 1959; New York Times October 26, 1958; New York Times Book Review, September 30, 1990; Punch November 14, 1979; Spectator April 12, 1957; September 9, 1978; Washington Post Book World, September 10, 1978; July 12, 1981.

KEILLOR, GARRISON (GARY EDWARD) (August 7, 1942–), American novelist, essayist, scriptwriter, and short story writer, was born in Anoka, Minnesota, the third of the six children of Grace (Denham) Keillor and John Keillor, a railway mail clerk and carpenter. Although his mother, a member of the Plymouth Brethren, brought him up in the strict ways of her sect—no dancing, drinking, or card playing—Keillor, even while chafing under the limitations of his upbringing, managed to find pleasure and amusement listening to the parables people told at Sunday meetings. As David Sexton said in his 1986 *Times Literary Supplement* review of *Lake Wobegon Days*, Keillor found "a series of wonderfully comic responses to the problem posed by a Protestant that 'in some ways we were meant to be here' when 'here' is a nowhere like Lake Wobegon." (Lake Wobegon being the name Keillor applies to his generic Minnesota hometown). In Keillor's "manifesto of resentments," according to Sexton, his progenitors taught him: "'When the going gets tough, the tough get going,' teaching me to plod forward in the face of certain doom."

Keillor's given name was Gary, but he decided to change it: in the eighth grade when he began submitting poems to his school paper boys weren't supposed to write poetry, as he told Diane Roback in *Publishers Weekly*, so he became Garrison, "a name that meant strength." Shy and socially withdrawn as a youngster, he early took to reading in the bathroom and in closets to avoid his mother, who believed his rightful place was outdoors. His parents, who "weren't much for literature," and whose reading tastes were limited to such popular magazines as *Reader's Digest* and *American Home*, were dismayed when Keillor discovered the pleasures of reading the *New Yorker* as an adolescent. As he put it in *Happy to be Here*, "They were dead set against conspicuous wealth, so a magazine in which classy paragraphs marched down the aisle between columns of diamond necklaces and French cognacs was not a magazine they welcomed into their home." Keillor admired the magazine's writers, particularly Thurber, Liebling, Perelman, and E. B. White. "They were my heroes . . . and in my mind they took the field against the big mazumbos of American Literature, and I cheered for them. I cheer for them now."

Besides reading and writing, Keillor's chief interest as a boy was listening to the radio. One of his favorite programs was hosted by Cedric Adams, a local announcer and laid-back commentator who ruminated about life in the Midwest while boosting the bread sales of his sponsor. Keillor later adapted Adams's low-keyed style to

GARRISON KEILLOR

the comic aura of the radio program "A Prairie Home Companion," which he created. Another favorite, destined to become equally influential, was "Grand Old Oprey", which featured hillbilly singers, fiddlers, and bumpkin comedians and was broadcast live on Saturday nights from Nashville, Tennessee.

While pursuing a B.A. degree at the University of Minnesota in Minneapolis, where he enrolled in 1960, Keillor spent much of his time writing and editing for the student literary magazine. He earned money for his college expenses by parking cars and by staff announcing for the campus radio station. Before graduating from the university in 1966, he married a fellow student, Mary Guntzel. Afterwards, having taken a bus to the East to try to win employment with a major magazine—and failed—he resumed his job as a broadcaster for the radio station of the University of Minnesota. He also began working on a novel and on humorous stories he hoped to sell to the *New Yorker*.

In 1968, Minnesota Public Radio hired him to host a three-hour morning classical music show. Keillor then dreamed up the idea of Lake Wobegon, the mythical hometown of the radio show he was to launch, "A Prairie Home Companion." Other ideas for the show occured to him when the *New Yorker* (which had begun publishing his stories in 1969) sent him to Nashville to write an article on the Grand Old Opry in 1974. Nashville stirred memories of the broadcasts he had enjoyed as a boy, and by the time he returned to Minnesota he had all the ideas he needed for the show's ingredients: country and folk spon-

sors; stories; parodies of old-time radio drama and serials; and the "News from Lake Wobegon." The president of Minnesota Public Radio approved Keillor's idea and "A Prairie Home Companion" was broadcast on a network of thirty upper-Midwest public radio stations.

Appealing at first to a handful of devoted local admirers, Keillor's radio show grew in popularity, eventually attracting listeners across the country. In 1980 it was syndicated nationwide, and in 1981 it received the George Foster Peabody Award for Broadcasting. Acting as host for such regulars as autoharp player Stevie Beck, the bluegrass band Stoney Lonesome, and Butch Thompson and his trio, Keillor also enlivened the weekly broadcasts with his trademark opening song "Hello Love," his monologues about Lake Wobegon's inhabitants, and the commercials for the "sponsors" (Ralph's Pretty Good Grocery, the Chatterbox Cafe, Bob's Bank, Jack's Auto Repair, and Powdermilk Biscuits—"made from whole wheat raised by Norwegian bachelor farmers . . . so you know they're not only good, they're also pure mostly—the biscuit that gives shy persons the strength to get up and do what needs to be done." Among the characters Keillor invented for his mythical hometown were Father Emil, according to *Current Biography* "the archtraditionalist pastor of Our Lady of Perpetual Responsibility Church, whose voice can be heard wafting from the confessional on Saturdays ("Oh, you didn't!") and Senator Knute Thorvaldson, "an unelected citizen named Senator by his mother because she thought it had sort of a ring to it."

One reviewer, commenting on the program for *Christian Century*, made the point that "the news [Keillor] brings is good because it is funny, but not funny in a mean or loud manner. In his humor is the recognition that there is something that heals and unites us even in the most absurd events we encounter." David Black commented in *Rolling Stone* that the program "doesn't have to range far to hit home. In some hidden chamber of our hearts, most of us, no matter where we live, are citizens of Lake Wobegon, where 'all the women are strong, all the men good looking and all the children above average.'"

In 1982 a collection of pieces Keillor had written for the *New Yorker* came out in a book entitled *Happy to Be Here*. According to the *Dictionary of Literary Biography Yearbook*, many of these pieces "show the witty and urban Keillor rather than the wistful, wandering storyteller in exile from Lake Wobegon, where 'smart doesn't count for very much.'" Doug Thorpe, in the *Christian Century*, noted that his favorite stories in the book had "little to do with radio":

one of them, "Found Paradise," is about writing, and "the yearning for the quiet country life . . . It is also, along the way, a fine parody of various latter-day Thoreaus. Out on the farm, the story-teller keeps a journal ('forty-eight animals seen today before lunch, of which all but six were birds, most small and brownish') . . . What he finds . . . is what one usually does find if one spends some time on a Minnesota farm during the winter." Roy Blount, in the *New York Times Book Review,* found that "Keillor's stuff is calmly, acrobatically droll, yet makes no bones about its fondness for decency and its distaste for bullies."

Keillor said of his next book, *Lake Wobegon Days: Recollections of a Small American Town,* that he had written it to get himself back to being a writer. "Even when I began publishing with the *New Yorker* in 1970 I was still torn between radio, which is improvisational and colloquial and more intimate and sentimental to me, and my other writing, which tended to be a little drier, a piece of craft." The book, which traces the history of his mythical Lake Wobegon from the 1830s was described by Veronica Geng in *New York Times Book Review* as "a genuine work of American history:" Lake Wobegon joins Thurber's Columbus as an an absurd definition of a very real Midwest . . . The 19th century section . . . fixes graphically in one's mind, like a swerving arrow on a schoolbook map, the force that will sustain the town—a force Mr. Keillor defines as a 'form of voluntary socialism with elements of Deism, fatalism, and nepotism.'" David Sexton commented in the *Times Literary Supplement* that Keillor's style is "habit-forming . . . rhythmic, resourceful and particular. . . . Keillor's active sense of grievance about his upbringing prevents complacency or vacuous nostalgia. . . . [He] has a faculty of seeing as both the child he was and the adult that the child became, at once naive and disenchanted, blithe and rueful."

Keillor's novel *WLT: A Radio Romance,* although comic rather than tragic, has a dark edge. *New York Times* reviewer Anne Bernays said: "I ended up wishing Mr. Keillor had let me laugh more . . . . [H]is feelings about radio—even as we once knew it—are so cheerless." The novel, which chronicles the rise and fall of a successful radio station in Minneapolis, was described by the *Times Literary Supplement* reviewer, Roz Kaveney, as "an elegy for the America of small towns and cheap filling breakfasts which comes somewhere in the mythic history of the United States between covered wagons and the shopping mall." While admiring Keillor's "eye for absurdity and pomposity," and the "several levels of irony" that are

"characteristic of Keillor's work," she found the book enjoyable, "an elegy for something that did not entirely die," although Keillor "never more than nudges his readers toward a judgment or an interpretation."

Keillor has received several awards and honors. Besides winning the George Foster Peabody Broadcasting Award in 1980 for "A Prairie Home Companion," he also received the 1985 Edward R. Murrow Award for service to public radio; a *Los Angeles Times* Book Award nomination in 1986 for *Lake Wobegon Days;* and a Grammy Award for best nonmusical recording in 1987 for *Lake Wobegon Days.* In 1990 the American Academy of Arts and Letters awarded him their Gold Medal for Spoken Language. John Hollander, giving the citation, spoke of Keillor as "a satirist too gentle for savage indignation and too honorable to desist from it, a teller of his own tales in the purest of vernaculars that the linguists call General American dialect, he has added to that literary map of fictional places—Winesburg, Ohio, Tilbury Town, Spoon River—which we all use in our own quest for the nature of American communitas."

After eleven years of marriage to Mary Guntzel, and the birth of their child, Jason, Keillor's first marriage ended in divorce in 1976. He later married Ulla Skaerved, a Dane, after leaving his long-time companion and producer Margaret Moos. He moved away from Minnesota in the mid 1980s, first to Denmark, and then to Manhattan, where he began a new radio show, "American Radio Company," which was very similar to "A Prairie Home Companion," occupying the same time slot and providing "News from Lake Wobegon." Asked about how Midwesterners might view his move to the East Coast, Keillor responded, "I think people there feel the same way as if I had dyed my hair purple."

In 1993, however, after the breakup of his marriage, Keillor returned to the Midwest and settled in an isolated country retreat in Wisconsin near the Minnesota border. His break with New York became all the more final when he stopped writing for the *New Yorker* after almost twenty-five years (the reason, it was reported, was his disapproval of the policies of the new editor, Tina Brown). He continued broadcasting, however, returning to his show's original title, "Prairie Home Companion." Some of his old "sponsors," such as Powdermilk Biscuits disappeared (perhaps temporarily), but others, such as Bertha's Kitty Boutique, remained in place. Although Minnesotans were reluctant to forgive his desertion of his home state for the "big time" of New York, he has apparently proved that "you can go home again."

The Book of Guys, a story collection featuring such male icons as Earl Grey and Don Giovanni, won praise from most reviewers, many of whom, oddly enough, were female. Susan Jeffreys, writing in the *New Statesman & Society*, said, "Keillor puts on the mantle of guyness, with its repeating pattern of male bonding and rugged manly embraces and camps around it . . . Keillor's style has evolved so that it suits both print and radio and it has now, happily, become impossible to read him without hearing that voice in your head." Lisa Zeidner, calling *The Book of Guys* Keillor's best work since *Lake Wobegon Days*, commented in the *New York Times Book Review*, "The most substantial tales aren't really about manhood at all but the arbitrariness and absurdity of modern success, especially in show business."

PRINCIPAL WORKS: G. K. the DJ, 1977; The Selected Verse of Margaret Haskins Durber, 1979; Happy to Be Here: Stories and Comic Pieces, 1982; Lake Wobegon Days: Recollections of a Small American Town, 1985; Leaving Home: A Collection of Lake Wobegon Stories, 1987; We Are Still Married: Stories and Letters, 1989; WLT: A Radio Romance, 1991; The Book of Guys: Stories, 1993.

ABOUT: Contemporary Authors 117, 1986; Contemporary Authors New Revision Series 36, 1992; Contemporary Literary Criticism Volume 40; Current Biography Yearbook 1985; Scholl, P.A. Garrison Keillor, 1994. *Periodicals*—New Statesman & Society January 17, 1994; New York Times November 29, 1991; July 4, 1993; December 12, 1993; March 27, 1994; New York Times Book Review August 25, 1985; November 10, 1991; Times Literary Supplement March 7, 1986; January 17, 1992.

KENNELLY, BRENDAN (April 17, 1936–), Irish poet, novelist, and dramatist, writes: "I was born in 1936 in the village of Ballylongford in Count Kerry, Ireland, twenty years after the Easter Uprising, which was followed by the Civil War, the War of Independence and the infamous Black-and-Tan outrages committed against the ordinary people of Ireland. So when I was growing up, talk of these momentous events was common in the village. As well as that, I had the advantage of being reared in a pub. Every night the men came in (women only rarely entered pubs in those days) and drank Guinness, beer, and, on rare occasions, whiskey. And almost every night, they sang the songs which they'd inherited from their families. There was a lot of talk and a lot of singing. I grew up in a world of voices, the voices of men, and sometimes of women, talking of history, telling stories, singing songs, tracing close and re-

BRENDAN KENNELLY

mote family and interfamily relationships, enjoying gossip and scandal, giving accounts of those young men and women who'd emigrated to England and America and who occasionally returned with their own stories of these distant countries. England, though the traditional enemy, was a generous source of employment; and America was, quite simply, the land of hope, a country where a man's work 'got the money and the recognition it deserved.'

"It seemed totally natural to me, therefore, to write ballads and songs; and I wrote them always about people, their lives, children, work, games, plans to live at home or plans to emigrate. So, from an early age, fourteen or fifteen, I was writing ballads in the style of the ballads I heard around me. And I wrote them for particular people. One man told me that a song I wrote for him would 'soften the pain of exile.' To this day, I believe poetry is produced by the poet *for other people*, to express vague or definite feelings in clear, accurate language, to give a bit of sweetness to hearts and minds calloused or soured with living, to enable men and women to make and to enjoy quick, surprising connections between themselves and, perhaps, parts of their own lives which they've forgotten, or parts of the lives of others which they may not have been bothered to recognise. Poetry is, above all, a singing art of natural and magical *connection* because, though it is born out of one's person's solitude, it has the ability to reach out and touch in a humane and warmly illuminating way the solitude, even the loneliness, of others. That is why, to me, poetry is one of the most vital treasures that humanity possesses; it is a bridge between separated souls. Poetry is the opposite of war and terrorism, which divide people for generations. Yet poetry will sing of terrorism and war, as it will sing of anything which the poet is capable of experiencing. By 'experiencing' here, I mean the poet's ability to enter into the darkness not only of his own life, but the lives of others both living and dead. A poem must be able to sing of the festive lights in the city streets at least as convincingly as it must sing of the darkness of the graves of men and women long forgotten. One of the surest signs of poetry is its spirit of daring and fearlessness; no love is beyond its celebration; no atrocity is beyond its scrutiny; no goodness will totally overwhelm it; no evil render it mute. Poets may be killed off by themselves or others, but the daring spirit of poetry never dies. Poets matter only insofar as they embody something of that daring spirit.

"To be born in Ireland is to inherit not only one of the most beautiful little countries in the world, but also an entire legacy of prejudices, hatreds, clichés, and an impressive supply of apparently invincible ignorance. I've tried to love and celebrate this beautiful land, and to confront that savage legacy, in my poetry. Historical prejudice is still a vehement Irish cancer. In *Cromwell*, a long poem, I tried to grapple with the complexities of that cancer in brutally simple language. And in *The Book of Judas*, a four-hundred- page epic poem, I sought to examine and present the Irish manifestation of that sickness which frequently masquerades as civilization and culture in our Western world. In Ireland, Judas and Cromwell are not merely damned; they are irredeemable. My purpose was to let them speak for themselves because I believe that in poetry nobody, no matter how outcast and hated, should be denied a voice. To me, poetry is the ultimate democracy, made possible by a lifetime's dedication and skill.

"I've published over twenty books of verse, that is, I've spent almost forty years trying to understand, express, celebrate, and criticize the life of which I am a tiny, bewildered and obstinately articulate part. I am grateful if one line of mine, one image, will help to clarify, even for a moment, the bewilderment of another human being. The bridge I mentioned is built of such moments."

———

In 1989 a reviewer in *Choice* described Brendan Kennelly as "a very good poet, perhaps the best at the moment in the Republic of Ireland." He is a prominent figure on the Dublin literary scene, the recipient of honors (the AE Memorial Award in 1967, the Critical Special Harveys Award in 1988, the *Sunday Independent–Irish Life* Award for poetry in 1991, and an honorary doctorate from Trinity College in Hartford, Connecticut, in 1992), popular for his lectures, and poetry readings, and appearances on Irish television, and widely known for his editions of the *Penguin Book of Irish Verse* and his essay collections *Ireland Past and Present* and *Landmarks of Irish Drama*. In recent years there have also been critically successful stagings of his adaptations of Greek tragedy—*Antigone* in 1986, *Medea* in 1988—and his dramatization of his own long poem *Cromwell* in 1986. Although he has traveled and lectured abroad, including a visit to Japan in 1992 and guest professorships in the United States at Barnard College in 1971 and Cornell and Swarthmore in 1971–1972, Kennelly has received relatively little critical attention outside Ireland.

With the publication of *A Time for Voices*, a selection of his poems from 1960 to 1990, and *The Book of Judas*, a massive poetic work, however, Kennelly has emerged as an authentic and powerful voice not only of his own country but of human conditions everywhere. Kennelly's poetic voice has been compared to a ventriloquist's: speaking through the poet are multitudes. He assumes identities and their voices in a deliberate effort of distancing himself, "liberating myself from my self." He writes in the preface to *A Time for Voices*: "I believe poetry must always be a flight from this deadening authoritative egotism and must find its voices in the byways, laneways, backyards, nooks and crannies of self . . . a poet, living in his uncertainties, is riddled with different voices, many of them in vicious conflict." The result is poetry that is candid and often brutally outspoken. Reviewers have sometimes complained of the roughness of the work, its looseness and carelessness in rhymes and meter, and excesses of language. Peter Porter wrote of *Cromwell* in the *Observer* in 1987: "Kennelly has always been a most unpolished writer, and his verse is as knockabout as it ever was." In an essay in *Tradition and Influence in Anglo-Irish Poetry*, Edna Longley, generally an admirer, finds *Cromwell* abounding in "catalogues, accumulations, bad taste, bad jokes, bad language, melodrama, shock tactics, grotesque disproportions, hyperboles, going over the top." Along with Patrick Kavanagh (1905–1967), the celebrated Irish poet whom he much admires, Kennelly would probably agree that poetry "is a dangerous thing" and does not offer quick and easy rewards.

As an Irish poet who has chosen to remain in Ireland, Kennelly is acutely sensitive to his country's tragic past and its troubled present. In "My

Dark Fathers," the only one of his own poems that he included in the *Penguin Book of Irish Verse*, he writes of the terrible suffering in the great famine that ravaged Ireland in the mid-19th century and his conviction "that the past is a savage educator, capable of defining the present with brutal precision":

> Skeletoned in darkness, my dark fathers lay
> Unknown, and could not understand
> The giant grief that trampled night and day,
> The awful absence moping through the land.

Kennelly refuses to reject the heritage of English culture and comes from an Irish tradition that combines the Gaelic with the Anglo-Irish." . . . The imagination has nearly always brought them closer together so that now, in retrospect, the cultures they both produced may be seen as a compact imaginative unity," he writes in the introduction to the Penguin anthology.

A Catholic himself, Kennelly is critical of the church, believing it a "male-infested institution." It is less the institutional church, than "the mothering-smothering faces in Irish society" that Kennelly criticizes.

In the preface to his *Selected Poems* Kennelly acknowledged the responsibility of the poet to explore and celebrate "the sad farce of Irish censorship, the modern middle-class commandment to complacency and swinish apathy, Joyce's nightmare, the ferocious bitterness of many Irish poets and artists I have met. . . . " These are the conditions that would evoke his later ambitious poems *Cromwell* and *The Book of Judas*. In these Kennelly explores what he calls, in his preface to *Judas*, "the full, fascinating complexity of a man I was from childhood taught, quite simply, to hate." Neither poem is a defense of its main character, but both are attempts to portray the Irish soul—spiritually haunted by the image of Judas, historically by the image of Cromwell.

In *Ireland's Literature* Terence Brown describes *Cromwell* as "collage of speeches, letters, historical fragments, legends, jokes, satires, and personal poems." There are some 250 poems, mainly lyrics, many of sonnet length, with occasional rhyme. It is conceived as a dialogue between England, in the person of Cromwell, and Ireland, whose spokesman is one M(ichael) P(atrick) G(usty) M(ary) Buffún, Esq., "who is all of us." Although Kennelly did extensive historical research for the poem, he blithely defies chronology and piles up anachronisms. Buffún imagines "Oliver / Buying a Dodge, setting up as a taxi-driver." The historical Cromwell is at one point the manager of a football club (the

Drogheda United) and at another drug-addicted Vietnam veteran. The result is disquieting but very powerful. Brown believes that *Cromwell* confronts the nightmare history of Ireland "with a liberating authenticity." Under Cromwell's leadership atrocities are committed upon the Irish people, but he is also seen as a driven and complex human being with "a truly passionate sense of mission and purpose." He is simply another dimension of Irish history. Kennelly describes him in a note as "the paradigm of a power, an egotism hard to understand and impossible to measure." The poem itself, Brown argues, "attempts a shaman-like act of purgation, an imaginative exorcism of demonic possession, a breaking of the spell." For Edna Longley *Cromwell* is "a therapeutic primal scream . . . Kennelly understands that you don't exorcise the curse of Cromwell merely by cursing Cromwell." Giles Foden noted in the *Times Literary Supplement* in 1990, "What marks Kennelly out as a writer of extreme psychological subtlety is the give in his treatment of Cromwell: an exacting judgement on the historical truth is tempered with mercy in the shape of comedy."

The Book of Judas is not an attempt to redeem the character but to imagine him in the full complexity of his being. Kennelly asks: "How must men and women who . . . must absorb the full thump of accusation without the hope of reply, who have no voices because we know 'they're beyond all hope,' feel in their cold, condemned silence? In *The Book of Judas* I wished to create the voice of a condemned man writing back to me, trained and educated to condemn him." The poem is divided into twelve parts, each a collection of short lyrics, sonnets, with occasional and irregular rhyme and frequently corrosive wit. Speaking as the modern calculating poet, Judas describes "My Production Notebook":

> To get a proper understanding of the event
> Which I foresaw would matter much to men
> Though a few among them grasped what it meant
> I kept a production notebook on the crucifixion
> I wanted, above all, to get the details right.
>
> Fascinating work, I chose samples of the mob's faces,
> I noted exactly how the hammers fitted into
> The honest fists of those who drove the nails home
>
> For a pittance. To grasp the drama, my production notebook
> Is vital. You may consult it at the University
> Of Texas: they bought it for an undisclosed sum.

Kennelly's Judas lives in Jerusalem but also in Dublin, in Vietnam, and in Nazi Germany. He is intimately acquainted with "the poor, the sick, / the inexplicably shivering, the blacks, the Irish, the AIDS/Lot, starving millions. . . . " ("A

Voice at Last"). It is from his very humanity that ultimately a kind of redemption is born. In the closing poem, "The True Thing," Judas confesses to "yearning occasionally, nevertheless, for dialogue with God," after which "anything might happen":

I can even imagine a poet starting to sing
In a way I haven't heard in a long time.
If the song comes right, the true thing may find a name
Singing to me of who, and why I am.

Kennelly, the son of Timothy and Bridget (Ahern) Kennelly, attended St. Ita's College in Tarbert, County Kerry, from 1948 until 1953. In 1961 he received a B.A., with honors in English and French, from Trinity College, Dublin. He began his graduate studies in England at the University of Leeds, which is the scene of his novel *The Florentines*, but returned to Trinity where he completed his M.A. in 1963 and a Ph.D. in 1967. Since 1963 he has taught English literature at Trinity, moving up in the ranks from junior lecturer to professor of modern literature, a post he has held since 1973. He married Margaret O'Brien in 1969; they have one daughter.

PRINCIPAL WORKS: *Poetry*—(with R. Holzapfel) Cast a Cold Eye, 1959; The Rain, The Moon, 1961; The Dark about Our Loves, 1962; Green Townlands, 1963; Let Fall No Burning Leaf, 1963; My Dark Fathers, 1964; Up and At It, 1965; Collection One: Getting Up Early, 1966; Good Souls to Survive, 1967; Dream of a Black Fox, 1968; Selected Poems, 1969; The Voices, 1973; Shelley in Dublin, 1974; A Kind of Trust, 1975; New and Selected Poems, 1976; Islandman, 1977; The House That Jack Didn't Build, 1982; Cromwell, 1983; Moloney Up and At It, 1984; A Time for Voices: Selected Poems 1960–1990, 1990; The Book of Judas, 1991. *Prose*—Journey into Joy: Selected Prose, 1994. *Novels*— The Crooked Cross, 1964; The Florentines, 1967. As editor—The Penguin Book of Irish Verse, 1970, rev. ed. 1972, rev. ed. 1981; Ireland Past and Present,1986; Landmarks of Irish Drama, 1988.

ABOUT: Brown, T. (ed.) Ireland's Literature: Selected Essays, 1988; Brown, T. and N. Grene (eds.) Tradition and Influence in Anglo-Irish Poetry, 1989; Contemporary Authors New Revision Series 5, 1982; Contemporary Poets, 5th ed., 1991; Dictionary of Literary Biography 40, 1985; Kenneally, M. (ed.) Cultural Contexts and Literary Idioms in Contemporary Irish Literature, 1988; Pine, R. (ed.) Dark Fathers into Light: Brendan Kennelly, 1994. *Periodicals*— Antigonish Review Autumn 1990; Choice February 1989; Irish Literary Supplement Fall 1984; Spring 1990; Irish Review Autumn 1990; Observer October 11, 1987; March 1, 1992; Poetry Ireland Review Summer 1984; Times Literary Supplement December 15, 1966; November 9, 1967; February 16, 1973; August 17, 1990.

KIDDER, TRACY (November 12, 1945–   ), American journalist, editor and short story writer, was born in New York. His father, Henry Maynard Kidder, was an attorney; his mother Reine Tracy Kidder, a high school English teacher. After attending Andover, Kidder received an A. B. in 1967 from Harvard, where he started writing short stories. An early story, "The Death of Major Great," was to win second prize (1974) in the "First" contest, sponsored by the *Atlantic Monthly*, where he has long been a contributing editor. After his graduation from Harvard, Kidder served in the army in Vietnam as an intelligence officer. In 1971 he married Frances T. Toland; they live in western Massachusetts.

When he returned from Vietnam, Kidder concluded that writing was the only thing he wanted to do. He then received a fellowship which enabled him to attend the University of Iowa Writers Workshop for three years, obtaining his M.F.A. in 1974.

In 1974 *The Road to Yuba City: A Journey into the Juan Corona Murders* was published. Somewhat reminiscent of *In Cold Blood*, by Truman Capote, *The Road to Yuba City*, parts of which first appeared in the *Atlantic Monthly*, is an almost day-by-day account of the 1971 trial of Juan Corona, accused of having killed some twenty-five migrant farm workers in northern California. Utilizing the techniques of a skilled observer and interviewer which he was to refine in his later works, Kidder attached himself over a period of four months to the participants in the trial and investigated the environment in which the events took place. He hopped a freight train to Yuba City and met an assortment of interesting vagrants and migrant workers along the way; he thinned peach trees side by side with the regular farmworkers; he visited the local saloons and absorbed gossip about the trial and about more mundane matters. Kidder then portrayed the bungling sheriff, the arrogant defense attorney who badgered state witnesses and inexplicably refused to call any witnesses of his own, and the impossibly stubborn juror who claimed to have been pressured by her colleagues into voting for a conviction. Kidder traveled to Guadalajara, Mexico, to interview Corona's shadowy brother Natividad, who may have been implicated in the crimes. He took a trip back east to Frankfort, Kansas, where he visited with a sister of one of the victims and sat in on a seance in which the murdered man denounced his killer.

The book was praised in *Library Journal* because it "answers some of the previously unanswered questions about this strange crime." According to *Best Sellers*, Kidder's "stories of seamy   characters   are   interesting   and

TRACY KIDDER

fascinating." *Publishers Weekly* found that "the writing is plain, the presentation skillful, the story, at times, as tense as good detective fiction." Despite its merits, *The Road to Yuba City* did not reach many readers or reviewers—perhaps, Kidder acknowledged in a November 1981 *New York Times Book Review* interview, because he "was unable to penetrate Corona's psyche the way Truman Capote or Norman Mailer penetrated the psyches of the murderers they wrote about."

Soul of a New Machine, a book about the computer industry—surprising because, as a Harvard undergraduate, Kidder had meticulously avoided any courses smacking of science or technology—was enormously successful, and Kidder received both the Pulitzer prize and the American Book Award. As he told Lee A. Daniels in a 1989 interview in the *New York Times Book Review*, he had turned his journalistic talent to "the little things around us, the small gestures, that add up to life," choosing to write "about nonfamous people at work."

Soul of a New Machine is a detailed account of "Eagle Project," undertaken by Data General Corporation (DGC), in Westborough, Massachusetts, to develop—in the face of seemingly impossible deadlines and other constraints—a new minicomputer. At the same time the book offers a history of computers in general and provides the nonspecialist reader with what a reviewer in *Scientific American* called "a pithy insight into just what a computer is." Because of the fierce competition between DGC and Digital Equipment Corporation, as well as the internal rivalry

between Eagle and another DGC group working in North Carolina on a different computer, the project was conducted in a kind of cloak-and-dagger secrecy. To write the book, Kidder, so to speak, infiltrated DGC for two years, spending eight months in the basement, where much of the work went on after midnight. Kidder thinks the engineers accepted him and patiently answered his questions because they were pleased that an outsider was interested. "They believe that what they do is elegant and important," he told the interviewer for the *New York Times Book Review*, "but they have the feeling that no one else understands or cares."

The main participant in Eagle is the enigmatic leader of the project, Tom West, a man given to taking risks. West conveys "the intensity of someone who's weathering a storm and showing us the way out." West, like Chuck Yeager in Tom Wolfe's *The Right Stuff*, is the embodiment of "a mythos around an almost larger-than-life figure," one of "the space-age craftsmen, the Cathedral builders of today," according to *English Journal*. Jeremy Bernstein said in the *New York Review of Books*, "One gets caught up in the project. The machine becomes a living entity." The reward, in West's view, is "pinball. . . . You win with this machine, you get to build the next." The leaders of Eagle "are portrayed as eccentric knights-errant, clad in blue jeans and open collars, seeking with awesome intensity the grail of technological accomplishment," Samuel Florman observed in the *New York Times Book Review* (August 1981). In the *Journal of American Studies*, Richard T. Brucher placed the Eagle engineers—particularly their leader, West—in the cultural tradition of Emerson, Thoreau, and Whitman. West seeks an "assertion of personal identity within the environment of business and technology."

House chronicles the planning and construction of a new home in Amherst, Massachusetts. As *Time* noted, Kidder interlaces his immediate subject with information about significant cultural and class differences in American society, as well as "vestpocket essays on architecture and the lumber business; insights into bidding, building techniques, and the pleasures of physical labor." We learn, for example, about postmodernism, the "baloon frame," and pouring the cellar floor. Even as routine a subject as building contracts assumes dramatic interest:

The written agreement separates emotions from transactions. If you put your deal in writing, you can head off misunderstandings and deter malfeasance. Those are the old and enduring promises. Americans have always believed in them, and in every era significant numbers of people have prepared for the construction of houses as they have prepared for death, by getting their wishes down in writing.

In the *Christian Science Monitor*, James Kaufmann commented that *House* is more than "a matter-of-fact picture of so many blueprints, hammers, and nails, but a really complex drama of human interactions with enough emotional energy to satisfy any playwright." Kidder sees the building of a house as nothing less than "an icon of the American dream."

Among Schoolchildren, Phyllis Theroux wrote in the *New York Times Book Review*, deals with "groups of people struggling against the odds to put something valuable together. *Among Schoolchildren* is about one woman's struggle against the odds to keep something valuable—20 children—from coming apart." That woman is Chris Zajac, fifth-grade teacher in Kelly Elementary School in Holyoke, Massachusetts. "We like to generalize about education," Kidder told the *Times* reviewer, "and look for grand solutions, often forgetting that there's something very compelling about what goes on in a classroom. . . . I wanted to write about a particular situation . . . and let the point come through that teachers matter, but they can't do it all." Accordingly, Kidder sat in on Mrs. Zajac's classes for the whole academic year, observing her at close range both inside and outside the classroom and recording her interactions with the generally disadvantaged children (mainly Puerto Rican) who live in what he calls "The ultimate rigged life in a rigged world."

Most critics agreed that the strength of *Among Schoolchildren* is its emphasis on the particulars of Chris Zajac's classroom—what Marie Ponsot, in *Commonweal*, called its "'dailiness.' . . . Modestly [Kidder] offers no big ideas about pedagogy or education politics. He draws no conclusions. The concreteness of his anecdotal portrait has the readability and convincing detail of all narrative." Kidder, despite his occasional forays into such issues as educational theory and the demographic and social history of Holyoke, told Jim Bencivenga, an interviewer for the *Christian Science Monitor* (1989), that he does not use much of "the exterior stuff." And yet, the absence of "exterior stuff" and Kidder's concentration on "dailiness" have led a few critics, including some of the book's admirers, to express reservations. As John R. Alden noted in the *Wall Street Journal*, "The most upsetting behavioral problem in Mrs. Zajac's class is resolved by the school principal midway through the book, and most of the other potentially dramatic situations Mr. Kidder sets forth are never explored." Herbert Kohl, in a review for the *Nation*, was disturbed by what he perceived as Mrs. Zajac's

inability to go beyond the curriculum, question her methods, or think globally about education. A "semitragic figure" driven by the fear of chaos, she becomes something of an authoritarian who feels compelled to stick to the rules so as to maintain control at any cost. Therefore, in Kohl's view, Kidder "leaves the reader with a dangerous romanticization of one way of teaching—an uncritical way that shuts off creativity and turns away from solving the problems of educating the poor."

Moving from schoolchildren to the other end of life's spectrum, Kidder turned in his next book, *Old Friends*, to America's aging population. As in his earlier works, he chose a single representative example and proceeded to explore it at length and in depth over a whole year. The old friends of the title are two residents of a Massachusetts nursing home, Lou and Joe, who share a room. Around them and their fellow residents Kidder details the daily routines, the small pleasures and larger despair of the lives of those who are waiting to die. David Gates observed in *Newsweek* that *Old Friends* is "devastatingly depressing yet profoundly humane." Kidder refuses to soften or sentimentalize his subject. He acknowledges that for some there may be "successful aging" ("often depicted in photographs of old folks wearing tennis clothes"), but he also emphasizes that such an image "leaves out a lot of people . . . Ultimately, of course, it leaves out everyone."

Because Kidder characterizes Lou and Joe and the other residents so deftly, however, he tends to shift the balance away from the focal issue, the problem of aging in America. As a seasoned "new" journalist, Kidder gives his readers an intimate insight into the lives of these people. But, as Scott Donaldson wrote in the "Chicago Tribune Books": "Unlike some of the more egregious practitioners of the new journalism, he does not intrude and has no attitude beyond compassion."

PRINCIPAL WORKS: The Road to Yuba City: A Journey into the Juan Corona Murders, 1972; The Soul of a New Machine, 1981; House, 1985; Among Schoolchildren, 1989; Old Friends, 1993.

ABOUT: Contemporary Authors 109, 1983. *Periodicals*—Architectural Record May 1980; Best Sellers December 1, 1974; (Chicago Tribune) Books September 19, 1993; Christian Science Monitor July 10, 1982; October 4, 1985; September 8, 1989; Commonweal November 3, 1989; English Journal December 1982; April 1990; Journal of American Studies December 1985, 325–336; Library Journal January 15, 1975; August 1981; August 1985; Nation February 15, 1986; November 6, 1989; New Republic November 13, 1989; New Statesman March 19, 1982; New York Review of Books October 8, 1981; New York Times Book

Review August 23, 1981; November 29, 1981; October 6, 1985; September 17, 1989; October 3, 1993; Newsweek October 4, 1993; Psychology Today December 1985; Publishers Weekly October 18, 1974; Scientific American October 1981; Time October 14, 1985; Wall Street Journal November 8, 1985; August 25, 1989; Washington Post Book World September 9, 1981.

BARBARA KINGSOLVER

KINGSOLVER, BABRARA (April 8, 1955–), American novelist, and writer of short stories writes: "I grew up in a rural Kentucky county that lies, both geographically and economically, between the affluent farms and the hardscrabble coalfields. It was a land of one-stoplight towns and labor-intensive farming, where cash was generally short; everybody knew everybody's business and people depended explicitly on family and neighbors for their survival. When I think about the themes to which my writing always returns—the valuable complexities of relationships and community responsibility—I recognize the worth of my childhood in this place.

"I like to write about the sort of people who would not think of their lives as the material of literature, but who rise to the difficult occasions of their lives with humor and inspiring resourcefulness. Our literary tradition tends to glorify individual action, and define heroism as something that rides in on a horse from the far horizon, but in my life I've rarely seen it happen that way. More often than not, I think, heroism is banged together with the help of friends using tools that were lying around the basement or the kitchen.

"My childhood world was constrained in the way that small-town childhoods are, but it held the infinite possibilities of the alfalfa fields and wooded hills surrounding our backyard. My parents taught me the names of trees and wildflowers, and allowed my siblings and me the exquisite luxury of bringing home turtles, orphaned rabbits, snakes, caterpillars that metamorphosed before our eyes, and jars of lightning bugs that lit our bedroom on summer nights. My experience was also opened by my family's summer vacations in a station wagon, and by the books that lined our home and came regularly on the Bookmobile. I read the encyclopedia, field guides, and every novel that crossed my path. I read *Little Women* and wanted to be Jo, the maverick girl who cut off her hair and had an opinion about everything on earth.

"For my seventh birthday I received a Five Year Diary, which I filled up in one year, and I've kept a journal consistently since then. In adolescence I began to experiment with poetry and fiction, but I did not, and would not for nearly twenty more years, think of myself as a writer. I didn't know any writers, and didn't imagine that the beautiful books I read could have been produced by an ordinary person like myself. But I felt (and still feel) a powerful compunction to nail down the experience of my life through writing, a process that feels something like trying to nail a river to its banks, to hold it still long enough for me to take a good look and try to understand it.

"In high school, I became aware of the inescapable boundaries of class, gender, and race in a small southern town; I couldn't have named these things, but couldn't have failed to know them, either. The kids from town, whose parents were merchants or civil servants, did not associate with those who rode in on the bus and so often had to miss school during tobacco-stripping season. The school was racially integrated when I was in second grade, but the town itself was still perfectly segregated in an obvious way. And fully a quarter of my female classmates were pregnant or already mothers by the age of eighteen. I felt a strong desire to see something more of the world.

"In 1973 I went to DePauw University, in Indiana, and learned about everything I could: music, literature, chemistry, biology (my eventual major), Asian history, and how to organize a moratorium on classes to protest the bombing of Vietnam. The latter was an important part of my education; we witnessed an immoral event, we protested it, and it ended. Though I know the causality was more complex, I still came away with a sense that I could engage my own conscience in the events of the world and participate in social change. I've been trying to do that ever since, as a human rights activist, an environmentalist, a mother, and as a writer. The belief that one can personally improve the world is now considered unfashionably naive, I know. But I believe it anyway, because it gives me a consistent sense of direction and the possibility of a happy life.

"In my adult life I lived in several countries and earned a graduate degree in evolutionary biology before settling permanently in Tucson, Arizona. I supported myself with many kinds of work before it dawned on me that books could be written by people like me. I'm as grateful for my diverse employment history and education as I am for my Kentucky childhood. My fiction is never explicitly autobiographical; it strikes me that using real people and their lives for my own designs would be a kind of thievery. Instead, I invent characters whose troubles and dreams resemble my own and those I've witnessed; I place them in a setting that distributed wealth, quiet desperation, and a lot of joyful noise; then I encourage them to face their problems in interesting and mostly honorable ways.

"My point of origin in writing is almost always theme, rather than character or incident, because I think there is no point in bringing another book into the world unless it's going to be about something important. I don't mind being thought of as a political writer. Fiction has the power of creating empathy, and gloriously—a political act."

Barbara Kingsolver is the daughter of Virginia (Henry) Kingsolver and Wendell R. Kingsolver, a country doctor whose needier patients sometimes paid their bills with squash or melons. Trained in classical piano as a child, Kingsolver went to DePauw University on a music scholarship, but eventually switched to biology. She went on to earn an M.S. in biology from the University of Arizona (in 1981), and pursued her research specialty—the social lives of termites—to the brink of a doctoral dissertation before deciding against an academic career. Presenting her thesis committee with an elaborate white lie about her need to support a disabled relative, she extricated herself from her academic obligations and took her first writing job—as a technical writer for the university. "Although it wasn't perhaps the most creative kind of writing," she told the *New York Times Book Review* in 1988, "it was really good training, because I learned to just sit at a desk and write eight hours a day."

Her training as a scientist notwithstanding, Kingsolver has had an abiding interest in literature. "Eudora Welty, Carson McCullers and Flannery O'Connor were the stars in my sky as a child," she told *Publishers Weekly* in 1990. Later influences include Doris Lessing, Ursula LeGuin, and William Faulkner—the only male author in her literary pantheon. Having already written a number of short stories (including a prize-winning entry published in a Phoenix alternative paper), she turned in earnest to fiction writing in 1985. Pregnant and suffering from chronic insomnia, she sequestered herself in a closet and began composing what would become her first novel—*The Bean Trees.*

The Bean Trees is narrated by Taylor Greer, a young Kentucky woman raised by a single mother in extremely modest circumstances. After graduating from high school and working for several years as a hospital lab technician, she buys a dilapidated Volkswagen and heads west, hoping to escape the fate of her cohorts—poverty, pregnancy, and marriage to a local boy with a dead-end job. Starved for sleep and short of cash, she stops one night to eat at a seedy, out-of-the-way diner in Oklahoma. As she is pulling out of the parking lot, a woman from the restaurant deposits a swaddled Indian baby on the seat of her car, saying, "Take this child." In the brief conversation that followed, Taylor learns only that the child belongs to the woman's dead sister, that it's "got no papers," that "[t]here isn't nobody knows it's alive, or cares," and that it was "born in a Plymouth." Before Taylor has a chance to demur, the woman drives off and disappears into the night, leaving her with a child she never asked for.

Unable to decide on any other course of action, Taylor decides to keep the child—a baby girl, she discovers—and continue her journey west. She names the silent baby girl with the tenacious grip Turtle. Taylor's car makes it as far as Tucson, Arizona, and there she decides to settle. Responding to a newspaper ad, she moves in with Lu Ann Ruiz, a young mother recently separated from her Mexican-American husband and, like Taylor, a native of Kentucky. Lu Ann's pessimism and lack of self-esteem contrast, often hilariously, with Taylor's plucky indomitability; the two women, each with a young child, establish their own makeshift, matriarchal menage. They converse in the patois of rural Kentucky, using such expressions as "I'll swan" (I do declare) and "dumb as a box of rocks." Another major figure in Taylor's life is her employer, Mattie, a widow in late middle age. In addition to being the proprietor of Jesus Is Lord Used Tires, Mattie is a clandestine activist in the sanctuary movement, an underground network providing shelter for Latin American refugees. Taylor's education in the ways of the world is furthered through friendship with two of Mattie's charges, Estevan and Esperanza, who have fled torture and repression in Guatamala. Taylor must come to terms with the reality of human rights abuses closer to home when X rays reveal that Turtle had been beaten (and probably sexually abused) in the first months of life.

Despite its attentiveness to the horrors of life in contemporary America and elsewhere, *The Bean Trees* is hardly a depressing novel. Each of the major characters, while struggling to overcome appalling circumstances, is a testament to the resiliency—and variety—of life. Turtle, the once-abused and abandoned child, whose early vocabulary consists almost wholly of the names of vegetables and flowers, most clearly exemplifies the novel's affirmation of life's regenerative possibilities. "*The Bean Trees* is as richly connected as a fine poem," Jack Butler wrote in the *New York Times Book Review* (1988), "but reads like realism. . . . It is the southern novel taken west, its colors as translucent and polished as one of those slices of rose agate from a desert rock shop." Kingsolver's depiction of strong, quirky women living independently made *The Bean Trees* especially attractive to feminist reviewers, among whom it created a minor literary sensation. Margaret Randall, writing in the *Women's Review of Books*, hailed it as "a first novel that's fast reading but long staying. . . . In style and vision," Randall noted, "she has written a book all her own, and with a deep female consciousness that feels like bedrock when put up against some of the preacher, more explicitly feminist works." In a *Ms.* magazine review entitled "A Major New Talent," Karen Fitzgerald wrote: "*The Bean Trees* covers expansive territory—literally and figuratively. Yet, despite the large sweep of the canvas, the characters remain firmly at the novel's center." Fitzgerald lauded Kingsolver for creating characters who could voice feminist ideas without becoming mere "mouthpieces of the party line."

Within just two years of her auspicious literary debut, Kingsolver published three more works: a collection of short stories, a nonfiction book, and a second novel. Reviewing *Homeland and Other Stories* in the *New York Times Book Review*, Russell Banks commented: "Of the twelve stories in this first collection . . . , all are interesting and most are extraordinarily fine. Barbara Kingsolver has a Chekovian tenderness toward her characters." In *Holding the Line*, a book she began writing in the early 1980s, Kingsolver chronicles the central roles played by women in the fractious 1983 labor dispute between Arizona mine workers and the Phelps Dodge Copper Corporation.

Animal Dreams, her second novel, is narrated by Codi Noline, a medical school dropout whose overwhelming sense of purposelessness prompts her to return to her hometown of Grace, Arizona. There she takes a teaching job and does what little she can for her father, an aging physician displaying early symptoms of Alzheimer's disease. Codi's aimlessness stands in stark contrast to the political commitment of her sister Hallie, who does agricultural work in war-torn Nicaragua, and whose voice emerges only in the long letters she writes home. Critical response to the novel, while generally favorable, was not as warm as that which greeted *The Bean Trees*. In the *New York Times Book Review*, Jane Smiley questioned Kingsolver's decision to make the uncommitted character the narrator of such an overtly political novel. Still, Smiley saw the work as an attempt at a new kind of political expression. "Unlike some other recently published novels that have broad scope," she noted, " . . . *Animal Dreams* is not Apocalyptic. . . . Barbara Kingsolver is one of an increasing number of American novelists who are trying to rewrite the political, cultural, and spiritual relationships between our country's private and public spheres. . . . Like others who are looking for a new approach, . . . Kingsolver prefers to concentrate upon particulars."

In her third novel, *Pigs in Heaven*, a sequel to *The Bean Trees*, Kingsolver examines what can happen when the moral claims of an individual conflict with the claims of a community. Turtle, now six years old and the legally adopted daughter of Taylor Greer, is the focus of this conflict. On a visit to the Hoover Dam with Taylor, Turtle saves a man's life by being the only witness to a freak accident. The publicity attending this incident brings Turtle to the attention of Annawake Fourkiller, an attorney for the Cherokee nation, who decides to launch an investigation into the circumstances surrounding the girl's adoption. Fourkiller then advances the claim that the Cherokee people—not Taylor Greer—are the rightful guardians of Turtle. "Possessed of an extravagantly gifted narrative voice, [Kingsolver] blends a fierce and abiding moral vision with benevolent, concise humor," Karen Karbo wrote in the *New York Times Book Review*. "Her medicine is meant for the head, the heart and the soul—and it goes down dangerously, blissfully, easily." Laura Shapiro, in *Newsweek*, while noting that "the denouement relies on a somewhat unwieldy coincidence," nevertheless concluded that "*Pigs in Heaven* succeeds on the strength of Kingsolver's clear- eyed warmhearted writing and irresistible characters." *Pigs in Heaven* was Kingsolver's first unqualified commercial success, spending more then eleven weeks on the *New York Times* best seller list.

Kingsolver has set most of her fiction in the America West, but her vision transcends regionalism. "We all have so much common ground," she remarked to a *Newsweek* interviewer. "We belong to the same species, have pretty much the same dimensions, the same food-chain position. When you reduce it, we all need the same things to survive."

Barbara Kingsolver is divorced from Joseph Hoffmann, whom she married in 1985. She lives with her daughter Camille in Tucson.

PRINCIPAL WORKS: *Novels*—The Bean Trees, 1988; Animal Dreams, 1990; Pigs in Heaven, 1993. *Short stories*—Homeland and Other Stories, 1989. *Nonfiction*—Holding the Line: Women in the Great Arizona Mine Strike of 1983, 1989. *Poetry*—Another America Otra America (With Spanish Translations by Rebecca Cartes), 1992.

ABOUT: Contemporary Authors 134, 1992; Contemporary Literary Criticism 55, 1989. *Periodicals*—Ms. April 1988; New York Times September 1, 1993; New York Times Book Review April 10, 1988; June 11, 1989; September 2, 1990; June 27, 1993; Newsweek July 12, 1993; Publishers Weekly August 31, 1990; Women's Review of Books May 1988.

W. P. KINSELLA

KINSELLA, W(ILLIAM) P(ATRICK) (May 25, 1935–), Canadian novelist and writer of short stories writes: "I was raised in unusual circumstances. My father (John Matthew Kinsella, 1896–1953) was an American who settled down late in life in Canada. He was a building contractor, but when the depression came along there were no buildings to build and he was too proud to accept relief, which was what welfare was called in those days. He sold his house in the city of Edmonton, Alberta, and bought a stony and useless quarter-section of farmland in an isolated area of Northern Alberta, which is where I spent the first eleven years of my life.

"I was an only child. The nearest neighbors were miles away and the nearest neighbors with children were I don't know where, because I seldom saw other children while I was growing up. My education consisted of correspondence courses, supervised by my mother (Mary Olive Elliot Kinsella, 1903–). I had to create all my own entertainment, which I feel had a good deal to do with my becoming a writer, because from an early age I was required to use my imagination—to bring to life imaginary playmates, to create exotic lives for my pet cats.

"Though we were only sixty miles from Edmonton, Alberta, we may as well have been 6000, the isolation was so complete. We had nothing mechanical on the farm, no tractor, no

electricity or plumbing. We traveled by horse and sleigh, horse and buggy, or just plain horse. Alberta is known for nine months of winter and three months of poor sledding.

"The one luxury we enjoyed was a subscription to a weekend edition of a Toronto newspaper. The papers arrived a month or so late, but it didn't matter as time meant little to us. The weekend newspaper did contain a short novel and several short stories, which were often read aloud to me. My parents, though of limited education, were readers and my father, particularly, read and reread aloud the few books we owned.

"I'm one of these people who woke up at age five knowing how to read and write, and I've been writing ever since. I had no role models. Received no encouragement to be a writer. My parents were so scarred by the depression their only advice was to get a steady, depression-proof job, probably in the civil service. We didn't study any fiction in high school, though I did have an excellent high school English teacher (Ethel Anderson), who taught me the importance of expressing myself in clear, straightforward, standard English.

"I published my first stories immediately after high school. But then I married and my daughters were born, and except for a few pieces of free-lance journalism, I spent the next fifteen years at a series of evil jobs in order to keep food on the table for my young family.

"In 1967 I opened a restaurant in Victoria, B.C., and after three years it was successful enough that I was able to find time to take a creative writing course at the University of Victoria. I was ravenous for an audience. My instructor (Derk Wynand) had one filer exclusively for the other 15 plus members of the class and one larger folder exclusively for me. I was turning out a ten to twenty-page story every week. I eventually sold my business and attended university full time, receiving a B.A. in creative writing in 1973. I found a mentor in short fiction writer W. D. Valgardson, who was able to put me on the right track by pointing out that I warmed up for a page or so before starting my stories and wound down for another page after finishing. I stopped doing that and I've sold everything I've written ever since.

"I went to graduate school at the Iowa Writers Workshop, where I received an M.F.A. in 1978. I was 42 in 1977 when my first book *Dance Me Outside* was published. I then taught for five unhappy years at the University of Calgary, which I always refer to as Desolate U, before my novel *Shoeless Joe*, published in 1982, opened all the doors of international literature to me, and gave me the freedom to quit teaching and write full time.

"I now have close to twenty books published and several more written. The movie *Field of Dreams* (1989) opened up many more doors for me. I loved the movie—most writers are not happy with what Hollywood does with their work, and with good reason. In bad hands *Field of Dreams* could have been just another car-chase movie, but Phil Alden Robinson, who both adapted and directed the movie, was so in love with the concept that he wanted to create something wonderful, and I believe he did.

"I consider myself a storyteller. A fiction writer's duty is to entertain. If I can write on a second or third level, occasionally slipping into something profound or symbolic, so much the better. But storytelling as entertainment dates to the days of the caveman when Ugh would stand up at the campfire and say, 'Listen to me! I want to tell you a story about the bear I killed this afternoon.' If Ugh wasn't a good storyteller everyone would sink off to their caves and he would be left alone. The same thing applies to fiction writers today. Either tell a fast-paced entertaining story or do so without an audience.

"Some of my nonbaseball writing has been criticized by the highly dangerous *Trendinistas*, the Hitleristic advocates of political correctness, concerning the nonissue of appropriation of voice. Every fiction writer may write from the point of view of any person in or out of the world, at any time, under any circumstances. The issue is not discussible.

"I consider myself a humorist. My work has been described as 'good-natured antiauthor-

itarianism,' with which I tend to agree. I love to poke fun at all the areas of society that take themselves too seriously—academics, religious leaders, politicians, bureaucrats. My heroes are often overwhelmed by the complexity of the world around them and long for simpler explanations. They often find, or appear to find, a structure in baseball that acts to anchor them in a world that otherwise too swiftly passes them by.

"Why baseball? I believe it is the open-endedness of the game that makes it so conducive to fiction writing. The other sports are twice enclosed, first by rigid playing boundaries, then by time limits. As we all know there are no time limits on a baseball game, and on the true baseball field the foul lines diverge forever, eventually taking in a good part of the universe. There is theoretically no distance that a great hitter couldn't hit the ball or a great field runner run to retrieve it. This makes for myth and for larger than life characters, two things fiction writers are always searching for. In *The Iowa Baseball Confederacy* I have a fielder who runs from Iowa to New Mexico chasing a fly ball. This kind of fanciful happening is almost impossible when writing of basketball, football, or hockey, which is why there has been quite a bit of good baseball fiction and virtually nothing of quality about the 'enclosed sports.'

"I've learned to be a reader-performer of my own work, and travel extensively making appearances all over North America. My daughters Shannon, Lyndsey, and Erin are the joys of my life. My wife, Ann Knight, could not be a more loving and supportive partner. She manages to help me keep my hectic life in perspective."

———

W. P. Kinsella spent much of his young adulthood in such decidedly nonliterary pursuits as selling insurance, managing a credit agency, running a pizza restaurant, and driving a taxi. He gained critical recognition with his first collection of stories, *Dance Me Outside*. Each of the collection's seventeen stories is narrated by Silas Ermineskin, an eighteen-year-old Cree Indian living on an Alberta reservation. The stories are at once humorous and melancholy, their atmosphere punctuated by Ermineskin's idiosyncratic, often fractures, syntax. Taken as a whole, the stories provide a bittersweet glimpse into the lives of contemporary reservation Indians as they try to get along in the Anglo world.

Critics applauded Kinsella's refusal to idealize the Cree, or to demonize the Caucasians. In a review of *Dance Me Outside* in *Fiddlehead*, Anthony Brennan wrote, "Kinsella's book . . . is all the more refreshing because it quite consciously eschews ersatz heroics and any kind of nostalgic, mythopoeic reflections on a technicolor golden age." George Woodcock, reviewing the collection in the *Wascana Review*, noted: "Laughter and evasion have always been excellent means of cultural survival, and in the stories which form *Dance Me Outside*, W. P. Kinsella deploys those elements with a virtuosity that reminds one of Hasek's use of fictional mockery as a social weapon in *The Good Soldier Schweik.*"

Kinsella has published several subsequent collections narrated by the fictional Cree, Silas Ermineskin. These include, *Scars, Born Indian*, and *The Moccasin Telegraph and Other Indian Tales*. In a *New York Times Book Review* notice of *The Moccasin Telegraph*, Jodi Daynard wrote: "Unsentimentally poignant, full of the energy of drama and folk tales, these marvelous stories go far in dispelling many lingering myths and misconceptions about North American Indians—none greater, perhaps, than the one that says they have no sense of humor."

While Kinsella established his literary reputation with his stories about the Cree Indians of Alberta, he is best-known for his baseball novel *Shoeless Joe*, the motion picture adaptation of which, *Field of Dreams*, was one of the most successful films of 1989. The novel had its beginnings as a short story, "Shoeless Joe Jackson Comes to Iowa," which was featured in the story collection of the same title. In that story, an Iowa farmer named Ray Kinsella heeds the call of a mysterious voice that instructs him to build a baseball diamond in his cornfield. "If you build it," he is assured, "he will come." He, in this case, is shoeless Joe Jackson, star of the World War I-era Chicago White Sox. Jackson and a number of his teammates were accused of intentionally losing the 1919 World Series, an episode infamous in sports history as the Black Sox scandal. In addition to being visited with public disgrace, Jackson was barred from baseball for the rest of his life. It is Iowa farmer Ray Kinsella's mission to resurrect Jackson and the rest of the 1919 White Sox for a game that will restore them to greatness.

After the collection *Shoeless Joe Jackson Comes to Iowa* was published, Kinsella was contacted by a young editor who was eager to see him expand the title story into a novel. For the novel, he left his short story more or less intact, using it as an opening chapter. Several characters not found in the original short story appear in *Shoeless Joe*. Paying homage to one of his own literary idols, Kinsella introduces J. D. Salinger as a fictional character. In the novel, Ray Kinsella hears a second voice, which commands him to "Ease his pain." Understanding that the voice is referring to Salinger, Kinsella brings the reclusive writer from his New England home to Boston's Fenway Park to see a baseball game.

In his consideration of the novel in *Modern Fiction Studies*, Neil Randall found Kinsella's invocation of J. D. Salinger to be perfectly apposite. "The novel's effect on us is precisely that which the fan attributes to the writings of J. D. Salinger ," Randall noted. "*Shoeless Joe* is a moral book, but it does not bludgeon its morality into us." Indeed, Salinger's fiction may well have provided W. P. Kinsella with the inspiration for the name of his novel's protagonist, Ray Kinsella; a character by that name appears in Salinger's 1947 short story, "The Girl in 1941 with No Waist at All." Salinger's celebrated novel *The Catcher in the Rye* introduces a Richard Kinsella; in *Shoeless Joe*, Ray Kinsella has a twin brother Richard. "I didn't know I was going to use Salinger," W. P. Kinsella remarked in his interview with *Publishers Weekly*. "It was just something in the back of my mind. I like being audacious."

In the magically real world of *Shoeless Joe*, the ostensibly illogical union of Ray Kinsella's family, J. D. Salinger, and the motley crew of long-departed baseball stars is the basis for many long meditations on love, literature, baseball, and life. Kinsella has always insisted, as he did to *Publishers Weekly*, that "*Shoeless Joe* isn't a novel about baseball. . . . It's a story about the power of love in all directions." The novel won favorable notices from critics, many of whom professed a general indifference to baseball and baseball fiction. Reflecting on the infectious enthusiasm of Ray Kinsella's baseball talk, Maggie Lewis wrote in the *Christian Science Monitor* (1982), "It was enough to make this reviewer, whose only contact with the game is the memory of being hit on the head with a softball she was supposed to catch, love baseball herself for a while. This is a convincing novelist." In addition to being one of the best-selling novels of 1982, *Shoeless Joe* received several prizes, including a Houghton Mifflin Literary Fellowship, the Books in Canada First Novel Award, and the Canadian Authors Association Prize.

The novel was not, of course, without its critics, the most scathing of whom was probably the *Washington Post's* Jonathan Yardley, who called it "a book of quite unbelievable self-indulgence." For William Plummer in *Newsweek* who commented that "the language sometimes melts in the hand rather than the heart." He added, however, that "such complaints seem mean-spirited, tin-eared, in the face of the novel's lovely minor music."

The short story collections *The Thrill of the Grass* and *The Further Adventures of Slugger McBatt*, and the novels *The Iowa Baseball Confederacy* and *Box Socials* are among Kinsella's other baseball fictions. The protagonist of the *Iowa Baseball Confederacy* is endowed with encyclopedic knowledge concerning a defunct baseball league, a league no one else recalls and about which no records exist. Theodore Roosevelt and Leonardo da Vinci are among the novel's characters, the latter descending from the heavens in a hot air balloon to inform onlookers that he is the inventor of baseball. Frank Loreto, like other reviewers, noted the novel's similarities to *Shoeless Joe*, but said in *CM* that the "summer dreamlike quality" of the earlier novel here takes on "more of a nightmarish tinge."

Box Socials is a coming-of-age story narrated by young Jamie O'Day, and set in the hinterlands of Alberta in the mid-1940s. The novel's baseball players—far from the glamour of the big city major leagues—represent teams from six small, poverty-stricken Alberta towns. In the *New York Review of Books*, Stephen Jay Gould wrote: "I can't remember when a book of this genre made me laugh so much, but *Box Socials* contains little about baseball, except as a device linking Kinsella's accounts of life, love, and gossip in hamlets literally off the map." Charles Fountain, reviewing *Box Socials* noted in the *Christian Science Monitor*: "There is great magic in Kinsella's work. . . . The magic in Kinsella's stories, however, is not the baseball, but rather incandescent use of language."

PRINCIPAL WORKS: *Short Stories*—Dance Me Outside, 1977; Scars, 1978; Shoeless Joe Jackson Comes to Iowa, 1980; Born Indian, 1981; The Ballad of the Public Trustee (chapbook) 1982; The Moccasin Telegraph and Other Indian Tales, 1984; The Thrill of the Grass, 1984; The Alligator Report, 1985; Five Stories (chapbook) 1986; The Fencepost Chronicles, 1987; Red Wolf, Red Wolf, 1987; The Further Adventures of Slugger McBatt: Baseball Stories, 1988; The Miss Hobbema Pageant, 1990; The Dixon Cornbelt League and Other Baseball Stories, 1993. *Novels*—Shoeless Joe, 1982; The Iowa Baseball Confederacy, 1986; Box Socials, 1992. *Poetry*—The Rainbow Warehouse, 1989. *Nonfiction*—The Spirits Soar: The Art of Allen Sapp, 1990.

ABOUT: Contemporary Authors New Revision Series 35, 1992; Contemporary Literary Criticism 27, 1984; 43, 1987; Who's Who in Canadian Literature 1985–1986, 1985. Periodicals—American Film May 1989; Books in Canada November 1984; Christian Science Monitor July 9, 1982; June 29, 1992; CM July 1986; Commonweal July 11, 1986; Fiddlehead Fall 1977; Film Comment May/June 1989; Modern Fiction Studies Spring 1987; Newsweek August 23, 1982; New York Review of Books November 5, 1992; New York Times Book Review September 2, 1984; April 20, 1986; Prarie Schooner Spring 1979; Publishers Weekly April 16, 1982; Village Voice December 4, 1984; Wascana Review Fall 1976; Washington Poet March 31, 1982.

KITO MORIO (pseudonym of Saito Munekichi) (1927–), a Japanese novelist, was born in Tokyo, the son of the psychiatrist and distinguished poet Saito Mokichi. His father, one of the first Japanese to study psychiatry in Germany and Austria, headed an important mental hospital in Tokyo. He was also celebrated in Japan as a gifted poet noted for his modernizing of the ancient Japanese *waka* tradition of thirty-one-syllable poetry, since early times the form of verse most employed in the Japanese court tradition. Kita Morio followed both directions of his father's career, although most of what he has written is fiction rather than poetry.

Raised in a cosmopolitan and highly cultivated family (later to figure in his novel *The House of Nire*), Kita originally planned to become an entomologist, but under his father's influence he switched to medicine, entering Tohoku University in 1948. He completed his medical degree in 1953 and practiced both on the staff of his father's hospital and in other mental clinics as well. Meanwhile, he was beginning his career as a writer. In 1954 he published, at his own expense, his first novel *Yurei* (*Ghosts*). The novel, described by Julian Loose in the *Times Literary Supplement* as "a number of lyrical fragments," than which Loose said it would be "hard to imagine a text more quintessentially Japanese. . . . saturated with images of the ephemeral: the silvery dust left by a butterfly's wings. . . . " Evoking some aspects of the author's childhood, it is the story of the coming of age of a young man during the 1930s and 1940s. Left without family after the death of his father, the abandonment by his mother of her children to relatives, and the death of his sister, he seeks to recapture a sense of his lost family. "The narrative, only just discernible, traces the way a series of small epiphanies prompt the hero to recall his earliest, apparently forgotten years. Driven by the need to discover some image of his dead mother, he brings a new sense of urgency to the familiar Proustian imperative to revive the vague and fading past," Loose said. *Ghosts* bears many traces of Kita's own intimate and formative experiences.

Kita established a firm literary reputation in 1960 with two novels of widely different natures. One, the first of a continuously popular series of humorous books, was *Dokutoru Manbo* kokaiki (*Dr. Manbo at Sea*). The book grew out of Kita's experiences as a ship's doctor in 1958 and 1959, on a fishing-resources survey that took him through the Indian Ocean and as far as Europe. This lighthearted but realistic account of the adventures of the luckless Dr. Manbo, clearly Kita's persona, won him a wide audience and launched a series of "Manbo books," among them *Dokutoru Manbo tochû gessha* (Dr. Manbo gets down on the way, 1966), *Dokutoru Manbo seishunki* (A record of Dr. Manbo's youth, 1968), *Manbo Shuyuken* (Manbo's excursion ticket, 1976), and *Manbo muykyo* (The place where manbo walks in his sleep, 1978), among many others.

Vastly different in subject and spirit was his short novel *Yoru to kiri no sumi de* (In a corner of the foggy night, 1960). The book, which deals with the moral crises faced by German doctors in mental hospitals who were forced by the Nazis to conduct experiments on their patients, was well received and won the prestigious Akutagawa Prize.

Well read in modern European literature, Kita was especially interested in the writings of Thomas Mann, whose great family history *Buddenbrooks* was a distinct influence on his own ambitious *Nireke no hitobito* (1964, *The House of Nire*), which won another major literary award, the Mainichi Prize. The book is altogether original, however, based loosely on his own family history. It chronicles three generations of the Nire family, beginning with the patriarch Nire Kiichiro, founder of the Nire Hospital. He sends his son, Tetsukichi, a character certainly modeled on Kita's father, to study medicine, in Germany. In turn his son Shuji, who appears to be the author's persona, becomes involved in the vicissitudes of life on a desolate Pacific island during World War II.

These men, representing three generations, provide the central core around which revolves a huge cast of characters—family members, servants, patients in the hospital, friends—all drawn with humor but with compassion and sensitivity as well. Their lives are played out against the vividly realized background of Japan in the years between 1918 and 1946. Kita's treatment of the closing period of the war is particularly satiric, and it may well be that these sections of the novel were meant by the author to serve as a commentary on the naive enthusiasms of his father, who supported the military war efforts with considerable enthusiasm. The role of the women in the book is extremely important. In particular, Momoko, Dr. Nire's third daughter, is a free spirit who, forced by family pressure to marry a man for whom she feels no affection, marries again for love when her first husband dies. Given the strict attitudes of the time, she is never reconciled with her parents.

The English translation of *Nireke no hitobito* was published in two volumes, *The House of Nire* and *The Fall of the House of Nire*. Phoebe-Lou Adams, in the *Atlantic*, found the first part of the Nire history a realistic and slyly humorous depiction of Japanese family life and called the second part, covering the war and its aftermath, "a convincing and touching picture of how ordinary Japanese citizens saw the war and what they suffered from it." In *World Literature Today* David G. Goodman agreed that the first volume was "an endearing combination of humor and compassion," while the second "conveys valuable insight into how the Japanese experienced the 'dark valley' of the second world war." Goodman also suggested that the Nire saga has interesting autobiographical significance because it reflects the conflict within Kita's own life between the demands of his two careers as novelist and as physician: his family. . . . "

In 1966 Kita published a novel, *Shiroki taoyaka na mine* (White graceful peak) which drew on his experiences as an attending physician for a mountain-climbing expedition in northern India. This account chronicles the sense of beauty, and of fear, that men feel before the face of the great forces of nature. Kita's text is prose, but with powerful lyrical overtones.

Kita has also written in a genre he describes as "nursery tales for adults." These short and touching morality tales have been collected as *Sabishii Osama* (The lonely king, 1969), *Sabishi kojiki* (The lonely beggar, 1974), and *Sabishii himemgimi* (The lonely princess, 1977). Other works of a lighter nature which have won him a large popular audience include *Yasashii nyobo wa satsujin oni* (The gentle wife a devilish killer, 1986) and *Dai Nippon supaman* (Superman of Great Japan, 1987).

Of a more serious nature is an ambitious work dealing with Japanese settlers in South America, covering the decades between the Meiji Period and Japan's defeat in World War II in 1945. Kita went to Brazil in order to carry out the research needed for this lengthy historical novel. Published under the omnibus title *Kagayakeru aoiki sora no shita de* (Beneath the brilliant azure sky), the book appeared in two parts—the first in 1982, which carries the action forward into the 1920s, and the second in 1987. Some reviewers noted that Kita's earnest style betrays his diligence in studying historical sources, but the eloquent plainness of his style and the exciting plot he created have held the attention of readers.

Kita has consistently shown a wide range of interests and of writing styles. His background in medicine and in international travel sets him apart from many of his more introverted contemporaries among Japaneses writers. Nevertheless, in bringing these qualities to his best work, Kita has been able to remain an author whose works have now beguiled, and instructed, two generations of readers.

Kita Morio lives in Tokyo, with his wife Yokoyama Kimiko whom he married in 1961, and their children.

PRINCIPAL WORKS IN ENGLISH TRANSLATION: (tr. D. Keene) The House of Nire, 1984; (tr. D. Keene) The Fall of the House of Nire, 1985; (tr. D. Keene) Ghosts, 1991.

ABOUT: Kodausha Encyclopedia of Japan, 1984. Periodicals—Atlantic November 1984; June 1985; New Yorker January 14, 1985; August 12, 1985; Publishers Weekly March 22, 1985; Times Literary Supplement August 7, 1992; World Literature Today Autumn 1985.

*KOLÁŘ, JIŘÍ (September 24, 1914–), Czech poet and artist was born in Protivín in southern Bohemia. His father was a baker, his mother a dressmaker. He went to school in Protivín and in the mining and industrial town of Kladno. At fourteen he began training in cabinetmaking. During the 1930s he worked as a casual laborer—a contruction worker, truck driver, watchmaker, nurse, waiter, and cabinetmaker. Totally self-taught in both literature and art, Kolář discovered poetry when he read the lyrical poems of Jaroslav Seifert (who won the Nobel Prize for literature in 1984). Seifert worked in traditional modes, but it was his passion for human justice that espcecially inspired Kolář. At about the same time he discovered avant-garde poetry, finding a library copy of the Italian Futurist poet Emilio Marinetti, going on from there to the French poets Mallarme and Apollinaire and then to James Joyce and T. S. Eliot. He told Charlotta Kotik, "From the beginning, my concern was to find the interfaces between the fine arts and literature. All previous attempts in this direction seemed insufficient to me and, above all, not consistent enough." Another early discovery for him was the poetry of Americans, such as Walt Whitman and Edgar Lee Masters, whom he later translated into Czech, both poets little known at that time in Czechoslovakia.

By the middle 1930s Kolář was living in Prague and working not only as a poet but as an artist in collage, a medium in which he found he could come as close as possible to realizing his goal of fusing the word and the image. His aim, Kotik writes, was "to cut through all the unconscious layers of connections which we carry in our minds—the connections of our pictorial and semantic imaginations." He had his first exhibition of collages at the Mozarteum in Prague in 1937, four years before he collected his first book of poetry Křestný list (Birth certificate, 1941), a collaboration with the well-known Czech poet František Halas and the critic Jindřich Chalupecký. Although more conservative reviewers dismissed it as a mere imitation of voguish dadaism and surrealism, Chalupecký defended it as a healthy invasion of "real and rich reality." Kolář was in fact condemning—with irony, grotesque humor, and street language that parodied traditional forms—"the Parnassism and artificiality" of a considerable part of European poetry at that time. He was trying to reinvigorate Czech poetics with his own imaginative but basically plebeian and working-class background.

A few months after the publication of Kolář's first book Skupina 42 (Group 42), the leading avant-garde movement at that time started its activity. According to their theoretician Chalupecký, "Surrealism in its orthodox form is not sufficient any more." They therefore took over what they considered the most valuable component of surrealism, "the miraculousness of ordinary things," and concentrated on "the mythology of modern man," on the metaphysics of "the world in which we are living"—our urban civilization "abandoned by religion," in which man is "a tragic hero between God and nothingness," who "feels his own self and never understands." After the Communist takeover of Czechoslovakia in 1948, the writers belonging to group 42 were no longer allowed to pursue their program. They published little and often devoted themselves to translating. Among those who were altogether erased from literature was Chalupecký himself, who had been an outspoken critic of establishment art.

Kolář's next two books of poetry, Ódy a variace (Odes and variations, 1946) and Limb a jiné básně (Limb and other poems, 1946), were written during World War II. In them he fully developed what he had invented in the distinctive poems of Křestný list. Chalupecký characterized them as "manifestos of group aesthetics": the first of them (with quotations from Henry Miller, Joyce, T. S. Eliot, Hermann Hesse and Kafka) is dedicated "To my friends from Group 42", and the other to Chalupecký. Kolář's poems are epic and dramatic, and testify to the fact that under the influence of Edgar Lee Masters he epitomized people's lives in character portraits. The poems are often dramatic monologues or di-

°kole AHZH, YI zhee

alogues condensed tragedies or comedies which resemble Robert Browning's. One work presents several variations of a single story.

Kolář's *Sedm kantát* (Seven cantatas, 1945), celebrating the end of the war, shares the idealistic illusions of many poets about the Soviet Union and a happy future: "it will be necessary to start again, again from the beginning, oh, youth!" Like Sandburg, Kolář celebrates the common people, who are "good, pure and simple." (At the time, he and Jiří Kotalík were translating Sandburg, whose *Ocel a dým* (*Smoke and Steel*) appeared in 1946; the Czech translation *Lid, ano, lid!* (*The People, Yes!*), made by Arnošt Vaněček, had been published in 1945.) The verse *Dny v roce* (Days of the year, 1948) and the prose *Roky v dnech* (Years of the days, 1992) are arranged like a "diary." As one of the two epigraphs says, coincidence was to help him to achieve a truthful account of one year. The texts were natural and spontaneous; as the other epigraph says, "Oh, by no means prose. I took everyday speech to help me." The poems as well as the prose contain accounts of Czechoslovakia and also France and Germany. The postwar traumas in the lives of individual people as well as in the situation in Czechoslovakia are the subjects. (Some of these images would be used by Kolář later in his absurdist plays.) The childlike optimism of *Sedm Kantát* vanishes. In its place he expresses a loss of faith in poetry, often citing Chalupecký's statement: "Poetry has fallen far behind visual art, not to speak of music." That is why he resolved to move beyond Poe, Mallarmé, Apollinaire and the surrealists, rejecting the "Parnassian and artificial" literature of his time as morally incompetent and outdated. Kolář drew radical conclusions from the condition of society, art, and literature. Following the devastation of World War II he embraced the avant-garde position of rigid standards, and the need for action.

The diary *Očitý svědek* (The eyewitness, published in Munich in 1983), written between February and December of 1949, follows the line of the two earlier books. It is written in prose as well as verse. The author's doubts about his own way of writing, which did not bring him freedom, grew stronger:

I am like a worm cut into halves,
in front of whom they put mud
to have somewhere to wriggle, somewhere not to end.

Kolář expressed moral skepticism about his situation: "Each sacrifice, as the old used to say, on the altar of justice, honesty and freedom is futile, foolishly futile."

Prométheova játra (Prometheus's Liver, writ-ten 1950, published in Czech in Toronto in 1985 and in Prague in 1990) is probably the saddest of all Kolář's books. It reflects the author's despair and fear in a period of the most rigorous Stalinism in Czechoslovakia, when Kolář and his works came under severe criticism. In its time the book was intended for the author's friends only and when a copy was found in the flat of Professor Václav Cerný, a well-known dissident, Kolář was imprisoned for nine months. A part of this work, *Jásající hřbitov* (A jubilating cemetery), contains several excerpts from the author's diary written in verse and in prose from January to December 1950; the other parts contain collage-like adaptations of texts of other authors and Kolář's variations of satirical stories. This remarkable book is overloaded with ideas and daring literary experiments and gives evidence of the emotional crisis Kolář was undergoing during this period.

In 1957, however, at the time of the political thaw, Kolář wrote two treatises in verse on poetry, *Mistr Sun o básnickém uměnñ* (Master Sun on the Art of Poetry) and *Nový Epiktet* (New Epictetus, published in 1968), which display his renewed self-confidence as a poet. The first was based on a 2,500 year-old handbook on military art, the other on texts of moral philosophy. For Kolář poetry is realized through the "master-disciple" relationship for which easy-to-remember aphoristic expressions are well fitted. He favors an imaginative and witty style, free of the adornments and conventions of a stifling past tradition.

In the years 1954 to 1957 Kolář wrote several books of poetry: *Cerná lyra* (The black lyre), *Návod k upotřebení* (Instructions for use), *Marsyas* (Marsyas), *Z pozustalosti pana A* (From the legacy of Mr. A.), *Vršovický Ezop* (Aesop from Vršovice), and *Ceská suita* (The Bohemian suite). A selection from these books was published in 1966; they were published in their entirety in 1993. The poems introduce lines of poetry (Whitman, for example) and prose pieces from other authors, ranging from ancient times (Pliny the Elder, Tacitus, old China) through accounts of concentration camps during World War II. *Ceská suita*'s poems are created from the texts of Czech writers dating from the 1800s to the 1930s. Most of them testify to human misfortune, poverty, misery, and anger, but some are simply sharply focused, ironical stories. The remaining books of poetry belonging to this group contain sprightly, sometimes parodic, poems written mostly in an argot or slang.

In 1957 Kolář wrote, "Since Eliot's *The Waste Land*, poetry has not advanced a single centimetre." From this he drew a lesson: he gave up more conventional poetry and devoted himself to experimental poetry and visual art. He wrote "evident or "concrete poetry, in which letters or objects, instead of words, become units from which the poems are constructed. An example is his "Bird in Space," inspired by Brancusi's sculpture of that name: a poem made up entirely of the name "brancusi" broken up into units to reproduce the shape of the piece. In such poetry Kolář achieves his purpose in collage, liberating words from their conventional meanings ("I have always been concerned with separating things from the context of their conventional symbolic meaning," he has said.), breaking down language and reassembling it in new forms, transforming poetry into visual art and art into poetry.

Parts of Kolář's collections were published under the title *Básně ticha* (Poems of silence, 1965 and 1966). After that he published *Návad k upotřebení* (Instructions for Use, 1969). It contains poems—"instructions for actions"—accompanied by the author's collages:

SONNET
We take a novel
we haven't read
cut off the spine
remove the pagination
and jumble up the pages
In this disorder
we then read the book
and in fourteen lines
write what it's all about

In 1958 Kolář finished two absurdist dramas in the manner of Samuel Beckett: *Chléb náš vezdejší* (Our daily bread, published in 1991) and *Mor v Athénách* (Plague in Athens, published in 1965). They are plays about the manipulability of people, about monotony, violence, and evil. Both have a silent overture performed by clowns and are assembled like collages, making use of texts from various periods as he had in earlier works. Already in Cerná lyra, it is apparent that Kolář believes that "drama has not advanced since Shakespeare" and that his problem is not to write "better," but "differently."

In *Odpovědi* (Answers, written in 1973, published in Cologne in 1984 and in Prague in 1992) Kolář formulated his views on literature, art, culture, and society, along the lines of his earlier "diary-like" books. When he gave up writing conventional poetry, he had achieved, he said, all he could. He had modified the heritage of the Czech avant-garde, which appeared to him too negative and dependent on the symbolist pols. Kolář is a poet of classic harmony and serenity, affirming love and absurdity, and shunning morbidity.

Kolář is an important translator from English (in addition to Whitman and Masters he has translated Tennessee Williams and Edward Albee). From French he translated Beckett's *Waiting For Godot*, Saint-John Perse, and Roger Garaudy. He has also written books for children; some of them, in collaboration with Josef Hiršal, adapt traditional themes (Aesop, Eulenspiegel, Baron von Münchhausen; the wise men of Schildau; Paleček, the clown of the Czech king George); and some of them rank among the best books of humor and nonsense poetry in Czech literature (for example, *Nápady pana Apríla* [Inventions of Mr. April-Fool] 1961).

One of the most significant Czech intellectuals of his time, Jiří Kolář influenced both literature and art. From the 1950s to the 1970s he was a strict arbiter of one Prague circle of writers and artist; his views exerted influence also on other writers, including Bohumil Hrabal, Václav Havel, and Ludvík Vaculík. A radical explorer, Kolář assumes that "after Joyce, an artist must take an interest in everything." His ideal is "not to carry on with something that has already been discovered." On the contrary, the artist has to "do things differently—and run away from what he knows how to do." Most of his books have been translated into French and some also into German, English and Italian.

PRINCIPAL WORKS ON ENGLISH TRANSLATION: Poems *in* Williams, E. (ed.) An Anthology of Concrete Poetry, 1967; (tr. G. Theiner) Two poems *in* Theiner, G. (ed.) New Writing in Czechoslovakia, 1969; Jiri Kolář: Transformations (catalogue of an exhibition at the Albright-Knox Gallery in Buffalo, New York) 1978.

ABOUT: Contemporary Artists, 2nd ed., 1983; Current Biography Yearbook 1986; Digby, J. The Collage Handbook, 1987; Kotik, C. *in* Jiri Kolář: Transformations, 1978. *Periodicals*—Art News November 1975; Arts Magazine September 1975; National Observer November 1, 1975; New Yorker October 27, 1975; Studies in Twentieth Century Literature Spring 1985.

KRIEGEL, LEONARD (May 25, 1933–), American essayist, memoirist, and novelist, writes: "I was born in the heyday of the depression, of Eastern European immigrant parents, and lived what I look back on as an idyllic childhood in the North Central Bronx. The summer I was eleven, I contracted polio at an upstate camp, my first time away from home. I spent the next two years in an orthopedic hospital trying to learn to live without the use of my legs. More than anything else, that experience formed me—both as a man and as a writer. A number of critics have spoken of my 'obsession' with be-

LEONARD KRIEGEL

ing crippled and what the reality of it created in my life. And a good deal of my writing has been structured around the aftereffects of polio. I'm not certain 'obsession' is a good description. I myself, in an essay called 'Writing the Unlived Life,' speak of how it was a polio virus that 'gave me a writer's voice. For it was that virus which taught me how to see and what to look for. And it was that virus which forced me to recognize that in writing about who I was and how I lived, I was still speaking for that eleven-year-old boy, the *who* I should have been and the *how* I might have lived.' But no writer is formed solely by a single event, no matter how traumatic. I'm also very much a product of a time and place, New York of the forties and fifties. It has always seemed to me that New Yorkers are among the truest regional writers in the nation, rivaling southerners for the sense of place they bring to their work. One of the best things I've ever read about writing is Hemingway's insistence that good writing begins with a sense of geography. A lot of bad writing probably begins there, too, but I think of myself as a writer whose imagination has been nurtured by the streets and angles of New York. Even when what I write is set elsewhere, it remains a product of a New York sensibility. Of course, the writers I learned from were not necessarily New Yorkers: Faulkner and Hemingway are first in line, and Jim Farrell (who seems to me a writer who gave many of us permission to look at where we were and why we were writing) and the early Bellow and Mann and Proust and more recently Mailer and Updike.

"For me, it's the sentence that creates good writing. It's always been the sentence. And I'm willing to forgive quite a bit for the sake of a good sentence. It's what I still like about my first book, *The Long Walk Home*, even though a good deal else about that book embarrasses me today. And it's what I like in the book of mine that is still my own personal favorite, *Notes for the Two-Dollar Window*, part-fiction, part-memoir, and rooted to the sentence from first page to last. It's the sentence that brings me into my books, whether the book is a novel about the rise and fall of a Jewish Communist labor leader, *Quitting Time*, or a polemic about manhood in America, *On Men and Manhood*, or a collection of autobiographical essays, *Falling Into Life*.

"I've made my living as a teacher of literature at the City College of New York since 1961. I've been the recipient of three Fulbrights, a Guggenheim, a Rockefeller, and, more recently, a Rifkin Fellowship. Writing and literature have been very good to me. But deep down I'd still like to get even with that virus, if for no other reason than that the virus is 'still the mote in my eye, still forcing me to look where I didn't plan to look and to see what I did not think I wanted to see. And the reason, finally, why I write.'"

———

Leonard Kriegel's first book is a deeply felt record of the catastrophe that was to be the single most important force in the author's personal and professional life. "I wrote *The Long Walk Home*," Kriegel says in "Writing the Unlived Life," "because I sensed that unless I wrote it I could no longer live with what the virus had done to me. But in the process of writing I discovered that I had consciously condemned myself never to live without what it had done. An exchange had been made—the virus had my legs; I had its sight."

The Long Walk Home details the author's experience at the New York State Reconstruction Home in West Haverstraw, New York ("the Rock," as it was called by Kreigel and the other victims): his painful progression from endless immersions in the pool to mastery of the wheelchair and, finally, to the braces and crutches that would be his permanent companions. Kriegel also felt a special personal link with Franklin D. Roosevelt, who fought the same virus: "I wasn't sure about God. . . . But I was sure about the President. . . . He was an easy god to worship." Especially painful is his account of his Bar Mitzvah at West Haverstraw, surrounded by a bewildered, but well-meaning family trying to ward off the fear that his disease might be some sort of divine punishment: "I would have to stand before them, before all of them, acknowledging my crime, my guilt, offering a sad imitation of manhood in exchange for the absolution of pity."

The turning point in Kriegel's battle occurred after his release from the West Haverstraw facility, while he sat one day at the window of his Bronx apartment intensely watching a street game of stickball and fantasizing about his future. "And then the myths dropped away forever, to die permanently in a sudden burst of anguish and despair. Because *I was a cripple.* Nothing but a cripple. . . . That was all—so simple, so brutal, a truth, the kind of truth I had never before permitted to invade my consciousness, a total candor that came with all the shock impact of an idea what was to embed itself permanently within the boundaries of my existence. I was a cripple." At that moment was born a new will to drive himself mercilessly as to achieve, to "get even." It remained for his wife-to-be Harriet Bernzweig who, in the words of the book's dedication, "crippled the myth of my cripple," to teach him how to channel his rage and "just be."

Working Through: A Teacher's Journey in the Urban University is an autobiographical memoir and social commentary based on Kriegel's career as student and/or teacher in five distinctive New York Institutions: Hunter College, Columbia University, New York University, Long Island University and City College. As an undergraduate at Hunter, where he was a member of the first coeducational class (the college had previously only admitted women), Kriegel acquired a love of literature and "a need to be useful, a service mentality that remains something I still find myself fighting as a teacher." His one year as a graduate student at Columbia engendered outrage at the "puffy ostentation" of a faculty that cared only for research and approached students with a "benevolent regality." "It was at Columbia that I first learned how dangerous the academic world would actually be. For it can destroy in the name of enlightenment and corrupt in the name of truth." It is possible, as Morris Dickstein wrote in the *New York Times Book Review*, that Kriegel, in this "piece of sustained loathing," cannot "sort out his private misery at Columbia from the near fatal flaws of graduate education everywhere." In any case, at New York University, where he received his Ph.D. in American studies, Kriegel enjoyed the "slight touch of raunchiness" and lack of intellectual pretension: "No one saw himself here as a guardian of the culture, and this helped make it a less uncomfortable place than Columbia." After a year of teaching at Long Island University Kriegel joined the faculty of City College (of the City University of New York). With time out for Ful-

brights (two in the Netherlands, one in France), he remained there until his retirement in 1993.

For Kriegel, City College was a microcosm of New York and of urban America in general as it underwent sweeping ethnic and intellectual transformations from the 1960s through the 1980s. And yet, as Daniel Coogan noted in *America* (1972), Kriegel "recognizes the perils of politicizing the university. . . . He deplores the substitution of a phony 'relevance' as the touchstone of a curriculum in place of the old solid values." "Where others," Dickstein observed, "have charged forward with ideological blinders, Kriegel employs a novelistic touch to render the feel and complexity of the great changes that have swept the metropolitan university."

Notes for the Two-Dollar Window: Portraits from an American Neighborhood is also a personal memoir, in part fictional, about Kriegel's periodic visits to his old neighborhood in the Bronx, a community that he came to reassess with eyes sharpened by the polio virus that had crippled him. The title, with its evocation of the racetrack, is an apt metaphor for the desperation that afflicted so many in the neighborhood, "the virus of penny-ante gamblers" struggling to escape from the working class, "to hit it big, to seize a certain glamour from life." The book consists of three chapters of the author's personal reminiscences (each entitled "Going Home"), alternating with novella-like autobiographies that are separately narrated by three characters (presumably in their forties) who reflect the ethnic diversity of the neighborhood: a sensitive high school dropout, Dominic (Italian);Audrey, an Irish hooker; and the author himself, Lennie (Jewish). The three protagonists are what Vivian Gornick characterizes in the *New York Times Book Review* as "the walking wounded—Lennie literally crippled, Dominic and Audrey soul-crippled." Lennie's friend Cliff draws up lists of some neighborhood people who "made it" (mostly small time). "I tell myself," Lennie observes, "that I will write and offer him a different list. The remnants, the suicides, and the leftovers, still dreaming on this and other parkways."

In addition to the three extended portraits, *Notes for the Two-Dollar Window* contains a number of vivid shorter sketches: Kriegel's venerable grandmother, whose gnarled and aged hand "possesses life, a breath of emancipation"; Uncle Morris, expert handicapper and militant left-winger, "who used to come home from the fur market with the *World-Telegram* in one hand and the Communist *Daily Worker* in the other, the one to maneuver the line at the track, the other to maneuver the world"; Little Sammy, faithful "guardian of the corner" and symbol of the dying Jones Avenue, who inexplicably commits suicide; and Gunner, the neighborhood fighter doomed to failure by an easily damaged glass jaw. Vivian Gornick emphasized the "dignified simplicity" with which Kriegel brings his characters to life: "A melancholy sweetness, alive and to the touch and having to do with time and place, runs through these pages; and out of this sweetness drift sorrow and love."

On Men and Manhood opens with a poignant account of Kriegel on crutches as he painfully struggles to join his two-year-old son on the beach. Sinking helplessly in the sand, he is forced to reconsider his role as a man and to reflect upon the changing ideal of manhood in American culture. The traditional values associated with manhood have, in Kriegel's view, been challenged in recent years by blacks, homosexuals, and feminists. Kriegel examines manhood in the context of several American classics, including the novels of Cooper and the autobiographical writings of Ben Franklin, U. S. Grant, and Henry Adams. He writes with sadness about his hero Hemingway, who, for all his famous bravado, failed to live up to his own self-created myth, "a pathetic victim of the very virtues he stood for." A chapter is devoted to sports. "The athlete," Kriegel writes, "may be a contemporary hero, but he is not necessarily a model of manhood. . . . A man is not just the sum of his physical effort, after all." In films, Kriegel traces the Hollywood image of the hero from John Wayne's mythic Ringo Kid (*Stagecoach*) through a new character type, the private eye, as represented by Humphrey Bogart and Robert Mitchum, and Terry Malloy, the Marlon Brando character in *On the Waterfront* who maintains a sense of outlawry even though "there is no respectable world for him to work against." Finally, the notion of the hero is drastically redefined in *Coming Home*, in which Jon Voight plays a crippled Vietnam war veteran, By 1978, Kriegel observes, Freud had descended over Hollywood and lent sophistication to its idea of manhood. Kriegel notes similar alterations in society's attitudes toward homosexuality and also observes that black men in America attained in the 1960s a stronger sense of manhood—though, he writes, they have, like their white counterparts, become "victims of shriveled times and expectations."

Reviewing *On Men and Manhood* for the *Nation*, Jean Bethke Elshtain commented on what she perceived as a sexist perspective in the book. "Much of the struggle, quest, mastery Kriegel insistently subsumes within 'man' and 'manhood' are human experiences shared across sexes." She also objected that the book implies that female identity is "a lower achievement, of meaner purpose than the male." But Sanford Pinsker, in the *New England Quarterly*, called *On Men and Manhood* "a tough-minded, independent, and important book." Vance Bourjaily, in the *New York Times Book Review* (1979), praised Kriegel as "a Socratic teacher inviting debate, raising questions, offering clarification. He has written a book to be read slowly, in agreement or disagreement, one that provokes a restless urge to amplify."

Quitting Time retraces the rise and fall of the fictional Barney Kadish a Jewish immigrant from Odessa who becomes a Communist labor organizer in the first half of the 20th century. Barney is at the side of the great union leader John L. Lewis as they organize a sit-down strike at the General Motors plant in Flint, Michigan. At the peak of his career Barney becomes president of the (fictional) United Garment Workers of America. In the 1950s he is forced to testify before a Congressional committee investigating Communist influences on the labor movement. He dies of a heart attack in Albuquerque, New Mexico, abandoned by the labor movement, as well as by his beloved Communist Party. The novel opens with Barney's death, and his life is revealed in retrospect through four separate accounts narrated by those closest to him: two coworkers, his wife, and his mistress.

In Barney Kadish, described by the reviewer for *America* as "an authentic hero of the working class," Kriegel has epitomized the turbulent history of the American labor movement and brought to life a "fascinating portrait of our collective past." Fiercely committed to the twin causes of organization and revolution, Barney fails as husband and father, and commits acts of shocking cruelty. He explains away Stalin's atrocities and justifies his own rejection by the party:

> "The forces of history. That's what you never understand, No man is worth a damn. Of course, the party doesn't care about me. That its glory, its strength. It uses what it can use. Then discards it. Like an old shoe. . . . There's no morality in our business. . . . A radical learns. First he learns that there is no God and then he learns that there is no people either and finally he learns that there's nothing but the self he's already given to the cause."

Quitting Time was praised by the *Library Journal* as "a compelling novel," that presents an "unsentimental portrait of the American labor movement." "At its best," the reviewer for the *Nation* (1982) wrote, it "has the visceral thrill of heroic stories passed down from generation to generation. . . . Leonard Kriegel writes beautifully of ordinary people who see history as their personal crucible. He writes with grace and uncommon courage."

Kriegel returned to memoir writing with the fourteen essays that make up *Falling into Life*. In his remarkable introduction, he acknowledges "an unstifled rage, a rage born of absence and framed by longing. . . . Over and over again, I thrust myself against a writer's memory and an eleven-year-old boy's ambition The one guards my sense of the way life was; the other grinds me against possibilities never realized, the things I could never do growing greater and greater as they are ransomed by my imagination. . . . A man can meet himself even on his way down. And these essays, written over the past decade, were for me a way of meeting myself." In the words of Steven Slosberg in the *New York Times Book Review*, "the joy and the rage of surviving polio dominate these pages as they have dominated . . . Kriegel's life."

In the title essay, Kreigel shows how falling is not just a metaphor but, literally, a skill the cripple must painfully master in order to survive. "*You let go! And there it is!* Yes, and you discover not terror, but the only self you are going to be allowed to claim anyhow." One day, in November 1983, the inevitable happened. He fell on a wet sidewalk on 14th Street and could not pick himself up. The experience drove home a sense of symmetry, of closure. "When the day comes, I want to be able to fall into my life." Another essay, "Invisible Shadows", contrasts the way two of the author's favorite cities, San Francisco and Paris accommodate (or fail to accommodate) wheelchairs: "If San Francisco had humanized a physical handicap, Paris magnified it into something thoroughly European." Two of the pieces, "Writing the Unlived Life" and "From the Burning Bush," shed valuable light on Kriegel's search for a literary identity. "Unfortunately for me," he confesses in the latter essay, "I find myself both primarily an autobiographical writer and a writer whose books do not sell. . . . I want writing about my life to be an act of vengeance upon a universe unaware of that life's very existence." In the final essay, "In Kafka's House," through the terrifying metaphor drawn from Kafka's tale of Gregor Samsa's metamorphosis into a gigantic insect, Kriegel writes about his friend Michael, a minister crippled by disease, who, because he is a disgrace to his family, is kept locked inside his room. He lies on the floor in his own dirt. Thinking about Michael, Kriegel reflects, "makes me want to howl like a wounded animal, to stick my hand through the glass. . . . I have created a life, built it piece by piece. And I can be thrust aside, locked away, made susceptible to the same terror as Michael. I shiver as I envision myself in Michael's place. Reeking of humiliation, imprisoned by those one loves, tested by calculating

malevolence." Having lived himself in Kafka's House since age eleven Kriegel acknowledges that he is destined to remain there forever. "And residence there made unforgettable the terror of someday finding myself helpless, bound to the obligations of others as I twist and squirm in my mind. To endure is not enough. I know that, now that I have lived long enough in Kafka's House to understand that the past expects the future."

Falling Into Life was hailed by Ivan Gold, in *Forward*, as a set of "elegantly conceived and forceful essays," and Art Winslow, in the *Nation*, was impressed by the fact that Kriegel's writing has been "purged of easy sentiment about 'overcoming challenges.'"

On August 24, 1957, Kriegel married Harriet May Bernzweig. The Kriegels, who live in Manhattan, have two children.

PRINCIPAL WORKS: *Nonfiction*—The Long Walk Home, 1964; Edmund Wilson, 1971; Working Through: A Teacher's Journey in the Urban University, 1972; Notes for the Two-Dollar Window: Portraits from an American Neighborhood, 1976; On Men and Manhood, 1979; Falling into Life, 1991. *Fiction*—Quitting Time, 1982. *As editor*—The Essential Works of the Founding Fathers, 1964; (with A. Lass) Stories of the American Experience, 1973.

ABOUT: Contemporary   Authors   1984. *Periodicals*—America October 14, 1972; July 24, 1982; Best Sellers May 1, 1964; Commonweal October 27, 1972; August 13, 1976; Criticism Fall 1972; Forward May 3, 1991; Jerusalem Post July 21, 1991; Library Journal May 1, 1976; October 15, 1979; March 1, 1982; Nation September 21, 1964; October 2, 1972; December 22, 1979; May 29, 1982; December 30, 1991; New England Quarterly June 1980; New Statesman April 18, 1980; New York Times Book Review November 19, 1972; April 18, 1976; December 9, 1979; June 23, 1991; Sewanee Review Spring 1991; South Atlantic Quarterly Summer 1972.

LEAVITT, DAVID (June 23, 1961–), American short story writer and novelist, was born in Pittsburgh, Pennsylvania, the son of Harold Jack Leavitt and Gloria (Rosenthal) Leavitt. The youngest of three children, he grew up in Palo Alto, California, where his father taught organizational behavior at Stanford University and his mother was a part-time political activist. After receiving a B.A. in English from Yale in 1983, he worked briefly as a reader and editorial assistant for a New York publisher. Leavitt has been a full-time writer since the age of twenty-three, when he published his first collection of short stories, *Family Dancing*.

In 1983, while still a senior at Yale, he published his short story "Territory" in the *New*

DAVID LEAVITT

Yorker. "Territory" quickly became something of a literary cause célèbre. It was the first New Yorker short story with explicitly homosexual characters. Neil, a young homosexual man from an affluent family; Barbara, Neil's mother; and Wayne, Neil's lover. After living in New York for several years, Neil has returned to his childhood home in northern California for a visit. There, Neil and his mother await the arrival of Wayne. Although Neil has long ago declared his homosexuality to his parents, he has never introduced a significant partner; consequently, Wayne's arrival reignites long-buried tensions between Neil and his mother. Neil's father is alluded to only in passing; as in so many of Leavitt's stories, the father is "away," this time on business. It is the complex interplay between Neil and his mother—an understanding, politically liberal woman pushed here to the limits of her tolerance—that is the central focus of the story, and which sparks the deepest, most ambivalent emotions in Neil.

"Territory" is one of the nine short stories in Family Dancing, Leavitt's highly praised first collection. While a number of the stories feature homosexual characters, Leavitt addresses a variety of concerns, most of them—as the title story suggests—having to do with domestic crises: cancer, divorce, and the exploitation of vulnerability. In the world of Leavitt's stories, the individual can rarely find stability, security, or honesty in his own family. In most of the stories, mothers suffer while fathers are absent, callous, or both. In "The Lost Cottage," for example, parents on the verge of a divorce decide to spend

one last summer together at their Cape Cod cottage. While the decision is ostensibly made for the sake of the children, the "children" are all adults with lives and jobs of their own.

Family Dancing was nominated for a National Book Critics Circle Award and a PEN/Faulkner award. "Counting Months," a story about a day in the life of a woman dying of cancer, won an O. Henry award in 1984. "David Leavitt has a genius for empathy," Wendy Lesser wrote in the New York Times Book Review" (1984) of Family Dancing. According to Lesser, "Mr. Leavitt captures, as few writers can, the self-preserving distance between even the most intimate parents and children." Interestingly, Lesser found that, given his penchant for empathy, "the young people in his fiction are the least convincing." In the New York Review of Books, Darryl Pinckney commented, "Leavitt is best with a small cast, when not too many sides of the repetitive story clamor to be told." He deemed "Territory" "the most assured story in the volume." Although Martha Ullman West, in the San Francisco Review of Books hailed Leavitt as "a master craftsman," she objected that "the author's treatment of the characters is so controlled and so dispassionate that these stories become literary exercises—excellently performed, but ultimately unmoving."

Homosexuality, but one of several concerns in Leavitt's early stories, comes to the fore in his first novel, The Lost Language of Cranes, in which most of the major characters are homosexual. Philip, the novel's twenty-five-year-old protagonist, works at a low-level editing job in Manhattan, but his major preoccupation is finding romance. This he finds in the person of Eliot, with whom he falls in love. Rose and Owen Benjamin, Philip's parents, are enmeshed in personal and financial difficulties; the most startling of these is that Owen himself has been conducting a secret homosexual life for years. The novel chronicles and contrasts "the coming out" of Owen and Philip, father and son. As in earlier Leavitt stories, it is the mother, in this case Rose Benjamin, who is left alone to sort out the consequences. "Rose is a wonderful character," Phillip Lopate noted in the New York Times Book Review (1986). "Mr. Leavitt's empathy extends less to his male characters than to his female ones, especially older women. We are left with the paradox of a novel in which the most sympathetic character is a heterosexual woman who resists the homosexuality of her men."

The novel's title is derived from a case history discovered by Eliot's roommate, Jerene, a Ph.D. student in developmental psychology. Fascinated by the subject of personal languages, Jerene reads the story of a boy brought up in isolation near a building site; instead of imitating human speech and motion, the boy bases his language on the sounds and movements of construction cranes. In the *New Republic*, Adam Mars-Jones wrote, "The lost languages theme is loudly, even portentously sounded, but it is not actually integrated with the narrative in any way." While Mars-Jones conceded that Leavitt's prose is "sometimes beautifully tailored," he concluded that the emotions he aims for at this stage of his career are still strictly off-the-rack." In the *New York Times Book Review* Phillip Lopate took a similar view of the novel. "Mr. Leavitt's sense of pacing, his graceful sentences and his storytelling ability dovetail nicely," he wrote. "On the other hand, the book *feels* young—experientially thin, intellectually timid, contrived, erratic and, understandably, not yet wise. *The Lost Language of Cranes* was made into a BBC television movie which aired on PBS in the United States in 1992.

Perhaps because he was so young when his first book was published, Leavitt has often been viewed as a kind of spokesman for his generation. In 1985 he published an essay, "The New Lost Generation," in *Esquire*; F. Scott Fitzgerald and William Styron had earlier published assessments of their generations in the same magazine. Leavitt characterized his generation as "Tail End. We have always been the tail end—of the sixties, of the baby boom." In that essay, Leavitt addressed what Phillip Lopate would later criticize, in his review of *The Lost Language of Cranes*, as the yearning for "domestic snugness." Contrasting his generation to that of his brother and sister (nine and ten years older than he), Leavitt noted: "Rather than move, we burrow. We are interested in stability, neatness, entrenchment. We want to stay in one place and stay in one piece, establish careers, establish credit." According to Leavitt, members of his generation could not express the same outrage as their older brothers and sisters had concerning an issue like nuclear holocaust. "We do not go crazy, because for us the thought of a world with no future . . . is completely familiar; is taken for granted; is nothing new." Explaining his generation's inability to "think beyond the moment," Leavitt wrote, "This blind spot has more to do with our attitude toward the nuclear family than with nuclear disaster. . . . "

Indeed, political concerns of any sort—unless they relate to family crises—are almost wholly absent from Levitt's early work. He has been faulted for his apparent disengagement from the concerns of the larger world. In "Post-Counterculture Tristesse," an essay which appeared in *Commentary* and was primarily de-voted to an anylysis of Leavitt's early work, Carol Iannone wrote that "our younger writers do not, for the most part, challenge the terms of our liberated culture. Accepting these terms as given—even at times celebrating them—they devote themselves instead to spare, taut chronicles of the sundry tribulations that are the by products of personal and cultural expansion."

Equal Affections, Leavitt's second novel, is another chronicle of a disintegrating family. At the center of the story is Louise Cooper, a middle-aged woman dying of cancer. Her family consists of a neglectful husband and two grown children—both of them homosexual. Leavitt's own mother died a slow and agonizing death from cancer. Although he denies that any of his work is specifically autobiographical, he told *Publishers Weekly*, "The enormity of that experience cannot be minimalized. It has gone into all of my work." Reviewing *Equal Affections* in the *Times Literary Supplement*, Jonathan Keates observed that while Leavitt has been placed in the "'Gay Writers' file, his concerns are a good deal less restricted than that implies."

Discussing his second short story collection, *A Place I've Never Been*, with a *Publishers Weekly* interviewer, Leavitt remarked, "My first three books were The Early Work, and the new one is the first book of The Middle Years." There is, nonetheless, considerable continuity between *A Place I've Never Been* and *Family Dancing*. Celia Hoberman, a character in "Dedicated" (*Family Dancing*) appears again in the title story, "A Place I've Never Been." In the latter story, she is one side of a triangle which includes her best friend (a homosexual man) and her friend's lover, who is HIV-positive. Leavitt's earlier silence on the subject of AIDS had aroused the ire of some homosexual activists and critics. Confronting those critics in his *Publishers Weekly* interview, Leavitt commented: "I don't think it's fair to say that writers have an obligation to write about any particular subject. A write's only obligation is to write well." "*A Place I've Never Been* is a substantial and impressive collection," James Lasdun wrote in the *Times Literary Supplement*. "It doesn't depart from the first book so much as consolidate what was already there."

Leavitt's third novel, *While England Sleeps*, a reminiscence by the narrator, Brian Botsford, an upper-class English dilettante writer, begins in 1936 and unfolds in England and Spain in the era of the Spanish civil war. When the story opens at a communist meeting in London, Botsford meets Edward Phelan, an earnest young working-class man with whom he promptly begins an affair. When Botsford is distracted by a wealthy woman (he needs money), Phelan, in a fit of jealousy, enlists in the International Brigade and goes off to fight in Spain.

The novel takes its title from George Orwell's *Homage to Catalonia*, a memoir of the Spanish civil war which describes "the deep, deep sleep of England" during Hitler's rise to power. "This is an ambitious novel," Penelope Lively wrote in the *New York Times book Review* (1993). "It requires strong literary nerve for a young American writer to set a story in the England of the late 1930s. . . . " In his *New York Times* review, Christopher Lehmann-Haupt commented, "It is to the novel's particular credit that it climbs out of its preoccupation with sex and makes a significant comment on the political issues of its time."

At the same time that Leavitt was being commended for at last addressing issues of the wider world, his novel became mired in controversy. Even before publication, he had been prohibited from using lines to the song "All of Me"; the song's publisher did not like the context in which Leavitt used it—men dancing and a homosexual love scene. More significantly in October 1993, the British poet Stephen Spender brought a lawsuit against the book's publisher, Viking. He claimed that *While England Sleeps* is a thinly disguised pornographic account of his own life, and that it breached the copyright of his memoir, *World Within World* (1951) and violated his "moral right" to his own work. Leavitt did not disguise the fact that his book was inspired by incidents in Spender's life, and he claimed that he had not listed Spender's memoir in his acknowledgments only on the advice of Viking's lawyers.

In February 1994 Spender's lawsuit was settled, with Viking agreeing to stop the sale of the book in England (it had already sold over 30,000 copies in the United States) until Leavitt removed or revised several pages of sexually explicit scenes. According to his publisher, these would be "minor modifications."

PRINCIPAL WORKS: *Short stories*—Family Dancing, 1984; A Place I've Never Been, 1990. *Novels*—The Lost Language of Cranes, 1986; Equal Affections, 1989; While England Sleeps, 1993.

ABOUT: Contemporary Authors 122, 1988; Contemporary Gay American Novelists, 1993; Contemporary Literary Criticism 34, 1985; Schumacher, M. Reasons to Believe, 1991. *Periodicals*—Commentary February 1987; Esquire May 1985; New Republic November 17, 1986; New York Review of Books May 29, 1986; New York Times July 22, 1991; June 24, 1992; June 30, 1993; October 14, 1993; October 27, 1993; December 1, 1993; February 17, 1994; New York Times Book Review September 2, 1984; October 5, 1986; February 12, 1989; August 26, 1990; October 3, 1993; New York

Times Magazine April 3, 1994; Publishers Weekly August 24, 1990; San Francisco Review of Books January–February 1985; Studies in Short Fiction Winter 1991; Times Literary Supplement June 9, 1989; February 8, 1991.

LEFFLAND, ELLA (November 25, 1931–), American novelist and writer of short stories writes: "I was born in Martinez, California, a small oil refining town near San Francisco. My parents were from Denmark, so I grew up in a European household. I never felt entirely American, but I had a strong feeling for the town I lived in—its hills and creek, its eucalyptus trees and its bay. I was drawing pictures of these things already when I was very small, and at about the age of nine I began to write stories. The characters in these stories were the dogs and cats of the neighborhood, the horses and cows that grazed in the hills, and the sea gulls and wild ducks that inhabited the tule marshes. Animals had a deep meaning for me as a child, as they still have, but after a while I began to write about human beings. These were usually undergoing horrible shipwrecks in the South Seas, riding troikas through wild Siberian blizzards, or feverishly painting masterpieces in squalid Parisian garrets. It was only when I grew older that the less extraordinary lives of my neighbors and other townspeople became interesting to me. These people were eventually those on whom the characters in my first novel, *Mrs. Munck*, and in the later *Rumors of Peace*, were based.

"When I was fourteen I submitted my first short story to a magazine. The story was about a man trying to reach his dying child in a Siberian blizzard, handwritten, as I had no typewriter and the magazine was the *New Yorker*. Although the rejection slip disappointed me, it made no dent in my self-confidence. This was to change over the years. I do not think the cumulative demoralization of rejection slips can be exaggerated. I remember my feeling of fruitless effort when I would lay the pages of a many-times submitted story on the ironing board and press out the creases and wrinkles before sending it off again.

"And yet the hard core of self-certainty, the unshakable belief in one's own work, which is essential to any writer, was never dented beyond repair. My first short story was accepted when I was in my middle twenties, interestingly enough by the *New Yorker*, achieving some sort of full circle. This time the story was not about a Siberian blizzard but a bleak, snow-covered Germany.

"A few years after graduating in 1953 from

ELLA LEFFLAND

San Jose State College, where I majored in art,
I had spent a year in Europe, hitchhiking and
staying at youth hostels. Most of the stories later
collected in *Last Courtesies* were based on my
experiences during this and a second stay in Europe.

"The jobs I held over the years were varied.
Some were boring to the point of deadliness—
picking the stems from grapes on a cannery con-
veyer belt, filing folders in an insurance office,
filing folders at a television station. Others were
fascinating—selling brooms from door to door,
working as a mess girl aboard a Norwegian
tramp steamer, as city hall reporter for a legal
newspaper, and as copy editor for northern California's black newspaper.

"During those years I wrote and painted
whenever I could—nights, weekends, and in the
solid chunks of time that elapsed between jobs.
I wrote two long novels, neither of which, when
finished satisfied me sufficiently to submit. The
third, *Mrs. Munck*, I did submit, and it was published in 1970.

"Since then, I have been able to write without
the impediment of outside jobs. Even so, I am
very slow, given to endless revision. The next
novel came out four years later, and the next five
years after that, and the last novel, *The Knight,
Death and the Devil*—which required a great
deal of research—took eight years to write. At
present I am working on a novel that also involves historical research, but I trust the book
will not demand quite as long a stint.

"My writing habits are pretty simple. On the
backs of old manuscripts I either write in longhand or use my hardy little manual typewriter
which I have had for years. I like to block out
everything from the outside world for days at a
time, weeks if possible, and live entirely inside
what I am writing. I believe that there is a strong
'underwater' element in the process of writing,
that the creation of a story or novel partakes
more of the unconscious and indefinable than it
does of the explicable. What can be explained
can be taught, which is why writing cannot be
taught except in the realm of the technical. I do
not enjoy writing, it is like an obsessional love affair fraught with misery.

"I live in San Francisco, and like to swim in
the bay."

Ella Leffland's first three novels and her first
collection of short stories were small and quiet
critical successes. Reviewers marked her as a
writer of dark, intense vision who specialized in
the study of lonely, alienated people—cruelly
victimized women and pathetically redundant
old men and women (*Mrs. Munck*), young people living on the perilous margins of San Francisco hippie society in the 1960s (*Love Out of
Season*), a girl coming of age in small-town
America during World War II (*Rumors of
Peace*). She went on to write a massive fictional
biography of Hermann Göring in *The Knight,
Death and the Devil*. The fact that she undertook the project with no formal training as a historian and little knowledge of German yet
produced a novel that, in the judgment of David
Kaufman in the *Nation*, "has the sweep of a
tome by Tolstoy and the engaging impact of
Dickens" reflects Leffland's independence of
spirit and her uncompromising faith in the novel
as a medium for working out "the complexities
and incongruities" of human character.

Mrs. Munck, her first published novel, introduces a richly complex character, the fiercely independent Rose Munck, who plans a deadly
revenge on a man who had seduced and abandoned her, leaving her penniless with a baby she
accidentally kills. Years later, widowed after a
loveless marriage, she becomes the caretaker of
her seducer, now a helpless old man unwanted
by his own children. In a taut, suspenseful narrative, Rose makes no appeal for sympathy. She recalls her childhood in a bleak farm home where
her parents never expressed their feelings for
each other or for her. Hungry for their attention,
she would often be disobedient in an outright bid
for punishment: "Not just a slap or a cuff—that
was everyday—but a real thrashing they would
put their souls into, because it would mean that
they had finally seen me, not as somebody who

did the chores, or as a female offspring to be married off in due course, but as me, Rose, a free spirit, who did strange, terrible things on her own." At seventeen she leaves home and defines her future character:

> And suddenly I knew it was good to be a person of my nature—extreme in everything, somehow merciless if touched wrong—but to be a woman, too; that was always going to be hard. Because all around you, in the very air, was the expectation that you lose yourself in the desires of others, and to deny this was considered a terrible kind of irresponsibility, almost . . . a cry against nature. But all the same it was good that I was as I was.

Christopher Lehmann-Haupt, in the *New York Times* (1970), called *Mrs. Munck* "a powerful dramatization of an oppressed woman's plight and revenges—a novel straight out of the tradition of the Brontës and Thomas Hardy." He recognized in it the power of redemption that reveals itself in Rose's inability finally to kill her enemy, now her helpless victim. In this novel, as in her later ones, Leffland fixes her characters firmly within a moral framework and makes her readers see them, unloved and unlovable as many of them are, with sympathy and compassion. "Miss Leffland's authorial presence," John Romano wrote of her stories in *Last Courtesies* in the *New York Times Book Review* (1980), "is distinctly caring. She lends great authority of feeling to the people whom, through the act of fiction, she befriends." Leffland believes that fictional characters must inhabit a universe in which morality has an important place. Characters cannot defy moral imperatives, unless those imperatives implicitly exist, Leffland thinks, in contrast to Joyce Carol Oates, whose twisted personae cannot be judged by standards of basic decency and humanity.

Lehmann-Haupt was less enthusiastic about *Love Out of Season*, the story of a love affair foredoomed both by the pressures of the San Francisco counterculture of the 1960s and by the temperamental conflicts of the lovers themselves. In his *New York Times* (1974) review he suggested that where in *Mrs. Munck* Leffland "allowed her imagination to run riotously free," in the later novel she undertook "to chain her imagination to specifics . . . It hasn't worked; the specifics have produced trivialities." She appeared to him to be so intent here on portraying her central characters in precise psychological detail that their actions became predictable. Other reviewers had similar reservations. C. J. Felsenthal, in *Library Journal* (1974), found that the relationship of the lovers "like their lives and the times, is often beautiful but ultimately scarred and unfulfilled." For this reviewer *Love Out of Season* was "ponderous and unresolved,

but too beautifully written and insightful to pass up." The reviewer for *Choice*, however, commented that thanks to Leffland's "mature and critical vision" the characters transcended their time and place and assumed universality.

Rumors of Peace, a novel that Leffland admits is "about ninety-five percent" autobiographical, turns refreshingly away from the isolation and alienation of the characters in her earlier books to focus on a child growing up in a working-class and loving family in Mendoza, a small California town like Martinez, Leffland's birthplace, near San Francisco. Its central character, Suse, is a bright, imaginative child moving no more painfully than most other children into adolescence and maturity. The time is World War II, and the bombing of Pearl Harbor is just about to shatter the complacency of Americans, especially those on the West Coast, with the prospect of their vulnerability to enemy attacks. Suse listens to reports of death and destruction in foreign cities and her inflamed imagination brings the war home to her. In due course she develops her precocious intelligence and sensitivity as she undergoes the normal experiences of young Americans—friends, an awakening interest in sex, and a growing curiosity for learning. Narrated by Suse as a memory exercise, the novel evokes the spirit of a tranquil, small-town childhood: "We had an old yellow train depot, a long tarry wharf, and a large white ferry. We had a stone courthouse with a dome, an L-shaped Woolworth's with creaking floors, and a small dim library that smelled of flour paste. We had a tule marsh, eucalyptus groves, and tall scruffy palms, and we had steep dry hills that you could slide down on a piece of cardboard."

Reviewers were for the most part enchanted with the quiet charm of *Rumors of Peace*. In the *New York Times Book Review* (1979) Daphne Merkin compared it to "stepping into a Norman Rockwell painting" and ranked it with "those deceptively guileless novels like *A Member of the Wedding* and *To Kill a Mockingbird*." Linda Osborne in the *Washington Post Book World* recognized "Leffland's concern with the nature of moral growth," as she traces Suse's "increasingly complex, human view of life," with war not merely the background but "an open metaphor for that growth."

The stories collected in *Last Courtesies* reflect the widening of Leffland's vision. Her characters are now as often literally, as they were earlier figuratively, uprooted and displaced. Even in the title story, set in San Francisco, the central character, a genteel widow struggling to preserve the values of an earlier day, helplessly confronts a brutal and violently changing and disintegrating society. Several of the stories are set in Europe, a continent seen not through conventional tourists' eyes but through those of Europeans or of lonely American visitors discovering the darker side of their own characters as foreigners in alien lands. Katha Pollitt, in *Saturday Review*, was struck by Leffland's "singleness of vision. What interests her in all her stories is the loneliness at the heart of human relations, connections missed and broken." Once again she treats her lonely eccentric, in some cases psychotic, characters with compassion, but there is also a strong moral thrust in these stories—what Dorothy Wickenden, in the *New Republic*, described as "an insistence that to see oneself as the victim rather than the agent of one's fate can be a dangerous form of self-indulgence."

In a certain sense Leffland's earlier writings, though mainly confined to the American scene, were preparation for her vastly ambitious novel *The Knight, Death and the Devil*. As the daughter of Danish immigrants she had a strong bond with Europe even before she traveled abroad. Growing up during World War II, she followed events in Japan and Nazi Germany with avid interest. Young Suse's story in *Rumors of Peace* indeed might be read as a domestic history of the war, every stage in her development finding its parallel in the catastrophic events going on in Europe and Asia. For some reason it was Hermann Göring among all the Nazi leaders who most fascinated her. She told an interviewer in 1992: "He embodied all the mysteries that are involved in actions that are deplorable, carried out by people who were neither sadists nor psychopaths." The more she read about him, the more complex and ambivalent he emerged. It was the very humanity she saw in him—a man who participated in some of the most inhuman acts in all human history—that drew her to the subject. Like the knight depicted in Albrecht Dürer's engraving, a favorite of Göring's that always hung in his study, he seemed to be riding to his doom in a dark twisted forest with Death accompanying him on one side and the Devil on the other. Essentially an ordinary man, typical of the Junker class into which he had been born, loving his country, food, art, and his family in just about that order, he was, as Leffland saw him, the chief and perhaps the most chilling example of what Hannah Arendt called "the banality of evil" implicit in Nazism. "I don't think I'd have written a book about Goebbels or Hitler. They didn't represent the human situation, and I felt that Göring did."

In choosing to write fiction, or more precisely what she calls "a historical biographical novel," Leffland acknowledged that if the mysteries of Göring's character were to be adequately explored, the novel was a better medium than factual biography: "But if the novel offers a dimension of human truth which the work of history cannot, it will fall short of its purpose unless it is rooted in fact as a plant is rooted in the soil." Accordingly, Leffland spent years of research in the records of Nazism. The background to the novel is a story itself, beginning with Leffland's brief visit in 1977 to Neuhaus, the small town in Bavaria where Göring spent his early years. She described her experiences in an article in the *New York Times Book Review*, "Has Anybody Here Seen Göring?" (January 21, 1990). At the time of her first visit she spoke no German and the citizens of Neuhaus spoke no English. On her return to the United States she began studying German and reading everything she could find on Nazi Germany. By 1979 when she returned to Germany, she was well launched into her research. She visited every town and city that had figured in Göring's life; she studied old newspapers, memoirs, diaries, and—most important for her purposes—she sought out and interviewed people who had known Göring—among them Albert Speer, the former minister of armaments; Adolf Galland, a former commander of the Luftwaffe; and a nephew of Göring's. Her richest source of information was Hitler's former bodyguard Werner Hohmann, "with whom I had numerous long conversations." Though at first hostile and unforthcoming, Hohmann gradually softened and, she recalls in her *Times* article, appeared to have "amorous designs" on her. "Nothing was overt, but I sensed it." Through him Leffland enriched her portrait with details of Göring's daily life and habits, his family relations, and the sheer "ordinariness," as she perceived it, "of life during the war."

The novel begins with Göring in his cell in Nuremberg awaiting trial for war crimes and ends with his suicide shortly before his scheduled execution. The intervening 700 pages are Göring's memories, as Leffland weaves together the strands of Germany history in the first half of the 20th century, introducing all the prominent political figures of the period and a host of characters—both real and fictitious—whose lives were in some way connected with Göring. "The historical aspect is occasionally a little lumpy," Peter Bricklebank wrote in *Library Journal* (1990), "but the insights of a fine novelist . . . more than redress the balance." Although "there are longueurs in the novel where her research slows and interrupts the narrative," overall, "Leffland's imagination and language soar," according to Herbert Mitgang, writing in the *New York Times* 1990. Thomas Keneally, in the *New York Times Book Review* (1990), observed that "the authoritative quality of . . . Leffland's writing" and her "narrative energy in handling the Göring enigma carry the novel and make it a considerable success. It is as if her velocity as a narrator sweeps the book's faults in her wake." If in the end she fails to convey more than the "predominantly external" quality of Göring's life, David Kaufman wrote in the *Nation*, his deterioration "is as palpable as Germany's loss of the war."

Ella Leffland is the daughter of Sven William (an automobile painter) and Emma (Jensen) Leffland. She lives in San Francisco when she is not traveling in Europe. She received Excellence in Literature awards from the Commonwealth Club of California for *Mrs. Munck* in 1970 and in 1975 for *Love Out of Season*, which also received the California Literature Medal in 1974. Her short story "Last Courtesies" was an O. Henry selection in 1977.

PRINCIPAL WORKS: *Novels*—Mrs. Munck, 1970; Love Out of Season, 1974; Rumors of Peace, 1979; The Knight, Death and the Devil, 1990. *Short stories*—Last Courtesies and Other Stories, 1980.

ABOUT: Contemporary Authors New Revision Series 35, 1992; Contemporary Literary Criticism 19, 1981; Dictionary of Literary Biography Yearbook 1984, 1985. *Periodicals*—Choice December 1974; Library Journal August 1974, February 1, 1990; LIT: Literature Interpretation Theory 3, 1991; Nation June 18, 1990; New Republic December 13, 1980; New York Times August 10, 1970; September 5, 1974; March 14, 1990; New York Times Book Review July 22, 1979; October 5, 1980; January 21, 1990; February 11, 1990; Publishers Weekly February 2, 1990; Saturday Review September 1980; Washington Post Book World July 29, 1979.

L'ENGLE,   MADELEINE   (Madeleine L'Engle Camp) (November 29, 1918–), American novelist, writes: "I was born in New York City shortly after the armistice that ended the war that was supposed to end all wars and I was born into a century of total war; many of them in the name of religion or freedom or people or democracy and war gets more and more abhorrent. My parents [Charles Wadsworth and Madeleine Barnett Camp] were both highly literate people whose friends were mostly artists, and so I grew up knowing that it is a right and good thing to try to express your feelings about the world and its problems in story. That, indeed, story is the only real vehicle the human being has to struggle to find out the truth in life.

"I lived in New York until I was twelve. Then we moved to Europe to try to find a place where

MADELEINE L'ENGLE

my father could breathe. He was mustard-gassed in that First World War, and it took him until I was nearly eighteen to finish coughing his lungs out. In Europe we lived in an old château that hadn't been altered since the eleventh century. There was no oven, only a huge fireplace with a spit for roasting oxen. I took it for granted that except in the big cities most people didn't have indoor plumbing and that you got a pitcher of water in the morning and that was the water for the day.

"We came back to the United States for me to finish high school in Charleston, South Carolina, and then I went on to Smith College and back to my beloved New York City as fast as I could get there. With the exception of some years spent in rural New England while my husband and I were raising our children, my life has been spent in New York. After college I went to work in the Broadway theater which is a wonderful school for a writer. I made lifelong friends there. While I was playing in *The Cherry Orchard*, I met my husband, Hugh Franklin, and married him in *The Joyous Season*. We had forty good years together for which I will always be grateful.

"Since I traveled a lot as a child, I acquired a taste for it. I still love to travel and see other people and other lands and other ways of living. I don't believe that writers can write about places they haven't seen. I couldn't have written *The Love Letters* or *The Arm of the Starfish* without going to Portugal, or *A House Like a Lotus* without going to Greece or Cyprus. As for Meg's trips to other galaxies and Polly O'Keefe's visit to an

Indian tribe who lived on this continent 3,000 years ago, my own experience certainly comes into those too, and other writers will certainly understand how. Last winter I had the privilege of visiting Antarctica, so it is no surprise that a large portion of my new Vicky Austin book is set on that fascinating continent.

"For the past several years I have been living with my college-going granddaughters who have been doing a good job of bringing me up. We have a golden retriever and three cats of indeterminate heritage, though one is pure white and beautiful."

The diversity of Madeleine L'Engle's prodigious output- ience fiction, fantasy, suspense, plays, poetry, essays, memoirs, and so on—makes it difficult to place her in any one genre or to describe her as a writer for any one age group. It is young people and adults who love children's literature, however, who are her most enthusiastic readers. Approximately half of L'Engle's works are considered juvenile titles, and *A Wrinkle in Time* has remained a popular children's book since its publication in 1962.

There is certainly nothing easy about her themes. "L'Engle's writings reflect her passionate concern with major aspects of life," Marygail Parker wrote in the *Dictionary of Literary Biography*, "a happy family life, the right and responsibility of the individual to make choices, the art of writing, death, and God." Despite the weight of such topics, L'Engle's approach is one of optimism, as Parker goes on to point out: "No matter how difficult a theme L'Engle writes of, or what personal or universal crisis her characters face, there is an underlying joy in her books, a feeling that her characters will eventually make the best choices."

L'Engle describes herself as totally committed to writing, which she started at the age of five. During adolescence, however, writing took on a special dimension in her life. Finding herself at a school where whe was unpopular, she escaped into her imagination by composing poems, stories, and novels. As an adult author, L'Engle finds her childhood experiences much more than just memories. "When I am writing about a fourteen-year-old girl I will not succeed unless I am, during the time of writing, Madeleine: fourteen," she writes in her memoir *The Irrational Season*. "The strange wonder of it is that I am also Madeleine: fifty-seven, with all the experience I have gained in the intervening years. But I am not, in the ordinary sense, remembering what it was like to be fourteen; it is not something in the past; it is present; I am fourteen."

After taking her B.A. in 1941, L'Engle lived in New York, trying unsuccessfully to publish in magazines that paid their contributors. She did manage to place some work in little magazines. This in turn brought her to the attention of several publishers, one of which (Vanguard) published her first novel in 1945. *The Small Rain* draws on L'Engle's experiences in boarding schools and the theater—much of her fiction is tinged with autobiography—to tell the story of a young woman whose passion for the piano is an escape from the darkness of her boarding school. In 1982 L'Engle continued the heroine's story in the sequel *A Severed Wasp*.

The Small Rain was a success; *Ilsa*, her second adult novel, was not. In 1949 she published her first children's title, *And Both Were Young*, about boarding school life. The *New York Times* named it one of the Ten Best Books of the Year, but following the publication of her third adult novel, L'Engle entered a low period in her publishing history, when she could sell nothing. Her fortieth birthday proved a turning point, for on that day another manuscript was rejected and she decided to cover her typewriter for good. In her memoir *A Circle of Quiet*, she recalls walking around the room crying: "Suddenly I stopped, because I realized what my subconscious mind was doing while I was sobbing: my subconscious mind was busy working out a novel about failure." Knowing then that she had no choice in life but to write, she uncovered the typewriter.

The publication of *Meet the Austins* in 1960 opened the next, and most important phase, of L'Engle's literary career. The Austins are a classic nuclear family. Twelve-year-old Vicky Austin narrates the story, which begins with the family's normal happy household cacophony. Soon, however, L'Engle introduces an event which makes it clear that this is not material for a television sitcom of the period. A phone call brings the news that the husband of Mrs. Austin's best friend and a coworker have been killed in an airplane crash. When the widowed friend arrives at the Austins for a visit, she brings the orphaned daughter of the deceased coworker. Maggy, a spoiled, attention-grabbing ten-year-old, soon disrupts the household, until the love and understanding of the Austins prevails. According to May Hill Arbuthnot and Zena Sutherland in *Children and Books*, "*Meet the Austins*, a family-centered book, was one of the first since *Little Women* to handle the death of a loved one so well," although it was the subject of death that had scared publishers away from L'Engle's manuscript. *Meet the Austins* was named an American Library Association Notable Book.

This early Austins story seems dated by today's standards; some reviewers in the 1960s were also critical of L'Engle's idealization of family life, although the book's charms eventually won the day. L'Engle followed with more stories about the Austin family: *The Moon by Night*, *The Young Unicorns* (a *Book World* Spring Book Festival Honor Book and one of *School Library Journal*'s Best Books of the Year), and *A Ring of Endless Light* (an ALA Notable Book and a Newbery Honor Book).

L'Engle's fascination for science fiction and fantasy is rooted deep in her past, in her lonely childhood. During her college years, she turned to "more realistic fiction, and found that it was not sufficiently real. Her discoveries of reality came from writing sci-fi or fantasy. Unfortunately for many publishers, L'Engle's discoveries, as expressed in her first science fiction book, *A Wrinkle in Time*, were beyond their vision; the manuscript was rejected twenty-six times in two years for a variety of reasons. The story could not be squarely placed in either the science fiction or fantasy genre. There were questions as to who the audience would be. Some publishers felt the book was too difficult for young readers.

A Wrinkle in Time is the story of three children: Meg Murry, her younger brother Charles Wallace, and Calvin O'Keefe, a popular athlete at Meg's high school. Mr. Murry, Charles and Meg's father, is a scientist on a secret mission to explore the existence of a tesseract—that is, a wrinkle in time. Led by the mysterious cosmic trio of Mrs. Whatsit, Mrs. Which, and Mrs. Who, the children travel to the planet Camazotz, where Mr. Murry is a captive. During their trip the children learn of a great evil power that is besieging the universe. When the children arrive on Camazotz, they discover a world where everything is exactly alike. As John Rowe Townsend noted in *Written For Children*, the "zombie population of a planet called Camzotz" is an aspect of "evil (evil being the extermination of individuality)." The children find out that the evil power is a desembodied brain named It. The naked intellect, according to L'Engle, is a destructive force, unless emotion softens hard reason. Meg realizes that she can combat It and rescue her party from their dire predicament through the power of love.

In a *National Catholic Reporter* interview, L'Engle said that *A Wrinkle in Time* was "based on Einstein's theory of relativity and Planck's quantum theory. It's good, solid science, but also it's good, solid theology. [It's] my rebuttal to the German theologians [who] attack God with their intellect on the assumption that the finite can comprehend the infinite, and I don't think that's possible." *A Wrinkle in Time* won the coveted Newbery Medal in 1963.

L'Engle was unable to match the success of *A Wrinkle in Time* in her companion books, although all have been well received. In *A Wind in the Door* Charles Wallace suffers from mitochondritis—the destruction of farandolae, tiny creatures in the blood. The journey to help him takes Meg and Calvin into inner space inside the boy's body. Robert Bell, in the *School Librarian*, called it L'Engle's "most virtuoso performance in fantasy to date," but admitted that the "book will not be for every child; a good many will find it puzzling." Meg is married and pregnant in *A Swiftly Tilting Planet*, which finds Charles Wallace and a unicorn named Gaudior traveling through time trying to save the world from a mad dictator. "Unfortunately, the different episodes are not well integrated, and the author's tendency to philosophize interrupts the smooth flow of the narrative," Karen M. Klockner wrote in the *Horn Book Magazine*. "Characterization, though, is carefully handled, and if the book is flawed on a structural level, it is impeccable on an emotional one." Meg and Charles Wallace's younger twin brothers, Sandy and Dennys, are the protagonists in *Many Waters*, in which time travel, mythical beasts, and fantastic people again abound.

Another popular and critically acclaimed series centers on the O'Keefe family: Polly, Charles, and their scientist parents (Meg and Calvin from the *Time Fantasy* series.) The emphasis of *The Arm of the Starfish*, *Dragons in the Waters*, *A House Like a Lotus*, and *An Acceptable Time* is a romantic suspense in exotic locales, although in the fourth novel, L'Engle returns to time travel. The series is marked by intricate plots, religious themes and symbolism, colorful characters, and a fast pace, which in the hands of a lesser author might be too much.

In addition to books, L'Engle's work has appeared in such publications as *Commonweal*, *Christianity Today*, and *Mademoiselle*. She still lives part of the year in her New York City apartment and continues to write, teach, and make speaking tours.

Madeleine L'Engle's husband, Hugh Franklin, died suddenly of cancer in 1986 after forty years of marriage. "We are not supposed to get over our greatest griefs," she said. "They are a part of what makes us who we are."

PRINCIPAL WORKS: Novels—The Small Rain, 1945 (reissued as Prelude, 1968); Ilsa, 1946; And Both Were Young, 1949; Camilla Dickinson, 1951 (reissued as Camilla, 1965); A Winter's Love, 1957; Meet the Austins, 1960; A Wrinkle in Time, 1962; The Moon by Night,

1963; The Arm of the Starfish, 1965; The Love Letters, 1966; The Young Unicorns, 1968; Dance in the Desert, 1969; The Other Side of the Sun, 1971; A Wind in the Door, 1973; Dragons in the Waters, 1976; A Swiftly Tilting Planet, 1978; The Anti-Muffins, 1980; A Ring of Endless Light, 1980; A Severed Wasp, 1982; A House Like a Lotus, 1984; Many Waters, 1986; An Acceptable Time, 1989; The Glorious Impossible, 1990; Certain Women, 1992. *Short Stories*—The Twenty-Four Days Before Christmas: An Austin Family Story, 1964; The Sphinx at Dawn: Two Stories, 1982. *Memoirs*—A Circle of Quiet, 1972; The Summer of the Great-Grandmother, 1974; The Irrational Season, 1977; Walking on Water: Reflections on Faith and Art, 1980; Two-Part Invention, 1988. *Nonfiction*—Everyday Prayers, 1974; Prayers for Sunday, 1974; Ladder of Angels: Scenes from the Bible Illustrated by the Children of the World, 1979; And It Was Good: Reflections on Beginnings, 1983; Dare to Be Creative, 1984; (with A. Brooke) Trailing Clouds of Glory: Spiritual Values in Children's Books, 1985; A Stone for a Pillow: Journeys with Jacob, 1986. *Poetry*—Lines Scribbled on an Envelope and Other Poems, 1969; The Weather of the Heart, 1978; A Cry Like a Bell, 1987. *Plays*—18 Washington Square, South;: A Comedy in One Act, 1944; The Journey with Jonah, 1967. *As editor*—(with W. B. Green) Spirit and Light: Essays in Historical Theology, 1976.

ABOUT: Arbuthnot, M. H. and Z. Sutherland Children and Books, 1981; Authors in the News 2, 1976; Children's Literature Review 12, 1976 Contemporary Authors New Revision Series 3, 1981; 39, 1992; Contemporary Literary Criticism 12, 1980; Dictionary of Literary Biography 52, 1986; Gillespie, J. And D. Lembo Introducing Books: A Guide for the Middle Grades, 1970; Gonzales, D. Madeleine L'Engle, 1991; Huck, C. S. Children's Literature in the Elementary School, 1976; Kingman, L. (ed.) Newbery and Caldecott Medal Books: 1956–1965 with Acceptance Papers, Biographies and Related Material Chiefly from the Horn Book Magazine, 1965; Meigs, C. (ed.) A Critical History of Children's Literature, 1969; Newquist, R. Conversations, 1967; Nodelman, P. (ed.) Touchstones: Reflections on the Best in Children's Literature, vol. 1, 1985; Something About the Author 27, 1982; Twentieth-Century Children's Writers, 1989; Twentieth-Century Science-Fiction Writers, 1986; Townsend, J. R. A Sense of Story: Essays on Contemporary Writers for Children, 1971; Townsend, J. R. Written For Children: An Outline of English-language Children's Literature, rev. ed. 1974; Viguers, R. Margin for Surprise: About Books, Children, and Librarians, 1964. *Periodicals*—Horn Book Magazine October 1978; Junior Bookshelf August 1966; National Catholic Reporter June 20, 1986; School Librarian September 1975; School Library Journal March 1968.

LEWIS, BERNARD (May 31, 1916–), American historian, was born in London, England, the son of Harry Lewis, a businessman, and Jane Levy Lewis. He was educated at the University of London, receiving a B.A. in history

with first-class honors in 1936. A year later he took a diploma in Semitic studies at the University of Paris and in 1939 was awarded a Ph.D. in Islamic history at the University of London. In 1938 he was appointed assistant lecturer in Islamic history at London University and became lecturer two years later. To prepare himself for Islamic studies he became proficient in several languages including Arabic, Turkish, Persian, and Urdu.

Lewis says he was attracted to Islam and the Middle East out of "idle curiosity." His original intention was to become a lawyer; but as his interest in the Middle East increased, his interest in the law lessened. Within the field of Islamic studies Lewis concentrated initially in medieval Islamic history, and his doctoral thesis reflected this interest.

Published in 1940, as *The Origins of Ismailism: A Study of the Historical Background of the Fatimid Caliphate*, Lewis's thesis probed the origins of Ismailism. In medieval Islamic society a series of sects arose that challenged orthodox teachings. The Ismailis were one of these and gained considerable influence as the result of their relationship with the powerful Fatimid dynasty in Egypt. According to Lewis no investigation had been done on the origins of the Ismaili movement since the late 1880s. In the meantime new material had become available and this warranted a new study.

Lewis's book was published hastily. World War II loomed, and Lewis wanted to conclude the work before war began, even though he admitted that it was incomplete. As he states in the preface to the 1975 reprint: "There was the temptation—very great to a young man—of a book to be published. The temptation was all the greater in that the alternative was indefinite postponement to a future which at the time seemed very uncertain both for the author and for the world in which he lived."

As time went by the work began to attract notice, particularly in India, where scholars were studying the Ismaili movement. One of these was Vladimir Ivanov, who took issue with Lewis's main thesis in a book published in 1942. Lewis paid little attention to Ivanov's comments. After the war, his scholarly interests had changed, and he no longer looked to refute the opposition nor, for that matter, wanted to complete his investigation. Despite its incompleteness, however, Lewis's slim volume won for its author a reputation as a first-rate Islamic scholar.

During World War II Lewis served in the British army for a time and later was assigned to the Foreign Office, where his language skills and knowledge of the Middle East made him a valuable assistant. After the war he returned to the University of London, where he became Professor of Near Eastern History at the early age of thirty-three. He remained in this post for twenty-five years, interrupted only by visiting professorships in the United States. A distinguished teacher and mentor to hundreds of students from all over the world, he left England permanently in 1974 for Princeton University, where he served as Cleveland E. Dodge Professor of Near Eastern Studies until his retirement in 1986.

Lewis's output, spanning a period of over fifty years, has been extensive in his chosen field of Islamic history. The bibliography in a festschrift in Lewis's honor comprises twenty-eight books written, edited, contributed to, or translated by Lewis through the year 1988. The list of periodical articles numbers close to 200. The works vary from scholarly disquisitions to polemics. They have been translated into at least seventeen languages. Overarching his writing effort has been Lewis's service as a principal editor and contributor to the new edition of the authoritative *Encyclopedia of Islam* since its inception in 1954. This encyclopedia is an important reference work on Islamic subjects in the English language.

Lewis's first important book, and perhaps his best-known, is *The Arabs on History*, which has gone through several reprintings, the latest in 1993. Addressed to beginning students of the Islamic peoples, the volume traces clearly and concisely the place of the Arabs in world history, their achievements, and the salient characteristics of their development. Most of the book deals with the period up to the 11th century, the time of Islamic hegemony. Only eighteen pages are devoted to the period from the Ottoman conquest in 1517 to the book's conclusion in 1950.

The Arabist Philip Hitti acknowledged in *Speculum* that Lewis's work was "reliable." However, his overall assessment was not a glowing one. In her long review of the work in *Middle East Journal*, Nabia Abbott of the University of Chicago's Oriental Institute was rather neutral in her evaluation. Nonetheless, the work has stood the test of time and today enjoys a high reputation as a first-rate interpretive study of the Arabs.

After World War II, Lewis's concerns moved away from medieval Islam to the Ottoman period of Turkish history. In 1949 he was afforded a rarely given opportunity to do research in the Turkish archives, and he returned to Turkey in the late 1950s to continue his research. These travels provided the framework for what is argu-

ably his most influential book, *The Emergence of Modern Turkey*. Here Lewis traces the influences that have produced modern Turkey: the decline of the Ottoman Empire, the Western influence on reform in the 19th century, the conflict between modernist and traditionalist elements, and the Turkish republic to the year 1950. In the second part, Lewis concentrates in greater detail on four aspects of reform: the move from Islam and the Ottomanism to the concept of nationhood, changes in the theory and practice of government, Islam versus secularism, and changes in the economic and social order. Finally, Lewis analyzes the Turkish democratic revolution and assesses its achievements.

The editors of *Foreign Affairs 50-Year Bibliography* (1972) stated that the book was the best introduction to modern Turkey for the layman and "commands the respect of the specialist. . . . Professor Lewis' erudition is solid." William Plowden, in the *Spectator*, wrote that the "book will probably become indispensable." Hugh Seton-Watson, in *Encounter*, observed that Lewis's thesis was "brilliantly explained and presented," and H. N. Howard in the *Annals of the American Academy of Political and Social Science* said that the book "is one of the very basic studies, and will, without doubt, become the standard work in the field." It did, indeed, become the standard work but is today coming under increasing challenge by younger scholars. Turkey has remained an important subject of Lewis's scholarship.

In *The Middle East and the West*, Lewis addresses the encounter between Islam and the West. He begins by defining the Middle East historically, geographically, and culturally. After this, he explains what the West means to Middle Easterners, discussing Western influence and domination over the affairs of the region. Next, he deals with three political and intellectual movements: a liberal/socialist tendency, a nationalist trend, and Islamic fundamentalism. Finally, he examines the role of the countries of the Middle East in world affairs and considers Western policy toward these countries.

In *Political Science Quarterly*, Wayne Wilcox termed *The Middle East and the West* "one of the finest interpretive introductions to the Middle East yet written for a Western audience." Walter Laqueur, in the *New York Review of Books*, called it "the best short book on the Middle East. . . . a work of the highest level combining elegance of style with an easy mastery of the subject."

The Muslim Discovery of Europe considers contacts between Islam and the Christian West from the seventh through the early 19th centuries in all their aspects: religious, social, economic, cultural, diplomatic, and military. These contacts are considered from the Muslim point of view. Both worlds displayed misunderstanding and hostility in their interaction. "While Europeans were inquisitive about the Middle East, Muslims were uninterested in and, with the exception of technological developments with military applications, uninformed about European languages, culture, and religious denominations," Joseph Gardner commented in *Library Journal.*

Lewis examines Muslim indifference toward the West, observing that even as the West became more secular and provided Muslims with the opportunity to unlock the secrets of its knowledge without jeopardizing Muslim religious teachings, the indifference persisted. Unlike Edward Said, who criticized "Orientalism" as studies lending a racist and demeaning tone to scholarly discourse, Ernest Gellner, reviewing *The Muslim Discovery of Europe* for the *New Republic,* called it an "elegant, richly documented, well-presented volume" and said the most interesting part "consists of speculations concerning why . . . Orientalism, warts and all, should in the end have been so incomparably richer than Occidentalism."

In *Race and Color in Islam* Lewis seeks to dispel the myth that there is an absence of racial bias in Islamic countries. He refers to the *Arabian Nights,* the Muslim classic in which blacks rarely appear as rising above the role of menials. While acknowledging that the Koran repudiates racial prejudice, Lewis points out that attitudes began to change in Islam not long after Muhammad's death in 632. Lewis details instances of racial prejudice in Islamic society; but he concludes that Islam never practiced the deeper racial separation that existed in South Africa and in the United States. In his later study *Race and Slavery in the Middle East* Lewis expands on his earlier work, reaching the same basic conclusions.

One work in the Lewis corpus, *Islam and the Arab World,* brought to the fore a body of criticism engendered by younger Arab scholars against Western Islamic specialists. A large, illustrated volume, it consists of thirteen chapters by distinguished scholars covering a number of aspects of Islamic civilization. Lewis edited and introduced the work. The emphasis and approach are in the traditional vein of Western Islamic scholarship. Some reviewers contended that the work is condescending and portrayed Muslims as an undeveloped, backward people. Notwithstanding this criticism, the work has had many defenders.

The Jews of Islam and *Semites and Anti-Semites: An Inquiry into Conflict and Prejudice* cover the interplay of Jews and Muslims from the creation of Islam to the 20th century. Rather than a chronological survey of Jews in the Islamic world, *The Jews of Islam* is, according to Norman Stillman writing in the *New York Review of Books* (1984), "a conceptual study that examines the fundamental social and mental structures underlying Muslim attitudes toward the Jews and their treatment of them, as well as the Jews' own responses. . . ." Stillman says Lewis is careful "not to create the false impression of timeless, static patterns." B. B. Lawrence, however, criticized in *Choice* Lewis's "carping tone" in compiling negative Muslim attitudes toward Jews without "even a skeletal explanatory model or interpretive thesis." Ernest Gellner, reviewing *Semites and Anti-Semites* in the *Times Literary Supplement,* also felt this volume lacks a central thesis: It "provokes no argument." For Gellner the book lacks a "general theory, diagnosis or recommendation." He lauds its "elegance and passion," but comments that if it were not for Lewis's erudition "one might compare this with some civil service brief." Gellner disagrees with Lewis's implication that because Jews did not suffer unduly in Islamic societies they felt no need to migrate.

In his introduction to the Lewis festschrift, Charles Issawi commended "Lewis' outstanding qualities—the exceptionally wide range of his languages, his great knowledge of so many aspects of Middle Eastern history and culture, his capacity for apprehending the essence of a problem and understanding the interrelationships of its parts, and the felicity of his terse, subtle, and precise style. It is these qualities that make him the outstanding historian of the region."

Islam and the West, published in 1993, is an examination of "encounters, the confrontations of Muslim peoples and the West; the western perception of Islam . . . ; and the political culture of Islam, dealing with questions of state and religion, Islamic movements and secularism," according to Ira Lapidus in the *New York Times Book Review.* In part a rebuttal to Edward Said and others who question Western motives for interpreting the Middle East, this book displays Lewis's enormous learning—"his deep knowledge of Arabic philology, his masterly acquaintance with the history and culture of the Middle East, and his intimate familiarity with the relations of East and West," as Lapidus characterized it. He faults Lewis, however, for abstracting "concepts from the real-life situations in which they take their actual meaning." Although Lapidus maintains that Lewis's historical vision is an "antagonistic one," he concludes that "he is correct in many of his responses and shows that his opponents go too far in their effort to undermine the credibility of traditional Western learning." Shaul Bakhash, in the *New York Review of Books* (1993), agreed that in "examining the broader, orientalist scholarly tradition, Lewis, unlike his critics, does not take a monolithic view. . . . that the imperial impulse and the lack of appreciation of Islamic (and other non-European cultures) permeated all of Western culture."

Bernard Lewis has received many honors for his scholarship. He has been named an honorary fellow to several prestigious learned societies, including the British Academy, the Royal Historical Society, the Turkish Historical Society, the American Academy of Arts and Sciences, and the American Philosophical Society. He has served as a long-term member of the Institute for Advanced Studies at Princeton. He holds many honorary degrees from institutions in the United States and abroad.

Lewis is divorced and has a son and a daughter. He maintains an office in the Department of Near Eastern Studies, Princeton University.

PRINCIPAL WORKS IN ENGLISH: The Origins of Ismailism: A Study of the Historical Background of the Fatimid Caliphate, 1940; Turkey Today, 1940; British Contributions to Arabic Studies, 1941; A Handbook of Diplomatic and Political Arabic, 1947; The Arabs in History, 1950; Notes and Documents from the Turkish Archives: A Contribution to the History of the Jews in the Ottoman Empire, 1952; The Emergence of Modern Turkey, 1961; Istanbul and the Civilization of the Ottoman Empire, 1963; The Middle East and the West, 1964; The Assassins: A Radical Sect in Islam, 1967; Race and Color in Islam, 1971; Islam in History: Ideas, Men, and Events in the Middle East, 1973; History—Remembered, Recovered, Invented, 1975; studies in Classical and Ottoman Islam: Seventh to Sixteenth Centuries, 1976; (with A. Cohen) Population and Revenue in the Towns of Palestine in the Sixteenth Century, 1978; The Muslim Discovery of Europe, 1982; The Jews of Islam, 1984; Semites and Anti-Semites: An Inquiry into Conflict and Prejudice, 1986; The Political Language of Islam, 1988; Race and Slavery in the Middle East, 1990; Islam and the West, 1993. As editor—Land of Enchanters: Egyptian Short Stories from the Earliest Times to the Present Day, 1948; (with P. Holt) Historians of the Middle East, 1962; (with P. Holt and A. Lambton) The Cambridge History of Islam, 2 vols., 1970; Islam from the Prophet Muhammad to the Capture of Constantinople, 2 vols., 1974; Islam and the Arab World, 1976 (in U.K.: The World of Islam: Faith, People, Culture). As editor and translator—Diwan, Poems in Arabic, Persian, Turkish, and Hebrew: Eighth to Eighteenth Centuries, 1981; (with B. Braude) Christians and Jews in the Ottoman Empire, 2 vols., 1982; (with E. Leites and M. Case) As Others See Us: Mutual Perceptions, East and West, 1985; Islam and the West, 1993.

ABOUT Blackwell Dictionary of Historians 1988; Bosworth, C. E., et al. The Islamic World from Classical to Modern Times: Essays in Honor of Bernard Lewis, 1989; Contemporary Authors 118, 1986; Encyclopedia Judaica 1971; Foreign Affairs 50-Year Bibliography, 1972; International Who's Who 1992–93; Who's Who 1993; Who's Who in America 1992–1993. *Periodicals*—Annals of the American Academy of Political and Social Science March 1962; Choice January 1985; Encounter December 1961; History: Reviews of New Books April 1985; Library Journal September 1, 1982; Middle East Journal Summer 1951; Nation July 27, 1964; New Republic August 16, 1982; August 23, 1982; New York Review of Books April 2, 1964; October 25, 1984; October 7, 1993; New York Times Book Review May 30, 1993; Political Science Quarterly September 1965; Spectator July 14, 1961; Speculum July 1951; Times Literary Supplement August 22, 1986; Virginia Quarterly Review Winter 1985.

*L'HEUREUX, JOHN (CLARKE) (October 26, 1934–), American novelist, short story writer, and poet, writes: "I was born in South Hadley, Massachusetts. My father was an engineer and my mother a concert pianist who gave up playing—I'm not sure why. I have an older brother, a civil engineer employed as a lumberjack. In his sixties my father began to paint in oils, brilliantly, I think.

"I attended public schools, trained as an actor, and performed briefly on stage and television. After two years at Holy Cross College, I entered the Jesuits. I did so on the grounds of coldest reason: I felt it was the best and most generous thing I could do with my life and so I did it. I found religious life extremely difficult and, I suppose, rewarding: I was ordained a priest and remained a Jesuit for a total of seventeen years. In 1970, however, I requested laicization, which was granted in 1971. I left the Jesuits because of difficulties with the vow of obedience. I wanted to be my own man, make my own decisions, and not feel guilty about doing so. I have never regretted leaving.

"The Jesuits gave me an enviable classical education—I was the last generation whose classes were taught in Latin—and allowed me to survive as a writer. I worked as an editor at the *Atlantic* while still a Jesuit and upon leaving the Jesuits taught American literature and fiction writing at Tufts, Harvard, and for the past twenty years at Stanford University. I am married to Joan Polston, a teacher and writer, and we live in Stanford, California.

"My writing extends far back into my Jesuit life. My first four books—poetry—were exercises in small, working taking the metaphor as far as it would go, exorcising anger, desire, desperation, love, coping with God and his odd

°luh ROO

JOHN L'HEUREUX

ways. My later books of short fiction (*Family Affairs, Desires, Comedians*) are, in a way, extensions of these poems. The stories explore the mysterious and ironic interventions of God in our lives, the range of the suprarational, the rag and boneyard of the heart.

"In my early novels (*Tight White Collar, Jessica Fayer*), it seems to me I'm searching for something larger than the self, something or someone to give allegiance to, some persuasive reason to go on living. *The Clang Birds* is a satiric version of this search. My more recent novels are concerned with the problems of sanctity in a post-Christian world. In *A Woman Run Mad*—in Angelo—I've tried to create the reluctant saint, sanctified almost despite himself and his promiscuity. In *An Honorable Profession*—in Miles—there is the blundering saint, saved and perhaps ennobled by the thing he runs from, the thing he fears most in himself. And in *The Shrine at Altamira*—in both father and son—there is the saint unaware, who does not care about God or salvation or anything else, but who nonetheless gives everything, even his life, in a single and apparently senseless act of love.

"This description of my work may sound solemn and pretentious, an attempt to give some form and significance to what I've been doing with my life. In fact, all these books are a pack of lies intended to entertain and illumine and dismay, and—for myself—to explore the shape of mystery that lies behind the few things I know.

"My next three novels—barring mental collapse or divine and whimsical intervention—will retreat from themes that explore ultimates to the more mundane grounds of (1) academe and the preposterousness of human wishes; (2) marriage, desire, and self-delusion; (3) the crucial mid-life discovery that everything is not enough. This latter book I envision as a moral thriller. I have completed a novel, 'Lies,' to be published posthumously.

"The few who are interested may now prepare my obituary. I suggest: 'He wrote too early and too late. He sacrificed his life on the altar of his books but was never convinced the sacrifice was worthy or worth it. He meant well, but doesn't everyone? And he loved well. He suffered no pain without complaint.'"

John L'Heureux is the son of Wilfred L'Heureux and Mildred (Clarke) L'Heureux. He earned a bachelor's degree and two master's degrees (one in English and one in philosophy) before studying for the priesthood at Woodstock College in Woodstock, Maryland, where he received a Licentiate in Sacred Theology in 1967. His four books of poetry and his memoir, *Picnic in Babylon: A Jesuit Priest's Journal, 1963–1967*, were all completed before he left the clergy in 1971. His first two poetry collections received generally favorable notices. Praising *Rubrics for a Revolution* in the *New York Times Book Review* (1967) James Dickey observed: "He is a religious poet, indeed a priest, but with a refreshing difference. His feeling for sacramental relationships has nothing of the owlish or scholastic; it is a form of worship that includes, as most religious verse does not, humor and a very wide latitude of tolerance." His next two poetry collections, which examine both religious and secular themes, fared less well with reviewers.

L'Heureux's first two novels, *Tight White Collar* and *The Clang Birds*, were published quite soon after his laicization and contain caustic portraits of Catholic clergymen. Both received mixed reviews. *Tight White Collar* is the story of one day in the life of a self-absorbed young priest who returns to his family's home to attend the wake of a distant relative. Doris Grumbach, in *America* (1972), wrote that although she admired L'Heureux's poetry, the novel was a disappointment: "For me the story itself fails in interest and in what Henry James demanded in fiction: intensity. . . . the novel has parts but no convincing whole." *The Clang Birds* is a satirical look at a small band of radical and sexually active priests who leave their order to form a commune devoted to protesting the war in Vietnam. In the *New York Times Book Review* (1972), Martin Levin praised

L'Heureux's "at once splenetic and sympathetic" way with his characters, and the novel's "dazzling juxtaposition of ironies." At least one reviewer displayed overt hostility toward L'Heureux's early fiction. Reviewing *Tight White Collar* and *The Clang Birds* in *Commonweal* (1972), Ralph McInerny commented: "His novels do not suggest that the religious vocation is, while difficult, a worthy ideal of pursuit. . . . There is little point in discussing the massive lapse in taste and tact and charity these novels represent."

Soon enough, however, L'Heureux began winning acclaim for his short fiction, sometimes from the same reviewers who had dismissed his early novels. In a *New Republic* review of his first short story collection, *Family Affairs*, Doris Grumbach wrote: "I suspect short fiction is his métier. . . . He can fix a situation to the page with a few sentences and then expand it, explore it, bring it to an inevitable conclusion—often by the use of a fine moment of epiphany—without striking a single false note." Although L'Heureux sketches a variety of characters, the travails of priests and ex-priests figure prominently in both *Family Affairs* and *Desires*, his second collection of stories. In the *New York Times Book Review* (1981) Johanna Kaplan hailed the stories in *Desires* as "oblique, ironic moral fables . . . written in a spare, elegant and witty prose."

Comedians, his third collection of short fiction, was also widely praised. "God's meddling in our lives seems as good a phrase as any to describe what is at the heart of L'Heureux's stories," Joseph A. Appleyard wrote in an *America* (1990) review of the collection. In one story, "The Comedian," a female stand-up comic finds herself unexpectedly pregnant. Afraid that the baby will destroy her career as a performer, she plans to have an abortion. A miraculous occurrence, however, dissuades her from going through with the abortion: she, and she alone, can hear a voice singing from her womb. Ironically, the child is born mute. L'Heureux, Greg Johnson noted in the *Georgia Review*, "writes devastating moral allegories that dramatize with equal passion the chaotic reality of his characters' 'profane' lives and their unappeasable longings for spiritual redemption."

Part thriller and part novel of ideas, *A Woman Run Mad* is set primarily in Boston and chronicles the tragic intersection of four damaged lives. J. J. Quinn is the novel's principle character, and perhaps its most unappealing one as well; an aspiring novelist, he is depressed because he has failed to receive tenure at Williams College. His wife, Claire, has a successful academic career, but little else. Both Quinn and Claire are lapsed Catholics, and both are extremely insecure—Quinn because of his stalled career and a permanent scar on his upper lip, and Claire because of her lifelong weight problem. Quinn, a sexual naif, intent upon gaining experience he might incorporate into his novel, becomes involved with Sarah, a mentally unstable Boston Brahmin. Sarah's secrets include the fact that she has murdered a former lover and is undergoing intensive psychiatric treatment. Angelo, Sarah's live-in caretaker, is a promiscuous homosexual, and an avid reader of Kierkegaard and Iris Murdoch. Angelo exemplifies L'Heureux's unorthodox concept of sanctity. When Quinn makes it clear that he intends to leave Claire, she is consumed by jealousy and becomes the "woman run mad," concocting a fiendishly brutal scheme that leaves Quinn and Angelo dead, and points to Sarah as the prime suspect in their murder.

Aware perhaps that the sensationalistic and melodramatic aspects of his novel might overwhelm his larger purpose, L'Heureux included the following prefatory note to *A Woman Run Mad*: "This book is not, in essence, about sex or murder but about the restlessness that drives us on to fabricate our lives and—willy nilly—to accomplish our fates."

John Gross, in the *New York Times*, expressed the confusion felt by other readers as to what precisely L'Heureux was trying to do in this novel: "At the very least, the book qualifies as a superior suspense story, but is it anything more?" Gross's final assessment was that the novel "reads like a blueprint for an obsession rather than the obsession itself." Richard Eder, in the *Los Angeles Times Book Review* (1988), wrote: "*A Woman Run Mad* is quirky and unbalanced. . . . Its excesses at the end hardly seem excessive, and that is the author's remarkable achievement." In the *New York Times Book Review* (1988), Richard P. Brickner deemed *A Woman Run Mad* "unlike any novel I know. Its events are freshly peculiar. . . . not always believable, but . . . always pleasurably unpredictable." Brickner termed the book's major characters "convincing and engrossing" but "never banal." He concluded that "unusual intelligence and personality are alive throughout the book."

Violence and sexual obsession are also central in L'Heureux's novels *An Honorable Profession* and *The Shrine at Altamira*. In the former novel, a popular high-school English teacher, Miles Bannon, befriends a seventeen-year-old male student who has been beaten and raped by a group of athletes. When the boy commits suicide, Miles finds himself at the center of a firestorm of controversy. In *The Shrine at Altamira*, which, Kathryn Harris wrote in the *Los Angeles Times Book Review* (1992) is "[p]erhaps his most ambitious novel . . . [and] also his most successful," a father sets fire to his young son, but is eventually forgiven by the boy. "But Mr. L'Heureux's intention is not to milk a hideous domestic tragedy of its horror," Patrick McGrath commented in the *New York Times Book Review* (1992). "Instead, by means of a fastidious precision in the rendering of his characters' lives and souls, he makes the point that an act of almost unimaginable evil can arouse pity both for perpetrator and victim once we recognize the forces shaping and driving their behavior."

"A recurring theme in L'Heureux is sex as a metaphor for something bigger for which the human heart longs," Michael J. Farrell noted in the *National Catholic Reporter*. L'Heureux told Farrell that he considers himself "puritanical." "The whole idea of being a writer is to get out of oneself and into another hide," he remarked. Although no longer a priest, L'Heureux still writes from the point of view of a believer. In his discussion with Farrell, L'Heureux noted, "I have no doubt there is such a thing as grace, and I do believe there is a God. All my characters agitate because they are not as convinced as I."

PRINCIPAL WORKS: *Poetry*—Quick as Dandelions, 1964; Rubrics for a Revolution, 1967; One Eye and a Measuring Rod, 1968; No Place for Hiding, 1971. *Novels*—The Clang Birds, 1972; Tight White Collar, 1972; Jessica Fayer, 1976; A Woman Run Mad, 1987; An Honorable Profession, 1991;The Shrine at Altamira, 1992. *Short stories*—Family Affairs, 1974; Desires, 1981; Comedians, 1990. *Memoir*—Picnic In Babylon: A Jesuit Priest's Journal, 1963–1967, 1967.

ABOUT: Contemporary Authors New Revision Series 23, 1988; Contemporary Literary Criticism 52, 1989; Who's Who in America, 1994. *Periodicals*—America June 10, 1972; June 9, 1990; Commonweal November 24, 1972; June 17, 1988; Georgia Review Winter 1990; Los Angeles Times Book Review January 17, 1988; April 19, 1992; National Catholic Reporter May 11, 1990; New Republic September 14, 1974; New York Times January 8, 1988; New York Times Book Review June 11, 1967; October 8, 1972; April 12, 1981; January 31, 1988; January 27, 1991; May 2, 1992; Poetry April 1972.

LI ANG (Pseudonym of Shi Shuduan)

(1952–), Taiwanese novelist, short story writer, and journalist, is best known for her vast output of writings on women's issues and her fictional explorations of sex as a metaphor for human relationships in general. A native of the port city of Lugang in central Taiwan, Li Ang was born to a wealthy family with talented children. In an 1984 interview, she said of herself: "I am probably one of those 'prodigies who failed to develop into a major talent.' I have two older sisters who are prominent writers, Shi Shu and Shi Shuqing. Also, I grew up in Lugang, a unique town. I read many fairy tales and memorized lots of traditional poems when I was very young. I started my first novel when I was only in the second year of junior middle school . . . In my first year of senior middle school, I wrote *Hua Ji* (translated as "Flowering Season") which became my first published work."

The stories from this early period were mainly psychological explorations of female consciousness, they showed influences of the young author's readings in existentialism. *Hua Ji*, a first-person narration of "a now lost radiant youth," describes a young girl's vivid fantasies about possible rape as she rides on a bicycle on her way to pick out a Christmas tree. Nothing happens at the end of the story—"But had I really hoped for something to happen?" the girl asks herself. "I'm not sure." Another outstanding work of this period, *You Quixian de Wawa* ("The Curvaceous Dolls") explores the world of a young woman obsessed by the female body. It centers on breasts, represented by a series of beautiful dolls described in voluptuous detail.

In 1970 Li Ang left her native Lugang for college in Taipei, the capital, and entered into a new phase of development. Between 1973 and 1974, she launched *Renjian Shi* (Man's World), a series of stories in which she planned to expose male chauvinism and demolish all the manifestations of sexual taboos in the society. The title story "Renjian Shi" was concerned not so much with the brief sexual encounter between two youngsters in a dormitory as with the tragic innocence of the girl and the harshness of the school authorities, who promptly expell the two students after the girl "confesses." Li Ang was shocked when a flood of letters from readers attacked her for her openness about juvenile sex. Two other well-known stories in the series, "Zuo Ye" (Last Night) and "Mo Chun" (Lost Spring), carry explicit and even clinical depictions of sex as joyless, sordid, and guilt-ridden, bringing nothing positive to the men and women desperately seeking involvement. The stories reflect the repression of erotic feelings in Chinese society at large.

In 1975, Li Ang left Taiwan for studies in North America. She earned an M.A. degree in theater from the University of Oregon in 1977 and returned to teach at the Chinese Academy of Culture in Taipei. The short stories collected in *Aiqing Shiyen* (The Love Test) and *Tamen de*

Yenlei (Their Tears), published in the productive period between 1978 and 1981, were mainly concerned with the breakdown of communication between people owing to psychological and societal barriers.

In 1983 *Sha Fu (The Butcher's Wife)*, undeniably Li Ang's most important work to date, received first prize in the annual fiction contest sponsored by *Lianhe Bao* (United Daily News). Afterward, Li Ang again found herself the target of attacks for "immorality." In her preface to the English edition of *The Butcher's Wife*, Li Ang reveals the genesis of the story. At a friend's house in California in 1977, Li Ang came upon an old news item about the sensational murder of a man by his wife in Shanghai in the 1930s. "What drew me to this particular story of husband killing was the fact that it was not just another case of adultery. In traditional Chinese society, any woman who kills her husband is presumed to have done so because of an extramarital affair . . . no other interpretation is possible." In this particular case, however, "the accused murderess insisted that she had killed her husband only to escape his abuses. . . . Thus," Li Ang pointed out, "instead of being just another in a long line of women labeled promiscuous by society, the husband-killer in this case was a woman who had suffered the oppression of traditional society." Its appeal to Li Ang was immediate, and she decided to use the news item as a basis for a story. But knowing nothing about Shanghai, she moved the background to her hometown of Lugang, a small town that retained the flavor of "old Taiwan." "And so," Li Ang writes, "the basic elements of a sensational murder case that had actually occurred in Shanghai were transported to Taiwan and transformed into a story of old Taiwanese society."

The Butcher's Wife is a gripping story centered on Lin Shi, an ignorant peasant girl driven by circumstances to husband killing, the worst offense in the spectrum of female offenses. Daughter of a destitute mother who had been banished by her clan for promiscuity (she was caught exchanging sex for balls of rice), Lin Shi is married off by her clan to Chen Jiangshui, a pig-butcher in Lingang. Helpless in a hostile environment dominated by supersition and gossip, Lin Shi is subjected to nightly rape by her brutish husband. For Chen, the sexual plunge is identified with the plunge of his butcher's knife: "This was Chen Jiangshui's moment. As the knife was withdrawn and the blood spurted forth, he was infused with an incomparable sense of satisfaction. It was as though the hot steam coursing through his body was converted into a thick, sticky white fluid spurting into the shadowy depths of a woman at the climax of a series of high-speed thrusts. To Chen Jiangshui, the spurting of blood and the ejaculation of semen had the same orgasmic effect." Finally, in a deathly trance after particularly vicious bout of psychological and physical abuse, Lin Shi kills her husband with his own butcher's knife and dismembers his body as he had done his pigs. Set in an indeterminate time, *The Butcher's Wife* transcends the particulars of Taiwanese society to expose the "timelessness" of an entrenched traditional culture that enslaves women. It strikes a universal chord with its powerful depiction of sexuality as a form of male dominance. Li Ang has said: "I cannot deny that I approached the writing of *The Butcher's Wife* with a number of feminist ideals, wanting to show the tragic fate that awaited the economically dependent Taiwanese women living under the rules of traditonal Chinese society. But as I wrote, I found myself becoming more and more concerned with larger issues of humanity, such as hunger, death, sex. What I want to emphasize here is that the ultimate concern of a piece of 'feminist literature' is, after all, human nature."

Li Ang's next major was the novella *An Ye* (Dark Nights), which moves from the nativist world of fishermen and peasants she depicts in *The Butcher's Wife* to a cosmopolitan circle of businessmen, journalists, and members of the educated elite, along with their wives and mistresses. The intricacies of lust and love, of buying and selling, are portrayed through a dialogue between two men, Mr. Huange, an industrialist on the verge of bankruptcy, and Dr. Chen, a philosopher and founder of a so-called Morality Research Institute. Dr. Chen reveals to Mr. Huang his wife's infidelity, his close friend's betrayal, and other sordid affairs going on behind his back. He urges Mr. Huang to expose these acts as manifestations of a larger social ill, even at the risk of losing his own business—to pass the test of integrity, so to speak. It transpires, however, that Dr. Chen is just seeking to manipulate Mr. Huang for his own selfish ends. Thus the framework of the story, on the verge of achieving a moral center, falls apart to expose an incurably diseased world of male dominance and manipulation. *An Ye* has some of Li Ang's most moving female characters: the neglected wife Mrs. Huang, who discovers sexual satisfaction outside marriage only to be betrayed by her lover, and the sexually liberated Miss Ding Xinxin, secretly plagued by anxieties to marry and "settle down."

Apart from writing fiction, Li Ang is also involved in journalism, writing on feminist issues. She runs a weekly column in *Zhongguo Shibao* (China Times) called "Nuxing de Yijian" (Women's Opinions), where she keeps in touch with readers and writes on problems in love, marriage, sex, family, chastity, work, children, adultery, divorce, friendship, and other concerns. These piquant and immensely popular weekly articles have been published in book form—*Nuxing de Yiji* (Women's Opinions, 1984) and *Zouchu Anye* (Out of Dark Nights, 1986).

Famous in Taiwan since the 1970s, Li Ang's fiction has been published in mainland China since the 1980s and is an important influence, especially on women writers.

PRINCIPAL WORKS IN ENGLISH TRANSLATION: *Novel*—(tr. H. Goldblatt and E. Yeung) The Butcher's Wife, 1986. *Short stories*—(tr. H. Goldblatt) "Flowering Season" *in* The Chinese PEN, Summer 1980; (tr. H. Goldblatt) "The Curvaceous Dolls" *in* Renditions 27–28, Spring–Fall 1987; (tr. H. Goldblatt) "A Love Letter Never Sent" *in* Duke, M. S. (ed.) Worlds of Modern Chinese Fiction, 1991.

ABOUT: Duke, M. S. (ed.) Modern Chinese Women Writers: Critical Appraisals, 1989; Goldbaltt, H. (ed.) Worlds Apart: Recent Chinese Writing and its Audience, 1990; Martin H. and Kindley, S. (eds.) Modern Chinese Writers: Self-Portrayals, 1992. *Periodicals*—Los Angeles Times November 17, 1987; Modern Chinese Literature 3, Spring–Fall 1987; 4, Spring–Fall 1988; New York Times Book Review December 28, 1986.

*LINDGREN, TORGNY** (June 16, 1938–), Swedish novelist, poet, and dramatist, was born in the province of Västerbotten in the northern part of Sweden. He grew up in the hamlet of Raggsjö, where his parents were farmers, and attended the Teacher Training College in Umea, graduating as an elementary school teacher in 1959. Later he qualified as a secondary school teacher. In 1965 he published his first book, a collection of poems. After the publication of his first novel in 1973, he left his profession as a teacher and became a full-time writer.

Lindgren was strongly influenced in his childhood by the Free Church religious life of Raggsjö. It was a harsh, strict Old Testament faith, and he was often frightened by the fiery sermons of itinerant preachers. His father was the children's Sunday school teacher and a gifted storyteller, as were also his mother and grandmother. As a result, Lindgren grew up in a culture of oral storytelling that proved fundamental for his own writing. He insists on the oral quality of his texts, speaking them aloud during the writing process. Ideally, they should be read aloud.

In the 1970s, Lindgren was politically active as a member of the Social Democratic Party, and

TORGNY LINDGREN

political themes permeate his works of that period: *Dikter fran Vimmerby* (Poems from Vimmerby), 1970; *Hur skulle det vara om man vore Olof Palme?* (What would it be like to be Olof Palme?, poems), 1971; *Skolbagateller medan jag försökte skriva till mina överordnade* (School trifles while I was trying to write to my superiors, short stories), 1972; *Övriga fragor* (Remaining questions, novel), 1973; *Hallen* (The hall, novel), 1975; and *Brännvinsfursten* (The aquavit king, novel), 1979. During this time Lindgren also wrote a number of radio plays.

Lindgren had not been a member of any church since he was about twelve years old. At that time his father had become an atheist and the family had left the Free Church community. In 1980, however, Lindgren joined the Catholic Church, and a significant shift became apparent in his writing, where the emphases moved from politics to religion, from social issues to the inner life of the individual. In his novel of 1981, for example, *Skrämmer dig minuten* (Does the minute frighten you?) the living Catholicism of one of the main characters is confronted by the secularized Protestantism of a clergyman of the Swedish church, dramatizing, to some degree at least, Lindgren's own religious struggle.

His novel *Ormens väg pa hälleberget* (1982, *The Way of a Serpent*) introduces a new dimension to his works and reflects the pronounced influence religion has had on him. For the first time he writes about the Västerbotten of his childhood. The language of the novel is colored by the terse idiom of these northern parts. As in the Icelandic sagas, words are few and heavy

*LIND grin, TORN yee

with meaning; silence talks. The author now also draws from the wells of oral storytelling of his childhood. In this novel, set in the second half of the 19th century, the narrator is a young man called Jani. He mourns for his mother Tea, his sister Eva, and his wife Johanna, who died as a result of the wickedness of the landowner and shopkeeper Ol Karlsa and his son Karl Orsa. Jani's story begins when his family lose their land and become leaseholders, constantly in debt to Ol Karlsa and his son; it ends with the catastrophe in which Jani's wife and children die, leaving him alone with his questions to God, whom he addresses throughout the book.

The Way of a Serpent bears a heavy stamp of determinism. Described in metaphoric language, Karl Orsa appears as a cruel and incomprehensible God. This may have its roots in the sermons on predestination and the last judgment that had frightened Lindgren as a child. In addition to the severe image of God represented by Karl Orsa, there is also a compassionate God to whom one may pray for help. This is the women's God—Tea's, Eva's, and Johanna's. They also have a lighter view of life than Jani, finding pleasure and hope in music. He cannot understand their courage and joy in living in the midst of darkness. Jani resembles Job in the Old Testament. Like Job, he defies the injustice of God, who has bereft him of all that made life worth living. Unlike Job, he does not in the end submit in humble silence to God's power and holiness. He obstinately continues to question God even after the final catastrophe—questions that reverberate in the reader's mind.

The publication of *The Way of a Serpent* in *Merab's Beauty* brought Lindgren to the forefront of Swedish writers. Bengt Holmqvist, one of the Swedish reviewers, was impressed with the aphoristic and lyrical qualities of Lindgren's language, praising especially his ability to create a rounded portrait of the evil Karl Orsa: "With swift and expressive traits he draws the picture of a man who is unhappy and lonely. . . . You remember Tea and Eva, the 'light music' in their mind that almost conquers the evil. But you remember their tormentor too, his anguish and his monstrous innocence."

Ulla Sweedler in *Library Journal* called *The Way of a Serpent* a "darkly shimmering jewel" and commented that all the stories in *Merab's Beauty* are "written in an archaic northern dialect with biblical overtones, impossible to reproduce in English. Nevertheless, the translation allows the magic and power of these moving tales to come through."

The short stories of *Merabs skönhet* (1983, translated as *Merab's Beauty and Other Stories*,

including three stories from *Legender* [1986]) have the same setting as *The Way of a Serpent* and are told in the same dialect-colored language. In "The Stump Grabber," the frightening and paradoxical image of God is similar to that in *The Way of a Serpent*. Jacob Lundmark's struggle with the stump of an old giant pine reminds us of the struggle of another Jacob with an angel in the Old Testament. When at the end Jacob Lundmark receives a blow that kills him, it is not clear—as A. G. Mojtabai pointed out in the *New York Times Book Review*—whether he "is felled by the might of an ancient tree, or by the slight turning of his head in response to his wife's call":

> But within him all he saw was Gerda, and he was bursting with her voice and her words, the eagerness and anxiety and warmth, her fondness for him that was so great that there were almost tears in her voice, so that when he fell headlong he did not grasp what it was that was happening, he did not realize what had befallen him. What it was that struck him like the hand of God's wrath and tore his breast open and killed him, if it was the winch, or if it was the almost unbearable heat of love, there are words that are like glowing coals, dearest love Jacob, you must be careful.

Mojtabai termed "creation as a continuing process" the dominant motif of the stories and added, "This vision of mutability has nothing to do with the world of capricious transformation and the luxuriance and dazzle that characterize magic realism. There is not the faintest hint of magic in . . . Lindgren's writing, only the most wide-eyed realism." Speaking of characters whose lives are a continuous struggle for survival in the harshest of climates, Mojtabai said, "There is scarcely a creature that moves through the pages of this beautiful, disturbing God-haunted book who is not clothed with spiritual power."

The events in Lindgren's next novel, *Bat Seba* (1984, *Bathsheba*), take place in Israel in the 10th century B.C. The protagonists are King David and his wife Bathsheba, although Lindgren has changed them considerably from the biblical story, giving Bathsheba a major role in the course of events, whereas in the Bible she appears only marginally. In the beginning of the story David is strong and powerful. As the years pass and David gets older, he also becomes more passive and indecisive, while Bathsheba grows in power and energy. In Lindgren's version, Bathsheba is the one who secretly plans every event of the story and makes it happen. At the end of the novel the relationship between David and Bathsheba is the opposite to what it was at the beginning: David is now weak and dying, while Bathsheba, as the Queen, has absolute power.

David's image of God—the God that he himself incarnates in the novel—is the Old Testament male God, sometimes cruel and inhuman, whose love is incomprehensible and crushingly heavy, but who sometimes manifests himself as the good shepherd. Bathsheba, on the other hand, is portrayed as a modern woman, free to question everything, even the Lord that David constantly invokes. A token of Bathsheba's rebellion against his male image of God is her own little house god of fig tree wood. She has cut off its enormous phallus, which had reached to its chin and constantly made it topple over. "It does not need one," she says. "Its godly strength is contained within itself."

Theological issues permeate this novel in the recurring question "What is the nature of the Lord?" In the first chapter King David answers the question, in the last chapter Bathsheba. On both occasions, the answer is, "He is like me." The answer ties the end of the story to its beginning. The circularity is the main motif of the book. The context in which that answer is given in the last chapter is the opposite to the context in the first chapter. In the beginning of the novel, when David answers, "He is like me," it is only a few minutes after he has nearly crushed Bathsheba under his weight, in what might well be described as a rape. At the end of the story, when Bathsheba gives him the same answer, she is tenderly warming him as he lies dying in his bed. This expresses the author's view of God as *Coincidentia oppositorum*, the unity of opposites.

Reviewing *Bathsheba* and *Merab's Beauty* in the *Times Literary Supplement* (1989), Clive Sinclair suggests that the two books be read in conjunction. There are profound similarities, though the novel is set in a biblical environment that would seem very far from the Swedish setting of the stories. The Västerbotten land of *Merab's Beauty*, says Sinclair, "with its harsh pastures and haunted forests, possesses a divine vindictiveness no less terrible than the burning wilderness of the Middle East. So it is hardly surprising that Lindgren's prose constantly echoes its biblical prototype—read as a realist text in those parts—or that his protagonists develop a pantheistic attitude towards their surroundings."

In *Ljuset* (1987, *Light*), the polarity of order/disorder is the principal theme. The story takes place in Västerbotten in the fourteenth century. A terrible epidemic, referred to as the Great Sickness, ravages the hamlet of Kadis and kills nearly all its inhabitants. Only seven people survive. The main characters are Könik the carpenter, his wife Eira, and his old friend Önde. After the death of the priest the chapel stands deserted. Together Könik and Önde assume the task of burying the dead, but they encounter fearful problems in their efforts to follow the ritual that only the priest knew.

A sense of God's absence pervades the story. When Könik occasionally goes into the empty chapel, he is aware of "how dreadfully absent something indeterminate actually was, something that they missed painfully and bitterly, yet which, precisely because of that absence and emptiness, almost made its presence felt so tangibly that it could be touched with the hand." The feeling of emptiness is connected with the disorder that marks everyday life after the plague has done its work. Indispensable knowledge has gone into the grave with those who possessed it. Whole families have died, but their houses, animals, and other belongings remain, creating a state of unnatural abundance in the community. In the dilemma between, on the one hand, the duty to take care of the animals and property, and, on the other hand, the feeling that it is not right to take possession of other people's belongings, Könik is the one who suffers most from the inevitable uncertainty about what is right or wrong.

One consequence of the chaotic conditions of life in post-plague Kadis is the disappearance of Kare, the newborn son of Könik and Eira. On the symbolic level, Kare is an image of Jesus Christ. His disappearance is another manifestation of the absence of God. Words of consolation for the despairing parents are uttered by a stranger who visits Kadis, claiming that he is an emissary from the king. In answer to Eira's conviction that her son will come back one day, he says, "Everything returns. . . . Everything reverts to its origins. There is a time for breaking up and a time for dispersing, but also a time for returning and coming back."

In the last chapter Kare does indeed come back to his parents. A priest comes back, too, and the deserted chapel resumes its former role. On the symbolic level, these events point out that the Christian faith may be true, but Lindgren leaves the reader with the ironic implication that this novel is a tall tale; no truths are given. The story does not end in salvation; life goes on in a realm of uncertainty, change, and ambiguity—in a created world of fiction.

This blurring of the borderlines between reality and fiction, between truth and falsehood—a postmodern trait in Lindgren's prose—is even more conspicuous in the novel *Till sanningens lov* (1991, *In Praise of Truth*). These two novels, *Light* and *In Praise of Truth*, by their metafictional qualities show a certain affinity to postmodernism, but they can also be read as Catholic novels, written by an author who is deeply interested in the rich intellectual tradition of Catholicism from Thomas Aquinas to modern Catholic theology. On this level, the metafiction of Lindgren's two latest novels turns out to be the adequate way of describing the world that God created, the realm where human beings in their imperfection, placed between angel and beast, can never distinguish between truth and falsehood and cannot see God—except in some rare moment of mystical transcendence.

The main theme in *In Praise of Truth* is the question of what is true and what is false. The impossibility of distinguishing these opposites from each other is manifested in the story when an authentic Dardel painting of the Virgin is duplicated by an art forger who is such a great artist himself that he is able to make an exact copy of the original. The author's ironic play with the polarity between falsehood and truth permeates the text throughout and reaches a climax at the end of the story that reminds the reader of that most falsified of all literary genres, romantic popular fiction with its traditional happy ending. However, all ironic reservations aside, the last chapter might be interpreted as a story of death, followed by salvation in the life hereafter. Read on this level, the happy ending takes place out of this world—which would be in accordance with the epigraph of the novel, a quotation from a prose poem by Charles Baudelaire: "Anywhere. Anywhere. If only it is out of this world."

Lindgren lives in the little town of Vimmerby, in the southern part of Sweden. His wife, Stina Lindgren, is the principal of the senior high school at Vimmerby. They have three children. Lindgren has received a number of literary awards, among others Prix Fémina (France) 1986 and the Prize of Övralid (1989). In 1990, he was appointed honorary doctor at the University of Linköping. Since 1991 he has been a member of the Swedish Academy.

PRINCIPAL WORKS IN ENGLISH TRANSLATION: (tr. T. Geddes) Bathsheba, 1989; (tr. T. Geddes) The Way of the Serpent, 1990; (tr. M. Sandbach and T. Geddes) Merab's Beauty and Other Stories, (including "The Way of a Serpent"); 1990 (tr. T. Geddes) Light, 1992; (tr. T. Geddes) In Praise of Truth, 1994.

ABOUT: Contemporary Authors 136, 1992. *Periodicals*—Globe and Mail (Toronto) August 13, 1988; Library Journal January 1990; Los Angeles Times Book Review March 4, 1990; New York Times Book Review March 11, 1990; Publishers Weekly May 3, 1993; Times Literary Supplement July 14, 1989; January 1, 1993; March 25, 1994; World Literature Today 61, 2, 1987; 62, 4, 1988.

LINNEY, ROMULUS (ZACHARIAH)

(September 21, 1930–   ), American playwright and novelist, writes: "I was an actor before I became a writer. At Oberlin College, in the 1950s summer stock and at the Yale Drama School, I acted a great range of good parts, thinking I would never want to do anything else. Then I got drafted and two years in the Army brought about a personality change. I returned to Yale, became a director in the theater, moved to New York and then, in what seemed further confusion, began to write fiction. One novel turned out well, however, got published, and after a second, I wrote a play, which got produced. Since then I have written one other novel and many plays, which I sometimes direct.

"My work falls into three categories: historical, Appalachian, and personal. I turn, it seems, from one to the other, writing from my childhood memories of North Carolina, from very strong emotional feelings about historical figures somehow connected to family memories, and from episodes in my own life.

"My plays have benefited a great deal by the spread of American theater out of New York and into the rest of the country via our resident theaters. While my work has been done often and well in New York, since most of it is nonurban in nature, it has appealed to many audiences outside the city. I have enjoyed this very much. In the 1991–1992 New York season, the Signature Theatre Company did a retrospective of five plays of mine, which was a high point in my career, bringing about the publication of two anthologies of my work and an Obie for Sustained Excellence in Playwriting.

"I was born in Philadelphia, Pennsylvania, in 1930, spent my childhood in Boone, North Carolina, my youth in Madison, Tennessee, and Washington, D.C. I now live in New York City, and I teach playwriting and fiction at Columbia University and at the University of Pennsylvania.

In spite of his having received many honors—among them two Obies (in 1980 for *Tennessee* and in 1992 for Sustained Excellence in Playwriting), awards from the National Endowment for the Arts (1974) and the Guggenheim Foundation (1980), the Mishima Prize for Fiction (1981), and the American Academy and Institute of Arts and Letters Award in Literature (1984)—Romulus Linney, as Don B. Wilmeth wrote in 1989, "remains a largely unknown major American playwright." His work has fared better in New York's Off-Broadway theaters and in university and regional theaters than on the commercial stage.

ROMULUS LINNEY

If there is a unified theme in Linney's many and varied plays, ranging in genre from farce to stark tragedy, and in subject from grandiose historical figures like Frederick the Great to illiterate dirt farmers living in the back hills of Appalachia, it is probably the burden of the past that haunts and shapes the lives of all humankind. Usually victims of their own failures to understand and master the religious, social, or personal pressures that control them, his characters grope with the possibilities in a series of dramatic confrontations: Frederick the Great with his domineering, tyrannical father; Lord Byron with the daughter he abandoned and the men and women he used sexually; American army brass with the ghastly carnage of the Vietnam War; a pious and half-educated southern mother with the children she loved but destroyed.

The Sorrows of Frederick, Linney's first major play, was described by Mel Gussow in a *New York Times* review of a revival of the play in 1991 as "an ambitious attempt to reveal the humanity shrouded by history [that] offers a psychological portrait of a totally obsessive personality." Opening with the great military leader as an old man suffering, one of the characters says, "from dropsy, gout, and a mouldering disposition," mourning the death of a pet dog while he casually sends his soldiers out to be slaughtered in battle, it moves in a series of flashbacks through Frederick's unhappy life. The play was written in the 1960s but did not reach off Broadway in New York until 1976, when Mel Gussow described it in the *New York Times* as "not primarily an epic about war and power

plays, but an interior psychological drama about what goes on in the crumbling mind of a philosopher-king." In the *New York Times* Alvin King praised a 1985 revival "as an evening of high theater, a powerful play of panoramic sweep, political intrigue, historical interest and contemporary resonance—a work of psychological insight and universal pertinence." Probably the most successful productions of the play were in Europe—in Düsseldorf and in Vienna in 1970.

Linney's single Broadway venture was a short run of *The Love Suicide at Schofield Barracks* in 1972. The play was a bold experiment in contemporary realism mixed with the symbolism of Japanese Noh drama. During his service in the U.S. Army from 1954 to 1956, Linney had visited Japan and become fascinated by the styled action and characters of classic Japanese theater. In *The Love Suicide* the two central characters, a U.S. Army general and his wife, never appear. Their story is dramatized in the testimony of witnesses to a bizarre episode in which the couple, wearing Japanese robes and masks, staged a bloody protest against the Vietnam War by destroying themselves publicly in an act of ritual murder-suicide. Reviews of the Broadway production were negative. For Clive Barnes in the *New York Times* (1972), "the construction of the play was clumsy, and the writing only rarely rose above sincerity to any point of eloquence." Others recognized the intelligence and strong conviction behind the composition of the play but found it simply unstageable. B. H. Fussell wrote in the *Hudson Review* that "the playwright has set himself an impossible task . . . what might work in fiction cannot work here, for the crucial event of the general's suicide . . . takes place before the play begins, so that the General can exist for us only as an abstraction." Revived in 1991, with Linney himself as director, the play appeared to have benefited by some revision. "Though problems of credibility remain," Mel Gussow wrote in the *New York Times*, the emphasis was shifted to the witnesses, "those who have been influenced by the life and death of the couple." Gussow saw it now as a precursor to Linney's play of 1990, *2*, "a work that deals more perceptively with questions of conscience," specifically the guilt of Hermann Göring, the Nazi "number 2" man after Hitler, on trial for war crimes at Nuremberg.

Linney's frankly literary plays were never destined for commercial success. He dramatized and combined in one play two novels by Henry Adams about political life in Washington during the presidency of U. S. Grant—*Democracy* and *Esther*. Under the title *Democracy* the play was produced in Richmond, Virginia, in 1974, in

Milwaukee a year later and off Broadway in New York in 1992. The sensitive and intelligent women who are the central characters of Adams's novels retain their integrity in Linney's sympathetic dramatic portraits.

More daring was Linney's attempt to give dramatic life to the most romantic and irreverent of poets in *Childe Byron*. The framework of the play if Byron's relationship with his only legitimate child, Ada, to whom he appears as a ghost in 1852 when she is dying of cancer. A series of short scenes moves back and forth from Ada's bedroom where she is writing her last will and testament to episodes in his stormy life. Linney crowds into the play a breathless survey of Byron's adventures and escapades, often quoting from his poetry. *Childe Byron* was enthusiastically reviewed in *Variety* as "a brilliant, witty searing work, that seeks and finds the man behind the romantic legend." Its most ambitious production was in New York in 1981, directed by Marshall W. Mason and starring William Hurt as Byron and Lindsay Crouse as Ada. In contrast to the generally favorable response the play had in regional theaters and in a Young Vic production in London the same year, it received a chilly reception from the New York reviewers. Frank Rich dismissed it in the *New York Times* as "a comic-book version of the life of Byron . . . a sporadically amusing but mostly ludicrous retelling" of Byron's life.

Linney was more successful with his imaginative recreation of the lives of literary women in *Three Poets*, which he directed for an off—Broadway production in 1989. The play introduces three writers—the twentieth-century Russian poet Anna Akhmatova; Komachi, a ninth-century Japanese poet; and the Saxon nun Hrosvitha, who wrote religious plays in the early Middle Ages. All were women who struggled against tyranny in one form or another but never abandoned their pursuit of their art. Linney told an interviewer for the *New York Times*, "I'm not writing about what you're supposed to think of women, but what you really think of them. The thing I find interesting is that women don't get credit for doing surprising things."

Linney's southern plays are drawn out of his own southern family background in which, from childhood, he cultivated "an ear for speech," a speech colored and enriched by the Bible. "In the South the King James language is still in vogue," he says. "In the church you get it all messed up, but it's still around." He is especially fascinated by the myths and folklore that are mixed with religious teaching in the fundamentalist sects of Appalachia. In plays like *Holy Ghosts* (1974), which deals with snake handlers

in a small Pentecostal church, he treats his characters with humor but also with compassion. John Simon noted in *New York* magazine his "steering clear of both condescension to and idealization of his characters." Mel Gussow praised his "rich Faulknerian sense of humor. In the best tradition he is a local colorist, taking regional characters and showing us how their lives are inextricably bound up with land, family and ancestral roots."

Two of Linney's most admired plays are adaptations of his own novels about life in the South. *Heathen Valley*, his first novel, was based on stories he had heard in his boyhood about a mission sent to a remote mountain community in western North Carolina, so isolated that it had forgotten its Protestant religious practices. In Linney's novel as Episcopalian bishop and his hired man try to restore morality and order to the community with dire results. Published in 1963, *Heathen Valley* impressed reviewers. V. A. Bradley wrote in the *San Francisco Chronicle*: "Linney's portraits of the rugged, sometimes comical, sometimes pathetic mountain people are done with scrupulous honesty and a sense of living history." *Library Journal* found the characters "carefully and sympathetically drawn, and the plot . . . credible and fascinating." The stage version of the novel was produced in 1988 in Boone, North Carolina, only a few miles from where the events that inspired it had actually taken place, and won an award from the American Critics Circle Association as the best play produced outside New York City that season; it was published in *Best Plays of 1987–1988*.

Slowly by Thy Hand Unfurled, Linney's second novel, is the diary of a semi-educated, devoutly religious 19th-century woman. Disarmingly simple as narrative, her account gradually reveals a complex and emotionally troubled mother who damages the lives of her children and everyone around her. Millicent Bell, in the *New York Times Book Review*, praised Linney's characterization of a self-deceiving woman: "he shows a first-rate talent for defining not only a representative but a personal reality." For David Galloway, in the *Southern Review*, the novel was a "tour de force"; its central character, he wrote, has been "etched with a vividness that sheds a weirdly engrossing light on the ambiguities of love and human responsibility." Adapted for the stage as *A Woman Without a Name*, it was produced in 1992 as part of the Signature Theater Company's cycle of plays by Linney. Mel Gussow's *New York Times* (1992) review praised the skill with which the playwright, using a bare stage and "laconic dialogue," constructed "a psychological drama with insightful undertones about how people can damage one another" and created a character who "becomes an individual of very human dimensions."

Although some of Linney's plays approach "Southern Gothic" in their dark, brooding intensity, he has tapped a rich vein of humor in his shorter plays—some, like the prize-winning *Tennessee*, are genial folktales about mountain people; others, like the one-acters *Laughing Stock* (1984) and *Pops* (1986), deal with sibling rivalry, the frustrations of would-be writers, young lovers, and late-blooming love. His 1987 novel *Jesus Tales* brings together some folktales inspired by his reading of the Gospels, the New Testament Apocrypha, and a collection of Italian folktales about the marriage of Joseph and Mary, Jesus' birth and childhood, his meeting with his disciples, and "his walk around the world." These are funny but never profane or sacrilegious stories that emphasize the human side of Jesus. Reynolds Price, who wrote a foreword to the book, noted that Linney deserves the gratitude of readers "for inventing a whole possible wing in the old house of Jesus' name and nature: a laughing god, approachable and tangible, mining our world with the sly cherry-bombs of his love and care." Some of these tales had earlier been the subject of plays by Linney, among them *Old Man Joseph and His Family*, staged off-Broadway in 1978.

Only one of Linney's plays, *The Captivity of Pixie Shedman*, might be described as autobiographical—to the extent at least that its central character is a struggling young southern playwright and novelist transplanted to New York, where he is haunted by the ghost of his grandmother. But all of his plays in one way or another reflect facets of his life. He has acknowledged that his relationship with his father (also named Romulus Zachariah Linney) is reflected in *The Sorrows of Frederick*, his temporary alienation from his daughter in *Childe Byron*, and his knowledge of the rural South in his many southern plays. Shaping all his work is his lifetime dedication to the theater itself. After his graduation from Oberlin in 1953, he enrolled in the Yale School of Drama. He interrupted his studies for two years of military service but returned to Yale to complete his M.F.A. in 1958. Except for time out to write his novels, he has worked steadily as a director and actor or taught drama. In 1960 he was a stage manager for the Actors Studio; in 1961 he taught dramatic arts at the University of North Carolina in Chapel Hill; in 1962 he was director of fine arts at North Carolina State University in Raleigh. More recently he has taught at Princeton, Connecticut College in New London, the University of Pennsylvania, and in New York City at Brooklyn and Hunter Colleges

and at Columbia University, where since 1992 he has been professor of theater arts. He has also written an opera libretto, *The Death of King Philip*, with music by Paul Earls, produced in Boston in 1979, and has written for television and films.

Linney has been twice married and divorced and has two daughters, Susan and Laura; the latter played Ada in *Childe Byron* when she was a student at Brown University.

PRINCIPAL WORKS: *Plays*—The Sorrows of Frederick, 1966; The Love Suicide at Schofield Barracks, 1973; Democracy, 1976; Holy Ghosts, 1977; Old Man Joseph and His Family, 1978; Tennessee, 1980; The Captivity of Pixie Shedman, 1981; Childe Byron, 1981; El Hermano, 1981; Laughing Stock (*includes* Goodbye Howard, F. M., Tennessee) 1984; Sand Mountain (*includes* Sand Mountain, Matchmaking, Why the Lord Comes to Sand Mountain) 1985; A Woman Without a Name, 1986; Pops, 1987; Heathen Valley, 1988; Ambrosio, 1993. *Collections*—Six Plays, 1992; Romulus Linney: Seventeen Short Plays, 1992. *Novels*—Heathen Valley, 1963; Slowly by Thy Hand Unfurled, 1965; Jesus Tales, 1980.

ABOUT: Contemporary Authors 2, 1967; Contemporary Dramatists, 4th ed., 1988; Contemporary Literary Criticism 51, 1989; McGill, R. O. (ed.) Notable Names in the American Theatre, 1976; Who's Who in the Theatre, 17th ed., 1981; Wilmeth, D. B. *in* Kolin, P. C. (ed.) American Playwrights Since 1945, 1989. *Periodicals*—Appalachian Journal Fall 1988; Christian Science Monitor January 12, 1970; Hudson Review Winter 1973; Library Journal June 1962; New York August 24, 1987; New York Times February 10, 1972; February 25, 1976; February 27, 1981; March 3, 1985; October 14, 1986; August 9, 1987; December 3, 1989; May 20, 1991; October 17, 1991; February 2, 1992; New York Times Book Review August 15, 1965; New Yorker February 11, 1991; San Francisco Chronicle July 12, 1962; Southern Review Summer 1968; Studies in American Drama 2, 1987; Variety May 25, 1988; Village Voice April 28, 1992.

LISH, GORDON (JAY) (February 11, 1934–) American novelist, short story writer, editor, and teacher, was born in Hewlett, New York, the son of Philip Regina (Deutsch) Lish. He attended the University of Arizona at Tucson, from which he graduated cum laude in 1959; in 1960 he did graduate work in literature at San Francisco State College. He worked in radio broadcasting and as an English teacher at Mills High School in San Mateo, California, between 1960 and 1963, when he joined the staff of Behavioral Research Laboratories in Menlo Park. From 1966 to 1969 he worked as an editor for Educational Development Corporation in Palo Alto, for whom he compiled the first work

GORDON LISH

published under his name, *New Sounds in American Fiction*, an anthology of contemporary short stories accompanied by analytical notes and questions for students and an audiotape of the authors reading and commenting on their own work. During this period he also edited a journal, *Genesis West*, and published several short works under pseudonyms.

According to Tom Wolfe, who contributed a preface to the 1973 collection of short stories that Lish had printed in *Esquire* magazine, *The Secret Life of Our Times*, Lish's decision to work in California had been inspired by his reading: "At the age of twenty-two he read Jack Kerouac's *On the Road* and bolted out of some perfectly sane place such as Tucson, Arizona, to head off to North Beach in San Francisco in order to find the book's hero, Dean Moriarty . . . Soon Lish himself became a character in the last days of the Beat movement and the early days of the psychedelic movement. From his cottage . . . he managed to inflame the literary egos of both groups by founding a magazine called *Genesis West*." Wolfe's half-serious account of Lish as a man so obsessed with fiction that he willingly confuses it with life is consistent with what Lish said in his foreword to the same collection:

> I was never a shy child, but I did feel alone. Jack Armstrong and Captain Midnight kept me company when I was a boy. I thought they lived in the radio—I mean inside the Emerson that stood on the table by my bed. . . . Reading began when I was about fifteen and in and out of school and generally falling behind. . . . I was always very competitive, so I just got to reading competitively. I would read a thing if no one I knew had heard about it, teachers most of all.

Lish makes clear, later in this foreword, that he regards the writing of fiction as an enactment of the writer's search for truth, and that this process, and the person who engages in it, should be treated with the utmost seriousness:

> I believe in the beatitudes of genius, and I think the next best thing to discovering something not commonly known is knowing someone who did. It is my ardent proposition that the writers presented here, in the works of fiction shown, have each discovered something not commonly known. I also propose that these writers went through some bad times to find out, which opinion is the organizing principle of this collection, in case you were wondering.

These intensely and unashamedly subjective attitudes to fiction, which some might consider an inappropriate grounding for critical discrimination, served Lish well as an editor and as a champion of writers. His passionate conviction of the importance of writing was also evident many years later in the letter he wrote in 1990 to prospective students in his New York City writing school. In this he advertised the course by calling attention to its rigors: "Newcomers could not possibly know how arduous, how taxing an experience awaits them." Lish intended to circulate this letter only among a small group of prospective students, but it caught the attention of the editors of *Harper's* magazine, who printed long passages from it in the December 1990 issue, thereby setting in motion a lengthy process of litigation in which Lish sued the magazine's editors for copyright infringement, false representation, libel, and "tortious infliction of emotional distress." Lish won his suit and was awarded a small sum of money in damages, but the repercussions of the case, which centered on the right of a magazine to print what Lish claimed was a private letter, sparked a debate about First Amendment rights. Although the attorney for *Harper's* argued that Lish's letter was in fact "a piece of promotion," the court's decision upheld the author's copyright on what it regarded as a private communication. But in the *New Yorker* (October 19, 1992) it was pointed out that the most serious issue for Lish himself was the fact that those who meant to hold him up as a figure of ridicule had attacked the very basis of his life, which is an absolute identification with words as he said, "My sentences are all I have. My life has always been an engagement with words. I do not have very much of a physical life. I write, I edit, I teach. And in all of these activities the focus of my attention is sentences. Sentences are continuous with my inmost being. . . . "

The claim that Lish makes to very radical identification with the act of writing fiction also appears in the preface he wrote to the textbook anthology of short stories he compiled in 1969. There he makes a clear distinction between writing, which he identifies with life itself, and "commentary, conversation, and analysis," which are "beside the point, if not downright hostile to the interests of literature." The "significance" of a work "will always be greater than the sum of its parts," and an "editor who reduces that synthesis to its individual parts . . . uncreates the work, accomplishes the destruction of its total effect and the confusion of its truth."

According to Michael Schumacher, who included a profile of Lish in his book *Reasons to Believe: New Voices in American Fiction*, Lish's compulsions and self-promotion on behalf of writers (he calls himself "Captain Fiction") have always won him detractors, but also an equal number of admirers who respect his tireless dedication. Many notable writers, including Barry Hannah and T. Coraghessan Boyle, have testified to his influence on them, and many literary careers, including that of Raymond Carver, have benefited from his work as an editor at *Esquire* magazine and later at the publishing house of Alfred Knopf, where he acquires fiction and, since 1987, has edited *The Quarterly*, a journal of short fiction.

In the arena of literary politics in which he has become a major figure, Lish sees himself, as a champion of the underdog in writing as in life in general. He acknowledges in the autobiographical statement he contributed to Schumacher's book, that he will go out of his way to publish an unknown writer in preference to an established one because he believes, in some way that he does not define, that emergent writers "are telling us their truths": "So I feel that the work I do, as an editor and teacher, has a dire necessity about it, and I feel that my energy for it, and my impatience with those who do not honor the same object, grows out of my feeling that the writers whom I publish are in the prospect of saving people's lives. Art can do that for us." During a time when literary discussion had often valued the critical as much as the fictional process and asserted the reader's claim to a role in the creation of fiction, Lish's stance, though self-aggrandizing and vulnerable to mockery, is outstandingly simple and forthright.

In his essay "The School of Gordon Lish," in *An Artificial Wilderness*, Sven Birkerts asserts that by virtue of his influence as an editor and teacher, Lish has created a coterie of distinctive writers whose style is characterized by "disembodied characters who move about in a generic sort of present." Joe David Bellamy, writing in the *Mississippi Review* in 1986, makes the even stronger claim that Lish is a "cultural commissar" promoting an aesthetic that he identifies with Republican conservatism on the grounds that both dwell only on externals rather than causes of behavior. In Birkerts' more complex view the writers whom Lish champions display a variety of styles, but have in common an indifference to social context: "What has passed into their fiction . . . is a total refusal of larger social connection . . . Among these writers a centripetal isolation prevails; the world never extends illusionistically beyond the cast assembled on the stage. This might explain why so many of these books are slight. The writers have shorn themselves, or they have been shorn of, a central resource."

Lish's own fiction exemplifies the traits that Birkerts observes in his protégés: terse colloquial speech, repetitive monologues, and an absence of imagery and social setting. Much of his writing consists of the voice of a single obsessional character who conjures up a scene or single incident in monologue, as in his first novel *Dear Mr. Capote*. The anonymous narrator, a neighbor of Truman Capote's, professes to be a serial murderer, claiming to have killed twenty-three women, and has been inspired to disclose his obsession by reading Capote's *In Cold Blood*, an account of a series of murders. The entire book is a letter, written overnight by the murderer, who threatens to kill more people if Capote fails to win him a book contract and a film deal, which the murderer covets as an inheritance for his son. For some reviewers, including Stanley Ellin in the *Washington Post Book World* (1983), this work is a "wonderful addition to the literature of mass murder"; a masterful exercise in ventriloquism that achieves its effects by mimicking the banal locutions of everyday speech. For Eliot Fremont-Smith, in the *Village Voice*, however, the exercise of creating the illusion that a semiliterate madman was speaking was less worthwhile: "As far as I can make out, whacko turns out be whacko, and the reader ends up with no clues at all as to what isn't."

This eccentric first novel was followed by a collection of Lish's stories *What I Know So Far*. These, as the novelist Ann Tyler pointed out in the *New Republic* (1984), "seem less stories than 'turns,' in the theatrical sense. The author steps forward, presents a little piece, and retreats." She finds this collection, in contrast to the novel *Dear Mr. Capote*, which brings its protagonist to life, "peculiarly distant." Other reviewers were impressed by Lish's dexterity, especially in the literary satire "For Jerome—With Love and Kisses," which places the parents of several contemporary Jewish writers together in a Florida condominium bemoaning their inability to make contact with their children. In the opinion of Dennis Drabelle, reviewing the collection in the *Washington Post Book World* (1984), "other stories in the collection are irritatingly obscure. Owing to the excessive archness of their narrative voices, they manage to fall on their faces and make the reader feel clumsy."

In the novel *Peru*, as in *Dear Mr. Capote*, the narrative consists of a single obsessional voice— the thoughts of a middle-aged man who recalls killing a playmate in the sandbox when both were six years old. The narrator recalls the details of this incident in the first quarter of the novel in a way that suggests, by its realistic detail, that the speaker is either psychotic or pleading with the reader to accept his version of events. The remainder of the novel consists entirely of broken fragments of recollection interwoven with brief observation of the circumstances that inspired the narrator to collect his childhood memories—perhaps in an attempt to exorcise them. Stephen Dobyns' review of the novel in the *New York Times Book Review* (1986) asks the author's purpose and concludes that "the book isn't about the murder or the quirky personality of the young Gordon but just memory . . . how we become the creatures we become. . . . the result is not a pleasant book, but it's obsessive and obsessions remain fascinating." Martha Bayles's comments in the *New Republic* (1986) suggest, on the contrary, that this work has aimed beyond the mere effort to create a plausible and frightening obsessional character and has something much more important to illustrate about the nature of memory and the part that unresolved conflicts play in our adult lives: "The link with larger horrors is made plain when Gordon identifies what he sees on TV with that hour which, for him, has never stopped occurring." This interpretation, however, implies that the work is an allegory about contemporary violence, a dimension that Lish's unwavering concentration on an individual's memory seems to resist.

After the success of *Peru*, Gordon Lish's work failed to win critical approval, possibly because his attention has focused only on the rather narrow world of his own experience, becoming a paradigm of the faults of his own school of writing. *Mourner at the Door*, a collection of short pieces, was dismissed by Josh Rubins in the *New York Times Book Review* in 1988 as "the flotsam and jetsam of a would-be writer's notebook," while its successor, *Extravaganza*, a humorous book was reviewed by Robert F. Moss in the same issue: "Gordon Lish seems to dream of creating mysterious and profound works of art and slipping into the ranks of literary celebrities." *My Romance*, a frankly autobiographical novel,

is a transcription of Lish's rambling reflections, delivered at a writers' conference, in which he explores his sense of guilt at his father's death and his reactions on leaving *Esquire* for the publishing house of Alfred Knopf. In *New York Times Book Review*, Jodi Daynard assumes that Lish has abandoned all efforts to be read: "We come away feeling that *My Romance* doesn't really need us. Make no mistake about it: this is a one-man show."

PRINCIPAL WORKS: Dear Mr. Capote, 1983; What I Know So Far, 1984; Peru, 1985; Mourner at the Door, 1988; Extravaganza, 1989; My Romance, 1991; Zimzum, 1993. *As editor*—New Sounds in American Fiction, 1969; The Secret Life of Our Times: New Fiction from "Esquire," 1973; All Our Secrets Are the Same: New Fiction From "Esquire," 1977.

ABOUT: Birkerts, S. An Artificial Wilderness: Essays on 20th-Century Literature, 1987; Contemporary Authors 117, 1986; Contemporary Literary Criticism 45, 1987; Schumacher, M. Reasons to Believe: New Voices in American Fiction, 1988; Who's Who in America 1992-1993. *Periodicals*—Antioch Review Fall 1986; Winter 1986; Winter 1988; Fall 1990; Winter/Spring 1992; Summer 1992; Winter 1993; Commonweal September 11, 1987; Esquire March 1989; Gentleman's quarterly May 1989; Harpers December 90; Nation November 16, 1992; December 28, 1992; New Republic May 28, 1984; May 5, 1986; New York Times Book Review April 17, 1977; June 12, 1983; April 22, 1984; February 2, 1986; April 3, 1988; June 4, 1989; New Yorker October 19, 1992; Publishers Weekly May 13, 1983; February 22, 1991; December 7, 1992; August 31, 1992; January 25, 1993; Review of Contemporary Fiction Fall 1988; Summer 1989; Fall 1991; Time March 10, 1986; Vanity Fair June 1991; Village Voice May 31, 1983; April 29, 1986; Washington Post Book World June 5, 1983; May 20, 1984.

LIVELY, PENELOPE (MARGARET LOW) (March 17, 1933–   ), British novelist and short story and children's fiction writer, was born in Cairo, Egypt. Her parents were Roger Low, a manager in the National Bank of Egypt, and the former Vera Greer. She had no formal education until after her parents' divorce, when she went to live with her paternal grandmother in London in 1945 and spent five unhappy years in a boarding school in Sussex. Lively's teachers failed to encourage the keen interest in history she had developed while living in Egypt, and, indeed were "sternly anticultural," as she described them. Her curiosity survived, however, and she went on to study modern history at St. Anne's College, Oxford. After her graduation in 1954, she remained in Oxford as a research assistant. She met Jack Lively, a research fellow at St. Anthony's College, and they were married in

PENELOPE LIVELY

1957. Their daughter Josephine was born in 1958, and their son, Adam, in 1961.

Lively's original intention was to write social history, but as a mother who read, she has said, "inordinately" to her children, she came to feel that her particular interests might be better explored in books for children. Her central preoccupation is the relationship between past and present, and these works, with their element of fantasy, allowed her to delve into how memories are constructed and distorted. Lively's reputation as a children's writer was quickly established, and in 1973 she won Britain's highest award for children's literature, the Carnegie Medal, for *The Ghost of Thomas Kempe*. For *A Stitch in Time* she received the Whitbread Award. In the late 1970s, however, she decided to start writing fiction for adults. As she said in an interview in *Horn Book*, adult characters are able to consider the past "in the context of a lifetime rather than in the context of history." This personal sense of the past, she believes, constantly interacts with and alters the present, the individual's perceptions of life, of self, and of others. Significantly, the first book she wrote for adults, a work of nonfiction, was a study of landscape history titled *The Presence of the Past*.

The Road to Lichfield, Lively's first novel, is the story of a married woman living an uneventful life, whose assumptions about her own past are destroyed when her father, James Stanway, becomes terminally ill. Between her visits to him in a Lichfield nursing home, she spends some time at his home and falls in love with his neighbor. Sorting through her father's papers, she is shocked to discover that he too had been involved in an extramarital affair. As Ellen Pall noted in the *New York Times Book Review*, some fourteen years after the book's original appearance in England, "Lively skips easily from character to character, recording the thoughts of each. . . . Some of the best passages detail the dreamy recollections that alternately torment and comfort Stanway as he drifts in a solitary, feverish fog." Pall terms the novel "a pleasant book—too pleasant, perhaps. . . . In the end, *The Road to Lichfield* is itself subject to the altering effects of the present. . . . In the glare of . . . Lively's later accomplishments . . . it looks a bit pale and slight." "Recollection," the authorial voice observes, "can sometimes be more real than experience."

In *Treasures of Time*, Lively's second novel, a family is again coming to terms with the past and with the illusory nature of memory and of identity. When a celebrated archaeologist dies, a television company decides to make a documentary about his life and work. Each member of his family contributes to the construction of a profile of the man, and each version is different. In the process, several character sketches emerge. His daughter, scarred by her own perceptions of the past, is so defensive that her fiancé is finally unable to marry her. His widow is beautiful, insensitive, and selfish. Her husband's death—and later, the death of her invalid sister—force her, in a series of flashbacks, to examine her past. But the question, ultimately, remains: can the truth about the past ever be established? As another character points out: "What you feel about what you see depends not on what it is but who you are." Lively won a National Book Award for *Treasures of Time*, and her technical artistry and skilled characterization were universally admired. Some reviewers, however, felt that the book suffered from a certain glibness and, more importantly, a premature ending. In Susan Hill's view, in *Books and Bookmen*, "*Treasures of Time* is enjoyable, perceptive, shrewd, but it collapses badly, and scurries towards a rather arbitrary conclusion."

Judgement Day centers on Clare Paling, an intelligent, agnostic young woman who disrupts the sleepy village of Laddenham when she moves there with her husband and two children and becomes involved with a pageant that the church committee organizes. As is characteristic in Lively's novels, it is told from several different viewpoints. History is embodied by a 14th-century wall painting of Judgement Day in the church. A sense of violence escalates as the novel progresses, as people of differing ages and social classes are forced together in a common endeavor, and old and new interact uneasily. Their own

"Judgement Day" arrives when an airplane crashes into a crowd, a local boy is killed by a lorry, and young vandals desecrate the church on the eve of the pageant. Reviewers found *Judgement Day* impressive—as technically assured as Lively's earlier novels and particularly fascinating as a study of class conflict in 1970s' England. The theme in this novel differs from her other works in that her concern is with the difficulty of believing in a God who would allow terrible tragedies to occur. Clare calls herself "a hostage to fortune," and asserts her own belief in nothing more than "blind fate." Lively has sometimes been criticized for the prominence of philosophical platitudes. Increasingly, however, she has built her message into the substance of a novel, rather than articulating it through the medium of a character's discourse.

In *Next to Nature, Art*, Lively's aim is to satirize the pretensions of a group of artists who run a "creative study centre" in an 18th-century manor in Warwickshire. The authorial voice is entirely absent, and the visitors to the facility are themselves unaware of the shallowness of their hosts. Gradually, it becomes apparent that the "faculty" are utterly lacking in both skill and integrity. Reviewers found this attack on the materialism and artificiality of modern life elegant, incisive, and more amusing than anything Lively had written before: "Her satire is direct and believable, the wit is profound," Bryn Caless commented in *British Book News*.

Perfect Happiness is a novel about a woman's fierce expression of bereavement, as she struggles to come to terms with the death of her husband. Happiness, she realizes, is in the past: "Perfect happiness, past perfect, pluperfect." Like the central character in *The Road to Lichfield*, she discovers information about the past which deeply upsets her, and like Clare Paling in *Judgement Day*, she has to conclude that "life cannot be arranged and does not make sense." Ultimately, she learns to control her grief and to order her memories so that they sustain rather than destroy her. Reviewers found Lively's ability to deal with the painful subject of loss and grief neither depressing nor sentimental: "In very tricky terrain for a novelist, she never puts a foot wrong," John Mellors wrote in the *Listener*, and the *Spectator* (1983) declared the novel "a considerable triumph."

According to Mark, whose title is an ironic echo of the Gospel, is a novel about a biographer. Mark Lamming, researching the life of what Richard Holmes, the biographer, writing in the *New York Times Book Review*, called "an off-off Bloomsbury author of the 1920's, Gilbert Strong" (both Lamming and Strong are fiction-al), falls in love with his subject's granddaughter and runs off with her, only to be "retrieved" by his wife. Holmes notes that "up to a point [Lively] takes her biographer sympathetically and even seriously." He believes that the book has "elegance," but for him there is a certain satirical quality in how any novelist views a biographer, the novelist being able to " 'establish control,' " while the biographer challenges the novelist with "narrative power and the subtlety of relations between subject and investigator, story and storyteller." He associates Lively with Philip Roth and other novelists who have poked some fun at the biographer as "a convenient intellectual fall guy: hopelessly bookish, nastily inquisitive, vicarious and thoroughly untrustworthy with emotional property (don't leave him near a diary, a desk or a granddaughter) . . . perpetually liable to betray true love for true literature . . . " Holmes summed up the book as "understated, thoughtful and gently mocking."

In 1987 Penelope Lively was awarded the Booker-McConnell Prize for her novel *Moon Tiger*. Like *Judgement Day*, it deals with the transitory nature of human happiness; as in *The Road to Lichfield*, an approaching death brings about a reevaluation as versions of history are imposed on the present. Claudia Hampton, the dying woman, shares with the protagonist of *Perfect Happiness* a fragile sensibility, detailed in impressionistic bursts. But here, as J.K.L. Walker points out in the *Times Literary Supplement* (1987), Lively has "taken a pair of scissors to conventional chronological narrative." Different voices, flashbacks, and flashforwards combine to create a complex layering of consciousness. "The method allows the cool analytic tone and the sense of the past which characterize . . . Lively's earlier work to be brought overtly to the fore, and the modish disjunction and distancing are lent plausibility by making Claudia a historian, who, as she lies dying in a hospital room, contemplates her life within the context of the age," Walker noted. Gradually, a comprehensive view of Claudia's life is constructed: her childhood, her incestuous relationship with her brother Gordon, and a desultory affair with the father of her disappointing daughter, Lisa. "Shake the tube and see what comes out," she says, and from this kaleidoscope narrative a central scene emerges, of occupied Cairo and the desert campaign, during which Claudia is working as a press correspondent. She falls in love with a young tank commander, who will be killed in action. The symbol of their love is the Moon Tiger, a mosquito repellent that burns beside their bed throughout the night, turning to ash by morning. This image is recalled at the end of the novel, as Claudia slips away: "The sun sinks and the glittering tree is extinguished. The room darkens again. . . . It is empty. Void."

The strongest passages, according to most reviewers, deal with the brief love affair Claudia experienced in Cairo during World War II with the doomed young officer. "Claudia mourns most of all . . . that she and Tom would be strangers now. She has gone on without him, and he will always be young and innocent, 'shut away beyond a glass screen of time,'" Anne Tyler said in the New York Times Book Review. She called Moon Tiger "a fine, intelligent piece of work, the kind that leaves its traces in the air long after you've put it away."

Lively was thought to have exhausted her theme in Passing On, which is about three middle-aged siblings coming to terms with the death of their overbearing mother. City of the Mind, in contrast, was well received. It focuses on a successful architect who wanders in solitude throughout London, communing with the history encoded in its buildings and streets. His peregrinations involve the architect with a love interest and a villainous developer, but Gary Krist, in the New York Times Book Review, characterized the novel's substance as a "dynamic interaction of mind and stones." He pointed out that "it is . . . as philosophical dialogue that the novel succeeds best." Because, in his opinion, Lively is "expert at discovering the universal that lurks on every street corner," she explores how attempts to impose order on the world by building cities or mapping the universe "reveal as much information about the ordering minds as they do about the world being ordered."

Cleopatra's Sister is a romantic adventure story set in the fictional country of Callimbia, once ruled by Cleopatra's sister Berenice, in which Lively returns to a consideration of fate. The consensus of reviewers was that it lacked originality, spontaneity, and descriptive power.

Like her novels, Penelope Lively's short stories explore the complex relationships between past and present, the randomness of fate, and the continuity of memory. In her first collection, Nothing Missing But the Samovar and Other Stories, which won the Southern Arts Literature Prize, her concern is to expose the shallowness of modern society, its obsession with material wealth and its irreverence for the riches of antiquity. In "Interpreting the Past," an emotionally disturbed archaeologist shatters the skeleton of a baby in a hysterical effort to "wipe the slate clean." "Party" centers on an elderly widow who finds that she has nothing in common with the socially ambitious young people she meets at her daughter's party and instead settles down to

making model airplanes with her grandson. Reviewers praised Lively's easy, unobtrusive style, John Mellors commenting in the Listener on her "knack of effacing herself," like the spinster in another story who studies the walkers in Hyde Park as invisibly as "an inquisitive ghost."

Some of Lively's short stories are miniatures that are enlarged in the novels. "The Art of Biography," in her second collection, Corruption and Other Stories, concerns a biographer who becomes obsessed with his subject—a theme developed in her novel According to Mark. "The Ghost of a Flea" is about a woman's near madness and the effect it has on the people around her. Lively experiments at times with technique and subject matter in this collection, but generally reviewers preferred her more characteristic pieces. "Grow Old Along With Me; The Best Is Yet to Be," which some considered her best story, depicts a young couple whose deep respect for antiquity is disturbed when they come across two pensioners passionately embracing in a Saxon church. Frances Hill, in the Spectator, found these stories "beautifully written, full of irony and gentle, pointed humor and perfect description."

Pack of Cards and Other Stories, which followed, was an unusually varied collection, unified by Lively's abiding concern with the vacuity and greed which, in her view, typify modern British society. Jay Parini, in the New York Times Book Review, described the thirty-four stories as "a virtual anthology of contemporary British types: the Reactionary Englishman Abroad, the Bemused Grandmother, the Female Academic, the Bright Young Thing, the Middle-Aged Housewife in Psychological Trouble. But her favorite is the Young Intellectual Man, who reappears in several key places." He concluded that the volume is "an abundantly rich collection. . . . Penelope Lively writes beautifully, with meticulous detachment."

Penelope Lively lives in Oxfordshire and London with her husband, who is a professor of politics at the University of Warwick and the author of books on political theory. She is a member of PEN and of the Society of Authors, and a Fellow of the Royal Society of Literature. In 1989 she received an O.B.E. In 1994 she published Oleander, Jacaranda, a memoir of her early years in Egypt.

PRINCIPAL WORKS: Juvenile—Astercote, 1970; The Whispering Knights, 1971; The Driftway, 1972; The Wild Hunt of the Ghost Hounds, 1972 (in U.K.: The Wild Hunt of Hagworthy); The Ghost of Thomas Kempe, 1973; The House in Norham Gardens, 1974; Boy Without a Name, 1975; Going Back, 1975; A Stitch in Time, 1976; The Stained Glass Window, 1976; Fanny's Sister,

1976; The Voyage of QV66, 1978; Fanny and the Monsters, 1979; Fanny and the Battle of Potter's Piece, 1980; The Revenge of Samuel Stokes, 1981; Fanny and the Monsters and Other Stories, 1982; Uninvited Ghosts and Other Stories, 1984; Dragon Trouble, 1984; A House Inside Out, 1987. *Novels*—The Road to Lichfield, 1977; Treasures of Time, 1979; Judgement Day, 1980; Next to Nature, Art, 1982; Perfect Happiness, 1983; According to Mark: A Novel, 1984; Moon Tiger, 1987; Passing On, 1989; City of the Mind, 1991; Cleopatra's Sister, 1993. *Short stories*—Nothing Missing But the Samovar and Other Stories, 1978; Corruption and Other Stories, 1984; Pack of Cards and Other Stories, 1986. *Nonfiction*—The Presence of the Past: An Introduction to Landscape History, 1976. *Memoir*—Oleander, Jacaranda, 1994.

ABOUT: Blain, V. et al. (eds.) The Feminist Companion to Literature in English, 1990; Buck, C. (ed.) Bloomsbury Guide to Women's Literature, 1992; Children's Literature Review 7, 1984; Contemporary Authors 29, 1990; Contemporary Literary Criticism 32, 1985; Contemporary Literary Criticism Yearbook, 1987; Current Biography Yearbook 1994; Dictionary of Literary Biography 14, 1983; Egoff, S. A. Thursday's Child: Trends and Patterns in Contemporary Children's Literature, 1981; Rees, D. The Marble in the Water: Essays on Contemporary Writers of Fiction for Children and Young Adults, 1980; Todd, J. (ed.) British Women Writers: A Critical Reference Guide, 1989; Townsend, J. R. A Sounding of Storytellers: New and Revised Essays on Contemporary Writers for Children, 1979; Who's Who 1994. *Periodicals*—Books and Bookmen September 1979; British Book News September 1982; Encounter February 1984; Horn Book June 1973, August 1973, February 1978, April 1978; Listener January 25, 1979; September 22, 1983; New Welsh Review Spring 1990; New York Times Book Review January 5, 1986; April 17, 1988; May 21, 1989; February 17, 1991; September 1, 1991; April 25, 1993; June 12, 1994; Publishers Weekly March 25, 1988; Spectator November 22, 1980; September 17, 1983; March 17, 1984; May 23, 1987; Time May 2, 1988; Times Literary Supplement July 14, 1972; April 6, 1973; July 16, 1976; November 21, 1980; October 19, 1984; May 23, 1986; May 15, 1987; April 5, 1991; April 23, 1993.

LOVELACE, EARL (July 13, 1935–), Trinidadian novelist, playwright, and journalist is considered a major writer in the recent West Indian literature that examines the evolution of West Indian identity and culture. Richly symbolic and descriptive, Lovelace's works are set in Trinidad and narrated in the local vernacular. Writing primarily for the Caribbean reader, Lovelace is concerned with preserving and validating West Indian culture and tradition. Dealing with the issues of city life versus country life, progress versus innocence, colonialism versus liberation, and Western culture versus native culture, Lovelace believes that the artist in West

EARL LOVELACE

Indian society is leading a battle against the influences of the West. Through their works, West Indian artists challenge their communities to maintain a sense of self and cultural identity that is not dependent upon or defined by outside forces.

Lovelace was born in Toco, Trinidad, and grew up in Tobago and Port of Spain. After working as a proof reader and later for the Department of Agriculture in Trinidad, he came to the United States in 1966 to study at Howard University in Washington, D.C. He has taught at Virginia Union University in Richmond, Virginia, Federal City College in Washington, D.C., and John Hopkins University in Baltimore. He was writer-in-residence at the University of Iowa from 1980 to 1981. He returned to Trinidad and has lectured at the University of the West Indies, in St. Augustine, living with his wife and three children in the remote and somewhat primitive village of Matura. Lovelace has preferred to live in the unspoiled country, and this preference for rural living is reflected in his works.

"In the rural communities people have an identity. Everybody knows you," he told H. Nigel Thomas in an interview for *World Literature Written in English* in 1991. "The city situation is really where you begin to search for identity on the individual level." He continued: "The whole political structure, the colonialists' stronghold, was in the cities. The country was where the plantations were located, where the colonists didn't live, but where the folk lived. That resulted in two things: one . . . is that it is where the native culture flourishes, and that is why you find there a greater support system; and it's not just people sticking together under oppression, it's a togetherness because of the values of the culture."

Lovelace's first novel, *While Gods Are Falling*, explores the ruinous effects of urban life. The main character, Walter Castle, moves to the city after he becomes unable to support his family. In this "dark, poisonous and stinking, something like a sore in this city," Walter, along with the other fragmented individuals, seeks to rediscover his manhood. Lovelace has admitted some dissatisfaction with his first novel, although it was awarded the British Petroleum Independence Literary Award in 1965. "The first novel was diffuse, I think," he told Thomas. "This doesn't excuse it. I wrote it quickly. It never got properly revised."

Lovelace describes his second novel, *The Schoolmaster*, as "less diffuse." "I wanted to be strict and quite controlled," he explained to Thomas. "And at the same time, you could see signs of wanting to break out of these controls, but I never did break out. . . . And here I was, I think, beginning to break out by becoming very disciplined rather than being loose."

The Schoolmaster is set in Kumaca, a village which Kenneth Ramchand described in his introduction as "on the fringes of the world and the twentieth century." Disorder comes to the community under the guise of progress—a schoolmaster who arrives to establish a school, and a shopkeeper who fills his shop with Western goods while slowly buying up the villagers' land. The schoolmaster, a product of an urban education, has rejected his cultural traditions and adopted city ways. The shopkeeper tantalizes the villagers with nongrocery items, gradually exciting in them a taste for modern luxuries.

Lovelace points out that people's response to progress determines whether or not they will survive it. "The broader world impacts on us," he told Thomas. "The question is how we deal with it. This is where there is the need to have a self to engage these outside forces that are constantly influencing us. There's a strong need for a Caribbean self in which we would be more linked than we are now. It is so important that we have a spiritual self to guide us in our contacts with the rest of the world. . . . "

The Dragon Can't Dance, a critically successful novel, is the story of migrants from the rural community of Calvary Hill who move to the city. With no wealth or material possessions, the characters struggle to find acceptance in a society that prizes money and objects. Music, violence, rebellion, or masquerading at Carnival are their means of affirmation. "All we thinking about is to show this city, this island, this world, that we is people," one character, Aldrick, says. "Not because we own anything, not because we have things, but because we is."

The Wine of Astonishment was Lovelace's first novel to be published and widely reviewed in the United States. It continues the thematic issue of simple, rural values and traditions versus the dictates of modernization. The residents of Bonasse have been prohibited from practicing their Spiritual Baptist religion, viewed as an uncivilized form of worship by the colonists. (A ban on the Spiritual Baptist Church had been passed in 1917 in Trinidad and Tobago.) The novel examines the effect of this ban on the lives of the villagers. A young, educated villager, Ivan Morton, chooses to accept the ban because he sees it as a way to become more like the whites. The village stick fighting champion Bolo, however, violently rejects the law and views it as an attempt by the oppressors to rob the people of their identity and culture. According to Thomas, in *World Literature Written in English*, Bolo "challenges the community to stand up to him, hoping that it will begin to reverse the destruction of its values. He teaches with the terror he inflicts on the villagers the implication of the new values. . . . " Eventually, the villagers find themselves torn between the Western values that Morton promotes and the native traditions that Bolo seeks to preserve.

Reviewers of *The Wine of Astonishment* were especially impressed with its strong characterization and its evocation of Trinidadian speech. "Lovelace writes with such fidelity to emotional traits," Julius Lester observed in the *New York Times Book Review*, "that we know these people as ourselves. . . . *The Wine of Astonishment* is . . . a sustained prose poem molded from the lyricism of everyday speech and life; it is a powerful, moving tale."

Lovelace again deals with the issue of preserving cultural values and remembering one's roots in his collection *Jestina's Calypso and Other Plays*. Jestina is an unattractive woman who falls in love with her pan pal, a Trinidadian who has moved to America. Rather than send him a photo of herself, she sends him a picture of a pretty friend. He plans to return to Trinidad and arranges to meet her at the airport. Jestina, meanwhile, agonizes over the meeting and desperately hopes that he will see beyond her physical appearance and be able to say, "This is my woman. This is my island with the bruises and sagging breasts." He, however, is unable to overlook her ugliness and rejects her. To Lovelace, Jestina is symbolic of the values and culture of Trinidad. When her lover rejects her, he, in effect, rejects his homeland.

Cherishing native culture and traditions is Lovelace's major concern. The challenge for the West Indian or blacks everywhere is in finding liberation in that which has been the cause of their oppression—their blackness. As he explained to Thomas: "It's more than putting on the trappings of blackness. It's the values we live by. I think that our main problem so far is that we have little spiritual understanding of what it means to be black. . . . Our difficulty here is our experience of enslavement and the feelings we came out of it with. . . . If we look at the values that have emerged from our folk culture, we will see in it a great deal that is positive. Our trouble is that we tend to see it solely in terms of loss. In spite of the horrors of enslavement . . . we have gained from the experience."

PRINCIPAL WORKS: *Novels*—While Gods are Falling, 1965; The Schoolmaster, 1968; The Dragon Can't Dance, 1979; The Wine of Astonishment, 1982. *Plays*—Jestina's Calypso and Other Plays, 1984. *Short stories*—A Brief Conversion and Other Stories, 1986.

ABOUT: Contemporary Authors 77–80, 1979; Fifty Caribbean Writers, 1986; International Authors and Writers Who's Who, 1991–1992; Rachmand, K. *introduction to* The Schoolmaster, 1968; Thorpe, M. *introduction to* The Wine of Astonishment, 1982; Writer's Directory, 1994–1996. *Periodicals*—Library Journal November 1, 1984; New York Times Book Review January 6, 1985; World Literature Today Autumn 1984; World Literature Written in English Spring 1991.

LUKACS, JOHN (January 31, 1924–), American historian, writes: "I was born in Hungary (Budapest). I doubt that I am less self-centered than other writers and scholars, but I do find it difficult to write about writings of mine that have been published. One of these reasons is my phobia of being repetitious; and my *Confessions of an Original Sinner*, while not a real autobiography, does contain the history and the evolution of my work. I shall, however, attempt to sum up what I consider to be the essential, and possibly unusual, conditions (and perhaps also the purposes) of my writing. The first, in chronological order, is my desire at an early age (when I was still a student in Hungary, and a desire still largely unchoate then) to find, and eventually produce, something like a new kind of history that would necessarily incorporate some of the finest qualities of great prose literature. This need involves a certain mastery of

JOHN LUKACS

style but, more important, the kind of profound understanding of people and places and times that we find, here and there, in some of the pages of great novelists (though not among the famous practitioners of historical novels whose genre I regarded and regard as outdated). The second condition of my life and work is that my formative years coincided with the Second World War and its aftermath in Hungary, that is, in the middle of Europe; and that, as an early opponent of Communism, foreseeing the eventual imposition of a Communist government on Hungary, I decided to flee my native country and family early, in 1946, fortunately assisted by some Americans and able to come to the United States.

Contrary to the majority of people at that time I believed that Russian and Communist rule in Hungary would last at least fifty years (I was ten years off, thanks to God). But more important for the purpose of these pages (and of my then decision) was my knowledge of English, propagated by my mother from the age of five, and including two summer semesters in schools in England before the war. Even before my arrival in the United States I was disinclined to seek a career of an émigré historian who, in imperfect English, would attempt to interpret the history and politics of his homeland to Americans. This accorded with the advice given to me by an eminent scholar, before I was to leave Hungary, to avoid involvement in émigré affairs in the United States. Thus I chose the task of becoming an English-speaking historian, hoping to develop eventually a good English style of my own. Even today, after fifteen or sixteen books, I take some pleasure when men and women whose writing I esteem write or say generous things about my style. I have not renounced my native country; I speak Hungarian fluently, and I had the occasion, especially lately, to make some small but significant contributions to Hungarian history and scholarship. But my main language (including the language in most of my dreams) has become English. This may also correspond to the fact that I have taught history in a small Catholic college in Philadelphia for the past forty-five years not destined to move further; that both of my wives (the first of my wives died tragically young) have been Americans of English ancestry, both with an extraordinarily wide literary culture; and that I have chosen to lead a quiet private life in Chester County, Pennsylvania, on the same land where I have been living for nearly forty years (where I also participate, officially and privately, in township and county affairs on occasion). The third condition of my writing is a philosophical one. Beginning in 1955, I saw the need and the opportunity for the proposition of a new historical philosophy (the very obverse of a philosophy of history) which, after more than a decade of hard work, I set forth in *Historical Consciousness*, and which I regard as my most important, though least known, book—also because many of its tenets have been incorporated in many of the different historical works that I have written, perhaps especially in the structures of *The Last European War, 1939–1941* and in *Outgrowing Democracy: A History of the United States in the Twentieth Century*. Since this series is about authors rather than about historians, allow me to add that, in my opinion, my relatively best written books are my *Philadelphia, Patricians and Philistines, 1900–1950*; *Budapest, 1900*; *Confessions of an Original Sinner*; and *The Duel*. My best written articles (though not my most important ones) appeared in the *New Yorker* in 1985 and 1986. (I have not written for the *New Yorker* since those years.) I find it agreeable that some of my books have been translated into many foreign languages (even though their translations are often wanting.")

———

Probably the most frequently recurring word in reviews of John Lukacs's books is "provocative," reflecting the complex and controversial character of his thinking. Writing in the *American Historical Review* of one of Lukacs's early books, *The Decline and Rise of Europe*, E. C. Helmreich complained of "sweeping generalizations, a good number of which are debatable," but concluded that "the

broad observations do not detract [from], but rather add zest to his arguments." A few years later, in the *Journal of Modern History*, Georg G. Iggers pronounced his *Historical Consciousness* "a thought-provoking even if disturbing and not wholly convincing work," and Thomas Molnar, in *Book World*, while complaining of the same book's looseness of organization, noted that Lukacs has "more knowledge, culture and insight than most of his academic colleagues." Joseph Sobran, reviewing *Confessions of an Original Sinner* in the *National Review* (1990), observed that Lukacs "has written some of the most thought-provoking historical studies of the last generation . . . [but] he is unclassifiable." In another review in the *Christian Science Monitor*, Leonard Bushkoff called that volume "pessimistic and provocative . . . magnificent writing but perverse, wildly eccentric opinions." And as late as 1993, in the *National Review*, Conor Cruise O'Brien summed up the ambivalence of readers: "Whether or not we accept all of Lukacs' insights, we surely have to recognize, as we read *The End of the Twentieth Century*, that we are in the presence of one of the most powerful, as well as one of the most learned, minds formed by that century. It is an ominous sign of the state of our culture, as the century nears its end, that John Lukacs is relatively little known."

Lukacs has pursued his early resolution "to produce something like a new kind of history," humanistically rather than scientifically based, in an era when the "new" history was moving in the opposite direction. "The proper study of history," he wrote in *Historical Consciousness*, "includes, principally, persons rather than economic units." The title of this volume, along with its subtitle "The Remembered Past," implies a rejection of the quantitative historical methodology that emerged in the twentieth century as a "social science." "Historical consciousness," on the contrary, assumes history as "a form of thought . . . a historical kind of philosophy" (but not, Lukacs cautions, a philosophy of history, which fails to recognize "the myriad, uncategorizable varieties of past human experience"). He opts for a historical philosophy,

> concentrating on the historicity of problems and of events, assuming the uniqueness of human nature anew, presenting no new definitions, no freshly jigsawed categories, emphasizing the existential—and not merely philosophical—primacy of truth: a more mature achievement of the human mind than even the mastering of certain forces of nature through the scientific method, and certainly more mature than the simplicist conception of causalities.

In his reading of the physicist Werner Heisenberg's writings, particularly his *Physics and Philosophy* (1958), Lukacs discovered a correspondence or "potential harmony" between the physicist's principle of uncertainty or indeterminacy and historical thinking. In Heisenberg he found confirmation of his own belief in the illusory nature of "factual" truth and his distrust of the Cartesian separation of the world into subjects and objects. Challenging the whole concept of scientific objectivity, Lukacs writes, "[T]here may be such a thing as human evolution, but perhaps only in the sense of the evolution of our consciousness—an evolution which, if determined at all, is determined from the inside."

Lukacs writes history as a Christian (he is Roman Catholic) humanist. He draws freely on his own experience both as a European who lived through, and witnessed firsthand, the Nazi and Communist eras in Western Europe, and as an American living in postwar, then post–cold war, American society. All his books, he says in the introduction to *Confessions of an Original Sinner*, share his conviction "that the most important matter in this world, and perhaps especially in our times, is what people think and believe and that the material conditions of their lives (and the very material structure of their world) are but consequences of that. Thus this book is in accord with the practice I followed in my other, very different books, its principal content being the history of my thoughts and beliefs."

Lukacs describes those beliefs candidly as reactionary: "A reactionary considers character but distrusts publicity; he is a patriot but not a nationalist, he favors conservation rather than conservatism; he defends the ancient blessings of the land and is dubious about the results of technology; he believes in history, not in Evolution." Indeed, it is "devolution" that Lukacs observes everywhere in the 1980s and early 1990s: "A decline of taste and judgment, of truthfulness and reason . . . together with the disappearance of the last vestiges of aristocratic values and standards." In *The End of the Twentieth Century* he foresees "the rising threat of barbarism and barbarians within our cities and nations, internal challenges, of savagery to our domesticity, inspired and spawned by some of the features and institutions and popular culture of our modern civilization itself."

The Modern Age, which began about the time of the Renaissance, is approaching its end. As the millennium year 2000 approaches, Lukacs is not alone in such pronouncements, nor is he alone in citing specifically as coming to their end: "The expansion of Europe. The conquests of the white race. The colonial empires . . . Liberalism. Humanism. Bourgeois culture . . . The Newtonian concept of the universe and of physical reality. The ideal of scientific objectivity. The Age of the Book." But he is not writing a jeremiad nor prophesying an Armageddon. The values he sees dying, he writes, "were created by and incarnated in institutions that still exist and function, but in ever more different ways and for different purposes; and many of them have become antiquated and scelerotic."

Many of the political developments of the early 1990s have confirmed Lukacs's observations. The collapse of Communism, and the retreat of Russia from Eastern Europe, which he foresaw in articles written as early as 1980, has not led to liberal democracy in the former U.S.S.R. nor in its former satellites. Rather, he observes in *The End of the Twentieth Century* a reemergence of nationalism—"the most powerful political force in the world." Hitler and Stalin had been the supreme nationalists of their time. Sweeping through Europe is a new nationalism, with "appeals to trivial and racial ties," that threatens to become "a new Barbarism." Writing the conclusion of *The End of the Twentieth Century* in 1992, Lukacs observed: "What is already happening in Eastern Europe (consider but the Yugoslav crisis as I write this) is not only the dismantling of Yalta—that is, of the results of the Second World War. Here and there we see the dismantling of Versailles, of the results of the First World War. Indeed, the twentieth century is over."

Early on in his career as a historian, John Lukacs had impressed his reviewers with the breadth of his reading, not only in historians ancient and modern, but literature in every imaginable genre: allusions to Sir Walter Scott, Jane Austen, Stendhal, Goethe and Trollope abound in his work. Discussing *Historical Consciousness* in the *Sewanee Review* in 1969, Russell Kirk had pronounced him "a bold and daring scholar . . . in the line of Tocqueville and Burckhardt." More than a decade later, in an essay aptly titled "Returning Humanity to History" (in *Intercollegiate Review*), Kirk again emphasized the uniqueness of Lukacs's contribution to the writing of history: "What we find in Lukacs then is not some new philosophy of history, but instead a fresh approach to the character of historical consciousness, illuminated by humane letters, psychology, and natural science."

Lukacs holds diplomas from Cambridge University and from the University of Budapest. He has been professor of history at Chestnut Hill College, Philadelphia, since 1947 and has had visiting professorships at La Salle College in Philadelphia, and at Columbia, the University of

Pennsylvania, the Johns Hopkins School of Advanced International Studies, the Fletcher School of Diplomacy, and Princeton. In 1964–1965 he was a Fulbright professor at the University of Toulouse, and in 1991 he was a visiting professor at the University of Budapest. He was president of the American Catholic Historical Association in 1977. Among other academic honors he has a doctorate from La Salle University (1989), and in 1991 he was awarded the Richard Weaver Prize of the Ingersoll Foundation for his book *The Duel*, a study of the critical eighty days in the early summer of 1940 when Hitler and Churchill made decisions that determined the outcome of the Second World War. Lukacs's first wife, Helen Elizabeth Schofield, whom he married in 1953, died in 1970. They had two children. In 1974 he married Stephanie Harvey. They live in Chester County, Pennsylvania, where he is a member of the Planning Commission.

PRINCIPAL WORKS: The Great Powers and Eastern Europe, 1953; A History of the Cold War, 1961; The Decline and Rise of Europe, 1965; A New History of the Cold War, 1966; Historical Consciousness: The Remembered Past, 1968, enl. ed. 1985, rev. ed. 1994; The Passing of the Modern Age, 1970; The Last European War, 1939–1941, 1976; 1945: Year Zero, 1978; Philadelphia: Patricians and Philistines, 1900–1950, 1981; Outgrowing Democracy: A History of the United States in the Twentieth Century, 1984; Budapest, 1900: A Historical Portrait of a City and Its Culture, 1989; Confessions of an Original Sinner, 1990; The Duel: Hitler vs. Churchill 10 May–31 July 1940; The End of the Twentieth Century; and the End of the Modern Age, 1993; Destinations Past, 1994. As editor—de Tocqueville, A. The European Revolution and Correspondence with Govineau, 1959.

ABOUT: Contemporary Authors New Revision Series 17, 1986; Lukacs, J. Confessions of an Original Sinner, 1990; Who's Who in America, 1995. Periodicals—American Historical Review July 1967; American Scholar Winter 1984–1985; (New York Herald Tribune) Book World November 10, 1968; Christian Science Monitor July 12, 1990; Continuity: A Journal of History Fall 1981; Dissent October 1971; Intercollegiate Review 16, 1980; Journal of Modern History March 1970; Modern Age Winter 1985; National Review June 25, 1990; March 29, 1993; New York Times January 26, 1993; New York Times Book Review May 20, 1990; February 7, 1993; Sewanee Review April 1969.

*LUSTIG, ARNOST (December 21, 1926–), Czech novelist and short story writer, who now lives in the United States, was born in Prague to Emil and Therese (Lowy) Lustig. He had his early schooling in Prague. Because he

ARNOST LUSTIG

was a Jew in a country at that time dominated by the Nazis, he was denied the opportunity for further academic education and was apprenticed to a tailor and decorator. In 1942 he was sent to the notorious "model ghetto" concentration camp of Terezin and thence to the death camps of Auschwitz (where his father died in the gas chambers) and Buchenwald. In 1945 he escaped from a German death train taking him to Dachau. Later that year, when the war ended, he began studies at the College of Political and Social Sciences in Prague, graduating in 1951 with an M.A. degree. From 1948 to 1956 he was a correspondent for the Czechoslovak Radio in the Israeli-Arab war and elsewhere in Europe, Asia, and North America. After that he worked as a reporter and producer for Czechoslovak Radio; in 1958 he was an editor of the weekly *Mladý svět* (Young World), and from 1960 to 1968, a scriptwriter for the Czechoslovak State Film Studios. After the Soviet takeover in 1968, however, Lustig's works were banned, and he left Czecholslovakia for Yugoslavia and then Israel. In 1970 he emigrated to the United States where he joined the International Writers Program at the University of Iowa for a year. After teaching for two years at Drake University in Des Moines, Iowa, he became professor of literature at American University in Washington, D.C. He has also lectured and taught as visiting professor of literature and film at several other universities. Married in 1949 to Vera Weislitz and the father of two children, he lives in Washington, D.C.

When Lustig began writing fiction in the

°LOO stik, UR nohsht

1950s Czech literature was in a period of decline, but with the relaxing of Communist controls it had a renaissance with new trends even in minor genres such as the short story, novella, reportage, and sketch writing. Writers began to assimilate and expatiate on the horrors of World War II. Early on reviewers recognized in Lustig's works an authenticity and immediacy that was rare and powerful. They had a quality of journalism that, though occasionally "flat and understated" (as Abraham Rothberg wrote in the *Southwest Review*), added to their appeal.

By 1958 the Czech critic Milan Jungmann noted the psychological one-dimensionality of Lustig's characters, which the author created "so that he could send them to hell that he has prepared for them." At the same time Jungmann wrote of Lustig's existentialism. The theme of all of his works can be expressed as: "What is at the bottom of man, what remains of him when he is alone, alone against evil, horror, pain and night—and finally when he is alone against death?"

Lustig's work has a purpose—to witness and testify—in order to fulfill what he regards as his obligation to the Holocaust dead. As Ernest Pawel observed in the *New York Times Book Review* in 1979: "Other survivors—Elie Wiesel, André Schwarz-Bart, Michel del Castillo—have dealt with childhood in the camps. But Mr. Lustig attempts to show not only how these youngsters died or survived, but how some of them managed to live, even to retain their humanity."

In *Noc a naděje* (1957, *Night and Hope*), a collection of short stories, Lustig's aims are fully developed. Czech reviewers had high praise for the book and Lustig emerged as a leading author of the liberal "new wave." The short stories take place mainly in a ghetto and depict what appears to be "an ordinary life" which suddenly becomes disrupted. Lustig's feeling for victims of Nazi violence, especially children and old people, for the way everyday life in the ghetto is by its very nature deformed, and for the way its ordinariness absorbs violence, is palpable. His characters reveal themselves in their action. One of them asks: "Who knows what people are like under the husk of rudeness or of despair where only they can see, and sometimes, perhaps, not even they themselves. Where, then, are the boundaries that differentiate people?"

A second collection of short stories *Démanty noci* (1958, *Diamonds of the Night*) was conceived as a sequel to *Noc a naděje*. While in the earlier book Lustig was primarily concerned with themes, this one puts greater emphasis on plot and characters. Lustig centers his attention on children (the "diamonds of the night" who

represent hope). Some of these short stories became famous: for example "Tma nemá stín" ("Darkness Casts No Shadow"), an open-ended story about two Jewish boys who escape from a deportation train. (This story was separately published in an enlarged version in 1991.) Another story, "Sousto" (A bite to eat; translated as "The Lemon"), is about a boy who removes his dead father's gold filling to trade it for a lemon to ameliorate the lots of his sick and starving sister and mother. Another, "Bílý," (White; translated as "The White Rabbit") is about a boy who wants to show a rabbit to a sick girl to make her happy, but he finds out that she has disappeared. Though short story collections, both books resemble novels: their theme is the progress from "night" to "hope."

In 1959 Lustig published another collection, *Ulice ztracených bratří (The Street of Lost Brothers)*. It includes a short story "Muj známy Vili Feld" (My acquaintance with Willi Feld) which he expanded into a novel in 1961. The collection contains stories of people living in the postwar period, but their fates have been molded by their wartime experiences, their lives maimed and their souls scarred. Lustig sees those deformations as characteristic of the present condition of humanity: "The longer I am in the world, the more clearly I see that the time of concentration camps has not come from nowhere and has not disappeared into nowhere. Man under pressure, on the boundary between existence and non-existence, is man of the present time."

Lustig's best work treating this theme is *Dita Saxová* (1962, *Dita*; also translated as *Dita Saxová*), a novella taking place between 1947 and 1948. The title character is an eighteen-year-old Jewish girl, left orphaned by the war and shaken by its horrors. A sensitive lover of art and a romantic dreamer, she sets herself the task of believing that "Life is not what we want but what we have. . . . " She moves in an enclosed society of Jews who are, like Dita, scarred by the war, traumatized and lost. Reading her favorite book, a symbolic novella *Krysař* (The rat catcher) by the Czech writer Viktor Dyk, she experiences, and also reflects upon, the fatality of her life. The book ends with Dita's death—a fall from a mountain in Switzerland—which may well be a suicide. This novel and the short stories in *Ulice ztracených bratří* are existentialist studies of people who "came back from the war too young to be left to their own devices, and yet too old to suffer anyone to look after them." *Nikoho neponížíš* (1963, Nobody will be humiliated, translated as *Indecent Dreams*) comprises four long short stories about people who dared actions inevitably brought about their deaths during the war or at its end. *Modlitba pro Kateřinu Horovitzovoú* (1964, *A Prayer for Katerina Horovitzova*), is set in a concentration camp. Nominated in the United States for a National Book Award in 1974, it details the fate of a group of American Jews arrested by the Nazis while vacationing in Italy and promised liberty if they will bribe their captors. At Auschwitz their paths cross with a young Polish girl who dates, finally, to act—killing a German guard—while the others remain passive victims.

Lustig's long short story "Bílé břízy na podzim" (White birches in the fall, 1966) takes place in one of the rear units of the Czech army where "class enemies" served in the Communist detention centers during the 1950s. Told almost like a folk ballad, it is the love story of a nineteen-year-old boy and a seventeen-year-old prostitute with the cruel military atmosphere and the young lovers' tale starkly contrasted.

Hořká vuně mandlí (The bitter smell of almonds, 1968) contains four short stories; in the first two Lustig deals with the massacres of Jews in concentration camps and in the other two stories he shows Germans executing their deserters at the very end of the war and Czechs eagerly seeking revenge.

Most of the copies of *Miláček* (Darling, 1969), the last of Lustig's books published in Czechoslovakia after the "Prague Spring," were destroyed by the authorities. *Miláček*, Lustig's first novel, takes place during the first Israeli-Arab war in the 1940s and tells the story of two men courting one woman.

In the years following his leaving Czechoslovakia, Lustig revised some of his older works and regrouped some of his short stories into newly arranged collections for their translations into foreign languages.

Lustig's first book written in exile was the novella *Nemilovaná* (*Z deníku sedmnáctileté Perly Sch.*) (*The Unloved: From the Diary of Perla S.*). It was published in Toronto in 1979 and in Prague in 1991. It is a diary of a seventeen-year-old girl forced into prostitution at Terezin while she waits for her inevitable death in the gas chambers. In the postscript Lustig poses one of the questions his book endeavors to answer: "What should one do when one sacrifices his body in order to save his soul?" Lustig offers no answers, but in the honesty and simplicity of Perla's record he achieved in a work of fiction something like the effect of Anne Frank's diary. Peter Lewis wrote in *Stand* that "Perla's ability to rise above the situation, to remain sane and retain her humanity in the face of institutionalized insanity and inhumanity, gives the novel a positive force."

Lustig writes about women with particular sympathy and sensitivity. He centers on the way they assert and preserve their femininity under the most terrible conditions, but he does not idealize them, portraying their weaknesses as well as their strengths.

Several of Lustig's stories have been filmed in Czechoslovakia—among them *Démanty noci* (*Diamonds of the Night*) in 1964, directed by Jan Němec; another film dealing with a different theme from the same book, *Transport z ráje* (Transport from paradise), directed by Zybněk Brynch, was released in 1963. *Dita Saxová*, directed by Antonin Moskalyk, was filmed in 1967.

Josef Skvorecký, the Czech novelist who emigrated to Canada, ranks Lustig with Milan Kundera, Ludvik Vaculík, and Ivan Klíma among those who wrote in a spirit of renewed hope after the horrors of the Holocaust and World War II, only to find their hopes crushed by the Soviet invasion of 1968. With the restoration of democracy in this country in 1989, however, Lustig's books are again being published and widely circulated there, and he is appreciated, Skvorecký says, "[not] only because he depicts the Jewish tragedy better than most; he is remarkable because the tragedy of a specific people becomes, in his fiction, the tragedy of man. And that, to my mind, is the sign of great literature."

PRINCIPAL WORKS IN ENGLISH TRANSLATION: *Short stories*—(tr. I. Unwin) Diamonds of the Night, 1962 (new translation by J. Němcová, 1978); (tr. G. Theiner) Night and Hope, 1962; (new translation by J. Němcová, 1976); short story *in* Otruba, M. and Pesat, Z. (eds.) The Linden Tree, 1962; short story *in* Czech and Soviet Short Stories, 1967; short story *in* Glatstein, J. (ed.) Anthology of Holocaust Literature, 1969; short story *in* New Writing in Czecholslovakia, 1969; short story *in* Burke, J. F. (ed.) More Tales of Unease, 1969; (tr. J. Němcová) Darkness Casts No Shadow, 1976; Indecent Dreams, 1988; The Streets of Lost Brothers, 1990; (tr. T. Whipple) "Colette" *in* Kenyon Review, Spring 1991. *Novels*—(tr. G. Theiner) Dita Sax, 1966 (tr. as Dita Saxová ny J. Němcová, 1979); (tr. J. Němcová) A Prayer for Katerina Horovitzova, 1979; The Unloved: From the Diary of Perla S., 1985.

ABOUT: Brent, J. *foreword to* The Street of Lost Brothers, 1990; Contemporary Authors 69–72, 1978; Contemporary Literary Criticism 56, 1989; Contemporary World Writers, 2nd. ed., 1993; Encyclopedia of World Literature in the 20th Century, rev. ed., III, 1983; Mikailovich, V. D. (ed.) Modern Slavic Literatures, III, 1976; Skvorecký, J. *afterword to* Indecent Dreams, 1988; Tucker, M. (ed.) Literary Exile in the Twentieth Century, 1991. *Periodicals*—Choice Fall 1974; New England Review Fall 1990; New York Times Book Review October 21, 1973; March 18, 1979; January 19, 1986; June 19, 1988; Observer February 1966; Proteus

Spring 1974; Publishers Weekly February 21, 1977; Southwest Review Winter 1974; Stand Autumn, 1986; Times Literary Supplement February 3, 1966; World Literarture Today Winter 1978, Autumn 1986.

MacINTYRE, ALASDAIR (CHALMERS)

(January 12, 1929–   ), British-American philosopher, was born in Glasgow, Scotland, to Eneas John and Margaret (Chalmers) MacIntyre, both physicians. He received a bachelor's degree from the University of London and master's degrees from Manchester University and Oxford University. He lectured at Manchester University and Leeds University and was a research fellow at Nuffield College, Oxford, from 1961 to 1962. From 1963 to 1966 he was a fellow and preceptor in philosophy at Oxford. In 1966 he became professor of sociology at the University of Essex. MacIntyre came to the United States in 1969 and taught at Brandeis University, Boston University, Wellesley College, and Vanderbilt University. In 1988 he was appointed McMahon/Hank professor of philosophy at the University of Notre Dame in Indiana. MacIntyre married Ann Perry in 1953. They were divorced in 1963 and that same year he married Susan Margery Willis. That marriage ended in divorce in 1977 when he married Lynn Sumida Joy. He has two daughters from his first marriage and a son and daughter from his second.

With the publication of *After Virtue* in 1981, MacIntyre emerged as one of the most provocative ethical philosophers and social critics in English-language philosophy. His earlier books, such as *Marxism, An Interpretation* and *Marxism and Christianity* reflected a commitment to Marxism. In *After Virtue*, Aristotle replaced Marx, and in subsequent books such as *Whose Justice? Which Rationality* and *Three Rival Versions of Moral Enquiry* his version of Aristotelianism has been reinforced by the synthesis of Aristotle and traditional Roman Catholic doctrine achieved by Thomas Aquinas and known as Thomism. Throughout his writings he has been a consistently trenchant critic of the ethical assumptions and social tendencies of modern liberal society.

In *After Virtue: A Study in Moral Theory*, MacIntyre's contention is that the ethical project of the 18th-century Enlightenment, the attempt to give moral values a purely naturalistic or rationalistic justification, was doomed to failure. The failure, he argues, has in effect been institutionalized in modern liberal societies, where moral language largely consists of fragments of earlier traditions that have been lost or submerged, and where a fragile bureaucratic unity, in which rules have replaced values and virtues, has been substituted for the unity of tradition and community. For MacIntyre, contemporary moral language is an inflated currency, without a sound basis in a traditional ethical culture, and it both masks and, in its incoherence, reveals an underlying moral anarchy that is inevitably leading to social disintegration.

Much of *After Virtue* takes the from of a history of ideas. The Enlightenment, in MacIntyre's view, went wrong when it discarded the traditional conception of morality based on a set of virtues, which received its definitive formulation in Aristotle's *Ethics.* For Aristotle, a virtue was a trait that advanced the individual toward the inherent good or purpose, the "final cause," of humanity. Enlightenment philosophers, seeing that the emergent modern scientific method, notably in Newtonian physics, did without the final causes of medieval Aristotelian cosmology, purged inherent goods and purposes from their discussions of ethics. They instead spoke of natural moral sentiments or natural rights. Kant tries to posit moral principles as necessary correlates of practical reason, and Bentham tried to bind the individual pursuit of pleasure to the "greatest happiness for the greatest number."

According to MacIntyre, all these efforts were bound to fail because there can be no objective ethical obligation unless it is anchored in the conception of a final purpose or good for human life. Thus Enlightenment ethics gradually sank into 20th-century morass of emotivism and relativism—the position that moral evaluations are expressions of simple preference or feeling, and that statements of value should not be mistaken for statements of fact. MacIntyre maintains the Nietzsche, alone among major modern ethical philosopher, saw this failure clearly, and tried to make the best of it, offering an ethic of radical individualism, in which the strong, self-sufficient individual creates his or her own values and by doing so in some sense creates himself or herself. Nietzsche is therefore the only real alternative to Aristotle, but a society based on Nietzschean willfulness and self-assertion must eventually collapse into anarchy.

This is just what is happening, MacIntyre argues, in modern liberal societies, which have become dominated by three types—the bureaucratic manager, the aesthete, and the therapist—and which embody a discordant mix of individual moral subjectivity, bureaucratic rationality, and remnants of lost ethical vocabularies. At the end of the book he holds out little hope for our civilization:

> What matters at this stage is the construction of local forms of community within which civility and the intel-

lectual and moral life can be sustained through the new dark ages which are already upon us. And if the tradition of the virtues was able to survive the last dark ages, we are not entirely without grounds for hope. This time however the barbarians are not waiting beyond the frontiers; they have already been governing us for some time. And it is our lack of consciousness of this that constitutes part of our predicament. We are waiting not for Godot, but for another—doubtless very different—St. Benedict.

Most critics did not follow MacIntyre in his call for a new monasticism or a new Aristotelianism, but all praise *After Virtue* for its provocative brilliance or argument and erudition. Writing in the *New Statesman*, Steven Lukes called it an "exhilarating and richly rewarding book" that "through a series of sketches (of Homeric Greece, of Athenian society and the plays of Sophocles, of medieval conflicts, of Benjamin Franklin and Jane Austen)" tells "an overall story of moral concepts and their place in social life." But for Lukes, the inexorability of this transformation as conceived by MacIntyre—as a precipitous moral decline—involves him in a "deep inconsistency." If the morality of virtues, given authority by being rooted in a traditional community, "is genuinely *lost*, as he says, the possibility of the rational justification it provided is no longer available. . . . How then can MacIntyre as philosopher *appeal to* the 'genuine objective and impersonal standards' embodied" in that tradition? "Not only is the argument inconsistent," Lukes continued, "it is also circular. How can he justify *choosing* Aristotle against Nietzsche other than by criteria furnished by Aristotle and unmasked ny Nietzsche? What justifies his account and catalogue of the virtues if not the evaluations deriving from a lost teleogical morality of virtue? Why are 'utility' and 'rights' moral fictions but not the human *telos* and the 'common good'? In short, his argument assumes the truth of his conclusions. . . . [the book] is, however, fresh, original, and full of incidental insights . . . This is unquestionably one of the most lively, interesting and provocative books in social theory to have appeared for at least a decade."

In her review of *After Virtue* in the *Times Literary Supplement* (1981), Philippa Foot called it a "pervasively nostalgic book" whose invocation of lost "moral consensus, tradition, locality, community, and social authority" will "sound familiar, but MacIntyre is in fact an idiosyncratic philosopher and sociologist with a special thesis of his own." She found his account of the unintelligibility and confusion of modern moral language compelling, but she was not convinced by his claim to have argued his way out of the confusion: "MacIntyre believes by producing a new and defensible Aristotelianism he has defeated Nietzsche. He thinks that he has shown that the individual is not his own moral authority as Nietzsche believes, since 'the conception of a good has to be expounded in terms of such actions as those of a practice, of the narrative unity of a human life and of a moral tradition.' As a claim to have given some general account of the concept of a good this is absurd in the context of the arguments actually offered in the book. Nietzsche could reply that no one knew better than he did the good of submitting to the laws of an art, and that the unity of a life was just what a strong man would create by the disciplining of is desires."

Foot concluded that the book was well worth reading and pondering even though MacIntyre had failed to offer rigorous arguments for his traditionalist position: "Whether MacIntyre could develop some strong and radical theory from his present starting points is really hard to tell on the evidence offered in this book. For although he says many true things he is here basically operating on credit, while the cruel fact about philosophy is that its only currency is cash . . . A reader interested primarily in finding a new moral theory may be disappointed. But if he will settle for the pleasures of intricate construction, lively argument, . . . and the skilful use of a wealth of reading in philosophy, sociology and literature he will be well served."

In a long and sympathetic essay in the *New York Review of Books*, J. M. Cameron conceded that any summary of *After Virtue* may "make MacIntyre sound like a romantic, a praiser of the far away and long ago, one who wishes to put us all to sleep under the rule of pope and emperor." But Cameron stressed the nuances in MacIntyre's view of the past, including Aristotle: "There is passion in the book, above all in what he writes about Greek, Icelandic, and Gaelic epic; the ethos of the heroic cultures he evidently finds close to his own feeling about human life, though of course he doesn't deny the limitations of this ethos. He has some important reflections on tragedy and its pertinence to ethics, especially in what he has to say about Aristotle, whose view that all conflict is in principle eliminable from human life is shown to involve a misreading of the Greek tragedians."

"The completed picture contains many puzzles," Cameron admitted. "One question is how far the variety of human life and possibility can be brought within such an account." But Cameron found MacIntyre's approach to answering this question persuasive and the book important for its value as provocation alone: "Many will hate the book and its line of thought, finding it 'reactionary' and unenlightened. But it is something to have a book, devoted to certain quite central technical philosophical questions, which is likely to produce so passionate a response."

MacIntyre's next book, *Whose Justice? Which Rationality?*, elaborated on his conception of rationality as grounded in social and intellectual tradition. This is actually a divergence from Aristotle, who grounded both reason and ethical ends in biological human nature. MacIntyre, still working in an Aristotelian framework, denied that rationality could have any universal basis; it can only exist within a specific tradition—the Aristotelian tradition being the one he has chosen to reason within. In the *New Statesman* Steven Lukes restated his view that *After Virtue* had left MacIntyre caught in a dilemma, invoking as a philosopher principles inherent in a tradition that he has shown as a historian to be lost. The new book, Lukes thought, had failed to rescue him. "Does *Whose Justice? Which Rationality?* show the way out, or back? Far from it. Indeed, it only sharpens the dilemma by offering an account of rationality, as tradition-bound, which itself only serves to reinforce the inaccessibility to post-Enlightenment thought of the very case MacIntyre seeks to make." Lukes noted MacIntyre's sardonic view that modern liberalism has failed to recognize that liberalism itself is not based on the illusory universal standards of rationality that it invokes, but is just another "community of pre-rational faith" whose "parish magazine," as MacIntyre puts it, is the *New York Times*, read by the "affluent and self-congratulatory liberal enlightenment" whose clergy are lawyers. Lukes concludes by saying that MacIntyre's position, offering no neutral ground for a rational assessment of competing traditions, or for debate between them, could only persuade the "co-habitants of his Aristotelian-Augustinian-Thomist tradition."

This was perhaps demonstrated in the conservative *National Review*, where Thomas Fleming strongly endorsed MacIntyre's defense of tradition: "The individual-as-such is the fantasy of liberal who have failed, after two centuries of effort, to realize their grand system of a world without superstition, prejudice, and traditional piety . . . Making moral sense of the world turns out to depend not upon what we can glean from the pages of John Rawls and Robert Nozick, but upon our allegiance to the blood of our ancestors and the faith of our fathers. . . . MacIntyre might not care for their company, but intelligent conservatives cannot afford to ignore the most subversive conservative thinker since T. S. Eliot and Richard Weaver."

MacIntyre's next major work, *Three Rival Versions of Moral Inquiry*, a revision of the Gifford Lectures he delivered at Edinburgh in 1988, extended the basic historical scheme of *After Virtue*, tracing three moral traditions—the liberal progressive, the Nietzschean-genealogical, and the Aristotelian-Thomist. The book cogently demonstrates the incompatible approaches of the three traditions. For instance, liberalism defines itself in terms of progress toward universal truth and humane institutions. The Nietzschean—like Nietzsche himself or Michel Focault—would "unmask" this notion of progress as nothing but a disguise for the will to power of certain groups or professions. By offering a "genealogy" of values like truth, progress, and humanitarianism, the Nietzschean attempts to show how these abstractions conceal and underlying self-assertive desire for dominance and control. The Thomist, in turn, would say that this skeptical unmasking is itself a mask for pride and a corrupted individual will.

In the *New York Times Book Review*, Jenny Teichman wrote that "MacIntyre tends to exaggerate the difficulties of reconciling conflicting conceptual schemes. For instance, he simply ignores this bits of philosophy in which real and universally acknowledged progress has occurred." She conceded, however, the acuteness of his historical considerations, notably "the chapters on the development of Christian philosophy between Augustine and Duns Scotus." In the *New Statesman* (1990), Alan Ryan described the book as a new opportunity for MacIntyre "to assault his old enemies—secular rationalists, liberals and social democrats, analytical philosophers, and anyone who thinks that 20th-century cosmopolitan societies are an improvement on pre-modern, confessional communities. If his positive allegiances have varied a good deal—Anglican, Trotskyite, now apparently Thomist and Roman Catholic—his antipathies have not. Nor has he been blind to the irony of the fact that is only in the age of the intellectual supermarket that his own career would have been possible, picking off the shelves one large anti-liberal scheme after another, while all the time deploring the existence of intellectual supermarkets that don't come down firmly in favour of one doctrine or another." But while many readers of MacIntyre will find his views, as summarized by Ryan, alarming—"the role of authority in setting limits to enquiry is essential; the intellectual and moral virtues cannot be sharply differentiated, seeing how the perversion and corruption of the human will lead men away from the truth; philosophy is practiced as a craft, so that it is essentially learned by imitation at the feet of master craftsmen, and by the same token it is essentially tied up with tradition, and the task for the individuals is not to buck the tradition but to strengthen it"—his positions are not, Ryan concluded, as repressive as they might sound. "MacIntyre simply wants there to be several different sorts of university, some liberal but less complacently so than present, some vividly Nietzschean and subversive, others built around an authoritative faith. They should then try to find some common setting in which they can argue the superiority of their own intellectual habits over those of their rivals. It sounds good fun—but not very unlike what goes on in America higher education at present, and terribly, terribly liberal."

PRINCIPAL WORKS: The Unconscious: A Conceptual Analysis, 1958; Difficulties in Christian Belief, 1959; Marxism, An Interpretation, 1963; Marxism and Christianity, 1968; Herbert Marcuse: An Exposition and a Polemic, 1970; Against the Self-Images of the Age, 1971; After Virtue: A Study in Moral Theory, 1981; Whose Justice? Which Rationality? 1988; First Principles, Final Ends, and Contemporary Philosophical Issues, 1990; Three Rival Versions of Moral Enquiry, 1990.

ABOUT: Contemporary Authors 118, 1986; Horton, J. and Mendus, S (eds.) After MacIntyre, 1995; Who's Who, 1994; Who's Who in America, 1994. Periodicals—America November 14, 1981; Commentary June 1988; Commonweal May 20, 1988; National Review May 13, 1988; New Republic June 6, 1988; New Statesman September 4, 1981; August 19, 1988; August 17, 1990; New York Review of Books November 5, 1981; New York Times Book Review August 12, 1990; Philosophical Review July 1983; Times Literary Supplement September 25, 1981; July 8–14, 1988; Yale Law Review January 1983.

MACKAY, SHENA (June 6, 1944–   ) Scottish novelist, short story writer, and poet, was born in Edinburgh. Her parents, Benjamin Carr Mackay and Morag (Cramaichel), went south to England while she was young; she was educated at Tonbridge Girls Grammar School and Kidbrooke Comprehensive School. (The latter at that time was famous as a model Comprehensive.)

She began to write when she was fifteen years old, and at nineteen published the astonishingly sophisticated two-novella volume *Dust Falls on Eugene Schlumberger and Toddler on the Run.* This, like all her other earlier books, has now been reprinted. But it was with the novel *Dunedin* in 1992—and the *Collected Stories* which followed it—that her reputation as an accomplished writer was finally confirmed.

Early on in her career, Mackay developed her unique prose voice, which the (London) *Daily*

SHENA MACKAY

Telegraph aptly described in a revise of *Music Upstairs* in 1965, as "scruffy, sweaty, shapeless, desultory, vivid, and heavy with inchoate poetry of adolescence. . . . " In 1971 the *New Statesman* called her "The supreme lyricist of daily grot." Having achieved a style so clearly her own, MacKay has not shown a sign of having strained for it, or of overwriting. But, although her work was widely praised it was only after her 1990s reprints and new books that serious critics have begun to examine Mackay's achievement, in both novel and short story, in any proper depth. In 1994, discussing *Dreams of Dead Women's Handbags*, her collection of short stories written over twenty years, Katharine Weber observed, in the *New York Times Book Review* that the book is "further evidence of Mackay's startling precocity . . . it also displays the more recent, elegant work of a developed writer who has continued to fine tune her distinctive voice over an unusually broad range."

Writing in the *Daily Mail* about MacKay's first book, Kenneth Allsop managed to list most of the adjectives that she would in due time earn from reviewers: "Macabre, zany, scoffingly droll, sadly beautiful, widly funny, glitteringly stylish. . . . She stands on her own." Although the surface of her prose does sparkle, it is by no means merely comic, or just "good fun." Far from being black humored she is, more properly and critically considered, a writer who hovers deliberately, and with much concealed art, between the tragicomic, as in *Dunedin*, and the comitragic, as in *Redhill Rococo.* As Martin Seymour-Smith put it: "She is like Schubert in the sense that, when you are actually listening to him, you think he must be the best."

Much of Mackay's accomplishment seems to be already present in her more youthful work. Always an expert, and funny, explorer of the quotidian lives of helpless and often penniless people who feel vaguely oppressed and unfulfilled, she specializes, in novels as in short stories, in giving poetry and, therefore, significance to lives which would be condemned out of hand by sociologists or theorists as lumpen. This is salient in, for example, the sad and sordid world in which her early novel *Music Upstairs* is set: "Sometimes at nightfall or in a storm, as autumn became cold, Earls Court Road seemed to steam; dark faces suddenly flashing in doorways, hands, whistles, cars stopping, breath hanging in the air above groups on the pavement or a snatch of perfume from people hurrying to cold orgies by the electric fire."

With *Redhill Rococo* this note deepened, since the zany protagonist, who has served a prison term for armed theft, is skillfully shown not be the psychopath for which society takes him, but, rather, a harmless fantasist whose flounderings reflect the true values (or, rather, lack of them) of his society. This is all done in farcical terms, but there was a moving and lyrical subtext: unlike the early Evelyn Waugh, Mackay does not use her characters to illustrate an underlying pessimism; all of them, however ridiculous their behavior, matter. Thus, although she is a critic of society, Mackay never withdraws compassion.

In *Dunedin*, a novel much more ambitious in scope, the comedy is preserved intact, but the psychological note is deepened. The book opens in New Zealand in 1909—an era subtly and skillfully evoked—to show Scottish Presbyterian minister Jack Mackenzie enjoying the all the pleasures (botanical and carnal) of Dunedin while his wife suffers. After the vessel that brought the Mackenzie family to the "New World" has sailed into the harbor, "Jack Mackenzie was the first passenger ashore: he had determined from the moment the ship left Glasgow that he should be, no matter who he had to elbow out of his way." Fascinated with the vegetation of the region and the nubile Maori girls—especially a housemaid, Myrtille—he ignores his homesick wife and tyrannizes over his children.

The portrait of Mackenzie, in many ways a monster, does not spare him because Mackay is never sentimental, and never spares anyone; but it is none the less a tour de force of sympathetic imagination, and one which seemed to some critics to be salutary in its peculiarly forceful and essentially feminine nonjudgmentalism. "Had he been a religious man, the minister would have been awestruck by the wonders of God's creation, which he observed from the deck; as a sensualist who had entered the Church at his father's behest and who nourished an amateur passion for the natural sciences, he performed his duties with more enthusiasm for marine life than for worship."

The novel shifts in time to contemporary London, in which Mackenzie's grandchildren recreate his sins in a search for authentic love. The moving ending of this novel is, in particular, a model of restraint and poetry of style: "There was no rainbow the day the Mackenzies set sail from Dunedin, nobody on the quay to wave them off . . . Jack Mackenzie, who had wanted a botanical specimen to be named after him, *Mackenzie officionalis*, had after all left behind something that might bear his name, but he did not know it, and neither, yet, did Myrtille."

Dunedin seemed to Martin Seymour-Smith to be "a major novel in a sense hardly achieved in Great Britain today." Lorna Sage, in the *Times Literary Supplement*, remarked that Mackay "writes about South East London with such penetrating familiarity and ingenuity that it becomes the focus for a whole world of dreams and disasters and guilty histories." She concluded that Mackay's "lightness of touch . . . lets you levitate out of the horrors, without in the least obscuring them."

The most obvious influence on Mackay the storywriter is Katherine Mansfield, but that influence is never obtrusive. In the *Listener* in 1967, Brigid Brophy commented on Mackay's stories: "Her beautiful prose isolates homely objects into disconcertingness, and her macabre, overwhelmingly original imagination blooms into sheerly surrealist images caught in midmetamorphosis." It is this capacity for the macabre and the disconcerting that has been missed by many reviewers of Mackay's books, since they have tended to concentrate on the sheer pleasure afforded by her deceptively engaging style. Mackay's own book reviews for the *Sunday Times* are themselves also deceptive: appearing to be homely appreciations of her contemporaries, they are in fact often sharply critical (but not malicious), although in an entirely unobstrusive manner. Mackay does not like to "have it in" for anyone, since, as her writings tell us, she regards everyone as an unfair victim of life.

For a time Shena Mackay, who lives in Norwood in South London, was married to Robin Brown. She has three grown-up daughters. She has taught creative writing and often gives public readings of her work.

PRINCIPAL WORKS: *Novels*—Dust Falls on Eugene Schlumberger and Toddler on the Run, 1964; Music Upstairs, 1965; Old Crow, 1967; An Advent Calendar, 1971; A Bowl of Cherries, 1984; Redhill Rococo, 1986; Dunedin, 1993. *Short stories*—Babies in Rinestones, 1983; Dreams of Dead Women's Handbags, 1987; Laughing Academy 1993; Collected Stories, 1994. *As editor*—Such Devoted Sisters: An Anthology of Stories, 1993.

ABOUT: Contemporary Authors 104, 1982. *Periodicals*—Daily Mail July 3, 1964; Listener June 15, 1967, July 8, 1971; New Statesman June 12, 1964, July 2, 1971; New York Times Book Review December 18, 1994; Newsweek January 17, 1966; Observer June 11, 1967; Times Literary Supplement June 15, 1967, July 2, 1971; July 10, 1992.

CHARLOTTE MacLEOD

MacLEOD, CHARLOTTE (November 12, 1922–), American mystery novelist, writes: "Born in Bath, New Brunswick, Charlotte Mac-Leod became an illegal alien six months later, when her parents emigrated to Boston, Massachusetts. Now living in Maine, she manages to keep one foot on either side of the border, writing mystery novels set in New England under her own name and Canadian mysteries as Alisa Craig. By the end of the 1994, she will have published twenty-nine adult mysteries, eleven for young adults, a biography of Mary Roberts Rinehart, a short story collection, and two anthologies.

"Coming from a family of storytellers, CM began to write almost as soon as she learned to read, and had her first story, a mystery, published in a local paper when she was in grade 6 at the Bicknell School in North Weymouth, Massachusetts. Thanks to the superb English curriculum in the Weymouth Public Schools at that time, she was graduated with a sound knowledge of what seem to be the lost arts of grammar, spelling, and composition. The words 'literate' and 'erudite' frequently appear in reviews of her work, although her next step was to enroll in the School of Practical Art, now the Art Institute of Boston, with the intention of learning to illustrate the books she had always meant to write. When offered an assistant's job at the Tufts Library in Weymouth, she took it and continued her art studies in evening classes.

"This was wartime; workers in every field were scarce. After a year and a half at the library, she was offered a job as staff artist in the advertising department of a Boston-based grocery chain. She soon began writing copy as well as doing artwork. She also became an American citizen. In 1952 she joined N. H. Miller & Company in Boston as copy chief, served as an account executive and vice president, and became a part-time consultant when her writing career absorbed more and more of her time.

"Her first signed piece appeared in *Yankee Magazine*, December, 1963, and was followed by other short stories and nonfiction pieces in American and foreign publications. Her first book-length young adult mystery was published in 1964 and soon went out of print, as have all the juveniles that followed.

"CM's first adult mystery appeared in 1978 from Doubleday Crime Club and brought her immediate recognition as a fresh voice in the field. Her serial characters have become intimate acquaintances of readers in many countries. As Alisa Craig, the author reflects her Canadian heritage in characters such as Detective Inspector Madoc Rhys of the Royal Canadian Mounted Police and members of the Grub-and-Stake Gardening and Roving Club of Lobelia Falls, Ontario. All her adult mysteries are in print.

"She is a charter member of Crime Writers of Canada and cofounder and former president of the American Crime Writers League, has won five American Mystery Awards—three as MacLeod, two as Craig—A Nero Wolfe Award, and two Edgar nominations. She received her Lifetime Achievement Award at Bouchercon XXIII in Toronto, October 1992."

"Charlotte MacLeod's best-known fiction emphasizes the orderly world vital to cozy mysteries," Jane S. Bakerman writes in

Twentieth-Century Crime and Mystery Writers.
"Moreover, her stories reveal that sweet dispositions, good food, and loyalty are the basic necessities for a happy marriage. Coupling this
philosophy with clever plots and plenty of humor has netted her a host of fans and a sound
reputation." Marcia Muller, in *1001 Midnights,*
agrees with this description of genteel mayhem:
"The mysteries of Charlotte MacLeod are of the
'bloodless' type: while murders abound, bloodletting is never described in all its painful ugliness. MacLeod writes with wry wit and style,
and her plotting is competent. If there is any
fault with the . . . series she has authored, it is
that many of the characters are somewhat emotionless and so eccentric that the books do not
seem very realistic. If, however, you are in the
mood for an enjoyable, humorous, and 'civilized'
murder mystery, little can beat MacLeod's
work."

MacLeod's sleuth Peter Shandy made his debut in the 1978 *Rest You Merry* (clever titles are
a MacLeod trademark). Shandy is a professor at
Balaclava Agricultural College in Massachusetts,
and a cocreator of the internationally famous
Balaclava Buster rutabaga; the dust cover of her
fourth Shandy mystery, *Something the Cat
Dragged In,* proclaims him the "Hercule Poirot
of the turnip fields." His first case begins with
the death of Jemima Ames, assistant librarian
and chairperson of the Christmas Eve Grand Illumination of the Balaclava Crescent Committee. After being hounded by Ames to decorate
his home for the Illumination, Shandy goes
slightly mad and overloads his home with gaudy
and tacky Christmas trappings. Now he finds
Ames in his living room: "The assistant librarian
was dead, no question about that. She was lying
on her back, looking up at him with the same
cold, fishy stare he'd seen when she handed him
the bouquet cut from detergent bottles. Her
mouth was slightly open, as though she might be
about to deliver one last exhortation about the
duty of a Crescent resident, but she never
would." Although the police and campus security believe that Ames was accidentally killed by
a fall from a nearby stepladder, Shandy believes
it is murder and successfully pursues the killer.
The book also introduces Helen Marsh, who will
become Shandy's wife. Throughout the series, as
Bakerman notes, the Shandys "are surrounded
by a fairly wide range of characters, most, like
publicly blustery, privately biddable President
Thorkjeld Svenson, easily recognizable types.
Peter and Helen are also, however, blessed with
some wonderful old friends, such as Catriona
McBogle, a writer whose 200-year old . . .
Maine home is very like MacLeod's own." The
theft of antique weather vanes is the unusual

premise of *Vane Pursuit,* the Shandys' seventh
mystery. *Publishers Weekly* called it the
"ultimate in escapism: an utterly hilarious albeit
totally unbelievable caper that MacLeod . . .
fans will savor."

Perhaps MacLeod's best and most popular series character is Sarah Kelling, a member of Boston Beacon Hill society. Bakerman points out
that the "Kellings' numbers are legion; many of
their fortunes are vast, and while their eccentricities are pronounced, those who aren't out-and-
out villains constitute a likable crowd prone to
discovering corpses and falling in love—
intensely, vocally, joyously in love." *The Family
Vault,* Sarah's first case, finds her in her twenties
and married to her fifth cousin, Alexander, who
is some twenty years her senior. The story begins
with the opening of the Kelling family vault for
the interring of Great-Uncle Frederick. What is
found inside is the body of Ruby Redd, a burlesque queen with a link to Alexander's wild
past; Sarah is soon wondering if Alexander could
be the killer. "It seemed rotten to go snooping
behind her husband's back, yet one could hardly
march up to him and ask point-blank, 'Did you
murder Ruby Redd?'" The mystery not only
leads Sarah into the family's past, but places her
in danger and leaves her widowed. Marcia Muller, however, notes that throughout her trials Sarah "keeps her wits and her sense of humor, and
emerges the woman she has only hoped to be."

As the series progresses, Sarah is courted by
Max Bittersohn, a private investigator specializing in art theft. The couple marry, have a child,
sleuth together, and occasionally sleuth apart.
Sarah is featured in *"A Cozy for Christmas,"* included by MacLeod in the short story collection
Mistletoe Mysteries; Max gets a chance to display
his own specialty in *The Convivial Codfish.* Together they solve the case of *The Recycled
Citizen,* in which a worker at the Senior Citizens'
Recycling Center is murdered and heroin is discovered in his collection bag. "Max and Sarah,
and various interesting kin eventually figure
things out, though without much trouble or dramatic tension," a *Library Journal* (1988) review
noted. "Solving the mystery evolves into a game
for the good-hearted rich with nothing better to
do. Shallow characterizations, somewhat disjointed narrative, meaningless plot." *Library
Journal* (1990) had kinder words for MacLeod
after Sarah, Max, and cousin-in-law Theonie
help Emma Kelling deal with "strange events,
attempted theft, and a sodden body" at a Main
retreat in *The Gladstone Bag*: "Tongue-in-cheek
eccentricities, the usual casual but astute deduc-
tions, and a certain luxuriousness of language
make this a most welcome addition to the Mac-
Leod canon."

Under the pseudonym Alisa Craig, MacLeod first reflected her "Canadian heritage" in the 1980 *A Pint of Murder*, featuring Detective Inspector Madoc Rhys of the Royal Canadian Mounted Police and his wife Janet. The following year she used the Craig nom de plume to introduce the Grub-and-Stake Gardening and Roving Club of Lobelia Falls, Ontario, in *The Grub-and-Stakers Move a Mountain*. The Rhyses and the Grub-and-Stakers are as adept at solving murders as their New England counterparts, and there is no lack of MacLeod's trademark wit, intriguing plots, and eccentric characters. "Though the supporting figures MacLeod/Craig introduces sometimes tend to be reminiscent of one another and though humor and action dominate characterization, all of her characters are memorable; all are interesting, and their expected foibles, actions, and reactions provide ample amusement and escape," Bakerman concludes. "Their peculiarities distance readers so that the emotional cost of eavesdropping on these murderous adventures is very low whereas the profit—entertainment—is very high."

In addition to novels, Charlotte MacLeod has contributed stories and articles to such publications as *Good Housekeeping*, *Yankee*, *Alfred Hitchcock's Mystery Magazine*, and *Cricket*.

PRINCIPAL WORKS: *Novels*—Rest You Merry, 1978; The Family Vault, 1979; The Luck Runs Out, 1979; (as Alisa Craig) A Pint of Murder, 1980; The Withdrawing Room, 1980; (as Alisa Craig) The Grub-and-Stakers Move a Mountain, 1981; (as Alisa Craig) Murder Goes Mumming, 1981; The Place Guard, 1981; Wrack and Rune, 1982; The Bilbao Looking Glass, 1983; Something the Cat Dragged In, 1983; (as Alisa Craig) The Terrible Tide, 1983; The Convivial Codfish, 1984; The Curse of the Giant Hogweed, 1985; (as Alisa Craig) The Grub-and-Stakers Quilt a Bee, 1985; The Plain Old Man, 1985; The Corpse in Oozak's Pond, 1986; (as Alisa Craig) A Dismal Thing to Do, 1986; The Recycled Citizen, 1987; (as Alisa Craig) The Grub-and-Stakers Pinch a Poke, 1988; The Silver Ghost, 1988; The Gladstone Bag, 1990; (as Alisa Craig) Trouble in the Brasses, 1989; Vane Pursuit, 1989; (as Alisa Craig) The Grub-and-Stakers Spin a Yarn, 1990; An Owl Too Many, 1991; The Resurrection Man, 1992; (as Alisa Craig) The Wrong Rite, 1992; (as Alisa Craig) The Grub-and-Stakers House a Haunt, 1993; Something in the Water, 1994. *Short stories*—Grab Bag, 1987. *As editor*—Mistletoe Mysteries, 1989; Christmas Stalkings: Tales of Yuletide Murder, 1991. *Juvenile*—Mystery of the White Knight, 1964; (as Matilda Hughes) The Food of Love, 1965; Next Door to Danger, 1965; (as Matilda Hughes) Headline for Caroline, 1967; The Fat Lady's Ghost, 1968; Mouse's Vineyard, 1968; Ask Me No Questions, 1971; Brass Pounder, 1971; King Devil, 1978; We Dare Not Go A-Hunting, 1980; Cirak's Daughter, 1982; Maid of Honor, 1984. *Nonfiction*—Astrology for Skeptics, 1972.

ABOUT: Pronzini, B. and Marcia Muller. 1001 Midnights: The Aficionado's Guide to Mystery and Detective Fiction, 1986; Something about the Author 28, 1982; Twentieth-Century Crime and Mystery Writers, 1991. *Periodicals*—Library Journal January 1988; February 1990; Publishers Weekly February 3, 1989.

MANEA, NORMAN (July 19, 1936–   ), Romanian-born fiction writer and essayist writes: "I was born in Suceava, Bukovina (between 1775 and 1918 part of the Habsburgic Empire). I first discovered my 'identity' when I was deported, in 1941, with my family and with the entire Jewish population of Bukovina to the concentration camp of Transnistria, in Ukraine.

"I returned to Romania with the surviving members of my family in April 1945. I still remember the most important gift which I was given at that time. It was a book of Romanian folktales. It was a magical encounter: the word as miracle, the moment when I fell in love with books. But soon after I had already entered the rigors of a society that tried to annihilate any kind of identity. After graduating, in 1954, from the High School (*Liceu*) in Suceava, I studied at the Institute of Construction, in Bucharest, at the Faculty of Hydrotechnology, graduating in 1959 with a master's degree in engineering.

"In the 1950s, literature in Romania was ruined by 'socialist-realism,' books and literary magazines were flagrantly manipulated as political tools. For this son betrothed too early to reading, to dreams and the queernesses of ideas, the parents wished a trade. Concrete, protective, sure. To top it all, I had the bad luck of being a very good student and a good mathematician. I paid dearly for this tormenting disguise, working for more than fourteen years as an engineer. I wonder if I really played this role, so estranged I felt, and I wonder how many individuals were in each of us in that socialist system of mystification. During my entire postwar life in Romania I had searched, thanks to reading and writing, for an inner resistance, against often unbearable external pressure. It is hard to believe that in a totalitarian society the 'I' could survive, and yet interiority was a mode of resistance. The 'I' remains even in the totalitarian environment where external pressures are always dangerous, perhaps especially there, the site of a clash between the centripetal necessity to preserve the secret, codified identity and the centrifugal tendency toward liberation.

"I tried to resist the outside pressure through my own immersion in writing, that 'walling in' of the self in a mental project where advancing into the unknown of sought-after beauty be-

NORMAN MANEA

comes so *real*, so immediate, that the dark, false, inconsistent reality surrounding you loses impact. I started to publish in the so called 'liberalization' period, in the mid-60s, in an avant-garde magazine, *Povestea Vorbii*, (Tale of the Word, or Proverb) which was suppressed after six issues. I avoided Party affiliation and my position in Romania's socialist literary life was perhaps peculiar and not at all comfortable. My work was an irritant to the authorities because of the implied and overt social criticism, of my themes and even my style.

"My first story *Fierul de călcat dragostea* (Ironing love), published in 1966, was an erotic and anxious story. I was trying to reestablish the natural theme and language, in a period when, though "liberalization" had started, literature was still forced to be political, moral, and accessible. Of course, the press instantly attacked my text. *Plicul Negru* (The Black Envelope), my last novel published in Romania, in 1986, was a dark allegory of daily life under Ceaușescu in its phase of extreme misery and terror. It was a time when the 'esthete' writer, even if pessimistic and modernistic, but estranged from the explosive social theme of the moment, was officially encouraged. The Romanian language allows the punning reference to *est* (east) in the word *estetica*. As I often said in Romania, all around Eastern Europe 'aesthetics' had become 'East-ethics.' As one can see, I evolved 'aesthetically' with the system, but in the opposite direction. When the political idealization of the activist as a sort of ideological colonizer of daily life was demanded, with solutions fitting all occasions, I

was trying to write about childhood, illness, love, anxiety, death. When such themes became possible, with the immediate social sphere and its political implications now interdicted, I wrote again on tabooed subjects. Autocracy gives rise to a peculiar literature. I was obsessed with the pathology of 'depersonalization' in the socialist universe of mediocrity, with the disruption of values and lives, but also with the deep need to know what had been lost without ever having been possessed. Irony, sarcasm, and the grotesque seemed the most suitable tools to investigate and reveal the corrupting reality, pervaded by apathy, decay, and perfidy. The main character in all my books is an *outsider* and alienation penetrates the psychological texture of all my writings. My struggle with the censor never stopped whenever I published a new text or a new book, whether with a political theme or deprived of it. And yet I published in this Byzantine 'real socialism' 10 volumes (short fiction, novels, essays). The literary / aesthetic traces of the war with the censorship are, unfortunately, lasting. An 'aesthetic of mutilation' (and an East-ethic as well) has resulted in all socialist countries from the confrontation with our omnipotent, shrewd, and cynical adversary. It is not by chance that comments printed in an interview of mine in the literary magazine *Familia* in 1981 pleading for integrity and a moral stance from writers, particularly from whose who showed themselves only too ready to do the regime's handiwork, provoked a prolonged press campaign against me, with anti-Semitic accents.

"The communist authorities withdrew in 1986 the Literary Prize which I was awarded by the Writers' Union of Romania. In 1986 I left Romania for West Berlin, where I was awarded the DAAD Grant for the year 1987 (Berliner Künstlerprogramm). In 1988 I came to the United States with a Fulbright Scholarship.

"For the mature adult, exile reformulates tardily the premise of initiation and becoming, putting into question all the steps of the past experience. And for a writer, to be exiled also from his last refuge, his placenta—language—represents the most brutal and irredeemable discentering of his being. Writing *On Clowns* in the United States, as in former times when I was writing other books—especially when I wrote, in Romania, *Anii de ucenicie ai lui August Prostul* (Auguste the Fool's apprenticeship years)—I had plenty of occasions to think about the process of formation through deformation, about the conflict between individual aspirations and the oppressive, stifling pressure of society.

"I was pleased and encouraged, of course, by the publication, reviews, prizes, and new friends in the West. Since I left Romania my short fiction and essays have been translated into more than ten languages. Finally, one feels not only the curse, but also the privilege, of being an exile, this strange *honor*, with its doubts and never-ending apprenticeship, its emptiness and richness, the unfettering of one self and clash within ourselves. It embodies not only the wounds of liberty, but also the main contradiction of our time, the contradiction between centrifugal, cosmopolitan modernity and the centripetal need (or at least nostalgia) for belonging."

In 1992, in the *New York Times Book Review*, Philip Roth described Norman Manea as "mild, reserved, anxious, at times a bit timid. He does not strike even himself, I believe, as the ideal writer to have been pitted against perhaps the most vicious dictatorship of the last forty years." As Roth reminded his readers, however, it is precisely the vulnerability of the survivors that is their triumph; "no moral endeavor is more astonishing," Roth wrote. The particular horror of the Ceaușescu regime in Romania was its banality, the grinding down of the human spirit by bureaucracy, petty tyranny, inefficiency, and plain stupidity. Manea captures the essence of this sterile society in his story "The Trenchcoat": "The waiting lines for bread plus toilet paper plus rubber bands plus plus plus. The loused-up public transportation and the poorly lighted streets and the badly heated apartments and the armed patrols, and the neuroses and the illegal abortions and nationalism and the demolition of the lovely old residential neighborhoods. . . . "

Growing up as a Jewish child in the Nazi-dominated Romania of World War II, Manea was exposed to greater physical risks than in his mature years when Nazism was superseded by a Communist dictatorship. But the mind- and spirit-numbing Ceaușescu regime was a formidable threat to him as an intellectual and a writer. John Updike wrote of Manea in the *New Yorker*: "A childhood in a Nazi internment camp yielded, with scarcely a pause, to a youth under an imposed Communism; an evil fairy tale became a grotesque circus." Manea early recognized the perils of a police state, the compromises that, he writes in the author's note to *On Clowns: The Dictator and the Artist*, "gradually destroy his [the writer's] integrity, and thus his identity. . . . In a lifelong attempt to avoid these kinds of traps, I have developed a firm skepticism toward political kitsch and a constant suspicion of its manipulative labels."

The stories in *October, Eight O'Clock* trace the painful education of a young child moving into adolescence and maturity during the period in which Manea was growing up in Romania. The "evil fairy tale" of his childhood informs "The Sweater," told in the voice of a half-starved boy in a disease-ridden Nazi camp where the sweater once worn by a little girl who had died of fever becomes an image of terror to the boy who inherits it. "Each day stalked us. We forgot the days; we waited, listening for the maddening fury of the night. The time we lived in pursued us; there was nothing to be done. Time itself had sickened, and we belonged to it." The nightmare of his childhood also haunts "Proust's Tea," in which starving women and children await deportation in a railway station. A relief worker offers the boy a mug of hot tea and a biscuit, releasing his memories of home and his grandparents. "There are, then, certain gifts whose only quality and only flaw is that they cannot be exchanged for anything else." In subsequent stories the child grows up, marries, becomes a writer—but he is scarred by his past, spied on by his janitor, frustrated by bureaucratic rules.

Unlike the subjective autobiographical stories of *October, Eight O'Clock*, the four novellas that comprise *Compulsory Happiness* are somewhat more objectively observed portraits of life under Ceaușescu. The first and most powerful of these, however, "The Interrogation," evoked comparison by several reviewers with Kafka's work because the political prisoner-victim here confronts mysterious, inexplicable changes in her existence. At first she is treated brutally—beaten, stripped naked, her head shorn. "To humiliate, intimidate, destroy," in Manea's phrase, is the purpose of such treatment. But suddenly she is given a bath, food, warm clothing, and brought before an Inquisitor, an intellectual who "can't stand violence . . . a sensitive soul." In a rambling monologue that lasts for hours, he reveals the full evil of the Party—their hatred of intellectuals, "of anyone connected with books. . . . They wouldn't be capable of understanding how unreal a real book can be! How real a still unwritten book can be, as long as its contents exist—virtually—in the mind of at least one person."

The literal torture in "The Interrogation" finds its counterpart in the frustration and monotony of life in "A Window on the Working Class." Waking up in the morning his characters "grope, haggardly, in terror of a new day. Shower, black coffee. Wide awake, sluggish, alert, groggy, sitting in front of their cups. Already belonging to this new day, no way out, none." The bureaucrats who work in a government office in "Composite Biography" and criticize everyone who lapses from "ideological correctness" and the dinner guests in "The Trenchcoat" who live under the shadow of state security agents are sharply satirized. For all their horrors, the Romanian dictator and his police state are also absurd, comic in the dark mood of modern-day political satire. "Manea . . . writes about the soul's deterioration under chronic deprivation, about a political and social system in which every person and every situation is always suspect, about people who are tortured. These are the century's classic themes, but . . . Manea's voice is radically new," Lore Segal said in the *New York Times Book Review*.

Manea's most powerful indictment of Ceaușescu and his followers is in his essay "On Clowns: The Dictator and the Artist." He takes his inspiration from the films of Charlie Chaplin (*The Great Dictator* in particular) and the Italian director Federico Fellini in which clowns play the roles of both hero and villain and the political state is a circus. The artist assumes the role of clown as a protective mask. In the 1981 interview to which Manea refers above (reprinted in *On Clowns*) he said: "The artist cannot 'dignify' officialdom by opposing it in a solemn fashion, because that would mean taking it too seriously, and inadvertently reinforcing its authority, thus acknowledging that authority. He pushes the ridiculous to grotesque proportions, but artistically, he creates . . . a surfeit of meaning." Manea assumed this role in a satirical series he called *Anii de ucenicie ai lui August Prostul* (Auguste the Fool's apprenticeship years), collecting clippings from the jargon-filled periodicals of the years 1949 to 1965, "To suggest the atmosphere in which a young man— who is rather open, vaguely melancholic, probably intelligent, thirsting for culture, art, anything that might transcend the constraints of daily life—might have been able to shape or misshape his character."

The ultimate absurdity is recounted in his essay "Censor's Report," on how the censors challenged his manuscript of *Plieul Negru* (The Black Envelope). Under pressure from his publisher Manea rewrote the book with "ambiguous solutions" in order to "subtly undermine the censor's demands." As he notes in the essay: "It is at this point that this inevitable duplicity weighs heavily on the captive writer." Manea's sweetest revenge is in printing the censor's report itself, revealing without comment its utter absurdity. Nevertheless the experience of censorship and compromise was the final blow. Having lived since 1981 in imminent danger of arrest and imprisonment, Manea applied for a travel visa in 1986, three years before the Ceaușescu regime was overthrown. "How could one 'resist' in this world of the absurd?" Manea asks in another essay in *On Clowns*, "The History of an Interview." "Isn't every attempt to be authentic, to rehabilitate the truth, inevitably prey to manipulation and defacement?"

Manea challenges his readers with a style that seems purposely oblique. There are passages that read like prose poems: "the sky glints like a new knife . . . the parks rustle with tangos . . . the beach lies dead under a grayish sky." For John Updike this was a fault, but he reminded his readers that the stories had been published originally in Romania in 1981 at the height of Communist power. Manea had to answer to the censor for his work, and "veiled language" was the only means through which he could express himself. The reader also detects in this guarded style the author's self-defense against the full horrors of his experiences. Furthermore, as John Bayley pointed out in writing of *October, Eight O'Clock* in the *New York Times Book Review*, the occasional "overkill" may be the result of translations (many of the English-language versions of his work have been made from French and German translations) and / or Manea's "own linguistic consciousness. Romanian is a Romance language, rich with Central European borrowings but related principally to French and Italian, and its weakness from a writer's point of view may be the natural indulgence of fine writing." Marguerite Driou wrote in *World Literature Today* in 1991 of a French translation of his stories: "Were it not for the great beauty of the writing, the pain inflicted by the reading of these brilliant pieces could be prohibitive."

The Black Envelope, Manea's fifth book, is "set against the repressions and deceptions of the Ceausescu regime in the 1980s" according to *Publishers Weekly*. A man who has descended from being a teacher, a highly respected position, to being a receptionist in a hotel takes a vacation when he learns he may lose even that lowly job. He embarks on a series of investigations, one of them "for the head of a nefarious association of deaf and mute people, whose physical disabilities mirror the moral ailments of Communist Romania." The *Publishers Weekly* reviewer concluded that although somewhat " gnomic," the "frequently beautiful language (even in translation) and the distinctive melancholy humor of Manea's voice amply reward a diligent reader's concentration." Larry Wolff, in the *New York Times Book Review* noted that "Manea's novel proposes an evil continuity from the murderous anti-Semitism of the war years to the more general persecutions of the Communist regime." Manea's novel, he concluded, "offers striking images and insights into the recent experience of Eastern Europe—'our own unlikely parts, with their ultra-coded laughter and tears, which are missing from the map of the world.'"

Louis Begley, a Holocaust survivor himself, pointed out in the *New York Review of Books* that Manea had set out "to elucidate the meaning of survival . . . the result of survival being an existence deprived of freedom and hope, bounded by the catastrophes of the Holocaust and the totalitarian state." The question, Begley wrote, is "whether life in such conditions is worth the effort it takes to live it." Begley finds the answer in the last lines of "Proust's Tea": "If later, I lost anything, it was precisely the cruelty of indifference. But only later, and with difficulty. Because, much later, I became what is called a feeling being."

PRINCIPAL WORKS IN ENGLISH TRANSLATION: *Fiction*—(tr. C. Golna, A. Hollo, M. Soceanu Vamos, M. Bleyleben, and M. Dorian) October, Eight O'Clock, 1992; (tr. L. Coverdale) Compulsory Happiness, 1993. *Nonfiction*—(tr. A. Bley-Vroman, C. Golna, and A. Hollo) On Clowns: The Dictator and the Artist, 1992; (tr. P. Camiller) The Black Envelope, 1995.

ABOUT: Tucker, M (ed.) Literary Exile in the Twentieth Century, 1991. *Periodicals*—(Jewish) Forward June 26, 1992; Los Angeles Times May 23, 1993; Nation October 12, 1992; New Criterion October 1992; New Republic June 1, 1992; New York Review of Books September 24, 1992; New York Times June 8, 1993; New York Times Book Review June 21, 1992; May 30, 1993; June 25, 1995; New Yorker November 7, 1992; Publishers Weekly May 22, 1995; Times Literary Supplement December 6, 1991; October 22, 1993; April 29, 1994; Washington Post May 17, 1992; World Literature Today Spring 1990, Summer 1990, Summer 1991.

MARKÓ, BÉLA (September 8, 1951–), Hungarian (Transylvanian) poet, was born in Tîrgu-Mureş. (Kézdivásárhely) where his father, an agronomist, taught at the agricultural school. His mother, Berta Bedó, had worked for the postal service before her marriage, but afterwards stayed home to raise two sons. While themselves already urban, both parents came of Székely peasant stock, the grandparents having been farmers of moderate means. Markó's roots thus are in the Székely segment of Hungarians in Romania. The Székelys, a people closely related to the Hungarians, were given the task of protecting the borders and of serving in the van- and rear guards of the armies, comprising one of the "nations" that guided the political fortunes of Transylvania into modern times. In the multiethnic society of Romania, and particularly of Transylvania, such a background leaves its mark more than class, religion, or politics. Markó attended schools in his native city and in 1970 enrolled at the Babes-Bolyai University in Cluj (Kolozsvár). Having been interested in literature since childhood—he had written poems and published in juvenile anthologies—he studied Hungarian and French.

After graduation, Markó was sent to Sîntana de Mureş (Marosszentanna) as a French teacher. In 1976 he became an editor at the periodical *Igaz szó* (True Word) and moved to Tîrgu-Mureş, where he has lived since. He married Enikó Molnos from Oradea (Nagyvárad) in 1973 and they had two children.

At *Igaz szó* Markó started a new periodical to give a voice to younger writers and contemporary literary products, but it lasted only a short while before the censor intervened. Although his activities were concentrated on literature, he did not escape the attention of the Romanian dictator Ceauşescu's secret police. But compared to the treatment of some of his fellow writers, he considered his interrogations hardly worth mentioning. Significantly, his 1984 volume *Talanítás* (Libera; literally deprivation or nothingness) was interdicted: nothing could be written about it; it was forbidden even to mention the work. Similarly, his 1980 text on Hungarian literature for twelfth-grade students was proscribed in 1983. As a vindication of sorts, after the fall of Ceauşescu the text was reissued and again used.

With the deepening of cultural repression in Ceauşescu's Romania, Markó had difficulty in providing a literary and stylistic background to the study of literature in the strictly censored texts and curricula of the day. He therefore turned his regular feature article on literature and the schools into a series of poetic critiques. The experience, he pointed out to Tibor Keresztúri in an interview in 1990, was useful for him; he had to provide an outline of the whole of Hungarian literature and, at the same time, he could develop his own poetic aesthetics. The poem, he concluded, cannot be removed from its context. The poet, his age, his community cannot be ignored. He learned that literature cannot be created in isolation: "It is not worthwhile to step out of tradition. You have to submit yourself to this centuries-old stream so that it can sweep you towards 'new waters.'" He asserted: "there is a unified Hungarian tradition, and we [Transylvanians] also are a part of this." During the years at *Igaz szó* he continued writing and twelve volumes appeared by 1989. With the publication of *Mindenki autóbusza* (Everybody's bus) in Hungary he was more widely recognized. In 1990 he received the Füst Milán prize and in 1991 the Déry Tíbor award—both prestigious Hungarian literary awards.

The repressive Romanian dictatorship was somewhat relaxed during his adolescence and youth, enabling him to become a member of the newly revived Gábor Gaál Literary Circle and serve as its president from 1971 to 1973. The association proved to be one of the most important opportunities for his generation, for it gave them a chance not only to work in the literary and cultural sphere but to prepare—even if indirectly—for public life.

December 1989 brought significant changes in his life as well as in the fate of his country. He was among the protesters at Tîrgu-Mureş and became a member of the county's first revolutionary council. With four colleagues he founded the Hungarian Democratic Alliance of Romania in Maros County. Becoming more and more involved in politics, he was elected president of the Alliance. He also stood for elections to parliament and was sent to Bucharest as a senator by the region. In 1993 he was reelected. Of his political goals he has said: "My program is, I believe, not a personal but a common one: it seeks to assure the independence of the Hungarians in Romania, including the support for various forms of autonomy." This is not far from his poetic goals, for he has stated that in Eastern and Central Europe the poet has always been called upon to be a politician as well, "perhaps because even in the darkest years an inner resistance forced the writer to his calling. This is not a personal merit. Simply, true literature is always in opposition." Markó believes there is a need for literature to recapture its full heritage. This may not happen until later, "when the Hungarians of Transylvania have a healthy, functional literary and artistic milieu that progresses through 'natural breaths' and an even rhythm. And this is the result of an appropriate institutional structure. It is possible that by the time we reach that stage, the poem will no longer have the same import, or it will have merely the same importance that it does in western Europe: the occasional treat of humanistic intellectuals."

In 1974, while he was still a student, his first volume of poems, A Szavak városában (In the City of Words) appeared. The poems already manifest a command of image and metaphor to convey the yearnings of a generation whose life was circumscribed by the restrictions of the regime. "Egyszerú vers" (Simple song) closes with this poignant quatrain in E. M. Basa's translation:

Boys, while we were playing grown-up,
Someone absconded with the toys.
Does it not cause you pain, that nothing else
Is left, but to declare ourselves adults?

The dreams of youth do not lead to the actions of manhood; instead, manhood looms threaten-

ingly: ambitions, innocence, dreams all must be put aside. Nature is central in his poetry, and it is used both to suggest limitless possibilities and the deadening weight of the "Cultural Revolution" that shattered the illusions of freedom tantalizingly dangled in the late 1960s. In "Ének" (Song), love seems to inspire him with possibilities expressed in two exquisite images: a fish flinging itself out of the water to encompass the world and a star swaying on a thread that twangs, and falls against the silence as the silken thread breaks. The possibilities, of course, are deceptive. An even more telling indictment is given in "Kitömött madarak" (Stuffed birds) where he intimates that it only needs the dripping of a faucet, the slamming of a door, or the rustle of paper for the birds to remember the babbling of a brook, or the frightening sounds of the forest that will send them flying:

Open the windows!
And now, softly, count to a hundred!
Behind the dusty glass eye
That other one will gleam.

He uses the bird again as a symbol for the dehumanization of man by the regime in "A felboncolt madár" ("The Dissected Bird").

Even in this early work Markó's talent and a sense of his poetic mission were recognized. "Markó is already an accurate chronicler of the mood of the age," Árpád Farkas concludes rather obliquely in a review, although in introducing Markó Farkas had recognized that the young poet followed the tradition of the committed poets who "thought in terms of nation and nationality" as he sought to "make tangible the unattainable."

Markó's second volume Sárgaréz erszak (Yellow brass season), was seen as the work of a "secretive" poet who did not wish to share his life with the reader. The poems, written between 1974 and 1976, seem to focus on means and methods rather than actions or emotions. Attila Mózes's critique dances around the analysis of the poet's theme, probably to avoid the censor's veto: "If the poet, forced to be expository, attempts to cheat the reader of this, he does so because the spectacle—the subject of his own poetry—does this to him also." Markó, the reviewer concludes, reaches his goal after all: what he once glimpsed as a vision and saw in its fullness becomes the one possible explanation of his text. But the vision cannot be revealed: it can only be hinted at and circumscribed. The poems thus become expressions of possibilities that cannot be reached and of grotesque realities. For example, in "Szerelmes vers" (Love song) he describes two lovers embracing in a snowy landscape. The awkwardness of the situation reaches beyond the moment:

in this embrace encumbered by great-coats
in this ponderous bears' dance
in this cumbersome pattering
bending over each other
yet not reaching each other . . .
as we love each other
now forever in a fever
forever in a bears' dance
forever in great coats

—tr. E. M. Basa

In *Lepkecsontváz* (Butterfly-skeleton, 1980) Markó introduces the legend of the secretive poet. The critic János Székely called him a moving target that the reviewer cannot shoot down. The mask adopted in this volume, Markó was later to explain, is part of the dramatic dynamism between poet and poem. The free verse was seen by some as a betrayal of the Transylvanian heritage of traditional forms, but others recognized the value of experimentation with modern forms. In spite of the avant-garde tone, Markó did not abandon the themes of his earlier poetry. Surviving the tyranny of the dictatorship with a sound mind, he noted in a 1990 interview in *Alföld*, meant commitment to the same cause: all agreed that what existed could not be endured and that a new kind of society had to be constructed. "At my writing desk, I could be my own lord," Markó stated. "And poetry is not only a refuge; it is also a possibility for action."

Two volumes appeared in quick succession: *Az Örök halasztás* (Eternal procrastination, 1982) and *Szarkatelefon* (Magpie telephone, 1983). Free verse is still the dominant genre and the poet still seeks to express that which is not permitted to be stated. But he begins to realize that "one cannot live one's life in metaphors," and the images seem to have lost some of their earlier force. In "A szüntelen ellenszélben" (In the unceasing headwind) he gives voice to the poet who must create against all odds.

Talanítás finally brought the wrath of the state down on Markó. Here he comes closest to "setting down not only external reality, but the mood that seeks to fade, the emotions sentenced to die, the words choked inside, hidden faith and patience which one could marshall against the force that sought to homogenize all, the world of 'talanítás.' " The word itself was coined by Markó to suggest the state of deprivation. It is a word, as Vilmos Ágoston points out, that implies much, yet remains undefinable in concrete terms. In the world of "talanítás" someone is always being deprived of something, regardless of whether that something is of value to him or not. In these poems everything turns to dust and eternal winter seems to rule. The sense of negation is distilled in the title poem:

. . . to distribute the liberating tools for
to consider the security of the liberators against
that they may peacefully liberate when
that they may productively liberate where . . .

to liberate, -berate, -berate
liberating, -berating, -berating
liberators, -berators, -berators
we liberate, we -berate we -berate

—tr. S. Csiffary

By 1987 Markó was experimenting with new avenues of expression. While he always held the same poetic values, the means to their expression differed, and so at this time he turned to a more classical vein. *Friss hó a Könyvön* (Fresh snow on the book) is a collection of sonnets and coincides with the Hungarian postmodern movement. But Markó does not really follow that school: he believes in a progression of styles as the prerogative of the poet, but not in a hierarchical value system.

Another volume, *Egó évek* (Burning years) appeared in 1989, containing poems written between 1984 and 1987. These echo the mood of the 1982 and 1983 volumes and of *Talanítás*, where there is no escape from the omnipresent oppression except into oneself: "Do not wander! Do not travel! Do not hope!" he exclaims in the poem that takes the first phrase as its title:

Hide in your house! . . .
so that whoever
searches for you in boots and with dirty fingernails
will cry out . . .
there is nowhere to fly
there is nowhere to run to
there is nowhere to crawl to
only inward! and inward! and even further inward!
so that he will cry, scream, grovel
who reaches with covetous fingers
to inventory your desk, your drawers
the lap of your lover.

—tr. E. M. Basa

Retreat into an interior world is also at the heart of his *Mindenki autóbusza* (Everybody's bus) which appeared in Hungary as a sign of the considerable liberalization of literary policy there by 1989. While works by some Transylvanian authors had been recognized—for example, Andras Sütó's later dramas were given their first productions in Hungary, and periodicals such as *Alföld* published selections from this literature—the publication of a book that forced the acceptance of Hungarian literature as part of the common literary heritage in Transylvania caused a minor sensation. These poems could not be labeled "Romanian." They were universal and they were Hungarian. Not insignificantly, the change in literary policy allowed Markó the recognition he feared might never come. Now his words would be no more "a blind man's mirror."

Klara Szeles, in her review of *Mindenki autóbusza*, notes that until recently Hungarian literature in Romania was, in Markó's own word, "ghettoized." The language of the poems, she says, seems to be motivated by "a sense of responsibility stricken by the knowledge of impotence. The message is one of encouragement without the depreciation of danger."

Tibor Zalán's review in *Könyvvilág* (Bookworld) similarly appreciates Markó's craftsmanship: "He seeks, beyond the harmony of words, an individual philosophy and a resigned peace, who sets as his goal a seemingly serene reflection, independent of the ever-increasing weight of external circumstances." Zalán emphasizes Markó's ability to use poetry as a means of preserving his wholeness and integrity: "When he looks up, he sees his own fate in the stars; when he looks before his feet, his life flashes by on the blade of grass, and his death swings softly upon it."

In the cycle of sonnets entitled "Költók koszorúja" (Wreath of poets) Markó uses the sonnet to dissolve "the bounds of time. . . ." He "steps out of the moment into the vista of the centuries of Hungarian literature," Szeles writes. The sonnet of course is a lyric, and as such it is a personal expression. Markó makes the sonnets into monologues that fit the ostensible speaker, whether Janus Pannonius in the 15th century or Miklós Radnóti in the 20th, yet they also speak for himself. Included in this full cycle of 100 sonnets are some from earlier volumes, but they are fitted organically into the structure that closes with fourteen tributes to Hungarian poets and a fifteenth, which expresses Markó's own ars poetica.

Throughout the years of oppression Markó was fully aware of the game he played with the authorities. Noting that the censors feared stylistic innovations even more than variations on traditional garb, he poured into the sonnet thoughts that were forbidden in Transylvania in the 1980s. In a country and at a time when the Hungarian population was forbidden to use its own language, when its schools and cultural institutions were being closed, when its history was falsified to make people feel like strangers in the land of their birth, and when official policy hinted that they should simply disappear, this poetic appeal to all-but-buried emotions was powerful. The concept of homeland (*haza*) gains new meaning in these poems, shedding the clichés of government propaganda. In the opening poem, "Janus Pannonius," the great Renaissance humanist struggles with the problem of where his true home lies:

I live as a Hungarian, and now I still do not know

whether this raw region, where my mouth is still sweet from my mother's milk, is my home

or if I am merely at home here?
—tr. E. M. Basa

PRINCIPAL WORKS IN ENGLISH TRANSLATION: (tr. N. Kolumban) "Fall cleaning" in Massachusetts Review, Winter 1991/1992; (tr. S. Csiffary) "The Dissected Bird" in Visions International 41, 1993.

ABOUT: Basa, E. M. Béla Markó's "Költók koszorúja": A Personal Commitment to Humane Values, Modern Language Association Conference, New York, 1992; Basa, E. M. *introduction to* Papers are the Poems of Béla Markó, American Hungarian Educators' Association Conference, College Park, Maryland, 1993.

MARTIN, VALERIE (METCALF) (March 14, 1948–   ), American novelist, and writer of short stories writes: "I was born in Sedalia, Missouri. Sedalia was my father's hometown to which he had returned with his family, my mother and older sister, after World War II. During the war he had served in the merchant marines. After three or four years of working as a traveling liquor salesman, he made the decision to go to New Orleans, where my mother's family lived, and to seek employment with a shipping company. We moved to New Orleans when I was three and stayed there. Eventually my father became a captain for Lykes Brothers Shipping Company. He was an infrequent but nevertheless impressive presence in our house.

"I attended public grammar schools in New Orleans, followed by a Catholic girls' high school run by Carmelite nuns. Though I was not a Roman Catholic, I became interested in Catholicism and particularly in books about the lives of the saints. Our school library had a large selection of hagiography which I read avidly. I was impressed by the writings of St. Theresa of Avila and St. Francis of Assisi. New Orleans has a large Roman Catholic population (my mother had been raised Catholic but left the church when she married my father), and it was easy to find statues and paintings of the various saints, of angels, devils, and other miraculous creatures. My taste for the mystical and fantastic was also nourished by stories of the city itself, of voodoo and slavery, of the big plantations north and south of the city, of pirates, aristocrats, and the early settlers of New Orleans, many of whom had only come to avoid a prison sentence. The lush physical environment of the city, with its florid vegetation, strange, often dangerous wildlife (alligators, rats, swarms of plague-bearing mosquitoes) also acted on my imagination, resulting in a sensibility that could be described as Gothic,

VALERIE MARTIN

though it still seems to me a fairly realistic, practical take on what is actually out there.

"In 1964 I went to the University of New Orleans, at that time a new college housed in an abandoned naval base near Lake Pontchartrain. After graduating I was employed by the Louisiana Department of Public Welfare, processing applicants for food stamps. I spent one year in graduate school at Louisiana State University in Baton Rouge, where I learned it was possible to obtain an M.F.A. degree in creative writing, a relatively new degree program, which was offered at only a few universities, none of them near my home. I was curious about the Northeast. Like many a southerner, I believed it to be a place of great intellectual superiority and cultural activity. I applied to the University of Massachusetts at Amherst where I was accepted and where I spent two years overcoming with ease my feelings of inferiority.

"In the years following my graduation from the University of Massachusetts in 1974, I took various teaching positions, at the University of New Orleans, New Mexico State University in Las Cruces, and the University of Alabama at Tuscaloosa. I also worked for the welfare department again, and as a waitress and a clerk in a children's bookstore. Between 1974 and 1984 I wrote five books: *Set In Motion* and *Alexandra*, published in 1978 and 1979 by Farrar, Straus and Giroux; *A Recent Martyr* and *The Consolation of Nature*, published much later in 1988 and 1989 by Houghton Mifflin, and 'The Perfect Waitress,' which was never published. In 1985 I moved back to New England to take a teaching

position at Mt. Holyoke College. There I wrote two novels, 'The Earth as Seen from the Moon,' which has never been published, and *Mary Reilly*, which was published by Doubleday in 1990. In 1988 I took a teaching position at the University of Massachusetts in the writing program from which I had graduated and where I am presently employed.

"I have been married and divorced twice, and have one daughter, Adrienne Metcalf Martin, who was born in 1975."

The influence of Valerie Martin's formative years in New Orleans is evident throughout her fiction, not only in the setting of several of her novels but in the atmosphere that pervades her narratives, linking setting to theme. The oppressive heat and humidity of the city and its decaying buildings lends a gothic aura to Martin's contemporary stories and reinforces the polarities in her fiction: danger / safety, fear / consolation, evil / good, darkness / light. Her novels and short stories present protagonists struggling with the tensions implicit in these contrasts.

Valerie Martin's early short story collection *Love* is informed by a theme that is consistent in her subsequent fiction—people trapped in darkness that often masquerades as light who find that true illumination is both costly and rare. The opening line of the title story, "The man I am talking to wants to kill me," reflects the element of psychological tension often characteristic of Martin's protagonists. In "Love" a social worker imagines the threat presented by the black, male client she is interviewing: "We have a table between us but it's a small table and he could grab me by my hair and pull me forward easily, turning my body away as he pulled me by the hair so that I could be stretched backward across the table and he could bring the blade down along my throat."

That the encounter proves harmless, that rather than inflicting harm, the client saves the woman from a serious fall, does not mitigate the woman's conviction about the adversarial nature of the relationship. It is as though an inherent quality of love that exists among people is continually negated by the climate of suspicion in which both the social worker and her client are forced to live.

The darkness Martin explores in *Love* is most evident in "Surface Calm," the story of Ellen, a young wife who copes with the tension of her husband's absence on a business trip through progressive episodes of self-mutilation. The sense of hidden depths that can erupt in an outwardly controlled life is also at the heart of the protagonist's crisis in *Set in Motion*, Martin's first published novel. The narrator, Helene Thatcher, is a New Orleans social worker, but the professional competence she displays helping others masks her inability to extricate herself from damaging relationships with three destructive men. Reviewing *Set in Motion* for the *New York Times*, Anatole Broyard commented that "Martin's characters seem to have passed beyond disillusionment into a deeper stratum of behavior." *Kirkus Reviews* reported that "Martin truly, acutely involves us with every pitch and toss of a lady straining to keep an even keel. . . . She coolly and efficiently traces the waterbug skittering in and around contemporary psychic hurts."

Helene Thatcher's interior darkness is magnified in the setting of Valerie Martin's second novel, *Alexandra*. The story is narrated by Claude, an unremarkable, middle-aged government worker whose attraction to the enigmatic Alexandra results in his abandonment of his job and city apartment to accompany the young woman deep into the bayou to the estate of her pregnant, very rich, and equally enigmatic friend Diana. In reviewing *Alexandra* for the *New York Times*, Francine du Plessix Gray concluded: "Valerie Martin's finest attribute is her skill in creating psychological atmosphere through a detailed depiction of place. Her description of the oppressive, subtropical Louisiana landscape is continuously suggestive of . . . dark currents of violence and unsolved crime. . . ."

Claude's renunciation of his life in New Orleans to follow the quixotic Alexandra is similar to Helene's attraction to the disturbed males in *Set in Motion*. The characters' dissatisfaction with the stable and ordinary lives they lead is reflected in the somewhat aberrant relationships they seek. In a *Publishers Weekly* interview, Valerie Martin commented on this aspect of her fiction: "I think my books mostly have to do with a search for another kind of reality besides the mundane everyday existence of the characters. It's a notion of liberation from the self, which we tend to seek in different places, in love and sex, for instance." With Helene and Claude, Martin explores psychic territory that will be common to the protagonists in her subsequent novels.

Another authorial interest evident in the early stories of *Love* is in the evocation of the numinous, most explicitly in "Messengers." In that story, three creatures appear to a man at breakfast one morning and announce that he is about to have the worst day of his life. He hides the incident from his wife and attributes it to a hallucination, which he plans to report to a psychiatrist when he gets to work. Before he can make that call, he is summoned to the hospital. His wife, injured in an accident, is suffering pain that physicians are unable to alleviate. Tortured by his wife's cries of agony, the man is again visited by his three messengers who tell him to burn his house, "burn everything." When he does this, his wife lapses into unconsciousness, finally relieved of her pain. Soon the doctor announces that there is no hope, and the man is visited by a blissful awareness of his wife's presence that "flooded through him like a flash of light, leaving a sweet taste in his mouth, a warm lassitude in his limbs, and an unfathomable serenity in his chest."

The juxtaposition of horror and spiritual transcendence in "Messengers" is central to Martin's third novel, *A Recent Martyr*, a starkly graphic yet symbolic narrative. The novel details the sadomasochistic affair between a married New Orleans woman, Emma Miller, and Pascal Toussaint. Their decadent liaison is mirrored in a deteriorating city whose citizens are threatened by a virulent plague. Through Pascal, Emma meets Claire, a young woman who had entered a cloistered religious order but has been sent home to reconsider her vocation. Claire expresses her desire for sainthood with a fervor that even the nuns find disquieting. She is the martyr of the title, later murdered in an incident of apparently random violence. Claire's death seems to be symbolic of the futility in trying to cloister oneself from the ordinary and the "horror" that is, in Martin's perspective, inherent in the physical world.

Earlier in the novel, when the plague causes the city to impose a quarantine, the two women are isolated together apart from Pascal, and Emma becomes fascinated with the idealistic Claire. In her affair with Pascal, Emma reported that she discovered "the sweet and unexpected horror of [her] own nature." But Emma's identification of Claire as an image of her better self enables her eventually to leave Pascal and resign herself to the ordinary life she had been unconsciously seeking to transcend through that liaison. As the novel ends, Emma describes the recovering city: "The future holds a simple promise. We are well below sea level, and inundation is inevitable. We are content, for now, to have our heads above the water." These words are equally self-referential, expressing the temporary equilibrium that is the best a Valerie Martin protagonist can achieve. In Martin's world, "inundation is inevitable." Danger and horror are inherent parts of the human condition, and contentment is at best momentary. In the work of another author, the elements of erotic fear and physical violence in the novel might have been sensational. But, as Carolyn Banks explained in the *New York Times Book Review*: "We are told these things . . . in Emma's voice, always steady, clear, elegant and direct. This places all that the novel contains—the heavily symbolic, the wildly coincidental, the lurid, the hideous—in high relief."

In 1988, Martin published her second short story collection, *The Consolation of Nature and Other Stories*, a volume that the author originally titled "Dead Animal Stories." While the original title may be infelicitous, it is accurate, for the stories in this collection focus on the deaths of animals and the epiphany those deaths engender for the human protagonists. Some characters recognize their own spiritual death in the physical death of an animal; for other protagonists the animal is emblematic of the negative forces of life that, however frightening, can be controlled. The rat that besieges a family in the title story exemplifies such negative forces. When the animal is finally killed, the child Lily thinks about its meaning: "She wasn't certain that he wouldn't seek her out again, but, she thought, he would never again seek her in that particular form. His menace had quite gone out of that form. . . . She returned to her bed, possessed of a strange fearlessness; it was as insistent as her own heartbeat, and as she drifted off to sleep it swelled and billowed within her and she understood, for the first time, that she was safe."

The rat in "The Consolation of Nature" that threatens the young girl's sense of safety will recur in a formative experience for Mary Reilly, the title character in Martin's fourth novel. However, "The Parallel World" also provides a gloss on the horror that is a characteristic element in Martin's fiction. Less a short story than an extended reflection, "The Parallel World" is narrated by a woman who longs to be absorbed into nature. It culminates when she wakes to a monstrous reflection, "for in the mirror she finds, beneath her eyelids, two wide, cold, black discs where her eyes should be, two insect eyes many-faceted and terrifying." However, "though she is a horror, she is not afraid, for this is her secret: she exists inside another woman, a very ordinary woman with an ordinary face."

This is a basic Valerie Martin theme. In *Alexandra* and *Set in Motion*, the protagonists mask the face of horror in their mundane lives but are nevertheless attracted to its revelation. In *A Recent Martyr*, Emma is drawn to the horror of the hidden self in her affair with Pascal and only retains equilibrium through association with Claire.

In 1988, John Irwin Fischer described Valerie Martin as "a major writer on the verge of being famous." That description seemed prophetic two years later when her fourth novel, *Mary Reilly*, resulted in Martin's first commercial success. The novel was reviewed in *Time* and *Newsweek* and its author profiled in *Harper's Bazaar* and interviewed by Dulcy Brainard for *Publishers Weekly*. In *Mary Reilly*, her first novel set outside of 20th-century New Orleans, Valerie Martin seems to have charted a new course. But her retelling of the Jekyll and Hyde story from the perspective of the housemaid is another expression of her consistent themes. As Michiko Kakutani pointed out in a *New York Times* review, "An obsession with the conflict between good and evil, reason and irrationality; a melodramatic use of horror; a preoccupation with man's bestial impulses and the natural dangers that lurk around the edges of our fragile civilization— each of these aspects of 'Dr. Jekyll and Mr. Hyde' can also be found in the work of Valerie Martin, a writer who has specialized in creating modern tales of gothic suspense."

In *Mary Reilly*, Martin's effective use of atmosphere to render the characters' psychological states is evident in the aura of the Jekyll household with its reticent master and mysterious assistant, all enveloped in the dense and persistent London fog. Martin's interest in the horror she sees within the apparently ordinary person provides her with a natural affinity for Robert Louis Stevenson's tale of the unfortunate Jekyll who unwittingly released the horror of Hyde, but she focuses the reader's attention on the hidden depths of the demure housemaid, Mary Reilly, unnamed in the original story. Mary's eventual discovery of the truth about Jekyll's nemesis provides an intriguing narrative framework in which Martin depicts the struggle of the housemaid to transcend the horrors of her past. Abused as a child by a brutal, alcoholic father, Mary Reilly has been in service since the age of twelve and has learned that there is safety in keeping "one's place" in the servant hierarchy. But she imperils that safety in her developing attachment to her solicitous employer.

With Mary, Martin explores the complexity in the tension between good and evil. The sober housemaid rigorously follows the rules of propriety for servants. But the kindly attentions of the beleaguered Jekyll rouse the housemaid's sentiments, and, in her devotion to her master, Mary transcends the limits of servile decorum and ultimately, she is discovered in a compromising situation that bodes ill for her future in service. Ironically, it is not the stereotypically evil Hyde but the benevolent Jekyll who creates problems for Mary. As Martin commented in an interview, one of her goals was to get beyond Stevenson's rather reductive notions about the nature of good and evil: "I don't believe one can be simply a force for good. . . . That's a kind of vanity. It's Jekyll's undoing." However, it is not only Stevenson's notions that are undercut in this novel but Mary's naive expectation that she can find a place of safety in the world. In Valerie Martin's fiction, danger is an ever-present reality.

A fiction as haunting and atmospheric as Valerie Martin's almost invites cinematic treatment. *Mary Reilly* was adapted for film. Its successor, *The Great Divorce*, is also cinematic—at least in its origins. Several reviewers of the novel noted its similarities to a cult film of 1942, *Cat People*. That film is set in New Orleans and has for its central character a young woman who is the victim of an ancient family curse, under which from time to time she becomes a black leopard preying on her rival. Martin's more ingenious and ambitious novel consists of three parallel narratives, all linked by a common motif—a black leopard. The principal story involves a New Orleans zoo veterinarian trying to salvage her marriage of twenty years. Her husband, infatuated with a younger woman, is writing a book about a 19th-century New Orleans belle who ripped out her abusive husband's throat, claiming that her spirit had been possessed by a black leopard. The third story centers on the veterinarian's assistant, a woman going over the edge, who wants to turn into a wild cat. Unrelated—or artificially related—as these stories seem at first, Michiko Kakutani observed in the *New York Times* (1994) that "Martin orchestrates their confluence with . . . verve, an air of authority that makes even their most implausible adventures feel emotionally vivid and real." Robert Houston, in the *New York Times Book Review* (1994), declared the book's controlling metaphor—divorce—is a preoccupation of Martin's in the sense that "divorce, from nature and from our own nature, is a central, irreversible attribute of civilization. . . . " and "in such a world, small victories for reconciliation, however futile, are worthy sources of comfort."

PRINCIPAL WORKS: *Short stories*—Love, 1977; The Consolation of Nature and Other Stories, 1988. *Novels*—Set in Motion, 1978; Alexandra, 1979; A Recent Martyr, 1987; Mary Reilly, 1990; The Great Divorce, 1994.

ABOUT: Contemporary Authors 85–88, 1980; Gandolfo, A. Testing the Faith; The New Catholic Fiction in America, 1992. *Periodicals*—Contemporary Literature 34, 1993; Extrapolation 34, 1993; Harper's February 1990; Kirkus Reviews April 15, 1978; Louisiana Literature 5, 1988; Newsweek March 12, 1990; New York Times June 23, 1978; January 26, 1990; February 18, 1994; New York Times Book Review August 5, 1979; June 7, 1987; January 31, 1988; February 4, 1990; March 13, 1994; Publishers Weekly April 10, 1978; February 9, 1990; Southern Review 24, 1988; Time February 19, 1990; Times Literary Supplement June 1, 1990; Washington Post March 4, 1990.

MASTERS, OLGA (LAWLER) (May 28, 1919–September 7, 1986), Australian novelist, short story writer, and journalist, was born to Leo and Dorcus (Robinson) Lawler in Pambula on the south coast of New South Wales. They were a poor family living in a small rural community. Olga was the second of eight children and was responsible for younger siblings and for home duties from an early age. Growing up in the great economic depression in Australia of the late 1920s–1930s, she was sensitive to the trauma and demoralization of men and women who were unable to find work and feed their families. The farming area was blighted by drought and overrun with rabbits; the people, especially the women, ignorant of family planning, suffered accordingly. Masters's later fiction documents family dynamics and the economic victimization of women with relentless clarity and irony. She wrote, for example, in *Amy's Children*: "Ted Fowler left his wife Amy and the children when the youngest, another girl, was a few weeks old. The infant was sickly. The Great Depression was in a much more robust state."

Olga Lawler was educated at St. Joseph's convent school and at the Cobargo public school; for economic reasons she was forced to leave school in 1934. In 1935 she worked as a cub reporter on the *Cobargo Chronicle*, which she later described in a short story, "Here Blue," in *The Rose Francier*, as " a good bi-weekly newspaper." When this work ceased, she went to Sydney where she worked as a clerk in a menswear store and factory. The experiences of these years are reflected in "Leaving Home" in *The Home Girls*, where a teenager growing up in a country town protests:

> All her youth spent with no money of her own, no job but helping a mother around the house, nothing to go to but the Berrigo show, and the Berrigo Sports and the Agricultural Ball where Berrigo's idea of decoration was to pile the stage with potatoes, pumpkins and marrows and cross stalks of corn around the walls! You felt like you were dancing in the farm sheds.

These early years shaped Masters's fiction, but it was not until she was fifty-eight years old that she began to write and publish her short stories and novels.

In 1939, when she was sharing lodgings with her sister in Sydney, Olga Lawler met a young teacher, Charles Masters, whom she married in 1940. Charles Masters's teaching positions took them to a variety of country towns in New South

Wales over the next ten years, and Masters later noted wryly, as Julie Lewis wrote in her biography, *A Lot of Living,* "she found herself returned to the situation from which she had fought to escape"—many pregnancies, little money, the demanding duties of a headmaster's wife in small country towns. She managed nevertheless to assert her independence. At thirty-five, after the birth of her sixth child, Masters began working as a part-time journalist, first in the timber town of Urbenville, then in Lismore, for the *Northern Star.* She wrote news of country life, reporting on cooking contests, needlework exhibits, and women who managed small businesses, for many years, but she did not write stories under her own name until the 1970s, when they began to appear in the *Manly Daily* in Sydney. In the introduction to a collection of her journalism, *Reporting Home,* published many years later, Deirdre Coleman noted that "during 1979, the International Year of the Child, she wrote a staggering number of articles about homeless and foster children in the Manly Warringah area. She never ceased to champion the struggle of working wives and mothers. Although acutely aware of the need to see the family as necessarily subject to the larger cultural and political forces, she strongly supported women who defended their families against outside intervention, particularly the tribes of 'experts'—the professional doctors, psychologists, social workers and child care specialists."

Masters's reputation was made with a collection of short stories, *The Home Girls,* and confirmed by her later fiction. There were early stories published in the *Cobargo Chronicle,* newspaper articles, a radio play, and a stage play in the 1970s. Between 1977 and 1981 she won nine prizes for her short stories; in 1983 she received a National Book Council Award for *The Home Girls.* Her last novel, *Amy's Children,* along with a collection of short stories and a collection of her journalism, were published posthumously after Masters died of a brain tumor in 1986.

The title story of *The Home Girls* is about foster children. In place of proper names, and the individuality they confer, her characters are designated as "the fat one," "the thin one," "the visitor," or "the foster mother." The sister of the host mother, who is the only person named, observes after witnessing the children's departing protest—lurid bathroom graffiti—"I'd kill you if I had you." To which the "fat one" replies: "Yes . . . and the 'thin one,' sounding as if they'd heard it before." The story emphasizes the gulf between the anxious foster mother's dutiful "doing everything [she] could" and genuine love. In the departing car, the children, who

have an acute sense of their dispensability, have already created a fiction out of their past experience. The implicit text speaks of the vulnerability of both children and adults beneath their overt insensitivity. It is the unspoken messages of the narrative that linger in the mind.

The short stories and novels that followed have the force of lived experience: Masters's own, as a woman, wife, and mother living in rural towns in New South Wales, and her working experience as a journalist. But the imaginative power of her fiction transcends social realism. Her writing is notable for its directness, economy, and psychological subtlety. Her characters reveal themselves through particularities of vocabulary, juxtapositions of dialogue, deft manipulation of imagery, and a carefully conveyed sense of repressed potentialities. Masters is funny, wise, compassionate, and wry as she observes, records, and comments on her life and times. She does not waste words: "In the middle of December the fourteenth child was born. I lived but Sarah didn't," she writes in "The Boy With Two Birthdays" (in *The Rose Fancier*). Her imagery is poetic but usually drawn from domestic life. She writes in "A Lovely Day" in *The Rose Fancier:*

The day was like a newly bathed baby. You would expect to hear it chuckle as a baby does when tickled with a towel. It had the fresh smell that soap has and a sprinkle of powder scented with lavender. A steel grey cloud had opened a slit of an eye and beamed some orange light on the houses packed together on the eastern hill. The gardens looked fresh from the bath too, which was not all that surprising because there had been a heavy dew. The tops of shrubs were smeared with a fine netting, as if someone had dipped a brush in a bucket of cobwebs and painted over them.

Deirdre Coleman attributes much of Masters's artistry to her career as a journalist. "[T]he continuity between journalism and fiction manifests itself in the desire to make a story, to develop the germ of a human interest assignment, no matter how unpromising at first sight, into an economical and satisfying narrative. . . . [W]hen one considers the powerful economy of Masters's fiction, newspaper work taught her the value of the old journalistic adage on length: 'just give it what it's worth.'"

Masters shows great awareness of sexual politics in many short stories and in her novels. In *Loving Daughters,* two sisters become rivals for the attention of a young unmarried clergyman who comes to their small town. Depending on his choice, one of the sisters will be cast as the lifetime housekeeper for their widowed father and their brothers; the other will escape to become the housekeeper of the parish. Howard Frank Mosher, reviewing the novel in the *New*

York Times Book Review referred to "the sly—and often comical—eroticism that pervades the entire novel." Mosher notes that the clergyman, after his marriage, is "always on the lookout for the main chance" and "has a scheme that in one way or another will serve nearly everyone's most private interests (especially his own). In fact, the single life of the woman he didn't marry may . . . turn out to be . . . livelier than her brief, disappointed courtship." Terming *Loving Daughters* a "subtly passionate novel," Mosher concludes that by "refusing to idealize the Herberts and their idiosyncratic neighbors, Olga Masters achieves an unusually honest empathy with them." As Masters states (in *Rooms of Their Own*): "All my writing is about human behaviour. There's not much drama, no great happenings in it. No violence. It's about the violence that's inside the human heart, I think, more than anything else."

A seminar devoted to the works of Olga Masters was organized by the University of Wollongong in 1988. The papers presented, collected under the title *Olga Masters: An Autumn Crocus*, were published in 1990.

PRINCIPAL WORKS: *Short stories*—The Home Girls, 1982; A Long time Dying, 1985; The Rose Fancier, 1988. *Novels*—Loving Daughters, 1984; Amy's Children, 1987. *Journalism*—Reporting Home, 1990. *Play*—A Workingman's Castle, 1989.

ABOUT: Coleman, Deirdre *introduction to* Reporting Home, 1990; Contemporary Authors 121, 1989; 135, 1992; Daniel, H. The Good Reading Guide, 1989; Ellison, J. Rooms of Their Own, 1986; Lewis, J. A Lot of Living, 1991; McGraw, W. and Sharrad, P. (eds.) Olga Masters: An Autumn Crocus, 1990. *Periodicals*—Australian Literary Studies May 1987; Commonwealth Essays and Studies Spring 1991; New York Times Book Review May 16, 1993.

MAY, ROLLO (April 21, 1909–October 22, 1994), American writer and psychologist, sometimes called the father of American existentialist psychotherapists, was born in Ada, Ohio, but spent most of his boyhood in Michigan. The second child and eldest son of Earl and Matie Boughton May, he was later to say that he had felt closer in childhood to his father, a field secretary for the YMCA, than to his mother, who had named him after "Little Rollo," the hero of a series of character-building books for children. In an interview in the *New York Post* in 1972, May recalled having hated his "sissy" name and feeling that his Victorian mother did not find him "acceptable." He pictured himself as a loner in childhood. He had, however, he said, enjoyed athletics, particularly swimming.

ROLLO MAY

May began college at Michigan State but soon transferred to Oberlin, where he majored in English and minored in Greek history and literature, subjects which were to interest him all his life. After obtaining a B.A. degree in 1930, he went to Salonika, Greece, where he taught English for three years at Anatolia College. During his two summer vacations abroad he visited Vienna to attend seminars conducted by the psychoanalyst Alfred Adler and to study painting with Joseph Binder. Adler, who had challenged Freudian theory by stressing the importance of social and cultural elements in human development, was one of the first psychologists to have an impact on May's thinking.

Still uncertain what he wanted to do with his life, May returned to America in 1933 and enrolled in the Union Theological Seminary in New York, not with the aim of becoming a preacher or YMCA secretary like his father, but to continue what had already become for him an avid quest to know more about the human condition. His studies were interrupted for two years when his parents divorced and he felt obliged to return home to look after his younger siblings, but he returned to Union and earned his bachelor of divinity degree in 1938. The theologian Paul Tillich, who was one of May's teachers in his final years at Union and who had recently written two books dealing with the religious and cultural dilemmas facing 20th-century man, impressed him deeply. Although May abandoned the ministry after two years of leading a Congregational parish in New Jersey, he found inspiration in Tillich's ideas, which borrowed widely from depth psychology, existentialist philosophy, and art history, and the two men remained friends throughout Tillich's lifetime. May's first two books, *The Art of Counseling: How to Gain and Give Mental Health*, and *Springs of Creative Living: A Study of Human Nature and God* were published during this time.

The eighteen-month period that May subsequently spent at a sanitarium for tubercular patients in upstate New York was a turning point in his life. Having contracted tuberculosis in his early thirties and been given a fifty-fifty chance of survival, he learned to face life at the sanitarium, as he put it later, through having to face death. Realizing that his recovery depended less on medical care than on his own struggle against death, he came to believe, as other existentialist thinkers had before him, that man's will was centrally important in determining his destiny. Later, as a therapist, this same idea inspired some of the techniques he devised for treating patients.

At some point while working as a minister in New Jersey, May apparently came to the conclusion that he could more effectively help people with their problems as a psychologist than as a preacher. By this time he had not only read widely in psychology but had also, during the two years he'd spent at home after his parents' divorce, worked as a counselor to male students at Michigan State College. After leaving the sanitarium at Saranac, although not fully recovered, he worked as a student counselor at City College in New York while studying for a doctorate in clinical psychology at Columbia University. He earned his Ph.D. from Columbia in 1949.

The Meaning of Anxiety, May's doctoral dissertation, was published the following year. In this erudite but plainspoken book May attempted to synthesize the thinking of the many hundreds of American and European writers who had impressed him—such psychologists as Freud, Harry Stack Sullivan, and Fromm, and such philosophers as Tillich, Kierkegaard, and Nietzsche, as well as poets and novelists from ancient to modern times—while framing their ideas within a context of his own. The basic question he asked, after defining the differences between neurotic and normal anxiety, was this: How can modern people constructively use the normal anxiety-creating situations that everyone in the 20th century faces? His contention that all of us live in a world where the old values have been eroded and nothing any longer is certain was not new; others had been saying the same thing for some time. May's contribution was to put his ideas into psychological language that the ordinary person could understand, to suggest

that acknowledging anxious feelings rather than denying them could lead to an enrichment of human experience. Anxiety, he believed, when it is denied and defended against, as in the case of neurotics, leads to an impoverishment of personality; but anxiety, when confronted, opens people up to the world and leads to creative endeavor.

Before graduating from Columbia, May had joined the faculty at the William Alanson White Institute of Psychiatry, Psychoanalysis and Psychology in New York and had begun treating patients there. In *Man's Search for Himself*, which came out in 1953, he commented that his patients were making him aware that a chief problem in modern living was a feeling of "emptiness," the experience of feeling powerless to do anything effective about one's life or the world one lives in. May claimed that the same emptiness was felt by people who *had* "adjusted" and were not neurotic. Normal anxiety, he insisted, cannot be avoided; all of us in the mid-20th century share a wanting to be liked, accepted, and approved of, and when we lack this approval we feel threatened. But if we try only to fit in, we will in the end be resigning ourselves to disappointment, frustration, and finally to apathy; and in apathy there is no possibility of feeling and facing anxiety. "Our task, then, is to strengthen our consciousness of ourselves, to find centers of strength within ourselves which will enable us to stand despite the confusion and bewilderment around us."

How should this be achieved? May's answer was through courage—"an inward quality, a way of relating to oneself and one's possibilities" through moving from the "protecting realms of parental dependence to new levels of freedom and integration." In acquiring freedom, there would always be for the individual the risk of being ostracized, but this was the risk that must be taken; adaptation to the expectations of others was a false choice, undermining courage and leading to dependence on others' convictions.

Reviewers joined in hailing May's book as a valuable contribution to contemporary social thought. A. P. Davies, in the *New York Times* (1953), commented: "Most of this diagnosis has been made before, but seldom, if ever, with such persuasive clarity. . . . It analyzes life as we are living it, and the analysis is truthful and profound."

Another of May's books to reach a wide audience, *Love and Will*, published in 1969 while the author was a practicing psychoanalyst in New York City, repeated many of the themes he had introduced earlier, but this time he focused on the 1960s: the "banalization" of love in literature and art, people's preoccupation with sex as a substitute for real feeling, arising from a "nothing matters syndrome." As a continual observer of contemporary life, May viewed the 1960s in America as a time when despite the advantages of greater freedom, "anxiety and guilt have increased." "Making oneself feel less in order to perform better" had become the standard, he felt, and the violence of those who felt disoriented and helpless had surged in to fill the emptiness. John Leonard, in the *New York Times* (1969), reported enthusiastically that the book ought to lead "any list of important books published in 1969."

May's next book, *Power and Innocence*, evoked criticism from a few theologians. His definition of innocence—or, as he called it, pseudo-innocence—as a "common defense against admitting or confronting one's own power," a wanting to believe in one's virtue, led to the objection in *Commonweal* that "the only positive purpose this book can achieve is to sow the widest possible moral confusion." But May's chief point, "that innocence in our day is the hope that there are no enemies, that we can move into a new Garden of Eden, a community characterized by freedom from all want," posed challenging questions for others. William Hamilton, in the *Christian Century*, commented: "At the bottom of this wise, humane and admirable book rest two quite terrifying questions: Is America possible? Is Christianity possible?" May's observation that a new generation of Americans was turning its back on history, believing itself capable of discovering all the answers, affronted his deeply held belief in the Western humanist tradition that had nourished him. Commenting on the 1960s "innocence of believing that somehow one escapes the tragedies and complexities of life simply by being simple," he wrote: "It is an antihistorical viewpoint to insist that the mere fact of having been born a generation later guarantees any rightness in itself."

In *The Courage to Create*, May stressed one of his favorite themes, namely that creativity is a fundamental expression of a human drive to fulfill one's highest potential, not a compensatory or neurotic adaptation. *Freedom and Destiny* focused on another of May's basic concepts, that an individual is not truly free unless able to accept the limitation imposed by destiny. *The Discovery of Being: Writings in Existential Psychology*, published in 1983, brought together several essays in which the author examined the theoretical and cultural roots of existential psychology. "Any therapist is existential," May argued, "to the extent that, with all his knowledge of transference and dynamisms, he is still able to relate to the patient as one existence communi-

cating with another." He likened his own crisis at the tubercular sanitarium to the crises his patients were going through, pointing out that their "adjusting" to life's problems was "exactly what a neurosis is . . . a necessary adjustment by which a person's centeredness can be preserved, a way of accepting *nonbeing* in order that some little *being* may be preserved." May stressed that what patients needed above all from therapy, if they were to arrive at a state of "being" rather than "nonbeing," was an "experience" of relationship with the therapist rather than cut-and-dried interpretations. His reception from the press was favorable but moderate. Marvin Geller, in *Science Books and Films*, commented that while the book would "serve as an excellent general introduction" to the ideas underlying existential psychotherapy, it would probably "disappoint those in search of techniques and principles." Another writer, in *Choice*, felt the book was "vintage Rollo May" and would be found "illuminating and uplifting by some undergraduates."

The Cry for Myth, published in 1991, devotes much space to analyzing the meaning of many of the great myths which have come to us through literature, past and present—the search through Hell into enlightenment in Dante's *Inferno*, modern man's problem in living in Ibsen's *Peer Gynt*, the myth of power in Marlowe's and Goethe's different renderings of *Faust*, among others. For May, all myths carry the values of a society and help the individual to find a sense of identity. But today "most of us have been taught to think only in rationalistic terms," so we stress objective facts while turning our backs on those myths which point up the "quintessence of human experience, the meaning and significance of human life." Pointing out that children use myths to formulate a personal pattern and a way of life, he says that when children grow up in a mythic vacuum, and therefore in an ethical rootlessness, they have no basis for making sound judgments. "Myth and self-consciousness are to some degree synonymous." Lacking sustaining ethical myths, many people today in America make "heroes out of gangsters," clinging to the idea of "rugged individualism" and viewing perpetual change as the only important value. Basing his ideas in part on an observation of his patients, May postulates the need for rediscovering "myths which can give us the psychological structure necessary to confront widespread depression."

The Cry for Myth, Irvin Yalom, a noted psychiatrist and author, commented on the book's jacket, encapsulates "Rollo May's ability to transform the timeless wisdom of myth into a timely and brilliant commentary upon both contemporary culture and psychotherapy. The book is lucid, deep, powerful, and above all, wise. In a most effective manner he harnesses the power of myth and brings it to bear upon the struggle of the single individual to grow, to change and to heal."

May received many awards for his writings and contributions to science. Chief among them: in 1954 he won the annual award from the New York Society of Clinical Psychologists for outstanding contribution to the profession and science of clinical psychology; in 1970 he was awarded Phi Beta Kappa's Ralph Waldo Emerson Award for humane scholarship; in 1971, New York University honored him for distinguished contributions, and the American Psychological Association for distinguished contribution to the science and profession of clinical psychology. Most recently he received the Gold Medal of the American Psychological Society. He was a member (and past president) of the American Psychological Association, a fellow of the American Foundation for Mental Health, the National Council on Religion in Higher Education, and the Society of Arts, Religion, and Culture, a part of the William Alanson White Psychoanalytic Society.

May was married twice—first to Florence De-Frees in 1938, later in 1971 to Ingrid Scholl. Both marriages ended in divorce. He has three children, all by his first marriage.

PRINCIPAL WORKS: The Art of Counseling: How to Gain and Give Mental Health, 1939; The Springs of Creative Living: A Study of Human Nature and God, 1940; The Meaning of Anxiety, 1950; Man's Search for Himself, 1953; Existential Psychology, 1961; Psychology and the Human Dilemma, 1967; (with L. Caliger) Dreams and Symbols, 1968; Love and Will, 1969; Power and Innocence: A Search for the Sources of Violence, 1972; Paulus: Reminiscences of a Friendship, 1973; The Courage to Create, 1975; Freedom and Destiny, 1981; The Discovery of Being: Writings in Existential Psychology, 1983; My Quest for Beauty, 1985; (with A. Maslow and C. Rogers) Politics and Innocence: A Humanistic Debate, 1986; The Cry for Myth, 1991. As editor—(with E. Angel and H. Ellenberger) Existence: A New Dimension in Psychiatry and Psychology, 1958; Symbolism in Religion and Literature, 1960.

ABOUT: Contemporary Authors 111, 1984; Current Biography Yearbook 1973; Holbrook, D. New Dimensions in America: Rollo May et al, 1988. Periodicals—Choice November 1983; Christian Century March 11, 1970; Commonweal February 9, 1973; Journal of Counseling and Development April 1989; New York Times January 4, 1953; December 24, 1969; Science Books and Films May–June 1984.

McCARTHY, CORMAC (July 20, 1933–), American novelist, was born Charles McCarthy in Providence, Rhode Island, the oldest son of Charles McCarthy and Gladys McGrail. McCarthy grew up in Tennessee, where his father, a lawyer, worked for the Tennessee Valley Authority. Most of what is known of McCarthy's early life is derived from a brief autobiographical note printed on the dust jacket of his first novel, The Orchard Keeper. From this we learn that he grew up in rural surroundings near Knoxville, finished high school in 1951, and then attended the University of Tennessee briefly before dropping out and wandering the country. In 1953 he enlisted in the air force for four years, two of which were spent in Alaska, where he relieved the tedium of service life by reading widely. In a New York Times Magazine interview in 1992, one of the very few this intensely private writer has granted, we also learn that McCarthy returned to the University of Tennessee in the late 1950s, but dropped out again to live a hand-to-mouth existence in Chicago and New Orleans. He has been married twice: first to Lee Holleman, by whom he has a son, Cullen, and then to an English pop-singer, Annie DeLisle, from whom he is divorced.

It was not until 1992 with the publication of All the Pretty Horses, McCarthy's sixth novel, that he won the National Book Award, popular readership, and entered the best-seller lists, but his work has received enthusiastic critical acclaim since the appearance of The Orchard Keeper. The prizes and grants that he received for this novel, including awards from the American Academy of Arts and Letters, the William Faulkner Foundation, and the Rockefeller Foundation, sustained him during the writing of Outer Dark, his second novel, and later awards, including the prestigious MacArthur Foundation grant, which he received in 1981, have helped McCarthy live apart from the literary establishment. He never reads from his work, has never taught or lectured, shuns the company of other writers, and has avoided journalism as a means of support. Since 1976 he has lived in El Paso, Texas—"the best-kept secret in American letters," according to Newsweek. As Denis Donoghue observed in New York Review of Books in 1993: "McCarthy may be a recluse, but he is a famous one."

By his account, McCarthy began work on The Orchard Keeper in 1959 while still a student at the University of Tennessee, "but the necessities of life delayed its completion." In 1964 it caught the attention of Albert Erskine, the editor of William Faulkner, Malcolm Lowry, and Ralph Ellison. Erskine immediately recognized McCarthy's talent and continued to champion

CORMAC McCARTHY

his work for twenty years, despite the poor sales of his novels. Prepublication comments on *The Orchard Keeper* from such senior figures of the literary establishment as Malcolm Cowley and Ralph Ellison went beyond the gracious encouragement often extended to young writers. Cowley wrote: "[McCarthy] tells a story marvelously, with a sort of baresark joy as he rushes into scenes of violence. He loves the countryside and makes us feel how a poor boy grew up loving it." It is clear in hindsight that the novel contains all the strengths of McCarthy's later writing, especially his unusual ability to control and harmonize two distinct styles: the laconic, pithy speech of rural characters, and a lyrical narrative voice that is replete with bookish but aptly chosen diction and underlines the realism of the dialogue:

> They sipped their wine with the solemnity of communicants, troglodytes gathered in some firelit cave. The lamp guttered in a draft of wind and their shadows, ponderous and bearlike upon the wall, heaved in unison.

The novel is set in the Tennessee hills during Prohibition, and describes in a seemingly anecdotal way the life of a teenage boy, John Wesley Rattner, who observes and occasionally converses with two older men: Marion Sylder, a carefree bootlegger, and Arthur Ownby, an Appalachian mountain man and sage who lives alone with his aging hound in a remote cabin and clashes with authority when he shoots up a government water tank with his shotgun. The scene in which Ownby's cabin is surrounded by officers sent to capture him is the earliest instance of McCarthy's ability to describe violent

action with a gripping intensity that belies a contradictory tendency in his writing, often complained of by critics who find his descriptions of nature overwritten and literary.

Another persistent feature of McCarthy's work, a preoccupation with motiveless killing, is evident in what might be regarded as the book's central episode, a fight between Sylder and a threatening hitchhiker that ends in Sylder's panicked efforts to dump his nameless opponent's corpse in a disused reservoir. Ownby's discovery of the body, and his preoccupation with its unburied, unshriven, anonymous state, haunts both him and the reader and constitutes a connecting thread in what might otherwise seem a rambling narrative of scenes from rural boyhood.

The Orchard Keeper is not so much a novel in the conventional sense as it is a collection of scenes united by a common purpose whose presence is strongly felt but difficult to articulate precisely. McCarthy's allegorical, implicitly religious purpose does not become clear until the very end of the novel when Rattner muses on the gravestone of a relative:

> The dead sheathed in the earth's crust and turning the slow diurnal of the earth's wheel, at peace with eclipse, asteroid, the dusty novae, their bones brindled with mold and the celled marrow going to frail stone, turning, their fingers laced with roots, at one with Tut and Agamemnon, with the seed and the unborn.

Out of the novel's context, where this literary authorial tone is juxtaposed with authenticating realism, such writing seems pretentious, and has made McCarthy vulnerable to insinuations that he is a kind of minor, latter-day Faulkner; an heir to the Southern Gothic tradition of grotesque heightened realism. Comparisons with Faulkner, however, are both apt and misleading. Like Faulkner, McCarthy has an enormous vocabulary that serves, especially in descriptions of landscape and animals, a rich diction that could not possibly belong to his protagonists and can therefore seem imposed on the narrative in an effort to wring symbolic significance out of common events. Such flaws can be found in all his novels, but are invariably offset by the sheer variety of the novelist's range of effects, and the convincing realism of his dialogue, which gives many of his scenes the permanence of first-rate genre painting. Unlike Faulkner, McCarthy does not attempt a wide social canvas, and evolves all his generalization through close observation of behavior. Even his minor characters convince us with brief gestures. Nonetheless, McCarthy writes within a literary tradition dominated by Faulkner and Flannery O'Connor that had made the South an exotic locale, intensely civilized and yet peopled by grotesque exotics whose inner tensions threaten to break at any moment into inexplicable violence. Like O'Connor and Faulkner, McCarthy can also be very funny, as in a lengthy scene from *The Orchard Keeper* in which a bar, crudely constructed on the edge of a ravine, breaks loose from its foundations and deposits its drunken patrons into the undergrowth. Vital and uproarious though this scene is, it is clear that the rural drunks are suffering an appropriate fate, one that is not explicitly religious but carries elements of moral judgement.

The allegorical and apocalyptic undertones of McCarthy's writing are most evident in *Outer Dark* and *Child of God*, which added greatly to McCarthy's critical reputation but for the most part repelled the general reader. Both of these intense narratives are driven by a malignant and unrelieved sense of the immanence of evil and the futility of a Greek tragedy, and with no greater sense of the possibility of redemption or forgiveness. Culla and Rinthy Holme are brother and sister and the parents of a son whom Culla delivers in an abandoned shack and then leaves in the woods. A sinister, prowling tinker who has been spying on the couple discovers the infant and gives the child to a nurse. Rinthy, suspecting that her child is not dead, searches for the tinker while Culla in turn searches for her. Their efforts to expiate their guilt are futile; Rinthy only discovers bones, while Culla's roamings lead him to a nightmarish encounter with a blind beggar who is stumbling toward a swamp "out of which reared only the naked trees in attitudes of agony." The point seems to be that a crime against nature has been committed, and that the world is transformed by it into an allegorical landscape that resembles the Hell painted by Hieronymus Bosch, in which the creatures are fictitious but rendered in fine realistic detail.

Surrealism, a heightened perception that expresses itself in the realistic depiction of a world that is not, in fact, real, but impresses the viewer wit its solidity, describes McCarthy's style at its most extreme. And yet, like all his work, *Outer Dark* is full of descriptions of the natural world so interesting that it compels attention to other aspects of the writer's vision that are less palatable. The psychiatrist and critic Robert Coles, McCarthy's most determined advocate, admits that "there are moments in this sad, bitter, and literally awesome book when only an exceptionally gifted and lyrical writer could take his audience's attention for granted."

Child of God, McCarthy's third novel, is equally dark and associated its author still more firmly with the Southern Gothic tradition. The backwoods protagonist Lester Ballard, evicted from his home following his father's suicide, becomes a necrophiliac murderer. In his inexplicable compulsions and his conviction that he is blessed, he is reminiscent of Flannery O'Connor's characters, whose actions, though violent and perverse, and perfectly consistent with their weird natures. This novel, the most disjointed and episodic that McCarthy has written, drew virtually no praise and did little to create an audience for his much better received next novel, *Suttree*.

Several reviewers have assumed, with good reason, that *Suttree* is autobiographical, and that McCarthy began to write it while still a student. This very long and very dense novel, which is almost Dickensian in its sheer variety of characterization and wealth of observation of a world that is exclusively urban rather than rural, reveals the author's acquaintance with the degraded, marginal side of Knoxville, Tennessee. It is peopled with an enormous cast of poor whites and blacks, whores, junk dealers, fishermen, ragpickers, railwaymen, and other sad outcasts of a world whose only palliatives are cheap alcohol and greasy food. Everything in *Suttree* is polluted, dirty, and ruined by the sense of loss and failure, including the eponymous hero, and ex-husband, ex-father, and formerly respectable citizen whom the local sheriff, overcome by a sense of disgust, gives five dollars to leave town on the bus. Suttree's profound alienation, which renders him an entirely passive observer of misery, pushes him to the very bottom of existence, where he ekes out a living as a fisherman on the Tennessee River. The river is the most explicit symbol in a richly symbolic novel:

> Bearing along garbage and rafted trash, bottles of sun-cured glass wherein corollas of mauve and gold lie exploded, orangepeels ambered with age. A dead sow pink and bloated and jars and crates and shapes of wood washed into rigid homologues of viscera and empty oil-cans locked in eyes of dishing slime where the spectra wink guiltily. One day a dead baby. Bloated, pulpy rotted eyes in a bulbous skull and little rags of flesh trailing in the water like tissuepaper. Oaring his way lightly through the rain among these curiosa he felt little more than yet another artifact leached out of the earth and washed along, draining down out of the city, that cold and grainy shape beyond the rain that no rain could make clean again.

The measure of McCarthy's skill is that he makes this utterly degraded world compelling and even beautiful, especially when it is closely observed by the hero, who is the most complex, intelligent, and reflective of his characters. Suttree has chosen his marginal existence and joins it willingly, yet preserves a sympathy for his fellow men that invests all the characters, however pitiable, with dignity. The novel also contains

McCarthy's first comic character, Gene Harrogate, a young man whose compulsive urge to survive by stealing draws him into numerous grotesque predicaments that both amuse and attract the reader. Although, death is always present in the novel, and Suttree's own near-demise from typhoid is presented in overwhelming detail, the value and persistence of life is affirmed. Bleakness is often relieved by black humor, as in a scene where one of Suttree's friends pesters him into helping to bury his dead father in the river so that the state authorities will not discover that his mother has been drawing welfare on a six-month-old corpse. It seems that the novelist's intention, expressed through his detached yet sympathetic hero, is to cast aside the civilized trappings of life in order to discover that it is, after all, worth living. In this context, McCarthy's celebrated ability to evoke the literal world is no longer merely decoration to his narrative; it works as a demonstration of the pleasure of living, and is also integrated with the thoughts of his educated hero. Suttree is evidently an ex-Catholic, like McCarthy himself perhaps, and the novel is replete with religious allusion that never obtrudes as a theme, but seems to underscore the possibility of hope.

Blood Meridian, or The Evening Redness in the West, marks a departure in McCarthy's work that coincides with his move from Tennessee to Texas and the West, the setting both of this novel and *All the Pretty Horses*. Both are Westerns based loosely on historical incidents, but neither recalls that well-worn genre in more than setting, and neither could be called a historical novel. The first concentrates relentlessly, in a plot charged with violent incident that never stops moving, on the actions of a small group of sociopaths who, in the lawless territory of Northern Mexico in the 1850s, engage in a brief career of murder and robbery. Since these outlaws are so completely devoid of any human feeling it is both surprising that McCarthy can render their actions interesting, and irrelevant to accuse the book of nihilism. It seems intended as a bravura exercise, a tour de force of brutality that forces the reader to examine any pleasure one might feel in reading it. Vereen Bell reads the book as an extended comment on the futility of human values, which are constantly held up to casuistic ridicule by the book's central, Satanic character, Judge Holden, who denies that anything in the world is mysterious and regards all human actions as merely contingent. The senseless violence of the book, which exists, as always in McCarthy's work, against a setting of extraordinary natural beauty, supports Bell's thesis that all McCarthy's writing is part of a dialectic in which good struggles against evil. The novel

could be read in those terms as an ironic parody: a Western in which the judge leads the forces of evil, and evil triumphs.

All the Pretty Horses, the first of a projected trilogy of novels, is McCarthy's first truly popular book, but contains all his distinctive strengths of economical characterization, eloquent and realistic dialogue, vivid action, and painstakingly precise evocation of landscape. What redeems this novel from earlier charges of literary obscurity and nihilism is the unabashed romantic heroism of the plot and the attractiveness of the protagonist, John Grady Cole, a sixteen year-old Texas rancher who rides into northern Mexico in 1950 to seek his fortune with a friend, Lacey Rawlins. Cole is escaping from a broken family and the constraints of fenced land in order to find himself and to test his assumptions and his powerful sense of honor and decency against a world that turns out to be implacably hostile. Seen from a completely detached perspective, McCarthy's plot, which involves Cole in a murder, a tragic love affair, and a desperate fight for survival in a Mexican jail, is the fabric of pulp fiction. Like the heroes of many lesser writers, Cole fights his way back to his homeland bearing numerous bodily and mental scars, but there is no happy ending: all that Cole preserves from his adventures is his life and his integrity, and both are seen, by comparison with the landscape and the passage of time, as ephemeral qualities:

> . . . he held out his hands as if to steady himself or as if to bless the ground there or perhaps as if to slow the world that was rushing away and seemed to care nothing for the old or the young or rich or poor or dark or pale or he or she. Nothing for their struggles, nothing for their names. Nothing for the living or the dead.

In the *New York Review of Books* in 1993 Denis Donoghue observed that McCarthy's strength as a novelist is in his vision of nature, of which he writes "with reverence and wonder." It is a raw nature, untouched by human presence, where indeed relationships, especially within a society, appear to be simply beyond the stretch of McCarthy's imagination. *All the Pretty Horses* goes awry, Donoghue suggests, when his characters enter "civil life," as John Grady Cole does when he falls in love with an aristocratic young Mexican girl: "[McCarthy] is best with what nature gives or imposes, rather than with the observations of culture." When he attempts to bring his characters into a society, Donoghue concludes, "McCarthy is writing adrift from his talent."

With the publication of *The Crossing*, the second in the Border Trilogy but not a sequel to the earlier novel, in 1994, McCarthy appears to have confirmed both the enthusiastic expectations of his admirers and the suspicions of those who consider his work overrated. Robert Hass, in the *New York Times Book Review*, hailed *The Crossing* as even better than *All the Pretty Horses*: "a miracle in prose, an American original." To the host of literary giants to whom McCarthy had already been compared from Cervantes and Dostoevsky to Hemingway and Faulkner, Hass added some well-known film directors like John Ford, Sam Peckinpah, and Sergio Leone, proclaiming McCarthy "a writer who can plunder almost any source and make it his own." Set in Mexico and the Southwest in the late 1930s, *The Crossing* has for its central character another young man, Billy Parham, who is on a literal and, of course, a kind of mystical quest. The challenges are even more formidable than those in *All the Pretty Horses*. Billy resolves to return a wolf that he has trapped to her native Mexican mountain home—a by-now familiar man-versus-nature theme in McCarthy. Symbolically Billy's adventures are a rite-of-passage. When he returns from Mexico to find his parents murdered and the family's horses stolen, he and his younger brother begin another quest—this one for revenge and justice—which is also a test of their emergent manhood.

The novel is long and episodic, some of it a string of seemingly unrelated scenes, encounters with all manner of colorful people—cowboys, peasants, gypsies, itinerant preachers. "The book teems with action," Hass wrote, "and with spectacle and surprise." As with his earlier novels, admirers of *The Crossing* were impressed with McCarthy's skills both as storyteller and as literary stylist. Hass described his prose as "firm, faintly hypnotic," and traced McCarthy's influences back to Joyce, Hemingway, and Gertrude Stein. Michiko Kakutani, in the *New York Times*, mentioned "isolated moments of emotional grandeur," although she considered the novel a failure. "However different their circumstances, almost all these people speak in the same portentous, prophetic terms," sounding sometimes "like bad Faulkner crossed with bad Thomas Wolfe," she noted.

Denis Donoghue concluded that although McCarthy may have "gone awry" in the projected trilogy, he is a writer of importance, "one of those . . . who exhibit in their truest work . . . a refusing imagination: it refuses to give credence to the world as it has come to be in its personal, social, and political forms. . . . In McCarthy's fiction the world is nature, deserts, mountains, rivers, snow, and lightning, and he writes of it in that character with reverence and wonder."

PRINCIPAL WORKS: *Novels*—The Orchard Keeper, 1965;

Outer Dark, 1968; Child of God, 1974; Suttree, 1979; Blood Meridian, of The Evening Redness in the West, 1985; All the Pretty Horses, 1992; The Crossing, 1994. *Play*—The Stonemason, 1994.

ABOUT: Bell, V. M. The Achievement of Cormac McCarthy, 1988; Coles, R. Farewell to the South, 1972; Coles, R. That Red Wheelbarrow: Selected Literary Essays, 1988; Contemporary Authors New Revision Series 10, 1983; Contemporary Literary Criticism 57, 1990; Dictionary of Literary Biography 6, 1980. *Periodicals*—Journal of the Appalachian Studies Association, 3, 1991; New York Review of Books June 24, 1993; New York Times January 20, 1979; June 21, 1994; New York Times Book Review September 29, 1968; April 28, 1985; May 17, 1992; New York Times Magazine April 19, 1992; Sewanee Review Fall 1970; Spring 1979; Southern Literary Journal Spring 1983; Spring 1985; Fall 1991; Southern Quarterly Fall 1990; Southern Review Spring 1990.

McCORKLE, JILL (COLLINS) (July 7, 1958–), American novelist and short story writer, was born and raised in Lumberton, North Carolina. Her father, John McCorkle, was a postal worker, and her mother, Melba Ann a medical secretary, Jill McCorkle grew up in a story-telling extended family. Her grandmother's tales impressed her in particular and still influence her writing. Despite her family's strong oral tradition, McCorkle put her own stories into writing even as a child. She also immersed herself in books early on and recalls reading and rereading *The Diary of Anne Frank* and *Where the Red Fern Grows*.

McCorkle majored in English at the University of North Carolina at Chapel Hill. She studied creative writing with authors Lee Smith, Max Steele, and Louis Rubin, all of whom encouraged her to become a writer. After receiving a B.A. with highest honors and the Jessie Rehder Prize from Chapel Hill in 1980, she earned a master's degree in writing at Hollins College the following year.

At Hollins, McCorkle began her novel *The Cheer Leader*, a first-person narrative by Jo Spencer, a southern girl who seems to lead a perfect life. As Jo recounts her childhood, however, she discloses an inner world of isolation and self-doubt. Even in grade school she struggles with a fragile identity and feelings of inadequacy: "I am upset in this class picture because I feel that I do not fit in. It is an odd thing, because outwardly, I fit in; I am one of the most popular girls in the fifth grade . . . " During high school, a miserable relationship with an older boy intensifies Jo's sense of betrayal, vulnerability, and detachment. Her misery only deepens in college, until she become anorexic and frighten-

JILL McCORKLE

ingly isolated. By the end to the novel, three years later, her recovery is progressing slowly.

McCorkle sent *The Cheer Leader* to Louis Rubin, who liked it as well that he added it to the list of his new publishing house, Algonquin Books. To support herself, she taught language arts at a junior high school in Florida, then worked as an acquisitions librarian at Florida Institute of Technology. during that time she wrote *July 7th* which follows a town full of characters in Marshboro, North Carolina, on one hot, fateful summer day. Sam Swett, a twenty-one-year-old aspiring writer, begins the day in a drunken stupor, dumped by the trucker who had given him a ride. By the end of the day, he was witnessed both the common circumstances and exceptional events of several households and seen how these shared experiences bond families and neighbors. Moreover, Sam has found a lodestar in Corky Revels, a quiet young women who gently dispels the illusion of uniqueness that has left him disconnected and confused:

> He watches her sleeping, her chest and stomach moving up and down slightly with her breath, the slight jerks and twitches of her hands and feet. It is as if everything is clearing up now and he has not felt so good and safe, so sure of himself in ages. Slowing he lifts her head and slips out from under her, kneels by the side of the bed and gently places her head back on the pillow.

Once again, McCorkle sent her work to Louis Rubin. He was so impressed by *July 7th* that he decide to publish it along with *The Cheer Leader*. This unusual debut enabled reviewers to compare the novels and measure McCorkle's

growth as an author. Like Annie Gottlieb, writing for the *New York Times Book Review*, many other reviewers found *The Cheer Leader* "a good but familiar first novel that shows glimmers of wicked talent." *July 7th*, however, impressed reviewers with its idiosyncratic characters and unexpected yet believable twists of plot. Ursula Hegi, in the *Los Angeles Times*, noted that while McCorkle's ambitious efforts at "multiple points of view" make the beginning of the book appear fragmented, McCorkle's characters eventually "emerge and become more complex, their voices more distinctive."

McCorkle returned to Chapel Hill in 1984, hoping to get a job teaching creative writing at her alma mater. In the meantime she worked as a secretary at the university's medical school and met her future husband, Dan Shapiro. McCorkle wrote her third novel in Boston, where her husband completed his medical training. *Tending to Virginia* features Virginia Suzanne Turner Ballard, who runs away from her adult life during a broiling North Carolina summer. Her world has become unbearable constricted by a difficult pregnancy, her despair at an upcoming move to Richmond, and discord with her preoccupied husband. Back in her hometown, she falls ill from toxemia and gives herself up to the ministrations, stories, and nonstop chatter of her grandmother, great-aunt, mother, and cousins. The family stories reveal that Virginia's foremothers endured endless work and emotional and physical pain without forfeiting their sense of humor, ability to love, and willingness to accept and move on. Virginia returns to her own home with the realization that she has the resources to cope with childbirth and motherhood, her marriage, and a move to an unknown place.

The book drew widely differing responses from reviewers. In the *Christian Science Monitor* Diane Manuel praised McCorkle's characterization, colloquial dialogue, and technical range. Novelist Alice McDermott noted in the *New York Times Book Review* that "the charters are "so full of life, so full of stories to tell," that the book almost overflows with them: "It is as if . . . McCorkle, finding herself with this cast over marvelously rich, garrulous, complex women . . . south to contain them in a conventional tale of a young woman's coming of age. When they would not be contained, she simply threw up her hands and let them keep talking. It was a wise decision." The *New Republic*'s reviewer, Pearl K. Bell, however, disparaged these "torrents of trivia and McCorkle's indifference to "literary shape, to the pace and the development a story requires." McCorkle herself realized at the outset that the book essentially had no plot and anticipated some negative criticism.

Even so, she commented in an interview in *Southern Review*: "I felt that some extensive plot would really muddy up what I was trying to do. When I was working on the novel I kind of felt like you could take these women, and maybe put six chairs on the stage, and rely on their voices."

In her next novel *Ferris Beach* McCorkle again populates a small southern town with idiosyncratic characters. The book's main character, Katie Burns, gives a first-person narration of the events overtake the residents of Fulton, North Carolina, throughout her 1970s childhood and adolescence. Katie also describes her inner world, which revolves around her romanticized view of her cousin Angela. Angela not only lives in Ferris Beach, a resort town that seems exotic and exciting to the sheltered Katie, but has a mysterious past that embodies everything Katie's mother wants to protect her from. In an interview with *Publishers Weekly*, McCorkle summed up *Ferris Beach* as "a mood swing book. It's funny, I think, but it has sad parts too, and I believe I straddled the line that kept it from being melodramatic."

As Ron Loewinsohn pointed out in the *New York Times Book Review*, *Ferris Beach* resembles *The Cheer Leader* in that both are coming-of-age stories. Yet *Ferris Beach*, Loewinsohn asserted, treats the same theme "at an impressively higher level of accomplishment—technically, thematically and psychologically." Reviewing the novel in *Vogue*, Florence criticized McCorkle's reliance on popular culture icons, such as brand names or rock songs, to set a scene or describe a character. King found that McCorkle writes best when she avoids these "analogies on the cheap."

McCorkle's fifth book, *Crash Diet*, is a collection of eleven stories, most of which first appeared in literary magazines. The title story chronicles the fall and rise of Sandra, whose husband leaves her one morning "before I'd even had the chance to mousse my hair. . . . " After a miserable spell of compulsive shopping and self-starvation, she emerges strong and competent. Luci, the main character of "Man Watcher," is self-reliant and savvy, especially when it comes to men. She reels off the categories she places men in, adding: "I've though of publishing a book about it all, all the different types of the species. You known it would sort of be like Audubon's bird book. I'd call it Male Homo Sapiens: What You Need to Know to Identify Different Breeds." In *New Stories from The South* McCorkle described how the character of Luci seemed to emerge full-blown, without warning: "I was driving home from work one day and while at a stoplight the story began:

What's my sign? Slippery when wet . . . I had no idea where the piece would go, only that I had stumbled upon a voice I wanted to follow. . . . I wrote all the way, nearly illegible scribbles on a pad in the passenger seat. . . . By the time I got to the computer, Luci had said everything she needed to say and worked herself full circle to a natural ending."

Reviewers responded enthusiastically to Luci and McCorkle's other heroines. Greg Johnson summarized *Crash Diet* in the *Georgia Review* as energetic, funny, and a showcase for strong, resilient women. McCorkle's pitfall, Johnson noted, is that all of her jaunty, first-person narrators tend to sound alike. He wished she would "slow down, shape her narratives more carefully, give more consideration to language—for at her best she is a fine writer indeed. . . . " Yolanda Manora pronounced the stories "appealing and diverse" in *Southern Living*, adding that they ring true.

In addition to *Crash Diet* and her full-length works, McCorkle has written many short stories that have appeared in the *Atlantic, Southern Review, Seventeen*, and several anthologies. She has taught writing at the University of North Carolina at Chapel Hill and at Duke, Harvard, and Tufts universities. McCorkle and her husband have two children.

PRINCIPAL WORKS: *Novels*—The Cheer Leader, 1984; July 7th, 1984; Tending to Virginia, 1987; Ferris Beach, 1990. *Short stories*—Crash Diet, 1992.

ABOUT: Contemporary Authors 121, 1987; Dictionary of Literary Biography Yearbook 1987; Ravenel, S. (ed.) New Stores from The South; The Year's Best, 1993. *Periodicals*—Christian Science Monitor January 5, 1988; Georgia Review Summer 1992; Los Angeles Times November 15, 1984; New Republic 29, 1988; New York Times Book Review October 7, 1984; October 11, 1987; October 7, 1990; June 14, 1992; Publishers Weekly October 12, 1990; Southern Living November 1992; Southern Review Winter 1990; Vogue October 1990.

McCULLOUGH, DAVID (GAUB) (July 7, 1933–),

American historian, biographer, lecturer, and editor, was born in Pittsburgh, Pennsylvania, the son of Christian McCullough, a businessman, and Ruth (Rankin) McCullough. He was educated at Yale where he studied, among other subjects, portraiture—but not history, the field in which he was later to achieve renown. In 1954 he married Rosalee Ingram Barnes; they had five children. McCullough worked as a writer and editor for *Time* from 1956 to 1961, the U.S. Information Agency from

1961 to 1964, and the American Heritage Publishing Company from 1964 to 1970. Since 1970 he has been a free-lance writer specializing in American history. He began working in educational television in 1984 as host of the PBS series "Smithsonian World"; for one of these programs, an interview with Anne Morrow Lindbergh, he received an Emmy Award. Since 1988 McCullough has been the host to the PBS series "The American Experience."

McCullough, whom Esther Fein described in a *New York Times* 1992 interview as "a tall and elegant man, funny and charmingly polite," chose to write in an office behind his home on Martha's Vineyard on a manual typewriter. Writing without the aid of a more modern machine, he said, is not an affectation. "I like the tactile part of it. I like rolling the paper and pushing the lever at the end of the line. I like the bell that rings like an old train. It's a great piece of machinery. I even like crumpling up pages that don't work . . . I don't like the idea that technology might fail me." While working on his biography *Truman*, he read every page of it aloud to his wife, and she read each one back to him. "You can hear things that you cannot see," he explained, "redundancies, awkward expressions. Painters often look at their work in the mirror because you can see flaws that you don't see looking straight at a canvas."

Each of McCullough's books, focusing on a specific period in American history, owe much to his earlier interest in portraiture and painting; in each he is concerned, just as a painter is, with detail, color, and composition. As many reviewers have pointed out, McCullough makes much of the drama of whatever event he is describing, giving lively portraits of all the participants. Eugene Roston, in the *Times Literary Supplement*, describes *Truman* as being like "a comfortable Victorian three-decker novel. There are two plots, a hero and heroine, and a glittering cast of characters ranging from Dean Acheson, Churchill and General Marshall to the Pendergasts and General MacArthur, as well as a splendid collection of Shakespearean clowns." McCullough, who once compared his history-writing with 19th-century novel-writing, would have no disagreement. *Truman*, he said, is not "just for the Arthur Schlesingers and the academics," but for everyone who knew the man or someone like him.

McCullough's first book, *The Johnstown Flood*, about the 1889 deluge that smashed through Johnstown, Pennsylvania, killing over two thousand people, alerted readers that here was a writer who could transform scholarly research into what Allan Nevins called "one of the most vivid and gripping pieces of narrative writing that I have ever read." Nevins' comment was apt; beginning as a novelist would, McCullough sets the scene for his book in nineteenth-century Johnstown when life there meant "a great deal of hard work for just about everybody." People had the feeling that they were getting somewhere; progress was being made in every field of endeavor; it was a time of hope. The men of the South Fork Fishing and Hunting Club—men such as Henry Clay Frick, Andrew Carnegie, and Andrew Mellon—who were ultimately responsible for the tragedy, rightly regarded themselves as leaders in this great era of progress. But in McCullough's opinion, they made "two crucial mistakes." In order to improve conditions for their club, which was situated on a lake high above Johnstown, they "had tampered drastically with the natural order of things. They had ravaged much of the mountain country's protective timber, which caused dangerous flash runoff following mountain storms; they obstructed and diminished the capacity of the rivers; and they had bungled the repair and maintenance of the dam," which broke during the terrific storm of 1889, causing the deluge. "Worst of all they had failed—out of indifference mostly—to comprehend the possible consequences of what they were doing, and particularly what those consequences might be should nature happen to behave in anything but the normal fashion, which, of course, was exactly what was to be expected of nature." A reviewer for *Time* described *The Johnstown Flood* as "meticylously researched," and the *New York Times* reviewer called it "a superb job, scholarly yet vivid, balanced yet incisive."

For *The Great Bridge*, McCullough's history of the building of the Brooklyn Bridge, the author grew a beard in order to feel and look like one of the book's heroes, Washington Roebling. As in his previous book, he spent much time setting the background for this enormous project. John Roebling, Washington Roebling's father and the designer of the bridge, is depicted as a driven, hard-working nineteenth-century man who lived at a time when the Suez Canal was being constructed in Egypt, the Mont Cenis Tunnel was being blasted beneath the Alps, and in America the Union Pacific was laying track at a rate of eight miles a day. His son carried on his father's work, battling both corrupt politicians and the bends which crippled him for life. McCullough's vision of this age of optimism in American history, when Americans were convinced that anything that could be imagined could be accomplished, is the background for the momentous—and tragic—fourteen years of the bridge building, when lives were lost and

Tweed machine politicians, as well as reformers, contributed to the problems. In the words of Lewis Mumford, McCollough's picture of the times offers "a Balzacian wealth of detail," replete with "shifty villains like Boss Tweed" and Washington Roebling's wife Emily, "a veritable Florence Nightingale of engineering."

Having mastered the technical details of engineering, McCullough went on to write *The Path Between the Seas*, about the creation of the Panama Canal. In his preface he writes that the canal "was far more than a vast, unprecedented feat of engineering. It was a profoundly important historic event and a sweeping human drama . . . it represented the largest, most costly single effort ever before mounted anywhere on earth . . . Great reputations were made and destroyed. For numbers of men and women it was the adventure of a lifetime." Besides being a best-seller, *The Path Between the Seas* won practically every major award as the best book of the year, 1978, on foreign affairs and history—the National Book Award for History, the Francis Parkman Prize, the Cornelius Ryan Award, and the Samuel Eliot Morison Award.

One early and ardent advocate for the building for the Canal, Theodore Roosevelt, became the subject of McCullough's next book, *Morning on Horseback*. Once again his canvas is larger than a single portrait. "My intention was not to write a biography . . . What intrigued me was how Theodore Roosevelt came to be." Accordingly, McCullough offers a rich study of the Roosevelt family and of the era in which young Theodore came to maturity. Drawing on unpublished letters and journals as well as published records, McCullough produced what R. A. Brown described in *Library Journal* as "a new and more meaningful type of biographical writing . . . a stimulating book that will appeal to the general reader even as it offers a new model to the biographer." *Mornings on Horseback* won the American Book Award for biography in 1982 and was a nominee for the Pulitzer Prize in biography.

Truman, on which McCullough worked for ten years, became an overnight best-seller. Based on extensive interviews and a wealth of research material, the book provides an intimate glimpse into the life of America's thirty-third president. Starting off with Truman's origins in the expansive world of the Missouri frontier, McCullough chronicles his boyhood days in Independence, Missouri, his work as a bank clerk in Kansas City, his ten-year stint working on the family farm, his experience as a combat artillery officer during World War I, his marriage to Bess Wallace in 1919, and the failed business venture he engaged

in; then, as preparation for the political life Truman would afterwards assume, McCullough tells the story of his association with the Democratic Kansas City Pendergast machine, which was responsible for Truman being elected a judge for the county court, a U.S. senator, and finally, in 1944, Roosevelt's vice president. In telling the story of Truman's origins and early years, McCullough strongly emphasizes his subject's moral values. He quotes Truman's statement, "Since childhood at my mother's knee, I have believed in honor, ethics and right living as its own reward," and shows repeatedly how Truman lived up to these precepts despite his association with the crooks in the Pendergast machine. Indeed, as many reviewers have noted, a main thesis of this book centers on Truman's determination to do what was right for the country rather than to bolster his own self-esteem.

In recounting Truman's presidential achievements, McCollough makes a compelling case for his assessment that the man was "a figure of world stature, both a great man, and a great American President." Alan Brinkley, in the *New York Times* (1992), makes the point that McCullough's biography may be the culmination of Truman's rehabilitated reputation. Like most reviewers of the book he found it a "warm, affectionate and thoroughly captivating biography," while acknowledging that many scholars would not "find much engagement in the debates over such highly charged questions as the decision to use atomic bombs on Japan, the origins of the cold war, the motives for the North Korean invasion of South Korea in 1950, and Truman's policy in Vietnam." But McCullough, Brinkley concedes, was less interested in policy and politics than in Harry Truman himself.

McCullough would agree. While preparing himself to write the book he began each day with a brisk early-morning walk, just as Harry Truman had, in order to get a feel for the man. In his interview with Esther Fein in the *New York Times*, he commented that he works *in* a book rather than *on* a book; he soaks up information so that he can imagine himself at the place in history and in the shoes of the people he is writing about. The greatest challenge in writing history or biography, McCullough told Fein, is "not doing the research. The most difficult thing is to capture the tension and drama of the events as they felt at the time . . . Harry Truman was a 19th-century man and I decided I would proceed as a great 19th-century biographer would, or as Dickens would."

A few reviewers dissented from the general praise *Truman* received. Ronald Steele, in the *New Republic*, called the book a "1,000 page valentine," and entitled his review "Harry of Sunnybrook Farm." While it is true that McCullough's admiration for Truman does take center stage in his biography, the author is not lacking critical acumen. At one point he comments that Truman's answers to questions, even complicated ones, were "nearly always direct and assured, plainly said, and followed often by a conclusive and 'that's all there is to it' . . . when in truth there may have been a great deal more to it."

Brave Companions: Portraits in History is a collection of short essays that McCullough published over twenty-year period in *American Heritage, Audubon, Life,* the *New York Times Magazine,* and *Smithsonian.* Some came out of his research for his books; others are indeed portraits (he calls them "figures in a landscape") of distinguished Americans—among them Harriet Beecher Stowe, Louis Agassiz, Alexander von Humboldt, and Frederic Remington. In his introduction to the volume he sums up his attitude toward his work: "It is a shame that history is ever made dry and tedious, or offered as a chronicle almost exclusively of politics, war, and social issues, when, of course, it is the full sweep of human experience: politics, war, and social issues to be sure, but also music, science, religion, medicine, the way things are made, new ideas, high attainments in every field, money, the weather, love, loss, endless ambiguities and paradoxes and small towns you never heard of. History is a spacious realm. There should be no walls."

McCullough, a family man, dedicated each of his books to his wife or to one another of his children. He lives and works in West Tisbury, Martha's Vineyard, where he also pursues his interest in sketching and painting.

PRINCIPAL WORKS: The Johnstown Flood, 1968; The Great Bridge, 1972; The Path Between the Seas: The Creation of the Panama Canal, 1977; Mornings on Horseback, 1981; Brave Companions: Portraits in History, 1992; Truman, 1992. As editor—(with C. L. Sulzberger) American Heritage Picture History of World War II, 1967; Smithsonian Library, 6 vols., 1968–1970.

ABOUT: Contemporary Authors New Revision Series 31, 1990; Current Biography Yearbook 1993; McCullough, D. introduction to Brave Companions, 1992; Who's Who in America 1990–1991. Periodicals—Library Journal May 15, 1981; New York Times June 21, 1992; August 12, 1992; New York Times Book Review June 21, 1992; Publishers Weekly June 8, 1992; Time April 19, 1968; Times Literary Supplement November 27, 1992.

McGRATH, THOMAS (November 20, 1916– September 20, 1990), American poet and novelist, was born on a farm near Sheldon, North Dakota, into an Irish Catholic family. He was the oldest of the six children of Catherine (Shea) and James Lang McGrath, a farmer, and he grew up in the hard-living and hardworking tradition of farm families of the Midwest in the 20th century. After finishing elementary schools and high in Sheldon, young McGrath worked at a variety of laboring jobs to pay for his college education at Moorhead State in Minnesota and at the University of North Dakota, from which he received a B.A., with election to Phi Beta Kappa, in 1939. In the same year he was named a Rhodes Scholar, but the outbreak of World War II prevented his going to England. Instead he accepted a scholarship from Louisiana State University, a school he chose not only because its environment differed totally from the rugged country where he had grown up, but also because of its excellent English faculty. At LSU he studied under Cleanth Brooks, who encouraged his interest in poetry, and he met Alan Swallow, who was just beginning his own career as a publisher of American poetry. McGrath's first publication, in 1940, was a modest pamphlet, *First Manifesto,* that was also the first publication of the Alan Swallow Press.

By this time, aroused by the widespread suffering in the depression and by the struggle against fascism in Europe, McGrath turned to radical politics. This was, to some extent, a natural evolution from his boyhood in North Dakota, where populist politics flourished and itinerant farm workers had introduced him early on to working-class struggles. In 1940, having completed his M.A. at LSU, he became an instructor in English at Colby College in Waterville, Maine. One year of academic life in a remote New England town left him restless and dissatisfied. He gave up teaching and went to New York City, where he plunged into political activism, taking factory jobs and working as a in labor organizer on the New York waterfront. In 1942 McGrath entered the U.S. Army and was posted to the Aleutian Islands, where he served until 1945. On his discharge from the service he returned to New York to rejoin the dockworkers in their struggles to establish a union in the crime-ridden and often violent atmosphere of the waterfront—an experience he described in detail a decade later in his novel *This Coffin Has No Handles.* But in 1947, learning that his Rhodes Scholarship would expire if he did not assume it immediately, he went to New College, Oxford. Here he spent a year steeping himself in modern poetry—Auden, Day Lewis, MacNeice, Spender, as well as Eliot and Pound—and the literary

THOMAS McGRATH

criticism of the Marxist Christopher Caudwell, who had been killed in the Spanish Civil War. He left Oxford without taking a degree and drifted about Europe until 1950 when he returned to the United States to take a teaching position at Los Angeles State College of Applied Arts.

McGrath had joined the Communist party in his college days. He stayed in it longer than many of his contemporaries; but, as Frederick C. Stern suggested in an article in the *North Dakota Quarterly* in 1982, McGrath was a communist, not a Communist, independent of the rigid Party line. Stern quotes him: "When anyone asks my politics, I tell them 'Unaffiliated far left.'" Unlike committed party liners, McGrath seasoned his politics with humor, describing himself as a cofounder of the Ramshackle Socialist Victory Party, known by its initials R.S.V.P. Although he drifted away from the Party during World War II, he remained active in radical labor movements and never repudiated the cause of revolution. As late as 1987 he told an interviewer in *Triquarterly*: "I am still a revolutionary, absolutely, no less than ever . . . I don't think I've ever lost any sense at all of what I wanted: to try to get as much in the world as I could to move." Idealism strong enough to be called romanticism was a major component of his politics, and he paid a high price for his convictions. In April 1953, at the height of the anti-Communist hysteria of McCarthyism, McGrath was called before the House Committee on Un-American Activities. He refused to cooperate on grounds of the First, Fourth, and Fifth Amendments to the Constitution, citing his responsibilities as a teacher: "To cooperate with this committee would be to set them [his students] an example of accommodation to forces which can only have, as their end effect, the destruction of education itself." He also cited his responsibility to the community of radical poets from Blake and Shelley to García Lorca: "I do not wish to bring dishonor upon my tribe."

McGrath's refusal to testify brought him prompt dismissal from his teaching post and blacklisting everywhere. From 1954 to 1960 he went from job to job, teaching in small private schools, working in a factory, and writing screen documentaries, television scripts, and children's books. Throughout this period he continued to write poetry but could find publication only in small presses and little magazines. In the more open atmosphere of the 1960s, however, he was able to resume his academic career. He was assistant professor of English at C.W. Post College on Long Island from 1960 to 1961. In 1962 he moved west to North Dakota State University at Fargo as assistant professor of English. In 1967 he returned to the college where he had begun his own studies, now Moorhead State University, where he remained until his retirement in 1983. In these later years McGrath had the satisfaction of recognition from distinguished sources—an Amy Lowell traveling scholarship in 1965–1966, a Guggenheim Fellowship in 1968, and grants from the National Endowment for the Arts (1974) and various Minnesota arts programs. In 1981 he received an honorary Doctorate of Literature from the University of North Dakota. During the 1980s he was also the subject of two honorary issues of literary journals—the *North Dakota Quarterly* in 1982 and *Triquarterly* in 1987, as well as a collection of tributes in Frederick C. Stern's *The Revolutionary Poet in the United States: The Poetry of Thomas McGrath* in 1988.

In 1990 McGrath died in Minneapolis, where he had lived since his retirement, as the result of injuries suffered in a fall nearly a year earlier. He was survived by his third wife, Eugenia Johnson, from whom he was estranged, and by a son, Thomas. This was the Tomasito, a child born late in McGrath's life, who inspired some of his most beautiful lyrics, including the poem "You Taught Me" from *Passages Toward the Dark*:

All those years, alone,
Married to the intense uninteresting life
And, until you came, Tomasito,
I didn't even know my name!

Although highly esteemed by many of his

contemporaries, Thomas McGrath is little known and appreciated on the wider scene of contemporary American poetry. McGrath was never a part of a literary establishment. Some have suggested that this neglect was the result of his radical politics. Kenneth Rexroth wrote in the *New York Times Book Review* in 1965: "It is the other people's opinions which have kept him from being as well known as he deserves, for he is a most accomplished and committed poet." Frederick C. Stern, in the *Southern Review* in 1980, wrote that "McGrath's radicalism has overshadowed his outstanding qualities as a contemporary poet of the first rank," but he reminded his readers that McGrath "is not *just* a 'red' poet" any more than were Hugh MacDiarmid, Pablo Neruda, or Salvatore Quasimodo.

McGrath was distinguished from other polemical poets by his devotion to his craft. He felt that it didn't matter how much of a revolutionary he was, if he could not express it in well-wrought poetry. From his earliest work he showed an attention to the "art" of poetry that is strikingly absent from most political verse and that probably alienated him from a larger reading public. In "Ars Poetica; or, Who Lives in an Ivory Tower," published in *Longshot O'Leary's Garland of Practical Poesie*, a volume prized by his more radical readers, he expresses the frustration of the poet in a society that craves escape in illusions:

Nobody wants your roundelay, nobody wants your sestina,
Said the housewife, we want Hedy Lamarr and Gable at the
    cinema,
Get out of my technicolor dream with your tragic view and
    your verses;
Down with iambic pentameter and hurray for Louella Parsons.

Even in political rage McGrath rarely lost his often grisly sense of humor—as in the title "Poor John Luck and the Middle Class Struggle; or, The Corpse in the Bookkeeper's Body" of in "A Little Song about Charity":

The boss came around at Christmas—
Oh smiling like a lamb—
He made me a present of a pair of gloves
And then cut off my hands—
Oh and then cut off my hands.

He was steeped, as well, in a Roman Catholic heritage from which he derived a great deal of his imagery, pitying the bookkeeper John Luck who "wakes up feeling that his youth has gone away. / Over the Eucharist of toast and coffee / He dreams of a Jerusalem where he was happy. . . . " Mourning his brother Jimmy, killed

in World War II, he writes: "The desperate laws of human motion / Deny innocence but permit salvation."

As McGrath's poetry matured it became more complex, with long lines and often difficult, though rarely obscure, images drawn from a variety of sources—classical mythology, Native American lore, the Bible, contemporary social issues, and his personal life. He described his longest and most ambitious poem, *Letter to an Imaginary Friend* ("I have been working on only one poem throughout my life"), as "pseudo-autobiography," and indeed the poem omits almost no detail of his life, physical, intellectual, and spiritual, from his earliest childhood memories to the mid-1980s. It swings back and forth from North Dakota to Louisiana, New York, and California, to the Aleutians, Greece, and Spain: "I do not know what end that journey was toward / But I am its end." The "I" of the poem, however, as in Walt Whitman's *Leaves of Grass* (to which it is often compared), is not so much the poet as his persona. "It is not simply autobiography," McGrath wrote. "I am far from believing that all parts of my life are meaningful enough to be usable in the poem. But I believe that all of us live twice; once personally and once as a representative man or woman. I am interested in those moments when my life line crosses through the concentration points of the history of my time. *Then* I live both personally and representatively."

In *Letter to an Imaginary Friend*, according to J. P. White, in the *New York Times Book Review* in 1991, McGrath "created a new form that might be called historical lyricism." He favored a long six-beat line, frequently broken into shorter units, but he varied the rhythms and even included passages of prose: "In the last analysis I was more interested in the cadence than the line, but as the poem progresses the autonomy of the line becomes assured—as I think it should be for the general welfare of American verse." White deemed *Letter* "quite possibly this century's most pervasive and entertaining poem about struggles for . . . social change." Parts I and II move swiftly through specific episodes in the poet's life. Though these are presented as fragments of memory, they adhere in the consciousness of the poet:

North Dakota
   is everywhere.
   This town where Theseus sleeps on his hill
Dead like Crazy Horse.
   This poverty.
   This dialectic of money—
Dakota is everywhere.
   A condition.
   And I am only a device of memory
To call forth into this Present the flowering dead and the

living
To enter the labyrinth and blaze the trail for the endur-
ing journey
Toward the round dance and commune of light. . . .

In Parts III and IV the poet assumes the mystical role of shaman, drawing on history, myth,
Hopi legend, and Christianity, pursuing a quest
for the Kachina, the god who will bring a new
world:

Time!—to change angles and angels and to reinstate
Cham, Amoymon, Marx, Engels, Lenin, Azael,
Stalin, Mahazael, Mao, Sitrael—Che-Kachina–
O yield up the names of the final Tetragrammaton!–
Time! To make sacred what was profane! Time! Time!
Time!
    to angelize the demons and the damned. . . .

McGrath said that the poem "is as open as it arrived and as open as I could make and allow it
to be." The abrupt transitions, he explained, are
"the kinds of cuts, jump cuts and dissolves which
most readers will be familiar with from old
films—and from new films since Godard—and
which have been a part of poetry long before
film." The poet Diane Wakoski commented in
the *Georgia Review*: "*Letter to an Imaginary
Friend* is an epic poem about the Christ child
figure of the poet Thomas McGrath grounded in
his Midwestern landscape but using the range of
Western myth from Orphic tradition to Hopi
prophecy. It glorifies the natural landscapes of
North Dakota, the agrarian community, and the
work ethic and depicts the fragmentation of
modern civilization as well as a vision of wholeness to be restored in a new poetic world."

McGrath's works, his novels in particular,
have received little public attention. Though not
published until 1984, the earlier of them, *This
Coffin Has No Handles*, was written in 1947, not
long after he had worked in New York during
the longshoreman's strike. Developed in a series
of interior monologues that shift from one character's unconscious to another's, the novel is a
graphic account of one week of the strike, incorporating as fictional characters some of the people he known on the waterfront. Although it
depicts a brutally violent reality, *This Coffin
Has No Handles*, nevertheless, emerges as the
work of a poet. "I was born at the age of
eighteen," the narrator says. "It happened in a
little fracas in Detroit which never even became
a strike. I got a wallop with a policeman's billy,
and I sprang, miraculously, fully formed from
my own head, like Athena being born from the
brow of Jove. An immaculate conception, gestation, parturition, and all done in the twinkle of
a nightstick." He walks through the city, a witness to its despair: "At Times Square they are un-
locking the cage, but already the desperate early

ones have crawled into the lions' den and the
snake pit, spreading the elastic bars . . . Some
with champagne, some with a can of smoke, investigate the pressures on the floor of the alcohol
sea, but all these are the Old China Hands in the
spreading Asia of a lost continent."

The almost literal nightmare of the city becomes a symbolic nightmare in McGrath's second novel, *The Gates of Ivory, The Gates of
Horn* (the title comes from the *Aeneid*, in which
ivory represents "deluding lies" and horn is
truth). Published in 1957 and, according to the
dust jacket, "highly influenced by McGrath's experience with the House Un-American Activities
Committee hearings during the 1950," this is a
futuristic novel, set in a dystopia not unlike the
society in George Orwell's *1984*. The central
character, the Investigator, works for a faceless
bureaucracy where there is no tolerance "for the
idiosyncrasies of individuals," where ownership
of most books is unlawful, and the state motto is
"One nation indivisible with efficiency and punishment for all." Increasingly disenchanted with
this society, the Investigator, until now a loyal
citizen, suspects that he himself is the victim of
a conspiracy, but his friend tells him that he is
a victim of his own will: "Man wants to be free.
He may not know exactly what he means by being free, but that's what he wants. You and your
kind have turned society into a man-trapping
machine, a real paranoid circus. There's only
one end for something like that: after you get all
the seditioners, you'll start trapping yourselves."

In 1989 McGrath was the subject of a three-
act play, *The Grass Eats Horse*, by Eric Blau. It
was given several public readings in New York
City at the church of St. Mark's-in-the-Bowery.
McGrath's last book was the posthumously published *Death Song*, a collection of short lyric poems, which J. P. White described in the *New
York Times Book Review* as "by far the most intimate, affectionate and vulnerable of all [his]
work." Summing up his achievement, White
called him "the essential modern American poet
of witness and community."

PRINCIPAL WORKS: *Poetry*—First Manifesto, 1940; To
Walk a Crooked Mile, 1947; Longshot O'Leary's Garland of Practical Poesie, 1949; Witness to the Times,
1953; Figures from a Double World, 1955; Letter to
an Imaginary Friend, 1962; New and Selected Poems,
1964; Letter to an Imaginary Friend, Parts I and II,
1970; The Movie at the End of the World, 1973; A
Sound of One Hand, 1975; Open Songs, 1977; Trinc,
1979; Waiting for the Angel, 1979; Passages Toward
the Dark, 1982; Echoes Inside the Labyrinth, 1983;
Longshot O'Leary Counsels Direct Action, 1983; Letter to an Imaginary Friend, Parts III and IV, 1985; Selected Poems, 1938–1988, 1988; Death Song, 1991.
Novels—The Gates of Ivory, The Gates of Horn, 1957;

This Coffin Has No Handles, 1984. *Children's books*—About Clouds, 1959; The Beautiful Things, 1960.

ABOUT: Contemporary Authors New Revision Series 6, 1982; Contemporary Literary Criticism 28, 1984; Contemporary Poets, 5th ed., 1991; Gibbons, R. and T. Des Pres (eds.) Thomas McGrath: Life and the Poem, 1992; Something About the Author 41, 1985; Stern, F. C. (ed.) The Revolutionary Poet in the United States: The Poetry of Thomas McGrath, 1988. *Periodicals*—American Poetry Review January–February 1987; May–June 1989; Georgia Review Winter 1989; New York Times September 22, 1990; New York Times Book Review February 21, 1965; March 10, 1990; March 10, 1991; North Dakota Quarterly Winter 1982; Winter 1985; Winter 1987; Winter 1990; Prairie Schooner Spring–Summer 1981; Southwest Review Winter 1980; Triquarterly Fall 1987.

McPHERSON, JAMES ALAN (September 16, 1943–), American short story writer, essayist, and editor, and one of the most highly acclaimed African American fiction writers of his generation, was born and raised in Savannah, Georgia, the son of James Allen McPherson and Mabel (Smalls) McPherson. Although it was a segregated city, rife with racial prejudice and animosity, the Savannah of McPherson's childhood was also something of a multicultural melting pot, a confluence of English, French, Spanish, Amerindian, and African-American influences. McPherson came of age during the turbulent and transformative years of the black civil rights movement. By his own account, he has been a direct beneficiary of landmark court decisions and legislation mandating the integration of schools, housing, and employment.

"In 1954, when Brown v. Board of Education was decided, I was eleven years old," McPherson wrote in an *Atlantic* magazine essay. "I lived in a lower-class black community . . . , attended segregated public schools, and knew no white people socially." He and his family did, however, have contact with the white community. His father was at one time the only licensed black master electrician in the state of Georgia, and his mother was a domestic worker in white households; as a boy, McPherson worked in a Savannah grocery store serving mostly white customers. He has always been quick to acknowledge the harrowing realities of racism, even the subtle distinctions based on "gradations of color" among blacks. Yet he recalls that during his youth, "there was a great deal of optimism, shared by all levels of the black community. . . . there was a belief in the idea of progress. . . . Though ours was a limited world, it was one rich in possibilities for the

future." The title of the *Atlantic* essay in which these recollections appear—"On Becoming an American Writer"—is revelatory, and perhaps faintly ironic. Like his literary mentor Ralph Ellison, McPherson is an unflinching chronicler of the prejudices that divide Americans, but he is determined, at the same time, to delineate the possibility of a uniquely "American" culture—one that is neither "black" nor "white," and which transcends ingrained ideas about race and ethnicity.

In 1961, having received a low-interest National Defense Student Loan, McPherson enrolled in Morris Brown College, a small black institution in Atlanta. For several summers during college, he worked as a dining car waiter for the Great Northern Railway Company. The job provided him with the opportunity to travel, mainly between Chicago and the Pacific Northwest. He was deeply affected by his visit to the 1962 World's Fair in Seattle, Washington, where the theme of the American exhibit, he recalls, was inspired by Walt Whitman's *Leaves of Grass*: "Conquering, holding, daring, venturing as we go the unknown ways." After attending Morgan State College in Baltimore, Maryland, in 1963 and 1964, he returned to Morris Brown, receiving his B.A. there in 1965. He began writing short fiction in college. Exhilarated by his travels and by the promise of the civil rights movement, he submitted his first short story to a contest sponsored by the *Reader's Digest* and the United Negro College Fund. The crudely typed manuscript was lost. His career as a fiction writer, therefore, launched with the publication of his second story, "Gold Coast," which won first prize in a fiction contest sponsored by the *Atlantic* magazine in 1965.

In 1965, a critical year in the history of the black civil rights movement in America, marking the assassination of Malcolm X in Harlem and the "Freedom March" from Selma to Montgomery, Alabama, led by Martin Luther King Jr., James McPherson graduated from college and published a prize-winning short story. He was admitted to the Harvard Law School, as well. Attending law school in cosmopolitan Cambridge, Massachusetts, he became friendly with people from diverse backgrounds, both black and white, students and nonstudents. During his second year at Harvard, he landed a job as a janitor in a Cambridge apartment building. "There I had the solitude, and the encouragement, to begin writing seriously," he noted in the *Atlantic*. That same year, he began toying with the idea that the Fourteenth Amendment to the U.S. Constitution, the so-called "equal protection amendment," might be more than simply "a legislative instrument devised to give former slaves legal equality with other Americans." Examining how the "basic guarantees" of the Bill of Rights had been incorporated into that Reconstruction-era amendment, McPherson began to detect "the outlines of a new identity." This yearning for a "new identity" was prompted by very real conflicts in his own life. The pressures of trying to maintain friendships with people of widely divergent backgrounds and points of view, he observed, "introduced psychological contradictions that became tense and painful as the political climate shifted. . . . I had to force myself to find a basis other than race on which such contradictory urgings could be synthesized. I discovered that I had to find, first of all, an identity as a writer, and then I had to express what I knew or felt in such a way that I could make something whole out of a necessarily fragmented experience."

Hue and Cry, McPherson's first collection of short stories, appeared not long after his graduation from Harvard Law School in 1968. "It is my hope," he wrote in the book's dust jacket notes, "that this collection of stories can be read as a book about people, all kinds of people. . . . As a matter of fact, certain of the people happen to be black, and certain of them happen to be white; but I have tried to keep the color part of most of them far in the background, where these things should rightly be kept." Most of the stories in *Hue and Cry* are narrated by working-class blacks, and many appear to be based on the author's personal experiences; they are not, however, strictly autobiographical, for McPherson always maintains a certain critical distance from his characters. In "A Solo Song: For Doc," an elderly black dining car waiter recounts for a young co-worker his glory days of service on the Chicago to Seattle trains. The main subject of his reminiscence is a deceased black waiter whose dexterity and sly amiability earned him the moniker "Doc Craft." Like the narrator, Doc was a "Waiter's Waiter" of the "Old School." Unlike the young temporary waiter in the story—the narrator calls him "summer stuff"—Doc derived complete satisfaction, indeed, his entire identity, from the expert practice of his trade. Doc's devotion to his craft is eventually no match for a rule-book-wielding inspector, who is intent upon getting rid of the older union waiters. Doc dies shortly after being forced to retire, and his death signals the demise of the entire "Old School." The prize-winning story "Gold Coast," also included in *Hue and Cry*, is narrated by an aging white janitor working in a once-fashionable building near Harvard Square.

Hue and Cry was widely praised by both black and white reviewers. Ralph Ellison, the black writer with whom McPherson is often compared, noted on the book's back cover: "With this collection of stories, McPherson promises to move right past those talented but misguided writers of Negro American cultural background who take being black as a privilege for being obscenely second-rate and who regard their social predicament as Negroes as exempting them from the necessity of mastering the craft and forms of fiction." In the *Saturday Review*, Granville Hicks observed: "Unlike certain other black writers, McPherson does not find it necessary to go into spasms of indignation every time he describes an act of discrimination. He is acutely aware of the misery and injustice in the world, and he sympathizes deeply with the victims whether they are black or white." Irving Howe, writing in *Harper's*, echoed those sentiments: "James McPherson had a strong sense of injustice . . . and he knows how disproportionately large a share of that injustice black men must bear; yet he manages to take human beings one at a time, honoring their portion of uniqueness." *Hue and Cry* earned McPherson a National Institute of Arts and Letters award in literature in 1970.

McPherson has been a contributing editor with the *Atlantic* since 1969. His fiction and nonfiction have also appeared in *Callaloo*, *Esquire*, and the *New York Times Magazine*. Although trained as a lawyer, McPherson chose to teach writing and literature. Since earning an M.F.A. from the University of Iowa in 1969, he has taught at the University of Iowa Law School (as a writing instructor), the University of California at Santa Cruz, Morgan State, and the University of Virginia. He was named a Guggenheim fellow in 1972–1973, and since 1981 has taught at the Iowa Writers Workshop in Iowa City.

Elbow Room, his second collection of short stories, was awarded a Pulitzer Prize in 1978. A number of the stories—"The Story of a Dead Man," "The Story of a Scar," and "The Silver Bullet"—focus solely on the experiences of black people. Yet, as the title of the collections suggests, the stories in *Elbow Room* deal with characters trying to makespace in their lives, space in which to forge identities based on something other than racial stereotypes. The title story describes the early married life of Paul Frost and Virginia Valentine, an interracial couple living in San Francisco. Sensitive and intellectually inclined, Paul is a white man from a small town in Kansas. Virginia, originally from rural Tennessee, "joined the Peace Corps and took the poor man's grand tour of the world." Although black in appearance, she is the product of black, white, and Cherokee blood lines. "Elbow Room" is narrated by an anonymous black friend of the couple. The narrator's highly subjective account is complicated by italicized editorial comments, such as: "The above section is totally unclear. It should be totally unclear. It should be cut."

Concluding a laudatory notice of *Elbow Room* in the *New York Times Book Review*, Robie Macauley noted, "A fine control of language and story, a depth in his characters, humane values, these are a few of the virtues James Alan McPherson displays in this fine collection of stories." A *New Yorker* reviewer hailed McPherson as "one of those rare writers who can tell a story, describe shadings of character, and make sociological oberservations with equal subtlety." In his *Nation* essay "Black Writing in the 1970s," Robert Bone wrote, "McPherson's respect for his craft, as well as his courage in choosing the road less traveled, have justified a major claim on our attention."

In addition to publishing short stories and essays, McPherson has coedited *Railroad: Trains and Train People in American Culture*. He has also contributed to such volumes as Nick A. Ford's *Black Insights* and Alex Harris's *A World Unsuspected*, a collection od autobiographies by southern writers. While McPerson is undoubtably one of the most respected black fiction wtiters of his generation, his reputation still rests on a small body of work. In 1981 he recieved a MacArthur Foundation award, which allowed him to reduce his teaching schedule and concentrate primarily on writing. He is reportedly at work on a novel.

Asked by the *New York Times Book Review* in 1984 to name the "writer of writers" who had influenced his work, McPherson, not surprisingly, cited Ralph Ellison, author of *Invisible Man*:

I have learned to listen for true voices, those that are not often found on the printed page. . . . In 1970 I met and began a friendship with Ralph Ellison. He was then under attack by black nationalists and was defending himself by affirming ideas that no one else, including whites, seemed to believe in—that something called America *did* exist; that it had a culture; that black Americans were, by our unique history and special contributions and the quality of our struggle, heroic; that self-imposed segregation, especially of the imagination, was a mistake."

PRINCIPAL WORKS: *Short stories*—Hue and Cry, 1969; Elbow Room,1977. *As editor*—(with M. Williams) Railroad: Trains and Train People in American Culture, 1976.

ABOUT: Beavers, H. Wrestling Angels into Song: The Fictions of Ernest J. Gaines and James Alan McPherson, 1994; Contemporary Authors New Revision Series 24, 1988; Contemporary Literary Criticism 19, 1981; Dictionary of Literary Biography, 1985; Wallace, J.

The Politics of Style: Language as Theme in the Fiction of Berger, Mc Guane, and McPherson, 1992. *Periodicals*—Atlantic December 1978; Ebony December 1981; Harper's December 1969; Modern Fiction Studies Spring 1988; Nation December 16, 1978; New York Times Book Review September 25, 1977; May 13, 1984; New Yorker November 21, 1977; Saturday Review May 24, 1969; Studies in Short Fiction Fall 1988.

MEYERS, JEFFREY (April 1, 1939–), American biographer, editor and educator, was born in New York City to Rubin, a clothing industry worker, and Judith Meyers. He grew up in Forest Hills. In 1959 he received his bachelor of arts in English literature from the University of Michigan. Following a year at the Harvard Law School, he switched to the graduate school of the University of California, Berkeley, where he received his Ph.D. in English in 1967.

Meyers has held various teaching positions in the United States interrupted by periods of residence and writing abroad. From 1963 to 1965 he taught English at the University of California, Los Angeles. There followed a year as lecturer in the University of Maryland Far East Division in Tokyo. Upon his return to America in 1967, he joined the faculty of Tufts University where he remained through 1971. Tired of the student riots and campus upheavals that began in the 1960s, according to Mark Allister in the *Dictionary of Literary Biography*, he left teaching for a three-year hiatus devoted to full-time writing in Europe, first in Malaga, Spain, and then in London. Back in America in 1975, he joined the English faculty at the University of Colorado in Boulder.

As Mark Allister summarizes his literary career: "Meyers began writing primarily as a literary critic who used biography to explicate literary texts, and he has since become a biographer who interprets literature." Most of Meyers's earlier books are thematic collections of essays on miscellaneous writers, to some of whom he subsequently devoted full biographies. In *Fiction and the Colonial Experience*, based on his doctoral dissertation, he explores "the cultural conflict that develops when Europe imposes its manners, customs, religious beliefs, and moral values on an indigenous way of life," as seen in the writings of Rudyard Kipling, E. M. Forster, Joseph Conrad, Joyce Cary, and Graham Greene. "Aesthetic analogies" between visual and verbal imagery are brought out in *Painting and the Novel*, a series of explications of works from Hawthorne's *The Marble Faun* to Lampedusa's *The Leopard* in which art plays a significant part. *Married to Genius* compares the experiences of spouses of great writers (e.g., Tol-

JEFFREY MEYERS

stoy, Conrad, Shaw, Katherine Mansfield, Virginia Woolf) with the aim of establishing "relationships between aesthetic and marital responsibilities." Such modern classics as *The Picture of Dorian Gray, The Immoralist, Death in Venice*, and *Remembrance of Things Past* are brought together in *Homosexuality and Literature, 1890–1930*.

Some reviewers of these composite studies thought Meyers's criticism sound but unoriginal, and complained of their loose organization, arbitrary choice of subject, and lack of clear focus. The solidly researched and more substantial and better organized biographies that followed gained him a wider readership.

In his introduction to *The Craft of Literary Biography*, a collection of essays by fellow practitioners, Meyers defines the successful biographer as "an investigative reporter of the spirit." In his own contribution to this volume, recalling the extensive and intensive research that culminated in his biography of Wyndham Lewis (*The Enemy*), he affirms that the biographer ideally "should combine the passion for learning about his subject and the period in which he lived with the detective's monomaniacal delight in facts for their own sake." In reaction against modern scholars who deny that it is possible to enter a writer's mind and content themselves with compiling "facts and externals"—he refers specifically to Carlos Barker, the biographer of Hemingway, and Bernard Crick, the biographer of George Orwell—Meyers sets down his own program: "When [the biographer] has finished his research, contemplated his discoveries, and understood the intellectual and emotional life of his subject, he must be able to fit everything he has learned into a meaningful pattern and satisfy his readers' natural curiosity about the life of an extraordinary person."

Meyers's own literary investigative reporting has been confined with one exception (Poe) to 20th-century figures whose careers are copiously documented. Moreover, his subjects were not only extraordinary, but aberrant in one way or another, whether as outsiders (Conrad, T. E. Lawrence), and he betrays a special penchant for self-destructing geniuses (Poe; Katherine Mansfield, his only female subject; Robert Lowell, Randall Jarrell, Theodore Roethke, and John Berryman, who are treated together in *Manic Power*; Ernest Hemingway; and Scott Fitzgerald). He tales a "monomaniacal delight" in questing after his quarries. His research on Katherine Mansfield took him to New Zealand—which trip, he claimed cost him more than he made from the book, though it was financed in part by lectures at the University of Auckland. Part of the preparation for his biography of D. H. Lawrence involved his absorbing the atmosphere around Nottingham, even descending over nine hundred meters into a mine shaft "carrying a battery lamp and wearing a gas mask" in order to relive the experience of Arthur Lawrence, the novelist's father. His passion for concrete fact extended in the case of Wyndham Lewis not only to listening to records of that writer-painter's voice, but holding his preserved brain in his hand.

In *The Biographer's Art*, another collection he edited, Meyers singles out George Painter's *Marcel Proust* as a model biography for treating that writer's works "as a part of, not a supplement to," his life. Painter, however, deliberately eschewed contact with anybody associated with Proust, whereas survivors, including immediate family when available, have provided what Meyers regards as the lifeblood of his biographies. (The acknowledgements that preface all of his biographies cover several pages.)

It has been observed that Meyers tends to go over ground already traversed by others—none of his biographies can be characterized as a "first"—a practice he justifies by his diligent pursuit of new primary sources. For his biography of Katherine Mansfield, for example, he had access to then-unpublished correspondence in the process of being edited and interviewed writers close to her: David Garnett, Christopher Isherwood, Frank Swinnerton, and Dame Rebecca West. With Wyndham Lewis his intention was, by means of various documents, including medical records, to dispel "the fog of rumour and half-proved fact, of conflicting statements and pure fantasy" that had distorted other accounts. His biography of D. H. Lawrence emphasizes more than his predecessors did the early influences of coal mining and Congregationalism, and casts further light on the circumstances surrounding the suppression of *The Rainbow* and Lawrence's art exhibitions. He has turned up more detail on Hemingway's war adventures and discovered a previously unknown involvement with the FBI. He has tracked down new information about Joseph Conrad's Polish background, his youthful activity in Spain and in the Malay Archipelago, and revealed for the first time an autumnal romance with the American journalist Jane Anderson.

More than one reviewer has remarked on the brisk pace of Meyers's output. David Gates, in his review of *Edgar Allan Poe: His Life and Legacy* in *Newsweek*, went so far as to dub him a "crank-'em-out-biographer." Critical reception of virtually all of the biographies has diverged widely. In the *New York Review of Books*, (1991) Noel Annan praised the biography of D. H. Lawrence for its dispassionateness and scrupulous weighing of evidence. However, Annan made clear in this same review that his was a minority report, citing colleagues who thought the writing "cold, simplistic, plodding," and the matching of fictitious chracters and real-life people "mechanical." A kind of left-handed compliment was paid by Julain Symons, in the *Times Literary Supplement*, where he wrote, "Taken as a whole, this robust, energetic book is probably the best biography [of Lawrence], adding, "It will make him no new friends, but perhaps we should not be sorry about that."

A similarly mixed response greeted *Hemingway: A Biography*. "Myers's evocative descriptions of the places . . . that Hemingway practically made his own, his informative discussion of Papa's espionage activities . . . during World War II . . . all contribute the feeling that this biography will establish itself as the definitive biography for some time to come," Bruce Allen wrote in the *Christian Science Monitor* (1986). But Raymond Carver, in the *New York Times Book Review* (1985), noted a mean-spirited quality: "Adulation is not a requirement for biographers, but Mr. Meyers's book fairly bristles with disapproval of its subject. What is especially disconcerting is his strong belief that [Hemingway] never matured as an artist . . . sounded repeatedly as one reads dazedly on." Some have questioned the value of Meyers's fresh archival diggings, such as the reviewer of the Joseph Conrad biography for the *Economist*: "Though Mr. Meyers deserves honor as a prospector, he brings to the surface not gold

but iron pyrites." Others have complained that he dredges up too much dirt; for example, Michiko Kakutani, in the *New York Times* dismisses his biography of F. Scott Fitzgerald as mere "pathography" (borrowing a term coined by Joyce Carol Oates) "All in all, an ugly and superfluous book about a major artist who deserves a better biographical fate."

Inevitably Meyers's books have been assessed alongside the work of previous biographers. The Hemingway biography was conceived specifically in reaction against what Meyers considered the inadequacies of Carlos Barker's monumental study, but the critical court was divided on the comparative merits of the two. Whereas in the judgment of Raymond Carver, "there was little in Meyers' book that Baker didn't say better," and Baker showed more understanding of Hemingway, Arthur Waldhorn, in the *Library Journal*, and Robert Gorham Davis, in the *New Leader*, thought Baker the more sensitive writer, but found Meyers's portrait more candid.

Meyers's Conrad biography had a formidable rival in Frederick Karl's massive one published in 1979. To Joyce Carol Oates, in the *New York Times Book Review*, Meyers's book "is never less than a workmanlike amalgam of known and new material; at its best, it is sensitively written, and clearly inspired by great admiration for its subject." She adds that there are many occurrences of "déjà vu" in Meyers's narrative which affect the reader "like hearing another time an old and cherished family anecdote."

One reviewer of the Poe biography, David Gates in *Newsweek*, remarked that Meyers did not sufficiently justify a new biography of "this most tormented of literary souls" coming so close upon the heels of the well-received one by Kenneth Silverman. However, Arthur Krystal, in the *Times Literary Supplement*, remarked that Meyers, "untempted by psychoanalytic theories, better conveys Poe's acrimonious, often absurd literary travails" and provides a fuller account than Silverman of his reputation and influence.

Meyers's virtues and shortcomings as a biographer are perhaps best summarized in John Pfordresher's assessment of the D. H. Lawrence book in *America*. To him it is "a succinct, factual narrative of events," which "vividly evokes the settings of Lawrence's peripatetic life" but "largely avoids the ultimate challenges of the biographer, the discernment of the fundamental contours in a life, the definition of crucial moments of choice and development." Depending on their predilections, reviewers have tended to commend Meyers for his efficient marshaling of his material and fact-filled, straightforward, jargon-free writing style, or to fault him for emphasizing the more sordid aspects of his subjects' lives and inadequately accounting for their literary achievements.

Concurrently with his better-known works, Meyers has edited critical evaluations of modern writers, including some of those he has treated, and contributed numerous reviews to literary periodicals. He has received Fulbright, Guggenheim, and American Council of Learned Society Fellowships, and in 1983 was elected a Fellow of the Royal Society of Literature. While in Japan in 1965, he met and married Valerie Froggatt, a graduate of Cambridge University and a teacher of English, to whom he has dedicated several of his books. Their daughter was born in 1972.

PRINCIPAL WORKS: Fiction and the Colonial Experience, 1973; The Wounded Spirit: A Study of "Seven Pillars of Wisdom," 1973, rev. ed. 1989; Painting and the Novel, 1975; A Fever at the Core: The Idealist in Politics, 1976; Homosexuality and Literature, 1890–1930, 1977; Married to Genius, 1977; Katherine Mansfield: A Biography, 1978; The Enemy: A Biography of Wyndham Lewis, 1980; D. H. Lawrence and the Experience of Italy, 1982; Disease and the Novel, 1880–1960, 1985; Hemingway: A Biography, 1985; Manic Power: Robert Lowell and His Circle, 1987; The spirit of Biography, 1989; D. H. Lawrence: A Biography, 1990; Joseph Conrad: A Biography, 1991; Edgar Allan Poe: His Life and Legacy, 1992; Scot Fitzgerald: A Biography, 1994. As editor—George Orwell: The Critical Heritage, 1975; Wyndham Lewis: A Revaluation, 1980; Hemingway: The Critical Heritage, 1982; D. H. Lawrence and Tradition, 1985; The Craft of Literary Biography, 1985; The Legacy of D. H. Lawrence: New Essays, 1987; Robert Lowell: Interviews and Memoirs, 1988; The Biographer's Art, 1989; Graham Greene: An Evaluation, 1989; T. E. Lawrence: Soldier, Writer, Legend, 1989.

ABOUT: Contemporary Authors 73–76, 1978; Contemporary Literary Criticism 39, 1986; Dictionary of Literary Biography 111, 1991. Periodicals—America June 7, 1980; Christian Science Monitor April 15, 1986; April 22, 1991; Economist June 29, 1991; Library Journal November 15, 1985; November 1, 1989; May 15, 1990; October 15, 1991; National Review December 31, 1987; New England Quarterly December 1988; New Leader December 16 & 30, 1985; New Republic December 2, 1985; New Statesman December 15, 1978; New Statesman & Society October 16, 1992; New York Review of Books June 12, 1986; January 17, 1991; New York Times October 21, 1985; April 15, 1994; New York Times Book Review November 17, 1985; April 14, 1991; Newsweek October 17, 1992; Times Literary Supplement July 19, 1985; September 7, 1990; November 15, 1991; October 16, 1992; Virginia Quarterly Review Autumn 1992.

MILLER, SUE (1943–), American novelist, writes: "I was born on the South Side of Chicago, the second child of four. My family ecclesiastical to its roots—my father, a church historian, was also an ordained minister, as were both my grandfathers and several great-grandfathers and great-great grandfathers and so on back through the generations. More importantly for me, my parents struggled consciously to make their lives meaningful in terms of what they saw as Christian witness—to pacifism, to racial equality; and though I don't see a direct embrace of religion among my siblings and the cousins in my generation, I'm aware in myself anyway, of a tendency towards self-examination and examination of others—intention, meanings, scruples, ethics— that seems to connect directly to that, has served me well as a writer.

"For about twenty years, my father taught at the University of Chicago. I went to a public grammar school in Hyde Park. I was a reader, a painter, an inventor of solitary projects, the quiet child in a fairly boisterous family. I went to a private girls' school, now defunct, for high school. I was writing poetry and stories all the time I was growing up, mostly derivative, though decreasingly sappy as time went on. At sixteen, after my junior year of high school, I began Radcliffe College.

"I was, simply, too young to have done this. Overwhelmed, I stumbled unhappily around Harvard for four years, taking comfort mostly in love of music—rock and roll, the blues, the folk music of the early sixties—and a string of boyfriends. I wrote fiction again only in my senior year of college, and it was in no way noticed or remarked on, with good reason.

"I graduated at twenty and was married two months later. In the early years of my marriage, while my husband went to medical school, I got a degree to teach high school English and did that briefly. I worked at a Head Start program— again, briefly. I got a job as a research assistant in psychology, as a cocktail waitress, as a model. My husband and I separated for a short time. I also wrote a very bad, short novel during this period, which I've since destroyed.

"In 1968 my son Ben was born, and I didn't write more than a few pages of fiction a year for the next seven or eight years. I was separated from my husband for a second, final time in 1970, divorced several years later. For the years after my separation, I worked in a day care and supplemented my income by renting rooms out in my house. In 1977–1978, I began writing again in earnest and for the first time with a sense of commitment and conviction, as well as a growing excitement in my own ability, it

SUE MILLER

seemed to me, to respond to some of the formal demands of writing—to understand something of how fiction worked.

"In 1979 I won a fellowship to the creative writing program at Boston University which paid me almost as much as I'd been earning in day care. I quit my job and enrolled. At the end of that year I won a Henfield Award, which let me take time to finish another novel, one I'd been working on sporadically for four or five years. It was never published. I'd begun by now to have a few stories accepted at literary magazines—*Ploughshares* and *North American Review*—and from this time on was able to get teaching jobs in various writing programs in the Boston area, stringing together a livelihood as an adjunct professor or lecturer at Boston University, Tufts, Emerson, Harvard Summer School, MIT—frequently several places simultaneously.

"In 1983 I won a Bunting Fellowship at Radcliffe College, and in 1984 a grant from the Massachusetts Arts Council. These allowed me to stop teaching entirely for one year and to work only half the time the following year. During this period of freedom, I wrote *The Good Mother*, a novel in which a woman comes to understand something about who she is by losing custody of a child. It was published in 1986 to very positive reviews and wide sales, and was translated and published in eight or ten different countries. In 1987, a collection of stories I'd written before and during the writing of *The Good Mother* was published. It's titled *Inventing the Abbotts*.

"By now I'd begun to work on *Family*

Pictures, relying on my own memories of growing up in Chicago, and on a lot of reading about the sixties about autism. The book traces the experiences of a family with an autistic child, examining the impact of his presence on various members as they change and grow. It was published in 1990, was nominated for a National Book Critics Circle Award, and has also been widely translated. I've finished work on a novel, *For Love*, the spring of 1993.

"I married for the second time in 1984. My husband is the writer Douglas Bauer. We live in Boston, Massachusetts."

Published in 1986, Sue Miller's first novel, *The Good Mother*, exhibited the realistic style and concern for family life and morality which would be evident in all of her work. In the novel, recently divorced Anna Dunlap is struggling to create a satisfying life for herself and her four-year-old daughter, Molly, separate from her controlling family and her dull ex-husband, Brian. She becomes immersed in an intense relationship with an artist named Leo who embodies all the enthusiasm and eroticism that Brian lacked. For the first time, she finds sexual fulfillment, genuine happiness, and "the euphoric forgetting of all the rules." But her world is torn asunder when Brian, claiming that Leo had molested Molly, tries to wrest custody of the child away from Anna, asserting that she is a negligent mother because she created a sexually open environment which allowed it to happen. During the ensuing custody battle, Anna must choose between her erotic love for Leo and her maternal love for Molly and determine exactly what a "good mother" is. The complexity of the issue involved made the novel one of the most talked about of the year, and it became one of the rare first novels to have an extended stay on the bestseller list.

Many reviewers noted the parallels between Anna Dunlap's dilemma of being torn between lover and child and that of Anna Karenina. According to Josephine Humphreys in the *Nation*, Miller complicates the issue by mutating the question "whether a woman can lose her child if the man she loves makes a mistake, and how hard she will fight to defend him." Humphreys felt that the novel was extraordinary because "Anna doesn't fight at all. She betrays Leo instead of defending him. . . . Anna knows Leo is not to blame—but she blames him, losing her child and her integrity at once, and for no great cause." Because Anna is "human rather than heroic," Humphreys continued, "the novel is all the more disturbing and powerful." Reviewers also complimented Miller's careful observation and evocation of the relationship between mother and child. In the *Chicago Tribune*, Catherine Petroski commented that Miller "has an eye for the perfect detail to crystallize the emotional impact of the character's situation." Although most reviewers found the book remarkably accomplished for a first novel, Jonathan Yardley wrote in the *Washington Post Book World* that it suffered from some typical first-novel failings such as "a self-absorbed first-person narrator, labored expository passages, prose that reaches for an excess of lyricism, and a plethora of extraneous detail," but he suggested that the novel redeemed itself through Miller's "willingness to cope with serious, complex issues, and a sincerity that is genuinely appealing." Yardley also asserted that while Miller "has woven [thematic] material quite successfully into her story, she insists on examining it didactically as well, apparently not trusting the reader to discover it on his own." Miller herself pleads guilty to such charges. In *Publishers Weekly* she stated, "It *is* a didactic book and finally that's the kind of person I am and that's the kind of writer I am."

In the ten short stories in *Inventing the Abbotts*, Miller again examines some of the moral quandaries of domestic life. In the title story, a young man watches his elder brother attempt to escape their family's low social class by having relationships with each of the three daughters of a wealthy man. The boys' mother also observes the affairs from afar, realizing that her son's life is empty and that she cannot help him. According to Roz Kaveney of the *Times Literary Supplement* this was the collection's most powerful story because it "is as much that of the boys' relationship with each other and with their mother as it is of their acquisition of a sense of the world from the Abbott girls. The myth is none the less powerful, and it links effectively, because understatedly, with *The Great Gatsby* : rich girls still don't marry poor boys, and their refusal to do so still sparks a real style of alienated but vigorously moral utterance." In most of the stories, Miller dealt with her more characteristic theme of sexual relationships, but Kaveney believes that Miller "tends to trivialize them, particularly when sexual and parental loyalties conflict." In the *New York Times Book Review*, Penelope Miller remarked that Miller often explains too much, losing the power of understatement. She nonetheless admired Miller's ability to "come up with some rewarding moments of authenticity" and present "adolescent anguish manifesting itself as truculence and apparent social barbarity."

Family Pictures spans 40 years in the lives of the Eberhardts, a middle-class Chicago family.

Miller explained in an interview with *Newseek* that she wanted the book "to be about a whole family almost as a character, and to trace the way everybody contributes to this mutual reality." Nina, the fourth of six children of David and Lainey, is a photographer and the primary narrator. As if looking at snapshots in a family album, Nina recalls specific events from her childhood that reveal the subtle effects of the presence of Randall, the autistic third child, on the entire family.

In the *New York Times Book Review*, Jane Smiley praised the ease of Miller's writing, noting that she "shifts into and out of four different points of view, jumps backward and forward in time, raises complex themes again and again in order to redefine and reconsider them." The result, Smiley believed, was "a work whose cumulative insight blossoms into wisdom and whose steady focus on a single family reveals much of what there is to know about the American middle class in the middle of our century." Other critics felt that, while Miller has an excellent eye for detail, the novel was too long, too diffuse, and had too much explanation. In the *Times Literary Supplement*, Jane O'Grady complained that "intriguing themes and ideas . . . are frustratingly taken up and dropped, remaining undeveloped like some of the scene-setting anecdotes." O'Grady observed that the novel "has some promising ingredients—childhood remembered, sibling intimacy, present wisdom's vantage-point on the past," but concluded that "as a whole it is less than the sum of its moving parts." Christopher Lehmann-Haupt wrote in the *New York Times* that Miller "is particularly good at dramatizing scenes of domestic chaos and the complex interplay of adults and children." Yet he also noted that the "measured pace does get tedious at times; there's not always enough going on beneath the surface to justify the length of the story." While crediting Miller's meticulous observation and "powerfully drawn scenes," Crystal Gromer remarked in *Commonweal* that "the novel as a whole is curiously mechanical" and that the excess of explanation makes the book "wearying." "Reading *Family Pictures* is a little like sitting around the Thanksgiving Day table, too full, listening to the endless stories that are supposed to enable you to catch up on what other family members are doing—all the while the Macy's Day Parade or football games drone on in the background, and it is only four o'clock in the afternoon," Gromer concluded.

Miller told an interviewer for the *New York Times Book Review*, in 1993 that her novel *For Love* is her attempt "to write a book about what it's like to fall in love now," now being an analytical age in which, however, "we still harbor romantic illusions of love." In the novel, Lottie Gardner, a middle-aged free-lance writer, returns to her childhood home shortly after her second marriage, to help her brother, Cameron, prepare their mother's house for sale now that she has entered a nursing home. Cameron has been involved in a long-term affair with a neighbor who comes from more upper-class family than theirs and with whom he and Lottie had gone to high school. Lottie compares Cameron's dramatic, romantic relationship with her own more staid marriage to Jack, an intelligent, patient man. Cameron's affair eventually causes the death of a young woman, a tragedy in which all are complicit, but none to blame. "This is the kind of extreme twist of plot that has unmoored many a story and led it into melodrama, but in Ms. Miller's hands, the actions leading up to the accident are so intricately examined that the story becomes a vivid allegory for all the harm that love can bring," Ron Carlson wrote in the *New York Times Book Review*. Carlson also observed that the novel is permeated with Miller's "trademark realism." Carlson notes that "the fabric of her world has even more threads per inch than John Updike's. She maps emotional terrain carefully, precisely, graphically, with a grit and grace." According to Christopher Lehmann-Haupt in the *New York Times* (1993), "it is the mounting complexities of situations, not their resolution, that interest Ms. Miller." Lehmann-Haupt noted that Miller "doesn't win all the gambles she takes. . . . There are scenes of such detail that the reader loses the story's drift. The promised violence aborts awkwardly and anticlimactically. But then that's what happens in life. And it is the singular virtue of Ms. Miller's richly textured fiction that it captures the randomness and awkwardness and asymmetry of life."

Sue Miller is the daughter of James Hastings Nichols, a professor of church history who taught at the University of Chicago Divinity School and later at the Princeton Theological Seminary. She earned a B.A. in English literature from Radcliffe in 1964. She also received a master's degree in early childhood education from Harvard and a degree in creative writing from Boston University.

PRINCIPAL WORKS: *Novels*—The Good Mother, 1986; Family Pictures, 1990; For Love, 1993. *Short stories*—Inventing the Abbotts, 1987.

ABOUT: Contemporary Literary Criticism 44, 1986; Pearlman, M. Listening to Their Voices: Twenty Interviews with Women who Write, 1993. *Periodicals*—Chicago Tribune April 27, 1986; Commonweal October 12, 1990; Nation May 10, 1986; New York Times April 30, 1990; April 5, 1993; New York Times Book Review May 24, 1987; April 22, 1990; April 11, 1993; Newsweek April 30, 1990; Publishers Weekly May 2, 1986; Times Literary Supplement July 17, 1987; December 21, 1990; Washington Post Book World May 4, 1986.

MILLETT, KATE (September 14, 1934–   ), American feminist writer, was born Katherine Murray Millett in St. Paul, Minnesota, the second of three daughters of James Albert Millett and Helen (Feely) Millett. When Millett was fourteen, her father abandoned the family, leaving her mother to support the children. Although Millett's mother was a college graduate, rampant sexual discrimination in the postwar job market led to her being offered only such employment as demonstrating potato peelers. She eventually found a job selling insurance, but unlike the male salesmen who received wages, she was compelled to work solely on commission. In her first year, Millett's mother earned only $600. "Yeah, we went hungry," Millett recalled in an interview with Helen Dudar in the *New York Post*. "We lived on fear largely."

After attending Catholic schools as a child, Millett enrolled in the University of Minnesota, where she earned a B.A. in English, magna cum laude, in 1956. She then studied at St. Hilda's College at Oxford University, where in 1958 she received a postgraduate degree in English literature with first-class honors. Upon her return to the United States, Millett briefly taught English at the University of North Carolina, but after deciding to become an artist, she moved to New York, supporting herself by working as a file clerk and a kindergarten teacher in Harlem. In 1961, she moved to Japan, where she spent two years studying sculpture. After she returned to New York, she taught at Hunter College and Barnard and entered a Ph.D. program at Columbia University.

During this period at Columbia, Millett became politically active. She was involved in the peace movement, joined the Congress of Racial Equality, and was a founding member of the New York Chapter of the National Organization for Women, becoming the fledgling organization's educational chairperson. Also at Columbia, she became an organizer for students' rights, women's rights, and abortion reform. Her support of these causes as well as her participation in the 1968 student strike at Columbia led to her dismissal from her teaching post. Shortly thereafter she began working on what became *Sexual Politics*, her doctoral dissertation about the politics of female subjugation and the means by

KATE, MILLETT

which literature promotes sexual inequality, which earned her a Ph.D. with distinction in 1970. Her dissertation was published as a book that same year and became a best-seller.

Sexual Politics is now regarded as the first major work of feminist literary criticism and a feminist classic. In the book, Millett first establishes gender as a "status category with political implications" in which women are essentially viewed as property in a patriarchal system that keeps them economically and culturally dependent and submissive. She argues that the concepts "masculine" and "feminine" are societal constructs rather than biological truths and that they have continued to hold sway because they are purported to be "natural." Millett provides considerable background on the women's liberation movement that began in the 19th century and the corresponding intellectual backlash that occurred when women succeeded in achieving reforms. In particular, she dismisses Freud's theories as an attempt to maintain male dominion by centering on the powers of male sexuality while reducing female sexuality to a passive function of anatomy. Using textual analyses, she also demonstrates how the works of D. H. Lawrence, Henry Miller, and Norman Mailer both reflected and influenced cultural attitudes. She places them in a misogynist and patriarchal literary tradition in which women are mere objects in men's power fantasies.

Although some, particularly male, reviewers criticized what they deemed Millett's stridency and overstatement of her case, most recognized *Sexual Politics* as an intelligent, scholarly work that broadened the realm of discourse about feminism. In the *New York Times Book Review* Jane Wilson hailed the book as "original and useful," remarking that "Millett's oblique approach to the problem of women's liberation— concentrating on the incidence of sexism in literature, as opposed to life—made cooler and somewhat more productive discussion possible." Although Jonathan Yardley complained in the *New Republic* that the book "is too long, too discursive, too arbitrarily organized, and its lapses into doctrinaire silliness are maddening," he concluded, "on balance it is an impressive, sober, provocative study." In the *New York Times*, Christopher Lehmann-Haupt was less equivocal, assessing the book as "supremely entertaining to read, brilliantly conceived, overwhelming in its arguments, breathtaking in its command of history and literature, filled with shards of wit and the dry ice of logic, and written with such fierce intensity that all vestiges of male chauvinism ought by rights to melt and drip away like so much fat in the flame of a blowtorch."

The success of *Sexual Politics* caused the media to adopt Millett as the spokesperson for the feminist movement. She appeared on the cover of Time magazine and was widely interviewed and frequently challenged. After acknowledging her lesbianism in response to a direct question during a speech at Columbia, she faced additional criticism by those who felt that her admission diminished the authority of *Sexual Politics*. Frustrated by her inability to control her own image, she began keeping copious notes about her life. She decided that the best way of dealing with the tumult was "to treat my own existence as documentary."

The result was her first autobiographical work, *Flying*, in which she reported upon her work, her love affairs, her friendships, and her mother's hostile reaction on learning of her lesbianism. Although Millett's discussion of the personal ramifications of acknowledging her homosexuality fascinated some reviewers, most also found the book self-indulgent and arduously long. Describing *Flying* as "a cry of pain," Jane Wilson remarked in the *New York Times Book Review* (1974) that "it is not mere justification that Millett seeks. She is after absolution as well, empathy, approval and admiration, and her demanding neediness hounds the reader from the beginning to the end of this marathon essay in self-absorption." Although Muriel Haynes wrote in the *New Republic* (1974) that the book "demands of the reader an analyst's endurance," she found Millett herself appealing. "An intelligent, gutsy, loving woman, full of self-hate and a passionate longing for acceptance, her genuine suffering reflects the damaging confusions of

American culture in transition," Haynes wrote. Haynes also praised Millett's gift for character, although she felt that Millett lacked the detachment to use such skills to create literature. Dissenting from these views was Annette Kolodny, who argued in *Contemporary Literature* that Millett succeeded in creating a new form of autobiography that offered a new view of female narrative. Kolodny noted that if treated "as an ongoing reading experience, rather than measured against a Procrustean bed of received expectations to which it was never meant to conform, *Flying* reveals its own internal organizing principles, as it explores the many-layered associative intertwinings of consciousness, memory, and image." Millett's second memoir, *Sita*, in which she recounts her dying love affair with the eponymous Sita, was notable at the time for being one of the rare realistic depictions of a lesbian relationship, but it received generally scathing reviews because of its excessive detail and what Sara Sanborn, in the *New York Times Book Review* called her "self-seriousness," which enables her to believe that "her personal doings are important to the rest of us."

Millett turned away from autobiography but maintained an intensely personal narrative approach with *The Basement: Meditations on a Human Sacrifice*, the story of Sylvia Likens, a 16-year-old whose torture and murder Millett had been obsessed with since its occurrence in 1965. With gruesome detail Millett reports the brutal events leading up to the killing, as she argues that Sylvia was killed because of her femaleness. Millett looks at the situation through Sylvia's eyes as well of those of Gertrude Baniszewski, the woman who was paid to board her and who, along with three of her seven children and two other neighborhood children, was convicted of the murder. Although most reviewers were unconvinced by Millett's central thesis that Sylvia died because of her sex, many nonetheless regarded it as her most powerful work. "The writing is fully ripened, rich and dense, sometimes spilling out in torrents," Anne Tyler commented in the *New Republic* attributing this to the book's long gestation period. Tyler concluded, "It is an important study of the problems of cruelty and submission, intensely felt and movingly written." In the *New York Times Book Review* Joyce Carol Oates remarked on the depth of Millett's empathy, writing: "There is something mesmerizing about another's obsession." While complimenting Millett's own voice and descriptions of the torture as "forceful and intelligent," Oates felt that Millett's stream-of-consciousness renderings of Gertrude's and Sylvia's minds "have the effect of flattening out and even trivializing the horror."

Going to Iran chronicled Millett's trip there in 1979, shortly after the shah was overthrown, to work on behalf of women's liberation. The book provoked mixed responses. In the *Nation*, Fred Halliday called it "astute, vivid and angry," while in the *New York Times Book Review* Clifford D. May renewed old charges that Millett's writing is muddled and is "only about Kate Millett," and judged that the book "does not succeed as travel writing, political analysis, current history or journalism."

Millett returned to overt autobiography in 1990 with *The Loony-Bin Trip*. Having been diagnosed as manic depressive in 1973, she was prescribed lithium, which she ceased taking in 1980 because she felt that the side effects stifled her creativity. Her friends and family grew concerned about what they deemed her erratic behavior and attempted to have her institutionalized to force her back on lithium. Although she managed to evade her friends' attempts, after exhibiting odd behavior at an airport in Ireland, she was taken to a hospital where she was heavily drugged, isolated, and treated like a "defective child." Following her release, she returned home and suffered severe depression before finally going back on lithium. Throughout the book, Millett argues that psychiatry is authoritarian and the mania is creative. Many reviewers found Millett's descriptions of institutionalization and her own illness disturbing and illuminating, comparing the work to Ken Kesey's *One Flew over the Cuckoo's Nest*. Chris Savage King judged Millett's testimony powerful, noting in the *New Statesman & Society*, "Writing like a forest fire in full blaze, she lays into psychiatry and the prejudices of the terminally normal with the scorching fury she brought to *Sexual Politics*." Yet like many other reviewers, King noted that "her final conclusions are disappointing. Madness exists, insanity doesn't; do away with drugs and psychiatry." Joy Williams was harsher, remarking in the *Chicago Tribune*: "The book actually is quite incoherent; there seems a disinclination here to focus, to shape a truth. . . . There is no sense of the mind examining itself, of the judgment of the present upon the past."

In *The Politics of Cruelty: An Essay on the Literature of Political Imprisonment*, Millett surveys contemporary incidences of state torture and, using both literary and documentary sources, ruminates on the psychology of the torturer and the tortured. Although reviewers pronounced many of her points valid and her descriptions gruesomely evocative, some considered the book an awkward assemblage of material and found her analyses somewhat superficial.

Millett entered another searching examination into the meaning of her own life in *A.D.* a memoir centering on her relationship with her rich, cultured, and snobbish aunt who sent her to study in England but broke with her when she discovered that Millett had lied when she promised to renounce her lesbianism. Elizabeth Gleick, reviewing the memoir in the *New York Times Book Review*, deemed its style "flood-of-consciousness" and noted the absence of "the rigorous prose of . . . Millett's *Sexual Politics*, or the politically charged, confessional writing in *The Loony-Bin Trip*." Gleick concluded: "Missing, too, is any vivid sense of an outside world, of what it was really like to be a lesbian in the 50's or an artist on her own in New York."

Millett has also written *The Prostitution Papers*, an examination of the experiences of prostitutes, and she wrote and directed the documentary film *Three Lives* (1971), about three people's experiences as women in America. Millett divides her time between New York City and a Christmas tree farm near Poughkeepsie, New York, which she runs as a women's artists colony. Millett was married to Japanese sculptor Fumio Yoshimura from 1965 to 1985, when the couple divorced.

PRINCIPAL WORKS: Sexual Politics, 1970; The Prostitution Papers, 1971; Flying, 1974; Sita, 1977; The Basement: Meditations on a Human Sacrifice, 1980; Going to Iran, 1982; The Loony-Bin Trip, 1990; The Politics of Cruelty: An Essay on the Literature of Political Imprisonment, 1994; A.D., 1995.

ABOUT: Contemporary Authors New Revision Series 32, 1991; Contemporary Literary Criticism 67, 1992; Current Biography Yearbook 1971; Pollack, S. and Knight D. D. (eds.) Contemporary Lesbian Writers of the United States, 1993. Periodicals—Chicago Tribune June 3, 1990; Contemporary Literature Autumn 1976; Nation April 17, 1982; New Republic August 1, 1970; July 6, 1974; July 7, 1979; New Statesman & Society October 11, 1991; New York Post August 1, 1970; New York Times August 5, 1970; August 6, 1970; New York Times Book Review June 23, 1974; May 29, 1977; September 9, 1979; May 16, 1982; August 13, 1995.

MITCHELL, ADRIAN (October 24, 1932–), British poet, dramatist, and novelist, was born in London, the son of James Mitchell and Kathleen (Fabian) Mitchell. His father was a scientist, his mother a teacher. He was educated at Greenways School and at Dauntsey's School, both in Wiltshire, before completing his National Service in the Royal Air Force (1951–1952). In 1952 he entered Christ Church College, Oxford University, where he was literary

ADRIAN MITCHELL

editor of *Isis* magazine (1954–1955). Also at Oxford, he became acquainted with such poets as Alan Brownjohn, George Macbeth, Geoffrey Hill, A. Alvarez, and Elizabeth Jennings. His first publication was a pamphlet which appeared in 1955 as part of the Fantasy Poets series edited by George Macbeth and Oscar Mellor.

After leaving Oxford, Mitchell worked as a reporter on the *Oxford Mail* from 1955 to 1957, and then on the *London Evening Standard* until 1959. He has also contributed columns and television and record reviews to various other London publications including the *Sunday Times*, the *Daily Mail*, *Woman's Mirror*, the *Sun*, the *Guardian*, *Peace News*, and *Black Dwarf*. His journalistic experience influenced his writing: both his drama and poetry incorporate styles of news presentation to heighten the immediacy of their impact. Early in his career Mitchell was known chiefly through his poetry readings, which formed part of the Hampstead Poets and Live New Directions movements. He gained wider recognition when he won the Gregory Award for Poetry in 1961.

In an interview in *Contemporary Poets*, Mitchell said of his own work and career: "Politically speaking, it was poetry as much as anything else that pushed me first in the direction of left-wing political action (in which I include committee work, demonstrating, envelope-addressing as well as poetry) . . . Every revolution so far has had its own songs and poems. That contribution towards changing the world may be very small, but the smallest contribution helps when it's a matter of changing the world. I think a poet, like any other human being, should recognize that the world is mostly controlled by political forces and should become politically active too."

In Mitchell's first long volume of poems, *Poems*, published in 1964, he articulates his belief that war is the ultimate expression of society's systemic brutality. Governments and institutions are invidious, individuals victims of their calumny. A self-avowed hater of the obscure and the esoteric, Mitchell keeps his poems short pointed and readily understandable, using such devices as easily recognized rhyme schemes and rhythmic repetitions to communicate his message to those who may not otherwise read poetry.

Mitchell deliberately presents his poems and dramas as revolutionary acts, savaging established conventions and expectations. His poetry, some of it tightly structured, some spilling out in loose free-flowing patterns akin to jazz improvization, expresses the rage of the fully committed. His dramas are often semi-improvisatory collaborations, aiming at a spontaneous interaction between performers and audience. Mitchell considers his poetic ancestors to be Wilfred Owen, Walt Whitman, Kenneth Patchen, Alex Comfort, Bertolt Brecht, Samuel Beckett, John Arden, Allen Ginsberg and most of all, the radical antiauthoritarian William Blake, the subject of his full-length play *Tyger*. He has himself been acknowledged as a precursor of and father-figure to Liverpool poets Adrian Henri, Roger McGough, and Brian Patten, who endow their public readings with the power of protest and rebellion.

Always angered at the sight of human suffering, Mitchell has written many repeated antiwar tirades such as "Chile in Chains," "Tell Me Lies About Vietnam," "On the Beach at Cambridge" and "The Dust." Strongly influenced by Blake's *Songs of Innocence and Songs of Experience*, Mitchell writes many of his poems as songs, often using them as musical inserts in his plays to lend particular emphases to character and action. Jazz, blues, and American popular culture in general, including pop art, have influenced all of Mitchell's work. He incorporates conversational language, raw emotion, and colloquial tone and diction into his writings.

In 1964 Mitchell wrote the verse adaptation for the English translation of Peter Weiss's *Marat/Sade* and in 1966 he shared the PEN translation prize for this work. His association with Peter Brook, who directed the celebrated stage and film productions of Weiss's play, led to Mitchell's writing seven songs for *US*, produced by Peter Brook for the Royal Shakespeare Company. These songs became the first poems in Out Loud, perhaps Mitchell's best-known work, articulating an undiluted antiestablishment stance and vitriolic opposition to the war in Vietnam. They also represent Mitchell's most oral poetry—most effective when read, as the title suggests.

Mitchell is credited with singlehandly inventing some of the bromides of the 1960s. In one poem from Out Loud, "To You," he writes "We must make love/ instead of money." In such poems Mitchell strives for the spontaneity and anarchic wildness achieved by his poetic forebears:

On William Blakes's birthday we're going to free you,
Blast you off your platforms with a blowtorch full
of brandy
And then we'll stomp over to the House of Parliament
And drive them into the Thames with our bananas.

Anthony Thwaite, writing in the *New Statesman*, has argued that Mitchell's poems presuppose "a youngish, leftish, protest prone audience . . . They are clear, direct, funny, warmhearted and eloquent. They are also sometimes obvious, banal, whimsical, and too genially sure of a welcome: the Queen, the bourgeoisie, the term 'critic' and the word 'peace' invite responses which can too easily be satisfied. It will be a pity if Mitchell's real talent for making poetry public is crudified and dissipated by an audience that too readily sits there waiting for him to hit old targets."

Mitchell's play *Tyger*, with a musical score by Mike Westbrook, has been praised for its innovation and its attempt to extend the notion of the musical. It has also been criticized as uneven, naive, and pandering to an audience already sated with television, pop music, and gutter press.

Mitchell has not articulated his hatred for what he perceives as a hypocritical and brutally conservative society in any way that particularizes, differentiates, and calibrates the scale of his judgment and response. However, it would be reductive to accept the familiar conclusion that his work is naive, simplistic, and dated. His 1989 collection *Love Songs of World War Three* brings together a formidable body of poetry previously set to music, and is based upon the contention that World War Three is in fact the continual warfare perpetuated in various countries throughout the world since 1945. This is not a dated perspective. In this volume he uses poetry, drama, and song to express a righteous anger that grows out of his abiding concern for humanity:

We have one choice to work at building heaven
And when we die, we're making room for someone . . . after death, what's left of us?

The results of our works and our lives
Whatever we created for the people
And marks of our love and hate in those who survive.

While Mitchell has broken no new ground in poetic technique, he has been part of a movement that has developed poetry as a dynamic dimension of popular culture.

Mitchell is also the author of three novels (and one novel adapted from a play). As urgent as his poetry and drama, they have received praise for their more inclusive approach to politics. The discipline of the novel form lends an organizing coherence to Mitchell's display of rhetorical forms. Poetry and jazz improvization are fused in his first novel, *If You See Me Comin'* which focuses on the fortunes of a blues singer. Political irony is granted extended development in the *The Bodyguard*, a psychological study of a self-congratulating fascistic thug. Speech, dream, interviews, letters, news items and fragmented thoughts are combined with narrative description in *Wartime* to embody the efforts of a political radical to defy the crushing demands of a reactionary society.

In addition to his writing, Mitchell has also made his living teaching and advising. He was instructor at the University of Iowa, Iowa City (1963–1964), and Granada Fellow in the Arts, University of Lancaster (1967–1969). He was Fellow at University Center for the Humanities, Middletown, Connecticut (1971–1972); resident writer, Sherman Theatre, Cardiff (1974–1975); visiting writer, Billericay Comprehensive School, Essex (1978–1980); Judith E. Wilson Fellow, Cambridge University (1980–1981); and resident writer, Unicorn Theatre for Young People, London (1982–1983). He received the Eric Gregory Award for Poetry in 1961, the PEN prize for translation in 1966, and the Tokyo Festival Award for Television in 1971. In 1988 he became a Fellow of the Royal Society of Literature.

PRINCIPAL WORKS: *Poetry*—Poems, 1955; Poems, 1964; Peace is Milk, 1966; Out Loud, 1968, Ride The Nightmare: Verse and Prose, 1971; Cease-Fire, 1973; (with John Fuller and Peter Levi) Penguin Modern Poets 22, 1973: The Apeman Cometh, 1975; The Annotated Out Loud, 1976; For Beauty Douglas: Collected Poems 1953–1979, 1982; Nothingmas Day, 1984; On The Beach At Cambridge: New Poems, 1984; Love Songs of World War Three (collected song lyrics) 1989; Adrian Mitchell's Greatest Hits, 1991; *Plays*—The Ledge, 1961; The Persecution and Assassination of Jean-Paul Marat as Performed by the Inmates of the Asylum of Charenton under the direction if the Marquis De Sade, 1964; The Magic Flute, 1966; US, 1966; The Criminals, 1967; Tyger: A Celebration of the Life and Work of William Blake, 1971; Tamburlaine the Mad Hen, 1971; Man Friday, 1973; Mind

Your Head, 1973; The Inspector General, 1974; A Seventh Man, 1976; Houdini: A Circus Opera, 1977; White Suit Blues, 1977; Uppendown Mooney, 1978; The White Deer, 1978; In the Unlokey Event of an Emergency, 1979; Hoagy, Bix, and Wolfgang Beethoven Bunkhaus, 1980; Peer Gynt, 1980; The Mayor of Zalamea; or, The Best Garrotting Ever Done, 1981; Mowgli's Jungle, 1981; You Must Believe All This, 1981; The Wild Animal Song Contest, 1982; Child's Christmas in Wales 1983; a Dream, 1983; Life's a Dream, 1983; Animal Farm, 1984; C'mon Everybody, 1984; The Greatest Theater of the World, 1984; The Government Inspector (revised version if the Inspector General), 1985; The Tragedy of King Real, 1985; The Pied Piper, 1986; Satie Day/Night, 1986; The Last Wild Wood in Sector 88, 1987; Mirandolina, 1987; Love Songs of World War Three, 1988; Anna on Anna, 1988; Fuente Ovejuna, 1988; Women Overboard, 1988; The Patchwork Girl of Oz, 1988; The Tragedy of King Real, 1989; *Screenplays*—Marat/Sade, 1966; Tell Me Lies (lyrics only) 1968; The Body (commentary), 1969; Man Friday, 1976; The Tragedy of King Real, 1983; *Radio Play*—The Island (libretto) 1963. *Television Plays*—Animals Can't Laugh, 1961; Alive and Kicking, 1971; William Blake [documentary] 1971; Man Friday, 1972; Somebody Down There is Crying, 1974; Daft as a Brush, 1975; The Fine Art of Bubble Blowing, 1975; Silver Giant, Wooden Dwarf, 1975; Glad Day, 1979; You Must Believe All This, 1981; Juno and Avis, 1983. *Fiction*— If You See Me Comin', 1962; The Bodyguard, 1971; Wartime, 1973; Man Friday, 1975. *Juveniles*— The Adventures of Baron Munchausen, 1985; The Baron Rides Out, On the Island of Cheese, All at Sea, 3 vols, 1985– 1987; Leonardo, The Lion From Nowhere, 1986; Our Mammoth, 1987; Our Mammoth Goes to School, 1988; Rhinestone Rhino, 1989.

ABOUT: Contemporary Authors 33–36, 1978; Contemporay Poets, 5th ed., 1991; Dictionary of Literary Biography 40, 1985; Who's Who 1993. *Periodicals*— Best Sellers August 15, 1970; Book World July 28, 1968; Canadian Literature Autumn 1983; Library Journal January 1, 1983; London Magazine June 1968; August 1968; New Statesman March 22, 1968; July 30, 1971; Observer August 2, 1970; August 30, 1970; Observer Review March 3, 1968; Plays and Players September 1971; January 1987; Stage November 2, 1972; Times (London) July 15, 1985; December 21, 1985; January 11, 1992; Literary Supplement October 29, 1982; November 23, 1984; December 19, 1986; October 9, 1987; October 23, 1987; May 22, 1992; Variety August 11, 1971. RTYTS

MITCHELL, JOSEPH (QUINCY) (July 27, 1908–), American journalist and essayist, whose stories on the bizarre and eccentric aspects of New York life have identified him solidly with that city, is actually a native of Fairmont, North Carolina, a tobacco and cotton farming community. He is the son of Averette Nance Mitchell, a cotton buyer ("cotton buyers always considered themselves superior to the rest of the world," his son once commented), and Elizabeth Amanda (Parker) Mitchell; his family had farmed land in the region since before the American Revolution. Mitchell attended the University of North Carolina from 1925 to 1929, was a reporter on the undergraduate newspaper, and wrote several short stories. One of these, "Cool Swamp and Field Woman," was published in the *New American Caravan* in 1929. A regional story, done in a consciously lyrical style, it owes much to his fellow southerner William Faulkner and also to James Joyce, one of his favorite authors.

Having decided that he wanted to be a reporter—specifically, a political reporter—Mitchell came to New York, arriving the day after the stock market crash. His first job, for a few months in 1929–1930, was as a legman covering crime stories in Brooklyn for the *New York World*. ("The only kind of crime I liked was gangster funerals and they threw a lot of big ones that year.") He then went to the *New York Herald Tribune* for a year (1930–1931), covering city news; Harlem was his favorite beat and, as he put it, "fascinated by the melodrama of the metropolis at night," he would wander the Harlem streets "discovering what the depression and the prurience of white men were doing to a people who are 'last to be hired; first to be fired.'" In 1931, after an interlude at sea working as a deckhand on a freighter bringing pulp logs back from Leningrad, he joined the *New York World-Telegram* and worked as a reporter for the next seven years. In 1931 he married Therese Dagny Engelsted Jacobsen (d. 1980), a photographer whose pictures illustrate his first book, *My Ears Are Bent*. They had two daughters.

Mitchell got his first byline in 1933 and began to do feature stories and interviews; he was assigned, for example, to cover the trial of Bruno Hauptmann, accused kidnapper of the Lindbergh baby. The trial was a "mess," he concluded, and "there will never be anything like it again, God willing. That is the way I feel about many of the stories I have worked on." In the course of his newspaper assignments he found that he was "tortured by some of the fanciest ear-benders, including George Bernard Shaw and Nicholas Murray Butler, in the world, and I have long since lost the ability to detect insanity." Despite this statement, the key to Mitchell's writing has always been his ability to draw people out, and his recognition that "the best talk is artless, the talk of people trying to reassure or comfort themselves." Such disclosures come from the introductory sketch in *My Ears Are Bent*, a collection of his *Herald Tribune* and *World-Telegram* pieces and earliest articles for

the *New Yorker* magazine—for which he started writing in 1938. The ear-benders also included drunks at the Broken Leg and Busted, a saloon in Harlem; the fan dancer Sally Rand; the Harlem religious leader Father Divine; a woman prizefighter; and "Miss Mazie," a Bowery movie theater ticket seller and one-woman rescue squad. He wrote also of homeless women in Bowery shelters and patients in a veterans' hospital; the scene on Coney Island, along Hester Street and at the Battery; and a trip aboard the old Albany Night Boat.

Since 1938 Joseph Mitchell's writing life has been wholly associated with the *New Yorker*; his published books—*McSorley's Wonderful Saloon, Old Mr. Flood, The Bottom of the Harbor*, and *Joe Gould's Secret*—are collections of the stories he wrote for the magazine. Those who read his Profiles, Reporter at Large pieces, and other sketches as they appeared (there have been something like forty-six of them in all) will have lists of favorites that have haunted them over the years. There was his classic, "The Old House at Home" (1940), about McSorley's, the oldest bar in New York. There were his reports about oyster fishing in New York harbor, rats on the waterfront, bands of gypsies in the city, and the Mohawk Indians, "who have no fear of heights and work as riveters on skyscrapers and bridges," and came to live in downtown Brooklyn. ("The Mohawks in High Steel," written in 1949, was reprinted in 1960 as the introduction to Edmund Wilson's *Apologies to the Iroquois*.) There were the unforgettable portraits of (among many others) a nine-year-old genius, Philippa Duke Schuyler; Jane Barnell, a.k.a. "Lady Olga," the bearded lady; and Mr. Flood, a semifictional composite of several Fulton Fish Market men, to whom Mitchell gave his own birth date. He wrote on his own tastes in food and literature and above all his own love for old New York. And there was "Professor Sea Gull," the bibulous, garrulous (and ultimately crazy) Joe Gould whose story fascinated Mitchell for twenty-two years. Brendan Gill, in his memoir *Here at the New Yorker*, states that "in the opinion of many . . . the finest writer on [the magazine] is Joseph Mitchell." Noel Perrin, in the *Sewanee Review*, has called him "one of the great essayists of our time." Characteristically, he achieves his effects with deliberate pacing, working with simple declarative sentences and a leisurely, often digressive accretion of details. Very much in the manner of the 18th-century writer Daniel Defoe, journalism becomes an art in Mitchell's hands. There are intimations of change and death in many of his pieces, but perceived as part of existence, never sentimentalized, and frequently lightened by lyrical divagations on the sights and smells and gustatory delights of his city. He writes, for example, in "Up in the Old Hotel," "Every now and then, seeking to rid my mind of thoughts of death and doom, I get up early and go down to the Fulton Fish Market." And in the introduction to "Mr. Hunter's Grave" (1956), he writes about Staten Island oystermen: "When things get too much for me, I put a wild-flower book and a couple of sandwiches in my pockets and go down to the South Shore of Staten Island and wander around awhile in one of the old cemeteries down there."

Gill's book, published in 1975, gives glimpses of Mitchell at work and among his peers in the milieu he had by then inhabited for almost forty years: "In the offices of the *New Yorker* is a long corridor off which Joseph Mitchell, Philip Hamburger, and a couple of dozen other writers and editors have their bleak little ill-painted cells. The silence in that corridor is so profound and continuous that Hamburger long ago christened it Sleepy Hollow." In his own austere, but tidy, cell Mitchell "gouged out" his work; the verb is Gill's, and he justifies it by a description of Mitchell's notorious slowness. Where once he took mere months to finish a piece, he began to take years (the six essays reprinted in *The Bottom of the Harbor* represent twelve years of work): "One consequence of that long period of composition is the interest it arouses among his editors and fellow-writers; everyone speculates about the nature of the piece . . . and about when it may be handed in." As to the finished product, Gill concludes that "if Mitchell worried less . . . and were less miserable in the long-drawn-out process of accumulating his inimitable prose, the results might be to that degree less joyous and carefree-seeming. For what we read . . . has the air of having sprung by the happiest chance, with no effort, from a playful superfluity of energy and talent on the part of the writer; not a groan in it anywhere." From their days on the *World-Telegram*, Joe Mitchell and that other quintessential *New Yorker* reporter A. J. Liebling had been close friends, and they regularly sallied forth together from their respective offices in search of sustenance and inspiration, working out what Christopher Carduff refers to in *The New Criterion* as their aesthetics of New York low life.

In 1942 Mitchell did a short profile of the celebrated Greenwich Village bohemian and freeloader Joe Gould. A man who claimed to be a poet and to be able to understand the language of sea gulls (and had tranlated Longfellow's poetry into sea gullese), he was writing "An Oral History of Our Time," which he estimated to be already over nine million words long. "Professor Sea Gull" was followed in 1964 (seven years after

Gould's death) by a two-part profile, "Joe Gould's Secret." It is much different from anything else Mitchell ever wrote—in great contrast, for example to the writing in *The Bottom of the Harbor*, about which Brooks Atkinson, in the *New York Times* (1960), said: "Although the author is the least described of its characters, his talent for self-effacement is creative. It represents enthusiasm that is muted in style but eloquent in understanding. It represents purity of perception." Although there is usually no sign of authorial intrusion in his essays, this one is self-conscious and introspective, revealing how much the reporter had become involved in and affected by his subject's life—to the point that his obsession with finding the hidden manuscript of the "Oral History" brought back a memory of his own unwritten novel. Unfailingly respectful of everyone else he wrote about, Joe Mitchell seemed frightened of Joe Gould and driven to uncharacteristic exasperation. Christopher Carduff (and other critics) suggests that Mitchell's long silence thereafter had much to do with how Gould had taken him over and worn him out, that the evanescent "Oral History" was a "nightmare vision" of his own oral history of a fading New York scene.

"Joe Gould's Secret" was Mitchell's last piece for the *New Yorker* (appearing in the issues of September 19 and 26, 1964), but he never officially resigned or retired. After the publication of the three articles in book form, as *Joe Gould's Secret*, in 1965, Mitchell became almost forgotten (except by die-hard old *New Yorker* fans), the more so as he refused to allow—for reasons he kept to himself—the reprinting of his books. Roy Blount, in the *Atlantic*, speculated that Mitchell's encounters with Gould "may have deconstructed [his] sense of character," and that he allowed his work to disappear from sight because he realized that the style and content of his reporting had gone out of fashion. The city had changed, so had social attitudes. The marginalized—circus freaks, alcoholics, down-and-outers—were no longer "good copy" but were recognized as having serious problems. On the other hand, William Zinsser, in his *American Scholar* article, credits Mitchell with having anticipated the New Journalism of the 1960s; and Gill slyly suggests that he was writing "faction" long before Truman Capote's *In Cold Blood*. George Core notes that Mitchell's best pieces, though based on real scholarship and undistorted reporting, partake of the quality of fiction, and that the writer himself, in fact, always called them "stories." Malcolm Cowley, in a 1943 *New Republic* review of *McSorley's Wonderful Saloon*, contrasted Mitchell's work with Dickens's novels, noting that "you might say that he tries . . . to achieve the same effects with the grammar of hard facts that Dickens achieved with the rhetoric of imagination."

In 1992 (again with no reason given) Joseph Mitchell broke his long silence and allowed his books—with the exception of *My Ears Are Bent*—to be reissued. The one-volume collection *Up in the Old Hotel* takes its title from a 1952 piece about the ghostly, dust-laden rooms above Sloppy Louie's fish restaurant on South Street, once a hotel for steamship passengers. The story is a paradigm of Mitchell's "haunted" work, as Luc Sante called it in the *New Republic*. Sante notes the "necrological aspect" of many of the inclusions, so often about survivors and the last days of New York traditions: shad netting, beefsteak dinners, gin mills. In "Mr. Flood's Party," from 1945, the nonagenarian Mr. Flood reflects about his favorite food: "I love those good old oyster names. When I feel my age weighing me down, I recite them to myself and I feel better. Some of them don't exist any more. The beds were ruined." But the writer himself is by no means opposed to change. As he told a *New York Times* interviewer in 1992, he was in favor of admitting women to McSorley's men-only sanctum. Asked about recent changes at the *New Yorker*, he replied that "the idea of a woman [Tina Brown] being editor . . . pleases me very much. Actually, I wouldn't be surprised if the *New Yorker* changes her as much as she changes it."

In the "Author's Note" prefacing *Up in the Old Hotel*, Mitchell defines the essential quality in his writing. "In going over these stories," he tells us, "I was surprised and pleased to see how often . . . graveyard humor turned up in them. . . . I was pleased to discover this because graveyard humor is an exemplification of the way I look at the world. It typifies my cast of mind." He also indicates the influences on this "cast of mind": Joyce's *Finnegans Wake* ("I must've read it at least half a dozen times"); and the morbidly comic engravings of the Mexican artist José Posada, first seen tacked on the walls of the artist Frida Kahlo's hotel suite when, as a *World-Telegram* reporter, Mitchell went to interview her in 1933.

Mitchell was elected to the National Institute of Arts and Letters in 1970. His memberships in other organizations are a key to his enthusiasms. He served on the restoration committee of the South Street Seaport Museum from 1972 to 1980, and from 1982 to 1987 was a member of the New York City Landmarks Preservation Commission. A former vestryman (1978–1984) of Grace Church in Manhattan, a church particularly associated with old New York and Edith Wharton, he has been a member of the Century Association since 1966 and belongs to the Society of Architectural Historians, the Friends of Cast-Iron Architecture (of which he was a founder), the James Joyce Society, and the Gypsy Lore Society (in England). He divides his year between the Greenwich Village apartment where he has lived since the 1940s and his farm in North Carolina where—an avid naturalist—he has undertaken a reforestation project. Brendan Gill quotes Tim Costello, proprietor of Costello's, a (long-gone) Third Avenue bar that was a favorite New York writers' hangout, as saying of Mitchell: " 'He's a great one, Joe is, for pawin' over other people's fallin'-down properties. If he ever disappears, start lookin' for him under fifty foot of brick, with a rusty fire escape on his chest and a pleased smile on his face.' " At the age of eighty-six he had not yet disappeared, and in fact told his *New York Times* interviewer that he was working on a book about his favorite haunt, the Fulton Fish Market, and—somewhat mysteriously—"a complicated biography of a woman about town."

In 1993 Joseph Mitchell's *Up in the Old Hotel* won the Brendan Gill Prize, an award given by the Municipal Arts Society of New York to the creator of a work of art best exemplifying the city's energy and creative spirit.

PRINCIPAL WORKS: My Ears Are Bent, 1938; McSorley's Wonderful Saloon, 1943; Old Mr. Flood, 1948; The Bottom of the Harbor, 1960; "The Mohawks in High Steel" *in* Apologies to the Iroquois (by Edmund Wilson) 1960; Joe Gould's Secret, 1965; Up in the Old Hotel and Other Stories, 1992.

ABOUT: Contemporary Authors 77–80, 1979; Core, G. "Stretching the Limits of the Essay" *in* Butrym, A. J. (ed.) Essays on the Essay: Redefining the Genre, 1989; Gill, Brendan Here at the New Yorker, 1975; North Carolina Authors: A Selective Handbook, 1952. *Periodicals*—American Scholar Winter 1993; Atlantic August 1992; Book Week September 19, 1965; New Criterion November 1992; New Republic July 26, 1943; October 5, 1992; New York Times April 24, 1960; August 16, 1992; Newsweek|August 10, 1992; Sewanee Review Spring 1983; Times Literary Supplement September 4, 1992.

MO, TIMOTHY PETER (December 30, 1950–   ) English novelist, journalist, and critic, was born in Hong Kong, the son of a Cantonese father, Peter Mo Wan Lung, and an English mother, Barbara Helena Falkingham. He was educated at the Convent of the Precious Blood, Hong Kong; Mill Hill School, England; and St. John's College, Oxford, where he took a B.A. and won the Gibbs Prize for 1971.

Timothy Mo is best known for novels that combine comedy and seriousness of purpose to articulate the lives of those who live at the boundaries of national culture, caught between the parochial and the international. He draws significantly upon personal experience to construct narratives that chart the typical and the unexpected in the experience of confronting alien cultures and adapting to them. His particular gift, for a Western audience, lies in his capacity to speak for those encountering Western characteristics, either in their own country as affected by colonialism and imperialism, or abroad, in England, adapting to the expatriate experience with bewilderment, humor, and resignation. Mo is most admired as a novelist of cultural overlap and interchange, confrontation and mutual ignorance.

Mo's first novel, *The Monkey King*, was well received by reviewers. Its portrait of expatriate Hong Kong culture won favorable comparison with V. S. Naipaul's early descriptions of Asian society in Trinidad, particularly *A House for Mr. Biswas*. *The Monkey King* draws upon the complications of the urban and international intensity of Hong Kong. Wallace Nolasco, the central character, part Chinese, part Portuguese, has come from Macao to live and work in Hong Kong. He is in business with Mr. Poon, an operator comfortable on both sides of the law. Reluctantly, Wallace agrees to marry Mr. Poon's daughter and move in with the entire Poon family. They are resentful of him as a cultural outsider and, despite his own ethnicity, he is generally disdainful of them as Hong Kong Chinese. After some years of attempting to succeed in Mr. Poon's empire, Wallace is sent to a provincial estate in the New Territories on the Chinese mainland where he is forced to accommodate himself to Chinese culture and deal with the practicalities of daily rural life. He becomes involved with the local powers-that-be, such as the village headman, and embroiled in a feud over the drainage of paddy fields and the siting of shrines in accordance with traditional concepts.

Wallace successfully turns exile to entrepreneurial advantage. He is invited back to Hong Kong to become the heir to the Poon business empire. At the novel's close, Wallace, like the mythical Chinese monkey king, triumphs by his wit and accepts commitment and responsibility. He has also become a significant part of the business culture he has hitherto disdained. The book is full of unresolvable irony. Mr. Poon's house "house furnished in two basic styles, classical Chinese and government surplus;" a daughter-in-law of Poon's, Fong, fails in a classically Chinese suicide attempt, sustaining only minor injury. However, she receives serious fractures and a concussion when the ambulance attendants drop her on the staircase. Mo investigates the persistent frictions that occur at points of interface and overlap between cultures with the intelligence to perceive their significance and the wit to let contradiction stand as a cultural icon in itself.

With his second novel, *Sour Sweet*, Mo again supplies an internal perspective on an unfamiliar social setting. However, he shifts the action away from the Far East to London, producing a vivid contrast between location and action, between 1960s England and a self-contained, traditional, and alien society functioning within it. The novel centers upon a Chinese family: Chen, the husband and father who works as a waiter in a restaurant in London's Chinese quarter; his wife Lily, a woman of demure and retiring aspect but great inner strength; their young son Man Kee, Lily's sister Mui; and, later in the novel Mui's illegitimate daughter and Chen's father. While the family struggles to find identity and money in London, they continue to look to Hong Kong for cultural authenticity and authority. Chen maintains serious relations only with other Chinese, while Lily bases her life upon the values learned in China as a child and finds no reason to change. Through misunderstandings and inevitable collisions, the family becomes a nexus for the contradictory pattern of expatriate experience: the absurdity of cultural inflexibility interwoven with the irrevocable consequences of chosen actions, and the irreconcilability of new options and the power of old duties.

To pay his father's hospital bills in China Chen takes out a loan from the Hung 'Family,' the local representative of the Triad Societies of London, a group much like the Mafia. In fear of being unable to repay the loan, Chen decides to leave the Chinese quarter. The family moves to the suburbs where Chen opens a 'take-away' Chinese restaurant. But the day inevitably comes when Chen must repay his debt to the Hung Family. The repayment of the debt costs Chen his life. Mo seems to be suggesting that the immigrant experience is less about shaping character than about bringing characteristics already held to the fore. Chen, eager to adapt, cannot learn to drive; Lily, reluctant to adapt but alert and ambitious, not only learns but realizes that the power of bribery is as strong in England as in Hong Kong. Mo highlights the pain and comedy of ordinary life in an alien land.

An Insular Possession is a long novel, meandering from 1833 to 1841, from the battles between the Western trading companies in South China and the Chinese authorities, into the First

Opium War, and then on to the lease and settlement of Hong Kong. Eschewing linear narrative, however, *An Insular Possession* is built as an agglomeration of excerpts from diaries, lengthy letters, and long parodic selections from newspaper such as the conservative, pro-British *Canton Monitor* and its rival *Lin Tin Bulletin*, founded by two young Americans opposed to British manipulation of the opium trade.

The novel is a species of imaginative history, crowded with learned passages on the coming of steam, essays on painting, recipes for the practice of heliogravure, fables told to personages and the rumors of events in the United Kingdom and the United States, the industrial revolution, and advances in weaponry. The book seems to vary its identity at every turn: part novel, part narrative history, part documentary history, part travelogue, part chronicle. The use of so many devices lends a sense of magnitude, of epic, and gives the novel an enormous range.

The reviewers for the *Economist* termed *An Insular Possession* "acute and brutal" as a "study of the opium trade in the 1830s," but found that "the book's wobbly balance between fact and fiction" is too weighty a cargo. Brian Martin, in the *Spectator*, called it "a marvellous, monumental achievement, highly intelligent, witty, and having the gravitas of true historical insight." However, Hermione Lee, writing in the *Observer*, stated, "By the end we have collected a compendium of alternative ways of representing history, and a conclusion which underlines the self-conscious methodology of the whole." She goes on to question Mo's wisdom in choosing an alienating mock-heroic manner that compounds the insistence on artifice, and the "yards and yards of portentous pronouncements, flat talk and stiff correspondence." She concluded, "It makes a daring and confident journey, but not all of its readers are going to get to the finish."

With *The Redundancy of Courage*, Mo moves his scene to the eastern half of a small island to the north of Australia, called Danu. Here, Adolph Ng, of Chinese origin but Canadian educated, leads a quiet existence as a hotel owner. He and his friends Rosa Soares, Maria Nolasco da Silva, Raoul Garcia, and Martinho Oliveira, take part in formulating the policies of the newly formed government, FAKOUM, of their newly independent homeland. The apparent comfort of their situation is destroyed when Danu is invaded by its neighbors, the Malais, who set up a brutal military dictatorship. Adolph escapes to the hills and joins FAKINTIL, the military wing of FAKOUM, led by Osvaldo Oliveira. The ensuing guerrilla warfare, in which Adolph Ng becomes closely involved, blurs all previous boundaries and compromises all previous assumptions. People undergo startling transformations and new alliances are forged in the most unlikely circumstances. Family members become enemies and children learn to become soldiers. Previous distinctions between courage and cowardice, generosity and betrayal, sacrifice and complacency, truth and partiality begin to disappear. Mo uses an ingenuous first-person narration in order to combine a simplicity of perspective, a fast-moving narrative, and spontaneous humor, all with the urgency of a thriller. But *The Redundancy of Courage* is conceived on a more ambitious scale. Like *An Insular Possession* it examines the results of a confrontation between ordinary people and their own national, and violent, history.

The novel is particularly contemporary, however, in its concentration upon the significance of communication: "so long as mouths move, words are said, statements issued, then anything can be justified . . . The reality is separate from the words." It is also particularly postmodernist in the ambiguity of the narrator's point of view. He is the only historian of this small and bloody war, yet he is no historian at all, shifting his emphases and perspectives to suit his interests. Adolph Ng decides that the individual courage and commitment lead to the deaths of his friends and fellow fighters mean nothing because when ordinary people are involved "there's no such thing as a hero—only ordinary people asked extraordinary things in terrible circumstances—and delivering." Individual deaths are insignificant because another "fuzzy-haired Messiah" will always turn up.

Adolph Ng is in fact a traitor: the traitor as historian. When captured by the Malais, he informs for all he is worth and wins for himself enough credit and time for a passport to exile. And yet, he *is* qualified to speak for Danu—he was there, and on the front line. His chameleonlike and opportunist nature reveal the partial and corrupted nature of history. War is daily life rather than a story of it. There are no resolutions; the war does not end; there are not culminating victories or defeats; the book only finishes. Lorna Sage commented in the *Times Literary Supplement* that Mo's "is action-writing of a high order, and gruelling to read because it refuses to allow the actors heroism or villainy of (even) a decisive historical role."

Timothy Mo's first novel, *The Monkey King*, won the Geoffrey Faber Prize for 1978. His second, *Sour Sweet*, was short-listed for the Booker McConnell Prize and the Whitbread Prize in 1982, and won the Hawthornden Prize. His third novel, *An Insular Possession*, was also short-listed for the Booker Prize, in 1986. In 1992 Mo received the E. M. Forester Award in Literature from the American Academy and Institute of Arts and Letters. Timothy Mo has also written for such publications as the *New Statesman*, *Boxing News*, and the *Times Educational Supplement*. He lives in London and describes his recreations as scuba diving, weight training, and gourmandizing.

PRINCIPAL WORKS: Novels—The Monkey King, 1978; Sour Sweet, 1982; An Insular Possession, 1986; The Redundancy of Courage, 1991.

ABOUT: Contemporary Authors 117, 1986; Contemporary Literary Criticism 46, 1988; Ramraj, V. The Interstices and Overlaps of Cultures, 1991; Who's Who 1993. *Periodicals*—Books and Bookmen November 1978; July 1982; Hudson Review Winter 1986; Listener May 8, 1986; New Republic May 11, 1987; New Statesman April 23, 1982; May 9, 1986; July 14, 1988; New York Times Book Review March 31, 1985; April 19, 1987; Spectator July 8, 1978; May 10, 1986; Sunday Times (London) July 23, 1978; September 17, 1978; April 25, 1982; October 3, 1982; May 11, 1986; April 14, 1991; September 29, 1991; Times (London) July 27, 1978; May 8, 1986; Times Literary Supplement May 7, 1978; July 7, 1978; May 9, 1986; April 19, 1991; Washington Post March 31, 1985; World Literature Today Autumn 1979; Summer 1981; World Press Review August 1991.

MARY MORRIS

MORRIS, MARY (May 14, 1947-), American novelist, and short story and travel writer writes: I was born in the Midwest and grew up outside of Chicago, in northern Illinois, along the banks of Lake Michigan. My grandparents were Russian Jews who had emigrated to Chicago during the pogroms of the late 1800s. Though I grew up in a world that was safe and suburban, I have always felt a deep sense of my Russian heritage and of the immigrant experience. The Midwest where I grew up was a place of cornfields where I rode horses, the beaches of Lake Michigan, the bluffs and ravines I wandered along. From an early age I explored the world where I lived and intended to stay. But for various reasons, including some complex ones surrounding family and a need for flight, I wanted to travel. The Midwest, someone once said, is a good place to be from, and I have long felt a kinship with Willa Cather and Fitzgerald. Both wrote movingly about the Midwest. Both left it.

"I have always been drawn to stories and I think perhaps that the short story is my natural genre. When I was a girl, my father made up stories so that I could go to sleep at night and I still remember them and have, in fact, written some

down. My maternal grandmother to whom I was quite attached was also a great teller of tales and she told me family lore, though I feel certain she made most of it up.

"I began writing stories when I was a girl and I had one teacher—Miss Dorsch who influenced me. When I was in third grade, she told my mother that I would be a writer. During recess when others went out to play, she let me stay inside if I had a story to complete. Life only seemed to come together for me in stories and in journeys and those two 'narratives'—one of the mind and the other of the road—have shaped my life.

"My mother had always wanted to travel. Once she was invited to a Suppressed Desire Ball and she made herself a costume of the world. I have written about this in *Nothing to Declare*, my travel memoir about Mexico. Whenever she could my mother took me on journeys. On my journeys and in general in my life, I kept journals and in these journals I outlined my stories. I began to write poetry in high school and wrote through college. In college I also wrote several novels and short stories, none of which I published. For years I felt a woman could not really be a writer and have what might be called a normal life. That is, the lives of women writers I had read about didn't lend themselves to this possibility. But in graduate school a poet who knew I was a graduate student in comparative literature insisted that I read my poems out loud at a reading, though he didn't even know if I had any poems. He insisted so vehemently that I finally read three poems which then someone else urged me to send to the *Columbia Review*, which they published.

"I soon realized that I didn't want to complete my graduate degree. I wanted to write fiction. I began to write and send short stories out and several were published in good magazines. Then in 1979 David Godine offered to publish my first collection, called *Vanishing Animals and Other Stories*. It is essentially a book about growing up, starting in the Midwest and ending in the East.

"My concerns as a writer have evolved from examining family, childhood, memory, and the Midwest into a broader spectrum, encompassing a larger look at the world. In *The Bus of Dreams* I wrote stories based upon my travels through Latin America and in *The Waiting Room* I examined the effects of the Vietnam War on one Midwestern family, in particular a sister and her damaged brother. In my two travel memoirs I have tried to look at the way women move through the world. I have one book to complete in a trilogy of travel books about this. *Nothing to Declare: Memoirs of a Woman Traveling Alone* examines my experiences as a single woman alone in Latin. America *Wall to Wall: From Beijing to Berlin By Rail* deals with a search for roots and home. And the third one whose working title is "The Pure Light: Travels with My Daughter in the Southwest will look at the mother/daughter relationship in the context of Indian America.

"As I said above, travel seems to shape my writing and writing seems to inform my travels. My next three books will basically all have to do with the American experience—something I haven't explored. The American dream in all its illusions, what it is really like being an American. *A Mother's Love* is the story of a woman, abandoned by her mother when she is a girl, who has a child as a single parent. But it is really an attempt to examine the American family.

"I do not really know why journeys and writing have gone hand in hand for me, but somehow they feed one another and I don't seem able to do without one or the other. For now, though I seem to be staying put. Or perhaps it is just a different kind of journey. I am married with one child and we live in Brooklyn."

Mary Morris's first short story collection, *Vanishing Animals*, is primarily concerned with memories of youth. The stories deal with such subjects as adolescent infatuation, family vacations, and guilt over the dismissal of a servant, yet they are not coming-of-age stories. The characters' reminiscences, although objective, convey lingering uncertainty about the events and

about life. Anne Tyler observed in the *Washington Post Book World* that some of the stories "take satisfaction in inconclusiveness, in the fact that the world today is neither black nor white but a particularly interesting (even beautiful) shade of gray." Tyler also complimented "the delicate click of the exactly right, coolly appropriate detail upon the page," but noted that some of the "stories stretch too mightily toward the mythical." According to Tyler, Morris was most effective when dealing with commonplace surroundings, where "there are intimations, entirely natural and unstrained, of an echoing, mysterious world just beneath the prosaic surface."

Crossroads, Morris's first novel, concerns the efforts of Deborah Mills to regain her equilibrium after her divorce. When she meets Sean Bryant, she must deal with the wounds from the breakup and her ambivalence about again allowing herself the security of a relationship. Hesitantly, she moves towards Sean, learning about herself and her own strength in the process. In the *New York Times Book Review* Susan Isaacs praised Morris's "talent for depicting ordinary Americans living through difficult times."

In 1985 Morris returned to short fiction with *The Bus of Dreams*, a series of stories that displays her trademark concerns—travel and inconclusiveness. Eve Ottenberg wrote in the *New York Times Book Review* that in the stories "everything is deliberately left suspended. No action really progresses. We start and finish in the middle." Morris nevertheless depicts the disillusionment of her characters and the emotional resonance of seemingly unimportant occasions. Although Jonathan Penner pointed out in the *Washington Post Book World* Morris's "utilitarian prose," he also lauded her sophistication and versatility.

In *The Waiting Room*, Morris chronicles the lifelong mourning of three generations of women. Having just completed medical school, Zoe returns to her hometown to visit her brother, Badger, who had fled to Canada to escape the Vietnam War and is now in a mental hospital nearly comatose following a drug overdose. Badger's condition reunites Zoe with her mother and grandmother, and they recall events from their past. Only by acknowledging her connection with these other waiting women can Zoe avoid the inertia of "the waiting room." Zoe's mother, June, had endured a lifetime of waiting for the emotional healing of her husband, who returned from World War II deeply disturbed. Zoe's grandmother, Naomi, is haunted by the memory of her childhood in Russia, where she was buried alive by her mother to protect her from the anti-

Semitic violence of the Cossacks. According to Wendy Brandmark of the *Times Literary Supplement* (1990), "The mad yet lucid letters from Zoe's brother which preface but also illuminate these flashbacks are beautifully done, but the hypnotic, incantatory effect of much of the writing, the repetition from one sentence to the next of some phrase or word, can be tiresome." Bret Lott, in the *New York Times Book Review* (1989), observed that the novel becomes an "interesting fable" because "the imagery and symbolism of magic realism is married to intensely minimalist prose. . . . Morris uses a daring mix, combining the stark sentence we've come to expect of contemporary literature . . . with startling images—ghosts here and there, sobs heard from hundreds of miles away hair growing Rapunzel-like on a dead man's head."

A Mother's Love, published in 1993, concerns the struggles of Ivy, an unmarried woman living in Manhattan, to raise her child alone after unintentionally becoming pregnant. Although the father claims to have no interest in being a parent, he occasionally returns offering Ivy frustratingly fleeting glimpses of emotional and financial sustenance. Following her son's birth, Ivy becomes isolated, and her loneliness and exhaustion are exacerbated by her memories of being deserted by her own mother when she was seven. Roxana Robinson remarked, in the *New York Times Book Review* that Ivy's "passivity makes her problematic as a heroine. We can't help observing that Ivy's trancelike and self-destructive inertia is responsible for her plight, most evident in her determination not to consider the emotional and financial consequences of her pregnancy until after her child is born. . . . The risk is that we lose some sympathy for Ivy, which does happen. But the benefit is that Ms. Morris has a chance to tell a haunting tale."

Morris's travel writing is at least as accomplished as her fiction, and in her mind, the two forms are very similar. For Morris, traveling is as much a journey into the self as it is a journey into a faraway land. As a result, she told *Publisher's Weekly*, "I think my fiction and nonfiction get blurred together in readers' minds. It may be that the parts people think are the most autobiographical are the least so, and the parts they think are the least (true) may—on another, disguised level—be the most faithful."

In 1978, disappointed with her life in New York, Morris headed for Mexico because, she told the *Chicago Tribune* in 1988, "I wanted to see a way of living. I wanted to see a people. I wanted to see something I just had never seen before." Her account of that trip, *Nothing to De-*

clare: Memoirs of a Woman Traveling Alone, was not published until ten years later. The book describes the year she spent living in a slum in a small Mexican town where she became close friends with Lupe, an illiterate mother of six. Despite their cultural differences, Morris discovered that Lupe was a nurturing influence with whom she had much more in common than she had thought possible. Morris later recalled: "One of the things I really learned was the value of people, the simplicity of friendship. I reorganized my priorities down there. You realize, for the Mexicans, friendship, family, children: Those are the things that really matter." During her stay, Morris also roamed throughout Mexico and into Guatemala, Nicaragua, and Honduras, maneuvering around the pitfalls presented by unfamiliar countries and predatory men. According to Morris, she meant the title, "Nothing to Declare," to be a metaphor for leaving behind both "physical baggage and maybe kind of an inner baggage we carry with us such as dependency—wanting somebody to take care of us." Moreover, the subtitle is a "a metaphor for the way women are living their lives in the post-feminist, post-60s generation. That there are choices; there are options. A lot of them are lonely options, or alone options, that don't necessarily mean you have to be lonely."

In the *New York Times Book Review* (1988), Molly Peacock called *Nothing to Declare* "a union of a travel book and a journey into the self. The vibrancy of this union is on every page of her memoir-cum-travelogue, which tells with generous clarity the story of a woman who locates parts of her nature, which have been denied by her familiar surroundings, in the unfamiliar, deprived, dangerous and beautiful locales." Peacock also describes the book as "a true story and an artfully told one, combining the narrative ease of fiction with unexpected, unwhole, awkwardly (coincidental real experience."

Wall to Wall: From Beijing to Berlin by Rail, Morris's memoir of her journey on the Trans-Siberian Express, was another amalgam of spiritual journey and travelogue. In describing the trip, she displayed what John Maxwell Hamilton, in the *New York Times Book Review* (1991) called "a novelist's gift for characterization." Hamilton marveled at her ability to "find interesting people in a closet." In the *Times Literary Supplement* (1992), Sofka Zinovieff observed that Morris's "elegant descriptions of the people and places she encounters are both poignant and amusing." She also noted Morris's talent for evoking "a constant sense of discovery" and concluded, "It has become apparent in this beautifully written book that the significance was quite clearly in the search and the journey, not the destination."

Mary Morris was born in Chicago, Illinois, the daughter of Sol Henry Morris, a businessman, and Rosalie (Zimbroff) Morris, a homemaker. After receiving a B.A. from Tufts College in 1969, she went to Columbia University where she earned an M.A. in 1973 and a M.Phil. in 1977. Since 1980, she has been teaching creative writing at Princeton University. She has also taught at New York University and served as writer-in-residence at American University and the University of California, Irvine. She has received grants from the National Endowment for the Arts and the Guggenheim Foundation. Morris lives with her daughter, Kate, and her husband, Larry O'Connor, a Canadian writer, in Brooklyn, New York.

PRINCIPAL WORKS: *Novels*—Vanishing Animals and Other Stories,1979; Crossroads, 1983; The Bus of Dreams and Other Stories, 1985. The Waiting Room, 1989; A Mother's Love, 1993. *Short Stories—Nonfiction*—Nothing to Declare: Memoirs of a Woman Traveling Alone, 1988; Wall To Wall: From Beijing to Berlin by Rail, 1991. *As editor*—(with Larry O'Connor) Maiden Voyages: Writings of Women Travelers, 1993.

ABOUT: Contemporary Authors 132, 1991. *Periodicals*—Chicago Tribune July 10, 1988; Kirks Reviews January 15, 1988; Los Angeles Times April 15, 1988; New York Times Book Review March 13, 1983; August 18, 1985; May 1, 1988; July 2, 1989; June 9, 1991; April 25, 1993; Publishers Weekly March 15, 1993; Times Literary Supplement April 27, 1990; March 6, 1992; Washington Post Book World December 23, 1979; July 14, 1985.

*MUDIMBE, V. Y. (December 8, 1941–) Zarian (Belgian Congo), philosopher, novelist, and poet writes: "By the time I was seven, I knew I would choose the life of a thinker. Reflecting back on my life, I can say that there are many similarities between the life of a Benedictine monk and that of a university professor. My earliest influences were within the Benedictine order to which I belonged in the late fifities. I entered the Benedictine Seminary when I was nine and had no contact with anyone, including my family, outside this world. At about the age of twelve, one monk originally from Czechoslovakia, Ladislas Poucek, Dom Maur, introduced me to philosophy. He encouraged us to have a motto and mine was "Etiam Omnes Ego Non" which essentially means that even if all those around you insist on something as truth, if you are not convinced, then you should oppose them. Later on, as a young man, I was particularly in-

fluenced by another Benedictine monk, Jean-Marie de Caters, Dom Théophanes, who was my spiritual director and my confessor. By the time I was 15, I had decided to become a monk.

The similarity I find between the life I almost embarked on and the life-course I utlimately adopted is to be found in the patience required, a ritual regularity which encourages a disciplined mood and tradition of reproduction. Ultimately, however, a combination of the political crisis in Rwanda and another one, Vatican II, in the Catholic Church provoked my decision to leave the Benedictines in the early sixties.

In terms of my intellectual orintation, I was originally majoring in Economics at Louvanium University in Kinshasa when I had the opportunity to meet a Belgian professor, Anne-Marie Poucet. She convinced me to major in philosophy and letters, and, thanks to her, I changed to philosophy and letters. As a consequence of that choice, I met a magnificant person, Professor Willy Bal, who simply invented me. He became my mentor at the University of Louvain in Belgium where I studied philosophy with a focus in Romance Studies.

Actually, my father dreamed of having a son who would become an engineer. Of course this was his desire for himself, but for one year, I studied engineering to prove to myself that I could do it successfully. Although I took a degree in economics, it did not really interest me. At the time, however, I thought it would provide me with the best means to serve my country. It was never my intention, after all, to leave Zaire. Yet today I can say that I am a nomad and am quite comfortable with this. If asked what does it mean to be an African, I must respond, "What is Africanness?" In general, I have an aversion to essentializing oneself, although I do believe that in order to transcend differences—racial and others—one must know they exist.

For me there is no contradiction between writing novels and writing books in philosophy. In fact, I had a wonderful model in Jean-Paul Sartre who was unusual in the tradition of philosophy. He wrote complicated philosophical books, theorizing about the human condition and, at the same time, he wrote novels and plays in which one finds a concrete illustration of his theoretical ideas and positions. My first three novels were purely theoretical exercises but the last one, *Shaba Deux*, which is about a woman, might be the most subjective of my novels. In fact, as a result of this novel, I was invited once to a conference and when I arrived the participants were shocked to discover that the author was a man.

My favorite writers are René Descartes and

°moo DIM bay

Jean-Paul Sartre but, I must admit, that I always travel with San Antonio or Agatha Christie. I have grown increasingly fascinated by the capacity of evil and disturbed to conclude that some people are almost naturally bad people. Why and how this is so is something I cannot understand unless they are sick. Yes, I would accept the sickness but evil for its own sake is something for which I have found no reasonable explanation.

At present, I am completing several books which will be published over the next two years. The most recent, *The Idea of Africa*, completes a project that began with *The Invention of Africa* in 1988 and signifies the end of theorizing about the truth premises through which Africa was invented as a field of study and colonized as an object of domination. This will be published about the same time as, *Les Corps glorieux des mots et des êtres* which is my intellectual biography. I am also currently assembling five lectures which I gave at the University of London in 1993 and these will appear uder the title, *Tales of Faith*. Finally, I am editing an exciting project, *the Encyclopedia of African Religion and Philosophy*.

Evaluating my own work recently, I came to the conclusion a year ago that I was becoming somewhat repetitive. Taking into account the fact that I have not been back to Africa in over ten years and my research has been conducted in libraries, I decided that, at least for the next few years, I should abstain from writing on Africa. I intend to return to a reflection on philosophy and metaphysics. Of course, this will not prevent me from teaching about Africa—my problem is about writing as an arm-chair anthropologist. My students sometimes ask me about my views on teaching and I enjoy their reaction when I respond that for me teaching is an occupation like carpentry—I try to do the job as competently as a carpenter does his. This absence of sentimentality is, perhaps, a mark of my Benedictine past.

The "crossroad," Kenneth Harrow has written, "is Mudimbe's definition of the present moment in African history." In this light, the best framework for grasping the Zairian writer V. Y. Mudimbe's work in literature and the history of philosophy is to see him as one of the most prominent figures in what has come to be called, since Paul Gilroy's study, the "Black Atlantic." The Black Atlantic delineates a geography linking Africa, Europe, the Caribbean, and the Americas, along the lines of the West Africa diaspora to all the regions bordering the Atlantic Ocean—a history of trade, conquest, colonial settlement, plantation slavery, urban migration, and (accompanying all these events) cultural contacts of the deepest kind. Gilroy establishes a cultural unit-in-diversity for the Black Atlantic.

The concept of the Black Atlantic provides an approach to the historical sources of Mudimbe's vision, his literary and political aesthetic; and in addition it allows us to see Mudimbe's own work as a formative contribution to Black Atlantic discourse. His novels *Before the Birth of the Moon* and *The Rift* explore the postmodern urban worlds of African political and intellectual elites—Kinshasa, an elaborate melange of Brussels and Paris in which African, European, and American expressive forms are juxtaposed. From the other pole of his career, Mudimbe's regular review essays for the international journal *Transition* shows the Atlanticist range of his topics, from Cameroon and South Africa to Martinique and Nicaragua, from the Paris of Foucault and Bourdieu to the London of Martin Bernal and the New York of Edward Said.

Mudimbe's major philosophical works, such as *The Invention of Africa* and *Parables and Fables*, trace an archaeology of intercultural relations in the domain of African philosophy, as against European Africanist discourse. In this way, Mudimbe's scholarly work—which in general comes after his fiction—offers a kind of answer to the Black Atlantic dilemmas faced by his fictional characters, some of whom, like the historian Nara in *The Rift* or the revolutionary priest Pierre Landu in *Between the Tides*, are fully conscious of the paradoxical quality of their lives. Nara's "rift" [*l'écart*] and Pierre's "tides" [*les eaux*] are both metaphors for "double consciousness." The Zairian critic Kankolongo Mbuyamba, writing about Nara, put it this way: "The 'rift' is finally this outdistancing of the human community, this desire to change first oneself and then one's life-world." In this conception, the rift is the endangered condition of the African oppositional avant-garde, intellectuals at once alienated and committed.

Mudimbe's critical work in philosophy occupies this rift—for Nara, the place of a mysterious early death—and works with the same political will to change which animates Pierre, also a spiritual casualty. Both rift and tide, as geological metphors, refer to the Atlantic basin itself, which historically intervenes in any effort at a simple account of African experience. The Black Atlantic is always marked by division. A sign of Mudimbe's feeling about this is his fondness for placing epigraphs in classical Greek at the entrances of his African books.

Yet Mudimbe's focus and identification remain African, as is reflected in a typical evaluation of his work, by Bernadette Cailler: "Mudimbe will be remembered as one of the leading African theoreticians and scholars of his generation." The Atlantic journey does not abandon its starting-point. In this regard, Mudimbe could be ranged alongside the anglophone philosopher Kwame Anthony Appiah, whose *In My Father's House* reframes his earlier philosophical investigations in African autobiography, as Mudimbe frames his later philosophical work in African poetry and fiction. Mudimbe and Appiah, both followed the route of intellectual migrancy from Africa through Europe to the United States, where until recently they were colleagues at Duke University.

Mudimbe's role in the contemporary understanding of the Black Atlantic is central: his work can be read as a kind of extended travel journal on the diasporic route triangulating Central Africa, francophone Europe, and the United States. This passage, since he is an academic, is a passage through texts, through discourse, through the archive. (He did actually publish in France in 1976 a notebook of his first academic journey through the United States, *Carnets d'Amérique*. The image of passage—currents or flows of people, goods, finances, gods, wars, images, and ideas—runs through his life and work. His enormous list of publications shows a similar tendency to voyage intellectually from one field to another, including (roughly in order) poetry, linguistics, the literary essay, fiction, philosophy, theology, and social science. Mbuyamba's insight into Nara could be extended to Nara's creator; an "outdistancing" is the mark of Mudimbe's whole career, and in this he joins a whole visionary company of African writers.

A highly intellectualist style marks the francophone culture which nurtured Mudimbe. Mudimbe exemplifies the mandarin—the savant who deploys a magisterial synthesis of discourses—and gives his voice in the Atlantic chorus a certain French accent. In his *mandarin* guise he is quite distinct from the more rough-and-tumble style of African literary intellectuals of anglophone expression. A "rift" of another sort comes into view in this contrast between francophone and anglophone linguistic and cultural traditions in African writing and criticism, a rift equally evident in the trilingual, tricultural Caribbean. Mudimbe's contributions to *Transition*, however, reflect the overcoming of this split, perhaps a result of residence in the United States.

A characteristic of Mudimbe's work in many genres is its unpredictability over time. Bernard Mouralis finds that his work as a whole "tries to give a meaning to the unintelligible and, in so doing, to erase in some measure the scandal it represents." But Bernadette Cailler disputes that view of "smooth links between the essayist, the poet, and the novelist": "I think that the upsetting, dissonant, unresolved aspects of Mudimbe's work may very well constitute the burning core of his creativity," she remarked. Many critics call attention to the meaning of style itself in his work. Lilyan Kesteloot, writing of *The Rift*, points to "a more intellectual, more sophisticated direction in which style plays a more active role and becomes an instrument of liberation." Much the same could be said of the glinting, ironic subtexts in Mudimbe's scholarly prose. In that he resembles both the metropolitan Sartre, Lévi-Strauss, and Foucault, and his Congolese fellow-novelist Sony Labou Tansi—as well as postmodernist African writers in English such as Ben Okri. Irony, or, in Kenneth Harrow's view, oxymoron, is the sign of the historical dilemma of Mudimbe's generation; like Wole Soyinka, Harrow writes, Mudimbe "sees only the end of the road, the way forward blocked. He refuses any satisfied, static position as complacent . . . Oxymorons, after all, are figures of unresolved struggle." Cailler speaks of a different kind of stylistic struggle when she says of his latest novel *Shaba Deux*: "As years go by, it seems to me that Mudimbe has been purging his style of all unessential ornaments . . . reading his latest work is like contemplating a face who beauty would rest exclusively on its bone structure." Mudimbe has noted here that he intends "to return to a reflection on philosophy and metaphysics," and perhaps in that work the "bone structure" of his writing will stand out in even bolder relief.

PRINCIPAL WORKS: *Fiction*—Before the Birth of the Moon, 1989; Shaba Deux, 1989; Between the Tides, 1991; The Rift, 1993. *Poetry*—Déchirures, 1971; Entretailles/Fulgurances d'une lézarde, 1973. *Philosophy, History, Linguistics*—L'Autre face du royaume, 1973; Etude Semantique, 1979; L'Odeur de pére, 1982; The Invention of Arfice, 1988; The idea of Africa, 1988; Fables and Parables, 1991.

ABOUT: Cailler, B., Rigby, P., Kesteloot, L., in The Surreptitious Speech: Présence Afrícaíne and The Politics of Otherness, 1992; Harrow, K. W., Thresholds of Change in Africa Literature, 1994; Mouralis, B., V. Y. Mudimbe ou le discours, l'écart et l'écriture, 1988; Ngate, J., Francophone African Fiction, 1988. *Periodicals*—Annales de la Faculté des Lettres et Sciences de Yaounde, 1985; Callaloo, 1992; Französísch Heute, December 1985; Génève-Afrique, 1976. L'Afrique Littéraíre, 1981; Nouvelles du sud, 1985; Research in African Literatures, 1993; UNESCO Courier, March 1990; Zaïe-Afrique avril 1980.

*MUKHERJEE, BHARATI (July 27, 1940–), Indian-born fiction writer, essayist, and educator, was born in Balygunge, a prosperous middle-class section of Calcutta. Her parents, Sudhir Lai and Bina (Chatterjee) Mukherjee, were Brahmins, an exalted status that sheltered Bharati and her two sisters from the tremendous upheaval of the 1940s, when India was being torn between colonialism and independence. "We were born," Mukherjee remarked in *Days and Nights in Calcutta*, "both too late and not late enough to be real Indians." She recalled being chauffeured to school and shutting out Calcutta's ugly reality. "The ride . . . is very long, and the cityscape unusually unpleasant, I learned very quickly, therefore, to look out of the window and see nothing."

In 1948 Mukherjee's father, a chemist, moved with the family to London and, later to, Basel, Switzerland. Returning to Calcutta in 1951, the girls entered Loreto Convent School. In 1958 the family settled in Bardoa. Mukherjee received a B.A. from the University of Calcutta in 1959 and an M.A. from the University of Bardoa in 1961. With the support of her family, she then left India and, eager to become a writer, journeyed to the United States to enroll in the University of Iowa Writers Workshop, receiving an M.F.A. in 1963 and a PH.D. in 1969. At Iowa she married (September 19, 1963) Clark Blaise, an "American-raised Canadian" and himself a writer and professor. The marriage produced two sons, Bart and Bernard.

After teaching briefly at Marquette University in Milwaukee and the University of Wisconsin in Madison, Mukherjee moved with her husband to Canada, becoming a Canadian citizen in 1972. From 1966 to 1978 she taught at McGill University in Montreal and soon launched a literary career. But Mukherjee was unhappy in Canada, where she encountered racial discrimination and hostility to cultural assimilation. "I was refused service in stores," she told Alison Carb in *Massachusetts Review* 1988–89 . "I would have to board a bus last when I had been the first on line. I was followed by detectives in department stores who assumed I was a shoplifter or treated like a prostitute in hotels. I was even physically roughed up in a Toronto subway station." Mukherjee also felt out of the Canadian literary mainstream, seeing herself, she said in *Days and Nights in Calcutta*, as "a late-blooming colonial who writes in a borrowed language (English), lives permanently in an alien country (Canada), and publishes in and is read, when read at all, in another alien country, the United States." In 1979 Mukherjee—for her own self-preservation, she says—moved to the United States, where she has taught at Skidmore Col-

BHARATI MUKHERJEE

lege, Queens College, Columbia University, City University of New York, and the University of California at Berkeley. In 1989 she became an American citizen. "I had moved," she says in the introduction to *Darkness* her first collection of stories (dedicated to Bernard Malamud), "from being a 'visible minority' against whom the nation had incited its less-visible citizens to react, to being just another immigrant." She now considers herself an American writer, her characters often reflecting this experience of moving "away from the aloofness of expatriation to the exuberance of immigration." In *The Tiger's Daughter* Mukherjee's first novel, Tara Banerjee, a graduate student married to an American novelist, revisits her native Calcutta alone. To quote *Library Journal*, Tara (like Mukherjee) has committed "class-heresy" in contracting her own marriage. Her Brahmin family and childhood friends are hopelessly blind to India's misery and violence, which threaten their very existence as a privileged class. "They were locked in a private world of what should have been and they relished every twinge of resentment and defeat that time had reserved for them."

The national dilemma of the Bengali Brahmins is reinforced on a personal level in Tara's experiences and reactions. As John Spurling wrote in the *New Statesman*, she "is made to register the frailties and contradictions of her ancestral way of life. . . . " while trying to adapt to America, she cannot relinquish her deeply rooted traditions and is troubled by her country's intractable problems. He husband David cannot gauge her spiritual crisis. "I miss you very much," he writes. "But I understand you have to work this out. I just hope you get it over with quickly. . . . The Mets are doing badly." Tara "could never tell David that the misery of her city was too immense and blurred to be listed and assailed one by one. That it was fatal to fight for justice; that it was better to remain passive and absorb all shocks as they came." This passivity helps explain an important event that occurs late in the book: Tara's half-willing acquiecence in her bloodless seduction by P.K. Tuntunwala, s strong political leader who would millitantly enforce the status quo.

Although the novel ends with an eruption of not unexpected brutality (Tara sits locked in a car watching helplessly as an old friend is beaten to death in a riot). *The Tiger's Daughter*, as pointed out in *Newsweek* and by other reviewers, is "built on understated irony and wit." At a picnic on her fathers factory grounds, Tara listens to purportedly serious talk about the servant crisis:

> They did not mind the servants's stealing a little from the days grocery total, but the did mind their joining the Domestic Workers' Union. In their agitation they exchange new stories about rape and riot.
> They reminded each other that Mrs. General Pumps Gupta had been abused twice on her way to the Metro Cinema in recent months. . . . "How is it the lower classes have such a good time? It's just us people who have to suffer!"

In *Days and Nights of Calcutta*, Mukherjee recounts a visit with a Marawi woman who lamented that for her "even reading a book is considered criminal. . . . They think education gets in the way of husband worship." Mukherjee later cried. "I was writing a second novel *Wife*, at the time, about a young Bengali wife who was sensitive enough to feel the pain, but not intelligent enough to make sense out of her situation and break out. The anger that young wives around me are trying so hard to hide had become my anger. And that anger had washed over the manuscript. I wrote what I hoped would be a wounding novel."

The protagonist of *Wife* is Dimple Dasgupta, an immature and self-conscious young Bengali woman hoping for an exciting marriage. But the best her parents can arrange is a match with Amit Basu, an engineer with whom Dimple emigrates to New York. Like her expatriate Indian friends in New York, she finds the adjustment to America difficult. Amit can not understand her vague needs. More important, even as a child in India, Dimple (like Tara's Bengali friends in *The Tiger's Daughter*) saw America from the perspective of romantic illusions promoted in popular magazines and on television. Mukherjee

consistently distances the reader from Dimple. "She thought she might have been a better person, a better wife at any rate, if she could have produced more glamorous leftovers." She has sexual relations with an American man thereby acting out an exciting scenario previously experienced vicariously through soap opera heroines. In a truly bizzare effort to relieve frustrations and add spice to a dreary live, Dimple thinks—seriously, it appears—about nine melodramatic ways to commit suicide. But these grandiose schemes are instantaneously deflated by Mukherjee's ironic tone:

> Later she thought of two more ways to die. One was to stand under a warm shower and slice open the jugular, though it would mean having to ask Amit where the jugular vein was, exactly, and he might get suspicious. . . .
> The other was to squat near the kitchen cabinet where the cleaning fluids were, select an aerosol can of pesticide, open her mouth wide, aim and spray for a very long time. She speculated if the pesticides came in different scents—peppermint, wild cherry, lemon—like chewing gum. It was important for the body to look and smell good when it was discovered. . . .

Unable to distinguish make-believe from reality, Dimple in the end performs a horrifyingly brutal act. She has duplicates the violent images absorbed from the television screen as well as from the mean streets of New York.

Wife, Krishna Baldev Vaid wrote in *Fiction International*, "transcends its ostensible occasion on the wings of its excoriating irony and luminously icy insights." The *Washington Post Book World (1975)* called it "a funny but upsetting account of the conflict of western and Indian cultures, and of modern and old-fashioned traditions of female destiny. . . . " But for some reviewers, Dimple's motivation is not persuasive. The *MS.* reviewer did not accept her schizophrenia; and others argued that Dimple is not represented as a victim of society's pressures, but is simply a sick and troubled woman.

In 1973, after a serious car accident and fire, Mukherjee and Blaise made a yearlong visit to India (their sons spent most of the year in a European school). Blaise took the trip "to understand my marriage"; Mukherjee, to revisit her childhood and, if possible, integrate her Indian identity into her life in Canada. The sabbatical was chronicled by Mukherjee and Blaise in independent journals, and then published in 1977 as *Days and Nights in Calcutta*. The contrast between their perspectives is striking. As Sloan Allen wrote in the *Saturday Review*, "Blaise . . . discovers a magic that enfolds reality in myth and ennobles Bengali life through a love of culture." Mukherjee "becomes angry and sad. For her fondly recalled traditions now mask fear and oppression—especially of women." She realized that she could not go home again. "The year in India had forced me to view myself more as an immigrant than an exile. . . . The India that I had carried as a talisman against icy Canada had not survived my accidental testings. I would return . . . but in future visits India would become just another Asian country with too many agonies and too much passion, and I would be another knowledgeable but desolate tourist."

Soon after becoming an American citizen in February 1988, Mukherjee noted in the *New York Times Book Review* that, having been a "psychological expatriate" in Canada for fifteen years, she was now an immigrant. She urged young immigrant writers to start writing out of their rich *American* experiences. "We're all here, and now, and whatever we were raised with is in us already. . . . Turn your attention to this scene, which has never been in greater need of new perspectives. . . . We may look a little different, and carry different sounding names, but we mustn't be seduced by what others term exotic." *The Tiger's Daughter* and *Wife* had shown the beginnings os the process whereby one sheds the burden of exile and attempts to come to terms with a new life. In Mukherjee's two published collections of short stories, *Darkness* and *The Middleman*, the effort continues; and in her third novel *Jasmine* the immigrant, after a heroic struggle against formidable odds, is at last on the verge of establishing herself psychologically in the American mainstream.

Some stories in *Darkness* were written in Canada, but most of them in Atlanta in 1984, when Mukherjee was writer-in-residence at Emory University. In "The World According to Hsu," a Canadian husband and his Pakistani wife Ratna vacation on an island where they become "prisoners of an unreported revolution." Despite the danger, Ratna feels more welcome there than in her future home Toronto, where Indians are regularly abused. "Tamurlane," a story about illegal Indian immigrants working in a Toronto restaurant, ends in a bloody encounter with the Mounties. "Isolated Incidents" portrays a would-be writer trapped in a dead-end job at the Human Rights Office while her friend lives the glamorous life of a pop star. The strength of *Darkness*, Hope Cooke wrote in the *New York Times Book Review* (1986), "comes from an accumulation of privately realized, often partly blindly realized, experiences."

The Middleman and Other Stories, winner of a National Book Critics Circle award for fiction, depicts immigrants from a number of countries—India, Trinidad, Afghanistan, Sri Lanka, Vietnam—who, with varying success, are "trying on their new American selves," as Mukherjee said in a *New York Times Book Review* interview in 1988. They have "broken away from their cultural and historical roots," the *Times Literary Supplement*'s reviewer wrote; "stranded between two worlds," they struggle for survival. The narrator in *Middleman*—most of the stories are told in the first person—is a gun runner in Latin America who lives dangerously but remains uninvolved: "I have no feelings for revolution, only for outfitting the participants." The heroine of "A Wife's Story," a professional who has emigrated to New York, is visited for two weeks by her Indian husband. He does not suspect that she has a lover. Staring in the mirror at her naked body, she acknowledges how she has changed. "I stand here shameless in ways he has never seen me. I am free, afloat, watching somebody else." In "Orbiting" a young Italian-American woman brings her new lover, an Afghan "from a culture of pain," to Thanksgiving dinner with her family. In "Fathering" the hero tries to maintain a balance between his mistress and his Vietnamese daughter, who is lacerated by terrible memories and hatreds: "Something incurable is happening to my women." "The Management of Grief," inspired by the crash in 1985 of an Air India flight over Ireland with 329 aboard (mostly Canadian Indians), is a poignant yet bitter exploration of the ways of coping with bereavement. (The crash had also been the subject of a second nonfictional collaboration betweens Mukherjee and Clark Blaise, *The Sorrow and the Terror*.) Reviewers generally found *The Middleman* superior to *Darkness*. Jonathan Raban wrote in the *New York Times Book Review* (1988) that Mukherjee has "not only enlarged her geographical and social range . . . but she has greatly sharpened her style," a style characterized in the shington Post Book World (1988) as "indelibly, effortlessly American."

Mukherjee's third novel, *Jasmine*, derives in part from a story of the same name in *The Middleman*, about an illegal Indian immigrant from Trinidad (via Canada) who works as an au pair for an Ann Arbor professor and is seduced during his wife's absence. The protagonist, Jane Ripplemeyer (one of the several names she assumes), lives in Baden, Iowa, with her disabled middle-aged lover Bud, whose child she carries. (Bud had been crippled by an assailant's bullet.) They have adopted a troubled young man, a Vietnamese teenager. Jane recalls how as "Jyoti," a seven-year-old in Hasnapur, in the Punjab, she had learned from an astrologer that she would be widowed and exiled—a prophecy fulfilled when her husband Prakash was killed by a terrorist bomb as they were about to emigrate to Florida. She resolved to carry on as "Jasmine," the new name Prakash had given her.

Jasmine's adventures in America are so numerous that some reviewers, among them John Skow in *Time*, considered the novel too slight for the vast weight it must bear. She arrives illegally, is raped in a cheap Florida motel, and then stabs her rapist to death. She is sheltered by a benevolent Quaker woman, who helps her get to New York where, like Jasmine in the short story, she becomes an au pair, this time for the family of a Columbia professor. Taylor Hayes, with whom she falls in love. But later she runs away to Iowa, where she meets Bud and embarks upon what seems to be yet a new life as "Jane." Her succession of names—Jyoti, Jasmine, Jase, Jane— represents the bold transformation through which, according to Michael Gorra in the *New York Times Book Review* (1989), "she has redefined herself as an American." At the end of the novel she makes what the *New Yorker* reviewer called an "abrupt change of plans . . . jarring and unconvincing" but "in keeping with her nature": she leaves Bud and heads out west to join Taylor. "I am not choosing between men." Jane says. "I am caught between the promise of America and old-world dutifulness." As a logical step in Mukherjee's personal and artistic development, *Jasmine*, in Gorra's words, "stands as one of the most suggestive novels we have about what it is to become an American." The process is enormously difficult, as Rashni Rustomji-Kerns suggested in the *Massachusetts Review*: "(Mukherjee's) characters remind one of circus performers, a combination of tightrope walkers and trapeze artists, as they search for secure, even familiar, places they can claim as their home. . . . They try to transcend the isolation of being a foreigner not only in another country but also in their own cultures."

Mukherjee has taken a firm stand in the controversy over ethnicities in literature. At a meeting of the Association for Commonwealth Literature and Language held in Graz Australia, in June 1993, which she attended as a "minority" writer from the United States, she condemned the "ghetto of hyphenated identity" and the artificial separation imposed by a "multicultural mafia" upon non-white, non-European/North American writers. "I am an American writer in the American mainstream. trying to extend it," she said. The extent of her success in doing precisely that may be measured by the favorable reception given he 1993 novel *The Holder of The World*. Her narrator is a young woman, Beigh Masters, investigating the background of a fabulous diamond. She comes upon a three-hundred-year-old portrait identified as Hannah Easton, born in Puritan Salem in 1670. A rebel at heart

Hannah had married an English gentleman-pirate, traveled with him to India, and ultimately became the lover of an Indian prince, by whom she had a daughter. Structured as a framework but far more integral to the novel is the story of the modern-day narrator, herself a descendant of Salem ancestors and the lover of a computer scientist who is an East Indian.

Ranging in time over three centuries, in a scene from Moghul India to Cambridge, Massachusetts, and in genre from historical romance to science-fiction (the computer becomes an instrument in Beigh's research into the past), Mukherjee even dares to introduce a subtext inspired by Hawthornes *The Scarlet Letter*, with Hannah and her half-Indian child returning to Salem and sharing a mystical identity with the indomitable Hester Perynne. A novel of vast ambition and bold imagination, *The Holder of the World* was highly praised by reviewers in both England and the United States. Claire Messud, in the *Times Literary Supplement*, hailed it as "a triumph of the imagination and a project of unflagging interest . . . an alternative history which could revise forever the imaginative relations between immigrants and 'natives' in Mukherjee 's America; it also provides a wonderful story." The African-American writer K. Anthony Appiah, in *The New York Times Book Review* admired the novel's rich detail and judged it "brilliantly conceived, finely written, sustained from the first page to the last. Mukherjee, reviewer's agreed, had moved beyond the conventional historical novel, succeeding in the wish, as she told an interviewer in the *New York Times Book Review*, "to bring the world into the 300-page novel without losing the complexity. What novelists have the power to do is to imagine the inner life of people who acted out the facts of history. And do it with the sympathy for every side."

PRINCIPAL WORKS: *Novels*—The Tiger's Daughter, 1972; Wife, 1975; Jasmine, 1989; The Holder of the World, 1993. Short stories—Darkness,1985; The Middleman and Other Stories, 1988. *Nonfiction*—(with Clark Blaise) Days and Nights in Calcutta,1977; The Sorrow and the Terror: The Haunting Legacy of the Air India Tragedy, 1987.

ABOUT: Contemporary Authors 107, 1983; Contemporary Literary Criticism 53, 1989; Current Biography Yearbook 1992; Dictionary of Literary Biography 60, 1987; Whos's Who in America, 1990–191. Mukherjee, B. and C Blaise, Days and Nights in Calcutta, 1977; Nelson E.S. Bharati Mukherjee, 1993; Nelson E. S. (ed) Reworlding: The Literature of the Indian Diosporo, 1992; Ross R. L. International Literature in England, 1991. *Periodicals*—Antioch Review 34, Spring 1976; Canadian Literature Fall 1986; Christian Science

Monitor, January 27, 1972; Fiction International 4/5, 1975; Library Journal, March 1, 1972; Massachusetts Review 29, 1988–1989; Ms, October 1975; New Republic, April 14, 1986; New Statesman, July 6, 1973; New York Times Book Review January 2, 1972; January 12,1986; June 19, 1988, August 23, 1988; September 10. 1989; October 10, 1993; New Yorker October 2, 1989; Newsweek January 17, 1972; Saturday Night October 1975; Saturday Review February 5, 1977; Time September 11,1989; Times Literary Supplement June 29, 1973; July 21–27 1989; April 27, 1990; July 23, 1993; November 12, 1993; Washington Post Book World January 9, 1972; May 18, 1975; July 3, 1988.

MULDOON, PAUL (June 20, 1951–   ), Irish poet, was born in Portadown, County Armagh, Northern Ireland. He grew up near a village called The Moy, which is frequently mentioned in his poetry. His mother, Brigid (Regan), was a teacher, while his father, Patrick Muldoon, worked on the land as a laborer and as a commercial grower of mushrooms. Both were Roman Catholics, and Paul, who attended St. Patrick's College in Armagh, was brought up in their faith. At St. Patrick's he learned Gaelic, in which he started to write poetry. Although he judged his efforts in this language to be clumsy and ineffectual and soon switched to English—whose literature he had been eagerly absorbing—the experience of working in the more ancient language had a profound effect on his later poetry.

From St. Patrick's Muldoon went on to Queen's University in Belfast, where he met the group of Ulster poets with whom, as a younger representative, he is associated: notably Michael Longley and Seamus Heaney, the latter of whom was his tutor. The éminence grise behind all these poets, however, was the English critic and poet Philip Hobsbaum, then teaching at Queen's, who had been a founder-member of the conservative, so-called Group, and who founded a similar one when in Belfast. But the major influence upon Muldoon's work has always been Louis MacNeice. Muldoon also read Auden, Frost, and Edward Thomas with keen attention. At first, he has said, he thought that Yeats "was God"; but that is common to young Irish poets, and his interests soon concentrated upon those whom he himself could hope to emulate.

After receiving his B.A. degree, Muldoon went to work for the BBC in Northern Ireland. He was a radio and television producer there for thirteen years. Muldoon published his first full collection, New Weather, when he was barely twenty-two. It was taken unusually seriously even by those who, like Hugo Williams in

Poetry, were highly critical of it; Williams found the poems "rather iced with their own talent," and thought that the poet's "detached virtuosity [sat] uneasily on the shoulders of a twenty-two-year-old, distracting one's attention." Other readers have suggested that Muldoon was a rather artificial poet. The complaint has been repeated about Muldoon's later collections: Mules, Why Brownlee Left, Quoof. "Occasionally, his metaphors are simply facile," Dillon Johnston commented in an otherwise favorable review of New Weather in Shenandoah. And Colin Falck, reviewing Mules in the New Review, found that the poems "rather often [had] a way of misfiring or seeming a bit of a try-on." On the other hand, as Seamus Heaney argued in an essay in Selected Prose, what Muldoon has to say is "constantly in disguise."

Richard Tillinghast, however, reviewing Annals of Chile in the New York Times Book Review, commented on the antecedents to the book: "Muldoon established himself earlier, however, in five books from the '70's and 80's, as a poet capable of writing startling and delightful short poems. 'Quoof,' the title poem of a 1983 volume . . . demonstrates his love of the recherche word and the private language, which possess the power both to seduce and to create distance." He quoted "Quoof" to demonstrate Muldoon's skill at employing half-rhymes and assonances:

How often have I carried our family word
for the hot water bottle
to a strange bed,
as my father would juggle a red-hot half-brick
in an old sock
to his childhood settle.

In Eire-Ireland in 1977, Roger Conover suggested that readers found in Muldoon "the articulation of a deeper structure of which the texture is only the outer skin." An English critic, Andrew Motion, reviewing the third book, Why Brownlee Left, in the New Statesman, wrote that a "child-begetting poem suggests that Muldoon's simplicity isn't quite what it seems . . . Can it avoid being written off by the self-irony it generates?" The long poem "Immram," in that same collection, Motion judged "much the best poem Muldoon has written," adding, "It's as if Raymond Chandler had recast a chunk of Coleridge's notebooks." The poem had been inspired by a medieval legend of a young hero, Mael Duin (a Gaelic form of the name Muldoon), who is seeking to avenge his father's murder. In pursuit of his quest he has a series of fantastic adventures culminating in an encounter with an old hermit, who appears to be the American millionaire-eccentric Howard Hughes, with a passion for Baskin-Robbins ice cream. In a typical episode of the poem, the hero finds himself in New York:

> Steel and glass were held in creative tension
> That afternoon in the Park.
> I strode through the cavernous lobby
> And found myself behind a nervous couple
> Who registered as Mr. and Mrs. Alfred Tennyson.
> The unsmiling, balding desk-clerk
> Looked like a man who would sell an alibi
> To King Kong on the Empire State Building,
> So I thought better of passing the time of day.
> I took the elevator all the way.

Alan Hollinghurst, writing in *Encounter* in 1981, dissented from the generally favorable reception of the poem: " 'Immram' plays an extravagant (Chandleresque) narrative on the Joycean subject of a boy's search for his father. Muldoon's poetic personality, from his first book . . . on, has been a cross of the coarse-grained and the aesthetical, and he makes something at once robustly humorous and calculatedly fine from his extended exploration of a purely personal fiction. It is a *tour de force* which leads nowhere, and can seem to gain its technical exhilaration from a recognition of its final pointlessness: the story is a compound of bravura and bravado and is performed above an inevitable and baffling vacuity."

Overall, however, reviewers were impressed with the increasing maturity and technical mastery of the poems in *Why Brownlee Left*. The sonnet that gives the book its title, "Why Brownlee Left," was called "brilliant" by Lester I. Conner, in the *Dictionary of Literary Biography*, who found reference in it to Muldoon's first marriage and divorce, a matter he "prefers not to discuss . . . beyond what may be implied in his poetry." The poem begins: "Why Brownlee left, and where he went / Is a mystery even now." Brownlee, a reasonably successful farmer, should have been contented with his life, but one day he went out to plough and simply disappeared:

> By noon Brownlee was famous;
> They had found all abandoned, with
> The last rig unbroken, his pair of black
> Horses, like man and wife,
> Shifting their weight from foot to
> Foot, and gazing into the future.

Discussing the absurdist word plays in *Quoof* ("mischievous scribbling in the margins of English," John Herrigan called them in *London Review of Books*), Muldoon's next full-sized collection, in *Encounter*, John Mole praised his "high-gloss technique" and "dazzling accomplishment," but called the poet's "obscurity . . . often downright teasing." Is the reader, he asked, "being led by the sensitive tip of his nose?" Neil Corcoran, in the *Times Literary Supplement*, declared of the poems in *Quoof* that they "delight in a wily, mischievous, nonchalant negotiation between the affections and attachments of Muldoon's own childhood, family and place, and the ironic discriminations of a cool literary sensibility and historical awareness." The *Choice* reviewer declared that *Quoof* shows "the poet . . . as [a]. . . . kind of shaman, weaving textures of deft language. . . . Seamus Heaney and others work in that genre, and there is more of interest to savor in Muldoon's forte: a witty and intriguing disposition of what is often hermetic if not surreal."

Neither the *Selected Poems: 1968–1986*, nor later collections have yet really settled the question of just how substantial, as distinct from clever, a poet Muldoon is. In his review of *Madoc: A Mystery* in the *New York Review of Books*, John Banville said: "I have to confess that I really do not know what to make of *Madoc*. . . . [Muldoon] is at once an artist of great gaiety and of high seriousness, and in his best work these two qualities are inextricably combined. *Madoc*, however, is a little too playful in its profundities. . . . " The poem "Madoc" incorporates the stories of a legendary Welsh prince who came to America 300 years before Columbus and a utopian community planned by the poets Coleridge and Southey in America. "While Southeyopol never materialized, . . . Muldoon invents its story, weaving into it bits of Lewis and Clark's expeditions, Burr's treason, Byron's sexual exploits," and a search for the lost Welsh tribe founded by Madoc, according to Ellen Kaufman in *Library Journal*. Critics, as well as readers, almost invariably find Muldoon's style ravishing and clever. Lachlan Mackinnon, in the *Times Literary Supplement*, said of *Madoc*: "Muldoon's reinvention of himself as an American writer is a source of vast entertainment. . . . Words melt into each other and human distinctions into fruits in quasi-Ovidian metamorphoses." Mackinnon commented that Muldoon "shows us a mind at work, teasing, improvising, listening, reading, loving, and his apparently impersonal narrative turns out to be a winning self-portrait."

Other critics have commented, some not as favorably, on the intellectual workout Muldoon's writing gives the reader. Kieran Quinlan, discussing *Selected Poems* in *World Literature Today*, while acknowledging Muldoon's newly acquired "extreme confidence," commented that many poems were "not easily accessible," and that "more recent poems . . . suffer . . . from requiring a detailed knowledge of both half-forgotten and all-too-familiar political contexts."

In *The Annals of Chile*, according to Richard Tillinghast, "a fascination with Native American culture recurs, as it has in most of his poetry. One of the best poems in the collection, however—"Incantata," termed by Tillinghast a "gritty, rhapsodic elegy to the Irish artist Mary Farl Powers"—is so Irish as to contain Gaelic phrases. Tillinghast, although unable to follow many of the allusions, said he was "glad to be reminded in so forceful and full-throated a voice that art 'builds from pain, from misery, from a deep-seated hurt, / a monument to the human heart / that shines like a golden dome among roofs rain-glazed and leaden.'"

Muldoon has edited the *Faber Book of Contemporary Irish Poetry*, written a television play called *Monkeys* (produced in 1989), and provided the libretto for Daron Hagen's 1989 opera *Shining Brow*, based on a love affair between Frank Lloyd Wright and the wife of one of his clients. Muldoon was praised for downplaying the melodrama; but, wrote Patrick Smith in the *Times Literary Supplement*, he finally "overweighted" it "with an intellectualism and a lyricism that the music cannot sustain." However, he did mention that those who had known Frank Lloyd Wright were well satisfied with its accuracy.

Muldoon was Judith E. Wilson Fellow at Cambridge University (1986–1987), Writing Fellow at the University of East Anglia (1987), and Visiting Professor at both Columbia and Princeton (1987–1988). Since 1990 he has taught at Princeton. He received the Eric Gregory Award in 1972 and the Faber Memorial Prize in 1982 for *Why Brownlee Left*. He married Jean Hanff Korelity in 1987. In 1994 he was awarded the T. S. Eliot Prize of the Poetry Book Society for *The Annals of Chile*.

PRINCIPAL WORKS: *Poetry*—Knowing My Place, 1971; New Weather, 1973; Spirit of Dawn, 1975; Mules, 1977; Names and Addresses, 1978; Immram, 1980; Why Brownlee Left, 1980; The O-O's Party, 1980; Out of Siberia, 1982; Quoof, 1983; The Wishbone, 1984; Selected Poems: 1968–1986, 1987; Madoc: A Mystery, 1990; Shining Brow, 1993; The Annals of Chile, 1994; New Weather, 1994 The Prince of the Quotidian, 1994; *As editor*—The Scrake of Dawn: Poems by Young People from Northern Ireland, 1979; The Faber Book of Contemporary Irish Poetry, 1986; The Essential Byron, 1989.

ABOUT: Contemporary Authors 129, 1990; Contemporary Literary Criticism 32, 1985; Contemporary Poets, 5th ed., 1991; Dictionary of Literary Biography 40, 1985; Hoffenden, J. Viewpoints: Poets in Conversation, 1980; Heeney, S. Preoccupations: Selected Prose 1968–1978, 1980; Poets of Great Britain and Ireland Since 1960, 1985. *Periodicals*—Chicago Review 35 1985;

Choice May 1984; Contemporary Literature Fall 1987; Eire-Ireland 10:2 1977, Summer 1978; Encounter February–March 1981, March 1984; Library Journal April 1, 1991; London Magazine October 1977; London Review of Books February 16, 1984; December 20, 1990; New Review September 1977; New Statesman September 26, 1980; New York Review of Books May 30, 1991; Poetry June–July 1973; Shenandoah Summer 1974; Stand 22 3, 1981; Times Literary Supplement May 14, 1989; October 12, 1990; World Literature Today Winter 1989.

*MÜLLER, HEINER (January 9, 1929–   ), German playwright, poet, essayist, story writer, translator, and stage director, was born in Eppendorf, Saxony. His father, an office worker, was arrested in 1933 for his activities as a small functionary of the German Social Democrat party and put in a concentration camp; after his release he was unemployed, and in 1941 was sent to France in a disciplinary battalion. During these years, the family lived with Heiner Müller's grandparents in Mecklenburg, where he attended local schools from 1935 on. In 1945 he was drafted into the Reich's work service and became a prisoner of war of the Americans for a brief period. Very much aware of the catastrophe brought about by Nazism and living in the Soviet occupied sector of Germany when the war ended, Müller turned to socialism as the only promise of genuine freedom. His father, harassed by the Soviet occupation authorities and expelled from the newly formed SED (Socialist Unity Party), moved to the West where he was later joined by his wife. Heiner Müller, however, chose to stay and initially participated enthusiastically in the socialist reconstruction of East Germany. He eventually finished high school, worked for some time in a library, and moved to East Berlin.

From 1950 to 1956, Heiner Müller earned his living as a journalist writing for several East German newspapers and for the Writers Union of the German Democratic Republic (GDR). During this period he also wrote his first literary works; i.e., poems, stories, anecdotes, and dramatic scenes. He began in 1955 with his *Produktionsstücke* (Production Plays), early drafts of *Germania Tod in Berlin* (1978, *Germania Death in Berlin*) and *Philoktet* (Philoctetes, 1965). From 1956 to 1958 he wrote *Der Lohndrücker* (The Scab) together with his wife Inge, and *Die Korrektur* (*The Correction*). He became a free-lance writer in 1959.

The 1960s and 1970s were fraught with personal tragedies and professional difficulties: his wife Inge, who had had a history of mental illness, committed suicide in 1966. In 1961, his

*°MYOO lur, HYnur

comedy, *Die Umsiedlerin* (The Woman Who Resettled), a play that did not comform to dogmatically defined Socialist Realism, was discontinued following its premiere, and Müller was excluded from the Writers Union. For some time then he translated and adapted classic Greek tragedies as well as plays by Shakespeare; as he put it in retrospect: "In the early sixties you could not write a play about Stalinism. You had to resort to this type of model if you wanted to ask real questions." In 1965, the Central Committee of the Socialist Party criticized him severely for yet another play, *Der Bau* (The Construction Site), the production of which did not come about until 1980. In the 1970s he turned once again to topics directly addressing specifically German problems—"die deutsche Misere" (the German calamity) as he put it—in plays such as *Die Schlacht* (1975, *The Battle*) and *Germania Tod in Berlin*. In 1973 he was attacked for his adaptation of *Macbeth*, which allegedly smacked of "Geschichtspessimismus" (historical pessimism). Müller worked as stage director for the Berliner Ensemble from 1970 to 1976 having been restored to favor by the Party. He collaborated on an opera libretto with Ginka Tscholakowa, whom he married in 1970. From 1976 on, he was an artistic consultant to the Berliner Volksbühne; since his exclusion from the Writers Union and the 1965 Party reprimand, his own plays, however, were mostly premiered in the West. In the academic year 1975–1976, Müller was writer-in-residence at the University of Texas in Austin and traveled widely in the United States and in Mexico.

Only after his international reputation had established Müller as Germany's most important playwright did the GDR become more tolerant toward him. As Müller put it somewhat wryly: "Quality is your best weapon." In the 1980s he was able to stage some of his plays even in the GDR, such as *Der Auftrag, Erinnerung an eine Revolution* (1984, *The Tasks*) and *Macbeth*, both at the Volksbühne in Berlin in 1980 and 1982 respectively. The HOT-theater in The Hague launched its "Heiner Müller Project" in 1983 with ten productions of his plays by theaters in Belgium, Bulgaria, West Germany, and the Netherlands; companies from Müller's own country were refused permission by the GDR authorities to travel to Holland—one of them, Berlin's Volksbühne, which was to perform Müller's own production of his play *Macbeth*. In 1984 he collaborated on the German contribution to Robert Wilson's megaproject "CIVIL warS," both in Los Angeles and in Cologne. As Carl Weber remarked in 1984, "These incidents . . . emphasize that his work and his positions are inseparable from the schizophrenia of today's partitioned Germany." Müller's two-volume edition of translations and adaptations of Shakespeare plays was published in 1985. In 1990 Heiner Müller became President of the Academy of the Arts of the GDR. The same year, the Frankfurt "Experimenta," the largest retrospective ever of a single writer in Germany, was dedicated to him. Leading theater companies from East and West Germany presented nearly forty different productions of his works in addition to ballets, operas, lectures, and concerts based on his texts. More than twenty thousand spectators attended the events. In 1993 he directed a new production of Richard Wagner's *Tristan* in Bayreuth.

Müller has been the recipient of a number of prizes: together with his wife Inge he received the Heinrich Mann Prize in 1959; subsequent prizes and honors include the Erich Weinert Medal (1964), the Lessing Prize (1975), the Mülheim Dramatists Prize (1979), and the Georg Büchner Prize (1985). Together with composer Heiner Goebbels he was also awarded the highly prestigious Hörspielpreis der Kriegsblinden (1986).

Heiner Müller is recognized as one of the most important and controversial playwrights of our time. Violently attacked in his own country in the past, he has come under attack from some Western critics as well who, following the fall of GDR socialism and the opening of the Berlin Wall, consider his dramatic oeuvre ideologically obsolete. However, many theater critics and stage directors consider Müller "the best we have got," the most significant German playwright since Brecht. Starting in Brecht's footsteps, he eventually rejected most of Brecht's models and proceeded to create his own paradigm of theater. According to him, theater must interfere with the social process, and it also depends on the active participation of the audience if it is to do justice to its function as a "laboratory of social imagination." Müller has influenced not only younger writers such as Thomas Brasch, Stefan Schütz, and Volker Braun but also painters, composers, and choreographers. Müller's texts—with their multiple meanings, their rich associations, and their highly complex structure—have called for ever new interpretations. Shakespeare, Büchner, Brecht, Artaud, Beckett, Genet, and Mayakovski as well as classic Greek and Roman drama have all left their imprint on his plays. The influence of traditional subjects, myths, and motifs does not end with his translations and adaptations but permeates his entire work.

Müller's work is a genuine "work in progress." The search for new forms of expression and permanent experimentation are his postulates:

"Art . . . is parasitical if it can be described with the categories of a given aesthetics." He has rewritten his plays many times, expanded them, presented new versions and variations on his major themes, and recycled what he calls his "left-overs." Cautiously, then, his plays can be divided into four distinct groups: 1) the Production Plays which developed out of Brecht's Epic Theater; 2) a sequence of plays exploring Brecht's model of the *Lehrstück* (didactic play); 3) history plays; and 4) essentially monologic role texts registering subjective consciousness.

Müller's Production Plays were a genre favored by official cultural policies in the GDR during the 1950s; these are texts aimed at motivating the population to improve production and lift standards. Müller's plays, however, are not propaganda pieces pitting worker-heroes against equally clear-cut class enemies; rather, they explore the effects of change on the daily lives of ordinary people critically, presenting characters caught in and torn by the struggle "between the old and the new." In *The Scab*, which emulates Brecht's epic mode, Müller focuses on the political activist and his position between the party and the workers. Balke, a mason, repairs a faulty furnace in record time. While the officials celebrate him as a model worker, his colleagues feel he is betraying them, lowering wage levels by establishing higher norms for a particular job. In *The Correction*, too, Müller points out the contradictions between production pressures and private interests. *Die Umsiedlerin* deals with the transition in agriculture towards collective farming and, far from offering idealizing agro-prop, reveals opportunism, corruption, and the deep rift between the old farmers and the new settlers. In *Der Bau*, Brigadier Barka says: "My life is bridge construction. I am the pontoon between the Ice Age and the Commune." The construction of the bridge becomes the metaphor for socialist society under construction, for "the society in transition." The line was later paraphrased by an angry Erich Honecker, leader of the GDR, as proof of negative trends in the contemporary cultural scene: "Our reality is seen only as 'the ferry between the Ice Age and Communism.'" Although Müller considered his Production Plays as a means of influencing audiences, he was not really concerned with generating populist appeal. His style is characterized by rhythmic language, the briefest of scenes, and a syntax reminiscent of Hölderlin's translations from ancient Greek; in other words, it is a style far removed from the aesthetics of Socialist Realism.

In his sequence of *Lehrstücke*, which includes adaptations from the Greco-Roman tradition in the 1960s, Müller expressed once again, albeit indirectly, his opinions regarding the GDR. Based on Sophocles' play, Müller's *Philoktet*, for instance, is a parable about the problem of appropriate political action and shows how individual happiness in disregarded in the process of instituting a collectivist society. *Mauser*, based on a theme from Brecht's *The Measures Taken*, is a *Lehrstück* experiment constituting a radical critique of Brecht's model and ideology. In Müller's opinion, Brecht not only posed the questions but also forced answers and easy solutions on the material. *Mauser*, on the other hand, is—in Müller's own words—"a movement into a space, with questions for which I have no answers." The densely constructed and highly poetic text presents only two characters, A and B, and a Chorus. It raises the question of whether the revolutionary cause justifies the cruelty of political means: "Why the killing and why the dying / If the price of the Revolution is the Revolution / If those to be freed are the price of freedom?" For Müller, however, death does not signal the end; and in his "Note" to *Mauser* he provides an indirect answer after all: "For something to come, something must go; the first shape of hope is fear; the first appearance of the new: Horror." Müller abandoned the form of the *Lehrstück* for some time to come. As far as the GDR was concerned, Müller had reached the depressing conclusion that "the socialist revolution is stagnating" and that "it has become impossible to imagine utopia within the historical process. Nowadays utopia is situated beyond or apart from history, beyond or apart from politics."

Müller's plays from the 1970s, some of which he had begun in the 1950s, corroborate what he had said early on: "The terror I write of is from Germany." His increasingly radical understanding of German history is paralleled by his aesthetic experimentation. The heaped-up rubble of German history finds its formal equivalent in the montage of disparate fragments that has come to characterize his plays. The tradition of the linear fabric is broken. Montage, "fast forward," fragmentation of scenic events, the dissolution of an all-embracing plot for the sake of autonomous single scenes: these are the characteristics of Müller's "open form" in his later plays. *The Battle* is Müller's earliest attempt to work through the "fascist trauma." An answer to Brecht's *Fear and Misery of the Third Reich*, *The Battle* is a collection of short playlets about life in Nazi Germany, as Brecht's play was, yet the five "scenes from Germany" present Müller's very different view of the German "collective mind" during Nazi rule, which Brecht misunderstood, according to Müller, because he was blindfolded by Marxist textbook ideology. The play dramatizes the rise and fall of the Third

Reich as the eternal return of the joy of destruction and self-destruction. History as a slaughterhouse is also the topic of *Germania Death in Berlin*, which Müller worked on from 1956 to 1971. It is, according to Carl Weber, "one of the first experiments in European drama which responded to what might be called a 'postmodern sensibility.'" A phantasmagoria of violence with clown routines, grotesque parodies, nightmarish horror scenes, and pantomimes of cruelty, the play represents a turning point in Müller's work, being his first effort at a genre he later elected to name "synthetic fragments." According to Müller, "fragments have a special value today because all the coherent stories we used to tell ourselves to make sense of life have collapsed." His "fragments," of course, are painstakingly crafted texts, "synthesized" from often widely diverse constituents. In *Germania Death in Berlin*, flashbacks from two thousand years of German history—the suppression of the Peasants' Revolt, the Thirty Years' War, the invasion of Napoleon, the triumph of Prussian militarism, the rise to power of the Nazis—are paralleled with scenes from the early period of the GDR state, thus making evident the continuation of destructive forces from the dark past in the present. *Leben Gundlings Friedrich von Preussen Lessings Schlaf Traum Schrei. Ein Greuelmärchen* (1977, *Gundling's Life Frederick of Prussia Lessing's Sleep Dream Scream: A Horror Story*) culminates in an American dream scene: the 18th-century German dramatist Gotthold Lessing together with Nathan and Emilia Galotti, the protagonists from Lessing's two most famous plays, meet the last American president, who is a faceless robot, before they are all destroyed by the white light of what seems to be a nuclear explosion. The text contains allusions to the American Indian movement and other aspects of contemporary American society. But Müller also delves back into German history: the "horror story," framed by the life of Gundling, a humiliated scholar at the court of Frederick William of Prussia, and by the petrification of Lessing, a classic who is resigned to obscurity because he has had no impact, describes not only the dangers of a dialectic of the Enlightenment and the perversion of absolutist rationalism but also the hostility towards intellectuals in 18th-century Prussia. At the same time, it is an attack on the repression of intellect in GDR Socialist Realism. Müller's plays on Germany have been criticized for their alleged historical pessimism, their defeatism, and their macabre doomsday atmosphere. But by presenting haunting images on stage, Müller wants to force his spectators to deal with the suppressed past, believing that we must know history to rid ourselves of its obsessions.

In the last years, Müller has written only sporadically, concentrating instead on his dramaturgy. He has become increasingly interested in a "theater without text" and he has summarized this aesthetic program as follows: "Bodies and their conflicts with ideas are thrown onto the stage." Which character says something has become more and more random. His last plays are characterized by a near total absence of scenic action, dialogue, and fully written parts. These are substituted for by monologues with an intricate web of quotations and associations. Beginning with *Hamletmaschine* (1977, *Hamletmachine*), a somber monologue that GDR critics considered a "failure" marred by "defeatism without perspective" but which others have recognized as his masterpiece, this tendency has found its climax in *Bildbeschreibung* (1985, *Explosion of a Memory/Description of a Picture*). Müller remarks in the postscript to *Bildbeschreibung*: "The action is optional since its consequences are past, explosion of a memory in an extinct dramatic structure." *Hamletmachine*, "the shrunken head of the Hamlet tragedy," as Müller called it, is the 8-page condensation of a 200-page play first written in the 1950s. It is a variant of the Hamlet story set in a communist country after Stalin's death. A drama about the son of a high party functionary whose father died under obscure circumstances, yet later received a state funeral, according to Carl Weber it represents "Hamlet in the Hungary of 1956." In a conversation about the text Müller said that while he was writing the play, there was no historical substance for real dialogues, but that "it became, more than ever anticipated, a self-critique of the intellectual. . . . The Ophelia character is a criticism of Hamlet, consequently a self-critique; it contains autobiographical material dealing with the man-woman relationship of today." As for its title, Müller said in an interview: "The title *Hamletmachine* was an accident. There was a project to print all of my texts that had to do with Shakespeare. We racked our brains for a title and hit upon 'Shakespeare's Factory' since I found that quite smart. And there was this play I had no title for and since I wanted an illustration from a book by Duchamp for the edition, the title *Hamletmachine* resulted automatically. That was eventually interpreted: Hamletmachine equals H. M. equals Heiner Müller. I carefully disseminated this interpretation." Müller no longer believes in keeping himself, the writer, outside of his texts in a detached position, and nowhere is this more evident than in *Hamletmachine* when a photo of the author is torn up on stage. Tearing his own photo was a forceful way of talking about himself, a powerful metaphor of the author's view of himself: "At bottom, playwrighting always means to me that a picture is torn, a picture of myself too. In one play one picture is torn, from this a new picture originates. And that has to be torn again. That is actually the process." In *Wolokolamsker Chaussee* (1988, *Volokolamsk Highway*) a cycle of performance texts, Müller returned to the *Lehrstück*, a model he had explored thoroughly during the 1960s, but which he now reshaped. In a 1986 interview, three years before the opening of the Berlin Wall, he explained: "I think something is turning around now, something has to change direction. The situation is rife with changes. This is the moment when one can learn again, when one must learn. And so this play-model Lehrstück becomes timely again."

In 1991 Müller directed a production of *Mauser*, which included four other Müller plays, at the Deutsches Theater in Berlin. Müller feared efforts on the part of the West Germans to obliterate the communist past, as he felt that they had obliterated the Nazi past. John Rouse commented in *Theatre Journal* that this production was part of Müller's effort to keep the past alive: "Müller . . . wants to keep the past uncovered, to keep raising the dead to disturb the living: 'One must accept the presence of the dead as dialogue partners, or dialogue disrupters—future arises only out of the dialogue with the dead.' "

Carl Weber has remarked that "there is hardly another contemporary author and surely no dramatist who has changed, so often and so drastically, the poetic and dramaturgic paradigms in his work as Müller." Nevertheless, certain themes and subjects can be traced in all his writings: "The often fatal contradiction between an accepted task or mission of a social, usually revolutionary, kind and the committed individual's desire or claim to achieve personal, often sensual, fulfillment in life are at the center of much of Müller's work. Among themes he has dealt with again and again are utopia versus despair and idealistic or romantic notions of humanity's progress shattered by the brutal realities of our 'prehistory,' as Müller calls all human history until the present. This ideology can be expressed as shrouding the primeval urge of violence—the remnant of mankind's barbarian past."

It has been pointed out that despite their cynicism and gloom, Müller's works are not unredeemably bleak, and it is with good reason that he has been called an optimistic nihilist. While presenting endgame rituals and setting figures against the background of a threatening, dehumanized historical process, his plays are still endgames of *hope*. Like all art, they "must awaken the yearning for another state of the world, and this yearning is revolutionary."

PRINCIPAL WORKS IN ENGLISH TRANSLATION: *Plays*—(tr. C. Weber) The Hamletmachine and Other Texts for the Stage, (includes The Correction, Hamletmachine, and Gundling's Life Frederick of Prussia Lessing's Sleep Dream Scream: A Horror Story), 1984; (tr. C. Weber) Description of a Picture/Explosion of a Memory and The PAJ Casebook: Alcestis *in* Performing Arts Journal 10: 1, 1986; (tr. C. Weber) Explosion of a Memory (includes Germania Death in Berlin and Explosion of a Memory/Description of a Picture), 1989; (tr. C. Weber) The Battle (includes The Scab, Mauser, and The Battle), 1989. *Nonfiction*—"To Use Brecht without Criticizing Him Is to Betray Him," *in* Theater 17:2, 1986; (tr. B. and C. Schütze) Germania, 1990.

ABOUT: Allen, P. Heiner Müller's "Wolokolamsker Chaussee": Confronting the Past with Poetic Counterstrategies, 1991; Botterman, J.C. Hegemony and the Subaltern: End of History in Heiner Müller's Theater, 1988; Cambridge Guide to World Theatre, 1988; Contemporary Foreign Language Writers 1984; Contemporary World Writers, 2nd ed., 1993; deLaurentis, T., et al. (eds.) The Technological Imagination: Theories and Fictions, 1980; Encyclopedia of World Literature in the Twentieth Century, rev. ed., II 1981; Fabioan, B., et al. (eds.) Shakespeare: Text, Language, Criticism: Essays in Honor of Marvin Spevack, 1987; Hartigan, K. V. (ed.) Text and Presentation, 1989; Hartigan, K. V. (ed.) Within the Dramatic Spectrum, 1986; Huyssen, A. After the Great Divide, 1987; Kleber, P. and Visser, C. (eds.) Re-Interpreting Brecht, 1990; Mandel, O. Philoctetes and the Fall of Troy: Plays, Documents, Iconography, Interpretations, 1981; McGraw-Hill Encyclopedia of World Drama, 1984; Mews, S. (ed.) "The Firsherman and His Wife": Günter Grass's The Flounder in Critical Perspective, 1983; Orr. J., et al. (eds.) Terrorism and Modern Drama, 1990; Oxford Companion to German Literature, 1986; Oxford Companion to the Theatre, 1983; Sebald, W. G. (ed.) A Radical Stage: Theater in Germany in the 1970s and 1980s, 1988; Teraoka, A. A. The Silence of Entropy or Universal Discourse: The Postmodernist Poetics of Heiner Müller, 1985; Who Is Who in the Socialist Countries of Europe, 1989. *Periodicals*—Art and Cinema 1:1, 1986; Brecht Yearbook 17, 1992; Canadian Theater Review 64, 1990; Colloquia Germanica 21:1, 1988; Drama 153, 1984; German Life and Letters 28, 1974–1975; German Quarterly 59:1, 1986; Gestus 1:3–4, 1985–1986; 3:1, 1987; Minnesota Review 8, 1976; Modern Drama 23:4, 1981; 31:3, 1988; 35:4, 1992; New German Critique 2, 1974; 8, 1976; 16, 1979; 50, 1990; New German Review 5–6, 1989–1990; New Literary History 23:4, 1992; New Perspectives Quarterly 10, 1993; New Republic 194, June 16, 1986; 202 April 24, 1990; New Statesman and Society 3, 1990; New York May 19, 1986; New York Times July 8, 1990; Paragraph 14:3, 1991; Performing Arts Journal 10:1, 1986; 11:2, 1988; 12:2–3, 1990; Seminar 28:2, 1992; Shakespeare in Southern Africa 3, 1989; Studies in Twentieth Century Literature 5:1, 1980; Text and Performance Quarterly 11:1, 1991; Theater 17:2, 1986; 19:3, 1988; Theatre Journal 39, 1987; 43, 1991; 45, 1993; World Literature Today 55:4, 1981.

*MUNIF, ABDELRAHMAN (May 29, 1933–), Jordanian-born Arabic-language novelist living in Damascus, Syria, began his career as a writer of Arabic fiction relatively late in life. His work over the last decade and a half has established him as one of the most prominent and accomplished of contemporary Arab novelists. Furthermore, his family background, academic training, and personal experiences—particularly that of exile—have provided him with a unique vision through which to project in his fiction the issues that confront not only the Arab world but the world as a whole: the delicate balance between the needs of humankind in the modern era and the preservation of the environment; and the continuing problem of human brutality, whether on the local or international level.

Munif was born in Amman, the capital of Jordan; his father was Saudi and his mother Iraqi. After secondary school education in Jordan, he enrolled in law school in Baghdad, but was expelled for political activities in 1955. He continued his studies in Cairo before moving to Yugoslavia in 1958 to complete a doctoral degree in petroleum economics. For a while, he worked as an oil economist in Syria, but in 1972 he moved to Lebanon. His first novel, *Al Ashjar wa-ightiyal Marzuq* (The trees and Marzuq's assassination) was published in 1973. In 1975 he traveled to Baghdad where he was appointed editor of the journal (in English) "Oil and Development." During his time in the Iraqi capital, Munif formed a close friendship with the great Palestinian litterateur Jabra Ibrahim Jabra (b. 1919). Jabra encouraged Munif in his writing career, and their mutual interest in the potential of the Arabic novel was to take the form in 1982 of a jointly written, *'Alam bi-la khara' it* (World without maps), which, besides its interesting mode of composition, is itself an accomplished contribution to the library of metafictional works in Arabic in that it incorporates within its story the process of writing a novel. In 1981 political factors seem to have impinged on Munif's career once again, making it necessary for him to leave Iraq; he moved to Boulogne, France, where he devoted his energies entirely to fictional writing. In 1986 he left France for Damascus, Syria, where he and his wife took up residence.

Munif's first published writings, were concerned with the crisis of the intellectual in the modern Middle East. In *Al-Ashjar wa-ightiyal Marzud* the central character, Mansur, returns from Europe to become a university professor but finds himself caught up in the societal consequences of Israel's 1967 victory. In *Sharq al-Mutawassit.* (East of the Mediterranean, 1977) the reader is confronted by one of the most harrowing depictions of prison life and torture

in the whole of contemporary Arabic literature. Rajab Isail is imprisoned for "political activities" in an unnamed country; upon his release, he is allowed to travel to France to study, but it is then his family's turn (in the person of his brother-in-law) to be harassed by the secret police. Rajab is forced to return home and dies in prison.

In 1978 Munif published the first of what was to be a series of works that took as their theme a topic clearly very much the concern of an oil economist: the fragile environment of the Middle East desert countries and the impact of human civilization—especially the discovery of oil—on that environment and those who live in it. *Al-Nihayat* (1978, *Endings*), is a most unusual work. Moving the setting of the Arabic novel far into the desert of an unnamed country in the Middle East, the narrator begins by introducing us through an almost anthropological analysis to the people of the village of al-Tibah and to their continuing struggle against the onslaught of drought and deprivation. Few characters have names because the portrait is one that comprises the entire community. Gradually, however, the story does focus on the fate of a single and singular individual, 'Assaf, the socially gauche hunter who serves as the guardian of the wildlife that lies within the reach of the village's fragile environment. In an insane gesture to the traditional demands of hospitality, 'Assaf takes a group of city folk out hunting, and they are trapped in the middle of the desert by the onset of a huge sandstorm, a situation that Munif describes in a passage of unparalleled vividness. 'Assaf dies and is mourned by the entire village in a remarkable evening, during which the villagers exhibit their skill as storytellers by narrating a whole series of tales about animals. On the following day a chastened community buries its unusual hero and faces its uncertain future. Munif's concerns with politics, the development of oil, and the dire effect that humans have on the environment are carried forward into his next novel, *Sibaq al-masafat al-tawilahhlah ila al-sharq* (Long-distance race: A trip to the East, 1979). Here an actual historical event, the nationalization of oil in Iran during the premiership of Mussadegh (1951), becomes the starting point for a fictional exploration of power and influence as seen through the filter of Peter MacDonald, a British agent whose reports both supply the reader with information about events and also show MacDonald's host of prejudices against the Middle East and its inhabitants.

This burst of creative output in fictional form makes it abundantly clear that even though Munif may have begun to write fiction relatively late in life, the medium provided him with the most appropriate outlet for his personal interests

*MOO neef, ab dul RAH mun

and concerns. These early works show an author experimenting not only with the more obvious fictional expressions of important topics but also with different modes of narrative structure and style. It seems reasonable to suggest that his exploration of all these aspects of fictional writing constituted a precedent for what has emerged as the most elaborate project yet undertaken in the realm of the Arabic novel, the gigantic quintet of works subsumed under the general title *Mudun al-milh* (Cities of Salt). The titles in the series are as follows: *Al-Tih* (The desert, 1984; translated as *Cities of Salt*); *Al-Ukhdud* (1985, *The Trench*); *Taqasim al-layl wa-al-nahar* (1988, *Variations on Night and Day*); *Al-Munbatt* (Hobbled, 1988); and *Badiyat al-zulumat* (Desert of gloom, 1988). Events are not treated chronologically, and indeed it is a major part of the author's plan that each work should address its period of time and its primary topic in a different way. The principal location is the city of Mooran, and it did not require a great deal of effort on the part of readers of the Arabic novel to glean that this was a thin disguise for Riyad and that the series of novels was nothing less than an in-depth investigation of the modern development of the state of Saudi Arabia (an association that was also not lost on the authorities in Saudi Arabia itself, who immediately banned the series and withdrew Munif's Saudi passport). In this context, it is important to note that, Munif insisted that the work is fiction and vigorously resists attempts at direct association of events and characters in the novels with the "facts" of history. "Munif is attempting nothing less, than the grand oil novel of the Arabian Peninsula and the Persian Gulf," Fouad Ajami wrote in the *New York Times Book Review* of the series.

In the first volume, a Bedouin community lives a life of prepetroleum innocence in the area to the south of the Gulf. The narrator conveys in his accounts all the bewilderment that the community feels at the sudden intrusion of foreigners, who poke around in the earth and then come to the region in droves to set up shantytowns and totally destroy the traditional lifestyle of the inhabitants. Mutib who first watches in anger as his community and way of life is destroyed and then disappears, riding off into the desert on his camel, assumes mythic proportions. Perhaps the most remarkable feature of this particular novel, replicated to some degree in the others as well, is Munif's deliberate reliance on the techniques of the traditional storyteller. If Western fiction aspires to economy and efficiency in its narrative expectations, no such principles govern the way in which Munif's narrators unfold their tale. These storytellers narrate in an unhurried fashion; if there is more than one version of a particular event, each one has to be given its due. Ocasionally a preference for one over another may be ventured, but more often than not the reader is left with several possibilities, a situation that provides an authentic insight into the psychology of a traditional society. By introducing a traditional feature of storytelling into modern Arabic fiction, Munif has made a truly innovative contribution.

The second volume in the series, *The Trench*, provides a stunning portrait of the development of the city of Mooran itself, as profiteers from the Middle East and elsewhere congregate there to take advantage, at least initially, of the rulers' inexperience in order to turn a traditional town into a modern city. Chief among the perpetrators of entrepreneurial activities is the redoutable doctor, a Syrian, who uses his position as medical adviser to inveigle his way into the confidence of Sultan Khazael, a man similar to King Saud. The picture conveyed is not a pretty one, nor is that of the chaos surrounding the earlier career of the ruler's father, Sultan Khureybit, the founder of the state, who resembles King Ibn Saùd.

The Trench opens:

> Mooran seemed sunk, early that spring, in a meditative silence, as if the city had nothing on its mind. But a sharp eye saw, in this silence, expectancy and signs of unease. The calm was deceptive and would end abruptly, as if it had never been.

Mooran is awaiting the death of Sultan Khureybit, the man who has created the state. At the end of this volume, the doctor, who has just married his daughter to Sultan Khazael, Khureybit's successor, experiences another expectant silence:

> The doctor was bewildered. From the rear balcony, in an effort to prove his importance and nonchalance, he moved from one chair to another, looked at the trees and at the sky. . . . He . . . retreated into the house to look hatefully at the telephone. He wanted it to ring, but the silence in the house compounded the stolidity of the instrument until it seemed like death.

When the awaited bulletin comes it announces the removal of Khazael and his replacement by Prince Fanar. The doctor is put on a plane for exile. "And still Mooran listened expectantly, and waited," the novel ends.

Tribal rivalries, battles, and internecine squabbles in the royal palaces turn the third volume, (*Variations on Night and Day*), into something like a war narrative, whether the fighting occurs on the battlefield itself or within the ever-expanding family in the harem:

> If it had nothing to do with the Sultan or one of his close

wives, though the degree of closeness was generally not spelled out, whether in terms of seniority or blood or the number of sons she had given him, sometimes for reasons that no one was aware of, it remained a secret between the Sultan and that woman—otherwise the war that broke out especially among powerful women, might rage on uncontrolled, with no one knowing where it would lead. It began with whispers from one bedchamber to another, from one wing of the palace to another, then took the form of coldness in relations followed by a breaking off of relations, until it escalated to the exchange of accusations, until at times one of them was dead.

The fourth volume, *Al-Munbatt*, takes us back once again to Sultan Khazael, living in exile in Germany, and to his obnoxious adviser, Dr. Mahmalji. The Sultan is advised to abandon his long-time counselor and does so, in the process divorcing Dr. Mahmalji's daughter and ordering her to return to her father's house. The doctor is left to contemplate his fall from grace in Switzerland, and his misery is only compounded when his daughter commits suicide and his son decides to side with the new ruler of the kingdom. The title of the final volume in the quintet does not promise a happy ending to this saga. It goes back in time to follow the career of Khazael's brother and replacement, King Fanar, who is later assassinated. Once again, the reader is presented with a relentless accumulation of stories of cruelty, venality, and corruption detailed on a vast scale.

Mudun al-milh is perhaps rivaled only by Najib Mahfuz's Cairo Trilogy in the sheer breadth of is vision and in its total commitment to reflect in fiction the foibles of mankind against the backdrop of the march of time and the processes of change, both of which Georg Lukacs identified as organizing principles of the epic novel. Munif has shown a remarkable ability to vary his style and narrative method to produce a group of works that, while focused on a single region and a specific time frame, still display a rich variety of approaches. In all of them, however, the motivations of the participants in the narrative are complex enough to demand a hearing, sometimes from unlikely angles.

Ajami viewed Munif's accomplishment as somewhat less than successful, however: "From the sprawling cycle of novels you come out shortchanged. . . . Instead of the storyteller's inventiveness you end up with the lament of an Arab nationalist." Despite Ajami's patent political disagreements with Munif, however, he acknowledged that at his best, "Munif can take you all the way back to the bleak desert world . . . before the age of oil . . . " and allow the reader "to know something of the desert itself, of its hold on its people."

In 1991 Munif returned to a theme of primary concern to him: the status of intellectuals and writers in the Middle East and the freedom of the individual. His novel of 1977, *Sharq al-mutawassit.* (East of the Mediterranean) opens with a statement of the Declaration on Human Rights, and *Al-an . . . huna aw Sharq al-Mutawasit maratan ukhra* (Now. . . . here, or east of the Mediterranean once again) also begins with quotations, including one from the famous Egyptian mystic, al-Sharani (d. 1565): "If you spot a policeman sleeping when he should be praying, don't bother to wake him up. If he does so, he'll just start hurting people," Political oppression continues in the Middle East, that area depicted with deliberate imprecision by Munif as being to "the East of the Mediterranean," and he shows characteristic courage in addressing the topic head on. As the prominent Syrian dramatist Sa'dallah Vannus said about Munif's 1991 novel, "It tears the silence apart and proclaims the scandal as it is: these countries that constitute prisons in themselves are a scandal; these citizens who serve as jailers are a scandal; Middle Eastern history itself is a prison steeped in scandal."

The novel has always been potentially, a revolutionary, even a dangerous, genre. Abdelrahman Munif's own peripatetic life demonstrates this truth. His works stand not only as symbols of the novel's crucially important role in the Arab world but, as Edward Said of *Cities of Salt*, "the only serious . . . fiction that tries to show the effect of oil, Americans, and local oligarchy on a Gulf country."

PRINCIPAL WORKS IN ENGLISH TRANSLATION: Munif (tr. P. Theroux) Cities of Salt, 1987; (tr. R. Allen) Endings, 1988; (tr. P. Theroux) The Trench, 1991; (tr. P. Theroux) Variations on Night and Day, 1993.

ABOUT: Allen, R. The Arabic Novel: An Historical and Critical Introduction, 1982; Allen, R. (ed.) Modern Arabic Literature (Library of Literary Criticism), 1987. *Periodical*—New York Review of Books March 26, 1992; New York Times Book Review October 27, 1991; World & I February 1989.

*MURAKAMI HARAKUI (January 12, 1949–   ), expatriate Japanese novelist, short story writer, translator of American Contemporary fiction, and jazz aficionado, was born in Kyoto and bears no relation to the well-known writer and multimedia artist Ryu Murakami (1952–   ). Designated the leader of Japan's literary "Brat Pack" by the *New York Times* reviewer Herbert Mitgang, Haruki Murakami is associated with the new wave of Japanese writers who emerged in the 1980s. His following is primarily composed of *shinjinnrui* ("new human beings"), Japan's young and affluent postwar generation.

*moo ruh KAH mee, huh ROO kee

MURAKAMI HARAKUI

Departing from earlier literary traditions, Murakami rejects the aestheticism, formalism, and nationalism that pervade the works of Yasunari Kawabata, Junichiro Tanizaki and Yukio Mishima. Instead, Murakami explores his Japanese identity in an untraditional way. His colloquial language, stylish plots, nihilistic themes, and emphasis on a trendy consumer culture have attracted his *shinjinrui* readership. As Murakami's English translator Alfred Birnbaum explains: "Kitsch and hype are everywhere on the page. Noticeably absent is any mourning for lost innocence; gone are the conflicts between traditional and contemporary values."

An only child, Murakami was raised in Ashiya, a suburb of the commercial port city of Kobe, by parents who taught Japanese literature at the high school level. His father had been a Japanese soldier based in southern China during World War II and his authoritarian manner alienated him from his son. Murakami's parents were not unusually strict, but life in a traditional Japanese household stifled Murakami and caused him to retreat into his music and books. The relationship between Murakami and his parents deteriorated over the years and resulted in almost total estrangement.

During Murakami's youth, Japanese society was recovering from the aftermath of World War II. American television, music, and films that accompanied the postwar Occupation became important forces in Japanese society, and for the youth generated a particular attraction to American pop music and cultural icons of 1960s. The pervasiveness of American culture

was at once appealing and yet subversive—older people preserved the group-oriented values and refined formalities of traditional Japan; young people, displaced and disaffected, were attracted to America's celebration of the individual and displays of flamboyant tastes.

Like most of his contemporaries, Murakami identified with this Americanized environment. "I am of the generation of Elvis Presley, the Beach Boys, and 'Peter Gunn,'" hence stated. American shows like "Father Knows Best" contributed to his visions of America's rich and casual life-style. In a 1992 *New York Times Book Review* interview with American writer Jay McInerney—who has written in a manner similar to Murakami about things Japanese—Murakami reflected: "American culture was so vibrant back then, and I was very influenced by its music, television shows, cars, clothes, everything. That doesn't mean that the Japanese worshiped America, it meant that we just loved that culture. It was so shiny and bright that sometimes it seemed like a fantasy world."

Fantasy for Murakami first came in the form of foreign literary landscapes. In a seemingly deliberate act of rebellion against his father's interest in Japanese literature, he claims not to have read a Japanese novel until he was sixteen years old, instead turning to Japanese translations of works by Balzac, Stendahl, and Dostoevski. After studying English in junior high and high school, he frequented used-bookstores for American novels and struggled through the English prose. At school he served as editor in chief of the Kobe High School newspaper; at home he escaped to a world of adventure and lonesome heroes in the detective novels of Raymond Chandler and Ross Macdonald, into the hapless romanticism of F. Scott Fitzgerald, or into science fiction. Murakami has compared the impact of these American writers on his life and works to that of the Argentine author Manuel Puig, whose childhood exposure to Hollywood movies also informed his identity as a writer.

In 1968, Murakami entered the prestigious Waseda University in Tokyo, where he studied drama and film. The turbulence of the era's student protest and financial difficulties prolonged Murakami's studies. At last in 1975, he produced a graduation thesis on the journey motif in American films. Although he had hoped to become a film director after graduating from college, he has since refused to adapt his writings to film, believing that "it's enough for a book to be a book." Writing also appealed to Murakami during his university days, but he felt that he lacked the skills required to write fiction.

Although Waseda was not a center of the radical student of the time, Marxist ideology was popular on most campuses, and in 1969 Waseda students instigated a five-month strike on campus. Police were eventually called upon to end the strike, at which point a violent confrontation ensued. Although self-described as "a rebel", Murakami never became a student activist. But like most Waseda students, he sympathized with the goals of the student movements and his political consciousness was shaped by the uprising at Waseda. Alfred Birnbaum believes that his "hard-boiled" style resulted from the failure of the protests and Murakami's subsequent cynicism and disillusionment.

Murakami married fellow Waseda student Yoko Takahashi in 1971. In 1974, they opened Peter Cat, a small jazz club located on the outskirts of Tokyo near an American military base. Catering to students and American soldiers, the bar not only became the couple's livelihood for the seven years it was in operation, but also served as an arena in which to advance their shared interest in American jazz and pop music. When local jazz groups were not performing on the bar's miniature stage, the two played recordings by John Coltrane and other jazz musicians of the time.

Particularly because of his estrangement from his parents, Murakami shares an almost symbiotic relationship with Yoko. He once said: "Japan was a male-dominated country. I didn't like that. I and my wife are equal partners working together. My parents loved me, and I had a happy childhood, but when I became 18 or 19, I was not happy with it. Maybe my father was too strong. So I found the way I am happy with." Murakami and his wife share many of the same interest and are constant companions. They have no children. Despite the wealth and fame that Murakami has acquired since his publications in the late 1970's, he and Yoko live in relative austerity. His youthful looks and stylish clothing belie a modest, soft-spoken, intensely private person whose lifestyle does not imitate the materialistic addictions of characters in his novels.

Murakami's decision to return to writing occurred during his years at the Peter Cat. The sudden realization that he had a story to tell has been compared to religious inspiration or the achievement of satori, a Zen term meaning spiritual enlightenment. Although Murakami claims not to write autobiographically, the opening passage of his earliest acclaimed novel *Kaze no uta o kike* (*Hear the Wind Sing*, 1979) can be read as a personal testimony. He writes: "when it came to getting something into writing, I was always overcome with despair. The range of my ability was just too limited. . . . For eight years

I was caught in that dilemma. . . . Now I think I'm ready to talk." Murakami himself describes the novel as "a young-man, things-are-changing kind of novel" set during "the age of counterculture" and strongly influenced by Richard Brautigan. In translation, the protagonist's casual, slangy voice is reminiscent of Salinger's Holden Caulfield.

Brautigan, Raymond Carver and Kurt Vonnegut are among the primary writers who, Murakami acknowledged, have influenced his writings. In addition to being a best-selling writer, Murakami has enjoyed a successful career in translating contemporary American fiction and his selectiveness in choosing to translate authors whose styles appeal to him also reveals others who have influenced his style. He has introduced works of Carver, F. Scott Fitzgerald, John Irving, Paul Theroux, Truman Capote, Tim O'Brien, and Tobias Wolff to Japan. Murakami is so celebrated by Japan's younger generation that people will purchase these translations simply because his name is attached to them.

Murakami's immersion in American literature through the years has produced a style and a voice severed from both Japanese tradition and expectation. As he told *Publishers Weekly* in 1991: "You have to know that the writing in Japan for Japanese people is in a particular style, very stiff. If you are a Japanese novelist you have to write that way. It's kind of a society, a small society, critics and writers, called high literature. But I am different in style, with a very American atmosphere. I guess I'm seeking a new style for Japanese readership, and I think I have gained ground. Things are changing now. There is a wider field." In cultivating this new field of experience, Murakami's second novel *1973 nen no pinboru* (*Pinball, 1973*) builds upon *Hear the Wind Sing*. The novel captured Kodansha Publisher's Shinjin Bungaku Prize, awarded to the best newcomer in literature. In it Murakami created an otherworldly atmosphere in which his characteristic themes of alienation, estrangement, dysfunctional families, and self-centeredness reappear.

Hitsuji o meguru bòken (1982, *A Wild Sheep Chase*) marks the turning point in Murakami's life when he gave up his jazz club in order to write full-time. Murakami considers this works his first novel because he felt joy and ease in writing the story. Critics concurred with his personal feeling of accomplishment when they awarded the novel the Noma Prize for new writers. Young Japanese readers found Murakami's contemporary language refreshing and stylish, whereas older readers responded with contempt because of his blatant disregard for traditional

literary tastes. *A Wild Sheep Chase* is also notable as the first of Murakami's works to be translated into English. Although overall the 1989
translation did not sell well in the United States,
it received positive reviews and was included on
some Western best-seller lists.

The novel's postmodern plot centers on a
young, world-weary advertising copywriter who
embarks on an adventure of the mythic, mysterious, and fantastic, after his friend "the Rat"
sends him a photo of sheep. Sheep become a recurring motif until "the Boss," a sinister prototype of a right-wing politician, blackmails the
copywriter into searching for a supernatural
sheep that possesses human minds. The quest
leads and his girlfriend, an ear model who doubles as a call girl and proofreader, to Hokkaido,
where after a series of ordeals, the mystery of the
sheep unfolds. In the end, the sheep assumes un-
determined symbolic proportions. Murakami insists that the sheep cannot be explicitly attached
to a symbol because, much in the vein of automatic writing, the image was derived from his
unconscious.

The anonymous narrator in *A Wild Sheep
Chase* is Murakami's trademark protagonist—a
likeable, thirtyish, divorced professional, who
enjoys drinking, smoking, and sex and has a keen
memory of trendy pop culture from his 1960s
university days. He is a Tokyo Everyman or the
ideal antihero. Echoing Murakami's other rootless, unambitious protagonists, he says:

> What have I got to feel threatened about? Next to noth-
> ing. I broke up with my wife, I plan to quit my job today,
> my apartment is rented, and I have no furnishings worth
> worrying about . . . I've made no name for myself,
> have no social credibility, no sex appeal, no talent . . .
> In a word . . . I'm an utterly mediocre person. What
> have I got to lose?

The narrator also suffers chronic loneliness that,
according to Hosea Hirata, a professor of modern Japanese literature at Princeton who knows
Murakami, accounts for the "'cool' point of view
in his books . . . It comes from how he grew up,
how he kept his distance from what was surrounding him."

Stylistically, the chapters in *A Wild Sheep
Chase* are short and develop according to
Murakami's preference for unfolding his stories
as he goes along. The result is a tour de force,
employing techniques ranging from allegory,
parody, fantasy, symbolism, realism, and folktale to modern movements of absurdism, surrealism, detective noir, techno pop, and postwar
cynicism. Although reviewers censured the English translation for its "plethora of
Chandlerisms" and slangy American style,
Murakami's intention was to modernize Jap-

anese syntax and to reconstruct the Japanese language for more universal understandings and
appeal.

Awarded the renowned Tanizaki Prize in
1985, *Sekai no owari hàdo-boirudo wandàrando*
(*Hard-Boiled Wonderland and the End of the
World*) preserves Murakami's crisp, readable
prose in a merging of mind and identity, science
and humanity, and dream and utopia. The novel
features   two   stories—"Hard-Boiled
Wonderland"   and   "End   of   the
World"—narrated by dual protagonists. Both
are reminiscent of the young, aimless and lonely
narrator in *A Wild Sheep Chase*, but the first
narrator in this novel is entangled in a high-tech
factional war in futuristic Tokyo and identifies
himself as *boku* (I, familiar) in the original text,
while the second narrator is distinguished as
watashi (I, formal) and finds himself the only
one able to read books on dreams in a walled
town of mindless, shadowless people and dying
unicorns. The worlds intertwine until the
"Hard-Boiled Wonderland" of data and computers converges into its grim manifestation of
prosperity—the world of mindless people dying
unicorns or Murakami's vision of the world.
Rather than escaping the disorder at the end of
the world, the narrator resolves to stay in the
world of the mindless and the dying and tend to
their deprivations.

After the success of *Hard-Boiled Wonderland
and the End of the World*, the intrusiveness of
fame prompted Murakami and his wife to leave
Japan. They first lived on a Greek island from
1986 to 1989, then in Athens and in Rome. In
1991, Murakami accepted a position as visiting
fellow in East Asian Studies at Princeton University, which was followed by an invitation from
the University of California at Berkeley in the
fall of 1993. Although willing to meet with students in Japanese literature programs to discuss
his works, he rarely lectures, refuses broadcast
interviews, and lives outside the literary mainstream.

In Japan, Murakami's fifth novel, *Noruei no
mori 1987*, (*Norwegian Wood*) sold over two
million copies and qualifies as his most popular
novel to date. Despite the novel's domestic success, Murakami and his publishers considered
the plot too "simple" and "sentimental" for ex-
port and *A Wild Sheep Chase* was selected instead for Murakami's first translation onto
English. To be sure *Norwegian Wood* adheres to
a more conventional plot than is generally expected from Murakami and tells a tale about a
romantic relationship between a 1960s college
student and a young woman suffering from depression. Besides the obvious references to the

Beatles' song in the title, allusions to Fitzgerald, Hemingway, Salinger, and Chandler pervade the text; the only Japanese writer refered to, Dazai Osamu, is considered outside the mainstream like Murakami.

Selling over one million copies within six months the 600-page novel *Dansu, dansu, dansu* 1988 (Dance, dance, dance) was presented as a sequel to a *Wild Sheep Chase* with the narrator reappearing as a hack writer in Tokyo. The opening of the novel recapitulates scenes in Hokkaido when the ear-model girlfriend has disappeared and shifts into a dizzying array of events in which the narrator encounters numerous beautiful, mysterious women. The advice to the protagonist—"Dance. You gotta dance. As long as the music plays. Don't even think why. Start to think, your feet stop. Dance so it all keeps spinning."—elucidates an allegorical parallel between Japan's modern wasteland and the aging of the aimless protagonist that Murakami sets up in the novel. The dancing motif as well as the title of Dansu, Dansu, Dansu like *Norwegian Wood*, grew out of a popular song this one performed by the Dells.

After *Murakami Haruki zensakuhin 1979–1989*, an eight volume collection of his works, was issued in 1990–1991, Murakami's first collection of short stories *The Elephant Vanishes* (1993) was published. The collection includes seventeen imaginative and humorous short works, among them the title story "*Zo no shometsu*" (1985) and some translations which were originally published in *The New Yorker*. Most stories are set in Tokyo and environs, although the cultural references are almost exclusively American. This "hybrid of tradition" is evidenced by references to such persons and things as Allen Ginsberg, Len Deighton, Meryl Streep, Candace Bergen, Clarence Darrow, Julio Iglesias, Willie Nelson, Adidas T-shirts and Silly Putty. The first culturally specific term, "Tokyoite," that affirms that the stories occur in Japan, does not appear until the eleventh page of the collection.

The parade of brand-name products in *The Elephant Vanishes* is present in all of Murakami's works. With the exceptions of place names and certain foods, he constructs contemporary Tokyo around American consumer clutter. Hamish Hamilton, in the *New Statesman & Society* has cited Murakami's preoccupation with American consumerism as "cultural name dropping," Cecilia Segawa Seigle in *The Journal of Asian Studies* calls it "self-conscious Westernization," and Masao Miyoshi refers to it as commercial fabrications for "foreign buyers." One of Japan's most important postwar writers

Kenzaburo Oe remarked that Murakami's works fail to "go beyond their influences on the lifestyles of youth to appeal to intellectuals in the broad senses with models for Japan's present and future." They make up "an exceedingly self-conscious representation of contemporary cultural habits" and an American influenced writing style that is "not really Japanese." But in his interview with Jay McInerney, Murakami explains that "what I wanted was first to depict Japanese society through that aspect of it that could just as well take place in New York or San Francisco. You might call it the Japanese nature that remains only after you have thrown out, one after another, all of those parts that are altogether too 'Japanese'. That is what I really want to express. . . . I would like to write about Japanese society from the outside. I think that is what will increasingly define my identity as a writer."

Although his style has been criticized as nonliterary and lightweight, Murakami believes that he writes simply and lucidly for a 20th century readership that has become accustomed to the visual quality and explicitness of modern television, radio, movies, and sports entertainment. Moreover, Murakami's translated works have expanded the breadth of Japanese literature available in the West from the traditional tone of Murakami, Kawabata, and Tanizaki to the universal voice emanating from Murakami's style and subject matter. "My intuitive sense," Hosea Hirata predicted, "is that Murakami's works will survive. I think he has captured the spirit of a generation, and at the same time he articulates, in a very culturally understandable way, a unique culture that is growing in Tokyo."

PRINCIPAL WORKS IN ENGLISH TRANSLATION: Novels—(tr. A. Birnbaum) Pinball, 1973, 1985; (tr. A. Birnbaum) Hear the Wind Sing, 1987; (tr. A. Birnbaum) Norwegian Wood, 1989; (tr. A. Birnbaum) A Wild Sheep Chase, 1989; (tr. A. Birnbaum) Hard-Boiled in Wonderland and the End of the World, 1991; Dance, Dance, Dance, 1994. Short stories—(tr. K. Flanagan and T. Omi) "On Meeting My One Hundred Percent Woman One Fine April Morning" In Mitsios H. (ed.) New Japanese Voices: The Best Contemporary Fiction from Japan, 1991; (tr. A. Birnbaum) "TV People" in Birnbaum, A. (ed.) Monkey Brain Sushi: New Taste in Japanese Fiction, 1991; (tr. A. Birnbaum and J. Rubin) The Elephant Vanishes, 1993.

ABOUT: Contemporary World Writers, 1993; Who's Who in Japan 1991–1992; Miyoshi, Off Center, 1991: *Periodicals*—Esquire September, 1991; Far Eastern Economic Review August 9, 1990; Houston Chronicle April 4, 1993; Independent October 13, 1991; Japan Quarterly October–December 1992; Japan Times November 23, 1986; Journal of Asian Studies February 1990; Los Angeles Times Magazine December 8, 1991;

New Statesman & Society October 18, 1991; New York Times June 17, 1991; New York Times Book Review December 3, 1989; July 8, 1990; September 15, 1991; September 27, 1992; March 28, 1993; May 12, 1993; January 2, 1994; New Yorker December 4, 1989; Publishers Weekly September 20, 1991; Review of Contemporary Fiction Summer 1990; Summer 1992; Times Literary Supplement November 11, 1993; World Literature Today Spring 1993.

NAMJOSHI, SUNITI (April 20, 1941–), Indian-born poet, satirist and fabulist writes: "I was born in Bombay, but never really lived there. I grew up in Pune, in "Punya-nagar," Poona, the city of virtue, the seat of the Peshwas, the place where the best Marathi is spoken, and in Phaltan, one of the princely states in Western Maharashtra, though boarding school was in the Himalayan foothills and later in a valley in the south. My father, Manohar Namjoshi, was a test pilot. He won all the races, he did aerobatics and he made headlines. He was killed when his plane crashed on December 11, 1953. My mother, Sarojini (Naik Nimbalkar), was/is a princess. (The princely states have been abolished.) I'm not entirely sure what the effect of having such glamorous parents was. Children are inclined to see their parents as more than life-size anyhow, and when everyone else seems to corroborate this, it becomes harder perhaps to stop seeing them as gods, heroes, giants. Certainly the death of my father was traumatic for all four of us (my brothers, my sister, and me): gods don't fall. The other two figures of mythic proportions are Goja and my grandmother. Quite a lot is known about my grandmother, the late Laxmi Devi Naik Nimbalkar, Ranisaheb of Phaltan (b. 17 Nov. 1901, d. 18 Nov. 1984). She was like a Niagara of energy, a green waterfall. Much less is known about Goja Kate. Servants don't have their photographs taken, their births aren't registered, records aren't kept. She was as straight and tough as the trees with black trunks and silver thorns (babul) that grown in the harsh, dry landscape of the Deccan plateau. No, not literally. She was bent over and had lost one eye. I haven't yet been able to write about Goja. I used some details of life with my grandmother in The Mothers of Maya Diip and dedicated the book to her. I think it would have amused her, though perhaps the lesbian aspects of my writing would have displeased her. The work is a dystopian satire after all, and isn't really concerned with character development.

"In a country where there are a great many poor people, it's not difficult for even a child to realize that the probability of being born relatively rich is very small, and that perhaps it's like

SUNITI NAMJOSHI

winning a lottery ticket—it doesn't have much to do with merit, or, for that matter, the lack of it. The notion of reincarnation I never took very seriously as a child, and later it seems to me only a very powerful metaphor. Am I not a Hindu then? Do I not come from a Hindu background? Of course I do. Perhaps the problem with the Hindu ideal of detachment is that it can so easily turn into indifference and resignation. Similarly, the problem with the Christian notion of compassion is that it can lead so easily to a glorification of suffering for its own sake and turn into pity, which is disrespectful to others, and into self-pity, which is disrespectful to oneself. The ideas themselves and the questioning of these ideas obviously come from two different traditions, but then that's what happens if one grows up in India as part of the Hindu mainstream, and at the same time one is educated in English. I did not leave India until 1968; I was 27. Since then I've lived in the West, mostly in Canada, where I taught at the University of Toronto, and for the past five years (written in 1992) in England. I visit India once a year.

"Because of India: Selected Poems has short introductions to each of the ten sections, which explain the context in which the fables or poems were written, i.e, the ideas that were influencing me at the time and the ideas that I was trying to work out. One changes, of course; one looks back on an array of past selves; one even recreates the past selves. The perspective is different, or perhaps what I mean is that the laws of perspective don't necessarily hold: the distant past may not be distant. And the perspective on the future also changes, though I am not quite sure how. At present I live in Devon with my partner, Gillian Hanscombe. I'd like to do some good work."

In *Feminist Fables* Suniti Namjoshi reworks traditional fairytales and myths of Eastern and Western cultures. One of these is "The Lesson," her own version of "The Emperor's New Clothes," in which a little girl sees the Emperor marching naked in the streets. She comes home and, removing all her clothes, announces to her mother that she is an emperor. "Don't be silly darling," her mother replies. "Only little boys grow up to be Emperors. As for little girls, they marry Emperors; and they learn to hold their tongues, particularly on the subject of the Emperor's clothes."

It is against precisely such sentiments that Namjoshi's work is directed. She is a feminist but not a polemicist. In resorting to imaginative literature, myth, and folklore, she ahs found a genre that allows her freedom to explore feminism in timeless and universal terms. The writers who have most stirred her imagination are Swift and Lewis Carroll, brilliant satirists whose absurdist logic illuminated the darkest corners of human ignorance and prejudice. "For me Swift was a great myth-maker. Every line of *Gulliver's Travels* spills over with the inventiveness of his imagery." Her enthusiasm for Lewis Carroll began with her respect for him as a mathmatician. Mathematics appeals to her, Namjoshi (who majored in the subject in college) has written "because it makes beautiful patterns within self-contained systems."

Namjoshi is a transplanted Indian living in Western society, a feminist and an lesbian in a world that remains essentially male-dominated. She identifies herself with "the other other"—the outsider, if not the pariah of conventional thinking. Although she has been publishing her poetry since 1967, it was not until she discovered her audience that she understood her function as a writer. That audience is outside the heterosexual patriarchy whose language has been the voice of English poetry. In an essay "Who Wrongs you, Sappho?" (published in *Out of the Margins*) Namjoshi and Gillian Hanscombe argue that as lyric poets they inherited a body of conventions, traditional images, and associations, assumptions in a poem, for example, that "I," the lover, is male and "you," the beloved, is female. Writing now at last as lesbians—"We can speak in public. That means we can take the central 'I' and 'you' of the language of lyric poetry to mean ourselves, without compromise." She writes (with Hanscombe in *Flesh and Paper*):

We can compose an ocean if we like;
deck it about with sand dunes, a
mountain or two, some trees.
Or we can compose ourselves.
But a politics? To invent, just we two,
a view? How to think? What to do?
And a country?

Namjoshi's early poetry reflects a painful struggle for self-identity. After taking a B.A. (1961) and an M.A 91963) at the University of Poona, she worked for five years in the Indian Administrative Service. She enjoyed her work at first but found living in an Establishment atomosphere frustrating. In 1968 she came to the United States for graduate study in public administration oat the University of Missouri. Here she suffered what she calls a severe case of culture shock." Sensitive to racism and her alienation as a foreigner, she moved on to Canada where she took her Ph.D. in English literature at McGill University in 1972 with a dissertation on Ezra Pound. She accepted an appointment in the English Department of Scarborough College of the University of Toronto and made her home in Canada for the next several years. Her poetry, which began appearing in Canadian journals and anthologies, won her grants from the Ontario Arts Council and the Canada Council.

During these years Namjoshi came to terms with her lesbianism. She described the struggle in *More Poems* in "Pinocchio," written in the late 1960s, recalling the wooden doll in love with the ivory doll but too shy to dance with her:

. . . If we should stumble
And clutching one another, discover
We're neither wood nor ivory, they'd switch on
The lights and the children would scream
And we would have to move
To the other side of the curtain.

She was also still haunted by the memory of her father's death: "Where is my father? / In the sky, a personal star, / shedding / effulgence." In "Discourse with the Dead" (published in *The Authentic Lie*) she attempts to deal with her grief: "I am not sure what the political implications of all this are for me as a feminist," she wrote the poem in *Because of India*. "For the child, for his daughter, his only crime was that he died. For the woman writing the poems, the central task was to clarify and shape the raw material of the grief of the child."

By the early 1980s Namjoshi was ready to declare herself a feminist but confessed to reservations: "I don't like being an activist. It frightens me, it doesn't suit my temperament." She channeled her feelings into *Feminist Fables*. "For me, they were a way of exploring feminist ideas and their implications for the patterns I have inherited through the mainstream literary tradition. The knowledge that an audience existed to whom I would make sense made all the difference. It released my imagination to try to make the patterns that were authentic to me." Kathleen Jamie wrote in the *Times Literary Supplement*, reviewing a reprint of the fables in 1990, that they show "the same satisfying growth of confidence and technical ability as does the rest of her work: a greater ease with cultural shifts, an assuredness which allows Namjoshi to dive deeper as she comes to terms with and celebrates her own sex and sexuality."

Woman, Namjoshi discovered in her study of Indian folklore, is the traditional "carrier of culture" as mother and storyteller, handing on her heritage to her children. *The Conversations of Cow*, a short and witty myth of her own creation, incorporates Indian lore by introducing the goddess Bhadravati who assumes the form of a Brahmin cow but in this story is a very human creature who can change identities at will. She lives in Canada, drinks scotch and water from a finger bowl, and speaks a colloquial American English. She acts as a mentor to the confused young woman who narrates the story and takes her to visit a "Self-Sustaining Community of Lesbian Cows" where, as Makarand Paranjape wrote in *World Literature Today*, she learns "that she is not determined by those markers that society uses to designate and manipulate identity; she can be anything she chooses to be . . . This is a story of learning and growing into greater self-acceptance and wisdom."

In contrast to the broadly comic spirit of *The Conversations of Cow*, *The Mothers of Maya Diip*, which Namjoshi herself describes as a dystopian satire, explores the problems of a matriarchal society. The astringent tone is introduced with the opening epigraph from Lewis Carroll: "'But what would you do if you were the Red Queen?' Alice replies, 'I would make everybody behave themselves.'" Set in an Indian state where "a matriarchy bloomed unashamedly," ruled by "the happy line of competent queens," Maya Diip proves to be less than idyllic. When they reach the age of fourteen, boy children are milked of their semen so that the colony may survive and then drowned. There is rivalry for the succession, rivalry with a neighboring maleaudroid society, and nonconformists are shunned. Yet the visiting "outside" who questions this authoritarian rule comes in the end to accept it and takes on the responsibility of leadership.

Namjoshi is neither bitter nor dogmatic. In her poetry she has creates female Calibans and female Frankenstein-creatures, complex figures who are justly angry and rebellious. But in most of her writing, especially in her prose fables, her feminism displays the wit, wisdom, and compassionate understanding that transcend sexism. An example from *Feminist Fables is "The Doll"*:

> Two little girls are making a doll. It's a male doll. It's made out of sticks. Perched on the sticks is a round stone. that is its head. The doll is fragile.

A boy comes along. He stares at the doll. The little girls tell him that the name of the doll is Brittle Boy. The boy gets mad. He smashes the doll. The two little girls get very angry. They would like very much to smash the boy, But they say to themselves that the boy is fragile. They pick up the sticks and start over.

PRINCIPAL WORKS: *Poetry*—Poems, 1967; More Poems, 1970; Cyclone in Pakistan, 1971; The Jackass and the Lady, 1980; The Authentic Lie, 1982; Fron the Bedside Book of Nightmares, 1984; (with G. Hanscombe) Flesh and Paper, 1986. The Blue Donkey Fables, 1988; *Prose*—Feminist Fables, 1981; The Conversations of Cow, 1985; The Mothers of Maya Diip, 1989. *Poetry and prose*-Because of India: Selected Poems and Fables, 1989.

ABOUT: Aaron J., ed. Out of the Margins: Women's Studies in the Nineties, 1991; Contemporary Authors 113, 1985; Nelson, E., ed. Reworlding: Literature of the Indian Diaspora, 1992; Nelson E., ed. Writer of the Indian Diaspora, 1993; Warland, B., ed. In/Version: Writings by Dykes, Queers and Lesbians, 1991. *Periodicals*—Canadian Literature Summer 1985; Times Literary Supplement September 14, 1990; World Literature Today Winter 1991.

NISSENSON, HUGH (March 10, 1933–), American novelist, and short story writer and journalist writes: "I was born a Jew in Brooklyn, New York. My mother was also born in Brooklyn; my father came to New York with his family from Warsaw in 1907, when he was seven, and grew up on the Lower East Side. He was a self-educated and eloquent man, who through all my childhood told me stories about his life. His narrative gift aroused in me a love of the American vernacular. I used his voice as the model for the narrator of my first novel *My Own Ground* which begins: 'In the summer of 1912, when I was fifteen years old, Schlifka the pimp offered me ten bucks to tell him when Hannah Isaacs showed up in the tenement on Orchard Street where I lived.'

"My Father loved and feared God; my mother is an atheist. I was twelve years old when the concentration camps were opened. I glimpsed

HUGH NISSENSON

hell in the newsreels but kept my faith. The mystical rabbi of *My Own Ground* has a vision of it back in 1912: 'The War of Gog and Magog is coming, and one of the soldiers of Edom will ride in a black car, and in the field on his left will be a big ditch, filled with dead Jews.'

"I lost my faith covering the Eichmann trial in 1961 for *Commentary* magazine. Till then, I had believed that God manifested himself in history. The stories I heard in the courtroom changed my mind. I couldn't reconcile my ideas about God with the fate of European Jewry under the Nazis.

"Loss of faith in a personal God is a major theme of my work. Twain, Melville, and Hemingway influenced me as a kid. I'm one of those American writers who's obsessed with the presence of evil and the absence of God. I first wrote about such things in two volumes of short stories, *A Pile of Stones* and *In the Reign of Peace*, a memoir, *Notes from the Frontier* and journals published in various magazines. In 1988, I collected a group of stories and journal entries set in Europe, Israel, and the United States between 1900 and 1987 and brought them out in one volume, *The Elephant and My Jewish Problem*. I realize in retrospect I spent thirty years writing one book, in which the Holocaust is a unifying element.

Arnost Lustig, professor of literature at American University, wrote: '*The Elephant and My Jewish Problem* may be the most accomplished literary work, the most eloquent literary testimony of Jewish destiny to appear in this century.'

"Race-hatred, mass deportation and genocide are major themes of my second novel, *The Tree of Life*, which takes place on the Ohio frontier during the War of 1812. It's narrator-protagonist is an ex-Congregational minister—a prototypical modern intellectual—who, like the Jewish hero of *My Own Ground*, loses his faith but comes to celebrate life in a world without God.

"Those two novels and the one I'm now (1992) writing called *The Song of the Earth*, which takes place in the 21st century, will eventually be a trilogy about American spiritual quests.

"It's painful for me to make a book; each takes years. I count myself an old-fashioned Modernist, who remains committed to making the novel new. The biographer and historian David McCullough wrote: '*The Tree of Life* is one of the most powerful, original, and disturbing books I have read in a long time. Hugh Nissenson has caught the voice of the old-time diary keeper just exactly. It's uncanny, marvelous, so direct and deceptively simple that you know what pains he has taken. The book is a work of art and no one who reads it will ever forget it. With a second reading, the impact is even stronger. It's like Picasso, often hard to take, but vivid and unforgettable in a way all its own.'

"As I grow older, I play more with the forms of the novel. In the last decade, I've taken to illustrating my novels and incorporating my drawings, paintings, and poems into their structure. I use these ostensibly disparate components as narrative elements. I'm a storyteller who seeks to make readers feel the astonishment, terror, and delight I experienced while listening to my father when I was a kid.

"I've been married since 1963 to Marilyn Claster Nissenson, who's also a writer. She and our daughters, Kate and Kore, make it possible for me to celebrate life in a world without God."

In 1987 the New York Public Library sponsored a series of lectures on "The Art and Craft of Religious Writing." Speakers included David Bradley, Frederick Buechner, Mary Gordon, Allen Ginsberg, Jaroslav Pelikan, and Hugh Nissenson—all of them characterized by William Zinsser in his introduction to *Spiritual Quests*, a collection of these lectures published in 1988, as "writers whose work is nourished by religious concerns . . . on a pilgrimage to find the source of their faith as individuals and of their strength as artists."

Ironically, Nissenson's loss of faith may have given his work a direction and dimension it would not otherwise have had. As Cynthia Ozick observed in a review of his short story collection

In the Reign of Peace, in the *New York Times Book Review*: "Hugh Nissenson possesses what can be called the theological imagination . . . He is the first American Jewish writer to step beyond social observation, beyond communal experience, into the listening-place of the voice of the Lord of History."

Whether writing about the Jew in Eastern European shtetls, the immigrant Jew on New York's Lower East Side in the early 20th century, the contemporary Jew in an Israeli Kibbutz, or a New England Protestant ex-clergyman on the American frontier in 1812, Nissenson has had one major purpose. "One of the things I address again and again," he told Mervyn Rothstein in an interview in the *New York Times* in 1988, "—I have no solutions, I'm not a philosopher, all I can do is dramatize—is the idea of the immense component of evil, and radical evil, in the human mind." Nissenson told Rothstein, "I think that what interested me so profoundly is the desire to take this experience and transfigure it through language into something which perhaps is beautiful, into something which perhaps has a form and shape."

Cynthia Ozick and other reviewers of Nissenson's fiction have commented on the leanness and stark simplicity of his prose. It is a quality derived from his journalism and carried over into his fiction. *Notes from the Frontier*, for example, is his straightforward, eyewitness report of life in a Kibbutz in 1965 and during the Arab-Israeli war of 1967. This unadorned style is equally effective in his fiction—"meticulous stories," Ozick said, "perfected, polished, as a result often radiant. The strength of Nissenson's prose is not what he puts in—the clear dialogue avoids idea-mongering, and there is on luxuriant visual or verbal surface to this fiction—but in how he omits." His stories are told swiftly, often in the form of a journal entries or memoirs, with enigmatic, inconclusive conclusions: "What good can come of it?" one story ends ("The Throne of Good"); in another an old Jew who has seen the corpses of Syrians and Jews killed in war reads a psalm for comfort: "And do you know something? I believe it. I'm sixty-six years old. I've been around, but I believe it. He sees everything . . . He never sleeps. One forgets. It wouldn't be so sad if I believed He was asleep" ("Going Up").

In 1965 Nissenson's first collection of short stories, *A Pile of Stones* won the Edward Lewis Wallant Award as the year's best book of American-Jewish significance. The stories in this early collection both reflect and anticipate the theme of his work, what has been called "the problem of belief." They are set in early 20th

century Poland where Jews were powerless but still possessed by their faith; in modern Israel where Jews who rebel against their suffering and hardships by denying their religion must confront the vacuum of their denial, and in America where Jews prosper and drift away from their traditions but still carry the burden of their faith. Dominating these stories is the omnipresent Jewish self-consciousness that is epitomized in the ethnic joke of the title of Nissenson's later collection of stories and essays, *The Elephant and My Jewish Problem*: "The zoology class is assigned a paper on the elephant. The Englishman writes 'Hunting the Elephant.' The Frenchman writes 'The Love Life of the Elephant.' The Jewish student turns in a paper, 'The Elephant and the Jewish Problem.'" Although the problem of belief may be more acute for the Jew who has suffered centuries of persecution than for others, in Nissenson's treatment it also has universal application. Lawrence I. Berkove wrote in an essay in *Critique* in 1978: "In these stories of the Jewish spirit, no doubt some of the best ever written by an American Jew, Hugh Nissenson has achieved a rare blending of beauty and power. Successful first as literary portraits of human beings, they are also movingly affirmative of Jewish tradition. In the best tradition of Judaism, they illustrate how much Jews have to say about being human."

While covering the Eichmann trial for *Commentary* in 1961, Nissenson met the Jewish theologian and philosopher Martin Buber, who articulated for him the complexity of a religion that sees good and evil alike as subsumed in one deity. "We Jews do not admit a dualistic explanation of evil. We don't believe in Satan. God has a demonic aspect." Buber cited Isaiah: "I make peace and create evil." He argued therefore that young Jews like Nissenson, then twenty-eight, must assume the burden of "wrestling with God." Although Nissenson's faith could not survive the witness of the Holocaust, he continues to wrestle with God, pursuing his spiritual quest with the unanswered question asked by a nonpracticing Jew he met in Israel: "You'd think that by now we'd be finished with Him once and for all. But is it possible to create a humane civilization without Him?"

Nissenson explores this question in his novels as well as in his short stories. *My Own Ground* is the first-person narrative of a young orphaned Jew newly arrived in America who must fend for himself in the sordid, poverty-ridden slum of New York's Lower East Side in the early 1900s. He is a witness to and register of both the demoralization and the exaltation that emerge in his characters—some reduced to crime and prostitution, others struggling in sweatshops to make a better life. The growing boy's religious faith is sorely tested, but his basic decency and humanity survive. Some reviewers of *My Own Ground* were troubled by its stark realism and by the flat, unemotional voice in which the story is told. Margot Lester wrote in the *Jewish Quarterly*, "This evocation of the Lower East Side is quite without sentimentality, recognizing human degradation and violence, and might at first seem only a sharp, pornographically frank, disheartening tale." She found the novel redeemed, however, by "the transforming power of the imagination." Its climax is the narrator's nightmare, a literary descent into hell, through which the boy, now an elderly man living a tranquil life in upper New York State, exorcises the evil he had experienced in his youth. "The world of our fathers has been transformed into a Freudian nightmare," Christopher Lehmann-Haupt wrote of the novel in the *New York Times*. He too complained of "the flatness of the prose and hollowness of the characters," but concluded that "this failure is of little moment when you consider the subtle complexity of Mr. Nissenson's dream . . . and its eloquent message that neither the promise of heaven above nor that of paradise below can serve to provide meaning to life. We must stand on our 'own ground.'"

In *The Tree of Life* Nissenson seemed to be moving as far away from his own ground as history and geography would take him. But the perilous existence of the 19th-century American Christian settler on the frontier parallels that of the 20th-century Jew in a modern-day Israeli Kibbutz. Nissenson's novel, however, never attempts to exploit relevance. Probably its most remarkable feature is its appearance of absolute authenticity. Told in the form of a journal by a Harvard-educated former Congregationalist minister, a lonely, heavy-drinking widower who gradually builds a new life in the wilderness, *The Tree of Life* is the product of four years of dedicated research and writing. Nissenson literally reconstructed the past, traveling to Ohio to visit the scene and comb the records of the Ohio Historical Association. He handled and used the tools and weapons his characters would have used; he wore their clothes and even camped out in the woods, duplicating their lives to the last detail. Though his narrator-protagonist, Thomas Keene, is highly educated, reads Greek and Latin, writes poetry, and has "a passion to draw" (the novel is illustrated with Nissenson's own striking, primitive-style paintings and drawings), he confines his journal to a minimal, near-documentary account of daily life—from his bookkeeping records to his strictly circumstantial accounts of the community's activities, his intimate sex life, his love for a young widow, and

the harrowing encounters with the local Delaware tribe. "Rarely have plain, homespun sentences been asked to shoulder such weight," Christopher Lehmann-Haupt wrote in the *New York Times*. For Paul Grey in *Time*: "Nissenson has created an apparently loose, formless work that is poetic in its artful selectivity. Scarcely a word is wasted." Yet within these limits Nissenson explores profound issues—Keene's loss of religious faith ("Within a year I learned I could live without God"), his regeneration as he discovers faith in his fellow humans, his experience of what Grey describes as "the American dream and its attendant nightmare." The novel is short but fragmentary; connections are not always immediately clear. "One reads *The Tree of Life* like a poem," Walter Clemons wrote in *Newsweek*, "submitting to compressed utterances that our own imaginations must connect and interpret. This is work, but it's both rewarding and moving."

The son of Charles Arthur and Harriette (Dolch) Nissenson, Hugh Nissenson grew up in Brooklyn and in Manhattan, where the family moved when he was nine years old. He graduated from Swarthmore College in 1955, with election to Phi Beta Kappa, and worked at odd jobs in journalism, among them a stint as copy boy at the *New York Times*. In 1961 he received a Wallace Stegner Literary Fellowship at Stanford. In 1962 he married Marilyn Claster, who was working as a television writer and producer. With her support and some assistance from his parents he became a full-time writer, publishing short stories and articles in the *New Yorker*, *Harper's*, *Commentary*, and other popular magazines. Although collections of his short stories were well received by reviewers, it was not until he published *The Tree of Life* that he received any wide recognition. That novel, a nominee for the PEN/Faulkner and the American Book awards, had enthusiastic reviews and sold so well that within a year of its publication it had three printings. Nissenson lives and works in an apartment on Manhattan's Upper West Side filled with his drawings and paintings and the artifacts he collected for *The Tree of Life*—animal skins, Indian headdresses and masks, flintlock rifles, buckskin clothing, and a tomahawk. "I'm sure I'm the only Jewish writer in history who learned how to throw a tomahawk," he told an interviewer for *House and Garden* in 1985.

PRINCIPAL WORKS: *Short stories*—A Pile of Stones, 1965; In the Reign of Peace, 1972. *Journalism*—Notes from the Frontier, 1968. *Selections*—The Elephant and My Jewish Problem: Selected Stories and Journals, 1988.

ABOUT: Contemporary Authors New Revision Series 27,

1989 Contemporary Literary Criticism 4, 1975; 9, 1978; Dictionary of Literary Biography 28, 1984; Nissenson, H. The Elephant and My Jewish Problem, 1988; Nissenson, H. Notes from the Frontier, 1968; Zinsser, W. (ed.) Spiritual Quests, 1988. *Periodicals*—Chicago Tribune Book World December 11, 1988; Critique 20, 1978; House and Garden November 1985; Jewish Quarterly Autumn 1976; New York Times October 14, 1985; January 4, 1989; New York Times Book Review March 19, 1972; December 11, 1988; February 12, 1989; Newsweek November 18, 1985; Publishers Weekly November 1, 1985; Studies in Short Fiction Summer 1973; Time October 21, 1985; Wall Street Journal January 23, 1986; Washington Post Book World December 2, 1985; January 8, 1989.

LARRY NIVEN

NIVEN, LARRY (LAURENCE VAN COTT) (April 30, 1938–), American science fiction novelist, writes: "1973 or thereabouts: Harry Harrison wanted biographical glimpses of his authors for an anthology. He wasn't satisfied with mine. He tried to get me to rewrite it. 'Let's have a look at the real Larry Niven!'

"I told him that none of my life is public property until I say it is.

"I'm not sure whether I was right or wrong. Some of my life goes into my books. Not all. My computer erases my mistakes; my false starts and half-written stories remain secret, and that's just fine by me.

"Well, let's try again.

"I knew it long ago: I'm a compulsive teacher, and can't teach. I lack at least two of the essential qualifications:

I cannot suffer fools gladly. The smartest of my pupils would get all my attention, and the rest would have to fend for themselves. And I can't handle being interrupted.

"Writing is the answer. Whatever I have to teach, my students will select themselves by buying the book . And nobody interrupts a printed page!

"I knew what I wanted when I started writing. I had daydreamed all my life, and I'd told stories too. Now the daydreams were shaping themselves into stories. I wanted to share them.

"The laws of astrophysics imply worlds stranger than any found in fantasy.

"I longed to touch the minds of strangers I would never see, and show them the wonders in my imagination.

"I wanted to be a published science fiction writer, like Poul Anderson and Jack Vance.

"I wanted a Hugo Award!

"Getting rich formed no part of that. Science fiction writers didn't get rich. I used money to keep score: how many people had I reached?

"I had my Hugo Award (or Science Fiction Achievement Award) three years after I sold my first story. Within the science fiction field one becomes a Grand Old Man fast. Now what?

"Now become a better writer. My writing had flaws, and I knew it. The worst was that I could not write about the things that hurt me most. Read my earlier novels and you find that nobody ever gets sick!

"My wife and I spent the last half of 1988 crippled. My knee eventually healed. An operation repaired Marilyn's back. We're back in shape for hiking. But I'm feeling old. My first 'known space' short story in fifteen years was set in a 'gray singles' bar. . . .

"Marrying Marilyn in 1969 changed my life, but not my career. That changed when I began writing with Jerry Pournelle.

"He's more organized than I am, more of a businessman. 'I'll make you rich and famous,' he said.

"I'm already rich,' I said.

"He got me into sailing and hiking. I had seen laziness as a pleasant life-style. That changed.

"He knows history and politics, and will lecture on any excuse. I listened. I needed his knowledge for the novels we were writing. He intends to drag humankind to the stars, kicking and screaming if necessary. Presently he talked me and Marilyn into hosting a gathering of the top minds in the space industry in an attempt to write a space program, with goals, timetables, costs.

"The Citizens Advisory Council for a National

Space Policy met five times over many years, for harrowing three-day weekends. The attendees include spacecraft designers, businessmen, NASA personnel, astronauts, lawyers. Adding science fiction writers turns out to be stunningly effective. We can translate: we can force these guys to speak English. We've had some effect on the space program . . . not enough, but some.

"I've been writing with a computer for fifteen years, ever since Jerry Pournelle talked me into it. He's since become the Users Column for BYTE magazine. What I do is, buy what Jerry Pournelle tells me to.

"At first I was calling Jerry at any time of the day or night to describe what the machine had done to me. Now . . . I remember typewriters. I remember typing whole pages to make two or three corrections; I remember Liquid Paper and scissors and scotch tape. A word processing program is a magic typewriter. Writing a first draft is almost as much work as it used to be—the computers don't do *that* yet!—but subsequent drafts are so easy that I find myself rewriting every time I read a passage over.

"I was raised in a drinking family. I've had to quit: I developed an allergy.

"Writing can be lonely, but it doesn't have to be. I've written with a variety of collaborators. I can interact with readers at science fiction conventions, and I get a constant stream of letters form strangers.

"Steven Barnes—another collaborator who teaches several varieties of martial arts—has repeatedly persuaded me and Marilyn to upgrade our exercise routines. I'm on yoga now.

"My present career goal is to save civilization and make a little money.

"Civilization takes a lot of saving. Fortunately humans are builders. Destruction is so much easier than creation that the world would be nothing but rubble if it were otherwise.

"I still have trouble talking about myself."

————

Some of Larry Niven's life is now public property. He was born in Los Angeles and raised in Beverly Hills. His parents are Waldemar Van Cott Niven, a lawyer, and Lucy Estelle Washington (Doheny) Niven. After attending Hawthorne Public School in Beverly Hills and Carpinteria School for Boys, he entered the California Institute of Technology in 1956, but was undone scholastically by a used bookstore wellstocked with science fiction magazines. He did try again, this time at Washburn University in Kansas, and earned his B.A. degree in mathematics in 1962. His psychology minor later proved beneficial to his fiction. A year of graduate work in mathematics at the University of California, Los Angeles, ended in 1963, when he decided to become a science fiction writer.

While supporting himself with a trust fund left by a great grandfather in the oil business, Niven went through the usual cycle of rejection slips. In 1964 he placed a short story titled "The Coldest Place" in December issue of If magazine. His first novel, World of Ptavvs, was published in 1966. The "ptavvs" in the title are inferior beings/slaves, and the enslavement of the earth is what the alien Kzanol, the last Thrint from the planet Thrintun, intends. Kzanol has the power of mind control, but his human protagonist, Larry Greenberg, has had his own minor telepathic powers boosted so that he can perform memory exchanges. A human memory transfer with the alien miscues and Greenberg ends up with more than Kzanol's memories. He now identifies himself as Kzanol inhabiting the substandard body of a human. One strength of the story is the dual alien and human perspectives. Eventually Greenberg recovers his own identity and plans to use his power for more alien contacts.

From the World of Ptavvs, Niven began to construct his elaborate, far-reaching history of the future, which he calls Known Space.

Four major themes have been noted in Niven's work: the interrelationship of human and alien civilizations; his interest in the psychic powers of the human being, however limited these may be; and fantasy, primarily involving time travel. Of Niven's use of fantasy, John J. Pierce writes in The New Encyclopedia of Science Fiction: "His work is distinguished by its carefully thought out, thoroughly detailed, farout ideas, but his imaginings, even his fantasies, are rationally explained." Niven's fourth major theme is his faith in the ultimately beneficial effects of technology.

After World of Ptavvs, Niven used both novels and short stories to continue his Tales of Known Space, from the early centuries of humankind's interplanetary outreach to a thousand years into the future. Ringworld—arguably Niven's best novel and winner of a Nebula Award, an Australian Ditmar Award, and his second Hugo Award—was published in 1970 and places the saga in the 31st century. Here Niven creates an artificial planet shaped like a massive hoop around a distant sun. "I myself have dreamed up an intermediate step between Dyson Spheres and planets," he says. "Build a ring 93 million miles in radius, one Earth orbit, which would make it 600 million miles long. . . . We wouldn't even have to roof it over. Put walls a thousand miles high at each rim, aimed at the sun, and very little of the air will leak over the edges. The thing is roomy enough: three million times the area of the Earth. It will be some time before anyone complains of the crowding." Ringworld is inhabited by various and sundry barbaric cultures and races, who have forgotten the long-dead builders of their world and the technology that made it possible. When an exploration team of two humans and two aliens crash-lands on the planet, the newcomers must journey across its width to safety.

Although *Ringworld* was successfully self-contained, Niven succumbed to fan pressure and ten years later published a sequel. In his dedication to *The Ringworld Engineers*, he alludes to the vast popularity of the original: "I have never stopped getting letters about it. People have been reading *Ringworld*, and commenting on the assumptions, overt and hidden, and the mathematics and the ecology and the philosophical implications, precisely as if it were a proposed engineering project and they were being paid to work." William J. Laskowski, Jr., in *Twentieth-Century Science-Fiction* calls *The Ringworld Engineers* a "grand, unifying coda to Known Space in which all the loose threads are gathered up and connected. Some readers found it unsuccessful, perhaps because the characters seem to be shadows of their former selves, and some of the unification forced. Yet read together, the novels furnish a fitting capstone to one of the most popular series in recent science fiction."

Niven has created other popular histories of the future, including the Leshy Circuit series, and, since the mid-1970s, has embarked on a string of successful collaborations with Jerry Pournelle and Steven Barnes, among others. In *The Mote in God's Eye*, Niven and Pournelle together entered classic science fiction territory, writing about the first contact between humans and aliens (here the Moties). Gerald Jonas, in the *New York Times Book Review*, was impressed by the authors' credentials, but little else: "Twenty pages into their novel, I found myself asking . . . 'Could this be a put-on?' Five hundred pages later, I reluctantly concluded that it was not. What (they) have done is to graft a serious 'first-contact' novel onto a laughably bad space opera. . . . The 19th century flavor in Niven's and Pournelle's Galactic Empire does not work as allegory or parody; it simply represents a failure of imagination." John Clute and Peter Nicholls, in *The Science Fiction Encyclopedia*, disagreed, calling it a "giant, spectacular tale with all the trappings: space-opera shenanigans, aliens with unhealthy proclivities to hide, galactic aristocracies, and so forth." Perhaps the highest praise came from the noted science fiction writer Robert Heinlein, who stated on the book's cover that it was "possibly the finest science fiction novel I have ever read."

Niven's wish for a Hugo Award has been granted more than once. In addition to one for *Ringworld*, he has received Hugos for his short stories "*Neutron Star*" (1967), "*Inconstant Moon*" (1972), and "*The Hole Man*" (1975), and his novelette "*The Borderland of Sol*" (1976). He and his wife Marilyn Joyce Wisowaty live in Beverly Hills.

PRINCIPAL WORKS: *Novels*—World of Ptavvs, 1966; A Gift from Earth, 1969; Ringworld, 1970; The Flying Sorcerers, 1971; Protector, 1973; (with Jerry Pournelle) The Mote in God's Eye, 1974; (with Jerry Pournelle) Inferno, 1976; A World Out of Time, 1976; (with Jerry Pournelle) Lucifer's Hammer, 1977; The Magic Goes Away, 1978; The Patchwork Girl, 1980; The Ringworld Engineers, 1980; (with Steven Barnes) Dream Park, 1981; (with Jerry Pournelle) Oath of Fealty, 1981; (with Steven Barnes) The Descent of Anansi, 1982; The Integral Trees, 1984; (with Jerry Pournelle) Footfall, 1985; (with Jerry Pournelle and Steven Barnes) The Legacy of Heorot, 1987; The Smoke Ring, 1987; (with P. Anderson and D. Ing) The Man-Kzin Wars, 1988; (with Steven Barnes) The Barsoom Project, 1989; (with D. Ing, Jerry Pournelle, and S. M. Stirling) The Man-Kzin Wars II, 1989; (with P. Anderson, Jerry Pournelle, and S. M. Stirling) The Man-Kzin Wars III, 1990; N-Space, 1990; (with Steven Barnes) Achilles' Choice, 1991; (with Jerry Pournelle and M. Flynn) Fallen Angels, 1991; The Man-Kzin Wars IV, 1991; Playgrounds of the Mind, 1991; (with Steven Barnes) The California Voodoo Game, 1992; (with Jerry Pournelle, S. M. Stirling, and T. T. Thomas) The Man-Kzin Wars V, 1992; (with Jerry Pournelle) The Gripping Hand, 1993. *Short Stories*—Neutron Star, 1968; The Shape of Space, 1969; All the Myriad Ways, 1971; The Flight of the Horse, 1973; Inconstant Moon, 1973; (with J. Brunner and J. Vance) Three Trips in Time and Space: Original Novellas of Science Fiction, 1973; A Hole in Space, 1974; Tales of Known Space, 1975; The Long Arm of Gil Hamilton, 1976; Convergent Series, 1979; Niven's Laws, 1984; The Time of the Warlock, 1984; Limits, 1985. *As editor*—The Magic May Return, 1981; More Magic, 1984.

ABOUT: Barron, N. (ed.) Anatomy of Wonder: A Critical Guide to Science Fiction, 3rd. ed., 1987; Contemporary Authors New Revision Series 14, 1985; Contemporary Literary Criticism 8, 1978; Del Rey, L. The World of Science Fiction: 1926–1976: The History of a Subculture, 1980; Dictionary of Literary Biography 8, 1981; Gunn, J. (ed.) The New Encyclopedia of Science Fiction, 1988; The Science Fiction Encyclopedia, 1979; Twentieth-Century Science-Fiction Writers, 1991; Who's Who in America 1995. *Periodicals*—New York Times Book Review January 12, 1975.

NOCHLIN, LINDA (January 30, 1931–), American art historian, and critic was born in Brooklyn, New York, the daughter of Jules and Elka (Heller) Weinberg After graduating with a bachelor's degree in philosophy from Vassar College in 1951, she went to Columbia University, receiving an M.A. in English in 1952. The following year she began studying at New York University's Institute of Fine Arts. Upon completion of her dissertation, "The Development and Nature of Realism in the Work of Gustave Courbet," in 1963, she received her doctorate in art history.

In her dissertation, she discussed the complex style and content of many of Gustave Courbet's major works while also putting him in political and social context's. By doing this, she established a pattern that would continue in her work. Rather than confining herself to the traditional formalist analysis of art, she has borrowed ideas and methods from literary criticism, sociology, and history. She examined the effect of the French Revolution of 1848 on Courbet and showed his affinity with provincial, rural people, thereby making Courbet and his work part the social history of 19th-century France. When her dissertation was published in 1976, Gabriel P. Weisberg of the Art Bulletin suggested that many of her assertions and interpretations had withstood the test of time. He wrote the "her definition of the characteristics of Courbet's Realism and her discovery of his popular sources made possible new discriminations and a new assessment of Realism."

What became Nochlin's lifelong interest in Courbet had been aroused in 1953 when she read an article by Meyer Schapiro entitled "Courbet and Popular Imagery." She told Art News that "Schapiro's brilliant study showed political content could emerge from folk art and other neglected forms." Courbet and the realist were also compelling to her because of "the oppressive political climate in this country in the 1950s, as borne out by the Army-McCarthy hearings. . . . I was anxious to bring together my political concern with my art history." With Schapiro's encouragement, she published an article in 1967 showing that Courbet had borrowed a popular image of the Wandering Jew and used it as the basis of a painting from 1854, The Meeting, which depicts Courbet meeting his patron. For this article, Nochlin won the Arthur Kingsley Porter Prize from Art Bulletin for the best article by a scholar under forty.

Although showing some signs of the interdisciplinary nature of her later work, Nochlin's writing during the 1960s was traditional in form. Her first book, Mathis at Colmar, is a detailed analysis of Mathias Grünewald's Isenheim Altar-

LINDA NOCHLIN

piece. Although in her explanations she stayed primarily within the conventional formalist confines of art history, she used all of the available analytical tools and types of critical language. In 1966, she edited two of a series of books to be used in teaching undergraduate art history courses. Impressionism and Post-Impressionism, 1874–1904: Sources and Documents and Realism and Tradition in Art, 1848–1900: Sources and Documents was acclaimed for Nochlin's choice of material and enlightening editorial comment.

By the beginning of the 1970s, Nochlin's interest became more focused. Energized by the political changes resulting from the women's liberation movement, she began applying feminist critique in her work, becoming one of the first practitioners of feminist art history. For Nochlin, the purpose of feminist art history is not to add women to the canon of great painters, but as she explained in the introduction to her 1988 book, Women, Art, and Power, "to reveal the structures and operations that tend to marginalize certain kinds of artistic production while centralizing others." This was not a simple task because "in 1970, there was no such thing as feminist art history: like all other forms of historical discourse, it had to be constructed. New material had to be sought out, a theoretical basis put in place, a methodology gradually developed." In 1969 Nochlin taught a semester at Vassar on women and art, the first of its kind ever offered. The following year she published a pioneering article, "Why Have There Been No Great Women Artists?" (Art News, January

1971) Her answer was that it was not because of any innate differences in ability or mental processes between men and women, but that institutions, educational systems, and other societal conditions prevented women from becoming great artists. Because women were educated to be mothers, it was unlikely that many would disregard social expectations in order to enter the public realm of an artist. Even if a woman had been willing to do this, she did not have access to the art schools where she would gain expertise at depicting the nude, a necessary skill for great artists before the 20th century.

The article was and remains controversial, even within feminist circles. In the *Nation*, Maureen Mullarkey remarked that "Nochlin follows her fine discussion of the fallacy of so-called masculine and feminine styles within the contradictory suggestion that no appropriate 'language of form' exists for women." If traditional definitions of the art are based on male subjectivity, then Mullarkey continued, Nochlin is saying that "women should not be judged by 'male' standards of quality. By insinuating a false opposition between women's abilities and concepts of quality, the argument is protectionist and retrograde." Others objected to her claim that there had been no great female artists. Many readers however, found the article galvanizing. "By simply posing the question in gender terms," wrote Eunice Lipton in the *Women's Review of Books*, "Nochlin audaciously threw open a firmly closed art-critical door to women."

In her 1971 book *Realism*, Nochlin made full use of her integrated approach to the study of art, incorporating sociological, scientific, philosophical, and literary methods of criticism along with stylistic and formalist analysis. In *Artforum*, Carol Duncan noted that because Nochlin treats "art as a human activity intricately bound up with social, political and cultural history," she is in the minority of art historians. "The more familiar and established modes of inquiry today treat art as a set of highly limited problems involving mainly formal and iconographic solutions," continued Duncan. Nochlin defined realism as the dominant stream in European art from the 1840s to the 1870s, in which the artist tried to represent accurately and objectively the world within the context of 19th-century life. Although the realists strived toward scientific truth, Nochlin argued that, like everyone else, they were products of their time and that this influenced their new style and unusual subject matter. Nochlin uses the term more broadly than do many scholars, placing Manet and the Impressionists under the realist umbrella because of their confrontational relationship with bourgeois society and traditional artistic ex-

pectations. Although Duncan found this a useful way of viewing 19th-century artistic developments, Keith Roberts, writing in *Burlington* thought that the book suffered "from the lack of the central analysis of the differences between the works of Courbet" and those of later artists such as Manet, Degas, and the Impressionists.

Because of the vast amount of material on this period, Nochlin used a thematic rather than chronological arrangement in her study. While some reviewers found this a convenient way of understanding realist concerns, others thought it made the book redundant. Cindy Nemser of *Arts Magazine* objected that each chapter "was written as a separate complete essay for various specific occasions and that these essays have been thrown together as a book." Yet Nemser also remarked that it was a "truly admirable and absorbing exposition of a highly complex and confusing subject" which Nochlin approached "with enthusiasm, élan, and originality." Nochlin's most important achievement with this book, Nemser argued, was that she placed realism "in the universal context unfortunately missing from most art historical writing today."

Throughout the 1970s and 1980s, Nochlin devoted herself to teaching, writing articles on realism and women, and editing books. The first of these books, *Women as Sex Object: Studies in Erotic Art 1730–1970* . . . contained one article by Nochlin in which she argued that art with erotic implications is always erotic for men only because woman lack an accepted language of erotic imagery. To demonstrate this, she changed the gender in a photograph of naked women. The result, rather than being erotic, was merely humorous. According to Lise Vogel's review in the *Art Journal*, Nochlin's essay was the only one in the book that was "self-consciously feminist." Vogel argued that Nochlin's answer to the lack of female erotic imagery was an "unimaginative reversal of sex roles" which, by making the man the sex object, maintained "a world of alienated and objectified sexual relations."

Nochlin also collaborated on two major exhibition catalogs in this period, *Women Artists: 1550–1950* in 1976 and *Courbet Reconsidered* in 1988. In the essay she contributed on Courbet, she used gender studies to analyze and suggest allegories for Courbet's *Painter's Studio*. While crediting the rigor and substance of Nochlin's work, many reviewers found her essay overly rhetorical and abstract, with the writer for *Virginia Quarterly Review* accusing her of "academic overinterpretation." In the introduction to *Art and Architecture in the Service of Politics*, a collection of essays which she coedited with Henry Millon, Nochlin questioned the political purposes of art, wondering if there is any fundamental difference between art used to further liberal goals and that is used to further reactionary causes and whether politically radical art is sometimes given undue credit for being formally innovative.

Women, Art, and Power and *The Politics of Vision* are collections of essays dating from 1965. In *Women, Art, and Power*, she retraces her involvement in the development of feminist art history. Although the essays are on diverse subjects, she explains in her introduction that they achieve unity because of "a consistent critical attitude toward the practice of mainstream art history" which, she contends, is still very resistant to feminists criticism. For Nochlin, feminist art history is inherently radical. She wrote in the introduction that it "is there to make trouble, to call into question, to ruffle feathers in the patriarchal dovecotes. It should not be mistaken for just another variant of or supplement to mainstream art history. . . . [it] is a transgressive and anti-establishment practice, meant to call many of the major precepts of the discipline into question."

While acknowledging Nochlin's role in creating feminist art history, reviews of the two books were mixed. Some critics argues that she was too dogmatic. Maureen Mullarkey reviewing *Women, Art, and Power* in the *Nation* noted that in Nochlin's early work, her "intelligence is sharply focused and the commentary is lucid and authoritative," and her "engagement with her sources was paramount." Mullarkey complained, however, that since the mid-1970s, Nochlin's "attention has shifted to a facile orthodoxy that decrees its own conclusions with scant help from her material." In *Art in America*, Brooks Adams cited Nochlin's "brilliant, energetic, searching prose style," but found that her writing contained excessive jargon and was too rhetorical. Still, Adams noted, Nochlin's ability to derive political content from a painting using ideas taken from literary criticism and sociology has been a very powerful addition to the study of art history. Norman Bryson wrote in the *Times Literary Supplement* that the common thread running through *The Politics of Vision* was "a commitment to understanding art as a social and political activity, rather than timeless self-expression." He also praised the way she views social history, not as a backdrop to art, but "as a force that influences even such apparently formalist aspects as a choice of colours or the handling of line and volume." It is this ability to move easily between detailed explication of painting and social history that he believes is one of Nochlin's major strengths.

Nochlin's research includes a study of the representation of bath time in 19th-century France, further work on Courbet, and a study of the representation of women in French art. Nochlin taught art history at Vassar from 1963 to 1979. In 1980, she moved to the Graduate Center of the City University of New York, where she taught until 1990. She is currently a professor at Yale University. Her first husband, Philip Nochlin, a professor of philosophy, died in 1960. She married Richard Pommer, an architectural historian, in 1968. She has one daughter from each marriage. Among her many honors are a nomination for the National Book Award for *Realism*, a Woman of the Year award from *Mademoiselle* magazine in 1977, and Fulbright, Guggenhiem, and National Endowment for Humanities fellowships.

PRINCIPAL WORKS: Mathis at Colmar: A Visual Confrontation, 1963; Realism, 1971; Gustave Courbet: A Study of Style and Society, 1976; (with A. S. Harris) Women Artists: 1550–1950, 1976; (with S. Faunce) Courbet Reconsidered, 1988; Women, Art, and Power, and Other Essays, 1988; The Politics of Vision, 1989; As editor—Impressionism and Post-Impressionism, 1874–1904: Sources and Documents, 1966; (with T.B. Hess) Women as Sex Objects: Studies in Erotic Art, 1730–1970, 1972; (with Henry Millon) Art and Architecture in the Service of Politics, 1978.

ABOUT: Contemporary Authors New Revision Series 6, 1982. *Periodicals*—Art Bulletin June 1978; Art in America May 1990; Art Journal Summer 1976; Art News December 1988; Artforum May 1973; Arts Magazine September/October 1972; Burlington Magazine May 1973; Nation December 19, 1988; Times Literary Supplement December 27, 1991; Virginia Quarterly Review Spring 1989; Women's Review of Books April 1989.

*NOOTEBOOM, CEES (July 31, 1933–   ), Dutch poet, novelist, playwright, travel writer, translator, and essayist, was born in The Hague, the Netherlands. He was eleven years old when his father died during a bombing raid in World War II. When his mother remarried, he was sent to various boarding schools run by Franciscan and Augustinian monks because he could not get along with his stepfather. This late introduction to Roman Catholicism contributed to a lasting fascination with religion, its decorum, tradition, and history, as well as to a genuine attraction to the closed world of monasteries. But the young Nooteboom was expelled from all these boarding schools and never finished high school. He has always thought of himself as "someone who did not belong to anything," a trait he shares with many of his fictional characters.

*NOH ti bom

CEES NOOTEBOOM

His first novel, *Philip en de Anderen* (1954, *Philip and the Others*) was inspired by a long hitchhiking trip he took through Europe. The work, which was immediately well received, betrays very little of the experiences of a youth who had witnessed the war as a child, and who had grown up without a father. The novel is above all a celebration of the imagination and of its power to transform the world. Filled with stories and flashbacks, the novel follows the capricious twists and turns in the road of young Philip as he pursues a young Laotian girl, the first of many women in Nooteboom's writings to embody creative vision: "You are afraid because your world, your safe world in which you were able to recognize things has gone, because you now see that things became created anew every moment and that they are alive. . . . And what you see, what people like you see, is dead. Dead." His journey of self-discovery and initiation concludes with an innocent optimism that is extraordinary for a postwar novel: "I reflected that the loveliness of the world begins anew with each new person, that it cannot be explained, and that, as my uncle Antonin Alexander said, 'a paradise lives beside it.' " Nooteboom later expressed embarrassment about "the forever-lost blend of impossible innocence, dreampower, and blissful inexperience" of this early work.

And indeed, his next novel, published almost ten years later, reflects the crisis of an imagination questioning its own powers of transformation. *De Ridder is Gestorven* (1963, *The Knight Has Died*), no longer represents the spontaneous outpourings of a young writer; rather, the work bears witness to the self-reflexive doubts of a novelist distrusting the very medium of his art. The joy of living is pitted against the art of writing and the most creative writers in this novel end up dead. The plot itself is shaped with mirrors and reflections: The main narrator writes a book about his dead friend, André Steenkamp, the knight, who, in turn, was writing a novel about an author who dies before completing his work. This interaction between fiction and reality, with the more realistic, outer narrator confronting and correcting the imagination of the romantic André Steenkamp, created an echo chamber within the novel as a whole: "And so I sit here, with eternally receding writers, mine and his, who die with other writers at their heels who then complete their books, but who die, with other writers at their heels who then complete their books, but who die, etcetera." The two protagonists are mirror figures, writers who wage battle against their reversed reflections and defend opposing views of the creative process. On trial is the nature of the imagination itself as it succeeds in transforming the real stuff of life into the stuffed life of the planned novel. Surrounded by cardboard characters, postcard sunsets, and painted monuments, Steenkamp, the knight in an all-too-fictional setting, dies of an excess of creative vision and of a lack of reality. But even with the protective shields of multiple frames, with the proliferation of writers and readers, and with the outer narrator ridiculing the knight's romantic vision, it is still Steenkamp's poetic perspective and charged vision that permeates the novel.

Nooteboom himself has pointed to the real crisis behind this work: "Whoever does not know *The Knight Has Died* does not know what kind of a writer I am." Though the work received less favorable reviews, both in his native country and here ("uncharacteristically humorless," Linda Simon wrote in the *New York Times Book Review* in 1990), this novel, with its structure of conflicting narrative voices and frames, is also the first, and most anguished, step towards that later works of metafiction, a genre which in Nooteboom's case is biographical in origin. The writer's virus examined in *The Knight Has Died* kept Nooteboom from completing another novel for seventeen years, until 1980, when he published the much celebrated *Rituelen* (*Rituals*). During those years, Nooteboom took on many different roles: as manager of the career of his wife, a popular singer; as a successful writer of travel articles for Dutch magazines; as a translator; as a songwriter; as a reporter chronicling the student revolution in Paris; as a husband going through divorce; and, as a poet giving voice to his many different selves.

Rituals is set in Amsterdam between 1953 and 1973 and features as an unlikely hero Inni Wintrop. A dilettante of independent means, Inni writes a horoscope column, follows the stock market, and occasionally deals in paintings. Described as "a hole, a chameleon, a being that could be given content, complete with attitude and accent," Inni Wintrop is a man without any firm convictions, open to many points of view, at once immune *and* vulnerable to the chaos of modern life. His choices stand in contrast to those of Arnold Taads and his son Philip, whose lives are anchored by firm principles, rigid discipline, and pronounced ideologies. Arnold Taads, Inni's early mentor, leads a life dominated by blocks and rituals; he adheres to a daily routine that punctuates the loneliness of a life without love. Once a champion skier, alone in the beauty of a pristinely white world, Arnold ends up a frozen corpse found in an isolated Alpine valley.

This need for order, beauty, and perfection is even more pronounced in the fate of the son Arnold refused to acknowledge, Philip Taads. His head shorn like a monk, and his thoughts shaped by Buddhism, Philip shares with his father the desire for an absolute purity and the disdain for a life that is haphazard and unpredictable. Philip too dies a lonely death, a suicide by drowning that is compared to a bottle of poison dissolving in the ocean. In contrast to Philip and Arnold's deadly need for discipline and order, Inni Wintrop thrives on the chaos of modern life. He takes delight in chance encounters on the streets of Amsterdam, and he discovers that only through women can he unlock the mystery of the world:

> 'I'm Petra,' she said. On this rock, this soft, round rock, he thought later, he had built his church. For there was no doubt about it—on that day women had become his religion, the center, the essence of everything, the great cartwheel on which the world turned.

Rituals, the first of Nooteboom's novels to appear in the U.S., became an immediate success. Like Inni, who survives his own suicide, the narrator in *Rituals* presents the unusual perspective of someone who has gone to the vanishing point and back, offering a point of view that is both passionate *and* distant.

In his next novel, *Een Lied van Schijn en Wezen* (1981, *A Song of Truth and Semblance*), narration itself is once more at stake, with two Dutch writers defending divergent views on the art of writing. Distancing himself from "the other writer" who defends the tradition of realist fiction, the main writer, who comes closest to Nooteboom's own voice, questions the very division between fact and fiction:

> It still seemed to him that he himself was the fictitious character, a person in a story. He had always had this feeling, even when not writing, and he knew it would always be so. He did not believe it had anything to do with Borges, Pessoa, or any other literary masters; theirs were mere constructions.

The novel shuttles back and forth between the writers discussing the craft of fiction, and the actual work of fiction that gradually takes shape in the imagination of the main writer. This simple frame sets into motion a series of echoes and reverberations in which the bloody world of dreams and fiction, filled with corpses, battles, nightmares, and passions, overshadows the paltry world of theoretical discussions that constitute the realm of reality in this novel. The ending especially is testimony to Nooteboom's reversed perspective on the semblance of what is real, for the invented characters survive the very destruction of the manuscript that brought them to life. This short work presents a more mature and philosophical view on the primacy of the imagination already explored in his first two novels. Had Nooteboom's knight been allowed to survive, he could have written *A Song of Truth and Semblance*.

Nooteboom's next novel, *In Nederland* (1984, *In the Dutch Mountains*), begins with a playful variation of a fairy tale: "Once upon a time there was a time that some people say is still going on." The novel is again a split-level narrative, intertwining the world of Tiburón, a chatty "inspector of Roads" in Zaragoza, with that of the fiction he is writing. His profession of building roads spills over into his hobby of writing, and he enjoys the art of digression in both. Literally squeezed into the tiny frame of a classroom desk, Tiburón rewrites Andersen's fairy tale of "The Snow Queen", now set in a legendary United Netherlands that is split apart between the flat North beautiful, perfect, absolute, abstract) and a fictitious, mountainous South (rugged, unpredictable, recalcitrant, and corrupt). Just as Tiburón enjoys moving in and out of his narrative desk, and in and out of his story, he takes delight in transferring Andersen's perfect characters, Lucia and Kai, from their fairy tale world in the North to the unpredictable and hazardous narrative roads of the South. Tiburón's imaginative playground is that threshold where the friction between map and territory is apparent, where the model, the map, the norm, the fairy tale, rub against a defiant reality. This short metafictional novel not only undermines the conventions and codes of the fairy tale, it also highlights, via Tiburón's detours in Zaragoza, the way in which fairy tales can structure the real world. With its many shifts in perspective, with its maddening proliferation of models, mirrors, reflections, and doubles and with its constant reshuffling of the maps that organize the narrative terrain, this slender work succeeded in establishing Nooteboom's reputation as a novelist with a unique voice. Bernard Levin, reviewing *In the Dutch Mountains* in the *(London) Sunday Times*, wrote: "Grasping the essence of this book is like grabbing a fistful of water from a stream. . . . *In the Dutch Mountains* is the brilliant and original fruit of a deep (and well-read) imagination."

In *Het Volgende Verhaal*, (1991, *The Following Story*), the narrator is Mr. Herman Mussert, a Dutch teacher of classics with the nickname of Socrates. The theme of this work is Nooteboom's most ambitious to date: the enigma of death. As the teacher is dying in his bed in Amsterdam, he is also waking up in Lisbon in the very bed in which he once committed adultery. Like Kafka's K., he "wakes up" to the strangeness of his own condition. This Dutch approach to the idea of a metamorphosis casts doubts upon the clear-cut division between life and death, and reality, longing and being. Death is erased and replaced by the idea of eternal change, a metamorphosis best exemplified in the splendid passage on the love life of the carrion beetles, the subject of a time-interval movie shown in the biology class visited by Socrates. These "gravedigger beetles," as they are called in Dutch, slowly sculpt a dead rat into a round ball of soft flesh; they then mate and leave this carrion ball for their offspring to feed on: "Spring, but in the class the notion of death has sneaked in, the connection between killing, mating, gorging, changing, the voracious, moving chain with teeth that is life." The brief moment separating life from death is here expanded into a large narrative voyage that takes both the reader and the teacher beyond the point of no return. As the teacher approaches his own death and gradually (and literally) disappears from view, he starts to tell "The Following Story," addressing his favorite pupil.

This short work was received with great enthusiasm in Germany and received many awards, including the selection of the Book of the Month Club in England. *Publishers Weekly* called *The Following Story* a "semi-surreal, elegantly lyrical, enchanting but baffling postmodernist fable." Penelope Fitzgerald, in the *New York Times Book Review* (1994) commented, "Nearly all the British reviewers of this translation by Ina Rilke were struck by the book's elegance and consciousness and its bitter humor. . . . Nooteboom . . . told an interviewer . . . in London that it covered the final two seconds of a man's life." Fitzgerald concluded that the "details of Mussert's daily life are brilliantly placed—even his cat is unforgetta-

ble—and beneath the self-deprecating, dry, rueful schoolmaster's voice you can feel the fury and melancholy only just under control." She expressed disappointment in the ending, however: "The ship of death, as a metaphor, creaks."

It is not accidental that Mussert in *The Following Story* turns to travel writing for extra money. For many years, Nooteboom's primary source of income for his writing came from his travel articles. Since 1963 he has edited and published eleven volumes, some of which are dedicated to one country only, such as *Berlijnse Notities* (*Berlin Notations*), bearing witness to the unification of Germany, and *De Omweg naar Santiago* (*The Detour to Santiago*), which reflects his lifelong fascination with Spain. As a traveler, Nooteboom is above all a philosopher, taking advantage of the distance to come closer to that strange substance of human nature. His favorite landscapes are barren, unforgiving, and absolute in their emptiness. Many of the later travel publication are accompanied by photographs taken by his companion and friend Simone Sassen.

Although he has had considerable success with his fiction and his travel writings, Nooteboom considers himself foremost a poet. He has published ten books of poetry, including one collection of his poems in 1978, a selection from which is being translated into English. While it is true that many of the themes of his fiction first find expression in his poetry, there is also a great distance between the light-footed, ironic narrators at ease with their craft in the novels, and the more mystical perspective of Nooteboom as a poet alone with his language. If Nooteboom identifies most with this more solitary and serious voice, it is perhaps because most of his work originates from the distance of a poet's point of view, one who is looking back at the world from the vanishing point.

PRINCIPAL WORKS IN ENGLISH TRANSLATION: *Novels*—(tr. A. Dixon) Rituals, 1983; (tr. A. Dixon) A Song of Truth and Semblance, 1984; (tr. A. Dixon) In the Dutch Mountains, 1987; (tr. A. Dixon) Philip and the Others, 1988; (tr. A. Dixon) The Knight Has Died, 1990; (tr. I. Rilke) The Following Story, 1994. *Nonfiction*—(tr. A. Dixon) Unbuilt Netherlands: Visionary Projects by Berlage, Ond, Duiker, Van den Broek, Van Eyck, Herzberg, and Others (ed. C. deJong, F. den Oudsten, and W. Schilder) 1985.

ABOUT: Contemporary Authors 124, 1988. Doctoral dissertations—Beukes, J. "The Narrative Figure in the Novels of Cees Nooteboom," University of South Africa, 1987; Spahr, H. "Writing on the Threshold," University of California at Berkeley, 1988. *Periodicals*—Chicago Tribune August 1, 1990; New York Times Book Review October 11, 1987; September 9, 1990; October 16, 1994; San Francisco Chronicle August 12, 1983; November 1, 1987; Publishers Weekly November 1, 1987; August 22, 1994; Sunday Times (London) May 24, 1987; Times Literary Supplement January 21, 1994.

OAKESHOTT, MICHAEL J(OSEPH) (December 11, 1901–December 18, 1990), British political scientist and educator, was characterized by Robert Grant of Glasgow University as "probably the greatest . . . political philosopher in the Anglo-Saxon tradition . . . certainly the most original, the most cultivated, and the most wide-ranging." He was born in Chelmsfield, Kent, the second of the three sons of Joseph Francis and Frances Maude (Hellicar) Oakeshott. Both of his partners were cultured, though not affluent, and dedicated to public service. His mother, a London vicar's daughter, studied nursing and commanded a small military hospital during World War I. His father, the son of a Newcastle postmaster, was a civil servant in the Inland Revenue Department (eventually rising to the position of principal), and a member of the Fabian Society, through which he became friendly with George Bernard Shaw.

Oakeshott's education in England and Germany brought him into contact with a variety of literary and philosophical traditions. With his father he read Montaigne, who became one of his favorite writers. An early formative influence was St. George's School in Harpenden, which he entered at the age of eleven. He described school as "a world of remarkable personalities, each very different from the others . . . a place surrounded by a thick firm hedge, and inside this hedge was a world of beckoning activities and interests." Oakeshott said of his education, "Religion did not appear as a set of beliefs, but as a kind of *pietas*; morals was knowing how to behave; Florentine and Pre-Raphaelite art was on the walls," but Robert Grant writes that Oakeshott was directed to the philosophy of Kant and Hegel, two pivotal figures in his first book, *Experience and Its Modes.*

In 1919 Oakeshott entered Gonville and Caius College in Cambridge, where he read history, with emphasis on the history of political thought. He subsequently pursued his interest in philosophy and theology in Germany, attending lectures at Marburg, where Martin Heidegger was on the faculty, and Tübingen. At this time he also steeped himself in German literature, particularly Hölderlin, Nietzsche, and Burkhardt. While on hikes through the countryside with the Wandervogel, a student group devoted to nature worship, he became imbued with a love of isola-

MICHAEL J. OAKESHOTT

tion and the outdoors which he retained through life.

After teaching English in a secondary school, Oakeshott took up a fellowship in 1927 at Gonville and Caius, where he taught modern history and became interested in the writings of Francis Herbert Bradley, a leading idealist philosopher. *Experience and Its Modes*, Oakeshott's first book, which grew out of his lectures at Cambridge, bears, according to his testimony, the dual impress of Hegel's *Phenomenology of the Spirit* and Bradley's *Appearance and Reality*. "Philosophical experience . . . I take to be experience without presupposition, reservation, arrest, or modification," he wrote in the preface. "Philosophical knowledge is knowledge which carries evidence of its own completeness." While he believed that philosophical experience was holistic (akin to Hegel's Absolute), he divided the study of it for analytical purposes into "modes" (a term from Spinoza, adapted by Bradley, signifying mental sets, or aspects of reality): history, which views the world under the aspect of the past; science, under quantity or regularity; and practice (which subsumes religion, morals, law, and politics), under desire or value. In later writings he added an aesthetic mode, poetry, answering to the basic human need for contemplation and delight.

Another product of Oakeshott's early teaching at Cambridge is a textbook, *The Social and Political Doctrines of Contemporary Europe*, undertaken at the behest of his colleague Ernest Barker as a guide for formal courses in political thought as well as for study groups. With an introduction by Oakeshott, it presents documents fundamental to the then five leading systems of government in England and on the continent—representative democracy, Catholicism, communism, fascism, and national socialism. This anthology proved to be in sufficient demand in American universities to call for the publication of an enlarged edition in the United States.

Oakeshott's academic career was interrupted by World War II. He joined the army immediately upon the outbreak of hostilities in 1940 and served until the end of the war as commander of an intelligence gathering unit in Holland known as "Phantom," whose mission was to determine if enemy targets were successfully hit by British artillery fire. One of his subordinates, the journalist Peregrine Worsthorne, testified to Oakeshott's "self-effacement . . . the quiet efficiency of his administration, and . . . mastery of everyday battlefield practicalities." A lasting effect of Oakeshott's war years was respect for the intuitive wisdom possessed by the field officer, versus the mere "technical knowledge" acquired by the enlisted civilian—a distinction central to his ideas on government and social policy. This experience also convinced him that the military organization model was inappropriate for the peacetime state with its more multivariate ends.

Upon resuming his teaching post at Cambridge after the war, Oakeshott renewed his interest in Thomas Hobbes, begun in the 1930s. Shortly thereafter he brought out his scholarly edition of *Leviathan*, which he lauded in his introduction as "the greatest, perhaps the sole, masterpiece of political philosophy written in the English language." He was impressed in particular by the breadth of vision of this treatise, concerned not merely with "means and ends," but encompassing "the entire conception of the world that belongs to a civilization." Hobbes to him combined, in the right proportion, compassion for humanity with hardheadedness, viewing life "not as a feast, or even a journey, but as a predicament." While universal in application, *Leviathan*, Oakeshott points out, confronts problems specific to its times; just as Plato's *Republic* grew out of the decline of Athenian democracy, Hobbes's book addressed the conflict between liberty and authority aggravated by the restoration of the British monarchy. The pithy introduction to Oakeshott's edition was subsequently reprinted, along with some of his other pieces on the philosopher, in *Hobbes on Civil Association*.

In 1947, Oakeshott, along with several colleagues, launched the *Cambridge Journal* and soon became its general editor. This journal, which ceased publication in 1952, was the outlet for essays later reprinted in one of his key books, *Rationalism in Politics*, as well as "The Universities," which reappeared in his last collection, *The Voice of Liberal Learning*. During his postwar Cambridge years, he also reviewed books on philosophy for the *Cambridge Review*, and contributed articles on Hobbes and Bentham to *Scrutiny*, and influential critical review edited by F. R. Leavis (whom apparently he never met).

In 1951 Oakeshott accepted the chair of political science at the London School of Economics. This appointment to a school reputed to be a "breeder of radicals" stirred up academic circles at the time. The institution had been founded by Sidney Webb along with other Fabians, including Oakeshott's father. Among the famous figures associated with it were Bertrand Russell and Clement Attlee. Moreover, the immediate predecessor in his chair was the eminent socialist theorist Harold Laski, a complete antithesis to the ivory-tower conservative that Oakeshott was by now reputed to be. Students were soon prepared for an unpartisan and iconoclastic approach to their field by Oakeshott's famous inaugural lecture "Political Education" (later reprinted in *Rationalism in Politics*), in which he likened the state to a boundless sea, and political activity to a sailing ship without anchor or harbor. His subsequent lectures undermining "rationalism" (i.e., political nostrums) and puncturing the pretensions of ideologues were cryptic and provocative. They irritated some, but, in general, attracted large audiences both within and outside his teaching department. Nonspecialists, reportedly, were particularly impressed by his lucid, eloquent expounding of recondite political doctrines. He remained at the London School of Economics until his retirement in 1968.

A *Times* leader entitled "Pragmatic Thatcherite," which appeared shortly after Oakeshott's death, characterized him as "nothing less than the chief reanimator of conservatism after the long dominance of socialism over political theory in 20th Century Britain," but his political position cannot be so easily pigeonholed. In *Our Age: Portrait of a Generation*, Sir Noel Annan places Oakeshott and his Cambridge colleague F. R. Leavis among "the Deviants"—those who "dismissed the received wisdom of the world of affairs." His empirical stance was announced immediately in his inaugural lecture: "Political activity comes first and a political ideology follows—not the other way around." Here he was applying to the world of affairs one of the central tenets of the philosophy of idealism; namely, that reality is identical with experience, not distinct from it (contrary to the teaching of, for example, Plato and Descartes). Hence Oakeshott rejected political programs based on abstract theories or "external" sanctions of any kind. Favoring the Hobbesian ideal of "civil association" over what he called "enterprise association" (under which he included managerial forms of government), he was actually as critical of the paternalism of conservative ministries as he was of state socialism.

The emphasis that Oakeshott placed on tradition and practice- what Aristotle called *phronesis*, or the pooled wisdom of enlightened minds—in guiding political action has led some scholars, notably Paul Franco, to identify him with liberalism, *phronesis* being close to the principle of consensus that lies at the heart of democracy. In his introduction to *The Social and Political Doctrines of Contemporary Europe*, Oakeshott does praise representative democracy, if in a qualified way, as the least authoritarian of those forms of government he surveyed and "having the advantage (denied to all the others save Catholicism) of not being the hasty product of a generation but of belonging to a long and expressive tradition of thought." Having "shown itself capable of changing without perishing in the process," Oakeshott continues, democracy "contains, I believe, a more comprehensive expression of our civilization," characteristically adding that "it is by no means either a complete or a satisfactory expression as it stands."

A view of life as an open-ended quest, never completed and never perfected, pervades Oakeshott's writing. "Philosophical reflection is recognized here as the adventure of one who seeks to understand in other terms what he already understands . . . in short a well-considered intellectual adventure recollected in tranquillity," reads his introduction to his most compact and abstruse book, *On Human Conduct*, published seven years after his retirement. This sense of tentativeness, of seeking without predetermined goals, also informs his definition of politics in "Political Education" as "the activity of attending to the general arrangements of a set of people whom chance or choice has brought together." As with philosophical speculation and political activity, the writing of history was for Oakeshott a form of refined induction: "the art of understanding men and events more profoundly than they were understood when they lived or happened." Consistent with his antirationalism, he disavowed any historical "laws," or any didactic role for history, which to him "consists of making sense of the evidence, making it cohere"; the historian merely establishes "subsequents" as "plausible consequents." (*On History And Other Essays*).

"Political education is not merely a matter of coming to understand a tradition," Oakeshott affirmed in his inaugural address at the London School of Economics, "it is learning how to participate in a conversation . . . at once an initiation into an inheritance in which we have a life interest, and the exploration of its intimations." In a lecture delivered at the University of Manchester in 1959, he conjectured, "Indeed it seems not improbable that it was the engagement in this conversation (where talk is without a conclusion) that gave us our present appearance, man descending from a race of apes who sat in talk so long that they wore out their tails." (*The Voice of Poetry in the Conversation of Mankind*). "Conversation" is a term that recurs in his writing, signifying the dialectical play of minds that for him was fundamental to human intellectual advancement. "University education is neither a beginning nor an end, but a middle," he said in a review essay, "The Universities." This conviction is expanded in his last book, *The Voice of Liberal Learning*. In the essay that heads this collection, "A Place of Learning" (first presented at the centennial of Colorado College in 1974), he visualized the university as a disseminator of culture, "a continuity of feelings, perceptions, ideas, attitudes, and so fourth, pulling in different directions, critical of one another, and contingently related to one another, so as to compose, not a doctrine, but what I shall call a conversational encounter." Furthermore:

> Ours, for example, accommodates not only the lyre of Apollo, but also the pipes of Pan, the call of the wild; not only the poet but also the physicist; not only the majestic metropolis of Augustan theology but also the 'greenwood' of Franciscan Christianity.

On his retirement, Oakeshott was lauded in a festschrift put together by admirers from various disciplines for his attempt "to achieve the most comprehensive understanding of experience possible," Rarely participating in public life, he was known mainly among academics, and his prestige among them was slow in spreading. *Experience and Its Modes*, regarded as a masterpiece, took thirty years to sell out an edition of 1,000 copies. He was unpretentious, even demurring at the festschrift produced in his honor. His canon includes the mischievously titled *A Guide to the Classics; or, How to Pick the Derby Winner*, written in collaboration with a Caius colleague, Guy Griffith, a racing enthusiast. This book is said to have shocked puritanical Cambridge, to Oakeshott's amusement. (Noel Annan has pointed out, however, that Oakeshott likens the racetrack, with its options and unpredictability, to the open state, and the Jockey Club to "civil association" governed by "the rule of law.") In another relaxed mood, he contributed to the BBC series "Imaginary Biographies" a talk on "The Servant Girl Who Burnt Carlyle's Manuscript." At a banquet in New York to celebrate the *National Review,* recalled William Buckley, its editor, in his obituary notice, Oakeshott whispered to the young lady seated next to him, "Just call me Mickey." During his last years he was the center of a drinking, dining, and discussion society at Caius College, where he enjoyed conversations with young students late into the night.

Oakeshott died at his home in Dorset, survived by his second wife Esther O'Neill, an artist, and a son from his first marriage (his first wife died in the 1950s). Andrew Sullivan reported in his obituary in the *New Republic* that villagers who read the death notices in the London papers "were surprised to learn that their neighbor, the sprightly reclusive octogenarian who drove an MG sports car, and who lived in a rustic cottage on the edge of a quarry, had been regarded as one of the most original political philosophers of the century." Sullivan summed up Oakeshott's life as "poetic, not prosaic. His conservative politics were not a means to repress man's exuberance, but a way to allow it to flourish when politics ends. In this way he was out of his time, but also curiously at home in it, a wild flower planted among our wheat."

PRINCIPAL WORKS: Experience and Its Modes, 1933; (with Guy T. Griffith) A Guide to the Classics; or, How to Pick the Derby Winner, 1936; The Voice of Poetry in the Conversation of Mankind, 1959; Rationalism in Politics, and Other Essays, 1962; Hobbes on Civil Association, 1975; On Human Conduct, 1975, On History and Other Essays, 1983; The Voice of Liberal Learning: Micheal Oakeshott on Education (ed. Timothy Fuller) 1989. *As editor*—The Social and Political Doctrines of Contemporary Europe (with preface by F. A. Ogg) 1942; Hobbes, T. Leviathan, 1946.

ABOUT: Annan, Noel. Our Age: Portrait of a Generation, 1990; Cowling, M. Religion and Public Doctrine in Contemporary England, 1980; Franco, P. The Political Philosophy of Michael Oakeshott, 1990; Grant, R. Oakeshott (Thinkers of Our Time), 1990; Greenleaf, W. Oakeshott's Philosophical Politics, 1966; King, P. and B. C. Parekh (eds.) Politics and Experience: Essays Presented to Michael Oakeshott on the Occasion of His Retirement, 1968. *Periodicals*—American Scholar Summer 1975; Summer 1991; British Journal of Political Science 9, 1975; Cambridge Journal 2, 1948–1949; Cambridge Review 55, 1934; Commentary 61, 1976; Encounter 28, 1967; Journal of Politics 21, 1959; 38, 1976; 41, 1979; Modern Age 29, 1985; National Review January 28, 1991; New Republic May 6, 1991; New York Times December 22, 1990; Partisan Review 44, 1977; Political Theory 4, 1976; Times (London) December 22, 1990.

OBA, MINAKO (1930–   ), Japanese novelist and writer of short stories writes: "Most of my childhood was spent in wartime. First the Manchurian Incident of my toddler years. This led to the Sino-Japanese War, which began the year of my first going-to-school, and finally the Pacific War, declared when I was in the fifth grade.

"The predominant image of girlhood is young men marching off to war, and tearful young wives and mothers waving good-bye. The newspaper and radio showered us with reports of glorious victories against our enemies, but even a child like me knew better than to harbor high hopes. Children usually see through the lies fed them by their elders, although they do not always say so.

"The wartime propaganda fostered my distrust of anything that tries to sound plausible. It is almost physical reaction of rejection that was implanted in me when I was very young.

"I was a precocious child, to be sure. I was reading adult books by the end of my grade school years, and even during the war, I was reading classical prewar literature. This may have contributed to my critical way of thinking, but it did not need a precocious reader to see the sad despondency of the adults around us. I am sure that this despondency is an unforgettable childhood impression shared by everyone in my generation.

"At the height of the Pacific War, schoolchildren were taken out of school and sent to work in military plants. At thirteen, I was working a grueling twelve-hour shift interrupted by a single short rest period. But my appetite for books was as voracious as ever, so that an air raid was a welcome disruption, for we could rest from our hard labor as we crouched in wheat fields while enemy planes passed overhead, and I could read a few pages of the forbidden Western novels that I kept hidden in my pocket.

"Then came the Defeat, and we children were treated to an astonishing metamorphosis on the part of our elders. Militarists, politicians, and teachers who had been heaping abuse on everything English or American a few months before were suddenly staunch supporters of democracy. This did not make me feel so much angry as sorrowful about human nature. Believe nothing, believe no one but yourself. Reject authority. These were the lessons taught me by war and defeat.

"The climax of my war experience came the summer of my fourteenth year, in the aftermath of the atomic bomb in Hiroshima. I came face to face with science's dream come true, and it seemed to me that the Bomb showed us exactly where the inordinate greed of mankind would eventually lead us. The war was ended, but was there a future beyond it?

"It seems to me that all living creatures, even we humans, are endowed with an instinct that tells us what to do for self-preservation. How otherwise could we have survived for so long? Today, we all seem to be preoccupied with worrying about the future. Technology, once our greatest hope, seems to us to have turned traitor and become a major threat to our environment. However, these forebodings may be a gift from heaven, sent to save us. Some call it despair, but despair may be our very hope. In any case, I find it preferable to hope with no hope of fulfillment. I might even add that such despair has come to be the main theme of my writing.

"In 1949, I entered a women's college in Tokyo. Later I married [Toshio], and in 1959, my husband's job took us to Alaska. There, I truly enjoyed our life on the last frontier, where my eyes feasted on precious remnants of untouched nature, and I learned a great deal from the culture of the Alaskan Indians and their way of living with nature.

"Until then, I had always written, but had never been published. The first work I sent out into the world was "Sanbiki no Kani" "The Three Crabs" written in the forests of southeastern Alaska. In 1968, this story was awarded the Akutagawa Prize, and thus began my life as a writer.

"In 1970, I returned to Japan. Since then, I have done a great deal of traveling and crossed many borders, but everywhere I go, I have almost always found more comfort in the universality of our humanity, then bewilderment of perturbation at our differences. In fact, as I grow older, it seems to me that not only the boundaries between different cultures, but also those between animals and plants and mankind, are fairly vague and inconsequential.

"I did not appear in this world from nowhere. I stand here with my two eyes, my mouth and nose, my two legs. I walk, I speak, I think human thoughts and dream human dreams, but I do not do these things by *my* power alone. It is generations and generations of ancestors—perhaps even the genes of prehuman life—that act through me, speak through me, think through me. What we call history is only a blink of an eye in the long chain of genes being handed down from generation to generation. I guess that I am a repository for these countless generations of life. I am not merely the result of my own petty experience or my own trivial thoughts as an individual."

Minako Oba's writing combines the artistry of a poet, a painter, and a stage actress, with the subversive spirit of a cultural critic and a comparativist, and the flair of a fairy-tale raconteur. What is more important, underneath the narrative surface of vulnerability, cynicism, anarchy, and subversive intent lurks the spirit of playfulness, the ludic. In this respect, she stands apart from other modern Japanese writers, both male and female. This element of the ludic also marks a territory most unfamiliar to and often overlooked by Japanese literary critics in their discussions of Oba's works. Many male critics, unaware of their own misreading of her texts, are baffled by her unfettered imagination.

Her female characters speak their mind in dialogues and dramatic monologues that are continually interrupted by the intrusion of an omnipresent authorial voice. Ideas and musings, sometimes lofty, sometimes verging on the absurd, merge and clash in comic, free-for-all repartee. This admixture of the serious and the ludic, the earthy and the lyrical, provides a continual source of entertainment, and constitutes the life blood of her writing.

Oba bares her soul by introducing the reader to a diverse group of characters whose points of view alternate with those of a protagonist and an omnipresent narrator through digression and free association. The fluidity of this narrative voice coupled with a poetic rhythm of narration creates a sense of perpetual movement in and out of the present and the past.

For example, in *Urashima-so* (The Urashima Plant, 1977), Oba models the female protagonist, Yukie, after a familiar Japanese folktale figure, Urashima Taro: He saves a turtle harassed by children on the beach, and is carried by the grateful creature to the Dragon Palace in the deep ocean. After a long enchanting stay at the Palace, Urashima Taro asks for permission to return to his homeland. The Dragon king gives him a *tamatebako* (a Pandora's box) as a farewell gift with the strict instruction never to open it. Once back on the shore, confronted with alien surroundings and unable to contain his numbing sense of abandonment, he ignores the king's warning and opens the box. Out comes a puff of curling white smoke and Urashima Taro turns into an old man with white hair. Yukie, Oba's Japanese female Rip Van Winkle who visits Japan after eleven years of living in the United States, is an uninvited guest in her own native land, a medium through whom Oba analyzes Japan's recent past, which closed with the dropping of the A-bomb on Hiroshima. It is clear that the atomic bomb serves as the correlative for her *tamatebako*, the unknown, destructive nature of the future of civilization and humankind.

The "plot" in her tales is life in its broadest, all-inclusive sense, life on this planet, in a universe where every wild creature, human, and plant, is inextricably interconnected. Her early stories deal with absence of this interconnectedness; in other words, the cost of human life in isolation, the desolation of disconnectedness with nature. "Nature" in Oba's lexicon is antiromantic and Zen-Buddhistic. For example, in "The Three Crabs," the story that won the coveted Akutagawa Prize in 1967, Oba depicts with relentless realism the boring life of Yurie, who happens to be a housewife, totally disconnected from a life force, sexual or spiritual, a woman on the run from a sterile, meaningless relationship with her husband sent abroad by his company (shosha-man), from her young daughter with whom she cannot communicate, and from friends who force upon her a routine of insipid socializing day in and day out. Oba superimposes the image of the fertile sea upon that of the dryness of sand which gets into the heroine's shoes as she walks absentmindedly on the beach. The cynicism displayed in this story is as gritty as the sand itself.

In her 1975 work *Garakuta Hakubutsukan* (The Junk Museum), one can see that Oba relishes the release of her pent-up energy as a Japanese woman who is denied self-expression and assertiveness. A delightful by-product of her Alaskan odyssey, the novel presents Oba, the cross-cultural social critic, at her best. Her style is invariably tongue-in-cheek; her tone witty, wise, merciless, yet forgiving. Her female characters, often full of the venom of sarcasm, spew spiteful yet realistic comments about the Japanese, humankind, modern society in general, and civilization.

Another example of such a satirical exercise is *Naku Tori no* (Birds Crying, 1985), a winner of the Noma Literary Prize. The spaecy novelist in this autobiographical work begins to write fiction as a housewife because "she could no longer stand not being able to tell anyone what was really on her mind. For too long she had kept things to herself. Every day of the year, without batting an eye, she uttered things that were not really what she wanted to say. She had continually lied to herself. But what almost drove her mad was the fact that people could never discern what was really on her mind; her deceptions didn't bother them at all." To borrow Lionel Trilling's words in *Beyond Culture*, Oba has a woman's "quarrel with civilization," asking "every question that is forbidden in polite society. It asks us if we are content with our marriages, with our family lives, with our professional lives, with our friends." Oba's answer seems clear: Women are doubly discontent-ed. This is where her feminist, revisionist inclination lies.

Among the issues of polite society that Oba takes up time and again are the meaninglessness of conventional man-woman relationships and motherhood, areas which have almost always been defined and investigated by men from a male perspective. Yet, for women writers, these areas still remain controversial, as women often find themselves devaluing the feminine perspective on these intimate subjects. Oba demonstrates in her tales an unrepentant, undaunted feminist spirit, forever challenging the structure of patriarchy as it is. This penchant for taboo breaking is not only limited to female characters, but often appears in male characters. For example, in *Funakui-mushi* (The Ship-Eating Worms, 1969), a harsh indictment of the conventional virtues of saintly motherhood and maternal love is spelled out by a male florist.

"The Smile of a Mountain Witch" ("Yamauba no bish-o," 1979) explores this same theme but Oba provides a twist by portraying the classic example of a codependent housewife whose sole role is that of reproduction: she performs "mothering" to perfection for her infantile husband and children, and sacrifices her entire life for the causes of motherhood and being a wife. This masterpiece of satire is double-edged: it produces the effect of either pity or anger depending upon the reader's response to the fate of the mountain witch-turned-human.

Japanese male critics often argue that the key to being a successful male writer is how well he can describe a woman, and by the same token, they say a successful woman writer must be able to portray a man competently. In this respect Oba seems to take the Japanese male critics by surprise with her unabashed descriptions of the male body. As in "Sea-Change" ("Tank-o," 1978), they are always clinical, precise, and devoid of romantic sentiment. In this story the sexual norms of a heterosexual relationship are turned upside down in a ménage à trois, between two men and a woman. The boundary separating sexual domination from erotic power becomes blurred in Oba's playfulness. The woman finds male obsessions amusing: "Why, in heaven's name, did this possession of theirs, this smooth, blood-filled projection, oblige them to boast of it so insistently and at such length, or to explain it away in such apologetic, almost tearful detail? Almost certainly, it was because the most important vital participant, the woman who received its benefits or its evil effects, didn't even look as it properly, much less subject it to detailed inspection."

This realistic portrayal of a man-woman relationship seems to endorse the definition of what Adrienne Rich once wrote in regard to the orphaned heroine in *Jane Eyre*: her "deternmined refusal of the romantic." In a scene in *O jo no Namida* (The Tears of a Princess, 1988), typical of Oba's style of handling gender relationships, the middle-aged widowed protagonist, Keiko, after having a gin and tonic with one of her tenant neighbors, Mr. Smith, becomes very vivacious: "Keiko was laughing under the magnolia tree. Immediately her lips were covered. While a thick, wet sarcocarp continued to suck at her, she kept one of her eyes open to steal a peek at the moon through the branches of a cassia tree that grew almost on top of the magnolia. His beard pricked her skin like the thorns of a sea urchin." The image of a Madam Butterfly pining for a Pinkerton never enters the world of Oba's tales.

Propositions central to her argument in "a discussion of men by women," which is also the title of a collection of her essays (1982), are what Susan Fraiman calls the "doubled view of women as agents as well as victims," and the yin-yang dyad as a fusion of complementarity and interchangeability between genders. For example, the middle-aged Yurie in *Kiri no Tabi* (The Journey through the Mist, 1976–1980), Oba's other autobiographical fiction, declares that women and men are like the opposite poles of a magnet: "If both poles, the male and female sexes, successfully come into contact, we get a quiet stability, but if they do not meet and stay parallel to one another, the situation remains unstable, frustrating, and one begins to hate the other. But, even if these opposites fail to come into contact, the situation won't be as bad as when there is unipolarity. It will not create any energy, everything will be suspended in midair." What is implied in this statement is a strong sense of equality between genders despite their sexual differences, a point Japanese patriarchal society has yet to embrace. Oba's unconventional outlook on men and women extends to a definition of a happy marriage: It means a situation in which a couple who, despite their freedom to be able to divorce at any time, has no desire to get one."

In addition to elements of the ludic, the painterly, and the poetic, another distinct characteristic of Oba's style has its origin in her early exposure to and love of the world's best fairy tales. The surrealistic, magical, dreamy tone and texture in "Fireweed" ("Higusa," 1969), *Katachi mo Naku* (Amorphous, 1982), "Candle Fish" ("Rosokuzakana," 1975), "The Pale Fox" ("Aoi Kitsune," 1973), and even "The Ship-Eating Worms," seem to demonstrate Oba's refusal to compartmentalize life into the rigid categories of reality and fiction. What she fears is a world devoid of imagination and creative power. She also finds the human trait to classify people strictly by nationality as misguided, since it tends to encourage racist behavior. He writing is an attempt to come to terms with her own vulnerability, to explore the possibilities of humanism by embracing the universe, the world, and humanity in their wholeness.

The unnamed female narrator in "Candle Fish," in telling the life story of her Russian friend, Olga, automatically takes up the role of a raconteur, purposely blurring the line between reality and dream. Also related to this technique is Oba's use of allegory. In "Boshi" (A Hat, 1981), a girl's hat serves to suppress her assertiveness, intuition, imagination, intellectuality, and self-identity. The irony of the situation is that the girl's oppressors are her mother and grandmother, who together assist in the molding of the little girl's personality.

Besides writing novels, short stories, and poetry and retelling fairy tales, Oba has also penned a fascinating biography of the founder of Tsuda Women's College, her alta mater. At the age of seven, Umeko Tsuda was sent to America by the newly formed Meiji (1868–1911) government in 1871 as part of the educational Japan was undertaking. She returned to Japan after eleven years with a B.S. degree from Bryn Mawr College. The basis if this literary biography are hundreds of letters Umeko wrote to her American foster mother, Adeline Lanman, which were accidently discovered in the attic of the college in 1984. The work is more than a biography; it is an intimate dialogue between two women of kindred spirit: Oba who lived in Sitka, Alaska, for eleven years, and Umeko, who had to relearn the language, customs, and manners of her own "native" country. Umeko's sober observations of Japanese and American societies are equally matched with Oba's own interpretations of America as a temporary resident and Japan as a returnee.

In *Mukashi Onna ga Ita* (Long Ago, There Was a Woman, 1994), Oba makes a bold adaptation of one of Japan's most celebrated works, *The Tale of Ise* (903 a.d.), a collection of episodes that revolves around an archetypical Japanese amorous hero. The title of the Oba version paraphrases the opening sentence of each episode in the classic tale: "Long Ago, There Was a Man." Oba, who has openly acknowledged her debt to the Japanese classics and her female predecessors in Heian literature (859–1300 A.D.), has successfully reinvented the episodic format to highlight the age-old battle of the sexes with wit, humor, satire, and playfulness, creating a delightful context where both genders are fair game.

Minako Oba is the eldest daughter of Saburo and Mutsuko Shiina. She received a B.A. from Tsuda Women's College in Tokyo in 1953, and has also studied art at the University of Wisconsin at Madison and painting at the University of Washington. She was a writer-in-residence at the University of Iowa and Rutgers University, and has given numerous lectures in the United States. Since 1987 she has shared with Taeko Kono the honor of being the first women to serve on the Akutagawa Prize Selection Committee. *Katachi mo Naku* (Amorphous) has been translated into German and published by Insel. Her autobiography, *Mai e Mai e Katatsumuri* (Dance, Dance, Snails, Up to the Sky, 1984), is also forthcoming in German.

PRINCIPAL WORKS IN ENGLISH TRANSLATION: (tr. S. Kohl and R. Toyama) "The Three Crabs" *in* Japan Quarterly 25, 1978; (tr. J. Bester) "The Sea Change" *in* Japanese Literature Today 5, 1980; (tr. M. Chambers) "Fireweed" *in* Japan Quarterly 18, 1981; (tr. N. M. Lippit) "The Smile of a Mountain Witch" *in* Stories by Contemporary Japanese Women Writers, 1982; (tr. Y. Tanaka and Hanson) "The Three Crabs" *in* This Kind of Woman: Ten Stories by Japanese Women Writers 1960–1976, 1982; (tr. S. W. Kohl) "The Pale Fox" *in* The Showa Anthology 2, 1985; (tr. T. Genkawa and B. S. Tomoyoshi) "The Repairman's Wife" (chapter two of *The Junk Museum*) *in* The Kyoto Collection: Stories from the Japanese, 1989; (tr. S. M. Lippet) "Bird Song" *in* Review of Japanese Culture and Society 4, 1991; (tr. Y. Tanaka) "Candle Fish" *in* Unmapped Territory: New Women's Fiction from Japan, 1991; (tr. J. Cohn) "White Wind" *in* Manoa: A Pacific Journal of International Writing 3, 1991; (tr. M. N. Wilson and M. K. Wilson) Chapter one (excerpt from *Birds Crying*) *in* Chicago Review 39, 1993.

ABOUT: Wilson, Michiko Niikuni. "Oba Minako" *in* Japanese Women Writers: Bio-Critical Sourcebook, 1994; Wilson, Michiko Niikuni. "Becoming, or (Un)Becoming: The Female Destiny Reconsidered in Oba Minako's Narratives" *in* Schalow, P. G. and Walker, J. A. The Woman's Hand: Gender and Theory in Japanese Women's Writings, forthcoming.

O'BRIAN, PATRICK (1914–   ), Irish novelist, short story writer, biographer, and translator, was born to a well-to-do Irish Catholic family and raised in Ireland and England. Relatively little is known about his life. Until the early 1990s, when his Aubrey/Maturin sea novels gained a substantial international readership, O'Brian gave no interviews at all; even when he did begin talking to interviewers, he was reluctant to divulge any personal details. "About my books, that's all that I think the public has, in its

PATRICK O'BRIAN

normal way, to know," he told Francis X. Clines in a rare interview with the *New York Times* in 1993. "My private life is by definition, private." He insisted that those authors we know least about—such as Homer—are the ones we absorb most purely.

A few facts about O'Brian's life have emerged. The fortunes of his once affluent family declined drastically during the Great Depression. His natural mother died when he was quite young, and he was partly raised by a stepmother, who was English. A chronic lung ailment often kept him out of school, and he received much of his early education at home. Despite his illness, he did enjoy outdoor sports: horse riding, hunting, and —most significant for his later fiction— sailing, to which he was introduced as a boy. The natural sciences and the classics were the focus of his formal education, and he attended the Sorbonne for a time. He was rejected for active service in World War II, but drove ambulances during the London blitz; later he served with an Allied intelligence unit connected to the French Resistance. Offered a job in the Paris embassy after the war, he chose instead to become a fiction writer, and set out in search of an isolated and inexpensive place of residence. He spent a brief period in Wales, which is the setting for his first novel, *Testimonies.* Since 1949, O'Brian and his English-born wife, Mary, have lived in the south of France.

While O'Brian was largely unknown to American readers until the early 1990s, he has published more than twenty novels, several collections of short stories, and two well-received biographies—one of Pablo Picasso and the other of Joseph Banks, the English botanist and adventurer who sailed with Captain Cook. O'Brian is also a prolific translator. A talented linguist, he speaks French, Spanish, Catalan, Italian, and (a middling) Irish; as readers of his novels soon discover, he also knows his Latin.

Although his first novel, *Testimonies*, did not reach a large audience, it was widely praised by reviewers. Set in the rugged farmlands of northern Wales, and narrated in the first person from three different points of view, the novel tells the tragic love story of an unlikely couple: an Oxford don who has given up his teaching post and the wife of a Welsh farmer. In a *Partisan Review* essay in which he found fault with Steinbeck's *East of Eden* and Hemingway's *The Old Man and the Sea*, Delmore Schwartz had extravagant praise for *Testimonies*. Comparing the novel to "a great ballad or a Biblical story" and to the poetry of W. B. Yeats, Schwartz noted, "The reader, drawn forward by lyric eloquence and the story's fascination, discovers in the end that he has encountered in a new way the sphinx and riddle of existence itself." An upsurge of interest in O'Brian's work led W. W. Norton to reissue *Testimonies*.

O'Brian's second novel, *The Catalans*, while not a critical failure, did not win the acclaim that *Testimonies* had. Throughout the 1950s and 1960s, he produced a steady stream of novels and short stories; these received less and less critical attention in Great Britain, and almost none in the United States. At the end of the 1960s, with all his previous novels out-of-print, O'Brian published *Master and Commander*, a historical novel about British seamen set in the early 1800s. It was not his first sea novel, nor was it widely reviewed. Nonetheless, it was a breakthrough of sorts. Whether or not he originally intended the novel to be part of a series, it became the first installment of a now long-ongoing nautical epic. These novels have brought O'Brian from obscurity to near cult status and to the threshold of literary celebrity.

In *Master and Commander*, O'Brian introduces Jack Aubrey and Stephen Maturin, and two characters whose names are most often used to identify the series. Their somewhat unlikely friendship is the centerpiece of the entire series, and both are central characters in all of the novels. The interplay of their contrasting styles and sensibilities often propels the narrative. Jack Aubrey, a career Royal Navy man who receives his first command in *Master and Commander*, is a staunch English patriot; he reveres George III and Lord Nelson above all mortals. Tall, stout, and bluff, Aubrey is of decidedly limited intelligence, except in matters of sailing and naval warfare.

Stephen Maturin, a physician and naval intelligence operative of mixed Irish and Catalan ancestry, is an altogether more complex character. Although Maturin is an Irish nationalist, his hatred of Napoleon has prompted him to make common cause with the English. The erudite Maturin is an accomplished surgeon, a dedicated naturalist, and a linguist, as well as the author of learned tracts, such as "Thoughts on the Prevention of Diseases Most Unusual Among Seamen." In his learning and range of interests, he bears a more than passing resemblance to Joseph Banks, whose work he cites frequently. In the course of the series, Maturin, prone to insomnia and melancholy, succumbs to and later conquers an addiction to laudanum; thereafter, he seeks solace in coca leaves. Throughout the series, Maturin plays another role: that of the bewildered "lubber." while Jack Aubrey and the rest of the crew communicate in an often daunting nautical jargon, Maturin (like most readers) has to be constantly reminded of such things as the location of the mizzen topgallant.

For a time, Aubrey and Maturin are both in love with the same woman. The two men also, have in common a love of music, which brings them together in *Master and Commander*. At a performance of Locatelli's Major Quartet at the Governor's House in Minorca. Aubrey's off-tempo flailing provokes Maturin to remark, "If you really must beat the measure, sir, let me entreat you to do so in time, and not half a beat ahead." At the brink of a duel, Aubrey ends up hiring Maturin as his ship's surgeon instead. Music remains a part of their world; both are avid, if not particularly accomplished, musicians: Aubrey on violin, Maturin on cello.

O'Brian followed *Master and Commander*, a modest success, with *Post Captain, H.M.S. Surprise, The Mauritius Command*, and *Desolation Island*. The series format has allowed O'Brian to incorporate his own interests—in sailing, natural history, and psychology—into bracing adventure stories set against a background of historical events. O'Brian has attempted to re-create shipboard life in the Royal Navy in the era of the Napoleonic Wars. "A novelist must know everything about his time," O'Brian told *New York Times Magazine* interviewer Mark Horowitz in 1993.

The Aubrey/Maturin novels have been compared to C. S. Forester's Horatio Hornblower series. Describing the Aubrey/Maturin novels in a *Times Literary Supplement* review of *The Mauritius Command* in 1977, T. J. Binyon wrote that while O'Brian's novels might lack "the mythopoeic quality of the Hornblower cycle, Aubrey and Maturin are subtler, richer items; in addition Patrick O'Brian has a gift for the comic which Forester lacks." In the eyes of most reviewers, O'Brian's interest in character and psychology distinguishes his work from that of Forester, whose primary concern was adventure.

The early Aubrey/Maturin novels created something of an underground sensation, winning praise from fellow novelists such as A. S. Byatt, Iris Murdoch, and Robertson Davies. Sales of the novels were steady in Great Britain, but the American publisher dropped the series after the fifth novel, *Desolation Island.* For more than a decade, none of the Aubrey/Maturin novels were available in the United States. That changed when Norton decided to publish *The Letter of Marque*, the twelfth novel in the series. At the same time, Norton began reissuing the first eleven novels in paperback, and the entire series became more popular in America. Norton has published "The Patrick O'Brian Newsletter," in which the author himself answered readers' questions about the more arcane aspects of his novels.

In the *London Review of Books*, Peter Campbell commented on *The Thirteen Gun Salute* (appropriately enough, the thirteenth novel in the series), "O'Brian is a master of the narrative action, but he has sustained interest through this long sequence of novels by expanding the genre to which they belong—the sea story of the Napoleonic Wars—so that it can include much else besides." In the *New York Times Book Review* in August 1991 Thomas Flanagan characterized the Aubrey/Maturin series as "novels of extraordinary, quirky attractiveness, oblique and complicated charm, and a rich and reliable intelligence."

There has long been a coterie of British O'Brian enthusiasts, centered mainly in Oxford. These include T. J. Binyon, Iris Murdoch, and her husband, the essayist and critic John Bayley. In an especially laudatory review in the *New York Review of Books* in 1991, Bayley wrote that "the most striking thing about the series is the high degree of fictional reality, of Henry James's 'felt life,' that it has managed to generate. . . . And no other writer, not even Melville, has described the whale or the wandering albatross with O'Brian's studious and yet lyrical accuracy." Bayley also hailed O'Brian's elaboration of "fictional surfaces": "The reader today has become conditioned, partly by academic critics, to look in Melville and Conrad for the larger issues and deeper significances, rather than enjoying the play of life, the humor and detail of the performance. Yet surface is what mat-

ters in good fiction. . . . O'Brian has contrived to invent a new world that is almost entirely in this sense a world of enchanting fictional surfaces, and all the better for it. As narrator he never obtrudes his own personality, is himself never present in the role of author at all. . . . "

"It is not for plot that you read his books," Christopher Lehmann-Haupt wrote in a *New York Times* review of *The Wine-Dark Sea* in 1993." "Instead what you savor is the byplay between the two friends." The "two friends" have often been compared to another famous duo—Sherlock Holmes and Dr. Watson. John Bayley remarked in the *New York Times Magazine*: "Aubrey and Maturin are the converse of Holmes and Watson. In O'Brian the leader is the less intelligent one, while the follower is the clever one." In a review of *The Wine-Dark Sea* in the *Times Literary Supplement* (1993) J.K.L. Walker, echoing this point, noted, "Watson . . . is in command here, while Holmes is below reassembling some poor fellow's skull; but that in itself is a sort of insight."

In his consideration of O'Brian novels (particularly *The Wine-Dark Sea*) in the *New Yorker*, Charles McGrath called them "classic examples of the English comedy of manners." McGrath maintains that the novels are genre entertainments: "The Aubrey novels provide all the satisfactions—and all the limitations—of genre writing. "They're formulaic in a way that's both predictable and reassuring. . . . But what they almost never do is what truly great literature does—that is, disquiet you or threaten your preconception. . . . they're escape reading in the best sense."

The time span of the novels has extended over the Napoleonic era from 1800 to 1814, and the scenes have ranged all over the globe. Inevitably, the question arises as to when and where the series will end. John Bayley considered this issue in his *New York Review of Books* essay in 1991: "In strict terms of time and sequence the war against Napoleon should now be over. . . . But O'Brian has cunningly allowed history to expand, as it were, so that his own episodes can continue while the larger process marks time." As Charles McGrath pointed out in the *New Yorker*, O'Brian has addressed this dilemma through his characters, though perhaps in a different context. In *The Nutmeg of Consolation*, the fourteenth novel in the series, Nathaniel Martin, ship's chaplain and assistant surgeon, reflects on a novel written by a friend: "As for an end, are endings really so very important? Sterne did quite well without one. . . . And there is at least one Mozart quartet that stops without the slightest ceremony: most satisfying when you get used to it." O'Brian himself, though far from young, shows little inclination to stop writing about Jack Aubrey and Stephen Maturin. "They turn in my mind constantly," he told Francis X. Clines of the *New York Times* in 1993.

PRINCIPAL WORKS: *Novels*—Testimonies, 1952 (in U.K.: Three Bear Witness); The Catalans, 1953; The Frozen Flame, 1953; The Golden Ocean, 1957; The Unknown Shore, 1959; Richard Temple, 1962. *Aubrey/Maturin novels*—Master and Commander, 1969; Post Captain, 1972; H.M.S. Surprise, 1973; The Mauritius Command, 1977; Desolation Island, 1979; The Fortune of War, 1979; The Surgeon's Mate, 1980; The Ionian Mission, 1981; Treason's Harbor, 1983; The Far Side of the World, 1984; The Reverse of the Medal, 1986; The Letter of Marque, 1988; The Thirteen Gun Salute, 1989; The Nutmeg of Consolation, 1991; The True-love, 1992; The Wine-Dark Sea, 1993; The Commodore, 1995. *Short stories*—The Last Pool and Other Stories, 1950; The Walker and Other Stories, 1955 (reissued as The Road to Samarcand, 1976); Lying in the Sun and Other Stories, 1956; The Chian Wine and Other Stories, 1974. *Biographies*—Pablo Ruiz Picasso: A Biography, 1976; Joseph Banks: A Life, 1987. *Naval history*—Men-of-War, 1974. *As editor*—A Book of Voyages, 1947. *As translator*—F. Mallet-Joris, A Letter to Myself, 1964; H. Noguères, Munich 1965; F. Mallet-Joris, The Uncompromising Heart: A Life of Marie Mancini, 1966; S. de Beauvoir, A Very Easy Death, 1966; M. Goudeket, The Delights of Growing Old, 1967; M. Mohrt, The Italian Campaign: A Novel, 1967; C. Malraux, Memoirs, 1967; L. Bodard, The Quicksand War, 1967; J. Kessel, The Horsemen, 1968; S. de Beauvoir, Les Belles Images, 1968; B. Fay, Louis XVI, or, The End of a World, 1968; S. de Beauvoir, The Woman Destroyed, 1969; R. Guillain, The Japanese Challenge, 1970; H. Charrière, Papillon, 1970; S. de Beauvoir, The Coming of Age, 1972; M. Ivanov, The Assassination of Heydrich, 27 May 1942, 1973; H. Charrière, Banco: The Further Adventures of Papillon, 1973; S. de Beauvoir, All Said and Done, 1974; S. de Beauvoir, When Things of the Spirit Come First, 1982; S. de Beauvoir, Adieux: A Farewell to Sartre, 1984; J. Lacouture, De Gaulle: The Rebel 1890–1944, 1990.

ABOUT: London Review of Books January 25, 1990; Natural History May 1993; New York Review of Books November 7, 1991; New York Times November 1, 1993; November 14, 1993; New York Times Book Review January 6, 1991; August 4, 1991; April 30, 1995. New York Times Magazine May 16, 1993; New Yorker October 18, 1993; Partisan Review November-December 1952; Publishers Weekly October 26, 1992; Times Literary Supplement June 24, 1977; July 2, 1993.

ODA MAKOTO (June 2, 1932–), Japanese essayist, novelist, and political activist, was born and raised in Osaka—a city so devastated by conventional bombing during World War II that it was not seriously considered as a target for either of the atomic bombs. Oda was in his first year of middle school when the war ended in 1945. Although, along with many Japanese, he had suffered hunger, displacement, and air raids in the last months of the war, Oda recalls that he reacted to Japan's defeat with "neither joy nor sadness," a remark that already points to the adult Oda's estranged relationship with the ideas of state authority and national identity. Nonetheless, the surrender and all it implied about his country's reputed superiority certainly made an impression on the adolescent Oda. He put his feelings into writing when he precociously embarked on a writing career. While still in high school he wrote and had published a novel entitled *Asatte no shuki* (Notes on the day after tomorrow, 1951), in retrospect a work of juvenilia but which at the time attracted attention and marked Oda as someone to watch as a writer of promise.

In 1952 he entered the University of Tokyo and selected the uncommon major of classical Greek, although in fact he spent most of his time writing fiction. Upon graduation he supported himself as an English teacher until, in the spring of 1958, he won a Fulbright Scholarship to study at Harvard. Returning home in 1960 via Canada, Mexico, and India on the proverbial "dollar-a-day" budget, he arrived just in time to participate in the most radicalizing events of his generation, namely the mass demonstrations, which eventually turned into riots, in Tokyo against the renewal of the United States-Japan Security Treaty. Typical of the post-Second World War Japanese intellectuals attracted to the cultural and social idealism of the United States yet disillusioned by the abuses of American power and wealth, Oda had no problem opposing what was widely seen as the imposition of American imperialism over Japanese sovereignty; even then in Oda's mind, there was apparently America the "country" and America the "state," and the distinction has remained a crucial one for him and indeed for his generation of left-wing Japanese intellectuals.

Oda's fame increased when he wrote an entertaining travelogue account of his extensive and, for the time, exceedingly rare international travels, *Nan de mo mite yaro* (I'll give anything a look, 1961). This best-seller established Oda's fame as a writer and his credentials as a social critic, as well as his claim to be a spokesman for a postwar generation ready to rejoin the world outside of Japan. Prominent novelist Oe Kenzaburo lauded it for its frankness, and it marked Oda's entry into that clique of intellectuals who were liberal or leftist critics of the United States but were nonetheless steeped in and dedicated to the celebrated American—specifically, Kennedyesque—ideals of individual freedom and social egalitarianism.

Oda soon completed another novel, *Amerika* (America, 1962), the story of a Japanese trading company employee sent to business school in the American South. His mission is to help pave the way for his company's expansion into the American market, but what happens instead is that this employee forsakes his identity as a company man and consequently "finds himself" through his interaction with American friends, his participation in the civil rights movement, and an affair with a white woman. He comes to view life in Japan as unacceptably straitened— he not only turns down the hand of his company president's daughter in marriage, but he seems to have irrevocably decided to stay in America forever, as an "American." In a remark typical of the novel, the hero says, "I want to be myself . . . I want to live my own life my own way." Such freedom is equated in Japan with the American identity; *Amerika* struck a responsive chord in its readers, despite the continuing resentment of the United States after the Security Treaty riots. The dream of an unencumbered life in America was one shared by many of Oda's generation, as was the realization that such freedom was not always enjoyed by the citizens of America's client states elsewhere in the world, or even by all Americans.

In one short essay Oda is quite candid about his obsession with America, an obsession that led to this novel's writing:

No doubt I wanted to possess my own "America." Ever since I can remember I have always had "America" in front of me. . . . In the deepest recesses of my mind— no, my body—"America" has always existed. The "America" of skyscrapers, the "America" of the Texas desert, the "America" of small Midwestern towns . . . the "America" of Vietnam, the "America" of Son My, white "America," black "America," yellow "America" . . . all the "Americas" deep inside me intertwined and mixed together. Nonetheless, there has always been one wall over there, one that I would, should I give it a name, would have to be my "America." Yet that, probably, is in fact my very own self.

In the spring of 1965, Oda was one of the founding intellectuals of the League of Citizens Movements for Peace in Vietnam (Betonamu ni heiwa o! Shimin Rengo), more familiarly known in English by the acronym, Beheiren. The umbrella organization for the anti-Vietnam war movement in Japan, Beheiren repudiated the notion of a "leadership" but was, in fact, coordi-

nated largely by Oda. He led the organization in often dramatically subversive activities. Soon recognizing the need to go beyond simply educating the Japanese public on the issues at stake in Vietnam, Beheiren went so far as to set up antiwar underground cells on American military installations in Japan, and even to assist U.S. soldiers who wished to desert. Beheiren was from the start an organization that engaged "America" far more than it did "Vietnam." Addressing his role in encouraging U.S. Army desertions, Oda has said: "I could sympathize easily with the young American draftees because I had been in the United States. I saw the draftees as victims of their own government as well as aggressors against the Vietnamese." In other words, Oda's actions in Beheiren both undermined and bolstered his "America." He worked against government policy while helping individual Americans victimized by that same policy. He was able both to assert his values of self-determination for the Vietnamese, and to put himself in a position to help Americans be, in his view, more genuinely American.

At the same time, within Beheiren Oda was able to put into practice his theory of the individual's relationship to power. The "young American draftees" were perfect examples of that relationship; but so were the Japanese people themselves. Oda wrote:

[O]ur country was a kind of "forced aggressor" in the [Vietnam] war. Because of the security treaty, Japan had to cooperate with the American policy of aggression. In this sense Japan was a victim of its alliance with that policy, but it was also an aggressor toward the small countries in Indochina.

Once Beheiren officially disbanded, Oda continued to hone his theory of the complicated and ambivalent nature of modern citizenship by exploring the specific relations between Americans, Japanese, and other Asians. He translated into Japanese, for example, Seymour Hersh's book about the massacre at my Lai, an American work by an American author about an atrocity perpetrated against Asians. It in a book that is both English and Japanese translation powerfully contrasts the naiveté of U.S. soldiers with the depravity of their actions. But only in the Japanese edition does one read of a translator, Oda Makoto, who identifies with both Hersh and the Vietnamese villagers massacred by Lieutenant Calley and his company. What is so fascinating, as well as horrible, Oda writes in his introduction, is Lieutenant Calley's very ordinariness. Victimizer, victim, and even the reader are construed as potentially interchangeable identities. Unlike many Japanese intellectuals, for whom their Japanese identity is crucial to the way they choose to interpret the world, Oda Makoto looks upon such national labels as statist impositions.

Oda's consistent interest in the relations between victimizer and victimized—actually, the relations between each individual's role as both victim and victimizer, subsumed in Oda's term "complementarity"—was inspired by his own wartime experiences in Japan and fueled by his experiences as both purveyor and critic of American values in the postwar period. In the same essay where he writes that "it is impossible to speak of the experience as victim without including the experience as victimizer," Oda reminisces about his childhood:

> Having endured the Osaka air raids on three occasions in my youth, I later became obsessed with curiosity about how the scene must have looked from the air, from the perspective of victimizer. I embraced that strange curiosity for twenty-one years after the war, but I only understood its true meaning in the library of a small, rural college in the United States. There, when I saw a *New York Times* news photo, my heart leapt. The caption read, "Osaka Air Raid." I realized that I had been under all that smoke, and in that instant I relived my own experience as victim, and that of each of my countrymen. On second thought, I saw that photo itself was unimpressive, nothing but tall, black columns rising into the air. It was just an abstract, impersonal picture of smoke—the sort I had glanced indifferently at in the past. If we were to carry this indifference a step further, is it clearly distinguishable from the indifference displayed by the pilot as he calmly drops bombs, calling forth a hell of suffering and smoke?

Oda's ease in regarding himself as both the subject and the object of the exercise of alienated violence replicates his duality as both a Japanese and an Americanized intellectual. This stimulates his desire to make plain the interrelations between this version of history, which mutually implicates both sides of his own experience and that of Japan versus America. "The Ethics of Peace" was written in 1968 at the height of Oda's involvement with another war. But the questions he asked then, seem to be the ones he sought to explore the most fully in his novel about the atomic bomb, written over a decade later. *Hiroshima* (Hiroshima, 1981; translated as *The Bomb*) is the work in which he most thoroughly seeks not so much to compare and contrast notions of victim and victimizer as to embody them in the lives of the American, Japanese, and other characters. *The Bomb* is the response to the need noted by Oda with frustration some dozen years earlier:

> Why have we no records of wartime experience as victimizer? Not objective, third-person accounts, but personal records similar to all those relating experience as victim. If that's too much to ask, just a collection of candid war stories, blurted out to close friends after a couple of beers, would do. When placed side by side with all those experiences as victim (they might be written by the same people) their intertwining complicity would become clear.

This "intertwining complicity" is in fact the theme of *The Bomb*. Unlike any other work of Japanese atomic-bomb literature, Oda's novel seeks to retell the events of August 6, 1945, as an example of how many peoples, not just the Japanese, are governed by the dictates of the modern state telling us which side we are on, when in fact the issue of "sides" is too complex to allow an unambiguous resolution. As a work written by a Japanese who saw the Osaka air raids from the earth rather than the sky, *The Bomb* is also a criticism of Japan's unwillingness to confront its own responsibility.

An American airman, Joe Clancey, taken prisoner outside of Hiroshima when his plane is shot down, is blinded and disoriented by the atomic bombing. Joe stumbles through hot rubble. His body feels as if burdened with a heavy weight. The darkness seems infinite, and he is unable to gauge the passage of time. The world, he intuits, is destroyed; he knows he is in a sea of fire, corpses, fragments of tile. Only gradually does his sight, and his ability to infer from what he increasingly senses, return; and it is accompanied by a growing incredulity. If only he knew what time it is, he says to himself, he could go on living. Miraculously, he finds a watch; its hands, however, have stopped at eight-fifteen. As his consciousness grows acute, so does his awareness of exhaustion and thirst. "Give me water," he moans repeatedly as he nears the center of the city—the center where so many of the novel's characters earlier strolled—and encounters more fire, more dead. Some of the corpses— no, surely their ghosts, Joe reasons—move towards him. They are so horribly disfigured they must come from another world; then Joe realizes he looks no different himself.

One of the "ghosts"—one who reminds him of the Indians back in the American Southwest— sees that Joe, despite his disfigurement, is not Japanese. "You American!" he gasps, and soon word spreads that the enemy is there among them. Many "ghosts" start to move towards Joe; a voice from Joe's life back in the desert warns him to run, run as fast as he did on the desert plain of White Sands. But Joe is simply unable to summon such energy.

> It was too late to do anything. The ghosts were coming to attack a ghost. They were summoning what little strength remained in their bodies to pounce upon him, another ghost. The dying ran over the dead—the dead over the dying—in getting to him. Using all his might he tried to push through them to run away, but the ghosts kept piling atop themselves in wave after wave, and he was unable to move at all underneath the weight of the heap. . . . Only the dead were within the flames. They

were the only ones left behind. Both the ones trying to finish one off, and the one trying not to let that happen, were piled up like so much garbage in the dark depths of a hell burning high with crimson flames; both died excruciating deaths even as they lived by struggling with each other with what little strength remained in their moribund state. He had now closed both of his eyes, but he thought he could see clearly how it all looked. His progressively weak consciousness of himself ("I . . . ") and his words that would follow (" . . . am here for what . . . ?") changed to take a plural subject ("We . . . "). Those were the final words that passed through his mind. A rain began to fall upon the heap of garbage. It was a rain like black mud.

Oda accomplishes here something without precedent in Japanese atomic-bomb literature. The selection of an American as his narrator of the atomic explosion may seem insensitive, but for Oda the line of demarcation is between the interchangeable states of victimhood and non-victimhood, not between "American," "Japanese," or any other variety of reified national identity. For him to have chosen a character to represent Hiroshima who is not Japanese is in effect to make the atomic bombing less a "Japanese" event and more a "historical" event that should resist any one nation's, as opposed to any one individual's, claim to a unique victimization.

For Oda and others in Japan, the paradox of efficacious action in the world has never resulted in a withdrawal from it. In his life as well as his writings, Oda has always, if sometimes artlessly, struggled to elucidate those conditions he firmly believes do make for real differences not only in the way we interpret the world, but in the way we live it. In the late 1980s Oda considered running on the Socialist Party ticket for mayor of Tokyo. Similarly, *The Bomb* is a novel which grapples sincerely with a problem many other writers in various ways have sought to minimize, even explain away; namely, how can we conceptualize our humanity, on a planet over which hover weapons of a complexity that renders anachronistic older notions of accountability? In Oda's replay of recent history one finds a dismantling of the ideas perhaps once thought securely fixed: the idea of victim and victimizer, of peaceful uses of nuclear energy and the belligerent ones, of the citizen of one nation-state and another, of intellectual and worker.

PRINCIPAL WORKS IN ENGLISH TRANSLATION: *Novel*—(tr. D. H. Whittaker) The Bomb, 1990. *Nonfiction*—"The Meaning of Meaningless Death" *in* JSPIJ 4, August 1966; "Making Democracy Our Own" *in* Japan Interpreter 6, Autumn 1970; "The Ethics of Peace" *in* Koschmann, J.V. (ed.) *Authority and the Individual in Japan: Citizen Protest in Historical Perspective*, 1978.

ABOUT: Havens, T. Fire Across the Sea: The Vietnam War and Japan 1965–1975, 1987; Treat, J. W. *Writing Ground Zero: Japanese Literature and the Atomic Bomb, 1994.*

OKRI, BEN (March 15, 1959–), Nigerian-born novelist, short story writer, and poet who lives in London, was born in Minna, Nigeria, to Grace and Silver Okri. His father was a lawyer who trained in London and later worked in Lagos, the Nigerian capital, where much of his son's fiction was to be set. A member of the Urhobo people from the delta region of southern Nigeria (not one of the three principal ethnic groups in the country), Okri began school in London, where he remembers his law-student father working in a Camberwell launderette to support the family. He returned to schools in the delta at Sapele and Warri, also attended Christ High School in the university town of Ibadan, and later went on to the University of Essex.

Okri's childhood was marked by the Nigerian civil war (the Biafran War), which took one million lives between 1967 and 1969. He was moved to a village where warplanes flew over the classrooms, and where, he told, a London Times interviewer, "my education took place simultaneously with my relations being killed," with "friends who one day got up in class and went out to fight the war." Some of his best short fiction refers to the war, usually from a child's point of view. In "Laughter Beneath the Bridge," in *Incidents at the Shrine*, the boy narrator is left waiting to be picked up at his boarding school after civil war has broken out, and he huddles with two companions "waiting for the bombs to fall." His mother eventually reaches the school, and their nightmare truck journey home takes mother and son through roadblocks and brutal interrogations where speaking the wrong language means rape or death. The child's views of war, and Okri's characteristic political irony, are distilled in the slogan painted on the lorry: "The Young Shall Grow." This story, and others like "The Shadow of War" in *Stars of the New Curfew*, are not necessarily autobiographical, but his elegiac images of violence and military abuse of power make the work "speak eloquently and movingly for a whole generation," according to Biodun Jeyifo in the *Lagos Guardian*, and "perfectly capture the emotional temperature of that turbulent country," as Sylvester Onword remarked in the *Times Literary Supplement*. One who has "heard the dead singing," as he says in his poem "An African Elegy," Okri also writes about war in a way that brings out what one poem calls "an undeserved sweetness," and he believes—as he says in "On a Picture of a South African Street," a poem for the South African struggle in *An African Elegy*—that "Love and agony can light / The future."

He began writing very early, finishing his first novel, *Flowers and Shadows*, at the age of nineteen. Working as a clerk in Lagos after high school, he wrote fiction under his desk while supposed to be writing letters to paint distributors. Going home on the crowded evening buses he would see the hot commuters frowning and laughing at his pieces in the evening paper—on "vicious landlords, water tanks, and bad roads"—and he slowly came to believe that his fiction could have the same impact on people as direct reportage. "Then one of my stories grew longer and longer . . . It became *Flowers and Shadows*." But his first literary efforts were "over a hundred poems" (though his impressive first volume of poetry, *An African Elegy*, was not published until 1992), and he also worked in painting, sculpture, and theater. "In fact, we did everything," he says of his Lagos circle; "it was a very interesting period to be young and to fall in love with art and literature and music . . . In our worldview, creativity is a river. We don't perceive that talent comes in units, like 'She's a writer' or 'She's a painter' . . . You do it because something is starting to sing in you."

His second novel, *The Landscapes Within*, traces the lively adventures of a young painter in a poverty-stricken city compound, its fascination with the portrait of the artist as a young man balanced by the young Okri's fascination with the city itself. The Ghanaian critic Abioseh Porter remarked in *World Literature Written in English* that this novel's dialogue has "a particularly Lagosian flavor," and its hero Omovo, unlike Stephen Dedalus in Joyce's Dublin, is happy to be one of the Lagos poor himself. "Ghetto-dwellers are the great fantasists," Okri told the *Times* interviewer in 1986. "There was an extraordinary vibrancy there, an imaginative life. When you are that poor, all you've got left is your belief in the imagination." Omovo becomes a painter, but Emokhai and Marjomi, the down-and-out friends of "In the City of Red Dust" (*Stars of the New Curfew*), also dream their picaresque way through hunger, unhappy sex, and the obscene waste of the state governor's birthday ceremony with "the gentle ferocity of spirit" that Emokhai loves in his wasted friend. As the story brings a wild day to a close, "listening to music, Emokhai rolled up, while Marjomi watched the sky. They smoked the marijuana from the governor's secret farms quietly into the night of the red city."

Okri left Lagos for England in 1978 and stayed, studying at The University of Essex and returning to London to write—about Nigeria. "The main attraction of England is that it gives distance and perspective," he told the *Times* interviewer, and he has often returned to Nigeria. "Africa is the only place I really want to write about. It's a gift to the writer." His fiction bears this out, though his collection of poems, *An African Elegy*, draws more on his English life. At first London was poverty and sleeping on office floors, but in 1984 one of his few stories about London, "Disparities" (*Incidents at the Shrine*), was selected by Peter Ackroyd in the PEN New Fiction contest. *Incidents* won the 1987 Commonwealth Prize for Africa and the *Paris Review* Aga Khan Prize for fiction. Now seen both in Africa and internationally as one of the most interesting of a new postmodern generation of African writer, Okri published his first book in the U.S., *Stars of the New Curfew*, in 1988, and these successes were capped by his major work to date, the brilliant novel *The Famished Road*, which was awarded the Booker Prize in Britain.

The Famished Road astonished critics with its scale, ambition, risk-taking, and strangeness. The title comes from a poem by Wole Soyinka, for whom the road is a central archetype: "May you never walk / When the road waits, famished." The walker on Okri's road, Azaro, is an *abiku*, a famished spirit-child, one destined, in Yoruba thought, to die in infancy and be reborn to the same mother over and over again—a powerful representation of both infant mortality and the repetitiveness of desire. But Azaro is determined to resist his fate, and to fight off the seductive calls of his siblings in the spirit world. The novel's air swarms with these hyperreal spirit forms in beautiful and grotesque shapes and colors, a feature seen before in Okri's fiction but never to this degree; he breaks definitively here with naive realism and conventional novel form. The novel's length and episodic plot create a hallucinatory repetitiveness in which the reality of the spirit world supersedes ordinary consciousness for Azaro, within whose point of new the reader mostly remains. Around Azaro spin the events of this world, focused—as in *The Landscapes Within*—on the ordinary life of Lagos ghetto-dwellers, especially his parents and the sinister shaman Madame Koto, whose bar Azaro frequents. But the heart of the book, as in Chinua Achebe's masterpiece *Arrow of God*, is the hero's struggle with his gods, the more moving because this hero is a child.

At the same time, a political allegory emerges through the *abiku* figure. Okri has a poem called "Political Abiku," in which the *abiku* becomes a politician who makes his mother / country suffer his birth again and again as he returns to power "With executions on his fingers / With numberless deaths / As his ring of pearls." A second *abiku* child in *The Famished Road*, Ade, summarizes its allegory in a turn quite different from the poem's: "Our country is an *abiku* country. Like the spirit-child, it keeps coming and going. One day like Azaro it will decide to remain." Azaro's spiritual displacement from a world dominated by corrupt power is thus an enabling strength, as much for his country as for himself. His visions resemble the "landscapes within" of the painter Omovo and Jeffia's mother in *Flowers and Shadows* in becoming a source of renewal.

Anderson, the hero of Okri's story "Incidents at the Shrine," finds the same kind of renewal in his return to the ancestral village shrine of which his uncle, the Image-Maker, says: "The world is the shrine and the shrine is the world." This essentially shamanistic conception of the imagination has much in common with such Native American fiction as Leslie Marmon Silko's *Ceremony*. It is a conception of historical change and personal transformation as one, and Okri's remarkable prose takes the reader inside the child-shaman's agonized journey. *The Famished Road* is a kind of translation of what Okri calls the "sea of narratives and myths" in African life into a new form of fiction and, at the same time, in the great scenes of the distribution of tainted powdered milk by the Party of the Rich and the uprising that ensues, a satirical horror show in which the political monsters if the city show themselves as all too real.

Okri is a postcolonial writer like V. S. Naipaul, Michelle Cliff, and Salman Rushdie in his cultural migrations back and forth between center and periphery, and his work has been best understood by those with a feeling for his African literary lineage as well as his postmodern aesthetic. Annoyed (as Toni Morrison was for her novel *Beloved*) by the tedious comparisons with Latin American magic realism in Western reviews of *The Famished Road*—as if García Márquez had established once and for all the fictional idiom of all "Third World" writers—Okri has rightly insisted on the Nigerian specificity of his work, its roots in the African urban lifeworld, the realist force of its spirit imagery in local belief. The African-American critic Henry Louis Gates Jr. has pointed to Okri's descent from a particular line of Nigerian writing, the Yoruba novel (D. O. Fagunwa in Yoruba, Amos Tutuola in English), and to Okri's deep affinities with Wole Soyinka, whose plays, novels, and poetry are steeped in Yoruba thought, and whose formal innovations in drama Okri is carrying into fiction. Gates notes that Okri's use of Yoruba

thought is literary, a kind of conceit, not something learned at his mother's knee (although he is a fluent Yoruba-speaker).

Okri's African affiliation is also stressed by Abioseh Porter, who shows how *The Landscapes Within* is a significant rewriting in a more spirited and undefeated mood of Ayi Kwei Armah's Ghanaian classic of the urban postindependence blues, *The Beautyful Ones Are Not Yet Born*, an even more significant influence on Okri's novel than James Joyce. There are many other echoes of and homages to earlier African writers in Okri, including the tragic lyricism of the Nigerian poet Christopher Okigbo, and the tradition of political satire that has flourished in the Francophone novels of Sembene Ousmane, Mongo Beti, and, in Okri's own generation, Sony Labou Tansi. Tansi and Okri, both devoted to a figurative style and nonlinear narrative, mark a new postmodern moment in African fiction, and yet both are saturated in the work of their predecessors. The African literary tradition itself is sufficient to account for a work like *The Famished Road*, while at the same time it draws on similar narrative resources better known in the West, like *The Satanic Verses*, Charles Johnson's African-American novel *Middle Passage*, or the work of García Márquez. Okri's work has a flavor at once African and cosmopolitan, postcolonial and postmodern.

Kwame Anthony Appiah, philosopher and critic, commented in the *Nation* that the significance of *The Famished Road* is "the energy of this rendering of the spirit world . . . linked to, and sometimes in tension with, his exile's passion for the project of Nigerian national politics." Gates too stressed, in the *New York Times Book Review*, under the brilliant prose, the political allegory, the "vision of contemporary political liberation" Okri shares with the preceding African generation, especially the Kenyan Ngugi wa Thiong'o. Gates observed that *The Famished Road* "succeeds magnificently in telling a story heretofore untold in English, and it does so in a bold and brilliant new way." Even if its length and its occasional need to name its message too explicitly have bothered some, most British and U.S. reviewers have agreed that the novel is a new kind of masterpiece, and that Okri is one of the most interesting writers now working in English. But in 1993 Okri's novel *Songs of Enchantment*, a sequel to *The Famished Road*, was found by Michael Gorra, writing in the *New York Times Book Review*, to be too loosely structured and repetitive. He wondered if the book's "scenes" might "be outtakes from a single, enormously long manuscript . . . whose best pages became *The Famished Road*."

The poetry in *An African Elegy*, however, confirms Gates's and Appiah's judgment. Okri read the title poem in his acceptance speech for the Booker Prize. It gives the key of his work in its movement from the plangent "mystery of our pain" (the suffering of underdevelopment, the agony of African politics) to "our music": "That is why our music is so sweet. / It makes the air remember." In Okri's music, personal memory and a people's history "sing and dream" together under the sign of hope. As "An African Elegy" concludes: "The ocean is full of songs. / The sky is not an enemy. / Destiny is our friend." This conviction allows him to live in and sing both Lagos, the "darkening city of all our loves," and London, its history "laughing all around us like ghosts / Who do not believe in the existence / Of men." Okri's work, like Michelle Cliff's and Salman Rushdie's, is that spirit laugh, a rueful shrug at the late-capitalist cities scattered across the globe in which he insists we must, nevertheless, "reclaim our lives."

PRINCIPAL WORKS: *Novels*—Flowers and Shadows, 1980; The Landscapes Within, 1982; The Famished Road, 1991; Songs of Enchantment, 1993. *Short stories*—Incidents at the Shrine, 1986; Stars of the New Curfew, 1988. *Poetry*—An African Elegy, 1992.

ABOUT: Los Angeles Times Book Review September 24, 1989; Nation August 3, 1992; New Statesman and Society July 29, 1988; New York Times Book Review June 28, 1992; October 10, 1993; Times (London) July 24, 1986; Times Literary Supplement April 19, 1991; Washington Post August 7, 1989.

TOBY OLSON

OLSON, TOBY (MERLE THEODORE)

(August 17, 1931–) American poet and novelist, writes: "I was born in Berwyn, Illinois, near Chicago, but left there at age eight for California. My family headed west because of my father's ill health, my mother working all the while to support us (my sister, Jill, my brother Jack, and I), and when California didn't help, we moved to Bisbee, Arizona, where I completed two years of high school, then back to Illinois, where my father died when I was seventeen.

"My travels continued after his death, the end of high school, and two years working in a gas station, freight house, and factory: California again, San Diego, where I joined the navy and worked as a medical corpsman on terminal cancer wards, then Corpus Christi, Texas, where I was a surgical technician. Back to Illinois, a year in civilian hospitals, then Occidental College in Los Angeles (English and philosophy, work at an industrial medical clinic where I also lived), then marriage and divorce, graduate school in New York, then finally to Philadelphia, where I currently live.

"Travel as a theme has been constant in my writing, the loss of place and people and the nostalgic wish for return. I began writing poetry in Texas, then in my first novel, *The Life of Jesus*, attempted to put the past and my father behind me. I was raised in a Catholic family, and that novel places the Holy Family as an idea analogue to my own: the pure mother and the weak father, the son as a wanderer.

"While in college at Occidental in the mid-sixties, I spent time in Aspen, Colorado, where I met some of those writers whose work and lives pointed me in the direction I still head: Paul Balckburn, Robert Creeley, Donald Barthelme. Later, it was Robert Coover's work that showed me a way into fiction, as did the novels of Lawrence and Faulkner, two writers who still stand as my models.

"After college, while living in New York City, I continued with poetry, but began to drift more firmly into fiction. I married Miriam Meltzer shortly after moving there in 1965, then in 1975, after graduate school and years of teaching at Long Island University, the New School for Social Research, and Friends Seminary, I was fortunate enough to find a place for myself at Temple University in Philadelphia, where I still teach English. A place on Cape Cod as well, North Truro, where I have begun most everything I've written since 1970, sitting before the same window, looking out at the bay and a changing landscape.

"I believe I owe my novels to the years of writing poetry that preceded them, though I've never been concerned with writing the 'poetic' novel. It has been language though, and an attention to details that has kept me going, feeling (with fiction as with poetry) that the expressed world is always more interesting than explanations of it. In *Seaview*, for example, my concern was with the ways people behave and feel in the face of terminal illness, rather than with some analysis of the significance of their thoughts and actions. This attitude may find its clearest articulation in *Dorit in Lesbos*, in the character of Edward Church, a painter who wishes to get more 'deeply' into his subjects, only to discover later that it's 'the surface of the world, where all beauty resides.'

"For me, poetry is no less than good talk about important things, fiction is invention, though both ways of writing may lead to the truth.

"I've tried to tell the truth in what I've written. I've tried then to celebrate that truth, and in these terms I find no important difference between the writing of poetry and prose."

Few contemporary writers have more easily bridged the distance between poetry and fiction than Toby Olsen. Gilbert Sorrentino wrote of Olson's novels, in *Review of Contemporary Fiction* in 1988: "All the action in his work takes on a splendor rooted in his need to describe. But the description in itself is a description not of an act, but of the ritual of which the act is celebratory . . . each detail of the ephemera of 'everyday life' attracts the author's complete attention and is proffered with the utmost care."

Like William Carlos Williams and Paul Blackburn, poets who have served as models for him, Olson's is a sharply focused "unliterary" poetry with the diction and rhythms of everyday speech that derives its power from its clear-eyed observation of the depths beneath the surfaces of experience. In an early poem, "Getting It Down on Paper" in *Changing Appearance*, he remembers his father, whose long, crippling illness continues to haunt him:

I am now 10 years distance
from the age of my father's death,
and tho he spent 15 years in dying
I am strong of body
and have 5 years on him.
My clearest memory
of my father is his climbing a walnut tree
in El Monte California
because the nuts within reach were diseased,
and there were good ones on the higher limbs.

His father struggles painfully up the tree, "his crutches against the trunk." And then the poet

recalls a murderer condemned to death whom he once visited in San Quentin prison:

My father was like a dead man for 15 years,
and in the process of his own dying
killed each of us a little.
Seeing my friend in San Quentin
is like seeing a dead man,
tho he has 15 years on my father.

The poem concludes:

I remember my father in that rotting tree,
going after a few lousy walnuts at the top,
his struggling and the diseased limbs.
I think (given the circumstances)
San Quentin
is as good as any place to die.

In an interview with Douglas Gunn in *Review of Contemporary Fiction* in 1991, Olson said that in everything he has written, "I've been aware of this filter of memory, this way in which the past can become story." His first novel, *The Life of Jesus*, lives up to its subtitle, "An Apocryphal Tale," because it is a memory exercise enlarged to the grand mythic framework of its title. It begins as a first-person narrative by an imaginative young Catholic boy growing up in California. Participating in the nativity service in his parish church, he identifies with Jesus: "It was Christmas morning. When Jesus was born, I was there." The boy, son so a carpenter, grows up more and more absorbed into the psychic and literal life of Jesus, worshiping his mother as the Virgin, resenting his father. As an adult he relives the experiences of Jesus, including the Passion and the union with his "real father" in another world. Of "this wonderfully imaginative and risk-taking novel," Judith Perkins wrote, in *Review of Contemporary Fiction* in 1991, "Olson uses the paradigm of Jesus's journey through the acceptance of life, suffering, and death toward his father to encapsulate his story of a son's initial estrangement from his father . . . and their final peaceful communion in a world of repose."

In all his later writing, Olson told Gunn, he has been conscious of personal memory. "So long as there has been a ground of direct, conventional reality, the exaggeration that memory can provide seemed possible. Fantasy is not aside from us, after all, but *in* us, and as such has power, can define us." His novels after *The Life of Jesus* have had ordinary mortals for characters, contemporary settings, and rich (overrich some of his critics have said), realistic, circumstantial detail—the moment by moment and movement by movement accounts of golf games in *Seaview*, of body massage by a professional masseur in *Utah*. But they are also dreamlike and visionary. Robert Creeley writes, in *Review of Contemporary Fiction* in 1991: "In these complexly echoing novels there is a pervasive sense of what has happened, of a web to be somehow recognized beyond the simple terms of overt relationships. Thus there are many caves, pockets, places of dreamlike, almost absent, containment, which are never more emphasized, paradoxically, than when the persons themselves are seemingly most substantial."

Each of Olson's novels takes the form of a journey or quest toward some goal—the solution of a mystery, an escape from some threatening danger, simply the desire to begin life again. Always, however, the journey leads the principal character to a rediscovery of his past.

Seaview, the novel for which Olson won the PEN/Faulkner award, centers on a cross-country journey as Allen drives his cancer-ridden wife Melinda from California to Cape Cod, her childhood home, where she wishes to die. Along the way he makes a little money working on golf links and plays golf with an almost ritualistic intensity. He delivers drugs for a dealer in order to get laetrile for Melinda. The novel reaches its climax in nightmare violence on a golf course, but not before it also reaches moments of transcendence as Allen, Melinda, and a wise old American Indian who has joined them explore the American West and their own pasts. The PEN/Faulkner award citation for *Seaview* read in part: "Everything in this brilliant, meditative vision of America is there to be lost as the characters, shaped by a state-of-not-knowing, acknowledge their emblematic roles and rehearse their leave-taking."

The visionary quality of the last sections of *Seaview* dominates the whole of *The Woman Who Escaped from Shame*. Even the identity of the narrator is uncertain because there are interlocking narratives and a mystery so dense that its resolution involves a series of breathtaking coincidences. Linsey Abrams wrote of the novel, in Review of Contemporary Fiction in 1991, "the more knowledge we accumulate in the book, the less sure we are of its meaning." In one passage Olson writes that as his narrator tells his story, he "realized how strange it was and he also realized he wasn't sure of all of it, not even those parts he had been involved in. He kept feeling he was missing things, leaving them out, forgetting them . . . he was not sure of the time of things." Nevertheless, Olson manages to engage his readers completely as his questing hero, Paul Cords, a young medical technician on a holiday jaunt to Mexico, gets embroiled with a gang of pornographic filmmakers. The transforming agent here is a tiny palomino horse used in these films.

Cords rescues the horse from her exploiters and nurses her back to health, as in a less literal sense he also attempts to rescue a prostitute who loves him. The redeeming feature for Paul Cords in this novel of brutality and the exploitation of the innocent is the love he both gives and receives.

In *Utah* the rootless, lonely narrator David, whose wife has disappeared and whose closest friend has just died of AIDS, travels from California to New York and ends up finally in Utah, where he finds not only his wife but a new love: "I had headed into Utah for answers to both relationships, but once there it had become not future revelations that held me but the quality of immediate ones, relationships that in this place had a way of remaining jettisoned from the past."

In *Dorit in Lesbos* a businessman pursues the mystery of the disappearance of his uncle, a painter, in a quest that takes him from California to a Chicago suburb to the Greek island of Lesbos. Although in outline the plot sounds like a conventional mystery story, Olson's attention is directed far more immediately to the mystery of artistic creativity than to a missing uncle. As Sven Birkerts remarked in the *New York Times Book Review*: "The novel has set its sights on the more ineffable stuff of human relations. Its mystery element is more out of the tradition of James—that's Henry, not P. D." In the letters of the uncle the reader finds the key not only to his disappearance but to Olson's own goals as a novelist: his desire, as the painter writes, to discover "the life of the body under the skin, ways to reveal, that make the inside real on the outside."

Writing of Olson's poetry some years earlier in the British journal *Poetry Information*, Robert Vas Dias observed, "It is a voice that speaks of the love of the world, that supplies no ready and facile answers to the emotional turmoil of human relationships, that speaks with humour and candour of sexuality, that is not condescending to any form of human experience, that acknowledges doubt and confusion, that deals uncompromisingly with the difficulties of living as it does with its joys." It is a comment that applies equally to Olson's fiction.

Toby Olson received a B.A. from Occidental College in 1965 and, in 1967, an M.A. from Long Island University where he taught English from 1966 to 1974. He was writer-in-residence at the Friends Seminary in New York from 1974 to 1975, when he joined the English faculty at Temple University. He has also taught at the New School for Social Research (1967–1975) and at the Aspen Writers Workshop (1964–1967). He has had fellowships from the National Endowment for the Arts (1985), the Guggenheim Foundation (1985), and the Rockefeller Foundation (1987). In addition to the PEN/Faulkner he has had awards for his fiction from Temple University (1990) and PENN/Book Pennsylvania (1990). He has coedited *Writing Talks*, a book about methods of teaching writing (1983). His first marriage to Ann Yeomans in 1963 ended in divorce in 1965. He married Miriam Meltzer, a social worker (and professor), in 1966. They live in Philadelphia

PRINCIPAL WORKS: The Brand, 1969; The Hawk-Foot Poems, 1969; Maps, 1969; Worms Into Nails, 1969; Pig's Book, 1970; Vectors, 1972; Fishing, 1973; City, 1974; The Wrestlers and Other Poems, 1974; Changing Appearance: Poems 1965–1970, 1975; Home, 1976; Three and One, 1976; We Are the Fire, 1984; Unfinished Building, 1993. *Novels*—The Life of Jesus: An Apocryphal Tale, 1976; Seaview, 1982; The Woman Who Escaped from Shame, 1986; Utah, 1987; Dorit in Lesbos, 1990.

ABOUT: Contemporary Authors Autobiography Series 11, 1990; Contemporary Authors New Revision Series 9, 1983; Contemporary Literary Criticism 28, 1984; Contemporary Poetry, 5th ed., 1991; Polak, M. L. The Writer as Celebrity, 1986. *Periodicals*—New York Times Book Review June 19, 1983; June 1, 1986; August 9, 1987; April 22, 1990; Poetry Information Winter 1976–1977; Review of Contemporary Fiction Fall 1988; Summer 1991.

*ORTESE, ANNA MARIA (1915–   ), Italian novelist and writer of short stories, writes: "At the beginning of the First World War—the period in which I was born—social discrepancies, in Italy as in many other parts of the world, were not, I believe, as painful as they are today. Above all, they were not so conspicuous. My family, a total of nine persons which included six children, lived a highly modest life, partially in poverty, in the southcentral region of the country and was surely no stranger to economic hardship, but we didn't really notice it. At least the children didn't. So even in spite of having been born into very uncomfortable circumstances, often sad, and marked above all by a great void of culture and security, I wasn't aware of it, and perhaps didn't suffer from it, up until adolescence. And at that point, the center of my life came to be occupied by other problems, which quickly coalesced into only a single problem: the problem of self-expression. The primary problem of survival—the universal problem, so to speak, which moreover was to tarry at my side throughout the whole of my life—flanked this second and equally serious problem, making it at times more intricate, and at others more simple. There were even moments when I managed to believe that

ANNA MARIA ORTESE

self-expression was my only problem; but then I'd be forced to admit that the other problem remained as well. Both of them, now, like Poe's famous raven, have taken up permanent residence on the threshold of my life. My life has become their home.

"But what is the nature of this problem of self-expression which can prove so strong as to be able to vie with the problem of survival itself, and for all of a span, by now, of forty or fifty years? Today we are wary of discussing such things, since they don't seem sufficiently 'democratic'—as the phrase currently runs. And yet if democracy is ever to prove its worth as the tool most suited for creating a certain happiness, I believe that the problem of self-expression—the problem of achieving a true individuality—may well have to occupy the very first place, and with reference to people in general.

"Self-expression: a child ordinarily achieves self-expression by means of drawing, playing, fantasizing, and running, and even by inventing another 'I' which offers protection from the world. Adolescents are apt to turn their attention to the ins and outs of much more sophisticated techniques, desiring to translate the act of self-expression into the production of something factual they can call their own. If such adolescents have been blessed with adequate education, their researches will be crowned with success, and the creative 'I' will experience harmonious growth. But this period in which the adolescent wants to give autonomous form (autonomous and therefore new) to what she or he feels is highly delicate, and things can also go quite

°or TAY zay

wrong. The world can overwhelm such a boy or girl with its own cultural models; or models may prove to be wholly lacking, as is typically the pitfall in highly impoverished societies. The adolescent runs the risk, in the first case, of being brainwashed and enslaved; or in the second of being set adrift into a course of distorted development. The present-day world of childhood and adolescence is full of such boys and girls—encaptived by society's values in the wealthy countries, and abandoned to their own devices in the poor ones. . . . But here, for a moment, I have to go back to what I understood at fifteen years of age—and still today understand—by self-expression, the field of which, for me, is centered quite precisely on the written page.

"I don't want to dwell on any deeply personal feeling—or, worse, on any self-satisfied feeling—that might hover at the edges of what I mean by 'self-expression.' So I do better to think of self-expression as a value that mediates knowledge and 'intelligence' rather than the life of the feelings: I see it as concerned with discerning things in terms of their *logical* order rather than with any of the vanity of finding oneself, like a mirror, in the midst of them. I have used the word *things*. And as a curious faculty peruses and presents us with things in their countless number, manifest variety and endless mutability, this word little by little fills up with a special air or meaning. Its meaning is involved—as far as I myself am concerned, or as far as my experience is concerned—with what I'd refer to as 'strangeness.' And there you have it. If I had to offer a definition of everything that surrounds me—things, in their infinitude, and the feelings through which I grasp them, and this by now for something on the order of half a century—I could hinge it on no other word: strangeness. My writings reflect the desire—indeed the painful urgency—to render this feeling of strangeness.

"For adults—or among highly cultivated peoples—the whole world is the world of the obvious, of the commonplace. So human beings apply their labels to everything—pricing and, whenever need be, describing the merchandise. This is a *field*, this is the *ocean*, this is a *horse*, this is your *mother*, this is the *national flag*, these are two *boys*. But for children, or adolescents, and as well for a certain sort of artist—less often for writers—that's not the way things stand. Wherever they go, everything shines with a light that betrays no origins. Everything they touch—that flag, that horse, that ocean—is vibrant with electricity and leaves them wonderstruck. They understand what adults have ceased to understand: that the world *is a heavenly body*; is a heavenly body; that all things within and beyond that world are made of cosmic matter; and

that their nature, their meaning—except for a dazzling gentleness—is unsoundable."

(From *Micromega*, May 1990. tr.—Henry Martin)

In 1987 Lawrence Venuti, in the *New York Times Book Review*, observed that among the paradoxes of Anna Maria Ortese's life is the fact that although she has received several important literary awards, including the Viareggio Prize for *Il mare non bagna Napoli* (1953, *The Bay Is Not Naples*), and the Strega Prize for *Poveri e semplici* (The poor and the simple, 1967), "her books have been more often praised than read, and she continues to live in near poverty . . . alienated from an Italian reading audience that for the most part prefers American best sellers." One reason for this lack of recognition may be that Ortese uneasily straddles the literary genres of social realism and fantasy. Uncompromising in her humanitarian idealism ("un culto umanamente evangelico," as Lorenza Farina described Ortese's convictions in *Letture* in 1983), she has been sorely tested by circumstances, including early poverty, the repressive Fascist state in which she came to maturity, the devastation of World War II, and the chaotic political and economic history of postwar Italy. Ortese confronts these conditions, sometimes with accurately observed, almost journalistic reporting, sometimes with rage and impassioned rhetoric, and sometimes in the guise of fable and allegory. Her response has been consistently sensitive and sympathetic to the weak and the poor, in a lean and graphic prose that, Farina writes, "has penetrated into the secrets of the heart of man."

Ortese was self-educated, reading everything she could find in Italian and foreign literature, delighting especially in the imaginative writings of Edgar Allan Poe and Hans Christian Andersen and in the adventures of Robert Louis Stevenson. She spent her early years in southern Italy and in the Italian colony of Tripoli in Libya. From 1928 until the outbreak of World War II she lived in Naples, where she began her literary career with poems and short lyric prose sketches. Some of the latter were published in the prominent journal *L'Italia letteraria* and came to the attention of Massimo Bontempelli, a writer famous for his stories of *realismo magico*. He encouraged her to collect her work in *Angelici dolori* (Angelic sorrows) in 1937. Partly autobiographical, partly dreamlike and surrealistic, these early writings set a pattern for Ortese and brought her critical praise.

When the war ended, she moved to Milan, where she published fiction and journalism in prominent newspapers and magazines, among them *Oggi* and *Il Mondo*. She twice won the Premio Saint Vincent for her newspaper work, in 1952 and 1955, the second for her reports on a visit to the USSR for *L'Europeo*.

A bold and articulate feminist long before the women's movement had made any inroads in Italy, Ortese was sensitive to the oppression of women both within their families and in society as a whole. The poverty that pervaded Italian life in the South and the exploitation of labor in the North victimized women. Whether writing journalistic reports on the squalor and hardships of life among the poor or converting these conditions into exotic fables, Ortese was uncompromising in her anger at social injustice and her compassion for its victims. Like Bettina, the writer-heroine of *Poveri e semplici*, who lives a bohemian life in Milan, Orese's goal has been "to work for humanity by means of my writing. To collaborate for the peace and betterment of mankind. This, I believe, is the duty of writers."

The Bay Is Not Naples is a representative collection. The stories are set in the South but, as Nicola Chiaromonte observed in a review of the book in the *New Republic*: Ortese's remarks about the struggle between Nature and Reason in the South could well apply to the moral and cultural situation in Italy as a whole." Chiaromonte admired her candid descriptions of Neapolitan life—"the real merit of the book"—and was impressed with her "passionate and forceful writing." Her vision of postwar Naples, much of the city in ruins from aerial bombardment, its populace impoverished and demoralized, is unsparing. She wrote in "The Sea and Naples":

> Neapolitans have never been what you might call really happy, and their blood seemed to have become black and congealed; their mildness and childlike simplicity shattered . . . Their well-known vivaciousness was now a form of restless anxiety, and their superficial gaiety concealed a wild melancholia, a sinking sensation of defeat and the end of everything they knew.

In "A Pair of Glasses," a desperately poor family (two of the sisters "so resigned to the miseries of this life that they intended to take the veil") cannot afford glasses to correct the near-blindness of a little girl. A bitter and overworked maiden aunt sacrifices her life savings for them, but as the delighted child puts on the glasses for the first time, she will see a world that, as one character says, "she had better not see." In another story, "Family Scene," an unmarried older sister runs a shop of her own and still dreams of marriage, but realizes that she cannot escape her responsibilities to her family:

> Like a drag horse, feeling the load pile up on the wagon behind him and his legs faltering, but unable to turn his gentle eyes to look back at his burden, so she did not see from what direction this weight of other lives was de-

scending upon her. All she knew was that she must carry it.

In contrast to the realism of *The Bay Is Not Naples* is *L'iguana* (1965, *The Iguana*), a novel that is part political allegory and part pure romantic fantasy. It begins in contemporary Milan, where a wealthy young nobleman assists his mother in buying up real estate for villas and hotels, seeking out "still intact expressions of what they understand as 'nature,' believing it a mixture of freedom and passion, with not a little sensuality and a shade of folly, for which the rigors of modern life in Milan seem to make them thirst." But the idealistic count is "basically indifferent to the very idea of possession, as though the true meaning of life had to lie in something else." Sailing away on his yacht, he discovers that "something else" on an uncharted island off the coast of Portuagal. There he meets another aristocratic but impoverished young man and his brothers, who employ as a house servant an iguana. This creature, the count gradually realizes, in spite of her reptilian features, is a young girl. Abused and overworked, she is the victim of her employers' exploitation, and the count resolves to rescue her. Her true identity and the true nature of the characters around her remain mysterious. The count, increasingly fascinated by her, is eventually drawn to his death, and the mystery remains unsolved. But as is characteristic of Ortese's fiction, social realism and fantasy mingle freely. Before his death the count has a moment of illumination:

> Then he felt that these voyages are dreams, and iguanas are warnings. That there are no iguanas, but only disguises, disguises thought up by human beings for the oppression of their neighbors and then held in place by a cruel and terrifying society. He himself had been product and expression of such a society, but now he was stepping out of it. This made him content.

The Iguana was followed by a number of critically esteemed books, among them *Il porto di Toledo: Ricordi della vita irreale* (The port of Toledo: Memories of an unreal life, 1975), an ambitious reworking of her lyrical and fabulous tales in *Angelici dolori*, and *Il capello piumato* (The plumed hat, 1979), a sequel to her *Poveri e semplici*, with young idealists in postwar Milan still engaged in a brave but ultimately futile struggle to reform society. *The Iguana*, however, remains the book that best defines the haunting and impressive quality of Ortese's work, summed up in the response of the count to his host's request for a definition of realism: "It is an art of illuminating the real. But people, unfortunately, don't always affirm the awareness that reality exists on many levels, and that the whole of creation, once you analyze the deepest level of reality, isn't real at all, and simply the purest and profoundest imagination."

PRINCIPAL WORKS IN ENGLISH TRANSLATION: (tr. F. Frenaye) The Bay Is Not Naples, 1955; (tr. H. Martin) The Iguana, 1987; (tr. H. Martin) A Music Behind the Wall, 1994.

ABOUT: Bloomsbury Guide to Women's Literature, 1992; Encyclopedia of Continental Women Writers, 1991; Encyclopedia of World Literature in the 20th Century, rev. ed., 1983. Periodicals—(in Italian) Letture: libro e spettacoli December 1983; New Republic October 5, 1953; New York Times Book Review November 22, 1987.

RON PADGETT

PADGETT, RON (June 17, 1942–), American poet, translator, and editor, was born in Tulsa, Oklahoma, "an average type place" as he described it to Edward Foster in an interview in *Talisman*. His father, he recalls, was a bootlegger (Oklahoma was a dry state until 1959) who bought liquor in neighboring Missouri and sold it to Oklahomans: "He made a *good* living that way, but he did have a reputation as a criminal." He had many friends among the police, however who "knew he was not a bad guy." Nor did he set a bad example for his son. "The only way I've been able to explain it to myself is to think about the image of my father as an outsider, a dashing figure who was willing to defy the social and legal conventions to do what he thought was right, and to that I link the image of the romantic poet, a Rimbaud-type figure. . . . " Years later Padgett dedicated his collection *Tulsa Kid* to his father.

Young Padgett was an average student but an omnivorous reader. He began writing poetry at about the age of thirteen and received some encouragement from a high school teacher. He also began to study French and discovered the poetry of Rimbaud and Baudelaire that was to shape his own poetic interests in the future. At fifteen he had a part-time job in a bookstore and took advantage of the inventory to discover literary journals like the *Evergreen Review* and emerging young writers like LeRoi Jones (Later Amiri Baraka) and Frank O'Hara. While working in the bookstore he met the poet Ted Berrigan, then a student at the University of Tulsa, with whom he and fellow Tulsan artist Joe Brainard were later to collaborate on "a fugitive work," *Some Things.*

By the time Padgett came east to study at Columbia University in 1960 he had fairly well determined the vocation that he has since followed. Initially attracted to Columbia by the fact that

Allen Ginsberg and Jack Kerouac had both studied there, he took his freshman humanities course and an American literature course with the poet Kenneth Koch, met poets, like Jones and Lorenzo Thomas, whose works he had discovered in Tulsa, and was soon in the center of the flourishing New York School, as it has been called, of poets and artists centered in the East Village and at the Church of St. Mark's-in-the-Bowery. There, with poetry readings and workshops and the presence of such famous poets and artists as Auden, John Ashbery, Frank O'Hara, and Jim Dine, Padgett found a congenial base for the development of his own talents.

Padgett did not neglect his academic education. He received his B.A. from Columbia in 1964 with distinction, winning both the George E. Woodberry award and the Boar's Head Poetry Prize. From 1965 to 1966 he studied in France on a Fulbright grant, theoretically at the Sorbonne but practically on his own. In Paris he discovered poets and artists with whom he felt a particular affinity—Guillaume Apollinaire, Pierre Reverdy, Blaise Cendrars, Max Jacob, Max Ernst, and Man Ray. These were not his contemporaries; most of them were associated with the avant-garde of World War I and the 1920s, but, as Padgett told Foster, he identified with them as "outsiders": Apollinaire and Cendrars not French by birth, Jacob a Jew converted to Catholicism, Reverdy not a Parisian but a provincial from the south of France. They had all too, like Padgett, been involved with painting and had lived most of their lives on very little money, "close to the bone."

Padgett's translations from the French have been praised for both their accuracy and their freshness and spontaneity: a combination of qualities that often eludes even the most experienced translators. Their success is in large measure owing to his personal identification with the writers he is translating. Blaise Cendrars, in particular, whose *Complete Poems* he translated for the University of California Press, appealed to him for "his good-humored orneriness, his outlaw sensibility, and his informality, all of which seemed so American." In his preface Padgett describes his experience in translating one of Cendrars's poems, "Easter in New York." At first he found its tricky rhyme scheme and its serious themes beyond his grasp. But suddenly one day he "had a breakthrough. . . . Some passages did not some easily, and I hope that an occasional awkwardness will be camouflaged by some equally awkward moments in the original that are clearly intentional—they reinforce the poem's sincerity (if one can accept the idea that artfulness can be sincere). In any case sincerity is crucial here, for the poem works only if the reader believes the poet."

Influential as French culture has been on him, Padgett has never lost what he calls his "Arkansas Ozark roots." The surrealist poet Reverdy was one of Padgett's special enthusiasms and Padgett was influenced by him. His poetry is very obviously different from Reverdy's, however. Though he has often worked in close collaboration with other writers (Ted Berrigan, Tom Clark, Tom Veitch), Padgett has his unique voice. "The work of others," he told Foster, "was more sophisticated, urbane and witty. But my work was quick and light, with a lot of the cowboy- hillbilly that was natural to my feelings. . . . "

Padgett's unique and natural voice is often disarmingly childlike: as in "Chocolate Milk," from *Tulsa Kid*:

Oh God! It's great!
to have someone fix you
chocolate milk
and to appreciate their doing it!
Even as they stir it
in the kitchen
your mouth is going crazy
for the chocolate milk!
The wonderful chocolate milk!

Such poetry reflects Padgett's commitment to teaching young children. He participated for many years in community education programs. From 1969 to 1976 he worked in the New York City Poets in the Schools project, and from 1976 to 1978 he lived in small towns in South Carolina working with that state's Art Commission. On his return to New York in 1978 he directed the St. Mark's Poetry Project for three years, and since 1982 he has been director of publications for the Teachers and Writers Collaborative. Much of his work has been with inner-city children. In these experiences, he writes in his essay "Among the Blacks": "I first felt the joyous relaxation of being blind to color." Having grown up in segregated Tulsa, he knew black people only as hired help; he also knew no Catholics or Jews. In New York, he writes, he discovered "not a melting pot . . . but a mixing bowl, with a startling variety of races." Padgett found his own identity in just such a mixture:

I wish the entire world were made of pieces interchangeable among all puzzles. I like to be at home among Vermont loggers, Scottish aristocrats, Colombian housemaids, and Chinese photographers. I love it when people very unlike me like me. So because I can't switch races or pretend I don't come from a particular social class, I yearn for those moments when the other person looks at me and sees a man around forty, tall, slender, with short silver hair and wearing wire-rimmed glasses for eyes that look straight out, and likes the fact that I too am different.

Childlike sometimes but not childish, Padgett's poems have a quality that David Shapiro described in *Talisman* as "opague zaniness." His quirky humor ranges from surreal-dada—"It's pancake time in Greece, huge/flapjacks draped over the countryside" (from *Triangles in the Afternoon*)—to puns and word plays—"Later, you beat me to a pulp magazine" (from *In Advance of the Broken Arm*); "A Venetian blind/ They brought me up" (from *Bean Spasms*). There is often striking sense in his nonsense, as in "The Giraffe" from *Tulsa Kid*:

The 2 f's
in giraffe
are like 2 giraffes
running through
the word giraffe
The 2 f's
run through giraffe
like 2 giraffes

and "Haiku" also from *Tulsa Kid*:

First: five syllables
Second: seven syllables
Third: five syllables

And the absurd can mask genuine feeling, as in the first of his "Three Little Poems" from *Toujours L'Amour*:

I call you on
the phone &
we chat, but
the way tele
is missing from

'phone is the
way it makes me
feel, wishing
the rest of
you were here

Sometimes, David Lehman writes in his review of *Great Balls of Fire* in *Poetry*, Padgett
oversteps "the thin line between brilliance and
mere cleverness . . . sometimes too cute, too
gimmicky, too instantly avant-garde. . . . Generally, however, to use one of the poet's favored
constructions, Padget's poems, pistol-epistles,
playfully prance a pun upon the pretty, permis-
sive page."

In most of Padgett's collaborations with others, logic is abandoned completely. *Supernatural
Duet*, for example, is "a shared work" in which
minimal poems, actually a few unrelated words
by Clark Coolidge, are printed within a box
frame with a caption by Padgett underneath.
One page, for example, has only the words *to,
and*, and *felt* in a box, with the caption, "An invisible employee decides to impersonate the
company president." In *Sufferin' Succotash*,
Padgett offers a number of plays on the word
sensation to comic-strip illustrations by Joe Brainard. With Jim Dine he tells stories in pictorial
images. In all the collaborations Padgett is as
much an artist as his artist-collaborator is a poet.
These works are the extremes in which the poet
seems to be stretching out beyond language for
the pure vision of color achieved in abstract art.
In a far more direct expression of this aim in
"The 26 Letters" in *Tulsa Kid*, he sees himself,
the working poet, at the typewriter, struggling
to compose a poem that seems to be turning into
an abstract painting:

with a head cold and a beard
and some tortoise-shell spectacles
attached to my head,
not a bad guy really,
a touch of Sad-Sack tonight,
a bit of red and green tomorrow
with a long streak of blue into the future
with orange and black zigzags along the sides.

In "Song" from *Tulsa Kid*, another poem that
might be taken as a statement of his poetic credo, Padgett writes:

Learning to write,
be a good person and get to heaven
are all the same thing
but trying to do them all at once
is enough to drive you crazy

When Padgett's collection, *New and Selected
Poems: 1963-1992* came out, the *Publishers
Weekly* reviewer commented on Padgett's poet-
ry: "Images veer off in every direction and

themes go adrift in streams of consciousness, but
the results never fail to excite, as Padgett bends
to various purposes observation and language. . . . "

Padgett is married to Patricia Mitchell; they
have one son, Wayne, and live on what Padgett
calls "the uptown fringe of the Lower East Side"
in New York City. He has received awards from
the Poets Foundation (1964, 1969), the
American Academy of Arts and Letters (1966,
1971), and the Translation Center of Columbia
University (1976) and received the New York
State Council of the Arts Translation Grant
(1983). He held a National Endowment for the
Arts translation fellowship in 1983 and a Guggenheim fellowship in 1986.

PRINCIPAL WORKS: *Poetry*—Some Thing, (with Ted Berrigan and Joe Brainard), 1964; In Advance of the Broken
Arm, 1964; Sky, 1966; Bean Spasms: Poems and Prose,
(with Ted Berrigan), 1967; Tone Arm, 1967; 100,000
Fleeing Hilda (with Joe Brainard), 1967; Bun (with
Tom Clark), 1968; Great Balls of Fire, 1969, Rev, ed.,
1990; Sweet Pea, 1971; Sufferin' Succotash (with Joe
Brainard), 1971; Poetry Collection, 1971; Back in Boston Again (with Ted Berrigan and Tom Clark), 1972;
Oo LaLa (with Jim Dine), 1973; Crazy Compositions,
1974; Toujours l'Amour, 1976; Arrive by Pullman,
1978; Tulsa Kid, 1979; Triangles in the Afternoon,
1980; (with Trevor Winkfield) How to be a Wood-
pecker, 1983; (with Trevor Winkfield) How to Be
Modern Art, 1984; Light as Air, 1989; The Big Something, 1990; New and Selected Poems: 1963-1992,
1995. *Novel*— (with Tom Veitch) Antlers in the Tree-
tops, 1973. *As editor*—(with David Shapiro) An Anthology of New York Poets, 1970; (with Bill Zavatsky)
The Whole Word Catalogue 2, 1976; (with Nancy Larson Shapiro) The Point: Where Teaching and Writing
Intersect, 1983; The Complete Poems, by Edwin Den-
by, 1986; Handbook of Poetic Forms, 1987; The
Teachers & Writers Guide to Walt Whitman, 1993.
Translations—The Poet Assassinated, by Guillaume
Apollinaire, 1968; enlarged edition, as The Poet Assas-
sinated and Other Stories, 1985; Dialogues with Marcel
Duchamp, by Pierre Cabanne, 1971; (with David Ball)
Rldasedlrad les Dlcmhypbdf, by Valery Larbaud,
1973; (with Bill Zavatsky) The Poems of A.O. Barna-
booth, by Valery Larbaud, 1974; Kodak, by Blaise
Cendrars, 1976; Complete Poems, by Blaise Cendrars,
1992. *Other*—(with J. Dine) The Adventures of Mr.
and Mrs. Jim and Ron, 1970; Among the Blacks: Two
Works with R. Roussel, 1988; Pantoum, 1988; Blood
Work, 1993; Educating the Imagination, 1994.

ABOUT: Contemporary Authors New Revision Series 30,
1990; Contemporary Poets, 5th ed., 1991; Dictionary
of Literary Biography 5, 1980; Kostelanetz, R. (ed.)
The New American Arts, 1965; Padgett, R. Among the
Blacks, 1988. *Periodicals*—New York Times Book Review March 31, 1968; September 19, 1976; Poetry December 1968; January 1972; Publishers Weekly July
31, 1995; Talisman Fall 1991; World Literature Today
Autumn 1985.

PAGELS, ELAINE HIESEY (February 13, 1943–), American religious scholar and historian, was born in Palo Alto, California, to William McKinley Hiesey, a research biologist, and Louise Sophia (Van Druton) Hiesey. "My father . . . had no use for religion, and I was brought up without," she recalled to an interviewer for *Publishers Weekly,* "and you know how children become fascinated with things they are not supposed to." Her interest in religion was further aroused through her involvement with an evangelical group during her early teens, when she was drawn by "the emotional power of the music."

She received her B.A. (1964) and M.A. (1965) from Stanford University, where her study in particular of ancient Greek history served as a bridge to the interpretation of the New Testament. She did not continue her studies immediately, however. Instead, she went to New York to join the Martha Graham modern dance studio. She found it "exhilarating, but it was the life of a nun," she told Jenny Schuessler in *Publishers Weekly.*

In 1965 she entered the graduate program in the history of Christianity at Harvard University. Here she had an opportunity to work under two distinguished professors of religion, George MacRae and Helmut Koester, who directed her to the ancient Gnostic texts known as the Nag Hammadi Codices. They had been discovered only twenty years earlier and were still being translated and interpreted by a team of scholars sponsored by UNESCO. Pagels then embarked on what proved to be her own area of specialization.

The Nag Hammadi codices were discovered in Egypt in 1945. The fifty-two texts making up these papyri were written in Coptic, subsequently dated by scholars from 350 to 400, but identified as translations from earlier Greek originals related to Christian scriptures.

When these manuscripts were sold on the black market by antiquities dealers in Cairo, they came to the attention of Egyptian government officials, and eventually most of them were deposited in the Coptic Museum in Cairo. However, one of the codices was smuggled out of Egypt and offered for sale in the United States. This text seized the interest of Gilles Quispel, a historian of religion from Utrecht. In tracing some missing pages from this codex to manuscript in the Coptic Museum in Cairo, Quispel aligned it with a Greek *Gospel of Thomas* that had been discovered in the previous century, thereby establishing the connection between the Nag Hammadi Codices and Gnostic Christianity. By 1952, following upon a compli-

ELAINE PAGELS

cated series of intrigues, the codices were nationalized by the Egyptian government. For the next twenty years, as Pagels related in the introduction to her book *The Gnostic Gospels,* they became "the focus of intense personal rivalries among the international group of scholars competing for access to them."

Pagels's own entry into the field came about through her doctoral dissertation, completed in 1970 under the direction of Helmut Koester, for which she learned the Coptic language. In this dissertation, *The Johannine Gospel in Gnostic Exegesis: Heracleon's Commentary on John,* published as her first book, and based on a fragmented text by a disciple of a leading Gnostic teacher named Valentines, Pagels began what was to become an extended inquiry into why Gnosticism eventually was condemned as a heresy by Orthodox Christianity. The Gnostics clashed with mainstream Christians from the outset, as Pagels shows, by their claim to special insight into the meaning of the Gospels (Valentines, the teacher of Heracleon, professed secret knowledge gained from a follower of Saint Paul). Fundamentally, the Gnostics denounced the reading of Christ's revelation by the majority of their Christina contemporaries (whom they preferred to as *hoi polloi,* or "the many") as naive and too preoccupied with the historical reality of Jesus. The far-reaching historical consequences of this exclusiveness on the part of the Gnostics, together with their recondite symbolic interpretations of Christ's message, are explored in Pagels's later books.

In 1970 Pagels took up her first teaching post,

at Barnard College, where she remained until 1982, becoming head of the department of the history of religion. During this period, she benefited from association with members of the Columbia New Testament Seminar and from colleagueship in particular with Theodore Gaster, a scholar of Eastern religions. At this time she also joined the team of scholars translating and editing the Nag Hammadi papyri for publication and journeyed to Cairo both to meet archaeologists and to study the original texts. A National Endowment for the Humanities summer grant in 1973 and a Mellon Foundation grant to attend the Aspen Institute for Humanistic Studies during the following summer provided the leisure to write her next scholarly monograph, *The Gnostic Paul: Gnostic Exegesis of the Pauline Letters*. In this hermeneutic study, Pagels presents evidence that, although many commentators on Paul stress his opposition to "the Gnostic heresy," he, like, Jesus, came to be read symbolically by Valentines and his students. As with the Gospels, Valentines opposed the literal reading of Acts and the Epistles, contending that Paul too chose to hide his meaning in parables. The text under study here, *The Interpretation of Knowledge*, was subsequently absorbed into the scholarly collection known as the Coptic Gnostic Library, (as Codes XI, 1), with introduction and notes by Pagels. For the general reader, her findings were expanded into her first book for the general reader, *The Gnostic Gospels*.

"I had to write this book. It was kind of an obsession," Pagels told the interviewer for *Publishers Weekly* shortly after the publication of *The Gnostic Gospels*. She had "always been attracted to the heretical," but a particular incentive to popularize her research was that, despite the publication in 1978 of an English translation of the Nag Hammadi Library, these Coptic texts had not stirred up the interest aroused by the later discovery in Israel of the Dead Sea Scrolls. Pagels saw herself as opening up the Gnostic writings to "intelligent readers who were not specialists," just as Edmund Wilson had so successfully done with the Qumran scriptures. Actually, she tried out portions of the book in advance for various audiences. For colleagues, the first four chapters were published earlier in more technical form in journals of theology and festschrifts. The third, and most controversial, chapter ("God the Father/God the Mother") was first delivered as a lecture before a woman's group at Barnard who had requested her to speak on the relation of her work to feminist interests. The first four chapters were introduced in condensed form to a wider readership through the *New York Review of Books* (October 25, November 8, November 22, December 6, 1979).

The basic thesis of *The Gnostic Gospels* is that the clash between the Gnostic Christians and the Orthodox Christians during the 2nd century had political as well as theological significance. Fundamentally, according to Pagels, Gnosticism was deemed detrimental to the survival of the Church as an institution: its rejection of the bodily resurrection of Jesus denied the sacramental principle and the apostolic succession basic to Church doctrine; its form of worship—rotating of religious offices to avoid any kind of hierarchy, and admitting women to priestly functions—subverted patriarchal and episcopal authority; its elitism—the claim to "secret" knowledge available only to initiates—ran counter to efforts of the church fathers to build a "universal" church. A possible explanation for the Nag Hammadi find offered by Pagels is that these texts were concealed to protect them from the anathema issued by Bishop Athanasius of Alexandria in 367 against all "apocyphal books" with "heretical" tendencies.

The Gnostic Gospels succeeded in reaching beyond the confined circles of historians of religion and archaeologists. At the extreme, perhaps, was an article in *People*, "Jesus Kissed Mary Magdalene on the Mouth: The Gnostic Gospels Could Rewrite Religious History," prompted by one of the more erotic-sounding of the texts, which this magazine chose not to interpret symbolically. Fellow scholars, while praising the author for her deftly assimilated erudition and lucid writing, were more skeptical about the cogency of her historical argument. "There is much in the book that is both true and insightful," wrote Pheme Perkins in *Commonweal*, but the review went on to criticize the author for hasty generalization and insufficient allowance for diversity among the defenders of orthodoxy. Others thought that Pagels exaggerated the feminist sympathies of the Gnostics and made them out to be more protoliberal than her evidence warranted. Hyam Maccoby, in *Commentary*, considered it "a useful but flawed interim report, a guide to the many fascinating possibilities that have been opened up, but a guide that should be consulted with caution." *The Gnostic Gospels* received both the National Book Critics Circle Award for criticism and the American Book Award.

Since 1982, Pagels has been on the faculty of Princeton University as Harrington Spear Paine Professor of Religion. The previous year, soon after she began work on a new book, the MacArthur Foundation, as she said, "astonished" her with a fellowship that gave her five years free for research and writing. This grant culminated in the publication of *Adam, Eve, and the Serpent*, in which she carried forward her study of the history of Christianity to its establishment as a state religion under the emperor Constantine and the consolidation of its doctrine by Augustine.

Pagels writes in the introduction to *Adam, Eve, and the Serpent*, "What I intend to show in this book is how certain ideas—in particular ideas concerning sexuality, moral freedom, and human value—took their definitive form during the first four centuries as interpretation of the Genesis creation stories, and how they have continued to affect our culture and everyone in it, Christian or not, ever since." Concurrent with the evolution of the Christian movement from persecuted sect opposed to imperial authority to established Church of Rome (in turn condemner of Gnosticism, among other heterodoxies), Pagels traces the transformation of Christian doctrine from affirmation of moral freedom to the Augustinian emphasis on bondage to sin and corruption. This shift in the reading of the Book of Genesis, she believes, corresponds with Augustine's own conversion from paganism to Christian asceticism. The most disputed contention in this book is that the triumph of Augustinianism sanctioned the power of the emperor because of sinful citizens' incapacity to govern themselves. In the concluding chapter, however, Pagels concedes that beyond this "social control" explanation, the Augustinian doctrine won out because it answers to a basic human need for people to blame themselves rather than external causes for their misfortune. W.H.C. Frend reviewing *Adam, Eve, and the Serpent*, concluded in *New York Review of Books*: "Basic causes of our present moral confusion have been laid bare as no one has done before. Elaine Pagels has shown that historical theology is no ivory tower and its scholars have an urgent and relevant message for our time." Declaring that the book "contains not a wasted sentence," the reviewer for the *Economist* commended Pagels's "rare combination of formidable knowledge and easy fluency."

In 1969, Elaine Hiesey, as she was then, married Heinz Pagels, a theoretical physicist on the faculty of Rockefeller Institute, and a highly praised author. In 1980 a son Mark was born to the couple, and they also adopted two children named Sarah and David. An ardent mountaineer, Heinz Pagels was killed on July 24, 1988 in a fall from Pyramid Peak in Colorado. *Adam, Eve, and the Serpent* came out shortly before the fatal accident, and special acknowledgment is made to Heinz Pagels "for reading the manuscript and offering excellent criticism." The book is dedicated to "our beloved son Mark," who had died the previous year.

In *The Origin of Satan* Pagels went on to confront the Christian invention of the devil. The first Jewish Christians, according to Pagels, would have liked to "demonize" the Roman authorities, but fearing their power, directed their wrath at the Jewish majority who did not join them. Thus was Christian characterization of Jews as killers of the messiah born. Pagels does not term this attitude "anti-Semitism" because, she told Jenny Schuessler in *Publishers Weekly*, "What I'm talking about in the book is really intra- Jewish conflict. . . . What was absent from Egyptian, Greek or Roman anti-Semitism was the idea that we are God's people and if you are not with us you are following evil. And once you add this, you have a particularly difficult and dangerous perception."

Norman Cohn commented in the *New York Review of Books* that rather than "a social history of Satan," as Pagels termed her work, *The Origin of Satan* is a more modest "account of how early Christians "defamed rival or hostile groups by labeling them servants or allies or worshipers of Satan." Cohn dubbed the work "original and adventurous" for its convincing demonstration of the long tradition of demonization in the Christian canon, especially how the authors of the canonical gospels, albeit unintentionally, created the "stereotype of the demonic Jew."

PRINCIPAL WORKS: The Johannine Gospel in Gnostic Exegesis: Heracleon's Commentary on John, 1973; The Gnostic Paul: Gnostic Exegesis of the Pauline Letters, 1975; The Gnostic Gospels, 1979; The Gnostic Jesus and Early Christian Politics, 1981; Adam, Eve, and the Serpent, 1988; The Origin of Satan, 1995. *As contributor*—The Dialogue of the Savior (Nag Hammadi Codex III, 15, 1984). *As editor*—(with John B. Turner) The Interpretation of Knowledge: A Valentinian Exposition on the Anointing, Baptism, Eucharist A and B (in Nag Hammadi Codices XI, XII, XIII, 1990).

ABOUT: Contemporary Authors New Revision Series 24, 1988; Who's Who in America, 1992–1993; *Periodicals*—American February 16, 1980; December 3, 1988; Atlantic February 1980; Chicago Tribune March 13, 1980; Christian Century July 30–August 6, 1980; Commentary June 1980; December 1988; Commonweal November 9, 1979; October 21, 1988; Economist August 6, 1988; Journal of Ecclesiastical History April 1, 1991; National Review November 7, 1988; New Republic August 8–15, 1988; New York Review of Books June 30, 1988; September 21, 1995; New York Times Book Review January 20, 1980; August 21, 1988; People November 12, 1979; Publishers Weekly October 15, 1979; July 31, 1995; Rolling Stone March 6, 1980; Times Literary Supplement March 21, 1980; December 2, 1988.

*PAGIS, DAN (October 16, 1930–July 29, 1986), Israeli poet and literary scholar, was born in Raduz, Bukovina (Romania), and emigrated to Israel (then Palestine) in 1946. His father had left Europe for Palestine when Pagis was four years old; that same year his mother died, and he was raised by his grandparents in a secular, German-style cultural environment. At the age of eleven Pagis was imprisoned in a German work camp for four years. Upon arriving in Israel, Pagis met his father again, but they were not reunited. Young Dan lived and studied in kibbutz boarding school. Later he became a member of a kibbutz where he served as a teacher. In 1949, only three years after his first acquaintance with the Hebrew language, Pagis published his first poems in which he established his particular poetic language, a fusion of modern, colloquial Hebrew with classical texts, and introduced his main motifs: personal and universal displacement. In 1956 Pagis lived in Jerusalem, where he studied at the Hebrew University. Awarded a Ph.D. degree, in 1972 he joined the faculty as a professor of Hebrew literature. Pagis was visiting professor at the Jewish Theological Seminary of America in New York; he also lectured at the University of California in San Diego and in Berkeley, and at Harvard. He was married and had two children.

As a literary scholar, Pagis was acclaimed for his research in medieval and Renaissance Hebrew poetry, and was recognized particularly for formulating an ambitious literary theory of Hebrew secular poetry in Spain and for reclaiming the tradition and contribution of the Jewish poetry of Italy and incorporating it into the canon of literary study. His Hebrew scholarly works include Shirat David Rogel (The Poetry of David Vogel, 1966), Shirat Levi Ibn Altabban of Saragossa (The Poetry of Levi Ibn Altabban of Saragossa, 1968), Shirat Ha'hol Ve'torat Ha'shir Le'moshe Ibn Ezra U'vnei Doro (Secular Poetry and Poetic Theory of Moses Ibn Ezra and His Contemporaries, 1970), Hidush U'masoret Be'shirat Ha'hol (Change and Tradition: Hebrew Poetry in Spain and Italy, 1976), Hebrew Love Poetry From Spain, Italy, Turkey and Yemen (in English, 1979) and Al Sod Hatum, (The Literary Riddle, 1986).

Pagis published five volumes of poetry in his life. A sixth appeared posthumously, and in 1991 a volume of his collected poems was published, including some new and unfinished manuscripts. In 1973 he published his only children's book, Ha'beitzh She'hithapsa (The Egg Who Masqueraded), illustrated by the poet himself. In the field of modern Hebrew poetry, Pagis holds a central position both as one of the poets of immigration and survival, as well as one of the leading modernists. He is associated with the poetic revolution of the 1960s, writing a lean, unadorned, and emotionally controlled style of lyrical expression. Robert Alter pointed out, in his introduction to Points of Departure, that Pagis should not be "pigeonholed" as a poet of the Holocaust: "In fact his imaginative landscape extends from the grim vistas of genocide to the luminous horizon of medieval Hebrew poetry in the Iberian peninsula . . . Pagis' own poetry, of course, is necessarily more understated and more controversial than the medieval texts he has studied, but in its distinctively modern idiom it, too, is a self-conscious demonstration and affirmation of what the poetic imagination can do."

Pagis's typical poem consists of a single, relatively short, terse, and often witty stanza, emotionally compact and intense. Several of his major poems, such as Shneim Asar Panim Shel Izmargad ("Twelve Facets of an Emerald") Mo'ach ("Brain"), and Akeivot ("Traces)," are sequences of such stanzas, untitled and enumerated, organized around a theme or a symbol. The predominant mood is somber and dry, often conveying a sophisticated ironic distance, particularly in the poems relating to the Holocaust. Yet there is a range of tonal variation, including humor, playfulness, and a limited measure of sentimentality. Generally, the narrative voice is intellectual and detached, giving the poems an air of almost scientific objectivity, communicating a sense of distance and displacement and a lurking, bitter pessimism. In the later part of his life he wrote short prose-poems and a prose sequence grouped in an unfinished manuscript titled Abba (Father), where the sarcasm gives way to confession, intimacy, and sentiment.

The worldview expressed in Pagis's collected poetry is underlined by the fundamental recognition of the absence of a rational, consistent equilibrium in the human condition and the persistent need to confront the archetypical existence of evil, embodied finally in the inevitability of death. This finality is a given that casts an onerous shadow over human life. The boundaries between life and death, therefore, become obliterated, and the transfer from one state to the other is viewed as technicality which lies in the power of Time.

Time is the dominating motif of this poetry. The hands of the clock, the hourglass, and the dial are central metaphors. "I do not know what might happen in the years gone by, what was already forsaken by the coming moment", he writes in Michtav (Letter, 1964), thus fusing the past with the present and the future into one ominous, meaningless tense. The titles of Pagis's books demonstrate his preoccupation with the various dimensions of this motif.

His first Volume, *Sh'on Ha'Tzel* (Shadow Dial, 1959; distinguished from sundial) established this centrality of time by the metonymy of its title. The poems revolve around related images: the seasons of the year as cycles of burial and as entombments of the past; as symbolic rootless tree; the dominant metaphor of an ever-turning wheel as the representation of life; depiction of people as they are constantly engaged in departures and impossible returns; lost childhood; and death as the determinant of life itself. In *Shir* (Poem), he writes: "Everything which bursts / ripens in its time, / descends and submerges / downward into its primeval bosom; / like a tree which drops / its fruit in the earth of its roots."

The second collection, *She'hut Meucheret* (Late Leisure, 1964), includes poems about mythic and historic heroes such as Robinson Crusoe, William Shakespeare, and the Jewish legendary Honi, who imprisoned himself in an imaginary circle of time and space, imploring God for rain. The fragmentation and eradication of individual identity is another aspect of the time motif expanded in this volume. "Whom did you live until now / And how did you find the strength to unload your foreign self?" he asks in this second collection, *Hevel Ma'tu'ach* ("Tight Rope", 1964), and also: "It is me, am I still alive?" ("Ata Holech"; "You are Going", and reiterated in the title of the poem *"Kvar Hai'ity Beterm Ani"* ("Already I Was Before I Am"). The repeated themes of photographs in the album and pages from a diary are attempts to recapture the self in its various lifecycle stages. At the same time, these images function as disguised and futile exercises in confronting his own missed and abused childhood. He also uses the metaphor of the wheel, the notion of futile reincarnations and the idea of metamorphosis which is indicated by the title of his next collection *Gigul* (Transformation, 1971).

Although the themes seem to be repeated here, the language is less formal. Dialogues are introduced and the poems rely less on images and metaphors. The apocalypse of the Holocaust is central in this volume. The use of dialogue, "distanced and multiple voices," Alter pointed out, "is linked with an impulse to pull apart the basic categories of existence and reassemble them in strange configurations that expose the full depth of the outrage perpetrated. It is as though time and space . . . man and God, self and other, body and soul, had been run through a terrific centrifuge to be weirdly separated out, their positions disconcertingly reversed."

In Pagis's third volume history, evolution, accumulated human knowledge, and the notion of a civilized culture are aspects of the time motif, negating the possibility of a fulfilled or wholesome existence. This is poignantly stylized in the poem *"Ish Ha'me'arot Shotek"* ("The Caveman Is Not About to Talk") in which the narrator imagines his great-grandchildren's children finding his skull, trying to learn about their ancestor. But he is deliberately silent, warm, and calm, as if he was "Never expelled from Mama's cozy womb." The evolution of the self, then, is but another path of horror, since, with the passage of time, one is removed from the unique and singular moment of peace which occurs only prior to birth.

In addition to this expression of universal and existential angst, the irony and the detachment in Pagis's poetry are clearly shields and defenses against the unbearable pain of personal memory. These devices underwent several changes during the poet's career, moving from the hermetic and enigmatic quality of his earlier writings to a certain degree of self-exposure and biographical reference in his later work. The essence of the earlier poems with their use of a distanced narrator, mythic archetypes, and concise language, is encapsulated in "Written in Pencil in the Sealed Railway-Car" included in Lawrence Langer's *Admitting the Holocaust*:

> here in this carload
> i am eve
> with abel my son
> if you see my other son
> cain son of man
> tell him that i
>
> —tr. S. Mitchell

Pagis's universe includes the first family, of which two members are captives in a death train, while the other two, Adam and Cain, are implied to be either victims or murderers. Written as the desperate last act of Eve, the archetypical mother, the message is found by an unidentified survivor—the implied narrator, perhaps—who could be either Adam or Cain. The message is incomplete, possibly because the train stopped before Eve could write her last word. The poem evokes the language of amulets, particularly and ironically the ancient amulets placed under the heads of women at childbirth as a plea for life. The message itself, however, arrives at a dead end: identity, the definition and the existence of the self, is annihilated. The reader is then led to read the poem again in a cyclical movement which establishes the perpetuity of murder and death as the defining characteristic of human existence. The poem's vocabulary is significant: Among the words in this poem (and its title), only three are not biblical or liturgical in origin: *pencil, carload* and *railway*. These are also the longest words, which, ironically, represent achievements of human endeavor since Genesis. Pagis thus implies that humanity improved the means of death by sophisticated technology and multiplied the original crime through greater efficiency. The longest line is the title, containing Jewish liturgical terminology associated with the Jewish New Year and the Day of Atonement. "written and sealed" are from the prayers for life, since, according to Jewish belief, one's future is determined, written, and sealed in heaven on those days.

Gigul also includes the autobiographical sequence *Akevot* ("Traces," or footprints, trails, and remnants), in which Pagis confronts personal memory and eventually comes to terms with the progression rather then the regression of time, and with the acceptance of his own life as an evolutionary process. Shimon Zandbank, a leading Israeli critic, indicated that in these poems Pagis had moved from his earlier focus on fixed and static images in the tradition of Rilke, to dynamic and intellectual symbolism in the tradition of Paul Valery, particularly to the latter's work "Roman d'un cerveau" from which, apparently Pagis drew the title for his next collection.

This fourth volume, *Moach* (Brain, 1975), is marked by the expansion of a theme which was introduced earlier in Pagis's poetry: nonhuman figures such as elephants, mosquitos, flies, petrified creature, and snakes, which inhabit a metaphoric laboratory for the study of evolution, survival, and eternity. Next to the chapter "*Bistiarium*" ("Bestiary") is the group of poems called "*Tikey Hakira*" ("Investigation Files"), centered on the ironic attempt to uncover truth and true identity. These, side-by-side with poems in which he uses the language of physics and scientific inquiry, mark the poetic style of *Moach* as in these lines from "Twelve Faces of the Emerald":

> You will never find the secret of my power.
> I am I: crystallized carbon
> with a very small quantity
> of chromium oxide
>
> — tr. S. Mitchell

Milim Nirdafot (*Synonyms*), published in 1982, introduces Pagis's first direct reaction to the reality of the State of Israel. Here he focuses on the Lebanon War, mastering his powers of irony and sarcasm. Taking a political and ideological stand, he questions the validity of the cultural heritage and the moral value system of the people as they turn, in his view, from victims to victimizers. Though just a small part of the book,

these poems, revealing a political rather than an ideological or detached attitude, brought Pagis more public attention than had his earlier more private and subjective poetry. From the ahistorical beginnings of his first volume, he moved to the reclaiming of personal memory, and finally into confrontation with the present as a historically significant moment.

PRINCIPAL WORKS: *Poetry*—(tr. S. Mitchell) *Points of Departure*, 1981; (tr. S. Mitchell) *Dan Pagis: Selected Poems*, 1972; (tr. S. Mitchell) *T. Carmi and Dan Pagis: Selected Poems*, 1976; (tr. S. Mitchell) *Variable Directions*, 1989. *Essays*— Hebrew Poetry of the Middle Ages and the Renaissance (foreword R. Alter) 1991.

ABOUT: Alter, R.I. *introduction to* Points of Departure, 1981; Rosenthal, M. L. *introduction to* T. Carmi and Dan Pagis: Selected Poems, 1976. *Periodicals*—Hebrew Annual Review 8, 1984; Literature and Theology 7, December 1993; New York Times Book Review November 12, 1989; Prooftexts 10, 1990; Style 22, Spring 1988; Translation Review 32-33, 1990.

*PAMUK, ORHAN (1952–   ), Turkish novelist, was born in Istanbul. Although Pamuk is reticent about the details of his life, he writes: "My family is secular, positivist, and in favor of Westernization. My grandfather became wealthy building railroads, and my grandmother read us the 'atheistic' poems of Tevfik Fikret—the turn of the century utopian individualist Turkish poet, whose earlier poems condemn all aspects of traditional morality in Ottoman institutions, chief among them being religion, and whose subversive verses were read as the credo of new ideals, such as humanism, pragmatism, and the power of reason to transform the world."

Pamuk continues: "In my childhood, I personally observed and lived through the transformation of the traditional Ottman family in the 'modern, West-oriented' bourgeois family when my own family moved from the great house into an apartment building, which I subsequently wrote about in my first novel, *Cevdet Bey and Sons*. My grandfather, my father, and uncle were all civil engineers. After finishing Robert College in Istanbul, I followed in their footsteps by attending the Istanbul University School of Technology to study architecture (1970–1974), but I did not graduate. So that I would have a university degree, I took the course in journalism at the University of Istanbul, but, in fact, all I did in those four years was to live at home with my mother and write *Cevdet Bey*. During the ten years (1972–1982), which were somewhat dark and unhappy, I did nothing but write thousands

ORHAN PAMUK

of pages, none of which I could get published. Then, suddenly, my work began to catch on and to bring, within the Turkish framework, fame and fortune, which was amazing to me."

Pamuk has published five major novels. His massive first novel, *Cevdet Bey ve oğullari* (1982, *Cevdet Bey and Sons*), narrates the three-generation saga of a wealthy Istanbul family. Formally, it employs the strategies and procedures of European realism, along the lines of Thomas Mann's *Buddenbrooks*, but Pamuk's novel is in itself the culmination of the modern Turkish novel, since its antecedents and destination are particularly and peculiarly Turkish. Here is the work of a master fiction writer learning his craft, cutting his teeth on something as colossal as the end of the Ottoman Empire and the onset of the Turkish revolution. The details of the narrative are consonant with a society forging a new consciousness while looking back on the remnants of the rich tapestry of their former lives, abandoned for the sake of modernity and westernization.

Cevdet Bey (whose elder brother was a real Young Turk intent on stirring up political and personal trouble for its own sake) represents the generation of polite, goal-oriented, benign patriarchs who took their responsibility to their extended families seriously while they basked in and insisted on being served with utter devotion. The sons, one of whom goes off to the hinterlands of Anatolia to build a railroad while the other follows in his footsteps to discover the tug of the heartland, consider themselves accountable not only to their family but to the nation.

Yet they must also define themselves as individuals. They use the poet Tevfik Fikret's Anglo-American ideals of individual liberty, enterprise, sense of personal responsibility, dignity, and integrity in their quest for self.

Pamuk's second novel, *Sessiz ev* (1983, *House of Silence*), has been compared with the work of William Faulkner and Virginia Woolf. In its French translation as *La Maison du silence* it won the Prix Medici as the best novel of 1988. Told from five different points of view, it covers a week spent by three upper-class, but deeply disaffected, siblings at their dying grandmother's country house, where their uncle, a dwarf, attends on the old Ottoman lady. The eldest is a corpulent and overindulgent professor of history whose interests lie in the local archives, where he digs up old stories concerning land deeds, legal dissensions, and all sorts of mayhem that now read like found art, or gems he can polish and hold up to the light. The middle grandchild is the sister, whose consciousness is kept repressed (honoring the fictional convention that requires the female to remain mysterious and elusive); she is a university student and involved in leftist causes. The youngest, in his last year at the American prep school in Istanbul, hopes to escape to the United States, where he plans to graduate from an Ivy League university and join the economic power elite on Wall Street.

Their background is filled out by the nonagenarian grandmother, reminiscing to herself about her late physician husband who at the turn of the century had been exiled to this little town by the Young Turk administration for his divergent politics. The old woman hated her husband's reform-minded efforts to write the first Ottoman encyclopedia intended to teach and civilize his countrymen, and, worse, she hated his philandering with the housemaid, which produced two illegitimate sons: first, the dwarf who serves as her majordomo (and as the novel's fourth point of view); the second, a cripple who sells lottery tickets to make a living. The fifth point of view belongs to the crippled uncle's son, a high school dropout with a deep grudge against the well-heeled relatives from Istanbul. He is involved with right-wing terrorist activities and sees himself as doing something momentous which will attract the attention of the world. He first develops a crush on the leftist university coed, stalks her all through the week, and finally approaches her, only to be called a "fascist maniac." In a rage, he beats her to death.

The consciousnesses of the five narrators are forged by the predominant values of their particular circumstances. Set during a particularly dark period in recent Turkish history (1981), when generations and ideologies clashed often physically and violently, *House of Silence* depicts a house where the family members keep quiet but go for each others' throats with their silent internal monologues. It is ultimately a metaphor for Turkey. The silent house is laden with its past and divided against itself: the legitimate and illegitimate. No one achieves individual excellence in Turkey; one can only drown the pain in alcohol, in exile, in nursing grudges, in megalomaniac dreams, and in silence that is akin to death.

Although Pamuk's early work has its roots in modernist novels, his later fiction can be considered postmodernist. His third book, *Beyaz kale* (1985, *The White Castle*), masquerades as a historical novel in which the two protagonists are mirror images of one another, doppelgängers—one of whom is ostensibly Ottoman, the other Venetian—but in fact they serve as a metaphor for the dissolution of one self into another, which is one of Pamuk's major themes. The book has garnered critical acclaim in the West not only because it provides an entry into contemporary Turkish literature, but because it is part of a discourse that transcends national boundaries, ideological underpinnings, and psychological verity, as well as manners and morals; rather, it is concerned with philosophical and aesthetic themes of a timeless, metapersonal literature.

The unnamed Venetian narrator begins by describing how he was captured by Ottoman corsairs, shipped back to Istanbul, and thrown into the dungeons. He avoids a hard time by pretending to be a physician and, after impressing the Pasha who owns him with his medical knowledge, he is saved from prison by being presented as a slave to a royal scholar, called the Hoja (teacher), who, to the narrator's astonishment and horror, resembles him so much that the two are identical—a perception never acknowledged by the Hoja. The two teach other everything that they know: "'Everything' meant all that I'd learned in primary and secondary school; all the astronomy, medicine, engineering, everything that was taught in my country." Then they begin to teach the adolescent Sultan, in an effort to bring enlightenment to the empire by enlightening the sovereign who will one day rule single-handedly. They have only partial success because the only thing that the little Sultan truly desires is for them to build him a war machine which will help conquer an impregnable, shining white castle in Europe called "Doppio." The war machine they build is too encumbered with its own clumsiness to succeed, and the campaign fails. At the end the narrator says that the Hoja, pretending to be the narrator,

goes to Italy to assume the Venetian's identity. The narrator says that he himself, having "become" the Hoja, has stayed on in a little town not too far from Istanbul.

"The passion that steadily drives the tale is intellectual and philosophical," John Updike wrote in the *New Yorker* "concerning the interplay of East and West—of fatalistic faith versus aggressive science—and at a deeper level, the question of identity." Pamuk would certainly agree with Updike on the question of identity, but, in Pamuk's own words, "the critical approaches to my work which unnerve me are concepts like 'East versus West.'" Paul Berman wrote in the *New Republic*: "One of the appeals of Pamuk as a novelist is that he invites this sort of daffy speculation, not explicitly, but by the substance of what he writes. Possible interpretations bubble up spontaneously from his pages. There are novelists who entertain us with their inventiveness and novelists who entertain us with our own inventiveness. Pamuk, with his easy Cartesian cerebralness, manages to do both."

Although his readers may think that the Ottoman and the Venetian are "real" and separate characters, Pamuk makes clear that his Venetian comes from fictions about Venetians. Nor is his Ottoman "real," but an amalgam of popular images of Ottomans. The narrator, neither European nor Asian, is unbounded; his two identities are often indistinguishable, merging into a single one. It is the reader, in the act of reading, who frees the soul from its slavery to a fixed persona, because it is only in reading that one can be "oneself and also another." This is a major theme in Pamuk's work. Behind his fiction there is a wondering adolescent who seeks to resolve the polarities of his imagination, personified in this novel by the charming adolescent Sultan who, although the sovereign of the largest empire in the world, is still capable of being awed and thrilled by the mysteries of the universe.

Only when the characters—both really aspects of the writer—reluctantly reject their own adolescent yearnings to be someone else, or acknowledge their failure to be purely themselves, do they achieve fulfillment. In *The White Castle* one character says of his doppelgänger: "I loved him the way I loved that helpless wretched ghost of my own self I saw in my dreams, as if choking on the shame, rage, sinfulness, and melancholy of that ghost . . . And perhaps most of all I loved him with the stupid revulsion and stupid joy of knowing myself." Jay Parini pointed out, in the *New York Times Book Review*, that one does not read *The White Castle* to find out what life was like in the 17th-century Ottoman Empire. He suggested that the author "places his narrative in a slightly disorienting, dreamlike zone simply to point up the fictional aspect of the narrative."

Kara kitap (1990, *The Black Book*), the most complex of Pamuk's novels, is set in modern-day Istanbul. Pamuk says his interest lay less "in representing life in Istanbul" than in "searching for a 'texture' appropriate to life as it is lived there." In *The Black Book* the influences on Pamuk's fiction of both Western and Eastern cultures are conjoined. It is couched in the conventions of the popular mystery novel, but its subtext is cosmic. In it, a lawyer's wife, who is also his first cousin, vanishes into the maze of Istanbul. Has she left him? Or is she playing a game of hide-and-seek? She may be with her half-brother, the narrator's cousin Jelal, a famous columnist who writes for a popular daily and also seems to be missing. The narrator searches through Istanbul for his lost love, and is thereby lured into mysteries that are as much mystical as they are literary, cultural as well as universal, idealized as well as deceptive. The protagonist's anguish over his absent wife recalls Marcel's despair over the disappearance of Albertine in Proust's *The Sweet Cheat Gone*; there are also echoes of 17th-century mystic poet Sheikh Galip's verse novel (*Love and Beauty*), and other works of Eastern mysticism.

This intricate play of texts and metatexts, the doubling back and forth of identities, makes *The Black Book* Pamuk's most accomplished novel, a success in his homeland as well as abroad where, like *The White Castle*, it has been widely translated. Pamuk's themes are found not only in the postmodernist fiction of the West, but they appear with equal power and intensity in traditional and mystic thought in the East. Playing upon the paradoxes of Sufi mysticism, Pamuk sees the Self as the Ultimate Mystery and the lawyer's quest for his beloved wife as another stage in the Sufi quest for union with God, a process that involves transcending the Self to become Another. If writing is a self-centered occupation, then reading is learning to become Another, that is, the author. "What is reading but acquiring someone else's memory bank?" By the same token, identity is simply a construct of the imagination, and love is a product of literary fictions. Writing fictions is mirroring fictions written by others.

Chapters depicting the search for the lost wife are interspersed with columns ostensibly written by the missing cousin, the celebrated journalist. The lawyer-sleuth traverses the city to find his wife, studying minutely all the signs and significations, and, after holing up in the missing cousin's apartment, he goes through the columnist's entire literary output, totally acquiring the writ-er's memory banks; he even "becomes" the columnist and takes over the column when the real columnist is gunned down by a disgruntled fan. The beloved wife is also finally found in the dead man's company, alas, also killed by a bullet meant for her celebrated brother.

In a world of appearances, surfaces, mirrors, and photographs Pamuk remains skeptical about the ability to "know." Pamuk does not suffer from the anxiety of influence. He cherishes, in fact, imitation, whereby his hero surpasses his boundaries, speaking to his lost wife, his Beatrice who guides the passage of his soul, through a device as vulgar as the mystery novel, into the luminous world of metaphysical fiction:

> I looked in the mirror and read my face. My face was the Rosetta stone I had deciphered in my dream. My face was a broken tombstone . . . My face was a mirror made of skin where the reader beheld himself; we breathed through the pores in unison: the two of us, you and I . . . I was the resourceful and melancholic hero in the book you read; I was the explorer who in the company of his guide who speeds along marble stones, tall columns and dark rocks, climbing stairs that led up the seven heavens replete with stars, toward those condemned to a fretful life underground; I was the hard-boiled detective who calls out to his sweetheart on the other end of the bridge across the abyss, "I am you!"

Terming *The Black Book* an "exercise . . . not for the faint of intellect," Robert Houston in the *New York Times Book Review* commented that it places the reader "in the world of those thousand and one nights in which life is sustained only by the endless telling of story after story plucked from . . . the garden of memory—without which one ceases to exist." But Houston added that the novel "has a political dimension . . . a running commentary on Turkey—Istanbul in particular—and its multiple identities, on its legacy of despotism and rebellion, on its ancient internal battles between East and West, between past and present." Houston thought Pamuk failed in that dimension: "To a visionary, there may well be other Istanbuls behind the quotidian one, but that 'real' city where the book began, with all its supposedly real people, still makes its demands. To the extent that . . . Pamuk ignores those demands, he loses and frustrates his reader, and damages his novel."

In the process of writing *A New Life*, his 1994 novel, Pamuk, master of fictional device, commented, "My basic concern now is language." The book begins with a sentence that resonates with the first sentence of the paragraph from *The Black Book* quoted above: "I read a book one day and my life was completely transformed." The book in *A New Life* is so luminous that it illuminates the reader's face. Here the narrator is the reader of the book. A voice whose source is Dante's *La Vita nuova* (*The New Life*) begins to flow, miraculously, in Turkish, transformed, different, and yet the same. The narrator begins to stay up all night to copy the book in longhand into his own notebook. He falls in love with a girl who had also read the book, loses her even before he can tell her he loves her, and takes off looking for her on dangerously dilapidated buses driven recklessly over treacherous country roads where accidental death is not only contingent, but necessary to maintain the questing spirit, which, as Dante says, "hath its dwelling in the secretest chamber of the heart."

In 1988, Pamuk was a visiting writing fellow at the University of Iowa's International Writing Program, and a visiting scholar at Columbia University where, in his cubicle at the Butler Library, he wrote the first half of *The Black Book*. Today, he lives in Istanbul with his wife, a historian, and their daughter, overlooking a shimmering, expansive view of the Bosporus.

SARA PARETSKY

PRINCIPAL WORKS IN ENGLISH TRANSLATION: *Novels*—Cevdet Bey and Sons; House of Silence; (tr. V. Holbrook) The White Castle, 1990; (tr. Güneli Gün) The Black Book, 1995; A New Life. *Screenplay*—The Hidden Face, 1991.

ABOUT: Contemporary World Writers, 2nd ed., 1993. *Periodicals*—Choice October 1991; Christian Science Monitor April 12, 1991; Library Journal February 15, 1991; New Republic September 9, 1991; New York Times Book Review May 19, 1991; January 15, 1995; New Yorker September 2, 1991; Times Literary Supplement October 12, 1990; World and I June 1991; World Literature Today Winter 1992.

PARETSKY, SARA (June 8, 1947–), American writer of detective stories writes: "Sara Paretsky grew up in eastern Kansas where she attended a two-room country school, playing third base for their baseball team in 1959–1960. Her first published writing, which appeared in the magazine *The American Girl* when she was eleven, told a tale of surviving a tornado with her schoolmates.

"After receiving a B.A. from the University of Kansas in political science, Ms. Paretsky moved to Chicago in 1968. While at the University of Kansas, Ms. Paretsky chaired the first University of Kansas Commission on the Status of Women. The commission study on career decision making by women students was used by the United States Department of Labor in evaluating needs for affirmative action in higher education.

"She got her Ph.D. from the University of Chicago in 1977, writing on 'The Breakdown of Moral Philosophy in New England before the Civil War.' Perceiving a complete lack of academic jobs for historians, Ms. Paretsky bowed to the inevitable, returned to school, and received an M.B.A. from the University of Chicago in 1977.

"After a decade of jobs ranging from bottle washing in a science lab to managing conferences on employment problems, and including several years as a secretary, Ms. Paretsky joined CNA Insurance in 1977. She worked there for nine years as a marketing manager, running advertising and direct mail.

"Since leaving CNA in 1986, Ms. Paretsky has worked full-time as a writer. Her novels, *Indemnity Only, Deadlock, Killing Orders, Bitter Medicine, Blood Shot, Burn Marks,* and *Guardian Angel,* all feature V. I. Warshawski, a woman detective who lives and works in Chicago. Like V. I., Ms. Paretsky has the misfortune to be a fan of the Chicago Cubs. Both women also share an interest in singing. All resemblance ends with those points.

"In 1986 Ms. Paretsky helped found Sisters in Crime, an organization to promote women writers, editors, reviewers, and booksellers in the suspense field. Ms. Paretsky was the organization's first president. It now has over a thousand members in the United States, Canada, Britain, Europe, and Japan.

"In 1976, Ms. Paretsky married Courtenay Wright, professor of physics at the University of Chicago. The two live in a Victorian house on Chicago's southeast side with their faithful golden retriever Cardhu."

She is one of hard-boiled crime fiction's first feminist detectives, and her name—Victoria Iphigenia Warshawski—is evocative of her unique combination of strengths and vulnerabilities. Her first name suggests the 19th-century British monarch whose long reign coincided with dramatic transformations in social life and saw the rise of startling new theories in science, politics, and economics. Her middle name recalls the tragic plight of Agamemnon's daughter (as related by Euripides and other dramatists), who was sacrificed by her father so that he could gain a favorable wind to sail his ships into battle. Married once to a lawyer, she is not divorced, lives alone, and cherishes her privacy and independence. She has a law degree herself (from the University of Chicago), and has worked as a public defender. Her instinct for action and her taste for danger have led her to forsake the law for the life of a private investigator. She doesn't hesitate to carry (and use) a gun when she needs one. A regular jogger and karate adept, she keeps herself in top shape. Her devotion to the Chicago Cubs and classical music is equally fervent. Unlike most fictional detectives, she grows a little older in each novel. She is an ever-developing character.

In her first novel, *Indemnity Only*, Paretsky eschewed original research and put her criminals in a world she already knew well—the insurance industry. In that novel, Warshawski's search for a missing person quickly turns into a murder investigation, in the course of which she has to go up against student radicals, shady insurance agents, and assorted underworld types.

Like most fictional detectives, V. I. Warshawski is both insider and outsider. What separates her from the run-of-the-mill fictional investigator (aside from the fact that she's a woman) is that the bad guys she pursues are not the usual array of psychopaths, terrorists, and low-lifes. Warshawski uses her knowledge as an insider and her perspective as an outsider to attack corporate or institutional crime. In each of her cases, no matter how mundane they appear at the outset, she uncovers some substantial corporate misconduct or an uncomfortably close nexus between corrupt corporate practices and the machinations of organized crime. In Paretsky's second novel, *Deadlock*, Warshawski investigates corruption in the Chicago shipping business. In *Killing Orders*, she discovers a connection between big business, organized crime, and the Catholic Church. *Bitter Medicine* finds the detective on the trail of criminal malpractice at a Chicago hospital.

In a review of *Bitter Medicine* in *Newsweek*, Laura Shapiro wrote, "Paretsky's work does more than turn a genre upside down: her books are beautifully paced and plotted, and the dialogue is fresh and smart. As for V.I. Warshawski, . . . she's the most engaging woman in detective fiction since Dorothy Sayers's Harriet Vane. . . . "

"I don't think in any way you ever avoid being political," Paretsky told Laura Shapiro in a 1988 *Ms.* magazine interview. "Even if you just look at one of those slam-gang murder mysteries, it's political in the sense that people are either buying into certain attitudes toward women or helping to bail out of those attitudes. But I don't want to be on a soapbox as a writer, because I think the quickest way to kill your fiction is to be writing sermons with it." The only daughter of a college professor and a librarian, Paretsky says that she strove for academic and professional achievement as a means of asserting her equality with her brothers. "I grew up in a family where girls became secretaries and wives, and boys became professionals," she told *Ms.* "I wasn't expected to have talents."

Paretsky was actively involved in the abortion rights movement in the early 1970s. In the 1980s she joined the board of the Chicago chapter of the National Abortion Rights Action League. "I think reproductive freedom is the most fundamental freedom," Paretsky told *Ms.* Helping to organize Sisters in Crime in 1986 has been her other major feminist involvement, because of a perceived need. She found that while women wrote almost half of published mysteries, major reviewing venues devoted only about six to thirteen percent of their reviews to mysteries written by women.

Paretsky's efforts as a writer have not gone unrewarded. Most of her novels have been warmly received by critics. In 1985 she won an award from Friends of American Writers for her novel *Deadlock*. *Ms.* magazine named Paretsky one of its Women of the Year for 1987. In 1988 she won a Silver Dagger award form the British Crime Writers Association for her novel *Blood Shot*. In that novel, V. I. Warshawski returns to her old Chicago neighborhood to investigate a chemical magnate responsible for toxic pollution and murder. Reviewing *Blood Shot* in the *New York Times Book Review*, Marilyn Stasio observed: "The author characteristically fuels her sociologically informed mysteries with . . . anger, inviting the reader to share her outrage over corporate America's profit-dictated cynicism toward workers, products and the environment. While splendid, her detective's ethical fulminations are only one side of her firebrand personality. . . . But she does her best and boldest work to date in creating a criminal investigation that is a genuine heroic quest."

V. I. Warshawski's "heroic quest" continues in Paretsky's later novels. In *Burn Marks*, she takes on a most formidable opponent—the Cook County Machine. In *Guardian Angel*, we see Warshawski breaking into offices and sorting through mountains of paper and computer printouts in an effort to penetrate a scheme that includes the manipulation of junk bonds and the looting of a pension fund. The V. I. Warshawski of *Guardian Angel* is nearing forty, and trying not to worry about growing older. *New York Times* reviewer Christopher Lehmann-Haupt found *Guardian Angel* "the richest and most engaging yet of Ms. Paretsky's thrillers." He reserved special praise for Paretsky's detective, "a radical loner who loves to shake up the Establishment. Her greatest appeal . . . is her willingness to defy decorum and raise absolute hell in defense of her outrage."

Not every reviewer has been enthralled by Paretsky's work. In a *Times Literary Supplement* review of *Guardian Angel*, Mary Beard found the novel overlong, "with about as much wit as the average fraud trial itself," and too saturated with local Chicago color. Beard deemed the contrast between V. I. and earlier heroines like Sayers's Harriet Vane "superficial." According to Beard, "V. I. may live in a world that makes Harriet Vane's type of radicalism look quaint; but in the end she is just one more plucky little woman taking on the nasty criminal world of men."

When asked in 1988 whether she planned to continue writing about V. I. Warshawski indefinitely, Paretsky replied, "I certainly want to keep writing about her, but I hope to do some other kinds of books as well." Although she has yet to publish a non–V. I. novel, Paretsky has edited *A Woman's Eye*, a collection of twenty-one mystery stories by Antonia Fraser, Sue Grafton, Amanda Cross, Paretsky herself, and other women writers. Paretsky sold the film right to the V. I. Warshawski character to Tri-Star Pictures in 1985. Although the 1991 film *V. I. Warshawski* starring Kathleen Turner, was not a critical or popular success, selling the film rights allowed Paretsky the freedom to pursue writing full-time.

In an overview of Paretsky's work in *Artforum*, Alice Yaeger Kaplan wrote, "V. I. Warshawski is a vital new addition to feminist fiction." Kaplan lauds Warshawski for the types of cases she takes and for her derring-do in the violent inner city. She concludes: "Paretsky is writing novels where a woman claims her right to the city, her right to her body, her right to feel. Fiction isn't all that's at stake."

PRINCIPAL WORKS: *Novels*—Indemnity Only, 1982; Deadlock, 1984; Killing Orders, 1985; Bitter Medicine, 1987; Blood Shot, 1988 (in U.K.: Toxic Shock); Burn Marks, 1990; Guardian Angel, 1992; Tunnel Vision, 1994. *As editor*—A Woman's Eye, 1991.

ABOUT: Contemporary Authors 125, 1989; 129, 1990; Current Biography Yearbook 1992. *Periodicals*—Artforum January 1990; Ms. January 1988; New York Times January 27, 1992; New York Times Book Review October 9, 1988; Newsweek July 13, 1987; Times Literary Supplement June 5, 1992.

PARINI, JAY (LEE) (April 2, 1948–), American novelist, biographer, poet and critic, writes: "I was born in a small town near Scranton, Pennsylvania. When I was four, I moved to Scranton itself, where my mother had grown up and where my maternal grandparents still lived. I went to the same little elementary school that my mother had attended.

"My grandparents on my father's side were Italian immigrants, and my grandfather was 'a character.' He was basically a gambler, though he dabbled in other forms of corruption. My maternal grandfather was a repairman for the telephone company. Neither of my parents finished high school, but my father did manage to get a high school diploma and become an insurance salesman for Prudential and, later, an ordained Baptist minister. (His conversion to fundamentalist Christianity was a big event of my early childhood.) I grew up listening to my father read the King James Version aloud: my first genuine literary experience. I also listened to my mother's wonderful family stories: she was born a storyteller.

"I decided to become a poet when, in the ninth grade, I first read Robert Frost. I also wrote stories and read such writers as Poe, Dickens, and Sir Walter Scott. At Lafayette College, where I entered as a freshman in 1966, I had to work especially hard to overcome rather poor high school training. It wasn't until my junior year abroad at the University of St. Andrews in Scotland that I really 'found' myself as a student of literature. I met a young don there, Tony Ashe, who inspired me and encouraged me immensely.

"Returning to Lafayette for my senior year, I was taken under the wing of James Lusardi, an English professor. He read my poems with amazingly close attention, and I leaped forward as a writer. I returned to St. Andrews for graduate studies, finishing a B.Phil. in 1973 with a thesis on [Gerard Manley] Hopkins and the poetry of meditation. I then wrote a doctoral thesis on Theodore Roethke that was eventually pub-

JAY PARINI

lished as *Theodore Roethke: An American Romantic*. It was during these years—1968–1975—that I found my 'voice,' which derived from Hopkins, Yeats, Eliot, Frost, and such contemporaries as Roethke, Heaney, and others. I favored, and still favor, a poetry that is alliterative, musical, physical (i.e., image-centered), and meditative. I am essentially an Emersonian, reading nature as a symbol of the spirit.

"My first book of poems was *Singing in Time*, an apprentice volume published by a small Scottish press. But my first 'real' book was *Anthracite Country*, which Random House published in 1982. Those autobiographical, anecdotal, and highly lyrical poems still seem very true and good to me. I always love to read them aloud.

"I taught at Dartmouth College from 1975 to 1982, and these were important years for me—personally and as a developing writer. I came under the influence of my friend and Vermont neighbor, Robert Penn Warren, who made a huge impact on my notions of what a poem looked like. I also used Warren as a model of the poet-novelist-critic that I wanted to become.

"I began writing novels at Dartmouth, publishing an immature first novel called *The Love Run* in 1980. A better novel was *The Patch Boys*, in which I return to the anthracite region of my boyhood in a novel that's told in the first person by a narrator who is, in spirit, much like my adolescent self. That novel is set in 1925, and it has its origins in my father's younger days on the banks of the Susquehanna River.

"In 1981 I married Devon Jersild, herself a writer, and we have had two children: Will

(born in 1982) and Oliver (born in 1985). Devon and I moved to Middlebury, in Vermont, in 1982, where I took a job at Middlebury College.

"The poems that came after *Anthracite Country* were less what might be called image-centered lyrics and more in a 'philosophical' or meditative vein. I found my voice opening up, the lines becoming more flexible, the music more inward. The volume that resulted from these years was *Town Life*, which concludes with a sequence of essayistic, meditative poems of medium length (3–4 pages). These poems reflect my experience of fatherhood and marriage and record my impressions of living within small communities in New England and Italy (where I spent stretches of time during these years).

"During 1986 I spent six months in Amalfi, in southern Italy. There I met Gore Vidal, the novelist and essayist, who became a friend. (I have edited a volume of essays on his work: *Gore Vidal: Writer Against the Grain*.) Vidal's interest in history spurred my own, and I wrote *The Last Station* between 1986 and 1989. This novel meditates on the last years in the life of Leo Tolstoy, and it is told from six different viewpoints. I loved writing this book, and I think it shows. The book has a curious effect: calm, idiosyncratic, obsessive. I often call it my 'cubist novel' because of the kaleidoscopic effect of the various narrators and the cutting back and forth in time.

"My fourth novel, *Bay of Arrows*, follows the lives of Christopher Columbus and his 20th-century dharma-heir: Christopher Genovese, a middle-aged professor at a small Vermont college. This satiric novel alternates between the 15th and 20th centuries, finding parallels, echoes, resemblances. Though largely an academic novel in the tradition of Kingsley Amis and David Lodge, there is a touch of Daniel Defoe in the second half of the novel, which takes place in the Dominican Republic. The book was written very quickly, with a lot of energy and concentration. I think the feverish quality of its writing is reflected in the prose, which is more 'crackling' on the surface than *The Last Station*.

"I move moving from form to form, writing poetry and fiction in my best hours, which are usually the morning hours. In the afternoons and evenings, when I feel the urge, I write essays and reviews—mostly as a way of clarifying my thoughts on various aspects of contemporary culture or politics. I have also, in the past year [1992], put a lot of time into editing *The Columbia History of American Poetry* and its sister volume, *The Columbia Anthology of American Poetry*. I look ahead to more poems, more novels, and whatever else happens to light my mind for a period of days, weeks, or months."

Jay Parini's parents, Leo J. Parini and Verna Ruth (Clifford) Parini, though both from the Scranton area, were from strikingly dissimilar ethnic backgrounds. His father came from a family of Italian immigrants; his mother, of English descent, was raised among working-class WASPs. As a child, Parini recalls feeling "tugged (not torn) between two worlds," and attributes his own sensitivity to issues of class to his lower-middle-class Scranton upbringing. At Lafayette College, where he toyed briefly with the idea of a career in law or politics, his worldview underwent a substantial transformation. The boy who had led a pro-Vietnam War rally in high school became an active opponent of the war, a conversion effected in part by a Noam Chomsky essay he read in *Ramparts*.

Parini's sensitivity to class distinctions is evident in his first novel, *The Love Run*, in which an ardent but rather doltish working-class youth kidnaps a wealthy and beautiful Dartmouth coed and tries to convince her to marry him. While the union is clearly an ill-fated one, it does cause the coed to sever her ties with her stolid Dartmouth boyfriend. From start to finish, the novel is a ruthless lampoon of a shallow, status-obsessed college community. *The Love Run* was poorly received and was at least partly responsible for Parini's failure to earn tenure at Dartmouth. In an interview with *Publishers Weekly*, he characterized the atmosphere there in the late 1970s as "right-wing, smelly, snobby, deeply anti-intellectual and misogynistic."

The poems in *Anthracite Country* display an assortment of poetic tastes and influences, from Roman lyric poetry to European and American poetry of the 19th and 20th centuries. In a prologue, "The Sabine Farm," he invokes the memory of the Roman lyric poet Horace; in so doing, he compares the modern poets of New England to Horace on his Sabine farm and draws an extended analogy between the tilling of farmland and the cultivation of a poetic landscape: "My friend, we follow in the Roman colter's / wake in our own ways, not really farmers, / but poachers on the farm Maecenas / granted." In later poems, about the coal mines of northeastern Pennsylvania, he compares the excavation of rock to the process of digging up and recovering memory. In the title poem, "Anthracite Country," he writes: "Rich earthwound, glimmering / rubble of an age when men / dug marrow from the land's dark spine, / it resists all healing. / Its luminous hump cries comfortable pain.

Reviews of *Anthracite Country* were consistently favorable. "In Jay Parini America has a poet whose impulses are classical, while his matter is immediate and personal," Anne Stevenson wrote in the *Times Literary Supplement*. Detecting the strong influence of the Irish poet Seamus Heaney (particularly his *Death of a Naturalist*), Stevenson concluded that Parini had not yet found his own voice. "If he goes on to develop his own voice—a voice which begins to emerge in *Anthracite Country*—he may well lead a number of potentially 'classical' poets out of the wilderness," she wrote.

In the *Yale Review* Louis Martz, on the other hand, concluded his notice of *Anthracite Country*: "But these masters are absorbed: Parini has achieved his own voice." Martz was particularly impressed by Parini's poems of childhood, such as "Playing in the Mines," which, he noted, "develops the memory of a childhood fear into a rich complex of implications and ambiguities." That poem reads, in part, "Never go down there, fathers told you, / over and over. The hexing cross / nailed onto the door read DANGER, DANGER."

The Patch Boys, Parini's second novel, tells of the coming of age of Sammy di Contini in 1925 in a coal-mining town. James D. Bloom, in the *New York Times Book Review* (1986), noted that *The Patch Boys* "covers the familiar working-class territory explored by Henry Roth, James T. Farrell and . . . others. . . . Parini evokes creditably an ethnic coming-of-age." Frank Perry, in *Voice of Youth Advocates*, wrote, "Sammy's handling of his troubles and his acceptance of Vincenzo as big brother and union leader of this 1925 Pennsylvania mine town elevate this novel . . . above typical coming-of-age stories."

In an essay published in *Christian Century* not long before the appearance of *Town Life*, his third collection of poetry, Parini compares the act of writing poetry to prayer and notes that both can result in "what Christians call grace." His conclusions are distinctly Emersonian: "Grace is a relation, a point of contact between God and the human mind which is realized only through the direct mental and emotional actions of meditation (whether in prayer or writing). . . . The poet's whole being is focused, in the act of composition, on the concrete reality of the poem. Likewise, in prayer or meditation, the whole of the person is brought into focus on the divine realities."

In a review of *Town Life* in the *Christian Science Monitor*, Thomas D'Evelyn noted: "At a time when poetry dithers at the margins of the arcane or the trivial, Jay Parini hits the mark. In doing so, he shatters some critical categories such as modernism and postmodernism." Another laudatory review came from W.C. Hamlin in *Choice*, who wrote, "Overall, the poems offer a marvelous diversity of imagery and form and attest greatly to the illusion of artlessness and freedom born of total control."

D'Evelyn singled out the poem "At the Ice Cream Parlor." "Study the poem and it will just be there for you, like your own room when you turn the lights on," D'Evelyn wrote. In the concluding stanza, the narrator declares, "I'm happy to believe that every object / may well have the chance to change its name, / to clarify its essence and become / more like itself than nature will allow / in these rough drafts, these early versions / of that fabled state, the life to come.

The Last Station, Parini's novel about the last days of the novelist and moral philosopher Leo Tolstoy, is set on Tolstoy's estate, Yasnaya Polyana, where a great number of his followers had gathered to dedicate themselves to poverty, chastity, and simplicity. The estate became the site of a ferocious power struggle, most notably between Vladimir Chertkov, Tolstoy's principal disciple, and Sofya Andreyevna, Tolstoy's wife, who wanted to maintain control over the valuable copyrights on her husband's work.

While in Naples in the mid-1980s, Parini discovered a memoir by Valentin Bulgakov, Tolstoy's last personal secretary, and realized that virtually all of the members of Tolstoy's inner circle had kept diaries. As he told *Publishers Weekly*: "I said to myself, 'Omigod—everybody was keeping diaries and recording the last year in Tolstoy's life!' His last year struck me as an ideal vehicle for exploring the thing that I'm most interested in: the radical subjectivity of experience, and the impossibility of arriving at anything like objective truth." He thus tells the story of Tolstoy's last year in "cubist" fasion, incorporating the points of view of six of the diarists. Parini's own voice emerges clearly only in the short poems he intersperses throughout the text.

The Last Station was acclaimed by reviewers. In the *New York Times Book Review*, Miranda Seymour characterized it as "one of those rare works of fiction that manage to demonstrate both scrupulous historical research and true originality of voice and perception." In the *Times Literary Supplement*, John Bayley noted: "*The Last Station* is an unexpectedly successful and subtle masterpiece which, as used to be said of Pushkin, may at first seem simple and banal but comes to reveal an ever-deeper distinction and *warmth* of meaning." Comparing Parini's novel favorably to such works as *The Good Soldier* and *The Alexandria Quartet*, *Nation* reviewer David Kaufman wrote, "*The Last Station* becomes an ideal vehicle for pursuing the modernists' obsession with perspective, and for demonstrating

that truth is addressable only as a multifacted phenomenon."

By contrast, Parini's fourth novel, *Bay of Arrows*, was something of a critical failure. *New York Times* reviewer Michiko Kakutani called the novel's protagonist, Christopher Genovese, "one of the more irritating fictional characters to come along in a long time." According to Kakutani, the novel fails as satire because the analogy between Christopher Genovese and Christopher Columbus "never comes off."

In addition to his steady output of poetry and novels, Parini is a prolific writer of short critical essays and magazine pieces. These have appeared in periodicals as diverse as *Interview*, *Mother Jones, Horizon*, and the *Hudson Review*.

PRINCIPAL WORKS: *Poetry*—Singing in Time, 1972; Anthracite Country, 1982; Town Life, 1988. *Novels*—The Love Run, 1980; The Patch Boys, 1986; The Last Station, 1990; Bay of Arrows, 1992. *Criticism*—Theodore Roethke: An American Romantic, 1979. *Textbook*—An Invitation to Poetry, 1987. *Biography*—John Steinbeck, 1995. *As Editor*—(with R. Pack and S. Lea) The Bread Loaf Anthology of Contemporary Poetry, 1986; (with R. Pack) The Bread Loaf Anthology of Contemporary Short Stories, 1987; (with R. Pack) The Bread Loaf Anthology of Contemporary Essays, 1989; (with R. Pack) Writers on Writing, 1991; (with R. Pack) Gore Vidal: Writer Against the Grain, 1992; (with R. Pack) Poems for a Small Planet: Contemporary American Nature Poetry, 1993; The Columbia History of American Poetry, 1993; (with R. Pack) American Identities, 1994.

ABOUT: Contemporary Authors 97–100, 1981; Contemporary Authors Autobiography Series 16, 1992; Contemporary Literary Criticism 54, 1989. *Periodicals*—Choice May 1988; Christian Century September 30, 1987; Christian Science Monitor February 17, 1988; Nation June 18, 1990; New York Times August 28, 1992; New York Times Book Review December 28, 1986; July 22, 1990; September 20, 1992; Publishers Weekly July 20, 1990; Sewanee Review Summer 1983; Times Literary Supplement August 27, 1982; December 28, 1990–January 3, 1991; Voice of Youth Advocates December 1986; Yale Review October 1982.

PARKER, ROBERT B(ROWN) (September 17, 1932–), American detective novelist, was born in Springfield, Massachusetts, the son of Carroll Snow Parker, a telephone company executive, and Mary Pauline (Murphy) Parker. He received his B.A. from Colby College in Waterville, Maine, in 1954, after which he served for two years with the U.S. Army in Korea. In 1957 he received an M.A. in literature from Boston University. Between 1957 and 1962, Parker was a technical writer for Raytheon Company, an

ROBERT B. PARKER

advertising writer for the Prudential Insurance Company, and a partner in his own advertising firm, Parker-Farman Company.

Parker began his sixteen-year academic career in 1962, when he became a lecturer in English at Boston University, and went on to teach at other colleges. He joined the faculty of Northeastern University in Boston as an assistant professor in 1968, rising to the position of full professor in 1976. Parker earned his Ph.D. in literature from Boston University in 1971. He claims to have written his dissertation, "The Violent Hero, Wilderness Heritage and Urban Reality: A Study of the Private Eye in the Novels of Dashiell Hammett, Raymond Chandler, and Ross Macdonald," in just two weeks. Discussing the thesis with Amanda Smith of *Publishers Weekly* in 1988, Parker remarked, "It went directly from my typewriter to microfilm unseen by the human eye."

Despite his denigration of the thesis and his many derisive comments regarding the academic profession, Parker clearly felt that his advanced degrees enhanced his work as a novelist. He did not enjoy teaching, however. In 1979, when he was sure that he could earn a living as a full-time writer (he'd already published five Spenser novels and a number of other books), he left teaching for good.

Parker began writing his first novel, *The Godwulf Manuscript*, soon after receiving his Ph.D. The novel introduces Spenser (he is never given a first name), a tall, burly, Boston-based private eye. An ex-policeman, ex-boxer, and bona fide gun-toting tough guy, Spenser is also a gourmet

cook, an amateur sculptor, and a reader of serious literature whose speech is sometimes larded with literary allusions. Like Chandler's detective Marlowe, Parker's Spenser is itself an allusion; the English poet Edmund Spenser's greatest work, *The Faerie Queene*, is an allegorical epic poem which examines knightly codes of honor and the meaning of moral virtue—focal concerns for Spenser the detective.

In *The Godwulf Manuscript*, Spenser is hired by a local university to investigate the disappearance of a priceless 14th-century illuminated manuscript. What at first appears to be a case of simple theft is revealed to be at the center of a complex web of crimes, including murder and extortion. Perhaps a reflection of Parker's distaste for academia, the villain is a scrawny, demented professor of medieval literature.

In *Sons of Sam Spade*, David Geherin notes the "striking similarities" between *The Godwulf Manuscript* and the novels of Hammett, Chandler, and Macdonald. "What is surprising, however," Geherin writes, "is the extent to which he has managed to stake out for himself an original claim to the territory already overrun by would-be successors to the three earlier masters of the hard-boiled detective novel."

Parker has aknowledged his debt to Chandler and the extent to which Spenser was based on Marlowe. In a 1991 interview, Parker told Joseph A. Cincotti of the *New York Times Book Review*: "Originally, Spenser came out to be the second coming of Philip Marlowe, and in the early books I made every effort to write just like Raymond Chandler. . . . The degree to which those early books are different is the degree to which I failed in my attempt."

In Parker's second novel, *God Save the Child*, Spenser's search for a missing boy leads him to a drug ring. It is the first of several novels (*Early Autumn* and *Ceremony* are others) which highlight a special concern of Spenser's: care and protection of the most vulnerable of innocent victims—children.

In *Mortal Stakes*, Spenser is hired by the Boston Red Sox to investigate their star pitcher, who is suspected of being involved with gambling. Although he finds that the pitcher is involved with illegal gambling, Spenser opts to save the man and his wife from a vicious blackmailer. He is forced to deal here with a morally complex situation, in which the distinction between right and wrong is not always the same as the distinction between legal and illegal. *Mortal Stakes* is the first novel in which Spenser's love interest, Susan Silverman, figures prominently. In subsequent novels, Spenser's relationship with this intelligent and independent woman is explored in ever greater depth. Unlike most other detectives in hard-boiled fiction, whose love lives are peripheral (if they exist at all), Spenser's ongoing relationship with Susan Silverman is an integral aspect of many of the novels. Peter Gorner suggested in a 1982 *Chicago Tribune* profile that Parker used his wife as a model for Susan. Parker has tended to agree with that assessment.

Parker's fourth novel, *Promised Land*, which finds Spenser in search of the kidnapped wife of a wealthy builder, won an Edgar Allan Poe Award. Although it was Parker's first novel to gain widespread public attention, it was not a favorite among all critics. In *Sons of Sam Spade*, Geherin commented: " . . . despite the acclaim it must be admitted that the novel is something of a disappointment, and its failures are in areas that, ironically, were responsible for the success of the first three novels. Parker's strength has never been in his plotting, and the shaky plot of *Promised Land* confirms this." On the other hand, Geherin does go on to praise Parker's incorporation of "personal drama, psychological insight, and social commentary into a serious exploration of contemporary American values."

In addition to being the first Spenser novel with an international setting, *The Judas Goat* marks the beginning of Spenser's collaboration with Hawk, a taciturn, muscular black man whose absolute allegiance to Spenser is far greater than his allegiance to the law. In *Promised Land*, Hawk appears as the hit man who is hired to kill Spenser, but refuses. Although as a team the two men work synergistically, Hawk is, in many respects, the antithesis of Spenser. In their book *Private Eyes: One Hundred and One Knights, A Survey of American Detective Fiction*, Robert A. Baker and Michael T. Nietzel write: "Parker has been criticized for Hawk, who some see as a subtly racist creation, made to do the dirty work which Spenser avoids. Parker maintains that Hawk represents an archetypal pattern in American myths—the dark companion of the white hero, Jim and Huck Finn, Tonto and the Lone Ranger. . . . However, the ultimate reason for Hawk's creation is that he illuminates and elevates Spenser. Hawk is in every way the opposite of Susan except for one quality—they both like Spenser. Hawk and Susan represent the extremes of Spenser's personality and . . . they help establish Spenser as the larger-than-life hero Parker intends him to be."

Spenser's tender side, especially toward women and children, is never far from view. In the novel *Early Autumn*, Spenser takes care of a fifteen-year-old boy whose parents are engaged in a furious custody battle. Reviewing the novel in

the *New York Times*, Anatole Broyard observed that "the private eye has come a long way from the dissolute days when he was a hell-raising, hard-drinking womanizer with a license to carry a gun. . . . In spite of Spenser's baby-sitting, he's a pretty rough customer and *Early Autumn* mixes violence and compassion in a better-than-average way."

Parker's skillful pairing of "violence and compassion" in the character of Spenser is a purposeful attempt to create a new kind of hard-boiled hero. In his interview with *Publishers Weekly*, Parker said of Spenser: "He's the evolutionary descendant of the frontier hero, who is an evolutionary descendant of the chivalric hero. . . . What makes him interesting is the struggle for his autonomy; for Spenser, it's a continuing struggle. Part of the reason he has to struggle is that he has allowed himself to be in love and to care. The struggle between care and commitment and autonomy lends tension to the form."

In *The Widening Gyre* (the title is from Yeats's poem "The Second Coming"), the character of Susan Silverman is given an added dimension as she embarks on a new career, returning to Harvard to get her Ph.D. in psychology. In *Playmates*, Parker again turns his attention to corruption in sports, and Spenser investigates a point-shaving scandal involving a Boston area college basketball team. In the *New York Times Book Review* in 1989, R.W.B. Lewis observed: "Robert B. Parker established such an elevated standard with his first four novels, through *Promised Land* in 1976, that it would have been virtually impossible to keep it up. The level was impressively high, though, through five or six more titles, by which time it was clear that we were witnessing one of the great series in the history of the American detective story. But then, in the opinion of some, a decline set in. *A Catskill Eagle* in 1985 was an overlong chase-and-rescue story with a double-digit body count and Susan Silverman as the temporarily willful damsel in distress. . . . *Crimson Joy* barely escaped the banal. The striking recovery of power in *Playmates* is all the more a matter for wonder and rejoicing."

In *Poodle Springs*, Parker collaborated with a deceased mentor. From "The Poodle Springs Story," a fragment of a novel left unfinished by Raymond Chandler at the time of his death, Parker picked up the story as the voice of Philip Marlowe. Before his death, Chandler had married Marlowe off, and moved him out of his natural habitat in Los Angeles and into Palm Springs. Because he finds the town to be a nearly endless parade of sybaritic women walking well-manicured dogs, Marlowe contemptuously refers to the place as "Poodle Springs." Assessing Parker's contribution, Lloyd Rose wrote in the *Atlantic*: "His setting is no longer a cramped, chilly eastern city but a spacious, hot place. . . . Like Chandler's finest work, *Poodle Springs* has a haunted quality that comes from somewhere beyond the plot, a sense of things gone fundamentally wrong. . . . *Poodle Springs* is a novel in its own right—Chandler's vision carried further than he carried it, and not betrayed but realized." Ed McBain, in the *New York Times Book Review* (1989), agreed: "At his very best, Mr. Parker sounds more like Chandler than Chandler himself—but with an edge the master had begun to lose in the waning days of his life."

Parker paid further homage to his mentor in *Perchance to Dream: Robert B. Parker's Sequel to Raymond Chandler's The Big Sleep.* "Parker starts strongly," Martin Amis wrote in the *New York Times Book Review*, "and for a while *Perchance to Dream* trundles along with more uncomplicated thrust than Chandler ever cared to generate. . . . But the denouement is a chaos of tawdry short cuts," with a Marlowe who grins and preens and jollies things along. This guy talks too much," Amis concluded.

Spenser has not aged appreciably since the mid-1970s, but his cases and concerns do reflect a changing American social reality. In *Double Deuce* (1992) Spenser investigates a conflict between rival gangs in a Boston housing project. Loren D. Estleman, in the *New York Times Book Review*, faulted Parker's attempt to replicate black street dialect, but found *Double Deuce* to be "a lean welterweight of a book. . . . The prose is taut, the language spare and to the point."

"I don't know any crooks or wiseguys," Parker told the *New York Times Book Review* in July 1991. "I don't know anything about fingerprinting or ballistics or any of that stuff, and if you're any good you can fake most of that. I don't do research." Parker eschews extensive rewriting and revision as well. In an essay written with Anne Ponder for Robin Winks's collection *Colloquium on Crime*, Parker described his method. "My books are seldom edited. . . . I don't believe that editing produces fiction; it only improves it. My artistic judgement is finished when the last pages leave my typewriter."

In *Colloquium on Crime*, Parker wrote: "Crime and its solution or even crime and punishment are not the central issues. Spenser is more and more interested in matters of the human behavior (such as honor and love) and steadily less interested in the conventional metier of detective fiction. In each book there is

some matter of mortal significance and that is what justifies what might be considered ethically realistic behavior patterns on Spenser's part."

With *All Our Yesterdays*, published in 1994, Parker may be said to have redeemed himself from the charge of being a weak plotter. Not a Spenser novel, *All Our Yesterdays* intertwines the stories of two families for three generations, beginning with the love affair of Conn Sheridan, wounded in 1920 in the Irish Troubles, and the married American Hadley Winslow, who nurses him back to health. Conn later enters a loveless marriage in America, as does his son. The last Sheridan, Chris, is destined, however, as his father wishes, to break the chain: "Be something decent. Have some land. Dogs." Christopher Lehmann-Haupt wrote in the *New York Times* that "despite [its] dark cynicism," this novel of "blasted lives ends on a note of uplift . . . short of being romantically sentimental" but which gives "the reader the savor of a happy, hopeful ending."

Outside the novel, *Three Weeks in Spring* has been Parker's most noteworthy and popular book. Written with his wife, Joan (Hall) Parker, the book recounts her ordeal with breast cancer, from which she eventually made a full recovery. The Parkers were married in 1956. They have two sons and live in Cambridge, Massachusetts.

Parker's books have spawned a number of spin-offs, the most notable of which is the television series "Spenser: For Hire," which ran during the mid-1980s. Outside the United States, Parker's work is most popular in Japan, where a line of men's cosmetics, Spenser's Tactics, has appeared. Film rights to many of the novels have been sold.

PRINCIPAL WORKS: *Novels*—(Those marked with an asterisk (°) are not part of the "Spenser" series.) God Save the Child, 1974; The Godwulf Manuscript, 1974; Mortal Stakes, 1975; Promised Land, 1976; The Judas Goat, 1978; °Wilderness, 1979; Looking for Rachel Wallace, 1980; Early Autumn, 1981; A Savage Place, 1981; Ceremony, 1982; °Love and Glory, 1983; The Widening Gyre, 1983; Valediction, 1984; A Catskill Eagle, 1985; Taming a Sea-Horse, 1986; Pale Kings and Princes, 1987; Crimson Joy, 1988; Playmates, 1989; The Early Spenser: Three Complete Novels: The Godwulf Manuscript, God Save the Child, Mortal Stakes, 1989; (with R. Chandler) °Poodle Springs, 1989; Stardust, 1990; Pastime, 1991; °Perchance to Dream: Robert B. Parker's Sequel to Raymond Chandler's The Big Sleep, 1991; Double Deuce, 1992; Paper Doll, 1993; Walking Shadow, 1994; °All Our Yesterdays, 1994. *Short story*—Surrogate: A Spenser Short Story, 1982. *Nonfiction*—The Violent Hero, Wilderness Heritage and Urban Reality: A Study of the Private Eye in the Novels of Dashiell Hammett, Raymond Chandler, and Ross Macdonald (Ph.D. dissertation) 1970; (with others) The Personal Response to

Literature, 1970; (with P. Sandberg) Order and Diversity: The Craft of Prose, 1973; (with J. Marsh) Sports Illustrated Weight Training, 1974, rev. ed. 1990; (with Joan Parker) Three Weeks in Spring, 1978; Mature Advertising: A Handbook of Effectiveness in Print, 1981; The Private Eye in Hammett and Chandler, 1984; Parker on Writing, 1985; (with J. Parker and W. Strode) A Year at the Races, 1990.

ABOUT: Baker, R. and Nietzel, M. Private Eyes: One Hundred and One Knights, A Survey of American Detective Fiction, 1922–1984, 1985; Contemporary Authors New Revision Series 26, 1989; Contemporary Literary Criticism 27, 1984; Current Biography Yearbook 1993; Geherin, David Sons of Sam Spade: The Private Eye Novel in the 70s, 1980; Twentieth Century Crime and Mystery Writers, 2d. ed., 1985; Who's Who in America 1990–1991; Winks, Robin (ed.) Colloquium on Crime: Eleven Renowned Mystery Writers Discuss Their Work, 1986. *Periodicals*—Atlantic October 1989; Chicago Tribune August 30, 1982; New York Times January 21, 1981; November 3, 1994; New York Times Book Review April 23, 1989; October 15, 1989; January 27, 1991; July 28, 1991; May 31, 1992; Publishers Weekly July 8, 1988.

PARKS, GORDON (November 30, 1912–   ), American photographer, film director, writer, and composer, was born in Fort Scott, Kansas, the youngest of the fifteen children of Sarah Ross Parks and Andrew Jackson Parks, a tenant farmer. The author has described in several memoirs the rage he felt at growing up black and poor in rural America as well as the many pleasures he shared with his family during his earliest years. His parents' "love and common sense," he states in Voices in the Mirror, "thwarted fate's attempt to wipe me out." Giving special credit to his strong-minded Methodist mother, he recalls her reminding him, after he had been taunted by some white boys, that only a minority of whites hated blacks. "And those that do are in such bad trouble with themselves they need pitying." He has also recalled an older brother stopping him from committing an act of violence by suggesting that if he was "going to fight the world," he should fight it with his brain, not his fists.

Following Parks's mother's death when he was fifteen, he was sent to Minnesota to live with an older sister, but within a few months his brother-in-law threw him out on the streets to fend for himself. Working at first as a weekend dishwasher, often sleeping in trolley cars while finding shelter in a pool hall by day, Parks was eventually reunited with his family in St. Paul, but this phase of his life did not last long. Having become "devoted to [his] restlessness" and feeling an "intense fear of failure" and a need to explore all possibilities ("every tool shop of my mind," as he put it), he soon returned to his nomad existence. For a time, while still attending high school, he took a menial job in a prestigious club in St. Paul where he had "the opportunity to observe what success was supposed to be, and to learn the rules I needed to know if I waned to claim success." He began to read more but soon afterwards, as a result of the depression, he lost his job, quit high school, and found work as a piano player in a brothel, where for a time he composed love songs and learned to play the trumpet.

Anxious to explore other possibilities, and "desperate to get out of St. Paul," he hopped a freight car to Chicago where he worked briefly as a janitor in a flophouse. The experience was not a happy one, and Parks was grateful when a relative helped him return to St. Paul where he took a low-level job in a hotel dining room. A white bandleader heard him play one of his songs on the hotel piano and offered him a job as a vocalist and composer in his band, which was traveling east to Harlem. When this band broke up in Harlem in 1933, Parks joined the Civilian Conservation Corps. That same year he married Sally Alvis, a young woman from St. Paul.

Waiting for his first child to be born, Parks remembered that "I was overjoyed, even though I wasn't yet prepared for fatherly responsibilities. I was still growing, still galloping about chasing things." By this time he was living with his in-laws in St. Paul, while working as a waiter at the Curtis Hotel and trying to promote his songwriting. After his first child was born he got a job as a waiter on a railroad line that ran between St. Paul, Chicago, and Seattle. Observing on this run "how the rich lived," he made an effort to overcome his wife's growing discontent with his wandering ways by buying her an expensive coat. "She looked gorgeous in it. . . . But I was just trying to keep our marriage from falling apart."

While working on the railroad Parks became interested in photography. In magazines he found on the train he came across photographs of migrant workers which impressed him. A newsreel he saw in a Chicago movie house, lauding the cameraman's achievement, further fueled his decision to become a photographer; thereafter, during layovers in Chicago, he began visiting the Art Institute to study paintings of Monet, Renoir, and Manet. He bought his first camera at a pawnshop for $7.50 (calling it his "weapon against poverty and racism"), but soon afterwards was fired from his job after a violent quarrel with the dining car steward. More bad news awaited him when he returned to St. Paul. His wife had left him, and though they were subsequently reunited, the same strains that had led to the first separation were to resurface later, and in 1961 to end in divorce.

The years between 1938 and 1961 increasingly brought Parks the success he had set his heart on. In 1938 he had his first photography exhibit in the window of the Eastman Kodak store in Minneapolis. Marva Louis, wife of the prizefighter Joe Louis, after seeing some fashion photographs he did for Frank Murphy's women's store in St. Paul, advised Parks to move to Chicago, where he attracted a clientele of society women who wanted their portraits done. In 1941 his exhibit of ghetto scenes at Chicago's South Side Community Art Center won him a Julius Rosenwald fellowship and an opportunity to move to Washington to work as an apprentice in photography under Roy Emerson Stryker at the Farm Security Administration. In 1944 he moved his family to Harlem and did free-lance work for *Glamour* and *Vogue* magazines while joining a photographic team that Stryker was heading at the Standard Oil Company. And in 1948 Parks won a staff position with *Life* magazine for which, during more than two decades, he did pictorial reports on a variety of subjects— sports, fashion, politics, crime, and racial segregation in the South—as well as writing biographical studies of Stokely Carmichael, Malcolm X, and Muhammad Ali. In 1961, on an assignment to document poverty in Brazil, he met Flavio, a slum child who was dying of asthma; his photo essay on this boy and his family inspired large donations, as a result of which Parks was able to bring Flavio to a clinic in America for treatment.

In late 1962 a fellow *Life* photographer who had heard Parks talk about his Kansas childhood urged him to put these reminiscences down in writing. The result, with the help of an editor, became his first work of fiction. *The Learning Tree*, which was described by a *Time* reviewer as "unabashed nostalgia . . . blended with sharp recollections of staggering violence and fear," was a popular success and was translated into nine languages. Three years later Parks followed this up with *A Choice of Weapons*, a memoir describing the years he had struggled to earn a living after his mother's death.

As a result of his success with *The Learning Tree*, Parks was invited to adapt, direct, and compose the score for a film version of the book, which came out in 1969. He had had earlier experience in filming, having made three documentaries on black ghetto life for National Education Television and a short documentary about the Brazilian boy Flavio, but had never

before been involved in a major studio production. His first Hollywood effort was praised by some commentators for its "wonderful humanism" and "images of startling beauty," but was soundly criticized by others for "clichés," "melodramatics," "over-glamorized photography," and "a lot of softness around the edges." Joseph Morgenstern, writing for *Newsweek*, found the film "all bound up with nostalgia for a vanished land in which barefooted farm boys could do cartwheels through unbounded fields of yellow flowers." Nevertheless, he gave Parks credit for creating an "astoundingly even-tempered piece of autobiography."

Parks next went on to direct *Shaft* in 1971, and *Shaft's Big Score* in 1972, two melodramatic crime films written by Ernest Tidyman which feature a black detective. Film reviewers used phrases such as "wittily enjoyable," "lively," and "rousing and entertaining" to describe Parks's directing, at the same time finding fault with his failure to make his characters more credible. Richard Combs, writing for *Films and Filming*, commented that "away from the areas of battle" in *Shaft* "the sense of personal relations tends to be trite and awkward." Parks's 1976 film, *Leadbelly*, also received mixed reviews, with commentators praising the film for its visual effects, while criticizing it for being "smooth, eager to please, defused," and "sanitized."

During the years of Parks's growing success as a filmmaker, his marital difficulties accelerated. After his divorce from Sally Alvis in 1961, Parks married Elizabeth Campbell, a much younger woman. Then, after nine years of marriage, he divorced her and married his Chinese-American editor at Harper and Row, Genevieve Young. This marriage too was to end in divorce in 1979. As Parks was later to write in *Voices in the Mirror*, "Sometimes I am inclined to think that ambition carved my image out of stone; that the persistence of it crushed Sally, Elizabeth and Genevieve under its weight." Also in 1979 Parks went through what he called the "moment every parent dreads," the news that his son Gordon had been killed in a plane crash while directing a film in Africa. Parks told the bearer of the news to "save a part of him to spread on Kilimanjaro."

To Smile in Autumn, Parks's second book of autobiography, celebrates his years of achievement from 1943 to 1979. Parks wryly notes in this memoir that "in escaping the mire [of poverty and racism], I had lost friends along the way . . . In one world I was a social oddity. In the other world I was almost a stranger." Mel Watkins, in the *New York Times Book Review*, commented that Parks emerges in this memoir "as a Renaissance man who has resolutely pursued success in several fields. His memoir is sustained and enlivened by his urbanity and generosity."

In his third memoir, *Voices in the Mirror*, Parks raises the question, "Why have I undertaken so many professions? . . . In my formative years I was ill-prepared and I tried to make up for that by exploring every possibility. If one failed me I turned to another, but I was never just a dabbler. I gave all of myself to every effort, and I still do. . . . I'm still occupied with survival; still very single-minded about keeping my life moving—but not for fame or fortune. I simply want to stay alive to learn more about the world we live in." Michael Eric Dyson, in the *New York Times Book Review*, found this book Parks's "most poignant self-portrait." Another *New York Times* reviewer, Andy Grundberg, described the book as "compelling" because of "the density of [the author's] experience. . . . One marvels that he has been able to find the time to write about his life while he has been busy living it." Yet reflecting on Parks's "central emotional paradox: that part of him loathes the very society in which he has found success after success," Grundberg concludes, comparing Parks's memoir with Wright Morris's *Will's Boy*, which "like his career, lacks a clear center. His forays into music, film and writing are discussed, but the psychological needs they fill are not."

Gordon Parks has frequently described himself as being driven by a need, as an African American, to overcome prejudice and succeed in a white world. He might justifiably argue that he has nevertheless met his own goals, which have not included delving into the sort of depths and subtleties of the works of America's more prominent black authors.

Besides being a Rosenwald Foundation fellow, Parks's awards and honors have also included: Photographer of the Year, Association of Magazine Photographers; Frederic W. Brehm Award, 1962; Mass Media Award, National Conference of Christians and Jews, for outstanding contributions to better human relations, 1964; Carr Van Adna Journalism Award, University of Miami, 1964; Spingarn Medal from the National Association for the Advancement of Colored People, 1972; Christopher Award, 1980, for *Flavio*; President's Fellow Award, Rhode Island School of Design, 1984; Kansan of the Year, Native Sons and Daughters of Kansas, 1986. He has received honorary degrees fron Fairfield University (1969), Boston University (1969), Macalaster College (1974), Colby College (1974), and Lincoln University (1975), as well as awards from the Syracuse University School of Journalism (1963), the University of Miami (1964), the Philadelphia Museum of Art (1964), and the Art Directors Club (1964, 1968).

PRINCIPAL WORKS: *Novels*—The Learning Tree, 1963; Shannon, 1981. *Poetry*—Gordon Parks: Whispers of Intimate Things, 1971; In Love, 1971; Moments without Proper Names, 1975. *Screenplay*—The Learning Tree, 1968. *Nonfiction*—Flash Photography, 1947; Camera Portraits: The Techniques and Principles of Documentary Portraiture, 1948; A Choice of Weapons, 1966; A Poet and His Camera, 1968; Born Black, 1971; Flavio, 1978; To Smile in Autumn, 1979; Voices in the Mirror, 1990; Arias in Silence, 1994.

ABOUT: Contemporary Authors New Revision Series 26, 1989; Contemporary Literary Criticism 16; Current Biography Yearbook, 1992; Dictionary of Literary Biography 53, 1984; Parks, G. A Choice of Weapons, 1966; Parks, G. To Smile in Autumn, 1979; Parks, G. Voices in the Mirror, 1990; Who's Who in America 1990–1991. *Periodicals*—Newsweek August 11, 1969; New York Times January 8, 1991; New York Times Book Review December 9, 1990; Time September 24, 1963.

PAULIN, TOM (THOMAS NEILSON)

(January 25, 1949–), British poet, critic, and playwright, described by critic John Haffenden as "one of the most intelligent and accomplished poets to have emerged from the North of Ireland in recent years," was born in Leeds, the son of a school headmaster. Through his mother, Paulin was descended from "strenuous Ulster Scots"; at the age of four he was taken to Belfast, where he grew up, attending the Rosetta Primary School and the Annadale Grammar School. An important clue to Paulin's later attitudes—he has always been considered by his contemporaries to be well to the left of center—is that while still at school he belonged to a Trotskyist organization. He has admitted disaffection from the Unionist culture of Northern Ireland, having felt it claustrophobic and corrupt. Trotsky has remained a frequent presence in his work, and in certain respects Paulin, fond by his own account of "terse fricatives," has never given up his conscious rebelliousness. But, as he told John Haffenden in 1980: "If I were to be identified with a particular political attitude or philosophy, I'd be upset. I'm not a Marxist, for example, and I don't have any ideological axe to grind."

Paulin went on to take first-class honors in English literature in 1971 from Hull University (at which Philip Larkin, whose political views he was to attack vigorously, was then the librarian). He then did research at Lincoln College, Oxford, where he gained a bachelor of letters in 1973. He has since lectured in English at the

University of Nottingham, whose location he characteristically described as "between the civil lawns of the south and the brick mills of the authentic north."

Paulin's first published book was a critical study, *Thomas Hardy: The Poetry of Perception.* Unlike the polemical prose and verse that followed it, this somewhat muted study received little attention and is seldom discussed in the context of its subject, who does not perhaps lend himself particularly well to treatment of a political nature. However, the collection of poems which came soon afterward, *A State of Justice,* was very widely read, especially for a first volume, and, on the whole, acclaimed for its great promise. For Paulin, as his anthology *The Faber Book of Political Verse* later made clear, poetry is political or it is nothing. *A State of Justice* is mainly directed at the British policy in Northern Ireland of "retributive justice." Separated by "that stretch of water" a British soldier sails to Northern Ireland, in the poem "States," to confront the impossible challenge of bringing peace with the instruments of war:

> Any state, built on such a nature,
> Is a metal convenience, its paint
> Cheapened by the price of lives
> Spent in a public service.

The most persistent complaint about this book, as about all of Paulin's poetry, was expressed by Anne Stevenson in the *Listener* in 1977: "sometimes he pares his poems down to the point of obscurity." But Stevenson admired the poetry as a whole and added that the "best poems suggest that the differences between the rich and the poor in Ireland can be taken as an allegory of the relationship between England and Ireland itself." The book established him as the most interesting of the crop of "Ulster poets" since the earlier advent of Seamus Heaney.

In the context of what he called Paulin's "obsession" with justice, Andrew Motion commented in the *New Statesman,* on *The Strange Museum* that in it "he is even more determined"; but "his two overriding preoccupations," Motion suggested, have now become "love and history." Dick Davis, reviewing the same volume in the *Listener* in 1980, was more reserved, anticipating those later critics who have found Paulin's insistent politicizing a hazard to his poetic achievement; he judged the book "good for its dour kind," but vitiated by Paulin's resistance to the "blandishments" of art: "I would give in to those blandishments, Mr. Paulin," he advised.

Liberty Tree began to divide reviewers, though none failed to pay tribute to Paulin's capabilities. Donald Campbell in *British Book News,* while finding all the poems in the collection "absorbing" and "demanding," thought them "never completely accessible" and sometimes "infuriating." Dick Davis, again in the *Listener* (1984), found the "language . . . pitched as a relentless attack on complacency," and, while intense, "finally wearying."

In 1993 Paulin published his *Selected Poems 1972–1990,* which drew from his first two major collections and from *Fivemiletown* published six years earlier. Robert Potts, in the *Times Literary Supplement* (1993), noted a "change of heart," beginning around 1980, from "critical unionism" to "a non-sectarian republicanism." "With the dialectical freedom of the later work," Potts half complained, "came an increased employment of dialect words . . . looking very like a conscious political strategy," yet with "a singing warmth." Potts felt that for "all the poignant, blocked stand-offs of his poems," Paulin had "developed an endearing and effective vehicle for his political commitments." But Paulin's politics appear to be increasingly Utopian in a situation which seems as yet to have no solution. The problem, as Neil Cameron suggested in *Contemporary Poets,* is that his strategy is to be deliberately obscure, "to withhold definition or resolution and to open instead into the allusive, the suggestive, the metaphoric and the emblematic." However, in his later collections—*The Liberty Tree,* for example—Paulin seems to be moving away from the tough, bitterly ironic mood of the early poems. Using the symbol of the juniper, a tree that survives in the coldest and most unwelcoming natural surroundings, in "The Book of Juniper," he observes that "it keeps a low profile / on rough ground." In Northern Ireland, he writes, "it is the only / tree of freedom / to be found." And in "To the Linen Halls" he affirms a solidarity that transcends politics:

> After extremity
> art turns social
> and it's more than fashion
> to voice the word *we.*

We can move on from the past and devise "a form / and a control

> Our shaping brightness
> is a style and discipline
> that finds its tongue
> in the woody desk-dawns
> of fretting scholars
> who pray, invisibly,
> to taste the true vine
> and hum gently
> in holy sweetness.

The question of precisely in what direction

Paulin's poetry is moving remained unresolved in his 1994 volume *Walking a Line*, the title of which, Lachlin Mackinnon wrote in the *Times Literary Supplement*, suggests the ambiguity of the poet's position. "When . . . Paulin escapes his burden of responsibility," Mackinnon commented, "he reminds us what a marvelous poet he has it in him to be; but that a fifth collection should seem only promising reminds us of what a difficult route he has taken."

Paulin's critical writing arouses passionate feelings, as all vigorous criticism must. The major collections are *Ireland and the English Crisis* and *Minotaur: Poetry and the Nation State*. The essays of the first book, all of them brilliantly and vivaciously written, describe how writers such as Joyce, Auden, and Paulin's own Irish contemporaries react to politics. It also contains a vigorous and influential attack on structuralism and deconstruction; that is, on some modern academic critics' dehumanizing insistence upon reducing poetry and novels to mere "texts." There are illuminating essays on William Trevor, D. H. Lawrence, and, more controversially, one extolling the novels of the popular thriller writer John le Carré.

Minotaur, more mature and closely argued, is undoubtedly Paulin's most substantial and challenging contribution to modern critical thinking. His Minotaur is "the monster that hides deep in the labyrinth of official lies, inert language and myths of national destiny." This Minotaur, suggests Paulin, "is a stirring of English spirit against . . . repression." Edward Said noted in the *London Review of Books* what goes into giving "*Minotaur* its breadth and passion—Paulin cares about human enlightenment and emancipation. Underlying his essays is the steadily unfolding grand narrative of the struggle to achieve justice, freedom and knowledge. That he discerns it so unfailingly in the broad features as well as the hints, ellipses and figures of the books he reads testifies to what an extraordinary student he is on the unending contest between life and literature." Simon Carnell in the *New Statesman & Society* commented on "Paulin's radical distrust of all forms of romantic authority, including the vatic authority of the poet." He sees the book's primary value in "Paulin's driven and astute belief in the vital connection between responsibility to the living word and responsibility for the kind of society in which we live."

Among pieces on John Clare, Christina Rossetti, and Emily Dickinson, in *Minotaur* there is one here on Philip Larkin which Claude Rawson, in the *Times Literary Supplement* in 1992, called "extremely acute and delightfully conducted." There may be some irony intended in the last phrase of this judgment, for the essay became notorious for its unfashionably hostile attitude toward certain aspects of Philip Larkin's work—in particular toward his allegedly spurious patriotism and xenophobia. This essay, and subsequent acrimonious correspondence about Larkin in the *Times Literary Supplement* stimulated a new interest in Larkin.

In addition to poetry and criticism, Paulin has written plays—in particular an adaptation of Sophocles' *Antigone*, titled *The Riot Act* (successfully produced in Belfast in 1984)—and, in addition to *The Faber Book of Political Verse*, has edited (with Peter Messent) an edition of *Selected Tales* by Henry James. In 1983–1984 he was visiting lecturer at the University of Virginia at Charlottesville. His poetry has received the Eric Gregory Award (1976) and (jointly) the Somerset Maugham Award (1978), and in 1982 he won the Geoffrey Faber Memorial Award. Paulin is widely regarded as the most important political poet in Great Britain since the early Auden.

PRINCIPAL WORKS: *Poetry*—Theoretical Locations, 1975; A State of Justice, 1977; Personal Column, 1978; The Strange Museum, 1980; Liberty Tree, 1983; The Argument at Great Tew, 1985; Fivemiletown, 1987; Selected Poems 1972–1990, 1993; Walking a Line, 1994. *Plays*—The Riot Act: A Version of Sophocles' Antigone, 1985; The Hillsborough Script: A Dramatic Satire, 1987; Seize the Fire: A Version of Aeschylus's Prometheus Bound, 1990. *Criticism*—Thomas Hardy: The Poetry of Perception, 1975; A New Look at the Language Question, 1983; Ireland and the English Crisis, 1984; Minotaur: Poetry and the Nation Sstate, 1992. *As editor*—The Faber Book of Political Verse, 1986; Hard Lines 3 (with F. Dubes and I. Dury), 1987; The Faber Book of Vernacular Verse, 1990.

ABOUT: Contemporary Authors 128, 1990; Contemporary Literary Criticism 37, 1986; Contemporary Poets, 5th ed., 1991; Dictionary of Literary Biography, 1985; Dunn, D. (ed.) Two Decades of Irish Writing: A Critical Survey, 1975; Haffenden, J. Viewpoints: Poets in Conversation, 1980; King, P. R. Nine Contemporary Poets: A Critical Introduction, 1979; Poets of Great Britain and Ireland Since 1960, 1985. *Periodicals*—British Book News October 1983; Irish Literary Supplement Spring 1985; Listener April 14, 1977; June 5, 1980; July 19, 1984; London Review of Books October 4, 1984; February 7, 1985; April 9, 1992; New Statesman April 4, 1980; February 14, 1992; New York Times Book Review April 17, 1988; Poetry Nation 7, 1980; Times Literary Supplement April 4, 1980; July 30, 1982; September 2, 1983; June 29, 1984; October 19, 1984; April 19, 1985; May 23, 1986; January 24, 1992; May 7, 1993; July 8, 1994.

*PAVIĆ, MILORAD (October 15, 1929–), Serbian novelist, short story writer, poet, and literary historian, was born in Belgrade into a distinguished family of writers. He graduated from the University of Belgrade and received his Ph.D. in literary history at the University of Zagreb. After teaching literature for several years at the universities of Novi Sad and Belgrade, he lived as a free-lance writer in Belgrade. A member of the Serbian Academy of Science and Arts, he has received many literary awards.

Pavić started out as a poet. His collections of poems, *Palimpsesti* (Palimpsests, 1967), and *Mesečev kamen* (Moon's stone, 1971), were followed by books of short stories, *Gvozdena zavesa* (The iron curtain, 1973), and *Konji svetoga Marka* (The horses of St. Mark, 1976). He published three more collections of short stories and a play. In these works one can discern the main characteristics of his later works: a merging of fantasy and reality, expressed in an impeccable and controlled style. In the course of his career he also published several well-received monographs of literary history, shedding new light on Serbian writers from the baroque period. No doubt, his broad erudition has enabled Pavić to develop his writing skills.

In an interview, Pavić explained some of his basic views on literature and writing. According to him, literature should have no boundaries; the more it is accepted all over the world, the higher the value it has. An ideologically tainted literature loses its value if it lacks artistic excellence. Fantastic literature is no less realistic than so-called realistic literature. Furthermore, we do not need a new way of writing literature but a change in our way of reading literature. All these ideas are not revolutionary or even entirely new (Borges comes immediately to mind), but they have been instrumental in bringing a new spirit into Serbian literature.

It was with his novels that Pavić became known beyond the borders of his native land. His first novel, *Hazarski rečnik* (1984, *Dictionary of the Khazars*), is a gold mine for interpreters of literature. The author himself invites speculation when he says, "Each reader will put the book together for himself, . . . and, as with a mirror, he will get out of this dictionary as much as he puts into it." The novel rests on a false premise— the existence of a Khazar dictionary, allegedly printed in 1691 by Daubmannus, an obscure printer in 17th-century Prussia. In fact, there was no such dictionary, and the author's claim that his novel is an attempt to reconstruct the original dictionary serves only as a pretext for writing the novel. Obviously, his intentions lie elsewhere, deftly camouflaged by an intricate net of myths, legends, stories, quasi-historical

documents, and a thousand-and-one nights' revelry. Such qualities help us appreciate the philosophical, religious, cultural, and aesthetic underpinnings of the novel, which has received accolades all over the world.

In the novel there is no distinct line separating reality from fantasy. The two spheres are constantly interchanged and their borderlines deliberately blurred. Characters change their appearance and reappear, easily recognizable, as someone else. The reason for all these transformations is the author's belief that reality and fantasy are of equal validity and that one does not exist without the other. The same can be said about dreams. Pavić borrows the lines from a fictitious dictionary: "A dream is a garden of devils, and all dreams in this world were dreamed long ago. Now they are simply interchanged with equally used and worn reality." This explains the role of the dream hunters, who have the capacity to "read other people's dreams, live and make themselves at home in them, and through the dreams hunt the game that was their prey." At least half of the happenings in the novel take place either in dreams or dreamlike hallucinations, which prompted Robert Coover to say in the *New York Times Book Review* that Pavić "thinks the way we dream." And if this frustrates the reader at times, "the impression of frustration fades before the enchantment of the quest," Paul Grey remarked in *Time*.

Our inability to know and acquire the historical truth at all times is also an important factor. Historical fact and legend are intertwined and of equal validity, leading to an abundant mixture of historical and fictitious characters. The same can be said about the seekers of the solution to the Khazar enigma, some of whom are known scholars while others are invented tools in the author's game. The historical uncertainty about the actual fate of the Khazars is the best argument for Pavić's contention that historical facts often elude us and that this is probably just as well. The lines between the past, present, and future are also blurred. The characters move from one century and geographical region to another, not only in imagination or in dreams, but matter-of-factly.

The *Dictionary* is pervaded with relativity. The story is told in three versions—the Christian in the Red book, the Islamic in the Green, and the Hebrew in the Yellow. One has to accept the author's belief that many other questions besides the Khazar question, be they historical, philosophical, or ethical, can be approached from several angles. Relativity is manifested in the asynchrony, in the mixture of races and cultures that are not normally mixed (the involvement of the Serbs in the Khazar question, for example), and in the seemingly incongruous reappearance of characters at unexpected time and places. Princess Ateh, one of the characters, has different names, four states of consciousness, and seven faces; she is both beautiful and not beautiful. She never dies, thus making death itself relative. Similarly, the true "Khazar face" is also hard to pinpoint, as is the nature of the passage of time. The author suggests that the novel can be read any way the reader pleases—horizontally (reading the same entries in all three books); vertically (following the events through history), from the beginning or from the end; or from anywhere, even diagonally.

The novel invites some age-old questions: What is the truth, and how can it be obtained? By mixing philosophical, historical, and cultural issues with a suspenseful yarn (including several murders) and lively, utterly modernistic narrative techniques (which go back to his favorite literary period, the baroque), Pavić has created "the first novel of the twenty-first century," as Philippe Tretiak called it in *Paris Match*. Robert Coover, ranking Christina Pribicevic-Zoric's translation with Gregory Rabassa's of *One Hundred Years of Solitude* and William Weaver's of the works of Italo Calvino, termed it "quite stunningly brilliant."

Milorad Pavić's second major novel, *Predeo slikan čajem* (1988, *Landscape Painted with Tea*), has provoked as lively a reaction as did *Dictionary of the Khazars*. It is comparable to the *Dictionary* in several ways. The *Dictionary* is subtitled "a novel-lexicon in 100,000 words," and *Landscape* "a novel for the lovers of crossword puzzles." In both novels Pavić suggests new ways of reading, in line with his dictum of how a book should be read. Here, one can read the way a crossword puzzle is solved—horizontally or vertically. The horizontal reading reveals the plot; the vertical, the characters. However, the closest parallel between the two novels is found in Pavić's removal of the boundaries between then and now, here and there, and fictitious and real characters.

Somewhat more rooted in our own time and place than the *Dictionary*, *Landscape Painted with Tea* presents Atanas Svilar (alias Razin), a Serb of Serbian-Russian parentage, as a minor architect in the postwar Yugoslavia and as a highly successful pharmaceutics businessman in the United States. The Serbian-Russian-American connection is one of the many puzzles in the novel. Pavić includes instructions on "how to solve this book," paralleling the instructions for a crossword puzzle, but like so much in Pavić's world, this is not to be taken literally.

Svilar joins the revered Serbian monastery of Khilandar on Greece's Mount Athos, where he hopes to lead a solitary life in prayer. Having taken monastic vows there, he learns that there are two kinds of monks—those who live and pray alone (idiorhythmics), and those who lead a communal life and work together (cenobites). Svilar discovers that although by disposition he is an idiorhythmic, as an architect he would be destined to live and work with others. He has to change his name, language, nationality, and residence if he wants to pursue his architectural profession, just as an idiorhythmic monk intent upon changing his monastic ways is required to transfer to the cenobite monastery and vice versa. He is warned by monastic elders, however, that "he who cures himself of himself will perish." Svilar is determined to try anyway. In the process, he adopts the name of his father, a Russian professor of mathematics, Fyodor Alekseyevich Razin. He leaves the monastery, emigrates to America, adopts the English language, and climbs to the pinnacle of financial success. He also takes to America his beautiful Serbian lover, Vitacha Milut, who becomes a famous opera singer. Toward the end of his life, however, Svilar pines for his homeland and for the happiness of his youth, a yearning symbolized by his three notebooks adorned with landscapes painted with tea. He realizes that his marriage to Vitacha has failed (she bears him no children), assumes again the name Svilar, and returns to his homeland in order to buy some children from his former friends. Failing that, he returns to America and builds for himself three exact replicas of Josip Broz Tito's palaces. The notebooks with the landscapes represent Svilar's enduring Serbian personality, as present before his American adventure and after his disillusionment with success. The symbolic function of the landscapes holds the novel together.

This is only a skeletal outline of the plot. Like the *Dictionary*, *Landscape* has many riddles, traps, and ambiguities. And like the earlier novel, it has two possible endings, the male and the female, depending on the reader's sensibilities. Some of the riddles are the allusions to Tito, the stories within the novel, the meaning of the names, the role of the devils, and the solution of the crossword puzzle. The best approach to these riddles is not to see them as indispensable keys to the meaning of the novel, but as integral components of Pavić's baroque and fantastic style. In the last analysis, it is the reader who seals the fate of all the characters.

Landscape Painted with Tea is distinguished not only by an unusual plot and characters, but also by striking metaphors, similes, paradoxes, hyperboles, maxims, and other tropes. Pavić also uses a method called "defamiliarization" (making strange), defined by the Russian formalist critics of the 1920s, in which a writer makes the familiar seem strange in order to capture the reader's attention and enhance his awareness. As a result, we encounter "a delightfully bewildering array of characters and situations and a bevy of literary and folkloristic genres and motifs from Serbian and Greek traditions," as J. M. Foley described it in *Choice*.

Pavić told Judith Shulevitz in an interview in the *New York Times Book Review* that *Landscape* "speaks deeply—allegorically, even prophetically—about the fate of Yugoslavia." The transformations of the protagonist—from architect to monk to capitalist, even from male to female and back—presage the twists and turns in the modern struggles in Eastern Europe. "States, political institutions, whole nations are divorcing themselves from their present loves and marriages and returning to former affections. Whole nations are moving from one place to another. Many states are changing sex," Pavić said.

The failed architect apprehends that "two winds could not be in the same place at the same time, nor could Svilar be a solitary and a builder at the same time. He simply did not belong to the architects, and he was not preordained to build." Jonathan Baumbach in the *New York Times Book Review* praised the translator's rendering: "There is hardly a page in Christina Pribicevic-Zoric's elegant translation from the Serbo-Croatian without some risky, improbable image that offers us the pleasure of being taken by surprise by something we are flattered to believe we knew all along. Presumed subjects peel away from . . . Pavić's novel like the skins of an onion. . . . [B]eneath those anecdotes is the issue of form in the guise of novel-as-crossword puzzle and beneath the issue of the puzzle is the reader as subject and beneath the issue of the reader, beneath all the other issues, is language. . . . As with all great writers, writers who transform our way of reading . . . Pavić's real subject—his, if you will, illicit love—is words, words that cross the page into sentences and paragraphs and stories. . . ."

Pavić's third novel, *Unutrašnja strana vetra ili roman o Heri i Leandru* (1991, *The Inner Side of the Wind; or, The Novel of Hero and Leander*), again offers innovative approaches to the reading of a novel, both playful and tricky. The trick here is that the book can be read from the front or the back, depending on whether one wants to read the story of Leander or of Hero first.

This is the love story of Hero and Leander, but they live in different centuries and countries. The two novels contained in this book are actually one, but they present two angles of the same story. The metaphor of the inner side of the wind (which is made possible when the wind blows in the rain) is used by the author to indicate two kinds of prophecies—the more expensive ones that see several hundred years ahead, and the cheap ones for the immediate future. In turn, Pavić uses this device to connect two lovers from different periods, Leander from Greek mythology and Heroneja from our time. They are united in death, just as the legendary Hero and Leander were united when he drowned swimming across the Hellespont to her and she leapt into the sea and drowned herself from grief. By using an ancient myth but connecting centuries and continents, Pavić renews the myth and makes it alive and relevant today. The love story takes on a fresh, intriguing angle, just as the wind does when it has an inner side.

Together with such writers as Borges, Cortázar, and Eco, Pavić has charted new territories in modern fiction. Pavić's enduring motivation, however, seems to be the beguilement of the reader. As W. S. Di Piero commented in the *New York Times Book Review*, for Pavić, "tale-telling is a comic affliction. His characters burst into story the way musical comedy characters burst into song. . . . He dissolves the crystalline structure of conventional storytelling into fluid competing versions of truth. But he also possesses an ironist's supreme ability both to operate and witness his own narrative contraptions." Di Piero concluded that "the teller will always somehow shape the tale to the moment—the cultural, sexual, political moment—in which it is retold."

PRINCIPAL WORKS IN ENGLISH TRANSLATION: *Novels*—(tr. C. Pribicevic-Zoric) Dictionary of the Khazars, 1988; (tr. C. Pribicevic-Zoric) Landscape Painted with Tea, 1990; (tr. C. Pribicevic-Zoric) The Inner Side of the Wind; or, The Novel of Hero and Leander, 1993.

ABOUT: Atlantic November 1988; Booklist October 15, 1988; September 1, 1990; Chicago Tribune Books November 6, 1988; Choice June 1989; November 1991; Esquire November 1990; Hudson Review Summer 1989; Autumn 1991; Kirkus Review September 15, 1988; September 1, 1990; Library Journal November 15 1988; Listener February 16, 1989; London Review of Books June 1, 1989; Nation December 5, 1988; New Republic December 19, 1988; New Statesman and Society February 10, 1989; New York Times November 23, 1988; New York Times Book Review November 20, 1988; November 12, 1989; December 16, 1990; June 13, 1993; Publishers Weekly May 13, 1988; August 12, 1988; September 8, 1988; Quill & Quire January 1989; Sunday Times (London) February 12, 1989; Time December 5, 1988; Times Literary Supplement

March 3, 1989; May 17, 1991; Ulbandus Review 1987; Voice Literary Supplement March 1992; Washington Post Book World November 13, 1988; November 18, 1990; World & I November 1988; January 1989; World Literature Today Autumn 1984; Winter 1986; Spring 1989; Winter 1990.

ERNST PAWEL

PAWEL, ERNST (January 23, 1920–August 16, 1994), American (German-born) novelist, biographer, and translator writes: "I was born in Germany, left that country in 1933 when Hitler came to power, drifted about Europe as a refugee for a few years, reached the U.S. in 1938 and joined the army in 1942. I served in Africa, Italy, and Yugoslavia with the OSS and subsequently attended the New School for Social Research, where for reasons no longer very clear to me I obtained my B.A. in 1948.

"My first novel, *The Island in Time*, published in 1951, dealt with the Holocaust survivors. Survival in the American corporate structure—which I observed for many years from a distance and with a measure of amusement—was the theme of my novel *From the Dark Tower*, while *In the Absence of Magic* presented the fictional portrait of one of Freud's disciples trapped in the ambiguities of his American exile.

"While working as an editor and translator for a major life insurance company, I contributed numerous articles and reviews to the *New York Times*, the *New Republic*, the *Nation*, *Commentary*, *Partisan Review*, *Midstream*, *Judaism*, and others. My award-winning biography of Franz Kafka was published in 1984 by Farrar, Straus & Giroux under the title *The Nightmare of Reason*. The same publisher brought out my biography of Theodor Herzl, *The Labyrinth of Exile*, in December 1989. I have since completed another novel and am currently working on several major projects."

The title of Ernst Pawel's biography of Zionist leader Theodor Herzl, *The Labyrinth of Exile*, might serve as a description of Pawel's own early life. In the interval between leaving Nazi Germany and immigrating to the United States in 1938, Pawel's parents, Paul and Flora (Breslauer) Pawel, moved their family to Yugoslavia. Croatian and Macedonian demands for independence from Yugoslavia culminated in the 1934 assassination of King Alexander, plunging the young country into turmoil. The Pawel family's departure from the country was opportune, for Yugoslavia was allied with or controlled by the Nazis for much of World War II. Ernst Pawel returned to Yugoslavia during the war as a member of the Office of Strategic Services (OSS), the intelligence unit that was the precursor to the Central Intelligence Agency (CIA). Using his ability to speak Serbo-Croatian and his firsthand knowledge of Central Europe, Pawel worked in conjunction with the anti-Nazi Yugoslav Resistance.

Pawel managed to escape the tyranny of Hitler's Germany and the concentration camps which killed so many other Jews. Yet he grew up in the very shadow of the Holocaust and bore direct witness to the Nazi depredation of Europe. Though he was not a religious Jew, Pawel chose to highlight the struggles of Jews in each of his books, fiction and nonfiction. He dealt explicitly with the consequences of the Holocaust in his first novel, *The Island in Time*, about a group of Jews interned on an island off the Italian coast and awaiting passage to Israel. Reviews of the novel were mixed. While Robert Pick in the *Saturday Review of Literature* found it "a competent piece of fiction, though burdened quite heavily with reflections of no particular originality or depth," *Nation* (1951) reviewer Harvey Swados hailed it as "a distinguished novel and an auspicious beginning of a literary career."

Pawel's second and third novels deal with Jews living in America. *From the Dark Tower* is a portrait of Abe Rogoff, a New York insurance company executive whose boss's suicide impels him on a journey of self-discovery. In the *Saturday Review*, David Carp wrote: "Pawel's fine book has a dark, strong taste and it ought to keep you awake nights. If you care at all about the human condition you must read it." The protagonist of *In the Absence of Magic* is a retired psychoanalyst who is lured back into practice by a former patient. "The two opposing characters are obviously meant to symbolize some of the larger issues of our times," Barbara Schiller wrote in the *New York Herald Tribune Book Review*, "and they are more successful on this level than they are as mere human beings."

The Nightmare of Reason is a biography of Franz Kafka, a seminal author whose works presaged the nightmare atmosphere the Nazis brought to Europe. Pawel's selection of Kafka was not haphazard; the affinities between the biographer and his subject are quite striking. The most obvious similarity is ethnicity; both men were born and raised in Eastern European Jewish families. More notably, both men pursued literary lives while working for insurance companies. Kafka, trained as a lawyer, composed almost all of his major fiction while he was an executive for the Prague-based Workmen's Accident Insurance Institute from 1908 to 1922. While Pawel worked as a writer, editor, and translator for the New York Life Insurance Company from 1946 to 1982, he wrote and published his first three novels. A visit Pawel and his wife made to Prague, her birthplace, in the late 1970s piqued his interest in writing about Kafka. "That brief visit gave me the inspiration to write the biography," Pawel told *New York Times Book Review* interviewer Herbert Mitgang in 1984. "I began to collect material, went to the archives of the National Library in Jerusalem, and interviewed several of Kafka's friends—survivors who had ended up in Israel."

"No life of Franz Kafka could have been written . . . had it not been for the vision and courage of Max Brod," Pawel wrote in the preface. "It was he who twice rescued Kafka's work, first from physical destruction, later from indifference and oblivion." Pawel made extensive use of Kafka's voluminous diaries and correspondence, subjecting these sources to a rigorous comparison with the known facts of Kafka's life. *The Nightmare of Reason* does not purport to offer new readings of Kafka's fiction. Rather, Pawel sets out to provide readers with a new perspective on Kafka's professional, private, and family life. As George Gibian noted in the *Nation* (1984): "Pawel concentrates not on the literary and philosophical aspects of Kafka's writings but on their social and ethnic background. He gives us a history of the German-speaking Jews of Prague going back to the eighteenth-century Hapsburg monarchs, and provides us with statistics about the German, Czech and Jewish segments of the population of Bohemia."

The Nightmare of Reason seeks to dispel, or at least to analyze, certain myths that have long surrounded Kafka. In a *New York Times Book Review* essay on Kafka (published in 1983, shortly before his book appeared), Pawel attacked the notion that Kafka's employment with the Workmen's Accident Insurance Institute was mindless drudgery: "The fact is that Kafka had a distinguished career as an expert in the prevention of industrial accidents, notably in Bohemia's thriving lumber industry."

Kafka's reputation as a failure with the opposite sex stems in part from his five-year engagement to and impassioned correspondence with Felice Bauer, a Berlin woman he barely knew. According to Pawel, however, there were other women: "He had an apparently quite satisfactory year-long liaison in his student days, and his later passionate involvement with the luminous Milena Jesenska and the devotion of Dora Dymant . . . provide abundant evidence of his capacity to love and be loved."

Kafka's bad relationship with his father was chronicled in painful detail in his diary. While Pawel acknowledges the "subjective truth" of Kafka's feelings, he sees the situation in the Kafka household as being one of mutual fear: "Hermann Kafka was a highly problematic candidate for apotheosis at best and clearly far more in awe of his overeducated son than the son was of him."

Pawel also affirms the prescience of certain of Kafka's writings: "*In the Penal Colony* anticipates *Eichmann in Jerusalem* and the banality of evil by more than half a century, and *The Trial* can be read as, among many other things, a preview of totalitarian justice. . . . " But he prefers to see Kafka as a writer who is part of our time. "Kafka the centenarian is our contemporary," he wrote in the *New York Times Book Review*. "This does not mean that he was ahead of his time but that he perceived its sickness with a lucidity that helped to kill him in the prime of life. He himself laid no claim to the mantle of prophet, saint, visionary or anything other than writer in search of the truth. Such truths as he found must be sought in his work."

The Nightmare of Reason won several literary prizes, including an Alfred Harcourt Award in biography and a *Los Angeles Times* book prize. It was also a finalist for the American Book Award in nonfiction. The book was critically acclaimed; Jim Miller in *Newsweek*, for example, termed it "a masterpiece—brilliantly written, thoroughly researched, richly imagined." In a front-page notice of *The Nightmare of Reason* in the *New York Times Book Review* (1984), Leonard Michaels called it "a superlative biography of Franz Kafka."

John Updike provided a more mixed assessment of the book in the *New Yorker*. "*The Nightmare of Reason. . . . ,*" he wrote, "is full of information and intellectual energy and should be read by everyone who cares about Kafka." On the other hand, Updike expressed reservations about Pawel's style: "[O]ne wishes that Mr. Pawel had found a slightly different tone in which to write. His prose, like his title, comes on too strong; his literary voice, as it details the earthly adventures of his delicate, almost unfailingly tactful protagonist, echoes at times the 'booming parade-ground voice' of that much-maligned father Hermann Kafka." Updike concluded, "Kafka's life, so intimately bound up with his work, fascinates us, it may be, unduly, at the price of a certain coarsening."

The *Times Literary Supplement*'s Martin Swales wrote: "Pawel indeed has telling points to make about the spiritual and social context of Kafka's life. . . . Yet the centre of Kafka's life, the life that was literature, somehow eludes his grasp."

Theodor Herzl was the subject of Pawel's second biographical study, *The Labyrinth of Exile*. Born in Budapest, Hungary, in 1860, the aristocratic Herzl made a reputation for himself in Vienna, first as a playwright, and later as an editor and journalist. In 1894, he covered the trial of French Army Captain Alfred Dreyfus, a Jew accused of treason. Convinced that European anti-Semitism was rampant and unalterable, Herzl devoted himself completely to what he saw as the only solution—the establishment of a separate Jewish state.

In writing his biography of Herzl, Pawel's intention was to find a new perspective on a man whose life had already been recounted many times. Reviewing *The Labyrinth of Exile* in the *Washington Post Book World*, Ronald Sanders noted: "There have been biographies of Herzl before, but Ernst Pawel . . . has faced the challenge with remarkable skill. . . . One of the noteworthy aspects of Pawel's book is its lack of hero-worship, and the frank acerbity of his studies of Herzl's clumsy work for the theater." In the *New Leader*, Yehudah Mirsky wrote: "Herzl emerges from the pages of this superbly written and immensely thoughtful biography as both child and fool, a seriously flawed man. But it is a measure of Ernst Pawel's deep humanity and wonderful sense of irony that he also understands the historical circumstances that helped his subject translate infantile obsessions into a political program offering promise to a confused, embittered people."

"*The Labyrinth of Exile* is a modern biography," Peter Loewenberg wrote in the *New York Times Book Review*. "It transcends the early hagiographies of Herzl. . . . But despite clearly portraying all of Herzl's shortcomings, Mr. Pawel admires the spirit of this proud nation builder, the force of his creative will and the hope that inspired first tens, then hundreds, finally thousands of followers to build a Jewish state." In his review of the book in the *New York Times*, Herbert Mitgang put it more succinctly, concluding: "Pawel's biography of the 'first Jewish soldier in modern times' helps to explain Israel's existence—and attitudes—today."

Pawel died in 1994. An autobiography, *Life in the Dark Age*, and *The Poet Dying*, the story of Heine's last years, were published after his death. Heine, exiled in Paris, lay dying for the better part of eight years, and Pawel includes a selection of poems that Heine wrote about death and dying. "On the subject of the dying itself—or rather of the life that constituted it—Pawel is informative and imaginative," Gabriele Annan wrote in *New York Review of Books*. Annan found "Pawel's insights into Heine's character . . . convincing" but noted that "what interests him most about the poet is his Jewishness." Annan observed, however, that Pawel defines Heine "neatly as 'rebel rather than revolutionary,' and recognizes that 'most of his quarrels with zealots of one stripe or another ultimately came down to personality clashes.' Pawel's position is like a kindly tutor's. . . . " The *Publishers Weekly* reviewer found *The Poet Dying* "a penetrating study of the great poet."

PRINCIPAL WORKS: *Novels*—The Island in Time, 1951; From the Dark Tower, 1957; In the Absence of Magic, 1960. *Biographies*—The Nightmare of Reason: A Life of Franz Kafka, 1984; The Labyrinth of Exile: A Life of Theodor Herzl, 1989; The Poet Dying: Heinrich Heine's Last Years in Paris, 1995; Life in the Dark Age (autobiography), 1995. *As translator*—(with L. Varese) Violent Ends (by G. Simenon) 1954; Five Operas and Richard Strauss (by L. Lehmann) 1964; The Great Debate: Theories of Nuclear Strategy (by R. Aron) 1965.

ABOUT: Contemporary Authors 131, 1991. *Periodicals*—Commentary November 1984; February 1990; Nation July 7, 1951; August 4–11, 1984; New Leader December 11–25, 1989; Newsweek June 18, 1984; New York Herald Tribune Book Review May 22, 1960; New York Review of Books August 10, 1995; New York Times December 15, 1989; New York Times Book Review July 3, 1983; June 10, 1984; December 31, 1989; New Yorker June 18, 1984; Publishers Weekly July 31, 1995; Saturday Review June 15, 1957; Saturday Review of Literature July 7, 1951; Times Literary Supplement October 5, 1984; Washington Post Book World December 17, 1989.

PEARSON, T(HOMAS) R(EID) (March 27, 1956–   ), American novelist, was born in Winston-Salem, North Carolina, the son of Thomas Elwood Pearson, a safety engineer, and Sarah Anne (Burton) Pearson. He grew up in Winston-Salem and studied English and American literature at North Carolina State University in Raleigh. After receiving his M.A. in 1980, Pearson spent one year teaching at a junior college in Raleigh. He then enrolled in a doctoral program at Pennsylvania State University. Pearson began work on what would become his first novel while at Penn State, though he found himself thoroughly indifferent to much of his course work. He left the university after only one year and returned to the Raleigh area, where he went to work with a friend who was a carpenter and house painter.

Pearson had begun writing fiction when he was around eighteen years old, and soon found that rejection notices became a way of life, although he had followed what he thought were literary trends. Once back in North Carolina, however, Pearson abandoned his previous notions about what publishers wanted, focusing instead on writing stories that he would like to read. He gathered material from what he considers to be his own natural milieu, rural Southern culture. From 1981 to 1984, he lived in a small town some twenty miles from Raleigh. There he devoted the early morning hours to writing (rising at five-thirty each morning to get in four hours of work) and eked out a living as a painter and carpenter.

He completed his first novel, *A Short History of a Small Place*, in 1982. The novel is set in the fictional North Carolina town of Neely and narrated by fifteen-year-old Louis Benfield Junior, who relates anecdotes, tall tales, and gossip he has heard from various townspeople, chief among these Louis's own father and Mrs. Philip J. King, the quintessential nosy neighbor. Much of their talk concerns the life and death of Miss Myra Angelique Pettigrew, a wealthy spinster whose suicide has created an unprecedented stir in Neely. But the numerous lengthy digressions touch on myriad subjects having nothing to do with Miss Pettigrew.

The *Virginia Quarterly Review* ran excerpts of *A Short History of a Small Place* in 1983, but Pearson still had great difficulty finding a publisher for his novel. A New York literary agency rejected the book but invited him to submit "something else sometime." The something else he sent them was his second novel, *Off for the Sweet Hereafter*, which he had completed in 1984. A publisher then brought out the two books in the order in which they were written.

T. R. PEARSON

A Short History of a Small Place garnered some critical acclaim, though reviewers varied in their assessment of Pearson's achievement. *Kirkus Reviews* prudently concluded: "Overall, this is a promising, if not fully accomplished, first effort by a talented writer, to whose future offerings one looks with hope." In the *Washington Post Book World*, Jonathan Yardley wrote, "*A Short History of a Small Place* is an absolute stunner, the work of a writer who may be young but whose command of his material never falters, who knows exactly what he is doing and does it with the sure hand of one far older and more experienced." Christopher Lehmann-Haupt, in the *New York Times* (1985), was more tempered in his praise: "Some readers will be charmed to the point of falling in love with Mr. Pearson's prose. Others will begin after a while to sense the tedium of self-indulgence. This reviewer ended up at a point somewhere in between—where he laughed out loud every now and then, but also found himself occasionally gritting his teeth."

Pearson's second novel, *Off for the Sweet Hereafter*, is also set in Neely, and its plot hinges on the death of one of the town's citizens. Unlike the earlier novel, however, *Off for the Sweet Hereafter* concentrates almost exclusively on the unsavory escapades of a few of the town's lowlifes. The novel's main character is Raeford Benton Lynch, an antisocial cipher, who "never has done a great deal with himself, until he hires on with a grave-moving crew and meets hot-blooded Jane Elizabeth Firesheets, whose charms lead him to a life of crime," according to Ann Fisher writing in *Library Journal*.

In the *New York Times Book Review*, Anne Tyler lauded Pearson's digressive prolixity: "That his narratives are more often attempts at narratives, proposing to tell a certain story but veering helplessly at every fork in the road to scoop up other stories that strike him as equally worthwhile, is partly what makes them so funny." Tyler found that the "style itself is the book's biggest joke; the first sentence is 407 words long." Other critics expressed less patience for Pearson's brand of storytelling. "Should you venture into this verbal swamp," George McCartney wrote in the *National Review*, "you'll find little more than a gaseous parody of the Bonnie-and-Clyde story entangled in a marsh of good-ole-boy digressions about local grotesques." Tyler, on the other hand thought the characters had "the swarming entangled look of the crowd in a Breughel painting, but each face stands out separately, innocent and endearing."

Pearson and his friend Dona Cunningham have completed a screenplay based on *Off for the Sweet Hereafter*.

Most of Pearson's reviewers, both friendly and hostile, have remarked upon the similarities between his labyrinthine prose style and that of William Faulkner. Faulkner is indeed one of Pearson's principal literary influences, as are Flannery O'Connor, Mark Twain, and Laurence Sterne. In a 1986 interview with Sam Staggs of *Publishers Weekly*, Pearson acknowledged the influence of *Tristram Shandy* on his own prose style, which he described as "put together with very loose sentence structure; it's so dense, and the sentences get longer and longer. I find it easier when I write just to keep going. I can always stick a 'that' or a 'which' in there and all of a sudden I've got a whole new direction to go in."

The Last of How It Was completes a loosely bound trilogy of works set in Neely. As in *A Short History*, Louis Benfield Junior and his Daddy are central characters. The novel consists almost wholly of Daddy's anecdotes and reminiscences on a broad range of topics, including murder, adultery, and homosexuality in prisons. In the *New York Times Book Review* (1987), Patricia Henley wrote: "William Styron once told the *Paris Review*, 'A great book should leave you with many experiences, and slightly exhausted at the end.' *The Last of How It Was* does that indeed."

After completing *The Last of How It Was*, Pearson quit (at least temporarily) the fictional landscape of Neely, North Carolina; each of his subsequent novels is set in the South, though not necessarily in his home state. Reviewers have continued to find his prose style the most arresting element of his fiction. Of his fourth novel, *Call and Response*, the *New Yorker* critic wrote,: "Above all, Mr. Pearson is a writer of sentences—long, baroque, ornate, and colloquial—in the manner of William Faulkner, though to an effect he might characterize as 'purely otherwise entirely.'"

The protagonist of Pearson's fifth novel, *Gospel Hour*, is a doltish lumber worker, Donnie Huff, who survives a logging accident during which he nearly drowns. His ambitious and unscrupulous mother-in-law senses an opportunity: proclaiming his survival a "miracle," she sends him out on the revival circuit to preach the gospel and accumulate as many donations as possible. Huff's ineptitude and his mother-in-law's stark venality fuel the novel's black comedy. "There are some stupendous laughs in *Gospel Hour*," Judith Freeman wrote in the *New York Times Book Review* (1991). "T.R. Pearson has written a very funny book and at the same time has called a certain kind of religion to account for its harsh and greedy fraudulence."

Roz Kaveney noted in the *Times Literary Supplement*, "*Cry Me a River*, his sixth novel . . . is another tale of mayhem, doomed love and the things single people do on dull evenings; the narrator is a . . . police patrolman investigating the death of a colleague . . . who carried a Polaroid of an unknown naked woman in his wallet." She found that all of Pearson's work has a suggestion of something more serious. "Pearson's rambling narratives tell us the whole story but not the whole truth." She termed his "most impressive achievement" the narrator's "baffled near-comprehension of what he is too limited ever to know."

In his *New York Times Book Review* notice of *Cry Me a River* William T. Vollmann wrote: "T.R. Pearson does not write like Faulkner. . . . His language is rarely sensuously elliptical—the opposite, in fact: it is conceptually precise, and beautifully so." Vollman concluded that "Beneath its whodunit disguise, *Cry Me a River* is a minor *Middlemarch* in its vivid delineation of a large gallery of complex, driven figures. Although . . . Pearson . . . give[s] us a perfunctory, obligatory denouement, you'll find no suspense, no burning gunpowder narrative trail. . . . [T]his novel is about two-thirds digressions by weight and the digressions are delicious . . . best . . . compared to chocolates. . . .

Pearson moved to New York City in 1985, soon after the publication of his first novel. The move had no perceptible impact on his choice of subject matter or on his style; in fact, Pearson relished the opportunity to write about the South from a distance. "It's easier to draw away and look back, rather than being in the middle of it," he told Sam Staggs in *Publishers Weekly.* "I can see things more clearly." More recently, however, Pearson returned to the South and settled in Carroll County, in southwestern Virginia.

PRINCIPAL WORKS: A Short History of a Small Place, 1985; Off for the Sweet Hereafter, 1986; The Last of How It Was, 1987; Call and Response, 1989; Gospel Hour, 1991; Cry Me a River, 1993.

ABOUT: Contemporary Authors 130, 1990; Contemporary Literary Criticism 39, 1986; Harris, A. (ed.) A World Unsuspected: Portraits of Southern Childhood, 1987. *Periodicals*—Kirkus Reviews April 15, 1985; Library Journal June 1, 1986; National Review December 5, 1986; New York Times June 20, 1985; January 23, 1986; New York Times Book Review July 7, 1985; June 15, 1986; November 1, 1987; April 7, 1991; April 11, 1993; New Yorker September 4, 1989; Publishers Weekly June 20, 1986; Time July 14, 1986; Virginia Quarterly Review Autumn 1991; Washington Post Book World June 16, 1985; Winston-Salem Journal July 14, 1985.

URSULA PERRIN

PERRIN, URSULA (June 15, 1935–), American (German-born) novelist, writes: "My first language was not English but German. I was born in Berlin, Germany. My parents emigrated to the U.S. in April 1938. They sailed from Bremerhaven aboard the luxury liner *Queen Mary* and I still have a photo, taken in the ship's dining room, of my mother and my father in party hats while the kid (me—I was an only child) digs an anticipatory spoon into something new called *grapefruit.* I've hated grapefruit ever since, and the recurrent dream that I've had since childhood is of a giant green (probably North Atlantic) wave, about to roll over my life. Despite the party hats, there was nothing frivolous about my family's exit from Germany. They were running for their lives.

"My mother was born in Peenemunde, a sleepy German resort town on the Baltic Sea, where, during World War II, the first V-2 rockets were developed and tested. Her family name was Kemp, her mother's family was Schoenfeld. Both families could trace their lineage back to the thirteenth century, when that part of Germany was called a *Mark,* or border area, and was fortified against the 'infidel' tribes, particularly the Slavs. In college my special interest was medieval history. Reading the chronicles of thirteenth-century East German monks was like reading about the American 'Wild West.' Raids, fortifications, horses, board sidewalks, mud!

"My father's family, the Gutmanns, had emigrated from Russia to Germany early in the nineteenth century. My father fought in World War I on two fronts, and later supported himself, a sister and an aunt, while going to medical school. In the late 1930s, when the Nazi government began their economic and social campaign against Jews, my parents decided to emigrate—my father was Jewish (my mother was not). They went to New York City, and after my father passed the New York State Medical Boards they moved to Amsterdam, New York, a small town on the Mohawk River, in upstate New York. Deep, snowy winters, blissful sunny summers! I can claim a reasonably happy childhood although, obviously, life was full of anxieties for a small refugee family living in an upstate town without other family or friends. Looking back, I'm astonished at their bravery. My parents insisted on being 'real Americans,' which meant reading the newspapers, voting, and taking part in the life of the community. Although they had a large library of German books, we all read mainly in English. By the time I was nine I was reading and enjoying Jane Austen, the Brontës, and anything else I could find.

"One night in 1945 I went to 'the early show' at the Rialto Movie Theater with my mother—school night, special treat. That night, they showed the first newsreels of the concentration camps. The theater was full of people, and completely silent. On the way home I asked my mother why people would do anything like that. My mother answered that 'human beings are the worst of the beasts'—an answer I didn't grasp at the time. A few months later, my father heard from the International Red Cross that his younger sister had died in a concentration camp. After that, he was always angry . . . or reading. My mother read, too, constantly—in my mind I still hear her beautiful crystalline laugh as she turns a page. I think the most constant theme in my fiction has been the liberating power of art and the human imagination. All my life I've known that animals speak to each other but the ability to hope, plan, and live another life while reading or writing a novel seems to me a uniquely bestowed gift—an utterly human mode of survival.

"In August of 1956 I was married to Mark Perrin. While he went to medical school, I taught history but I knew I wanted to write. Between 1960 and 1964, I produced three children (Tom, Chris, Nick) and my first novel which (luckily) no one published. My first 'real' novel, *Ghosts*, was published in 1967.

"I've always made it a goal to write honestly, as a human being living a very full life in the tumultuous twentieth century. My favorite novelist is Vladimir Nabokov. My pet peeves are Freudians and deconstructionists. I think 'writing degree zero' makes about as much sense as 'how many angels can dance on the head of a pin?' *All* writing is subjective. So what? English literature ought to be taught by people who love language instead of sociology majors with tin ears. Politically, I think socialist, and vote Democrat. I work actively for New Jersey's beautiful but battered environment. Current reading: *Who Will Tell the People* by William Greider. At the age of fifty I took up horseback riding and am now very involved with 'Zimilie's Andante,' an elderly but still elegant thoroughbred. I am still married to husband number one—my friend and lifelong companion. I am a feminist but think that all of us, male and female, need to be more generous and nurturing, to each other and to the world. If there were another twenty-four hours in my day I would organize a business devoted to the sale and distribution of good 'little-press' fiction. My life has been dedicated to reading and writing and I still believe in the magical power of words—to enlarge, to enrich, to enchant."

Ursula Perrin's novels are reconstructions of the lives of mature, married women who reflect on their past, their relationships with men, their friendships with other women, and their present situation. Every one of Perrin's books has earned lavish critical praise, but she has not enjoyed great commercial success.

Ghosts was heralded as an unusually good first novel. It focuses on one woman, Eleanor Munson, a married college graduate with children, who reflects on the maturing process: "how life goes on endlessly turning, birth to death, death to birth. . . . how just living can grind you down small." Her story begins when she is nine years old in a bedroom of a large family house in upstate New York. Her sister is crying, her father, a doctor, is out on his rounds; outside, her mother is mowing the lawn. As the day progresses, it becomes clear that her brother, who was in Europe with the army, has been killed. The Munson family contain their grief silently, so that the "ghosts" of the past are never properly laid to rest. In a typical adolescent manner, Eleanor observes with interested detachment the strange behavior of adults. She has problems of her own, because her boyfriend is of the wrong class, and in the end she rejects him.

Although the subject matter of *Ghosts* is grim, Perrin's realistic evocation of teenage turmoil is written with humor, and Eleanor herself is witty, quirky, and optimistic. The book was praised for its accuracy and simplicity, its poignancy and readability. The author's spare, straightforward style was universally admired. Jane Oppenheim, writing in *Bestsellers*, stated that Perrin had "achieved much in this little novel."

A decade after *Ghosts, Heart Failures* appeared. The story is narrated by Dr. Nell Dreher Kurtz Calverson, like Perrin the daughter of German émigrés, the father a doctor, who grew up in upstate New York. Nell meets her childhood friend Carrie when her former husband, now married to Carrie, is injured in a car crash and brought to the hospital where she works. As he lies in a coma, the women piece together their past lives, their friendship with each other and with Mina, the reckless poet who also fell in love with Carrie's charming but selfish husband, and later committed suicide. Nell's second marriage has also failed, and in the course of the narrative there is a good deal of reflection on the state of her present relationship with another man.

With skill, and the same spare, economic style she employed in *Ghosts*, Perrin packs a huge amount of plot into a short novel. Nell's memories, which are reported in third-person form, contain revealing, epiphanic episodes. *Heart Failures* is literate, intelligent, alluring and amusing. It was, in the opinion of a reviewer for *Publishers Weekly*, written by "a born storyteller," whose "quiet, lovely novel is poignant, probing, compassionate."

Perrin's third novel, *Unheard Music*, is a retrospective chronicle of the life of forty-year-old Antonia Haseltine. While at college, Antonia meets Charity Mullet, an unbalanced girl whose wealthy parents died violently when she was eleven years old. As Tonia graduates, finds employment as a secretary, and pursues an operatic career, the hapless Charity enters and reenters her life. Tonia abandons her singing career in order to marry a successful suburban doctor upon whom she is miserably dependent, and with whom she is bored and frustrated: "He did the money, she did the house and kids." After an affair with another doctor, she is abandoned by her husband, and her eldest child is killed in an accident. Finally, Tonia achieves self-realization. Humor pervades this ostensibly bleak tale, which, according to Susan Fromberg Schaeffer in the *Chicago Sunday Times*, embodies a universal "truth, beautifully perceived, wonderfully articulated." Like its predecessors, the novel is an account of limitation, which many women readers can readily recognize and understand, an account which is "marvelously true and therefore heartbreaking," Schaeffer wrote. Perrin's ear for dialogue is accurate, her vision tragic and also ironic, and her writing considered, as always, entirely engaging.

In *Old Devotions*, Perrin unfolds the story of the friendship between Isabel Schliemann, a mediocre novelist with a failed marriage and a dull career, and Morgan Whiteside, a successful stage manager. When Morgan develops leukemia, Isabel falls in love with her husband, and is forced to reexamine her life and her motivations, the restrictions that "old devotions" and emotional laziness have imposed on her. Perrin's usual themes, an unhappy marriage, a frustrated career, a crisis of health, and the inextricable intertwining of women's lives and loves—are treated with characteristic irony and realism. Reviewers praised Perrin's perception, the grace of her prose, and the depth of her characterization. Some felt that *Old Devotions* was her best novel to date. In the opinion of Betty Leighton in the *Winston-Salem Journal*, the novel had more subtlety and sensitivity than Perrin's earlier work. There are no easy answers, Leighton observed, and the unexpected is always to be expected: "The mystery of human nature abounds, which is to say that her novels are real."

Perrin again juxtaposes two women protagonists in *The Looking-Glass Lover*. Barbara Bigelow, the narrator, is a poor teacher and novelist living in New Jersey. She has been deserted by her alcoholic husband and her children have left home. Her cousin, Claire Parker, is a wealthy, apparently happily married, sophisticated writer of short stories. Barbara wants everything Claire has, including her husband, a doctor, and is unaware that Claire is fundamentally unfulfilled. Her son had been killed in a car crash, she is suffering from writer's block, and she does not love her husband. Finally she leaves him to Barbara, and embarks on a doomed affair with Barbara's former lover. Absorbing one another's lives, the two women eventually distinguish their own, independent identities.

Some reviewers found the literary device of the mirror in *Looking-Glass Lover*, the way in which the women's lives constantly reflect one another, contrived and superficial. Others were unhappy with Perrin's tendency to produce two-dimensional and unlikable male characters. In general, however, the novel was well received as another warm, witty, and well-written account of quiet female despair. In the words of a reviewer for *Publishers Weekly* (1989), "Perrin's books . . . get better each time out."

Ursula Perrin's parents were Max Gutmann and the former Gretchen Kemp. She became a naturalized American citizen in 1944, and received a degree from Smith College in 1956. A member of the Author's Guild and the Author's League of America, she lives in Summit, New Jersey.

PRINCIPAL WORKS: *Novels*—Ghosts, 1967; Heart Failures, 1978; Unheard Music, 1981; Old Devotions, 1983; The Looking Glass Lover, 1989.

ABOUT: Contemporary Authors 101, 1981. *Periodicals*—Bestsellers April 1, 1967; Chicago Sunday Times November 15, 1981; January 23, 1983; Chicago Tribune November 22, 1981; Kirkus Reviews July 15, 1978; May 15, 1989; Library Journal June 1, 1989; Los Angeles Times November 20, 1981; February 20, 1983; New York Times Book Review August 20, 1989; Publishers Weekly September 15, 1978; November 19, 1982; June 9, 1989; Winston-Salem Journal February 6, 1983.

PERRY, ANNE (October 28, 1938–   ), British mystery novelist writes: "I was born in London, England, a few months before the war, and spent the first years of my life there, although I was evacuated a couple of times, for short periods. My schooling was very interrupted, both by frequent moves and by ill health, but I do not feel as if I have been deprived because of it. I read a great deal, and had parents who gave me time and attention. There was always discussion in the house, and as far as I can recall, no subject was forbidden.

"Because much of my education was acquired haphazardly, there are some rather large gaps in it, and some odd additions. I loved translations from the classical Greek and Latin, histories, drama especially, legends, and poetry. I do not think I have changed much!

"There was never anything I seriously wished to do except write, but I was very late in actually

ANNE PERRY

putting pen to paper, rather than merely dreaming about it and visualizing stories in my head. And when I did begin, it took me ten years before my first book was accepted, by which time I was in my mid-thirties.

"During those ten years I wrote historical novels, heavy in politics, intrigue, and battles, and my own philosophies. Some of them I care about very much still, and will rewrite with stronger plotting and character, and I hope get published. Two I have already rewritten, particularly one set in the early Inquisition in Aragon, 1484, told from the point of view of the Inquisitor. It is his voyage of discovery about himself, his faith and the nature of free agency. The other is set in the French Revolution. I have already done that three times, and am about to do it a fourth, with far more character and plot which is fictional rather than the factual events (which to me are fascinating), but I realize for a novel I need more new plot.

"I began writing mysteries set in Victorian London on a suggestion from my father as to who Jack the Ripper might have been. I found I was not interested in that particular question, but totally absorbed by what happens to people under the pressures of investigation, how old relationships and trusts are eroded, and new ones formed. *The Cater Street Hangman* was accepted, and I continued to write about the characters involved.

"Over the years I have expanded my canvas, listened to a great deal of constructive help and criticism, and endeavoured to broaden out of strictly mystery genre into writing a novel which happens to include a mystery. I believe there is very much which can be said in this format. It is the eternal conflict of ethics, questions of cause and effect, complicated morality, the subtler reasons why people do things, individual's and society's structure and responsibilities. There is no reason why serious thoughts cannot be raised by a story which involves a gripping plot about characters we like. A good novel is written on many levels.

"I began the Monk series in order to explore a different, darker character, and to raise other questions about responsibility, particularly that of a person for acts he cannot remember. How much of a person's identity is bound up in memory? All our reactions, decisions, etcetera spring from what we know, have experienced. We are in so many ways the sum of all we have been!

"I have also written two parts of an epic fantasy trilogy which I began when my agent said to me that I had a better book in me than I had so far written, because I always held something back, 'pulling my punches.' She told me to do something entirely for myself, regardless of whether I thought it would sell or not. Indulge myself. I thought for a long time as to what kind of a story I wanted—war story, mystery, love story, etcetera. I realized what I really wanted, for the heart and the gut, was a quest, a search for truth. It is now written, although it is not yet accepted, and contains love, adventure, philosophy, imagination, and I believe is the best thing I have done, perhaps because it is the most sincere, and the most thoroughly thought through.

"The sequel is written, and I have the third on the 'back burner' in my mind. It is my highest ambition to write something which would enrich as others and I have been enriched and inspired by the writers of the past."

Anne Perry told Helga Borck and GraceAnne A. DeCandido in *Twentieth-Century Crime and Mystery Writers* that she enjoys the Victorian for "its dramatic contrast between upstairs and downstairs, manners, morals, the splendour and squalor so close to each other, the value of reputation." She also noted that the period trappings, the "long gowns, fog, hansom cabs, etc., the necessity of extraordinary manners, double standards, etc. are fun!" Perry's novels have been highly praised for their vivid and authentic recreation of Victorian England. Borck and DeCandido, however, offer the reminder that "these are not light-hearted romps through Victorian rose gardens. . . . Perry's interest lies in showing how individuals in a restrictive society with rigid notions of status and propriety may respond to pressures to conform, and how society in turn protects its interests in the face of deviation or rebellion."

Most reviewers have found Perry's three-dimensional characters worthy of the realistic, consistent settings she creates for them. Above all, they are not modern people simply placed in the past, but are true inhabitants of their era. "For a plot to be powerful, the reader has to believe that all the characters would really behave as they do," she said in the *Writer* in March 1991. "The moment something does not make sense, the spell is broken." Perry therefore finds it useful to create first a one-page biographical sketch for each character who has more than a bit part; here she notes everything from family background and social status to fears and obsessions. She also stresses consistency between personality and physical appearance, and believes it is better to allow characters in effect to describe themselves: "The feelings characters express and the words they choose are very strong indicators of personality, and much sharper to the reader than descriptions of vices, virtues, wit, gentleness, etc." Another reason Perry's characters are more complex and interesting than many other series characters is that she allows them to develop from book to book. In another article in the *Writer* in October 1993, she pointed out that series characters like Miss Marple and Hercule Poirot "do not noticeably progress or have any personal life outside the plot of the current story. Others, whom I personally admire more, grow, have changing relationships, and inhabit a world of places and events that also develop. Dorothy Sayers's Lord Peter Wimsey is an excellent example of the latter type."

Published in 1979, *The Cater Street Hangman* was the first of Perry's popular Victorian mysteries featuring the genteel Charlotte Pitt and her husband Thomas, an inspector with the London police. Part of the plot concerns the courtship between Charlotte and Thomas. Charlotte is marrying beneath her class, while her sister Emily will marry above hers. Borck and DeCandido point out that from book to book "one watches the Pitts adjust to marriage, produce children, move to larger quarters and acquire a maid. This is in contrast to, and in occasional conflict with, the more privileged lives of those among whom Charlotte and Emily pursue their investigations, and indeed of Emily herself." Their connections gain the sisters entry into London's best society, a subtle, intricate world largely inaccessible to the streetwise Thomas. This is not to say that Thomas approves, or sometimes even knows, about the covert sleuthing of his wife and sister-in-law. And it is this parallel investigating of the same crime by the two Pitts

that gives Perry's plots their variety and intricacy.

Perry's second Pitt mystery, *Callander Square*, offers early proof that her intention has never been to write lighthearted Victorian romps for the squeamish. Here the grisly crime is infanticide as two dead babies are discovered in the fashionable Callander Square neighborhood. *Library Journal* reviewer H. C. Veit praised Perry for creating a "story of sin and scandal, of which adultery is the least. . . . The characters are particularly strong and lively and the story is full of authentic atmosphere."

Not even the Pitts themselves are immune to tragic scandal. In *Cardington Crescent* Emily, Charlotte's sister stands accused of the murder of her husband, whose affair with Emily's young cousin was hushed but known.

In 1990, after ten Pitt novels, Perry's interest in exploring a "different, darker" Victorian character led to *The Face of a Stranger*, her first William Monk mystery. Rosemary Herbert, in the *New York Times Book Review* noted that in the Pitt series "while the issues differed . . . the format was familiar; the novels were constructed to a satisfying blueprint, with the wife infiltrating society in aid of the police inspector's competent investigations of middle- and low-brow life." Herbert then goes on to point out that *The Face of a Stranger* represents both a natural progression in Ms. Perry's concern with social issues and a significant development away from the formulaic. In fact the novel is a classic example of the book that turns the author's recognized strengths in an entirely new direction."

William Monk is a London police detective but, as the novel opens, he is in a hospital after a traffic accident has left him an amnesiac. When he returns to the department, he must not only learn about himself, but also deal with a particularly ticklish mystery: the sensational murder of Major the Honorable Joscelin Grey, a popular Crimean war hero. The case will require Monk to delve into the secrets of a noble family; he suspects that his superior, the crafty Runcorn, hopes that he will fail. Monk is faced with the double bafflement of a difficult investigation and piecing together the puzzle of his own identity. But there is more to Perry's plot than just murder and revelations. According to Herbert, Perry brilliantly "extends Monk's amnesia to encompass his awareness and understanding of much of the social and political climate of his day, thereby using his unbiased perspective to examine tragedies like child prostitution and the horrors of the Crimean War . . . with new eyes."

Perry followed this successful Inspector Monk

debut with *A Dangerous Mourning*, in which the widowed daughter of a seemingly impeccable aristocratic family is found stabbed to death in her bed. As Ann Arensberg, in the *New York Times Book Review* (1991) so grimly put it, when Monk begins his investigation "family secrets and civil corruption come spilling out like maggots in a garbage pit." She also writes that Perry "still seems genuinely outraged by an era in which pious ideals masked inhuman callousness" and "of all the evils the most intolerable to Ms. Perry is the dependency of women." To quote one of the novel's women characters: "Men dislike agitation and anything that detracts from a woman's image as serene, dependable, innocent of all vulgarity or meanness, never critical of anything except slovenliness or unchastity, and above all never contradictory towards a man." Arensberg, however, feels that this time Monk's investigation "takes a back seat to the family melodrama and the feminist message."

Perry has continued the Monk series with *Defend and Betray* and *A Sudden, Fearful Death*. A dissenting voice was raised to the chorus of praise for Perry's work by Thomas Boyle in a review of *A Sudden, Fearful Death* in the *New York Times Book Review*. He termed the novel "a miasma of narrative infelicities that makes one yearn for a revival of the *real* Victorian practitioners of unreadable melodrama. . . . Much of its difficulty seems centered on the unfocused character of Monk. . . . A detective with a shattered memory who thinks in overheated, equally shattered prose is a most unpromising guide through a suspense thriller. Moreover, the mystery of Monk's 'dark fear' of his past is never resolved . . . leaving one to wonder why it is introduced. . . . "

That somewhat prescient comment by Boyle antedated the release in 1994 of *Heavenly Creatures*, a film that purports to tell the story of a passionate friendship between Pauline and Juliet, teenagers in New Zealand. The film climaxes with the murder of Pauline's mother by both girls. Publicity surrounding the film forced Anne Perry to reveal that she was the real Juliet and had served five years in prison for the crime after a 1954 trial. Perry told John Darnton in a 1995 interview in the *New York Times* that her participation in the murder was the payment of "a debt of obligation because Pauline had written letters to her when she was confined to a sanitarium." Darnton continued: "Attempts to distinguish between right and wrong preoccupy her writing. A sense of persecution threads through her conversation, and expressions of remorse are not volunteered. But she says she accepted responsibility for her deed after a few

months in prison. . . . " Perry explained her publicity tours and television interviews thus: "The reason that I'm sticking my head over the parapet at all is that other people have made such a noise."

PRINCIPAL WORKS: *Novels*—The Cater Street Hangman, 1979; Callander Square, 1980; Paragon Walk, 1981; Resurrection Row, 1981; Rutland Place, 1983; Bluegate Fields, 1984; Death in the Devil's Acre, 1985; Cardington Crescent, 1987; Silence in Hanover Close, 1988; Bethlehem Road, 1990; The Face of a Stranger, 1990; A Dangerous Mourning, 1991; Highgate Rise, 1991; Belgrave Square, 1992; Defend and Betray, 1992; Farriers' Lane, 1993; A Sudden, Fearful Death, 1993; The Hyde Park Headsman, 1994; The Sins of the Wolf, 1994; Traitor's Gate, 1995; Cain His Brother, 1995.

ABOUT: Contemporary Authors New Revision Series 22, 1988; Twentieth-Century Crime and Mystery Writers, 1991. *Periodicals*—Library Journal March 1, 1980; New York Times February 14, 1995; New York Times Book Review November 18, 1990; October 20, 1991; October 17, 1993; Writer March 1991, October 1993.

PESETSKY, BETTE (BLOCK) (November 16, 1932–), American novelist, writes: "I was born in Milwaukee, Wisconsin. I was a child of the Midwest and a child of the depression. I grew up hearing anecdotes about what was called 'better times.' I ran the streets of working-class neighborhoods—a life that I had been born into—and for me those were the 'better times.' Growing up in the Midwest in those years was exciting—a period of surging changes and political experiments. The Milwaukee I knew had a Socialist mayor, and we all believed that poverty was only temporary. The secure middle-class life that my parents had known was over by the time I was born, and like many families in those years ours became occasional transients in search of work, and we circled the Midwest. Ultimately my parents returned to St. Louis, where my father had been born.

"Libraries were the most important places in the world to me. All the books I wanted were free and that along with the occasional dime for admission to a Saturday afternoon movie seemed to make life complete. Since poverty for my parents was a state of mind and the American dream always beckoned, they never accepted that I was most completely a child of my neighborhood. By the time I reached junior high school, I had discovered a way to live. I could write and perhaps was saved.

"I studied chemistry in college as well as literature, because depression children need the security of a way to make a living. Yet for

BETTE PESETSKY

graduate education, I gleefully went to the Writers' Workshop at the University of Iowa where, surrounded by people who wrote, I began to consider the possibilities of a life in which that could be the primary goal. There were few writing workshops at universities at that time and I learned how to exit with fierce competition and criticisms, and how to toughen my skin. Yet practical necessities intervened and I spent many years afterward doing medical editing and working as a ghostwriter. But my stories gradually accumulated. And by the late 1970s I began to be published in literary magazines.

"I am very interested in the rhythm of language and believe that sentences have a beat of their own. I'm a ruthless rewriter and a pruner. I read my work out loud to myself searching for the essence of a particular sentence, its resonance.

"*Stories Up to a Point*, my first collection of short stories, was published in 1982. Its critical reception was deeply satisfying to me. I was exploring the lives of contemporary women and how they survived in society. My novel *Author from a Savage People* was published in 1983. Who owns art? Who gets the credit? It was the story of a woman ghostwriter whose work has won a Nobel Prize for a man named Quayle. *Digs*, a novel published in 1984, continued my interest in defining art. It was essentially the story of an attempt to dig up a beautiful apartment house that was designed to promote perfect living. Can the way one lives be art? Four years later I published *Midnight Sweets*, a novel about a woman who makes cookies and sees this skill as

artistry as the heroine searches for a perfect cookie, one that would resonate with meaning. It was also for me a way of defining how one values woman's work.

"My second collection of short stories, *Confessions of a Bad Girl*, published in 1989, contains a series of connected stories about a brother and sister who survive the indignities of a fractured family. In 1991 I published the novel *The Late Night Muse*, which was perhaps for me the most difficult book I have written because I tried to create as a heroine a modern poet. For a woman to be taken seriously as an artist I fear that she must adopt a suitable facade—she must in effect look the part. My heroine failed that test and had to succeed on her own terms.

"I am a frequent contributor of book reviews to newspapers and periodicals. I am an insatiable reader—I read contemporary fiction, poetry, biographies, history. If I had to declare a main interest it would be how women fit into society— and how best to explain and describe their lives."

The daughter of Louis Block, a small-business owner, and Rose (McKnight) Block, Bette Pesetsky earned a B.A. at Washington University in St. Louis in 1954, and an M.F.A. in creative writing at the University of Iowa in 1959. In 1956 she married Irwin Pesetsky, a professor of anatomy.

Pesetsky's short fiction began appearing in the *Cimarron Review, Kansas Quarterly*, and other small literary journals in the late 1970s. Recognition for her efforts soon followed, and she received a creative writing fellowship from the National Endowment for the Arts (1979–1980) and a writing grant from the New York Council on the Arts (1980–1981). With the blossoming of her literary career, Pesetsky has been in demand as a teacher and lecturer; she has taught at Fordham University, the Iowa Writers' Workshop, and other universities, and in 1985 served as dean for faculty research at Adelphi University in Garden City, New York.

Almost all of Pesetksy's fiction focuses on the travails of contemporary women. Her heroines, many of whom are locked in a perpetual struggle to find their places in society, suffer the indignities of marital infidelity, illness, and violence, and are often overwhelmed by feelings of uselessness, boredom, and isolation. The fifteen short tales in her critically acclaimed first collection, *Stories Up to a Point*, are concerned with the shattered lives of middle-aged women. Pesetsky's prose is lean and stark, and dialogue is minimal. Gail Gilliland noted in the *Philadelphia Inquirer* that "all, but two of the stories are narrated by the I, as if *I* am in fact the only person to whom I can speak, the only one who will really listen. . . . " Many of Pesetsky's narrators search in vain for some continuity in their lives. Cleaning out the apartment once occupied by her grandparents, the narrator of "The Hobbyist" discovers that her grandfather's lifelong hobby was collecting samples of dust from various locations, which he put in bottles and labeled; the narrator's husband, however, wants the dust—tangible pieces of the past—out of their house. In "From P Forward," which refers to the collection's title, the narrator's search for continuity takes the form of a compulsion to create graphs of special occasions. Translating a fact or event into a given point, P, she remarks, "Anything was possible from P forward."

"With their compactness, their flat tone," David Quammen wrote in the *New York Times Book Review*, "*Stories Up to a Point* read like telegraphic dispatches from the battlefield of modern life. . . . Generally these women sound shell-shocked. But the messages are clear. They carry, some of them, important news from the front." *Times Literary Supplement* reviewer David Montrose found in Pesetsky's stories the influence of Donald Barthelme's style: "Pesetsky has borrowed Barthelme's method but not his madness, eschewing the surreal for a firm attachment to the quotidian. . . . Neurotic, lonely, sad, Pesetsky's women endure lives of quiet desperation and write anxious, jerky prose. But they occupy no world apart; theirs is the one we inhabit. . . . " In the *Georgia Review*, Doris Grumbach commented, "I admire the strong silences that exist among the words, between the sentences, and hover everywhere over the events in Bette Pesetsky's *Stories Up to a Point*." Grumbach's only reservation was that Pesetsky's "prose leaves large air holes through which, if one happens to put the book down in mid-story, memory escapes."

May Alto, the protagonist of Pesetsky's first novel, *Author from a Savage People*, is a brilliant but disgruntled ghostwriter, tired of others always getting credit for the work she does. A man named Quayle wins a Nobel Prize largely on the strengths of the enigmatically titled *Eine Leerstelle*—German for "an empty space"—a book written by May. May proceeds to concoct an elaborate blackmail scheme, threatening to expose the fraudulent Quayle unless he gives her not only the prize money, but the prize itself and all the accouterments of his life, including the human.

In *Harper's*, Frances Taliaferro wrote, "Questions of art and authenticity, delirium and reality, hover at the sharp edges of this eccentric novel, but the central conflict remains the war between men and women, and the outcome is unclear." *New York Times* reviewer Christopher Lehmann-Haupt conceded that the novel's plot may "sound a bit far-fetched, especially the idea of awarding the Nobel Prize to a two-book author who sounds like a cross between Kahlil Gibran and Lewis Mumford. But in the world created by Mrs. Pesetsky's mordant, hallucinatory prose, such extremes seem not only possible but also downright plausible." In the *New York Times Book Review* (1983), Timothy Foote agreed that it was "hard to accept, even in fantasy," that an author as "insignificant" as Quayle could win a Nobel Prize. "Naturally," Foote wrote, "the condition of the ghostwriter has not been overlooked in modern fiction. . . . But no one so far has tried what Bette Pesetsky gets away with in this savage, funny small novel— that is, using ghostwriting as a metaphor to dramatize the view that women do most of the work of creation while men (unfairly) get most of the credit."

The four narrators of Pesetsky's second novel, *Digs*, become obsessed with a gigantic hole in the ground. Walter and Sara Simon, a middle-aged New York couple, came into an inheritance and move into a farmhouse several hours outside the city. Walter soon begins an extensive excavation in search of the magnificent apartment house built by an old utopian community once resident on the site. The enormous hole he digs exerts a strange power and becomes the very center of his life, disrupting his relationships with his wife and sons. "The depth and complexity Pesetsky's earlier narratives seem to be searching for are in full bloom in *Digs*," Michael Feingold wrote in the *Village Voice*. "The immaculately terse, hard-edged sentences that have made her writing a model of austere clarity from the start are still present, but the monochrome, depressive feeling that often accompanied her arias for solo voice has been replaced by the rich sonorities and twisting rhythms of a quartet."

The sources, nature, and consequences of female creativity are recurring themes in Pesetsky's fiction. May Alto, in *Author from a Savage People*, is a creative artist who works incognito; her greatest work has been expropriated by men. Sara Simon, in *Digs*, is a painter whose work undergoes a strange transformation after her husband embarks on his quixotic excavation. Christopher Lehmann-Haupt noted in the *New York Times* that "when Sara Simon threatens to fulfill herself as an artist . . . the vital world of the novel comes to a stop. As . . . Pesetsky has said several times before with her fiction, the world as it exists cannot tolerate female artists—

or, to put it the other way around, when a female artist emerges, the world as it is must end."

Theodora Waite, the principal character in Pesetsky's third novel, *Midnight Sweets*, is a woman who has built a successful financial empire on the basis of one seemingly insignificant creative talent—baking cookies. "*Midnight Sweets*, like its heroine," David Leavitt wrote in the *New York Times Book Review* in 1988, "is gentler, less astringent; the fine sense of irony that is Ms. Pesetsky's special gift is leavened by an enriching sympathy and a willingness to let the sadness of certain lives speak for themselves." One of the five novels nominated as Best Book of 1988 by the *Los Angeles Times*, *Midnight Sweets* was also listed as one of the notable books of 1988 by the *New York Times Book Review*.

Pesetsky's fourth novel, *The Late Night Muse*, also earned a mention as one of the *New York Times Book Review* notable books of the year 1991. Its protagonist, Bernadette, is a prolific but largely unrecognized thirty-seven-year-old poet dying of an unnamed neurological disorder. As her death approaches, she becomes increasingly obsessed with her own posthumous reputation. With the little time left to her, she embarks on a methodical quest for literary immortality. She names a literary executor, one of her cousins, and sets out to amass and collate every scrap of paper related to her literary life. She also begins a journal, a sort of guide for her literary executor, in which all the loose ends of her life and work will be tied together.

Eric Kraft, reviewing the novel in the *New York Times Book Review*, commented, "As she has come to define herself in terms of her work, Bernadette has come more and more to dread interruptions and the people who bring them." When her husband insists that they go to a party, she falls and knows that it is the beginning of the end. She becomes completely dedicated to her work. But what she leaves, according to Kraft, is "hurried, vague and sly . . . a sketch, not a portrait. Still, *The Late Night Muse* is disturbing and valuable as a cautionary tale, a fable for poets. The lesson: Skip the party and write the poems. It's later than you think."

In *Cast a Spell*, a woman's creativity is devoted to magic tricks. Known as Miz Magic, star of a children's television show, she is the subject of an exposé by her cousin; as Shelby Hearon observed in the *New York Times Book Review*, "When all is told in *Cast a Spell*—and all is always told in . . . Pesetsky's wry, dry tales—the conclusion seems as surprising as the hidden mirror, the false bottom and the concealed compartment that permit the magician's tricks."

Many reviewer's have commented on the obvious depth of Pesetsky's talent, depth some feel she has not yet plumbed. However, Frederick Busch, in the *Southern Review*, found intent in what Pesetsky has done: "She is, on the whole, not passionate in her prose; it is precise, ironic, smart. It comments, with what you feel is keen accuracy, on lamentation and delight—but it doesn't generate delight or misery: it is the prose of experience already over, not in process."

PRINCIPAL WORKS: *Short stories*—Stories Up to a Point, 1982; Confessions of a Bad Girl, 1989. *Novels*—Author from a Savage People, 1983; Digs, 1984; Midnight Sweets, 1988; The Late Night Muse, 1991; Cast a Spell, 1993.

ABOUT: Contemporary Authors 133, 1991; Contemporary Literary Criticism 28, 1984; Dictionary of Literary Biography 130, 1993. *Periodicals*—Georgia Review Fall 1982; Harper's April 1983; Los Angeles Daily News December 1, 1991; Nation June 11, 1983; New York Times April 18, 1983; November 2, 1984; New York Times Book Review February 14, 1982; March 27, 1983; November 13, 1988; November 3, 1991; Philadelphia Inquirer February 10, 1982; Southern Review Spring 1991; Times Literary Supplement September 10, 1982; Village Voice November 13, 1984.

PETERS, ELIZABETH(pseudonym of BARBARA[GROSS] MERTZ) (September 29, 1929–), American detective story writer, writes: "I spent the earliest years of my life in a small town in Illinois—and when I say 'small,' I mean fewer than 2000 people. It was an idyllic sort of existence, I suppose, except for a few minor disadvantages like a nationwide depression and the fact that my hometown had no library. Luckily for me both my parents were readers. From my mother and a wonderful great-aunt I acquired most of the childhood classics and a few classic mysteries. My father's tastes were somewhat more eclectic. By the time I was ten, I had read (though I won't claim to have understood) Mark Twain, Shakespeare, Edgar Rice Burroughs, *Dracula*, and a variety of pulp magazines, to mention only a few. I can't emphasize too highly the importance of this early reading experience—its diversity as well as its extent. I will not claim that a writer must also be a compulsive reader, but it certainly helps.

"When I was in fourth grade we moved to a suburb of Chicago and I discovered the public library. I read everything I could get my hands on, but I didn't begin writing until I was in high school. Oak Park-River Forest High School was one of the finest public institutions in the country. I was majoring in history, but I had a minor

ELIZABETH PETERS

in English, and among the courses I took was one in creative writing. It may well be that the first seeds of a desire to write were planted during that course, when my teacher called me out of another class (a definite no-no in those days) to ask whether I had—unconsciously, of course—plagiarized the sonnet I had handed in the day before. That sonnet is the only thing I've ever written that has appeared in a respectable literary magazine. We sent it to *Saturday Review*, asking readers whether they could identify it. They couldn't. It was my own—such as it was.

"I didn't want to be a writer, though. I wanted to be an archaeologist. After graduating from high school I went to the University of Chicago—not because it had a world-famous department of Egyptology, but because it was close to home and I had received a scholarship. My mother went back to teaching to help out with expenses, and I worked every summer and part-time during the year. Practicality was the watchword; I was supposed to be preparing myself to teach—a nice, sensible career for a woman. I took two education courses before I stopped kidding myself and headed for the Oriental Institute. I got my doctorate there when I was twenty-three.

"Much good it did me. (Or so I believed for many years.) Positions in Egyptology were few and far between, and in the post-World War II backlash against working women, females weren't encouraged to enter that or any other job market. I recall overhearing one of my professors say to another, 'At least we don't have to worry about finding a job for her. She'll get married.' I did. And they didn't.

"While I was raising my children—the most challenging, tiring, rewarding, demanding job in the world—I still wanted to be an archaeologist. I had, however, become addicted to mystery stories, and finally decided I would try to write one. It was awful. The second was awful too. I rather enjoyed the process, though, and kept on scribbling. My husband's job sent us to Germany for two years; the additional leisure (for we were able to hire household help) and the stimulus of travel abroad allowed me to produce a book that finally aroused some interest in publishing circles. It didn't sell, but it got me an agent. Exasperated by his inability to sell the book, which he had liked, he demanded, 'Can't you write something else besides mystery stories?' Thus my first book to be published was not a thriller but *Temples, Tombs, and Hieroglyphs: A Popular History of Egyptology*. It was followed by *Red Land, Black Land: Daily Life in Ancient Egypt*. Finally that degree had 'paid off,' in a way I never expected. I am modestly proud of the fact that those two volumes are still in print almost thirty years after they were written.

"Finally, in 1966, I managed to get a mystery novel published. *The Master of Blacktower* appeared under the pseudonym of Barbara Michaels. I have written approximately twenty-five mysterysuspense novels under the Michaels name and another two dozen under my second pseudonym, Elizabeth Peters. (The ostensible reason for using pseudonyms is that readers need to distinguish the various types of books written by a single author: Mertz writes nonfiction on archaeology; Michaels writes thrillers, many with a supernatural element; and Peters focuses on mystery-suspense. I find the various names a horrible nuisance, but apparently readers do see a difference between the productions of these personae.)

"It has taken me over a quarter of a century to realize that I love to write, and that this is what I should have focused on from the beginning. If I were superstitious, which I am not—and if there were not so many examples that prove the contrary—I would fancy that fate somehow pushes us into the kind of life that is best for us. I am still fascinated by Egyptology, and I have used my training, not only in the nonfiction books and articles I have produced, but in what is probably my most popular mystery series, written under the Peters name: the saga of Victorian archaeologist Amelia Peabody, who has been terrorizing 19th-century England and Egypt through seven volumes (so far). The research necessary for these books is a joy in itself, and the characters have become almost frighteningly real to me.

"The research skills I learned can be applied to any field; I have used them to collect background material for novels that deal with the Peasants' Revolt, Etruscan archaeology, vintage clothing, the Risorgimento, the Chartist movement, and innumerable other subjects. Accuracy is very important to me as a novelist; not only does my own professional pride demand it, but I have many readers whose expertise is at least as great as my own. They can and do chastise me when I make mistakes. To err is human, but to err through carelessness or laziness is inexcusable.

"The craft of writing delights me. It is impossible to attain perfection; there is always something more to be learned—figuring out new techniques of plotting or characterization, struggling with recalcitrant sentences until I force them to approximate my meaning. And nothing is ever wasted. Everything one sees and hears, everything one learns, can be used.

"At the present time [1992] I am living alone, except for various animals, in an old farmhouse in the Maryland countryside. My children are grown and married, with children of their own. I have three lovely granddaughters, one of whom is already writing mystery stories. I have never been able to understand how people can complain about being lonely or bored; there are so many interesting things to do, so many fascinating people to know. I love my work, and I hope to go on doing it till I drop at the age of 99. In my spare time I collect vintage clothing, cats in all forms, and a variety of other unnecessary objects. My hobbies include gardening, sewing (especially the construction of Victorian costume), reading, music, embroidery, and long conversations with fellow mystery writers."

As Elizabeth Peters—a pseudonym created by combining the first names of her daughter and son—Barbara Mertz has created three particularly colorful women: Dr. Victoria Bliss; Jacqueline Kirby; and her best-known and most interesting character, Amelia Peabody. Mertz introduced Peabody in the 1975 mystery *Crocodile on the Sandbank*. Set during the Victorian period, the story is told by thirty-two-year-old Amelia, whose domineering father has just died. Amelia, a self-proclaimed "spinster," declares: "Why should any independent, intelligent female choose to subject herself to the whims and tyrannies of a husband? I assure you, I have yet to meet any man sensible as myself." That philosophy eventually changes when she travels to Egypt and meets the irascible Radcliffe Emerson, an archaeologist on a dig. Ame-

lia's trip produces much more excitement than just meeting her future husband. The uncovering of a lost tomb and a two-thousand-year-old walking mummy add to what Susan Dunlap, in *1001 Midnights*, called a "wonderfully amusing romp."

Throughout the series Peabody and Emerson continue to call each other by their surnames; Dunlap describes their union as a "Tracy-Hepburn relationship," and points out that Amelia is "exceptionally well educated, full of endurance, and never, never forgoes her principles. Peters's skill is in keeping the friction inherent in this situation amusing, yet making the characters just realistic enough to be credible and immensely likable . . . it is the interchange between the characters that is the delight of the book."

And then there is the Peabodian wit. In another dire predicament in *The Snake, the Crocodile and the Dog*, Amelia quips: "I closed my eyes and clung to Emerson. We would die in one another's arms, as he had once proposed. The idea did not appeal to me any more now than it had on that occasion." The Peabody-Emerson team is later expanded to include their precocious son Walter, better known as Ramses. Together they continue their efforts to protect the heritage of ancient Egypt from plunderers, with Amelia becoming "that one woman outpost of Empire in Victorian England," to quote the dust jacket of *The Curse of the Pharaohs*.

Peters's penchant for exotic locales is also evident in her Victoria Bliss series. Dr. Bliss is an American art historian who often finds herself matching wits with thieves and other rapscallions of the art world. In certain novels, like *Street of the Five Moons*, *Silhouette in Scarlet*, and *Trojan Gold*, she is joined by Sir John Smythe, himself and art thief, with whom she has a complex relationship. Another Peters character is Jacqueline Kirby, a librarian and later a novelist. In *The Murders of Richard III*, Peters presents an interesting variation on an old mystery theme, when Kirby is invited to a party at an English country house. The variation is that the quests are supposed to act like members of Richard's court, which inspires a murderer to use historical methods to dispatch victims.

Mertz has been equally successful and prolific as Barbara Michaels, starting with *The Master of Blacktower*. In an interview in Kathryn Falk's *Love's Leading Ladies*, Michaels admits that it was "very derivative, but very educational, because I learned a lot about plotting and character development. I also learned that writing is hard work!" Joanne Harack Hayne in *Twentieth-Century Romance and Historical*

Writers places Michaels's novels in two categories: historical romance—although Mertz might object to the word "romance"—and those dealing with the supernatural. Hayne, however, wonders if Michaels is uncomfortable with the latter. "Imbued with the author's characteristic intelligence, these are, on the whole, rather less satisfying works, perhaps because the element of pastiche is missing," she writes. "The best of the Michaels novels are those with a historical setting (*Wings of the Falcon*), or those in which a historical background figures prominently (*Wait for What Will Come*). Those which take place in the present, but in which supernatural events are rooted in history to legend (*Ammie, Come Home*), are more convincing than those in which the supernatural is a literal element of the plot."

As both Michaels and Peters, Mertz is known for her meticulous research; it is especially delightful when she chooses a theme that corresponds with one of her own personal interests, such as Egyptology and the Amelia Peabody series. Her interest in antique clothes, for example, adds fascinating detail to *Shattered Silk*, in which a young woman, reeling from the break-up of her marriage, encounters murder, ghosts, and romance in Georgetown. In *Vanish with the Rose*, a woman takes a job for which she is unqualified as a landscape architect at the last place her missing brother was seen. "There's a creaky old house, a ghost (or perhaps more than one), a 100-year-old murder, and a drunken would-be killer," according to *Library Journal.* "Not quite as good as *Ammie, Come Home* . . . or *Be Buried in the Rain* . . . but close. Lots of gardening detail makes things even more interesting."

Reviewers agree that Mertz's strong women characters are central to her appeal. Writing in the *Washington Post Book World*, Sarah Booth Conroy describes these women as "characters who burst forth their corsets of self-doubt and outside denigration, and learn to make it on their own or as equal partners with their lovers. All are opinionated, independent, strong, brusque, suspicious, quick to take offense, slow to ask for help and funny. The stories are really about liberation." Mertz would agree; in *Love's Leading Ladies*, she describes them as "intelligent, independent women who fall into the hero's arms *only* because they fall in love. They don't need men for financial or emotional support. They are capable of making it alone and would rather be alone than settle for second best. Not all my heroines marry the heroes."

Despite this emphasis on strength and independence, Mertz is not impressed with the hard-boiled female detective genre. "It amazes me to hear these books called realistic," she told *Library Journal.* "For the women I know, real life consists of dealing with the butcher or plumber. Very few women are trained in karate or in handling a gun. I like to write about ordinary women who are faced with a situation where they have to show gumption, courage, and wit. I don't find these other characters particularly valid feminist figures. That's not my kind of feminism, and I'm a proud feminist."

Barbara Mertz was born in Canton, Illinois, to Earl Gross, a printer, and Grace Tregellas Gross, a teacher. She earned all of her degrees from the University of Chicago—Ph.B., 1947; M.A., 1950; Ph.D., 1952. She was married to Richard R. Mertz, a professor of history, from 1950 until their divorce in 1968.

Barbara Mertz was awarded the first Anthony Grand Master Award for her contributions to the field of romantic suspense.

PRINCIPAL WORKS: *As Barbara Michaels*—The Master of Blacktower, 1966; Sons of the Wolf, 1967 (reissued as Mystery on the Moors, 1968); Ammie, Come Home, 1968; Prince of Darkness, 1969; The Dark on the Other Side, 1970; Greygallows, 1972; The Crying Child, 1973; Witch, 1973; House of Many Shadows, 1974; The Sea King's Daughter, 1975; Patriot's Dream, 1976; Wings of the Falcon, 1977; Wait for What Will Come, 1978; The Walker in Shadows, 1979; The Wizard's Daughter, 1980; Someone in the House, 1981; Black Rainbow, 1982; Dark Duet, 1983; Here I Stay, 1983; The Grey Beginning, 1984; Be Buried in the Rain, 1985; Shattered Silk, 1986; Search for the Shadows, 1987 (in U.K.: Search the Shadows); Smoke and Mirrors, 1989; Into the Darkness, 1990; Vanish with the Rose, 1992; Houses of Stone, 1993. *As Elizabeth Peters*—The Jackal's Head, 1968; The Camelot Caper, 1969; The Dead Sea Cipher, 1970; The Night of Four Hundred Rabbits, 1971 (in U.K.: Shadows in the Moonlight); The Seventh Sinner, 1972; Borrower of the Night, 1973; The Murders of Richard III, 1974; Crocodile on the Sandbank, 1975; Legend in Green Velvet, 1976 (in U.K.: Ghost in Green Velvet); Devil-May-Care, 1977; Street of the Five Moons, 1978; Summer of the Dragon, 1979; The Love Talker, 1980; The Curse of the Pharaohs, 1981; The Copenhagen Connection, 1982; Silhouette in Scarlet, 1983; Die for Love, 1984; The Mummy Case, 1985; Lion in the Valley, 1986; Trojan Gold, 1987; The Deeds of the Disturber, 1988; Naked Once More, 1989; The Last Camel Died at Noon, 1991; The Snake, the Crocodile and the Dog, 1992. *Nonfiction as Barbara Mertz*—Temples, Tombs, and Hieroglyphs: The Story of Egyptology, 1964, rev. ed. 1978; Red Land, Black Land: The World of the Ancient Egyptians, 1966, rev. ed. 1978; (with R. Mertz) Two Thousand Years in Rome, 1968.

ABOUT: Contemporary Authors New Revision Series 11, 1991; Falk, K. Love's Leading Ladies, 1982; Pronzini, B. and Muller, M. 1001 Midnights: The Aficionado's

Guide to Mystery and Detective Fiction, 1986; Something About the Author 49, 1987; Twentieth-Century Crime and Mystery Writers, 1991, Twentieth-Century Romance and Historical Writers, 1990. *Periodicals*—Bestsellers 4, 1990; Library Journal July 1992; Washington Post Book World June 11, 1989.

PHILLIPS, CARYL (March 13, 1958–), British (West Indian–born) novelist, dramatist, and essayist writes: "I was born in St. Kitts, West Indies. St. Kitts was, at this time, a British colony. My parents migrated to England in the same year, and I was brought up in Leeds.

"As a schoolboy, I always enjoyed writing and reading, but it was not until I was a student at University that I decided I wanted to become a writer. At this stage the only form with which I was familiar was the theatre, having directed a number of plays as an undergraduate. So I began my writing life as a playwright, but with a desire that I might one day write prose.

"In 1985 I published my first novel, *The Final Passage*. Since then my dramatic work has taken second place to my prose. These days I also teach both literature and creative writing, and this leaves even less time for anything but prose. But I do intend to continue to work in drama.

"I am not particularly interested in trying to detect any dominant themes or ideas in my writing. There are others, who are better qualified than I am, who can do this. Suffice to say, I live, I read, and I write. In that order."

———

In 1992 Caryl Phillips told an interviewer for the *Caribbean Review of Books*: "For me there was never any nostalgic or remembered Caribbean, it was a Caribbean that I've had to discover, and, I think, being born in the Caribbean, and the quest to return to the Caribbean, the desire to be here, has made me a writer." Reared and educated in England, he has reversed the pattern of most transplanted writers who move from their native lands to alien cultures—V. S. Naipaul, for example. Naipaul, in Phillips's opinion, rejected his West Indies heritage and chose to live in England, "writing in an oppositional tradition; in the tradition of those who would seek to bury us West Indians under the full weight of their assumed cultural superiority." Phillips, however, describes his goal as "in some small way to be contributing to the development of a relatively youthful Caribbean literature, rather than being merely an exotic adjunct to English literature."

The conflict of two cultures—European and Afro-Caribbean—has produced "a sense of

CARYL PHILLIPS

otherness" which he acknowledges may have "destabilized me slightly," but it has also produced the tensions out of which his writing has emerged. In his nonfiction *The European Tribe*, Phillips confronted that "otherness" directly. The book was inspired by his reactions on his first return to St. Kitts, where he still had family but "felt like a transplanted tree that had failed to take root in foreign soil." He set out then on a voyage of self-discovery in Europe: "I knew I would have to explore the European Academy that had shaped my mind. A large part of finding out who I was would inevitably mean having to understand the Europeans." In a journey that mingled the subjective with attempts at objective reporting on the countries he visited, Phillips found racism everywhere—in personal encounters and in the general insensitivity of Europeans to minority peoples. As a personal expresssion, *The European Tribe* is an understandably angry book, but reviewers complained of the strident rhetorical overlay. Andrea Lee wrote in the *New York Times Book Review*, that Phillips breaks "with disconcerting frequency into simplistic didacticism. . . . but when he abandons rhetoric he creates disturbingly powerful images. . . ." Ashok Bery, in the *Times Literary Supplement* observed that "there are plenty of things to be angry about," but pointed out that Phillips "engages only intermittently with the people he meets, the countries he passes through, and even with himself."

Since 1988 Phillips has had a house on St. Kitts where he lives part of each year. He says, however, that he could not live there all the time. He has formed attachments in Britain and, in recent years, the United States, and acknowledges that such wider cultural experience "has enabled me to develop in some ways." His first two novels are studies of the impact of emigration and deracination upon the islanders. By far the more bleak and despairing of them is *The Final Passage*, in which a young island woman of mixed race, Leila, helplessly in love with a feckless islander, marries him only to suffer neglect, abuse, and virtual abandonment by him after they have emigrated to England. The man, Michael, is perhaps representative of the loss of spirit inbred in the islanders after generations of slavery and colonialism. Apart from drink, sex, and speeding on his motorbike, he has no reason to exist. Unwilling to do hard menial work, he is idle and irresponsible. Already the father of a child by another woman, he takes no responsibility for his child by Leila. "Since individuals like Michael are unaware of the impersonal forces that have damaged their lives," Charles Sarvan and Hasan Marhama suggest in an essay on Phillips in *World Literature Today*, in 1991, "they continue the pattern: irresponsible, violent, fantasizing, trying to find temporary escape from a reality they do not comprehend and cannot combat. It is the reader who reaches an understanding."

The Final Passage may be read as a novel of exile; *A State of Independence* is a novel of return. Its central character, Bertram Francis, returns to his native Caribbean island after twenty years in England. He had gone abroad full of hope with a scholarship, but once there he lost interest in his studies and simply drifted from job to job: "England just take me over . . . Nothing happened to me in England, you can believe that? A big rich country like that don't seem to have make any impression on me. I might as well have left yesterday for I just waste off all that time.'" With the exception of a woman he had once loved, no one else on the island, even his mother, seems to have a place for him in their hearts or their lives, and he thinks of returning to England. The island has just received its independence and is in the throes of political pride and confusion. A bartender tells him: "'We living on an island where the typists can't type, where we have power cuts all the time, the movies pirated on ZYZ still have the New Jersey logos on them, the sea has sewage accidentally discharged into it, we have twenty-four hour bars that close, and the roads still breaking an axle every day.'" Although Andrew Salkey, reviewing the novel in *World Literature Today*, found it "a very, *very* bleak novel indeed, allegorizing, I think, accurately a densely bleak Caribbean," *A State of Independence* ends on a

note of promise with Bertram finding his own "state of independence." He watches a worker threading wires on telephone poles, "as though trying to stitch together the island's villages with one huge loop." It gives him a sense of purposeful resolve—"to imagine how he might cope, were he to make peace with his own mediocrity and settle back on the island."

The novel that most dramatically reflects the tensions in Phillips's own perceptions—and the possibility of transcending them—is *Higher Ground*, three seemingly unrelated stories that share a common theme. The first of these, "Heartland," is narrated by an African who works in the slave trade, and is patronized by the whites because of his command of English but despised by his own people. ("I merely survive and if survival is a crime, then I am guilty.") The second, "Cargo Rap," leaps ahead into the 20th century. Its narrator, Rudy, writes a series of letters from prison, where his efforts to win parole are constantly frustrated. Like the speaker in "Heartland," he is a captive and also like him, he is self-educated and uncommonly articulate. His letters, addressed to family and outsiders who organize a campaign to free him, trace a gradually accelerating political consciousness that leads him finally to madness. Sarvan and Marhama suggest a link to George Jackson, whose prison letters were collected in *Soledad Brother* in 1970. But Jackson's violent death in prison is not echoed in what happens to Rudy, whose sanity, rather than his life, is terminated. For Sarvan and Marhama the story is "a work that is disturbing in more ways than one."

The focus shifts quite stunningly in the third story, "Higher Ground," to a white woman, a Polish refugee from the Holocaust, who finds herself alone in England after being deserted by a white lover. She has a brief and tender affair with a man from the Caribbean, but he too leaves her to return to his homeland. The transference of the black experience of alienation and misery to a white Jewish woman is deliberate. Finding little or no representation of the suffering of his own people in the media, Phillips writes in *The European Tribe*, "I vicariously channelled a part of my hurt and frustration through the Jewish experience."

In all of Phillips's work slavery, literal and/or figurative, forms what Oliver Reynolds, in a review of *Crossing the River* calls his "presiding consciousness and conscience." As in *Higher Ground*, this book brings together stories from the past—a slave ship in 1752; an American plantation owner seeking a former slave in Africa in the 1840s; a love affair during World War II between a young Englishwoman and a black

American soldier. His stories, Reynolds writes, "derive . . . their moral power from a depiction of human goodness surviving degradation." This essentially philosophical theme unites past and present, black and white, slave and those who live in the illusion of freedom. It receives its most ambitious and dramatic treatment in his novel *Cambridge*. Once again he justaposes two unlikely characters whose paths cross with ironic and tragic consequences. The first narrator is a thirtyish Englishwoman, Emily Cartwright, who travels to the West Indies to oversee her father's plantation. She plans to return to England in a few months and enter a loveless marriage with a much older man, but while on the island she has a passionate affair with the plantation overseer, who is later murdered by a slave he has been abusing. The other narrator is that slave, Cambridge, now awaiting execution for the crime. Educated in England where he lived as a free man and became a missionary, he was betrayed into slavery.

Probably the most remarkable feature of the novel is the authenticity of these two voices. Emily's is a carefully cultivated English with which she reveals her own repressions and her deeply ingrained prejudices: "I was also aware that the highest position on which a sable damsel could set her sights was to become the mistress of the white man"; "The slaves ceased their Sisyphean labours. . . . "; "We all hope to welcome the day when liberty shall rule over an ample domain, but at present the white man's unfitness for long toil under the rays of a vertical sun would appear to go some way to justify his colonial employment of negro slaves, whose bodies are better suited to labour in tropical heat." Cambridge's is a self-consciously elevated speech reflecting his study of the Bible and his pride and dignity even when he is reduced to the ignominy of slavery: "I earnestly wished to imbibe the spirit and imitate the manners of Christian men, for already Africa spoke to me only of a barbarity I had fortunately fled"; "In one moment of weakness I called upon God's thunderous avenging power to direct the sudden state of death to myself, rather than permit me to become a slave and be passed from the hand of one man to another like a sack of grain, but the Lord, in His mercy, chose to spare me." Phillips did long and painstaking research for *Cambridge*, reading 19th-century novels, letters, journals, and accounts of travel to the Caribbean, which helped him to understand the period, and its cultural trappings. The result was pronounced a success by the reviewers. George Garrett, in the *New York Times Book Review*, hailed the novel as "a triumph of Caryl Phillips' craft and art . . . Now with *Cambridge* he takes a firm step toward joining the company of the literary giants of our time." For Maya Jaggi, in the *Times Literary Supplement*, "*Cambridge* is a masterfully sustained, exquisitely crafted novel. Through its multiple ironies and fertile ambiguity, it offers a startling anatomy of the age of slavery and of the prejudices that were necessary to sustain it."

Crossing the River consists of a prologue and four narratives. In the prologue a father bemoans having sold his three children to slave traders. The subsequent narratives detail the lives of two of the children, as well as those of the captain of a slave ship and a black G.I. in World War II England, depicting the two hundred and fifty years of the African diaspora. The father—who has had to say "The crops failed. I sold my children. I remember."—returns at the end to say, "I have listened. To reggae rhythms of rebellion and revolution dipping through the hills and valleys of the Caribbean. I have listened. To the saxophone player on a wintry night in Stockholm. A long way from home. For two hundred and fifty years I have listened."

Nicholas Lezard in the *London Review of Books* noted Phillips's gift for "accomplished ventriloquism. . . . a near-perfect pastiche of 18th and 19th-century English." Lucasta Miller, in the *New Stateman & Society*, praised the "author's capacity to create characters who invite real imaginative empathy." She judged Phillips's exploration of black and white relationships "nuanced, humane and sympathetic" and praised his "deep awareness of the historical process." In the *New York Times Book Review*, Janet Burroway pointed out that in *Crossing the River* Phillips deals with one of his overriding concerns: the message that "the diaspora is permanent, and that blacks throughout the world who look to Africa as a benevolent fatherland tell themselves a stunted story. They need not to trace but to put down roots."

Phillips has written plays for stage, screen, and radio. Three of his plays have been staged—*Strange Fruit* in Sheffield in 1980, and *Where There Is Darkness* and *The Shelter* at the Lyric Theatre in London in 1982 and 1983 respectively. *Strange Fruit* is a domestic drama of the conflict in a West Indian family living in England; the ambitious mother wants her sons to settle and prosper there, but the sons are drawn to their West Indian heritage. *Where There Is Darkness*, like the novel *A State of Independence*, deals with the problem of a West Indian planning to return home after twenty-five years in England; and *The Shelter* is a powerful two-character drama set in the first act, in the 18th-century, when a white woman and a black man finding themselves cast up on a desert island, lovers as we gradually discover, reach a crisis in their relationship. In his introduction to this play on interracial love, Phillips alludes to the classic example in drama, *Othello*: "In Africa I was not black. In Africa I was a writer. In Europe I am black. In Europe I am a black writer. If the missionaries wish to play the game along these lines I do not wish to be an honorary white, and do the state some service, for that tough taskmaster, history, has shown us the folly of such deceit."

Phillips's work has won him several honors and awards—the Malcolm X Prize for Literature for *The Final Passage* in 1985, the Martin Luther King Memorial Prize for *The European Tribe* in 1987, the Young Writer of the Year Award of the (London) *Sunday Times* in 1992, and that same year a Guggenheim Fellowship. He has taught writing in universities in India, Sweden, Canada, and England, and since 1992 he has been writer-in-residence at Amherst College in Massachusetts.

PRINCIPAL WORKS: *Fiction*—The Final Passage, 1985; A State of Independence, 1986; Higher Ground: A Novel in Three Parts; 1989; Cambridge, 1991; Crossing the River, 1993. *Nonfiction*—The European Tribe, 1987. *Drama*—Strange Fruit, 1981; Where There is Darkness, 1982; The Shelter, 1984, 1984; The Wasted Years (radio play) 1985; Playing Away (screenplay) 1987.

ABOUT: Phillips, C. The European Tribe, 1987. *Periodicals*—Callaloo Summer 1991; Caribbean Review of Books February 1992; Encounter May 1987; Kunapipi (Aarhus, Denmark) 9, 1987; 11, 1989; London Review of Books September 23, 1993; New Statesman & Society May 21, 1993; New York Times Book Review August 7, 1987; February 16, 1992; January 30, 1994; New York August 10, 1992; Times Literary Supplement April 10, 1987; March 15, 1991; May 14, 1993; World Literature Today Autumn 1985; Winter 1987; Summer 1990; Winter 1991.

PHILLIPS, ROBERT S(CHAEFFER) (February 2, 1938–), America poet, fiction writer, critic, and editor, was born in Milford, Delaware. He grew up in Laurel, Delaware, a community he considered culturally stifling. His father, T. Allen Phillips, was trained as a metallurgical engineer, but taught chemistry and physics at the local high school until he retired. His mother, Katheryn Schaeffer Phillips, was born in the Blue Ridge country of Virginia, considered socially above Laurel. Phillips's poem "Vertical and Horizontal" expresses his mother's discontents as well as his father's indifference to them. To supplement the family income, his mother wrote the weekly society column for the town paper.

ROBERT S. PHILLIPS

Phillips developed an early interest in music, learned to play the piano, and often traveled to Philadelphia or Wilmington on his own to attend concerts. Later, in high school, he formed his own dance band, which had a one-hour live program on a local radio station. Phillips received some of his education, from the town's fine public library. On Saturdays he devoured the poems of Wordsworth, Longfellow, and other 19th-century authors, as well as *the Catcher in the Rye* and *The Naked and the Dead*.

In high school, art displaced music as Phillips's major interest. Though he had planned to attend Pratt Institute to study painting, late in his senior year Phillips "felt much too ignorant to began to specialize so early." Instead, he chose to follow a liberal arts program at Syracuse University, where he helped pay his expenses by playing the piano in the dining hall. While an undergraduate, Phillips began writing seriously in Syracuse's crative writing program. Two of his classmates were Joyce Carol Oates, who became a lifelong friend, and Judith Bloomingdale, who became his wife. Phillips continued his education at Syracuse on the graduate level, aided by a teaching assistantship. After trying to cope with the "mountain of paper" created by three sections of freshman composition, Phillips decided not to pursue an academic career. Nevertheless, he thoroughly enjoyed graduate school, particularly his contacts with the poet Delmore Schwartz, whom he found to be a brilliant teacher and fascinating conversationalist. In graduate school, Phillips also published his first poems.

While waiting for Judith to finish her graduate studies, Phillips worked as assistant director of admissions at Syracuse. They were marrried in 1962, after she graduated. Moving to New York shortly after, Judith worked as an editor and Phillips began a career in advertising, in which he was to advance eventually to the position of vice president and creative director of J. Walter Thompson, Inc., a large advertising agency. At the same time, he published his first book of poems, *Inner Weather*, establishing the pattern of a double vocation. With the arrival of their son Graham in 1967, the Phillips family moved to Westchester County, and Phillips began the routine of commuting to New York City from the suburbs, which was interrupted only by a two-year stay in Germany in 1971–1972. Commuting to work, Phillips suggests, "may account for the prevalence of poetry over prose in my oeuvre; it was easier to write a short poem on the train than to juggle the manuscript of a novel."

Two months after their return from Germany in 1972, where Phillips had worked in an advetising agency, personal tragedy entered their lives; Judith Phillips had a stroke. Not only did this end her writing career, but her long illness shifted the responsibility of raising their son and maintaining the household to Phillips's shoulders. Sometime during his period of crisis Phillips stopped playing piano because he felt the joy had departed from his life.

In an interview with Jerome Mazzaro in *Modern Poetry Studies*, Phillips justified his career in advertising by describing it as "a good alternative to teaching for a writer. . . . Everything one says about a product . . . must be said in seventy words or less. This is a terrific discipline." He also pointed out that the "can write just about anywhere."

Robert McPhillips pointed out in the *Dictionary of Literary Biography* that if Phillips has never received the level of recognition that he deserves as a writer, it may be because he was "slow to establish himself strongly in any single genre." Phillips apparently refuses to be categorized in terms of a single genre, describing himself to Mazzaro as "a writer, not as a poet or critic or fiction writer." Between his first two volumes of poetry, *Inner Weather* and *The Pregnant Man*, he published works of criticism, a biography, and a volume of short stories, *The Land of Lost Content*, based on life in his hometown. This was followed over twenty years later in 1992 by a second volume, *Public Landing Revisited*. The choice of subject of his critical work *The Confessional Poets* in 1973 reflects the influence of poets like Robert Lowell and Sylvia Plath on his own development. As he told Mazzaro: "I must say that the so-called confessional

poets helped liberate my poetry," by making it more personal and autobiographical.

Phillips described *Inner Weather* as a work of "unassimilated influences," paticularly those of John Crowe Ransom, and has "always felt its publication was premature." However, Phillips considers *The Pregnant Man* to be "the cornerstone" of his poetry: "The book established the style and voice and many of the subjects of all that was to follow." The most enthusiastic review, by Joyce Carol Oates in the *New Republic*, recommended the book to feminists because in it Phillips demonstrates that "'feminine' sensitivity (and indeed, suffering) is hardly the exclusive lot of women." (The most important influence on this second book of poetry Phillips attributes to Erica Jong.) Phillips deliberately overturns the conventional sexual roles: " . . . my several pregnant men . . . are all fecund receptacles." Most poignant of these may be "The Invisible Man":

No one looks up
when I come into a room.
Someone sits down on me
when I occupy a chair.
People stretch on top of me
when I lie in bed.
I am an invisible man.
My words, empty cartoon balloons.

My motives, totally transparent.
But there are advantages.
I don't worry about a wardrobe.
When poeple don't know your're there,
it doesn't matter which suit
you wear. Sometimes I like
being an invisible man.
I can eavesdrop on all,

observe all idiosyncrasies. . . .

This self-description is followed by a plea to be "filled in":

Of course, you could help.
You could acknowledge my present,
come at me with your crayon set.
Look: Scribble in my hair, my eyes,
my mouth, limb my body's tree.
Give some color to my life.
I'm a person! (That too is a dream.)

Though his men may be "pregnant," Phillips insists that his book "is not about that now fashionable subject androgyny."

Phillips's third poetry collection, *Running on Empty* was popular because of its strong personal emotional content. The title poem, his most frequently autobiologized piece is one of several in the book dealing with Phillips's family life; it reflects his love of driving the family car to no particular destination: "I just had to drive, to get somewhere, to ward off my boredom." But at the same time the poem makes a strong comment on the nature of his relationship with his father.

> As a teenager I would drive Father's
> Chevrolet crosscountry, given me
>
> reluctantly: "Always keep the tank
> half full, boy, half full, ya hear?"—

In the poem the boy defies his father's injunction, drives on Empty "mile after mile, faster and faster" until his luck runs out:

> I stranded myself only once, a white
> night with no gas station open, ninety miles
>
> from nowhere. Panicked for a while,
> at a standstill, myself stalled.
>
> At dawn the car and I both refilled.
> But Father, I am running on Empty still.

The last lines suggest what is confirmed elsewhere in "The Whip" and "once"—that Phillips learned to survive despite the lack of his father's love.

In *Personal Accounts*, Phillips included new and selected poems from his previously published volumes, arranged not chronologically, but by topical "chapters" in each of which the poems express his continuing concerns. As Phillips describes them, "These chapters included poems on childhood in Delaware, middle age, lives of great artists, our travels in Europe, works of art, parts of the body, and, above all, survival. A good embodiment of this theme is found in 'the Stone Crab' . . . "

> Delicacy of warm Florida waters,
> his body is undesirable. Once giant claw
> is his claim to fame, and we claim it,
>
> more than once. Meat sweeter than lobster
> less dear than his life, when grown that claw
> is lifted, broken off at the joint.
>
> Mutilated, the crustacean is thrown back
> into the water, back upon his own resources.
> Once of nature's rarities, he replaces
>
> an entire appendange as you or I
> grow a nail. . . .
>
> Something vital broken off, he doesn't
> nurse the wound; develops something new.

From the appearance of *Inner Weather*, critics have commented on Phillips's technical facility. "Every poem I write," Phillips told Mazzaro, "has definite form. Each poem seems to come out in form, to take its own form before I give it one. . . . " He justified his use of form: "I think one of the prime responsibilities of an reasons for art is to give coherence to the incoherence of life—to order the daily disorder." Even in his free verse, Phillips detects a definite ordering rhyme. Enjambment coupled with the pun is his favorite device: "I use puns the way some poets use rhyme. They punctuate, they underscore, and hopefully they give second meaning."

Phillips insists that he does not deliberately write humorous poetry: "I never consciously set out to write a funny poem or even a funny line. But things often come out that way. Humor is part of the world of my imagination, I guess— one of the tools or weapons that I use to mine or fend off the real world, perhaps." Confirming also the elements of nostalgia, exuberance, affection, and mystery in his work, Phillips told Mazzaro: "My work is marked by its pursuit of the world *that could be* as well as by the world that is. Certainly many of the images are unreal or surreal." Phillips also pointed out that he had been influenced by the writers of the four Gospels: "I am, if nothing else, a Christian poet, as unfashionalbe as that may be today . . . New Testament thought and Old Testament language have been important influence . . . and the authors of The Book of Common Prayer. . . . "

His personal literary acquaintances are many, and these friendships have resulted in literary projects for and about them. He has edited works by other writers: William Goyen, Denton Welch, and Noël Coward. As literary executor of the estate of Delmore Schwartz, he published two volumes of Schwartz's letters, a collection of his essays, a book of poems, and a book of verse plays. Joyce Carol Oates remains "a loyal friend and a soul mate." Their friendship has been carried on largely through letters, and Phillips presented Syracuse University wth his half of their correspondence. Of his nonliterary friends, the artist Deloss McGraw has had several shows of paintings based on "The Wounded Angel," one of the poems in *Personal Accounts*. A separate edition of the poem, published in 1986, contains McGraw's etching.

Phillips has had numerous essays, interviews, and reviews published in periodical such as the *Paris Review*, the *Ontario Review*, *Modern Poetry Studies*, and the *Hudson Review*. He has also published two volumes of fiction, *The Land of Lost Content* and *Public Landing Revisited*, short stories set in a small town, "Public Landing." Although he insists that the characters "for the most part were totally imagined," he admits that a few were inspired my people he had known in Laurel, Delaware, his boyhood hometown. He does not offer a sentimental or sympathetic portrait of small-town life. "H. L. Mencken would have loved and applauded Phillips' depiction of the New South," Robert Emmet Long observed in the *Saturday Review*.

In 1987 Phillips received an Award in Literature from the American Academy and Institute of Arts and Letters. In addition, he has received fellowships from Yaddo, the Dierassi Foundation, and the MacDowell Colony. He has also served as professor of English and director of the Creative Writing Program at the Unviersity of Houston.

PRINCIPAL WORKS: *Poetry*—Inner Weather, 1966; The Pregnant Man, 1978; Running on Empty, 1981; Personal Accounts, 1986; The Wounded Angel, 1986; Face to Face, 1992; Breakdown Lane, 1994. *Fiction*—The Land of Lost Content, 1970; Public Landing Revisited, 1992. *Criticism*—Aspects of Alice: Lewis Carroll's Dream Child, 1971; The Confessional Poets, 1973; Denton Welch, 1974; William Goyen, 1979. *As editor*—Moonstruck: An Anthology of Lunar Poetry, 1974; Last and Lost Poems of Delmore Schwartz, 1979, 1989; Collected Stories of Noël Coward, 1983; Letters of Delmore Schwartz, 1984; The Stories of Denton Welch, 1985; Delmore Schwartz, The Ego Is Always at the Wheel: Bagatelles, 1986; Triumph of the Night: Tales of Terror and the Supernatural, 1989; Delmore Schwartz and James Laughlin: Selected Correspondence, 1991; Delmore Schwartz, Shenandoah and Other Verse Plays, 1991. *Other*—The Achievement of William Van O'Connor, 1969.

ABOUT: Contemporary Authors Autobiography Series 13, 1991; Contemporary Authors New Revision Series 8, 19983; Contemporary Literary Criticism 28, 1984; Dictionary of Literary Biography 105, 1991. *Periodicals*—Modern Poetry Studies Autumn 1978: New Republic December 9, 1978; Publishers Weekly April 25, 1994; Saturday Review May 1, 1971.

PILCHER, ROSAMUNDE (SCOTT) (September 22, 1924–), British novelist and short story writer was born in Lelant, Cornwall. When her father, Charles Scott, a British civil servant, was posted in Burma, her mother remained in England, having decided that Cornwall was a good place to bring up children. Lelant, where Rosamunde was born in a boardinghouse, is a small coastal village three miles from St. Ives, a community of free-spirited artists and writers. In St. Ives, which later became the fictional Porthkerris in Pilcher's best-selling novel *The Shell Seekers*, the family did their shopping and Pilcher went to school. Despite the often acute shortage of money while she was growing up, Pilcher told Amanda Smith of *Publishers Weekly* that she remembers her life in Cornwall, running wild over the beaches, picnicking and swimming, as "great fun—it was a lovely place to live."

Pilcher's writing career began a the age of seven when she overheard her mother describing how her friend Dorothy Black supplemented her army officer husband's salary by writing stories for the *Ladies Home Journal*. Pilcher told Amanda Smith that from that moment on, she saw writing as the ideal answer to the problem of how to become economically self-sufficient and at the same time to enjoy the satisfcations of family life—"one would get married and write little stories and be independent." A solitary child, Pilcher began filling exercise books with plays and stories. She was encouraged in this activity by her father, who returned to England in 1938 to take up a career as journalist. When she was eighteen, and on active duty with the Women's Royal Naval Service (1942–1946); one of Pilcher's stories was accepted for publication after years of rejection. In part because of this exacting apprenticeship, Pilcher never again in the course of her writing career received a rejection slip.

In 1946, shortly after her demobilization at the end of World War II, Pilcher married Graham Hope Pilcher, a Scottish war veteran, and moved to his family home in Invergowie, outside Dundee, Scotland, where she still lives. In this environment, in which there was more affluence than the one in which she had grown up, she found her lack of economic independence a disadvantage. While her husband was employed in the local jute factory, where he became a director and eventually president, Pilcher resumed her writing on a typewriter abandoned in the attic by her mother-in-law. Her first publisher was Mills and Boon, for whom, as she told Amanda Smith, she wrote, under the name of Jane Fraser, "sort of mimsy little love stories," because most publishers of hardback novels were not interested in light romantic fiction. Pilcher explained that she avoided the big magazines, even though they paid very well, because she found it boring to conform to their standards—no divorce, no this, no that."

When Pilcher was fifty, her career reached a turning point. She acquired a more helpful agents, left Mills and Boon, moved to Collins, and eventually to St. Martin's Press, who bought all of Pilcher's back books. At the same time, Pilcher began an association with *Good Housekeeping*, to which she sold more stories than did any of their other writers within the same decade. As Pilcher explained to Smith, she felt free at last from the restrictions of writing romantic fiction and able to turn to more realistic subjects that represented her true interests. She began to write "books about real life, people being unfaithful, loving and not loving and marrying the wrong person—the sort of grotty things that happen, as well as funny things."

Over the years, in addition to her writing career, Pilcher has reared four children, two girls and two boys, and maintained a large garden and a spacious house, where she often entertains. Consequently her writing has had to fit into the lives of those around her, and has been done in the kitchen or in one of the children's bedrooms. She continues to write on an old manual typewriter, after finding an electric one impossible. As she described those years to Smith, "It was a great life with all these little children and this wonderful thing of being able to earn." Personally modest about her attainments, she favors jeans and ratty cardigans and enjoys rambles in the fields near her home.

Though Pilcher is honest about writing for profit, she takes her craft and her readers seriously. While insisting that her work is not autobiographical, she told Smith that she does not write anything that she has not actually experienced. She feels that the writer must know the people and experiences in any work "from the bones out," and credits interruptions in her work schedule with allowing her time to become intimately familiar with her characters and their circumstances. When necessary, as in the case of the references to art in *The Shell Seekers*, she verifies her material with research.

The inspiration for her novel, *The Shell Seekers*, came from an article she read in *Harper and Queen* about the lives of upper-class people "who lived immensely Bohemian, very democratic, extremely hospitable lives." This reminder of the Bohemian residents of St. Ives, plus a long-standing desire to write about the boredom of civilian life during World War II, were given impetus by her editor at St. Martin's Press, who wanted a "big, fat novel for women, a good read." Although she admitted to Laurel Graeber, in an interview for the *New York Times*, that in *The Shell Seekers* she "had put a lot of myself down on paper," Pilcher at the same time denied that the novel is based on her life. Rather, the free-spirited heroine of *The Shell Seekers*, Penelope Keeling, is the woman Pilcher would like to have been, and writing about her was a "bit of wish fulfillment."

Pilcher's novels have been well received in the United States. Maeve Binchy, in the *New York Times Book Review* described *The Shell Seekers* as a deeply satisfying story, written with love and confidence." Stressing the importance of the central character, Binchy writers: "This is Penelope's book. It's the story of a woman who must have been like a lot of other people. Her ordinariness is what gives her strength and defines her." yet at the same time, the book "scans a time of hugh importance and change in the world"—World War II. Binchy measures the

success of this book by the fact that "a reader can be carried for more than 500 pages in total involvement with Penelope, her children, her past and the painting that hangs in her country cottage."

Pilcher's best-selling novel *September*, set in Scotland, was described by Belva Plain in the *New York Times Book Review* as giving the reader "a comfortable pleasure" through its description of the "interlocked lives of Violet Aird and her family and friends, with their numerous scandals and conflicts." The reviewer is content to overlook what she feels is "an overabundance of trivia, too many and too lengthy descriptions of clothing and interior decorations" for the sake of the character of Violet Aird, which is at the heart of the story.

There is a certain condenscension among reviewers of Pilcher's fiction, a tendency to dismiss it as escapist reading. But such an attitude misses the sturdy common sense and realism that inform her work. She has a healthy senbse of the challenges of writing and takes satisfaction in the growing seriousness with which her novels are taken.

PRINCIPAL WORKS: *Novels*—A Secret to Tell, 1955; April, 1957; On My own, 1965; Sleeping Tiger, 1967; Another View, 1969; The End of the Summer, 1971; Snow in april, 1972; The empty House, 1973; The Day of the Storm, 1975; Under Gemini, 1976; Wild Mountain Thyme, 1978; The Carousel, 1982; Voices in Summer, 1984; The Shell Seekers, 1987; Coming Home, 1995. *Novels as Jane Fraser*—Half-Way to the Moon, 1949: The Brown Fields, 1951; Dangerous Intruder, 1951; Young Bar, 1952; A Day Like Spring, 1953; Dear tom, 1954; Bridge of Corvie, 1956; A Family Affair, 1958; A Long Way from Home, 1963; The Keeper's House, 1963. *Short stories*—The Blue Bedroom and Other Stories, 1985; Flowers in the Rain and Other Stories, 1991. *Plays*—The Dashing White Sergeant, (with C. C. Gairdner), 1955; The Piper of Orde (with C. C. Gairdner); The Tulip Major, 1957.

ABOUT: Contemporary Authors New Revision Series 27, 1989; Twentieth-Century Romance and Historical Writers, 2nd ed., 1990. *Periodicals*—New York Times Book Review February 7, 1988; May 6, 1990; People Weekly May 28, 1990; Publishers Weekly January 29, 1988.

PIPES, RICHARD (EDGAR) (July 11, 1923–   ), American historian of Russian history, writes: "I was born in the Silesian town of Cieszyn, Poland. My father, a businessman, born in Lwow had been raised in Vienna and served in the Polish Legions during World War I. My mother was a native of Warsaw. During my childhood our household was bilingual, and I

RICHARD PIPES

spoke both Polish and German. In 1928 we moved to Warsaw.

"I recall an ordinary and happy childhood, not particularly disturbed either by the depression or the rise of Nazism. Adolescence brought with it, besides the usual psychological turmoil, a sudden awareness of the outside world and, above all, of music and art. My first passion was music and I seriously trained to be a composer and conductor: on the eve of World War II I was about to begin the study of counterpoint. But even before the war had interrupted my musicological studies, I realised that my talents were mediocre and turned my attention to the history of painting. At fifteen I began a monograph on Giotto.

"On September 1, 1939, the Germans bombed Warsaw and after that nothing was ever the same. We survived the siege of the city and spent one month under German occupation. My father managed to procure forged passports which allowed us to leave Poland on a German troop train for Italy. The trip was not without mishaps which could have ended tragically. We spent seven blissful months in Italy, where I continued studying the old masters and learned the language. In June 1940, as Italy was about to enter the war, we fled to Spain, and from there, by way of Portugal made our way to the United States, where we landed on my seventeenth birthday.

"I had nothing else on my mind but university studies. My father, who had managed to take some money out of Poland before the war, had very little to spare. I wrote on penny postcards

to one hundred colleges asking for fellowships and part-time employment. Muskingum college in Ohio offered me both and I spent two and a half years there. In 1943 I was inducted into the air force, which sent me to Cornell to study Russian. On being discharged three years later I enrolled at Harvard for a doctorate in history.

"My original intention at Harvard was to combine history, art, and philosophy, but the requirements for a higher degree demanded rather narrow specialization. I chose Russia as my principal field and soon found myself completely caught up in the subject. My doctoral dissertation dealt with Marxism and nationalism. On completing my degree in 1950 I was appointed an instructor in history and literature at Harvard. In 1958 I was given tenure. I never left Harvard.

"My first book, *The Formation of the Soviet Union*, published in 1954, dealt with the nationality problem during the Russian Revolution. I believe I was the first scholar in the United States to study this topic. Even so, I decided to give it up in favor of Russian political thought and institutions, which struck me as revealing extraordinary continuity. The fruit of these inquiries was *Russia under the Old Regime* (1974). Since that time, I have focused on the late 19th and early 20th centuries in Russia. The main results of these studies have been *The Russian Revolution* (1990) and *Russia Under the Bolshevik Regime*. The three volumes form something of a trilogy. I have not yet decided what I shall turn my attention to next, but it may well be a subject outside the Russian field.

"In 1981–1983 I served as director of East European and Soviet Affairs in President Reagan's National Security Council. It was a unique experience for a historian which taught me a great deal about politics and politicians and significantly influenced my views of the past.

"Although my entire professional life has been devoted to the study of politics, my early passion for art has not abated. It finds expression in an aesthetic approach to the writing of history with strong attention to narrative structure and the human dimension of events. I dislike 'social scientese,' which dominates the profession, and feel greater affinity for writers and artists than fellow-historians. I also have an aversion for intellectuals who claim omniscience and consider themselves superior to ordinary human beings. I feel best in our summer house in New Hampshire. I am happily married."

Because Russian history, Richard Pipes's specialty, has long been an ideological battleground, Pipe's various political activities, undertaken in the service of conservative, anti-communist organizations, are especially noteworthy. In 1976 he was chairman of "Team B," an intelligence review board of Soviet specialists created by then CIA director George Bush. In addition to his work on President Reagan's National Security Council, Pipes was a member of Reagan's State Department transition team. In 1988 he was chairman of Republication presidential candidate Robert Dole's U.S.-Soviet Relations Task Force. Since 1977 he has been a member of the executive committee of the Committeee on the Present Danger, an anticommunist organization. He is also a member of the Heritage Foundation and the Council on Foreign Relations. In a 1988 column in *U.S. News and World Report*, Michael Kramer called Pipes "the Sovietologist most worth listening to" and the "grandfather to the American right's hard line."

Pipes's scholarly work in Russian history is wide-ranging; it includes a two-volume intellectual biography of the Russian economist and historian Peter Struve (1870–1944) as well as *Survival Is Not Enough*, a book of policy analysis that warned of an inherently expansionist Soviet empire. At the heart of his historical work, however, are the three volumes which, taken as a whole, constitute a comprehensive history of Rusia and the Soviet Union through the middle of the 20th century: *Russia under the Old Regime, The Russian Revolution*, and *Russia under the Bolshevik Regime.*

Russia under the Old Regime treats more than ten centuries of Russian history, ending in the 1880s during the reign of Tsar Alexander III. It was then, according to Pipes, that "the ancien régime" in the traditionally understood sense died a quiet death in Russia. . . . , yielding to a bureaucratic-police regime which in effect has been in power there ever since." Unlike the historians who sought the roots of 20th-century totalitarianism in Western ideas—i.e., Marxism and Nazism—Pipes turned his attention to "Russian institutions." Most reviews of the book were favorable. Writing in the *Times Literary Supplement*, John Keep commented, "*Russia under the Old Regime* is a study in depth—learned, judicious, witty and full of common sense—in which the wisdom of the standard authorities blends with new insights gained from a knowledge of total power as it manifests itself in our era." Similarly, it was praised in *New York Review of Books* as "an excellent introduction, painstaking and enjoyable. . . . "

In the *New York Times Book Review* (1975) Adam Ulam wrote of *Russia Under the Old Regime*: "A work of historical synthesis of this kind calls for intellectual boldness and erudition, gifts with which the author is abundantly endowed. But it also requires a sense of proportion and precision, and it is on this count that we begin to run into some trouble." Ulam faulted Pipes for such rash pronouncements as: "One can state categorically that not one great Russian writer, artist, scholar or scientist of the old regime placed his work in the service of politics; the few who did were without exception untalented third-raters." Ulam cites Dostoyevsky and Turgenev as two writers of overtly political novels who were not certainly not "third-raters."

In the introduction to *The Russian Revolution*, Pipes writes, "This book is the first attempt in any language to present a comprehensive view of the Russian Revolution, arguably the most important event of the century." His account begins in the late 1890s, when large-scale revolts swept through Russian unversities, and ends in 1918, with the outbreak of the civil war and the execution of Tsar Nicholar II and his family. In the course of 842 pages, he provides detailed accounts of the 1905 and 1917 revolutions. Stressing the continuity in Russian history, he further elaborates his thesis (from *Russia under the Old Regime*) that the roots of Russian totalitarianism, which found its full expression under Stalin, can be found in the "partrimonialism" of the old regime. Most importantly, Pipes sees the Bolshevik seizure of power in November 1917 not as a popular insurrection, but rather as a coup d'état orchestrated by a small band of fanatical utopians led by Lenin.

Pipe's account contradicts not only the official Soviet version, but also that propounded by many Western historians. Determined to refute both resoundingly, Pipes lays the blame for the atrocities of the Soviet regime squarely on the shoulders of Lenin, his lieutenants, and his successors. Pipes is opposed to all theses that view Stalinism as a betrayal or aberration of an idealistic revolution. For Pipes, the Bolshevik seizure of power led inexorably to the horrors of Stalinism. His book is dedicated simply "To the victims."

Published in 1990 in the wake of Gorbachev's reforms and on the eve of the total unraveling of the Soviet Union, *The Russian Revolution* was received with respect but also considerable reservation by reviewers. It was described by Geoffrey A. Hosking in the *Times Literary Supplement* as "the first full-scale single-volume narrative of the Russian revolution," it was praised for its scholarship, but its continuity thesis—in Hosking's words, the belief that "the root of the Communist evil lies as much in the Russian heritage as it does in Marxism"—was challenged. Hosking found the book "erudite . . . lucidly and elegantly written . . . but not quite the 'comprehensive view of the Russian Revolution' Pipes promises in the preface." In the *New Republic*, Terrence Emmons pondered the question of the continuity theory: "Pipes' evolutionary view of history in general, and of Russian and Soviety history and culture in particular, has led him, I believe, to underestimate Russia's historical capacity for radical change." He questioned whether Pipes's "rigid notion of continuity in Russian history" will contribute to our understanding of the enormous changes that were taking place and would continue to take place in the 1990s.

Pipes concluded his history of the Russian Revolution with *Russia under the Bolshevik Regime*, published in 1994. Covering a period of civil war and political chaos up to Lenin's death in 1924, he arranges his material topically rather than chronologically, focusing on the economy, the civil war, the emergence of totalitarianism, and the famine of 1921 ("the greatest disaster in European history until then, other than those caused by war, since the Black Death.") Communism, Pipes believes, was a failure in every area: "perhaps the most pernicious idea in the history of human thought, that man is merely a material compound, devoid of either soul or innate ideas, and as such a passive product of an infinitely malleable social environment." It is Pipes's thesis—challenged by other historians but strongly argued by him—that although Lenin's rule might have been less overtly tyrannical than Stalin's, it neverlessless "insured that the man who controlled the central party apparatus controlled the party and through it, the state. And that was Stalin."

Like the two earlier volumes, the third impressed reviewers with its passion and conviction, as well as with the breadth of Pipes's knowledge of Russian history. As Geoffrey A. Hosking observed in the *Times Literary Supplement*: "this volume is driven by a moral vision which rightly insists that communism was a new and terrifying form of political evil, both precursor to and first embodiment of the various forms of twentieth century totalitarianism." But, Hosking added, with its sweeping judgments and "onesided" approach, the book "fails to do justice to what recent research has made possible"—specifically the role of workers, peasants, and soldiers in the shaping of events, and the emergence of local nationalism within the U.S.S.R—factors that led finally to the collapse of the Communist regime. In the *New York Times*, Christopher Lehmann-Haupt, who found Pipes's overall approach "a reward" for the read-

ers, acknowledged that Pipes's conservatism commits him to a less than "benevolent outlook" on the Russian Revolution. Nevertheless, Pipes tells "a great story in the most theatrical terms possible," according to Lehmann-Haupt. "Regardless of ideological bias, you cannot help but be caught up by his account of the struggle for the dying Lenin's mantle."

Pipes's *The Russian Revolution* and *Russia Under the Bolshevik Regime* were combined into *A Concise History of the Russian Revolution*. The *Publishers Weekly* reviewer termed the volume the "single most readable, useful and illuminating chronicle of the revolution and its aftermath" and praised the "remarkably vivid, compelling narrative" which "turns up fresh insights on every page."

Richard Pipes has received honorary degrees from Muskingum College (LL.D., 1988) and Adelphi University (D.H.L.., 1991). He had Guggenheim Fellowships in 1956 and 1975, and was Walter Channing Fellow at Harvard in 1990–1991. since 1965 he has been a Fellow of the American Academy of Arts and Sciences. Appointed Baird Professor of History at Harvard, he lives in Cambridge, Massachusetts. He married Irene Eugenia Roth in 1946; they have two sons.

PRINCIAL WORK: The Formation of the Soviety Union: communism and Nationalism, 1917–1923, 1954, rev. ed. 1964; Karamzin's Memoir on Ancient and Modern Russia, 1959; Social Democracy and the St. Petersburg Labor Movement, 1885–1897, 1963; (with W. Langer et al.) Western Civilization (2 volumes) 1968; Europe Since 1815, 1970; Struve: Liberal on the Left, 1870–1905, 1970; Russian under the Old Regime, 1974; Struve: Liveral on the Right, 1905–1944, 1980; U.S.–Soviet Relations in the Era of Detente, 1981; Survival Is Not Enough: Soviet Realities and America's Future, 1984; Russia Observed: Collected Essay on Russian and Soviet History, 1989; The Russian Revolution, 1990; Russia under the Bolshevik Regime, 1994; A Concise History of the Russian Revolution, 1995. As editor—The Russian Intelligentsia, 1961; (with J. Fine) Of the Russe Commonwealth (by G. Fletcher) 1966; Revolutionary Russia, 1968; P. B. Struve: Collected Works in Fifteen Volumes, 1973; Soviety Strategy in Europe, 1976.

ABOUT: Contemporary Authors 21–24, 1977; Who's Who in America 1990–91. *Periodicals*—Nation February 18, 1991; New Republic November 5, 1990; New York Review of Books April 17, 1975; New York Times March 14, 1994; New York Times Book Review July 13, 1975; October 7, 1990; Publishers Weekly August 21, 1995; Times Literary Supplement June 20, 1975; February 1, 1991; May 20, 1994; U.S. News and World Report July 11, 1988.

PIRSIG, ROBERT M(AYNARD) (September 6, 1928–   ), American novelist, was born in Minneapolis, Minnesota, the son of Maynard E. Pirsig, a professor and later dean of the Minnesota Law School, and Harriet (Sjobeck) Pirsig. He enrolled in the University of Minnesota at the age of seventeen, but quit in 1946 to serve a two-year hitch in the U.S. Army. After receiving his B.A. from the University of Minnesota in 1950, he traveled to India to study philosophy at Benares Hindu University. In 1954, Pirsig returned to the Midwest and married Nancy James. Over the next several years, he lived in Nevada and New Mexico, earning a living as a journalist, a science writer, and an industrial-advertising writer. He received an M.A. in journalism from the University of Minnesota in 1958 and began teaching English composition at Montana State College (now University) in Bozeman the following year. It was during this period that his serious disenchantment with modern values began, and he undertook a systematic investigation of "quality," a concept that figures prominently in his books.

Pirsig enrolled in a doctoral program at the University of Chicago in 1961. He financed his studies by teaching rhetoric to undergraduates. While in Chicago, he was plagued by emotional disorders, which culminated in his being hospitalized in a state mental institution. The agonies of this critical period in Pirsig's life reverberate like a haunting refrain throughout his first and most celebrated book, *Zen and the Art of Motorcycle Maintenance*.

Pirsig left Chicago without his doctorate, and from 1963 to 1967 he worked as a technical writer for various electronics firms in and around Minneapolis. In 1968 he traveled from Minneapolis to California by motorcycle with his twelve-year-old son Christopher. This journey forms the narrative skeleton of *Zen and the Art of Motorcycle Maintenance*. When Pirsig began to write about the trip, he thought he was writing a travel essay. The essay soon grew into a literary hybrid of mammoth proportions—part autobiography, part disquisition on values, and part novelistic travel book.

In a 1984 essay in the *New York Times Book Review*, Pirsig recalled the difficulty he had publishing what became one of the most successful books of the 1970s: "Certainly no one could have predicted what has happened. Back then, after 121 editors had turned us down, one offered a standard $3,000 advance. He said the book forced him to decide what he was in publishing for and added that, although this was almost certainly the last payment, I shouldn't be discouraged. Money wasn't the point with a book like this." *Zen and the Art of Motorcycle*

ROBERT M. PIRSIG

Maintenance, however, became a surprise best-seller, attaining the status of a cult classic.

On one level, the narrative is simple. A man and his son travel from Minneapolis to San Francisco. The man has a wife and another son at home in Minneapolis, though the reader learns almost nothing about them. Two friends on another motorcycle accompany the man and his son as far as Montana, but they too have very little bearing on the story. The man and boy travel alone after Bozeman, Montana, and since they are riding together on one motorcycle and are wearing helmets, there is little opportunity for dialogue or interaction between them on the road. They confront no physical danger; nor do they have any unforeseen adventures.

In *Zen and the Art of Motorcycle Maintenance* (*ZAAMM*, for short), the action—to the extent that there is any—is largely a vehicle for ideas, a spur for the father/narrator's philosophizing. Early on, the narrator noted the conflict between nature and technology, between man and machine; these basic observations are the starting point for a series of philosophical monologues, or what the narrator calls "Chautauquas." Through these Chautauquas, the narrator investigates the idea of "quality" (that is, values) using illustrations from such activities as motorcycle maintenance and teaching freshman rhetoric. For Pirsig, the study of quality *is* the study of values; the book's subtitle is *An Inquiry into Values*. That Pirsig's real interest in *ZAAMM* is something other than Zen or Motorcycles per se is made clear in the "Author's Note." After noting that the book is "based on actual occurrences," Pirsig writes: "Although much has been changed for rhetorical purposes, it must be regarded in its essence as fact. However, it should in no way be associated with that great body of factual information relating to orthodox Zen Buddhist practice. It's not very factual on motorcycles, either."

In the course of the extended Chautauquas, the narrator is constantly grappling with his shadowy alter ego, Phaedrus. Although he is a vehicle for philosophic inquiry like Plato's Phaedrus, Pirsig's Phaedrus is also the power of insanity, the potential recrudescence of the mental processes that led to the asylum. Robert Adams, writing in the *New York Review of Books*, noted that "'Phaedrus' represents the ghost that the present mature narrator must track down and lay. . . . " Adams termed Pirsig "a stunning writer." "The real test of a prickly, rankling book like ZAAMM," he added, "lies in its enduring power to disquiet. One can guess that even if the intense and confused metaphysics should pall . . . the wonder and fear of the novel would remain." He ascribed this effect as one "that grows, not simply out of effect making, but from quiet and deft prose on seemingly impersonal topics."

Writing in the *New Yorker*, George Steiner noted that "Pirsig's work is, like so much of classic American Literature, Manichaean. It is formed of dualities, binary oppositions, presences, values, codes of utterance in conflict. . . . Phaedrus is hunting the narrator. He is, at one level, the secret sharer, the intense questioner, the compaction of pure intellect. He has sprung directly out of the Plato dialogue that carries his name, and the device of having a living being pursued by a shadow out of Plato is by itself enough to certify Pirsig's strength, his mastery over the reader." Steiner concluded his review of ZAAMM by comparing it favorably to perhaps the greatest of American novels: "A detailed technical treatise on the tools, on the routines, on the metaphysics of a specialized skill; the legend of a great hunt after identity. . . . the analogies with *Moby Dick* are patent. Robert Pirsig invites the prodigious comparison."

Pirsig was divorced from his first wife in 1978, and married Wendy Kimball, a writer, soon after. In November of 1979, his oldest son, Christopher, was murdered in San Francisco as he left the Zen Center, where he was a student. It was Christopher who had accompanied Pirsig on the cross-country motorcycle odyssey. In his 1984 essay in the *New York Times Book Review*, Pirsig reflected on his son's death: "Where did Chris go? . . . He was a real, live person, occupying time and space on this planet, and now suddenly, where has he gone to? Did he go up the stack at the crematorium? Was he in the little box of bones they handed back? Was he strumming a harp of gold in some overhead cloud? None of these answers made any sense." When his new wife became unexpectedly pregnant, she and Pirsig had all but decided to go ahead with an abortion; Pirsig was in his fifties and had not recovered from the death of his son. A sudden revelation made him change his mind. "I said, 'Wait. Stop. Something's wrong.' What it was was unknown, but it was intense, and I didn't want it to continue. It was a really frightening thing, which has since become clearer. It was the larger pattern of Chris, making itself known at last. We reversed our decision and now realized what a catastrophe it would have been for us if we hadn't." Pirsig's daughter, Nell, was born in Sweden.

Pirsig's second book, *Lila*, which appeared seventeen years after ZAAMM, is, in many respects, a sequel. Subtitled *An Inquiry into Morals*, the novel finds a Pirsig-like character named Phaedrus living comfortably off the proceeds of a successful book, sailing his small boat around America. A storm on the Hudson River forces Phaedrus into a dockside bar near Kingston, New York. There he meets Lila, a heavy-drinking, middle-aged woman who has had serious psychiatric problems, and has once worked as a prostitute. After a drunken evening, Phaedrus consents to take Lila as far as New York City. Although they are completely mismatched, each finds something fascinating about the other. When an acquaintance of Phaedrus tells him that Lila is "a very unfortunate person of very low quality," Phaedrus is piqued, and he decides to devote his journey with Lila to deciphering her latent "quality." In a 1991 *New York Times* article on Pirsig, Roger Cohen noted Pirsig's description of quality as "a characteristic of thought and statement that is recognized by a nonthinking process. Because definitions are a product of rigid, formal thinking, quality cannot be defined." Pirsig told Cohen, however, that the answer to questions about quality contained in *Lila* is "The dynamic quality each person senses is universal, but the static patterns each person has vary." Pirsig says of Lila, "There is something ferociously dynamic going on with her." Cohen comments that the "dynamic for . . . Pirsig, is liberating, universal and the fount of the new; but it can also quickly degenerate into chaos if not held in check."

Reviewing *Lila* in the *New York Review of Books*, where years earlier he had reviewed *Zen and the Art of Motorcycle Maintenance*, Robert Adams commented on *Lila* that in pursuing the nature of Dynamic Quality, "Pirsig comes up with a particularly heavy-handed version of Social Darwinism. . . . [S]omewhere on the way Dynamic Quality has derailed the mental traveler." Adams concluded that: "Some of the vitality of *ZAAMM* remains in *Lila*, though the dynamism of the motorcycle is sorely missed. . . . When not entangled in his private arguments, Pirsig writes crisp, descriptive prose . . . "

In the *New York Times Book Review*, Richard Restak wrote, "*Lila* is a marvelous improvisation on a most improbable quartet: sailing, philosophy, sex and madness."

After many itinerant years, Pirsig has settled "somewhere in New England," where he jealously guards his privacy. In a 1991 interview with the *New York Times*, he said of *Lila*, "I refused to end the book optimistically because life does not end optimistically, and to paint it optimistically is to paint it falsely." Acknowledging the delicacy of his novel's theme, he conceded that he still had more work to do "on where exactly love fits in to the Metaphysics of Quality."

PRINCIPAL WORKS: *Novels*—Zen and the Art of Motorcycle Maintenance: An Inquiry into Values, 1974; Lila: An Inquiry into Morals, 1991.

ABOUT: Contemporary Authors 53–56, 1975; Contemporary Literary Criticism 4, 1975; 6, 1976; Something About the Author 39, 1985. *Periodicals*—Harvard Educational Review February 1975; New Republic June 27, 1974; New York Review of Books June 13, 1974; December 19, 1991; New York Times October 8, 1991; New York Times Book Review March 30, 1975; March 4, 1984; October 13, 1991; New Yorker April 15, 1974.

STEPHEN POLIAKOFF

POLIAKOFF, STEPHEN (December 14, 1952–   ), British playwright, was born in London to Alexander Poliakoff, a Russian born businessman and inventor, and Ina (Montagu) Poliakoff, an actress before her marriage. His paternal grandfather, an electronics expert, had brought his family to England in 1924 to escape the growing anti-Semitism in the U.S.S.R. His maternal grandmother, Firenza Montagu, had two plays produced on the West End in the 1920s.

Poliakoff grew up in a middle-class home, with two younger sisters. He wrote a novel at the age of fourteen, and began to write plays while attending Westminister School One of these, Granny, involved a series of bizarre and vicious tricks played on various unsuspecting adults by a sadistic teenager. Obviously influenced by the works of Harold Pinter and Joe Orton, the play showed a strong dramatic sense and a flair for colorful, often humorous, dialogue. Poliakoff or-

ganized a public production of the piece in 1969, which resulted in an introduction to literary agent Margaret Ramsay, who accepted the sixteen-year-old as a client. He attended Cambridge University, but found the tradition bound atmosphere stifling and depressing, and left after two years to become a play reader for the Hampstead Theatre Club. Another of his Westminister plays, *Day with My Sister*, in which a neurotic young man keeps his younger sister a virtual prisoner, was produced professionally at the Traverse Theatre in Edinburgh in 1971.

Poliakoff has described his early work as "urban canyon" plays, which depict the confusiong and alienation of young people in modern society. In 1972, *Pretty Boy* had a single tryout performance at the Royal Court Theatre. Again there are Pinteresque overtones, as a group of friends, led by an agggressive and emotionally disturbed twenty-year-old, plan various acts of vandalism to shock and frighten their neighbors. All their plots eventually come to nothing, however. Critics hailed the youthful playwright's ability to portray a sense of anarchy and casual violence among young people, but they also pointed out weaknesses in both plot development and characterization which continued to be evident in several of his later plays.

Other Poliakoff plays depicting this subculture appeared at various London venues in the early 1970s. In September 1974, *The Carnation Gang* was produced at the Bush Theatre Club. It tells the story of twin brothers in their mid-twenties who run a profitable business selling drugs to teenagers. Among their clients is a trio of young hoodlums, who try unsuccessfuly to force the brothers to give them free dope. There are explicit scenes of drug-taking, which led some critics to see the play as either an attack on the drug culture or a plea for toleration of it. Others thought it pointed up the gulf between wealthy, well-educated people who can break the law with relative impunity, and those in the lower strata who resort to violence to achieve their ends. There was general agreement that the play was "entertaining and gripping theatre . . . although it came to no real conclusion."

Clever Soldiers opened in 1974 in London, and brought Poliakoff broad public notice. The play takes place during World War I, with scenes shifting back and forth between Oxford and the front. Teddy is an officer with a public school and Oxford background; he treats war as a game, and is so disturbed by the mindless obedience of his subordinates that he deliberately goads one of the soldiers into attacking him in order to establish some kind of human contact. Another aspect of the class conflict is dramatized in taunting conversations between Teddy and David, his Oxford tutor, whose working-class background has made him bitter toward those in the privileged ranks. As with his earlier plays, critics appreciated Poliakoff's skill in depicting class differences with dramatic immediacy, but deemed the message somewhat muddled. Some reviewers also found his portrayal of the period unconvincing, although others praised the realism of his scenes in the trenches.

Hitting Town is a one-act play in which a brother and sister wander aimlessly through a provincial English town. They visit a fast-food shop, amuse themselves by telephoning obscene comments to a radio call-in show, and go to bed together. While some critics emphasized the incestuous relationship, most reviewers focused on the boredom and despair of life in a depersonalized urban society where flouting convention is one means of protest. The play was mounted at the Bush Theatre Club in April 1975.

Heroes, originally titled *Berlin Days*, continues the examination of class collisions. Julius is an aspiring artist living on a comfortable allowance. He becomes infatuated with Rainer, a young man with strong fascistic leanings, and deserts an older friend in order to go off with Rainer to join a fascist group and "clean up" the country. The play was produced in July 1975 at the Royal Court Theatre Upstairs to largely negative reviews. One critic called it a rehash of *Clever Soldiers* and *Hitting Town*, while others complained that the play veered fuzzily between pre-Hitler Germany and England of the mid-1970s.

In March 1976, *City Sugar* became the first play of Poliakoff's to reach the mainstream West End. Leonard Brazil is a popular disc jockey who despises himself, his on-air music, and his audience, so he takes out his frustration by browbeating his staff and insulting his listerners. The plays's climax centers on a pop music contest that Brazil has rigged so that Nicola Davies, one of his Vacuous teenybopper fans, will become a finalist who Brazil can humiliate in the deciding round. Critical reaction was almost universally favorable, with reviewers citing Poliakoff's ability to portray the sorry state of contemporary popular taste and the emptiness of success with wit and occasionaly poignancy. The play toured other cities in Great Britain and Europe, and came to New York in June 1978. Poliakoff won the *Evening Standard's* Award for Most Promising Playwright of 1975, and he was appointed Writer in Residence at the National Theatre for 1976–1977.

Strawberry Fields, a title based on the Beatles' song, opened to mixed notices in March 1977. Two young right-wing zealots drive around England seeking financial support for a revolution to cleanse the country of pollution, immigration, and communism. During their travels, Charlotte and Kevin pick up an old fashioned liberal named Nick, who is attracted to the couple but soon realizes how dangerous they are. When he tries to dissuade them from their violent plans, Charlotte shoots him. A New York production of *Strawberry Fields* was mounted in May 1978 to run simultaneously with *City Sugar*, and Poliakoff came to New York to work with the producers on his two American premieres. Tish Dace, in the *Soho Weekly News*, said that Poliakoff's "sense of construction is almost as sure as his ear for dialogue, his depiction of barely restrained impulses toward savagery is searing and certain, and his perceptions of nurturing of such capacities in the human soul is terrifying."

Shout Across the River was presented in London in 1978 and in New York in 1980. It takes place in South London, where a fifteen-year-old girl humiliates her timid mother in a variety of bizarre episodes. Reviews were generally negative on both sides of the Atlantic, most saying that the actions of both mother and daughter were ambiguous and inexplicable, signifying confusion on the part of the playwright rather than his characters. *American Days* opened in London in 1979 and came to New York in 1980. A recording industry executive viciously insults three young rock singers during an audition, but the teenagers have the spunk to stand up against his abuse. Once again, reviewers noted the thinness of the plot but praised the play's tension and energy.

Poliakoff's next play, *The Summer Party*, was offered in *Crucible Theatre*, Sheffield in 1980. It deals with a hugh outdoor pop concert at which the singers fail to appear. The impresario works frantically all night long to keep the audience calm, and the crisis is finally solved at dawn by a chief constable who tells the cheering crowd that they are about to witness the miracle of sunrise. The critics had a field day lambasting the play, calling it heavy and half-baked trivia compared to the raw slices of life that were offered in *Hitting Town* and *City Sugar*.

Favourite Nights opened in 1981. It concerns an English instructor for foreign businessmen who also acts as their escort in the evening. She takes one of her pupils to a casino, where it turns out that she is a self-destructive gambler with serious emotional and financial problems. The play was criticized for its meandering reprise of Poliakoff's familiar themes, until it finally came to grips with the central character's addiction.

In the early 1980s, Poliakoff departed from his "urban canyon" pieces to write what he described as "European" plays. *Breaking the Silence*, which was presented by the Royal Shakespeare Company in 1984, is based on the experiences of Poliakoff's family in postrevolutionary Russia. The play opens in 1920, when the aristocratic family of Nikolai Pesiakoff has been forced to exchange their dacha for an abandoned railroad car, the domicile that goes with Pesiakoff's new job as Inspector of Telephones on the Northern Line. Pesiakoff refuses to take the work seriously, and neglects his new duties in order to work on an invention for sound motion pictures. (Poliakoff's grandfather, Nikolay, was working on such an invention when he left the Soviet Union). His wife and the family maid decide to fabricate figures and reports to fool the authorities, whereupon Mme. Pesiakoff discovers that she enjoys her new responsibilities and the freedom from the traditional restraints surrounding women of her class. Meanwhile, their resentful son deliberately smashes a shipment of lenses needed to complete his father's invention. The play ends in 1924, when Stalin comes into power, and in a tense final scene the family escape to England. *Breaking the Silence* earned Poliakoff some of the best reviews of his career. Critics praised the sensitive and touching details, as well as the satirical description of the Soviet bureaucracy and the tension of the political situation.

In *Coming in to Land*, directed by Peter Hall in 1987, Poliakoff switched his focus from Soviet to British bureaucracy. He also contrasted traditional British reserve with the "more hungry, less inhibited European experience." The plot centers on a Polish visitor's efforts to remain in Eng-land, after having spent years nursing her dying father in Warsaw, by inventing a story of her narrow escape from political oppression, which is immediately picked up by the media. In the climactic scene, a smug and manipulative immigration officer tries to discredit her account, which grows more elaborate as the cat-and-mouse game proceeds. Reviewers tended to think that play overwritten and lacking in genuine emotion.

Playing with Trains, presented in 1989, concerns a successful inventor-businessman engaged in various research projects and development schemes who rides roughshod over colleagues, government officials and family, until he loses an important libel suit. His business ventures collapse, and his life goes downhill. The last scene takes place in his run-down flat, where he achieves a shaky reconciliation with his daughter. Richard Davenport-Hines expressed the general critical opinion when he wrote in the *Times Literary Supplement* that "Stephen Poliakoff is a dramatist who excels at portraying people misleading and hurting one another, but is invariably embarrassing when he turns to soapbox punditry. His power but also his weakness are shown to full effect in his latest play."

In 1991, Poliakoff wrote *Sienna Red*. It is a modern Benedick-Beatrice romance set in a warehouse, which also comments on "junk taste." The play had a national tour in 1992, but did not appear on the West End.

In 1977, the BBC produced Poliakoff's television drama, *Stronger than the Sun*. Like Karen Silkwood in America, the play's heroine makes a futile effort to publicize the dangers of nuclear energy. The drama received generally favorable reviews, especially for its "thriller" aspects, although some critics thought the polemics overshadowed the personalities. "Caught on a Train," an award-winning 1980 BBC telecast, presents the east-west clash in a gentler context, when an Englishman's orderly life is upset by a chance meeting on a train with an old German aristocrat played by Peggy Ashcroft. *Blood Kids* (ATV, 1980) offers another view of the urban scene, as two boys scheme to see the inside of a police station by saying that one has stabbed the other. *She's Been Away*, with Peggy Ashcroft as an inmate of a retirement home, received a Venice Film Festival Prize in 1989. Michael Ratcliffe commented in the *Observer* that Poliakoff's screen and television dramas have "strong, spare scripts which support visual narratives of great boldness from which one retains, years later, resonant and vivid images of individual helplessness and distress."

Poliakoff turned his hand to directing his own

films with *Hidden City*, which opened in London in 1987. The plot turns on affair between a middle-class professional man and a waiflike young woman who claims to be searching for secret government films. Eventually they find a series of underground tunnels, and the film proves to be a record of an official experiment that misfired. Reviewers found the movie very uneven, and *Variety* reported that it had many good ideas that were never fully developed, resulting in "an overlong film with too many storylines. . . . that rambles along with an air of self-importance."

Close My Eyes, a 1991 film written and directed by Poliakoff, returns to the subject of incest. A brother and sister, estranged since childhood, meet during an abnormally hot English summer and slide into an affair. The relationship, like the heat wave, lasts all summer, until Natalie decides to withdraw and Richard tries and fails at suicide. A subplot concerns Richard's equally futile efforts as a government regulator to make unscrupulous housing developers conform to environmental standards. Reviews were mixed, some praising its "visceral energy," others complaining that it was filled with "ludicrous banalities."

Poliakoff married Sandy Welch in 1983, and the couple have one son and one daughter. He is a prolific and intense writer, often working eight hours a day stopping only to eat. He claims that he works best under pressure of a contract or a deadline or an opening night. Poliakoff told an interviewer in *Drama* in 1987: "I don't write about issues, but about characters. . . . Through their lives I hope I throw shafts of light onto something larger."

Poliakoff is regarded as one of the foremost playwrights of the post–John Osborne generation. He had been particularly successful in capturing the disillusionment and hopelessness of many young people living in depressed urban environments in the 1980s, especially when exacerbated by economic and social class differences, which has led some adolescents to an infatuation with fascism. His writing has been called overly pessimistic and inconclusive—a criticism he denies, although he sees much that is wrong with society and is still unsure of the remedy—but even Polikaoff's harshest critics admire his adroitness at building suspense through the use of characters and situations that project an undercurrent of menace.

PRINCIPAL WORKS: Hitting Town and City Sugar, 1976; Strawberry Field, 1977; American Days, 1979; Shout Across the River, 1979; The Summr Party, 1980; Favourite Nights and Caught on a Train, 1982; Breaking the Silence, 1984; Runners and Soft Targets, 1984;

Coming in to Land, 1986; Playing with Trains, 1987; Plays (incudes Clever Soldiers, Hitting Town, City Sugar, Shout Across the River, American Days, Strawberry Fields), 1989; She's Been Away and Hidden City, 1989; Close My Eyes, 1991; Sienna Red, 1992.

ABOUT: Contemporary Authors 106, 1982; Contemporary Literary Criticism 38, 1986; Dictionry of Literary Biography 13, 1982; Hayman, British Theatre Since 1955, 1979; Kerensky, O. The New British Drama, 1977; Who's Who 1993. *Periodicals*—Drama: The Quarterly Review 163, 1987; Modern Drama 27, December 1984; Observer (London) September 1, 1991; Soho Weekly News June 15, 1978; Stage and Television Today Jun 17, 1982; November 1, 1984; Theatre Journal 45, May 1993; Times Literary Supplement December 15, 1989; Variety May 27, 1987.

PORTER, HAL (HAROLD EDWARD)

(February 16, 1911–September 29, 1984), Australian novelist, short story writer, poet, and playwright, was born in the Melbourne suburb of Albert Park. His father, Harold Owen Porter, was a railway engine-driver and his mother, Ida Ruff, had been a tailor before her marriage. Hal was the first of their six children. He grew up and was educated in the Gippsland town of Bairnsdale, about which he later wrote and illustrated a book. After completing secondary school, he took a primary teacher's certificate and studied drawing at the National Gallery in Melbourne. He taught for several years in the primary schools, then had a resident mastership at Queen's College in Adelaide in 1941 and went on to teach senior English at Prince Alfred's College in 1942. When World War II ended he spent a year in Japan teaching children of the Australian Occupation Forces. He began publishing short stories in magazines in the late 1930s, but did not become a full-time writer until he was fifty.

Porter characterized himself as a watcher, an "extra," a spectator or "joker" who, like Socrates before him, was preoccupied with "many wonders and none of them more wonderful than man." As he explained in an essay, "Answers to the Funny, Kind Man" (published in *Southerly* in 1969):

> Man means men, women and children, and their cats and cattle and catastrophes, superb slums and bashed-up abbeys, gardens and bomb-droppings, off-moments and on-moments, glamorous vices and threadbare virtues, blood-chilling nobilities and heart-warming blunders, their charm and wickedness, their unending variety and fatiguing sameness, their alarming depth and their more alarming shallowness.

Such a passage demonstrates why Hal Porter's biographer Mary Lord called him "the odd-

HAL PORTER

man-out of Australian literature." A cynic and iconoclast, he entertained no illusions about himself or his art, comparing writers to freaks who "displayed their special abnormalities for money." He was a complex personality, critical and uncompromising. A heavy drinker, he was an enigma to his friends, who were fascinated, loyal, and supportive, but often appalled at his behavior. As a stylist and literary craftsman, however, Porter has few equals in modern Australian literature. That he is so little read outside Australia—especially in contrast to his contemporary Patrick White, who won the Nobel Prize for literature in 1973—may be his own choice. Although a number of his stories are set in Europe and Japan, Porter was primarily a regional writer, concentrating with fierce intensity upon the territory he knew best, southern provincial Australia. But, again like Patrick White, he rejected the straightforward and sometimes pedestrian realism of much Australian regional writing. His method, rather, was to reconstruct observable reality in such a way as to reveal another reality below the visible surface. Adrian Mitchell wrote (in the *Oxford History of Australian Literature*) that Porter tried "to establish an elaborate surface by the massing of detail, the observable or remembered features of an actual world . . . and then to reveal, or suggest, the presence of something furtive, if not evil, just below the surface, the social or individual truths that are kept out of sight, the secrets of character."

Porter's reconstitutions of historic times, celebrations of particular times, and preoccupation

with individuals trapped within the confines of their era, while often historically accurate, transcend mere nostalgia. He invariably has more complex agendas. In the story "Uncle Foss and Big Bogga" the narrator observes: "As I grow older I am increasingly fascinated by the interlocking circles which link past to present, a remoter past to a less remote. One has constantly to revalue the quality of appearances, to give a testimony at seven thirty-two one considered grotesque at half past seven." In "Country Town" a mature man returns to his hometown to confront not only its changed condition but the distance between his current perception and the formative views which once defined him. Marvelously, the extant top halves of a street's stone buildings remain as a comment on renovations made in the 1950s to the lower stories, providing a visual metaphor for the town's, and the narrator's, fall from grace. The story documents the coming to consciousness of transformation as "Life dwindles to life": the man revisits a room in a house central to his childhood, which has loomed large in his consciousness. Now it is subdivided, relocated by the exigencies of rental in a modern world where the old ways exist only in memory. The fate of country towns around Australia and the demise of a 19th-century way of life are suggested.

Porter often re-creates the painful process of acquiring knowledge. His short story "First Love" portrays a boy's disillusion, as his obsession with the photograph of a woman long-loved is cured by a confrontation with the real embodiment of life and change. In "Everleigh's Accent" the narrator, a commercial traveler playing the role of professional man of the world, is upstaged by the performance of a younger man whose disguise eventually slips to reveal the racism of the community. Porter's characters adopt masks for all occasions feigning indifference, pseudosophistication, corruscating or frenetic gaiety, deliberate harshness, overt sentimentality, nostalgic indulgence, sexual innuendo, or frank confessing, as if demonstrating that, as he wrote, "time does not alter men—but simply unmasks them."

Porter is an intrusive author, prompting the reader to ensure that his sense of pathos or irony is not lost. For example, in "Brett," the narrator/traveler/aesthete "discovers" a living replica of Bronzino's painting of Eleanor da Toledo, only to have her speak with a broad Australian accent and volubly express her need to cheat the Italian authorities to obtain money. She is, however, a new breed of innocent abroad:

> She hadn't come to Italy to dislike it; its inhabitants had taught her to. She felt blameless, she'd earned her fare

over; was paying her way, working her way, conning her way, when all else failed, through an Old World she'd been lured into visiting by gilded legends, propaganda ablaze with seductive adjectives. She'd been taken by the mirage of civilizations accounted superior to her own country's, of breath-taking landscapes strewn with gorgeous cities and enchanting villages alive with diverting and decorative people. She had been too ingenuous to believe, had not lived long enough to learn, that the Utopias of the pamphlets are what one does one's best to avoid.

Despite his worldly-wise stance, the narrator, fresh from a renewed acquaintance with DaVinci's *Last Supper* and longing for the relief of placid "beauty that is feud's aftermath," is confronted by his Australian traveling companion's sheer vitality, which is invigorating despite her "impercipience." Brett is too homesick to see Italy, and the narrator is both touched and saddened by his distance from her pragmatic view of Europe as "an elaborate piece of machinery set up to bilk and pillage the tourist." What separates them is not only age, but an Age and an entire way of viewing the relationship between Australia and Europe.

In the long run, Porter seems to be suggesting, the modern age has defeated itself. It is not so much that he idealizes the past, but that the present, in his view, has failed to realize its promise. History, as he defines it in *Bairnsdale: Portrait of an Australian Country Town*, is "a broken looking-glass in the remaining fragments of which enough of former eras is reflected to make us doubtful if our own era is in all ways an improved one." In his first novel, *A Handful of Pennies*, for example, he casts a cold eye on post-World War II attempts to introduce democracy into what had been a largely feudal Japan. "Occupation Democracy," he observes at the beginning of the novel, "is Delusion's son, the weak uncle, the sponsor of no Christ but of guilds of Pontius Pilates." The plot emphasizes the clash of cultures and the failure of relationships: "The Westerners in occupation not only corrupt the vanquished Japanese, each corrupts the other and himself." Yet it is not nostalgia for the past that Porter expresses. He observes with equal cynicism the harsh realities of 19th-century Australia in what is regarded as his best novel, *The Tilted Cross*. Van Dieman's Land, where the novel begins, is "an ugly trinket suspended at the world's discredited rump"; Hobart Town is "a town of the dispossessed, half its creatures criminal, half its creatures lower class or middle class. It was the privy of London; it was indeed a miniature and foundling London, a Johnny-come-lately London, turnkey-ridden and soldier-hounded, its barracks and prisons imprisoned between a height of stone and a depth of water." The central character is closely modeled on the British artist Thomas Griffiths Wainewright, whose paintings were once exhibited at the Royal Academy. Driven by scandal to exile as a ticket-of-leave man (parolee) in Australia, he becomes, in Porter's novel: "An elegant, defiant husk whose wit and anguish were alike mummified, whose wine of life was almost drawn . . . an almost empty plate from which time had gobbled the juicier delicacies and gnawed at the bones."

Porter took many of his characters directly from life, and he filled his writings with data, keen observation, and infinite detail. But, as most of his critics have noted, what is remarkable about his work is his style. "So extraordinary is the range of his vocabulary," Adrian Mitchell wrote, "so elaborate his familiarity with ornamental detail, and so precise his eye (and ear) for the bizarre, the extravagant, the vulgar and the exotic, the comic and the malicious, the *outré*, that the material substance of his work is largely overwhelmed, and the manner rather than the matter of his writing fixes itself as the centre of attention."

Porter's success as a playwright—his plays often produced on stage in Australia—was also a matter of "manner rather than matter." His plots were dismissed as melodramatic or formulaic, and his characters as stereotypical, but his gift for wordplay and incisive dialogue served him well. Mary Lord noted that he himself regarded his plays as mere potboilers which he could knock off in a few weeks. "Any play I write," he said, "is, largely, based on an idea for a novel there's no time (and no *strong* inclination to make time) to work on."

The same gift of elegance of style marked the relatively small amount of poetry that Porter published. He took the writing of poetry far more seriously, however, than playwriting, and worked on his poetry over the course of his career. Many of his poems are "dramatic"—vignettes in verse reflecting his pervasive irony and wit. He catches the bitter essence of a broken love affair in "Alexandria Tea Room":

An East-of-Suez ceiling fan, stopped dead
some hot, F. Scott Fitzgerald afternoon
says ten-to-nevermore above your head
while you, you bitch, and I do good-bye's deed,
stir stillborn tea with an unsilver spoon.

He elegizes the lost past, at the same time as he ponders sardonically on Australian provincialism, in "An Australian Graveyard":

All hereabout anachronism's rife.
The landscape plays at Constable and Gray
With hedgegrow, hawthorn, far-off farm-house roof;

A lowing herd to wind its text-book way;
A ballad graveyard, hackneyed rhyme of yew,
Headstones set elegiacally askew.

Probably Porter's best work, and the books for which he will be longest remembered are his three volumes of autobiography, most notably the first of these, *The Watcher on the Cast-Iron Balcony.* Mary Lord warned that there are disparities between the facts of his life and the selective versions he publishes in these volumes, but nowhere is his eye for telling detail better served. In *The Paper Chase,* his second autobiography, covering his young manhood and his experiences as a teacher during the depression he is an accurate and keenly sensitive chronicler of his times:

> . . . It is impossible not to know that many of my pupils live on the bread-line, it is impossible not to observe the home-cobbled shoes, the darned elbows of boys' jumpers—heather-mixture jumpers just too tight and short of sleeve, the don't-be-ashamed-of-a-patch trousers and turned collars, the chapped patent-leather belts and scrubbing-board-dimmed colours of girl's dresses, their skirts homemade from some obviously adult material. No-one is, however, not neat; there are speckless fingernails and polished shoes: no-one gets emaciated; all are ebullient and happy-go-lucky, or undetectedly pretend to be so.

But it is in the first volume, *The Watcher,* which recalls his earliest years, that Porter shines. In that "pre-six" era, he claims, he has no distinct visual memory of his parents, but what emerges is something far more profound:

> I remember the face of Father's gold pocket-watch, and the hairline crack across its enamel, but not his; I remember exactly the pearls and rubies in Mother's crescent brooch but not her eyes. . . . I do remember his fatherliness and her motherliness, essences informed by their youth and vitality and simplicity in which I have every trust. Fatherliness, motherliness, youth, vitality, and simplicity I would not now trust for a moment. Each can destroy. Each helps destroy my parents; each helps them lay waste about them.

For much of his later career Hal Porter lived in a caravan on his sister's farm at Garvoc. His marriage, to Olivia Parnham, a model, in 1939 ended in divorce five years later. He died in Ballarat at the age of seventy-two, after lingering for fourteen months in a coma, of injuries he had received when he was knocked down by a car. In its obituary, the *London Times* called him "one of Australia's most distinguished writers."

PRINCIPAL WORKS: *Novels*—A Handful of Pennies, 1958; The Tilted Cross, 1961; The Right Thing, 1971. *Short Stories*—Short Stories, 1942; A Bachelor's Children, 1962; The Cats of Venice, 1965; Mr. Butterfry and Other Tales of New Japan, 1970; Selected Stories, 1971; Fredo Fuss Love Life: Short Stories, 1974; The

Clairvoyant Ghost and Other Stories, 1981. *Poetry*—The Hexagon, 1956; Elijah's Raven, 1968; In an Australian Country Graveyard, 1974. *Plays*—The Town *in* Kippax, H. G. (ed.) Three Australian Plays, 1963; The Professor, 1966; Eden House, 1969. *Autobiography*—The Watcher on the Cast-Iron Balcony, 1963; The Paper Chase, 1966; The Extra, 1975. *Miscellaneous*—Stars of the Australian Stage and Screen, 1965; The Actors: An Image of New Japan, 1968; Bairnsdale: Portrait of an Australian Country Town, 1977; The Portable Hal Porter (Lord, M., ed.) 1980.

ABOUT Capone, G. Incandescent Verities: The Fiction of Hal Porter, 1990; Contemporary Authors 114, 1985; Contemporary Authors New Revision Series 3, 1981; Contemporary Novelists, 3d ed., 1982; Kramaer, L. *introduction to* Hal Porter: Selected Stories, 1971; Lord, M. Hal Porter, 1974; Man of Many Parts, 1993; Oxford History of Australian Literature, 1981; Penguin New Literary History of Australia, 1988; Porter, H. The Watcher on the Cast-Iron Balcony, 1963; Porter, H. The Paper Chase, 1966; Porter, H. The Extra, 1975. *Periodicals*—Australian Literary Studies 7, 1975; Meanjin 25, 1966; Times (London) October 2, 1984.

*POSSE, ABEL (January 7, 1934–), Argentine novelist, writes (in Spanish): "I was given life in Córdoba, a city in the interior of Argentina, a miraculous occurrence, like every birth, the central motif of every celebration, apart from all the ordinary events, horrific and delightful, of what we call life. My mother came from an old landed family in Tucumán. My father was the son of an Italian immigrant who must have come to Argentina to flee the European chaos. I was raised in an upper middle-class home in Buenos Aires. I went to the best schools in my country, institutions that seemed to have no success in destroying my fantasy life. I became a lawyer and then turned myself into a diplomat.

"My father idolized culture. From childhood I remember having heard him say, to my surprise, that he would prefer that his son be a poet rather than a dentist or a soldier. Aware of all the risks, he nevertheless preferred eagles to oxen. Since my early youth I have believed myself a writer and profited by the opportunity to grow up in the marvelous Buenos Aires of thirty of forty years ago, where every café was a school of literature or philosophy; it was a cosmopolitan city with Spanish, Italian, German, Jewish, and even Latin American parts. It was the time of Perón and Evita, and also of an outburst of talents, such as Borges, Enrique Molina, Julio Cortázar, and Alejandra Pizarnik. As young writers, we had every imaginable philosophical optionn from Buddha to Taoism to revolution-

ABEL POSSE

ary Marxism and Freudianism. For young novelists the most important influences came from Russian literature, from German, and from the North American novelists, already seemingly becoming an extinct species in the face of the decadence in English-langugre literature. I refer to William Faulkner, John Dos Passos, Caldwell, Thomas Wolfe, and others.

"Ostensibly to study, but impelled more by a lively curiosity, I lived for four years in Europe, mainly in Paris and in Germany. Returning to Argentina, I embarked upon a diplomatic career, (in contrast to my father, I felt that to permit oneself to be a poet one must first be something of a dentist). I planned long autobiographical novels as an exorcism. At the urging of friends of Borges and Ernesto Sábato, I published my first works. When I lived in Moscow, I finished my novel Los Bogavantes, which had been bubbling up in me for ten years. It synthesized the experience of Paris in the 1960s, and conveys the adventures of Che Guevara in America and the impact of the May revolution in '68 in Europe. I entered that novel for the famous Planeta Prize in Spain, but it was eliminated by Franco's censors. A prestigious failure opens the doors of the literary life to us as a good prize does. That book was to be my first novel. It was published in Buenos Aires in 1970.

"From my experiences in Moscow between 1967 and 1970 came another novel. I believe I felt at the time that the only formative task of a writer is to find his true voice, which is very difficult to hear. It is heard when one's style encompasses the greatest possible part of one's character, humor, and tragic experiences, as well as legitimate ambitions and crazy dreams. I believe that after having lived in Peru I was finding that voice in historical novels or those with a historic pretext, such as Los Perros del Paraíso [The Dogs of Paradise] and Daimon, the novels that have since had fifteen translations into foreign languages, and the only ones published in English. I believe in literature as a profound but silenced and marginal expression of our life, and as a product of intimacy, but one certainly with few roots in the publishing experience, fame, or the literary subculture of our time. Nevertheless, that marginal expression occupies a vast space in our lives (one could say the same of love or of religion).

"I have a stirring and at the same time happy exterior life. That preserves for me the necessary intimacy for that literary life, which emerges as a creation of language and from adventures in the imagination and the search for beauty. I have lived and live most of my life in Europe, 'from the Atlantic to the Urals.' Paris, Venice, Seville, Tübingen, Moscow, Prague, Jerusalem, and Lima are the cities of my long worldly and existential journey.

"In my ongoing search for a voice, I have had literary recognition, which always surprised me because I have never taken part in political groups, brotherhoods, or the publishing establishment. (In Argentina I can perfectly well be considered a marginal writer.)

"Among those prizes, the most important has been the international Romulo Gallegos Prize, which is given every five years to the best novel written in Spanish. I have also been awarded the international Diana Prize of Mexico for my novel on Nazism, and, recently, the international V. Centenario Prize in Spain for the novel El largo Cabeza de Vaca caminante, in which I recount the voyage of Cabeza de Vaca and his black assistant, the true discovers of the states of Mississippi, Louisiana, Texas, Arizona, New Mexico, and part of California. Do North Americans know that? He was an Andalusian Catholic who befriended a black North African. . . .

"I contribute to newspapers in Spain and Latin America. I trust I have been able to write something that succeeds in the intention to 'narrate history from an alternative viewpoint,' according to a critic in the Washington Post.

"In my life I have experienced several episodes of such gravity, or so insupportable, that I have not wanted to continue living. In those horrible moments—apparently, for the most part fragile and marginal—religious feelings, cosmic intuitions, and the verses of poets have been the only things that have helped me to endure, to support, and even more, to be able to *celebrate* existence. For me, writing is much more than writing my books or having the appearance of being a writer. It is my consciousness of being alive. I am above all, a 'worker' for the consciousness of everyone."

—tr. S. Yampolsky

Abel Posse has revealed little of his private life to interviewers, but has opened out his imagination in his novels—or rather he has allowed it to burst open, spewing its seed like a ripe tropical fruit. He told Magdalena García Pinto in an interview (in Spanish) in *Revista Iberoamericana* in 1989 that he had decided to abandon the *porteño* (Buenos Aires) writing of his first two novels, *Los Bogavantes* and *La boca del tigre*. The *porteño* writer is one who "is formed more by ideas on life than by direct or aesthetic experience of life and of language. That is the problem with the literature of Buenos Aires, which can culminate in the writing of a Borges, or can fall by the wayside, useless to anyone."

His own voice came to him after reading the Cubans, particularly José Lezama Lima, but it was from a sojourn in Peru that he captured what he believes is his true style—a telluric voice deriving from the Inca experience. García Pinto asked him what caused the change in his vision, and he replied, "I saw for the first time the reality of America in all its profundity. In all of Argentina, even on the highest level of life, you don't see that; but I encountered it in an old civilization—the Inca civilization. . . . a universe full of restraints, profundities, and the mystery of the Inca world. The Andean world was for me a tremendous aggregation of spiritual wealth. . . . and that became the basis of my books, the part that integrates the vision of the conquered. For that reason I say that in 1492, October 12th, it was the Americans who discovered Europe."

Although Posse's novels take a dim view of arbitrary authority, and certainly seem to have a leftish cast, he claims no particular politics. "I was an independent anarchist, like all writers," he told García Pinto of his years in Europe. With regard to America, he prefers to view it as "a great upheaval . . . a continent in formation that can be seen almost geologically . . . a volcano." In the ferment and chaos, Posse finds the source of his inspiration.

Published in Spanish in 1978, *Daimon* was the second of Posse's novels to be translated into English, after *The Dogs of Paradise*, published in Spanish in 1983. It was with *Daimon* that Posse found the technique that he was to call his own—a surreal use of historic figures to unite the past with the present. Posse told García Pinto that *Daimon* is the story of "el conquistador loco (the mad conquistador), the conquistador who remains with us in America because the idea of authority and power in this continent comes to us from the mad conquistador and not from the holy conquistador; it is the image invented by Spain to support genocide. . . . [T]here is a constant play of anachronisms: the past and the present are mingled in a circle of time. And, in fact, one of the characters comes to live 400 years." Posse sees no difference between the arbitrary brutalization imposed on the natives by the conquistadors and modern military dictatorships. It makes no difference whether the power is exercised by a 400-year-old man or a 40-year-old.

Lope de Aguirre, the mad conquistador, makes a pact with the devil in *Daimon*. He is cruel, greedy, and faithless. Posse says of him in a prologue, "*It seems that he believed solely in the will to power, the revels of war, the heat of delirium (lethally disdaining those who disagreed or were lukewarm).*" Lope de Aguirre is the murderer of thousands, among them his fifteen-year-old daughter. Nevertheless, he is called "The Old Man" and his erotic adventures and ability to recharge his own vision inspire a certain sympathy in the reader, perhaps deriving from Aguirre's sensitivity to atmosphere. Aguirre's utterance on seeing Machu Picchu: "Final palace of the seen world, periphery of the absolute. Celestial geometry that, blinded, we once scorned . . . ! Here is a permanence of words and stone. All life, a shock of stone petals. . . . " This vision is vouchafed to him in the novel, "109 years before the official discoverer for the white race, Professor Hiram Bingham of Yale University, USA." That scene takes place in 1802, but in the time of Hiram Bingham the still-living Aguirre "slipped back into gloom like Monday on a government job. . . . He felt that nothing was so dark and deep as the anguish of the modern city, where our solitude and anonymity are myriad in the thousand unknown faces that pass us on the street; one mirror of indifference." Clearly, the myriad brutalities of which Aguirre is guilty do not impede his sensitivity to the lost beauty of the Inca past and the degrading impositions of modernity.

Posse told García Pinto that *Daimon* and *The Dogs of Paradise*, the story of Columbus, are parts of a trilogy. The last part, dealing with the Jesuit missionaries to the New World, is called *Los heraldos negros*, which is the title of one of César Vallejo's greatest books of poetry. *The Dogs of Paradise*, like *Daimon*, is a disorienting plunge into "the eternal return," according to its author, who sees in the 1492 voyage of Columbus to America the origins of the torture and death endemic to Latin American politics, in Ferdinand and Isabella's reign the source of fascist dictatorship, and in the Spanish Inquisition the seeds of religious intolerance that continue to bear fruit. In *Choice*, J. Shreve said, "*Posse* irreverently depicts a world of greed, hypocrisy, and machination not unlike our own."

The language that Posse uses to depict that world, however, is not the bland language of bureaucracy and hypocrisy, but the florid rhetoric of magical realism, termed "verbal excess and page-by-page delirium" by Alexander Coleman in the *New York Times Book Review*. Referring to Alejo Carpentier's complaint about the surrealists' "bureaucracy of the marvelous," Coleman said that "Posse had magical talents indeed, but . . . the implacable prestidigitation in *The Dogs of Paradise* . . . might . . . elicit the same weary plaint from even the most benevolent reader today." Gordon Brotherston, in the *Times Literary Supplement*, however, deems Posse's "deftness in plot-control and turn of phrase" the signs of a master craftsman. "Columbus emerges as 'seriously subversive, a mystic without temporal loyalties' who may serve as a kind of hero among the dog-angels of his discovered paradise."

Posse told García Pinto that he was using an expressionist technique: "While impressionism may be better for minutely conveying the lyrical, expressionism is like a blow that can deliver an annihilating vision to an outside observer. There is a phenomenon of alienation. And I wanted to re-create the surprise of the European, of the conquistador, before that burgeoning American universe: the waterfall, the volcano, the marvelous jungle, the strange birds. I needed to have recourse to the poetic."

Elzbieta Sklodowska, in *Romance Quarterly*, placed Posse's writing not in the realm of magic, but in that of parody: "*The Dogs of Paradise* seems brilliantly to paraphrase that idea found throughout the works of Marx that every recurrence of an event of a historical personage results irremediably in its abasement, from the sphere of the tragic to the petty universe of farce. The re-creation of history in the space of a piece of writing is, inevitably, parodic."

Whether considered poetic or parodic, Posse's prose is always fervid. "America is burning, Lope! This is the hour of nations, don't you see? . . . Just betray that pack of parasitic rascals!," The Evil One exhorts Aguirre in *Daimon*. Everything that happens prefigures the larger betrayals that are to come in both the New World and the Old. When Lipzia, the Jewish

"crusader for culture," is accused of alchemy, he "felt the horror of all imminent pogroms (like the premonition of an earthquake)." Aguirre asks Lipzia if his alchemy is real and he answers, "The gold you've got . . . is only a figure of speech. There's gold, yes, but it's spiritual. The quest has transformed you. Resurrection, rebirth . . . Then you possess the power to see gold in anything and everything, or in gold see mud, as you like. This is invincible power: not dependent on reality."

The thread that runs through *Daimon* and *The Dogs of Paradise* is that of transmutation: not the alchemy that "works lead" to turn it into gold, but the alchemy of delirium. Posse's is a vision that merges the mud of evil with the gold of sanctity, the past with the present, the dead with the living, and enables the reader to enter the magic of seamless combination and recombination that is "the eternal return."

PRINCIPAL WORKS IN ENGLISH TRANSLATION: (tr. M. S. Peden) The Dogs of Paradise, 1989; (tr. S. Arvio) Daimon, 1992.

ABOUT: *Periodicals*—Choice 27, 1990; New York Times Book Review March 18, 1990; December 13, 1992; Times Literary Supplement June 29, 1990. *In Spanish*—Revista Iberoamericana 55, 1989; Romance Quarterly 37, 1990.

POTTER, DENNIS (CHRISTOPHER GEORGE) (May 17, 1935–June 7, 1994), British dramatist, novelist, television and screenwriter, and nonfiction writer, was born and raised in a small and cramped cottage at Joyford Hill, Coleford, Gloucestershire, in the Forest of Dean, a coal-mining community such as that in which many of his works are set. His father, Walter, was a coal miner. His mother, Margaret Constance (Wales) Potter, had been born and raised in London. He started school at Christ Church Village School, Coleford, but transferred to St. Clement Danes Grammar School in London when his family moved for two years to the Hammersmith area, which became the setting for some crucial scenes in his plays. After a crash language course during his National Service, he became a Russian-language clerk in the War Office. He won a scholarship to New College, Oxford, and in 1959 received an honors B.A. in philosophy, politics, and economics; at university he edited *Isis* and in his senior year wrote *The Glittering Coffin*, a critique of the university, metropolitan culture, and the English social system. Also in 1959 he married Margaret Morgan, a journalist. They had two daughters and a son.

In his mid-twenties Potter developed psoriatic

DENNIS POTTER

arthropathy, a particularly severe form of arthritis causing intense skin irritation and joint stiffening, which often left him bedridden. He began writing professionally in order to support his family and considered his disease an "ally" that shaped his life. Potter served on the current affairs staff of the British Broadcasting Corporation (BBC-TV) from 1959 until 1961, when he left to join the *London Daily Herald* as a feature writer and television critic. During this time he also wrote sketches for *That Was the Week That Was*, a television series (seen in the United States) that made sport of the week's news. In 1964 he became an editorial writer for the *London Sun* but resigned that same year to become a free-lance writer and to run (unsuccessfully) for the House of Commons as a candidate of the Labour Party from East Hertfordshire.

In his writing career Potter pushed to the limits the possibilities of narrative in novels and performance arts, while simultaneously attracting a mass audience. Although his fusion of fantasy and reality exhibits the meticulous specificity of naturalist writing, he called his work "non-naturalism" and readily admitted to a desire to break rules in order to advance the arts. His writing frequently provoked outrage not only for its unorthodox forms, which make strong demands on readers and viewers, but for its provocative examinations of love and sexual relations, sin, politics, and the decay of English culture.

Although most have not been seen in the United States, his television dramas have reached larger audiences than his printed works, their re-

ception often straddling a thin line between notoriety and acclaim. *Stand Up, Nigel Barton*, canceled by the BBC in 1964 for its contemptuous treatment of parliamentary democracy and televised the following year in a slightly rewritten form, was later incorporated with *Vote Vote Vote for Nigel Barton* and produced at the Bristol Old Vic in 1968. Inspired by Potter's experience in running as a Labour candidate for a safe Tory seat in Parliament, it is the sour but honest story of a miner's son who discovers that in a class-conscious nation principle must be sacrificed in the pursuit of power. *The Confidence Course* (first televised in 1965) brought threats of a lawsuit from the self-improvement programs of the Dale Carnegie school. In *A Beast with Two Backs* (1968), based on actual events in the Forest of Dean in the 1890s, a girl is murdered by her seducer and a performing bear is stoned to death.

After the audacious *Son of Man* (1969), which portrayed Jesus Christ as a hippie carpenter, Potter was threatened with prosecution for blasphemy. *Only Make Believe* (1973), in which an angel copulates with a bored housewife, was attacked for indecency. *Schmoedipus* (adapted from a novel by Angus Wilson and televised in 1974) and the play derived from it, *Track 29* (1988), openly portrayed incest. And *Brimstone and Treacle* (commissioned in 1975 and televised in 1987) was banned by the BBC for eleven years for its portrayal of a brain-damaged girl who is cured after being raped by the devil. It was adapted for the stage (Sheffield, 1977) and later became a motion picture with Denholm Elliott, Joan Plowright, and Sting. In *Dalhousie Review* Paul Delany quoted from Potter's introduction to the play: "we cannot even begin to define 'good' and 'evil' without being aware of the interaction between the two." Delany called Potter a "fervent but totally unorthodox" Christian and quotes him as saying that "we must live inside the iron cage of morality and necessity, for fear of the worse horrors outside it." In a profile in the *New York Times Magazine* Alex Ward commented on the tension throughout Potter's works "between puritanism and intellectual adventure, between wishing for a sort of orthodoxy and yet wishing for anarchy." He quoted Potter as observing, "The dominant motif in nearly all my work is of someone saying, 'God, are you there? And if not, why not?'"

Controversial as Potter's television plays were, they were praised for their daring and their masterly technical skill. *Blue Remembered Hills*, which won BAFTA's Best Drama Award in 1979, met the daunting challenge of casting adults in the roles of young children without condescending cuteness. *Blade on the Feather*, an outspoken attack on Britain's privileged classes, telecast in the United States in 1984, was a thriller that, John J. O'Connor remarked in his *New York Times* review, "takes on the proportions of a John le Carré thriller as arranged by Harold Pinter."

Although Potter's television miniseries were equally daring in theme and even more revolutionary in form than his individual programs, they advanced television arts so substantially that they brought him more acclaim than complaint, especially in the United States. Potter's fondness for Hollywood musicals inspired *Pennies from Heaven* (first televised in 1978), which follows the pursuit of happiness of a sheet-music salesman in the 1940s. Arthur Parker (played by Bob Hoskins) seeks a life as sweet as that in sentimental popular music, but his libidinous urges betray him and he is hanged for a murder he did not commit. In the series, sober or somber characters startle viewers by lip-synching upbeat popular songs, and in that spirit, Potter brings the hanged Parker back from the dead for a happy ending. The highly acclaimed series won BAFTA's Best Writer Award, Most Original Production Award, and Broadcast Press Guild Awards in 1978. Potter also wrote the script and received an Academy Award nomination for a Hollywood film version (1981) starring Steve Martin. In the *Times Literary Supplement* Russell Davies echoed the feelings of many viewers of *Pennies from Heaven*: "The cheap little tunes on its soundtrack . . . were perceived in some fragmentary way as immune from mortal decay. . . . there was something, some primeval chirp in these silly old refrains, that kept hope alive. . . . Every song embodied a declaration of faith by the beleaguered playwright."

Potter's greatest success was his six-part *The Singing Detective*, directed by Jon Amiel and starring Michael Gambon (televised on BBC in 1986 and on PBS in the United States in 1988). Philip Marlow, a pulp-detective novelist hospitalized for psoriatic arthropathy, retreats into what at first seems pathological fantasy, becoming the hero of his first novel. He relives or rewrites the events of his own life, past and present, as a bizarre tragicomedy in which, for example, he can put into perspective a cadre of solemn and pessimistic physicians when he pictures them singing "Dem Bones, Dem Bones, Dem Dry Bones." Much of the effect on the viewer is subliminal, as time sequences are rapidly juggled, unrelated sounds are connected to wrong images, real characters become fictional and fictional characters become all too real in settings of pre–World War II in England. Potter used physical illness as a metaphor for moral dis-

array, and Marlow holds on to his sanity, empowers his sickly self, and restores his health by his imaginative rewriting of events.

As Paul Delany noted in *Dalhousie Review*, Potter constantly reworks "unresolvable contradictions between child and adult, past and present, belief and scepticism, fantasy and reality." The series was widely acclaimed. John J. O'Connor, television reviewer for the *New York Times*, observed of its virtuosic juggling: "Layer is placed upon layer, interweaving and overlapping, until Marlow is finally realized whole and inevitable. It is an astonishing tour de force." Vincent Canby, *New York Times* film reviewer, asked, "Is the year's best film on TV?" He answered his own question, declaring that if *The Singing Detective* were a movie it would be "one of the wittiest, wordiest, singingest-dancingest, most ambitious, freshest, most serious, least solemn movies of the year. . . . of a density more often associated with the literary form than with the cinematic . . . a writer's movie" that "set a new standard for all films."

The Singing Detective was awarded the Gold Medal for Best Mini-Series at the New York Film Festival in 1987. Viewers were especially touched by the sensitive portrayal of the young Marlow—a coal miner's son in an idyllic countryside who adores his father but is wrested from his innocent illusions and thrust into a sinful and disease-prone world. Potter at one time declared that Marlow's illness was the only autobiographical aspect of the story, but the work was so effectively wrought that most viewers chose to believe otherwise.

Potter's third miniseries, *Christabel* (first televised in 1988), an adaptation of Christabel Bielenberg's *The Past Is Myself*, silenced some who had complained of the inaccessibility of his previous series and those who faulted his unsympathetic portrayals of women. *Christabel* is the autobiographical account of a woman who married a German citizen jailed for an attempt to assassinate Adolph Hitler. In *American Film* Graham Fuller said that *Christabel* showed "how far decent people will be pushed before they fight back. Rare for Potter, it's also a celebration of married love and a woman's self-determination."

As a novelist, Potter was noted for his black humor and abrasive dialogue, his intertwined narratives and subtle ideas, but his novels have not had the critical or public success of his television writing, despite his utilization in them of television devices such as voice-overs, dissolves, and flashbacks. *Hide and Seek*, a book about writing a book, is a complex story about a novelist who discovers that he is a manipulated character in a novel by another writer, who also turns out to be fictitious. A third author (representing Potter) appears to be responsible but may also be merely another puppet. *Blackeyes* focuses on men's exploitation of women in the person of a writer who uses as material the life of his much-abused niece. (A four-part adaptation, directed by Potter, was televised by the BBC in 1989.) Reviewing *Ticket to Ride* in the *London Review of Books*, John Sutherland noted Potter's debt to themes of film noir: "guilty paid-for sex in hotels, doubles, the indelible residues of childhood guilt, love, murder, and the insubstantiality of middle-class decencies."

Potter also wrote original screenplays and adaptations for motion pictures. These include the screenplay for *DreamChild* (released in 1985), *Gorky Park* (released in 1984), *Track 29* (a screenplay based on *Schmoedipus*, released in 1988) and *Secret Friends* (released in 1992), which he wrote and directed. For television he wrote screenplays for *The Mayor of Casterbridge* (adapted from Thomas Hardy's novel, televised in 1978) and *Tender Is the Night* (adapted from F. Scott Fitzgerald's novel, televised in 1985), and other adaptations.

Increasingly troubled by ill health, Potter nevertheless worked at a prodigious pace in the last years of his life. In 1992 he went to New York to participate in a program, "The Television of Dennis Potter," sponsored by the Museum of Television and Radio. Here, while deploring the hucksterism of American commercial television and the deteriorating quality of British television, he affirmed his faith in the medium, stating as his credo: "A confidence in common culture, an assumption that people are very much brighter than the market men say they are, that something in them is capable of responding to things that are very complex." In 1993 he wrote a film, *Midnight Movie*, and a television play, *Lipstick on Your Collar*. Diagnosed as suffering from inoperable cancer in February 1994, he worked with even greater determination to complete two more television plays. "My only regret," he told Melvyn Bragg in a television interview only weeks before his death, "is if I die four pages too soon. If I can finish, I'm quite happy to go." Fortified by painkillers but even more by an indomitable will, Potter completed the work before his death, at his home, near Ross-on-Wye. His wife, Margaret, who had nursed him through years of illness, had died of cancer only a week earlier. His obituary in the *New York Times* on June 8 printed a statement from an interview Potter had given in 1989: "For me, writing is partly a cry of the soul. But at the same time I'm bringing back the results of a journey many people don't get the chance to make, to whatever hinterland it is where all those dark figures jibber and jeer and fly at you."

PRINCIPAL WORKS: *Television plays*—"Vote Vote Vote for Nigel Barton" (revised version incorporating "Stand Up, Nigel Barton") *in* The Nigel Barton Plays: Two Television Plays, 1967; Son of Man, 1970; "Follow the Yellow Brick Road" *in* The Television Dramatist, 1973; "Joe's Ark" *in* The Television Play, 1976; Brimstone and Treacle, 1978; Sufficient Carbohydrate, 1983; Waiting for the Boat (three plays), 1984; The Singing Detective, 1988. *Novels*—Hide and Seek, 1973; Pennies from Heaven, 1982; Ticket to Ride, 1986; Blackeyes, 1987. *Nonfiction*—The Glittering Coffin, 1960; The Changing Forest: Life in the Forest of Dean Today, 1962.

ABOUT: British Television Drama, 1981; Contemporary Authors 107, 1983; Contemporary Authors New Revision Series 33, 1991; Contemporary Dramatists, 1973; Contemporary Literary Criticism 58, 1990. *Periodicals*—American Film March 1989; Critical Quarterly Winter 1987; Dalhousie Review Winter 1988–1989; London Review of Books November 1986; New Statesman & Society November 24, 1989; New York Times January 6, 1988; July 10, 1988; January 12, 1992; January 18, 1992; June 8, 1994; June 9, 1994; July 30, 1994; New York Times Book Review October 15, 1989; New York Times Magazine November 13, 1988; Plays and Players April 1987; Times Literary Supplement December 25, 1981.

POWNALL, DAVID (May 19, 1938–), British novelist and dramatist, was born in Liverpool, the son of a dockworker. He attended Lord Wandsworth College, a British public school, on a scholarship for war orphans, and Keele University, where he received an honors B.A. in English and history. Still influenced by his working-class background, he made the practical decision to become a trainee in personnel for the Ford Company in Dagenham. He worked there from 1960 to 1963, writing a novel (which was never published) in his spare time. He married Glenys Elsie Jones in 1961.

In 1963, with a wife and young son to support, he took a job in personnel with an Anglo-American copper mining company in Rhodesia (now Zambia and Zimbabwe). There, in some company-run theaters established to entertain the staff, he discovered his interest in theater production and playwriting. He returned to England in 1969, determined to become a writer. His marriage was dissolved in 1971, and he devoted himself to full-time work with regional theatrical groups in Lancashire, and to writing for stage, radio, and television. He started his own theater touring company, Paines Plough, for which he also wrote. Though mainly a playwright and novelist, Pownall has written a pan-

DAVID POWNALL

tomine, short stories, children's stories, and a book about the part of Lancashire in which he lives, called "Between the Ribble and the Lune," which is part local history, part travel guide, and part memoir.

Pownall attests that his immediate surroundings affect his work, both in subject matter and style, and indeed several of his plays and novels obvious connections with his own experiences. His first published novel, *The Raining Tree War*, took African liberation as its main subject, proving, according to Peter Ackroyd, in the *Spectator*, that "you could be funny about the black Africans without being patronising or even bigoted." It is a theme that recurs in his second novel, *African Horse*, and the play *Motorcar*, both of which have been admired for their sharp satirical humor. Of *African Horse*, H. B. Mallalieu wrote in *Stand*, that "There is a hero, Hurl Halfcock, whose search for his identity gives a narrative continuity, yet it is not so much him we remember as the atmosphere in an emergent black nation as self-seeking, as ridiculous, as incompetent as its former rulers. In spite of the craziness, the goonery, the cruelty even, a compassion comes through."

Closer to home, Pownall directed his satirical attention to a small theatrical company and the struggles of its resident playwright in *God Perkins*. The novel, which certainly drew on his own experiences, was unconventional in plotting and only slightly bound by the conventions of narrative. In the words of Peter Prince, in the *Times Literary Supplement*, it was a "freewheeling farce." However, Prince found it

less effective than Pownall's earlier works of satire: "We need to be able to trust a satirist's skill, everyday perceptions—otherwise it is difficult to follow him confidently into his large fantasies. I am not sure . . . Pownall earns that basic confidence." *Light on a Honeycomb* also drew on Pownall's observations of the home scene—the industrial North of England—here reduced to a near madhouse of farce. There is both a literal insane asylum, run by a mad Dr. Zander, and a metaphorical one involving an industrialist and radicals of all sizes and shapes. The book had a mixed reception, with many reviewers finding it weakened by farcial "overkill."

With *Beloved Latitudes*, regarded by many as his best novel up to that time, Pownall returned to the African scene with a sensitive story of the close relationship between an African dictator and his English friend and adviser.

In his later novels, Pownall has enlarged his literary canvas to include historical figures—real and imaginary—from ancient times to the near present. He uses historical settings as a backdrop against which to place characters who reflect on the changing social, political, and philosophical moods of their given times. In *The White Cutter*, the protagonist is a stonemason ("white cutter") who works on the great cathedrals of the 11th century. It is a time of changing and developing styles of architecture, and huge building programs, and according to Pownall, the period when the Albigensians flourished and then were destroyed by war and inquisition. Pownall's protagonist, Hedric Herbertson, born into the faith of the Albigensians, writes a memoir destined to be burnt immediately on completion in fulfillment of the penance imposed on him for killing his much loved father. His interest is in the impetus that drove the architects and masons who worked on these immense cathedrals. The plot itself is both straightforward—in that it follows the rather improbable life of Hedric as he is initially brought up by his father, left with monks, taken up by the powerful of the land (including Henry IV, Simon de Montfort, and Master Henry de Reyns, the royal architect), becomes at one point the companion of Roger Bacon, and at another meets Robin Hood in Sherwood Forest—and also quite involved as discussions of philosophy, natural science, politics, and religion absorb Hedric and mold his carving as much as his views.

The novel elicited varying reactions. Patricia Hampl, in the *New York Times Book Review*, commented on the "real passion and keenest insight of the novel . . . the intellectual and spiritual longing for the elusive future we now inhabit, and the desperation this blind longing engenders." She suggested that the "historical novel bears an oddly fraternal relationship to science fiction, which would seem to be its opposite. The historical past, as far as fiction is concerned, is as much up for grabs as the future. And like most science fiction, *The White Cutter* is fundamentally about a world, and is less successful in its creation of individual character. It is also about how a prevailing consciousness commands actions and decides fates. . . . best read . . . as a meditation on the interior strivings that have brought Western civilization to its future. That is, to our present." In contrast, Phoebe-Lou Adams in the *Atlantic*, declared it "such a tangle of theology, heresy, secret dealings, and double identities that its culmination with Robin Hood in Sherwood Forest becomes simply absurd, although the tone of the book indicates that the author had serious meaning in mind."

This fascination with the way ideas dictate actions and how views of history may affect the present is wittily explored in one of his plays, *Richard III, Part Two*. Here Pownall takes the events of three different years and weaves them together into a complex and funny play. The years in question are 1984, 1948, and 1484, and the action moves freely between them aided by careful doubling of roles, according to which George Orwell and Richard III are doubled, as are two Frances Lovells (one born in 1950, the other in 1450) and two George McMasters (born in 1951, and 1451 respectively). The plots concern the publication of *1984*, the Orwell novel; the invention of a board game called Betrayal, based on the supposed events of Richard III's reign, and some events of 1484, chief amongst which is the commissioning and execution of a stained-glass window for Berkhamsted Castle. The attitudes being explored in the play are put forward close to the beginning as Orwell states:

> History is a law, like gravity. There is no greater power in the human present than the human past. The present *is* the past. . . . Stage One—you make up a story for propaganda purposes. Stage Two—you deliberately believe that story yourself. Stage Three—you force yourself to forget that you created it. Stage Four—you accept it as history. So history is plastic. Its patterns are in a state of constant disturbance.

It is this "state of constant disturbance" that seems to intrigue Pownall and which he demonstrates and partakes of in much of his work. Such explorations are not without humor, however. *Richard III, Part Two* in particular is full of wordplay, such as the moment when Chrysostom, the man employed to make a church window, and therefore, in more ways than one, an image maker, introduces himself to Richard III:

"Sire, it is a pleasure for the world's best stained glass window maker to meet the world's most blood-stained widow maker." Meanwhile, 1n 1984, the new board game, Betrayal, is launched. Its inventors hope that it will rival Monopoly, but discover that it has a flaw: players get too involved and take the thing too seriously, refusing to leave when tempers become frayed, forgetting that it is only a game; playing at the possibilities of betrayal too easily leads to enacting them.

Pownall's inventiveness is displayed again in *Elgar's Rondo*, a play that deals with the life of the noted British composer Sir Edward Elgar in the years between 1911 and 1918, using the rondo of the third movement of his Second Symphony as both symbol and structure. Reviewing a production at the Swan Theatre in Stratford-upon-Avon in 1993, Robert Meikle commented in the *Times Literary Supplement*: "Sometimes the most interesting dramatizations. . . . are those that dare to speculate beyond faithful adherence to the evidence." Elgar also furnished matter for Pownall's radio play *Elgar's Third*, in which the composer painfully struggles to write a symphony while he lies dying of cancer. The plays ends with his death: "Bury me where the hares run and have to stop. Never let me go."

The combination of historical, philosophical imagination and the desire to enact that imagination through the often fictionalized and frequently unheroic (yet not unadmirable) personal histories of recognized figures is perhaps the hallmark of Pownall's writing in all genres. It is seen again in *The Sphinx and the Sybarites*, a novel which revolves around a celebration of the hundredth birthday of the Greek philosopher Anaximander. In an act of what Mary Bears called, in the the *Times Literary Supplement* "blatant fictionality" Pownall not only displaces the date of such a celebration by roughly twenty-five years to place his party in about 510 B.C., but also "challenges that sense of respectful awe that marks most modern discussions of these early Greek philosophers." This challenge consists mostly of presenting the uncouth behavior of these esteemed ancients, in particular their sexual victimization of the seer Kallias. Bear dryly remarks, "Greek philosophers at play." Yet it is not all highbrow pornography; once again Pownall fills his text with intricacies and informed historical details, using them to explore the consequences of intellectual change for the individual.

Even when writing what purports to be a simple guide to a carefully defined part of Lancashire, this habit of describing through individuals dominates. *Between the Ribble and* the *Lune* is a series of personal recollections and insights into Pownall's own history, intermingled with accounts of local events and personalities, such as Thomas Coulston, who built the house Pownall bought and whom Pownall holds responsible for one of the ghosts, the Lady in White, who now haunts it. Extrapolating gleefully from a line in Coulston's will—"I give and bequeath unto my dear wife all my wines and liquors"—Pownall creates a brief domestic history, ending with "the clanking of empties as Mrs. Coulston bemoans her lot." He is equally wry at this own expense, such as when he describes the slow process of furnishing a house of many rooms with goods bought entirely at auction. The success of fitting out the whole place for eighteen pounds is further illuminated by the vow never to attend another auction: " . . . sitting in a crowd which is picking over the remains of other people's lives is a poor way to spend even February." At the end of the book Pownall mentions "a sense of not quite belonging, an edginess, a resistance to being absorbed, or settling down and admitting—this is it, I stay here. It might be that it is a war generation, born into a disturbed time. Perhaps the world offers too much."

Pownall has written well over thirty plays, most of them produced by small theater companies in Lancaster, some also in London and Edinburgh. He has also writen a number of radio and television plays. He received the John Whiting Award for drama in 1982 and the Giles Cooper Award in 1982 and again in 1986. In 1972 he married Mary Ellen Ray, an American actress. They have a son.

PRINCIPAL WORKS: *Novel*—The Raining Tree War, 1974; African Horse, 1975; God Perkins, 1977; Another Country, 1978; Light on a Honeycomb, 1978; Beloved Latitudes, 1981; Master Class, 1983; The White Cutter, 1988; The Gardner, 1991; Stagg and His Mother, 1992; The Sphinx and the Sybarites, 1993. *Short stories*—My Organic Uncle, 1976. *Plays*—Music to Murder By, 1978; An Audience Called Edouard, 1979; Motorcar/Richard II, Part Two, 1979; Master Class, 1984. *Nonfiction*—Between the Ribble and the Lune, 1980.

ABOUT: Contemporary Authors 89–92, 1980; Contemporary Literary Criticism 10, 1979; Contemporary Novelists, 4th ed., 1986; Dictionary of Literary Biography 14, 1983. *Periodicals*-Atlantic April 1989; Listener March 17, 1977; June 15, 1978; New York Times Book Review February 26, 1989; Observer June 30, 1974; July 27, 1975; September 19, 1976; March 27, 1977; June 26, 1977; January 1, 1978; March 16, 1994; Spectator July 6, 1974; July 26, 1975 October 2, 1976; March 12, 1977; June 17, 1978; Stand 17, 1976; Times Literary Supplement August 2, 1974; July 25, 1975; September 24, 1976; March 11, 1977; June 30, 1978; November 5, 1993.

PRICE, RICHARD (October 12, 1949–), American novelist and screenwriter, was born in the Bronx, New York. His father was a window dresser, and his mother became a bank teller. His upbringing was lower-middle-class; the Bronx neighborhood where he spent the first eighteen years of his life was in an ethnically mixed neighborhood—part white Catholic, part Jewish, and part black. "It wasn't the South Bronx, but it wasn't suburbia either. It was kind of clean-cut poverty," Price told the *Nation* in 1977. Emulating his grandfather, Price began composing stories and poems at a young age. "My first inspiration was my grandfather, the factory-worker-poet Morris Price," he recalled. "I used to see his poetry in YMHA journals when I was nine or ten, and convinced myself that it looked easy." Even the physical act of writing presented a challenge to Price, however, whose right side is partially paralyzed due to cerebral palsy. Today, he writes as he always has, using a pen, a legal tablet, and his left hand; the resulting scrawl is then sent to a typist or word processor.

After graduating from Bronx High School of Science, Price won a partial scholarship to Cornell University. He was the first member of his family to attend college. At Cornell he majored in labor relations and studied creative writing (under Ronald Sukenick); he also joined the Students for a Democratic Society (SDS). After receiving his B.S. in 1971, he considered attending either law school or graduate school. Like the protagonist of his novel *The Breaks*, Price was placed on the waiting list at Columbia Law School but was not finally admitted. Price opted to enroll in Columbia University's M.F.A. program in creative writing. In 1973 he spent one term at Stanford University, which had awarded him a Merriless Fellowship in fiction-writing, and returned to Columbia with the beginnings of what would soon become his first novel. The work so impressed two of his Columbia professors that they put Price in contact with a literary agent.

That novel, *The Wanderers*, was published when Price was only twenty-four years old and still a student at Columbia. The book consists of twelve loosely connected vignettes, all of which are set in the early 1960s and depicts the social, sexual, and domestic tribulations of The Wanderers—a gang of Bronx teenagers, most of them Italian-Americans. Critical response to the novel was overwhelmingly favorable. *Chicago Sun-Times* reviewer Rick Kogan hailed *The Wanderers* as "one of the few powerful and worthwhile novels of the year." In his *Times Literary Supplement* notice of the novel, John Lahr wrote, "There have been stunning books about ghetto life, but Richard Price's *The Wanderers* finds its own place among the chronicles of urban turmoil by focusing on a white community . . . in housing projects on the outskirts of the bourgeois dream."

Price's appeal can be attributed to his emotionally realistic portrayal of alienated urban youth, and his skillful re-creation of the 1960s era. In *Rolling Stone*, Michael Rogers commented, "These kids live in housing projects in the Bronx, run in gangs, rumble with car aerials and straight razors, and in general lead lives sufficiently grim to make the small-town pranks and repressed sexuality of the *American Graffiti* crew look like material for Hans Christian Andersen."

"Comparisons with James T. Farrell . . . are inevitable because Price sets his young characters in a naturalistic world where environment shapes and often dooms them, and he writes very traditional narrative," brooks Landon observed in the *Dictionary of Literary Biography*. However, when asked in 1983 about his own early literary influences, Price responded, "The two books that opened my eyes were *Last Exit to Brooklyn* by Hubert Selby, Jr. and *The Essential Lenny Bruce*." Selby became one of Price's earliest and most ardent champions. In the *New York Times Book Review* in 1974, Selby observed: "*The Wanderers* is an outstanding work of art because . . . Price never imposes himself on the reader. His dialogue is musically true and emotionally correct."

In his second novel, *Bloodbrothers*, Price concentrates on conflicts within a blue-collar Italian-American family in the Bronx. Eighteen-year-old Stony De Coco wants to work with abused children but is subjected to relentless pressure to join his father and uncle in the electricians' union. Reviewing *Bloodbrothers* in the *Village Voice*, Eliot Fremont-Smith wrote: "The novels considerable force also derives from its authenticity: Price clearly knows what he is talking about, both the surface detail and the feelings roiling just beneath. He is sharply observant of these, understanding, not patronizing." In his *New Statesman* review of *Bloodbrothers*, British novelist and critic Julian Barnes called the book, "a smart, professional example of the post-Selby genre of lower-depths chic."

Price received his M.F.A. from Columbia in 1976, having already published his first novel and completed his second. Although he values his own writing education and has taught creative writing at several universities (SUNY–Stony Brook, New York University, and Yale among them), Price remains dubious about the value of creative-writing majors for undergraduates. "Someone who wants to be a writer shouldn't major in writing," he told the *Saturday Review*. "If a kid wants to go to college and be a writer someday, he should be a history major or a psychology major, not an English major. The worst thing in the world is to read Henry James and then go home and try to write your own stuff."

Price's third novel, *Ladies' Man*, was his first to be set outside the Bronx. It is narrated by Kenny Becker, a thirty-year-old door-to-door salesman living on the Upper West Side of Manhattan. When his longtime girlfriend deserts him, Becker embarks on a frenzied week of bar hopping, the details of which are seldom pleasant. "Though its gaminess will offend many readers," Laura Mathews wrote in the *Atlantic Monthly*, "*Ladies' Man* is a remarkably sustained portrait of a present-day underground man."

Not long after the completion of *Ladies' Man*, Price found himself facing a new problem—drugs. Describing that period of his life in a *New York Times* article (June 13, 1993), Price wrote, "Part of the reason I was falling apart as a novelist was that I had developed a drug problem, and so I gave up on novels, thinking 'Well, if I'm a drug addict, I might as well be a screenwriter. I have to do something that doesn't require so much brains.'" Although he had intended only a brief hiatus from writing novels, he ended up spending most of the 1980s as a Hollywood screenwriter. His scripts include *The Color of Money* (nominated for Best Screenplay, 1986), *Life Lessons* (the Martin Scorsese segment of *New York Stories*), *Sea of Love*, *Night and the City*, *Mad Dog and Glory*, and the screen adaptation of his novel *Clockers*. Price's first two novels have been made into films, though he did not write the scripts. "I think people in Hollywood saw in my writing an easy transfer to script style," he told *Publishers Weekly*. "They thought I had potential as a screen writer because my books were like screenplays already." While his screen writing has brought him great financial rewards, and even increased critical respect, Price remains deeply ambivalent about Hollywood. "Ultimately, the drugs were very easy for me to give up; the screenplays were harder," Price wrote in the *New York Times*. "The screenplays and the whole world around them became new addictions." Although Price has characterized Hollywood as the town of "Hurry up and wait" and maintains that "a screenwriter is a craftsman," not an artist, he continues to work as a scriptwriter, in part, no doubt, for the money, and part to offset the loneliness of novel writing.

Price published only one novel during the 1980s, *The Breaks*. Peter Keller, the twenty-three-year-old protagonist of the novel, is a recent college graduate who ends up back at his alma mater, where he gets involved in a messy love triangle. "*The Breaks* is far from perfect," Josh Rubins wrote in the *New York Review of Books*. " . . . But, with undercover craft and psychological sophistication made nearly invisible, Price has given uncommon weight and reach to a belated story of growing up."

Price's fifth and most ambitious novel, *Clockers*, appeared almost a decade after *The Breaks*. The action in each of Price's first four novels unfolds in a milieu intimately associated with the author's own past. In *Clockers*, Price steps far outside his previous fictional terrain, though he covers no great geographical distance in order to do so. The novel's world is that of the clockers—street-level crack cocaine dealers— and the narcotics and homicide detectives whose (mostly Sisyphean) job it is to police them. Most of *Clockers* takes place in Dempsy, New Jersey, a fictional town modeled on Jersey City but representative of many medium-sized American cities gripped by drugs, crime, unemployment, and despair. "I wanted to create a generic mid-sized city that could just as easily be East St. Louis or Akron or Tampa, any place that's got 300,000 angry people in it," Price told Janet Maslin in the *New York Times* in 1992.

Clockers focuses on two characters in this swarming milieu. Strike is a nineteen-year-old mid-level street dealer in the ninth month of a career that rarely lasts longer than six. Estranged from his family, bossing a crew of unreliable "clockers" for a shrewd and treacherous overlord, he is a morose but conscientious young man, afflicted with a nervous stammer and an ulcer. His opposite number, Rocco Klein, is a middle-aged Jewish homicide detective nearing the end of a long and frustrating career in law enforcement, with family problems of his own. The plot revolves around one of Klein's cases, the murder of a dishonest dealer. When Strike's brother confesses to the crime, Klein cannot believe him—the brother, Victor, has a legitimate job, a family, and a clean record. Convinced that the confession is phony, Klein embarks on a personal crusade to save Victor and convict Strike (who is, the reader knows, innocent).

Price spent months researching the novel, spending time with both cops and drug dealers. To ingratiate himself with the dealers, he sometimes gave them money, sometimes books. "This one drug dealer said to me," Price told the *New York Times*'s Bruce Weber, "'the scariest thing to a kid out here on the streets is not drugs, AIDS, guns, jail, death. It's words on a page.'" Into what is essentially a straightforward murder-mystery plot, Price has incorporated a wealth of information concerning police procedure and the often complex rituals of addicts and dealers. As Price told Janet Maslin: "You don't have to write about the coffee mug between your cupped palms. . . . There's a whole world out there in which you can find yourself by losing yourself."

"The signal achievement of *Clockers* is to make us feel the enormous power of these giants that are drugs, alcoholism, poverty," Christopher Lehmann-Haupt wrote in the *New York Times* (May 28, 1992), while Jim Shepard, in the *New York Times Book Review* (1992), noted, " . . . perhaps the novel's most impressive accomplishment is the sheer amount of exposition it deploys and controls without ever losing its narrative drive." In the *Nation* (1992), Gerald Howe compared *Clockers* favorably to Tom Wolfe's *The Bonfire of the Vanities*, another sprawling novel of social realism, albeit with a far more genteel cast of characters. "On balance *Clockers* brilliantly revives a strain of American social fiction that runs from Dreiser's *An American Tragedy* to Wright's *Native Son* and James T. Farrell's Studs Lonigan trilogy. In this ugly time, when the white middleclass and the black urban poor seem to be inexorably drifting apart, Price's selection of subject matter and his bold acts of novelistic sympathy and penetration have true social import."

While Price's choice of subject matter in *Clockers* may be viewed as either timely or provocative, Price himself has little desire to preach politics through his fiction. In an interview with the *Saturday Review* he expressed these sentiments: "I don't have a political stance in my fiction because I can't stand proselytizing of any kind. But I do think all art is political; any sort of vision of the way things are is a political statement. . . . If there's any political element in my books, it's that I want to create an awareness that certain people exist. . . . Let me just put them down on paper so the reader can see them and decide who they are."

PRINCIPAL WORKS: The Wanderers, 1974; Bloodbrothers, 1976; Ladies' Man, 1978; The Breaks, 1983; Clockers, 1992.

ABOUT: Contemporary Authors New Revision Series 3, 1981; Contemporary Literary Criticism 6, 1976; 12, 1980; Dictionary of Literary Biography Yearbook: 1981, 1982. *Periodicals*—Atlantic Monthly October 1978; Chicago Sun-Times March 31, 1974; Nation June 11, 1977; June 1, 1992; New Statesman May 20, 1977; New York October 27, 1986; New York Book Review of Books March 31, 1983; New York Times May 28, 1992; June 2, 1992; September 6, 1992; March 21,

1993; June 13, 1993; New York Times Book Review April 21, 1974; June 21, 1992; New Yorker October 5, 1992; People Weekly November 27, 1992; Publishers Weekly May 4, 1992; Rolling Stone May 9, 1974; Saturday Review March / April 1983; Times Literary Supplement May 30, 1975; Village Voice April 26, 1976.

*QUIGNARD, PASCAL (April 23, 1948–), French novelist and critic,writes (in French): "I was born in Verneuil-sur-Avre (Normandy). both of my parents taught classical literature. I am the third of four children. My father came from a family of organists, and my mother from a family of Sorbonne professors. I spent my entire childhood in the devastated port city of Le Havre, running among the ruins, the rats, and the newly renovated buildings. My elementary school classes were held in a wooden hut, which had a coal-burning stove in the middle of the room.

"I completed my secondary studies at the Lycée de Sèvres. My mother was the director of the bilingual school there. My father was the secretary general of the International Center for Pedagogical Studies. He then became the principal of the Lycé de Sèvres. Madame de Pompadour had formerly lived in the headmaster's official suite; it was crammed with blue Sèvres. I fled. I worked as a salesman at a bookstore in Dieppe. I worked on the organs in Ancenis.

"I completed my university studies at the University of Paris at Nanterre, where I obtained a *diplôme* in 1968, and my *Licence de philosophie* in 1969. Daniel Cohn-Bendit was a fellow student. My teachers were Emmanuel Levinas and Paul Ricoeur. I began to publish my work in the journal *L'Ephémère* in 1968, with the kind help and encouragement of Louis-René des Forêts, Michel Leiris, Paul Celan, André du Bouchet, Henri Michaux, and Pierre Klossowski.

"I have completed scholarly work of textual editing (Maurice Scève), and translated works from Greek, Chinese, and Latin (Lycophron, Damaskios, Kong-souen Long, Porcius Latro, Albucius Silus). I have taught at the University of Paris at Vincennes (medieval and Renaissance studies) and at the Ecole Pratique des Hautes Etudes (origins of old romances). I was hired as reader at Editions Gallimard in 1969, appointed to the editorial board in 1976, and to the board of directors in 1989. A fervent musician, I have continued to sing and to play the piano, the organ, the violin, the viola, and the cello. I was named consultant to the Center for Baroque Music in 1988, chairman of the Concert of Nations in 1991, and chairman of the Baroque Festival

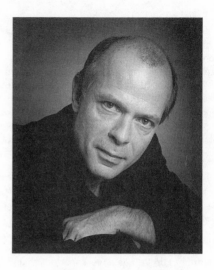

PASCAL QUIGNARD

of Versailles in 1992."

—tr. N. Lewis

Best known outside France as the author of the novel *Tous les matins du monde*, on which Alain Corneau's 1991 film was based, Pascal Quignard has written many other works of fiction, poetry, criticism, and scholarship. His critical writing has focused on such diverse subjects as Sacher-Masoch, 17th century music and painting, and Chinese culture. His erudition, broad humanistic knowledge, and unique style are impressive. Among French reviewers of his work, Gilles Anquetil, in *Le Nouvel Observateur* of November 29, 1990, wrote: "Literary collector of curios . . . , Quignard loves constantly to imagine the life or death of his nocturnal companions as seen through trivial and incongruous trifles, debris, and minute details, as if to say that the truly secret is always concealed in those things which we don't even bother to examine. In *Albucius*, Quignard magnificently praises what he calls 'the beauty of sordid things.' The permanent collision of beauty and filth, science and savagery, silence and noise is a literary technique which is his alone."

Patrick Kéchichian, in *Le Monde* of August 7, 1992, observed of *Albucius*: "Pascal Quignard, whose ability to invest distant or hidden historical or geographical situations with his imagination . . . , creates subtle literary images under the cloak of an icy and impeccable style, in which the classicism of the writing balances the unbridled and bloody nature of the story."

°kee NYAHR

Tous les matins du monde (1991, *All the World's Mornings*) unites in a short and spare narrative two of Quignard's passions—his love for the baroque and his love for music. Its French title is taken from a line that appears near the end of the novel: "Tous les matins du monde sont sans retour" ("All the world's mornings are gone without recall.") Like most of his fiction, it is as much a philosophical essay and a work of history as it is a novel. The story of a choir boy who leaves the church of Saint-Germain-l'Auxerrois when his voice changes and finds a new vocation as a composer and virtuoso of the viol began in Quignard's biographical essay on the historical musician Marin Marais (1656–1728), a work of scholarship embellished with imaginary details and philosophical commentary, first published in his collection *La leçon de musique* (The music lesson, 1987). In 1989 Quignard met the film director Alain Corneau at a recital of baroque music in Paris, and about a year later Corneau asked him to write a script for a film on French baroque music. Knowing nothing about the technique of screenwriting, Quignard offered to write a novel which might be adapted for a film. He had meanwhile been introduced to the music of Marin Marais's teacher, Monsieur de Sainte Colombe, a master of the viol. Quignard developed his novel around these two great musicians, inventing a story of a highly conflicted master-pupil relationship. In his tale Sainte Colombe, a widower grieving for his wife, leads a secluded life in the country, devoting himself to his music, his two daughters, and ghostly visitations from his dead wife. He is reluctant at first to accept Marin Marais into his household because, as he says of the young man, he is "a music maker but not a musician." Unlike the idealistic and dedicated Sainte Colombe, Marin Marais seeks royal patronage and becomes a court composer. His master quarrels bitterly with him, but Marais continues to meet secretly with his daughter, whom he seduces and leaves pregnant. Years later, the daughter dead by suicide, Marin Marais returns, hoping to get more music from Sainte Colombe's. In a final scene of reconciliation they play together Sainte Colombe's composition "Tears":

As the song of the two viols rose in the air, they looked at one another. They were weeping. The light coming into the hut through the skylight in the roof had become yellow. While their tears rolled slowly down their noses, their cheeks, their lips, they at the same time kept smiling at one another. It was dawn before Monsieur Marais returned to Versailles.

Tous les matins du monde was a best-seller in France. The film, released in 1992, an almost literal translation of the book to the screen, was enriched with a musical sound track of compositions by Marais, Sainte Colombe, Couperin, and Lully; with painterly settings (showing particularly the influence of Georges de la Tour, on whom Quignard has written a book); and performances by Gerard Depardieu as Marin Marais and Jean-Pierre Marielle as Sainte Colombe. It was a critical success only in the United States, but in France it was astonishingly popular and credited with creating an explosion of interest in French baroque music.

An English translation of *Le Salon de Württemberg*, an earlier novel of Quignard's that had been a best-seller in France in 1986, was published in 1991. Musical sensibility figures prominently in this novel too, but its setting is contemporary. Like the characters in *Tous les matins du monde*, the young hero, Charles Chenogne, plays baroque music on the cello and viola da gamba. His friend Florent is an artist in his own fashion, an archivist and collector. Denied love by his mother and confused in his identity as the son of a French mother and a German father, Charles falls in love with his friend's wife and runs away with her—a betrayal not without similarity to Marais's seduction of his master's daughter in *Tous les matins du monde*. In this novel too the betrayal and rift in the friendship is at last transfigured in a reconciliation several months before Florent's death in an automobile accident. Charles mourns for him and undergoes a series of crises through which he comes finally to a better understanding of his life.

Memory is the medium through which Charles explores his past, seeking to define himself in the present. But memory, as Charles recognizes, is unreliable: "But I pursue these memories in vain, like the words people say they have on the tip of their tongue." At other times he is resigned to the fact that we change our memories to suit others or ourselves. As Claudia Roth Pierpont observed in her review of *The Salon in Württemberg* in the *New Yorker*: "Quignard's chosen ancestor is surely Proust, whose great themes and melodies are evoked again and again, in an act of homage which itself seems part of a tradition, like the *Apothéose* that Couperin composed for Lully, or the *tombeau* that Ravel composed for Couperin: a celebration at once full-hearted, modestly scaled, and determinedly the work of its own time and author."

PRINCIPAL WORKS IN ENGLISH TRANSLATION: (tr. D. Applefield) Excerpt from Petits traités *in* Literary Review Spring 1987; (tr. B. Bray) The Salon in Württemberg, 1991; (tr. J. Kirkup) All the World's Mornings, 1993.

ABOUT: *Periodicals*—Choice July–August 1991; Library

Journal December 1990; New York Times November 8, 1992; New Yorker October 7, 1991; Review of Contemporary Fiction Summer 1988; Spring 1991.

QUINDLEN, ANNA (July 8, 1953–), American journalist and novelist, was born in Philadelphia, Pennsylvania, the oldest of five children of Robert V. Quindlen, a management consultant, and Prudence Quindlen, a homemaker. With an Irish father and an Italian mother, she grew up in a traditional Catholic environment in the suburbs of Philadelphia and West Virginia. She attended Catholic schools, where, she said, her teachers were "well-educated and intellectually rigorous" priests and nuns from the liberal wing of the Church who exposed her to a wide range of ideas about Catholicism. Her interest in writing had emerged by the time she was in high school, where she became the editor of the school newspaper.

Quindlen attended Barnard College, receiving a B.A. in English literature in 1974. At Barnard, her study of the novels of Charles Dickens made a significant impression on her. "He wrote with such eye for detail," she recalled in an interview with *Writer's Digest.* "What I learned most from reading Dickens is that telling detail makes a book by itself, telling detail is the root of all good writing. And my work as a newspaper reporter positively reinforced the necessity of detail." While still in college, Quindlen was able to use these lessons, achieving success in both fiction and reporting. She landed her first paying newspaper job at the age of eighteen, and *Seventeen* magazine published her first story when she was a college junior. Although her original ambition was to write fiction, she decided that being a reporter was more practical. "I went into newspaper writing to support my fiction habit," she explained in an interview with *Publishers Weekly.* "But I found it was more fun than anything in the world, that it was an end in itself, and also that it would be good for me as a fiction writer." Upon graduation, she began working full-time for the *New York Post*, where she had worked part-time during college.

In 1977, Quindlen joined the staff of the *New York Times* as a general assignment reporter, spending much of her time covering City Hall. By 1981, she had convinced her editors to assign her the coveted "About New York" column, making her, at the age of twenty-eight, the youngest person ever to write it. Quindlen found the column both stimulating and edifying. She told Chris Lamb of *Editor & Publisher*, "I developed a voice of my own without using the first

ANNA QUINDLEN

person and I developed the ability to come up with column ideas." Two years later when she was promoted to deputy metropolitan editor, she became one of the highest ranking women on the paper. After her second child was born, she decided it would be a convenient time to pursue her goal of writing a novel, so she resigned her position. She continued to write free-lance for the *Times*, however, producing essays for the "Hers" column. These columns became so popular that competing newspapers offered her staff positions, causing the *Times* to counter with an offer of a permanent weekly column in which she would be free to write about any subject.

Quindlen's "Life in the 30's" column became so popular that within two years it was being syndicated in sixty newspapers. "Life in the 30's" was deeply personal, often dealing with marriage, motherhood, and her inner doubts and concerns from the perspective of a modern feminist Catholic. For many people, she became the voice of the baby boom generation, as readers responded with empathy to her honesty and her direct style. In 1988, a selection of these columns was collected into *Living Out Loud*. According to Margot Slade, the editor of the column, Quindlen's popularity was due to her candor. Slade remarked, "It's as if, by revealing so much of herself, she gives readers permission to explore their innermost selves." Sybil Steinberg wrote in *Publishers Weekly* that Quindlen "has a gift for turning the quotidian into the existential, the mundane into the meaningful. The commentators, however, found her intense introspection self-absorbed." Karen Lehrman commented in the *New Republic* that "in her 'Life' columns, Quindlen suffered from the customary myopia that afflicts confessionals. Self-analysis parading as generational analysis can't help being presumptuous." Lehrman also complained that Quindlen sometimes seemed to be "trying to shock *New York Times* readers with her 'femaleness,' her daring intimacy. Exhibitionism was a way of establishing the common woman's touch; no subject was too personal to discuss."

Quindlen herself grew tired of the self-disclosure, and in December 1988, much to the disappointment of her loyal following, she stopped writing the column in order to complete a novel. In an interview with *Commonweal*, she explained: "I had told people about how my children were delivered, about what it was like when my mother was dying, about my father. It wasn't just that I was in the spotlight, it was like I was in the spotlight naked." Despite discussing so many personal topics, Quindlen claimed that she never revealed all of herself. She said in *Editor & Publisher*, " 'I know that people thought they were getting 100% of the life of Anna Quindlen, but they were really only getting about 70%.'"

After Quindlen had taken only about a year off, the *New York Times* once again lured her back, this time with the offer of a biweekly column on the Op-Ed page. To her "Public & Private" column, which she began writing in early 1990, Quindlen brought a personal response to public issues such as abortion, the Persian Gulf War, and AIDS. "I think of 'Public & Private' as a synthesis of [my first] two columns," she told Chris Lamb in *Editor & Publisher*. "I came to the realization that there were certain public issues that were most usefully dealt with within some sort of framework of at least my private beliefs, if not my private life." Rather than analyzing domestic or foreign policy, in "Public & Private" Quindlen puts policy in human terms, discussing the recession from the perspective of a checkout clerk or a war from the view of a soldier's child. Patricia Morrisroe observed in *New York* magazine that "Quindlen is particularly adept at zeroing in on small details—what she once described as 'the tiny dots that, taken together, make up the pointillistic picture of our lives.'" Karen Lehrman of the *New Republic* concurred: "Humanizing political issues . . . is a worthy and often neglected pursuit and Quindlen is quite good at it," adding that the "colorful reporting" of her pieces is "a welcome departure from the often dry policy memoranda that accompany them on the page." Lehrman noted, however, that "either Quindlen will generalize from a specific incident (elevating the private to the public), or she will take an important issue like the budget or the recession and tell us what ordinary people think, or more accurately, feel about it (reducing the public to the private)." As a result, Lehrman believes, Quindlen offers little in the way of logic or analysis. "She is a remorseless sentimentalist," Lehrman continued, "who ends up trivializing matters of considerable importance." In 1992 Quindlen received the Pulitzer Prize for commentary in recognition of her columns on abortion, the Persian Gulf War, and the confirmation hearings of Supreme Court Justice Clarence Thomas. A year later, Quindlen published *Thinking Out Loud: On the Personal, the Political, the Public and the Private*, a compilation of many of her Op-Ed page columns.

In Quindlen's first novel, *Object Lessons*, she did not stray far from the preoccupations of her newspaper columns. "I can't think of anything to write about except families. They are a metaphor for every other part of society," she explained in *Publishers Weekly*. *Object Lessons* was autobiographical to the extent that it was about a Catholic girl of Irish-Italian heritage growing up in the suburbs in the mid-1960s. Told from the perspective of twelve-year-old Maggie Scanlon, the book chronicles a tumultuous summer during which her grandfather, the domineering patriarch of the family, has a stroke, her teenage cousin becomes pregnant, and her mother almost has an affair. In the *New York Times Book Review* Anne Tyler credited *Object Lessons* with being "intelligent, highly entertaining and laced with acute perceptions about the nature of day-to-day family life." Tyler thought Maggie was a particularly vivid character, and described the novel as "a coming-of-age story, an acccount of how one young woman decides who she's going to be for the rest of her life." Tyler also noted that, although the book "succeeds because of its close attention to character," it lacks narrative momentum because of Quindlen's frequent use of flashbacks. In the *New York Times* (1991), however, Maureen Howard complained that Maggie's character was uneven, saying that her voice "swings from stunning innocence to savvy, from girlish summary to Quindlenian aphorism."

Quindlen's 1994 novel, *One True Thing*, deals with the death of a mother from cancer and her daughter's conversion from being the daughter of her father, a shallow man of literary pretensions, to being the daughter of her mother, a "woman of the heart." Lynne Sharon Schwartz, writing in the *New York Times*, termed the novel "thoroughly considered" and found its appeal in its "intelligence, its nowadays unconventional moral rigor," but, although she appreciated its detailed portrait of death and dying, she thought it lacking in "literary style, subtlety and a certain intelligence." Frederick Busch commented in the *New York Times Book Review:* "The banality of the language is matched by the banality of the ideas it expresses."

Anna Quindlen lives in Hoboken, New Jersey, with her husband, Gerald Krovatin, a criminal-defense attorney, and their children, Quindlen, Christopher, and Maria. Although in the past she has avoided remaining in one job for a long period of time, "Publc & Private" seems to offer her sufficient latitude to maintain her interest. "It really seems to me that the nineties is going to be a time when the issues that I care about most passionately are going to be at the forefront of American consciousness," Quindlen said in an interview with *Commonweal.* "I think child care and family planning and abortion and homelessness are some of those things that are really going to be some of the most pivotal issues of the next ten years and I certainly feel I can go on writing about them forever."

PRINCIPAL WORKS: *Nonfiction*—Living Out Loud, 1988; Thinking Out Loud: On the Personal, the Political, the Public and the Private, 1993. *Novels*—Object Lessons, 1991; One True Thing, 1994.

ABOUT: Contemporary Authors 138, 1993. *Periodicals*—Commonweal February 14, 1992; Current Biography April 1993; Editor & Publisher November 30, 1991; New Republic June 10, 1991; New York December 24–31, 1990; New York Times April 18, 1991; September 13, 1994; New York Times Book Review April 14, 1991; September 11, 1994; Newsweek April 4, 1988; Publishers Weekly March 15, 1991; Writer's Digest March 1993.

*RADICHKOV, YORDAN (October 24, 1929–), Bulgarian author of short stories, novels, travelogues, motion-picture scripts, and plays, was born in the village of Kalimanitsa, located in the western part of the Balkan range. His father was a farmer, who also worked as a mason to supplement the family income. His mother was a homemaker and helped with the farm. She was also a midwife and practiced some folk medicine. After finishing the school in Kalimanitsa, Radichkov attended the high school in the town of Berkovitsa, from which he graduated in 1947.

"For twenty-two years," he told Lyubomira Parpulova Gribble in an interview (published in 1978 in the Bulgarian magazine *Septemvri*), "I lived in a village." This period ended in 1951 when he became regional correspondent for the newspaper *Narodna mladezh* (National youth).

A year later he moved to the capital, Sofia, to work as an editor for the same paper. From 1955 until 1959 he worked for the newspaper *Vecherni novini* (Evening news). In 1962, after several years on the screenplay board of the Bulgarian Cinematography Company (1959–1962), Radichkov was appointed editor in the leading Bulgarian literary paper *Literaturen front* (Literary front), where he stayed until 1969. In 1962 he became a member of the Union of Bulgarian Writers.

During the 1960s Radichkov was not only directly involved in the institutions of literature, but also found the unique style that earned him national and international recognition as the most original and interesting prose writer in contemporary Bulgarian literature. It was his eighth book, *Svirepo nastroenie* (Violent mood, 1965) which surprised the readers with its boldly innovative imagery and mode of narration. By that time Radichkov had already published *Gorda Stara planina* (The proud Balkan Range, 1956), *Sŭrtseto bie za khorata: Sotochinski razkazi* (The heart beats for the people: Stories from Sotochino, 1959), *Prosti rŭtse* (Simple hands, 1961), *Obŭrnato nebe* (The sky upside down, 1962), *Planinsko tsvete* (A mountain flower, 1964), *Sharena cherga: Razkazi za detsa* (A multicolored rug: stories for children, 1964), and *Goreshto pladne: Razkazi* (Hot noon, 1965). *Gorda Stara planina* is a collection of journalistic sketches which the author himself does not consider part of his literary works. Therefore, his career as a writer of fiction begins with the appearance of *Sŭrtseto bie za khorata*. This book, as well as the three other collections of short stories that followed it, was written in a rather traditional manner. All four books were favorably received by both the literary critics and the general public and praised for their finely crafted details, strong lyrical prose, and intense dramatic conflicts, but they did not break any new literary paths.

The next two books, although still dominated by the traditional mode of narration, show some of the features which later became Radichkov's trademark—namely, unusual characterization, mythical images, and extensive digressions from the main story. Intended for children, *Sharena cherga* presents the author with the opportunity to play with naive imagery, unorthodox plotting, whimsy, and absurdity. The subtitle of the other book is *Razkazi* (Short stories), but it actually contains three novelettes: *Goreshto pladne, Posledno lyato* (Last summer), and *Privŭrzaniyat balon* (The Tied balloon). Disregard for the canonical literary genres is another characteristic of vintage Radichkov. The change in the mode of narration can be seen also in the

*ruh DEECH kuv, your DAHN

increasingly prominent mixture of realism and myth. For instance, in "Goreshto pladne" the river is, at first, a real part of the landscape, but once it threatens the life of a boy trapped in the foundations of a bridge, it assumes symbolic properties, no longer the beautiful village river, but now a serpent from hell.

Svirepo nastroenie fully displays Radichkov's unique vision of the world. The action takes place in Cherkazki, an imaginary village located in the vicinity of his native Kalimanitsa. However, Cherkazki in *Svirepo nastroenie* is very different from its essentially realistic namesake in *Goreshto pladne.* This time the reader sees a surrealistic universe in which a pig plows into the sky faster than Halley's comet ("Svirepo nastroenie"), a peasant's dog eats up his master and the story itself ("Kucheto zad karutsata"; The dog behind the cart), and a rifle fires and blows the village and its inhabitants to pieces ("Studeno"; Cold).

During the next decade-and-a-half the new mode of narration completely dominated Radichkov's prose: the short stories in *Vodoley* (Aquarius, 1967), *Nie, vrabchetata* (We, the sparrows, 1968), *Baruten bukvar* (The gunpowder ABC book, 1969), *Kozheniyat pŭpesh* (The leather melon, 1969), *Choveshka proza* (Human prose, 1971), (Plyava i zŭrno (Chaff and grain, 1972), *Kak taka* (How come?, 1974), and *Malko otechestvo* (A small fatherland, 1974); the novelettes *Kozyata brada* (Goat's beard, 1967), *Vyatŭrŭt na spokoystvieto* (The wind of calm, 1968), *Skalni risunki* (Rock drawings, 1970), *Spomeni za kone* (Memories about horses, 1975), and *Shest malki matryoshki i edna golyama* (Six small Matryoshkas and a big one, 1977); the novels *Vsichki i nikoy* (Everybody and no one, 1975), and *Prashka* (Sling, 1979); and the travelogue *Neosvetenite dvorove* (Unlit courtyards, 1965).

Critics frequently call Radichkov's fiction "kaleidoscopical." Indeed, he seems deliberately to be avoiding any likeness of a unified and steady point of view. He attributes the discourse to different narrators and combines various voices (first-person narratives of educated city dwellers, ordinary townsfolk, and peasants from remote villages). Although his imagination is the ultimate source of the fantastic imagery, he emphasizes its ties with the folk beliefs and narratives of his native village. The original and amusing play of fictional images and realistic referents often results in absurd statements and situations.

The story "Tenets" ("The Sprite") is an excellent example of this "kaleidoscopical" and absurd vision of the world. A peasant catches a jay and brings it home where his wife is weaving on a loom and a pot of corn is simmering on the stove. Immediately after that a series of amazing occurrences begins. As he walks to the barn, some invisible creature snatches the bucket from his hand, milks the cow, and brings the milk home, then puts more wood into the stove, cleans the snow from the roof, chops wood, feeds the pig, and gets into the loom and weaves all night. The peasant feverishly tries to find the cause of all this and recalls various folk beliefs about supernatural beings. He consults with his wife, a true connoisseur of village lore, but nothing fits the case. Finally, it dawns on them that this is a sprite, namely, "a person who had not gone anywhere when he died [perhaps a hundred or five hundred years ago], but had remained on earth." In the last part of the story, the reader learns that the sprite kept working for the couple. At first the husband worried that the sprite might make sexual advances toward his wife, but after a while he decided that the creature "wasn't the sort to try anything." At this point, the writer interferes directly, announcing that he, too, wanted to have a sprite. He followed the advice of the peasant: caught a jay, boiled some corn, and left his typewriter in the room. Then he went hunting with the peasant. The sprite came and wrote the story "Tenets." The writer only took "the liberty of offering it to the reader." Since then, the sprite writes everything for the author, while he enjoys life. This short, first-person narrative creates a parodic slant by proving wrong the expectations of the reader about the omniscient narrator.

Unlike the benevolent *tenets*, who is taken directly from the folk demonology of the real Kalimanitsa, the other major mythical inhabitant of Cherkazki, the all-devastating *verblyud*, is Radichkov's own creation ("Verblyud"). In general, he likes to bring together totally opposite concepts and to explore the consequences of such unconventional unions. The contact between urban civilization of the technological era and the rural way of life and its traditional ideology is one of his favorite themes.

His treatment of the politically charged topic of antifascist resistance in *Baruten bukvar* is also very unconventional. It is not suprising that the book stirred up strong controversy. Hard-liners were incensed because they did not find there the well established clichés of Socialist Realism, according to which the main character had to be either a dedicated Communist or a politically neutral person who enthusiastically embraces Communist ideology at the end. Liberal critics defended the author, pointing out that his general attitude toward the resistance was positive and emphasized the high literary quality of the work.

"Yamurluk" ("The Cloak") is a representative sample of Radichkov's unorthodox treatment of an orthodox topic. It also presents still another feature typical of Radichkov's narrative style during the 1960s and '70s—namely, the open ending with the possibility of multiple interpretations. The story, a first-person narrative by Lazarus, a poor middle-aged peasant, revolves around his shepherd's cloak. It starts with a lengthy discourse about the sheep from which the fleece was sheared, the selection of the wool, the weaving of the material, the making of the cloak, and the cases in which it proved to be superior to the German-made mackintosh of his neighbor Tseko, nicknamed Twin Storks, after the identifying symbol of the German company Solingen, whose tools he praised incessantly. One morning, as Lazarus is harvesting corn, a young man with feverish eyes, armed with a rifle and a hand grenade, suddenly appears from the mist. He takes Lazarus's cloak and disappears into the forest. Lazarus realizes that this is a partisan; i.e., an antifascist guerrilla fighter. He is terrified that the partisan will kill him, or that Twin Storks, who works nearby, will notice them. Later he agonizes over the thought that if the partisan were captured, the police would recognize his coat and execute him as a collaborator. When the Communist-led political coalition takes power, the partisans come to the village. The fellow with the cloak is among them. Lazarus embraces "the man and the cloak." It is not clear whether he rejoices just because the fear for his own life is finally gone or he is glad to see the young man alive as well. In any case, Lazarus corrects neither the partisan's assumption that he celebrates the political victory, nor Twin Storks' conclusion that he has been helping the partisans all the time.

Since the early 1980s, Radichkov's manner of writing has developed along new lines. He is relatively more explicit and direct, and a new issue, the preservation of nature and wildlife, has been the central topic of many of his later works. Short stories and novelettes continue to be his favorite genres. He published ten more collections of such works: *Luda treva* (Wild grass, 1980), *Pedya zemya* (A span of land, 1980), *Nezhnata spirala* (The tender spiral, 1983), *Po vodata* (On the water, 1983), *Verblyud* (Verblyud, 1984), *Izpadnali ot karutsata na boga* (Things that have fallen off God's cart, 1984), *Skakalets* (Grasshopper, 1984), *Skandinavtsite* (Scandinavians, 1985), *Tenekienoto petle* (The little tin rooster, 1985), *Khora i svraki* (People and magpies, 1990). He also wrote one more novel, *Noev kovcheg* (Noah's ark, 1988), and a second travelogue, *Malka severna saga* (A small northern saga, 1980).

Radichkov's travelogues deserve special mention, since by definition they should be closer to a documentary than to fiction. However, with Radichkov the facts are often submerged into the absurd and richly ornamental style of his fiction. The first travel book, *Neosvetenite dvorove*, offers a highly original picture of Siberia as seen during his trip in 1965. The second, inspired by a 1979 journey to Sweden, has a stronger lyrical current, but its imagery is less exotic and surprising. Radichkov's screenplays are also closely related to his other writings. In fact, each of them is an adaptation from his book *Goreshto pladne*. *Goreshto pladne* (1965) and *Posledno lyato* (1973) were both made into motion pictures that won national and international awards. For censorship reasons, the movie made from *Privŭrzaniyat balon* (1967) was withdrawn and did not appear in theaters until 1990.

The relationship between his plays and prose works is equally close. With the exception of *Zhelyaznoto momche* (Iron boy, 1967), Radichkov's plays—*Sumatokha* (Confusion), *Yanuari* (January), *Lazaritsa* (Lazarus treed), *Koshnitsi* (Baskets), and *Obraz i podobie* (Image and likeness)—were both critical and popular successes, although they are unconventional and seem to defy all rules of dramatic art. A family penchant for theater emerges in that Radichkov's son, Dimitur is a theater director, and his daughter, Roza, is a drama critic.

Radichkov has close family ties and a number of autobiographical details are directly introduced into his fiction. His wife, Suzi, a former journalist, is Jewish. He was very deeply attached to his mother Mladena, who lived with his family in Sofia for many years. Both of his grandsons are named, in traditional Bulgarian fashion, after him (the granddaughter is named for his wife). His travel abroad (the U.S.S.R., Sweden, the United States, France, Italy, Poland, Czechoslovakia, Germany, Brazil) is connected exclusively with his literary career. He is the recipient of the highest Bulgarian literary award and of foreign honors, including the Italian international prize for literature, Grinzane Cavour. His works have been translated into many languages (English, French, German, Italian, Spanish, Russian, Swedish, Polish, Hungarian, etc.). A considerable number of Radichkov's stories and some of the plays have appeared in English in various periodicals, but only a few of them are published in book form. *Hot Noon*, translated by Peter Tempest in 1972, has a misleading title because its content is different from that of his *Goreshto pladne* (Hot noon, 1965). The English edition includes the stories "Hot Noon," "The Leather Melon," "The Sprite," "Full of Hoping," "The Cloak," and "The Gunpowder ABC Book."

PRINCIPAL WORKS IN ENGLISH TRANSLATION: *Short stories*—(tr. P. Tempest) Hot Noon, 1972. *Play*—(tr. E. J. Czerwinski) Lazaritsa *in* Slavic and East European Arts, Summer 1987.

ABOUT: Black, K. L. (ed.) A Biobibliographical Handbook of Bulgarian Authors, 1981; Dictionary of Literary Biography, 1995 147; South Slavic Writers, ed. Vasa D. Mihailovich. *Periodicals*—Delos Winter 1988–1989; World Literature Today Winter 1990.

RASPUTIN, VALENTIN (GRIGOREVICH) (March 15, 1937–), Russian writer of novellas, short stories, and ethnographic studies, as well as environmental activist and publicist for conservative nationalist causes, was born to a family of hunters and farmers in Atalanka, a village on the Angara River in Siberia. His father, who worked in agriculture and logging and was in combat in World War II, served time in prison for alleged carelessness with government money. As a result, his mother and grandmother—with their stories of village life and folklore—were the dominant influences in his childhood. Rasputin remained in the village until 1948 when his mother sent him to Ust-Uda, a town thirty miles away, to complete his schooling. In 1961, Atalanka, like many villages along the Angara, disappeared beneath the waves of the reservoir formed by a massive hydroelectric project. Rasputin's comment that he is "from the ranks of the drowned" gives a sense of the enormity of this loss for him personally and as a child of Siberia, whose environment and traditions were constantly under attack during the Soviet period. The author has said that whenever he thinks back to his childhood, he always remembers the shores of the Angara next to his native village, "with the islands across the water from me and the sun setting on the opposite shore. I've seen many objects of beauty both natural and man-made, but I will die with that picture before me which is dearer to me than anything else in the world. . . . It is how I see my homeland."

From 1954 to 1959 Rasputin studied history and literature at Irkutsk University; he seriously intended to become a teacher and says that he entered the literary world by accident. When he did not receive a stipend one year, his friends found him work on a local newspaper, and from the second half of the 1950s until the mid-1960s he worked as a journalist for several newspapers and for Soviet television. He was sent all over Siberia to gather material for stories promoting the "radiant future" that Moscow had planned for this region. He also began publishing short stories in regional journals beginning in 1961 with

"Ia zabyl sprosit'u Leshki" ("I Forgot to Ask Lyoshka").

Rasputin was first identified as a rising talent by the historical novelist and Siberian patriot Vladimir Chivilikhin (1928–1984) at a 1965 seminar for young writers in the Siberian city of Chita. Chivilikhin was impressed by the short stories he saw and pressed the Writers Union to grant Rasputin early admission, even before he had published his first book. Rasputin gratefully refers to Chivilikhin as his "literary godfather." It is important to realize that between 1934 and 1985 the government-sponsored Writers Union controlled all aspects of the literary and personal lives of its members from publication fees to living quarters. To give some sense of the varied texture of cultural life in the Brezhnev years (1964–1982), during the same week that union officials were out in Siberia shaping Russia's literary future, back in Moscow Alexander Solzhenitsyn's archive was seized, and, in a separate incident, Andrey Sinyavsky and Yuly Daniel were arrested after they were discovered to be the authors of supposedly "anti-Soviet" works published abroad under the pseudonyms of Tertz and Arzhak.

The best of Rasputin's journalism appeared in two collections in 1966: *Kostrovye novykh gorodov* (Campfire tenders of new cities) and *Krai vozle samogo neba* (The land next to the sky). The latter book, with its colorful descriptions—some, like "Starukha" (The old woman), lightly fictionalized—of the nomadic Tofalarians of Siberia's Sayan Mountains, shows Rasputin's interest in the traditions of the indigenous peoples of Siberia, soon to be supplemented by an even deeper interest in the region's long-time Russian inhabitants. This was followed in 1967 by his first story collection, *Chelovek s etogo sveta* (A person from this world), which includes the frequently anthologized "Vasilii i Vasilisa" ("Vasili and Vasilisa") and reworked versions of his early fiction.

The year 1967 also saw the appearance of *Dengi dlia Marii* (*Money for Maria*), the first of the four novellas that made Rasputin one of the best-known writers in the Soviet Union. All of these short novels take place in Siberia and are focused on an imminent crisis in a peasant family or an entire village. In *Money for Maria*, the author is concerned with the community's reaction when one of its members is unfairly charged with embezzling government money. Maria has reluctantly agreed to run the local store; when an inspector discovers a shortfall of a thousand rubles, even he sees that this is due to Maria's trustful nature and lack of education. Nevertheless, she is given only five days to replace this considerable sum, and the narrative follows the efforts made by her husband Kuzma to press fellow villagers and family members to help Maria avoid a prison sentence. The ending is left open as Kuzma approaches their last hope—his brother in the city. Rasputin sees this as the type of incident that exposes moral relationships and the secret depths of the human character. Attention is paid to the decline of the peasant community and the gap between urban and rural life, favorite themes in the author's subsequent fiction and nonfiction writing.

In *Poslednii srok* (1970, *Borrowed Time*), Rasputin focused on Anna, an old woman on her deathbed. As Anna remembers her long life, her children respond in a variety of ways to her final illness; in the end they impatiently disperse on the eve of her death. Rasputin is particularly drawn to the depiction of older village women— often the sole inhabitants of villages depleted by collectivization, war, and the postwar flight to urban areas—as the repositories of a vanishing peasant culture. Russian critics noted the author's skill in capturing the quality of these lives, and the colorful peasant language that had been virtually absent from Russian literature since 1934. Some lauded this demonstration of the richness of Russian language and culture; others objected to what they saw as the elevation of substandard language and marginal characters.

In 1945, the young Rasputin saw a captured army deserter led through his village, and this traumatic memory serves as the basis for the 1974 novella *Zhivi i pomni* (*Live and Remember*). Although there is an extensive body of fiction about wartime Russia, this work is daring in its expression of sympathy for the dilemma faced by the deserter, Andrei Guskov, but even more so for the tragic choice his wife Nastyona must make. If she fails to secretly help her husband, who had deserted in order to visit her, he will quickly perish in the Siberian forest, but by helping him she is risking the loss of a community totally committed to the war effort. When she becomes obviously pregnant, a decision can no longer be put off and she commits suicide. Rasputin's affection and respect for his heroine is the most moving aspect of this strongly written narrative. We are uncertain of Andrei's fate, knowing only that Nastyona's death has temporarily delayed his capture. This short novel, more than any of Rasputin's other works, resonates with the influence of Dostoyevsky. Rasputin has said that he was "strongly attracted by the intensely psychological nature of Dostoyevsky's work, the passions of his characters, and his ability to tell all there is to tell about a person."

The watery demise of Rasputin's own birthplace spurred him to write a trio of stories about communities drowned by the floodwaters of progress. The first of these is "*Vniz i vverkh po techeniiv*" (1972, "Downstream"), which follows an urban-based writer's lyrical digressions as he floats down the Angara River on a steamer that will take him to his family, who have been relocated after the destruction of their village. *Proshchanie s Materoi* (1976, *Farewell to Matyora*) is the second part of this trilogy and probably the best-known of all Rasputin's works. The year after it appeared he won the U.S.S.R. State Prize for Literature. *Matyora* focuses on an island village on the very eve of the flooding, when its 300-year existence is coming to an end before the villagers' eyes. Once again, it is the older women who are the central and most positive characters, with Darya Pinigina as the moral compass of her community, its memory and conscience. Rasputin's narrator says that every Russian village has someone with Darya's qualities and that when one such leader dies, "her place will immediately be taken by another woman who has grown old, strengthening her position among the others with her firm and just temperament." Darya worries not only about the displacement of the living, but even more about the abandonment and "drowning" of the generations of villagers who rest in Matyora's cemetery. Darya's careful preparation of her family home for its "funeral" is one of the most powerful scenes in postwar Russian literature. As the novella comes to an ambiguous close, Darya and a few friends defiantly remain in the sole standing structure (everything else has been burned down by government workers to clear the location) while the people sent from the mainland to remove the old people forcibly drift helplessly in the fog that has enveloped the island. A film of *Farewell to Matyora* was made by Elem Klimov in 1981. The film version omitted the novella's most controversial character, a catlike island spirit, invisible to human eyes, who is called the Master.

Rasputin's four novellas placed him firmly in the front ranks of the school of literature known as village prose (c. 1956–1980), which had begun in the thaw period of the 1950s with criticism of collective-farm management but which went on to lyrically recall the more traditional countryside of the writers' childhoods. Ignoring many important conventions of the official Socialist Realist literary model, writers like Fedor Abramov, Vladimir Soloukhin, Viktor Astafiev, and Vasily Belov evoked a past that was radiant, but they also displayed an underlying anxiety and anger about the fate of peasant Russia. In the 1960s and 1970s, certain works of rural literature were criticized for what were said to be patriarchal, anti-Soviet values. In the post-Soviet period village prose has been interpreted—often inaccurately—as a seedbed for Russian chauvinism. The fact that these rural writers were able to publish much of what they wrote during the "years of stagnation" attests to the quality of their prose (in contrast in Socialist Realism), which appealed to critics and readers, and to latent nationalism in government circles. Rasputin is considered one of the finest stylists of this movement, who was best able to capture the nuances of contemporary rural speech without turning his works into mere transcripts. His work is strong narratively and he is credited with helping to reintroduce interior monologue to Soviet prose fiction. Rasputin's female characters are especially well written.

While it is the four novellas that made Rasputin famous, he is also widely respected for his shorter works such as "Vasilii and Vasilisa," "The Old Woman," "Uniz i vverkh po techniiu" ("Downstream"), "Uroki frantsuzsrogo" (1973, "French Lessons"), "Vek zhivi" (1981, "You Live and Love"), and "Pozhat" (1985, "The Fire"). If *Farewell to Matyora* of 1976 signals the beginning of the end of the village prose movement, then "The Fire" of 1985, which completes the Angara trilogy, marks the onset of *glasnost* literature. The author fulfills a promise he made after *Matyora* to "follow" his characters to the new settlements to see what their lives would be like there. Not only have the old villages disappeared beneath the waves, but the whole way of life that accompanied agricultural work has also disappeared, and the fire that rages through the logging settlement illuminates the lack of any community feeling. "The Fire" is the most pessimistic of Rasputin's stories, and the last important work of fiction written before the author began to concentrate on nonfiction genres.

Rasputin had begun his career as a journalist, and returned to an elevated form of journalism in the early 1980s. His essays are a powerful combination of the polemical and the lyrical; his favorite subjects have been the environment (especially concerning Lake Baikal), and ethnography (the history of Russians in Siberia). Since the mid-1980s he has also written about Russian spiritual and cultural history with many profiles on Siberian writers. All of these subjects come under what Rasputin and other contemporary writers have called "the ecology of culture."

Before the Gorbachev era Rasputin was known as a writer of lyrical fiction and a fearless environmental activist. After 1985 he became more active politically, writing polemical articles in favor of nationalist causes, speaking out at writers' congresses, signing open letters on political subjects, and serving as a representative in the Russian parliament and as a member of Gorbachev's inner council in 1990. Just as he had refrained from joining the Communist Party during the Brezhnev era, subsequently Rasputin kept clear of direct involvement with ultranationalist groups like Pamyat, but has remained active in the conservative branch of the Russian Writers Union. His signing of the chauvinistic "Letter of the 74 Russian Writers" in March 1990 and controversial remarks made during an interview with the *New York Times* (January 28, 1990) began to alter Rasputin's reputation at home and abroad and left him open to a charge of anti-Semitism, which the writer vigorously denies, saying that he has been regularly misquoted and quoted out of context. He and his supporters say that he is driven by the pain he feels at the disintegration of Russia and its people during his lifetime.

Rasputin's wife Svetlana is a teacher of mathematics; they have a son Sergey and a daughter Maria. When not in Moscow on literary or other business, he makes his home in Irkutsk with frequent trips to villages along the Angara and to the shores of Lake Baikal. The most dramatic personal event in the writer's life came in March 1980 when he was viciously beaten by thieves in his Irkutsk apartment building. It took several operations over the next few years before he was able to write full-time again, and when he did, the luminous atmosphere of his earlier work had disappeared, whether for personal or political reasons.

Valentin Rasputin's career has taken several distinct turns thus far. Beginning as a regional journalist, he next became a leading writer of lyrical fiction and a major talent of the village prose movement, and then one of Russia's most prominent and controversial essayists. Because of his negative comments on Soviet Jews, he gained a notoriety in the West rather than fame as a writer of novellas. Like a number of literary figures before him—Dostoyevsky, for example, in *The Diary of a Writer*—his artistic sense is not matched by political wisdom. But if Rasputin's political vision has been clouded, his artistic vision in such works as *Farewell to Matyora* astonishes the reader with its confidence and beauty. At the height of his fictional powers, he helped to demolish Socialist Realism and he brought to Russian readers powerfully lyrical stories about their native land.

PRINCIPAL WORKS IN ENGLISH TRANSLATION: *Novellas*—(tr. A. Bouis) Live and Remember, 1978 (reissued, 1992); (tr. A. Bouis) Farewell to Matyora, 1979 (reissued, 1991); (tr. K. Windle and M. Wettlin) Money for Maria and

Borrowed Time, 1981. *Short stories*—"French Lessons" *in* Soviet Literature no. 1, 1975; "I Had to Say Goodbye to Matyora" *in* Soviet Studies in Literature, Summer 1978; "The Swans on the Nepryadva" *in* Soviet Studies in Literature no. 9, 1980; "Vasili and Vasilisa" *in* Soviet Studies in Literature no. 3, 1980; (tr. V. Brougher and H. Post) "Downstream" *in* Contemporary Russian Prose, 1982; "The Human Race is not Accidental" *in* Soviet Studies in Literature no. 7, 1983; "Rudolfio" *in* Kenyon Review no. 3, 1983; "The Fire" *in* Soviet Studies in Literature no. 7, 1986; (tr. A. Myers) You Live and Love and Other Stories, 1986; (tr. G. Mikkelson and M. Winchell) Siberia on Fire, 1989. *Nonfiction*—"To Be Oneself" *in* Soviet Studies in Literature, Winter 1977–1978.

ABOUT: Brown, D. *in* Russian Literature and Criticism, 1982; Contemporary World Writers, 2nd ed., 1993; Dunlop, J. *in* Russian Literature and Criticism, 1982; Gillespie, D. Valentin Rasputin and Soviet Russian Village Prose, 1986; Kasack, W. *in* Dictionary of Russian Literature Since 1917, 1988; Mikkelson, G. *in* Studies in Honor of Xenia Gasiorowska, 1983; Mikkelson, G. and Winchell, M. *foreword to* Siberia on Fire, 1989; Oulanoff, H. *in* Handbook of Russian Literature, 1985; Parthé, K, *foreword to* Farewell to Matyora, 1991; Parthé, K. *foreword to* Live and Remember, 1992; Polowy, T. The Novellas of Valentin Rasputin, 1989. *Periodicals*—Canadian Slavonic Papers 22, September 1980; 28, 1986; Choice May 1990; Modern Language Review April 1985; New York Review of Books March 15, 1990; February 14, 1991; New York Times May 3, 1981; December 23, 1981; July 29, 1990; New York Times Book Review May 10, 1987; December 17, 1989; New York Times Magazine January 28, 1990; People April 6, 1987; Quinquereme 9, 1986; Russian Language Journal 114, 1979; Russian Review January 1994; Scottish Slavonic Review 8, 1987; Slavic and East European Journal 31, 1987; Soviet Literature July 1986; Soviet Studies in Literature 14, Summer 1978; 17, Summer 1981; World Literature Today 53, 1979; 54, 1980; 60, Winter 1986; 64, Summer 1990.

*REVUELTAS, JOSÉ (SÁNCHEZ) (20 November 1914-April 14, 1976) Mexican novelist, playwright, film scenarist, and short story writer, was born in Durango to José Revueltas Gutiérrez, a grocer, and Romana Sánchez Arias. He had three siblings who grew up to be prominent in the arts in Mexico: Silvestre, a musician; Fermín, a mural painter; and Rosaura, an actress. The family moved to Mexico City when José was six, and he attended the Colegio Alemán, a prestigious private school. In 1924 his fathers death plunged the family into poverty, and José had to go to public school and later to work in a hardware store instead of attending high school. At this time he was radicalized by listening to lectures and attending demonstrations under the aegis of Manuel Rodríguez, a Marxist. His leftist leanings were solidified when he was arrested in a demonstration at the age of fourteen. He was sent to a harsh federal reformatory and then to a reform school, the first in a series of incarcerations. The reform school was the mildest, allowing him to read and study, but imprisonment put an end to his formal education. His real education had come, he later claimed, from his readings in his father's library and the Biblioteca Nacional.He became a member of the Communist Party two years after his first incarceration..

By the time Revueltas was twenty-one, he had done two terms in the Islas Marías, a penal colony, sentenced for his participation in workers' strikes. Upon his release from the Islas Marías in 1935, the Mexican Communist Party named him a delegate to the Seventh World Communist Congress held in the Soviet Union. His participation in the Congress lasted five months. Although Revueltas was expelled from the Mexican Communist Party in 1943 and again in 1960, he never wavered in his commitment to the principles of Marxism, and remained one of his country's foremost theoreticians of radical politics, in the words of Sam Slick.

Revueltas married Olivia Peralta in 1937 and had four children with her before their divorce in 1947. He began to publish short stories and wrote his first novel "El quebranto" (The surrender), based on his experiences in the federal reformatory. It was stolen before it could be published. His first published novel *Los muros de agua* (1941, Walls of water) explores the brutalizing dehumanization of life in Islas Marías. Revueltas depicts "a world that assaults the mind and spirit and drives people to suicide, perversion, and incredibly inhuman acts," Sam Slick said. "The effective portrayal of this inferno is effortlessly executed by Revueltas. The author claimed, however, that his true experiences in the Islas were worse than those depicted. . . . "

The year 1943 marked the appearance of Revueltas's most famous, although not necessarily his best, novel, *El luto humano*, which was translated into English in 1947 by H.R. Hays as *The Stone Knife* and in 1990 by Roberto Crespi as *Human Mourning*. *Human Mourning* takes place in the aftermath of the Mexican Revolution. An infant dies, and her mother sends her husband, the dead child's father, to seek a priest to attend to the last rites. Although the priest the man goes for is, as expected, Roman Catholic, Revueltas merges the father's need for a priest with the archaic rites of the Mexican past:

> Always a priest at the hour of death. A priest who cuts out the heart from the chest with that stone knife of penitence, to offer it, as did the ancient priests on the sacrificial stone, to God, to God in whose bosom the idols had

been pulverized and their earth scattered, imperceptible now in the white body of divinity.

On his journey to find the priest, the father has a revelation:

An unexpected idea surged in his head in the middle of the night: the last sacrament, the final communication of sins, the last oil, the holy oils of the King of the Jews, was nothing other than immortality itself. Because death only exists without God, when God does not see us die. But when a priest arrives, God sees us die and He forgives us. He forgives us our life, the life He is about to snatch from us.

Before finding the priest, Ursulo, the father, has inadvertently acquired the company of a hired assassin, Adán. The priest has a flash of memory back to the Cristero War, a revolt of Catholic militants against separation of church and state from 1926 to 1929, after he sees Adán. He recalls how, from the hiding place where he cringed, he saw Adán murder the leader of the Cristeros—after the Cristero leader had asked for a cease-fire.

Ursulo treks back over the perilous, storm-drenched terrain with the assassin and the priest to where his wife and a few other peasants are getting drunk in mourning. Each has memories and consciousness which connect them to each other, to the epochal events that preceded the story, and to a larger whole of which each is a symbol. The little group is trapped by raging flood waters, and after a few days the circling vultures have their prey:

A second *zopilote* [vulture] descended and then a third. Huddled together, they coldly and calculatingly sized up the situation as if nothing could possibly be hidden from them, not even thoughts, as if they were masters of destiny. . . . The *zopilotes* knew all the secrets of the heart. Who had paid any attention to them before, when they would circle meekly and with quiet rhythm high in the skies so far away? Nevertheless, there always exists a bond of reciprocal vigilance and hatred between them and man.

The vultures are located at one extreme and man at the opposite. Man goes toward them and before he dies defends himself with the land or fire. The vultures wait. Their turn is written. . . .

This simple plot serves as the framework around a complex series of flashbacks, meditations, and streams of consciousness that encompass all of Mexico—its myth, history, and present reality, which is Revueltas's "cosmic, ahistorical, totalizing vision of Mexico," according to Slick. The novel emphasizes the immediate historic precursors of its story—the Revolution, the Cristero War, and a strike by the workers on a Federal Irrigation System project. Slick called the novel "an investigation into the soul and psyche of the

Mexican," and maintained that the "confusion and corruption" implicit in the Revolution and the Cristero War influenced Revueltas's idea that it was"as if to live Mexico's history is to be contaminated spiritually and emotionally."

Octavio Paz contributed a preface to *Human Mourning*, the first part of which consists of a review of the book that Paz wrote in 1943. The second part is a reconsideration from 1979, when Paz was already considered a great man, on his way to winning the Nobel Prize, and Revueltas was dead. In 1943, Paz noted a sacral element in *Human Mourning*: "Adán, an assassin who believes himself to be the incarnation of Fate, and Natividad, an assassinated leader, symbolize, very religiously, the past and future of Mexico." Paz saw the religious element as "a baptism that combines, together with the rites of agricultural fertility, the ancient baptism of the Aztecs and that of the Christians." In his reconsideration, however, Paz chose to view Revueltas as a Marxist who was unable to leave the Christian element out of his work because he possessed "a vision of Christianity within his Marxist atheism." Paz believed that "Revueltas lived Marxism as Christianity, and that is why he lived it, as Unamuno would put it, as agony, doubt, and negation." Paz thought Revueltas was able to integrate the Christian element into his belief system and his writings because "for Christianity, Jesus' incarnation and sacrifice are facts that are both supernatural and historical. Divine revelation not only displays itself in history, but it also is the testing ground for Christians: souls are won and lost here, in this world. The Marxist Revueltas assumes, with all its consequences, the Christian legacy: the weight of men's history. . . . The connection between Christianity and Marxism is history. . . . "

For Raymond Leslie Williams, writing in the *American Book Review*," as the novel progresses, the discourse moves from blatantly Christian to blatantly Marxist. Unfortunately, both these languages are occasionally heavy handed. . . . " Williams faults not Crespi's translation, deeming it "fine," but an overly ponderous effort by Revueltas to "universalize the situation." Similarly, David Unger, in the *New York Times Book Review*, noted that the characters "are both real and symbolic" but "never manage to come sufficiently alive. . . . Revueltas overwhelms the reader with rhetoric and polemics, with images and memories, often carelessly piled on, and much of the book's action is internalized."

Human Mourning, considered a seminal example of the "new novel" in Mexico, won the Mexican Prize for Literature. The book's heterodoxy, however, contributed to Revueltas's expulsion from the Mexican Communist Party.

Revueltas worked in films and theater during the rest of the 1940s. He was active in La Linterna Mágica (The Magic Lantern), a prominent avant-garde theater group, and was one of the founders of El Insurgente, an independent group with Marxist tenets. Later he helped to found the Partido Popular (People's Party), another left-wing group outside the Communist Party. During the 1940s and 1950s Revueltas produced *Los días terrenales* (Earthly days), *En algún valle de lágrimas* (In a certain vale of tears), *Los Motivos de Caín* (The motives of Cain), and *Dormir en tierra* (Sleeping on shore) —works famous throughout the Spanish-speaking world, but never translated into English. They garnered for him Mexico's top literary prize, the Xavier Villaurrutia. He traveled to the Soviet Union and to Cuba several times, serving in 1968 as a judge for the Cuban Casa de las Américas literary prizes.

Los días terrenales, (1949, Earthly days) Revueltas's third novel, according to Ignacio Trejo Fuentes, marked both an ideological and formal break with his previous writings. "The language of *Los días terrenales* runs the gamut from that of the billboard writer to that of the most vacuous bourgeois sympathizer of the Communist Party." Characters in Mexico City, the first urban setting that Revueltas used, stroll about, discussing the Party propaganda that they are disseminating, which supplies the the propaganda aspect. Another character, a "caricature of bourgeois morality and decadent life-style," according to Slick, is supplied with sexual fantasies—the fantasies of those who can afford to have them. Trejo Fuentes pointed out that in *Los días terrenales* Revueltas was severely criticizing the dogmatism of the Mexican Communist Party, "for which rebellion he found himself obligated to withdraw the book from circulation."

In 1968, long-simmering tensions in Mexico, erupted in mass demonstrations and protests. With the student movement in the vanguard, demonstrators demanded greater participation in Mexican political and economic life. As he had been all his life, Revueltas was a leader and organizer, particularly in supporting the Mexican Student Movement. In October 1968 police shot into a crowd of student demonstrators on the Tlatelolco plaza in Mexico City. For his participation in the events of 1968, José Revueltas, who only the previous year had been awarded Mexico's greatest literary prize, was arrested and thrown into the notoriously horrible Lecumberri prison, later closed after another writer, José Agustín, served a term and publicized the condi-

tions there. Revueltas was not tried until nearly two years later, at which time he was sentenced to a term of sixteen years. He was released in 1971, after his health had deteriorated rapidly in prison.

He was divorced from María Teresa Retes in 1971, and in 1973 married Ema Barrón. Revueltas also had a lover in Cuba by whom he had a child. He continued to travel to Cuba and to write, producing several books and a play, before his death in 1976. Octavio Paz summed up Revueltas as having "intuitively and passionately, in a movement of return to the oldest part of his being, consulted religious answers mixed with the millenary ideas and hopes of the revolutionary movement. . . . His religious temperament led him to communism, which he saw as the road of sacrifice and communion; that same temperament, inseparable from the love of truth and goodness, led him at the end of his life to the criticism of bureaucratic 'socialism' and Marxist clericalism. . . . Living with himself was not, for Revueltas, less difficult than living with his communist comrades. . . . He lived his internal contradiction with loyalty: his atheistic Christianity, his moribund Marxism."

Revueltas can be said to have owed ultimate fealty only to his art. His journals were published in 1987. In them he had commented in 1961 (to describe the psychology of Jacobo, a character in *Los errores*):

I have never thought about my age except in relation to death. Or, in other words, in the context of the time when I can still dispose of my affairs and complete some projects, before incapacity, followed by the final defeat. . . . This business of not feeling my age, then, becomes a bit grotesque and to my own eyes seems ever more foolish, ridiculous, and inhibiting. I was thinking a great deal about the problem and suddenly a paragraph from Somerset Maugham's journal came to me. He says: "A novelist . . . must not grow up completely. He must interest himself to the end in matters that he might have outgrown." . . . Although the preceding could be taken as advice, it hardly applies to the personal, private, biographical life of the writer. It refers to a literary posture, to one's attitude toward the writer's tools, but not to what a novelist of 47 years must cling to *more than his own business.* My tragedy is fundamentally that *I do not wish to grow up* and continue to behave in a childish manner. . . .

—tr. S. Yampolsky

Octavio Paz concluded that "Revueltas, in the name of Marxist philosophy, undertook an examination of conscience that Saint Augustine and Pascal would have appreciated. . . . "

PRINCIPAL WORKS IN ENGLISH TRANSLATION: (tr. R. Crespi) Human Mourning, 1990.

ABOUT: Flores, A. Spanish American Authors: The Twentieth Century, 1992; Slick, S. José Revueltas,

1983. *In Spanish*—Escalante, E., ed. Los días terrenales, 1991; Revueltas, J. Las evocaciones requeridas (Memorias, diarios, correspondencia), 1987; Torres M., V. F. Vision global de la obra literaria de José Revueltas, 1985; Trejo Fuentes, I. Revueltas en la mira, 1984.

REWALD, JOHN (May 12, 1912–February 2, 1994), American art historian and curator, whose documentary histories of impressionism and postimpressionism are considered two of the great 20th-century works of art scholarship, was born in Berlin, the son of Bruno A. and Pauline (Feinstein) Rewald. During and after World War I the family led a nomadic existence, living for a time in Sweden and Argentina, and finally settling in Hamburg. Rewald studied at the University of Hamburg for one semester in 1931 under the renowned art historians Erwin Panofsky and Fritz Saxl. He then went on to study medieval art at the University of Frankfurt am Main. In 1932 he entered the University of Paris, intending to study Romanesque and Gothic architecture; but—as a result of a trip to Provence—he became interested in the work of Paul Cézanne. Although the Sorbonne then offered no courses in modern art, he was eventually allowed to do a thesis on Cézanne, and became a *docteur ès-lettres* in 1936. Prohibited, as an alien, from teaching or holding a museum post, Rewald stayed on in France as a free-lance writer, and published numerous articles and several monographs on such artists as Cézanne, Gauguin, and Maillol. In 1939 he was imprisoned for three months as an enemy alien. By 1941 he had obtained a visa to enter the United States, where he became a citizen in 1947.

Rewald's doctoral dissertation, *Cézanne et Zola* was published in Paris in 1936 and was awarded the Prix Charles Blanc of the French Academy. It was revised and enlarged three years later as *Cézanne: Sa vie, son oeuvre, son amitié pour Zola* (Cézanne: His life, his work, his friendship with Zola). Meantime, in 1937, he edited a volume of Cézanne's *Correspondance*, which was translated into English as *Paul Cézanne: Letters*; a fifth, revised edition was issued years later, in 1984. Cézanne, the precursor of modern painting, was to remain Rewald's greatest interest throughout his career. His dissertation was eventually translated, after the war, as *Paul Cézanne: A Biography*. Fifty years after the publication of the original French text, Rewald reworked and expanded the English version; the new edition—according to John Golding in the *Times Literary Supplement*—"reads as freshly and compulsively as ever, largely because of his original decision

to let the contemporary documents and evidence speak for themselves." If the analysis of the paintings, however, is "serviceable rather than inspired," no one else has "identified with the artist and caught him whole" in the same way. *Cézanne: A Biography* (a slight change in title had been made) won the 1986 Mitchell Prize, given annually for "an outstanding contribution in English to the study and understanding of the visual arts."

Upon arriving in the United States, Rewald worked first for the Weyhe Gallery in New York, then was employed by the War Department as a translator. In 1943 he began his lifelong association with the Museum of Modern Art as guest curator. One of his first American publications was the translation of his monograph *Georges Seurat*, a work he had begun in Paris in 1938. Writing in the *Nation*, the art critic Clement Greenberg praised "the objectivity, coolness, and carefulness of research [which] show how facts about art should be presented." At the same time he acknowledged that Rewald was more concerned with giving an account of Seurat's life, the development of his ideas, and contemporary reactions to his pointillist innovations than with visual analysis.

The documentation of art was always Rewald's subject rather than matters of technique or visual effect. The Seurat monograph is also another instance of Rewald—with his passionate devotion to scholarship—turning back in later years to correct and augment one of his earlier works. In this case, the revised edition, *Seurat: A Biography*, came out four years before his death. Reviewing it in the *Times Literary Supplement* in 1991, John Leighton declared that what had been, when it first appeared, an invaluable introduction to a then not well-known postimpressionist, was now an essential reference book, with its updated references and bibliography. He continued: "Rewald's text stands up well to the test of time although it now seems rather brisk and concise for its expanded format."

The first of Rewald's two major works was *The History of Impressionism*, which he compiled with the help of a grant from the Museum of Modern Art and which was published by the museum. Now considered a classic in the field, magisterial in its scope and complexity of detail, it is at the same time a truly readable narrative, written in the third of the languages at Rewald's command and one in which he always demonstrated a remarkably lucid, flowing style. As he remarked to a *New York Times* interviewer in 1983: "I prefer to write in English. I find the . . . vocabulary much richer." His account of the art world between 1855 and 1886 considers the paintings of the era in their historical contexts, describes the progress of a number of artists simultaneously, and—by means of the copious and aptly chosen illustrations—brings together works done by different painters within the same time period. Such an approach, the author noted, might not do justice to individual works, "but once they have been given their place in [the] whole, it will become easier for others to explore them more completely."

Alan Bowness, in the *Times Literary Supplement* (March 28, 1986), testified to the success of Rewald's aim. *The History of Impressionism*, he concluded, "revolutionized the study of the subject. It would be hard to exaggerate its originality and authority, or the debt that all those who have since worked on French nineteenth-century painting owe to its author." Rewald's quotations of the artists' own comments (in letters, diaries, notebooks), of exhibition catalogue notes, of contemporary reviews—much of this material not previously available in English—provide essential documentation. So generous is this provision, in fact, that museum director James Johnson Sweeney complained in the *New York Times* in 1946 that "Rewald's text suffers from a fault very similar to that which marked orthodox Impressionist painting. Its surface is too active: it is overrun with anecdote and quotation. And there is too little substantial criticism beneath it." The first revised edition of Rewald's book was even richer in content. In the *Saturday Review*, Robert Melville regretted that "he has not put a check on his somewhat conventional enthusiasm for Impressionism, his sentimental regard for the painters, and his contempt for art critics. Although he never tampers with his source material or with facts as such, his interjections frequently constitute a subjective interference." The *Times Literary Supplement* review of the fourth revised edition in 1974 was celebratory, however. "The richness of its documentation, and the clarity with which it traces the complex interrelationship between the Impressionist painters, provide a model against which any writer on the subject has to measure himself."

The sequel, *Post-Impressionism: From van Gogh to Gauguin*, had meanwhile appeared. Similar in intent and format, it too was published under Museum of Modern Art auspices. In this other major opus, Rewald identifies and characterizes the many movements, hitherto not clearly defined, that succeeded impressionism. The time frame here is 1886 to 1893, from van Gogh's arrival in Paris to Gauguin's return from his first trip to Tahiti. Recognizing that if he concentrated on accounts of individual artists he would lose sight of the complicated whole, "that criss-cross of ideas, that overlapping of episodes which make these years so fascinating," Rewald compromised in his approach. He would focus on certain key figures and, as it were, allow others to "revolve around them." As he notes further in his introduction, it would "distort" history, however, to single out artists we now think of as key figures but who were unknown in their day, and remain silent about the artists and events their own contemporaries thought far more important. A wealth of documentary information fills this gap and—as in *The History of Impressionism*—forms the core of the book. As Rewald explains, rather than mechanically presenting this assemblage of documents and testimonials, "I have endeavored . . . to organize this vast material in a way I thought most appropriate to the subject—a way that is true to history." Included are many previously unpublished statements, and others never before translated into English or retranslated more successfully by Rewald himself. A chapter on the contemporary symbolist movement in literature ("1886-1890: Symbolists and Anarchists from Mallarmé to Redon") enhances the work as a general cultural history of the period. Certain artists are mentioned only in passing, Rewald's intention having been to treat such painters as Toulouse-Lautrec, the Nabis, and Cézanne more fully in a succeeding volume to be called "Post-Impressionism—from Gauguin to Matisse." This book was never completed, however. As they stand, his two existing surveys of late 19th-century art form the basis of much recent scholarship on the subject. As Michael Kimmelman, chief art critic of the *New York Times*, summed it up in 1994: "One way or another, every scholar of late nineteenth-century French art had to contend with [Rewald's] writings."

Over the years, the historian contributed a substantial body of articles and reviews to all the major art journals. A number of these, going back several decades and scattered among not easily accessible sources, were brought together in the companion volumes *Studies in Impressionism* and *Studies in Post-Impressionism*, edited by Irene Gordon and Frances Weitzenhoffer. In some cases the latter contributed new translations of the French originals; some articles, too, have been updated by the author. A particularly graceful gesture: each of the essays has been reprinted with a dedication to a colleague; for example: "Cézanne and His Father" to the collector Paul Mellon; "Some Notes and Documents on Odilon Redon" to Alfred Barr, former director of the Museum of Modern Art and one of Rewald's sponsors for entry into the United States; "Seurat: The Meaning of the Dots" to Meyer Schapiro, the celebrated professor of art history at Columbia University.

"Reading Rewald is always like reading a book one cannot put down," Eugene V. Thaw remarked in the *New Republic* in 1986. He singles out "Theo van Gogh as Art Dealer," one of the eight pieces in the postimpressionist volume, as "an enormously valuable contribution to the history of taste as well as a mine of information on the van Gogh family." This nearly book-length (108-page) article originally appeared in the *Gazette des Beaux-Arts* in February 1973. Among the fifteen pieces gathered in the impressionist volume are a lengthy and seminal study of Degas and his family in New Orleans (a connection that had great effect on the painter's character and his work), and several Cézanne studies.

Rewald's last writings were concentrated on Cézanne. His catalogue raisonné of the artist's watercolors includes exhaustive entries that provide a veritable anthology of pertinent quotations from earlier commentators, and a checklist of Cézanne exhibition to reproductions of all the artist's work in this genre. "In [Rewald's] carefully written introduction" to the catalogue, Eugene Thaw noted in the *New Republic* in 1984, he "gives the most lucid account yet published of the development of Cézanne's watercolor style, its relationship to his paintings, and to his search for truthful sensations before nature, and to the ultimate critical acceptance and appreciation of the master's achievements. . . . " According to Sir Lawrence Gowing in the *Times Literary Supplement* (1985), this "study of the place that watercolour took in Cézanne's development and his legacy . . . is perhaps the most enjoyable and informative thing that [Rewald] has ever written. The great oeuvre catalogues are the enduring pillars of artistic life, and this one will remain unshakeable." The volume was undertaken as a revision of the watercolor section of the catalogue raisonné of all Cézanne's work that had been begun by the Italian art historian Lionello Venturi in the 1930s; Rewald was to have followed it by a catalogue of the paintings in oil—an enormous enterprise left unrealized. Among the other projects on which Rewald was working at the time of his death was an edition of Gauguin's letters.

In 1979 Rewald gave the Andrew W. Mellon lectures at the National Gallery of Art in Washington; they were the basis of his book *Cézanne and America: Dealers, Collectors, Artists and Critics, 1891–1921*. Working from a vast array of contemporary reviews, memoirs, and personal correspondence, Rewald put together an immensely erudite yet highly readable story of the role the American art world played in establishing Cézanne's reputation as the father of modern art. Part of his Mellon lecture material was used

again—in condensed form—in the 1986 Walter Neurath Memorial Lecture delivered at the University of London and printed in book form as *Cézanne, the Steins and Their Circle*.

In addition to his status as a writer, Rewald was a prominent figure in the art world as a teacher of art history and curatorial advisor. Although he never held a full-time appointment at the Museum of Modern Art, he served as curator of the exhibitions devoted to Bonnard (1948), the Fauves (1952), and the Symbolists: Odilon Redon, Gustave Moreau, and Rodolphe Bresdin (1961), and contributed to the attendant catalogues. In 1977 he worked with William Rubin, then director of painting and sculpture at the museum, and Professor Theodore Reff of Columbia University on the landmark exhibition of Cézanne's late paintings. In 1983 Rewald was appointed an honorary trustee of the museum. He was a visiting professor at Princeton University in 1961, taught at the University of Chicago from 1963 to 1971, and was Distinguished Professor of Art History at the Graduate Center of the City University of New York from 1971 to 1985, when he retired as emeritus professor. Upon his retirement the John Rewald Professorship was established in his honor. For many years (1948–ca. 1966) he served as the curator of John Hay Whitney's private collection, advising on purchases as well as on donations to museums; major acquisitions of modern French paintings by the National Gallery, Yale University, and the Museum of Modern Art are credited to Rewald's recommendations. He acted also as an advisor to Paul Mellon on his collection of modern French art. For his outstanding achievements in this area Rewald was given an award by the Art Dealers' Association of America in 1983.

In 1954 John Rewald was created a chevalier and in 1986 was promoted to officer of the French Legion of Honor, and distinguished as "a national treasure of France." In 1979 he became a commander of the French Order of Arts and Letters. As a result of his efforts in the 1950s to save Cézanne's studio in Aix-en-Provence from destruction, the city made him an honorary citizen in 1984 and also named a street after him. Rewald was married three times; his only child (of his first marriage) Paul died in 1976. Rewald, who lived in New York and in the south of France, died in New York.

PRINCIPAL WORKS: Pissarro, 193-?; Gauguin, 1938; (tr. P. Montagu) Maillol, 1939; (tr. L. Abel) Georges Seurat, 1943 (reissued as Seurat: A Biography, 1990); (with M. Wheeler) "Modern Drawings" *in* Modern Drawings (ed. M. Wheeler) 1944, 3rd ed. 1947; The History of Impressionism, 1946, rev. and enl. ed. 1980; (tr. M. H. Liebman) Paul Cézanne: A Biography, 1948 (rev. and

exp. ed. reissued as Cézanne: A Biography, 1986);
Pierre Bonnard, 1948; Aristide Maillol, 1861–1944,
1950; Edgar Degas, 1834–1917, 1950; Camille Pissarro
(1830–1903) 1954; Paul Gauguin (1848–1903) 1954;
Seurat (1859–1891) 1954; Post-Impressionism: From
van Gogh to Gauguin, 1956, 2nd ed. 1962, 3rd ed.,
rev., 1978; Sculptures and Woodcuts of Reder, 1957;
Camille Pissarro, 1963; Giacomo Manzù, 1967; "The
Last Motifs at Aix" in Cézzane: The Late Work. [Es-
says by Theodore Reff and] others, (ed. W. Rubin)
1977; Paul Cézanne, the Watercolors: A Catalogue
Raisonné, 1983; Studies in Impressionism (ed. Irene
Gordon and Frances Weitzenhoffer) 1986; Studies in
Post-Impressionism (ed. Irene Gordon and Frances
Weitzenhoffer) 1986; Cézanne, the Steins and Their
Circle, 1987; Cézanne and America: Dealers, Collec-
tors, Artists and Critics, 1891–1921, 1989. Exhibition
Catalogues—Homage to Paul Cézanne (1839–1906)
1939; "An Introduction to the Fauve Movement" in
Les Fauves 1952–1953, 1952; Seurat and His Friends,
1953; "Odilon Redon" in Odilon Redon—Gustave Moreau—Rodolphe   Bresdin,   1961;   "Maillol
Remembered" in Aristide Maillol: 1861–1944, 1975.
As editor—(tr. M. Kay) Paul Cézanne: Letters, 1941,
5th rev. and aug. ed. 1984; (tr. L. Abel) Camille Pissarro: Letters to His Son Lucien (with L. Pissarro), 1943,
rev. and enl. ed. 1981; Paul Gauguin: Letters to Am-
broise Vollard and André Fontainas, 1943; The Woodcuts of Aristide Maillol: A Complete Catalogue, 1943;
(tr. J. Coleman and N. Moulton) Degas: Works in
Sculpture, a Complete Catalogue, 1944 (rev. ed. reissued as Degas: Sculpture, the Complete Works, 1956);
Renoir Drawings, 1946, rev. ed. 1958; Gauguin Drawings, 1958; (with F. Weitzenhoffer) Aspects of Monet:
A Symposium on the Artist's Life and Time, 1984.

ABOUT: Contemporary Authors New Revision Series 5,
1982; Oxford Dictionary of Art, 1988; Who's Who in
American Art, 17th ed., 1991. Periodicals—Nation
December 25, 1943; New Republic September 10,
1984; June 30, 1986; New York Times December 8,
1946; May 6, 1983; April 16, 1989; February 3, 1994;
Saturday Review May 19, 1962; Times Literary Supplement May 3, 1974; March 22, 1985; March 28,
1986; December 5, 1986; February 15, 1991.

*RIBEIRO, JOÃO UBALDO (January 23,
1941–   ), Brazilian novelist, short story writer,
and journalist, was born on the island of Itaparica, off the coast of Salvador, the capital city of
the northeastern state of Bahia. While Ribeiro
was an infant, his parents, both lawyers, moved
the family to the neighboring state of Sergipe,
but returned to Bahia when he was eleven years
old. As a young man, Ribeiro was active in the
effervescent cultural scene of Salvador in the
early sixties. His group included Gilberto Gil,
Caetano Veloso, Calazans Neto and Glauber
Rocha, all of whom were to become prominent
in music, the visual arts, and filmmaking. After
graduating from the University of Bahia College

JOÃO UBALDO RIBEIRO

of Law, Ribeiro attended the University of
Southern California, where he completed a master's degree in political science and public administration. Upon his return to Brazil, Ribeiro
taught briefly at the Federal University of Bahia, but the academic life did not seem to have
much appeal for him. He settled down on Itaparica, and resumed his pursuit of what has
turned out to be a very successful dual career as
a creative writer and journalist. Despite being
one of the most celebrated living fictionists in
Brazil, Ribeiro has remained committed to journalism, a lifelong devotion that dates back to his
twenties, when he started contributing to local
newspapers in Bahia. He currently writes a regular column for O Globo, a national newspaper
published in Rio de Janeiro by the largest media
conglomerate in Brazil.

Although Ribeiro is a cosmopolitan, urbane
man who has traveled abroad extensively and
has recently moved his primary residence from
Itaparica to Rio de Janeiro, his fiction draws
heavily on the raw materials from northeastern
Brazil, particularly from his native Bahia. Yet
Ribeiro's fiction transcends the narrow confines
of regionalism. Ribeiro is not primarily concerned with what is supposedly typical of the region, and therefore does not place emphasis on
recording its popular traditions or depicting its
landscapes. Instead, he utilizes regional material
as a springboard for a consideration of larger
questions. These include controversial national
issues, such as class differences, government ineptitude and corruption, the fragility of political
and social institutions, the fallacy of Brazilian ra-

cial harmony, and the unfinished definition of Brazilian identity, as well as topics of universal significance, such as the follies of the human condition and the capacity of human beings both to inflict and to endure pain.

As is the case with other writers of his generation, Ribeiro displays in his works a profound awareness of the past and present history of Brazil. Nevertheless his fiction does not passively mirror Brazilian history over the past quarter of a century. Skeptical about the ability of historiography to provide a full account of reality, he aims to create through his fiction alternative voices that supplement and at times challenge the perspective of official history.

Ribeiro wrote his first novel, the semi-autobiographical *Setembro não tem sentido* (September has no meaning, 1967), when he was only twenty-one, but was unable to find a publisher until several years later. Focusing on the adventures of a group of young Bahian intellectuals, this novel already contains some of the qualities that would become his trademarks, such as his mastery of narrative technique, elegant style, and satirical wit. *Setembro não tem sentido* is a good example of Ribeiro's sensitivity to the mental context of historical events. Set against the background of the institutional crisis brought about by President Jânio Quadros's abrupt resignation on August 25, 1961, after only seven months in office, it records the anxiety, insecurity, and hopelessness of Ribeiro's generation, faced with the unstable political and economic situation that would eventually lead to the military takeover of April 1, 1964. But the novel also possesses an uncanny prophetic quality. While capturing the mood of the early sixties, it forecasts the growing discouragement Brazilians would experience as the 1964 regime became increasingly repressive in the late sixties and early seventies. In fact, not long after the novel's publication, the hard-liners staged a successful "coup within the coup" on December 13, 1968, starting the suffocating years of repression aptly known as the *sufoco* (1968–1974).

Ribeiro's second novel, *Sargento Getúlio* (1971, translated by the author as *Sergeant Getulio*), and *Vencecavalo e o outro povo* (Overcomes-Horses and the other people, 1974), a collection of five interconnected short stories, are representative cultural products of Brazil in the early seventies. During this period, the darkest days of the authoritarian military regime, writers and other artists had to resort to allegory, symbolism, and experimental techniques in order to elude the constraints of ubiquitous censorship. Written in a harsh poetic prose, *Sergeant Getulio* is structured as a rambling monologue by the title character, a ruthless gunman who has been hired by a political boss to capture and deliver one of the boss's enemies. Ordered by his boss to set the prisoner free when political conditions abruptly change, Getulio refuses to bend and vows to carry out his assignment even as federal troops are sent to relieve him of the prisoner, pursue him through the backlands, and eventually kill him. Getulio is a paradoxical figure whom the reader learns both to loathe and to admire. He is capable of the most savage actions against others, but at the same time he possesses the stature of a tragic hero who remains blindly faithful to his principles and whose unshakable sense of duty stands above opportunism and political expediency. Thematically and formally, *Sergeant Getulio* is Ribeiro's most subversive work. The novel was published at the height of the "economic miracle" of the early seventies, when the government concocted such slogans as "No one can hold this country back," "Let's move ahead, Brazil," and "Brazil, love her or leave her" in order to project the image of a peaceful, harmonious, and united country and thus to divert attention from some of the worst political repression in Brazilian history. Getulio's cold-blooded cruelty explodes, however, the myth of Brazilian benevolence, which was an essential component of the government's propaganda. Furthermore, in acknowledging the existence of violence in Brazilian society, the novel makes an indirect commentary on the brutal methods used by the military government's repressive apparatus, which included the torture of many of the regime's opponents. At the same time, Getulio's refusal to compromise his moral values, no matter how warped they may seem, and his resolve to stand up to authority can be viewed as an indictment of all those who, through silence and fear, acquiesced in the tyranny of the military rulers. Finally, the striking narrative technique employed in the novel violates the reader's expectations of time and space, and thus functions as a structural correlative of the theme of violence. One of the most impressive achievements in recent Brazilian literature, *Sergeant Getulio* was turned into an award-winning film in 1983.

Vencecavalo e o outro povo is an irreverent and iconoclastic satire that addresses in a mock-heroic tone a variety of topics of national interest, ranging from government corruption and ineptitude to Brazil's status as a postcolonial, economically dependent country. The stories also poke fun at many aspects of the Brazilian national character, including Brazilians' proverbial ability to improvise solutions for the stickiest situations. Published when censorship was just beginning to be relaxed after the hard-liners were replaced by moderates in the mid-1970s, this work relies on parody, allegory, and a Rabelaisian delight in linguistic excess to create an antihistory of Brazil that demystifies and deconstructs official history.

Ribeiro's more recent works bespeak the growing liberalization that started in the late seventies and continued into the "New Republic," which began after the military surrendered control of the government in January of 1985. *Vila Real* (1979; Vila Real) rejects the symbolism and stylization of the two preceding works and deals in a straightforward manner with the struggle of a group of backlanders against an all-powerful company. Such a candid treatment of a controversial social topic would have been inconceivable during the more repressive years of the military regime. Ribeiro's next two works, *Viva o povo brasileiro* (1984, translated by the author as *An Invincible Memory*) and *O sorriso do lagarto* (1989, *The Lizard's Smile*), reflect the uncertainties faced by Brazilians over the past decade, during which new hope has alternated with increasing doubts about the prospects for the country, particularly after the failed attempts of the first civilian administration to control inflation, improve social conditions, and restore confidence in government.

An Invincible Memory is arguably Ribeiro's most ambitious work. In this massive historical novel Ribeiro creates a composite of Brazilian society since colonial days. The action consists of a series of interconnecting subplots that focus on the intersections between the personal and familial histories of dozens of characters from every social stratum and with every racial mixture to be found in Brazil. Ribeiro also brings in references to a host of popular traditions, most notably those of Afro-Brazilian origin, but manages to avoid mere local color by weaving them into the fabric of the narration. Such is the case with the religion known as *candomblé*, whose deities, or *orixás*, intervene on behalf of Brazilians as they are about to succumb to their Paraguayan enemies. In the mold of the classic historical novel, imagined situations are intertwined with well-known historical events like the Farroupilha Revolution (1835–1845), a rebellion in Brazil's southern most state of Rio Grande do Sol against the imperial government, and Brazil's bloody war against Paraguay (1865–1870). Yet *An Invincible Memory* is not a traditional historical novel. It is, rather, an exemplar of a new kind of historical fiction, which emerged in Brazil at the time of the political liberalization in the mid 1970s and has continued to flourish. These novels combine a renewed confidence in fiction as a means to recover the past, particularly from an alternative perspective to that of official history, with an awareness of the textual nature of history, and a self-conscious recognition that history and fiction are human constructs. Deliberately shunning linearity, the narrator of Ribeiro's novel carries the reader back and forth between Bahia, Rio de Janeiro, Lisbon, Paraguay, and the "pampas" of southern Brazil over a time span ranging from 1647 to 1977. Thus the reader is compelled constantly to establish connections between the bits of information gradually provided by the narrator and to assume a more active role than that of the reader of most histories or historical novels. Involving the reader is crucial to Ribeiro's project. From as early as the epigraph ("The secret of Truth is as follows: there are no facts, there are only stories"), the novel casts doubts on absolute truths, proposing, instead, the existence of a repertoire of competing interpretations of the world, all potentially valid and equally partial, including the reader's own. At the same time, the active participation demanded from the reader also suggests that the past and the present exist in a dialectical relationship, so that the present can only be understood via the past, whereas, in turn, the past acquires its meaning through its reflection in the present. Though the past cannot be scientifically reconstructed, but only interpreted, it is necessary to look into the past in order to make sense of the apparent chaos of the present. It is not surprising, then, that in creating this vast panorama, Ribeiro comments on different aspects of Brazilian life. His main targets are the pretentious upper classes, whom he chastises with his typically caustic humor for aping European tastes and fashions, for displaying prejudice and contempt for the lower classes, and for desperately trying to conceal any tinge of black blood in the family line, a quixotic task in a racially diverse society. The oppressed lower classes fare much better in the novel. As suggested by the Portuguese title, they are presented as the strongest and most authentic element in Brazilian society. Identifying the "people" as a potential source of renewal, the novel ends on a mild note of hope, typical of the optimism that characterized the advent of the "New Republic."

John Gledson, reviewing *An Invincible Memory* in the *Times Literary Supplement*, called it "a vivid evocation of Brazil in one of its heartlands" and observed that this "very rich and courageous novel. . . . manages to retain its unity while including the disparate elements thrown up by slavery, whose brutality Ribeiro neither ignores nor exploits." He termed Ribeiro's English translation almost wholly successful, "no small feat, given [its] linguistic wealth." Mary Morris, in the *New York Times Book*

Review like Gledson, compared *An Invincible Memory* unfavorably to *One Hundred Years of Solitude* and found it unsuccessful, terming it "a novel of ideas told by a student of history." Luiz Fernando Valente, in *World Literature Today*, agreed with Gledson's favorable view of the novel, calling it "a monumental achievement."

This optimism is noticeably absent from *The Lizard's Smile*. In this somber and bitter novel, Ribeiro relies on parodies of soap operas, pornographic films, and popular fiction to tell the story of a society that has lost its moral bearings. The narrative centers on João Pedroso, who has given up his career as a biologist to become a fishmonger in Itaparica, but it also touches on a gallery of Bahian characters. All of them become witnesses to disturbing transformations in the natural world while faced with distressing occurrences in their private lives. The pervading atmosphere of evil, disease, and decadence represents a literary counterpart to the aimlessness of the José Sarney government (1985–1990), and reflects the pessimism brought about by the worsening economic crisis of the late 1980s. The novel was adapted into an acclaimed miniseries produced by the Globo television network.

Ribeiro has been successful in other genres besides the novel and the short story. His two children's books, *Vida e paixão de Pandonar, o Cruel* (Life and passion of Pandonar, the cruel, 1983) and *A vingança de Charles Tiburone* (Charles Tiburone's revenge, 1990), have been highly praised by educators. In *Política* (Politics, 1981, revised 1986) Ribeiro strives to define and explain in relatively simple language the meaning of such concepts as the state, government, and citizenship. Written during the political liberalization of the early 1980s, this work became a best-seller when a revised edition was published as a Constituent Assembly began drafting a new constitution for Brazil in the mid-1980s. Ribeiro has also been a practitioner of what is known in the Portuguese-speaking world as the *crônica*, a "sketch," generally written colloquially, but possessing a definite literary quality, in which the line between fiction and journalism is blurred. Many of his best *crônicas* were collected in *Sempre aos domingos* (Always on Sundays, 1988).

Some of Ribeiro's recent projects have included the adaptation of fictional works for television, including his own. Although Ribeiro has published no major novels since 1989, he has continued to write both fiction and nonfiction, and has retained a large and loyal readership. Ribeiro is generally regarded as one of Brazil's most important living writers, as attested by his easy election to the Brazilian Academy of Letters in 1994.

PRINCIPAL WORKS IN ENGLISH TRANSLATION: *Novels*—(tr. J. U. Ribeiro) Sergeant Getulio, 1978; (tr. J. U. Ribeiro) An Invincible Memory, 1989 (in U.K.: Long Live the People); (tr. C. E. Landers) The Lizard's Smile, 1994. *Short stories*—(tr. J. U. Ribeiro) "Alaindelon de la patrie" *in* Massachusetts Review, Fall/Winter 1986; (tr. J. U. Ribeiro) "It Was a Different Day When They Killed the Pig" *in* Colchie, T. (ed.) Hammock beneath the Mangoes: Stories from Latin America, 1991.

ABOUT: Contemporary Authors 81–84, 1979; Contemporary Literary Criticism 10, 1979; Contemporary World Writers, 2nd ed., 1993; Dictionary of Brazilian Literature, 1988; Encyclopedia of World Literature in the 20th Century, rev. ed., 1993. *Periodicals*—Hispanic American Historical Review August 1979; Latin American Research Review 1, 1993; Library Journal March 15, 1989; Modern Fiction Studies Autumn 1986; New York Times Book Review April 9, 1978; April 16, 1989; Times Literary Supplement October 6, 1989; World Literature Today Spring, 1990.

RICE, ANNE (October 4, 1941–   ), American novelist, was born Howard Allen O'Brien—she adopted the nickname Anne in the first grade—in the Irish Channel section of New Orleans, the second of four daughters of Howard O'Brien, a postal worker, and Katherine (Allen) O'Brien. Rice's childhood was passed in an atmosphere of creative freedom. In an interview with the *Washington Post*, she recalled, "My sisters and I grew up like the Brontë sisters. . . . We had complete fantasy worlds with ongoing characters." Her father, in his spare time, was a sculptor, an unpublished poet and fiction writer. He read to his children from Shakespeare, Poe, and Oscar Wilde. He also took Anne on history walks through New Orleans' famous cemeteries, with their disquieting combination of the beautiful and the bizarre. She came to love the cemeteries, a fact that will come as no surprise to her readers. In Katherine Ramsland's *Prism of the Night: A Biography of Anne Rice*, Rice acknowledges her debt: "My father was a terrific influence on me. He was always reading and writing. I see elements of his story [a fantasy titled *The Impulsive Imp*] that later appeared in my work. He was living proof that a person could write."

Rice also owes a creative debt to her mother. Katherine O'Brien was a skilled storyteller who enjoyed telling ghost stories despite the fact that she was afraid of the dark. Rice remembers that "when it came to accomplishments in the world, to manner of dress, to intellectual curiosity or achievements, she gave me a sense of limitless power. She put no premium at all on conformity."

Perhaps Rice's most deeply felt early influ-

ANNE RICE

ence, however, was the city of New Orleans itself, with its atmosphere of sultry sensuality and
decay. "Steamy, dark, and mystical, home to
voodoo queens, jazz musicians, and gamblers,"
as Ramsland describes it, "the essence of the 'Big
Easy' in those years was not easily grasped in rational terms." Rice was also influenced by her
Catholic upbringing, which together with the
general exoticism of New Orleans gave her the
feeling of being an outsider and pulled her toward writing about outcasts.

Anne Rice was not quite fifteen when her
mother died from the effects of alcoholism. Rice
was devastated by the loss. According to Ramsland: "Eventually her inner world would unfold
in novels that revealed the need to regain her
mother's presence and a desire to conquer death.
Many of Anne's early themes would involve
young people suffering through sudden change,
tragic mother figures, or the doomed embrace of
a mother and child lost together, juxtaposed
against immortality and other forms of power
and triumph."

Howard O'Brien remarried in 1957 and six
months later moved the family to Richardson,
Texas, a Dallas suburb. Despite the shock of this
dramatic change in environment, Rice came to
love her new life, if not Texas itself. The beatnik
movement was spreading across the country and
Rice's best friends were a group of nonconformists, in keeping with her growing reputation as
a "weirdo." She became the features editor of
the Richardson High School student newspaper.
The editor was Stan Rice, a year behind her in
school, and the man she would later marry.

After graduation she attended Texas Woman's University in Denton. It was a time of continuing emotional and intellectual change. She
had begun to question the tenets of Catholicism
in high school, and now her doubts turned to
conviction. "My faith just went," she told Susan
Ferraro of the *New York Times Magazine.* "It
struck me as really evil—the idea you could go
to hell for French-kissing someone. . . . I didn't
believe God existed." She became interested in
existentialism and read Nietzsche and Kierkegaard, whose works the Church condemned.
Her sexuality was also developing. One aspect of
this was a growing interest in and empathy with
homosexuals, especially gay men.

Rice transferred to North Texas State University, where Stan had also enrolled. Her stay at
State was short-lived; having just turned nineteen she moved to San Francisco and found work
as a claims processor in an insurance office. The
apartment she shared with a girlfriend became
a hangout for an artistic, creative crowd.

Eventually her romance with Stan took hold
and he proposed by letter. They were married
in Texas in 1961 and moved to San Francisco,
where they found themselves living in the heart
of the burgeoning counterculture movement.
They began studies at San Francisco State College (now University) and took their degrees—
hers in political science—in 1964. Rice began
graduate courses in art—later switching to German and then creative writing—and finally began to put her thoughts and fantasies on paper,
producing several short stories and two novellas—one pornographic, one a romance. In 1965
she published her first short story, titled
"October 4, 1948"—the date of her seventh
birthday—in the college magazine *Transfer.* In
it a young girl explores an abandoned New Orleans' mansion, only to find that it isn't haunted.
Already Rice's evocative prose is in evidence:
"the tinkertip of change on the galvanized table
top" and "nets of spiders and fragments of their
unstuck victims."

The Rices' first child, Michele, was born in
1966. Anne began studies at the University of
California at Berkeley, but soon returned to San
Francisco State. She continued writing, delving
again into pornography. As a child she had had
fantasies of sadomasochism and the fascination
remained. "The images obsessed her," Ramsland
points out, "and would acquire intensity and
greater dimension as she realized the social prejudice that reserved symbolic sexual violence as
a turn-on exclusive to males. She knew what excited her and was not about to allow anyone to
tell her differently." It was also a time when Rice
experienced a growing interest in her roots. "I

began to be haunted by the past," she told Bob Summer of *Publishers Weekly* in 1988. "I . . . began reading everything I could find about Louisiana."

In 1972 the Rices' world was shattered when their daughter died of leukemia. At first they sought to relieve their pain with alcohol. Finally Anne turned to her writing. In 1968 she had written a short story about a vampire and, with the encouragement of a friend, decided to build upon it.

What followed was a "white heat" of creativity, as she finished the novel in a little over five weeks. It was called *Interview with the Vampire*, the first of her Vampire Chronicles. It is set in 19th-century New Orleans. The vampire Louis tells an interviewer: "I was a twenty-five year old man when I became a vampire and the year was seventeen ninety-one." Louis relates how the vampire Lestat turned him into one of his kind, remembering the eroticism of the experience: "The movement of his lips raised the hair all over my body that was not unlike the pleasure of passion." Louis and Lestat occupy a town house, where Louis's overwhelming craving for blood causes him to attack a five-year-old girl named Claudia—the Rices had sometimes called their daughter Michele Claudia. Claudia, who also bears a physical resemblance to Rice's child, becomes a vampire. She and Louis are later pitted against Lestat, and travel to Europe in search of their roots and the meaning of their existence. Eventually Claudia is destroyed. In the first version of the story she remains immortal. "There was initial comfort in that," Ramsland comments, "but it produced a psychological backlash. A year later with the rewrite, Anne was further removed. She was more inclined to get on with her life and allow Michele to die." In her interview with Susan Ferraro, Rice discussed that psychological backlash: "I almost died myself and went kind of crazy. . . . If somebody is meant to die and you don't do it, you're really risking your well-being at the end of the book." Despite this trauma, Ramsland reports that Rice insists that any resemblance between Michele and Claudia was superficial.

It doesn't take the reader long to realize that *Interview with the Vampire* is not a rehash of the one-dimensional vampires made famous in B-movies. "Rice turns vampire conventions inside out," Ferraro stated in the *Times* interview. "Her immortals enjoy looking at themselves in mirrors, do not flinch before crucifixes and ignore garlic. They avoid the dark decay of the grave and slurp their bloody draughts in splendor; they wear fine clothes and enjoy fine art. Impotent, they are somehow also bisexual." Rice places her readers in the unnerving position of sympathizing with the vampire rather than the victim. "They are lonely, prisoners of circumstance, compulsive sinners, full of self-loathing and doubt," Ferraro concluded. "They are, in short, Everyman Eternal."

Published in 1976, *Interview with the Vampire* went on to sell well over a million and a half copies. Critical reaction was intense, pro and con. "What makes *Interview* so bad is not that the erotic content is so explicit," Edith Milton declared in a blistering *New Republic* review, "but that the morbid context is so respectable. . . . Death is made sexual here as blandly as if it were just another preference." Leo Braudy, in the *New York Times Book Review*, concluded that "there is no story here, only a series of sometimes effective but always essentially static tableaus out of Roger Corman films, and some self-conscious soliloquizing out of Spiderman comics, all wrapped in a ballooning, pompous language." Those in Rice's corner were just as adamant in their praise. *Wall Street Journal* reviewer Edmund Fuller found it a "quite stunning debut. . . . It is hard to praise sufficiently the originality . . . Rice has brought to the age-old, ever popular vampire tradition; it is undoubtedly the best thing in that vein since Bram Stoker, commanding peer status with *Dracula*." Given the novel's tremendous popularity, it is not surprising that in 1993 it was made into a film with Neil Jordan as director and Tom Cruise in the role of Lestat.

For her next two novels, Rice put vampires aside, but not her fascination with outcasts. *The Feast of All Saints* is set in the New Orleans of the 1840s and concerns the *gens de couleur libre*, or free men of color—the mulattoes, quadroons, and octoroons, who were neither white nor black. Despite the intellectualism and refinement of their culture, they were shunned and disfranchised by the whites, as well as hated by the black slaves. Rice's third novel, *Cry to Heaven*, tells the story of two castrati of 18th-century Italy. Castrati were males who were castrated as youths so they could permanently sing soprano—"children mutilated to make a choir of seraphim, their song a cry to heaven that heaven did not hear," Anne Rice calls them. Reviews for both books, as with *Interview*, were mixed. Although some consider them her best work, neither book achieved the commercial success of the first.

After the publication of *Cry to Heaven*, Rice wrote for *Redbook* and *Vogue* and began writing under two pseudonyms. As A. N. Roquelaure she published *The Claiming of Sleeping Beauty*, the first of a trilogy re-creating the Sleeping

Beauty fairy tale as unbridled pornography. Rice is quoted in *Current Biography* as saying that her aim was to "write the kind of delicious S & M fantasies I'd looked for but couldn't find anywhere." Under the name Anne Rampling, she published a pornographic love story titled *Exit to Eden* and *Belinda*, which Gerri Hirshey, of *Rolling Stone*, called a "*Lolita* of the 1980s."

Meanwhile, Lestat (from *Interview*) continued to develop in her imagination. In *The Vampire Lestat* he is revived in 1985 by a rock band called Satan's Night Out, who move into the house next to the one under which he slumbers. Eventually he becomes a double outsider, vampire and motorcycle-riding rock star, but first Rice tells his story beginning with his youth in 18-century Paris. She also includes long digressions into the world of vampire lore. In the *New York Times* (1985), Michiko Kakutani judged this "vampire sociology . . . more compelling than the rest of the novel." She was far less enthusiastic about Lestat's vampire version of soul-searching: "his rather heartfelt attempts to come to terms with his anomalous condition . . . are buried under heaps and heaps of wordy philosophizing about good and evil, heaven and hell, and even more wearisome meditations about the nature of Beauty and Truth." Kakutani compared reading the novel to "spending an entire day in a museum featuring only works by Henry Fuseli—all hung in heavy, gilt frames decorated with curlicues and malicious cherubs. By the end, you're reeling from both the strangeness and the surfeit of ornamentation." Nina Auerbach, in the *New York Times Book Review* (1985), disagreed, calling the novel "ornate and pungently witty. In the classic tradition of Gothic fiction, it teases and tantalizes us into accepting its kaleidoscopic world. Even when they annoy us or tell us more than we want to know, its undead characters are utterly alive. Their adventures and frustrations are funny, frightening and surprising at once."

The Vampire Lestat became a best-seller and created much anticipation for the promised continuation of the Vampire Chronicles. *The Queen of the Damned* was described by Kakutani, in the *New York Times* in 1988, as a "sort of *Paradise Lost* of the vampire kingdom, detailing the genesis of these creatures, their fall from grace, and their precarious fate in the world at large, in the past, the present, and future." The novel also became a tremendous best-seller. In 1992 Rice followed with *The Tale of the Body Thief*. Lestat returns and his feelings of doubt and loneliness lead to an unsuccessful suicide attempt. He agrees to change bodies with a body thief, accepting the risk so that he can spend a short time as a mortal. *Times Literary Supplement* reviewer Anne-Marie Conway found that the story "rarely fails to grip, though it lacks the coherence and sensuality that made Rice's *Interview* . . . so appealing. Its strength lies in the way the novel raises, and rephrases, some of the old questions about evil."

Rice's forays into the supernatural are not limited to vampires. In 1989 she published *The Mummy; or, Ramses the Damned*, reviving the long dead pharaoh as Dr. Ramses in Edwardian London. Seeking to satisfy his ancient lust, Ramses brings his beloved Cleopatra back from the grave. Given Rice's track record, it is not surprising that it became a paperback best-seller. It is also not surprising that reviewers were strongly divided. Most reviews were positive, but others considered it her weakest novel. A *Publishers Weekly* review was especially sharp, calling it a "potboiler" that "avoids character and plot development, larding largely lifeless, sloppy prose with a surfeit of epiphanies and calamities."

It was generally agreed that Rice came back strongly the following year with *The Witching Hour*; some even called it her finest work. The Mayfairs, generations of female and male witches, are at the center of what Patrick McGrath, in the *New York Times Book Review* (1992), called "this huge and sprawling tale of horror." Ramsland points out that the "Mayfair witches are designated, one per generation, as the beneficiaries not only of the legacy but also of the powers of 'the man.'" His name is Lasher, a bisexual spirit/demon "who gives the witches gifts, excites them sexually, and protects them. Exactly who or what he is provides the central mystery of the novel." For Rita Mae Brown, in the *Los Angeles Times*, "*The Witching Hour* unfolds like a poisonous lotus blossom redolent with luxurious evil. . . . Anne Rice writes with hypnotic power. . . . It will delight the senses."

In 1993 Rice continued her saga of the Mayfair witches with *Lasher*. Beautiful Rowan Mayfair, queen of the coven, is irresistibly attracted to Lasher, but eventually flees from him, taking their child, one of a "brood of children born knowing, able to stand and talk on the first day." What follows is a haunting, unsettling tale of escape and pursuit through worlds both human and demon.

Anne and Stan Rice live in the Garden District of New Orleans with their son Christopher.

PRINCIPAL WORKS: *Novels*—Interview with the Vampire, 1976; The Feast of All Saints, 1979; Cry to Heaven, 1982; (as A. N. Roquelaure) The Claiming of Sleeping Beauty, 1983; (as A. N. Roquelaure) Beauty's Punishment, 1984; (as A. N. Roquelaure) Beauty's Release, 1985; (as Anne Rampling) Exit to Eden, 1985; The Vampire Lestat, 1985; (as Anne Rampling) Belinda,

1986; The Queen of the Damned, 1988; The Mummy; or, Ramses the Damned, 1989; The Witching Hour, 1990; The Tale of the Body Thief, 1992; Lasher, 1993.

ABOUT: Contemporary Authors New Revision Series 12, 1984; Contemporary Literary Criticism 41, 1987; Current Biography, 1991; Ramsland, Katherine Prism of the Night: A Biography of Anne Rice, 1991. *Periodicals*—Los Angeles Times November 18, 1990; New Republic May 8, 1976; New York Times October 19, 1985; October 15, 1988; New York Times Book Review May 2, 1976; October 27, 1985; November 4, 1992; New York Times Magazine October 14, 1990; Publishers Weekly October 28, 1988; May 5, 1989; Rolling Stone November 20, 1986; Times Literary Supplement December 11, 1992; Wall Street Journal June 17, 1976; Washington Post November 6, 1988.

RICE, EDWARD (1918–), American journalist, travel writer, biographer, and photographer, was born in New York, the son of Edward and Elizabeth Rice. He attended Columbia University with the class of 1940, then worked as an editor at *Collier's* magazine, and later spent several years writing scripts for documentary films. He was the founder and editor in chief of *Jubilee* magazine, which published the work of W. H. Auden, Jack Kerouac, and Mother Teresa in the 1950s and 1960s. The author of hundreds of magazine articles, Rice traveled extensively in Asia, Africa, Latin America, and the South Pacific, both as a journalist and as a preparer of photographic medical reports for the United Nations.

Rice's first book, *The Man in the Sycamore Tree*, is a biography of the writer and heterodox Catholic religious thinker Thomas Merton. A convert to Catholicism, Merton became an ordained priest and a member of the austerity-minded, silence-bound Trappist monks. *The Seven Storey Mountain*, an autobiographical work written during his early years in the Trappist monastery, remains his most famous and popular book; but Merton was also a poet and essayist as well as the author of works of social and religious criticism. The title *The Man in the Sycamore Tree* refers to a passage in St. Luke in which Zacchaeus, because of his short stature, climbs a sycamore tree in order to get a better view of Jesus. Far from being an academic biographical study, *The Man in the Sycamore Tree* is a highly personal account of the life of a man Rice considered a close friend and mentor. The two men had met in the late 1930s when both were students at Columbia University. Their friendship endured until Merton's untimely death by accidental electrocution in Thailand in 1968. Rice's brief text is supplemented by photo-

EDWARD RICE

graphs, reminiscences by Merton's friends, and by Merton's own drawings and poems.

Reviewing the book in *Commonweal*, James Forest wrote, "It is most vivid, with a Henry Miller energy and abruptness, especially in telling something of that period of life that apparently (but not by Merton) was much expurgated in *The Seven Storey Mountain*. . . . " The *New York Times Book Review* (1970) concurred: "*The Man in the Sycamore Tree* . . . is a fascinating supplement to Merton's own portrait of himself and his times—times of social unrest, war, student agitation, intellectual and religious ferment—times very much like our own."

Rice and Merton shared an interest in Indian life, religion, and customs; yet Rice's preoccupation with that part of the world is not directly attributable to his friend's influence. "I have had a life-long interest in India, going back to my childhood," Rice told one interviewer. "One of my favorite uncles . . . went out at the age of eighteen for a ten-year stint on the rubber plantations, and was a great influence on me." During one of his many trips to the subcontinent, Rice interviewed and photographed scores of Indian youths. Some of these portraits appear in his photoessay *Mother India's Children*, which the *New York Times Book Review* named one of the Outstanding Books of the Year in 1971.

In his review of *Mother India's Children* in the *New York Times Book Review*, J. Anthony Lukas wrote: "In this extraordinary book, Edward Rice has cut through 'the teeming masses.' With his camera and typewriter and his fresh sensibilities, he has plucked out 21 young Indians and made us see them in all their stubborn, idiosyncratic individuality." The aim of Rice's project was to illustrate the similarities between Indian and American youths, not to highlight their many obvious differences. "What pleased me most was discovering how 'real' the young Indians are," Rice commented. "Even with the lack of facilities that we take for granted, their lives are, in most cases, full, varied, and interesting. . . . The same life force that animates and excites young Americans is present but in a very different context."

A Junior Literary Guild selection, *Mother India's Children* was designed primarily, but not exclusively, for younger readers. Rice is the author of a number of other books for young people. Like most of his other works, these are based primarily on his travels. *The Ganges: A Personal Encounter* explores the cultural significance of India's sacred river. Rice's other books for younger readers include *Ten Religions of the East*, *Babylon, Next to Nineveh*, and *Margaret Mead*, a biography of the anthropologist.

In *John Frum He Come*, Rice turned his attention to the cargo cults of the South Pacific islanders. As Rice explains in his introduction, "Loosely defined, Cargo is the belief that someday the people of this or that place—the locale is most often the South Pacific—will be given certain material goods now possessed by whites and denied to the black and brown man by white selfishness. Belief in Cargo first arose in the 19th century, when Europeans began to appear in numbers in the South Pacific." John Frum is the name of one elusive cargo "messiah." Although John's existence has never been verified to the satisfaction of outside observers, his cult has flourished on Tanna, a small island in the New Hebrides chain, since before World War II. For Rice, who admits to "a built-in bias," the truth of the cargo cultists' claims is less significant than what those claims reveal about the relationship between the "developed" and the "underdeveloped" world. Toward the end of his book, Rice writes, "John lives in the hearts and minds and souls of the Tannese. Whether or not he is physically present, he is very much a spiritual and psychic reality."

A reviewer for the *New Yorker* was pleased by Rice's nonanthropological approach in *John Frum He Come*: "It is quite a wonderful book, written by a man who, although a conscientious reporter and researcher, makes no pretension to scholarship or, above all, to objectivity. He is angry at the callous and persisting exploitation of the native people of the South Pacific—at the theft of their lands by white men, their virtual economic enslavement, the stamping out of their ancient cultures."

Journey to Upolu is Rice's biography of the poet and novelist Robert Louis Stevenson. Rice follows the ailing, itinerant Scotsman's travels through Europe, America, and finally the South Seas, where Stevenson spent his last years on the Samoan island of Upolu. Critical reaction to the book was mixed. *Christian Science Monitor* reviewer Alex Johnson wrote, "Anyone brought up on Stevenson's classic adventure stories will enjoy the unusual and perceptive insight which Mr. Rice has to offer." Less favorable was *Choice*: "Stevenson wrote well; it is a pity that he should fall into the hands of a man who writes as poorly as Rice. . . . "

Captain Sir Richard Francis Burton, a biography of the 19th-century British soldier, diplomat, author, and adventurer, has been by far Rice's most successful book to date. In *Burton*, Rice discovered a subject who was almost larger than life. Even the subtitle of Rice's book—*The Secret Agent Who Made the Pilgrimage to Mecca, Discovered the Kama Sutra, and Brought the Arabian Nights to the West*—only hints at the diversity of Burton's talents, the epic dimensions of his many adventures, and the prodigiousness of his appetites. "If a Victorian novelist of the most romantic type had invented Capt. Sir Richard Francis Burton," Rice writes in his introduction, "the character might have been dismissed by both the public and critics in that most rational age as too extreme, too unlikely."

"In a sense I grew up on Burton," Rice told Mervyn Rothstein in a *New York Times* interview in 1990. "I first started reading him when I was thirteen years old." Of his other work, Rice noted, "Everything I did was a preparation for Burton." Despite his long immersion in the subject matter, the project did not proceed smoothly. After Rice had put seven years of work into the book, his editor at Random House was fired and the manuscript was "lost in the shuffle." The book was eventually published by Scribner's, and became Rice's first best-seller.

Burton was rewarded with critical as well as public acclaim. In the *New York Times Book Review* (1990), Anthony Burgess wrote: "Mr. Rice's telling of the tale—an odyssey really, of the travail and travels of this body and of the unquenchable urge to get at the truth of life that rode above the tale—is first-class. It excuses those of us too lazy or too television-soaked to get at Burton himself by giving us a terse summary of a strange life." In the *Wall Street Journal*, David Shribman noted: "Rice helps us see that Captain Sir Richard Francis Burton breached barriers, not only in Europe's far-flung colonies but in England itself. For all his excesses, some of them deplorable, Burton was a man of adventure—but his achievement (and Edward Rice's) is that his adventures thrill us still."

"Although this is not the definitive biography, it is an amazing story and Burton and Rice combine to tell it very well," Robert Irwin wrote in the *Washington Post Book World*. But Irwin faulted Rice for making exaggerated claims about Burton's translations. "Rice's account of Burton's achievement as translator of the *Arabian Nights* is simply contentious," he wrote. "It cannot be true, as he claims, that it 'is due to him that the work in general, and especially certain of the stories like "Aladdin" and "Ali Baba and the Forty Thieves" became such a standard item in the early reading of Western children.' Gibbon, Wordsworth, Coleridge, Dickens and Newman—to name a few children with greatness ahead of them—came to these stories without any help from Burton."

In *Captain Sir Richard Francis Burton*, Rice allows his subject to speak for himself by providing generous citations from Burton's writings. In his conversation with Mervyn Rothstein, Rice remarked, "Previous biographers made the claim that Burton wasn't sure of his identity, that he was always searching for the real Burton. But he knew who Richard Francis Burton was. You can't go to any of the dangerous places he went to, embark on any of the adventures he undertook, without being sure of yourself. He knew he was going to be better than the other guy—stronger, smarter, more courageous."

PRINCIPAL WORKS: *Biography*—The Man in the Sycamore Tree: The Good Times and Hard Life of Thomas Merton—an Entertainment with Photographs, 1970; Journey to Upolu: Robert Louis Stevenson, Victorian Rebel, 1974; Captain Sir Richard Francis Burton: The Secret Agent Who Made the Pilgrimage to Mecca, Discovered the Kama Sutra, and Brought the Arabian Nights to the West, 1990. *Nonfiction*—John Frum He Come: A Polemical Work About a Black Tragedy, 1974; Eastern Definitions, 1978. *Juvenile*—Mother India's Children: Meeting Today's Generation in India, 1971; The Five Great Religions, 1973; The Ganges: A Personal Encounter, 1974; Marx, Engels and the Workers of the World, 1977; Ten Religions of the East, 1978; Babylon, Next to Nineveh: Where the World Began, 1979; Margaret Mead: A Portrait, 1979; American Saints and Seers: American-Born Religions and the Genius Behind Them, 1982. *As editor*—Temple of the Phallic King (by P. Baba) 1973.

ABOUT: Contemporary Authors New Revision Series 1, 1981; Something About the Author 42, 1986; 47, 1987. *Periodicals*—Choice February 1975; Christian Science Monitor November 6, 1974; Commonweal January 22, 1971; New York Times September 18, 1990; New York Times Book Review December 13, 1970; May 2, 1971; May 20, 1990; New Yorker May 13, 1974; Victorian Studies Summer 1991; Wall Street Journal June 6, 1990; Washington Post Book World May 20, 1990.

RIEFF, PHILIP (December 15, 1922–   ), American sociologist and social theorist, was born in Chicago, the son of Joseph Gabriel and Ida (Hurwitz) Rieff. He received his B.A. in 1946 from the University of Chicago, where he was an instructor in sociology from 1947 to 1952. Before receiving his doctorate from the University of Chicago in 1954, he taught at Brandeis University from 1952 to 1958. He became an associate professor at the University of California, Berkeley in 1958. He was appointed a professor at the University of Pennsylvania in 1961 and became the Benjamin Franklin Professor of Sociology there in 1967. He has received numerous academic honors and fellowships, has taught at Harvard, Yale, Princeton, and Oxford, and was a consultant to the Planning Department of the National Council of Churches from 1961 to 1964. Rieff has one son, David, from his first marriage to Susan Sontag; he married Alison Douglas Knox in 1963.

Rieff's reputation as an important though little-noticed analyst of American society and Western society in general was assured by the publication of his first book, the paradoxically titled *Freud: The Mind of the Moralist*, which was immediately recognized as a major work, not only on Freud himself, but on the cultural tradition that he inspired. Here Rieff, as he states in his preface, tries "to show the mind of Freud, not the man or the movement he founded, as it derives lessons on the right conduct of life from the misery of living it." The aim of this book is to extricate Freud from the success of his own theory, because, as Rieff observes, "movements learn to speak more in the name of than with the voice of the founder." Freud's thought has been accepted into the mainstream of popular thought, he continues, owing to its ability to counsel us on subjects that were previously hidden or disregarded and to bring into the open what was previously thought unthinkable. The corollary of this revelation, however, is that because of his refusal to offer any prescription for mental health other than the discovery of the origins of behavior, Freud offers "none of the consolations of philosophy or the hopes of religion."

As the British psychologist D. W. Harding observed in the *Spectator*, Rieff brings the insights of a sociologist and philosopher, not the empirical questioning of a scientist, to his subject. He is not concerned, therefore, about whether Freud was correct in the details of his observations about human behavior, because he believes in the general validity of Freud's pessimistic conception of humanity. Rieff's primary concern is the implications of Freud's thought and the destructive effect these have had on traditional systems of thought and belief, which have given way, during the 20th century, to the concept of "psychological man . . . the dominant moral type of Western culture." It is this individual's tendency, Rieff believes, to relate all public questions not to received traditions of communal morality, but "to himself and his own emotions." Rieff calls attention throughout his study to the fact that Freud was troubled by the outcome of his own discoveries and continually speculated on their implications for social behavior. He points out that Freud did not recommend an unconditional release of human energy and was both a critic of repressive social interdictions and their defender:

> If Freud takes sides against culture, it is only for therapeutic purposes. He believes no more in instinct than in culture; for his day and age he sought only to correct the imbalance between these two main categories of moral life. He is the architect of a great revolt against pleasure, not for it. He wrote no briefs for the pleasure principle. Rather he exhibited its futility. It is toward the reality principle that Freud turns us, toward the sober business of living and with no nonsense about its goodness or ease.

Before applying his exegesis of Freud to the theories of society outlined in *The Triumph of the Therapeutic*, Rieff edited a ten-volume standard edition *The Collected Papers of Sigmund Freud* in 1961, appending to each paper notes and commentary that trace the evolution of his thought.

Rieff regards himself, he writes, in the preface to *The Triumph of the Therapeutic*, as one of "those intellectuals, whether of the left or right, whose historic function it has been to assert the authority of a culture organized in terms of communal purpose, through the agency of congregations of the faithful." The issue he faces in this, his central credo and major book, is how to define our culture in the absence of any institutional authority based on faith; and to ask whether, following the defeat and dispersal of past ideals of behavior, "our culture can be so reconstructed that faith—some compelling symbolic or self-integrating communal purpose—need no longer superintend the organization of personality." He is attempting to define for "psychological man"—in Freudian terms a creature sublimating the id to serve the controlled commands of the civilized ego—a social theory that reconciles any opposition between human nature and the social order, but does so without recourse to the "moralizing function of our past." Rieff, whose mind is deeply stocked with literary images of society, constructs his opening chapter, "Toward a Theory of Culture," around two quotations from Yeats: the first, from "The Second Coming," a vision of a "rough beast" that "slouches toward Bethlelem"; the second, from

"A Prayer for My Daughter," foresees a union between the self and heaven in which "The soul recovers radical innocence / And learns at last that it is self-delighting, / Self-appeasing, self-affrighting, / And that its own sweet will is Heaven's will. . . . " Although he does not quote a third poem by Yeats, Rieff's perception of the time in which he lives seems to match the poet's description of the chaos surrounding the political struggles of Easter 1916, in which the best of society "lack all conviction," while the worst "are full of passionate intensity."

Despite the breadth and audacity of its attempt at cultural summary, *The Triumph of the Therapeutic* is reticent about solutions to the problems it describes, which concern the individual's efforts to find ways of recognizing the goals of self-fulfillment within the boundaries of social responsibility. Rieff never answers his own urgent question: "In what does the self now try to find salvation, if not in the breaking of corporate identities and in an acute suspicion of all normative institutions?" However, a partial answer seems to lie in his account of "responsible psychotherapists" who "continue to struggle confusedly to discover their own proper attitude toward renunciatory moral demand systems even as the normative character of their abandonment has altered both the theoretical and working conditions of clinical practice." Rieff is conscious that, in the climate of relativism and respect for individuality that now prevails, the search for a single binding synthesis is disabled by the very conditions that make it necessary: "Our cultural revolution does not aim, like its predecessors, at victory for some rival commitment, but rather at way of using all commitments, which amounts to loyalty toward none. By psychologizing about themselves interminably, Western men are learning to use their internality against the primacy of any particular organization of personality."

Although, as Rieff recognizes in his allusions to his intellectual forebears, it is the responsibility of the social theorist to offer truths that bind society, he is more an observer of ideas than a proponent of any particular idea. His function seems rather to define the intellectual origins of "therapeutic man," whose identity, according to Rieff, began to be formed during the French Revolution but is fully depicted in the work of Freud, who conceived the understanding of the self as humanity's primary goal in a world in which "there seems little likelihood of a great rebirth of the old corporate ideals. . . . By this time men have gone too far, beyond the old deception of good and evil, to specialize at last, wittingly, in techniques that are to be called, in the present volume, 'therapeutic,' with nothing at stake beyond a manipulable sense of well-being." It is a measure of Rieff's acumen that he foresaw, more than twenty years before the end of the cold war, that the rebellion of Russian intellectuals against the constraints of state ideology presaged the eventual collapse of Soviet social order in the face of the influence of the West and its message of self-realization.

The durability and invincibility of what Rieff calls "the therapeutic outlook" is virtually guaranteed because "men will have ceased to seek any salvation other than amplitude in living itself." In such a climate, Rieff believes, all creeds have equal validity "to enhance the interest of living freed from communal purpose," and hence we have entered a kind of religion of fulfilled self in which "We are, I fear, getting to know one another." The only redemptive possibility that Rieff saw in 1966 was offered by Martin Luther King, whom he described as the principal spokesman for a movement for "the conservation of inherited culture" against "vastly superior numbers of nominally Christian (or Jewish) barbarians." As King emerged as the leader of American Christians, Rieff noticed, however, a trend that bears out his main contention, that society was drifting toward a moral anarchy of individualism: "For the American Negro has been a focus for releasing images in the dominant white culture. Affluent white society, as it grows more affluent, may draw nearer their idea of the Negro as a model enjoyer of the relaxed life, but that idea is profoundly prejudicial to the renewal sought by the religious leadership, black and white." As Rieff predicted, such a renewal did not take place, and another kind of social consciousness—insistence on respect for cultural diversity—has confirmed the rightness of another of his diagnoses: "What culture has ever attempted to see to it that no ego is hurt?"

After describing the foundations of revolt against doctrinal authority and the lack of any compensating sense of communal responsibility, *The Triumph of the Therapeutic* proceeds to explain the use made of Freud's thinking by Carl Jung, Wilhelm Reich, and D. H. Lawrence, all of whom attempted to build philosophical systems on the foundation of psychoanalytic theory, and to attack the connections between conventional morality and a culture of which they disapproved. The book ends where it began with the observation that what society can collectively regard as moral "becomes and remains self-evident only within a powerful and deeply compelling system of culture." In the absence of such a system, Rieff believes, what was once a by-product of striving after communal goals—a sense of personal well-being—has become an

end in itself. Reviewers of *The Triumph of the Therapeutic*, who included Philip Rahv and Robert Coles, did not take issue with the premises or the terms of Rieff's argument, which they apparently found unassailable. Rahv and Coles did disagree, however, about the effectiveness of Rieff's style, which Coles, in the *New York Times Book Review*, found "sharp, witty, passionate, and at all times strikingly aphoristic." Rahv, on the other hand, found Rieff's language a "non-conductor" and his constant pursuit of aphorisms an obstacle to thought rather than an effective tool of analysis.

Fellow Teachers is a lengthy meditation on the role of the teacher in higher education that grew out of an invitation Rieff received to lecture at Skidmore College in 1971. In this book, which is not divided topically or by chapters, Rieff elaborates on the central proposition that the teacher in a post-Freudian age should maintain an objective distance from both society and social theory in order to place students in a stance of uncommitted, inquiring neutrality: "There is no Method for achieving the proper distances of feeling intellect; there is an institution within which we can keep trying. Only in our schools can our students hope to achieve a humane and proper distance from the social struggles in which they may be—need be—otherwise engaged. . . . Our second pedagogic responsibility is to keep our ideas to ourselves . . . for as long a time as the disciplined ego will allow." The "feeling intellect" is a detached quality of mind more easily defined by negatives than by practical explanation. We learn from *Fellow Teachers* that it is not preaching, nor espousing any particular doctrine, but Rieff offers no detailed observation of such an intellect in action. His thoughts, like Freud's, seem ambivalent about all cultural systems; always examining social theory with a passion for sympathetic explication, but always falling short of discipleship. Reviewing the book in *Commonweal*, Victor Ferkiss disagreed with Rieff's Freudian view that culture is becoming destabilized because people are unwilling to sublimate their desires, but he wrote favorably: "Much of what Rieff says is stimulating and worth saying: his shock at the ignorance of students and his anger at their desertion by their teachers, and also his condemnation of abortion, his arguments for capital punishment, and his deflation of the pretentious claptrap of black militancy." In the last analysis, however, all that is left after various targets have been destroyed, Ferkiss observes, "is rage and pride."

Rieff published no book in the years between the appearance of *Fellow Teachers* and *The Feeling Intellect*, a collection of his essays made by Jonathan Imber, a former student. Imber sheds no more light than his mentor on what constitutes the act of teaching, but compliments Rieff on his ability to "unpack" the thought of others, and offers a generalization on the present state of higher education: "The quiet life of teaching, the life necessary for feeling intellect, is a foreign, forgotten thing. That life has been replaced by the pursuits of soft money and hard science, each transforming itself into the other. The most ambitious and occasionally most talented flee teaching first in search of promotions awarded for anything but teaching. Beneficient foundations and government confer awards that degrade teaching further." *The Feeling Intellect*, which consists of four loosely arranged sections entitled "Freud and Psychoanalysis," "Religion and Politics," "Intellectuals and Education," and "Character and Culture," should have been more selectively edited, wrote Frank Cioffi in his *Times Literary Supplement* review. Cioffi dismisses Rieff's views on higher culture as "bromides," and finds his resistance to the current broadening of cultural standards insensitive and narrow-minded. Above all, he takes Rieff to task for lacking a rationale for much of his disdain for popular culture, and for "throwing aphorisms" at genuine problems. Cioffi suspects that Rieff "just likes being stern and prohibitive even when he is unclear as to the rationale."

Two reviewers who explicitly identify themselves with Rieff's thinking and characterize their points of view as "conservative" take an entirely opposite stance to that of Cioffi. Jerry Muller, writing in *Commentary* under the heading "A Neglected Conservative Thinker," admits that Rieff's writing "merits translation into English" but justifies this difficulty by describing it as "aphoristic, allusive, and ironic." His point that Rieff is a Socratic teacher is an interesting one that unfortunately can only be demonstrated by representing his conversation. In reviewing the entire span of Rieff's career, Muller notes that Rieff disclaims any original thoughts, and sees himself only as one who has sought for viable systems of thought amongst the ideas of others. This search has resulted in a sense of "higher" as opposed to "lower culture," which is characterized by the enactment of each and every fashionable impulse, a phenomenon to be blamed on the authority of "therapy and analysis," whose aim is to deconvert people from their respect for inherited commands without "offering compelling reasons of its own for moral behavior." Christopher Lasch, whose own writings on cultural and moral degeneration are better known than Rieff's, reviewed *The Feeling Intellect* with great respect in *New Republic*

(1990), shedding light on Rieff's gradual disappearance from public view following *The Triumph of the Therapeutic*. Lasch pointed out that in *Fellow Teachers* Rieff treats any kind of public pronouncement, especially an interview, as an entertainment, and prefers to see his teachings disseminated in the university. The danger in Rieff's efforts to replace religious faith with faith in the secular institutions of higher learning, Lasch noted, is precisely that faith and the "moral laws that mankind makes for its own governance" cannot finally be equated.

PRINCIPAL WORKS: Freud: The Mind of the Moralist, 1959, rev. ed. 1961; The Triumph of the Therapeutic: Uses of Faith After Freud, 1966; Fellow Teachers: Of Culture and Its Second Death, 1973; The Feeling Intellect: Selected Writings (ed. J. Imber) 1990. *As editor*—The Collected Papers of Sigmund Freud, 1961; On Intellectuals, 1969.

ABOUT: Contemporary Authors 49–52, 1975. *Periodicals*—American Journal of Sociology November 1959; Commentary February 1991; Commonweal May 3, 1974; Contemporary Sociology September 1991; New Republic March 19, 1966; November 19, 1990; New Statesman February 20, 1960; New York Times March 22, 1959; New York Times Book Review February 6, 1966; Saturday Review April 11, 1959; Spectator February 12, 1960; Times Literary Supplement January 11, 1991; Virginia Quarterly Review Summer 1992; Yale Review June 1959.

*RIVE, RICHARD (MOORE) (March 1, 1931–June 4, 1989), South African writer of fiction, essays, and plays, was born in District Six, a Cape Town slum, to Nancy (Ward) Rive and a black American father. Because his maternal grandfather had been white, he was classified under South Africa's racial laws as "coloured": "a term I find offensive," he observed in his autobiography *Writing Black*, "implying inferior to Whites and superior to Blacks." Although poor, Rive's family lived in "shabby respectability": that is, "I wore shoes to school, a mark of great social distinction," and he attended an Anglican church regularly. As a child he had little exposure to the cruelty of apartheid but was sensitive to the well-meaning but patronizing attitude of social workers who would "invade" the neighborhood and "smother us with love, good will, and dripping-wet charity." He attended the local schools where he excelled in athletics as well as academic studies and won a scholarship that enabled him to go to a municipal high school and from there to Hewat College of Education, from which he received a teacher's diploma in 1951. He taught English and Latin at South Peninsula High School in Cape Town and later joined the

RICHARD RIVE

faculty of Hewat College as a lecturer in English. At the time of his death he was head of the English Department at Hewat.

From early childhood Rive was an avid reader, devouring everything from comic books to Shakespeare, Sir Walter Scott, and Dickens. These classics were of course by white writers: "Books were not written about people like me. Books were about a White Deerslayer who was condescending towards a Red Indian Chingakook. They were about a White Huckleberry Finn who was condescending towards Nigger Jim." It was his reading of Alan Paton's *Cry, the Beloved Country* and his discovery of black writers—Americans like Langston Hughes, Richard Wright, and Countee Cullen and the black South African Peter Abrahams—that awakened him as a writer. "I was now able to analyze my own situation through theirs, rationalize my own situation through theirs. I could break with my literary dependence on descriptions by White Folks and the ways of White Folks. Native son had come of age," he said in *Design and Intent in African Literature.*

Rive began publishing short stories under the name Richard Moore in local periodicals. In 1955 he won a short story contest with "Dagga Smoker's Dream," a graphic portrait of a man on a drug high, which brought him to the attention of a number of prominent black African authors—Alex La Guma, Ezekiel Mphahlele, Lewis Nkosi—and sympathetic white authors such as Nadine Gordimer and Alan Paton. Especially helpful to him was Jack Cope, editor of the journal *Contrast*, who published some of his early

work and singled him out as a promising young talent. Unable, however, to find a publisher in South Africa, he published his first book of short stories, *African Songs*, in East Germany in 1963. Reviewers such as Berndt Lindfors in *Books Abroad* recognized his promise: "Often, by repeating certain phrases, images or musical refrains and by skilfully orchestrating them as leitmotifs within a story, Rive achieves unusual lyrical and rhythmical effects. But stylistic virtuosity does not save all of the stories. A number, especially some of those protesting against racial attitudes and racial policies in South Africa, are too loud to be finely drawn." Also in 1963 Rive edited and contributed four of his own stories to *Quartet: New Voices from South Africa*, published in the United States with an introduction by Alan Paton. The other contributors were Alex La Guma, James Matthews, and a South Afrikaaner, Alf Wannenburgh. Rive's stories were "Strike," in which some young blacks nervously prepare for a protest strike; "Resurrection," told from the point of view of a dark-skinned woman who had a white father and now bitterly resents her mother for bringing her into a world where she is denied privileges enjoyed by her light-skinned siblings; "No Room at Solitaire," an ironic episode in which a white innkeeper turns away a black couple in an analogue to the Mary and Joseph story; and "Rain," set in a fish-and-chips shop where the white owner offers some kindness to an unhappy young black woman. Characteristics of Rive's later fiction emerge in these early stories—compressed narrative, crisp dialogue, irony, and often wry humor. He later dramatized some of his stories for stage and radio presentation.

Rive was awarded a Farfield Foundation Fellowship in 1963 on which he traveled extensively in Africa, Asia, and Europe studying contemporary African literature. He became increasingly aware of the frustrations of the black South African writer. Forbidden publication at home and facing threats of imprisonment, many writers went into exile abroad. Their work, recognized and applauded outside Africa, was unknown to the audience who should have been reading them. At home the black writer was like Ralph Ellison's Invisible Man, read only by a few sympathetic white liberals who could afford to buy foreign editions.

Unlike many of his fellow writers, Rive chose to return to South Africa after his travels aboard. He continue to teach and to write, publishing his first novel, *Emergency*, in London in 1964. The book centers on three days of the Sharpeville riots of March 1960, during which the South African government used brutal force to put down demonstrations against apartheid. The central character, and clearly the author's persona, is a coloured schoolteacher, Andrew Dreyer, who finds himself torn between his natural desire for a quiet life of teaching and writing and the pressures to join his people in their struggle for freedom. He comes under police surveillance not only because he is educated and has friends in the African Union, but because he is having a love affair with a white woman also active in the struggle against apartheid. Reluctantly but inevitably Andrew is caught up in the violence. "There comes a point," he says, "when human nature can stand injustices no longer." His white friends urge him to leave the country, but he resolves to stay: "If there is another march on Cape Town, I shall be in it. I want to live my own life. I have reached the stage where I am prepared to ignore any legislation that denies me the right to go where I please, to love the girl I love, and to think the things I think." *Emergency* was banned in South Africa, but it brought Rive favorable attention in Europe and the United States. When finally published in South Africa in 1986 it was hailed as a powerful record of a young man's awakening to action. One reviewer called it "the finest Bildungsroman in our national literature."

In 1965 Rive came to the United States on a Fulbright scholarship to study in New York at Columbia University, where he received an M.A. in 1966. He renewed contact with many prominent black writers whom he had met during his earlier travels in Europe and England and came to know Harlem at first hand. When he returned to Cape Town in 1967 he took a B. Ed. at the University of Cape Town which certified him to teach at the college level. Resolved now to make his career in teaching and writing, Rive decided to work for a Ph.D. degree in England. In 1971 he received a junior research fellowship from Magdalen College, Oxford, where he spent the next three years. For his dissertation subject he chose the white South African writer Olive Schreiner, whose novel *The Story of an African Farm*, originally published in 1883, had become a classic, and whose later work was outspokenly critical of the treatment of blacks and coloreds in South Africa. Rive pursued his research on Schreiner beyond the Ph.D., conferred in 1974. In 1979 he received a grant to travel to the University of Texas at Austin where he studied the Schreiner archive in preparation for a scholarly edition of her letters, the first volume of which was published in 1988. Rive came back to the United States again in 1987 as visiting professor at Harvard University, offering a course in literature by nonwhite South Africans.

At no period in his life did Rive question his decision to make his permanent home in South Africa He felt he belonged there despite his identity as "an unenfranchised Black suffering under a policy of racial discrimination, born and nurtured in a notorious slum in a beautiful city in a bigoted country," as he said. Ironically, Rive's choice was not received favorably by some of his peers. His independence, his firm rejection of what he considered the narrowly ethnic philosophy of negritude as itself a form of racism, and his continued emphasis on Western or predominantly white culture even while he refused to submit to the humiliations of apartheid, put him in an ambivalent position. Invited to lecture on African poetry at a writers' conference in Berlin, he affirmed that "African poetry and indeed all of African literature can only be understood in terms of universal creativity, without any allowances or concessions." Poets should be appreciated, he argued, "for their poetic worth, not for their pigmentation. Their colour (much as it does affect them) is incidental to the quality of their verse."

Rive discussed the dilemma of the black African writer in an article, "Storming Pretoria's Castle—to Write or Fight," in the *New York Times Book Review* (January 17, 1988). The title alluded to a poem by the black South African poet Arthur Nortje, who had died in 1970—"For some of us must storm the castle / some define the happening." As early as 1965, Rive wrote, he had been singled out for criticism by Lewis Nkosi for staying behind and working within the system. Nkosi argued that if black writers chose to remain in South Africa, they should renounce literature temporarily and devote their energies to politics and the struggle for freedom. In the early 1980s, as that struggle intensified, a group of black writers had withdrawn from the Johannesburg chapter of PEN because, Rive wrote, "they objected to the fact that the Organisation contained White members." In the Untied States, the African Literature Association voted to deny membership to any resident of South Africa "on the grounds that all who live here are in some way collaborating with the apartheid regime." Rive resented these charges bitterly: "It is impertinent to suggest that a writer's literary credentials should be dependent on how often he can throw stones at white policemen."

Though it was Rive's choice to "define the happening" in his teaching and writing rather than to "storm the castle," he became increasingly sensitive to his ethnic identity. By giving his autobiography the title *Writing Black* in 1982 he rejected the ambiguous term "coloured." "I have been forced into the position of having to call myself a black writer," he wrote in an essay, "The Black Writer in South Africa." Nevertheless, he continued:

I do not see myself as being in the process of abandoning my non-racial stand. It becomes a matter of definition and clarification. I see "black" as politico-economic rather than ethnic. When I call a literature "black" I imply that that literature emanates from a people who are unenfranchised and discriminated against because of the colour of their skins. Such a literature must differ in texture and quality from that emanating from a people who have the vote, suffer no discrimination and are in a power position because of the colour of their skins.

In an interview in 1989; Rive affirmed his independence once again, although he acknowledged that his views had alienated him from a younger, more radical generation: "The one thing I can assure you of, and it must make me very unpopular: I refuse to write to a march or to a tune, and I refuse to have an organisation, no matter what organisation, telling me what to write. I haven't written anything in my life which hasn't attacked apartheid, racialism." And when asked how he felt about "being a voice from the past, or a voice in the present," he replied, "I'm a voice of the future as well."

Rive was not destined for a personal future, however. In June of 1989 he was found murdered in his home, brutally stabbed and beaten, his furniture oveturned and his car missing. There was no further report on the circumstances of his death nor of the arrest of his killers.

Rive did not leave a substantial body of fiction behind him: three short novels and a number of short stories, some of them only brief sketches. His early success may not have worked entirely in his favor. Recognized as a gifted young writer by black South African writers such as Ezekiel Mphahlele, fiction editor of the influential journal *Drum*, Rive achieved international recognition as well, and translation into several European languages. Langston Hughes included his work in his anthology *An African Treasury* in 1960, before his talent had an opportunity to mature. After the publication of *Emergency* in 1964 he devoted more of his time to lecturing and attending literary meetings at home and abroad than to writing. In an obituary article on Rive in *Current Writing: Text and Reception in Southern Africa* in October 1989, Stephen Gray wrote: "Discovered fatally young, overpraised and undervalued in the 1950s, Richard certainly had career difficulties. Harassment and bannings stopped Richard in his tracks, just as firmly as apartheid stopped his athletic career. But his talent, perhaps scenting some new underground thrust for liberation, did surface again. In the '80s he could not stop writing, and rewriting, his past, feeling the future close."

In 1986 Rive had published what many of his readers regard as his finest book, *"Buckingham Palace," District Six*, a novel developed in a series of episodic short sketches. As in most of his fiction, the characters and situations here are drawn from his own life. "Buckingham Palace" was a slum in Cape Town inhabited by blacks, coloureds, and Asians. It was the slum were Rive himself had grown up—rowdy, colorful, a mix of poor but respectable working-class families, petty thieves, con men, and prostitutes all living together more or less happily, "an island in a sea of apartheid." For Rive the book was an exercise of memory, all the more poignant because in 1965, by edict of the government, District Six was declared an area for white housing. The residents were evicted, the district bulldozed and razed. When the adult Rive returned to his neighborhood he found a pile of rubble, "a lunar landscape" where there had once been life: "There are those of us who still remember the ripe, warm days. Some of us still romanticise and regret when our eyes travel beyond the dead bricks and split tree-stumps and wind-tossed sand." While there is no violence or overt brutality in the book, Rive offers a powerful indictment of a system that creates such havoc in a small community. A white landlord who is a Jewish refugee from Nazi Germany shares the outrage of the residents and defies the government edict. In Germany, he recalls, he was treated as an *untermensch*: "But I cannot forget what they did to us in Germany. So my heart is with all the *untermenschen*, whoever and wherever they are." The novel could easily have slipped into political polemic, Robert L. Berner commented in 1987 in his review in *World Literature Today*, but he concluded that *"Buckingham Palace* is a work of art because it is filled with rich human content. Rive's last line, about a flame which 'flickered some time determined to stay alive,' is an eloquent tribute to his faith in the ultimate triumph of the humanism that informs his beautiful novel."

Reviewers found Rive's *Emergency Continued*, published only a few months before his death, an earnest but overly self-conscious novel. It takes up the story of Andrew Dreyer, now middle-aged and married to a woman of his own race, living comfortably as a secondary school teacher. But the emergency of 1985, the strike of black students in protest against apartheid, forces him once again to confront his ambivalence. He compares himself to Hamlet, irresolute yet forced to act. He is all the more troubled because his young son has become involved in the demonstrations and faces arrest. As Dreyer, who is writing a novel even as he recounts his experiences, observes: "The black youths of today are different from what we were yesterday. We were a generation that grew up in a climate of less overt discrimination which was more institutionalised than constitutionalised." He finds himself alienated from his son and once again his life is disrupted by the violence that surrounds him. Maya Jaggi commented in the *Times Literary Supplement* that "Rive succeeds in dramatising the tensions between older black South Africans and a more militant 'apartheid generation' who have grown up fearless, having nothing to lose. He also involved the reader in the debates of the black community over tactics. . . . " By his own quiet tactics Rive contributed to the ongoing process of liberation from apartheid that he was never to see.

PRINCIPAL WORKS: *Fiction*—African Songs: Short Stories, 1963; Emergency, 1964; Advance, Retreat: Short stories (Ill. C. Skotnes) 1983; "Buckingham Palace," District Six, 1986; Emergency Continued, 1989. *Collected Works*—Selected Writings: Stories, Essays, and Plays, 1977. *Autobiography*—Writing Black, 1982. *Nonfiction*—(with T. Covzens) Seme, 1992. *As editor*—Quartet: New Voices from South Africa, 1963; Modern Africa Prose, 1964.

ABOUT: Contemporary Authors 128, 1990; Contemporary Authors New Revision Series 27, 1989; Daymond, M. J. (ed.) Momentum: On Recent South African Writing, 1984; Dorsey, D. F. (ed.) Design and Intent in African Literature, 1982; Rive, R. Writing Black, 1982; Zell, H. M. Bundy, C., and Coulon, V., (eds.) A New Reader's Guide to African Literature, 2nd ed., 1983. *Periodicals*—African Literature Association Bulletin 15, 1989; Books Abroad Spring 1965; Contrast: South African Literature Journal December 1980; December 1983; December 1985; Current Writing: Text and Reception in Southern Africa October 1989; New York Times June 5, 1989; New York Times Book Review October 4, 1987; January 17, 1988; January 7, 1990; August 25, 1990' Times Literary Supplement August 2, 1991; World Literature Today Summer 1982; Autumn 1987.

ROBISON, MARY (REISS) (January 14, 1949–), American novelist and short story writer, was born in Washington, D.C., to Anthony Cennomo, an attorney, and F. Elizabeth Reiss, a psychologist. She grew up in Ohio along with five brothers and two sisters. Her childhood was chaotic and she ran away from home twice as a teenager, once to Florida in search of Jack Kerouac. Her earliest writing took the form of journals and diaries, and, throughout her adolescence, poetry. Instead of going to college, she told *Ms.* magazine, she "fell in and out of marriage," had two daughters, and "was bad and wild and had to be kept sedated much of the time." Although some reviewers assume that her work is largely autobiographical, according to Robison "[i]t's pretty much whole-cloth inven-

MARY ROBISON

tion. I'm afraid of autobiography and fond of my family. I'm not ready to write them really."

Robison writes short stories and novels that present a spare, prosaic, funny view of contemporary American life, particularly within families. Because of her lean, dispassionate style, she has often been compared to fellow writers Raymond Carver, Ann Beattie, Bobbie Ann Mason, and Frederick Barthelme. Despite her early forays into writing, she did not begin to think of herself as a serious writer until she entered the graduate writing program at Johns Hopkins University in Baltimore. She has high praise for that program, and singles out writer/teacher John Barth for his inspiration and encouragement. After completing her master's degree at Johns Hopkins in 1977, she received fellowships from the Yaddo Writers and Artists Colony in 1978, the Bread Loaf Writers' Conference in 1979, and the Guggenheim Foundation in 1980–1981. During those years, she also taught at a number of colleges and universities, including Ohio University at Athens, the University of Southern Mississippi at Hattiesburg, and the University of North Carolina at Greensboro.

Robison's first major publication was *Days*, a collection of twenty stories, eight of which first appeared in the *New Yorker*. These stories clearly display the hallmarks of her style: exactitude, spareness, humor, incisive dialogue, and quietly desperate people. "Pretty Ice" limns a graduate botany student who is so isolated by his work that he cannot stop analyzing the disastrous effects of an ice storm long enough to see its beauty. His fiancée finally admits what she has long known: she cannot spend her life with someone whose world view is as narrowly defined as plant taxonomy. In "May Queen," a seemingly innocent religious ceremony ends with the May queen, sixteen-year-old Riva, nearly immolated after a holy candle sets her clothes on fire. Her father's subsequent words of comfort sound so banal that she finally asks him to shut up.

Reviewing *Days* in *Fiction International*, Elizabeth Inness-Brown praised Robison's stories as "clean, flat, accurate, full of dialogue, and nearly emotionless. . . . " Inness-Brown noted, however, that the stories tend to flatten out when read consecutively, distorting rather than clarifying these glimpses of contemporary life. *New York Times* (1979) reviewer Anatole Broyard found Robison's fiction puzzling. Focusing as it does on life's inscrutability and pointlessness, he wrote: "Her stories are a form of affirmative action in defense of the poverty of experience. Life is less a luxury boutique of sensations than a thrift shop of ambiguities and ambivalences." In *Critical Survey of Short Fiction*, Patrick Meanor suggested that the characters in *Days* fear change to the point of paralysis and thus doom themselves to lives of ennui and self-deception. This quality in Robison's work reminded Meanor of James Joyce's *Dubliners*, as well as of stories by Raymond Carver and Ann Beattie. Despite its dark theme, however, he pointed out that *Days* contains great humor, which some "overly serious" reviewers miss altogether.

In 1981, Robison published her first novel *Oh!*, which chronicles a few weeks in the lives of the Clevelands, a midwestern family. Cleveland *père*, a retired millionaire, owns a corporation that peddles soda, miniature golf, and fast food. His grown children, Howdy and Maureen, live at home, along with Maureen's preadolescent daughter, Violet. They spend their idle days in passive, depressed states. Cleveland has long indulged his lethargic, sponging children because they grew up without a mother. Howdy and Maureen have always believed that she disappeared almost twenty years earlier to get away from their father. When they finally learn the truth about her absence, the ensuing emotional chaos drives Cleveland to shove them out into the world.

Despite its bleakness, *Oh!* struck readers as a comic, strangely buoyant novel. The *New Yorker* praised its boiled-down prose and colloquial dialogue. Beneath a satirical "situation comedy" surface, "Robison is trying to show us how the incredibly complicated dance of family life works, how it balances love and hate, respect and contempt, humor and self-righteousness, wisdom and foolishness." Dulcie Leimbach, reviewing the novel in *Ms.*, also found Robison's take on American family life insightful and funny. John W. Aldridge, however, viewed the novel more harshly in his study *Talents and Technicians: Literary Chic and the New Assembly-Line Fiction*. Aldridge asserted that Robison exerts no control over her characters, having instead an "almost narcissistic relationship" with them. Since they delight her in and of themselves, she doesn't bother to give them personal histories or meaningful actions. The truth about the Clevelands' mother comes too late to endow the family's dysfunction with any significance, Aldridge contended. "The novel becomes, therefore, a chronicle of attractively zany but unmotivated behavior brought to a climax by the introduction of an overly melodramatic deus ex machina."

Like her previous work, Robison's second story collection, *An Amateur's Guide to the Night*, focuses on American families stumbling within constricted lives and fractured relationships. The characters lead "attenuated lives," Michiko Kakutani observed in the *New York Times*. "There are few clues to people's motivations, little narrative exposition and a willful resistance to interpretation of any kind." The title story is about a high school student whose unbalanced mother constantly invades her daughter's world, which the daughter escapes by stargazing through her telescope. In "The Dictionary in the Laundry Chute," a mother and father discuss their grown daughter, who suffers from alcoholism and eating and sleeping disorders, while a psychologist attempts crisis intervention in another part of the house. The father grossly simplifies both his daughter's illness and his own responsibility, insisting that the solution lies in merely stopping her drinking, forcing her to take her pills, and fattening her up.

In the *Hudson Review* Dean Flower praised *An Amateur's Guide to the Night*'s skillful dialogue, but complained that Robison's stories are inconclusive; "[I]n the end we are left entirely to our own conclusions. My own is that if these stories are indeed meant to be some kind of guide to the night, Robison has not made it dark enough for us to need one." Frances Taliaferro, in the *New York Times Book Review*, thought Robison's second collection more substantial than *Days*. While some of the stories seemed meaningless to Taliaferro, others impressed her with their wisdom and humor: "[Robison] seems to me not so much a maker of cultural documentaries as a free-lance pathologist who takes her little emotional biopsies in clean slices wherever she finds symptoms of unease." In a *Village Voice* review, David Leavitt admired *Amateur's Guide* for its precision, humor, dialogue, and urgency and hoped that it would earn the critical and popular acclaim enjoyed by Robison's contemporaries, like Raymond Carver and Bobbie Ann Mason.

Robison's third collection of stories, *Believe Them*, indicates a shift in the author's technique and perspective in that she uses more first-person narration and explores the processes by which people awake to self-responsibility. For example, in "Seizing Control," growing children get their first real taste of independence by breaking every parental rule they can think of. In "Trying," Bridie, a wisecracking, token liberal student at her Catholic high school, realizes that she has much in common with the very conservative Sister Elspeth, who has giantism. As Bridie acknowledges, she and Elspeth are misfits, yet they keep struggling to effect change.

Believe Them was well received for its balance and variety. Larry McCaffery, reviewing the collection in the *New York Times Book Review*, detected a more upbeat tone and less bitter humor in the eleven stories. McCaffrey acknowledged that Robison's "restraint and refusal to supple her incidents with a more dramatic shape occasionally produce stories that evoke a sense of 'So what?'" Nevertheless, he appreciates "her intuitive feel for the surrealistic dimensions of American life that lie barely concealed under the ordinary."

Subtraction, Robison's second novel, follows Paige Deveraux, poet and Harvard professor, as she tracks down her roving husband Raf. She finds him in an alcoholic torpor in Houston, where she attempts to rehabilitate him and their marriage. They drink heavily, their marriage founders, and they drift aimlessly back to New England. At the end, Paige and Raf are reunited, on the road without a destination but apparently together for the long haul:

> I studied him. Below his black hair the fine bones of his skull were modeled by the white cabin light. His good eye was a pool of shadow. I thought: generic man, perfect man. I thought how even when Raf was dead-still, he had an intensity out of which someone could interpret a world.

By the time this reconciliation takes place, however, Douglas Bauer, in the *New York Times Book Review* (1991), found that he no longer cared about the main characters: "Yet at the book's end one feels only—past any interest and without the least concern—that they deserve each other." In the *Antioch Review*, Jon Saari admitted that while Raf's appeal eluded him, he did find the novel "compelling," thanks to Robison's ability to "[pare] down language, situation, and character to their most emotive."

Mary Robison is married to writer Jim Robi-

son and has two daughters. She has taught creative writing at Harvard University, the College of William and Mary, Bennington College, Oberlin College, and the University of Houston. Her work has been published in the *New Yorker* and *Esquire* and short fiction anthologies including *Best American Short Stories 1982* and *Masters of Life and Death*. In addition to short stories and novels, she has also written screenplays.

PRINCIPAL WORKS: *Novels*—Oh!, 1981; Subtraction, 1991. *Short stories*—Days, 1979; An Amateur's Guide to the Night, 1983; Believe Them, 1988.

ABOUT: Aldridge, John W. Talents and Technicians: Literary Chic and the New Assembly-Line Fiction, 1992; Contemporary Authors 116, 1986; Contemporary Literary Criticism 42, 1987; Contemporary Novelists, 5th ed., 1992; Dictionary of Literary Biography 130, 1993; Magill, F. (ed.) Critical Survey of Short Fiction 1991. *Periodicals*—Antioch Review Summer 1991; Fiction International 12, 1980; Hudson Review Summer 1984; Ms. July 1981, New York Times June 2, 1979; November 15, 1983; New York Times Book Review November 27, 1983; July 31, 1988; February 24, 1991; New Yorker December 21, 1981; Village Voice January 10, 1984; Vogue June 1984.

ROIPHE, ANNE (December 25, 1935–   ), American novelist and essayist, was born in New York City to Blanche Phillips Roth and Eugene Roth, a lawyer. She obtained a B.A. degree at Sarah Lawrence College in 1957 and married Jack Richardson in 1958, by whom she had a daughter. Four years later, after a divorce from Richardson (in 1963), she married a psychoanalyst, Herman Roiphe, who had two daughters from a previous marriage. She and her husband, who has since become codirector of the Infant Intervention Center at Mt. Sinai Hospital in New York, subsequently produced two daughters of their own. Although Roiphe has not described her novels as autobiographical, all of them provide evidence of the themes and issues that have preoccupied her during her extensive writing career, and at least one of them has been described by reviewers as confessional.

Modern woman in one sort of family crisis or another is the focus of Roiphe's novels (the earliest written in 1967). The tensions between a mother and daughter (a theme which would recur in later novels as well) are explored in *Digging Out*, which presents a daughter's reflections on her rich, Jewish family as she sits by the bed of her dying mother. While her mother is being buried, the daughter muses that our "tribe does not take kindly to defection, but now that

ANNE ROIPHE

my mother was going into the ground I could leave them chanting in the temple."

In Roiphe's second novel, *Up the Sandbox!*, the familial focus switches to a young married woman torn between her own needs and those of her husband and children. Despite finding satisfactions in her domestic life, she frequently indulges in fantasies of an alternative lifestyle which would offer her the freedom to go to Vietnam, spend a night with Fidel Castro, or join a group of black militants and blow up the George Washington Bridge. Nora Sayre, in *New York Times Book Review*, noted that the book quickly became "a Rorschach test for many readers: Some see a character who yearns for liberation, while others insist that she's afraid of it." One reader belonging to the second category commented in the *Village Voice* that the novel "affirms over and over that the rewards of caring full-time for children, are real and fulfilling, and that . . . the liberated life is a doomed one for women, fraught with disappointment and disaster." Nevertheless, the book, which established Roiphe's reputation as a novelist of considerable talent, received many favorable reviews and was made into a film with Barbara Streisand in 1972.

Long Division follows the journey of a wife (who has been deserted by her husband) as she drives to Mexico with her daughter to obtain a divorce. The wife's frenzied voice in the opening chapter sets the tone of the book: "What I'm doing in this car flying down these screaming highways is getting my tail to Juarez so I can legally rid myself of the crummy son-of-a-bitch who

promised me a tomorrow like a yummy fruitcake and delivered instead wilted lettuce, rotted cucumber, a garbage of a life. I'm not going gently into this divorce, but yelling and kicking all the way with blood and skin under my fingernails and hate balled up inside like a gallstone fouling up my vital functions." Fantastic fantasies, not unlike those in *Up the Sandbox!*, become realities here: in one incident, the daughter is kidnapped by gypsies; in another, she falls into a vat of chocolate in a Hershey, Pennsylvania, chocolate factory; still later, mother and daughter meet up with a group of outwardly smiling senior citizens who plot to keep them under lock and key. The wife/narrator intersperses these bizarre happenings with comments on contemporary America, reflections on the horrors of history, and lamentations that she is a Jew without a clan. According to Nora Sayre, in *New York Times Book Review* Roiphe's prose is "exhilarating throughout." She has "the voice of an urban nomad who truly respects the ridiculous."

The author's fourth novel, *Torch Song*, met some negative and some favorable reviews. It was described by Julian Moynahan in the *New York Times Book Review* as being "about an awful marriage that lasted at least six years, producing a single child (out of virtually no sexual embraces), and an immense amount of misery and misbehavior." Moynahan judged the narrator "fundamentally dishonest in explaining why she got and how she stayed married until the day the man walked out." Laurie Stone wrote in the *Village Voice* that the novel "crucifies an already much tortured form—the confessional novel." Karl Miller, in the *New York Review of Books*, also labeled the book confessional but found the author's portrait of the artist/husband genuinely interesting and her use of Thomas Mann's story *Tonio Kröger* a useful device for exploring the nature of a modern artist: "In *Torch Song*, as in *Tonio Kröger*, normality triumphs . . . The relationship breaks up, and the book ends by the sea, as does Mann's story, in a jolly, healthy atmosphere of children, fishing, and suntans, with [the narrator] married happily ever after to a kind, potent pediatrician." Concluding that Roiphe's "conception of normality seems very unappealing," this critic nevertheless found the book written "with a good deal of journalistic force."

Roiphe's next two books were nonfictional. *Generation Without Memory*, which came out in 1981, is a collection of essays (many of which she had written for magazines or presented at public forums) on Judaism and cultural assimilation. Four years later she and her analyst husband published *Your Child's Mind: The*

Complete Guide to Infant and Child Emotional Well-being. In a preface describing her amateur interest in child development and her "affection for her mate's field of interest," she writes that their five daughters "have suffered from our divorces and from other mistakes that we, despite all good intentions, could neither foresee nor avoid. . . . We have been through some bad times that temper our memories of the glorious and triumphant occasions. . . . We have been bruised in the fray—and that made us wiser and possibly better able to combine our intellectual knowledge and our skills in a way that might be meaningful to other parents."

In *Lovingkindness* Roiphe returned to fiction. The story, about a modern American single parent struggling to come to terms with her rebellious daughter, was inspired by a true-life tale told to her by a woman at a Jewish feminist gathering. Roiphe told an interviewer for the *New York Times Book Review* in 1987 that she identified in her book with both characters: "It would be nice if one could have two lives and really be both. . . . Maybe that is why we have children." The daughter of this novel is no mere ordinary rebellious child of the sixties. She dyes her hair various shades of pink and red, involves herself with numerous self-serving male partners, has three abortions, and along the way has her back tattooed with a picture of a rattlesnake. Frequently telling her mother that she has never felt loved, appreciated, or guided, she finally finds peace in the all-absorbing religious rituals of a fundamentalist Israeli yeshiva. The challenge for the intellectual, feminist mother who has never ceased loving her daughter is in coming to accept the fact that the daughter's choice is right for her and more than that, a spiritual affirmation, an antithesis to her own worship of the rational. Blanche d'Alpuget, in the *New York Times Book Review*, commented that Roiphe brings to the drawings of her main character such a depth of insight that the denouement—the reverse of what I wanted to happen—lifted the book from its pages, exhilarated me with its elegance."

Roiphe's next book, *A Season for Healing*, contains her reflections on the Holocaust. "As an American Jew," she wrote, and "as a mother who wants her children's children to survive. . . . I could not stop thinking about what the events of 1941–1945 meant. . . . How can we make sense of our history, and what can we do to make the future better?" Finding the Jewish response to the Holocaust in the post-Holocaust world threatening, because of its emphasis on the Holocaust's uniqueness, she argues that this stance implicitly denies the wrongs that other groups have suffered and has already led to revivals of

anti-Semitism. Her central point, that all groups ought now to recognize the need for a "season for healing," is essentially a plea for empathy: each of us, from whatever background (whether black, Arab, or otherwise) should develop a capacity for understanding, since history has shown that no one group is unique in its suffering. Berel Lang, in the *New York Times Book Review*, (1988) found the issues Roiphe addresses "unquestionably important," while questioning several of the author's points (for instance, that black anti-Semitism stems from a Jewish emphasis on the Holocaust). She also questioned Roiphe's assumption that "a person or group can at will take on another's memories and give up its own . . . Even if her assumption here were true. . . . it would not follow that Jews are somehow obligated to alter their conception of self and history."

Roiphe's most ambitious novel is *The Pursuit of Happiness.* The number of characters one meets in this tale of five generations of immigrant Jews and their offspring is so prodigious that there is sometimes a problem remembering their names. Beginning in 1878 in Poland and ending in the present, the book (as Amy Wallace described it in the *New York Times Book Review* in 1991) "bounces back and forth in time" and includes "countless deaths and births and injuries and affairs and shames and secrets." On one level about an immigrant family that starts out poor but ends up acquiring a fortune, the novel's deeper implications have to do with ambivalence within families and, as Roiphe puts it, with "the dips and swings" of morality—"how it sways and jitterbugs through the generations." Although Wallace in her review found the book's "plethora of characters" confusing, she also admitted to growing fond of the author's "sprawling family of sufferers and strivers."

In 1979, Roiphe told an interviewer that Doris Lessing had been the writer who had influenced her most. "What her books are about—what's she doing—is what I've always wanted to do." At the same time she voiced the opinion that all relationships are ambivalent: "I'm sure that if you're tied to someone by virtue of love, there have to emerge the pulling-away feelings which have to do with anger and hate. One needs to know only a little about adolescence to know precisely what that's all about . . . One of the reasons I wrote about it is that it was one of those things we were not supposed to say, and I've always wanted to write about precisely the things that you're not supposed to say."

Roiphe lives with her husband on the Upper West Side of Manhattan. Her daughter Katie Roiphe is the author of *The Morning After: Sex,*

Fear, and Feminism on Campus, published in 1993.

PRINCIPAL WORKS: *Novels*—(as Anne Richardson) Digging Out, 1967; Up the Sandbox!, 1970; Long Division, 1972; Torch Song, 1977; Lovingkindness, 1987; The Pursuit of Happiness, 1991; If You Knew Me, 1993. *Nonfiction*—Generation Without Memory, 1981; (with Dr. H. Roiphe) Your Child's Mind: The Complete Guide to Infant and Child Emotional Well-being 1985; A Season for Healing, 1988.

ABOUT: Contemporary Authors 89–92, 1980; Contemporary Literary Criticism 3, 1975; 9, 1978. *Periodicals*—New York Review of Books February 3, 1977; New York Times November 10, 1993; New York Times Book Review November 5, 1972; January 9, 1977; August 30, 1987; November 13, 1988; July 21, 1991; Village Voice January 3, 1977.

RORTY, RICHARD (October 4, 1931–), American philosopher and educator, was born in Chicago, the son of two political journalists, James Hancock and Winifred (Rauschenbusch) Rorty. One of his books—*Contingency, Irony, and Solidarity*—is dedicated "in memory of six liberals: my parents and grandparents." His maternal grandfather was Walter Rauschenbusch, a liberal Protestant theologian eminent in his time. Both of his parents contributed to the *Nation* and other radical publications during the depression years. His father, at first active in Communist-front organizations, became an ardent participant in the anti-Stalinist Trotskyite movement along with a friend, the philosophy professor Sidney Hook. Hook was a stellar influence on Rorty during his early years ("a man upon whose knees I was bounced," he later recalled), directing him in particular to Hook's mentor John Dewey, a philosopher whose sagging reputation Rorty subsequently did much revive.

"Precocious, bookish, and nearly friendless" during his young adolescence, in the words of L. S. Klepp, who interviewed him for the *New York Times Magazine*, Rorty floundered throughout his early school years; eventually, after skipping several grades, he entered the University of Chicago at the age of fourteen. Following some attempts at writing poetry, in which he was discouraged by his father, he decided at the age of seventeen, prompted by Sidney Hook, to become a philosopher. He received his B.A. from the University of Chicago in 1949, at the age of eighteen. His postgraduate degrees are from Yale (M.A, 1952; Ph.D, 1956).

Rorty's academic career began at Yale, where he taught in the philosophy department from 1955 to 1956. After a year of military service, he was appointed an assistant professor of philosophy at Wellesley College, where he remained from 1958 to 1961. He moved by invitation to Princeton, then recognized as the center of analytic philosophy, which had become Rorty's specialization. His years at Princeton were spent "poking at linguistic and logical conundrums," as he told Klepp, editing as his first publication a collection of articles under the title *The Linguistic Turn*. He rose to the rank of full professor by 1970, but growing increasingly restive under the constrictions of traditional philosophy, he found himself out of sorts with his colleagues. "They started telling graduate students, 'It's a waste of time to do your dissertation under Rorty,'" he recalled, and he came to be regarded as "some sort of a crank."

Rorty's rift with his academic associates came to a climax in 1979 when, as chair of a meeting of the Eastern branch of the American Philosophical Association, he cast a clinching vote leading to the election of a candidate opposed, as he had come to be, to the analytical school. In this same year he published his iconoclastic *Philosophy and the Mirror of Nature*, in which he advocated the "setting aside" of the central concerns of philosophy from the ancient Greeks through Kant. In 1982, he joined the faculty of the University of Virginia at Charlottesville as Kenan Professor of Humanities. This title reflects his break with the "old" philosophy as well as the wide-ranging intellectual interests that have made him—in the words of one of his admirers, Adolph Gottlieb—"the most talked about outside of philosophy departments" of American philosophers (*New York Review of Books*, June 2, 1991).

Philosophy and the Mirror of Nature, Rorty's seminal book, created a stir in philosophical circles because it undermines two concepts focal to Western thought: dualism (the mind-body dichotomy associated principally with Descartes) and realism (the assumption of "external" truth independent of a thinking mind, whose origins go back to Plato). For Rorty, philosophy advances not by offering new answers to old questions, as once assumed, but by posing new questions. He regards the traditional vocabulary of epistemology and metaphysics to be as outmoded for the modern age as was the terminology of Scholasticism to the thinkers of the Enlightenment. The three most important philosophers of our century for him are Wittgenstein, Heidegger, and Dewey—"edifying" in his terms rather that "systematic" philosophers, all three having rejected the traditional "ocular image" of the mind as "a mirror of reality." These three philosophers are "anti-representational" (another of Rorty's key terms) in that they recognize "the nation of knowledge as accurate representation made possible through special mental processes needs to be abandoned." Dewey is extolled in particular for having "constructed a new kind of society," dominated not only by "the ideal of objective cognition" but by "aesthetic advancement." Fundamental to the reconstituting of philosophy for postmodern times, according to Rorty, is some adaptation of William James's pragmatism, which views truth as "what it is better to believe." Knowledge is not "a means of getting reality right," but "acquiring habits of action for coping with reality."

One of the reviewers of *Philosophy and the Mirror of Nature*, Ian Hacking, pointed out, in the *New Republic*, its "internal paradox . . . a death-of-philosophy book [that] doubles interest in all kinds of philosophy." Typical of the general response was that of Quinton Skinner, in the *New York Review of Books* in 1981, who found it a "disturbing and brilliantly argued book," but felt that the author's insistence on "all our claims to knowledge" being "nothing more than claims about existing canons of argument" ignored the success of scientific theories in explaining and controlling the phenomena of nature. In his *Times Literary Supplement* review in 1980, the philosopher Charles Taylor, like Rorty a dissident from the analytical school, considered his first book "ambitious and important" by placing modern philosophy in historical perspective, but objected to the wholesale rejection of "super standards."

Rorty's theories have since been widely disseminated through conferences in America and abroad (six to eight annually by his estimate). Consequently, the books that followed *Philosophy and the Mirror of Nature* bring together lectures and papers, some delivered orally at various symposia, others previously published in philosophical journals or collections. Generally they expand or refine his pluralistic philosophical position, which has been labeled New Pragmatism.

The Consequences of Pragmatism, made up of essays written between 1972 and 1980, is introduced by one of Rorty's most famous paradoxes: "Pragmatists are saying that the best hope for philosophy is not to practice Philosophy." Not to practice Philosophy seems to involve for him the jettisoning of universals: "They [Pragmatists] think that it will not help to say something true to think about Truth, nor will it help to act well to think about Goodness, nor will it help to be rational to think about Rationality." The age-old Platonic division between appear-

ance and reality is to Rorty a Gordian knot which the philosopher severs simply by denying that there is "an invidious distinction to be drawn between kinds of truths." In effect, Rorty refuses to separate, in Plato's terms, opinion from knowledge. In his philosophy, all our received "truths" are time-bound; we cannot shed our cultural, linguistic, and historical traditions ("step outside our skins," in Rorty's words) to arrive at something absolute.

Reviewers of *The Consequences of Pragmatism* were for the most part dazzled and amused, but left up in the air. "The essays are sometimes witty and possess a sophistication not dependent on technical jargon," wrote Jerome Miller in *America*, but he was concerned for the consequences of a philosophy "that would release action from normative values." The British philosopher Anthony Quinton, considering this later book alongside *Philosophy and the Mirror of Nature* in the *Partisan Review* in 1984, observed that much as Rorty calls for a revolution in philosophy, "its specific consequences, apart from fairly gestural references to conversation and cultural criticism, are left wide open."

As Quinton indicated, Rorty sets great store by dialogue among intellectuals (using the term "conversation" somewhat in the way it was employed by the political philosopher Michael Oakeshott, much admired by Rorty). Quinton also anticipated Rorty's turning to literature rather than to philosophical discourse for guidance. *Contingency, Irony, and Solidarity*, the book that followed *Consequences of Pragmatism*, is the product of Rorty's years as a MacArthur Prize Fellow (1981–1986), which "made it easy for me to branch out into new areas of reading and writing." The essays that make up the book were originally delivered as lectures at University College, London, and Trinity College, Cambridge. Their general theme is announced by the epigraph of the book, taken from Milan Kundera's *The Art of the Novel* : "The art born as the echo of God's laughter, the art that created the fascinating imaginative realm where no one owns the truth, and everyone has the right to be understood." The title *Contingency, Irony, and Solidarity* refers to the centrality of chance in human affairs, the recognition that no one individual's sense of truth is "intrinsic" or self-sufficient, and the striving of humanity towards "fellow feeling" through the imagination. "The process of coming to see other human beings as 'one of us' rather than as 'them' . . . is a task not for theory, but for genres such as ethnography, the journalist's report, the comic book, the docudrama, and especially the novel," reads the introduction. "That is why the novel, the movie, and the TV program have, gradually but steadily, replaced the sermon and the treatise as the principal vehicles or moral change and progress."

The ideal of what Rorty calls in a key essay "Self-Creation and Affiliation" is exemplified notably by Nietzsche and Proust, "paradigm nonmetaphysicians" who succeeded in transforming themselves and their universe—Nietzsche by reacting against and redescribing people whom he met in books, Proust by recreating people whom he had met in the flesh.

Rorty singles out George Orwell as the type of compassionate novelist (akin to Dickens) who brings us in touch with the suffering of human beings we might not otherwise get to know. Among other writers admired by Rorty are Henry James and Vladimir Nabokov, who make us aware of the cruelty that civilized people perpetrate on each other. Julian Bell observed in the *Times Literary Supplement* in 1989 that human life "is, for Richard Rorty's purposes, a never completed effort at self-creation. Everyone tries to weave a coherent story about what he is out of the materials that chance has given him. From the world-transforming terms of the genius to the 'private poem' of the lunatic, all are searching for a personal symbolic order. . . . For an intellectual such as himself, the principal materials to hand are books"

As Kai Nielsen noted in his book *After the Demise of the Tradition*: "Richard Rorty has had a not inconsiderable influence both within philosophy and in certain intellectual circles outside of philosophy." In 1982 a series of interdisciplinary seminars centered on *Philosophy and the Mirror of Nature* was conducted by the School of Economic and Social Studies of the University of East Anglia; the papers were published eight years later in *Reading Rorty*, allowing for an assessment also of his subsequent writings. Alan R. Malachowski, the editor, characterized Rorty's criticism of the traditions of philosophy as "peculiarly rich." Participants in the symposia found his ideas challenging, but a number felt that he misrepresented the philosophers whom he opposed. Bernard Williams was skeptical about his ideal of a nonprofessional philosopher, "a new Renaissance polymath doing literary criticism in the morning, history in the afternoon, and doing them in the spirit of Nietzschean gaiety." Reacting to Rorty's idea of the humanities as mental release, Michael Fischer, the only literature professor in the group, likened Rorty's conception of literary culture to "a visit to a pre-school playroom." Rorty in turn has written that literary theorists are in danger of taking philosophy too seriously. One traditional function of the philosopher that he has served is that of gadfly.

Rorty was married to Amelie Oksenberg from 1954 to 1972, when they were divorced. In 1972 he married Rosalind Varney. He has a son, from the first marriage, and a daughter and a son, from the second, to whom his books are variously dedicated. The University of Virginia continues to be his academic base, and he lives in Charlottesville, but has had numerous visiting professorships in America and Europe. Apart from his controversial books, he is a prolific writer and reviewer for philosophical and literary journals, and a contributor to published symposia.

PRINCIPAL WORKS: Philosophy and the Mirror of Nature, 1979; Consequences of Pragmatism, 1982; Contingency, Irony, and Solidarity, 1989; Objectivity, Relativism, and Truth, 1991; Essays on Heidegger and Others, 1991; Rorty and Pragmatism: The Philosopher Responds to His Critics, 1995. *As editor*—The Linguistic Turn: Recent Essays in Linguistic Method, 1967; (with E. Lee and A. Mourelatos) Exegesis and Argument: Studies in Greek Philosophy Presented to Gregory Vlastos, 1973; (with J. Schneewind and Q. Skinner) Philosophy in History: Essays in the Historiography of Philosophy, 1984. *As contributor*—The Tanner Lectures on Human Values, 13, 1992.

ABOUT: Bhashkar, R. Philosophy and the Idea of Freedom, 1991; Contemporary Authors New Revision Series 9, 1983; Klepp, L. S. "Every Man a Philosopher-King" in New York Times Magazine December 2, 1990; Kolenda, K. Rorty's Humanistic Pragmatism, 1990; Reading Rorty, (ed.) Malachowski, Alan 1990; Nielsen, Kai. After the Demise of the Tradition, 1991; Who's Who in America, 1992–93. *Periodicals*—America February 19, 1983; American Philosophical Quarterly January 1984; British Journal of Aesthetics October 1990; Chicago Review 38, 1992; Clio Winter 1984; Summer 1989; Critical Inquiry Winter 1990; International Philosophical Quarterly September 1983; June 1984; Journal of Aesthetics and Art Criticism Summer 1986; Spring 1989; Journal of Philosophy December 1990; Los Angeles Times Book Review December 1982; Modern Language Notes December 1990; New Republic October 17, 1981; New York Review of Books March 19, 1981; April 28, 1983; New York Times Review of Books March 19, 1981; April 28, 1983; New York Times Book Review June 6, 1991; Partisan Review 51, 1984; 58, 1991; Raritan Summer 1990; Times Literary Supplement December 26, 1980; July 15, 1983; December 6, 1985; January 7, 1986; November 24–30, 1989.

ROSE, PHYLLIS (October 26, 1942–   ), American biographer, literary critic, and essayist, was born in New York City, one of the three children of a teacher, Minnie (Selesko), and Eli Davidoff, an attorney. She received a B.A. from Radcliffe College in 1964, an M.A. from Yale University in 1965, and a Ph.D. from Harvard University in 1970. In 1965 she married Mark

PHYLLIS ROSE

Rose. She began her teaching career as an instructor at Yale in 1969, became an assistant professor of English at Wesleyan University the same year, and since 1981 has taught at Wesleyan as a full professor. Her marriage to Mark Rose, from whom she has a son, Ted, ended in divorce in 1975.

Rose first came to literary prominence with the 1978 publication of her widely acclaimed biography of Virginia Woolf, *Woman of Letters*. Published three years after her divorce, the book was inspired by a rereading of Woolf's novels, and a rethinking of Woolf's role as a feminist. In a thought-provoking preface to the book, Rose comments that previous biographies of Woolf have made too much of her illness, intellectual aloofness, and suicide—too little of her great artistic talent, resilience, productivity, and "emotional resonance." Exploring Woolf's novels, letters, and diaries, with a focus on the novelist's inner life, Rose clarifies the difficulties Woolf faced in discovering her identity while liberating herself from the Victorian mores of her patriarchal family. As Rose puts it, Woolf's "core of strength and vulnerablility, of self-containment and resentment, of charm and anger," made her in some ways "the most sophisticated spokeswoman that feminism has ever had . . . To examine her life is to examine the dynamics of a miracle."

While several reviewers noted that the biography made no attempt to reveal new facts about Woolf's life, almost all were impressed by Rose's fresh approach to her subject. She "illustrates the problems still facing women of achievement,"

Frank Kermode wrote in the *New York Review of Books*; her book is "admirable," her view of Woolf "extremely sympathetic and balanced." Margaret Drabble, in the *New Statesman*, concurred, finding in Rose's portrait "considerable insight" into Woolf's attitude to herself as a woman. The reviewer for *Publishers Weekly* commented: "Rose . . . succeeds brilliantly . . . thinks clearly, evaluates perceptively and writes well. Her engrossing study explores and explains Woolf's deepest concerns, the inner conflicts and attitudes that shape her works as they mirror her life."

In her next book, *Parallel Lives: Five Victorian Marriages*, Rose returned to a theme she had touched on briefly while writing about Woolf—that to some extent we all impose a "narrative form onto our lives" and that this narrative will determine what shape our lives will take. Applying this idea to the disparate or similar narrative constructs each partner brings to a marriage, she decided to explore the unions of five notable Victorian writers (Thomas Carlyle, John Ruskin, John Stuart Mill, Charles Dickens, and George Eliot) with a focus on the changing balances of power within each union. "Happy marriages," Rose comments in a prologue, "seem to me those in which the two partners agree on the scenario they are enacting"—and in her book she warmly describes George Eliot's union with George Henry Lewes, and John Stuart Mill's with Harriet Taylor as examples. By contrast, the "unhappy marriages" of Charles Dickens, Thomas Carlyle, and John Ruskin, described in the book in equally vivid detail, seem to Rose the unfortunate consequence of "two versions of reality" that conflict.

Although some reviewers of *Parallel Lives* were critical of the author's central theme and focus, almost all were impressed by Rose's vivid storytelling. Nina Auerbach, in the *New York Times Book Review* (1983), commented that the marriages Rose describes are "told compellingly," but wished Rose had explored more about the points of view of Effie Ruskin, Harriet Tayor Mill, and Catherine Dickens. Patricia Blake, in *Time*, observed that reading *Parallel Lives*, while "not a pleasant experience," was a "compelling one"; in her opinion the Victorian giants depicted by Rose "prove too large to be contained by a single formula." She nevertheless found the book a "lively study."

Rose's next published work, *Writing of Women: Essays in a Renaissance*, is a collection of essays about women authors and their biographers. Described in *Library Journal* as a book which contains "marvelous biographical tidbits" but lacks "theoretical coherence," this work received less critical attention than the two preceding it. Catherine Bancroft noted in the *New York Times Book Review* that "Rose is finicky about biographies of writers she admires" while welcoming biographies of writers who have not previously been considered as suitable subjects. She praised the book, however, as engrossing.

In 1989 Rose published a second full-length biography, *Jazz Cleopatra*, about Josephine Baker, the black jazz dancer who became an international sensation in the 1920s and 1930s. "My interest" in Baker, Rose wrote in an article for the *New York Times*, began "when I felt my life had become predictable and boring. The only kind of music I could listen to was jazz, because I never knew where it would go next. I thought that Baker—whose moves in every sense seemed unpredictable, whose whole life seemed a jazz improvisation—was a subject I could spend time with and be psychically nourished by the contact." When Rose saw a photograph of Baker in a beaded dress, crossing her eyes and making fun of herself, she felt that here was a "vitality, spontaneity, fearlessness and joy I very much wanted to appropriate." She discovered a focus for her biography when she realized that her own late 20th-century enchantment with Baker mirrored the enthusiasm white people had felt about African-Americans in the 1920s.

In her book Rose explores Baker's celebrity in its historical and cultural context, describing the singer's rise from poverty in St. Louis to her success as a singer and dancer in Paris during the 1920s and 30s, her role as a World War II resister, and her later activities as a civil rights activist. Mavis Gallant, writing in the *New Republic*, commented that "Rose's sections on Europe's discovery of black American dancers and musicians . . . are among the most rewarding in her book." *Jazz Cleopatra* received high praise from Jim Haskins, who commented in the *Los Angeles Times Book Review* that it was "the finest and most insightful book that has yet been written on the phenomenon that was Josephine Baker," and from Ishmael Reed, who wrote in the *Washington Post Book World* that anyone "interested in an artist who had a significant impact upon the world's culture" would find the book "a must." But the book was not universally applauded. James R. Mellow wrote in the *New York Times Book Review* (1989) that "much of the commentary is intriguing, but it tends to create the suspicion that Baker's long career as an entertainer lacks substance enough for a serious study. At times, particularly in the earlier chapters of the book, Baker simply disappears behind the sociological scenery." And Lynn Garafola, in the *Nation*, found the book a "failure on nearly every count . . . Revealing

only a superficial grasp of Baker's many worlds . . . this . . . is an embarrassment to a scholar of Rose's reputation. . . . She gives jazz hardly a mention . . . seems indifferent" to the role of race in Baker's life, treats Baker's childhood poverty superficially, and above all doesn't understand Baker's art.

Rose has said about her approach to writing biography that she places the facts of people's lives into new contexts; she uses a theoretical or intellectual construct and tends to emphasize issues in her subjects' lives that have been important in her own.

Her personal approach extends also into her writing of essays, a collection of which has been published in her most recent book, *Never Say Goodbye*. While some reviewers of Rose's essay collection have delighted in her insight and wit, others have commented that she is at her best as a biographer. Steven Slosberg, in the *New York Times Book Review* observed that when Rose "removes herself from an essay—pieces about lawsuits and literature and about a woman who abets the assassination of a Nicaraguan general come to mind—her commentary is more driven and satisfying."

Rose has been awarded several honors and awards. Her first book, *Woman of Letters*, was nominated for a National Book Award in 1978. In addition, she has received grants from the National Endowment for the Humanities, the Rockefeller Foundation, and the John Simon Guggenheim Memorial Foundation. In 1991 she married Laurent de Brunhoff, an artist and author, and went to live with him in Middletown, Connecticut.

PRINCIPAL WORKS: Woman of Letters: A Life of Virginia Woolf, 1978; Parallel Lives: Five Victorian Marriages, 1983; Writing of Women: Essays in a Renaissance, 1985; Jazz Cleopatra: Josephine Baker in Her Time, 1989; Never Say Goodbye: Essays, 1991. As editor—The Norton Book of Women's Lives, 1993.

ABOUT: Contemporary Authors 135, 1992; Rose, P. Never Say Goodbye, 1991; Who's Who in America 1992–93. *Periodicals*—Library Journal April 1, 1985; Los Angeles Times Book Review November 12, 1989; Nation February 5, 1990; New Republic November 6, 1989; New Statesman November 3, 1978; New York Review of Books November 21, 1978; New York Times March 10, 1991; New York Times Book Review November 13, 1983; June 23, 1985; November 5, 1989; Publishers Weekly March 24, 1991; Washington Post Book World October 15, 1989.

RUSS, JOANNA (February 22, 1937–),
American science fiction novelist, short story
writer, and essayist was born in New York City,
the daughter of two school teachers, Evarett I.
and Bertha (Zinner) Russ. Both of her parents
were of Jewish ancestry, and both were avid
readers. Raised in the Bronx, Russ began to write
at the age of five, receiving ample encouragement from he parents, especially her mother.
"She was the literary person," Russ recalled in an
interview with the *New York Times Book
Review* in the 1988. She credits her mother with
introducing her to literature written from the female point of view. Russ was an exceptional student, gifted in both the arts and the sciences. In
1953, during her senior year in high school, Russ
was a winner of the Westinghouse Science Talent Search. At Cornell University, where she received her B.A. in 1957, she studied literature
and writing. Vladimir Nabokov was one of her
professors there. She published her first science
fiction short story in 1959, and in 1960 earned
an M.F.A. in playwriting from the Yale School
of Drama.

In a *New York Times Book Review* interview,
Russ stated that she considers most of her work
"experiments in fiction." Although most science
fiction writers come from a science background
and develop their writing skills, Russ arrived at
science fiction from literary interests, with some
bent towards science.

Russ began her teaching career at Queensbo-
rough Community College in New York City in
1966, and has taught at Cornell, the State University of New York at Binghamton, and the
University of Colorado. Since 1977, she taught
literature and writing at the University of Washington in Seattle.

Space flight, time travel, and alternate worlds
figure prominently in much of Russ's work. Yet
her brand of science fiction bears little resemblance to that of most of her cohort, the vast majority of whom are men, and in whose stories
women—if they appear at all—are usually depicted as space-suit-clad damsels in distress.
Russ's women are strong, often aggressive, and
always complexly motivated. Like Ursula Le
Guin, a writer with whom she has often been
compared, Russ uses science fiction scenarios (in
which literally anything is possible) as a platform for the exploration of, among other things,
the nature of sexual identity, the conflict between the sexes, and the role of environment in
shaping character and awareness. In one of her
early essays, "What Can Heroines Do?—or,
Why Women Can't Write," Russ argues that female fictional characters are almost invariably
portrayed as reactive, relegated to passive roles
and awaiting the actions of men. If Russ's

JOANNA RUSS

"fictional experiments" have one overriding
goal, it is to confront the stereotype of the weak
and passive woman with female protagonists
who are strong, complex, and engaged in the
creation of their own realities.

In *Picnic on Paradise*, her first novel, Russ introduces Alyx, one of her most memorable heroines. A Mediterranean Greek woman from 1500
B.C., Alyx has rejected the sexual and economic
roles available in her own world and has chosen
to be a petty thief. One day, she is accidentally
transported four thousand years into the future
by a shadowy organization known as Trans-
Temporal. She is then assigned to lead a group
of tourists across Paradise, an ice-covered recreational planet beset by economic warfare. In
that first novel, Russ articulates a number of
themes that recur throughout her later work: the
necessity of acting in and for the present, the
complex dynamics in the struggle between men
and women, the ever-present conflict between
the self and others, and the challenge of creating
one's own life and facing one's own death in a
universe without God. Russ chronicles the further adventures of her heroine in the collection
Alyx, which includes short stories, a novella, and
the novel *Picnic on Paradise*.

Russ' former teacher Vladimir Nabokov is one
of the dedicatees of her second novel, *And Chaos
Died*. Jai Vedh, the novel's protagonist, is an
Earthman shipwrecked on a planet whose inhabitants have highly developed psychic powers. As Jai learns to develop his own psychic
powers, he finds that the confusion that has always plagued him is greatly reduced. Although

he is a male protagonist (somewhat remarkable in a Russ novel), he is undoubtedly an outsider, set apart by his homosexuality and his disgust with the decadent and materialistic society on Earth. One of the principal themes of *And Chaos Died* is the contrast between matter and spirit, and how people have so often made the former antagonistic toward the latter.

Russ won her first Nebula Award in 1972 for the short story "When It Changed." The story is set on Whileaway, a future world on which all males have fallen prey to a mysterious sex-linked plague, leaving a population consisting entirely of women and girls. It was included in Harlan Ellison's collection *Again, Dangerous Visions.*

The future world of Whileaway appears again in *The Female Man,* Russ's third and best-known novel. Steeped in controversy since its publication, the novel has served as a rallying cry for feminists of various stripes. Essentially plotless, the novel is an extended meditation on the question of female identity. The reader of *The Female Man* is presented with five different points of view, each of which offers trenchant commentary on the lives of women. All of the voices belong to women, and four of them have names beginning with the letter "J." Janet, the protagonist of the story "When It Changed," lives on all-female Whileaway. Joanna hails from a contemporary Earth society much like America in the late 1960s. Jeannie lives in an alternate present-day Earth, one where the depression never ended and World War II has yet to take place. Jael is from a future world on which the battle of the sexes has escalated into full-scale open warfare. Each of these four, linked as they are (one even has the same first name as the author), are really different manifestations of the same woman. In addition to the four "J" characters, there is one omniscient narrator, whose point of view encompasses and blends all the voices into the whole, which makes up the universe of the novel.

Critical reaction to *The Female Man* spanned the gamut from hosannas to expressions of outright bewilderment. In an essay in *Science Fiction Dialogues,* June Howard discerned a new trend in imaginative literature: feminist science fiction. "The increasing influence of women writers and of what we might call women's issues on science fiction has been noticeable since 1968. Science fiction is valuable for feminists as a means of uncovering what is latent in our reality, and focusing a new kind of criticism on it." Howard deemed *The Female Man* "an important work of feminist science fiction" which "defies summary." Lyman Tower Sargent detected many of the same feminist attributes in

the novel. In an essay which appeared in the volume *Women and Utopia,* Sargent noted: "The Female Man is a strong, clear, angry statement of radical feminism stressing the damage done to women by our social arrangements. It also provides a picture of a good society, Whileaway, where there are no men."

In the *New York Times Book Review* Gerald Jonas complained that the novel "plays with a marked deck of alternative universes. . . . " Jonas claimed not to be disturbed by Russ's feminism, but only by her method of presentation. "With her obvious grasp of the biological givens and her command of so many science fiction weapons, Russ might have produced a truly provocative study of 'woman's fate,'" he wrote. "Unfortunately, she keeps slipping into the easy rhetoric of mainstream feminist tracts." Michael Goodwin, who reviewed *The Female Man* for *Mother Jones,* had perhaps the most complex reaction to the novel. After denouncing it as "not a novel" he wrote: "It's unfair, it's maddening, it's depressing. I hated it for months after I read it." Yet Goodwin conceded a year after first reading the novel, "*The Female Man* remains perfectly clear in my mind—seductive, disturbing and hateful." He concluded that its impact made the book "an important one."

On Strike Against God [not science fiction] is narrated by a middle-aged feminist English professor who details the discovery of her own lesbianism. *Village Voice* reviewer Robert Morales contended that the high quality of Russ's prose "places her in a minority within a minority of people who write fiction with a feminist consciousness—she can write."

Russ is also a notable essayist and critic. Her work has appeared regularly over the years in such journals as *Extrapolation, Science Fiction Studies,* and *Magazine of Fantasy and Science Fiction* (where she was a book reviewer from 1966 to 1979). In her book *How to Suppress Women's Writing,* Russ has taken on a subject at the very center of her intellectual concerns. Surveying the history of Western (mostly English-language) literature, she finds that men have traditionally suppressed women's art by resorting to what she labels "Glotolog" methods, that is, "Information control without direct censorship." As Russ herself notes, her study is more "a sketch of an analytic tool" than a full-fledged history of the suppression of women's art. In *Modern Fiction Studies,* Kristine Ottesen Garriagan commented: "Relatively little is original about Russ's arguments. Aside from vivid personal anecdotes, many of her examples are well worn. . . . What handsomely redeems Russ's book, however, is its wit, economy, and moral energy."

The Hidden Side of the Moon, Russ's fourth collection of short stories, brings together twenty-seven of her tales of horror, science fiction, and fantasy written between the late 1950s and the mid-1980s. Despite the abundance of science fiction and genre pieces, *Times Literary Supplement* critic Colin Greenland concluded: "Russ's domain is inner space, not outer. . . . The book opens and closes with some startling experiments in feminist autobiography. . . . In between, the collection is rich and remarkable, but rather literal in its organization." In the *New York Times Book Review*, John Clute offered high praise for one of those experiments. According to Clute, "Russ is a major writer within the science fiction genre, and beyond it."

In a detailed overview of Russ's work in *Women Worldwalkers*, the science fiction writer Samuel R. Delany notes that many of the most serious writers is the genre "consider Russ's work in one way or another a touchstone in the science fiction field. . . . By *touchstone* I mean that all of us are convinced *some* process inchoate to the writing of science fiction is occurring in Russ's work at about the highest concentration available to a currently working science fiction writer." The poet and novelist Marge Piercy shares Russ's feminist perspective, though not her bent for science fiction. In a critique of Russ's first four novels in the *American Poetry Review*, Piercy wrote: "All of Joanna Russ's novels are interesting beyond the ordinary. They ask nasty and necessary questions. . . . They offer a gallery of some of the most interesting female protagonists in current fiction, women who are rarely victims and sometimes even victors, but always engaged sharply and perceptively with their fate."

PRINCIPAL WORKS: *Novels*—Picnic on Paradise, 1968; and Chaos Died, 1970; The Female Man, 1975; We Who Are About to. . . . , 1977; The Two of Them, 1978; On Strike Against God, 1979; (with J. Tiptree) Houston, Houston, Do You Read?, 1989. *Short stories*—Alyx, 1976 (in U.K.: The Adventures of Alyx); (with J. Saxton) Womanspace: Future and Fantasy Stories and Art, 1981; The Zanzibar Cat, 1983; The Hidden Side of the Moon, 1988. *Nonfiction*—How to Suppress Women's Writing, 1983; Magic Mommas, Trembling Sisters, Puritans and Perverts: Feminist Essay, 1985. *Juvenile*—Kittatinny: A Tale of Magic, 1978.

ABOUT: Barr, M. and Smith, N. (eds.) Women and Utopia: Critical Interpretations, 1983; Bleiler, E. (ed.) Science Fiction Writers: Critical Studies of the Major Authors from the Early Nineteenth Century to the Present Day, 1982; Contemporary Authors New Revision Series 11, 1984; Contemporary Literary Criticism 15, 1980; Dictionary of Literary Biography 8, 1981; Palumbo, D. (ed.) Erotic Universe: Sexuality and Fantastic Literature, 1986; Weedman, J. (ed.) Women Worldwalkers: New Dimensions of Science and Fantasy, 1985; Wolfe, G. (ed.) Science Fiction Dialogues, 1982. *Periodicals*—American Poetry Review May–June 1977; Modern Fiction Studies Summer 1984; Mother Jones August 1976; New York Times Book Review May 4, 1975; January 31, 1988; Times Literary Supplement May 12, 1989; Village Voice April 15, 1981.

RYBCZYNSKI, WITOLD (March 1, 1943–) Canadian writer and architect, writes: "I was born in the city of Edinburgh in 1943. My parents, who had left Poland in 1939, were both serving in the Polish Free Forces stationed in Scotland. They stayed in England after the end of the war, and emigrated to Canada in 1953, settling in the province of Quebec. My primary and secondary schooling in England and Canada was entrusted to Jesuits; I have been told that it shows. I studied architecture at McGill University in Montreal, where I returned to teach in 1973, specializing in the design of minimum-cost housing for developing countries. This work absorbed me for fifteen years and took me to Mexico, Central America, Africa, India, Southeast Asia, and China. The son of central Europeans in Britain, an English-speaker in predominantly French Quebec, a white Westerner in the Third World—I naturally learned to look at things as an outsider. Whatever I have to contribute as a writer owes much to this vantage point.

"I started writing in 1977, almost by chance. I had written an article critical of the small-is-beautiful movement for a small Californian journal, and an American editor asked if I would be interested to expand it into a book. To my surprise, and perhaps his, I said yes. The result was *Paper Heroes: A Review of Appropriate Technology*, and three years later *Taming the Tiger: The Struggle to Control Technology*. These books were not widely reviewed and found only a small audience but I was satisfied—I was becoming a writer.

"It is trite to say that a single event has changed one's life, but in my case it's true. My book, *Home: A Short History of an Idea*, a chronicle of the evolution of domestic comfort, was a critical and a commercial success. Nominated for the Governor General's Literary Award and the L.A. Times Book Prize, and a winner of the QSPELL Prize and the Prix Paul-Henri Lapointe in Quebec, it has been translated into nine languages. *Home* not only brought me readers but also the opportunity to publish essays and reviews. In 1988 I became architecture critic for *Wigwag*, a new American monthly general in-

WITOLD RYBCZYNSKI

terest magazine (which ceased publication in February 1991), and my essays began to appear regularly in the *New York Times*, the *New York Review of Books*, and the *Alantic Monthly*; I also began to review for the *Washington Post*, the *New York Times*, *Newsday*, and the *Times Literary Supplement*. *The Most Beautiful House in the World*, an architectural autobiography that describes the design and construction of the house that my wife, Shirley Hallam, and I built in rural Quebec, appeared in 1989. It was at this time, I believe, that I began to think of myself as a writer who architected, rather than as an architect who wrote.

"I am not sure how I would categorize my writing. It is certainly nonfiction, but with a strong autobiographical bent. Scholarly sometimes, but never academic. It is intended to inform, challenge, and entertain the reader. If I say that I admire the writing of J. H. Huizinga, V. S. Naipaul, Jonathan Raban, John Lukacs, Paul Theroux, Annie Dillard, and Zbigniew Herbert, I suppose I'm also saying that the act of writing, as well as the subject, is important to me. I agree with Milan Kundera, who has been quoted as saying that the writer's purpose is not to preach a truth but to discover a truth. All my books begin with that premise: I know something, but I don't understand it. Writing is, for me, a way of trying to fathom the world.

"I continue to teach, although on a reduced scale, and I devote most of my time to writing, of which I do a great deal. Although my subject is often related to architecture, buildings, and cities, it seems periodically to expand into other areas of culture and everyday life. *Waiting for the Weekend* (1991) is a history of leisure and free time. A collection of my essays titled *Looking Around: A Journey Through Architecture* appeared at the end of 1992.

Once a full-time architect and teacher who did some writing on the side, Witold Rybczynski has become a full-time writer who does some architecture and teaching on the side. "I think I'm a better writer than an architect," he told an interviewer from the Canadian magazine *Enroute* in 1990. "By temperament I'm not suited to be an architect. To have to deal with so many people. A writer needs only an editor and he's your ally." Although he had a strong interest in writing during his years at Loyola College High School in Montreal, he felt obliged to train for a profession. "The notion of being a writer wasn't an option," he told *Publishers Weekly*. "It wasn't something I considered in terms of a career. A career meant going to university—essentially, it meant a professional career." He attributes this feeling, at least in part, to being the son of immigrant parents who were themselves professionals. His father, Witold K. Rybczynski, was an engineer, and his mother, Anna (Hoffman) Rybczynski, was a lawyer. Being the son of immigrant parents, he noted, "There's a certain pressure on you to capitalize on all this sacrifice that has put you through high school or university."

His early book *Taming the Tiger* is a historical examination of social attitudes toward technology. Rybczynski detects the roots of a widespread contemporary misunderstanding of the very nature of technology in the Luddites and other "machine-bashing" movements of the industrial revolution, as well as in the attitudes of such 19th-century writers as William Morris and Henry David Thoreau. "The perception of technology as a *thing* rather than as an *activity* is common enough in our own culture," Rybczynski observes. Viewing technology as a "thing," he argues, breeds not only fear, mistrust, and oversimplification, but tends to obfuscate any discussion about technological innovation by shrouding the process itself in mystery. "Technology begins not with the tool," he writes, "but with the human imagination, and the acts of imagining, inventing, and using tools and machines are human acts. . . . Moreover, since technology is a *human* activity, it is thus part of human culture and hence reflects the human preoccupations of its time."

In the foreword to his book *Home: A Short History of an Idea*, Rybczynski reports that lacunae in his own education impelled him to investigate the history of domestic comfort. "During the six years of my architectural education the subject of comfort was mentioned only once. . . . It was curious omission from an otherwise rigorous curriculum; one would have thought that comfort was a crucial issue in preparing for the architectural profession, like justice in law, or health in medicine." *Home* is part history and part polemic, with "comfort" serving as a unifying motif throughout. In tracing the evolution of domestic comfort from the Middle Ages to the present day, he takes careful stock not only of architectural design and central heating, but also of such amenities as furniture, clothing, and interior ornamentation. "The first use of 'comfort' to signify a level of domestic amenity is not documented until the eighteenth century," he notes. Sir Walter Scott and Jane Austen, two English novelists, were among the first writers to use "comfort" and "comfortable" in the sense these words are now understood.

As a polemic, *Home*'s overriding objective is to upbraid modernist architecture for neglecting people's desire for comfort. While the idea of comfort may have been slow to catch on, by the 19th century it was the sine qua non of the bourgeois household. Many modernist architects of the 20th century, in a rebellion against bourgeois tradition, sought to streamline exteriors and eliminate clutter and ornamentation from interiors. Among the most eminent of these modernist architects was the Swiss-born Le Corbusier, who conceived of the house as "a machine for living in." It is Le Corbusier (the pseudonym of Charles-Édouard Jeanneret) who is the main target of Rybczynski's attack. Of particular interest to Rybczynski is Le Corbusier's austere "New Spirit" pavilion, a prototype home that was unveiled at the 1925 Exposition Internationale des Arts Décoratifs et Industriels Modernes in Paris. Coming down squarely in favor of comfort, Rybczynski writes in the concluding chapter of *Home*, "What is needed is a reexamination not of bourgeois styles, but of bourgeois traditions." This would mean, among other things, "returning to house layouts that offer more privacy and intimacy. . . . What is needed are many more small rooms . . . to conform to the range and variety of leisure activities in the modern home."

Reviewing the book in the *New Yorker*, John Lukacs noted that, compared to other recent critiques of modernism, "*Home: A Short History of an Idea* is serious, historically minded, and exquisitely readable. It is a triumph of intelligence." In the *New York Times Book Review*, William Gass called *Home* "a book of great interest and instruction." According to

Gass, "Rybczynski is particularly good at describing the effects, and sometimes the surprising ineffectuality, of invention. . . . " Nonetheless, Gass felt that Rybczynski's "malice against the 'modern'" had pointed "his book in the wrong direction." Gass wrote, "The book's treatment of its arch-villain, Le Corbusier is hardly fair." In the *New York Review of Books*, Diane Johnson wrote, "His . . . aim is to rebuke modern architecture—modernism, which we might have thought was a dead horse anyway. . . . "

In *Waiting for the Weekend*, a philosophical-historical inquiry, Rybczynski examines the role and meaning of leisure in human affairs, and looks at various ways in which societies have divided the cycles of work and leisure. Noting that the day, the month, and the year are all (originally, at least) based on natural cycles, he asks, "What does a week measure? Nothing. At least, nothing visible. No natural phenomenon occurs every seven days. . . . The week is an artificial, man-made interval." While the seven-day week has comparatively ancient roots, the idea of the weekend, particularly as a two-day period of sanctioned leisure, is of modern origin. In the *Oxford English Dictionary* Rybczynski discovers that the word "week-end" first appeared in the print in an English magazine in 1879.

Much of *Waiting for the Weekend* is devoted to a consideration of how people conceive of and use this abundant "free time." "This is a vast topic," Eugen Weber wrote in the *Times Literary Supplement*. "Rybczynski handles it by focusing on the week, specifically on the tail that has come to wag it: 'how the weekend became the chief temporal institution of the modern age.'" Although he had specific quibbles with Rybczynski's analysis of leisure, Weber urged readers, "Buy the book. . . . It will fit fine into a weekend." In the *New York Times Book Review*, Laura Shapiro suggested that *Waiting for the Weekend* "should have been packaged with a porch swing and a glass of lemonade." Like Weber, she found that Rybczynski had not takes sufficient account of all those unable to benefit from increased leisure, particularly women. Shapiro's major criticism of the work, however, was that Rybczynski "puts forth no major argument here, no unusual insights, not even much of a thesis." In the *New York Times*, Christopher Lehmann-Haupt, on the other hand, remarked that when "Rybczynski is puzzled by something, he starts asking questions so obvious that few people have thought to ask them before."

Looking Around is a collection of essays on various architectural topics. Many of the essays originally appeared in such publications as *Wigwag*, the *New York Review of Books*, and *Art & Antiques*. In *Maclean's*, Pamela Young wrote: "Many architects begin their careers designing houses and other small projects; the successful ones generally move onto large, lucrative commissions. But the home has remained Rybczynski's primary interest." In 1990, for example, Rybczynski and his colleague Avi Friedman introduced the Grow Home, an inexpensive town house. Concerning the essays, Young remarked, "Most of the pieces in *Looking Around* are well-researched and thoughtful, but a few have a dashed-off quailty."

Although he has devoted an entire book to the uses and meaning of leisure, Rybczynski himself admits to having no hobbies—other than reading a great deal—and has little interest in taking vacations. On vacation, he told *Publishers Weekly*, "I don't know what to do with myself. I guess I fit the profile of a workaholic." But for Rybczynski, work itself is a recreation. In *The Most Beautiful House in the World*, a book he describes as "architecture masquerading as autobiography," he tells how he built a weekend house for himself and his wife in rural Quebec. Begun as simply a shed for his boat, it grew in a leisurely fashion—like the book itself, which ranges over a variety of subjects literary, architectural, historical, mythical. The result was a house that for him at least is the most beautiful in the world, reminding readers, as Martin Filler observed in the *New York Times Review of Books* "of what a house can be as wish-fulfillment of our deepest feeling about life."

PRINCIPAL WORKS: Low Cost Technology Options for Sanitation: A State-of-the-Art Review and Annotated Bibliography, 1979; Paper Heroes: A Review of Appropriate Technology, 1980; Taming the Tiger: The Struggle to Control Technology, 1983; Home: A Short History of an Idea, 1986; The Most Beautiful House in the World, 1989; Waiting for the Weekend, 1991; Looking Around: A Journey Through Architecture, 1992; A Place for Art: The Architecture of the National Gallery of Canada, 1992.

ABOUT: Contemporary Authors 110, 1984; Who's Who in America 1992–1993. *Periodicals*—En Route October 1990; Maclean's November 30, 1992; New York Review of Books December 4, 1986; February 1, 1990; New York Times August 8, 1991; New York Times Book Review August 3, 1986; May 21, 1989; August 18, 1991; New Yorker September 1, 1986; Publishers Weekly July 25, 1991; Times Literary Supplement December 20, 1991.

SAFIRE, WILLIAM (December 17, 1929–), American journalist, essayist, and novelist, was born in New York City, the youngest of the three sons of Ida Panish Safir and Oliver Safir, a successful thread manufacture. (Safire added a final vowel to his name in the 1950s to make spelling match pronunciation.) When he was four years old, his father died of lung cancer, leaving the family pinched but not poor. According to his older brother Leonard, young William was "bounced around a lot" as a boy; he lived through some "tough times." But his widowed mother's teaching that what her sons had in the world was "blood and friendship" made a strong impression. Safire is known for being steadfastly and unwaveringly loyal to friends. He began dreaming of becoming a writer at an early age. When he was ten, he started sending "long and funny letters" to his brother in the army. At the Bronx High School of Science and later at Syracuse University, he wrote essays and short stories for the school papers. Safire had entered Syracuse on a scholarship, but two years later he dropped out to work for Tex McCrary, a columnist for the New York *Herald Tribune*, a host on a radio show, and a dabbler in Republican politics. Bill ran into McCrary, his brother Leonard has said, "at the impressionable age when fathers normally help sons."

In 1952 McCrary, having decided to promote Dwight D. Eisenhower for the presidency, approached Safire with a suggestion: how would he like to volunteer to head the Madison Square Garden rally to bring Eisenhower home from Europe to run for president? Safire replied that he was already working twelve to fourteen hours a day, but McCrary, a tough, demanding taskmaster, won him over. Safire worked on the rally, and as he was to say later, the job made him realize that "This is what it's all about. From what I could see, you could get a bunch of people together, whip up the press and have some impact." It was his initiation into politics.

In 1959 Safire met Richard M. Nixon in Moscow. By that time he had become a public relations agent for All-State Properties, a company that had built a typical American split-level house for a trade-show exhibit. Nixon, then the vice president, was the trade show's official host in Moscow, and was taking Nikita Khrushchev around the fairground. Safire managed to get the two into the kitchen his split-level house, take photographs of the two leaders discussing American kitchens. His first impression of Nixon, an impression that has never left him, was that the then vice president was "terrific . . . He really stood up to Khrushchev. He decided then and there to work for Nixon for president, and although Nixon lost the 1960

WILLIAM SAFIRE

presidential race and subsequently a gubernatorial race in California, Safire continued to regard him as the best hope for a Republican White House comeback. During the 1968 presidential campaign Safire took a job as speechwriter for Spiro Agnew, and for several years thereafter was a senior speechwriter for Nixon at the White House. He resigned this job in 1973, When the Watergate scandal broke, to take a job as Washington, D.C., columnist for the *New York Times*. Soon afterward he began writing an "On Language" column for the *New York Times Sunday Magazine*.

Safire, who regards himself as a libertarian conservative, was completing *Before the Fall: An Inside View of the Pre-Watergate White House* when Nixon resigned. He had some difficulty getting the book published and cheerfully acknowledges that he could have won "an unpopularity contest at the *Times* for saying that "Watergate was no big deal, that everybody did it." Fond of describing his role as commentator as "the greatest job in the world," allowing him the freedom to say anything he wants, he was undoubtedly neither surprised nor dismayed when *Before the Fall* received mixed reviews. Walter Clemons, in *Newsweek*, found the book "a puffy, lightweight concoction, served up for the faithful," and complained of Safire's defense of Nixon. In the *Atlantic*, Richard Todd gave the book credit for contributing interesting data on the Nixon administration's penchant for thinking of the world as "us against them," while Daniel Schorr, in the *New York Times Book Review*, concluded: "If Nixon gets the kind of under-

standing he wants, this book will surely have helped a lot."

In an interview he gave for *Playboy* in 1992, Safire aired his views on Watergate, repeating many of the opinions he had expressed earlier in his columns for the *Times*. "Nixon," says Safire, "made some very terrible blunders," but the wiretapping he was accused of "took place under Roosevelt, Kennedy and Johnson" first. "The break-in of Ellsberg's doctor's office was a criminal offense. It was wrong" he continued, but "not unprecedented . . . I think the facts speak very loudly that the Kennedy Justice Department bugged and tapped Martin Luther King, that the Johnson Adminstration carried out a plan for the containment and repression of dessent . . . I just want to make two points here. One, everybody did it is no excuse. But there's also no excuse for denying that everybody did it. And two, I've denounced the intrusion into personal privacy in the Nixon years. I've denounced it preceding it, and I've denounced it subsequent to it . . . I just don't think you can say it was invented by Nixon."

Safire's political books and columns continue to arouse debate and controversy. Some commentators, like William Greider in the *Washington Post*, decry the author's penchant for expressing "outrageous opinions," while conceding that Safire is "sometimes persuasive and always provocative." A more partisan reader, William F. Buckley Jr., wrote in *New York* that Safire's Op-Ed pieces in the *Times* are "sassy, entirely self-assured, tough, great fun to read . . . He is, I think, entirely fearless." Paul Gray, in *Time*, noted that Safire's twice-a-week columns "continue to display reportorial zeal and refreshing unpredictability." It was on the basis of his columns on Bert Lance, a close associate of President Jimmy Carter, that Safire received the Puletzer Prize for distinguished commentary in 1978.

The author's books on language, most of them collections of his "On Language" columns for the *New York Times Magazine*, have aroused less controversy—a majority of reviewers finding Safire's love of language contagious and his comments stimulating and entertaining. David Thomas observed in his review of *I Stand Corrected*, in the *Christan Science Monitor*, that "Safire may be the closest we have to a clearinghouse for hearing, seeing, and testing how we're doing with the language."

Safire has also written two novels. His first, *Full Disclosure*, depicts a fictional American president who has become disabled from a bump on the head. At issue are presidential politics and the possible abuse of the Twenty-fifth

Amendment concerning disabled presidents. The book was praised by many for its entertainment value, derided by others for being cynical and long-winded. John Kenneth Galbraith, in the *New York Times* noted that Safire was "casual in his economics" but brilliant in depicting people who are "sharply and distinctively etched as to speech, political style and personal behavior. They are always interesting, they are frequently funny, and most are deeply unattractive." Safire's second novel, *Freedom*, about Lincoln's political role during the early Civil War years, was criticized for being overlong and paying too little attention, as C. Vann Woodward put it in the *New York Review of Books*, "to the impact of slavery and the complexities of race." In the *New York Times* (1987), William McFeely complained that Safire "sometimes accepts shopworn stereotypes . . . where a fresh novelist's eye would have been welcome." Other reviewers, however, praised the book. Walter Shapiro, in *Time*, judged it "sprawling and ungainly but nonetheless fascinating."

The First Dissident: The Book of Job in Today's Politics reflects Safire's lifelong fascination with the man who challenged God's "moral mismanagement of the universe." Safire writes: "This puzzling and infuriating biblical character has haunted my life." As he sees it, the message of the Book of Job is "not that we should accept the dictates of Fate, but rather that we should object to Authority's injustice or unconcern, and assert our morality as best we can." The author of the *Book of Job*, "Poet-Job," was being "irreverent and daringly subversive"; he was in fact the first dissident. Safire views the moment when Job finally submits to God's will as neither a surrender nor an act of patient resignation but an affirmation that confrontation can lead to real contact between master and subject, and can thus inspire leaders and free people everywhere to discuss their political differences. He writes: "You may or may not find the answer by demanding to know, but you will surely never find the answer by fearing to ask." Safire did solid research for the book, citing biblical scholars who question the authenticity of the happy ending (Job being rewarded with new riches) to bolster his own speculation that Poet-Job may have bowed to the wishes of ancient editors who wanted to repress the book's message of dissidence in order to appease popular religious sentiment.

Nicholas Lemann, in the *New York Times* in 1992, found Safire's depiction of Job as a rebel more convincing than his idea that the *Book of Job* has "specific political application today . . . His central message . . . doesn't seem to have

risen inexorably from his reading of the Book of Job, but rather to be something he already believed and sought biblical support for." Concurring, *Newsweek*'s Kenneth Woodward judged the book "sometimes wise and frequently witty" but hardly a guide for voters and politicians in Washington.

Safire lives with his British-born wife Helene, a jewelry designer, and their two Bernese mountain dogs in a Georgian house in Chevy Chase, Maryland. Their children, Mark and Annabel, have left home to pursue their separate careers. Known as a charming and gracious host, Safire continues to relish his chosen role as maverick and provocateur. Speaking of the meaning of his life, he said, "I think I was put here to object, to cry, to prod, to challenge, to educate myself and to teach as much as I can . . . I think I've been given a fantastic opportunity and a great forum to open up some minds and to go against some grains and to share the pleasures of contrarianism."

PRINCIPAL WORKS: *Nonfiction*—The Relations Explosion, 1963; (with M. Loeb) Plunging into Politics, 1964; The New Language of Politics, 1968 (3rd. published as Safire's Political Dictionary, 1978; revised as Safire's New Political Dictionary, 1993); Before the Fall: An Inside View of the Pre-Watergate White House, 1975; On Language, 1980; Safire's Washington, 1980; What's the Good Word?, 1982; (with Leonard Safir) Good Advice, 1982; I Stand Corrected, 1984; Take My Word for It, 1986; You Could Look It Up, 1988; Language Maven Strikes Again, 1990; Words of Wisdom, 1990; Coming to Terms, 1991; The First Dissident: The Book of Job in Today's Politics, 1992. *Novels*—Full Disclosure, 1977; Freedom, 1987.

ABOUT: Contemporary Authors New Revision Series 31, 1990; Contemporary Literary Criticism 10, 1979; Who's Who in America 1992–1993. *Periodicals*—Atlantic July 1975; Christian Science Monitor December 31, 1984; New York Times Book Review February 23, 1975; December 21–28, 1992; New York Review of Books September 24, 1987; New York Times June 12, 1977; August 23, 1987, November 5, 1992; Playboy October 1992; Newsweek March 3, 1975; November 9, 1992; Time February 12, 1990.

SAHGAL, NAYANTARA (PANDIT) (May 10, 1927–), Indian novelist and journalist, writes: "I was born in Allahabad, in what was then British India, and my family was actively involved in the nonviolent civil disobedience campaigns to free India from British rule, a fact that made politics the central focus of my consciousness as a child. I grew up in an environment where political happenings illumined and intensified whatever went on around us, for it

NAYANTARA SAHGAL

was a time when every issue was a political issue, political events merged with private lives, and personal and political fates were inextricably bound. My first book, an autobiography called *Prison and Chocolate Cake*, published in 1954, was a recollection of this childhood, of life in a family of rebels against empire who had to spend much of their time away from home, at work or in jail, and a father who died in 1944 of his last imprisonment under the British.

"I did not set out to write 'political' fiction. I have no ideology except a vague sort that feels uncomfortable with title and privilege, with kings, queens, and political dynasties. I have used political settings and events in my novels because these happen to be the outer focal points that trigger my imagination, and also because I think we gain or lose significance in our relationship to events. It has been natural for me to try and trace in human terms the implications of what happens to us politically. And besides, politics was for so long dictated by the colonial regime's view of us that I have found it satisfying, artistically and personally, to redress the balance by giving it Indian expression and interpretation.

"Freedom in all its forms, especially the uses and misuses of power that deprive people of it at the national or domestic level, remains a continuing awareness with me, both in my newspaper commentary and in novels that reflect the idealism of an emergent nation and record its progressive decay and destruction. As part of this commitment I was for several years a vice president of the People's Union for Civil Liber-

ties, founded in 1977, to create an awareness of human rights in the country and provide suitable help and support when these are violated.

"I prefer to think of myself as having a sense of history rather than politics, which to my mind is the ancient and culturally complex mix that has gone into the making of every Indian. I am interested in the kind of people this has made us and the qualities of character it has fostered. Passivity, for example, may be a strength and an active choice among people who live where invasion and occupation have been the pattern, because it may be their best chance of remaining whole. The influence of Hinduism on character interests me, too, for though we are not all Hindus, it is the dominant religion and for good or ill it is responsible for the social and psychological atmosphere we all live in.

"If I am not gender-conscious in an obvious sense, it may be because my upbringing took equality entirely for granted. It was the men in my family who were feminists, urging the women to step out and fulfill their potential, so that two of them achieved international political stature, one as a prime minister, one as a diplomat and first woman president of the U.N. General Assembly. This may be why my fictional women are stronger and fitter for battle than my men, and have to be, to survive in a society where the cult of virtue (female) and honour (male) still prevails, and domestically it is still a man's world.

"I went to schools in India and to Wellesley College in the United States where I took a degree in history. During a research scholarship at the Radcliffe (now Bunting) Institute, Cambridge, Massachusetts, I wrote a study of Indira Gandhi's political style, published as *Indira Gandhi: Her Road to Power*. As a Fellow of the Woodrow Wilson International Center for Scholars, Washington, D.C., I wrote *Rich Like Us* (Sinclair Prize for fiction in Britain, Sahitya Akademi Award in India). As a Fellow of the National Humanities Center in North Carolina I wrote *Plans for Departure* (Commonwealth Writers' Prize for Eurasia). In 1990 I was elected Foreign Honorary Member of the American Academy of Arts and Sciences, Cambridge, Massachusetts. During 1990 and 1991 I served on the jury of the Commonwealth Writers' Prize. I live in Dehra Dun, India, with my husband, E. N. Mangat Rai."

———

The "family of rebels against empire" of whom Nayantara Sahgal writes so proudly above included some of the most prominent names in modern Indian history—her mother Vijaya Lakshmi (Nehru) Pandit, who was Indian ambassador to the United States and president of the United Nations General Assembly from 1953 to 1954; her uncle Jawaharlal Nehru, a leader of India's struggle for independence and prime minister; and her cousin, Nehru's daughter, Indira Gandhi, also prime minister of India.

In her novels Nayantara Sahgal has drawn on that rich heritage and on her own active career as a journalist-observer of Indian politics. She has been especially sensitive to the condition of Indian women emerging from a rigidly confining social structure into a modern society. Her novels cover the span of 20th-century Indian history from the eve of World War I through the declining days of British imperial rule, into the stormy early years of independence and partition after 1947 and the struggle, in the last quarter of the century, to preserve democracy under threats of autocracy and bitter religious and ethnic conflicts.

As Nayantara Pandit recalls in her autobiography *Prison and Chocolate Cake*, she and her two sisters "grew up at a time when India was the stage for a great political drama, and we shall always remain a little dazzled by the performance we have seen." Their father, Ranjit Sitaram Pandit, a scholar of Sanskirt, was as determined as their activist mother that his daughters should not be educated in "the vast concentration camp," which was India as they saw it before independence. Educated, therefore, abroad, Nayantara received her B.A. from Wellesley College in 1947 and returned to India at the moment it had achieved its freedom from British rule. Fired by the idealism that Mahatma Gandhi inspired in so many millions, she looked forward to the restoration of India's "inward" as well as its outward freedom. "The survival of India's people can matter only as long as her spirit survives—" she wrote in *From Fear Set Free*, the second volume of her autobiography, "the spirit of Gandhi, and older than this, the fathomless spiritual reservoir from which he drew his faith and inspiration." But her own career ambitions emerged slowly. Her first marriage, in 1949, to a businessman, Gautam Sahgal, from which three children were born, proved unsatisfactory. They were divorced in 1967. Her husband's interests, generally conventional and apolitical, clashed with her own desire for active engagement in her country's affairs. She turned to writing as an outlet, producing two volumes of autobiography and novels that Jasbir Jain, who has written a book on her work, called "emotional autobiographies." These early novels cannot, however, be described as self-pitying or self-indulgent, and their central characters are more often men than women. Nevertheless they reflect Sahgal's increasing consciousness that the enforced passivity of women is unnatural and has no place in the new India.

From her first novel, *A Time to Be Happy*, Sahgal confronted the sweeping changes in society that political independence demanded. The prosperous Indian businessman-protagonist gives up his comfortable life in a shallow, and Anglicized Indian society to follow Gandhi and work with the poor. His decision is paralleled by the choice of an unhappily married wife of an Anglicized civil servant to leave her home and work in the rural villages. The actions of these characters represents a political ideal that is developed more fully in Sahgal's subsequent novels. *This Time of Morning* is more overtly political with its two leading male characters representing the factions in the Congress Party.

With *Storm in Chandigarh*, Sahgal emerged as a hard-hitting political novelist. Her convictions tend toward socialism, but she firmly rejects Communism which, she said in a lecture in 1978 (published in K. A. Paniker's *Indian Renaissance* in 1983) "has everywhere institutionalized authoritarianism." Chandigarh, a model city designed by Le Corbusier, is the scene of violent clashes that arose when the Punjab was divided into two states—Punjab and Hariyana. Sahgal writes in *Storm in Chandigarh*: "The map of India, once a uniform piece of territory to administer, was now a welter of separate, sensitive identities, resurrected after independence. Psychology seemed to play as important a part in understanding them as did history, geography, and economics." Sahgal dramatizes her political theme with a love story involving another unhappily married woman and the young civil servant who comes to Chandigarh on a peacemaking mission. Some reviewers found the book too heavily journalistic with passages of clumsy exposition and awkward shifts in narrative point of view. But the *Times Literary Supplement*'s reviewer conceded that though mainly "quality journalism," *Storm in Chandigarh* offered "tantalizing hints of that rarest of birds, the political novel that is both political and a novel"; and Stuart Hood, in the *Listener*, found it "a novel which handles with equal assurance the workings of politics and the mechanisms of the human heart."

Although all of these novels portray women sympathetically (even the passive, self-centered, and self-satisfied wives of the Indian business and civil service classes are seen as the products of a stifling system), her first woman protagonist did not appear until *The Day in Shadow*, in which a courageous woman leaves her selfish husband and, under the harsh terms of the divorce she is granted, must support herself and her large family. Martin Levin, in the *New York Times Book Review*, admired this enlightened, strong-willed woman, noting that Sahgal "has written no feminist polemic, but a lively explication of the Indian socio-political scene in terms of character."

A woman plays an even more important role in *A Situation in New Delhi*, in which the sister of an idealistic prime minister who has recently died becomes involved with a British journalist who is writing his biography. Around the time this novel was published, Sahgal became persona non grata in India for outspoken criticism of the authoritarian rule of Prime Minister Indira Gandhi. A longtime contributor to Indian political journals, Sahgal had often been critical of her cousin for having "fundamentally different" values from her father and his successor, Lal Bahadur Shastri. "It became obvious after 1969," Sahgal wrote in *Indira Gandhi: Her Road to Power*, "that Mrs. Gandhi, who saw herself as a humanist and a democrat, did not in any sense partake of the democratic faith her father had held and served." When Mrs. Gandhi proclaimed an emergency in 1975, she assumed complete control over the government. Elections were postponed; thousands were imprisoned without trial, and a rigid censorship was imposed. Thanks to a fellowship from the Radcliffe Institute at Harvard, Sahgal came to America in 1976. At Cambridge she wrote *Indira Gandhi's Emergence and Style*, which she later expanded into *Indira Gandhi: The Road to Power*. Especially interesting is Sahgal's account of the close bond between her mother and her brother, Nehru. Theon Wilkinson observed, in *London Magazine*: "Nayantara Sahgal is no ordinary observer; the family relationship is significant for although it does not detract from this carefully constructed and objectively researched study, it explains the vehemence with which she expresses some of her views and the touching glimpses behind the veils of history from letters between her mother, Mrs. Pandit, the sister of Nehru, and the great man himself."

Sahgal's later fiction has shown a maturing talent, better integrating political and narrative themes. *Rich Like Us*, set in the period of the Emergency, is an attack on the corruption of business and political interests. It has two strong women characters—the narrator, Sonali, a young Indian civil servant, and Rose, an older Englishwoman, a Cockney, married to a wealthy but now helplessly ill Indian businessman. Sonali observes with dismay the effects of the Emergency: "We knew this was no emergency. If it had been, the priorities would have been quite different. We were all taking part in a thinly disguised masquerade, preparing the stage for family rule. And we were involved in a conspiracy of silence. . . . " The real victim of that conspiracy is Rose, who is murdered when she begins to question the family's dishonest business practices. But Sonali is so disgusted by the spectacle of cruelty and violence that she escapes to the past, giving up her job to devote herself to the study of 17th-century India, in one of its most glorious and creative periods. Kate Cruise O'Brien, in the *Listener*, pronounced *Rich Like Us* "readable and startlingly intelligent," and Maria Couto, in the *Times Literary Supplement*, wrote that it "offers a cohesive and intimate portrait of the intrigues of power . . . [although] it is unable to attempt a resolution of the conflict between culture and technology."

Plans for Departure moves back to 1913–1914 in a story that has Europeans for its central characters—a Danish suffragette who has come to India on a spiritual quest and an English magistrate whose wife has mysteriously disappeared. John Mellors noted in the *Listener* that Sahgal, both a political journalist and an imaginative storyteller, here allowed the storyteller a free hand—with happy results: "a subtle, sharply imagined novel, skillfully plotted and elegantly written."

Mistaken Identity, set against the political background of 1929 when the Anglo-Indian government harshly repressed dissidents, is primarily a portrait of a singularly disaffected young Indian, a poet of sorts, from a distinguished family, who returns from a trip to Europe to be arrested on suspicion of treason. Politically apathetic and totally innocent of the charges, he is jailed under appalling physical conditions but survives after three years in prison, retaining his sense of humor and awakening at last to India's need for independence. He marries a woman who is a political activist but remains himself "a quiet home-loving man. I'm at home writing for hours every day." In this novel Sahgal appears at last to have achieved a successful balance of politics, narrative skill, and sensitive characterization. Maurya Simon praised *Mistaken Identity*, in the *New York Times Book Review*, as "an intriguing novel, one that offers rare and moving insights into the intersection of personal and national destinies."

PRINCIPAL WORKS: *Novels*—A Time to Be Happy, 1958; This Time of Morning, 1965; Storm in Chandigarh, 1969; The Day in Shadow, 1972; A Situation in New Delhi, 1977; Rich Like Us, 1985; Plans for Departure, 1985; Mistaken Identity, 1986. *Nonfiction*—Prison and Chocolate Cake, 1954; From Fear Set Free, 1962; A Voice for Freedom, 1977; Indira Gandhi's Emergence and Style, 1978; Indira Gandhi: Her Road to

Power, 1982; (with E. N. Mangat Rai) Relationship Extracts from a Correspondence, 1994.

ABOUT: Chew, S. and Rutherford, A. (eds.) Unbecoming Daughters of the Empire, 1993; Contemporary Authors New Revision Series 11, 1984; Contemporary Literary Criticism 41, 1987; Dhawan, R. K. (ed.) Commonwealth Literature 1, 1989; Gupta, G. S. Balarama (ed.) Studies in Indian Fiction in English, 1987; International Who's Who of Women, 1992; Jain, J. Nayantara Sahgal, 1978; Kirpal, V. (ed.) The New Indian Novel in English, 1990; Nasta, S. (ed.) Motherlands, 1991; Ross, R. L. (ed.) International Literature in English, 1991; Sahgal, N. Prison and Chocolate Cake, 1954; Sahgal, N. From Fear Set Free, 1962. Periodicals—Listener May 29, 1969; July 11, 1985; London Magazine June–July 1977, June 1978, March 1986; New York Times Book Review September 24, 1972; July 9, 1989; Times Literary Supplement July 12, 1985; World Literature Today Winter 1991.

SALTER, JAMES (June 10, 1925–), American novelist and writer of short stories writes: "In childhood my teachers were women and I remember only one or two. In boyhood they were men, born at the end of the 19th century, who had attended, for the most part, Eastern colleges and universities. They were individuals of strong principle. The tone of the school was essentially Anglo and the underlying philosophy was that we were responsible for our own destinies, with obligations to society and the relatively privileged class from which we came. There was none of Buechner's or Ibsen's determinism. We were not what irresistible societal forces made of us but rather what we would make of ourselves. This was in spite of the Second World War, already started in Europe, and the tremendous slaughters and murder which were to be part of it. In the morning, in the auditorium, we sang *Men of Harlech* with its dauntless words, *surging, foemen, glory,* and also *Roar, Lion, Roar* and *Lord Geoffrey Amherst.*

"What effect this had on others, I do not know. I remember a youth of no forebodings. Poetry, football, and the esteem of friends were the things of importance then. Years later when I read Gunter Grass's *Cat and Mouse* I recognized, with only a few alterations, the tone of my own boyhood.

"My father had gone to West Point and, following in his rather illustrious footsteps, I went there myself. I ended up in the air force and was sent to the Pacific a few months after the war was over. During the Korean War I came back to Japan and the Far East and flew in combat. Sometime about then, in an unrecalled bookstore, I came across a copy of *The Town and the City* by John [Jack] Kerouac whom I recognized

from the sensitive jacket photograph as the football player and sometime writer I had last seen ten years before when we were at prep school. This was his first novel, before he became mythicized. Despite its being imitation Thomas Wolfe, that he had written it filled me with envy. He was twenty-seven or twenty-eight years old; I was twenty-five. I had never been able to rid myself of a feeling that the life I was leading, with all its manliness and movement, was in the end somehow perishable and what Kerouac had done was not. He had done something essential, made something out of all he had known.

"And so I began to tunnel beneath my career like a man in prison camp, at night, working tirelessly with the dream of a daring and solitary escape. The tunnel was, of course, a book. I had already tried to write one, as well as stories, and failed. This time I made it through. It was a novel about flying in Korea called *The Hunters*. At the time of its publication, in 1957, I resigned my commission and in a house by the river, about twenty miles from New York, not even knowing the neighbors, settled down to write. It was the world of the suburbs, comfortable and removed. The city was nearby, however. For nearly ten years I went in to various inexpensive rooms there to work, interrupted by a year in France when, during the Berlin Crisis, Kennedy called up the reserves.

"This year in France, stationed near a provincial town, Chaumont, was like a great song of farewell. Everything was part of it. I spoke some French, I had friends in Paris, I somehow came into possession of a grand car. There was even a serious illness and a long, semi-delirious stay in an empty hospital. I flew as often as I could, knowing this was the last time.

"From this year came the first real book, *A Sport and a Pastime*, little noticed when it appeared and treated uneasily by reviewers, but of a different order than the two previous novels. It was meant, a bit like some books of Henry Miller or Genet, to open the door to repudiated things which continue to ravish us, to illuminate an illicit world more pure than our own. It was written visually as was the next, *Light Years*, published in 1976. I was now past my forties and for some years had also been writing films, at first ambitiously, then out of habit, then to get by. I was frequently in Europe, being put up in fine hotels and accomplishing very little. Art consoles but I became uncertain that movies had this power and I drifted away from them in the early 1980s without regret.

"Fortunately, an exceptional small publishing house, North Point Press, came into existence in about 1980 and I was favored in being one of their writers. Over the years I was probably admired as much for that as for anything I had written.

"I think writing is in decline, not in its quality but in its importance. People's hearts, especially those of the young and promising, seem to beat to something different now. Language—and that means, finally, civilization—has less value. This is neither good nor bad, it is beyond such judging; it is historic. Nevertheless real writing will always mean something.

"For the most part my sense of order in life has been created by books and by nature. Names that are important to me are Cavafy, Chekhov, Berryman, Nabokov, Turgenev, and Babel. Of my own few books, the best are *A Sport and a Pastime*, which seems to me to have clarity and an esprit, and *Light Years*, which is melancholy but also more nourishing. I would like to have done other things in life but it is difficult to imagine not writing."

——————

"A well-kept literary secret": so Adam Begley characterized James Salter in the *New York Times Magazine* in 1993. By then in his midsixties, author of six books and several screenplays (including Robert Redford's 1969 production of *Downhill Racer*), he is one of a number of American writers who enjoy prestige but are not famous, whose books receive critical acclaim but sell only modestly. Salter works slowly and meticulously with concern for the perfection of his prose. He has won important literary honors—a grant in 1984 from the American Academy and Institute of Arts and Letters, inclusion of several of his stories in the *O. Henry* and *Best American Short Story* annuals, the PEN/Faulkner award for his *Dusk and Other Stories* in 1989—enough to bolster his own faith in his work. When Edward Hirsch, interviewing him for the *Paris Review* in 1993, asked him why he writes, Salter replied: "Because all this is going to vanish. The only thing left will be the prose and poems, the books, what is written down. Man was very fortunate to have invented the book. Without it the past would completely vanish, and we would be left with nothing, we would be naked on earth."

A relatively late starter in fiction writing, Salter brings to his work the rich experience of an early career in the military, travel, and adventures. Born in New York City as James Horowitz, Salter received his early education at the Horace Mann School, after which he entered West Point. "To enter you passed, that first day, into an inferno," he recalled in an essay, "A Soldier's

Memories," in *Esquire* in 1992. The unrelenting discipline of a cadet's life was a trial for him, but he passed the qualifying examinations for the army air force. In the course of his training he crashed his plane into a house on May 8, 1945, V-E Day. By a stroke of incredible good fortune, the family and their friends were celebrating V-E Day and the return of a son. They went outside to view what they thought was an aerial salute, while the plane demolished part of the house. Luck stayed with him in his service in the U.S. Air Force. He flew one hundred combat missions during the Korean War and remained in the service as a squadron leader in Europe until 1957 when he resigned his commission, with the rank of major, to become a full-time writer.

By that time Salter has discovered the theme that was to dominate his writing: the pursuit of perfection, sometimes in acts of extraordinary physical bravery (like combat flying in his early novels or mountain climbing in the later *Solo Faces*), more often in coming to terms with the circumstances of one's individual life. Recalling his experiences as a fighter pilot many years later, he wrote in "A Single Daring Act,": an essay in *Grand Street*

> When I returned to domestic life I kept something to myself, a deep attachment—deeper than anything I had known—to all that had happened. I had come very close to achieving the self that is based on the risking of everything, going where others would not go, giving what they would not give. Later I felt I had not done enough, had been too reliant, too unskilled. I had not done what I set out to do and might have done . . . But it had been a great voyage, the voyage, probably, of my life.

Salter's first two novels, *The Hunters* and *The Arm of Flesh*, drew on his air corps experiences in Korea and in postwar Europe. Like most first novels, they were largely ignored by reviewers and allowed to go out of print. Obliged to earn a living, he began to work on television documentary films and on screenplays.

With *A Sport and a Pastime*, Salter firmly established himself as a writer. Margaret Winchell Miller wrote, in the *Hollins Critic*, that the book "reveals his two most compelling gifts: a poet's ear for lyricism and an obsession with the power of desire." Like all his protagonists, the central figure here, Philip Dean, a Yale dropout traveling in Europe, yearns for perfection, absolute fulfillment which, in this novel, he finds not in hazardous adventure but in the pursuit of an idealized physical love. The scene is France, where Salter sets an idyllic mood from the outset with a train journey from Paris into the countryside:

> Green, bourgeoise France. We are going at tremendous speed. We cross bridges, the sound short and drumming. The country is opening up. We are on our way to towns

where no one goes. There are long wheat-colored stretch-es and then green, level land, recumbent and rich. The farms are built of stone. The wisdom of generations knows that land is the only real wealth, a knowledge that need not question itself, need not change. Open country flat as playing fields. Stands of trees.

Taking his title from the Koran ("Remember that the life of this world is but a sport and a pastime"), Salter describes in explicit detail the love affair between the young American and an eighteen-year-old working-class French girl whom he meets in a café. Although it is ostensibly Dean's story—for all its eroticism, a sweetly sad romance—the novel acquires greater depth in its narrator, who is never named. He is a passive observer, significantly a photographer by vocation but more like a voyeur in his knowledge of the intimacies of his characters' lives. Indeed, it becomes apparent before the novel ends that he is living vicariously and possibly only imaginatively in their love affair: "I am myself as an *agent provocateur*, or a double agent, first on one side—that of truth—and then on the other. . . ." He knows that for himself there is only frustration: "To begin with, no matter what I do, I can never recover everything . . . I am only the servant of life. He [Dean] is an inhabitant . . . I am afraid of him, of all men who are successful in love."

A Sport and a Pastime won praise from several reviewers. Webster Schott, in the *New York Times Book Review*, found it "a tour de force in erotic realism, a romantic cliff-hanger, an opaline vision of Americans in France." He considered it a "minor" work, "with a jagged, Hemingwayesque style," but also "a direct novel, not a grimy one. Salter celebrates the rites of erotic innovation and understands their literary uses." The reviewer in *Time* detected the influence of the French *nouveau roman* of Alain Robbe-Grillet in shaping the dreamlike memory effects of the book: "This curiously distilled method of storytelling proves effective and makes something lyrical of a rather commonplace romance."

Light Years, Salter's next novel, received more critical attention, though again sales figures were unimpressive. Salter speculated to Adam Begley that two unfavorable notices in the *New York Times* and the *New York Times Book Review* discouraged sales. Ironically, these reviews objected to the very quality that attracted other reviewers to the novel—the painterly elegance of Salter's prose, which struck Robert Towers, in the *New York Times Book Review*, as "fine" writing and "strained lyricism." Adam Begley describes it as "a lush mail-order catalogue, a dazzling display of polished surfaces." *Light Years* is the record of a marriage so seem-

ingly perfect that it is inevitably doomed. Set in contemporary suburban New York and Europe, it introduces a "happy" family—a successful architect, his beautiful and intelligent wife, their charming daughtesr—all living in an exquisitely furnished and situated house on the banks of the Hudson River. With the effects of an Impressionist painter (appropriately the cover illustration in the North Point reissue of the novel is Pierre Bonnard's *The Breakfast Room*) Salter evokes, Sven Birkerts wrote, the "texture, tones, and silences of the calm and abundance of family life . . . [and] a feel for a milieu and its rites." Some readers were reminded of the nostalgia for lost golden days that F. Scott Fitzgerald evoked in *The Great Gatsby* and *Tender Is the Night*. Salter himself told Edward Hirsch: "The book is the worn stones of conjugal life. All that is beautiful, all that is plain, everything that nourishes or causes to wither . . . It is about the sweetness of those unending days."

In 1977 the actor-producer-director Robert Redford asked Salter to write a screenplay on mountain climbing. To prepare for the assignment, Salter took up mountain climbing himself, with the result that although the screenplay was rejected, he was able to turn his experiences into a novel, *Solo Faces*. His hero was based on the real-life American climber Gary Hemming, but thanks to his own knowledge of climbing, he produced a book of stunning authentic detail. *Solo Faces* emphasizes the risks and rigors but also the sheer aesthetic delight of climbing, of which he says, "the most hazardous attempt is made beautiful by its rightness, even if it means falling to one's death." He continues:

The rock is like the surface of the sea, constant yet never the same. Two climbers going over the identical route will each manage in a different way. Their reach is not the same, their confidence, their desire. Sometimes the way narrows, the holds are few, there are no choices—the mountain is inflexible in its demands—but usually one is free to climb at will. There are principles, of course. The first concerns the rope—it is for safety, but one should always climb as if the rope were not there.

Over the years Salter has published many articles and short stories in the *New York Times*, the *Washington Post*, *Esquire*, *Vogue*, *Grand Street*, the *Paris Review*, and other journals. His prize-winning *Dusk* collects eleven short stories, several of these set in Europe and drawn from his own experiences in travel and filmmaking abroad. Salter's favorite among them is "American Express," in which he tellingly characterizes the "Yuppie" generation—in this instance, young partners in a New York law firm: "The city was divided . . . into those going up and those coming down, those in crowded restaurants and those on the street, those who waited and those who did not, those with three locks on the door and those rising in an elevator from a lobby with silver mirrors and walnut paneling." They travel to Europe in luxurious style, but one of them begins to sense the emptiness of their lives. At the end of the story he looks out of his hotel window at a young Italian driving by and reflects: "He was going to get the rolls for breakfast. His life was simple. The air was cool and pure. He was part of that great, unchanging other of those who live by wages, whose world is unlit and who do not realize what is above."

Salter, who received an M.A. from Georgetown University in 1950, has lectured on writing in the United States, Europe, and Japan, and has taught at the Iowa Writers Workshop. In 1993 he was preparing his memoirs, parts of which have appeared in *Esquire* and *Grand Street*, for publication. An early marriage, from which he has two children, ended in divorce. Since the mid-1970s he has lived with the writer Kay Eldredge. They have one son and, when not traveling, divide their time between homes in Aspen, Colorado, and Bridgehampton, Long Island, New York.

PRINCIPAL WORKS: *Novels*—The Hunters, 1957; The Arm of Flesh, 1960; A Sport and a Pastime, 1967; Light Years, 1975; Solo Faces, 1980. *Short stories*—Dusk and Other Stories, 1989. *Nonfiction*—The Water's Edge (ill. S. Gall), 1995.

ABOUT: Birkerts, Sven American Energies: Essays in Fiction, 1992; Contemporary Authors 73–76, 1978; Contemporary Literary Criticism 7, 1977; Contemporary Novelists, 3rd ed., 1982; Singer, A. E. (ed.) Essays on the Literature of Mountaineering, 1982. *Periodicals*—College English January 1988; Esquire December 1992; Grand Street Spring 1990; Hollins Critic February 1982; New York Times Book Review July 27, 1975; February 21, 1988; New York Times Magazine October 28, 1993; Paris Review Summer 1993; Publishers Weekly May 31, 1985; Vanity Fair June 1985.

SANCHEZ, SONIA (September 9, 1934–   ), American poet, playwright, educator, and political activist, was born Wilsonia Benita Driver in Birmingham, Alabama, the daughter of Wilson L. Driver and Lena (Jones) Driver. When Sanchez was one year old her mother died; subsequently her grandmother, whom she called Mama, helped with her care. "My grandmother was tough and spiritual enough to never let white people touch me," Sanchez stated in an interview with Zala Chandler in *Wild Women in the Whirlwind*. "If they attempted to touch my

SONIA SANCHEZ

sister or me, she would always respond, 'Don't touch them! These are mine. Don't take the power from them at all!'"

Sanchez was six when her grandmother died. She told Chandler, "I think it's significant to mention that after Mama's death, I had started to write poetry, these little ditties, because I had started to stutter and found it difficult to communicate with people. . . . Because I couldn't communicate well I retreated to books and to writing. And I spent a lot of time in solitary."

In 1943 Wilson Driver moved his family to Harlem. Sanchez earned her B.A. in political science at Hunter College in 1955, followed by postgraduate work at New York University. There she studied poetry under Louise Bogan and was encouraged to pursue a career as a writer. Sanchez began to publish poetry in small magazines and in black periodicals at a time when the United States was entering a period of tremendous social and cultural upheaval. Barbara Christian, in her *Black Feminist Criticism*, described the rise of the Black Power Movement in the 1960s: "There was a renewed interest in African and Afro-American history and culture and a corresponding contempt for whites. Poets saw themselves as revolutionaries in the service of their community." Christian considers Sanchez, along with Nikki Giovanni and Carolyn Rodgers, as part of that "cultural nationalist thrust," and writes that "their works called upon black women to heal themselves by asserting their pride in black beauty and by reassessing their relationship with black men, a relationship continually distorted by a racist society." In her interview with Chandler, Sanchez declared: "To have discovered oneself in the 1960s . . . was almost like being reborn. You could be your natural self. What a relief from a peculiar kind of bondage that was there, that we were involved in. It means that we now had more time to do some things with our heads, with our brains."

Sanchez's commitment to the black liberation struggle led her to join other activists in demanding, and ultimately establishing, black studies programs on college campuses. Kalamu ya Salaam commented in the *Dictionary of Literary Biography* that Sanchez was determined to stand up and be counted and consistent in advocating revolution in this country and abroad. As part of her ongoing commitment to causes of justice, Sanchez supports various national and grassroots organizations and movements.

It is not surprising that Sanchez the writer and Sanchez the activist are almost indissoluble. "The poet is a creator of social values," she states in her preface to Haki Madhubuti's and David Williams's essays in *Black Women Writers*. She goes on to observe that the "power that the poet has to create, preserve, or destroy social values depends greatly on the quality of his / her social visibility and the functionary opportunity available to poetry to impact lives." Madhubuti pointed out that Sanchez "writes poetry that is forever questioning Black people's commitment to struggle." This can take many complex forms, such as the struggles between African Americans and whites, between African Americans themselves, the struggles within oneself, between the sexes, and cultural struggles. "Her poetry cuts to the main arteries of her people, sometimes drawing blood, but always looking for a way to increase the heartbeat and lower the blood pressure," Madhubuti wrote. "Her poetry, for the most part, is therapeutic and cleansing."

In 1969 Sanchez published *Homecoming*, her first book of poetry. "Sanchez's early voice was one of militant blackness," Kalamu ya Salaam pointed out. "Her poetic style was brief, razor sharp, and full of scorn and invective for 'white America.'" In "For Unborn Malcolms" she writes:

its time
   an eye for an eye
   a tooth for a tooth
   don't worry bout his balls
they al
   ready gone,
   git the word
out that us blk / niggers
   are out to lunch
and the main course
is gonna be his white meat.
   yeah.

For David Williams the "verse of *Homecoming* is speech heightened by a consciousness of the ironies implicit in every aspect of Black existence. The poems read like terse statements intended to interrupt the silence that lies between perception and action." In the title poem, Sanchez "presents the act of returning home as a rejection of fantasy and an acceptance of involvement."

i have returned
leaving behind me
all those hide and
seek faces peeling
with freudian dreams.
this is for real.

Williams wrote that Sanchez had been "one of those 'hide and seek faces' on the outside, looking in at the niggers; in the real world she is now a nigger":

black
niggers
   my beauty.

Williams noted that "this, the climax of the poem, is the real homecoming," and mentioned the "new resonance" acquired by the poem's opening lines:

i have been a
way so long . . .

One of the most distinctive elements in Sanchez's poetry is her use of African American speech, which gives some of her work the cutting immediacy of street talk. Madhubuti commented on Sanchez's respect for the power of this language and recognized her as responsible, more than any other poet, for "legitimatizing the use of urban Black English in written form." In "To Blk/Record/Buyers" she declares:

don't play me no
righteous bros.
   white people
ain't rt bout nothing
no mo.
   don't tell me bout
foreign dudes
   cuz no blk/
people are grooving on a
sunday afternoon

Sanchez writes the kind of poetry that almost demands to be read aloud. According to Kalamu ya Salaam, she "developed techniques for reading her poetry that were unique in their use of traditional chants and near-screams drawn out to an almost earsplitting level. The sound elements, which give a musical quality to the intellectual statements in the poetry, are akin to West

African languages; Sanchez has tried to recapture a style of delivery that she felt had been muted by the experience of slavery." The music analogy is appropriate. Her poems often create a feeling of spontaneity akin to a jazz solo. Her father was a musician and took her to hear jazz greats, such as Billy Eckstine, Billie Holiday, and Art Tatum. She also credits Malcolm X as a major influence. "A lot of our words and language came from Malcolm," she is quoted as saying in *Black Literature Criticism*. "He was always messing with the language and messing with people, and sometimes in a very sly kind of way demanding things of people and also cursing people out."

As the radicalism of the 1960s passed into the 1970s, the struggle turned to empowerment. "We couldn't just keep on saying that America is racist, America is racist," Sanchez commented to Zala Chandler. "We had to start talking about what we were going to do about it." In 1973 Sanchez published *A Blues Book for Blue Black Magical Women*, which *PHYLON* writer George E. Kent called a "mountain-top type of poem." Sanchez told Chandler: "I attempted to speak about both the political part of us and the personal. . . . I wanted us to know that in order for us to be effective political people, we must be in control of the personal." For Sanchez *A Blues Book* was about memories and their use:

        as i entered into my
        young womanhood i became
        a budding of laughter. i
        moved in liquid dreams
        wrapped myself in a
        furious circuit of love
        gave out quick words
        and violent tremblings
        and kisses that bit
        and drew blood
        and the seasons fell
        like waterfalls on my thighs

Kent called it the "poetic rhythms of one who has climbed from the valleys and is now calling others up from the low, the misted flats."

In 1973 Sanchez also published *Love Poems* which, according to Kalamu ya Salaam, "reads like a slide show of Sanchez's emotional life." Madhubuti agreed, calling these "introspective and meditative" poems a "startling and profound departure from Sanchez's other books." In "July" the poet asks:

        i wonder what it is
        to be old
        and swallow death each day
        like warm beer

Williams commented that in *Love Poems* Sanchez widened her range of imagery, moving

from the harshness of urban reality to "images of trees, flowers, earth, birds, sea, and sky" dotting the verse. Williams, however, made it clear that Sanchez is "very far from using them to suggest an idyllic universe." In "Old Words" the poet laments:

        this earth
        turns old
        and rivers grow lunatic
        with rain. how i wish
        i could lean in your cave
        and creak with the winds.

During the 1970s Sanchez also emerged as a playwright, probing the same difficult and painful issues as in her poetry. In *Sister Son/ji* and *Uh Huh; But How Do It Free Us?* she writes of the subservience of women in the liberation movement, as well as of the physical abuse many of them suffer. She has also published several children's books. As she told Claudia Tate in *Black Women Writers at Work*: "I do think that it's important to leave a legacy of my books for my children to read and understand; to leave a legacy of the history of black people who have moved toward revolution and freedom; to leave a legacy of not being afraid to tell the truth. . . . We must pass this on to our children, rather than fear and victimization."

The year 1981 was an important one in Sanchez's literary career for it marked the appearance of *I've Been a Woman: New and Selected Poems*. "This collection is the history of Sanchez as poet—the poet consistently at her best, spanning the entire range of her talent," Madhubuti wrote. He called the collection "river-like and thirst-quenching. . . . containing landscapes and mountains with few valleys." In 1985 Sanchez won the American Book Award for the poems in *homegirls & handgrenades*. As a political landscape, however, the 1980s were a dangerous period in Sanchez's view. "There is a growing mood at all levels of America that says that they can treat us any old kind of way again," she observed in her interview with Chandler. She questioned the notion that economic power is a panacea for African Americans "Being rich without real power means nothing."

Added to Sanchez's multifaceted life is her role as educator. In addition to being an international lecturer, she has taught at the Downtown Community School in San Francisco, San Francisco State University, the University of Pittsburgh, Rutgers University, Borough of Manhattan Community College, Amherst College, and the University of Pennsylvania, and she is a tenured professor at Temple University in the Department of English / Women's Studies. She is also a contributing editor for both

Black Scholar and *Journal of African Studies*. In addition to publishing in periodicals, her work is included in many anthologies. As an Egyptologist, she was a contributor to Ivan Van Sertima's *Black Women of Antiquity*.

PRINCIPAL WORKS: *Poetry*—Homecoming, 1969; Liberation Poem, 1970; We a BaddDDD People, 1970; A Blues Book for Blue Black Magical Women, 1973; Love Poems, 1973; I've Been A Woman: New And Selected Poems, 1981; homegirls & handgrenades, 1984; Under a Soprano Sky, 1987. *Plays*—Sister Son/ji *in* Bullins, E. (ed.) New Plays from the Black Theatre, 1969; The Bronx Is Next *in* Davis, A. and Redding, S. (eds.) Cavalcade: Negro American Writing from 1760 to the Present, 1971; Uh Huh; But How Do It Free Us? *in* Bullins, E. (ed.) The New Layfayette Theatre Presents: Plays with Aesthetic Comments by Six Black Playwrights, 1974. *Juvenile*—It's a New Day: Poems for Young Brothas and Sistuhs, 1971; The Adventures of Fathead, Smallhead, and Squarehead, 1973; A Sound Investment and Other Stories, 1979. *Nonfiction*—Ima Talken bout the Nation of Islam, 1972; Crisis in Culture: Two Speeches, 1983; Van Sertima, I. (ed.) Black Women of Antiquity, 1988. *As editor*—Three Hundred and Sixty Degrees of Blackness Comin' at You, 1971; We Be Word Sorcerers: 25 Stories by Black Americans, 1973.

ABOUT: Black Literature Criticism 3, 1992; Blackshire-Belay, C. A. (ed.) Language and Literature in the African American Imagination, 1992; Braxton, J. M. and McLaughlin, A. N. (eds.) Wild Women in the Whirlwind: Afra-American Culture and the Contemporary Literary Renaissance, 1990; Christian, B. Black Feminist Criticism: Perspectives on Black Women Writers, 1985; Contemporary Authors (on CD-ROM), 1994; Dictionary of Literary Biography 41, 1985; Evans, M. (ed.) Black Women Writers, 1950–1980: A Critical Evaluation, 1984; Gates, H. L. (ed.) Reading Black, Reading Feminist, 1990; Hartigan, K. V. (ed.) The Many Forms of Drama, 1985; Inge, T. B. (ed.) Southern Women Writers: The New Generation, 1990; Notable Black American Women, 1992; Parini, J. and Millier, B. C. (eds.) The Columbia History of American Poetry, 1993; Tate, C. Black Women Writers at Work, 1983; Weixlmann, J. and Baker, H. A., Jr. (eds.) Black Feminist Criticism and Critical Theory, 1988. *Periodicals*—Indian Journal of American Studies July 1983; Melus 12 Fall 1985; PHYLON: The Atlanta University Review of Race and Culture June 1975.

SANCHEZ, THOMAS (February 26, 1944–), American novelist, was born in Oakland, California, to a Spanish father, Thomas Louis Sanchez, and a Portuguese mother, Geraldine (Brown) Sanchez. Three months before Sanchez was born, his father died in World War II. During much of Sanchez's childhood, his mother worked in canning factories, as did his grandmother, whom he credits with fostering in him a love of language and literature. Sanchez told Kay Bonetti in the *Missouri Review* that although his grandmother never learned to read or write, "She developed a sense of the oral; she developed a sense of storytelling. . . . She'd throw some verbs up in the air like they were a pizza pie and they would come down as a cherry pie. The postman and the neighbors would come along to have a cup of coffee in my grandmother's kitchen and stay for hours upon end."

When his mother became severely ill, Sanchez was sent to the St. Francis School for Boys in Watsonville, California, which he described as "a combination orphanage and boarding school and reform school. Most of the children there were either very poor children or orphans. There were Chicano children, there were American Indians, there were black children. It was a true American melting pot." It was in this school that Sanchez began his intense involvement with Native American culture. In addition to the Indian students, there was one old man who, Sanchez recalls, "was sort of a father to us all and in a spiritual way touched something in me and showed me a different consciousness. It was almost as if he was living in another dimension." After high school, Sanchez studied literature at a local community college and worked on ranches in the Sierra Nevada mountains, where he continued to live among Native Americans, including some from the Washo tribe. He also worked as a truck driver, a laborer, a carpenter, and a gardener to support himself while writing fiction.

The history and culture of the Washo Indians was the subject of his first novel, *Rabbit Boss*, which he began writing while working on a cattle ranch at the age of twenty-one. He continued working on the novel while attending San Francisco State University, where he earned a B.A. in 1966 and an M.A. in 1967. He taught at San Francisco State until 1969, when there was a strike involving students and teachers, during which he witnessed a SWAT team descend on the campus and beat students on the steps of the library. The violence deeply disturbed Sanchez, who had been very involved in the antiwar movement and in the civil rights movement as a member of CORE and SNCC. He told Bonetti: "I remember quite vividly this image of the blood flowing down the steps and thinking what a profound irony: that inside all the learning is locked up and outside we are clubbing the youth of this country. At that point I decided that the only way to survive would be to leave America to complete *Rabbit Boss*." He moved to Spain, where he lived in the mountains and continued writing.

A pattern of self-imposed exile and intense re-

flection on America defines Sanchez's work. The
seven-year period during which he wrote *Rabbit
Boss* required an immense personal commitment. "When you move so deeply into a novel
that its consciousness takes over your
consciousness," Sanchez has said, "it begins to supersede your own life":

> It devours you, it consumes you, it takes over your sub-
> conscious, it takes over your dream state. I would wake
> up in the middle of the night gnashing the insides of my
> cheeks with nightmares. I had placed a comma in the
> wrong place for the character who existed eighty years
> ago, and since that comma was in the wrong position in
> the sentence—that's not where that man would have
> stopped to take a breath—I had betrayed that character,
> which meant I had betrayed the chapter which meant
> I had betrayed the entire novel and all of those years
> were worthless. I would wake up with blood in my
> mouth and spit it out into a bowl.

In Sanchez's vision of America, the destruction of the Washo Indians was linked to the Vietnam War: "For me, the beginning of trying to
deal with the war in Vietnam was to re-create
the beginning of a war that took place on the
western continent of the United States—the war
against the indigenous peoples." In Sanchez's
epic re-creation of the Washos' encounters with
white Americans—beginning in 1846 with a
Washo, Gayabuc, witnessing the cannibalism of
the Donner party—the destructive power of
American expansion is shown through the clash
between a spiritual Native American culture
and a violent, materialistic culture that ultimately degrades and destroys it. Gordon Burnside
wrote in the *New York Times Book Review*: "As
Sanchez tells it, the safely familiar exaggeration
of American frontier humor turns itself inside-
out and reappears as the secret language of demons. This is the novel that Mailer's *Why We
Are in Vietnam* was meant to be."

Rabbit Boss interweaves the stories of four
generations of Washos, each the inheritor of the
once-respected title of Rabbit Boss, which is
passed down from father to son. By the 1950s,
the role of Rabbit Boss, which once included
great spiritual power such as the ability to hunt
animals in one's dreams, has been reduced to
plebeian service to the whites. Gayabuc's great-
grandson, Joe Birdsong, is told by his brother-in-
law, Felix:

> How can you compare yourself to them that did some-
> thing, something noble. You! You're nothing but a straw-
> hat, a hired Indian with a rifle, hired by a whiteman to
> keep the rabbits from chomping up all his range grass or
> his stupid cattle from fallin into their holes and breakin
> a leg that holds up all those pounds of money meat.
> You're a hired game warden, you ain't even that, you're
> just an exterminator.

Scenes of atrocities committed against Indians

are interspersed with lyrical portrayals of tribal
life. The reviewer for the *Times Literary
Supplement* wrote: "Few have shown more startlingly and with such a wealth of anthropological knowledge the clash between the Indian life,
so rich in myth and a sense of the numinous, and
the incoming White settlers, who are shown as
being at the best obtuse and crassly materialistic
and at worst, to modify Wallace Stevens's
phrase, diners off human heads." Complimenting Sanchez's "controlled use of language," the
writer observed: "Their incompatibility is shown
through the use of vocabulary. The Indians in
control of their relationship with Sky, Sun, Bird
and Woman are given an exalted art-language,
at times close to self-parody." The reviewer in
Time was more critical of Sanchez's rendering
of the Indians' thought and speech, calling it "a
portentous lingo that just does not work."

Most reviewers, however, found the overall
achievement stunning. Although some critics
agreed with H. L. Van Brunt's judgment in the
Christian Science Monitor that *Rabbit Boss* was
"overlong and diffuse," most expressed incredulity that a young, first-time author had produced
a novel of such power and complexity. Phoebe-
Lou Adams wrote in the *Atlantic* that Sanchez's
grim themes are presented "through a dazzle of
lively episodes, shifting points of view and time,
and convincing characters. The work is a first
novel; it reads like the work of an expert
veteran."

Sanchez's second novel, *Zoot-Suit Murders*, a
mystery set in Los Angeles during World War
II, was a less ambitious effort. Sanchez used the
tension between Mexican-Americans and those
who suspected them of disloyalty as a backdrop
to the story. This tension ultimately exploded in
the "Zoot-Suit Riots" of 1943, in which mobs of
sailors set upon men wearing zoot suits, the favored attire of Chicano gang members, beating,
stripping, and shaving them. The novel centers
on Oscar Fuss, an undercover agent sympathetic
to the city's Hispanic residents, who investigates
the murder of two FBI agents and the fascist and
communist groups attempting to infiltrate the
barrio. Although John Thomas Stovall in the
Chicago Tribune, called *Zoot-Suit Murders* "a
vivid tale of political intrigue and romance,"
most reviewers were less enthusiastic. Kenneth
Paul, in the *Christian Science Monitor*, bluntly
concluded that "the dialogue is bad," and the
book was generally considered more superficial
in its construction and its treatment of social issues than the painstakingly wrought *Rabbit Boss*.

With *Mile Zero*, published more than a decade later, Sanchez received acclaim for another
extremely ambitious novel. Like *Zoot-Suit*

Murders, Mile Zero weaves the turbulent social issues exposed in a particularly revealing time and place into the plot of a mystery, but this time the issues were far more numerous and broader in implication. After spending five years writing the novel with a California and Mexico setting, Sanchez passed through Key West and suddenly felt the book's themes crystalize. "I had really been trying to put together a novel that would fuse the Vietnam generation with the post-Vietnam generation, but somehow the voices weren't coming," Sanchez told Stephanie Strom in the *New York Times Book Review* in 1989. Key West offered the opportunity to present the intersection of powerful images, from Haitian refugees to space shuttle launches to the flood of drugs and drug money. "These three things forged in my mind a new metaphor, and I realized that the themes of the novel I had been carrying around for all those years had finally coalesced in some hard voices speaking to me in soft, fresh language. It was the language of the new American experience."

One of the novel's central voices is that of St. Cloud, a burned-out Vietnam War activist who is described as trying to "wash away in a sea of alcohol . . . a war he couldn't forget, a war no one else remembered except those who fought in it or against it." St. Cloud is drawn into an attempt by Justo Tamarindo, a Cuban-born policeman who is a pillar of strength and decency, to prevent the deportation and certain death of a Haitian refugee with AIDS. While St. Cloud attempts to recover from losing his wife to lesbianism, Justo fights off the temptation to commit adultery and searches for a mysterious killer named Zobop, who leaves visionary, voodoo-inspired notes warning of environmental apocalypse.

Erica Abeel, in the *New York Times Book Review*, compared Sanchez's new book favorably with *Rabbit Boss*: "That book, it is now clear, was only a warmup for the dazzling achievement of *Mile Zero*. Mr. Sanchez's new novel is marked by the same commanding sense of place, the same mix of politics and poetry. But *Mile Zero* is more shapely, leaner and free of *Rabbit Boss's* diffuseness and longueurs." While others admired the book, particularly its evocative rendering of Key West, some felt that it fell short of its prophetic, epic goals. Ralph Novak wrote in *People*: "Sanchez has said that he intended this novel to 'unravel my own generation.' As it happens, while he's no more lacking in talent and literary resources than he is in ambition, this seems more like a beautifully written mystery than it does a generation-defining opus."

The novel's plethora of characters and themes permits many different interpretations. Sanchez said in the *Missouri Review* of the book's critical reception: "It's as if I've written twelve different books. Every single review focuses on a different character, a different element, a different slant—a mystery novel, a love story, a novel of the occult, a holy terror of a book." Sanchez is more than happy to let people take what they can from his work. He told Bonetti: "I don't really see a novelist in the role of a teacher. Perhaps not even as a seeker. I think that if you actually can give life to a book, that *perhaps* that life will touch other lives in a meaningful way, but only *perhaps*. Writing a novel is a fabulous act of arrogance. If I'm going to place a novel before someone and it takes them five or seven hours or twenty hours to read, I want to make certain that I'm placing before them the very best that I'm capable of, something that I've thought out in every single word, with every single line. It must have a purpose and a value. Otherwise, I would not offer it."

In addition to his three novels, Sanchez is the author of the nonfiction book *Native Notes from the Land of Earthquake and Fire*. He has received fellowships from the Guggenheim Foundation and the National Endowment for the Arts. He has one child, Dante Paloma, from his marriage to Stephanie Dante.

PRINCIPAL WORKS: Rabbit Boss, 1973; Zoot-Suit Murders, 1978; Mile Zero, 1989. *Nonfiction*—Native Notes from the Land of Earthquake and Fire, 1979 (reissued as Angels Burning: Native Notes from the Land of Earthquake and Fire, 1987).

ABOUT: Contemporary Authors New Revision Series 2, 1981. *Periodicals*—Atlantic June 1973; Chicago Tribune December 10, 1978; Christian Science Monitor July 18, 1973; January 17, 1979; Missouri Review XIV, no. 2, 1991; New York Times Book Review March 10, 1974; October 1, 1989; People October 16, 1989; Time July 30, 1973; Times Literary Supplement March 1, 1974.

SANTMYER, HELEN HOOVEN (November 25, 1895–February 21, 1986), novelist, essayist, teacher, and librarian, attained literary fame with her fourth book . . . *And Ladies of the Club.* While the monumental historical novel and the octogenarian novelist appeared to have burst on the publishing scene in 1984, both had existed quietly long before their celebrity. *Ladies* had evolved over a 20-year period only to languish after its publication by a university press in 1982. Santmyer, at eighty-six, had devoted much of her adult life to chronicling late

HELEN HOOVEN SANTMYER

19th- and early 20th-century Ohio life in fiction and nonfiction works, to some critical but little public or commercial success.

Santmyer's perennial affiliation with Ohio began in Cincinnati, where she was born to Joseph Wright Santmyer, a traveling drug salesman and later manager of a rope manufacturing company, and Bertha (Hooven) Santmyer. Both her parents came from venerable Ohio clans whose Republican-Presbyterian orientation later manifested itself in her writing. Santmyer and her family, including her younger siblings Philip and Jane, moved to Xenia, Ohio, around the turn of the century. She subsequently spent the greater part of her life in the small southwestern Ohio town, using it as the setting and often the subject of her novels and essays.

Although herself an unladylike tomboy, the young Santmyer revered a select group of ladies who belonged to Xenia's Women's Club. This literary forum, whose members shepherded the town's social and cultural activities, later provided the framework and central characters for *Ladies*. Santmyer frequented the library established by the Women's Club and became an avid reader from a young age. She particularly admired Louisa May Alcott and made up her mind to write books for children.

Soon after receiving a bachelor of arts degree from Wellesley College in 1918, Santmyer moved to New York City with hopes of becoming a writer. Her early efforts did not earn enough to support her, however, and she took a secretarial job at *Scribner's Magazine*. In 1921, Santmyer returned to Xenia, where she taught

English and began her first novel, *Herbs and Apples*. From 1922 to 1924, she taught literature at Wellesley and finished her book.

Sixty years later, Santmyer fittingly described *Herbs and Apples* as "for the most part autobiographical." It tells the story of Derrick Thornton, an Ohio girl who has yearned to become a writer since childhood. She goes to college and then moves to New York to fulfill her literary aspirations. After her young man dies in World War I, Derrick loses her hunger for renown and chooses instead to be satisfied with the "herbs and apples" of life in her Ohio hometown.

The novel received cautious praise. Reviewers found fault with its sluggish pacing and overabundance of detail but attributed these problems to Santmyer's inexperience. Some critics saw genuine promise in her characterization and occasional inspiration: "[S]cattered through this oddly compounded book are passages of a breath-taking delicacy and poignancy, of insight and power beyond cavil," the *New Republic*'s reviewer noted.

Just before the book's publication, Santmyer went to Oxford University to study literature. She received a bachelor of literature degree in 1927 and returned again to Ohio, where she wrote her second novel, *The Fierce Dispute*. Although she set this book in familiar Xenia, the characters and events were foreign to her own experience—created, she said, "out of thin air." The "fierce dispute" is between the mother, Hilary, and grandmother of a little girl named Lucy Ann. Hilary has alienated her mother by marrying an Italian musician who soon abandons his wife and young daughter. She takes Lucy Ann back to the old family mansion in Ohio and quickly locks horns with her mother, who wants to stifle Lucy Ann's innate musicality. In the end, the dispute is resolved when the grandmother reluctantly yields to the child's natural talent.

Reviewers of *The Fierce Dispute* commended its framework and premise but thought Santmyer failed to make the most of its plot. Despite this inadequacy, she was praised for her ability to set a gloomy and haunted atmosphere, her clear and straightforward prose, and her convincing portrait of the lonely, delicate Lucy Ann. As before, reviewers agreed that Santmyer's work showed promise.

In the early 1930s, Santmyer moved with her parents to Orange County, California. While there, she composed two essays about Xenia but realized once more that her writing would never provide a living. After the family moved back to Ohio, she became dean of women and head of the English department at Cedarville College, a Presbyterian school near Xenia. She worked at the college until 1953, when it came under Christian fundamentalist direction, then spent the remainder of her nonliterary career as a reference assistant at the Dayton and Montgomery Public Library. During this time, two of her essays—"Cemetery: A Reminiscence" (1956) and "There Were Fences" (1961)—appeared in the *Antioch Review*. She eventually wrote several other pieces, all of which a friend submitted to Weldon Kefauver, an editor at the Ohio State University Press. Kefauver "realized with the very first paragraph that [he] had something extraordinary in [his] hands" and published the collection as *Ohio Town: A Portrait of Xenia* in 1962.

In *Ohio Town*, Santmyer conducts a meandering tour, beginning at "The Courthouse" to expound on Xenia's recorded and remembered history and stopping by the "School" to revisit her grandmother's childhood as well as her own. She ends the tour at "Four Corners," where the crossroads lead out of town, explaining, perhaps, why she herself chooses to remain behind:

[Xenia] encourages no glamorous illusion that life was once wholly fair; it is a background that makes no demands on its children; it does not sustain in them any extravagant hope. In these streets, under these roofs, they are free to dream their dreams in peace; they are free also to forget them when they must, without bitterness, and to accept instead the humdrum daily life of the generations of mankind. . . .

Reviewing *Ohio Town* in *History News*, James Iverne Dowie commended Santmyer's "veritable genius for developing historical narrative through sensitive descriptions of familiar landmarks." Eldon Hill, in the *Indiana Magazine of History*, admired her "retentive memory" and "quick eye for the interesting anecdote" as well as her literary style. Nevertheless, he considered her "somewhat carried away with her subject" at times, as when comparing Xenia to "even Illyria and Elsinore." The *Washington Post*'s John Baskin thought Santmyer's narrative too often lapsed into a tedious catalog of information, but enjoyed her "decorous, measured, and somewhat distant" language. The collection won the Florence Roberts Hood Memorial Award from the Ohioana Library Association in 1964.

Santmyer retired in 1960 and pursued her interests in gardening, antique collecting, and travel with her longtime friend Mildred Sandoe. She also began to work intensively on a new novel, *. . . And Ladies of the Club*. Although she wrote the nearly 2,000 page manuscript in approximately fifteen years, in effect she had been researching it all her life, as she said in the introduction to the 1985 edition of *Herbs and Apples*:

For as long as I can remember I was collecting scraps of information and putting away bits that I had heard discussed around the dining table in my home, and making notes from books about the Civil War and the long span of years from then until the early 1930s . . .

Santmyer set her story in exactly that time period, beginning in 1868 and ending in 1932. *Ladies* opens with the founding of the Waynesboro Women's Club in a fictional small town modeled on Xenia. The narrative is structured around the Club and its members, who have determined to "meet at intervals and promote an interest in culture—in letters, in poetry—at least in a small group." *Ladies* focuses on two of the Club's founders. Their personal stories, interwoven with Waynesboro's collective history, unfold slowly and methodically until 1932, when the last charter member of the Club dies. The novel fluctuates between the minute details of domestic and community life and the momentous social, political, and economic changes of post–Civil War, pre–New Deal middle America.

Santmyer finished *Ladies* in the mid-1970s and sent the lengthy manuscript to Weldon Kefauver at the Ohio State University Press. At his suggestion, she spent several years cutting approximately 600 pages. Finally published in 1982, *Ladies* won Santmyer the Ohioana Book Award in Fiction but otherwise made very little impact, selling mostly to libraries and garnering only regional reviews.

A dramatic turnaround in the novel's fortunes occurred two years later when the book came to the attention of a literary agent who arranged its republication by G.P. Putnam's Sons, which assured its popularity. As a best-seller, the novel was widely reviewed. Its stunning commercial success struck some critics as more noteworthy than the book itself. *Newsweek*'s Gene Lyons unhesitatingly categorized *Ladies* as a "publishing" rather than "literary" event. Michael Malone explained in the *Nation* that *Ladies* had "legs," which "means [it] will walk briskly off the shelf to the cash register. . . . " *Ladies'* length and extensive detail divided reviewers. "[W]hile this book is a prodigious feat of endurance and, in a way, an act of bravery," Malone remarked, "the result is work and not art." In the *New York Times Book Review*, Vance Bourjaily observed that "[it] is details that give the book charm." Some reviewers were disturbed by the author's outdated sensibilities, however. "It's not shocking that [Club members] are snobs and bigots; what's remarkable is that their creator displays not a particle of irony about it . . . ," Gene Lyons remarked in *Newsweek*.

Santmyer herself responded to the furor over her book with considerable equilibrium. "I tried to make the atmosphere true," she explained, "but nothing hysterical." Although eighty-eight years old, in failing health, and living in a nursing home, she gave interviews to *Life*, *People*, and other magazines. In reply to the suggestion that *Ladies* was a rebuttal to Sinclair Lewis's caustic novel *Main Street*, she asserted: "My book was something I had been planning to do most of my life. Lewis wrote his version [of small-town middle-America] and I wrote mine."

As a result of *Ladies'* success, Santmyer received an honorary doctorate in humanities from Wright State University, the (Ohio) Governor's Medal, and induction into the Ohio Women's Hall of Fame. The novelist unexpectedly found herself in illustrious company when a local scholar organized a conference called "Perspectives on "Small Town" Life: Lewis, Dickens, and Santmyer . . . " in January 1985.

Santmyer died of emphysema in 1986. Ironically, the success that came just before her death finally established her as a writer. All three of her earlier books were reprinted; *Herbs and Apples* and *Ohio Town* in some cases received better notices than *Ladies*. Another, semiautobiographical novel, *Farewell, Summer*, which Santmyer believed "must have been lost a long time ago," was discovered and published posthumously in 1988. She also left behind an unpublished mystery novel, "The Hall with Eight Doors."

PRINCIPAL WORKS: *Novels*—Herbs and Apples, 1925; The Fierce Dispute, 1929; . . . And Ladies of the Club, 1982; Farewell, Summer, 1988. *Nonfiction*—Ohio Town: A Portrait of Xenia, 1962.

ABOUT: Contemporary Authors 118, 1986; Contemporary Literary Criticism 33, 1985; Current Biography Yearbook 1985; Dictionary of Literary Biography Yearbook 1984; Major 20th-Century Writers, 1991. *Periodicals*—American Spectator November 1984; CLA Journal June 1986; History News November 1964; Indiana Magazine of History March 1963; Life June 1984; Nation July 21–28, 1984; National Review October 5, 1984; New Republic January 6, 1926; New York Times February 22, 1986; New York Times Book Review June 24, 1984; Newsweek June 18, 1984; Notes on Contemporary Literature September 1985; People Weekly July 16, 1984; Washington Post September 2, 1984.

SARAMAGO, JOSE (November 16, 1922–), Portuguese writer, was born to José de Sousa and Maria (da Piedade) Saramago in Azinhaga, in the province of Ribatejo. Of humble origin, he was forced to abandon school in order to

JOSE SARAMAGO

earn his living. He held various manual jobs before becoming a journalist, translator, and writer. Success came late in life, but since 1979, Saramago has devoted himself entirely to writing, a rare privilege for any Portuguese author. His works include plays, chronicles, poetry, short stories, travelogues, libretti, and diaries. Both at home and abroad, however, he has made greatest impact as a novelist. Now widely translated, he was won an impressive list of awards and distinctions and is recognized as one of the most interesting and influential novelists writing in Europe today. Remarkably varied in theme and inspiration, Saramago's major works bear all the hallmarks of great fiction. Like the great 19th-century novelists he favors a broad canvas which allows him to explore every conceivable facet of human experience. A deep love and knowledge of his native Portugal goes hand in hand with a keen awareness of cultural differences beyond the Iberian peninsula.

Saramago was in his fifties when he wrote his first novel, *Manual de Pintura e Caligrafia* (1977, *Manual of Painting and Calligraphy*), which conveys from the outset his constant preoccupation with the relationship between life and art. The narrator is the anonymous H, a second-rate artist commissioned by a wealthy client to paint a family portrait. H reflects on the artist's struggle to survive in a world of material bourgeois values; he clings to his ideals in a society obsessed with status and affluence. H's penetrating eye begins to disturb his sitters and the more he works on the portrait the deeper the animosity and resentment which come to the surface. H's portrait leaves his sitters feeling uncomfortably exposed. H comments: "I believe biography is to be found in everything we do and say, in our every gesture, in the way we sit, the way we walk and stare, the way we turn our head or pick up an object from the floor. And that is what the painter must try to capture." H's reflections on people and things within his immediate circle of friends and acquaintances soon expand into a more searching analysis of wider issues concerning aesthetics and ethics. Diary entries made by H during a tour of Italian museums and art galleries confirm the painter's belief that the critic's role, whatever his medium, is not merely to observe but, above all, to understand. Serious and biting in turn, Saramago can elicit overwhelming perceptions about fate and circumstance from the most banal details. The commission is abruptly canceled and financial compensation offered, but H prefers to keep his unfinished portrait and go unpaid rather than sacrifice his principles. An artist's integrity is seen to be much more important than material rewards. The novel also heralds a new era in Portugal, as the dictatorial regime of Salazar collapses and the people rebel.

The following year Saramago published a collection of short stories entitled *Objecto Quase* (1978, *Quasi Object*) which confirmed that he is no less adept and versatile when dealing with the tensions of shorter narrative forms. Three of the six stories are sociopolitical allegories that show his incomparable skill in expanding a metaphor and weaving myriad associations around some obsessive image. The chair, for example, in "A Cadeira" symbolizes the dramatic demise of Salazar when a cerebral hemorrhage in 1968 effectively terminated his political career. Witty and provocative, these political allegories convey all the horror and fear engendered by oppressive and unnatural forces. Other stories in the collection strike contrasting moods and tonalities. The extinction of "O Centauro" (The Centaur) is described with unbearable pathos, while "Desforra" (Revenge) exemplifies the moving lyricism in Saramago's writing, which mitigates even the most acerbic of his observations about the human condition.

Saramago's second novel, *Levantado do Chão* (Raised from the Ground), 1980, which he himself defined as a "social novel," exposes further the sinister methods of repression practiced during the period of dictatorship (1932–1968). It covers a dark chapter in Portugal's history, which silenced writers and opponents of the regime.

Two years later, Saramago established his reputation internationally with *Memorial do Convento* (1982, *Baltasar and Blimunda*), which many critics consider to be his greatest achievement. The novel takes a satirical view of power and politics in Portugal during the first half of the 18th century. Evoking an age of pomp and ceremony when Portugal still had considerable influence in Europe, Saramago pillories both the monarchy and the Church for their vanity and greed while thousands of ordinary men and women suffered poverty and hardship in order to satisfy the whims of kings and prelates who ruled by force and the cruel instrument of the Inquisition. This questioning account of human fortunes in 18th-century Portugal is centered on the one hand on dreamers and visionaries like Padre Bartolomeu Lourenço de Gusmão, who invented a flying machine in the form of a huge bird, and, on the other, on the haunting love affair between a disabled ex-soldier, Baltasar Mateus (nicknamed Seven Suns because he can see only in the light), and the mysterious Blimunda (also known as Seven Moons because she can see in the dark), who has inherited her mother's Jewish blood and clairvoyant powers. Baltasar and Blimunda represent two vastly different worlds locked within the same historical reality. Richly textured with multiple layers of meaning, this is a novel in the grand manner.

Saramago's next novel, *A Jangada de Pedra* (1986, *The Stone Raft*), speculates on the dramatic separation of the Iberian peninsula from the rest of Europe when a crack suddenly opens down the entire length of the Pyrenees. This inexplicable phenomenon allows the author to voice his own misgivings about the excessive influence of France, Germany, and England over European politics and to launch a vigorous defense of smaller and poorer nations within the Community. The panic that ensues as the Iberian peninsula floats off into the Atlantic has elements of farce and pathos. Politicians and bureaucrats are thrown into confusion by this unexpected threat to their fortunes, experts and advisers consult their textbooks in vain for feasible explanations, while ordinary men and women try to make a new life for themselves amidst the chaos. Predictably enough, the latter reveal greater resourcefulness in coping with change than the powerful and privileged.

O Ano da Morte de Ricardo Reis (1984, *The Year of the Death of Ricardo Reis*), is rightly considered to be Saramago's most ambitious novel to date. Set in Lisbon in the 1930s, the novel probes every imaginable aspect of Portugal's history and culture by means of lengthy dialogues between the fictional narrator Ricardo Reis, newly returned from political exile in Brazil, and Portugal's most celebrated poet, Fernando Pessoa (1888–1935). Ricardo Reis, which was one of Pessoa's actual pseudonyms, is in Saramago's novel a monarchist and a doctor. Reis learns of Pessoa's death on his arrival in Lisbon, but Pessoa does not completely fade away from the world until nine months later. When he dies for the second time, he takes Reis with him.

As in all of Saramago's novels, poetry and reflection overlap. Pessoa and Reis are to some extent mirror images of the author himself, who reminds the reader: "We all suffer from some essential malaise, inseparable from what we are . . . because of that malaise we are so little, because of it we succeed in being so much." Saramago sees the world as one great theatrical arena where men and women play out games of life and death, each and every one of us irresistibly drawn to our own destiny. Intimations of transience, solitude, and nothingness remind us that human existence is at once prodigious and tragic. The vision of mankind presented here is complex and all-embracing. An astute observer of human foibles, Saramago guides us through the ages of man as his characters bare their souls and eventually discover that "human nature with its endless contradictions and misunderstandings is not to be trusted." A master of satire, he has an unsparing eye for the sham and hypocritical. Things human and divine are challenged, complacent values overturned. The author's portrait of Lisbon in 1936 has been compared with Flaubert's descriptions of Paris in 1848 and Joyce's vision of Dublin at the turn of the century. Shaun Whiteside, in the *New Statesman & Society*, called *Ricardo Reis* "a novel of ideas, subtly textured and rich in symbolism, written in a style redolent of the age of high modernism. . . . Giovanni Pontiero deserves to be applauded for capturing the novel's many different levels of discourse." In the *Times Literary Supplement*, Gabriel Josipovici found not only Pessoa behind the novel, but also Borges, although he deemed Saramago's style and his concerns very much his own: "a dense yet flexible style with long paragraphs, frequent shifts from third to first person, and no punctuation, apart from full stops and commas. In Giovanni Pontiero's versatile translation it comes over with authority, leaving you feeling that this is the only way to convey the world. . . . [T]he ending, when Pessoa, his nine months up, calls on Reis to lead him in turn to the cemetery, takes on an eerily mythic quality because it is so underwritten."

More solemn in tone, the *Historia do Cerco de Lisboa* (The History of the Siege of Lisbon, 1989) finds Saramago at his most philosophical and introspective. Closer to essay than fiction with its dense speculations, this thought-provoking perusal of Portugal's cultural past engages in a subtle game of counterpoint between the real and the imaginary, between history and literature.

O Evangelho segundo Jesus Cristo (1991, *The Gospel According to Jesus Christ*) is his most controversial novel. This powerful and moving account of Christ's earthly mission, from Bethlehem to Gethsemane, makes a spirited attack on traditional interpretations. Saramago faithfully traces out the key episodes in the Gospels, but bland, edifying narration is replaced with startling intimacies about the main protagonists in the greatest of all dramas. The emotional and spiritual ties between Jesus and his parents, between God the Son and God the Father, are ambivalent, tense, and often hostile. A troubled Jesus implacably questions the role he has been coerced into playing. An uncompromising champion of mankind, Saramago's Christ challenges Divine Authority, exposes the dubious nature of Providence, and mocks God's justice. As his end approaches, Jesus acknowledges that he has learned as much from Satan as from God. Thirty-three years on Earth have not been enough to ask all the questions or to receive any of the answers he so badly needed. God the Father, as portrayed by Saramago, is intransigent to the point of irrationality, his designs obscure to the point of perversity. In the final confrontation between Father and Son, Jesus has to be satisfied with "the only reply silence can give." Radical skepticism has rarely been voiced with such passion and poetry. John Butt remarked in the *Times Literary Supplement* on the wit that embellishes the novel, but said that "as Jesus' life approaches its terrible climax, the narrative acquires dignity and authority. The last chapters contain pages of great power, everywhere enhanced by an elegant and limpid translation" by Giovanni Pontiero.

Convinced that the writer's task is "to enlarge the world," Saramago explores every possible facet of human experience. Human destiny is a central issue in each of his novels, for he sees humankind as a remarkable species which only needs the right conditions in which to achieve its true potential. As a novelist, Saramago has no desire to be detached or impassive. For him, the writer is biased and should show his hand. Fluent and persuasive, Saramago passes effortlessly from description to commentary, from philosophical conceits to popular wisdom, from elaborate metaphors to simple human statements. Traditional elements of symmetry and counterpoint are combined with avant-garde techniques. Punctuation is strictly limited to commas and full stops in order to emphasize the oral nature of his prose and create what he himself has defined as *"uma corrente continua"* (a continuous flow) in the verbal music.

The Italian composer Azio Corghi composed a three-act opera based on the text of *Baltasar and Blimunda* which has been performed in Milan, Lisbon, and Turin. Saramago's play *In Nomine Dei*, also set to music by Corghi, was staged at Münster to commemorate the Anabaptist revolts in 1532–1535.

In 1994 Saramago had two more novels planned for publication: *Ensaio Sobre A Cegueira* (Essay on Blindness) and *O Livro das Tentações* (The Book of Temptations). Haunted by the idea that "the works of man are ever incomplete," he writes with the energy of a writer half his age, as if rediscovering with each new book that writing is a truly passionate way of living one's life.

PRINCIPAL WORKS IN ENGLISH TRANSLATION: *Novels*—(tr. G. Pontiero) Baltasar and Blimunda, 1987; (tr. G. Pontiero) The Year of the Death of Ricardo Reis, 1991; (tr. G. Pontiero) Manual of Painting and Calligraphy, 1994; (tr. G. Pontiero) The Stone Raft, 1994; (tr. G. Pontiero) The Gospel According to Jesus Christ, 1994. *Short stories*—(tr. G. Pontiero) Quasi Object, 1995.

ABOUT: Contemporary World Authors, 1993. *Periodicals*—Bulletin of Hispanic Studies (Portuguese issue) May 1994; Cultura Spring 1993; Independent Saturday Review (London) July 31, 1993; Nation May 16, 1994; New Statesman & Society August 28, 1992; New York Review of Books October 24, 1991; P.N. Review 16, no. 4, 1989; Times Literary Supplement December 5, 1988; September 11, 1992; October 22, 1993.

SAYLES, JOHN (THOMAS) (September 28, 1950–), American novelist, short story writer, filmmaker, playwright, and actor, was born and raised in Schenectady, New York, the son of Donald John Sayles, a teacher and school administrator, and Mary (Rausch) Sayles, also a teacher. By his own admission, Sayles was a "jock" at Schenectady's Mount Pleasant High School, where he earned letters in four sports. Notwithstanding his athletic prowess, he found that he was more of a "natural" at fiction writing. In a *New York Times Book Review* essay in 1981, he recalled: "I liked writing stories for class assignments and was pretty good at them. It was like getting a high grade for lying. I wrote a lot of rip-offs of Jack London or of 'The Untouchables' on TV. . . . " Never having met a writer, Sayles assumed that people wrote only "for fun," as he did. "I never thought about being a writer as I grew up; a writer wasn't something to *be*. An *out*fielder was something to be." It was the summer before he entered college, when he read Nelson Algren's novel *Somebody in Boots*, that Sayles first considered the possibility of writing his own book.

JOHN SAYLES

At Williams College Sayles majored in psychology because, as he put it in the *New York Times Book Review* in 1981, "I liked reading case histories and seeing films about animals' sex problems." An often indifferent scholar, he devoted much of his time to shooting pool and watching movies. Although he took few English courses, he did begin reading voraciously; he enrolled in creative writing classes in order to get his "grade-point average high enough to stay in school." After graduating from Williams in 1972, Sayles held a succession of low-paying, menial jobs: he worked as a nursing home orderly in Albany, as a day laborer in Atlanta, and as a meat packer in a Boston sausage factory. In his spare time he continued to write short fiction, which he submitted to magazines he had seen listed in the back of an *O. Henry Prize Stories* collection. At first, because he was unfamiliar with many of the periodicals he wrote to, he accumulated a steady stream of rejection notices. Then, in 1975, his short story "I-80 Nebraska"—a piece written almost entirely in truck drivers' CB argot—was published by the *Atlantic* and awarded an O. Henry prize.

Sayles completed his first novel, *Pride of the Bimbos*, while laid off from his meat packing job and collecting unemployment insurance, which he has called "my first and last grant for the arts." The central character, Midget "Pogo" Burns, is the extremely diminutive shortstop for the Brooklyn Bimbos—a five-man exhibition softball team touring the carnival circuit in rural Georgia, playing their games dressed in women's clothes. "In this comic first novel . . . John

Sayles does not just ask that disbelief be willingly suspended; he wants it lynched," a *Time* magazine reviewer said. Most critics commended Sayles for having produced an original treatment of an admittedly well-worn theme: American manhood and the perils of machismo. "Sayles's particular strength," Raymond Solokov wrote in the *New York Times Book Review*, "is to force us to care about his freaks and nonentities."

Sayles followed *Pride of the Bimbos* with *Union Dues*, the only novel to be nominated for both the National Book Award and the National Book Critics' Circle Award in 1977. Set in the late 1960s, the novel traces the flight of Hobie McNatt, who runs away from his home in the West Virginia coal country to search for his older brother, a burned-out Vietnam veteran. Arriving in Boston, Hobie takes up residence in a radical commune. His father, Hunter McNatt, although embroiled in an ongoing union dispute back home, sets out for Boston to rescue his wayward son. By placing Hobie, a West Virginia coal miner's son, in a totally unfamiliar milieu—that of the largely middle-class, college-educated New Left—Sayles is able to provide a nuanced examination of American class distinctions. While Sayles is rarely judgmental toward his characters, the middle-class revolutionaries in *Union Dues* emerge as fanatical and manipulative. Numerous critics have remarked upon Sayles's sensitive and authentic portrayal of working-class Americans; the unmasking of class distinctions figures prominently in much of his best work, both fiction and film.

In the *New Republic*, Bruce Allen wrote: "I could not keep myself from racing through the final chapter. . . . Not many novels, or novelists, can overpower you that way." Edward McConville, in the *Nation* (1977), called *Union Dues* "a disturbingly well-written novel" and "quite simply, the best book of its kind since Harvey Swados's *On the Line.*"

Union Dues was sold through a literary agency with connections to the Hollywood film industry. This provided Sayles, a movie devotee who aspired to become a screenwriter, with an entrée to the business. Moving to Santa Barbara, California, he was hired by Roger Corman, whose New World Pictures specialized in low-budget genre movies. Sayles cut his teeth as a screenwriter on such New World B pictures as *Piranha*, *The Lady in Red*, and *Battle Beyond the Stars*. Although he was soon much in demand as a scriptwriter and "script-doctor," Sayles was increasingly frustrated because so much of what he wrote never appeared on the screen. He financed his first independent film, *The Return of the Secaucus Seven*—which he wrote, directed, edited, and acted in—with money saved from studio scriptwriting assignments and royalties from his novels. Shot on location in New Hampshire and completed for a total budget of only $60,000, the film depicts a weekend reunion of seven former political activists, all of them around thirty years old and struggling to define themselves in adult roles. While it was warmly received and achieved some commercial success (it has since become a cult favorite), *The Return of the Secaucus Seven* did not lead to an immediate offer to do a studio-backed project.

Lianna, Sayles's second independent film, received mixed reviews, but established Sayles as a writer and director unafraid to confront issues that are usually anathema to Hollywood studios. Without resorting to sensationalism, *Lianna* portrays an unhappy young wife's awakening lesbianism. Meanwhile, Sayles had earned widespread critical acclaim for his short story collection *The Anarchists' Convention*. *Washington Post Book World* reviewer Garrett Epps praised Sayles's "unerring ear for American speech" and his "tremendous gift for characterization." However, two plays by Sayles, *New Hope for the Dead* and *Turnbuckle*—both performed at New York City's Boat Basin Theatre in 1981—were critical and commercial failures.

In 1983, still in his early thirties, Sayles was a recipient of a prestigious MacArthur Foundation grant, sometimes referred to as the "genius award." The five-year stipend, which provided $35,000 in tax-free income annually, allowed Sayles more latitude to pursue his independent film projects.

The Brother from Another Planet, the first film he completed after receiving the award, is a comic send-up of science fiction movies and a decidedly unconventional social satire. The title character, a runaway slave from a distant world, is marooned in a poverty-stricken, drug-infested section of Harlem. Pursued by interplanetary bounty hunters, he attempts, with often hilarious results, to blend in with the local human population. Aside from being mute and having clawlike toes, the extraterrestrial "brother" is indistinguishable from an ordinary human black man. He does, however, possess at least one special power: he can heal people's wounds and repair machinery with a single touch of his finger. While the film was not a critical success, its offbeat comic charm made it a commercial success, at least by the standards of low-budget independent films. In the *Nation*, Andrew Kopkind commented, "[Sayles's] one-man alternative cinema is a real treat, and if you watch closely, he can make Hollywood disappear."

With his next two films—both of which were written years before being produced—Sayles turned his attention to historical subjects. *Matewan* focuses on a bloody conflict between coal mine owners and union activists in a West Virginia town in 1920. In *Thinking in Pictures*, a nonfiction book, Sayles analyzes the making of *Matewan* from start to finish, providing a host of technical material, the complete screenplay, as well as details on such matters as fund-raising and assembling a cast. His next picture, *Eight Men Out*, is a dramatization of the "Black Sox Scandal," in which members of the Chicago White Sox baseball team conspired with oddsmakers and gamblers to throw the 1919 World Series.

Los Gusanos, Sayles's third and most ambitious novel, was twelve years in the making. While all of the major characters are fictional, the novel is grounded in real historical incidents, in this case the experiences of Cuban exiles living in Miami, Florida. *Los Gusanos*, Spanish for "the worms," is the derogatory appellation Castroites apply to those Cubans who left the island nation in the wake of the 1959 revolution. Sayles recalls being intrigued by the plight of the Miami Cubans even as a child, when he would visit his grandparents' home in Florida. As he remarked to a *New York Times Book Review* interviewer in 1991, he wrote the book to answer the questions, "Who are these people, and what do they think about?" He drafted a plot outline in the late 1970s, but wrote the bulk of the novel in the two years prior to its publication. In the intervening decade, he learned Spanish, interviewed Cuban exiles, and immersed himself in Cuban and Cuban-American literature, working on the novel between film projects and during two prolonged Writers' Guild strikes.

While *Los Gusanos* contains dozens of characters and multiple points of view, Sayles concentrates throughout on the experiences of one family. The novel opens in Miami in 1981. The de la Penas, once well-to-do cattle ranchers in the central Cuban province of Camagüey, have fallen on hard times. Scipio, the family patriarch, is confined to a Miami nursing home, mute and helpless after suffering a massive stroke. One of his two sons was killed in the disastrous 1961 Bay of Pigs invasion. The other son has disappeared into the underworld. Marta de la Pena, the only daughter, is a nurse in the facility where Scipio teeters on the brink of death. Withdrawn, beautiful, and proud, Marta—who has spent most of her life in the United States, but still remembers her Cuban childhood—devises a paramilitary plot to strike out against Castro and to restore her family's honor. Marta recruits "El Halcón" (the falcon), a murderous ex-military

man from the Batista regime, for her desperate, ill-fated mission.

"To me," Sayles told *Progressive* magazine, "the important spectrum in *Los Gusanos* is not right-wing or left-wing, because most of the people are right of center. It's between 'believers' and 'cynics.' A lot of what I'm dealing with is how do you still act once you know too much to be a true believer."

Los Gusanos is replete with chunks of untranslated Spanish, particularly dialogue, which Sayles included to provide a more realistic rendering of the colloquial mix of English and Spanish spoken by many Cuban émigrés. "Some may be alarmed at the audacity of a white boy from Schenectady daring to presume to write knowingly about such an insular community," Randall Kenan wrote in a *Nation* (1991) review of the novel. "But Sayles's portrait of a community in exile and a Cuba decades gone hums with a conviction that cannot be dismissed lightly." Jay Cantor, himself the author of a fictional biography of Che Guevara, noted in the *New York Times Book Review* (1991): "Like the American novel's grand progenitor, *Moby Dick*, this book has a rich mix of ethnicities and races. . . . *Los Gusanos* is an energetic, fierce, melodramatic and ironic adventure novel; like poetry and opera war comics, another thing that history becomes."

Sayles never intended to make *Los Gusanos* into a film. "This has twenty or so points of view," he told the *New York Times Book Review*. "Any movie would be a reduction." In the past, Sayles rarely worried about distinctions among different media and genres. As he noted in his 1981 *New York Times Book Review* essay: "The various forms of writing I've done, from *Union Dues* to the screenplay for *Alligator* [a 1980 film directed by Lewis Teague], have never seemed that different to me." Indeed, Sayles's versatility and independence make him virtually one of a kind among his artistic contemporaries. *American Film* contributor Thulani Davis observed: "He's an accomplished novelist, and he makes his own movies—exercising total control over both kinds of work. And he still has time to develop shows for television and to write the occasional screenplay for somebody else." His 1992 film *Passion Fish*—about a crippled ex-soap opera star and her black caretaker—won widespread critical acclaim, even from reviewers that had formerly been dismissive of his work. "He had emerged as the rarest of American filmmakers," Andrew Sarris wrote in *Film Comment*, "one who understands the subtler overtones of class distinctions, social injustices, and economic inequalities. . . . "

Based in Hoboken, New Jersey, throughout much of the 1980s, Sayles and his longtime companion and collaborator Maggie Renzi moved to an upstate New York farm in the early 1990s. "Conversation is what I'm ambitious about," he told the *Progressive*. In an interview with *Sight and Sound*, he remarked: "A lot of my movies are about community. Their culture is an attempt at community culture rather than mass culture. . . . I'm aware of mass culture, and I'm aware that I'm part of it. The stuff I do goes into theatres, it's advertised, I do interviews. But I want my work to be about it, but not necessarily of it."

PRINCIPAL WORKS: *Novels*—Pride of the Bimbos, 1975; Union Dues, 1977; Los Gusanos, 1991. *Short stories*—The Anarchists' Convention and Other Stories, 1979. *Nonfiction*—Thinking in Pictures: The Making of the Movie Matewan, 1987. *Films written and directed by Sayles*—The Return of the Secaucus Seven, 1980; Lianna, 1983; Baby, It's You, 1983; The Brother from Another Planet, 1984; Matewan, 1987; Eight Men Out, 1988; City of Hope, 1991; Passion Fish, 1992. *Other screenplays*—Piranha, 1978; The Lady in Red, 1979; Battle Beyond the Stars, 1980; Alligator, 1980; (with T. Winkless) The Howling, 1980; (with R. Maxwell) The Challenge, 1982; Enormous Changes at the Last Minute, 1983; The Clan of the Cave Bear, 1984; Wild Thing, 1987; Breaking In, 1989; A Safe Place, 1993. *Plays*—New Hope for the Dead, 1981; Turnbuckle, 1981.

ABOUT: Contemporary Authors New Revision Series 41, 1994; Contemporary Literary Criticism, 7, 1977; 10, 1979; 14, 1980; Current Biography Yearbook 1984; Dictionary of Literary Biography, 44, 1986; World Film Directors, Vol. II, 1988. *Periodicals*—American Film May 1986, June 1991; Film Comment May/June 1993; Nation October 22, 1977; October 6, 1984; June 24, 1991; New Republic September 17, 1977; New York Times August 2, 1990; New York Times Book Review September 14, 1975; September 6, 1981; November 29, 1987; June 16, 1991; Progressive November 1991; Rolling Stone September 8, 1977; Sight and Sound September 1993; Time July 7, 1975; Washington Post Book World August 24, 1975; April 29, 1979.

SCHAMA, SIMON MICHAEL (February 13, 1945–   ), American historian and educator, was born in London to Arthur Osias Schama, a textile merchant descended from Jewish spice traders in Smyrna, and Clare (Steinberg) Schama, whose ancestors were timber farmers in Lithuania. His paternal grandparents had emigrated from Romania to England. Schama recalled his boyhood in post–World War II London, born "the night we bombed Dresden" in a street that had been destroyed by V-2's and "playing soccer in the weedy ruins." The family

SIMON MICHAEL SCHAMA

was peripatetic, moving about in rhythm with his father's varying fortunes: "cricket matches and houses by the sea alternated with cramped apartments in London." Arthur Schama had many cultural interests. To him the son attributes the awakening of his historical curiosity—stimulated at first by visits to English monuments and old houses—as well as a love of the theater and a relish for language and eloquence.

Schama entered Christ's College, Cambridge University, already determined to study history for his first tripos (freshman and sophomore years); but, in deference to his parents' wishes, he agreed to switch to law for his third and fourth year program. However, the influence in particular of the eminent historian J. H. Plumb, who early recognized his student's intellectual brilliance and linguistic gifts, set him on his professional path.

During his undergraduate years Schama's academic career was nearly blighted when, to the disappointment of his mentor Plumb and to his own humiliation, he was awarded merely upper second-class honors instead of the first-class that everybody expected of him. Plumb tried in vain to get the grade reconsidered. Some years later it was discovered that Schama had been the victim of an academic vendetta; a disciple of the historian Sir Herbert Butterfield, a rival out to undermine Plumb's standing, had managed to become a part of Schama's examination committee and had deliberately downgraded his papers. But the candidate meanwhile had more than made up for this setback by taking a "star first" on his second tripos. As a result, he was offered a teaching fellowship at Christ's College immediately upon receiving his B.A. in 1966 at the age of twenty-one. His M.A. followed in 1969.

For ten years (1966–1976) Schama was director of studies in history at Cambridge, followed by a shorter tenure (1976–1980) as tutor in history and lecturer at Brasenose College, Oxford. Here he met and married an American geneticist, Virginia Papaioannu, who subsequently became a professor of anatomy and pathology at Tufts Medical College. They have two children, Chloe and Gabriel.

In 1980 Schama moved to the United States to take up an appointment at Harvard as Mellon Professor of Social Sciences and also became a senior associate at the Center for European Studies. At Harvard Schama acquired a reputation as something of an enfant terrible among academic graybeards. "He had quite a stage presence," according to former student Peter Spiro, a foreign-policy analyst in Washington, D.C. Another student, the television writer Louise Campbell, remembers him as a "a kook, a breath of fresh air, very bubbly." Generally he attracted large numbers of undergraduate students with his unorthodox teaching methods, lecturing without notes in a manner reminiscent of an evangelical preacher, employing visual aids generously. At the same time he was challenging and demanding in his graduate seminars.

Schama's charismatic personality has been backed up by substantial innovative scholarship. "The most famous historian of his generation" according to the New York Observer, he is one of the few to have reached best-seller status. His books ranging over Palestine, Holland, France, and America and through the centuries defy specialization. They have in common, in his words, "the formation of national identities, the way in which people recognize themselves as part of a historical community."

At the time he came to Harvard Schama was the author of two conventional monographs known mainly to specialists. One of these had developed out of his seminars in Jewish intellectual and social history at Cambridge—Two Rothschilds and the Land of Israel, a densely packed reconstruction of the part played by the French philanthropist Baron Edmond de Rothschild and his son James in the late 19th- and early 20th-century settlement of Palestine. This book was commissioned by a descendant, the banker Lord Victor Rothschild, who provided Schama access to the files of the Jewish Colonization Association. Schama acknowledges also the inspiration of his father, "a passionate enthusiast of Jewish history," who had died a few

months before the publication of the book. This study was preceded by Patriots and Liberators, which traces the transformation of the Batavian Republic from a "semi-fief" of France into the Independent Kingdom of Holland after the French Revolution. This first book, for which Schama learned Dutch in order to delve into untapped archives in The Hague, was awarded both the Wolfson Prize for History in 1977 and the Leo Gersoy Prize of the American Historical Association in 1978.

In the preface to Patriots and Liberators, Schama expresses gratitude to his mentor Plumb for teaching him that "history must at least strive to be an art before it can pretend to be a science." Plumb also encouraged him to move beyond the traditional preoccupations of historians with politics and war. When he returned to Dutch history in The Embarrassment of Riches, the book by which he first reached a wide readership, it was with an enlarged cultural context. Pushing back his investigation to Holland's "Golden Age" of the 17th century, which had left behind a rich graphic record of its everyday life, Schama prepared himself by an intensive course in what he refers to as "the history of art history." This program included not only close study of the paintings and prints of the period, but modern inconographic theory as well. His students were offered such novel courses as "Pieter Breughel and Northern Humanism" and "Art and Allegiance in the Baroque."

In The Embarrassment of Riches, which originated in the Erasmus Lectures on the Civilization of the Netherlands delivered at Oxford in 1978, Schama characterizes Dutch culture as "an allegiance that was fashioned as the consequence, not the cause, of freedom, and that was defined by common habits rather than legislated by institutions." This collective mentality was shaped, as Schama reconstructs it, both by the historical circumstances of the Dutch, having wrested themselves free of foreign domination (Spain), and by their "moral geography," their sense of being surrounded by a sea which they had conquered and which had made them prosperous. The epigraph of the book, taken from John Calvin's Commentary on Genesis—"Let those who have abundance remember that they are surrounded by thorns"—sets the pattern of the interlocking chapters that follow in which contradictory elements in the Dutch temperament are reconciled: piety amidst worldliness, provinciality united with cosmopolitanism, thrift alongside ostentation, the burgher dwelling inside the patrician. Works of art—paintings, sculpture, monuments, emblems, prints—are profusely reproduced as manifestations of the manners, morals, and social assumptions of the age.

The Embarrassment of Riches was hailed by John Gross in the *New York Times* as "history on a grand scale," but others were qualified in their praise. The opulent, colorful writing, which led Harold Beaver, in the *New York Times Book Review* (1987), to liken the book to "a fascinating panorama as busily animated and skillfully composed as scenes by Frederick Avercamp and Jan Steen," overwhelmed some reviewers. John Huxtable Elliott, for one, while noting, in the *New Republic* (1987), the author's acute eye for the apt, pictorial image went on to remark that with the "baroque profusion" of detail the reader may find himself "submerged beneath a cascade of words, witticisms, and illustrative examples." Art historians complained that Schama had stressed the topicality of the paintings he discussed while scanting the traditions behind them. Some social historians questioned whether the picture portrayed here of the effect of Dutch affluence could stand for the entire society. Schama seems to anticipate such an objection in his introduction, where he points out that the culture of 17th-century Holland was a widely shared one; barriers between the elite and the masses had broken down through a common religion, genre paintings, and the dissemination of cheap books and prints. At any rate, the book became "an event in historical studies," as Jonathan Israel predicted in the *Times Literary Supplement*, public response calling for six printings.

More controversy greeted Schama's next book, the equally mammoth-sized *Citizens: A Chronicle of the French Revolution*, published two years later to coincide with the bicentenary of the Fall of the Bastille. This study had its inception in a seminar on the biographical approach to history conducted at Balliol College by Richard Cobb, which Schama contends taught him to see the Revolution "not as a march of abstractions and ideologies, but as a human event of complicated and often tragic outcomes." Hence private life alternates with public life in this narrative account enlivened with pen portraits of famous as well as obscure people involved in these calamitous events. As with *The Embarrassment of Riches*, the art of the period—the paintings of David and contemporaries as well as cartoons and pornography—is invoked to yield its polemical messages. Much is made too of the newly emergent mass media—pamphlets, newspapers, and public oratory.

Lawrence Stone, reviewing *Citizens* in the *New Republic* (1989), was impressed with its "coruscating brilliance" and "dazzling display of erudition and intelligence," but some fellow historians took issue with what Stone refers to as the "unusual stress on the sheer ferocity and brutality of the events," and the revisionist stance in general. The Revolution for Schama—far from the progressive, populist movement of received tradition was retrograde, actually halting the process of "modernization" that had already been launched under the monarchy. Rather than advancing the cause of liberty and equality, "for one year, it practiced representative democracy; for two years, it imposed coercive egalitarianism. . . . But for two decades its enduring product was a new kind of militarized state." Specialists in the period, while conceding some validity to Schama's interpretation, felt that his reading of the events was one sided and blinkered. According to Eugen Weber in the *New York Times*, "nowhere more than here does [Schama] challenge enduring prejudices with prejudices of his own." Colin Jones, in the *Times Literary Supplement* (1989), detected in this "top-down rather than bottom-up" view of the Revolution inconsistency, confusing chronology, shrill pamphleteering, and even, towards the end, signs of hasty writing. Some reviewers were bothered by what seemed its arbitrary conclusion at the height of the Reign of Terror in 1794 before the Revolution reached its culmination. Nevertheless, *Citizens* proved a popular success. It subsequently received Britain's National Cash Register (NCR) Book Award for Nonfiction, and was designated Book of the Year in 1990 by the *Yorkshire Post*.

Meanwhile Schama accepted an invitation by the editors of the British literary magazine *Granta* to contribute a sketch titled "The Many Deaths of General Wolfe," hero-martyr of the battle for Quebec on the Plains of Abraham in 1759, commemorated in the idealized painting by Benjamin West. Out of this so-called "experiment with historical narrative" germinated *Dead Certainties (Unwarranted Speculations)*, made up of two "historical novellas," the second and longer one taken up with the murder of Dr. George Parkman by John Webster, a professor of chemistry at the Harvard Medical School, a case that rocked Boston in 1849. Schama was led to investigate this crime because the victim was an uncle of the historian Francis Parkman, one of his sources on the death of Wolfe. Tenuous as the link seems between these two tragic events, the various received accounts of both being riddled with contradictions and unresolved mysteries, they served the author as complementary illustrations of the elusiveness of truth. While drawing on primary sources from the library and archives of the Massachusetts Historical Society, Schama admitted that he indulged his imagination to flesh them out—particularly in a purported eyewitness report of General Wolfe's death by a soldier, and a reconstructed dialogue between two key figures in the Parkman trial.

Propelled by the fascinations of a detective story, Schama's "experiment" could be enjoyed, as it was by many, as a "rattling good read," in the words of Roy Porter in the *New Statesman & Society*, but in the opinion of a number of historians this hybrid of fact and fiction fell between stools. "The detail is marvelous. But too many details obscure and cloy. And I am not sure that the central message they are intended to embroider is as important or as sound as Schama supposes," observed Linda Colley in the *Times Literary Supplement* (1991). For Gordon S. Wood, his harshest critic, writing in the *New York Review of Books* (1991), Schama's "violations of the conventions of history writing actually puts the discipline of history at risk." Schama took opportunity to defend his approach at a crowded lecture in the auditorium of the New York Historical Society in the fall of 1991. "So far from the intellectual integrity of history being policed by the protocols of objectivity, distance, and scientific dispassion," he declared on this occasion, "its best prospects lie in the forthright admission of subjectivity, immediacy, and literary imagination." Invoking Henry James's *The Sense of the Past* in the afterword of *Dead Certainties*, he wrote of historians in general: "We are doomed to be forever hailing someone who has just gone around the corner and out of earshot."

"*Landscape and Memory* . . . seeks to uncover the memories, myths, and cultural associations with which the inhabitants of the West over the past two or three millennia have perceived and shaped the natural world around them," according to Keith Thomas in the *New York Review of Books*. In *Landscape and Memory* Schama tries to cast light on the ways in which the myth as a way of regarding and explaining the world lingers in todays's views of nature. Divided into sections on Wood, Water, and Rock, the book contains an enormous variety of history and anecdote, including the story of Schama's ancestors. Thomas concluded that no summary could convey "the riches of this book. . . . the brio and hilarity with which it is written . . . its narrative excitement; or . . . the long gallery of eccentrics and visionaries whose idiosyncrasies the author seizes upon with such relish."

In 1992, Virginia Papaioannu ("Ginny," to whom *The Embarrassment of Riches* is dedicated) was offered a professorship of genetics and development in Columbia's College of Physicians and Surgeons, and when the university authorities learned who her husband was, Schama

was invited to join the faculty as Old Dominion Professor of Humanities, an appointment that enables him to teach both in the history and art history departments. His new academic base, he has remarked, "is the farthest thing imaginable from an ivory tower. It's more of a bloodied grand dame." His book, *Landscape and Memory*, combines his fields of scholarship. It has been contracted by BBC for adaptation as a television film with the author serving as narrator.

PRINCIPAL WORKS: Patriots and Liberators, 1977; Two Rothschilds and the Land of Israel, 1979; The Embarrassment of Riches: An Interpretation of Dutch Culture in the Golden Age, 1987; Citizens: A Chronicle of the French Revolution, 1989; Dead Certainties (Unwarranted Speculations), 1991; Landscape and Memory, 1995. *As editor*—(with E. Homberger and W. Janeway) The Cambridge Mind, 1970.

ABOUT: Contemporary Authors New Revision Series 39, 1992; Current Biography Yearbook 1991; International Who's Who 1991–1992. *Periodicals*—American Historical Review December 1979; American Spectator September 1989; Commentary July 1979, September 1982; Encounter August 1989; Harvard Magazine November–December 1991; History Today December 1987; Journal of Modern History March 1993; New Republic August 24, 1987; April 17, 1989; June 3, 1991; New Statesman November 24, 1978; New Statesman & Society June 7, 1991; New York Observer September 27, 1993; New York Review of Books January 21, 1988; April 13, 1989; June 27, 1991; September 21, 1995; New York Times March 15, 1989; April 27, 1989; May 9, 1991; New York Times Book Review May 15, 1977; December 13, 1978; July 5, 1987; March 19, 1989; May 12, 1991; New York Times Magazine September 8, 1991; New Yorker September 24, 1987; April 17, 1989; Publishers Weekly May 17, 1991; Time April 17, 1989; Times Literary Supplement November 20–26, 1987; July 21–27, 1989; June 14, 1991.

SCHELL, JONATHAN (August 21, 1943–   ), American journalist and historian, was born in New York City, the youngest of the three children of Marjorie Bertha Schell and Orville Schell. Although his parents eventually divorced, his father, a partner in the law firm of Hughes, Hubbard & Reed, a one-time president of the City Bar Association, and an early opponent of the Vietnam War, must be considered a centrally important influence. Orville Schell, while belonging to the world of Wall Street, was anything but a conventional lawyer. He was active in human rights, including service as chairman of Americas Watch, a human rights organization monitoring Latin America and the Caribbean, and often traveled abroad to investigate human rights violations. In the late 1960s he marched in peace parades and helped organize a group of 1,000 lawyers who marched on Washington to protest the American military campaign in Cambodia. Thus it was hardly surprising that Jonathan Schell began his writing career by exposing the cruelties that American troops were inflicting on the Vietnamese people, nor that he went on to castigate government policy during the Nixon administration, and finally to question the American government's nuclear policy. As his editor at the *New Yorker* put it, "The Constitution [has been] his touchstone; he went back to it for inspiration time after time. He approached each new situation with his historical perspective and his particular political vision intact."

Educated at the Dalton School in Manhattan, the Putney School in Vermont, and Harvard College, Schell graduated magna cum laude in 1965. He spent the next year at Harvard studying Far Eastern history and the year following studying Japanese in Tokyo. In 1967 he joined the *New Yorker* magazine as a writer and editor; in 1969 he became the chief writer for the magazine's "Notes and Comment"; many of his books first appeared there in serialized form. After working for the *New Yorker* for twenty years, Schell became a visiting professor, first at Emory University, then at New York University's School of Journalism. He was the Ferris Professor at Princeton for a term in late 1988. He then became a columnist for *Newsday*.

On his way home from Tokyo in early 1967, Schell stopped off in Vietnam "with a vague ambition of doing some writing." Having managed to get himself accredited as a correspondent for the Harvard *Crimson*, he was aboard one of the U.S. helicopters that made the assault on the village of Ben Suc. From this position he watched the village being taken, the inhabitants forcibly removed, and their houses burned, bulldozed, and bombed. His first book, *The Village of Ben Suc*, which was initially serialized in the *New Yorker* and which vividly describes the military maneuvers he witnessed, is a scathing indictment of the unnecessary damage and cruelty the U.S. forces inflicted on Vietnamese civilians—an indictment achieved by simple reporting, letting the events speak for themselves. John Mecklin, writing for the *New York Times Book Review*, commented that the book was "brilliant" and "extraordinarily persuasive" but also "slanted journalism, mainly because of its multitudinous sins of omission . . . The book makes no effort at all to relate the performance at Ben Suc to the monstrous handicaps that plague the United States effort in Vietnam . . . It should be read with the caveat that it tells only a small part of the story, but it nevertheless performs a public service in suggesting how poorly American military commanders . . . understand the nature of Asian guerilla warfare." Comments such as this one, both praising and questioning Schell's views, were repeated with each book Schell published, and the author remained a much lauded but also controversial writer.

His next book, *The Military Half: An Account of the Destruction in Quang Ngai and Quang Tin*, was again based on personal observation. This time the pilot of the plane he flew in had the job of locating targets for jet fighter-bombers; the pilot was to determine which villages—seen from 1,500 to 5,000 feet above—were friendly and which were not. The ultimate results of these sightings were massive air strikes—bombings, napalm drops, and strafing. Schell writes that seventy percent of the villages in Quang Nagi were obliterated, and that forty percent of the population was removed to refugee camps. Reviewers of the book were once again divided in their responses—Steven Schueller commented in the *National Review* that Schell "witnessed action in a limited area," while Jonathan Mirsky pointed out in the *Nation* that the wide-scale destruction that Schell described was common, and that he knew no book which had made him angrier and more ashamed of the American intervention.

Turning next to the Nixon administration in *The Time of Illusion*, Schell argues that this administration ushered in "a new form of rule in which images were given precedence over substance in every phase of government." Nixon, Schell argues, believed that he could control and manipulate public opinion and acted to "compose scenes rather than to solve real problems"; he perceived all opposition as part of a unified conspiracy against presidential authority and accordingly set out to assume dictatorial powers and "make war against Americans." The greater illusion of his administration and of those just preceding it, Schell maintains, was to assume that America's "credibility" with the rest of the world depended on its maintaining an *appearance* of power. Peter Prescott, reviewing the book for *Newsweek*, found it "overlong, repetitious, ill organized and intemperate, which is not to say that it is not entirely correct. Schell's graceful sentences nearly mitigate the rage with which he writes; his ironic juxtapositions nearly persuade me to accept his argument as fact. And yet his assumption of insidious design calls for more evidence." Nevertheless, he found the book a "genuine chiller, if only because it reminds us of how far Nixon succeeded in dismantling our government and Constitution before Watergate."

Schell's next two books, *The Fate of Earth* and *The Abolition*, focus on the nature of the nuclear threat and how that threat might be averted. Once we recognize, Schell argues in *The Fate of the Earth*, "that a holocaust *might* lead to extinction we have no right to gamble, because if we lose, the game will be over, and neither we nor anyone else will ever get another chance . . . We have no choice but to address the issue of nuclear weapons as though we knew for a certainty that their use would put an end to our species." After explaining how atomic bombs are made and how widespread use of them would lead to human extinction, Schell discusses our responsibility to future generations and argues that the theory of mutual deterrence cannot be relied on to prevent nuclear war; only the establishment of a world government and the abolition of sovereign states can avert a nuclear catastrophe. Following up on this theme in *The Abolition*, Schell suggests "a way of abolishing nuclear weapons that does not require us to found a world government, which the world shows virtually no interest in founding," and proposes that the weapons now in existence should be abolished.

Reviewers of the two books were more favorable to the first than the second. Obviously, on such a momentous issue as nuclear policy, there was bound to be controversy among political analysts, some of whom found Schell's solutions vague and naive. But Schell also had many supporters—among them Max Lerner, who predicted in the *New Republic* that *The Fate of the Earth* would become "the classic statement of the emerging consciousness." Harrison Salisbury commented that the book was the most important one of the decade, "perhaps of the century." And in the opinion of Walter Cronkite, the book was "one of the most important of recent years. If it can do for the nuclear sanity movement what Rachel Carson's *Silent Spring* did for the environment movement, there still may be hope to save our civilization." *The Fate of the Earth* received several awards, among them the Melcher Book Award and the Los Angeles Times Book Award. It was nominated for the Pulitzer Prize, the National Book Award, and the National Book Critics Award.

Schell's method in *History in Sherman Park* is less polemical than reportorial. This time he begins by visiting a neighborhood in Milwaukee in order to understand the views of voters during the 1984 Reagan-Mondale presidential campaign. A young college-educated, married couple of working-class background and their neighbors, relatives, and friends provide the main material for his discussion about how middle Americans are responding to a new era of

politics. What he finds is a profound transformation of American life. "The dissolution of neighborhoods . . . is accompanied by a dissolution of political ties. Replacing the ties based on community . . . are ties created by the television set." Watching television, one image being immediately replaced by another, Schell maintains, Americans become forgetful and, worse, capable of substituting one idea for another in rapid succession so that different ideas are entertained at the same time and no one idea can outlast the moment or make an enduring impression. In the postwar period, we have been spared real pain while wars, revolutions, and famines have become in every sense "living room" events for us. Despite Schell's caveat, the heart of *History in Sherman Park* is more compassionate than divisive; the author's understanding of the individuals he interviewed takes on a novelistic coloring as he attempts to comprehend the problems at confront each family, and how work, family, and community life have changed in America.

Observing the Nixon Years brings together the many essays about Vietnam and Watergate that Schell wrote for the *New Yorker*'s "Notes and Comment" from 1969 to 1975. Covering the period from Nixon's inauguration through his resignation and the fall of Saigon less than a year later, Schell discusses Nixon's strategy of Vietnamization, ostensibly designed to train the South Vietnamese to defend themselves, but in effect making the war more palatable to protesters by reducing American casualties. Nixon's strategy worked for a time, helping to create public apathy about the war—but in fact, Schell points out, the slow withdrawal of American troops under Vietnamization increased the level of American violence. As American soldiers left for home, the air force augmented its attacks over North and South Vietnam, and also over Cambodia. Schell depicts the air war as cowardly and indiscriminate. "Never," he says, "has a nation unleashed so much violence with so little risk to itself. It . . . involves us all in the dishonor of killing in a cause we are no longer willing to die for." In late chapters discussing Watergate, Schell sounds the themes of arrogance in the executive branch and of public apathy. His indictment of the Nixon administration, and of Nixon himself, found favor among a number of writers and even among a few politicians. Senator Paul Simon called *Observing the Nixon Years* a "great book," observing that Schell was "absolutely on target." Robert Heilbroner thought Schell's pieces were "as fierce as razor blades," finding them "a record of a terrible time in America," and applauding them for their reaffirmation of "the essential principles of

American virtue." David Oshinsky, in the *New York Times Book Review*, said that "even today one can admire the originality of these essays, their eloquence and plain good sense," William Shawn, editor of the *New Yorker*, commented in a preface to the book on "the unexpectedness of [Schell's] turn of thought. He is constantly saying what has not been said before."

Schell has won many grants, honors, and awards, in addition to the awards and nominations given him for his most acclaimed book, *The Fate of the Earth*. He was a Guggenhiem Fellow in 1989 and a MacArthur Foundation Grant winner during the same period. The American Academy and Institute for the Arts and Letters gave him an award for literature in 1973. He was made a Doctor of Humane Letters at Saint Xavier College in 1985, and his Notes and Comment for the *New Yorker* were awarded the George Polk Award in 1976. Schell lives in New York City with his wife, Elspeth Schell, an elementary school teacher, and his three children, Matthew, Phoebe, and Thomas.

PRINCIPAL WORKS: The Village of Ben Suc, 1967; The Military Half: An Account of the Destruction in Quang Ngai and Quang Tin, 1968; The Time of Illusion, 1976; The Fate of the Earth, 1982; The Abolition, 1984; History in Sherman Park, 1987; The Real War, 1988; Observing the Nixon Years, 1989.

ABOUT: Contemporary Authors New Revision Series 12, 1985; Contemporary Literary Criticism 35, 1985; Current Biography Yearbook, 1993. *Periodicals*—Nation August 5, 1968; National Review March 25, 1969; New Republic April 28, 1982; New York Times June 19, 1987; New York Times Book Review October 29, 1967; April 9, 1989; Newsweek January 12, 1976; Publishers Weekly April 21, 1989.

SCHNACKENBERG, GJERTRUD (CECELIA) (August 27, 1953–), American poet, was born in Tacoma, Washington, the youngest of four daughters of Doris (Strom) and Walter Charles Schnackenberg. The family is of Norwegian origin. Her father, who died in 1973, was a professor of Russian and medieval history at Pacific Lutheran University in Tacoma. He was a man of wide-ranging interests in history, religion and art, to whose memory she paid tribute in the poem "Walking Home." in *Portraits and Elegies*: "I never knew / A man who loved the world as much as you, / And that love was the last thing to let go." While still an undergraduate at Mount Holyoke College, Gjertrud Schnackenberg began writing poetry, and before she received her B.A., summa cum laude, in 1975, she had published in literary journals

GJERTRUD SCHNACKENBERG

and had twice received the Glascock award for poetry (1973 and 1974). Mount Holyoke awarded her an honorary doctor of letters in 1985. During the late 1970s her work appeared in the *Mississippi Review*, *Poetry*, *Ploughshares*, and *Kenyon Review*. She held fellowships from the Mary Ingraham Bunting Institute of Radcliffe College (1979–1980), the Bread Loaf Writers Conference (1981), and the Ingram Merrill Foundation (1981–1982). Since publication of her first collection in 1982, her poetry has appeared in the *Atlantic*, the *Paris Review*, the *Yale Reviews* the *New Yorker*, and other venues, and she has had further recognition including, in 1983, the Lavan Younger Poets Award of the Academy of American Poets and the Rome Prize in Creative Literature, awarded jointly by the American Academy and Institute of Arts and Letters and the American Academy in Rome. She spent the academic year 1984–1985 in Rome on an Amy Lowell Travelling Scholarship in Poetry. In 1986 she had a National Endowment for the Arts fellowship in poetry, and in 1987–1988 she was a Guggenheim Fellow and artist-in-residence at the American Academy in Rome. In 1989 she received the Brandeis University Creative Arts Award citation in poetry. She has given readings and lectures at a number of American colleges and universities and at the Library of Congress, the Folger Shakespeare Library, the New York Public Library, and the Institute of Contemporary Art in London. She is married to the philosopher Robert Novick, who teaches at Harvard.

The three slender volumes of verse that

Gjertrud Schnackenberg published in the decade 1982 to 1992 reveal not only the growing maturity of voice and vision one expects in any developing young poet, but, more remarkably, as David St. John wrote in the *Antioch Review* of her first book, *Portraits and Elegies*, a poet "writing in the traditional forms who also has in her grasp both powerful subject matter and the intelligence to command her technique." Her use of traditional rhyme and meter has led some critics to assign her to the New Formalism, but such narrow classification misrepresents her poetry, which adheres to no strict literary ideology or poetics. Rather, she works independently within the wide framework of traditional humanism. Without comparing their poetry in any specific detail, Phoebe Pettingell, writing in the *New Leader* in 1985, cited Schnackenberg and Amy Clampitt as poets "who represent change in current poetic style. They both recognize a universe of ideas outside their own personal impressions and treat form as an enhancement and delight, rather than a trap."

Portraits and Elegies received wide and generally very favorable attention. Reviewers were especially impressed with the young poet's mastery of her technique and with her sense of history. The "portraits" include a narrative poem, "Darwin in 1881," and a series of poems, "19 Hadley Street," that trace the history of a house and its inhabitants back to 18th-century New England. Emblematic of this domestic history in "The Paperweight" is a glass globe that holds a small house in a snowy scene:

Beyond our lives, they laugh, and drink their tea.
We look at them just as the winter night
With its vast empty spaces bends to see
Our isolated little world of light,

Covered with snow, and snow in clouds above it,
And drifts and swirls too deep to understand.
Still, I must try to think a little of it,
With so much winter in my head and hand.

In "Darwin in 1881" the naturalist, living his last year of life withdrawn from society, is a redundant Prospero returned from his island to Milan: "Breaking his wand, and taking off his robe: / Knowledge increases unreality." Her Darwin wanders about his house at night and awaits death: "Now, done with beetle jaws and beaks of gulls / And bivalve hinges, now, utterly done, / One miracle remains, and only one."

The most moving of her elegies in this first volume is for her father. In "Laughing With One Eye," three days after his death, she sits in the kitchen looking at an old-fashioned planter's clock and recalls childhood fishing trips with him:

. . . We watch the black
Waters together. Our tennis shoes are damp.
Something moves on your thoughtful face, recedes,
Here, for the first time ever, I see how,
Just as a fish lurks deep in water weeds,
A thought of death will lurk deep down, will show
One eye, then quietly disappear in you.
It's time to go. . . .

. . . You start to row, the boat
Skimming the lake, where light begins to spread.
You stop the oars, mid-air. We twirl and float.

Gazing now at the fanciful design of the kitchen clock, she closes: "Clock hands sweep by it all, they twirl around, / Pushing me, oarless, from the shore of you."

History—universal, natural, and personal—dominates in all these poems. "[S]he makes us aware of the *idea* of the past," David St. John wrote, "and of the way a past, a history, resounds within and intrudes upon the present." Richard Howard, in the *Nation*, observed that Schnackenberg's "learning" in a few instances "drowns out the life beneath the words," and he noted "an overeagerness to rhyme," but he was impressed with "the carefully concocted necromancy which is most of this fine book."

History also figures in many of the poems in her second collection, *The Lamplit Answer*. "Kremlin of Smoke" is a fictional portrait of young Chopin, playing in an elegantly furnished drawing room in Paris where he learns of the Russian conquest of Warsaw. While he entertains "millionare guests" who "fling a kremlin of smoke overhead, / Dome upon dome, rising up to the mauve-tinted heaven / Of trompe-l'oeil clouds," episodes from his early life in Poland come back to haunt the artist who has made the choice to dedicate his life to art instead of politics. The fantasy of fairy tales takes on the quality of nightmare in "Imaginary Prisons," its title inspired by Piranesi's engravings of cavernous prisons ("one prison engineered within another"). In Schnackenberg's version of "Sleeping Beauty," "failed princes" are "hidden in the brambles . . . / Entangled in their struggles with the briars." But, balancing these dark images, in other poems Schnackenberg reveals a playful lightness, with outrageous rhymes in the spirit of Byron in *Don Juan*. "Love Letter" is addressed to a lover who has gone to Hawaii:

The days stack up like empty boxes stored
In ever-higher towers of cardboard
Swaying in senseless-lost-time's spooky attic.
I'll give the -atic rhyme another try.
To misconstrue the point-of-view Socratic,
Life is a painful stammered-out emphatic
Pronunciation of the word Goodbye.

The Lamplit Answer convinced Robert McDowell, in the *Hudson Review*, that "she is capable of successfully making any type of poem she sets her mind to." Peter Stitt, in the *Georgia Review*, was similarly impressed: "This is a cunning volume, containing poems as objectively beautiful as they are conceptually intriguing."

After the singular success of these first two collections, Schnackenberg appears to ave suffered a period of writer's block. With the publication of *A Gilded Lapse of Time* in 1992, however, her reviewers noted a new and fresh spirit in her work. In this, "her darkest and yet most radiant book," William Logan wrote in the *New York Times Book Review*, her poems "have a leisurely grandeur; they are written in a melodic free verse . . . Less controlled by form than her earliest work, they show an unusual concern with the market of mind and religion, the movement of mind and philosophy." Her early intimations of Christianity—explored in "Supernatural Love" in *The Lamplit Answer* where, as a four-year-old child, she confuses the definition of the flower *carnation* with the *incarnation* of Christ—develop into a profound and moving expression in this later volume. The title poem, "A Gilded Lapse of Time," is a visionary impression of the city of Ravenna. The poet speaks in her own voice as the modern visitor before whose eyes the three most striking sites of Ravenna—the mausoleum of Galla Placidia, the church of San Vitale, and Dante's tomb—transcend historical time, uniting classical antiquity and medieval Byzantium with the timeless suffering and regeneration of the human spirit. The poet begins her visit with a sense of personal loss, like Dante entering the dark wood of his Inferno: "When love was driven back upon itself, / When a lapse, where my life should have been, / Opened like a breach in the wall. . . . " The mausoleum of Galla Placidia, now incongruously bordered by an industrial zone, startles the visitor with its dazzling mosaics, "the whirl of gold" that draws the eye upward, "Where God is a word written into the ceiling / Under planets shining even by day. . . . " She observes the marvelous detail of the mosaics:

Stags whose horns flash as they bend to drink,
Peacocks taking refuge at the springs,
Lambs with drops of water on their muzzles,
Doves mesmerized at the edge of a bird bath. . . .

She then follows the historical trail to the church of San Vitale, as light and open as the mausoleum is dark and enclosed. Looking up at the mosaics in the apse here, representing Jesus blessing the waters, she has her own moment of transcendence:

. . . there the *imago Dei* wavers
Above the flooded, inaccessible crypt. . . .

Messiah, do not withdraw your hand from me.
Messiah, looking back where we have gathered
On the stone floor—looking through crazed gold,
As if you'd raised yourself to gaze at us,
Astonished, through a broken window's heart.

Proceeding then to Dante's tomb, "In a whirl of rain / That hurls itself from that age to my feet," she makes the final link of history, religion, and art, so that when she returns to her hotel room and looks out over the night sky, she can see

That point at which the fixed stars
Twinkle in translations,
Where one motion and another cross,
Where east and west mingle
With unfamiliar orbits and constellations
Before which we could grow
Forgetful, as if our lives and deeds
No longer mattered—were it not that
We still hear that weeping there below.

Art—in mosaics in Ravenna, in religious paintings everywhere in Italy, in poetry—is the agency that links time and cultures. These are, in Phoebe Pettingell's words in the *New Leader* (1992), the themes of *A Gilded Lapse of Time*: "human creation versus the work of God, the impact myth has on real events, the relationship between love and art, the existence of evil." That evil figures prominently in the last poem of the volume, "A Monument of Utopia," an homage to the Russian poet Osip Mandelstam, who died in one of Stalin's labor camps. The poem begins with a vision of a time "when poetry will no longer / Be a door fallen open upon / A dangerous conversation," a time "when, once having spoken, / A man will be allowed / Simply to resume growing older."

A Gilded Lapse of Time is probably Schnackenberg's most personal expression to date of her feelings about poetry. She refuses to theorize or engage in polemics, preferring to allow her work to speak for itself. However, in a prose essay on Paul's Epistle to the Colossians, contributed to Alfred Corn's collection of contemporary writings on the New Testament, *Incarnation* (1990), she defined her poetic principles in unmistakable terms. Tracing on an ancient Roman map the route that Paul would have taken on his journey from Ephesus to Colossae, she writes:

The sight of the Roman road system, sketched out in its totality on a map, is nearly as telling and as exciting to me as the sight of verses on a page. Like lines of poetry, the Roman roads are lines humming with communications, lines of awesome directness and force, lines that cut through confusion, connecting distant objects and events; like lines of poetry, the roads flow with multiple associations and images, they are open to all subjects, they break through borders and boundaries, they take the highest way, affording the largest views; like lines of poetry, the roads, in all the rhythms of their branchings, favor change, variation, mental evolution, and they culminate, finally, in a mind of self-portrait . . . the empire's self-portrait. . . . And, like lines of poetry, the Roman roads have a depth to their foundations that, finally, we cannot touch, foundations bound to crumble away or dissolve at our probing, backward into a time gulf.

PRINCIPAL WORKS: Portraits and Elegies, 1982; The Lamplit Answer, 1985; A Gilded Lapse of Time, 1992.

ABOUT: Contemporary Authors 116, 1986; Contemporary Literary Criticism 40, 1986; Contemprary Poets, 5th ed., 1991; Dictionary of Literary Biography 120, 1992. *Periodicals*—Antioch Review Spring 1983; Georgia Review Summer 1985; Hudson Review Winter 1986; Nation March 20, 1982; New Leader September 23, 1985; November 30, 1992; New York Times Book Review November 15, 1992.

JOANNA SCOTT

SCOTT, JOANNA (June 22, 1960–), American novelist, writes: "I grew up in Darien, Connecticut, a suburb of New York City. My ambivalence about the town might explain, to some extent, why I tend to avoid contemporary settings and locate my fictions either in history or outside of a specified time. The privacy preserved by the hedges and stone walls of Darien helped me to grow comfortable with solitude, but this same privacy depends upon exclusion and shamefully circumscribed experience. Early on, fiction made it possible for me to discover, and invent, past secrets hidden behind the great pretenses of language.

"Once I left Darien for college in 1978, I indulged my restlessness and for four years moved between different schools and cities. I attended Trinity College in Hartford for three semesters, left there and enrolled at Barnard College, left there after a year to study at the Barbieri Center in Rome, returned to New York and worked for six months as a proofreader for a news syndicate. I finished at Trinity in the summer of 1982.

"That summer I moved back to New York City and found a job as an assistant at a literary agency in Greenwich Village. I typed letters, read manuscripts, and answered the phone for the two women who, three years later, would become my agents. Evenings I sat at my typewriter, a pink brute of a machine I'd bought secondhand with my first week's salary. I began to think of writing as *work*, with its own distinct responsibilities and risks and pleasures. But committed work requires time, and I didn't have enough of that, so after a year I left my job at the literary agency and moved to Providence to attend the Graduate Writing Program at Brown University.

"During my two years at Brown I studied with Robert Coover, Susan Sontag, and John Hawkes. In the last story I wrote in graduate school, I threw over the attenuated ironic style that I'd been honing for two years and took on a voice radically different from my own. This story, narrated by an old man, became the opening chapter of my first novel, *Fading, My Parmacheene Belle*. I discovered that I could wander not only through fictional worlds but through a wealth of marvelous, antiquated information as well. Before I even realized I was writing a novel, I had saturated the prose with metaphors borrowed from fishing and soon found myself pouring over 19th-century game-fishing manuals to find out more about the lore of the sport.

"I moved to Rochester, New York, in 1986 and began my second novel, *The Closest Possible Union*, inspired by a cabin boy's account of an illegal slave ship's middle passage. Here, in an attempt to narrate a boy's confused responses to the brutality he's witnessed, I mix dream and history, sometimes making them indistinguishable.

"I received a Guggenheim Fellowship to work on my third novel. In *Arrogance*, based loosely on the life of the painter Egon Schiele, I fracture the biography into different narratives. The closer my fictional approximation to history, the more I find myself wanting to weaken the tyranny of fact. And yet my imagination continues to thrive upon the secrets and eccentricities of past lives. *Arrogance* was published in 1991. I've recently [1992] completed a collection of short fiction, *Various Antidotes*; some of the pieces in the collection draw from the actual history of medical research, and some invent a history.

"I have taught at the University of Maryland and Princeton University. I am currently an associate professor of English at the University of Rochester. I received a MacArthur Fellowship in 1992. I am married to James Longenbach, a literary critic and poet. Our daughter Kathryn was born in August 1991.

Joanna Scott was born in Greenwich, Connecticut, the daughter of Yvonne (DePotter) Scott, a psychologist, and Walter Lee Scott. Her intriguingly titled first novel, *Fading, My Parmacheene Belle*, published when she was still in her twenties, earned widespread critical acclaim for its mythic emotional intensity and its startlingly idiosyncratic language. The novel's nameless narrator, an irascible old backwoods fisherman, has just lost his wife of fifty-three years. He leaves the funeral service before its completion and, in a fit of rage, hurls a chair at his sole surviving progeny—a mentally retarded son whose very disability the old man construes as a cosmic commentary on the burdensome state of his marriage. Fearing that he has killed his son, the old man sets out on a journey of resolution, determined to discover the truth about his life and marriage.

The old man is beset by many questions about the woman he has always called simply "the wife." He wonders, for example, whether Gibble, his wife's cousin, manipulated him into marrying her. Now that she is dead, he sometimes refers to "the wife" as his Parmacheene Belle, the name of a particularly effective fly-fishing lure. Indeed, the old man thinks about life almost entirely in terms of piscatorial metaphors. With the "fading" of his Parmacheene Belle, he is bereft, embittered, and seized with a raging desire to confront his own true self. Near the beginning of his journey, he meets up with a runaway teenage girl, whom he dubs "the mermaiden." Although this dissolute young waif is the antithesis of every woman he has ever known, he is drawn to her by a combination of parental and carnal instincts. Together, they embark on a circuitous and often dreamlike expedition toward the sea, and "the wife's" old home.

"[If] one were to strip this story of its language," Christopher Lehmann-Haupt wrote in the *New York Times* "there would not be much original about it." Nonetheless, Lehmann-Haupt conceded that "the mad eloquence of the old narrator redeems *Fading, My Parmacheene Belle*. A blend of the bucolic and the biblical, it achieves its own peculiar tragicomic vision."

Chicago Tribune Books reviewer Catherine Petroski agreed: "Reading *Parmacheene* is like encountering a new strain of English, one that has its own grammar and logic and lexicon, and as we absorb the rules of the old man's language, we are drawn into his world." Another admirer, David Profumo, writing in the *Spectator*, touted the novel's "unrelenting prose that is by turns precise and visionary." Elaine R. Ognibene, in *Belles Lettres*, offered a harsher perspective: "Scott's first novel, though highly inventive as well as intelligent and clever in its sustained use of fishing metaphors, disappoints because her main character is unsympathetic, and her message is finally unclear." Scott's narrator, Ognibene noted, "fails to discover the truth about his family or himself. . . . he lacks the ability to grow in wisdom, human sympathy, or love."

Scott's second novel, *The Closest Possible Union*, is the story of a nightmarish voyage on the *Charles Beauchamp*, an illegal American slave ship posing as a whaler. Tom Beauchamp, the fourteen-year-old narrator, is the son of the ship's owner and the apprentice to its captain. Tom's account of the ship's voyage—from New England to the west coast of Africa, and on to South America—is a phantasmagoric mélange of half-remembered dreams and grisly recollections. Reactions to the novel were mixed. Although he praised Scott's "truly marvelous sense of language," in the *New York Times Book Review*, Robert Houston concluded: "[Tom] remains part of a cerebral construct, a pawn of the book's overheated symbolism . . . It is as if the author were so afraid of foundering on the reefs of historical romance that she seldom allows her readers a good look at the land."

Arrogance, Scott's third novel, examines the brief but tempestuous life of the Austrian expressionist painter Egon Schiele, who died in 1918 at the age of twenty-eight in the worldwide Spanish influenza epidemic. It is the first of Scott's novels to be based, if only loosely, on the life of a real historical figure. Unlike her previous novels, both of which are narrated in the first person and unfold in more or less chronological sequence, *Arrogance* is told from multiple points of view and eschews any semblance of chronology. An opening scene depicts the young adult Schiele in 1912, imprisoned—he pretends not to know why—for painting young girls in suggestive poses. The novel then zigs and zags backward and forward in time to scenes of Schiele's childhood (he was terrorized by an alcoholic father who burned his drawings), his apprenticeship, and his brief, contentious career. What emerges is the portrait of an arrogant, reckless, and often childlike individual—an artist so utterly convinced of his own talent and destiny that he casts aside friends and critics alike. Schiele's character is limned by, among others, his mother, his sister, his mistress, and by Schiele himself, with excerpts from his diaries. His milieu—fin de siecle Vienna—is carefully and lovingly rendered, making the city and its inhabitants as central to the story as Egon Schiele.

"With this, her third novel," Hunter Drohojowska wrote in a front-page notice of *Arrogance* in the *Los Angeles Times Book Review*, "Scott emerges as a writer who should not be ignored." According to Drohojowska, "One of the most satisfying aspects of *Arrogance* is her treatment of Schiele's art—which many an art critic might envy." By concentrating so heavily on "the supporting characters" and the "Austrian setting," Drohojowska noted, Scott "prevents a reader from becoming engrossed in the story: sympathy for Schiele is derailed repeatedly by asides and observations. But this is clearly the author's intention, and those detours become enjoyable in themselves." In the *New York Times* (1990), Michiko Kakutani also remarked upon the lack of "narrative drive or tension to the book" that results from its "montage, jump-cutting" approach to Schiele's life. "The effect, rather," Kakutani wrote, "is musical: assorted voices . . . giving us their impressions of Schiele, while recurring emotions . . . are coolly orchestrated to produce an impressionistic portrait of his world." Scott Bradfield, in the *New York Times Book Review* (1990), found the novel "often bulky with exposition, and perilously short on active characters and dramatic scenes. However, like Schiele's art, Joanna Scott's literary materials . . . are deployed in sensuous, provocative patterns. They resound with rich experience and intriguing perceptions." In the *Times Literary Supplement*, Neil Taylor thought *Arrogance* irreparably marred by its lack of "sustainable characters." "As her earlier work demonstrates," he noted, "Scott can adopt an assumed voice and fill a novel with it. . . . Here, however, the multivocal structure confuses and the ambition to outdo both biography and the novel seems, if not arrogant, then foolhardy at least."

The eleven stories in *Various Antidotes*, Scott's first collection of short fiction, are all concerned, in one way or another, with troubled characters involved in scientific experiments based on the prevailing theories or myths of their day. Some of the protagonists, such as the American mental-health reformer Dorothea Dix, and the French patriot Charlotte Corday (who stabbed revolutionary leader Jean-Paul Marat to death in his tub), are real historical figures. Others, such as the microbe-obsessed main character in "Concerning Mold Upon the Skin, Etc.," are

purely fictional. "Although some of the stories in this book rely too heavily on their simple oddness to capture one's attention," Michiko Kakutani wrote in the *New York Times* "Ms. Scott's skills as a writer help to redeem even the weakest tales. . . . [her] gifts turn what might have been just an eclectic collection into a fascinating little museum of human behavior." In the *New York Times Book Review* George Garret deemed *Various Antidotes* "purely and simply wonderful," and noted that there is no "typical" Joanna Scott story. "Clearly . . . Scott is a truly gifted and highly original artist. There are only a few working American writers who can do similar things with the short story form. . . . "

PRINCIPAL WORKS: *Novels*—Fading, My Parmacheene Belle, 1987; The Closest Possible Union, 1988; Arrogance, 1990. *Short stories*—Various Antidotes, 1994.

ABOUT:Contemporary Authors 126, 1989; Contemporary Literary Criticism 50, 1988. *Periodicals*—Belles Lettres September–October 1987; Chicago Tribune Books March 8, 1987; Los Angeles Times Book Review August 12, 1990; New York Times March 26, 1987; July 13, 1990; February 1, 1994; New York Times Book Review April 14, 1988; August 19, 1990; March 6, 1994; Spectator April 9, 1988; Times Literary Supplement July 28, 1991.

SCOTT, NATHAN A(LEXANDER), Jr.

(April 24, 1925–), American critic and theologian, writes: "Though my baccalaureate was not formally awarded by the University of Michigan till January 1944, I completed my undergraduate studies in Ann Arbor at the end of the summer of 1943, and that autumn I entered Union Theological Seminary (New York) as a candidate for the bachelor of divinity degree. I had already come to be greatly fascinated by the early books of Reinhold Niebuhr and was eager to be in his classroom and to win a fuller grasp of the main contours of his thought. So I went on the New York City in September of '43, and over the next two years I was simply drunk with the excitements engendered by all that I was encountering in the lectures and seminars of Niebuhr and Paul Tillich and Richard Kroner and various others in the Union faculty of that period. Then in the course of time, remarking the resoluteness with which Niebuhr was undertaking to relate theological perspectives to the social-political dynamic of the time and Tillich was undertaking to relate theological perspectives to philosophical culture, I, at some undatable moment, began to feel that perhaps my own vocation might be that of reckoning with the literary culture of the modern scene and of at-

NATHAN A. SCOTT, JR.

tempting to disclose the manifold ways in which it, too, may be illumined by a theological perspective. It was such an ambition that shaped my doctoral studies at Columbia, and it has been to this kind of effort that my professional life has ben devoted over the past forty years.

"I cannot here attempt to trace out the various shifting patterns of emphasis that may be found in the twenty-six books I have written and edited and in the sizable body of essays I have contributed to symposia and journals, but these mutations in any event will perhaps be more authoritatively defined by others. Suffice it to say that I have constantly kept the conviction (as I said in the preface prepared for a book of 1958, *Modern Literature and the Religious Frontier*) that 'the literary intelligence, is by far the best intelligence of our time, better than the philosophic intelligence, better than the social-scientific . . . and better . . . than the theological." And in dealing with a variety of modern writers (Dostoyevsky, Hardy, Kafka, Lawrence, Eliot, Hemingway, Beckett, and many others), I have often been eager to suggest something like the assertion made by that famous aphorism in William Blake's *The Marriage of Heaven and Hell* which says: 'The tygers of wrath are wiser than the horses of instruction.' Or, if they have not been wiser, I have wanted at least to urge (as I said in the 1958 preface) that they 'seem to have traveled farther than most of . . . us and seem to have thrust us more exactly upon the centers of . . . [what is problematic in our lives] than any other class of [modern intelligentsia] . . . has succeeded in doing.'

"I should say, however, that for me it is unimaginable that any such claim might be sustained in relation to the House of Criticism in our period, for, though distinguished people are at work there also, the main drift of things in that quarter has lately been so much toward proclamations of 'the death of the author' and the dissolution of the literary work into the indeterminate deeps of *intertextualité* that the 'poem' is no longer seen to promise any kind of meditation at all of the 'world.' As we are told by the New People, the poem exhibits nothing more than a play of tropes whose mercuriality forbids any text being read as a version of the *logos*: which is to say that what is denied is the possibility of finding a work of literary art to present a coherent account of human experience. And this represents a *trahison des clercs* with which I have not been inclined to make any kind of common cause.

"Perhaps I may be permitted also to say in a final addendum that, among my various books, my favorites are *The Broken Center: Studies in the Theological Horizon of Modern Literature*; *Negative Capability: Studies in the New Literature and the Religious Situation*; *The Wild Prayer of Longing: Poetry and the Sacred*; *Three American Moralists: Mailer, Bellow, Trilling*; *The Poetry of Civic Virtue*; *The Poetics of Belief*; and *Visions of Presence in Modern American Poetry*.

In an early article, "A Neglected Aspect of the Theological Curriculum" (*Journal of Religious Thought*, Autumn–Winter 1949–1950), Nathan Scott characterizes himself as a Christian apologist, not in the sense of defending a theistic view of the world, but rather in spelling out "the implications of the Christian revelation for the rational understanding of the world and our experience in it." He has turned to men of letters, particularly to major 20th-century figures, as crucial witnesses to this insight; but, as he points out in his preface to *Modern Literature and the Religious Frontier*, unlike such religious-minded writers as T. S. Eliot, W. H. Auden, and Allen Tate, who have moved from aesthetic problems to religious ones, Scott's spiritual journey has moved him in the opposite direction. In the preface to a later book, *Negative Capability*, he accounts for the closer attention paid to the modern cultural scene in the great centers of theological study as an increased sense on the part of Christian educators that "the Holy and the Sacred are to be encountered in historical reality." He singles out as a guiding principle behind his own writing Paul Tillich's pronouncement in *The Protestant Era*: "Religion is the substance of culture, and culture the form of religion."

Scott was born in Cleveland, Ohio, to Nathan A. Scott, a lawyer, and Maggie (Martin) Scott. During his early childhood the family moved to Detroit, where he received his first schooling. From 1940–1941 he attended Wayne State University before being admitted, at the age of sixteen, to the University of Michigan, which granted his B.A. in 1944. His subsequent earned degrees were a bachelor of divinity from Union Theological Seminary (1946) and a doctorate in literature from Columbia University (1949). Teachers on the Columbia faculty whom he recall as especially influential were John Herman Randall, Jacques Barzun, and Lionel Trilling.

Scott's first professional appointment was as dean of chapel at Virginia Union University (1946–1948). Since then he has held a series of teaching posts bridging theology and literary study. From 1948 to 1955 he was on the faculty of Howard University, eventually becoming director of the General Education Program in the Humanities. In 1955 he was appointed an assistant professor in the Divinity School of the University of Chicago, where in 1972 he was named Shailer Matthews Professor of Theology and Literature. During this period he also coedited the *Journal of Religion* published by the Divinity School. His teaching at the University of Chicago was interrupted by visiting professorships at the University of Michigan and John Carroll University. From 1965 to 1972 he was a senior fellow of the School of Letters at the Indiana University. Concurrently, he was ordained a priest of the Episcopal Church in 1960, and from 1967 to 1976 served as canon theologian of the Cathedral of Saint James in Chicago. In 1977 he moved to the University of Virginia as William R. Kenan Professor of Religion and professor of English.

"I should like to define my *genre* by way of saying that these pages constitute an essay in philosophical anthropology," Scott writes in the preface to his first book *Rehearsals of Discomposure: Alienation and Reconciliation in Modern Literature*. Here he employs "anthropology" in its religious signification: the origin and nature of man in relation to God. "If this book cannot lay claim to the fullest significance for *aesthetic* discussion, it may have an *existential* validity," he further suggests in its preface. The four authors discussed in this book exemplify aspects of the fundamental dislocation of the modern writer from his civilization: Franz Kafka representing "cosmic exile"; Ignazio Silone, "alienation from the modern community"; D. H. Lawrence,

"ontological solitude"; T. S. Eliot alone having reached "the most controversial, and what is, in my view, the most complete strategy of reconciliation in recent literature." *Rehearsals of Discomposure* was generally welcomed for the novelty of its standpoint and the wide reading distilled on its pages, though the reviewer for the *Times Literary Supplement* complained about Scott's "abstract jargon" and his "rather indiscriminate eclecticism in quotation from other critics."

Scott's subsequent prolific output has been made up mainly of collections of lectures and essays in religious and literary journals in which he explores the current cultural condition. Such titles as *Modern Literature and the Religious Frontier*, *The Broken Center: Studies in the Theological Horizon of Modern Literature*, *Craters of the Spirit: Studies in the Modern Novel*, *Negative Capability: Studies in the New Literature and the Religious Situation*, *The Unquiet Vision: Mirrors of Man in Existentialism*, and *The Wild Prayer of Longing: Poetry and the Sacred* reflect Scott's concern for the spiritual angst of modern writers and his forays into the ground where religion, aesthetics, and psychology meet. Among individual figures, he has contributed monographs on two exemplars of "alienation" who wrote in French, Albert Camus and Samuel Beckett, to the series Studies in Modern European Literature and Thought (edited by Erich Heller). He has also found religious significance in a "muscular" writer like Ernest Hemingway and a cynical one like Nathanael West. In other books he has grouped writers in unique juxtapositions: Norman Mailer (whom Scott labels "our Whitman"), Saul Bellow (recorder of "the phenomenology of selfhood"), and Lionel Trilling (representative of "anxious humanism") come together as *Three American Moralists*; T. S. Eliot, André Malraux, and W. H. Auden are the quintessence of *The Poetry of Civic Virtue*.

Basic to all of Scott's critical writing is his conviction that creative writers have a contribution to make to the spiritual and intellectual life of their times. In *Modern Literature and the Religious Frontier*, he takes issue with T. S. Eliot's famous declaration (in the essay "Shakespeare and the Stoicism of Seneca") that the poet is not a thinker. For related reasons, he opposed the emphasis of the then fashionable New Critics on form over content in literature, which to Scott minimizes "the controlling effect upon the creative process of the writer's ideas and beliefs." Scott was drawn more to religious writers like the Catholic critic Jacques Maritain with his concept of "imaginative prehension," and the heterodox Jewish theologian Martin Buber who introduced the idea of an "I-Thou" dialogue between man and God. In *The Poetics of Belief*, the 19th-century critics Coleridge, Arnold, and Pater are brought together with representative 20th-century figures George Santayana, Wallace Stevens, and Martin Heidegger to testify that "finally there is no separating the poetic and the imaginative from the reflective and the metaphysical."

The "shifting patterns of emphasis" and "mutations" that Scott alludes to in connection with his own body of critical writing are summed up by Diane Apostolos-Cappadone, in the journal *Horizons*, as a movement from "texts which explicitly raise questions of estrangement and alienation" to those which "present a vision of sacramental grace." This judgment seems to be confirmed by Scott's affinity for poets of spiritual feeling like Hopkins, Eliot, Stevens, Frost, and Roethke. Apostolos-Cappadone accounts for this change of perspective by the influence on Scott of Heidegger's vision of "literature as a creative expression of life," which, in her opinion, took over from that of Tillich's more existentialist outlook.

"By any account Nathan Scott must be reckoned one of the most extraordinary educators of twentieth-century America," in the words of Anthony C. Yu, a colleague from the University of Chicago, in his introduction to *Morphologies of Faith*, a collection of essays honoring Scott on his retirement as William R. Kenan Professor of Religious Studies at the University of Virginia in 1990. As intermediary between the worlds of Protestant Christianity and secular humanism, Scott has found a wide audience through courses of lectures at numerous universities and theological seminaries. He has also received many honorary degrees. Among the offices he has held is the presidency of the American Academy of Religion, and he is a Fellow of the American Academy of Arts and Sciences.

In 1946 Scott married Charlotte Hanley has been since 1976, University Professor of Commerce and Education at the University of Virginia. They have two children.

PRINCIPAL WORKS: Rehearsals of Discomposure: Alienation and Reconciliation in Modern Literature, 1952; Modern Literature and the Religious Frontier, 1958; Albert Camus, 1962; Reinhold Niebuhr, 1963; Samuel Beckett, 1965; The Broken Center: Studies in the Theological Horizon of Modern Literature, 1966; Ernest Hemingway, 1966; Craters of the Spirit: Studies in the Modern Novel, 1968; Negative Capability: Studies in the New Literature and the Religious Situation, 1969; The Unquiet Vision: Mirrors of Man in Existentialism, 1969; Nathanael West, 1971; The Wild Prayer of Longing: Poetry and the Sacred, 1971; Three American Moralists: Mailer, Bellow, Trilling, 1973;

The Poetry of Civic Virtue: Eliot, Malraux, Auden, 1976; Mirrors of Man in Existentialism, 1978; The Poetics of Belief: Studies in Coleridge, Arnold, Pater, Santayana, Stevens, and Heidegger, 1985; Visions of Presence in Modern American Poetry, 1993. *As editor*—The Tragic Vision and the Christian Faith, 1957; The Climate of Faith in Modern Literature, 1964; The New Orpheus: Essays toward a Christian Poetic, 1964; Forms of Extremity in the Modern Novel, 1965; Four Ways of Modern Poetry, 1965; Man in the Modern Theatre, 1965; The Modern Vision of Death, 1967; Adversity and Grace: Studies in Recent American Literature, 1968; The Legacy of Reinhold Niebuhr, 1975.

ABOUT: Contemporary Authors New Revision Series 20, 1987; Living Black American Authors, 1973; Page, J. and Roh, J. (eds.) Selected Black American, African, and Caribbean Authors, 1985; Who's Who in America, 1991–1993; Who's Who in Religion, 1985; Yu, A. C. *introduction to* Morphologies of Faith: Essays in Religion and Culture in Honor of Nathan Scott, Jr., 1990. *Periodicals*—Books Abroad Winter 1970; Christian Century February 19, 1969; May 6, 1970; January 2, 1974; June 1, 1977; September 25, 1985; Commonweal April 1, 1977; November 1, 1985; Comparative Literature Spring 1968; Georgia Review Summer 1969; Horizons Fall 1983; Journal of Religion April 1986; Time Literary Supplement July 24, 1953; Virginia Quarterly Review Autumn 1968; Summer 1977.

SCRUTON, ROGER (February 27, 1944–   ), British philosopher, critic, and novelist, writes: "I was born in Buslingthorpe, Lincolnshire, in 1944, while my father [John Scruton] was serving in the Royal Air Force, and my mother [Beryl Hayes Scruton] was billetted on a local farm. In order to fetch the midwife, my father was forced to walk fifteen miles through heavy snowdrifts. He never forgave me. Not did he forgive me when, in later years, my successful rise through the grammar school system (the family had settled by then in Buckinghamshire) proved too great an affront to his working-class sensibilities. Not that he was working-class; but it was the affectation of the time to claim to be so if one had the remotest chance of carrying it off; and, as the child of a drunken layabout with far more children than he could count, my father had some claim to the title. By his own efforts he managed to become a primary school teacher, and a local figure of some renown. But the estrangement between us lasted for the rest of his life. I admired his intelligence and public spirit; I learned from him much about England, the countryside, and socialism. But I was never able to feel at home where he was, not even while my mother—a gentle and self-effacing person—was alive. Her death destroyed our family, and the three children went their separate ways—my sisters to marriage and childbearing, I to my books.

ROGER SCRUTON

"I gained a scholarship to Cambridge, to read natural sciences. But already my main love was literature, and in deciding to read philosophy I was greatly influenced by my discovery of Rilke, Spengler, and Nietzsche. I had also acquired an intense love of music, which had an added attraction for me in that my father hated no sound more than the sound of my piano playing. Among our near neighbours were the intensely musical children of a Viennese exile, son of a once well-known psychiatrist; together we played through the repertoire, on whatever instruments we could muster. I also learned to accompany lieder, and to this day Schubert's songs serve as my paradigm of artistic achievement.

"I had many friendships at Cambridge, though I was not happy there. My solace was writing: poetry, for the most part, of an embarrassing awkwardness. On obtaining my degree, I decided not to continue my studies, but to go to France, where I had to the opportunity to spend a year as *lecteur* in the university college of Pau. I had already formed a great attachment to France through visits to Paris and friendships formed there with painters and literary 'exiles' from Britain and America. I now took the opportunity to learn the language, to read widely in its glorious literature, and to write the novel that I had conceived during my student years. The novel was, of course, a failure. But I met the girl who was to become my wife, in my one short-lived attempt at matrimony.

"France in the mid-sixties was an important experience for another reason. It provided my first encounter with student Marxism and with the spirit of universal rebellion which was eventually to explode into action in 1968. I conceived a fierce admiration for everything that the student activists opposed: for General de Gaulle in particular, whose unique combination of political authority and literary refinement impressed on me a wholly new ideal of human conduct. As to Marxism, I could not say quite what was wrong with it. But a few months in Italy persuaded me that Marxism is the enemy of Western culture and the true cause of Italy's incredible intellectual decline in recent decades.

"I returned to Cambridge at last, took up my philosophical studies, and began to write the kind of dry academic rubbish that philosophers must write if they are to obtain a university position. I am not proud of this; nor am I proud of the fact that I stayed thereafter in the academic world, moving first to a fellowship at Peterhouse, and then to Birkbeck College in London. However, I never regarded my academic career as my principal employment and was glad to be living in a great city, in which the *odium theologicum* of the academy counted for nothing. I read for the Bar and acquired through the study of law a grounding for my own increasingly conservative opinions. I worked for a while as a conveyancing clerk and wrote more widely, fiction and journalism. And in due course I began to involve myself in politics. Perhaps the most interesting part of my life to date has been the experience of the underground universities of Eastern Europe, which—in conjunction with a few friends—I supported during the late seventies and eighties. Following my arrest in Czechoslovakia in 1985 I was no longer able to travel to that country, which I had grown to love. But the happiest of all recent experiences has been that of witnessing its final liberation and regaining the ability to visit friends whom I had once met in secret but who now run the show.

"I first began to write in a way that pleased me in the late seventies, with *The Aesthetics of Architecture*, a book in which I threw off the shackles of academic philosophy in order to say something pertinent about the human condition. This has been followed by a variety of publications: essays, studies, novels, and stories. My first published novel, *Fortnight's Anger*, was well received, and I still have a fondness for it. It portrays a state of mind of extreme disorientation; but it is a state that inhabits *two* minds and can only be understood in terms of the relation between them. Shortly after publishing this book I became known as an outspoken conservative. Since then many reviews of my work have been hostile. I have tried not to be deterred by this, and to continue in my principal project, which is to marry imaginative literature and philosophical speculation and to use both to express an unfashionable vision of society. Of my more recent writings, I believe that the novel *Francesca*, which contains a sympathetic portrait of my father, and the story 'A Dove Descending,' succeed in conveying the peculiar experience of modern England that haunts me in my work.

"Not surprisingly, my social and political writings seem to be more popular in Eastern European countries than they are at home and have appeared in several of the local languages. Their principal value, it seems to me, is that they try to give conceptual clarity to an outlook that is too often seen as a matter of inarticulate sentiment. For the last ten years, as founder and editor of the *Salisbury Review*, I have learned much about the difficulties of expressing a conservative philosophy that is something other than free-market economics. Intellectually this has been extremely rewarding; and the hostility provoked among my immediate colleagues has taught me how very much more interesting the world is outside the academy than in it. I have now moved to the country, to divide my time between writing and the care of horses.

"Among those who have influenced me in recent years I should mention the art critic Peter Fuller, whose recent death in a car crash deprived me of a spiritual companion whose thoughts I valued all the more because his political sympathies were so opposed to mine. I have also learned much from modern English composers, such as Robin Holloway and David Matthews, who represent an undimmed ideal of artistic integrity, in a sphere where frauds and imposters have recently tended to prevail. Among living authors I have a high regard for Peter Porter, for Vikram Seth, whose *Golden Gate* was unjustly neglected by the prize-giving committees, and for J. F. Boylan, who is probably as crazy as I am."

In *The Redefinition of Conservatism*, Charles Covell aligns Roger Scruton with "Thinkers of the New Right" (in a group that includes John Casey, Maurice Cowling, Shirley Letwin, and Michael Oakeshott), placing him at the opposite pole from *Thinkers of the New Left*, the title of one of Scruton's own books. He is better characterized by John Dunn who reviewed *Thinkers of the New Left* in the *Times Literary Supplement*, as "an interesting philosopher of aesthetics, and a forceful and accomplished philosophical expositor." While he came to public attention as a vehement polemicist for the conservative position, Scruton's vast and versatile output actually encompasses metaphysics, aesthetic theory, ethics, politics, art, architecture, literature, linguistics, music, film, photography, and the psychology of sex, besides the fiction which he gives priority, though it is not as well known in America as are his other writings.

Scruton's first book, *Art and Imagination*, grew out of his doctoral dissertation presented at Jesus College, Cambridge, where he had already received his B.A. (1965) and M.A. (1967). Among his examiners was the philospher Stuart Hampshire, but in the preface to the book he acknowledges in particular the influence of Kant (the first philosopher, he points out, to have made aesthetics a distinct sphere of thought) and Wittgenstein. Characterized by its author as "an account of aesthetic experience in terms of an empiricist philosophy of mind," *Art and Imagination* distinguishes aesthetic judgments which engage our "sense of what is right or appropriate" from moral judgments which involve the conscience and imply sanctions. Defining "aesthetic perception" as the imaginative contemplation of an object "for its own sake," Scruton proceeds in this treatise to an examination of the fundamental idiom of the arts—representation, expression, and symbolism.

The Aesthetics of Architecture, the book by which Scruton "threw off the shackles of academic philosophy," is concerned, as was its predecessor, with "certain mental capacities—capacities for experience and judgment," but he addresses himself this time to "the aesthetics of everyday life" as embodied in our concrete environment—in a dual sense. While assuming the utility of the architect's product, Scruton departs from the functional theorists in his emphasis on "foresight," looking to the future, rather than merely to the immediate purpose of the structure. "Durability," in Scruton's view, is what distinguishes architecture from mere building. While as abstruse as *Art and Imagination*, the later book is more accessible to the general reader, its theories spelled out with specific examples, enhanced by attractive photographic illustration.

Scruton has affirmed that analytical philosophy, the field in which he was trained, is worthless "until connected to critical intelligence in the fields of human value." His conviction in particular that the arts and the social sciences are intertwined is explicit in the introduction to *The Politics of Culture*, one of his collections of essays: "The political spirit . . . is a spirit that concerns itself with culture, and with the institutions and practices through which culture is upheld."

Scruton's central political position is enunciated in *The Meaning of Conservatism*, the book that followed *The Aesthetics of Architecture*. Here he undertakes to demonstrate that conservatism, contrary to its critics, is an attitude both systematic and reasonable, but "rendered feeble and confused by the attempt to dilute it with doctrines of American liberalism." Like fellow conservative Michael Oakeshott, a strong upholder of custom and the rule of law in the governance of human affairs, Scruton locates the basis of the conservative attitude towards the body politic in "the persistence of civil order," supported on the three legs of authority, allegiance, and tradition. In opposition to the social contract theory associated with Hobbes and Locke, he finds an analog for the state in the family, both social units arising out of "natural necessity," not choice. Obligation among citizens as among kin, it follows, is founded not on justice, but on respect, the real basis of authority. Allegiance, for Scruton, derives from the assumption that society transcends a mere aggregate of its constituents; hence his antipathy to liberalism, which to his mind elevates individual liberty above the good of the whole. The power of tradition as he conceives it—making "history into reason"—joins his political theory to his aesthetics, the conservative principle for him reaffirmed by contemporary writers like James, Conrad, Yeats, Eliot, and Joyce, who have made modern consciousness "part of a tradition of artistic expression" which they have revivified.

Scruton has been praised by fellow philosophers for his incisive analytical mind. To Christopher Norris, he "stands in a line of conservative critic-philosophers from Burke to T. S. Eliot who valorize the aesthetic by placing it beyond the reach of ideological technique." However his attempts to apply his humanistic ideals to the social realm have not in general been welcomed by professional political scientists and economists. His assumption that the test of time necessarily validates institutions has been called into question, as have his unqualified justification of "civil order" and his sweeping suspicion of any kind of government "interference" in human affairs. "Like so many high tories, he cannot resist a certain lingering affection for dead dictators, a certain wooliness when dealing with present problems," observed the anonymous reviewer of *The Meaning of Conservatism* in the *Economist*. "Traditional conservatism is an important doctrine. It does not benefit from being fitted out in periwig, knee-breeches, and velvet boots."

In 1982 Scruton launched the *Salisbury Review* to articulate the conservative position, heretofore, in his opinion, too much the province of "laborious works of political science" or "light-hearted journalism." A collection of essays from the *Review* under the title *Conservative Thoughts* confronts such touchy issues as the Soviet threat, the Welfare State, the new polytechnic universities, and the impact of immigration from East Asia on the secondary schools. A connecting thread is exposure of the fallacies of socialism and the excesses of populism. Among the contributors are Friedrich A. Hayek, John Casey, Ray Honeyford, and J. Enoch Powell. Vaclav Havel, whom Scruton met in Czechoslovakia, speaks for the dissidents of Eastern Europe in "Politics and Conscience," an address intended for an honorary doctorate at the University of Toulouse which he was unable to attend (he was a state prisoner at the time). Intended as a platform to answer his critics, this journal made Scruton more vulnerable to attack. According to his testimony, the *Review* was "severely persecuted," one contributor having been forced to resign from his position, others threatened with dismissal, while a substantial number had lecture engagements canceled. At various "intellectual show trials," the editor further laments, his colleagues have been denounced for "chauvinism," "fascism," or "racism." Fighting back personal attacks, he won libel suits against the British Broadcasting Corporation in 1986 and the *Observer* in 1988.

Concurrently with editing and writing for the *Salisbury Review*, Scruton made further contributions to philosophy, notably a history, *From Descartes to Wittgenstein*, as well as monographs on Kant and Spinoza. He is probably best known in the Unites States for *Sexual Desire: A Moral Philosophy of the Erotic*, in which he offers a phenomenological analysis of the sexual act that Richard A. Shweder described in the *New York Times Book Review* as "a brave, deliberately provocative, and excessively illiberal first step toward restoring the body as a moral universe to our collective consciousness." Most reviewers, however, agreed with Roz Kaveney when she said in the *New Statesman*, "The prevailing tone of his book is one of spite . . . toward lives he does not understand and wishes to remould. . . . full of wilful misstatements of fact and misinterpretations of texts. . . . "

Scruton has been prolific also as a contributor to books by others (e.g., *Conservative Essays*, edited by Maurice Cowling) in addition to writing for literary periodicals. *The Politics of Culture* brings together his essays on such varied subjects as the psychology of R. D. Laing, the theories of Buckminster Fuller, deconstruction and criticism, and the fiction of Graham Greene. A later collection under the title *The Philosopher on Dover Beach* ranges through Hegel, Oswald Spengler, modern drama ("Pinter, Stoppard, and

Beckett") and modern art ("Picasso and the Women"). "I hope that these essays may offer some partial vindication of the culture of Europe and the moral sense that speaks through it," he writes in the preface. "And I hope that some of my readers will take heart, recognizing that there is a way out of the barrenness of modernism, and that it is a way not forwards into the unknown, but backwards into the familiar." Among his works of fiction, *Francesca*, centering on a young writer who breaks away from the influence of his crusty schoolmaster father with Marxist leanings, is of autobiographical interest. The stories that make up the volume titled *A Dove Descending* involve various aspects of "loss and deception"; reflecting Scruton's interest in dissident movements is the nightmarish "The Seminar," set in Czechoslovakia during the Soviet occupation. In an article "What is Right?" (*Times Literary Supplement*, April 3, 1992), intended as a rebuttal to Steven Lukes, a leading proponent of the Left, he took special satisfaction in the downfall of Communism in Czechoslovakia as lending support to his political position.

From 1969 to 1971, Scruton was a resident fellow at Peterhouse, Cambridge. He joined the faculty of Birkbeck College, University of London, as lecturer in philosophy in 1971, where he has been professor of aesthetics since 1985. In 1978 he was called to the Bar, Inner Temple. His marriage in 1973 to Danielle Lafitte was dissolved.

PRINCIPAL WORKS: *Aesthetics and philosophy*—Art and Imagination, 1974; The Aesthetics of Architecture, 1979; From Descartes to Wittgenstein: A Short History of Philosophy, 1981; Kant, 1982; The Aesthetic Understanding: Essays in the Philosophy of Art and Culture, 1983; Spinoza, 1986; Sexual Desire: A Moral Philosophy of the Erotic, 1986; Modern Philosophy: An Introduction and Survey, 1994. *Politics*—The Meaning of Conservatism, 1980; A Dictionary of Political Thought, 1982; Thinkers of the New Left, 1986; A Land Held Hostage: Lebanon and the West, 1986. *As editor*—Conservative Thoughts: Essays from the Salisbury Review, 1988; Conservative Texts: An Anthology, 1991. *Fiction*—Fortnight's Anger, 1981; A Dove Descending and Other Stories, 1991; Xanthippic Dialogues: A Philosophical Fiction, 1993. *Collected Essays and reviews*—The Politics of Culture and Other Essays, 1981; Untimely Tracts, 1987; The Philosopher on Dover Beach, 1990.

ABOUT: Contemporary Authors New Revision Series 16, 1986; Covell, C. The Redefinition of Conservatism, 1986; Norris, C. The Contest of Faculties: Philosophy and Theory after Deconstruction, 1985; Who's Who, 1991. *Periodicals*—British Journal of Aesthetics July 1992; Economist November 1, 1980; Encounter September/October 1986; Journal of Aesthetics and Art Criticism Spring 1985; National Review October 20, 1988; New Statesman March 14, 1980; New York Review of Books December 18, 1986; New York Times Book Review March 23, 1986; July 26, 1987; February 27, 1991; Southern Review November 1984; Times Higher Education Supplement October 17, 1986; July 22, 1988; Times Literary Supplement February 28, 1986; April 14, 1986; August 18, 1988; July 20, 1990.

SCUPHAM, (JOHN) PETER (February 24, 1933–   ), British poet and small-press publisher, was born in Liverpool. His parents were Dorothy (Clark) and John Scupham, head of Educational Broadcasting for the British Broadcasting Corporation. He was educated at the Perse School, Cambridge (1942–1947), St. George's School, Harpenden (1947–1951) and at Emmanuel College, Cambridge (1954–1957), from which he graduated with an honors B.A. in English. After graduation he became a schoolteacher and in 1961 was appointed had of the English Department at St. Christopher School, Letchworth, in Hertfordshire. Between leaving school in 1951 and going up to Cambridge in 1954, Scupham did his National Service with the Royal Army Ordance Corps. He married Carola Nance Braunholtz, a teacher, in 1957; they have four children.

Scupham's first full-scale volume was *Prehistories*, published in 1975, but he was already known as the author of five smaller pamphlets or collections, the earliest of which was *The Small Containers*. Of these, *The Snowing Globe* had been the most substantial. From the start it was evident that he was a traditional poet rather than an innovator, and that he enjoyed writing poetry to a set of complex rules—"a game of knowledge," a phrase he quoted with approbation from Auden, who, indeed, has been one of the chief influences upon him. Others whom he especially acknowledges are Norman Cameron (whose bite and irony, however, he lacks), James Reeves, Louis MacNeice, Richard Wilbur, and John Crowe Ransom. His aims have continued to be to make good sense and to achieve elegance rather than passion. He is generally regarded in Great Britain as a distinguished and painstaking poet, capable of playing elegant games, although not one of much originality. A poet with whom he has much in common is his British near contemporary Jon Stallworthy, He shares Stallworthy's liking for neatness, his attachment to the past, his concern with World War I, and his rootedness in the poetry of older 20th-century generations.

The Hinterland was his most discussed collection. A sequence of fifteen sonnets, in which the poems are linked together by their first and last lines, gives the book its title and was the feature of the book seized upon by most of its reviewers. Craig Raine, in the *Observer*, compared it to "a constriction suit"; but Colin Falck, writing in the *New Review*, also found it to be self-injuriously overcontrived, adding that he approved of readers who "suspect that this may be the kind of foolery that gets poetry a bad name." John Cotton however, in *Contemporary Poets*, called it a "dazzling technical feat" such that "it has beguiled critics from the quality of the work itself." He quotes these lines from it in his approval:

Where blood and stone proclaim their unities
Under the topsail vagueries of green
Works the slow jostle of the small debris. . . .

Cotton (himself a poet with similar tendencies) gives a valuable summary of Scupham's poetry as a whole. Following upon his remarks on the title poem "The Hinterland," he wrote: "While it is true that Scupham's poetry can be so loaded with meaning, overtones, and allusions that it reminds one of those great summer bees freighted with rich pollen; he has done the art some service in reminding us that technical excellence and true feeling are not inimical."

A powerful example is from *The Hinterland*, Sonnet 6, on the dead of World War I, with its refrain "The unfleshed dead refusing to lie down":

'The sons of men, snared in an evil time,'
Whose luck ran out, whose claim was disallowed—
The poplars all are felled: not spared, not one—
Who lies in France under a criss-cross shroud?
A great space, and young voices echoing.
What inch of sunlight gilds their vanishings?

Scupham's lack of directness, so that feelling in him becomes artifice, has engendered a feeling among readers that poetry is with him not much more than a "game." Scupham does, however have his genuine admirers, such as Neil Powell, who wrote in the *Dictionary of Literary Biography* that Scupham enjoys "the support of some leading magazine editors, a distinguished publisher, and a loyal readership. . . . [H]is greatest asset is that deep cultural-historical taproot, so unusual and so welcome at a time when English poetry can seem to be a rather shallow-rooted plant."

At the beginning of the 1990s Scupham published *Watching the Perseids* and his *Selected Poems*. Reviewing both volumes in the *Times Literary Supplement* (1991), Michael Walters wrote that "animating" *Watching the Perseids* was "the vigour of a dying generation"; of the selection, he remarked that it was "excellent," and

that it confirmed Scupham's reputation. The poems in *Watching the Perseids* are elegiac, haunted with ghosts of the past—Edwardian England, his childhood, the deaths of his parents: "I watch you turning into memory, / becoming something far too sharp and clear." But, as in "Watching the Perseids: Remembering the Dead," they resist self-pity, balancing skeletal morbidity with a sense of magic:

The Perseids go riding softly down:
Hair-streak moths, brushing with faint wings
This audience of stars with sharp, young faces,
Staring our eyes out with such charming brilliance
• • •
They are the comet's tail we all must pass through
Dreamed out into a trail of Jack O'Lanterns . . .

The rituals of dying and death are affirmed in their healing power by nature:

We wait for last words, ease the rites of passage,
The cold night hung in chains about our questions,
Our black ark swinging lightly to its mooring.

In a *Times Literary Supplement* review of *The Ark* in 1995, Neil Powell assessed Scupham's career to date: "Readers of Scupham's earlier poetry tended to be either beguiled or exasperated by a sort of linguistic playfulness which relished arcane and archaic locutions, and blitzed out despair with bursts of furiously willed good humor." Summing up the early poems, Powell quotes a line from *The Small Containers*: "His words all lean sideways, blown by his eloquence." Emerging in the later work, Powell suggests, are "uncompromisingly bleak themes . . . it is his intimacy with despair which validates his fragile celebrations." In *The Ark*, he concludes, Scupham "[lets] loose an accumulation of wisdom, anger, grief; the result is a collection of extraordinary honesty and power, tempered by generosity and brightened by moments of utterly bogus charm."

As owner since 1974 of the Mandeville Press, Scupham produces (with the advice of John Cotton, Neil Powell, John Mole, and others of like mind) fine editions of contemporary poetry. Powell describes his work as a teacher as "successful and highly original."

PRINCIPAL WORKS: *Poetry*—The Small Containers, 1972; The Snowing Globe, 1972; Children Dancing, 1972; The Nondescript, 1973; The Gift: Love Poems, 1973; Prehistories, 1975; (with N. Powell and G. Szirtes) A Mandeville Troika, 1977; The Hinterland, 1977; Megaliths and Water, 1978; Natura, 1978; Summer Palaces, 1980; (with J. Mole) Christmas Past, 1981; Transformation Scenes, 1982; Winter Quarters, 1983; (with J. Mole) Christmas Games, 1983; (with J. Mole) Christmas Visits, 1985; Out Late, 1986; (with J. Mole and M. Norman) Winter Emblems, 1986; (with J. Mole

and M. Norman) Christmas Fables, 1987; The Air
Show, 1988; (with D. Tull) The Bells of Lyonesse,
1988; (with J. Mole and M. Morman) Christmas Gifts,
1988; (with D. Tull) Duffy & the Devil, 1989; (with J.
Mole) Christmas Boxes, 1990; Watching the Perseids,
1990; Selected Poems 1972-1990, 1990; The Ark,
1994.

ABOUT: Contemporary Poets, 5th ed., 1991; Dictionary
of Literary Biography 40, 1985. *Periodicals*—Agenda
(London) Autum 1988; Barriers Down (Brownbread
Street) 78, 1989; Encounter 62, March 1981; Observer
23, November 1977; New Review November 1977;
Phoenix 9 (Stockport, Cheshire) Winter 1972; Teacher
(London) March 2, 1973; Times Literary Supplement
May 23, 1975; November 21 1977; September 5 1986;
May 13 1988; March 1 1991; February 3, 1995.

ALLAN SEALY

SEALY, ALLAN (1951–), Indian novelist
and writer on travel, writes: "I was born in Allahabad into an Anglo-Indian family, one of two
children. Our childhood was spent in small
towns across the state of Uttar Pradesh in whose
police force my father was an officer. Our early
education was managed by my mother, a
trained teacher. Later my sister and I were sent
to boarding school in the state capital Lucknow.
I grew to dislike my school, a place at once stately and boorish, and returned home for three
months in the year with a sense of deliverance.
Ours was not a bookish house, but when I was ten
my parents bought, at what must have been a
considerable expense, a children's encyclopaedia
in which I spent whole stretches of my holidays.
After seven years at La Martinière, Lucknow, I
went to St. Stephen's College at Delhi University, where I read English literature and first tast-
ed freedom of mind and body. In my final year
a doubtful assessment in the English novel paper
cost me my first division—and may have determined my career. I had strong and untested
opinions.

"There was no money in the family for an education abroad, but a chance award of the annual St. Stephen's exchange scholarship took me to
the Honors College at Western Michigan University. I came of age in America, but appear to
have spent my time there studying Asia. During
that time our family emigrated to Australia,
where I joined them, but after a year my parents
returned to India, settling in the foothills of the
Himalayas in Dehra Dun, a city I came to think
of as my home town. I taught briefly at the University of Sydney before travelling to Canada,
where I wrote a doctoral dissertation at the University of British Columbia on the Caribbean
novelist Wilson Harris, a man whose work and
friendship I value and whose writerly career re-

mains an inspiration. While writing my thesis I
had already begun what was to turn into my first
novel; I completed the thesis in the knowledge
that I would never use my doctorate.

"My first novel, *The Trotter-Nama*, was the
work of seven years. It tells the story of the An-
glo-Indians, assembled as a single family, the
Trotters, whose rise and decay spans two hundred years. As I set out to write, I was acutely
conscious that the novel form was a European
import. To counter its foreignness I cast about
for an Asiatic form, and found it in the *nama* or
medieval chronicle. The nama's baggy, wayward, and slightly windy manner encouraged
the numerous digressions by which my own story proceeded; what began as a flavouring became part of the book's structure, that of a
discursive comic epic in prose—with Indian
roots.

"*Hero*, my next novel, took a dim and eventually black view of the contemporary national
scene, where film stars turned politicians and
politicians tinsel gods. Their shadowy goings-on
suggested a masque, and I found a modern Indian equivalent in the now hallowed Bombay formula movie. The book goes from 'Song' and
'Dance' through such chapters as 'Fight,' 'Rape,'
and 'Chase,' back finally to 'Song' and 'Dance.'

"My new book is a travelogue, an account of
a journey from arctic Canada to tropical Mexico,
From Yukon to Yucatan. I made the journey a
year before the Columbus quincentenary and
intended to retrace the original peopling of the
Americas across the land bridge from Asia. The
actual journey took me from the Eskimo to the

Maya, but I was also interested in more recent arrivals. The book is subtitled 'A Western Journey'; it looks at the notions and relics of the frontier, and examines on the way my own encounter with a larger West. *From Yukon to Yucatan* mirrors a geopolitical shift—the vertical integration of the three countries of North America—that shakes the old east-west, coast-to-coast assumptions of North Americans. The travelogue becomes a skein of voices as the people I met on the road speak of themselves and their neighbours, north and south.

"I am now [1993] at work on a Himalayan valley novel, a quiet book of much narrower compass.

"I am married to a New Zealander; we have just adopted a little girl."

If there is a single theme informing I. Allan Sealy's rambling and extravagant first novel, *The Trotter-Nama*, it is displacement. The author's own background is not fixed territory—Anglo-Indian, American, Canadian—and his literary imagination has its roots in a tangle of clashing cultures. In the novel, 18th-century Justin Trotter, the French-born patriarch of the Trotter dynasty, has fought in the British colonial army, made a fortune in India, and built himself a vast estate, Sans Souci, in Nakhlau, a city very like Lucknow, where Sealy went to school, "[f]ate having cast my lot in three separate lands of Europe, America and Asia (four, if the Africa of my getting be counted) and brought me at last to this place which I have come to consider my very home. . . . " He has sired a line of descendants of mixed race—mostly dark-skinned, but fiercely British in their loyalties. Characteristically, they have mismatched eyes, one blue, one brown, "looking in two directions, toward past and future . . . floating above two worlds." As Justin reflects:

> But what is this India? Is it not a thousand shifting surfaces which enamour the new comer and then swallow him up? It allows him the many titles of victory while obliging him to accept a single rigid function, that of conqueror. The very divisiveness that allowed him in enmeshes him. How is he to grasp what cannot be held—what in fact holds him fast?

Almost two centuries after Justin's death (by falling out of a balloon of his own design), his seventh-generation descendant Eugene Aloysius Trotter, flying home to India from his world travels, carries his manuscript of the family chronicle. Eugene—candid, funny, happily self-centered—earns his living by forging Indian miniatures. In him the Trotter line has apparently reached its inglorious end:

> "The late Mr. Trotter," my favourite dentist used to call me. His daughter was less charitable. "Lenten Trotter" was her choice, and when I asked her why, she said: "Well, corpu-lent, flat-ulent, indo-lent." She thought the *indo*-lent was especially apt even though I said: "I'm half *Anglo*, you know."

In the present, almost fifty years after India's independence from Britain, the Trotter estate, Sans Souci, has fallen into neglect and all that remains is a shabby hotel. The Trotters have scattered all over the world, but the survivors have not lost their zest for life.

Sealy is one of a number of contemporary Indian novelists who have adapted an essentially European literary genre, the family saga novel, to a vastly different culture and sensibility. They have turned from the almost documentary realism of the great 19th-century novels to an imaginative, even fantastic, vision of their own family histories. The term "magical realism," used most often to describe the writings of such Latin American novelists as Gabriel García Márquez, is equally appropriate when applied to such writers as Amitav Ghosh, Shashi Tharoor, Sealy, and—most obviously—Salman Rushdie, who set the pattern with his *Midnight's Children* in 1981. In the unabashed liberties they take—parody, digressions, deliberate anachronisms, exuberant language, and arbitrary shifts in time, place, and point of view—they recall an earlier heritage of Rabelais and Laurence Sterne. But mingled with what appears as eccentricity and self-indulgence is the sharp and often chilling reality of contemporary events in India and the burden of the colonial past that Indians still carry.

The Trotter-Nama won the Best First Book Award of the Commonwealth Writers' Prize in India in 1989. Typical of the reviewers' reactions was Tony Jesudasan's enthusiastic appraisal in the *Indian Express*: "Sealy's novel heralds a turningpoint in Indian-Anglo literature. At a time when fiction of the fabulist genre is fashionable, *The Trotter-Nama* stands out as an original. Sealy's quirky humor is bizarre and exuberant, his prose intense and eclectic." Less approving was the novelist Bharati Mukherjee, in the *Washington Post Book World*, who called the novel "clever" and "occasionally . . . hilarious," but took a dim view of Sealy's style: "tiresome, show-offy, obese," as Sealy "indulges in bombastic parodies and tired literary mannerisms." A similar judgment was made by Timothy Mo, in the *New York Times Book Review*: *The Trotter-Nama* depends heavily on wit and words, but this is a desperately hard act to bring off, and talented as Mr. Sealy is, he often stumbles."

Sealy's virtuosity, most reviewers agreed, was

a mixed blessing. While praising the novel's "ebullience and complexity," as did Linda Conrad in *Writers of the Indian Diaspora*, they complained of its excesses. For Firdaus Kanga, in the *Times Literary Supplement*, it was "a torrent of fantasy which ended up clogging the narrative with the silt of a too rich imagination." Kanga wrote that in Sealy's second novel, *Hero*, a shorter and more sharply focused book, "he seems to have his hands more firmly on the sluices of his creativity." *Hero* is set in present-day India and uses the theme of filmmaking and stardom as a metaphor for the troubled and complex political history of India in recent years: "We have more film stars-turned-politicians than any country on earth . . . Film star to politician: strange, retrograde metamorphosis. As if a butterfly should turn into a caterpillar."

The speaker, and narrator of the novel, who calls himself Zero, is the loyal and self-effacing friend and aide of Hero, a superstar of the Indian film industry. "The fact was he had . . . presence. Massive presence, which did attract by some cosmic gravity, or maybe simple mathematics, people who were nothing. I should know, I, Zero, felt myself elevated from a cipher in his company." Hero plays swashbuckling roles in scenarios that Zero writes, cynically aware of their absurdity.

> There was money in them, not a lot but enough. Friends will taunt me about the expense of spirit, but there was nothing real to write about. Real misery was all around me, but the moment you wrote about it, it became abstract, painfully abstract. Scripts were solid objects; the streets were unreal, and scrofulous besides.

Thanks to his charismatic presence Hero becomes a political leader, exploiting essentially the same techniques of illusion that film uses to make himself a dictator.

There is much carefully targeted political satire in *Hero*. Linda Conrad writes: "*Hero* highlights the vicissitudes of a post-colonial country adapting to Westminster democracy." Sealy continues to write in the witty and free-wheeling manner that characterizes *The Trotter-Nama*, with asides and a running series of directions to remind readers that the story is being told in the form of a filmscript, and may have only as much credibility as the kind of scenarios he had been writing for Hero. But a harsher spirit, a colder realism pervades the novel: "The rights of man! In this country we hadn't yet plumbed the depths of his wrongs." Hero is assassinated; Zero becomes an exile in Canada; and the novel ends on a sobering note: "Sometimes I am visited by a sadness that I shall not live to see our second moment in history—that I was not born back

then, when we were something, or forward then, when we will be something again. Not a power, or a force, but simply a people who do things right, who have faith in themselves."

PRINCIPAL WORKS: The Trotter-Nama, 1988; Hero, 1991; From Yukon to Yucatan, 1994.

ABOUT: Contemporary Literary Criticism 55, 1988; Nelson, E. S. (ed.) Writers of the Indian Diaspora, 1992. *Periodicals*—Indian Express January 1, 1989; New York Times Book Review February 28, 1988; Observer February 10, 1991; Times Literary Supplement March 1, 1991; Washington Post Book World April 3, 1988.

SEIDEL, FREDERICK (LEWIS) (February 19, 1936–), American poet, was born in St. Louis, Missouri, to Jerome Jay Seidel, a business executive, and Thelma (Cartun) Seidel. He attended the St. Louis Country Day School from 1948 to 1953, then entered Harvard University, from which he received his B.A. in 1957. Seidel grew up in a background of comfort and affluence, but his early years were marked by the tragedy of his mother's mental illness and her lobotomy. As he wrote in "The Beast Is in Chains," "My father saying, 'What should we do?' / I was fifteen, my mother forty-three / 'This will be our decision.'" In "Wanting to Live in Harlem," he describes how, as an American Jew coming of age while the Holocaust raged in Europe, he was also haunted by a sense of guilt for his own security and well-being:

> I had given up violin and left St. Louis,
> I had given up being Jewish,
> To be at Harvard just another
> Greek nose in street clothes in Harvard Yard.
> Mother went on half dying.
> I wanted to live in Harlem. I was almost unarmored . . .

In his student days Seidel published some poems in the *Harvard Advocate*. After completing his degree he worked for a year (1960–1961) in Paris as an editor of the *Paris Review*, of which he remains an advisory editor. In 1960 he married Phyllis Munro Ferguson; they had two children and were divorced in 1969.

Seidel's activities on the *Paris Review* and the publication of his poems in a number of prominent literary journals—*American Poetry Review, Evergreen Review, Hudson Review, Partisan Review, Poetry* and others—won him early recognition among poetry readers. With his first collection, *Final Solutions*, however, he also won attention as the center of a censorship controversy. The poems had received the Helen Burlin Memorial Award of New York's YM-

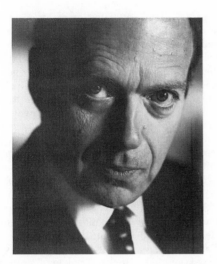

FREDERICK SEIDEL

YWHA Poetry Center while still in manuscript, and they were scheduled for publication as a book. On the advice of their attorneys, the Poetry Center and the publisher demanded that one of the poems, "Americans in Rome," be withdrawn because of the possibility of a libel suit (it contains unflattering references to a prominent Catholic clergyman). When Seidel refused to remove the poem, the sponsors withdrew the award. The judges who had originally selected the manuscript—Louise Bogan, Stanley Kunitz, and Robert Lowell—protested vigorously, and the volume, including the controversial poem, was published by another publisher, Random House.

With Robert Lowell's endorsement on the dust jacket and an enthusiastic review by Louise Bogan in the *New Yorker, Final Solutions* received more critical attention than most first works of poetry. There was an inevitable backlash of adverse reviews, mainly on the grounds that Lowell's influence was all too evident in the poems. James Dickey's opinion, in the *New York Times Book Review* was the most severe: "The diction is the same as Lowell's, as are the historical references, the inflated hortatory style, which manages to be at the same time mockurgent and pompous, arrogant and self-pitying, and worst of all, the systematic and somewhat callous use of personal confession as a device to produce awed silence in the reader who is supposed to sit humbly, his critical faculties turned to dust, in the presence of The Truth." Louise Bogan's *New Yorker* review, appearing about a month later, was an almost point-for-point re-

buttal to Dickey. She was impressed with Seidel's passion ("He radiates heat") and his technique: "The terrifying aspects of the experiences he describes are outlined with clinical precision by means of the rightness of his epithets and of his nouns and verbs, which can be tender as well as shocking. He is a master of metaphor. And each poem is compressed straight up to, and sometimes beyond, the limits of comprehensibility—not as a truth but for a purpose . . . And there is not a trace, throughout the book, of the usual slick response of cold coarseness or gratuitous brutality."

There was an almost twenty-year gap between Seidel's first volume and his second, *Sunrise*. During that period he had polished his technique and, as Denis Donoghue noted in the *New York Review of Books*, he had found his own voice: "Lowell and Yeats are incorporated so fully in his language that they are no longer present as separable excitements." His vision had broadened to range beyond the personal to the public scene: the assassinations of the Kennedys, the civil rights movement, the Vietnam War, the drug plague, the Manson murders, and the alienation of a generation of young people. His poems became even more "difficult": dark, bitter, surreal at times, always challenging. *Sunrise* won the Lamont Poetry Prize of the Academy of American Poets in 1980, and in 1981 the National Book Critics Circle Award and the *American Poetry Review's* poetry prize. Lawrence Joseph, in the *Nation*, summarized his achievement: "For all the power and allure of its subject matter, Seidel's poetry isn't easy . . . In the tradition of difficult modernism, he challenges his reader to learn how to read him . . . The propulsion toward the aesthetic during a time of brutal social insensitivity makes *Sunrise* quite a book."

Slim as the collection is, *Sunrise* contains some of Seidel's most admired verse—a coolly satirical exercise in celebrity name dropping in "Pressed Duck," in which, at a party given by the famous New York restaurateur Elaine, the poet recalls himself as a young man:

Elegant and guileless

Above our English clothes

And Cartier watches, which ten years later shopgirls

And Bloomingdale's fairies would wear,

And the people who pronounce chic *chick.*

Also singled out for praise (Denis Donoghue called it "a love poem as touching as anything I have read in years") was "The Soul Mate," which begins:

Your eyes gazed
Sparkling and dark as hooves,
They had seen you through languor and error.
They were so still. They were a child.
They were wet like hours
And hours of rain.

The occasion of the long, forty-stanza title poem "Sunrise" was the death of a friend in Australia. The poet confronts his grief in cosmic terms, spanning the distance between himself in New York and the grievously injured friend in Perth and everything in between from ancient Egypt to space flight. "Sunrise" holds its readers with striking metaphors and deeply felt emotion:

The gold watch that retired free will was constant dawn.
Constant sunrise. But then it was dawn. Christ rose,
White-faced gold bulging the horizon
Like too much honey in a spoon, an instant
Stretching forever that would not spill. . . .

The critical reception of *Poems 1959–1979* and *These Days: New Poems* in 1989 confirmed the judgment of his earlier reviewers that Seidel was a powerful presence in contemporary poetry but was also a poet of disturbingly uneven quality. In 1963, in *New York Herald Tribune Books*, Stephen Stepanchev had detected a potential trap in Seidel's obsessive sense of the cruelty and evil in the world: "the structure of the poems is relatively weak and tends to disintegrate in the 'meaninglessness' that is at the center of the poet's vision." Writing of *These Days* in *Contemporary Poets*, Martin McKinsey complained of entropy in the poems: "Previously the centrifugal energies of Seidel's imagination had been held in check, barely, by the harness of stanza and occasional rhyme; his latest poems veer between a flatly rhyming formalism and somewhat diffuse, fugue-like improvisations." Sven Birkerts, in the *New Republic*, acknowledged the striking talent displayed in some of the poems in *These Days*, but, while praising the "moments of great power and eloquence," he objected to "terms of reference . . . just too private for the uninitiated reader." In the *New York Times Book Review* Don Stap remarked on the "surreal mindscape" of Seidel's poems of despair in *These Days*: "The voice speaking to us—suffocating in a private malaise—can only record confusion and distress. Nevertheless, if we cannot comprehend the poem, we want at least to apprehend it, to grasp its experience. . . . " Some of the poems in the collection, Stap wrote, "have no weight, no center, nothing to hold on to."

Reviewing *My Tokyo*, the poet's 1993 volume, Daniel J. Guillory remarked in *Library Journal* on Seidel's "grotesque and disturbing juxtaposi-tions. . . . the near-extinction of American bison and the death of a prostitute, a Concorde jet and the Chartres cathedral, the horrors of the Pol Pot regime and the death of poet Sylvia Plath. . . . Seidel is fascinated by the heroic scale of evil in the 20th century. . . . Stalin, Hitler, concentration camps, and nameless battles where the 'bloated corpses lie like sausage on fire.'" In *Poetry* Calvin Bedient also commented on the violence contained in Seidel's images, referring to "Seidel's Ninja-style attacks on innocent contentment," which, in his opinion, "would amount to little without the inspired malice and pathos of his inventions. . . . "

Seidel lives in New York City, on the Upper West Side, but spends considerable time abroad. He is interested in filmmaking; *Afraid of the Dark*, a film he wrote with Mark Peploe, was released in 1991. He has been an "occasional lecturer" at Rutgers University in New Jersey since 1964.

PRINCIPAL WORKS: Final Solutions, 1963; Sunrise, 1980; Men and Women: Selected Poems, 1984; These Days: New Poems, 1989; Poems 1959–1979, 1989; My Tokyo, 1993.

ABOUT: Contemporary Authors New Revision Series 8, 1983; Contemporary Literary Criticism 18, 1981; Contemporary Poets, 5th ed., 1991; Dictionary of Literary Biography Yearbook 1984. *Periodicals*—American Poetry Review May–June 1982; Library Journal August 1993; Nation September 24, 1990; New Republic April 23, 1990; New York Herald Tribune Books August 11, 1963; New York Review of Books August 14, 1980; New York Times Book Review September 1, 1963; September 21, 1980; October 14, 1990; New Yorker October 12, 1963; Poetry March 1994.

SELZER, RICHARD (June 24, 1928–), American physician and writer of essays, memoirs, and short stories, was born in Troy, New York, the second of the two sons of Gertrude Schneider Selzer, an amateur music hall singer, and Julius Louis Selzer, a family doctor. His interest in medicine, nourished both by his father and by the depression-ridden city in which he grew up, began early. As Selzer was to put it in his 1992 memoir *Down from Troy*, the city was "rampant with alcoholism, venereal infections and malnutrition . . . Birth defects were common and tuberculosis endemic." As a youngster he studied pictures in his father's medical textbooks, sounded out words that fascinated him (such as *cerebellum* and *carcinoma*), and spent hours listening on the staircase above his father's office to the sounds of pain and suffering that drifted upwards. Although seldom allowed into the sickroom when he accompanied his father on house calls, he used every opportunity to become an acute observer and questioner. The day would come, his father predicted, when he would learn to love wounds, tumors, and festering sores—and indeed, as Selzer was later to write, "The vivid colors, odor and shape" of wounds "appeal to the sensual mind" and carry with them "the glorious possibility of being healed." He was to learn too that "disease raises the sufferer, granting him . . . an intimate vision of life, a more direct route to his soul."

While the boy was learning from his father a physician's "passionate interest in craft," he was also learning from his mother the very different craft of a music hall "artiste" who knows she must move audiences with drama, display, and suspense. Gertrude Selzer, who, her son says in Down from Troy, was given to wearing "scarves of crushed silk, floating stoles and floppy hats," and who sang—not only on stage, but at home while doing the dishes—with the "flamboyant personality of a diva," convinced herself that her younger son, an avid reader from an early age, was destined to become a writer. While Selzer's father used every opportunity to encourage the boy's interest in medicine, her mother used all her wiles to encourage his passion for literature. Young Selzer, who soon sensed that his parents, in their conflicting ambitions for him, were actually battling one another, was torn: devoted to both, he did not want to have to choose between them.

Selzer's father's death of a heart attack when the boy was twelve marked a turning point in his life. As he was to write in Down from Troy: "It was then and there that I gave myself to medicine the way a monk gives himself to God. Not to have done so would have seemed an act of filial impiety." Meantime he continued to be an avid reader. As a boy, his favorite books had been Greek myths, fairy tales, and Aesop's fables; as he grew older he turned to the Iliad and the Odyssey, and to Edgar Allan Poe, Robert Louis Stevenson, Sir Walter Scott, and Rafael Sabatini. His early interest in literature was also stimulated by his frequent visits to a nearby tavern, a place he had gotten to know when his father had sent him there on errands to patients. Here among drunks and derelicts, Selzer listened spellbound to Duffy, the local bard, whose "genius" for spinning yarns he likened to Homer's. Later he was to write that Duffy taught him that "suspense, humor, and the grotesque" could all be "instruments of illumination."

After finishing high school, Selzer enrolled at Union College in Schenectady, and then, after completing his B.S. degree in 1948, at Albany Medical College—both choices made so that he could continue to live near his mother when she needed him. When one of his supervisors scornfully asked him if he was a mother's boy, Selzer candidly admitted that he was. His straightforward honesty, seen here in the larger context of human concern, was to become a hallmark of his dual career as surgeon and writer. As one of the nurses who assisted him while he was practicing surgery said of him, he was the most attentive and caring surgeon" among the doctors with whom she worked. Selzer's more modest estimation of his medical career has been that "surgeons suffer, and are afraid," and sometimes "they fail."

After receiving his M.D. degree from Albany Medical College in 1953, Selzer enrolled at the Yale University School of Medicine to begin his internship and residency. He married Janet White in 1955, and that same year his studies were interrupted when he was recruited for military service in Korea. While tending American soldiers and Korean refugees and peasants there, he contracted malaria and amoebic dysentery, afterward spending more than a year in Japan to recuperate. He returned to Yale to complete his residency, began a private practice in general surgery in 1960, and in 1961 accepted a job at Yale as an instructor in surgery, eventually rising to the position of assistant professor, a position he held for twenty years.

Selzer turned to writing in 1968; until this time he had confined his love of language to fabricating stories for his children. He began by writing a short story based on the biblical tale of Jonah and the whale, but soon switched to writing horror stories—having always, as he put it, been drawn to the "macabre and the grotesque." Ellery Queen's Mystery Magazine launched his writing career in 1971 by publishing a story entitled "A Single Minute of Fear," which was described by the magazine's editor as "filled with suspense and a growing sense of terror." In 1972 Esquire magazine began publishing nonfiction pieces by Selzer that combined the author's experiences as a surgeon with his extensive knowledge of literature and myth. Selzer, who has said that he began writing "to give pain a name," found an outlet in these early stories for his love of style and drama and what one of his critics was later to describe as his "need to grapple physically with the grotesque."

Selzer's first book, Rituals of Surgery, a collection of fictional pieces, was published in 1974, but only a few critics reviewed it. However, his second, Mortal Lessons: Notes on the Art of Surgery, a collection of his Esquire pieces and some autobiographical essays, received dozens of reviews in newspapers and periodicals. Most were favorable; for example, Peter Stoler, writing in *Time*, thought that would-be surgeons should read the book because it would force them "to think about the morality of medicine" and might make them genuine healers. One dissenting view came from Peter Prescott, who wrote in *Newsweek* that Selzer "aims to shock," and that his anecdotes were "grisly."

Selzer's next collection of essays, *Confessions of a Knife*, includes numerous stark details of a surgeon's work; it was described in 1979 by *Newsweek*'s reviewer, Elizabeth Peer, as "not for the squeamish." Commenting that Selzer "forces us to look at what is fearsome and disgusting" and "to view human decay as invested with sensuality, irony, bathos, low comedy, and high terror," she concluded that through "dwelling on the mechanics of death, he celebrates life." Yet a few, like Christopher Lehmann-Haupt, in the *New York Times*, were less impressed; in his view, "there may be some beauty in the way Dr. Selzer writes about these encounters with sickness and death, but to me the art of them seems gratuitous."

In *Letters to a Young Doctor*, Selzer once again uses case histories, parables, and reflections as examples of human suffering, failure, and triumph. Doctors, patients, staff, and families all become transcendent metaphors for the human condition. Whether they fail (as when a dying woman rejects her husband's comfort by calling out the name of her lover) or succeed (as when two sisters who have been violent antagonists are reconciled when one acts as the midwife to the other's illegitimate child), they are all seen as protagonists in the larger context of Everyman's journey through life. In the view of Diane Ackerman, reviewing *Taking the World in for Repairs* in the *New York Times Book Review* in 1986, Selzer is a scientist "searching for romance, myth, faith and all those other ephemera we throw into a poke and call meaning." The author, she concluded, has "a surgeon's cunning and a stylist's zest."

Selzer's later books have been *Imagine a Woman*, a book of short fiction; his memoir *Down from Troy*; and *Raising the Dead*, an account of his near-death from Legionnaires' disease in 1991. Merrill Joan Gerber, in the *New York Times Book Review*, commented that in the first of these books, "Selzer abandons the measured tone of his scientific observations and speaks with a wilder voice—deeply emotional, frankly melodramatic and notably unmodern . . . His heroes and heroines fight for their lives in a nether world of bogs and bat caves and garbage dumps, doing battle with evil forces in the guise of psychoses, incurable diseases, poverty, radioactive debris and overwhelming grief. Medicine is not an answer to their despair, and sometimes it is the cause of it." Conceding that the author has enormous compassion and is "a master of description," with the power to "evoke primal feelings and fears," she nevertheless regrets that a reader attending to this group of stories "is denied the triumph of discovery because clues that might have been deftly placed are announced with fanfare."

Susan Cheever, who reviewed Selzer's memoir *Down from Troy* in the *New York Times Book Review*, saw the author as driven by childhood demons, "a man on a lonely, yearning quest for something he cannot even define. His world is filled with monsters and death . . . [His] prose swoops and dives, occasionally veering into humor . . . zooming down into despair and back again." And, like other critics before her, Cheever concluded that Selzer writes "in arresting, idiosyncratic and lyrical prose" and "immerses us in the facts we all know but hate to admit."

Selzer has received honorary degrees from several universities and colleges—among them the University of Pennsylvania Medical College, Georgetown Medical School, and Albany Medical College. He won the Pushcart Prize for fiction in 1982, the American Medical Writer's Award in 1983, and a Guggenheim Fellowship in 1985. He has been described as short and slim, unassuming, friendly and genuinely interested in the people around him. Selzer has said of himself that he is "profoundly religious despite an oft-professed atheism," and that he views his life "as a blend of passion and affliction, a combination that has driven Western civilization." He and his wife of more than forty years live in New Haven.

PRINCIPAL WORKS: Rituals of Surgery, 1974; Mortal Lessons: Notes on the Art of Surgery, 1977; Confessions of a Knife, 1979; Letters to a Young Doctor, 1982; Taking the World in for Repairs, 1986; Imagine a Woman, 1990; Down from Troy: A Doctor Comes of Age, 1992; Raising the Dead: A Doctor's Encounter with His Own Mortality, 1993.

ABOUT: Contemporary Authors New Revision Series 14, 1985; Current Biography April 1993; Who's Who in America 1990–1991. *Periodicals*—New York Times August 27, 1979; New York Times Book Review October 5, 1986; July 18, 1990; July 26, 1992; New York Times Magazine September 22, 1991; Newsweek January 24, 1977; September 3, 1979; Time January 24, 1977.

*SEROTE, MONGANE WALLY (May 8, 1944–   ), A South African poet, novelist, essayist, and spokesperson on culture for the African national Congress, writes: "I was born in Sophiatown, Johannesburg. I left Sophiatown with my mother when I was small to settle in Alexandra township. I grew up and lived here until 1974 when I left South Africa to study for my M.F.A., which combined writing and filmmaking.

"Before I left South Africa, during and after my school days, I worked as a gardener, mechanic, and at a bottle store as a packer, at a calendar factory. Most times I learnt from the streets of Alexandra. By 1974 when I left South Africa I was working as a copywriter, at an advertising firm called J. Walter Thompson. By then, I had also worked in the ANC [African National Congress] underground for which I was detained in 1969 for nine months in solitary confinement. When I was released in 1970, my first book, *Yakhal'inkomo*, was published. I was by then working with people like Stephen Bantu Biko, with whom I nurtured a warm friendship, which led us to talk endlessly, into the early hours of the morning for days on end, about our country. It is these discussions and through endless reading that I became more and more convinced that I must become a fighter against apartheid. But also, it is my close association with the likes of Biko, Pityana, Joyce Sikhakhane and others, which created a deep curiosity among us to know our country. We travelled its length and breadth and met people from different parts of our country and from different backgrounds. Nothing could convince one more about the cruelty and brutality of the apartheid system against the black people.

"I was by this time convinced that if I wrote, and wrote as honestly as I could, I would contribute to the fight against the evil of the apartheid system. I saw, I heard, I experienced, and I was the more outraged by my country. So I wrote. In 1974, I left. I lived in New York from 1974 to 1977. Martin Luther King was dead and so was Malcolm X. Vietnam and the civil rights movement had died down. America was incredibly quiet and I knew it was not innocent. So I travelled; I kept late nights talking. I heard once that James Baldwin, answering a question about this quietness, said: 'I am not a repentant son . . .' I agreed totally with him—I was not a repentant son. I found that to be an apt answer for the restlessness in me.

"June 1976 happened in South Africa. In a sense it was not any surprise for me. I always knew that the authorities in South Africa would not hesitate to kill a thousand or a million or more black children if they are left to do it. It is this and the fact that I was unrepentant and

I must say fearful of all this that made me persevere to explore human relations by writing. Poetry, in 1976, seemed to burst at the seams, unable to contain the bulge of the implications of human relations. I thought I would make films, but in the meantime, I thought I should write novels, short stories, plays, and might return to poetry some time.

"When I reached Botswana from the United States in 1977, we founded Medu Arts Ensemble. I met good men like Tim Williams, Mandla Langa, and Thami Mnyele, and women like Teresa Devent. I was then given the opportunity to work in photography, painting, filming, theatre, writing, and music.

"Thami Mnyele was killed by SADF [South African Defence Force] in 1985 in Botswana. One of South Africa's best painters went just like that. I was a fully fledged member of ANC by this time. The ANC gave me a chance to travel, to meet people, to question political systems of the whole world, to seek the best solutions to what boils down to human relations. I worked in various structures of the African National Congress, including the underground structures and Umkhonto we Sizwe. I was lucky; I met and many times discussed with men and women I admire most like Oliver R. Tambo, Raymond Mokoena, Cassius Make, Joe Jele, Florence Mphosho, Thabo Mbeki, and some young, dedicated men and women who were not reluctant to discuss this elusive issue: human relations.

"I left Botswana in 1986, for Britain. I worked there in the ANC office as a cultural attaché, having been the head of the African National Congress Department of Arts and Culture since 1983. For the first time I looked Europe in the eye. Europe, like America, has shown how civilization can contribute to human relations. It is here that some of the most important experiments on human relations take place: the rights of women, the rights of gays, the rights of the disabled, the rights of children. I saw also educated men and women in large numbers. I had come from where the uneducated are in the majority. I saw communication systems function at their best: planes, trains, ships, buses, taxis, phones, faxes, computers; human beings were willing to reach out. The West in my view has missed the boat despite the achievements in communication—it knows very little about human relations.

"I was absolutely shocked by the rumblings of the beginnings of the fall of the Eastern bloc. Up until then, my optimism was based on the fact that there was an opposite to capitalism. Apartheid, being a brainchild of capitalism, is evil. Europe and America convinced me. The eventual fall of the Eastern bloc is, in my view, one of the most terrible human tragedies to happen in history. Capitalism cannot be the option left us for human relations. That was why I was apprehensive, pained, and uncertain because of this find when I left London in 1990 for Johannesburg, after sixteen years of being in exile.

"I am back in South Africa now [April 1993]. I am heading the Department of Arts and Culture of the African National Congress once more. I listen. I watch. I ask. I give my view. I have not stopped writing. I must find a better way of asking: what is human nature and human relations? I must write. I watched the bombardment of Iraq on television. I watched Mandela and de Klerk put the future of our country to the nation, and as foolish as this may sound, I kept thinking, a prisoner and his jailer are talking. It seems a very difficult issue for me to handle. How does one forget that a large chunk of one's life was spent in jail, sent there by the same man who argues about freedom with one? But as they were talking at CODESA, I was conscious of the fact that since that time when Mandela announced the suspension of armed operations, violence, organized political violence was spreading in South Africa. I could not help but want to know who, between them, was talking about the future of all South Africans. F. W. de Klerk was not. He was always unable to do so. He was trapped in the issues of constituency. And his constituency is that spoiled, backward, individualistic, and power-hungry tribe, called the white South African. On the other hand, in spite of the history and track record of the ANC, on matters of nonracialism, democracy, Mandela was not able to convince this white tribe of Africa that he meant that South Africa had no choice; it had to be nonracial. This is very important. White people in this country are unable to listen to black people. What must Mandela do? I ask and ask.

"What must we as South Africans do to arrive at a common national consciousness? A consciousness which will oppose violence and not seek to know whether it is blacks, whites, Xhosas or Zulus who are the victims? What must we do to arrive at this consciousness?"

––––––––––

The numerous critical studies of Mongane Wally Serote's work, made from very different perspectives, agree that he is one of the leading writers of his generation in South Africa. The basis for this judgment is in the first place his poetry, particularly the four volumes published in the 1970s, when (along with Mtshali, Ndebele, Sepamla, Gwala and others) he led a resurgence of black poetry that ended the relative silencing of black writers during the repressive 1960s. His novel *To Every Birth Its Blood* has also been considered a major work of South African fiction; and his collection of essays, *On the Horizon*, represents his importance as a thinker about politics and culture in the African National Congress, whose Department of Arts and Culture he has headed.

Serote's career began in the radical nationalism of the Black Consciousness Movement, led by Steve Biko, to which his poetry of the 1970s lent a powerful voice. He has written of the slogan "Black man you are on your own" that it is "the political commitment that informed our writing at that point": "We were writing for black people and we were saying it is very important that black people talk among themselves about how they were going to liberate themselves." Moving away from the patronage of the well-intentioned, liberal, white, English-speaking establishment that dominates South African culture, this poetry needed to address such topics as black rage: "i understand alas i do understand / the rage of a whiteman pouring petrol on a black child's face" ("Poem on Black and White"). In the last lines of "That's Not My Wish," while Serote still has much to say to non-black readers, his horizon (like that of the African-American poet Audrey Lorde's essay "The Uses of Anger") is essentially the psychosocial well-being of the black community: "To talk for myself, / I hate to hate, / But how often has it been / I could not hate enough." The principle of black autonomy and coming to voice emerges in the much-quoted epigrams of another poem:

> White people are white people,
> They are burning the world.
> Black people are black people,
> They are the fuel.
> White people are white people,
> They must learn to listen.
> Black people are black people,
> They must learn to talk.

Oswald Mtshali's book of verse, *Sounds of a Cowhide Drum*, which was taken up by white readers to great acclaim just before the appearance of Serote's *Yakhal'inkomo*, had nothing like this. Mtshali's plangent ironies and images, according to the poet and critic Njabulo Ndebele, lacked the black voice and address that Serote took over from predecessors like James Matthews, and "merely confirmed the fact of oppression without offering a challenging alternative. Our poetry, however, should go beyond the confirmation of oppression to reveal the black man's attempt to re-create himself." This self-creating dynamic of Black Consciousness gives a different dimension to a poem like "City Johannesburg," which white readers might otherwise mistake for elegy (the title *Yakhal'inkomo* refers to the cry of slaughtered cattle). When Serote speaks there of going back "to my love, / My dongas [ditches], my dust, my people, my death, / Where death lurks in the dark like a blade in the flesh," it is not only the poverty and danger but the creative force of his urban black community which is invoked; the title also refers to a famous solo by the Johannesburg saxophonist Mankunku Ngozi.

Serote's first books plunged into a confessional intimacy about black township life that was not particularly mediated for white readers, as in his Alexandra poems, about the bulldozed township of his childhood, where the obsessive image of violated women stands for the whole community: "i cannot look / for your legs are chained apart / and your dirty petticoat is soaked in blood"; "i heard a man weep like a woman giving birth / while he pleaded for his life" ("Another Alexandra"). The novelist and critic Mbulelo Mzamane also points to Black Consciousness as the basis of Serote's unsparingly critical, didactic poems like "My Brothers in the Streets" which are "very functional in purpose. They are meant to transform Black society by curing it of its social illnesses. . . . The constructive self-criticism . . . is an outcome of Black Consciousness." The poem ends:

Oh you black boys,
Who spill blood as easy as saying 'Voetsek' ["Bug off!"]
Listen!
Come my black brothers in the streets,
Listen,
It's black women who are crying.

Similarly, a short poem in homeless children in *Tsetlo* ends with an image which summons the community to heal itself: "this small boy will die one day / his lips stuck together, glued by the glue he smokes."

Although Serote was awarded the literary establishment's Ingrid Jonker Prize in 1973, some conservative white critics were put off by a poetry so decisively addressed to a black readership; the complex reception of Serote's poetry is part of the tense relationships that made up apartheid society itself. But the white poet Douglas Livingstone's reading of the early poems is alive to both the "sensibilities" and the "circumstances" that produced them: "His pitch or tone of voice, in his best work, is tragically resonant, deeply felt and very sad." The poem Serote addressed to his friend, the poet Don Mattera ("For Don M.—Banned") is an example:

it is a dry white season

dark leaves don't last, their brief lives dry out
and with a broken heart they dive down gently headed
for the earth
not even bleeding.
it is a dry white season brother,
only the trees know the pain as they still stand erect
dry like steel, their branches dry like wire,
indeed, it is a dry white season
but seasons come to pass.

This poem invoked the Afrikaner novelist André Brink, whose novel of the radicalization of an Afrikaner schoolteacher (and the film Euzhan Palcy made of it) is entitled *A Dry White Season*.

Nadine Gordimer's shrewd, empathetic comment on Serote's poetics resembles Livingstone's, but is more alive to the political background, and raises the question of language: "There is a piercing subjectivity in his work, in which 'black as struggle' becomes at times an actual struggle with the limits of language itself." Mzamane points out that these "limits" were often simply the exclusion of black speech from South African poetry, a limit Serote crossed by employing "township colloquialisms through direct transliteration. . . . The simplicity and effective tone of his language . . . are intended to make his appeal to the Black community as broadly based as possible." This commitment to black speech finds diverse expression, as in the urgent political rhetoric of "Time Has Run Out," or the parallel cadences of oral poetry in "City Johannesburg" and "Alexandra" ("Jo'burg City, you are dry like death, / Jo'burg City, Johannesburg, Jo'burg City"), or the jagged musicality of township jazz in "Waking Up. The Sun. The Body." Often Serote's black vernacular idiom gives the poetry a realist quality at odds with elegiac lyricism. Looking at the poem "Mama and Child" (from *Tsetlo*) in the broader context of the African and Caribbean race-conscious poetics of negritude, Clive Wake felt a sharper edge in Serote. Contrasting the poems realism with the idealizing lyricism of Senghor's poem "Femme Noire," Wake noted in *Research in African Literatures* "a greater affinity with the Césairian brand of negritude, with its great directness and simple anger." The anger is even more direct in the later *No Baby Must Weep, Behold, Mama, Flowers* and "Time Has Run Out" (whose long "epic" forms also echo Césaire's verse), as when racist whites are named "the gods of destruction . . . / bloody-footed / things who have forgotten how to kiss."

Without abandoning his original commitment to black autonomy, Serote moved after the late 1970s towards the Marxist-inflected, democratic, nonracial humanism of his ANC affiliation. Ndebele had already said at an early black students' conference that "the struggle is more than a racial one, it is also a human one." Serote speculated in his 1988 essay "Post-Sharpeville Poetry: A Poet's View" (printed in *On the Horizon*) that "perhaps Black Power, like soap, has washed away the shame of those who were black, and ashamed of that fact. Like soap, that poetry is finished, it has done its job. Screaming poetry has rendered its poets hoarse, and those who write swearing poetry must only be a bit embarrassed by it now. South African poetry has . . . emerged revitalized from its past. It has struggled with the struggling people of South Africa to become part of humanity." *To Every Birth Its Blood* in some ways chronicles this shift, which many writers made about the same time, partly in response to the deepening of the liberation struggle after the Soweto revolt of June 16, 1976. Kelwyn Sole commented in *Research in African Literatures*: "The events of 1976 have a powerful implied presence as a fulcrum in this narrative, transforming the agonized subjective narration of Tsi Molope in the first section of the novel into a more objectified focus on the activities of a group of revolutionaries afterward." The second part of the novel is a new "plot" not yet found in Serote's poetry up to that point, but Tsi's flowing interior monologue in the first part, often carried by a jazz-based improvisational style (and full musical references), stems directly from the long, declamatory lines of *No Baby Must Weep* and *Behold, Mama, Flowers*. Those volumes were also distinguished by a broader range of reference than township life, in part because their author was living in New York, Botswana, and London; and this perspective (especially a Pan-Africanist, socialist, and anti-imperialist politics) is carried through into the novel. Published in South Africa (where it was banned at first) England, and the United States, *To Every Birth Its Blood* has been widely read internationally as a chronicle of the South African "world of burdened, complex people struggling to give life to something new," as William Finnegan wrote in the *New York Times Book Review*.

The shift, or evolution, in Serote's work from 1971 to the 1990s is typical of the fusion of a more inward-looking 1970s Black Consciousness, led by students, with the energy of the much broader 1980s mass movement, led by the new black trade unions and the nonracial, ANC-aligned coalition called the United Democratic Front (UDF). His choice to move from writing to organizational work with the ANC in exile is also part of the experience of his generation (the poet Mandla Langa, for instance). Now, with a new long poem, *Third World Express*, and his influential position in cultural policy in the new majority-ruled South Africa, Serote is poised to embark as a writer on the most fateful moment of his generation's history, as they attempt to transform apartheid into a democratic culture.

PRINCIPAL WORKS: *Poetry*—Yakhal'inkomo, 1972; Tsetlo, 1974; No Baby Must Weep, 1975; Behold, Mama, Flowers, 1978; The Night Keeps Winking, 1982; Selected Poems, 1982; Third World Express, 1992. *Novel*—To Every Birth Its Blood, 1981. *Essays*—On the Horizon, 1990.

ABOUT: Alvarez-Pereyre, J. The Poetry of Commitment in South Africa, 1984; Barnett, U. A. A Vision of Order, 1983; Campschreur, W., and Divendal, J. Culture in Another South Africa, 1989; Contemporary Poets, 5th ed., 1991; Daymond, M. J., and Jacobs, J. U. Momentum, 1984; Gordimer, N. The Black Interpreters, 1973; Lindfors, B. South African Voices, 1973; Ndebele, N. S. The Rediscovery of the Ordinary, 1991; Shava, P. V. A People's Voice, 1989; Trump, M. Rendering Things Visible, 1990; White, L. and Couzens, T. Literature and Society in South Africa, 1984; Zell, H. A New Reader's Guide to African Literature, 1983. *Periodicals*—Bloody Horse 1981; diacritics Spring 1992; Journal of Southern African Studies October 1982; New Classic 1975, 1976; New York Times Book Review May 7, 1989; Research in African Literatures Spring 1985; Spring 1988; Staffrider April–May 1981.

*SETH, VIKRAM (June 20, 1952–), Indian poet, novelist, and travel writer, was born in Calcutta to an upper-middle-class Hindu family socially much like the families who people his novel *A Suitable Boy*. His father, Premnath Seth, was a business consultant to a Czech shoe manufacturer in Calcutta. When Vikram was two years old, his father was transferred to London by his employer, and there his mother Leila Seth (her maiden name was also Seth), began to study law. On the family's return to India in 1957, his mother continued her law practice and became the first woman to serve as chief justice in the High Court of Delhi. Like many other comfortably established Indian families, they gave their son an "English" education, sending him first to a boarding school, Welham, where he excelled in mathematics, and then to the exclusive Doon School, where again he won distinction as a scholar, though not as a school athlete. He returned to England to study philosophy, politics, and economics at Corpus Christi College, Oxford, taking a B.A. with honors in 1975 and an M.A. in 1978.

Although he had elected to specialize in economics, young Seth pursued many other interests at university, including the study of Chinese, in which he became relatively proficient, and the writing of poetry. In 1975 Seth began graduate work at Stanford University. The experience

°SATE, VEE krum

of a totally new and, for him, liberating environment in California was a transforming one. In particular he found direction for his poetry in tutorials in creative writing. Working with the poets Donald Davie and Timothy Steele, Seth developed an interest in formal verse, rhyme, and regular meter. His primary concentration, however, remained economics, in which Stanford University awarded him an M.A. in 1979, and he began research for a doctoral dissertation on the subject "Seven Chinese Villages: An Economic and Demographic Portrait."

With grants from Stanford and the Ford Foundation, Seth spent two years, 1980 to 1982, in China at Nanjing University. In the summer of 1982 he embarked on an adventurous overland journey home to India via Tibet and Nepal. Traveling by rail occasionally, but more often hitchhiking truck rides or simply on foot, he had the rare opportunity to study the varied cultures of China and northern India. The journey was not without risks and physical hardships and the maddening frustrations of political bureaucracy, with long waits for visas and clearance papers. But Seth was amply compensated by the warmth and friendliness of the people he met along the way and—not surprisingly, since he carried a copy of Lao-Tze's writings with him—by a few moments of transcendence. One such experience was on the border between China and Nepal when he paused to watch a waterfall and reflected on water as a unifying element of all living things:

> I will during my life be certain to drink some molecules of the water passing this moment through the waterfall I see. Not only its image will become a part of me; and its particles will become a part not merely of me but of everyone in the world. The solid substances of the earth more easily cohere to particular people or nations, but those that flow—air, water—are communal even within our lives . . . It is this visible movement of water, whether of the concentric ripples on a lake, or of the "sounding cataract" falling whitely into chaos, that informs the purity of a uniform element with the varying impulse of life.

Seth recorded these travel experiences in a journal which he published in 1983 as *From Heaven Lake: Travels Through Sinkiang and Tibet*. The book, illustrated with his own photographs, was well reviewed and won the Thomas Cook Travel Book Award for 1983. Richard Cobb, in the *Spectator*, found it "wonderfully visual and with an acute sensitivity to speech, gesture and stance. It is beautifully written, always in a low key, and is enlivened by a gentle and kindly humour." Other reviewers noted its excellent reporting on the effects of the Cultural Revolution, then in its waning years; these remote regions; and the political tension between China and Tibet.

Seth's exposure to Chinese culture has been a shaping force in his poetry. His collection, *The Humble Administrator's Garden*, echoes traditional Chinese poetry not only in its title but in the delicacy and simplicity of his language and imagery. The eponymous Humble Administrator is in direct line of descent from the classic Chinese lyric poet Wang Wei, whose poems Seth translated in a collection, *Three Chinese Poets* (the others are Li Bai and Du Fu). Seth's own poems preserve the Far Eastern sense of formality, within a western model—the Shakespearean sonnet. His Mr. Wang strolls through his garden proudly observing its beauties and choosing to forget the "somewhat dubious means" by which he had acquired the money to plant it:

> The Humble Administrator admires a bee
> Poised on a lotus, walks through the bamboo wood,
> Strips half a dozen loquats off a tree
> And looks about and sees that it is good.
> He leans against a willow with a dish
> And throws a dumpling to a passing fish.

A few of the poems in this collection are unrhymed and more open in form. Emotion is pure and restrained, as in "The Accountant's House," in which a family mourns the death of a son but remains warm and friendly to a visitor:

> Yet they laugh, yet they laugh, these lovely people,
> And he clicks his abacus and she gives me a towel and
>   the two girls
> Smile shyly, boldly at the stranger and the father
> Discussing matters of much importance together.

Some of the poems in *The Humble Administrator's Garden* have American settings and treat domestic life, business machines, and, in one instance, a California food delight, "Abalone Soup":

> The gourmet's edelweiss, of the four A's
> Of California—asparagus,
> Ab, avocado, artichoke—you raise
> Our palates to the most vertiginous
> Conception of sublimity. . . .

Seth displays a similarly wide range of interests in his later collection, *All You Who Sleep Tonight*. The influence of Chinese poetry persists in a number of descriptive lyrics, as in "Night in Jiangning":

> A glass of tea; the moon;
> The frogs croak in the weeds.
> A bat wriggles down across
> Gold disk to silver reeds.
> The distant light of lamps.
> The whirr of winnowing grain.
> The peace of loneliness.
> The scent of imminent rain.

Much of this is light verse. But there are also po-

ems that reflect on the bitter realities of war—
the Holocaust ("Work and Freedom," in which
a Nazi officer at Auschwitz rationalizes his grim
duties but dimly perceives that he too is a prisoner of his conscience), the atomic bombing of Japan ("A Doctor's Journal Entry for August 6,
1945," which reads in part: "Silence was common to us all. I heard

I have to speak—I must—I should—I ought . . .
I'd tell you how I love you if I thought
The world would end tomorrow afternoon.
But short of that . . . well, it might be too soon.

In an even lighter spirit are the fables and
folktales of *Beastly Tales from Here and There*,
a collection of stories from India, China, Greece,
Russia, and Seth's imagination. Written in rhyming tetrameter couplets and illustrated with
whimsical drawings by Ravi Shankar, this volume seems intended for children; but, like most
folk literature, it can be converted to subtle and
sophisticated adult satire. Retelling the classic
Tortoise-Hare tale, for example, Seth has the silly, vain hare profiting from the publicity of losing her race: "Soon she saw her name in lights
/ Sold a book and movie rights."

Seth had won early recognition as a writer of
technically expert but essentially light verse, but
he launched his major literary career with an
ambitiously conceived poetic opus—a full-
length verse novel about contemporary
American life, *The Golden Gate*. With some 1,
300 pages of more than 8,000 tetrameter
rhymed lines, the book was a bold venture into
a rarely used narrative form. Seth's principal inspiration was Charles Johnston's translation of
Pushkin's *Eugene Onegin*, the great 19-century
verse novel. He was also of course well schooled
in the whole tradition of English narrative verse
in rhyme from medieval epics to Butler's
Hudibras and Pope's *The Rape of the Lock*. The
novel's closest ancestor, after Pushkin, was Byron's *Don Juan* with its breathless pace and its
occasionally outrageous rhymes (Seth rhymes
"iguana / sultana," "Onegin / Reagan"). Seth
writes with a facility that appears spontaneous,
but in fact the novel is carefully plotted and attempts to capture the whole restless, direction-
less spirit of 1980s life among the well-to-do
young professionals labeled "yuppies." *The
Golden Gate* is named for the bridge and for the
city of San Francisco where it takes place. Gore
Vidal gave it a dusk jacket endorsement as "the
great California novel," but its setting is confined to one particular city and—in the early
1980s—its burgeoning environs:

. . . Silicon Valley
Lures to ambition's ulcer alley

Young graduates with siren screams
Of power and wealth beyond their dreams,
Ejects the lax, and drives the driven,
Burning their candles at both ends.
Thus files take precedence over friends. . . .

The central character among the five principal characters is a young computer expert ("He
thought of or-gates and of and-gates / Of ROMS,
of nor-gates. . . . "), good-looking and successful, but a latter-day Onegin, alienated, unable to
make a commitment of love. His friends, equally
successful in their careers, include two women
to whom he is attracted—a Japanese-American
artist and a lawyer—and two men, one Catholic,
one Jewish, who have a brief homosexual affair.
All the characters are sensitive to social and political causes—nuclear disarmament, environmental preservation, civil rights. Indeed, their
(and Seth's) endorsement of such causes offended one reviewer, Carol Ianone, in *Commentary*,
who objected to "Seth's trusting subscription to
current orthodoxies." Other reviewers, however,
judged the book on its literary merits—for the
most part favorably. For Thomas M. Disch, in
the *Washington Post Book World* (1986), "*The
Golden Gate* is a thing of anomalous beauty. . . . Seth writes poetry as if it has not been
written for nearly a century—that's to say, with
the intention that his work should give pleasure
to that ideal Common Reader for whom good
novelists have always aspired to write." For John
Gross, in the *New York Times*, it was a literary
curiosity that manages to skirt but never fall into
the traps of sentimentality and banality: "Here
and there *The Golden Gate* is too cute for its own
good; occasionally inspiration falters or we become aware of an emotional soft center. But for
the most part the poem is a splendid achievement, equally convincing in its exhilaration and
its sadness." John Hollander, in the *New
Republic*, hailed the book as "most unqualifiedly
marvelous . . . an astounding achievement . . . a tour de force of the transcendence
of the mere tour de force."

The phrase "tour de force" is even more appli-
cable to Seth's first novel in prose, *A Suitable
Boy*, a work of formidable proportions that
somehow also managed to engage readers on the
level of simple, forthright (some have suggested
"old fashioned") narrative. Advanced publicity
emphasized the size and weight of the novel—1,
349 pages, with Seth proclaiming in his rhymed
dedication "Buy me before good sense insists /
You'll strain your purse and sprain your
wrists"—and its sweeping coverage of life in India in early postcolonial days of the 1950s. Comparisons to the great panoramic novels of the
19th century—*Les Misérables*, *War and Peace*,

Middlemarch—were inevitable and perhaps, in the critical long run, more damaging than helpful. Essentially, *A Suitable Boy* is a domestic novel centering on four families—three Hindu, one Muslim. Although there are panoramic scenes—religious processions, political crises (a few characters are from real life, among them Prime Minister Nehru), riots—the book focuses, as its title suggests, on the search for a suitable husband for an intelligent young Hindu woman with a mind of her own. She rebels against the choice of her equally strong-minded mother, becomes infatuated with a romantic young Muslim, flirts pleasantly with a young writer, and ultimately settles down with a "suitable" businessman who, at least, is of her own choice. Not surprisingly, some reviewers found *A Suitable Boy*, in Richard Jenkyns's words in the *New Republic* "a decent, unremarkable, second-rate novel . . . after 1,300 pages the feeling still persists that it is a little thin." In the *New York Times Book Review*, Robert Towers called Seth "a sentimental bourgeois realist with a taste for scrupulous documentation." His characters, Towers wrote, "are conventionally conceived, well drawn and sufficiently interesting in their social and familial roles; none, I predict, will continue to haunt our memories." Anita Desai, a novelist who also writes about contemporary India, observed, in *New York Review of Books*, that "for all the breadth and scope of the author's intention, there is at the heart of his work a modesty that one would have thought belonged to the miniature, not the epic scale." Seth is more successful, she suggested, in the humorous domestic scenes of the novel than in the dramatic ones, but she emerged from her reading of *A Suitable Boy* with a feeling of awe about Seth's readers: "amazed at their ability to read some 1, 400 pages so easily, and awed, of course, by Seth's having written them with seemingly equal ease."

In spite of the many serious and tragic episodes that take place in the background of *A Suitable Boy*, Seth himself establishes a tone of geniality and humor that tends to undermine the ambitious aims of his novel. The character of Amit Chatterji, the English educated young poet who is in the process of writing a long novel, is clearly his persona. He is a thoroughly amiable young man, gifted but almost self-deprecatingly modest. Asked by a member of an audience to whom he is reading his poetry why he rejects Bengali, "your mother tongue," for English, he replies "that his Bengali was not good enough for him to be able to express himself in the manner he could in English. It wasn't a question of choice." Besides, he says, "'We are all accidents of history and must do what we are best at with-

out fretting too much about it.'" Asked about the report that he is writing a very long novel, he replies:

> "Oh, I don't know how it grew to be so long . . . I'm very undisciplined. But I too hate long books: the better, the worse. If they're bad, they merely make me pant with the effort of holding them for a few minutes. But if they're good, I turn into a social moron for days, refusing to go out of my room, scowling at interruptions, ignoring weddings and funerals, and making enemies out of friends. I still bear the scars of *Middlemarch*."

Since 1987 Seth has made his home in India. He lives with his parents in Noida, a suburb of New Delhi. After spending six years writing *A Suitable Boy*, Richard Woodward reported in the *New York Times Magazine* in 1993, he wants to write plays—"which take less time and are very intense and put me in touch with people." He has reacted to the publicity and the $1.1 million advance he received from publishers in India, Britain, and the United States with characteristic diffidence. "My main motivation," he told Woodward, "is not to get bored. I am just hoping I get a vaguely maverick reputation."

PRINCIPAL WORKS: *Poetry*—Mappings (chapbook), 1982; The Humble Administrator's Garden, 1985; All You Who Sleep Tonight, 1990; Beastly Tales from Here and There, 1991. *Novels*—The Golden Gate (verse), 1986; A Suitable Boy, 1993. *Travel*—From Heaven Lake: Travels Through Sinkiang and Tibet, 1983.

ABOUT: Contemporary Authors 127, 1989; Contemporary Poets, 5th ed., 1991; Dictionary of Literary Biography 120, 1992; Kirpal, V. (ed.) The New Indian Novel in English: A Study of the 1980s, 1990; Nelson, E. S. Writers of the Indian Diaspora, 1993. *Periodicals*—American Poetry Review November–December 1986; Commentary September 1986; New Republic April 21, 1986; June 14, 1993; New York Review of Books May 27, 1993; New York Times April 14, 1986; New York Times Book Review May 9, 1993; New York Times Magazine May 2, 1993; Publishers Weekly May 10, 1993; Spectator December 17, 1983; Times Literary Supplement September 21, 1990; March 19, 1993; Vanity Fair May 1993; Washington Post Book World March 23, 1986; July 22, 1990.

SHAARA, MICHAEL (JOSEPH) (June 23, 1929–May 5, 1988), American novelist and short story writer, was born in Jersey City, New Jersey, the son of Michael Joseph and Alleene (Maxwell) Shaara. An Italian POW during World War I, the elder Shaara emigrated to the United States, where he became a trade union representative and once worked as campaign manager for Congressman Peter Rodino. Alleene Shaara was a southerner who counted Thomas Jefferson

and "Light-Horse Harry" Lee among her ancestors. In high school, young Shaara excelled as both a scholar and an athlete. He earned his B.A. from Rutgers in 1951, and did graduate work at Columbia University and the University of Vermont.

Shaara's first published story, "All the Way Back," appeared in *Astounding Science Fiction* in 1951. He had originally written the story for an undergraduate writing seminar at Rutgers. "I gave it to the professor," Shaara recalled, " . . . and three weeks later he gave it back to me, looking down on me with sad distaste, and he said, 'Please don't write this sort of thing. Write *literature.*'" Undeterred, Shaara continued to write as he pleased throughout his career. In a 1982 interview with Michael Kernan in the *Washington Post*, Shaara remarked: "I've written all kinds of things in thirty years. I write whatever comes to mind, I've never written for a buck. Never stayed in one field. I write for the fun of it, and I don't think of the reader." Perhaps because of this uncompromising attitude, the fact that he "never stayed in one field," and his inability to get along with literary agents (he had at least twelve), Shaara's path to literary recognition was a tortuous one.

His idols were Ernest Hemingway and John O'Hara. Like them, Shaara strove to be a robust man of action (and a dedicated literary craftsperson) as opposed to a detached, theoretical observer. By his own account, Shaara's early career highlights more than fulfilled this ideal. He worked as a merchant seaman and served as an army paratrooper with the 82nd Airborne Division. In the mid-1950s he was a police officer in St. Petersburg, Florida. Following in the footsteps of his four uncles, he even tried his hand at professional boxing, winning seventeen of his eighteen fights. Shaara's own accounts, however, were not always reliable. His obituary in the *Washington Post* reported that he had told more than one interviewer about the tragic early death of his son, who was very much alive.

In 1961 Shaara began teaching literature and creative writing at Florida State University in Tallahassee. After suffering a heart attack, he wrote an article about the experience, "In the Midst of Life," which won an award from the American Medical Association. A popular and dedicated teacher, Shaara was voted outstanding teacher of the year by Florida State students in 1967. Most significantly, it was during his tenure at Florida State that Shaara completed and published his first novel, *The Broken Place*.

The story of Tom McClain's journey of self-discovery, *The Broken Place* takes its title from a passage in Hemingway's *A Farewell to Arms*:

"The world breaks everyone and afterward many are strong at the broken place. But those that will not break it kills." Not surprisingly, both soldiering and boxing figure prominently in the novel. A Korean war hero who has miraculously escaped death while on patrol, Tom McClain returns to college but quickly realizes that he is no longer fit for the routines of academic life. He loves a woman, but cannot settle down with her. Driven by an inexplicable inner rage and unable to make plans for his future, McClain sets out for Singapore with an old army buddy. They pass through a variety of exotic locales, including the Holy Land and the Himalayas. On a remote mountain road in the Himalayas, McClain's friend is stricken with meningitis and dies.

Distraught, he returns home, this time to pursue his first love, boxing. The nature and dimension of McClain's inner rage emerge with the revelation that McClain has killed another man in the ring. Shaara describes in detail the brutality and agony of the boxer's life. During his final fight, he is dealt a crushing blow that leaves him so badly injured he will never fight again.

In the *New York Times Book Review* (1968), Richard Rhodes remarked, "The author spars like Hemingway through much of this first novel about a soldier-prizefighter. . . . " He noted that "McClain's is a rare sickness, and more rarely still does someone write it truly . . . Shaara generates fits of murderous rage at least as well as Hubert Selby Jr., and somewhat better than Truman Capote. Having done so, he seems ready to explain McClain's violence away. But answers proliferate in his search for them, and we get so many that none is conclusive."

Shaara's second novel, *The Killer Angels*, won considerable critical acclaim, including the 1975 Pulitzer Prize for fiction. The novel chronicles four days in the summer of 1863 when the Gettysburg campaign culminated in the ferociously bloody Battle of Gettysburg, during which the Confederate and Union armies lost more than 20,000 men. The story of the battle is told from the point of view of Northerners and Southerners in alternating chapters. Colonel Joshua Lawrence Chamberlain, a Bowdoin College professor turned soldier, and General John Buford are the principal narrators for the Union army. Robert E. Lee, already withered and fragile from the heart ailment that would eventually kill him, and Lieutenant General James Longstreet tell much of the Southerners' story. In preparation for the novel Shaara read letters and diaries written by participants and reconnoitered the terrain of the Gettysburg battlefield repeatedly, both on the ground and from the air, flying his own plane.

Thomas Lask, reviewing *The Killer Angels* in the *New York Times* shortly after it was awarded the Pulitzer Prize, said: "Shaara's narrative conveys the drama, the courage and the heartbreak of those days. . . . [But] his fictional touches do not add much to the dimensions of the men we know. Their character as underlined rather than deepened. . . . Gettysburg is such a dramatic story that no one who comes near covering it within the compass of a book can fail. . . . But *The Killer Angels* is not proof positive that the historian need make way before the more spacious art of the novelist."

Not long after completing *The Killer Angels*, Shaara had a severe accident in Florence, Italy, where he was teaching a group of Florida State students. As he told *Washington Post* interviewer Kernan: "I bought a Vespa because I couldn't afford the gasoline. I'd never had an accident, I've flown planes for twenty years. But I cracked up. Don't remember any of it. Hit the back of my head. I was unconscious five weeks. They didn't figure I was coming out and brought me back to the States as totally and permanently disabled." It took some months for Shaara to regain his sight and hearing and for his multiple fractures to heal. Aside from leaving him with a form of dyslexia, the accident and his long recuperation resulted in his divorce from Helen Krumweide, his wife of twenty-nine years.

In the interval between his recuperation from the accident and his untimely death in 1988, Shaara published one more novel and a collection of short stories. His novel *The Herald* is about a radiation plague created by a brilliant geneticist who has been deeply influenced by Friedrich Nietzsche's doctrine of the Superman. In order to build a utopia on Earth, a world devoid of people with any trace of genetic weakness, the scientist invents a radiation machine that has the capacity to destroy weaker individuals while leaving genetically superior ones unaffected. The novel's main character, an airplane pilot, becomes suspicious when he is unable to make radio contact with the control tower of Jefferson City, Georgia. When he lands and inspects the airport, he quickly realizes the reason for the mysterious silence: everybody is dead. Heading into town, he meets a contingent of soldiers and decides to join them in their search for the source of the disaster. He begins the search in earnest, but soon enough comes to relish the benefits of the plague. In the nearly deserted town he finds a woman who has survived the radiation while locked in jail. Virtually alone in the ravaged town, they enjoy an Edenic, if evanescent, love affair. Before he is killed, the scientist reveals the location of a second radiation machine, even deadlier than the one that has devastated Jefferson City. After his lover is shot and killed, the pilot takes it upon himself to activate this second, most lethal radiation device.

A problematic allegory fitting neatly into no genre, *The Herald* was largely ignored by mainstream literary critics, although it was widely reviewed by science fiction magazines. In a brief review in the *Washington Post Book World* Maude McDaniel noted, "This beautifully written, finely failed novel begins as mesmerizingly and authentically as any such novel I have ever read but starts to lose it all halfway through—about the time the characters go with the flow, like tourists at a summer resort, in the middle of fifty-five square miles of dead bodies."

Soldier Boy is a collection of Shaara's short stories, and includes many of his best science fiction works from the 1950s.

Michael Shaara died of a heart attack at his home in Tallahassee at the age of fifty-eight. *For the Love of the Game*, a novel he completed shortly before his death, appeared posthumously. The novel focuses on the thoughts and memories of Billy Chapel, an aging major league baseball player, as he pitches his final and greatest game. Although Shaara told his 1982 *Washington Post* interviewer about a planned novel on the life of William Shakespeare, he never published such a work.

PRINCIPAL WORKS: *Novels*—The Broken Place, 1968; The Killer Angels, 1974; The Herald, 1981; For the Love of the Game, 1991. *Short Stories*—Soldier Boy, 1982.

ABOUT: Contemporary Authors 102, 1981; 125, 1989; Contemporary Literary Criticism 15, 1980; Dictionary of Literary Biography Yearbook 1983, 1984; Who's Who in America 1986–1987. *Periodicals*—Atlantic Monthly August 1981; New York Times May 10, 1975; May 9, 1988; New York Times Book Review April 7, 1968; October 20, 1974; Publishers Weekly April 12, 1991; Washington Post September 29, 1982; May 7, 1988; Washington Post Book World August 2, 1981.

SHAMMAS, ANTON (1950–), Israeli poet, novelist, and journalist of Arab Christian origins, was born in Fassuta, an Arab village in Northern Galilee, to Hamna Shammas, a third generation Fassutian, and Elaine Bita, a Lebanese, who came to the village in the late 1930s as a French teacher. In 1962 the family moved to Haifa. Shammas graduated from an Israeli high school in which Jews and Arabs remained segregated and then studied at the Hebrew University in Jerusalem.

In the 1970s, Shammas edited a literary journal, *Ashark*, in which he published Arabic translations of modern Hebrew literature. In

1974, he edited a bilingual literary collection titled *In Two vioces*, prepared especially for a binational meeting of Israeli and Arab writers. Shammas himself is an accomplished translator in both languages. He produced an excellent translation of Emile Habiby's *The Pessoptimist*, and his bilingual version of Beckett's *Waiting for Godot*, which was staged in the Haifa Theatre, was well received. In 1975 Shammas was awarded a creativity grant by the Tel Aviv Foundation for Literature and Arts and in 1980 he received the Prime Minster's award in recognition of his creative work. Shammas worked as a producer of programs in Arabic for Israeli television and as a reporter and columnist for the popular Tel Aviv weekly *Ha-Yir.* In 1988 Shammas moved in Ann Arbor to teach at the University of Michigan. He had published articles on the Israeli-Palestinian conflict in such publications as the *New York Review of Books, Harper's,* the *New York Times Magazine,* and others.

Shammas has not camouflaged the complexity of his situation as an Israeli Arab, deeply rooted in the cultural landscape of the predominantly Jewish Israel. He spoke openly against the Israeli occupation of the West Bank and Gaza Strip. In his *Ha-Yir* column, Shammas endorsed David Grossman's series about the situation in the West Bank (later published in a book titled *The Yellow Wind* in its English translation), praising the forceful capability of Grossman's reportage to "convince the unconvinced, the dreaming and the naive, that have not yet learned to ask the right questions about this sullied and sullying occupation."

Shammas does not limit his criticism of the State of Israel to the problem of Palestinian refugees. In his *New York Review of Books* article "The Morning After," which was translated into Hebrew and reprinted in the Israeli press, Shammas, with considerably irony, warns the future Palestinian state not to fall into the pitfall of racist oppression, which has plagued Israeli democracy. The source of contention lies in the definition of Israel as a Jewish, rather than an Israeli, state. This position engenders and legalizes discriminatory treatment of citizens other than Jews. The Law of Return which grants all Jews (and only Jews) immediate citizenship upon immigration to Israel epitomizes the discrimination in the Israel political system. As an Israeli Arab, Shammas feels a second-rate citizen. The acuteness of the sensibilities involved was demonstrated in the almost four-year-long, highly publicized controversy between Shammas and A. B. Yehoshua, one of the most prominent left-wing Israeli writers. Shammas rejected indignantly Yehoshua's view of the future Palestinian state as a homeland of Israeli Arabs. As an Israeli

citizen, Shammas considers Israel his homeland, where he should be treated as an equal.

Courageous involvement in political polemics, however, constitutes only one facet of Shammas's extraordinary personality. His literary work, written practically in its entirety in Hebrew, determines Shammas's outstanding position in the Israeli cultural milieu. His first book of poetry, *Krikha Kasha* (Hardcover, 1974), was praised for its control of the language, its sophisticated, multileveled meaning, and the ease with which the poet interlaces imagery from both Old Testament and New Testament. As Curtis Aronson notes in *Modern Hebrew Literature,* "[F]rom his Hebrew poetry, [Shammas] is seen to be an extremely careful poet who is sensitive to the use of Hebrew for his poetry . . . *Krikha Kasha* is among the better books of Hebrew poetry to appear recently."

Shammas second volume of poetry, *Shetah Hefker* (No-Man's Land, 1980), focuses on the search for identity. Critics detected an affinity with Israeli poets such as Amir Gilboa, Nathan Zach, and Dan Pagis, who had to deal with their sense of acute estrangement produced by their detachment from their childhood surroundings. The motif of alienation, suggested by the image of no-man's land, runs throughout the poems. It emerges especially in the poem about Isaac where the poet's voice does not identify with either Jacob or Esau, but epitomizes isolation and loneliness. The volume met with favorable critical response. Alex Zahavi, in *Modern Hebrew Literature,* maintained that "none of [Shammas's] peers among Hebrew poets has succeeded in achieving his level of poetical expression and the complexity and richness."

That Shammas is capable of transforming the complexity of his particular political situation into art became evident with the publication of his novel, *Arabeskot* (1986, *Arabesques*). The novel presents a complex, intricate plot. It is, in part, the saga of Shammas's Arab Christian family, which settled in the early 19th century in Fassuta. The sections titled "The Tale" tell the story of the family from the Ottoman and British rule of Palestine to the Israeli conquest in 1948 and the Israeli occupation of the West Bank and Gaza Strip in the 1967 war. The "Tale" sections intersect with the autobiographical "The Teller" sections, which focus on the author's stay in Paris and on his participation in a writing program in Iowa City. The family saga and the author's story are interrelated thematically through the narrator's search for his lost cousin, Michael Abyad, whose original name—Anton Shammas—the narrator bears. The ties with Michael, which were severed as a result of the Israeli conquest of Fassuta in 1948, are eventually reestablished in a dramatic meeting of two cousins in Iowa City.

For the most part, the novel met with critical acclaim. Shammas was praised for his narrative abilities as well as for his masterful Hebrew. "It is an Israeli Hebrew work in every respect," Yael Lotan wrote in her review of the novel in *Modern Hebrew Literature*, "The average Israeli reader will feel close to the book and to its characters." Dov Vardi remarked in *World Literature Today* that Shammas's "mastery of Hebrew matches that of most writers in Hebrew today." In the *New York Times Book Review*, William Gass compared Shammas's narrative and style with that of Gabriel García Márquez, stating that "the real aim of this impressively beautiful piece of prose is the discovery and definition, even the creation, of a self, not merely an account of a self already made."

Not all reviewers, however, found the unusual form of the novel acceptable or meaningful. The transitions between the saga and the postmodernist fragmentation of the autobiographical sections evoked resistance. While he admires the quality of Shammas's Hebrew, Hillel Halkin, in the *New Republic*, thought the parts of "The Teller" confusing, "a flat exercise in literary modernism . . . spoiling a little masterpiece." Irving Howe, in the *New York Review of Books*, at first "happily yielded to Shammas's charm," but then discovered that he was not charmed by the segments dealing with Paris and Iowa City, which he considered "certainly inferior to those set in the Galilee and the West Bank." Israeli reviewers, such as Dan Laor and Dan Miron, agreed that the family story was superior to the autobiographical account. Rachel Feldhay Brenner, in her *PMLA* article, pointed out that the seemingly incongruous stylistic and formalistic combination represents the fragmented personality of the protagonist seeking wholeness in a work of art which will combine the Hebrew language with the Arab tale.

To fathom the complexity of Shammas's situation, the reader must listen to the writer himself. In an answer to queries about his own self-image after the publication of *Arabesques*, Shammas confessed: "I chose to identify myself as an Israeli-Palestinian writer, which is an impossible combination. Such self-definition stands in opposition to everything, including myself: it signifies de-Judaization, de-Zionization of the Jewish State by instilling an Israeli-national content to the word Israel and, at the same time, it places emphasis on the Palestinian entity as an ethnic dimension, equal to that of the Jew . . . It was a kind of inter-cultural translation—the Arab

Galilean identity, translated to Arab-Israeli identity, which got translated to Palestinian identity in Hebrew letters and finally to Israeli-Palestinian identity. Despite all the obstacles and thanks to Hebrew."

Arabesques was included among the top sixteen books of the year by the *New York Times Book Review* in 1988.

PRINCIPAL WORKS IN ENGLISH TRANSLATION: (tr. Y. Lotan) "Arab Walls, Reflecting Change" *in* Harper's, November 1987; (tr. V. Eden) Arabesques, 1988.

ABOUT: Contemporary Literary Criticism 55, 1989; JanMohammed, A. R., and Lloyd, D. (eds.) Nature and Context of Minority Discourse, 1990; Raraz-Rauch, G. The Arab in Israeli Literature, 1989. *Periodicals*—American Book Review January–February 1990; Choice October 1988; London Review of Books January 5, 1989; Modern Hebrew Literature 1974; 1980; 1987; New Republic May 2, 1988; New York Review of Books April 14, 1988; New Yorker October 17, 1988; PMLA May 1993; Times Literary Supplement November 18, 1988; World Literature Today Winter 1988; Summer 1989.

SHIELDS, CAROL (WARNER) (June 2, 1935–), American novelist, short story writer, playwright, and poet, sends the following to *World Authors*: "I was born in Oak Park, Illinois, the youngest of three children. I attended public schools in Oak Park, graduating from Oak Park High School in 1953. In 1957 I graduated from Hanover College, Hanover, Indiana, with a bachelor of arts degree, majoring in English, minoring in history. Literature and history, and the place where these two intersect, have continued to interest me. I worked on school newspapers and literary magazines in school, but I had no very clear idea about becoming a writer. Indeed, becoming a writer seemed as remote and impossible as becoming a movie star.

"In 1957 I married a Canadian, Donald Hugh Shields, and immigrated to Canada. I've lived at various times in Vancouver, Toronto, Ottawa, and am now [1994] settled in Winnipeg where I am an associate professor of English at the University of Manitoba. I have also spent five or six years in England and France, and for the last twenty-five years I've spent my summers in France.

"In 1975 I completed a master's degree at the University of Ottawa, specializing in Canadian literature; my thesis, entitled *Susanna Moodie, Voice and Vision*, published in 1977, is a theme study of the works of Canadian pioneer writer Susanna Moodie.

"I am the mother of five children, which was

CAROL SHIELDS

one of the reasons my writing life began rather late. In 1972 my first book of poems, *Others*, was published by Borealis Press in Ottawa, and this volume was followed by another, *Intersect*, in 1974.

"Around this time I decided to write a novel. My first effort failed, but I was encouraged to try again; this second novel, *Small Ceremonies*, was published in 1976 and won the Canadian Author's Association Prize for the best novel of the year. My second novel, *The Box Garden*, published in 1977, is really a companion novel to the first. Both these novels are set in Canada.

"In 1988 I published a novel called *Happenstance*, set in Chicago, and two years later published a companion novel titled *A Fairly Conventional Woman*. These two novels have recently been reissued in the U.K., U.S. and Canada in a single back-to-back volume.

"Frustration over a novel-in-progress made me turn to short fiction writing, and in 1985 a volume of short stories, *Various Miracles*, was published in Canada, later by Penguin in the U.S. The troublesome novel finally found its form, and was published in the United States and Canada under the title *Swann*, and in the U.K. under *Mary Swann*. This novel was nominated for Canada's Governor General's Award and won the Arthur Ellis Award for the best crime novel of the year.

"A second collection of short stories, *The Orange Fish*, was published in Canada and the U.S. in 1989. In 1991 I published an epistolary novel, *A Celibate Season*, with coauthor Blanche Howard. A novel titled *The Republic of Love* was published in 1992, a joint venture between Random House Canada, Viking U.S., and Fourth Estate of England. This novel was short-listed for the Guardian Fiction Prize. A third volume of poetry, *Coming to Canada*, was also published that year by Carleton University Press. "A new novel, *The Stone Diaries*, was published in the U.K. and Canada in 1993, and in the U.S. in 1994. It was short-listed for the Booker Prize and won Canada's Governor General's Award. It also won the Manitoba Book of the Year Award and the Canadian Booksellers' Award. Two plays, *Departures and Arrivals* (1990), and *Thirteen Hands* (1993), have been published by Blizzard Press.

"My novels have been translated into twelve languages. All my books are in print today. *Swann*, *The Republic of Love*, and *The Stone Diaries* have been optioned for film, and I am now writing the film script for *The Republic of Love*.

"In 1990 I won Canada's Marian Engles Ward.

"If I have a life theme, it is the necessity of telling our life stories, particularly the lives of women."

———

Although Carol Shields's work focuses on women characters and, more often than not, has love relationships at its center, it is, to quote British novelist Anita Brookner reviewing *The Stone Diaries* in the *Spectator*, "of an altogether superior kind" to "women's novels." Domestic life is simply an area in which her broadly human concerns are worked out. A lifelong feminist but also, and perhaps primarily, a humanist, she told an interviewer for *West Coast Review* in 1988: "I wanted to write the kind of novel I couldn't find on the library shelf . . . about the kind of women I knew, women who had a reflective life, a moral system, women who had a recognizable domestic context, a loyalty to their families, a love for their children."

Shields's small audience reads her for the sheer pleasure of her wit, her ingenuity in plotting—creating surprise and excitement out of the most ordinary of everyday experiences—and the subtle complexities of her seemingly ordinary characters. As Abby H. P. Warlock noted in *Canadian Women Writing Fiction*, hers is "a humanist approach which blurs both [Canadian and American] national boundaries and, in postmodern fashion, the lines separating literary genres. She depicts people who, although fallible and aware of the 'unknowability' of others, are fully, generously drawn and develop an increased awareness, however, imperfect of their identities and of their relationships to family and community."

There is considerable virtuosity behind the apparent simplicity of Shields's fiction. A single human life unfolds itself in the course of a short story to reveal layers of complexity unrealized by the character herself or by those around her. For example, Girlie Turner in "Mrs. Turner Cutting the Grass" (in *Various Miracles*) is a fat old woman, a widow living alone. She irritates her younger, environmentally conscious neighbors because she sprays pesticide on her lawn, looks ridiculous in her shorts and halter, and annoys them with her boisterous cheeriness. To them she lives a life of absolute banality. They know nothing of her stormy past in which she was seduced, forced to leave her hometown under a cloud of scandal, drifted about the country, had a baby that she abandoned, and finally returned home to marry and settle down. In later years, living on a small income and contented with her life, she travels occasionally with her sisters: "She and Em and Muriel have been to Disneyland as well as Disneyworld. They've been to Europe, taking a sixteen-day trip through seven countries." On a visit to Japan they are noticed by another American tourist—a professor who is a frustrated poet. He makes them the unknowing subject of a satirical poem that brings him fame: "The poem was not really about the Golden Pavillion at all, but about three midwestern lady tourists who, while viewing the temple and madly snapping photos, had talked incessantly and in loud, flat-bottomed voices about knitting patterns, indigestion, sore feet, breast lumps, the cost of plastic raincoats and a previous trip they had made together to Mexico." In nonjudgmental terms Shields evokes compassion for this woman who has herself been so cruelly judged by others. The story ends: "She cannot imagine that anyone would wish her harm. All she's done is live her life. The green grass flies up in the air, a buoyant cloud swelling about her. Oh, what a sight is Mrs. Turner cutting her grass and how, like an ornament, she shines."

Shields's poetry has a similar simplicity and lightness that conceal more profound and emotionally stirring themes. In "Mother" from *Intersect*, writing about a woman with a passion for moving her furniture about the house on sleepless nights, she might almost be describing the effects of reading her fiction:

In the morning we found
the amazing corner, startled by pure
circuits of light we'd never
seen before, pleasing
elbows of space and new shapes
to fit into   bringing us
closer to rebirth

than we ever
came   in all those years.

It was through poetry that Shields discovered her passion for writing. Although she had been scribbling stories and poems since childhood, she had no thoughts of a career in literature until, at the age of thirty, she read the British poet Philip Larkin, whose honesty and directness of expression inspired her. She began publishing her poems in the *Canadian Forum*, and a few years later her first novel appeared. Poetry quite literally figures in one of her most successful novels, *Swann* (published in the U.K. as *Mary Swann*), a skillfully plotted novel about the pursuit of the elusive life and even more elusive manuscripts of an obscure woman poet, Mary Swann, "the Emily Dickinson of Upper Canada," who had been murdered and dismembered by her husband, who then shot himself to death. Grisly as this sounds, *Swann* is a sly comic satire on academic scholarship—a subject Shields knows from her own experience of writing a master's thesis on Susanna Moodie. It is also a lighthearted love story about a brilliant young feminist scholar, author of a doctoral dissertation that incredibly becomes a best-seller, *The Female Prism*. She is recovering from a divorce and finding a new love, and in the course of her research on Mary Swann she encounters an assortment of colorful characters—a small town librarian, an aged journalist and publisher, a successful but painfully insecure biographer.

In *Swann* Shields boldly confronts the problem of showing as well as telling by offering samples of Mary Swann's poetry. If no Emily Dickinson, the laconic and self-taught Mary Swann is nevertheless a reasonable facsimile:

A morning and an afternoon and
Night's queer knuckled hand
Hold me separate and whole,
Stitching tight my daily soul.

Swann was highly praised by reviewers for its wit and ingenuity. Phoebe-Lou Adams, in the *Atlantic*, applauded its "well-drawn characters, expert writing, and silky malice." Norman Sigurdson, in *Quill and Quire*, wrote that Shields "seems to have taken the best from her previous work—the close attention to detail, the compassion for ordinary folks leading humdrum lives—and refined and clarified it into a more sophisticated and satisfying entertainment." The only reservation expressed by some reviewers was over what they considered its overly ingenious narrative structure. The novel is divided into five parts—one for each of the principal characters and a final section written as a report on a scholarly meeting, "The Swann Symposium," in the form of a film script with director's notes. The denouement involves a wild slapstick chase that reminded even the admiring Sigurdson of "a badly written episode of television's 'Murder, She Wrote.'" For Josh Rubins, in the *New York Times Book Review* (1989), "the initial inspiration flattens out quickly. As satire, *Swann* remains mild and obvious, without the buoyancy or savage wit of top-notch academic watchers from Kinglsey Amis to Malcom Bradbury." For other reviewers, however, this authorial device was part of the whole parodic nature of the novel. As Clara Thomas pointed out, in an article in the periodical *Room of One's Own*, this last section of *Swann* is "a large bonus of fun in the postmodern critical theory style," a deconstruction of the plot, with the characters finally uniting in an attempt to reconstruct the missing poems.

Shields's playfulness with the conventions of narrative is evident in much of her later writing. As its subtitle indicates, *Happenstance: The Husband's Story; The Wife's Story* is a novel comprising two novellas arranged not sequentially but from front to back and from back to front so that they end in the middle of the book. Essentially it is one story of a middle-aged American couple who separate for a week while she, a talented designer, attends a crafts conference where she discovers her new independence, and he, a historian, loses his faith in the work that has engaged him for so many years. Their marriage is shaky but it survives. "The double structure of the narrative actually achieves a genuine intra-subjective novel," Isobel Armstrong wrote in the *Times Literary Supplement*, "where two independent subjects exist, not the solipsist modern subject and its distant objects."

Far less intricate but still unusual is the plotting of *The Republic of Love*. Here Shields tackles an unabashedly conventional love story and invigorates it by placing her characters in a crowded world of family, friends, ex-wives, discarded lovers, and work. The heroine is a folklorist writing a book on mermaids. The hero is a radio talk show host. They do not even meet until well beyond the middle of the novel, but when they do, they fall wildly in love. As Shields observes in an authorial aside: "We turn our heads and pretend its not there, the thunderous passions that enter a life and alter its course. Love belongs in an amorous operetta, on the inside of a jokey greeting card, or in the annals of an old-fashioned poetry society." The fact that she can convince her readers—and her reviewers—of the possibility of two ripely middle-aged people falling rapturously in love is testimony to Carol Shields's powers. Peter Kemp, in the *Times Literary Supplement*, found it "a love story that is enticingly seductive," a novel that restores credibility to a discredited genre. For Elinor Lipman, in the *New York Times Book Review*, *The Republic of Love* is "a touching, elegantly funny, luscious work of fiction." And Carolellen Norsky, in *Quill and Quire*, allowed that "if such a story is sentimental, it is tempered by a narrative voice that is wry and wise, and given to lovely, luminous observation."

The Stone Diaries—with enthusiastic reviews and, in Britain, a nomination for the prestigious Booker Prize and in the U.S., the Pulitzer Prize in 1995—established Carol Shields in the first rank of Canadian-American-British women novelists. This novel is another of her celebrations of what Anita Brookner calls "an unremarkable life." Framed by an authorial voice, it is a record from her birth to her death in her eighties—in the form of letters, diaries, even family photos (some from museums and antique shops, other from Shields's own family album)—of the long and undramatic but not uneventful life of Daisy Goodwill Flett—"Everywoman," Jay Parini called her in the *New York Times Book Review* (1994). Daisy herself is totally unself-conscious about the meaning of her life: "She just lets her life happen to her," one of the characters observes. Her mother dies in giving her birth, her father—a stonemason by trade—gives her to a neighbor to raise. She grows up in Winnipeg, has an unhappy early marriage, a happy second marriage to a botanist, raises her family, is reunited with her father, grows old and dies. Interviewed by Mel Gussow in the *New York Times* after winning the Pulitzer Prize, Shields told him that she "worried that the story was thin on plot." But she was reassured by a statement by Patrick White who made plot subsidiary to "life going on toward death." She "relaxed into that quotation. . . . 'It's always seemed to me that this was the great primordial plot: birth, love, death.'" Parini noted that the absence of conventional plot "does nothing to diminish the narrative compulsion of this novel. . . . Carol Shields has explored the mysteries of life with abandon, taking unusual risks along the way. *The Stone Diaries* reminds us again why literature matters."

The quilt maker in *Happenstance*, the woman who "discovers that she is an artist and nothing in her life has prepared her for that knowledge," according to Gussow, is like Shields, for whom "writing is like quilt making and the important thing is in the creating. 'I always feel like I'm making something when I write a book, an artifact . . . and that's where the pleasure is.'"

PRINCIPAL WORKS: *Novels*—Small Ceremonies, 1976; The Box Garden, 1977; A Fairly Conventional Woman,

1980; Happenstance, 1980; Swann: A Mystery, 1989 (in U.K.: Mary Swann); (with B. Howard) A Celibate Season, 1991; The Republic of Love, 1992; The Stone Diaries, 1993. *Short stories*—Various Miracles, 1985; The Orange Fish, 1989. *Poetry*—Others, 1972; Intersect, 1974; Coming to Canada, 1992. *Plays*—Departures and Arrivals, 1990; Thirteen Hands, 1993. *Nonfiction*—Susanna Moodie: Voice and Vision, 1977.

ABOUT: Contemporary Authors 81–84, 1979; Hughes, K. J. (ed.) Contemporary Manitoba Writers, 1990; McMullen, L. (ed.) Re(Dis)covering Our Foremothers, 1990; Pearlman, M. (ed.) Canadian Women Writing Fiction, 1993; Singley, C. J., and Sweeney, S. E. (eds.) Anxious Power: Reading, Writing, and Ambivalence in Narrative by Women, 1993. *Periodicals*—Atlantic August 1989; New York Times May 10, 1995; New York Times Book Review August 6, 1989; March 1, 1992; March 27, 1994; Publishers Weekly February 28, 1994; Quill an Quire November 1987; March 1992; Room of One's Own (Carol Shields Issue) 13, 1989; Spectator September 4, 1993; Times Literary Supplement March 1, 1991; March 20, 1992; August 27, 1993; West Coast Review Winter 1988.

SILKO, LESLIE MARMON (March 5, 1948–   ), poet and novelist,

was born in Albuquerque of Laguna Indian, Mexican, and white ancestry. She grew up at Laguna Pueblo in west-central New Mexico. Silko's great-grandfather, Robert Marmon, and his brother Walter first came to Laguna in the 1870s. They settled in the pueblo, and both eventually served as governor. A number of different peoples live at Laguna—Hopi, Zuni, Navajo, and whites, among others—but the Laguna have a strong sense of their particular identity, and Silko's mixed-blood ancestry was a source of some pain and embarrassment in her youth. As she puts it in *Voices of the Rainbow*:

> My family are the Marmons at Old Laguna on the Laguna Pueblo reservation where I grew up. We are mixed bloods—Laguna, Mexican, white—but the way we live is like Marmons, and if you are from Laguna Pueblo you will understand what I mean. All those languages, all those ways of living are combined, and we live somewhere on the fringes of all three. But I don't apologize for this any more—not to whites, not to full bloods—our origin is unlike any other. My poetry, my storytelling rise out of this source.

Silko graduated from the University of New Mexico in 1969. While in college she married Robert Chapman. The couple had a son and were later divorced. She spent three semesters in law school at the University of New Mexico before devoting herself to writing. She married John Silko in 1971, and had a son in 1972.

Silko's first publication was *Laguna Woman* in 1974, a collection of poems. Although it is incommon for most novelists to be successful as poets, it is the rule rather than the exception for Native American writers. In addition to Silko, N. Scott Momaday, James Welch, Louise Erdrich, and Gerald Vizenor are Native American writers who began as poets and became successful both as poets and novelists.

Silko's poetry is distinguished by its vivid images, as in "Poem for Myself and Mei: Concerning Abortion":

> The morning sun
> coming unstuffed with yellow light
> butterflies tumbling loose
> and blowing across the Earth

Her imagery takes the reader by surprise, with its unusual juxtapositions and mordant wit, as demonstrated by "Indian Song: Survival":

> I have slept with the river and
> he is warmer than any man.
> At sunrise
> I heard ice on the cattails.

On the basis of *Laguna Woman*, Silko won the poetry award from *Chicago Review*, and the Pushcart Prize for poetry in 1977.

In 1977 Silko published her first novel, *Ceremony*, in which she stretches the conventions of the modern American novel by adding a mythic dimension. Myth is frequently employed in modernist literature, but Silko goes further than many of her predecessors. Novelist and critic Louis Owens, himself a Native American, makes the distinction: "Silko moves far beyond anything imagined by T. S. Eliot when he wrote of the usefulness of mythological structures in literature. Rather than a previously conceived metaphorical framework within which the anarchy and futility of 'real' (as opposed to mythic) existence can be ordered, as often occurs in modernist texts, mythology in *Ceremony* insists upon its actual simultaneity with and interpretation into the events of the everyday mundane world."

In other words, it is a work in which the events of traditional tribal myths occur again in a contemporary realistic setting. Kiowa novelist N. Scott Momaday desribes the form as a "telling," and employs it in his book *The Ancient Child*, which is based on a myth of a boy who turns into a bear.

The Laguna myths Silko employs tell of the origin of a severe drought, and what tribal culture heroes have to do to bring back rains and fertility to the land. These myths bear a strong resemblance to European myths in which a country becomes a drought-stricken wasteland because of the condition or conduct of a king, who needs help to restore fertility to the land.

The protagonist of *Ceremony* is Tayo, a veteran who returns from fighting in the Philippines in World War II a victim of what would be called today posttraumatic stress syndrome. Military doctors cannot cure him, so Tayo finally goes to a Navajo healer, Betonie, who performs a complex set of rituals, and sends Tayo on a quest to retrieve his uncle's cattle. Tayo's task is a difficult and dangerous one: he has to outwit the white cowboys who are holding the cattle, and a set of malevolent Native American veterans who practice witchcraft. Tayo gets the cattle back with the help of a mysterious figure, Ts'eh Montano. It is ambiguous whether Ts'eh is human or divine. When Tayo completes his task, the rains come, the land blooms, and his sanity is restored.

Ceremony has aspects of a naturalistic protest novel with a Native American veteran as protagonist, who, in the words of what has become a cliché, "can die for his country, but not live in it." The archetype is based on Ira Hayes, the Pima marine who raised the American flag on Iwo Jima and then died in a ditch, drunk, on the reservation after the war. Most of the works that employ such archetypal protagonists end tragically. Viewed from that standpoint, the ending of *Ceremony* is a surprise. But although Silko is consciously setting forth the plight of the modern archetype, she is also hearkening back to Laguna myths, which end with the triumph of the hero. The source of evil in the book is witchcraft, what Lagunas call "the witchery." It is the ultimate source of atomic testing in the New Mexico desert, and even the source of the existence of white people themselves. According to Laguna myth, witches invent whites as part of a contest to determine who can do the worst evil.

In 1981 Silko published *Storyteller*, which combines autobiographical reminiscences, traditional Laguna myths, poems, and short stories. The importance of telling stories to impose order on the world is a major theme in Silko's writings. The title story is about the conflicts of cultures, and the difficulties of cross-cultural understanding. The heroine, an unnamed Eskimo woman, lures a white storekeeper out onto thin ice which he falls through to his death. She is motivated by revenge, because an earlier storekeeper had sold poisonous alcohol to her parents. Witnesses to the drowning testify that the storekeeper's death looked like an accident; he was crazed with lust, chasing the woman across the frozen river. The woman insists on taking credit for his death, claiming it was premeditated. She feels that this is the only way to make sense of her life and to honor her parents. The fact that the storekeeper who killed her parents and the ones she kills are different men is irrelevant—both are "Gussucks," Caucasians, and therefore equivalent in her eyes.

The best-known story in the collection is "Yellow Woman," since reprinted with a group of critical essays in a series on women writers. The story makes use of the Laguna myth of Yellow Woman, a woman abducted by a kachina (spirit). In Silko's story the nameless heroine, a Laguna woman with a husband and baby, goes off willingly on a two-day affair with a cattle rustler named Silva who may or may not be Navajo. Silva tells the heroine that she is Yellow Woman, and must follow him. The woman has opportunities to leave Silva, but chooses not to. When Silva kills a white rancher, the heroine runs off, returning to her village. She plans to tell her husband that she has been abducted. The story treats a number of Silko's favorite themes: parallels between life and mythology, the power of story to shape perceptions of reality, and the legitimacy of sexual freedom for women.

In 1983 Silko received a grant from the MacArthur Foundation and set to work on her magnum opus, *Almanac of the Dead*, a 750-page jeremiad about the impending collapse of European civilization in North America. The title refers to a pre-Columbian Meso-American notebook, a few fragments of which have survived and been smuggled north by fugitive slaves escaping from the Spanish. The almanac has passed into the hands of Lecha, a mixed-blood spiritualist who has been translating the text, a mixture of Native American glyphs, Spanish, and Latin, into English. Many of the remaining fragments are cryptic: "Black Zip whistles a warning. He is the deer god. In the year Ten Sky, the principal ruler is Venus." But the general drift is clear enough—the almanac predicts an apocalypse: "This world is about to end."

The title *Almanac of the Dead* figuratively refers to the whole book, a series of narratives about the walking dead of North America, and warnings concerning the impending destruction of European civilization on the continent. The book is a vast *summa decadentia*, a blanket indictment of Mexican and American culture featuring a huge cast of characters, most of whom are totally corrupt, which for Silko means homosexual as well as financially and politically dishonest. Virtually every white male in the book—as well as many of the Native Americans and Mexicans—is homosexual. The most degenerate of a very unsavory lot are Judge Arne, who has sex with his basset hounds, and a pornographer and drug dealer named Beaufrey who produces in utero videos of fetuses cringing from scalpels during abortions.

Silko is sympathetic to a degree to Marx, though this is qualified by her distaste for the "immense crimes" of his followers, Stalin and Mao. The problem with Marx, for her, is that he too is European, and so Marxism has a "bleak future on American shores." The Americas can only be cleansed by a return to the indigenous religions, the Meso-American cults of the sacred macaw and the giant stone snake.

The climax of the book comes when a small group of "eco-warriors" called "Green Vengeance" blow up Glen Canyon Dam in northern Arizona, the first shot in the war to take over North America by indigenous people and their allies. After 700 pages of portraying homosexuals as evil, Silko allows one a role in this heroic enterprise. A gay activist ill with AIDS, he leaves a manifesto urging his stricken brothers to "go out while you're still looking good and feeling good," urging them to join the armed struggle to "avenge gay genocide by the U.S. government!"

The book ends with the holy war in a very early stage, but there are hopeful signs for the indigenous peoples: throughout the West buffalo herds are increasing, and white farmers are disappearing. The Ghost Dance of the late 19th century didn't end with the massacre at Wounded Knee: it just went underground. The spirits that the Indians have been praying and dancing for are working to bring about the prophecies of the old almanac.

Silko's apocalyptic fantasy ignores the fact that the Meso-Americans who will take over North America were in pre-Columbian days not only as culturally sophisticated as the Spanish who conquered them, but also as bloodthirsty, intolerant, and imperialistic. All in all, however, *Almanac* is a very powerful book, in which Silko identifies many of the ills that afflict American society. If novels are to be judged on literary rather than political grounds, this is a gripping narrative, with vividly rendered characters. Silko's view of life is complex, though occasionally alarming, and she renders her conception in powerful language. *Almanac of the Dead*, Elizabeth Tallent wrote in the *New York Times Book Review* (1991), "burns at an apocalyptic pitch— passionate indictment, defiant imagery, bravura storytelling."

Silko is a provocative writer, whose works often seen to assault the reader. In her sardonic humor, her depiction of the underside of American life, particularly the scenes involving drugs and homosexual sex, she is reminscient of William Burroughs, whom she describes as "one of [her]

heroes." Silko has taught from time to time during her career, first at Navajo Community College, then the University of New Mexico, and finally the University of Arizona. She lives in Tuscon, Arizona, and writes full-time.

PRINCIPAL WORKS: *Novels*—Ceremony, 1977; Almanac of the Dead, 1991. *Poetry*—Laguna Woman, 1974. *Short stories*—Storyteller, 1981. *Other*—The Delicacy and Strength of Lace (letters to and from James Wright), 1985; Sacred Water (narratives and pictures), 1994.

ABOUT: Contemporary Authors 122, 1988; Contemporary Literary Criticism 23, 1983; Contemporary Novelists, 4th ed., 1986; Fleck, R. Critical Perspectives on Native American Fiction, 1993; Graulich, M. (ed.) "Yellow Woman": Leslie Marmon Silko, 1993; Larson, C. American Indian Fiction, 1978; Lincoln, K. Native American Renaissance, 1983; Nelson, R. M. Place and Vision: The Function of Landscape in Native American Fiction, 1993; Owens, L. Other Destinies, 1992; Rosen, K. Voices of the Rainbow, 1995; Velie, A. Four American Indian Literary Masters, 1982. *Periodicals*—Harper's June 1977; New York Times Book Review June 12, 1977; May 24, 1981; December 22, 1991; Southwest Review Spring 1979.

SINCLAIR, CLIVE (JOHN) (February 19, 1948–), British novelist, short story writer, and journalist, writes:

"Let me begin with the question a colleague put to Cynthia Ozick. When did you begin to write?"

"What was her reply?"

"She said that she did not begin, that she was born writing. Were you?"

"No. If anything, I was born with a knife and fork in my hands. The year, incidentally, was 1948. The place, London. My parents would stand over me chanting, 'Eat. Eat.' (They still do.) I learned to reply very early. I suspect that my first words were, 'No, no!' On the other hand I did not begin to read and write until quite late. But once I did books provided me with a vivid social life."

"Hence *Bibliosexuality*, the title of your first novel. Literature as a substitute for living."

"You are jumping the gun."

"Right. Were you an only child?"

"No. I have a brother."

"Is he a writer too?"

"No. He works with the criminally insane."

"There is a difference?"

"I'll make the jokes. To answer your question more seriously than it deserves; writers possess a sense of guilt."

"You do not see yourself in the prophetic tradition? Or at least as a moral scout for humanity?"

"Hardly. At best I see myself as a seducer."

"Ah. *Bibliosexuality* again."

"Please. Allow me to reach puberty."

"Okay. Let's talk about your schooling."

"I learned nothing at school. My formal education began in 1966, when I went to the University of East Anglia. Actually this is not strictly true. I learned two things at school; how to pass exams, and how to lead a secret life. At the same time I met some good people, who remain my closest friends."

"Would you say that you had an unhappy childhood?"

"On the contrary, I was very happy. At least until the age of eleven. My parents were always trying to induce me to play with cousins. But I remained obstinately asocial. They had more success when they introduced me to art and soccer. Every Saturday afternoon in the season my father would take me to a local Jewish soccer team called Wingate Football Club. That's where I learned about Jewishness; not in *cheder.*"

"You have written about Wingate Football Club more than once."

"Indeed. There is an entire story on the subject, as well as an ersatz history of the club in my second novel, *Blood Libels*. They are true in spirit, if not in fact."

"Jewishness is obviously important to you. Could you say why?"

"Look, my situation is hardly unique. I am an atheist, but am happy to call myself a Jew. It remains my culture, albeit in translation. It is also my magma, the stuff that engages me imaginatively. There is also the matter of Israel (another child of '48). It is my platonic ideal; a country willed into existence. (Its politics are another matter, of course.) Compared to that miracle, my efforts will always be puny. Nevertheless, I try to make my own little world with words. It is a Jewish tradition, begun by the God in whom I do not believe."

"When did this modest effort commence?"

"It began with letters to my friends from East Anglia (and later from the University of California at Santa Cruz, where I was a graduate student for a year). Indeed, one of my best friends, to whom I still write, insists that letter writing is my true métier. Be that as it may I wanted a larger audience than one. My first novel was published in 1973. *Hearts of Gold*, a book of stories followed in 1979 (the same month as my marriage). That marks the true beginning of my literary career."

"*Hearts of Gold* won the Somerset Maugham Award. But it has also been called a collection of evil little fictions. Not without reason. Why are you so attracted to the unwholesome?"

"At the beginning of *The Turn of the Screw* Henry James describes a little boy who awakens from a nightmare and calls for his mother. He doesn't want to be comforted, rather he wants her to share his fear. I resemble that little boy."

"You have spent a further year in America as a Bicentennial Arts Fellow (during which time your own son was born), you have been the British Council Guest Writer-in-Residence at the University of Uppsala in Sweden, and you have travelled extensively in the Americas, Europe, and Israel. Are these wanderings incidental or essential?"

"The latter. My writings are an attempt to distill the essence of other places. To make myself temporarily at home."

"Has your work been translated?"

"Yes. Into several languages. The more obscure the language the better I like it. So long as the book is in English I feel compelled to improve upon it. Even in print it remains unfinished. But when it is in Bulgarian, Hebrew, or Japanese, it becomes a completed work of art; mine, yet beyond my reach."

In Clive Sinclair's short story "Scriptophobia," the narrator, a writer, is asked by his mother: "'Why don't you write something nice about the Jews for a change?'" He replies: "'There are plenty of others to do that . . . Besides, you are confusing fact with fiction. I write stories.'"

Sinclair cites with some pride a reviewer's comment that his stories are "evil little fictions." In fact, the reviewer (Victoria Glendinning, in the *Times Literary Supplement*) called them "evil, entertaining little fictions"—a fine ambiguity that characterizes much of Sinclair's work. To the extent that he is iconoclastic, irreverently satirical, and totally uninhibited in his choice of language and subject matter, Sinclair might agree that his stories are "evil." But in rejecting "nice" writing—about Jews or any other subject—he has a precedent not only in many of his older contemporaries—among them I. B. Singer, Philip Roth, Saul Bellow, Woody Allen—but also in *tzimtzum*, which, he points out in his story of that title, is "the cabbalistic doctrine which explains creativity as a synthesis of good and evil."

From his first novel, *Bibliosexuality*, published when he was twenty-five, Sinclair has teased, puzzled, and, depending on their sensibilities, offended or delighted his readers. As its title suggests, the novel connects literature with libido—a concept certainly not invented by Sinclair but exploited by him to the fullest. Bibliosexuality is "the intercourse between writer and reader." He defines it more fully in a scholarly appendix to the novel as "a disorder of the senses in which an unnatural relationship with a book is either strongly desired or obstained. . . . This psychological complex is invariably accompanied by a peculiar sensitivity to words, and by a conspicuous delight in the sensual and orgasmic possibilities of language." His central character, David Drollkind, in the throes of composing both a novel and a thesis ("Towards a Jewish Tradition in American Literature"), is suffering from writer's block. The narrator, a sympathetic observer, is a "bibliotec" ("The literary world is divided into those who are bibliosexuals and those who are bibliotecs, and just as the great detective chases the master criminal, so the bibliotec pursues the bibliosexual"). Perhaps closest in spirit to Sinclair here is Vladimir Nabokov ("himself a notorious bibliosexual," Sinclair writes), but he also acknowledges the bibliosexuality of the Gothic novel, of Edgar Allan Poe's stories, Bram Stoker's *Dracula*, Henry James's *The Turn of the Screw*, and J. M. Barrie's *Peter Pan*. As Malcolm Bradbury pointed out in an essay in *No, Not Bloomsbury*, Sinclair's games-playing with such literary masters "exposed the twenty-five year old author to harsh comparisons." At best, his first book won the dubious compliment of "clever." Bradbury, like most other reviewers, found it "a little bit too much of a single extended verbal pun."

In the years that followed, Sinclair published two volumes of short stories, *Hearts of Gold* and *Bedbugs*, that won him substantial recognition, including a Bicentennial Arts fellowship from the British Council in 1980, a Somerset Maugham Award from the Society of Authors in 1981, and in 1983 a citation from the British Book Marketing Council as one of the top twenty young British fiction writers currently publishing. Short stories gave Sinclair an opportunity to range widely over many genres from fable to parody, from burlesque to erotic fantasy, and to indulge his passion for language. Bradbury wrote: "Stylistically playful, the stories are at the same time stylistically serious, and an energetic assimilation of several literary traditions as well as of the major paradoxes of literary presentation—if you can imagine a Borgesian Joseph Heller or Nabokovian Isaac Bashevis Singer, you start to reach into Sinclair's very distinctive tone."

Although Sinclair's work resonates with literary echoes like those cited by Bradbury, it remains distinctive. He plays multiple roles with many voices. In some stories he is the self-hating Jew obsessed with survivor guilt, the schlemiel, a sexual bumbler, victimized by his own ineptness. In others he is a Hollywood private eye,

Joshua Smolinsky, who speaks in the terse accents of Raymond Chandler or Dashiell Hammett: "I drive nonstop to Las Vegas in my old Volkswagon . . . The motel, forming a rebus from Paradise, called itself the Pair of Dice. The air-conditioning in my room doesn't work, making it hotter than hell inside." He describes a character in *Hearts of Gold*: "Life had given him a thirty-year head start on his latest wife who had yellow hair that was whipped up like a piece of confectionary." Another Smolinsky story, "The Incredible Case of the Stack o' Wheat Murders," begins with the detective engaged in conversation with Sir Isaiah Berlin about Bakunin and other famous terrorists. Still others are perversely moral fables: "Genesis," which opens in the museum of the La Brea tar pits in Los Angeles, involves an angel trapped on earth who says: "I have flown out of the shadows into the substance of your world. Where I dwell we are free from the contagion of language, our feelings float through the empyrean like balloons in a comic book."

Like other Jewish writers—Singer, Roth, and Bernard Malamud—Sinclair has used the absurdist fable to ultimately serious ends. Bradbury noted that underneath his mockery, he is "more assertively the Jew in the age of Zionism, guilty, corrupt, and hungry for absolution." An example is "The Evolution of the Jews," which begins, "'Remember you are a Jew,' my father said when I was old enough to stand on my own four feet." The narrator turns out to be a giraffe, a member of the lost tribe of Israel. "What proof can I give? For starters, there's the statue of Moses wearing horns. Just like mine. Put the rest down to evolution." While the giraffe's long neck for viewing distant dangers and his four legs for speed in escaping them are natural adaptations, he suffers terrible anxieties: "I dreamed of pogroms, of massacres, of trials, of tortures. I hear the cruel laughter of antisemites." He is saved, however, from the perils of the wilderness when he is captured by a group of Jews who take him to a zoo in Israel. Because they speak only Hebrew and he only Yiddish, they cannot communicate, but they treat him royally. Nevertheless, he is unhappy. He fears the future, the inevitability of anti-Semitism. "But in Israel I am dumb."

Sinclair's ambivalence about the State of Israel is reflected in a nonfiction book, *Diaspora Blues: A View of Israel*, on the conflicting feelings of Jews living outside Israel toward that country (he regards himself as "an inside-outsider"), and in two seriocomic novels, *Blood Libels* and *Cosmetic Effects*. In *Blood Libels* the meek and mild Jake Silverstone, born in the year Israel was born and literary editor of the *Jewish Voice*, becomes, through a series of farcical and macabre adventures, involved in the Israeli invasion of Lebanon. The juxtaposition of the comic grotesque plot and the grimly serious history is not easy to accept; most reviewers found the book entertaining but also troubling. "In *Blood Libels*," Linda Taylor wrote in the *Times Literary Supplement*, "Clive Sinclair has assembled the Jewish anomaly: at odds with the old Judaism, ambivalent towards the new Zionism . . . More funny than sad, more ironic than tragic, the novel presents the story, rather than the history of statelessness."

In *Cosmetic Effects* Sinclair's sexually tormented antihero, a lecturer on film at a British university, goes to Israel, ostensibly to advise on the making of a "matzoh-ball Western" based on the story of King David. Between frantic sexual activity and Arab–Israeli politics, he has a difficult time of it. Some reviewers questioned what Dennis Drabell, in the *Washington Post Book World*, called the author's "plague-on-both-your houses" attitude and his making light of profoundly serious issues. But, Drabell concluded, these shortcomings "scarcely detract from the novel's taut prose, skilled pacing and pervasive multifaceted intelligence. *Cosmetic Effects* is a disarmingly entertaining novel."

Sinclair carries his black whimsy to its furthest extreme in *Augustus Rex*, which is narrated by Beelzebub, Lord of the Flies, who bids for the soul of the Swedish playwright August Strindberg (who died in 1912) by offering him resurrection in 1961. Since Strindberg was not only a notorious misogynist but also an outspoken anti-Semite, we are assured of Beelzebub's triumph and the playwright's eternal damnation as a buzzing fly: "Only you can release him from this eternal torment, dear reader; but first you have to know which fly to swat."

As literary editor of the *Jewish Chronicle* from 1983 to 1987, Sinclair encouraged the publication of Israeli books in England, though he reported, in an article in *Modern Hebrew Literature* (Fall/Winter 1991), that, with the exception of Amos Oz and most recently David Grossman, "Israel does not enjoy most favoured nation status in England's green and pleasant land any more than it does, say, in Sweden." Sinclair himself has made a contribution to England's and America's knowledge of modern Yiddish literature with his short but critically acclaimed study *The Brothers Singer*. "This is a book about literary relationships," Sinclair wrote; but in fact one of the chief merits of the book is his use of autobiographical material not only of the two celebrated brothers, Israel Joshua Singer, author of *The Brothers Ashkenazi*, and

his even more celebrated brother Isaac Bashevis Singer, but also of their much neglected sister Hinda Esther (later Esther Kreitman). Sinclair drew upon her autobiographical novel *Deborah*, as well as Joshua's memoirs and Bashevis's personal recollections. In 1978 he had a long interview with Bashevis in his New York apartment. The result was an eminently readable book, faulted by some reviewers for its lack of scholarly thoroughness but praised for its sympathetic overview of two distinguished literary careers. S. S. Prawer observed, in the *Times Literary Supplement* (1992), that Sinclair's experience as a novelist was helpful in bringing to life the family members and details of their lives in Poland and New York: "their fortunes in peace and war are told vividly and economically, but always in such a way that we see their connection with the literary output which clearly prompted Sinclair to write his book."

Sinclair regularly contributes book, theater, and film reviews to the *Times Literary Supplement* and other periodicals. He also reports on his travels to Israel, the United States, and Eastern Europe. In 1991 he described for the *Times Literary Supplement* his participation in a writers' conference in Belgrade where he observed the tensions, especially among Jewish intellectuals torn between their memories of Croatian persecution during World War II and present-day Serbian aggression. He lives in St. Albans, in Hertfordshire, with his wife, a teacher, and their son. Sinclair has a B.A. (1969) and a Ph.D. (1983) from the University of East Anglia.

PRINCIPAL WORKS: *Novels*—Bibliosexuality, 1973; Blood Libels, 1986; Cosmetic Effects, 1990; Augustus Rex, 1992. *Short stories*—Hearts of Gold, 1979; Bedbugs, 1982; For Good or Evil, 1992. *Nonfiction*—The Brothers Singer, 1983; Diaspora Blues: A View of Israel, 1987.

ABOUT: Bradbury, M. No, Not Bloomsbury, 1987; Contemporary Authors 127, 1989. *Periodicals*—Nation November 19, 1983; New York Times Book Review September 14, 1986; Times Literary Supplement April 29, 1983; September 13, 1985; January 16, 1992; Washington Post Book World July 22, 1990.

SINGER, PETER (ALBERT DAVID) (July 6, 1946–   ), Australian philosopher, writes: "I was born in Melbourne, Australia, as part of the postwar baby boom. My parents were Viennese and Jewish; they had left Austria as soon as Hitler annexed it and gone wherever they could get an entry permit. So I was brought up in what was still essentially an Anglo-Saxon culture with a

PETER SINGER

high regard for common sense and a disdain for pretentious ways of thinking and obscure ways of speaking. But at the same time, from my family and their friends I absorbed an orientation towards European ways of living and thinking. I also grew up with a deep sense of the evil of racism, and a personal involvement in the tragedy of the Holocaust. Of my grandparents, I knew only my mother's mother. She survived the war and came to Australia; my other grandparents died in Nazi camps.

"I might have followed my father into business, or my older sister into law; but somehow I got sidetracked into philosophy and ethics, where I remain. Most of my writing has been directed towards issues of both philosophical and practical interest. I try to write as simply and directly as possible, so that my readership is not restricted to academics.

"I am best known for writing *Animal Liberation*, a work that gave its name to a worldwide movement. The essential philosophical view it maintains is simple but revolutionary. Species is, in itself, as irrelevant to moral status as race or sex. Hence 'speciesism' is as objectionable as racism or sexism. Nor should we exclude beings from equal consideration on the grounds that they fall below a given level of intelligence or rationality. On the contrary, the only justifiable limit to our moral concern is the limit of sentience, or the capacity to feel pleasure or pain. If beings lack this capacity, then we cannot affect their lives, for better or worse, from their own subjective point of view, because they have no such point of view. As long as beings are capa-

ble of feeling pleasure or pain, they have interests, and we do wrong when we give their interests less consideration than we give to the similar interests of members of our own species. Taken seriously, this conclusion requires radical changes in almost every interaction we have with animals, including our diet, our economy, and our relations with the natural environment.

"To say that this idea is revolutionary is not to say that no one had ever thought of it before me. Similar ideas can be found, for instance, in Henry Salt's *Animal Rights*, first published in 1892. I owe my awareness of the issue to some of my fellow students at the time when I was studying philosophy at Oxford University. (Before then, my ideas about animals were entirely conventional, and I had never been—and still am not—an 'animal lover.') My particular contribution was to state, clearly, rigorously, and in modern terms, the case for extending equal consideration to nonhuman animals. That the time was ripe for such a restatement can be seen by the fact that people all over the world have responded positively to *Animal Liberation*, and have changed their diet and their lives as a result. I find this pleasing, not only because of its positive practical consequences, but especially because it proves that ethical reasoning can have an impact on the world.

"My view on a broader ranger of issues can be found in *Practical Ethics*. Here the treatment of animals receives its proper place as one among several major contemporary ethical issues. I approach each issue by seeking the solution that has the best consequences for all affected; and by 'best consequences' I mean that which satisfies the most preferences, weighted in accordance with the strength of the preferences, and over the long run. Thus my ethical position is a form of preference utilitarianism.

"In *Practical Ethics* I apply this position to such issues as equality (both between humans, and between humans and nonhuman animals); abortion; euthanasia and infanticide; the obligations of the wealthy to aid those living in poverty; the refugee question; environmental concerns, especially the preservation of wilderness; and the obligation to obey the law. (This list describes the contents of the second edition; the first edition was a little narrower in scope.)

"A nonspeciesist and consequentialist approach to these issues leads to striking conclusions. It offers a clear-cut account of why abortion is ethically justifiable. (I show that opponents of abortion rely on an indefensibly speciesist evaluation of human life.) The consequentialist approach also condemns our failure to aid those in desperate need, when we have a considerable surplus of wealth.

"Some of my conclusions disturb and shock people. In Germany and Austria my advocacy of active euthanasia for severely disabled newborn infants has led to the cancellation of conferences at which I had been invited to speak, and on other occasions I have been shouted down, and once even had my glasses smashed. Perhaps it is only to be expected that there should be heated opposition to an ethic that challenges the generally accepted superiority of human beings, and the traditional view of the sanctity of human life. Nevertheless, I deplore the intolerance and lack of respect for freedom of speech shown by those responsible for this opposition. I find dismaying their refusal even to discuss my views with me. I also regret the misrepresentations of my views that they have purveyed to others, including those with disabilities. Those who read my works—and not just a few sentences taken out of context—can easily see that my ethical approach cannot pose any threat to people, whether intellectually disabled or not, who are capable of enjoying their lives (by their own criteria) and of wanting to go on living."

Peter Singer, in addition to being the author of numerous books on subjects ranging from animal rights to human genetic engineering, is an internationally known lecturer, a seasoned activist, and, what is perhaps most remarkable in an age of strictly academic specialists, a trained philosopher with a genuinely public following. He is the son of Ernst Singer, a coffee and tea importer, and Cora (Oppenheim) Singer, a medical doctor. After receiving his secondary education at Scotch College in Melbourne, Singer earned his B.A. (1967) and M.A. (1969) from the University of Melbourne.

His attitudes toward animals and animal rights underwent a sea change in 1970, when he encountered a group of vegetarian philosophy students at Oxford University. He received his B.Phil. from University College, Oxford, in 1971, and remained there as a lecturer from 1971 to 1973. He began work on *Animal Liberation*, still his most famous book, during his last year at Oxford; the book grew out of an article ("Animal Liberation") he published in the April 5, 1973 issue of the *New York Review of Books*. While teaching at New York University as a visiting associate professor in 1973–74, he completed his research on factory farming and animal experimentation.

Singer always intended *Animal Liberation* to be more than a series of academic musings. In the opening passage of his preface to the book, he sounds a clarion call to potential activists:

"This book is about the tyranny of human over nonhuman animals. . . . The struggle against this tyranny is a struggle as important as any of the moral and social issues that have been fought over in recent years." Singer's well-documented exposé of the systematic horrors of factory farming and his carefully reasoned refutation of what he has labeled "speciesism" make *Animal Liberation* a potent combination of journalism and philosophy. "Peter Singer is as far from a 'philosopher's philosopher' as one can get . . . ," the philosopher C. G. Luckhardt wrote approvingly of *Animal Liberation* in the *New York Times Book Review*. Luckhardt lauded Singer for avoiding "arcane and technical issues" and for "getting philosophy back into the marketplace."

Another reviewer who found much to admire in *Animal Liberation* was Murray Polner, who wrote in the *New Republic*, "Singer . . . has written an extraordinarily persuasive book, part tract, part systematic analysis, irreverent, questioning, surely unsettling, a bit emotional at times perhaps but throughout a striking account of the perpetual discrimination practiced against animals, a bias he characterizes as 'speciesism.'" In the *Village Voice*, however, Richard Goldstein expressed specific quarrels with *Animal Liberation*, most of them having to do with Singer's "methodology" and his "lack of social logic." Nonetheless, Goldstein concluded: "This is an important book, first because it reveals . . . the rough beast of self-interest which motivates all human society. Second, because it offers solutions . . . in a spirit of mercy so touching and disquieting that one can only marvel at the persistent power of compassion."

Animal Liberation has been translated into eight languages, including Finnish and Japanese; it has had a worldwide impact on both the movement for ethical vegetarianism and the campaign to halt animal experimentation. While the book has certainly come to occupy a central place in the animal rights movement, Singer himself is dubious whenever his (or anyone else's) book is referred to as a "bible." "I don't believe in bibles: no book has a monopoly on truth," he wrote in the preface to the new edition of *Animal Liberation*. "In any case, no book can achieve anything unless it strikes a chord in its readers."

The appearance of the revised edition of *Animal Liberation*, to which Singer added new material on animal experimentation, provoked an angry response from some scientists. In a letter published in the *New York Review of Books* (1992), three University of California, Berkeley physiologists contended that in his zeal to convince readers of the suffering inflicted upon animals by human researchers, Singer "uses the techniques of propagandists, but he masquerades them in the guise of responsible scholarship. . . . " They accused Singer of selecting research projects "that can be exploited for maximal emotional impact" and protraying them as the norm. Singer concluded his point-by-point rebuttal of their argument by writing that "it is noteworthy that [the writers] do not object to a single description of an experiment. Nor do they challenge the fairness of even one of the quotations I have taken from the many journal articles in which experimenters describe the suffering they themselves have inflicted upon animals. . . . That they say nothing against my accounts of the nature of experimentation on animals can therefore be taken as a reluctant endorsement of the accuracy of this damning material. For that I thank them."

In 1977 Singer joined the philosophy faculty of Monash University, in suburban Melbourne. Since 1983 he has served as director of the university's Centre for Human Bioethics. In such works as *Practical Ethics*, *The Expanding Circle*, and *Making Babies* (originally published as *The Reproduction Revolution*), Singer attempts to apply ethical (or moral) solutions to such divisive issues as abortion, euthanasia, and infanticide. Throughout these works he is concerned with examining the moral dilemnas posed by such now widespread technologies as in vitro fertilization. In his lengthy and detailed consideration of *Practical Ethics* in the *New York Review of Books* in 1980, H.L.A. Hart detected flaws in Singer's application of utilitarianism to certain problems, but praised the author's scholarship and vision: "Singer's book is packed with admirably marshaled and detailed information, social, medical, and economic. . . . " In a review of *The Expanding Circle* in the *New Republic* R. M. Hare wrote, "Only those who have tried to do it know how difficult it is to write, as Peter Singer has, in a way that can be understood by any intelligent person and yet goes to the heart of the subject."

Singer's advocacy of euthanasia for severely disabled infants (argued in *Practical Ethics* and elsewhere) has provoked a firestorm of criticism, the expression of which has not been confined to the letters columns of scholarly journals. Not surprisingly, the storm has been most intense in the German-speaking countries, where discussion of euthanasia inevitably prompts memories of the Nazis—notorious for their barbarous murder of the sick and helpless. In May 1991, after his scheduled speech on animal rights at the University of Zurich had been drowned out by protesters chanting "Singer raus!" ("Singer out!"),

Singer was assaulted by a man from the audience. In a *New York Review of Books* essay in 1991, he recounted and analyzed the history of the bitter opposition to his work in the German-speaking nations. Many of his most vociferous detractors, he noted, were ignorant of his work, ideas, and background. They were unaware of his groundbreaking work in animal rights, thought that he was associated with the extreme right wing, and, perhaps worst of all, had no idea that his parents were Austrian Jews who lost many family members to the Holocaust. "In contrast to the Nazi ideology that the state should decide who was worthy of life," Singer wrote, "my view was designed to reduce the power of the state and allow parents to make crucial life and death decisions, both for themselves and, in consultation with their doctors, for their newborn infants."

Singer eats no meat and avoids using products made from animals, including those developed through animal research. Believing that the rich have an ethical obligation to help the poor (and realizing that rich is a relative term), he routinely donates between ten and twenty percent of his salary to such organizations as Community Aid Abroad. According to Singer's demanding ethic, which he has admitted to following only imperfectly, even the simple act of eating out poses a dilemma. "Given that there are people who are in much greater need of money than my family and I are," he told an interviewer from *HQ* magazine, "and given that there are reasonably efficient ways of getting them assistance through organisations like Community Aid Abroad, I think you can say that every time I take my family out to a restaurant and spend, say, $80 on a meal for the four of us instead of giving that money to Community Aid Abroad, then I have done something that is ethically dubious."

Singer married Renata Diamond in 1969; they have three daughters.

PRINCIPAL WORKS: Democracy and Disobedience, 1973; Animal Liberation: A New Ethics for Our Treatment of Animals, 1975, rev. ed. 1990; Practical Ethics, 1979; (with J. Mason) Animal Factories, 1980, rev. ed. 1990; Marx, 1980; The Expanding Circle: Ethics and Sociobiology, 1981; Hegel, 1982; (with D. Wells) Making Babies: The New Science and Ethics of Conception, 1984 (in U.K.: The Reproduction Revolution: New Ways of Making Babies; (with H. Kuhse) Should the Baby Live?, 1985; (with T. Carney) Ethical and Legal Issues in Guardianship Options for Intellectually Disadvantaged People, 1986; (with L. Gruen) Animal Liberation: A Graphic Guide, 1987; (with B. Dover and I. Newkirk) Save the Animals, 1991. *As editor*—(with T. Regan) Animal Rights and Human Obligations: An Anthology, 1976, rev. ed. 1989; (with W. Walters) Test-Tube Babies: A Guide to Moral

Questions, Present Techniques, and Future Possibilities, 1982; In Defence of Animals, 1985; Applied Ethics, 1986; (with H. Kuhse et al.) Embryo Experimentation, 1990; A Companion to Ethics, 1991.

ABOUT: Contemporary Authors New Revision Series 8, 1983; Current Biography Yearbook 1991; International al Who's Who 1991–1992, 1991. *Periodicals*—Christian Science Monitor May 23, 1987; HQ Magazine (Sydney, Australia) Winter 1992; New Republic May 29, 1976; February 7, 1981; New York Review of Books May 15, 1980; August 15, 1991; November 5, 1992; New York Times Book Review January 4, 1976; Village Voice March 22, 1976.

SLAVITT, DAVID R(YTMAN) (pseudonyms HENRY SUTTON, DAVID BENJAMIN, HENRY LAZARUS, LYNN MEYER) (March 23, 1935–), American poet, novelist, and translator, writes: "I suppose the most striking thing about my literary career is its diversity, which I attribute to my early teachers and role models. At Andover, I studied with Dudley Fitts, and along with everything else he taught me, there was the unspoken and perhaps even unintended suggestion that one wasn't a full member of the culture if one didn't do at least a little translating. Then, at Yale, working with such masters as Robert Penn Warren and Richard Sewall, I got the idea that the different genres were all valuable and interesting ways to explore various aspects of the world and of my own inner self. I have also been quite lucky, contriving against very long odds to make a living from writing, and this has extended the range of my interests to include a fair amount of journalism as well as a number of calculatedly commercial works of fiction.

"That these commercial novels have been pseudonymous generally requires a word of explanation. My impression was that Graham Greene's gesture of labeling certain works as 'entertainments' never quite worked. But it seemed to me that commerce offered its own solution. Everyone knows that Omega makes Tissots, Longines makes Wittnauers, and Chrysler makes Plymouths. What could be more convenient? Besides, in 1967, I had a small highbrow, low-revenue novel that was about to appear, at last, in the United States, having already been published in London. This was the same season as *The Exhibitionist* was scheduled to appear, and my impression was that, given the choice of two books by the same author, booksellers would tend to order the one with the large advertising and publicity budget and ignore the other. The pseudonym, then, also served to protect *Rochelle*, at least for the moment.

DAVID R. SLAVITT

"Otherwise? My life is mostly in my work, in the poems, stories, novels, and—particularly—the translations. I did the Virgil—the *Eclogues* and then the *Georgics*—back when I was at the apex of my commercial career, and those poems are, in my reading anyway, contemplations about the literary life and, more generally, about labor, which is one of the great subjects but one that very few poets since Virgil have addressed. I also had the impression that these were undervalued poems of Virgil's, that they had been nudged away from the focus of our attention by the extraordinary vitality of the *Aeneid.* I turned later on to Ovid's poems of exile, the *Tristia* and the *Letters from the Black Sea*, and then to Seneca's tragedies of blood and pain. These darker works were comfortable masks to put on, or say personae, by which I could allow some part of my grief at my mother's murder—during a burglary, in 1982—to express itself. That loss is also the real subject of *Lives of the Saints*, and, indeed, of *The Hussar.*

"My children have all graduated from their expensive schools, so there is no compulsion for me to perform any further acts of commerce. I write, now, only to please myself and in the hope that there may be a few friends who approve of what I do. Their tiny numbers are unimpressive to New York trade publishers, but my friends at John Hopkins University Press and at Louisiana State University Press continue to support my work. Indeed, with Leslie Phillabaum at LSU, my relationship is now one of thirty years' duration, which is extraordinary in contemporary American publishing.

"I am reaching that stage in my life and career when, among other things, I am occasionally occupied with the renewing of copyrights (under the old law). It is a kind of milepost. I shall be sixty in a very few years. And before my sixtieth birthday, I shall have published my fiftieth book, which seems a great many (most of them are out of print). But then, because there are too many books in the world, only the good ones are ever remembered. And this is a mercy, one gentle aspect of an otherwise rough-and-tumble business that is already working to my advantage. My Henry Sutton exploits have not so much been forgiven by the middlebrows as they have been forgotten. I can look at the bookcase with all my work in it and, in my better moods, persuade myself that some of it is pretty good."

———

Born in White Plains, New York, David Rytman Slavitt is the son of Samuel Saul Slavitt, an attorney, and Adele Beatrice (Rytman) Slavitt. He attended public schools until the age of fifteen, when he was enrolled in Phillips Andover Academy in Massachusetts. There, under the tutelage of the poet and classicist Dudley Fitts, he began writing verse. At Yale, from which he graduated magna cum laude in 1956, Slavitt was a Scholar of the House and succeeded William F. Buckley Jr. as anchorman of the debate team. Instead of going on to law school, as his father had wished, Slavitt earned an M.A. (1957) in literature from Columbia University, after which he spent an unsatisfying year teaching English at Georgia Tech. From 1958 to 1965, he was employed by *Newsweek* magazine, chiefly as a book and film reviewer. Although he has held teaching posts at various universities over the years, Slavitt has essentially earned a living as an independent writer since the mid-1960s.

Considering the diversity and prodigiousness of Slavitt's literary output—a dozen collections of poetry, nearly thirty novels, a host of translations from the Latin, as well as miscellaneous works of nonfiction and drama—he has attracted relatively little critical attention. This neglect is attributable, at least in part, to his unabashed exploitation of the commercial novel as a means of subsidizing his more purely literary work, and to his undisguised contempt for those who preside over what he has derisively labeled the "Quality Lit Biz." His first collection of poetry *Suits for the Dead*, which appeared while he was still with *Newsweek*, marked Slavitt as a serious and decidedly noncommercial writer. It thus came as something of a shock to reviewers when, several years later, Slavitt—using the pseudonym Henry Sutton—published *The*

Exhibitionist, a calculatedly commercial novel that became a best-seller. His next two Sutton novels, *The Voyeur* and *Vector*, also became best-sellers. Between 1967 and 1980, Slavitt published a total of nine manifestly commercial novels under four different pseudonyms—Henry Sutton, Lynn Meyer, Henry Lazarus, and David Benjamin. During that same period, he continued to publish serious fiction, poetry, and translations under his own name.

Anagrams, one of his early novels, satirizes the absurd goings-on at a campus-sponsored literary festival. The protagonist, Jerome Carpenter, is a poet who earn a living peddling plagiarized dissertations to aspiring academics. In the *New York Times Book Review*, Michael Mewshaw wrote: "Books by David Slavitt aren't actually reviewed. Critics seize upon them as opportunities to snipe at him for his histrionic disdain of them. Muggers, sex maniacs and murderers may find forgiveness, but there's no sympathy for Slavitt, who committed literary sacrilege by making fun of what he calls the Quality Lit Biz—and, worse yet, making money by making fun. . . . A talented comic novelist, he tossed off . . . a trio of bestselling potboilers that filled his enemies with outrage and envy, and his coffers with coin of the realm." As for *Anagrams* itself, Mewshaw lauded the book's "dozens of grotesquely funny scenes," but found the story to be "slender and at times creaky," and the characters "curiously flat."

Slavitt pays particular attention to the professions of his characters; consequently, his novels are filled with facts and information. In *Anagrams*, *Cold Comfort*, and *The Cliff*, the focus is on academic life. *Jo Stern* deals with the publishing industry, examining a successful female author who greatly resembles Jacqueline Susann. But Slavitt has ranged far beyond the worlds of academia and publishing. His best-seller *Vector* looks at scientists engaged in bacteriological warfare experiments, while *King of Hearts* concerns transplant surgery. *The Idol* provides an insider's view of the Hollywood movie industry. The main character in *Lives of the Saints* is a reporter for a supermarket tabloid.

Notwithstanding the number and diversity of his novels, poetry remains at the center of Slavitt's literary enterprise. His fifth collection, *Vital Signs: New and Selected Poems*, brings together almost 200 pieces of his best work from the first fifteen years of his career. Vernon Young, in the *Hudson Review*, was struck by the versatility of Slavitt's poetic voice: "He inhabits history and the world of poetic forms as playfully as an otter its fluvial element; with no audible panting, he commands a diversity of stanzaic constructs and syllabic linecounts, tosses off ballads, sestinas, sonnets, *ottava rima*, dramatic monologues in unrhymed strophes of varying meters. . . . I don't know if anyone recognizes that in Slavitt Americans have their own Cavafy, their own Auden." Reviewing the collection in *Poetry*, Robert Holland commented: "Though he is no Yeats or Stevens, Slavitt speaks with his own quiet authority, from a relaxed, almost homely stance. And though he is not . . . blazing new trails in American poetry, his poems have a classical quality which makes innovation seem merely irrelevant." However, in the *New York Times Book Review* (1975), Helen Vendler found little to admire in *Vital Signs*: "[A] dreadful flatness and didacticism dooms all of Slavitt, whose tedious parameters offer no surprises, whose learning remains poetically inert, and whose new poems are, if anything, less interesting than his earlier ones."

In the *Virginia Quarterly Review*, Henry Taylor noted: "From the beginning, Slavitt's poetry has been characterized by profound wit, neoclassical attention to form, and a generous erudition. [He] is also a master of tonal variety; within the same poem he can make shifts of tone which most poets would find too risky."

In the title poem of his later collection *Crossroads*, Slavitt imagines the tiny Polish village from which his ancestors emigrated:

> I see that dour landscape clearly, although
> I've never been there. It could be from a story
> we tell to children—but then, on second thought, no.
> Why should we have them worry
> as we do? Nothing remains of that crossroads
> hamlet.

In *Crossroads*, Bruce Bennett wrote in the *New York Times Book Review* (1994): "David R. Slavitt . . . relies chiefly on a ruminative, elegiac mode reminiscent of W. H. Auden's. Like Auden, . . . he is an adept practitioner of formal verse; many poems rhyme or off-rhyme and are shaped as traditional stanzas, but the effect remains low-key and unobtrusive."

Eight Longer Poems, Slavitt's 1990 collection, has four poems that deal with history and myth. Richard Moore, reviewing the volume in *American Book Review* wrote, "The darker emotions abound. . . . and . . . when we look into the horrors and absurdities of recorded and mythical history, we mainly find clearer and less inhibited images of what lies buried but undead in ourselves." Moore was particularly taken with Slavitt's Vlad the Impaler, "the most enduring symbol for the horror and foreboding that seem to have inhabited him. . . . " In *America*, Robert E. Hosner remarked that "the lines of epic and personal history often intersect . . . *Eight*

Longer Poems chronicles the development of an artist who has a poet's ear [that] can 'hear what dead voices whisper' and a poet's voice that can sing with astonishing conviction and clarity."

Slavitt, an accomplished Latinist, has won considerable acclaim as a translator of Virgil, Ovid, and Seneca. His *The Eclogues and the Georgics of Virgil* is at once a translation and an imaginative reinterpretation of Virgil's work. Slavitt devised a novel perspective on Virgil's *Eclogues*, which have traditionally been viewed only as exemplary works of pastoral poetry. When he first read the *Eclogues*, he noted in his preface, "They were a babble of unconvincing shepherds." He went on to ask, "If you were ever a living, breathing poem, what could you conceivably have been about?" Slavitt's answer was daringly original. "Indeed," he wrote, "the lit biz is a primary concern of the *Eclogues*. No writer who has ever raged at agents, editors, publishers, critics, other writers, or the public can fail to recognize in these extraordinary poems the anguish Virgil felt, the compassion, or the hope."

The poet, novelist, and critic George Garrett has been one of Slavitt's most consistent champions. In his book of critical essays *My Silk Purse and Yours*, Garrett had high praise for Slavitt's work as both poet and translator: "Slavitt is a poet of very considerable gifts and accomplishment—and, if truth could somehow ever be known in this era of hype, false images, and inflated reputations, a major poet, to be counted among the few and best of those writing poetry in our language. That he should have managed to achieve a great translation [*The Tristia of Ovid*] and restoration of the work of a master from another time is at once appropriate and astonishing."

Since 1991 Slavitt has been a lecturer in English and classics at the University of Pennsylvania. He lives in Philadelphia with his second wife, Janet Lee Abrahm, a physician.

PRINCIPAL WORKS: *Poetry*—Suits for the Dead, 1961; The Carnivore, 1965; Day Sailing and Other Poems, 1969; Child's Play, 1972; Vital Signs: New and Selected Poems, 1975; Rounding the Horn, 1978; Dozens, 1981; Big Nose, 1983; The Walls of Thebes, 1986; Equinox and Other Poems, 1989; Eight Longer Poems, 1990; The Gift, 1993; Crossroads, 1994. *Novels*—Rochelle; or, Virtue Rewarded, 1966; Feel Free, 1968; Anagrams, 1970; ABCD, 1972; The Outer Mongolian, 1973; The Killing of the King, 1974; King of Hearts, 1976; Jo Stern, 1978; Cold Comfort, 1980; Ringer, 1982; Alice at 80, 1984; (with B. Adler) The Agent, 1986; The Hussar, 1987; Salazar Blinks, 1988; Lives of the Saints, 1989; Turkish Delights, 1993; The Cliff, 1994. *Pseudonymous novels*—(as Henry Sutton) The Exhibitionist, 1967; The Voyeur, 1968; Vector, 1970; The Liberated, 1973; (as Lynn Meyer) Paperback

Thriller, 1975; (as Henry Lazarus) That Golden Woman, 1976; The Sacrifice: A Novel of the Occult, 1978; (as David Benjamin) The Idol, 1979; The Proposal, 1980. *Short stories*—Short Stories Are Not Real Life, 1991. *As translator*—The Eclogues of Virgil, 1971; The Eclogues and the Georgics of Virgil, 1972; The Elegies to Delia of Albius Tibullus, 1985; The Tristia of Ovid, 1986; Ovid's Poetry of Exile, 1989; Seneca: The Tragedies (2 vols.) 1992–1993; The Fables of Avianus, 1993; The Metamorphoses of Ovid, 1994. *Nonfiction*—(with P. Secord and C. Backman) Understanding Social Life: An Introduction to Social Psychology, 1976; Physicians Observed, 1987; Virgil, 1991. *Drama*—King Saul, 1967; The Cardinal Sins, 1969. *Opera*—(with L. Pickett and F. Wiseman) Welfare: The Opera, 1992. *As editor*—Land of Superior Mirages: New and Selected Poems of Adrien Stoutenberg, 1986; (with S. Palmer Bovie) The Complete Roman Drama, 1992–1994.

ABOUT: Contemporary Authors Autobiography Series 3, 1986; Contemporary Authors New Revision Series 41, 1994; Contemporary Literary Criticism 5, 1976; 14, 1980; Contemporary Poets, 5th ed., 1990; Dictionary of Literary Biography 5, 1980; 6, 1980; Garrett, G. My Silk Purse and Yours, 1992; Garrett, G. (ed.) The Writer's Voice: Conversations with Contemporary Writers, 1973. *Periodicals*—America December 15, 1990; American Book Review January/March 1991; Hudson Review Winter 1975–1976; New York Times Book Review September 5, 1971; September 7, 1975; April 17, 1994; New Yorker January 29, 1990; Poetry February 1977; Virginia Quarterly Review Spring 1990.

SMILEY, JANE (September 26, 1949–   ), American novelist and short story writer, was born in Los Angeles, to James Laverne Smiley, a career army officer, and Frances Nuelle (Graves) Smiley, a journalist. She grew up in St. Louis, Missouri, where her mother, who had tried to write novels, passed on her love of literature to her. Smiley wrote a novel as her senior thesis for her B.A. degree in English at Vassar College in 1971. This experience convinced her that writing prose should be her life's work, and she later recalled in a *New York Times Book Review* interview in 1989, that, "I knew this was for me, this creation of worlds."

In the early 1970s, she began graduate study at the University of Iowa, taking an M.A. in 1975, an M.F.A. in 1976, and a Ph.D. in 1978. She received a Fulbright fellowship in 1976 to do research in Iceland for her doctoral dissertation in Old Norse literature. She was taken with Old Norse literature because it had an extremely dark view of the world, but was, at the same time, quite comical. While in Iceland, she became fascinated by stories of Eric the Red and his 10th-century Norse colonizers of Greenland. Although she knew at the time that she wanted to write a novel on the subject, she felt that it was

JANE SMILEY

too complex an undertaking for a first novel. Instead she decided to write about the more familiar territory of contemporary America to gain "practice and technical skill," she told Marielle Thiebaux in *Publishers Weekly*. In fact, a variety of subjects and settings were to be used in her novels. Michiko Kakutani in the *New York Times* called her "most definitely a fox," meaning one of those writers who push "their talents in as many directions as possible, continually reinventing their styles and continually looking for new subjects."

Her first two novels, *Barn Blind* and *At Paradise Gate*, are realistic and focus on the strains within families in middle America. *Barn Blind* tells the story of Kate Karlson, the mother of four teenagers, who is so obsessed with raising horses and making her children championship equestrians that she is blind to their emotional needs. The book is replete with details about horsemanship and ranch life. Michael Malone of the *New York Times Book Review* called it a "pastoral novel" with a "rich, drowsy pace." He also complimented Smiley's authentic evocation of familial relationships, saying that she "handles with skill and understanding the mercurial molasses of adolescence, and the inchoate, cumbersome love that family members feel for one another."

In *At Paradise Gate*, the three middle-aged daughters of Anna Robison have gathered to visit their dying father, Ike. Rather than being a comfort to their mother, however, the daughters renew old rivalries and reawaken tensions in their parents' marriage. The rancor causes the unsentimental Anna to reexamine her life and her difficult marriage to Ike. According to Valerie Miner in the *New York Times Book Review* the novel is "not so much about Ike's death as about Anna's life—a retrospective on her difficult past and a resolution of her remaining years." Miner concluded that "Anna's tart honesty and acute consciousness hold the book together when the story line dwindles."

Duplicate Keys is a mystery set in Manhattan, but the characters are all transplanted midwesterners and she again carefully evokes place through the use of telling detail. At the outset of the novel the police are questioning a librarian named Alice about the murder of two of her friends. Because the story is told from Alice's perspective, the crimes are soon relegated to the background as Smiley explores the relationships among a group of friends. The murders are actually ancillary. "More important and far more compelling," noted Lois Gould in the *New York Times Book Review* (1984), "is the anatomy of friendship, betrayal, the color of dusk on the Upper West Side, the aroma of lilacs in Brooklyn's botanic garden, of chocolate tortes at Zabar's." Laura Marcus concurred in the *Times Literary Supplement*, saying that in Smiley's exploration of trust and maturity, she "demonstrates a considerable sensitivity in the treatment of love and friendship, displacing the forensic impulse into an analysis of feeling and emotion." Marcus also remarked that Smiley cleverly correlated detective work and personal wisdom. "The title refers not only to the running motif of stolen and borrowed keys, of changing locks too late," she wrote, "but also the question of the dangers and the delights involved for women in opening up their lives to others."

The Age of Grief, Smiley's next book, was a collection of five short stories and a novella, a literary form that she considers "more meditative" than the novel or short story. The novella is "great for going deeply into one theme," Smiley told Laurel Graeber in the *New York Times Book Review*, and its shorter length makes it more likely to maintain the reader's interest when the author is being "contemplative." The title novella is narrated by David Hurst, a dentist with three young daughters who believes that his wife is unfaithful. Although David wants to confront her, he is unable and unwilling to, instead sinking into depression. Anne Bernays wrote in the *New York Times Book Review* that "'The Age of Grief' has the compactness of a short story, the density and expansiveness of a novel. It is a shameless, unblinking look at the sort of emotional accommodation made by partners in even the best marriage." Two of the short stories in the collection received O. Henry Awards and one received the Pushcart Prize; like the novella,

most of the stories focus on the sorrows and strains of marriage. Roz Kaveney observed in the *Times Literary Supplement* that the events in these stories "are entirely in keeping with [Smiley's] strong vein of social realism, but they have too a quality of the unpredictable, a quality which gives an uninsistent but pervasive sense of the pain and surprise which lie beneath even the most conventional of lives." *The Age of Grief* was nominated for the National Book Critics Circle Award for fiction in 1987.

In 1988, Smiley published *The Greenlanders*, the long and complex historical novel about the Norse colony in 14th-century Greenland that she had first conceived over a decade earlier. In imitating the restrained style of Norse sagas, Smiley interweaves historical and fictional characters in hundreds of small episodes. As ferocious battles and arduous travels are intermixed with mundane births and deaths, the numerous plots overlap to tell the story of the small community that is in decline and will soon disappear. Critical responses to what Howard Norman in the *New York Times Book Review* (1988) called "a prodigiously detailed, haunting novel" were glowing. Norman wrote: "Given the vast template of History, it is impressive how . . . Smiley is able to telescope certain incidents, unravel personalities in a few paragraphs, [and] delve into a kind of folkloric metaphysics." He also noted that although extinction is the overarching theme of the book, "the cadences of day-to-day village life, the larger social dynamics as well as the domestic particular comprise the true riches of *The Greenlanders*." Verlyn Klinkenborg observed in the *New Republic* that *The Greenlanders* has "the nearness of contemporary fiction." Many reviewers also admired the disciplined style that Smiley used to evoke the somberness, stoicism, and fatalism of the Greenlanders. Norman remarked that "each page seemed to correspond, decade by decade, if not breath by breath, with the slowly evolving Greenlandic tragedy." Klinkenborg agreed, commenting that although the book is grim, "in its austerity and the caliber of its art it is jubilant."

With *Ordinary Love & Good Will*, Smiley returned to writing novellas about modern life. "Ordinary Love" is the story of fifty-two-year old Rachel Kinsella, whose seemingly perfect husband absconded with their five children to England after he discovered that she was having an affair. On the twentieth anniversary of the breakup of her marriage, three of her children visit her. Rachel has always felt responsible for her divorce, but has never explained the circumstances of it to her children. When she confesses her infidelity, they respond mildly at first, but then recount some disturbing events in their own lives with their father. Rachel ultimately concludes that she has given her children "the two cruelest gifts I had to give . . . the experience of perfect family happiness, and the certain knowledge that it could not last." In the companion novella, Bob Miller, a Vietnam veteran, is living on a self-sufficient farm with his wife Liz and their young son Tommy. Without a car, telephone, or television and with the ability to grow or make everything they need, they live in complete isolation except for Tommy's attendance at school. Bob's egotistical obsession with living in this world that he has created makes him oblivious to the desperate effect of the isolation on his son until Tommy reacts with appalling aggression towards a black girl at school, ultimately causing Bob's expulsion from his Eden.

Many reviewers complimented Smiley's use of domestic detail and understatement to illustrate emotional and psychological states. "The language of home is slow, meditative, satisfyingly physical," wrote Valerie Miner in the *Women's Review of Books*. According to Josephine Humphreys in the *New York Times Book Review* (1989), Smiley's novellas "are shaped with a constant overseeing intelligence, with full sympathy for humanity's tendency to destroy its own best visions." Although egocentricity is often a destructive force for Smiley's characters, Humphreys noted that the protagonists are usually "reflective, in spite of their blind spots." It is by becoming aware of their ignorance that the characters gain wisdom. "Both novellas end with a chastened, richly incomplete consciousness of how we live and what we want," Humphreys wrote.

In *A Thousand Acres*, the events of life on a family farm in Iowa are played out against the backdrop of *King Lear*. Larry Cook, the owner of a large successful farm, decides to transfer ownership of it to his three daughters, Ginny, Rose, and Caroline. When Caroline, the youngest daughter, who has left the farm to become a lawyer in the city, hesitates and expresses doubts about the wisdom of the decision, her father cuts her out of the inheritance. After the father retires, he becomes increasingly restless and volatile, eventually descending into madness. Meanwhile, as the family's cohesiveness and the farm crumble, Ginny gains awareness of herself, and she and Rose reveal their long-held secret that their father sexually abused them.

Most reviewers commended Smiley's use of *King Lear* as innovative rather than derivative, and she was awarded the 1992 National Book Critics Circle Award and the Pulitzer Prize for fiction. Smiley "doesn't lean against Lear for support," wrote Ron Carlson in the *New York Times Book Review*. Instead, she "takes the truths therein and lights them up her way, making the perils of family and property and being a daughter real and personal and new and honest and hurtful all over again." Diane Purkiss concurred in the *Times Literary Supplement* observing that "Smiley makes the silences of *King Lear* a metaphor for the unspeakableness of incest and rape. Her feminist rewriting of Shakespeare's plot replaces the incomprehensibly malign sisters with real women who have suffered incomprehensible malignity." In the *New York Times*, Christopher Lehmann-Haupt complained, however, that "it seems too much to have made Larry Cook a sexual abuser of Ginny and Rose in their childhood. Lear himself is hugely egotistical, but to push his selfishness into pathological monstrosity insults him retroactively and robs him of majesty." Others felt that the incest was a harrowing yet vital part of the story. Purkiss commented that "Larry's ownership and rule extends to his adolescent daughters' bodies; he owns his acres and his family. His apparent renunciation of the land forces Ginny and Rose to try to come to terms with his possession of their selves." Filled with vivid details of farm life and domestic routines, the book, according to Martha Duffy in *Time*, conveys an "exact and exhilarating sense of place, a sheer Americanness that gives it its own soul and roots." *A Thousand Acres* also reaffirmed Smiley's ability to illuminate family strife. She "brings us in so close that it's almost too much to bear," Ron Carlson wrote. "She's good in those small places, with nothing but the family, pulling tighter and tighter until someone has to leave the table, leave the room, leave town."

Moo is an academic novel set in a large agricultural college in the Midwest known as Moo U. Cathleen Schine in the *New York Review of Books* commented on the essential ingredients of such a novel: the "race for tenure and sex and grants and love and grades and enlightenment. . . . the . . . discrepancy between the spiritual aspirations of those who still absurdly cling to spiritual aspirations and the bureaucratic pettiness and institutional banality of the framework within which they absurdly cling. . . . " Schine remarked that although the academic novel is almost always a satire, "incredibly *Moo* is not a satire. Smiley subverts satire, making it sweeter, and ultimately more pointed. She has written a generous and, therefore, daring book." Michiko Kakutani in the *New York Times* deemed *Moo* "uproariously funny and at the same time hauntingly melancholy," and while Smiley "uses these people to gently send up some of the current trends in higher education—including political correctness, multicultural studies and deconstruction—she turns out to be less interested in social satire, as such, than in the simple spectacle of ordinary human beings succumbing to greed, power, hope, envy and love."

Jane Smiley joined the English department at Iowa State University in Ames in 1981. In addition to her fiction, in 1988 Smiley also published *Catskill Crafts: Artisans of the Catskill Mountains*, about the handmade crafts and techniques of both longtime practitioners and recent arrivals in the Catskills. Her third husband, Stephen Mortensen, is a screenwriter. They live in Ames with her two daughters, Phoebe and Lucy, from her second marriage.

Smiley, when asked if she ever faced dry periods in her writing, told Nadine Broznan in the *New York Times* that after she bought a horse, "there has been basically a trough ever since. There is nothing I would rather do than ride the horse, and it has interfered with my career." Most readers would take that with the grain of salt with which she meant it.

PRINCIPAL WORKS: *Novels*—Barn Blind, 1980; At Paradise Gate, 1981; Duplicate Keys, 1984; The Greenlanders, 1988; A Thousand Acres, 1991; Moo: A Novel, 1995. *Novellas*—Ordinary Love & Good Will, 1989. *Short stories*—The Age of Grief, 1987. *Nonfiction*—Catskill Crafts: Artisans of the Catskill Mountains, 1988.

ABOUT: Contemporary Authors New Revision Series 30, 1990; Current Biography Yearbook 1990. *Periodicals*—New Republic May 16, 1988; New York Review of Books August 10, 1995; New York Times October 31, 1991; March 21, 1995; April 22, 1995; New York Times Book Review August 17, 1980; November 22, 1981; April 28, 1984; September 6, 1987; May 15, 1988; November 5, 1989; November 3, 1991; Publishers Weekly April 1, 1988; Time November 11, 1991; Times Literary Supplement August 24, 1984; March 18, 1988; October 30, 1992; Women's Review of Books April 1990.

*SORESCU, MARIN (February 19, 1936–), Romanian poet, playwright, prose writer, and essayist, °° was born in the village of Bulzeşte in the province of Dolj, a mostly agricultural region in southern Romania due west of the capital, Bucharest, and bordering on the Danube. His father, Ştefan, a peasant who loved to read and also composed verse as an avocation, died at the age of forty-four when the future writer was three years old, leaving his mother, the former Nicoliţa Ionescu, with six children. Sorescu, the second youngest, attended primary school in his village and secondary schools first in Craiova, the closest city, then, after a post–

MARIN SORESCU

World War II educational reorganization, in a nearby village before finally transferring to a military school in Predeal in the Carpathian Mountains. There, for the first time, his aptitude for literature became recognized. From 1955 to 1960, he attended the University of Iaşi in northeastern Romania (Iaşi is the commercial and cultural center of Moldavia). In 1960, after first spending three years as a Russian language and literature major, he graduated with a degree in philology from the Romanian department, doing a diploma paper on the poetry of the highly influential 20th-century poet and man of letters Tudor Arghezi. At the university, Sorescu distinguished himself as a writer, making his debut in print in 1959 in the literary magazine *Viata studenteasca* (Student Life), for which he became an editor upon graduation and moved to Bucharest. The year after, Sorescu married Virginia Şeitan, and in 1963 he became editor of the important literary journal, *Luceafărul* (Lucifer); the Sorescus still live in Bucharest. In 1966, he became editor in chief at Animafilm Cinematographic Studios and in 1978 of the venerable review *Ramuri* (Branches). In 1990 he founded a new journal, *Literatorui* (The Writer), and became director of the Romanian Writer Publishing House.

The year 1964, which saw the publication of Sorescu's first book, *Singur printre poeţi* (Alone among poets), a volume of parodies and pastiches mostly written during his university years, ushered in a short burst of remarkable achievement both for Romanian literature in general and also for Sorescu, one of the young writers

°saw RES coo, mah REEN

most responsible for the creative outpouring. Among his most important books of poetry that followed in rapid succession are *Poeme* (Poems, 1965), *Moartea ceasului* (The Death of the Clock, 1966), *Tinereţea lui Don Quijote* (The Youth of Don Quixote, 1968), *Tuşiţi* (Cough, 1970), *Astfel* (And So, 1973), and *Suflete, bun la toate* (Soul, good for everything, 1972). Other notable Sorescu volumes include *La lilieci*, the peasant-dialect volumes of pastoral works about Romanian village life (To the lilacs, vols. 1–4, 1973, 1977, 1980, 1988), *Sărbători itinerante* (Itinerant feasts, 1978), *Fîntîni în mare* (Fountains in the sea, 1982), *Apă vie, apă moartă* (Water of life, water of death, 1987), *Ecuatorul şi polii* (The Equator and the poles, 1989), and *Poezii alese de cenzură (Poems selected by censorship, 1991).* The play *Iona* (*Jonah*), his first published theater piece, came out in book form in 1968, the year of its initial performance in Bucharest under Andrei Şerban (within four years, it had also been given in Paris, Munich, Zurich, Poland, and Finland), and Sorescu has published dramatic writing at a steady pace since, mostly in literary reviews. In 1974, five plays were collected under the title *Setea muntelui de sare* (The Thirst of the Salt Mountain), including *Iona* and *Paracliserul* (*The Verger*), which, with *Matca* (1975, *The Matrix*), form a trilogy which was published in England in 1985 under the same title as the 1978 Romanian collection. In 1980, the volume *Teatru* (Theater) included *Răceala* (A cold) and *A treia ţeapă* (The third stake), the former of which was published in a dual-language, Romanian–English volume in 1979, and the latter in English in 1987 as *Vlad Dracula the Impaler.* Sorescu's *Vărul Shakespeare* (Cousin Shakespeare), fragments of which had appeared in literary journals in 1988, was in rehearsal in Craiova at the time of the revolution in December 1989; it came out in book form with two other plays in 1993. Sorescu has also published two novels. In 1977 he published *Trei dinţi din faţă* (Three front teeth), a nearly 500-page volume despite some 150 pages having been cut by the censors, and in 1981, *Viziunea vizuinii* (The vision of the burrow). He has also published five collections of essays, including a prize-winning volume of criticism; a book of translations of Pasternak; and four works for children. There have been a number of selected editions of both poems and plays as well, and in 1990, the poet published volume 1 of a Definitive Edition of his works, *Poezii* (Poems). Two critical volumes on Sorescu have appeared in Romania.

Sorescu has traveled widely abroad for literary congresses and festivals; he has won residency fellowships in the Iowa International Writing Program, and literary awards not only in his native country (including Writer's Union Prizes for both poetry and drama and the Romanian Academy award) but also in Italy (the Gold Medal at Naples, 1970, and "Le Muze" prize in Florence, 1978), Spain ("Fernando Riello" poetry prize at Madrid, 1983), and Austria (Herder Prize, Vienna, 1991). He is a corresponding member of the Mallarmé Academy in Paris as well as a member of the Société des Auteurs Dramatiques et des Compositeurs there, and corresponding member of the Romanian Academy and the European Academy of Science, Art, and Humanities.

As a poet, Sorescu is best known for his teasing, ironic, sometimes resigned or melancholy, but nonetheless often charming parables and deadpan absurdities. His style is straightforward, largely antimetaphorical and antilyrical (though he has written a surprising number of formal, rhymed, sometimes sentimental short poems in regular stanza patterns). The surface of his poetry is cool in its emotion, at times minimalist, with a flat vocabulary that is not immune to colloquialisms and that one translator, Michael Hamburger, in the introduction to *Selected Poems* recognized as "transparent," "low-mimetic," and "deeply subversive of the attitudes of mind on which it usually rests." But the anecdotes and brief monologues that make up many of his poems turn, in a moment of surprise, into canny and suggestive extended metaphors and wry, fantastic allegories. In the introduction to *Let's Talk About the Weather*, the English poet Jon Silkin praised Sorescu's "metaphysical imagination" and "an unlikely coupling of this mode with sensuous power," noting the "purity of outline" of his imagery, which "has what Eliot in his remarks on Jonson's poetry termed 'profile.'" In his 1968 afterword to *The Youth of Don Quixote* Sorescu himself defined poetry's function most of all as a form of "knowledge": the writer, who "is either a thinker or nothing," dispenses what the poet called elsewhere "the bitter medicines of life." Sorescu's irony and satire frequently bear this out in the aim of their aesthetic play, which is intellectually rather than verbally stimulating; nonetheless, at its sharpest his work is much more than merely didactic. Indeed, in the surprising, often unsettling shifts and complex intersections of perspectives and the speaking persona's disingenuous, sophisticated simplicity, as Seamus Heaney noted in the introduction to *Hands Behind My Back*, most of all it gratifies: "It teaches and delights, but not in that order: the delight takes precedence."

This style, as Hamburger remarked, like that of many East European poets after World War II, represents a "clean break" with "Romantic-Symbolist assumptions." Superficially, it seems broadly surrealistic, but it aims at conscious truths, not the freeing of the subconscious. Its themes usually derive from the realms of the social, philosophical, and logically critical rather than amid buried psychological strata. Thus Sorescu's rebel Job, perhaps a kind of emblem of Romantic angst and inward suffering—

Covered with sores,
Far more sores than dung,
Though there was god's plenty of that, too,
Since he had picked the hugest dung heap

—is so comically pathetic that God, too (though perhaps only Job's echo) cannot help respond by questioning the source of his suffering. The poet's pervasive irony can be fierce and polemical in its unstated intentions, for which ambiguity and oblique implication are the opening toward publicly unutterable subtexts. Thus, in "Icarus," a modernization of a Greek tale, Sorescu's unheroic protagonist's fall, hardly tragic in image, is his nation's:

Our Icarus
Cannot fall from high above
(The ceiling will prevent him)
But when he does fall,
He goes straight to the heart of the problem.

And when a tearful Lazarus, "taking the trouble to die once more" in "The Ground," is horrified that he is to be buried again, it is hard not to read his horror as an unwillingness to be reborn in totalitarian Romania's soil, though the implications remain general and existential:

"By no means in the ground!"
He mumbled faintly.
"Anywhere you want, except in the ground."

"The ground brings you back to life!
It heaves you into life again,
It contrives somehow
To raise you from the dead!"

A central strategy of many East European writers was the protective coloration of indirection and seeming irrelevant fabulation. It is not for nothing that a primary inheritance for Sorescu was Romanian involvement in the European avant-garde so crucial to the surreal, to dada, and to the absurd (the writers Urmuz, Tristan Tzara, and Eugène Ionesco all were Romanian). Adam J. Sorkin, writing in the *Literary Review* on the importance of Sorescu's ironic postures as a model for dissidence under censorship, likened the poet's sardonic, parabolic conceits to the Soviet bloc's self-preservative, antigovernment humor: "They have the extreme compression of the best political jokes that circulated throughout the satellite nations—black humor for a black hole."

Both in what the poet Nina Cassian in *Parnassus* termed the "homeopathic pills" of Sorescu's corrective metaphysical wit and in his quiet, lyrical sensibility (which can seem almost as stealthy in its tenderness), the mark of a Sorescu poem is usually brevity. The poet himself has written "Poetry must be concise, almost algebraic." In speaking in particular about his major books of the middle to the late 1960s, which derived from a period of deep inward crisis during which he felt his inspiration at a halt, he again returned to this dictum: "The language is uncomplicated, almost algebraic, deprived of ornaments and 'poetic' words, because I simply had no intention of publishing these poems. I meant each of them to be a will." The legacy, however, is rich and varied. It ranges from cynicism and the direct railing at modernity in "We Never Wonder," where the opening jadedly exclaims,

We never wonder at anything anymore.
Wonder has finally been eliminated,
An atavism which brought us too near the ape. . . .

and the ending is openly sarcastic,

We never wonder at anything,
We're part of uninterrupted progress. . . .

to the comic multiplication of defamiliarized mythos and playful mockery at human nature in "Adam," where the first man imitates God as creator (not unlike a poet) and so enjoys making things, in this case new Eves from his ribs, "his intercostal seraglio," that

Then the Creator raised his eyebrows
At Adam's too handy fruitfulness.
He summoned him for sentencing, divinely gave him hell,
And purged him from Paradise
For the sin of surrealism.

It can span from depiction of the dead end of self-disdain in "The Snail," who "stares / Into himself" in "Cosmological disgust," to genuine celebration of vitality and nature's generation in "Leda," who sleeps with all "the world's things":

What an easy, splendid catch,
This Leda!
Ah, that's why the world itself
Stays so beautiful, so sweet.

Other poems present a rich and graceful homage to admired predecessors, celebrating in particular Shakespeare and Romania's great 19-century poet Mihai Eminescu in "Shakespeare" and "They Had to Have a Name," the latter one of the most famous recent poems in Romania. And as with his irony, the poet's sense of mystery can vary greatly—for example, from the troubling to the magical. In "Only Night," human beings "must take after the bats," for "The wings of the future beat / Only at night," but in "Like a Pastel," a muted love poem,

Trees sprout feathers in their roots,
Birds keep us in mind
In their flight through the air.

Poems like "Adam," "Leda," "Job," "Ulysses," "The Two Thieves" (who were beside "the Great thief," "the one in the middle") and "The Great Blind Man" (about Homer's reincarnation with a different talent that "Sets astir our blood," no longer bard but masseur) suggest in miniature some of Sorescu's major subjects in his plays, which in their greater thematic ambition transform amused, or bemused, incredulity and keen comic amazement into dismay and muted tragic wonder at life's woe. Cassian has distinguished the plays from the poetry: "Sorescu uses a lot of ideas in his poems, where he improvises, and in his plays, where he elaborates and achieves greater profundity." The critic Virgil Nemoianu, who places Sorescu in the dramatic tradition of Giraudoux and Christopher Fry, in the *Times Literary Supplement* found his "cleverly balanced" reactions to his world and its terrors (both existential terrors, those of the human condition, and more local ones, those of the police state) at their best in the plays, which he terms "masterpieces of allusion and adroit manoeuvring." Indeed, except for one episode in 1981 when he was sentenced to three months of house arrest following the Ceauşescu dictatorship's decision that the transcendental meditation movement was a plot against the state, Sorescu remained out of trouble with the political regime, neither falling into sycophantism and servility, nor gambling on open protest and resistance. His technique of displacing the contemporary into the historical and mythical (both biblical and classical) was both a defense and, more to the point, stimulation to his imagination. In the playwright's preface to *Vlad Dracula the Impaler*, Sorescu comments: "For the dramatist, history is like a bone to a dog. It arouses that state of covetous exaltation, the eyes grow larger at such a heap of facts and ready-made dramas, all senses are alerted. Inspiration wets the lips and wags its tail; the marrow of life stands before it—enticing it."

"Man is matter and nature is—history," says The Turk, who with The Romanian is one of the two impaled victims (or, it is suggested, a succession of interchangeable victims) who open the play, at the close of which Prince Vlad has a third, huge stake erected between the two, who are still waiting to die at the end of act 5. At the play's end, Vlad, about to impale himself on the third stake, and recognizing his own cruelty, which he attributes to the nature of the times, speaks of his entrapment in what the author called in his preface "[t]he chain of symmetries and asymmetries" of history and politics, as well as his mixed innocence ("everything I did was for the good of the country") and guilt ("I've dispensed justice in this country in great detail. Only one remained unpunished"). His death is a self-sacrifice, a self-crucifixion for a people who are themselves trapped in the unmotivated terror of history. Dennis Deletant insists in his introduction that Sorescu's Vlad Dracula has nothing to do with Bram Stoker's, and Western popular culture's, vampire. Sorescu's Vlad is strongly based in historical fact, but the character is rendered complicated. His savagery, in which he gloats at first, is not the play's subject, but more like a sign of (or tragic flaw engendering) his downfall as part of historical and plot necessity. As a whole, Deletant notes, the play becomes "an allegory for the fear and fatalism that characterises the Romanians"—the latter element of cultural character placing the work in the context of a long tradition of stories going back through national folklore to ballads such as the "Mioriţa" (The ewe-lamb).

Marguerite Dorian in *World Literature Today* observed that Vlad Dracula is one of the writer's "gallery of heroes, stemming from a philosophical family of defeated rebels who leave behind them the open wound of their existence and a painful immortality that haunts us." The three earlier plays that makes up the trilogy *The Thirst of the Salt Mountain* are thus about what the author calls "an immense abstract thirst." In these monodramas, he notes, "My characters are irrevocably contemplative, forever unprotected in life, entirely unarmed from a pragmatic point of view." In *Jonah*, the title character, in the belly of the whale, tries to cut his way out only to find the whale swallowed by another, bigger whale, "an endless row of bellies"; in the end, he must slice open his own gut in order to attain freedom. In *The Verger*, the play Sorescu considered "closest" to him, the verger climbs scaffolding in his insane, self-appointed task of blackening—historicizing—the walls of the new cathedral. If Jonah's search is "on the horizontal," the verger's is "on the vertical," but in the end he is destroyed, too, in self-immolation. The heroine in *The Matrix*, Irina, transcends both death (of her father, then her own implicit demise) and flood with the act of birth and, in the heavily symbolic conclusion, mounting the coffin and raising her infant above the water just about to drown her.

Marin Sorescu continues to be a productive, popular, and always interesting writer, with an increasingly international profile. Seamus Heaney pointed out that, behind Sorescu's "throwaway charm and poker-faced subversiveness, . . . there is a persistent solidarity with the unregarded life of the ordinary citizen, a willingness to remain at eye-level and on speaking terms with common experience and to salute the stamina that goes into maintaining individual identity and self-respect in the very humblest of people." In a similar vein, Nemoianu wrote in the *Times Literary Supplement* that Sorescu "represents the voice of a community," one that "has had to respond to sore trials and pressures without recourse to heroics. . . . "

In the 1990s, in a second public career, Sorescu has begun to flower as a painter. He had been working seriously for at least a decade, particularly since the brief period in the early 1980s during which he could not publish. Recently, he has had one-man exhibitions in museums in major Romanian cities. In 1993, Sorescu joined the government as minister of culture.

PRINCIPAL WORKS IN ENGLISH TRANSLATION: *Poetry*—(tr. R. MacGregor-Hostie) Rame / Frames (bilingual ed.), 1972; (tr. S. Deligiorgis) Postface from Tinereţea lui Don Quijote *in* 46 Romanian Poets in English, 1973; (tr. S. Deligiorgis) Don Quijote's Tender Years, 1979; (tr. M. Hamburger) This Hour (chapbook), 1982; (tr. J.R. Colombo and P. Negoşanu) Symmetrics, 1982; (tr. M. Hamburger) Marin Sorescu: Selected Poems, 1983; (tr. A. Deletant and B. Walker) Let's Talk About the Weather . . . and Other Poems (intro. J. Silkin), 1985; (tr. D. Constantine et al.) The Biggest Egg in the World, 1987; (tr. J. Deane) The Youth of Don Quixote, 1987; (tr. G. Dragnea, S. Friebert, and A. Varga) Hands Behind My Back: Selected Poems (intro. S. Heaney), 1991. *Drama*—(tr. S. Deligiorgis) Răceala / A Cold (bilingual ed.), 1978; (tr. A. Deletant and B. Walker) Jonah, The Verger, and The Matrix *in* The Thirst of the Salt Mountain, 1985; (tr. D. Deletant) Vlad Dracula the Impaler (intro. D. Deletant), 1987.

ABOUT: Contemporary World Writers, 2nd ed., 1993. *Periodicals*—Concerning Poetry Fall 1984; Literary Review Fall 1991; Parnassus: Poetry in Review 1993; Times Literary Supplement May 18, 1994; October 9–15, 1987; World Literature Today Winter 1985; Spring 1988; Winter 1989.

SPACKMAN, W(ILLIAM) M(ODE) (May 20, 1905–August 3, 1990), American novelist and literary critic, was born in Coatesville, Pennsylvania, the son of George Harvey Spackman, an executive, and Alice Pennock (Mode) Spackman. As a Princeton undergraduate he was editor of the *Nassau Literary Magazine*, but was

removed from that post when the university president deemed his Joycean prose "sacrilegious and obscene." Graduating cum laude in 1927, Spackman went on to Balliol College, Oxford University, as a Rhodes scholar, and later returned to Princeton to earn an M.A. After a brief stint as an instructor of classics at New York University (1930–1931), he was a copywriter and account executive for various New York public relations firms, a radio writer, and a Rockefeller Fellow in opinion research at Columbia University. From the late 1930s until 1953, he was associated with the University of Colorado, Boulder, first as director of public information and then as an assistant professor of classics. Thereafter he devoted himself to literary work and architecture, a lifelong avocation. He spent his later years in Princeton, New Jersey, dying there of cancer at the age of eighty-five.

Spackman's literary career was an unusual one. He was nearly fifty years old when he published his first novel, *Heyday*; by the time his second novel appeared, twenty-five years later, he was over seventy. And although he went on to complete only a handful of novels—most of them quite brief—he earned critical acclaim (fervent, if not widespread) as a distinctive and accomplished prose stylist. In 1984 the American Academy and Institute of Arts and Letters presented him with the Howard D. Vursell Memorial Award for "work that merits recognition for the quality of its prose style." Spackman once remarked that his "only real literary interest [was] the high-style novel." Aesthetic considerations—attention to language, structure, and style—always take precedence over ideas, plot, and character in Spackman's novels. Usually considered a novelist of manners, he concentrates above all on the romantic obsessions and foibles of the rich and wellborn. His lush, carefully constructed, often formidable prose is infused with classical allusions and untranslated snippets of Latin, Greek, French, and Italian. A "classicist," he wrote in his acknowledgements to his collection of essays, *On the Decay of Humanism*, "would not have to deface his pages with translation if the world were properly run. . . . "

In *Heyday*, published in the 1950s but set primarily in the 1930s, Spackman pays tribute to his own generation, whose young adulthood coincided with the Great Depression. Comparing the intent of his novel with that of F. Scott Fitzgerald's short story "Babylon Revisited," Spackman called *Heyday* "the spiritual biography of a generation, . . . a statement about the young American upper class in that era of its disaster, the 1930s." The novel's narrator, Webb Fletcher, is, like Spackman, a member of the Princeton class of 1927. His reminiscences, many of them centering on erotic adventures in Greenwich Village, are touched off when he learns of the death, in World War II combat, of his cousin and classmate Mike Fletcher.

Reviewers' reactions to the novel were mixed. In a mostly favorable review of *Heyday* in *Commonweal*, William Pfaff noted that, for the most part, "the story is an impassioned involvement in the past, sometimes quite moving, sometimes just a bit silly. It is quite erotic, . . . occasionally to a faintly absurd degree. And it is always very readable." In the *Saturday Review*, James Kelly praised the novel but found that it did not live up to its "elaborate intentions": "If Max Bodenheim, Scott Fitzgerald, and Ezra Pound had at one time pooled their forces (shocking thought) to write a definitive Depression Novel, the chances are it would have turned out something like this parodiable amalgam of classical allusions, large social observations, and explicit sexual vignettes. As a one-man tour de force, *Heyday* is remarkable." Nonetheless, Kelly insisted, "It is not enough. . . . His people have small significance beyond their assigned roles as erotic symbols."

An Armful of Warm Girl, Spackman's second novel, takes place in 1959 and recounts the amorous and gustatory adventures of Nicholas Romney, a well-heeled, fifty-year-old Philadelphia banker whose wife suddenly and unexpectedly has requested a divorce. Leaving his palatial Pennsylvania estate in disgust, Nicholas goes to New York and sets about wooing Victoria, a married woman with whom he had an affair some seventeen years earlier. Nicholas is in turn himself wooed by Morgan, a twenty-year-old actress who may or may not be his illegitimate daughter. Only slightly younger than the protagonists of *Heyday* (he is a member of the Princeton class of '31), Nicholas has impeccably refined tastes in art, cuisine, and literature. He lunches on such delicacies as "glazed crème de cervelle" and recites Ovidian couplets in Latin. Essentially, he is a civilized libertine. Moral conflict, or any search for "answers," is alien to him. Driving to Boston to visit his son, Nicholas muses:

What was this business of homilies anyhow but mankind's fatuous and age-old yearning for the Book of Answers! There never had been answers; never would be; merely a linguistic mistake of Greek philosophy's we'd taken over, that if the word existed the thing it denoted existed too. Why, the only serious desiderata for a normal Indo-European are a pretty girl within grabbing range, a dazing drink, and somebody to knock down. Hymns of self-praise or self-pity on these topics are standard too, being in fact our literature. But answers, no.

"At last," Frances Taliaferro wrote in a *Harper's* review of *An Armful of Warm Girl*, "after all the novels of fornication, a novel of seduction. The title is far too cute for the contents: Spackman is a very Fabergé among novelists, and this novel is not fluffy but mannered, elegant, enameled." Hailing Nicholas Romney as "the most original literary creation of the decade," Taliaferro concluded, "Only a barbarous Boeotian could fail to be tickled by the amorous intricacies of this delightful book." Hardly less enthusiastic about the novel was *New York Times* (1978) reviewer John Leonard, who wrote that "not much happens in *An Armful of Warm Girl*, and yet everything happens: romance, wit, intelligence, geniality, culture without the politics that spoiled it after 1959, sex without tears, [and] a genuinely lovable character. . . ."

An Armful of Warm Girl established Spackman's literary reputation, and set the tone for his subsequent novels. A love triangle, involving two women and one man, is a recurrent motif in his fiction. *A Presence with Secrets* again focuses on the lives and loves of a wealthy libertine—Hugh Tatnall, a famous American painter living in Florence. Jean Strouse wrote in *Newsweek*, "A sense of humor about sex is a rare thing in contemporary writing, and Spackman drenches these dalliances in laughter and light." *Village Voice* reviewer Edmund White made a similar observation: "Spackman's lovers do not suffer. . . . [his] characters reveal what people feel when love is free, uncoded."

A Difference of Design, Spackman's fourth novel, is explicitly modeled on Henry James's *The Ambassadors*. The protagonist, Sather (reminiscent of James's Strether), is a wealthy middle-aged American businessman sent to Paris by a mother who fears her son is too deeply involved with a Frenchwoman. In the course of the novel, two women, both in their twenties, fall madly in love with Sather. Even while praising Spackman's sensuous, finely crafted language, a number of reviewers faulted the book's lack of passion. The "real shortcoming" of the novel, according to Guy Davenport in the *Sewanee Review*, "is that it dispenses with . . . the very quality that makes James's version of the story so powerful: a sense of the conflict between the potential individual destinies of the Americans in Europe and the mundane social destinies designed for them by the American back home. There simply are no individual personalities in the book capable of engaging the interest of a mature reader."

In the *New York Times* (1983), Anatole Broyard conceded that "[e]verybody seems to admire W. M. Spackman's novels," but added that "his love lacks the sadness and pain that makes us believe in it." Stephen Koch observed in the *Washington Post Book World* (1983): "I have no objection to . . . Spackman finding his poetry in the lightweight language of the upper crust, but as his reputation grows, I think the shallowness of his sources is worth noting. . . . Finally this gossamer has been spun from little more than the asinine lockjaw drawls of Muffy and Wingate III. If it is high style, it it also high Prep." Comparing Spackman, somewhat invidiously, with Nabokov, Koch further noted: "People die in Nabokov. In Spackman, all adored, they drift. . . . to my mind [Spackman's novel] lacks passion, and lacking passion, truth."

Love affairs are again at the center of the short comic novel *A Little Decorum, for Once*, the last of Spackman's works to appear during his lifetime. Observing that the novel is "virtually plotless," Christopher Schemering wrote in the *Washington Post Book World* (1985): "Spackman . . . is such an eccentric stylist that he may be considered an acquired taste. . . . The characters' exchanges are so long and dense and intricate that it's easy to get lost in all the verbal haranguing." Wendy Lesser's remarks in the *New York Times Book Review* might be applied to any of Spackman's fictions: "Reading *A Little Decorum, for Once* is a bit like sitting in a cafe and overhearing a rather pretentious but nonetheless fascinating conversation at the next table. On the one hand, you can't believe that people really talk like that. On the other, you're thrilled at having acquired this stolen bit of 'real life.'"

PRINCIPAL WORKS: *Novels*—Heyday, 1953; An Armful of Warm Girl, 1978; A Presence with Secrets, 1980; A Difference of Design, 1983; A Little Decorum, for Once, 1985. *Essays*—On the Decay of Humanism, 1967.

ABOUT: Contemporary Authors 81–84, 1979; 132, 1991; Contemporary Literary Criticism 46, 1988. *Periodicals*—Commonweal March 27, 1953; Harper's April 1978; High Plains Literary Review Spring 1989; Los Angeles Times August 10, 1990; New York Times April 10, 1978; June 16, 1983; August 9, 1990; New York Times Book Review October 20, 1985; Newsweek January 12, 1981; Saturday Review February 21, 1953; Sewanee Review Winter 1984; Village Voice January 14–20, 1981; Washington Post August 11, 1990; Washington Post Book World August 14, 1983; November 10, 1985.

SPURLING, HILARY (FORREST) (December 25, 1940–), British biographer, critic, and editor, was born in Stockport, England, the daughter of G. A. Forrest, a judge, and E. M. Armstrong Forrest, a teacher. After receiving her bachelor's degree from Somerville College, Oxford, in 1962, she worked for the *Spectator* as arts editor and theater critic from 1964 to 1970 and as literary editor from 1966 to 1970. Since 1970 she has been a free-lance writer. She married John Spurling, a playwright, on April 4, 1961; they have three children.

Although she has a variety of titles to her credit, Spurling's most important accomplishments thus far have been two literary biographies, which she skillfully researched and wrote. The first of these has as its subject the idiosyncratic English novelist Ivy Compton-Burnett and was published in England in two volumes: *Ivy When Young: The Early Life of I. Compton-Burnett, 1884–1919* in 1974 and *Secrets of a Woman's Heart: The Later Life of I. Compton-Burnett, 1920–1969* in 1984. The American edition includes both volumes under the title *Ivy: The Life of I. Compton-Burnett*. The title of the second of these literary biographies, published in England in 1990 as *Paul Scott: A Life*, was lengthened in the American edition to *Paul Scott: A Life of the Author of the Raj Quartet* in 1991, in recognition of the great popularity of the television series dramatizing these novels, *The Jewel in the Crown*. So anxious was the American firm of W. W. Norton to publish this second biography that, as its editor reported, "we bought this work before we saw one word on paper—not even a proposal." The finished product, she said, "more than fulfilled my expectations."

Despite the vast disparity between them in almost all respects, including the matter and style of their individual works, the subjects of the two biographies presented a similar challenge to their biographer—both Ivy Compton-Burnett and Paul Scott led lives outwardly dull and without interest to the general reader. To illustrate, the setting of the second half of Compton-Burnett's biography, from 1920 to her death in 1969, remains, with very few and brief interruptions, the austere flat in Braemar Mansions in South Kensington where she lived with her companion Margaret Jourdain and wrote her claustrophobic novels. In refusing to write her memoirs, she offered this justification: "I have had such an uneventful life that there is little to say."

Paul Scott's life had, for the most part, the same sedentary character. Aside from his three years in India during World War II, when he served as an officer in the air supply branch of the Indian army, Paul Scott seldom left London

HILARY SPURLING

and never moved more than a few miles from the modest house in which he was born in 1920. Despite marked literary and academic talents, he was forced by his family's financial straits to leave school at the age of fourteen and go to work as an accountant. Upon leaving the army he resumed the life of a businessman in order to support his wife and two daughters, working first for a publishing firm and then as a literary agent. Meanwhile, at the expense of his family life, he subjected himself to the hard discipline of learning the craft of writing in his spare time; not until 1960, at the age of forty, did he cut himself free from all other professional responsibilities to devote himself single-mindedly to writing. He liked to quote Faulkner's comment that the biography of a novelist should consist of just seven words: "He wrote the novels and he died."

Reviewers agreed that Spurling has succeeded in making these two lives of absorbing interest to even the casual reader. In his review of the second volume of the Compton-Burnett biography in the *Times Literary Supplement*, A. N. Wilson wrote of Spurling: "She has made one of the most fascinating of modern biographies out of what must have been one of the most boring of all modern lives." Gabrielle Annan, in the *New York Review of Books*, described the biography as capable of being read "purely for pleasure and almost as a novel—a Victorian novel . . . It is a marvelous book, intelligent, gripping, funny, and fastidiously well written." After confessing herself no fan of Ivy Compton-Burnett, Joyce Carol Oates, in the *New York*

Times Book Review, nevertheless hailed Spurling's biography as "wonderfully readable."

Of the Paul Scott biography, reviewers had much the same thing to say. Kennedy Fraser wrote in his *New Yorker* review that "in many ways, this biography reads like a novel." J.K. L. Walker, in the *Times Literary Supplement* (1990), suggested that the biography can be "read as either an exemplary or a cautionary tale of a writer's life. That Scott's personal dramas were largely internal and on the face of it drably domestic makes the success of this biography all the more noteworthy."

Though both subjects presented their biographer with puzzles that needed to be resolved in the telling of their stories, these puzzles arose for different reasons. As Ivy Compton-Burnett's biographer, Spurling had to contend with a serious lack of her subject's personal papers, journals, or diaries. After describing her as the "English Secret," Joyce Carol Oates explains: "When she died at the age of 85, in 1969, her personal papers filled only half a shoebox—and were not very personal at that." In addition, Compton-Burnett, who was well known for being uncommunicative as well as for frustrating her admirers with banal conversation, often made misleading and unreliable references to her past, which it became her biographer's duty to clarify and correct. For example, Spurling makes it clear that she was not descended from the 17th-century divine Gilbert Burnet, bishop of Salisbury; that the Compton-Burnetts were not landed gentry but farm laborers; that her physician father could not have studied in Vienna with Freud because the founder of psychoanalysis was only nine at the time; that there was no basis for Compton-Burnett's blaming her unsatisfactory first novel *Dolores* on the interference of her brother Noel. Spurling used as source material for the first volume of her biography the account of their lives given from memory by Ivy's two surviving sisters, which she obtained in personal conversations with them. Though Spurling had access to the accounts of numerous witnesses of Compton-Burnett's later life, she found their impressions often vague and contradictory. As a result, Spurling concluded that "the only hope of solving the many puzzles . . . lay in some attempt to see what Ivy saw in her own heart." As Gabrielle Annan observed in her review, "Spurling set out to discover what it was by relating the life to the work," quoting "so much and so well that one gets a Compton-Burnett anthology thrown in with the life." However, Spurling did not read the novels for information about what really happened in Compton-Burnett's life; this would have been pointless in any case since, as A. N. Wilson explained, in Compton-

Burnett "the habits of distortion, affectation, and creation were ingrained." On the contrary, Spurling shows convincingly that her fiction was not based on her life, but that she often lifted her plots from trashy late-Victorian novels. Nor does she attempt to identify the characters with real life people, an identification that Compton-Burnett would seem to have forbidden with the comment: "People in life hardly seem to be definite enough to appear in print." Instead, the use that Spurling makes of Compton-Burnett's fiction is to evoke from it, with great sensitivity, her thoughts and feelings, and in this way she succeeds in re-creating "what Ivy saw in her own heart."

Like Ivy Compton-Burnett's, Paul Scott's life was relatively featureless. Unlike Compton-Burnett, however, the intensely private Paul Scott left a rich legacy of personal papers and more than 6,000 letters. Exploring this resource, in which Scott expressed the emotions he failed to express in direct, personal contact with people, Spurling found herself once again puzzled, particularly as she found traces of an aspect of Scott's life that he had kept carefully hidden, even from his family. She described her discovery to Chris Goodrich in an interview in *Publishers Weekly*: "It was a series of shocks. I had been told his life was too dull to write, but the more I found out about [his sexuality], the harder it was to avoid." The need to confirm her suspicion of Scott's homosexuality took Spurling to Tasmania to visit an old friend of Scott's; there they "talked all day for two weeks," and she read still another cache of Scott's letters. Once she had established his homosexuality and identified the incident that forced him to suppress it, Spurling confronted the puzzle of Scott's lifelong preoccupation with India. Ultimately she was able to see Scott's homosexuality as crucial to his art and its suppression as coloring his life and determining his view of the relationship between colonizer and colonized in Anglo-India. As Michael Gorra wrote of *The Raj Quartet* in the *New Republic*, Scott presented, through the British officer Ronald Merrick, a repressed homosexual, his view of the British rule in India as "the repressed homoeroticism of empire." This sexual repression emerges as sadism in the behavior of the racist Merrick, and since he represents the Raj, it is as a sadistic, racist exercise of power that Scott identifies the British presence in India, thus indicting the British for the moral failure to govern India with justice and to relinquish the reins of government to the Indians in a responsible way. Gorra identifies Spurling's uncovering of this connection between Scott's sensibility and his Indian subject as her greatest achievement. As Spurling described Scott's sensibility, "He un-

derstood both the authoritarian and the suppressed, the bully and the victim, and he understood it in his heart."

A few reviewers of these biographies had reservations. Julian Symons, in the *London Review of Books*, found the Scott biography "much too long." Kennedy Fraser faulted Spurling for her "failure to understand that the disease of alcoholism" was responsible for Scott's destructive behavior toward his family. Michael Gorra suggested: "It's one of Spurling's few weaknesses that she says little about Scott's reading," while claiming that Scott became a "formidably knowledgeable Imperial historian." Nigel Cross wrote in the *New Statesman*: "If Hilary Spurling has a fault, it is in glossing over this negative reaction of [the critics] which might have helped to explain Ivy Compton-Burnett's enduring lack of popularity." Joyce Carol Oates expressed a regret that Spurling "avoids entirely an analysis of English literary politics." Gabrielle Annan in the *New York Review of Books* complained that the biography of Compton-Burnett contains too much detail about the antecedents of figures of minor importance.

Despite these qualifications, the overall judgment of Spurling's work remains that expressed by Mollie Panter-Downes in the *New Yorker* in 1985: "exhaustive, brilliant biography."

PRINCIPAL WORKS: *Biography*—Ivy: The Life of I. Compton-Burnett, 1984 (in U.K.: published as 2 vols.: Ivy When Young: The Early Years of I. Compton-Burnett, 1884–1919 *and* Secrets of a Woman's Heart: The Later Life of I. Compton-Burnett, 1920–1969); Paul Scott: A Life of the Author of the Raj Quartet, 1991 (in U.K.: Paul Scott: A Life). *Nonfiction*—Handbook to Anthony Powell's Music of Time, 1977; Elinor Fettiplace's Receipt Book: Elizabethan Country House Cooking, 1986. *As editor*—Mervyn Peake: Drawings, 1974.

ABOUT: Contemporary Authors New Revision Series 25, 1989; International Authors and Writers, 1986; 1989; Who's Who, 1985; 1988; Writers' Directory, 1986; 1988. *Periodicals*—London Review of Books July 19–August 1, 1984; October 25, 1990; New Republic May 20, 1991; New Statesman June 15, 1984; New Statesman and Society November 2, 1990; New York Review of Books December 20, 1984; New York Times Book Review December 9, 1984; June 23, 1991; New Yorker November 4, 1985; 1991; Publishers Weekly March 1, 1991; Times Literary Supplement June 8, 1984; November 2, 1990.

STERN, DANIEL (January 18, 1928–), American novelist and essayist, writes: "I was born in New York City, on the Lower East Side. My mother was born in New York, my father was an immigrant from Hungary. My father

DANIEL STERN

loved music and used to stand in line for hours to get into the Metropolitan Opera, only to stand through an entire performance. So it is not surprising that I was given music lessons; the cello was the instrument. It took me to the High School of Music and Art and on the road with Charlie Parker right after graduation. I skipped college and became a musician.

"I then did a one-year stint in the army, though World War II had ended, and when I came back I joined the Indianapolis Symphony Orchestra. There, I rented a room in the home of an old woman, a Christian Scientist. I was lonely and out of my loneliness I began to write short stories. When I returned to New York at the end of the orchestra's season my uncle, a dentist who played the viola and wrote short stories, suggested I join him in taking a course in short story writing at the New School for Social Research. The first story I read aloud, called "Conversation in Prague" (I had never been to Prague) received loud applause from the class. After that, I never looked back. I switched to a course in novel writing and began my first novel. The teacher was also editor-in-chief of Bobbs-Merrill publishers, and he accepted the book for publication. I was twenty years old and, now committed to being a serious writer, I gave up being a professional musician. My second novel was published while I was on a Huntington Hartford fellowship in California. My third novel, *Miss America*, was published by Random House. It has been optioned for motion pictures many times, but the film has never been made.

"All this time I was teaching myself the craft of fiction writing. By the time the 1960s arrived I had also taken up writing advertising copywriting to earn a living.

"I wrote a novel about Holocaust survivors, *Who Shall Live, Who Shall Die*, which was published by Crown Publishers in 1963. (In 1975 this book won the International Prix du Souvenir, given by the Bergen Belsen society and awarded by Elie Wiesel, chairman of the prize jury.) I count this as the beginning of my serious writing. 1963 was an important year for me: I was married to Gloria Branfman in November of that year. In 1968 I adopted her son, Eric.

"From 1963 through 1969 I had a rapid rise in advertising, from copywriter to senior vice-president at McCann-Erickson, to worldwide vice-president of advertising and publicity for Warner Bros. motion pictures. This was also a very productive time for me as a writer. In 1967 my novel *After the War* was published, and *The Suicide Academy* was published in 1968.

"In 1969 a long romance with the academic world began when I was invited to Wesleyan University by Prof. Ihab Hassan, a critic with a great interest in postmodern fiction. I became a fellow of the Center for the Humanities and later was visiting Professor in Letters and English at the College of Letters.

"Two years later, having moved to Hollywood for the job with Warner Brothers, I completed *The Rose Rabbi*, a kind of sequel to *The Suicide Academy*, which McGraw-Hill published in 1970.

"The need to experiment with the conventional form of the novel came to me late: with my sixth and seventh novels, *The Suicide Academy* and *The Rose Rabbi*. This last was written while I was vice-president at Warner Bros., writing one page a day, relentlessly, regardless of the extreme pressures of the movie world.

"When I left that world, I began a novel dealing with it, *Final Cut*—begun in East Hampton, Long Island, after I left Hollywood, and finished in Paris where my wife and I went to live for that fall and winter. It was published in 1975 by Viking. I became vice-president of advertising and promotion for the CBS television network in 1979, and at that time completed my eighth novel, *An Urban Affair*—a return to the lyrical novel of ideas, which was published in 1980.

"Then, in 1986, I began writing a series of stories in a new form I called *Twice Told Tales* (after Hawthorne). In these stories I would take a major text of literature, psychology, or philosophy and weave a narrative in which the text played a central part. These were published in book form by the Paris Review Press and received enthusiastic reviews. Foreign rights were sold to France and Brazil. One novella in the collection, 'The Psychopathology of Everyday Life by Sigmund Freud: A Story,' received the John Train Humor award from the *Paris Review*. Another story, 'The Interpretaion of Dreams by Sigmund Freud: A Story,' won an O. Henry Award and was published in the *Best American Short Stories*, 1987. The entire collection won the 1990 Rosenthal award for literary distinction given by the American Academy and Institute of Arts and Letters.

"While working at a new job, director of humanities at the 92nd Street Y in New York, I persisted in this new form. I chose six other texts, as varied as 'A Hunger Artist,' by Franz Kafka, and *The Communist Manifesto*, by Karl Marx and Friedrich Engels, and wrote the sequel, *Twice Upon a Time*, which was published by W. W. Norton in 1992. The book was received even more enthusiastically than *Twice Told Tales*. One story' 'A Hunger Artist by Franz Kafka: A Story, won a second O. Henry award, and was nominated for the Magazine Association Awards for 1993, and selected for the Pushcart Prize Anthology. In 1992 I was appointed Distinguished Professor and holder of the Cullen Chair in English at the University of Houston."

Daniel Stern first earned widespread critical attention with his sixth novel, *The Suicide Academy*, an ambitious work combining realism and allegory. A private institution financed by contributions from its clients, the suicide academy of the title is in the business of providing one day of intensive counseling to those considering self-murder. The novel covers one eventful day in the life of the academy's director, Wolf Walker—a man peculiarly fitted to his task because of his upbringing among a rebel sect of Hasidic Jews, who revere the will of the individual above all other human attributes. In providing its services, the academy is supposed to remain neutral, counseling its clients on the pros and cons of suicide, but never intervening in their decision-making process. This aspect of the academy's mission is a persistent bone of contention between Walker and his assistant, an anti-Semitic black man named Gilliatt. Charging that Walker has consistently favored life over suicide, thus undercutting the academy's chief source of financing, Gilliatt has filed a number of formal complaints against his boss. Walker is beset by other problems as well: both his pregnant girlfriend and his ex-wife are contemplating suicide. By the end of the novel, the academy—set in a snow-drenched New England landscape—goes up in flames, while Walk-er, undeterred, announces his intention to found another academy elsewhere.

In his book *Contemporary American Literature, 1945–1972*, Ihab Hassan considers Stern's work in the context of the Jewish novel, noting that *The Suicide Academy* "creates a metaphor of the contemporary world, balanced intricately in the dance of affirmation and denial, hovering in the dialogue of Black and Jew. The atmosphere of 'para-reality,' funny and darkly scintillant, leaves the reader with a brilliant sense of himself." That sense of "para-reality" led others, such as Lucy Rosenthal in the *Washington Post Book World*, to deem *The Suicide Academy* "an anti-novel." Critical reaction to the novel seemed to vary in proportion to the reviewer's judgment as to how well Stern had melded allegorical themes and realistic prose narrative. In a glowing review in the *Village Voice* (and later in her collection *In Favor of the Sensitive Man*), Anaïs Nin wrote: "The novel leaps from metaphysics to pugilism, from literature to jealousy, from race prejudice to mythology, from mental acrobatics to physical exertion to sensual adventures, disguising wisdom under its agilities. The central juggler never misses." Hailing the novel as an "antidote" to the "plague of hatred" affecting American society, Nin concluded: "*The Suicide Academy* is ultimately the book of a poet, which means he flies at an altitude above the storms of destruction, above neutrality, above indifference, and therefore beyond death."

In the *Nation*, Shaun O'Connell wrote: "The leap from realism to allegory is often sudden, not always convincing. . . . Stern would have it both ways, but often his realism and allegory work to diminish each other." Acknowledging the centrality of suicide as a theme of contemporary literature, Richard Rhodes noted, in the *New York Times Book Review*, that "Stern deals with this theme in the abbreviated, allegorical manner of Jorge-Luis Borges and Samuel Beckett. . . . " But Rhodes, like O'Connell, found Stern's approach to his subject less than successful: "Where Borges is gnomic but lucid, Stern is private and opaque. . . . He never really establishes his academies as believable institutions. They are only stage sets, and stage sets cannot . . . stand for the human universe the academies are supposed to represent."

Stern won high praise for his novel *Final Cut*, in which Ezra Marks, a former Kennedy aide turned marketing and demographics whizz, goes to Hollywood to help determine the ultimate shape of a *Woodstock*-like documentary called "Festival." Calling it "a novel rich in theme and character," David Freeman noted, in the *New York Times Book Review* (1975), that "*Final Cut* is more complex than a roman à clef of the author's days at Warner Brothers. . . . Stern writes more from his insight than his own biography." In *Commonweal*, Robert Phillips remarked, "Stern, as many before him, employs Hollywood as a microcosm of the American dream gone wrong, of the debasement of art in favor of commerce."

Stern had already published nine novels before issuing his first collection of short fiction, *Twice Told Tales.* "With a bold and witty hand," Norma Rosen wrote in the *New Leader,* "Stern weaves his stories in and about the imprint of their famous predecessors, allowing his themes of illusion and reality, displacement and recovery, to ricochet in countless ironies off the originals." In the *North American Review*, Perry Glasser observed: "Daniel Stern is not writing derivative work. All these stories are insightful, engaging, tales that take off from their namesakes with complete originality." Like *Final Cut* and some of Stern's other works, the stories in *Twice Told Tales* are concerned with the problematic nature of the artist's role in a society ruled by commercial imperatives. As Ann Arensberg wrote in the *New York Times Book Review* (1989): "When art has become peripheral to profits, how, [Stern] asks, does an artist, in particular a writer, stay on course and keep the faith?"

Attempting to answer this question, Stern first refers the reader back to an earlier, perhaps more innocent time, before the American literary scene had been thoroughly corrupted by commerce. In the collection's opening piece, "The Liberal Imagination by Lionel Trilling: A Story," Katherine Eudemie, a young novelist from the Midwest, enamored above all with the New York Jewish literati, immerses herself in Trilling's salon. Despite the stunning success of her first novel and her one produced play, Eudemie is unable to get any of her subsequent work published; she plunges into a deep depression, and eventually kills herself. Katherine Eudemie reappears in the collection's final story, "The Psychopathology of Everyday Life by Sigmund Freud," in which she will die of cancer rather than by her own hand. Still frustrated by her failure to publish a second novel, she is now studying to become a therapist. With increasing frequency, she begins committing a series of what Freud termed "parapraxes," small slips or errors which reveal an individual's true unconscious desires. First she leaves her copy of Freud's famous book in the restaurant she frequents—a New York literary hangout called the Russian Rendezvous. Next, it is her four-year-old daughter, Tulip, whom she leaves behind in the restaurant's cloak room. Abandoned by her mother, the child takes up residence in the Russian Rendezvous, where she receives French lessons from Eugène Ionesco, dancing instruction from Balanchine, and soon becomes the darling of many of the other regulars.

In the *New York Times Book Review*, Ann Arensberg expressed surprise that *Twice Told Tales* was Stern's first short story collection, noting that "the short form seems to be an ideal showcase for his dramatic gifts: his flair for dialogue and scene-crafting and his talent for infusing satire with mercy. . . . Literary life, according to Mr. Stern's reckoning, may have collapsed in the mid-1970s. But he holds out hope that the virus of integrity continues to breed underneath the rubble."

Twice Upon a Time, Stern's second collection of stories, was also well received. Judith Dunford wrote, in the *New York Times Book Review*, that "he snakes the inspiring story in and out of his own fiction, uses it to color the situation, makes the story itself a character as well as a metaphor. . . . Stern's stories have powerful endings. Like the musician he is . . . , he can draw everything together to swell into a resounding coda. In the silence that follows, you can hear the sound of your own pulse."

PRINCIPAL WORKS: *Novels*—The Girl with the Glass Heart, 1953; The Guests of Fame, 1955; Miss America, 1959; Who Shall Live, Who Shall Die, 1963; After the War, 1967; The Suicide Academy, 1968; The Rose Rabbi, 1971; Final Cut, 1975; An Urban Affair, 1980. *Short stories*—Twice Told Tales, 1989; Twice Upon a Time, 1992.

ABOUT: Contemporary Authors New Revision Series 5, 1982; Hassan, I. Contemporary American Literature, 1945–1972: An Introduction, 1973; Nin, A. In Favor of the Sensitive Man and Other Essays, 1976; Who's Who in America 1992–1993. *Periodicals*—Commonweal June 20, 1975; Nation October 21, 1968; New Leader May 15–29, 1989; New York Times Book Review October 6, 1968; May 18, 1975; June 18, 1989; September 27, 1992; North American Review December 1990; Village Voice October 10, 1968; Washington Post Book World September 1, 1968.

STORR, (CHARLES) ANTHONY (May 18, 1920–   ), British psychiatrist and writer on psychology, was born in Bentley, England, the son of Vernon, a clergyman and official of Westminster Cathedral, and Katherine Storr. He attended Winchester College, a distinguished private school, and studied medicine at Christ's College, Cambridge University, and the Westminster Hospital Medical School in London. After qualifying as a physician he trained as a psychiatrist at the Maudsley Hospital in London. Between 1947 and his retirement from practice in 1984

ANTHONY STORR

he served in a succession of posts in London and Oxford, and also maintained a private practice between 1950 and 1974. He was a lecturer in psychiatry at Oxford University between 1974 and 1984 and has served as a consultant in psychiatry and psychotherapy to the Oxford Health Authority. He is a fellow of Green College, Oxford University, a fellow of the Royal Society of Literature, and a member of the New York Academy of Sciences. Storr's first marriage, in 1942 to Catherine Cole, by whom he has three daughters, ended in divorce. He married Catherine Barton (née Peters), a lecturer in English at Somerville College, Oxford University, in 1970.

In addition to his active career as a practicing and teaching psychiatrist, Anthony Storr's writing on the nature of the mind has made a major contribution to the psychological study of human achievement in the arts and sciences. His earliest books—on the personality, sexual deviation, aggression, and destructive impulses—all written while working in the field of mental health, were primarily aimed at an audience of medical professionals, but his study of the creative process *The Dynamics of Creation*, published in 1972, and his brief summary of the work of Jung in the following year presage his work for the general reader written since his retirement from practice in 1984. Storr's later writing is notable for the insight he brings to subjects that have formerly been the province of literary critics, historians, and philosophers. His books on Jung and Freud elucidate the celebrated disagreement between the two founding fathers of modern psychology; *Solitude* (or *The School of Genius*) discusses the solitary nature of individual creativity and fulfillment; and the collection of essays *Churchill's Black Dog* takes up the question "What internal dynamic forces impel men and women to devote so much time and energy to creative invention?" Extending a train of thought begun in the essay "The Psychology of Symbols," which appeared in *Churchill's Black Dog*, Storr, an amateur musician, has also tackled the notoriously difficult problem of the relation between music and meaning in *Music and the Mind*.

Storr's early training in medical science is the foundation of his inquiries, but the insights that he brings to personality from a psychological perspective are invariably tentative and avoid the dogmatism and tendentiousness that he attributes to Freud's interpretations of the etiology of neuroses. He is sympathetic to Freud's efforts to instate psychoanalytical procedure as a scientific discipline but firmly believes, as he writes in the essay "Why Psychoanalysis Is Not a Science":

> Although some of the hypotheses of psychoanalysis can be treated scientifically, that is, subjected to objective assessment and proved or disproved in the same fashion as scientific hypotheses in other fields, this is only true of a minority. For most of the hypotheses of psychoanalysis are based upon observations made during the course of psychoanalytic treatment, and psychoanalytic treatment cannot be regarded as a scientific procedure.

Storr dismisses the claims of psychoanalysis to represent empirical truth but has a profound regard for it as an interpretive system that can assist people to make sense of their own lives. He stresses, therefore, in his commentary on Freud, that it was not Freud's objective to "cure" his patients, but rather to use their cases as evidence to support his ideas. Storr makes clear when writing on Freud and Jung that both men devised their methods of psychological analysis in order to make sense of their own lives and that both should therefore be regarded as creators of interpretive, heuristic systems rather than as scientists. Although psychoanalysis is not a "hard" science, Storr adds, "this does not mean it should be dismissed as hopelessly subjective." He concluded that "the practice of psychoanalysis demands of the analyst all the intuitive, empathic understanding which he can muster."

One of the most important tasks that Storr sets himself as an interpreter of personality and commentator on psychoanalytic theory is to dispel the commonly held notion that psychoanalysis offers any kind of objective truth. He believes that Freud's insistence that his work was scientific was unfortunate, and points out that the development of his ideas was probably distorted by the fact that Freud had very little contact with psychotic patients, and that his experience as a practitioner, even with the neurotic patients he preferred to treat, was surprisingly limited. In Storr's view Freud's very ambition, his desire to show that all behavior proceeded from suppressed infantile instincts, caused much of the later dissension among his followers and the division of his school into competing sects. The consequence has been that the uses of psychoanalysis as a humane, professional discipline have been obscured by false claims for its validity as a universal system of belief: "The appeal of psychoanalysis, the fact that it became a movement rather than remaining a type of medical treatment for neurosis, surely derives from its claim to explain so much. Psychoanalysis lacks many of the features usually associated with religion, but, in a secular age, in which those who could not subscribe to the old faiths often felt rootless and insecure, psychoanalysis offered an explanatory system which was eagerly embraced as a substitute." Despite his considerable differences from Freud and his acknowledgement that his own thought has more in common with that of Jung, whose speculations on the spiritual aspects of human nature fascinate him, Storr concludes his summary of Freud's influence by testifying to his vast contribution to the progress of human understanding, especially to the irreversible changes that he brought to the understanding of sexuality and criminality. "It was Freud," he says, "who taught us how to listen."

Storr recognizes that both Freud and Jung sought transformative theories of human nature, and that their observations of particular people may be accused of falsity without cost to the essential truth or general validity of their propositions. Looking at Storr's work as a whole, it appears that although he feels more drawn to the work of Jung, in whose methodology he was trained, no particular school of interpretation claims his exclusive allegiance. It is clear from *The Art of Psychotherapy*, described by Storr as "an introduction . . . aimed primarily at postgraduate doctors who are embarking on specialist training with a view to becoming psychiatrists," that he is a pragmatist whose interests have gradually begun to focus on the unique dynamics of individual personalities. Storr's urbane discussion of the art of psychotherapeutic healing, which continually returns to the principle that psychotherapy is a personal interchange whose success depends on a rapport between patient and therapist, serves as a general apology for a relatively new branch of medicine as "the art of alleviating personal difficulties through the agency of words and a personal, professional relationship." When dealing, in his chapter on "Interpretation," with the question of what causes maladaptation to the circumstances of life, and the origins of neuroses, Storr observes from his standpoint as a therapist: "In practice, questions of origin turn out to be much less important that the existential question of what the patient is actually doing in the here and now . . . the therapist can never fully determine how much of the patient's adult personality is the result of early damage and how much to indefinable genetic causes." By abandoning the question of origin so frankly, Storr acknowledges his limitations as an original thinker, but also advertises his strengths as a synthesizer of ideas about the personality, and explains why he is such a convincing guide to the mysterious process of creation.

In the first book in which he considered human nature as a whole, *The Integrity of the Personality*, Storr stresses that all psychotherapy is influenced by the therapist's own beliefs, and that complete objectivity is therefore unachievable. Such skepticism not only leads him to approve of Freud's injunction that the analyst should never offer practical advice to the patient but also gives him the sense that all nonpsychotic personalities have their own internal logic whose intricacies can never be completely understood. The danger of a doctrinaire approach, therefore, is that no view of a personality that is completely dependent on a preexisting theory can possibly take account of individual needs. This belief inevitably sets Storr apart from colleagues who have espoused one or another line of thinking. Although he is generous in his recognition of his peers, especially the British psychologists D. W. Winnicott and John Bowlby, he implies that no theory or system of analysis holds all the answers and insists that no theory can ever be scientifically proved. Hence, perhaps, his almost exclusive concentration in his later writings on the nature of individual personalities, and his absorption in the question of why some people, despite or because of the oddity of their personalities, are able to perform extraordinary feats of creativity.

The School of Genius, despite its urbane, measured style, is a contentious book that takes issue with what Storr regards as the prevailing psychological orthodoxy of our time—the view that successful personal relationships are the sine qua non of human happiness. This belief, which colors a great deal of contemporary psychotherapy, is ultimately descended, as Storr makes clear in his book on Freud, from the master's conviction that man is an instinctual creature who sublimates his infant desires in mature relations with other adults. Through the work of Melanie Klein and other psychologists who have worked on "object relations theory," notably Storr's prominent contemporary John Bowlby, the forming of familial and social bonds has taken a central position in psychotherapy. It is Storr's conviction, founded on the observation of genius, that many people seek happiness in isolated work and that solitude is an undervalued state that should not be regarded merely as the absence of fulfillment:

> It is not only men and women of genius who may find their chief value in the impersonal rather than the personal. I shall argue that interests . . . play a greater part in the economy of human happiness than modern psychoanalysts and their followers allow. . . . We must all have known people whose lives were actually made worthwhile by such interests, whether or not their human relationships were satisfactory. . . . The burden of value with which we are at present loading interpersonal relationships is too heavy for these fragile craft to carry. Our expectation that satisfying intimate relationships should, ideally, provide happiness and that, if they do not, there must be something wrong with those relationships, seems to be exaggerated.

Characteristically, Storr is not challenging one absolute with another, but trying to redress an imbalance. Love and friendship are not our sole sources of happiness, he points out, nor is creative endeavor "invariably an alternative to human relationships." Creative work does not necessarily exclude the emotional satisfaction of marriage and friendship, nor vice versa. Taking his cue from the historian Edward Gibbon's remark that "solitude is the school of genius; and the uniformity of a work denotes the hand of a single artist," Storr explores the ways in which individuals work in solitude to achieve integration of thought, answering the demands of conflicting and separated ideas rather than those of fellow beings.

Many of the writers and scientists to whom Storr refers in his exploration of the need for solitude were people whose upbringing did not encourage the forming of personal attachments for later life. Kipling, Isaac Newton, Franz Kafka, and Immanuel Kant, to name a few of the numerous examples Storr cites, endured childhoods that might well have led to miserable lives. In all these cases, however, the absence of qualities that are normally deemed healthy led to extraordinary creative efforts. The art of Kafka, one of Storr's prime examples, could be described as pathological, but Kafka's stories succeed in transforming neurosis into art. This view of artistic creation does proceed from Freud's view that all artists are essentially neurotic, but Storr regards this as a reductive view, and explains that he is more in sympathy with Jung, who focused

his attention on the spiritual, rather than the physical, side of human nature. By addressing the question of artistic creation from the standpoint of a psychiatrist, Storr brings new interest to a question first raised by Plato and Aristotle, whether the vision of the poet should be regarded as an outcome of a kind of madness, or whether, on the contrary, art offers new, profoundly sane, integrations of experience.

The capacity to balance the competing claims of the conscious and unconscious depends, Storr observes, on acting upon the promptings of the unconscious in a way that Freud would have characterized as infantile regression. Apparently, and especially in creative people, the search for subjective fulfillment in the external world fosters individuality. "Learning, thinking, innovation and maintaining contact with one's inner world are all facilitated by solitude." Storr does not deny that in many of the geniuses he studies the reasons for solitude were pathological, and that therefore Kafka's stories and Beethoven's late quartets were "biologically adaptive" means of survival, but he also means to correct an imbalance that is relevant to common humanity by pointing out that most of us, at one time or another in our lives, are condemned to solitude, and would therefore be unwise to seek our fulfillment exclusively in human relations. He ends the book with the humane but inconclusive thought: "The happiest lives are probably those in which neither interpersonal relationships nor impersonal interests are idealized as the only way to salvation."

Anthony Ryle, reviewing *The School of Genius* in the *Times Literary Supplement* regarded Storr's discussion as "a symptom of the over-extension of psychoanalytic concepts," and accused him of reducing psychoanalytic authorities to "straw men." He also complained that psychoanalysis presents a restrictive vision only to those who, like Storr himself, are a part of its intellectual tradition, and that Storr does not take into account the social and cultural conditions in which artists create. But, as he observed in contradiction to his own view, these concepts have indeed become a part of "general culture," and Storr, by concentrating exclusively on individuals, does not imply that there is a necessary correlation between genius and childhood unhappiness.

Ryle's complaint about the absence of cultural reference in Storr's analyses is partly answered by Storr's next book, *Churchill's Black Dog*, which can be regarded as a series of long footnotes to his work on solitude. Here Storr gathers essays on writers, scientists, musicians, and the politician Winston Churchill, and examines the psychopathology of each, while also making general observations in the essay "The Sanity of True Genius," in which he examines the opposing views of genius as sanity and madness. He allies himself with the point of view of Charles Lamb, who observed that "it is impossible for the mind to conceive a mad Shakespeare." His studies of a number of creative minds results in the view that creativity is not a product of neurosis or psychosis, but rather a defense against them. There is actually, then, a negative correlation between the unhappiness of geniuses and their work, because these people sought affirmation in the impersonal act of creation.

Storr devotes a good deal of the latter portion of his work on solitude to discussions of Brahms and Beethoven, revealing an interest in both the symbolic meaning of music and the inner lives of composers that is treated at length in *Music and the Mind*. He describes this book as "an attempt to discover what it is about music that so profoundly affects us, and why it is such an important part of our culture." Christopher Longuet-Higgins's *Times Literary Supplement* review, which condescendingly referred to Storr as "a sensible chap," nonetheless complimented him for "a resolute and wide-ranging attempt to define the significance of music in scientific, philosophical, aesthetic and even religious terms." The challenge Storr takes on when venturing outside his profession into fields where he is vulnerable to the objections of specialists is that of advancing the understanding of the general reader. He does not, as Anthony Ryle complained, explain how works of genius were created, but he does, by daring to examine the lives of creative people, extend the reader's expectations of what it is to be "sane."

PRINCIPAL WORKS: The Integrity of the Personality, 1961; Sexual Deviation, 1965; Human Aggression, 1968; Human Destructiveness, 1972; The Dynamics of Creation, 1972; Jung (Modern Masters Series), 1973; The Art of Psychotherapy, 1980; Solitude: A Return to the Self, 1988 (in U.K.: The School of Genius); Churchill's Black Dog, Kafka's Mice, and Other Phenomena of the Human Mind, 1989; Freud (Modern Masters Series), 1989; Music and the Mind, 1992. As editor—The Essential Jung, 1983.

ABOUT: Contemporary Authors New Revision Series 17, 1986; Current Biography Yearbook 1994; Who's Who 1994. Periodicals—Commonweal February 24, 1989; Economist March 12, 1983; Hudson Review Autumn 1989; New Republic October 14, 1972; New Statesman September 22, 1972; New York Review of Books December 14, 1972; February 23, 1973; New York Times Book Review February 25, 1973; June 27, 1976; October 5, 1980; November 8, 1981; October 2, 1988; March 5, 1989; Newsweek December 28, 1992; Times Literary Supplement September 22, 1972; September 14, 1973; May 9, 1980; August 5, 1988; September 1, 1989; U.S. News & World Report September 12, 1988; Village Voice Literary Supplement November 1990.

STRAUB, PETER (FRANCIS) (March 2, 1943–   ), American novelist and poet, was born in Milwaukee, the son of Gordon Anthony Straub and Elvena (Nilsestuen) Straub. An academically gifted child who taught himself to read around the age of five and displayed an early talent for writing, Straub received his high school education at the Milwaukee Country Day School. He entered the University of Wisconsin with the intention of studying both literature and medicine. "In college, I wanted to be a doctor—a literary doctor like William Carlos Williams," he told *Publishers Weekly* in 1983. "Then reality intervened. I discovered I had no gift for science and became an English major. I thought I'd become a college professor. And, after I could admit to myself that what I chiefly wanted to do was write, I thought I'd be a professor who writes books. I expected to have one of those raffish, wandering academic lives."

After receiving his B.A. in English from the University of Wisconsin in 1965, Straub enrolled in the graduate English program at Columbia University. In 1966 he earned his M.A. (with a thesis on William Carlos Williams) and married Susan Bitker, a counselor. Not knowing exactly what to do with his life, he returned to Wisconsin, where he took a job teaching English at his alma mater, the Milwaukee Country Day School. After three years, Straub was ready for a change. "I grew bored. If I'd stayed, I'd have become a gravy-stained old teacher with a beat-up car and an alcohol problem. It seemed like a kind of death, and I had to escape. So we went to Ireland to live, and I became a graduate student."

Straub began working toward his Ph.D. in the fall of 1969 at University College, Dublin, where his advisor was the literary critic Denis Donoghue. In Dublin he wrote poetry and started a doctoral thesis on Victorian literature and D. H. Lawrence. Disputes with Donoghue over the direction of the thesis, and a desire to pursue his own writing, prompted Straub to abandon his academic work in 1972. *Ishmael* and *Open Air*, two collections of his poetry issued by the Irish University Press, appeared during this period. But Straub was still dissatisfied; his longtime ambition had been to write a novel, and it was to that task that he applied himself soon after severing his ties with the university. His first novel, *Marriages*, is about an American businessman living in London and conducting an adulterous affair. While it received some praise from critics, most notices were mixed and sales were poor.

After the publication of *Marriages*, Straub moved to London, where he immediately set to work on a second novel and supported himself by writing short fiction for British women's magazines. His stories were sometimes rejected for being overly literary, and Straub soon realized that if he was going to achieve popular success as a novelist his work would have to have more commercial appeal. Straub's agent, noting the author's proclivity for taut, suspenseful prose, suggested that he write a Gothic novel. Thus it was *Julia*—his third novel, but only his second to be published—that launched his career as a writer of horror fiction.

Set in the Kensington district of London, *Julia* is the story of a woman tormented to the point of suicide by a ghost who exploits her crushing guilt over the death of her son. "In the last resort *Julia* . . . [succeeds] in the brutal business of delivering supernatural thrills," Michael Mason wrote in the *Times Literary Supplement*. "[Straub] has thought of a nasty kind of haunting, and he presses it upon the reader to a satisfying point of discomfort." While reviews of the book were mixed (*Listener* reviewer John Mellors called it "an overcooked and indigestible blood-pudding of a book"), *Julia* did well enough for Straub to turn his back on the women's magazines and concentrate all his energies on writing novels. *Julia* was adapted into an undistinguished film, *The Haunting of Julia*, in which Straub had no hand.

Straub followed *Julia* with *If You Could See Me Now*, a Gothic novel set in the American Midwest. Miles Teagarden, the novel's protagonist, is a literature professor who returns to his native Wisconsin, where he is haunted by the malevolent spirit of a female cousin whose death was both violent and mysterious. "*Julia* and *If You Could See Me Now* established Straub's primary fictional pattern of depicting the horrors of guilt in characters who explore the past to understand the present," Patricia L. Skarda wrote in the *Dictionary of Literary Biography Yearbook 1984*. "*If You Could See Me Now* works rather well," Peter Ackroyd wrote of the novel in the *Spectator*. Noting that the question of "reality," even for "straightforward novelists," has become less and less a straightforward matter, Ackroyd observed, "The book quite carefully evokes the real world of everyday folk, while at the same time intimating—through dreams, metaphors and analogies—the existence of a superior reality which can occasionally be understood. . . ."

Straub first met the best-selling horror fiction writer Stephen King in London in 1976 or 1977, after King had written a jacket blurb for *Julia*. He credits King with helping him to overcome some of his staid, conventional literary tendencies. As he told *Publishers Weekly*: "Steve showed me that the rules—the idea that you should hint at something but must break off before you actually present the reader with it— don't apply. That you could show the thing itself—the terrifying, awful, perhaps cornball, thing itself, and as long as you did it in big, bright primary colors, and with all the conviction you could summon up, the reader would be so astonished that he would experience delight." In writing his next novel, *Ghost Story*, Straub made a conscious effort to apply King's dicta, while at the same time showing the influence of literary masters of the Gothic. Describing his goals to Thomas Lask in the *New York Times* in 1979, Straub remarked: "I want to take the old standards and explode them, to make them more gorgeous, to work from the real to the unreal and still make the narrative exciting."

Set in Milburn, a fictional town in upstate New York, *Ghost Story* recounts the fate of five respectable, elderly residents. In addition to their status as pillars of the community and their membership in the Chowder Society (a group that convenes to tell ghost stories), the five men share responsibility for a murder. When the ghost of their long-dead victim appears, she pursues the men relentlessly, destroying them one by one. In the *New York Times Book Review* Gene Lyons commented: "[In writing *Ghost Story*] Peter Straub quite clearly wishes to have it both ways: to make a hit at the checkout counter and in the English department as well. For besides nightmares, apparitions, werewolves, bloodletting viragos and hosts of the undead, . . . Straub has summoned up the literary shades of Hawthorne, Poe and Henry James in an attempt to dignify and provide a respectable context for his long and complicated book." Lyons felt that "up to a point, . . . Straub succeeds in both ways." *Ghost Story* earned enough money for Straub and his wife to move back to the United States. The film version of *Ghost Story*, however, which discarded most of the novel's strengths in favor of gory special effects, was a critical and commercial failure.

Straub completed his next novel, *Shadow Land*, at the Victorian mansion he had bought in Westport, Connecticut, upon his return to the United States. The story of a boy's encounter with a magician, the novel steps back from the explicit ghoulishness that made *Ghost Story* so popular and concentrates instead on a more insidious, psychological brand of horror.

Straub recovered his commercial stride quickly enough with his next novel, the best-selling *Floating Dragon*. In this book, the people of Hampstead, Connecticut, are beset by two lethal "dragons." The first is a deadly gas leak from a local chemical warfare plant, and the other is a protean supernatural monster, the latest in a long line of evil spirits to have plagued the town. *Floating Dragon* elicited a mixed response from critics. "Unfortunately," Barbara Righton wrote in *Maclean's*, "at the end of *Floating Dragon*, the reader is no wiser. The evil remains ephemeral, the ghost nameless." In the *Times Literary Supplement*, Alan Bold wrote, "*Floating Dragon*. . . . represents a new level of sophisitication in the Gothic novel. . . . The novel is sustained with great skill as the battle between good and evil is impressively, if agonizingly, stretched out over the disturbingly supernatural plot."

Straub and Stephen King decided to collaborate on a novel long before they actually got around to doing so. "Steve proposed to me," Straub told *Publishers Weekly* in 1984. "That was in 1978, very late at night, in the house I had in London. I think he just said, 'Why don't we collaborate on a book sometime?'" Both writers had conflicting contractual obligations that delayed the start of the project until 1982. Then, after completing an outline, King (in Maine) and Straub (in Connecticut) wrote alternate sections of the narrative on linked word processors.

Their finished work, *The Talisman*, is a picaresque horror–fantasy novel that borrows liberally from past and contemporary American fiction and film. The hero, twelve-year-old Jack Sawyer, embarks on a cross-country quest for the Talisman, a magical device that will cure his mother's lung cancer. In the course of his perilous journey from New Hampshire to California, Jack must pass in and out of the Territories, a mysterious alternate world inhabited by menacing and succoring figures. Predictably enough, critical reaction to the novel was lukewarm, and sometimes even hostile. Sales, however, were nothing short of phenomenal.

Not all reviewers dwelt on the book's weaknesses. In *Esquire*, screenwriter Barney Cohen identified three indispensable elements of the horror genre, whether fiction or film: suspense, shock, and revulsion. "*The Talisman* isn't faked," Cohen observed. "Straub and King have all three elements down, and all the permutations are figured into the mix."

Straub's second (and previously unpublished) novel, *Under Venus*, is one of the three selections in *Wild Animals*, which also contains the previously published novels *Julia* and *If You Could See Me Now*. Horror of a decidedly unsuperna-

tural nature is the subject of his 1988 novel *Koko*. In it, a group of Vietnam veterans fly to Southeast Asia to discover whether an old comrade is behind a string of grisly slayings. "In this fable of men undone by the ultimate horror, evil is anything but banal," Richard Fuller wrote in the *New York Times Book Review*.

Tom Pasmore, the protagonist of Straub's novel *Mystery*, has a near-death experience at the age of ten, and later, as a teenager, finds himself involved in an unsolved murder case that leads him to clues about his own identity. In the *Washington Post Book World*, Robin Winks wrote: "Peter Straub writes blockbuster novels, the kind that are at the heart of a commercial publishing house's fiction list. . . . *Mystery* is a superb example of this form of publishing, and it is also, on balance, a fine justification for it."

With *The Throat* in 1993 Straub brought *Koko* and *Mystery* into a trilogy for which this latest novel provided, in Frank Wilson's judgment in the *New York Times Book Review*, a "very impressive finale." Tom Pasmore returns to solve a series of murders in a small town in Illinois. Reviewers noted with approval the seriousness of the novel and the high quality of the writing. Wilson wrote: "What gives *The Throat* its particular resonance is that its underlying theme seems to have less to do with sublunary crime and criminals than with the more transcendent mystery of moral contagion, the permanent scars it can inflict and the curious bonds it causes to be formed."

Houses Without Doors is a collection of Straub's short stories, most of which focus on doomed aberrant, or psychologically crippled men. The collection's title is from the Emily Dickinson poem that begins, "Doom is the House without the Door—." "The surprise of *Houses Without Doors* is the suppleness of its best prose, the delicacy of its plotting and its psychological acuity," Christopher Lehmann-Haupt wrote in the *New York Times*. "These stories shift in their coloring with the sinister effect of sunshine on oily water." Patrick McGrath was another admirer of the collection. In the *Washington Post Book World*, he concluded, "*Houses Without Doors* is a big, generous collection, and it demonstrates that in hands like Straub's the horror genre is quite sufficiently supple, and versatile, to attack complex themes with vitality, sophistication and wit."

Even Straub's detractors are willing to admit that he is far from a run-of-the-mill horror writer. As Walter Kendrick noted in the *New York Times Book Review*, "To aficionados of horror and fantasy, . . . Straub is known as the thinking man's Stephen King—a more slowly paced, more polished writer who wants his prose to be savored rather than gulped down."

PRINCIPAL WORKS: *Poetry*—Ishmael, 1972; Open Air, 1972; Leeson Park and Belize Square: Poems 1970–1975, 1983. *Novels*—Marriages, 1973; Julia, 1975 (reissued in U.K. as Full Circle, 1977); If You Could See Me Now, 1977; Ghost Story, 1979; Shadow Land, 1980; Floating Dragon, 1983; (with S. King) The Talisman, 1984; Wild Animals: Three Novels (contains Under Venus, Julia, If You Could See Me Now) 1984; Blue Rose, 1985; Under Venus, 1985; Koko, 1988; Mystery, 1989; Mrs. God, 1990; The Throat, 1993. *Short stories*—The General's Wife, 1982; Houses Without Doors, 1990.

ABOUT: Contemporary Authors New Revision Series 28, 1990; Contemporary Literary Criticism 28, 1984; Current Biography Yearbook 1989; Dictionary of Literary Biography Yearbook 1984; The Penguin Encyclopedia of Horror and the Supernatural, 1986; Who's Who in America 1992–1993. *Periodicals*—Esquire November 1984; Listener February 26, 1976; Maclean's March 14, 1983; New Statesman and Society December 7, 1990; New York Times April 27, 1979; December 24, 1990; New York Times Book Review April 8, 1979; October 9, 1988; December 30, 1990; June 27, 1993; Newsweek December 24, 1984; Publishers Weekly January 28, 1983; May 11, 1984; Spectator July 9, 1977; Times Literary Supplement February 27, 1976; March 11, 1983; Washington Post Book World April 8, 1979; February 11, 1990; October 28, 1990.

SÜTO, ANDRÁS (June 17, 1927,–), Hungarian dramatist, essayist, and short story writer, was born in Pusztakamarás in Transylvania. His father András and his mother, the former Berta Székely, were of peasant background, and he was the first in his family to receive higher education. From his school days at the Bethlen Gábor Collegium in Aiud (Nagyenyed) he considered himself a spokesman for his family, his community, the Hungarians of Transylvania, and indeed of all Hungarians in Romania.

The historical connections of his birthplace and youth left a lasting impression on him: the 19th-century writer Zsigmond Kemény is buried in Pusztakamarás, and a descendant of his helped equip young Süto for school when the time came. As Süto himself writes in "Anyám könny˝u álmot igér" (My mother promises light dreams, 1970), he hails from "the very center of the hilly region of Transylvania called Mez˝oség, forty kilometers from Kolozsvár (Cluj), sixty from Marosvásárhely (Tîrgu Mureş) far from the arteries of railroads and intellectual life, in the dried-out valley of former marshes, lakes and wetlands." The unity of Süto's work is ensured by the bond to this region, its people, and his own childhood memories. Furthermore,

his art is one that seeks and creates the home: it confronts estrangement and isolation. The intimacy of the family is a motif found is all of his work.

At the Reformed Collegium in Cluj, Süto was drawn into the leftist circle whose members were the foremost literary figures among contemporary Transylvanian intellectuals. While still in secondary school, he worked as a reporter for the daily *Világosság* (Light). He married Éva Szabó in 1949; they later had two sons. At the time Süto worked for *Falvak népe* (People of the Village) of which he became editor in chief in 1950. From 1955 to 1957 he was deputy chief editor of *Igaz szó* (True Word) in Tîrgu Mureş and in 1957 he became editor in chief of *Uj élet* (New Life). Between 1973 and 1981 he was vice president of the Writers' Federation of the Socialist Republic of Romania and in 1979 he won the Herder Prize in Vienna.

Like most of his contemporaries Süto participated in the reorganization of democratic institutions after the fall of Ceauşescu in December 1989, becoming active in the Democratic Association of Hungarians in Romania. On March 15, 1990, a Romanian nationalist attacked Süto and other leaders of the association in the riots at Tîrgu Mureş; he escaped with his life, but lost an eye as a result of the beating he sustained. In spite of this, he did not retire from public life but continued to write, to lecture, and to serve on the editorial board of several journals.

True to his determination to become a writer from 1949 onward, Süto produced a steady stream of short stories, dramas, essays, and diaries—a blend of sociographical essay and historical meditation. *Hajnali gy˝ozelem* (Victory at dawn), *Anikónéném felébred* (My Aunt Anikó wakes up, 1950), and *Az uj bocskor* (The new sandal, 1954), longish short stories published independently, only highlight the material that appeared in periodicals. In 1950 *Mezitlábas menyasszony* (Barefoot bride), a reworking into drama of an earlier story, was performed at the request of the peasants of Kendilona who had provided the basic materials for the drama. In 1953, his first collection of short stories, *Emberek indulnak* (Men set out), appeared, quickly followed by *Egy pakli dohány* (A package of tobacco) in 1954. His works began to appear in Romanian also, and in 1953 and 1954 he won state prizes. The 1950s thus opened up new possibilities as Süto was hailed as the representative of the best in the new Hungarian literary movement both at home and abroad.

Until 1956 Süto accepted his role as spokesman for the Hungarians in Romania more or less in cooperation with the authorities, and did not at first examine the darker side of socialism. The Hungarian Revolution of 1956, its condemnation and the repression of the Hungarian minority that followed it in Romania, made him examine his work more closely. In the humorous short stories of the 1950s he criticized the excesses of the new regime at a time when censorship made any obvious form of condemnation impossible. Soulless bureaucracy and uninspired ideology are his particular targets. The 1959 series of essays, "Tün˝odés magunk fölött" (Ponderings about ourselves), addresses the role of the writer as spokesman for his countrymen living not only in minority status but under increasing oppression in their homeland. But Süto moves beyond local concerns to champion the rights of all men bound by a common race, language, religion, or ideology against the racism and intolerance of those who hold power. Süto has been led by his mother's admonition, "If you would write about us, son, write the truth," even when the setting and ideas have transcended the world of his Pusztakamarás society.

The question Süto asks in his later essays and dramas is How can this—or any ethnic group—survive? How can a minority retain its cultural roots and yet become fully integrated into the majority population? What, in fact, can guarantee the rights of individuals against tyranny, of minorities against intolerance? The notes to one of his latest plays make clear the way in which he uses his work to examine these truths. *Alomkommandó* (The dream commandant), a play within a play, draws parallels between the fate of Jews in Auschwitz and the tyranny of Ceauşescu in Romania. His play, Süto states, is not merely a memoir of the past; it was written under the "triple constraint" of past, present, and future. The lesson of Auschwitz has been lost and "those dedicated to power and racism . . . again let loose the bloodhounds of prejudice and the myth of blood which does not tolerate Reason . . . or Differences." Such thinking is only a short step to the conviction that "second-class" races or nations and second-class citizens are superfluous. On October 19, 1991, when the play could finally be performed in Tîrgu Mureş, he reasserted his belief in the timelessness of his dramas: "their timeliness could not cease because the conditions—for example, the trampling underfoot of human rights—is not necessarily a fleeting phenomenon . . . degradation and chauvinistic hatred continues to ravage steadily. For how much longer?"

This message is already found in Süto's seminal essay, "Anyám könny˝u álmot igér." While ostensibly concerned with the fate of his people in Pusztakamarás, Süto shows that their concerns are universal concerns. Even in the face of offi-

cially sanctioned lies, he must speak the truth. For this, he chose a genre that is a blend of essay, diary, and sociographical report. Its language is intimate yet sonorous, playful yet with echoes of biblical dignity. Anecdotes, interviews, essays, letters, and idylls are juxtaposed skillfully.

Using a stream of consciousness technique Süto presents associations and connections in order to make the reader realize a truth which he himself has gained at some expense. In addressing the concerns of the Hungarian community in Romania, as of all minorities, he recognizes that human rights and linguistic rights are essentially one, and the writer has a duty to make others aware of the character-forming quality of the mother tongue, the right and duty of memory, and the survival of the community. Süto's works examine two related problems: survival and the duty of the individual in the face of tyranny.

In later essays he often chooses historical settings to comment on contemporary affairs. Thus, in the essay "Perzsák" (The Persians, 1973), as in the drama which evolved from this, *A Szuzai menyegz˝o* (The wedding feast of Susa, 1981), he condemns Alexander the Great's attempt not only to conquer the Persians but to make them into Greeks. As long as a common language serves the goals of communication and commerce and does not impose its exclusivity it is a blessing. When it betrays this role, it becomes a curse, he notes in the essay.

Two important collections of essays, *Istennek és falovacskák* (Gods and Wooden Play Horses, 1973), and *Nagyenyedi f˝ugevirág* (Fig-tree flower of Nagyenyed, 1978), both ostensibly a series of travel essays subtitled "essay, travel meditations," showed Süto's increasing concern for the fate of his mother tongue in his homeland. He argues for the preservation of the multicultural and multilingual heritage of Transylvania and mutual respect for all of the peoples who have formed that society. The title essay of the latter takes as its starting point his arrival at the famous school in 1940, but the lessons of tolerance and exhortation to vigilance in the preservation of humane values is directed at the increasingly repressive regime which sought to eradicate both personal freedoms and the cultures of minority populations, attacking the Hungarians with particular severity. The closing of Hungarian schools and linguistic persecution form the basis of the "complaint" Süto delivers in his imagination to Gábor Bethlen, founder of the school in the 16th century and prince of Transylvania, who had guaranteed religious freedom and who had supported all the peoples of his land equally: Bethlen had ordered the translation of the Bible into Romanian, thus giving them an entree into Renaissance scholarship shared with other nations of the region. But in the 20th century, the Romanian government seeks to deny even the spoken word. Force, whether from the Hungarian or the Romanian part, is equally condemned.

Engedjétek hozzám jönni a szavakat (Allow the words to come to me, 1977) is an "essay novel" which Süto wrote to teach his grandson an appreciation for his mother tongue and the secrets of his heritage: "What can a nation or a generation expect from its writers, if not precisely this faithfulness to the community: the exposure of our problems even from storehouses whose gate is barred by No Trespassing signs." In a narrative that covers two and a half years of the child's development, far-reaching associations are woven as the grandfather presents the world to his grandson through the discovery of the word. "He can only take possession of the world," Süto writes, "—be it only a broken piece of pottery—if he has named it."

The last years of the 1960s and the early '70s were a period of liberalization in Romania during which dramatists, too, were allowed to learn from Western models and authors could explore stylistic and thematic areas that had been taboo. Hungarian drama in Romania at this time was distinctly intellectual and historical; the ideas that had lain unexpressed, and which still could arouse the disapproval of the authorities, were presented obliquely. Süto's drama tetralogy examines whether modern man—individually or as part of a community—can fulfill his role so that he is true to his own nature and yet remain a part of a larger community and serve the advancement of humanity. True human values, Süto argues, respect both the individual and the community, and the community must respect the individuals who compose it.

Egy lócsiszár virágvasírnapja (1973, *The Palm Sunday of a Horse Dealer*) received its inspiration from Kleist's *Michael Kohlhaas* and presents the tragedy of a man who seeks justice for himself and his family. Süto's hero becomes a reluctant rebel as he slowly comes to realize the emptiness of law when its sole function is to defend those in power. In *Csilag a máglyán* (*Star at the Stake*) he reaches into the fratricidal history of the Reformation to argue against tyranny. John Calvin, the liberal student, becomes the tyrant who sends his friend Servetus to the stake because Calvin can only accept one truth, and one power: his own. Though the scene is set in the 16th century it hauntingly echoes conditions in Romania in Ceauşescu's days.

Kain és Abel (1978) and *A Szuzai menyegz˝o*

also examine the questions of power, law, and justice, and the way in which these abstracts, personified in the modern state—particularly the totalitarian state—affect the individual and the community of individuals who stand opposed to these forces. In the former play, Cain is presented as an independent man who retains his dignity in adversity while Abel is both servile and cowardly. In this drama the motif of a lost Eden, which Cain feels it to be his right to know and to regain, also speaks to Hungarian audiences who are treated as aliens in their own homeland. As Adam says in a bitter outburst to the Lord: "My son did not seek to sit in your place. He did not assault you, but only wanted to preserve himself, and his own view of the condition and obligations of man . . . You could also have said wisely, *different* from that which you imagined. We all turned out to be different. After all, even your grasses, your birds, your cedar trees all show the beauty of variety, and then why not man!"

In notes written for performances of the play, Süto commented in 1979 that while of biblical inspiration, the play is certainly contemporary in its message. In 1983 he expanded on this idea: "In my work, *Kain és Ábel*, I sought to call in testimony the joy and drama of the head raised high." Finally, in March 1989, when sending his best wishes for the Hungarian Regional Theater in Slovakia from Budapest, he wrote: "I think that perhaps the miracle will happen . . . that is, the Hungarians living in Marosvásárhely and those in Komárom will turn with the same thought and unite in a common human endeavor to express their shared dream: the ideal of the raised head which even in our minority status is a *sine qua non* of our collective survival." Similarly, he points out that in *A Szuzai menyegz˝o* human values are pitted against a tyrant who wishes all to conform to his wishes: "A spiritual kinship links us together as we again take note of the nature of power. For in this drama . . . the intoxication of power plays games with a patient humanity."

Süto's insistence on the dignity of the individual and the rejection of a regimented, artificially homogenous society had deep roots in Transylvanian tradition. As he noted when acceptingd the Herder prize in 1979: nations can best contribute to universality with the values of their own uniqueness. The preservation of individuality, therefore, means the enrichment of universal values in all ages.

As a Hungarian writer in Romania, Süto has inevitably become a political writer in a society that sought to eradicate all minorities. A product of the fruitful symbiosis that had characterized

Hungarian and Romanian relations when political powers did not make an issue of differences, Süto's world writings embody the best of that which this region has to offer in a world fragmented by prejudice.

PRINCIPAL WORKS IN ENGLISH TRANSLATION: (tr. J. Brogyányi)Star at the Stake *in* Modern International Drama no. 13, Spring 1980; The Palm Sunday of a Horse Dealer *in* Drama Contemporary: Hungary, 1991; "At the Graveside" *in* The New Hungarian Quarterly 24, 1991.

ABOUT: Contemporary World Writers, 1993. *Periodicals*—Irish University Review Autumn 1987; New Hungarian Quarterly Summer 1988; Summer 1990.

*SZULC, TAD (July 25, 1926–   ), American (Polish-born) journalist, writes: "I was born in Warsaw, Poland, dispatched to a boys' prep school in Switzerland (Le Rosey) at the age eleven—I started to learn foreign languages there—then spent the first year of World War II in the South of France, and the next five years in Rio de Janeiro, Brazil, where I went to high school and university.

"This background served beautifully, as it turned out, for a career in journalism that now spans nearly a half-century—and for a lifetime of writing books, teaching, appearing on radio and TV, and the like.

"My first serious job in journalism was with the Associated Press and Agence France Presse in Brazil. In 1948 (the year I married my wife, Marianne), I went to work for the United Press in New York, covering the United Nations (where it helped to be totally fluent in English, French, Spanish, Portuguese, and Polish and somewhat fluent in Italian, Czech, and Russian). In 1953, I joined the *New York Times*, in whose service I remained for twenty years, mostly as a foreign correspondent in Southeast Asia, Latin America, and Western and Eastern Europe, and diplomatic reporter in Washington, D.C. I covered guerrilla wars in Asia, revolutions against five dictators in Latin America, the Cuban Revolution, the Bay of Pigs, the Cuban missile crisis, the U.S. intervention in the Dominican Republic, the loss of four U.S. hydrogen bombs in Spain, the Soviet invasion of Czechoslovakia, attrition wars in the Middle East, the diplomacy of the Vietnam war . . . All together, I have reported from eighty-seven foreign countries, traveled with Presidents Kennedy and Nixon and Pope Paul VI, and knew most of the key statesmen and adventurers of that era.

"From 1973 until the present time, I have

TAD SZULC

functioned as an independent writer, contributing to the *National Geographic Magazine*, the *New Yorker*, the *New York Times Magazine*, *Foreign Policy Quarterly*, *New York Magazine*, *Parade*, the *Smithsonian*, the *New Republic*, *Playboy*, *Rolling Stone*, etc., etc. For my journalistic work, I have been awarded Columbia University's Maria Moors Cabot Gold Medal, Sigma Delta Chi's Distinguished Service Award, and six Citations for Excellence from the Overseas Press Club of America.

Three of my sixteen books—*Fidel: A Critical Portrait*; *The Illusion of Peace*; and *Then and Now—How the World Has Changed Since World War II*—received the Overseas Press Club's award for best book on foreign affairs.

"I am knight of the French Order of the Legion of Honor and of the Dominican Republic's Order of Sanchez Y Mella. I hold the honorary degree of Doctor of Humane Letters from the American College of Switzerland. I was Visiting Professor in Public Diplomacy at the Fletcher School of Law and Diplomacy (1979)."

———

Although Tad Szulc is the winner of numerous journalism awards and has earned a reputation as a consummate investigative reporter, he is uncomfortable with the designation "investigative reporter." He regards the expression as a redundancy.

Szulc's early books focus on Latin America and the Caribbean, where he was a reporter for the *New York Times*. When Fidel Castro came to power in Cuba in 1959, Szulc was there on assignment. He was first introduced to Castro by veteran *Times* correspondent Herbert Matthews; the three men spent an entire night talking in the kitchen of what was then the Havana Hilton. Szulc is often credited with breaking the story of the Bay of Pigs invasion, an unsuccessful 1961 attempt by United States–trained guerrillas to topple Castro's government. He is one of the few journalists to have witnessed Castro's Cuba both in its early days and in the 1980s.

Working in collaboration with Karl E. Meyer, another reporter, Szulc wrote *The Cuban Invasion*, the first comprehensive account of the ill-fated United States–sponsored incursion. In parceling out blame for the reasons behind the mission's failure, Szulc and Meyer point primarily toward the CIA and the Joint Chiefs of Staff. They do not, however, come to any firm conclusions regarding the morality of the invasion itself. "In the main, . . . this is a hard-boiled book about a hard-boiled scheme," Richard Dudman wrote in the *New Republic*. "As such, it deals only lightly with the moral question involved in the invasion plan."

In *Innocents at Home*, written after a five-year absence from the United States, Szulc examines American politics and culture in the 1970s. Although he found poverty on the rise and equality of opportunity on the decline, he ended his book on an optimistic note: "So long as America remains a revolutionary society—revolutionary in the sense of seeking change and searching for new truths—and so long as we accept that confrontations among us are as inescapable as they are necessary, then I feel certain that We Shall Overcome, and that this will come in our time."

The Illusion of Peace, one of Szulc's longest and most ambitious books, is a comprehensive accounting of Richard Nixon's foreign policy. While he is highly critical of the role played by National Security Adviser (and later Secretary of State) Henry Kissinger, Szulc argues that Nixon was the author of his own foreign policy. Reviewers praised Szulc's in-depth treatment of Nixon's policies toward Vietnam, the Middle East, the Soviet Union, and China; however, many of those same reviewers decried the author's lack of commentary on the events he describes in such detail. As Alex Beam noted in an otherwise favorable review in the *Nation*, "Szulc is long on narrative and short on analysis." According to Richard H. Ullman, in the *New York Times Book Review* (1978), Szulc's book suffered from a lack of documentation and "scholarly apparatus." "*The Illusion of Peace* is absorbing, even compelling reading," Ullman

wrote. "Much of its information is new, sometimes startlingly so. But it is information often impossible to evaluate. . . . Often a reader does not know whether a quoted person is central or peripheral, a friend of the Administration or an enemy."

Szulc's best-known book, or at least the one which has generated the most commentary, is *Fidel: A Critical Portrait*, a biography of Cuban leader Fidel Castro. The Overseas Press Club named it the best book on foreign affairs in 1986 (and had earlier given the same award to *The Illusion of Peace*.) The contentious critical reaction to the book surprised no one, least of all Szulc. Ever since Castro's guerrilla victory over Batista in 1959, and his subsequent declaration of Marxist principles, Castro had been a divisive figure, especially (but certainly not only) among Western intellectuals. Everything about him—his ideology, his stewardship of Cuba, even his seemingly larger-than-life personality—has been the subject of acrimonious debate.

Szulc was attracted to the idea of writing about Castro because relatively little was known about his life. After making a survey of world leaders in the mid-1980s—Ronald Reagan, Margaret Thatcher, Helmut Kohl, and François Mitterand (whom Szulc knows well)—Szulc decided that Castro was simply the most interesting among them.

Over the course of one month in 1985, Szulc conducted five extended conversations with Castro. He was also granted access to a substantial number of Cuban government documents. Szulc devotes fully two-thirds of *Fidel* to an examination of Castro's life, politics, and relationships prior to 1959. "I would like to think that this book reflects in its structure the evolution of Castro, and more space is dedicated to his early, settling years because that is what is least known about him," Szulc told *Publishers Weekly*. Claiming that he was not "trying to discover the fate of the Cuban Revolution," Szulc further asserted, "Since the late '60s and early '70s, the man really hasn't changed that much."

Szulc contends that a careful analysis of one of Castro's speeches, the one popularly referred to as "History Will Absolve Me," is essential to any understanding of the development of his political thought. Arrested after his July 26, 1953 raid on the Moncada barracks outside Santiago de Cuba, Castro spent more than two months in solitary confinement. When he at last came before the tribunal, which sentenced him to fifteen years in prison, Castro delivered this rousing, two-hour speech, in the course of which he discussed the English and French Revolutions, and invoked Rousseau, Saint Thomas Aquinas, and, of course, Cuban independence leader José Martí. "Condemn me, it does not matter," Castro concluded. "History will absolve me."

Szulc cautions that there is a certain futility in trying to determine precisely when Castro made his conversion to Marxist-Leninist principles. Szulc disagrees with those who claim that Castro was a Communist even before the aborted Moncada raid, and with those who claim that Castro was pushed into Communism (and alliance with the Soviet bloc) solely or primarily by United States policies. As nearly as Szulc can determine, Castro made the decision that his revolution would be a Communist one in the spring of 1958. Because he did not reveal this to the world until 1961, he has often been charged with treachery and duplicity. One of the most startling revelations of Szulc's book is that the CIA helped to finance Castro's guerrilla movement in 1957 or 1958.

"I know I will have antagonized everyone— the pro-Castro people and the anti-Castro people," Szulc told *Publishers Weekly*. "My name is mud in Havana and mud in Miami." Pondering Castro's reaction to the book (he did not see it until it was released to the public), Szulc remarked, "I don't think I'll ever go to Cuba again—because I don't think they'll let me in after this book."

Reviewing *Fidel* in the staunchly anti-Castro *National Review*, Tom Bethell found Szulc's stance toward Castro anything but confrontational. "Despite his subtitle, *A Critical Portrait*," Bethell wrote, "Szulc worships Castro too much to bother with his defects." Szulc's greatest error, according to Bethell, was his omission of any detailed consideration of the "Cuban Gulag" and Castro's generally ruthless treatment of dissidents. *Nation* reviewer George Black, from a different political perspective, complained of the book's "numbing lack of drama and a rather more surprising dearth of original information."

In a long consideration of the book in the *New Republic*, French writer K. S. Karol lauded Szulc's impeccable credentials as a reporter of Latin American affairs, but disagreed fundamentally with his central thesis, "which is that Castro was 'almost a Communist' as early as 1948, and that he decided in 1958, . . . alone and in the absence of pressure from abroad, to create a Communist regime in Cuba." Disagreements aside, Karol concluded, however, that "a judicious reader . . . will find much to appreciate in this lively book." In the *New York Times Book Review*, Stanley Hoffmann found *Fidel* full of useful information about its subject, but regretted Szulc's decision to devote the bulk of his book to Castro's early life.

More recently, Szulc has published *Then and Now: How the World Has Changed Since World War II* and *The Secret Alliance*, a history of how Israel has rescued persecuted Jews from around the world since World War II. *Then and Now* is a broader study, which takes into consideration historical, political, and cultural trends throughout the postwar world. Reviewing it in the *New York Times Book Review*, Anthony Howard wrote: "In its scope and range, the book . . . is a tour de force—matched only by Paul Johnson's *Modern Times*. . . . Whereas . . . Johnson belongs to the right, . . . Szulc comes across as a defiant '60s American liberal, though one very much of the pragmatic school."

Szulc's Polish birth gave him extra insight for explaining the background of Pope John Paul II. Greatly influenced by Polish history, Karol Jozef Wojtyla, the man who became Pope John Paul II, is a " master of" the theater and oratory that carry Polish history from generation to generation, according to Margaret O'Brien Steinfels who reviewed *Pope John Paul II* in the *New York Times Book Review*. "Martyrdom and suffering are the lifeblood of Poland's history and the keynotes of the Pope's life," she noted. "The Pope as depicted by . . . Szulc is devout, intelligent, warm, humorous and hospitable . . . yet he seems wilfully blind to some of the church's most pressing issues" as Szulc depicts him. Steinfels faulted Szulc for skimming over theological issues, making the biography, otherwise excellent, "like a biography of Einstein without physics."

PRINCIPAL WORKS: Nonfiction—The Twilight of the Tyrants, 1959; New Trends in Latin America, 1960; (with K. Meyer) The Cuban Invasion: The Chronicle of a Disaster, 1962; The Winds of Revolution: Latin America Today and Tomorrow, 1963; Dominican Diary, 1965; Latin America, 1965; The Bombs of Palomares, 1967; Czechoslovakia Since World War II, 1971; Portrait of Spain, 1972; Innocents at Home: America in the 1970s, 1974; The Illusion of Peace: Foreign Policy in the Nixon Years, 1978; Then and Now: How the World Has Changed Since World War II, 1990; The Secret Alliance: The Extraordinary Story of the Rescue of the Jews Since World War II, 1991. Biography—Compulsive Spy: The Strange Career of E. Howard Hunt, 1973; Fidel: A Critical Portrait, 1986; Pope John Paul II, 1995. Novel—Diplomatic Immunity, 1981. As editor—The United States and the Caribbean, 1971. Juvenile—The Invasion of Czechoslovakia, August, 1968; The End of a Socialist Experiment in Freedom, 1974; The Energy Crisis, 1974, rev. ed. 1978.

ABOUT: Contemporary Authors New Revision Series 23, 1988; Who's Who in America 1992–1993. Periodicals—Nation May 20, 1978; January 24, 1987; National Review February 13, 1987; New Republic

May 21, 1962; January 19, 1987; New York Times
Book Review June 18, 1978; November 30, 1986; May
14, 1995; Publishers Weekly December 5, 1986.

*TACHIHARA, MASAAKI (January 6,
1926–August 12, 1980), Japanese novelist, was
born in Korea. His father had once been a government bureaucrat, possibly a soldier, but became a priest associated with the ancient Zen
temple Hoteiji at the time of Tachihara's birth.
In 1932, when Tachihara was six years old, his
father committed suicide. His mother later remarried and moved to Japan. Tachihara continued to live in Korea with an aunt and uncle until
1937 when he went to Japan to live with his
mother's new family in Yokosuka. Tachihara's
early education was a mixture of traditional Zen
training encouraged by his father and modern
Japanese schooling insisted on by his mother. He
was discouraged from continuing his Zen training by his father's suicide and thwarted in his attempt to get the best possible modern education
because of his Korean heritage, which caused
him to experience deep discrimination in Japan.

Faced with a turbulent family situation and
the disruption caused by World War II and social discrimination, Tachihara made a decision
to devote himself to the pursuit of art and beauty, particularly as these are found in the Zen-
based culture of medieval Japan. It was almost
as though he was determined to become more
familiar with Japanese culture than the Japanese, as though by being Korean he had to
prove himself. We see this view worked out artistically in the story "Tsurugigasaki" (1965,
"Cliff's Edge"), where the hero turns away from
the political and social implications of Japan's
loss of the war and the consequent independence
of Korea as a nation. Bereft of family and country, the hero devotes himself to the pursuit of art
and beauty just as Tachihara did in his personal
life.

The postwar years were particularly chaotic
ones for Tachihara. Although he had entered the
prestigious Waseda University in 1945, he was
asked to leave the school in 1947 because he was
spending all his time writing and never attended
classes. In the meantime he had married Yone-
moto Mitsuyo, his childhood sweetheart, and
with the birth of their son he had a family to support. Unable to get a job because of discrimination against Koreans, Tachihara managed to
scrape together a living by selling articles on the
black market. Although much of his time during
this period was spent drinking and carousing,
Tachihara was also studying the traditions, history, and aesthetics of the medieval No theater, an

MASAAKI TACHIHARA

endeavor which was to form an important basis
for much of his later writing. He was also interested in modern literature as well and was reading the works of Ernest Hemingway and T. S.
Eliot. He was especially interested in Eliot's
views on the importance of tradition and saw a
similarity between the poet's views and those expressed by the 15th-century No dramatist Zeami
Motokiyo.

This convergence of modern and traditional
values centered on the aesthetic traditions of the
No theater can be found expressed in a number
of his works including "Takigino" (1964,
"Torchlight No"), Kinuta (The Fulling Block,
1973), and Mai no Ie (The performers, 1971).
The story "Takigino" has its setting in contemporary Japan and depicts the superficiality and
bankruptcy of modern academic and intellectual endeavors. In contrast to this is the rich cultural heritage of the No tradition, which is
perceived to be out of date and irrelevant to the
modern world. The heroine's decision to choose
a lover's suicide reflects her despair over the failure of her marriage, but at a deeper level it also
provides Tachihara with the means to explore
the medieval concept of horobi no bi, the beauty
of destruction, or the nobility of failure. In this
regard, far from being the alien, Tachihara is the
interpreter and preserver of Japanese values
which the Japanese themselves are in danger of
losing. Not surprisingly, perhaps, Tachihara had
trouble getting "Torchlight No" published, partly because he himself was an unknown writer at
that time and partly because editors felt the story was too old-fashioned with its focus on the No

°tah chee HAH ruh, mah sah AH kee

theater and love suicide. Nevertheless, once the story saw print in the literary journal *Shincho* (New Tide), it was highly acclaimed, nominated for the Akutagawa Prize, and it established the author as a new voice on the literary scene.

The following year Tachihara's writing took a new direction with the publication of "Cliff's Edge." Although one may see elements of a No play in the way this work is constructed with its re-creations of scenes from the past, the author deals with his own experiences as a person of Korean heritage living in wartime Japan. Here, in one generation, the father rejects Japan and devotes his life to the cause of Korean nationalism and succeeds at the expense of his family, while the uncle commits himself to the cause of the Japanese Imperial Navy and thus to Japan's wartime aspirations. With the loss of the war, the uncle dies. In the next generation, the older son, Ichiro, although living in Japan, will not compromise with Japanese culture and dies. The cousin, Kenkichi, will not compromise Japanese culture by accepting Koreans, and he too dies. Finally, only Jiro remains because he has been able to make the compromise and to accept Japanese culture. "Cliff's Edge" was also nomimated for the Akutagawa Prize, but again failed to win it. Although not strictly autobiographical, this work deals with Tachihara's deep concern with what is means to be a Korean in Japanese society. Autobiographical writing forms one important strand of the author's complete oeuvre. In *Utsukushi Shiro* (Beautiful Castle, 1968), Tachihara serves as a spokesman for the experiences of his generation in postwar Japan. This was a generation that was shaped by the militaristic and nationalistic education system of prewar and wartime Japan, but it was also a group too young to have been conscripted and shipped overseas for combat duty in the war zones. At the same time, this generation had completed its education before the postwar reforms were instituted and so knew nothing of that experience of a freer educational climate. In short, these people were educated for a world that no longer existed once their education had been completed. Finally, in *Fuyu no Katami ni* (Winter Profile, 1975), the author recapitulated his autobiographical experiences and yet, as critics have pointed out, he did not stick to the literal facts, but created a fictional autobiography. In a real sense he created his own persona through this work.

Although Tachihara never won the Akutagawa Prize for so-called "pure" literature, in 1966 he won the Naoki Prize for popular fiction with the publication of the story "Shiroi Keshi" (White Poppy). Here was recognition and acclaim for his skill as writer, but not necessarily the sort of recognition he sought. Tachihara responded by saying that his goal as an artist was not to create either "pure" literature or "popular" literature, but rather to maintain his own integrity as an artist in pursuit of his own vision of beauty. He put the literary world on notice that despite receiving this award he was not about to play the role of a conventional popular novelist and should not be regarded in that way.

Throughout the remainder of his career Tachihara explored Japan's rich cultural heritage and sought to preserve traditional values by adapting them to the needs of contemporary society. When such adaptation was not possible, he was willing to show the conflict between traditional and contemporary values. This position is reflected in the novel *Yume wa kareno wo* (1974, *Wind and Stone*). As is so often the case in Tachihara's writing, the central character is a woman and the story deals with her dilemma. In this case Mizue is the archetypal Japanese woman of postwar Japan. Her husband is the second son of a family that owns a meat processing company, which provides him with the wealth and leisure to dabble in artistic things about which he has no real understanding or competence. They have two children, a boy and a girl, and a fine suburban home. Mizue is a poster-perfect image of postwar Japan; she has realized the dream that everyone is seeking. Yet despite the material wealth and creature comforts this life provides, Mizue loses her complacency and comes to feel dissatisfied with her spiritual and emotional emptiness. Her husband calls in a landscape architect to build a traditional Japanese garden for their new home. Mizue is attracted by the creative energy of the architect and becomes involved in an affair with him. In the end, she feels she cannot abandon her husband and children, but neither can she endure the meaningless futility of this life once she realizes there can be something more. When her husband learns of the affair, he tries to destroy the garden, but finds that art cannot be destroyed, only rearranged. Tachihara's message is that Japan as a nation has achieved economic preeminence, but the people have become spiritually bankrupt by abandoning or ignoring their rich cultural heritage. The novel not only explores this issue of the loss of spiritual values, it also quotes frequently from traditional manuals on the art of garden building and is at one level virtually an essay on the aesthetics of the Japanese garden.

In addition to fiction, Tachihara also wrote extensively on art and aesthetics, most notably a collection of essays on Japanese gardens located in and around Kyoto. He also wrote about ceramics and about the No theater. The results of these scholarly investigations were reflected in his fiction. The effect this had on Tachihara's art is that while the plot lines may sound like soap operas dealing with adultery and betrayal, the issue he raises is really the search for meaning and spirituality in modern Japan, and the content of his work is deeply colored by the author's scholarly research on Japanese traditions.

Having at last achieved recognition as a writer, in 1968 Tachihara was invited to serve as editor in chief for a revival of the influential literary journal *Waseda [Bungaku]* (Waseda University Literature). Although he was initially reluctant to undertake this job because he had dropped out of the university without graduating, the two years he served in this position were ones of great dedication and gave him the opportunity to significantly shape the direction of contemporary Japanese literature by recognizing and publishing the work of aspiring writers.

During the last decade of his life Tachihara traveled extensively in Europe, China, and Korea. The travel writing in which he details these experiences forms another major strand in his literary production. Just as his other work has contrasted traditional and contemporary Japanese values, these works contrast Japanese values and viewpoints with those of Europe and mainland Asia.

Although heavily engaged in travel writing and editing, Tachihara continued to write fiction. At the time of his death of cancer in the summer of 1980, he was at work on a major novel based on the life of Zeami Motokiyo, which would have provided another extensive exploration of Japan's medieval aesthetic traditions.

PRINCIPAL WORKS IN ENGLISH TRANSLATION: *Novel*—(tr. Stephen W. Kohl) Wind and Stone, 1992. *Short stories*—"The Path to the Tea Room" *in* Chanoyu Quarterly, 1977; (tr. S. W. Kohl) Cliff's Edge and Other Stories (includes "Cliff's Edge," "Torchlight No," and "The Archer"), 1980.

ABOUT: Kodansha Encyclopedia of Japan, 1993; *introduction to* Cliff's Edge and Other Stories, 1980.

TALLENT, ELIZABETH ANN (August 8, 1954–   ), American essayist, short story writer, and novelist, has become known for her intimate, incisive portrayal of contemporary people and places. Drawing on her anthropological training and strong sense of place, Tallent evokes the portentous details of everyday life. Although her lucid depiction of the American Southwest suggests she has always lived there, Tallent was born in Washington, D.C., and raised in a sub-

ELIZABETH ANN TALLENT

urb of Peoria, Illinois. Her father, William Hugh Tallent, worked as a research chemist in both government and private sectors. Her mother, Joy Redfield Tallent, a speech therapist, stayed home with Elizabeth and her younger sister and brother.

Tallent went to college at Illinois State University at Normal, where she majored in anthropology. She never considered becoming a writer during her undergraduate days, but does remember feeling "an affection for writers uncommon in an anthropologist," as she commented in a *Saturday Review* interview. In 1975, she received her degree and got married, intending to begin graduate work in southwestern archaeology at the University of New Mexico. As she and her new husband, Barry Smoots, approached the campus, however, she made a last-minute decision to forgo graduate school. The couple settled in the Santa Fe area and Tallent began writing stories, inspired in part by her old discipline. "Archeologists look at physical evidence of a life that has permanence, a context, intricacy," she once explained. "That's what I'd like in my writing."

In 1980, Tallent sold her first short story, "Ice," to the *New Yorker*. Her story "Why I Love Country Music" appeared in the 1981 edition of *The Pushcart Prize*, an anthology that honors outstanding fiction published in little magazines. "Ice" was selected for *The Best American Short Stories 1981* by editor Hortense Calisher, who recalls in her introduction how the story compelled her with its "suspending magic. . . ."

Soon after Tallent's successful debut as a story writer, she published a collection of essays, *Married Men and Magic Tricks: John Updike's Erotic Heroes*. In the preface, Tallent describes feeling "drawn toward whatever seemed to me, within Updike's fiction, most strikingly curious or beautiful or lively, and I have often valued impulse over consistency, so that this work cannot claim to be either methodical or comprehensive." Nonetheless, she argues that a principal thesis applies to all Updike's work: his male heroes are modern-day Adams, caught between a need for secure domesticity and a desire for the risky adventure of adultery. "So the place of man," Tallent writes, "between innocence and alarmed knowledge, is as precarious as it ever was in Eden."

Despite her prefatory disclaimer, Tallent received some unfavorable criticism for the superficial quality of her work. Elizabeth Prioleau commented in *American Literature* that while Tallent offers beautiful prose and genuine insights, she fails to fully decipher the complicated sexual code in Updike's novels. Prioleau further criticized Tallent's omission of notes, her apparently arbitrary selection of novels to discuss, and the order in which she discusses them. A reviewer for *Choice* noted the absence of index and bibliography, but praised Tallent's prose style and original perspective.

Tallent's foray into literary analysis did not interrupt her fiction writing. She continued to produce stories and she sold several, mainly to the *New Yorker*. In 1983, Knopf published *In Constant Flight*, a collection of her early works, including the previously acclaimed "Ice" and "Why I Love Country Music." All eleven stories portray incongruous pairs of people who cling to each other in a world of miscommunication and alienation. In "Asteroids," the young daughter and girlfriend of a divorced man abide by one another during his prolonged absence. "The Evolution of Birds of Paradise" centers on a retired professor and his daughter-in-law who share not only a house but also a pained apprehension of the other's most private failures. Reviewers of *In Constant Flight* praised Tallent's finely wrought details, arresting images, and elegant prose. While faulting the stories' abstractions, unfathomable metaphors, and overdone attempts at originality, they predicted that Tallent would mature into a fine writer.

Tallent's early characters live in such diverse places as San Francisco, Boulder, and Albuquerque and travel the world from the American middle west to Peru. In her later work, she has favored southwestern settings. "There's a different quality of life here. Everything is extraordi-

narily defined," Tallent observed in the *New York Times Book Review*, adding that she tries to bring this clarity to her writing. Her affinity for the Southwest, particularly New Mexico, is vividly revealed in her first novel, *Museum Pieces*. The book's title refers both to the objects created by Clarissa, a painter, and retrieved by Peter, an archaeologist, and to the shards of their broken marriage. As they try to find the centers of their separate lives, their twelve-year-old daughter Tara balances perilously between them. Peter has moved out and lives among artifacts and beer cans in the basement of the museum where he works. Clarissa appears more stable but also feels dislocated. Going home one evening, she realizes that she "will have to face the empty house alone. That's the part she hates. The rooms that darkness alters slightly, the clutter of Tara's room, the spokes of her bicycle in the hallway, the dusty spines of Peter's books unclaimed on the shelves."

Museum Pieces impressed writer Louise Erdrich, in the *New York Times Book Review*, as "a sure-handed extension of Elizabeth Tallent's short stories. She has kept the humor and immediacy, the telling quirks, the odd and inventive bits of circumstance, while at the same time rendering her characters in deeper tones." In the *Hudson Review*, Wendy Lesser, on the contrary, felt that *Museum Pieces* lacked the substance and self-propulsion appropriate to its length. Nevertheless, she praised Tallent's command of details and her ability to "formulate the exact linguistic expression of a state of mind." *New York Times* reviewer Michiko Kakutani saluted Tallent's insightful treatment of Tara and her best friend and attributed the book's slow pace to "the sense of drift and impermanence that haunts the grownups [and children]."

In her sensitive depiction of Tara in *Museum Pieces*, Tallent ventures into a new realm, one she explores further in her next collection, *Time with Children*. In the title piece and three other stories, an American husband and wife living in London finally abandon their adulterous brinkmanship because of the innocent intercession of children. "Black Holes" conveys the sad resignation of a little girl who assumes that she must live alone now that her father and stepmother have a new baby. Tallent continues to emphasize place, notably in a series of stories about a couple whose marriage threatens to disintegrate after they buy an isolated, ramshackle house outside of Santa Fe. One of these stories, "Favor," was selected for *The Best American Short Stories 1987*. In the contributors' notes, Tallent comments that many of her works "seem to me to be about how land or a house belongs to someone, or how some*one* belongs to someone, and what two people, if they "belong together,' must exclude; not only that, but how those two people interpret belonging, what responsibility it entails for them, and how it feels to them. That is the crux for me: how it feels to them. I sometimes imagine that writing a story is a way of setting up a field of details such that the feeling you are chasing can play over and through those details."

In a *Times Literary Supplement* review, Isabel Fonseca noted that this attention to detail in *Time with Children* tends to overwhelm within a single story but that "cumulatively [Tallent's] precision lends a vibrancy to concerns that could easily seem trivial." Tallent's women characters all struck Fonseca as cynical, savvy, and faithful to lost causes. Fonseca construed both this continuity and the reappearance of characters as practice for a promising novel. *Library Journal* reviewer Mary Soete found the western settings, strong women, marriage, and infidelity reminiscent of *Museum Pieces*. "The beauty of Tallent's prose," Soete remarked, "focuses the clarifying light of heartache on emotional dilemma and dislocated lives."

In *Honey: Stories*, Tallent revisits some of the families featured in *Time with Children*. She continues to investigate the relationships and day-to-day lives of couples, parents and children, and divorced spouses. For instance, "Prowler" concerns a man who suddenly grants his ex-wife partial custody of their son after he breaks into her apartment and finds irrefutable evidence of her vulnerable, endearing motherhood. In "Kid Gentle," a young woman gropes for ways to relieve the estrangement and hollowness she feels after a miscarriage.

Jay Parini observed, in the *New York Times Book Review* (1993), that Tallent presents marriage as "a kind of crucible in which one is tested and tempered." Her use of language, attention to nuance rather than plot, and insight into ordinary lives reminded Parini of John Updike's work. Although Tallent sometimes overextends her descriptions, he concluded that her stories are "full of wisdom and, finally, the kind of tender grace that has become her trademark."

Tallent's stories have been published in a wide variety of periodicals and included in several anthologies. She has received many honors and awards, notably a 1983 National Endowment for the Arts fiction fellowship, an O. Henry Award (1984), and inclusion in the PEN Syndicated Fiction Project (1985), which publishes outstanding short stories in newspapers throughout the United States. In addition to fiction, Tallent has written reviews for the *New York Times Book Review* and other publications and contributed articles on Santa Fe art collectors, gal-

leries, and historic landscapes to *Architectural Digest*. She has established a second career as a writing instructor, teaching at the University of California at Irvine in 1986, the University of Nevada at Reno in 1987, and the University of Iowa and Iowa Writers' Workshop in 1989. In 1990, she was appointed to a teaching position in the English Department at the University of California at Davis. She lives in Davis and Little River, California, with her son Gabriel.

PRINCIPAL WORKS: *Novel*—Museum Pieces, 1985. *Short stories*—In Constant Flight, 1983; Time with Children, 1987; Honey: Stories, 1993. *Nonfiction*—Married Men and Magic Tricks: John Updike's Erotic Heroes, 1982.

ABOUT: Contemporary Authors 117, 1986; Contemporary Literary Criticism 45, 1987; Dictionary of Literary Biography 130, 1991. *Periodicals*—American Literature March 1983; Choice January 1983; Hudson Review Autumn 1985; Library Journal October 15, 1987; New York Times March 30, 1985; New York Times Book Review April 7, 1985; November 7, 1993; Publishers Weekly September 6, 1993; Saturday Review May/June 1985; Times Literary Supplement July 8–14, 1988.

TAN, AMY (February 19, 1952–   ), American novelist, short story writer, and essayist, was born in Oakland, California, the only daughter of the three children of Chinese immigrants—Daisy Ching and John Tan, a Beijing-educated electrical engineer and Baptist minister. Her parents met in China and emigrated in the late 1940s to California, where they married and began raising a family. They moved frequently while the author was growing up, living in Oakland, Fresno, Berkeley, and various suburbs of San Francisco before settling in Santa Clara. Tan, who experienced this early period in her life as one of constant adjustment, has said that she reacted by living in her imagination. Wanting to blend into the American culture, she felt caught by the clash between her own wishes and those of her parents. At the age of eight, when she won an essay contest, she began dreaming of writing fiction, knowing that her parents wanted her instead to become a neurosurgeon and part-time concert pianist—and to speak perfect English while retaining her identity. She later recalled having grown up with a sense of shame and self-hatred, a feeling that was hardly mitigated when in adolescence her older brother and father both died of brain tumors.

Shortly afterward, in 1968, her mother moved with Amy and Amy's younger brother John Jr. to Europe, finally settling in Montreux, Switzer-

AMY TAN

land. It was at this time that Tan's determination to resist the strictures of her upbringing erupted into open adolescent rebellion, doing "a bunch of crazy things. My mother . . . thought I should be even better as a daughter because of what had happened to her family. Instead, I just kind of went to pieces." Among other things her mother broke up her relationship with a man who was involved in drug dealing by informing on the man to the police and then driving Tan to meet him. "Seeing him no longer had anything to do with rebellion and I realized I wasn't interested anymore," she told an interviewer for the *Toronto Globe and Mail.*

Tan's mother, a part of whose tragic early life is told in the author's second novel, *The Kitchen God's Wife*, must be counted not only as a central influence in Amy Tan's life but the muse of much of her writing—even though it took Tan a long time to realize how much her mother's stories about growing up and marrying a first husband in China had sparked her own creative imagination. Tan's maternal grandmother, living on an island off the coast of Shanghai, had been ostracized after a wealthy womanizer forced her into concubinage by raping her. After the grandmother committed suicide, Tan's mother married an abusive man and had three daughters; though she eventually obtained a divorce and escaped to the United States, she had to abandon the daughters, who remained in the custody of the brutal first husband. "My mother could never talk about any of this, even with her closest friends," Tan told a *Life* interviewer. When Daisy Ching Tan finally did confide her

life story to her daughter, and Tan reassured her that she understood, the mother burst out: "How can you understand? You did not live in China then. You do not know what it's like to have no position in life . . . We had no face! We belonged to nobody! This is a shame I can never push off my back."

Tan's eventual discovery of the facts of her Chinese heritage, enhanced by a trip she took with her mother to Beijing in 1987, finally reconciled her to her origins. As she put it in the 1991 *Life* magazine interview: "This (now) is the picture I see when I write. These are the secrets I was supposed to keep. These are the women who never let me forget why stories need to be told."

But the road that led from Tan's early rebellion to her eventually becoming a writer of short stories and novels, and reconciling with her mother, was a difficult one. After the year she spent in Europe as an adolescent, during which time Tan finished high school, she and her mother and brother returned to the San Francisco Bay area. It was her mother's idea to enroll her, in 1969, as a premed student in Linfield College, a Baptist institution in Oregon, but after two semesters Tan followed her Italian-American boyfriend, Louis DeMattei, to San Jose City College, where she changed her major to English and linguistics—a change that enraged her mother and led to an estrangement between the two for six months. She married DeMattei in 1974 shortly after earning a B.A. at San Jose State University; she later obtained an M.A. degree in linguistics. Then, after working briefly toward a doctorate at the University of California at Santa Cruz and at Berkeley, she dropped out in 1976 to become a language-development consultant to the Alameda County Association for Retarded Citizens before switching into business writing in the early 1980s. Still a rebel, she began writing nonfiction as a free lance after being told by her boss that writing was her worst skill and she should hone her talents toward account management.

Tan was so successful as a business writer that she was soon able to establish a business of her own. "My mother started feeling that maybe I was doing okay for myself when I became successful as a freelance business writer and my husband and I were able to buy her a place to live in," Tan has said. "That's really what success is about in Chinese families—it's not success for yourself, it's success so you can take care of your family."

But Tan was dissatisfied, feeling that she had not yet found her own voice. She was measuring success by the number of clients she had and how much money she was making, sensing all this time that her priorities had become distorted. In 1983 she entered therapy, feeling that she had become a workaholic, but she quit after a few months when she discovered that her therapist was interested only in hearing about the events that had made her miserable in childhood. Thereafter, she became her own therapist, reading fiction by Eudora Welty, Flannery O'Connor, Alice Munro, and Louise Erdrich, and then writing her own first short story, "Endgame," about a precocious young chess champion who has had a stormy relationship with her overprotective Chinese mother. After joining a fiction writers' workshop run by the novelist Oakley Hall, Tan rewrote her story, which was published in *FM* magazine and reprinted in *Seventeen*. Molly Giles, a Flannery O'Connor Award–winner, who had guided Tan's rewrite, sent the story to literary agent Sandra Dijkstra, who decided after Tan had written a second story, "Waiting Between the Trees," to represent her. Dijkstra, who was favorably impressed by Tan's writing, requested synopses for several more stories and then proceeded to try to market the collection as a book. Not really thinking that there was a chance of the book's being published, Tan accompanied her mother to visit her half-sisters in Beijing.

Meeting her half-sisters and getting to know China for the first time was a turning point in her life. "It was instant bonding," Tan has said. "I found something about myself that I never knew was there." On returning to San Francisco, she joined a new writers' group and was happily surprised to learn that Dijkstra had meantime obtained a commitment from Putnam's to pay her a fifty thousand dollar advance for a book, which was to be composed from the stories she had previously written plus several more. "[I wrote the additional chapters] very quickly because I was afraid this chance would just slip out of my hands," Tan has said. "I'd light incense, put on certain music, and start to imagine myself in another world. I conjured up people to come and tell me their stories. Then I'd enter that other world and hours would go by and I'd forget everything else."

Tan's first novel, *The Joy Luck Club*, was published in March 1989. Constructed as a series of short vignettes, the book explores the generational and cultural differences that separate four American-born daughters from their Chinese mothers. Throughout the novel, the various mothers and daughters attempt to articulate their concerns about the past and present and to understand how their different lives have affected their relations with one another. Among the many reviewers who praised the book, Orville Schell, in the *New York Times Book Review*,

was perhaps the most laudatory. "In the hands of a less talented writer," he wrote, "such thematic material might easily have become overly didactic, and the characters might have seemed like cutouts from a Chinese-American knockoff of *Roots*. But in the hands of Amy Tan, who has a wonderful eye for what is telling, a fine ear for dialogue, a deep empathy for her subject matter, and a guilelessly straightforward way of writing, they sing with a rare fidelity and beauty. She has written a jewel of a book." Although a few reviewers reacted less favorably, feeling that the book was lively but not profound, *The Joy Luck Club* attracted a large readership and for several months was on the *New York Times* best-seller list. In November 1989, Tan became a finalist for the National Book Award for fiction and was nominated for the National Book Critics Circle Award. She received the Bay Area Book Reviewers Award for fiction and the Commonwealth Club Gold Award. Since then, *The Joy Luck Club* has been translated into seventeen languages. It was made into a very successful film in 1993, with a screenplay by Tan. The film was directed by the Chinese-American filmmaker Wayne Wang and it was the first "mainstream-American" film with an all-Asian cast.

Tan's second novel, *The Kitchen God's Wife*, published in 1991, tells the life story of Jiang Weili, who grew up in China in the 1920s, married an abusive husband, lived with him and her son throughout World War II, then finally escaped to America to join and marry the Chinese-American man she had fallen in love with during the war. The daughter she raises in America, wanting only to be assimilated, at first knows nothing of her mother's story; but after hearing it, she becomes reconciled to her Chinese origins. An underlying theme of the book is the inhumanity of women's lives in 19th-century China. Tan, who had started and abandoned several other novels before settling on this one, has credited her mother as the inspiration for her second work of fiction. She remarked to Jonathan Mandell in an interview in *New York Newsday*, "When my mother read *The Joy Luck Club*, she was always complaining to me how she had to tell her friends that, no, she was not the mother or any of the mothers in the book . . . So she came to me one day and she said, 'Next book, tell my true story.'" Tan told Mandell that "the most terrible things that happened to [Jiang Weili] happened to my mother. And I left out things that were even worse . . . (and changed things, and added things.) I think one of my mother's great despairs was that she went through such a horrible life and nobody had compassion for her. Nobody understood."

Many reviewers of the book were favorably impressed. Josephine Humphreys, in *Chicago Tribune Books*, wrote that the book "can be read and reread with enormous pleasure" and that the final reconciliation of mother and daughter proves the "usefulness of story-telling as a way of thinking, a way of evaluating the human experience." Pico Iyer, in *Time*, commented that "Tan has transcended herself again, triumphing over the ghosts . . . raised by her magnificent first book." A few reviewers had reservations, among them Christopher Lehmann-Haupt, in the *New York Times*, who expressed the opinion that while the book was entertaining in many respects, it was "also cliched and predictable." He found the cruel husband of the book, Wen Fu, to be "a man of such one-dimensional malevolence that one can only regard him as a caricature," and lamented that the portraiture "shrinks . . . Tan's story to the moral dimension of pop fiction."

Tan's *The Moon Lady*, illustrated by Gretchen Schields, is a departure from her earlier books. It has been described as a picture book for children aged seven through eleven, derived from a story in *The Joy Luck Club* and given a happy ending. Ellen Schecter, in the *New York Times Book Review* (1992), commented that the book was an "invitation to young readers to attend a long-ago autumn moon festival in China," and that "Schield's vigorous illustrations capture the mood and tone of the story." Nevertheless, Schecter found "structural flaws in the first and last pages, which are also marred by stilted dialogue and spurious morals . . . *The Moon Lady* can stand alone without the extra baggage of flashback and update."

Amy Tan lives in San Francisco with her husband, Louis DeMattei, a tax attorney. She enjoys playing the piano and drawing; her favorite sports are skiing and playing billiards.

PRINCIPAL WORKS: The Joy Luck Club, 1989; The Kitchen God's Wife, 1991; The Moon Lady, (ill. G. Schields), 1992; The Chinese Siamese Cat (ill. G. Schields), 1994.

ABOUT: Contemporary Authors 136, 1992; Current Biography Yearbook, 1992; Who's Who in America 1995. *Periodicals*—Chicago Tribune Books June 9, 1991; Life April 1991; New York Newsday July 15, 1991; New York Times June 20, 1991; New York Times Book Review March 19, 1989; November 8, 1992; September 5, 1993; Time, June 3, 1991; Toronto Globe and Mail June 25, 1991.

TANNER, TONY (PAUL ANTHONY) (March 18, 1935–), British literary critic and reviewer, was born in Richmond to Arthur Bertram and Susan (Williamson) Tanner. After completing his secondary education at Raynes Park County Grammar School, he went to Jesus College, Cambridge, where he received both an M.A. and a Ph.D. in English. Except for periods of study and teaching abroad, Tanner has been associated with Cambridge University all his professional life—as fellow of King's College since 1960, university lecturer from 1966 to 1980, reader in American literature from 1980 to 1989, and since then professor of English and American literature. He was an American Council of Learned Societies Fellow at the University of California in Berkeley in the academic year 1962–1963 and had a fellowship at the Center for Advanced Studies in Behavioral Sciences at Stanford in 1975, as well as visiting lectureships over the years at Northwestern, Emory, and other American universities.

Specializing in 19th- and 20th-century English and American literatures, Tanner is best known to students and general readers in the United States and Great Britain for his critical introductions to English and American authors and his introductions to particular texts ranging from the novels of Jane Austen and Charlotte Brontë to those of Melville and Henry James. If his work to to be categorized, it belongs to the once honored but now underappreciated genre of belles lettres rather than to literary criticism per se. As David Bromwich observed in the *New Republic* of Tanner's monograph *Jane Austen*: "One can read for pages at a stretch with the pleasant sense of overhearing a reader talking to other readers. In short this is the sort of intelligent study of a single author's views that has become uncommon in recent criticism. It is genuinely introductory as well as genuinely searching."

In his preface to *Scenes of Nature, Signs of Men* Tanner speaks of his "ongoing interest and pleasure" in American literature, awakened in 1958 when he first visited the United States and began writing on Henry Adams and Mark Twain. This interest was inspired by Henry Nash Smith, the distinguished Mark Twain scholar under whom he studied at the University of California at Berkeley.

The direct result of those early studies was *The Reign of Wonder: Naivety and Realism in American Literature*, in which he traced the influence of American transcendentalism, specifically the conception of a universal Nature, from Emerson and Thoreau to such 20th-century figures as Gertrude Stein, Sherwood Anderson, and Ernest Hemingway. The sense of wonder, Tanner suggested, in its variety of shapes and forms, was shared by writers as diverse as Mark Twain and Henry James and continued to dominate the imaginations of writers as contemporary (in 1965) as J. D. Salinger. Tanner's thesis, David Daiches wrote in *Encounter*, "is not, of course, new, but the intelligence and perceptiveness with which . . . Tanner has developed and illustrated it help to make his book a stimulating invitation to reconsider this aspect of American literature."

Tanner continued to work on American writers, producing a book on Saul Bellow and later one on Henry James. In 1971 he published *City of Words*, a study of American fiction from 1950 to 1970. Fascinated by what he perceived as a paradox in the American literary imagination, Tanner argued that American novelists have been torn between a dread of total loss of identity and the threat of the domination of one's identity by some rigid outside force. In his introduction he writes: "I shall try to show that there is an abiding dream in American literature that an unpatterned, unconditional life is possible, in which your movements and stillnesses, choices and repudiations, are all your own; and that there is also an abiding American dread that someone else is patterning your life, that there are all sorts of invisible plots afoot to rob you of your autonomy of thought and action, that conditioning is ubiquitous." To meet this challenge the writer creates his own identity by his special use of language and becomes preoccupied with "a general self-consciousness about the strange relationship between the provinces of words and things, and the problematical position of man, who participates in both." The writer is, as it were, a citizen of "the City of Words." Having long recognized "how tenuous, arbitrary, and even illusory" language is in its efforts to communicate reality, novelists of the mid-20th century create their identities by manipulating language to their own ends. Tanner examines some twenty American authors—such well-established figures as Bellow, Roth, Mailer, Malamud and, in the early 1970s, Pynchon, Hawkes, and Gaddis. Reviewers singled out as probably the best chapter in the book his discussion of Ralph Ellison's *Invisible Man*, which, "so far from being limited to an expression of an anguish or injustice experienced peculiarly by Negroes," Tanner writes, "was quite simply the most profound novel about American identity since the war." The reviewer in the *Times Literary Supplement* wrote of *City of Words*: "The analysis of the anxieties and fears surrounding the question of identity is most perceptive." But Tanner's overall views on language struck this reviewer as "a disappointment . . . due mainly

to the author's uncritical approach—a suspension of judgment which he justifies as essential to the appreciation of diversity and variety." Jonathan Raban, in the *New Statesman & Society*, found the book impressive in its scope but "oddly brittle [with] all the flash and parry, the taste for provocative intellectual games and puzzles, the passionate enthusiasm for what's new, of a packed undergraduate course in the hands of a hard-headed good talker."

Tanner continued his studies in American literature with *Henry James: The Writer and His Work*—actually an extension of his interest in the late-19th-century English novel as well. Like much of his other work, this book is a collection of previously published pieces, in this case three pamphlets he had written for the British Council publications. While it was hailed by J. J. Benardete in *Choice* as "a splendid brief introduction to James," it had a chilly reception from Nina Baym in the *New England Quarterly*, who found the plot summaries "slovenly work" and Tanner's whole approach "reductive and patronizing." The extremes with which reviewers have received Tanner's work in recent years reflect the gulf between the generalist reader and the specialist scholar-critic. Increasingly Tanner's work has come under attack for the very qualities that have appealed to popular readers: it is easily accessible, provides summaries without delving deeply into critical questions, and offers "short cuts" to literary study. This is not to suggest, however, that Tanner ignores the latest trends. In *City of Words* he acknowledges his indebtedness to Vladimir Nabokov's "lexical playfulness" and to Borges's ventures into games of the imagination. He shows familiarity with the radical intellectuals who influenced the 1960s—McLuhan, Marcuse, Wilhelm Reich—and in later writings Tanner paid his dues to literary theory without embracing it. He says of Jacques Derrida, for example, (in a book review in the *Times Literary Supplement* in 1992): "At times he meanders into self-parody and undeniable silliness, . . . but at times he worries his inquiries and meditations through to tracts of thought which have never been opened up before, and brilliant propositions and formulations which can radically change and enlarge our sense of the wonder of reading and writing."

In *Scenes of Nature, Signs of Men* Tanner collected his essays, lectures, and radio talks ranging over twenty-five years on American literature. The unifying theme of the book is his sheer pleasure in that literature: "From this point of view," he writes in his preface, "it is at once something of an act of homage and a small repayment of a debt of gratitude." His subjects range here from 19th-century figures—Henry Adams, Walt Whitman, Stephen Crane, Mark Twain—to contemporaries—Don DeLillo, William Gass, John Barth, and Thomas Pynchon. Barbara Fisher, in the *New York Times Book Review*, had high praise for the book: "As always . . . Tanner is sensitive, subtle, surprising. He is not bound by critical theories." She especially approved "his most dazzling essay," "Games American Writers Play," where, she wrote, he "relates the post-modernists' nonrealistic, nonreferential novels to play, games and a spirit of carnival." (Tanner uses "carnival" as it was defined by Michael Bakhtin—the liberation of the spirit from all rigid forms.) As has become almost typical of the reception of his books, *Scenes of Nature, Signs of Men* also evoked much cooler response. Harold Beaver characterized it, in the *Times Literary Supplement* (1988), as a "mere torso," a selection from previously published essays and lectures dating back to 1961. But Beaver conceded that "with a barrel as rich as his, even such a miscellaneous volume is well worth having. It represents the whole range of American literature."

Tanner by no means confined his studies to American literature. *Adultery in the Novel: Contract and Transgressions* is a foray into comparative literature with essays on what he considers "three key novels of adultery"—Rousseau's *La Nouvelle Héloïse*, Goethe's *Elective Affinities*, and Flaubert's *Madame Bovary*. He centers his attention primarily on novels of bourgeois family life because it is there that adultery becomes rebellion against society's values and codes of behavior. He writes:

> What kind of imagination did the family stir and nourish? Apparently complicit with "the sanctity of the family," the centrality of marriage, and the authority of the Father, the novel has, in fact, in many case harbored and decorously celebrated quite contrary feelings. Very often the novel writes of contracts but dreams of transgressions, and in reading it, the dream tends to emerge more powerfully.

Tanner wrote *Venice Desired* for the Blackwell Series on Cities. As a literary scholar he studies the "textualizing of a city," showing how the most romantic of cities has been "depicted, deployed, dramatized—perhaps reinvented, metamorphosed or transfigured in selected writings." He ranges widely among British (Byron), American (James, Pound), and continental writers (Proust, Sartre, Rilke, Mann)—all of whom found in Venice "an ambiguous object of desire, both aesthetic and erotic, both tempting and dangerous." Once again reviewer reaction swung from enthusiasm—as exemplified by T.

L. Cooksey, in *Library Journal*, who found the book "a witty, erudite and often exuberant examination"—to acerbity—as demonstrated by Geoff Dyer's remarks, in the *New Statesman & Society*, that Tanner "does not write in clichés, he thinks in them—but this undertaking is jeopardised by the fact that his over-literariness comes close to rendering him sub-literate."

Tanner has been married since 1979 to Nadia Fusini. He lists his recreations in *Who's Who* as travel and talk.

PRINCIPAL WORKS: The Reign of Wonder: Naivety and Reality in American Literature, 1965; Saul Bellow, 1965; City of Words: American Fiction 1950–1970, 1971; Adultery in the Novel: Contract and Transgressions, 1979; Thomas Pynchon, 1982; Henry James: The Writer and His Work, 1985; Jane Austen, 1986; Scenes of Nature, Signs of Men, 1987; Venice Desired, 1992. *As editor*—Austen, J. Mansfield Park, 1966; Henry James: Modern Judgments, 1968; James, H. Hawthorne, 1968; Austen, J. Sense and Sensibility, 1969; Austen, J. Pride and Prejudice, 1972; Brontë, C. Villette, 1979; James, H. Roderick Hudson, 1981; Melville, H. Moby Dick, 1988; Melville, H. The Confidence Man, 1989; Emerson, R. W. Essays and Poems, 1992.

ABOUT: Contemporary Authors 85–88, 1980; Who's Who 1984. *Periodicals*—Choice April 1986; Encounter October 1965; Library Journal September 15, 1992; New England Quarterly March 1986; New Republic May 18, 1987; New Statesman & Society March 19, 1971; June 19, 1992; New York Times Book Review June 19, 1988; Times Literary Supplement July 16, 1971; June 19, 1988.

*TANSI, SONY LABOU (SONY, MARCEL) (June 5, 1947–June 14, 1995), African playwright and novelist, was born in Kimwanza, Zaire, of a Zairian father and a Congolese mother. His father moved him from a Belgian missionary education in local languages to the then French Congo on the other side of the river so the boy would learn French. Sony describes the method: any pupils who used their own language in class or made a mistake in French had a foul-smelling "Symbol" hung around their necks, which they passed on only when—as the "Watcher"—they could catch another unfortunate pupil in a mistake. Not surprisingly, in later life Sony would say that a principal intention in his work is to develop, "in the French tongue, our *own* language." His traumatic launching into the French of the colonizer gave way to nearly twenty plays and novels especially known for their decolonized French, a syntax and vocabulary full of "puns, surprising abbreviations, a continuous intrusion of the oral into the written," as one critic put it; while J.-P.

°TAN zee, SON nee la BOO

Morel, in a review in *Le Matin*, admired him for writing French "with such an instinct for the nuances of the language." He went to high school in the capital, Brazzaville ("that ancient capital of France," he later called it, sadly or mockingly: it had in fact been the capital of French Equatorial Africa in colonial times), and completed his education at the Ecole Normale Supérieure d'Afrique Centrale. He became a high school teacher of French and English in several provincial centers.

As a teacher, Sony worked somewhat subversively with the student's creativity, through student newspapers and theater groups. The authorities often greeted these labors with censorship, which Sony anticipated by calling the newspaper *The Voice of Silence*. Eventually he made his way to Pointe Noire, where he taught English at the Collège Tchicaya-Pierre, and then to Brazzaville, where he worked as an administrator in several ministries. His work is full of hilarious satire of bureaucratic mentality and language, for which his own practical experience may well have been the source; an old fisherman in *L'Anté-peuple* (*The Antipeople*) remarks that "The only blood circulating now is the blood of paper documents." He first wrote poetry, but finding it hard to publish even with a preface by Senghor, he turned to fiction and drama. In one year, his first play (*Conscience de tracteur* [Tractor Consciousness]), first novel (*La Vie et demie* [A Life and a Half]), and a novella (*Le Malentendu* [The Misunderstanding]) were published, and both the novel and the novella won literary prizes in France. The same year in Brazzaville, he founded, and still directs, one of the best-known theater troupes in Africa, the Rocado Zulu Theatre, which took his plays to Dakar, Paris, and New York (where George C. Wolfe directed), and established his international reputation. In 1985 there were three of Sony's plays being staged at the same time in Paris theaters, and he has consistently won prizes at international festivals from 1978 to the present; among them are the 1982 Inter-African Theatre Prize for his troupe, the 1983 Grand Prix de l'Afrique Noire for the novel *L'Anté-Peuple*, and in 1988 the Ibsen Foundation Prize, given by the drama critics of Paris, and the First Prize at the International Festival of Francophone Cultures.

He has been described since he began publishing as a "leader of the new generation of francophone writers in sub-Saharan Africa." The Zairian critic Georges Ngal, a professor at the Sorbonne, links Sony with Henri Lopès among African writers in French as creators of "a new literature which corresponds to the new political realities" of the second postindependence generation. Lopès introduced Sony's first play by distinguishing what this writing had in view: "not a story of exotic Africa nor of that of the griots; not . . . local color; it's a way of telling us that heroes, leaders, scholars aren't enough for the great advance [*Grande Marché*] of Africa; we need also and above all masters of thought and feeling." They looked to such predecessors of the 1960s as the Malian Yambo Ouologuem and the Ivoirian Ahmadou Kourouma, says Ngal. To these names should be added, from his own generation, Calixthe Beyala and Werewere Liking, whose novels and plays, with a women's perspective on sexual politics, breathe the same postmodern atmosphere as Sony's "antipeople"; he is also much influenced by his great Congolese precursor Tchicaya U Tam'si, particularly Tchicaya's later work like the fantasmagoric novel *Les Méduses* (The Madman and the Medusa). Ngal derives the "new tone" of Sony's generation from the figure of the African teacher (*didacteur*), with his or her "clowning, cracking jokes, fantasticality, grotesquerie, and burlesque." Ngal quotes Sony's phrase for this new tone: *tropicalités*, the writing of "tropical violence." Like anglophone writers of the same generation such as Ben Okri and Salman Rushdie, he is often compared to the magical realists of Latin American fiction, especially Gabriel García Márquez. In this vein, he has referred to the writer's task as "my job of being mad but clearheaded [*dingue sans déconner*]." The African-American critic Eileen Julien, the leading authority in English on Sony, comes to a similar conclusion; she writes in her book on orality in African novels that his "impulse is to empower . . . through a tradition of ridicule and fable."

The strong emotional palette of this *tropicalité* stems largely from Sony's obsessive sense—from his vantage point in central Africa—of world historical crisis, the threat of "nuclear suicide and chemical death," as Christian Descamps wrote in his review of the novel *Les Sept Solitudes de Lorsa Lopez* (The Seven Solitudes of Lorsa Lopez) in *Le Monde*. "We are the children of *Cosmocide*," Sony wrote in 1979. Africa's place in this ecologically and politically convulsive world is suggested by the image of the volcano; in his preface to the novel *Les Yeux du volcan* (The Eyes of the Volcano), he said: "Africa is a volcano. The whole world is another volcano. Our peoples are volcanoes and their eyes are watching us." He spoke, in an interview published under the title "Breaking through Words" ("Casser les mots"), of a transnational way of thinking which his work is designed to strengthen: "Today, to speak of the universal is not only a right but a duty. . . . Nations have created a national consciousness, and now people must acquire an international consciousness." Consistent with his postnationalism, Sony's notion of culture and civilization makes them equivalent to a posture of "listening to the Other" (*IL'écoute de l'autre*) and the "negotiation" of difference: "It is for this that I write," he says in the same interview. Breaking through a dangerously outmoded nationalism thus corresponds to his "breaking" of forms, styles, genres, and literary language itself: "It has always been thought that Africa was a civilization of the word," he said in the epigraph to *Les Sept Solitudes*: "I assert the exact opposite: we are really the civilization of silence. A crossblood silence [*silence métissé*]." This manifesto announces defamiliarization and cross-cultural hybridity as markers of a new aesthetic. In *La Vie et demie*, Eileen Julien points out, Sony "abandons the canons of realism that governed fiction in the 1950s and 1960s," producing a fictional landscape of "grandiose Rabelaisian numbers" like the 12,711 books which appear praising a dictator after his death, outsize character having sex with fifty virgins on national television, or the same or bringing to his political career "his eighteen outstanding qualities as a former cattle thief." This novel, particularly rich in satire even for Sony, includes in the goings-on at His Excellency's palace (*le palais excellentiel*, he puns in French) a political party named PPUDT (*pute* is French slang for "prostitute"); 228 national holidays, including one honoring spermicide and another the President's chameleons; a nonsense language—known only to the Heaven-Sent Guide—in which the second article of the Constitution is written; and the banning of the words "hell" and "pain" from the nation's lexicon. The novel, Julien concludes, is "a discourse about the betrayal of discourse."

Against the neocolonial and neotraditional absurdities of official discourse (a thinly disguised reference to the Mobutu regime in Zaire) is ranged a "beautiful battalion of spray-painters [*pistolétographes*]," who paint even the palace walls with the slogan of the revolutionary Martial: "I will not die this death." Sony has said that while he does not like war he adores "combat," because for him it contains "the essential dynamism of the universe, that is, contradiction and questioning" (one of his characters, a scholar, speaks of being "crucified on a giant question mark"). The novelist as *pistolétographe*, he enlists laughter in this combat in what Julien calls a "liberating strategy" of *La Vie et demie*. She quotes Mikhail Bakhtin on laughter to illustrate the method: "Laughter demolishes fear and piety before an object, before a world"—even such a fearsome world as Mobutu's Zaire, with its Western backing.

Laughter and Sony's other extravagant literary effects defend the psyche against the surreal or numbing harshness of real events. Despite their antinaturalist aesthetic, many of his works are in fact based on specific happenings. He said of *La Vie et demie*, for example, that it was "a sort of cruel fable" written in anger at a particularly bad moment in 1977 just after some friends had been killed. *L'Anté-peuple* too was based on the story of a friend from Zaire, a refugee in Pointe Noire, who had been falsely accused of the murder of a young woman. Similarly, *Les Sept Solitudes de Lorsa Lopez* began with a real event, the sight of a body, surrounded by a crowd waiting for the police, which lay outside the Brazzaville hospital where his wife worked. It is the deaths, the State murders, that most emgage his imagination; and the political lying, indifference, amnesia, and devastation of language and public culture they entail inspire writing which the writer describes as deliberately provocative: "You can't make an omelette without breaking words [*casser les mots*]. . . . I write to make people feel fear and shame." *L'Etat honteux* (State of shame) "was inspired by Mobutu's speeches. He's a man with a certain magic in his words." Laughter functions here as a kind of anti-magic breaking the words of power, the shamanistic charisma of writing exerted against the aura of official culture, or what often figures in Sony's work as "the capital"—the hypertrophied State, the overdeveloped, parasitic city. The South African novelist Lewis Nkosi pointed out in the *Times Literary Supplement* that African literary modernism, for complex reasons, "entailed an immediate conflict with postindependence governments"; one of Nkosi's examples, the Zimbabwean Dambudzo Marechera, was a contemporary and kindred spirit of Sony Labou Tansi. As a leading member of the African avant-garde, Sony shows that the idiom of modernism—satiric fable, inventive excess, the style of *casser les mots*—is as effective a weapon against the parasitic State as the critical realism of his Senegalese predecessor Sembene Ousmane.

It is often argued against (post)modernism, as a heavily intellectualist tradition, that it marginalizes African writers in their own societies and implies writing for an international audience instead. This explains the turning to theater and cinema of many African writers, Sony among them. Sony refuses to define an African theater or a Black theater, or to enter a competition with European theater on its own terms. Like many postcolonial writers, he believes instead that "what's needed now is to imagine a world theater in which African theater will find its place," side-stepping the colonial polarity between the bounded cultures of center and periphery. His troupe performs in Western capitals and villages in the bush, where they gather spectators by such methods as rushing through the village miming a hunt (some actors are dogs, some the prey, some the hunters), until the onlookers are seduced into becoming an audience.

While the plays share themes and inventiveness of language with his fiction, Sony has said that the center of theater is the actor, and the performative style of his theater stresses surprise, timing, changes of tempo, and sudden, bewildering shifts in perspective, so that the act of performance itself mimes something essential in Sony's worldview: actors "play with life in a permanent dialogue with suicide: as soon as they mount the stage, they must kill a part of themselves." Bernard Magnier said of *La Parenthèse du sang* (Parentheses of Blood) that the characters, though they change names, roles, and even the status of being alive or dead, "remain the symbols or spokespeople of those who, victims or perpetrators, live the oppression of their daily reality"—especially its instability.

The "new political realities" Georges Ngal sees at the heart of Sony's novels also animate his plays: the "parentheses" which enclose life and death, for example, are figured in the play as handcuffs (the condemned are handcuffed even to plan a wedding), a chilling image of the security Sate reminiscent of the Eastern European theater of the absurd. In the more realist manner of the play *Je soussigné cardiaque* (I, the Undersigned, Heart Patient), the secretary Hortense says straightforwardly: "What a country! Before independence it stank of the White. Today it stinks again. Of the Black. In every office. The others played against us the card of the skin. Today, 'our own' do it from the heart. They mistreat us as though they had our permission. It's worse." The Old Man, the ambiguous savior or Noah-figure of *Conscience de tracteur*—a play which uses the conventions of science fiction— kills 14, 278 people in order to regenerate them as the New Man "cured of his heart and reason . . . [who] will have the soul and the consciousness of a tractor." He is opposed in the play by a more conventional villain, the General Leiso; but few would wish a victory for either side.

Sony's plays produce a kind of political vertigo in which skepticism is the only reliable anchor. The Old Man says as much: "We have to work with our own silence, our own disorderliness of the body, the furious cadence of doubt." But for Sony "work" remains an ethical imperative, and extreme bewilderment is matched by extremes of inventiveness from his actors on the edge, dialoguing with "permanent suicide."

Like the plays, Sony's novels embrace marginality and displacement from "the capital" as the place of an alternative vision, and even more as the place where sanity and a respect for life can flourish. The plot of *The Antipeople* removes the hero Dadou from his post as president of a teachers college in Zaire to the life of a refugee in a fishing village and among the urban destitute across the river. A drinker like Malcolm Lowry's consul in *Under the Volcano* (the *tropicalités* of Lowry and Sony have sometimes been compared), Dadou is sent on an estranging journey, a shaman's preparatory vision-quest. Typically of Sony's heroes, no climactic vision is ever grasped; Dadou's culminating act is to assassinate a State and Party official during mass in the cathedral, a gratuitous act of little political or cosmic significance, though it is ordered by a vague "Resistance" consisting of groups of the dispossessed and outlawed with no visible program.

The real point of Dadou's ordeal is what he comes to see along the way, in passages that combine a poetics of the river landscape with sexual lyricism. Dadou's alliances are with the river and river people, and with women like Rita (who "swam like a dream of bronze in the turbulent water of the Congo"), the militant Yéaldara, and his wife, whose letters he reads after her death. In the riverine world, where "time came and withdrew, full of events which consumed so many friends, so much knowledge, so much hope, so much strength," Sony defines a margin where the program of modernism may pass for political hope, where writing, like the river, "remained. The sky remained." Dadou's fullest moments are lived in a fluid world, "those liquid moments where everything becomes liquid. Liquidity in thought, word, and deed." The old fisherman Amando in *The Antipeople* gives this metaphysical commitment to sweeping re-vision a more historical edge: "In ten or twenty years, you know, our children will hate the soldier [*le béret*] as we hated the colonizer. And a new decolonization will commence. The most important, the first revolution: the heart, the brain, against the soldier." Sony here allies himself with all those heterogeneous forces in African politics and civil society who press against "recolonization" and for renewal, revision, an open-ended revolution.

Les Sept Solitudes de Lorsa Lopez endorses Fartamio Andra's maxim in the novel: "Enigma is the most beautiful explanation of the world." She urges this against the hunt for explanations by 800 Western scientists encamped on the Ile des Solitudes, looking for reasons why the coastal cliffs around Valancia and Nsanga-Norda groan as a portent before dreadful events like Lorsa

Lopez's murder of his wife. If this novel is the explanation of its central event (as plots usually are), then Sony's point seems to be that no event can be disconnected from any other as cause and effect; each "explains" all, all explain each, or none explain any—and what remains is narrative itself, or pure chronicle. The novel does take the form of an "annals"—a nonexplanatory kind of history—of the coastal town of Valancia. It is a set of stories not causally linked, though sharing the same enigma; the "decapitalization" of Valancia, as by orders of the government the site of the capital is moved to Nsanga-Norda. (Literally moved: gardens, bridges, the fifteen Arcs de Triomphe, the nine Towers of Babel, the bones in the cemetery of Harma Hozorinte, and all.) This decapitalization is echoed in the decapitation of Estina Benta, the assassination of Estina Bronzario (the "head" of the women in Valancia), and the death of Fartamio Andra (of the line of "Founders" of the town). These stories of the deaths of powerful women are told by the female narrator Gracia, who at the end removes herself (the fountainhead of the narrative) from Valancia to Nsanga-Norda—which has itself become removed, submerged by a freak invasion of the sea. Gracia delivers the crowning paradox: "We come into the world to *name*: but woe to her who names her loss or her shame" (as Gracia has done throughout her tale of the fall of women). The novel ends, as Gracia contemplates the sea like Dadou contemplating the Congo River, in an elegy of the liquid world: "Still before us lies the profound beauty of things: if the sea has swallowed Nsanga-Norda, it is no less beautiful for that, the riddle of its robe studded with insects and night-birds, stirred by the deadly uproar of the waves. To die in that night. Rejoin Nsanga-Norda. The sea!" If the sea, like the river and the volcano, represent what the author's preface calls "the silence of History," the stories of Gracia and the other "children of Cosmocide" are speech as counterpoint to that silence.

Counterfactual, fabular narrative continues in *Les Yeux du volcan*, which takes leave of fictional realism altogether, with its events which may or may not have taken place; its explosion of characters into shape-shifting identities with fantastic names like Alvano Salvo do Moesso-Nsa, Tristansio Banga Fernandez, or the Reverend Father Luxor Sadoun ("based in Indiana"); and its images of gigantic horses of different colors parading through the town (Sony has said that his favorite reading is The Book of Revelations). The title is a password—"The eyes of the volcano are watching you"—exchanged among members of a fabulous conspiracy of ancient, disillusioned ex-colonels trying in their uncoordinated, at times farcical way, to restore decency

to the country. According to Sony, it takes place in Brazzaville, a city whose hybrid "place names are tragically fragile, in the wait for an ultimate and improbable revolution." The trickster-shaman emerges fully into the foreground of this novel as the controlling figure of Sony's imagination; not only in major characters like the colossus Affonso Sombro, who oversees events in the first half of the tale, or Benoit Goldmann (a "Hercules in bronze" with blue eyes who reads Genesis aloud to avoid sex with his wife, Alleando Calero), but in the omnipresent crowd of townspeople continually demonstrating, parading, or lining up to shake a hero's hands, and not least in the graffiti artists (like the spray painters of *La Vie et demie*) who convert Party posters and slogans into subversive jokes. Madmen abound, often bearers of wisdom, as when Colonel Claudio Lahenda announces to an enormous crowd, "Comrades, the revolution has been postponed." Lest this remind Western readers of the racist tradition of representing Africa as farce (as in Evelyn Waugh's *Black Mischief*), it should be said that Sony's use of humor—like Rushdie's—has an altogether different tone: self-critical, painfully corrective, serious at heart, and hopeful. *Les Yeux de volcan*, like *The Satanic Verses*, is postcolonial satire, not Swiftian nihilism. A poster-poem by Sombro ends: "Comrades / Don't shoot / The light," which could stand for Sony's confidence about the entry of writers into the combat between the soldier and the heart.

Tansi was found in Foufoundou, a remote village in Congo, by Howard French, a reporter for the *New York Times* in June 1995. Suffering from AIDS, he had left a hospital in Paris to seek healing in a traditional African setting, tended by a spiritual medium and practitioners of herbal medicine. His wife was with him, dying, but Tansi said the incantations and herbs had made him stronger. His son waited back in Brazzaville, endangered and under guard because his father had engaged "more and more in the country's increasingly tribal politics, even winning a seat in the National Assembly," French said. "Still full of combat, Mr. Tansi said he had finished a new work during his Paris stay, 'The Beginnings of Pain,' which he said his publishers had initially refused to publish because of what they saw as its excessively harsh tone toward France. . . . A new nonfiction work, 'La Cosa Nostra,' he said, would argue for a Marshall Plan for Africa."

A few days later, both Tansi and his wife were dead. The *New York Times* obituary by Randy Kennedy said his novels, "known for their biting satirical treatments of colonialist Africa and the dictators who arrived after independence" had made Tansi considered "Central Africa's greatest writer." *The Seven Solitudes of Lorsa Lopez* was to be published.

PRINCIPAL WORKS IN ENGLISH TRANSLATION: *Plays*—(tr. L. A. Veach) Parentheses of Blood, 1986; (tr. L. A. Veach) Afrique, 1987. *Novel*—(tr. J. A. Underwood) The Antipeople, 1988.

ABOUT: Brezault, A. and Clavreuil, G. Conversations congolaises, 1989; Herzberger-Fofara, P. Ecrivains africains et identités culturelles : entretiens, 1989; Higgins, L. A. and Silver, B. R. (eds.) Rape and Representation, 1991; Julien, E. African Novels and the Question of Orality, 1992; Zell, H. M. (ed.) A New Reader's Guide to African Literature, 2nd ed., 1983. *Periodicals*—Jenne Afrique May 11, 1988; Le Matin; Le Monde May 13, 1984; New York Times June 7, 1995; June 15, 1995; New York Times Book Review July 24, 1988; Présence Africaine 120, 1981; Recherche, Pédagogie, et Culture 68, October–December 1984; Research in African Literatures 20, Fall 1989; Silex 23, 1982; Times Literary Supplement July 15, 1988.

TEMPLETON, EDITH (April 7, 1916–   ), British novelist and short story writer, was born in Prague, into a wealthy landowning family. Her father was a doctor of technology who was awarded a gold medal from Emperor Franz Joseph for academic excellence. Templeton attended the French Lycée in Prague from 1931 to 1935, and then the Medical University of Prague from 1936 to 1937. After several short visits to Britain, she settled, at the age of twenty-two, first in Cheltenham and then in London. Her first husband, whom she married in 1938, was William Stockwell Templeton (divorced in 1947), and her second husband, whom she married in 1955, was Dr. Edmund Ronald, a cardiologist in India and physician to the King of Nepal. She has one son, Edmund, from this second marriage. Templeton lived with Ronald in Calcutta and while there met Nehru and the Dalai Lama. Since then, she has lived in Salzburg, Lausanne, Torremolinos, Estoril, and Italy, she speaks Czech, German, French and "fluent bad Italian, unfluent bad Portuguese." During World War II she drew on her medical training and her facility for language to work as a medical coder in the American War Office in the Office of the Surgeon General in Cheltenham and London (1942–1945). From 1945 to 1946 she served as a captain with the British Forces in Germany as conference and law court interpreter.

Templeton began writing early, when she was just four years old, and she had her first story published when she was ten, in the Sunday edition of *Prager Tagblatt*. Her first novel, *Summer in the Country* (U.S. title: *The Proper Bohemians*), was published in 1950. Her nomadic years had provided her with a sense of exile and of statelessness which became crucial to her authorial position. As the novelist Anita Brookner observed, in her introduction to a reissue of the novel in 1985: "[T]he state of exile in which she writes represents both her inner and her outer world; she has lived in many countries since she left her native Prague at the age of nineteen, and although equally at home, or not at home, in Paris, in Torremolinos, in Estoril, in Salzburg, in Katmandu, or . . . in Bordighera, she is at all times definitively removed from her birthplace and from the way of life to which she so constantly refers: the life of the country gentry of central Europe in the years immediately preceding World War Two." Writing out of a sense of exile provides Templeton with the space for ironic detachment. In all her novels she casts a cool, unsentimental eye over the social worlds she depicts. Her prose conveys a subtle sense of strangeness and foreignness essential to her aim, which is to depict "a world in which everything is foreign and everything had enormous style." It comes as no surprise, therefore, that Templeton's work has been compared to that of Turgenev, Jean Rhys, and Chekhov. Templeton's novels deal with a civilized—perhaps over civilized—society. As Brookner explained: "[A]lthough these novels are essentially novels of manners, they are also something more, for running beneath the social comedy, so beautifully conducted by all the principal players, there lies acts of madness, of revenge, and of revolt, resorted to in extreme moments, but—and this is the singular thing—never regretted. It is the strange completeness of these acts, and the density of the context in which they are committed, that give Edith Templeton's novels their unusual savour."

The plot of *Summer in the Country* has been compared to that of Chekhov's *The Cherry Orchard*. The narrative focuses upon a landowning family, the Birks, living in the castle of Kirna in central Bohemia. Family life and family matters are so centrally important to the Birks that outsiders have only a marginal status. A young lawyer who visits as prospective husband for one of the daughters is made nervously aware that he is an outsider, with no hope of ever being an insider. Even the millionaire Oscar Ritter, who has married Mrs. Birk's granddaughter Margot, is not accepted as one of the clan. Indeed he is doubly an outsider, being both not of the family, and—crucially in a social world where manners are all—not quite a gentleman. As a result he coolly disposed of, and Templeton's eccentric family resumes its "normal" life without a twinge of conscience. Most reviewers appreciated the spirited comedy of *Summer in the Country*, but some, like Hugh L'Anson Fausset in the *Manchester Guardian*, while acknowledging the echoes of Turgenev and Chekhov, complained of the absence of any "redeeming tenderness" in the book. James Kelly, in the *New York Times*, however, read it approvingly as a work of serious social criticism. "Going deeper into the novel," he wrote, "one discovers a brisk but sympathetic discourse upon human folly and the blind fanaticism of people determined to preserve an outmoded way of life."

Templeton's second novel, *Living on Yesterday*, again depicts a now-vanished wealthy Czech milieu where servants are vital, enmities and eccentricity thrive, and lavish décor and food are integral to the setting. Templeton makes full use of the metonymic potentials of the realist novel form to evoke society of faded elegance, decadence, and crumbling disarray:

> Although the library faced south and had three windows, it was a sombre room. The moss-green velvet hangings were never completely drawn aside, and the ruched and gathered tulle curtains, once white, were now so dusty that each fold was traced with a line of grey. The divan was draped with a persian rug and strewn with cushions of gold and silver brocade, the covers of which could easily have been identified by old friends of the family as being discarded ball dresses of the late lamented Mrs. Marek. The black bookcases reached to the ceiling and were filled in such a manner that the finely bound and gilt edged volumes stood on the upper and middle shelves, while the paperbacked and bedraggled books occupied the lower regions, irrespective of their contents. A settee and two armchairs of red repp were grouped in a corner near the stove round a table with a blue and red brocade cover trimmed with a tarnished gold fringe, and all the other stands and shelves and small tables in the room had similar brocade covers. Even the small and fashionable objects which litter a man's room, the case for playing cards and the brush for the card table, the appointments book and the blotter, were backed with brocade and enriched with gold braid. A lamp with a domed brown shade was suspended by brass chains from the ceiling like a sinister mushroom.

As in her first novel, a young woman married off to a wealthy husband to shore up the family finances revolts, with devastating results. In both novels, we sense that certain acts are irrevocable, and once committed, nothing can remain the same.

The Island of Desire, Templeton's third novel, remains focused upon a similar social milieu, the beau monde of Vienna and Prague. It vividly portrays a young girl's repressive social training now coupled with obscure erotic impulses: "a woman is a poor creature; what can she give but herself?" The novel charts the progress of Franciska's sexual and emotional voyage of self-discovery as she rebels against her worldly and decadent mother, leaves Prague to explore Europe, and finally commits herself to a disastrous marriage. As history repeats itself, her only escape is migraine (her mother's ailment), and a series of love affairs. Anita Brookner said in her introduction this novel is "succinct," "mordant," and "memorably unsentimental," and while *The Island of Desire* celebrates self-discovery, it is a self-discovery which is arrived at warily and is described in the briefest and most circumspect of terms.

The Surprise of Cremona, though a work of nonfiction, came as no surprise to Templeton's readers. It is an idiosyncratic travel book—witty, shrewdly observed, and totally self-indulgent. A chronicle of her visits to six Northern Italian cities—Cremona, Parma, Mantua, Ravenna, Urbino, and Arezzo—it fulfills her own prophecy, early in the book: "One day I will write an antiguide-book, in the same spirit as the medieval Popes set up anti-Emperors when the actual Emperor did not please them." As an "antiguide-book" *The Surprise of Cremona* registers the impressions of a sophisticated, worldly woman, comfortable in the language and the company of the colorful people she has a gift for discovering everywhere. She travels independently, with no rigid plan, and records miscellaneously her reactions to everything from baroque churches—

> Soon I feel dead tired and disgruntled and I think I have got the recipe by heart: one scroll up and one scroll down above the portal. Flank with two columns, crown same with twisted saint each. Finished. Next, please.

—to eating fettucine—

> At first I wind them round the fork and find that they behave like the crowds in the cathedral square in Parma: while one end is being wound up, the other end—which I believed already secured—strays loose and expects to make a comeback once more. I get tired and just shove them into my mouth. It is no use. A non-Italian cannot look dignified while eating pasta.

Italian travel figures in Templeton's next novel, *This Charming Pastime*, which follows an English woman in Sicily as she experiences passion, jealously, and her lover's sudden death. Published in 1955, this novel was her last for many years. She did not give up writing, however, but turned instead to short stories, which she published in a number of popular magazines in Britain and the United States—*Vogue, Holiday, Harpers*, the *Atlantic*, and the *New Yorker* among them.

A reissue of several of Templeton's novels in the mid-1980s and their favorable critical reception encouraged her to return to the novel form in 1992 with *Murder in Estoril*. Like her earlier work, this book evokes a peculiarly odd and morally ambiguous spirit. As Anne Duchene observed in the *Times Literary Supplement*: "[It] carries the quaint stamp of a writer not born among us and who has not lived among us or listened to us for a long time." Again there are resonances of the work of Jean Rhys, in its depiction of the female narrator's confused existence in a half-world of financial dependence on men and inevitable sexual exploitation. Yet, according to Duchene, the novel also postulates female submission to men, being "a high sexual fantasy" where the narrator finally encounters a man with a special voice, "the voice of authority, of the power to enforce obedience, of unquestioning mastery, or unassailable power."

Templeton, who lists her recreation in *Who's Who* as "travel, with the greatest comfort possible," lives in Bordighera, Italy.

PRINCIPAL WORKS: *Novels*—Summer in the Country, 1950 (reissued as The Proper Bohemians, 1952); Living on Yesterday, 1951; The Island of Desire, 1952; This Charming Pastime, 1955; (with A. Gould and C. Kentfield) Three: 1971, 1971; Murder in Estoril, 1992. *Nonfiction*—The Surprise of Cremona, 1954.

ABOUT: Brookner, A. *introduction to* The Island of Desire, 1985; Brookner, A. *introduction to* Summer in the Country, 1985; Contemporary Authors 53–56, 1975; Who's Who 1994. *Periodicals*—Times Literary Supplement May 15, 1992.

TESICH, STEVE (originally STOYAN) (September 29, 1942–   ), playwright, screenwriter, and novelist, was born in Uzice, Yugoslavia, to Radisa and Gospava (Bulaich) Tesich. His father was a professional soldier who fled to London during World War II to join the government in exile. The family was ignorant of his plans, and for years they assumed that he was dead. However, in 1957 he contacted them from the United States, and arranged for his wife and their two children to join him in East Chicago, Indiana, where he was working in a steel plant. The reunion was strained, since the family unit had been organized around the mother for so long. The father, who died in 1960, seemed distant, and the children could sense his unhappiness with his new life.

Young Tesich was an avid fan of American films, especially Westerns, and consequently looked forward to life in the United States, but the first year was very disappointing. East Chicago did not resemble the prairies of the films, and its pollution and dinginess made a depressing contrast to his hometown of Titovo Uzice (its new name under Marshal Tito). Moreover, Te-

STEVE TESICH

sich did not know any English and so was put back a few grades in school, which made him the butt of classmates' jokes. Encouraged by his mother and fascinated by the family comedies he watched on television, he learned enough English in a year to advance to his proper level in school and began to get excellent grades. Tesich later described his elation at this time as feeling something like "a tuning fork . . . that could respond to the language and the country." He was also impressed by the many nationalities who lived together peacefully, which he said could not happen in Yugoslavia.

In 1961, Tesich entered Indiana University in Bloomington on a wrestling scholarship. His interest soon switched to bicycle racing, a sport he still enjoys, and his team won the school's annual "Little 500" race. Tesich majored in Russian literature, was admitted to Phi Beta Kappa, and graduated in 1965. He won a scholarship to Columbia University in New York, where he continued his Russian studies, earning a master's degree in 1967. He enrolled in Columbia's Ph.D. program with an academic life in mind, but dropped out within a year when, after taking courses in playwriting and short story composition, his interest turned to creative writing. He took a job as a caseworker at the Department of Welfare in Brooklyn, so that he could write in his spare time. Rebecca Fletcher, another social worker, believed so strongly in his talent that she agreed to support them both while Tesich concentrated on his writing. The couple moved to Denver, Colorado, in 1970, and were married in the City Hall in 1971.

Tesich's first six plays all had limited runs off-Broadway in New York. His first offering, *The Carpenters*, opened in December 1970. Absurdist in style, it concerns the disintegrating Carpenter family, whose home is literally collapsing around them. The father is shocked to learn that his son plans to murder him and that the rest of the family is unconcerned. His journey of self-discovery leads him to realize that the harsh rules he has set for the family have ensnared him most of all. Reviewers did not care for the play's obvious symbolism, but they found it a very promising debut.

Lake of the Woods opened a year later, in December 1971. It told a similar but less cataclysmic story of a dysfunctional family trying to break out of its rut by taking an automobile trip to various scenic spots; but the "lake of the woods" has become a dry hole, and the other points of interest are in similar ruin. The family's woes pile up, culminating in the robbery of their car and its contents. However, the father welcomes this as a chance to search for a new reality divorced from empty words and promises. Reviewers praised the witty dialogue, but once again, they deplored the play's heavy-handed symbolism.

In his next play, *Baba Goya*, Tesich turned to quirky comedy, as he recounted the zany adventures of a lower-middle-class extended family consisting of orphans, bastards, standby husbands, a pseudo-grandfather, and a thief, all ruled by an earth mother named Baba Goya. This mixture of Ionesco, Sam Shepard, and *You Can't Take It with You* pleased most of the reviewers, who appreciated Tesich's lively comic spirit. After its initial run in May 1973, *Baba Goya* reopened as *Nourish the Beast* in October 1973 for fifty-four performances.

While at Columbia, Tesich had tried his hand at writing a "Russian" novel (which has never been published), but he drew on his Russian studies for a musical biography of Maxim Gorky, the Russian writer who died in 1936, possibly poisoned. With music by Mel Marvin and lyrics by Tesich, the play uses a trio of actors to show three aspects of Gorky's life: the nature-loving youth, the fierce and idealistic revolutionary, and the disillusioned, dying old man. When *Gorky* opened in 1975, reviewers were sharply divided about its merits. Some thought it a moving, serious play laced with "Gorkyesque" humor, while others considered it a confused and ponderous mixture of styles that veered from naturalism to fantasy and from documentary to stilted folk musical.

Passing Game, which was staged in 1977, features two unsuccessful actors whose guilt at their own failures has already caused them to harm, either physically or emotionally, their blindly adoring wives. The two couples have rented cabins in a deserted area of the woods, where the men hope that a mysterious stranger lurking in the area will murder the women. Self-loathing and bitter rivalry keep surfacing as the two men egg each other on while playing an impromptu game of basketball. The theme reminded critics of the works of Eugene O'Neill and Dostoevsky, but they felt that it was not developed successfully. The play was a milestone in Tesich's career, however, because it marked his first collaboration with Peter Yates, a director who would later work with the playwright on several movies.

In *Touching Bottom*, a trio of two-character short plays which opened in 1978, Samuel Beckett's influence is apparent. In *The Road*, a naive woman hitchhiking to "freedom" in the city meets a disillusioned man who is hitchhiking in the opposite direction, toward the country. *A Life* revolves around a confused old man sitting alone in a room as he tries to straighten out his muddled memories. In *Baptismal*, a widow and widower meet in a graveyard and endlessly repeat their marital vows and mistakes. *Touching Bottom* was greeted as a welcome return to Tesich's easy, absurdist humor in both characterization and dialogue.

Tesich also began to explore the film genre during the 1970s. He wrote six screenplays which created some interest but never attracted financial backing. At Peter Yates's suggestion, he combined two of these early scripts into *Breaking Away*, which Yates produced and directed in 1979. The comedy is often hilarious in its depiction of life in a midwestern college town, where there is a fierce rivalry between a quartet of working-class boys and a group of college students. The climax of the movie is a "Little 500" bicycle race between the two factions, which is won by one of the town boys. Several scenes drew on Tesich's own life as a steelworker's son and a racing enthusiast at Indiana University. *Breaking Away* was a critical and box office success, winning praise for its understanding of small-town life and its affectionate portrayal of the hero's family and friends. The movie won awards from the National Society of Film Critics for best film of 1979, the New York Film Critics' Circle for best screenplay, and an Oscar for best original screenplay.

In 1980, Tesich returned to the stage with *Division Street*, which opened in Los Angeles in May to rave reviews, and came to Broadway in October. The play's hero is a 1960s activist seen twenty years later, when he has become a middle-aged businessman living quietly in Chicago. Through a bizarre incident involving food poisoning, his picture appears in a newspaper with the result that all of his old friends and assorted other characters descend on him in a series of farcical situations. Reaction to the New York production was sharply divided. It was compared both favorably and unfavorably to a Feydeau farce, with some reviewers content to accept the play as a hilarious comedy, while others looked for a more honest ending than the flag-waving, "I-love-America" climax. The play closed after twenty-one performances. (In 1987, Second Stage in New York offered Tesich's revised version of *Division Street*, in which the hero does not find a new cause, but is left alone in his shabby apartment. Tesich changed the ending to make it less like his own wish fulfillment and more true to the characters.)

In the early 1980s, Tesich was also involved in two film productions: *Eyewitness* was shot in New York by Peter Yates, and Arthur Penn filmed *Four Friends* in Chicago. *Eyewitness* is a romantic murder mystery involving a television anchorwoman and a janitor who is secretly infatuated with her. When a murder is committed in his building, the janitor seizes the opportunity to meet his idol by pretending to have information about the killing, which predictably puts them both in danger. *Eyewitness* was released in 1981 to reviews that were sympathetic, but not particularly enthusiastic. Tesich's talent for creating oddball characters was praised, but the plot was generally considered to be too melodramatic and farfetched.

Four Friends, released late in 1981, was a return to the familiar world of *Breaking Away*, but with a much darker tone. It was clearly autobiographical, with a young Yugoslav hero, Danilo, who has come to America with his mother to be reunited with his steelworker father. Danilo has three friends, and the movie recounts their coming of age in the 1960s, but its main concern is Danilo's acceptance of the realities of American life as opposed to the immigrant's dream. Critical reception was mixed, but largely negative, on the grounds that the plot was contrived and obvious in its efforts to balance Tesich's optimism with Penn's pessimistic views.

Tesich's next screen project was an adaptation of John Irving's popular novel *The World According to Garp*. Tesich agreed to write the script because of his desire to work with the director, George Roy Hill, and because he discovered parallels between his own life and beliefs and those of the book's hero. Garp was raised by his mother, was a wrestler at school, became a writer, and, despite anxieties and setbacks, views life as a great adventure to be lived as fully as possible before one dies. The film was released in 1982 to mostly favorable reviews. It was praised for its fidelity to the spirit of the novel, even though Tesich had changed the focus somewhat from Irving's feminist approach and had glossed over some of the novel's more harrowing scenes.

Tesich's first published novel, *Summer Crossing*, which he had begun writing in 1980, also appeared in 1982. It had many autobiographical details, including the Midwest setting and its hero, Daniel Boone Price, a graduating high-school senior who was a member of the school's wrestling team. He longs to escape his unhappy home life, fearing that he will become like his bickering working-class parents, but escape is difficult because his father is dying of cancer and the boy has been smitten with love for a beautiful classmate.

Two Tesich films opened in 1985. In *American Flyers*, two brothers learn to understand each other in the course of a grueling bicycle race through Colorado. *Eleni*, the next Tesich-Yates collaboration, was based on Nicholas Gage's best-selling book about his return to Greece to search for the men who tortured and killed his mother during the Greek civil war. Both films met a negative critical response.

In 1989, after a nine-year absence, Tesich returned to the stage with a play that explored contemporary moral issues, both public and private. *The Speed of Darkness* premiered in Chicago before coming to Broadway in February 1991, where it ran for thirty-six performances. The title refers to the "speed of darkness" which at times "might even exceed the speed of light. It comes upon people and nations. . . . " In the play, a homeless Vietnam War veteran invades the prosperous midwestern household of a wartime buddy, and dark secrets gradually emerge that involve the family and a secret dumping site for nuclear waste. Most reviewers applauded the powerful message of the play, which was reminiscent of Ibsen and Arthur Miller, although they thought the action contrived and melodramatic.

Continuing his examination of today's moral climate, Tesich wrote *Square One*, in which a smug singer, a "state artist third class" in a Brave New World society, meets and marries a freethinking woman who refuses to ignore the suffering all around them. According to Tesich, "It used to be that the arts sounded the alarm, but now it's almost as if the arts have become an extension of the machine that's crushing us." The play received mixed reviews.

The protagonists of Tesich's third black comedy, *On the Open Road*, are two survivors, an intellectual and a thug, trying to escape from a war-ravaged land. It had its premiere in Chicago in 1992 and arrived in New York in 1993, where reviewers found it a disturbing combination of nihilistic humor and moral outrage.

Tesich became a naturalized citizen in 1961. He received a Rockefeller fellowship in 1972. The Tesichs divide their time between a Manhattan apartment and a one-room log cabin in Conifer, Colorado, where they have lived since 1974. Their daughter was born in 1989.

While Tesich's quirky humor and absurdist style have turned to darker subjects in recent years, traces of his early optimism and idealism remain. He examines society's ills with a sympathetic eye, and never gives up hope.

PRINCIPAL WORKS: *Plays*—The Carpenters, 1971; Nourish the Beast (Baba Goya), 1974; Gorky, 1976; Passing Game, 1978; Touching Bottom (includes The Road, A Life, and Baptismal), 1980; Division Street and Other Plays (includes Baba Goya, Lake of the Woods, and Passing Game), 1981; Square One, 1990; On the Open Road, 1992. *Novel*—Summer Crossing, 1982.

ABOUT: Contemporary Authors 105, 1982; Contemporary Dramatists, 4th ed., 1988; Contemporary Literary Criticism 40, 1986; Current Biography, 1991; Dictionary of Literary Biography Yearbook 1983, 1984; Who's Who in America, 1992–93. *Periodicals*—American Film March 1981; Back Stage March 8, 1991; Chicago Sun-Times April 16, 1989; Denver Post January 24, 1982; New York Times August 14, 1979; People May 12, 1980.

THAROOR, SHASHI (March 9, 1956–), Indian novelist and writer of short stories, writes: "Ever since my birth—to Indian parents in London—was marked by the casting of two mutually irreconcilable horoscopes, I have led a 'double life,' only one part of which has been devoted to writing.

"But it has been an important, even vital part. I wrote fiction from a very young age, my first story emerging when I was six. I was an asthmatic child, often bedridden with severe attacks, who rapidly exhausted the diversions available to me. Like every first child, I found few books on the family's shelves that appealed, and those I read inconveniently fast. Purchases were expensive and libraries limited: many let you borrow only one book at a time, and I had an awkward tendency to finish that in the car on the way home. Perhaps the ultimate clincher was that there was no television in the Bombay of my boyhood. So I wrote.

"I often had to sit up in bed to do so, but my

SHASHI THAROOR

imagination overcame my wheezing. My first stories were imitative school mysteries in the Enid Blyton tradition, but without the Enid Blyton flair. (My Indian equivalent of the Five Find-Outers and the Famous Five were the Six Solvers. They tracked down various villains in adventures with titles like "Solvers on the Trail" that nobody but my devoted father and a handful of friends ever read.) By the time I was nine I had discovered Biggles and was attempting to churn out heroic tales of wartime derring-do. Here I was more than derivative: I abandoned any patriotic pretensions and wrote about an RAF fighter pilot called Reginald Bellows. When the first instalment of 'Operation Bellows' appeared, in a Calcutta teen magazine, I was a month short of my eleventh birthday. I had found my métier.

"My next few stories remained imitative and inspired by my childhood reading. Finally, as I became a teenager, I started trying to depict the world I knew in India, and saw around me. Improbable fantasies about distant lands and times seemed suddenly less interesting than writing about people like myself, and the things that occupied our minds.

"The audience was ready-made: Indians who read Indian mass-circulation magazines. I was writing to be published and be read, not to pursue an obscure literary aesthetic. This in turn helped define the nature, and the limitations, of my early work. My stories (subsequently collected in *The Five-Dollar Smile*) largely reflect an adolescent sensibility: with one or two exceptions their concerns, their assumptions, their language, all emerge from the consciousness of an urban Indian male in his late teens.

"India is, of course, a vast and complex country; in Whitman's phrase, it contains multitudes. If the world depicted in my short stories was a very narrow slice of it, the scope of my first novel may have taken my writing to the other extreme. In *The Great Indian Novel* I attempted to reinvent the political history of 20th-century India through a recasting of characters, events and themes from the 2,000-year-old Indian epic the *Mahabharata.* I hoped in the process to cast a satirical light on the myths and legends of India's traditional culture as well as of its contemporary history. My second novel, *Show Business,* was, like its predecessor, also concerned with the kinds of stories a society tells about itself. In retelling, reinterpreting, and remaking national myths both ancient and modern, the two novels attempted an irreverent treatment of some fairly serious questions—the nature of India as society and nation, as well as the issues of destiny and predestination, reality and illusion, morality and human values, even karma and dharma. But the irreverence was essential, both because of its capacity to provoke and because I unashamedly want people to enjoy my books. I subscribe to Molière's credo, 'le devoir de la comédie est de corriger les hommes en les divertissant.' You've got to entertain in order to edify.

"The other feature of my writing that I hope readers will appreciate is the liberties I take with conventional narrative technique. The interpolation of verse (mock-epic doggerel in *The Great Indian Novel,* parodied film lyrics in *Show Business*) was a pleasurable stylistic device, as well as serving a literary purpose. The patterning of *The Great Indian Novel* after the structure of the *Mahabharata,* and the series of three interlocking narratives in each of the sections of *Show Business,* reflect my concern with the structure of the novel, and my belief that the manner in which the narrative unfolds is as integral to the work as the story it tells, and as essential to the experience of the reader.

"I have always seen myself as a human being with a number of concerns about—and responses to—the world, some of which I express in my work for the United Nations (over eleven years with refugees, now [December 1992] just over three on peacekeeping, where I lead the team at United Nations headquarters handling the peacekeeping operation in Yugoslavia) and some of which emerges in my writing. This is why, in my fiction so far, my concern has been more with the mores than the men, and less with the individual than the issues."

———

Shashi Tharoor's double life as a novelist and as a diplomat for the United Nations has served him well, having given him a unique perspective from which to view what he says is the principal inspiration of his writing—India: "what India is, what makes it what it is, the traditions that infuse the Indian consciousness." Although he writes in English and acknowledges English writers (everyone from P. G. Wodehouse to Graham Greene and George Orwell) as major influences on his work, Tharoor identifies himself unequivocally as an Indian. As he told an interviewer for *Gentleman* magazine in 1990: "I have always seen myself in the Indian context. In a sense you could say that I *chose* India because I prefer to have an Indian passport, even though, having been born in London, I still have and will always have the right to a British passport."

It follows therefore that Tharoor's first novel should have been "a satirical reworking" of the classic, 2,000-year-old Indian poetic epic the *Mahabharata.* With a title literally translated from Sanskrit (Tharoor writes, in a disclaimer for readers "who may feel, justifiably, that the work that follows is neither great, not authentically Indian, nor even much of a novel," that *Maha* means great and *Bharata* means India), *The Great Indian Novel* is at once an irreverent comedy and a serious portrait of a troubled country in the throes of self-definition. Its closest parallels are not in English literature but in contemporary political allegories like those of Gabriel García Márquez's *One Hundred Years of Solitude* and Salman Rushdie's *Midnight's Children,* writings that recast a nation's recent history as legend, thereby reclaiming the past even as they illuminate the rapidly developing events of the present.

For all its wit and irreverence, *The Great Indian Novel* has its foundation in serious scholarship. Tharoor's doctoral dissertation, revised and published in 1982 as *Reasons of State: Political Development and India's Foreign Policy under Indira Gandhi, 1966–1977,* is an exhaustive analysis of Indian politics in the decade dominated by Prime Minister Indira Gandhi, when the newly independent country experienced serious challenges to its democratic goals. Drawing upon public documents; the writings, speeches, and memoirs of many government officials; newspaper accounts; and interviews with people actively involved in politics, Tharoor is highly critical of Mrs. Gandhi, but, writing in 1980, before her assassination, he is cautiously hopeful that she will "transcend the dogmas of the past" and restore India's respected position in the international community. Tharoor's version of the *Mahabharata* is set in 20th-century India, but it is haunted by the ghosts of India's ancient past.

Near the end the narrator, an eighty-eight-year-old statesman who has been witness to the span of Indian history from pre–World War I colonialism to the withdrawal of British rule after World War II, and the bloodshed that followed the partition of India, describes his recent dreams:

> They were extraordinarily vivid dreams, in full costume and colour, with highly authentic dialogue delivered (for they were clearly set in the epic era of our national mythology) in Sanskrit . . . I dreamed in Sanskrit, and I dreamt of our traditions. Yet my dreams were populated not by Ramas and Sitas of your grandmother's twilight tales but by contemporary characters transported incongruously through time to the oneiric mythological settings.

The novel is boldly cynical—"They tell me India is an underdeveloped country. . . . Stuff and nonsense, of course. . . . India is not an underdeveloped country but a highly developed one in an advanced state of decay"—and iconoclastic. Mahatma Gandhi, for example, here called Gangaji, is an embarrassment: "The principles he stood for and the way he asserted them were always easier to admire than to follow. While he was alive, he was impossible to ignore; once he had gone, he was impossible to imitate." Along with Gandhi, many other prominent figures in Indian politics appear—Nehru, Mohammed Ali Jinnah, Lord and Lady Mountbatten, Indira Gandhi—all thinly disguised with names from the *Mahabharata* and all given equally satirical treatment. The epic framework is preserved with an omniscient narrator, Ved Vyas (the sage Vyasa in the *Mahabharata*) reciting his memoirs to a young secretary, Ganapathi (named for the elephant-god Ganesh to whom the original was dictated). The language of the novel ranges from contemporary journalese to the high-flying rhetoric of classical epic, and interspersed throughout the narrative are pages of rhymed verse—much of it doggerel—that parody the poetry of the original. The parodic mood is underscored by the titles of the various books that comprise the whole, among them "The Duel with the Crown," "The Son Also Rises," "Midnight's Parents," "Passages through India," "The Rigged Veda," and "The Bungle Book—or, The Reign of Error."

Inevitably *The Great Indian Novel* shocked and offended some Indian readers with its irreverence. As with other satirists, Tharoor's strongest defense was his passionate commitment to his subject. *The Great Indian Novel*, he told an interviewer for *Earth Summit Times* in 1992, "speaks for an India of multiple realities and of multiple interpretations of reality . . . My fiction is infused, in this sense, with the 'greatness' of India's cultural heritage, of Maha Bharata, a greatness that has emerged from the fusion of its myths with the aspirations of its history." For Edward Hower, reviewing the novel in the *Chicago Tribune*, "The effect is to humanize both historical and mythological figures. We need no special knowledge of India to find Tharoor's book fascinating." Hower's only reservation—one shared by other reviewers—was that at times "selfconscious literary wit is juxtaposed too closely with serious, sometimes tragic content, the impact of the serious material is diluted and the humor looks like schoolboy flippancy." Michael Gorra, in the *New York Times Book Review*, said that "nearly all of this is ingenious and some of it is inspired," but felt that overall, it made hard going for the reader, and Bharati Mukherjee, in the *Philadelphia Inquirer*, recognized Tharoor's promise and cleverness but found the length excessive and the wit too often self-conscious: "Tharoor attaches himself to the epic machinery of the *Mahabharata*, but he does so with a continual 'Get it?' 'Get it?' that annoys rather than dazzles." In contrast, Tapan Raychaudhuri remarked, in the *Times Literary Supplement*, that the "slightly camouflaged and highly idiosyncratic version of India's political history from the Champaran satyagraha to Indira Gandhi's last election victory" in the novel "never fails to hold our attention." Although critical of the use of characters borrowed from epic, Raychaudhuri noted that in *The Great Indian Novel*, "[t]he epic masks have . . . been borrowed . . . with delightful inventiveness."

The shift from the mythology of *The Great Indian Novel* to filmmaking in *Show Business* is less radical than it appears. The native Indian film industry is devoted largely to modern mythmaking, of which Tharoor gives several hilarious examples in the cliché-ridden scenarios he summarizes in *Show Business*. The narrator here is an Indian film star who turns briefly and disastrously to politics. As his father warns him, both film and politics "function amid fantasies, playing your assigned role in a make-believe India that has never existed and can never exist." Translating the "glamor and glitz" of the Hollywood (here called Bollywood) dream factory into Indian films produces a wildly incongruous product which the narrator and central character of the novel, Ashok Banjara, attempts to exploit to his own advantage. He tells his story as he lies dying in a Bombay hospital, terribly burned in an accident during filming. Although Ashok's circumstances are tragic, the story is as much comic.

Ashok's narrative is structured like a film in a series of "takes," each of which begins with the same sentence: "I can't believe I'm doing this."

Within each section, however, there are other speakers as well as extracts from film scripts and a gossip column, "Cheetah's Chatter," in *Showbiz* magazine. Ashok himself is a man lost in illusions:

Me, Ashok Banjara, product of the finest public school in independent India, secretary of the Shakespeare Society at St. Francis' College, no less, not to mention son of the Minister of State for Minor Textiles, chasing an aging actress around a papier-maché tree in an artificial drizzle, lip-synching to the tinny inanities of an aspiring (and high aspiring) playback-singer. But it *is* me, it's my mouth that's moving in soundless ardor, it's my feet that are scudding treeward in faithful obeisance to the unlikely choreography of the dance director.

A megastar dazzled by his own fame and prosperity, married to a beautiful former film star and father of triplets, he yields to every temptation, abandoning his youthful dreams of acting in serious drama like Pinter and Beckett ("there was no money in it, and not much recognition either"), he plays in trashy films, neglects his wife and family, becomes infatuated with a glamorous costar, sleeps with a loathsome but powerful gossip columnist, gets involved in political scandals—all at such a dizzying pace that it becomes impossible to distinguish the reality of his life from the films in which he is acting. At the end, with his life slipping away "like the wet sari of a dancing actress," Ashok acknowledges the futility of his existence—"I will be left holding nothing but my own emptiness." But he takes comfort in the knowledge that his films have served a purpose: "I have kept India awake by telling the nation it can dream with its eyes open. I have given each Indian the chance to reinvent his life, to thrill to the adventurous chase, to chase the unattainable girl, to attain the most glorious victory, to glory in the sheer joy of living."

In *Show Business*, Emily Mitchell wrote in *Time*, Tharoor "invents a fictional world that is a metaphor for deeper concerns." Among those concerns, Melissa Pearson wrote in the *Village Voice*, is free will: "Tharoor handles the Big Topic—the role of dharma, the belief in predestination that he suggests might also be a comic cop-out—without crushing his fragile characters."

Show Business is a far cry from what Tharoor describes as "an adolescent sensibility" displayed in the short stories collected in *The Five-Dollar Smile*, but even these early writings (one of them, "The Boutique," published when he was only fifteen) show promise of the concerned social satirist he was to become. Slight as the stories are, some of them reflect more serious ambitions. "The Death of a Schoolmaster" is based on memories of his maternal grandfather, a gentle scholar who lost most of the family's money to others "wiser in the ways of the world than he." The poignant title story of a young Indian orphan flying to the United States for a visit with charitable foster parents emerged directly from his own work with refugee children.

Tharoor's early schooling was in Bombay and Calcutta. He has a B.A. with honors in history from Delhi University and an M.A. and M.A. L.D. and Ph.D. from the Fletcher School of Law and Diplomacy at Tufts University. During his student days he free-lanced as a journalist and in 1976 won the Rajika Kripalani Young Journalist award. He has worked for the United Nations since 1978 in Geneva, Singapore, and (since 1989) New York. Tharoor has close ties to his family—his parents Chandra and Lily Tharoor, his two sisters, and his wife, Tilottama Tharoor, a journalist. They have twin sons, born in 1984, and divide their time between New York and India.

PRINCIPAL WORKS: *Novels*—The Great Indian Novel, 1989; Show Business, 1992. *Short stories*—The Five-Dollar Smile: Fourteen Early Stories and a Farce in Two Acts, 1990. *Nonfiction*—Reasons of State: Political Development and India's Foreign Policy under Indira Gandhi, 1966–1977, 1982.

ABOUT: Nelson, E. S. (ed.) Writers of the Indian Diaspora, 1993. *Periodicals*—Chicago Tribune Books June 16, 1991; Earth Summit Times September 14, 1992; Gentleman February 28, 1990; India Currents October 1992; Littcrit 14, 1991 (University of Kerala); New York Times February 13, 1990; New York Times Book Review March 24, 1991; September 27, 1992; Philadelphia Inquirer May 26, 1991; Time October 12, 1992; Times Literary Supplement September 8, 1989; Village Voice September 16, 1992; Washington Post Book World March 24, 1991.

THOMPSON, JIM (1906–1977), American novelist, short story writer, and screenwriter, was born James Myers Thompson in Anadarko, Oklahoma. Relatively little is known about his early life. As a young man, he held a series of grueling odd jobs, including roustabout, hotel bellhop, farmhand, and truck driver. He earned a bachelor's degree from the University of Nebraska, and in 1931 he married. During the depression, he was a director of the WPA Writers' Project in Oklahoma.

While many critics now regard him as an important American crime novelist, Thompson labored in virtual obscurity during his lifetime. At the time of his death, all twenty-nine of Thompson's novels were out of print; his work was known only among aficionados of hard-boiled crime fiction. Then, beginning in the mid-1980s, there was a remarkable resurgence of interest in Thompson. Black Lizard Press and Mysterious Press reissued most of his long out-of-print novels; one book, *The Rip-Off*, appeared for the first time. These attracted the attention of readers, critics, and, perhaps most significantly, filmmakers. Whether or not the popularity of Thompson's work will endure, the resurrection of his novels in the 1980s raises interesting questions about the dynamics of literary reputation.

The reasons for Thompson's erstwhile obscurity are readily comprehensible. First, there are his protagonists, almost all of whom are criminals of one sort or another; the worst of them are absolute monsters—murderous, amoral psychotics. As Peter S. Prescott noted in *Newsweek* in 1986: "The first thing to be said about Thompson is that his fiction resembles no one else's. The distinguishing marks of his novels are a high degree of death, a varying degree of comedy, some astonishing play with psychology, and—most important—the absence of any moral center at all." Moral resolution or anything resembling hope is hard to find in his work. "Typically, there are no winners in a Thompson novel," Lawrence Block wrote in the *New York Times Book Review* in 1990. "Even the innocent are guilty, and no one gets out alive." In addition to all of this, the format of Thompson's novels almost guaranteed his obscurity. All but a few of his books were issued as paperback originals; few of these, adorned as they were with lurid covers, ever attracted the notice of critics.

Thompson's early stories appeared in such "pulp" publications as *True Detective* and *Saga*. For a time, he served as editor in chief of *Saga*. At the same time that he was contributing stories to the pulps, Thompson worked as a journalist, writing for the *New York Daily News* and the *Los Angeles Times Mirror*. His first two novels—*Now and On Earth* and *Heed the Thunder*—both of which were published in hardcover, are conventional, mainstream fictions. *Nothing More than Murder*, his third novel, points to the influence of James M. Cain, a hard-boiled writer with whom Thompson has often been compared. It was not until the publication of his fifth novel, *The Killer Inside Me*, that Thompson presented the sort of protagonist for whom he would gain posthumous fame—a maniacally homicidal sheriff.

Max Allan Collins, one of Thompson's most perspicacious critical champions, contends that Thompson's work is significantly bleaker than even that of the so-called hard-boiled writers, whose stories of murder and mayhem were guided by a perceptible moral compass. In his essay "Jim Thompson: The Killers Inside Him," in *Murder Off the Rack*, Collins notes that Thompson makes even hard-boiled standard-bearers like James M. Cain and Raymond Chandler look soft: "The subject matter of Thompson's best books is so disturbing as to make Cain, the master of the 'tabloid murder,' seem a friendly spinner of tales."

This characterization of Thompson's work is nowhere more evident than in *The Killer Inside Me*. The novel is narrated by Lou Ford, the sheriff of a small but booming Oklahoma city. The opening pages of the novel reveal Ford to be well-liked and certainly amiable enough. But Ford is anything but an easygoing jokester; he soon reveals himself to be both a sadomasochist and a psychopathic killer. What perhaps most distinguishes Thompson from other crime novelists is his frequent use of the psychopathic killer as narrator. In so doing, he brings the reader one step closer to the killer's eerily deliberate thought process. One of the most shocking aspects of Ford's narration of *The Killer Inside Me* is his calm, almost methodical reflection on acts of unspeakable brutality. He himself refers to his homicidal impulse as "the sickness."

R. V. Cassill concluded that *The Killer Inside Me* is "worthy of being read as we read the very best modern novels." In "*The Killer Inside Me*: Fear, Purgation, and the Sophoclean Light" (an essay included in David Madden's *Tough Guy Writers of the Thirties*), Cassill argues that *The Killer Inside Me*, despite its obvious limitations as a genre work, is in fact an unflinching examination of the dark side of the American Dream. According to Cassill, "[I]n Thompson's hands, the mode of the paperback original, husks and all, turns out to be excellently suited to the objective of the novel of ideas. . . . Using the given idiom . . . Thompson makes a hard, scary Sophoclean statement on American success."

The Killer Inside Me brought Thompson to the attention of film director Stanley Kubrick, who called the novel "probably the most chilling and believable first-person story of a criminally warped mind I have ever encountered." Kubrick had plans to make a film based on the novel, but these never came to fruition. (In 1976, director Burt Kennedy released a film version of it with Stacy Keach in the role of sheriff Lou Ford.) Kubrick did, however, recruit Thompson to work as a screenwriter on two of his most highly regarded films of the mid-1950s: *The Killing* and *Paths of Glory*.

In "Jim Thompson: The Killers Inside Him," Max Allan Collins wrote, "Not all of Jim Thompson's books deal with murderers or psychopaths as their protagonists, but the best and most characteristic do." *After Dark, My Sweet* and *Pop. 1280* are two such "characteristic" works. *Pop. 1280*—which, Collins notes, "may be his best book,"—is similar in many ways to *The Killer Inside Me*. Like Lou Ford, the novel's narrator, Nick Corey, is a sheriff. Like Ford, Corey affects a simple, folksy manner to conceal his murderous cunning. Unlike *The Killer Inside Me*, which is unremittingly bleak and deadpan, *Pop. 1280* is suffused with a tone of black comedy. In the *New Republic*, David Thomson referred to the novel as Thompson's "comic masterpiece." Although he is every bit as murderous as Lou Ford, Nick Corey confronts his affliction differently. By the novel's end, he has convinced himself that he is Jesus Christ incarnate, placed on Earth for the specific purpose of shepherding souls to judgment. In *Coup de Torchon* (or, *Clean Slate*), his film adaptation of the novel, French director Bertrand Tavernier transplanted the murderous sheriff from a small town in the American South to a flyblown colonial outpost in French West Africa in the 1930s.

The Getaway, a 1972 film directed by Sam Peckinpah, was the first commercially successful adaptation of a Jim Thompson novel. *The Getaway* is the story of an ex-convict and his wife who collaborate in a violent bank holdup. The novel ends ironically: holed up in hellish underground caverns, the fugitives realize they are trapped, their "getaway" finished. In Peckinpah's movie, on the other hand, the couple (played by Steve McQueen and Ali MacGraw) escape across the border into Mexico. Thompson, who had nothing to do with the film, was reportedly unhappy with the new ending.

The more recent revival of Thompson's work, during the 1980s, culminated in a number of film adaptations. The most critically acclaimed, and popular, of these was Stephen Frears's 1990 film *The Grifters*. The protagonist is Roy Dillon, a small-time con man, or grifter, whose specialty is the short con. The two other principal characters are Dillon's mother, herself a con artist, and his scheming, unscrupulous girlfriend. The three characters entangle themselves in a web of deceit and thievery; although the novel (and the film) end in a murder, *The Grifters* never approaches the viciousness and brutality of such works as *The Killer Inside Me*. In fact, applying the criteria of Max Allan Collins (and others), *The Grifters* and *The Getaway* are hardly characteristic Thompson novels at all: both are narrated in the third person, and neither contains a psychopathic killer.

Reviewers gave *The Grifters* high marks for its faithful reproduction of the corruption-drenched atmosphere of Thompson's novel. In *Film Comment* (1990), Maitland McDonagh noted: "*The Grifters* is a pretty poor excuse for Jim Thompson novel. Not a dazzling psychopath in sight. . . . " Nonetheless, McDonagh hailed Frears's *The Grifters* as "a hell of a movie: cynical, tough-minded, and relentlessly mean—mean cruel and mean petty both."

Two other screen adaptations of Thompson novels appeared in 1990: *After Dark, My Sweet* and *The Kill-Off*. A number of other Thompson titles, including *Nothing More than Murder* and *South of Heaven*, were slated for production in the early 1990s. In addition, Michael J. McCauley published a full-length biography of the author, *Jim Thompson: Sleep with the Devil*. It is significant that McCauley is a filmmaker, and not a literary critic or a novelist; the revival of interest in Thompson's work seems to have been fueled as much by filmmakers as it has by critics.

Thompson, of course, never lived to see *The Grifters* made into a popular, commercially successful film; nor did he live to see the widespread discussion of his works in literary circles. What he would have made of such phenomena is anyone's guess. Reviewing McCauley's biography of Thompson in the *New York Times Book Review* in 1991, Michael Anderson wrote: "Thompson himself hooted at highbrow exegeses of his novels. . . . From *The Killer Inside Me* to *Pop. 1280*, Thompson's novels are still best enjoyed without frippery." Although Thompson never wrote a proper memoir, at least two of his novels—*Bad Boy* and *Roughneck*—contain a substantial amount of autobiographical information. By all accounts, Thompson was an alcoholic (an affliction he describes in frightening detail in several novels), and his later life was no easier than his youth. By the 1960s, he was forced to earn a living writing novelizations of movies and television shows.

Mystery writer Lawrence Block, in a *New York Times Book Review* retrospective of Thompson's work in 1990, wrote: "Jim Thompson, who received too little recognition during his lifetime, is getting rather too much of it now. So what? He still has things to tell us; his books are worth reading. Just keep in mind that it ain't Shakespeare." Even such ardent critical supporters of Thompson as Max Allan Collins readily admit the author's shortcomings and limitations. In his essay "Jim Thompson: The Killers Inside Him," Collins observed: "Thompson is not a writer whose work is readily accessible to most readers. For one thing, he is extremely uneven; his craft was only occasionally up to his genius."

PRINCIPAL WORKS: *Novels*—Now and On Earth, 1942; Heed the Thunder, 1946; Nothing More than Murder, 1949; Cropper's Cabin, 1952; The Killer Inside Me,

1952; The Alcoholics, 1953; Bad Boy, 1953; The Criminal, 1953; Recoil, 1953; Savage Night, 1953; The Golden Gizmo, 1954; A Hell of a Woman, 1954; The Nothing Man, 1954; Roughneck, 1954; A Swell-Looking Babe, 1954; After Dark, My Sweet, 1955; The Kill-Off, 1957; Wild Town, 1957; The Getaway, 1959; The Transgressors, 1961; The Grifters, 1963; Pop. 1280, 1964; Texas By the Tail, 1965; Ironside (novelization of television series), 1967; South of Heaven, 1967; The Undefeated (novelization of screenplay), 1969; Nothing But a Man (novelization of screenplay), 1970; Child of Rage, 1972; King Blood, 1973; The Rip-Off, 1989. Collected works—Hardcore, 1986; More Hardcore, 1987. Short stories—Fireworks: The Lost Writings of Jim Thompson (eds. R. Polito and M. McCauley) 1988.

ABOUT: Breen, J. and Greenberg, M. (eds.) Murder Off the Rack: Critical Studies of Ten Paperback Masters, 1989; Contemporary Literary Criticism 69, 1992; Hublin, A. Crime Fiction, 1749–1980: A Comprehensive Bibliography, 1984; McCauley, M. J. Jim Thompson: Sleep with the Devil, 1991; Madden, D. (ed.) Tough Guy Writers of the Thirties, 1968; Twentieth-Century Crime and Mystery Writers, 2nd ed., 1985. Periodicals—Film Comment September / October 1984; November / December 1990; New Republic April 15, 1985; New York Times Book Review October 14, 1990; May 19, 1991; Newsweek November 17, 1986; February 4, 1991; (Village) Voice Literary Supplement February 1982.

THOMPSON, LAWRANCE R(OGER) (April 3, 1906–April 15, 1973), American biographer and literary scholar, was born in Franklin, New Hampshire, to Roger Everett and Magdalena (Keller) Thompson. His father was a clergyman. Lawrance Thompson's New England heritage was to serve him well in the major work of his lifetime, his massive—and controversial—biography of Robert Frost. He began reading the poet in his student days. In 1926, a sophomore at Wesleyan University in Middletown, Connecticut, he heard Frost reading his own poems: "I remember that by this time I considered myself enough of an authority on Frost's poetry so that I expected I would know almost all the poems he would read." To Thompson's surprise, Frost read a poem that he did not know, "The Freedom of the Moon," in which the poet describes the changing images of the moon and concludes, "all sorts of wonders follow." From the moment he heard this poem, Thompson wrote, "I was not only a Frost admirer but also a Frost addict, without suspecting that my addiction would make all sorts of wonders follow."

Thompson recalled this experience many years later in an appendix to the third volume of his biography of Robert Frost. Here he treats the casual but, seen in hindsight, fateful circumstances that drew him into a close personal relationship with Frost and culminated in his appointment as his official biographer. After taking his B.A. in 1928, Thompson began graduate studies in English. He returned to Wesleyan as a teaching fellow in 1934 and continued to pursue his Frost "addiction," not only studying his poetry but also his publishing history. When Frost returned to Wesleyan to lecture in 1935, Thompson proposed an exhibition of his books at the university library. Frost was very cooperative, lending his manuscripts and rare editions, and Thompson prepared a catalogue that was the first chronological survey of the poet's work.

Thompson completed his graduate studies at Columbia University, receiving his Ph.D. in 1939. His special knowledge of bibliography brought him an appointment as curator of rare books and manuscripts at the Princeton University Library in 1937. In 1939 he became assistant professor of English, and Princeton remained his academic home until his death in 1973. On his return from service in the U.S. Naval Reserve (1942–1946), by this time a published author and the announced biographer of Robert Frost, he became associate professor and in 1951 professor of English. In 1968 he was appointed Holmes Professor of Belles Lettres. During these years Thompson traveled abroad as guest lecturer at the Salzburg Seminar in American Studies in 1954; the University of Oslo, also in 1954; the University of Puerto Rico in 1959; and the Hebrew University in Jerusalem in 1961 and 1962. He had fellowships from the Guggenheim and Ford foundations in 1946 and 1953, respectively, and the American Council of Learned Societies in 1966. Thompson married Janet McLean Arnold in 1945. They had four children.

Frost had long known of and appreciated Thompson's interest in his work. When in 1939 Robert Newdick, a professor of English at Ohio State University who had been planning to write a biography of the poet, suddenly died, Frost invited Thompson to his farm in Vermont and asked his suggestions for a new biographer. Thompson recommended three distinguished writers, all friends of Frost—Mark Van Doren, Bernard De Voto, and Louis Untermeyer. For his own reasons, Frost ruled them out and asked Thompson to undertake the task—"with the stipulation," Thompson recalled, "that no part of the proposed biography would be published during his lifetime. Until shortly before his death on 29 January 1963, he worked closely with me, and yet he gave me complete freedom to arrive at my own conclusions. He never asked to see any part of the biography."

Although Thompson devoted a major part of

his time in the remaining years of his life to the Frost project, spending hundreds of hours in conversation with the poet at home, and traveling with him, as well as exhaustively tracking down people who knew him and every detail of documentation connected with him, he continued his teaching career and he wrote a number of books and articles, not all of them associated with the poet. Almost all of Thompson's work, however, was on major American writers. His first book, *Young Longfellow, 1807–1843*, was based on previously unpublished material from the Longfellow archives and attempted to correct the austere, marmoreal image of the poet created by his earlier biographers. Thompson's interest, he wrote, was in "the colorful and impetuous personality of the poet in the vigor of his youth and early manhood." The book was well received, and Frost told Thompson that it had convinced him to designate him his biographer: "Your Longfellow book is enough 'evidence' for me."

A later and more controversial book was *Melville's Quarrel with God*, in which Thompson proposed the radical thesis that Herman Melville's writings mask a deep-seated anti-Christian bias. Admitting in his introduction that "my own bias is decidedly different from the bias of Herman Melville" and that he was at times "guilty of losing my detachment so completely as to evaluate Melville's viewpoint in terms of my own prejudice," Thompson argued that much of the author's rhetoric and imagery was designed to conceal his "heresy," his "misanthropic notion that the world was put together wrong and that God was to blame." Thompson offers daring but highly questionable conjectures—for example, that the title *Mardi* is a pun—"mar deity"—and that the ill-fated Pequod was named "to pique God." Although many Melville scholars were shocked by the book and challenged its theses, it remains an important work in literary scholarship—a provocative contribution to still unresolved questions about Melville's religious faith.

In 1942 Thompson published the first full critical study of Robert Frost's poetry, *Fire and Ice: The Art and Thought of Robert Frost*. Frost was by then a major figure in American literature, widely regarded as a poet of nature, writing an affirmative, uplifting poetry in simple, forthright language. Thompson was the first among many critics to come who detected a far darker and more complex vision in his work. His title, borrowed from Frost's own metaphoric title ("Some say the world will end in fire, / Some say in ice"), appropriately suggests his thesis: "Poems which seemed at first glance so very lucid and direct have often proved to possess facets and surfaces which catch the light in its purity and break it into myriad gradations of color. Beneath the intricate structures of Robert Frost's poetry may be found not only a wide technical range of intent and extent but also a spiritual depth of sight and insight." Thompson proceeds to analyze the poems in terms of theory (Frost wrote "without recourse to the fads and limitations of modern experimental techniques") and practice (Frost's emphasis on "the sound of sense," the integration of language, meter, and rhythm with the meaning of the poem). He discusses Frost's use of metaphor, irony, and satire, and his often subtle and playful humor, which has caused many misreadings of the poems. The final section of the book, "Attitude toward Life," anticipates to some degree what Thompson would explore at much greater length in the biography—"the mental, emotional and spiritual equipment" that made Frost the poet and the human being he was.

Certainly no earlier literary biographer, including James Boswell, who chronicled Samuel Johnson's life and conversation in exhaustive detail, lived longer with his subject than Thompson. The record of that association and of Thompson's change of heart toward Frost is preserved in the biographer's unpublished two thousand pages of "Notes from Conversations with Robert Frost," now in the library of the University of Virginia. Thompson had planned to write an account of his experiences to be titled "The Story of a Biography," but he died before even completing the biography itself. The notes give a fragmentary but detailed account of his gradual disillusionment with Frost as a man and of his painful struggle to continue working on the subject. Increasingly, he discovered inconsistencies and inaccuracies in Frost's account of his past and of his working habits. Frost claimed, for example, that he often wrote spontaneously, citing his celebrated "Stopping by Woods on a Snowy Evening" as a composition dashed off the spur of inspiration, "written with one stroke of the pen." Thompson discovered pages of draft manuscript of the poem, showing painstaking work and revision. The closer scrutiny he gave to Frost's embittered and domineering relationship with his wife, his children, and his friends, the more judgmental Thompson became. He felt himself betrayed by Frost at times, especially when the poet encouraged and cooperated with others who were writing books about him. His respect for the poet, however, if not for the man, was never diminished. From time to time Thompson had to remind himself of what Frost had once told an audience at one of his readings: "Trust me on the poetry, but don't trust me on my life." To reconcile these conflicting feelings,

Thompson sought to get beneath the surface, to write what Joyce Carol Oates, in commenting on more recent literary biographies, described as "pathography"—the study of the subject's "inner torments." In 1968, five years after Frost's death and two years after the publication of the first of the three volumes of his biography, Thompson wrote: "The ultimate problem of a Frost biographer is to see if the biographer can be enough of a psychologist to get far enough back into the formative years of Robert Frost to try to understand and explain what forces were operative, back there, to create the curious forms of neuroses which Robert Frost had to struggle with throughout most of his life. Of course such an approach on the part of the biographer is dangerous—very dangerous."

Fully aware of the risks, Thompson turned to the writings of Karen Horney, in particular her *Neurosis and Human Growth* (1950), for a "psychological framework" for the biography. He traced Frost's neuroses back to his unhappy childhood, his "recurrent self-doubt and intermittent lack of confidence," and his frustration in his early years with his failure to win recognition as a poet. The coldness and selfishness he displayed in his later life, Thompson inferred from Horney, was a protective mechanism, "masks" concealing his vulnerability. Donald G. Sheehy, who had written on Thompson's unpublished notes in *American Literature* and *New England Quarterly*, noted that the biographer suffered his own emotional conflicts in striving, not always successfully, for balance and objectivity in his biography of Frost. He quoted Thompson: "'It's easy enough to drag out all the faults of anyone. The point is that here was a man who actually achieved a well-deserved and lasting fame as an artist-poet; a man who in spite of his flawed human qualities, was at times extremely lovable; a man who, in spite of his meanness to so many people, really went out of his way to help certain people—and did help them. I must keep reminding myself of this.'"

That Thompson made strenuous efforts to be fair in his treatment of Frost is apparent in the introductions he wrote to the *Selected Letters of Robert Frost*, published a year after the poet's death, and to the first two volumes of the biography. He did not live to complete the third and last volume, in which he planned to adjust the balance. In 1971, he wrote to a friend and former student, Darcy O'Brien, who had expressed confusion and dismay after reading the portrait of Frost that emerged in volume 2: "You watch the neurotic and psychotic side of him develop and you can't help but have a sense of sympathy for the sadness of the circumstances which drove him into his neuroses and psychoses. . . . Stick

around until you read Volume Three. . . . and in my last chapter. . . . to be called 'The Summing Up,' I'm going to end up with praise for what is best and lasting in the poetry."

Nevertheless, the "demythicizing" of Frost began with the *Selected Letters*, a culling of more than four hundred from a collection of close to fifteen hundred letters. Their publication, *Newsweek*'s reviewer wrote, "must result in a drastic revision of the received myth. The erratic, flawed man who emerges from the letters is far more interesting than the visible 'mask,' as Thompson calls the Frost manner." Readers were therefore prepared for the publication of the first volume, *Robert Frost: The Early Years, 1874–1915*, in 1966. Although some reviewers detected "a troubling uncharitableness" (Benjamin De Mott in the *New York Herald Tribune Book Week*), the consensus was that Thompson had been eminently fair in his treatment of Frost and absolutely scrupulous in his documentation, some 128 pages of notes. "If the emphasis seems to be misplaced," Louis Untermeyer observed in the *Saturday Review*, "if there is little of the man who won friends with his native charm, his wry playfulness, and his stimulating intentness and interest, there is the most minute record of the course of Frost's wavering career."

The response to the second volume, *Robert Frost: The Years of Triumph, 1915–1938*, was strikingly different and ranged from enthusiastic praise (John W. Aldridge, in *Saturday Review*, called it "a work of brilliant scholarship and psychological portraiture") to outright condemnation ("In his harsh, distorted, and personally resentful view . . . Thompson sees only the determinations of a man who wanted fully to control his career and his public image," Richard Poirier wrote in *Robert Frost: The Work of Knowing*). Probably the most damaging judgment—on Thompson and on Frost alike—was Helen Vendler's in the *New York Times Book Review* (1970); she found the book "depressing reading . . . everything is flattened out into doughy prose . . . intellectually superficial." Primarily, she objected to the image of Frost that emerged: "a monster of egotism, a self-protective man leaving behind a wake of destroyed human lives." To some readers (notably Stanley Burnshaw in *Robert Frost Himself*), Thompson was guilty of nothing less than character assassination. Others more temperately suggested that Thompson's intentions were admirable but that "a certain literalness of mind" and clumsiness of writing made it impossible for him to capture the complexities of Frost's character. "And it is fair to say," William H. Pritchard wrote in *Frost: A Literary Life Reconsidered*, "that, for all his tireless fact-gathering, Thompson as a writer was not adequate to that subject." No reviewer, however, challenged the scholarship and comprehensiveness of *The Years of Triumph*, and it received the 1971 Pulitzer Prize for biography.

In August 1971 Thompson suffered a cerebral hemorrhage. He had by this time collected most of the material for his third volume, and with the assistance of Roy Winnick, a graduate student at Princeton, he wrote a rough draft of the book before he died of a brain tumor in April 1973. Because Winnick had worked so closely with him and had access to so much material, he was able to complete the third volume, *Robert Frost: The Later Years, 1938–1963*. Altogether the three volumes amounted to some two thousand pages with hundreds of additional pages of notes and indexes. *The Later Years*, with its portrait of the aged Frost, a revered national figure who had so movingly recited "The Gift Outright" at the inauguration of President John F. Kennedy in 1961, offers an even darker portrait of the poet and provoked even more controversy than had volume 2. Reviewing the book in the *New York Times Book Review*, David Bromwich expressed revulsion at Frost's character—"a more hateful human being cannot have lived who wrote words that moved other human beings to tears." A few weeks later the *Book Review* published two pages of letters, most of them angrily challenging not so much the book as Bromwich's response to it. In a brief rebuttal he wrote what may be the fairest assessment of Thompson's biography of Frost: "They seemed to me neither as masterpiece nor a travesty of their kind. The books are without psychological subtlety or penetration. But they are tolerably well written and they are scrupulous." They remain, furthermore, the fundamental and essential sources for our knowledge of the life of this major American poet.

PRINCIPAL WORKS: Young Longfellow, 1807–1843, 1939; Fire and Ice: The Art and Thought of Robert Frost, 1942; Melville's Quarrel with God, 1952; William Faulkner: An Introduction and Interpretation, 1963; Robert Frost: Vol. I, The Early Years, 1874–1915, 1966; Robert Frost: Vol. II, The Years of Triumph, 1915–1938, 1970; (with R. H. Winnick) Robert Frost: Vol. III, The Later Years, 1938–1963, 1977; Robert Frost: A Biography (one-volume condensation; ed. E. C. Lathem), 1981. *As editor*—(with E. C. Lathem) Robert Frost: Farm Poultryman . . . Contributions by the Poet, which appeared in Two New England Poultry Journals in 1903–1905, 1963; Selected Letters of Robert Frost, 1964.

ABOUT: Burnshaw, S. Robert Frost Himself, 1986; Contemporary Authors New Revision Series 10, 1983; Greiner, D. J. Robert Frost: The Poet and His Critics,

1974; Poirier, R. Robert Frost: The Work of Knowing, 1977; Pritchard, W.H. Frost: A Literary Life Reconsidered, 1984; Thompson, L. *appendix to* Robert Frost: The Later Years, 1977. *Periodicals*—American Literature October 1986; New England Quarterly June 1990; New York Herald Tribune Book Week November 13, 1966; New York Times April 16, 1973; New York Times Book Review August 9, 1970; January 16, 1977; April 3, 1977; March 11, 1984; Newsweek August 31, 1964; Saturday Review November 15, 1966; August 15, 1970.

*TOLSTAYA, TATIANA (NIKITICHNA)

(May 3, 1951–), Russian prose writer, was born in Leningrad (now St. Petersburg) into a family with one of the most prestigious of Russian literary genealogies. A distant relative of Lev Tolstoy, Tolstaya is the granddaughter of the novelist Alexei Tolstoy, the "Red Count," one of a handful of Soviet writers who achieved the status of "living classic" during the Stalin period for his epic works of Socialist Realism. Tolstaya's paternal grandmother, Natalya Krandievskaya, Alexei Tolstoy's third wife, was a poet and herself the daughter of a writer (Anastasya Krandievskaya) and a publisher.

Tolstaya has reacted negatively to commentators' inevitable references to her literary ancestry. "I hate being discussed as a relative of someone," she told Marta Mestrovic in *Publishers Weekly*. Yet she has also acknowledged the practical benefits of her renowned surname: "When people recognize your last name and because of that act accordingly . . . they will read your manuscript." More important, her literary forebears served her as models for the discovery of her own literary voice. She remarked to Catharine S. Nepomnyashchy in a personal interview translated by Nepomnyashchy: "I read a great deal both of Alexei Tolstoy and of my grandmother's poetry, and therefore saw how they lived through the period of the formation of their styles, how they searched for their own styles. . . . I saw the living process directly. Therefore when, let's say, many people ask whether the fact that my ancestors were famous hindered me. . . . It didn't hinder me at all. On the contrary, I felt them very deeply from inside—living people before a blank sheet of paper."

Tolstaya remembers her childhood spent as a "beloved child," one of seven siblings in a close family, as a happy time. "There was nothing awful, weighty, or sad in my childhood. But to make up for it in adulthood, on the contrary, a sad period came over me, a period of youthful depression—precisely because childhood was good, and when you begin to become an adult,

*tol STAH yuh, taht YAH nuh

TATIANA TOLSTAYA

you see that something good is missing. Childhood is missing. Therefore the clash came when childhood had already ended. But inside childhood there were no clashes or at least I don't remember them and they simply went away somewhere," she told Nepomnyashchy. Her father was a physicist with a facility for languages. From him Tolstaya learned both English and French. Aside from the educational advantages of her upbringing, Tolstaya's home life also accustomed her to an unusually critical vision of the Soviet regime. Born two years before Stalin's death, Tolstaya's early childhood coincided with the final years of the Stalin cult in Soviet society. Yet, as Tolstaya has observed, "I grew up in a family where there was no Stalin, and when I asked who Stalin was, I was answered that he was a tyrant and executioner."

Hardly surprisingly given this background, Tolstaya's "clashes" with the outside, "adult" world began in childhood. She started school in 1958, two years after Khrushchev's "secret speech" initiated the process of de-Stalininzation of Soviet society, which was accompanied by a relative relaxation of controls over culture. The legacy of Stalinism none the less remained, as Tolstaya recalled to Nepomnyashchy: "I attended school in the post-Stalin period, when almost all of the teachers were still Stalinists. But for some reason this didn't frighten or oppress me, rather I fought with them. This even forged my character, and I fought with them as only an eight-year-old child can. And it was the same in the older classes."

Tolstaya considers one incident that occurred when she was seven years old in particular a turning point. She remembered how she was taught in the first grade that "the city was full of spies. These spies were seeking the way to various secret enterprises—and everything was considered secret." One day she was playing in the courtyard outside her home and an old man and woman asked her how to get to the nearby botanical garden. Under the influence of what she had been taught in school, fearing the couple were "spies," Tolstaya sent them in the wrong direction. She immediately realized the absurdity of the paranoia instilled in her, but was too ashamed to call the old people back: "It was precisely from that moment I remember clearly that I began to hate the whole school system, all the lies, all the propaganda. . . . The sight of those unfortunate old people, whom I had sent in the opposite direction, walking away, made an indelible impression on me—I can see them to this day. I cannot forgive the school this. Although precisely after that it became clear to me, as if lightning had lit everything up in the darkness. And from that time I became a fighter." Because of her challenges to the "military discipline" of the school and to the stultifying official educational line taken there, Tolstaya claims, school authorities wanted to expel her but apparently were afraid to because her father was the son of a famous writer.

Tolstaya graduated from Special School 213 in Leningrad and went on to study in the philological department of Leningrad State University. She received her bachelor's degree in classical languages from that institution in 1974. In the same year she married Andrei Lebedev (now a renowned Hellenist), whom she had met when they were both students studying in the same department, and went to live with him in his hometown, Moscow. While she retained deep literary and emotional ties to Leningrad, Tolstaya told an interviewer in *Panorama* that she recognized the practical expediency of life in the capital: "It was uncomfortable to part with Leningrad, but Leningrad is not a very comfortable place. Moscow is also not the cheeriest of cities, but it was easier there and more peaceful in the dark years." She took a job at the Nauka (Science) publishing house and "put in time" there for eight years, she commented to Mestrovic. "There was a philosophy among intellectuals that we should graduate from universities, get our diplomas—then freedom starts! . . . In order to make a career, you had to establish relations with unpleasant people, and sometimes you had to join the Party. But if you wanted just to be free, you just chose the first job offered, and you could still be in the cream of intellectual society." Tolstaya, Lebedev, and their two sons paid a financial price for this relative freedom, however. At one point in the 1970s, the family was living on some ninety rubles a month—beneath the official poverty level. Tolstaya's efforts to gain some help for her family from the Fund to Aid the Children of Families of Classics were met, she told Nepomnyashchy, with "exceptional contempt, abuse, dissatisfaction, etcetera. But all the same toward the end of the year they allotted me seventy-five rubles. Our government receives millions on Alexei Tolstoy. . . . "

At the age of thirty-two, Tolstaya decided to try her own hand at writing and quit her job at Nauka. Speaking of her motivation for embarking on her new career, she has said that she began writing "because I got sick of reading. I didn't like this. I didn't like that. I grumbled mentally. And then on principle: 'Oh, you don't like it? Then try it yourself!'—so I went at it and tried myself." Her first story, "Na zolotom kryl'tse sideli" ("On the Golden Porch"), appeared in the Leningrad journal *Avrora* in 1983; it was followed in the same year by the publication of "Suidanies ptsitser" ("Date with a Bird") in the Moscow-based journal *Oktyabr'*. She published five more stories in Soviet journals in the succeeding two years. In January 1986 Tolstaya's story "Peters" was published in *Novyi mir*, the Soviet Union's most prestigious literary journal. She published six more stories in the same year, three in the relatively narrow-circulation *Avrora* and three in the December issue of *Novyi mir*. In 1987, not only did five more of her stories appear in various journals, but thirteen of her stories were collected in *Na zolotom kryl'tse sideli* (*On the Golden Porch*).

Given the bleak background provided by the Soviet literary scene in the pre-glasnost period, when most of the more talented older generation of writers had been forced into emigration, it is not surprising that the rich and exuberant verbal texture of Tolstaya's works, her distinctive voice, attracted the attention of critics. Leonid Bakhnov, a Soviet critic, went so far as to speak of the "Tolstaya phenomenon," observing: "For two or three stories to make a name for a writer—that has not been seen for a long time." Other critics echoed his excitement, commenting on the works Tolstaya had published through 1986.

Tolstaya's swift rise to national and, almost immediately thereafter, international prominence—due first and foremost to the fact that she arguably was and remains the most gifted Russian prose writer of her generation—was not without hindrance, drama, and controversy. While Tolstaya's first works appeared during the "period of stagnation," the bulk of her literary

publications belong to the glasnost period. Although her works are not political in any Western understanding of the word, they did present a challenge to the literary aesthetic, inextricably intertwined with the ideological co-optation of literature that prevailed in the Soviet Union in the early 1980s and the legacy of which persisted into the Gorbachev years and beyond. The formal complexity of her style, which went against the tradition of tendentious literature easily accessible to the mass reader, and her choice of "unsuccessful," marginalized "little people" as her central characters, which flouted the heroic optimism of most official writing, rendering her stories unpalatable or unpublishable from the point of view of some editors. Tolstaya told Nepomnyashchy, "Although there is nothing anti-regime in my stories, my style irritated official editors, while, on the contrary, some liked what I wrote a great deal, but knew that it was impossible to publish it." Editors rejected her stories, she told Olga Martynenko in *Moscow News*, "on the pretext that in our country there are no unfortunate people, there are no crazy people, there are no old women." Censorship, she commented to Nepomnyashchy, was arbitrarily applied: "My first story . . . went completely uncensored, there was nothing to censor there. It started with the second and the third; they began to pick at me. The funniest instance was with the story 'Date with a Bird,' because the struggle with drunkenness was being waged, and they wanted to throw out of the story words like 'bottle,' 'glass,' 'drank.'" Probably the most widely known instance of such meddling concerns the title of Tolstaya's story "Peters." A conservative editor at *Novyi mir* considered the original title, "This Wonderful Life" (which Tolstaya fought to retain until her resistance threatened to jeopardize the publication of the story), "a mockery of Soviet reality." The editor's rancor was clearly aroused by the seeming discrepancy between the "wonderful life" of the original title—which seemingly parodies the ideologically charged, upbeat titles of many Socialist Realist works—and the repeatedly thwarted attempts of the pitiful and unattractive central character to find happiness. Even Soviet critics favorably disposed to Tolstaya's writings at times seemed to have difficulty coming to terms with the complex interplay between the writer's multilayered narrative voice, her intricate verbal artistry, and her "unheroic" characters. Accustomed to literary works in which the line between "good" and "bad" characters was clearly defined, in which the authorial stance toward his or her personages was unambiguous and unmistakable, reviewers repeatedly raised the issue of whether Tolstaya did or did not "like" her characters.

The point, however, lies precisely in Tolstaya's refusal to pass judgment, or rather in her relocating of the question from the moral to the aesthetic sphere. In focusing her artistic attention precisely on those considered "unsuccessful" by the conventional standards of their society and who have therefore been largely overlooked in official Soviet literature—forgotten old ladies, unattractive and unloved women, ineffectual dreamers, and emotionally retarded adults—she reclaims them from oblivion, asserting that their stories are worthy of being told. The power of art, of storytelling—which presents the danger of seduction by illusion, but more often holds the promise of memory and preservation—runs as a leitmotif through her works and is in fact embodied in the luxuriant "excess" of her style, which implicitly counterposes the potentially redemptive richness of artistic expression to the bleakness of the reality it chronicles.

Since 1988, Tolstaya has taught at a number of American universities (the University of Richmond, the University of Texas at Austin, Texas Tech, Princeton, and Skidmore) and has lectured widely throughout the United States. She has taken up residence with her husband and one of her sons in the United States, although she continues to visit her homeland when her schedule allows. Tolstaya last published a new work of fiction in 1991. Since that time, she has regularly published journalistic articles, the bulk of them in English translation in such publications as the *New York Review of Books*, the *New Republic*, and the *Guardian*. She has proved herself a lively commentator on current events in Russia, and her outspoken views on American life, especially her attacks on American feminism, have generated controversy.

Uprooted by the uncertain economic and political situation in Russia and seeking new paths for her creative development, Tolstaya appeared in the 1990s to be in a period of transition both in her life and her work. Her works grew progressively longer, and she began a novel. Although the trajectory of her development as a writer was unclear, the quality and importance of the works she produced are beyond dispute. Arguably no Russian writer since Isaac Babel has laid such claim to mastery over the short story, and not in many years has Russian literature witnessed the emergence of such a vibrant new talent.

PRINCIPAL WORKS IN ENGLISH TRANSLATION: *Short stories*—(tr. N. Condee) "Sonia" *in* Newsletter of the Institute of World Affairs, no. 17, 1986; (tr. M. Zirin) "Date with a Bird," "Sonia," and "Peters" *in* Heritage and Heresy: Recent Fiction by Russian Women, 1988; (tr. J. Gambrell) "Fire and Dust" *in* Zalygin, S. (ed.)

The New Soviet Fiction, 1989; (tr. M. Zirin) "Peters" *in* Goscilo, H. (ed.) Balancing Acts, 1989; (tr. A. Bouis) On the Golden Porch, 1989; (tr. M. Zirin) "Night" Goscilo, H. and Lindsay, B. (eds.) *in* Glasnost, 1990; (tr. J. Gambrell) Sleepwalker in a Fog, 1992; (tr. S. McLaughlin) "Dear Shura" *in* McLaughlin, S. (ed.) The Image of Women in Contemporary Soviet Fiction: Selected Short Stories From the USSR, 1989.

ABOUT: Boym, S., Givens, J. R., Goscilo, H. and Ivanova, N. *in* Fruits of Her Plume: Essays on Contemporary Russian Women's Culture, 1993; Contemporary World Writers, 2nd ed., 1993; Goscilo, H. *in* New Directions in Soviet Literature: Selected Papers from the Fourth World Congress for Soviet and East European Studies, 1990; Goscilo, H. *in* Sexuality and the Body in Russian Culture, 1993; Ledkovsky, M. et. al. (eds.) Dictionary of Russian Women Writers. *Periodicals*—American Spectator January 1992; Atlanta Journal Constitution January 19, 1992; Boston Globe June 8, 1990; January 14, 1992; Chicago Tribune March 1, 1992; Choice December 1990; Guardian May 24, 1989; May 26, 1989; March 19, 1992; May 7, 1992; Houston Post September 17, 1989; Indiana Slavic Studies 5, 1990; Library Journal May 1, 1989; London Review of Books June 1, 1989; Los Angeles Times June 2, 1989; January 19, 1992; May 12, 1992; May 23, 1992; Los Angeles Times Magazine September 27, 1992; Midwest Quarterly Winter 1991; Moscow News February 22, 1987; no. 26, 1990; New Republic April 6, 1992; New York Review of Books June 1, 1989; May 14, 1992; New York Times April 25, 1989; April 30, 1989; May 9, 1989; January 3, 1992; March 17, 1992; New York Times Book Review April 30, 1989; January 12, 1992; Newsday April 30, 1989; Publishers Weekly January 1, 1992; Russian Language Journal, nos. 147–149, 1990; San Francisco Chronicle April 21, 1989; Slavic and East European Journal, no. 1, 1990; Slavic Review Summer 1988; Soviet Life January 1989; Studies in Comparative Communism, nos. 3–4, 1988; Slovo May 1990; Times Literary Supplement June 26, 1987; May 1, 1992; USA Today January 23, 1992; Washington Post April 18, 1988; May 28, 1989; April 25, 1991; February 9, 1992; Washington Times January 26, 1992; February 4, 1992; World Literature Today Winter 1993.

TOMALIN, CLAIRE (June 20, 1933–   ), British biographer, was born in London, the daughter of Emile Delavenay, a scholar, and Muriel Herbert, a songwriter. She was educated at Hitchin Girls' Grammar School, Dartington Hall School, and Newnham College, Cambridge, where she received her M.A. She married Nicholas Osborne Tomalin on September 17, 1955 (he died in 1973) and has one son and two daughters from this marriage. In 1993 she married the playwright and journalist Michael Frayn. Her recreational activities include traveling in Europe, gardening, and walking in Regent's Park, London.

CLAIRE TOMALIN

Tomalin began her career as a publisher's reader and editor at Heineman, Hutchinson and Cape, from 1955 to 1967. Then she moved to the *Evening Standard* in 1967. From 1968 to 1970 she worked as assistant literary editor of the *New Statesman*, becoming literary editor in 1974, a post she held until 1977. She began reviewing for the *Sunday Times* in 1977 and was its literary editor from 1979 to 1986. Tomalin reviews regularly for the *London Review of Books*, the *Times Literary Supplement*, the *New York Review of Books*, and *Sight and Sound*. Her stage play *The Winter Wife*, about Katherine Mansfield's last years, was performed at the Nuffield theater, in Southampton in 1991. She is a trustee of the National Portrait Gallery, a member of the Committee of the Royal Literary Fund, and a fellow of the Royal Society of Literature. In October 1985 Tomalin won libel damages in the High Court for an unfounded slur on her professional integrity published in *Private Eye*.

The Life and Death of Mary Wollstonecraft was the first of a series of well-received literary biographies which Tomalin has produced since 1974. This first book, a well-researched, calm, and sympathetic account of Wollstonecraft's often turbulent life, won the Whitbread award in 1974. Tomalin's individual approach is clear, even in this first book. In the (London) *Times*, Michael Ratcliffe described it as "a biography right outside the current fashion," being relatively short (less than 300 pages) and written by a busy literary editor and mother who acknowledged the labors of her babysitters at the beginning of the book. Tomalin's final judgment on

Mary Wollstonecraft is a model of balance and good sense: "She was tough. . . . If she was not the perfect heroine, she was at least an antiheroine to be reckoned with. She got herself an education as best she could, she wooed her own men, and was sometimes selfish and insensitive, sometimes comical. She endured ridicule and beat it down by sheer force of personality . . . and, while the world busied itself with great concerns, she spoke up, quite loudly, for what had been until then a largely silent section of the human race."

The Life and Death of Mary Wollstonecraft won the approval not only of general readers but of professional historians as well. In the *New Statesman*, J. H. Plumb pronounced it "a wise, penetrating, sympathetic biography of a remarkably complex woman . . . more than a biography : it illuminates the radical world of the 1780s and 1790s as few other books do." Richard Cobb observed, in the *Times Literary Supplement*, that if Tomalin began her book as a biography of a political radical and pioneering feminist, "what she has in fact produced is something far more interesting. Mary's claim to public recognition tends to be pushed into the background and what we read is a fascinating account of a twisted and difficult personality."

Shelley and His World maintained Tomalin's reputation for balanced and searching research on the life and work of literary figures. She was becoming well known for the pithy and puncturing comments that pepper her writing. David Williams noted, in the (London) *Times*, that of Shelley's poems "The Cloud," "To a Skylark," and "The Witch of Atlas" she wrote "dazzling exercises that do not invite too many re-readings." Her gift for making challenging writers accessible is evident in this work; as Williams said, "Claire Tomalin knows exactly where to pause and to praise, and I cannot think of a better short summing-up of a far from easy writer than this one." A. N. Wilson commented, in the *Times Literary Supplement*, that "she writes from the position of the ideal Shelley biographer: primarily as an admirer of his poetry but also with a genuine liking for the man which is not blind to the flaws in his nature. . . . "

Parents and Children is an anthology of long and thoughtful literary passages inviting the reader to consider the delights and terrors of the parent–child relationship. The collection is distinguished by Tomalin's adroit handling of her material, organizing her extracts in order to highlight the changes in attitude to the relationship which occurred through the centuries, and keeping her editorial tone "understanding but not indulgent, moved but not sentimental, critical but calm," as Janet Morgan commented in the *Times Literary Supplement* (1981). She termed it "a touching collection, most delicately assembled."

In 1983, Tomalin edited a collection of short stories by Katherine Mansfield, and then turned her biographer's eye upon Mansfield's life, publishing *Katherine Mansfield: A Secret Life* five years later. The book's major contribution to scholarship on Mansfield was to bring a feminist perspective to Mansfield's life. Acknowledging in her foreword the recent publication of two other biographies of Mansfield—Jeffrey Meyers's in 1978 and Antony Alpers's in 1980—Tomalin wrote: "One final point is that I am of the same sex as my subject. It may be nonsense to believe that this gives me any advantage over a male biographer. Yet I can't help feeling that any woman who fights her way through life on two fronts—taking a traditional feminine role, but also seeking male privileges—may have a special sympathy for such a pioneer as Katherine, and may find some of her actions and her attitudes less baffling than even the most understanding of men."

Sara Maitland, in the *New Statesman*, commented: "Although Tomalin has adduced considerable new evidence about the ins and outs of Mansfield's life, there is nothing here that will radically change the picture of Mansfield carried in people's minds from the previous biographies. Indeed, it quickly becomes clear that Tomalin does not want to explode the myth; she wants instead, to up-date it. The old myth of the 'suffering artist' is now united with the newer myth of the 'suffering woman.'"

Donna Rifkind complained, in the *American Scholar*, of the "creeping feminism" which "prevade[s] its pages. . . . Here and there throughout the narrative are hints [Tomalin] believes Mansfield ought to be considered something of an emblematic woman, that her faults ought therefore to be excused, and that only other women can be truly sympathetic to her fate. . . . "

In 1989 Tomalin visited the grave of Ellen Ternan in Southsea and noticed that time and neglect were rapidly obliterating it. "Quite soon, by the look of it, the grave was likely to disappear altogether. It seemed a good moment to start putting something on paper which might restore Nelly to visibility." Accordingly she tracked down the many papers, wills, photographs, playbills, and miscellaneous records that enabled her to give "invisible Nelly" a generous measure of visibility. Nelly herself, Tomalin wrote, "is not an important person. No one would have begun to think about her were it not

for Dickens, standing like a giant over the Victorian age." *The Invisible Woman: The Story of Nelly Ternan and Charles Dickens*, Tomalin won the NCR Book Award for 1992, as well as the Hawthorden Prize and the 1990 James Tait Black Prixe for Biography. She gives a gripping account of Dickens's secret twelve-year relationship with Ternan, which lasted from his forty-fifth year until his death in 1870. In her depiction of Nelly, Tomalin avoids the dichotomy of "mercenary minx" or "doll-like victim" which had divided previous biographers into opposing camps.

Reviewers appreciated the judiciousness and thoroughness with which Tomalin approached her subject. For John Sutherland, in *London Review of Books*, *The Invisible Woman* "reads as grippingly as a detective story. All the familiar material is brought together with much that is new and clinching." Michiko Kakutani agreed, in the *New York Times*, that she used "her gifts of sympathy and insight to flesh out the bare bones of her detective work [producing] . . . an absorbing book about a minor historical character, a character who helps to illuminate the life of a great artist and the life of her times."

Tomalin's *Mrs. Jordan's Profession: The Actress and the Prince*, tells the story of Dora Jordan, the great comic actress of the 19th-century British theater. Dora became the mistress of the future king, William IV. She lived with him and gave him ten children; yet she died alone, in obscurity, and when a biography of King William appeared in 1884, Dora's name did not even appear in it. As with her earlier biographies, Tomalin combines clarity with detailed research and a flair for gripping narrative.

Stella Tillyard, reviewing the book in the *New York Times Book Review*, noted that, unlike her famous male theatrical compatriots Edmund Kean and John Kemble, Jordan "has dropped out of our memories. . . . Tomalin's life, the first informed by feminism, reinstates her as a powerful woman as well as an extraordinary talent." Tillyard considered that the "most enthralling part of . . . Tomalin's book is a portrait of a powerful and independent woman at work, commanding large fees, confronting managers, bewitching audiences, making her own contracts and controlling her own purse. . . . a remarkable picture of life of a 'working mother' of 200 years ago. . . . Tomalin's . . . portrait of Mrs. Jordan as a loving mother and outstanding professional highlights not the tragic victim of male perfidy but the successful architect of all but the very end of her life."

PRINCIPAL WORKS: The Life and Death of Mary Wollstonecraft, 1974; Shelley and His World, 1980; Katherine Mansfield: A Secret Life, 1988; The Invisible Woman: The Story of Nelly Ternan and Charles Dickens, 1990; Mrs. Jordan's Profession: The Actress and the Prince, 1994. *Play*—The Winter Wife, 1991. *As editor*—Parents and Children, 1981; Katherine Mansfield: Short Stories, 1983; Virginia Woolf's Mrs. Dalloway.

ABOUT: Who's Who 1994. *Periodicals*—American Scholar August 1988; London Review of Books November 8, 1990; New Republic June 10, 1991; New Statesman September 6, 1974; October 30, 1987; New York Review of Books March 17, 1988; New York Times March 26, 1991; New York Times Book Review May 15, 1988; April 21, 1991; May 14, 1995; New Yorker July 22, 1991; Sewanee Review Summer 1992; Smithsonian January 1993; Studies in Short Fiction Fall 1988; (London) Times September 5, 1974; October 30, 1980; Times Literary Supplement September 12, 1980; September 11, 1981; November 20, 1990.

TREMAIN, ROSE (August 2, 1943–   ), English novelist, dramatist, and short story writer, was born in Fulham, London. Her father was the playwright Keith Nicholas Thomson, and her mother was the former Viola Mabel Dudley. They split up when Rose Tremain was ten years old, and the separation affected her deeply. She attended the Frances Holland School, and the Sorbonne in Paris, gaining a diploma in Literature in 1963. Returning to England, she obtained an honors degree in English Literature at the University of East Anglia, where she took classes with the novelist Angus Wilson.

Between 1967 and 1969 Tremain taught French and history at a primary school in London. She spent a further two years as an editor at British Printing Corporation Publications before resigning in 1971 to take up writing fulltime. In the same year she married Jon Tremain. They had one daughter, and were divorced seven years later.

Tremain's first two books were nonfictional. *Freedom for Women* grew out of her interest in the suffragette movement in Britain and America. In it she traces the development of the women's rights movement, and warns that apathy will lead to the reinstitution of former inequities. *Stalin* is a biography of the dictator, which avoids judgment while attempting to explain his motivations, particularly through reference to his childhood. These two carefully researched but outspoken works appeared only in the United States, not in Britain.

A marked feature of Rose Tremain's fiction is her use of protagonists whose ages and backgrounds bear no relation to her own. Her dismissal of the idea that a novel should simply describe the author's experiences is justified by

ROSE TREMAIN

her deeply sympathetic portraits of a great range of characters.

Sadler's Birthday is the story of a seventy-six-year-old retired butler who lives on the estate he inherited from his childless employers, after years of devoted service. Like most of Tremain's novels it is, in essence, a study of loneliness, of the insurmountable internal exile of the displaced outsider or misfit. Sadler spends his time reliving his past, and in a series of flashbacks we are introduced to all the people who have been important to him. Tremain tends to produce several complex portraits within a novel, and balances them with skill. As Susannah Clapp commented in the *Times Literary Supplement*, "each of its voices is fully, if briefly, realized." Sadler's mother was a country girl who was forced into domestic service to support her illegitimate son. His own employers live empty lives in a loveless marriage, until they are killed in a car crash on the way to see the coronation of Elizabeth II. There are the other servants, but most importantly there is Tom, a young cockney boy who was evacuated to the house during the war. Tom is the only person Sadler ever loved. There is eventually a physical relationship, but Sadler is broken by the boy's ultimate indifference towards him. His only relief comes at the end of the novel when, crowded about by the memories that spread through the deserted East Anglian mansion, he returns to his old bedroom. In this neglected room, a symbol of the past life he had attempted to lock away, he recognizes that his employers shared with him the experience of failure and lovelessness. Close to death himself, Sadler is left with the possibility of acceptance, if not happiness. Reviewers noted Tremain's affection for all of her characters and her insight into their predicaments. The reader's sympathy is held, and painful scenes are alleviated, by a gentle humor that, in Clapp's words, transforms "what could have been a wan comedy of mannerisms into a rich and informative novel."

Tremain's next novel was *Letter to Sister Benedicta*, in which wealthy, middle-aged Ruby Constad writes to the nun who had taught her in the convent school she attended in India. Ruby has been rejected by her dropout son and lesbian daughter, and her husband is dying after a stroke brought on by the behavior of his children. Ruby, like Sadler, is left to evaluate a life which is as bleak as his. Her husband is a domineering man and the marriage has been an unhappy one. It gradually emerges that her children, who never visit, have been lovers. She writes to Sister Benedicta, who may well be dead, because she has nobody else to address. Between visits to her silent husband, to Brompton Oratory, where she tries but fails to pray, and to Harrods department store, Ruby "confesses" the story of her life, her husband's adulteries and her own single, tentative infidelity. In spite of her unhappiness, she retains a fundamental capacity for humor, imagination, and love. Tremain was criticized for expecting readers to believe that such a woman would have allowed herself to be so misused and restricted. Her ultimate decision to return to India, "a mutilated land. . . . a country that is bleeding to death," also seems unlikely. John Mellors, in the *Listener*, found it "a rather unconvincing finale to an otherwise most impressive book."

By 1981, when *The Cupboard* was published, Rose Tremain had established herself as an accomplished author. Like *Sadler's Birthday*, *The Cupboard* deals with old age, and the social, physical, and psychological disintegration that accompanies it. Erica March is an elderly novelist who was once a committed political activist but, with love affairs and literary acclaim behind her, has done nothing for thirty years and is stagnating in a modern world that is without passion. When her mother is killed by a bull, she inherits a huge cupboard, which both frightens and comforts her, a womblike retreat that has the ambivalent connotations of both Sadler's bedroom and Ruby's convent. Her inevitable return to this confinement, however, signifies not a possibility of "rebirth," but death. The only other substantial character in the novel is Ralph Pears, an American journalist who is writing the story of Erica's life. Downtrodden and physically stunted, he is, like so many of Tremain's characters, in search of love and acceptance, but unable to reach out, to communicate this need to others. From Erica he expects inspiration, the escape from inadequacy which she cannot even afford to herself. When she has finished telling her story, she climbs into the cupboard and overdoses on sleeping pills.

Reviewers found *The Cupboard* well constructed, and as accurate in its depiction of human pain as the former novels, but they felt it lacked the conviction, range, plausibility, and humor that characterized her earlier work. Erica's story is told in question and answer form, and this inevitably seems artificial and becomes tedious, as do the protracted reminiscences and the extracts from her own novels that are included. Tremain's tendency to dismiss historical events with remarks such as, "There was so much misery in the Thirties," while insisting that public and private history are inextricably interlinked, has also been criticized. Helen Angel, writing in *British Book News* commented that "this novel is laboured and contrived."

Tremain's first collection of short stories, *The Colonel's Daughter*, fared a little better in that, while the quality of the stories was extremely uneven, a few were highly acclaimed. Tremain employs a large range of narrative strategies, from third-person storytelling to monologues and the interview structure used in *The Cupboard*. Every kind of relationship is explored, including the conflicts between parents and children, husbands and wives, homosexual lovers, and different social classes. Status and material welfare are common preoccupations for these characters whose outward civilities only tenuously control the intense and violent emotions that constantly threaten to erupt. In the title story, the rebellious daughter of a colonel robs her own ancestral home, setting off a chain of tragic events. "Autumn in Florida," which was considered one of the best of the collection's stories, centers on George and Beryl Dawes, whose hopes for their holiday of a lifetime end in humiliation and the exacerbation of the sense of mediocrity they were attempting to overcome. Critics found that here, and for example in "Wedding Night," and "My Love Affair with James I," Tremain had recovered both her wit and her self-assurance. "Dinner For One" and "A Shooting Season" were less admired because of a somewhat contrived sentimentality; the latter ends with a long-suffering wife declaring "Yes Marcus . . . there's always tomorrow." "Still," Caryn James remarked in the *New York Times Book Review*, "this is an extremely ambitious and largely successful collection." In 1984 it won the Dylan Thomas Prize for Short Stories. Tremain published her fourth novel in that year, having been listed in 1983 among the Best of Young British Novelists.

In *The Swimming Pool Season*, which won an Angel Literary award, Larry Kendall leaves Oxford for a small French village after the failure of his swimming pool business. When his wife, Miriam, returns to England and her mother's deathbed, he builds a pool in the village. It becomes an image of flow, of change, and an emblem of his own struggle for achievement. Again, several characters are introduced as the narrative moves between the two locations. Tremain's attention to detail and the inclusive sympathy with which she writes make each one real and important to the reader. Food is an important metaphor in this novel which is, as Jonathan Keates says in an article written for the *Observer*, "awash with gastronomy." Food variously comforts, delights, and betrays, building up into a symbolic framework of the need, the decay, and the longing that marks the lives of these people. As the imagery accumulates, the flow of changes moves them further away from their goals, making this ultimately another tale of universal exile. Everyone falls in love with the wrong person, and a witchlike local invokes bylaws to have the swimming pool, along with Larry's dreams, destroyed. Although reviewers found the detail at times overwhelming, and the overall effect diffuse, they recognized also a firm structuring, and the mature artistry with which Tremain produced this entertaining and assured narrative.

Tremain published a story for children, *Journey to the Volcano*, and a second collection of short stories, *The Garden of the Villa Mollini*, before her most successful novel appeared in 1989. *Restoration* was short-listed for the Booker Prize, and was the Sunday Express Book of the Year. Like *Sadler's Birthday* and *The Swimming Pool Season* it has a male protagonist, but the ease with which Tremain writes in the first-person from a male point of view, and her concentration on this single, and singular, viewpoint, endows the book with a pervasive, uniquely convincing masculinity. The character of King Charles II, to whose Restoration in 1660 the title refers, is also skillfully drawn. A delightful and entirely plausible mixture of cruelty, kindness, and impulsive wickedness, the king's presence is felt throughout the novel as both a symbol of this decadent age and a focus for all the admiration, fear, and affection of the hero, Robert Merivel.

Merivel is the son of a glovemaker to the king, lazy, promiscuous, and greedy. He is half-heartedly pursuing a medical career when his father decides to introduce him at Court. Accidentally "curing" one of the king's spaniels, he is installed there to care for the palace animals. A friendship develops between the two men, and in order to assuage the envy of his other mistresses the king marries Merivel off to his favorite, Celia. He is given an estate, wealth, and a knighthood on the understanding that his marriage never be consummated. Giving up his studies, Merivel adopts a lifestyle of extravagance and riotous debauchery. Depressed and demoralized by this aimless life, he finds himself falling in love with Celia. News of his feelings reaches the king, and he is immediately dispossessed.

Working with an old colleague at a lunatic asylum, Merivel attempts the "restoration" of his spiritual sanity. Eventually he gives in to temptation, however, and impregnates a female inmate. Shepherding her through the plague epidemic and the London fire of 1666, caring for her until she dies in childbirth, and for her daughter thereafter, he finally makes peace with himself and with the king. Tremain has effected her own restoration, according to Florence King in the *New York Times Book Review*, in returning the historical novel to its former, honorable position. King declares that this panoramic, yet finely detailed portrait of 17th-century England is "nothing less than superb."

Sacred Country, set in East Anglia is the story of Mary Ward, who makes a discovery on February 15, 1952 when she is six years old and living on her father's farm: "I am not Mary. That is a mistake. I am not a girl. I'm a boy." The novel follows her transformation into Martin, and the changes in the lives of her family and her neighbors. The novel musters a great gallery of characters, including a cricket bat maker who believes he has been reincarnated, and Walter, a butcher boy who wants to be a country and western singer. As Stephen Dobyns wrote in the *New York Times Book Review*, "The force of . . . Tremain's writing exerts absolute control over the world she has created. The crowd of characters is never a confusion. Instead, they perform an elaborate and exactly constructed ballet." Though each life is interlinked, each is also parallel and lonely. Happiness of a kind is achieved when Walter fulfills his ambition to reach Nashville, feeling "in a kind of heaven because of the colossal shine on things." Martin follows him to this "sacred country" and finds a "level place" working on a farm. Back in the fields he has, like Sadler, Ruby, and Erica, come full circle, but also moved on. *Sacred Country* is controlled and unsentimental, and in Dobyns' words "makes us look forward to . . . Tremain's other books with hungry pleasure."

Tremain has written several plays for radio and television. This work exhibits her characteristic concern with pain and lovelessness, as well as the comic detachment that is such an important feature of her writing. *Temporary Shelter* won a Giles Cooper Award for radio plays, and appeared in Methuen's *Best Radio Plays of 1984.* In 1994 she adapted *Scared Country* for a BBC television series. *Restoration* was filmed in 1994, with Robert B. Downey, Jr. playing Merivel. Tremain told an interviewer for the *New York Times* that she was not herself interested in writing the screenplay, but she did work on one of the drafts.

From 1979 to 1980 Rose Tremain was a fellow at the University of Essex. Since 1984 she has been teaching at the University of East Anglia in the creative writing course established by Malcolm Bradbury. Her second marriage, to Jonathan Dudley, ended in divorce. Having met the biographer Richard Holmes she is, she says in an interview given to the *Observer* in 1992, "very happy for the first time in years." She is a member of International PEN and the Royal Society of Literature.

PRINCIPAL WORKS: *Novels*—Sadler's Birthday, 1976; Letter to Sister Benedicta, 1978; The Cupboard, 1981; The Swimming Pool Season, 1984; Restoration, 1989; Sacred Country, 1982. *Short stories*—The Colonel's Daughter, and Other Stories, 1982; The Garden of the Villa Mollini, and Other Stories, 1986. *Radio plays*—The Wisest Fool, 1976; Blossom, 1977; Dark Green, 1977; Don't Be Cruel, 1978; Leavings, 1978; Down the Hill, 1979; Half-Time, 1980; Mother's Day, 1980; Temporary Shelter, 1984. *Television plays*-Halleluiah, Mary Plum, 1979; Findings on a Late Afternoon, 1981; A Room for the Winter, 1981. *Stage plays*—Yoga Class, 1984. *Juvenile*—Journey to the Volcano, 1985. *Nonfiction*—Freedom for Women, 1971; Stalin: A Biography, 1974.

ABOUT: Blain, V. et al., The Feminist Companion to Literature in English, 1990; Boylan, C. (ed.) The Agony and the Ego: The Art and Strategy of Fiction Writing Explored, 1993; Buck, C. (ed.) Bloomsbury Guide to Women's Literature, 1992; Contemporary Authors 97–100, 1981; Contemporary Literary Criticism 42, 1987; Dictionary of Literary Biography 14, 1983; International Authors and Writers Who's Who, 1993; Who's Who, 1994. *Periodicals*—British Book News March 1982; Harper's Bazaar April 1993; Listener April 19, 1979; New York Times August 21, 1994; New York Times Book Review July 24, 1977; May 27, 1984; April 15, 1990; April 11, 1993; Observer August 30, 1992; Publishers Weekly April 5, 1993; Sunday Times (London) March 10, 1985; Times Literary Supplement April 30, 1976; October 16, 1981; September 4, 1992.

*TSUJI, KUNIO (September 24, 1925–), Japanese novelist, short story writer, playwright, and critic, was born in Tokyo, the third son in his family. In accordance with traditional Asian astrological practices, his given name, Kunio, was derived from the Japanese numbers for the month and day of his birth. Tsuji has written about the timing of his birth: "If you divide the 20th century in half, then cut it in half again, you have the year of my birth, and the twenty-fourth of September that year was the day of the autumnal equinox, when day and night are divided equally. In the middle of the night separating September 23 and 24, just at the time when I was born, Venus moves from the house of Virgo to that of Libra. One quarter of the 20th century; the bisection of day and night; Libra; Venus—it seems to me that these phenomena are accurate descriptions of the nature of my writing."

Like many other Japanese writers of this century, including Yasunari Kawabata and Yasushi Inoue, Tsuji was born into a family that had long been engaged in the practice of medicine. The men in both his father's and mother's families, in Yamanashi and Kagoshima prefectures respectively, had been doctors for generations. His father, however, broke with the tradition and made his living as a journalist; he was also not without sympathy for the artistic life, having distinguished himself as a performer on a form of lute known as the Satsuma biwa.

When Tsuji was born, one elder brother had already passed away, and another died in 1928; the sister just before him also died in infancy. Two other sisters were born in 1929 and 1931. In 1930, the family moved to Nagoya when his father was transferred in his job, and they lived near Tsurumai Park. In retrospect Tsuji wrote: "Sahoko, the woman who would later become my wife, was born that same year on the 21st of November in the hospital right next to Tsurumai Park. It would seem as though, under the guidance of Venus, I was led all the way to Tsurumai Park to watch over the birth of my future wife."

In 1932 the family returned to Tokyo, and Tsuji entered elementary school at Akasaka that same year. In 1944, as the war situation worsened and the firebombings frequently ravaged Tokyo, the family was forced to evacuate the capital city and live in Yugawara, an area in the mountains south of Tokyo that boasts many hot springs resorts. In April 1944, after failing his entrance exams and spending an additional year of study in order to pass, Tsuji was admitted into the science department of the Matsumoto Higher School (in the prewar Japanese education system, a "higher school" was equivalent to the present-day university). Matsumoto, located in the mountains of Nagano Prefecture, was even farther from his home, and Tsuji had to move into the school dormitory.

Although science was his declared field of study, Tsuji wasted no time involving himself in literary pursuits. Only half a year after his admission into the school, he wrote the script for a play that was performed by residents in his dormitory. Perhaps, in fact, his heart was not much into his practical studies and was more taken by his literary pursuits, because in April 1945, Tsuji was dismissed for poor scholarship. There was, however, a positive benefit to be derived from this situation: by this point in the war effort, very few real classes were held at higher schools in Japan, and most able-bodied students were required by the military authorities to spend their days in various acts of labor service. Tsuji was able to avoid conscript labor because he had failed his school courses, although he continued to live at the dormitory. He spent his days founding a magazine that circulated through the dorm, sponsoring haiku poetry gatherings, and staging plays by Ibsen and Hauptmann.

In June 1945, Tsuji met one of his closest lifelong literary friends, Morio Kita, who moved into the dormitory after his family home in Tokyo was destroyed in a firebomb raid. The two young men hit it off immediately, partly because Kita (whose real name is Munekichi Saito) also came from a household that combined the medical and literary professions: his father was the renowned psychiatrist and poet Mokichi Saito. Tsuji and Kita encouraged one another in their literary pursuits, and the month the war ended, Tsuji published one of his compositions in the dormitory's literary magazine. With the end of the war, however, suffering from the efforts of poor nutrition, he returned to live with his family in Yugawara.

No sooner were classes resumed than Tsuji enrolled in the literature section at Matsumoto Higher School. He published frequently in the school newspaper, but then abandoned creative writing for a time to devote his full energies to the school's drama program. In 1947, he left the dormitory and took up lodgings at Asama Onsen, another hot springs town. He seldom attended classes, and once again was dismissed, this time, for poor attendance. In 1949, he moved back to Tokyo and in April entered the French literature department of Tokyo University, where he studied with Kazuo Watanabe, a renowned scholar and critic of French literature.

In 1950, Tsuji continued to attend classes while taking on a job in the advertising department at Minsei Diesel (which later became Nissan Diesel). He remained with the firm for seven years, but spent much of his leisure time around the dressing rooms of the Kagetsu Theater at Asakusa. He would often see the famed dilettante writer Kafu Nagai—who, though he spent much of his time frequenting strip houses, became something of an ironic cultural hero for refusing to write military propaganda during the war—entering the dressing rooms of the Rokku Theater next door. Tsuji's dream at this time was to write comedies in the style of Molière. He graduated from Tokyo University in 1952, writing his graduation thesis on Stendhal, and immediately thereafter entered the graduate school.

In April 1953, Tsuji was hospitalized for a month with an acute case of hepatitis. He had recovered sufficiently by June to marry Sahoko Goto, and the newlyweds settled in the Kokubunji suburb of Tokyo. The first of many summers was spent in Kita Yatsugatake, another mountainous part of Nagano Prefecture, in 1955; much of the writing of his first important work, *Natsu no toride* (Summer fortress) was done here.

In 1956, Tsuji became a part-time lecturer in the literature department of Gakushuin University. In September of the following year, he booked passage in the fourth-class section of a French ship and sailed to France, where he remained until 1961. One of the most important personal and intellectual influences on Tsuji during these years abroad was the friendship he formed with the leading Japanese philosopher Arimasa Mori, a specialist in French literature who shifted his interests to the study of Pascal and Descartes and introduced the writings of Sartre to Japan.

During this first of what would come to be almost annual sojourns in Europe, Tsuji traveled through Italy, Greece, Sicily, Spain, Germany, and Austria. This first trip also provided him with the final determination he needed to undertake his own career as a writer. In the summer of 1959, while standing on the Acropolis beside the Parthenon, he was deeply moved by his surroundings and felt as though he had found the motivation to begin creative writing again. Responding to that impetus, that fall he wrote "Mishiranu machi nite" (In an unfamiliar town) and sent it to Morio Kita. Kita gave this and three subsequent stories to Yutaka Haniya, one of the founding editors of the important postwar literary journal *Kindai Bungaku*, and a prominent critic and novelist. With Kita's support Tsuji's stories began to be published in that journal. In February 1961, he published "Seio no hikari no shita" (Beneath the light of Western Europe) in *Shincho*.

Tsuji returned to Japan on a French mail ship

in March 1961 and resumed his teaching position at Gakushuin University. In June, he published "Monogatari to shosetsu no aida" (Between the tale and the novel) in *Kindai Bungaku;* this became the first part of a study of the novel which he serialized in literary journals. In July, he accompanied Kita to pay his first call on Yutaka Haniaya, and thereafter became a regular visitor at Haniya's house.

Spurred by the reception of the short stories he had published, Tsuji began serialization of his first novel, *Kairo nite* (In the corridor) in *Kindai Bungaku.* In it a narrator who has discovered the letters and journals of a woman artist after her death attempts to reconstruct her life of loneliness and despair and the manner in which she turned fate to her advantage and found depth and meaning in her life. Tsuji received the fourth Kindai Bungaku Prize for this work, marking his debut in the literary world. He followed this well-received novel with a study of the painter Monet in 1964, and wrote the first and second drafts of *Natsu no toride,* which was finally published in 1966, the same year that he became associate professor at Rikkyo University.

The novel describes the experiences of a woman from an old established family who develops an attachment to the arts of the medieval period through her study of handwoven brocades, but disappears after her involvement in a lesbian affair in a foreign land.

In 1968, Tsuji published his full-length critical evaluation of the novel genre, *Shosetsu e no josho* (An introduction to the novel), distinguished both for its original appraisals of Rousseau, Proust, Thomas Mann, and other major writers, and for examining the ways in which Japanese writers from the 17th century to the present had sought to bring qualities of the premodern "tale" into the Japanese novel.

Also in 1968, Tsuji published *Azuchi Okanki* (A record of comings and goings to Azuchi; translated as *The Signore: Shogun of the Warring States),* which received the Geijutsu Sensho New Writers Prize. The only work by Tsuji translated into English at this point, *The Signore* is a historical novel set in one of the most popular eras for Japanese storytellers: the late 1500s, when a century of civil war and decentralized rule was finally coming to an end through the efforts of military warlords who have been labeled the "three unifiers." Tsuji's novel focuses upon the first of these military leaders, Oda Nobunaga (the "Signore" of the title), and his struggles to unify the nation and negotiate with the recently arrived Catholic missionaries and European traders. The persuasive power of the novel lies in Tsuji's choice of narrator: neither Japanese nor a missionary, the Italian seafarer who tells the story is able to comment dispassionately on both the strengths and the foibles of the Japanese warriors and the European proselytizers. Nobunaga is fascinated by this pilot's knowledge of guns and shipbuilding—skills the Japanese critically needed to compete with the encroaching Western powers. The narrator's neutrality gives him license to move freely between the two foreign camps, showing the reader both the machinations of the missionaries and the strategic brilliance of the Signore. His unique positioning allows the narrator to see through the armored layers of Nobunaga's power and discern the essential loneliness of this great leader: "In making himself impervious to human feelings, he chose a path fraught with every difficulty life could bring; and the further he walked along that path, the less he was understood by those around him." Van C. Gessel commented in the *San Francisco Review of Books* that "the subtle technique of speculative narration makes for a truly enjoyable reading experience. Stephen Snyder's . . . translation intensifies that pleasure."

In July 1968, Tsuji accompanied Haniya on a trip to Europe. After traveling through the Soviet Union, he returned to France. His experiences from this year of residence in Paris were eventually recorded in his *Monmarutoru nikki* (Montmartre diaries, 1974). He also began serialization of *Amakusa no gaka* (A Song of Solomon in Amakusa) and *Sagano Meigetsuki* (A record of the bright moon in Sagano). In September 1969, Tsuji returned to Japan and began the serialization of his novel *Haikyosha Yurianusu* (The apostate Julianus). The next year, 1970, he published a series of dialogues with Kita, a short story collection, and several stories. He began that year to spend each summer in the mountain resort area of Karuizawa to escape the heat of Tokyo.

In April 1972, Tsuji became professor at Tokyo University of Agriculture and Industry. He completed his novel Julian the Apostate, which was awarded the Mainichi Geijutsu Prize, and the first of six volumes in a series of his collected works was published. In October, he and Kita traveled through France, Italy, and Germany. He also began serialization of *Haru no taikan* (Coronation in spring), a portrait of Florence under the Medicis in the days of Botticelli. Between 1973 and 1974, five volumes of diaries he had kept of his year-long sojourn in Paris, titled *Pari no shuki* (Paris journal), were published. In 1973, his play *Poseidon Kamensai* (Masked festival of Poseidon) was performed by the Shiki Troupe, and published. In July, he traveled to Italy, France, and Germany, continuing what would become essentially an annual ritual for him: teaching and writing in Japan through the regular academic year, and spending spring and summer breaks in Europe. During a typical four months he spent in France in 1985, for example, Tsuji participated in two literary and cultural symposia, the first treating "Revolution in Contemporary Japanese Culture," the second a Franco-Japanese cultural summit.

Among his many varied publications in 1974, perhaps the most unusual was the serialization of 100 linked short stories, given the collective title *Aru shogai no nanatsu no basho* (Seven locales from a certain life). In April 1975 he accepted a position as professor in the literature department of Gakushūin University.

In 1976, Tsuji began his first newspaper novel serialization, *Toki no tobira* (The door of time), which appeared in the *Mainichi Shimbun* evening edition. His several journeys this year took him to Syria, the South Pacific, France, Greece, Yugoslavia, and China. *Natsu no umi no iro* (The color of the summer sea), a collection of linked stories, appeared in 1977, followed by completion of the novel *Haru no taikan*. His newspaper novel was also concluded, and in May he visited the Soviet Union and France.

Tsuji Kunio zen tampen (The Complete Short Stories of Tsuji Kunio) was published in 1978. In June 1980, after publishing a collection of essays of literary and aesthetic criticism, Tsuji began a year's sojourn in France. In the fall, he gave lectures on Japanese folklore in Paris, and from November 1984 to March 1985 he taught courses on Japanese literature in Paris.

An essay collection and a story collection appeared in 1981, and though he returned to Japan in June, he was back in France between September and October. His travels did not hinder his production; Tsuji has been prolific. More than fifty published volumes are credited to him. In 1983, for instance, his major publications included a full-length critical consideration of Thomas Mann and a story collection.

In 1985, the Bungakuza Theater troupe presented his play *Tenshitachi ga machi o yuku* (Angels are walking the streets). In 1986 he edited a six volume series titled *Seikimatsu no bi to yume* (Beauty and dreams in the fin de siècle). In 1988, Tsuji published two collections of linked stories, a volume of film criticism, a compilation of his university and public lectures, and finally completed the 100 linked stories he had started in 1974.

Tsuji has continued to write energetically and creatively, scrupulously avoiding the tendency among his countrymen to become entrapped in the writing of autobiographical fiction. His work, in fact, stands in stark counterpoint to the "I-novel" tradition of realism with its emphasis on the dark side of human behavior and the ugliness of everyday life, with little plot development. Tsuji, in contrast, has made significant attempts to restore the qualities of storytelling to the novel. As one of the first postwar Japanese writers to focus almost exclusively on non-Japanese characters and settings, Tsuji can be said to be one of the most erudite, cosmopolitan, and internationalized writers Japan has produced in the postwar period.

PRINCIPAL WORKS IN ENGLISH TRANSLATION: (tr. S. Snyder) The Signore: Shogun of the Warring States, 1989.

ABOUT: Kodansha Encyclopedia Japan, 1983. *Periodicals*—San Francisco Review of Books Fall 1990; World Literature Today Winter 1991.

*TSUSHIMA, YUKO (March 30, 1947–   ), Japanese novelist and short story writer, was born Satoko Tsushima in Mitaka, a suburb of Tokyo. She was the third and last child born to her mother, Michiko (Ishihara), and her father, whose real name was Shuji Tsushima, but who was best known as one of the most important novelists of modern Japan under his pen name, Osamu Dazai. When Satoko was born, her elder sister Sonoko was six years old, her brother Masaki three.

Dazai had been married once before, in the early 1930s to a geisha of whom he was enamored, but the relationship had been rocky, and they had tried to commit suicide together before parting ways. In a desperate attempt to help Dazai gain control of his meandering life, his family importuned Dazai's literary mentor, the famed novelist Masuji Ibuse, to find him a "normal" wife. Michiko Ishihara was a stable, intelligent schoolteacher from Yamanashi Prefecture who had the ability to tame some of Dazai's wildness, particularly during the war years, and Dazai even created some lovely modern recreations of classical fairy tales for his oldest daughter during the early 1940s. But not long after Japan's defeat in World War II, Dazai reverted to his old ways, slipping into adultery and drug abuse once again, and ironically, producing the novel that became emblematic of Japan's physical and spiritual defeat, *Shayo* (1947; translated as *The Setting Sun*). One of his mistresses gave birth to a daughter, Ota Haruko, just eight months after Satoko's birth. Haruko also became a writer.

About fifteen months after Satoko was born, Dazai made another in a string of despairing attempts to commit suicide—usually with a fe-

YUKO TSUSHIMA

male lover—and this time, June 13, 1948, he was at last successful. Dazai and a mistress drowned themselves in the Tamagawa Canal, not far from the family home, and their bodies were discovered there on the nineteenth, Dazai's thirty-ninth birthday. Tsushima, of course, has no memories of her notorious father—she has written virtually nothing of her impressions of him or his work; in a collection of stories called *Waga chichitachi* (Our fathers), the closest she comes to commentary on him is when one character, a mother, confesses to her seventeen-year-old daughter that her late father was not human but, in fact, a dog. But the manner of Dazai's life—fathering children with several different women and then abandoning them through his acts of dissipation—and the manner of his death—choosing water as the fateful instrument—have had an unmistakably profound impact upon her thinking and her writing.

Soon after her father's suicide, Tsushima moved with her family to live with a maternal uncle in another part of Tokyo. In April 1950, Tsushima was enrolled in a private nursery school near her home, where the emphasis was placed on music education, and in 1953, at the age of six, she entered an elementary school operated at the time by Tokyo Gakugei University. Her middle school was the Catholic-run Shirayuri Gakuen.

In 1960, shortly before Tsushima's thirteenth birthday, her elder brother Masaki died of pneumonia. Tsushima had been very close to this brother, who was afflicted with Down's syndrome and could not speak beyond the two-year-old level. The relationship was very important to her developmental years, and she has claimed that much of her childhood was spent devoid of verbal communication. Consequently, writing became for Tsushima a means of expressing her emotions after her brother was gone, and of making this "family secret" that haunted her something that no longer belonged to her alone. Several of her short stories feature this brother as an important character and symbol for the struggle to communicate, with both the living and the dead.

At the age of fifteen, in 1962, Tsushima advance to the high school at the Shirayuri Gakuen, and in 1965 she enrolled in the English literature department of Shirayuri Women's University. She wasted little time starting up a small coterie literary magazine, called *Yoseatsume*, distributed in mimeographed form, but it lasted only two issues. This did not discourage Tsushima's desire to write, however, and in October 1966 she received a school prize for an essay, "Gendai to yume" (The present age and dreams), whic was published in the university newspaper. Bored at school, she set up her own independent "seminars," organized a folksinging group to perform protest songs, and spent a good deal of time traveling, but ultimately she came to realize that writing was the form of escape most congenial to her nature.

The following year, Tsushima signed up with another literary magazine, *Bungei Shuto*, and in August published her first short story, "Aru tanjo" (A birth) in that magazine, using the pen name Aki Yuko. Setting the model for most of her later work, this story draws its materials from her own familial surroundings in its depiction of a father who feels personally responsible for the retardation of his three-year-old son and a seven-year-old daughter who cherishes her brother and cannot understand her father's feelings of guilt. Two other stories followed in the same magazine in 1968, both published under the pen name Ashi Yuko.

The first appearance of her present nom de plume, Tsushima Yūko, came as the byline of a story, "Rekuiemu—Inu to otona no tame ni" (Requiem—For a dog and an adult) that appeared in the important literary journal *Mita Bungaku* in January 1969, just two months before her graduation from college. Tsushima's senior thesis treated the Faust theme in the writings of Marlowe and Byron. Her personal reading during these years included a close examination of her father's writings, partly out of the desire to come to know the father she did not remember, but also out of the sense that, as his daughter, she had an obligation to understand his works better than anyone else. Tsushima also absorbed herself in reading Dostoyevski, James Joyce, Virginia Woolf, Faulkner, Poe, Jun ichiro Tanizaki, Kyoka Izumi, and Kanoko Okamoto.

She entered the graduate program in English literature at Meiji University in April 1969, but Japanese students of the day, following the example of their Western European and American peers, were rioting against the government and all other forms of social order. Tsushima, like most other students, used the unrest as an excuse to skip classes. Instead, she continued to publish short stories in various magazines. Within two years she had formally withdrawn from the university. In November 1969 she moved out of the family home and into her own apartment at Yoyogi. Of this period, the narrator of her 1983 short story "Yokushitsu" ("The Bath") remarks: "My mother and I had lived alone since I entered high school. . . . When I was 23, I left home to chase after a young man—not the one who became the father of my children. It wasn't that I was all that much in love with him; it was just that the thought of living enveloped in my mother's solitude, as if in a dark cloud, was frightening. Rather than feel sympathy for my mother's loneliness, I found myself stifled by it" (tr. J. M. Holman).

Tsushima took a job with the Hoso Bangumi (Broadcast Programming) Center in April 1960, but resigned the position in November when she married a man with connections in the Japanese theater world. Her first important literary work, a three-part piece given the overall title of "Shanikusai" (Carnival), was published in 1971; this, along with two earlier works, appeared in her first story collection, also called *Shanikusai*, in November of that year.

In January 1972, Tsushima moved back into her mother's house, and in May she gave birth to her first child, a daughter. Another story collection, *Doji no kage* (Shadows of a child), was published in March 1973; her first novel, titled *Ikimono no atsumaru ie* (The house where living things gather), which concerns a young woman's desire to see the country home where her father was raised, appeared a month later; the important novella *Mugura no haha* (Mother in creeping vines) appeared in 1974.

In 1975, Tsushima made her first brief trip overseas, spending a month in Paris. That same year, several of the short stories that are included in the translated collection *The Shooting Gallery* were first published in Japan. After *Mugura no haha* appeared in a collection with other stories at the end of that year, it was awarded the sixteenth Tamura Toshiko Prize for literature.

In 1976, Tsushima gave birth to her second

child, a son, Daimu (written with characters that mean "the great dream"). Tsushima has described this child's birth as resulting from a "marriage that had not passed through the legal formalities." Not long after Daimu was born, Tsushima went through what she has chosen to call "an ordinary divorce." Whatever she may have meant by that phrase, the challenges of raising two children without a father in a society like Japan's has formed the substance of much that Tsushima has written, and the motif of the absent father—one that has been familiar to her since shortly after her own birth—has brought distinction and depth to many of her stories and novels.

In 1977, Tsushima published the story "Kusa no fushido" ("A Bed of Grass"), which received the Izumi Kyoka Prize for that year. The story's narrator describes both the death of a retarded older brother and the estrangement she feels from her own mother: "I was in junior high school when my brother died. He was sixteen but was still a child. When the funeral was over and our normal life had resumed, my mother and I tried to avoid each other in the house. I felt uneasy being with her without my brother there. . . . I was afraid of touching the sadness of my mother, which I could not understand, and so I continued to ignore her. My father had died over ten years before in an accident. I was afraid I would be overcome by the deaths of my father and brother as my mother had been." (Trans. Y. Tanaka and E. Hanson) As will be made clear from subsequent details in Tsushima's life, the story also seems almost eerily prophetic, since the narrator goes on to give birth to a child who dies young. Also in 1977, with her daughter, she visited Buffalo, New York, where her maternal uncle was living. Tsushima's first essay collection, titled "Tomei kukan ga mieru toki" (When transparent space becomes visible), was published in August 1977.

Tsushima's most productive and impressive period of literary output began in 1978, with the publication of her acclaimed novel *Choji* (*Child of Fortune*), which received the Women's Literature Prize. It was her first important work translated into both English and French, and it is particularly moving in its depiction of Kōko, a woman whose relationships over time with three men have led to an abortion and the birth of a daughter by a man who is not the real love of her life. Kōko seems to feel that only by becoming pregnant again and producing a "child of fortune" can she bring order to the chaos of her relationships with men, but it proves a phantom dream.

A series of important literary prizes came to

Tsushima in the wake of *Child of Fortune*. Her 1979 story collection *Hikari no ryobun* (Realm of light) received the Noma Literary Prize for New Writers. A second seminal novel, *Yama o hashiru onna* (1980, *Woman Running in the Mountains*), combines Tsushima's focus on the mundane but ultimately defining incidents in the everyday life of a single mother. Her sensitive ability to use fragmented images of women in Japanese folklore underscores the emotional turmoil of those, like herself, who struggle against the stereotypes of women in Japanese society.

This novel was followed by *Moeru kaze* (Burning wind, 1980); *Suifu* (Ministry of water, 1982), in which Tsushima combines the watery suicide of her father with the ancient Japanese legend of an underwater Palace of the Dragon King; *Hi no kawa no hotori de* (Beside the river of fire, 1983); *Oma monogatari* (Tales of encounters with demons, 1984); and the story collection *Danmari ichi* (Silent traders, 1984), the title story of which received the Kawabata Prize and has been translated into English.

For an autobiographical writer such as Tsushima who relies heavily upon the pieces of her own life to provide the skeletons for her fictions, certain pivotal moments from that personal experience can literally overwhelm and come to dominate the substance of what she writes. Certainly the critical event that occurred in Tsushima's life in 1985 has become such an element in her literature. In March of that year her son Daimu, eight years old at the time, was at home taking a bath while Tsushima was in the adjoining room. Puzzled that he had stayed so long in the bath, she went in to find him unconscious in the tub, a smile on his face. She struggled to pull his body from the bath, but the boy was already dead. An autopsy concluded merely that the child had died of a "breathing spasm," but for his mother, the death remains "inexplicable." The extraordinary irony of losing both father and son in watery graves has not escaped her readers and critics.

Tsushima's first attempt to grapple in her fiction with this profound tragedy came in the tender, inventive novel *Yoru no hikari no owarete* (Pursued by the light of the night, 1986), which received the Yomiuri Literary Prize. Here, a woman who has experienced a loss like Tsushima's own begins the attempt to restore contact with the world around her not by means of her contemporary circle of friends or family, but by writing letters to a female author who lived a thousand years before and produced a tale of the Japanese court titled *Yoru no nezame* (Wakefulness at night). By corresponding with this wom-

an and retelling portions of her classical tale that have been lost, the narrator forms a bond of sorrow with the women of the past and tales some hesitant steps toward an acceptance and understanding of her experience.

Even more effective and poignant are the stories about her loss in *Yume no kiroku* (A record of dreams, 1988). The best story in this collection is "Hikarikagayaku itten o" (A single glittering point of light), which conveys both the inability of this mother to accept the fact that her son is dead and her frustration at being unable to convey the reality of her loss to others through the instrumentality of words. Tsushima's lifelong struggle to make words tools of expression, stemming back to her relationship with her retarded brother, is elegantly displayed in this story.

In 1990, Tsushima published the novel *Afureru haru* (Abundant spring), and in that year she was one of four Japanese writers invited to participate in the conference on literature sponsored in San Francisco by the Wheatland Foundation. (At that same conference, Tsushima's English translator, Geraldine Harcourt, received the foundation's prize for translation.) The novel *Oi naru yume yo, hikari yo* (O great dream, great light) appeared in 1991. She subsequently published *Kagayaku mizu no jidai* (The age of glimmering waters, 1994). Tsushima remains one of the most stimulating and challenging practitioners of the "I-novel" form of personal narrative in Japan today.

PRINCIPAL WORKS IN ENGLISH TRANSLATION: *Novels*—(tr. G. Harcourt) Child of Fortune, 1983; (tr. G. Harcourt) Woman Running in the Mountains, 1991. *Short stories*—(tr. G. Harcourt) The Shooting Gallery, 1988; Short story *in* Zyzzyva, Fall 1988; Short story *in* Tanaha, Y., and Hanson, E. (ed.) This Kind of Woman: Tens Stories by Japanese Women Writers, 1982.

ABOUT: Contemporary World Writers, 2nd ed., 1993; Masao, M. Off Ceater, 1991. *Periodicals*—New York Times March 23, 1991; New York Times Book Review July 24, 1988.

TUROW, SCOTT (April 12, 1949–), American novelist and lawyer, was born in Chicago, Illinois, the son of David T. Turow, a gynecologist, and Rita (Pastron) Turow, a teacher and writer of children's books. He spent his early years on Chicago's North Shore. When he was thirteen, the family moved to Winnetka, a Chicago suburb. Although he received a failing grade in freshman English at Winnetka's academically demanding New Trier High School, by his junior year Turow was writing regularly for the school newspaper, and eventually be-

SCOTT TUROW

came its editor. When he enrolled as a freshman at Amherst College, he had already decided that he was going to be a novelist. His mother urged him to prepare for a profession, preferably medicine, reminding him of the literary work of Doctors Anton Chekhov and William Carlos Williams. But Turow would have none of it. "[W]hen I went to Amherst I decided that I wasn't going to be a mere journalist," Turow told *Missouri Review* interviewer Kay Bonetti. "I wanted to be an *artiste* and a writer of fiction, and I began writing seriously then."

Turow was so intent upon pursuing a literary career that he completed a first novel, "Dithyramb," during his first year at Amherst. Only a few of his friends ever saw the novel, which was rejected by every publisher who read it. Turow was not, by his own admission, "one of the stars of the English department" at Amherst. He was, nonetheless, a voracious reader; Lawrence Durrell's *The Alexandria Quartet* and Robert Stone's *A Hall of Mirrors* are among the works that had the greatest influence on him as an undergraduate. During his senior year, he studied with the short story writer Tillie Olson. While still at Amherst, he had two stories accepted by the *Transatlantic Review*, one of which was published before he graduated.

After receiving his B.A. in English from Amherst in 1970, Turow moved to Stanford University, which had awarded him a graduate creative writing fellowship. At Stanford he completed a second, unpublished novel, "The Way Things Are," about a Chicago rent strike. "Writing 'The Way Things Are' was one of the more painful

experiences of my life," Turow told the *Missouri Review*. "I wanted desperately to be a great writer, and was, in some parts of 'The Way Things Are,' not even a remotely good one. I found that terribly painful." By the time he received his M.A. from Stanford in 1974, Turow was uncertain whether he could continue writing fiction.

In researching and writing about a rent strike, Turow was surprised to learn how intricate the relevant laws were, and even more surprised at how much the legal aspects of the story captured his imagination. At the same time, he and his wife (he had married Annette Weisberg, an artist, in 1971) were becoming more and more disenchanted with their lives in California. "There was incessant drinking and substance abuse, and marriages were falling apart all over the place," he told Paul Gray in *Time*. "Annette and I were newly married, and we decided to stay married. In that sense, California was too crazy for us." Fearing that his writing career was going nowhere, he decided, on the recommendation of some lawyer friends, to take the Law School Admissions Test. To his astonishment, he got an outstanding score. Although the University of Rochester had offered him a tenure-track position in the English department, Turow was tired of teaching and opted for a complete change of course. With acceptance letters from several top law schools, Turow chose Harvard.

When Turow wrote to his literary agent to inform her that he was going to law school and to thank her for her efforts to sell "The Way Things Are," her remarked that someone should publish a book about the law school experience from the student's point of view. Thinking that Turow was asking for the assignment himself, his agent took the idea to the Putnam Company, which quickly offered Turow a contract to write about his first year at Harvard Law School—one that proved to be extraordinary grueling, and during which he routinely worked between eighty and one hundred hours per week. He did the actual writing of the book during his first summer break, working from detailed diaries he had kept throughout the year. Since he was writing a critical assessment of academic practices at Harvard Law—both on the part of students and professors—Turow was careful to change the names of principal characters and create composites whenever possible.

Published as *One L* (the title refers to Harvard's designation for a first-year law student). while Turow was in his third and final year of law school, the book had an enthusiastic critical reception. Reviewing *One L* in the *New York Times Book Review* in 1977, Philip M. Stern wrote: "It is compelling in its vivid portrayal of the high-tension competitiveness of Harvard Law School and of the group madness it seems to induce in the student body. It is important because it offers an inside look at what law students do and don't learn and who they are and are not equipped to represent when they graduate."

After receiving his J.D. from Harvard in 1978, Turow returned to his native Chicago. He took a job with the United States Attorney's office for the Northern District of Illinois, where he assisted in the tax fraud prosecution of Illinois's attorney general, William J. Scott. A relatively inexperienced lawyer, Turow established his reputation as a crack litigator when he participated in Operation Greylord, a wide-ranging investigation into corruption in the Illinois courts, prosecuting Circuit Court Judge Reginald Holzer, who was convicted of soliciting more than $200,000 in bribes and was sentenced to eighteen years in prison.

Although he was finding success in a challenging and lucrative profession, Turow still yearned to write—and publish—a novel. During his first year at the U.S. Attorney's office, Turow used the time spent on his commuter train ride to begin to work on a new novel. Much of this writing would eventually find its way into his first published novel, *Presumed Innocent*. But the writing progressed slowly and had to be squeezed in between professional and family obligations. In addition, he began writing another novel. Even after he had settled on the plot, structure, and characters of *Presumed Innocent*, he decided that he still needed an uninterrupted block of time to complete the work. Following his wife's suggestion, he left his job at the U.S. Attorney's office in July 1986, giving himself three months to complete the novel before beginning a new job with the Chicago firm of Sonnenschein, Carlin, Nath and Rosenthal.

He finished the novel with time to spare. By the time he went to work for Sonnenschein, Carlin in late September, the finished manuscript of *Presumed Innocent* had already been in his agent's hands for several weeks. The novel soon became the object of a fierce bidding competition among various publishers.

The principal character and narrator of *Presumed Innocent* is Rusty Sabich, husband, father, and chief deputy prosecutor of Kindle County, a fictional jurisdiction highly reminiscent of Chicago's Cook County. The novel's plot hinges on the murder of Carolyn Polhemus, an independent single woman who is also a Kindle County prosecutor. Six months before her death, Polhemus and Sabich had had a brief, tumultuous affair, ended by Polhemus. Sabich's politically ambitious boss, unaware of the affair, and wanting to convict someone as quickly as possible, assigns Sabich to the case. When he unable to prosecute the case successfully, and when his affair with the murdered woman in revealed, Sabich himself becomes the prime suspect and must stand trial for murder.

Reviewers of the novel were especially impressed by Turow's dramatic and informative renderings of courtroom procedure. "From page one, the book consciously transcends the murder-mystery genre, combining whodunit suspense with an elegant style and philosophical voice," Anne Rice wrote in the *New York Times Book Review* (1987). She praised his painstaking, yet dramatic, delineation of legal complexities, but faulted the novel's surprise conclusion: "The crime as explained seems too calculated, too elaborate and too purely vicious to have been committed by the person in question."

In the *New York Review of Books*, Robert Towers wrote that "*Presumed Innocent* does not easily fit any preconceived notion of the suspense novel, literary or not." Towers gave Turow high marks for his depiction of the legal process: "[W]hat held me . . . was not suspense about the outcome or the danger to Rusty, but the legal lore—the insider's view of the craft of law—that Turow provides so skillfully and abundantly."

Newseek critic Walter Clemons found the novel's surprise ending to be one of its many strengths. "After the trial ends," he wrote, "Turow fingers a least likely suspect, right in the foreground, so surprising that it's a pleasure to retrack our way through the book to see how we were fooled."

The film version of *Presumed Innocent* (with which Turow had no direct involvement) was directed by Alan J. Pakula. It starred Harrison Ford.

The protagonist of Turow's second novel, *The Burden of Proof*, is Sandy Stern, who was first encountered in *Presumed Innocent* as Rusty Sabich's defense attorney. In the opening scene of *The Burden of Proof*, Stern returns home from a business trip to discover that his wife of thirty-one years has committed suicide. The story revolves around the criminal machinations of Dixon Hartnell, a high-rolling commodities trader who is Stern's brother-in-law and client.

The Burden of Proof. like *Presumed Innocent* before it, was a colossal popular success; among reviewers, however, it had few admirers. In the *London Review of Books*, John Lanchester commented, "You have to concentrate with the result that the novel's effort-to-reward ratio is disproportionately weighted on the side of effort." In the *New York Times Book Review*,

Peter Maas wrote: "I regret to report that if re-creating the strengths of *Presumed Innocent* was Mr. Turow's intent, he comes up short. . . . If you're an aficionado of soap opera, you'll proba-bly love *The Burden of Proof*." Robert Towers, in the *New York Review of Books*, found the novel's main problem to be one of subject mat-ter: "*The Burden of Proof* is extremely informa-tive on the subject of laws regarding futures trading—a subject some readers may find less enthralling than the laws regarding murder."

Even more intricately plotted that its two pre-decessors, *Pleading Guilty* proved, in the judg-ment of most of its reviewers, that Turow had not exhausted his material. In this tough-talking and fast-moving novel, the central character, Mack Malloy, a former policeman now practic-ing law (and sleuthing) in a huge corporate law firm, is investigating the disappearance of a col-league of very dubious character. Mack himself is a recovering alcoholic, unhappily married, and only too prone to compromising situations. With a prose that, Christopher Lehmann-Haupt wrote in the *New York Times*, "effectively catches the roar and murmur of big-city life" and a large cast of mainly unsavory characters, Turow showed his characteristic skills—what Lehmann-Haupt called "the almost too-dazzling plot tricks he tried to pull off in his earlier novels." But fellow-lawyer and novelist John Mortimer pointed out in the *New York Times Book Review* that with this third novel Turow shows himself "worthy to be ranked with Dash-iell Hammett or Raymond Chandler."

Turow's novels have led a surge in the public's interest in a new type of courtroom fiction. "As such, a new genre has been created," Esther B. Fein wrote in the *New York Times* in 1992. "Where once there was simply legal or court-room fiction, now there is a rapidly growing sub-category—legal fiction by lawyers."

Turow credits his legal education and his work as an attorney with changing his whole ap-proach to storytelling. As he told *New York Times Magazine* interviewer Jeff Shear in 1987: "What I learned by trying cases that I didn't learn by writing fiction was the level of detail you need to tell a story. How much people need to know. What details they will be satisfied not having." In his profile of Turow in *Time* in 1990, Paul Gray wrote, "He is the Bard of the Litigious Age, an expert witness on the technicalities of the current stampede to litigation and on the ethical and emotional conundrums that accom-pany it."

Turow remains committed to the idea of writ-ing popular fiction that is informative, challeng-ing, and entertaining. In his conversation with the *Missouri Review*, Turow remarked: "I don't believe that the role of literature has been histor-ically, or ought to be today, to confine itself to a tiny professional elite who are capable of un-derstanding it. . . . Storytelling is as innate to human experience as music, and some of us who write may feel a fundamental responsibility to recognize that and to seek as wide an audience as is possible." Still practicing law, though with a reduced caseload to allow more time for his writing, Turow views the law as being at the very heart of everyday experience, and thus a very worthy subject for novelists. As he told *New York Times* writer Esther B. Fein in a November 1992 interview: "I've tried to figure out what it means, that people are so interested in these nov-els about the law, and I think the reason is that the law remains our one universally recognized repository of values. The church is no longer the center of people's lives. . . . People's sense of community has been fractured. And so the law . . . seems to unite us as an embracing value."

PRINCIPAL WORKS: *Nonfiction*—One L: An Inside Ac-count of Life in the First Year at Harvard Law School, 1977. *Novels*—Presumed Innocent, 1987; The Burden of Proof, 1990; Pleading Guilty, 1993.

ABOUT: Contemporary Authors 73–76, 1978; Current Biography Yearbook 1991; Who's Who in America 1990–91. *Periodicals*—London Review of Books Sep-tember 13, 1990; Missouri Review no. 1, 1990; New York Review of Books November 19, 1987; August 16, 1990; New York Times February 9, 1992; July 20, 1992; November 11, 1992; June 3, 1993; New York Times Book Review September 25, 1977; June 28, 1987; June 3, 1990; June 6, 1993; New York Times Magazine June 7, 1987; Newsweek June 29, 1987; Pub-lishers Weekly July 16, 1987; Time June 11, 1990; Wall Street Journal August 1, 1991.

*UNO, CHIYO (1897–   ), Japanese novelist and publisher, was born in Iwakuni, a small town on the Inland Sea west of Hiroshima. Her father, Uno Toshitsugu, was the second son of a wealthy sake-brewing family. Never gainfully em-ployed, he spent much of his life in debauchery, dependent on his elder brother. Uno's mother, Doi Tomo, died of tuberculosis while Uno was still an infant. Toshitsugu, then forty-two, mar-ried the seventeen-year-old Saeki Ryû and sub-sequently fathered five more children. Uno's relationship with her step-mother was warm and nurturing, as Uno was more of an ally than a daughter. Both bore the brunt of Toshitsugu's ill humor. In 1912 Toshitsugu died of consumption, freeing his family from his tyranny but fettering them financially. Uno went to work as a teach-

*OOH no chih YO

CHIYO UNO

er's assistant upon graduation from the Iwakuni Higher School for Girls in 1914. A bright student herself, Uno enjoyed teaching, but her career was cut short when she was discovered in an affair with a fellow teacher. The resulting notoriety, and Uno's refusal to act chastened, forced her to leave Iwakuni. After a brief spell in Korea, Uno accompanied her maternal cousin, Fujimura Tadashi, to Kyoto and then to Tokyo where he entered the Law Division of Tokyo Imperial University. Uno was expected to serve Fujimura as a housekeeper but eventually found herself compelled by his dwindling finances to seek outside employment. She worked as a maid, a model, a bookkeeper, a babysister, and as a waitress at a fashionable café, where she met some of the luminaries on the literary scene. In 1919 she and Tadashi married and moved to Hokkaido, where he took a position at a bank.

Uno has since called her sojourn in Hokkaido the only time she led the life of a "normal woman." But normalcy was boring. To occupy herself Uno began to write. One of her stories "Shifun no kao" (Painted face) won first prize in a short story contest sponsored by the Tokyo-based journal *Jiji Shimpo* in 1921. Encouraged by her success (and by the money she won), Uno set to work on a longer piece, *Haka wo abaku* (Open the grave, 1922). Both stories were based loosely on Uno's experiences. The former, written with flippant casualness, concerns a poor yet ambitious waitress who tries unsuccessfully to compensate for her inferior clothing with elaborate cosmetics. The latter, in keeping with the socialist trend then popular in literature, describes the injustices a rural schoolteacher encounters.

Retrospectively unimportant, these two works nevertheless launched Uno's career. She left the boredom of Hokkaido, and her husband in the process, and returned to Tokyo, where she threw herself into the literary scene. Uno bobbed her hair, put away her kimono for Western dresses, and married again in 1924. This time her husband, Ozaki Shiro (1891–1964), was a writer like herself, though not nearly as successful. Uno Chiyo, given her beauty and propensity for sensationalism, was a writer in demand. She published frequently and widely. Many of her stories from this period describe country girls who search for fame and fortune in the big city only to have their hopes scuttled along the way by desperate brothers or unfaithful lovers. Before long Uno's stories turned more directly personal, as she began to relate the frustrations and uncertainties of a woman whose unconventional career overshadows her husband's. Ozaki could not long abide in Uno's shadow and by 1929 the two had divorced.

Uno was not to be alone long. In the spring of 1930 she began to live with a Western-style artist, Togo Seiji (1897–1978), whose attempted love suicide the year before had shocked Tokyo. Uno's five-year relationship with Togo inspired what is considered her first literary success: *Irozange* (1935, *Confessions of Love*. This novel-length work describes the series of affairs a self-centered Western-style painter enjoys before finding himself in an unsuccessful love suicide. Clearly based on Togo Seiji's experiences, the story is told by a first-person male narrator. Uno credits the success of the work to Togo's skill as a storyteller. (She claimed she wrote the story word-for-word as he had told it to her.) But later critics have suggested it was Uno's ability to depict so artlessly the sexual malaise of the times and to capture so thoroughly the self-consciousness of the male narrator that led to the success of the book. It was heralded as the finest romance to be written in the prewar period. And Uno Chiyo earned distinction as "a writer of illicit love."

Confessions of Love appeared just when Japan was heading into the Pacific War. Soon love stories of this variety were no longer tolerated by the militaristic government. Her next important work, thought also based on the stories told her by a male narrator, had a decidedly more subdued tone. "Ningyoshi Tenguya Kyukichi" (1943, "The Puppet Maker") describes the life and work of a carver of Bunraku puppets. The work is quiet and thoughtful, as Tenguya Kyukichi looks back over his eighty-six years in a small town on the remote island of Shikoku. At times Kyukichi is mournful: the art he has devoted his life to is destined to perish, and Kyukichi will leave no heirs. But the tale is also gently humorous, as Kyukichi relates his many "secrets" for a life well lived. Uno's greatest success in the work is that she was able to re-create Kyukichi's Shikoku dialect.

Uno's experiments with dialect led to *Ohan*, the work that is considered by most to be her masterpiece. Uno gained inspiration for *Ohan*, she has said, while she was in Shikoku interviewing the puppet maker. She stopped at a secondhand shop and the story the owner told her became the germ for *Ohan*. Despite this attribution, *Ohan* has roots in Uno's own life. The model for the wife, Ohan, is vaguely similar to Uno's own mother, Doi Tomo. And the setting for the story is clearly Iwakuni, though not the Iwakuni of the mid 20th century, but the town of Uno's memories. The story is simple: a man describes to his unseen interlocutor how he left his gentle wife Ohan to live with the brash and domineering geisha Okayo. Seven years later he meets his wife again, and they begin a secret liaison until circumstances (perhaps "fate") drive them apart. Like the earlier "Puppet Maker," it is not the story alone that is important but the way it is told. Uno carefully crafts a voice for her hapless narrator that echoes the mood and rhythms of the old Bunraku balladeers. She creates a dialect for her narrative by combining the regionalisms of Shikoku and Iwakuni and polishing these with the soft sophistication of Kyoto speech. All in all, hers is an artificial dialect but one that suggests the nuances and shadows of the old dramas. Critic Kobayashi Hideo (1902–1983) heralded Uno's narrative achievements by declaring: "With a compelling use of words that outlive their power as mere words, the author invents a storybook world of fantasy, rare among contemporary novels which have surrendered completely to fact." *Ohan* received the Noma Prize for literature in 1957 and the Association of Japanese Women Writers' Award in 1958. And with these distinctions Uno Chiyo proved that she was much more than "a writer of illicit love."

Ohan was barely 100 pages in length but it took Uno over ten years to complete (she began the work in 1947 but did not complete it until 1957). Her attention to the language of the work was certainly one reason for the delay. But Uno's complicated personal life was also a factor. Uno married once again in 1939. Her husband this time, Kitahara Takeo (1907–1973) was also a writer. Together they launched the literary journal *Buntai* (Literary Style). Just prior to her marriage, Uno had embarked on the publication of a woman's fashion magazine, Japan's first,

known as *Sutairu* (Style). She and Kitahara, in addition, opened a boutique of the same name which featured, among other "styles," kimonos of Uno's design. In 1952 the Style Company was charged with tax evasion, and Uno and Kitahara lost everything. The magazine folded in 1959; Uno and Kitahara divorced in 1964.

Uno's divorce from Kitahara Takeo inspired a new flourish of literary activity. In fact, all of her divorces and separations influenced her fiction, so much that Uno has stated: "No one is as fortunate as a woman writer. No sooner does she break up with a man than she can write about it all without the slightest sense of shame." Uno wrote about her relationship with Ozaki in "Tanjobi" (Birthday) and "Shitsurkau no uta" (Song of Lost Happiness), both written in 1929. When she and Togo separated she wrote "Wakare mo tanoshi" (Parting Pleasure, 1935) and "Miren" (Lingering Attachment, 1936). And, after her twenty-five year marriage to Kitahara ended, Uno was inspired to write a number of personal narratives. While most concerned her marriage to Kitahara, others looked back further still to her earlier relationships with Togo, Ozaki, her first husband Fujimura, and even her father. As personal and as painful as some of these stories are, they have been admired by critics for their perceived "objectivity." As Hagiwara Yoko has said: "I know of no other author who can describe the separation between a man and a woman with such freshness, with such a store of love. Women writers in particular write of the hatred they feel toward their men. To purge their hearts of any lingering affection, they spew a profusion of rancorous words throughout their works. . . . There is none of that in [Uno's works]."

Notable among the personal narratives Uno wrote following her divorce from Kitahara are: *Sasu* (1966, translated (in part) as "To Sting,") "Kono oshiroi ire" (1967, "This Powder Box") "Kofuku" (1970, "Happiness,"); *Aru hitori no onna no hanashi* (1971, *The Story of a Single Woman*): and *Ame no oto* (*The Sound of Rain*).

Sasu, a novella-length work in five parts (the third of which is translated), describes the collapse of the narrator's magazine empire as it parallels the collapse of her marriage and her realization that her youth is lost. The strength of the story lies in the portrayal of the narrator's self-discovery. At first she refuses to see her husband's infidelities. She refuses to admit that she is old. She catapults her magazine into disaster as she tries to bind her husband to her. But by the story's conclusion the narrator has "convinced" herself that she is happy to let her husband go. She busily, almost gaily, helps him pack and then sends him out the door, knowing he will not come back.

"Happiness" continues the narrator's resolve to see her life in a positive light. No matter what disappointments she may have met, she is determined to participate actively, even aggressively, in life. Uno's narrative approaches self-satire as the first-person narrator looks back over her life of adventure and mishaps and decides that it was a life well lived. The gentle self-mocker, tempered by an undercurrent of melancholy, earned this work high critical acclaim and Uno's second Association of Japanese Women Writers' Award.

"This Powder Box," though written shortly after Uno's divorce from Kitahara, concerns her relationship with Togo Seiji instead. Much more detached than her earlier stories, "This Powder Box" is double-voiced, as a contemporary narrator describes the actions of a younger self. The narrator enters a near dialogue with this younger self, challenging her to explain why she did as she did. *The Story of a Single Woman* takes Uno back even further, to her childhood and her relationship with her irascible father. Again the narrative is double-voiced and again the purpose of the undertaking seems to be a quest for self-understanding, self-legitimacy. *The Sound of Rain*, perhaps the loveliest and most lyrical of Uno's autobiographical works, brings us back to her relationship with Kitahara. Here she describes his death and her acceptance of her own frailty and loneliness. The quiet, almost mournful tone of this story—induced by the sound of the rain—has led critics to call it a "requiem."

By the early 1980s Uno had stopped writing fiction and concentrated instead on essays which depicted both her past experiences and her present observations. She eventually began serializing in the *Mainichi* newspaper a collection of memoirs, *Ikite yuki watashi* (I Will Go on living), which became a best-seller when issued in book form in 1983. The book was later made into a thirteen-part television series as well as into a stage play. The success of this book led to an Uno Chiyo revival of sorts. Most of her earlier works were reprinted and displayed prominently in book stores. *Ohan* was made into a major commercial film under the direction of Ichikawa Kon in 1985. Magazines and television talk shows vied with one another for interviews. And the *Mainichi* newspaper asked Uno to carry an Ann Landers–type advice column. In the midst of all this activity Uno was still able to manage her small kimono boutique and to continue writing, though her production was limited.

In her late nineties, Uno, although not in the best of health, maintained a disciplined writing schedule and published an essay or two a year.

She worked on a sequel to her volume of memoirs.

Time has tempered the assessment of Uno Chiyo's contribution to the Japanese literary tradition. She catapulted onto the scene as a tantalizing femme fatale—the value of her work hanging in the balance of her love life. But as she matured Uno proved that she was not just a sensationalist but a writer of worth. To her credit she has received the Twenty-eighth Academy of Arts Award (1972); the Third Order of the Sacred Treasure (1974); the Thirtieth Kikuchi Kan Prize for Literature (1982); and in 1990 she was named a "Person of Cultural Merit."

PRINCIPAL WORKS IN ENGLISH TRANSLATION: *Novels*—(tr. D. Keene) Ohan *in* The Old Woman, the Wife and the Archer, 1961; (tr. P. Birnbaum) Confessions of Love, 1989; (tr. R. Copeland) The Sound of the Wind, 1992; (tr. R. Copeland) The Story of a Single Woman, 1992. *Short stories*—(tr. Teshigawara Mitsugi) "Shopgirl" *in* Young Forever and Five Other Novelettes, 1941; (tr. P. Birnbaum) "Happiness" *in* Rabbits, Crabs, etc., 1982;) (tr. Kyoho Iriye Selden) "To Stab" *in* Noriko Mizuta Lippit and Kyoho Iriye Selden (eds.) Stories by Contemporary Japanese Women Writers, 1982; (tr. Yukiko Tanaha) "A Genius of Imitation" *in* To live and to Write, 1987; (tr. R. Copeland) "Suddenly a Spring Wind," 1989; (tr. R. Copeland) "The Puppet Maker," 1992; (tr. R. Copeland) "This Powder Box," 1992.

ABOUT: Copeland, Rebecca. The Sound of the Wind: The Life and Works of Uno Chiyo, 1992; Keene, D. "The Revival of Writing by Women" *in* Dawn to the West, 1984. *Periodicals*—Japan PEN News June 1966; Japan Quarterly April–June 1988; October–December 1992; New Yorker October 31, 1988; New York Times Book Review September 20, 1992; Times Literary Supplement March 16, 1990; December 4, 1992; Winds December 1989. All quotes are translated by Rebecca Copeland and reproduced from *The Sound of the Wind: The Life and Works of Uno chiyo*, 1992.

UNSWORTH, BARRY (FORSTER) (August 10, 1930–), British novelist, writers: "I was born in Wingate, County Durham, in the north-east of England, in 1930. Wingate was a coal-mining village and nearly all the men went to work in the pits. My father started out as a miner but he emigrated to the United States when he was nineteen years old and when he returned to England he went into the insurance business, thus breaking the mining tradition as far as my own family was concerned. It was this, more than anything, I think, that opened up different prospects of life for my brother and myself. I attended Manchester University between 1948 and 1951 and took a B.A. Honours degree in English. After that came two years of military service, compulsory in Britain in those days.

BARRY UNSWORTH

"My father died when I was nineteen and my mother five years later. There was thus a fairly early severing of family life. Coupled with this there was the breaking away from working-class background and local ties (very strong in mining communities). These circumstances combined to give me a feeling of being uprooted, of not quite belonging, which has continued up to the present and is one of the main elements in my sense of myself as a writer. Perhaps because of it I have had a rather wandering kind of life, living in various parts of England and also for long periods abroad, in France, Greece, Turkey, Sweden, Finland, and now Italy. I suppose I have become in the course of time an expatriate writer. These travels are reflected in my work in that it has a wide variety of settings, and ranges considerably in period, though the central sensibility, the narrative voice, is generally English.

"My first novel, *The Partnership*, was published in 1966 when I was already thirty-six years old, which makes me a late starter. In fact I had spent my twenties trying to write short stories. These were invariably rejected but I kept doggedly on until a friend advised me to try the longer form. This I did, and it suited me better. Since then, with very rare exceptions, I have written only novels. The first one was characteristic in that it was set in Cornwall, in the extreme south-west of England, which was as far away as I could get at the time. It was also characteristic in that, though it has a strong sense of landscape, of physical locality—and this has always been a very important component of fiction for me—I was somewhere quite different when I wrote it,

in Greece in fact. My next novel, *The Greeks Have a Word for It* was set in Athens, but by then I was living in Istanbul. . . . This is a pattern that has continued through the years not because of any deliberate policy on my part but simply by accident and the habit of travel.

"I have written ten novels so far [1994] and am at present wrestling with the eleventh. I don't find it gets any easier. The ones that stand out most in my mind, apart from the first, which is always exciting, are *Mooncranker's Gift* (1974), which was the first of my novels to be published in the united States and which won the Heinemann Award, given my the Royal Society of Literature; then *Pascali's Island*, which was my first venture into historical fiction and was subsequently made into a feature film; *Stone Virgin*, in which I experimented with different historical periods; and my most recent novel *Sacred Hunger*, which was co-winner of the Booker Prize for 1992 and has so far been translated into six languages.

"The main early influences on my work were Conrad and Golding among British authors and some of the American writers of the Deep South. An odd combination perhaps, but they are all writers who deal in extreme situations and this has been an enduring interest in my own fiction. I am a strong believer in the traditional virtues of the novel, sometimes these days regarded as old-fashioned: respect for the complexity of character, care for the physical background and a style that seeks to convey the truth of experience without posturing and pyrotechnics."

Barry Unsworth is the son of Michael Unsworth and the former Elsie Forster. He married Valerie Irene Moor on May 15, 1959, and the couple had three daughters. That marriage was dissolved, and Unsworth married a Finnish woman and went to live with her in Helsinki in 1989. The harsh winter and difficult language later drove Unsworth to move to Perugia, Italy, with his wife Aira

Unsworth began his career as a lecturer in English literature at Norwood Technical College in London in 1960. It is to some extent in his capacity as a teacher that he has traveled so widely, lecturing in Greece and Turkey.

Unsworth sees himself as a "symbolist realist." He is very much concerned with contemporary moral questions, which he believes are of fundamental importance to the novelist, but he rarely chooses to set his stories in a modern British location. Instead, an awareness of the complexities of modern life is reflected in the personal, ethnical, or political struggles of characters that are distant either in time or in geography. An acute sense of historical continuity, particularly in his more recent fiction, lends to Unsworth's novels a significance which is at once specific and universal.

An image that links all of Unsworth's work is the Fall of Man, the loss of innocence. This metaphor is often represented in terms of an actual fall or destruction. For example, in *Mooncranker's Gift*, James Farnaby notes that when "all the different persons I have been merge into an awful perception of what I am I fall backwards, flat on my back." The protagonist of *Pascali's Island* becomes obsessed with a Greek statue, and is attempting to steal it when he is discovered by the authorities. In the ensuing struggle the statue falls to the ground and is smashed. In *The Rage of the Vulture*, Henry Markham falls, literally and comically, for a young singer.

Reviewers were impressed with Unsworth's assured prose style and skillful psychological portraits of individualistic characters in these early novels. If his later novels—*Stone Virgin* for example—were found to be flawed, they were also considered more substantial, more involved than their predecessors. The Fall motif is elaborated in *Stone Virgin*, in which Simon Raikes is commissioned to restore a 15-century sculpture of the Madonna in a Venetian church. Working on the scaffolding, Raikes is in constant danger of losing his balance. As he cleans away the dirt from the Virgin, she begins to exert a strange influence over him, and he is compelled to begin a search that leads him to love and passion in the person of Chiara, a Venetian marred to a sculptor, and to the discovery that the Madonna's creator died in mysterious circumstances. Did he fall, or was he pushed into the Venetian waters?

Generally, reviewers found *Stone Virgin* a disappointment, ingenious and carefully researched, but lacking in tension and suspense. For Savkar Altinel, in the *Times Literary Supplement* it was "something of a let down." But Alison Fell in the *New Statesman*, found its strength in its observations of the basic issues of the sacred and the profane. It is, she wrote "a reflection on mediaevalism versus renaissance humanism, creators versus critics, and—last but not least—an elegy to Venice, its water and stone."

Sugar and Rum received similarly mixed reviews. As an in-depth psychological study of Clive Benson, a self-doubting author with a writing block, the novel was much admired. Some reviewers, however, felt that the ennui and lethargy afflicting the protagonist permeate the text to such an extent that the reader is also affected. The Fall comes in the form of a suicide jump that Benson witnesses at the beginning of the novel, a "gathering fall" which haunts him as he

struggles to make sense of such a "crude act of self-extinction" in relation to his own life.

Unsworth's major achievement came with his immensely successful *Sacred Hunger*, as co-winner (with Michael Ondaatie's *The English Patient*) of the 1992 Booker Prize. Both a story about England's slave trade during the 18th-century and a morality tale, the book draws clear parallels between what Unsworth sees as the disastrous consequences of the economic "hunger" of the century, and of governmental policies adopted in the 1980s: "Numbers of men are getting richer and greater numbers are getting poorer. Alas, both classes have greater expectations these days." He seeks to demonstrate that greed, in a sense, enslaves the masters by embroiling them in the vicious slave trade, and he explores large concepts such as justice and liberty.

The narrator is Matthew Paris, who takes a position as ship's surgeon on the *Liverpool Merchant* after his wife dies in childbirth. He watches the construction of the ship, during which a man falls to his death. He sails to Africa, where Captain Thurso, "a simple man, being an incarnation, really, of the profit motive," buys the slaves. When several of them become sick, Thurso drowns them in order to claim insurance—an incident based on fact—and Paris becomes increasingly disgusted at the way in which the slaves are treated. There is a mutiny, for which he is partly responsible, during which Captain Thurso is killed. The survivors set up an Eden-like colony in Florida, constructed on egalitarian principles, but Paradise is lost once again when greed—the "sacred hunger"—reasserts itself.

The outstanding feature of *Sacred Hunger* is its elegant, economical, smooth, and assured prose. Unsworth's blending of fact and fiction, image and allegory, in one scene after another, was praised in reviews as "seamless," as was the mass of meticulously researched historical detail. Mainly it is the moral thrust of the novel that was found impressive. Janet Barra, in the *New Statesman & Society*, called it "a novel of scarred idealism . . . an immense and impressive work." Herbert Mitgang, in the *New York Times*, called it a "remarkable novel in every way" written by "a master craftsman." In the *New York Times Book Review* Thomas Flanagan expressed the hope "that *Sacred Hunger* . . . resist that . . . ideological judgment" that Unsworth's psychic distance from the Africans is racist because, he concluded, it "is a book of grace and meditative elegance, and of great moral seriousness."

Unsworth's deep concern with moral issues is

also apparent in *Morality Play*, the story of a priest's joining a troupe of traveling players in 14th-century England during the time of the Black Plague. The priest, a fugitive who has left his parish, commits a further sin by appearing with the players. They try to get to the bottom of a murder by re-enacting the crime, leading them further into violations of custom and resulting in their imprisonment. The *Publishers Weekly* reviewer commented on "Unsworth's marvelously atmospheric depiction of the poverty, misery and pervasive stench of village life" and on his searching examination of "the chasm between appearance and reality and the tenuous influence of morality on human conduct."

Barry Unsworth lives in Perugia and enjoys gardening, birdwatching, and viticulture. A social democrat, and a member of the Church of England, he is a fellow of the Royal Society of Literature.

PRINCIPAL WORKS: The Partnership, 1966; The Greeks Have A Word for it, 1967; The Hide, 1970; Mooncranker's Gift, 1973; The Big Day, 1976; Pascali's Island (also published as The Idol Hunter), 1980; The Rage of the Vulture, 1982; Stone Virgin, 1985; Sugar and Rum, 1988; Sacred Hunger, 1992; Morality Play, 1995.

ABOUT: Contemporary Authors 25–28, 1971; Contemporary Literary Criticism 76, 1993; Who's Who 1994. *Periodicals*—Books March / April, 1992; New Statesman August 8, 1986; New Statesman & Society February 28, 1992; Newsweek January 28, 1983; New York Times December 23, 1992; New York Times Book Review January 11, 1981; March 13, 1983; April 6, 1986; July 19, 1992; Publishers Weekly August 21, 1995; Spectator August 24, 1985; Times Literary Supplement August 30, 1985; September 16–22, 1988; Washington Post January 24, 198; April 3, 1983; September 13, 1992.

VALAORITIS, NANOS (July 5, 1921–), Greek poet, prose writer, playwright translator and editor, writes: "I was born in Lausanne Switzerland of Greek parents, by the lake Lehman, where Lamartine wrote his famous poem 'The Lake,' in the city of Lausanne. I grew up in Athens where I went to high school and the first three years of University until the Germans shut it down during the Occupation. At that time in 1942–44, I witnessed the horrors of the war, the famished dying in the streets and carts filled with them outside the university morgue. My first poems had been published in 1939 in the modernist Greek review *Ta Nea Grammata* (New Letters). Premonitions of the experience lived a few year later made me write about the dead in World War I. Subsequently I escaped

NANOS VALAORITIS

from German-occupied Greece and went to Cairo and then London. At the time, between 1944 and 1948, I wrote most of the poems in my first collection *He Timoría ten Mágon*, (The Punishment of the Magicians), most of them reflecting indirectly the atmosphere of menace, terror, exile, bloodshed, civil war, but with a lyrical, 'Orphic' form, as the poet Apollinaire called it, which musical lines and language and an allusory modernist technique, which made these poems harmonious artificts, in the predominant style of contemporary poets of the war, such as Keith Douglas, Sidney Keyes, and the premonitory and elegiac poems of Dylan Thomas and W. H. Auden. While in London I translated and presented articles in British and French magazines on the new modernist poetry of Greece in the thirties and forties and first translations of the two Nobel Prize poets, George Seferis and Odysseus Elytis. This was the first appearance of Greek poetry on the international scene since, roughly, the end of the classical and postclassical (hellenistic) era. The fifteen enthusiastic reviews in the British press and magazines, with congratulations of T. S. Eliot, Edith Sitwell, and many others, attest to the success of these translations of Seferis and Elytis.

"After a brief return to Greece in 1953, I left for London and Paris where, after some studies in London University I enrolled in the Sorbonne—and followed Mycenian language and grammar, recently deciphered by Ventris. I then joined the French Surrealist group under André Breton and participated with my second, American, wife, Marie Wilson, a painter. (My

° val eh oh EYE tees, NAH noes

first wife was British actress, writer Anne Valery.) My Greek poet friends were mostly of the Surrealist trend, and I was on familiar ground. During those six years I wrote many plays in French, one of which, entitled *The Sundown Hotel* was performed. Another play, *The Log*, on the Greek myth of Meleager, was performed in Athens by the Art Theatre of Koun, and then staged at the Spoleto Festival by Giancarlo Menotti.

"On my return to Greece in the late fifties, the second collection of poems *Kentriké Stoa*, was published, with many poems from the previous decade, in a general climate of exile and discovery of new poetic horizons. My first poems appeared in translation in French, *Cahiers du Sud* (1948), and in Caress Crosby's *Folio*, in the early fifties, translated by Kimon Friar. Also *Botteghe Oscure*, Prince Caetani's review in Rome, published a London diary, 'Problems of an Empire'. In the later fifties and early sixties, It was published by various English and American reviews, *Poetry, Encounter, London Magazine*, etc. In the sixties (1963–1967) I edited and published the Greek literary review *Pali*, after my return to Athens. In the sixties I wrote poetry, criticism, novels, short stories, and oriented my poetry towards other more expanded experiments. I presented a lot of American poets in the review *Pali*, among them Allen Ginsberg, Philip Lamantia and Harold Norse, as well as Samuel Beckett, Octavio Paz, and French poets André Breton, Joyce Mansour, Jean Tardieu, and Alain Jouffroy. In 1968, I accepted an offer to teach at San Francisco State University.

"After the fall of the junta, during my return in 1975, I renewed my contract with Greek letters. New York, such as the *Anonymous Poem* (1974 and 1978) and *Ho Exchromus Stylographos*, (Colored Ballpoint) Ballpoint was written in California. Twelve more books of prose and poetry were published, written between 1961 and 1970. In English four books of poetry were published and some prose in critical articles. Also, I contributed to, and even coedited, some magazines, such as as *Bastard Angel, Manroot, Kayak, Channel*, and others.

"My style is one that tries to combine the outer world with the world of language, image, and imagination and make them stick, correspond and relate to one another, with flashing imagery, evoking distant vistas and perspective, on the one hand, while stating certain things I believe are significant, using modernist techniques of compactness, collage, association of ideas, sounds, and patterns, lists, formal designs and rhythms mainly iambic, in either blank or free verse. The importance of harmonious sounds takes precedence over subject and theme, but not atmosphere, in which every poem must be immersed in order to qualify as a poem. Occasional circumstantial poetry I have written (of place and time), but it's not my main preoccupation. The influence of dadaism, Surrealism, modernism, avant-garde experimentation leaves marks—as well as speech patterns that have an effect on audiences—broken rhythms, repetitions, breaks, variations. 'Language centered' poetry is closely related to mine, but I do not follow, either in prose or in verse, the nonreferential preference of many of these poets. However, I do believe that the language of poetry is a universe of its own, self-contained but which has to create a kind of versimilitude to experiences of emotion, place, mind, vision, so that what is said may be recognizably meaningful to the reader, as a total artifact."

An avowed surrealist and, according to Nikos Stangos, in the *Times Literary Supplement*, "one of the most innovative writers of his generation," Nanos Valaoritis (who is the great-grandson of a noted Greek poet, Aristotelis Valaoritis) has sought to liberate modern Greek literature from its classical past which had been largely appropriated by the West. His work, mainly short prose narratives and prose poems, is centered in the text, Stangos writes, "language and the behaviour of words. . . . His narratives, whether in verse or prose, are manic parables without a moral, riddles the answers to which are subverted by the intrusion of the absurd." He is an eclectic writer. Dawn Kolokithas commented in *Poetry Flash* that his prose has "an international quality," and she noted "a consonance between Valaoritis's prose and selected works by Borges, Kundera, Nabokov, Kafka, Calvino, Pavio, and Lagerkvist, not all of whom appear on Valaoritis's reading list. Moreover, there is a correspondence between the tropes in *My Afterlife Guaranteed* and Homer's myths, Zeno's Paradoxes, Goethe's tales, Flaubert's stories, and a host of others, with Lawrence Durrell's *Labyrinth, Tales from a Thousand and One Nights*, and even a little Robbe-Grillet for good measure."

Valaoritis's early prose-poems emphasized absurdist elements, often parodying the exploitation of populist demotic Greek culture. His primary concern was to radicalize the conservative Greek modernism of the 1930s and offer in its place cosmopolitanism, contemporaneity, and textuality. He refused to consider "Greekness" as a measure for aesthetic value and rejected European Hellenism which treats modern Hellas in a strictly rationalist context and dissociates it from ancient Greece altogether. For Valaoritis modern Greece retains many prevalent historical and cultural features of ancient and Byzantine culture, comprising an amalgam of ideas confusing to Western Europeans, one that combines paganism with Christianity, Eastern and Western elements, localism with cosmopolitanism, metaphysical abstraction with dialectical concretism.

Valaoritis reinterprets ancient mythology and modern demotic songs in terms of absurd images and irrational thought. In an essay entitled "Introduction to Greek Surrealism" he writes: "This reductive idea of Greece, which was forged by 'rationalistc' neo-classicism, is a prejudice which ignores all of the contradictory variety in a country which passes from myth to reason and from reason to mysticism in a movement that oscillates from one extreme to the other. Whether classicists like it or not, modern Greece is at the opposite pole from 'rational' Atticism. No, Greece is to the highest degree the land of the absurd, the senseless, and the imaginary." He once again redefines Greek orientalism, as Cavafy had earlier, finding a new place for the Turks, the Arabs, and the East. Legendary cities, such as Adana, Aleppo, and Beirut, map out the new surrealist utopia.

With *Kentriké Stoa* (Central Arcade) and *Estíes Agannis* (Sanctuaries of Microbes) Valaoritis goes further to encompass absurdist ideas and syntactical disorder. Here is, for example, the poem "The Contents": "In George appears: the weather's change / a 'why' / the skin of a crocodile / a movie advertisement / a pen / twenty-five drachmas / a fixed idea / God's happiness / his new shoes three millions of red hemispheres / his slippers / a glass of water / a revolver / a sporty t-shirt / a 'why' / a dog / a crocodile / a whale / a nineteenth-century politician's statue / various valuables / a 'why' the weather's change / a revolver / a pen / a fixed idea."

Valaoritis gives language the highest rank in the poem. He favors "alchemic automatic writing," liberated from syntactical and logical references. In "The Body Proper" automatic language is unfolded from image to image, from metamorphosis to metamorphosis in order to signify the nonsensical and the irrational, "Interpreters of poetry gigantic in their holy vestments interrogating things that never happened with the book wide open their handful full of sand their handful full of blood and the book being closed . . . " Freeing language from syntactical discipline, he allows it to explode, expressing the sociopolitical schizophrenia of Greece in the Cold War era.

In the prose-poem "The Woman of Constitution Square," from *Merikes Gynaikes* (Some Women), language reflects the irrational and uneasy political situation in Greece immediately after the military takeover of 1967–74: a period marked by censorship. In Kafkaesque style the speaking subject condemns the entire sociopolitical system. It is a delirious speech overflowing with paradoxical questions and dissociations of meaning, where the woman seeks her escape in becoming an androgyne, a shoe. In "WordsWomen" the becoming-Woman takes her most extreme position: she becomes the margin, the minimal edge of language possibilities. Words are opened to new possibilities, connected to schizophrenic flights, "using only words—keys—that open cupboards—shelves—drawers—linen chests—boxes—desks—bookcased-soapcases—trunks—bags—baggages—souls."

Valaoritis came to the United States with his wife and three children in 1968 when he joined the faculty of San Franciso State University to teach comparative literature and creative writing. After a two-year period aboard, 1975 to 1977, he returned to San Francisco State and became Professor Emeritus.

PRINCIPAL WORKS IN ENGLISH: Hired Hieroglyphs, 1970; Diplomatic Relations, 1971; Flash Bloom, 1980; (tr. M. Kitroeff and others) My Afterlife Guaranteed and Other Narratives 1990.

ABOUT: *Periodicals*—Journal of Modern Greek Studies May 1992; Journal of Modern Hellenism, October 1991; Poetry Flash, May 1991; Poetry Project, May 1991; Sepctator, February 23, 1991; Times Literary Supplement April 26, 1991;

*VIZINCZEY, STEPHEN (May 12, 1933–), Canadian novelist, essayist, and dramatist, was born in Kaloz, Hungary, the son of Istvan Vizinczey, a school headmaster and church organist, and Erzsebet (Mohos) Vizinczey. Istvan Vizinczey, a prominent antifascist, was murdered by a Nazi zealot when Stephen was only two years old. Stephen Vizinczey began writing poetry at an early age, and enrolled in the University of Budapest at sixteen. He later transferred to the National College of Theater and Film Arts, where he began writing plays. Three of his early dramas were banned by the Hungarian Communist regime. His first play, "The Paszti Family," about a Communist factory manager who kills himself, was suppressed for its antisocialist tendencies, as the regime deemed them. Suicide figures prominently in another of his banned student works, "The Last Word," in

*VI zin tsay

STEPHEN VIZINCZEY

which a crusading journalist, hounded by the authorities, is driven to self-destruction. That play was rehearsed and ready for its Budapest premiere when Vizinczey was summoned to the offices of the Ministry of Culture and ordered to hand over all copies of the script.

Despite having to endure considerable harassment, Vizinczey enjoyed some success as a young Hungarian playwright. His play *Mama* was broadcast by Radio Budapest in 1956, and was scheduled to be performed at the National Theatre.

Vizinczey, although at the brink of huge success, resented, as did most Hungarians, the political oppression to which they were subjected. Massive public demonstrations led to the elevation of Imre Nagy—a Communist who was, nevertheless, critical of Soviet control—to the Hungrarian premiership in the late 1956. Vinzinczey took part in the popular but ill-fated armed uprising against Soviet domination which followed. Soviet forces crushed the revolt and deposed (and later executed) Nagy. Tens of thousands of Hungarians, Vizinczey among them, fled into exile. Knowing only about fifty words of English, he arrived in Canada in 1957.

Never one to be content with modest dreams, Vizinczey aspired not only to speak English, but to write "immortal novels" in the language. He mastered his adopted tongue quickly and—impelled by the fear of starvation—soon found employment as a writer. Between 1957 and 1965, he worked as a scriptwriter for the National Film Board in Montreal, and later as a writer-producer for the Canadian Broadcasting Corpo-

ration (CBC). In 1960 he was the editor and cofounder of *Exchange*, a short-lived literary–philosophical journal. *Exchange* attempted, if only briefly, to unify the otherwise fragmented Canadian literary scene. The magazine folded when its backer, the son of a wealthy manufacturer, was threatened with disinheritance and withdrew his financial support. In 1961, Vizinczey became a naturalized Canadian citizen.

During his brief tenure at *Exchange*, Vizinczey got the idea for his first novel, *In Praise of Older Women*. Subtitled *The Amorous Recollections of Andras Vajda*, it is the story of a character whose background is not very different from Vizinczey's. Born in pre–World War II Hungary, Vajda endures the horrors of the Nazi and the Communists; he manages to find solace, however, in a seemingly never-ending series of sexual encounters. Like Vizinczey, he makes his way to Canada as a young man; at the time he is telling his picaresque tale, narrator Vajda is philosophy professor at the University of Saskatchewan. Although he is quite frank in presenting himself as a voluptuary and a libertine, Vajda is immune to the charms of young women and virgins. As the novel's title suggests, he is interested exclusively in mature and experienced women, those in their thirties and forties.

Vizinczey tried to interest a number of publishers in the work, but was dissatisfied with the only offer he received. Convinced that his novel was a great one, he then took a series of audacious steps: he quit his job and borrowed money in order to publish and promote the novel himself. His risky gambit paid off. *In Praise of Older Women* became a surprise best-seller, first in Canada, and later in Great Britain and elsewhere. It has been translated into German, Spanish, Portuguese, Swedish, Italian, and other languages, gone into forty printings in English alone, and sold more than three million copies worldwide. What is more the novel has won critical acclaim throughout the English-speaking world and beyond.

Writing in the Canadian periodical *Saturday Night* (1965), Kildare Dobbs noted his frequent discomfort with the "hornier-than-thou" attitudes of authors such as D. H. Lawrence, Henry Miller, and Norman Mailer. "One reason why *In Praise of Older Women* is so remarkable is that its narrator . . . doesn't share this attitude," Dobbs wrote. "His amorous recollections, set down with classic grace and concision, own up to as many failures as successes." Hailing the historical significance of the novel, Dobbs concluded, "I believe we have to go back to Boswell's *London Journal* to find anything that matches Vizinczey's book for freshness, candour and unaffected charm."

A number of reviewers compared Andras Vajda to Julien Sorel, the protagonist of Stendhal's novel *The Red and the Black*. For John Daniel, in the *Spectator*, Vizinczey's novel could not be favorably compared to Stendhal's work. "As it is," he wrote, "it eschews any serious Sorel-like purpose and intends to be more than it is: a buoyant diary of sex for sex's sake." For at least one reviewer, however, the novel succeeded as something more. After commenting on the book's bleak political backdrop, Marvin Mudrick wrote in the *Hudson Review*: "In Praise of Older Women is extraordinary in its modesty and buoyancy, its fearlessness and persistent unemphasized sadness. It comes to the boundaries of life, but only after alert and energetic explorations. . . . It is a good novel."

In 1978, thirteen years after the original publication of *In Praise of Older Women*, Robert Fulford, reassessing the novel and its impact in *Saturday Night*, wrote: "Curiously, the years have if anything improved it. The style in which [Vizinczey] wrote it seems even more cool and classic than it did in 1965, mainly because the period since then has brought us so many abjectly confessional, self-pitying, huffing-puffing sex novels." A film version of *In Praise of Older Women* was released in 1978.

Vizinczey's next book, *The Rules of Chaos*, is a collection of essays on literature, politics, and metaphysics. (The American edition of the book had the subtitle *Why Tomorrow Doesn't Work*.) The elusive nature of time, the futility of planning, and the predominance of chance in all events are the themes uniting most of the essays. The critical response to *The Rules of Chaos* was mixed. *Washington Post Book World* reviewer S. K. Oberbeck found the collection "a painfully diffuse foray into ontological deep-think," which reads at times "like Heisenberg for housewives . . . " Expressing the wish that Vizinczey would stick to novels and literary essays, Oberbeck concluded, "A Schopenhauer he's not." In *Canadian Forum*, George Jonas thought it difficult to determine "the ultimate validity" of Vizinczey's speculations regarding the nature of time and chance. Still, Jonas concluded, "The case he makes for it . . . is very strong, and it is presented in the same graceful and compelling style that made his first book . . . such a pleasure to read."

Vinzinczey spent twelve years writing and revising his second novel, *An Innocent Millionaire*. During much of that time, he was involved in a protracted legal dispute with Ian Ballantine, the publisher who had bought the American rights to *In Praise of Older Women*. Ballantine sold the novel to a small imprint created for Harold Robbins and other "potboiler" novelists. Vizinczey

was distressed that Ballantine's marketing of the book had kept it out of the hands of its natural audience—readers of literary fiction. In his suit, Vizinczey claimed that Ballantine had taken too large a share of the novel's foreign royalties and deprived him of income by remaindering the hardcover edition of the novel too soon.

Vizinczey channeled his considerable wrath—especially that related to his encounters with unscrupulous lawyers and publishers—into the writing of *An Innocent Millionaire*. "*An Innocent Millionaire* makes sense of what happened to me. . . . The idea of striving for something and succeeding," he told *Publishers Weekly*. Reflecting on his long period of litigation, he said: "The lawsuit was the best education of my life. I wouldn't have learned all the things I wrote about in *An Innocent Millionaire*, the many things about crooks and the way the law operates, if I hadn't gone through it." Perhaps for emphasis, Vizinczey added, "I didn't know evil people until I got involved with New York attorneys"—a somewhat startling claim considering his experience with two tyrannical regimes in Hungary.

An Innocent Millionaire is, in many respects, a roman à clef. An unsavory New York art dealer, for example, is named John Vallantine (remarkably reminiscent of Vizinczey's archnemesis Ian Ballantine). Mark Niven, the novel's protagonist, is the son of a rather unsuccessful touring actor. Since his parents have no money, he decided early on that he will have to make (or find) his own fortune. After he learns about the *Flora*, a treasure-laden ship which sank near the Bahamas in 1820, he devotes years to maritime research and becomes progressively more obsessed with the notion of recovering the ship and its treasure. In the course of pursuing his dream, however, he is waylaid by one wily rogue after another. Although he grows older and gains experience, Mark Niven remains innocent, idealistic, and incorruptible throughout the novel.

The original Canadian edition of *An Innocent Millionaire* was adorned with enthusiastic blurbs from such renowed authors as Graham Greene and Anthony Burgess. The actual critical reception of the novel, however, spanned the gamut—from high praise to dismissive indignation. "Pervaded by an acerbic wit, entertaining and uplifting, it offers a story that is worth dreaming about and worth thinking about," Jamie Conklin wrote in a review of the novel in *Quill and Quire*. In the *New York Times Book Review*, Sam Tanenhaus hailed it as "as rare accomplishment, a contemporary adventure told with style, wit and wisdom." .

Those critical of the novel most often focused

on its didacticism and its aphoristic style. "Like an emu, Stephen Vizinczey's second novel is impressive but flightless," Fraser Sutherland wrote in *Books in Canada*. According to Sutherland, a "compulsion to moralize at every opportunity creates a jerky cast of puppets manipulated by the author. Vizinczey's people do not live; they illustrate aphorisms." The *Times Literary Supplement* reviewer T. J. Binyon concluded that "Like Voltaire, Vizinczey tells a good story which slips easily down the throat; but, unlike *Candide, An Innocent Millionaire* proves to be eupeptic mush throughout."

Vizincey's second book of criticism, *Truth and Lies in Literature*, consists primarily of short book reviews, many of which original appeared in the London *Times*, the *Sunday Telegraph*, and the *Guardian*. The title essay, an abbreviated version of which appeared in *Harper's* (as "Engineers of Sham"), is an examination of literary misrepresentations of power. Vizinczey analyzes Herman Wouk's *The Caine Mutiny* and Herman Melville's *Billy Budd*, and concludes that both endorse a blind obedience to (often sadistic) power.

In the *Christian Science Monitor* Thomas D'Evelyn wrote, "The short literary review becomes an art form in the hands of Stephen Vizinczey." D'Evelyn had special praise for Vizinczey's treatment of works dealing with such 19-century French authors as Balzac and Stendhal (Vizinczey's literary idols). In his prologue to the collection, "A Writer's Ten Commandments," Vizinczey offers advice to writers and would-be writers: a sample is the seventh, "THOU SHALT NOT LET A DAY PASS WITHOUT RE-READING SOMETHING GREAT." Others, such as the fifth commandment, are more unusual: "THOU SHALT NOT BE MODEST." Under that heading, Vizinczey writes, "Small ambitions evoke small efforts. I never knew a good writer who wasn't trying to be a great one." Speaking with *Publishers Weekly*, Vizinczey remarked, "I think modesty is a fault . . . the powers-that-be want you to be modest, because if you are modest it's easier for them to handle you."

Vizinczey has been married to Gloria Fisher, an editor, since 1963. They have three children. In recent years he has lived in London.

PRINCIPAL WORKS: *Novels*—In Praise of Older Women: The Amorous Recollections of Andras Vajda, 1965, rev. ed. 1985; An Innocent Millionaire, 1983. *Criticism*—The Rules of Chaos; or, Why Tomorrow Doesn't Work, 1969; Truth and Lies in Literature, 1986.

ABOUT: Contemporary Authors 128, 1990; Contempo-

rary Literature Criticism 40, 1986. *Periodicals*—Books in Canada December 1983; Canadian Forum March 1970; Christian Science Monitor August 1, 1986; Harper's June 1886; Hudson Review Summer 1966; New York Times Book Review June, 16 1985; Publishers Weekly June 14, 1985; Quill and Quire November 1983; Saturday Night September 1965; May 1978; Spectator August 12, 1966; Times Literary Supplement April 15, 1983; Washington Post Book World July 19, 1970.

WAKEFIELD, DAN (May 21, 1932–), American journalist, novelist, and scriptwriter, was born and raised in Indianapolis, Indiana, the son of Ben H. Wakefield, a pharmacist, and Brucie (Ridge) Wakefield. As a student at Shortridge High School he was a regular contributor to the *Shortridge Daily Echo*, one of the nation's few high school dailies. Since he had already resolved to become a professional writer by the time he was in high school, Wakefield was encouraged to learn that Kurt Vonnegut, a Shortridge graduate (and *Daily Echo* contributor) some ten years his senior, had gone on to publish stories in national magazines. He finally met Vonnegut, by then a successful novelist, in 1963, and the older writer was later instrumental in helping Wakefield to publish his first novel.

After spending a year at Indiana University, Wakefield transferred to Columbia University in New York City in 1952. At Columbia, he studied American literature, wrote for the school paper, the *Daily Spectator*, and immersed himself in the bohemian literary life of Greenwich Village. Upon receiving his B.A. in 1955, he took a job as news editor at the *Weekly Packet* in Princeton, New Jersey. Later in 1955, he returned to New York to work as a research assistant for C. Wright Mills, his Columbia sociology professor. In Princeton, Wakefield met one of his journalist heroes, the columnist Murray Kempton, who helped him get his first magazine writing assignment. He was sent by the *Nation* to Sumner, Mississippi, to cover the trial of two white men accused of murdering Emmett Till, a black teenager who had whistled at a white woman. Other assignments for the *Nation* followed, included one in Israel in 1956. Between 1956 and 1962, Wakefield spent much of his time in the American South covering the civil rights movement for the left-liberal weekly. The subject of his first book, *Island in the City*, is New York's Spanish Harlem, where he lived for six months in 1957. His second book, *Revolt in the South*, grew out of his reporting on the civil rights movement.

A Nieman Fellowship in Journalism took Wakefield to Harvard University in 1963–1964.

DAN WAKEFIELD

Having fallen in love with the city of Boston, he decided to make his home there and began a long association with the Boston-based *Atlantic* magazine, then under the editorship of Robert Manning. His essays on literature, film, politics, and journalism appeared regularly in the *Atlantic*, and from 1967 to 1980 he served as a contributing editor of the magazine. Wakefield's journalistic pieces of the 1960s reflect a growing preoccupation with cultural commentary. *Between the Lines: A Reporter's Personal Journey through Public Events*, a collection of his articles originally published in the *Nation*, *Esquire*, *Playboy*, and other magazines, covers subjects ranging from the Newport Jazz Festival to the work of author J. D. Salinger. The book won accolades even from those critical of Wakefield's politics. "Not a mere scissors-and-paste job," G. M. Pepper wrote in the *National Review*, "the articles and essays are interspersed with commentary. . . . As for the articles themselves, great differences in political and general viewpoint would separate the author and, for instance, this reviewer, but they cannot diminish one's enjoyment." In order to write his highly impressionistic book *Supernation at Peace and War*, which originally appeared as the entire March 1968 issue of the *Atlantic*, Wakefield traveled throughout the United States and Canada interviewing dozens of people—draft resisters, soldiers, hippies, policemen, journalists, and government officials—gathering their thoughts on the war in Vietnam.

Wakefield had long aspired to become a novelist, and had made several false starts on novels

dating back to his years at Columbia. At the age of thirty-six, having published four book-length works of journalism, as well as several short stories, he decided to devote himself entirely to the writing of a novel. The result was *Going All the Way*, which chronicles the homecoming in 1954 of two veterans of the Korean War. They meet on a train and discover that they went to the same high school and are both returning to Indianapolis. They are, in many respects, an odd couple: Sonny is shy, unassuming, and sexually frustrated, while Gunner, a legendary high school athlete, now seethes with rebellious instincts. Both find themselves deeply alienated from the parochialism, bigotry, and materialism of their hometown culture. They spend much of the novel wandering aimlessly around Indianapolis, drinking heavily and searching for sexual companionship. Wakefield traces Sonny's musing early in the novel:

> The war wasn't really a war—a "police action" some of the papers called it—and nobody gave much of a damn about it except for the politicians and the military men and of course the guys who got drafted and all their relatives. Being a soldier in that half-assed war was like being on a team in a sport that drew no crowds, except for the players' own parents and friends.

Going All the Way was published when American forces were deeply mired in a seemingly endless war in Vietnam, and public skepticism regarding the United States' role there was increasing rapidly. The novel quickly became a national best-seller. "Its central subject—the baffled despair of two young men trying to reckon with middle class, material values in a world where they no longer suffice—is only beginning to emerge in our Gross National Consciousness," Robert Phelps wrote in the *New York Times Book Review*. "Next year, and the year after that, *Going All the Way* will seem even more pertinent than it does now."

Starting Over and *Home Free*, Wakefield's second and third novels, also focus on a crisis in American values. Phil Potter, the protagonist of *Starting Over*, is a divorced man in his thirties, a successful executive who once harbored ambitions of an acting career. His 1950s upbringing has provided him with few clues for dealing with life as a single man in the 1970s. Confused, anomic, and probably alcoholic, he drifts from one sexual encounter to another before settling into a serious relationship with another lost soul, a Boston divorcée. Reviewing the novel in *Newsweek*, Arthur Cooper commented: "Wakefield uses his gifts splendidly. . . . [His] style is understatement, using small gestures to depict large passions until a sigh can convey the force of a scream."

Home Free examines how the deterioration of American values affected members of the counterculture in the late 1960s and early 1970s. Gene, the novel's central character, wanders, seemingly without purpose, from one end of the United States to the other, trying all the while to decide what to do with his life. In the *New York Times Book Review* (1977), Anatole Broyard wrote: "In *Home Free*, Dan Wakefield sounds like a literary Rip Van Winkle. . . . [His novel] reads like a revival of Jack Kerouac, with more sex and drugs." Jerome Klinkowitz's was a more positive assessment. He wrote in the *New Republic*: "Few novelists are so well equipped to portray the emptiness these years amounted to, for Gene and for a lot more people than we'd care to admit." In *The New American Novel of Manners*, Klinkowitz further noted that *Going All the Way, Starting Over,* and *Home Free* "form a trilogy, especially when seen from the perspective of American manners. As the decades advance from the 1950s through the 1970s, Wakefield is critical of the general trend away from commitment and tradition toward a nebulous sense of personal freedom."

Wakefield's interest in television prompted him to write *All Her Children*, an appreciative, and at times adulatory, look at the daytime soap opera "All My Children" and its creator Agnes Nixon. Shortly afterwards, Wakefield got a chance to write for television himself. He had already done some rewrite work on his novel *Starting Over* before it was made into a film, but in 1976 he was given virtual carte blanche to create an original script for a television series. The result, "James at 15," an hour-long prime-time drama, was initially popular but was canceled after one full season on the air. Wakefield remained in Hollywood writing television movie scripts until 1980. His Hollywood experiences served as the basis for his comic novel *Selling Out*.

In 1980 Wakefield had a "spiritual crisis" that transformed his life. One morning, shortly before his forty-eighth birthday, he woke up screaming. Ostensibly a successful writer—he had been lauded as journalist, a novelist, and, most recently, as a screenwriter—he nevertheless realized that he was completely at sea, and quite miserable. Both of his parents had died within the past year. Earlier, he had undergone years of intensive psychoanalysis, which he now considered worthless. In a 1987 *New York Times Magazine* memoir, "My Six Years on the Couch," he wrote: "I was entrusting the most private and precious part of my life to someone who didn't like me and whom I neither liked nor trusted. I would never lie down on the couch again." Even worse, he had been drinking heavi-

ly and taking drugs for years, to the point where his health was almost ruined. Leaving Hollywood and returning to Boston, he started an exercise program, quit alcohol and drugs, and, most significantly returned to church for the first time in more than twenty-five years. Raised in the Presbyterian Church (he also had a grandfather who was a Baptist minister), Wakefield had been an avowed atheist since his student days in New York. With the rediscovery of his faith, he joined King's Chapel, a 300-year-old Unitarian church in Boston. There he enrolled in a course in writing a religious autobiography.

His book *Returning: A Spiritual Journey* grew out of the work he did in that class. "One of the reasons that the book was so intimate was that I was writing for the eight people in this class, all of them sharing these very deep experiences," Wakefield told a *Publishers Weekly* interviewer. More than simply a memoir of his own religious experiences, *Returning* is also a homage to various of his spiritual and intellectual mentors; he pays special tribute to Mark Van Doren, his literature professor at Columbia, and Dorothy Day, leader of the Catholic Worker movement. Not surprisingly, the book was well received by Christian reviewers. In *Commonweal*, Jane Redmont wrote: "In *Returning*, Wakefield is graphic but never self-indulgent. . . . This is no whitewashed, pious essay. Wakefield speaks of the mess of real life and the discovery of a God who is alive in the very midst of the mess."

Instead of relying strictly on his own memory in *New York in the Fifties*, Wakefield returned to many of his former New York haunts and interviewed writers, artists, and activists he had known since the 1950s. In an interview with the *New York Times* in August 1992, he commented: "I've always felt that this was one of the richest scenes or periods. The 50s were different from the 30s and 40s. There was a real upsurge after World War II, never a time when we had such a flowering of literature, theater, music and painting." Unlike many commentators, who view the 1950s primarily as a period of quiescence and conformity, Wakefield argues that the decade was one of significant artistic ferment, and was probably a crucial prelude to the more turbulent and politically active 1960s. "Well, an era doesn't go between even-numbered years," he said. "My 50s were from 1952 to 1963, from Eisenhower to Kennedy, some say to the first Beatles concert on Ed Sullivan's show in early '64."

In the *New York Times*, Michiko Kakutani wrote: "An odd jumble of autobiography, reportage and essayistic musing, *New York in the Fifties* often struggles to find a coherent tone. . . . somewhat strained interviews with prominent acquaintances like Allen Ginsberg and Norman Mailer jostle awkwardly for space with the author's own rambling reminiscences about his writing career, his love life and his psychic ups and downs." However, Kakutani felt that Wakefield "does succeed . . . in communicating his affection for a vanished time." While Kakutani found the interviews in the book "strained," in the New York Times Book Review (1992) Vance Bourjaily observed, "It is a privilege for the reader to listen in on these interviews; there's love and wisdom to be heard." In the Nation, Richard Lingeman, one of those Wakefield interviewed for New York in the Fifties, was also favorably impressed by the work. "Wakefield is really writing a memoir of his own life and, through his cohorts' shared memories, seeking to tap into the Zeitgeist," Lingeman said. "He has woven the various testimonials into a series of chapters and vignettes that cumulate in an orchestrated portrait of another time, another New York, which sometimes seems as quaintly remote as Samuel Pepys's London."

Wakefield is no longer cavalier about the hard-drinking image—so much a part of 1950s literary culture—that he cultivated for years. In the dust jacket photo of his novel Starting Over, he is posed drink in hand, seated before a row of liquor bottles. "I thought it was real glamorous to die young," he told Publishers Weekly in 1988. "I sure don't now."

PRINCIPAL WORKS: Journalism/nonfiction—Island in the City: The World of Spanish Harlem, 1959; Revolt in the South, 1961; Between the Lines: A Reporter's Personal Journey through Public Events, 1966; Supernation at Peace and War, 1968; All Her Children, 1976; The Story of Your Life: Writing a Spiritual Autobiography, 1990. Novels—Going All the Way, 1970; Starting Over, 1973; Home Free, 1977; Under the Apple Tree, 1982; Selling Out, 1985. Autobiography—Returning: A Spiritual Journey, 1988; New York in the Fifties, 1992. As editor—The Addict, 1963.

ABOUT: Contemporary Authors 21–24, 1977; Contemporary Authors Autobiography Series 7, 1988; Contemporary Literary Criticism 7, 1977; Klinkowitz, J. Literary Subversions: New American Fiction and the Practice of Criticism, 1985; Klinkowitz, J. The New American Novel of Manners: The Fiction of Richard Yates, Dan Wakefield, and Thomas McGuane, 1986; Who's Who in America, 1994. Periodicals—Commonweal May 20, 1988; Nation August 3/10, 1992; National Review May 17, 1966; New Republic March 19, 1977; New York Times May 29, 1992; August 27, 1992; New York Times Book Review August 9, 1970; May 8, 1977; May 12, 1985; June 7, 1992 New York Times Magazine December 20, 1987; Newsweek July 9, 1973; Publishers Weekly March 4, 1988.

WANG ANYI (1954–), Chinese novelist and short story writer, was born in Nanjing of literary parents (her mother is a well known novelist, Ru Zhijuan). Wang Anyi was brought up in affluence among cultural circles in Shanghai. She was sent down to the countryside during the Cultural Revolution at age sixteen, but being musical, she managed to join a provincial art troupe after two years of rural life, and finally made her way back to Shanghai to work for a children's magazine in 1978. The long letters she sent to her mother every Tuesday describing life at the grass roots was the first budding of her creative talent. Writing and publishing nonstop since the 1980s, Wang Anyi became one of China's best-known writers.

Drawing from the life she knew best, Wang's short stories of the early 1980s, collected in Liushi (Lapse of Time), portray with great sensitivity the humiliations and frustrations in the everyday lives of the back-alley residents of Shanghai. For this Wang Anyi has been acclaimed the writer of "Shanghai consciousness." The title story portrays Duanli, a strong woman of bourgeois background, who holds her family together through forty years of poverty and vicissitudes under Communism. It also incorporates lively descriptions of Shanghai life throughout the turmoil of revolution and reform.

Xiaobaozhuang (Baotown), an example of the school of fiction characterized as "seeking for roots," explores the mysterious ways in which a small village is linked to China's ancient roots by myth and legend, and presents the villagers as being defined more by tradition than by modern ideology. Baotown, a remote and isolated village, is a microcosm of human society. Its residents work hard, have few material possessions and barely enough to eat, but find escape from their humdrum lives in dreams. Although most of these dreams are doomed to frustration, they unite people in a common bond of hope. Tracing the history of their town back to a legendary origin, the Baotowners still live on "tall tales." A young would-be writer, whose nickname in the village is "Word Crazy," pesters an old soldier with questions about his heroic deeds in war. The soldier turns on him with an ironic question: if he is not writing his book for the government or the commune, nor for money (royalties having been abolished in the Cultural Revolution), "Then who are you writing it for?" The young man has no answer. He can only keep on writing

WANG ANYI

and heading every piece he writes with same motto: "An eagle can fly lower than a chicken, but a chicken can never fly as high as an eagle."

There is a cheering stoicism in these characters even when they confront suffering. Jonathan Mirsky remarked, in *New York Review of Books*: "Wang Anyi's quiet sense that there is a continuing Communist comedy to be observed in China sets her apart from her contemporaries." Not even a devastating flood can destroy the hope of these sturdy people. The console themselves that only three people died in it: "And at that they had been a lunatic, an old man and a child—indeed, the child could have lived but died trying to save the old man." And the dead child is made a hero by the state, bringing brief fame and honor to Baotown.

The stoical calm and passivity of these peasants is in striking contrast to the women characters who dominate in the third and, to date, most significant phase in Wang Anyi's career. In her Love Trilogy published in 1986 and 1987, she explores female sexuality with a candor that is rare in contemporary Chinese writing. She portrays sexual passion as irrational, sometimes even destructive. Significantly, her women emerge strengthened by their sexual freedom. *Huangshan zhi Lian* (*Love on a Barren Mountain*), the first of these books, ends in a suicide pact between adulterous lovers, but the woman is the "femme fatale," the stronger character. Similarly, in *Xiaocheng zhi Lian* (*Love in a Small Town*) the unmarried young woman, physically and emotionally stronger than her lover, ends up as a competent and confident single mother. The young woman in *Jinxiugu zhi Lian* (*Brocade Valley*) gains a new sense of identity through a fleeting extramarital affair. At the outset she is bored with her husband but happily engaged in her job as an editor: "It was only when she went out the door that her life started. Being at home was no more than a preparation for life, like being backstage before a performance." In this post–Cultural Revolution era, she relishes her professional life. Sent to represent her firm at a writer's conference in a beautiful mountain resort, she meets a writer and in this romantic setting, the Brocade Valley, they fall passionately in love. What many Western readers would regard as the conventional language of popular romances was exciting and erotic for Wang Anyi's Chinese public:

> At this moment they stopped feeling any sense of uneasiness or awkwardness. As darkness enveloped them, they had something to cover themselves with; they weren't naked any longer; they needn't feel ashamed. Also, the mountain had so much understanding of the human heart, and gazed down on them with such keen insight that there was no further need for evasion. Shedding their pretense, they felt relaxed, liberated, free.

There is no expression of morbid guilt. The woman returns to her husband and the narrator closes her story: "A story in which there is no story is finished."

Wang Anyi denies emphatically that she is a feminist because, she says, "One of the premises of feminism is to deny the distinction between men and woman." In an interview in *Modern Chinese Literature* in 1988 she told Wang Zheng that she believes that not all women are qualified to do important work and that many women are better off in the home caring for their children. Nevertheless, she said, in modern-day China "women play a great role in determining their own fate . . . When there are only two people, a man and a woman, Chinese men actually seem very weak. In fact the Chinese man is passive but likes to think of himself as aggressive."

Wang Anyi lives in Shanghai with her husband Li Zhang. In her 1988 interview she said that she was childless by choice. Regarded as a leading writer of the post-Mao generation, she has moved far from the socialist realism that dominated Maoist writing. Bonnie S. McDougall wrote in her introduction to *Brocade Valley*: "Her dedication to the ideals of individualism and self-respect produce female portraits of a depth and complexity rarely found in Chinese literature in any era."

PRINCIPAL WORKS IN ENGLISH TRANSLATION: *Short stories*-(tr. H. Goldblatt et al.) Lapse of Time, 1988; "Miaomiao" in Chinese Literature, Spring 1992. *Novels*—(tr. M. Avery) *Baotown*, 1985; (tr. E. Hung) *Love in a Small Town*, 1988; (tr. E. Hung) *Love on a Barren Mountain*, 1991; (tr. *Brocade Valley*, 1992. B. S. McDougall and C. Maiping).

ABOUT: Bloomsbury Guide to Women's Literature, C. Buck (ed.) 1992; Lu Tonglin, (ed.) Gender and Sexuality in 20th Century Chinese Literature and Society, 1993; Martin, H. and Kinkley, J. (ed.) Modern Chinese Writers: Self-Portrayals, 1992; Woh's Who in the People's Republic of China, 3rd ed., 1991; Widmer, E. and Wang D. Der-wei (eds.) From May Fourth to June Fourth: Fiction and Film in Wtentieth Century China, 1993. *Periodicals*—Modern Chinese Literature 4 1988;New York Review of Books October 26, 1989.

*WEIL, JIŘI (August 6, 1900–December 13, 1959), Czech fiction writer and journalist, was born in the village of Praskolesy near the town of Hořovice and died in Prague. His father was a joint owner of a firm producing picture frames. Weil attended grammer school in Prague and went on to study Slavonic philology and comparative history of literature at the Arts Faculty of Charles University. In 1928 he earned a doctorate for a thesis on Gogol and the 18th-century English novel. From 1922 to 1931 Weil worked as a translator at the press office of the Soviet embassy in Prague. After that he became a freelance writer and journalist. As a Jew he was forced into hiding during the Nazi occupation of Czechoslovakia (even pretending to have committed suicide). After the war he became an editor for a publishing house and from 1950 to 1958 he was a research worker at the Jewish State Museum in Prague.

Up to World War II, Weil devoted himself to left-wing political and cultural journalism and to establishing cultural contacts with the Soviet Union. He also made some minor translations from Lenin, Marx, Engels, and Stalin. A member of the Czech cultural avant-garde and a pioneer translator of modern Russian authors such as Mayakovsky, Pasternak, Gorky, and Tsvetayeva, he was the author of the pioneer survey *Ruská revoluční literatura* (Russian revolutionary literature, 1924), the compiler of *Sborník sovětské revoluční poezie* (Anthology of Soviet revolutionary poetry, 1932), and the author of other popularizing works about the Soviet Union. During the 1930s Weil worked in Moscow in the Czech division of the official Comintern publishing house and traveled to Central Asia. What he observed of Stalinism was enough to disillusion him, and he was expelled from the Party until he agreed to undergo indoctrination in a commune in Central Asia.

Weil's first novel. *Moskva—hranice* (From Moscow to the border, 1937), was written immediately after his return to Czechoslovakia from the U.S.S.R. and reflects his total disenchantment with Stalinism. Like André Gide's record of a similar experience, *Retour de l'URSS*, published in France just a year earlier, it generated much discussion among left-wing intellectuals; both books were banned after the Communist takeover of Czechoslovakia in 1948. *Moskva—hranice* is written in an unusual form for a novel. It is a semidocumentary, full of facts and eyewitness reporting, all but eliminating the conventional narrator and allowing the characters to speak for themselves. The story centers on two sincere, sensitive Czechs—Ri, wife of a Polish engineer, and Jan Fischer, a Communist intellectual. Ri comes to the U.S.S.R. prejudiced against Communism, but in the end she accepts her place in Soviet society; Jan Fischer is eventually expelled from the Communist Party, thus becoming a "nonperson," a "dead man." Weil fills the novel with lively action portraying the hectic, pulsating quality of life in the early days of socialism in the U.S.S.R., and the two protagonists encounter and collide with the many social and political experiments of the time. The ending—with the bourgeois Ri conforming to and the idealistic Jan Fischer rejecting Communism—came as a startling surprise to readers, especially because Weil had worked it out so logically and objectively.

In 1938 Weil finished *Dřevěná lžíce* (The wooden spoon), a sequel to *Moskva—hranice*. It was published posthumously in 1970 in an Italian translation and in Czechoslovakia not until 1992 in book form. The novel takes place mainly in the industrial region of Kirghizia against the background of the construction of a combine. The main characters are first in parallel. Later, the fates of the official Alexander Alexandrovich and of the Austrian worker Tony Stricker reverse themselves as the official, at first basking in glory, turns into a nonperson, and the worker, at first taken into custody, becomes almost a model worker—a hero.

Weil wrote his third novel, *Makanna—otec divu* (Makanna the father of miracles, 1946), in 1940. It is a historical novel about the false prophet and leader from the 8th century in Central Asia. Weil developed themes made famous in the early 19th century by the Irish Romantic poet Thomas Moore in his picturesque epic *Lalla Rookh* (1817) to conform to his own contemporary interests in history and literature. The novel is written like a journalistic report from a witness who evokes both the exotic appeal of the Orient and the political significance of the hero Makanna—a popular leader who becomes corrupted by his ambition and proves to be a false prophet. Weil treats his subject with full awareness of its psychological and sociological implications for his own time, but the novel is not a simple allegory of Nazism. A historical epic, it is laden with panoramic battle scenes and carefully researched miniatures of everyday life.

Many years later, in 1958, Weil published another historical novel, *Harfenik* (The Harpist), whose parallel main charcters are two Jews—a poor man and a factory owner. The novel takes place mainly in 19th-century Prague and is an interesting example of Weil's imaginative adaptation of the past to foreshadow and reflect contemporary issues. The novel portrays a collective hero—the workers in textile factories who confront corrupt and deceitful political and religious leaders. Although it displays Weil's originality at its best, the novel had a cool reception. The reason may be that the characters are not individualized. Weil stands apart from them, choosing the position of detached observer, depicting history and social movement in Kafkaesque states of hesitation and misunderstanding, and he shows these qualities as typical of the Czech nation.

Barvy (Colors, 1945) is Weil's first commemoration of the victims of World War II and of the German occupation of his country. It is a small collection of short stories that he wrote during the war, depicting the fates of the victims of the Holocaust and of the anti-Nazi resistance movement. The short stories are lyrical and subjective; their language is formal, and they read like allegories and parables. *Mír* (Peace, 1947) written sometime between 1938 and 1948, is another collection of short stories inspired by peripheral genres: travel sketches, reportage, and anecdotes. *Vzpomínky na Julia Fučíka* (Reminiscences of Julius Fucik, 1947) tells of Weil's contact with Julius Fucik, real-life hero of the Communist anti-Nazi resistance movement. The book testifies to Weil's concern with honest, absolutely objective reporting.

The first of the two novels that introduced Weil to the English-reading public was *Život s Hvězdou* (1949, *Life with a Star*, which takes place in Prague at the time of the Nazi occupation. (The title alludes to the Star of David that Jews were required to wear.) It is the story of Josef Roubicek, a lonely Jew—although *Jew*, like *Nazi* and *Prague*, is not used in the book. He has been a man who has known only "how to add up columns of figures," but now, trapped in the city, living in his lonely room, where he has destroyed everything so that "they" will not be able to profit by any of his possessions, he works as a gravedigger and roams about. His only compan-

ions are Tomas, a cat, and Ruzena, his lover, married to someone else and with him only in imagination. She has wanted him to flee with her, but he has not had the courage, and now skulks about the city, talking to Ruzena in his head and dreaming of and remembering how they danced together and went skiing in happier times. But Ruzena vanishes even from his dreams, and he learns that she and her husband have been shot. After the cat too is shot, Roubicek is completly alone when he receives the summons to the transport. He decides not to accept the summons, but hesitates:

> I began to hesitate because suddenly I felt very tired. . . . It would be better to give up, to disappear, to submerge myself among the hundreds of others going to their deaths. I would be all right; I would have peace; I would accept extinction without fear or shame. Instead the freedom I would now have to bear would be a heavy load. . . . Perhaps it would be better after all to become a number, a leaf carried by the wind until it falls to the ground and is trampled into the mud.

This cipher-like man in the unnamed city, facing deportation and death at the hands of an unnamed enemy, immediately overcomes his hesitation, however:

> . . . I had overcome death, and it was a good thing to overcome death. At that moment I knew whom to ask for advice. It was Ruzena who came to advise me that night, Ruzena whose advice I had rejected long ago. I knew I would accept it now. . . . Now I must follow Ruzena, as I should have done then. We would never again have to stand on the riverbank and say goodbye at the street-car stop. If I came to a decision now, we would go on together. Ruzena would always accompany me, and with Ruzena there was nothing to be afraid of.
>
> It was then, when the last sheets of my scribblings were burning in the stove, annulling the name of Josef Roubicek, that I understood that the Josef Roubicek who wanted to make excuses, to evade, and to dodge, only to avoid freedom, no longer existed and would never exist again.

The English translation of *Life with a Star* was initiated by the American novelist Philip Roth: "I first heard of *Life with a Star* in Prague in the early seventies, when I met the widow of the writer Jiří Weil. Weil hid from the Nazis during the war—most of the time, as I understand it, in the bathroom of the house of Vera Saudkova, Kafka's niece. The book is, without a doubt, one of the outstanding novels I've read about the fate of a Jew under the Nazis. I don't know of another like it." Roth wrote in the preface to the English translation by Rita Klímová with Roslyn Schloss that there were points of similarity between Isaac Babel and Weil: "Both became literary victims of socialist realism and political victims of Stalinism (and Stalinist anti-Semitism). And each lived through his lonely years as a writer and a man, unpublished, unread withdrawn, and silent. . . . "

Joseph Švorecký, the Czech novelist who now lives in Canada, wrote in the *New Republic* that this "extraordinary" novel "was certainly the first important work of Czech fiction to come out of the war. . . . There are some great fictions about the Holocaust, but I know of no novel like *Life with a Star*, in which the nightmare of the Final Solution is captured in such an indirect way, by the renunciation of the hellish effects of gas chambers, torture, and sudden death. It concentrates instead on the condition of anxiety before the step into the unknown and the unspeakable." The Czech critic Jan Grossman observed that the book is a picture of the absurdity which penetrated everyday life. "The absurd is more important than the horrifying. Absurdity is horror and pervertedness, rationalized, made banal, 'made commonplace'; as such it even penetrates the thoughts and actions of its victims and becomes established into a sort of convention because it follows convention."

Na střeše je Mendelssohn (*Mendelssohn Is on the Roof*), written some years earlier but published posthumously in 1960, was intended to be Weil's most ambitious novel. It cost him much effort; he spent several years working on it. At the request of the censors he added to it passages about the Communist resistance movement and the Soviet Army. The novel is composed of several streams of narrative about the tragic fate of Jews in occupied Prague and in the concentration camp Terezín, as well as about the Nazis, including their supreme commanders in Bohemia. At the same time Weil wrote with humor and a sense of the grotesque, to which especially the title bears witness.

In honor of a visit to Prague of a high-ranking Nazi officer, two workmen are ordered to removed the bust of the "Jewish" composer Felix Mendelssohn from the roof of the Municipal Building. There are no identifying names on the busts on the roof, so they do not know which one to remove: "This was a pretty mess. Nobody had ever told him, [a workman], what the statue of that Jew looked like. And even if they *had* told him, it wouldn't have done any good. The statues all loooked alike." Having taken a course in "racial science" in which noses were measured to determine race, the boss finally gives the order: "'Go around the statues again and look carefully at their noses. Whichever one has the biggest nose, that's the Jew.'" They find the biggest nose—which is on the statue of Richard Wagner.

Mendelssohn Is on the Roof, in contrast to the tightly constructed and intimate *Life with a Star*, has a wide canvas and a large cast of characters ranging from occupying Nazis to Jewish victims. Michael Hofmann in the *Times Liter-ary Supplement* called *Mendelssohn* "a wide-screen job with a Victorian or Edwardian proliferation of scenes and plots and characters. . . . leitmotivs of statues and rivers and music and well-researched details, . . . " John Bayley noted, in *New York Review of Books*, that although by the time he wrote the book, Weil had been expelled from the Communist Party, he was "using the novel for demonstrative and ideological purposes." Nevertheless, Bayley found it "a worthy predecessor of the more famous *Life with a Star*." Larry Wolff, in the *New York Times Book Review*, considered Weil "a powerful authorial presence [inhabiting] the characters in turn, pulling their puppet strings and then rushing on to the next figure in the gallery. . . . Jiri Weil was a writer who witnessed the worst of this century and testified to his experience in works of unflinching and astonishing literary vision."

Philip Roth, describing his reactions on first reading Weil's stories, said in the preface to *Life With a Star* that he "was stunned, not solely by the horrors they described but by the elemental means that served to communicate Weil's hatred for the Nazis and pity for their victims. They were stories conceived in rage and tears, then told with the matter-of-factness of the journalist and the disarming simplicity of the family anecdotalist. . . . and from the nature of those translations, Weil appeared to have been by nature a colloquial storyteller rather than a relently self-scrutinizing stylist of the minimalist persuasion."

Weil is a consistent representative of the experimental prose of the period from the 1930s to the 1950s—the period which suffered from discontinuity of cultural development. That is why Weil appears to many writers of the "new wave" as their direct predecessor.

PRINCIPAL WORKS IN ENGLISH TRANSLATION: (tr. R. Klimova with R. Schloss) Life with a Star, 1988; (tr. M. Winn) Mendelssohn Is on the Roof, 1991.

ABOUT: Roth, P. *preface to* Life with a Star, 1988. *Periodicals*—Library Journal June 1, 1989; February 15, 1991; London Review of Books August 6, 1992; New Republic September 4, 1989; New Statesman & Society December 1, 1989; New York Review of Books September 18, 1989; April 11, 1991; New York Times March 15, 1991; New York Times Book Review June 18, 1989; May 5, 1991; Times Literary Supplement December 8, 1989; February 14, 1992; World Literature Today Spring 1990.

WEISSKOPF, VICTOR (FEDERICK) (September 19, 1908–), Austrian-born American physicist, was born in Vienna, then the capital of the Austro-Hungarian Empire. He is the son of Emil Weisskopf, a lawyer and judge who achieved considerable success despite modest origins, and Martha (Gutt) Weisskopf. His parents were assimilated, and affluent, Jews for whom culture and education were extremely important. Victor Weisskopf began studying the piano at an early age and briefly considered a career as a concert pianist. It was science, however, that interested him the most. He was a talented student who sometimes displayed a streak of impudence. In his memoir *The Joy of Insight*, Weisskopf recalls that by early adolescence he already considered himself a socialist, "more interested in the future of the world than in the exploits of the kings and emperors of the past." When a history teacher reproached him for not knowing "a single date in history," Weisskopf replied, "'That's not true. I know all the dates. I just don't know what happened on any of them.'"

After completing his general education at the gymnasium, Weisskopf enrolled in the University of Vienna to study physics. In 1928, having exhausted the physics curriculum in Vienna, he moved to the University of Göttingen, in Germany. There he studied under Max Born, a pioneer in the nascent field of quantum mechanics, and wrote a dissertation on the ways in which atoms emit light. He received his Ph.D. in physics in 1931.

Soon after earning his doctorate, Weisskopf went to Leipzig to work with the German physicist Werner Heisenberg, a founder of quantum theory best known for his "uncertainty principle." He soon moved on to the University of Berlin, then home to many of the world's top theoretical physicists, to work as a research assistant to Erwin Schrödinger. In 1932 he traveled and lectured in the Soviet Union, and upon his return was awarded a Rockefeller grant. He chose to use the grant in Copenhagen, working with quantum mechanics pioneer Niels Bohr. In the course of his long career, Weisskopf met and worked with many illustrious physicists, though none had a greater impact on the development of his thought than Bohr. In *The Joy of Insight*, Weisskopf refers to Bohr as "my intellectual father."

In 1933, at the invitation of Wolfgang Pauli, Weisskopf went to work as an instructor at the Institute of Technology in Zurich, Switzerland. After a year in Zurich, he married Ellen Tvede, a Danish woman he had met in Copenhagen. Despite the growing political menace posed by the Nazis, Weisskopf published a number of important papers, including one on the structure of atomic nuclei with which, he recalls, "I became a member of the community of nuclear physicists."

By 1937 the mounting Nazi anti-Semitism had become impossible for Weisskopf to ignore, even though he himself was never persecuted and claimed, in *The Joy of Insight*, that he "lived a charmed life during the Nazi era." Invited to teach physics at the University of Rochester, Weisskopf and his wife came to the United States in September 1937. Eventually, he was able to bring all the members of his immediate family—his mother, brother, and sister—to America, thus sparing them from the Holocaust. In 1942 he became a naturalized citizen of the United States.

Early in 1943, Weisskopf was contacted by J. Robert Oppenheimer, the American physicist in charge of the atomic-energy research project in Los Alamos, New Mexico. Oppenheimer briefed Weisskopf on the American effort to develop an atomic bomb and urged him to come to Los Alamos to work on the project. At the research labs in Los Alamos, where the first bomb was actually built, Weisskopf became known as the "Los Alamos Oracle," due to his astounding ability to predict the results of experiments.

Although he later opposed the nuclear arms race, Weisskopf had relatively few qualms about his work at Los Alamos, particularly because it was then widely believed that German scientists were on the verge of creating their own bomb. In fact, Weisskopf has mainly fond memories of his time in New Mexico, surrounded as he was by many of the world's top physicists. "We were an unusual community," he wrote in *The Joy of Insight*, "an international crowd of extremely creative people, and even our informal social gatherings were extraordinarily stimulating and interesting." Despite his overall enthusiasm for the project, however, Weisskopf was critical of the decision to drop a second atomic bomb on Japan just three days after the first was dropped on Hiroshima. After World War II, Weisskopf declined to participate in any further nuclear weapons research. He was among the founders of the Association of Los Alamos Scientists (later known as the Federation of American Scientists), an organization devoted above all to educating the public about the dangers of nuclear weapons. He was also instrumental in founding the *Bulletin of the Atomic Scientists*, a monthly publication focusing on nuclear politics, arms control, and (later) environmental issues.

In 1946 Weisskopf joined the faculty of the Massachusetts Institute of Technology, where he became a popular professor known to students and colleagues alike as "Viki." From 1961 to 1966, he was the director-general of the Conseil Européen pour la Recherche Nucléaire, or CERN, the European organization for nuclear research, with headquarters near Geneva. He was head of the physics department at MIT from 1967 to 1974, after which he retired from active teaching. During his later years at MIT, he served as chairman of the high energy physics advisory panel of the Atomic Energy Commission. He was also a member of the American Academy of Arts and Sciences, and president of that organization from 1975 to 1979. Elected to the Pontifical Academy in 1976, he used his membership in that group to urge the pope to speak out publicly against the nuclear arms race. In addition to his membership in many professional organizations, Weisskopf has been the recipient of numerous awards and honors. Among these are the Max Planck Medal (1956), the Boris Pregel Prize from the New York Academy of Sciences (1971), the Enrico Fermi Award from the U.S. Energy Department (1988), and the Compton Award (1993). During the 1980s, Weisskopf was an outspoken opponent of President Ronald Reagan's Strategic Defense Initiative, popularly known as Star Wars. Along with Carl Sagan, Hans Bethe, and other prominent scientists, he was a contributor to *The Fallacy of Star Wars*, prepared by the Union of Concerned Scientists.

Weisskopf has written for physicists and serious students of the subject and for general readers with a strong interest in scientific issues. Virtually all of his many professional papers, of course, belong to the first category. His first book, *Theoretical Nuclear Physics*, written with *John Blatt*, is also of the first type; it was used as a standard university textbook for many years. Also belonging to the first category is *Concepts of Particle Physics*, a two-volume work written in collaboration with *Kurt Gottfried*. It is significant, especially considering Weisskopf's eminence in a rather abstruse field, that most of his other books are at least partially accessible to the general reader. This accessibility is not an accident.

The Privilege of Being a Physicist, a collection of essays written over a period of fifteen years, is an attempt to bridge the ever-widening chasm separating science from the rest of culture. The collection includes biographical sketches of two physicists Weisskopf knew well: Wolfgang Pauli and Werner Heisenberg. In such essays as "What Is an Elementary Particle?" and "The Origin of the Universe," he uses jargon-free, nonmathematical language (and a host of illustrations) to explain the major discoveries of 20th-century physics to general readers. In the essay "The

Privilege of Being a Physicist," Weisskopf notes, "Popularization of science should be one of the prime duties of a scientist and not a secondary one as it is now."

M. Mitchell Waldrop, reviewing *The Privilege of Being a Physicist* in the *New York Times Book Review* in 1989, found the essays to be "models of simplicity, conciseness and clarity. And taken together they provide a compelling, if perhaps unintended, portrait of the author: incisive, humane and joyful." Reviewers from more specialized publications were equally enthusiastic about the book. In *American Scientist*, Sidney D. Drell noted: "To be sure, an intelligent reader is called for—but certainly not an expert. . . . These essays are written for the amateur. And pleasure is what these essays provide—along with understanding." *Nature* (1989) reviewer John S. Ridden commented that "Weisskopf's responsibility has been fulfilled: in the book he continues to call for an end to the madness of nuclear weapons."

Weisskopf was already over eighty years old when he published *The Privilege of Being a Physicist*. His autobiography, *The Joy of Insight*, appeared shortly thereafter. That book served to reinforce his reputation as an elder statesman of science because he was, by then, one of the few refugee physicists from the World War II era still alive and writing. With few exceptions, the autobiography was warmly received by both scientists and lay critics. "*The Joy of Insight* is written with great charm, and shows Viki Weisskopf the human being even more than Weisskopf the great physicist," Hans Bethe wrote in *Physics Today* (1991). In *Nature* (1991) William H. Press noted, "Weisskopf is the very model of the modern, liberal, politically conscious and administratively adept, twentieth-century physicist, a major-domo of 'big science'. He did about everything there was to do, except make a major scientific discovery himself." Jeremy Bernstein, wrote in *New York Review of Books* (April 1991) "The autobiography, *The Joy of Insight*, is, as I expected, charming, and it is sometimes revealing, but it falls short of what I had hoped it would be." Bernstein, a former student of Weisskopf's, readily acknowledged that Weisskopf was "a master teacher" who deserves to be ranked with the century's top physicists. Nonetheless, he faulted Weisskopf for a persistent tendency to overlook the shortcomings and errors of others. "This quality no doubt makes for a more agreeable life," Bernstein noted, "but it tends to make an autobiography less than satisfying." Principally, Bernstein objected to Weisskopf's roseate assessment of Werner Heisenberg's role in the Nazi nuclear program. Although the German physicist never joined the

Nazi Party, he remained in Germany during the war and played a leading role in the German nuclear weapons program. In *The Joy of Insight*, Weisskopf suggests that Heisenberg purposefully delayed the project (by presenting German officials with misleading information, for example). Bernstein, however, argued that "Heisenberg's failure to make a nuclear weapon had nothing to do with lack of 'eagerness.'" Concluding his review of *The Joy of Insight*, and noting that it was written largely from memory, Bernstein wrote, "The problem is that much of his book is written as if it were history, and, in view of his eminence, people may well take it for history."

Nancy M. Haegel observed in *Commonweal*, "Weisskopf had the good fortune to come of age during the 'golden years' of modern physics and had the ability to take advantage of it." Having helped usher the world into the nuclear age, Weisskopf could not help reflecting on the virtues of a simpler time. "I have often thought that, given a choice, I would have liked to live as a scientist in the nineteenth century," he wrote in *The Joy of Insight*. "It was a time of opportunity and new beginnings in all areas of culture. It was a time of great optimism for a better future. It was a time of innocence without the terrible knowledge we now have of all the negative consequences of much of what began at that time."

PRINCIPAL WORKS: *Physics*—(with John Blatt) Theoretical Nuclear Physics, 1952; Knowledge and Wonder: The Natural World as Man Knows It, 1962; Physics in the Twentieth Century: Selected Essays, 1972; (with K. Gottfried) Concepts of Particle Physics: Volume I, 1984; (with K. Gottfried) Concepts of Particle Physics: Volume II, 1986; The Privilege of Being a Physicist, 1989. *Autobiography*—The Joy of Insight: Passions of a Physicist, 1991. As editor—(with M. Fierz) Theoretical Physics in the Twentieth Century: A Memorial Volume to Wolfgang Pauli, 1960; Nuclear Physics, 1963.

ABOUT: Contemporary Authors 107, 1983; Who's Who in America 1992–1993; Zuckerman, L. Star Wars in a Nuclear World, 1987. *Periodicals*—American Scientist July/August 1989; Commonweal December 20, 1991; Issues in Science and Technology Winter 1991–1992; Nature November 5, 1987; April 27, 1989; april 25, 1991; New York Review of Books April 11, 1991; June 27, 1991; New York Times Book Review May 14, 1989; March 24, 1991; Physics Today October 1991; February 1993; Science May 17, 1991; Wall Street Journal January 2, 1985; January 17, 1985; December 27, 1988.

WESLEY, MARY (June 24, 1912–), British novelist, born near Windsor in England, the daughter of Colonel Mynors and Violet (Balby) Farmar. She attended Queen's College, London, and subsequently the London School of Economics before going to work in the War Office from 1939 to 1941. She married Lord Swinfen in 1937, was divorced in 1944, and then married Eric Siepman, a writer, in 1951. She has three sons whom she says she sees rarely and for short periods to avoid the risk of boring each other: this belief in the need for mutually independent lives of parents and children is a motif throughout her novels. Her somewhat unusual life and easy articulation of slightly unorthodox views have made their way into her writing, as has her experience of living in London and continental Europe, as well as the West Country. London and the West Country in particular provide backgrounds for several of the books, while France is frequently invoked to add a touch of the cultured exotic. Her time as a member of the antique trade also leaves a light trace, as an appreciation of valuable objects, both aesthetic and in terms of canny investment, and the kind of people who notice and own them, are scattered liberally in several of her novels.

Although she had been writing fairly constantly since the late 1960s and had published several novels for children, she came to the fore in the 1980s, gaining a reputation as a popular romantic novelist who does not shirk direct language and earthy, often convoluted, plots. She herself is of the opinion that her "chief claim to fame is arrested development, getting my first novel published at the age of seventy." Certainly her age was much remarked upon in reviews of her first books, particularly of the first novel, *Jumping the Queue*, which has as its central character a woman, recently widowed, who is planning suicide, effected by swallowing lots of pills washed down with good Beaujolais and then swimming out to sea. The defense of voluntary euthanasia perceived in this novel, and the denial that a wish for death is necessarily a result of despair or ill-health, brought much controversy and publicity for Wesley, as well as the first of several television adaptations of her books. Throughout, Wesley has maintained that there was no autobiographical element in her books, though she has admitted to some colorful moment in her own life and tempts her audience to believe she took advantage of the changes wrought by the Second World War. As she told Barth Healey in the *New York Times Book Review* in 1992: "We were hit by the war when we were very young and it was awful—but it was also very exciting, and you behaved differently. You could even think of a divorce or leaving your husband or having an affair."

MARY WESLEY

Subsequent novels have been mainly romantic, though never straightforwardly so. She has a penchant for sensational plots, for example in *Not That Sort of Girl*, there is a subplot of incest between twin brother and sister. Prevalent among her qualities are ironic humor and sharp observation of social mores, coupled with a lack of overt comment, which draws criticism from those of her readers who seek direct social judgments. Her books tend to focus on a small group and their relations and interrelations over several years, frequently using the recollections of several characters. This results in a form of narrative that moves between times zones in an associative rather than strictly chronological way. She delights in almost impossibly complex situations, which gives rise to much comedy and some social satire. Her chosen cast are the better-off members of English families, her favored settings being small towns of the rural England of the Home Counties.

A Dubious Legacy concentrates on just such a family, beginning in 1944 when Margaret Tillotson is brought home by her new husband and promptly retires to bed. Alida Becker, in the *New York Times Book Review*, described Margaret Tillotson as "a character so wonderfully warped that she proves irresistible—to readers as well as to the members of her firmly rebuffed husband's makeshift social group." Patricia Beers was similarly enthusiastic in her review in the *London Review of Books*. She remarked that *A Dubious Legacy* "is not wholesome enough to be called a good yarn, I am glad to say, but it is absorbingly readable." A contrasting view is

voiced by Aisling Foster, who noted in the *Times Literary Supplement* that although "banality is sometimes a weakness in Wesley's universe, a 1950s setting for this novel *A Dubious Legacy* overcomes the problems," although "just occasionally, the author loses her grip on the story's postwar setting. References to au pairs, muesli, dinner in the kitchen, cholesterol and German language lessons for better business can be disorientating. Yet when she finally fast-forwards to 1990, her little England looks much the same . . . At this point one appreciates the deeper resonances of the title. Seeing such people hand on nothing more than a determination to remain in their niche does seem pretty dubious. What is unclear is whether their author thinks so, too."

Similar reservations about Wesley's style and ability were voiced by Lucasta Miller in the *New Statesman*. Miller commented that what "is strange about *A Sensible Life* is that it fails to make the most of potent mements. . . . Flora's story is disturbing, but Wesley seems almost unconscious of these elements." While Elizabeth Barry commented in the *Times Literary Supplement* (1990) that "admirers of Mary Wesley's particular brand of dashing romances" would not be disappointed since it shares with all her novels "a general atmosphere of playfulness as well as specific elements—such as the liberating effect of the Second World War on well brought-up English girls and the assertion of happiness in late middle age. Wesley's skill at organizing interconnected lives and loves, and her meticulous rendering of chit-chat, continue to appear effortless."

Wesley unites food and sex with a comic touch in *Harnessing Peacocks*, which centers on Hebe, a beautiful woman who supports her son and herself by cooking for wealthy women—supplementing that income by being the mistress of several men, the peacocks of the title. Both her careers call for careful scheduling and an unsentimental approach to life—an approach understood and shared by the women who hire her as part-time cook as an indulgence. *Harnessing Peacocks*, like her other books, assumes a certain type of educated audience—in this case one which does not need to have the myth of Hebe presented to it, though Wesley gets mileage out of some characters not knowing the classical myth, which allows for a repeated pun on Hebe as a bush, hastily corrected to "shrub." This cultured aura is part of the ambience of the novels, and often an element in the sex-cum-snob-appeal of the characters for each other. She writes, for example: "Further up the street Hannah restlessly debated whether she should marry George. She had planned to marry a man who pronouced regatta 'regattah.' George said 'regatter.'"

Later she interviews Ferry:

"Terry?"
"Yes?" . . .
"Say 'regatta.'"
"Regattah.' He was smiling. 'Received prounciation suit you? I regattah, you regattah, she begat her. . . . "

Needless to say it is Terry Hannah chooses in the end.

As Wesley continued to produce novels at a constant rate, some characters from earlier books reappeared in later ones, allowing for some play and association between novels. The popular appeal of these characters and the fact that her novels adapt well for television provide Wesley with a loyal and large audience.

PRINCIPAL WORKS: Jumping the Queue, 1982; The Camomile Lawn, 1983; Harnessing Peacocks, 1985; The Vacillation of Polly Carew, 1986; Not That Sort of Girl, 1987; Second Fiddle, 1988; A Sensible Life, 1990; A Dubious Legacy, 1992. *Juvenile*— Speaking Terms, 1968; The Sixth Seal, 1968; Haphazard House, 1983.

ABOUT: Contemporary Authors 49–52, 1975; Who's Who 1990–1991. *Periodicals*—London Review of Books July 26, 1990; March 12, 1992; New Statesman & Society March 16, 1990; New York Times Book Review July 8, 1984; June 12, 1988; July 30, 1989; July 29, 1990; November 8, 1992; Publisher Weekly July 6, 1990; Times Literary Supplement March 16, 1990; February 7, 1992; Women's Review of Books March 1991.

WETHERELL, W(ALTER) D(AVID) (October 5, 1948–), American novelist, short story writer and essayist, writes: "I began writing when I dropped out of college at nineteen, not seeing how anything I was learning there could contribute to the apprenticeship I knew I had to serve. What I didn't know was how long the self-teaching process would take—eight years really, until I had anything like a polished story. In the meantime I went through all sorts of jobs, false starts, career paths tentatively adopted then precipitously dropped, buying myself time to write, largely in summerhouses left vacant in winter and so rented cheap. Material and a wide range of it—that's what I was getting, half deliberately in the old hard-knocks manner, half by accident, while all along, to make sure there was no escape, I was burning each bridge that might lead to security and stability and all the other pitfalls I as a writer was determined to avoid. The one straight line during the swerves of these years were the stories I'd never stopped writing.

W. D. WETHERELL

"There was another reason behind this late bloom. Even as a beginner I was trying my wings with a wide variety of material, never happy unless I was taking risks, trying new styles handling subjects that by any sober criterion I had no business touching. Between this and a great deal of personal shyness (compared to me, Franz Kafka was a Rotarian), the fact that I grew up in an environment where art was foreign, the isolation and false starts I had to work through were perhaps more extreme than they otherwise might have been. But there you are. It was eight years before I published anything, a good many years after that before I met anyone who had read my work, even in manuscript; I had three books published before I met another author in the flesh.

"Perhaps as a result, in my fiction I try to speak for the loner, the person who sees things differently, for the person to whom fate and fortune have not been kind. I've also tried to show people caught up in the various winds that blow through our times, social, cultural, and most of all, historical. Some of these characters are chilled by the wind, surrender to it completely, but others, most in fact, fight back as best they can, even if they are defeated in the end. This note is particularly prominent in two stories I wrote when things began coming together for me: 'The Man Who Loved Levittown,' and 'Spitfire Autumn,' both of which cover forty years of postwar history, the former set in suburban Long Island, the latter in London.

"The other concern that seems to show up both explicitly and implicitly in all my work is art, or rather, the artist's view of the world, the responsibility this entails, the pains and rewards, most prominently in my novel *Chekhov's Sister*, which is my statement of artistic faith, one I wanted to make as extreme and passionate as I could.

"My first book was a novel *Souvenirs*, published in 1981. My first story collection, *The Man Who Loved Levittown*, won the 1985 Drue Heinz Literature prize and was published later that year. My second story collection, *Hyannis Boat and Other Stories*, was published in 1989; and the same publisher brought out *Chekhov's Sister* in 1990. I'm also the author of two essay collections, both revolving around fly-fishing and the natural world: *Vermont River* (1985) and *Upland Stream* (1991). In these last books are autobiographical passages, interesting only because autobiography is something I've never bothered with in fiction.

"I was born in Mineola, New York, and educated in the Garden City public schools. Since 1982, I've lived in Lyme, New Hampshire. I have a son, Matthew, and a daughter, Erin; my wife is Celeste [Tousignant] Wetherell.

"I've received grants from the NEA and the Rockefeller Foundation; my work has won the Drue Heinz Literature Prize, two O'Henry Awards and the National Magazine Award."

———

W. D. Wetherell's first collection of essays, *Vermont River*, begins: "The perfect river does not exist." This is a fisherman's discovery, but it is the writer Wetherell who converts his passion for fishing into an aesthetics and a metaphysics. "No river can match the rivers of our imagination," he continues. "We stock them with fourteen-inch trout that rise steadily to the fly, grace them with abundant shade and gentle breezes, preserve them from harm . . . There are no dams in our imaginary rivers. No pollution, no highways, no debris. They run unsullied between immaculate banks, our own inviolable preserve."

In *Vermont River* and its sequel, *Upland Stream*, Wetherell joins a goodly company of writers who have discovered a powerful link between fishing and the literary imagination—Melville, Hemingway, more recently Norman Maclean, to name only a few. Among this brotherhood he especially honors Anton Chekhov, whose memory he celebrates in his novel. *Chekhov's Sister*: "Chekhov would have been a good man to fish with—caring nothing for orthodoxy, whether in literature or fishing, and with that rare ability to forget he's a great man." Wetherell has fished the rivers and streams of

Vermont, New Hampshire, Montana, Nova Scotia, and Scotland partly in search of an answer to his young daughter's question, "Why fish?" The beauty of a trout on his line, he writes in *Upland Stream* in a kind of answer to that unanswerable question, "is like catching and holding a condensed length of spray." In "the wild upland of words," where he works, the writer's language is his rod and reel with which he struggles to catch the elusive idea. Fly-fishing is a physical experience, "uniting muscles and nerves in harmonious, graceful ways"; but, he claims in *Vermont River*, it is also cerebral, "depending on the thread of memory that links the fisherman standing in the river to the boy who dreamed of standing in the river."

Wetherell recalls in *Vermont River* that he has been fishing since he was fourteen. At nineteen he got a summer job selling fly-fishing equipment, a career that ended abruptly when, in his zeal for demonstrating his merchandise, he shattered an expensive fly rod. His first professional job after he completed his B.A. at Hofstra University in New York in 1973 was as editor of a fishing magazine which he prefers not to name. Carried over from his life into his fiction, fishing defines and shapes the destinies of some of his characters. "The Bass, the River, and Sheila Mant," one of the stories in his prize-winning collection *The Man Who Loved Levittown*, opens: "There was a summer in my life when the only creature that seemed lovelier to be than a largemouth bass was Sheila Mant." The narrator, then fourteen, had fallen madly in love with the seventeen-year-old and vastly more worldly Sheila. The doom of the romance is sealed from the moment she announces, "I think fishing is dumb," and he loses the prized bass he had accidentally hooked. The boy doesn't fully realize until some time later that his regret is not for Sheila but for the fish he lost that night. "There would be other Sheila Mants in my life, other fish, and though I came close once or twice, it was these secret, hidden tuggings in the night that claimed me, and I never made the same mistake again."

In most of Wetherell's stories, however, it is not fishing itself but the characteristics of the fisherman that shape human lives—patience, persistence even to the point of obsession, dedication to elusive and frustrating ideas, and memory that links present and past. The narrator of "The Man Who Loved Levittown" does not fish, but he clings to his idealized past with a persistence that becomes nearly self-destructive. Wetherell evokes a past that he is himself too young to remember, beginning his story just as World War II has ended and returning American veterans, eager to settle down with their young families, find acute housing shortages everywhere. Their salvation is the quickly built and inexpensive developments that sprawl out into the suburbs. One of the most famous of these is Levittown in Long Island, New York. Here the working-class narrator and his wife raise their family. With his wife now dead and his children and old neighbors moved away, he finds himself isolated, surrounded by unsympathetic young families who offer large sums for his house and make him feel like an interloper. But Levittown embodies his past and his pride, and he stubbornly resists all efforts to get him out:

> Here they are starting off where we finished, everything took us so long to get they have right away . . . You know what these kids who stayed on Long Island know? Shopping centers, that's it. If it's not in a mall they don't know nothing. And talk about dreams, they don't have any. A new stereo? A new Datsun? Call those dreams? Those aren't dreams, those are pacifiers. Popsicles! That's exactly what I feel like telling them. . . . You find your own dream, pal, you're walking on mine.

Essentially, all of Wetherell's characters, like the man who loved Levittown, are romantics doomed to frustration. In "North of Peach," a man who travels around the country in the cause of world peace, handing out leaflets to indifferent people, suffers painful humiliation in a small-town laundromat. In "Spitfire Autumn," an Englishwoman nurses a sentimental memory of dancing with the "Yanks" in World War II, when she was young and beautiful. In "Volpi's Farewell," a once famous opera singer helplessly watches his young son's crushing disappointment in puppy love even as his own attempts to remarry fail.

In spite of their melancholy, Wetherell's short stories have humorous insights into life and leave the reader as much impressed with the gallantry of the survivors as with their unhappiness. In *Hyannis Boat and Other Stories*, his second collection, his characters show equal resistance to disppointment and despair. An elderly woman on a day's outing in Vermont is thrilled by a visit to the home of President Calvin Coolidge in "Remembering Mr. C." A baseball player in the glory days of the Brooklyn Dodgers in "Brooklyn Wept" confronts his own aging, his declining skills, and the failure of his marriage, but out on the field he experiences a moment of transcendence as he looks up at the fans:

> The pops taking their kids by the hand, tugging them away from the hot dog vendors. The teenagers with their ducktail haircuts, Dodger jackets, pointy black shoes . . . Watching them I felt like I was part of Brooklyn, riding with its hope and joy, rooting from some nutty, unshakable loyalty deep down inside. It was a beautiful feeling to be part of. I had my ear tilted against the borough's heart.

Souvenirs, Wetherell's first novel, suggests even in its title the haunting presence of the past. It is the story of a woman who devotes her life to the care of her senile mother and prides herself on her work as a restorer of memorabilia: "The Past Patched Up! Scrapbooks Our Specialty! Old Uniforms Darned. Bootees Bronzed. . . . " The novel was little noticed by reviewers, and readers were unprepared for his boldly ambitious and—in the judgment of its reviewers—brilliantly executed second novel, *Chekhov's Sister*. Evoking a scene and a past far remote from his own—Yalta from the years just preceding the Russian Revolution through World War II—Whetherell even more daringly wrote parts of his novel in dramatic dialogue in the spirit of Chekhov himself. He tells the story from the point of view of Kumin, a young medical student and worshiper of Chekhov who first visits his home in Yalta early in the century. Here he meets Chekhov's sister, who has dedicated herself to her brother's memory. The young man stays on to help her, eventually becoming director of the museum: "For forty years he had been trying to find a common ground with the writer whose memory he had devoted his life to serving."

The novel moves back and forth in the lives of Kumin and Maria Pavlova, who has sacrificed her chances for marriage and even risked her life in her obsessive worship of her brother. She defies the mobs who attack the house in the revolution; she later battles the Communist bureaucracy to get support for her project. Her most threatening challenge is a Nazi officer in World War II, a fanatic admirer of Chekhov's plays, who tempts her to compromise with her principles by staging a production of *The Sea Gull* in the house. The interaction of the characters in the novel with the roles they play in the production is skillfully carried off. David Kaufman wrote in the *Nation*, "With an emphasis on Chekhov's subtlety and deadpan irony, Wetherell artfully duplicates Chekhovian effects while offering a breathtaking tale of his own, incorporating private intrigues and political subplots intermingled with real historical events . . . a major achievement and addition to contemporary literature."

The highest praise given the novel was that it was "Chekhovian." Wetherell directly incorporated scenes from *The Sea Gull*, and his mixture of fact and fiction is made at no sacrifice to the book as a work of the creative imagination. "The novel is full of echoes," Janette Turner Hospital wrote in the *New York Times Book Review* (1990), "as intricate in its patterns of repetition as a set of Chinese boxes." He poses, moreover, the profound moral question of whether art can transcend politics and, as David W. Henderson wrote in *Library Journal*, ["reminds] us of the power of art (unlike more formal histories) to get to the essence of things and to help us endure."

PRINCIPAL WORKS: *Novels*—Souvenirs, 1981; Chekhov's Sister, 1990; The Wisest Man in America, 1995. *Short stories*—The Man Who Loved Levittown, 1985; Hyannis Boat and Other Stories, 1989. *Essays*—Vermont River, 1984; Upland Stream, 1991. *Nonfiction*—The Smithsonian Guides to Natural America, Northern New England—Vermont New Hampshire, and Maine, 1995.

ABOUT: Contemporary Authors 138, 1993; Wetherell, W. D., Upland Stream, 1991; Wetherell, W. D. Vermont River, 1984. *Periodicals*—Library Journal March 15, 1991; Nation June 18, 1990; New York Times Book Review January 5, 1986; March 25, 1990; Publishers Weekly January 26, 1990; February 15, 1991.

KENNETH WHITE

WHITE, KENNETH (April 28, 1936–), British poet and writer of fiction, writes: "I was born in Scotland, in the city and Atlantic port of Glasgow, more specifically in its ill-famed quarter, the Gorbals: nutmeg-faced Lascar sailors, bearded streetsynagogue Jews, colourful Pakistanis, and a varied collection of local punters, bookies, flymen, and barfiends. On both sides (father, William McKenzie White, mother, Janet Downie Cameron), I come from families who drifted down from the north to the industrial belt at the end of the 18th century. My paternal grandfather was a strolling actor, publican, soldier, musician, and factory-worker, according to circumstances and opportunities. When I came on the scene, my father, who had been forced to leave school at fourteen, was working as a railway signal man in Glasgow, doing a great deal of reading, mostly in history and economics, during his nightshift. Around 1939, he and my mother decided it would be better to raise their children in a more natural context, so I was brought up on the west coast of Scotland, amid shores, moors, woods, and hills: that landscape marked me, just as much as the city images, and I've translated it into mindscape.

"I went to primary and secondary schools in Ayrshire, before going up to the University of Glasgow to study French and German, with Latin and philosophy on the side. After two years, since I was showing alarming signs of intellectual unrest, the German professor thought I'd better cool off, and suggested a break in Germany. I spent the year 1956–19557 in Munich, studying mainly German philosophy on my own, and living in a wooden shack on the banks of the quiet-flowing *Isar*. After another two years in Glas-

gow, I was lucky that one of my external examiners at the Honors examination was Enid Starkie, the Rimbaud specialist from Oxford. Anyway, the result was that, in addition to a double First, I ended up with a two-year postgraduate scholarship to anywhere I liked. I thought vaguely of Oxford and Harvard, but decided for Paris. I spent four years there, ostensibly working on a thesis on a poetry and politics in the context of surrealism, but in fact wandering around the city and beginning to write in my own way, notably a manuscript that was finally to be called *Incandescent Limbo*, as well as a book of essays variously entitled the *Legacy of Jude the Obscure*, or *Marx, Reich and the Third Eye*.

"I married Marie-Claude Charlut, late 1959. In 1961, we bought an old farmhouse in the Ardèche, south-east France, and spent a good part of every spring and summer there. Down there in the 'French desert,' I studied a lot of Far Eastern literature and thought, and wrote *Letters from Gourgounel*. In 1963, feeling I had unfinished business to do, I went back up to Scotland: taught modern French poetry at the University of Glasgow, set up a group called the Jargon Group devoted to 'cultural revolution' (no reference to Mao), and went on with my own writing. My very first book had been published in Paris, at the Mercure de France (*En toute candeur*, 1964), but my first English books, prose and poetry, came out from London (Jonathan Cape) between 1966 and 1968. By the end of 1967, I was back in France again. Britain seemed to me to have gone into a cultural slump from which it was not going to emerge for quite some time. When I presented my fourth manuscript in London, I was told it was 'great stuff,' but I should put it in the fridge for ten years, and in the meantime write a nice little novel to 'establish my reputation.' I said I didn't want to establish that kind of reputation. Another London publisher whom I went to see told me that I was definitely doing 'the real thing,' but that after all he was in the 'entertainment industry.' I said I liked to laugh as much as the next man, but that as a writer I didn't consider myself as part of the entertainment industry. That was the situation that was setting in: an industry of fast-food literature with, at the side, 'serious' writers all sounding as if they had gone through a creative writing course at the university and come out with quite good marks. Something a lot more radical and far-reaching had been going on in France. On the continent I felt that my intellectual family was Breton, Artaud, Daumal, Michaux.

"Back in France, I was just in time for the May '68 revolution, in which I participated, thereby losing the job I had at the university. Thereafter I spent nine years down there in the Pyrenees, publishing nothing, but writing away. As of 1970, I had a university job in Paris (I commuted every week from the Spanish border to the big city), and moved around a bit in Europe, in Asia (Hong Kong), Thailand, Japan) and America (from Montreal up to Labrador). I started publishing again in 1976 in Paris, with books (prose, poetry, essays) accumulated during the nine-years silence coming out at a rapid rate; to date about twenty full-length books in all. From the French, or sometimes from the original manuscripts, these books were translated into some other languages (German, Dutch, Spanish, Bulgarian, Polish. . . .) but were not appearing in English. I was in no hurry. In 1979, I defended a State Doctorate thesis in Paris on the theme of 'intellectual nomadism.' That same year, I took out French nationality papers (while not losing the British ones). And in 1983, I was appointed as professor to a newly created Chair of 20th-century Poetics at the Sorbonne: I do a course there on 20th-century American poetry and run a research seminar on 'world poetics.' That same year, I moved from the Pyrenees to the north coast of Brittany, where I now reside. Always this dialectic of being in touch with cities, but living on the periphery. . . .

"In 1989, I founded the International Institute of Geopoetics, and started up its review, the *Cahiers de Geopoetique*, which I continue to direct. In 1989, too, I renewed contact with English-language publishing. Since then, have appeared a collected longer poems, a collected shorter poems, three of the prose-narrative books I call way-books, but not yet the essay books. A very paradoxical situation is beginning to be cleared up. In some sense, I've lived in a kind of no man's land, with less and less respect for national contexts. That has its inconveniences: you are either totally neglected, or fired at from all sides. But at least you're not entrenched in convention, nor smothered in congestion. Anyway, whatever the outcome, here, in my outpost on the Breton coast, I get on with the work."

Like the Irish-born Samuel Beckett, Kenneth White, a Scot, has made his home and his literary career in France. In fact, however, he describes himself as "an intellectual nomad." As he wrote in *L'Esprit nomade*: "The intellectual nomad . . . leaves history's high road . . . and presses on into a landscape where sometimes there are no more roads . . . He must invent his geography for himself and more fundamentally, that deepening of geography which I have called geopoetics."

White combines the seemingly contradictory qualities of mystic and intellectual, his Celtic heritage, and wide reading in Eastern philosophies with his education in Western philosophy. "Nietzsche is the key philosophical foundation, the starting-point of White's work," Tony McManus wrote in *Chapman* in 1990. He embraces Nietzsche's nihilism as a necessary stage in the passage toward transcendence, clarity, or what, punning on his own name, he calls "le mode blanc"—absolute self-realization—in "At the Solstice" from *The Cold Wind of Dawn*:

I stand in my own inscrutable whiteness
and my heart is a blazing furnace
and I try to enlarge my soul
and I know that the deepest is the most alive
and I want nothing less than all.

White's work is rooted in the same force that impelled the English romantic poets and the 19th-century American transcendentalists—a determination to break free of the constrictions of modern urban industrial society. Glasgow, his birthplace, "with its bituminous deserts and its sinister fog," is emblematic of everything he has sought to escape. Melville, Emerson, Thoreau, and Whitman, all of them seeking oneness with the universe, served as models for him. He identifies with Melville's "ontological heroes," of whom he writes in *The Blue Road*, "There's a love of the world in them (as well as a disgust with what humanity makes of it), an immense, an *encyclopaedic* love, and an expense of their own persons that can amount to an ecstatic annihilation."

White writes both prose and poetry: the two forms moving in the same direction, with the poems, he says, "expressing more intense moments of concentration." Robin Fulton suggests that too often his poetry reflects "the mystic's pull towards wordlessness and the poet's ineradicable dependence on words." The challenge of communicating the abstract is also present in his prose, which is frequently indistinguishable from his poetry. But White rejects what he calls, in the preface to his prose work *Travels in a Drifting Dawn*, "the dreary and deadening" process of separating poetry and prose. Impressionistic and subjective as much of his prose is, it is also very much in touch with the earth. In a collection of his French-language essays, *La Figure du dehors* (The Outward Form, 1982), he writes, "If you want to renew your vision of things . . . it's a good idea to return to the landscape, where everything began." His several moves in the countryside of France and his frequent travels to the most isolated and remote areas of the world—the Hebrides, Labrador, northwestern Canada, northern Japan, southeast Asia—are results of that quest to reach into one's deepest roots in the universe.

White's first major prose work, *Letters from Gourgounel*, is a record of his life in a farmhouse in the south of France. "I was seeking a deserted place to center, from time to time, my life and my thought," he writes in *L'Itinérarie de Kenneth White* in 1990. "I found it in Ardèche, more precisely in the valley of the Baume in a place called Gourgounel." There White found an ideal spot for solitude and contemplation. But he also found sympathy with his sturdy neighbors, "a disappearing class . . . They hang on, but their old certainty and confidence has drained away . . . I do not idealize the peasants. But I would like to see a progress which was based on the substantial qualities of the human being rather than on the meaner ones." Alone but self-reliant, White repaired the dilapidated farmhouse and settled down to reading, reflection, and writing. In this simple life he achieved the transcendence he sought. As he sits under a plum tree:

> gazing at one particular branch which in itself concentrates all the richness and splendour I have come to feel in the world. . . . It is all the world I want, but I want it centered. I do not want merely to distract myself. I want to bring the whole world into myself, and into more than myself,—that plum branch there.

In a sense all of White's prose is travel writing, with journeys into remote parts of the world and journeys into his own psyche. *Pilgrim of the Void: Travels in South-East Asia and in the North Pacific* begins with his early awakening to

Eastern culture through his boyhood reading in the *Upanishads* and the *Tao te ching*. While studying philosophy in Munich in the 1950s he discovered the Japanese writings of Dôgen, Bankei, and Hakuin, which "hit my brain like lightning." He did not travel to the East until the early 1970s. His experiences there, as recorded in *Pilgrim of the Void*, are, not unexpectedly, spiritual: "It's neither a book about the East, nor a book about Buddhism, it's a book about a landscape—mindscape in which you no longer feel the need to talk about Buddha or whatever at all, you live it in and for yourself." But he also reports on the social and physical conditions of life around him with exuberant realism:

> We go to the grocery store kept by a Chinese family. Floor of beaten earth well swept. The woman offers tea and bananas. There's a Meo girl (black bodice, blue skirt, red sash, black leggings, thick silver ring round the neck) at the table, feeding noodles to an infant. Her dark full breasts show clearly through the slit in her bodice. She's not overwashed, but looks healthy as hell.

White's poetry displays the same eclecticism that marks his prose, alternating between such diverse and contradictory influences as Walt Whitman's free form and the Japanese tanka and haiku, Eastern Mysticism and Scottish regionalism. He writes in the Japanese-influenced "Obscure," in *Handbook for the Diamond Country*:

> Golden eagle
> red deer
> would be
> almost too much
>
> I'll settle for
> this arctic moss
> on the rock's
> obscure face

His Scottish aspect is paramount in "Walking the Coast," in *The Bird Bath*

> though I think too at times
>   of Donnacha ban nan Orain
>   whose wife
>   was a dandy whisky distiller—
> and of Alasdair MacMhaigstir Alasdair
>   the man who wrote the *birlinn*—
>   and of Iain MacCodrum nan Ron
> who wrote the rabelaisian
>   *Oran na Muice*
> and who chose an enormous and amorphous
> lump of gneiss
>   for his gravestone. . . .

White is an iconoclast, largely ignored by critics of the English literary mainstream, although since 1990 he has been enlarging his English readership. His most appreciative audience is in France, where he has received numerous honors, including the Grand Prix du Rayonnement Français of the French Academy for his work as a whole in 1985; in 1986 he was named Chevalier de l'Ordre des Arts et des Lettres; in 1987 he won the the Prix Alfred de Vigny. He has been the subject of many articles in French art and literary journals and of more than a dozen thesis at the University of Paris and elsewhere. In an homage to him collecte under the title *Kenneth White: L'Homme et l'Oeuvre* and published in 1987, Robert Brèchon expressed poetically White's importance as a liberating spirit, particularly to the French: "It has been twenty years since the wandering poet has appeared among us, / heralding a springtime for culture. / His welcome affirms that his coming has met expectations. / His success in the very domain / where system—Marxist theory,/psychoanalystic dogma, structuralist method—/has for so long caused intellectual terror to reign, / has been one of the signs of a thaw. / But the nature of poets makes them answer questions with more questions. / In his books, where mingle poems, / essays and travel notes, / Kenneth White does not himself posit a truth. / He opens a path. He extends / a thread for finding a way out of the labyrinth."

PRINCIPAL WORKS (IN ENGLISH): *Poetry*—Wild Coal, 1963; En toute candeur (poetry and prose, bilingual French-English), 1964; The Cold Wind of Dawn, 1966; The Most Difficult Area, 1968; The Bird Path: Collected Longer Poems, 1964–1988, 1989; Handbook for the Diamond Country: Collected Shorter Poems 1968–1990, 1990; In the Sand Parishes, 1990. *Nonfiction*—Letters from Gourgounel, 1966; Travels in a Drifting Dawn, 1989; The Blue Road, 1990. *Fiction*—Pilgrim of the Void, 1992.

ABOUT: Contemporary Poets, 5th ed., 1991; Fulton, Robin. Contemporary Scottish Poetry: Individuals and Contexts, 1974; Hamburger, M. The Truth of Poetry, 1969; White, K. The Blue Road, 1990; White, K. Letters from Gougounel, 1969; White, K. Pilgrim of the Void, 1992; White K. Travels in the Drifting Dawn, 1989. *Periodicals*—Chapman January 1990; Scotsman December 1, 1983; Times Literary Supplement October 20, 1989.

WHITNEY, PHYLLIS A(YAME) (September 9, 1903–　), American novelist and short story writer (adult and juvenile), Yokohama, Japan, the daughter of Charles Joseph Whitney and Lillian (Mandeville) Whitney. After living in Japan, where Charles Whitney was an American shipping line representative, the family moved to the Philippines and then to China, operating hotels in both countries until her father's death. Phyllis Whitney was fifteen when she came to

the United States with her mother, who was terminally ill with cancer; they lived in Berkeley, California, and San Antonio, Texas. When her mother died two years later, she went to live with an aunt in Chicago, where she graduated from McKinley High School in 1924. Lacking money to attend college, she worked at the Chicago Public Library and then in bookstores while dabbling in writing. It took her four years to place her first work, a short story, in the *Chicago Daily News*. Over the next three years she sold four stories to pulp magazines and Sunday school publications, which led her ino the field of children's writing. Whitney's first book, *A Place for Ann*, was a juvenile title published in 1941. From 1942 to 1946 she was children's book editor at the *Chicago Sun* and held the same position at the *Philadelphia Inquirer* from 1947 to 1948. She also taught juvenile fiction writing at Northwestern University, Evanston, Illinois, in 1945, and at New York University from 1947 to 1958.

For over thirty years, the careers of Whitney the children's author and Whitney the master of adult romantic suspense were entwined. Since the late 1970s her output has been mostly adult. Her juvenile fiction falls into two categories: novels about growing up and mysteries. Whitney addressed serious issues like racial prejudice, divorce, stepfamilies, and the plight of migrant workers. Given the nomadic nature of Whitney's own childhood, it is not surprising too that dislocation and the longing for domestic stability are among her favorite themes. In 1975 Whitney described her characters to *Parade* magazine as "out solving their own problems. They've always been women's libbers because I've always been a liberated woman . . . I've always done whatever I've wanted to do."

Whitney's first adult novel, *Red Is for Murder*, published in 1943, was a conventional mystery. Will Cuppy in the *New York Herald Tribune Weekly Book Review*, called it a "nicely written and sufficiently exciting yarn about two murders at . . . . a Chicago department store." Overall it was not "sufficiently exciting" enough to lure Whitney away from her successful juvenile career. She did not return to adult writing until the mid-1950s, but by the 1960s and 1970s she had become a best-selling writer of romantic suspense.

Settings are just as important in Whitney's adult novels as in her juveniles. According to Nancy Regan, in *Twentieth Century Romance and Historical Writers*, she chooses locales "for their romantic possibilities. Yet she avoids the predictably romantic American locations, those places which resonate loudest in the American psyche: the South, Los Angeles, New York." Whitney's young women find themselves enmeshed in danger in the Catskills, the Hamptons, New England, New Jersey, and the Poconos. Not all her suspense is domestic. Turkey, Japan, England, and the Caribbean are some of the exotic locales she has used. In *Listen for the Whisperer* a young woman journeys to Norway in search of her reclusive actress mother, who bore her illegitimately and then abandoned her. "This is a strongly plotted novel, and the background material on Norway is excellent," Marcia Muller wrote in *1001 Midnights*. "Whitney has the ability to make her reader see the scenery, feel the crispness of the air, taste the national foods; this wonderfully titled book makes the reader feel he has really been there."

Whitney's adult books are formulaic, and her readership knows exactly what to expect, while eagerly anticipating the details. Whitney calls this the "dear familiar landscape," and, judging by her popularity, it is not a familiarity that breeds boredom.

In *Hunter's Green*, *Best Sellers* reviewer Sr. M. Marguerite, RSM, found all the "required ingredients" for a typical gothic novel: "an ancient and history-crammed English estate; a gruff, dedicated and misunderstood owner; an elderly woman, a few characters that may or may not lead the reader to guess which one is the villain; and of course, a newcomer, an outsider, innocent and victim of intrigue." Sr. Marguerite noted, "One must admit that though the pattern is in general as unvarying as the rules for a sonnet or the recipe for a cake, there are always fresh approaches and the reader's attention is held."

In some of her later work, Whitney has attempted to bring modern issues to her tried-and-true format with mixed results. In 1984, Jane Stewart Spitzer wrote of *Rainsong* in the *Christian Science Monitor*, that current moral standards and the gothic formula don't mix. "The contemporary aspects of the plot and some of the characters' involvement in the music industry, in drug use, and in illicit sexual relationships are superimposed over the traditional elements—assumed identities, a past tragedy, and a brooding mansion, and a heroine in distress," she stated. "The effect is jarring, and *Rainsong* simply doesn't work. The contemporary aspects rob the story of any possible fairy-tale qualities the traditional elements might provide." But certain basic elements of Whitney's fiction seem to be timeless in their appeal. In her 1992 novel *The Ebony Swan*, Whitney again takes the reader to that "dear familiar landscape." After the death of her father, Susan Prentice returns to her childhood home, where she witnessed her mother's death in a fall twenty-five years before. What she encounters are people fearful of what she will remember, and the possibility that her mother's death was not an accident. In a starred review, *Publishers Weekly* called it one of her best efforts: "The suspense never falters, and Whitney wonderfully enriches her storytelling with the lush background of tidewater Virginia and well-integrated historical commentary."

Phyllis Whitney has been the recipient of numerous awards and honors, including the Agatha Award from Malice Domestic Teapot, and two Edgar Allan Poe awards from the Mystery Writers of America for best juvenile mysteries in 1960 (*Mystery of the Haunted Pool*) and 1963 (*Mystery of the Hidden Hand.*) She was also named grand master by the Mystery Writers of America for ther lifetime achievements. A widow, she lives near her daughter in Nelson Country, Virginia. Her manuscript collection is housed in the Mugar Memorial Library at Boston University.

PRINCIPAL WORKS: *Juvenile novels*—A Place for Ann, 1941; A Star for Ginny, 1942; A Window for Julie, 1943; The Silver Inkwell, 1945; Willow Hill, 1947; Ever After, 1948; The Mystery of the Gulls, 1949; Linda's Homecoming, 1950; The Island of Dark Woods, 1952 (reissued as Mystery of the Strange Traveler, 1967); Love Me, Love Me Not, 1952; Step to the Music, 1953; A Long Time Coming, 1954; Mystery of the Black Diamonds, 1954 (in U.K.: Black Diamonds); Mystery on the Isle of Skye, 1955; The Fire and the Gold, 1956; The Highest Dream, 1956; Mystery of the Green Cat, 1957; Secret of the Samurai Sword, 1958; Creole Holiday, 1959; Mystery of the Haunted Pool, 1960; Secret of the Tiger's Eye, 1961; Mystery of the Golden Horn, 1962; Mystery of the Hidden Hand, 1963; Secret of the Emerald Star, 1964; Mystery of the Angry Idol, 1965; Secret of the Spotted Shell, 1967; Secret of Goblin Glen, 1968; The Mystery of the Crimson Ghost, 1969; Secret of the Missing Footprint, 1969; The Vanishing Scarecrow, 1971; Nobody Likes Trina, 1972; Mystery of the Scowling Boy, 1973; Secret of the Haunted Mesa, 1975; Secret of the Stone Face, 1977. *Adult novels*—Red Is for Murder, 1943 (reissued as Red Carnelian, 1968); The Quicksilver Pool, 1955; The Trembling Hills, 1956; Skye Cameron, 1957; The Moonflower, 1958 (in U.K.: The Mask and the Moonflower); Thunder Heights, 1960; Blue Fire, 1961; Window on the Square, 1962; Seven Tears for Apollo, 1963; Black Amber, 1964; Sea Jade, 1965; Columbella, 1966; Silverhill, 1967; Hunter's Green, 1968; The Winter People, 1969; Lost Island, 1970; Listen for the Whisperer, 1972; Snowfire, 1973; The Turquoise Mask, 1974; Spindrift, 1975; The Golden Unicorn, 1976; The Stone Bull, 1977; The Glass Flame, 1978; Domino, 1979; Poinciana, 1980; Vermilion, 1981; Emerald, 1983; Rainsong, 1984; Dream of Orchids, 1985; The Flaming Tree, 1986; Silversword, 1987; Feather on the

Moon, 1988; Rainbow in the Mist, 1989; The Singing Stones, 1990; Woman Without a Past, 1991; The Ebony Swan, 1992. *Nonfiction*—Writing Juvenile Fiction, 1947, rev. ed. 1960; Writing Juvenile Stories and Novels: How to Write and Sell Fiction for Young People, 1976; Guide to Fiction Writing, 1982.

ABOUT: Contemporary Authors New Revision Series 25, 1989; Contemporary Literary Criticism 42, 1987; Current Biography 1948; Gleasner, D. Breakthrough: Women in Writing, 1980; The Junior book of Authors, 1951; Pronzini, B. and Muller, M. 1001 Midnights: The aficionado's Guide to Mystery and Detective Fiction, 1986; Something About the Author 30, 1983; Twentieth Century Children's Writers, 1983; Twentieth Century Crime and Mystery Writers, 1991; Twentieth Century Romance and Historical Writers, 1990. *Periodicals*—Best Sellers May 1, 1968; Christian Science Monitor April 6, 1984; New York Herald Tribune Weekly Book Review November 28, 1943; Parade November 2, 1975; Publishers Weekly May 4, 1992.

TOM WICKER

WICKER, TOM (THOMAS GREY) (pseudonym PAUL CONNOLLY) (June 18, 1926–), American journalist and novelist, writes: "I was born in the railroad town of Hamlet, North Carolina (population about 4,000), the son of a railroad conductor for the Seaboard Air Line (now about three mergers back) and an ambitious mother. My parents were not well-educated but they encouraged my sister and me to read, as they did. In my youth, this resulted primarily in my reading from cover to cover each edition of the *Saturday Evening Post*, which we received in the mail every Monday, and all the historical novels I could find in the Hamlet Public Library.

"These early reading habits led on to a much broader experience. Today, I consider myself reasonably well read, and have a particular fondness for Mark Twain, Faulkner, Conrad, Henry James, Jane Austen, García Márquez, and Graham Greene. Reading, it seems to me, as widely and as hungrily as possible, is the proper education of a writer.

"At Hamlet High School, in the early '40s, I was on the staff and subsequently the editor of the mimeographed *Sandspur*, our school newspaper, and discovered that the class papers I often had to write usually got good grades. I decided then that I would be a writer; and I have had no other ambition. At first this one rose only to the level of hoping to have a story appear someday in the *Saturday Evening Post*. (Never fulfilled; the *Post* did later publish some journalist's articles of mine, but no fiction.)

"I attended the University of North Carolina at Chapel Hill, first in the old Navy V-12 unit during World War II, later as a civilian. I was too devoted to good times to work on the *Daily Tar Heel* or the campus literary publications, but I still wanted to write; I found my favorite course in Professor Phillips Russell's creative writing class—part of the journalism department, where I eventually took my major.

"After graduation, I had to earn a living, particularly after I was married to Neva McLean on August 20, 1949—even more particularly after our two children, Cameron, a daughter, and Grey, a son, were born in 1954 and 1959. So I embarked on a career in journalism that led from the weekly *Sandhill Citizen* (circulation 1, 800) in Aberdeen, North Carolina, in 1949 to the *New York Times* in 1960. In between, I worked for the *Robesonian* (circulation 5,000), an afternoon daily in Lumberton, North Carolina; the North Carolina State Board of Public Welfare (as public relations director); the Winston-Salem, North Carolina, *Journal*; and the *Nashville Tennessean*. I was recalled to Korean War duty in the U.S. Navy (1952–1954) and served as ensign and lieutenant (junior grade) in Japan.

"I worked for the *Times* from 1960 until my retirement on December 31, 1991, at age 65, by which time I had been divorced (in 1973) and remarried (in 1974) to Pamela Hill, a talented producer of television documentary films. Throughout, I kept up my efforts to write fiction, working often early in the mornings before punching the clock for an employer and on weekends and holidays. This was not so much a matter of necessity as of ambition; and I have always believed that people can find the time to do what they *really want to do*.

"As a consequence, over the years, I have published nine novels and five books of nonfiction, all written in addition to my work as a journalist—which culminated in my writing a political column for the *Times* from 1966 through 1991. It is for this column, rather than my books, that I am primarily known.

"Reviewers and I generally agree that my best book was *A Time to Die*, a journalist's account of having been one of the outside negotiators during the doomed Attica prison revolt in 1971. I was able, in this work, to bring a novelist's technique to a journalist's observations—with better results, I believe, than either might have achieved alone.

"My novels have not been so well received. Critical reception has been mixed, suggesting that I tell a good story, write arresting dialogue, but tend to depict 'wooden characters who seldom come alive. My only best-seller was *Facing the Lions*, which remained on the *Times* best-seller list for 18 weeks, rising to third place.

"I hold, against the grain of my literary time, that fiction should primarily be narrative; its primary concern is *the story to be told*, with its consequent effects on the reader's emotions—the evocation of his or her pity or hatred, hope or despair, love, terror, compassion. The most direct appeal of fiction, as of all art, is to the senses.

"At age 66 (in 1992), with this idea firmly held, and if—as we say down South—the creeks don't rise, I plan to write one more book of nonfiction and several more novels. In retirement from journalism, I also am trying to learn how to write a screenplay, as the movies seem to me to have become the dominant medium of storytelling."

Although Tom Wicker is known primarily as a journalist and a columnist for the *New York Times*, he published six novels before writing his first nonfiction book. Three of his early thrillers—*Get Out of Town, Tears Are for Angels*, and *So Fair, So Evil*—were published under the pseudonym Paul Connolly. *The Kingpin* and *The Devil Must*, the first two novels on which he put his own name, appeared during his tenure at the *Winston-Salem Journal*.

As a staff reporter on the Washington bureau of the *New York Times* from 1960 to 1964, Wicker traveled the country covering congressional races and presidential appearances. Wicker was the only *New York Times* correspondent present in Dallas, when President John F. Kennedy was assassinated there on November 22, 1963. He filed his 106-paragraph account of the episode from a phone booth at the Dallas airport.

Wicker's first book of reportage, *Kennedy Without Tears*, is a recapitulation of his coverage of the Kennedy White House. While that book received only mixed reviews, his next effort, *JFK and LBJ: The Influence of Personality Upon Politics*, was more successful. In it, Wicker advances the thesis that the personality of a strong, individualistic leader is often the decisive factor shaping the politics of an era. Reviewing *JFK and LBJ* in the *New Leader*, Michael Janeway commented: "More successfully than in his earlier *Kennedy Without Tears*, Wicker combines the commanding overview of an historian with the earthy frankness of a working reporter. He is neither sentimental nor bitter."

Facing the Lions, Wicker's first novel to enjoy widespread critical and popular acclaim is an overview of the complex interplay between politics and journalism in Washington, D.C. Appropriately, the novel's two main characters are a senator and a reporter. Hunt Anderson is a charismatic southern senator who bears a more than passing resemblance to the Tennessee politician Estes Kefauver. Journalist Rich Morgan, like Wicker, is a son of the smalltown South. Trapped in a crumbling marriage, Morgan is tormented by what he perceives to be the triviality of his chosen profession. Jonathan Yardley wrote in the *Washington Post Book World*, "Tom Wicker has accomplished a rare and wholly laudable feat: he has written a novel about Washington in which the people are more important than the politics." Patrick Anderson noted in the *New York Times Book Review*: "The trap that undoes most journalists who turn to political fiction is that, trained to deal in external facts, they are unable to deal in internal truths; they understand process but not people. Wicker has seen this trap and avoided it. . . . *Facing the Lions* is . . . one of the best political novels you will ever read."

After prisoners at the Attica State Correctional Facility in New York rose up and took hostages in 1971, Wicker was among those "outsiders" invited by the prisoners to take part in the Citizen's Mediation Committee. The group attempted, without much success, to act as an intermediary between the prisoners and the authorities. The affair ended catastrophically, with more than forty hostages and inmates killed. In *A Time to Die*, Wicker intersperses an analysis of what went wrong at the prison with recollections of his own southern childhood. Throughout the book, he refers to himself in the third person, as "Wicker." Reviewing *A Time to Die* in the *New York Times Book Review*, Kurt Vonnegut Jr. noted, "He gives us within a single volume an objective account of a massacre, a melancholy autobiography and a demonstration of how difficult it is for a careful and experienced journalist to write angrily." Most reviewers lauded the book as a substantial achievement. In the *Nation* (1975), Robert E. Walters found Wicker a bit too lenient toward New York governor Nelson Rockefeller, whose "refusal to go to Attica when matters were at a stalemate was a prime factor in the slaughter." Walters concluded, however that "*A Time to Die* is an excellent and gripping account of a massacre that dramatized some appalling weaknesses in the fabric of our society." In the *New Republic*, Kay Boyle wrote: "Wicker's contribution to an understanding of the tragedy of Attica does not lie in his Faulkneresque excesses of rhetoric. . . . Wicker's contribution lies in his depictions of the various prison officials, as well as of Rockefeller's representatives, and also in his credible (if at time uncharitable) analyses of his fellow members of the observers' committee."

Wicker's book was not, of course, without its detractors. Conservative critic M. J. Sobran Jr., deriding Wicker's sympathy for the prisoners' plight, labeled him a "a sucker for the rebels." In his notice of *A Time to Die* in the *National Review*, Sobran wrote, "Wicker's fatuity makes this a terribly silly book, but his virtues make it moving; and the combination makes it embarrassing."

A Time to Die and Wicker's *New York Times* columns established him as one of America's most eminent liberal journalists. As a syndicated columnist with a uniquely prominent and influential platform—the Op-Ed page of the *New York Times*—Wicker has come under fire from critics on both the left and the right. A 1985 Wicker column critical of the Sandinistas prompted Alexander Cockburn to write in the *Nation* "Hypocrisy and misrepresentation . . . marked Tom Wicker's column in the October 21 *New York Times*, apropos the Nicaraguan emergency decree. My respect for Wicker took a severe plunge some time ago, after he started parroting the Reagan Administration's views about the late great Grenadian Maurice Bishop. But this time, Tom, it's all over between us." More frequently, Wicker has been assailed from the right. Rankled by Wicker's insistence that the late American sinologist Owen Lattimore had not been a Communist, conservative columnist William F. Buckley Jr. wrote in the *National Review* in 1989, "I assume that a Communist is pro-Communist, though . . . Wicker sometimes sounds as though it would be an act of McCarthyism to impute pro-Communism to Stalin, let alone Gorbachev."

In *One of Us: Richard Nixon and the American Dream*, which is more a consideration of Nixon's career in the overall context of American politics than a biography of the man, Wicker comes to an unexpected and unorthodox conclusion: Nixon's real accomplishments lay in the realm of domestic affairs, not foreign policy, the area in which he is usually given the most credit. "When I began," Wicker told *New York Times Book Review* interviewer Hal Goodman in 1991, "I also accepted the conventional view that foreign policy was Nixon's strong point. But I came to the conclusion that with the exception of the opening to China, Nixon's performance in foreign policy was not all that impressive." In the *New York Times Book Review*, Godfrey Hodgson wrote, "Wicker's knowledge, insight and fairness have enabled him to transcend the scuffle between the friends and the foes of Richard Nixon and to see him, instead, with all his strengths and weaknesses, as a more representative and a more tragically interesting figure than either the implausible heir of Metternich or the dark creation of liberal paranoia."

While the tone of *One of Us* is hardly adulatory, it is a far cry from the sometimes harshly critical posture columnist Wicker had taken vis-à-vis President Nixon. In his conversation with Goodman, Wicker called many of his scathingly anti-Nixon columns of the 1960s and 1970s "overstated and indignant." Wicker had himself been on Nixon's "enemies list" and was a contributor to the volume *White House Enemies: Or How We Made the Dean's List*. Thus, more than one reviewer of *One of Us* was startled, even dismayed, to find Wicker, Nixon's erstwhile nemesis, speculating about the former president's greatness. "In anointing Nixon as 'great,'" Stanley J. Kutler wrote in the *Christian Science Monitor*, "Wicker necessarily minimizes Watergate, more or less rationalizing the president's actions as something 'everyone' did. Historians will not dismiss Watergate as lightly."

Completed shortly after his retirement from the *New York Times*, Wicker's novel *Donovan's Wife* centers on the spectacle of a sleazy no-holds-barred Senator campaign. In the *New York Times Book Review* Linda Wertheimer called it "a bitterly funny look at . . . politics . . . today." She commented that in "the world of *Donovan's Wife*, candidates are chosen because they are photogenic, issues are picked by pollsters, and politicians with vestigal convictions are urged to forget their toy hired handlers. . . . Wicker has created a cartoonish political campaign and just barely beat the politicians to it." Max Boot, in the *Christian Science Monitor*, remarked that agree or not, "oldstyle campaigns were more honorable than today's variety . . . *Donovan's Wife* is a highly readable, sometimes savage satire on today's 'sleaze' politics."

Wicker has indicated that he intends to continue writing novels; these may or may not be bound by the conventions of his past work. "A columnist is not necessarily required to look ahead ten years and think that what he's going to think," Wicker told interviewer Hal Goodman in their discussion of *One of Us.* Tom Wicker the novelist might well claim this same freedom.

PRINCIPAL WORKS: *Novels*—Kingpin, 1953; The Devil Must, 1957; The Judgment, 1961; Facing the Lions, 1973; Unto This Hour, 1984; Donovan's Wife, 1992; As Paul Connolly—Get Out of Town, 1951; Tears Are for Angels, 1952; So Fair, So Evil, 1955; *Nonfiction*—Kennedy Without Tears: The Man Beneath the Myth, 1964; JFK and LBJ: The Influence of Personality Upon Politics, 1968; (with others) White House Enemies: Or How We Made the Dean's List, 1973; A Time to Die, 1975; On Press, 1978; One of Us: Richard Nixon and the American Dream, 1991.

ABOUT: Contemporary Authors New Revision Series 21, 1987; Contemporary Literary Criticism 7, 1977; Current Biography Yearbook 1973; Who's Who in America 1992–1993. *Periodicals*—Christian Science Monitor March 27, 1991; October 1, 1992; Nation April 26, 1975; November 2, 1985; National Review April 25, 1975; August 18, 1989; New Leader May 20, 1968; New Republic March 15, 1975; New York Times November 17, 1992; New York Times Book Review June 3, 1973; March 9, 1975; March 10, 1991; October 25, 1992; Newsweek February 25, 1991; Southern Literary Journal Fall 1986; Washington Post Book World June 3, 1973.

WIGGINS, MARIANNE (November 8, 1947–), American novelist and short story writer, was born in Lancaster, Pennsylvania, one of two daughters of John Wiggins and Mary Klonis. Her father was a farmer who worked in a gorcery store after losing his land, but his primary vocation was preaching in the church that his father had founded, characterized by Wiggins in an interview with *Publishers Weekly* as "a Bible-beating, reactionary kind of church." Wiggins described her father, who eventually committed suicide, as "a man who was repressed in every way—didn't drink, didn't smoke, and yet . . . he chose to marry an exotic woman." Wiggins's mother was from a Greek immigrant family and was of the Greek Orthodox religion. After being raised as a fundamentalist Christian until she was nine, Wiggins was baptized into her mother's faith. "I left those wooden pews for rooms full of icons and incense and men in robes," Wiggins recalled.

Wiggins was a sickly child and spent long, bedridden hours reading books. Reading the

MARIANNE WIGGINS

works of Eugene O'Neill convinced her to become a playwright, and she began writing plays in high school. Following her high school graduation in 1965, she married Brian Porzak, and they moved to Europe, where he was employed as a film distributor. According to Wiggins, after three years in Europe "I felt I had fallen one step outside my generation. I wanted to be back in the States." Three years after they returned, she and her husband divorced. Wiggins, who by that time was twenty-three and had a three-year-old daughter, had never before supported herself. She began working as a typist in a stockbrokers' firm in White Plains, New York, and after four years, she herself became a stockbroker, the only regular, fulltime job she has ever held.

During this period, she wrote *Babe*, her semi-autobiographical first novel about a single mother. Her comic second novel, *Went South*, centers on Megan, a woman in her early thirties with a young daughter who, unhappy with her ridiculous husband and bored with her life in rural New Jersey, learns to take control of her life. The reviewer in *Publishers Weekly* wrote, "The portrait of this wife and mother beset, the bonds she struggles against, the small risks that lead to bigger ones, is sharply and perceptively drawn."

Wiggins's third novel, *Separate Checks*, was more innovative and attracted more critical attention. It was composed of a series of stories written by Ellery McQueen (the daughter of a mystery writer) as therapy while she is recovering from a nervous breakdown. In an effort to sort through her dysfunctional family, she writes about her aunts and cousins, all of whom are slightly off kilter. In the *New York Times Book Review* Judy Bass observed that the novel "resembles Sylvia Plath's *The Bell Jar* gone haywire" and complained that it lacked "cohesion, lucidity and poignancy." Although acknowledging the book's awkward construction, Mary Kathleen Benet was nonetheless more favorable in the *Times Literary Supplement* calling the writing "modern and knowing" and crediting Wiggins's facility with description. Around this time Wiggins met Salman Rushdie, whom she was to marry in 1988.

Herself in Love, Wiggins's first short story collection, was notable for the complexity and diversity of the works and the thoughtfulness and verve of the writing. In the *Times Literary Supplement*, John Clute noted that many of the characters are in some way exiled. "Dense, spiky, guarded and extremely competent, these tales speak in barbed, self-sufficient rhythms of making a life in strange surroundings," he wrote. While praising the sharpness of Wiggins's prose, he also observed that "at times the urge to create tales of a self-sufficient compression leaves a sense of almost inextricable knottedness, or of a sleight-of-hand virtuosity that demands rereading without necessarily rewarding it." In the *New York Times Book Review*, Jonathan Penner complimented Wiggins's ability to "choose words as one might draw rare fabric over bathed skin," but complained about obscurity of the stories and the difficulty in unraveling the characters' relationships. Nonetheless, he concluded that the works arise "from a questing mind. Their greatest merit is their exclusion of unexamined language. One warms to their originality even while wishing it lay more in discovery, and less in invention."

The germ of *John Dollar*, Wiggins's next novel, arose from her rereading of William Golding's *Lord of the Files*. She thought, "Girls wouldn't do it this way," she recalled in an interview with the *New York Times Book Review*. As a result, she decided to write "a kind of female *Lord of the Flies*. And I wanted it to be about the British form of empire." In the novel, set in 1919, a group of British families living in Burma set out to rename an island in honor of King George. They hire as their guide a sailor named John Dollar. After a tidal wave, some girls are stranded on an island with Dollar, the only adult survivor, who has become paralyzed from the waist down. In creating their own society, the girls develop rules and rituals, particularly with regard to Dollar, whom they make into a Christ-like figure. The girls are driven mad after witnessing cannibalism, which they eventually mimic, eating pieces of Dollars's legs in a religious ritual. Wiggins told Caryn James in a *New York Times* interview that cannibalism "is the ultimate taboo masked in all our religious rituals, particularly Christianity, the body of Christ, taking the bread and wine. The men who thought up religion knew exactly what they were doing, playing on people's deepest fears." James termed the novel a "lyrical and effectively savage critique that means to undermine some foundations of western civilization—patriarchy, imperialism, colonialism and the rituals of Christianity."

Most reviewers found the novel highly effective, particularly in its ability to shock. Michael Gorra wrote in the *New York Times Book Review* that Wiggins has "a prose simultaneously spare and lush, as precisely opulent as a diamond solitaire—darting, telegraphic, cutting quickly from one scene, one tense, one point of view to another. That style gives the novel an almost cinematic speed and objectivity." Although Gabriele Annan complained in *New York Review of Books* that Wiggins's characterizations are often inconsistent and that her "prose is sometimes careless and sometimes overdecorated with adjectives like 'murrhine' and 'vitelline,'" she applauded her skill at evoking sensation. Annan remarked that Wiggins's special ability to cross "some kind of frontier of perception. . . . [She is] even more effective when she's dealing with horrors: she begins by making one's scalp crawl with physical revulsion, then leads one by an ever clammier hand into a state of existential shock." Writing in the *New Republic*, Anne Tyler noted how Wiggins uses humor to make the horror even more shocking observing that "you're reading cheerily along and you suddenly say, Wait. they did *what*? And you go back and read again to make sure, and the truth finally hits you with a sickening punch to the stomach. But precisely what gives the punch its oomph is that you were, indeed, reading *cheerily* along." Tyler also complimented Wiggins's "crip, firm, authoritative sentences" that leave one "feeling hammered and bruised by all that's happened," yet she concluded that the book is "oddly healing. When you set aside *John Dollar*, what hangs on is not the horror of the story but the pleasure in the way it was told, and an abiding respect for a next-to-impossible task most elegantly accomplished."

The publication of *John Dollar*, which had more publicity and a much larger print run than any of Wiggins's earlier books was soon overshadowed. Salman Rushdie had drawn the wrath of Muslim fundamentalists who believed that his novel, *The Satanic Verses*, was blasphemous. When Ayatollah Khomeini of Iran issued a *fatwa*, ordering the pious to kill him, Wiggins and Rushdie, who had been married about a year when the controversy erupted, went into hiding together, forcing Wiggins to cancel a tour promoting her own book. After five months during which they moved every few days, Wiggins reemerged in the world, denying rumors of marital difficulties, citing her desire to live a normal life and her need for more varied experiences to maintain her vitality as a writer, saying "If I had stayed in isolation, then isolation would have become our subject." By the time her next book, *Bet They'll Miss Us When We're Gone*, was published in 1991, the couple had announced they were divorcing. In the London *Times*, Wiggins criticized Rushdie, who was still in hiding, saying he was self-obsessed and thought only of his own career, rather than aligning himself with other persecuted writers.

Each of the stories in *Bet They'll Miss Us* is accompanied by the date and place of composition, which range from 1979 to 1990 in locations from the Virginia Tidewater to Amsterdam to London. The collection's most commented-upon stories were those that were the most obviously autobiographical, such as "Zelf-Portret," in which a woman, upon visiting Anne Frank's house, ruminates about being in hiding. In "Croesco i Gymru," the narrator, whose name is Marianne, writes, "We were on the lam in Wales, running through the Black Mountains like unarmed smugglers from the righteous with their guns." In the story, Wiggins offers intimate insight into a life in hiding, writing: "One night, watching news from elsewhere on the television, I saw the president of a bankrupt desert nation speak into a microphone while an English-accented male voice-over translated his, the president's, intent to send a black arrow of revenge from that distant desert into my husband's heart."

In the *New York Times Books Review*, George Garrett said that the stories demonstrated an "extraordinary variety and . . . an almost assertive virtuosity," but found a common thread in their themes of "memory, its persistence and failure," and "language, the magic and the mystery of words, of real and imaginary names." Michiko Kakutani was more critical in the *New York Times* (1991), complaining that the older stories seemed "like flimsy sketches," while the newer ones "are of interest only insofar as they illuminate the experiences of the author and . . . Rushdie. Though they succeed in communicating a mood and a state of mind, they do not stand up as independent fiction: they flirt willfully with the facts we've read in newspaper stories and would probably not mean much (or even make a lot of sense) to someone ignorant of the circumstances of the author's life." While

crediting the "clear, intelligent and effective" writing of "Croeso I Gymru," Jean Hanff Korelitz observed in the *Times Literary Supplement* (1992) that the volume "conjures the uncomfortable but unmistakable image of its author ransacking her files for a decade's worth of pieces, too many of which seem written in haste."

In 1989, Marianne Wiggins received grants from the National Endowment for the Arts and the Whiting Foundation. She has one daughter from her first marriage.

PRINCIPAL WORKS: *Novels*—Babe, 1975; Went South, 1980; Separate Checks, 1984; John Dollar, 1989; Eveless Eden, 1995. *Short stories*—Herself in Love, 1987; Bet They'll Miss Us When We're Gone, 1991.

ABOUT: Contemporary Authors 130, 1991. *Periodicals*—New Republic March 27, 1989; New York Review of Books June 15, 1989; New York Times February 28, 1989; April 4, 1990; June 14, 1991 New York Times Book Review April 8, 1984; October 18, 1987; February 19, 1989; June 30, 1991; Publishers Weekly June 13, 1980; February 17, 1989; Times (London) March 31, 1991; Times Literary Supplement November 2, 1984; May 22, 1987; March 6, 1992; Writer's Digest February 1991.

WILL, GEORGE F(REDERICK) (May 4, 1941–), American journalist and political commentator, was born in Champaign, Illinois, the son of Frederick L. Will, a professor of philosophy at the University of Illinois, and Louise Will, a high school teacher who later edited a children's encyclopedia. He had described his childhood as a happy time. A devoted fan of the Chicago Cubs, he was obsessed with baseball. Professional baseball has since become one of the defining passions of his adulthood, and Will has written extensively about the sport. As an undergraduate at Trinity College in Hartford, Connecticut, Will was the sports editor of the school paper; for the most part, he was an indifferent student. In a 1990 interview with *Publishers Weekly*, he admitted that "the spark didn't hit the kindling of intellectual life until the time between my junior and senior years in college." Like his parents, Will was a Democrat; even though he was too young to vote, he was cochairman of the Trinity Students for Kennedy in 1960. In his senior year, he became editor of the school paper.

After receiving his B.A. from Trinity in 1962, Will enrolled in Magdalen College, Oxford University. During his two years in England, Will's political philosophy underwent substantial transformation, his tepid liberalism evolving

GEORGE F. WILL

into devout conservatism. At Oxford he came into contact with disciples of Friedrick von Hayek, Milton Friedman, and other free-market economic theorists. The Berlin Wall was another significant factor in Will's conversion. Traveling in Berlin, he helped an East German man escape to West Berlin by supplying him with an American military uniform. While some of Will's later views are markedly heterodox for an American conservative, he was resolute in his anticommunism, and steadfast in his disdain for the Soviet Union.

In 1964 Will returned to the United States to pursue further graduate study at Princeton University, where he earned a Ph.D. in politics in 1967. His doctoral dissertation, "Beyond the Reach of Majorities: Closed Questions in the Open Society," is critique of the liberal ethic of absolute tolerance and prefigures much of his later work. Will taught political science briefly: at Michigan State University from 1967 to 1968 and at the University of Toronto from 1968 to 1969. In 1970, eager to take a more active part in politics, he joined the staff of Colorado Senator Gordon Alcott, then chairman of the Republican Policy Committee. While he was on Alcott's staff, he began publishing articles in William F. Buckley Jr.'s *National Review*. Will lost his staff position after Alcott was defeated for reelection in 1972. In 1973 Will became the Washington editor of the *National Review*, a post he held until 1975. During his tenure with the *National Review*, Will began contributing op-ed articles to the *Washington Post*; his *Post* column was nationally syndicated in 1973 and in

1974 it began appearing regularly, twice a week. Since 1976, he has been a contributing editor at *Newsweek*, where his now well-known biweekly column appears on the back page. In 1977 he was awarded the Pulitzer Prize for distinguished commentary.

In many respects, Will is part of a new breed of political commentators. For one thing, he has never worked as a "hard news" reporter. For another, he has not confined himself to print media, having long been a regular fixture on various television news and opinion programs. From 1979 to 1984, he was a panelist of "Agronsky and Company." In 1981 he began appearing regularly on ABC's "This Week with David Brinkley." The hour-long Sunday morning discussion show has made Will a household name even among non-newspaper readers. He has also been an occasional commentator for ABC's "World News Tonight." In at least one case, Will has blurred the distinction between political commentator and political actor. In 1980 he helped candidate Ronald Reagan prepare for debate against President Jimmy Carter. Will later appeared on television, praising Reagan's performance but neglecting to mention his own role as debate coach. While the incident provoked some accusations of conflict of interest, it did not diminish Will's prestige or influence.

Will's first two books, *The Pursuit of Happiness, and Other Sobering Thoughts* and *The Pursuit of Virture, and Other Tory Notions*, are both collections of his previously published columns. In his third book, *Statecraft as Soulcraft: What Government Does*, Will attempts to clarify the principles that underlie and guide his thought. In his preface, Will writes, "My aim is to recast conservatism in a form compatible with the broad popular imperatives of the day, but also to change somewhat the agenda and even the vocabulary of contemporary politics." Unlike most conservatives, who decry any manifestation of "big government," Will is a vigorous defender of the welfare state: "A welfare state is certainly important to, and probably indispensable to, social cohesion, and hence to national strength." Distinguishing himself also from conservatives of a libertarian bent, Will most emphatically believes that it is precisely the business of the government to legislate morality: "By the legislation of morality I mean the enactment of laws and implementation of policies that proscribe, mandate, regulate, or subsidize behavior that will, over time, have the predictable effect of nurturing, bolstering or altering habits, dispositions and values on a broad scale."

Will perceives a widespread social benefit in

a variety of laws—those mandating civil rights, as well as those restricting access to abortion, drugs, or pornography. Departing from his student philosophy at Oxford, and further separating himself from American conservatives, Will supports restraints on the free-market economy and favors higher tax rates for the well-to-do. Because he views all political choices as moral choices, he argues for a species of strong government conservatism, one which is necessarily concerned with the "inner lives" of citizens. This, in Will's estimation, is the essence of statecraft as soulcraft. Defending the concept, he writes: "My point is that statecraft *is* soulcraft. It is by its very nature. Statecraft need not be conscious of itself as soulcraft; it need not affect the citizens' inner lives skillfully, or creatively, or decently. But he added, "one thing that it cannot be, over time, is irrelevant to those inner lives."

Will espouses what he calls "a 'European' conservatism." Appropriately, the "heroes" of his book include such exemplars of the creed as Benjamin Disraeli, John Cardinal Newman, and, above all, Edmund Burke. Among Will's "villains" are such liberal individualists as Machiavelli, Hobbes, and Locke. While true conservatives, Will insists, have always endorsed a strong government in the service of a moral polity, the liberals have consistently derogated the coercive aspects of government as a necessary evil. Using Burke as his standard, Will concludes that, in America today, "there are almost no conservatives, properly understood."

Given Will's support for a strong, even paternalistic, government, it is not surprising that his book enraged some conservative reviewers. "This is conservatism, properly understood?" an irate and perplexed Joseph Sobran asked in the *National Review*. "I call it a toothless, coffeetable Toryism, nicely calculated for liberal consumption, but short on serious answers. . . . " Liberal reviewers were not pleased with *Statecraft as Soulcraft* either, though many accorded it some measure of respect. "What must be said in favor of George Will is that he stepped far outside the inch-wide range of normal political analysis in an attempt to explain our predicament," James Fallows wrote in the *Atlantic*. However, Fallows faulted Will on a number of fronts, primarily his inability "to explain what his high-flown concepts would mean when applied to real life." In the *New York Times Book Review* (1983), Michael J. Sandel lauded Will's attempt to integrate politics and morals. "Still," Sandel wrote, "*Statecraft as Soulcraft* leaves a lurking worry. Missing from it is any clear commitment to democracy."

Despite the mixed reception of *Statecraft as Soulcraft*, Will and his ideas continued to enjoy widespread prestige in the upper echelons of Republican politics throughout the 1980s. In a long and respectful assessment of Will's work in the conservative journal *Commentary*, James Nuechterlein noted that Will was usually at his best when writing columns dealing with specific issues. "His columns," Neuchterlein wrote, "taken together, offer a richer and more satisfactory (if less systematic) public philosophy than does his book. . . . *Statecraft as Soulcraft* too often lacks the anchor of particularity." With the rise of the campus "culture wars" of the 1990s, Wills's book, concerned as it is with political morality, once again became the focus of some debate. In his book *Politics by Other Means*, a critique of both conservative and radical social theorists, David Bromwich writes: "*Statecraft as Soulcraft* is a short and repetitious book. But it was taken seriously in the Reagan administration; and, since it comes as near as we are likely to get to a full statement of Will's creed, it is worth examining closely."

Despite his close ties to Ronald Reagan, Will became increasingly critical of the president toward the end of his second term. In *The New Season*, for example, a preview of the 1988 election, Will wrote disapprovingly of Reagan's mounting budget deficits and contended that the much-vaunted "Reagan Revolution" had never really occurred.

Professional baseball is the subject of *Men at Work*, Will's only nonpolitical book. He breaks the game down into four fundamental specialities and examines an exemplary practitioner of each: Orel Hershiser (pitching), Cal Ripken Jr. (fielding), Tony Gwynn (batting), and Tony La Russa (managing). In an enthusiastic notice of the book in *New York Review of Books* Stephen Jay Gould wrote: "I am a card carrying (dare I utter the word?) liberal, Will an equally self-identified writer of conservative bent. On baseball, however, we differ little. . . . "

In *Restoration: Congress, Term Limits, and the Recovery of Deliberative Democracy*, his eighth book, Will delineates a breakdown in the American political process whose symptoms include corruption, gridlock, and a crisis of confidence. While *Restoration* is less philosophically ambitious than *Statecraft as Soulcraft*, It is more focussed on specifics and more prescriptive. Will's essential recommendation is that Congress be reformed so that it can stand up to an overburdened and increasingly all-powerful executive branch. Fundamental to this reform, in Will's view, is the imposition of congressional term limits: he would allow no member of the House or Senate to serve longer than twelve years. One of the goals of term limits, as he conceives them, is the recovery of "deliberative democracy," a government in which representatives would not be forever at the beck and call of clamorous interest groups. In the *New York Times Book Review*, (1992), Joseph A. Califano noted: "*Restoration*, which roams across the lines of polemic, sermon and diatribe, is a biting, humorous and often perceptive shifting of much of the sand that fouls the national political machinery. . . . As a brief for term limits, however, . . . Will's book is far from persuasive."

In his review of *Restoration* for the *National Review* William F. Buckley, Jr. had lavish praish for Will's work both as a writer and a television commentator and called him "the most under-celebrated benefactor of the conservative movement in my lifetime," a "surpassingly brilliant polemicist," and a "consummate stylist." If, as Buckley claims Will is in some way "under-celebrated," he is certainly not underexposed. In his various capacities as columnist, television commentator, and friend to a variety of powerful public officials, George Will has attained a degree of influence (and fame and wealth) rare among contemporary journalists.

For his own part, Will is inured to the controversies and the criticisms of his work. Married since 1967 to Madelaine C. Marion and the father of three children (one of whom was born with Down's syndrome), Will lives in suburban Maryland. He is, in many ways, a determined antimodernist, and not only regarding art and literature; he writes his regular columns by hand, with a fountain pen. He does not view himself so much as an opinion maker as an opinion confirmer, noting that readers of op-ed columns have usually made up their minds. "My popularity derives chiefly from putting into words what people are already thinking," he told William A. Henry III in *Esquire*. " I do not change minds, because I preach to the converted. . . . Who would want to live in a country where journalists had real power, where poeple would be blown around like leaves by the gusts of public opinion? That would be a silly country."

PRINCIPAL WORKS: The Pursuit of Happiness, and Other Sobering Thoughts, 1978; The Pursuit of Virture, and Other Tory Notions, 1982; Statecraft as Soulcraft: What Government Does, 1983; The Morning After: American Successes and Excesses 1981–1986; The New Season: A Spectator's Guide to the 1988 Election, 1987; Men at Work, 1990; Suddenly: The American Idea Abroad and at Home 1986–1990, 1990; Restoration: Congress, Term Limits, and the Recovery of Deliberative Democracy, 1992; The Leveling Wind: Politics, Culture, and other News, 1990–1994. *As editor*—Press, Politics, and Popular Government (by R. Bartley and others), 1972.

ABOUT: Bromwich, D. Politics by Other Means: Higher Education and Group Thinking, 1992; Burner, D. and West, T. Column Right: Conservative Journalists in the Service of Nationalism, 1988; Contemporary Authors 77–80, 1979; Contemporary Authors New Revision Series 32, 1991; Current Biography Yearbook 1981; Grauer, N. Wits and Sages, 1984; Hoeveler, J. Watch on the Right: Conservative Intellectuals in the Reagan Era, 1991. *Periodicals*—Atlantic May 1983; Christianity Today July 13, 1984; Commentary October 1983; Esquire January 1987; National Review June 10, 1983; November 16, 1992; New Republic November 10, 1986; New York Review of Books October 11, 1990; November 19, 1992; New York Times Book Review July 17, 1983; September 27, 1992; Publishers Weekly March 16, 1990; Washington Monthly October 1987.

WILLIAMS, T(HOMAS) HARRY (May 19, 1909–July 6, 1979), American historian and biographer, was born in Vinegar Hill, Illinois, which he once described as located "an axe handle and a twist of tobacco" from the birthplace of Ulysses S. Grant, Galena, Illinois. William Dwight Williams, his father, who had at one time been a schoolteacher, was a sheep farmer. When his mother, Emeline Louisa Collins Williams, died, only two years after the boy's birth, his father moved with his son to Hazel Green, Wisconsin, in order to be near his family. There young Williams grew up under the watchful influence of his paternal grandparents. His father and his grandfather, both staunch liberals in the old midwestern Populist tradition, encouraged his reading, especially in history and the classics. After graduation from the local high school, he attended Platteville State College, a small teacher training college, completing his B.Ed. in 1931. With the country in the depths of the depression, he was unable to find a teaching position, and his father suggested that he take graduate courses at the University of Wisconsin. In 1932 he received his M.Ph. Degree and entered the doctoral program in American history. In 1936, still preparing his dissertation, Williams began teaching in the University of Wisconsin Extension Division. He took his Ph.D. in 1937, and a year later became an instructor in history at the University of Nebraska at Omaha. He remained there until 1941, when he joined the American history faculty at Louisiana State University. At LSU he became Boyd Professor of History in 1953, a post he held until his death in 1979. During these years Williams was a visiting professor at several universities, among them Colorado, Rhode Island, and Tulane. In the academic year 1966–1967 he was Harmsworth Professor of American History at Queen's College, Oxford. He had many academic honors, including degrees from Northland

College in 1953 and Bradley University. In 1957 he was awarded a Guggenheim fellowship. In 1937, while a graduate student, Williams married Helen M. Jenson, also a graduate student in American history. They were divorced in 1947, and in 1952 he married a colleague at Louisiana State University, Estelle Skolfield. They had a daughter.

Williams's Pulitzer Prize–winning biography of the flamboyant Louisiana governor and U.S. Senator Huey Long, who liked to call himself the "Kingfish," was the culmination of more than a quarter century of study of the history and politics of the American South. These studies began with his master's thesis on Benjamin Franklin Wade, one of the Republican radicals who had urged punitive measures against the South in the era of Reconstruction. His doctoral dissertation continued and expanded on this subject and was published in 1941 as *Lincoln and the Radicals*. Written in a lively and colorful style, the book displayed little sign of its academic origins, but its scholarship was impressive. "Aggressive, vindictive, and narrowly sectional," Williams wrote, "the radicals hated slavery with a bitter personal feeling. But more than slavery they hated its political representatives, the proud cavaliers who had dominated Congress in the fifties and who had scourged the sputtering radical minority with polished gibes." The only reservation expressed by some reviewers was that Williams drew too dark and unrelieved a portrait of these "Jacobins," as he called them. Nevertheless, it was agreed that *Lincoln and the Radicals* was a significant contribution to Civil War history. Even in this, his first book, Williams displayed a flair for dramatizing history that reflected his boyhood reading of historians like Thomas Macaulay and Thomas Carlyle. Concluding with Lincoln's assassination and the descent of the radical carpetbaggers upon the South, Williams wrote: "Hysteria and rage engulfed the country . . . As the fury of the people blazed higher, the Jacobin leaders again raised their cry for vengeance upon the South. Now there were none to oppose them. Ironically, Lincoln's death had killed also his policy of mercy. The vindictive spirit of the Jacobins became the faith of the nation."

The South, which was to be the center of Williams's future work, became his home in 1941 when he moved to Baton Rouge to teach at Louisiana State University. Thanks largely to the energies of Huey Long, who was assassinated in 1935, LSU had become a major southern university with a distinguished faculty and a thriving university press. Through a Yankee in an atmosphere still haunted by the spirit of the Confederacy, Williams was a popular teacher at LSU,

his course on the Civil War attracting many students, a number of whom went on to complete their doctorates under his direction. As a scholar who would increasingly turn his attention to Southern history, Williams was sympathetic but objective. Estelle Williams, his widow, wrote in her introduction to the *Selected Essays of T. Harry Williams*: "Although he loved the South, Harry could see its shortcomings. He had the advantage of an outsider's view of the region. But because he lived in the state through its transition from the Old South to the New South, he could look with pride and admiration upon the progress made by his adopted region, particularly on the racial question."

In 1948, the publisher Alfred Knopf suggested that Williams round out his Civil War studies with a book that was published four years later as *Lincoln and His Generals*. Thanks to his sense of the dramatic and his interest in human character, Williams managed to produce a book on military strategy that was also a popular success. It had a large sale in both hardcover and paperback editions and was a Book of the Month Club choice. The particular distinction of *Lincoln and His Generals* among the plethora of books on the Civil War is that it was the first to argue that the winning strategy was initiated not by the Union generals but by the president: "My theme is Lincoln as a director of war and his place in the high command and his influence in developing a modern command system for this nation." In what was "the first of the modern total wars," Williams argued, Lincoln was "a great natural strategist, a better one than any of his generals . . . [and] did more than Grant or any general to win the war for the Union." Allan Nevins, in the *Saturday Review*, judged *Lincoln and His Generals* "an able and fascinating book," and Jay Monaghan, in the *New York Times Book Review* wrote, "As a scholar . . . Williams has drawn his facts from fundamental sources, and as a story teller he displays a craftsmanship that holds the reader in suspense even when he knows exactly how the incident ends."

Regional history was the background for Williams's next major work, a biography of the Creole P.G.T. Beauregard—not a great general, in Williams's account, but a grim and purposeful soldier . . . the most colorful of all the Confederate generals. He had more glamor and drama in his Gallic-American personality than any three of his Anglo-Saxon colleagues in gray rolled into one." Concentrating as much on Beauregard's postwar history as a businessman and social leader in New Orleans as on his military career, Williams brought to life a much neglected figure and, even more important, threw light on the postwar economic history of the South.

Even after he began research for his major work, the biography of Long, Williams continued to write on military history. In 1956 he gave a series of lectures at Memphis State University, collected as *Americans at War: The Development of the American Military System*. Here, in three succinct essays he traces that system from its beginnings in the American Revolution through the Mexican, Civil, and Spanish-American wars up to the outbreak of World II.

Williams studied other Civil War generals in *McClellan, Sherman, and Grant* and Rutherford B. Hayes in *Hayes of the Twenty-Third*. All these works were based on original documents, letters, and diaries, and although their emphases were on military tactics, they were also notable for their incisive portraits of the generals themselves. One of his works-in-progress at the time of his death was *The History of American Wars from 1745–1918*, which was edited for publication by Estelle Williams.

Among the fascinations that the Old South had for Williams was its "romance," its isolation from the rest of the United States, "the Southern talent for fantasy" as he called it in a lecture in 1960 on "The Distinctive South." While the post–Civil War North moved into the modern world, "the South remained static, its economy and society not greatly different from the colonial period." With the emergence of backwoods political movements like Populism and Progressivism, however, in the 1890s, poor farmers and the working class began to challenge the entrenched political power of upper-class white society. It was out of such movements, Williams believed, that Huey Long emerged. That same lower-class constituency, aroused by the desperate economic conditions of the entire nation in the early 1930s, made his extraordinary career possible. In an address given at the Southern Historical Association in Atlanta in 1959, Williams placed Long squarely in the Populist tradition as a "mass leader" (he was using Eric Hoffer's classification here), a bold, brazen American political boss, not a potential fascist dictator: "It is possible that we have been too apologetic about and too patronizing toward all the Southern demagogues. Some of these were hopelessly confused and some were merely clowns. . . . But the best of them tried to do something for their people. . . . Bluntly, forcibly, even crudely, [Long] injected an element of realism into Southern politics. Above all he gave the Southern masses hope."

Williams had followed the career of Huey Long with interest even before he came to LSU, where many of his colleagues remembered Long well. Aware of new techniques of research that had developed in the Oral History project at Co-

lumbia University in the 1950s, Williams had the idea of recording the impressions of contemporaries of Long for a biography. In 1956, by coincidence, he received a letter from Long's son Russell, a U.S. senator himself, praising his biography of General Beauregard. Williams writes in the preface to *Huey Long: A Biography*, "I was so impressed by his appreciation of the scholarly approach to biography that I wrote to ask him if he did not think the time had come when an objective life of his father should be written." Long responded favorably and cooperated by suggesting the names of many of his father's associates whom Williams might interview. "I stressed to him that I would have to have an absolutely free hand in interpreting the facts." Long agreed, and Williams proceeded with the biography. It was not until 1964 that he was able to begin writing. He completed the 876-page book in 1968. On its publication in 1969 it became a national best-seller and in 1970 it won both the National Book Award and the Pulitzer Prize for biography. In his massively detailed account, Williams not only examined every record published or in manuscript that was available to him but, of equal and possibly even greater value, he interviewed some 300 living witnesses to Long's extraordinary life, ranging from personal friends and enemies to political colleagues, journalists, and virtually anyone he could find who had some connection with and memory of Long. The single exception was Huey Long's wildly erratic brother Earl, who himself became governor of Louisiana. Williams's mistake, he told Walter Clemons in an interview in the *New York Times Book Review* in 1969, was writing Earl long a formal letter requesting an interview: "I think that if I'd just barged into Earl's office, he would've told me whatever I wanted to know."

On a figure as controversial as Huey Long, scholarly detachment and dispassionate interest were difficult to maintain. Williams was candid about his own ambivalence. Freely admitting that Long was power-hungry and ruthless in his political dealings, Williams nevertheless confessed to a certain sympathy and respect for him. A writer of narrative, sometimes even anecdotal, history, Williams acknowledged that if he had a theory of history it was the "Great Man" theory articulated by Thomas Carlyle in *On Heroes, Hero-Worship, and the Heroic History*: "I believe," Williams wrote, "that some men, men of power, can influence the course of history. They appear in response to conditions; many give a new direction to history. In the process, they may do great good or evil or both, but whatever the case they leave a different kind of world behind."

Accordingly, as Williams told Clemons: "I started with a predilection for Huey, as a realistic operator who got things done that needed doing in a Southern state with a blind resistance to change. . . . I believe too . . . that certain men of power can change the course of history. I think Huey Long did that." From the opening chapter of the biography Williams portrays Long as a charismatic figure—"a pudgy pixie who could suddenly become a demon," a man set apart from others: "He excited people and he excited emotions, arousing in his relatively short but explosive career every feeling in the political spectrum—amazement and admiration, disbelief and disgust, love and hatred, and, with many individuals, cold apprehension." Williams was sensitive to the charges that as a contemporary of Hitler and Mussolini abroad and of Father Coughlin and Gerald L. K. Smith at home, Long cast a sinister shadow. The difference between Long and these men, Williams pointed out, was that Long made no appeal to racial bias and anti-Semitism. He declared his opposition to the Ku Klux Klan in unambiguous terms. "It was to help the people," Williams wrote near the end of *Huey Long*, "that Huey seized power and then more power. He was not a fascist and he did not want to become a dictator. But he had become obsessed with the conviction that he could not do what he had to do without reaching for more power. He could not tell himself whether he would ever have enough."

In the course of the book Williams traces the Long family history, Huey's boyhood, and emerging character in painstaking detail, recording every episode, however minor, that he could find in his subject's life. As Williams moves into the labyrinthine mazes of Louisiana politics and later on to the national political scene, the pace of his narrative accelerates. The technique of oral history gives the book an immediacy that is rare in political biographies.

E. M. Yoder, in the *Saturday Review*, was convinced that Williams "sustains his thesis that the man who dragged Louisiana kicking and screaming into the twentieth century is both misunderstood and underrated." Tom Wicker, in the *New York Times Book Review*, found the book "a monumental biography" that shows that "while the remarkable Kingfish may have been clown, menace, dictator, he was also a native political genius who was perhaps the only successful radical leader that American politics has produced." Wicker, however, regretted that the book was not more analytical and that it did not "shed much light on the origin and limits of Long's radicalism." The major limitation of oral history, as David Donald pointed out, is its inability to reveal the inner life of the subject.

"Despite Williams's researches, we are still puzzled as to what manner of man this was."

Williams responded to some of his critics in a lecture he delivered in 1977 to the American Historical Association. At that time he was planning to write a biography of Lyndon Johnson, a man to whom he was attracted, he said, as being, along with Lincoln and Long, "great power artists." He admitted to an admiration for such figures: "I like men who move things forward, who leave their world different, men who use power." To those who felt that Williams had not been sufficiently critical of Long, he responded that it was not the function of the biographer to make moral judgments: "His primary job is to try and get inside his subject's brain and to see the view of the world that person had."

PRINCIPAL WORKS: Lincoln and the Radicals, 1941; Lincoln and His Generals, 1952; P.G.T. Beauregard: Napoleon in Gray, 1955; (with R. N. Current and F. Friedel) A History of the United States, 1959; Americans at War: The Development of the American Military System, 1960; Romance and Realism in Southern Politics, 1961; McClellan, Sherman, and Grant, 1962; Hayes of the Twenty-Third, 1965; Huey Long, 1969; Selected Essays of T. Harry Williams (ed. E. Williams), 1983; The History of American Wars from 1745–1918, 1985. *As editor*—Selected Writings and Speeches of Abraham Lincoln, 1943; With Beauregard in Mexico, 1956; Abraham Lincoln: Selected Speeches, Messages, and Letters, 1957; Military Memoirs of a Confederate (by E. P. Alexander), 1962; Hayes: The Diary of a President, 1964.

ABOUT: Contemporary Authors New Revision Series 3, 1981; Dictionary of Literary Biography, 1983; Hesseltine, W. B. Sections and Politics, 1968; *preface to* Selected Essays of T. Harry Williams (ed. E. Williams), 1983. *Periodicals*—Nation November 3, 1969; New York Herald Tribune Book World November 1, 1969; New York Times Book Review February 24, 1952; November 2, 1969; Newsweek November 3, 1969; Saturday Review February 23, 1952; November 1, 1969.

WILSON, EDWARD O. (June 10, 1929–   ), American biologist, and educator, was born in Birmingham, Alabama, the only child of Inez (Freeman) and Edward Osborne Wilson, an accountant with the Rural Electrification Administration. His parents and teachers encouraged his early interest in the natural environment, and by the time he reached adolescence Wilson knew he wanted to become an entomologist. During his childhood, his father changed jobs often, living at various times in Washington, D.C., Florida, and Georgia, as well as in Alabama. For two years while they lived in Washington, Wilson made regular visits to the National Zoo and

EDWARD O. WILSON

the Smithsonian Institution, and when the family lived in Florida and Alabama he collected and studied insects. While he was a senior at Decatur Senior High School in Alabama, Wilson decided that he would specialize in the study of ants. Four years later, majoring in biology at the University of Alabama (class of 1949), he made his first contribution to science in a report on the fire ant, an imported insect that had become a pest in the Southeast.

After receiving an M.S. degree at the University of Alabama in 1950 and doing further graduate work at the University of Tennessee in 1950–1951, Wilson enrolled at Harvard University. While working there towards a Ph.D degree in biology, he took part in several field expeditions—to the Windward Islands and Mexico in 1953, to New Caledonia in 1954, and to Australia and New Guinea in 1955. He earned his Ph.D from Harvard in 1955. In 1956 he became an assistant professor of biology at Harvard, rising to become the Frank B. Baird Jr. Professor of Science in 1976. Since 1973 Wilson has also held the position of curator of entomology at Harvard's Museum of Comparative Zoology.

Long before Wilson published his first major book, *The Insect Societies*, in 1971, he had contributed many articles to scientific journals on social insects, principles of evolutionary theory, population ecology, and methodology of scientific classification. But it was *The Insect Societies* that first brought him to the notice of a wider audience. The reviewer for *Library Journal* called the book the "most masterful synthesis of knowledge of the social insects to appear in the last

half-century." Though not an easy book for non-scientific readers, it laid the groundwork for everything Wilson wrote later. Based on a thorough study of the biology and behavior of insect societies, it not only presents a vast amount of material previously published on the subject but incorporates this knowledge into the context of modern biology—from biochemistry to evolutionary theory and population ecology. In his conclusion, Wilson comments that "social insects have achieved most of the basic forms of learning employed by mammals." though they lack what is most visibly distinctive in the learning capabilities of the highest-level mammal societies. Thus, they are not believed to be capable of insight learning; they "apparently cannot duplicate the mammalian feat of reorganizing their memories to construct a new response in the face of a novel problem." They do not play, an attribute the author believes essential to social learning. They do not establish personal bonds, nor do they appear to recognize personal members of the group. Nevertheless, in the author's words, when the social insects *as a unit* are compared with nonhuman vertebrate society units, they "can equal or exceed the accomplishments" of the latter.

Having suggested in this first book that it should be possible to apply to vertebrate animals the "same principles of population biology and comparative zoology that have worked so well in explaining the rigid systems of the social insects," Wilson set himself the task of learning the vast literature on vertebrate social behavior. From this research, in 1975, came *Sociobiology: The New Synthesis*, in which the author, in a final chapter, suggested that since all social groups have learned to adapt to the environment by evolution, it should be possible to arrive at general principles concerning the biological properties of entire societies, including those of human beings.

Although *Sociobiology* was well reviewed in most scientific journals, it aroused a great deal of controversy in the wider community. Among those who protested, the Columbia anthropologist Marvin Harris and the Harvard biologist Richard Lewontin contended that, contrary to Wilson's view, cultural and environmental forces alone shape man's behavior. Undeterred, Wilson went on in 1978 to write *On Human Nature*, describing it as "an exploration," a work about science, not a work of science. In preparation for this book, Wilson read widely in the fields of human behavior and human civilization, then attempted to apply what he had recently learned to what he already knew about invertebrates and vertebrates. The time had come, he felt, to "close the gap" between what social scientists on the one hand, and biologists on the other, had been saying for some time in their own different ways. Could the natural sciences penetrate into the science of human behavior, involving the humanities and philosophy, he asked, and if so, how far?

Presupposing, as he does in the book, that "human emotional responses and the more general ethical practices based on them have been programmed to a substantial degree by natural selection over thousands of generations," he arrives at the speculation that "the general traits of human nature appear limited . . . when placed against the great backdrop of all other living species. . . . We are not entirely culture-bound . . . as some social scientists have maintained." One of our more problematical traits, for example, is innate aggressiveness, meaning not that this trait will develop in all environments but that it *will* develop in a specified set of environments. Culture plays a role here, giving the particular form to the innate predisposition to aggression. Therefore, with pacifism as a goal, it is up to scholars and political leaders, understanding that humans are programmed by natural selection to respond to the "imperatives of selfishness and tribalism," to "express this knowledge openly as part of a daily diplomatic procedure." Wilson expressed the hope that the widely separated fields of science and the humanities would eventually come together to help solve the great unsolved problems of the human race, and that scientific materialism would herald a new and "true sense of wonder . . . Unknown and surprising things await. They are as accessible (now) as in those days of primitive wonder when the early European explorers went forth and came upon new worlds."

Most reviewers found the book provocative and often persuasive, though some raised doubts about Wilson's hopes for solving the problem of human aggression, and others found Wilson's suggestion that scientific materialism might one day replace religion as a new enlightened mythology unsound. Nicholas Wade wrote in *New Republic* that this last particular idea was "grandiose and unappealing." Yet he too found the book "a splendid departure from the dead-hand canons of the scientific literature," pronouncing it clear, precise, and bold. When *On Human Nature* was awarded the Pulitzer Prize for general nonfiction in 1979, Wilson told an interviewer that "the Pulitzer is an affirmation that this is an important new area of thought. It's not necessarily a certification that I'm right, but an affirmation that this is an important thing we should be talking about."

Wilson's *The Diversity of Life* moves into a different domain—that of ecology; instead of confronting the idea, as he had previously, of how biology affects humans, the author this time questions how humans are affecting biology. While celebrating the diversity of life on earth, Wilson argues that humans appear to be on the verge of precipitating a biological disaster as great as any in evolutionary history. Because of the human population explosion of the late 20th century, causing a continually increasing need for new agricultural land and grazing pastures, man is wiping out species and ecosystems at an unprecedented rate. At the current rate of species extinction, Wilson argues, twenty percent of those species now existing will become extinct in the next thirty years. Why is this important? Because, says Wilson, many thousands of species that we take for granted, microbes included, contribute to the biological recycling processes that purge the air, soil, and water of toxins and wastes. Wipe out one of them and we may be endangering an entire ecosystem.

Once again Wilson's thinking aroused controversy. David Rapineau, reviewing the book in the *New York Times*, commented that "the real question, though . . . Wilson does not emphasize it, is not whether biodiversity is worth saving, but who is going to pay for it. For better or worse, most of the threatened species are in countries with few economic resources, countries where the concern for diversity is likely to be viewed as a luxury for the rich." John Teborgh, in *New York Review of Books*, made similar points, commenting: "Both the argument that diversity enhances the quality of life and the ethical argument that man has no moral right to permanently destroy nature are eternal and irrefutable . . . but they are tragically lacking in persuasive force in our materialistic world." At the same time, both reviewers found the book stirring, original, and fascinating. The general consensus among reviewers was that *The Diversity of Life* educates, illuminates, and offers hope despite its pessimistic message.

In 1994 Wilson published his autobiography, *Naturalist*, which David Campbell in *Natural History* termed "a rich and nuanced odyssey, a reminiscence on discovery, society, science, intellectual fortitude, and of memory itself." In it, Wilson details his rueful reactions to the controversy generated by his theory of sociobiology. For example, he dubs the episode when demonstrators, chanting "Wilson, you're all wet," dumped a pitcher of ice water on his head at a meeting of the American Association for the Advancement of Science in 1978, possibly "the only occasion in recent American history on which a scientist was physically attacked, however mildly, simply for the expression of an idea." He defends himself against the charges of genetic determinism, but maintains that although "people have free will and choice to turn in many directions, the channels of their psychological development are nevertheless—however much we might wish otherwise—cut more deeply by the genes in certain directions than in others." And, Wilson concludes, "I prefer those scientists who drive toward daunting goals with nerves steeled against failure and a readiness to accept pain, as much to test their own character as to participate in the scientific culture." He is obviously referring to himself, and he has been given the opportunity in full to test himself, a test which most would consider he has passed with flying colors.

Wilson has taught and lectured at many places beyond the Harvard University campus. In 1972 he was the Hitchcock Visiting Professor at the University of California at Berkeley; in 1976 he gave the Messenger Lectures at Cornell University; during 1977 he lectured at the University of Pennsylvania, John Hopkins University, Dartmouth College, and McGill Unversity; from 1978 to 1981 he was the Tarner Lecturer at King's College, Cambridge University. Among the awards he has received are the National Medal of Science, given to him by President Jimmy Carter in 1977; the Mercer Award and the Founders Memorial Award from the Ecological Society of America in 1971 and 1972; the Distinguished Service Award from the American Institute of Biological Sciences in 1976; the Leidy Medal from the Academy of Natural sciences in 1979; and the Sesquicentennial Medal from the University of Alabama in 1981. He has also received honoray doctorates from Duke University and Grinnell College and is a member of the American Philosophical Society, American Genetics Association, World Wildlife Fund, National Academy of Sciences, American Academy of Arts and Sciences, German Academy of Sciences, and the Society for the Study of Evolution.

Wilson married Irene Kelley, a secretary and research assistant, in 1955; they have one child, Catherine Irene Wilson, and live in Lexington, Massachusetts. In *Naturalist*, he says that the people he admires most are "those who concentrate all the courage and self-discipline they possess toward a single worthy goal."

PRINCIPAL WORKS: The Insect Societies, 1971; Sociobiology: The New Synthesis, 1975; On Human Nature, 1978; (with C. J. Lumsden) Genes, Mind and Culture: The Coevolutionary Process, 1981; (with C. J. Lumsden) Promethean Fire: Reflections on the Origin of Mind, 1983; Biophilia: The Human Bond to Other Species, 1984; (with B. Holldobler) Journey to the Ants, 1990; The Diversity of Life, 1992; Naturalist, 1994.

ABOUT: Contemporary Authors Autobiography Series 16, 1992; Contemporary Authors New Revision Series 16; Current Biography Yearbook 1979; Turner, R. (ed.) Thinkers of the Twentieth Century: A Biographical, Bibliographical and Critical Dictionary, 1983; Who's Who in American 1990-191. *Periodicals*—Library Journal January 15, 1972; Natural History December 1994; New York Times October 4, 1992; October 16, 1994; New Republic November 11, 1983; New York Review of Books November 5, 1992; Times Literary Supplement August 13, 1993.

WINNICOTT, D(ONALD) W(OODS)

(April 7, 1896–January 28, 1971), British writer, pediatrician, child psychiatrist, and psychoanalyst, was born and raised in a nonconformist household in Plymouth, England. His parents, believers in the Wesleyan tradition of religious independence, refused to impose overly strict rules and regulations on their son, and in so doing allowed him the freedom to grow and arrive at his own ways of thinking and doing. One of Winnicott's later memories of his father, who for a time was mayor of Plymouth, was that "once when I asked him a question that could have involved us in a long argument, he just said: Read the Bible and what you find there will be the true answer for you. So I was left, thank God, to get on with it myself." Winnicott also recalled that he first became interested in studying medicine when he was sixteen; while in the sickroom at his school, having broken his collar bone on the sports field, he decided that the only way out of having to depend on doctors was to become one himself. He became fascinated reading Darwin's *Origin of Species* because it "showed that living things could be examined scientifically" and that gaps in knowledge need not be intimidating.

Winnicott received a degree in biology at Cambridge, began his medical studies there, and completed them at St. Bartholomew's Hospital in London. In 1923 he was appointed consultant in childrens' medicine at the Queens's Hospital for Children and also at Paddington Green Childrens' Hospital, a position he held throughout his lifetime. That same year, having become interested in Freud's theories, he began postgraduate training at the British Psychoanalytical Society. Psychoanalytic thought, for Winnicott, linked the observations he had been making as a pediatrician with what he knew of biology. As he was to write later, "Psychoanalysis goes on where physiology leaves off." He was for a time a pupil of Melanie Klein, whose theories about child development influenced and enriched his own.

While practicing pediatrics and sharpening

his powers of observation, Winnicott had been quick to notice wide behavioral variations among the infants he treated. As each infant progressed from the first fist-in-mouth activities to the beginning attachment to a teddy bear, doll, or other toy, a few appeared fearful while most boldly accepted the challenge of exploring these new external objects. In many of the articles Winnicott later contributed to scientific journals, he was to focus on that period in an infant's growth *after* she has acquired some degree of trust in the mother (or other nurturing person) but *before* she has fully realized her as a being separate from and outside of herself. The healthy infant's play with a "transitional object" (such as a teddy bear) or with "transitional phenomena" (including hard toys, games, etc.) came to symbolize for Winnicott the infant's evolving but still immature ability to assert mastery over separations from the mother. At first clinging to an illusion of omnipotence based on a feeling of total union with the mother or other nurturing person, the infant gradually starts to see himself as a semiautonomous being within the "potential space" he creates between himself and her. As Winnicott put it in *Playing and Reality*:

> Transitional objects and transitional phenomena belong to the realm of illusion which is at the basis of initiation of experience. This early stage in development is made possible by the mother's special capacity for making adaptation to the needs of her infant, thus allowing the infant the illusion that what the infant creates really exists.

One of Winnicott's most important contributions to psychoanalytic theory evolved from his premise that "it is in playing and only in playing that the individual child or adult is able to be creative and to use the whole personality." In using the word creative, Winnicott refers to a human being's capacity for enjoyment—his aliveness and responsiveness—not to any special ability he or she may have.

The aggressive (even destructive) impulses that exist from the very beginning of the infant's life come to be tolerated and modified because the mother continues to provide adequate care. Thus, the infant who had begun to experience love and hate as a result of gratification and inevitable frustration may throw his first toy from him, maltreat it, subject it to infinite abuse, yet it remains whole, and a valuable part of himself and of the world he is beginning to experience, so long as he continues to feel trust in the person who cares for him. However, the toy will decrease in value if the mother fails in her nurturing role; if she loses interest in her child, the child will eventually lose interest in the "transitional object."

But what if the mother, for whatever reason, has been unable to provide what Winnicott terms a "facilitating environment"—if as a consequence, the infant has felt too anxious to enjoy creative playing? This was the question that confronted Winnicott when, as a practicing psychoanalyst, he began treating adults whose ability to be playful and to function autonomously had been damaged or impeded too early. He came to recognize such patients by their arid way of expressing themselves to him; instead of communicating spontaneously, they set up barriers, ruminating obsessively, or narrating the story of their lives without getting in touch with real feelings.

As might be expected, Winnicott came to view the space between himself and such patients as a potential playground, a space where playing (in the largest sense of the word) could begin to happen. As he put it in *Playing and Reality*, "Psychoanalysis has been developed as a highly specialized form of playing in the service of communication with oneself and others."

Using the analogy of the "good-enough" mother who first gratifies, then frustrates her infant by gradually withdrawing part of her attention, Winnicott stipulated that the analyst must play a double role for the patient who has been deprived at the earliest stage of his development. When such patients reach a state of regression and dependency, it will be necessary to "hold" them before gradually introducing reality, which always involves frustration and disillusionment. In the author's words "Whenever we understand a patient in a deep way and show that we do so by a correct and well-timed interpretation, we are in fact holding the patient."

While stressing that correct interpretations are essential to analytic work, Winnicott also makes clear that there are times when the analyst should make *no* interpretation at all. Knowing when to interpret and when not to presumes a knowledge of what emotional state the patient is in at each particular moment. In *Holding and Interpretation: Fragment of an Analysis*, published after the author's death, the reader is presented with a verbatim record of analytic sessions between Winnicott and a clinically depressed young man who came to him complaining of feeling unreal. As Dodi Goldman pointed out in *In Search of the Real*, Winnicott used aggression, as well as empathy, in accounting for a patient's ability to integrate: "Winnicott implies that unless one tolerates the ruthless side of one's character, it is impossible to have the full experience of the survival of the analyst. . . . Trust, in other words, is the confidence gained by the analyst's survival of the patient's destructiveness." By this the patient is able to affirm, rather than to try to eradicate, his own "realness."

Winnicott's empathy is also apparent in the lectures he delivered before mothers, teachers, and other nonprofessionals, and in the BBC radio talks he gave in the 1960s. Whenever he addressed mothers, Winnicott was particularly supportive and encouraging. In a talk he gave to the Nursery School Association of Great Britian and Northern Ireland in 1966, he said he had been "ragged somewhat" because of his often stated opinion that the ordinary mother is devoted to her infant.

> There are many who assume that I am sentimental about mothers and that I idealise them, and that I leave out fathers, and that I can't see that some mothers are pretty awful if not in fact impossible. I have to put up with these small inconveniences because I am not ashamed of what is implied by these words.

Over and over Winnicott stressed that the mother should not be interfered with in her maternal role. Having frequently observed that a mother given too many instructions can lose self-confidence, he urged her to enjoy herself, "enjoy being thought important. Enjoy letting other people look after the world while you are producing a new one of its members." Because he valued the "immense contribution" the ordinary mother makes to her child and to society (and wanted to persuade other to think the same), he worked at putting his theoretical thinking into plain everyday language, using metaphors that could be easily grasped—n one example likening the infant to a bulb in a window box while observing:

> You do not have to make the bulb grow into a daffodil. You supply the right kind of earth or fibre and you keep the bulb watered just the right amount, and the rest comes naturally, because the bulb has life in it. Now, the care of infants is very much more complicated than the care of a daffodil bulb, but the illustration serves my purpose because, both with the bulb and with the infant, there is something going on which is not your responsibility.

In 1923 Winnicott married Alice Taylor. She was more of a patient than a wife to him, but he did not divorce her until 1949, when he believed she would be strong enough to bear the separation. During the years of World War II, Winnicott worked as Psychiatric Consultant to the Government Evacuation Scheme in Oxford. He later met and married Clare Britton, a social worker with a special interest in the field of child care. Lacking children of their own, the couple nevertheless shared a deep mutual interest; from the perspectives of their different careers, each contributed to the other, the development of

children being the central interest of both. As many observers have noted, Winnicott had a special way with children. Children understood him; when he was with them he was wholly with them.

Besides serving on the staff of the Paddington Green Childrens' Hospital for all of his professional life, Winnicott also served on the training staff of the British Psychoanalytical Society for twenty-five years and was twice elected its president. He was elected a Fellow of the Royal College of Physicians, and president of the Pediatric Section of the Royal Society of Medicine.

Others psychiatrists in the first half of the 20th century have written profoundly about child development, and many have made an impact in analytic circles. It was Winnicott's special contribution to combine erudition with what many in his field have called a poetic and intuitive sensibility. His natural gifts as a writer and speaker made him widely influential, not just among analysts but among pediatricians, teachers, and nurses in Great Britain and the United States. For the American pediatrician Benjamin Spock, Winnicott "helped bridge the gap between pediatrics and child development." T. Berry Brazelton viewed Winnicott as a "major influence on all of us who have tried to bring emotional and behavioral issues into pediatrics." Another American pediatrician, Marshall Klaus, noting somewhat ruefully that Winnicott had grown up in prewar England "at a time of optimism and hope," makes the point that Winnicott "had a very different attitude about the father than is in vogue today. For Winnicott, the father is the protector and caretaker of the mother. He protects the mother so she can develop a close relation with the baby." Klaus valued Winnicott's contributions highly, observing that he wished he had been aware of Winnicott's insights while he was helping to rear his children and grandchildren. A social worker and colleague of Winnicott's, recalling the impact he had made on her life and work, remembered him as a man "of great charm and humour . . . He had that rare gift of concentration upon the person of the moment."

PRINCIPAL WORKS: Clinical Notes on Disorders of Childhood, 1931; The Child and the Family: First Relationships, 1957; The Child and the Outside World: Studies in Developing Relationships, 1957; Collected Papers: Through Paediatrics to Psychoanalysis, 1958; The Child, the Family, and the Outside World, 1964; The Maturational Processes and the Facilitating Environment, 1965; The Family and Individual Development, 1965; Playing and Reality, 1971; Therapeutic Consultations in Child Psychiatry, 1971; The Piggle: An Account of the Psycho-Analytical Treatment of a Little Girl, 1978; Deprivation and Delinquency, 1984; Holding and Interpretation: Fragment of an Analysis, 1986; Home Is Where We Start From, 1986; Babies and Their Mothers, 1987; The Spontaneous Gesture: Selected Letters of D. W. Winnicott (ed. F. R. Rodman), 1987.

ABOUT: Clancier, A. Winnicott and Paradox: From Birth to Creation, 1987; Davis, M. And Wallbridge, D. Boundary and Space: An Introduction to the Work of D. W. Winnicott, 1981; Goldman, D. In Search of the Real, 1993; Grolnick, S. The Work and Play of Winnicott, 1990; Hughes, J. Reshaping the Psychoanalytic Domain: The Work of Melanie Kleing, W. R. D. Fairbairn, and D. W. Winnicott, 1989; International Encycolpedia of Psychiatry, Psychology, Psychoanalysis and Neurology, 1977; Rudnytsky, P. L. (ed.) Transitional Objects and Potential Spaces: Literary Uses of D. W. Winnicott, 1993. *Periodicals*—Journal of Child Psychology and Psychiatry 12, 1971.

WINTERSON, JEANETTE (August 27, 1959–), English novelist, was born in Manchester, England, grew up in Accrington, Lancashire, and received her university education at St. Catherine's College, Oxford. Since one of Winterson's most notable characteristics as a writer is her ability to break down distinctions between objective and fictional truth, and between present and historical time, it is impossible not to read her first novel, *Oranges Are Not the Only Fruit*, which was published when she was twenty-six, as autobiography. The protagonist, who is named Jeannette, is the adoptive child of a Pentecostal Christian family dominated by her mother, a domineering figure who expresses continual frustration and surprise that the world outside her church does not conform to her impossibly narrow evangelistic vision. Jeannette lives within the constraints of church and home until, carrying out her mother's intentions that she become an evangelical missionary, she first converts and then has sexual relations with a young woman. When her guileless and guiltless action is condemned in church Jeannette is astonished, and ultimately forced to realize that the "love" she has been taught about is not the same kind of feeling she is experiencing.

This is, as the *Times Literary Supplement* reviewer observed, "a steely, dream revenge of a book, rich in malicious strategy . . . the most charming comeuppance a comic monster on the scale of Mother has ever had," but it is also one of the achievements of the novel to present the heroine's family in a convincingly realistic style that is not reductive or absurd. Consequently, Jeannette's discovery that she cannot live in their society is both joyful and sad; it carries the implication that the young woman has been kicked out of paradise into a world that is more complex than she, or her parents, imagined. The reader's sense that the novel recounts a real-life coming-of-age is confirmed by a *Sunday Times* London article in 1987 about Winterson in which she is quoted as saying: "My dad was employed in a TV factory, and my mum had her hobbies. She spent nearly all her day in church and looking after us. It was when I began to love another woman that the exorcism took place. I was appalled by the violence my lover and I experienced, and I could no longer be naive about the church and its goodness." Like her narrator, Winterson has worked as a waitress, ice-cream seller, and undertaker.

The theme of self-discovery dramatized in a realistic domestic setting by a young narrator who rejects parental values is the common stock of first novels about coming-of-age, and there are numerous British examples of the genre, but *Oranges Are Not the Only Fruit* made a sharp and lasting impression by the deftness of its comedy, the novelty of its style, and its treatment of female homosexuality. In addition to many favorable reviews it received the Whitbread Prize for the best first novel of 1985. As Gabriele Annan pointed out in the *New York Review of Books* in 1993, certain passages of the novel point to "future preoccupations": "sexual determination and personal freedom, and how to reconcile them." In a preface written for a new edition of her novel, Winterson acknowledges that her fiction is intended to challenge and question the definition of "love" offered by her upbringing: "*Oranges* is a threatening novel . . . It exposes the sanctity of family as something of a sham: it illustrates by example that what the church calls love is actually psychosis and it dares to suggest that what makes life difficult for homosexuals is not their perversity but other people's. Worse, it does these things with such humor and lightness that those disposed not to agree find that they do." The novel won an even wider audience in its television dramatization in 1990.

Winterson's later writing, especially *Sexing the Cherry*, often seems to be driving at a new and more comprehensive definition of love. This is not, as Gabriele Anna suggests "propaganda" for homosexuality, because it is much more complex than this term suggests; it is, rather, a generous and socially liberal recognition of the fact that sexual attraction and identity cannot be neatly divided into homo- and heterosexuality. *Written on the Body*, whose central subject is sexuality, is an episodic novel consisting partly of lyrical meditations that attempt to trace "a secret code" that determines our sexual attractions. The code is hard to interpret because it is laid down by nature, written by experience, and subject to the passing of time:

In silence and in darkness we loved each other and as I
traced her bones with my palm I wondered what time
would do to a skin that was new to me. Could I ever feel
any less for this body? Why does ardour pass? Time that
withers you will wither me. We will fall like ripe fruit
and roll down the grass together. Dear friend, let me lie
beside you watching the clouds until the earth covers us
and we are gone.

Such earnestly serious passages in Winteson's
work seem to avoid triteness because they are intense episodes in narratives that use many tones
of voice in a succession of swift changes of scene,
point of view, and time frame. Her approach to
narrative has been compared by some critics to
the "magical realism" of Latin American fiction
and to the confusion of historical with present
time that is found in the writing of her British
contemporaries Angela Carter and Peter Ackroyd. In *Sexing the Cherry* and *The Passion*,
which are both, in a partial sense, "historical
novels," Winterson often disrupts the reader's
sense of time by switching between historical
circumstance, contemporary characters, and the
timeless mode of myth.

Winterson's use of myths and fairy tales,
which appear in her first novel as commentaries
on the young narrator's developing consciousness and are even more evident in *Sexing the
Cherry*, have invited critical comparison with
Italo Calvino, wh frequently retold and adapted
myths to modern settings. A passage from Winterson's novel, *Boating for Beginners*, offers insight into the freedom she claims to conflate
various literary genres in her own narratives:

The Bible writers didn't care that they were bunching together sequences some of which were historical, some
preposterous, and some downright manipulative. Faithful recording was not their business; faith was.

In this same passage, however, Winterson makes
it clear that "believers are dangerous and mad
and can only be countered by creating rival
myths, such as those of the Romantic writers,
who "found their own fire." In *Boating for
Beginners*, which burlesques the Biblical story of
Noah's Ark, and also has a lot of blasphemous
fun with New Testament miracles, Winterson
seems to be exorcising her own Christian education in a spirit that recalls the Monty Python
treatment of Christ in the film *Life of Brian*. In
this novel, her games with literary allusion and
modern manners make her seem to be, as the
Times Literary Supplement reviewer remarked,
"bobbing in a sea of literature." In *Sexing the
Cherry*, however, she writes versions of fairy
tales and myths that recall tradition while rewriting it in a comic style that is not merely burlesque but, like her first novel, exposes cant,
undermines hypocrisy, and subverts sexual repression.

The Passion, Winterson's third novel, borrows
its setting from historical events—the retreat of
Napoleon's army from Russia—but is peopled
by fictional characters. Although the novel is intermittently convincing as a re-creation of the
past, Winterson, ranges freely between realism
and fantasy to relate the romantic love of a
young man who serves as Napoleon's cook for
the red-haired and web-footed daughter of a Venetian boatman. While comparing Winterson's
style to magical realism, David Lodge, in the
New York Review of Books, asserted that "she
has continued her own flight froma repressive
Christian upbringing by embracing the Romantic tradition of storytelling, the tradition of Poe,
Mary Shelley, and Emily Brontë." Whereas the
tradition of magical realism makes the familiar
world strange, Lodge noted that Winterson is
trying to create an entirely new, unfamiliar
world. This effort, he added, sometimes makes
Winterson a "slapdash, lazy, and derivative
writer," who is "lacking in the ironical self-
consciousness that saves a writer from bathos or
pretentiousness." But what redeems Winterson's
work from such faults, Lodge acknowledged, is
"an overwhelming impression of . . . remarkable self-confidence." At its best, her writing
"stares you down," and simply forces the reader
to allow incredible flights of fancy to pursue the
truths that Winterson is seeking. For the less
sympathetic reviewer in *Library Journal*, however, this novel, despite its virtues, was
"irritatingly inaccessible."

Sexing the Cherry, which is also a historical
novel, is a more controlled, and perhaps more
accomplished work, although here too Winterson departs from the standard orderliness of the
form to make excursions into anachronistic reverie and even introduces modern characters who
make irrelevant remarks on environmental issues that have no obvious connection with the
central themes of the novel. The more unified
effect of this novel is achieved by use of a principal narrator, the Rabelaisian Dog Woman, a gargantuan person who lives beside the Thames in
London in the 1640s and earns her living by
breeding hounds. With her adoptive son Jordan,
whom she rescues, Moses-like, from the river,
she witnesses the events of the English Civil
War, the Commonwealth of Oliver Cormwell,
and the eventual Restoration of the monarchy
under Charles II. The Dog Woman, far too large
to experience any kind of sexual relationship
herself, is an ironic observer of love, lust, and
perversity in others. In her hatred of Puritans,
who hypocritically repress others while concealing their own desires, she seems a surrogate for
Winterson herself, and more than one reviewer
remarked on the novel's misogyny. The earthy

comedy of the Dog Woman is counterpoised against the voice of her Jordan, a mystical, almost ethereal character who is apprenticed to the historical figure of John Tradescant, a notable early naturalist who served as the King's gardener and was responsible for introducing exotic fruit to England. As in her first novel, Winterson uses fruit as sexual symbol: a banana is a phallic symbol to the Dog Woman, and Tradescant, near the book's end, teaches Jordan how to graft a cherry tree. The cherry, which turns out to be female, serves as the author's metaphor for the indeterminateness of sexuality.

The second strain of narrative, almost entirely fairytale-like, is given to Jordan, who undergoes various adventures out of time, including a visit to twelve dancing princesses, each of whom has murdered her husband. The man's role, in which he sometimes wear women's clothes, is to dramatize the thesis laid down by Winterson in the epigraphs to the novel—that the constraints of time and matter are arbitrary: "The Hopi, an Indian tribe, have a language as sophisticated as ours, but no tenses for past, present, and future. The division does not exist. What does this say about time? . . . Matter, that thing the most solid and the well-known, which you are holding in your hands and which makes up your body, is now known to be mostly empty space. Empty space and points of light. What does this say about the reality of the world?" Whereas the Dog Woman remains firmly grounded, both physically and as a narrator, and nurtures Jordan, the boy defines himself by perpetually traveling to other places and time. This partnership of the gross with the ethereal has the effect of setting Winterson's preoccupations with the fluidity of time and ambiguity of gender against the background of an enjoyable tale whose events help to make metaphorical sense of her wilder flights of fancy. The Dog Woman's castrations of Puritans, for example, are counterpoised with a retelling of the myth of Orion and Artemis, in which Artemis kills the hunter-god after being raped.

Several reviewers of Sexing the Cherry called attention to the banality of Winterson's political and philosophical ideas, and in the New York Times Book Review Michael Gorra pointed out that "the kinds of material . . . Winterson uses—the feminist revision of fairy tales, the reliance on historical pastiche, an insistence on the subjectivity of all truth—have paradoxically become so fashionably familiar that they begin to seem the cliches of postmodernism." These faults, when added to the occasional triteness or false profundity that other critics have complained of, seem serious demerits, but even those who find Winterson's talents have not yet reached their full expression agree that her writ-ing is marked by an extraordinary, exuberant style of storytelling, and an "emotional intensity," as Michael Gorra puts it.

The quality of almost breathless exuberance and the fascination with ambiguous gender carry over into Winterson's fifth novel, Written on the Body, whose narrator's gender is never defined. After a succession of intense love affairs, the narrator falls in love with Louise, the wife of a doctor who offers the only hope of rescuing Louise from certain death from cancer. The rapidly paced episodic narrative, punctuated by the narrator's struggles to use language to define love, abruptly ends in a set of variations, each preceded by an excerpt from an anatomical textbook, on how love interprets a part of the body. This interlude, which interrupts the narrator's flight from Louise to a remote provincial restaurant, also occurs at a point when the narrator is being ardently pursued by the restaurant's owner. When the narrative resumes, the narrator is found with the restaurant owner in a rented cottage, but what seems to be the inevitable acceptance of the persistent suitor is ended by the unexpected appearance of Louise. The novel ends in an ecstatic rhapsody that, like passages of Winterson's earlier novels, questions the boundaries of time and space. As Gabriele Annan observed in the New York Review of Books, this seems to be a return to the autobiographical mode of her first novel, but "the new persona is more plaintive and given to self-pity, more sententious and preachy," which makes the novel "harder to like." This "is a pity," she adds, "because Winterson has a lot of talent."

While acknowledging Winterson's "originality . . . her distinctive mix of romanticism and irony, erudition and passion," Jim Shepard, in the New York Times Book Review, found Written on the Body weakened by lapses into sentimentality and cliché and by the narratpr's sexual ambiguity: "The author's refusal to identify the narrator's sex (though hints do begin to pile up that the voice is female) backfires as Ms. Winterson continually asserts the gesture's subversiveness, in a writerly way, each time another opportunity to release the information is neatly (and noticeably) avoided. Other attempts to rattle society's cage on the issue of sexuality fall short of illuminating as well." This opinion was shared by Anna Vaux, in the Times Literary Supplement, who complained also of a certain coldness in the novel: "There is something unpleasant at the centre of the book, some deep self-satisfaction behind all the mourning . . . something odd and self-indulgent about a sensibility that can dwell so much upon its own high passions while portraying the feelings of other characters in the book as one-dimensional or comic and easy to dismiss."

In 1990 Winterson received the E. M. Forster Award of the American Academy and Institute of Arts and Letters. The citation read: "So serenely confident is Jeanette Winterson's imagination that she is able to stand with one foot in the quotidian, essential to the true novelist, and the other foot in fairyland." Although she claims never to read reviews of her books, Winterson clashed openly with the press in 1994. Her novel of that year, *Art & Lies*—an eccentric and whimsical exercise of the imagination involving two women, a poet and a painter, and a man friend living in a decaying society—received what the *Times Literary Supplement* (July 8, 1994) described editorially as "one of the great critical roastings of modern times." In fact the *Times Literary Supplement's* reviewer, Lorna Sage, had been fairly even-handed in treatment of the book (June 17, 1994), judging it "safely good but not great—better than her last, *Written on the Body*, not as good as *Sexing the Cherry*." Sage observed, however, that Winterson herself has become a media personality, giving interviews on television and in the press that display "her particular style of self-promotion which says that if you don't adore her that means you're immune to art altogether."

PRINCIPAL WORKS: *Novels*— Oranges Are Not the Only Fruit, 1085; Boating for Beginners, 1986; The Passion, 1987; Sexing the Cherry, 1989; Written on the body, 1992; Art & Lies, 1994. *Essays*—Art Objects, 1995.

ABOUT: C. (ed.) Feminist Criticism: Theory and Practice, 1991; Contemporary Authors 136;, 1992 International Who's Who 199292. *Periodicals*—Chicago Tribune November 8, 1987; July 5, 1988; Hudson Review Winter 1991; London Review of Books September 14, 1989; Nation July 9, 1990; New Statesman & Society September 1, 1989; New York Review of Books September 29, 1988; March 4, 1993; New York Times April 27, 1990; New York Times Book Review November 8, 1987; August 7, 1988; April 29, 1990; February 14, 1993; Sunday Times (London) June 7, 1987; Times Literary Supplement March 22, 1985; November 1, 1985; June 26, 1987; September 15, 1989; September 4, 1992; June 17, 1994; July 8, 1994; Village Literary Supplement June 1990; Washington Post Book World May 13, 1990.

*XIAO QIAN (formerly spelled HSIAO CH'IEN) (January 27, 1910–   ), Chinese novelist, short story writer, essayist, translator, and journalist, writes: "I was born in Beijing of a Mongolian family. I studied in an American Presbyterian school, Truth Hall, where I worked half days, first as a milk deliverer then a rug maker. I was arrested by war-lord Chang Tso-lin as radical when I was sixteen. After ten months

in prison, where there was a fellow prisoner who was nine, I was released, but under house arrest in school. Then became an errand boy in Bei Hsin Publishing House, the earliest press issuing workss of the new literature. There I read profusely both Chinese and foreign literature. I adored Chekhov and Katherine Mansfield.

"In 1930, I became a freshman in the Catholic University (Fu Jen) inaugurated by the American Benedictines. There I published the English translation of three Chinese modern plays in the University's *Fu Jen Magazine* and helped Bill Alan, a young American, in running an English journal in Peking, *China in Brief*, in which I translated some pieces from the works of modern Chinese writers such as Kuo Mo-juo and Shen Tsung-wen. In 1933, I was transferred to Yenching University, established by American missionaries. There I met the journalist from Missouri, Edgar Snow, who taught me feature writing. It was then that I started writing short stories.

"In 1935, I became the literary editor of the *Takungpao* (now, *Dagongbao*) which was then known as the *Manchester Guardian* of China. I continued to write short stories and published a novel, *Meng zhi gu* (Valley of dreams, 1938), based on my tragic first love, which was made into a TV film in 1991.

"I started writing reportage in 1934 after a visit to Inner Mongolia. In the autumn of 1935, I covered the flood in Shandong and Jiangsu. Parts of those features I wrote have since been chosen by school textbook editors. In the spring of 1939, I wrote a number of features about the construction of the Burma Road, which later became the sole lifeline of China after the fall of Hong Kong in December 1941.

"I was invited to teach Chinese by the School of Oriental and African Studies (SOAS) of London University in the autumn of 1939 and boarded a French mailboat bound for Europe the day before the war in Europe was declared. While teaching, I was concurrently war correspondent in London for the *Takungpao*. I wrote profusely about the European war, particularly the blitzkrieg of 1940 in London. In 1942–1944, I did research on the modern English novel in King's College, Cambridge, and became a close friend of E. M. Forster. In the summer of 1944, I became a full-fledged war correspondent and joined the U.S. Seventh Army under General Patch. We advanced from France into Germany and I left them just as the battle for the Rhine started in order to proceed to San Francisco to attend the inauguration of the United Nations. After traveling all over America, I flew to Berlin to cover the Potsdam Conference and later the

Nuremberg trials. Then I did an eighteen-day trip on a jeep through the U.S. and French occupied zones from Munich to Paris.

"I came back to postwar China in 1946, serving as leader writer for the same paper and also professor of English literature at Fudan University in Shanghai. The year 1949 was a big crossroad for every Chinese intellectual. Being emotionally attached to my birthplace, I came back to Beijing. I first served as deputy chief editor of the English journal *People's China*, and later in the same post at the *Literary Gazette*. In 1957, I was predictably named as a rightist and exile to a state farm near Tangshan for three years. I returned to Beijing in 1961, demoted, and was allowed only to translate 18th-century works such as Henry Fielding and publish under a pseudonym.

"When the damned Cultural Revolution started in June 1966, I and my family were naturally among the first targets as class enemies. My house was completely ransacked and all my small collection of art was destroyed. In 1969, I was sent along with millions of intellectuals to the May 7th Cadre School in Hubei, which was a euphemism for labor reform. Three years after, I was sent back to Beijing to translate collectively works like Schlesinger's *A Thousand Days: John F. Kennedy in the White House*.

"My fate improved vastly after 1979 when I was rehabilitated and in 1985 made the director of the Central Research Institute of Culture and History. Accompanied by my wife Wen Jie-ruo, I have made ten foreign trips and renewed correspondence with some friends abroad, which was strictly forbidden before. The first foreign trip I made was to Iowa City, where I joined the International Writing Program under the directorship of the late Paul Engle. As a reward for my translation and production of Ibsen's *Peer Gynt* in China, King Olav V of Norway invited me to go to his country, where he received me and awarded me a medal.

"In addition, being the translator of some of the works of Henry Fielding, Charles Lamb, Ibsen, Upton Sinclair, Stephen Leacock, and Herman Wouk, I have published thirty-two books in Chinese of my original work, and wrote eight books in English, five of which were published in London. My first book was a study of book reviewing (1935), which was my thesis for the B.A.. The rest are mainly collections of short stories and essays. *Report On Life* (1947) is an omnibus of news features which has been reprinted by Taiwan in 1990. A number of my short stories were translated into English by myself and published in London by Allen and Unwin in 1944 under the title of *The Spinners of Silk*. That pub-lisher also published my book *Etching of a Tormented Age* (1941). My *China But Not Cathay, Dragonbeards Vs. the Blueprints*, and *A Harp With a Thousand Strings* were published by London's Pilot Press. *Traveller Without a Map* (my memoir, written in 1987) was translated by Kinkley and published by London's Hutchinson. The book has also been translated into Japanese by Maruyama Nabaru of Tokyo University.

"At present [1992] I am translating James Joyce's *Ulysses* with my wife. Although this monumental work of Western fiction was published in 1922, there is still no translation of it in China. There are two volumes of critical essays (in Chinese) on my works, one published in May 1992 commemorating the 60th anniversary of my literary career, when an exhibition was held in the Historical Museum in Beijing."

In his autobiography, *Traveller Without a Map*, Xiao Qian recalls with self-mocking humor and pathos the humiliation and physical abuse that he and his wife, Wen Jie-ruo, a specialist in Japanese literature whom he married in 1954, suffered during the Cultural Revolution. Their whole family (including their son and daughter and a son from an earlier marriage) were exiled to the country and forced to do strenuous labor. His health was severely and permanently damaged, but his spirit and energy never flagged. In 1979 he was officially rehabilitated, with a certificate that it had been "a mistake" to name him a rightist. His freedom of movement and access to acceptable living conditions were gradually restored. In recent years he has lived in a modest apartment in Beijing, and he has been free to accept foreign invitations, including participation in the International Writers Program at the University of Iowa in 1979. Since then he has traveled abroad many times to accept honors and deliver lectures.

Xiao has made up for the time lost during the Cultural Revolution; he has in spite of his failing health published a book every two years since 1979 and on average an article a month. To those who decry those twenty lost years he says: "When you're permitted to do nothing but lie, what's so bad about having your pen snatched away? . . . My silence kept me alive." Honored in 1992 for his sixty-year writing career with an exhibition of his works and the publication of a book of essays about him by some thirty Chinese critics, he was also at that time appointed director of the Central Research Institute of Culture and History in Beijing. "Strange to say," he wrote in 1992, "the last twelve years have been the most prolific period of my literary career.

Counting translations as well, I have done nearly a million words and practically all my books have been reprinted. Not many Chinese writers can say that. Simply because I have never attacked anyone who's been named 'class enemy,' I have a more smooth conscience, whatever the quality of my writing."

Xiao Qian's writing style is spare and lyrical. "Cut, cut, cut," he recalls the strictures of his teacher at Yanjing University, Edgar Snow. His own advice to writers is simply stated: "The key to finding both a topic and a style [is] in opening one's heart to the people." This principle, combining the directness and economy of journalism with the more enduring qualities of literature, is reflected in all his work and accounts for his popularity. Kenneth McLeish, reviewing *Traveller Without a Map* for the (London) *Sunday Times,* wrote: "The octogenarians who rule China now seem . . . to have spent their lives mistaking their underground bunker for the universe. If only they had lifted their heads, as Xiao did, they might have seen that there are horizons beyond the exercise of power, and that humanity is enhanced, not threatened, by taking in the view."

Traveller Without a Map broke new ground in China, where memoirs traditionally tend to obfuscate rather than reveal. Xiao Qian was a man who experienced the major cataclysms of his time, both in Europe and in China. In Germany as the Nuremberg trials were beginning after World War II, Xiao visited the concentration camp at Dachau. "The jeep passed through forests and Alpine villages on the way back," he writes. "I remained silent the whole way. When we reached . . . the press camp. . . . [d]inner was in the Austrian style . . . laid out colourfully on the plate . . . but I couldn't taste it. I kept staring blankly out the window at the lake water. That night I was visited by one nightmare after another. . . . At Dachau I had lost a good part of my faith in humanity."

Xiao retained most of his faith in the importance of tradition, and the need to keep in touch with his roots, however. Although he had traveled widely and known both the United States and Europe from having lived and studied there, when he was offered a university teaching post in England, he refused it. He was then forced to suffer denunciation, exile, hard labor, and near starvation during the Cultural Revolution. He writes at the conclusion of *Traveller Without a Map* that a man who predicted in 1961 that he would "run off to a foreign country" was "another who misunderstood us intellectuals . . . He was an artist himself . . . but he didn't know the first thing about his country's in-

tellectuals, what they aspire to, what they dream of, what touches their hearts or what stirs up their resentment. . . . Now I'm home again. . . . This is the place where my ancestors lived. . . . Its history flows in my veins. It's here that I intend to grow old and here that I'll perform my last small labours."

PRINCIPAL WORKS IN ENGLISH TRANSLATION: Etching of a Tormented Age, 1941; China But Not Cathay, 1942; The Spinners of Silk, 1944; The Dragonbeards Vs. the Blueprints, 1944; A Harp with a Thousand Strings, 1946; How the Tillers Win Back Their Land, 1951; Chestnuts, 1984; Semolina and Others, 1984; (tr. J. C. Kinkley) Traveller Without a Map 1990.

ABOUT: *Periodicals*—China Daily (Beijing) November 9, 1993; Chines literature, 1984; Chinese Literature, 1984; The Daily Telegraph (London) January 5, 1990; Guardian (London) May 30, 1991; The Listener June 7, 1990; Observer (London) May 20, 1990; South China Morning Post (Hong Kong) August 9, 1990; The Sunday Times (London) June 3, 1990; World Literature Today Winter 1990.

YANG LIAN (1955–), Chinese poet, now living in the United States, is one of the group of unorthodox young poets to emerge in the late 1970s. They are generally known as the *Today* group, from the journal *Jintian,* in which their first poems were published. Their writing is loosely identified as the "Misty," or "Obscure," school of poetry for its "modernist" bent, and is internationally recognized as the most vibrant poetry coming out of China, though many of the group are now living abroad. Of this group, Yang Lian stands out for his deep sense of tradition and original use of historical material.

Born in Berne, Switzerland, where his parents were stationed as diplomatic personnel, Yang Lian spent his childhood in the western suburbs of Beijing near the ruins of Yuanming Yuan, the European palace of Emperor Qianlong, which was burnt down by the invading armies of the West in 1860. He haunted the ruins, first as a child, and later in the 1970s when the ruins were the gathering place of the *Today* group. The ruins of Yuanming Yuan, with its associations both to death and destruction and to the meeting of East and West, came to be one of the central symbols in Yang's poetry. In his much quoted poem *"Zibai"* (Apologia) from the poetic sequence *Binghu Zhi Zhong* (Bell on The Frozen Lake), he evokes the stone of the ruins, especially the half-buried sundial, emblem of China's former greatness, and makes the imagist leap to his own role as poet:

Let this mute stone

Attest my birth
Let this song
Resound
In the troubled mist
Searching for my eyes

. . .

I come to this ruin
Seeking the one hope that has illumined me
Faint star out of its time
Destiny, blind cloud
Pitiless chiaroscuro of my soul
No, I have not come to lament death! It is not death
has drawn me to this desolate world
I defy all waste and degradation—these swaddling
clothes
Are a sun that will not be contained in the grave. . . .

In my premature solitude
Who knows
The destination of the road singing into the night
To what shore its flickering ghostfires lead?
A secret horizon
Ripples, trawls distant dreams
Distant, almost boundless.

Only the wind rousing a song
In place of the broken sundial in the earth
Points to my dawn . . .

A formative influence on Yang Lian was his early training in classical Chinese poetry. His father had made him memorize poems by the hundreds before he entered primary school. This classical grounding accounts for his attention to form and tonal patterns, a meticulousness unique to Yang among his peers. Another influence was modern and contemporary Western poetry, which Yang had read widely in translation. He had also collaborated on Chinese translations of T. S. Eliot's *Four Quartets*, poems by Dylan Thomas and Robert Bly, and Yeats's *A Vision*. He dipped into Western resources for techniques of self-exploration and was evidently influenced by the symbolic systems of William Carlos Williams and Ezra Pound in his own poetic sequences.

Yang Lian's poetry is imbued with a sense of history and cultural tradition. He draws inspiration from China's geological remains and artifacts, the concept of yin and yang, the symbolic systems embodied in the ancient classic texts, the religions and rituals of Tibet and other ethnic minorities, as well as the everyday life and struggles of ordinary men and women caught in social and political movements beyond their control.

As Yang said in *Renditions* 19/20, "Tradition is an eternal present; to neglect it is to neglect ourselves. We should, in the course of creation and criticism, begin from an exploration of the 'intrinsic elements' of tradition, absorb them into our poems, and then enrich that tradition with our creations . . . The more of tradition we can lay claim to in this way, the more distinctive will be our realization of our own creative and innovative mission, and the greater will be our place in history." One much quoted poem *Dayanta* (Great goose pagoda), in the *Taiyang* sequence meditates on the Greater Wild Goose Pagoda in Xi'An, a landmark in this ancient capital:

Here I have been made to stand, immobile,
For a thousand years
In China's
Ancient capital
Upright like a man
Sturdy shoulders, head held high,
Gazing at the endless golden earth.
I have stood here
Immobile as a mountain
Immobile as a tombstone
Recording the travail of a nation.

. . .

I stand here like a man
A man of immeasurable suffering, dead but obstinately upright.
Let me destroy this nightmare at last,
(And realign the shadow of history.

. . .

I shall raise the children
High, high, laughing for joy to the sun.

As embodied in the image of the "dead" pagoda lifting up laughing children to the sun, Yang Lian sees change as one of the intrinsic elements of history. He was also influenced by the ancient Taoist text *I Ching (Book of Changes)* in developing his own conception of change.

In the sequence *Tian Wen* (Heavenly Questions, 1984), there is a clear analogy with the poem of the same title by Qu Yuan. Familiar to all Chinese by lore and legend, Qu Yuan is a tragic statesman / poet who lived more than two thousand years ago; banished from the court, he cries out to heaven in his anguish and sets out on a quest. Yang Lian draws inspiration from *Tian Wen* to emphasize his exalted vision of the poet as mover and shaker for change, as well as seer and prophet:

I am a poet
I will the rose to bloom and it blooms;
. . .
I will return, reopen the furrow of suffering,
Begin to plough this land deep in snow.

All the elements of tradition for Yang Lian came together in the exotic *Norlang* (1983), named after the male Tibetan deity Norlang, with the Potala Palace as dominating image. Here Yang Lian rediscovers Tibet as a spiritual center. He explains in his notes to the reader: "This is the plateau of our lives. Suffering imbues it with magic. The wasteland draws us toward the divine. It is timeless—on the far horizon ancient civilization descends like the setting sun. It leaves only its ancient wisdom, at dusk, at midnight, suspending the tilting constellations, illuminating the mystery of the universe."

Other poetic sequence such as *Dunhuang* (1982–1983), referring to the site of ancient Buddhist frescoes, *Banpo* (1982–1984), referring to the Neolithic site near the ancient capital of Xi'an, and *Flux* (1985) explore into myths, rites, history, and reality for a key to a new modern Chinese consciousness. As the writer himself claimed: "Each poem becomes an exploration into the human experience and the ability to express it."

Though condemned by the official press, Yang Lian is widely read and admired in China. In 1989 he and his wife and child left China. They lived in New Zealand and Australia before settling in the United States. Even in exile he continues to influence young poets in China, and his writings reflect his deep concern for his fellow Chinese still in the homeland. The events of June 1989 in Tiananmen Square left him in despair of ever returning, and his fears were confirmed when, in December 1989, the Chinese government banned all future publication of his work.

PRINCIPAL WORKS IN ENGLISH TRANSLATION: *in* Renditions, Spring 1983; *in* Renditions Autumn 1983; Selections *in* Soong, S. C. and Minford, J. (eds.) Trees on the Mountain: An Anthology of New Chinese Writing, 1984; Barme, G. and Minford, J. (eds.) Seeds of Fire: Chinese Voices of Conscience, 1986; (tr. U. of Hong Kong) In Symmetry with Death, 1989; (tr. M. Lee) Masks and the Crocodile, 1990; Morin, E, (ed.) The Red Azalea: Chinese Poetry Since the Cultural Revolution, 1990; Yeh, M. (ed.) Anthology of Modern Chinese Poetry, 1992; Barnstone, T. (ed.) Out of the Howling Storm: The New Chinese Poetry, 1993.

ABOUT: Martin, H. (ed.) Contemporary Chinese Literature: The Cologne Workshop, 1986; Lee, M. *introduction to* Masks and the Crocodile, 1990; Goldblatt, H. (ed.) Worlds Apart: Recent Chinese Writing and its Audience, 1990; Yeh, M. Modern Chinese Poetry: Theory and Practice, 1991.

*ZAGAJEWSKI, ADAM (June 1945–), Polish poet and essayist, was born in Lvov, a city in eastern Poland which in September 1939, as a result of the Molotov-Ribbentrop Pact, became a part of the Soviet Ukraine. In the summer and fall of 1945, a large part of the Polish population from Lvov and the surrounding area was resettled in Upper Silesia, from which the German population was being expelled. Zagajewski's family settled in Gliwice (Gleiwitz), before and still a major center of coal mining in Poland. He has confronted the memory of his adolescence and youth in the sketch *Dwa miasta* (*Two Cities*, 1992). Janusz Drzewucki, reviewing this work in the Polish periodical *Twórczość* in 1992, wrote:

ADAM ZAGAJEWSKI

"Gliwice is the city of the childhood and school years of the future author of 'Komunikat' (The Communique) and of 'Sklepy miesne' (Butcher Shops), of 'Świat nie przedstawiony,' (The Unrepresented World), and the co-founder of the poetry group 'Teraz' (Now). Gliwice in *Two Cities* reveals itself as a symbol of unsurpassed obscurantism, of Socialist hopelessness and Communist poverty. It turns out to be a symbol of historical injustice." Lvov, on the other hand, the city of his birth, although actually unremembered, takes mythical dimensions and becomes the symbol to Zagajewski of prewar Polish culture, refinement, and beauty.

The young Zagajewski began his university studies at the Jagiellonian University in Cracow in 1963. He studied Polish literature and Western philosophy and nurtured his talent for poetry. During these years he gave particular attention to the great masters of 20th-century prose, Bruno Schulz and Witold Gombrowicz. He read and studied the poetry of his older contemporaries Czesław Miłosz, Tadeusz Rózewicz, and Zbigniew Herbert. In 1968, Zagajewski became an inadvertent participant in politics. His friend Czesław Miłosz speaks of him as a member of the "angry" generation of 1968. (Stanisław Barańczak also belongs to this group.) This generation had much to be angry about in light of the suppression of dissent in Poland, and the crushing of what had been called "Socialism with a human face" in Czechoslovakia when Soviet tanks entered Prague in August 1968. His poetry for a time expressed his strong commitment to politics. In the 1970s Zagajewski's political engagement diminished, and he gave his poetic muse a new voice. Even the titles of his collections suggest a move away from topical issues: *Ciepło, zimno* (Warm, cold, 1975), *Drugi oddech* (The second breath, 1978) and *Cieńka kreska* (A thin line, 1983). Around this time he began to acquire an international reputation, and in 1979 he was invited to West Berlin to the Berliner Künstlerprogramm, where he had been preceded by his friend, the poet Zbigniew Herbert. Zagajewski returned to Poland in September 1981, three months before the proclamation of martial law on December 13, 1981, under General Jaruzelski. He left Poland the following year to live in Paris, where he has lived ever since, making annual visits to the University of Houston to teach spring semesters in its creative writing program.

Zagajewski started publishing in Poland in the late 1960s and early 1970s. His first published book was *Komunikat* (The communique, 1972). Starting with the 1980s, most of Zagajewski's work appeared in Polish émigré publishing houses in London and Paris. Around the same time publishers issued translations of his work in the book market, first in German (*Polen: Staat im Schatten*; [Poland: Nation in the Shadow] 1981) and in Hebrew, later also in other languages. Since the mid-'80s Zagajewski's poetry has been translated into English, and in recent years individual poems have been published in a variety of American periodicals: the *New Republic, New York Review of Books, Partisan Review, Paris Review, TriQuarterly*, and others.

Zagajewski speaks with a muted voice, and his flashes of imagery display a brilliant capacity for sight and cognitive association. He probes the essential nature of things, admitting freely that it remains a mystery to him, yet he sees in all things a strange interrelationship and multifariousness. Fascinated in recent years by the interrelationship of language and ideology, he has gone through what he calls a "definitive process of linguistic reorientation." "Freedom," he has written, "would certainly also have to be a freedom from words, which bind, and from friends who unwisely demand loyalty. Should it really turn out to be just such a deception as disgraced death? Should I really turn into a prisoner of freedom?"

His personal freedom is certainly Zagajewski's most precious possession. He resents the coercive notion that one must be attuned to the major historical movements of the times. He said in "Ode to Plurality," as translated by Joachim T. Baer:

Whoever listens to the news does not know that
Nearby in the garden, wet from the rain
A small gray cat is out for a walk and enjoys itself
Wrestling with the hard stems of the grasses.

This short poem, dedicated to Zagajewski's friend Adam Michnik, a brilliant critic of the political establishment, strikes the reader both with its unusual and vivid image (the small cat *wrestling* with the hard stems of the grasses) and its direct and unpretentious language. In "Ode to Plurality" in *Tremor* Zagajewski also says:

I don't understand it all and I am
even glad that the World like a restless
ocean exceeds my ability
to understand the essence of water, rain,
of plunging into Baker's Pond, near
the Bohemian-German border, in
September 1980, a detail without any special
meaning, the deep Germanic pond.

• • •

. . . Who has once met
irony will burst into laughter
during the prophet's lecture. Who once prayed
with more than just a dry mouth
will remember the presence of the strange echo
coming from a wall. Who once
was silent would rather not talk
over dessert. And who was struck
by the shock of love will return to his books
with an altered face.

. . . .

Peace, thick nothing, as full of sweet
juice as a pear in September.

. . . .

A poem grows
on contradiction but it can't cover it.

In the poem "Do Lwowa" ("To go to Lvov"), widely admired for its beautiful imagery, he uses the city of Lvov as a symbol of his total immersion in memory and dreams. Rich in images, the poem concludes with a comparison of Lvov to a peach: "Go to Lvov, after all it exists, / quiet and pure as / a peach. It is everywhere." We can read various things into the image "there was always too much of Lvov," repeated three times. Was it "too much" of this world's goods, objects, old-fashioned people, ancient architecture, too much form, or too much matter? The wealth of it all suggests the joy of abundance, of a cornucopia of unending delights, which only partially existed in reality but has now been transformed and given a place in the imagination, where it is much greater than it likely ever was in reality—like Jerusalem, a city of enormous imaginative pull, from whose protective walls its citizens were expelled to wander the face of the earth, a city containing thousands of years of history and embracing various civilizations. Lvov, too, lay at the crossroads of civilizations (West and East European). As in Osip Mandelstam's and William Butler Yeats's poetry dedicated to Byzantium, past and present are transcended, transformed into what philosophers have called the *nunc stans*, the "eternal now."

Osip Mandelstam figures in one of Zaga-

jewski's poems in *Tremor*: "In the Encyclopedias, No Room for Mandelstam." The poem is an
example of Zagajewski's art at its best: incongruities, paradoxes, illogical associations, staccato
phrases run together in unbroken sequence, a total absence of punctuation. Yet it clearly expresses Zagajewski's love and admiration for
Mandelstam:

> You close a book it sounds like a gunshot
> White dust from the paper tickles your nose a Latin
> evening is here it snows nobody will come tonight
> it's bed-time but if he knocks at your thin door
> let him in

The question of the form of things and the
concomitant struggle with eternal chaos, and
how to find a middle ground between these two,
has been a profound artistic problem for Zagajewski. The conclusion of his collection of essays,
Solidarity, Solitude (original Polish edition
1986), reads as follows: "For an instant the sky
is clear, but this doesn't last long; a squadron of
cumulus clouds shows itself shyly and grows like
a flagship, approaches, one hears sails flapping,
the shouts of sailors, whistling ropes. I know that
God would have to be both form and
formlessness." In these five essays ("Sèvres";
"The High Wall"; "Solidarity, Solitude"; "The
Little Larousse"; "Flamenco") the author tries to
come to terms with the absurdity of his time (he
encapsulates it in the opposition of two
phrases—the "negative" spirit vs. the excessively
"positive" spirit) and juxtaposes such incongruities as the inhabitant of the island of Grenada
who had copied the statutes of the Communist
Party of the Soviet Union against the quiet of a
Sunday afternoon in Sèvres: "Silence reigns in
Sèvres. It is Sunday: families emerge from their
shelters and go to the yellow woods where they
will walk slowly, step by step, looking back for
the children, the dogs, the titmice and robins."
Zagajewski has a synthesizing imagination. He
looks for unity and form even in chaos. Like the
English metaphysical poets, he attempts to bring
together the apparent contradictions of life.
"When Brueghel painted the falling Icarus
(which Auden wrote about so beautifully)," he
writes, "the sailors in the passing galley, the
plowman, bird, the trees maintained an imperturbable indifference. Many more indifferent
things have entered our lives. Tobacco leaves are
drying. The wind rocks a TV antenna." At the
conclusion of his essay "The Little Larousse" he
compares the artist to an observer standing
"before a painting in a museum": "There exist
two treasures, two forces very similar to one another and at the same time quite different. One
is fixed in the world itself, in people who act,
struggle, love. Its author is God. The other mean-

while expresses itself in pictures, books, in music,
films—and is an echo of the first. Its author is
people. Solitude is the quiet zone between two
tumults." Solitude is thus the unifying force that
allows all things to flow together.

It is this realm of solitude, "between two
tumults," that Zagajewski's collection of poetry,
Canvas, explores. The canvas is the poet's metaphor for life:

> I stood in silence before a dark picture
> . . .
> but it had turned into the world.
> I stood in silence before the dark canvas,
> . . .
> of moments of helplessness
> and my chilly imagination
> that's the tongue of a bell,
> alive only when swaying,
> striking what it loves,
> loving what it strikes,
> and it came to me that this canvas
> could have become a winding-sheet, too.

Reviewing *Canvas* in the *New Republic*, Robert Pinsky summed up Zagajewski's work:
"Unlikely as it may seem, the poems of the Polish poet Adam Zagajewski, wonderful in themselves, may also suggest ways to think about
American culture. Zagajewski's shrewd, clear,
passionate poems have a distinctive way of
touching the relation of historical reality to the
lives of individuals, and to art. And because he
writes in the language of a country that has seen
itself as small, often defeated, but innately noble
and even aristocratic—a nation unified by
shared religion, art, historical knowledge—the
contrast alone should interest us. . . . And
moreover he is good; the unmistakable quality
of the real thing—a sunlike force that wilts cliches and bollixes the categories of expectation—
manifests itself powerfully through able translation, both in . . . *Tremor* and . . . in *Canvas*."
In December 1991, responding to a survey
among prominent authors by the *Times Literary
Supplement* as to the single book of the year that
had most impressed them, Leon Wieseltier
named Zagajewski's collection of essays
Solidarity, Solitude, writing: "Zagajewski's
themes are old ones, but they are treated unsentimentally and in the name of no political party
or cultural cause: how to reconcile the obligation
to others with the need for isolation in the higher
spiritual regions, how to protect ecstatic experience from its own indifference to ethics; how to
keep history at bay even as you struggle to fix it,
and to move it along . . . [He] is decent but interested in more than decency; humane, but not
a worshipper of humanity. He is, in short, a liberal with a fascination for transcendence. Not an
easy course, but a rich and honest one."

PRINCIPAL WORKS IN ENGLISH TRANSLATION: (tr. R. Gorczyński) Tremor: Selected Poems, 1985; (tr. R. Gorczyński, B. Ivry, and C. K. Williams) Canvas, 1991; (tr. L. Vallee) Solidarity, Solitude: Essays, 1991; (tr. L. Vallee) Two Cities: On Exile, History, and the Imagination, 1995.

ABOUT: Birkerts, S. The Electric Life: Essays on Modern Poetry, 1989. *Periodicals*—New Republic January 6–13, 1986; January 25, 1993; New York Review of Books August 1991; New York Times Book Review February 16, 1986; Newsweek July 7, 1986; Times Literary Supplement March 27, 1987; October 8, 1993; World Literature Today 66, no. 4, 1992.

Acknowledgements

The lines from the poem "Black-Footed Ferret Endangered" are from *Darwin's Ark* (Indiana University Press, 1984) by Philip Appleman

The lines from the poem "Remembering the Great Depression" are from *Summer Love and Surf* (Vanderbilt University Press, 1968) by Philip Appleman

The lines from the poem "Lighting Your Birthday Cake" are from *Let There Be Light* (HarperPerennial, 1991) by Philip Appleman

The lines from the poem "Slave-hands" are from *El Central: A Cuban Sugar Mill* (Avon Books, 1984) by Reinaldo Arenas, translated by Anthony Kerrigan

The lines beginning "Once I goosestepped . . . " and the lines from the poem "The Answer" are from "The August Sleepwalker" (New Directions, 1988) by Bei Dao, edited and translated by Bonnie S. McDougall

The lines beginning "'It seems to me now . . . '," "Here's absinthe." and "Doctor Quackenbush" are from *Complete Poems* (Bloodaxe, 1988) by Martin Bell

The lines from the poems "Golden State IX," "California Plush," "The War of Vaslav Nijinski," the lines beginning "Without a body . . . " the lines beginning " . . . I am now reading" are from *In The Western Night* (Farrar, Straus & Giroux, 1990) by Frank Bidart

The lines from "The Rocklestrake" were originally printed in *Rocklestrakes* (Outposts, 1960) by David Black

Lines from the poems "Kew Gardens," "The Hands of Felicity," "Melusine," "From the Privy Council," and "Notes for Joachim" are from *Collected Poems 1964–1987* (Polygon, 1991) by David Black

The lines from the poems "I Believe," "Bitter Body," "Purity, I Know," "So Must I Wait," "Portrait," "Ballad," and the lines beginning "White bodies of poplars . . . " by Ana Blandiana were translated from the original by Adam J. Sorkin

The lines from the poem "An Irish Childhood in England," "Suburban Woman," "Mastectomy," "Night Feed," and "Outside History" reprinted from *Outside History: Selected Poems 1980–1990* with permission of W.W. Norton & Company, Inc. Copyright © 1990 by Eavan Boland

The lines from the poem "That the Science of Cartography is Limited" and "What Language Did" are from *In a Time of Violence* (W.W. Norton & Co., 1994) by Eavan Boland

The lines of the poem from "The Fourth Monkey" are from *Life Sentence* (W.W. Norton & Co., 1991) by Nina Cassian

The lines from the poem "I understand it as a kiss" are from *My Wicked, Wicked Ways* (Random House, 1992) by Sandra Cisneros

The lines beginning "in the inner city . . . ," "Listen children," "come home from the movies" and the poems "After Kent State" are reprinted from *Good Woman: Poems and a Memoir 1969–1980* copyright © 1987 by Lucille Clifton. Reprinted by permission of Boa Editions Limited.

The lines from the poem "White Lady" are from *Quilting* (BOA Editions Limited, 1991) by Lucille Clifton

The lines from the poems "Getting Past the Past" and "Chinese Porcelains at the Metropolitan" are from *All Roads at Once* cpyright © Alfred Corn, 1976

The lines beginning "Biography repeats itself . . . " are from *A Call in the Midst of the Crowd* copyright © by Alfred Corn 1975, 1976, 1977, 1978

The lines from the poem "At the Grave of Wallace Stevens" are from *The Various Light* copyright © by Alfred Corn, used by permission of Viking Penguin, a division of Penguin Books USA Inc.

The lines from the poem "1992" are from *Autobiographies* (Viking Penguin, 1992) by Alfred Corn

The lines from the poem "The Thirty Year Old Body" and the lines from an untitled poem beginning "Let me confess . . . " are by Daniela Crăsnaru translated from the original by Adam J. Sorkin

The lines beginning "Ah, how I hate this place . . . " are by Daniela Crăsnaru and were translated by Ioana Ieronim and Adam J. Sorkin

The lines from the poem "Indigo Violet" are from *Letters From Darkness* (Oxford University Press, 1991) by Daniela Crăsnaru, translated by Fleur Adcock

The lines from the poem "Shadow of Lightening" are from *Omneros* (Invisible City/ Red Hill Press, 1978) by Mohammed Dib, translated by Eric Sellin

The lines from the poem "Walls" are by Mircea Dinescu from *15 Young Romanian Poets* (Eminescu Publishing House, 1982) translated by Lilliana Ursu

The lines from the poem "Dance" are by Mircea Dinescu and translated from the original by Adam J. Sorkin

The lines from the poem "Not Today" are by Mircea Dinescu from *ShiftingBorders: East European Poetry of the Eighties* (Fairleigh Dickinson University Press) edited by Walter Cummins

The lines from the poem "Poetics" are from *This Kind of Bird Flies Backward* (Totem Press) by Diane di Prima

The lines beginning "All hereabout anachronism's rife . . . " are from *An Australian Country Graveyard and Other Poems* (Thomas Nelson, 1974) by Hal Porter

The lines from the poems "For Unborn Malcolms," "Homecomming," and "To Blk/Record/Buyers" are from *Homecomming* (Broadside Press, 1968) by Sonia Sanchez

The lines beginning "as i entered into my . . . " are from *A Blues Book for Blue Black Magical Women* (Broadside Press, 1973) by Sonia Sanchez

The lines from the poems "July" and "Old Words" are from *Love Poems* (Third Press, 1973) by Sonia Sanchez

The lines from the poems "The Paperweight" and "Laughing with One Eye" are from *Portraits and Elegies* (David R. Godine, 1982) by Gjertrud Schnackenberg

The lines from the "The Love Letter" are from *The Lamplit Answer* (Farrar, Straus & Giroux, 1985) copyright © 1985 by Gjertrud Schnackenberg

The lines from "A Gilded Lapse of Time" are from *A Gilded Lapse of Time* (Farrar, Straus & Giroux, 1992) copyright © 1992 by Gjertrud Schnackenberg

The lines beginning "Where blood and stone proclaim . . . " and the lines from Sonnet 6 are from *The Hinterland* copyright © 1977 by Peter Scupham. Reprinted by permission of Oxford University press.

The lines fromn the poem "Watching the Perseids: Remembering the Dead" are from *Watching the Perseids* (Oxford University Press, 1990) by Peter Scupham

The lines from the poems "Wanting to Live in Harlem," "Pressed Duck," "The Soul Mate," and "Sunrise" are from *Poems 1959–1989* copyright © 1989 by Frederick Seidel. Reprinted by permission of Alfred A. Knopf, Inc.

The lines beginning "White people are white . . . " and the lines from the poem "AnotherAlexandra" are from *Yakhal'inkomo* (Renoster, 1972) by Mongane Wally Serote

The lines from the poem "For Don M.—Banned" are from *Tsetlo* (Donker, 1975) by Mongane Wally Serote

The lines beginning "The Humble Administrator admires a bee . . . " and the lines from the poems "The Accountant's House" and "Abalone Soup" are from *The Humble Administrator's Garden* (Carcanet Press, 1985) by Vikram Seth

The lines from the poems "Night in Jiangjing" and "A Doctor's Journal Entry for August 6, 1945," are from *All You Who Sleep Tonight* (Alfred A. Knopf, 1990) by Vikram Seth

The lines beginning " . . . Silicon Valley / Lures . . . " are from *The Golden Gate* (Random House, 1986) by Vikram Seth

The lines from the poem "Mother" are from *Intersect* (Borealis Press Ltd., 1974) by Carol Shields

The lines from the poems "Poem for Myself and Mei: Concerning Abortion" and "Indian Song: Survival" are from *Laguna Woman* Greenfield Review Press, 1974) by Leslie Marmon Silko

The lines from "Crossroads" are from *Crossroads: Poems by David R. Slavitt* (Louisian State University, 1994) copyright © by David R. Slavitt

The lines beginning "Covered with Sores . . . " and the poems "We Never Wonder," "Leda," and "Like a Pastel" by Marin Sorescu were translated from the original by Adam J. Sorkin and Linda Vianu and are unpublished

The lines from the poem "Icarus" are from *The Literary Review* (fall, 1991) by Marin Sorescu, translated by Adam J. Sorkin and Linda Vianu

The lines from the poem "The Ground" are from *American Poetry Review* (Nov/Dec 1991) by Marin Sorescu translated by Adam J. Sorkin and Linda Vianu

The lines from the poem "Adam" are from *Poultry: A Magazine of Voice* (3rd series, 1992) by Marin Sorescu, translated by Adam J. Sorkin

The lines from the poem "At the Solstice" are from *The Cold Wind of Dawn* (Cape, 1966) by Kenneth White

The lines from the poem "Obscure" are from *Handbook for the Diamond Country: Collected Shorter Poems 1968–1990* (Mainstream, 1990) by Kenneth White

The lines from the poem "Walking the Coast" are from *The Bird Bath: Collected Longer Poems, 1964–1988* (Mainstream, 1989) by Kenneth White

The lines from the poems "Apologia" and "Great Goose Pagoda" are from *Trees on the Mountain: An Anthology of New Chinese Writing* (Chinese University Press, 1984) by Lian Yang edited by Stephen C. Soong and John Minford

The lines beginning "I am a poet . . . " are from *Tian Wen* (1984, Heavenly Questions) by Yang Lian

The lines from the poem "Ode to Plurality" are by Adam Zagajewski and were translated by Joachim T. Baer

The lines from the poems "Ode to Plurality" and "In the Encyclopedias, No Room for Mandelstam" are from *Tremor: Selected Poems* by Adam Zagajewski, translated by Renata Gorczyński. Translation copyright © 1985 by Farrar, Straus, & Giroux.

The lines beginning "I stood in silence before a dark Picture . . . " are from *Canvas* by Adam Zagajewski, translated by Renata Gorczyśki, Benjamin Ivry, and C. K. Williams. Translation copyright © 1991 by Farrar, Straus, & Giroux.

Picture Credits

Abish, Walter: photo by Cecile Abish; *Aleshkovsky, Yuz*: courtesy of the author; *Al-Kharrat, Edwar*: courtesy of the author; *Anaya, Rudolfo*: courtesy of the author; *Anthony, Piers*: photo by Mrs. Anthony; *Antunes, António Lobo*: photo by Secker & Warburg; *Appleman, Philip*: courtesy of the author; *Archer, Jeffrey*: photo by Terry O'Neill; *Arenas, Reinaldo*: photo by Almendros.

Bailyn, Bernard: courtesy of the author; *Banville, John*: Secker & Warburg; *Barker, Clive*: photo by Bridgette Jouxtel; *Baudrillard, Jean*: compliments of Verso; *Baumbach, Jonathan*: courtesy of author; *Bei Dao*: courtesy of New Directions; *Bell, Madison Smartt*: photo by John Stoddard; *Bell, Martin*: courtesy of Bloodaxe Books; *Benchley, Peter*: © Tracy Benchley; *Benford, Gregory*: courtesy of Bantam Books; *Benítez-Rojo, Antonio*: courtesy of Amherst College; *Bennett, Alan*: photo by Tom Miller; *Binchy, Maeve*: Liam White photography; *Black, David*: courtesy of the author; *Blandiana, Ana*: courtesy of Thomas Austin; *Boland, Eavan*: courtesy of the author; *Bosse, Malcolm J.*: photo by Lori Mack; *Bradley, Marion Zimmer*: © Jerry Bauer; *Brandys, Kazimierz*: Louis Manier; *Brin, David*: © Jerry Bauer; *Brown, Rita Mae*: photo by Mark Homan; *Bufalino, Gesualdo*: photo by Giuseppe Leone; *Buruma, Ian*: © Jerry Bauer; *Busch, Frederick*: photo by John Hubbard.

Cannadine, David N.: photo by Eaden H. Lilley; *Cantor, Jay*: photo by Jerry Cantor; *Can Xue*: courtesy of author; *Carpelan, Bo*: courtesy of Carcanet Press; *Cassian, Nina*: courtesy of the author; *Chabon, Michael*: photo by E. J. Camp; *Cherryh, C. J.*: © Tau Celti Inc.; *Cheuse, Alan*: photo by Joel Foreman; *Cisneros, Sandra*: © Rubén Guzmán; *Clancy, Tom*: photo by John Earle; *Clark, Mary Higgins*: photo by Bernard Vidal; *Clifton, Lucille*: photo by Michael Glaser; *Codrescu, Andrei*: photo by S. F. Tabachnikoff; *Corn, Alfred*: photo by Christopher Corwin; *Craig, Gordon A.*

Dagan, Avigdor: courtesy of author; *Dahl, Robert A.*: photo by Michael Marsland; *Danto, Arthur C.*: © 1994 Anne Hall; *Davis, David Brion*: courtesy of author; *Degler, Carl N.*: courtesy of Stanford University; *Delbanco, Nicholas*: courtesy of author; *Dickstein, Morris*: © Dorothy Alexander; *di Prima, Diane*: © Sheppard Powell; *Dixon, Stephen*: photo by Meredith Waddell; *Dobyns, Stephen*: photo by Margot Balboni; *Doerr, Harriet*: photo by Thomas Victor; *Dorfman, Ariel*: © Thomas Victor; *Dorris, Michael*: photo by Louise Erdrich; *Draper, Theodore*: © Terry Barnum; *Duberman, Martin*: © Gene Bagnato.

Ehrenreich, Barbara: © 1993, Sigrid Estrada;

Ekström, Margareta: © Jan Eve Olsson; *Elliott, Janice*: courtesy of author; *Estleman, Loren D.*: photo by Deborah Morgan; *Exley Frederick*: photo by Mark Jury.

Fainlight, Ruth: courtesy of author; *Farmer, Beverley*: courtesy of author; *Fish, Stanley Eugene*: © Barney Cokeliss; *Fleming, Berry*: courtesy of Second Chance Press.

Galeano, Eduardo: Amilcar Pertichetti; *Galvin, Brendan*: courtesy of author; *Gates, Henry Louis Jr.*: courtesy of author; *Gébler, Carlo*: © Nick Cook; *Ghosh, Amitav*: photo by Ulf Anderssen; *Gibson, William*: photo by Sigrid Estrada; *Gildner, Gary*: courtesy of author; *Gilroy, Frank D.*: courtesy of the author; *Grafton, Sue*: photo by Michael Goldman; *Greenblatt, David*: courtesy of author; *Greer, Germaine*: © Nick Cook; *Grimes, Martha*: © Isolde Ohlbaum; *Grossman, David*: © Fialho 1993; *Gurganus, Allan*: photo by Beckett Logan.

Hadas Rachel: photo by Chip Simons; *Hamilton-Paterson, James*: photo by Jane Brown; *Hanrahan, Barbara*: courtesy of author; *Hardison, O. B. Jr.*: photo by Stavros Moschopoulos; *Harris, MacDonald*: © Jerry Bauer; *Harrison, Barbara Grizzuti*: courtesy of author; *Heinesen, William*: photo by Jacob Maarbjerg; *Hillerman, Tony*: photo by Tom Lazarevich; *Hirsch, E. D.*: © Mimi Levine 1987; *Hirsch, Edward*: courtesy of author; *Hogan, Desmond*: courtesy of author; *Holden, Ursula*: courtesy of author; *Holmes, Richard*: courtesy of Hodder Stoughton; *Hongo, Garrett*: photo by Gary Teptev; *Hove, Chenjerai*: courtesy of Heinemann; *Howatch, Susan*: photo by Barbara Pollard; *Howe, Tina*: © J. P. Laffort/Sygma; *Hwang, David Henry*: photo by Michael Ramaos.

Isaacs, Susan: © Ingrid Estrada; *Iser, Wolfgang*: courtesy of author; *Ishiguro, Kazuo*: © Nigel Perry.

Jacobsen, Rolf: photo by Tom A. Kolstad; *Janowitz, Tama*: photo by Josef Astor; *Johnson, Charles*: © Jerry Bauer; *Joseph, Jenny*: photo by Stuart Redler; *Just, Ward*: photo by Sarah Catchpole.

Kadare, Ismail: photo by Caroline Forbes; *Kagan, Jerome*: courtesy of Howard University, News Office; *Kapuściński, Ryszard*: © Czeslaw Czaplinski; *Kauffman, Janet*: photo by Dick Schwarze; *Keillor, Garrison*: photo by Carmen Quesado; *Kennelly, Brendan*: courtesy of author; *Kidder, Tracy*: photo by Gabriel Amadeus Cooney; *Kingsolver, Barbara*: © Seth Kantner; *Kinsella, W. P.*: photo by Scott Norris; *Kriegel, Leonard*: © Layle Sibert.

Leavitt, David: photo by Marion Ettlinger; *Leffland, Ella*: courtesy of author; *L'Engle,*

Madeleine: © Sigrid Estrada; *L'Heureux, John*: photo by Chuck Painter; *Lindgren, Torgny*: photo by Ulla Mantan; *Linney, Romulus*: © Susan Johann; *Lish, Gordon*: photo by Bill Hayward; *Lively, Penelope*: courtesy of Walker Books Ltd.; *Lovelace, Earl*: courtesy of Henmann; *Lukacs, John*: courtesy of author; *Lustig, Arnost*: courtesy of author.

Mackay, Shena: courtesy of Moyer Bell; *MacLeod, Charlotte*: courtesy of author; *Manea, Norman*: courtesy of author; *Martin, Valerie*: photo by Thomas Victor; *May, Rollo*: © W. W. Norton; *McCarthy, Cormac*: photo by Marion Ettlinger; *McCorkle, Jill*: photo by Bernard Thomas; *McGrath, Thomas*: photo by Michael Hazard; *Meyers, Jeffrey*: © Jerry Bauer; *Miller, Sue*: © Jerry Bauer; *Millett, Kate*: © W. W. Norton; *Mitchell, Adrian*: photo by David Silltoe; *Morris, Mary*: photo by Thomas Victor; *Mukherjee, Bharati* : photo by Tom Victor; *Murakami, Haruki* : courtesy of the author.

Namjoshi, Suniti : © Marty Crowder *Nissenson, Hugh*: courtesy of author; *Niven, Larry*: photo by Greg Preston; *Nochlin, Linda*: courtesy of author; *Nooteboom, Cees*: photo by Simone Sassen.

Oakeshott, Michael J.: photo by Angus McBean; *O'Brian, Patrick*: © Rex Features; *Olson, Toby*: photo by Robert A. Lisak; *Ortese, Anna Maria*: photo by Paola Agosti.

Padgett, Ron: photo by George Tysh; *Pagels, Elaine Hiesey*; *Pamuk, Orhan*: courtesy of author; *Paretsky, Sara*: courtesy of author; *Parini, Jay*: photo by Miriam Berkley; *Parker, Robert B.*: photo by John Earle; *Pawel, Ernest*: © Jerry Bauer; *Pearson, T. R.*: photo by T. E. Pearson; *Perrin, Ursula*: courtesy of author; *Perry, Anne*: courtesy of author; *Pesetsky, Bette*: courtesy of author; *Peters, Elizabeth*: © Creative Force Photography; *Phillips, Caryl*: © Jerry Bauer; *Phillips, Robert S.*: photo by Geoffrey Kerrigan; *Pipes, Richard*: photo by Jane Reed; *Pirsig, Robert*: photo by Wendy Pirsig; *Poliakoff, Stephen*: photo by Mark Gerson; *Porter, Hal*: courtesy of author; *Posse, Abel*: photo by Ernesto Monteavaro; *Potter, Dennis*: © BBC Enterprises Ltd; *Pownall, David*: courtesy of the author.

Quignard, Pascal: courtesy of the author; *Quindlen, Anna*: photo by Joyce Ravid.

Ribeiro, João Ubaldo: © Jerry Bauer, *Rice, Anne*: photo by Mary Ellen Mark; *Rice, Edward E.*: courtesy of Dorling Kindersley Inc.; *Rive,*

Richard: photo by Douglas Reid-Skinner; *Robison, Mary*: photo by James Robinson; *Roiphe, Anne*: © Thomas Victor; *Rose, Phyllis*: photo by Rollie McKenna; *Russ, Joanna*: photo by Hannah Kanzell; *Rybczynski, Witold*: photo by Gerd Ludwig.

Safire, William: photo by Nancy Crampton; *Sahgal, Nayantara*: courtesy of author; *Sanchez, Sonia*: photo by Marion Ettlinger; *Santmyer, Helen Hooven*: courtesy of Knowledge Ideas & Trends, Inc.; *Saramago, Jose*: photo by S. Fischer; *Sayles, John*: photo by Robert Marshak; *Schama, Simon Michael*: photo by Ginny Papaioannou; *Schnackenberg, Gjertrud*: © Robert Nozick, *Scott, Joanna*: © James Montanus/University of Rochester; *Scott, Nathan A., Jr.*: courtesy of author; *Scruton, Roger*: courtesy of author; *Sealy, I. Allan*: photo by Luke Strongman; *Seidel, Frederick*: © Douglas Brothers; *Shields, Carol*: courtesy of author; *Singer, Peter*: courtesy of author; *Slavitt, David R.*: courtesy of author; *Smiley, Jane*: photo by Steve Martensen; *Sorescu, Marin*: photo by Virginia Sorescu; *Spurling, Hilary*: photo by R. Cohen; *Stern, Daniel*: courtesy of author; *Storr, Anthony*: photo by Stephen Markeson; *Szulc, Tad*: courtesy of author.

Tachihara, Masaaki: courtesy of Wasenda University; *Tallent, Elizabeth Ann*: photo by Mark Kane; *Tan, Amy*: courtesy of G. P. Putnams Sons; *Tesich, Steve*: courtesy of the author; *Tharoor, Shashi*: photo by Ajay Malik; *Tolstaya, Tatiana*courtesy of the author; *Tomalin, Claire*: courtesy of author; *Tremain, Rose*: courtesy of the author; *Tsushima, Yuko*: photo by Keiko Susaki; *Turow, Scott*: photo by Skrebneski.

Uno Chiyo: © Peter Owen Ltd; *Unsworth, Barry*: courtesy of the author.

Valaoritis, Nanos: © Chris Felver; *Vizinczey, Stephen*: photo by Sally Soames.

Wakefield, Dan: photo by Theresa Mackin; *Wang Anyi*: photo by Dana Gluckstein; *Wesley, Mary*: courtesy of Overlook Press; *Wetherell, W. D.*: courtesy of author; *White, Kenneth*: photo by Tarre-Claude White; *Wicker, Tom*: courtesy of author; *Wiggins, Marianne*: photo by Elena Seibert; *Will, George F.*: © Capital Cities/ABC Inc.; *Wilson, Edward O.*: courtesy of Harvard University Press.

Zagajewski, Adam: photo by Virginia Schendler.